Advances in Consumer Research

Volume XXII   Editors: Frank R. Kardes, Mita Sujan

International Standard Book Number (ISBN): 0-915552-34-5

International Standard Serial Number (ISSN): 0098-9258

Frank R. Kardes and Mita Sujan, Editors

Advances in Consumer Research, Volume 22

(Provo, UT: Association for Consumer Research, 1995)

Cover Design by Michael Balint

Preface

The twenty-fifth Annual Conference of the Association for Consumer Research (ACR) was held at the Boston Marriott Hotel Copley Place in Boston, Massachusetts on October 20-23, 1994. This volume (Vol. 22) contains papers that were presented at this conference and session summaries.

Forty-three members of the Association served on the Conference Program Committee. These individuals contributed many ideas that shaped the content of the conference. These individuals also served as the review board for the selection of special sessions. Another 217 members of the association served as reviewers for competitive papers and research notes. The reviewers were prompt and thorough, and their efforts greatly enhanced the quality of the conference. Many of the reviewers also contributed by serving as session chairs or discussants.

Our colleagues submitted 174 competitive papers, 71 special session proposals, and 30 research notes for peer review: 89, 40, and 30 of these, respectively, were accepted for presentation in Boston, and for inclusion in this volume. A new attendance record was set: 640 colleagues attended the twenty fifth Anniversary ACR conference. This level of intellectual commitment to the ACR conference by both presenters and attenders bodes well for the future of consumer research.

We wish to thank Alice M. Tybout, the President of ACR, for asking us to serve as co-chairs/co-editors. We also wish to thank former ACR President and current Executive secretary, H. Keith Hunt, for selecting the conference site and for handling innumerable emergencies with grace and style. We also thank the 1993 ACR Co-chairs, Chris T. Allen and Deborah Roedder John, for their invaluable advice and assistance. Thanks are also due to Jeff Inman, who developed the program for matching submissions with reviewers. We also thank Jim Muncy and Steve Barnett for preparing this volume for publication, and we thank Michael Balint for the cover art. Finally, We wish to thank the arrangements committee and our doctoral students for helping the conference to run so smoothly.

We are pleased to have had the opportunity to help provide a forum for the high level of research activity and scholarship evident at the conference, and we hope that we have contributed, in some small way, to facilitating the remarkably rapid growth of the field of consumer behavior. May the next 25 years be as stimulating and productive as the previous 25 years.

Frank R. Kardes, University of Cincinnati
Mita Sujan, Pennsylvania State University
1994 ACR Co-chairs/Co-editors

Conference Committee

REVIEWERS

ERRATUM

Due to an oversight on the part of the first author, the name of the second author was omitted from the following article. The proper citation is:

Severson, H.H. and A. Benthin (1993), "Adolescents' Perception of Risk: Understanding and Preventing High Risk Behavior," in *Advances in Consumer Research*, eds. L. McAlister and M. L. Rothschild, Ann Arbor , MI: Association for Consumer Research, 177-182.

Table of Contents and Conference Program

ASSOCIATION FOR CONSUMER RESEARCH
ANNUAL CONFERENCE

OCTOBER 20-23
BOSTON MARRIOTT HOTEL COPLEY PLACE
BOSTON, MASSACHUSSETTS

```
┌─────────────────────────────────────────┐
│          THURSDAY, OCTOBER 20           │
│                                         │
│       ACR EXECUTIVE BOARD MEETING        │
│              10;00 - 5:00               │
│                                         │
│              REGISTRATION               │
│               4:00 - 8:00               │
│                                         │
│                RECEPTION                │
│               5:30 - 7:30               │
└─────────────────────────────────────────┘
```

```
┌─────────────────────────────────────────┐
│           FRIDAY, OCTOBER 21            │
│                                         │
│       JCP EDITORIAL BOARD MEETING        │
│               7:15 - 8:15               │
│                                         │
│              REGISTRATION               │
│        7:30 - 11:30 and 2:00 - 5:30      │
│                                         │
│                SESSION 1                │
│               8:15 - 9:45               │
└─────────────────────────────────────────┘
```

1.1   *Special Session*: **Consumer Promotion and Brand Loyalty: Information Processing Perspective**

Chair: France Leclerc, MIT
Discussant: Leigh McAlister, University of Texas

1.2   *Special Session*: **Reference Effects in Dynamic Marketing Mix Environments: Insights from Decision-Making Research**

Chairs: Deborah J. Mitchell, Temple University
                Sankar Sen, Temple University

1.3   *Special Session*: The Cumulative Effects of Advertising Repetition on Product Beliefs and Attitudes Under Low Involvement

Chair: Scott A. Hawkins, University of Toronto
Discussant: Alan G. Sawyer, University of Florida

1.4   *Competitive Paper Session*: New Directions in Consumer Measurement

Chair: Haim Mano, University of Missouri, St. Louis
Discussant: Barbara Bickart, Rutgers University

1.5   *Competitive Paper Session*: **Customer Satisfaction: Implications for Analysis and Action**

Chair: George Belch, San Diego State University
Discussant: Mickey Belch, San Diego State University

1.6   *Special Session*: **Peaks and Flows: Intense Joys and Optimal Experiences in Consumption**

Chair: Ruth Ann Smith, Virginia Polytechnic Institute and State University
Discussant: Linda Scott, University of Illinois

1.7   *Special Session*: **Individual Differences as Moderating Variables: Issues in the Development and Use of Personality Variables**

Chairs: David J. Moore, University of Michigan
          Pamela M. Homer, California State University, Long Beach
Discussant: Douglas M. Stayman, Cornell University

Self-Referencing and Attitude Change Processes: Insights from a Dispositional Approach
    Curtis P. Haugtvedt, Ohio State University
    H. Rao Unnava, Ohio State University
    W. Blair Jarvis, Ohio State University

Emotional Intensity: An Individual Difference Perspective
    David J. Moore, University of Michigan

FRIDAY, OCTOBER 21

SESSION 2
10:00 - 11:30

2.1   *Special Session*: **The Maintenance of Positive Self-Evaluations: In Search of a Motive Underlying Some Consumption Related Behaviors**

Chair: Harish Sujan, The Pennsylvania State University

Confluence of Self Processes
    Abraham Tesser, University of Georgia

The Role of Goal-Directed Emotions in the Self-Regulation of Action
    Richard P. Bagozzi, University of Michigan
    Hans Baumgartner, The Pennsylvania State University
    R.G.M. Pieters, Tilburg University

When Silence Hurts: The Role of Loneliness in Object Relations and Consumption
    R.G.M. Pieters, Tilburg University
    Harish Sujan, The Pennsylvania State University

2.2   *Special Session*: **The Determinants of Choice Deferral**

Chair: Joel Huber, Duke University

Deciding Not to Decide in Sequential Search Among Choice Sets
    Robert J. Meyer, University of Pennsylvania
    Brian Peterson, University of Pennsylvania

The Effect of No Purchase Option on Preferences Among Alternatives
    Ravi Dhar, Yale University
    Itamar Simonson, Stanford University

The Meaning of a "None" Response in Commercial Studies Using Choice-Based Conjoint
    Joel Huber, Duke University
    Jonathan Pinnell, IntelliQuest

2.6 *Special Session*: Perspectives on the "New Sociology" of Consumer Research: Addressing the Structure/Agency Dilemma

Chairs: Douglas E. Allen, The Pennsylvania State University
Paul F. Anderson, The Pennsylvania State University

2.7 *Competitive Paper Session*: Advertising Execution and Programming Context Effects

Chair: Meryl Gardner, University of Delaware
Discussant: James Kellaris, University of Cincinnati

FRIDAY, OCTOBER 21

LUNCH
11:45 A.M. - 1:45

BUSINESS MEETING

PRESIDENTIAL ADDRESS
Alice M. Tybout
"The Value of Theory in Consumer Research"

FRIDAY, OCTOBER 21

SESSION 3
2:00 - 3:30

3.1   Special Session: New Directions in Behavioral Decision Theory: Implications for Consumer Choice

Chair: Ravi Dhar, Yale University

Special Session Summary

The Construction of Preferences
        Itamar Simonson, Stanford University
        Amos Tversky, Stanford University

Ownership Effects in Consumer Choice
        Sankar Sen, Temple University
        Eric J. Johnson, University of Pennsylvania

Consumer Self-Control through Purchase Quantity Rationing
        Klaus Wertenbroch, University of Chicago

The Effect of Common and Unique Features in Consumer Choice
        Ravi Dhar, Yale University
        Jim Sherman, Indiana University

3.2   Competitive Paper Session: Schema Congruity and Categorization

Chair: Cynthia Huffman, University of Pennsylvania
Discussant: Ronald C. Goodstein, UCLA

3.3   Special Session: Tell Me Again Why I Should Listen to You?: Source Effects Revisited

Chair: Nancy Artz, University of Southern Maine
Discussant: Elizabeth J. Wilson, Louisiana State University

Special Session Summary

Voice Intonation and Intensity as Antecedents of Source Credibility in the Advertising Context
        Claire Gélinas-Chebat, University of Quebec, Montreal
        Jean-Charles Chebat, University of Quebec, Montreal

Whitewater Framed by Canyon Walls: Playing Games in Nature
    Eric J. Arnould, California State University, Long Beach
    Linda L. Price, University of Colorado

Playing with Play, Games within Games: How Baseball Spectators Reconstruct Professional Baseball
    Douglas B. Holt, The Pennsylvania State University

"Guess What I Paid for This" and Other Games Bargain-Hunters Play
    Robert M. Schindler, Rutgers University

3.7   *Competitive Paper Session*: Green Marketing: Science and Practice

Chair: Robert W. Veryzer, Rensselaer Polytechnic Institute
Discussant: Edward F. McQuarrie, Santa Clara University

> # FRIDAY, OCTOBER 21
>
> ## SESSION 4
> ## 3:45 - 5:15

4.1   *Special Session*: Understanding Consumer Decision Processes Using Verbalization Data: Substantive and Methodological Perspectives

Chairs: Gabriel J. Biehal, University of Maryland
                Dipankar Chakravarti, University of Arizona
Discussant: Eric J. Johnson, University of Pennsylvania

The Impact of Concurrent Verbal Protocols on Encoding and Retrieval
    Reshma H. Shah, University of Pittsburgh
    Robert J. Gilbert, University of Pittsburgh
    C. Whan Park, University of Pittsburgh

4.2   *Special Session*: New Directions in Exploring the Interface of Consumer Cognition and Motivation

Chair: S. Ratneshwar, University of Florida
Discussant: Jerome B. Kernan, George Mason University

4.3   *Special Session*: Consumers' Anticipations in Decision Making

Chair: Michel Tuan Pham, Columbia University
Discussant: Andrew Mitchell, University of Toronto

Aboriginal Consumer Culture
> Russell W. Belk, University of Utah
> Ronald Groves, Edith Cowan University
> Per Ostergaard, Odense University

Australian Aborigines and the Dreaming: The Meaning of Land and Aboriginal Culture
> Ronald Hill, Villanova University

Observers Observed: Researcher Behavior and Imagination in the Odyssey Downunder
> Per Ostergaard, Odense University
> Kim Bridge, Edith Cowan University
> Noel Bridge, Edith Cowan University

4.7   *Competitive Paper Session*: **Phenomenological Perspectives and Issues**

Chair: Eric J. Arnold, California State University, Long Beach
Discussant: Eva M. Hyatt, Appalachian State University

Perceiving What Package Designs Express: A Multisensory Exploratory Study Using Creative Writing Measurement Techniques
> Jeffrey F. Durgee, Rensselaer Polytechnic Institute
> Gina Colarelli O'Conner, Rensselaer Polytechnic Institute

4.8   **ACR 1995 Program Committee Meeting**

Chairs: Kim Corfman, New York University
                    John Lynch, University of Florida

FRIDAY, OCTOBER 21

**ACR 25th Anniversary
Celebration Meeting and Reception
5:50 - 8:00**

SATURDAY, OCTOBER 22

**SCP EXECUTIVE COMMITTEE MEETING
7:15 - 8:15**

**REGISTRATION
8:00 - 11:30**

**SESSION 5
8:15 - 9:45**

5.1   *Special Session*: Other-Than-Conscious Consumer Information Processing: Empirical Examinations of an Emerging and Controversial Topic (Part I)

Chairs: Susan E. Heckler, University of Arizona
                 Stewart Shapiro, University of Baltimore
Discussant: Arthur Reber, City University of New York, Brooklyn

5.2   *Competitive Paper Session*: Brand Exposure, Retrieval, and Choice

Chair: Pallab Paul, University of Denver
Discussant: Carolyn L. Costley, University of Miami

5.3   *Special Session*: Self-Referencing: An Examination of Antecedents, Consequences, and Role in Message Processing

Chairs: Jennifer Edson Escalas, Duke University
                 Parthasarathy Krishnamurthy, The Pennsylvania State University
Discussant: Patricia Linville, Duke University

The Process of Becoming Homeless for Families on AFDC
        Renya Reed, Villanova University
        Ron Hill, Villanova University

Roles of Low Income Husbands and Wives in Making Financial Decisions
        Roger Baran, DePaul University

Effects of the New FDA Rules for Food Labels on Disadvantaged Consumers
        Anusree Mitra, The American University
        Manoj Hastak, The American University
        Gary T. Ford, The American University
        Debra Jones Ringold, Willamette University

5.7   *Competitive Paper Session*: Personal Values and Consumption

Chair: Robert J. Fisher, University of Southern California
Discussant: George W. Brooker, Central Washington University

SATURDAY, OCTOBER 22

SESSION 6
10:00 - 11:30

6.1   *Special Session*: Other-Than-Conscious Consumer Information Processing: Empirical Examinations of an Emerging and Controversial Topic (Part II)

Chairs: Susan E. Heckler, University of Arizona
                    Stewart Shapiro, University of Baltimore
Discussant: Arthur Reber, City University of New York, Brooklyn

Nonconscious Processing of Covariation Information: Empirical Evidence of Attitude Change
        Susan E. Heckler, University of Arizona
        Christopher P. Puto, University of Arizona

Implicit Preferences for Novel Stimuli
        Arthur S. Reber, City University of New York, Brooklyn
        Diane Zizak, City University of New York, Brooklyn

Preattentive Processing: The Effects of Unattended Information on Consideration Sets
        Stewart Shapiro, University of Baltimore
        Deborah J. MacInnis, University of Arizona
        Susan E. Heckler, University of Arizona

6.2 **Special Session:** The Constructive Nature of Consumer Response to Differential Product Advantages

Chair: Ziv Carmon, Duke University
                 Stephen M. Nowlis, Washington State University
Discussant: Robert J. Meyer, University of Pennsylvania

Consumers' Underestimation of their Willingness to Pay for Quality
       Ziv Carmon, Duke University
       Itamar Simonson, Stanford University

The Effect of Response Mode on Consumer Decisions Involving Overall Brand Quality, Price and Product Features
       Stephen M. Nowlis, Washington State University
       Itamar Simonson, Stanford University

The Effects of Advertising on Benefits Consumers Choose and on their Price Sensitivity
       Anusree Mitra, American University
       John G. Lynch, University of Florida

6.3 **Special Session:** Schema Incongruity: A Multidimensional Perspective Involving Advertising Schema, Self-Schema, and Product Schema

Chair: Kalpesh Kaushik Desai, University of Texas

Multiple Product Incongruities and Schematic Changes
       Kalpesh Kaushik Desai, University of Texas at Austin
       Esra Gencturk, University of Texas at Austin
       Linda Rochford, University of Minnesota, Duluth

Can Ad Design Influence Consumer Perceptions? The Congruity of Ad Layout with Product Positioning
       Joseph C. Nunes, University of Chicago
       Joan Meyers-Levy, University of Chicago
       Laura Peracchio, University of Wisconsin, Milwaukee

Mismatches Between Self-Schemas, Endorser Schemas, and Product-User Schemas
       Katryna Malafarina, University of Minnesota
       Barbara Loken, University of Minnesota

The Relationship Between Brand Extension Incongruity, Consumer Involvement, and New Product Evaluations
       Eyal Moaz, Northwestern University
       Alice M. Tybout, Northwestern University

6.4   *Special Session*: The Brand as a Character, a Partner and a Person: Three Perspectives on the Question of Brand Personality

Chairs: Jennifer Aaker, Stanford University
                  Susan Fournier, Harvard University
Discussant: Kevin Lane Keller, Stanford University

6.5   Research Note Session

Chairs: Maryon F. King, Southern Illinois University
                  France Leclerc, MIT
                  Deborah L. Marlino, Simmons College
                  Howard Marmorstein, University of Miami
                  William J. Qualls, MIT
                  Cliff Schultz, Arizona State University
                  Deepak Sirdeshmukh, Case Western University
                  Gerald Smith, Boston College

6.6   *Special Session*: Interactive Marketing Technologies: Implications for Consumer Research

Chair: John Deighton, University of Chicago
Discussant: Jonathan Frenzen, University of Chicago

Consumers and the Emerging Interactive Communications Infrastructure
      Christopher Meyer, Mercer Management Consulting

Constructing Virtual Relationships
      John Deighton, University of Chicago
      Kent Grayson, London Business School

How Interactive Technologies are being Implemented: Design and Measurement Issues
      Rishad Tobaccowala, Leo Burnett Inc.

6.7   *Competitive Paper Session*: Belk's Legacy: Materialism, Possessions, and Compulsions

Chair: Robert E. Kleine III, Arizona State University
Discussant: Larry D. Compeau, Clarkson University

SATURDAY, OCTOBER 22

LUNCH
11:45 - 2:45

PRESENTATION OF AWARDS

ACR FELLOW ADDRESSES
Russell W. Belk
Morris B. Holbrook
Jacob Jacoby
(Articles Located at Beginning of *Proceedings*)

7.4   *Competitive Paper Session*: Involvement and Persuasion: New Perspectives and Issues

Chair: Peter Bloch, University of Missouri
Discussant: Pamela M. Homer, California State University, Long Beach

7.6   *Special Session*: New Directions in Affect and Consumer Satisfaction

Chair: Richard A. Spreng, Michigan State University
Discussant: Robert B. Woodruff, University of Tennessee

7.7 *Competitive Paper Session*: Cross-Cultural Perspectives in Consumer Research

Chair: L.J. Shrum, Rutgers University
Discussant: Dogan Eroglu, Georgia State University

SATURDAY, OCTOBER 22

SESSION 8
4:45 - 6:15

8.1 *Special Session*: A 20 Year Retrospective on the Journal of Consumer Research

Chair: Valerie Folkes, University of Southern California
Discussant: Jerome Kernan, George Mason University

Panelists: James Bettman, Duke University
              Ron Frank, Emory University
              Harold H. Kassarjian, UCLA
              Richard Lutz, University of Florida
              Kent Monroe, University of Illinois
              Brian Sternthal, Northwestern University

8.2 *Special Session*: Experiments with Social Networks and Social Boundaries

Chair: Peter Reingen, Arizona State University
Discussant: Dawn Iacobucci, Northwestern University

8.5 *Competitive Paper Session*: **Information Search and Utilization**

Chair: Sundar Narayanan, University of Illinois
Discussant: Tina Keisler, Rutgers University

8.6 *Special Session*: **New Research on Limited Cognitive Capacity: Effects of Arousal, Mood, and Modality**

Chair: Nader T. Tavassoli, University of Minnesota
Discussant: Dipankar Chakravarti, University of Arizona

8.7 *Competitive Paper Session*: **Consumer Satisfaction: Cognitive and Affective Dimensions**

Chair: Akshay R. Rao, University of Minnesota
Discussant: Narasimhan (Han) Srinivasan, University of Connecticut

---

SATURDAY, OCTOBER 22

JCR EDITORIAL BOARD MEETING
6:30 - 8:00

RECEPTION
6:15 - 8:00

SATURDAY, OCTOBER 22

ACR 25TH ANNIVERSARY CELEBRATION
10:00 - 11:30

ACR 25th Anniversary Celebration

Chair: Jerome B. Kernan, George Mason University

SUNDAY, OCTOBER 23

SESSION 9
8:30 - 10:00

9.1   *Special Session*: **Divergent Perspectives on the Role of Prior Knowledge in Consumer Information Search and Processing (Part I)**

Chair: Christine Moorman, University of Wisconsin
Discussant: Wesley Hutchinson, University of Florida

9.4   Competitive Paper Session: Customer-Salesperson Relationships

Chair: John C. Mowen, Oklahoma State University
Discussant: Susan P. Mantel, University of Toledo

9.5   Competitive Paper Session: Children as Consumers

Chair: M. Carole Macklin, University of Cincinnati
Discussant: Debra L. Stephans, Villanova University

9.6   *Special Session*: Product Design, Aesthetics, and Consumer Research

Chairs: Robert W. Veryzer, Jr., Rensselaer Polytechnic Institute
                 Molly Eckman, Colorado State University
                 Janet Wagner, University of Maryland
Discussant: Morris B. Holbrook, Columbia University

9.7   *Special Session*: Toward the Development of Relationship Theory at the Level of the Product and Brand

Chair: Susan Fournier, Harvard University
Discussant: Gerald Zaltman, Harvard University

SUNDAY, OCTOBER 23

SESSION 10
10:15 - 11:45

10.1   *Special Session*: Divergent Perspectives on the Role of Prior Knowledge in Consumer Information Search and Processing (Part II)

Chair: Christine Moorman, University of Wisconsin
Discussant: Wesley Hutchinson, University of Florida

Affect-Driven Distortion of Product Information in Consumer Information Search and Processing Activities
> J. Edward Russo, Cornell University
> Victoria Husted Medvec, Cornell University

The Moderating Effects of Information Search Environment Characteristics on Expert Judgments
> Mark T. Spence, Southern Connecticut State University
> Merrie Brucks, University of Arizona

Subjective and Objective Knowledge and their Consequences: Limits of Experimental Approaches
> David Mothersbaugh, University of Pittsburgh
> Lawrence Feick, University of Pittsburgh
> C. Whan Park, University of Pittsburgh

10.2 Competitive Paper Session: Interdisciplinary Approaches Toward Understanding the Elderly Consumer

Chair: Charles M. Schaninger, SUNY Albany
Discussant: Rose L. Johnson, Temple University

10.3 Special Session: Sad, Glad, and Mad: The Revealing Role of Emotions in Consumer Rituals

Chair: Julie A. Ruth, University of Washington
Discussant: Elizabeth C. Hirschman, Rutgers University

Special Session Summary

A Theoretical and Interpretive Exploration of Ambivalence Within the Context of the Wedding
> Tina M. Lowrey, Rider College
> Cele Otnes, University of Illinois

Funerals: Emotional Rituals versus Ritualized Emotions
> Larry Compeau, Clarkson University
> Carolyn Nickolson, Clarkson University

When Receiving a Gift is Associated with Negative Emotions: Violations of Scripts, Audience, and Artifacts
> Julie A. Ruth, University of Washington
> Cele Otnes, University of Illinois
> Fred Brunel, University of Washington

10.7   *Special Session*: **Ethical Issues in Consumer Research: Consumer and Researcher Perspectives**

Chair: Jill Gabrielle Klein, Northwestern University
Discussant: Alan R. Andreasen, Georgetown University

PRESIDENTIAL ADDRESS
The Value of Theory in Consumer Research
Alice M. Tybout, Northwestern University

INTRODUCTION

Presidential addresses to this body have traditionally called for setting our sights higher, achieving more, exhibiting greater creativity and, in general, having a greater real world impact. These are appropriate topics for a forum such as this one and, during this conference, you will no doubt hear a variety of opinions about how these goals might be best achieved, for one constant in ACR is a diversity of points of view. My remarks will focus on the value of theory in advancing understanding of consumer behavior.

Many factors have figured in the development of ACR. One factor was the interest in theory that emerged in the wake of scathing critiques of business school curricula that were published in 1959. Funded by the Ford Foundation and the Carnegie Foundation, these critiques instructed business schools to "stop teaching descriptive material and start emphasizing theory and research" (Kernan 1994, p.2; also see Shimp 1993). In response, behavioral scientists interested in understanding the processes underlying human behavior began to focus their attention on *consumer* behavior. ACR was created as a forum for these academicians to interact with each other and with practitioners and public policy makers in their quest to better understand consumers.

Twenty-five years later seems to be an appropriate time to ask, where has the quest for theory led? Some observers contend that progress has been negligible. They echo sentiments expressed earlier in ACR's history when when such critics charge that we have borrowed theories without enriching them with insight unique to the consumer behavior context in which we operate, that our theories are impoverished and microscopic in their scope, and that the theories we do have are ill-tested and, as a result, are of little practical value. Still other observers have gone so far as to question whether theoretical, scientific knowing is distinct from other types of knowledge.

Before we heed any call to abandon the pursuit of scientific theory and to embrace some other approach, we need to scrutinize the source of our dissatisfaction. Much of this dissatisfaction is due to the confounding of the logic or philosophy of science with the sociology and psychology of science; we fail to distinguish between the progress that science has the potential to make and the circuitous route by which science often proceeds because of the behaviors of scientists. Although progress has not been linear, and consumer research can be accurately characterized as focusing more narrowly than might be desirable, there *is* evidence of impressive theoretical progress. Moreover, if progress is to remain our goal, it is an illusion to think that there is a viable alternative to the scientific pursuit of theory. What are sometimes presented as alternatives are, in reality, simply weaker versions of the traditional scientific approach. Greater progress in the next 25 years requires not abandoning theory, but rather requires a better understanding how to judge and apply theory.

---

[1] I owe a great debt to my colleagues and doctoral students (present and past) in the marketing department at Northwestern University for providing a supportive and intellectually stimulating environment. Special thanks are given to Bobby J. Calder and Brian Sternthal, who shared in the development of many ideas expressed in this address and who provided detailed feedback on earlier versions of this paper.

As a starting point in developing this thesis, consider the following five true-false items about theory and procedures for testing theory.

T or F   1) Progress can be increased by abandoning theory or by pursuing a different level of theory than we have sought in the past.

T or F   2) It is possible to render a unique explanation for a simple (two-level) main effect.

T or F   3) Certain measures and data collection procedures must be followed when testing a theory if theoretical progress is to be made.

T or F   4) Predictions constitute more rigorous tests of theory than postdictions.

T or F   5) A well-designed study will provide theoretical insight and will allow generalization of the effects observed to a real world situation of interest.

I'll return these items later in my remarks. For the moment, let me indicate that there is substantial disagreement about whether the correct response to these statements is true or false. To resolve this disagreement, let me begin by discussing theory and theoretical progress in consumer research.

THEORY AND THEORETICAL PROGRESS IN CONSUMER RESEARCH

Confusion about theory is reflected in the paradoxical uses of the term. Theory refers to specific, scientific principles that are used to explain a set of real-world phenomena. Theory also refers to guesses or conjectures that may be in opposition to reality (as in the case of statements such as, "well that's true in theory, but not in practice"). It is no wonder that misunderstandings of theory abound!

For the purpose of today's remarks, I will use the term theory with reference to a hypothesized set of relationships or a nomological network linking abstractions known as constructs. The constructs and the relationships between them cannot be observed. Instead, the adequacy of a theory is assessed in relation to observations about real-world phenomena, with preference given to the theory that can account for phenomena most parsimoniously. Thus, the goal of theory is ultimately a highly practical one; to enable us to explain and to predict the world in which we live.

Although a theory may gain acceptance, it always remains a "work in process," because new observations have the possibility of contradicting a preferred theory and prompting its revision or replacement. It is in this manner that scientific knowledge is seen as offering the *possibility* of progress.

While progress is a possibility, it has recently been argued the sociology of science makes this possibility remote at best. The contention is that, in reality:

Ego-involved Theorists persevere indefinitely in the face of Theory-disconfirming results. Theory 'tests' are so imperfect

FIGURE 1

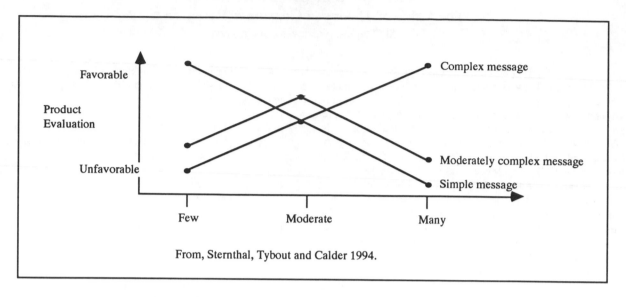

From, Sternthal, Tybout and Calder 1994.

that they can always be written off. When consumer behavior Theories are 'tested,' they do not get better or even change. And, Theory-oriented consumer researchers neither replicate their findings nor systematically investigate the range and limits of their work. (Wells 1993, p. 497).

To assess the validity of this analysis, let us turn to the specific body of theory that has been the focus of much attention within ACR. A substantial portion of consumer research has focused upon how individuals acquire and use information in making consumption decisions. Has theorizing on this topic evolved in the past 25 years?

In 1970, Berlyne proposed a two-factor theory that predicted a nonmonotonic relationship (inverted U) between stimulus familiarity and liking. This outcome is predicated on the assumption that early exposures to a stimulus lead to positive habituation due to a reduction in uncertainty, whereas later exposures result in tedium due to satiation.

In 1979, Cacioppo and Petty offered a more detailed view of the process underlying the nonmonotonic relationship proposed by Berlyne. They reasoned that exposures affect the time to think about the stimulus and, thus, the content of thoughts that people generate. This initial Elaboration Likelihood Model offered a robust explanation, accounting for many findings in the psychology literature and in the consumer behavior literature.

In the past five years, the Elaboration Likelihood Model has been extended and modified by consumer researchers. While the elaboration construct offers an explanation of persuasive message processing and attitudinal effects, it does not enable anticipation of *when* elaboration will enhance persuasion and *when* it will undermine it. To address this limitation the notion of resources as the engine that fuels elaboration was introduced. The idea is that persuasion is maximized when the resources required for message processing are matched by those available: too few resources inhibit message processing and too many prompt idiosyncratic thinking—in both instances reducing the processing of the message and thus its persuasive impact (Anand and Strenthal 1990). The theory that elaboration results in the greatest persuasion when resource requirements and demands are matched provides a cogent account for a wide range of repetition effects reported in the literature.

But progress did not stop here. There is a recurrent finding of a null effect of repetition when complex stimuli composed of ads and programming or editorial material are used. These outcomes have been construed by some investigators as evidence that theory fails to offer meaningful application. However, there is emerging evidence that we can explain the moderating role of contextual factors on repetition effects by viewing elaboration not as a single notion but as being of two distinct types. One type of elaboration bolsters the retrieval of the target object and its category membership and, a second type of elaboration helps distinguish the target object from its alternatives.

Thus, in the past 15 years we have extended the initial idea that persuasion is based on elaboration first by introducing antecedent resource conditions to anticipate the impact of elaboration and, more recently, by distinguishing two types of elaboration that can account for the effects of context on the persuasiveness of a message. This is impressive theoretical progress.

And just as important, from a practical perspective, we have progressed from being able to account for the effect of the repetition of a single ad to being able to explain the impact of repetition and a host of others variables that represent the same construct in a complex settings that reflect everyday situations! Consider as an example the industry practice of theater testing to assess the effectiveness of alternative advertising executions. The typical theater test exposes people to three repetitions of alternative ads and compares the effectiveness of these ads in terms of recall and brand preference. The assumption is that is that the ad that results in greater recall and brand preference in the theater test also will be the ad that is the more effective under natural viewing conditions, even though natural conditions may involve higher levels of repetition. However, current theorizing about information processing suggests that such an assumption is only justified if the two ads are similar in their comprehension difficulty. If, instead, one ad is more complex than the other, the simpler ad may dominate at moderate levels of repetition and this pattern may be reversed when repetition is higher, as illustrated in the graph (Figure 1). Thus, theory informs practitioners about factors that must be taken into account in constructing and interpreting research intended for specific application.

FIGURE 2
Levels of Abstraction in Research

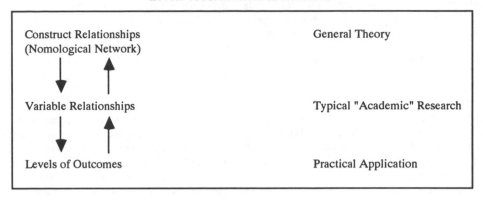

In addition to enhancing understanding of the relationship between repetition and persuasion, theorizing about elaboration and cognitive resources also can explain phenomena such as when and why vivid messages have their impact, when the use of color in ads is likely to have greater impact than black and white ads and when the reverse is true (Meyers-Levy and Peracchio, in process), and when self-reference is an effective message device and when it is not (Burnkrant and Unnava, in press). And, the theory has been enriched by these efforts to expand the set of phenomena for which it accounts.

Of course, these advances in understanding consumer information processing have not been the result of one researcher or one study. Rather, such progress reflects the effectiveness of the larger, scientific process.

While you might agree that the stream of work just described does indeed represent significant progress, it is still reasonable to ask why we haven't made more progress both within the specific realm consumer information processing and within the more general domain of understanding consumers' behavior and consumption experiences. My view is that the preoccupation with variables and procedures in judging theoretical explanations of phenomena has been a major impediment to our progress.

ASSESSING THEORY

To elaborate on this view, it is necessary to distinguish three levels of abstraction that may be employed in interpreting research. As depicted in the diagram (Figure 2), the first, most concrete level reflects an interest in the particular outcome(s) observed. The theater testing of ads described earlier represents such a situation. The ad sponsor is interested in determining which ad is more effective so that the more effective ad can be aired. Although some implicit (or even explicit) theoretical notions may have contributed to the design and to the testing of the alternative ads, it is the outcome observed in the theater test, and not any theoretical notion, that the researcher seeks to generalize.

This type of ground-level effects generalization is typical in many business settings. Firms and managers adopt procedures and techniques that have been shown to be effective in specific case examples often with little scrutiny of the underlying assumptions and the appropriateness of these assumptions to the situation of application. Thus, firms have embraced downsizing, out-sourcing, TQM, benchmarking, re-engineering, and delighting customers (though not necessarily in that order! see Iacobucci, Grayson, and Ostrom 1994).

An alternative, more abstract interpretation of research occurs at the level of variable relationships. Here, the goal is to identify those variable relationships that are robust and to confirm a particular interpretation of such relationships.

Historian Frank Sulloway's research on the role of birth order in historical events has been featured in the general media recently and can serve as an illustration of this approach (Stiff 1994). Sulloway's thesis is that birth order is a critical determinant of one's willingness to embrace radical ideas. The priviledged status of first borns is argued to result in their being conservative and favoring the status quo. By contrast, latter borns, who are less advantaged, are reasoned to be more open-minded, innovative, and rebellious than first borns. In an effort to confirm this hypothesis, Sulloway analyzed a database profiling 6,000 influential historical figures, including Voltaire, Darwin, Lenin, and Einstein. His findings indicate that birth order is superior to other variables, such as social class, in accounting for how people respond to radical new ideas. This confirmation is viewed as especially powerful because it is based on so many observations.

Many studies in consumer research also reflect an interest in identifying and interpreting general variable relationships. For example, research might be conducted to examine the relationship between the presence or absence of pictures and persuasion. The notion might be that pictures reinforce an auditory message, enhancing learning and, thereby, increasing persuasion. This hypothesis could be confirmed by a study demonstrating that an ad with a picture resulted in more persuasion than an ad without a picture. Support for the hypothesis would be bolstered, however, if a manipulation check revealed that the picture was perceived to reinforce the message, if recall measures showed improved performance when a picture was present, and if cognitive responses indicated more positive thoughts when a picture was present. These additional opportunities to confirm would be viewed as making the interpretation rendered more convincing.

Interest in variable relationships is understandable; variables are the currency of theory. However, efforts to equate a variable with particular construct are inappropriate. If a variable were always related to a particular construct, there would be no need for constructs. A single variable may operationalize a variety of different constructs or different levels of a single construct as a function of the people, setting, and time being examined. For example, a picture may serve to repeat or reinforce a message, but a picture may also usurp resources and prompt idiosyncratic thoughts or emotions.

To illustrate the complexity of the variable-construct relationship, let us return to Sulloway's birth order research. Birth order is an intriguing variable because it has a substantial impact on one's life experience. However this impact implies that birth order captures many concepts; not merely one's investment in the status quo. Indeed, Sulloway acknowledges this fact in offering an explanation for the finding that first borns, who are argued to be conservative, dominated the French Revolution. He attributes this outcome to a second construct, first borns' tendency to be "tough-minded," and suggests that tough-mindedness is a factor when "extended revolutions lead to terror." Thus, the challenge is to identify the most *appropriate* interpretation of variable relationships. This requires moving to the level of general theory and adopting parsimony, rather than confirmation, as the criterion against which theory tests are judged.

Despite the requirement that explanation be in terms of nomological networks of constructs and not in terms of variable relationships per se, there is much resistance to moving to this, highest level of abstraction. Why? From a sociological perspective, remaining at the variable or near-variable level enables numerous experts or leaders to coexist, albeit each in very narrowly defined areas. This serves a practical purpose of accommodating the tenure review process, which at most major institutions requires that a candidate be a leader or expert in some defined area. Thus, our field includes as experts in variables such as repetition, source credibility, attitude-toward-the-ad, and so on.

From a psychological perspective, focusing on variables and procedures fosters the (comforting) illusion that one can know the value of a study before the data are collected. It also provides an easy means for evaluating others' research; if the interpretation of the variables is similar to that in prior research and if all the manipulation checks and so-called process measures are in place, the study is viewed as lacking any "fatal flaw." A practical problem is that studies examining trival or near-tautological hypotheses, as well as ones in which the outcomes are dictated by the procedures (i.e., studies in which subjects seem to have no degrees of freedom), will yield confirmations of these hypotheses (see Wallach and Wallach 1994). This implies that an additional criterion must also be invoked. A common approach is to assert that the research somehow be "interesting." This too is an easy judgment to render; one simply introspects on whether the research results are reconcilable with, but not identical to, the point of view held prior to reading the research. Notice, however, that such judgments are idiosyncratic because they are tied to one's personal knowledge base. It is impossible for researchers to know what will be viewed as "interesting" by a set of reviewers in advance of receiving their opinions.

In short, focusing on variables and confirmation may serve sociological and psychological needs, but in so doing, we depart from the logic of science and, thereby, abandons the possiblity of progress. Instead of confirming an interpretation or attempting to divine what will be "interesting" to an as yet selected set of reviewers, we should strive to select the *best* explanation available at a point in time. This implies the criterion parsimony.

A parsimonious interpretation of data can only be achieved through the application of convergence or triangulation procedures. These procedures require multiple variable-level operationalizations of each construct being examined. While the need for triangulation is well-known and widely endorsed, in practice researchers often present construct-level interpretations that rest on a single operationalizations. This cannot be justified.

While multiple variables are required, convergence procedures are indifferent to whether these measures include manipulation checks and so-called process measures. Nor is it an issue whether the experimenter measured or manipulated the independent variables. Convergence can be achieved either by multiple dependent measures or by multiple independent variables.

What matters is whether the pattern of results on *whatever* measures are available (from new research and evidence previously reported) can be interpreted uniquely at a theoretical level. This can only be determined after the fact and by examining the data, not by examining the procedures and measures per se. (Unless, of course, the hypothesis is a tautology.) If a uniquely parsimonious interpretation is offered, then the research makes a contribution to knowledge and the theory is accepted until such time when a more parsimonious alternative or an equally parsimonious but more encompassing alternative becomes available. (See Sternthal, Tybout, and Calder 1987 for an extended discussion of these issues.)

An interesting and, to some, a counterintuitive by-product of how theoretical progress is made is that prediction holds no advantage over post hoc explanation (See Sternthal et al. 1987; 1994; Brinberg, Lynch, and Sawyer 1992). Indeed, just the opposite may be argued to be the case; post-hoc explanation is to be preferred.

When a prediction is tested, the opportunity to assess whether alternative explanations offer as good accounts for the data as the favored view is limited. When tests are post hoc, rival explanations have had such an opportunity. Brush (1989) illustrates this point when discussing two types of evidence for Einstein's theory of relativity: light bending which was predicted before it was observed, and Mercury's orbit which was explained after it was observed:

> rather than light bending providing better evidence because it was predicted before the observation, it actually provides less secure evidence for that very reason....Because the Mercury orbit discrepancy had been known for several decades theorists had already had ample opportunity to explain it...and had failed to do so...Light bending, on the other hand, had not previously been discussed theoretically...but now that the phenomenon was known to exist one might expect that another equally or more satisfactory explanation would be found (p.1126).

Recognizing the irrelevance of when an explanation for data is developed, prominent psychologists such as Daryl Bem (1987, 1991) argue that, when writing a research report, it is perfectly appropriate, and may even be desirable from a communication standpoint, to present as hypotheses notions that were developed after the data were collected. To some this seems heretical; it misleads the reader by implying prediction when the reality is postdiction (Kerr 1994). But this view rests on a false assumption, fostered by a confirmation orientation, that a variable represents a particular construct and, therefore, the failure of a variable to behave as anticipated is newsworthy. If the fact that variables can represent *many* constructs is acknowledged, then deducing the construct operationalized by the variable after the fact is necessary and certainly does no harm to theoretical progress. Moralistic or other non-scientific concerns must be invoked in any attempt to justify a preference for prediction.

Thus, I believe that one reason that we have not seen more theoretical progress because we have not paid enough attention to what theory requires. Too often we have been focused on variables and procedures per se and not on how these variables and procedures inform us about abstract relationships between constructs. For greater progress we must shift our focus to a more abstract, theoretical level and hold our research to the single criterion of identifying a uniquely parsimonious explanation, at least for the moment. We should strive for theories that are universal in the sense that when we become aware of the limits of our theories this should be taken as an opportunity to modify or replace the theory with one that is again encompassing.

It would be naive to ignore the sociological and psychological pressures that sometimes run counter to the logic of science. In fact, it may even be worthwhile to make responses to such pressures the subject of theoretical examination, for they are nothing more than additional data points to be explained. But recognition of these influences in no way implies that they offer a viable alternative to the logic of science in pursuing the goal of progress. If we are seeking progress, there is no alternative to parsimony in judging our theoretical explanations.

You may have observed that I have made only passing reference to how the phenomena that we attempt to explain are documented. Perhaps your awareness of my own style of research and the language of "theory testing" have created the impression that my remarks are primarily applicable to experimental data. I do not believe this to be the case. The criterion of a uniquely parsimonious interpretation can be applied to explanations of ethnographic data, scanner data, and so on. Indeed, as indicated earlier, I am not aware of any other criterion that could be applied appropriately if our goal is progress in understanding.

THEORY IN USE

Beyond changing the way in which we value and assess theory, our progress will be enhanced by broadening the phenomena we attempt explain, as several previous ACR presidents have argued eloquently. This is because failures are more likely than successes to spur theory revision or the development of new theory. (Though, we cannot know which new phenomena will be especially enlightening in this respect a priori.)

But, in attempting to apply existing theory to specific circumstances that may be of interest, it is important to recognize that the central benefit of theory, its relevance across specific circumstances, implies that theory can only anticipate general patterns of relationships. And, translating these relationships into predictions relevant to a particular set of circumstances will likely require numerous assumptions about which constructs and the level of these constructs that are represented by the variables of interest. Further, if assumptions about how the variables map onto constructs are erroneous, even a good theory will make inaccurate predictions. The establishment of a construct-variable link necessarily must rely on empiricism.

These limitations are at the core of many criticisms regarding the value of theory. What good is theory if all it can offer is imprecise (relational) prediction that rests on assumptions about variable-construct relationships, which could be wrong? Theory doesn't seem to get us very far. Why not go "direct," stay at the level of the variables, and skip the abstraction to theory.

The answer is, of course, that there is no escaping the need for theory. How does the researcher know which aspects of any given situation should be studied and which might reasonably be ignored? The researcher's logic for believing that selected variables might affect purchase behavior constitutes a theoretical explanation of the variable relationships. This theory too often remains implicit and untested when more explicit consideration would seem to be beneficial. As evidence for this point, recall the theater testing of commercials discussed earlier.

Thus, when substantial resources are at stake, theory application is served by additional research that examines the calibration of the theory the situation. In such research, the theory is:

... unfolded or re-expanded; that is, the compressed general statement that constitutes the theory must be supplemented with detailed information about the special case (Gell-Mann 1994, p.77).

While using theory may be seen as requiring too many assumptions, assumptions are unavoidable. Theory forces us to be more explicit about these assumptions and thereby, increases the likelihood that the reasonableness of those assumptions will be considered in light of prior research and with concern for the real-world conditions to which the theory is being applied.

It has been suggested that there is an intermediate ground of theory somewhere between abstract, universal theory and variable-level description (Wells 1993). Indeed, this is probably descriptive of the theories that we actually have. But application is not served by striving for explanation at this level. When limits to a theory are identified, future application is better served by revising the theory in the direction of universality than by delimiting its boundaries more narrowly. For example, if one attempts to explain persuasion in terms of consumers' ability and motivation to engage in various types of cognitive elaboration, one has no basis for saying that the relationship applies to, say, advertisements presented on television but not via direct mail advertisements or to advertisements for nondurables but not to advertisements for durables. Such a view confuses variables with constructs. And if the *constructs* cannot account for phenomena within the domain of the theory, then the theory is of questionable value on the very grounds that it is *not* universal (i.e., it cannot explain relevant phenomena).

I believe that our field would benefit from more efforts to develop and test theory-based interventions or applications (see Calder, Phillips, and Tybout 1981). In constructing such interventions, attention would center on the variable-construct mapping, with the construct-to-construct mapping assumed to be accurate. To avoid extreme particularism, such applications would strive to address problems that might emerge in a variety of situations. For example, one might compare alternative, theory-based strategies for combatting various types of rumors or one might explore alternative campaigns for charitable donations.

Separating theory testing and theory application is predicated on the notion that it is difficult to *design* research that is optimal for both goals. The goal of rigorously assessing theoretical deductions and the goal of generalizing to a particular real world situation typically are served by different choices with respect to the research setting, subjects, and independent and dependent variables (see Calder et al. 1981). Thus, it is necessary to give priority to *either* theoretical or problem-solving goals in a particular study. Contrary to what we are told or may wish; we can't have it all—at least not all at once.

In this regard, I am reminded of an article that I read several years ago. In it the author discussed the interaction between the various roles that women play; worker, wife, mother, daughter, friend etc. She noted that the roles allow women to express different, complementary aspects of their personality. But the roles can also compete for attention and, thereby impair performance. This point was illustrated by describing a situation in which a woman was physically in the workplace but mentally elsewhere during an important staff meeting. Where was she? She was busy making a mental list of tasks related to her other roles, as wife/mother/daughter/friend and so on. Few among us, regardless of gender, have escaped this experience. It is simply a fact of busy rich lives. But don't we enjoy what we are doing more when we immerse ourselves in it for the moment? And might not this idea be applied to our research? We would do well to focus sometimes on assessing theory and other times on using theory in an effort to solve important problems in the real-world.

Thus, I suggest that the goal of better theory is also served by distinguishing between studies that have as a primary goal theory testing and studies that have as their primary goal theory application. Each has value, each may inform the other, but it difficult to design research that optimizes both. More generally, I borrow the words of Speck:

> Science is served in many ways: By intelligent discussion and fresh proposals, by the extension or completion of previously presented theories, by the fair-minded and unflinching evaluation of current proposals, by justly protesting, blowing the whistle, and pointing out that this kingly theory or that is not wearing a shred of evidence, by sometimes synthesizing and sometimes isolating, by daring to be explicit and—ironically—by daring to be suggestive. It is when scientists and philosophers of science cannot make up their minds as to which role they are playing or—what is worse—try to fill several roles at one, that matters go awry. Then the Ivory Tower and the Tower of Babel sound disturbingly alike. (Paul Surgi Speck as quoted in Hunt 1993, p. 176)

THEORETICAL CREATIVITY

Whether focusing on a theory or on solving a problem, we need to foster creativity. As discussed earlier, too often we are hidebound by our desire for concreteness and specific procedures; we define the phenomena to be explained and/or what would constitute an adequate explanation far too narrowly. A classic puzzle illustrates this well. If you have never seen this puzzle take a moment to try it.

Draw no more than four straight lines (without lifting the pencil from the paper) which will cross through all nine dots.

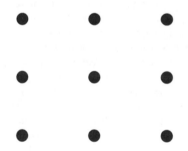

Once you know the trick, that there is no reason to be confined by the imaginary boundary around the perimeter of the puzzle, the solution becomes easy (see a, Figure 3) If fact, it is possible to solve the puzzle with only three lines if you also reject the notion that the lines must go through the center of the dots (b). And if you are willing to fold the paper in a complex manner (c) or cut the paper and paste the dots in a row, (d) one line will do quite nicely. Or, easier still, as one ten year old suggested, just get a very fat writing "apparatice (sic)" (Adams 1986, 24-32).

The problem is that too often we fail to think outside of the box when defining the phenomena to be explained or the problem to be addressed. Evidence of this is everywhere. Ph.D. students who collect data for the first time are often stumped when they obtain significant but unanticipated results. It is not that the results are uninterpretable or uninteresting. Often they are at least as interesting as what was expected and they *can* be explained. But the explanation cannot emerge until one abandons the original frame or expectations.

Thus, we must ask ourselves, what are the *real* constraints we face in our research? When developing an explanation, the phenomena to be explained (not the procedures and measures per se) represent the only relevant constraint. When applying theory, the theory itself, as well as any practical constraints on implementation warrant consideration.

How can we eschew inappropriate constraints on our theoretical creativity? Some insight is suggested by reflecting on the people and situations in which we observe creative insight. I have noticed that, in seminars, the most profound questions are not necessarily asked by the people who are most knowledgeable about the particular topic. An intelligent, highly motivated audience member from another, related field is often able to seize on the key issues or assumptions that should be debated while the so-called experts are buried in details. In a very different realm but a similar manner, children's *lack* of detailed knowledge enables them often to pose profound questions, as any parent has experienced.

Should we turn our research programs over to people in other areas or our children? Perhaps that's not such a bad idea. But before we do that, we might try training ourselves to think more abstractly and relationally, seeking parallels across seemingly disparate phenomena. Many exercises and techniques exist that encourage more abstract thinking (e.g., Adams 1986). No doubt you are generally familiar with many of these tools and may even have some colleagues who supplement their faculty income by training groups of executives to solve problems through brainstorming, synectics, and the like. Yet too often, creativity training (ironically) sees its primary application in business settings. When we attempt theoretical research we run for the safe "box" of previously used variables, procedures, and explanations. We decry the absence of more strict replications (which, in fact, are technically impossible to conduct and are inherently less informative than conceptual replications). To make more progress, must break out of our theoretical boxes.

CONCLUSION

In summary, let me return to the true-false items presented earlier. As you have probably inferred by now, I believe that the correct answer to each item is "false," that these are myths about theory and procedures for testing theory.

Myth 1: Progress can be increased by abandoning theory or pursuing a different level of theory than we have sought in the past.

Reality: There is no alterative to theory, there are only alternative theories.

Myth 2: It is possible to render a unique explanation for a simple (two-level) main effect.

Reality: Theoretical explanations cannot be tied to any single variable, they are inherently abstract and can only be inferred by employing convergence or triangulation procedures.

Myth 3: Certain measures or data collection procedures must be followed when testing a theory if theoretical progress is to be made. The absence of these measures or procedures constitutes a "fatal flaw."

FIGURE 3

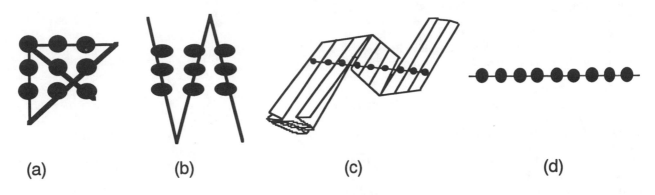

(a)   (b)   (c)   (d)

Reality: While *multiple* measures are required for convergence or triangulation on theoretical constructs, any set of multiple measures, collected by any combination of methods can be adequate for assessing theory. The only fatal flaw is the presence of rival, equally parsimonious interpretation. (Though an inspection of procedures may offer insight as to *why* you failed to arrive at a unique explanation.)

Myth 4: Predictions constitute more rigorous tests of theory than postdictions.

Reality: When a theoretical explanation is developed is immaterial to its rigor. Parsimony can occur at any point in time.

Myth 5: A well-designed study will provide theoretical insight and will allow generalization of the effects observed to a real-world situation of interest.

Reality: Theory testing and generalization typically imply different choices regarding the subjects, the setting, and the selection of independent and dependent variables. Thus, a particular study should give clear priority to one of these goals.

Although I contend that we have made significant theoretical progress in certain areas of consumer research, junior researchers have no reason to fear that all or even most of the important questions have been answered. At the same time, there is reason to believe that we can make substantial progress in the next 25 years. A starting point for this journey is to abandon the myths that I have outlined. Instead, focus on the true nature and value of theory.

Consumer research offers a rich context in which to assess the robustness of explanations developed elsewhere. And, there is less need to focus on a narrow set of variables than there might be in a more mature, more densely populated discipline (for sociological reasons). We have greater opportunity to pursue integration of theories and convergence through creative application of methods.

To harness our potential, it may be opportune for teams of consumer researchers focus on specific consumption related issues or problems in the marketplace, with the goal of designing and testing theory-based interventions. There have been impassioned calls for such efforts (Hirschman 1989, Andreasan 1991), but to date progress has been limited to an exchange of ideas in ACR sessions and has not been translated into any hands-on projects. Such projects would be one means of operationalizing the theoretical creativity that I referred to earlier, a Consumer Behavior

Odyssey of a different sort. Possible topics need not be limited to, but might include, exploring the impact of technology on consumer behavior or examining programs intended to reduce dysfunctional consumption behaviors.

One final comment. After my reference to Sulloway's birth order findings, some of you may have been ruminating about whether I am a first born or a latter born. On the one hand, you might reason that some of my views, say that post hoc explanations have the same status as a priori ones, are unconventional, implying that I am a latter born. On the other hand, you might reasonably interpret the general tenor of these remarks as an appeal to traditional values of theory and science, and, thereby, infer that I must be a first born. Therein lies the problem. It is possible for me to hold both views that are unconventional and ones that embrace the status quo, but I cannot be both first born and latter born—at least not in this lifetime. Thus, birth order (or any other variable) can never provide a satisfactory explanation for my attitudes and behaviors...... however, for the record, I'm a first born.

Thank you for this opportunity to speak to you.

REFERENCES

Adams, James L. (1986), *Conceptual Blockbusting*, Reading MA: Addison-Wesley.

Anand, Punam and Sternthal, Brian (1990), "Ease of Message Processing as a Moderation of Repetition Effects in Advertising," *Journal of Marketing Research*, 27 (August), 345-53.

Andreasen, Alan (1992), "A Social Marketing Research Agenda for Consumer Behavior Researchers, " in *Advances in Consumer Research*, Vol. 20, eds. L. McAlister and M. L. Rothschild, Provo, UT: Association for Consumer Research, 1-5.

Bem, Daryl (1987), "Writing the Empirical Journal Article," in *The CompleatAcademic: A Practical Guide for the Beginning Social Scientist*, eds M. Zanna and J. Darley, New York: Random House, 171-201.

Bem, Daryl (1991), "Writing the Research Report," *Research in Methods in Social Relations*, (6th Edition), eds. C. Judd, E. Smith, and L. Kidder, Fort Worth, TX: Holt 453-476.

Berlyne, Donald E. (1970), "Novelty, Complexity, and Hedonic Value," *Perception and Psychophysics*, 8, 279-89.

Brinberg, David, Lynch Jr., John G., and Sawyer, Alan G. (1992), "Hypothesized and Confounded Explanations in Theory Tests: A Bayesian Analysis," *Journal of Consumer Research*, 19, 139-54.

Brush, Stephen G. (1989), "Prediction and Theory Evaluation: The Case of Light Bending," *Science*, 246, 1124-9.

Burnkrant, Robert E. and Unnava, H. Rao (in press), "Effects of Self-Referencing on Persuasion," *Journal of Consumer Research.*

Cacioppo, John T. and Petty, Richard E. (1979), "Effects of Message Repetition and Position on Cognitive Response, Recall, and Persuasion," *Journal of Personality and Social Psychology*, 37 (January), 97-109.

Calder, Bobby J., Phillips, Lynn W., and Tybout, Alice M. (1981), "Designing Research for Application," *Journal of Consumer Research*, 8, 197-207.

Gell-Mann, Murray (1994), *The Quark and the Jaguar*, New York: W. H. Freeman and Company.

Hirschman, Elizabeth (1990), "Secular Mortality and the Dark Side of Consumer Behavior: Or How Semiotics Saved My Life" in *Advances in Consumer Research*, Vol.18, eds. R. H. Holman and M. Soloman, Provo, UT: Association for Consumer Research, 1-4.

Hunt, Shelby (1993), *Modern Marketing Theory: Critical Issues in the Philosophy of Marketing Science*, Cincinnati, OH: South-Western Publishing Co.

Iacobucci, Dawn, Grayson, Kent, and Ostrom, Amy (1994), "Customer Satisfaction Fables," *Sloan Management Review*, Summer, 93-96.

Kernan, Jerome (1994), "Declaring a Discipline: Reflections on ACR's Silver Anniversary," in *Advances in Consumer Research*, Vol. 22, eds., F. Kardes and M. Sujan, Provo, UT: Association for Consumer Research.

Kerr, Norbert (1994), FRCRP Project, Department of Psychology, Michigan State University, East Lansing, Michigan 48824.

Meyers-Levy, Joan and Peracchio, Laura (in process), "Understanding the Effects of Color: How the Correspondence Between Available and Required Resources Affects Attitudes," *Journal of Consumer Research.*

Shimp, Terence (1993), "Academic Appalachia and the Discipline of Consumer Research," in *Advances in Consumer Research*, Vol. 21, D. Roedder John and C. Allen, Provo, UT: Association for Consumer Research, 1-7.

Sternthal, Brian, Tybout, Alice M. and Calder, Bobby J. (1994) "Experimental Design: Generalization and Theoretical Explanation", in *Principles of Marketing Research*, ed. R.P. Bagozzi, Cambridge Mass.: Blackwell Publishers, 195-223.

Sternthal, Brian, Tybout, Alice M. and Calder, Bobby J. (1987), "Confirmatory versus Comparative Approaches to Judging Theory Tests," *Journal of Consumer Research*, 14 (June), 114-25.

Stiff, David (1994) "Blame the Birth Order for History's Revolts, This MIT Scholar Says," *Wall Street Journal*, August 23, 1994 1, 8.

Wallach, Lise and Wallach Michael A. (1994), "Gergen Versus the Mainstream: Are Hypotheses in Social Psychology Subject to Empirical Test?," *Journal of Personality and Social Psychology*, 67, 2, 233-242.

Wells, William D. (1993), "Discovery-oriented Consumer Research," *Journal of Consumer Research*, 19 (March), 489-504.

ACR FELLOW'S ADDRESS
Awards, Rewards, Prizes, and Punishments

Russell W. Belk, University of Utah

In the year I have had to reflect on the honor of the ACR Fellow's Award, I have come to realize that awards are a very special type of consumer good. Not only are awards rare and momentous, but we can neither purchase them nor plan their acquisition. In one view awards are a ritual distinction bestowed by an organization that seeks to convey honor and prestige to selected individuals and by so-doing gain a certain prestige and legitimacy from the honorees who accept these distinctions (Goode 1973). As an alternative to such reciprocal exchange, awards may also be more one-sided agapic gifts of love and respect. By choosing to analyze such awards and related phenomena in this address, I do not mean to behave ungraciously like the teacher played by Sidney Portier in the film *To Sir With Love* (Clavell 1967) who receives a love note from a student, only to pedantically and dispassionately correct its grammar and return it to the love struck but now shattered young girl who had penned it. Therefore please allow me to begin by saying "thank you!". This is a profound honor for which I am deeply grateful.

Having said that in all sincerity, I should also share with you the fact that the title I initially had in mind was "Awards and Why I Hate Them." The impetus for this investigation was my curiosity about my own behavior; specifically the certain knowledge that once I get the award plaque home, no one will see it again. It will instead enter the recesses of a filing cabinet where it will join a small number of miscellaneous trophies I have been fortunate enough to receive as an adult. For some time this resting place has seemed natural and right to me, but until the last few years I have not known why. Now I think I can understand my uneasiness with awards at several different levels. By exploring the roots of my uneasiness in the following analysis of awards, rewards, prizes, and punishments, perhaps I may stimulate other consumer researchers to take an interest in these significant but largely neglected aspects of consumption.

CONCEPTS

Rewards and Punishments

In behavioral learning theory rewards and punishments are positive and negative reinforcements used for shaping behavior. A behavior may also automatically bring it's own rewards and punishments as when we try a new food and learn that it tastes good or bad. But I am concerned here with rewards and punishments actively used to achieve a purpose. I am most interested in the macro impacts of material reinforcers including self-rewards and self-punishments.

A reward or punishment is always contingent; it is provided, promised, or threatened contingent upon the performance of a behavior someone deems desirable or undesirable. Prominent consumer behavior examples include giving or denying treats to our pets, children, students, and other small animals over whom we exercise authority. Generally the reward or punishment follows or is concurrent with the behavior. If the behavior is instead in the future, the reward is offered as an incentive or bribe (Noonan 1984). A promise or threat of a future reward or punishment may be used as an incentive or disincentive to mold behaviors, as when children are told that they had better be "good" or else Santa Claus will not bring them gifts or will even punish them instead.

Some reinforcers are inherently positive or negative, but in many cases their valence is socially constructed. Thus Tom Sawyer (Twain 1958) was able to frame whitewashing a fence as desirable by promising it as a reward for those friends who first did favors for Tom or gave him their valuables. Similarly, in the Frederick Pohl (1983) story, "The Midas Plague," in a future world of abundance, consuming becomes a punishment so that those who are "poor" are forced to consume more opulently and lavishly. One of the inadvertent consumer socialization outcomes of using rewards is the valorization of the reward and depreciation of the behavior required to achieve it. For instance, if we insist that our children finish studying before they can watch television, we disparage studying as onerous and venerate television viewing as desirable. Similarly, if we tell children they cannot have dessert unless they eat their vegetables, this valorizes desserts as something good and denigrates vegetables as a necessary evil.

Prizes and Awards

We can reward or punish ourselves as well as those who are dependent on us, but prizes and awards can only be conferred by others. We don't generally compete with others for rewards and punishments, but we do so for prizes and awards. For most of us prizes and rewards are also received less frequently than rewards and punishments. If a reward or punishment is generally deserved, a prize or an award may or may not be, with the selection of the recipients sometimes being determined by chance. Prize is a more generic term that brackets awards in this respect and may range from winning a lottery or sweepstakes that is totally subject to chance, to winning a competition where the outcome is based strictly on performance. Falling between these extremes, awards tend to have elements of both chance and performance. This is because award recipients are usually selected by judges based on subjective performance criteria.

The "contest system" (Gouldner 1965) in which prizes and awards are the payoff for success in competition with others, might be thought of as the dominant motivational model in Western society. But it is not the only one. One alternative is a cooperative system in which we jointly help each other rather than compete. The family is based on these principles as is the ideal of academia as a community of scholars. A second alternative motivational system included in McClelland's (McClelland, Atkinson, Clark, and Lowell 1953) conception of achievement motivation is competition against a self-imposed standard of excellence. In this case we compete, but only against ourselves and our internal standards. And a third alternative is competition against an external standard in a system that Ernest Thompson Seton called honor by standards (Mechling 1987). The President's fitness award to all children who qualify is an example. Unlike the contest system, none of these alternatives sets up a zero sum game in which one person's gain is another's loss.

UNDERLYING PARADIGMS

1. Instrumentalism

Behind awards, rewards, prizes, and punishments, the underlying model of human behavior is generally instrumental, egoistic, controlling, patriarchal, and positivistic. We behave as we do in order to increase chances for awards, rewards, and prizes and in order to decrease chances for punishments. We compete with others to win awards and prizes, and winning matters a great deal. According to this paradigm the key behavioral motives are seeking pleasure and avoiding pain; the pleasure principle tempered by the reality principle; an hedonic calculus seeking to maximize net pleasure. And the key to altering the behaviors of others who are so-motivated is selectively administered reinforcement. Osborne (1985) summarizes concerns with such reinforcement:

> One concern is that, if people are frequently rewarded, they will behave appropriately only when they are paid to do so. Some believe that reinforcing practices may interfere with the development of spontaneity, creativity, intrinsic motivational systems, and other highly valued self-determining personality characteristics. Others even consider the deliberate use of reinforcement as deceptive, manipulative, and an insult to the personal integrity of human beings (p. 988).

Therefore rewarding students for good grades with money, treats, food, or other perks, as is done by some school systems, local businesses, teachers, and parents, may kill interest in learning rather than encourage it (Kohn 1993). Moreover, resentment and reactance may result when others try to alter our behavior. An illustration is seen in foreign aid payments that, far from generating good will and gratitude, stimulate feelings of helplessness, dependency, and anger (Dillon 1968). These criticisms most clearly involve consumers in individualistic and materialistic cultures in which material rewards and punishments are employed to mold behavior. Besides elevating or lowering the esteem in which we hold the consumer goods used as reinforcers, the common use of material and monetary reinforcers has a secondary effect of reinforcing materialism and endorsing the view that happiness is something that can be purchased in stores. DeLong (1991) and Holbrook (1993) suggest that in celebrating the merchandize given as prizes, television game shows also stimulate and reinforce consumer culture.

Because awards are less directly contingent than rewards, their effect in reinforcing behavior is also less direct. Rather than strengthening the behavior that is thought to have led to the award, the recipient may instead celebrate by indulging in self-rewards. Furthermore, there may be an over-justification effect such that what was once done spontaneously for the sheer internal joy of doing it, comes to be seen as work done for external awards and as therefore contemptible (Deci 1971). We may also experience attention and envy that we neither sought nor desire. Or we may feel undeserving of the award; we are instead guilty impostors who, more sincerely than Wayne and Garth, believe that "we are not worthy" (Spheeris 1992). Future productivity, risk-taking, and creativity may also be impaired because, in symbolic self completion terms, we now enjoy the self-esteem connoted by *having* the award and feel that it is therefore less necessary to pursue self-esteem by *doing* the things that led to the award. There may be an accompanying feeling that our goals have been accomplished and that now there is nothing left to achieve. Accordingly, Wicklund and Gollwitzer (1982) report that the receipt of a Nobel prize typically signals the decline of the recipient's productivity. In all of these cases the gift of an award may be a Trojan horse that destroys our initiative for further achievements.

The award may also fail to benefit and may even harm the conferring organization. Like high value merchandise coupons given as purchase incentives, we may become less rather than more loyal to the organization that makes the award, since we can now rationalize that we only participated in the organization is for its

awards or prizes. Furthermore, awards can sometimes be corrupt, unfair, or a mere mutual admiration society distributing awards among an in-group in control of the organization. Poor selection of award recipients or too many such rewards may devaluate the organization rather than increase it's prestige and legitimacy. Following a race without beginning, end, or fixed course, and in this respect like most academic award competitions, the Dodo in *Alice's Adventures in Wonderland* (Carol 1930, p. 34) announced that "*Everybody* has won, and all must have prizes." Yet, if awards are to remain symbols of achievement in competition against others, this clearly can't be the case. Awards must be scarce to be valuable (Lynn 1992; Thierry 1992), even if that scarcity must be invented (Xenos 1989). As Klapp (1991) notes, the inflation of symbols, like the inflation of money, lessens these symbols' worth, sometimes to nothing.

From a societal perspective, awards reinforce competition. Even though awards are essentially nontangible, the pursuit of such honors is very much a part of the competitive distinction seeking found in materialism (Kassiola 1990). Although there have been attempts to develop non-competitive games (e.g., Mechling 1987; Orlick 1978) most societies prefer masculine games with winners and losers (Gilligan 1982). But this can breed envy, resentment, and discontent, especially where the awards are thought to be distributed unfairly. The possibility of discrimination, the sapping of initiative, and the precipitation of performance geared only to those criteria used in selecting award recipients, are other potential negative social consequences of awards. And to the extent that awards increase competition both the quality of research and scholarship and feelings of cooperation and communitas within a community of scholars may be harmed (Axelrod 1984; Hyde 1983). These are some, but not all, of the reasons why I dislike awards.

2. Self-Reinforcement

This second model is most germane to self-reward and punishment. Self reinforcement is demonstrated in some experiments by an animal that repeatedly pecks at a key or pushes a bar to produce pleasurable sensations in the brain. As Clement (1985) notes, human consumption areas potentially involving self-reinforcement include alcoholism, drug abuse, dating, impulse control disorders, physical exercise, and smoking. We might add to this list compulsive buying (O'Guinn and Faber 1989), gambling (Burns, Gillett, Rubinstein, and Gentry 1990), impulsive buying (Rook 1987), eating disorders (Grunert 1993), therapeutic self-gifts (Mick and DeMoss 1990), collecting (Belk forthcoming), and conspicuous consumption (Mason 1981). All of these behaviors involve dosing ourselves with self-administered consumption-based sources of anticipated pleasure and thereby reinforcing and learning associated behavioral patterns. As virtual reality becomes more of a reality, we are reminded of Nozick's (1974, pp. 42-45) question of whether we would indefinitely plug in to a hypothetical machine capable of giving us any experience we wished. Hopefully not, for if we do we will become the button-pecking lab animals of learning studies.

Besides positive self-reinforcement, we may occasionally also use negative self-reinforcement. We may chastise ourselves or do mild penance for "bad" behavior. The day after we over-eat or over-drink, we may fast, abstain, exercise vigorously, or complain that our body is suffering the consequences of our overindulgence. We may also try to reduce our excessive consumption through a rhetoric of self-control (Ainslee 1985; Hoch and Lowenstein 1991). The rhetoric of self-control versus self-indulgence appears to be a pervasive one in consumption, regardless of whether we focus on sexual consumption (Laqueur 1992), food consumption (Bordo

1990), or the various consumption habits and patterns perceived to affect our health (Crawford 1984). In each case we frame indulging or denying ourselves rewards as a battle for self-control. If controlling others has sinister connotations, controlling self is seen as virtuous in many cultures.

3. A Balance Sheet Model

Although the precedents go back farther in time and the practice is more universal, I once suggested that when we learn as children that there is no Santa Claus, we become our own Santa Claus and begin to reward ourselves (Belk 1987a). This tendency is recognized in recent work on reward self gifts (Mick and DeMoss 1990; Mick forthcoming; Sherry, McGrath, and Levy forthcoming). While rewards are not the only type of self-gift, we use things from the small rewards of a soft drink if we finish grading five more papers, to a new car if we graduate from college, in order to delay gratifications and give ourselves an additional reason for accomplishing something. This parallels the Puritanical achievement-oriented view of the way the world works: good things come to those who persevere and put work before pleasure. Thus when we eat dessert, we believe not only that we are getting the last course of the meal, but also our just desert—that which we deserve for eating the healthy but less sweet foods that preceded it. The longer postponement of Christmas gift-opening in higher social class households, supports the assumption that there are class differences in this tendency to delay gratifications, at least in Western cultures (Löfgren 1993; Searle-Chatterjee 1993).

A total model of individual justice would also demand that we punish ourselves when we are "bad." In many societies unearned rewards are seen as tainted with evil, just as the blame-the-victim phenomenon helps to preserve the myth that people always "get what's coming to them." If we don't get our deserved rewards and punishments now, we may believe we'll get them later in heaven, hell (multiple hells in Buddhism), or a future life (McDannell and Lang 1988; Tiger 1992). In the West, these beliefs are based on an Old Testament patriarchal God who rewards and punishes, as Garrison Keillor (1990) illustrates:

> It's a primitive sense of justice: you do bad, and your Creator smacks you one—but there it is. One day you're daydreaming at the wheel, you smash into someone's rear end. She gets out of her car, looks at the busted taillight, and smiles. She's relieved; she says, "Well it could've been a lot worse." You've just run into a guilty person. She did something in the past twenty-four hours that made her think the universe would land on her with both feet. She'd be covered with boils, wrapped in burlap, sitting in the ashes, flies on her, and lightning coming closer and closer, but all it is is a taillight. Not bad. She smiles and drives away. Now you start to feel guilty (pp. 104-105).

The perspective Keillor illustrates is that of sin and guilt. While not all cultures agree on what is sinful, all of the world's major organized religions invoke a notion of sin that precipitates either guilt or more collective shame (Fürer-Haimendorf 1974). And although sin has lost some of its power in a secular age (Menninger 1973), it has not disappeared (Capps 1993). But the contemporary Western God and Santa Claus have lost their earlier punitive characters (Belk 1993), and we too shy away from punishing ourselves, at least by willingly engaging in aversive behaviors in order to suffer. We may sometimes give to charities out of feelings that we have more than we deserve, but it is more common that we only delay or deny self-rewards. In one characterization,

self-punishment is neurotic or even psychotic masochism (Johnson 1987). Moreover, as a part of a society that has learned the deficit spending pattern of consumer debt, we may be more inclined to pay for our self-rewards with *future* "good" behavior. Thus the rationalization that an ice cream sundae is something I deserve, because I'm going to start dieting tomorrow. Pre-Lenten celebrations of Mardi Gras and Carnival invoke this principle as well. Similarly, we tend through prayers and entreaties to make bargains with God that "I will be good or do penance or give to the poor or make a sacrifice *IF* God will first grant my wish."

We may either self-administer anticipated pleasures when we feel we need them (the self-reinforcement model) or when we feel we deserve them (the balance sheet model). As with receiving awards, rewards, prizes, and punishments doled out by others, an alternative regulating theoretical principle to that of self-administered need-based pleasure is that of deservingness or justice: do we experience positive and negative outcomes in a way or with a result that is perceived as deserved or fair? A variety of related psychological perspectives have been advanced to predict interpersonal behaviors based on such perceptions. These include distributive justice, equity theory, belief in a just world, procedural justice, social comparison, relative deprivation, and entitlements (see Cohen 1979 and Furby 1986). While these theoretical perspectives have generally been applied to an array of interpersonal problems including relative income satisfaction, attitudes toward welfare, and prejudice against AIDS victims (e.g., Easterlin 1973; Furnham and Lewis 1986; Murphy Berman and Berman 1991), there is no reason why their underlying notion of fairness might not be employed intrapersonally in what might be thought of as a balance sheet model of self-reward based on perceptions of our own deservingness. The important difference is that intrapersonal deservingness does not depend upon a comparison to others (see Kassiola 1990). The principle of deservingness is a consistent theme in research on self-gifts as rewards. Some likely reasons are considered in what follows.

Self-rewards based on a subjective personal balance sheet are not self-reinforcements but rather self-compensations in order to restore perceptual equity between rewards received and rewards deserved. Thus we might see the compensatory consumption (Grønmo 1984) of status mobility-blocked blue collar workers (Chinoy 1955) or yuppies (Belk 1986), and affection-blocked food consumers (Grunert 1993) or collectors (Muensterberger 1994), as involving consumption-based efforts to redress perceived imbalances between our own deservingness and the total externally administered rewards and punishments we receive. For example, when we have raised and educated our children we may feel we deserve a luxury automobile or a foreign vacation. We are likely to feel freer and more absolved of guilt for spending money on ourselves when we feel we lack the rewards we deserve. When we have worked hard or achieved a goal we may feel we deserve a break today at McDonalds. We may more readily accede to the biblical-sounding Chivas Regal injunction to "Reward Thyself." In the art world we sometimes ask ourselves, "Am I good enough to own this painting?" (Greenspan 1988). And when we feel we have been unjustly abused by the world, we may feel that we owe ourselves a drunk (Spradley 1970) or a looted television (Fiske 1994). We may disguise self gifts as gifts to our house, our car, or, as with Alice in Wonderland promising to buy her feet new boots every Christmas, even as gifts to our own anthropomorphized body parts—which after all deserve rewards even if we don't. Successful male executives sometimes "trade-up" to the so-called trophy wives they feel they deserve. In popular love stories, women are often found to expect material luxury to be bestowed upon them for being "good" partners (Perebinossoff 1974). Some conspicuous consumers and collectors appear to be compensating for reward deprivations experienced traumatically during childhood (e.g., Muensterberger 1994).

People have long recognized that it is not a totally just world, prompting concepts like original sin to reconcile bad things happening to good people (e.g., Kushner 1983). One way to attempt reconciliation in a materialistic, individualistic society is to take matters into our own hands and try to provide self-compensation through consumption. If God is dead and Santa is a fiction, we'll reward ourselves. Because the balance sheet view of self-reward is intrapersonal, it is not appropriately modeled as the zero sum game characteristic of the interpersonal models. Even with resources shared among family and friends, rather than allocating rewards to others versus self, we may be embrace an ethic of care (Gilligan 1982) when we view these others as parts of our aggregate extended selves (Belk 1988). When we want our children to have more than we had, or when we enjoy our friend's and spouse's success, this too may be seen as a compensatory self-reward that is vicariously enjoyed. And if someone from our department, institution, or research paradigm receives an award, we too may share in this award's compensatory benefits.

Some objections might be raised to the balance sheet model. Research by Prentice and Crosby (1987) suggests that the notion of deservingness is seen by consumers as highly relevant in a work context, but not very relevant in the contexts of home and family. The same is true of Fine's (1980) research on the allocation of food within poor families in India, in which deservingness also was not found to be very relevant. But these involve interpersonal rather than intrapersonal deservingness. However, if over time we become more narcissistic or more cynical about the correspondence between external rewards and deservingness (e.g., Gamson 1992; Martindale 1982), we may become less insistent upon applying these principles through self-administered rewards and punishments. There are also likely cultural, temporal, class, and gender biases in our concepts of justice (Furby 1986). And it may be that self-administered rewards cannot fulfill what is perceived as due from the parental source of childhood deprivations (Shabad 1993). Thus research needs to assess the applicability of such a balance sheet model intrapersonally across different time periods, cultures, people, and injustices.

One clue to the viability of the balance sheet model as a cultural ideal for consumer behavior comes from stories about the attainment of wealth, riches, and consumer goods. Consistently these stories tell a similar moral tale, whether they derive from Aesop's *Fables*, *Grimms' Fairy Tales*, Jewish folktales (Drory 1977; Jason 1988), comic books (Baker 1975; Belk 1987b), the Bible (Brams 1989; Gieze 1992), buried treasure legends (e.g., Foster 1964; Hurley 1951; Lindow 1982), or the stories of Horatio Alger, Jr. (e.g., Coad 1972; Lindberg 1979; Scharnhorst 1976). Collectively these moral tales tell us that rewards in the form of wealth, treasures, possessions, and happiness will be ours if we follow a few basic rules:

Don't be greedy or miserly	Do good deeds
Don't be immodest	Do suffer in silence
Don't cheat	Do keep promises
Don't yield to temptation	Do work hard
Don't be unkind or seek revenge	Do care for others and be generous.

Many such stories involve siblings or a husband and wife who show opposite regard for these rules. When the rules are broken, rather than reward, punishment invariably results and the one who ruthlessly seeks riches by any means available ends with less than he or she began and possibly loses his or her life. The tales are resolved by creating a more just material world in which being a moral person leads eventually to material rewards and being an immoral person leads to material calamity. However, it should be noted that deservingness is rewarded and undeservingness punished by *external* forces: spirits, magic, or God—more morally principled forces than Adam Smith's invisible hand of the market or Charles Darwin's survival of the fittest. While Mick (forthcoming) calls reward self-gifts Puritanical, the Puritans too saw rewards as signs of God's blessing. Ironically in moral tales, those who consistently try to *internally* reward themselves rather than give to others, lose all and are punished for their greed. This may seem to suggest that the balance sheet model may be problematic at the individual consumer level of action. But what is punished is not using self-rewards to bring about justice as balance sheet theory requires, but rather using self-rewards in spite of undeservingness in order to solely pursue self-interests.

The key plot device in these stories is to set up obvious injustice and right it. When the poor, but honest, caring, hardworking, and generous characters in the stories are ultimately rewarded, they are then able to indulge themselves as they deserve. But no more indulgence than they deserve is tolerated. Nor may they change character and neglect the traits that made them deserving initially. If they become selfish, lazy, greedy, uncaring, or vengeful, their treasure must also be forfeit in order to restore balance. An illustration of a number of these principles is found in the misogynist Brothers Grimm tale of "The Fisherman and his Wife." A poor but hardworking, modest, and kind fisherman who lived with his wife in a hovel by the sea one day caught a talking flounder who was really an enchanted prince. Hearing the fish talk, the fisherman recognized his uniqueness and let him go. But when the man returned home, his wife demanded that he go back to the sea and ask the flounder to replace their hovel with a pretty cottage. The husband reluctantly did so and returned home to find a beautiful cottage furnished with food, gardens, and farm animals. Nevertheless, his wife was soon dissatisfied and urged her husband to go to the flounder again and ask for a big stone castle. This too was granted with a castle full of beautiful tapestries, rich carpets, crystal chandeliers, delicate foods, and costly wines. But his wife quickly grew dissatisfied again and had her husband demand of the flounder that she be king. Upon returning home the fisherman found that his wife was king, the castle was bigger, and the furnishings were made of marble, gold, and diamonds. Next his wife had him demand that she be Emperor and then Pope. Each time more sumptuous treasures, courtiers, and privileges resulted. At last the fisherman's wife persuaded her reluctant husband to ask the flounder that she be made Lord of the Universe. At this the flounder balked and returned the fisherman and his greedy wife to their hovel. While this tale invokes the sexist stereotype of woman as insatiable consumer, it illustrates the moral that greed, immodesty, and yielding to temptation inevitably lead to ruin. And the misogyny of the story is engagingly debated and redressed by Günter Grass (1978) in his inventive novel *The Flounder*, based on this fairy tale (see also Corbett and Rives 1991). In both stories, while the fisherman's generosity and humility initially result in favors via the *deus ex machina* of the enchanted fish, ultimately the scale tips too far and fortunes are again reversed. Until that point is reached however, self-reward through magical consumption is granted as something that is deserved. The more people have suffered unjustly, the larger will be their eventual reward. Like the Beatitudes, numerous Cinderella tales invoke a similar deservingness model and promise that justice will ultimately prevail and that indulgent but deserved self-reward is justifiable so long as it does not become over-reward (e.g., Bettelheim 1976; Fohr 1991; Philip 1989). The Platonic and Aristotelian ideal of the golden mean carries a related message of moderation, but it fails to embrace the notion of deservingness or justice. Future consumer research might profitably explore the degree and conditions under which as consumers we tend to behave according to this balance sheet model.

THE DEEPER REASON I HATE AWARDS

Although some general disadvantages of awards to recipients, awarding organizations, and society have been discussed, they do not reach to the real reason that I hate receiving rewards. It is not out of any false modesty or bitterness or belief that my work is not award-worthy. But it does stem from a balance-sheet-based belief that I do not deserve awards. I believe the reason lies in my childhood. When I was perhaps 14 and my brother 12, we had high ambitions. We were going to be the first college graduates in the family; he wanted to be an architect and I wanted to be a geologist. We had a fairly intense sibling rivalry and because I was older I was usually more successful. Nevertheless we both collected a small array of ribbons from various competitions, which we proudly displayed in little wall frames we each made to show them to best advantage on our bedroom wall. It happened that one of the educational toys we requested and received from our parents about that time was a "black light" kit, complete with powders, crayons, minerals, and paints that were visible only under the appropriate wavelength ultraviolet light. One day, in an unforgivable act, I took one of these crayons and wrote on my brother's ribbons the words "Booby Prize." The captions were not very visible in normal light, but we both knew the words were there. It was a cruel vandalism that had the desired effect of angering my brother and making him cry. Yet I had still not apologized four years later when my brother died in what may or may not have been a suicide. So, you see, I don't deserve this award or any other, no matter how much I may treasure it. Therefore as a small act of contrition, I would like to accept this Fellows Award on behalf of my brother David. It is he who is deserving, not me.

As an addendum, I recall that someone (Otnes 1994) once told me that I have a tendency to cite a lot of references. *Mea Culpa* (Enigma 1990). But in coming to realize the source of my uneasiness with awards, I think I have also come to realize the source of this citation propensity. I have been careful, overly carefully no doubt, to try to now give credit where credit is due for prior achievements and ideas. In this same spirit, it is only appropriate to end by thanking the many people to whom I have been a son, brother, husband, father, friend, student, teacher, research partner, and colleague. I have learned much from you. Thank you all. I hope that someday I can better balance the scales by giving back as much as I have received.

REFERENCES

Ainsley, George (1985), "Beyond Microeconomics: conflict Among Interests in a Multiple Self as a Determinant of Value," in *The Multiple Self*, Jon Elster, ed., Cambridge: Cambridge University Press, 133-175.

Axelrod, Robert M. (1984), *The Evolution of Cooperation*, New York: Basic Books.

Baker, Ronald L. (1975), "Folklore Motifs in Comic Books of Superheroes," *Tennessee Folklore Society Bulletin*, 4 (December), 170-174.

Belk, Russell W. (1986), "Yuppies as Arbiters of the Emerging Consumption Style," *Advances in Consumer Research*, Vol. 13, ed. Richard J. Lutz, Provo: Association for Consumer Research, 514-519.

Belk, Russell W. (1987a), "A Child's Christmas in America: Santa Claus as Deity, Consumption as Religion," *Journal of American Culture*, 10 (Spring), 87-100.

Belk, Russell W. (1987b), "Material Values in the Comics: A Content Analysis of Comic Books Featuring Themes of Wealth," *Journal of Consumer Research*, 14 (June), 26-42.

Belk, Russell W. (1988), "Possessions and the Extended Self," *Journal of Consumer Research*, 15 (September), 139-168.

Belk, Russell W. (1993), "Materialism and the Making of the Modern American Christmas," in *Unwrapping Christmas*, Daniel Miller, ed., Oxford: Oxford University Press, 75-104.

Belk, Russell W. (forthcoming), *Collecting in a Consumer Society*, London: Routledge.

Bettelheim, Bruno (1976), *The Uses of Enchantment: The Meaning and Importance of Fairy Tales*, New York: Alfred A. Knopf.

Bordo, Susan (1990), "Reading the Slender Body," in Mary Jacobus, Evelyn Fox Keller, and Sally Shuttleworth, eds., *Body/Politics: Women and the Discourses of Science*, New York: Routledge, 83-112.

Brams, Steven J. (1980), *Biblical Games: A Strategic Analysis of Stories in the Old Testament*, Cambridge, Massachusetts: MIT Press.

Burns, Alvin C., Peter L. Gillett, Marc Rubinstein, and James W. Gentry (1990), "An Exploratory Study of Lottery Playing, Gambling Addiction and Links to Compulsive Consumption," in *Advances in Consumer Research*, Vol. 17, Marvin E. Goldberg, Gerald Gorn, and Richard W. Pollay, eds., Provo, UT: Association for Consumer Research, 298-305.

Capps, Donald (1993), *The Depleted Self: Sin in a Narcissistic Age*, Minneapolis, MN: Fortress Press.

Carroll, Lewis (1930), *Alice's Adventures in Wonderland*, (original 1897), London: Macmillan.

Chinoy, Ely (1955), *Automobile Workers and the American Dream*, Boston: Beacon Press.

Clavell, James [director] (1967), *To Sir With Love*, RCA/ Columbia (based on the novel by Edgar R. Braithwaite, Englewood Cliffs, NJ: Prentice Hall, 1959/1960).

Clement, P. W. (1985), "Self Reinforcement," in *Baker Encyclopedia of Psychology*, David G. Brenner, ed., Grand Rapids, MI: Baker Book House, 989-990.

Coad, Bruce (1972), "The Alger Hero," in *Heroes of Popular Culture*, Ray B. Browne, Marshall Fishwick, and Michael T. Marsden, eds., Bowling Green, OH: Bowling Green University Popular Press, 42-51.

Cohen, Ronald L. (1979), "On the Distinction Between Individual Deserving and Distributive Justice," *Journal for the Theory of Social Behaviour*, 9 (July), 167-185.

Corbett, Lionel and Cathy Rives (1991), "'The Fisherman and His Wife' The Anima in the Narcissistic Character," in *Psyche's Stories: Modern Jungian Interpretations of Fairy Tales*, Vol. 1, Marray Stein and Lionel Corbett, eds., Wilmette, IL: Chiron Publications, 103-120.

Crawford, Robert (1984), "A Cultural Account of `Health': Control, Release, and the Social Body," in John B. McKinlay, ed., *Issues in the Political Economy of Health Care*, New York: Tavistock, 60-103.

Deci, Edward L. (1971), "Effects of Externally Mediated Rewards on Intrinsic Motivation," *Journal of Personality and Social Psychology*, 18, 105-115.

DeLong, Thomas A. (1991), *Quiz Craze: America's Infatuation with Game Shows*, New York: Praeger.

Dillon, Wilton (1968), *Gifts and Nations: The Obligation to Give, Receive, and Repay*, The Hague: Mouten.

Drory, Rina (1977), "Ali Baba and the Forty Thieves: An Attempt at a Model for the Surface Level of the Reward-and-punishment Fairy Tale," in *Patterns in Oral Literature*, Heda Jason and Dimitrii M. Segal, eds., The Hague: Mouton, 31-48.

Easterlin, Richard A. (1973), "Does Money Buy Happiness," *The Public Interest*, 30, 3-10.

Enigma (1990), "Mea Culpa," *MCMXC a.D.*, London: Virgin Music (Composers Curly M.C. and David Fairstein).

Fine, Seymour (1980), "Toward a Theory of Segmentation by Objectives in Social Marketing Objectives," *Journal of Consumer Research*, 7 (June), 1-13.

Fiske, John (1994), "Radical Shopping in Los Angeles: Race, Media and The Sphere of Consumption," *Media, Culture & Society*, 16 (July), 469-486.

Fohr, Samuel Denis (1991), *Cinderella's Gold Slipper: Spiritual Symbolism in the Grimm's Tales*, Wheaton, IL: Quest Books.

Foster, George M. (1964), "Treasure Tales and the Image of the Static Economy in a Mexican Peasant Community," *Journal of American Folklore*, 77 (303), January-March, 39-44.

Furby, Lita (1986), "Psychology and Justice," in *Justice: Views from the Social Sciences*, Ronald L. Cohen, ed., New York: Plenum, 153-203.

Furnham, Adrian and Alan Lewis (1986), *The Economic Mind: The Social Psychology of Economic Behavior*, New York: St. Martin's Press.

Fürer-Haimendorf, Christopher von (1974), "The Sense of Sin in Cross-Cultural Perspective," *Man*, 9 (December), 539-556.

Gamson, Joshua (1992), "The Assembly Line of Greatness: Celebrity in Twentieth-Century America," *Critical Studies in Mass Communication*, 9 (March), 1-24.

Giese, Ronald L., Jr. (1992), "Qualifying Wealth in the Septuagint of Proverbs," *Journal of Biblical Literature*, 111 (Fall), 409-425.

Gilligan, Carol (1982), *In a Different Voice: Psychological Theory and Women's Development*, Cambridge, MA: Harvard University Press.

Goode, William J. (1973), *The Celebration of Heroes: Prestige as a Social Control System*, Berkeley: University of California Press.

Gouldner, Alan (1965), *Enter Plato: Classical Greece and the Origins of Social Theory*, New York: Basic Books..

Grass, Günter (1978), *The Flounder*, Ralph Manheim, trans., London: Pan Books (original 1977).

Greenspan, Stuart (1988), "Am I Good Enough to Own This Painting?," *Avenue*, 12 (February), 88-94.

Grønmo, Sigmund (1984), "Compensatory Consumer Behavior: Theoretical Perspectives, Empirical Examples and Method-ological Challenges," in *Marketing Theory: Philosophy, History and Sociology*, Paul F. Anderson and Michael J. Ryans, eds., Chicago: American Marketing Association, 184-188.

Grunert, Suzanne C. (1993), "On Gender Differences in Eating Behavior as Compensatory Consumption," in *Gender and Consumer Behavior Second Conference Proceedings*, Janeen Arnold Costa, ed., Provo, UT: Association for Consumer Research, 74-87.

Hoch, Stephen J. and George F. Lowenstein (1991), "Time-Inconsistent Preferences and Consumer Self-Control," *Journal of Consumer Research*, 17 (March), 492-507.

Holbrook, Morris B. (1993), *Daytime Television Game Shows and the Celebration of Merchandise: The Price is Right*, Bowling Green, OH: Bowling Green University Popular Press.

Hurley, Gerald T. (1951), "Buried Treasure Tales in America," *Western Folklore*, 10 (3), July, 197-206.

Hyde, Lewis (1983), *The Gift: Imagination and the Erotic Life of Property*, New York: Random House.

Jason, Heda (1988), *Whom Does God Favor: The Wicked or the Righteous? The Reward-and Punishment Fairy Tale*, Folklore Fellows Communications No. 240, Alan Dundes, Bengt Holbek, Lauri Honko, Matti Kuusi, and Anna Birgitta Rooth, eds., Helsinki: Suomalainen Tiedeakatemia.

Johnson, Glenn M. (1987), "Self-Punitive Habit Syndrome: A Theoretical Model and Cognitive-Behavioral Intervention Strategy," *Journal of Cognitive Psychotherapy*, 8 (Fall), 171-182.

Kassiola, Joel Jay (1990), "Materialism and Modern Political Philosophy," Chapter 8 in *The Death of Industrial Civiliza-tion*, Albany, NY: State University of New York Press, 125-149.

Keillor, Garrison (1990), *Leaving Home*, London: Penguin Books.

Klapp, Orrin E. (1991), *Inflation of Symbols: Loss of Values in American Culture*, New Brunswick, NJ: Transaction Publishers.

Kohn, Alfie (1993), *Punished by Rewards: The Trouble with Gold Stars, Incentive Plans, A's, Praise, and Other Bribes*, Boston: Houghton Mifflin.

Kushner, Harold (1983), *When Bad Things Happen to Good People*, New York: Avon.

Laqueur, Thomas W. (1992), "Sexual Desire and the Market Economy During the Industrial Revolution," in Domna C. Stanton, ed., *Discourses of Sexuality: From Aristotle to AIDS*, Ann Arbor: University of Michigan Press, 185-215.

Lindberg, Stanley W. (1979), "Institutionalizing a Myth: The McGuffey Readers and the Myth of the Self-made Man," *Journal of American Culture*, 2 (Spring), 71-82.

Lindow, John (1982), "Swedish Legends of Buried Treasure," *Journal of American Folklore*, 95 (377), 257-279.

Löfgren, Orvar (1993), "The Great Christmas Quarrel and Other Swedish Traditions," in *Unwrapping Christmas*, Daniel Miller, ed., Oxford: Oxford University Press, 217-234.

Lynn, Michael (1992), "The Psychology of Unavailability: Explanations for Scarcity and Cost Effects on Value," *Basic and Applied Social Psychology*, 13, 3-7.

Martindale, Don (1982), "Mute Inglorious Miltons: A Plea for the Study of Unacknowledged Genius," *International Social Science Review*, 57 (Summer), 138-144

Mason, Roger S. (1981), *Conspicuous Consumption: A Study of Exceptional Consumer Behavior*, Westmead, England: Gower.

McClelland, David C., John W. Atkinson, Russell A. Clark, and Edgar L. Lowell (1953), *Achievement Motivation*, New York: Appleton.

McDannell, Colleen and Bernhard Lang (1988), *Heaven: A History*, New Haven, CT: Yale University Press.

Mechling, Jay (1987), "The Manliness Paradox in Ernest Thompson Seton's Ideology of Play and Games," in Gary Alan Fine, ed., *Meaningful Play, Playful Meaning*, Champaign, IL: Human Kenetics Publishers, 45-59.

Menninger, Karl (1973), *Whatever Became of Sin?*, New York: Hawthorne.

Mick, David Glen (forthcoming), "Self-Gifts," in Cele Otnes and Richard Beltramini, eds., *Gift Giving: An Interdisciplinary Anthology*, Bowling Green, OH: Bowling Green University Popular Press.

Mick, David Glen and Michelle DeMoss (1990), "Self-Gifts: Phenomenological Insights from Four Contexts," *Journal of Consumer Research*, 17 (December), 322-332.

Muensterberger, Werner (1994), *Collecting, An Unruly Passion: Psychological Perspectives*, Princeton, NJ: Princeton University Press.

Murphy-Berman, Virginia A. and John J. Berman (1991), "Perceptions of Justice and Attitudes Toward People with AIDS: German-U.S. Comparisons," *Social Behavior and Personality*, 19 (1), 29-38.

Noonan, John T., Jr. (1984), *Bribes*, New York: Macmillan.

Nozick, Robert J. (1974), *Anarchy, State, and Utopia*, New York: Basic Books.

O'Guinn, Thomas and Ronald Faber (1989), "Compulsive Buying: A Phenomenological Exploration," *Journal of Consumer Behavior*, 16 (September), 147-157.

Orlick, Terry (1978), *Winning Through Cooperation*, Washington, D.C.: Acropolis Books.

Osborne, S. R. (1985), "Reinforcement," in *Baker Encyclopedia of Psychology*, David G. Brenner, ed., Grand Rapids, MI: Baker Book House, 986-988.

Otnes, Cele (1994), personal communication.

Perebinossoff, Philippe (1974), "What Does a Kiss Mean? The Love Comic Formula and the Creation of the Ideal Teen-Age Girl," *Journal of Popular Culture*, 8 (4), 825-835.

Philip, Neil (1989), *The Cinderella Story*, London: Penguin Books.

Pohl, Frederick (1982), "The Midas Plague," in *Midas World*, New York: St. Martin's Press, 5-74 (original 1954).

Prentice, Deborah A. and Faye Crosby (1987), "The Importance of Context for Assessing Deservingness," in *Social Comparison, Social Justice, and Relative Deprivation: Theoretical, Empirical, and Policy Perspectives*, John C. Masters and William P. Smith, eds., Hillsdale, NJ: Lawrence Erlbaum Associates, 165-182.

Rook, Dennis (1987), "The Buying Impulse," *Journal of Consumer Research*, 14 (September), 189-199.

Scharnhorst, Gary F. (1976), "The Boudoir Tales of Horatio Alger, Jr." *Journal of Popular Culture*, 10 (1), 215-226.

Searle-Chatterjee, Mary (1993), "Christmas Cards and the Construction of Social Relations in Britain Today," in *Unwrapping Christmas*, Daniel Miller, ed., Oxford: Oxford University Press, 176-192.

Shabad, Peter (1993), "Resentment, Indignation, Entitlement: The Transformation of Unconscious Wish into Need," *Psychoanalytic Dialogues*, 3 (4), 481-494.

Sherry, John F., Jr., Mary Ann McGrath, and Sidney J. Levy (forthcoming), "Egocentric Consumption: Anatomy of Gifts Given to the Self," in John Sherry, ed., *Contemporary Marketing and Consumer Behavior: An Anthropological Sourcebook*.

Spheeris, Penelope [Director] (1992), *Wayne's World*, Paramount Pictures.

Spradley, James P. (1970), *You Owe Yourself a Drunk: An Ethnography of Urban Nomads*, Boston: Little, Brown.

Thierry, Henk (1992), "Payment: Which Meanings Are Rewarding?," *American Behavioral Scientist*, 35 (July), 694-707.

Tiger, Lionel (1992), *The Pursuit of Pleasure*, Boston: Little, Brown and Company.

Twain, Mark [Samuel Clemens] (1958), *The Adventures of Tom Sawyer*, New York: Dodd, Mead (original 1896).

Wicklund, Robert A. and Peter M. Gollwitzer (1982), *Symbolic Self-Completion*, Hillsdale, NJ: Lawrence Erlbaum Associates.

Xenos, Nicholas (1989), *Scarcity and Modernity*, London: Routledge.

Seven Pieces of Wisdom on Consumer Research From Sandy, Quarter, Tommy, Matthew, Paul, Dave, and Dolly: A Love Letter To ACR

Morris B. Holbrook, Columbia University[1]

Once a year, my wife Sally and I devote a long evening to watching the Academy Awards Ceremony, a television extravaganza viewed by literally a billion people worldwide (Levy 1990). Typically, these Oscar Awards drag on for three or four hours amidst endless introductions, special announcements, sappy acceptance speeches, and bad jokes from some famous movie or TV personality like Bob Hope, Johnny Carson, Billy Crystal, or Whoopi Goldberg. It would be hard to argue that this program represents anything other than the lowest common denominator in schlock mass-oriented low-brow pop culture. Yet—invariably—by the end of the night, at least once or twice, I find myself sitting there with a little tear trickling down my cheek.

Why do I find the Academy Awards so moving? Why does Hollywood's crowd-pleasing celebration of itself tap some deep well of emotion within me? The answer, I think, is that I have always dimly sensed how nice it would feel to be honored in that sort of way.

By contrast with the motion-picture industry, the teaching profession rarely inspires one's bosses, colleagues, or audiences to say "good work" or "nice going" or "thank you." So receiving the ACR Fellows Award is probably the closest I shall ever come to winning an Oscar. And this occasion has made me extremely happy, proud, and grateful.

How do I plan to demonstrate this gratitude? The answer is that I want to share seven pieces of wisdom that people have been kind enough to bestow upon me over the years. I would like to take this opportunity to pass them along to others. For the most part, these pieces of wisdom do not come from books—at least not from marketing books or consumer-research journals. Rather, they come from the common fund of experience in the world around us and are part of the folk culture in which we live. All the more reason why someone should perhaps write them down before we forget their importance and they disappear forever in the sands of time.

ONE

The first piece of wisdom I wish to mention comes from my father Sandy and takes us back about forty years to Christmas 1954 when, at age eleven, more than anything else in the world I wanted my parents to give me a chemistry set. As I recall, the one I wanted was produced by a company called Gilbert and came in an eye-catching wooden box complete with all sorts of powders in little bottles, test tubes, beakers, a mortar-and-pestle, and even a small microscope. Using this marvelous equipment, a kid could while away many happy hours doing things like combining phenolphthalein with potassium chloride and watching the resulting solution turn bright red. I believe the whole thing cost about $39.95 and could be ordered direct from the F.A.O. Schwartz catalogue.

My mom bought the chemistry set that I wanted so badly and hid it in the guest-room closet upstairs. I know this because I used to devote the first weeks of December to inspecting the Christmas

gifts that she had carefully hidden in this manner. So, as the twenty-fifth of December approached, I eagerly anticipated all the fun I was going to have with my new toy.

Meanwhile, my father Sandy had other plans. Sandy was a physician in Milwaukee and was therefore intimately familiar with beakers, flasks, test tubes, mortars, pestles, microscopes, and rare powders in little bottles. Apparently, Sandy took one look at the cleverly packaged chemistry set that my mother had purchased, did a quick mental calculation, and computed that its entire contents were worth about four dollars and sixty three cents. As a trained practitioner, Sandy knew that for $39.95 he could put together a vastly superior set of beakers, flasks, tubes, and powders. And this is exactly what he proceeded to do.

Unbeknownst to me, Sandy copied down a list of each item in the chemistry set that I wanted so much, went to the nearest drug-supply house, and purchased better versions of everything in the package. Instead of little imitation beakers and flasks, he got nice big vessels of the type that a real pharmacist would use. Instead of tiny bottles of sulfur and acid, he got big jars reminiscent of what you would find in an apothecary. Instead of the tinny little microscope supplied with the toy chemistry set, he included a powerful one that my grandfather had used in his own medical practice—one that I have always kept, that has become an antique, and that is probably worth hundreds of dollars today.

But when Christmas morning arrived, when I put on my navy blue bathrobe and furry slippers to join my parents for the annual present-opening ceremony, and when I found this assemblage of chemicals and other laboratory gadgets, I felt an overwhelming sense of disappointment. True, I could easily see that every single item in my father's lovingly assembled collection was superior to the corresponding item in the toy chemistry set. But Sandy had failed to notice that there was just one crucial ingredient missing— namely, an instruction book.

For the next several months, I spent countless hours in the basement of our house systematically finding out what happens if you use your magnificent mortar and pestle to mix various chemicals together in various combinations and then heat them up. Mostly what happens is that you get some truly dreadful smells. Often, these mixtures catch on fire or explode. Sometimes, they form such a tough crust on the inside wall of the test tube that you have to throw it away. Also, if you put a beaker under cold water while it is still hot, it will surely shatter. And if you try to ram some glass tubing through the hole in a rubber stopper without first warming the rubber and oiling the tubing, it will break and plunge into the base of your thumb and leave a scar that will prevent you from playing tenths on the piano even forty years later.

These, I suppose, were all valuable lessons. But the most important lesson by far lay in the significance of the difference between a chemistry set put together by a toy manufacturer and a collection of authentic chemicals and real laboratory equipment assembled by a genuine physician. The point, of course, is that— like my father's well-intentioned but somewhat misguided Christmas present—*science does not come with an instruction book.*

Only toy science comes with instructions included. In real science, you must figure out the rules for yourself and you must endure a lot of bad smells, dangerous explosions, crusty messes, broken glass, and bloody fingers. But if this is true, how should we scientists proceed? This question brings me to the second piece of

[1]Morris B. Holbrook is the Dillard Professor of Marketing, Graduate School of Business, Columbia University, New York, NY 10027. The author thanks his colleagues at ACR for the privilege of contributing this paper. He also gratefully acknowledges the support of the Columbia Business School's Faculty Research Fund.

wisdom that I would like to offer, one that comes directly from my cat.

TWO

Before he recently died of old age, Quarter the Cat shared our New York apartment for eighteen years, during which time he enlightened us on a variety of topics, one of which bears directly on the question at hand and concerns the ways in which cats differ from dogs (Holbrook 1993a).

Briefly, dogs are obedient; they aim to please their masters; they want to do what we want them to do; they wish to follow the rules. In short, they are *DOG*matic. If there were an instruction book for pets, dogs would gladly live by those guidelines.

By contrast, cats are independent; they aim to please nobody but themselves; they really do not care what others think; they are indifferent to the whole concept of rules and regulations. In short, from the viewpoint of the dog fancier, they are *CAT*astrophic. If there were an instruction book for pets, cats would insist on ignoring it completely.

Quarter the Cat exemplified this attitude to a highly refined degree. If you called his name, Quarter absolutely would not come—unless he was hungry, in which case he would come whether you called his name or not. If you scolded Quarter for eating leaves from the dracaena on Monday, he would devote all his energies to eating some more leaves as soon as you left the apartment on Tuesday. If Quarter wanted to jump out of the fifth-floor window and live to tell about it, Quarter jumped and Quarter lived—both of which he did one evening when he was just a kitten.

So—like all cats—Quarter followed a simple but powerful philosophy that constitutes our second piece of wisdom: *Do what you want.* For consumer researchers as well as cats, this tenet has an immediate corollary: Satisfy your curiosity. Explore ceaselessly. Never stop poking your nose into anything that interests you. Show some respect for the first person who had the courage to eat an artichoke.

In the absence of an instruction book for science, these strike me as good principles for the consumer researcher to live by. Do what you think is important. Investigate the issues that matter to you. Insist on setting your own priorities. As the anthropologist Joseph Campbell put it in his conversations with Bill Moyers, "Follow Your Bliss" (Campbell and Moyers 1988). Or, as urged by Lorna Catford and Mike Ray, "Do What You Love, Love What You Do" (Catford and Ray 1991, p. 67).

But this advice immediately raises another tough question—namely, if we behave in this manner, how do we know when we have got it right? And this issue brings me to a third piece of wisdom, one given to me by my old piano teacher.

THREE

Tommy Sheridan is a great jazz pianist with the technique of an Oscar Peterson, the refinement of a Bill Evans, and the audience rapport of a George Shearing. But, rather than seeking the limelight and traveling extensively, he has lived happily as a devoted family man in Milwaukee and has dedicated his life to helping fortunate students like me share his boundless enthusiasm for jazz. Tommy has taught by example. And his example has conveyed the importance of finding joy in what you do. Those who delight in ACR trivia will find that a conference proceedings Beth Hirschman and I edited fifteen years ago is dedicated to Tommy Sheridan (Hirschman and Holbrook 1981).

One day, I came to Tommy with a question about an unusual chord progression I had devised that seemed to depart from the rules for harmonic substitutions he had been showing me. I played him a little passage that contained my musical discovery, mentioned how it violated the accepted doctrine on permissible chord changes, and asked him if it was okay to do something like that. Tommy cheerfully replied, "It sounds good, doesn't it?" "Yes," I said, "I guess so." "Well," Tommy said, "If it sounds right, it *is* right."

Thirty-five years later, I found the same thought attributed to Duke Ellington: "If it sounds good, it *is* good" (quoted by Feather 1956/1958, ed. 1993, p. 61). The sociologist David Sudnow (1978, ed. 1993) uses similar logic to teach novices to play the piano, claiming that "no one...needs to read music to pick out a melody" because "people can hear their own bad notes" (Miller 1993, p. 9). And during a tense scene from the movie *In the Line of Fire*, John Malkovich asks Clint Eastwood to "name one thing that has any meaning in your life"—to which Clint replies, "I play the piano."

But, beyond such anecdotal support, many consumer researchers will be reassured to find comparable views enunciated by one of our favorite neopositivistic philosophers of science—namely, the late Sir Karl Popper. In his intellectual autobiography entitled *Unended Quest* (Popper 1976)—just after explaining the principles of falsificationism and using these to discredit Freud, Marx, and some other major thinkers as "unscientific" (p. 52)—Sir Karl announces that "in all this, speculation about music played a considerable part" (p. 53). He speaks feelingly of his admiration for Schubert, Brahms, and Bruckner and of his dislike for Wagner, Richard Strauss, and Schoenberg. He then launches into an eighteen-page account of how this interest in music influenced his philosophy.

In general, Popper (1976) suggests that his experience with music shaped his ideas on "the logic of discovery" or what he calls "an objectivist epistemology" (p. 55). More specifically—Sir Karl emphasizes "an interpretation of the difference between Bach's and Beethoven's music" (p. 60), claiming that this comparison prompted his deepest insights into the nature of an objectivist epistemology: "It was to distinguish the two distinct attitudes of Bach and Beethoven towards their compositions that I introduced...the terms 'objective' and 'subjective'" (p. 61). Beethoven followed the subjective route because he "made music an instrument of self-expression" (p. 61). But Bach operated "like a scientist" to create "objective music" (p. 64).

We might wonder in what sense music could be "objective." Popper's answer hinges on his conception of falsifiability:

> According to my objectivist theory...the really interesting function of the composer's emotions is not that they are to be expressed, but that they may be used to test the success of the fittingness or the impact of the (objective) work: the composer may use himself as a kind of test body, and he may modify and rewrite his composition...when he is dissatisfied by his own reaction to it.... he will in this way make use of his own reactions—his own "good taste" (p. 67).

Here, clearly, Popper assumes that Bach and other composers conjecture that something will sound good, write it down, play it, listen to it, and thereby test it on themselves. If they like it, they consider it corroborated or at least not falsified. In the words of Bach's son Carl Philipp Emanuel, "A musician cannot move others unless he, too, is moved" (quoted by Blum 1994, p. 25).

An exception that proves the rule occurred when jazz pianist Dave Brubeck studied briefly with the famed atonal composer Arnold Schoenberg. In Brubeck's words,

> I brought him a piece of music I'd written.... He said, "That's very good. Now go home and don't write anything like that

again until you know why everything is there. Do you know now?" he asked. I said, "Isn't it reason enough if it sounds good?" He said, "No, you have to know why." That was my last lesson with Schoenberg (quoted by Lyons 1980, pp. 208-209).

Schoenberg himself had a complex theory of how music should be constructed, no matter how bad it sounded. Those who agree with his views should be strapped to a chair and forced to listen to his excruciatingly ugly *Pierrot Lunaire* all the way through.

Jule Styne—a more tuneful composer who wrote the music for such memorable songs as "Bye Bye Baby," "Guess I'll Hang My Tears Out to Dry," "The Things We Did Last Summer," "I Fall In Love Too Easily," "Just In Time," "Make Someone Happy," "The Party's Over," and "Time After Time"—passed away on September 20, 1994. The *New York Times* reported his death as a featured story on the front page and gave him six-and-a-half feet of column space (Blau 1994), followed by a special tribute in the Arts and Leisure section two Sundays later (Holden 1994). By contrast, when Sir Karl Popper had died three days earlier at the age of ninety-two, the *Times* had buried this news on page 54 in a brief notice that ran only twenty-one inches. The *Times* quoted Sir Karl as claiming that "next to music and art, science is the greatest, most beautiful and most enlightening achievement of the human spirit" (Associated Press 1994, p. 54). Next to music and art..., indeed.

In other words—to paraphrase Sir Karl, to echo Duke Ellington, to clarify David Sudnow, to extend Clint Eastwood, to honor C. P. E. Bach, to contradict Arnold Schoenberg in favor of Dave Brubeck or Jule Styne, and to ratify Tommy Sheridan—*if it sounds right, it is right.*

FOUR

Suppose that you happen to agree with the three pieces of wisdom proposed so far. You realize that science has no instruction book. Therefore, you decide to do what you want. And you hope that you will recognize what is good by what sounds right. Further suppose that you happen to make such a discovery. The next question is what you should do with it.

Here, I wish to draw on a fourth piece of wisdom dispensed by someone whom I shall call The Unknown Respondent. This anonymous person participated in a survey conducted by my wife Sally for her doctoral dissertation in clinical social work. At the end of Sally's questionnaire, in a space designed for open-ended comments, The Unknown Respondent wrote, "This study sounds interesting. *Don't hide your light under a bushel.*"

Neither Sally nor I had heard this expression before, but it certainly sounded like good advice to the social scientist. Once you think you have found some truth, don't be bashful. Get out there and talk about it. Present it at a conference. Send it to a journal. Publish it.

Nonetheless, we continued to wonder where the expression came from. One day, I ran across the same figure of speech in a 1949 movie called *A Letter To Three Wives.* So we knew that it did exist in the vernacular, at least back in the 1940s. We therefore continued to search for its source. Indeed, I developed the habit of asking almost everybody I ran into if they had ever heard the phrase or could tell me where it originated. No one had and no one could.

Finally, one of our more religious friends suggested that it sounded like something from *The Bible.* This hint sent me to a colleague whose husband has a degree in theology and who ultimately provided our answer. It turns out that the expression comes from a highly reputable source—namely, Jesus Christ. It appears in the midst of the passage from *St. Matthew* (Chapter 5) that

recounts the famous Sermon on the Mount. Soon after the familiar part about the poor being blessed in spirit and the meek inheriting the earth, shortly before the well-known references to committing adultery in your heart and turning the other cheek, Christ says:

14 Ye are the light of the world. A city that is set on a hill cannot be hid.

15 Neither do men light a candle and put it under a bushel, but on a candlestick; and it giveth light unto all that are in the house.

He then follows with words so important that they have been incorporated into Christian church services all around the world:

16 Let your light so shine before men, that they may see your good works, and glorify your Father which is in heaven.

So this strikes me as excellent advice that we have acquired on good authority. Translated into the context of my present theme, Christ Himself suggests that—after we have given up on finding an instruction book for science, done what we want to do, and found something that sounds right to us—we should put it on a candlestick and let this light so shine before both men and women that they may see our good work. In other words, we should show it to the world by publishing it.

FIVE

This is the point at which we encounter the problems posed by reviewers, editors, and publishers. I have spoken on this topic before (Holbrook 1986) and shall not now repeat myself on the ethical problems that infect the review process (Holbrook 1994) except to mention that some recent motion pictures have treated relevant publishing-related themes.

First, the film based on Stephen King's novel called *Misery* tells the story of what can happen when authors fall under the sway of their readers in general or under attack by their critics in particular. James Caan plays the part of a writer held captive by Kathy Bates. In a brilliant Oscar-winning performance, Ms. Bates undergoes a cinematic transformation from the role of an adoring fan to that of a vicious reviewer who ultimately destroys the author's work. *Misery* thereby illustrates the damage that can occur when reviewers and other critics pursue their tasks too aggressively.

Second, in *Husbands and Wives*, Woody Allen—who has proclaimed to the world in real life that he feels no need to honor society's generally accepted views on ethical propriety—casts himself as a professor who teaches across the street from Columbia University at Barnard College. Then, in *Manhattan Murder Mystery*, Woody works as an editor at a well-known publishing company in New York.

Third, another film deals even more directly with the essence of the publishing business. It stars Michelle Pfeiffer and Jack Nicholson in the title role of *Wolf.* Below the surface of the rather conventional werewolf story, this movie suggests the lupine qualities of rapacious ferocity needed to succeed in this line of endeavor.

In sum—at the hands of reviewers, editors, and publishers—even good work is likely to receive savage treatment. Indeed, it often appears that *the better the work is, the more likely it is to be mistreated.*

This fifth piece of wisdom surfaces in a recent commentary by Joshua Gans and George Shepherd (1994) entitled "How Are the Mighty Fallen: Rejected Classic Articles by Leading Economists."

Gans and Shepherd chronicle stories told in self-reports collected from numerous economic scholars who have won the Nobel Prize or the John Bates Clark Medal but whose most influential papers have initially been rejected with amazing regularity and apparent injustice. These abused economic geniuses include such prominent figures as Paul Samuelson (on general equilibrium models), James Tobin (on probit regression), Franco Modigliani (on his consumption function), Gary Becker (on competition and democracy), Robert May (on chaos theory), Robert Lucas (on rational expectations), Gerard Debreu (on technological change), Kenneth Arrow (on inventories), and George Ackerlof (on the market for lemons). One noteworthy expression of outrage comes from James March:

> I have certainly had articles rejected.... I recall on one occasion a referee filing a two paragraph commentary...suggesting (in the first paragraph) that the key theorem involved was trivially obvious and (in the second paragraph) that it was wrong. I thought on the whole that he ought to choose (quoted by Gans and Shepherd 1994, p. 174).

The point is that even masterpieces by Nobel laureates routinely get trashed in the review process. Hence, our fifth piece of wisdom is clearly articulated by Paul Samuelson:

> Yes, journals have rejected papers of mine, some of them later regarded as "classics."... the quality of papers of mine at first rejected is not less than the quality of papers accepted at once (quoted by Gans and Shepherd 1994, pp. 165-166).

SIX

How, one might ask, can we possibly find happiness in a world where reviewers, editors, and publishers constantly torment us with the threat of rejection? I once proposed an answer to this question (Holbrook 1989) by suggesting that we should emulate the example of J. S. Bach in anticipating Popper's advice by writing cantata after cantata until he finally got it right in *Ein feste Burg ist unser Gott* or *A Mighty Fortress Is Our God* (Cantata #80) and in *Herz und Mund und Tat und Leben* with its wonderful chorale movement that we call "Jesu, Joy of Man's Desiring" (Cantata #147). Or we should follow Mickey Mantle, on damaged knees, limping to the plate again and again to try for just one more home run. But, in an ironic sort of postmodern reflexivity, my comments on Bach and Mantle were themselves declared unpublishable. Also, since then, I have recalled that Bach borrowed the theme for *A Mighty Fortress* from Martin Luther, who had based it on a song that German students used to sing while getting drunk in the beer halls. And, amidst great publicity, my hero Mickey Mantle has spent part of the past year trying to dry out at the Betty Ford Clinic (Brady 1994). So the old question still haunts us: After losing the instruction book, doing what we want, getting it to sound right, trying to show it to the world, and suffering the inevitable slings and arrows of outrageous fortune, where can we turn for comfort?

I believe that a partial answer—which I offer as our sixth piece of wisdom—comes from an experience I had in Fifth Grade when our English teacher conducted some classes on business writing. As an exercise, we all completed an assignment in which we wrote away to large corporations requesting various sorts of free materials. Our teacher selected the letter by Dave Smith (fictitious name) as the best in the class—except for one minor problem near the end—and read the entire communication out loud:

Dear Sirs [remember this was 1953],

I am a student in the fifth-grade class at the Milwaukee Country Day School and am interested in your company and in the work that you are doing in the production of automobiles.

I would be grateful if you could please send me your annual report and any other available information describing your business, such as relevant photographs or other free materials.

Thank you in advance for your kind consideration.

Love, Dave

The teacher viewed Dave's closing salutation as a tragic flaw in his letter, but I have always considered it the letter's crowning glory. Dave's ending seemed to imply that—even in the world of business—*love is a relevant concept*. Unintentionally, he echoed the thoughts of many great writers through the ages—from Saint Thomas Aquinas to Dante to James Joyce to John Lennon and Paul McCartney. In short: "Love is all you need."

The aforementioned Sermon on the Mount clearly anticipated the inequities of the review process when it emphasized this sixth piece of wisdom:

> 44 But I say unto you, Love your enemies, bless them that curse you, do good to them that hate you, and pray for them which despitefully use you, and persecute you.

Paradoxically, following the advice of Christ can get you in a whole lot of trouble. Indeed, as He Himself found out, placing an emphasis on love almost guarantees that some people will treat you badly.

For example, this strategy ensured my rejection from the Harvard Business School. In its MBA application form, Harvard asked for a personal essay on the candidate's three most valuable qualities. I suppose they expected things like (1) the ability to remain clear-headed while negotiating multi-million-dollar corporate mergers; (2) the overwhelming motivation to succeed financially; and (3) the unquenchable desire to donate large sums of money to one's alma mater. Unfortunately for me, I mentioned the capacity to love as a characteristic that I considered worthwhile. Somewhere, even today, a retired Harvard admissions officer probably collapses in helpless laughter whenever he recalls this incident. At any rate, the Harvard Business School responded to my misguided plea for agape by rejecting me and recommending that I gain maturity by joining the Army. By the way, this was in 1965—at the height of America's military build-up in Viet Nam.

So Harvard taught me that love is not necessarily a virtue admired by all. Nonetheless, we might aspire to the spirit implied by that business letter written long ago and signed "Love, Dave." Many of my marketing colleagues have probably been surprised to find my letters closing with the words "Love, M——." But, if you've been wondering, that's what I learned in my fifth-grade English class.

SEVEN

Some people probably think that all this sounds rather sentimental. Indeed, sentiments, emotions, or feelings—as opposed to mere sentimentality—pervade consumption experiences in ways that lie very close to my heart as a consumer researcher. For example, recent work with Robert Schindler has focused on the role of nostalgia in consumer behavior. And nostalgia depends at least partly on sentiment in the form of a bittersweet longing for the past (Holbrook 1993b; Holbrook and Schindler 1991, 1994).

These intertwined themes of love, sentiment, and nostalgia return, circle-like, to the place where I began—namely, to a concern for awards ceremonies in general and for the Oscars, Emmys, Grammys, and ACR Fellows Awards in particular. Surely, we have all noticed how the phenomenon of nostalgia has surfaced in our contemporary popular culture, especially at some of the recent Grammy Award celebrations (Holbrook 1993c).

A couple of years ago, Natalie Cole revived an old song called "Unforgettable" that her father Nat had first recorded in 1951. Ms. Cole's new performances of this and other nostalgic favorites won a total of seven Grammy Awards in 1992, including the three Grammys for record, song, and album of the year (Pareles 1992).

Something similar happened again this year when Whitney Houston reached back to a song written and recorded by Dolly Parton in 1974. Ms. Houston included it in the soundtrack for her film *The Bodyguard*, which promptly became the best-selling movie soundtrack of all time, the most popular recording of 1993 (ten million copies sold), and winner of the 1994 Grammy Award for album of the year, with Whitney's performance of Dolly's old song also receiving Grammys for best female pop vocal and record of the year (Pareles 1994).

To conclude by returning to my opening theme and its connection with the awards ceremonies, the words of Dolly Parton's song convey my gratitude for the Fellows Award, express how I feel toward my friends at ACR, and reflect what I now offer as my seventh, final, and most personal piece of wisdom. To quote Dolly:

I hope life treats you kind.
And I hope you have all you dreamed of.
And I wish you joy and happiness.
But, above all this, I wish you love.
And....

Well, *you all know the rest*.

REFERENCES

Associated Press (1994), "Sir Karl Popper Is Dead at 92...," *New York Times*, (September 18), 54.

Blau, Eleanor (1994), "Jule Styne, Bountiful Creator of Song Favorites, Dies at 88," *New York Times*, (September 21), A1, D19.

Blum, David (1994), "Emotions Can Be Dangerous Or Be Put to Expressive Use," *New York Times*, Arts and Leisure Section, (January 16), 25.

Brady, Erik (1994), "The New Chapters in Mantle's Life," *USA Today*, (June 10), 2C.

Campbell, Joseph and Bill Moyers (1988), *The Power of Myth*, New York, NY: Doubleday.

Catford, Lorna and Michael Ray (1991), *The Path of the Everyday Hero: Drawing on the Power of Myth to Meet Life's Most Important Challenges*, Los Angeles, CA: Jeremy P. Tarcher.

Feather, Leonard (1956/1958, ed. 1993), *The Encyclopedia Yearbooks of Jazz*, New York, NY: Da Capo Press.

Gans, Joshua S. and George B. Shepherd (1994), "How Are the Mighty Fallen: Rejected Classic Articles by Leading Economists," *Journal of Economic Perspectives*, 8 (Winter 1994), 165-179.

Hirschman, Elizabeth C. and Morris B. Holbrook (ed. 1981), *Symbolic Consumer Behavior*, Ann Arbor, MI: Association for Consumer Research.

Holbrook, Morris B. (1986), "A Note on Sadomasochism in the Review Process: I Hate When That Happens," *Journal of Marketing*, 50 (July), 104-108.

Holbrook, Morris B. (1989), "Some Words of Inspiration on Research, Religion, Bach, and Baseball," *ACR Newsletter*, (March), 1-3.

Holbrook, Morris B. (1993a), "Comments on the Report of the AMA Task Force on the Development of Marketing Thought," in *Enhancing Knowledge Development in Marketing: Perspectives and Viewpoints*, ed. P. Rajan Varadarajan and Anil Menon, Chicago, IL: American Marketing Association, 19-23.

Holbrook, Morris B. (1993b), "Nostalgia and Consumption Preferences: Some Emerging Patterns of Consumer Tastes," *Journal of Consumer Research*, 20 (September), 245-256.

Holbrook, Morris B. (1993c), "On the New Nostalgia: 'These Foolish Things' and Echoes of the Dear Departed Past," in *Continuities in Popular Culture: The Present in the Past & the Past in the Present and Future*, ed. Ray B. Browne and Ronald J. Ambrosetti, Bowling Green, OH: Bowling Green State University Popular Press, 74-120.

Holbrook, Morris B. (1994), "Ethics in Consumer Research: An Overview and Prospectus," in *Advances in Consumer Research*, Vol. 21, ed. Chris T. Allen and Deborah Roedder John, Provo, UT: Association for Consumer Research, 566-571.

Holbrook, Morris B. and Robert M. Schindler (1991), "Echoes of the Dear Departed Past: Some Work in Progress On Nostalgia," in *Advances in Consumer Research*, Vol. 18, ed. Rebecca H. Holman and Michael R. Solomon, Provo, UT: Association for Consumer Research, 330-333.

Holbrook, Morris B. and Robert M. Schindler (1994), "Age, Sex, and Attitude Toward the Past as Predictors of Consumers' Aesthetic Tastes for Cultural Products," *Journal of Marketing Research*, 31 (August), 412-422.

Holden, Stephen (1994), "The Master of Dramatic Truth," *New York Times*, Arts and Leisure Section, (October 2), 6.

Levy, Emanuel (1990), *And the Winner Is...: The History and Politics of the Oscar Awards*, New York, NY: Continuum.

Lyons, Len (1980), *The 101 Best Jazz Albums: A History of Jazz On Records*, New York, NY: William Morrow and Company.

Miller, Russell (1993), "Play 'Misty' (Again and Again) for Me," *New York Times*, Arts and Leisure Section, (November 7), 9.

Pareles, Jon (1992), "Cole's 'Unforgettable' Sweeps the Grammys," *New York Times*, (February 26), C15.

Pareles, Jon (1994), "Top Grammys to Houston; 5 for 'Aladdin,'" *New York Times*, (March 2), C15, C22.

Popper, Karl (1976), *Unended Quest: An Intellectual Autobiography*, La Salle, IL: Open Court.

Sudnow, David (1978, ed. 1993), *Ways of the Hand: The Organization of Improvised Conduct*, Cambridge, MA: M.I.T. Press.

FELLOW'S AWARD
Ethics, Morality and the Dark Side of ACR: Implications for our Future[1]

Jacob Jacoby, New York University

"But above all things, truth beareth away the victory."
Inscription over the entrance
to the Main Branch of the
New York Public Library.

First, let me add my own personal note of congratulations to Morris Holbrook and Russ Belk, whose election as ACR Fellows was long overdue.

Today, I'll be using some personal experiences to illustrate a problem that affects us all and which, if not recognized and treated, is likely to render ACR not credible as the voice of scholarly consumer research.

In the process, I'll be speaking bluntly about things that are unpleasant—ethics, or the lack thereof, on the part of some respected members of ACR. Beyond describing what I believe to be instances of scholarly misrepresentation and plagiarism by prominent ACR members, I'll also be discussing things like arrogance, hypocrisy and the abuse of power at ACR. Of course, any who are offended by my remarks can always bring me up before ACR's Ethics (nee Professional Affairs) Committee. Oops, I forgot—though, as President, I made certain that ACR had such a committee (see Friedman, 1977a, 1977b; Jacoby, 1977), it was disbanded several years afterward.

So without an Ethics Committee or Code of Ethics, I guess anything goes, doesn't it? Though some within ACR apparently operate as if this were the case, I don't and won't. That is why the Address, along with its appendices, document what I have to say. As these appendices are too extensive to be included in the ACR Proceedings, I've brought along copies for each ACR member in the audience.[2] Clearly, I am prepared to back up and take full responsibility for everything I say. My purpose is not to embarrass anyone, though, in the process, this may occur. Rather, through providing concrete, real-life examples, my objective is to rouse sentiment and spur action toward much needed reform within our discipline generally, and specifically within ACR. Why? Because it is in our own self-interest to do so; not doing so will only diminish us individually and collectively as the voice of consumer research.

WHAT IS MEANT BY "ETHICS"?

Ethics has been defined in various ways. According to Webster's New Collegiate Dictionary, ethics is "the discipline dealing with what is good and bad with moral duty and obligation;" essentially, it is a "set of moral principles or values" (Merriam-Webster, 1977, p. 392). Moral, in turn, is defined as "of or relating to principles of right and wrong in behavior" (p. 748). As it permeates everything I am about to say, let me re-state this point: **At core, ethics is about principles of right and wrong behavior.**

What does this mean in practical terms? Specifically, how do we know or determine just what is right and what is wrong? There are some guidelines. At least since Socrates, Plato and Aristotle,

fairness and justice have been accepted cornerstones of what is right; unfairness and injustice are understood to be wrong. Another cornerstone is each individual's right to be treated with dignity and respect (Engel et al., 1993, p. 817). Though it is not always fail-safe, perhaps the best rule of thumb for someone trying to distinguish right from wrong is to apply the Golden Rule, namely, "Do unto others as you would have them do unto you." "At its heart, the Golden Rule calls for moral and ethical reasoning to be based on the highest principle that the rights of others should be *paramount* to our own" (Engel, et al. 1993, p. 817; italics supplied). In my experience, the best way to apply the rule is to treat it as a negative, namely, "Don't do unto others what you would NOT want them to do unto you."

THE B-A DISTINCTION

Ever since joining academia, I've heard colleagues hold forth on the purported big difference between the ethics of academicians vs. those in other arenas, particularly in business or law. The argument goes something like this: Though there are some bad apples, the proportion of unethical people in academia is trivial relative to the proportion found in business. (A version of this argument may be found in Holbrook, 1985; see Jacoby, 1985, for a contrasting point of view.) This thesis can be depicted by the two overlapping normal distributions in Figure 1, with the shaded portion representing academia's rotten apples.

Well I'm here to tell you that the B-A distinction is a BAD distinction. Widely reported scandals at leading academic institutions (e.g., Stanford University, The University of Michigan, Rockefeller University) over the past few years suggest that rotten deeds and apples may flourish in the academic orchard. As the findings by Swazey et al. reveal, the patterns of ethical misconduct in academia "do not support the `bad apple' explanation that is often proffered to account for scientific misconduct" (1993, p.550).

Not only does the myth of superior ethics among academicians have no basis in fact but, as will be documented below, given this organization's cavalier attitude toward ethics, the entitlement to presume ethical superiority is a particularly erroneous and unhealthy fiction when applied to ACR. This presumption blinds us to seeing and accepting the obvious, namely, that our continued inattention to ethics is unwarranted; it also may actually encourage the development and growth of rotten apples capable of ruining the entire orchard.

ETHICS IN ACADEMIA

Ethics pertain to every aspect of academia. This is especially true for the scholarly research enterprise. Thus, it is surprising how few and far between are scholarly articles on ethics in our discipline. Little has changed in the 20 years since Tybout and Zaltman observed: "The extant marketing literature is ... silent on ethical issues when compared to other disciplines in the social sciences..." (1974, p. 357). Since then, some work has focused on ethics outside of academe, specifically, the ethics of marketing managers and corporate marketing researchers (e.g., Akaah and Riordan, 1989; Ferrell and Gresham, 1985; Ferrell and Skinner, 1988; Ferrell and Weaver 1978; Hunt et al. 1984; Smith and Quelch 1993). This parallels the emphasis in our introductory consumer behavior texts where, if discussed at all, the focus is generally on the interface between consumer researchers and the public beyond (e.g., Engel

---

[1]The author appreciates the reactions to an earlier version of this manuscript provided by Jerry Olson (Pennsylvania State University), Jonathan Weiss (New York) and two friends who prefer to remain anonymous.

[2]Copies of the appendices are available upon request.

FIGURE 1
The B-A Distinction: Mythical Form

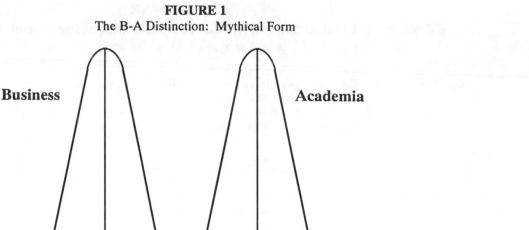

The Ethics Continuum

et al. 1993, Ch. 24; Wilkie, 1990, Appendix 21-B). In an interesting reversal, one paper has even considered the ethical beliefs of the final consumer (Muncy and Scott 1992).

As to work conducted on ethics within the academic setting, the overwhelming majority of articles have focused on ethical issues surrounding human subject research (e.g., Misra, 1992; Sojka & Spangenberg, 1994; Toy, Olson and Wright 1993; Tybout and Zaltman 1974). Few have considered ethics within academe or among the community of academic scholars (Belch, 1993; Holbrook, 1993). Though much can be said regarding unethical conduct by department chairmen and deans, our present focus is on the conduct of ACR members as these reflect the discipline of consumer research. In the process, I'll be describing five cases involving scholarship (Cases 1,2,3,4 and 7) and three involving the governance of ARC (Cases 5, 6 and 8).

Ethics within the Community of ACR Scholars:

The National Academy of Sciences (1992) has clustered ethical problems involving scientists into three categories. The most serious category, termed Misconduct in Science, includes "fabrication, falsification or plagiarism in proposing or reporting research" (see Swazey et al. 1993, p. 542). The cases discussed below focus on one or more of these issues.

Walter Massey, a former Director of the National Science Foundation, observed: "Few things are more damaging to the scientific enterprise than falsehoods—be they the result of error, self-deception, sloppiness and haste, or, in the worst case, dishonesty. It is the paradox of research that the reliance on truth is both the source of modern science... and its intrinsic fragility" (Massey, 1992; Swazey et al. 1993, pp. 552-3).

It is likely that there is hardly an actively publishing scholar alive today (including this author) who has not, at one or more times in his or her career, spoken, written or published some falsehood. In the overwhelming majority of cases, for any one of a number of reasons,[3] I suspect these incidents are innocently and unknowingly committed by the individual. In my opinion, ethical aspects surface only when there is good reason to believe that, at the time the act was

committed, the person either knew, or had exceptionally good reason(s) to know, that what he was doing was somehow in error. In instances of plagiarism, the persons committing the plagiarism must clearly be aware that the person from whom they are plagiarizing was the one to have developed those ideas and/or crafted that language.

While scholars sometimes unknowingly misrepresent another's work, misrepresentation takes on ethical overtones when there is strong evidence (such as the scholar's own prior or contemporaneous published writings) to indicate that the person knew or had good reason to know that how he or she was representing the other's work either was not accurate, was not in fair balance, or was likely to mislead a not insubstantial number of readers into extracting a false implication.

In my opinion, the same applies when author B neglects to cite earlier work by author A when that work is materially and directly relevant to the issue at hand and citing it would cause author B to modify claims made in his or her own writings. Of course, no one can be aware of all the directly relevant and potentially relevant work by others. It is only when there are strong reasons to believe that author B knew or had good reason to know about this other work, yet decided not to mention it, that ethical overtones arise. This can happen when that author's own contemporaneous published writings, or that person's direct access to other information, indicates that he knew or had good reason to know he was omitting reference to another's work that would make his own writings either false, inaccurate, "not in fair balance" or likely to mislead.

---

[3]Several years after publication of an article on which I was the junior author, I found that a portion of one sentence in a section drafted by the senior author had been taken from another's writings. Though frightened for my academic life (I was an untenured Assistant Professor at the time), I wrote the editor of the journal explaining what had happened and offering to make amends. His decision was to let the matter drop.

Case 1: Mis-characterizing a Published Work: In the first case, by publishing an article that mis-characterizes my research in an area where I do research and consulting, this person made it appear that my research was so stupidly conceived and designed that it deserved being highlighted as a prime example of a "scandalous error." I'm referring to the survey I designed and conducted for Kraft, Inc., that was submitted as evidence in the Federal Trade Commission v. Kraft (1991).

All parties involved in the dispute, including Kraft, agreed that calcium was material to (i.e., impacted upon the purchase decisions of) consumers of Kraft's Singles processed cheese (see Jacoby and Szybillo, 1995). Thus, the purpose of my research was **not** to determine whether **the presence of calcium** was material to consumers. Rather, it was to determine whether consumers thought **the difference in calcium** between that contained in 5 oz. of milk vs. that contained in 3.5 oz. of milk was material. By analogy, this is comparable to asking someone who was considering buying a pen not whether the $4.79 price of the pen was material, but whether the 10-cent difference in price between $4.79 and $4.89 would have a material impact on their purchase decision. Yet directly under the title "The Scandalous Record of Avoidable Errors in Expert Evidence Offered in FTC and Lanham Act Cases," this ACR member misrepresented my research by writing: "In another example of avoidably erroneous evidence, Kraft, Inc. tried to establish that **the presence of calcium** is not regarded as material by consumers who purchase cheese" (Preston, 1992, p. 57; bolding supplied).

One might be inclined to excuse this mis-characteri zation as an innocent mistake were it not for evidence that, in my opinion, indicates this author knew or should have known it was a misrepresentation when submitting his article for publication. In a co-authored article appearing a scant three pages earlier, he had written: "We posit that the best test of materiality entails comparing the importance of the implied falsity with that of the truth, much as Jacoby did when he asked consumers whether **the difference in calcium** would cause them to continue or stop buying Singles" (Richards and Preston, p. 54; bolding added). The TV example provided in his very next paragraph further demonstrates his clear understanding that the materiality issue, and Kraft's survey of it, revolved around the question "Is the difference in calcium material?," not "Is calcium material?"

Some may think this is really something too small to complain about.[4] Again, I ask you to consider the Golden Rule: What if it was your work that was being inaccurately represented in a way that then made it seem so stupid and so wrong that it warranted being called a "scandalous error?" Would you like working decades to establish a reputation as a competent researcher, only to see that reputation tarnished by another researcher who, though he knew or should have known that what he was publishing incorrectly described what you had done, still went on to misrepresent your work so that he could label it scandalous? I suspect you would not like it at all and, like me, would feel that, if there was anything

scandalous about the matter, it was the conduct of this mis-characterizer. Please understand that regardless of the rationale or qualifications that person might later use to justify his actions (see Appendix A), since his misrepresentation was published in one of our more highly regarded journals, he never will be able to prevent others who read his misrepresentation and, not knowing it to be such, accept it as true from making similar aspersions about the quality of my work in their own writings.

I submit that, whether by intent or sloppy scholarship, incorrectly representing what someone else has written not only qualifies as unethical conduct by a scholar (see the definition provided by the National Academy of Sciences, 1992), but also violates ethical "principles of right and wrong behavior" as these are generally understood and accepted by society at large.

Case 2: "Deception Via Omission" I: While the above (Case 1) reflects misrepresentation by referring to something I did write, I believe the next two cases reflect misrepresentation arising from failing to do so. Were this to occur in advertising, those familiar with FTC policy (as is the author involved in Case 2; see Richards, 1990, pp. 30-31) would label it an instance of what the FTC "deception via omission." Those more familiar with Food and Drug Administration policy (see Sections 502n and 1.105 of the Federal Food, Drug and Cosmetics Act, 1962) would recognize it as being misleading by virtue of "lacking in fair balance."[5] Regardless of what term is used, I think the behavior in each case reflects unethical scholarship.

Case 2 involves a monograph which its author writes was "intended to serve as a reference for behavioral scientists interested in studying issues related to deception in advertising" (Richards 1990, p. 178). In a passage that indicates he was aware of and had read our most recent published work on this subject, this author compliments Jacoby and Hoyer (1987) for "offering the most comprehensive and insightful view to date of the relationship between comprehension and mediated communications" (Richards, 1990, p. 84). Yet when he subsequently (on pages 104-109) summarizes and critiques prior definitions of deceptive/misleading advertising, strangely for a work claiming to "serve as a reference for behavioral scientists," he neglects to mention the comprehensive definition of deceptive/misleading advertising we provided (Jacoby and Hoyer 1987, pp. 54-62) in the same chapter that he so nicely lauded twenty pages earlier (on p. 84). Instead, he cited and attacked the definition I had developed twelve years earlier (Jacoby and Small, 1975) and long since revised. Perhaps he did this so he could then look good demolishing a "straw man;" perhaps he did this so that, by not having acknowledged the Jacoby and Hoyer (1987) definition which would have refuted his point, he was able to assert: "*Without exception* they [i.e., the prior definitions] fail to explain whether their intent is to define deception or deceptiveness ..." (p.104; italics added); perhaps he omitted reference to our work so that he would not have to explain why his definition (Richards, 1990, p. 109) had so many elements in common with ours (Jacoby and Hoyer, 1987, p. 59-62).

Regardless, because we explicitly stated that our thinking had been substantially revised since publication of Jacoby and Small

---

[4]Science, as the pursuit of truthful knowledge, and scientists operate on the assumption that the scholarly research we read has been truthfully gathered and truthfully reported. If we can't assume the truth and accuracy of what is written, then we have no foundation and everything crumbles. Thus, whether as a result of sloppy scholarship, fraud, misrepresentation, etc., a scholar who publishes untruths injures all stakeholders. Like pregnancy, truth in scholarship is an all or nothing affair. Those willing to excuse "a little" dishonesty, misrepresentation, etc. are on a slippery slope and place the integrity of the entire scholarly enterprise in jeopardy.

[5]By example, an ad for a prescription drug that cited only the studies showing it had a positive effect while failing to also report studies showing it had a negative effect would be deemed by the FDA as "not in fair balance." Similarly, an ad that cited a researcher's early work in support of a drug but failed to also cite the fact that that same researcher later revised his opinion or obtained new data that modified or contradicted his earlier findings would also be deemed to be "lacking in fair balance."

(1975) twelve years earlier,[6] it would be hard for anyone reading our 1987 treatment not to understand that our 1975 conceptualization was no longer one we accepted. This would be especially true for someone sufficiently knowledgeable to be writing a reference work on the subject of deceptive advertising who also claimed to have read our 1987 chapter.

Though our 1975 treatment clearly labeled what was and was not a dictionary definition, it was virtually impossible for anyone reading our 1987 work to extract the implication that the dictionary definition we supplied was one and the same as, or substitutable for, the definition of deception used by regulators (1987, pp. 54-55). Yet despite the fact that he knew or should have known our thinking had substantially changed and that we had provided such clarification, this author (Richards, 1990) presented our outdated views as if they were our most recently published views. Referring to our 1975 treatment, he then went on to write:

> Although the authors chose a dictionary definition of *deception*, and may not themselves be confused about its legal implications, **it seems ironic that in an article about misleading advertising they should mislead their readers.** (Richards, 1990, p. 22; bolding supplied).

Let me assure you that my 1975 piece was not written to mislead readers nor is there any shard of evidence that it misled anyone. Yet instead of writing that he thought our article "**might** mislead readers," and without providing any evidence to support his assertion, the language this person chose to use implied we actually had misled readers. While it may be permissible for scholars to give things a particular "spin," it is not permissible for them to misrepresent another's work. As the very point at issue had been clarified in our 1987 work—a work this author (Richards, 1990) claims to have read—we consider it "scandalous" that he would use language asserting we had misled readers (when we hadn't), yet fail to note that the point he was railing against had been clarified in our subsequent writings, which he himself (as a scholar compiling a "reference" work) claims to have read. I guess it is fair for me to say "it seems ironic that in a book about deceptive advertising the author should, via omission and not being in fair balance, deceive his readers."

Would you like someone who, via omission, in your opinion clearly misrepresented your work and then characterized it as something done to "mislead readers?" I suspect not. Do you think this is how that author would have appreciated having his work handled had the positions been reversed? I think not.

The bottom line is that he (Richards) had ample reason to know and should have known we had substantially revised and clarified our earlier thinking. Since he should have been aware of this and also claimed to be writing a "reference" work on the subject, it was incumbent upon him to note our revised thinking. Doing otherwise reflects "insufficient or misleading reporting" and "inappropriate citation," two of 21 "transgressions of scientific integrity" identified and discussed at a 1991 conference on promoting integrity in behavioral science research (Adler, 1991). Moreover, these infractions are equivalent to "deceptive via omission" and "misleading by not being in fair balance," concepts central to this author's area of expertise.

Case 3: "Deception Via Omission" II: This next case is especially interesting. As explained below, it involves four co-authors, only one of whom I have reasons to believe knew or should have known about, but did not cite, directly relevant work that would have made null and void the paper's claim of having developed something completely new.

Since virtually all here are scholars with an understanding of the rules of the game, let me pose the following for your consideration. Suppose I had written a widely distributed and cited paper claiming that a procedure I developed was a new and original "first of its kind" contribution. Suppose, further, that not only were there relevant prior publications in core psychology journals indicating that someone else had developed and used virtually identical procedures years earlier, but there were a number of reasons to believe I knew about this earlier work, yet chose to make no mention of it in my paper. Were I to do such a thing, how would you characterize my behavior?

With these questions serving as background, consider the following from a widely circulated and cited working paper (Johnson, Payne, Schkade and Bettman, 1989). In the introduction, entitled "Background," the authors write:

> **As an alternative to simple information boards** and difficult to use eye movement recording, **we propose a new methodology for monitoring information acquisition behavior.** That methodology uses computer graphics to display information which is accessed using a computer-based pointing device called a "mouse." (p. 3; bolding supplied)

One interpretation of this passage (or the entire paper) is that the only new development being claimed was the use of a "mouse" as a pointing device, not the entire system. Yet such an interpretation does not seem to fit well with the language used. By comparing the new procedure to "simple information boards," these authors generate the pragmatic implication (Harris and Monaco, 1978) that there were no other previous instances where computers have been used to study consumer information acquisition. Why else would they be positioning their procedure as "an alternative to simple information boards"? Relatedly, note the following promise made in the Abstract:

> This report documents a procedure for monitoring the information acquisition stages of decision behavior. .... The **relationship of the procedure to other process tracing techniques is discussed.** (Bolding supplied.)

Yet when it comes to fulfilling this promise to describe the relationship of their procedure to other process tracing techniques, the authors provide only the following sentence:

> There are a number of computer-based pointing or position entry devices such as a lightpen, joystick, directional cursor keys, and mouse. (p. 4)

Beyond acknowledging these general possibilities, nowhere do they cite or refer to any previous decision making research that used a micro-computer controlled pointing device as part of a system offering a number of flexible graphics and data recording routines—again reinforcing the pragmatic implication that there must be none such. Yet consider the following appearing in the *Journal of Applied Psychology* (Jacoby, Mazursky, et al. 1984, p. 535):

> All information was stored in a Cromemco Z-2H microcomputer .... Respondents commenced their ... decision ... by communicating with the computer via a light pen attached to a color video monitor. After an initial series of person-

---

[6]After referring to both Jacoby and Small (1975) and Jacoby, Hoyer and Sheluga (1980), we state: "Our current views reflect evolution and change." (Jacoby and Hoyer, 1987, p. 55.)

machine inter–actions to review the task instructions and rules, two "menu" lists were displayed—one containing the names of the eight stocks, and the other being a list of 26 fundamental factors .... The analyst was permitted to access only a single piece of information at a time .... Accessing of the information was accomplished by touching the screen twice with the light pen—once to identify the stock for which the information was being requested and a second time to identify the fundamental factor[7]—and the desired information appeared on the screen almost instantly. After acquiring this first item of information, the computer inquired whether the analysts wanted to make a best buy recommendation at that point or wanted to acquire additional information. If the analyst replied that he or she wanted to acquire additional information, the two lists were displayed again, and the analysts used the light pen to indicate which item of information he or she next wished to consider. Each analyst continued in this way until the point at which he or she felt ready to make a "best buy" recommendation. This, too, was indicated via the light pen.

A nearly identical description was provided in 1985 in the inaugural issue of *Computers in Human Behavior* (Jacoby, Kuss et al., pp. 101-102). These procedures were again described in a 1987 *Journal of Experimental Social Psychology* article (Jacoby, Jaccard et al., pp. 150-151, 160). Although not described there in any great detail, a fourth paper based on the same procedures as the *JAP* and *CHB* papers (Jacoby, et al. 1986) appeared in *Advances in Consumer Research*. The three articles published in recognized peer review journals all confirm that others not only developed and used, but were the first to publish articles using a "computer- controlled pointing device" and set of procedures offering "a number of flexible graphics and process tracing techniques" for studying information acquisition. However, even had they not come across any of these articles, as the factors described below indicate, one of the co–authors had considerable reason to know about our procedures and developments. Hence, there was no justification for co–authoring a paper claiming to be the first to develop and use a "computer-controlled pointing device" and set of procedures offering "a number of flexible graphics and process tracing techniques" for studying information acquisition.

Based upon the numerous experiences I've had conducting deceptive advertising surveys submitted as evidence in litigated matters, I can assure you that if we applied the same procedures in this instance as are routinely used to assess deceptive advertising (e.g., showing the Mouselab passages noted above or, for that matter, the entire paper to a randomly selected group of scholars from related social science and/or management disciplines and then asking them questions to learn the meanings and inferences they extracted from exposure to this paper), we would find that regardless of whether it was the authors' intent to confine their claim to the mouse and nothing else, "a not insubstantial proportion"—at least 15% to 20% and probably more than that[8]—would come away believing either that: (1) the authors of the Mouselab paper were the first to develop and use computers, in contrast to "simple information boards," to study consumer information acquisition, and/or (2) they were the first to use a "computer-controlled pointing device" and set of procedures offering "a number of flexible graphics and process tracing techniques," and/or (3) that no other similar "com-

puter-controlled pointing device" or procedures offering "a number of flexible graphics and process tracing techniques" had previously been described in the literature.

Prompted by matters to be described below (in the section entitled "Ethical [Mis-?]Conduct by ACR Executive Committees"), I wrote to the senior author of this paper explaining my beliefs and requesting an explanation. This led to an exchange of correspondence which eventually culminated in a face-to-face meeting. My recollection is that the following points surfaced during these exchanges. Both the Jacoby and Payne teams seem to have developed computer IDBs at approximately the same time, circa 1975-76. However, articles describing the Jacoby team's use of an advanced system equivalent to the Mouselab appeared years before the Payne team's published descriptions and, to the extent the authors knew about them, should have been noted in that section of the Mouselab paper that promised to compare the Mouselab to other comparable procedures. As doing otherwise would reflect instances of "insufficient or misleading reporting" and "inappropriate citation" (Adler, 1991), future work by the Mouselab authors would not lay claim to being the first or only such procedure and, as necessary, would include appropriate citations.

It is important to emphasize that the issue is not that knowledge of the Jacoby team's efforts assisted the Johnson– Payne team in any way to develop or refine the Mouselab. There is nothing that gives me reason to believe, nor should there be anything in what I have written that gives anyone else reason to believe, that the Mouselab procedures were not developed totally and completely independently of anything that my colleagues and I had developed and done. Rather, the issue is that one of the four authors knew or had exceptionally good reasons to know about the Jacoby team's related developments; hence, this person should never have co–authored a paper which claimed that the procedures being described therein were unique and without precedent.

Specifically, it should be obvious that I thought highly enough of Jim Bettman to (a) invite him to Purdue in 1975 where he gave a colloquium to the psychology faculty on his work, (b) to, at that time, show him the IDBs I had developed and was using in my research and (c) to share my early data with him (see Bettman and Jacoby, 1976). At the 1976 and 1977 ACR conferences, I also shared with him information regarding our computer–IDB developments which, for its time, was informaiton I believe was noteworthy for those working in this area.

Jim Bettman was also a member of the six person 1979 National Science Foundation Advisory Panel connected with a $353,000 grant (NSF PRA 79–20585) awarded to Jim Jaccard and me for the purpose of studying consumer information accessing with respect to technologically complex products. Like others on the panel, in 1979, Jim was sent a copy of the full proposal for his comments and reactions. That proposal described the new procedures and equipment we would be using — procedures that,

---

[7]Instead of having to touch the screen twice, as with the "menu" format described above, a series of studies conducted during 1980-1982 used a "blank matrix" format that required touching the plasma screen only once.

[8]The FTC has determined that ads were deceptive when as few as 9% have been misled. Some examples are: 13% (in Elliott Knitwear Inc. 59 FTC 893; 1961); 14% (in Benrus Watch Co. 64 FTC 1018, 1032; 1964); 10%-15% (in Firestone Tire & Rubber v. FTC 481 F.2d 246, 249; 6th Circuit; 1973); 9%-10% (in ITT Continental Baking Co. 83 FTC 865; 1973); and 14% (in Bristol Myers et al. 85 FTC 688; 1975). Based upon the dozens of deceptive advertising cases in U.S. District Courts in which I've been involved, I can safely say that the Federal courts use essentially the same criterion level, i.e., levels of at least 15% to 20% are usually sufficient for a court to reach a finding of deception.

unknown to me and apparently also to them, were in virtually every essential respect equivalent to that being independently developed by the Mouselab team (specifically, Johnson and Payne).

Finally, the 1985 article that appeared in *Computers and Human Behavior*, as well as the empirical protion of the 1987 article that appeared in the *Journal of Experimental Social Psychology*, had initially been submitted to the *Journal of Consumer Research* in mid–1984. While I have no idea which members of the 1984 Editorial Board served as reviewers, it must have been individuals with expertise in the information processing realm. Regardless, in his capacity as *JCR*'s co–editor at the time, Jim sent me a November 16, 1984 rejection letter which indicated he had read my manuscript (which detailed my development of "computer graphics to display information which is accessed using a computer–based pointing device" and how I was using these procedures to study security analyst decision making) and the 16 pages of reviewer comments. As the reviewer comments clearly indicate, the computer procedures were described in considerable detail. Reviewer B even wrote: "Cut Back! Who cares what type of microcomputer it was stored on?"

In other words, there are several strong reasons underlying my belief that, by 1986, when Jim Bettman became a co–author on the Mouselab paper, he either knew or should have known about the Jacoby team's developments.[9] The fact that it was "only a working paper" did not prevent its authors from citing and widely disseminating it so that the information contained therein could influence the thinking and writing of others.

Case 4: Unintended Plagiarism: Next is a case of actual plagiarism, though I suspect the authors were well- intentioned and never realized it as such. Webster's "New Collegiate Dictionary" (1977, p. 877) defines "plagiarize" as **"to pass off the ideas ... of another as one's own,"** and to **"present as new and original an idea or product derived from an existing source."** Now consider the following.

Not satisfied with what I found in the texts of the time, in 1968 I began developing a definition of consumer behavior which I then presented in a working paper devoted to the subject (Jacoby, 1969a) and in a talk delivered at the 1969 American Psychological Association's annual convention. I spent the next five years fleshing out the definition and its implications before proposing it in my 1974 Presidential Address to APA's Division of Consumer Psychology (Jacoby, 1975) and, again, in my 1975 Presidential Address to ACR (Jacoby 1976a). This definition achieved wider dissemination through my chapters in the *Annual Review of Psychology*, and the *Handbook of Industrial and Organizational Psychology* (Jacoby, 1976b,c). In other words, by the end of 1976, I had invested an appreciable amount of intellectual effort to develop this definition, craft the particular language used to describe my thoughts, and to develop and articulate the ideas in the several pages that accompanied and explained the components of this definition. Without the accompanying elaboration, the basic definition was as follows: "Consumer behavior is the ...

---

[9]Following a conversation I had with JIm Bettman and Eric Johnson on the morning of October 23, 1994, the day after this Address was delivered, I revised the Address to further clarify the bases for my views on this matter. I invited them to comment upon these revisions and I also offered to mail, at my expense, a copy of this revised section on Case 3, along with a set of any contrasting comments that they might prepare, to all those on ACR's list of conference attendees. They declined to accept either of these invitations and indicated they might consider providing their views on this matter in another forum.

acquisition, consumption, and disposition of goods, services, time and ideas by decision making units (e.g., individuals, families, firms, etc.)" (Jacoby, 1975a, p. 1).

Comparing this definition to those in the texts of that era, one can readily see that this synthesis represented a unique and substantially more comprehensive definition of consumer behavior than any proposed to that point in time.

Now consider the following from a book published two years later. In the Preface to the book, and with no quotation marks or any attribution to my prior work, the editors define "consumer and industrial buying behavior" as the ...

acquisition, consumption, and disposition of goods, services, time and ideas by decision making units or buying centers (Woodside, Sheth, and Bennett 1977, p. ix).[10]

Upon not seeing any quotation marks or attribution to some other source, readers not aware of the original source of these ideas would likely believe this definition was created by the book's editors. Presuming they are themselves ethical scholars, they would then begin attributing this definition to these editors in their own writings.

Let me note that these authors (Woodside, Sheth and Bennett) were kind enough to use and correctly cite some of my other ideas on this very same page and, had they recognized what they were doing, I firmly believe they would have used quotation marks or made some other appropriate attribution. However, regardless of how innocent the deed or well-intentioned the imitation, I suspect most in this audience would have felt similarly unhappy to have their hard work made to appear as if it were the work of others. According to the long-standing canons of scholarly ethics, as the one who had devoted the time and intellectual effort to developing this definition, I deserved to be accorded the recognition for this, not have it made to appear that it was the work of others.

I'll be describing one more example of scholarly misconduct where, in my view, a series of eight letters prior to its occurrence made the plagiarism deliberate and deceitful. However, since my decision to report this case (Case 7) comes only as a consequence of other events, its description is being delayed until after these other events can themselves be described.

I'm sure many here can attest that the few examples of misconduct I've described are by no means isolated examples within our discipline. My purpose, however, is not to focus on these individuals or their actions. Rather, it is to focus on ACR itself. To paraphrase the Bard, "Somthing is rotten in ACR" and if we fail to correct the problem, I am certain that ACR will come to be viewed as a rogue organization by other social scientists.

ETHICAL MIS(?) CONDUCT BY ACR'S GOVERNANCE

One might think that, regardless of how they might behave or misbehave as individuals, when those at ACR whom we honor and trust with elected office come together to discharge their official duties, one could expect there would be no such misconduct. Well I'm sorry to have to disabuse you of this fairy tale, "knights in white armor" wish-it-were-so–but–it's-not, notion. As I show below,

---

[10]For any who think a string of 14 **words** is trivial, consider that a computer program used in the bio-medical sciences for detecting fraud works on strings of 30 **characters**, and data obtained from the application of this program have been successfully used in prosecuting cases of plagiarism. (See Hilts, 1992).

ACR Executive Committees have accepted and acted on the basis of slander, ACR Presidents have used disrespect as official ACR policy, and both have compounded and perpetuated injustice in an errant attempt to "save face." None of these behaviors are anything that those who engaged in these actions would appreciate experiencing themselves.

The ACR Fellow Award:

Consider the ACR Fellow Award. Though up to three such awards can be made in any one year, including the trio of Belk, Holbrook and Jacoby, in the fifteen years since its inception, the various Executive Committees have elected 16 Fellows, an average of slightly more than one per year. In founding the Award, the minutes of the 1978 ACR Executive Committee state that the Award is to be given for **"significant impact on scholarly work in consumer behavior."**[11] This raises two questions: What constitutes "scholarly work?" How do you gauge "impact?"

Assessing a scholar's contribution is by no means an easy task and there exist varying approaches for doing so. Because it is the one traditionally used in faculty promotion and tenure meetings, the approach we are all familiar with is to consider the number and type of publications a person has and where these have appeared. There are reasonably well-known pecking orders: for example, publishing work in a discipline's rigorously reviewed vanguard journals is accorded the highest esteem and considered to reflect the highest level of scholarly contribution; things like editing books are considered of lesser value. However, while the traditional approach may provide some idea of the extent of a scholar's contribution, it does not tell you anything about the **impact** of that body of work, specifically, whether these contributions have influenced anyone else in the field or beyond— which, after all, is how knowledge in any scientific discipline advances.

Publications do not necessarily translate into impact. For example, approximately half of all articles published in the physical and biological science's most rigorous journals during the five year period from 1981 through 1985 were **never** cited in the five years after their publication (see Cote et al. 1991, p. 402). From this it seems reasonable to deduce that these articles had little, if any, impact. Scientific contribution is not about publications; it's about influencing thought and advancing the field.

With the above serving as background, let me make some highly immodest observations, the reason for which will soon become obvious. Consider, first, the *Journal of Consumer Research,* for the past twenty years, the journal regarded as the most rigorous and prestigious in our field and the only one ACR sponsors. According to Hoffman and Holbrook (1993), at the end of its first fifteen years, I was the most cited researcher by the 41 other most published authors in *JCR.* (Examination will reveal this was also true in 1979 and again in 1984, after *JCR*'s first five and first ten years of existence.) As testimony to the good company I'm in, after fifteen years, the second and third most cited contributors were Morris Holbrook and Russ Belk, respectively.

Since many articles on consumer behavior are published in the *Journal of Marketing* and *Journal of Marketing Research*, some might ask: "What happens when these other primary sources are

considered?" According to Cote, Leong & Cote (1990), based on citations to articles published in *JCR, JM* and *JMR* during the twenty year period from 1966 through 1986, I am the second-most cited person across the more than 1400 journals that comprise the *Social Science Citation Index.* Only Paul Green, someone generally viewed as being a statistician and methodologist more than a consumer researcher, ranked higher (thereby effectively making me the most frequently cited consumer reseacher during this twenty year period). Again, both Morris and Russ are not far behind (see Appendix B).[12]

Of course, knowing that, as compared to articles in other disciplines, those in marketing have a more rapid "death rate" (Goldman, 1979), those with a "what have you done for me lately?" perspective would point out that high cumulative citation rates after 15 years may reflect many early citations which have begun to wane in later years. Accordingly, consider the recently published *Handbook of Consumer Behavior* (Robertson and Kassarjian, 1991). This compendium is promoted as representing "a current account of what is known about consumer behavior" (p. vii). As its editors write, the 16 "chapters represent the conceptual underpinnings of the consumer behavior discipline as it currently exists" (p. vii). Presumably, the greater the number of chapters that cite a person's work, the broader and more lasting has been that person's contribution to and impact upon the field. Once again, the trio of Holbrook, Belk and Jacoby rank right up there; the only ACR Fellow to have his work cited in more chapters is Jim Bettman.

Some might ask: What about contributions to ACR in particular? Consider what the editors of the *Index* covering the first ten years of *ACR Proceedings* wrote: "We began to wonder who, in fact, are the greatest contributors to the ACR Proceedings. Counting all listings in this index ... the clear winner was Jack Jacoby. He had published 22 separate entries..." (Kassarjian and Orsini 1980, iii). Next came Rich Lutz, Jerry Olson and Jag Sheth, each with 12 entries.[13] With six additional entries in the *Index* compiled to cover

---

[11] If anything was ever voted on and approved by the membership, it was this language. More recently, the Calls for Nominations have omitted the "significant impact on scholarly work" phrase and instead stated that the Fellow Award is to be given for "a long period of productivity and contribution." If you will, please ponder for a moment the phrase "a long period of productivity and contribution." Just what does this mean or encompass? I return to this question anon.

[12] Like any form of measurement, impact assessment via citation frequencies is not perfect. However, as it more closely reflects the ultimate criterion of interest for a scholar (namely, what has been the impact of his work on scholarly contributions to the discipline?), it would seem to be at least as good an indicant of a scholar's contribution over time than simply noting the number of publications that a person has had. In my opinion, aside from being as comfortable as an old shoe, the reason why many academic departments in business schools continue to rely on the number and type of publications and choose to not augment this traditional approach with a concurrent assessment of impact is that (a) the latter is relatively new, (b) the latter requires more effort than simply looking at a vita or writing others for "outside letters," and (c) while impact usually requires a period of years to be evidenced, given the "up or out" fast track that promotion and tenure committees generally must operate on, there is little time for impact to be manifested. Having said this, it is interesting to note that many more academic departments in the physical, biological and behavioral sciences rely on citation counts as compared to academic departments in business schools.

[13] One of my 22 entries was my ACR Presidential Address (Jacoby, 1976a) which, if I'm not mistaken, is still the only ACR Presidential Address to subsequently undergo peer review and then be published in one of our leading journals. As Keith Hunt later wrote in an ACR Newsletter, by subsequently garnering the American Marketing Association's "Maynard Award" for being judged the best contribution to marketing theory published in the *Journal of Marketing* in 1978, this address brought kudos to ACR.

the subsequent five years (see Curren et al., 1984), my 10 contribution "lead" over all other contributors widened. In other words, at the end of ACR's critical, formative first 15 years, based upon the record established of contributions made specifically at ACR conferences and published in ACR's Proceedings, no other ACR member had contributed as much as had I.[14]

Given this record of "significant impact on scholarly work in consumer behavior," how come it took the unanimous recommendation of at least six different ACR Fellows Nominating Committees (and the corresponding rejection by five different ACR Executive Committees) dating back to 1981 for me to be elected a Fellow—an award established for the sole purpose of honoring precisely such impact? Puzzling, isn't it, how someone could rank first in terms of being cited in *JCR* during the first 15 years of its existence, be the first ranked consumer researcher over a 20 year span in having the work he published in the field's three most prestigious journals cited in the 1400-plus representing the best of all the other social sciences, and rank first in the number of contributions to the ACR Proceedings during ACR's first 15 years—yet be repeatedly rejected for ACR Fellowship, an honor ostensibly bestowed for just such contributions.

Given spans of 15 and 20 years, it is not like these contributions could be considered a flash in the pan. Given that we are speaking about what have traditionally been recognized as the three most prestigious journals regularly publishing scholarly consumer research, it is not like these contributions were somehow mysteriously hidden from view. So how come it has taken this long for them to be recognized? What is the explanation? The answer has direct and significant implications for each and every one of you and especially for the credibility and integrity of this organization.

Case 5: When Petty Politics Became Accepting and Taking Official Action Based on Unsubstantiated Falsehoods: From 1981 through 1990, I know of at least three occasions when I was nominated for the ACR Fellows Award; I believe there were other occasions that I cannot document and probably yet others of which I am not aware. I was also nominated again in 1991, 1992, and 1993.[15] According to ACR's Rules of Procedure, being elected a Fellow requires that the Nominating Committee be unanimous in sending any candidate's name forward to the Executive Committee. This means that on each of the six (or more) times my name came before the Executive Committee, I had received the unanimous endorsement of the Nominating Committee; yet except for the last, on each previous occasion I was voted down. Since the only legitimate basis for granting or denying anyone this award revolves around that candidate's body of scholarly contributions and the impact these have had on the field, and on nothing else, and given my above-documented contributions to the discipline generally and this organization in particular, I was puzzled by these repeated rejections. "Petty politics" I told myself.

The longer I was denied election to ACR Fellow, the more it began to hurt, the more I felt alienated from and by this organization, and the more I felt the need to understand what was going on. During the 80s, I rationalized that, outspoken as I tend to be, I must have said or done something that antagonized one or more of those voting. However, since (except for Keith Hunt) the composition of the Executive Committee changes over the years, I eventually

---

[14]Hindsight being what it is, I now recognize that sending good material to ACR (before having tried top-notch journals) was not a good idea, as it has led to oblivion for much of that work. Regardless of the uniqueness or quality of such material, scholars who publish in journals often don't consider it worthwhile reviewing what has appeared in *ACR Proceedings*. As but a few examples:

In reviewing Multi-Method Multi-Trait matrices in consumer research, Bagozzi and Yi (1991, p. 427) write: "Despite the importance of construct validation, the MMMT design has been used infrequently in consumer research. Only a few studies using the MMMT procedure could be found in [the first 17 years of] *JCR*....Also, very few related consumer research studies could be found in the *JMR* over its 26 years." Perhaps thinking it unlikely there would be any such piece in the *ACR Proceedings*, these authors overlook the detailed account of two such studies in ACR's Third Annual Conference *Proceedings* (Jacoby, 1972).

In similar fashion, Rentz (1987, p. 19; and Peter, 1979, before him) contend that "generalizability theory has largely been overlooked in marketing." Yet both overlook a generalizability study presented at ACR's 1977 conference and then published in our *Proceedings* (Jacoby et al. 1978). In fairness to Peter, his review included only *JMR* (for the years 1972- 1976), *JCR* (1975-1977), *JM* (1974-1976), the *AMA Proceedings* (1974-1976) and the *ACR Proceedings* (1974-1976). My point? Simply that, even 10 years after it appeared as the earliest series of a "multifaceted generalizability approach" (Peter, 1979, p. 12) in the consumer literature, it was still relatively unique. Making Jacoby et al. (1978) an *ACR Proceedings* contribution reflected a lack of "publishing strategy wisdom" on my part.

Probably my greatest lack of good judgment in this regard came in making Jacoby, Chestnut, Weigl and Fisher (1976) an *ACR Proceedings* contribution. I had mistakenly assumed that there was little need to submit to a journal what, for its time, was a groundbreaking paper describing the Information Display Board research my collaborators and I were doing, as colleagues recognizing that it could certainly have been published in *JCR* or *JMR* would cite it when appropriate. Since the Behavioral Process approach had already been presented in an article in *JCR* (Berning and Jacoby, 1974) and also in a special issue of *Communication Research* devoted to consumer research (Jacoby, 1975b), I felt "being first" had already established and there was no need to send the Jacoby, Chestnut et al. paper to a journal. Instead, to go along with my ACR Presidential Address that year, I decided it would be nice to present this research at the 1975 ACR Conference. As they say, the rest is history. Others have apparently failed to understand that, except for its having been translated from a horizontal to a vertical axis, the IDB was essentially the same procedure used by Berning and Jacoby (1974). Regardless, by contributing this to an *ACR Proceedings* rather than sending it to a journal, I opened the door for others to begin crediting Payne (1976) or Bettman and Kakkar's (1977) modification of what I had shared with Bettman as having introduced this approach and procedure into the consumer literature.

The bottom line implication may be that, despite what the annual Call for Papers says about sending your better work to ACR and having it published in the *ACR Proceedings*, don't, as that may be the fast track to oblivion.

[15]To substantiate a point made below, copies of Jerry Olson's 1991 and 1993 nomination letters are provided in Appendix C.

discounted this hypothesis.[16] It was clear that something beyond petty politics was involved.

After the 1991 Fellows Nominating Committee's unanimous recommendation was rejected for at least the third time in a decade (and Jerry Olson's "Don't sweat it Jack; it's only a matter of time" became less comforting), I finally became curious enough to see if I could learn what was going on. First I called the Chairman of the 1991 Nomination Committee who told me that, though he and his committee were strongly positive in their nomination, he didn't have a vote on the 1991 Executive Committee and, though he was personally disturbed by what he observed, he couldn't tell me what went on. So I called someone on the Executive Committee whom I hoped might be willing to share with me some small inkling—anything that would give me some insight.

This "source" turned out to be more forthcoming than I had ever expected. I was at first shocked, then angered, to hear that the reason I was being "blackballed" had absolutely nothing to do with my "body of contributions" (which, according to this source, all on the Executive Committee agreed merited the award). Rather, it had to do with what I interpret as illogical and malicious slander emanating from who knows where that, without any effort at verification, was apparently being condoned, accepted and used as the basis for a decision each time my nomination came before the Executive Committee. These allegations were that:

1. Some of my published research has been funded by contracts from industry. This research appears to have been "slanted," that is, used in a manner that "some see as supporting the interests of business clients at the possible expense of consumers."

2. At times, I have quarreled with colleagues. More seriously, this includes "quarreling over who should receive credit for academic achievements."

3. I consult, "make a lot of money" and live well. For some, this "consulting appears to interfere with [my] continuing to make contributions to the field."

I won't take the time here to address these allegations; my full reply to Numbers 1 and 3 are set forth in the redacted version of a 46 page letter provided here as Appendix D. As for quarreling with others, I think the Cases I've described provide some understanding of the kinds of scholarship that makes me "quarrelsome," and would give any scholar cause to become "quarrelsome."

Regardless, even if true, these allegations in no way undo my "body of contributions" or "the impact these have had on scholarly research within the field." Thus, they provide absolutely no legitimate basis for rejecting my nomination—at least not according to the official Minutes of the 1978 Executive Committee that established the award, nor according to anything else that has ever been formally stated and since become member-approved policy.

Whether you are being voted on for the ACR Fellow Award, being voted on for promotion or tenure, or anything else you value, please think of a committee that votes on whether you receive somthing the record strongly suggests you have earned. Would you appreciate this committee accepting and acting on the basis of

malicious slander about you without first trying to obtain clarification from others in a position to know the particulars or, better yet, without giving you an opportunity to explain or reply? Would you appreciate being repeatedly denied an honor you had earned for reasons having nothing to do with the officially stated policy regarding the purpose for which that honor is to be accorded? Did the members of those early Executive Committees do unto another something they themselves would not want done unto them had the roles been reversed?

Case 6: Disrespect as Official ACR Policy: To stimulate some semblance of conscience and reason among the ACR governance, I began writing what became the earlier referred to 46 page single–spaced letter addressing these allegations, portions of which are provided in Appendix D. To insure I was accurately describing what my source had told me, I sent that person successive drafts of the letter, each of which was followed up with an extended phone conversation. Satisfied that I was describing my source's account of the meeting accurately, on January 28, 1992, the final version of the letter (which also raised a number of important policy and governance questions for the Executive Committee to consider; see Appendix D, pages 38-39 and 43-44), was sent to all members of the 1991 Nominating Committee as well as to the ACR President.[17] My January 29th cover letter to the ACR President (see Appendix D) contained several additional questions directed specifically to him, as follows:

In the event that the Executive Committee does not go along with the request that it re-establish an ethics committee then, as a dues-paying member of ACR in good standing, I'd appreciate answers to the following questions:

1. For what reason was ACR'S Professional Affairs Committee disbanded? How did it come to be disbanded? When did it happen (i.e., who was ACR's President at the time)?

2. Are ACR committees able to be disbanded without a vote of the general membership? If so, should this be so?

3. Given that we no longer have a Professional Affairs Committee charged with handling ethical disputes, is the full Executive Committee prepared to do so? If so, as I would like to have some issues considered, what are the procedures, rules and mechanisms for doing so?

I quess these questions must be either very tough or very inappropriate because, though I received a March 2nd letter acknowledging

---

[16]To infer from this that Keith was responsible is equivalent to saying that, since the same man got drunk on scotch and water one night, bourbon and water the next night, and vodka and water the third night, drinking water causes drunkenness.

[17]Of all the Executive Committee members who voted on my nomination that year and then received a copy of my January 28, 1992 letter, only Kent Monroe, a gentleman as well as a scholar, called to apologize. Morris Holbrook, a member of the Nominating Committee, also sent me a very kind and empathic letter which included some of the data from his forthcoming article (Hoffman and Holbrook, 1993).

Note, also, that shortly after my letter was distributed, I received a concerned call from my source asking if I had threatened or initiated a suit against ACR for slander. As I told my source, that course of action had never entered my mind. When I asked from where did this new rumor come, the source replied that another Executive Committee member had called cautioning my source to keep quiet about the Executive Committee's deliberations because of a concern that they might be sued. Presumably others on the Executive Committee received similar calls.

his receipt of my letters, I never received a return letter or so much as a phone call in answer to my questions (see Appendix D). After several months of non-response, I sent several follow-up letters;[18] these yielded no response whatever. Recall that a cornerstone of ethics is the right that each of us has to be treated with dignity and respect (see Engel et al, 1993, p. 817). Was this ACR President "Doing unto others as he would have them do unto him?" I think not.

I ask you: How would you feel if, as a dues-paying member in good standing, you had written asking the ACR President legitimate questions regarding ACR's functioning that were of concern to you, yet never received a substantive reply? When I served as ACR President, it never would have occurred to me to be so impolite and disrespectful a representative of this organization as to ignore the letters of **any** dues-paying member, much less a founding member and past-President—and when I hadn't received any answer to my questions by the time of ACR's 1992 Annual Conference in Vancouver, I told this outgoing ACR President so at that conference. Confirming what my source had told me eight months earlier (see Footnote 17), this past-President's reply amounted to: We don't want to talk to you about it and we especially don't want to put anything in writing because we're concerned you

---

[18]Consider the following from my letter of May 16, 1992 (see Appendix D):

".... This caused me to once again wonder why any ACR member should be in the dark regarding the criteria used for determining ACR Fellow status.

Accordingly, please consider this letter to fall under the "press your concerns" rubric. Though I recognize that, without consulting the ACR Executive Committee, you are not yet in any position to answer the questions posed on pages 38-39 and 43-44 of my January 28th letter to the ACR Fellows Nominating Committee, I want to emphasize that I remain intensely interested in having these questions answered. I also think that, in one form or another, these answers should be communicated to the ACR membership at large."

Also consider the following from my letter of September 3, 1992 (see Appendix D):

"... my January 28th letter raises a number of questions regarding the meaning of the Fellow Award and the criteria used for bestowing this award. For the good of the organization, I believe it is important that these questions be discussed, answered and this information communicated to the membership at large.

Like other dues-paying members in good standing, annually, I receive a form requesting that I fulfill a responsibility of ACR membership by submitting the names of worthwhile Fellow nominees. Heretofore, when considering whom I might nominate, I was under the impression that the Award was conferred for making contributions to ACR and to the discipline that advanced scholarly thought, research and practice. I was also of the belief that factors other than these were irrelevant. However, upon learning what kind of issues became the focal point of discussion at last year's meeting, it may be that I have been mistaken. Accordingly, I would like some clarification so that I can responsibly fulfill this obligation of membership. I suspect that I am not alone in this regard; there must be other ACR members who need and would appreciate such clarification as well.... Just what are the objectives of and criteria used in bestowing the ACR Fellow award? I am open to the possibility that the award doesn't represent what I (and, I am sure, many others at ACR) think it does. But, then, what does it represent?"

might sue.[19] To this very day, two years later, my questions about fundamental governing policies of ACR have yet to be answered.

Their unwillingness to answer my legitimate questions only fueled my frustration and anger. I also took their unfounded concern to mean that they had some inkling that, were I to sue, their behavior would necessarily be exposed for others to see and understand for what it was. Thus, even were I to mount and lose such a suit in court, the ACR Executive Committee had more to lose in ACR's court of public opinion.

These experiences made me realize several other things, paramount among these being that I was dealing with at least some members of the Executive Committee who, while intellectually sophisticated, apparently also happened to be ethically deficient. Being able to hide behind veils of secrecy, their actions not subject to independent review, they seemed able to get away with doing virtually anything—including accepting and acting on slanderous charges that amounted to character assassination. Rather than conjure up images of knights draped in white robes acting as defenders of the faith (as I'm sure many of us are inclined to view our elected officials), I began seeing their actions as more akin to that of the white knights of the Ku Klux Klan. Just like the KKK, in trampling on the rights of those with little or no recourse to defend themselves, they had apparently convinced themselves that the rumors and slander they themselves were hearing and accepting represented "truth" and thus justified their actions.[20]

Case 7: Plagiarism, Blatant and Deceitful: My frustration gave way to anger, then to resolve, then to action. The most immediate action I took brings me to describing the case I referred to earlier of what I believe was deliberate and deceitful plagiarism that occurred more than twenty years ago which has helped this person reap many tangible rewards, including being elected an ACR President and ACR Fellow. Having not done so for more than twenty years, it could not be more obvious that I never intended, nor would now be making this matter public knowledge had it not been for what I learned was being said about me behind closed doors at ACR Executive Committee meetings. But with ACR having disbanded its only mechanism for independent review and my having no other place to go to get a fair hearing on Executive Committee conduct, I felt enough was enough. If they were going to listen to and base their official decisions on unfounded slander about me behind closed doors, yet not even grant me, a dues-paying member, the respect of answering my legitimate questions regarding how they were governing this organization, then I was going to

---

[19]Perhaps in an attempt to be kind, Andreasen also told me that, because they felt I had "so much more to contribute," the Executive Committee hoped I would become active again in ACR. Surprising, isn't it, how people engaged in the study of human (consumer) behavior seem not to understand one of the most fundamental set of concepts our texts tell us underlies most human behavior, namely conditioning and extinction. Kick someone in the stomach often enough and, instead of giving you "more," if he doesn't have to return to take more abuse, he won't.

[20]This seems analogous to Rosenblatt's (1994) description of the psychological mechanisms tobacco executives use in order "to live with themselves" and not be concerned that what they do causes serious harm to others. Rosenblatt (1994) contends they must be in denial. "to be in denial implies that one may not be held accountable, in psychological terms, for one's actions." "Individually, they ... create their own moral universe of explanations and justifications" (p. 36).

confront them with a case that, in my opinion, amounted to flagrant and deceitful plagiarism and see what, if anything, they would do about it.[21] Through this I hoped they would see the problem in terms of the broader issues involved and, as a consequence, move ACR in a direction that would culminate in the re- establishment of an ACR Ethics Committee.

Briefly, under the pretense of co–authoring a paper, a former ACR President obtained copies of my unpublished working papers and related notes. Only after receiving these materials (but never providing me with copies of his own, as we had agreed), did he inform me he was also thinking of preparing a "light weight piece of 10–12 manuscript pages" for submission to "a second rate journal" as a sole–authored paper. That so–called light weight piece was then published not in any "second rate journal," but in the most prestigious journal in the field at that time, the *Journal of Marketing Research* (Kassarjian, 1971). Further, despite having written that his behavior with respect to my unpublished ideas and writings would be as pure as the driven snow (for example: "Let me assure you that I am quite scrupulous about plagerizing" [sic]; and my paper would "avoid including any of the concepts you and I will introduce later" in our co– authored piece), and without my knowledge or permission, he had lifted and used ideas, phrases, and complete sentences from my unpublished working papers. Some of my ideas and language appeared in his article without quotation marks or any attribution to indicate its source (namely, Jacoby 1969a, 1969b). As an example, compare the following:

Statistical techniques...are applied and anything that turns up looking halfway interesting furnishes the basis for the discussion section. (Jacoby, 1969b)

Statistical techniques are applied and anything that turns up looking halfway interesting furnishes the basis for the discussion section. (Kassarjian, 1971, p. 416)

Aside from what I believe amounts to irrefutable evidence of duplicity in the eight letters exchanged (e.g., the frequent promise that none of my ideas or writings would be used), what makes the actual lifting of concepts and words difficult for the casual reader to detect is the fact that Jacoby is sometimes cited. However, as the APA Code of Ethics (1992, p. 1609) complete standard regarding plagiarism states: "Psychologists do not present substantial portions or elements of another's work or data as their own, **even if the other work or data source is cited occasionally"**[22]

---

[21] Even then, before bringing this matter to the Executive Committee, via a series of letters during March 1992, I leaned over backward to first give this person an opportunity to forestall any action by making amends. Though I proposed some ways in which this might be accomplished to our mutual satisfaction, I gave him every opportunity to suggest others. As he was unwilling to make **any** amends, I reluctantly brought the matter to the ACR Executive Committee for action. Recognize that there might not have been any reason to make this matter public had I been able to have this matter heard and resolved by an ACR Ethics Committee.

[22] One cannot reach an informed judgement based on the brief account provided here. In addition to the working papers, the file consists of eight letters exchanged between Kassarjian and Jacoby from June 16 to December 15, 1970, 23 pages of correspondence between this author and Kassarjian during the month of March 1992, and the 15 pages (complaint plus cover letter) sent to Alan Andreasen, the ACR President, on March 30, 1993.

As it would require going through the entire 12-page March 30, 1992, complaint and related documents filed with the Executive Committee for me to give you a full appreciation of the apparent perfidy and deceitfulness involved in what I believe is this person's plagiarism, I will spare you that here. Suffice it to say that I believe the evidence is abundant and irrefutable that this plagiarism was both deliberate and deceitful. That person's own letters suggest that, at the time he did so, he knew he was plagiarizing.[23] After the fact, he tried to excuse his behavior by telling me he was compelled to do so because he felt he needed one more sole-authored refereed publication to insure his promotion to full professor.[24,25]

This article (Kassarjian, 1971) went on to become one of the most highly cited and reprinted classics in our field. Of the 2,700 substantive articles published in *JM, JMR* and *JCR* for the years 1965-1986, this article was among the 35 articles to be "most cited" in all the other 1400 (ca.) journals comprising the social science literature (Cote et al., 1990). Sometimes, it is cited specifically for the ideas I believe were purloined from my working paper. As we all know: "Plagiarism, the appropriation of another author's words or ideas, is a much despised crime in the academic world, where intellectual property is the basis for advancement" (Hilts, 1992, p. C1). As explained in my March 30, 1992 complaint to the ACR Executive Committee, though he profited from using my words and ideas (i.e., my intellectual property), by publishing my unpublished

---

[23] "Finally, concerning our paper on personality. I have run into a dreadful snag on this that may have some ethical overtones. I got myself into a corner." From Kassarjian's letter to Jacoby of November 17, 1970.

[24] It is interesting to contrast the manner in which my material is treated by Kassarjian (1971) with the ethical way in which the exact same unpublished material was treated by Engel, Kollat and Blackwell (1973, p. 652).

[25] If you can get away with it once, why not twice? Compare the following two sets of passages. In each case, the first passage is the original from Holsti, the second passage from Kassarjian. Though the first passage from Kassargian (1977) refers to Holsti, it uses no quotation marks, leaving the reader to imply that it was Kassarjian who originated the thoughts and crafted the language he was reading. The second passage from Kassarjian (1977) makes no mention whatever of Holsti (1968).

Set 1: **The sentence "These clandestine Soviet actions on the imprisoned island of Cuba will not be tolerated by the American people," contains assertions about three nations. The coder must be able to reduce this sentence into its component themes before they may be placed in proper categories.** (Holsti, 1968, p. 647).

...the sentence "These clandestine Soviet actions on the imprisoned island of Cuba will not be tolerated by the American people," contains assertions about three nations. The coder must be able to reduce this sentence into its component themes before they may be placed in proper categories (Holsti, 1968). (Kassarjian, 1977, p. 12).

Set 2: **The core of each General Inquirer system of content analysis is a dictionary in which each entry word is defined with one or more "tags" representing categories in the investigator's theory. (Holsti, 1968, p. 665)**

material, he effectively prevented me from reaping any benefit from my own scholarship.[26]

On August 31, 1992, I received ACR's official reply (see Appendix E) stating: "The Board of Directors of the Association for Consumer Research has given considerable thought" to the matter and "concluded it would be both inappropriate and undesirable for the Association of Consumer Research to formally intervene in this case." Of the five reasons given for the Board's decision, two merit special note:

"2. As of this date, ACR has not committed itself to serving in any fashion as a watchdog over the ethical behavior of individuals undertaking 'consumer research' whether ACR members or not....

3. ACR has not adopted any standards for any type of ethical behavior in consumer research and/or publication. Thus, evaluation of the merits in this case would be impossible absent preordained standards."

As I said earlier, with no rules to guide our conduct and no penalties for misbehavior, this apparently means that "anything, including plagiarism, goes at ACR." Further, the organization that claims to be the legitimate voice of scholarly consumer research, by definition and the choice of its governance, is essentially an ethi-

---

The core of each General Inquirer System of content analysis is a dictionary in which each entry word is defined with one or more "tags" representing categories as ordinarily used in content analysis. (Kassarjian, 1977, p.15).

Even when one acknowledges the original source by what, at best, is an ambiguous reference, according to any any credo of scholarship, re-stating 47 words in a row without placing quotation marks around that passage constitutes plagiarism. Using 26 words in a row without quotation marks or any acknowledgment of the original source constitutes plagiarism. (For any who think strings of 47 and 26 **words** are trivial, consider that a computer program used in the bio- medical sciences for detecting fraud works on strings of 30 **characters** each, and that data obtained from the application of this program have been successfully used in several court cases of plagiarism. See Hilts, 1992). Think of what we teach and expect from our students, much less our scholars. Such "scholarship" is, in my opinion, sham scholarship amounting to fraud, something for which I have flunked students out of class and out of school. Those taking the time to compare Kassarjian (1977) with Holsti (1968) will find numerous other striking similarities (in phrases, sections, section headings), confirming that what I firmly believe was Kassarjian's pilfering of Jacoby's intellectual property was not an isolated instance. I sometimes think I bear some responsibility for this pilfering of Holsti's words, as had I blown the whistle on Kassarjian's earlier pilfering of Jacoby, this 1977 plagiarism of Holsti might never have happened.

[26]Within 48 hours after delivering this Address, a number of people mentioned that, without access to the original correspondence between Jacoby and Kassarjian and the working papers in question, it is difficult to render a fully informed judgment. After all, the portions quoted here may have been taken out of context. Accordingly, copies of these material are available to ACR members who request them, in writing from the author.

cally lawless organization that won't do anything about plagiarism or other instances of scholarly misconduct by its members. Is that what we want? Like many others, if I can't trust a "scholar" to behave ethically and abide by time-honored, well-understood and widely accepted canons of scholarly ethics, then I can't trust anything that person has published and **I begin to have serious doubts about trusting the discipline that tolerates such behavior and publishes such work.**

"In addition to the specialized knowledge and techniques that distinguish them, academic disciplines have distinctive cultures— that is, particular beliefs, norms, values, and patterns of work and interpersonal interaction that affect the behavior within the discipline" (Swazey, et al. 1993, p. 551). What kind of "distinctive culture" do we have? What kind of "distinctive culture" do we want to be known as having? If we continue to cling to our misguided, nul-policy of "anything goes," how do you think ACR will come to be viewed by the other social sciences and the scholarly organizations that represent them? I submit that the credibility and reputation of any disciplinary organization that tolerates such behavior will be as substantial as the proverbial grains of sand running through our fingers.

I wrote back telling this ACR President that, under the circumstances, I understood the Board's unwillingness to rule on the matter (letter of September 9, 1992; Appendix E). However, while I don't consider their failure to render a decision in this matter unethical, there is still something about their behavior that smacks of moral cowardice, especially from a President who, in his "President's Column" in ACR's Newsletter, had just a few months earlier written: "ACR is an agency for advancing an academic discipline... through **collective attention to ... research issues and the preservation of standards in the field**" (Andreasen, 1992, p. 3, bolding supplied).

Regardless, I felt that I had accomplished my objective. As stated in my September 9th letter, this was to: "ask the Board to ponder the following: Why does it deem it inappropriate to hear and decide upon allegations of misconduct in this context, yet is not similarly reluctant to consider undocumented and slanderous allegations made during its deliberations in regard to ACR Fellow nominees? Stated somewhat differently, if the Board is unwilling to hear evidence when documents are produced and all parties to a dispute are available for questioning, then how does it justify giving rumor and half-truths any credence whatsoever when the person who is the object of the allegations isn't given an opportunity to address these allegations? Fairness suggests one can't have it both ways. The same standards should apply."

Case 8: Compounding Injustice: Saving Face or Eventual Disgrace?: A few weeks later, the 1992 Executive Committee had the opportunity to redeem prior injustices. Instead, it behaved in the tradition of its predecessors. Apparently thinking more of appearances rather than acting forthrightly to rectify a wrong, they heaped insult upon injustice, thereby, in my opinion, disgracing themselves and the organization they represented. In this respect, the academicians who were behaving as this organization's "executives" exhibited behavior that was no different from what sometimes happens in industry and government.

Specifically, beyond the January 28, 1992 letter (see Appendix E) and my subsequent attempt to redress the old wrong (Case 7, including the aforementioned letter of September 9, 1992, see Appendix E), my only other reaction to the events that transpired at ACR's 1991 Executive Committee meeting was to ask Jerry Olson to re-submit my name to the 1992 Fellows Nominating Committee. I naively hoped that my January 28th and September 9th letters would help those on the incoming 1992 Executive Committee recognize that how my nomination had been treated in the past amounted to a miscarriage of justice. Moreover, to insure that they had evidence enabling them to render an informed judgment on whether my contributions had exerted a "significant impact on scholarly work in consumer behavior," I made certain that they knew of the findings reported in Cote et al. (1990) and Hoffman and Holbrook (1993). Surely, I thought, what more evidence could they want of a long period of sustained contribution to, and impact upon, scholarly research in this discipline? Given that up to three fellows could be elected each year and feeling there could no longer be any rational, logically defensible argument that would stand in the way, I went to the October 1992 Vancouver conference reasonably confident that the 1992 Executive Committee would finally elect me a Fellow.

Perhaps you can imagine how I felt when Bill Wells, as Chairman of the 1992 Fellows Nominating Committee, stood up to announce that the Executive Committee had elected only one Fellow that year—Rick Bagozzi. Of course Rick deserved being elected a Fellow![27] But as the Executive Committee could elect up to three Fellows each year, upon hearing that, even after the events of the previous year and the evidence of scholarly impact in their possession, my time had still not come, I began to feel it never would. The hurt was deep and tears welled up in my eyes. Past-President Bob Pratt, sitting next to me, saw my reaction and leaned over to ask what was wrong. When I explained, he offered to see what, if anything, he could find out. He later called to tell me that, from what he could learn, the 1992 Executive Committee decided not to elect me a Fellow because doing so would imply they had been pressured, among other things, by my letters of January 28th and September 9th.

More than a century ago, the English statesman, William Gladstone, noted: "Justice delayed is justice denied" (Edwards, 1957, p. 326). I wonder if, in reaching their decision, the Executive Committee believed the "costs" they might incur in electing me a Fellow (i.e., "not wanting to feel or appear pressured" to act ethically) far outweighed the "costs" or injustice that was being done to me?[28] I tend to doubt it. Rather than using their chance to right a wrong, the 1992 Executive Committee compounded it.

Once again, I had cause to wonder about the ethics—that is, the ability to discern right from wrong and act accordingly—(or lack thereof) of an ACR Executive Committee. While I didn't appreciate either the slander condoned or behavior exhibited by earlier Executive Committees, perhaps these might have been excused as being a function of their not having relevant and reliable information. But, despite now undeniably having such information, by perpetuating the injustice, in my opinion, the 1992 Executive

Committee disgraced both itself and the organization it represented. I was confident that these people had done unto another that which they would definitely not like done unto them and from that point onward lost all respect for those who were party to that action.[29]

Later that afternoon, Bill Wells took me aside during a break to tell me that, though I hadn't been elected a Fellow that year, if I kept a low profile, didn't write any more letters and just "cooled it" for a year, while there were no guarantees, he felt very confident there was "at least a .9 probability" of my being elected a Fellow in 1993. I believe he was surprised when this angered rather than pleased me. Not only did I believe the award was long overdue and that the 1992 Executive Committee had just acted out of spite rather than any concern for "Doing unto others as they would have wanted done unto them," but as I told Bill, this meant that each time I looked into the mirror during that year, I would be seeing the face of a hypocrite who had quietly accepted injustice just so that he could reap a reward[30] at the end of the tunnel—and I didn't think I could do that. While it was politically smart not to "rock the boat," to be elected a Fellow even partly because of such political acumen would only reinforce the fact that the award had indeed become "political."

When "Enough" became "Enough!!!": Octobers '92 through '94

I spent the next few days thinking long and hard about what Bill had said and even drafted a letter explaining to him how, if senior people were not willing to take a stand against ethical misconduct among ACR's constituents and the possible abuse of power being committed on ACR's behalf, the problem could get worse and ACR would deserve whatever unethical behavior it was getting—but then thought better of it and threw the letter in the trash. Instead, I decided that, while heeding Bill's advice, I would spend the year using a low-profile approach to try and expose the hypocrisy. At the end of that year, and regardless of whether or not it resulted in my ever being elected an ACR Fellow, I would initiate a high profile approach to try and help ACR's members understand that is was in their own vital self interest to take a stand against ethical misconduct by those within.

---

[27] In announcing Rick's election, above and beyond his meritorious accomplishments as a scholar, Bill stressed that Rick was "a role model." Wondering where I stood on this dimension, the first though that crossed my mind was that, at that very moment, four of the top twenty marketing departments in the country were either chaired by my students (Jerry Olson at Penn State and Wayne Hoyer at Texas) or by students on whose Doctoral Committees I served (Don Lehmann at Columbia and Jim Ginter at Ohio State). Two of my students (Leon Kaplan and George Szybillo) had been elected President of the American Psychological Association's Division of Consumer Psychology (Division 23); another (Jerry Olson) had been elected President of ACR.

[28] In contrast: "At its heart, the Golden Rule calls for moral and ethical reasoning to be based on the highest principle that the rights of others should be *paramount* to our own" (Engel, et al. 1993, p. 817; italics supplied).

[29] My January 28, 1992 letter noted: "Depending upon what happens as a consequence, there may come a need for wider dissemination of this information" (Appendix D, p. 42). I had hoped that, being put on notice, these ACR officers would finally treat me fairly and with dignity. However, subsequent events (described above in Cases 6 and 8) showed these individuals unwilling to treat me with the same dignity and respect they would have wanted accorded to themselves. When, after being asked to cease unjust actions regarding an individual, the injustice persists, those involved need to understand that they may eventually be held accountable for such injustice. These people may now recognize that, in part, this address is a matter of an honorable person keeping his word. "Wider dissemination of this information," not a law suit, is what was promised and what is being delivered. Having said this, let me emphasize that the more important objective of this address is to focus on what I perceive to be the root problem at ACR that enables injustice and questionably ethical practices to flourish, namely, governance by cliquish in-groups coupled with the absence of a fully functioning ACR Code of Ethics and Ethics Committee.

[30] An award that, in the hands of ACR's skilled alchemists was, in my opinion, being turned from gold into lead.

The ACR Newsletter as a Lid-lifting Device: An announcement by the ACR Newsletter editors at the 1992 conference gave me one way to be proactive in a low profile sort of way. Noting that, beyond the "News & Notes" kind of material, members were not submitting substantive items, the editors encouraged contributions from the members. Though I had doubts about whether they would publish what I had in mind, I did view their solicitation as an opportunity to begin lifting the lid—by publishing some data of which the Executive Committee was aware, but which were not in general circulation.

Though many must have thought my 1993 Newsletter piece on "'Scholarly impact' in consumer research: Evidence of convergent validity" (see Appendix F) was immodest, perhaps it will now be understood that my basic purpose in submitting this item was so that I could raise, then answer the question: "How does being among the most published and most cited JCR authors relate to receiving the ACR Fellows Award?" (p. 18). I was hoping that at least some would be shocked to learn that, for an award ostensibly being given for "significant impact on scholarly work in consumer behavior," the answer was "Hardly at all!".[31] Perhaps some will now appreciate that Peter Wright's (1994) reaction reflected neither a rejoinder nor self-aggrandizement, but the anguish of another soul who had made many substantial and significant contributions to this discipline and organization, only to be repeatedly passed over when it came to handing out the cookies.

Taking "Low Profile" to "No Profile": On the flight home, I thought of another way that, while heeding Bill's advice, would eventually expose the hypocrisy; it was to carry this "low profile" notion a step further than I'm sure he intended. Not only would I not write letters to any ACR officials, but (other than the aforementioned Newsletter piece) I was determined not to publish anything during that entire year. This way, if elected a Fellow in 1993, as did in fact happen, as my vita would reflect not a single new entry above and beyond that present the year before, the 1993 Executive Committee's own actions would be testimony to the fact that I just as well merited this honor in 1992.[32] Further, anyone who came to learn about what had transpired would be able to recognize that, when they had an opportunity to redress a long-standing wrong, more concerned with "saving face," those on the 1992 Executive Committee instead chose to bring shame to the organization by compounding the injustice. Having thought about it for two years now, placing myself in their shoes, I still cannot fathom a single defensible reason that any member of the 1992 Executive Committee could give that would excuse or justify the actions at that meeting. If there is one, I would love to hear it.

The Scholarly Literature on Ethics and Justice: This "low profile year" was also used to begin acquainting myself with the scholarly literature on ethics. Equally meaningful is the related body of writings on the topic of justice, defined as "the relationship of obligations and entitlements between the individual and the group" (Deutsch and Steil, 1988, p. 3). Two articles in particular provided me with an understanding of why I was feeling as frustrated, angry and depressed as I did over events at ACR; I recommend both (Deutsch and Steil, 1988; Leventhal et al. 1980) to you very highly. Restraining my enthusiasm to quote almost everything, please consider a few relevant items.

The first explains why, at this point, I happen to be more sensitive to these issues than most; basically, it is because I am someone who was affected by the injustices of the system. If and when your turn comes, you, too, are likely to become more sensitized to issues of ethics and justice.

[Unless directly affected,] An individual may often give little thought to questions of fairness.... Unless fairness is important to him, he won't bother to evaluate the fairness of distributions or procedures. (Leventhal et al. 1980, p. 198).

Now consider the following:

...violations of our conceptions of justice presents a twofold threat: It challenges and weakens the moral base of our community and it brings into question the evaluative framework that provides a foundation for our individual and social actions. (Deutsch and Steil, 1988, p. 4).

The sense of injustice can be elicited or intensified by the timing of distribution of a social good ....[as when] the honor is too long delayed in relation to the achievement (Deutsch and Steil, 1988, p. 6).

The victim suffers the loss of a desired outcome, a threat to self esteem, and possible derogation from peers. (Deutsch and Steil, 1988, p. 8).

I also obtained an understanding of what made the injustice so odious and insidious—it was because it was all being accomplished behind closed doors under the guise of "following fair procedures."

...the appearance of fair procedures can mute the protest over unfair outcomes by masking the underlying unfairness. (Deutsch and Steil, 1988, p. 8)

Quasi-fair behavior is that which may superficially resemble fair behavior but which stems from motives unrelated to fairness. Quasi-fair behavior is motivated by pragmatic goals rather than moral concerns. Such behavior may seem to be motivated by a concern for fairness, but is actually tactical in nature and serves other ends. (Leventhal et al. 1980, p. 211-212).

A final quote explains why I found the 1992 Executive Committee's actions so reprehensible, why the conversation with Bill Wells hurt so much, and why I felt compelled to respond:

The experience of an injustice that is not acknowledged and responded to by one's fellow group members is apt to leave one feeling very alien and alienated from one's group; similarly, if one does **not acknowledge and respond to an injustice one has experienced, one will be alienated from oneself** (Deutsch and Steil, 1988, p. 4; bolding supplied).

This is probably nowhere as true as when applied to injustice that strikes at the core of one's reputation. I think it was Jerry Olson who, in 1991 or 1992, turned me on to a little book containing 511

---

[31]Specifically, at the time the Newsletter note was written, only two of the twelve people to be elected an ACR Fellow were among Hoffman and Holbrook's empirically generated list of 42 most published and most cited JCR authors (Paul Green, who ranked 4th, and Jim Bettman, who ranked 6th).

[32]Olson's 1991 and 1993 Nomination letters were virtually identical. Also recognize that the 1993 Executive Committee that finally approved my election consisted, for the most part, of the same people that had rejected my nomination in 1992. With absolutely no additional evidence of scholarly contribution or impact, why did these people vote for me in 1993?

suggestions on how to live a happy and rewarding life. Instruction 421: "Take care of your reputation. It's your most valuable asset" (Brown, 1991).

The Lesson Imparted by Dr. Rees: During this period I came across a very powerful and insightful article by Dr. Thomas D. Rees showing why it is important and just how one might go about protecting one's reputation. A New York surgeon whose distinguished career had spanned more than three decades and had earned him a very successful medical practice, Dr. Rees described how that practice, and he himself, were nearly destroyed by malicious, untrue rumors. In Dr. Rees' words:

> My personal struggle with the effects of a malicious rumor gave me deep empathy for others who have had their lives marred by lies. I learned that rumors are indeed powerful weapons in the hands of those without conscience. I learned that such ruinous gossip must be dealt with vigorously, aggressively and immediately. [Waiting] until things blow over is a ruinous approach. Those who promote lies do not stop unless they are threatened with exposure and humiliation. (1993, p. 32)

Reading Dr. Rees' account of his experiences reinforced my resolve to begin exposing some of the unethical behavior and scholarly misconduct I've experienced. For me, the catharsis would come not from getting things off my chest, but from having these incidents help others to understand why it vital for ACR to become proactive in regard to safeguarding its reputation and that of the individuals who constitute its membership. Sad to say, but the cases mentioned above represent only the tip of my personal iceberg; I've heard enough stories from others to know that there are many other such icebergs floating in this same sea.

Re-forming and Reforming ACR: My experiences with the conduct of certain ACR members and especially ACR's governance also made it abundantly clear that when those who succeeded my Presidency disbanded ACR's Ethics (nee Professional Affairs) Committee, they had taken an exceedingly unwise action. Without such a committee, ACR lacks anything to serve the Safeguard and Appeals functions Leventhal et al. (1980) identify as being essential to the survival of any social system (see "Where does ACR go from here?" section below). The above experiences furthered my resolve to invest energies helping ACR members understand why, as a matter of their own self-interest, they had to consider re- establishing an ethics committee.

As an initial effort, I interested three other ACR past-Presidents (Holbrook, Olson and Wilkie) in joining me in a session on "Ethical issues in consumer research" for the 1993 ACR Conference.[33] As part of my presentation, I took the liberty of conducting some exploratory research using the audience as respondents. Twelve types of behavior were described and, for each, respondents were asked to indicate (a) whether the behavior was ethical or not, and (b) whether it would be something appropriate for an ACR Ethics Committee to consider (questionnaire and data are available from the author).

Disregarding for the moment the fact that it was a small (n = 37) and unrepresentative sample, the findings revealed striking agreement on a number of issues. Reflecting issues touched upon above, consider the following examples:

Behavior #1:
ACR establishes an annual "Best article" award for papers published in the ACR Proceedings, then gives the award based on its assessment of the author's personality.

Thirty of 36 respondents to this question (83.3%) rated the behavior as "unethical" (16) or "highly unethical" (14); most (27; 75%) thought it would be something appropriate for an ACR Ethics Committee to consider. (If one substituted "Fellow Award" for "Best article," I suspect the results would not be too different.)

Behavior #2:
ACR member publishes a paper in which he presents an idea or procedure as being new and original, despite knowing that virtually the same idea or procedure was developed and published years earlier by others in journals not typically read by ACR members.

Thirty-six of 37 respondents to this question (97.3%) rated the behavior as "unethical" (12) or "highly unethical" (24); most (22; 59.5%) thought it would be something appropriate for an ACR Ethics Committee to consider.

For both behaviors, there was substantial agreement that the behaviors in question were unethical (83.3% and 97.3%, respectively) and were ones that would be appropriate for an ACR to consider (75% and 59.5%, respectively). Several of the other asked-about behaviors were associated with even higher levels of agreement (see Appendix G). Such widespread agreement suggests that, as ACR members share similar values and norms, developing an acceptable Code of Ethics should not be too difficult. However, these data were gathered from a small and unrepresentative sample.

Projectably Pervasive: My exploratory study led me to a design and conduct a more comprehensive and projectable survey of ACR members (n = 185; 92% academicians). The pattern of findings was very similar. While a fuller report is being prepared for submission elsewhere, a few of the findings are of particular interest in terms of issues discussed above.

One section of the questionnaire asked respondents to complete the following task: "Below is a list of illustrative behaviors that might become the focus of an ethical misconduct complaint. In each case, please suppose that the complaint involved an ACR member, and the work in question has been published in an ACR-sponsored publication.... Which, if any, do you consider to be a matter warranting ACR attention?" Using a six-point scale ("definitely does not...," "probably does not...," "uncertain," "probably does...," "definitely does warrant ACR attention," and "no opinion"), respondents were asked to evaluate 19 different potential complaints about an ACR member. The percentages answering "Definitely..." and "Probably does warrant ACR attention" for some issues of current interest are provided in Table 1. Based upon these data[34] (which reflect high levels of agreement and parallel high agreement found on a variety of other issues), one can infer that ACR members share a common set of norms and values regarding scholarly ethics and believe ACR should become more active in monitoring ethical matters within the discipline.

---

[33]One anonymous reviewer justified his "reject" recommendation by writing: "I realize that politics may preclude this. But this strikes me as a 'bull' session by the 'old boys.'"

[34]The fact that 50.3% apparently do not view failure to use quotation marks around sentences as unethical suggests that some may not understand this behavior is a fundamental form of plagiarism. On the other hand, nearly nine in ten understand that to have "received another's unpublished notes and ideas and, **without permission**, published these before the original author could do so" represents unethical behavior.

TABLE 1
Selected behaviors warranting ACR attention

Defnt'ly %		Prob'ly %	Potential Complaint
27.0		36.8	claimed as "new and original" an idea or procedure, while knowing that virtually
	63.8		the same idea or procedure had already been published elsewhere by others.
22.7		27.0	failed to place quotation marks around sentences taken directly from the
	49.7		written work of others.
68.3		20.0	received another's unpublished notes and ideas and, without **permission**,
	88.3		published these before the original author could do so.
44.3		27.0	knowingly and in print, for the purpose of establishing a "straw man" that could
	71.3		easily be attacked, substantially misrepresented another scholar's work.

FIGURE 2
The B-A Distinction: Reality

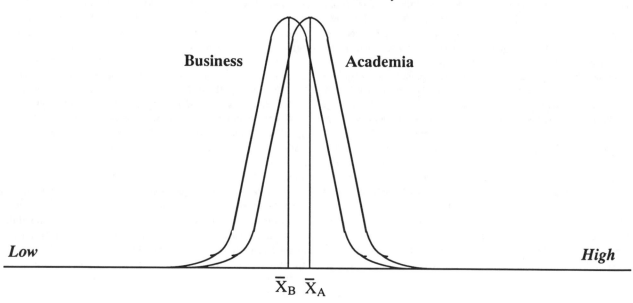

Business **Academia**

Low *High*

$\overline{X}_B$ $\overline{X}_A$

The Ethics Continuum

THE B-A DISTINCTION REVISITED

The cases described above, all involving respected ACR members, are but a few of the many examples of unethical and questionably ethical behavior I've personally experienced. If I were to include the many other examples told to me by the colleagues and graduate students who experienced them—incidents of deliberate acts of what Morris calls the three F's, fabrication, falsification and fraud, and the three P's, prevarication, plagiarism and profiteering (Holbrook, 1994, p. 568)—my knowledge of such incidents increases manyfold.

The bottom line is that we have a situation here of the academicians within ACR's pot calling those in other kettles black.

I submit that if there is indeed a B-A distinction, its practical significance is nil and most likely corresponds to that depicted in Figure 2. There are good, less good and downright rotten apples in every bunch; in most instances, the means and distributions are probably about the same. So before anyone here begins pointing fingers at others, make sure that you **and the organizations to which you belong and which you support** are, at the very least, to the right of the mean of that other group's distribution. These days, I seriously doubt that ACR members can do this vis-a-vis the business sector. That's because, in an effort to control and weed out bad apples, at least many firms and organizations have developed and adopted codes of ethics. That's more than we can say about ourselves. If we can't clean up our own house, we have no moral basis for criticizing others whose homes might contain similar garbage. Academicians, heal thyselves.[35]

Accordingly, unless you have access to a fount of data not otherwise available, I suggest you reject any stereotype that holds business people are less ethical than ACR scholars. Not only are such stereotypes unworthy of social scientists, but they clearly are not valid. Try not to forget that, for many of us, the business people we know best are our spouses—including those whose spouses are therapists "in business" for themselves. They are also our parents, grandparents, children, favorite aunts, etc. Recognize that good people do not automatically become unethical when they join industry. As would a true scholar, get the facts and evaluate each case on its own merits.

And just because an academician works with those in industry, don't automatically assume that that person's behavior must be unethical or is being done to satisfy evil purposes. Earlier I mentioned Peter Wright as one who has too long been denied the ACR Fellow Award. In my opinion, another whose contributions surely warranted his being elected an ACR Fellow long ago is Jagdish Sheth. From what I understand, the fact that he is also a successful businessman has been the main reason for denying him this honor. If this is indeed the reason, this shames us all.

And for those who cannot forsake their deeply ingrained anti-business sentiments, here's something to ponder. In addition to being an academician whose publications in our core journals garnered more citations in those journals than any other consumer researcher for a period of at least 15 years, I am also a successful businessman and damn proud of it. I come by my business success honestly and ethically, and I challenge any who would besmirch my reputation as an honest and ethical businessman to put up or shut up.

WHERE DO WE GO FROM HERE?

Recognize that the least costly, least risky and easiest thing for me to have done today was to graciously thank all involved in electing me a Fellow,[36] give an address on some facet of science that I had all along envisioned would mark my election as an ACR Fellow,[37] then sit down. Since I've been elected a Fellow, why

---

[35]"Many at ACR call for vigilance, followed by the hot pursuit and prosecution of those who practice deceptive advertising, including advertising that is 'deceptive via omission.' I support this sentiment. But why stop there? Why not be as vigilant and demanding when it comes to scholarly articles that engage in similar deception? Fair is fair. Why not turn the same spotlight on ourselves?" (Jacoby, 1992; letter of January 28, see Appendix D).

[36]Actually, I **am** very grateful, especially to those former and present students and collaborators who have helped bring me to this point, and especially to Jerry Olson who kept sending in those nomination letters and, when they inevitably failed, tried to keep my spirits up.

[37]Instead of talking about ACR as an organization as had the five prior chief executives (two Chairmen of the Advisory Council and three Presidents), my ACR Presidential Address was the first to focus on the scientific aspects of the emerging consumer research discipline (see Jacoby, 1976a, p.1, footnote #2). The twenty or so Presidential Addresses since then have generally followed this tradition. Though some might call me a contrarian, at this point in ACR's development, I believe it more important to turn the organization's focus inward to consider the way in which it is being governed (misgoverned?).

dredge up past history? Why stick my neck out? Why risk alienating so many "powerful" people? Why risk unpleasant repercussions and retaliation?[38] There are a number of reasons.

Why am I Speaking Out?

First, being elected a Fellow is far and away inconsequential relative to safeguarding my name and reputation. As a by-product of raising these issues, one effect will be to address what apparently are some long- standing rumors shared and spread by a number of people in this organization. I also wanted to confront head on any whispers that might arise, now or later, to the effect that I condoned "the system" or was elected a Fellow as payment for maintaining a low profile and not making waves.

By speaking as candidly as I have, I probably alienated and angered some in the room today. If so, then perhaps they can understand that I felt at least as alienated and angered by their actions toward me. Regardless, I don't believe I will have alienated any who are concerned with behaving ethically and being part of an organization that operates in like fashion. To my way of thinking, making oral statements or even writing about ethics means very little if, when elected to a position of authority and trust, you "do unto others what you would not like them to do unto you." In other words, I only risk alienating those whose opinions and attitudes I no longer care about or respect.[39]

In contrast, I know I don't risk alienating Jerry Olson, Wayne Hoyer, Gita Johar, Mimi Morrin, Zeynep Gurhan and Alfred Kuss, who are in the audience, or a number of others not here today. For those who might want to know what kind person I am, I suggest you speak to the people who know me best—my former students (all of whom worked for years as my "subordinates" and hence were vulnerable to any unethical whims I might have had or actions I might have taken) and frequent collaborators—and find out. If anything, I believe they will see this talk as providing a demonstration of behaving ethically and, when one can, confronting injustice in the scholarly organizations one holds dear. As such, they will understand my behavior as another instance of mentoring and serving as a role model.

A related reason for speaking out stems from a sense of responsibility and obligation. True, I risk repercussions and retaliation by those whom I've identified. However, if senior scholars can't talk out about questionably ethical conduct and misconduct within our community, then what hope is there for more junior scholars who witness and often bear the brunt of such unethical behavior (see Swazey et al. 1993, pp. 550-52)?

Another reason has to do with combating the smug sense of self-righteousness that many academicians in this organization seem to have vis-a-vis the ethics of those in other sectors. Look around the room. What do you see? A room full of people with superior ethics? If you believe this, then as people presumably

---

[38]It is probably inevitable that I will experience some shunning, ostracism, greater criticism of my scholarly work, etc., on the part of those identified herein and their colleagues, friends, etc. Though it would be difficult to discern, one would hope that the repercussions would not extend to retaliation via unethical practices when those named or their colleagues, friends, etc., serve as editors and reviewers of manuscripts.

[39]As documented elsewhere (Jacoby, 1977), during my tenure as ACR President, I didn't just talk about the need for greater attention to ethical matters by ACR and its members; I devoted considerable time and effort to insuring that ACR instituted an Ethics Committee.

practiced in scientific thinking, where is your evidence? And if you have no evidence, then come sit with me for a few more days, so that I may share some of my experiences and those of others whose sad stories I've heard—like the graduate student whose major professor took his term paper, then published it as his own; like the grad student whose research supervisor instructed him to count the answers to all the questions on crossed out pages of a questionnaire as valid data (i.e., to fabricate data); like the author of an "intro consumer" text telling me that the author of another "intro consumer" text had plagiarized his work; like the department chairman who diverted departmental resources for his own use; like the department chairman who awarded departmental summer assistantships to his own children; like visiting professor from a distant country who, after accepting a summer teaching job over the phone, is told upon his arrival that he would be paid 15% less than was agreed upon; like department chairmen and deans who while courting you, smile, lie to your face, shake your hand on a deal, then after you've arrived, have convenient memory lapses;[40] etc.; etc.; etc. Wake up! Academicians can be just as rotten, sleazy and slimy as any other group of people; there are rotten apples in every bunch.

Yet another reason for speaking out is that getting the award is far and away not as important as getting a meaningful award. Frankly, if it's going to be treated like a political football by those who happen to temporarily have the authority to grant it, then I don't want it—just as I wouldn't want an award from any other organization I did not respect.

All of which brings me to the most important reason why I have spoken out as I have. I am convinced that ACR needs a fundamental overhaul, especially vis-a-vis ethics; this address is an act of moral conscience designed to move the organization in this direction. I am hoping that Deutsch and Steil are correct when they write:

> By raising to consciousness the discontent and sense of injustice, a powerful and persisting energy for change is activated. (1988, p. 17).

What I have said thus far is prologue to what I would like to say regarding the future of ACR.

Where does ACR go from here?

Let me ask you a question: Can you name any other scholarly organization that's been around for 25 years, that is as large as or larger than ACR, that professes to be the voice of a scholarly discipline—and that has no Code of Ethics? I can't. History reveals that, as part of their evolution and maturation, and in order to maintain credibility both inside and outside the field, organizations purporting to represent scholarly disciplines develop a focus on the ethical issues surrounding their discipline. Consumer research is a maturing area of scientific inquiry. Where is such emphasis within ACR? Our credibility as an organization claiming to represent the discipline is limited by the integrity of our members (and their research practices) and institutions. By not developing vehicles for handling ethical issues that surface in these regards, our credibility is left open to question. Academicians are no different from anyone else. Without policies to prevent and punish abuse, it is apparent that some will try to get away with as much as they can for as long as they can.

Perhaps stimulated by my letters (particularly those of January 28 and 29, 1992; see Appendix D), the Executive Committee issued

a call in the December 1992 ACR Newsletter for volunteers to serve on a task force to examine "whether ACR should have any role in establishing and/or monitoring professional standards in the field of consumer behavior" (Smith, October 7, 1993, p. 2; see Appendix H). A six person committee was formed with Craig Smith as Chair.

Craig solicited letters from each of the committee members, then wove these various perspectives into a report (see Appendix H). This report was submitted to and considered by the ACR Board of Directors at its October 7, 1993 meeting. As Craig later wrote to his committee (October 21, 1993 letter; Appendix H): "our report to the ACR Board meeting resulted in a heated discussion," the net result of which was that "there was not sufficient support to justify" proceeding any further. "My interpretation of the response to our proposals is that the timing is not right. Maybe there is never a right time for this sort of initiative; but, quite frankly, it is simply not going to happen right now."

Reasons for NOT developing a Code of Ethics and establishing an Ethics Committee. In his October 21, 1993 letter, Craig identified five concerns expressed at the October 7th Board of Directors meeting. These were:

1. "An ethics code/committee may create a litigious climate if not a legal nightmare. Some participants spoke of their adverse experiences of these mechanisms in other contexts."

Over the past 30 years, I've belonged to a number of scientific and scholarly organizations, serving in a variety of official capacities in several of these. Not once have I ever known the presence of Codes of Ethics or Ethics Committees to "create a litigious climate." Think about it. Would you say the presence of a Code of Ethics has made the American Marketing Association, the American Psychological Association, the American Sociological Association, the American Association for Public Opinion Research, etc., any more litigious than those same organizations would have been without a Code of Ethics? I sincerely doubt it. A lesson to be learned from Dr. Rees' experiences is to ask the people claiming to have knowledge of "adverse experiences ... in other contexts" to document their "experiences"—and if they cannot or will not, to please shut up and sit down.

2. "Other mechanisms/avenues for redress are already available for many of the issues identified; for example, litigation for breach of copyright."

According to the illogic involved in this argument, no scholarly organization needs a Code of Ethics. Further, those proposing this argument disregard the fact that not every instance of unethical scholarly conduct warrants or is capable of being litigated. Regardless, litigation is time consuming, expensive (costing more than most scholars are willing or capable of paying), and has many associated indirect costs. For these reasons alone, it is usually the course of last resort.

Further, as evidenced by Case 3, some instances of questionably ethical conduct by a scholar may involves that scholar's **unpublished** works. As suggested by Case 7, some plagiarism may involve a scholar pilfering ideas and language from someone else's **unpublished** works. Does this mean that, to be safe from such pilfering, we now need to begin copyrighting all our working papers? And suppose I had copyrighted my working papers and decided to file a law suit against Kassarjian. Given that it would be difficult to show he profited monetarily or I sustained monetary damages as a consequence of what I believe was a case of intellectual theft, what could I hope to gain? On the other hand, consider the time, energy and financial resources I would have had to

---

[40]"Power — the ability to do others great harm ... — can induce widespread amnesia, it appears" (Bhide and Stevenson, 1990, p. 123).

expend.[41] Though litigation sounds like an easy solution, it is far from that.

Moreover, many infractions tend to be subtle, seemingly minor and often done in ways that are not readily recognizable. That is probably why they escape the attention of journal reviewers who, like most scholars reading a scholarly paper operate on the assumption that what they are reading is an honest and truthful description. As a result, the victim has difficulty addressing these instances. For example, how was I to address the "scandalous" example in Case 1? As it was all accomplished via a single phrase within a single sentence, was I to write and submit a one or two paragraph rejoinder? Would the editor have published such a "piece" if I had, or is it more likely I would have been told it was a small point and, unless I had more to say, not worth publishing? And suppose the senior author of the Mouselab paper decided not to follow through on his promise that he would immediately revise the Mouselab working paper and, when relevant, would acknowledge my directly related and prior work in future scholarly writings? How am I to address this?

True, other organizations to which many ACR members belong have Codes of Ethics and Ethics Committees, thereby offering other avenues for redress. But some ACR members belong only to this organization.[42] Moreover, as illustrated by Case 2, some problems involve work not published under the auspices of any scholarly organization. From whom should the aggrieved party seek redress under these circumstances? And if the incident involves something that happened under our auspices (e.g., misrepresentation in an article published in our Proceedings or in *JCR*, a journal we sponsor), why can't we take responsibility for policing our own?

Moreover, in those instances where the question of ethical misconduct involves concern with the governance and policies of this organization, why should an ACR member with a legitimate gripe be expected to go elsewhere?

3. "It is safer to rely on trust in the people to carry out ACR duties and to let the market work where this fails; for example, one would not work again with a co-author who cheated in some way and word got around."

This argument sounds very much like "trust big brother." But what are you supposed to do when you find big brother is the problem and, based on what you've experienced, can't be trusted to behave ethically?

Regardless, if there are any on the Executive Committee who truly believe and accept this argument, then they must certainly understand this Fellow Address to be a concrete manifestation of my trying to make sure the "word got around;" as such, I'm certain they support my speaking out so frankly.[43] However, based on my experience, I think if you tell others that someone else plagiarized or misrepresented your work, rather than getting the problem

solved, you place yourself in jeopardy of being branded by those without the facts (or interest in acquiring the facts) as someone who "quarrels with others over contributions" (see Case 5).

I believe that relying on a strategy of "getting the word around" will be as effective as relying on the tooth fairy to deliver a present. The notion that "trust is enforced in the marketplace through retaliation and reputation" and "if you violate a trust, ... others are likely to stop doing business with you," as Bhide and Stevenson note (1990, p. 122), "sounds plausible enough until you look for concrete examples." "More damaging to the moralists' position is the wealth of evidence against trust. Compared with the few ambiguous tales of treachery punished, we can find numerous stories in which deceit was unquestionably rewarded" (Bhide and Stevenson, 1990, p. 122).

Trust breakers are not only unhindered by bad reputations, they are usually also spared retaliation by those they injure.... attacking a more powerful transgressor is considered foolhardy.... if you are an employee and your employer breaks promises, you usually don't retaliate....

Where power doesn't protect against retaliation, convenience and cognitive inertia usually do. Getting even can be expensive; even thinking about broken trusts can be debilitating.

Retaliation is a luxury you can't afford, respondents told us. ... "It's a realization that comes with age: retaliation is a double loss. First you lose your money; now you're losing time."... Without convincing proof of one-sided fault, you'll get a reputation for vindictiveness and scare even honorable men and women away from establishing relationships. (Bhide and Stevenson, 1990, p. 125-26).

4. "The impact of an ethics code/committee on the character of ACR; the preference for an informal organization, not a bureaucracy like AMA."

This argument is nothing but a giant smokescreen. Consider the experiences of the American Psychological Association, an organization with more than 78,000 members (which works out to being approximately 50 times the size of ACR) and another 40,000 student affiliates. The most recent report of its Ethics Committee (1994) notes that a total of 66 cases were opened during all of 1993. The overwhelming majority of these involved matters of psychotherapy and therapeutic practice (see Table 4, p. 661). In all, only five complaints involved any of the 10 categories listed under "Inappropriate research, teaching or administrative practice." Of these, two involved controversies over authorship or credit, three involved controversies over supervision or termination. There were no complaints involving improper research, plagiarism, or biased data. Table 2 compares these data to that reported for the years 1991, 1992 and 1993 (see APA Ethics Committee, 1993, Table 4, p. 815).

Disregarding the "supervision/termination" supervisor vs. subordinate category, it can be seen that, with a complaint rate of only 7 cases over four years involving alleged misconduct in regard

---

[41]At the time, as an untenured Assistant Professor in a School of Humanities and Social Science, with loans to pay, a wife not yet working, and two children under the age of two, I could hardly make ends meet, much less afford a law suit.

[42]When Kassarjian decided to ignore my 1992 request for justice, I turned to the American Psychological Association, only to be told that he had dropped his membership years earlier and, hence, no case could be opened on the matter. (See Appendix E, letter dated April 14, 1992.)

[43]If not, perhaps they will at least appreciate that I am not speaking "behind people's back" or hiding behind closed doors. Rather, I am expressing my thoughts and feelings openly and am willing to stand behind my words and take the consequences — which is more than can be said about how some at ACR prefer to operate.

TABLE 2

Number of each type of case opened by the American Psychological Association during the years indicated
(See APA, 1993, 1994)

Cases per year:

	1990	1991	1992	1993
Authorship controversies/credits	0	2	1	2
Plagiarism	1	0	0	0
Improper research	0	0	1	0
Biased data	0	0	0	0
Supervision/termination	4	3	1	3

"research, teaching or administrative practice," APA's administrative/ bureaucratic workload is hardly overwhelming. If we can assume that consumer researchers are inclined to be no more nor less ethical than psychological researchers, so that on a percentage-per- member basis the same case load should apply, we can project ACR as having to contend with appreciably less than one case every few years.[44] This could hardly be termed a bureaucratic nightmare, especially when considered relative to what ACR and the discipline would stand to gain.

On the other hand, reflect for a moment on "the impact that **not** having an ethics code/committee would have on the character of ACR." It would grant license to those who engage in dishonest (or "sloppy") scholarship to continue operating as they have, in reckless disregard of well- established norms and canons of ethical scholarship. It would serve notice to other scholarly organizations that we are not willing to stand behind the scholarship and truthfulness of what our members publish in our publications and beyond. It would tell the outside world that we are an ethically lawless organization not willing to accept the responsibilities that go along with claiming to be the voice of a scholarly discipline. Is that what we want?

5. "Guidelines may restrict individual freedom: `I don't want to be governed.'"

Who does? But we all, professors included, have to grow up sometime. Individual freedom is not absolute. Even our First Amendment Right to "Freedom of Speech" is not absolute. Try yelling "fire" in a theatre or saying "I have a gun" in an airport terminal. Try telling a judge he has no right to issue a "gag order," or a government employee that he cannot be prohibited from divulging this country's secrets. Consider the 1988 "gag rule" formulated by Pres. Ronald Reagan's Department of Health and Human Services which "prohibited physicians in federally funded clinics from telling women that abortion was a legal option ... [Instead] Women who inquired about the procedure were to be told that the clinic did not consider abortion to be an appropriate part of family planning.'" (NY Times, 1994, A16). There are also laws against free speech when that speech is slanderous. Perhaps the

only absolute right we have is our right to "equal justice" (and in those states that have a death penalty, it is clear that the right to justice even supercedes the right to life).[45] At ACR, the emphasis on "equal justice" relative to that placed on "free speech" seems to be reversed.

And while some on the Executive Committee might not like it, what would the members like? Two questions near the end of the "Projectably Pervasive" study (see "When `enough' became `enough'!!!," above) provide some indication. These two questions and the corresponding data are summarized in Table 3. As these data show, 80% (four out of five) respondents said they were in favor of ACR developing and publishing a Code of Ethics and 66% (two out of three) were in favor of ACR establishing an Ethics Committee to hear complaints that ACR may receive regarding its members.

Yet despite what appears to be shared norms and strong support for such actions, the ACR governance has not seen fit either to discuss this matter with the membership or submit it to a membership vote. What is going on here? Do we really need or want a paternalistic governance imposing its will on the membership on an issue that is not only of considerable concern and importance to the discipline, but one on which there apparently exists widespread member convergence on positions contrary to that prevalent among the governance?

Suppose we had a debate on the issue. What would that debate show? Among other things, it would expose the pros and cons of our taking such actions. As we've already considered some (all?) of the cons,[46] let's consider some of the pros.

---

[44]This assumes that "word got around" that ACR had a Code of Ethics and an Ethics Committee intent on dispensing appropriate penalties for violations and, knowing this, ACR members would become as careful in their scholarly writings as APA members apparently are in theirs.

[45]The author thanks his daughter, Robin, for bringing the relative importance of these rights to his attention.

[46]Within hours of this Address, a few senior ACR members told me that this talk took a lot of the "fun" out of research for them. For the record: I am not against fun. By renting a room, spending $100 of my own money and inviting "more than 100 of my closest friends" to a party at ACR's second annual conference at the University of Chicago, I think I began what has evolved into ACR's Thursday night receptions. Though it may be viewed as such by some, it needs to be remembered that ACR is not a social club, but a scientific organization. Yes, it's not like the old days — but kids and teenagers grow up. As a maturing scholarly organization, when there is a conflict, trustworthy science needs to prevail, or we really have no basis for claiming legitimacy as a scientific organization.

TABLE 3

ACR Members' sentiments on ACR developing a Code of Ethics and establishing an Ethics Committee (n = 185)

"We recognize there has not yet been a thorough discussion of the pros and cons. However, as you have now had some exposure to the kinds of issues that might come before ACR, we would like a sense of how you are `leaning.' In general how do you feel about ACR developing and publishing a Code of Ethics?"

43.2%	strongly favor
37.3	leaning in favor
8.6	neutral
5.4	leaning against
5.4	strongly against
0.0	no opinion/don't know

"Separate from developing a Code of Ethics, how do you feel about ACR establishing an Ethics Committee to hear complaints that it receives regarding ACR members?"

27.6%	strongly favor
38.4	leaning in favor
13.0	neutral
9.7	leaning against
10.3	strongly against
1.1	no opinion/don't know

Reasons FOR developing a Code of Ethics and establishing an Ethics Committee. "Members of a group who share common norms also share common obligations to protect these norms and respond to their violations" (Deutsch and Steil, 1988, p. 4). In other words, freedoms and rights bring with them corresponding obligations and responsibilities (Wilkie, 1990, Appendix 21-B). We can't continue to enjoy our freedoms while irresponsibly shirking our obligations—at least not continue to do so and also believe we warrant respect.

Consider Schein's work on "the psychological contract." When an individual joins an organization, both parties enter into a "psychological contract" (Schein, 1965, p. 11). "The notion of a psychological contract implies that the individual has a variety of expectations of the organization and that the organization has a variety of expectations of him. The expectations ... involve his whole pattern of rights, privileges, and obligations.... [one of which is that the organization will] insure that he will not be taken advantage of." And how do they accomplish this? By establishing fair and effective processes for the allocation of rewards and punishment.

"Effective allocation processes are essential to the survival of a social system" (Leventhal et al. 1980, p. 174). According to these authors, two of the seven components required for effective allocation processes are "Safeguards" and "Appeals."

Safeguards. Some procedures serve as safeguards which ensure that agents who administer the allocative process are performing their duty properly. Other safeguards deter opportunistic individuals from obtaining rewards ... illicitly. In both cases, the procedures call for monitoring the behavior of individuals and applying sanctions when violations occur.

Appeals. Social systems usually contain some form of grievance or appeal procedures... (Leventhal et al. 1980, p. 170-71).

With specific respect to scholarly organizations, Swazey et al. (1993, p. 547) note: "The ways in which suspected misconduct and other ethical problems are dealt with ... are crucial to the integrity of research and scholarship, and they may help shape the values, the attitudes and the behavior of trainees." On the other hand, here is a prescription for disaster: "Environments that foster expectations of retaliation, coupled with low levels of exercised collective **responsibility for the conduct of colleagues** ... raise grave concerns about the willingness and ability of academic research communities to govern ..." in a way that insures the integrity of their enterprise (Swazey et al., p. 449; bolding supplied). This echos what Lanberth and Kimmel conclude: scientists "**collectively** assume responsibility for the knowledge that they generate **through scientific and interdisciplinary organizations**" (1981, p. 78; bolding supplied). Establishing a Code of Ethics to govern scholarly research practices within the domain of consumer research is **our** responsibility, no-one else's.

Both as individuals and collectively, want to be a positive role model? Then don't shove ethical problems under the carpet. Want to show that ethics matter? Then take a stand. In informing the ACR Professional Standards Task Force of what transpired at the October 7, 1993 Board meeting, Craig Smith wrote: "The Board and closely associated ACR members are focused on the specific complaints of Jack Jacoby which may or may not be a sound basis for evaluating our proposals ..., but are influencing the decision nonetheless" (Appendix K, October 21, 1993 Memorandum, p. 2). This suggests they think ethics are Jack Jacoby's issue, not everybody's issue. Perhaps, behaving like children, they are blind to the fact that spinach is good for them. Regardless, they seem not to understand that developing a Code of Ethics to govern our scholarly research practices is our responsibility as scientists.

This I do know: "Justice is itself the great standing policy of any civil society; and any departure from it, under any circumstances, lies under the suspicion of being no policy at all" (Burke, 1899, 438-9). Recognize that choosing not to act in this regard, in effect, is an ethical statement. It means you accept and condone the present, ethically lawless system of "Anything goes." Those who do should not be surprised when they later get what they deserve.

So, aside from feeling real good about yourself, what are the benefits ACR would derive from developing a Code of Ethics and establishing an Ethics Committee? I see at least seven: clarifying expectations, fairness, accountability, role modeling, credibility, a decrease in unethical practices, and the avoidance of hypocrisy and shame.

1. Clarifying expectations: As Schmeisser (1992, p. 7) notes, codes of ethics are "intended to clarify the expectations of professional conduct ... and to affirm that the profession intends and expects its members to recognize the ethical dimensions of their practice."

An example of clarifying expectations that pertains to two of the above–cited cases, consider the following passages from pages 292–294 of the APA *Publications Manual*:

Different scholarly disciplines have different publication styles. In contrast, there are basic ethical principles that underlie all scholarly writing. These longstanding ethical principles are designed to achieve two goals:

1. To ensure the accuracy of scientific and scholarly knowledge and

2. To protect intellectual property rights.

Quotation marks should be used to indicate the exact words of another....

Psychologists do not present substantial portions or elements of another's work or data as their own, **even if the other work or data source is cited occasionally.**[bolding supplied]

The key element of this principle is that an author does not present the work of another as if it were his or her own words. If an author models a study after one done by someone else, the originating author should be given credit.

Plagiarism can be subtle and disguised as when the second author occasionally acknowledges or cites the origianl source. But as the above passsages indicate, such occasional reference to the original source is insufficient when the reader is left with the impression that some of the ideas and words taken from the original source were the second author's, not the original source. Of course, Kassarjian might contend he was unaware that occasional citing was insufficient — which is all the more reason why a Code of Ethics clarifying expectations is needed in this field.

2. Fairness: Probably not much more needs to be said than has already been said above. Those who still don't "get it," that is, understand that fairness and justice are at the core of all social enterprises, including the community of scholars, may be hopelessly and cortically ethically deficient (Blakeslee, 1994, pp. C1, C14).

3. Accountability: Both as individual scholars and when serving as representatives of this organization, ACR members need to be accountable for their actions in connection with this discipline and organization. If you don't want to be held accountable for a particular action, then don't do it. As part of this accountability, after 25 years, it's about time ACR developed and instituted appropriate safeguards and appeals mechanisms.

The governance of ACR offers various opportunities for questionably ethical practice, especially since a number of important decisions are reached behind closed doors.[47] When these involve actions of an ACR committee, the aggrieved party can bring the matter to the attention of the President and Executive Commit-

tee. But what does he or she do if the problem originates at the organization's highest level? To avoid creating the impression that ACR is an organization run by a coterie of insiders having little or no accountability, ACR needs a formally constituted body (e.g., an independent Ethics Committee at which appeals could be heard) to serve a checks-and-balances function.

4. Role modeling: Swazey et al. (1993, p. 547) note: "The ways in which suspected misconduct and other ethical problems are dealt with ... are crucial to the integrity of research and scholarship, and they may help shape the values, the attitudes and the behavior of trainees." Words are cheap. It's not sufficient to write or talk a good line about ethics if one then fails to behave accordingly. It sets a bad example for the kids.

5. Establishing Credibility: "It is my belief that unless we demonstrate a firm commitment to high ethical principles and practice ... our claim to legitimacy will always be open to serious question. Our credibility can only be as good as our integrity" (Jacoby, 1977, p. 256). As long as we refuse to accept any responsibility for what our members do in the name of our science, we remain nothing but a pretense for an organization having a legitimate right to claim it represents a scholarly discipline. As such, we would deserve and have no credibility.

6. Decrease in unethical practices: As Schmeisser (1992) suggests, among the most important benefits of a code of ethics, when coupled with enforcement procedures, is that it decreases instances of unethical behavior.

7. Avoidance of hypocrisy and shame: Those of us who continue to inveigh against the ethical failures of others (e.g., by railing against advertisers who are "deceptive via omission" and lawyers who "shade the truth") while tolerating such practices by ACR members should understand that this gives reason for others to consider us nothing but a bunch of smug, self-righteous hypocrites who obviously can't see beyond our myths and illusions.

Developing a Code of Ethics. Developing a Code of Ethics and set of enforcement policies will no doubt require dedicated time and effort (see Appendix H). At very least, it should entail broad member input.[48] It should also involve a review of what related social science organizations (e.g., APA, AMA, AAPOR) have developed. Here are some other suggestions.

---

[47]When an ACR member whose questionably ethical or unethical behavior causes another ACR member to bring the matter to the attention of an ACR President, Executive Committee or Board of Directors requesting them to consider the matter and take some appropriate action, one issue such an ACR President, Executive Committee or Board of Directors needs to be especially sensitive to is anything (e.g., friendships between the President or a member of the Executive Committee/Board of Directors and the alleged wrongdoer) that might create the existence or appearance of a conflict of interest.

[48]Saying that the members are always free to attend and speak up at the Thursday Executive Committee meeting before the start of each annual conference is no substitute. In any given year, the large majority of members do not attend the conference. Those that do attend generally arrive after the Executive Committee meeting takes place. If 15 people attend these meetings, that's a lot — and less than 1% of the membership. According to Don Lehmann only 2 people attended the 1994 Executive Committee meeting. Clearly, we need a more adequate forum for discussion and debate.

TABLE 4
ACR Members' sentiments on appropriate penalties for plagiarism (n = 185)

%	Acceptable penalty for plagiarism
8.6	No penalty or action should be taken.
29.2	The guilty party should receive a confidential reprimand from the Board of Directors (or the Executive Committee) on behalf of ACR.
36.8	As is done in some other scholarly organizations (e.g., the American Psychological Association), the person's name and infraction should be included in a confidential year-end letter mailed to all members noting all parties found to have engaged in ethical misconduct during the prior year and penalties imposed.
35.1	An announcement of the guilty party's name and ACR action (e.g., reprimand, censure, expulsion) should appear in the ACR Newsletter.
30.8	The person should be prohibited from holding or any elected office at ACR.
31.5	If elected or appointed an ACR office holder, that person should be required to resign.
30.3	If an ACR Fellow, the Fellow Award should be retracted.
29.2	The person should be expelled from ACR.

Do we consider ourselves scientists? The National Academy of Sciences has adopted a strict definition of misconduct in scientific research (*Nature*, 1992). Both the National Science Foundation and the Public Health Service define scientific fraud and misconduct as "practices that seriously deviate from community expectations." One would think that the expectations within ACR regarding honest scholarship and the proper citation of others creative contributions are not unlike those in the other, more mature behavioral sciences. If so, then as a Preamble, we should consider incorporating some or all of the NAS and/or NSF language.

As to specific standards, perhaps it would be helpful to start with APA's Code of Ethics (December, 1992, p. 1597-1611). After removing the nine standards dealing with psychotherapy, we could determine which of the six Principles and remaining 93 standards might be appropriate.[49]

Consider, also, doing research on the membership. One thing to find out is what, specifically, would be viewed as "practices that seriously deviate from community expectations?" Another is what penalties our members would consider acceptable for violations of each type of practice. The "Projectably Pervasive" study referred to above did this for several practices. Table 4 summarizes the findings for plagiarism. (Note: Respondents were asked to indicate "all those penalties you feel are appropriate;" hence, the percentages add to more than 100%.) From here it can be seen that the membership is not of an "off with their heads" mentality, though I suspect higher percentages would be obtained now as compared to when these data were collected.

In 1962, President John F. Kennedy promulgated a Bill of Consumers Rights that included, among others, the right to full and accurate information and the right to redress. While as members of American society, all consumers have these rights, at this very moment, consumer researchers as members of ACR do not. Apparently, we don't even enjoy the right to have our legitimate questions answered by those whom we elect to positions of authority and trust.

Since a Code of Ethics is likely to evolve over time, let's get something in place sooner rather than later and not hide behind the lame excuse "We wanted it to be complete/perfect before implementing anything." Let ACR not find itself in the position of an exposed plagiarist who may, too late, understand the full import of Tryon Edwards' observation: "Hell is truth seen too late; duty neglected in its season" (Edwards, 1957, p. 268).

Let Fellows Elect Fellows: It has always seemed strange to me that people who are themselves not Fellows should be the arbiters of which scholars are elected Fellows. Now that there are 14 living Fellows, as is done by all other organizations I know of honoring members through the election of Fellows, after the Nominating Committee has done its work, let ACR's Fellows handle the final stage of their own election. In the era of FAXing and conference calls, this should not pose insurmountable problems.

But whatever we do, let's at least get the criteria straight and applied uniformly and justly. This is an award made on behalf of the membership and supposed to reflect the organization as a whole. Accordingly, why shouldn't the membership play a role in identifying, clarifying and voting to approve these criteria? And if the membership is not given a say in the matter, then let the Board justify why it finds vagueness and "undefined" criteria preferable, so that the Call for Nominations for Fellows reads: "Although **the Board of Directors has deliberately kept the qualifications for the award undefined,**[50] it has been stipulated over the years that

---

[49]As possibilities, consider the following passages extracted from Principles B, "Integrity," and Principle C, "Professional and Scientific Responsibility" (see page 1599):

Psychologists seek to promote integrity in the science, teaching and practice of psychology. In these activities, psychologists are honest, fair, and respectful of others. In describing or reporting their qualifications, services, products, fees, research, or teaching, they do not make statements that are false, misleading, or deceptive. (From Principle B.)

Psychologists are concerned about the ethical compliance of their colleague's scientific and professional conduct. (From Principle C.)

---

[50]This seems to be a strange posture for social scientist to adopt. Think of the implications for science if we kept our concepts "undefined" before we went out to identify and measure exemplars of these constructs. According to the language found in the 1978 ACR Minutes, the founding fathers of the Fellow Award had a clear idea of what they wanted the award to represent.

the award is for a long period of productivity and contribution, not for a single or a few contributions to the field" (bolding supplied). Further, why is this "productivity" language different from the "significant impact on scholarly work in consumer behavior" language used upon founding the award? What are the implications of this subtle change? Regardless shouldn't the membership have a say in this?

By way of providing guidance, something for posterity, and further insuring a fair and effective reward allocation process, as do other scholarly organizations, let's consider having a description indicating why each elected Fellow merited the award published in the annual ACR Proceedings, either the year that Fellow is elected or when he/she delivers his/her Fellow's Address.

Where do individual ACR Members go from here?

I hope this Address adds to the motivation that I'm sure most ACR members have to think and behave ethically. When in doubt, think of applying the Golden Rule. Again, I've found the best way to apply this rule is to invert it and say: "Don't do unto others what you would not want them to do unto you." Another question you might ask: "Is it fair?"

Second, "ethics" is fast becoming a burgeoning arena for scholarship—so much so, that Larry Erlbaum (LEA Publishers) found a sufficient quantity of high quality work to initiate and sustain a new journal, *Ethics and Behavior*, now in its fourth year. Several other journals also focus on ethics. I hope this Address will stimulate some to consider doing research on this subject. Lord knows, there are many opportunities for such meaningful research in our field.

Third, I encourage each ACR member to expect ethical behavior; but if you experience unethical behavior, please consider speaking out. Though the current climate makes it easier to do so than it was in 1971, it's still not easy, especially when the guilty party is in a position of authority. I would only suggest that you keep as good records as you can and consider speaking out when there is no longer any danger of a Pyrrhic victory. As the Swiss Philosopher, Henry Frederic Amiel, noted: "Truth is not only violated by falsehood, it may be equally outraged by silence" (in Edwards, 1957, p. 688).

Where does Jack Jacoby go from here?

First, I want to let those who are wont to slander me know that, from this point onward, you better have hard evidence to back up what you say because I'm going to come after you with everything at my disposal including, if necessary, a law suit. Unfortunately, this blunt language seems to be the only kind that some at ACR understand.

Other than that immutable resolve, where I go from here depends, in part, what this organization does. One thing I will consider is whether this address (sans appendices) is published in full, or whether some reason will be concocted as to why it should not be published in its current, albeit controversial form. Any who might call for this address to be condensed or revised should keep the following in mind. Though page length restrictions apply to all other contributions to the ACR Proceedings, such restrictions have never been applied to the addresses of either Presidents or Fellows. Hence, any retroactive attempt to impose a requirement that this address be condensed or revised before it can be published should be recognized as an act of censorship not in keeping either with ACR precedent or the hallowed tradition of intellectual freedom.

More importantly, where I go from here depends on where ACR goes from here. As an organization without a Code of Ethics or Ethics Committee, I see parallels between ACR's current situation and organizations that have rules against accepting Jews, Afro-

Americans, etc. as members. It has become fashionable among those seeking elected office to say that they've come to understand that remaining a member of such organizations is morally wrong so that, after years of going along with these policies, they are dropping their memberships.

Well I'm not seeking any elected office either here or elsewhere. But I can no longer, in good conscience, remain a member of a scholarly organization, now celebrating its 25th year, that continues to reject the notion of developing and acting according to a Code of Ethics, and then compounds the problem by treating its rank and file members like children by denying them a vote on this issue. Like those who refused to invest in the stocks of firms doing business in South Africa or the tobacco or alcoholic beverage industries, unless there is positive action on the ethics front, I will no longer invest any resources in ACR—other than to take the time to resign. Specifically, if I see no movement in this direction by ACR's governance during the next 12 months, then considering it analogous to refusing to be associated with any other organization I believed was operating lawlessly and unethically, I will resign from ACR. I don't want my name listed as a supporter of an ethically lawless scholarly organization only to later be forced to give some lame excuse for having passively accepted its lawlessness.

Though I will feel sad about it, I will leave with my head held high, knowing that, (as a successful and ethical businessman,) for periods involving 15 and 20 years, I achieved a level of impact on scholarship in the field that few could match. My head will be held even higher knowing that I had done everything within my power, including incurring considerable financial costs and risking the wrath and retaliation of others, to help this organization behave responsibly in fulfilling rather than debasing its destiny as the voice of scholarly research on consumer behavior. Thereafter, whatever would be said about me by those here would not hurt, as I can only be hurt by those whom I respect. By its refusal to act responsibly, ACR would have demonstrated it no longer deserved my respect.

Fortunately, I don't think I will have to resign. Ever since serving on his doctoral committee, I've known Don Lehmann to be a straight-shooter and follower of the Golden Rule. I am certain he understands the merit of what I'm advocating and confident that, as incoming ACR President, he will help those who may not like this messenger or his style[51] understand that the substance of the message is something vital to their own interests. With that, ladies and gentlemen, colleagues all, I thank you for listening.

REFERENCES

Adler, Tina (1991), "Outright Fraud Rare, but not Poor Science,"*The Monitor*, (American Psychological Association), Vol. 22,p. 11.

Akaah, Ishmael P. and Edward A. Riordan (1989), "Judgments of Marketing Professionals about Ethical Issues in Marketing Research: A Replication and Extension," *Journal of Marketing Research*, 26 (1), 112-120.

American Association of Public Opinion Research (1991), *Code of Professional Ethics and Practices and AAPOR's Procedures for Dealing with Alleged Violations of the Code*. Ann Arbor: Michigan.

---

[51]For those who may think that this Address is "socially inappropriate" and may cause undesirable angst and conflict, I suggest they be at least as concerned with the scholarly practices and unfair organizational procedures at ACR that provide the wellsprings for this Address.

American Marketing Association (1987, Fall), "AMA Adopts New Code of Ethics," *Marketing Educator*, pp. 3ff.

American Psychological Association (1992a), "Ethical Principles of Psychologists and Code of Conduct." *American Psychologist*, 47 (12), 1597-1611.

American Psychological Association (1992b), "Rules and Procedures: Ethics Committee of the American Psychological Association." *American Psychologist*, 47 (12), 1612-1628.

American Psychological Association (1993), "Report of the Ethics Committee, 1991 and 1992," *American Psychologist*, 48 (7), 811-820.

American Psychological Association (1994), "Report of the Ethics Committee, 1993," *American Psychologist*, 49 (7), 659-666.

Andreasen, Alan R. (1992), "President's Column." *ACR Newsletter*. March.

Bagozzi, Richard P. and Youyae Yi (1991), "Multitrait-Multimethod Matrices in Consumer Research," *Journal of Consumer Research*, 17 (4), 426-439.

Belch, Michael A. (1993), "Discussant: Public Policy and Ethical Issues," unpublished remarks. (Noted in Allen, Chris T. and Deborah Roedder John, Eds., *Advances in Consumer Research*, 1994, 21, xxvi.)

Berning, Carol A. Kohn and Jacob Jacoby (1974), "Patterns of Information Acquisition in New Product Purchases,"*Journal of Consumer Research*, 1 (2), 18-22.

Bettman, James R. and Jacob Jacoby (1976), "Patterns of Processing in Consumer Information Acquisition," *Advances in Consumer Research* 3, 315–320.

Bettman, James R. and Pradeep Kakkar (1977), "Effects of Information Presentation Format on Consumer Information Acquisition Strategies," *Journal of Consumer Research*, 3 (4), 233-243.

Bhide, Amar and Howard H. Stevenson (1990), "Why be Honest if Honesty doesn't Pay?" *Harvard Business Review*, September-October, 121-129.

Blakeslee, Sandra (1994), "Old Accident Points to Brain's Moral Center," *The New York Times*, May 24, pages C1, C14.

Brown, H. Jackson Jr. (1991) *Life's Little Instruction Book.* Nashville, Tenn.: Rutledge Hill Press.

Burke, Edmund (1899), "Reflections on the Revolution in France,"*The Collected Works of Edmund Burke*, Vol. 3, 438-439.

Cote, Joseph A., Siew Meng Leong and Jane Cote (1990, August 10), "Assessing the Dissemination and Utilization of Marketing Research in the Social Sciences: A Citation Analysis Approach," Working paper, School of Business, Washington State University, Vancouver, Washington.

Cote, Joseph A., Siew Meng Leong and Jane Cote (1991), "Assessing the Influence of *Journal of Consumer Research*: A Citation Analysis," *Journal of Consumer Research*, 18 (3), 402-410.

Curren, Mary T., Tina Kiesler and Harold H. Kassarjian (1984), *Advances in Consumer Research, Index for Volumes 7-11 (1980-84)*. Provo, Utah: Association for Consumer Research.

Deutsch, Morton and Janice M. Steil (1988), "Awakening the Sense of Injustice," *Social Justice Research*, 2 (1), 3-23.

Edwards, Tryon (ed. 1957), *The New Dictionary of Thoughts: A Cyclopaedia of Quotations*, Standard Book Company. (Work originally compiled in 1852 and later revised and enlarged by C.N. Catrevas, Jonathan Edwards and Ralph Emerson Browns).

Engel, James F., David T. Kollat and Roger D. Blackwell (1973) *Consumer Behavior* (Second ed.). New York: Holt, Rinehart and Winston.

Engel, James F., Roger D. Blackwell and Paul W. Miniard (1993), *Consumer Behavior* (Seventh ed.). Fort Worth, Texas: Dryden Press.

Federal Trade Commission v. Kraft, Inc. (1991), Final Order. Docket No. 9208, January 30. Lexis 38.

Ferrell, O.C. and Larry G. Gresham (1985), "A Contingency Framework for Understanding Ethical Decision Making in Marketing." *Journal of Marketing*, 49 (3), 87-96.

Ferrell, O.C. and Steven J. Skinner (1988), "Ethical Behavior and Bureaucratic Structure in Marketing Research Organizations," *Journal of Marketing research*, 25 (1), 103-109.

Ferrell, O.C. and K. Mark Weaver (1978), "Ethical Beliefs of Marketing Managers" *Journal of Marketing*, 42 (3), 69-73.

Friedman, Peter Monroe (1977a), "ACR Standards for Professional Conduct in Consumer Research: Can we Get there from here?," In William D. Perrault, Jr. (ed.) *Advances in Consumer Research*, Vol. IV, 254-255.

Friedman, Peter Monroe (1977b), "Establishing Standards for Professional Conduct in Consumer Research: A Suggested Role for the Association for Consumer Research." In William D. Perrault, Jr. (ed.) *Advances in Consumer Research*, Vol. IV, 261.

Goldman, Arieh (1979), "Publishing Activity in Marketing as an Indicator of its Structure and Disciplinary Boundaries," *Journal of Marketing Research*, 16 (4), 485-494.

Harris, Richard J. and G. E. Monaco (1978), "Psychology of Pragmatic Implication: Information Processing Between the Lines." *Journal of Experimental Psychology: General*, 107 (1), 1 - 22.

Hilts, Philip J. (1992), "Plagiarists Take Note: Machine's on Guard," *The New York Times*, January 7; pp. C1, C9.

Hoffman, Donna L. and Morris B. Holbrook (1993), "The Intellectual Structure of Consumer Research: A Bibliometric Study of Author Co-citations in the first 15 years of *JCR*," *Journal of Consumer Research*, 19 (4), 507-517.

Holbrook, Morris B. (1985) "Why Business is Bad for Consumer Research: The Three Bears Revisited." In Elizabeth C. Hirschman and Morris B. Holbrook (Eds.) *Advances in Consumer Research*, 12, 145-156.

Holbrook, Morris B. (1994), "Ethics in Consumer Research: An Overview and Prospectus." In Allen, Cris T. and Deborah Roedder John (eds.), *Advances in Consumer Research*, Vol. 21, 566-571.

Holsti, Ole R. (1968), "Content Analysis," In *The Handbook of Social Psychology*, Vol. 2, Gardner Lindzey and Eliot Aronson (Eds.). Reading, Mass.: Addison-Wesley. Pp. 597-692.

Houlihan, Daniel, Lisa Hofschulte, Daniel Sachau, and Christi Patten (1992), "Critiquing the Peer Review Process: Examining a Potential Dual Role Conflict." *American Psychologist*, 47 (12), 1679-1681.

Hunt, Shelby D., Lawrence B. Chonko and James B. Wilcox (1984), "Ethical Problems of Marketing Research." *Journal of Marketing Research*, 21 (3), 309-324.

Jacoby, Jacob (1969a), "Toward Defining Consumer Psychology: One Psychologist's Views." *Purdue Papers in Consumer Psychology*, No. 101. (Presented as part of a symposium entitled "Towards a Definition of Consumer Psychology," American Psychological Association, 77th Annual Convention, Washington, D.C., September 4, 1969.)

Jacoby, Jacob (1969b), "Personality and Consumer Behavior: How NOT to Find Relationships," *Purdue Papers in Consumer Psychology*, No. 102.

Jacoby, Jacob (1972), "Opinion Leadership and Innovativeness: Overlap and and Validity," In M. Venkatesan (Ed), *Proceedings, Third Annual Conference*, The Association for Consumer Research, Vol. 2, 632-649.

Jacoby, Jacob (1975a), "Consumer Psychology as a Social Psychological Sphere of Action," *American Psychologist*, 30 (10), 977-987. (1974 Presidential Address to Division 23, The American Psychological Association.)

Jacoby, Jacob (1975b), "Perspectives on an Information Processing Research Program," *Communication Research*, 2 (3), 203-215.

Jacoby, Jacob (1976a), "Consumer Research: Telling it Like it is," *Advances in Consumer Research*, 3, 1-11. (1975 Presidential Address to the Association for Consumer Research. Condensed version published as "Consumer Research: A State of the Art Review," *Journal of Marketing*, 1978, 42 (2), 87-96.)

Jacoby, Jacob (1976b), "Consumer Psychology: An Octennium," *Annual Review of Psychology*, 27, 331-358.

Jacoby, Jacob (1976c), "Consumer and Industrial Psychology: Prospects for Theory Corroboration and Mutual Contribution," Marvin D. Dunnette (Ed.), *The Handbook of Industrial and Organizational Psychology*, Chicago: Rand-McNally, 1031-1061.

Jacoby, Jacob (1977), "History and Objectives Underlying Formation of ACR's Professional Affairs Committee." In William D. Perrault, Jr. (ed.) *Advances in Consumer Research*, Vol. IV, 256-257.

Jacoby, Jacob (1985), "The Vices and Virtues of Consulting: Responding to a Fairy Tale." *Advances in Consumer Research*, 12, 157-163.

Jacoby, Jacob (1993), "Ethical Issues in Consumer Research: Selected Remarks." Unpublished paper presented at the Annual Conference of the Association for Consumer Research. (See *Advances in Consumer Research*, 1994, Vol. 21, 565.)

Jacoby, Jacob, Robert W. Chestnut, Wayne D. Hoyer, David A. Sheluga and Michael J. Donahue (1978), "Psychometric Characteristics of Behavioral Process Data: Preliminary Findings on Validity and Reliability," *Advances in Consumer Research*, 5, 546-554.

Jacoby, Jacob, Robert W. Chestnut, Karl Weigl and William Fisher (1976) "Pre-Purchase Information Acquisition: Description of a Process Methodology, Research Paradigm and Pilot Investigation," *Advances in Consumer Research*, 3, 306-314.

Jacoby, Jacob and Wayne D. Hoyer (1987), *The Comprehension and Miscomprehension of Print Communications: An Investigation of Mass Media Magazines.* Hillsdale, NJ: Lawrence Erlbaum Associates.

Jacoby, Jacob, Wayne D. Hoyer and David A. Sheluga (1980), *The Miscomprehension of Televised Communications.* New York: The American Association of Advertising Agencies.

Jacoby, Jacob and James J. Jaccard (1984), "The Influence of Health and Safety Information of Consumer Decision Making Concerning New Technological Products," unpublished final report, National Science Foundation grant PRA 7920585.

Jacoby, Jacob, James J. Jaccard, Alfred Kuss, Tracy Troutman and David Mazursky (1987), "New Directions in Behavioral Process Research: Implications for Social Psychology," *Journal of Experimental Social Psychology*, 23 (2), 146-174.

Jacoby, Jacob, Alfred Kuss, David Mazursky and Tracy Troutman (1985), "Effectiveness of Security Analyst information Accessing Strategies: A Computer Interactive Assessment," *Computers in Human Behavior*, 1, 95-113.

Jacoby, Jacob, David Mazursky, Tracy Troutman and Alfred Kuss (1984), "When Feedback is Ignored: The Disutility of Outcome Feedback," *Journal of Applied Psychology*, 69, 531-545.

Jacoby, Jacob and Constance B. Small (1975), "The FDA Approach to Defining Misleading Advertising," Purdue Papers in Consumer Psychology, No. 146. A condensed version was published in *Journal of Marketing*, 1975, 39 (4), 65-68.

Jacoby, Jacob and George J. Szybillo (1995), "Consumer Research in FTC v. Kraft: A Case of Heads we Win, Tails you Lose?" *Journal of Public Policy & Marketing*, 14 (1), 1-14.

Jacoby, Jacob, Tracy Troutman, Alfred Kuss and David Mazursky (1986), "Experience and Expertise in Complex Decision Making," *Advances in Consumer Research*, 13, 469-472.

Johnson, Eric J., John W. Payne, David A. Schkade and James R. Bettman (1989), "Monitoring Information Processing and Decisions: The Mouselab System," unpublished manuscript. Center for Decision Studies, Fuqua School of Business, Duke University, Durham, North Carolina. February 14th.

Kassarjian, Harold H. (1971), "Personality and Consumer Behavior: A Review," *Journal of Marketing Research*, 8 (4), 409-418.

Kassarjian, Harold H. (1977), "Content Analysis in Consumer Research," *Journal of Consumer Research*, 4 (1) 8-18.

Kassarjian, Harold H. and Joseph L. Orsini (1980), "Preface" *Index: Association for Consumer Research Proceedings, 1970-1979.* Ann Arbor, Michigan: Association for Consumer Research. iii-iv.

Lamberth, John and Allan J. Kimmel (1981), "Ethical Issues and Responsibilities in Applying Scientific Behavioral Knowledge." Allan J. Kimmel (ed) *New Directions for Methodology of Social and Behavioral Science: Ethics of Human Subject Research.* San Francisco: Jossey-Bass. 69-79.

Leventhal, Gerald S., Jurgis Kazur Jr and William Rick Fry (1980), "Beyond Fairness: A Theory of Allocation Preferences," In Gerold Mikula (ed.) *Justice and Social Interaction*, Berne, Switzerland: Hans Huber.

Massey, Walter (1992), *National Science Foundation Annual Report, 1991.* Washington, D.C.: National Science Foundation.

Merriam-Webster (1977), *Webster's New Collegiate Dictionary*, Springfield, Massachusetts: G. & C. Merriam Company.

Misra, Shekhar (1992), "Is Conventional Debriefing Adequate? An Ethical Issue in Consumer Research," *Journal of the Academy of Marketing Science*, 20 (3), 269-273.

Muncy, James A. and Scott J. Vitell (1992), "Consumer Ethics: An Investigation of the Ethical Beliefs of the Final Consumer," *Journal of Business Research*, 24 (4), 297-311.

National Academy of Sciences (1992), *Responsible Science: Ensuring the Integrity of the Research Process.* Vol. 1. Washington, D.C.: The National Academy Press.

Nature (1992), "Defining Misconduct." April, Vol. 356, 73-731.

Peter, J. Paul (1979), "Reliability: A Review of Psychometric Basics and Recent Marketing Practices," *Journal of Marketing Research*, 16 (1), 6-17.

New York Times (1994), "The Gag Rule, Revisited," Editorial, Oct 24, p. A16.

Preston, Ivan L. (1992), "The Scandalous Record of Avoidable Errors in Expert Evidence Offered in FTC and Lanham Act Deceptiveness Cases." *Journal of Public Policy and Marketing*, 11 (2), 57-67.

Rees, Thomas D. (1993), "A Rumor of AIDS," *New York Magazine*, 26 (30), 26-32.

Rentz, Joseph (1987), "Generalizability Theory: A Comprehensive Method for Assessing and Improving the Dependability of Marketing Measures," *Journal of Marketing Research*, 28 (1), 19-28.

Richards, Jef I. (1990), *Deceptive Advertising*. Hillsdale, NJ: Lawrence Erlbaum Associates.

Richards, Jef I. and Ivan L. Preston (1992), "Proving and Disproving Materiality of Deceptive Advertising Claims," *Journal of Public Policy and Marketing*, 11 (2), 45-56.

Robertson, Thomas S. and Harold H. Kassarjian, eds. (1991), *Handbook of Consumer Behavior*, Englewood Cliffs, New Jersey: Prentice-Hall.

Rosenblatt, Roger (1994), "How do they Live with Themselves?" *New York Times Magazine*, (March 20); Section 6; 34-41, 55, 73-76.

Schein, Edgar H. (1965), *Organizational Psychology*. Englewood Cliffs, NJ: Prentice-Hall, Inc.

Schmeisser, Cynthia B. (1992), "Ethical Codes in the Professions," *Educational Measurement Issues and Practice*, 11 (3), 5-11.

Smith, Craig (1993), "Ethics and ACR: An Initial Report to the ACR Board of Directors from the ACR Professional Standards Task Force." Unpublished report discussed at the Annual Conference of the Association for Consumer Research. (Noted in Allen, Chris T. and Deborah Roedder John, Eds., *Advances in Consumer Research*, 1994, 21, 565.)

Smith, Craig and John A. Quelch (ed. 1993), *Ethics in Marketing*. Boston: Irwin.

Sojka, Jane and Eric R. Spangenberg (1994), "Ethical Concerns in Marketing Research," In Allen, Chris T. and Deborah Roedder John (Eds.) *Advances in Consumer Research*, 21, 392-396.

Swazey, Judith P., Melissa S. Anderson and Karen Seashore Lewis (1993), "Ethical Problems in Academic Research," *American Scientist*, 81, 542-553.

Thibaut, John and J. Walker (1975), *Procedural Justice*, Hillsdale, NJ: Lawrence Erlbaum Associates.

Toy, Daniel, Jerry C. Olson and Lauren Wright (1993), "The Role of Deception and Debriefing in Consumer Research," Unpublished paper. (Noted in Allen, Chris T. and Deborah Roedder John, Eds., *Advances in Consumer Research*, 1994, 21, 565.)

Tybout, Alice M. and Gerald Zaltman (1974), "Ethics in Marketing Research: Their Practical Relevance." *Journal of Marketing Research*, 11 (4), 357-368.

Wilkie, William L. (1990), *Consumer Behavior* (Second Edition), New York: John Wiley and Sons.

Woodside, Arch G., Jagdish N. Sheth and Peter D. Bennett (eds. 1977), "Preface," *Consumer and Industrial Buying Behavior*. New York: Elsevier North-Holland.

Wright, Peter (March 1994), "Scholarly Influence within the Field of Consumer Behavior," *ACR Newsletter*, pp 13-14.

Three parties requested the opportunity to respond to the published version of Professor Jacoby's fellow's address. The Board of Directors of ACR has published these responses along with Jacoby's address in these proceedings. Professor Jacoby requested, but was not granted, an opportunity to reply to the responses. The Board believes that the positions of the parties are adequately represented in the submissions contained in these proceedings.

A Perspective on Using Computers to Monitor Information Acquisition

James R. Bettman, Duke University
Eric J. Johnson, University of Pennsylvania
John W. Payne, Duke University

ABSTRACT

In this note, we reply to the section of Jacoby's 1994 Fellow Address (Jacoby 1995, pp. 24-26) focusing upon our acknowledgment of his prior work in our 1989 users' manual for the MOUSELAB system (Johnson, Payne, Schkade, and Bettman 1989). We dispute Jacoby's arguments; we believe that the development of computer-based information search procedures was part of the zeitgeist of the 1970s and 1980s and that many researchers, including Jacoby and us, made contributions to monitoring information acquisition.

We make four major points:

(1) Jacoby informed us of his allegations in correspondence in 1992, stating that "if you folks had *developed* such procedures prior to mid-1979, *used* them prior to 1980, and *published* articles in refereed journals describing these procedures prior to 1984 then, provided with some evidence of this, with deep humility and the utmost of sincerity, I would apologize profusely for bothering you with these two letters."

(2) We then wrote Jacoby, pointing out such prior publications as Payne and Braunstein (1978). He responded that "While I've seen occasional references to the 1978 Payne and Braunstein piece, I don't believe I ever read it... I agree that this sets the record straight about Mouselab and its relation to prior work... and do apologize if my earlier letters caused you concern."

(3) We cited the work of Jacoby and others (Payne and Braunstein 1978; Jacoby, Mazursky, Troutman, and Kuss 1984; Dahlstrand and Montgomery 1984; Brucks 1988) when we adapted part of our MOUSELAB manual for publication as an appendix in our 1993 book *The Adaptive Decision Maker* (Payne, Bettman, and Johnson 1993). We informed Jacoby in our 1992 correspondence of these upcoming citations, and the book appeared in 1993 well before the 1994 ACR Conference.

(4) We were therefore shocked to see Jacoby's charges repeated in his 1994 Fellow Address when he had stated in his correspondence with us that the matter was settled.[1]

FURTHER DETAILS

We now provide some further details about the above points. The essence of Jacoby's allegations (pp. 24-26, Jacoby 1995) is that we failed to explicitly reference previous research that used personal computers to study information acquisition behavior in our MOUSELAB systems manual (Johnson, Payne, Schkade, & Bettman

1989).[2] Jacoby argues that our manual implies "that there were no other previous instances where computers have been used to study consumer information acquisition" (Jacoby 1995, p. 24).[3]

Jacoby (1995) then references several papers by Jacoby et al. published in the period 1984-1987 and concludes that "the three articles published in recognized peer review journals all confirm that others not only developed and used, but were the first to publish articles using a "computer-controlled pointing device" and set of procedures offering "a number of flexible graphics and process tracing techniques" for studying information acquisition" (Jacoby 1995, p. 25). Jacoby then argues that Jim Bettman knew of this work since Jim was on a 1979 advisory panel for an NSF grant to Jacoby that resulted in the published papers from 1984-87 and Jim served as editor for a 1984 submission by Jacoby to the *Journal of Consumer Research* using this technique.[4] As we point out below, however, Bettman's exposure to Jacoby's work is irrelevant to our main points.

In our 1992 correspondence, Jacoby was informed that Payne had published an article in a refereed journal in 1978 that used a computer-based system to monitor the information acquisition behavior of decision makers (see Payne & Braunstein 1978, p. 555). Thus, six years before the peer reviewed publications referenced by Jacoby in his address, and before any exposure of Jim Bettman to Jacoby's work, Payne had published an article in a refereed journal using a computer-based approach to study the content, amount, and sequence of information acquisitions. In a companion working paper to Payne and Braunstein (1978), Payne and Braunstein (1977) describe a second system that used a wheel moving crosshairs as a pointing device and a computer-based information display board. That paper was referenced in Russo (1978, p. 569), a paper presented by Russo at a 1977 ACR special session in which Jacoby was a participant. The papers by Payne are also referenced in a published paper by Payne, Braunstein, and Carroll (1978, p. 35), which is a often-cited paper dealing with methods for exploring pre-decision behavior.

Given that Payne and Braunstein had published an article in 1978 that used a computer-based system to monitor information acquisition behavior, it seems difficult to argue that we were claiming that the use of computers to monitor information acquisi-

---

[1] Although we reference this 1992 correspondence throughout this reply, ACR chose not to publish appendices of correspondence. Copies of the entire correspondence are available from the authors upon request.

[2] It is important to recognize that the 1989 paper by Johnson, Payne, Schkade, and Bettman was written as a manual for the MOUSELAB computer program. Thus, the majority of the text is examples of how to program and use MOUSELAB.

[3] At the time Jacoby first made his allegations in 1992, he did not cite the most current version of the MOUSELAB manual, which was a 1991 version. That 1991 version contained many changes in wording from the 1989 version throughout the manual. Earlier versions of the manual than 1989 also exist.

[4] Bettman was indeed exposed briefly to Jacoby's proposal in 1979 and served as the editor for Jacoby's 1984 submission. Bettman served as the editor for hundreds of papers during his 6+ year JCR tenure; his memory of the Jacoby manuscript was limited to the notion that it studied security analysts.

tion was new in the mid to late 1980s. Our emphasis in our 1989 description of the MOUSELAB system is on the *use of a mouse as a pointing device*, and most of the introduction in the MOUSELAB manual concerns why a mouse is a superior pointing device. That was what we thought was new. That was why the system was called MOUSELAB! Extensive citing of prior work by Payne or anyone else did not seem relevant for a users' manual whose major purpose was to describe the features of the mouse-based system and how to use it.

In the 1992 exchange of correspondence that we refer to above and Jacoby refers to in his remarks (Jacoby 1995 p. 25), Jacoby wrote on June 2, 1992 that "if you folks had *developed* such procedures prior to mid-1979, *used* them prior to 1980, and *published* articles in refereed journals describing these procedures prior to 1984 then, provided with some evidence of this, with deep humility and the utmost of sincerity, I would apologize profusely for bothering you with these two letters." Johnson then sent Jacoby a letter and copies of Payne and Braunstein (1978) and the related unpublished paper by Payne and Braunstein (1977) on June 19, 1992. After receiving Johnson's letter and the copies of the papers, Jacoby wrote a letter to Johnson on July 7, 1992 in which he stated that "While I've seen occasional references to the 1978 Payne and Braunstein piece, I don't believe I ever read it. If I did, evidently I did not remember the use of a computer-based procedure for assessing information acquisition. Regardless, I agree that this sets the record straight about Mouselab and its relation to prior work... I appreciate the spirit in which your letter was written and do apologize if my earlier letters caused you concern." Interestingly, Jacoby stated in his April 16, 1992 letter to Johnson that "I have no question that you folks were the first to develop the "mouse" approach and are clearly entitled to claim being first in this regard."

The purpose of the paragraphs above is not to establish whether we were the first to use computer-based systems to monitor information acquisition behavior. Perhaps others used computer-based systems and pointing devices earlier than either Payne or Jacoby; certainly it was the obvious next step to develop computerized versions once Information Display Boards (IDBs) had been introduced (Wilkins (1967) had used IDBs as early as the 1960s), and many other clever computer-based approaches were also being used during the 1980s (e.g., Brucks 1985). It is our belief, indeed, that the zeitgeist of the information processing revolution made such approaches inevitable, and the nature of computer-based systems for monitoring information acquisition behavior became more sophisticated as computers became more sophisticated from the mid 1970s on. As an example of the effect of this zeitgeist, Jacoby states in his Fellow Address that "both the Jacoby and Payne teams seem to have developed computer IDBs at approximately the same time, circa 1975-76" (Jacoby 1995, p. 25) (Parenthetically, although Jacoby refers to the "Payne team," Payne's early work was his own; Johnson did not begin to work with Payne until roughly 1981, and Bettman did not begin to work with them until roughly 1983).

In the same July 7, 1992 letter in which Jacoby acknowledges that the record had been set straight about MOUSELAB and its relation to prior work, he asked that any future descriptions of MOUSELAB be more specific in referencing other work that used computer systems of various types to monitor information acquisition during decision making. In our 1993 book, *The Adaptive Decision Maker* (Payne, Bettman, and Johnson 1993), we did exactly that, describing the MOUSELAB system in an appendix and explicitly referencing Brucks 1988; Dahlstrand & Montgomery 1984; Jacoby et al. 1984; and Payne and Braunstein 1978 as examples of other computer-based information acquisition procedures. Jacoby was made aware of this forthcoming cite to his work

in *The Adaptive Decision Maker* by Eric Johnson in his letter of June 19, 1992. The book was published by Cambridge University Press in 1993, well before the October 1994 ACR Conference. We do not know why Jacoby failed to acknowledge this more recent 1993 description of MOUSELAB or the prior work we had brought to his attention.

Thus, we felt that the matter had been amicably resolved, privately and in good faith, in 1992. We were therefore shocked to see these charges repeated in Jacoby's Fellow Address, given the earlier statements in Jacoby's July 7, 1992 letter.

Jack Jacoby has made contributions to consumer research and to the development and use of information monitoring techniques in particular. We have acknowledged those contributions where appropriate in our own work for almost two decades. We believe that techniques for monitoring information acquisition are simply tools, and our greatest excitement in our work has come from using these process-tracing tools to uncover substantive results that help reveal the inner workings of decision processes.

REFERENCES

Brucks, Merrie (1985), "The Effects of Product Class Knowledge on Information Search Behavior," *Journal of Consumer Research*, 12 (June), 1-16.

Brucks, Merrie (1988), "Search Monitor: An Approach for Computer-Controlled Experiments Involving Consumer Information Search," *Journal of Consumer Research*, 15 (June), 117-121.

Dahlstrand, Ulf, and Henry Montgomery (1984), "Information Search and Evaluation Processes in Decision Making: A Computer Based Process Tracing Study," *Acta Psychologica*, 56, 113-123.

Jacoby, Jacob (1995), "Ethics, Morality, and the Dark Side of ACR: Implications for Our Future," in *Advances in Consumer Research, Volume XXII*, eds. Frank R. Kardes and Mita Sujan, Provo, UT: Association for Consumer Research.

Jacoby, Jacob, David Mazursky, Tracy Troutman, and Alfred Kuss (1984), "When Feedback is Ignored: The Disutility of Outcome Feedback," *Journal of Applied Psychology*, 69, 531-545.

Johnson, Eric J., John W. Payne, David A. Schkade, and James R. Bettman (1989), "Monitoring Information Processing and Decisions: The Mouselab System," Unpublished Manuscript, Center for Decision Studies, Fuqua School of Business, Duke University.

Payne, John W., James R. Bettman, and Eric J. Johnson (1993). *The Adaptive Decision Maker*, Cambridge: Cambridge University Press.

Payne, John W., and Myron L. Braunstein (1977), "Task Complexity and Contingent Processing in Decision Making: A Replication and Extension to Risky Choice," Unpublished Working Paper, University of Chicago.

Payne, John W., and Myron L. Braunstein (1978), "Risky Choice: An Examination of Information Acquisition Behavior," *Memory and Cognition*, 6 (5), 554-561.

Payne, John W., Myron L. Braunstein, and John S. Carroll (1978), "Exploring Predecisional Behavior: An Alternative Approach to Decision Research," *Organizational Behavior and Human Performance*, 22, 17-44.

Russo, J. Edward (1978), "Eye Fixations Can Save the World: A Critical Evaluation and a Comparison Between Eye Fixations and Other Information Processing Methodologies," in *Advances in Consumer Research, Volume V*, ed. H. Keith Hunt, Ann Arbor: Association for Consumer Research, 561-570.

Wilkins, L. T. (1967), *Social Deviance*, Englewood Cliffs, NJ: Prentice-Hall.

In Response to Jacoby
Harold H. Kassarjian, UCLA

The paper that has particularly disturbed Jacoby is a review article in which I discuss and evaluate some 100 papers on the topic of personality and consumer behavior. (Harold H. Kassarjian, Personality and Consumer Behavior, *Journal of Marketing Research*, 8 (November 1971), pp. 409-418.)

Jacoby is upset by one sentence that appears on the bottom of the first column of page 416. However, the paragraph that precedes and the one that follows that sentence are also relevant. Jacoby implies that he was not accorded sufficient credit for his contributions. In that sentence and the adjoining sentences I refer to Jacoby and reference his work a total of eight times - eight times in two paragraphs.

I ask you, the reader, to please turn to the article, particularly the bottom of the first column of page 416, and make up your own mind. I ask that you form your opinion based on the material itself. I think you will be amazed!

Since it may be difficult for many readers to access either my personality review article or Jacoby's working paper, both written more than a quarter century ago, I reproduce below the relevant paragraphs, word for word, punctuation mark for punctuation mark.

THE PERSONALITY AND CONSUMER BEHAVIOR ARTICLE

{Page 416} . . .

A third reason for the lackluster results in the personality and consumer behavior literature is that *many studies have been conducted by a shotgun approach with no specific hypotheses or theoretical justification.* Typically a convenient, available, easily scored, and easy-to-administer personality inventory is selected and administered along with questionnaires on purchase data and preferences. The lack of proper scientific method and hypothesis generation is supposedly justified by the often-used disclaimer that the study is exploratory. As Jacoby has pointed out [51, p.244]:

> Careful examination reveals that, in most cases, no a priori thought is directed to *how*, or especially *why*, personality should or should not be related to that aspect of consumer behavior being studied. Moreover, the few studies which do report statistically significant findings usually do so on the basis of post-hoc "picking and choosing" out of large data arrays.

Statistical techniques are applied and anything that turns up looking halfway interesting furnishes the basis for the discussion section [49].

An excellent example of the shotgun approach to science, albeit a more sophisticated one than most, is Evans' original study examining personality differences between Ford and Chevrolet owners. Jacoby, in an excellent and most thoughtful paper, noted that Evans began his study with specific hypotheses culled from the literature and folklore pertaining to personality differences to be expected between Ford and Chevrolet owners [49]. He then presented the EPPS to subjects, measuring 11 variables, 5 of which seemed to be measuring the variables in question; the remaining 6 were irrelevant to the hypotheses with no a priori basis for expecting differences. If predictions were to have been made on these six

scales, Jacoby says, they should have been ones of *no* difference. Using one-tailed tests of significance, since the direction also should have been hypothesized, 3 of the 5 key variables were significant at the .05 level and none of the remaining 6 were significant. In short, Evans' data could have been interpreted such that 9 of the 11 scales were "significant" according to prediction. Jacoby's interpretation leads to a conclusion quite different from Evans', that there are no personality differences between Ford and Chevrolet owners. Also, with a priori predictions, Jacoby did not have to pick and choose from his data, as Kuehn was forced to do in showing a relationship between "dominance minus affiliation" scores and car ownership [59].

. . .

REFERENCES

{Note: The *Journal of Marketing Research* style, 25 years ago, required that all references be numbered in alphabetical order and presented not by name in the text but by number in brackets. The following, from my article, are the references cited above.}

49. Jacoby, Jacob. "Personality and Consumer Behavior: How Not to Find Relationships," Purdue Papers in Consumer Psychology, N. 102, Purdue University, 1969.

51. _____ , "Personality and Innovation Proneness," *Journal of Marketing Research*, 8 (May 1971), 244-7.

59. Kuehn, Alfred A. "Demonstration of a Relationship Between Psychological Factors and Brand Choice." *Journal of Business,* 36 (April 1963), 237-41.

PURDUE PAPERS IN CONSUMER PSYCHOLOGY NO. 102

{Note: The following material written by Jacoby in 1969 is on the second page of a paper he has termed "PPCP # 102." The cite is number 49 above. The following is a word for word, punctuation mark for punctuation mark, presentation of the full paragraphs on page 2 of the 7 page text in that working paper. These are the paragraphs that Jacoby has claimed contain the copied material.}

{Page 2} . . .

Consider, for a moment, the typical study addressed to the personality-consumer behavior relationship. Investigators usually take a general, broad-coverage personality inventory and a list of brands, products, or product categories, and attempt to correlate subjects' responses on the inventory with statements of product use or preference. Careful examination reveals that, in most cases, no a priori thought is directed to *how*, or especially *why*, personality should or should not be related to that aspect of consumer behavior being studied. Statistical techniques, mostly simple correlation or variants thereof, are applied and anything that turns up looking halfway interesting furnishes the basis for the Discussion section. {Note that the quote is not exactly identical and hence I could not use quotation marks as demanded by Jacoby. I should have cited the source, which I did.} Skill at post hoc interpretation has been demonstrated, but little real understanding has resulted.

Many of these investigators seem to adopt the naive assumption that given both the general hypothesis (i.e., that consumer behavior is, to a certain extent, determined by the consumer's personality) and the availability of an easy-to-administer personality inventory, said inventory ought to differentiate among groups of consumers or the general hypothesis fails. Proceeding in such a manner and at such a level of generality, this expectation is quite unreasonable. It is no wonder that results obtained from such atheoretic, shotgun, correlational investigations have been inconclusive or mildly suggestive at best.

. . .

Please decide for yourself if plagiarism or unethical behavior has occurred. Thank you for your time and my apologies that it has been necessary to take up your time on all this.

Reply to Jacob Jacoby

Ivan L. Preston, University of Wisconsin

This responds to the references made to me by Jack Jacoby in the publication version of his 1994 Fellow Address. He said I misrepresented his research in the following statement in an article: "In another example of avoidably erroneous evidence, Kraft Inc. tried to establish that the presence of calcium is not regarded as material by consumers who purchase cheese." The reason for the misrepresentation, Jack said, is that "the purpose of my research was not to determine whether the presence of calcium was material to consumers. Rather, it was to determine whether consumers thought the difference in calcium [between two sources] was material."

To begin, my statement did not mention Jack explicitly. I mentioned no one but Kraft in the cited statement or elsewhere because I was describing Kraft's overall defense against charges by the FTC. That defense included but was not restricted to Jack's actions, and Jack had no overall role nor responsibility for the whole. Jack's survey was of course part of Kraft's defense. But it was not all of it, and Jack was not Kraft's only witness.

Although Jack's expertise was certainly solicited and used, the law firm that hired him and supervised his work had oversight over, and responsibility for, everything that he did. In turn, Kraft had oversight over, and responsibility for, everything that the law firm, as its agent, did. Everything Jack did, then, was what Kraft chose to have him do, and again, what Kraft did was more than what Jack did.

Accordingly, a mention of Kraft can scarcely be interpretable as an implied mention of Jack. Many readers could not have seen Jack identified because of not even knowing of his role in the case. And of those who did have such prior knowledge, many would also have known that the case consisted of other elements besides Jack's survey. Indeed, it would seem quite unlikely that those readers most sophisticated with legal cases in general or most informed about the Kraft case in particular would think that a reference to Kraft's defense must constitute a reference narrowly to only one element of that defense. Thus, while one of the commonsense expectations about a statement that offends a person is that it should identify that person, it would appear unlikely in the given context that my statement would be taken by any significant number of readers as identifying Jack specifically.

Jack says the reference elsewhere by a co-author and myself to an action taken in the Kraft case by "Jacoby" shows that I knew it was him all the time. Of course I knew of his participation, and in the co-authored piece we cited him by name because we specifically wanted to comment on what he did. In my own piece I did not.

Peripherally, Jack seems incorrect in describing my action as "Mis-characterizing a published work." I have never seen his survey in published form, nor known it to be published. I have never seen a copy of it in any form, but have only read what the legal decisions said about it.

My statement said that Kraft used "avoidably erroneous evidence," defined in my article as that which its submitter could predict in advance will be rejected in court because rejection of similar evidence had occurred earlier. I stand behind the statement, for it was surely within the legal expertise of Kraft's or its outside lawyers to know that similar evidence had been rejected before and therefore was subject to rejection again.

However, it was not within Jack's consumer behavior expertise to know that. The difference in type of expertise absolves him of any charge of error on the point while also amounting to still another reason why my statement is unlikely to be taken by readers as identifying him.

My basic reason for calling "avoidably erroneous" Kraft's contention (that a presence-of-calcium claim was not material) is reflected in the comment by the judge that it is a "common sense conclusion that ads which make nutrition claims, which are disseminated over an extensive period of time, and which help to increase sales, make claims which are material to consumers." That is not only commensensical, but the point had appeared previously at the FTC, even if not specifically concerning calcium in cheese. The judge said that Kraft commissioned a materiality survey despite that. He attributed the decision to Kraft, as do I.

I doubt that my statement would be considered offensive to Kraft in the context. Even if it were so to a researcher, it would not be to a law firm. Lawyers often take steps they know have failed in the past. Reasons for such actions are speculated upon in my article, and examples are given of such actions in advertising cases. I don't think lawyers should be allowed to do such things, but that's another topic.

Returning to Jack's objection that it was not the purpose of his research to examine the materiality of a presence-of-calcium claim, the initial decision shows that the judge interpreted him as showing an interest in that. Also, although Jack wrote that "All parties...agreed that calcium was material," the opinions of judge and commissioners and appellate court all appear to have interpreted Kraft as disputing that point.

The judge wrote that one of the purposes of Jack's survey was "to determine ... whether ... in general, calcium was claimed to be important by consumers in their decision to purchase Kraft Singles slices...." He probably thought that because Jack asked his subjects a question about the important of the presence of calcium apart from considering any difference in amounts available from different sources, "thereby showing," the judge wrote, "according to Dr. Jacoby, that calcium is, in fact, relatively unimportant to their purchase...." Thus while Jack's stated purpose was to examine the materiality of differences in calcium in different cheeses, he nonetheless offered on the basis of his survey evidence what the judge interpreted as a conclusion about the materiality of the presence of calcium.

"I reject his conclusion," the judge wrote, because, although Jack had emphasized that subjects rated various other cheese attributes as more important than calcium, they had also rated calcium as important (71% said "extremely" or "very" important). The Commission opinion said "We agree with the ALJ [judge] that the results of Kraft's materiality survey confirm the importance of calcium as a factor in consumers' purchase decisions...." Later the appellate court said "Kraft's arguments lack merit. The FTC found solid evidence that consumers placed great importance on calcium consumption...."

Overall, then, the case certainly discussed the materiality of the presence of calcium, and Jack's survey was in the middle of that discussion whether he intended it to be or not. If his stated intent was misunderstood, it was by the judge, commissioners, and appellate court. Perhaps it was difficult for those jurists to interpret a situation in which a party participated in an activity while claiming he intended not to. Meanwhile, there seems no doubt that Kraft involved itself with the materiality of the presence-of-calcium claim by intent.

In summary, Jack Jacoby involved himself, by legal conclusion although not by his stated intent, in the materiality of a presence-of-calcium claim. That involvement, however, was not "avoidably erroneous" to him, and for that and other reasons cited my statement was not about him. There would thus seem to be no basis for the statement to offend him.

Consumer Promotion and Brand Loyalty: An Information Processing Perspective

France Leclerc, M.I.T, Sloan School of Management[1]

This paper summarizes the contents of a special topic session. Papers were presented by Priya Raghubir and Kim P. Corfman (New York University); Bari Harlam (University of Rhode Island) and Barbara Kahn (University of Pennsylvania); France Leclerc and John Little (MIT Sloan School of Management). The session was chaired by John Little with Leigh McAlister (University of Texas at Austin) serving as a discussant.

In recent years, marketing expenditures on consumer promotions has grown dramatically. For example, manufacturers distributed 75 billion coupons in 1977, and 292 billion in 1991. As a result, a thorough understanding of the various impacts of consumer promotions is of considerable practical importance. Although much effort has been spent studying the effect of various types of promotions on brand choice behavior, very little is known about the process by which this type of marketing activity influences choice. This special topic seminar attempted to shed some light on this issue by presenting current research dealing with how consumers process information in a promotional context. A better understanding of this process should help enhance the effectiveness of consumer promotions.

At least two different approaches can be taken to improve our understanding of how promotion works. First, one likely way by which promotion can affect brand choice is through its effect on brand evaluation. Over the years, there has been considerable debate as to whether or not promotion negatively affect the evaluation of a promoted brand (see Davis, Inman and McAlister 1992 for a review). By identifying factors or characteristics of the promotion likely to moderate such an effect, one may be able to reconcile these conflicting results. Second, consumers have been shown to vary in their level of loyalty to a brand, this level of loyalty impacting to some extent consumer responsiveness to a promotion. By contrasting how consumers loyal to a brand and consumers who switch among a number of brands process information in the context of a promotional event, one may be able to identify systematic patterns differentiating the two groups. These are the two approaches that were discussed in the proposed session.

In the first presentation, Raghubir and Corfman proposed a theoretical model describing how consumers process promotional cues and make inferences about service quality. They proposed that the process of pre-trial attitude formation is mediated by attributions for a promotion, and is contingent on contextual factors including perceptions of the variability of quality within an industry, perceptions of how common it is to promote within an industry, and the past promotional frequency of the service firm. In one experiment, they demonstrated that across a range of industries, offering a price promotion on a service can unfavorably affect brand evaluations. This is particularly true when price promotions are uncommon in the industry, and consumers perceive the quality of firms in the industry to vary. Further, they showed that the effect of promotions on brand evaluations is mediated by the attribution made for the promotion. In a second experiment, within the context of the mutual fund industry, Raghubir and Corfman showed that consumers' judgments of potential risk, return and service quality of a fund are dependent on contextual factors including industry norms, and the fund's own historical promotion behavior. These results suggest that under certain conditions a price promotion can lead to inferences of inferior quality which may diminish the effectiveness of a given promotion.

The two other papers attempted to contrast the "information processing" of two types of consumers, those who are loyal to a brand and those who switch among a number of brands. They did so using two different approaches, one using a computerized display board to trace the information search patterns, the other inferring the information processing from the impact of different types of information on brand attitudes.

Harlam and Kahn hypothesized that consumers who switch among brands (variety-seekers) are less non-compensatory than loyal consumers in their brand choice process unless promotions are present in which case variety-seekers are more non-compensatory than loyals. Why? Because variety-seekers have a more difficult task than loyal consumers in choice situations. Variety-seekers need to select at least two acceptable brands for their consideration set while loyals are only required to choose one acceptable brand. Therefore, variety-seekers will be more exhaustive and deliberate when searching information about brands and they are more likely to make trade-offs when evaluating brands. However, when promotions are present, variety-seekers will be more likely to react to them (even in the absence of specific price knowledge about the brand) because variety-seekers have more flexibility due to their larger consideration set sizes. These hypotheses were tested using a computer-based choice experiments. Subjects first had the opportunity to access brand/attribute information. Then subjects made a series of hypothetical purchases. Throughout the purchase opportunities, there was a varying probability of a promotional offer. Search measures, information processing measures and logit-choice model results suggest that variety-seekers are less non-compensatory in their brand choice process than loyal consumers but that they are more non-compensatory in the presence of promotions. Finally, the results of a second experiment suggest that consumers react to promotional offer information and feature improvement information very differently; promotions are more likely to be treated as a signal.

The third paper also investigates the effect of brand loyalty on how consumers process information, this time, in the context of an FSI. Leclerc and Little proposed a conceptual framework based on current models of persuasion suggesting that for categories generating relatively high involvement, the more loyal consumers are to a brand (promoted brand or competitive brand), the less motivated they are in processing brand information. As a result, loyal consumers are less likely to be persuaded by an information-oriented ad than by an ad featuring an attractive picture. Alternatively, consumers that are not loyal to any brand are more likely to be persuaded by an information-oriented ad than an attractive picture. For categories that generate low involvement, an ad featuring an attractive picture is more likely to be effective than an information-oriented ad in persuading both loyal and non-loyal consumers. The predictions for the high involvement product categories were tested and supported in an experimental study. As additional support for the framework, a cross-sectional analysis of scanner data from 250 coupon events revealed that the amount of information in an ad had a significant effect on incremental sales for high involvement products but not for low involvement products.

Finally, Leigh McAlister who has made very important contributions to the field of promotion, closed the session by sharing her

[1]Author's notes: The author would like to thank the session participants for their contribution to this summary paper.

insights on the presented papers. In trying to integrate the three papers, McAlister proposed that in thinking about how consumers react to promotions, we may want to categorize industries on the basis of two of the factors proposed by Raghubir and Corfman, the extent to which there is variation in quality in the industry and the frequency of promotions in the industry. The results presented in this session as well as previous research seem to suggest that for industries with frequent promotions (as shown in Davis, Inman and McAlister 1992), promotions may have no impact on brand evaluation while for industries that promoted infrequently, then promotions would have a negative impact on brand evaluation and this effect would be maximized if there was quality variation in the industry. McAlister also suggested that one interesting avenue to pursue would be to investigate whether loyal consumers and switchers differ in their information search, promotional sensitivity and the extent to which brand evaluation is affected by promotions for these four types of industries.

Insight to this question can be gained by looking at the results of the last two papers. They suggest that in the context of a shopping environment where there is no promotion, consumers with low levels of loyalty search more than highly loyal customers. However, the opposite is observed when a promotion is offered on one brand. Alternatively, in the context of an FSI booklet, where to some extent every brand is promoted, consumers with low level of loyalty seem to process the information more thoroughly than highly loyal consumers just as they did in the shopping environment without promotion. One can speculate that expectation of a promotion, a factor suggested in the first paper as being a moderator of the effect of promotion on brand evaluation, may be at play here to some extent.

Overall, the session has extended the framework typically used in thinking about the effect of promotion on brand choice and brand evaluation in bringing in additional factors such as frequency of promotion and variation of quality in the industry as well as types of consumers as defined by level of loyalty.

REFERENCE

Davis, Scott, Inman J. Jeffrey and Leigh McAlister (1992), "Promotion Has a Negative Effect on Brand Evaluations—Or Does It? Additional Disconfirming Evidence". Journal of Marketing Research 23 (1), 143-149.

When Do Price Promotions Signal Quality? The Effect of Dealing on Perceived Service Quality

Priya Raghubir, Hong Kong University of Science and Technology
Kim P. Corfman, New York University

In this paper it is hypothesized and demonstrated that offering a price promotion on a service can unfavorably affect brand evaluations. This is particularly true when price promotions are uncommon in the industry and consumers perceive that the quality of firms in the industry varies. Further, it is demonstrated that the effect of promotions on brand evaluations is mediated by the attribution made for the promotion. Results from a laboratory experiment are reported.

It is universally acknowledged that sales promotions account for a large and increasing percentage of the marketing budget, and that they increase brand sales (e.g., Chevalier 1975, Neslin and Shoemaker 1989). It is less universally acknowledged that offering a price promotion can lead to unfavorable brand evaluations. On one hand, advertising gurus warn about the dangers of using sales promotions at the expense of advertising as part of a complete marketing strategy (Ogilvy 1963). On the other hand, marketing academics have searched, almost in vain, for a negative effect of sales promotions on brand evaluations (e.g., Davis, Inman and McAlister 1992).

In this paper we revisit the issue of whether offering a promotion affects brand evaluations and look at the conditions under which it might do so. We explore whether the effect of a promotion is moderated by industry factors—specifically, perceptions of how common it is to deal in a particular industry and the perceived range of quality among firms in the industry. We also examine whether the effect of promotions on brand evaluations is mediated by whether the promotion is attributed to brand-related vs. non-brand-related reasons.

LITERATURE

The literature on the effect of promotions on brand evaluations is surprisingly sparse and equivocal. The vast majority of prior literature that has assessed the effects of sales promotions on brand evaluations has studied the effect after product trial (Scott and Yalch 1980, Scott and Tybout 1979, Tybout and Scott 1983). Scott and her colleagues examined the effect of promotions on evaluations after subjects had tried the promoted brand. They found that promotions can positively or negatively affect brand evaluations, depending on a) whether subjects had examined the brand previously (Scott and Yalch 1980), b) when they thought about their behavior (Scott and Tybout 1979), and c) whether they had previous knowledge about the brand (Tybout and Scott 1983).

In the one study that examined the effect of exposure to promotions on pre-purchase brand evaluations, rather than the effect of promotions after product trial, Davis, Inman and McAlister (1992) found no evidence that sales promotions affect brand evaluations. Davis et al. (1992) initially measured brand evaluations for selected brands in eight categories of frequently purchased products. Three brands in each of four product categories (canned pasta, pain relievers, toothpaste, and toothbrushes) were promoted in rotation for three months. None of the brands in the other four product categories (microwaveable popcorn, saline solution, cereal, and mouthwash) was promoted during this period and served as a control. After three months, one brand each from the promoted and control product categories was evaluated by another group of subjects who had observed the brands over the experimental period.

Mean evaluations of promoted brands in the post-promotional period were not found to be lower than those in the pre-promotional period. Davis et al. (1992) conclude that their results provide "... evidence that promotion does not have a negative effect on brand evaluations" (p. 147).

One possible explanation for Davis et al.'s finding is that it was due to the kinds of products they studied. They looked at the effect of promotions on frequently purchased products. In the next section, we hypothesize that the effects of promotions on brand evaluations will depend on a) how common promoting is in the industry and b) the variability of brand quality in the industry. Frequently purchased packaged goods are, as a group, commonly promoted and do not have a high variation in quality among brands in each industry, which may explain why promotions in such categories do not lead to unfavorable brand evaluations. This paper examines variations in the perceived commonness of promotions and perceived variability of quality as they affect a promotion's influence on brand evaluations.

HYPOTHESES

It is theorized that the process of pre-trial attitude formation in response to a promotion is mediated by causal attributions (i.e., consumers assigning a cause) for the promotion. Attributions may be to the brand offering the promotion or to factors external to the brand, such as competition. The principles of attribution theory help predict the conditions under which the brand is implicated as the cause for a promotion. The attribution of a cause to "internal" (here, brand-specific factors) has been theorized to be a function of whether behavior conforms to what others do, traditionally termed the *distinctiveness* of the behavior (Einhorn and Hogarth 1986, Kelly 1967, 1972, Hilton and Slugoski 1986). In the promotions context, distinctiveness is determined by beliefs about the amount of promoting in the product category. The less common promoting is perceived to be in an industry, the more distinctive a promotion, and therefore, the greater the likelihood that a promotion offered by a specific brand in the industry will be ascribed to brand-related causes. Accordingly, we hypothesize that the locus of causality of a promotion is a function of the perceived amount of dealing within an industry:

H1: Causes of promotions are attributed to brand-related (vs. non-brand-related) factors more often when dealing is perceived to be uncommon in an industry than when it is perceived to be common.

An important question is whether a promotion is a positive or negative signal, across consumers, industries, brands, and types of promotions. There is far from unanimous agreement regarding the valence of a promotion. However, studies have either found negative or null effects of promotions on brand evaluations, rather than positive effects. The basis for theorizing that price promotions are negatively valenced derives from the price-quality literature. (For a review see Rao and Monroe 1989.) The monetary cost of a promoted brand is lower than it would be if the promotion had not been offered, because promotions reduce price or increase quantity for a given price. The price-quality literature has found that, on average, a lower price is a signal of inferior quality (Olson 1977,

Monroe and Petroshius 1981, Rao and Monroe 1989). Since price promotions reduce price and lower prices are associated with lower quality, there is reason to believe that price promotions also lead to inferences of lower quality. Lichtenstein, Burton and O'Hara (1989) found that brand-specific attributions for a promotion were negatively valenced, whereas reasons unrelated to the brand were positively or neutrally valenced.

Because dealing is a negative signal, when a brand is distinctive for promoting in an industry in which promoting is uncommon, the brand-related attributions (hypothesized in H1 as resulting from distinctiveness) are negative and result in brand evaluations more negative than if promoting were common and *non*-brand-related attributions had been made instead. Thus, causal attributions—whether the cause of the promotion is attributed to brand-related factors or non-brand-related factors—mediate the effect that the promotion has on brand evaluations.

H2a: Brands that promote less often than other brands in their industry are evaluated more favorably than the brands that promote more often than others.

H2b: The attributions for a promotion mediate the effect of promoting on brand evaluations.

There are situations in which the effect of promotions on brand evaluations is likely to be small or insignificant. If there is little perceived variation in quality among brands in an industry (e.g., airlines and many consumer packaged goods), consumers will have little need to use promotions as signals of quality. As discussed earlier, this may explain the null findings for effects of promotions in research that has studied frequently purchased consumer products, among which there may not be large perceived differences in quality.

H3: The lower the perceived variation in quality among firms in an industry, the smaller the effect of promoting on brand evaluations will be.

METHOD

Nine service industries were chosen to represent a wide range of service types. The industries chosen ranged from long distance calling to hair salons (see Table 1) and were expected to differ in terms of perceived commonness of dealing. For each industry, subjects read about a price promotion and answered the questions described below. The order in which the nine industries were presented was randomized for each subject.

Locus of Causality: Subjects were asked to rate what they thought was the single most important reason the promotion was being offered, on a 5-point scale anchored at 1 = "Due to competition," and 5 = "Due to the company."

Brand Evaluation: Subjects responded to two questions asking "If a _____ company offers a deal MORE (LESS) OFTEN than other companies, the quality of the service is ..." The responses were provided on a 5-point scale, anchored by 1 = "Definitely better," and 5 = "Definitely Worse."

Subjects also rated how personally interested they were in each industry and how important the quality of the service was to them on 5-point scales. All but one industry was rated above the midpoint on both interest and importance of quality. The exception was hair stylists whose mean interest rating is 2.82.

After they provided the above ratings by industry, subjects were asked to estimate the overall percentage of companies in each industry that offer promotions and the percentage that are of good quality.

Subjects were 29 undergraduates at a large northeastern university, who completed the task during one of their regularly scheduled classes.

Results

Hypothesis 1. It was expected that promotions were more likely to be ascribed to external (vs. internal/brand-related) reasons, the more common subjects believed promoting was in the relevant industry. At the industry level this is the pattern observed. (See Table 1.) In all industries in which the mean locus of causality is less than 3, i.e., the promotion is rated as more likely to be due to competition than brand-specific factors (7 out of 9 cases), the overall estimated probability of dealing is greater than 40%. In the two industries in which the overall estimate of dealing is under 40% (dental services and music shows), the mean locus of causality of the promotion is greater than 3 (3.50 and 3.66, respectively).

To check whether there is a statistically significant relationship between estimated probability of dealing and locus of causality, we combined observations across industries and subjects and regressed the locus of causality (dependent variable) on the estimated dealing percent (independent variable). The results of this univariate regression are significant ($R^2=0.12$, p<.001). The sign of the beta coefficient is negative, as hypothesized in H1, implying that the greater the estimated probability of dealing in the industry, the greater the attribution of the promotion to competitive factors.

Hypothesis 2a. H2a predicts that promoting more than others in an industry leads to less favorable evaluations. A MANOVA using ratings of the brand if it promoted more than (vs. less than) others in the industry was conducted for each of the service industries. We expected differences in ratings such that a brand would be rated worse if it promoted more often and better if it promoted less often than others in its industry. As can be seen from Table 1, the mean quality ratings of brands that promoted more often than others in their industry are consistently worse (lower numbers represent higher quality) and the differences are at least marginally significant in seven of the nine industries. Further, the absolute numbers indicate that the mean quality ratings for brands that promoted "more often" than others in their industries are above the mid-point (3) of the scale in all but one industry (health clubs). This means that on average subjects rated a brand as worse than others in its industry if it promoted more often than the other brands in the industry and rated it as better than the others if it promoted less often. This supports H2a.

Hypothesis 2b. H2b predicts that attributions mediate the effect of promoting on brand evaluations. To test this hypothesis, we treat each industry rating made by a subject as a separate observation and look only at the brand when it promoted more often than others in the industry. We ran a regression in which the dependent variable was the evaluation of the brand. The first independent variable is the promotion's locus of causality. The other is the estimated percent of firms in the industry that promote. Since we look only at brands that promote more than the others in the industry, this captures the distinctiveness of the promotion—the higher the percent of firms promoting, the lower the distinctiveness. Because attributions were hypothesized to mediate the effect of promoting on evaluations, we expected that the coefficient of the attribution variable (locus of causality) would be significant and the coefficient of the estimated percent of firms which deal would be lower than in a regression in which it was the only independent variable. This is the pattern of results. The regression is significant ($R^2=.12$, p<.001) and the effect of locus of causality is positive and significant ($\beta=.24$, p<.002), implying that when promotions were attributed to the competition, brand evaluations were more favorable. The coefficient for the estimated percent of firms that deal, is

TABLE 1
Mean Ratings of Causality and Valence of Promoting

Service industry	Locus of causality [1]	Promote more often [2]	Promote less often [2]	% Deal in Industry [3]
Credit cards	2.03 (1.21)	3.31 (0.81)	2.89 * (0.74)	77.07 (23.1)
Restaurants	2.93 (1.12)	3.50 (0.79)	2.21 ** (0.88)	50.20 (25.9)
Hair stylists	2.46 (1.29)	3.54 (0.74)	2.29 ** (0.85)	44.52 (23.6)
Dental services	3.50 (1.26)	3.71 (0.85)	2.64 ** (0.95)	25.33 (20.8)
Savings accounts	2.25 (1.32)	3.14 (0.71)	2.96 (0.64)	56.90 (30.0)
Music shows	3.66 (0.97)	3.48 (0.69)	2.76 ** (0.95)	38.74 (28.3)
Airline travel	1.86 (1.25)	3.48 (0.69)	2.76 ** (0.74)	82.29 19.1)
Health clubs	2.38 (1.24)	2.93 (0.59)	2.86 (0.58)	77.95 (15.4)
Long distance calls	1.96 (1.04)	3.39 (0.69)	2.79 ** (0.69)	88.75 (9.47)

[1] Numbers under 3 represent an external attribution, and those over 3 represent an internal attribution. Standard deviations are given in parentheses.

[2] Lower numbers represent better quality. * = $F_{(1,28)}$ significant at $p < .10$, ** = $F_{(1,28)}$ significant at $p < .01$. Standard deviations are given in parentheses.

[3] Numbers represent probability estimates and can range from 0 to 100. Standard deviations are given in parentheses.

negative and significant ($\beta=-.20$, $p<.01$), indicating that the more distinctive the promotion, the more negative the evaluation. However, the estimate is lower than in the regression that had percent of firms that deal as the only independent variable ($\beta=-.286$, difference=.08, $z=1.76$, $p<.05$). As hypothesized, it appears that the attributions for the promotion mediate the effect of the promotion on brand evaluations.

Hypothesis 3. H3 predicts that the lower the perceived variation in quality among firms in an industry, the smaller the effect of promoting on brand evaluations will be. Among the industries we examine there are none in which subjects felt quality is uniformly low. Thus, in our test of H3, the only kind of lack of variation in quality we examine is when quality is uniformly high. Our operational hypothesis is: brands that promote more often than other brands in their industry are evaluated better the larger the percentage of brands in the industry that are perceived as being of high quality. In other words, if quality in an industry is uniformly high, a brand that promotes more than others in the industry should be rated better than it would be were quality in the industry more variable. To test H3, we ran a univariate regression using only ratings of brands that promoted more often than others in their industries. The dependent variable is the brand evaluation and the independent variable is the estimated percentage of brands in the industry that are of good quality. The regression is significant ($R^2=.03$, $p<.05$) and the parameter estimate is negative (lower numbers represent better quality). Consistent with H3, this indicates that the more good quality brands there are perceived to be in the industry, the better the brand that promotes more than others is rated.

CONCLUSIONS

In this study we examined the effects of promotions on brand-related attribution and on brand evaluations in nine service industries. We found evidence that *a)* the higher the perceived amount of dealing in an industry, the more likely it is that attributions for the promotion will be to the brand, and *b)* a brand that promotes more often than others in its industry is perceived to be of poorer quality than others in the industry, while a brand that promotes less often is perceived to be of better quality. This was true across a variety of industries. Further, the effect of promotions on brand evaluations is mediated by attributions made for the promotion. We also found that the effect of promoting on brand evaluations is diminished when a high percentage of brands in the industry are viewed as being of high quality. This may explain the results of prior studies in which promotions were not found to have an effect on brand evaluations.

One of the limitations of this study is that whether the experimental brands promoted more or less often than other brands was more obvious than it normally would be to consumers. Therefore, we cannot rule out a demand effect explanation for the result that promotions have a negative effect on brand evaluations. However, it is less plausible that subjects guessed the other hypotheses. Future research manipulating the information value of a promotional signal under various situations would give us a better understanding of when and how price promotions affect brand evaluations, and contribute further to the reconciliation of conventional wisdom with the results of academic research.

REFERENCES

Blattberg, Robert C., and Scott A. Neslin (1990), *Sales Promotion: Concepts, Methods, and Strategies*, Englewood Cliffs, NJ: Prentice Hall.

Chevalier, Michel (1975), "Increase in Sales Due to In-Store Display," *Journal of Marketing Research*, 12 (November), 426-31.

Davis, Scott, J., Jeffrey Inman and Leigh McAlister (1992), "Promotion Has a Negative Effect on Brand Evaluations—Or Does It? Additional Disconfirming Evidence," *Journal of Marketing Research*, 29 (February), 143-8.

Dodson, Joe A., Alice M. Tybout and Brian Sternthal (1978), "Impact of Deals and Deal Retraction on Brand Switching," *Journal of Marketing Research*, 15 (February), 72-81.

Einhorn, Hillel J. and Robin M. Hogarth (1986), "Judging Probable Cause," *Psychological Bulletin*, 99 (1), 3-19.

Fiske, Susan T. (1980), "Attention and Weight in Person Perception: The Impact of Negative and Extreme Behavior", *Journal of Personality and Social Psychology*, 38, 889-906.

Gidron, David, Derek J. Koehler, and Amos Tversky (1993), "Implicit Quantification of Personality Traits," *Personality and Social Psychology Bulletin*, 19 (October), 594-604.

Hamilton, D.L. and M.P. Zanna (1972), "Differential Weighing of Favorable and Unfavorable Attributes in Impressions of Personality," *Journal of Experimental Research in Personality*, 6, 204-212.

Hilton, Denis J. and Ben R. Slugoski (1986), "Knowledge Based Causal Attribution: The Abnormal Conditions Focus Model," *Psychological Review*, 93 (1), 75-88.

Kelly, Harold H. (1967), "Attribution Theory in Social Psychology," in *Nebraska Symposium on Motivation*, Vol 15, ed. D. Levine, Lincoln, NE: University of Nebraska Press.

Kelly, Harold H. (1972), "Attribution in Social Interaction," in *Attribution: Perceiving the Causes of Behavior*, eds. E.E. Jones, D.E. Kanouse, H.H. Kelly, R.E. Nisbett, S. Valins, and B. Weiner, Morristown, NJ: General Learning Press.

Lichtenstein, Donald R., Scot Burton, and Bradley S. O'Hara (1989), "Marketplace Attributions and Consumer Evaluations of Discount Claims," *Psychology and Marketing*, 6, 163-180.

Monroe, Kent B., and Susan M. Petroshius (1981), "Buyer's Perception of Price: An Update of the Evidence," in *Perspectives in Consumer Behavior*, eds. Harold H. Kassarjian and Thomas S. Robertson, Glenview, IL: Scott, Foresman and Company, 43-55.

Neslin, Scott A. and Robert W. Shoemaker (1989), "An Alternative Explanation for Lower Repeat Rates After Promotional Purchases," *Journal of Marketing Research*, 26 (May), 205-13.

Ogilvy, David (1963), *Confessions of an Advertising Man*, New York: Atheneum.

Olson, Jerry C. (1977), "Price as an Informational Cue: Effects on Product Evaluations," in *Consumer and Industrial Buying Behavior*, eds. Arch G. Woodside, Jagdish N. Sheth, and Peter D. Bennett, New York: North Holland, 267-286.

Rao, Akshay R. and Kent B. Monroe (1989), "The Effect of Price, Brand Name, and Store Name on Buyer's Perceptions of Product Quality: An Integrative Review," *Journal of Consumer Research*, 26, 351-7.

Scott, Carol A. and Alice M. Tybout (1979), "Extending the Self-perception Explanation: The Effect of Cue Salience on Behavior," in *Advances in Consumer Research*, Vol. 6, ed. William L. Wilkie, Ann Arbor, MI: Association for Consumer Research, 50-54.

Scott, Carol A., and Richard F. Yalch (1980), "Consumer Response to Initial Product Trial: A Bayesian Analysis," *Journal of Consumer Research*, 7 (June), 32-41.

Taylor, Shelley (1991), "Asymmetrical Effects of Positive and Negative Events: The Mobilization-Minimization Hypothesis," *Psychological Bulletin*, 10 (July), 67-85.

Tybout, Alice M. and Carol A. Scott (1983), "Availability of Well-Defined Internal Knowledge and the Attitude Formation Process: Information Aggregation Versus Self-Perception," *Journal of Personality and Social Psychology*, 44 (3), 474-479.

Reference Effects in Dynamic Marketing Mix Environments: Insights from Decision-Making Research

Deborah J. Mitchell, Temple University
Sankar Sen, Temple University

As human beings, our judgments are based in subjectivity. Perception being only a bet on reality, seemingly inconsequential aspects of the environment have the power, at times, to drive cognition and affect in ways not expected, and perhaps not desired, by the individuals involved. Thus, whether or not we are happy and satisfied with ourselves (or others) depends on the current standard or reference point to which those lives are compared (Festinger 1954; Strack, Schwarz, and Gschneidinger 1985); mood and self-esteem can swing dramatically with a change in reference point. Research on wishful thinking has shown that when making judgments of likelihood, whether or not probabilities and outcomes are treated as independent varies with the valence and size of the outcome considered (Slovic 1974). Finally, whether or not we engage in certain behaviors, from voting to condom use, can vary depending on whether we frame events as potential losses or potential gains (Thaler 1993).

The pervasiveness of such effects has been demonstrated in the domain of consumer choice, as well. For example, product attribute descriptions, framed in a normatively equivalent manner, can change product preferences. Levin and Gaeth (1987) showed that consumers' preference for beef is greater when it is described as 75% lean than as 25% fat. In addition, how brands or alternatives are grouped and considered can set up different contexts which in turn will influence choice. For example, the composition of a consideration set can influence decision outcomes via attraction and compromise effects (Huber, Payne, and Puto 1982; Simonson and Tversky 1992). Relatedly, the order in which alternatives are considered can set implicit reference brands for the evaluation of subsequent alternatives, ultimately changing decision outcomes (Hauser 1986; Kahn, Moore, and Glazer 1992).

Given the vast number of demonstrations of context (or more specifically, reference) effects within psychology and consumer behavior, it is clear that context influences decision-making. In addition, it is clear that at times variations in context can lead to outcomes which appear to be non-normative. However, several important questions remain. First, what psychological processes underly these dramatic shifts? In addition, do such effects hold in dynamic, as well as static, environments?

Second, the great majority of research on context and reference effects has been done in strictly-controlled laboratory environments, using static decision tasks with alternatives described in a limited manner on very few attributes. Do findings based on such an approach generalize easily to more naturalistic settings?

Third, most research on reference dependence within marketing has looked at price as the key contextual cue. However, are evaluations of non-price attributes reference dependent as well? More generally, relatively little work has addressed the implications of such phenomena for managers. How should managers apply research findings on reference dependence? Clearly there are implications for the pricing strategist. But if these phenomena are as powerful and pervasive as the data suggest, there will be product strategy implications as well. Of course, providing managers with prescriptions for marketing mix applications may not be helpful if they themselves fall prey to context effects and biases in their strategic mix decisions.

This special topic seminar addressed these key theoretical and application questions related to demonstrations of reference effects in decision-making. Specifically, it brought together researchers from varied empirical and methodological backgrounds, working on primary, different but related, dimensions of reference dependence and marketing mix appplications. Collectively these studies (1) demonstrated new phenomena within the domain of context effects, and (2) linked basic research that has already been done with the theoretical contributions and marketing mix applications inherent in these papers.

In terms of session structure, the first three papers presented new findings from consumer decision-making research. The first paper, by Morwitz and Sen, was concerned with how consumers interpret changes in product strategy, and how these perceptions influence product preferences. Integrating work on intertemporal decision-making and reference dependence, the first experiment demonstrated loss aversion on several non-price attributes over time. In the second experiment, the processes underlying this effect were investigated further.

Next, O'Curry and Sheu examined the basic question of how internal reference prices are formed, particularly within product categories where there is heavy price promotion. The Strahilevitz paper examined how our experiences and expectations regarding different modes of acquiring consumer goods affects our preferences for them. The final portion of the session addressed one of our primary objectives, i.e., to examine how, or to what extent, managers can use these findings in making strategic marketing mix decisions. The Mitchell and Bhoovaraghava paper provided a demonstration of a heretofore unexamined context effect ('point of view'), using managers' product strategy decisions as input. In addition, a second study investigated the cognitive processes underlying this effect.

Special Session Summary
The Cumulative Effects of Advertising Repetition on Product Beliefs and Attitudes Under Low Involvement

Scott A. Hawkins, University of Toronto

The average North American consumer is increasingly bombarded with marketing information from a multitude of sources (Britt, Adams, and Miller 1972). Although some of this information is relevant to the consumer's immediate needs and receives careful scrutiny and consideration, the majority of marketing communications convey little or no relevant information and receive minimal levels of attention and evaluation (Bauer & Greyser 1968; Belch 1981). Nonetheless, repetition can have a variety of cumulative effects on consumer beliefs (Pechmann & Stewart 1989; Sawyer & Ward 1979) even under low-involvement conditions (Krugman 1965).

Advertisers have long been interested in the complex and subtle effects of repeated exposure to advertising. In order to properly allocate their advertising spending advertisers must determine how repetition affects consumers' product judgments. This session brought together three distinct streams of research that have identified significant effects of repetition on consumer judgments.

The first paper by Kirmani examined some of the implications for consumers' quality judgments suggested by economic signaling theory (Nelson 1974; Kirmani & Wright 1989; Kirmani, 1990). This framework suggests that increased advertising spending should lead consumers to infer that the advertised product is higher quality: Increased advertising spending reflects the manufacturer's belief that the product is high quality. Furthermore, the study examined the moderating role of two variables that might be important signals of manufacturers' advertising spending: level of repetition and the use of color in the ads. Results suggested that higher levels of repetition and the use of color v. black & white ads contributed to higher ratings of product quality. The impact of these variables on quality judgments appears to be mediated by subjects' judgments of the manufacturers' level of commitment to the brands. Finally, the author explored the implications of the results for various theoretical perspectives.

The second paper by Hawkins, Meyers-Levy, and Hoch extended the recent finding that repetition of messages increases individuals' beliefs in those messages (Hawkins & Hoch 1992). One of the concerns of any advertiser hoping to use repetition to change consumer beliefs is that consumers will become bored and even skeptical of messages at higher repetition levels. This study examined a commonly adopted solution to this wearout phenomenon: variations-on-a-theme advertising. Subjects saw and rated between one and four product feature claims that all suggested a common benefit. Each of the feature claims was repeated between one and four times. Results indicated that exact repetition of a single feature claim increases belief in that claim, but increasing the number of related claims does not increase belief in the feature claims. However, subjects are more likely to believe the general benefit claim (the benefit implied by the feature claims) as the number of related claims increases. Further analyses indicated that the impact of repetition on beliefs is mediated by the familiarity of claims. Finally, the implications of these results for theories of repetition-induced beliefs and for advertising strategy were discussed.

The third paper, by Haugtvedt and Schumann, explored some of the implications of a common advertising strategy: exposing consumers to varied executions (e.g. related product arguments) of

an advertising message (Schumann, Petty, & Clemons 1990; Haughtvedt, Schumann, Schneier, & Warren, 1994). Their study examined the effects of the argument strength and the order of presentation on persuasion. Results suggested that the argument strength had greater impact on attitudes when the order of the ads was varied than when the arguments were repeated in the same order. The authors suggest that this interaction reflects increased involvement and elaboration that is induced by varying the order of arguments. By using message characteristics (such as argument order), marketers can influence the degree of elaboration, which highlights the difference in the persuasiveness of the arguments.

The discussion by Sawyer emphasized the evolution in the study of effects of repetitive advertising. Research on repetitive advertising has shifted from a focus on whether repetition influences consumer responses to advertising (e.g., improving attitudes toward a brand) to understanding how the repetition might change attitudes (i.e., identifying important mediating factors). Although the three papers in this session adopt very different perspectives, they complement each other in suggesting important intervening variables in the impact of repetition on persuasion.

REFERENCES
Bauer, Raymond A. and Stephen A. Greyser (1968), *Advertising in America: The Consumer View*, Boston: Harvard University, Graduate School of Business Administration.

Belch, George E. (1981), "An Examination of Comparative and Noncomparative Television Commercials: The Effects of Claim Variation and Repetition on Cognitive Response and Message Acceptance," *Journal of Marketing Research*, 18 (August), 333-349.

Bornstein, Robert F. (1989), "Exposure and Affect: Overview and Meta-Analysis of Research, 1968-1987" *Psychological Bulletin*, 106, 265-288.

Britt, Stuart H., Stephen C. Adams, and Allan S. Miller (1972), "How Many Advertising Exposures Per Day?" *Journal of Advertising Research*, 12 (1), 3-9.

Haughtvedt, Curtis P., David W. Schumann, Wendy L. Schneier, Wendy L. Warren (1994), "Advertising Repetition and Variation Strategies: Implications for Understanding Attitude Strength" *Journal of Consumer Research*, 21 (June), 176-189.

Hawkins, Scott A. and Stephen J. Hoch (1992), "Low-Involvement Learning: Memory without Evaluation," *Journal of Consumer Research*, 19 (September), 212-225.

Kirmani, Amna and Peter Wright (1989), "Money Talks: Perceived Advertising Expense and Expected Product Quality," *Journal of Consumer Research*, 16, 344-353.

Kirmani, Amna (1990), "The Effect of Perceived Advertising Costs on Brand Perceptions," *Journal of Consumer Research*, 17 (September), 160-171.

Krugman, Herbert E. (1965), "The Impact of Television Advertising: Learning without Involvement," *Public Opinion Quarterly*, 29 (Fall), 349-356.

Pechmann, Cornelia and David W. Stewart (1989), "Advertising Repetition: A Critical Review of Wearin and Wearout," *Current Issues and Research in Advertising*, 11, 285-330.

Nelson, Philip (1974), "Advertising as Information," *Journal of Political Economy*, 82, 729-754.

Sawyer, Alan G. & Scott Ward (1979), "Carry-Over Effects in Advertising Communication," *Research in Marketing*, 2, 259-314.

Schumann, David W., Richard E. Petty, and Scott D. Clemons (1990), "Predicting the Effectiveness of Different Strategies of Advertising Variation: A Test of the Repetition-Variation Hypothesis," *Journal of Consumer Research*, 16, 192-202.

Using the Comparative Judgment Task in Consumer Research: An Illustrative Study

Madhubalan Viswanathan, University of Illinois
Terry Childers, University of Minnesota

ABSTRACT

Understanding how consumers represent product information in memory has been of interest to researchers in consumer behavior. Several techniques such as MDS and direct scaling have been used to map the representation of a product in consumer memory. This paper suggests the use of the comparative judgment task researched in cognitive psychology to study magnitude representations in consumer memory. Although comparative judgments have been studied in psychology, similar research on product dimensions has not been conducted in consumer research. Details of an experiment conducted to demonstrate the use of comparative judgments in marketing are reported followed by a discussion of extensions to consumer research.

Understanding how consumers represent product information in memory has been of interest to researchers in consumer behavior (cf., Johnson and Fornell 1987). Several techniques such as MDS and direct scaling have been used to map the representation of a product in consumer memory. Such techniques are very useful in marketing research as a means of understanding consumer perceptions of products. Researchers have pointed to the importance of understanding the storage of magnitudes[1] along attributes in the area of consumer decision making (Park 1978; Monroe 1973; Alba and Hutchinson 1987). This paper suggests the use of the comparative judgment task researched in cognitive psychology to study magnitude representations in consumer memory. Consumers often compare brands on attributes using product information that is available to them. Such comparisons of brands on specific attributes may be performed by consumers during judgment or choice (cf., Biehal and Chakravarti, 1982) or as a way of learning about various brands in the market place. Although comparative judgments appear to be of importance to consumer research and have been studied in psychology (cf., Banks, 1977), similar research on product dimensions has not been in consumer research with a few exceptions (cf., Viswanathan and Childers, 1992; Viswanathan and Narayanan, 1994). This paper aims to demonstrate the use of comparative judgments in consumer research. As mentioned earlier, a stream of research in cognitive psychology has focused on the process of making comparative judgments. Research on comparative judgments in cognitive psychology is reviewed. Details of an experiment conducted to demonstrate the use of comparative judgments in consumer research are reported followed by a discussion of extensions of this methodology to consumer research.

REVIEW OF RESEARCH ON COMPARATIVE JUDGMENTS

Comparative Judgments in Psychology

Comparative judgment tasks researched in cognitive psychology require subjects to compare stimuli along a dimension and make a judgment about the magnitudes of stimuli along that dimension. As an example, subjects may be required to identify the larger of two stimuli (such as an elephant and a mouse) on the basis of size or identify the larger of two digits. Psychologists have studied comparative judgments across a range of dimensions such as magnitudes of digits, sizes of objects, and pleasantness of stimuli (Banks, 1977; Parkman, 1971; Moyer and Landauer, 1967; Holyoak and Walker, 1976). Research on comparative judgments has led to several empirical effects including the symbolic distance effect and the semantic congruity effect (Banks, 1977; Holyoak, 1978; Jaffe-Katz et al.,1989; Moyer and Landauer, 1967). The symbolic distance effect demonstrates that decisions are made faster and/or more accurately when a pair of stimuli on some dimension are farther apart than when they are closer together. In a comparison task involving digits, the symbolic distance effect is manifest in the finding that a comparison between '1' and '100' is made faster (and/or more accurately) than a comparison between '1' and '3'. Therefore, the symbolic distance effect is the finding that the larger the distance between two stimuli on some dimension, the faster (or more accurate) the comparison between the two stimuli. This finding is interesting in that the speed or accuracy of comparative judgments may provide insight into the nature of representations of magnitudes in memory. The distance effect suggests that some notion of distance between stimuli characterizes the representation of magnitudes in memory that are used to make comparative judgments. The symbolic distance effect appears to be a very robust effect across different attributes.

Other effects include the semantic congruity effect which is the finding that if the instruction is congruent with the size of the digits, then the response to such decisions is faster. As an example, if a task requires a choice of the 'larger' item on a dimension such as size, decisions are faster for a pair of large stimuli than for a pair of small stimuli. In a task requiring subjects to identify the larger of a pair of digits, the semantic congruity effect is the finding that the comparative judgment is faster for a comparison between a relatively large pair of numbers such as '99' and '101 than it is for a relatively small pair of digits such as '1' and '3'. It should be noted that this effect occurs even though the differences between the pairs of stimuli in question are equal (i.e., 101 - 99=3 - 1=2). This effect appears to be very robust and has been obtained for different types of experiments (Banks et al., 1976).

Comparative judgments have also been used to study the effect of reference points. Holyoak (1978) studied reference points by using a task where subjects were required to identify one of two digits that were closer to a third digit (which served as an explicit reference point). The main finding was that the response time of comparisons increased with the distance between the two points and the reference point (with higher response time being an indicator of more difficulty in performing a comparison). Holyoak and Mah (1982) studied comparative judgments based on the distances between cities. They found that judgments were made faster when the stimuli were in the vicinity of a reference point than farther away from it. They suggest that people may be able to make finer discriminations in the vicinity of a reference point.

Comparative Judgments in Consumer Research

Research on comparative judgments has focused on the *process* of making comparative judgments. The comparative judgment task can be applied to a consumer setting where consumers compare brands along attributes and identify the larger or smaller of two brands on an attribute. In contrast to the focus in psychology on the

---

[1]The term, magnitude, is used here to refer to the location of a brand along an attribute or the attribute value.

Advances in Consumer Research
Volume 22, © 1995

comparative judgment task per se, the focus in consumer research can be broader by using comparative judgments to understand product representations in memory. An experiment was conducted in a consumer setting to illustrate the use of the comparative judgment task. The experiment is used as a basis for further discussion of extensions of this methodology to consumer research.

Adapted to a consumer decision making context, a comparative judgment task involves comparing a pair of brand names on a specified attribute in order to choose the larger or smaller of the two brands using magnitudes from memory. Using a setting where subjects are exposed to information on several brands along several attributes with the goal of making a choice or learning information, two hypotheses were developed about comparative judgments for illustrative purposes. These hypotheses related to the effect of processing goals, a factor that has been argued to be of importance in consumer research. Because a choice task requires consumers to differentiate between brands and choose a brand from among several alternatives, consumers may be more likely to compare brands along attributes during a choice task when compared to a learning task (cf., Biehal and Chakravarti, 1982). Therefore, they may be able to make faster comparative judgments following a choice processing goal when compared to a learning goal.

H1:   Faster comparisons will be made following a choice task when compared to a learning task.

The robust distance effect in psychology when translated to a consumer setting would predict that comparisons of pairs of brands on an attribute that are farther apart in magnitude (i.e., have greater distance between them on an attribute like gas mileage, such as a pair of brands with gas mileages of 32 mpg. and 20 mpg.) will be faster and/or more accurate than comparisons of pairs of brands that are closer in magnitude (i.e., have lesser distance between them, such as a pair of brands with gas mileages of 32 mpg. and 29 mpg.). Because choice processing is more likely to lead consumers to use magnitude information about brands and judge distances between brands along attributes, the distance effect is more likely to be found in comparative judgments following choice. However, because a learning task, unlike a choice task, does not require consumers to differentiate between brands in terms of distances between brands along attributes, the distance effect may be less likely to be found following learning when compared to choice.

H2:   The symbolic distance effect is more likely to be found following a choice task when compared to a learning task.

EXPERIMENT USING COMPARATIVE JUDGMENTS

Overview

In the experiment, subjects were exposed to brand information in the form of numerical or verbal labels with instructions to either make a choice or learn information. This initial task was followed by a distracter task involving pictorial information in order to remove the effects of short term memory and allow subsequent tests of long term memory without using verbal or numerical information. The initial choice or learning task was followed by a distracter task and then a comparative judgment task.

Stimulus Materials

Calculators were chosen as the product category because students, who were the participants in this study, are familiar with this product and are likely to own it (Biehal and Chakravarti 1983). Information was presented on four attributes chosen based on past research; number of functions, display width, battery life, and warranty length (Childers et al. 1991). Fictitious brand names were used to avoid differences in the level of prior knowledge about specific brands among subjects. Pilot tests were performed to assess various issues such as adherence to task instructions, knowledge about the product category, comparable levels of credibility of both numerical and verbal information, and processing of all pieces of information. Sixteen pieces of information (4 brands x 4 attributes) were used based on pilot tests. The magnitudes assigned to each brand along each attribute were chosen to cover the range of possible values. The actual numerical and verbal labels used were determined on the basis of a pretest.

A typical consumer setting using comparative judgments can involve presentation of brand information to subjects wherein factors to be studied are manipulated. The comparative judgment task can be used to assess pair-wise comparisons of brands along an attribute. By varying the magnitudes of brands along an attribute, it is possible to vary ordinal and interval distances between pairs. Therefore, manipulation of distances can be achieved for the various attributes. By arranging brands along an attribute continuum, ordinal or interval distances between brands can be varied. For example, using four brands (B1 to B4) on a five point continuum such that their values are 1, 2, 3, and 5, respectively, the ordinal distance between B1 and B4 is 3 while the interval distance is 4. The number of different levels of ordinal and interval distances are 3 and 4, respectively. In a subsequent comparative judgment task, the effects of various factors, such as the the the metric of the representations, can be evaluated.

The manipulation of attribute magnitudes in numerical and verbal forms was determined on the basis of a pretest using a cross-modal magnitude scaling procedure (cf., Lodge, 1981). Because the aim here was to manipulate the distances between labels, a pretest was required to understand how respondents perceive magnitudes conveyed by labels describing product attributes. A range of magnitude labels (i.e., 13 verbal and 13 numerical labels) for each of several attributes of calculators were estimated by subjects by using numbers (or drawing lines) such that the size of numbers (or the length of lines) indicated their subjective impressions of the magnitudes conveyed by these labels. The range of numerical labels, and the verbal anchors to be used for each attribute (such as "lengthy" for warranty length) were chosen on the basis of previous work (Childers et al., 1991). Thirteen verbal labels were chosen for each attribute by attaching a range of descriptors (such as "extremely") from previous research (Wildt and Mazis, 1978) to anchors specific to each attribute (such as "lengthy" for warranty length). Based on this analysis, five verbal labels were chosen for each attribute. Numerical labels equivalent to each of the five verbal labels were identified by interpolating the magnitudes assigned to the 13 numerical labels for each attribute. The set of five verbal labels and five equivalent numerical labels for each attribute represented a five point scale that covered the attribute continuum.

On the basis of the pretest and pilot tests, the set of brand-attribute information to be used in the experiment was determined. The brand names along with the chosen values along attributes warranty length, battery life, number of arithmetic functions, and display width, respectively, were as follows: (i) 'Baron' - Extremely brief, 40 hours, 120 functions, and Wide, (ii) 'Colony' - 18 months, 220 hours, Extremely low, and Extremely wide, (iii) 'Profile' - 36 months, 380 hours, Low, and Extremely narrow, and (iv) 'Angle' - 72 months, 3 hours, Neither low nor high, and Narrow.

Procedures

The experiment was conducted using Macintosh computers. Forty undergraduate students at a midwestern university participated in the experiment with twenty subjects assigned to each task. Subjects performed an exercise on the use of a Macintosh computer, were familiarized with attributes to be used, read instructions for each task, and were familiarized with brand names on which information would be presented. A brand-attribute matrix was used in this experiment where subjects could view information in any desired sequence. Brand names were presented along the horizontal axes and attribute names were presented along the vertical axes. Subjects were required to click a "mouse" on a particular cell to see a specific piece of information. At this point, they were exposed to a screen containing the brand name, attribute name, and value. They could return to the matrix by clicking on a portion of the screen. Subjects could exit the procedure only after seeing all 16 pieces of information to ensure exposure to all pieces of information. The initial choice or learning task was followed by a pictorial distracter task and then the comparative judgment task.

The comparative judgment involved presenting pairs of brands and requiring subjects to identify the larger (or smaller) brand on a specified attribute. Pairs of brand names can be presented on the left and right portions of screens of presentation. Some issues relating to the experimental procedures based on past research include (i) balancing the number of correct responses which require identifying the brand on the 'left' or the 'right' so that the apriori probability of correctly identifying a brand by guessing is 50%, (ii) balancing the judgment task in terms of identifying the 'larger' versus the 'smaller' brand either across attributes (i.e., using instructions to identify the 'higher' brand on some attributes and the 'lower' brand on other attributes) or within attributes (i.e., requiring subjects to identify the 'higher' brand for a set of trials and to identify the 'lower' brand for the same set of trials, preferably with a counterbalancing of the order of the two sub-tasks across attributes), and (iii) providing instructions separately for each attribute to familiarize subjects with idiosyncratic labels used for each attribute (for example, 'wider' versus 'narrower' for an attribute such as display width of a calculator).

Six pair-wise comparisons are possible between four brands along each attribute leading to a total of 24 trials for four attributes in the comparative judgment task. A pair of brand names were presented to subjects and they had to make comparative judgments from memory. Subjects were instructed to choose the larger of two brands for two attributes and the smaller of two brands for the other two attributes. The verbal labels used to instruct subjects were not "larger" and "smaller" but idiosyncratic to the attributes in question (i.e., "lengthier" for warranty length and so on). A pair of brand names were placed on the left and right side of the screen, respectively, and subjects clicked the mouse on the left or the right portion of the screen to indicate the larger/smaller of the pair. An attribute-based sequence of trials was used with 3 second masks between trials. Such a sequence allowed comparisons along one attribute at a time, and instructions specific to an attribute preceded the set of trials for that attribute in order to familiarize subjects with the labels used to describe it.

Data Analyses

Several dependent variables can provide valuable insights into magnitude representations in memory. The *accuracy* of comparative judgments provides an indication of the extent to which an attribute continuum is correctly represented in memory. *Speeds* of comparative judgments provide a means of assessing the accessibility of comparative or relational information. Following the logic

of the symbolic distance effect, inferences about the nature of magnitude representations in memory in terms of metric properties can be made based on trend analyses or regressions. Linear trend analyses (or regressions) can be performed on accuracy and response times as a function of ordinal (or interval) distances between brands. Significant linear trends may suggest that subjects store ordinal (or interval) level distances in memory. Significant linear trends using interval distances may suggest interval level properties which subsume ordinal level properties. However, if significant linear trends are obtained only for ordinal distances, this would be indicative of ordinal level properties at best. The data would also allow for an examination of more complex trends as a function of distances between pairs of brands.

The accuracy of responses and mean response times of correct responses were computed for each subject for each interval distance as well as each ordinal distance. Two (processing goal) by 4 (interval distance) factorial ANOVAs were performed on the mean response times and on mean accuracies. For the ANOVA on response times, the difference in response time across goal conditions was marginally significant ($F(1,38)=2.85$; $p<.10$) with faster responses for the choice condition (6.5 secs.) when compared to the learning condition (7.7 secs.), providing support for H1. For the ANOVA on accuracies, the difference in accuracies across goal conditions was nonsignificant ($F(1,38)=1.65$, $p>.05$) with only directionally higher accuracy for the learning condition.

The occurrence of a distance effect (i.e., higher accuracy and lower response time of comparisons with increasing distance) was assessed by examining mean accuracy and response time as a function of ordinal distance as well as interval distance and performing linear trend analyses. Using a 2 (processing goal) by 3 (ordinal distance) factorial ANOVA for response time, the main effect of distance was significant ($F(2, 76)=3.83$; $p<.05$) while the interaction between processing goal and distance was marginally significant ($F(2, 76)=2.93$; $p<.06$). Using a 2 (processing goal) by 3 (ordinal distance) factorial ANOVA for accuracy, the main effect of distance was significant ($F(2, 76)=5.43$; $p<.05$) as was the interaction between processing goal and distance ($F(2, 76)=3.75$; $p<.05$). Based on significant or marginally significant interactions, the mean accuracy and response times for each distance were examined and suggested linear, monotonic trends following choice, with decreasing response times and increasing accuracies with increasing distances (Figure 1, panels a and b). However, such monotonic trends were not found following learning (Figure 1, panels a and b). Linear trend analyses were performed in an attempt to quantify the results. The analyses produced significant linear trends for choice for accuracy ($F(1, 38)=14.28$; $p<.001$) and response time ($F(1, 38)=5.21$; $p<.05$). However, non-significant linear trends were obtained for learning for accuracy and response time. These results provide support for H2.

Analyses based on interval distances led to significant main effects of distance and significant interactions between processing goal and distance. Trend analyses based on interval distance were identical in terms of monotonic trends and significant linear trends following choice and non-monotonic trends and non-significant linear trends following learning with one exception (Figure 1, panels c and d). For response time, the interaction between task and mode was non-significant and the linear trend for learning was significant. Overall, the pattern of results appears to provide support for H2.

Both hypotheses were supported by the findings. These results provide interesting insights into how consumers represented magnitudes along attributes following learning versus choice tasks. First of all, the speed of comparative judgments provides insight

FIGURE 1
Results for Comparative Judgments

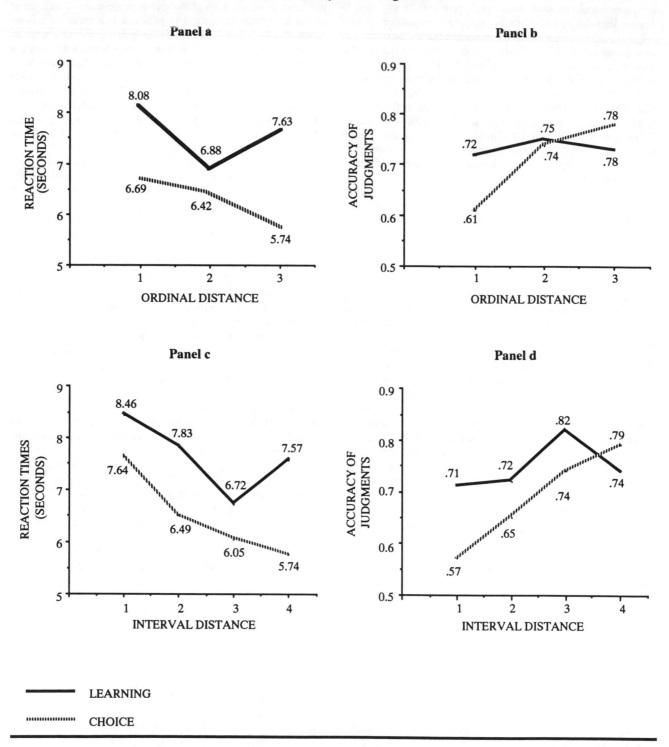

into the degree to which relational information on brands across attributes is accessible, with findings suggesting greater accessibility following choice. Such a result was expected because the choice task is likely to lead to comparisons between brands along attributes whereas the learning task requires only the memorization of individual information. Results based on accuracy point to the potential effect of processing goal on accuracy of comparisons. Although the effect was not significant, the results suggest that the choice task

actually led to higher accuracy at the largest distance (see Figure 1, panels b and d) whereas the learning task had higher accuracy at other distances. Perhaps, because large differences between brands along attributes are crucial in making a choice, consumers are likely to encode such information more accurately than small differences between brands, resulting in more accurate comparisons.

These distance effects offer insights into the nature of representation of magnitudes in memory, whether at ordinal or interval levels. The evidence for this experiment suggests that magnitude information may be stored at the interval level, particularly following choice. However, distance does not appear to play a role following learning perhaps because of the nature of the task which may lead to memorization rather than an understanding of magnitudes of brands.

POTENTIAL USES OF COMPARATIVE JUDGMENTS IN CONSUMER RESEARCH

Comparative judgment tasks may have several applications in consumer research. Alba and Hutchinson (1987) suggest that representations of dimensions may develop in two ways; through paired-associate learning and transitive learning. They also point out differences between partial and complete orderings of stimuli. Several such issues relating to magnitude representations can be tested using comparative judgments. Using dependent variables such as response time and accuracy of comparisons, comparative judgments following choice or learning tasks can be used to understand the effects of a range of factors such as processing goals, format of information presentation, and mode of information on the encoding of magnitudes on specific dimensions.

The empirical findings in psychology in terms of the symbolic distance effect, the semantic congruity effect, and reference point effects present interesting testing grounds for hypotheses in consumer research. The distance effect can be used as a means of understanding how consumers represent magnitude information in memory. The occurrence or non-occurrence of the distance effect for different types of distances (i.e, ordinal versus interval) may provide insight into the nature of representation of magnitudes in memory. The occurrence of the symbolic distance effect can be studied as a function of several factors. In this way, the nature of storage of magnitudes can be assessed. Similarly, the effect of task demands (such as asking subjects to identify the higher versus the lower on some attribute) and the effect of reference points could be studied. For example, comparative judgments of prices of brands can be used to research reference price information and its usage by consumers. Variants of the comparative judgment task can be used to assess several issues of importance in consumer research. Instead of comparing brands along a single attribute, comparisons across attributes for a particular brand can also be assessed. Comparative judgments within brands versus comparative judgments within attributes can provide a test of the strength of within attribute versus within brand linkages in consumer memory.

The comparative judgment task could also be used to assess comparisons between pairs of brands available in the market place. In addition to providing data on pairwise comparisons, the advantage in using response times is that perceptions of distances between brands can be inferred indirectly. Findings on the occurrence of the distance effect at the ordinal or interval levels can then be used to design appropriate response scales and data analyses. For example, in the experiment conducted here, it appeared that respondents were storing distances between brands at the interval level, particularly following the choice task. Knowledge of the ordinal versus interval nature of storage of brand information is crucial to the use of techniques such as MDS which assume certain metric properties. Further, data on comparative judgments can be used to represent brands along unidimensional (or multi-dimensional) space. Pairwise comparisons at the attribute level can be treated similar to pairwise comparisons of brands used as input to non-metric scaling. Comparative judgments across attributes can also be used to indirectly assess perceptions of covariation between attributes.

Whereas similarity judgments have been used in marketing at a brand level to assess "distances" between products, comparative judgments may be used to assess "distances" at the attribute level. The comparative judgment technique has advantages in allowing for the use of multiple dependent variables. This task appears to be face-valid because consumers often compare brands along single attributes and allows for the use of a sensitive dependent variable like response time. The comparative judgment task provides a means of indirectly inferring magnitude representations through accuracy and response time rather than requiring direct scaling by respondents (as in direct scaling). It also focuses on the attribute level and does not require inferences about dimensions (as in many applications of MDS). In conclusion, the comparative judgment task may be a useful methodology for understanding product representations in consumer memory.

REFERENCES

Alba, Joseph W. and J. Wesley Hutchinson (1987), "Dimensions of Consumer Expertise," *Journal of Consumer Research*, 13 (4), 411-454.

Banks, William P. (1977), "Encoding and Processing of Symbolic Information in Comparative Judgments," in *The Psychology of Learning and Motivation*, ed. G.H. Bower, New York: Academic Press, Vol. 11, 101-159.

Banks, W.P., M. Fujii, and F. Kayra-Stuart (1976), "Semantic Congruity Effects in Comparative Judgments, of Magnitude of Digits," *Journal of Experimental Psychology: Human Perception and Performance*, 2, 435-447.

Biehal, Gabriel and Dipankar Chakravarti (1982), "Information Presentation Format and Task Goals as Determinants of Consumers Memory Retrieval and Choice Processes," *Journal of Consumer Research*, 8, 431-41.

Biehal, Gabriel and Dipankar Chakravarti (1983), "Information Accessibility as a Moderator of Consumer Choice," *Journal of Consumer Research*, 10 (June), 1-14.

Childers, Terry L., Esra Gencturk, Akshay Rao, and Jan Shimanski, (1991) "An Empirical Examination of Consumer Memory: Evidence on Brand Organization and Verbal Versus Numerical Representation, Working Paper, University of Minnesota.

Holyoak, Keith (1978), "Comparative Judgments with Numerical Reference Points," *Cognitive Psychology*, 10, 203-243.

Holyoak, Keith J. and Wesley A. Mah (1982), "Cognitive Reference Points in Judgments of Symbolic Magnitude," *Cognitive Psychology*, Vol. 14, 328-352.

Holyoak, K.J., and Walker, J.H. (1976), "Subjective magnitude information in semantic orderings," *Journal of Verbal Learning & Verbal Behavior*, 15, 287-299.

Jaffe-Katz, A., Budescu, D. and Wallsten, T.S. (1989), "Timed magnitude comparisons of numerical and nonnumerical expressions of uncertainty," *Memory and Cognition,* 17 (3), 249-264.

Johnson, Michael D. and Claes Fornell (1987), "The Nature and Methodological Implications of the Cognitive Representation of Products," *Journal of Consumer Research*, 14 (September), 214-228.

Lodge, Milton (1981), *Magnitude Scaling: Quantitative Measurement of Opinions*, Beverly Hills, CA: Sage.

Monroe, Kent (1973), "Buyers' Subjective Perceptions of Price," *Journal of Marketing Research*, 10, 70-80.

Moyer, R.S., and Landauer, T.K. (1967), "Time required for judgments of numerical inequality," *Nature*, 215, 1519-1520.

Park, C. Whan (1978), "A Conflict Resolution Choice Model," *Journal of Consumer Research*, 5 (September), 124-137.

Park, C. Whan and V. Parker Lessig (1981), "Familiarity and its Impact on Consumer Decision Biases and Heuristics," *Journal of Consumer Research*, 8 (September), 223-230.

Parkman, J.M. (1971), "Temporal aspects of digit and letter inequality judgments", *Journal of Experimental Psychology*, 91, 191-205.

Wildt, Albert R. and Michael B. Mazis (1978), "Determinants of Scale Response: Label Versus Position," *Journal of Marketing Research*, Vol. 15 (May), 261-267.

70 / *Using the Comparative Judgment Task in Consumer Research: An Illustrative Study*

Park, C. Whan and V. Parker Lessig (1981), "Familiarity and its Impact on Consumer Decision Biases and Heuristics," *Journal of Consumer Research*, 8 (September), 223-230.

Parkman, J.M. (1971), "Temporal aspects of digit and letter inequality judgments", *Journal of Experimental Psychology*, 91, 191-205.

Wildt, Albert R. and Michael B. Mazis (1978), "Determinants of Scale Response: Label Versus Position," *Journal of Marketing Research*, Vol. 15 (May), 261-267.

Ranking: Is It Really Sequential Choice?

John A. Schibrowsky, University of Nevada
James W. Peltier, University of Wisconsin-Whitewater

ABSTRACT

Preferences generated by rank order tasks are typically assumed to be equal to those generated by choice tasks. This exploratory study reports the findings of an empirical investigation of this assumption. The results indicate that ranking and choice tasks result in differences in resulting preferences. In addition, two manipulations, requiring a justification and altering the information format, were investigated to determine their impact on resulting preferences. Requiring a justification of resulting preferences had a differential impact on ranking and choice tasks.

INTRODUCTION

Preference data is one of the primary tools employed in the development of marketing strategies. It is commonly assumed that each alternative has an underlying utility or expected value and that the consumer prefers the alternative with the highest value. This value maximization assumption (VM) is the cornerstone of the economic theory of the consumer, and is used extensively by theoretical and practical marketing researchers (Simonson and Tversky 1992). One principal ramification of the VM assumption is that preferences between alternatives are independent of the preference elicitation task employed. Tversky, Sattath, and Slovic (1988) refer to this proposition as procedural invariance: Normatively equivalent procedures should yield the same preferences.

One area of investigation of procedural invariance is the realm of response modes. To date, researchers investigating procedural invariance with regard to response modes have focused on the distinction between various rating and choice tasks (see Payne, Bettman, and Johnson 1992). The research suggests that rating and choice tasks result in differences in preferences (e.g., Einhorn and Hogarth 1981; Hansen 1976; Hogarth 1980; Huber et al. 1993; Slovic and Lichtenstein 1983; Tversky, Sattath, and Slovic 1988).

The relationship between preferences generated by ranking and choice tasks has received little attention. Ranking is typically assumed to be a method of eliciting sequential choices. The alternative that is ranked first is assumed to be the alternative that would be the first choice. The alternative ranked second is assumed to be the alternative that would be selected if the first choice is not available, etc. While the distinction between ranking and choice tasks to elicit preferences appears to be a simple substitution of sequential choices (ranking) for individual choices, research in the area of rating and choice tasks suggests that this assumption may be incorrect.

The research question addressed by this study was, "Do ranking and choice tasks result in similar preferences?" The experiment reported here had two purposes. First, it was designed to investigate the impact of ranking and choice tasks on resulting preferences. Second, it was designed to identify factors that affect ranking and choice tasks differently.

RANKING AND CHOICE

Individuals are often asked to rank order their preferences. For example, members of a marketing department are asked to rank prospective faculty candidates. A market researcher asks individuals to rank order their preferences for brands of laundry detergent. In each case, ranking is assumed to yield the same resulting preferences as those generated by an individual choice task. While recent findings (Ben-Akiva, Morikawa, and Shiroishi 1992) sug-

gest that this assumption may not be accurate for lower ranks (e.g. third or fourth), the assumption that the first ranked alternative would also be chosen as the most preferred alternative has not been explicitly tested.

In consumer research, ranking tasks are often used to determine preferences, especially when decompositional models of preferences are employed (e.g. Green and Srinivasan 1978). In a ranking task, an individual must determine his/her order of preference. From a measurement perspective this requires an ordinal information response.

While little is written about the underlying mental processes associated with ranking tasks, Desoto (1961) found that individuals have a preference for single orderings. This suggests that ranking processes are likely to be top to bottom or bottom to top oriented based on one key attribute. As such, the highest priced, highest quality alternative or the lowest price, lowest quality alternative is likely to be the first ranked alternative.

Choice tasks require a selection from a set of alternatives. This response mode is often employed in marketing research studies, based on the argument that choice is the actual task performed by the consumer when preferences are used to make a purchase (Bither and Wright 1977). This "realism" is not without a cost. When this preference elicitation task is employed, less information is gathered per respondent. From a measurement perspective, this task requires only a nominal information response.

Choice tasks are associated with a wide array of choice heuristics, designed to simplify the process by employing cutoff strategies and other noncompensatory processes (Gensch and Ghose 1992; Johnson and Russo 1981, 1984; Klein and Bither 1987; Olshavsky and Granbois 1979; Tversky 1972). Recently, tradeoff contrast and extremeness aversion have been identified as choice strategies (Simonson and Tversky 1992).

A better understanding of the relationship between preferences generated by ranking and choice tasks is important for two reasons. First, both, ranking and choice data, are often used by marketing researchers to obtain preference data (Huber et. al. 1993). This is based on the procedural invariance assumption. Second, ranking seems to be a very natural task (Desoto 1961). As such, it is likely to be common consumer activity, and needs to be investigated.

FACTORS AFFECTING RANKINGS AND CHOICES

In 1981, Hogarth and Einhorn noted that "the conditions under which judgments and choices are similar as well as different need to be better understood if a descriptive theory of judgment and choice is to be developed." One of the purposes of this study was to operationalize this challenge in a consumer setting. Two factors that merited investigation were information formats and justification.

Information presentation formats and justification were selected to be investigated in this study based on three criteria. First, a review of the literature suggested that these conditions might affect rankings and choices differently. Second, they did not change the utilities of the alternatives or the consideration set in any way. Third, they were conditions that might be manipulated by marketing researchers gathering preference data.

Information Format Effects.

Bettman and Kakkar (1977), Bettman and Park (1980), Johnson, Payne, and Bettman (1988), and Jarvenpaa (1991) showed that preference formation was sensitive to the way information was presented. Kahneman and Tversky (1979) hypothesized that judgment tasks are affected by the order in which the alternatives are evaluated. They referred to this phenomenon as "anchoring and adjusting." Lynch, Chakravarti, and Mitra (1991) investigated this phenomena in a consumer setting. It seems plausible that anchoring and adjusting might affect ranking tasks in the same way as rating tasks.

Also, choices have been shown to be affected by the frame associated with the consideration set (e.g., Simonson, 1989; Ratneshwar, Shocker, and Stewart, 1987). Simonson (1989) and Simonson and Tversky (1992) extended these findings to explain the way individuals evaluate the advantages and disadvantages of the available alternatives. They provide evidence that decision makers tend to avoid extreme alternatives. This is referred to as "extremeness aversion" (Simonson and Tversky 1992).

In summary, the research suggests that changing the order of the alternatives and making the middle alternative easier to identify might have a differential impact on rankings and choices. Specifically, in the centered/ordered condition (see Appendix A) subjects assigned to the choice task should be less likely to prefer the end alternatives (extremeness aversion), while subjects assigned to the ranking task should be more likely to prefer the end alternatives (top-down or bottom-up processing).

Justification.

Hagafors and Brehmer (1983) provided evidence that justification of one's judgments leads to a more analytic evaluative process, while the lack of justification leads to a more intuitive evaluation process. "One conception (of choice) asserts that much of the deliberation prior to choice consists of finding a concise inherent set of reasons that justify the selection of one option over others," (Slovic, Fischhoff, and Lichtenstein 1982). Tversky (1972) and Slovic (1975) used an "ease of justification" reasoning to explain the use of particular choice rules. This finding was also supported by Simonson (1989), who concluded that justification results in the use of easy to explain choice rules. He reported that attraction and compromise effects tend to be stronger among subjects who knew they would be asked to justify their selections.

These studies reflect the importance of considering justification in ranking and choice. It is logical to suggest that requiring a justification will affect rankings and choices in different ways.

HYPOTHESES

The literature review lead to the following testable hypotheses:

H1: The preferences obtained from ranking and choice tasks will be significantly different.

H2: The preferences obtained from centered/ordered and not centered/ordered product by brand matrices will be significantly different.

H3: The preferences obtained from subjects that were asked to justify their responses will be significantly different from the preferences obtained from subjects that were not asked to justify their responses.

In addition to these main effect hypotheses, the following interaction effects were proposed:

H4: The preferences obtained from the ranking and choice tasks will be affected differently by the centering/ordering manipulation.

H5: The preferences obtained from the ranking and choice tasks will be affected differently by the justification manipulation.

METHOD

Design and Subjects

The experiment employed a 2 tasks (ranking and choice) x 2 information structures (centered/ordered and not centered/ordered) x 2 levels of justification (required or not) factorial, between subjects design. A total of 370 subjects were recruited from those students enrolled in the various upper division business classes at a midwestern university.

Procedure

Eight questionnaires were prepared for the study, one for each experimental condition. All booklets contained the same warm-up exercise followed by one of two product matrices comparing five fictitious fast food restaurants on five attributes (no dominated alternatives)(see appendix A for the two different matrices), one of two tasks (ranking or choice), and a justification required or not. This was followed by a page of questions asking for information pertaining to manipulation checks and product usage.

Subjects were assembled in a classroom, randomly assigned to one of eight treatments, and given general directions concerning the procedure they were to follow. Subjects were told that they were taking part in a marketing research project sponsored by a fast food company contemplating moving into the local market. They were given as much time as needed to complete the questionnaire. Following the data collection task, subjects were debriefed and thanked for their participation.

Independent Variables

The subjects were asked to either rank order or choose among the alternatives. The particular ranking task employed in this study was as follows:

Rank order the restaurants shown above in terms of your preference in having the various restaurants close to your residence (1=most preferred through 5=least preferred).

The choice task used in this study was as follows:

From the alternatives shown above, choose the one restaurant you would most prefer to have close to your residence.

The information structure manipulation was accomplished by arranging information about the five fictitious fast food restaurants in two different ways. In the centered/ordered condition, the information was presented by ordering the restaurants from highest price to lowest price, and noting the middle value on each attribute. In the not centered/ordered condition, the information was presented in a random order with no indication of the middle alternative. Appendix A contains the two different product matrices.

The justification manipulation was accomplished with a question asking a portion of the respondents to explain the reasoning behind their rankings or choices. The subjects assigned to the justification condition, knew they would need to justify their responses before they made their ranking or choice.

TABLE 1

Data and Model Fit for H1

	N	P	Q	J	L	
RANK	61 (35)*	72(41)	37(21)	4(2)	2(1)	176
CHOICE	47(26)	75(41)	40(22)	10(5)	12(6)	184

MODEL	CHI-SQUARE CHANGE	DEGREES OF FREEDOM CHANGE	STATISTICALLY SIGNIFICANT
PREF=CONSTANT			
PREF=CONSTANT+TASK	11.38	4	P<.05

* PERCENTAGES IN PARENTHESES

TABLE 2

Data and Model Fit for H2

	N	P	Q	J	L	
CENTERED	62(31)*	81(41)	38(19)	9(5)	7(4)	197
NOT CENTERED	46(28)	66(40)	39(24)	5(3)	7(4)	163

MODEL	CHI-SQUARE CHANGE	DEGREES OF FREEDOM CHANGE	STATISTICALLY SIGNIFICANT
PREF=CONSTANT			
PREF=CONSTANT+CENTER	1.74	4	NO

* PERCENTAGES IN PARENTHESES

Dependent Variable

The dependent variables in this study were the resulting preferences generated by the different tasks. As such, this study employed a behavioral decision making or structural perspective rather than an information processing perspective (Johnson and Puto 1987).

The results were reported in percentages or probabilities of each of the alternatives being ranked or chosen as most preferred. Using this approach, the dependent variable was conceptualized as a series of log odds ratios of the probability of a subject choosing or ranking each of the alternatives as most preferred.

RESULTS

Since the dependent variable was multinomial and interactions were predicted, the data were analyzed using a multinomial logistic modeling method. Critical to the investigation was the measure of goodness-of-fit. A chi-square fit statistic was used to compare the various models' ability to account for the data. As a model's ability to account for the data increases, chi square also increases. In order to directly compare the "fit" of models, a nested model method was used. Basically, a model provided a better "fit" when the improvement in chi-square (given the change in degrees of freedom) was large enough to be significant at the p<.05 level.

Main Effects

These hypotheses predicted main effects associated with the task, information format, and justification manipulations. To test each of these hypotheses, a constants only model was compared to a model containing the hypothesized main effect.

Task Effects. H1 predicted that ranking and choice tasks would result in significantly different preferences. The results of the test of H1 are presented in Table 1.

They indicated that the inclusion of the task variable significantly improves the fit of the model (chi-square increased by 11.38 while the degrees of freedom were reduced by 4). This indicated that the preferences obtained from the ranking task were significantly different from those obtained from the choice task. Specifically, subjects assigned to the ranking task were more likely to prefer the high priced alternative (N), while subjects assigned to the choice task were more likely to prefer the lower priced alternatives (J&L). This finding supports H1.

Information Format Effects. H2 predicted that the centered/ordered and not centered/unordered presentation formats would result in significantly different preferences. The results of the test of H2 are presented in Table 2.

The inclusion of the centered/ordered variable did not significantly improve the fit of the model. This indicated that the differences in preferences obtained across the two conditions were not statistically significant. This finding does not support H2.

Justification Effects. H3 predicted that the justification manipulation would significantly affect preferences. The test of H3 is presented in table 3.

The addition of the justification variable did not significantly improve the fit of the model. This finding indicated that the preferences obtained across the two conditions were essentially the same.

TABLE 3
Data and Model Fit for H3

	N	P	Q	J	L	
JUSTIFIED	54(28)*	88(45)	43(22)	7(4)	4(2)	196
NOT JUSTIFIED	54(33)	59(36)	34(21)	7(4)	10(6)	164

MODEL	CHI-SQUARE CHANGE	DEGREES OF FREEDOM CHANGE	STATISTICALLY SIGNIFICANT
PREF=CONSTANT			
PREF=CONSTANT+JUSTIFY	5.75	4	NO

* PERCENTAGES IN PARENTHESES

TABLE 4
Data and Model Fit for H4

RANKING

	N	P	Q	J	L	
CENTERED	36 (38)*	40 (43)	16 (17)	2 (2)	0 (0)	94
NOT CENTERED	25 (30)	32 (39)	21 (26)	2 (2)	2 (2)	82

CHOICE

	N	P	Q	J	L	
CENTERED	26 (25)*	41 (40)	22 (21)	7 (7)	7 (7)	103
NOT CENTERED	21 (26)	34 (42)	18 (22)	3 (4)	5 (6)	81

MODEL	CHI SQUARE CHANGE	DEG OF FREEDOM CHANGE	STAT SIG.
PREF=C			
PREF=C+TASK	11.38	4	P<.05
PREF=C+TASK+CENTER	1.76	4	NO
PREF=C+TASK+CENTER+TASK*CENTER	4.92	4	NO

* PERCENTAGES IN PARENTHESES

Interaction Effects

Hypotheses, H4 and H5, predicted interaction effects between the centering/ordering manipulation and task and between the justification manipulation and task. A nested model method was employed to test these hypotheses.

Task by Centering/ordering Interaction. H4 predicted that the centered/ordered manipulation would affect preferences from ranking and choice tasks in different ways. To test this hypothesis, the main effects model was compared to the interaction model. The test H4 is presented in Table 4.

The inclusion of the task by centering/ordering interaction variable did not significantly improve the fit of the model. This implied that the centering/ordering manipulation did not have a differential impact on ranking and choice. These findings do not support hypothesis H4.

Task and Justification Interaction. H5 predicted that the justification manipulation would affect preferences from ranking and choice tasks in different ways. To test this hypothesis, the main

effects model was compared to the interaction model. The test H5 is presented in Table 5.

In the case of the justification manipulation, the inclusion of the task by justification interaction variable significantly improved the fit of the model (chi-square increased by 9.82, while degrees of freedom were reduced by 4). This indicated that the justification manipulation had a differential impact on ranking and choice. Specifically, the justification manipulation resulted in more ranking subjects (38% vs 33%), but fewer choice subjects (22% vs 44%) preferring the end alternatives. These findings support hypothesis H5.

DISCUSSION

The key finding of this study is that preferences obtained from the ranking and choice tasks were significantly different. Two points pertaining to these results need to be mentioned. First, it should be noted that the absolute magnitude of these differences was substantial. In the ranking task, 35% of the subjects preferred

TABLE 5
Data and Model Fit for H5

RANKING

	N	P	Q	J	L	
JUSTIFIED	34 (37)*	36 (39)	18 (20)	3 (3)	1 (1)	92
NOT JUSTIFIED	27 (32)	36 (43)	19 (23)	1 (1)	1 (1)	84

CHOICE

	N	P	Q	J	L	
JUSTIFIED	20 (19)	52 (50)	25 (24)	4 (4)	3 (3)	104
NOT JUSTIFIED	27 (34)	23 (29)	15 (19)	6 (8)	9 (11)	80

MODEL	CHI SQUARE CHANGE	DEG OF FREEDOM CHANGE	STAT SIG.
PREF=C			
PREF=C+TASK	11.38	4	P<.05
PREF=C+TASK+JUSTIFY	6.11	4	NO
PREF=C+TASK+JUSTIFY+TASK*JUSTIFY	9.82	4	P<.05

* PERCENTAGES IN PARENTHESES

---

alternative N; while in the choice task, 26% of the subjects preferred alternative N. Second, the result contradicts the procedural invariance assumption. With both tasks, the constraints of the situation and the utilities of the alternatives were identical. As such, VM would predict no differences in the preferences generated by the two tasks.

A review of Table 1 indicates that individuals asked to perform the ranking task were more likely to prefer alternative N (the high price) than the individuals performing the choice task (35% vs 26%). One appealing explanation is that subjects who were asked to rank the alternatives were more likely to use some type of "top to bottom" ranking rule.

The centered/ordered condition did not have a main or interaction effect on preferences. One possible explanation can be found in the manipulation check. In the centered/ordered condition 85% of the subjects were able to accurately identify the middle alternative, while in the not centered/ordered condition 66% of the subjects were able to identify the middle alternative. It is possible that the not centered/ordered condition was not complex enough to disguise the ordering of the alternatives. In addition, it should be noted that the two information structure manipulations were confounded in this study. It would have been interesting to have investigated them separately.

While the justification manipulation did not result in a main effect, the predicted interaction between task and justification was supported. For subjects assigned to the ranking condition, the justification manipulation increased the likelihood of preferring the extreme alternatives, N and L (33% vs 38%). For subjects assigned to the choice condition, the justification manipulation reduced the likelihood of selecting the extreme alternatives, N and L (45% vs 22%) and increased the likelihood of selecting the middle alternatives P, Q, and J (56% vs 78%). Perhaps the selection of these middle alternatives as most preferred in the justification condition was the result of some type of trade-off between quality and price. If so, this pattern of results supports Hagafors and Brehmer's (1983) findings that justification leads to more analytical and compensatory processing of evaluation information.

These results might also be explained by the "ease of justification" hypothesis forwarded by Tversky (1972) and Slovic (1975). For individuals assigned to the ranking task, the easiest rule to justify might have been a "top to bottom" ranking rule. For individuals assigned to the choice task, the easiest rule to justify might have been some sort of compromise or aversion to the extreme rule.

It should be noted that these "processing" explanations are conjecture, based on previous research and a qualitative review of the written justifications that subjects provided in the justification condition. However, the interesting and indisputable finding is that the justification manipulation resulted in more ranking subjects preferring the end alternatives and more choice subjects preferring the middle alternatives.

CONCLUSIONS

In summary, this study reports two critical findings for those researchers interested in ranking and choice. First, it was shown that ranking and choice tasks do not necessarily result in the same set of preferences. Second, asking individuals to justify their preferences affects ranking and choice tasks in different ways.

The results of this study have three important implications for marketing. First, this study sheds light on the distinction between rankings and choices. It enhances the work of consumer researchers that have shown that response modes impact resulting preferences.

Second, this study suggests that the mode of response used to elicit preferences and the degree to which individuals justify their preferences will impact their resulting preferences. This conclusion has implications for those researchers involved in preference research. The decision of the response mode used to reveal preferences is typically a function of the statistical methods to be employed. This study suggests that researchers need to recognize that this decision might affect the resulting preferences.

Third, this study has implications for new product development research. If consumers actually structure the evaluation of some new products as ranking tasks and others as choice tasks,

APPEDIX A
Centered/ordered and Not Centered/ordered Matrices

NOT CENTERED/ORDERED CONDITION	P	J	L	Q	N
PRICE OF A "TYPICAL MEAL" (approximately equal portions of hamburger, fries and shake)	3.05	2.25	1.85	2.65	3.30
NUTRITIONAL VALUE OF A "TYPICAL MEAL" (on a scale of 1 to 10, where 1=little or no nutritional value and 10=excellent nutritional value)	7	3	4	5	6
SERVICE (on a scale of 1 to 10 where 1=poor service and 10=excellent service)	7	5	3	6	9
MENU SELECTION — NUMBER OF ITEMS	41	33	28	31	38
OVERALL APPEARANCE OF THE RESTAURANT (on a scale of 1 to 10 where 1=poor and 10=excellent appearance)	6	5	4	7	8

****

NOT CENTERED/ORDERED CONDITION	N	P	Q	J	L
PRICE OF A "TYPICAL MEAL" (approximately equal portions of hamburger, fries and shake)	3.30	3.05	2.65 *	2.25	1.85
NUTRITIONAL VALUE OF A "TYPICAL MEAL" (on a scale of 1 to 10, where 1=little or no nutritional value and 10=excellent nutritional value)	6	7	5*	3	4
SERVICE (on a scale of 1 to 10 where 1=poor service and 10=excellent service)	9	7	6*	5	3
MENU SELECTION — NUMBER OF ITEMS	38	41	31	33*	28
OVERALL APPEARANCE OF THE RESTAURANT (on a scale of 1 to 10 where 1=poor and 10=excellent appearance)	8	6*	7	5	4

* underlined numbers indicate median or middle scores on each of the attributes considered.

predicting the success of new products might be improved if researchers take this distinction between ranking and choice into consideration in the product concept testing and product development stages of new product development.

REFERENCES

Ben-Akiva, Moshe, Takayuki Morikawa, and Fumiaki Shiroishi (1992), "Analysis of the Reliability of Preference Ranking Data," *Journal of Business Research*, 24, 149-164.

Bettman James R. and Pradeep Kakkar (1977), "Effects of Information Presentation Format on Consumer Information Acquisition Strategies," *Journal of Consumer Research*, 3, 233-240.

_____and C. Whan Park (1980), "Effects of Prior Knowledge and Experience and Phase of the Choice Process on Consumer Decision Processes: A Protocol Analysis," *Journal of Consumer Research*, 7, 234-248.

Bither, Stewart W. and Peter Wright (1977), "Preferences Between Product Consultants: Choices versus Preference Functions," *Journal of Consumer Research*, 4, 39-47.

DeSoto, Clinton B. (1961), "The Predilection for Single Orderings," *Journal of Abnormal and Social Psychology*, 62, 16-23.

Einhorn, Hillel J. and Robin M. Hogarth (1981), "Behavioral Decision Theory: Processes of Judgment and Choice," *Annual Review of Psychology*, 32, 53-88.

Gensch, Dennis H. and Sanjoy Ghose (1992), "Elimination by Dimensions," *Journal of Marketing Research*, 29, 417-429.

Green, Paul E. and V. Srinivasan (1990), "Conjoint Analysis in Marketing Research: New Developments and Directions," *Journal of Marketing*, 54, 3-19.

Grether, David M. and Charles R. Plott (1979), "Economic Theory of Choice and the Preference Reversal Phenomenon," *American Economic Review*, 69, 623-638.

Hagafors, Roger and Berndt Brehmer (1983), "Does Having to Justify One's Judgments Change the Nature of the Judgment Process? " *Organizational Behavior and Human Performance*, 31, 223-232.

Hansen, Fleming (1976), "Psychological Theories of Consumer Choice," *Journal of Consumer Research*, 3, 117-142.

Hogarth, Robin M. (1980), *Judgment and Choice*, John Wiley and Sons, New York.

Huber, Joel, Dick R. Wittink, John A. Fiedler, and Richard Miller (1993), "The Effectiveness of Alternative Preference Elicitation Procedures in Predicting Choice," *Journal of Marketing Research*, 30, 105-114.

Jarvenpaa, S.L. (1990), "Graphic displays in Decision Making-- The Visual Salience Effect," *Journal of Behavioral Decision Making*, 3, 347-62.

Johnson, Eric J., John W. Payne, and James R. Bettman (1988), "Information Displays and Preference Reversals," *Organizational Behavior and Human Decision Processes*.

Johnson, Eric J. and J. Edward Russo (1981), "Product Familiarity and Learning New Information," in *Advances in Consumer Research*, Vol.8, Kent B. Monroe (ed.) Ann Arbor Michigan: Association for Consumer Research.

_____and _____(1984), "Product Familiarity and Learning New Information," *Journal of Consumer Research*, 11, 542-550.

Johnson Michael and Christopher P. Puto (1987). "A Review of Judgment and Choice," *Review of Marketing*, Michael Houston, ed., American Marketing Association: Chicago IL, 236-292.

Kahneman, Daniel and Amos Tversky (1979), "Prospect Theory," *Econometrica*, 47, 263-292.

Klein, Noreen M. and Stewart Bither (1987), "An Investigation of Utility Directed Cutoff Selection," *Journal of Consumer Research*, 14, 240-256.

Lynch, John G., Dipankar Chakravarti, and Anuaree Mitra (1991), "Contrast Effects in consumer Judgments: Changes in Mental States or Rating Scales?" *Journal of Consumer Research*, 18, 284-297.

Olshavsky, Richard W. and Donald Granbois (1979), "Consumer Decision Making: Fact or Fiction," *Journal of Consumer Research*, 6, 93-100.

Payne, John, James R. Bettman, and Eric J. Johnson (1992), "Behavioral Decision Research: A Constructive Processing Point of View," *Annual Review of Psychology*, 43, 87-131.

Puto, Christopher P. (1987), "The Framing of Buying Decisions," *Journal of Consumer Research*, 14, 301-315.

Ratneshwar, Srinivasan, Allan D. Shocker, and David W. Stewart (1987), "Toward Understanding the Attraction Effect: The Implications of Product Stimulus Meaningfulness and Familiarity," *Journal of Consumer Research*, 16, 411-420.

Simonson, Itamar (1989), "Choice Based on Reasons: The Case of the Attraction and Compromise Effects," *Journal of Consumer Research*, 16, 158-74.

Simonson, Itamar and Amos Tversky (1992), "Choice in Context: Tradeoff Contrast and Extremeness Aversion," *Journal of Consumer Research*, 16, 158-74.

Slovic, Paul (1975), "Choice Between Equally Valued Alternatives," *Journal of Experimental Psychology: Human Perception and Performance*, 1, 280-287.

Slovic, Paul, Barruch Fischhoff and Sarah Lichtenstein (1982), "Response Mode, Framing and Information Processing Effects in Risk Assessment," in R. M. Hogarth (ed.), *New Directions for Methodology of Social and Behavioral Science: The Framing of Questions and the Consistency of Response*, San Francisco: Jossey-Bass.

Slovic, Paul and Sarah Lichtenstein (1968), "The Relative Importance of Probabilities and Payoffs in Risk Taking," *Journal of Experimental Psychology Monograph Supplement*, 78 (3), part 2.

_____and _____(1983), "Preference Reversals: A Broader Perspective," *American Economic Review*, 73 (4), 596-605.

Tversky, Amos (1972), "Elimination by Aspects: A Theory of Choice," *Psychological Review*, 79, 281-291.

Tversky, Amos (1988), "Context Effects and Argument-Based Choice," Paper presented at the Association for Consumer Research Annual conference, Maui, Hawaii.

Tversky, Amos, S. Sattath and Paul Slovic (1988), "Contingent Weighting in Judgment and Choice," *Psychology Review*, 95, 371-384.

Tversky, Amos, Paul Slovic, and Daniel Kahneman (1990), "The Causes of Preference Reversal," *American Economic Review*, 80, 204-217.

Toward the External Validity of the Information Integration Paradigm

Roger Marshall, Nanyang Technological University
Christina Kwai-Choi Lee, University of Auckland
Jennifer Yee Sum, University of Auckland

ABSTRACT

This paper reports an experiment conducted to test the external validity of the information integration paradigm. Consumers' decision processes are studied as they make quality judgements of orange juice in a naturalistic setting, with the information available controlled in a manner more typical of the market-place than in integration experiments reported thus far. An averaging model is supported.

Research in the area of impression formation has been dominated for the last two decades by the information integration approach of Norman Anderson and his associates. Information integration is a research paradigm which allows the researcher to study theoretical combination rules (model algebra) by examining actual combination rules (cognitive algebra) employed by experimental subjects as they make judgements in controlled conditions (Bettman, Capon & Lutz 1975). Based on the use of factorial ANOVA design, this theory has been extended to provide insights into an impressive array of domains of human judgement ranging from psychophysics (magnitude estimation) and decision theory to consumer attitudes (Cohen, Miniard & Dixon 1980).

The two integration models that have received the greatest amount of attention and have been most extensively tested are the adding and the averaging models (Anderson 1981). The averaging model depends on the postulation that the weight, or importance, of an attribute in the model varies according to the weights of the other attributes to be integrated. The adding model, on the other hand, assumes that the weight of each attribute is independent of the other attributes' impact. In short, adding implies a cognitive system in which "the more [items of information] the better", whereas averaging implies the contrary; where "more may not be better" (Shanteau & Ptacek 1983).

The results of the numerous studies conducted and reported in the psychology literature enable Shanteau and Ptacek to state with confidence that "...averaging is a very common psychological mechanism for consumer information processing" (1983, p.149). The relevance and importance of this statement to marketers and advertisers is significant; it is odd, then, that there is a relative paucity of reported research into consumer judgements using the integration paradigm. A comment to this effect was made by Troutman and Shanteau in 1976. Then, more than a decade after the technique was first introduced to the Journal of Consumer Research by Bettman et al. in 1975, Lynch also wrote that "in relatively few published articles in marketing and consumer research has the integration paradigm been used to study basic consumer judgement processes" (1985, p.2). There are, inter alia, two reasons for this apparent oversight.

The first is simply that there has been no perceived lacuna in the marketing and buyer behaviour literature. The additive model, and in particular that of Fishbein and Ajzen (1975) seems firmly ensconced. Moreover, a strong argument can be mooted that linear models such as Fishbein's fit the data so well that a barrier has effectively been placed in the way of further investigation into the processes of information integration (Anderson & Shanteau 1977). Markin (1980, p.320) wryly comments that consumer behaviourists are "loath to attack the gods of convention". A quick perusal of the current texts reveal that in the present context this is certainly the case; very few give more than a cursory mention of integration theory or averaging models of impression formation. (See, for example, Assael 1988; Bennett 1988; Engel, Blackwell & Miniard 1990; Howard 1989; Kotler & Armstrong 1989; Peter & Olson 1990.)

The second reason is altogether different, pertaining to specific criticisms of the technique. Many of the technical criticisms levelled have been answered more or less satisfactorily, but continue to provide material for debate. Unfortunately, the criticism of integration theory that is probably the most damning in the eyes of marketers remains unanswered - that there is little reported evidence available to show that the techniques can be applied in market-place conditions. Before this theme of external validity is further pursued, the basic integration technique under discussion is briefly revisited.

THE INTEGRATION PARADIGM

Research into attitude formation, human perception and judgement usually requires the use of some form of simple algebraic model. Anderson is no exception in this regard, and originally used algebraic methods to present his ideas (Anderson, 1965). Nevertheless, a graphical approach is conceptually easier to grasp, and so will be used here.

Anderson builds his substantive theory into the measurement technique, thus forming what he calls "functional theory" (Anderson 1974a). In practice, this involves asking respondents to provide judgements of series of stimuli on some scale, then decomposing these judgements mathematically to derive the rules used in their formation; an approach reminiscent of conjoint analysis.

To illustrate the idea, consider Figure 1A. Here, two attributes of some imaginary product have been varied over three levels to provide six combinations of information with which a subject can form a judgement of the product in question. The mean judgements of the sample group are plotted against values on the Y-axis; and the High, Average and Low values of one attribute joined. Note that the lines are parallel. That this is so is partly dependent on an underlying assumption of integration theory, that an item of judgement information retains a constant value when combined with other items of information. There is no interaction between the two lines, thus it can be stated that the judgements for each level are both consistent and independent.

Figure 1B shows the same plots, with an additional series representing the mean judgement of the group when presented only with information about the variable shown on the X-axis. The (dashed) line created by joining these new plots is obviously not parallel with the other two, and actually exhibits a crossover with one of them. As respondents have only been given one item of information, we can be sure that they have employed an additive paradigm in arriving at their judgement in this instance. The fact that the slope of the dashed line is steeper than that of the other two suggests that the integration of the extreme high and low value information has resulted in a judgement value closer to the mean; i.e. an averaging paradigm has been used when two items of information were integrated. More simply, "the addition of moderately polarized information to highly polarized information decreases the polarity of the response" (Anderson 1965a, p.397). In fact, although the cross-over effect is central to the proof of

FIGURE 1
Plotted judgements for an imaginary product

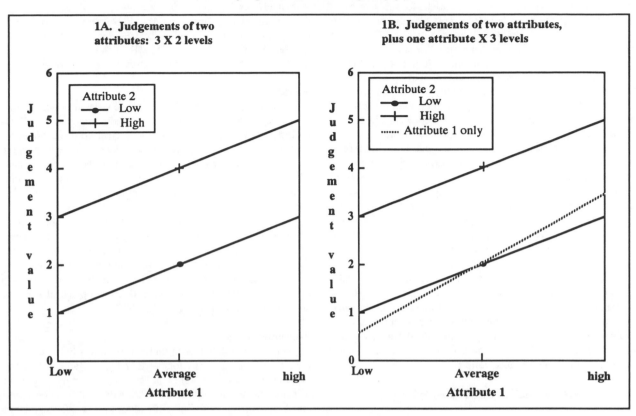

averaging, an actual crossover is not necessary; it is only necessary to show that the slope of the line is significantly steeper (Troutman & Shanteau 1976). ANOVA provides a useful and rigorous test of parallelism.

THE EXTERNAL VALIDITY OF INTEGRATION ANALYSIS

There are four major facets to the accusations of poor external validity of the integration paradigm; the artificial settings of most integration experiments to date, the almost exclusive use of pencil-and-paper tests in the reported integration literature, the problem of inference, and the use of procedural techniques that fall short of replicating marketing conditions.

With regard to the first charge above, Ebbessen and Konecni (1980) are vocal critics, claiming that the laboratory simulations that provide underpinning for the averaging model lack validity in real-world settings. Levin, Louviere, Schepanski and Norman (1983) rush to the defence of the technique, taking the line that generalizations from laboratory to market are justified in the light of the external validation provided for the results of a number of such studies. This is a little unconvincing for many consumer behaviour students and marketing practitioners, however; and even Levin goes on to sound a note of caution about expecting results acquired in the laboratory to be exactly duplicated in a naturalistic setting.

The use of paper-and-pencil tests refers to the prevalence of studies that present information to subjects as written statements rather than in the form of actual products with various (manipulated) attributes. Obviously, the former technique provides a much closer control of the information being manipulated, but raises the possibility that other variables not specifically included might yet inferentially affect the analysis.

Cohen *et al.* (1980) question the validity of the critical cross-over test of Anderson's theory along these same lines, by referring the readers to the experiment conducted by Troutman and Shanteau (1976). In this experiment, expectant parents were randomly offered a series of nine written descriptions of diapers; each description combined one of three levels of absorbency with one of three levels of durability. Quality ratings elicited from the subjects, along with ratings of products described by offering information on only one of the product attributes, suggested that an averaging model was being used in the judgement information-integration process. Cohen *et al.* suggested (page 39) that respondents' inferences about the missing attribute data accounted for the averaging. Levin et al. (1984) carried out an experiment of their own to validate Cohen *et al.*'s idea. Their research offers some support, in that "...inferences based on interstimulus relationships appear to occur only when the relationship between stimulus dimension is strongly established and when the missing information is deemed crucial to the required judgement" (p101).

In the market-place, of course, the marketer can rarely present attribute information in isolation. As well as the difficulty of using the crossover test in the face of possible inferences being made from the missing judgement dimension, there is an additional hazard. In the event that information items of minor importance are being manipulated, then the combination rules used to integrate them may be obscured from the researcher by stronger inferences drawn from the more important (non-manipulated) evaluative criteria.

The final external validity problem mentioned above relates to the procedural techniques used in a typical integration experiment.

Researchers such as Cohen *et al.* (1980) have criticized Anderson's experimental procedures contending that they create "a task context in which averaging becomes a heuristic for subjects to use" (p.165). Anderson has never failed to supply his subjects with clear instructions as to how to treat the given information. The instructions usually assure subjects that each attribute is as important as the other and that an equal amount of attention should be paid to each. "This is intended to help ensure the assumption of equal weighting, which is necessary for the parallelism prediction under the averaging model" (Anderson 1974b, p.264). Furthermore, the scales are firmly anchored and subjects are given practice runs in order to familiarize them with the use of a measurement scale.

In fact, these procedures are perfectly justifiable in the sense that integrationalists are not really concerned with the absolute utility ascribed to a particular stimulus by a particular individual respondent, but rather the way that utility is affected when the stimulus is combined with another. In practice too, failure to anchor the scale carefully may well be compensated for merely by enlarging the sample until a reasonable distribution around the judgement mean has been achieved. It is true, however, that consumers are not coached to make judgements about quality or value when selecting products in an everyday situation, neither do they necessarily assign equal weight to all of their evaluative criteria. Although it is reasonable to claim that specific targeted market segments may well have similar absolute values for a given attribute, and that consumers should need no coaching in assessing the quality of most commonly purchased items, the procedural question needs to be addressed in order to maximise validity.

THE PRESENT EXPERIMENT

Purpose

The purpose of the experiment described in this paper was to conduct an investigation of impression formation using the integration paradigm in a naturalistic setting, under conditions that would test the external validity of the model. This is to address the criticism that IIT experiments have been, for the most part, confined to unrealistic laboratory conditions. There is a trade-off between experiments undertaken in laboratory conditions and those totally based in market situations. To provide data that would allow the claim of true external validity for IIT techniques would call for consumption decisions to be made and analyzed, with money changing hands and all the usual market-place pressures, distractions and risks present. The experiments described here did not go that far, because the focus of interest was still the paradigm used to integrate information; and the maintenance of that focus demanded that a modicum of control be retained. The basic research task here was to ascertain whether or not information integration techniques are sufficiently robust that they could distinguish between adding or averaging processes even when subjects made their quality judgement of a consumer good within a more realistic market setting than has hitherto been used.

Method

The general design of this experiment is a 3 x 3, fully crossed, within-subject factorial, with 3 levels of orange juice purity (pure, watered and no information included (herein referred to as "not included")) and 3 levels of brand (Freshup, Woolworths and generic).

Sample

Judgements about perceived quality of orange juice were solicited from 25 women. More specifically, this quota sample consisted of mothers, who were house-persons of European descent, between the ages of 25 and 45 years, and had lived in Auckland (New Zealand) for at least five years. This forms a single-culture sub-set of a primary target market of the major producer and marketer of fruit juices in New Zealand, the New Zealand Apple and Pear Marketing Board (NZAPMB). (The customer profile and juice used in the experiment were provided by that organisation.)

Materials

The stimuli selected for the study consisted of six clear and three opaque, white plastic 1-litre bottles of orange juice, all with professionally-produced labels. Three clear bottles contained an orange juice of a heavy texture and density, in which orange sediment was clearly visible. Each of the three bottles carried either a Freshup, Woolworths or generic brand on their label. The other three clear bottles contained a thinner orange liquid, that had the appearance of a cordial rather than a pure juice, but bearing the same Freshup, Woolworths or generic brand label. The three opaque bottles bore identical labels but actually contained water to ensure an identical weight to the bottles filled with juice. The nine products thus created closely resembled typical supermarket products.

Respondents' perceptions of product quality were captured on a scale card created by drawing a line on a piece of card, and labelling the ends "$1.50" and "$3.50".

Procedure

Prior research had been undertaken to test brand names for their quality associations for the target group and to find their evaluative criteria for orange juice. An inspection of previous research and discussion with the NZAPMB identified price, purity and brand as the principal evaluative criteria. Once this was established, realistic purity and price levels were subjectively determined by scanning supermarket shelves. These attributes and levels were then pre-tested, until satisfactory separation of scale values was achieved, by conducting a series of 12 dummy-runs of the integration exercise with members of the public who fitted the description of the target group.

In a further pre-test survey, respondents were required to tick a box labelled "High quality", "Medium quality", or "Low quality" against each of three brands. The highest quality brand was the "Fresh-up" brand of the New Zealand Apple and Pear Marketing Board. A lower, but still positive, quality attribution was accorded to the housebrand of one of New Zealand's largest food chains, Woolworths. (Although unrelated to the Woolworth companies in the United States and Great Britain, the Australasian - and later New Zealand - Woolworths chain has developed from the same "dime-store" beginnings as the overseas counterparts.) The generic label in New Zealand carries a very low perception of quality (this has also been noted in previous published work, see Robertson and Marshall, 1987).

Thus nine "products" were created. A rich coloured juice and a watered, cordial-type juice with a Freshup, a Woolworths brand and no brand; and the three opaque bottles carrying the same three brand labels.

Interviews

Data collection took place mid-week in a busy shopping centre in an upper-middle class residential district. Full cooperation was received from the Management of the Shore City Shopping Mall in Takapuna, Auckland. The researcher introduced himself as a member of the University undertaking academic research. After potential subjects had been approached by the researcher and invited to participate, they were asked a short series of screening questions about their age, children and purchase frequency of orange juice, to ensure that they fitted the profile of the target group. No refusals were encountered.

Subjects were invited to sit on a chair in an alcove formed by potted plants at the foot of a stairway. Each interview was conducted one-on-one, although many of the women had small children with them. In these situations the child was given a small carton of orange drink to keep them occupied. The task was explained carefully, with the researcher checking frequently to ensure that the instructions were understood.

Quality ratings were eliciting from respondents in terms of the price that they believe to represent the quality of each alternative product, rather than a quality rating on some arbitrary scale. Thus the inference problem posed by the existence of evaluative criteria other than those manipulated in the experiment (brand and juice purity) is overcome by explicitly including all three evaluative criteria. Furthermore, it was thought that respondents should be able to use prices to reflect quality far easier than to record perceived quality on a 100-point scale; after all, there can be few people who do not frequently undertake this process during every-day shopping activities.

No preliminary training was given, but the end points of the scale were anchored to compensate for the somewhat small sample size. Anchors were placed by gaining agreement that the lowest quality 1-litre bottle of orange juice retailed normally for about $1.50, and the dearest, highest quality juice for about $3.50. The appropriate stimuli were inspected during this discussion. Subjects were told that they were expected to consider each bottle as it was presented, and call out a price that, in their view, reflected its quality. Instructions were given carefully, and subjects were asked to explain what they thought they had to do before the judgement task began, in order to ensure that the process was fully understood.

Quality judgements of each alternative were recorded by the researcher as they were called out by the subject. The subject held the scale card as a reminder, and their oral responses recorded by the researcher so that the respondents did not have access to the record of their earlier judgements. Respondents were allowed to hold and inspect the bottles one at a time, as they were presented in a different, predetermined, random order for each respondent. This is important, because if stimuli were presented in the same way on each occassion, then an order bias might develop which could offer an alternative explanation for the results. Respondents took readily to the judgement task, seemingly relating closely to the use of a price level to express their quality judgement. Using price in this way also avoided the need to prompt subjects to make quality rather than preference judgements. The whole judgement procedure rarely took longer than five minutes for each individual.

RESULTS

The data was analyzed using the established procedures of functional measurement. First, the data was plotted and visually scanned, then subjected to rigorous test by ANOVA. The purpose of the ANOVA test is three-fold. First, it is to rigorously confirm the existence or otherwise of parallelism between the judgement plots (a lack of interaction indicates parallelism). Second, a significant main effect does give an indication that the attributes selected were indeed relevant in the judgement process. Third, the comparative weights of the different attributes in the judgement can be calculated, to ensure that integration has actually occurred.

Anderson suggests that weights represent the salience or relevance of the judgement dimension (Anderson, 1981). In terms of IIT, analysis of two attributes both displaying equal but very small weighting would be meaningless (it doesn't matter how

people treat unimportant information). Similarly, if two attributes are combined, but one has a very low weighting and the other a very high, then the one could be overpowered to such an effect that the "integrated" judgement may show no difference to one in which only the high-weighted attribute is used (ie, no integration takes place). Assessment of the weights of information items can be made from a *post hoc* inspection of the ANOVA analysis. Because of the direct relationship between power and sample size, the F test gives no information about the strength of the effects in an ANOVA analysis (Keppel, 1973). Rao (1977) states that the relative importance of each attribute in an analysis of variance is best assessed from a comparison of the proportion of the sum of squares due to each attribute. It is the Hays formulation of omega squared (w^2) that is used as the primary indicator of weight in all the analyses that follow.

Under inspection by ANOVA, the 2 x 3 analysis of the plots for pure and watered juice over the three brands shows a significant main effect (F=39.07, p<.001, w^2=.67). In addition, the visual impression of parallelism is confirmed ($F_{(Pure \times Watered)}$=1.452, p=.237), demonstrating meaning consistency. There is evidence of unequal weighting, although not too severe to impair the results (w^2(Brand)=.18; w^2(Purity)=.49).

The main effect for the 3 x 3 analysis also shows an F value of 39.07 (p<.001, w^2=.42). Furthermore, the interaction between the watered juice and the juice in the opaque white bottles (giving no information about purity) is significant (F=5.9, p=.003). Thus the cross-over effect visible in Figure 2, suggesting averaging, is statistically significant.

DISCUSSION

The overall results obtained in the research lends clear support for averaging, and - by implication - the many studies that have found similar results for a host of decisions in the laboratory setting. This latter point is really the nub of the issue, because there is an abundance of published research work that has already led to generalizations being made about the use of averaging integration models; these generalizations have been strengthened by the present research, and hopefully made more meaningful to marketing readers. Even further, it is even possible that some review of Information Integration methods and the consequent development of an averaging judgement paradigm may be made in future marketing texts.

To really address the issue of external validy will call for further work along the same lines, but moving yet closer to the marketplace. Thus, perhaps, a situation might be contrived where consumers are observed using their own money to back their judgements of products decribed with different information on their labels. The control problems here, though, are formidable.

The practical implications of the support for averaging can be discussed at a general and specific level. Specifically, of course, the conclusion is very clear - Woolworths in New Zealand should note that using their own brand name for high quality merchandise will probably lower the quality perception of the good! In a more general sense, any marketer can fairly easily establish the evaluative criteria for his or her products or services, which can then be evaluated by a sample of the target market. In reality it is not always ethically or practically possible to manipulate the product attributes to the extent utilised in the present experiment setting; but certainly efforts should be made by marketers to change perceptions of marginally positive attributes, or to emphasize or de-emphasize relevant information accordingly.

For advertisers, the recommendation that flows from this work is to minimize advertised material to the principal benefits and not

FIGURE 2
Mean quality ratings of the sample for nine products

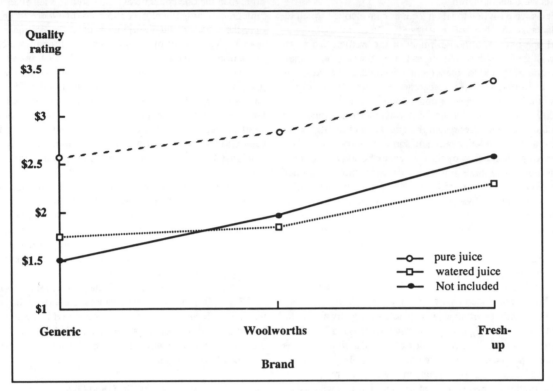

to lower overall attitudes with the inclusion of extra, less positive information about a product or service. This coincides with the old advertising maxim about effective messages containing a single, unique selling point, in that further information may detract from overall evaluation of the product unless the new information is at least as positive as the old.

The most important implication, within the present context, is that techniques of information integration seem sufficiently robust to cope with the unravelling of judgements made by consumers, even when those product evaluations are made in a realistic manner and within a naturalistic market setting. Even the potential problem caused by the unequal weighting of the attributes was insufficiently serious to invalidate the results. Thus, it does seem as if wider acceptance of IIT within the marketing community would be justified, at least on the score of external validity.

REFERENCES

Anderson Norman H. (1965), "Averaging Versus Adding As A Stimulus Combination Rule In Impression Formation," *Journal of Experimental Psychology*, 70 (4), 394-420.

_____ (1970), "Functional Measurement And Psychophysical Judgement," *Psychological Review*, 77 (3), 153-170.

_____ (1974a), "Algebraic Models In Perception," in *Handbook of Perception, Vol.II, Psychophysical Judgement and Measurement*, Edward C Carterette and Morton P. Friedman (eds), New York: Academic Press, 215-298.

_____ (1974b), "Information Integration Theory: A Brief Survey", in *Contemporary Development In Mathematical Psychology, Vol. 2*, Krantz D.H., R.C.Atkinson, R.D.Luce, P.Suppes (eds), San Francisco: W.H. Freeman and Company.

_____ (1981), *Foundation Of Information Integration Theory*, New York: Academic Press.

_____ (1982), *Methods Of Information Integration Theory*, New York: Academic Press.

_____ and Margaret A. Armstrong (1989), "Cognitive Theory And Methodology For Studying Marital Interaction", in *Dyadic Decision Making*, David Brinberg and James Jaccard (eds), New York: Springer-Verlag, 3-50.

Assael Henry (1988), *Consumer Behaviour And Marketing Action*, Melbourne: Thomas Nelson Australia.

Bennett Peter D. (1988), *Marketing*, New York: McGraw Hill Book Co.

Bettman James R., Noel Capon and Richard J. Lutz (1975), "Multiattribute Measurement Models And Multiattribute Attitude Theory: A Test Of Construct Validity," *Journal of Consumer Research*, 1 (March) 1-15.

Cohen Joel B., Paul W. Miniard and Peter R. Dixon (1980), "Information Integration: An Information Processing Perspective," *Advances in Consumer Research*, 7, 161-170.

Ebbersen Ebbe B. and Vladimir J. Konecni (1980), "On The External Validity Of Decision-Making Research: What Do We Know About Decisions In The Real World", in *Cognitive Processes In Choice And Decision Behaviour*, Thomas S. Wallsten (ed), Hillsdale, New Jersey: Lawrence Erlbaum Associates Publishers, 21-45.

Engel James, Roger D. Blackwell and Paul Miniard (1990), *Consumer Behaviour*, Chicago: The Dryden Press.

Fishbein Martin and Icek Ajzen (1975), *Belief, Attitude, Intention And Behaviour*, Reading, Mass: Addison-Wesley Publishing Company.

Hays, W. J. (1963). *Statistics for psychologists*. New York: Holt, Rhinehart, Winston.

Howard John A. (1989), *Consumer Behaviour In Marketing Strategy*, New Jersey: Prentice-Hall, Inc.

Keppel, G. (1973). *Design and analysis: A researcher's handbook*. Englewood Cliffs, NJ: Prentice Hall Inc.

Kotler Philip and Gary Armstrong (1989), *Principles Of Marketing*, New Jersey: Prentice-Hall, Inc.

Levin Irwin P., Jordan J. Louviere, Albert A. Schepanski and Kent L. Norman (1983), "External Validity Tests Of Laboratory Studies Of Information Integration," *Organizational Behaviour and Human Performance*, 31, 173-193.

Lynch John G. Jr. (1985), "Uniqueness Issues in the Decompositional Modelling of Multiattribute Overall Evaluations: An Information Integration Perspective" *Journal of Marketing Research*, Vol.22 (February), 1-19.

Markin Rom J. (1980), "The Role Of Rationalization In Consumer Decision Processes: A Revisionist Approach To Consumer Behaviour," *Journal of The Academy of Marketing Science*, 7 (4), 316-334.

Peter Paul J. and Jerry C. Olson (1990), *Consumer Behaviour And Marketing Strategy*, Homewood, Il: Irwin.

Rao, V. R. (1977). Conjoint measurement in marketing analysis. In J. N. Sheth (Ed.), *Multivariate methods for market and survey research* (pp. 257-286). Chicago, IL: American Marketing Association.

Robertson Kim R. and Roger Marshall (1987), "Amount of Label Information Effects on Perceived Product Quality and Effectiveness", *International Journal of Advertising*, London, Vol.6, No.2.

Shanteau James (1988), "Information Integration Theory Applied To Consumer Behaviour," in *Proceedings of the Division of Consumer Psychology 1987*, L.F. Alwitt (ed), Washington D.C.: American Psychological Association, 100-102.

Shanteau James and Charles H. Ptacek (1983), "Role And Implications Of Averaging Processes In Advertising," in *Advertising and Consumer Psychology*, Larry Percy and Arch G. Woodside (eds), Massachusetts: Lexington Books, 149-167.

Troutman C. Michael and James Shanteau (1976), "Do Consumers Evaluate Products By Adding Or Averaging Attribute Information," *Journal of Consumer Research*, 3 (September), 101-106.

_____ and _____ (1977), "Inferences Based On Nondiagnostic Information," *Organizational Behaviour and Human Performance*, 19, 43-55.

_____ and _____ (1989), "Information Integration In Husband-Wife Decision Making About Health-Care Services," in *Dyadic Decision Making*, David Brinberg and James Jaccard (eds), New York: Springer Verlag, 117-151.

Vaughan, G. M., & Corballis, M. C. (1969). Beyond tests of significance: Estimating strength of effects in selected ANOVA designs. *Psychological Bulletin*, 72(3), 204-213.

Using Computerized Response Time Measurement for Detecting Secondary Distractions in Advertising

Robert S. Owen, SUNY Oswego
Kenneth R. Lord, SUNY Buffalo
Martha C. Cooper, Ohio State University

Use of the secondary task technique in the measurement of the distraction potential of prospective media environments is advocated and briefly discussed. Although there are a variety of secondary task methods that can be used to detect and measure the various attention related constructs, the current discussion focuses on the "RT-probe" technique, whereby the response time (latency) to a secondary task is taken as an indicator of mental attention devoted to a primary task. The proliferation of microcomputers brings this method within reach of most advertising researchers, albeit with some cautions and limitations that are discussed.

INTRODUCTION

The notion that the human processing system has an asymptotic limit in "capacity" can be used as the basis for the investigation of such related constructs and processes as "attention", "elaboration", and "mental effort." For example, television viewing could involve substantial elaboration as viewers anticipate a conflict resolution or relate an episode to their own prior experiences (Lord and Burnkrant 1993). As more attentional capacity is absorbed by the task of program elaboration, a viewer would likely become less aware of or responsive to other stimuli (e.g., advertisements) in the environment. The observation that a person is less aware of or responsive to other "secondary" stimuli can be taken as an indication that the "primary" task of product comparison is attracting or requiring a greater amount of "mental attention". A measure of the amount of deterioration in responsiveness to "secondary" stimuli can be taken as an indicator of the amount of mental attention that program involvement and elaboration attracts or requires.

This so-called "secondary task technique" has been implemented in a variety of ways. One interesting variation on the general idea of the secondary task technique has been used by Children's Television Workshop, producers of *Sesame Street*, to test television shows on 3- and 4-year old children (Waterman 1990). Children in day-care centers were shown segments of the TV show under test while slides were concurrently projected on a screen next to the TV display. The ability of a TV segment to capture the "attention" or "involvement" of these preschool viewers is taken as a function of the attention that is given to the secondary (slides) vs. primary (TV show) task. In this use of a secondary task technique, the observation of lesser attention to the secondary task is presumed to indicate that the primary task is absorbing, consuming, or in some way requiring greater viewer attention.

The focus of the present report is more specifically on the use of the "RT-probe" form of secondary task technique in the measurement of capacity-related constructs such as attention, elaboration, involvement, mental effort, and such. In using the RT-probe technique, changes in reaction times (RT) to a secondary task are taken to indicate changes in the use of attentional resources that are devoted to performance of the primary task. Commonly available microcomputers can be used to measure and record reaction times.

Although this method is not new, it has never been adequately described with regard to how it is implemented and, importantly, how it is limited. The present report, then, is a synthesis of issues associated with the measurement technique, the necessary physical instrumentation, and limitations of the physical instrumentation and of the theoretical basis of the technique. The general basis of this technique is first discussed, followed by discussion of how computers can be implemented in using this method, of some limitations and cautions in making these uses, and of some limitations of the secondary task technique itself.

THE SECONDARY TASK TECHNIQUE AND THE RT-PROBE

One of the more common operationalizations in the investigation of the various attention-related constructs and processes has involved the so-called "dual-task" and "secondary task" techniques. Dual-task and secondary task techniques generally presume a processing system of resource limitations: the consumption of processing capacity by one task will leave less capacity for the processing of a second concurrent task. When both tasks attempt to concurrently consume more capacity than is available, the performance of one or both tasks must suffer. This will presumably result in the observation of degraded task performance.

A frequently used secondary task in laboratory settings in recent years has been the "RT-probe", in which subjects must press a hand-held switch button in response to an occasional flash of light or an audible click or "beep" sound. A degradation (increase) in reaction time (RT) to an occasional beep (the secondary task) during, say, the reading of a message or the viewing of a television program (the primary task) is taken as a quantitative measure of an increase in attention or mental effort devoted to the primary task. Points at which RTs greatly increase above "normal", usually accompanied by many "misses" (no response to the beep) or "false alarms" (response where no beep occurred), are taken to indicate degraded secondary task performance and as an indication that the primary task is consuming attentional resources near the capacity threshold. This presumably provides an indication of, say, points within a communication that consume more attention or require more effort to process, or of, say, mental comparisons that require more mental attention or effort. Secondary task performance changes, then, are taken to function as a probe into attentional resource consumption by the primary task.

Lord and Burnkrant (1993), for example, used the RT-probe to find apparently "high involvement" and "low involvement" segments within a suspenseful "Alfred Hitchcock Presents" television program. Longer RTs to an occasional audible beep were taken as an indication of higher viewer "involvement" with particular points within the program story. After the RT-probe had identified the location of the more and less involving segments of the program story, commercials could then be positioned within these apparently high involvement or low involvement segments of the program story. The objective was to investigate differences in recall and attitude change associated with advertisements that were shown at points of high vs. low program involvement.

Lord, Burnkrant, and Owen (1989) had found that longer RTs continued throughout television advertisements embedded within high involvement segments, but remained normal throughout the same advertisements positioned within low involvement segments. These longer RTs were taken to indicate that processing resources

Advances in Consumer Research
Volume 22, © 1995

were being consumed by program elaboration throughout advertisements positioned within high involvement program segments. Attitude and recall measures taken after the program viewing suggested that there apparently was some processing interference associated with commercials positioned within high involvement program segments.

Thorson and her colleagues (1985; 1987) have similarly used the RT-probe to investigate television viewer "attention". Moore, Hausknecht and Thamodaran (1986) have used the RT-probe in the investigation of "attention allocation" to the processing of compressed audio commercials. Britton and his colleagues have conducted a number of studies (1978, 1979, 1980, 1982) into the usage of "cognitive capacity" with differences in text complexity and structure. All of these uses of the RT-probe are based on the assumption that as the primary task consumes near the threshold of capacity, secondary task performance will be degraded due to a lack of sufficient reserve capacity.

USING COMPUTERS IN RT-PROBE MEASUREMENT

None of the above uses of the RT-probe secondary task technique required especially elaborate, specialized, or expensive equipment. Thorson et al. and Moore et al., for example, report using commonly available Apple II computers. Lord et al. used a Commodore C-64 computer. In the Lord studies, the built-in game ports were used to input both the beep sound stimuli from the video tape (recorded separately on one stereo track) as well as the hand-held button switches. The game port on the Commodore computer allows the input of analog signals (the beep sound) and allows as many as ten button switches to be attached simultaneously (i.e., ten subjects can be run in a single session). The button switches are simply substituted for the four direction switches and the fire button of a joystick. Note that the analog input does require some simple signal conditioning—it will not give good results if directly connected to the audio output of the video player.

Lord et al. also used the computer to dub the beep stimuli on the stimulus tape. The computer generated beep sounds (a pleasant "bing") that were randomly spaced between three and nine seconds apart—an average of 10 beeps per minute. These were recorded on one channel of the stereo audio track of the video tape. The reason that the spacing between the beeps was random, rather than maintained at a constant interval, was to minimize the possibility of automatism, i.e., so that subjects would not get acclimated to any particular pace in responding to the secondary task. The beeps were recorded on a stereo audio track separate from the program audio to simplify the task of detecting them with the computer equipment.

On playback to subjects, the computer was used to count beeps in the audio portion of the video program, thereby locating particular points in the program by beep number. The computer also measured the time between the onset of a beep and any button presses by subjects. The data that were saved, then, were the beep number, the subject identification number each time a new button press was detected (ten subjects could be run simultaneously), and the reaction time between the onset of the beep and each new button press.

Other commonly available, low cost microcomputers can similarly be used for these purposes. A low cost game port can easily be installed in an older, discarded IBM-PC, for instance. (Maybe the old beast has a clunky floppy drive and can't do Windows, but it can still make beep noises and can still count beeps and timer ticks—don't throw it away yet!) One limitation that many potential users might encounter, however, is that writing the machine-level software to read these inputs and to take measurements

of the time between the secondary stimulus input and the button press does require some specialized expertise.

COMPUTER JIFFIES AND TICKS AS TIMING DEVICES

Most microcomputers provide user-accessible time keeping functions known as "jiffy clocks" or "tick counters". In HyperCard on a Macintosh, a "tick" is an interval of time of nominally [1/60]-second in length, and on a PC-DOS or MS-DOS machine, a "tick" is an interval of time of nominally [1/18.2]-second in length. Note that ticks are not implemented or used in the same way on all computers. On an IBM-PC, for instance, the tick is derived from a periodically occurring event called an "interrupt", and the frequency of the occurrence of this interrupt can be altered through software (that is, it is possible to write software to "speed up" this tick rate, thereby allowing time measurements of finer resolution: cf., Buhrer, Sparrer, and Weitkunat 1987; Heathcote 1988; Sargent and Shoemaker 1984, p. 263). On a Macintosh, the higher frequency tick is derived from an interrupt generated by the periodically occurring CRT display refresh (Lane and Ashby 1987), and therefore cannot be altered. These periodically occurring interrupts are used primarily as reminders to an operating system to perform certain operations, such as to check the keyboard for new information and to increment the tick counter by one count for time keeping functions. The value in this tick counter is used by many operating systems to update the time-of-day clock and can usually be accessed by the user. An exception is the Macintosh, which does not use the tick counter to maintain its time-of-day clock (Harvey 1988, p. 471).

There are three potential problems associated with using tick counters for timing measurements. The first is that the performance of some operations can require that other operations be temporarily suspended, including updating the tick counter. Disk drive operation, for instance, will interfere with the tick counter on the Macintosh (Harvey 1988, p.471; Kieley and Higgins 1989). Under normal uses, the loss of a tick here and there is of little consequence. For scientific measurements, however, the loss of a tick here and there is an unacceptable source of systematic error in a short-interval measurement. As long as one has a knowledge of the interrupt structure of the particular operating system being used, however, such sources of systematic error can usually be avoided. (E.g., simply avoid using the disk drive in the middle of taking a timing measurement!)

A second potential problem associated with using tick counters for timing measurements is that most users cannot instantly read the time in a tick counter. A line of program in a higher-level language (e.g., BASIC) which reads the tick register may take tens of milliseconds to execute, and this amount of time can vary within the same program, making higher-level languages unsuitable in many applications (Dlhopolsky 1983a, 1983b; Dorfman 1987; Emerson 1988; Flexser 1987; Grice 1981; Kieley and Higgins 1989; Mapou 1982; Rayfield 1981, 1982). This unknown amount of processing overhead can be an unacceptable source of systematic error if a short-interval measurement is required.

A third problem associated with using tick counters for timing measurements is that they sometimes lack the proper amount of resolution for the uses that are made of them. Importantly, to display, analyze, or report a unit of, say, [1/18.2]-seconds as 0.055 seconds is at best misleading, giving the false impression that the measurement instrument was capable of resolving to the level of at least one millisecond. The actual unit of resolution is 55 times more crude, and any analysis using the decimalized value looses meaning (cf., Owen and Cooper 1990). The Moore et al. (1986) study is noteworthy in that these investigators appropriately analyzed and reported Apple II sixtieth-second ticks directly in units expressed as ticks, without unnecessary conversion to decimal form.

As an aside, it is perhaps useful to note here that a typical *fast* reaction time—when a person is in high arousal or a state of readiness to respond to a clear visual or audio stimulus—will be on the order of magnitude of about 2-tenth-seconds with a hand-held button switch. That is, this is the sort of reaction times that would be typical in an RT-probe secondary task when enough "capacity" is available to respond to the secondary task. As the primary task requires processing resources at a level that approaches capacity limits, reaction times can be observed to degrade to well over a second, with the longer reaction times likely to be "false alarms"; these longer reaction times are also accompanied by many "misses".

Although the 2-tenth-second level of reaction time might appear to be well within the abilities of computer ticks to detect, interest is often in the *difference* between various reaction times, which can be at the *hundredth-second* order of magnitude. The needs of the measurement task therefore require special consideration to determine if a tick-based timer is appropriate for the particular measurement task. Also note that some advise an additional order of magnitude in taking measurements (e.g., Owen and Cooper 1991), i.e., differences of hundredth-second levels should be measured and analyzed at millisecond levels, although this is not a universally accepted caution.

KEYBOARD AS A RESPONSE DEVICE

The method used to gather subject responses to the secondary stimulus also requires some scrutiny. Note, for example, that the closure of a switch on an IBM-PC keyboard cannot be instantly registered by the main processor. Keyboard switches are not directly connected to the keyboard cable; a processor within the keyboard first interprets which key is depressed from the matrix of switches and sends a correspondingly coded series of pulses through the keyboard cable (see Glasco and Sargent [1983] for a very thorough discussion). On a PC running under PC-DOS or MS-DOS, the computer checks, or "polls", for a signal from the keyboard about 18.2 times per second. Although it is possible for a knowledgeable programmer to have the keyboard polled at a faster rate, the keyboard itself can still take tens of milliseconds to output a signal in response to a keypress, and this amount of time has been found to vary between keyboards (Graves and Bradley 1987). Substituting the PC keyboard as an input device if millisecond-level reaction time measures are required is at best hazardous, and more precise and faster response devices should be used instead for this purpose (cf. Crosbie 1989). The Macintosh functions in a similar manner, except that the keyboard is polled at a rate of nominally 60 times per second, and a keypress can be detected by the keyboard in about 6 milliseconds (Lane and Ashby 1987).

As a general rule, older microcomputers in which the keyboard is contained in the same enclosure as the main processor do not operate in this way, allowing the keyboard to be sensed by the processor in real-time (i.e., usually within a few microseconds, discounting any mechanical latency of the switch itself). More specifically, the *memory-mapped* keyboard designs of many older microcomputers (e.g., Commodore C-64, PET, TRS-80, etc.) are better suited for high-resolution reaction time measurement. Due to the mechanical construction of the key switch, however, even these keyboards might sometimes (although very unlikely in advertising studies) not be suitable as response devices if millisecond-level response latency measurement is critical (Reed 1981). A variety of more appropriate or more desirable alternatives to the keyboard for real-time button-press detection exist (e.g., Creeger,

Miller, and Paredes 1990). Recall, for example, that Lord and Burnkrant (1993) and Lord, Burnkrant, and Owen (1989) used external button switches that were plugged in to the game (joystick) port of a computer. Game ports for IBM-PC computers are readily available for well under $50.

SOME LIMITATIONS IN USING THE RT-PROBE TECHNIQUE

There are some important limitations to consider in using the RT-probe technique. First and foremost, one has to be careful with assumptions regarding the particular construct that is presumably measured by any secondary task technique. A general discussion of attention and the secondary task technique can be found in Lynch and Srull (1982); Owen (1991) outlines a variety of concerns and cautions regarding the attention-related constructs. The point here is that constructs such as attention, elaboration, involvement, mental effort, and such, all seem to be related to the notion of "capacity", but the full relationship and distinction between such constructs is not yet clear. The RT-probe technique merely detects when capacity is near the threshold of being "swamped", and conclusions regarding any of a variety of capacity-related constructs always require careful scrutiny. Nonetheless, the fact that the secondary task technique does appear to detect *something* should encourage us to use this technique as long as it allows us to make useful inferences regarding an attention-related construct (cf., Navon 1984; Owen 1991).

Additionally, there is evidence that the human processing system consists of more than just a simple, single "capacity" resource (cf., Owen 1991). The fact that subjects in high attentional load conditions will respond to a secondary task beep after, say, a one second delay does itself suggest that there exists an auditory resource that can independently attend to and store incoming audio stimuli until a general purpose, main processor can attend to this new input. Nonetheless, that one second delay can be used as evidence that some sort of general, global attentional resource is being used more heavily. The point is that one must always maintain caution regarding conclusions that can be drawn about the use of processing resources.

A second caution regards some of the limitations of microcomputer equipment that might be used in making RT-probe measurements. These limitations are not necessarily severe, but the limitations of any measurement instrument must be understood whenever it is used to take a measurement. For example, most timing measurements that use an IBM-PC platform make use of an internal timer that "ticks" at a rate of nominally 18.2 times per second. Unfortunately, many examples can be found which express such "ticks" in decimal form, incorrectly implying millisecond-level resolution where the true level of resolution is closer to about a tenth-second order of magnitude. For example, the "timer" function in MS-DOS QBasic and GW-Basic, commonly misused in writing timing routines, misleadingly returns a continuous value in decimal form, but a simple "print timer" loop will return values at *increments* of nominally [1/18.2]-seconds.

Such limitations in the abilities of the available hardware, however, do not necessarily restrict the ability to conduct RT-probe research. If the expertise exists, special programming techniques (which might require the use of machine language) can be used to obtain measurements at much finer levels of resolution. Lord and Burnkrant (1993) and Lord, Burnkrant, and Owen (1989), for example, used machine language and built-in timing hardware that enabled a resolution of much better than 100 microseconds. For human reaction-time measurements, however, such fine resolution is, in many cases, not necessary. Moore et al. (1986), for example, reported RT-probe reaction time measures at the level of sixtieth-second ticks; the resolution of these tick units is adequate and appropriate for the particular task that was reported.

CONCLUDING REMARKS

The secondary task technique has seen more extensive use in engineering and cognitive psychology than in advertising. Greater use of the secondary task technique in advertising research is advocated, and it is hoped that the "how to" nature of the present report will encourage greater use in both experimental research and in field practice. The secondary task technique can be used in the study of a number of constructs, processes, and issues of relevance to advertising effectiveness, such as television program involvement, the attention-engaging capacity of a particular advertisement, and the quantity of "processing resources" that are required for such objectives as brand awareness, claim recall, message elaboration, or persuasion.

The RT-probe is a special form of secondary task that holds appeal in advertising research for several reasons. One feature of the RT-probe is that it can provide continuous yet relatively unobtrusive measures of attention consumption. That is, it enables the advertiser to pinpoint a particular segment of an advertisement or program/editorial environment in which greater or lesser attentional resources are being utilized. Used in conjunction with post-task paper and pencil instruments, the RT-probe can provide an objective measure of attention-related constructs and processes to assist in validation of subjective measures. The RT-probe is a form of secondary task which provides data in numerical form, enabling common statistical sorts of inferences.

Several cautions regarding the underlying theoretical assumptions of the RT-probe and the use of computers in response time measurement have been discussed. Although particular limitations in theory and in the level of software/hardware expertise of the research team must be important considerations in applying the RT-probe, the secondary task is a well established and respected method outside of the marketing and advertising disciplines. Dual-task and secondary task methods have been used effectively by experimental psychologists for over a century (e.g., Jastrow 1892; Welch 1898), and the RT-probe technique has been in use for at least two decades (e.g., Posner and Boise 1971). This technique has seen recent use in advertising and provides great promise in field and experimental work in the study of consumer advertising processing.

REFERENCES

Britton, Bruce K. and Abraham Tesser (1982), "Effects of Prior Knowledge on Use of Cognitive Capacity in Three Complex Cognitive Tasks," *Journal of Verbal Learning and Verbal Behavior*, 21, 421-436.

_____, Timothy S. Holdredge, Cheryl Curry, and Robert D. Westbrook (1979), "Use of Cognitive Capacity in Reading Identical Texts with Different Amounts of Discourse Level Meaning," *Journal of Experimental Psychololgy: Human Learning and Memory*, 5, 262-270.

_____, Robert D. Westbrook, and Timothy S. Holdredge (1978), "Reading and Cognitive Capacity Usage: Effects of Text Difficulty," *Journal of Experimental Psychology: Human Learning and Memory*, 4, 582-591.

_____, Robbie Zeigler, and Robert D. Westbrook (1980), "Use of Capacity in Reading Easy and Difficult Text: Two Tests of an Allocation of Attention Hypothesis," *Journal of Reading Behavior*, 12, 23-30.

Buhrer, Michael, Bernd Sparrer, and Rolf Weitkunat (1987), "Interval Timing Routines for the IBM PC/XT/AT Micro-computer Family," *Behavior Research Methods, Instruments, & Computers*, 19(3), 327-334.

Creeger, Carl P., Kevin F. Miller, and David R. Paredes (1990), "Micromanaging Time: Measuring and Controlling Timing Errors in Computer-Controlled Experiments," *Behavior ResearchMethods, Instruments, & Computers*, 22(1), 34-79.

Crosbie, John (1989), "A Simple Turbo Pascal 4.0 Program for Millisecond Timing on the IBM PC/XT/AT," *Behavior Research Methods, Instruments, & Computers*, 21(3), 408-413.

Dlhopolsky, Joseph G. (1983a), "Limitations of High-Level Microcomputer Languages in Software Designed for Psychological Experimentation," *Behavior Research Methods & Instrumentation*, 15(4), 459-464.

_____(1983b), "Machine Language Millisecond Timers for the Z-80 Microprocessor," *Behavior Research Methods & Instrumentation*, 15(5), 511-520.

Dorfman, David (1987), "Software Timing of Events in Cognitive Psychology Experiments," *Behavior Research Methods, Instruments, & Computers*, 19(2), 185-190.

Emerson, Phillip L. (1988), "TIMEX: A Simple IBM AT C Language Timer with Extended Resolution," *Behavior Research Methods, Instruments, & Computers*, 20(6), 566-572.

Flexser, Arthur J. (1987), "Accurate Display Timing Using an Enhanced BASIC for the Tandy Color Computer," *Behavior Research Methods, Instruments, & Computers*, 19(5), 457-459.

Glasco, David B. and Murray Sargent III (1983), "Using IBM's Marvelous Keyboard," *Byte* 9(5), 402-415.

Graves, Roger and Ron Bradley (1987), "Millisecond Interval Timer and Auditory Reaction Time Programs for the IBM PC," *Behavior Research Methods, Instruments, & Computers*, 19(1), 30-35.

Grice, G. Robert (1981), "Accurate Reaction Time Research with the TRS-80 Microcomputer," *Behavior Research Methods & Instrumentation*, 13(5), 674-676.

Harvey, Greg (1988), *Understanding HyperCard*. San Fransisco: Sybex.

Heathcote, Andrew (1988), "Screen Control and Timing Routines for the IBM Microcomputer Family Using a High-Level Language," *Behavior Research Methods, Instruments, & Computers*, 20(3), 289-297.

Jastrow, J. (1892), "The Interference of Mental Processes," *The American Journal of Psychology*, 4, 219-223.

Kieley, James M. and Timothy Higgins (1989), "Precision Timing Options for the Apple Macintosh Family of Computers," *Behavior Research Methods, Instruments, & Computers*, 21(2), 259-264.

Lane, David and Brad Ashby (1987), "PsychLib: A Library of Machine Language Routines for Controlling Psychology Experiments on the Apple Macintosh Computer," *Behavior Research Methods, Instruments, & Computers*, 19(2), 246-248.

Lord, Kenneth R. and Robert E. Burnkrant (1993), "Attention versus Distraction: The Interactive Effect of Program Involvement and Attentional Devices on Commercial Processing," *Journal of Advertising*, 22(March), 47-60.

_____, _____, and Robert S. Owen (1989), "An Experimental Comparison of Self-Report and Response Time Measures of Information Processing," in *AMA Educators' Proceedings: Enhancing Knowledge Development in Marketing*, Paul Bloom, Russ Winer, Harold Kassarjian, Debra Scammon, Bart Weitz, Robert Spekman, Vijay Mahajan, Michael Levy, eds., Chicago: American Marketing Association, 196-200.

Lynch, John G. and Thomas K. Srull (1982), "Memory and Attentional Factors in Consumer Choice: Concepts and Research Methods," *Journal of Consumer Research*, 9, 18-37.

Mapoou, Robert L. (1982), "Tachistoscopic Timing on the TRS-80," *Behavior Research Methods & Instrumentation*, 14(6), 534-538.

Moore, Danny L., Douglas Housknecht, and Kanchana Thamodara (1986), "Time Compression Response Opportunity in Persuasion," *Journal of Consumer Research*, 13(June), 85-99.

Navon, David (1984), "Resources - A Theoretical Soupstone?" *Psychological Review*, 91, 216-234.

Owen, Robert S. (1991), "Clarifying the Simple Assumption of the Secondary Task Technique," *Advances in Consumer Research*, 18, 552-557.

_____and Martha C. Cooper (1990), "Some Definitions and Issues in Measurement and Instrumentation," Working Paper Series of the College of Business #WPS 90-49. Ohio State University.

Posner, Michael I. and Stephen J. Boies (1971), "The Components of Attention," *Psychological Review*, 78(5), 391-408.

Rayfield, Frederick (1981), "Controlling Behavior Experiments with BASIC on 6502-Based Microcomputers," *Behavior Research Methods & Instrumentation*, 13(6), 735-740.

_____(1982), "Experimental Control and Data Acquisition with BASIC in the Apple Computer," *Behavior Research Methods & Instrumentation*, 14(4), 409-411.

Reed, Adam V. (1981), "On Choosing an Inexpensive Microcomputer for the Experimental Psychology Laboratory," *Behavior Research Methods and Instrumentation*, 12(6), 607-613.

Sargent, Murray III and Richard L. Shoemaker (1984), *The IBM Personal Computer from the Inside Out*, Reading, Mass: Addison-Wesley Publishing Company.

Thorson, Esther, Byron Reeves, and Joan Schleuder (1985), "Message Complexity and Attention to Television," *Communication Research*, 12(4), 427-454.

_____, _____, and (1987), "Attention to Local and Global Complexity in Television Messages," In *Communication Yearbook 10*, Ed. Margaret McLaughlin. Newbury Park, CA: Sage Publications, 366-383.

Waterman, Robert H. Jr. (1990), *Adhocracy: The Power to Change*, location unlisted: Whittle Direct Books.

Welch, Jeanette. C. (1898), "On the Measurement of Mental Activity through Muscular Activity and the Determination of a Constant of Attention," *American Journal of Physiology*, 1, 283-306.

The Four Faces of Aggregation in Customer Satisfaction Research

Michael D. Johnson, University of Michigan

ABSTRACT

This paper applies Epstein's (1980) four faces of aggregation to customer satisfaction research. While existing studies tend to focus on individual subjects and consumption experiences, there is a recent trend toward aggregation. Studying customer satisfaction in the aggregate (over subjects, occasions, stimuli, and measures) should result in more reliable empirical generalizations in an area where disparate empirical findings are common. The discussion illustrates the importance of taking a macro-psychological perspective on customer satisfaction where satisfaction is itself a cumulative, abstract construct on which a variety of products and services may be compared.

INTRODUCTION

Research on customer satisfaction relies heavily on the experimental tradition established in psychology. Satisfaction studies typically use individuals as the level of observation and often involve a limited set of both stimuli and product or service use occasions. This paper describes how this approach limits the ability of research to generate empirical generalizations regarding satisfaction. Using Epstein's (1980) "four faces of aggregation," it is argued that greater application of adequate sampling procedures over individuals, stimuli or situations, trials or occasions, and measures facilitates the establishment of generalizable results. Application of the four faces of aggregation in a customer satisfaction context requires that greater attention be paid to: (1) a market level or macro-psychological perspective on satisfaction, (2) defining satisfaction around customers' cumulative experience with a product or service to-date, and (3) operationalizing and modeling satisfaction accordingly.

Nature of the Problem

Although a volume of satisfaction experiments are reported in the literature, empirical generalizations remain elusive (see Yi 1991 for a comprehensive review). A number of studies support expectancy-disconfirmation as a principal determinant of satisfaction while others support direct effects of both performance and expectations on satisfaction. Given the range of performance and expectation related effects on satisfaction, the trend has been to include multiple antecedents in satisfaction models (e.g., Anderson and Sullivan 1993; Churchill and Surprenant 1982; Oliver 1993). However, the size of these effects varies widely across studies.

Endemic to this problem is the concern that experimental studies in the behavioral sciences are inherently limited in their ability to establish reliable generalizations (Ajzen and Fishbein 1974; Cronbach 1975; Epstein 1980; Greenwald 1975; Koch 1959). Epstein (1979, 1980) describes these limitations in his essays on the "stability of behavior," the key points of which are summarized here. One major limitation pertains to the issue of control. The purpose of experimentation is to provide a high level of control. However, adequate control in a behavioral study may be impossible given the wide range of variables that can not be controlled in any given experimental design (Campbell and Stanley 1963). A second limitation is that, when one attempts to increase experimental control in social science research, the result is often an increase in the problem one seeks to reduce. "The achievement of a small error term by controlling the variables that can be controlled magnifies the contribution of uncontrolled situation-specific variables no less than that of experimental variables" (Epstein 1980, p. 794). That is,

as one increases control, the effect of highly idiosyncratic or situational factors becomes even more salient which reduces generalizability.

Another limitation relates to the lack of effort expended conducting replication studies, and the relatively small proportion of such studies that are published (Greenwald 1975; Smith 1970). Unless an experiment demonstrates something different, rather than the same result in a different context or situation, it is considered uninteresting. Results that replicate across different contexts or situations are often judged as "not a sufficient contribution" to the field of consumer research. This response says, in effect, that consumer researchers are not interested in establishing empirical generalizations.

Epstein describes two solutions to these problems, the study of higher order interactions and the use of aggregation or sampling. The first, advanced notably by Cronbach (1957), is to pay greater attention to higher order interactions. Modeling individual difference, situation, and stimulus related interactions should, presumably, control for factors idiosyncratic to a particular study and allow researchers to look across studies to see common, generalizable effects. One problem with this solution again lies in the solution itself. "Once we attend to interactions, we enter a hall of mirrors that extends to infinity. However far we carry our analysis - to third order or fifth order or any other - untested interactions of a still higher order can be envisioned" (Cronbach, 1957, p. 119). Years later, it is not surprising that Cronbach (1975) was far more pessimistic in his evaluation of this solution. Epstein's second option is aggregation.

THE FOUR FACES OF AGGREGATION

Aggregation provides two important research benefits. It reduces error in measurement, and provides more generalizable results. Epstein describes four different forms of aggregation: (1) aggregation over subjects, (2) aggregation over stimuli and/or situations, (3) aggregation over trials and/or occasions, and (4) aggregation over measures. After describing the latter three points and their application to satisfaction research, the discussion will focus on aggregation over subjects as having particular relevance.

Aggregation Over Stimuli and/or Situations

A wealth of evidence demonstrates how laboratory findings vary widely from stimulus set to stimulus set and context to context. Nevertheless, many satisfaction studies continue to investigate a particular stimulus set or context, or a limited range of stimuli or contexts, relative to the domain to which the researcher wishes to generalize. Epstein argues that "the need for replication in various settings before a relationship can be accepted as of general theoretical interest can hardly be overstated" (1980, p. 799). As noted, researchers are often biased against replication studies. Aggregation over varying stimuli or situations *within* an experiment is one solution. That is, individual studies should seek a more broad based set of stimuli and situations as the basis for empirical study. This is not the same as Brunswik's (1947) concerns over the ecological validity of experiments. Rather, aggregation over stimuli and situations is seen as a way of increasing replicability and generality by canceling out uncontrolled unique effects.

It is not surprising that the satisfaction studies that do cut across a wide range of stimuli yield a similar, generalizable result. For example, Andreasen and Best (1977) examined customer

Advances in Consumer Research
Volume 22, © 1995

satisfaction and complaint data across 35 product and service categories and found greater satisfaction, on average, with products than with services. A primary reason for this difference is that it is inherently more difficult to provide consistent service quality than it is to provide consistent product quality (Grönroos 1984; Zeithaml et al. 1988). Service production involves more of the human resources of the firm and customers themselves. Not surprisingly, Fornell (1992) examined 32 Swedish industries and also found services lagging behind products on customer satisfaction.

Aggregation Over Trials and/or Occasions

Aggregating over trials and/or occasions serves the same purpose. It cancels out any uniqueness due to particular trials or occasions. Epstein groups trials and occasions together because they both involve aggregation over time. Yet aggregating over occasions is seen as more important. Aggregating over specific trials in an experimental session increases "concurrent" reliability. In contrast, aggregating over occasions cancels out incidental effects associated with particular occasions and thus increases "temporal" reliability. The personality literature offers an illustration, where Mischel (1968) notes the relative failure of measured personality traits to predict objective events or behaviors. The objective data in this case consists of single behavior observations or events, usually obtained in a laboratory. In four studies, Epstein (1979) argued and showed that the stability of such relationships can be demonstrated so long as the behavior is averaged over a sufficient number of occasions or events. Although personality traits are not strong predictors of what an individual will do on any given occasion or event, they predict an individual's behavior over several occasions quite well.

The application of occasion aggregation to satisfaction research centers on the distinction between "transaction specific" and "cumulative" satisfaction (Johnson, Anderson and Fornell 1995). Transaction specific satisfaction is a customer's evaluation of a particular product or service experience (Cronin and Taylor 1992). Cumulative satisfaction is the customer's evaluation of their entire purchase and consumption experience to-date (Johnson and Fornell 1991). Epstein's arguments suggest that adopting a more cumulative operational definition of the satisfaction construct will result in more generalizable findings. Oliver (1993) emphasizes that interest in satisfaction research stems, in large part, from the fact that most customer decisions are not initial decisions. Rather, they are decisions influenced by purchase and consumption histories. It is this history, or aggregation over occasions, that drives current and future behavior. An important implication is that aggregation over occasions should produce an operationalization of satisfaction that explains customer loyalty. This aggregation does not necessarily involve taking occasion specific measures and averaging them into an overall experience. It may consist of self-ratings by customers, on a single occasion, that are based on experiences gathered over a period of time.

Aggregation Over Measures

Aggregation over measures is commonplace in consumer research, and specifically research on customer satisfaction. The use of multiple measures to reduce measurement error in causal model estimations has become almost routine (e.g., Churchill and Surprenant 1982; Cronin and Taylor 1992; Fornell 1992; Oliver 1980; Westbrook and Reilly 1983). There is less consensus as to just what the multiple measures of satisfaction should be. Johnson and Fornell (1991) argue for an expanded view of these measures to properly tap cumulative satisfaction. Properly measured, this cumulative satisfaction allows for meaningful comparisons across very different individuals and product categories. Satisfaction,

viewed as an abstract construct, allows one to compare seemingly noncomparable products and services (Johnson 1984). Because this satisfaction is an overall evaluation of the customer's consumption experience (a.k.a. consumption utility), satisfaction measures should be chosen that reflect the inherently abstract nature of the construct.

Cumulative satisfaction should thus be operationalized as a latent variable or index using a variety of proxies. Specifically, measures that evaluate or compare performance relative to the different standards that customers use in the course of their purchase and consumption experience provide good reflective measures of latent satisfaction. Fornell (1992) uses three measures of satisfaction in the Swedish Customer Satisfaction Barometer (SCSB): overall satisfaction, confirmation of expectations, and the product's distance from the customer's hypothetical ideal product in the category. These same satisfaction measures are being used in the American Customer Satisfaction Index (ACSI) which is being developed by the National Quality Research Center at the University of Michigan. These measures offer different angles from which customers may express satisfaction. The satisfaction index is itself embedded in a system of cause and effect relationships where expectations and perceived performance affect satisfaction while satisfaction, in turn, affects complaining behavior or "voice" and loyalty or "exit." Importantly, this latent satisfaction index only extracts that portion of the disconfirmation ratings, satisfaction ratings, and ideal point ratings which all three measures have in common and which predicts customer behavior (Johnson and Fornell 1991).

One implication is that the satisfaction index is not confounded by either disconfirmation or performance. It is only the psychological difference between performance and expectations and between performance and the customer's ideal that are used as reflective measures of satisfaction. Another implication is that antecedent measures within a transaction or occasion specific view of satisfaction can be used to provide multiple indicators of cumulative satisfaction. On any given occasion, for example, expectancy-disconfirmation ratings and/or comparisons to an ideal product or service in a category are logical antecedent to satisfaction (Boulding et al. 1993). Across occasions, however, a broader, more abstract satisfaction construct is partially reflected in a subject's rating of performance versus expectations, performance versus their ideal, and overall satisfaction. Operationalizing satisfaction as an index based on the shared variance among these measures is thus consistent with a cumulative view of the satisfaction construct. Naturally, there is a trade-off inherent in this approach. Individual level process details are lost in favor of an approach that balances description *and* prediction.

Aggregation Over Subjects

Finally, aggregation over subjects is particularly interesting and relevant to customer satisfaction research. Averaging responses over a large sample of subjects increases the stability of findings and their generality. Epstein views aggregation over subjects as common practice in psychological research with proven value. Despite early research by Pfaff (1977; Lingoes and Pfaff 1972), this aggregation has only recently reemerged in customer satisfaction research.

Research on the "time series - cross section paradox" illustrates the value of aggregate level analyses (Adams 1965; Bouwen 1977; Katona 1979). This research examines the ability of consumers' attitudes toward the economy, as expressed in consumer confidence measures, to predict subsequent purchase behavior. Aggregate analyses show a clear attitude-behavior relationship; the more optimistic (pessimistic) customers are as a whole regarding economic conditions, the more likely they are to increase (decrease) their subsequent spending on major durables. Analogous relationships do not emerge from individual level data, where stated buying plans, not attitudes, predict individual purchase behavior.

Bouwen's (1977) study provides insight into this paradox. He introduced two important individual level variables that serve to either mediate or mask the attitude-behavior relationship in this context. One is the consumer's own base-level of optimism-pessimism toward the economy which must be controlled for. The other is the consumer's future time orientation, or the degree to which they plan their purchases into the future. Bouwen predicted an attitude-behavior relationship for those consumers with a future time orientation, controlling for individual differences in optimism-pessimism. His results reveal that a relationship between attitudes and behavior does emerge from individual level data once these variables are introduced. These results are important in that they support the argument that the predictive effect of attitudes observed in aggregate data has a parallel at the individual consumer level which is obscured by individual differences. Katona (1979) concludes that understanding the influence of attitudes on behavior is much simpler when studied in the aggregate where individual differences are often self-canceling random factors. With respect to satisfaction, another advantage of aggregating over subjects is the ability to focus on market segment level data and phenomena. Managers, product planners, and development teams typically focus on entire markets or market segments when making decisions that affect customer satisfaction.

One should not conclude that individual level studies should be replaced by aggregate studies. Rather, the discussion and research described here illustrates the value of augmenting existing individual level studies with studies based on aggregates. As Wärneryd (1988) observes, understanding what is possible is a prerequisite for prediction. Individual level studies provide a rich description of the types of phenomena that are *possible*. Aggregate level studies help us understand what is *probable*. It is also important to note that aggregating over individuals may be problematic unless one also aggregates over situations and/or occasions. As more subjects are aggregated into more and more reliable variable means, smaller differences are needed to find a statistically significant result. Minute, incidental differences may emerge that are specific to a particular situation or occasion. The implication for satisfaction research is straightforward. Aggregation over individuals is more valuable when satisfaction is defined and operationalized as cumulative (across occasions) rather than transaction specific (within a particular occasion). Otherwise, a highly context dependent result may appear to be more general than it actually is.

Emerging Generalizations

Recent studies using the SCSB data (Anderson, Fornell and Lehmann 1994; Fornell and Johnson 1993; Johnson, Anderson and Fornell 1995) illustrate the application of the four faces of aggregation to customer satisfaction. These studies examine market segment (firm) level satisfaction (aggregation over individuals). Satisfaction is defined, and measured, as cumulative in nature. Customers are asked to reflect back over their recent experiences when assessing performance and satisfaction rather than focus on a particular product or service encounter (aggregation over occasions). The analyses cut across a wide range of product-oriented to service-oriented industries (aggregation over stimuli). Finally, satisfaction is an index composed of a broad-based set of multiple measures (aggregation over measures).

Fornell and Johnson (1993) examined the effects of differentiation on satisfaction across industries. Differentiation, or the degree to which customers choose among predictably different options in an industry, is shown to have very systematic effects on aggregate expectations, perceptions of performance, and subsequent satisfaction. As differentiation increases, perceived performance increases which, in turn, increases aggregate satisfaction. Differentiation also increases customers' aggregate expected level of performance in an industry. Following Van Raaij (1989) and Katona (1979), these increased expectations have a separate positive effect on aggregate satisfaction. Overall the study supports the generalizability of basic marketing principles. That is, when a heterogeneous population of customers has a wider variety of predictably different options to choose from, satisfaction increases.

Anderson, Fornell and Lehmann (1994) focus on the recent debate regarding the financial payoff from increasing quality and satisfaction. As satisfaction increases, customer retention should increase thereby reducing one's marketing costs and increasing revenues. Thus satisfaction should increase profitability. Using ROA (return on asset) data in combination with the SCSB, their findings support a positive impact of customer satisfaction on profitability. Their results also call into question the traditional assumption that market share and profitability are positively related. In fact, they find a negative relationship; increasing market share may actually decrease satisfaction suggesting that they are not necessarily compatible goals.

In the third study, Johnson, Anderson and Fornell (1995) used the aggregate data to test alternative models of market level expectations, perceived performance, and customer satisfaction. The authors argued that aggregate performance expectations, like price expectations, should be largely rational in nature. Unlike price expectations, however, these performance expectations should remain adaptive to changing market conditions. Performance information is revealed over a longer time period than is price information making the aggregate performance expectations more adaptive. Their results support the adaptive nature of performance expectations. They also show that market level satisfaction, expectations, and perceived performance are relatively stable constructs over time.

Overall these studies suggest that an aggregate level of analysis provides a number of emerging generalizations. Providing a heterogeneous population of customers with a variety of predictably different options increases satisfaction. Because it is more difficult to differentiate a service, service satisfaction is generally lower than product satisfaction. Satisfaction, in turn, has a significant positive impact on customer retention and profitability. Increasing satisfaction may also be inconsistent with a firm's market share goals. Finally, aggregate performance expectations are not completely "rational" in a strict economic sense. Rather, they remain adaptive as performance information is revealed over time.

There are several directions for future research using aggregates in this area. One is the study of cross cultural differences in satisfaction. National satisfaction indices are now in place in Sweden, Germany and the U.S. while indices are being developed in Taiwan and New Zealand. The degree to which similar industries show similar levels of satisfaction across these cultures will provide an interesting test of the degree to which industrial organization variables versus cultural differences drive aggregate satisfaction. A second research direction is to explore those industrial organization variables, beyond differentiation, that likely affect aggregate satisfaction. A third research direction is to study performance drivers across industries and cultures. Specifically, to what degree does "fitness for use" or customization of a product or service affect aggregate satisfaction versus its reliability, or "things gone wrong."

CONCLUSIONS

As interest in customer satisfaction research continues to grow, researchers face an important choice. Some will choose to conduct experimental studies focusing on individual subjects, events, stimuli, and/or measures. These studies will provide a level of detail that is essential to our understanding of the nature and antecedents of satisfaction. At the same time, these studies will not necessarily generate empirical generalizations. To do so, researchers should also study satisfaction from an aggregate perspective. Using Epstein's (1980) four faces of aggregation, this paper argues that aggregation over stimuli, occasions, measures, and individuals will help provide empirical generalizations in this area. Existing studies of aggregate satisfaction reveal a number of these emerging generalizations.

Yet the implications of aggregation stem far beyond empirical findings. Taking an aggregate perspective on satisfaction affects how we conduct satisfaction research, how we define satisfaction, and how we measure it. Aggregation entails a market level or macro-psychological perspective on satisfaction. This satisfaction is defined as customers' cumulative experience with a product or service to-date. This, in turn, requires researchers to take a broad view of the measures used to operationalize satisfaction as an inherently abstract construct on which different people and product categories may be compared.

REFERENCES

Adams, F. Gerard (1965), "Prediction with Consumer Attitudes: The Time Series - Cross Section Paradox," *The Review of Economics and Statistics*, 4, 367-378.

Ajzen, Icek and Martin Fishbein (1977), "Attitude-Behavior Relations: A Theoretical Analysis and Review of Empirical Research," *Psychological Bulletin*, 84, 888-918.

Anderson, Eugene W., Claes Fornell, and Donald R. Lehmann (1994), "Customer Satisfaction, Market Share, and Profitability: Findings from Sweden," *Journal of Marketing*, 58 (July), 53-66.

_____and Mary Sullivan (1993), "The Antecedents and Consequences of Customer Satisfaction for Firms," *Marketing Science*, 12 (Spring), 125-143.

Andreasen, Alan R. and Arthur Best (1977), "Consumers Complain - Does Business Respond?," *Harvard Business Review*, July-August 1977, 93-101.

Boulding, William, Richard Staelin, Ajay Kalra, and Valerie Zeithaml (1993), "A Dynamic Process Model of Service Quality: From Expectations to Behavioral Intentions," *Journal of Marketing Research*, 30 (February), 7-27.

Bouwen, René (1977), "Anticipation and Realization: Attitudes and Buying Plans in the Future Time Orientation of Consumer Behavior," *Psychologica Belica*, 17 (2), 113-134.

Brunswik, Egon (1947), *Systematic and Representative Design of Psychological Experiments*, Berkeley: University of California Press.

Campbell, Donald T. and Julian C. Stanley (1963), *Experimental and Quasi-Experimental Designs for Research*, Chicago: Rand McNally.

Churchill, Gilbert A. and Carol Surprenant (1982), "An Investigation into the Determinants of Customer Satisfaction," *Journal of Marketing Research*, 19 (November), 491-504.

Cronbach, Lee J. (1957), "The Two Disciplines of Scientific Psychology," *American Psychologist*, 12, 671-684.

_____(1975), "Beyond the Two Disciplines of Scientific Psychology," *American Psychologist*, 30, 116-127.

Cronin, J. Joseph, Jr. and Steven A. Taylor (1992), "Measuring Service Quality: A Reexamination and Extension," *Journal of Marketing*, 56 (July), 55-68.

Epstein, Seymour (1979), "The Stability of Behavior: I. On Predicting Most of the People Much of the Time," *Journal of Personality and Social Psychology*, 37, 1097-1126.

_____(1980), "The Stability of Behavior: II. Implications for Psychological Research," *American Psychologist*, 35 (9), 790-806.

Fornell, Claes (1992), "A National Customer Satisfaction Barometer: The Swedish Experience," *Journal of Marketing*, 56 (January), 6-21.

_____and Michael D. Johnson (1993), "Differentiation as a Basis for Explaining Customer Satisfaction Across Industries," *Journal of Economic Psychology*, 14 (4), 681-696.

Greenwald, Anthony G. (1976), "An Editorial," *Journal of Personality and social Psychology*, 33 (1), 1-7.

Grönroos, Christian (1984), "A Service Quality Model and Its Marketing Implications," *European Journal of Marketing*, 18 (1), 36-44.

Johnson, Michael D. (1984), "Consumer Choice Strategies for Comparing Noncomparable Alternatives," *Journal of Consumer Research*, 11 (December), 741-753.

_____, Eugene W. Anderson, and Claes Fornell (1995), "Rational and Adaptive Performance Expectations in a Customer Satisfaction Framework," *Journal of Consumer Research*, forthcoming.

_____and Claes Fornell (1991), "A Framework for Comparing Customer Satisfaction Across Individuals and Product Categories, *Journal of Economic Psychology*, 12 (2), 267-286.

Katona, George (1979), "Toward a Macropsychology," *American Psychologist*, 34 (2), 118-126.

Koch, Sigmund (1959), "Epilogue," in S. Koch (ed.), *Psychology: A Study of a Science*, Vol. 3, New York: McGraw Hill.

Lingoes, James C. and Martin Pfaff (1972), "The Index of Consumer Satisfaction: Methodology," in M. Venkatesan (ed.), *Association for Consumer Research: 3rd Annual Conference Proceedings*, 689-712.

Mischel, Walter (1968), *Personality and Assessment*, New York: John Wiley.

Oliver, Richard L. (1980), "A Cognitive Model of the Antecedents and Consequences of Satisfaction Decisions," *Journal of Marketing Research*, 17 (November), 460-469.

_____(1993), "Cognitive, Affective, and Attribute Bases of the Satisfaction Response," *Journal of Consumer Research*, 20 (December), 418-430.

Pfaff, Martin (1977), "The Index of Consumer Satisfaction: Measurement Problems and Opportunities," in H. Keith Hunt (ed.), *Conceptualization and Measurement of Consumer Satisfaction and Dissatisfaction*, Cambridge, MA: Marketing Science Institute, 36-71.

Smith, N. C., Jr. (1970), "Replication Studies: A Neglected Aspect of Psychological Research," *American Psychologist*, 25, 970-975.

Van Raaij, Fred (1989), "Economic News, Expectations, and Macro-Economic Behavior," *Journal of Economic Psychology*, 10 (4), 473-493.

Wärneryd, Karl-Erik (1988), "Economic Psychology as a Field of Study," in W. Fred Van Raaij, Gery M. Van Veldhoven, and Karl-Erik Wärneryd (eds.), *Handbook of Economic Psychology*, Dordrecht, The Netherlands: Kluwer Academic Publishers, 2-41.

Westbrook, Robert A. and Michael D. Reilly (1983), "Value-Percept Disparity: An Alternative to the Disconfirmation of Expectations Theory of Consumer Satisfaction," in Richard P. Bagozzi and Alice M. Tybout (eds.), *Advances in Consumer Research*, Vol. 10, Ann Arbor, MI: Association for Consumer Research, 256-261.

Yi, Youjae (1991), "A Critical Review of Customer Satisfaction," in V. A. Zeithaml (ed.), *Review of Marketing 1990*, Chicago: American Marketing Association.

Zeithaml, Valerie A., Leonard L. Berry, and A. Parasuraman (1988), "Communication and Control Processes in the Delivery of Service Quality," *Journal of Marketing*, 52 (April), 35-48.

The Relationship Between Customer Complaints to the Firm and Subsequent Exit Behavior

Ruth N. Bolton, GTE Laboratories Incorporated
Tina M. Bronkhorst, GTE Laboratories Incorporated

ABSTRACT

This paper investigates the influence of customers' complaints to a service firm with their subsequent decision to exit from a relationship with the firm. The context is a longitudinal study of cellular communications customers' behavior. The study shows that overall satisfaction with a firm and customer complaint behavior are related to exit behavior. Furthermore, companies should strive to "get it right the first time" because the firm may not always be able to appease a complaining customer.

As part of a defensive marketing strategy, complaint management is designed to minimize turnover (Fornell and Wernerfelt 1987). Complaint management entails finding and correcting systemic causes of dissatisfaction rather than simply placating unhappy customers. Although there is a vast literature on customer complaining behavior, surprisingly few studies have investigated the relationship between customer complaints and turnover. This paper investigates the influence of customers' complaints on their subsequent decision to exit from a relationship with a firm.

BACKGROUND

Customer complaining behavior (CCB) has been defined as "a multiple set of behavioral and non–behavioral responses triggered by a dissatisfactory purchase episode" (Singh 1988, p. 94). A substantial body of research has focused on the nature and classification of these responses. Hirschman (1970) classified customers' responses to dissatisfaction as exit, voice or loyalty. In buyer–seller relationships, a customer may *exit* from a relationship with a firm by switching brands or service providers, or by reducing consumption levels. He/she may *voice* complaints to friends, third–party organizations (e.g., Better Business Bureau) or sellers (i.e., retailers or manufacturers). Lastly, a customer may choose *not* to act, thereby remaining *loyal*. In subsequent studies, market researchers have extended this classification scheme. For example, they have developed typologies that differentiate between public and private voice (Day and Landon 1977) and that discriminate among the objects toward which the response was directed (Singh 1988). A recent experiment provides empirical support for the validity and usefulness of Hirschman's taxonomy (Maute and Forrester 1993).

There is a vast—albeit fragmented—literature on voice responses (e.g., Strahle and Day 1985). In fact, Andreason (1988) estimates that there are over 500 studies on predictors of CCB responses—that is, studies investigating the dual questions of which customers complain and why. Several empirical studies have shown that customer dis/satisfaction is related to customer complaining behavior (Bearden and Teel 1983; Oliver 1980; Olshavsky and Miller 1972). Mediating variables include causal attributions about the service failure, attitudes and demographics, the costs and benefits of complaining frequency of interactions, the product/service context, and situational factors (Andreason 1977; Day and Landon 1977; Folkes 1984a; 1984b; Fornell and Didow 1980).

This paper investigates the relationship between voice and exit responses, focusing on complaints to the seller. Although voice and exit responses are frequently considered to be substitute responses to dissatisfaction, they may actually be complements. However, few studies have examined their relationship. In a notable excep-

tion, Solnick and Hemenway (1992) found that customers who register medical complaints are four and a half times more likely to leave their Health Maintenance Organization than customers who do not complain. Furthermore, in an early study, Gilly and Gelb (1982) established that customers who were more satisfied with the firm's response to their complaints were more likely to repurchase, and tended to have slightly higher re–purchase levels.

PROPOSITIONS

This study focuses on three facets of the relationship between complaints and exit behavior. First, it examines the relationship between the incidence of customer complaints and subsequent exit behavior. Then, it investigates how the nature of customer complaints mediates this relationship. Last, it looks at the potentially ameliorating effect of sellers' attempts at redress.

Complaints and Exit Behavior

By definition, CCB arises from product/service dissatisfaction. Prior studies have found that higher levels of dissatisfaction with the firm are associated with increased brand switching behavior (LaBarbera and Mazursky 1983) and exit intentions (Maute and Forrester 1993). However, there is little research relating customer dis/satisfaction to actual behavioral measures. Hence, our first proposition concerns the relationship between satisfaction and exit behavior.

P1: *Customers who have lower levels of overall satisfaction with the firm are more likely to exit.*

As discussed earlier, there is a paucity of studies about the relationship between voice and exit responses (Andreason 1985). However, Solnick and Hemenway (1992) found that patients who register medical complaints are four and a half times more likely to voluntarily exit from a Health Maintenance Organization.

P2a: *Customers who complain are more likely to exit than customers who do not complain.*

Although it is seldom discussed, an alternative form of exit behavior is a reduction in consumption levels. This behavior is particularly likely in monopoly conditions.

P2b: *Customers who complain will show a decrease in consumption levels relative to customers who did not complain.*

The Nature of Customer Complaints

In a study of credit card purchases by major oil company customers, Gilly and Gelb (1982) found that complainants are more likely to be satisfied by the company's response to monetary problems, and they are more satisfied if the percent received is higher. Thus, we might expect that they are less likely to exit.

P3: *Customers who complain about monetary loss (e.g., billing errors) are (a) more likely to be satisfied with the firm's response and (b) less likely to exit than customers who complain about other problems.*

Advances in Consumer Research
Volume 22, © 1995

Prior research has shown that customers' attributions about the stability, locus and controllability of product failure are useful in predicting expectancy reactions, marketplace equity reactions and anger reactions (Folkes 1984b). These effects should influence customers' satisfaction with sellers' efforts at redress. Customers should be less satisfied with sellers' redress of problems that are firm–related (i.e., the locus of the cause is within the firm) and when the firm has control over the reason for the product failure. Hence, they should be more likely to exit.

P4: *Customers who complain about problems that are firm related and within the firm's control are: (a) less likely to be satisfied with the firm's response and (b) more likely to exit than customers who complain about other problems.*

The Effect of Sellers' Attempts to Redress Complaints

From the standpoint of the firm, attempts at redress are designed to reduce the likelihood that a customer will exit. A variety of studies have investigated how the sellers' responsiveness to complaints affects complainants' satisfaction, perceptions of fairness, and so forth (e.g., e.g., Goodwin and Ross 1992; Smart and Martin 1992). There is less evidence about how sellers' redress efforts affect exit behavior. However, Gilly and Gelb (1982) found that the higher the degree of satisfaction with organization complaint response, the greater the likelihood of brand re–purchase. This finding may extend to other products.

P5: *The higher the degree of satisfaction with the firm's response to a complaint, the greater the likelihood that the customer does not exit.*

STUDY DESIGN

This study investigates customer voice and exit behavior in the rapidly growing cellular communications industry. Although customers have a month–to–month subscription relationship with their cellular provider, over 30% of the typical cellular providers' customers exit—either switching providers or discontinuing cellular usage—each year (Steuernagel 1992). Hence, the cellular industry provides a particularly appropriate context for an investigation of voice and exit responses.

In the customer complaint literature, studies have typically measured complaint *intentions* and re–purchase *intentions*. In contrast, this study measures actual complaint behavior and subsequent exit behavior by tracking customers who subscribe to cellular service from a large firm over an 18 month period. During January through March 1992, a probability sample of 3361 customers (who had subscribed for three months or more) were interviewed using a standard customer satisfaction survey questionnaire. (This survey is administered by a commercial market research supplier each quarter.) Selected items from the questionnaire are displayed in Exhibit 1. These data were merged with company billing records that capture customers' *subsequent* consumption behavior and exit behavior for the period January 1992 through August 1993.

Customer Satisfaction and Complaints. As shown in Exhibit 1, customers were asked to rate their overall satisfaction with the firm's service, to report their perceptions of any calls they made to customer service centers in the past three months, and to provide demographic information. Customer complaints were identified from a survey question about the purpose of calls to customer service centers (Q9h) administered prior to any decision to stay loyal or exit from the firm. "A question regarding your bill," "a problem with your cellular service," "a problem with your phone equipment," and "a problem with roaming" were categorized as complaints. Since billing questions typically involve queries about the accuracy/appropriateness of charges, it was assumed that billing questions were problems/complaints.

Customer Exit Behavior. Between January 1992 and August 1993, the company tracked these 3361 customers to determine whether (and when) they subsequently cancelled service. In addition, each customer's monthly billing records measured consumption levels by average minutes of use per month.

RESULTS

Complaints and Exit Behavior

To investigate the first two propositions, data from two groups were compared: customers who exited and customers who did not (i.e., customers who remained "loyal.") The relevant data are shown in Tables 1 and 2.

P1: *Customers who have lower levels of overall satisfaction with the firm are more likely to exit.*

To examine P1, the distributions of responses to the overall satisfaction question (Q1) for the two groups were compared using a chi–square test. The results indicate that we should reject the null hypothesis that there is no difference between the groups (χ^2=33.03, p<.001). For example, 83.1% of customers who were "very satisfied" subsequently remained loyal; whereas, 37.0% of customers that were "very dissatisfied" subsequently exited.

P2a: *Customers who complain are more likely to exit than customers who do not complain.*
P2b: *Customers who complain will show a decrease in consumption levels relative to customers who did not complain.*

The two groups' exit behavior were compared with a chi–square test. As shown in Table 2a, the results indicate that there is a significant difference between the groups (χ^2=7.16, p<.01). Customers who complained were more likely to have subsequently exited than customers who did not complain. This result supports P2a. The differences in the two groups' change in consumption levels were compared in the following way. As shown in Exhibit 1, customers' survey responses indicated whether they had called customer service "in the past three months." Since the interviews took place in January through March 1992, the time period during which the complaint was registered ("the past three months") roughly corresponds to the November 1991 through January 1992. The time period after which the complaint was registered roughly corresponds to March through May 1992. Hence, each customers' average monthly minutes of use was computed for the periods roughly "during" the complaint was registered and "after" the complaint was registered. Then, the difference between these two consumption levels was calculated for each customer. Average consumption levels decreased for both complaining and non–complaining customers due to seasonality. More importantly, the null hypothesis that the average change in the consumption levels of the two groups is equal could not be rejected (p=0.39). However, the direction of the effects is consistent with our proposition. As shown in Table 2b, complainants show an average decrease of 15 minutes/month whereas non–complainants show a decrease of only 11 minutes/month. In conjunction with P2a, these results suggest that cellular customers' complaints are more likely to be followed by cancellation of service than by reduced consumption levels.

EXHIBIT 1
Survey and Billing Items

1. Overall, how satisfied are you with the quality of services you receive from Company X? Are you (5) very satisfied, (4) somewhat satisfied, (3) neither satisfied nor dissatisfied, (4) somewhat dissatisfied, or (5) very dissatisfied?

9. Have you personally called Company X's customer service in the last three months?
   (Yes/No)

9c. Overall, how satisfied were you with the representative you spoke with? (Very satisfied . . . very dissatisfied)

9h. Generally, what was the purpose for this call? Verbatims coded as follows:

   A general question about your cellular service
   *A question regarding your bill
   *A problem with your cellular service
   *A problem with your phone equipment
   A change in service you requested
   A general question about your phone equipment
   A sales/marketing contact from XXX
   A question/information about roaming
   *A problem with roaming
   Other
   Don't Remember

15. Classification questions: age, education, income.

* Categorized as a customer complaint for analysis purposes.

TABLE 1
Overall Satisfaction with Firm and Exit Behavior

	Very Dissatisfied	Somewhat Dissatisfied	Neither	Somewhat Satisfied	Very Satisfied
No Exit	63.0%	71.5%	79.5%	79.3%	83.1%
Exit	37.0	28.5	20.5	20.7	16.9
Obs'ns	73	186	117	1155	1803

TABLE 2A
Customer Complaining Behavior versus Exit Behavior

	Voiced Complaint to Firm	Did Not Voice Complaint
No Exit	76.6%	81.3%
Exit	23.4	18.7
Observations	625	2736

TABLE 2B
Customer Complaining Behavior versus Minutes of Cellular Use

	Voiced Complaint to Firm	Did Not Voice Complaint
Change in Average Minutes of Use	−15.5%	−11.5%
Standard Error	1.9	5.0
Observations	610	2713

TABLE 3A
Billing Complaints versus Satisfaction with the Service Representative

	Very Dissatisfied	Somewhat Dissatisfied	Neither	Somewhat Satisfied	Very Satisfied	Obs'ns
Billing Complaints	9.2%	8.1%	4.0%	21.0%	57.8%	348
Other Complaints	10.3	4.4	1.8	19.1	64.4	273

TABLE 3B
Exit Behavior versus Billing Complaints

	Billing Complaints	Other Complaints
No Exit	78.8%	73.9%
Exit	21.2	26.1
Observations	349	276

This finding is not entirely surprising because customers can usually subscribe to service from another provider.

The Nature of Customer Complaints

Cellular customers may complain about three types of problems: billing, service and equipment problems. To investigate P3 and P4, we compare these different categories of complaints.

P3: *Customers who complain about monetary loss (e.g., billing errors) are: (a) more likely to be satisfied with the firm's response and (b) less likely to exit than customers who complain about other problems.*

This proposition is investigated by comparing the responses of customers who reported billing complaints to customers who reported other types of complaints. The null hypothesis that the two groups' satisfaction with the firm's handling of the complaint are equivalent is tested using their ratings of the customer service representative (Q9c). The data in Table 3a indicate that the null hypothesis cannot be rejected; there is no difference between the groups (χ^2=7.16, p<.15). In fact, 57.8% of respondents with a billing complaint were "very satisfied" with the service representa-

tive whereas 64.5% of respondents with other complaints were "very satisfied." This finding is inconsistent with P3a.

To examine P3b, the two groups' exit behavior is compared. As indicated in Table 3b, the null hypothesis that there is no difference between the groups cannot be rejected (χ^2=2.05, p<.15). However, customers who call with billing complaints tend to have slightly lower exit levels than customers who call about other problems. Considering the results from P3a and P3b together, customers seem to rate the firm's handling of billing problems as no better or worse than their handling of other problems. Hence, even though they typically receive adjustments from their bill, they are no more likely to cancel.

P4: *Customers who complain about problems that can be attributed to the firm and are within the firm's control are: (a) less likely to be satisfied with the firm's response and (b) more likely to exit than customers who complain about other problems.*

Since the cellular provider does not manufacture or sell equipment, customers are unlikely to attribute equipment problems to the firm, or to believe that these problems are within the control

TABLE 4A

Service Complaints versus Satisfaction with the Service Representative

	Very Dissatisfied	Somewhat Dissatisfied	Neither	Somewhat Satisfied	Very Satisfied	Obs'ns
Service Complaints	13.6%	5.1%	2.5%	21.2%	57.6%	503
Other Complaints	8.8	6.8	3.2	19.9	61.4	120

TABLE 4B

Exit Behavior versus Service Complaints

	Service Complaints	Other Complaints
No Exit	68.3%	78.6%
Exit	31.7	21.4
Observations	120	505

TABLE 5

Satisfaction with Service Representative versus Exit Behavior

	Very Dissatisfied	Somewhat Dissatisfied	Neither	Somewhat Satisfied	Very Satisfied
No Exit	75.0%	87.5%	79.0%	72.0%	77.7%
Exit	25.0	12.5	21.0	28.0	22.3
Observations	6	40	19	125	377

of the firm. However, service problems (e.g., dropped calls, static on the line) should be attributed to the firm and are within the firm's control. Hence, this hypothesis is investigated by comparing the responses of customers who reported service problems to customers who did not report service problems. As shown Table 4a, the null hypothesis that there are no differences between the groups cannot be rejected (χ^2=3.14, p= 0.534). Customers who complain about service problems have equivalent satisfaction levels to customers who complain about other problems.

To investigate P4b, the two groups' exit behavior is compared. The null hypothesis is rejected (χ^2= 5.72, p<0.02). Customers who complain about service problems are more likely to exit than customers who complain about billing or equipment problems. This result is intuitively appealing because these problems concern the "core service" of the firm.

The Effects of Seller's Attempt to Redress Complaints

To investigate the effects of the firm's handling of complaints, we examine the customer's perception of the sales representative (Q9c).

P5: *The higher the degree of satisfaction with the firm's response to a complaint, the greater the likelihood that the customer does not exit.*

As shown in Table 5, the null hypothesis that satisfaction with complaint handling and subsequent exit behavior are independent cannot be rejected (χ^2=4.54, p=0.338). Satisfaction levels for the service representative do not differ significantly between customers who exit and customer who remain loyal. This result demonstrates that the service representative cannot entirely forestall exit behavior by customers who have made a complaint.

DISCUSSION

This study shows a significant relationship between customer's overall dis/satisfaction with service and subsequent exit behavior. Customers who are generally dissatisfied with service are more likely to exit. Many companies regularly survey their customers and measure satisfaction levels across different operating units or geographic areas. These firms can target marketing and quality improvement programs at customer groups that report lower satisfaction levels, thereby maintaining the existing customer base, and potentially increasing profits. These profit increases may be substantial. In the cellular industry, for example, it is estimated to cost $600 to acquire a new customer and only $20 to *retain* an existing one (Steuernagel 1992). Consequently, it is far more profitable to retain existing customers than "replace" them.

Customers who contact a service company to voice a complaint are more likely to exit. This finding highlights the complementary nature of voice and exit behavior. Many companies believe that appropriate complaint handling can help them "recover" from customer complaints and retain customers. However, this study suggests that redress efforts are not always effective. Since redressing complaints to the customer's satisfaction is difficult the firm should "Get it right the first time" (Albrecht and Bradford 1990, p.101).

Unlike prior research, this study considered two forms of exit behavior: severance of the relationship with the firm (i.e., cancelling service) and a reduction in consumption levels (i.e., decreased minutes of cellular service use). Although customer complaints were not associated with significantly greater decreases in consumption levels, the direction of the effect was consistent with P2b. This finding is sufficiently interesting to warrant further investigation. Since the date of the complaint was unavailable, this study measured consumption levels before and after the customer's retrospective report of the complaint. In future research, it would be useful to examine consumption levels before and after the time that the complaint was registered at the firm.

Customers exit behavior varies depending on the nature of the complaint. When a disruption in core service is the source of the complaint, customers become dissatisfied and more likely to cancel. Customer expectations of ancillary services seem to be viewed less critically. Customers who report billing complaints do have slightly lower levels of exit (P3b).

The finding that customers who complained about service problems are more likely to exit than customers who complained about other (e.g., equipment) problems provides support for an attribution-based approach complaining behavior. Although this study does not measure attributions, customers are found to be more likely to exit due to problems that can be categorized as firm-related and within the firm's control. This result is consistent with studies of customer satisfaction and service quality (e.g., Bitner 1990). For example, Bolton and Drew (1994) found that satisfaction with a repair process depended on locus of responsibility for the problem (firm versus customer), and whether the problem was within the firm's control (i.e., non-equipment problems).

A firm's response to a complaint may not make up for the fact that a customer has been dissatisfied enough to voice a problem. Our investigation of P3a, P4a, and P5 all demonstrate that the service representative cannot necessarily "recover" from a complaint. Tables 3a and 4a both show more than 70% of respondents reporting that they were either "somewhat" or "very satisfied" with the service representative. As shown in Table 3a, customers are slightly more dissatisfied with firm's response to complaints regarding monetary loss than other types of complaints. Either service representatives are not be able to adequately address billing complaints, or customers may expect that the billing process should be "seamless" and resent billing errors and difficulties understanding the bill.

Managers may be somewhat surprised to find that, even when customers report that they are "very satisfied" with the customer service representative, they may still choose to exit (P5). There are two possible reasons for this result. First, not all complaints can be resolved by customer service representatives. Customers may perceive that the representative was courteous, knowledgeable and

helpful; yet ultimately, the firm may have been unable to redress the underlying problem. For example, certain intermittent but recurring problems (e.g., static on the line for a cellular communications provider) may be very difficult to resolve. Second, even if a complaint is satisfactorily resolved by the firm—possibly including monetary compensation for the disruption in service—the customer will not necessarily be satisfied with overall service. From the customer's standpoint, it would be preferable if there had not been a disruption in the first place. Again, there is support for this notion in the literature on customer satisfaction and service quality (Bolton and Drew 1992).

CONCLUDING REMARKS

Despite considerable research on customer complaining behavior, few studies have examined the relationship between customer complaint and exit behavior. Even fewer studies have examined actual behavior, rather than intentions. The results from this study suggest that voice and exit behaviors are complementary. The study shows that overall dis/satisfaction with a firm is related to exit behavior. For this cellular provider, efforts to redress customer complaints are not sufficient to forestall exit behavior. This finding is indicative of an inadequate complaint resolution processes, and may not necessarily generalize to all firms. For example, as earlier studies have shown, some industries are characterized by factors such as high switching costs that impede exit behavior in the short run. However, this study also shows that exit behavior is likely to follow a complaint—*even when the complaint is handled satisfactorily*. Thus, even firms with highly rated complaint handling processes should be concerned about forestalling complaints.

In this study, complainants show an average decrease of 15 minutes/month, whereas non-complainants show an 11 minute/month decrease. The difference is not statistically significant. However, in the cellular industry, there are frequently two providers in a market and switching costs are relatively low, so that customers may choose to exit rather than reduce consumption. Nevertheless, the relationship between complaint behavior and consumption levels is worthy of further study in other industries. Consumption levels are directly tied into a corporation's profits, and this "alternative" form of exit behavior could be a costly problem. Many service companies collect consumption data for billing purposes, enabling them to study this issue. Such efforts would be an important step in understanding the costs and benefits of complaint management.

In the customer satisfaction and service quality literature, researchers have begun to developed sophisticated multivariate models that relate these constructs to their antecedents (e.g., Bitner 1990; Bolton and Drew 1992). A similar effort is required in the customer complaining literature. The natural extension of the work reported in this paper is a multivariate model of the relationship between customer complaints and exit behavior, and their antecedents.

REFERENCES

Albrecht, Karl and Laurence J. Bradford (1990), *The Service Advantage*, Homewood, Illinois: Dow Jones–Irwin.

Andreason, Alan R. (1977), "A Taxonomy of Consumer Satisfaction /Dissatisfaction Measures," *Journal of Consumer Affairs*, 11 (Winter), p. 11–24.

_____(1988), "Consumer Complaints and Redress: What We Know and What We Don't Know," in *The Frontier of Research in the Consumer Interest*, E. Scott Maynes et al, eds., Columbia, MO: American Council on Consumer Interests, 675–722.

Bearden, William O. and Jesse E. Teel (1983), "Selected Determinants of Consumer Satisfaction and Complaint Reports," *Journal of Marketing Research*, 20 (February), 21–8.

Bitner, M. J. (1990). "Evaluating Service Encounters: The Effects of Physical Surrounding and Employee Responses," *Journal of Marketing*, 54 (2), 69–82.

Bolton, Ruth N. and James H. Drew (1994), "Linking Customer Satisfaction to Service Operations and Outcomes," *Service Quality: New Directions in Theory and Practice*, Roland T. Rust and Richard L. Oliver, eds., 173–200.

———and ———(1992), "Mitigating the Effect of Service Encounters," *Marketing Letters*, 3 (1), 57–70.

Day, Ralph L. (1980), "Research Perspective on Consumer Complaining Behavior," in *Theoretical Developments in Marketing*, C. W. Lamb and P. M. Dunne, eds. Chicago: American Marketing Association, 211–15.

———and E. Laird Landon, Jr. (1977), "Toward a Theory of Consumer Complaining Behavior," in *Consumer and Industrial Buying Behavior*, Arch G. Woodside, Jagdish Sheth and Peter Bennnet, eds., New York, NY: Elsevier–North Holland, 425–437.

Folkes, Valerie S. (1984a), "An Attributional Approach to Postpurchase Conflict Between Buyers and Sellers," in *Advances in Consumer Research*, 11, Thomas C. Kinnear, ed. Ann Arbor, MI: Association for Consumer Resarch, 500–503.

———(1984b), "Consumer Reactions to Product Failure: An Attributional Approach," *Journal of Consumer Research*, 10 (4), 398–409.

Fornell, Claes and Nicholas M. Didow (1980), "Economic Constrains on Consumer Complaining Behavior," in *Advances in Consumer Research*, 7, J. C. Olsen, ed., Miami, FL: Association for Consumer Research 318–23.

———and Birger Wernerfelt (1987), "Defensive Marketing Strategy by Customer Complaint Management: A Theoretical Analysis," *Journal of Marketing Research*, 24 (November), 337–46.

Gilly, Mary C. and Betsy D. Gelb (1982), "Post–Purchase Consumer Processes and the Complaining Consumer," *Journal of Consumer Research*, 9 (December), 323–328.

Goodwin, Cathy and Ivan Ross (1992), "Consumer Responses to Service Failures: Influence of Procedural and Interactional Fairness Perceptions," *Journal of Business Research*, 25, 149–63.

Hirschman, Albert O. (1970), *Exit, Voice and Loyalty*. Cambridge, MA: Harvard University Press.

LaBarbera, Priscilla A. and David Mazursky (1983), "A Longitudinal Assessment of Consumer Satisfaction/ Dissatisfaction: The Dynamic Aspect of the Cognitive Process," *Journal of Marketing Research*, 20 (November), 393–404.

Maute, Manfred F. and William R. Forrester, Jr. (1993), "The Structure and Determinants of Consumer Complaint Intentions and Behavior," *Journal of Economic Psychology*, 14, 219–47.

Oliver, Richard (1980), "A Cognitive Model of the Antecedents and Consequences of Satisfaction Decisions, *Journal of Marketing Research*, 17, 460–9.

Olshavsky, Richard and John A. Miller (1972), "Consumer Expectations, Product Performance and Perceived Product Quality," *Journal of Marketing Research*, 9, 19–21.

Singh, Jagdip (1988), "Consumer Complaint Intentions and Behavior: Definitional and Taxonomical Issues," *Journal of Marketing*, 52(January), 93–107.

———(1990), "Voice, Exit and Negative Word–of–Mouth Behaviors: An Investigation Across Three Service Categories," *Journal of the Academy of Marketing Science*, 19 (Winter), 1–15.

Smart, Denise T. and Charles L. Martin (1992), "Manufacturer Responsiveness to Consumer Correspondence: An Empirical Investigation of Consumer Perceptions," *Journal of Consumer Affairs*, 26, 104–128.

Solnick, Sara J. and David Hemenway (1992), "Complaints and Disenrollment at a Health Maintenance Organization," *Journal of Consumer Affairs*, 26 (1), 90–103.

Steuernagel, Robert A. (1992), "Limits to Growth," *Cellular Business* (July), 26–29.

A Contingency Framework for Predicting Causality Between Customer Satisfaction and Service Quality

Pratibha A. Dabholkar, University of Tennessee

ABSTRACT

There is extensive literature on customer satisfaction and service quality, but little investigation of the causal sequence between these two constructs. Past models of this sequence are based on unique conceptualizations of the constructs with little agreement on the issue. A contingency framework is presented wherein different causal sequences between customer satisfaction and service quality occur under different service situations. By examining the determinants of causality between satisfaction and quality, the framework enhances our understanding of the customer evaluation process. Furthermore, the different contingency-related sequences discussed in the framework are predicted to have varying effects on future customer behavior, thus being of critical interest to practitioners. An agenda for future research on causality between satisfaction and quality and its impact on customer behavior is outlined. Strategic implications for service design and employee training are suggested.

INTRODUCTION

Businesses today are well aware that they must satisfy customers and offer quality services in order to be competitively viable. For several years now service firms have been measuring customer satisfaction and service quality to gauge how well they are meeting customer needs. It is interesting that these measures of customer satisfaction and service quality are often used interchangeably (Cooper, Cooper, and Duhan 1989) indicating that practitioners may not see much difference between the two constructs. Consequently, there has been little discussion or research on the causal link between the constructs. Recently, however, researchers have suggested that the direction of the relationship between customer satisfaction and service quality be explored in order to increase our understanding of service evaluation processes used by customers (Bolton and Drew 1991; Cronin and Taylor 1992).

Some researchers (e.g., Iacobucci, Grayson, and Ostrum 1994) suggest that causality between customer satisfaction and service quality may be relevant only for an understanding of the consumer's evaluation but not necessarily for managerial considerations. It is true that practitioners are mainly concerned about customer satisfaction and service quality as *predictors* of customer behavior (Reichheld 1993) and not about the constructs themselves. This is certainly understandable; it is customer behavior, such as repeat purchase and word-of-mouth, that directly affects the viability and profitability of the firm. However, if the direction of the causal link between customer satisfaction and service quality were to lead to different customer behavior outcomes, this issue would have considerable managerial relevance in addition to enhancing our understanding of the process of customer evaluation.

The purpose of this paper is to propose a contingency framework where the causal link between customer satisfaction and service quality varies for each contingency and where it impacts customer behavior in different ways based on the causality. Such a framework would allow us to gain a deeper understanding of how customers evaluate services and to predict the type of evaluation processes that would lead to repeat purchases and customer loyalty.

BACKGROUND

There has been much recent debate regarding the overlap between the customer satisfaction and service quality constructs at the conceptual level and in terms of measurement (e.g., Bitner and Hubbert 1994; Dabholkar 1993; Iacobucci, Grayson, and Ostrom 1994; Parasuraman, Zeithaml, and Berry 1994; Spreng and Singh 1993). Researchers have proposed different conceptualizations of the two constructs and their relationship to each other. Most of these proposed relationships are dependent on the definitions of the constructs themselves. For example, some researchers (Bitner 1990; Oliver 1981; Parasuraman, Zeithaml, and Berry 1988) visualize customer satisfaction as experiential or occurring at the transactional level and service quality as an attitude at the global level; thus, they propose a causal link from customer satisfaction to service quality. Other researchers (Bolton and Drew 1992; Drew and Bolton 1991) point out that customers can and do evaluate service quality at the transactional level and customer satisfaction may be quite meaningful at the global level; therefore, they propose a causal link from service quality to customer satisfaction. Still others (Anderson and Sullivan 1993; Oliver 1993) view service quality as one of the antecedents of customer satisfaction and propose a link from service quality to customer satisfaction.

At first glance it may appear that the prediction of causality between customer satisfaction and service quality is merely academic and based superficially on the conceptualization of satisfaction and quality. However, most of this literature may be quite consistent if it can be drawn into a broad contingency framework. It is proposed that different conceptualizations of customer satisfaction and service quality are related to different contingencies. An understanding of these contingencies should allow us to predict the causal link between customer satisfaction and service quality across situations and to study the influence of this directionality on customer behavior.

DEVELOPING A CONTINGENCY FRAMEWORK

Evaluations of a service may occur prior to experiencing the service (based on word-of-mouth and/or promotion), during and immediately after a service experience, or after several experiences with a given service. In general, if a customer has not experienced the service, s/he could express an evaluation of service quality (based entirely on word-of-mouth and/or promotion) but satisfaction would be impossible to evaluate without experience (see Oliver 1993). Thus, causality between the two constructs is irrelevant prior to experiencing the service. Similarly, after experiencing several instances of the service delivery, the customer would integrate his/her evaluations of the service across all these instances and form an overall evaluation of service quality which would be very similar to his/her overall satisfaction with the service and both would evolve simultaneously over time. Thus, causality between the two constructs at the global level is also not relevant. When it comes to the actual service encounter, however, evaluations of quality and satisfaction may occur in different ways for different situations and different people. Here, causality could be quite meaningful especially if it impacts future customer behavior in different ways. Thus, the contingency framework is developed with a focus on specific service encounters.

There appears to be agreement in the literature that the evaluation of service quality is mainly cognitive (Bitner 1990; Parasuraman, Zeithaml, and Berry 1988), while the evaluation of customer satisfaction is a combination of cognitive and affective elements (Mano and Oliver 1993; Woodruff, Cadotte, and Jenkins

TABLE 1
Contingency Framework for Predicting Causality between Customer Satisfaction (CS) and Service Quality (SQ)

	SQ ⟶ CS	CS ⟶ SQ
nature of service experience	little or no emotion aroused	strong emotion aroused
zone of indifference	experience within	experience outside
essential aspects of service	present	absent
service enhancers	absent	present
type of service	e.g., grocery shopping	e.g., hospital emergency room
type of customer	cognitive	emotional
customer's mood	somewhat neutral	very good or very bad

1983; Yi 1990). Some researchers suggest that customer satisfaction is in fact mainly affective (Oliver 1989; Westbrook 1987), which would be particularly true for service experiences. This difference between the two constructs can be used to predict different causal links for different service experiences. It is proposed that for service experiences where cognitions are formed first, the causal link will be from service quality to customer satisfaction, provided that some type of affect follows the initial cognitions. However, if there is little or no affect following the cognitions in relation to the experience, there will be an overlap between the two constructs. Finally, if there is a strong emotional reaction to the service, this will influence later cognitions about the service, and the causal link will be from customer satisfaction to service quality. Even if initial cognitions are formed in assessing discrepancies in the service that lead to emotional reactions, these cognitions will take second place to the strong emotional reaction that would influence later cognitions about the service.

For example, a customer goes to the store where the service is fairly good (or somewhat substandard) and no unforeseen circumstances arise. There is little chance in this situation for strong emotion. The customer may say to him/herself "the service wasn't bad (or wasn't too good)" and then begin to feel good (bad) about it. This would mean that the customer evaluated the service quality at the cognitive level and then experienced satisfaction at the affective level based on the cognitive evaluation of service quality. Or, the customer may not feel good (or bad) about the service and may merely note at the cognitive level that the service was okay (or not). If service quality and customer satisfaction were to be measured in such situations, there would be no discriminant validity between the two constructs and no causal sequence. Now, if the customer goes to a service provider where something happens to delight (or disgust) him/her, this customer will experience strong emotion which would form a significant part of his/her satisfaction with the service experience. For the customer who is delighted, even if the rest of the service was not quite up to standard, the delightful aspect and the associated emotion will color cognitions that are subsequently formed about the service. In the same way,

if everything had been proceeding fairly well, but something happens to upset the customer, s/he will experience strong emotion (perhaps anger) and this will influence later cognitions about the service. Various situations where the two possible causal sequences are likely to occur are presented in Table 1.

Zone of Indifference
If the customer's evaluation of the service is within an acceptable range called the zone of indifference (Erevelles and Leavitt 1992), the customer is unlikely to experience strong emotion and the causal link will be from service quality to customer satisfaction. If on the other hand, the customer's evaluation of the service falls outside the zone of indifference, emotional reactions (delight or anger) are more likely (Bloemer and Poiesz 1989) and the causal link will be from customer satisfaction to service quality.

Early definitions of customer satisfaction have included an element of surprise (Oliver 1981). Customers are likely to be surprised if the service experience falls outside the zone of indifference. As Spreng and Droge (1994) point out, surprise, itself, although often included in lists of emotional reactions (e.g., Izard 1977), is not an emotion given that it can be both positively and negatively valenced. It is a cognition that acts as an emotion intensifier (Ortony, Clore, and Collins 1988). Thus, it is surprise that gives rise to strong emotion when the evaluation of the service is outside the zone of indifference and creates a feeling of strong satisfaction or dissatisfaction with the service. If the customer is not surprised, this indicates that the experience was within the range acceptable to the customer, who should therefore be able to rationally and cognitively evaluate the quality of the service.

Essential Aspects versus Service Enhancers
All services have certain aspects that are essential to the service and others that are not essential but enhance the service experience (e.g., satisfiers versus dissatisfiers, Cadotte and Turgeon 1988; core versus peripheral (factors), Iacobucci et al. 1994). If the essential factors are present, they are often not even noticed.

Customers expect to get medical attention at the doctor's, to reach the intended destination when taking a flight, and to have a place to park at any given service site. Such outcomes are not noticed because they are expected as a matter of course and when they are present, customers are likely to evaluate the service at a cognitive level. If, however, these factors are absent, i.e., the customer ends up not seeing the doctor, the flight is rerouted to another airport, or there is absolutely no parking available, the customer is likely to be upset. These experiences are outside the zone of indifference and will be noticed. They are likely to cause strong emotional reactions which will influence customers' subsequent evaluations of the service.

On the other hand, when service enhancers are absent, they may not be noticed, but if they are present, they will be. If the waiting time at the doctor's office is typical or the customers eventually find what they are looking for in the store, they may not be too concerned that the service could have been better. They did receive adequate service based on their expectations and they will therefore evaluate the experience cognitively. However, if the customer is called in to the doctor's examining room a minute after arrival and examined almost immediately or the store personnel go out of their way to help and find what the customer wants right away, the customer will feel very good about such experiences and will base subsequent cognitions on these feelings. Even if something else (minor) goes wrong during the service delivery, the good feelings will tend to override the evaluation of such discrepancies.

Type of Service

Some service situations themselves may be inherently more emotional than others, such as going to the hospital emergency room. In this case, the emotional evaluation of the service is likely to influence cognitions, and the directionality will be from customer satisfaction to service quality. Other services inherently will have low emotional possibilities such as shopping for groceries and customers will tend to evaluate such services cognitively. It may not be possible to neatly classify all service encounters into this dichotomy and hence, type of service should be viewed more as a continuum. Getting a haircut does not compare with the emergency room for emotional possibilities, but a bad haircut may be quite emotional for the customer and may influence subsequent evaluations of the service provider.

Type of Customer

Some customers may be more cognitive than others and be more likely to evaluate experiences rationally at the cognitive level. Individuals with a high need for cognition (Cacioppo and Petty 1984) tend to look for information and to think about different aspects of their experiences. Such customers will evaluate service quality first and then decide whether they are satisfied. Other customers may be more emotional and are likely to evaluate experiences at the emotional or feeling level. Individuals with a high affect intensity (Larsen and Diener 1986) tend to magnify their emotions and feel experiences more deeply than others. Such customers will experience (dis)satisfaction with the service at an emotional level and then form a judgment about the service based on this emotion.

Customer's Mood

The customer's mood in the service situation is also likely to influence causality between customer satisfaction and service quality. Even mild moods can have a significant impact on behavior and evaluation (Gardner 1985). If the customer is in a very bad (or good) mood it is likely that s/he will evaluate the service experience emotionally and the causal sequence will be from customer satisfaction to service quality. If the customer is in a somewhat neutral mood (recognizing that there is no such thing as a completely neutral mood), then s/he is likely to evaluate the service at a cognitive level and the directionality will be from service quality to customer satisfaction.

INTERACTION OF CONTINGENCY SITUATIONS

The situations discussed above and presented in Table 1 are not necessarily independent. In fact, there is likely to be considerable interaction among these factors, and the causal sequences are most likely to occur if there are several factors present. For example, if an emotional customer in a bad mood has a service experience which is outside (and below) the zone of indifference, the directionality will be from customer (dis)satisfaction to service quality and the effect will be quite strong. It may also be noted that there are other factors that may influence the sequence of evaluation of the service that are not indicated in Table 1 because these may not have a clear main effect on the sequence. For example, the shopping situation, i.e., whether one is shopping alone or with friends/family is likely to affect whether one reacts emotionally or not, but different people may react differently in such situations. Thus, the influence of the shopping situation on the directionality between customer satisfaction may be manifest only through interaction with other factors.

Three possible interactions of the factors listed in Table 1 are presented in Figure 1. In practice, many more such interactions are possible, but these three examples are quite representative of the gamut of possibilities and each is just a little different to suggest the range of influences on the directionality between customer satisfaction and service quality.

As seen in Figure 1A, customers who rate low (or high) on both need for cognition and affect intensity will not favor a particular sequence for forming evaluations of the service in terms of service quality and customer satisfaction. The constructs are likely to overlap in these two cases. The individual who is low on both factors may simply form an overall sense of satisfaction and quality and thus the two constructs will overlap. The individual who is high on both factors may think in great detail about each aspect of the service, but may simultaneously experience emotions about each aspect. Thus, this individual too will form evaluations of satisfaction and quality simultaneously, but the evaluations will be richer in content. Now, customers who have a high need for cognition and low affect intensity are more than likely to evaluate experiences cognitively and then decide if they are satisfied with the service or not. Thus, their evaluations will show a causal sequence from service quality to customer satisfaction. On the other hand, customers with a low need for cognition and high affect intensity are more than likely to evaluate experiences on an emotional basis and then form cognitions about the service based on these emotions. Thus, they will go from customer satisfaction to service quality.

The interactions in Figure 1B are a little more complicated. Here, if the essential aspects of a service are present and service enhancers are absent, the presence or absence of these factors is unlikely to be noticed and thus an emotional reaction is unlikely. The customer will first form cognitions about the service and the directionality of evaluation will be from service quality to customer satisfaction. If the essential aspects of a service and service enhancers are both present, the service enhancers will be noticed and their presence will be appreciated and will make customers feel good about the service, and in turn, influence cognitions about the service. Thus, the causal sequence of evaluation will be from customer satisfaction to service quality.

FIGURE 1
Interaction of Contingency Factors for Predicting Directionality between
Customer Satisfaction (CS) and Service Quality (SQ)

A. Type of Customer: Cognitive versus Emotional
Need for Cognition

		Low	High
Affect Intensity	Low	overlap of constructs	SQ -------> CS
	High	CS -------> SQ	overlap of constructs

B. Essential Aspects of Service versus Service Enhancers
Essential Aspects of Service

		Present (not noticed)	Absent (bad)
Service Enhancers	Present (good)	CS -------> SQ (good experience)	CS -------> SQ good/bad depends on service recovery)
	Absent (not noticed)	SQ -------> CS	CS -------> SQ (bad experience)

C. Zone of Indifference versus Customer's Mood
Zone of Indifference

		outside (below)	inside	outside (above)
Customer's Mood	very good	SQ -------> CS overlap, or mood change	CS -------> SQ or overlap	CS -------> SQ **
	somewhat neutral	CS -------> SQ or overlap	SQ -------> CS	CS -------> SQ or overlap
	very bad	CS -------> SQ **	CS -------> SQ or overlap	SQ -------> CS overlap, or mood change

** strongest links to future behavior

If the essential aspects of a service and service enhancers are both absent, the absence of the essential aspects will be noticed and this will be resented making customers feel bad about the service. This bad feeling will then influence cognitions about the service. Thus, the directionality of evaluation here will also be from customer satisfaction to service quality. Finally, if the essential aspects of a service are absent and service enhancers are present, both aspects will be noticed. While the customer may appreciate the presence of the service enhancers s/he will resent the absence of the essential factors. The reaction is therefore likely to be emotional and the causal sequence will be from customer satisfaction to service quality. Whether the overall experience is perceived as good or bad will depend on the service recovery process used to placate the customer about the missing essential aspects.

The last example of interactions (see Figure 1C) depicts three possible levels for each factor. A customer may be in a very good mood (e.g., elated), in a somewhat neutral mood, or in a very bad mood (e.g., upset). The service experience may be outside the zone of indifference (and below it) implying a really bad service experience, within the zone of indifference implying an acceptable service experience, or outside the zone of indifference (and above it) implying a really good service experience. The customer in the somewhat neutral mood who experiences a service within the zone of indifference is not likely to experience an emotional reaction. Instead the evaluation is likely to be cognitive and the directionality will be from service quality to customer satisfaction. If this customer's experience falls outside the zone of indifference, then given that expectations are not met (or are exceeded), it is possible that an emotional reaction will occur but this may be tempered by the customer's "normal" mood. Thus, we could expect a possible directionality from customer satisfaction to service quality or an overlap of the two constructs.

If the customer is in a very good or very bad mood, even if the experience is within the zone of indifference, the customer's mood is likely to temper the experience and evaluation will be mainly emotional. Thus, the causal sequence will be from customer satisfaction to service quality. It is possible, however, that the customer is able to prevent his/her mood from influencing the evaluation of the service recognizing that it was after all what s/he expected. In this case, there may be an overlap between service quality and customer satisfaction. If the customer in a very good (bad) mood experiences a service outside the zone of indifference and above (below) it, then the strong emotional reaction will be compounded by the customer's mood. The directionality should be from customer satisfaction to service quality and should strongly influence future behavior.

Finally, if the customer in a very good (bad) mood experiences a service outside the zone of indifference and below (above) it, there is a conflict between the initial feeling that the customer was experiencing and that caused by the service experience. In these situations, it is predicted that one (or more) of three things could happen. The customer in the very good mood will face the bad service philosophically and rather than get perturbed will evaluate it at a cognitive level, thus indicating a sequence from service quality to customer satisfaction. Similarly, the customer in the very bad mood will appreciate the excellent service, perhaps not enough to be jubilant, but still recognizing that it is more than s/he expected, and will evaluate it at a cognitive level, thus indicating a sequence from service quality to customer satisfaction. Or, in either situation, the customer may form both evaluations simultaneously resulting in an overlap of the two constructs. Alternatively, or in conjunction with either of these sequences of evaluation, the customer's mood may change from very good (bad) to somewhat neutral and perhaps even a little "down (up)" due to the service experience.

PREDICTING THE IMPACT ON CUSTOMER BEHAVIOR

As researchers we are interested in how the evaluation of service quality and customer satisfaction as well as the causal sequence of their formation influence subsequent customer intentions for repurchase. Under what conditions are repurchase intentions and loyalty strongest? When there is overlap between customer satisfaction and service quality in a given situation, it implies that the situation evoked little or no emotion (see Figure 2A). In this case, both evaluations are cognitive and while they could lead to future intentions, there is likely to be little commitment. When the evaluation of service quality takes place prior to the evaluation of customer satisfaction, and the customer then forms intentions for repurchase, the order of evaluation is cognitive, then affective, then conative, as predicted in traditional attitudinal models (see Figure 2B). Given that the evaluation is based on cognitions and then fortified by the affect that follows, the intentions should be well formed. Yet, the customer may be open to competitors' services if s/he has not yet tried them.

Lastly, when the evaluation of service quality takes place after the evaluation of customer satisfaction, this implies that there has been a strong emotional reaction to the service experience. It is commonly accepted that emotion is a much stronger predictor of behavior (Izard 1977; Westbrook 1987) especially when one is relatively new to the experience and still involved in the process of evaluation (Allen, Machleit, and Kleine 1992). Moreover, cognitions about service quality will be influenced by the emotion evoked during the situation and will be biased in one direction or another. The evaluation may not be as rational as in the earlier cases, but the impact on intentions should be much stronger including both direct and indirect effects (see Figure 2C). The models in Figure 2 extend Cohen and Areni's (1991) distinction between attitude as evaluative judgment and affect as a valenced feeling state by proposing three different possibilities in the sequence of evaluation formation and its impact on behavioral intentions.

From the provider's perspective, there are six possible outcomes for a service experience as presented in Figure 3. If there is an overlap between evaluations of satisfaction and quality and the customer receives a good (poor) service, this could be considered a good (poor) outcome. However, even in the case of the good outcome, there is much room for improvement because there is little commitment toward future behavior. If the causal sequence is from service quality to customer satisfaction and the customer has received good service, this should be considered a better outcome compared to the overlap situation (but not ideal). The customer is highly likely to come back, but s/he may try the competitors' services as well (Schlossberg 1993). The reason is that everything may have been done right, but the provider did not go the extra length to strike an emotional chord to win customer loyalty. For the same sequence, if the customer has received poor service, this should be considered a worse outcome compared to the overlap situation (but not terrible). The customer is highly likely not to come back, but then again, s/he may decide to give the firm a second chance given that this was a single occasion.

When the causal sequence for the evaluation is from customer satisfaction to service quality, and the customer has received good service, this is the *best* possible outcome for the firm. The customer will be delighted and is likely to be a customer for life (Schlossberg 1993). Having evaluated the experience on a highly emotional level, the customer will then translate this emotion to cognitions to become convinced to keep coming back. The *worst* outcome for the firm is if the customer receives poor service and evaluates the service emotionally. This customer is likely to be upset or disgusted, will form lasting cognitions based on this emotion, and will

FIGURE 2
Impact of Causality on Intentions

A. SQ / CS ————————> INT (corresponds to purely cognitive model)

B. SQ ———> CS ———> INT (corresponds to attitudinal model)

C. CS ———> SQ ———> INT (corresponds to emotion-driven model)
    ————————————————————>

FIGURE 3
Possible Outcomes for Service Experiences

Customer Perception

		Good Service	Poor Service
	overlap CS / SQ	Good Outcome	Worse Outcome
Causal Sequence	SQ -------> CS	Better Outcome	Worse Outcome
	CS -------> SQ	Best Outcome	Worst Outcome

be lost forever to the firm. This customer is also likely to engage heavily in negative word-of-mouth.

DISCUSSION

The literature on service quality and customer satisfaction does not appear to be in agreement regarding the causal order between these two constructs. Each researcher has his/her own conceptualization of these constructs and the directionality follows from this. At the same time, researchers realize that a causal order predicted entirely by suggesting that one construct is transactional and the other is global is somewhat arbitrary (e.g., Bitner and Hubbert 1994; Dabholkar 1993; Iacobucci, Grayson, and Ostrom 1994; Parasuraman, Zeithaml, and Berry 1994; Spreng and Singh 1993). Both service quality and customer satisfaction evaluations can occur at the transactional and the global level.

The contingency framework proposed in this paper attempts to show that different conceptualizations of customer satisfaction and service quality are indeed possible but under different contingencies. Researchers who predict that customer satisfaction leads to service quality are simply thinking about service situations where there is an element of surprise which enhances the emotion evoked by the encounter and colors subsequent cognitions about the experience (e.g., Bitner 1990; Oliver 1981; Parasuraman, Zeithaml, and Berry 1988). This view emphasizes the equivalence of satisfaction with experiential evaluation and of service quality with cognitions formed after the experience. On the other hand, those who predict that service quality leads to customer satisfaction are envisioning an attitudinal approach where cognitive evaluation precedes the formation of the associated affect. An example of this approach is the research on evaluations of telephone service (Bolton and Drew 1992; Drew and Bolton 1991) where cognitions appear to be formed first regarding the quality of the service and where the customer then decides whether s/he is happy with the service. In addition, the

proposed framework outlines the various situations under which these different conceptualizations are valid.

Having presented a contingency framework to show that the causal link between customer satisfaction and service quality varies according to the service situation and that the direction of the causal link influences future customer behavior, an agenda is suggested for future research. The contingencies presented in Table 1 (as well as other relevant contingencies) could be used to set up experiments where the effect of these factors or their interactions on the link between customer satisfaction and service quality (see Figure 1) can be investigated. Furthermore, the influence of this directionality under various contingencies on future customer behavior can also be investigated. However, such studies must deal with the issue of truly measuring emotion rather than measuring cognitions about emotion (see Allen, Machleit, and Kleine 1992; Oliver 1989). The use of critical incidents (see Bitner 1990; Bitner and Hubbert 1994) is another useful technique to determine the sequence between customer satisfaction and service quality. Yet another technique would be to monitor actual service delivery and/or the recovery process to determine emotional content and causal sequence and to decide which sequence leads to the strongest intentions regarding future behavior.

The framework presented in this paper also has several implications for practitioners. First, service firms should understand the three models presented for service evaluation (Figure 2), the six possible outcomes of service from the provider's perspective (Figure 3), and all the different contingencies (Table 1, Figure 1) where these evaluations and outcomes can occur. The firms should then train employees to provide the basic minimum service. For example, they can ensure that essential aspects of the service are present and that the service provided is within the zone of indifference for most customers. Firms should then motivate employees to strive for the best possible service delivery. For example, employees should try to provide service enhancers and strive to provide service above the zone of indifference. However, providing service at this level involves extra effort and cost, and is not always possible. Yet, if the customer is delighted, s/he is likely to become a customer for life. At the other extreme, employees must be trained to avoid the worst situation. If the customer is upset, s/he will be lost to the firm and may take other customers along through negative word-of-mouth. To avoid such situations, employees must take care of little problems and prevent a bad situation from getting worse. They must learn to judge situations especially for services with high emotional possibilities. Also, some customers are more emotional than others and employees must learn how to handle them. For services with little emotional possibility, the best approach is to offer efficient, effective services that will receive high cognitive evaluation.

REFERENCES

Allen, Chris T., Karen A. Machleit, and Susan Schultz Kline (1992), "A Comparison of Attitudes and Emotions as Predictors of Behavior at Diverse Levels of Behavioral Experience," *Journal of Consumer Research*, 18 (March), 493-504.

Anderson, Eugene W. and Mary W. Sullivan (1993), "The Antecedents and Consequences of Customer satisfaction for Firms," *Marketing Science*, 12 (Spring), 125-143.

Bitner, Mary Jo (1990), "Evaluating Service Encounters: The Effects of Physical Surroundings and Employee Responses," *Journal of Marketing*, 54 (April), 69-82.

_____ and Amy R. Hubbert (1994), "Encounter Satisfaction versus Overall Satisfaction versus Quality: The Customer's Voice," in *Service Quality: New Directions in Theory and Practice*, Roland T. Rust and Richard L. Oliver, eds., SAGE Publications, 72-94.

Bloemer, Jose M. M. and Theo B. C. Poiesz (1989), "The Illusion of Consumer Satisfaction," *Journal of Consumer Satisfaction, Dissatisfaction and Complaining Behavior*, 2, 43-48.

Bolton, Ruth N. and James H. Drew (1991), "A Multistage Model of Customers' Assessments Service Quality and Value," *Journal of Consumer Research*, 17 (March), 375-384.

Cacioppo, John T. and Richard E. Petty (1984), "The Need for Cognition: Relationship to Attitudinal Processes," in *Social Perception in Clinical and Counseling Psychology*, Vol. 2, R. P. McGlynn et al., eds., Lubbock: Texas Tech University Press, 113-140.

Cadotte, Ernest R. and Normand Turgeon (1988), "Dissatisfiers and Satisfiers: Suggestions from Consumer Complaints and Compliments," *Journal of Consumer Satisfaction, Dissatisfaction and Complaining Behavior*, 1, 74-79.

Cohen, Joel B. and Charles S. Areni (1991), "Affect and Consumer Behavior," in Handbook of Consumer Behavior, Thomas S. Robertson and Harold J. Kassarjian, eds., Englewood Cliffs, NJ: Prentice-Hall, 189-240.

Cooper, Ann R., Cooper, M. Bixby, and Dale F. Duhan (1989), "Measurement Instrument Development Using Two Competing Concepts of Customer Satisfaction," *Journal of Consumer Satisfaction, Dissatisfaction Complaining Behavior*, 2, 28-35.

Cronin, Joseph J., Jr. and Steven A. Taylor (1992), "Measuring Service Quality: A Reexamination and Extension," *Journal of Marketing*, 56 (July), 55-68.

Dabholkar, Pratibha A. (1993), "Customer Satisfaction and Service Quality: Two Constructs or One?" in *Enhancing Knowledge Development in Marketing*, David W. Cravens and Peter Dickson, eds. Chicago: American Marketing Association, 4, 10-18.

Drew, James H. and Ruth N. Bolton (1991), "The Structure of Customer Satisfaction: Effects of Survey Measurement," *Journal of Consumer Satisfaction, Dissatisfaction and Complaining Behavior*, 4, 21-31.

Erevelles, Sunil and Clark Leavitt (1992), "A Comparison of Current Models of Consumer Satisfaction/Dissatisfaction," *Journal of Consumer Satisfaction, Dissatisfaction and Complaining Behavior*, 5, 104-114.

Gardner, Meryl P. (1985), "Mood States and Consumer Behavior: A Critical Review," *Journal of Consumer Research*, 12 (December), 281-300.

Iacobucci, Dawn, Kent Grayson, and Amy Ostrum (1994), "The Calculus of Service Quality and Customer Satisfaction: Theoretical and Empirical Differentiation and Integration," in *Advances in Services Marketing and Management*, Teresa A. Swartz, David A. Bowen, and Stephen W. Brown, eds., Volume 3, JAI Press.

Larsen, Randy J. and Ed Diener (1986), "Affect Intensity as an Individual Difference Characteristic: A Review," *Journal of Research and Personality*, 21, 1-39.

Izard, Carroll E. (1977), *Human Emotions*, New York: Plenum.

Mano, Haim and Richard L. Oliver (1993), "Assessing the Dimensionality and Structure of the Consumption Experience: Evaluation, Feeling, Satisfaction," *Journal of Consumer Research*, 20 (December), 451-466.

Oliver, Richard L. (1993), "A Conceptual Model of Service Quality and Service Satisfaction: Compatible Goals, Different Concepts," in *Advances in Services Marketing and Management*, Teresa A. Swartz, David A. Bowen, and Stephen W. Brown, eds., Volume 2, JAI Press, 65-85.

_____ (1989), "Processing of the Satisfaction Response in Consumption: A Suggested Framework and Research Propositions," *Journal of Consumer Satisfaction, Dissatisfaction and Complaining Behavior*, 2, 1-16.

_____ (1981), "Measurement and Evaluation of Satisfaction Processes in Retail Settings," *Journal of Retailing*, 57 (Fall), 25-48.

Ortony, Andrew, Gerald L. Clore, and Allan Collins (1988), *The Cognitive Structure of Emotions*, New York: Cambridge University Press.

Parasuraman, A., Valarie A. Zeithaml, and Leonard L. Berry (1994), "Reassessment of Expectations as a Comparison Standard in Measuring Service Quality: Implications for Further Research," *Journal of Marketing*, 58 (January), 111-124.

_____, _____, and _____ (1988), "SERVQUAL: A Multi-Item Scale for Measuring Consumer Perceptions of Service Quality," *Journal of Retailing*, 64 (1), 12-40.

Reichheld, Frederick F. (1993), "Loyalty-Based Management," *Harvard Business Review*, 71 (2), 64-73.

Schlossberg, H. (1993), "Dawning of the Era of Emotion," *Marketing News*, 27 (4), 1.

Spreng, Richard A. and Cornelia Droge (1994), "A Comprehensive Model of the Effects of Expectations on Consumer Satisfaction, presented at the *Society for Consumer Psychology* Conference, St. Petersburg, FL, forthcoming.

_____ and A. K. Singh (1993), "An Empirical Assessment of the SERVQUAL Scale and the Relationship between Service Quality and Satisfaction," in *Enhancing Knowledge Development in Marketing*, David W. Cravens and Peter Dickson, eds., Chicago: American Marketing Association. vol. 4, 1-6.

Westbrook, Robert A. (1987), "Product/Consumption-Based Affective Responses and Postpurchase Processes," *Journal of Marketing Research*, 24 (August), 258-270.

Woodruff, Robert B., Ernest R. Cadotte, and Roger L. Jenkins (1983), "Modeling Consumer Satisfaction Processes Using Experience-Based Norms," *Journal of Marketing Research*, 20 (August), 296-304.

Yi, Youjae (1990), "A Critical Review of Consumer Satisfaction," in *Review of Marketing*, Valarie Zeithaml, ed., Chicago: American Marketing Association, 68-123.

Session Overview
Peaks and Flows: Intense Joys and Optimal Experiences in Consumption

Ruth Ann Smith, Virginia Polytechnic Institute and State University

This session was designed to systematically explore two distinct yet related intense emotional states that may occur during consumption. Consumption peaks, a type of peak experience (Maslow 1964), are consumption episodes in which a consumer experiences great joy and excitement. Flow (Csikszentmihalyi 1990) is an experiential state of enjoyment that is intrinsically rewarding and which is sought simply for the pleasure it brings. The central premise of the session was that peaks and flows constitute an essential benefit in many consumption experiences and as such are an important factor in a consumer's continuing involvement with an activity or attachment to an object. The objectives of the session were to: 1) conceptually clarify consumption peaks and flows and 2) explore their substantive effects on the consumption of both tangible products and intangible experiences by individuals and groups.

GOING WITH THE FLOW: COLLECTING AS AN OPTIMAL CONSUMER EXPERIENCE

Smith and Lee examined the role of flow in the consumption experiences of collectors. Following Csikszentmihalyi (1990), they conceptualized flow as an intensely absorbing optimal experience lying between anxiety-producing over-stimulation and boring under-stimulation. Congruence between the actor's skills and the demands of the task the actor is attempting to perform is an antecedent to this state. As a consequence of flow, the actor emerges as a more complex individual in the sense of being more highly integrated into meaningful human relationships and being more differentiated as a unique person. Smith and Lee hypothesized that if flow is an essential element in the consumption experiences of collectors, then collectors of an object would possess the antecedent match of skills to collecting task demands, experience optimality and absorption, and benefit from the consequences of individuation and integration to greater degrees than non-collectors.

The hypothesis was tested in the context of book collecting, and collectors' scores on measures of the relevant constructs were significantly higher than those of non-collectors (p<.001) except for absorption where no difference was observed. As the absorption measure did not differentiate between absorption with the experience of collecting books and absorption with the content of a book, it is likely that this exception reflected a methodological artifact of the research context. The overall pattern of results, however, was highly consistent with the hypothesis, suggesting that flow is an integral element in the consumption experiences of collectors.

VIEWS FROM THE MOUNTAIN TOP: THE LIVED EXPERIENCE OF CONSUMPTION PEAKS

Guiry and Lutz reported the findings of a two-stage investigation of consumption peaks. In the first stage, they used a structured instrument to identify the distinguishing characteristics of consumption peaks and flow relative to ordinary consumption. Novelty and communion emerged as the definitive aspects of consumption peaks, while absorption was characteristic of flow. Ordinary consumption exhibited none of these qualities. The second stage of their research employed depth interviews with five adult consumers to explore consumption peaks from a first-person perspective. Informants were asked to describe a consumption experience that

was particularly satisfying to them and that engaged them very intensely relative to an ordinary consumption experience such as one might have in a grocery store. The five informants described varied experiences including the serendipitous acquisition of tickets for a sold-out theater performance, purchasing and riding bicycles on the beach, a Colorado ski vacation, taping, watching, and visiting the production sets of daytime soap operas, and running.

The interviews reinforced the definitive characteristics of consumption peaks as being both novel and involving communion, either with other people, fictitious characters, or in a more metaphysical sense through communion with nature. In addition, the peak experiences described all shared the dimension that the actor learned something important during the consumption episode. The informants learned something about life in general, about themselves and their abilities and instincts, about other people, or acquired a new skill or competency. In the case of at least one informant, the learning was profound in the sense that it altered her life course. This element of learning suggests a close relationship between consumption peaks and flows despite their unique elements of novelty/communion and absorption respectively. That is, learning requisite skills is antecedent to attaining flow and consumption peaks encompass significant learning.

FLOW AND PEAK EXPERIENCE IN COMMITMENT TO A SUBCULTURE OF CONSUMPTION

Schouten and McAlexander reported on a five-year ethnographic study of consumption subcultures, or groups of people who organize themselves around certain consumption activities or the consumption of a particular brand or product. Although their research did not originally focus on consumption peaks and flows, depth interviews with Harley-Davidson and Jeep owners produced substantial evidence that these states perform important intrapersonal and social roles within a subculture of consumption. Moreover, peaks and flows result in enduring attitude change toward products and contribute to the development of brand loyalty among members of the subculture.

At the individual level, consumption peaks are novel or even unprecedented experiences that profoundly affect how a member of a consumption subculture views him or her self. A consumption peak often involves using a particular brand or product and leads to the forging of a new, stronger person-brand/product relationship. The brand/product may have originally been purchased out of a sort of terminal materialism (e.g. a Harley is purchased because it *is* a Harley), but following the consumption peak, the brand/product becomes instrumental to recreating the experience. Socially, a consumption peak may constitute the basis for one's status within the subculture of consumption. Further, these experiences are shared with other members in the form of narratives that may eventually attain legendary status. Both the intrapersonal and social dimensions of consumption peaks suggest their relationship to flow. That is, one experiences a consumption peak through a novel consumption episode which is later recreated and repeated by using the brand/product repetitively and by retelling the story of the experience. This repetition creates a deepening and refinement of the experience that leads to flow.

Advances in Consumer Research
Volume 22, © 1995

SUMMARY

The three presentations suggested both points of difference and similarity between consumption peaks and flows. Where consumption peaks encompass elements of novelty and communion, flows involve absorption. And, a consumption peak may be attained during one's first experience with a particular consumption episode but flow appears to be achieved through the repetition and recreation of the episode, either through individual performance or group interactions. Peaks and flows seem to share the common element of knowledge or learning. A peak often involves acquiring knowledge, while flow involves refining and fine-tuning skills. Moreover, both peaks and flows contribute to a consumer's sense of self and to the formation of meaningful relationships with others.

In her comments, Scott raised several questions that were not addressed in the research presented in this session. First, because so many products are consumed simply for the experiences they offer, rather than for utility or symbolism, the issue arises of how one might differentiate these experiences from peaks and flows. Reading a cheap spy thriller to take oneself out of the tedium of a long airplane trip, for example, is absorbing but probably does not qualify as a flow state. And, while drug use may be a novel experience involving elements of communion, it may not constitute a consumption peak. Further, she argued that both consumption peaks and flows may involve negative experiences although the session focused only on the positive. She suggested that consumption peaks and flows bring an experiential aspect to consumer research that is not captured by either a classic view of consumption as utility maximization or by a symbolic view of consumption as a social construct. As such, further exploration into the role of peaks and flows in consumption seems warranted.

REFERENCES

Csikszentmihalyi, Mihalyi (1990), *Flow: The Psychology of Optimal Experience*, New York: Harper and Row.

Maslow, Abraham (1964), *Religions, Values, and Peak Experiences*, Columbus: Ohio State University Press.

Individual Differences as Moderating Variables: Issues in the Development and Use of Personality Variables

David J. Moore, University of Michigan

The recent resurgence of interest in personality research in consumer behavior has been a result of careful conceptualizations and a stronger commitment to rigorous measurement (Bagozzi 1993). Indeed, the real contribution to be derived from personality concepts lies not in their power as predictors of main effects but rather in their power as moderator variables (Bagozzi 1993; Haugtvedt, Petty, and Cacioppo, 1992). As more and more consumer behavior researchers recognize the potential of personality variables in theory testing and applied research, it is important that certain basic guidelines and perspectives be made salient. Thus, one objective of this session was to provide researchers with examples of the development and the use of personality variables in a manner that enhances understanding of the basic underlying processes.

In the first paper of the session *"A General Approach for Representing Personality Constructs,"* Richard Bagozzi outlined the advantages and the limitations of representing a personality variable as a unidimensional or multidimensional construct. Results of analyses on the need for cognition construct (Cacioppo & Petty, 1982) were used to illustrate a unidimensional scale. Analyses on the Carver and Scheier's self-conciousness measure were used to illustrate a multidimensional scale approach. In addition to these illustrations, Bagozzi's presentation included a discussion of four levels of abstraction at which a given personality construct may be modeled.

The total aggregation model is the level at which the personality construct is represented as either a single composite made up of the sum of several items measuring that construct, or a single factor with each measure loading on that factor. The need for cognition was shown as a representation of total aggregation. The main advantages of the total aggregation model are its simplicity and its ability to capture the essence of the underlying meaning of a personality construct. On the other hand, the disadvantage is that it fails to represent the unique properties of subdimensions, if any, and overlooks both the differential dependence and the effects of subdimensions on other constructs of theoretical interest.

A second level of representation is the partial aggregation model where the dimensions of the construct are not formally modeled as indicators of it but rather are treated as separated subscales loosely tied to the overall construct, termed the discrete components case. Two approaches can be taken with discrete components. Either the items within the components are summed to form a total subscore or else the components are treated as individual factors with their respective items loading on them. The self-monitoring scale has been treated this way, where three lowly correlated dimensions have been identified: extraversion, other-relatedness, and acting ability.

The third level of representation is the partial disaggregation model. Here each dimension of the scale can be represented by a unique latent variable measured by a composite of items. The main advantage of this approach is the ability to specify and test for the existence of multiple dimensions of a personality construct. One unresolved issue associated with this approach is the method to be used to group items to form composite indicators.

The fourth level of representation is the total disaggregation model which is similar to the partial disaggregation model, but instead of using indicators comprised of composites of items, each item is employed as a measure of its respective dimension in a confirmatory factor analysis. In practice, this model can be unwieldly because of likely high levels of random error in typical items and the many parameters that must be estimated.

As illustrations, two well-known scales in consumer research were examined with the proposed framework. For the need for cognition scale, the 18 items from the shortened version were treated as indicators of a single latent variable in a confirmatory factory analysis on a sample of 1700 respondents. The model fit well and was found to generalize across gender, education, and age. For the self-consciousness scale, two composite indicators were formed as the sum of appropriate items on each of three subdimensions: private self-consciousness, public self-consciousness, and social anxiety. The partial disaggregation model was found to fit the model welll and to generalize across samples of Americans and Japanese consumers.

Having been exposed to Bagozzi's general framework for representing personality constructs, two relative new individual difference measures were presented- the Propensity to Self-Reference scale and the Affect Intensity Measure (Larsen and Diener 1987). Curt Haugtvedt introduced the Propensity to Self-Reference individual difference measure, a personality construct developed for use in attitude change and persuasion research. Theoretical justification for the scale was consistent with the perspectives outlined in a JCP article by Haugtvedt, Petty, & Cacioppo (1992)- that is, the idea that useful individual difference measures can be developed that mirror the impact of situational manipulations. The PSR scale was thus developed to reflect the kinds of processes associated with situational manipulations of self-referencing (e.g., Burnkrant & Unnava, 1989). His presentation included a brief discussion of the psychometric properties of the scale and the results of a study in which the scale has been used. Interestingly, this study revealed a curvilinear pattern of self-referencing effects. That is, the highest degree of message elaboration was oberserved at moderate levels of self-referencing. The results of the study thus have implications for resolving the seeming inconsistency between results previously reported by Burnkrant & Unnava (1989) and Sujan, Bettman, & Baumgartner (1993). That is, Burnkrant and Unnava (1989) found high self-referencing to be associated with high levels of elaboration whereas Sujan et al. (1993) found high levels of self-referencing to be associated with the lowest levels of elaboration. In summarizing his presentation, Haugtvedt discussed how self-relevant thinking was posited to play important and unique roles in persuasion processes and suggested that future consumer research might benefit by giving consideration to the theoretical as well as practical value of well-defined unidimensional personality constructs. He concluded his presentation by discussing research projects underway in which he is attempting to replicate the curvilinear pattern using three levels of a situational manipulation as well as assessment of attitude strength consequences of self-referencing processes.

The final paper of the session, *"Emotional Intensity: An Individual Difference Perspective"* by David Moore, demonstrated how the Affect Intensity Measure (AIM) can be used as an important moderator in explaining consumer response to advertising stimuli. The AIM is defined at the upper end of the continuum by those who experience their emotions with fairly strong intensity and

Advances in Consumer Research
Volume 22, © 1995

by those at the lower end of the continuum who experience their emotions mildly with only minor emotional responses (Larsen 1984). Even when exposed to similar levels of emotional stimulation, high AIM individuals are expected to manifest more intense emotional reactions than their low affect intensity counterparts, regardless of the hedonic tone of the emotion evoked (Larsen, Diener and Emmons 1986). However, when the stimulus is neutral or non-emotional, the significant differences between high and low AIM individuals are expected to disappear.

To offer further confirmation of the affect intensity hypothesis, Moore (1994) randomly exposed subjects to six public service TV ads (three negative emotional ads and three non-emotional). The results can be summarized as follows: (1) Significant differences in the intensity of emotional responses between high and low AIM subjects occurred only in response to the three emotional ads, but not in response to the non-emotional ads. (2) When exposed to emotionally charged advertising appeals, high AIM individuals reported significantly higher levels of emotional discomfort and lower levels of enjoyment than their low AIM counterparts; (3) Affect Intensity was significantly related to the affective component of the empathy scale, but showed no relationship to the cognitive component of the empathy contruct (Davis 1983). (4) High and low AIM subjects showed no significant differences in attitude toward ads which stimulated emotionally uncomfortable feelings. These results are consistent with previous findings of Larsen et al. (1987).

The studies reported by both Moore and by Haugtvedt demonstrated the fact that individual difference variables can offer additional insight to consumer researchers when these variables are linked to a rigorous theoretical framework. The work presented at this session underscored the notion that the real contribution to be derived from personality concepts lies not in their power as predictors of main effects, but rather in their role as moderator variables (Bagozzi 1993; Haugtvedt et al. 1992). The future contribution of personality research can be significantly enriched if more attention is given to the refinement of the dimensional structure of these scales along the lines suggested in Richard Bagozzi's presentation.

REFERENCES

Bagozzi, Richard P. (1993), "Assessing Construct Validity in Personality Research: Applications to Measure Self-Esteem, *Journal of Research in Personality*, 27, 49-87.

Baumgartner, Hans, Mita Sujan and James R. Bettman (1992), "Autobiographical Memories, Affect and Consumer Information Processing", *Journal of Consumer Psychology*, 1 (1), 53-82.

Davis, Mark, H. (1983), "Measuring Individual Differences in Empathy: Evidence for a Multidimensional Approach," *Journal of Personality and Social Psychology*, 44, 113-126.

Haugtvedt, Curtis P., Richard E. Petty, John T. Cacioppo (1992), "Need For Cognition and Advertising: Understanding the Role of Personality Variables in Consumer Behavior," *Journal of Consumer Psychology*, 1 (3), 239-260.

Larsen, Randy J. and Ed Diener (1987), "Affect Intensity as an Individual Difference Characteristic: A Review," *Journal of Research in Personality*, 21, 1-39.

The Maintenance of Positive Self-Evaluations: In Search of a Motive Underlying Some Consumption Behaviors

Harish Sujan, Penn State University

Social cognitive psychology has increasingly begun to investigate the motivational underpinnings of behavior and cognitions. Last year, in his address at ACR, Bagozzi (1993) urged an increased emphasis in consumer research on motivation and personality issues. This session was put together with the objective of furthering the goal of bringing motivation and personality research into the consumer domain.

Three presentations comprised the session. The first, taking about half the session time, was a presentation by *Abraham Tesser*, a psychologist at the University of Georgia, describing his *theory on self-evaluation maintenance*: an important goal that underlies human behavior. The second, taking about quarter the session time, was a presentation by *Rick Bagozzi* (work conducted with Hans Baumgartner and Rik Pieters) on *the effect of emotions in motivating behavior directed at achieving weight loss goals*. The third, taking about quarter the session time, was a presentation by *Rik Pieters* (work conducted with me) on *differences in consumption by lonely and non-lonely people*.

Abraham Tesser has proposed that people have a need to maintain a positive self-evaluation of themselves (Tesser 1988; Tesser, Millar and Moore 1988; Tesser and Cornell 1991; Tesser, Martin and Cornell 1993). A large number of theories exist relating to the self—there are so many theories about the self that one could call them a "self zoo"—but underlying several of these theories is the motive of protecting self-esteem. If one were to reason from Kurt Lewin's work on substitution, there are likely to be many alternative ways to achieve the higher order goal of maintaining positive self-esteem. Claude Steele's (1988) has identified external affirmation of one's important values (self-affirmation) to be a substitute for dissonance (a defensive reaction), that is under self-affirmation dissonance disappears. Steele has also identified that decreased learned helplessness reduces dissonance. Tesser's conclusion based on Steele's work is that apparently disparate psychological processes are guided by a higher order goal: self-esteem maintenance.

In research conducted with Dave Cornell (1991) he has extended Claude Steele's work by showing that unfavorable social comparison with a close other on an important attribute (self-esteem reduction) is compensated by self-affirmation (ratification of important personal values). Dave Cornell and he have also showed that favorable social comparison on an important attribute with a close other (self-esteem enhancement) reduces dissonance. This, they suggest, adds to evidence suggesting that qualitatively different processes—learned helplessness, social comparison, self-affirmation and dissonance—are all in service of the same goal, maintaining a positive self-esteem.

While concluding his talk, Tesser raised the question: "What is the common currency underlying these disparate processes?" Acknowledging that some psychologists disagree with his point of view, he suggested that emotion is the common currency—self-esteem maintenance is in service of staying in a positive affective state. So far his data has supported this hypothesis only for non-conscious affect (e.g., being exposed for milliseconds to facially expressed emotions); support had not been found for conscious affect or mood.

Rick Bagozzi, University of Michigan, (working with Hans Baumgartner, Penn State University, and Rik Pieters, Tilburg University), presented research on the role of goal-directed emo-

tions in weight control behavior. He suggested that the goal of maintaining or reducing body-weight results in anticipatory emotions that motivate instrumental behavior. Using longitudinal data collected in the Netherlands he suggested a classification scheme for anticipatory emotions, and reported findings on the effect of these emotional dimensions on goal directed behavior, achievement of the goal and emotional reactions to the outcome. Linking his work with Tesser's self-evaluation maintenance theory, he suggested that anticipatory emotions provide information (on self-esteem?) that motivate weight-loss behavior.

Rik Pieters, Tilburg University, (working with me), presented research on the role of loneliness in object relations and consumption. He suggested that three nodes on a triangle are the self, another person, and an object, and substitution exists between the self's relations with objects and other people. Using data collected in the Netherlands, he demonstrated this substitution by identifying that materialism (increased relationship with objects) correlates positively with loneliness (decreased relationship with other people). In another demonstration of this principle, using data collected in the U.S., he reported that lonely people, relative to non-lonely people, feel less positive affect when asked to think about the prospect of spending two months abroad in a place where it is hard to make friends. They are, however, able to restore their positive affect through thinking about possessions that they would buy and take with themselves. The substitutability of object and person, he suggested, may be (in keeping with Tesser) a result of there being alternative routes to self-esteem maintenance.

In an attempt at integration, *I* described a few taxonomies that exist for alternative consumption goals. I then suggested that shifting from one goal to another may cause a shift in attribute choice, brand choice and even product category choice; and consumers may be persuaded to shift goals if they believed that the alternative goal would be just as effective as their current goal in maintaining positive self-evaluation.

REFERENCES

Bagozzi, Richard P. (1993), "Personality, Motivation and the Self: New Directions for Consumer Research," ACR Fellow Address, *Association of Consumer Research Conference*, Nashville, TN, 8-11.

Steele, Claude M. (1988), "The Psychology of Self-Affirmation: Sustaining the Integrity of Self," in L. Berkowitz (ed.), *Advances in Experimental Social Psychology* (vol. 21), NY: Academic Press, 261-302.

Tesser Abraham (1988). "Toward a Self-Evaluation Maintenance Model of Social Behavior," *Advances in Experimental Social Psychology*, 21, pp. 181-227.

_____ , Murray Millar, and Janet Moore (1988), "Some Affective Consequences of Social Comparison and Reflection Processes: The Pain and Pleasure of Being Close," *Journal of Personality and Social Psychology*, 54 (No. 1), pp. 49-61.

_____ and David P. Cornell (1991), "On the Confluence of Self-Processes," *Journal of Experimental Social Psychology*, 27, 501-526.

_____ , Leonard Martin and David P. Cornell (1993), "On the Substitutability of Self-Protective Mechanisms," *Rineberg Conference of Motivation and Action*.

Special Session Summary
The Antecedents and Consequences of Choice Deferral
Joel Huber, Duke University

While a great many studies have explored the determinants of purchase decisions, relatively few have studied what brings a consumer to put off making a decision and fewer still the consequence of that indecision. There are two reasons why indecision has received relatively little attention. First, it is difficult to determine from sources such as scanner data when a deferral decision has been made. For example, how can one know whether a shopper leaving the supermarket without a box of cake mix has rejected all of the offerings, has simply not been in the market at all, has intentionally put off the purchase to ask for a spouse's advice on available brands or to otherwise obtain more brand information, or perhaps put off the purchase because this shopping trip was already straining the shopping budget? Second, while the factors that affect choice within a set generally can be adequately accounted for by the attributes of the alternatives, the decision to put off buying, say, a personal computer for home, is far more dependent on external factors such as income constraints, risk attitude, and the response to a neighbor's purchase.

Given the difficulty of defining and conducting research in the area, it is appropriate that the four papers in this session examine choice deferral through a variety of methodological lenses, each focusing on a different aspect of the phenomenon. The paragraphs below describe the research frameworks of each of these papers and summarize their major findings with respect to the deferral decision.

Robert J. Meyer's paper "Deciding Not to Decide in Sequential Search Among Choice Sets," examines choice deferral in an experimental gaming context. This procedure has advantages in that it is possible to contrast human behavior with optimal policy. MBA students are asked try to find the best backpacking tent as a function of its price, quality and weight. Each is shown a number of tents in a store and can choose one of those offered or move on. While searching is costless, once a store has been left, its options are no longer available, thereby creating an opportunity cost to delaying purchase. Respondents are given prior information about the number of stores in their shopping tour and the expected number of alternatives in each store.

The study uncovers several interesting findings with respect to the impact of set size, past set quality, and within-set contrast effects on choice deferral. Concerning set size, the study shows a general (and unexpected) bias towards shopping at too many stores compared to optimal, and particularly so in environments in which stores stock only one alternative. Thus, there is a particular aversion to making a final decision in lone-alternative stores. The study also finds that a high relative quality in the last store increases the likelihood of deferring choice in the current store. This makes sense. It would be particular hard to settle for an alternative worse than one rejected at an earlier store. Generally, the quality of offerings at the last store are likely to form important anchors in evaluating the quality of the current store.

Importantly, and in contrast with results of Tversky and Shaffir (1992) and Dahr (1992), the study does *not* find a within-store contrast effect. Neither the difference between the best and second best alternative in a store nor the presence of a dominant option significantly increases the likelihood to stop search. Thus these two aspects of choice difficulty appear not to affect choice deferral in this shopping game.

Another paper, "The Meaning of a 'None' response in Commercial Studies using Choice-Based Conjoint" by Huber and Pinnell

is also relevant to this issue of the impact of choice difficulty on decision deferral. Choice-based conjoint is similar to full profile conjoint, except that instead of ranking or rating individual profiles the respondent is asked to choose one from a small set of experimentally manipulated profiles. Choice deferral is commonly assessed by the inclusion of a "none" alternative, indicating that none of the alternatives in a given set is acceptable. Jon Pinnell at IntelliQuest has conducted more than 20 commercial studies of studies which include this default alternative. These studies enable the authors to determine the impact of choice difficulty, absolute choice quality, and respondent characteristics in bringing about the decision deferral in choice-based conjoint.

Choice difficulty is operationalized as an inverse measure of the standard deviation in the utilities of an individual's choice set, the smaller the variation in utilities the more difficult the decision. Logistic regression predicts choice of "none" as a function of the average quality of a choice set and the standard deviation of that quality (Huber and Pinnell 1994). In a study of over 300 computer buyers they show that the logistic weight predicting "none" is far greater for the standard deviation than the average utility of the alternatives in each set. This provides evidence for the importance of choice difficulty on choice-based conjoint. However, attempts to replicate the study with five other choice sets found greater weight for average quality over variability, reversing the finding in the first study that variability is more important than the mean. In these latter data sets, choice difficulty remains statistically significant, but appears to be a relatively unimportant element in the selection of the default.

How is the "none" response used in commercial studies? It would be very useful if it was a surrogate measure for potential demand measured in speed or volume of purchases. However, that interpretation has not found empirical support. A study comparing respondents' frequency of choosing "none" with their likelihood to purchase a computer within a three month period showed no relationship, and across a number of studies, direct questions measuring purchase likelihood or speed are consistently unrelated to each respondents propensity to use "none". However, while market demand appears not to be usefully related to choice of the default, it is related to the difficulty consumers have with the decision. That is, people who have less authority to make the decision, are in larger firms at which making a computer decision is more difficult, and have less information about it, tend to be more likely to choose "none."

The Dahr and Simonson paper, "The Effect of Forced Choice on Consumer Preferences" reverses the causal focus of the other two papers. Rather than attending to the antecedents of choice deferral, their paper explores the consequences of having a choice option on two well-known context effects. These context effects are the attraction effect (Huber, Payne and Puto 1982), which posits that the addition of an alternative to a choice set dominated by only one alternative will increase the share of the dominating alternative, and the compromise effect (Simonson 1989), which posits that choice share is biased towards the middle alternative in a set of three.

Dhar and Simonson find that the availability of a "None" option differentially affects these two context effects. The attraction effect is made stronger by the presence a default, while the compromise effect is made weaker. The authors speculate that the motivation for compromise is similar to the motive to use "none",

Advances in Consumer Research
Volume 22, © 1995

both reflect a cautious response to a difficult decision. By contrast, asymmetric dominance of the attraction effect provides a reason (albeit counter-normative) for choosing an object and thus gets one out of the need to use "none." These results begin an important process of elaborating on the different and diverse motives for constructed choices.

The final paper, by Greenleaf and Lehmann, "The Effect of Consumer Delay Time and Delay Reasons on Consumer Satisfaction," also looks at the consequences how long and why consumers delay - in this case on consumer satisfaction. Their project works with retrospective reports. They ask MBA students to think of a recent major decision (over $200) which they had delayed for at least one month before making the decision (Greenleaf and Lehmann 1994). They then are asked to think about the reasons for that delay and their eventual satisfaction with the selection, the process and the product chosen.

The authors propose that the relationship between delay time and satisfaction depends on the reasons why consumers delay. In its main effect, longer delay tends to decrease satisfaction. The reasons why consumers delay also affect satisfaction - some delay reasons tend to increase satisfaction, while others decrease it. However, consumers who delay for some reasons tend to be more satisfied as delay time increases, while consumers who delay for other reasons tend to be less satisfied as delay increases. Thus the answer to the question "What is the impact of delay time on satisfaction?" depends on why consumers are delaying.

For example, consumers tend have higher overall satisfaction when they delay to obtain more information. However, they tend to be less satisfied as the amount of time required to obtain this information increases - presumably because they want the information rapidly and easily and want to get on with selecting a brand. By contrast, delay to wait for prices to drop also tends to increase satisfaction, but here consumers tend to be more satisfied as this delay increases - presumably because it gives them time to find a better price. Such reasoning is speculative, necessarily so given the limitations of retrospective data. However, the ideas from such analysis can provide rich source of hypotheses that can be tested by the experimental methods of the first three papers. Thus, the struggle to understand choice deferral will necessary progress through the interaction of different research modalities.

REFERENCES

Dhar, Ravi (1992), "Investigation Context and Task Effects on Deciding to Purchase," Ph.D. Dissertation, University of California, Berkeley

Greenleaf, Eric A., and Donald R. Lehmann (1994) "A Typology of Substantial Delay in Consumer Decision Making," Working paper. Stern School of Business, New York University

Huber, Joel, John W. Payne, and Christopher Puto (1982), "Adding Asymmetrically Dominated Alternatives: Violations of Regularity and the Similarity Hypothesis." *Journal of Consumer Research, 9* (June), 90-98.

Huber, Joel and Jonathan Pinnell (1994) "The Impact of Set Quality and Decision Difficulty on the Decision to Defer Purchase," Working paper, Fuqua School of Business, Duke University.

Simonson, Itamar (1989), "Choice Based on Reasons: The Case of Attraction and Compromise Effects," *Journal of Consumer Research, 16* , 158-174.

Tversky, Amos and Eldar Shaffir (1992), "Choice Under Conflict: The Dynamics of Deferred Decisions," *Psychological Science, 3.6* (November), 358-361.

Role of Attitude Toward Brand Advertising on Consumer Perception of a Brand Extension

Jung S. Lee, Towson State University

ABSTRACT

This paper reports findings from an experiment that investigates the role of consumers' attitude toward the brand advertising (Aad) on the accessibility and perceived appropriateness of the brand attributes in their perception of a brand extension. The effect is examined either for a comparable extension (sneakers from denim clothing) or for a moderately noncomparable extension (perfume/cologne from denim clothing). Findings suggest that positive Aad significantly increases both the accessiblity and the perceived appropriateness of the brand attributes. The effect on the accessibility of the brand attributes is observed in a similar pattern for both comparable and moderately noncomparable extensions. The effect on the perceived appropriateness of the brand attributes occurs more consistently for a moderately noncomparable extension than for a comparable extension. Additional analysis indicates that Aad strongly influences consumers' overall attitude toward a brand extension, with the effect being greater for a moderately noncomparable extension than for a comparable extension.

INTRODUCTION

The purpose of this paper is to investigate the role of consumers' attitude toward the brand advertising on the way they relate a brand extension to the brand. Although the role of brand concept or brand attitude on consumer perception of a brand extension has been actively pursued during the past several years, few studies have investigated the impact of brand advertising on the process. Brand attitude and brand concept are relatively stable, yet they are affected by the current marketing communication environment. Consumers' response to brand advertising is likely to have a significant influence on their attitude toward the brand and the brand-salient concepts at the time of a brand extension, which, in turn, would influence their perception of the brand extension. Furthermore, it may have a direct effect, in addition to its mediated effect through the brand, to their perception of a brand extension.

It is reasonable to think that marketers try a brand extension instead of introducing a new brand, if they believe that consumers will relate a brand extension to their existing positive attitude and image of the brand. For example, the marketer of Ivory shampoo would hope that consumers who like Ivory soap would also like Ivory shampoo and associate it with the 'pureness' of Ivory soap. Thus, in general, the more consumers can associate a brand extension to the existing brand, the better it is.

Among different ways consumers relate a brand extension to the brand, the *amount* of brand attributes that become *accessible* when they think of a brand extension, and the *degree* to which those attributes are perceived to be *appropriate* for a brand extension are of special interest in this study. This is because they seem to represent two distinctively different ways consumers relate a brand extension to the existing brand.

Several studies in brand extension suggest that consumers' attitude toward the brand influences their overall evaluation of a brand extension through a process of 'affect transfer' when a brand extension is made to a highly similar category (e.g., Aaker and Keller, 1990; Park et al., 1991). However, few studies have investigated whether the overall attitude toward the brand (or toward brand advertising) influences the way consumers relate specific brand attributes to a brand extension.

Research on the role of affect on cognitive organization suggest that people's affective state (either from the context or from the stimuli) significantly influences the way they organize incoming information (e.g., Isen and Daubman, 1984; Murray et al., 1990). Research on affective response to advertising has shown that (1) attitude toward the ad indicates in part consumers' affective response to the ad (Batra and Ray, 1986), and that (2) a brand name, when cued later, can retrieve the affect associated with its advertising (Edell and Burke, 1992; Keller, 1987; Stayman and Batra, 1991). From this line of reasoning, it is speculated that the consumers' attitude toward the brand advertising may influence the way they make a sense of a brand extension later. Although the conceptual distinction between affect as a general feeling state and attitude as an overall evaluative predisposition is important (Cohen and Areni, 1990; Isen, 1984), it would be interesting to see if attitude toward the brand advertising (as an indicator of an overall affective response) has a significant impact on consumers' cognitive organization of brand attributes in a brand extension. It is not the purpose of the study to determine whether the effect is a consequence of pure affect or of attitude. Thus, the term 'affect associated with the ad' and 'attitude toward the ad' are used interchangeably in the current study.

Affect and Cognitive Organization

Research have shown that positive affect influences people's cognitive organization (see Forgas, 1991, for a review). However, there is little consensus about what these effects are and how they occur. First, the *state-dependency* model states that people in a positive state are *more* likely to selectively activate, attend to, store, and retrieve positive materials than those in a neutral mood are (Forgas and Bower, 1987). Second, the *cognitive flexibility* model states that positive affect facilitates people's access to both "proattitudinal" and "counterattitudinal" messages, depending on the goal of processing (Murray et al., 1990). This is because positive affect enhances cognitive flexibility, instead of state dependency. The *Cue-accessibility* model proposes that positive affect cues *more* material and *more diverse* material compared to neutral affect (Isen and Daubman, 1984).

Less is known about the role of negative affect on cognitive organization. Studies have shown that people under a negative mood engaged in more critical and systematic information processing, had a narrower latitude of acceptance, and formed a less inclusive category (see Schwartz and Bless, 1991 for a review). On the other hand, it has been also suggested that individuals' information processing might become less critical or systematic under a negative feeling state than under a neutral state (Cialdini, Darby and Vincent, 1973; Isen and Daubman, 1984). This reportedly is because people engage in an *affect repair* process when they experience a negative feeling.

Affect and biased inference-making

Other research has shown that positive affect influences the nature of inferences people make about given information, rather than its organization. For example, people in a positive state rated the same traits of a target person in a more positive way than those in a neutral state did (Kunda, 1987). It was suggested that this biased inference was due to "misattribution" of positive affect from the mood-eliciting stimuli to the object being evaluated (Schwarz and Clore, 1983). If misattribution is the underlying mechanism, it is likely to occur consistently under both positive and negative affect.

116

Moderated by Task Complexity

A question may be raised as to whether positive affect always influences cognitive organization or inference-making. Schwarz and Clore (1988) noted that judgments that were based on often-rehearsed and highly familiar information ("crystalized") were much *less* likely to be influenced by transient mood than were new, ambiguous, or difficult judgments. This reportedly is because there is less need for a complex cognitive context when the task is simple (Branscombe and Cohen, 1991). It has also been argued that the relationship between affect and cognitive organization is often meaning-specific. That is, affect influences the organization of the materials that are meaningfully related to the type of affect (see Isen, 1987, for a review). This finding may be applied to the role of affect on biased inference-making. That is, affect is most likely to bias the inference-making for those concepts that are meaningfully related to the object being evaluated.

When an evaluation task itself is complex, however, it becomes difficult to judge the relevance of the accessible concepts to the object being evaluated. Thus, affect may bias the inference-making rather consistently for all concepts activated in the context. For a relatively easy task, on the other hand, the effect is likely to occur to a greater degree for those concepts that are relevant to the object being evaluated. Thus, task complexity may moderate the influence of affect on biased inference-making, because it influences judgment on the concept relevance, which, in turn, moderates the extent of biased inference-making.

Implications for consumer perception of a brand extension

The findings on the role of affect on cognitive organization and biased inference-making seem to provide useful insights on the investigation of the relationship between consumers' attitude toward the brand advertising and their perception of a brand extension. First, findings on affect and cue-accessibility imply that consumers' attitude toward the brand advertising may influence the *accessibility* of the brand attributes when they think of a brand extension. Second, the discussion on biased inference-making suggests that attitude toward the brand advertising may also affect the *perceived appropriateness* of the brand attributes in a brand extension, as a specific type of inferences.

Furthermore, the extent of the effect may vary across different types of brand extensions. Past research in brand extension has defined an extension product as being either similar or dissimilar to the core product. The current study adopts a different view in which many extensions could be simply noncomparable to the brand to the ordinary consumers, unless external cues are provided that clarify the relationship. Thus, there could be comparable brand extensions that are easy to judge their relationship with the brand, and noncomparable brand extensions of which the judgments are more difficult.

Johnson (1984) defines product comparability as the degree to which two products are represented by the same set of attributes. Thus, a comparable extension is one that is evaluated by the same set of attributes as those of the core brand, although the relative salience of each attribute may vary between the two. A moderately noncomparable extension, on the other hand, refers to one that shares only a few of its salient attributes with those of the brand, while each product possesses unique attributes that are irrelevant to the other. A completely noncomparable extension is excluded in this study because it is unlikely for this type of extension to occur in a real situation.

HYPOTHESES

Based on the above discussion, the following hypotheses are made about the effect of consumers' attitude toward the brand

advertising (Aad) on the accessibility and perceived appropriateness of the brand attributes in their perception of a brand extension.

On Brand-Attribute Accessibility

H1a: The more positive consumers' attitude toward the brand advertising (Aad) is, the higher the accessibility of brand attributes is in their perceptions of a brand extension.

H1b: The effect of Aad on the brand-attribute accessibility is stronger for a moderately noncomparable extension than for a comparable extension.

On Perceived Appropriateness of Brand Attributes

H2a: The more positive consumers' attitude toward the brand advertising (Aad) is, the more they are likely to think that the brand attributes are appropriate for a brand extension.

H2b: The effect of Aad on the perceived appropriateness of the brand attributes is more consistent for a moderately noncomparable extension than for a comparable extension.

METHODS

Overview

Fictitious print advertisements were prepared for denim clothing (women's jeans, men's jeans, jackets). Two-thirds of the participants saw the ads and the remaining one-third were given the brand names only to form a baseline measure. Each participant was then asked questions about a future brand extension that is either comparable (sneakers) or moderately noncomparable (perfume/cologne) to denim clothing.

Pretest

A series of pretests were carried out to select the core product, two extension products and fictitious brands and ads.[1]

Stage One: Selecting core product and extension products. Denim clothing was chosen as a core product from which two different brand extensions would be made. It was selected because (1) denim clothing was a familiar product to the college students who would be the participants of the study, and therefore should facilitate their cognitive and affective responses to its advertisements; (2) jeans were rated on a moderate level of product involvement (an index of 99 based on Zaichkowsky's Product Involvement Inventory), thus it was likely to minimize the product involvement effect; and (3) jeans were associated with diverse attributes which made it easy for the experimenter to manipulate different attributes in its advertisements. Three different types of denim clothing, women's jeans, the men's jeans and the denim jacket, were used in the study.

Once denim clothing was chosen as the core product, a list was prepared that included product categories that varied in their shared attributes with the denim clothing. The list was presented to a group of 27 students who were from the same population group but independent from those participating in the main study. Students were first asked to write down all their thoughts, other than specific brand names, for each product in the list. They were then asked to rate the overall similarity of each product to each of the three types of denim clothing, and their subjective knowledge of each product and the three types of denim clothing (i.e., how much they thought

---

[1]Please contact the author for the further details of the findings.

they knew each product). The purpose of testing the overall similarity was to maintain a moderate level of similarity in both a comparable extension and a moderately noncomparable extension. Subjective knowledge of each product was measured to separate the comparability between denim clothing and a brand extension from the individuals' knowledge of each product independently.

Sneakers and perfume (or cologne when an extension was made from men's jeans) were chosen as a comparable and a moderately noncomparable extension, respectively, based on the analysis of the product association. Specifically, sneakers as a category shared the same attribute set as the denim clothing although some attributes were more salient in denim clothing than they were in sneakers and vice versa. Perfume/cologne, on the other hand, shared one of its most salient attributes, mystique, with that of denim clothing. But each also had unique attributes that were not comparable with the other. Overall, nine out of ten thoughts associated with denim clothing were also associated with sneakers, while less than half of them were associated with perfume.

A moderate level of similarity was maintained for both sneakers (4.68 on a scale of 1-7) and perfume/cologne (3.77). There was no significant difference in the level of subjective knowledge across the three types of denim clothing and the two extension categories (p>.05). Therefore, the difference in comparability is not from the difference in the participants' independent knowledge of denim clothing and sneakers (or perfume/cologne), but from their relationship to each other.

Stage Two: Selecting ad stimuli and brand names. Six print advertisements (two for each of the three types of denim clothing) were prepared either from unfamiliar magazine advertisements or from pictures that could be disguised as advertisements for denim clothing. It was important to use ads that were not familiar but looked real to the participants because their cognitive and affective responses to the ad were crucial measures in the study. The real brand names and any other written information were replaced with the prepared headlines using a computerized scanner.

Three fictitious brand names were borrowed from a previous study (Hitchon & Churchill, 1992). They were Belas, Komar and Jasil. Three random combinations were prepared between the three brand names and the three types of denim clothing to cancel out any difference that was uniquely associated with a specific brand name. The three combinations were then inserted to each of the six advertisement, thus creating a total of 18 ad stimuli. The ads were then developed into slides.

Procedure

A total of 132 communication major students from a large Midwestern University participated in the study in groups of three to seven. Each group was randomly assigned to one of the three orders of different types of denim clothing. Within each assigned order, each group was again randomly assigned to one of the three brand names. Once the participants were seated, the experimenter explained that they were participating in a part of advertising copy test for a national clothing company. They were told that the real brand names were replaced by fictitious names for confidentiality.

When an introduction was over, a slide of the advertisement corresponding to the assigned order was shown to the participants for 10-15 seconds. They were then asked to list all of their thoughts about the advertised brand. Participants' perception of the brand was then measured with a scale that included both salient and latent attributes of the brand. It was followed by a measure of their overall attitude toward the ad (Aad), attitude toward the brand (Ab), and familiarity with the ad.

The experimenter, then, briefly explained the concept of brand extension by saying, "it refers to a situation in which a company that currently makes a certain product with a brand name 'A' introduces a new product under the same brand name." Ivory shampoo and Honda lawnmower were presented as examples of brand extensions from Ivory soap and Honda automobile, respectively. Once all of the participants said that they understood the concept, they were told that a brand extension, either sneakers or perfume (cologne if the core product was men's jeans), would soon be introduced from the advertised brand of denim clothing. They were then asked to list all of their thoughts at the moment on the specified brand extension. This was followed by a scale-measure of the perceived appropriateness of the brand attributes for the brand extension. The items in the scale were the same as those used to measure their perception of the advertised brand. Next, their overall attitude toward a brand extension (Ab-ext) was measured, followed by their perception of the overall similarity of the brand extension to the advertised brand. The same procedure was repeated for the remaining two types of denim clothing. After subjects completed all three sections, they were asked what they thought the purpose of the study was; if they were aware of the stated purpose while answering the questions; and if they would write down more details if they did. Finally, they were debriefed and dismissed.

Measures

Subjects' *attitude toward the advertisement (Aad)*, was measured with six seven-point semantic differential items that were used in a previous research (Stayman & Batra, 1991). They are 'unpleasant-pleasant,' 'unfavorable-favorable,' 'dislike-like,' 'low quality-high quality,' 'worthless-valuable' and 'disagreeable-agreeable. Since these items were highly correlated with each other (Cronbach's Alpha=.96), the mean rating across six items was used as a single measure of individuals' attitude toward the advertisement. The same items were used to measure their *attitude toward the brand (Ab)*, and *attitude toward the brand extension (Ab-ext)*.

Accessibility of the brand attributes was measured from the participants' thought listing. Participants' thoughts on each brand extension was differentiated into individual thoughts and coded by two independent judges depending on whether each thought was based on the participant's prior description of the brand (brand-relevant thoughts), or on something else, including the unique attributes of extension category (brand-irrelevant thoughts). The inter-judge agreement was 86%. Disagreement was resolved by discussion, thus all thoughts were coded. Once the coding was completed, the number of brand-relevant thoughts in each subject's response was counted to be a single measure of his or her accessibility of brand attributes.

Perceived appropriateness of the brand attributes for a brand extension was measured by the participants' rating of a brand extension on a scale of six seven-point semantic differential items that represented the brand-salient attributes. Three of the six items in the scale were the salient attributes of the denim clothing that were also salient in the category of sneakers, but less so in the category of perfume/cologne ("intrinsic attributes"). They were: 'not durable-durable,' 'not lasting-lasting,' 'not built well-built well' (for women's jeans); 'uncomfortable-comfortable,' 'not easy to wear-easy to wear,' 'not relaxing to wear-relaxing to wear' (for men's jeans); 'not warm-warm,' 'not weather-resistant-weather resistant,' 'doesn't protect from the elements-protects from the elements' (for denim jacket). The inter-item reliability coefficients (Cronbach's Alpha) for each scale were .89, .92, and .75, respectively. The other three items in the scale were the salient attributes of the denim clothing that were also salient in the category of perfume/cologne more than in sneakers ("extrinsic attributes"). They are: 'gentle-bold,' 'unconfident-confident,' 'not sexy-sexy' (for women's jeans); 'soft-rugged,' 'weak-tough,' 'feminine-mas-

TABLE 1
Effects of Aad and Extension Comparability on the Number of Brand-Relevant Thoughts

HIERARCHICAL REGRESSION

Variable Order	R^2 Change	F Change	p
Order	.005	.59	.55
Aad	.04	9.64	.002
Comparability	.001	.001	.98
Aad x Comp.	.001	.002	.96
Overall R^2	.04		

	Comparable	Noncomparable
Positive	3.23	3.41
Negative	2.28	2.44

culine' (for men's jeans); 'not exotic-exotic' 'not mysterious-mysterious' 'timid-bold' (for denim jacket). The inter-item reliability coefficients (Cronbach's Alpha) for each scale were .76, .86., and .76. An average score across the three items in each scale was used as an index of the perceived appropriateness of brand attributes for a brand extension.

RESULTS

Treatment and Control Check

Order Effect. Because each participant saw three advertisements (one for each of the three types of denim clothing), it was suspected that the order of presentation might have a significant effect on the dependent measures in addition to the effects from the independent variables. Hierarchical regression analyses were carried out to test the main effect of the order and the interaction effect with the independent variables (Aad and extension comparability). The results showed that the main effect of order was significant for one of the dependent measures (perceived appropriateness of the extrinsic attributes). The interaction effect of the order with the independent variables was not significant for any of the dependent measures. Thus, the effect of order was removed first (co-varied out) before testing the effect of the independent variables in the analyses to test hypotheses.

Brand-attribute accessibility in no-ad exposure group. There was no significant difference in the number of brand-relevant thoughts between the two brand extensions among those who had not seen an ad. (X=2.09 for sneakers, X=1.51 for perfume/cologne, p>.05). Thus, it may be said that any significant differences in the accessibility of brand attributes between the two types of extensions among those who had seen an advertisement was not due to an inherent difference between sneakers and perfume/cologne as categories.

Hypotheses Testing

Effect of Aad and Extension Comparability on Brand-At-tributeAccessibility. H1a suggested that the more positive consumers' attitude toward the ad (Aad) was, the higher the accessibility of brand attributes was in their perception of a brand extension. A hierarchical regression analysis in Table 1 showed that Aad explained a small, but significant amount of variance in the number of brand-relevant thoughts the participants listed for brand extensions (R^2=.04, p<.01). On average, those who had a positive Aad (scored 5 or higher on a scale of 1-7) listed more brand-relevant thoughts

(X=3.32) than those who had a negative Aad (scored below 3 on a scale of 1-7) did (X=2.51). Therefore, H1a was supported.

It was also hypothesized (H1b) that the effect of Aad on the brand-attribute accessibility would be stronger for a noncomparable extension than for a comparable extension. The results showed that the interaction between Aad and the extension comparability was not significant (p>.05). That is, a positive Aad increased the number of brand-relevant thoughts to a similar degree for both comparable and noncomparable extensions. Therefore, H1b was not supported.

However, given the significant main effect of the Aad, the author was interested in examining whether the effect might have occurred differently across different levels of Aad (i.e., positive, neutral, negative). This was because the previous research on affect and cognitive organization suggested that the effect between positive and negative affect was not always symmetric. Furthermore, studies have shown that positive affect significantly increased cue-accessibility when the task was ambiguous, but not when it was easy. Thus, the average number of brand-relevant thoughts in each of the three levels of Aad was compared between a comparable extension and a noncomparable extension. The overall trend in Figure 1 showed that the effect of the Aad was mostly created by those who had a positive Aad as opposed to those who had a neutral Aad when a brand extension was made to a noncomparable category (X_{23}=3.41 vs. X_{22}=2.44).[2] Positive Aad little influenced the accessibility of brand attributes when the extension was made to a comparable category (X_{13}=3.23 vs. X_{12}=2.95). On the other hand, negative Aad decreased the accessibility of brand attributes over neutral Aad for a comparable extension (X_{11}=2.28 vs. X_{12}=2.95) while it had little influence for a noncomparable extension (X_{21}=2.73 vs. X_{22}=2.44). Therefore, there were some preliminary indications that (1) the effect of consumers' attitude toward brand advertising might have a nonlinear relationship with the accessibility of the brand attributes, and (2) the pattern of relationship might differ between a comparable and a moderately noncomparable extension.

Underlying process. Given that positive Aad increased the brand-attribute accessibility in consumer perception of a brand extension, an additional analysis was performed to determine if

---

[2]The first number in the subscript refers to the extension category (1=comparable, 2=noncomparable). The second number refers to the level of Aad-core (1=negative, 2=neutral, 3=positive).

FIGURE 1
Effect of Aad and Extension Comparability on the Number of Brand-Relevant Thoughts

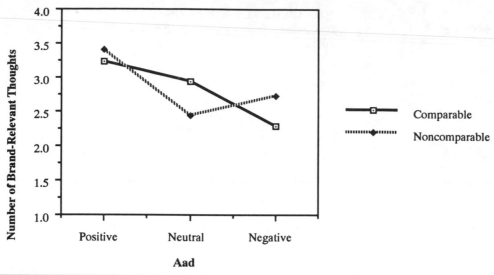

positive Aad increased the number of brand-relevant thoughts in part by increasing the number of thoughts on the advertised brand itself. That is, consumers who liked brand advertising might have had more thoughts on the brand to begin with. They were then probably better able to retrieve those brand-relevant thoughts later when they were asked to describe a brand extension.

A correlation analysis showed that the number of thoughts on the advertised brand was positively correlated with the number of brand-relevant thoughts on brand extensions (r=.41, p<.001). Aad, however, was *not* significantly correlated with the number of thoughts on the advertised brand (r=.07, p>.05). As a result, a hierarchical regression analysis showed that each of the two variables, the number of thoughts on the advertised-brand and Aad, had a unique and significant effect on the number of brand-relevant thoughts in brand extensions (Partial corr coeff.=.40, p<.001 for the number of thoughts on core-brand; Partial corr coeff.=.15, p=.05 for Aad). Therefore, Aad had a significant direct effect on the accessibility of the brand-attributes in consumers' perceptions of brand extensions.

Effect of Aad and Extension Comparability on Perceived Appropriateness of Brand Attributes. It was suggested that consumers' attitude toward the brand advertising would have a significant effect on the degree to which they thought the brand attributes were also appropriate for a brand extension. Specifically, it was hypothesized (H2a) that the more positive Aad was, the more consumers would think that the brand attributes were also appropriate for a brand extension. As expected, the more positive Aad was, the higher were the ratings on the perceived appropriateness of the brand attributes. Two separate hierarchical regression analyses (Table 2) showed that the main effect of Aad was overall strong and significant (p<.001) for the brand attributes whether they were category-congruent or category-incongruent. Therefore, H2a was supported.

It was also hypothesized (H2b) that the effect of Aad on the perceived appropriateness of the brand attributes would be more consistent for a noncomparable extension than for a comparable extension. Figure 2 shows the pattern of interaction. For a comparable extension, Aad had a differential influence on the perceived appropriateness of the brand attributes, depending on

their congruity with the category concept. It had a greater effect for the category-congruent attributes than it did for the category-incongruent attributes. For a noncomparable extension, on the other hand, Aad showed consistent effects on the perceived appropriateness of the brand attributes regardless of their congruity with the extension category. As a result, hierarchical regressions (Table 2) showed that the interaction between Aad and extension comparability was not significant for the category-congruent attributes (p>.05), but was significant for the category-incongruent attributes (p<.05). Therefore, H2b was supported.

Underlying process. Another issue of interest was the extent to which Aad had a direct effect on the perceived appropriateness of the brand attributes in a brand extension, and/or Aad had an indirect (i.e., mediated) effect through its effect on the brand itself. A separate analysis showed that Aad was positively correlated with the ratings of the brand attributes in the brand itself (r=.45, p<.001). That is, the more positive the participants' Aad was, the more they were likely to agree that the ad-claimed attributes appropriately described the brand. This, in turn, influenced the degree to which they thought that those attributes were also appropriate for the brand extensions. A hierarchical regression analysis was performed to see if the unique effect of Aad on the perceived appropriateness of the brand attributes in a brand extension remained significant after accounting for its effect on the brand itself. The result indicated that the unique effect of Aad became smaller, but remained significant even after accounting for its effect on the advertised brand (Partial corr coeff.=.11, p<.05). Therefore, Aad had both a significant direct effect *and* an indirect effect (through its influence on the brand) on the perceived appropriateness of the brand attributes in a brand extension.

Nonhypothesized Findings

Effect of Aad and Extension Comparability on Attitude Toward Brand Extension. Although no specific hypotheses were proposed, the effect of Aad on the participants' overall attitude toward the brand extension (Ab-ext) was also measured. The result suggested that Aad had a strong effect on their overall attitude toward the brand extension. The Aad explained more than a-third of the total variance in the overall attitude toward the brand

TABLE 2
Effects of Aad and Extension Comparability on the Rating of Perceived Appropriateness of Brand Attributes

HIERARCHICAL REGRESSION
(Category-Congruent)

Variable Order	R² Change	F Change	p
Order	.01	1.31	.27
Aad	.20	67.11	.001
Comparability	.001	.03	.86
Aad x Comparability	.001	.17	.68
Overall R²	.21		

	Comparable	Noncomparable
Positive	5.18	5.33
Negative	3.66	3.60

- -

(Category-Incongruent)

Variable Order	R² Change	F Change	p
Order	.01	1.62	.20
Aad	.11	32.28	.001
Comparability	.003	.98	.32
Aad x Comparability	.02	4.49	.04
Overall R²	.14		

	Comparable	Noncomparable
Positive	4.27	4.72
Negative	3.58	3.23

FIGURE 2
Effect of Aad and Extension Comparability on the Rating of Perceived Appropriateness of Brand Attributes
(Category-Congruent vs. Category-Incongruent)

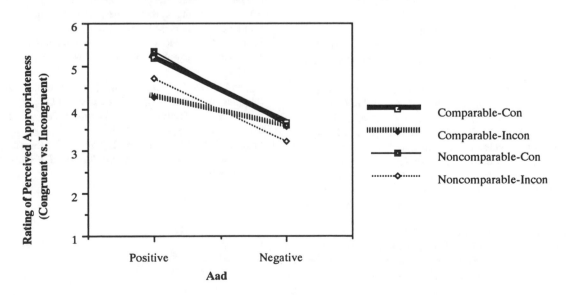

extension (R^2 change=.37, p<.001). Furthermore, the interaction between Aad and the extension comparability was significant (p<.05). That is, the overall increase occurred to a greater degree for a noncomparable extension than for a comparable extension. The average rating increased from 2.62 (among those who had a negative Aad) to 5.32 (among those who had a positive Aad) for a noncomparable extension, while it increased from 3.17 to 4.82 for a comparable extension.

DISCUSSION

Using fictitious brand names and realistic-looking advertisements may have overestimated, to some degree, the effect of advertising over a more stable effect of the brand itself. In addition, subjects were asked about a brand extension shortly after they gave their responses to the advertised brand. In the real world, there most likely will be a longer delay between consumers' exposure to brand advertising and to a brand extension. Thus, their responses to brand advertising may not be as salient in consumers' minds as they were in the current study. On the other hand, consumers are likely to be exposed to brand advertising more frequently in the real world. A previous study suggested that the frequency effect was stronger than the recency effect when there was a long delay between priming and an observation (Higgins, Bargh and Lombardi, 1985). Nevertheless, a future study may consider using a distraction task between participants' exposure to the advertisement and their response to a brand extension.

Within this and other limitations, findings from the current study seem to imply that consumers' attitude toward the brand advertising is important not only for the brand itself, but also for a future brand extension, especially when an extension is planned to a somewhat noncomparable category. Affect associated with the brand advertising shows a significant impact on they way consumers relate a brand extension to the brand, such as accessibility and perceived appropriateness of the brand attributes. Furthermore, the preliminary analyses suggest that the effect tends to occur to a greater degree (or more consistently) for a moderately noncomparable extension than for a comparable extension. These indications are consistent with the findings from previous research on the relationship between affect and cognitive organization. Therefore, consumers' attitude toward brand advertising may influence their perceptions of a brand extension in a similar way that an overall affective state influences individuals' cognitive organization.

REFERENCES

Aaker, David A. and Kevin Lane Keller (1990), "Consumer Evaluations of Brand Extensions," *Journal of Marketing*, 54 (January), 27-41.

Batra, Rajeev and Michael L. Ray (1986), "Affective Responses Mediating Acceptance of Advertising," *Journal of Consumer Research*, 13 (September), 234-249.

Branscombe, Nyla R. and Brian M. Cohen (1991), "Motivation and Complexity Levels as Determinants of Heuristic Use in Social Judgment," in *Emotion & Social Judgment*, ed., Joseph Forgas, New York: Pergamon Press, 145-160.

Cialdini, R. B., B. Darby and J. Vincent (1973), "Transgression and Altruism: A Case of Hedonism," *Journal of Experimental Social Psychology*, 9, 502-516.

Cohen, Joel B. and Charles S. Areni (1990), "Affect and Consumer Behavior," in *Handbook of Consumer Theory and Research*, eds. Harold Kassarjian and Thomas S. Robertson, Englewood Cliffs, NJ: Prentice Hall, 188-240.

Edell, Julie E. and Marian Chapman Burke (1992), "The Impact of Memorability of Ad-Induced Feelings: Implications for Brand Equity," in *Advertising and Building Strong Brands*, eds. David A. Aaker and Alexander L. Biel, in press.

Forgas, Joseph P. (1991), "Affect and Social Judgments: An Introductory Review," in *Emotion and Social Judgments*, (ed.), Joseph P. Forgas, New York: Pergamon Press, 3-29.

_____ and Gordon. H. Bower (1987), "Mood Effects on Person-Perception Judgment," *Journal of Personality and Social Psychology*, 53, 53-60.

Hitchon, Jacquelyn and Gilbert Churchill (1992), "To Be or What To Be: An Empirical Investigation of Metaphor Effects in Advertising Commercials," unpublished manuscript, University of Wisconsin-Madison.

Isen, Alice M. (1984), "Toward Understanding the Role of Affect in Cognition," in *Handbook of Social Cognition*, eds., Robert S. Wyer, Jr. and Thomas K. Srull, Hillsdale, NJ: Erlbaum, 179-236.

_____ (1987), "Positive Affect, Cognitive Process, and Social Behavior," in *Advances in Experimental Social Psychology*, ed., Leonard Berkowitz, New York: Academic Press. 20, 203-253.

_____ , and Kimberly A. Daubman (1984), "The Influence of Affect on Categorization," *Journal of Personality and Social Psychology*, 47 (6), 1206-1217.

Johnson, Michael D. (1984), "Consumer Choice Strategies for Comparing Noncomparable Alternatives," *Journal of Consumer Research*, 11 (December), 741-753.

Keller, Kevin Lane (1987), "Memory Factors in Advertising: The Effects of Advertising Retrieval Cues on Brand Evaluation," *Journal of Consumer Research*, 14 (December), 316-334.

Kunda, Z. (1987), "Motivated Inferences: Self-Serving Generation and Evaluation of Causal Theories, *Journal of Personality and Social Psychology*, 53, 636-647.

Murray, N. H., E. R. Hirt Sujan and Mita Sujan (1990), "The Influence of Mood on Categorization: A Cognitive Flexibility Hypothesis," *Journal of Personality and Social Psychology*, 59, 411-425.

Park, C. Whan, Sandra Milberg, and Robert Lawson (1991), "evaluation of Brand Extensions: The Role of Product Feature Similarity and Brand Concept Consistency," *Journal of Consumer Research*, 18 (September), 185-193.

Schwarz, Norbert and Herbert Bless (1991), "Happy and Mindless, But Sad and Smart? The Impact of Affective States on Analytic Reasoning," in *Emotion and Social Judgment*, ed. Joseph Forgas, New York: Pergamon Press, 55-71.

_____ and Gerald L. Clore (1983), "Mood, Misattribution, and Judgment of Well-Being: Informative and Directive Functions of Affective States," *Journal of Personality and Social Psychology*, 45, 513-523.

Stayman, Douglas M. and Rajeev Batra (1991), "Encoding and Retrieval of Ad Affect in Memory," *Journal of Marketing Research*, 28 (May), 232-239.

Effect of Cobranding on Consumer Product Evaluations

Clayton Hillyer, American International College
Surinder Tikoo, University of Connecticut

ABSTRACT

Cobranding, in which a product features more than one brand name, is being used increasingly by marketers. This paper uses current process models of attitude formation and change as an overall framework to discuss two important and interrelated issues with respect to cobranding: 1) how does cobranding influence consumer brand evaluations 2) and under what conditions is cobranding a useful brand strategy to adopt. The paper identifies and discusses the specific processes by which cobranding influences consumer product evaluations. This discussion is used to generate managerially relevant propositions about when cobranding will be an effective strategy to adopt.

INTRODUCTION

The practice of double branding products, in which a product features more than one brand name is known as cobranding. Kellogg's Pop Tarts with Smuckers preserves and Nabisco Cranberry Newtons with Ocean Spray Cranberries are examples of cobranding. A detailed discussion of the benefits of cobranding is provided by Norris (1992). There has been a significant increase in cobranded products in recent years, and most often these products have seen increased consumer acceptance after being cobranded (Wall Street Journal, August 3, 1993).

The cobrand (e.g., Kellogg's Pop Tarts with Smuckers Preserves) consists of a primary brand (PB - Kellog's Pop Tarts) and an associated secondary brand (SB - Smuckers Preserves). The SB is often an ingredient or component of the PB (e.g., Nabisco Cranberry Newtons with Ocean Spray Cranberries), but may also be part of the augmented PB (e.g., Honda Accord with a Motorola cellular phone). Marketers use cobranding to increase sales of the PB by enhancing consumer evaluation of the PB. To use a cobranding strategy effectively, marketers need to know the conditions under which cobranding can enhance consumer brand evaluations. Understanding how cobranding influences consumer product evaluation can help identify the conditions under which cobranding will be an effective strategy to adopt. There, however, has been little discussion in the marketing literature about cobranding.

This paper discusses two important and interrelated issues about cobranding: 1) how does cobranding influence consumer brand evaluations 2) and under what conditions is cobranding a useful brand strategy to adopt. The paper first discusses the likelihood that the input associated with the SB will be used; given that the input associated with the SB will be used, the paper uses current process models of attitude formation and change as an overall framework for understanding the nature of influence that cobranding has on consumer product evaluation. The paper then integrates findings from past research, within the context of the overall framework, to identify and discuss the specific processes by which cobranding influences consumer product evaluation. This integration is used to generate managerially relevant propositions about when cobranding will be an effective strategy to adopt.

Cobranding is used to strengthen the PB's competitive benefits, therefore the brand equity literature, which concerns itself with issues such as brand leverage, is relevant to the study of cobranding. In this study, we use insights from brand equity research, however, we do not use the brand equity research stream as the central framework. Marketing managers will want to use SBs that have favorable consumer associations, therefore an under-standing of brand equity is a prerequisite for cobranding. This paper focuses on developing a process-based framework that explains when and how a SB can contribute to strengthening a PB.

WILL THE SB HAVE ANY IMPACT?

For cobranding to influence consumers in any form, consumers must first use the information input associated with the SB. Feldman and Lynch's (1988) framework provides valuable insight into when the input associated with the SB will be used by consumers in judgement and choice tasks. According to the framework, the likelihood of the consumer using input A (the input associated with the SB) is a positive function of input A's accessibility in memory and its perceived diagnosticity and a negative function of the accessibility and diagnosticity of other inputs in memory. While this framework has been applied mainly to memory-based tasks, it is applicable to all inputs, whether or not the inputs are recalled or externally available.

Accessibility refers to the ability and ease with which a certain input can be acquired by the consumer, either externally or from memory. Accessibility is a necessary, but not always a sufficient condition. Accessible inputs must also be perceived as diagnostic. Diagnosticity refers to the perceived relevance of the input to the judgment or choice task. A diagnostic input provides information that can be utilized to further evaluate an alternative or discriminate among alternatives.

DEPTH OF PROCESSING AS A DETERMINANT OF COBRANDING EFFECTS

We suggest that the nature of influence that cobranding has on consumer evaluation and choice is dependent on the extent to which consumers process the information related to the SB. Recent process models of attitude formation and change provide a useful overall framework for understanding the influence of cobranding on brand evaluation. Both the Elaboration Likelihood Model (ELM) (Petty and Cacioppo 1986) and the Heuristic-Systematic Model (HSM) (Chaiken, Liberman, and Eagly 1989) posit two paths to persuasion and enhanced evaluation: (1) shallower processing (called peripheral route and heuristic-processing respectively) and (2) deeper processing (called central route and systematic-processing respectively). The key factors affecting the depth of processing are generally agreed to be the motivation to process (involvement), the ability to process (brand familiarity, expertise, intelligence), and the opportunity to process (noise, contingencies). In the next two sections we examine cobranding in the context of shallower and deeper processing.

COBRANDING AND SHALLOWER PROCESSING

Shallower processing suggests that consumers prefer to conserve their cognitive resources. Under shallower processing, cobranding can affect consumer product evaluation and choice in three different ways: (1) influence on composition of the consideration set, (2) halo effect, and (3) facilitate the use of heuristics. Each of these influences is primarily due to the increased accessibility of the input associated with the SB.

Inclusion in Consideration Set

A highly accessible SB can increase the accessibility of the PB through associative cuing in which the SB acts as a retrieval cue for the PB (Alba, Hutchinson, and Lynch 1991). This associative cuing can increase the likelihood of the consumer considering the PB. Research has shown that the inclusion of a brand in, and the size of, the consumer's consideration set is an important determinant of brand choice (Hauser 1978). It has also been shown that the presence of a brand in and the size of the consideration set can affect choice without altering brand evaluations (Nedungadi 1990). For the accessibility of the PB to increase through associative cuing, it is necessary that the SB be highly accessible and the evaluative dimension represented by the SB be salient. Moderating these factors in memory-based tasks is the strength of the association between the PB and the SB: a highly accessible SB can only serve as a retrieval cue for the PB if there is an established association between the two. Accessibility can also play an important role in stimulus-based decisions (e.g., walking down a supermarket aisle) by increasing brand recognition because of perceptual enhancement (Jacoby 1983). More accessible brand names and marks tend to be recognized first, especially if they are considered prototypical of the product category (Alba et al., 1991). Thus, a consumer's attention may be drawn first to a highly accessible SB displayed on the PB's packaging, which in turn, increases the likelihood of the PB's inclusion in the consideration set.

While the favorableness of the evaluation of the SB will often play a large role in ultimately determining brand choice, a negative evaluation of the SB doesn't necessarily deny inclusion into the consideration set, because both positive and negative brand names can be highly accessible. For example, consider a scenario where the SB is the only recognizable brand name among the cobrand and the other competitive brands. Even if the SB has a less than favorable evaluation, it may be the first, and only member of the consideration set when consumer motivation is low.

P1: The greater the accessibility of the SB, the more likely the PB will be a member of the consideration set.

P2: P1 will be moderated by the saliency of the dimension associated with the SB and the pre-existing association between the SB and PB for memory-based evaluations.

Halo Effect

According to Fazio (1986) the greater the attitude strength, the greater is the accessibility of the attitude object. Fazio describes attitude strength as the link between the attitude object and its evaluation, regardless of its favorableness. Highly accessible attitudes are retrieved spontaneously on the mere observation or mention of the attitude object. The retrieved affect toward the attitude object influences consumer perception by favoring attitude-consistent information and behavior (Fazio, Powell, and Williams 1989). The ELM suggests that the positive affect associated with the SB may be "transferred" to or "confused" with the affect associated with the PB.

In a cobranding context (shallower processing), the spontaneously retrieved affect associated with a highly accessible SB may, to some degree, transfer to the entire cobrand. One would expect this effect to be more likely when the consumer has no or a weakly held attitude toward the PB. For example, when a consumer evaluates an unfamiliar or less known brand of pop tarts cobranded with Smuckers real fruit filling, the affect generated from the brand associations for Smuckers will be associated with the evaluation of the entire product.

P3: The greater the accessibility and positive (negative) affect associated with the SB, the more (less) effective

cobranding will be because of a halo effect toward the PB.

Heuristics Favoring the PB

According to the HSM, consumers use accessible decision rules (heuristics) for interpreting information when their use can reduce cognitive effort while providing sufficient confidence (i.e., diagnosticity) in their application (Chaiken et al., 1989). In addition to generating a halo effect, a highly accessible SB may also lead a consumer to retrieve, with little or no effort, successful past decision heuristics associated with a highly accessible SB. Because the SB is highly accessible, these heuristics would probably come to mind before other heuristics. For example, heuristics based upon affect or brand familiarity should be readily accessible when the SB is activated in a consumer's memory.

The activation of these heuristics may make them attractive to the consumer. First, there is the familiar association between these heuristics and the SB, which is part of the cobrand. The notion of confidence in their applicability (i.e., diagnosticity) suggests that these heuristics are more attractive when the SB is perceived to be an integral part of the most desired benefits sought by the consumer from the cobrand.

Second, consumers are probably more willing to use heuristics associated with the SB because, under low involvement, consumers are more likely to be cognitive misers. In many low involvement purchase situations, the cognitive costs involved in retrieving/constructing alternative heuristics are greater than the perceived marginal gain, in better decision making, that will result from using these alternative heuristics compared to using the already accessible heuristics associated with the SB. For example, consider a consumer who chooses a household bleach by using a heuristic that specifies to choose the brand with which the consumer is most familiar. Now, when shopping for a ceramic tile cleaner, the consumer comes upon a tile cleaner cobranded with Clorox bleach. We argue that the brand familiarity heuristic that was used for the SB will be accessed and may be applied to the tile cleaner category. The consumer's actual use of the SB-related heuristic to evaluate the cobrand and its impact on the consumer's evaluation of the cobrand will be moderated by the degree to which the SB contributes to the benefits sought by the consumer from the cobrand.

P4: The greater the accessibility and favorableness of consumer associations of the SB, and the greater the SB's contribution to the benefits sought by the consumer, the greater the likelihood that the consumer will use heuristics that are associated with the SB.

Pairing the SB and PB entails pairing their respective brand equity/liability (the summary of their respective brand associations). Under shallower processing, the brand associations that comprise brand equity for the SB may influence the overall evaluation of the PB even though many of these brand associations may have little bearing on the PB's performance on the evaluative dimension associated with the SB.

When the brand associations of the SB are strong, the SB lends credibility to the PB by acting as an augmenting cue in consumer inferences and judgements. As a result, consumers may be more inclined to increase their acceptance of all of the PB's claims, because they may infer that a highly credible brand (high equity) would only allow itself to be associated with another "quality" brand. This effect is more likely to occur when the consumer also has strong brand associations of the PB.

When the SB does not have strong brand associations, especially when compared to the strength of the brand associations the consumer has for the PB, one would expect the opposite effect. The SB will serve as a discounting cue and cause the consumer to be less willing to accept PB claims. Here, the SB undermines the credibility of the PB and lowers the evaluation of the PB on dimensions other than the one associated with the SB. It should be noted that attributional processing, such as the one just described is classified as peripheral route processing (Petty, Unnava, and Strathman 1991). We, however, also recognize that depth of processing is a matter of degree rather than a dichotomy. Clearly, with respect to the effect of attributional processing discussed here, the consumer must reach some upper threshold within shallow processing at which he/she is motivated to engage in causal attribution.

P5: When the brand associations of the SB are favorable (unfavorable), cobranding will enhance (diminish) the evaluation of the PB on all salient dimensions, including evaluative dimensions not associated with the SB.

COBRANDING AND DEEPER PROCESSING

The expectancy-value model of consumer evaluations provides a useful model for understanding consumer evaluations under deeper processing (Fishbein and Ajzen 1975). The two components of the expectancy-value model are consumer evaluations (e_i) of salient product attributes and consumer beliefs (b_i) about the extent to which a particular brand possesses the salient attributes. According to the expectancy-value model, a consumer's evaluation of a brand is shaped by (1) the importance the consumer accords to an attribute currently under consideration, (2) the consumer's consideration of an attribute or attributes that were not previously considered, and (3) the consumer's beliefs about the extent to which a brand possesses the salient attributes. We believe these are important considerations related to the effectiveness of cobranding and discuss each in turn.

Importance Accorded to Salient Evaluative Dimensions.

With respect to the importance that consumers accord to an attribute, there is a difference between products for which consumers have well formed beliefs versus products for which consumers have less well formed beliefs. When consumers have well formed beliefs about attribute importance, saliency is thought to often correspond to their internal needs and motives. However, when consumers do not have well formed beliefs about attribute importance, research has shown that factors such as familiarity (Alba and Hutchinson 1987), repetition (Wright and Rip 1980), increasing the prominence of stimuli (Gardner 1983), priming (Herr 1989), and the presence of retrieval cues (Keller 1987) can increase salience by tapping or increasing the attitude strength of the attitude object.

Viewed in this light, it is easy to see how a SB may increase the saliency of the evaluative dimension associated with SB, especially if the SB is heavily advertised (repetition), is a market leader (familiarity), and is featured prominently in PB advertising, sales promotion, packaging, etc (prominence, retrieval cue, priming), especially when consumers do not have well formed beliefs about attribute importance. Marketers may gain by utilizing a SB that offers unique or superior performance on a evaluative dimension that has little impact on overall PB performance. Cobranding should be effective at increasing the saliency of evaluative dimensions regardless of their objective impact on product performance in product categories in which assessing brand performance is complex, problematic because of long-term effects and/or are ambiguous because there are no clear criteria with which to relate

attribute performance to overall performance. In these cases, consumers are likely to increase the salience of dimensions made more familiar and accessible by the presence of the SB.

It is important to note that the following propositions are moderated by the pre-existing association between the PB and the SB. Accordingly, until the association between the PB and SB is adequately established in the minds of consumers, cobranding will be more effective when the association is available externally during judgement or choice (stimulus-based) tasks.

P6: The greater the SB accessibility the more effective cobranding will be at increasing the salience of existing evaluative dimensions.

The salience of the evaluative dimension associated with the SB is determined, to a degree, by the accessibility of other inputs. Highly accessible salient cues have been shown to inhibit the recall of less accessible information (Alba and Chattopadhyay 1986). A highly accessible SB that acts as a retrieval cue for its associated evaluative dimension may also inhibit the recall of other evaluative dimensions. This inhibition effect is thought to be moderated by consumer knowledge (Alba et al., 1991). Consumers with extensive knowledge are less susceptible to inhibition in part-cuing tasks. Thus, the ability of cobranding to inhibit other evaluative dimensions would be greatest when consumers do not hold well formed beliefs and have relatively little product category experience.

P7: The greater the accessibility of the SB, the fewer other evaluative dimensions consumers will be able to recall, especially when they do not have well formed beliefs about attribute importance.

When consumers have well formed beliefs about the importance of a particular product attribute, the presence of the SB through cobranding is likely to be more effective for reinforcing already highly salient evaluative dimensions and less effective for less salient evaluative dimensions, because consumers are biased toward confirming their existing beliefs (Hoch and Deighton 1989). Confirmation bias implies that a highly accessible SB will receive even more attention because it provides information consistent with the consumer's beliefs about the importance of the attribute associated with the SB. Therefore, cobranding is an attractive strategy when the PB performs well on a sole or few primary salient evaluative dimensions and marginally on secondary evaluative dimensions.

P8: When consumers have well formed beliefs about the attribute importance of the PB, cobranding with a highly accessible SB will be more (less) effective at increasing the salience of evaluative dimensions that already have high (low or no) salience.

Non-salient Attributes become Salient

For the consumer to consider the attribute associated with the SB, that was not previously considered, requires that the associated dimension should become more accessible and also must be diagnostic. In this case accessibility is not a sufficient condition for increasing saliency, especially when the consumer has well formed beliefs regarding attribute importance.

Critical to diagnosticity is the perceived contribution of the SB to the overall utility or benefit of the PB, similar to the notion of "perceptual fit" in the brand equity research stream. Diagnosticity provided by the SB should be stronger the more the SB is perceived as a direct causal agent of highly desired consumer benefits. For consumers with well formed beliefs about attribute importance, cobranding would be better suited for introducing a new brand attribute (Crest toothpaste with Listerine) or brand variant (Kellog's Pop Tarts with Nutrasweet) because consumers are not likely to change their beliefs about existing evaluative dimensions. For consumers without well formed beliefs, cobranding appears suited for making almost any evaluative dimension salient for the same reasons as discussed with regard to Proposition 6.

P9: The more the SB's perceived contribution to the desired benefits provided by the PB, the more salient a previously non-salient attribute will become, given equal levels of accessibility.

Beliefs About Attribute Performance

Assuming accessibility and diagnosticity constant, the beliefs associated with the SB will also influence the evaluation of the PB. The best situation would be that beliefs associated with the SB be more favorable than the actual beliefs or inferred beliefs associated with the PB ($b_{SBi} > b_{PBi}$) on a particular evaluative dimension. This is possible if the SB is stronger than the PB on the evaluative dimension.

While changing beliefs about the attribute presence is probably the most intuitively effective way to enhance the evaluation of the PB, it is possible, given a distribution of consumer preferences, that some segment of consumers will not perceive the SB as improving the PB performance on that evaluative dimension. This is most likely to occur when the SB "replaces" an existing attribute that consumers were already satisfied with (attribute loyal or why fix it if it ain't broke?). In this case, there exists the possibility that cobranding may harm the evaluation of the PB because cobranding may evoke psychological reactance (Brehm 1966). Reactance theory posits that when a consumer feels their personal freedom (i.e., brand choice) is somehow being impinged upon or threatened, they react negatively toward the object and are motivated to restore their lost freedom. The intense reaction of brand loyal Coca-Cola drinkers to "New Coke" (and the loss of the "Old" Coke) has been cited as a case of consumer reactance (Mowen 1988).

As a response to this "unwanted" cobranding strategy and the loss of the original PB, these consumers are likely to lower their overall evaluation of the PB and possibly purchase the PB less often. For example, some consumers pleased with the performance of the Ford engine in the Ford Taurus may experience reactance at cobranding the Taurus with an engine manufactured by Mitsubishi, and therefore purchase a different model.

P10: When consumers hold similar or more favorable beliefs of attribute performance for the PB compared to the SB for a salient attribute prior to cobranding, cobranding may cause brand loyal consumers to lower their evaluations of the PB, especially if the non-cobranded product is not available after the introduction of the cobrand.

On the other hand, if the evaluative dimension represented by the SB is new and does not replace any existing beliefs, then consumers are not likely to experience reactance. Introducing low calorie Kellogg's Pop Tarts with Nutrasweet is less likely to evoke reactance if this is a new brand variant (low calorie).

P11: When consumers hold similar or more favorable beliefs of attribute performance for the PB compared to the SB and the evaluative dimension associated

with the SB was previously non-salient, then cobranding will not lower the evaluation of the PB.

The discussion up to this point has separated the effect cobranding has on beliefs (b_i) and saliency (e_i) for ease of presentation and because it is theoretically possible to enhance evaluations without changing beliefs. In reality, adopting a cobrand in many situations will affect the salience of an evaluative dimension and existing beliefs. Ideally, cobranding will increase the saliency of the evaluative dimension associated with the SB and lead to more positive beliefs regarding the performance of the cobrand on that evaluative dimension. An important question is whether these are independent effects or whether they result in a favorable interaction effect. Some current research suggests increasing the saliency of an evaluative dimension can also influence the performance of a brand on that evaluative dimension, even when the evaluation is based upon direct experience (Hoch and Ha 1986). While there is a need for more research in this area, increased saliency of an evaluative dimension may tend to amplify or polarize a consumer's belief regarding attribute performance because of increased attention and thought. Research has shown that increased levels of mere thought (i.e. self-persuasion) can lead to the polarization of evaluations under deeper processing (Chaiken and Yates 1985).

P12: The greater the joint accessibility and favorable (unfavorable) beliefs toward the SB, the more positive (negative) the ordinal interaction between the two factors, and the more positive (negative) the affect of cobranding on PB evaluation.

SUMMARY AND CONCLUSION

This paper discussed the influence of cobranding on consumer product evaluations. The influence of cobranding on consumer product evaluations will differ depending on whether the evaluation is characterized by high involvement (deeper processing) or low involvement (shallower processing). Under shallower processing, cobranding will change the likelihood of the cobranded PB being included in the consideration set, the halo affect associated with the SB will transfer to the cobrand, and the presence of the SB will facilitate the use of heuristics that are compatible with the consumer's behavior with respect to the SB. Under deeper processing, cobranding will lead to greater salience of the evaluative dimension associated with the SB, a change in beliefs about the extent to which the cobrand possesses the attribute associated with the SB, and make previously nonsalient dimensions salient.

Cobranding is one of the many different strategies that marketers can employ to make consumers evaluate their brand more favorably. This paper uses existing theoretical insights to provide normative guidelines about the conditions under which cobranding is an effective option. The discission in this paper compares a cobrand strategy to a no cobrand strategy. Within cobranding itself, the marketer will have to choose a SB among different candidate SBs. The financial and pricing aspects of a cobranding strategy, such as possible increases in cost have to be considered while evaluating the suitability of a cobranding strategy.

Present trends indicate that there will be a significant increase in cobranded products in the future, because of which the study of cobranding is a useful endeavor. Future research can test empirically the propositions developed in this paper. Cobranding, especially of the augmented type is akin to bundling. Research using a bundling perspective (such as used in research on pricing) can also be used to analyze cobranding.

REFERENCES

Brehm, Jack W. (1966), *A Theory of Psychological Reactance*, San Diego, CA: Academic Press.

Alba, Joseph W. and Amitava Chattopadhyay (1986),"Salience Effects in Brand Recall," *Journal of Marketing Research*, 23 (November), 363-369.

_____ and J. Wesley Hutchinson (1987),"Dimensions of Consumer Expertise," *Journal of Consumer Research*, 13 (March), 411-454.

_____, J. Wesley Hutchinson, and John G. Lynch, Jr. (1991), "Memory and Decision Making," in *Handbook of Consumer Behavior*, eds. Thomas Robertson and Horold H. Kassarjian, Prentice Hall: NJ.

Chaiken, Shelly, Alice Liberman, and Alice H. Eagly (1989), "Heuristic and Systematic Processing within and beyond the Persuasion Context," in *Unintended Thought*, eds. J. S. Uleman and J. A. Bargh, New York: Guilford Press.

_____, and S. M. Yates (1985),"Affective-Cognitive Consistency and Thought-Induced Attitude Polarization," *Journal of Personality and Social Psychology*, 49, 1470-1481.

Fazio, Russel H. (1986), "How do Attitudes Guide Behavior?," in *Handbook of Motivation and Cognition: Foundation of Social Behavior*, eds. Richard M. Sorrentino and Tory E. Higgins, New York: Guilford, 204-243.

Fazio, Russel H, Martha C. Powell, and Carol J. Williams (1989), "The Role of Attitude Accessibility in the Attitude-to-Behavior Process," *Journal of Consumer Research*, 16 (December), 280-288.

Feldman, Jack M. and John G. Lynch (1988),"Self Generated Validity and Other Effects of Measurement on Belief, Attitude, Intention, and Behavior, *Journal of Applied Psychology*, 73 (August), 421-435.

Fishbein, Martin and Izek Ajzen (1975), *Belief, Attitude, Intention and Behavior: An Introduction to Theory and Research*. Reading, MA: Addison-Wesley.

Gardner, Meryl Paula (1983)," Advertising Effects on Attributes Recalled and Criteria Used for Brand Evaluations,"*Journal of Consumer Research*, 10 (December), 310-318.

Hauser, John R. (1978),"Testing the Accuracy, Usefulness, and Significance of Probabilistic Models: An Information Theoretic Approach," *Operations Research*, 26 (May/June), 406-421.

Herr, Paul M. (1989),"Priming Price: Prior Knowledge and Context Effects,"*Journal of Consumer Research*, 16 (June), 67-75.

Hoch, Stephen J. and John Deighton (1989)," Managing What Consumers Learn From Experience," *Journal of Marketing*, 53 (April), 1-20.

Hoch, Stephen J. and Young-Won Ha (1986)," Consumer Learning: Advertising and the Ambiguity of Product Experience," *Journal of Consumer Research*, 13 (September), 221-233.

Jacoby, Larry L. (1983), "Perceptual Enhancement: Persistent Effects of an Experience," *Journal of Experimental Psychology: Learning, Memory, and Cognition*, 9 (January), 21-38.

Keller, Kevin L. (1987), "Memory Factors in Advertising: The Effect of Advertising Retrieval Cues on Brand Evaluations," *Journal of Consumer Research*, 14 (December), 316-333.

Mowen, John C. (1988),"Beyond Consumer Decision Making,"*Journal of Consumer Marketing*, 5, 15-25.

Nedungadi, Prakash (1990),"Recall and Consumer Consideration Sets: Influencing Choice Without Altering Brand Evaluations," *Journal of Consumer Research*, 17, 263-276.

Norris, Donald G. (1992),"Ingredient Branding: A Strategy Option with Multiple Beneficiaries," *Journal of Consumer Marketing*, 9, 19-31.

Petty, Richard E. and John T. Cacioppo, (1986) *Communication and Persuasion: Central and Peripheral Routes to Attitude Change*: New York: Springer/Verlag

Petty, Richard E., Rao H. Unnava, and Alan J. Strathman (1991),"Theories of Attitude Change," in *Handbook of Consumer Behavior*, eds. Thomas Robertson and Harold H. Kassarjian: Prentice Hall: New Jersey

Wright, Peter (1975),"Consumer Choice Strategies: Simplifying vs. Optimizing," *Journal of Marketing Research*, 12 (February), 60-67.

Wright, Peter and Peter D. Rip (1980),"Product Class Advertising Effects on First Time Buyers' Decision Strategies," *Journal of Consumer Research*, 7 (September), 176-188.

A Conceptual Framework for Analyzing the Impact of a Me-too Entrant on the Pioneer's Market Share

Jaideep Sengupta, University of California, Los Angeles

ABSTRACT

Earlier research has found that a pioneering brand attains a sustainable competitive advantage in relation to later entrants, especially me-too brands, by being identified as the prototype of the product category, and thus gaining in perceptual distinctiveness. However, is a prototype model of schemas always appropriate? Research in psychology and marketing points to the existence of an alternate model, namely, the exemplar model of schemas. This article discusses how the competing models can be used to arrive at diametrically opposite predictions concerning the effectiveness of a me-too strategy to counter a pioneer, and sets forth conditions under which each of these models is appropriate.

Marketing research on pioneering has traditionally examined the phenomenon from the firm's point of view (e.g., Robinson and Fornell 1985, Robinson 1988, Kalyanram and Urban 1992). Not much research has addressed the issue of pioneering from the consumer's perspective. A study by Carpenter and Nakamoto (1989; hereafter CN) represents an exception (see also Kardes and Kalyanram 1992). This study used an experimental approach and, based on a prototype model of schemas (Fiske and Taylor 1991), showed that pioneering advantages can result from the way consumers learn about brands and form preference structures. An important finding of this study was that me-too entrants actually ended up enhancing the pioneer's market share advantage by reinforcing the perception of the pioneer as the category prototype.

CN's paper raises an interesting question–is there an alternate learning process under which me-too entrants can actually *hurt* the pioneer, and if so, what are the conditions under which these alternate mechanisms prevail? This is a pertinent question, since pioneers often *do* fail (Golder and Tellis 1993), and a major reason for their failure would seem to be that later entrants can easily imitate the pioneer, at a low cost (Liebermann and Montgomery 1988, Kerin, Varadarajan and Peterson 1992, Golder and Tellis 1993).

Thus, although Carpenter & Nakamoto's (1989) proposed mechanism represents an important step in studying the consumer processes related to pioneering, a more complete framework would also explain why pioneering may not always be a successful strategy, and show how a me-too entrant may hurt the pioneer.

The goal of this paper, as a first step in ongoing research, is to provide such a conceptual framework, by presenting an alternate learning mechanism which explains how a me-too entrant could hurt the pioneer. CN used the prototype model of schemas as the theoretical foundation for their proposed learning mechanism. We use a competing model of schemas-the exemplar model-as the foundation of the alternate learning mechanism we propose.

We also present a set of propositions delineating the conditions under which these two alternative learning mechanisms will prevail.

WHY PIONEERING WORKS: CARPENTER AND NAKAMOTO (1989)

CN argue that the process by which consumers learn about brands and form preferences for them has an important role in creating an advantage for pioneers, and that this process has two components. First, in the early stages of many markets, consumers may know little about the importance of the product attributes or their ideal combination. Thus, a successful early entrant can have a major influence on how attributes are valued and on the ideal attribute combination. Coca-Cola, for example, may have had a significant impact in its early years on the formation and evolution of individuals' preferences for colas. This influence can shift individuals' preferences to favor the pioneer over later entrants, leading to a market share advantage for the pioneer. In essence, following successful experiences with the pioneering brand, buyers come to perceive the combination of attributes possessed by that brand as the ideal combination, an idea which is reinforced by advertising.

The above process represents the first component of CN's explanation of the pioneering advantage. However, this process in itself would not provide long term pioneering advantage, since later entrants would merely position themselves at the consumers' "ideal point" which has been created by the pioneer. The second component of CN's explanation, which we discuss below, is based on the notion that consumers hold schemas for a product category (Sujan 1985) and that pioneers are perceived as being 'prototypical' of the schema, thus giving them a sustainable competitive advantage.

The Prototype Model of Schemas

A schema is defined as a memory representation of a particular stimulus domain (Fiske and Taylor 1991). A schema contains information about the category it represents, and is often used to categorize a new stimulus. Thus a schema about the category 'colas' may contain attributes such as "carbonated", "sweet" etc., as well as the interrelationships between these attributes, and a new drink possessing these typical attributes may be categorized as a cola, without much effort.

However, it is not always clear which instances belong to a category; thus, baseball may be a good example of the category "games", but betting on the Super Bowl may not (Fiske and Taylor 1991). The perception that some instances are more typical than others leads to the basic idea underlying the prototype model; namely, that instances range from being quite typical to atypical, with a most typical or prototypical instance best representing the category. The prototype is the "central tendency" or average of the category members (Fiske and Taylor 1991).

People may never actually encounter their prototypes in real life because they are abstracted from experiences with examples. Even though none of the instances may itself be a perfect prototype, people abstract out the most typical or average features. Further, according to this model, a new instance is classified as being a member of the category following comparison only with the abstract prototype, not with 'real' examples or instances of the category.

A prototype may, of course, be a real example of the category as well, in the cases where a category instance gets so strongly associated with the category as to become the prototype for that category. In such a situation, new instances are classified following comparison with this real 'example' which happens to be the prototype. Other examples of the category are not used in the classification attempt For example, for some people, Coca-Cola may be the prototype for the category 'colas' and new instances will be classified following comparison only with this prototype. The prototype thus becomes highly salient and distinct in peoples' perceptions, and the other instances of the category are neglected in comparison.

CN use this version of the prototype model to explain pioneering advantage by suggesting that the pioneer has a unique distinctiveness derived from its being representative of the category, thus acting as the prototype for that category. Being perceptually distinct, the pioneer overshadows brands positioned nearby, especially me-too brands that often rely on the pioneer to establish their identity.

Since the pioneer acts as the prototype, any new entrant in that product category is compared to the pioneer, and the closer the entrant is positioned to the pioneer, the more it serves to reinforce the idea of the pioneer as the category standard. That is, a me-too entrant helps the pioneer to become even more strongly associated with the category in the mind of the consumer. In so doing, the me-too entrant helps the pioneer by reinforcing its identity, and at the same time, suffers from its own lack of a unique identity. Therefore, as long as ambiguity remains concerning an objective ideal point for the category, comparisons drawn between the me-too entrant and the pioneer invariably favor the pioneer.

For a similar reason, price-cutting by me-too brands has little impact on the advantage of the pioneer. Being closer to the pioneer, the me-too brand is less distinct than the pioneer, so any price reduction has a smaller impact than a similar price reduction by a more differentiated rival.

Pioneering brands, therefore, have a perceptually based competitive advantage based on their prototypicality, that insulates them from competitors and may actually *reverse* competitive forces. Attempts by a me-too to cut price and reposition toward the pioneer to "compete away" its high share *increase* the pioneer's advantage by increasing the pioneer's perceptual mass.

Based on the foregoing, CN suggest a strategy for a later entrant to overcome the pioneer's advantage. The principal competitive disadvantage for a later entrant lies in its lack of distinctiveness, especially if it is positioned as a me-too of the pioneer. A later entrant should therefore try to diminish the impact of the pioneer's distinctiveness and increase its own by moving away from the pioneer. By doing so, it can establish an identity for itself, and thus become perceptually more distinctive.

Further, if a brand does wish to use the me-too strategy, it would seem to make sense for it to copy a differentiated later entrant, rather than the pioneer. Positioning closer to a differentiated entrant helps develop recognition for the market segment and increases the relative prominence of both the distinctive entrant and its me-too. Furthermore, by decreasing the relative distinctiveness of the pioneer, this segmentation strategy increases the market shares of both the brands at the pioneer's expense. In other words, by copying a differentiated entrant, a competing perceptual mass is set up which can effectively challenge the pioneer's perceptual mass.

The ideas discussed above were verified experimentally by CN. To summarize, their key findings were, that given a product-market with ambiguous attribute weights and an ambiguous ideal point:

1. The more similar a me-too entrant to the pioneer, the more it helps the pioneer in terms of increasing share.
2. A price cut by a me-too does not hurt the pioneer as much as an equivalent price cut by a later entrant.
3. The market share advantage of the pioneer decreases as the similarity between the differentiated later entrant and its me-too increases.

The above results are based on a learning process which rests on the prototype model of schemas. It is important to remember that according to the prototype model, the different elements of a schema do not come easily to mind when thinking of the category; what does come to mind is a "typical" element of the category. Thereby, the ability to distinguish between different elements of the category is severely diminished, and only the prototype gains perceptual distinctiveness.

CN's results certainly seem counterintuitive to some extent. Given a rational consumer, one would expect a close imitator of the pioneer to reduce the pioneer's market share, not increase it. Similarly, a price-cut by the me-too should adversely affect the pioneer. Finally, if a later entrant has a me-too substitute, the pioneer should gain because the later entrant and its me-too will compete away each other's share. We propose to show that these results are predicted by an alternate learning process which is based on the exemplar model of schemas.

THE EXEMPLAR MODEL OF SCHEMAS

As a counterpoint to the prototype perspective, the exemplar approach (e.g. Brooks 1978; Hintzman 1986), suggests that one remembers separate instances (or exemplars) one has actually encountered, rather than some average prototype one has abstracted from experience. In this view, people categorize a new instance by seeing whether it resembles a lot of remembered exemplars from a category, rather than by comparing it with a single prototype. Thus, according to the exemplar view of schemas, a number of instances of a category (not just a single prototypical instance) can be highly salient perceptually and distinct in memory.

Fiske and Taylor (1991), in a concise review, note that the exemplar view has several advantages over the prototype view of schemas in being able to explain a number of schema-related issues with more ease. The exemplar view most directly accounts for people's knowledge of specific examples that guide their understanding of a category. For example, to refute an assertion that all luxury cars come with power windows, one may retrieve a specific counter-example from the category 'luxury cars'. This reliance on concrete instances suggests the idea of exemplars and supports the thesis that an exemplar viewpoint allows for the salience of different category members.

Further, people often know a lot about the possible variation of members within the category. A prototype theory cannot represent information about variability. However, it is easy to describe people's knowledge of such variation by positing exemplars. Again, such knowledge of variability implies that the consumer is in a position to retrieve specific examples of a category.

Within social cognition, the exemplar model is emerging as a powerful alternative to the prototype model (Smith and Zarate 1990). It has been used to explain how people make judgments about an individual from another culture (Read 1987), the effect of irrelevant similarities on judgments (Gilovich 1981), and facets of the ingroup - outgroup effect (Linville, Fischer and Salovey 1989).

In consumer research, a study of advertising schemas revealed that consumers contain specific examples of ads within a product category, rather than general rules for 'typical ads' (Goodstein, Moore and Cours 1992). In another recent consumer study, Basu (1993) found some evidence for the presence of prototype versus exemplar based processing under different informational conditions.

The accumulated evidence indicates that there is good reason to theorize about the exemplar model, although the prototype model has traditionally received more attention in schema research.

A key difference between the prototype model and the exemplar model (especially relevant in the context of the pioneering problem) is that the prototype model posits that the schema contains an abstract, global, generalized representation of the category, whereas the exemplar model suggests that the schema contains differentiated, individual instances of the category. If the exemplar model is the "true" one, then the different members of a category will all be salient, and similarities and differences between these members can easily be perceived.

Thus, if an exemplar model is a better representation than a prototype model of the way a majority of consumers view a product category, CN's hypotheses concerning the pioneering advantage may not hold true. If consumers recognize the different brands as distinct entities, as is the case under an exemplar viewpoint, the different examples of the category (i.e. the different brands) will all be perceptually salient and distinctive. Positioning a new entrant near the pioneer should not enhance the abstracted 'perceptual mass' of the pioneer, because such an abstraction only holds good under the prototype viewpoint. On the contrary, such an entrant will steal market share from the pioneer since consumers will perceive it as a substitutable brand. This adverse effect on the pioneer's share will be strengthened if the me-too is priced lower. Finally, if a later entrant competes with its me-too, the pioneer should gain by the competition between these two brands since the consumer is able to treat the brands distinctly and observe their similarities and differences, unlike in the prototype case where the later entrant and its me-too together form an abstract perceptual mass against the pioneer.

Based on the foregoing, we arrive at the following proposition which is the basis for our conceptual framework:

P1   If an exemplar model, as opposed to a prototype model, is the true representation of the consumers' learning process, then:
  A.   The more similar a me-too entrant to the pioneer, the more it hurts the pioneer in terms of market share.
  B.   A price cut by a me-too hurts the pioneer more than an equivalent price cut by a later entrant.
  C.   The market share advantage of the pioneer increases as the similarity between the differentiated later entrant and its me-too increases.

Simply put, our framework suggests that a prototype based learning process implies that a me-too entrant will help the pioneer, while an exemplar based learning process implies that a me-too entrant will hurt the pioneer.

The remainder of this paper discusses the moderating factors which determine when each learning model is appropriate.

PROTOTYPES VERSUS EXEMPLARS: A RESOLUTION

The set of moderating factors that follows has been culled from various streams of research in social cognition and marketing.

Order of Learning

Researchers have obtained exemplar versus prototype based processing by manipulating the way people learn initial information about the category. For example, in one study, subjects who learned about group prototypes before encountering individual group members engaged in more prototype based processing, relative to subjects who were given information about group members at the outset (Smith and Zarate 1990, see also Medin, Altom and Murphy 1984). In another study, Basu (1993) induced

prototype versus exemplar based processing by giving subjects a categorization rule or exposing them to a number of category exemplars, respectively.

In the consumer domain, it may happen that the consumer learns about the product category through a set of abstract attributes, or through experiences with various brands. In the latter case, the exemplar based model of schema representation and categorization should be more appropriate than the prototype model.

P2   If consumers' initial information about the product category comes through exposure to various brands, rather than to an attribute based category rule, the learning process will be based on the exemplar model, and a me-too entrant will hurt the pioneer. However, if the initial information about the category comes through an attribute based category rule, the learning process will be based on the prototype model and a me-too entrant will help the pioneer.

Amount of Elaboration Accompanying Learning

Another approach to resolving the prototype-exemplar debate suggests that the use of exemplars represents relatively elaborated processing. Along these lines, Fiske and Taylor (1991, pg. 116) observe, "the capacity and the motivation to be accurate or to focus on individuals would probably encourage exemplar-based processes over prototype-based processes." Supporting research has been done by Brewer (1988), who suggests that people start out by representing others in pictoliteral prototypes, and then move on to exemplars when they can individuate other people. Relatedly, Linville, Fischer and Salovey (1989) suggest that people use more exemplars to represent their own groups, and that therefore they can engage in more elaborate processing of own group members than of other group members.

The basic idea emerging from this approach is that exemplar-based models are more appropriate under conditions which encourage more elaborate processing (see, however, Kossan 1981 for another view). The exemplar representation of schemas and the consequent categorization process certainly seems to require people to put in more cognitive effort than does the prototype model, since, according to the exemplar model, people can distinguish between different instances of a category and keep them separate in memory, unlike in the prototype model wherein different instances get bound up into a single, fuzzy "prototype". Further, categorization in the exemplar model requires comparison with a number of exemplars, which seems to be cognitively more taxing than a comparison with a single prototype.

Thus, when category learning is accompanied by greater elaboration, a me-too entrant should hurt the pioneer, whereas under lower elaboration, a me-too entrant should help the pioneer.

In support of this idea, we should note that CN explicitly state that the mechanism they propose holds only when attribute weights and the ideal point are ambiguous, i.e., when product category knowledge is low. In terms of our framework, since lower category knowledge leads to lower elaboration (Sujan 1985), the learning process will be based on the prototype model, and the me-too will end up helping the pioneer, as found by CN.

Further theoretical support for elaboration as a moderating factor stems from the idea that under low elaboration conditions, consumers often rely on simple heuristics to guide their evaluations (Petty and Cacioppo 1986). Thus, the fact of a brand being a pioneer may itself be used as a positive heuristic. A me-too entrant will lend support to such a heuristic, leading to increased market share for the pioneer under low elaboration conditions. Under high elaboration, however, a more detailed evaluation will lead to the me-too threatening the pioneer's share, particularly if the me-too is lower priced, as is often the case.

Another stream of research lends weight to this perspective. CN's findings regarding the counterproductive impact of a me-too is very similar to the attraction effect, whereby a brand gains in market share when another brand that it asymmetrically dominates enters the choice set (Huber and Puto 1986). Ratneshwar et al (1987) found that increased knowledge regarding the product category diluted the attraction effect, a finding that is also predicted by our model. Increased knowledge produces greater elaboration (Petty and Cacioppo 1986), facilitating an exemplar based process which results in the me-too hurting the pioneer. In other words, the dominated brand might hurt the dominating brand instead of helping it.

Finally, Kardes and Kalyanram (1992), in discussing various order-of-entry effects, suggest that prior category knowledge and high category involvement should serve to decrease the pioneering advantage. Again, this is in line with our framework since both greater knowledge and involvement produce greater elaboration (Petty and Cacioppo 1986). Greater elaboration will lead to an exemplar based learning process, which implies that a me-too entrant will decrease the pioneering advantage.

The accumulated evidence leads us to the following proposition:

P3   When category learning is accompanied by greater elaboration, an exemplar based process ensues, and a me-too entrant hurts the pioneer. Lower elaboration facilitates a prototype based process under which a me-too entrant helps the pioneer.

Some of the pioneering literature provides additional empirical support for this proposition. For example, consumer goods have been shown to benefit more from pioneering, as compared to industrial goods (Robinson, 1988). In terms of our discussion, industrial goods are probably a more highly involving purchase than are consumer goods, because they usually represent a higher investment. As greater involvement leads to greater elaboration, we would expect the above result. Similarly, Robinson and Fornell (1985) in a study using the PIMS data, found that low cost consumer goods gain more from pioneering than high cost consumer goods; again, an expected result according to our proposition, since higher cost leads to higher purchase involvement, leading in turn to greater elaboration.

Lag Time for Me-too Entrant

Another important factor affecting the type of learning mechanism, and hence the degree of pioneering advantage, would seem to be the amount of time that elapses till a me-too enters the market. The longer the time the pioneer occupies a perceptual space on its own, the more the likelihood that it acquires the status of a category standard or prototype. Consumers get repeatedly exposed to the pioneer, through advertising, word of mouth, consumption experiences etc. causing the pioneer to significantly impact category learning (Kardes and Kalyanram 1992). However, if a me-too enters the market soon after the pioneer, there is still room in the consumers' perceptual space for another category instance, and an exemplar based learning process is more likely to occur, cutting the pioneer's advantage. Empirical support for this idea comes from studies by Kalyanram and Kardes (1992) who found that when subjects were given information about a set of brands sequentially,

the pioneer benefited; however, when the same information was given simultaneously across brands, this effect was wiped out.

P4   A low time lag between the pioneer and its me-too will lead to an exemplar based learning process, which implies that the me-too will hurt the pioneer. A high time lag between the pioneer and its me-too will lead to a prototype based learning process, which implies that the me-too will help the pioneer.

In conclusion, this paper has tried to present a conceptual framework for analyzing the impact of a me-too entrant on the pioneer, using the exemplar/prototype distinction as a theoretical basis. The framework has been used to delineate a set of factors which affect the learning process leading to pioneering (dis)advantage.

Future research should seek to carry out empirical tests of the framework presented here, and use the framework to uncover other factors that affect the impact of a me-too entrant on the pioneer.

REFERENCES

Basu, Kunal (1993), "Consumers' Categorization Processes: An Examination with Two Alternative Methodological Paradigms," *Journal of Consumer Psychology*, 2 (2), 97-121.

Brewer, Marilynn B. (1988), "A Dual Process Model of Impression Formation," in *Handbook of social cognition*, Vol.1, eds. Robert S. Wyer, Jr. and Thomas K. Srull, Hillsdale, NJ: Erlbaum, 1-36.

Carpenter, Gregory S. and Kent Nakamoto (1989), "Consumer Preference Formation and Pioneering Advantage," *Journal of Marketing Research*, 26 (Aug.), 285-298.

Fiske, Susan T. and Shelley E. Taylor (1991), *Social Cognition*, Reading, MA: Addison Wesley.

Gilovich, Thomas (1981), "Seeing the Past in the Present: The Effect of Associations to Familiar Events on Judgments and Decisions," *Journal of Personality and Social Psychology*, 40 (May), 697-808.

Golder, Peter N. and Gerald J. Tellis (1992), "Pioneer Advantage: Marketing Logic or Marketing Legend?" *Journal of Marketing Research*, 12 (May), 158-170.

Goodstein, Ronald C., Marian C. Moore and Deborah A. Cours (1992), "Exploring Advertising Schemas: A Multi-Method Investigation," paper presented at the American Marketing Association Winter Educators' Conference, San Antonio, TX.

Hintzman, D.L. (1986), "Schema Abstraction" in a Multiple-Trace Memory Model," *Psychological Review*, 93, 411-428.

Kalyanram, Gurumurthy and Glen L. Urban (1992), "Dynamic Effects of the Order of Entry on Market Share, Trial Penetration and Repeat Purchases for Frequently Purchased Consumer Goods," *Marketing Science*, Vol. 11 (Summer), 235-249.

Kardes, Frank R. and Gurumurthy Kalyanram (1992), "Order-of-Entry Effects on Consumer Memory and Judgment: An Information Integration Perspective," *Journal of Marketing Research*, Vol. 24 (August), 343-357.

Kerin, Roger A., Rajan P. Varadarajan and Robert A. Peterson (1992), "First-Mover Advantage: A Synthesis, Conceptual Framework and Research Propositions," *Journal of Marketing*, 56 (October), 33-52.

Kossan, N.E. (1981), "Developmental Differences in Concept Acquisition Strategies," *Child Development*, 52, 290-298.

Liebermann, Marvin B. and David B. Montgomery (1988), "First Mover Advantages," *Strategic Management Journal*, 9, 41-58.

Linville, P.W., Fischer, G.W., & Salovey, P. (1989), "Perceived Distributions of the Characteristics of In-group and Out-group Members : Empirical evidence and a Computer Simulation," *Journal of Personality and Social Psychology*, 57, 165-188.

Medin, Douglas L., Mark W. Altom and Timothy D. Murphy (1984) "Given Versus Induced Category Representations: Use of Prototype and Exemplar Information InClassification," *Journal of Experimental Psychology: Learning, Memory and Cognition*, 10(3), 333-350.

Petty, Richard E., and Cacioppo, John T.(1986), *Communication and persuasion: Central and Peripheral Routes to Attitude Change*, New York : Springer-Verlag.

Read, Stephen J. (1987), "Similarity and Causality in the use of Social Analogies, "*Journal of Experimental Social Psychology*, 23, 189-207.

Robinson, William T.(1988), "Sources of Market Pioneer Advantages: The Case of Industrial Goods Industries," *Journal of Marketing Research*, 25 (February), 87-94.

Robinson, William T. and Claes Fornell (1985), "Sources of Market Pioneer Advantages in Consumer Goods Industries," *Journal of Marketing Research*, 22 (August), 305-317.

Smith, Eliot R. and Michael A. Zarate (1990), "Exemplar and Prototype Use in Social Categorization," *Social Cognition*, 8 (3), 243-262.

Sujan, Mita (1985), "Consumer Knowledge: Effects on Evaluation Strategies Mediating Consumer Judgments. *Journal of Consumer Research*, 12, 1-16.

An Exploration of Triune Brain Effects in Advertising

Arjun Chaudhuri, Fairfield University
Ross Buck, University of Connecticut

ABSTRACT

A causal modelling approach is used to investigate the relationship of advertising strategies, ad-evoked thoughts and feelings and ad effectiveness. Results indicate that ad strategies are indirectly linked to ad effectiveness with the indirect path occurring through aspects of the "triune" brain, as measured by the CASC scale.

INTRODUCTION

According to MacLean (1990; 1973), the human brain is essentially a *"triune"* brain consisting of three independent yet interactive brain structures. Responses such as aggression, sex, striving for power, etc. constitute the workings of the *reptilian brain* (brain stem, mid brain, basal ganglia) that is part of our evolutionary heritage and that has evolved over millennia. Prosocial and individualistic feelings are generated in the limbic system or *old mammalian brain* and these function to preserve the species and the individual, respectively. The neocortex or *neomammalian brain* represents the last of the "three brains" and it is the center for higher order learning, language and sequential thought processes.

This study proposes to examine the nature of the advertising strategies that relate to the workings of the triune brain as measured during advertising exposure by the CASC (Communication via Analytic and Syncretic Cognition) scale (Chaudhuri and Buck 1994). Specifically, we investigate whether certain ad strategies are directly related to measures of advertising effectiveness such as "liking" or whether these ad strategies are indirectly linked to advertising effectiveness, *with the indirect path occurring through analytic (rational) and syncretic (emotional) cognitions*, as measured by the CASC scale. No specific hypotheses are presented since the scope of this study is exploratory in nature.

THEORETICAL FRAMEWORK

Syncretic and Analytic Cognition

Buck (1988) describes two types of cognition. The first is *syncretic cognition* or "knowledge by acquaintance," which cannot be described but is "known" immediately by the person and may consist of sensations, bodily symptoms, drives and affects, such as happiness, fear, anger, and disgust. This is the process of immediate and subjective experience which William James (1890) wrote about: "I know the color blue when I see it, and the flavor of a pear when I taste it....but about the *inner* nature of these facts or what makes them what they are I can say nothing at all" (p. 22).

In contrast to syncretic cognition, which is holistic, synthetic and right brain oriented, *analytic cognition* or "knowledge by description" is sequential, analytic and left brain oriented (Tucker 1981). While syncretic cognition is derived from direct sensory awareness, analytic cognition results from the interpretation of sensory data and involves judgements about phenomena. As Bertrand Russell (1912) observed, "My knowledge of a table as a physical object....is not direct knowledge. Such as it is, it is obtained through acquaintance with the sense-data that make up the appearance of the table" (p. 73-74).

Thus, the brain appears to involve two functionally different ways of knowing. Seen in this light, *emotion is a kind of cognition*: syncretic cognition which is the product of the reptilian and old mammalian brains (MacLean 1990), as typically processed by the right hemisphere. It constitutes general affects such as happiness, fear, anger, etc. and also such primal urges as the search for pleasure, power, sex, etc. Further, syncretic and analytic cognition are the direct outcomes of the advertising strategies discussed next.

Advertising Strategies

The effects of four different types of advertising strategies were examined in this study: product information strategies, spokesperson strategies, family appeals and status appeals. These four strategies are based on generally accepted theories of advertising and are expected to relate to analytic and syncretic cognitions as discussed below.

Systematic learning theories, under the traditional information processing paradigm in consumer behavior (Bettman 1979), view the consumer as an active processor of information. The generation of analytic cognitions is especially relevant to message elements in ads, which present *product information* in a favorable way. Lavidge and Steiner (1961) proposed a hierarchy of advertising effects in which attitude formation for a brand starts with beliefs, leads to overall evaluation and, finally, leads to behavior. According to Fishbein and Ajzen (1975) as well, a person's attitude is a function of his or her salient beliefs. This process of the creation of beliefs and judgements about brands is also the process of knowledge by description, which produces analytic cognition.

According to Chaiken (1980) persons process information in both systematic and heuristic ways. While systematic processing involves thoughtful, "mindful" analysis of the content of the ad, *heuristic processing* involves the use of simple heuristic cues in order to arrive at a conclusion (brand preferences, etc.). Thus, consumers may use simple decision rules such as buying a brand name; buying the brand advertised by an expert, attractive or trustworthy spokesperson; or buying the brand that most people use. Moreover, spontaneous affective cues, such as *spokespersons*, may elicit heuristic processing and generate syncretic cognition. Ray and Batra (1983) state that emotion laden stimuli in ads may create better message acceptance, since in a positive affective state, people tend to make speedier, less complex judgements. The use of visual, sensory, nonverbal imagery may discourage counterargument and analytic cognitions and facilitate persuasion via affective heuristic cues which generate syncretic cognition.

Pavlov (1927) and others (Watson and Rayner, 1920) in their classic experiments demonstrated that if two dissimilar objects are repetitively associated together in close contiguity to each other, the emotional response originally elicited by the unconditioned stimulus can, over time, be elicited by the conditioned stimulus alone. Thus, *classical conditioning* strategies result in syncretic cognition through the use of spontaneous (nonverbal) cues in the advertisement. Persuasion here is almost on a subliminal level and the attempt is to create involvement with the advertisement by using affect-laden appeals like *family appeals*, sex appeals, humor, etc. Repeated pairings of a brand with a favorable affective appeal, over time, transfers the affect to the brand itself.

Pechmann and Stewart (1989) describe the process of *vicarious learning* through advertising. Ads that portray reward or punishment for an actor due to use or non use of a particular brand arouse identification and emotion. The point is that humans construct beliefs, rules about which brands/products to use, based on emotional communication. The rewards/punishments meted out

TABLE 1
The Dimensions in the CASC Scale

Prosocial	Individualistic	Reptilian	Analytic
Happy	Angry	Sexy	Pros & cons of the brand
Proud	Afraid	Aggressive	Arguments for using or not using the brand
Hope	Disgusted	Envy	Think of facts about the brand
Affiliation	Irritated	Power	Real differences between the brand and its competitors

to the model in the ad are exemplified in the model's expressive behavior, such as facial expressions, etc. The process of observing (decoding) such emotional expression results in arousal and a vicarious sharing of the same subjective experience as undergone by the model in the ad. The consumer comes to associate the brand with the emotion generated (happiness, say) and sees the brand as the social instrument that obtains rewards and stays punishment. Thus, it is suggested that certain nonverbal cues, such as the delineation of social rewards and *status appeals* represent vicarious learning strategies that result in syncretic cognitions concerning the emotional benefits of advertised brands.

MEASUREMENT

The CASC Scale

The CASC (Communication Analytic and Syncretic Cognitions) Scale consists of items that investigate analytic and syncretic cognitions elicited by advertising (Chaudhuri and Buck 1994). It is a multidimensional scale (see Table 1) consisting of four subscales and, of these, one subscale contains analytic cognitive items, while the other three subscales ask for syncretic cognitive responses on the dimensions of reptilian, prosocial and individualistic feelings (MacLean 1990). CASC is a seven point paper and pencil scale anchored at two ends by "Not At All" and "A Lot" (see Appendix I). The general form of the scale is "Did the ad make you think/feel ...". In all there are sixteen items, four for each subscale. Coefficient alpha for the analytic subscale is highest at .96, followed by prosocial at .79, reptilian at .78 and individual at .70.

Advertising Effectiveness

Two single item responses served in this study to measure advertising effectiveness in terms of *"liking"* and *"buying"*. The items (seven point scale) were "How much did you like the ad?" and "Was the ad effective in leading you to buy the product?". We used both liking and buying in order to tap both the rational and emotional dimensions of attitudes, as discussed by Biel and Bridgwater (1990).

Likability has repeatedly been identified by practitioners to be a strong determinant of brand and commercial success (Haley and Baldinger 1991; McCarthy 1991; Biel and Bridgwater 1990) and ad effectiveness in terms of buying the product is clearly a worthwhile objective. Past research (Batra and Ray 1986; Edell and Burke 1987; Holbrook and Batra 1987) has also demonstrated that emotional responses are related to attitudinal measures of ad effectiveness similar to those used in this study and, accordingly, the multidimensional elements of the CASC scale can also be expected to predict ad effectiveness. It is also expected that advertising strategies (discussed next) will be *indirectly* related to liking and buying since ad strategies are expected to relate directly to analytic and syncretic cognitions, as discussed earlier.

Advertising Strategies

Table 2 provides the items which were used to operationalize product information, spokesperson strategies, family appeals and status appeals. Certainly, these are *not* the only viable operationalizations of the four ad strategies and they are not meant to be exhaustive of all advertising strategies. For instance, classical conditioning strategies could also be represented by sex appeals, humor, animals and other ad executions. The attempt here has been to measure *some* of the ad strategies that may be related to analytic and syncretic cognitions. In particular, family appeals were chosen since it is reasonable to expect that such appeals may be related to the "prosocial" syncretic cognitive subscale in CASC. Similarly, spokesperson strategies and status appeals may also be expected to relate to syncretic cognitions, while product information strategies should be related to analytic cognitions.

METHODS

Dependent Variables

This study used ads, rather than individuals, as the units of observation. This method of analysis has been in vogue in recent years (Holbrook and Batra 1987; Olney, Holbrook and Batra 1991; Stewart and Furse 1986), since it has more significance for advertising practitioners who have to consider the effects of individual ads. Accordingly, two hundred and forty advertisements were selected for analysis. Of these, exactly half were television ads and half were full page color ads from magazines. Ads were selected to represent a range of product categories in both print and TV. Ads in both media were also selected with the range of responses in the CASC scale in mind. Since this method of analysis involves the use of aggregative responses from individuals in order to arrive at scores for individual ads, subjects (or, more correctly, "raters" of analytic and syncretic cognitions) had to be recruited.

One hundred and twenty nine undergraduate communication students (64 male, 65 female) from a large state university in northeastern Connecticut provided analytic and syncretic cognitive responses, using the CASC scale, for the entire set of ads. Additionally, they provided responses on "liking" and "buying". Each subject viewed 10 television ads and read 10 magazine ads and provided their responses after each ad. A minimum of 10 subjects responded to each ad with regard to analytic and syncretic cognitions and ad effectiveness. Print and TV ads from the total pool were randomly assigned to sets of ten and two sets (one for TV and one for print) were randomly chosen by the researcher for any one group of subjects. In all, twelve groups responded to 240 ads in sets of 20 ads (10 for TV and 10 for print) per group. Subjects were randomly assigned to the groups and received course credit for their participation.

The procedures for obtaining responses to the ads were as follows. Subjects were told that we were interested in investigating the thoughts and feelings that are evoked by advertising and,

TABLE 2.
Advertising Strategy Items and Their Reliabilities

Item	Alpha
Product Information	
1. Extent of tangible brand benefits	.91
2. Extent of ingredients/components	.92
3. Extent of quality appeal	.89
Spokesperson	
4. Extent of a typical consumer	.94
5. Extent of spokesperson	.86
6. Extent of user satisfaction/loyalty	.79
Family Appeals	
7. Extent of family appeal	.98
8. Extent of special occasions	.96
9. Extent of children	.97
10. Extent of elderly people	.86
Status Appeal	
11. Extent of affluent setting	.97
12. Extent of desirable lifestyle	.87
13. Extent of social rewards	.45
14. Extent of others' approval/disapproval	.56
15. Extent of status appeal	.84

accordingly, they were to respond to the ads spontaneously, without too much deliberation. Subjects watched each of the television ads and responded after each ad. Similarly, they viewed copies of the magazine ads and responded after each ad and then went on to the next ad. Questionnaires were reverse ordered to obviate fatigue and order effects and the order of presentation of the ads was reversed for half of the subjects in each group.

Independent Variables

Eight judges (4 male, 4 female) were trained to rate the extent of the presence of the four advertising strategies and Table 2 lists these items, which were rated using a unipolar seven point rating scale, anchored by the points "None - - - A Lot".

All eight raters rated 40 (20 for TV and 20 for print) of the 240 ads. Next, 100 ads were rated by four of the raters and the remaining 100 ads were rated by the other four raters. Table 2 gives the reliabilities for each item across the first 40 ads. Note that only 2 of the items had reliabilities of less than .75. These items were dropped from further analysis, since they appear to have been inconsistently coded and may be considered to be non-reliable items on which raters did not always agree. For the remaining items, the mean of each item for every ad was derived from the scores by the individual raters and the mean was then assigned as the score for that item for the corresponding ad. Note from this, and the previous discussion, that the study uses independent samples of "judges" to arrive at the aggregative measures for the independent and dependent variables attributed to the ads. This is an extremely important precaution that guards against the kind of response bias that is likely to occur when the same sample provides both sets of measures.

ANALYSIS AND RESULTS

The final analysis used advertisements as the unit of analysis (N=240) and each ad was provided a mean score (compiled by using the mean of the individual subjects' scores) to represent the level of analytic and syncretic cognitions and liking and buying. Similarly, as discussed earlier, the mean of each ad strategy item was compiled from the individual ratings by the judges who rated the ads for advertising content. Thus, an aggregative data set was compiled for all 240 ads. Covariance structure analysis (using Lisrel VII) was employed to test this data set for the direct and indirect paths from the four advertising strategies to the two measures of ad effectiveness with the indirect paths occurring through analytic and syncretic cognitions, as measured by the four subscales of the CASC scale. Liking and buying were treated as single indicator variables, assumed to be measured without error. A marker variable strategy was used.

We first tested the just identified model specifying all possible paths between the constructs. Paths that were non-significant (t value<1.96, p >.05) were dropped from the model and Figure 1 presents the final or trimmed model showing only the significant paths between the constructs. The final model fits the data fairly well (Chi Square=376.57, d.f. 315, p=.01, GFI=.902, AGFI=.874, RMSR=.056). Although a non-significant Chi Square with a p value closer to .10 would have been more desirable, it was unnecessary to relax orthogonality constraints further since the goodness of fit indices were at an acceptable level. In fact, the calculation of other indices, as recommended by Bentler (1980), shows that the goodness of fit of the model is actually very good once we compensate for the high degrees of freedom (Tucker Lewis index=.985; Bentler Bonett index=.901).

Figure 1 and Table 3 provide the following results:

(a) *None* of the ad strategy variables are directly linked to advertising effectiveness in terms of liking and buying.
(b) However, *all* the ad strategy variables are directly related to one or more of the analytic and syncretic cognition constructs. Spokesperson strategies cause "individualistic" reac-

FIGURE 1
Final (trimmed) Model of Advertising Effects

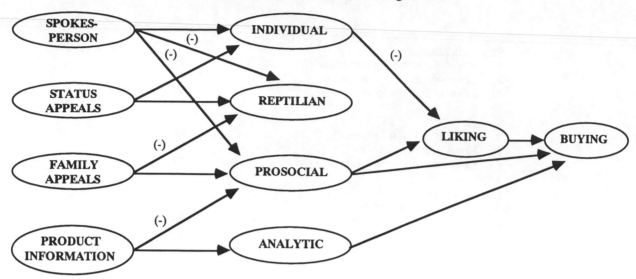

Note: 1. All paths shown here are significant (p<.05)
         2. (-) denotes a negative path coefficient

TABLE 3
Standardized Structural Coefficients
(Final Trimmed Model)

Product Info.	— — —	Analytic	.701
Product Info.	— — —	Prosocial	-.333
Spokesperson	— — —	Prosocial	-.270
Spokesperson	— — —	Individual	.294
Spokesperson	— — —	Reptilian	-.192
Family Appeals	— — —	Prosocial	.139
Family Appeals	— — —	Reptilian	-.308
Status Appeals	— — —	Individual	.188
Status Appeals	— — —	Reptilian	.336
Analytic	— — —	Buying	.489
Prosocial	— — —	Liking	.621
Prosocial	— — —	Buying	.241
Individual	— — —	Liking	-.291
Liking	— — —	Buying	.341

Note: all parameters shown are significant (t-value > 1.96; p < .05)

Variance Explained in the Dependent Variables

Analytic	Prosocial	Individual	Reptilian	Liking	Buying
.491	.203	.122	.268	.500	.527

tions (anger, etc.) and also predict an absence of "reptilian" and "prosocial" elements. Status appeals cause both individualistic and reptilian emotions. Family appeals cause prosocial feelings and an absence of reptilian feelings. Product information causes analytic cognitions and an absence of prosocial feelings.

(c) With one exception (reptilian), all of the analytic and syncretic cognitions are related to either liking or buying or both. Analytic cognitions are not related to liking for the ad but they are positively related to buying. The prosocial dimension of syncretic cognitions is positively related to both liking and buying, while the individualistic subscale is negatively related to liking. (d) It follows from (a), (b) and (c) that advertising strategies are *indirectly* related to liking and buying with *the indirect path occurring through analytic and syncretic cognitions.*

DISCUSSION

Our results indicate that spokesperson and status appeals both create "individualistic" reactions such as anger, disgust and irritation. Spokespeople, typical consumers relating their satisfaction with products, are also strongly conducive to an *absence* of positive emotional responses such as happiness, pride and hope. Of course, these strategies may still be effective in terms of other measures (say "recall") of ad effectiveness, which were not examined in this study. However, if the intention of the advertiser is to create a positive emotional bond between the consumer and the product, then this may not be the way to do it. Perhaps, this advertising format has become all too common and suffers from "wear out" so that spokespeople lack credibility.

While vicarious learning strategies (status appeals) were not significantly related to analytic or prosocial dimensions, there was a strong, positive and significant relationship with reptilian. This confirms Buck's (1989) assertion that emotional communication is *directly* accessible to an audience and does not require the intervention of analytic cognitions. Moreover, consistent with earlier studies (Zillmann and Bryant 1985), there is evidence here that the process of observational learning may be mediated by physiological arousal - recall that reptilian was composed of such elements as "aggressive" and "sexy". Vicarious learning strategies thus appear to have direct behavioral effects that are independent of the more knowledge - based ("cognitive" in the larger sense) factors such as analytic cognitions. More work needs to be done, perhaps using physiological measurements, to understand the spectrum of emotions and feelings that is gradually coming to "light" through research in this area. From this study we know that advertisements containing status appeals and depicting affluent and desirable lifestyles generate self reported physiological arousal and the emotions of power and envy.

Product information strategies generate analytic cognitions and discourage the occurrence of prosocial emotions. On the other hand, family appeals generate prosocial emotions and discourage reptilian feelings. These findings appear intuitively plausible and are in keeping with theoretical expectations and prior research. For instance, these findings corroborate the Fishbein model of reasoned action in which beliefs generate active information processing and they also indicate that classical conditioning strategies, such as family appeals, produce ad induced affect, i.e. affect induced from the executional elements in the ad.

Most importantly, there is considerable evidence in this study that analytic and syncretic cognitions *mediate* the effect of advertising strategies on proven measures of ad effectiveness such as liking for the ad and whether the ad is effective in terms of buying the product. *None* of the ad strategies were directly related to liking or buying, yet *all* were directly related to analytic and syncretic cognitions which, in turn, were almost always related to either or both liking and buying (see Figure 1). These findings corroborate the work of Holbrook and Batra (1987) and the present study extends their findings in the context of a larger number of ads, ads from both television and print, both analytic *and* syncretic cognitions and a rigorous causal modelling approach which simultaneously examines the effect of advertising strategies on a number of dependent variables.

In addition, the inclusion of the reptilian dimension substantially increases the range of affective responses that are usually considered to be relevant in advertising. This new category of responses may have special significance for advertising practitioners. Although advertising research has emphasized affect and cognition in forced exposure situations, the reality is that most actual advertising is conducted in situations of very low involvement (television viewing, for example) that may be more amenable to persuasion without the intervention of cognitive and attitudinal mediators. The results of this study show that even in forced exposure situations, reptilian types of evoked affect are not related to attitudinal measures of advertising effectiveness. Although there is no attempt in the present study to examine the further mechanisms by which reptilian feelings and desires may obtain their effect, nevertheless, it is the contribution of this paper to draw attention to the reptilian brain which may play a significant role in the advertising process.

REFERENCES

Batra, Rajeev and Michael L. Ray (1986), "Affective Responses Mediating Acceptance of Advertising," *Journal of Consumer Research,* 13 (September), 234- 249.

Bentler, Peter M. (1980), "Multivariate Analysis with Latent Variables: Causal Modelling," In *Annual Review of Psychology,* Vol 31, M.R. Rosensweig & L.W. Porter, eds. Palo Alto, CA: Annual Reviews.

Bettman, James R. (1979), *An Information Processing Theory of Consumer Choice,* Reading, MA: Addison-Wesley.

Biel, Alexander L. and Carol A. Bridgwater (1990), "Attributes of Likable Television Commercials," *Journal of Advertising Research,* 30 (3), 38-44.

Buck, Ross (1988), *Human Motivation and Emotion,* New York, NY: John Wiley.

_____(1989), "Emotional Education and Mass Media," In *Advancing Communication Science: Merging Mass and Interpersonal Perspectives,* R.P. Hawkins, J.M. Weimann, & S. Pingree, eds. Beverly Hills, CA: Sage Publications.

Chaiken, Shelly (1980), "Heuristic Versus Systematic Information Processing and the Use of Source Versus Message Cues in Persuasion," *Journal of Personality and Social Psychology,* 39 (5), 752-766.

Chaudhuri, Arjun and Ross Buck (1994), "Are Advertisers Using Brain Theory ? Introducing the CASC Scale," in *1994 AMA Winter Educators Conference Proceedings,* C. Whan Park and Daniel C. Smith, eds. Chicago, IL: American Marketing Association.

Edell, Julie A. and Marian C. Burke (1987), "The Power of Feelings in Understanding Advertising Effects," *Journal of Consumer Research,* 14 (December), 421-433.

Fishbein, M. and I. Ajzen (1975), *Belief, Attitude, Intention and Behavior: An Introduction to Theory and Research,* Reading, MA: Addison-Wesley.

Haley, Russell I. and Allan L. Baldinger (1991), "The ARF Copy Research Validity Project," *Journal of Advertising Research,* 31(2), 11-32.

Holbrook, Morris B. and Rajeev Batra (1987), "Assessing the Role of Emotions as Mediators of Consumer Responses to Advertising," *Journal of Consumer Research,* 14 (December), 404-420.

James, William (1890), *The Principles of Psychology,* Vol 1., New York, NY: Henry Holt and Co.

Lavidge, Robert J. and Gary A. Steiner (1961), "A Model for Predictive Measurements of Advertising Effectiveness," *Journal of Marketing,* 25 (3), 59-62.

MacLean, Paul D. (1973), *A Triune Concept of the Brain and Behavior,* Toronto: University of Toronto Press.

_____(1990), *The Triune Brain in Evolution: Role in Paleocerebral Functions,* New York, NY: Plenum Press.

McCarthy, Michael J. (1991), "Mind Probe," *The Wall Street Journal* (March 22), B3.

Olney, Thomas J., Morris B. Holbrook, and Rajeev Batra (1991), "Consumer Responses to Advertising: The Effects of Ad Content, Emotions, and Attitude toward the Ad on Viewing Time," *Journal of Consumer Research,* 17 (March), 440-453.

Pavlov, Ivan (1927), *Conditioned Reflexes. An Investigation of the Physiological Activity of the Cerebral Cortex,* London: Oxford University Press.

Pechmann, Cornelia and David W. Stewart (1989), "The Multidimensionality of Persuasive Communications: Theoretical and Empirical Foundations," in *Cognitive and Affective Responses to Advertising,* Patricia Cafferata and Alice M. Tybout, eds. Lexington, MA: Lexington Books.

Ray, Michael L. and Rajeev Batra (1983), "Emotion and Persuasion in Advertising," *Advances in Consumer Research,* 10, 543-548. Russell, Bertrand (1912), *Problems of Philosophy,* New York, NY: Oxford University Press.

Stewart, David W. and David H. Furse (1986), *Effective Television Advertising: A Study of 1000 Commercials,* Lexington, MA: Lexington Books.

Tucker, D. M. (1981), "Lateral Brain Function, Emotion, and Conceptualization," *Psychological Bulletin,* 89, 19-46

Watson, J.B. and R. Rayner (1920), "Conditioned Emotional Responses," *Journal of Experimental Psychology,* 3, 1-14.

Zillmann, D. and J. Bryant (1985), *Selective Exposure to Communication,* Hillsdale, NJ: Lawrence Erlbaum.

A Framework for Critiquing the Dysfunctions of Advertising: The Base-Superstructure Metaphor

Renee G. Lee, Virginia Tech
Jeff B. Murray, University of Arkansas[1]

ABSTRACT

It is widely acknowledged that advertising has potentially negative effects on individuals and society. However, these effects are relatively unexplored within consumer research, particularly the influence of advertising on consumers' constructions of reality. One of the reasons for this lack of attention is the need for a critical framework that is useful at the macro level of analysis. In this paper, the base-superstructure metaphor is discussed as a useful critical framework. First the framework is presented, then it is illustrated by discussing the role of advertising in society. The paper concludes by outlining the research implications of this framework.

INTRODUCTION

If we accept the call to be more critical of advertising (e.g., Pollay 1986), what kind of analytic framework would be useful? Pollay's (1986) survey of critics of advertising includes psychologists, sociologists, anthropologists, educators, communication specialists, philosophers, theologians, historians, and a number of other representatives of various traditions. Curiously, Pollay ignored an unorthodox Marxist perspective[2]. This is ironic since this perspective provides a useful defense to Holbrook's (1987) criticisms by: a) providing a critical view of advertising from a macro perspective; and b) recognizing that fundamentally advertising tends to reflect and reinforce the *status quo*. A common interpretation of this perspective or critical framework is often referred to as the *base-superstructure* metaphor.

The base-superstructure metaphor is associated with a critical-emancipatory sociology of knowledge. This view assumes that certain types of knowledge are selected and become dominant due to their consistency with existing social structures and relations. In other words, if ideas legitimate the existing power structure, they are more likely to be disseminated and therefore accepted. On the other hand, if ideas oppose the existing power structure, they are less likely to be disseminated and therefore will not be available for public debate.

The purpose of this paper is to present the base-superstructure metaphor in a way that is useful for analyzing the unintended consequences or dysfunctions of advertising. The paper also extends the work of researchers that have called for the critical assessment of ideology in our field (e.g., Anderson 1989; Belk 1986; Firat, Dholakia, and Bagozzi 1987; Hirschman 1993; Murray and Ozanne 1991, 1994a, 1994b; Murray, Ozanne, and Shapiro 1994).

This paper will first discuss the base-superstructure metaphor within the context of the sociology of knowledge. Second, the key dimensions of the metaphor will be described. This section includes discussion of the base, the superstructure, the connection between the base and superstructure, and the functions of this connection. Finally, the role of advertising in society will be discussed from this perspective. This section concludes with research implications of the base-superstructure metaphor.

CLASSICAL SOCIOLOGY OF KNOWLEDGE

The classical view of the sociology of knowledge assumes that all knowledge arises from a sociohistorical context. The sociologist of knowledge provides an account of the social construction of knowledge by investigating the relationship between knowledge and social influences. The sociohistorical context and knowledge are not considered reciprocal partners in this relationship but primacy is given to the concrete historical reality; the sociology of knowledge is "a theory of the relation of ideas and reality asserting the primacy of reality and the determination of ideas by reality" (Remmling 1973, p. xvii).

Karl Mannheim and Max Scheler are generally credited with the origination of the sociology of knowledge as a separate subdiscipline in 1924 (Remmling 1973). However, Karl Marx is often recognized as the intellectual precursor of these researchers. Remmling (1973, p. 135) refers to Marxism as the "storm center of the sociology of knowledge" since Marx was one of the first philosophers to assert the materialist position that ideas stem from the concrete reality of our lives.

Merton (1968) provides a useful framework for organizing and interpreting Marx's contribution to this field. According to Merton (1968), all approaches to the sociology of knowledge can be understood and compared by answering the following questions: What kinds of social and cultural factors exercise influence (i.e., the *base*)? What kinds of knowledge are open to sociological analysis (i.e., the *superstructure*)? What is the nature of the *connections* between knowledge and society? And what are the *functions* of these connections? (see Murray and Ozanne 1994b, p. 5).

In the next section we discuss an interpretation of Marx that provides answers to these questions. Together, these answers present an overview of the base-superstructure metaphor.

THE BASE-SUPERSTRUCTURE METAPHOR

The edifice-like metaphor of base and superstructure is used by Marx to suggest that the means and the social relations of production brought together in the wage relation (i.e., the base) shape the nature of the state and popular culture (i.e., the superstructure) (Larrain 1983). Thus, the metaphor is used to discuss the relationship between three general dimensions of society, whereby the state and popular culture arise from the base. From this perspective, social consciousness that may seem to result from the consumption of popular culture (e.g., TV, popular novels, advertising) is really the result of a particular economic structure. In other words, advertising is reflecting the type of social consciousness that is necessary for contemporary capitalism to survive. Critiquing advertising without taking into account the social totality is misdirecting our energies since it stems from the relations of production. These ideas will be discussed further in the last section. For now, it is important to discuss each dimension of the metaphor.

[1] The authors would like to thank Julie L. Ozanne and Chirs Toulouse for commenting on earlier drafts of this paper.

[2] Pollay (1986, p. 19) states: "While this study excludes the European Marxist tradition, the research process is otherwise a survey rather than a sampling, with no authors knowingly excluded."

The Base

A starting premise for Marx's sociology of knowledge is that "the production of ideas, of conceptions, of consciousness, is at first directly interwoven with the material activity and the material intercourse of men, the language of real life" (*The German Ideology Part I* 1965; Tucker 1978, p. 154). In other words, knowledge originates from those activities that are essential for the survival of the community. For example, the dominant knowledge consisting within hunting and gathering cultures results from the need to coordinate the hunt (i.e., the relations of production), as well as the knowledge needed to manufacture the equipment that is necessary for this activity (i.e., the forces of production). The social consciousness resulting from this knowledge will lead to rituals, dance, and religion that reinforce this mode of production. Similarly, the dominant knowledge consisting within corporate capitalism results from the need to coordinate activities within the firm (i.e., the relations of production), as well as the knowledge needed to manufacture the capital that is necessary for production (i.e., the forces of production). The social consciousness resulting from this knowledge will lead to ideology which legitimates nine-to-five lifestyles, certain kinds of leisure activities, family structure, forms of education, advertising, and so forth.

In his well known preface to *A Contribution to the Critique of Political Economy* (Tucker 1965, p. 4), Marx (1904) introduces the idea that knowledge and consciousness stem from material existence:

> In the social production of their life, men enter into definite relations that are indispensable and independent of their will, relations of production which correspond to a definite stage of development of their material productive forces. The sum total of these relations of production constitutes the economic structure of society, the real foundation, on which rises a legal and political superstructure and to which correspond definite forms of social consciousness. The mode of production of material life conditions the social, political and intellectual life process in general. It is not the consciousness of men that determines their being, but, on the contrary, their social being that determines their consciousness.

This quotation illustrates the materialist position that human thought is integrally related to social structures and that the relations of production constitute the foundation for the superstructure of ideas. Further, Marx's contention that social existence determines consciousness suggests that individuals' thoughts are influenced by the worldview that dominates their sociohistorical milieu. Thus, from this perspective, the same worldview that has influenced advertising has also influenced every other institution. For example, it is not unusual to hear a teacher state that the purpose of education is so students can get a good job, make a lot of money, and be able to buy nice things. To suggest that social consciousness stems from advertising is to credit this institution with excessive influence. In other words, advertising is just one piece of the puzzle. If consumers find aspects of advertising offensive, it is not due to unethical ad agencies, it may be due to the demands of a particular form of capitalism.

In sum, the base constitutes the relations and forces of production found in contemporary corporate culture (i.e., corporate capitalism).

The Superstructure

The notion of superstructure is used to indicate two dependent societal dimensions: the state and social consciousness (Larrain 1983). Social consciousness, in this context, refers to the consciousness of a class. Thus, it is ideological in the sense that it not only includes values, interests, opinions, and lifestyles, but also illusions or distortions. A more contemporary interpretation of this social or class consciousness would be *popular culture*.

Advertising is therefore an exemplary form of superstructural knowledge. It communicates the values, interests, opinions, and lifestyles necessary to fuel a materialistic economy based on overproduction, and at the same time distorts a clear picture of this society. Advertising presents a stereotypical view of the world (Holbrook 1987) by underrepresenting certain segments of society, neglecting important issues such as human suffering (McCracken and Pollay 1981, as cited by Holbrook 1987) and emphasizing beautiful sexy people living a life of conspicuous leisure. It is no wonder advertising encourages consumers to be happy ("celebrate the moments of your life"), to be in love ("so kiss a little longer"), to be materialistic ("the ultimate driving machine"), and to remain unpoliticized ("have a Coke and a smile").

Hamilton (1974, p. 35) has suggested that ideology can be most clearly understood as "systematically distorted knowledge"— *distorted* in that it represents and reinforces the current relations of production and therefore dominant groups. In other words, distortion does not mean a false reflection; it is distorted in the sense that the views of the dominant group are taken to be the general view.

> Marx insists that class relationships form the basic axis upon which ideologies find general acceptance in society. Thus ideology is, in an important sense 'illusory:' not in the sense that the content of idea-systems is a mere 'reflection' of material life and therefore is irrelevant to the activity of the subject, but insofar as ideas which are thought to be of general or universal validity are in fact the expressions of sectional class interests (Giddens 1971, p. 213).

Ideologies thus often serve to benefit dominant groups because the presentation of distorted versions of reality has a profound influence on consumers' interpretations and social constructions of reality.

The Connection

Most critiques of Marxism assume that Marx was an economic determinist and attack the perspective on grounds of economic reductionism (Larrain 1983). Clearly, it is easy to think of many superstructural examples that do not reflect the interests of the current mode of production. It is more useful to think of the relationship between the base and superstructure as *reciprocal*.

This means that although the economic base is a dominant force, the superstructure is capable of exercising reciprocal influence. For example, a superstructural value that legitimates the current mode of production is unabashed materialism (thus advertising resonates with this value). However, this value also leads to the eventual destruction of the environment. Since the destruction of the environment would also lead to the demise of capitalism, we are beginning to see aspects of environmentalism embraced by those that control the current mode of production and thereby reflected in advertisements. Thus we find two contradictory values currently embraced by the advertising community (i.e., materialism and environmentalism). This contradiction may lead to changes in consumption habits (a superstructural change), or to a change in how we manufacture and dispose of products (a change in the economic base). In addition, due to the emancipatory interests of some marketing managers, it is easy to find oppositional ideologies in advertising (e.g., Ben and Jerry's, The Body Shop, and Bennetons to name a few) (see Murray and Ozanne 1991).

These progressive advertisements that endorse alternative forms of social organization present an anomaly to the "economic determinist" position. A *reciprocal* position however anticipates some degree of opposition in every institution. This perspective does not assume that institutions (including advertising) are well-ordered monoliths, but that institutions are pluralistic, contradictory, dynamic, and characterized by conflict.

The Function

The function of the connection between the base and superstructure is to divert attention away from alternative ways of organizing the base. If the base is made to seem objective and static rather than a historical product, then ideas which legitimate it seem unbiased. In this sense, the function is *social control*. Media vehicles that are perceived as unbiased carriers of the message have successfully masked all connections to social interests and context. This masking will benefit those aligned with powerful interests. In other words, if the human relations represented in advertisements seem "normal" then they have persuasive power.

In this sense, *truth* and social control are interconnected. The values necessary to legitimize and maintain the current relations of production must be viewed as accurate descriptors of human nature. Thus, the *truth in advertising* legislation, beginning around 1910, was not brought about by social critics but by the advertising industry itself (Ewen 1976).

> Paul Nystrom, the consumer economist, noted approvingly in 1929 that 'the movement in the United States for truth in advertising has been sponsored by and promoted largely through advertising men' (Ewen 1976, p. 71).

Although the truth in advertising legislation made unlawful any claim which "contains any assertion, representation or statement of fact which is untrue, deceptive or misleading" (Ewen 1976, p. 71), it was equipped to deal only with denotated meaning. By not being able to confront connotated[3] meaning, these laws could not combat psychological manipulation. James Rorty attributed the following to the truth in advertising campaign: "Always tell the truth. Tell a lot of the truth. Tell a lot more of the truth than anybody expects you to tell. Never tell the whole truth" (as cited in Ewen 1976, p. 72). As Pollay (1986) makes clear, given that advertising is pervasive, persuasive, repetitive, developed by people very aware of issues surrounding attention and comprehension, and delivered to an audience that is born into a world saturated with it, it can be a powerful tool of manipulation.

In sum, the base consists of the relations and forces of production, the superstructure consists of the state and popular culture, the connection between the two is reciprocal, and the function of this connection is social control. The base-superstructure metaphor provides a useful framework for critiquing the role of advertising in American and international markets.

THE BASE-SUPERSTRUCTURE METAPHOR AND ADVERTISING

It is widely acknowledged that advertising has a potentially negative impact on individuals and society. Numerous consumer researchers have discussed the potential harmful consequences of advertising (c.f., Pollay 1986), but few have used a critical framework from which to develop a more conceptual argument. The base-superstructure metaphor represents one alternative. This framework can be used to examine the power of advertising ideology in the context of a particular political economy. Critics may be misdirecting their energies by taking advertising out of its social context for analysis. Criticism needs to focus on the social totality, the entire superstructure and the connections and functions with the base. In addition, the framework draws attention to contradictions and potential conflict between repressed and dominant groups.

Since young consumers are becoming increasingly detached from traditional sources of primary socialization (Pollay 1986) such as families, churches, and schools, advertising is emerging as a key vehicle for producing and reproducing ideology. Given that we are born into a world steeped in advertising, we tend to take the norms and values reflected in ads for granted.

> We do not ordinarily recognize advertising as a sphere of ideology....[Analyzing ads permits us to] explore how ideological assumptions [are] present in the ordinary discourses of daily life and, most importantly, that ideology [is] not merely the product of conspiracy or a ministry of propaganda—that, in fact, ideology is something we enter into and participate in (Goldman 1992, pp. 1, 9).

Goldman's passage underscores the argument that the dominant ideology communicated through advertising can have a profound influence on the construction of individual perceptions of reality. Although selective exposure (e.g., *zapping and zipping*) may decrease attention, from the base-superstructure perspective, the reason these companies are paying for particular TV shows is because they represent the same values as the commercials. From a postmodern perspective (e.g., Featherstone 1991; Turner 1991) zapping and zipping will only serve to further fragment the consumer, making them more vulnerable to ideology. Indeed, the most potent ads are rarely zapped, for example, Pepsi ads featuring Michael Jackson were zapped by only one to two percent of the audience (Kneale 1988).

The base-superstructure perspective suggests that advertising's power is analogous to the power Marx attributes to the ruling class, i.e., it exercises its power to influence the production and distribution of knowledge as a means of social control[4]—in order to serve its own interests. The messages of advertising serve the interests of the sponsors by constructing and idealizing those images that are consistent with the products being advertised.

> The class which has the means of material production at its disposal, has control at the same time over the means of mental production, so that thereby, generally speaking, the ideas of those who lack the means of mental production are subject to

---

[3] *Denotation* refers to the explicit or direct meaning or set of meanings of a word or expression—the literal meaning of a signifier. *Connotation* refers to the associated or secondary meaning of a word or expression in addition to its explicit or primary meaning—the "cultural baggage" of the signifier (see Berger 1984).

[4] It is recognized that the effect of advertising on individuals is not a uniform and unchanging phenomenon but a dynamic one, i.e., there are many who resist and contest advertising's social control function. However, while many will argue that they are personally immune to the effects of advertising, the pervasiveness of advertising makes it difficult to escape. In fact, Pollay (1986) suggests that immunity from advertising is a myth: "The myth of immunity from persuasion may do more to protect self-respect than accurately comprehend the subtleties and implications of influence" (p. 23).

it (Marx *The German Ideology Part I* 1965; Tucker 1978, p. 172-3).

Advertisements bombard consumers with the idea that acquisition can lead to a more desirable body, relationship, lifestyle, and so on. Ads construct and reinforce not only images, but values. Nowhere is the materialization of value more obvious than in the evolution of the desirable body.

It is here, in the complex tissues of biology, ideology, and consciousness, that the modern commodity aesthetic, and the incarnations of personal identity, uncomfortably—at times pathologically—mesh (Ewen 1988, p. 176).

The bodies of men and women, as reflected through advertisements, track the changes in the economic base since the early years of the twentieth century. For example, around the turn of the century, the ideal body for women reflected the tangible biases of landed value (Ewen 1988). A well-fed body meant material seclusion from scarcity and hard labor. Just as the architecture of the time took on a heavy, ornamented appearance, the cultured body took on a heaviness, wrapped in ornamented fashion.

For women—whose object-value was intimately tied to their reproductive capacities—a heavy bosom and stout hips were conspicuous elements of beauty (Ewen 1988, p. 177).

By the end of the First World War, demographic, social, and economic changes were bringing women into metropolitan life. Value was shifting from the tangible agrarian lifestyle to abstract, market value. Value was now understood not in terms of land, but exchange value and a "floating" currency. Architecture started to emphasize space rather than ornament.

As the dominant system of profitability was coming to rest on a foundation of thin air, the female body—along with other icons of the new order—followed suit (Ewen 1988, p. 178).

Over time, this ideology of thinness has become so entrenched in our everyday lives it has become a norm of beauty. Consumers seek to achieve this ideal through the purchase and consumption of diet and fitness products and services. For men, the ideal body reflects instrumental values set by the modern work discipline, the machine, and conspicuous leisure. Thus men feel constrained to join the legion of Sly Stallone wanna-bes. They join the ranks at the *Nautilus* assembly line, sweat on their own in-home *Soloflex*, and learn the language of hard bodies (e.g., reps, sets, and programs used to shape biceps, triceps, deltoids, abs, etc.). This example illustrates Goldman's notion of how consumers "enter into and participate in" ideology. Although advertising reinforces and perpetuates this ideology, the base-superstructure framework encourages us to think about the critique in more macro terms.

If the function of superstructural ideology is social control, advertising should reinforce the *status quo* and therefore existing inequities. For example, there have been numerous criticisms of the portrayal of women in advertising, such as charges that women have been depicted in narrow social and occupational roles, as sex objects, as subservient to men, and as not involved in important work or decisions (c.f., Courtney and Whipple 1983). From the perspective of the base-superstructure metaphor, these portrayals reflect the need for low-cost labor. If women perceive themselves to be inferior, they might agree to a lower wage for equal work. Empirical research has shown that stereotypical female portrayals can lower women's self-confidence and independent judgement

(Jennings Walstedt, Geis, and Brown 1980), inhibit women's achievement aspirations (Geis, Brown, Jennings Walstedt, and Porter 1984), reduce women's satisfaction with their physical attractiveness (Richins 1991), and ingrain children with more traditional (versus progressive or insurgent) attitudes toward women's societal roles (Pingree 1978).

Elderly people catch much of the brunt of the negative images—they are often portrayed as senile, stupid, or ornery (just think of ads for Wendy's and Denny's). On those occasions when they are portrayed in a positive manner, it is typically in a manner that is quite unrealistic for a majority of elderly consumers (e.g., portrayals of the elderly engaging in activities such as biking, sailing, and dancing are pervasive, while portrayals of others who may be confined to homes or hospitals are nonexistent). Again, in this situation advertising is reflecting the interests of the dominant relations of production. The elderly have used up their most productive years, thus from the standpoint of a particular political economy, there may be little value placed in this specific group.

In all these examples, advertising reflects a very narrow, and therefore distorted interpretation of reality. In this sense, advertising reinforces certain lifestyles and self-conceptions and thereby acts as an agent of social control. A critique of advertising needs to go beyond an analysis of the values inherent in the text, and investigate the historical connections to the economic base. The base-superstructure metaphor provides a critical framework that makes this possible.

SUMMARY AND CONCLUSIONS

From the beginning, ACR-*JCR* culture has been tightly linked to the business community (see Murray and Ozanne 1994a for a historical overview of these ties). For example, the Institute of Scientific Information classifies *JCR* as a "business" journal. Lutz (1989) notes that "this perception is commensurate with historical reality, with the majority of *JCR* authors, articles, and reviewers associated with the Marketing discipline" (p. viii). Although these connections have been very important for our discipline, they may have discouraged a more critical stance taken toward advertising and marketing strategy in general. Pollay's (1986) overview of how other disciplines have dealt with the topic of advertising increases awareness as to how uncritical we have been. If we are to become more critical, frameworks that help organize and direct research programs are needed. The purpose of this paper was to present and illustrate such a framework: *the base-superstructure metaphor*.

This metaphor encourages research on the historical connection between the relations and forces of production and advertising ideology. It also draws attention to the relationship between advertising and other institutions making up the superstructure of society. Since advertising can have such a powerful influence on consumers' construction and interpretation of reality, we should not accept the impact of advertising as inevitable. As consumer researchers and educators we can have an important influence on how future generations of marketing executives think about advertising. It is time to turn our critical imaginations toward this important topic.

REFERENCES

Anderson, Paul F. (1989), "On Relativism and Interpretivism—with a Prolegomenon to the 'Why' Question," in *Interpretive Consumer Research*, ed. Elizabeth C. Hirschman, Provo, UT: Association for Consumer Research, 10-23.

Belk, Russell W. (1986), "What Should ACR Want to Be When It Grows Up?" in *Advances in Consumer Research*, Vol. 13, ed. Richard Lutz, Provo, UT: Association for Consumer Research, 423-424.

Berger, Arthur Asa (1984), *Signs in Contemporary Culture*, Salem, WI: Sheffield.

Courtney, Alice E. and Thomas W. Whipple (1983), *Sex Stereotyping in Advertising*, Lexington, MA: Lexington Books.

Ewen, Stuart (1976), *Captains of Consciousness*, New York: McGraw Hill.

_____ (1988), *All Consuming Images*, New York: Basic.

Featherstone, Mike (1991), *Consumer Culture and Postmodernism*, Newbury Park, CA: Sage.

Firat, A. Fuat (1991), Nikhilesh Dholakia, and Richard P. Bagozzi (1987), *Philosophical and Radical Thought in Marketing*, Lexington, MA: Lexington.

Geis, F. L., Virginia Brown, Joyce Jennings Walstedt, and Natalie Porter (1984), "TV Commercials as Achievement Scripts for Women," *Sex Roles*, 10 (7/8), 513-525.

Giddens, Anthony (1971), *Capitalism and Modern Social Theory: An Analysis of the Writings of Marx, Durkheim, and Max Weber*, Cambridge: Cambridge University Press.

Goldman, Robert (1992), *Reading Ads Socially*, London: Routledge.

Hamilton, Peter (1974), *Knowledge and Social Structure: An Introduction to the Classical Argument in the Sociology of Knowledge*, London: Routledge and Kegan Paul.

Hirschman, Elizabeth C. (1993), "Ideology in Consumer Research, 1980 and 1990: A Marxist and Feminist Critique," *Journal of Consumer Research*, 19 (March), 537-555.

Holbrook, Morris B. (1987), "Mirror, Mirror, on the Wall, What's Unfair in the Reflections on Advertising?" *Journal of Marketing*, 51 (July), 95-103.

Jennings Walstedt, Joyce, Florence L. Geis, and Virginia Brown (1980), "Influence of Television Commercials on Women's Self-Confidence and Independent Judgment," *Journal of Personality and Social Psychology*, 38 (2), 203-210.

Kneale, Dennis (1988), "Zapping of TV Ads Appears Pervasive," *The Wall Street Journal*, April 25, p. 21.

Larrain, Jorge (1983), "Base and Superstructure," in *A Dictionary of Marxist Thought*, eds. Tom Bottomore, Laurence Harris, V. G. Kiernan, and Ralph Miliband, Cambridge, MA: Harvard University Press, 42-45.

Marx, Karl (1965 [1978]), "The German Ideology Part I," in *The Marx Engels Reader*, 2nd edition, ed. R. Tucker, New York: Norton.

Marx, Karl (1904 [1978]), "A Contribution to the Critique of the Political Economy," in *The Marx Engels Reader*, 2nd edition, ed. R. Tucker, New York: Norton.

McCracken, Grant W. and Richard W. Pollay (1981), "Anthropological Analyses of Advertising," Working Paper #815, Faculty of Commerce and Business Administration, University of British Columbia.

Merton, Robert K. (1968), *Social Theory and Social Structure*, New York: The Free Press.

Murray, Jeff B. and Julie L. Ozanne (1991), "The Critical Imagination: Emancipatory Interests in Consumer Research," *Journal of Consumer Research*, 18 (September), 129-144.

_____ and _____ (1994a), "A Critical-Emancipatory Sociology of Knowledge: Reflections on the Social Construction of Consumer Research," Working Paper, Department of Marketing and Transportation, University of Arkansas, Fayetteville, AR 72701.

_____ and _____ (1994b), "The Social Construction of Consumer Research," Working Paper, Department of Marketing and Transportation, University of Arkansas, Fayetteville, AR, 72701.

_____, _____ and Jon Shapiro (1994), "Doing Critical Research: Observations from the Front," Working Paper, Department of Marketing and Transportation, College of Business Administration, University of Arkansas, Fayetteville, AR 72701.

Pingree, A. (1978), "The Effects of Nonsexist Television Commercials and Perceptions of Reality on Children's Attitudes About Women," *Psychology of Women Quarterly*, 262-77.

Pollay, Richard W. (1986), "The Distorted Mirror: Reflections on the Unintended Consequences of Advertising," *Journal of Marketing*, 50 (April), 18-36.

Remmling, Gunter W. (1973), *Towards the Sociology of Knowledge: Origin and Development of a Sociological Thought Style*, London: Routledge and Kegan Paul.

Richins, Marsha L. (1991), "Social Comparison and the Idealized Images of Advertising," *Journal of Consumer Research*, 18 (June), 71-83.

Turner, Bryan S. (1991), *Theories of Modernity and Postmodernity*, Newbury Park, CA: Sage.

Establishing the Spokes-Character in Academic Inquiry: Historical Overview and Framework for Definition

Margaret F. Callcott, University of Texas at Austin
Wei-Na Lee, University of Texas at Austin

ABSTRACT

A growing interest in advertising spokes-characters as product presenters suggests the need to establish a foundation for serious academic inquiry in this topic area. The issues that emerge most often when considering how to direct research efforts in this topic area are related to character definition, i.e., how a character looks and acts in an advertisement. This paper briefly documents the history and evolution of advertising spokes-characters, and outlines two criteria that separate these images from other advertising trademark symbols. A multi-dimensional framework for spokes-character definition is then presented, which provides for definition along four parameters: the physical *Appearance* of the character, the *Medium* it appears in, advertising or non-advertising *Origin*, and spokes-character *Promotion* of the product (AMOP). Topics for future research are discussed.

INTRODUCTION

Advertising characters, which made their debut in the late 1800s in the form of registered trademarks, have long been important forces in advertising strategy and American culture. As trademarks, the advertising character's main function in the early twentieth century was to distinguish one product from another in a marketplace increasingly dependent upon mass produced goods. In a 1950 advertising handbook, Rogers elaborates on this point, defining the trademark as "any device that enables a purchaser to choose the goods he prefers from among competing articles, and to discriminate against those he dislikes or knows nothing of" (p. 77).

Many trademarks were also intended to give large companies a personality that people could connect with, a sort of substitute for the familiar faces of local merchants, from whom the majority of consumer products came before mass production and transportation (Morgan 1986). Marchand (1985) notes that although consumers appreciated the benefits brought on by industrialization, they resented the accompanying "indignities of scale." Accordingly,

> ...advertisers gradually observed and responded to a popular demand that modern products be introduced to them in ways that gave the appearance and feel of a personal relationship. People craved opportunities, through vicarious experience, to bring products within the compass of their own human scale (p. xxi).

In the interest of establishing this personal connection with consumers, many companies created characters to use as trademarks. These characters appeared in a variety of forms, including animals, objects, mythological figures, and humans. Usually the animals and objects were personified in some way to facilitate identification with the consumer. According to Morgan,

> People imbued the trademarks with all that they knew or felt about the business behind them, based on reaction to the package and trademark, experience with the product, and the messages and images given by advertising. If public reaction to the symbols was positive, manufacturers could count on a reliable base of business (p. 11).

Although ultimately responsible for selling products, it is evident that advertising characters appearing at the turn of the century played a significant role in gaining consumer trust for new products produced far from the point of purchase. In many cases consumers began to feel that they had a personal relationship with these characters, and advertisers were mindful of this advantage when developing characters to represent their brands.

Advertising characters have maintained a continuous presence in the American marketplace as product endorsers, symbols of company/brand continuity, and objects of nostalgia. During the past decade, a handful of significant campaigns have highlighted the ongoing appeal and versatility of advertising characters. For example, the successful union of Schultz's comic strip heroes with Metropolitan Life Insurance showed advertisers that characters could be used to promote serious products and services. Advances in animation technique that brought about the success of both "Roger Rabbit" (rotoscope) and the California Raisins (claymation), also compelled advertisers to take another look at the use of spokes-characters in advertising campaigns (e.g., Gales 1987; McBride 1991; Young 1989). The resulting surge in character advertising has been fueled even further by a rebirth in the classic animated film industry (e.g., Cole and Smilgis 1992; Pendleton 1990), the acceleration of licensed character marketing (e.g., Dallabrida 1993; Fahey 1991; Freeman and Fisher 1990), and increased attention to potential objects of baby boomer nostalgia (e.g., Barrier 1989; Garfield 1990).

Character advertising has also begun to attract attention as an avenue of academic inquiry. Stern (1988, 1990) explores the relationship between spokes-characters and allegorical figures in literary criticism. Callcott and Alvey (1991) present a spokes-character typology, which becomes the basis for research linking character type to product recall. Phillips (forthcoming) presents a different definition of advertising characters, which is adapted to a study of character meaning transfer in advertisements (Phillips 1993).

As interest in advertising characters continues to grow, the need to establish a foundation for systematic academic inquiry becomes more apparent. The issues that emerge most often when considering how to direct research efforts in this topic area are related to character definition, i.e., how a character looks and acts in an advertisement. The separate ad character definitions already presented in previous papers suggest that the foundation for ad character research must include a comprehensive definition that can accommodate a variety of research perspectives. This paper attempts to provide such a definition, based on a survey of over 700 ad character images from the past century of American advertising. The majority of these images were collected from the Center for Advertising History (Smithsonian Institution) in Washington, D.C., and the American Advertising Museum in Portland, Oregon. The resulting multi-dimensional framework for ad character definition is intended to serve as both a foundation and a catalyst for future research.

THE EVOLUTION OF THE MODERN SPOKES-CHARACTER

Literature that treats the subject at all – whether from a pragmatic or historical point of view – is consistently vague about what exactly constitutes an advertising spokes-character. Simply deciding what to call the advertising character is a devilish undertaking, since "advertising character" seems too broad, and "trade character" conjures up images of a bygone era, early in modern advertising history, when most advertising characters were registered trademarks for a brand and/or company. For many of the more recent characters, which are used for promotional purposes and never registered as legal trademarks (Phillips, forthcoming), the term "trade character" seems slightly misleading. Instead, the term "spokes-character" will be used in this paper, implying a relationship between imaginary advertising product endorsers and their human counterparts (spokes-persons), whose function is to speak for a product or provide some kind of visual demonstration (Stout 1990).

Technical Evolution

Part of the confusion in spokes-character definition stems from the fact that the means by which characters have been presented, along with the characters themselves, have evolved over time. The modern spokes-character has its roots in "human-interest" illustrations and trademark symbols used in early American advertisements. The appearance of illustration in advertising was rare until the advent of outdoor advertising posters in 1867, when the work of actual artists was "combined with advertising sense" in Europe (Presbrey 1929, p. 495). Before posters, illustrations were hampered in size and quality by the limitations of boxwood, the only wood available for woodcut reproductions. In the late 1840s, the use of pine for woodcut engraving made larger reproductions possible, and the use of human-interest illustrations evolved in outdoor advertising (Presbrey 1929). The pioneers of human-interest illustration are reportedly Macassar Oil for the hair and Nubian Blacking for boots, both English products. The Macassar ad contained a picture of a woman with hair reaching to the floor, while the Nubian ad showed a picture of a Negro grinning at his reflection in a recently polished boot. Presbrey (1929) notes that the latter picture "had an arresting quality and an interest that gave it dominance over the all-type sheets around it" (p. 494).

Another milestone in pictorial advertising occurred in 1887, when the English soap manufacturer, A.& F. Pears, used a painting of a young boy blowing soap bubbles in a magazine advertisement for Pears' soap. The advertisement elicited more interest than the news pictures in the magazine, prompting other goods manufacturers to begin hunting art for their own advertisements. The introduction of the halftone technique for photographic reproduction in 1892 provided human-interest characters with more "naturalness and greater emotiveness" than previous line drawings and woodcut engravings could (Presbrey 1929, p. 382). Advertisers thus began to make wider use of human-interest trademarks, especially adorable child characters, to appeal to children and women (Hornung and Johnson 1976).

Advances in photography, cinematography and animation had a significant impact on the way spokes-characters appeared in advertising. Spokes-characters presented via hand-drawn illustration were thus joined by live humans and animals photographed in costume or in character (e.g., Ronald McDonald and Morris the Cat). Characters were also presented via increasingly diverse methods of animation, including puppetry, stop-motion photography, rotoscope, claymation and, most recently, computer animation.

Historical Antecedents

In addition to their commercial roots as trademarks, spokes-characters owe much of their evolution to an historical fascination with personification. Personification, which is the representation of an object or creature as a person, is historically one of the most popular techniques used in the creation of advertising spokes-characters. The Michelin Man, created in France in 1897, was among the first personified spokes-characters. A host of industrially fabricated men, made of everything from paper to metal, followed in the footsteps of the man made of tires. Food and household items were also widely personified, e.g., Mr. Peanut and the Nick and Pull pencil characters. At least as popular as the personification of inanimate objects has been the personification of animals. Perhaps taking their cue from the rising popularity of comic strip and animated cartoon stars, early modern advertisers produced a number of walking pigs, rabbits, chickens and frogs, as well as employing celebrities like Buster Brown and Mickey Mouse.

Although undoubtedly sensing their appeal, the creators of the Michelin Man, Tony the Tiger, and the California Raisins may not have recognized that their creations mirrored a form of communication that has been an important part of various folklore traditions for centuries. However, a look at popular culture in various societies throughout history reveals a universal tendency to "humanize" animals, objects and concepts that are a part of everyday life. According to Gowans (1981), the pervasiveness of talking animals throughout our popular culture and commercial arts is the result of man's roots in the past. Talking animals are common in examples of early Japanese and Western medieval illustrations. Gowans believes these illustrations reflect a strong identity between humans and the animal kingdom in ancient times, and that "it's in part due to atavistic memories from this age that talking animals speak so effectively to our needs" (p. 205). Furthermore, Gowans asserts that "humor mouthed by animals is the safest way to assert values," because they allow us to "make jokes of what we are embarrassed to put plainly" (p.196). He notes that a good deal of traditional wisdom has been imparted by personified animals operating in cartoon worlds, where

> ... courage, loyalty, wisdom, and shrewdness win out often enough, stupidity and wastefulness and folly regularly enough get their just rewards, for songs and stories about funny animals to display a sanity conspicuously missing from the twentieth century's controlling ideology. Such illustration therefore does for our society what illustrative arts throughout history have done – keep before populations those values and attitudes necessary and unavoidable if society is to survive, however unspeakable they may temporarily be (p.197).

In a study of animal lore in English literature, Robin (1932) maintains that animal symbolism enters into all mythologies, citing as an example the dragon, which appears in the mythologies of ancient civilizations from China to Scandinavia. He outlines three ways in which animals have been employed in literature: (1) in description of their (real or supposed) form and habits; (2) as types of character or disposition in analogy or contrast with human nature; and (3) as sources of simile or metaphor to illustrate the phases of human life and experience. Robin goes on to point out that while detailed descriptions of animal life are comparatively rare in literature, due to a lack of information about real animal habits,

> ... there is a wealth of allusion to the supposed characters or dispositions of birds, beasts, and fishes. Many of these are

accepted as types of human qualities, and from the dawn of literature to the present day illustrations of human virtues and foibles have been drawn from animal lore. The lion has always typified strength, courage, and majesty; the fox stands for cunning, the ass and the goose for stupidity, the bee for industry and orderly government, the dove for meekness and constancy (pp.15-16).

Stern (1988) makes a similar observation concerning the supposed dispositions of animals found in advertising, noting, for example, the connection between tigers and the strength commonly attributed to them in our culture:

Tigers, for example, in cereal ads (Tony the Tiger) are associated with human strength, in gasoline ads (Exxon) with car strength ("Put a tiger in your tank"), and in financial services ads (The Boston Company Special Growth Fund) with financial strength ("Grow, tiger, grow!") (p.86).

Robin posits that the interpretation of the animal world inspired the fable, which we recognize today as a literary descendent of the oral stories told by many primitive peoples, most notably the Greek Aesop (circa 600 B.C.). He quotes a definition of the fable as relating an incident in which "beings irrational, and sometimes inanimate, are for the purpose of moral instruction feigned to act and speak with human interests and passions" (p. 16). Robin also points to animal use in allegory, most notably the bestiaries, in which the supposed nature of all known animals (and some imaginary ones) were described, followed by an explanation of their religious significance. He maintains that "natural history was ransacked for similes to illustrate in a mechanical way the most commonplace experiences and feelings of human nature" (p.19). In this way, animal lore was used to illustrate, compare and contrast all phases of human life.

Although the mode of transmission is far different in the modern era, using animals to illustrate human experience is still a vital element of popular culture. Personified animals such as Gertie the Dinosaur and Felix the Cat were among the first screen stars created through animation, and comic/cartoon history suggests that their popularity was due in part to human identification with character personalities. For example, in his historical analysis of the comics, Waugh (1947) concludes that "people read comics because they find themselves reflected in them," (p.353) and that "because people love to laugh at themselves, the [comic] strips are little mirrors which reflect their intimate habits and feelings..." (p.23). Similarly, Rosemond Tuve, in her book on allegorical imagery (1966), notes that the popularity of allegorical narratives hinged on peoples' tendency to see themselves in the stories:

It was clearly shared by mediaeval author and Renaissance imitator: the pleasure in pure seeing-of-similitude, taken in as immediately as an echo, while conceiving the literal story, as one sees a pebble under water with more significance than a pebble. Neither water nor pebble offers any great novelties; what pleases is merely to observe the nature of the world and correspondences one can see in it (p.10).

The human need to personify things, to give them a personality that can be identified with, extends beyond animals to abstract concepts and inanimate objects. Young children name their toys and attach personalities to them, taught to do so by Richard Scarry books and *Charlotte's Web* (White 1952), by *Mike Mulligan and His Steam Shovel* named Mary Ann (Burton 1939), *The Little*

Engine That Could (Piper 1961), and by countless numbers of television shows, advertisements and movies that personify animals and objects in numerous fantastic ways. By the time we reach adulthood, personification is ingrained in our psyche. In addition to our pets, we name our vehicles, our plants, our guns, and even our body parts, forever seeking to relate to them on some human level.

This need to place ideas and objects on a human level dates back to ancient times, when gods were created to personify abstract concepts such as strength and love, as well as little understood natural forces like sunshine and thunder. The personification of abstract concepts, especially those having to do with virtues and vices known to mankind, was also a hallmark of medieval allegory. Allegory comes from a Greek term meaning "other-speaking," and is defined in the Random House College Dictionary as "a representation of an abstract or spiritual meaning through concrete or material forms; figurative treatment of one subject under the guise of another; a symbolic narrative" (p.36). According to Lewis (1936), it is impossible to imagine the ultimate origin of allegory because "it is of the very nature of thought and language to represent what is immaterial in picturable terms" (p.44). Tuve (1966) devotes an entire chapter of her book entitled *Allegorical Imagery* to the debate surrounding allegorical definition, but for our purposes it is sufficient to say that allegorical communication often involves the personification of abstract concepts, such as time and nature, and conflict between these concepts (e.g., a battle between virtue and vice).

The importance of this material in understanding the function and appeal of advertising spokes-characters has recently been brought to the attention of consumer behaviorists by Barbara Stern. Stern links elements of medieval allegory – namely metaphor, personification, and moral conflict – to modern advertising strategy. She begins by making a compelling argument for the application of allegory in modern mass communication by comparing the medieval masses – "simple folk" who needed "simple lessons" in the form of allegorical moral instruction – to the modern mass market (Stern 1988). She goes on to identify two types of allegory that influence modern advertising: typology and reification (Stern 1990). The latter is of particular interest here because of its connection to personification. Reification allegory emphasizes conflict over allusion, and character over action. Personification is the main element in reification, and Stern points out that "any animal, vegetable, or mineral can be shown behaving the way humans do" (p.18). In a personified advertisement, consumers have the opportunity to get to know oral hygiene products, household cleansers, various food items and even a few pharmaceuticals on a first name basis. Reification may set up conflict between these characters, then highlight the brand as the solution to the problem. As an example of this application in advertising, Stern cites the now classic Alka-Seltzer commercial in which a man sits arguing with a personified version of his stomach, sitting opposite him in a chair. The man wishes to eat things which upset his stomach, and the conflict seems to defy resolution until Alka-Seltzer arrives to save the day. As demonstrated by this example, personification can serve as a humorous means of addressing somewhat taboo product areas, such as those dealing with human digestion and excretion.

SPOKES-CHARACTER DEFINITION ISSUES

From the preceding discussion, we can see that spokes-characters evolved from an interesting mixture of commercial necessity and human nature. It is also evident that advanced technology and other changes in American culture have affected spokes-character presentation since their introduction a century ago. A comprehensive definition must therefore be flexible enough

TABLE 1
Framework for Spokes-Character Definition

Parameters	Description			
Appearance	**Fictitious Human** *Actors* *Caricatures*		**Non-Human** *Animal* *Mythical* *Product Personification*	
Medium	**Print** *Illustration* *Photography*	**Film** *Animation* *Puppetry* *Live-Action*	**Radio** *Personas*	**Merchandise** *Premiums* *Character Licensing*
Origin	**Advertising** *Non-celebrity*		**Non-Advertising** *Celebrity*	
Promotion	**Active** *Speak for product* *Demonstrate product*		**Passive** *Symbolic*	

to accommodate the diversity found among 100 years of spokes-character advertising. The proposed Framework for Spokes-Character Definition (Table 1) attempts to fill this prescription by providing four parameters for character definition: the physical *Appearance* of the character, the *Medium* it appears in, advertising or non-advertising *Origin*, and spokes-character *Promotion* of the product (AMOP). Spokes-characters may be defined along all four parameters, or on any combination of parameters that is desired for research purposes.

Although this framework strives to be inclusive, there are two criteria that must be met for an advertising image to be considered a "spokes-character" within the AMOP parameters. First, a character must be used consistently in conjunction with the product it advertises. This excludes figures that appear in advertising as illustrations or graphic devices for a single ad or campaign. Secondly, the spokes-character must have a recognizable "character" or "persona." Webster's defines "character" as "a distinctive trait, quality, or attribute" (p.304). This means that an image must have an explicit personality or nature that is easily perceived by consumers.

Several abstract human figures used as logos and graphic devices fail to qualify as spokes-characters using these criterion. Smith (1993) devotes an entire book to the study of FLMs (Funny Little Men) popular in American advertising during the 1940s. Although their form was generally recognized by consumers as humorous, the lack of a recognized persona limits consumer involvement with several of these figures, thus creating a different dynamic from that created by spokes-characters. The exclusion of these figures is not to deny that consumers become attached to these images as well as to characters used in advertising (consider, for example, the nostalgic appeal of the Coke bottle). While commercial images of all types can promote product recognition, ad recall, and even gain nostalgic appeal, spokes-characters are unique in that they provide consumers with the opportunity to identify with a specific persona. Therefore, we would argue that commercial figures not meeting the above criteria of ad continuity and personality should be studied as symbols and not as "characters."

Appearance

Although spokes-characters have appeared in a mind-boggling array of forms, a basic distinction can be made between human and nonhuman spokes-characters. *Fictitious Human spokes-characters* may be pictured realistically through illustration or less so through caricature. Notable among realistic depictions are the Quaker Oats man, Betty Crocker, and the Morton Salt Girl. Although photography made it possible to present live versions of these characters long ago, their images have consistently been updated via illustration instead. One reason for this choice of presentation may be the desire to present ideals that "real" humans could not adequately represent. For example, General Mills' Betty Crocker, whose face appeared for the first time in 1936, was created to be the perfect picture of domesticity. Although Betty's image has since been updated five times, a public relations manager at General Mills points out that she has always been a reflection of the American homemaker. The use of illustration enables Betty to be "everywoman," that is, a composite of the female employees at General Mills, and of women all over America (Kapnick 1992). It also allows Betty's image, enhanced by consumer imagination, to remain untarnished through several generations. As one employee at the Madison Avenue agency Wells, Rich, Greene, says: "Betty was created to have exactly the qualities she's supposed to have. She's perfect" (Kapnick 1992, p. D1). The introduction of a real person in the role of Betty Crocker might conflict with existing consumer perceptions of this spokes-character.

Many human spokes-characters have also been presented in the form of caricatures, with the intent of producing more attractive and/or humorous characterization: ethnic figures (e.g., the Gold Dust twins), old men (e.g., Sunny Jim), and children (e.g., the Campbell Kids). Webster's (1983, p. 275) defines *caricature* as "the deliberately distorted picturing or imitating of a person, literary style, etc. by exaggerating features or mannerisms for satirical effect." Far from being unpleasant, the distortion of human characteristics often helps endear the character to the consumer in some way. The physical features that make personified animals and objects attractive, in particular those that render characters childlike, often make human caricatures more attractive to consumers as well.

Actors have also been used to further a spokes-character's image. Before the advent of television, several versions of Buster Brown and his dog Tige toured the country promoting the Brown Shoe Company (Company pamphlet), and Aunt Jemima was personified from her conception into the 1960s by three generations of African-American women (Marquette 1967). More recently, Kool-Aid, Ronald McDonald and the Fruit-of-the-Loom Guys populate our television sets. Less costume-dependent personas of our era include Madge (Palmolive), the Maytag Repairman, and Mr. Whipple (Charmin bathroom tissue).

Non-Human spokes-characters fall into one of three categories: Animals, Mythical beings, or Product Personifications. The degree of personification in animal spokes-characters varies widely, and can best be pictured on a continuum. Tony the Tiger, Smokey Bear and Joe Camel are among the most personified animal characters in that they closely resemble humans in their speech and/or behavior. Among the least personified is Morris the Cat, a real cat that has been given a specific personality that allows consumers to relate to him. Non-personified animals like the Bon Ami chick and the Sinclair dinosaur, are generally used because they possess well-known qualities that advertisers wish to associate with their products. For example, the Bon Ami chick is perceived as soft and gentle, qualities that the advertisers wish to associate with their cleansing powder, while the Sinclair Refining Company chose a brontosaurus "to dramatize the age and mellowness" of the crude oil they refined.

Mythical spokes-characters hail from a variety of literary and folklore traditions, and include giants (Green Giant), elves (Keebler), fairies (Coca-Cola's Sprite), mermaids (Chicken of the Sea tuna), genies (Mr. Clean), vampires (Count Chocula) and even Big Foot (Pizza Hut). Occasionally, mythical beings are created specifically for a product, as in the case of Kellogg's Big Mixx cereal, which featured "the legendary chicken/wolf/moose/pig of Yakima Valley."

Product Personification can take the form of the product, itself, or of some product-relevant concept. Modern food and household cleanser personifications like the California Raisins and the Dow Scrubbing Bubbles are the descendents of Mr. Peanut, created in 1916, and the Oxydol "Hustle-Bubble Suds," appearing in the 1940s. Product-relevant personifications – including the product's packaging or unique selling proposition – also have a long history in advertising. One of the most technologically advanced packaging personifications stars an heroic Listerine bottle that battles gum disease in a number of venues. After its boxing ring debut, the computer animated Listerine champion swung through a forest a la Tarzan, and most recently donned Robin Hood gear complete with bow and arrow to skewer plaque and gingivitis. Listerine's packaging predecessors include a dapper Clorox bottle in top hat and spats (circa 1940) and a looming bottle of Raid that sprays himself on hapless insects in Raid commercials (circa 1956). Examples of personified product-relevant concepts include the Domino's Pizza Noid (a personification of cold pizza that Dominos consistently foils) and the Glad-Lock Zipper finger, which personifies the bags' convenient closing mechanism.

Medium

The second parameter for spokes-character definition relates to the medium through which these characters are presented to the public. There are four basic media through which spokes-characters connect with consumers: print, film, radio and merchandise. As discussed above, spokes-characters appearing in *print* may be in the form of illustrations (realistic or caricature), or photographs. Spokes-characters appearing on *film* may be brought to life by some form of animation (cel, computer, stop-motion, etc.), puppetry, or live-action. Puppetry can be mechanized (e.g., the Energizer Bunny and Duracell robots) or hand-driven (e.g., the Hamburgler in McDonald-Land or the Zip-Lock Finger puppets). Live-action spokes-characters include humans and animals in costumes or in character (e.g., Ronald McDonald or Morris the Cat).

Although not a visual purveyor of spokes-character imagery, *radio* has created it's share of advertising personas, as well as contributing to the personas of existing characters. Betty Crocker was the star of daytime radio's first cooking show, which debuted in 1924 ("The Story of Betty Crocker"). Betty's subsequent radio performance in the 1950s network program, "Time for Betty Crocker," proved more popular than her concurrent television appearances, perhaps because consumers preferred to create their own visual image of "America's First lady of Food" (Heighton and Cunningham 1976). The key to distinguishing between radio personalities and actual radio spokes-characters is whether or not the character survives independent of the announcer. One 1946 advertising handbook notes that "if an outside representative is employed (to represent a store), it is well to give a fictitious name that becomes the property of the store, to prevent the announcer's taking to another employer any personal following built up" (McCormick, Everest and Bartlett 1946). In this way, announcers create a radio persona instead of achieving their own celebrity.

Finally, it is important to recognize the continuing popularity of spokes-character *merchandise*, which proliferates through promotional premiums and licensing. Several books have been written about the collectibility of advertising character merchandise, which became popular at the turn of the century with numerous Buster Brown and Campbell Kids products. Today, an entire catalog is devoted to Joe Camel merchandise, the Energizer Bunny offers beach towels and boxer shorts in his 1994 calendar, and members of the Dow Scrubbing Bubbles Tub Club can order a range of bathroom accessories (from towels to a shower radio) featuring the cherubic Scrubbing Bubbles. Although not advertising per se, merchandise featuring spokes-characters helps strengthen consumer awareness of the character, and presumably the brand. Spokes-character premiums are perhaps better at promoting brand awareness than other forms of licensed merchandise since proofs of purchase are often required in order to obtain them.

Because of the prevalence of character licensing, it is important to differentiate between a spokes-character licensed to endorse a product and a character licensed to appear on a product. According to Stout (1990), an endorsement requires a visual demonstration or verbal testimonial from the personality. Therefore, Bart Simpson and the California Raisins are not spokes-characters for T-shirts and lunch boxes just because they appear on them. Rather, Bart is a spokes-character for Butterfinger candy bars, a product he actually touts, while the Raisins are spokes-characters for the California Raisin Board.

Origin

Spokes-Characters can be further defined as having an advertising or non-advertising origin. Like their human counterparts, characters with a *non-advertising origin* can be classified as celebrities, that is, their notability is achieved through movies, comic strips and television, where they develop well-known personalities that can later be readily associated with a product. Examples of celebrity spokes-characters include Garfield for Embassy Suites and Alpo; Bugs Bunny for Holiday Inn and Astro World; and the Peanuts characters for Metropolitan Life Insurance. These characters are already widely known, and therefore may have many of the same characteristics as human celebrity endorsers, including the ability to attract attention and create a positive association for a product through a popular personality.

Non-celebrity spokes-characters are those characters with an *advertising origin*, that is, they were originally created strictly for advertising purposes. Exploratory research indicates that non-celebrity spokes-characters may be more effective than their celebrity counterparts because the identity they provide for a product belongs only to that product (Callcott and Alvey 1991). This eliminates the problem of character overexposure and subsequent consumer confusion over which product a popular celebrity character endorses. Instead, non-celebrity characters become almost "as one" with a product through repeated exposure over the years, often earning the support and trust of the American population.

Both celebrity spokes-characters and celebrity humans are related in that they provide ready-made images that advertisers borrow, with hopes of transferring something positive about that image to their products. In contrast, non-celebrity characters must be imbued with their own brand-appropriate image, preferably something that consumers find appealing, relevant to the product or company, and/or trustworthy.

Promotion

A final parameter for spokes-character definition concerns the way in which spokes-characters promote a product. *Active* promotion of the product involves speaking for the product or demonstrating the product in some way. Characters shown using the product (e.g., the Energizer Bunny and Joe Camel) or presenting it to the consumer (e.g., the Pink Panther for Owens-Corning insulation) qualify as active promoters even if they never utter a word on behalf of the product.

Passive promotion of the product is more symbolic in nature. For example, the Uneeda Biscuit Slicker Boy was created in 1898 to symbolize Uneeda's revolutionary moisture-proof packaging (Morgan 1986). The Morton Salt girl symbolizes the salt's unique selling proposition: that it won't become sticky in humidity (thus, "when it rains it pours"). The modern Quaker Oats Man lends only his countenance to advertising for Quaker Oats, symbolizing both the product's wholesomeness and its longevity.

It is important to note that the degree of activity a spokes-character exhibits can change over time. Many well-known advertising spokes-characters have moved back and forth between active promotion of a product and symbolic representation of tradition and continuity. The Quaker Oats man and Betty Crocker both actively promoted their products for many years before retiring to iconic status. The Campbell Kids and Elsie the Cow (both currently active) have also moved between active promotion and symbolic appearances on packaging and on the bottom of advertisements. This cycle may help to prevent character wear-out, while at the same time preserving consumer relationships with the characters.

CONCLUSION AND FUTURE RESEARCH DIRECTIONS

The use of spokes-characters as product presenters is a topic area rich enough to sustain numerous research efforts aimed at understanding the character's relationship to consumers and to the various products they promote. Key to the development of research in this area is the definition of advertising spokes-characters, which have been presented in numerous ways during the past century. Pursuit of an understanding of the spokes-character has potential to contribute to several areas of consumer behavior research, including source credibility, product involvement, nostalgia and symbolism.

The evolution and continued use of spokes-characters in advertising is indicative of an appeal that transcends changing consumer lifestyles and advertising trends. Although few research efforts have targeted the spokes-character directly, a number of studies provide clues to their appeal. Advertising research has concluded that positive attitudes toward advertising can lead to positive attitudes toward the brand (Lutz, MacKenzie and Belch 1983; Shimp 1981). Spokes-characters have also been linked to various forms of positive affect, including attractive colors and shapes (Lawrence 1986), humor (Kelly and Solomon 1975) and nostalgia (Stern 1988). Future research should include further exploration of the affective components of spokes-characters.

In addition, most of the research that addresses spokes-characters directly, has been concerned with their effects on youth (Hoy, Young and Mowen 1986; Van Auken and Lonial 1985). Very little research has explored the relationship between advertising spokes-characters and adult consumers, and the use of characters in trade advertising has never been examined. However, it is evident that spokes-characters have always had some appeal for adult consumers. An historical survey of spokes-characters reveals a number of industrial product personifications likely to have been used in trade publications (Callcott 1993). In addition, Callcott and Lee (forthcoming) find evidence that animated spokes-characters are appearing in television commercials aimed at adult audiences. Spokes-character relationships to various target audiences can be examined using content analysis of selected media containing characters, or by using established methods for measuring audience response. Cognitive responses to spokes-character advertising may lend weight to speculation about spokes-character impact on consumer attention and memory.

The four parameters presented here serve as a guide for focusing on key differences in spokes-characters, with respect to both consumer response and advertising effectiveness. For example, a previous study using spokes-character origin found that spokes-characters with an advertising origin elicited 70% correct product recall, while characters with a non-advertising origin elicited only 30% correct product recall (Callcott and Alvey 1991). A future study along the first two AMOP parameters (Appearance and Medium) might examine differences in consumer perception of human vs. non-human spokes-characters. It is possible that people respond differently to human characters in costume or in persona than to more fantastic animal and product personifications. Experts in both animation and advertising have alluded to the "suspension of disbelief" that allows people to accept product claims made by animated presenters (Baldwin 1982; Crafton 1982; White 1981). The degree to which suspension of disbelief mediates consumer acceptance of human vs. non-human characters and their product claims is a promising area for further study.

It is also likely that spokes-character success is in part product-dependent. The recent controversy surrounding Joe Camel indicates that many consumers feel it is inappropriate for spokes-characters to promote certain products. Even if "appropriateness" is not an issue, there may be differences in the types of products successfully promoted by spokes-characters versus other creative approaches. Furthermore, determining which spokes-character types work best for different products would be valuable insight for both advertisers and advertising practitioners. Several studies have reported on the significance of product/endorser congruence (e.g., DeSarbo and Harshman 1985; McCracken 1989). Future research might examine whether the same source effects apply to spokes-characters.

REFERENCES

Baldwin, Huntley (1982), *Creating Effective TV Commercials*, Chicago: Crain Books.

Barrier, Michael (1989), "Memories for Sale," *Nation's Business*, 77 (December), 18-26.

Brown Shoe Company pamphlet: "The Life and Times of Buster Brown."

Burton, Virginia Lee (1939), *Mike Mulligan and His Steam Shovel*, Boston: Houghton Mifflin.

Callcott, Margaret F. (1993), "The Spokes-Character in Advertising: An Historical Survey and Framework for Future Research," unpublished dissertation, Department of Advertising, College of Communication, University of Texas, Austin, TX 78712-1092.

_____and Patricia A. Alvey (1991), "Toons Sell... and sometimes they don't: An advertising spokes-character typology and exploratory study," in *Proceedings of the 1991 Conference of The American Academy of Advertising*, ed. Rebecca Holman, 43-52.

_____and Wei-Na Lee (1994), "A Content Analysis of Animation and Animated Spokes-Characters in Television Commercials," *Journal of Advertising*, 23 (December), 1-12.

Cole, Patrick E., and Martha Smilgis (1992), "Aladdin's Magic," *Time*, 140 (November 9), 74-76.

Crafton, Donald (1982), *Before Mickey: The Animated Film 1898-1928*, Cambridge, MA: The MIT Press.

Dallabrida, Dale (1993), "No boring burgers for Rocky J. and Bullwinkle," *Sunday News Journal*, Wilmington, DE, (March 28), E1.

DeSarbo, Wayne S., and Richard A. Harshman (1985), "Celebrity-Brand Congruence Analysis," in *Current Issues and Research in Advertising*, eds. J.H. Leigh and C.R. Martin, Jr., Ann Arbor, MI: Division of Research, Graduate School of Business Administration, The University of Michigan, 17-52.

Fahey, Alison (1991), "Hagar the Horrible roots for Pepsi," *Advertising Age*, 62 (July 1), 10.

Freeman, Laurie, and Christy Fisher (1990), "Popeye lends muscle to GH green seal," *Advertising Age*, 61 (June 25), 58.

Gales, Ron (1987), "Fateful attractions: Rollicking raisins and a manic noid," *Adweek*, (October 12), 54, 59.

Garfield, Bob (1990), "Revival Recap: How does the Buster Brown song go?" *Advertising Age*, 61 (July 30), 28.

Gowans, Alan (1981), *Learning to See: Historical Perspectives on Modern Popular/Commercial Arts*, Bowling Green, OH: Bowling Green University Popular Press.

Heighton, Elizabeth J., and Don R. Cunningham (1976), *Advertising in the Broadcast Media*, Belmont, CA: Wadsworth Publishing Company.

Hornung, Clarence, and Fridolf Johnson (1976), *200 Years of American Graphic Art: A Retrospective Survey of the Printing Arts and Advertising Since the Colonial Period*, New York: George Braziller.

Hoy, Mariea Grubbs, Clifford E. Young, and John C. Mowen (1986), "Animated Host-Selling Advertisements: Their Impact on Young Children's Recognition, Attitudes, and Behavior," *Journal of Public Policy and Marketing*, 5: 171-184.

Kapnick, Sharon (1992), "Commercial Success: These advertising figures have become American icons," *Austin American-Statesman*, (April 25), D1, D6.

Kelley, J. Patrick, and Paul J. Solomon (1975), "Humor in Television Advertising," *Journal of Advertising*, 4(3), 31-35.

Lawrence, Elizabeth A. (1986), "In the Mick of Time: Reflections On Disney's Ageless Mouse," *Journal of Popular Culture*, 20(2), 65-72.

Lewis, C.S. (1936), *The Allegory of Love*, London: Oxford University Press.

Lutz, Richard J., Scott B. MacKenzie and George E. Belch (1983), "Attitude Toward the Ad as a Mediator of Advertising Effectiveness: Determinants and Consequences," *Advances in Consumer Research*, Volume 10, Richard P. Bagozzi and Alice M. Tybout, eds., Ann Arbor, MI: Association for Consumer Research, 532-539.

Marchand, Roland (1985), *Advertising the American Dream: Making Way for Modernity 1920-1940*, Berkeley: University of California Press.

Marquette, Arthur F. (1967), *Brands, Trademarks and Good Will: The Story of the Quaker Oats Company*, New York: McGraw-Hill.

McBride, James (1991), "Animation American Style," *Back Stage/Shoot*, (March 15), 32-36.

McCormick, C.D., Philip J. Everest, and Kenneth G. Bartlett (1946), *Transit and Radio Advertising*, Scranton, PA: International Textbook Company.

McCracken, Grant (1989), "Who Is the Celebrity Endorser? Cultural Foundations of the Endorsement Process," *Journal of Consumer Research*, 16 (December), 310-321.

Morgan, Hal (1986), *Symbols of America*, New York: Penguin Books.

Pendleton, Jennifer (1990), "Animation: A Cartoon Comeback," *Knoxville News-Sentinel/Los Angeles Daily News*, (June 13), B1, B8.

Phillips, Barbara (1993), "The Role of Advertising Trade Characters in Forming Product Perceptions," unpublished thesis, Department of Advertising, College of Communication, The University of Texas, Austin, TX 78712-1092.

_____(forthcoming), "Defining Trade Characters and Their Role in American Popular Culture," *Journal of Popular Culture*.

Piper, Watty (1961), *The Little Engine That Could*, New York: Platt & Munk.

Presbrey, Frank (1929), *The History and Development of Advertising*, Garden City, NY: Doubleday, Doran and Company.

Robin, P. Ansell (1932), *Animal Lore in English Literature*, London: John Murray.

Rogers, Edward S. (1950), "What Makes a Good Trademark?" in *Advertising Handbook*, ed. Roger Barton, New York: Prentice-Hall, 73-89.

Rothenberg, Randall (1988), "A new career in sales for old cartoon stars," *New York Times* (May 23), D8.

Scarry, Richard (1969), *Richard Scarry's Great Big School House*, New York: Random House.

Shimp, Terence A. (1981), "Attitude of the Ad as a Mediator of Consumer Brand Choice," *Journal of Advertising*, 10 (June), 9-15.

Siegel, Seth, and Michael Stone (1990), "Classic, long-lasting properties the focus in today's licensing industry," 1990 Marketer's Resource Guide to Licensing, *Advertising Age*, (May 28), L-7.

Smith, Virginia (1993), *The Funny Little Man: The Biography of a Graphic Image*, New York: Van Nostrand Reinhold.

Stern, Barbara (1988), "Medieval Allegory: Roots of Advertising Strategy for the Mass Market," *Journal of Marketing*, 52 (July), 84-94.

_____(1990), "Other-Speak: Classical Allegory and Contemporary Advertising," *Journal of Advertising*, 19(3), 14-26.

"The Story of Betty Crocker," General Mills, Inc. pamphlet, 1992.

Stout, Patricia (1990), "Use of Endorsers in Magazine Advertisements," *Journalism Quarterly*, 67(3), 536-46.

Tuve, Rosemond (1966), *Allegorical Imagery: Some Mediaeval Books and Their Posterity*, Princeton, NJ: Princeton University Press.

Van Auken, Stuart, and Subhash C. Lonial (1985), "Children's Perceptions of Characters: Human Versus Animate; Assessing Implications for Children's Advertising." *Journal of Advertising*, 14(2): 13-22.

Waugh, Coulton (1947), *The Comics*, New York: Macmillan.

Webster's New 20th Century Unabridged Dictionary, Second Edition, New York: Simon and Schuster, 1983.

White, E.B. (1952), *Charlotte's Webb*, New York: Harper.

White, Hooper (1981), *How to Produce an Effective TV Commercial*, Chicago: Crain Books.

Young, Paul (1989), "Cartoon craze a boon for N.M. animation house," *Adweek*, XI (March 6), 1, 6.

Accessibility Effects on the Relationship Between Attitude Toward the Ad and Brand Choice

Cynthia B. Hanson, Greensboro College
Gabriel J. Biehal, University of Maryland

ABSTRACT

This study examines direct and indirect effects of attitude toward the ad (Aad) on brand choice, and the impact of brand information accessibility on the role of Aad in brand choice. The results show no direct effect of Aad on brand choice: the effect of Aad was completely mediated by brand attitude. Consistent with theoretical predictions, ad effects were more dramatic when brand information was less accessible. In fact, when brand information was highly accessible, Aad affected brand attitude but not choice outcomes.

INTRODUCTION

Over a decade of research supports the importance of a consumer's attitude toward an ad (Aad) in the formation of brand attitude and purchase intention. Brown and Stayman (1992) summarized the results of much of this research in their meta-analysis of Aad studies. Their analysis provides a comprehensive comparison of various models which have been proposed in the literature and identifies several moderating factors. It also serves to illuminate some important gaps in the Aad research both in terms of modeling the effects of Aad and identifying moderating factors. Specifically, most studies have used brand attitude or purchase intention as the outcome variable and, consequently, the effect of Aad on choice has not been fully explored. The distinction between brand attitude, purchase intention and choice is important when studying Aad, as Aad may have an effect on brand attitude without affecting choice behavior (Chattopadhyay and Nedungadi 1990); or, Aad may have a direct effect on choice in addition to the indirect effect through brand attitude (Biehal, Stephens, and Curlo 1992). Furthermore, although the consumer behavior literature shows that memory-based choice processes are very different from externally-based choice processes (Biehal and Chakravarti 1982), very few studies have looked at the impact of differences in brand attribute information accessibility on the role of Aad. Therefore, the purpose of this study is twofold. First, it investigates the direct and indirect effects of Aad on choice, attempting to replicate previous research findings. Second, it extends previous work by examining the impact of brand information accessibility on the role of Aad in brand choice.

CONCEPTUAL BACKGROUND

Attitude Toward the Ad

The most widely supported model of the role of Aad is the "Dual Mediation Hypothesis," first tested by MacKenzie, Lutz, and Belch (1986). This model proposes that both brand cognitions and attitude toward the ad directly influence brand attitude. In addition, Aad is shown as having an indirect effect, through brand cognitions, on brand attitude. This model has received extensive support in the literature (MacKenzie et al. 1986, Homer 1990, Brown and Stayman 1992).

However, using purchase intention rather than choice as the final outcome measure leaves open two possibilities. First, it is possible that Aad effects on brand attitude and purchase intention do not carry through to choice. The fact that attitudinal indicators, such as brand attitude and purchase intentions, do not always predict choice is well-documented in the consumer behavior and social psychology literature (Smith and Swinyard 1983, Fazio, Chen, McDonel, and Sherman 1982). Attitudes may not be reflected in choice for a variety of reasons, including situational factors, constraints, and lack of product involvement. Research by Fazio et al. (1982) suggests that attitudes which are not formed through direct experience may be more weakly associated with the object, less accessible in memory, and thus less likely to carry through to choice. Furthermore, attitude changes may not be reflected in choice behavior if they are not large enough to affect *relative* preferences among brands in the choice set. Research by Chattopadhyay and Nedungadi (1990) and Miniard, Sirdeshmukh, and Innis (1992) illustrates that advertising manipulations which significantly affect brand attitudes may not affect choice. Since most advertising managers are ultimately concerned with how their advertising affects choice behavior, it is important to measure choice in addition to attitudinal effects of advertising.

The second reason for extending the Aad models to choice concerns the direct versus mediated effects of Aad on choice. Baker and Lutz (1988) suggest that when two brands are similar, Aad may become a "tie-breaker." This implies that Aad has a direct effect on choice, not mediated by brand attitude. Although previous analyses have found no direct path from Aad to purchase intention, Biehal et al. (1992), in a study which included two very similar brands, did find a significant direct effect of Aad on choice. Therefore, the first research question to be addressed in this study is: does Aad have a direct or mediated effect on brand choice?

Accessibility as a Moderator of Aad Effects

Much of the research on the role of Aad has focused on identifying factors affecting the strength of the various model relationships, particularly the relative influence of brand beliefs and Aad (MacKenzie and Lutz 1989, Brown and Stayman 1992). One factor which has not received much attention, in spite of theoretical and empirical research showing its importance in affecting choice, is brand information accessibility. Biehal and Chakravarti (1982, 1986) showed that choice processing when all information is externally available differs in several respects from choice processing when some information is in memory. Chattopadhyay and Nedungadi (1992) did investigate the effect of accessibility on attitude toward the ad. However, their manipulation weakened the accessibility of ad cognitions while brand cognitions remained stable, resulting in a decline in the impact of Aad over time. In contrast, this study investigates the role of Aad when brand attribute information is less accessible.

Several theoretical frameworks of consumer judgment and choice highlight the importance of an input's accessibility in determining its impact on consumer judgment and choice (Baker and Lutz 1988, Feldman and Lynch 1988, Kisielius and Sternthal 1984). The Relevance-Accessibility Model (Baker and Lutz 1988) is particularly useful for examining the effect of accessibility on Aad, since it is specifically designed as a model of advertising effectiveness. According to the Relevance-Accessibility Model, given a sufficient level of involvement, the primary determinant of a consumer's brand response will be his or her cognitive structure, which is comprised of brand beliefs. However, if the brand attribute information is less accessible in memory, the importance of (stored) evaluative reactions to the ad increases. This implies that Aad will

Advances in Consumer Research
Volume 22, © 1995

have a greater impact on brand choice when brand attribute information is less accessible in memory. Therefore, the second research question addressed in this research is: does the role of Aad in choice depend upon the accessibility of brand attribute information?

METHOD

The findings reported in this paper are part of a larger study with additional conditions. Only the manipulations and procedures for the four conditions reported in this paper are described below.

Experimental Design

The experiment included two levels of brand attribute accessibility (high accessibility, i.e., information externally available during choice; and, low accessibility, i.e., information on some brands available only in memory) and two levels of ad picture (good and bad) for a target brand. Therefore, the study was a 2 X 2 between-subjects design.

Stimuli

Print ads for eight hypothetical brands of running shoes, labeled A through H, were constructed. Ads contained a headline at the top, a four-color photograph (approximately 6 inches square), and a short paragraph of ad copy at the bottom. The copy described the brands on four attributes, determined through pretesting to be salient features of running shoes: cushioning, durability, support, and color/style. Each attribute could have one of three performance levels. Exhibit 1 shows the brands and their features. The order in which features were presented in the ad copy was changed for each brand, to encourage subjects to read the entire ad copy. Brands were defined so that brands B (the target brand) and D would be the most likely choices. These two brands performed very well on cushioning and color/style, but subjects would need to trade-off B's superior durability against D's higher comfort level. Brands E through H were designed to perform worse than at least one of the brands A through D, so that in the high accessibility condition they were unlikely to be chosen.

Manipulations

Accessibility. One factor which has been shown to affect subsequent accessibility of brand information in memory is the amount of cognitive elaboration it receives at the time of encoding. The amount of cognitive elaboration, and thus the accessibility of brand attribute information, can be reduced by limiting the amount of time a consumer is given to examine an ad (Kisielius and Sternthal 1984). Therefore, we manipulated accessibility using a speeded learning task designed to represent a situation in which some brand attribute information is encoded fleetingly, without being evaluated or integrated to form attitudes. Pretesting showed that with thirty seconds to learn each ad, subjects were able to encode its information, but it was not very accessible. Further, self-report measures indicated subjects did not form overall brand evaluations.

Ad Picture. The quality of the ads was manipulated by varying ad pictures and headlines. The target brand had either a good ad or a bad ad (between subjects), and all other brands' ads were average. One good, one bad, and seven average ads were selected based on pretesting. The bad ad contained a picture of a man and a woman running. The woman was dressed as a leprechaun and the headline was "Go for the Gold." (This ad is reproduced in Biehal et al. 1992.) The good ad contained a picture of a lone man running on a rural road. The headline was "There is No Finish Line." All ad pictures were taken from magazines, either from old running shoe ads or from photographs of running events. Most headlines were written by the experimenter, although some were taken from the magazine picture captions. References to brand names were removed. Pretesting showed that subjects did not associate any of our fabricated ads with real brands.

Procedure

Figure 1 provides a flowchart of the experimental procedure. Subjects were given a package of eight ads, identified by the letters A-H. Subjects indicated their attitudes toward the eight ads. The ad copy at the bottom of the eight ads was replaced by x's during the ad rating task, to keep subjects from forming brand attitudes or engaging in choice processing.[1] Half the subjects saw a good ad for brand B (the target brand) and half saw a bad ad. After the ad rating task, the subjects returned the ads to the package and closed it. Then they read some background information on running shoes, explaining the four attributes used to describe the running shoes (cushioning, support, style/color, and durability).

The procedure then differed depending on the subject's accessibility condition. Subjects in the *high accessibility condition* were given a package of eight ads, which now contained brand attribute information on four features, in the form of ad copy, at the bottom of the ad. They then chose the brand they preferred. The eight ads were externally available, i.e., in front of the subjects, when they made their choices.

Subjects in the *low accessibility condition* were given a limited amount of time to learn the brand attribute information contained in the ads for the first four brands, A-D. After learning the ads the subjects returned them to the envelope and closed it. Then, low accessibility subjects were given recall and recognition tests to check the manipulation. After this, the low accessibility subjects received the ads for the second set of four brands and were asked to choose their most preferred brand from all eight brands, i.e., the memory brands, A-D, and the four external brands, E-H. Thus, low accessibility subjects had a mixed choice task.

As Figure 1 shows, after subjects made their choices, the procedure was the same for both groups. Subjects first returned all the ads to the envelope, and then indicated their brand attitudes toward their chosen brand and toward the target brand, B. Finally, subjects completed a questionnaire designed to measure task reactions and subject characteristics.

Measures

Brand choice was operationalized by having subjects circle the brand label (A through H) of their chosen brand. For purposes of this study, choice was dichotomized into chose/did not choose brand B. Attitude toward the ad was derived from an average of subjects' ratings on four 10-point scales: bad/good, dislike/like, uncreative/creative, boring/interesting. Brand attitude was derived from an average of subjects' ratings on four 7-point scales: bad/good, dislike/like, unpleasant/pleasant, poor quality/good quality. These scales were based on a review of existing research. Coefficient alpha was .94 for Aad and .95 for brand attitude, indicating acceptable levels of reliability for these scales (Nunnally 1978).

Subjects

The study involved 97 undergraduate students from the business subject pool at a large state university. Their ages ranged from

---

[1]Since the text of all ads was almost identical (only the attribute performance and statement sequence was varied) it should not have affected relative ad attitudes among brands. Therefore, although the Aad measure was based on the picture and headline, this should not have affected the results, and was felt to be necessary given the study design.

EXHIBIT 1
Brand Features

	Brand A	Brand B (Target)	Brand C	Brand D
Cushioning	Thick midsole cushioning for good shock absorption	Extra thick midsole cushioning for excellent shock absorption	Midsole cushioning for shock absorption	Extra thick midsole cushioning for excellent shock absorption
Support	Comfortable because of heel support	Very comfort. because of good arch and heel support	Very comfortable because of good arch and heel support	Extrm. comfort. because of excel. arch, heel, and instep support
Style/Color	2 colors and nylon uppers	Wide range of popular colors and uppers	Several popular colors and uppers	Wide range of popular colors and uppers
Durability	Very durable 12-14 months w/some maintenance	Extrm. durable 16-18 monthsw/ minimal maintenance	Durable 8-10 months w/careful maintenance	Very durable 12-14 months w/some maintenance
Sequence of attributes in ad copy	1,2,3,4	2,3,4,1	3,4,1,2	4,1,2,3

	Brand E	Brand F	Brand G	Brand H
Cushioning	Midsole cushioning for shock absorption	Midsole cushioning for shock absorption	Thick midsole cushioning for good shock absorption	Midsole cushioning for shock absorption
Support	Comfortable because of heel support	Very comfort. because of good arch and heel support	Very comfortable because of good arch and heel support	Comfortable because of heel suppport
Style/Color	2 colors and nylon uppers	2 colors and nylon uppers	Several popular colors and uppers	Several popular colors and uppers
Durability	Very durable 12-14 months with some maintenance	Durable 8-10 months with careful maintenance	Very durable 12-14 months w/some maintenance	Durable 8-10 months w/careful maintenance
Sequence of attributes in ad copy	4,3,2,1	3,2,1,4	2,1,4,3	1,4,3,2

19-40 years, with a mean of 22, and 56% were female. The subjects received extra-credit in exchange for their participation.

RESULTS

Manipulation Checks

Attitude Toward the Ad. Attitude toward ad B was significantly higher when ad B had the good picture versus the bad picture (7.44 versus 5.05, p<.001). A 2 X 2 ANOVA of attitude toward ad B with ad picture and accessibility showed only the ad picture main effect: accessibility had no main (p>.50) or interaction (p>.40) effect on Aad (see Exhibit 2). Attitude toward the other ads ranged from 5.22 to 7.29, with a mean of 6.19. Most importantly, Aad for brand D, the other likely choice candidate, was 5.99, which is significantly lower than the good brand B ad (p<.001), and significantly higher than the bad brand B ad (p<.001).

A series of regression equations (Baron and Kenny 1986) showed that Aad completely mediated the effect of the ad picture manipulation on brand attitude: 1) Ad picture significantly affected Aad (beta=.46, p<.01), 2) Ad picture significantly affected brand

FIGURE 1
Experimental Procedure

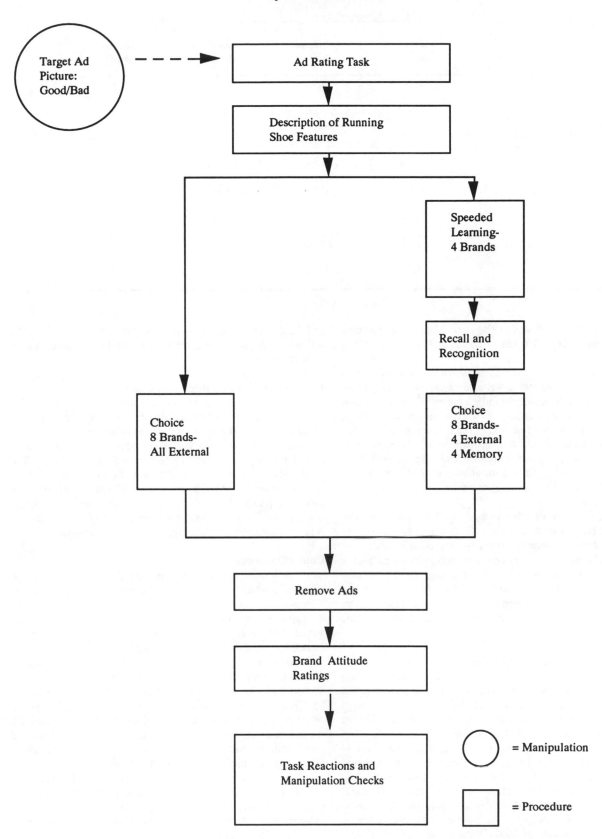

EXHIBIT 2
Summary Results

	Low Accessibility		High Accessibility	
	Good Ad (n=23)	Bad Ad (n=22)	Good Ad (n=26)	Bad Ad (n=26)
Aad	7.48	4.76	7.41	5.29
Brand Attitude	5.51	4.06	5.92	5.33
Choice Behavior Chose Target Brand (B)	47.8%	4.5%	61.5%	57.7%
Chose D	26.1%	31.8%	34.6%	26.9%
Chose A or C	8.7%	18.2%	0%	0%
Chose E-H	17.4%	45.5%	3.8%	15.4%
Total	100%	100%	100%	100%

attitude (beta=.21, p<.10), and 3) The effect of ad picture on brand attitude disappeared (p >.70) when Aad was included as a predictor of brand attitude.

Accessibility. First, recall was measured by giving low accessibility subjects four minutes to write down everything they could remember about each memory brand's features. Then, recognition was measured by presenting subjects with two descriptions of each memory brand's features (the text at the bottom of the ad), one correct and one incorrect, and having them indicate the correct one. The incorrect description was altered by increasing the level of one attribute and decreasing the level of another attribute. Ad picture recall was checked by having subjects write a brief description of each ad's picture.

Although 76% of the subjects recognized the correct description of brand B, none could correctly recall all four attributes. The average number of attributes correctly recalled was 1.82. The difference between recognition and recall scores indicates that the target brand information was available but not accessible (Thomson and Tulving 1970). The fact that 87% of the subjects were able to correctly describe the ad picture in an uncued recall task suggests that the ad picture was more accessible than the brand attribute information.

Overview of Experimental Outcomes

Exhibit 2 contains summary results for the experiment. Both the brand attitude and choice results indicate that the ad picture had more of an effect when brand attribute information for the target brand was not externally available. A 2 X 2 ANOVA of brand attitude showed a main effect of ad picture (p<.001), a main effect of accessibility (p<.01) and a marginally significant accessibility by ad picture interaction (p=.10), indicating that the ad picture manipulation had a greater effect on brand attitude in the low accessibility condition. Similarly, a logistic regression of brand B choice showed a significant effect of accessibility (p<.01), a significant effect of ad picture (p<.01) and a significant ad picture by accessibility interaction (p<.05). When accessibility was high, about 60% of subjects chose target brand B regardless of ad picture treatment. However, when brand attribute information was less accessible, 47.6% chose brand B when it had the good ad picture

and 4.5% chose brand B when it had the bad ad picture. The following analyses investigate more precisely the role of Aad in these outcomes.

Direct Versus Mediated Effects of Aad

The first research question was: does Aad have a direct or mediated effect on brand choice? In order to address this question, brand attitude was regressed on Aad, brand B choice was regressed on Aad, and brand B choice was regressed on Aad and the mediator (brand attitude) simultaneously (Baron and Kenny 1986).[2] The results showed that although Aad significantly affected brand attitude (beta=.42, p<.001), and Aad significantly affected choice (beta=.54, p<.05), Aad did not effect choice when the mediator, brand attitude, was included (beta=-.06, p>.80). Thus, the effect of Aad on choice was compeletely mediated by brand attitude.

Choice Outcomes

The second research question was: does the role of Aad in choice depend on the accessibility of brand attribute information? To answer this question we first consider the correlation coefficients for each accessibility group (Exhibit 3). It is clear that brand attitude (Ab), Aad, and target brand choice are all significantly related to one another, with one exception: the Aad-chose B correlation (r=.14) is not significant for high accessibility subjects. Thus, when subjects made their brand choice with all ad information externally available, Aad affected brand attitude but not choice (cf. Chattopadhyay and Nedungadi 1990). To see if the interaction between Aad and accessibility is significant, we ran an OLS regression model with target brand choice as the criterion, and brand attitude, Aad, accessibility, and the two-way interaction between accessibility and brand attitude and Aad as predictors (Exhibit 4). The overall model was significant (F(5,91)=16.1, p<.0001). The accessibility by brand attitude interaction was also significant (beta=-.65, p<.05): its negative sign reflects the fact that as accessibility decreases, so does the correlation between brand

---

[2]Logistic regression was used to analyze the choice equations in this section.

EXHIBIT 3

Correlation Matrices

	Low Accessibility (n=45)		High Accessibility (n=52)	
	Aad	Ab	Aad	Ab
Ab	0.43 [a]	1.00	0.41 [a]	1.00
Chose B	0.39 [a]	0.58 [b]	0.14	0.66 [b]

a. $p < .01$ b. $p < .001$

EXHIBIT 4

Results of Choice Regression Model

	Beta	t	Significance
Ab	0.80	6.28	.001
Aad	-0.16	-1.34	ns
Accessibility (A) [1]	0.10	0.33	ns
A x Ab	-0.65	-2.04	.05
A x Aad	0.45	1.76	.10

1. Coded: 0 = High accessibility, 1 = Low accessibility

attitude and choice. The accessibility by Aad interaction is marginally significant (beta=.44, p<.10): the relationship between Aad and choice is stronger when brand attribute information is less accessible.[3]

DISCUSSION

The following presents a summary and brief discussion of the key findings of our research on accessibility and Aad.

1. Under high brand information accessibility, Aad affected brand attitude but not choice outcomes. This finding underscores the importance of measuring choice as an outcome variable. Chattopadhyay and Nedungadi (1990) present a similar outcome (Aad affecting attitude but not choice) under different circumstances. As discussed previously, attitudinal indicators are not always reflected in choice, for a variety of reasons.

2. Aad had no direct effects on choice, under high or low accessibility. This finding contrasts with and represents a failure to replicate Biehal et al. (1992). One possible explanation for the different finding is that the current research involved eight hypothetical brands instead of four. With only four brands in the Biehal et al. (1992) study, the ad seemed to work as a tie-breaker, tipping the probability of choice for the target brand when it had the good ad. However, with eight brands in the current study, the bad ad may have drawn attention to the target brand, which was a logical choice based on features. Thus, the attention factor may have outweighed the bad ad factor.

3. Though the effect was not strong, Aad had more of an effect on choice under low accessibility, when subjects had to try to recall

ad and brand information in order to make their choice. This is consistent with several theoretical frameworks which predict that the likelihood that ad cognitions and ad attitude will be used in judgment and choice increases when the accessibility of alternative inputs, e.g., brand-related information, decreases (Feldman and Lynch 1988, Baker and Lutz 1988). Our findings can be contrasted with those of Chattopadhyay and Nedungadi (1992), who found that the effects of ad attitude dissipated after a delay. The key seems to be the relative accessibility of ad versus brand information. In our research, ad information (i.e., ad picture) was more accessible than brand information, as may be expected when the brand information is fairly complex and there is not much variance among brands. Therefore, the ad information had a significant effect on brand attitudes and choice.

In summary, it has been well-established through consumer research that externally-based choice processes are very different from memory-based choice processes. The research presented here shows that accessibility also affects the role of Aad in choice. Ad effects on choice were more dramatic when brand information was less accessible. In fact, in our research, ad attitude affected brand attitude but had no effect on choice outcomes when the subjects had all information in front of them when making their choices. Given the existence of a number of situations (e.g., catalogs, Yellow Pages) where choices are made based on externally available ad information, this finding deserves further attention.

REFERENCES

Baker, William E. and Richard J. Lutz (1988), "The Relevance-Accessibility Model of Advertising Effectiveness," in *Nonverbal Communication in Advertising*, Sidney Hecker and David W. Stewart, eds., Lexington, MA: Lexington Books, 59-84.

---

[3]Use of logistic regression increases the significance level of the accessibility by Aad interaction to $p < .14$.

Baron, Reuben M. and David A Kenny (1986), "The Moderator-Mediator Variable Distinction in Social Psychological Research: Conceptual, Strategic and Statistical Considerations," *Journal of Personality and Social Psychology*, 51 (6), 1173-82.

Biehal, Gabriel, Debra Stephens, and Eleonora Curlo (1992), "Attitude Toward the Ad and Brand Choice," *Journal of Advertising*, 21 (3), 19-36.

_____and Dipankar Chakravarti (1986), "Consumer's Use of Memory and External Information in Choice: Macro and Micro Perspectives," *Journal of Consumer Research*, 12 (March), 382-405.

_____and Dipankar Chakravarti (1982), "Information-Presentation Format and Learning Goals as Determinants of Consumers' Memory Retrieval and Choice Processes," *Journal of Consumer Research*, 8 (March), 431-41.

Brown, Stephen P. and Douglas M. Stayman (1992), "Antecedents and Consequences of Attitude Toward the Ad: A Meta-analysis," *Journal of Consumer Research*, 19 (June), 34-51.

Chattopadhyay, Amitava and Prakash Nedungadi (1990), "Ad Affect, Brand Attitude and Choice: The Moderating Roles of Delay and Involvement," in *Advances in Consumer Research Volume 17*, Marvin E. Goldberg, Gerald Gorn and Richard W. Pollay, eds., Provo, UT: Association for Consumer Research, 619-620.

_____and Prakash Nedungadi (1992), "Does Attitude Toward the Ad Endure? The Moderating Effects of Attention and Delay," *Journal of Consumer Research*, 19 (June), 26-33.

Fazio, Russell, Jeaw-Mei Chen, Elizabeth McDonel, and Steven Sherman (1982), "Attitude Accessibility, Attitude-Behavior Consistency, and the Strength of the Object-Evaluation Association," *Journal of Experimental Social Psychology*, 18, 339-57.

Feldman, Jack M. and John G. Lynch (1988), "Self-Generated Validity and Other Effects of Measurement on Belief, Attitude, Intention, and Behavior," *Journal of Applied Psychology*, 73 (3), 421-35.

Homer, Pamela M. (1990), "The Mediating Role of Attitude Toward the Ad: Some Additional Evidence," *Journal of Marketing Research*, 27 (February), 78-86.

Kisielius, Jolita and Brian Sternthal (1984), "Detecting and Explaining Vividness Effects in Attitudinal Judgments," *Journal of Marketing Research*, 21 (February), 56-64.

MacKenzie, Scott B. and Richard J. Lutz (1989), "An Empirical Examination of the Structural Antecedents of Attitude Toward the Ad in an Advertising Pretest Context," *Journal of Marketing*, 53 (April), 48-65.

_____, Richard J. Lutz, and George E. Belch (1986), "The Role of Attitude Toward the Ad as a Mediator of Advertising Effectiveness: A Test of Competing Explanations," *Journal of Marketing Research*, 23 (May), 130-43.

Miniard, Paul W., Deepak Sirdeshmukh, and Daniel E. Innis (1992), "Peripheral Persuasion and Brand Choice," *Journal of Consumer Research*, 19 (September), 226-39.

Mitchell, Andrew A. and Jerry C. Olson (1981), "Are Product Attribute Beliefs the Only Mediator of Advertising Effects on Brand Attitude?" *Journal of Marketing Research*, 19 (August), 318-32.

Nunnally, Jum C. (1978), *Psychometric Theory 2nd edition*, New York: McGraw-Hill Book Company.

Smith, Robert E. and William R. Swinyard (1983), "Attitude-Behavior Consistency: The Impact of Product Trial Versus Advertising," *Journal of Marketing Research*, 20 (August), 257-67.

Thomson, Donald M. and Endel Tulving (1970), "Associative Encoding and Retrieval: Weak and Strong Cues," *Journal of Experimental Psychology*, 86 (2), 255-62.

Memory-Based Product Judgments: Effects of Presentation Order and Retrieval Cues

Jong-Won Park, Korea University

ABSTRACT

This paper investigated the way in which the presentation order of information and a retrieval cue influenced product judgments when they were memory-based. Subjects in an experiment received a list of informational items with instructions to comprehend each item. The items were separately presented one at a time and the order of the presentation was varied. After receiving the information and a short delay, subjects were requested to form an overall evaluation of the product. At this time, some subjects received an informational item as a retrieval cue and others did not. Results suggested that the presentation order and the cue appeared to interactively influence recall of product information and hence, product judgments. Implications of these results for product impression formation and judgment are discussed.

Consumers often make a product judgment some time after they have acquired product information. Thus, their judgment is memory-based, i.e., based on product information available in memory (Lynch and Srull 1982; Alba, Hutchinson, and Lynch 1991). It has been suggested that consumers are likely to retrieve only a subset of information available in memory (e.g., Wyer and Srull 1989). This is often attributed to consumers' lack of ability to access all of the information they have acquired and stored in memory, and to their lack of motivation to do so. When incomplete retrieval takes place, it tends to show recency effects, i.e., retrieval is likely to be biased toward information that was received relatively recently (e.g., Anderson and Hubert 1963). On the other hand, retrieval of information is often facilitated when an appropriate cue is provided (e.g., Keller 1987). Then, it seems reasonable to suppose that judgments based on retrieved information would be influenced by both the presentation order of information and retrieval cues at the time of judgments. However, the exact pattern of such effects is not clear. The present research provides some insights into this matter.

BACKGROUND

Effects of Presentation Order of Information in Judgments

When consumers form a product judgment based on memory, the evaluative implications of information that is accessed from memory plays an important role (e.g., Kisielius and Sternthal 1984, 1986; Reyes, Thompson, and Bower 1980). Since information retrieval is unlikely to be exhaustive, the relative accessibility of product information in memory is critical (Feldman and Lynch 1988). Easier access to negative information could lead to an unfavorable evaluation of the product, whereas easier access to positive information could result in a more favorable evaluation. This means that the same set of information of a product in memory might create different evaluations about the product depending on the relative accessibility of positive and negative informational items in the set.

One of the well-recognized phenomena related to the information's accessibility and judgments is the recency effect (Feldman and Lynch 1988; Wyer and Srull 1989). It refers to the possibility that a judgment is more heavily influenced by recent information in memory than by earlier one (e.g., Anderson and Hubert 1963; Lichtenstein and Srull 1987). Such effect is typically observed when a judgment is formed some time after information is received and thus has to be based on the evaluative implication

of information in memory (e.g., Lichtenstein and Srull 1987). According to a general memory model proposed by Wyer and Srull (1986, 1989), recency effects are due to the relative retrieval advantage (or easier accessibility) of recent information compared to earlier one (see also Feldman and Lynch 1988 for a similar idea). When the processing goal at the time information is initially received is to simply learn the information (comprehension goal), each piece of information is encoded and stored as a separate unit into a "bin" in memory from the bottom up. If the contents of the target bin are searched at some later time, the search is assumed to proceed from the top down. However, memory search typically terminates without retrieving all items available in memory. This limited search is likely to result in a biased recall in favor of those near to the top of the bin (i.e., informational items that are received relatively recently). Consequently, judgments that are based on recalled information are likely to be primarily determined by the implications of those recent items (i.e., recency effects).

Recency effects in judgments are perhaps best documented in the study by Lichtenstein and Srull (1987). In their study, subjects received a list of both favorable and unfavorable behavior descriptions about a target person with an objective either to form an overall impression about the person or to comprehend the information. Some subjects received favorable information first and unfavorable information next, while others received the same set of information in the reversed order. After some delay, all subjects were asked to judge overall likability of the target person. Subjects who had received information with the comprehension objective showed strong recency effects in their likability judgments: the target's overall likability was made more favorably when favorable information was presented last than when unfavorable information last. However, such effects did not occur when subjects had the goal of impression formation at the time they received the information. Since there is often a delay between the time consumers acquire product information and the time they make a product judgment or purchase decision, as well as consumers typically learn various aspects of a product *over time*, recency effects are likely to occur in product judgment situations (Park and Hastak, forthcoming).

Effects of Retrieval Cues in Judgments

Realizing that information retrieval tends to be incomplete, marketing researchers have been interested in the way in which retrieval is assisted. One that has been widely investigated is the role of an external cue. The premise is that consumers may retrieve more information upon exposure to an external stimulus which activates memory nodes for product information. Several consumer researchers have found that such cues as verbal and visual information contained in the original ad facilitated retrieval of product information (e.g., Burke and Srull 1988; Costley 1992; Dick, Chakravarti, and Biehal 1990; Keller 1987, 1991; Lynch, Marmorstein and Weigold 1988). In the study by Keller (1987), for example, subjects were shown target ads in a competitive ad environment. Thus, the accessibility of the target information was not readily accessible. After a delay, subjects' memory for specific aspects of the target products were examined. Results showed that subjects who were provided with a retrieval cue produced a superior recall than those who were not given a cue.

Theoretically, a memory cue activates corresponding nodes in memory. From the activated memory nodes, some form of search for associated information through the network of memory traces

Advances in Consumer Research
Volume 22, © 1995

takes place. This enhanced search by a cue results in an increased recall. However, it should be noted that cues' effectiveness is not always apparent. First, it may depend on the accessibility of the information to be recalled (c.f., Alba and Chattopadhyay 1985; Keller 1987). If the information is readily accessible, an external cue may offer little additional help because there is no need for the cue. However, a cue can successfully facilitate recall if the information is relatively difficult to access. In other words, cueing difficult-to-access information will have a facilitation effect on recall, whereas cueing easy-to-access information may not. Second, a cue may interfere with retrieval of some of information in memory. Perhaps the best known example of such interference effect is the phenomenon of part-category cueing effects (e.g., Alba and Chattopadhyay 1985; Rundus 1973; Slamecka 1968, 1969). It refers to a possibility that external cues for information pertaining to a category in memory may inhibit recall of other information in that category. Further, interference can also occur between categories when they compete each other for recall. That is, an external cue for one category may interfere in the recall of members in the other category. If the accessibility of each category differs, however, the interference might be asymmetrical. Specifically, cueing a more accessible category inhibits the recall of members in a less accessible category, whereas cueing a less accessible category has little influence on the recall of the members in a more accessible category (e.g., Alba and Chattopadhyay 1985).

The above discussion of presentation order of information and a retrieval cue has some interesting implications for product judgments. Suppose that subjects receive a set of positive information and then a set of negative information of a product (positive-negative order) with an objective of comprehending the information. When they are later asked to form an evaluation of the product, they will have to retrieve information from their memory to make an evaluation. Then, the negative information (which is encoded relatively recently) is more likely to be retrieved and used for judgments, compared to the positive information. Thus, evaluations are likely to be made unfavorably (recency effects). If a retrieval cue is available at the time of evaluation, however, different evaluations may be generated. If the cue is relevant for the information that was encoded relatively early (i.e., positive information), it will facilitate the recall of early information. Consequently, evaluations are likely to be more neutral. If the cue is relevant for relatively recent items (i.e., negative information) instead, it may not facilitate the recall of recent items because the items are readily accessible without the cue's help. However, evaluations would still be affected by the cue (i.e., becoming more negative in this case) because the cue may inhibit the recall of positive items. In short, both early- and recent-cue alter recency effects in judgments, but through different effects on recall. This possibility was examined in the study to be reported below.

METHOD

Overview

Subjects received a large number of informational items about an automobile and were asked to comprehend this information. The information presented was the same in all conditions. However, the order with which the information was presented was experimentally manipulated. That is, some subjects received negative items first and positive items later (*positive-last conditions*), while others received the information in the reversed order (*negative-last conditions*). After receiving this information and a brief delay, subjects were asked to form an overall (memory-based) evaluation of the automobile. At this time, another manipulation (retrieval cue

factor) was introduced. Specifically, about half of the subjects were reminded of one of the informational items that they had received: either one of the items presented early (*early-cue conditions*) or one of the items presented later (*recent-cue conditions*). The remaining subjects did not receive such a retrieval cue item (*no-cue conditions*). Immediately after subjects formed and reported their evaluations, they were asked to recall as many informational items about the automobile they had received as possible.

Predictions

Since subjects were instructed to comprehend the informational items at the time they received the information, they presumably encoded and stored the items separately in memory without spontaneously forming an overall product evaluation (see Srull and Wyer 1989; Wyer and Srull 1989 for this assumption). Thus, when they were later asked to evaluate the automobile, they would have to retrieve the information from memory to use it as a basis for generating an evaluation. When there was no cue, we expected that information retrieval would be likely to be biased toward the "recent" items, and hence judgments to be subject to recency effects. That is, subjects in the positive-last conditions will produce more favorable evaluations of the product than those in the negative-last conditions. We also expected that providing a retrieval cue would alter this possibility through affecting retrieval. We first speculated that an early-cue would facilitate the recall of early items, without affecting the recall of recent items. Thus, recency effects in judgments would be mitigated. In contrast, a recent-cue would inhibit the recall of early items, without facilitating the recall of recent items. Consequently, recency effects would be strengthened. To state these predictions more formally:

H: When there is no cue available, product judgments would be influenced by presentation order (recency effects). If there is a cue which activates memory for early information, the judgments would be less affected by presentation order (less recency effects). This is through the facilitated recall of early information due to the cue. If a cue is relevant for activating memory for recent information, the judgments would be more heavily influenced by presentation order (stronger recency effects). This is through the inhibited recall of early information due to the cue.

Subjects and Design

One hundred and twenty-two male and female MBA students at a large university participated in the experiment as a part of a course requirement. Subjects were randomly assigned to each of the presentation order conditions (positive-last versus negative-last). Among them, 68 subjects received either an early-cue or a recent-cue, and the remaining subjects received no retrieval cue. All subjects received the same set of information which contained fifteen items total. These stimuli are described below.

Stimulus Materials

An automobile product was selected as the product to be evaluated. A large number of informational items were created on the basis of magazine advertisements and articles in *Consumer Reports*. The informational items described important attributes of an automobile such as power, comfort, safety, and economy. Based on a pretest, we finally selected seven positive items (e.g., "the anti-lock breaking system provides an excellent breaking power even at a slippery road" "a silent shaft reducing idling noise provides more interior quiet," etc.), five negative items (e.g., "the gas mileage is below average compared to other similar brands," "the interior space for the driver's seat is somewhat narrow," etc.), and three neutral items (e.g., "the industry average warranty period is provided," etc.).

Presentation Order

Subjects received a total of fifteen informational items. These items were presented in separate sheets with an interval of 15 seconds. The presentation order was systematically varied across subjects. First, we used ten items (five positive items and five negative items) to manipulate the presentation order. Some subjects received the positive items first and the negative items later (negative-last condition), while others received the information in the reversed order (positive-last conditions). In either case the serial position at which a given item was presented was counterbalanced across subjects. Thus, pooled over all subjects, the number of times a given item appeared at a particular serial position was the same for all of the ten items. Finally, we interspersed five filler items (two positive and three neutral items) before, after, and during the course of presenting ten test items. This was deemed necessary to make the presentation order manipulation less obvious (c.f., Lichtenstein and Srull 1987).

Retrieval Cue

After receiving the information and before making an overall evaluation of the product, subjects engaged in a 5-minute distraction task which was designed to eliminate a short-term memory effect. Then, an overall evaluation was requested and the manipulation of retrieval cue conditions was introduced. Specifically, some subjects were not provided with any retrieval cues at the time an overall evaluation of the product was requested (no-cue conditions). However, subjects in the cueing conditions received a retrieval cue. They were simply reminded of one particular item that was initially presented. Selection of the item was systematically varied depending on cueing conditions. For some subjects, the cue was one of the items that had been presented early (early-cue conditions). For others, it was the one that had appeared relatively recent (recent-cue conditions). However, selection of an item as the cue was counterbalanced across all conditions. In the cases of early-cue conditions, the cue always was the second item among those presented early. Similarly, the cue always was the forth item among those presented recent in the cases of recent-cue conditions. This ensured counterbalanced selection of an item as the cue because as explained previously, the serial position at which a given item was presented had been counterbalanced across subjects. Thus, pooled over subjects, the number of times a given item was used as the cue was the same for all of the ten items.

Procedure

The experiment was run during class time. At the beginning, subjects were told that (a) we were interested in how comprehension of product information would be influenced by the way in which the information was worded, (b) they would see product feature descriptions of automobile brands, (c) the brands were currently available in the market, and (d) that the feature descriptions were obtained from an article in *Consumer Reports*. We pretended that the informational items to be presented were about several brands of automobile. This was deemed effective to discourage subjects from forming an overall evaluation of the product on-line. Then, subjects were asked to rate each informational item in terms of how easily they could understand it. These instructions were followed by a list of the product information items. We presented the 15 informational items in the manner described earlier, one item at a time with an interval of 15 seconds.

After this and a 5-minute task unrelated to the present study, subjects were informed that the informational items they had received were actually about a single brand of an automobile, and then were asked to evaluate this brand in terms of overall quality. At this point, a retrieval cue was provided only for those in the cueing conditions. Subjects reported their evaluations on two 9-point scales ("bad"-"good", "dislikable"-"likable"). A recall task immediately followed this. Subjects were asked to recall as many of the informational items about the automobile as they could remember. Finally, subjects were debriefed and dismissed.

Scoring recalled items

Recalled items were scored according to a gist criterion by two independent judges. That is, items were scored as correct if they conveyed the same idea as the original item regardless of wording. In addition, partial credit was given when subjects recalled just the attribute name without specifying its evaluative content. Inter-judge agreement was 82.3%. (Disagreements were resolved through discussion.)

RESULTS

Overall Product Evaluations

We expected recency effects (or presentation order effects) on overall evaluations for no-cue conditions and recent-cue conditions, but not for early-cue conditions. To test this prediction, overall evaluations were analyzed as a function of presentation order and cueing.

Since the two scales used for measuring overall evaluations were highly correlated (r=.82), the average score was used for the analysis to be reported. Table 1 shows mean overall evaluation scores as a function of presentation order and cueing. A 2 by 3 ANOVA (presentation order by cueing) on these scores revealed a main effect for presentation order $(F(1,115) =7.20, p <.01)$. As expected, subjects in the positive-last conditions reported more favorable evaluations than those in the negative-last conditions (5.63 versus 4.83). The presentation order by cueing interaction was not significant (F<1). However, comparisons which examined the effect of presentation order under each cueing condition separately provided support for our expectation. First, when no cue was provided, product evaluations were more favorable in the positive-last conditions than in the negative-last conditions, showing a marginal recency effect $(t(115)=1.73, p<.10)$. Second, this recency effect was strengthened when a recent-cue was provided, confirming our expectation, $(t(115)=1.99, p<.05)$. Finally, as expected, this recency effect was removed when an early-cue was provided, $(t(115)=.868, p>.39)$. In sum, these results are consistent with the hypothesized effects of presentation order and retrieval cue on product evaluations.

Immediate Recall

Previous research suggests that immediate recall is a good indicator of the information that is retrieved and used for judgments especially when the judgments are computed based on information in memory (e.g., Lichtenstein and Srull 1985; see Hastie and Park 1986 for a review). Thus, we examined recall data to gain an insight into retrieval processes underlying recency effects we observed. Overall, relatively recent items were expected to be recalled better than earlier items. However, a retrieval cue would influence the recall. Specifically, it was expected that an early-cue would facilitate recall of early items without affecting the recall of recent items, but a recent-cue would inhibit recall of early items without helping recall of recent items to a meaningful extent.

TABLE 1

Overall Product Evaluations As a Function of Presentation Order and Cueing

Cueing	Presentation Order	
	Negative-last	Positive-last
No cue	4.87 (n=27)	5.76 (n=27)
Recent-cue	4.56 (n=17)	5.53 (n=17)
Early-cue	5.06 (n=16)	5.53 (n=17)

Note: n in each parenthesis indicates cell size.

TABLE 2

Immediate Recall Scores as a Function of Recall Type and Cueing

Cueing	Recall Type	
	Early items	Recent-items
No cue	2.0 (n=27)	2.4 (n=27)
Recent-cue	1.2 (n=17)	2.5 (n=17)
Early-cue	2.1 (n=16)	2.3 (n=17)

Note: n in each parenthesis indicates cell size.

In order to look at these hypothesized effects, we coded the recall of early items and that of recent items separately. The positive items recalled in the negative-last conditions and the negative items recalled in the positive-last conditions were counted for the recall of early items. The recall of recent items was calculated by counting the negative items recalled in the negative-last conditions and the positive items recalled in the positive-last conditions. Then, the recall scores were analyzed as a function of presentation order (positive-last/negative-last), cueing (no cue/recent-cue/early-cue), and recall type (early items/recent items). The last factor was a within-subject variable.

A 2 x 3 x 2 mixed ANOVA revealed three noticeable effects. First, a significant effect for recall type ($F(1, 116)=11.17$, $p<.001$) indicated a recency effect in recall. As expected, subjects recalled recent items more than early items (2.41 versus 1.80). Second, there was a recall type by presentation order interaction effect ($F(2, 116)=28.16$, $p<.001$). Early items were recalled better in negative-last conditions than in positive-last conditions (2.25 versus 1.36), whereas recent items recalled poorer in negative-last conditions than in positive-last conditions (1.36 versus 2.93). Interpreting differently, subjects recalled more positive items than negative items regardless of the presentation order. Finally, and more importantly, cueing by recall type interaction effect approached a significance ($F(2, 116)=2.97$, $p<.06$). Table 2 shows recall scores as a function of cueing and recall type. To further analyze this interaction, several mean comparisons were conducted on the recall of early items and that of recent items separately. First, providing a recent item as a cue did not significantly increase the recall of recent items (2.4 versus 2.5, $t(119)<1$), confirming our expectation. On the other hand, the recent-cue significantly suppressed the recall

of early items (2.0 versus 1.2, $t(119)=2.51$, $p<.05$). This also confirmed our expectation. Finally, results in the early-cue conditions were mixed. That is, an early-cue did not suppress the recall of recent items as expected (2.4 versus 2.3, $t(119)<1$), it did not facilitate the recall of early items either (2.0 versus 2.1, $t(119)<1$), disconfirming our expectation. However, the difference in recall of early versus recent items was negligible in the early-cue conditions ($F<1$).

Further Analysis

The previous analysis of overall evaluations revealed that recency effects (or presentation order effects) occurred in no-cue and recent-cue conditions, but not in early-cue conditions. It was assumed that these effects were mediated by retrieval of information during judgments. To further assess this mediation process, the difference score between the recall of positive items and that of negative items was calculated to be used as a covariate. If our assumption about the mediation is correct, recency effects on evaluations observed in the previous analysis should be eliminated when the covariate is introduced in the analysis. In fact, this was the case. First, an ANCOVA on overall evaluations as a function of presentation order and cueing with the covariate revealed a significant effect of the covariate in no-cue conditions ($F=18.25$, $p<.001$), in recent-cue conditions ($F=3.70$, $p<.06$), and in early-cue conditions ($F=10.893$, $p<.005$). More importantly, when the covariate was introduced, the presentation order effects (or recency effects) that were previously observed were successfully removed in no-cue conditions ($F=1.72$, $p>.19$) and in recent-cue conditions ($F<1$). These results indicate that as expected, recency effects on evaluations were mediated by the information recall during judgments.

DISCUSSION

Overall, the study provides reasonable support for the proposition that presentation order and retrieval cues would influence retrieval of information and hence, product judgments. This proposition was supported in analyses for overall product evaluations and in the mediation test. That is, recency effects emerged in no-cue conditions and were strengthened in recent-cue conditions. As expected, however, cueing early items in memory successfully eliminated recency effects. Finally, ANCOVA results suggested that recency effects in evaluations were mediated by the net valence of the information retrieved during judgments.

The recall data provided support for the hypothesized effects of a recent-cue. As expected, a recent-cue did not help recall of recent items but inhibited the recall of early items to a meaningful extent. Consequently, subjects in the recent-cue conditions showed a stronger recency effect in evaluations, as compared to those in no-cue conditions. In contrast, an early-cue did not have such inhibition effect on the recall of recent items. These results are consistent with previous studies. For example, Alba and Chattopadhyay (1985) found that cueing a member in a dominant (or easier-to-access) category inhibited the recall of members in a dominated (or difficult-to-access) category, whereas cueing a member in a dominated category had little influence on the recall of the members in a dominant category. In our study, the recent items and the early items constituted a relatively dominant (or easier-to-access) category versus a dominated (or difficult-to-access) category in memory. This was because the evaluative implications of early items and recent items were oppositely valenced, thus encoded differentially, although the items within each category may not have been clustered in a conventional network form (c.f., Klein and Loftus 1990). Consequently, cueing the dominant category (recent information) suppressed the recall of the members in the dominated category (early information), whereas cueing the dominated category did not decrease the recall of members in the dominant category.

Unfortunately, results do not provide unambiguous evidence for the effects of an early-cue on recall and judgments. As expected, an early-cue successfully eliminated the recency effects in evaluations. This result paralleled the negligible difference in recall of early versus recent items. Further, the cue did not suppress the recall of recent items, consistent with the notion of asymmetric interference effects. However, it did not facilitate recall of early items either, failing to support our expectation. Perhaps, the power to detect this effect was weak. Nonetheless, future research is warranted to resolve this ambiguity.

Finally, it is worth noting that our results have interesting implications for marketing managers. For instance, when marketers want consumers to retrieve as many features of their products as possible, they need to carefully select retrieval cues. If the cues selected by marketers happen to trigger memory node for highly accessible information, they might actually impair the overall recall by consumers. This is because the cues may only suppress less accessible information, while not facilitating highly accessible information. Thus, it is suggested to use such cues that might activate memory for relatively less accessible information. Another implication is related to competition in a retrieval set of brand names. Marketers certainly want their brands to be included in consumers' retrieval set. Our results suggest that both major and minor brands can be benefitted from such marketing practice as a point-of-purchase display (but for different reasons) in increasing their inclusion in consumers' consideration set. Minor brands can be benefitted from such marketing practice because it increases the chance that the brands will be retrieved for consideration during a purchase decision. However, major brands can also be benefitted

from it because it is likely to decrease the probability that other brands will be retrieved for consideration.

REFERENCES

Alba, Joseph W. and Amitava Chattopadhyay (1985), "Effects of Context and Part-Category Cues on Recall of Competing Brands," *Journal of Marketing Research*, 22 (August), 340-349.

Alba, Joseph W., J. Wesley Hutchinson, and John G. Lynch (1991), "Memory and Decision Making," in *Handbook of Consumer Behavior*, eds., Thomas S. Robertson and Harold H. Kassarjian, Englewood Cliffs, NJ: Prentice-Hall, 1-49.

Anderson, Norman H. and Stephen Hubert (1963), "Effects of Concomitant Verbal Recall on Order Effects in Personality Impression Formation," *Journal of Verbal Learning and Verbal Behavior*, 2 (5-6), 379-391.

Burke, Raymond, and Thomas Srull (1988), "Competitive Interference and Consumer memory for Advertising," *Journal of Consumer Research*, 15 (June), 55-68.

Costley, Carolyn L. and Merrie Brucks (1992), "Selective Recall and Information Use in Consumer Preferences," *Journal of Consumer Research*, 18 (March), 464-473.

Dick, Alan, Dipankar Chakravarti, and Gabriel Biehal (1990), "Memory-Based Inferences During Consumer Choice," *Journal of Consumer Research*, 17 (June), 82-93.

Feldman, Jack M. and John G. Lynch, Jr. (1988), "Self-Generated Validity and Other Effects of Measurement on Belief, Attitude, Intention, and Behavior," *Journal of Applied Psychology*, 73 (August), 421-435.

Hastie, Reid and Bernadette Park (1986), "The Relationship Between Memory and Judgment Depends on Whether the Judgment Task is Memory-Based or On-Line," *Psychological Review*, 93 (July), 258-268.

Keller, Kevin L. (1987), "Memory Factors in Advertising: The Effect of Advertising Retrieval Cues on Brand Evaluations," *Journal of Consumer Research*, 14 (December), 316-333.

_____(1991), "Memory and Evaluation Effects in Competitive Advertising Environment," *Journal of Consumer Research*, 17 (March), 463-476.

Kisielius, Jolita and Brian Sternthal (1984), "Detecting and Explaining Vividness Effects in Attitudinal Judgments," *Journal of Marketing Research*, 21, 54-64.

_____ and _____(1986), "Examining the Vividness Controversy: An Availability-Valence Interpretation," *Journal of Consumer Research*, 12, 418-431.

Klein, Stanley B. and Judith Loftus (1990), "Rethinking the Role of Organization in Person Memory: An Independent Trace Storage Model," *Journal of Personality and Social Psychology*, 59 (3), 400-410.

Lichtenstein, Meryl and Thomas K. Srull (1985), "Conceptual and Methodological Issues in Examining the Relationship Between Consumer Memory and Judgment," in *Psychological Processes and Advertising Effects: Theory, Research and Applications*, eds., Linda Alwitt and Andrew A. Mitchell, Hillsdale, NJ: Earlbaum, 113-128.

_____ and _____(1987), "Processing Objectives as a Determinant of the Relationship Between Recall and Judgment," *Journal of Experimental Social Psychology*, 23 (March), 93-118.

Lynch, John G., Jr., Howard Marmorstein, and Michael F. Weigold (1988), "Choices from Sets Including Remembered Brands: Use of Recalled Attributes and Prior Overall Evaluations," *Journal of Consumer Research*, 15 (September), 169-184.

_____and Thomas K. Srull (1982), "Memory and Attentional Factors in Consumer Choice: Concepts and Research Methods," *Journal of Consumer Research*, 9 (June), 18-37.

Park, Jong-Won and Manoj Hastak (forthcoming), "Memory-Based Product Judgments: Effects of Involvement at Encoding and Retrieval," *Journal of Consumer Research*.

Reyes, Robert M., William C. Thompson, and Gordon H. Bower (1980), "Judgmental Biases Resulting from Differing Availabilities of Arguments," *Journal of Personality and Social Psychology*, 39 (1), 2-12.

Rundus, Dewey (1973), "Negative Effects of Using List Items as Recall Cues," *Journal of Verbal Learning and Verbal Behavior*, 12 (1), 43-50.

Slamecka, Norman J. (1968), "An Examination of Trace Storage in Free Recall," *Journal of Experimental Psychology*, 76, 504-513.

_____(1969), "Testing for Associative Storage in Multitrial Free Recall," *Journal of Experimental Psychology*, 81, 557-560.

Srull, Thomas K. and Robert S. Wyer, Jr. (1989), "Person Memory and Judgment," *Psychological Review*, v.96, No.1, 58-83.

Wyer, Robert S., Jr. and Thomas K. Srull (1986), "Human Cognition in Its Social Context," *Psychological Review*, 93 (3), 322-359.

_____and _____ (1989), *Human Memory and Cognition in Its Social Context*, Hillsdale, NJ: Earlbaum.

Belief in Imitator Claims: The Role of Source Memory

Sharmistha Law, University of Toronto

ABSTRACT

This study investigates the effectiveness of imitator ads. Results suggest that imitator ads confuse subjects, as evidenced by low recognition rates compared to ads seen for the first time. Overall, subjects report a lower belief in imitator ads relative to novel ads. Memory for the source of an imitator ad is a major determinant of its believability. When subjects confuse an imitator ad with a similar ad seen previously, they express greater belief in it. On the other hand, when subjects correctly recognize an ad as an imitator, they are strongly skeptical of it. Marketers need to consider these findings, especially the effect of source memory, when implementing imitator strategies.

INTRODUCTION

In 1988, the Clearly Canadian Beverage Company introduced a transparent cola, portraying a pure, natural, environmentally conscious image. Its introduction was soon followed by Crystal Pepsi. In 1992, Colgate brought out a clear version of its Softsoap. A few months later, Procter and Gamble launched a clear version of Ivory (*The Globe and Mail*, 1994). Examples of such "me-too" products abound in today's marketplace. Imitation strategies include similar package designs, similar claims about product performance, or similar brand names. Competitor slogans and tag lines may also be mimicked. Creators of imitator ads attempt to position their product next to a more established brand in the hope that consumers will generalize attributes of the original brand (usually a leading brand) to their product (Foxman, Muehling, and Berger, 1990).

Imitation strategies can have harmful consequences for the consumer. Confused consumers may be at a physical risk when they unintentionally buy products other than the one they intended to buy. For example, when Lever Brothers introduced Sunlight dishwashing detergent, the package's similarity to Minute Maid lemon juice led several consumers (33 adults and 45 children in the state of Maryland alone) to mistakenly ingest Sunlight (Reiling, 1982). More generally, consumers who mistakenly buy me-too brands can suffer negative consequences if such products perform less well than the original brand. Therefore, from the public policy point of view, there is indeed a need for greater understanding of the factors that contribute to consumer confusion. Identification of these factors and the circumstances under which they operate will aid policy makers in reducing the detrimental effects of this marketing strategy.

Some critical questions for both marketers and researchers with respect to consumer confusion are: How do consumers react to imitator ads? Do advertisers benefit from using an imitator strategy? Or, do me-too claims hurt the product? This study addresses these questions by investigating the impact of imitator ads on consumer confusion and consumer belief regarding the claims.

CONSUMER BRAND CONFUSION

Empirical studies demonstrate that consumers become confused when there is a high degree of package similarity (e.g., Foxman, Darrel, Muehling, and Berger, 1990; Loken, Ross, and Hinkle, 1986; Ward, Loken, Ross, and Hasapopoulos, 1986), when copycat brands match the timing of the market leader's advertising (Trout and Ries, 1985 cited in Park and Hahn, 1991). For example,

Foxman et al. (1990) showed subjects slides of packages of well known consumer products. Subjects were shown a slide depicting packages of the original brand alongside five, physically similar imitator brands, and were required to identify the original brand. Results indicated that 17% to 27% of the subjects wrongly identified an imitator brand as the original brand.

An explanation for why consumer brand confusions occur is suggested by the phenomenon of category priming and the associated notion of assimilation effects (e.g., Herr, 1989; Herr, Sherman, and Fazio, 1983; Meyers-Levy and Sternthal, 1993). Higgins, Rholes, and Jones (1977) found that, subjects primed with exemplars of a particular category are more likely to use that category in evaluating a subsequently presented target stimulus. When the target stimulus closely resembled the previously presented object, subjects categorized the target as being the object previously presented.

The preceding discussion suggests that prior exposure to marketing claims will affect consumers' judgments of new claims and, consumer brand confusion will occur when a new imitator claim closely resembles the original claim.

CONSUMER BELIEFS AND THE EFFECT OF SOURCE MISATTRIBUTION

While confusion is clearly an important concern for marketers and consumers, little research has been done on the impact of brand confusion on product *evaluation*. On the one hand, brand confusion may lead to an increased false belief for imitator claims when the imitation goes undetected. On the other hand, consumers may become unduly skeptical or suspicious when a market leader's product claim is repeated by an imitator, thereby resulting in diminished belief in the claim.

Previous research has shown that the mere repetition of statements causes them to be rated as more valid than non-repeated control statements (e.g., Hasher, Goldstein, and Toppino, 1977; Bacon, 1979; Arkes, Boehm, and Xu, 1991; Schwartz, 1982), a phenomenon called the "truth effect." It is argued that subjects' sense of having seen the item before (i.e., feelings of *familiarity*) leads to heightened truth ratings (e.g., Bacon, 1979; Hawkins and Hoch, 1992). For instance, Hawkins and Hoch found that (a) repetition of marketing claims increased belief in the claims, and (b) statements perceived to be repeated, whether or not they were actually repeated, were given higher validity ratings than statements perceived to be non-repeated.

Law and Hawkins (1994), building on the truth effect research, investigated the role which memory for the source of the claim has on the subjects' belief regarding the claim. They demonstrated that the subjects' belief in a statement is influenced not only by their familiarity with it, but also by whether or not the second presentation is accompanied by a correct recall of the source of the prior experience. Amongst repeated items, those items which were misattributed to a source outside the experiment received the highest truth ratings.

Given the findings of Law and Hawkins (1994) that, *source misattribution* leads to increased belief in claims, it seems reasonable to expect this effect with respect to imitator claims. That is, the previous exposure to an original claim should result in feelings of familiarity with an imitator claim, and in the absence of correct recognition (that is, if subjects fail to recognize that their initial exposure to the ad had been associated with a different brand), subjects will judge the claim to be more believable than if they are able to accurately identify it as an imitator.

The purpose of this study is threefold: (1) to examine the level of confusion (that is, misrecognition) of imitator ads; (2) to assess the believability of imitator claims, and (3) to investigate the role of source misattribution on subjects' belief about imitator claims.

The preceding discussion leads to the following hypotheses:

H_1:   *Incidence of Confusion.* Imitator ads will lead to consumer confusion as reflected in a lower accuracy of recognition relative to other ads seen for the first time.

H_2:   *Belief in Imitator ads.* Subjects' beliefs in imitator ads will be different relative to other ads seen for the first time.

H_{3a}:   *Role of Source Memory.* Misattribution of the source of an imitator claim (that is, not realizing that this is an imitator claim) will increase subjects' belief in it.

H_{3b}:   Conversely, correctly recognizing an imitation claim will decrease subjects' belief in it.

Since subjects' level of fatigue and/or boredom may influence how they react to and process commercial messages, the relationship between arousal level and truth ratings was also examined in this study. To test our hypotheses, imitator ads were operationalized as ads which contained a plausible claim that had been previously presented with a different brand name.

METHOD

Subjects

Subjects were 35 undergraduate students who were enrolled in an introductory management course and took part for extra marks. They were run in small groups ranging in size from 2 to 7 with each group being randomly assigned to one of four separate booklet conditions (to be discussed shortly). Three subjects were excluded from the study as they failed to comprehend or act upon the instructions. One subject, who was able to guess the hypotheses of the study, was also excluded from the data analysis. Therefore, the hypotheses were tested with a total of 31 subjects.

Design

The study involved a 2 x 2 completely within subjects design. Session (Study vs. Test) and Claim Type (Original vs. Imitator claims) were the two repeated factors.

Stimuli Construction

The experimental stimuli consisted of fictitious marketing claims about brands and products. Two stages of pretesting were conducted to ensure that the brand names were familiar and the claims were plausible to Canadian consumers.

Pretest 1. This pretest was conducted in a sample of 15 subjects to identify familiar brand names. Brand names with an average familiarity of 2.5 or higher on a 5-point scale (1=Very Unfamiliar; 5=Very Familiar) were selected from a list of 112 names spanning 50 different product categories (e.g., shampoo, airlines, car rental companies). The mean familiarity rating for the chosen brands was 3.9.

Pretest 2. The selected brand names from Pretest 1 were then paired with fictitious statements to form plausible product related

claims. Some of these statements were from Hawkins and Hoch (1992). The plausibility of these claims were pretested using another 15 subjects. However, as one subject did not complete the questionnaire, the data analysis for the pretest was conducted using 14 subjects. Those statements with a mean truth rating of approximately 3.0 (on a 5-point scale with 1=Definitely False; 5=Definitely True), standard deviation of less than 1, and with a unimodal distributions were included in the experimental stimuli list. The mean plausibility rating and standard deviation of the statements included in the main experiment was 3.07 and 0.82, respectively.

The final test material consisted of 64 fictitious marketing claims. For each claim, two brand names (an original and an imitator) could be used interchangeably. Using these statements, 4 counterbalanced booklet types (A, B, C, D) were created. Each booklet had 32 Study items and 32 Test items. At Study, each subject saw a set of 16 new items (called *original*) which would be altered slightly and re-presented as *imitator* items; and a different set of 16 new items (called *new1*). At Test, each subject saw a set of 16 *imitator* items (which were ads corresponding to the originals seen at Study) and a different set of 16 items (called *new2*). The imitator ads were exactly the same claim as the original but with a different brand name.

To ensure the results of the experiment were free of any systematic bias due to the nature of the claims or the particular brand name, each statement occurred an equal number of times as an *original*, *new1*, *new2*, and an *imitator*. In addition, each brand name was paired an equal number of times with an *original*, *new1*, *new2*, and an imitator product claim. Subsequent analysis of the results showed no significant effect of booklet [$F(3,108)=0.78$, $p>.5$] and no significant interaction between booklet and item-type [$F(9,108)=1.16$, $p>.3$], confirming that the process of stimulus randomization had had its desired effect.

The Study list consisted of 70 product-related statements which were composed of the following: 16 *original* items; 16 *new1* items; 10 *buffer* items used to minimize recency and primacy effects; and 28 *filler* items included to increase the length of list. The Test booklet contained 50 product-related claims: 5 *buffer* items included to allow subjects to get acquainted with the task; 16 *imitator* items (corresponding to the 16 *original* items); 16 *new2* items; and 13 *filler* items. Table 1 describes the template of the Study and Test booklets.

Procedure

The Study consisted of three parts: Study, Filler, and Test. Subjects were told that the purpose was to assess the effectiveness of product claims. During the Study session, subjects were shown 70 claims for 10 seconds each (a time period determined on the basis of pretests) and asked to rate how true of false they thought each statement was (see Dependent Measures section for the scale used). Following this, there was a 20 minute interval during which subjects filled out a questionnaire for another study and completed a mental folding task. This part of the study served as a Filler task to minimize the effects of short term memory. At Test, subjects were told that they would see another set of marketing statements and would be required to respond to two questions. For each statement displayed, subjects were given 10 seconds in which to fill out the two dependent measures (to be discussed shortly). They were also instructed not to leave any questions blank.

Dependent Measures

In the Study session, subjects rated the truth of each item. For each item seen in the Test session, subjects first rated its truth and then indicated the source of their prior exposure to it.

TABLE 1
Study and Test Booklet Templates

Study Booklet	Test Booklet
Most of the profit for credit card companies comes from the fee imposed on merchants who accept the cards. [*Buffer*]	The price of reusable canvas bags has almost doubled since 1981. [*Buffer*]
British Airways has flown the greatest number of transcontinental passengers. [*Original*]	TWA has flown the greatest number of transcontinental passengers. [*Imitator*]
Six of CIBC Mutual Funds have been awarded AAA rating by Canadian Bond Rating Service. [*New1*]	Bausch & Lomb contact lenses come in 12 different colours. [*Filler*]
United Parcel Service delivers more packages than the U.S. Postal Office. [*Filler*]	Sears clothes dryers come with a moisture sensor which is more accurate than the thermostat. [*New2*]
Avis is the cheapest national car rental firm, and it also has the highest rate of customer satisfaction. [*Original*]	**Hertz** is the cheapest national car rental firm, and it also has the highest rate of customer satisfaction. [*Original*]

Belief in a Claim. Subjects' truth rating for each presented item was measured on a continuous 16 cm. Likert scaled anchored at "Definitely False" on the left, to "Definitely True" on the right. Belief in a claim was measured as the distance (in cms.) from the left hand side of the scale.

Source Attribution. In the Test session, after rating the truth of an item, subjects were asked to indicate where they had encountered the statement: *Before: from TV, magazine, friend, etc.* (that is, outside the experiment); *First Session* (that is, during Study); *Before and First Session*; or *Never*.

Incidence of Confusion. Confusion is considered to have occurred if a subject misidentified the source of a statement. In other words, if a subject indicated that an imitator statement had been seen during the Study phase or outside of the experiment or both, then that response would constitute an instance of brand confusion.

Other Measures. Mackay, Cox, Burrows, and Lazzerini's (1978) Arousal scale was adapted to measure subjects' self-reported activation once before the Study session and again after the Test session. Subjects were given a list consisting of the following adjectives: active, drowsy, vigorous, sleepy, aroused, alert, passive, lively, idle, stimulated, somnolent, tired, activated, sluggish, and energetic. They were instructed to respond to the scale as follows: 'definitely feel' (++), 'feel slightly' (+), 'do not understand or cannot decide' (?), and 'definitely do not feel' (-). The score for this scale runs from 0 to 15 with smaller numbers indicating greater fatigue.

RESULTS AND DISCUSSION

Incidence of Confusion

H_1 predicted that subjects would commit more errors in accurately recognizing imitator ads compared to new ads. To test this hypothesis, subjects' ability correctly classify imitator claims and new claims as never having seen before, was compared. Confirming H_1, subjects' recognition accuracy of *imitator* items was found to be significantly lower than that of *new2* items (mean correct recognition: 51% vs. 71%, p<.001). Indeed, accurate

recognition rate was almost at chance (that is, 50%) for the imitator ads, suggesting subjects' confusion with imitator claims.

Belief in Imitator claims

Consistent with H_2, subjects rated the validity of imitator ads significantly lower relative to new claims (see Figure 1). For each subject, we calculated a mean response to *original, new1, new2,* and *imitator* items. A within-subject ANOVA of these means revealed a significant effect of item type [$F(3,90)=15.40$, p<.001] such that *original* and *new1* items shown at Study and *new2* items shown at Test were evaluated as being more true than *imitator* claims displayed at Test ($M_{original}=9.28$; $M_{new1}=9.54$; $M_{new2}=9.1$; $M_{imitator}=7.91$). In addition, thanks to the extensive pretesting, no significant difference was found between the truth ratings of *original, new1,* and *new2* claims (p>.05).

These results suggest an overall detrimental effect of imitator ads on consumer belief. It appears that subjects are generally more skeptical of imitator claims compared to novel claims seen for the first time.

Role of Source Misattribution

The principal comparison of interest in this experiment was the role of source misattribution on the truth effect. H_{3a} predicted that copycat marketing claims thought to have been seen before (that is, misattributed) will be believed to be truer than would claims (correctly) identified as being new. A within subject ANOVA post-hoc blocked by source attribution, confirmed this hypothesis. There was a significant main effect of source attribution with the imitators thought to have been seen outside the experiment being rated highest in truth value [$F(2,53)=28.83$, p<.001].

Hypothesis H_{3b} predicted that a claim correctly recognized as being an imitator and hence attributed as being a new claim, would be less believable compared to a claim thought to be presented earlier. This hypothesis was confirmed. The mean truth rating means for the different source attributions along with a count of responses in each category were, in the order Never, First Session, and Before: 6.89 (n=31, SE=0.30), 8.36 (n=29, SE=0.39), and 10.07 (n=26, SE=0.44). See Figure 2. Post hoc comparisons revealed that these means were all significantly different at p<.01.

FIGURE 1
Truth Ratings for the Four Item Types

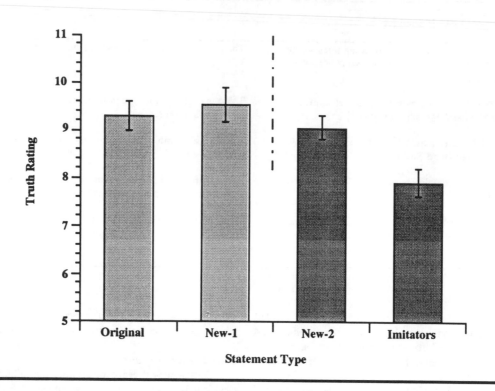

It is noteworthy that, when subjects are confused about the source of an imitator claim (that is, they fail to detect it is an imitation and attribute it to an outside source), they rate the statement to be truer. However, when they correctly recognize that the ad is an imitator, they rate it significantly lower. This finding qualifies the results reported in support of H_2 as it demonstrates that while consumers are generally skeptical about imitator ads, imitator ads which go undetected actually benefit from the sense of familiarity they induce in the consumer, and hence are rated more true compared to novel claims.

Measure of Fatigue

Truth ratings of new statements were found to be generally lower at Test than at Study (though not significantly so). It may be argued that fatigue or boredom, might be accounting for the differences in truth ratings across the experimental sessions. Two results rule out this interpretation. First, comparison of self-reported levels of arousal measured by the Arousal scale showed no significant difference across Study and Test [$t(30)=1.00$, $SE=0.77$, $p>.3$]. Second, the standard errors for the four item types were, in the order *new1, new2, imitators, originals*: 0.28, 0.21, 0.27, and 0.25, indicating low and equal variability around the performance means. These findings allow us to reject the possibility that ratings at Study were affected by subject fatigue or boredom.

CONCLUSION

Imitation advertising is a common occurrence in today's advertising campaigns. Results presented here replicate previous research by showing that imitator ads do indeed result in consumer confusion. Furthermore, this research shows that consumers' belief in imitator ads is influenced not only by their feelings of familiarity

with the message but also by whether or not the feeling is accompanied by recall of the source of the prior experience.

Particularly noteworthy is the finding that, when subjects misattribute imitator ads to a source outside the experiment, they judge them to be most believable. In contrast, when subjects are able to accurately identify an imitator ad, they tend to rate it significantly lower in validity relative to completely new ads. In sum, these results suggest that the use of "me-too" advertising is a double-edged sword. More specifically, imitation claims presented in an ad does not appear to always benefit from similarities shared with the original claims. It may be that an awareness that a presented claim mimics a previously shown claim functions as a "discounting cue" (Hovland, Lumsdaine, and Sheffied, 1949) which attenuates its believability. As the use of me-too claims increases, the users of these strategies need to be aware of the issues raised in this paper.

How imitator ads impact the image of the original brand has not been addressed in this study. It will be interesting to investigate if imitator advertising affects the believability of the claims made by the original brand. Also, it will be of interest to examine the effectiveness of imitator ads which, unlike the ones used in this study, claim the same benefit as an original brand but do not use identical wording.

Finally, in this study the imitator ads were seen soon after the originals whereas in the real world, days or even weeks may transpire between two such exposures. Viewing the imitator ads soon after exposure to the originals may have resulted in enhanced "discounting" as the originals may have been still fresh in the subjects' memory, leading the subjects to judge the imitators more severely than they normally would. Future studies can partially mitigate this concern by increasing the delay between Study and

FIGURE 2
Effect of Source Attribution on the Truth Rating of Imitator Claims

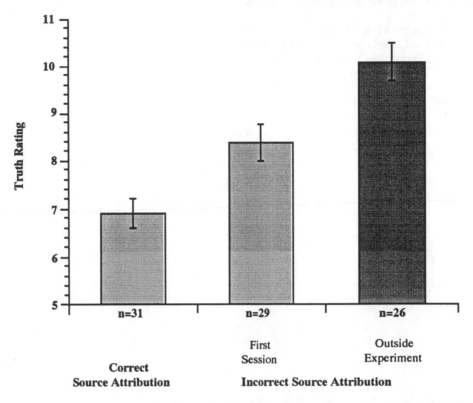

REFERENCES

Arkes, Hal R., Lawrence Bochm, and Gang Xu (1991), "Determinants of Judged Validity," *Journal of Experimental Social Psychology*, 27, 576-605.

Bacon, Frederick T. (1979), "Credibility of Repeated Statements: Memory for Trivia," *Journal of Experimental Psychology: Human Learning and Memory*, 5 (3), 241-252.

Burke, Raymond R., Wayne S. DeSarbo, Richard L. Oliver, and Thomas S. Robertson (1988), "Deception by Implication: An Experimental Investigation," *Journal of Consumer Research*, 14 (March), 483-493.

Foxman, Ellen R., Darrel D. Muehling, and Phil W. Berger (1990), "An Investigation of Factors Contributing to Consumer Brand Confusion," *Journal of Consumer Affairs*, 24 (1), 170-189.

Hasher, Lynn, David Goldstein, and Thomas Toppino (1977), "Frequency and the Conference of Referential Validity," *Journal of Verbal Learning and Verbal Behavior*, 16 (1), 107-112.

Hawkins, Scott A. and Stephen J. Hoch (1992), "Low-Involvement Learning: Memory without Evaluation," *Journal of Consumer Research*, 19 (September), 212-225.

Herr, Paul M. (1989), "Priming Price: Prior Knowledge and context Effects," *Journal of Consumer Research*, 16 (June), 67-75.

Herr, Paul M., Steven J. Sherman, and Russell H. Fazio (1983), "On the Consequences of Priming: Assimilation and Contrast Effects," *Journal of Experimental Social Psychology*, 19 (July), 323-340.

Higgins, Tory E., William S. Rholes, and Carl R. Jones (1977), "Category Accessibility and Impression Formation," *Journal of Experimental Social Psychology*, 13, 141-154.

Hovland, Carl I., Arthur A. Lumsdaine, and Fred D. Sheffield (1949), *Experiments in Mass Communication.* Princeton: Princeton University Press.

Law, Sharmistha and Scott A. Hawkins (1994), "Advertising Repetition and Consumer Beliefs: The Role of Source Memory," *Measuring Advertising Effectiveness.* NY: Lawrence Erlbaum (forthcoming).

Loken, Barbara, Ivan Ross, and Ronald L. Hinkle (1986), "Consumer confusion of origin and brand similarity perceptions," *Journal of Public Policy and Marketing*, 5, 195-211.

Mackay, Colin, Tom Cox, Grenville Burrows, and Tony Lazzerini (1978), "An Inventory for the Measurement of Self-reported Stress and Arousal," *British Journal of Social Clinical Psychology*, 17, 282-284.

Meyers-Levy, Joan and Brian Sternthal (1993), "A Two-factor Explanation of Assimilation and Contrast Effects," *Journal of Marketing and Research*, 30 (August), 359-368.

Reiling, Lynn (1982), "Consumer Misuse Mars Sampling for Sunlight Dishwashing Liquid," *Marketing News*, 3 (September), 1.

Test sessions or by collecting think-aloud protocols which would examine subjects' cognitive processing during exposure to the ads.

Schwartz, Marian (1982), "Repetition and Rated Truth Value of Statements," *American Journal of Psychology*, 95, 393-407.

The Globe and Mail (1994), "Why Outlook is Murkey for Clear Products," March 16.

Ward, James, Barbara Loken, Ivan Ross, and Tedi Hasapopoulos (1986), "The Influence of Physical Similarity Generalization of Affect and Attribute Perceptions from National Brands to Private Label Brands," in *AMA Educator's Proceedings*, Series Number 52, Terence A. Shimp et al. (eds.), Chicago, IL: American Marketing Association, 51-56.

Why Familiar Stimuli Are Better Liked. A Study on the Cognitive Dynamics Linking Recognition and the Mere Exposure Effect

Marc Vanhuele, Groupe HEC

ABSTRACT

If a brand that was advertised is encountered at a later point in time, the original presentation(s) to and evaluation of the advertisement—if ever formed—may not be retrievable from memory, but the brand itself may still look familiar, which may lead to recognition and liking. The cognitive dynamics underlying these effects are examined using a probabilistic model that describes the processes generating the recognition and liking responses.

INTRODUCTION

In the typical ad *pretest* design with recognition, all subjects are first exposed to the ad and after some retention interval receive a portfolio with a set of ads from which they have to select the one(s) they saw during the first phase of the test. In a recognition-based *campaign evaluation*, people are contacted on a random basis, presented with one or a set of ads, and asked whether they recognize the target ad(s). These two tests involve different types of recognition that may partly be affected by different factors because they depend on different cognitive processes. For that reason they may also have a different impact on evaluation and choice.

In the first type of recognition test the recognition question explicitly or implicitly refers to the episode in which the ad was originally presented. The respondent may then for instance recall the thoughts and evaluations she had during the initial presentation and based on this information confirm that she saw the ad during the first phase of the test. In the second type of test, usually no reference is made to a specific exposure. The recognition decision is, therefore, more likely to be based on a mere feeling that the stimulus is familiar. The respondent then infers from that feeling that she must have seen the ad before. Dual-process models of recognition make the distinction between the two bases of recognition illustrated here and label them retrieval and familiarity (Mandler 1980). Crucial for the present project is that these bases are independent pieces of information. Familiarity is not simply based on a "weaker" representation of the information in memory: the two types of recognition rely on different *qualities* of the memory representation.

The distinction between the two types of recognition memory has not yet been examined in our domain (cf., Taschian, White, and Pak 1988 and Alba and Hutchinson 1987 for perspectives on recognition). Our current recognition tests of ad and brand awareness, for instance, are almost exclusively focused on retrieval-based recognition. On the one hand, it may be argued that involvement in the typical advertising experiment and pretest is higher that in a natural context (cf., Hawkins and Hoch 1992) and that the frequency of retrieval-based recognition is therefore overstated. Consumers may in reality not be able or not be willing to find out why they recognize a brand. On the other hand, this focus on retrieval-based recognition may understate the impact of advertising (Pluzinski 1992).

Familiarity is evaluated positively, and this positive affect may be transferred to the familiar marketing stimulus (Janiszewski 1993), a phenomenon that is usually referred to as the mere exposure effect. It has been argued that familiarity and liking (in the mere exposure effect) in general covary because they share a common antecedent and are generated by similar cognitive processes (Anand and Sternthal 1991; Jacoby and Kelley 1987,

Janiszewski 1993). It will be argued here that retrieval-based recognition not only is not necessary for the effect, but even may counteract it.

The present project examines both the distinction between the two types of recognition memory and the link between familiarity-based recognition and the mere exposure effect. Even low-involvement advertising exposures may be sufficient to generate the effects studied here. To examine these relatively automatic (and maybe even unconscious) responses to advertising, a methodology is used that relies to a minimal extent on introspection and verbalization of the process that generates the responses. This methodology instead infers what the cognitive process must have been like to produce a certain set of responses.

TWO BASES OF RECOGNITION

Theories of recognition memory distinguish between two bases of recognition, *familiarity* and *retrieval*, that can contribute independently and additively to a recognition judgment (Mandler 1980). Noticing a given brand on the store shelves, for instance a brand in an infrequently purchased product category, may trigger a feeling of knowing that brand. This response is relatively automatic and effortless: the brand seems to "jump out" and present itself as familiar. As a result, we may decide that we recognize the brand. We may also, in addition, realize that we recently saw a commercial for that brand, and thus understand why the brand looks familiar. Retrieving scenes from that commercial then confirms our feeling of knowing the brand.

The two bases of recognition depend on different qualities of the memory representation. In Mandler's terminology, familiarity mainly results from *intraitem integration*, while retrieval is a function of *interitem elaboration*. The latter refers to the associations in long-term memory: when there are more and stronger associations to other stimuli and events, it is easier to recognize a target stimulus on the basis of retrieval. Intraitem integration is the extent to which the elements or features of a stimulus are integrated. Sheer exposure and repetition make the different elements of an item seem more coherent and integrated, and thereby make it look more familiar.

PERCEPTUAL FLUENCY: AN ANTECEDENT OF FAMILIARITY AND LIKING

Mandler leaves the issue of the psychological processes that generate feelings of familiarity unaddressed. Larry Jacoby and his colleagues (Kelley and Jacoby 1990; Jacoby, Toth, Lindsay, and Debner 1992) advance the notion that both familiarity and recognition should be conceptualized as inferences. Familiarity and the results of possible retrieval are among the cues that inform a recognition inference. A stimulus is judged old when it generates a sufficiently strong feeling of familiarity and/or when enough details about a previous occurrence can be retrieved. Familiarity itself is, at least partly, based on what Jacoby et al. define as "perceptual fluency", that is the ease with which a stimulus is processed perceptually. They also argue that affective evaluations may as well, at least in part, be based on perceptual fluency. This common antecedent may explain the link between familiarity and liking in the mere exposure effect. The argument is basically that perceptual fluency is a vague unspecific sensation that something is different about an item. This feeling may then be attributed to a range of qualities of the item, for instance that it is true, that it is fitting in a certain context, that it has been encountered before, or that it is likeable (cf., Anand and Sternthal 1991; Hawkins and Hoch 1992; Janiszewski 1993).

THE INVARIANCE OF FAMILIARITY-BASED RECOGNITION

The low-involvement nature of many advertising exposures and purchasing occasions may inhibit recognition by retrieval because there is an insufficient quantity and quality of processing, either of the original exposures to the advertisements, or of the later exposure to the product when an evaluation has to be made. The following review of factors that influence the two types of recognition confirms this idea but also suggests that the typical low-involvement ad exposure may still generate enough perceptual fluency for familiarity and a mere exposure effect.

Recent studies have found that quite a few factors influence recognition by retrieval but not recognition by familiarity. Gardiner and his co-workers found that recognition based on familiarity was not affected by levels of processing, dividing attention during study, passive reading versus actively generating the target information, and time delays of up to one week (see the summary of this work in Gardiner and Java 1991). On the other hand, each of those factors had a significant influence on recognition with retrieval: lower levels of processing, divided attention, passive reading, and a test delay lead to weaker recognition performance by retrieval. Jacoby and his colleagues (Jacoby et al. 1992) found that manipulating attention to the target stimuli during the recognition test and inducing different levels of processing affected recognition based on retrieval, but had no influence on familiarity-based recognition.

In summary, recognition by retrieval apparently depends on a minimum amount and certain quality of processing at exposure and test that recognition without retrieval does not require. Within a certain time frame, the latter type of recognition also shows little deterioration compared to the first type. Thus, the low-involvement conditions that characterize many advertising exposures may on the one hand lead to the inhibition of more conscious, deliberate attitude formation and retrieval, but on the other hand still generate familiarity, and a mere exposure effect. This also means that the conditions under which familiarity, as opposed to retrieval, becomes the dominant base in recognition should make the mere exposure effect a more important contributor to affect. With recognition based on retrieval, evaluations that were formed at the time of exposure are retrieved or new evaluations are formed based on retrieved information. These evaluations probably overwhelm the contribution of the mere exposure effect to affect. This hypothesis can be tested on any of the factors that have been shown to affect retrieval and not familiarity. In the present study one factor, the passage of time, is examined. A time delay between exposure and test should enhance the mere exposure effect, because such a delay has relatively little effect on familiarity and reduces the ability to retrieve. The test proposed in the next section not only tracks the size of the mere exposure effect over time, but also links the effect to the bases of recognition.

A MODEL OF DUAL-PROCESS RECOGNITION AND MERE EXPOSURE

Description

Assume that a person is presented with a set of previously encountered marketing stimuli and is asked to retrieve from memory her initial evaluation of those stimuli. The framework described in the previous section predicts that stimuli that were *liked initially* can be categorized again as liked on the test for three reasons:

- the initial evaluation is retrieved,
- the same evaluation is formed again, or
- the stimuli have become perceptually fluent and this fluency is interpreted as a positive evaluation (i.e., the mere exposure effect).

Stimuli that were *not liked before* may be categorized as liked as a result of the mere exposure effect. Detecting the impact of mere exposure on affect depends on two factors:

- perceptual fluency remains stable in the time frame considered—which is what we expect from research on the invariance of familiarity—, and
- retrieval is suppressed over time.

Assume now that the retrieval-of-evaluation test just discussed is combined with a "yes/no" recognition test. New and old stimuli are presented and subjects are instructed that when they give a positive recognition response, they also have to tell if they initially liked or disliked the stimulus. Figure 1 gives the processing trees that are hypothesized to underlie the response behavior for this task. For each type of stimulus (initially liked, initially disliked, and those that have not been seen before) there is a processing tree. The labels on the branches of the trees are the parameters representing the probability of the cognitive events described above. For each type of stimulus there are three possible responses ("Liked", "Disliked", and "Not Seen"). These responses are the result of the different cognitive events. R and F are the probabilities that retrieval and familiarity are sufficient for recognition responses, and PF is the probability that perceptual fluency is sufficient for a mere exposure effect. In the absence of retrieval and sufficient fluency, people have to resort to guessing to produce a response. In the first place they have to guess the exposure status and, in case they guess that the stimulus is old (which they do with probability g_s), also have to guess their initial affective reaction (they will guess it was favorable with probability g_l).

The model (and corresponding processing tree) represent how each response flows from a (series of) cognitive event(s). For instance, a *"like"* response for a *previously disliked* stimulus can result from two strings of events. In any case, a "like" response indicates that the initial negative evaluation was not retrieved from memory ($1-R$). The response can be either based on fluency or, in case there is insufficient fluency for a feeling of familiarity ($1-F$), on guessing. In the first case, the liking response would only be given if the item looks familiar (F) and generates sufficient perceptual fluency for a mere exposure effect (PF). In the second case, the response is the result of two guesses, first that the item has been seen before (gs), second that it was liked (gl). In mathematical notation:

$$P(\text{"}L\text{"}|NL)=(1-R)F*PF + (1-R)(1-F)g_sg_l$$

This equation also makes clear that the model (unlike what the tree representation may suggest) does not make any assumptions about the sequence of the different cognitive events. Similar descriptions and equations can be formed for each stimulus/response combination. This gives nine equations relating responses to parameters that represent hypothetical cognitive events.

As explained, conditions that have been shown to affect retrieval negatively but that leave familiarity intact should produce a stronger mere exposure effect. This prediction can be evaluated

FIGURE 1
Cognitive Processing Tree for Experiment

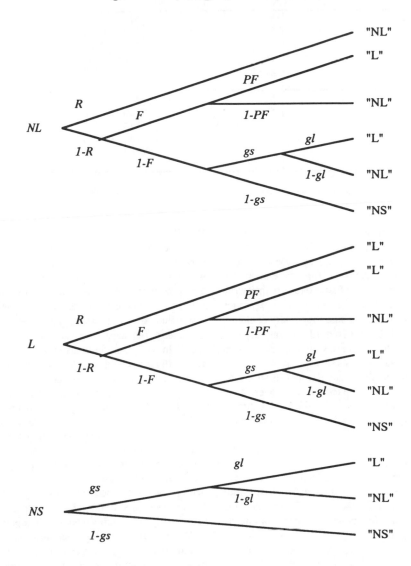

Legend: NL, L and NS refer to the initial evaluation that a subject gave for a stimulus (not liked, liked) and to the presentation status of the item (presented for the two previous cases or not see). "NL", "L", and "NS" are the possible responses during the test (did not like, liked, did not see). R, F, and PF are the probabilities of retrieval, familiarity, and mere exposure liking. gs is the probability that a subject guesses that a stimulus has been presented before. gl is the probability that a subject guesses that her initial affective response was favorable.

on the basis of a comparison of the estimates for the parameters R, F, and PF, for conditions that are and are not expected to reduce retrieval.

Parameter Estimation

Multinomial modeling is used to estimate the parameters (Batchelder and Riefer 1990). In short, the responses in the experiment described above are the result of a series of dichotomous events, and the 5 parameters are the probabilities of each event occurring. If responses for each stimulus type are independent and identically distributed across the three response types, the joint distribution of data for a given stimulus type is given by the trinomial model. Each p-value can itself be written in terms of cognitive parameters (cf., Eq. 1). If in addition there is indepen-

dence between stimulus types, then the complete data pattern can be described by the product of the three trinomial distributions. This product gives the likelihood equation that can be maximized to get the parameter estimates. Multinomial modeling, thus, basically infers the probabilities of a series of cognitive events from estimates of the response probabilities across a large number of stimuli. Comparing the corresponding parameters, especially R, F and PF, across different delay conditions that are expected to influence the likelihood of observing mere exposure effect is the objective of the following pilot study.

DESIGN OVERVIEW

Subjects were 42 undergraduate students. The study was presented to them as a search for the best-liked product logos. They

TABLE 1
Maximum-Likelihood Estimates (standard errors between parentheses)

Short Retention Interval	R	.5706 (.0187)
	F	.6333 (.0241)
	PF	.4565 (.0329)
	g_s	.1024 (.0109)
	g_l	.5125 (.0559)
Long Retention Interval	R	.2488 (.0339)
	F	.7607 (.0232)
	PF	.5248 (.0295)
	g_s	.1310 (.0180)
	g_l	.5870 (.0726)

received a folder with unknown trademarks and were asked to indicate which trademarks they liked or disliked. In order to enhance the statistical power of the analyses, they were asked for a roughly equal number of likes and dislikes. They were instructed to familiarize themselves with the full set first and to only then write down their evaluations. This gave each trademark two exposures during this phase of the experiment. In case they really could not make up their mind, they could check off a third, neutral, response alternative. Stimuli receiving this response were eliminated from the analysis. The evaluation task took about 7 minutes.

After a retention interval, subjects saw a folder in which the previously evaluated trademarks were mixed with new ones. They were asked for their recognition and for their initial evaluation in case they indicated they recognized the trademark. This phase took between 4 and 6 minutes.

Stimuli

A set of 81 unknown trademarks were collected from different published sources. To counterbalance item-specific effects, four different selections of 54 stimuli were made for the first phase of the experiment. The remaining 27 functioned as distractors in the folder used in the second phase.

Response Measures

In the first phase, responses were collected on a two-page list with 54 3-alternative scales ("liked", "?", "disliked"). In the second phase the experimenter checked off the responses to the 81 stimuli from a list. Subjects could answer with "liked", "did not like" or "did not see". This way of response collection prevented subjects from adjusting previous responses to end up with the desired number of responses in each category (they knew that of the recognized logos about half received a liking response in the first phase).

Independent Variable

The retention interval between the two phases was either about 30 minutes or 1 day. In both cases the recognition test came unanticipated to minimize the possibility of subjects memorizing the material and responses. Following the first phase, subjects were asked to make a choice between continuing the study right away (they anticipated a duration of 50 minutes) or returning the next day for a session of about 5 minutes. If they chose the second option, they would also enter a lottery for $175. Of the 42 subjects, 13 chose the second option.

Results

The parameter estimates are given in Table 1. Differences between the parameter estimates for the two retention intervals were tested by comparing the difference in likelihood-ratio statistics G^2 between the unrestricted model and a model that restricts the parameter of interest to be the same across the retention intervals. The values of the guessing parameters are not essential to the hypothesis, but have face validity and, thus, support the model itself. In both conditions the absence of retrieval and familiarity apparently is a reliable cue for the recognition judgment and when both are absent people rarely guess that a stimulus is old (g_s=0.10). Although the maximum-likelihood estimate is higher for the one-day delay (0.13 vs. 0.11), the difference is not significant (ΔG^2_1=2.01, p<.15). This result may indicate that even at the longer delay in this experiment, the presence or absence of familiarity and retrieval are still a strong informative cue in the recognition judgments. In case people guess they saw the stimulus before, the theory would predict that because there is no familiarity information, the level of perceptual fluency is also not sufficiently high to be a basis for a liking judgment. People are therefore expected to randomly pick a liking response. The parameter g_l is indeed close to 0.5 in the short-delay condition and that for the long-delay condition is not significantly different from the first (ΔG^2_1=0.56, p<.45). As hypothesized, the retention interval of one day considerably inhibits the possibility of retrieval (0.25 vs. 0.57, ΔG^2_1=74.04, p<.0001), compared to the 30-minute retention interval. Contrary to the predictions, however, the probabilities that perceptual fluency exceeds the decision criteria for familiarity and liking do not remain stable but increase (for F: ΔG^2_1=16.1 p<.0001; for PF: ΔG^2_1=4.52 p<.04). One possible explanation for these results is the small number of subjects in the long-delay condition. To check to what extent the responses of specific individuals (possibly outliers) drive the results, a jackknife-like estimation was carried out. The results were, however, confirmed. A second explanation is that familiarity was not always used as a cue in the short-delay condition (even though it would have been an informative cue) because retrieval was relatively easy. The familiarity (and mere exposure) parameter may therefore have been underestimated for this condition. A third explanation is that the specific model formulation adopted here drives the results. More research is needed on this explanation. Applying the procedure used by Jacoby (1992), however, led to the same substantive findings.

To conclude, the results of this pilot study certainly call for a replication study, and for experiments on the effect of other processing factors on the contributions of familiarity and retrieval to liking. More work is also needed on the role of the specific model used to estimate the results, and on the assumptions on which the model is based. Some of these assumptions may be testable independently of the model developed here.

CONCLUSION

There is almost no research in our discipline on the effects of low-involvement advertising exposures. Even the low-involvement conditions in the typical advertising response experiment "still seem reasonably involving compared with the natural conditions under which consumers inattentively process advertising information" (Hawkins and Hoch 1992, p. 14). In addition, most of our research methods and instruments are geared toward introspective verbal descriptions of cognitive and affective responses to advertising, and these may be less appropriate for studying low-involvement processes.

The theories presented here suggest that low-involvement exposures are conducive to a mere exposure effect, because even this type of presentation has been shown to enhance familiarity-based recognition, and because this type of presentation is expected to inhibit retrieval-based recognition. In addition, the passage of time makes it more likely to observe a mere exposure effect because retrieval, unlike familiarity, is suppressed over time. The present study presents an experimental procedure that not only tests the prediction for the effect of time on the mere exposure effect, but that also, and more importantly, allows to verify if and to what extent the effect is produced by the inhibition of retrieval and stability of familiarity over time. This procedure, which can be applied to examine a wide range of possible mediators of the mere exposure effect, has two important advantages. A problem with the explanatory variables in this research is that they usually have parallel effects. Familiarity and retrieval both lead to a positive recognition response, and the mere exposure effect and retrieval of a previous positive evaluation both lead to a liking response. A first advantage of the procedure developed in this paper is its power to separate the contribution of these different parallel factors to a given response. Second, because familiarity and mere exposure involve relatively automatic, and thus relatively unconscious processes, people may not be able to report on them. The procedure proposed here addresses this issue by inferring the probability that a response originated from a certain factor, instead of directly asking for the source of the response. The main contribution of the present study is the development of the combination of an experimental procedure and a multinomial model that allows us to study the dynamics underlying relatively automatic cognitive processes.

REFERENCES

Alba, Joseph W. and J. Wesley Hutchinson (1987), "Dimensions of Consumer Expertise," *Journal of Consumer Research*, 13 (March), 411-454.

Anand, Punam and Brian Sternthal (1991), "Perceptual Fluency and Affect Without Recognition," in *Memory & Cognition*, 19 (3), 293-300.

Batchelder, William H. and David M. Riefer, "Multinomial Processing Models of Source Monitoring," in *Psychological Review*, Vol.9, No.4, 548-564.

Gardiner, John M. and Rosalind I. Java (1991), "Forgetting in Recognition Memory With and Without Recollective Experience," in *Memory & Cognition*, 19 (6), 617-623.

Hawkins, Scott A. and Stephen J. Hoch (1992), "Low-Involvement Learning: Memory without Evaluation," in *Journal of Consumer Research*, 19 (September), 212-225.

Jacoby, Larry L. and Colleen M. Kelley (1987), "Unconscious Influences of Memory for a Prior Event," in *Personality and Social Psychology Bulletin*, Vol.13, No.3 (September), 314-336.

Jacoby, Larry L., Jeffrey P. Toth, D. Stephen Lindsay and James A. Debner (1992), "Lectures for a Layperson: Methods for Revealing Unconscious Processes," in *Perception without Awareness. Cognitive, Clinical, and Social Perspectives*, eds. Robert Bornstein and Thane S. Pittman, New York: The Guildford Press.

Janiszewski, Chris (1993), "Preattentive Mere-Exposure Effects," in *Journal of Consumer Research*, December, 376-392.

Kelley, Colleen M. and Larry L. Jacoby (1990), "The Construction of Subjective Experience: Memory Attributions," in *Mind & Language*, Vol.5, No.1, 49-68.

Mandler, George (1980), "Recognizing: The Judgment of Previous Occurrence," in *Psychological Review*, Vol.87, No.3, 252-271.

Pluzinski, Carol (1992), *The Partial Activation of Inaccessible Brand Names in Consumer Memory*, Working Paper Mark-92-9, Department of Marketing, Stern School of Business, New York University, New York, NY 10003.

Tashchian, Armen, J. Dennis White and Sukgoo Pak (1988), "Signal Detection Analysis and Advertising Recognition: An Introduction to Measurement and Interpretation Issues," in *Journal of Marketing Research*, Vol.15 (November), 397-404.

Perspectives on the "New Sociology" of Consumer Research: Addressing the Structure/Agency Dilemma

Douglas E. Allen, Pennsylvania State University
Paul F. Anderson, Pennsylvania State University

In recent years, consumer researchers have begun to return to the field of sociology, a discipline that proved to be particularly important during the early years of consumer behavior's growth. For more than two decades the dominant paradigms of cognitive and social psychology made important substantive and methodological contributions to our field while sociology's contribution remained relatively modest. In the interim, sociological theory was reinvigorated by both new approaches and the elaboration of extant paradigms by younger scholars.

This special session explored some of the implications that this "new sociology" has for the study of consumption. In particular, it focused on the structure/agency debate which has plagued the social sciences, and it introduced several contemporary theoretical frameworks designed to transcend this dualism. The general thesis is that sociology does not, as traditionally thought, focus solely on the role that external collectivities (structures) play in determining behavior. Rather, to fully explain behavior, it must take into account the individual-level perspectives (agency) that actors invest in their day-to-day interactions. The three presentations revolved around this central topic.

The first presentation by Craig J. Thompson and Diana L. Haytko addressed the traditional structure/agency dichotomy in their empirical study of fashion consciousness by employing the philosophy and methodology of hermeneutics. Thompson and Haytko argued that one's sense of fashion emerges out of the dialectic between shared cultural meanings (structural considerations) and the personal understandings (agency considerations) that individuals derive from the "fashion system". Through use of an iterative part-to-whole method of interpreting their data, the authors were able to place the individual level data that they derived from phenomenological interviews into the broader context of socio-cultural and reference group influences that help to shape personal perceptions.

In the second presentation, Aaron C. Ahuvia and Michael Bernard-Donals argued that extant methodologies used to assess the social impact of consumer exposure to various marketing-related texts (e.g., advertisements, films, television shows, etc.) tend to neglect the way in which a text is received by its audience. As a result it was argued that it is necessary to go beyond mere analysis of the text to understand the reader-level understandings derived from texts. The talk concluded with directions for future research in this area.

The third presentation by Douglas E. Allen and Paul F. Anderson was based on nine months of ethnographic research at a two-year business school. Based on this study, Allen and Anderson introduced a model of consumer choice designed to transcend the structure/agency dichotomy. This model viewed choice as a relationship between socio-historical factors practically inscribed in the consumer and socio-historical factors objectified in the form of the product. Implications that such a view of choice has for understanding decisions based on diffuse affective responses were discussed. Additionally, this conceptualization of choice was used to question what it means to "satisfy customer needs" in the context of the marketing of non-traditional goods or services (e.g., education, health care, etc.).

The Effects of Editorial Context and Cognitive and Affective Moderators on Responses to Embedded Ads

Keith S. Coulter, University of Connecticut
Murphy A. Sewall, University of Connecticut

This paper utilizes two experiments within a print media setting to examine the manner in which contextual involvement effects may be moderated by a number of key variables including affective tone of the article and ad (i.e. affective consistency), cognitive priming of relevant attributes, and involvement in the advertisement. Results indicate that editorial context involvement has a negative impact on attitude toward the ad (Aad). This relationship is moderated by the interactive effects of affective consistency and ad involvement. Cognitive priming was found to interact with editorial involvement in influencing attitude toward the brand, but not Aad. The results have important implications in terms of achieving the appropriate "match" between editorial content and advertising message.

In today's fast-paced, information-oriented world, advertisers are increasingly competing for consumers' attention. As advertising costs escalate, brand choices proliferate, and the consumer is bombarded by product claims within an ever broadening array of media channels, the advertising practitioner must be acutely aware of factors influencing message effectiveness. One of the factors that has received considerable attention in the literature is "editorial," "program," or "advertising" context (Lord and Burnkrandt 1993; Yi 1993; Norris and Colman 1992). The first term is generally applied to print media (e.g., Soldow and Principe 1981), whereas "program context" is more often applied to broadcast media (e.g., Murry, Lastovicka, and Singh 1992). "Advertising context" may be thought of as a generic term that is applicable to either print or broadcast media.

An important issue involved in decisions on the selection of an appropriate context for advertisements deals with the context's influence on ad and product evaluations. A number of studies suggest that ad context can influence the audience's perception of an advertisement, and thus, its effectiveness (Singh and Churchill 1987; Soldow and Principe 1981). Both program and editorial context have been examined in terms of a number of key variables including involvement (Lord and Burnkrandt 1993), program induced affect (Goldberg and Gorn 1987; Kamins, Marks, and Skinner 1991), program "liking" (Murry, Lastovicka, and Singh 1992), and cognitive and affective priming (Yi 1990, 1993).

This paper utilizes a print media setting to examine the manner in which contextual involvement effects may be moderated by a number of key factors including three of the variables listed above: 1) affective tone of the article and ad, 2) cognitive priming of relevant attributes, and c) involvement in the advertisement. While each of these variables has been examined individually, specific interaction effects have not been investigated. Further, this research extends the investigation of editorial context involvement effects to include not only measures of recall and recognition (e.g. Norris and Colman 1992) but also attitudes toward the ad (Aad) and brand (Ab).

PROGRAM OR EDITORIAL INVOLVEMENT

Program (i.e. broadcast) or editorial (i.e. print) context involvement refers to the degree of commitment of cognitive resources to the contextual material (Norris and Colman 1992; Soldow and Principe 1981). The negative impact of program involvement on commercial message processing has been demonstrated by a number of researchers (Bryant & Comiskey 1978; Soldow and Principe 1981). In these studies, television viewers demonstrated better recall of commercial content when they were less involved in the program. Lord and Burnkrandt (1988), who observed response times prior to and during advertising commercials, concluded that highly involving program content may induce viewers to commit a large proportion of available attention to its processing, thus reducing the efficiency with which they can encode and store information presented by a commercial. While high program involvement may effectively activate attentional resources, it may hinder viewers' ability to process an advertisement by directing those resources toward the contextual program stimuli at the expense of a shift in attentional focus toward the new (advertising) message. In a more recent study, Lord and Burnkrandt (1993) found that both program involvement and dramatic attentional devices used in television advertisements, based on their interaction with one another and with viewers' processing motivation, have the capacity to enhance or hinder the generation of viewer thoughts relevant to ad messages (i.e. ad cognitions).

The apparent disadvantage of high context involvement has also been demonstrated in studies using print media (i.e. editorial context). It would seem logical for this to be the case, since readers of print media have control over the speed of information processing. A magazine reader who is involved in an article can easily skip over any embedded advertisements and continue reading without any appreciable delay, thereby continuing to attend to the absorbing material basically without interruption. An involved television viewer, on the other hand, is forced to stop viewing the program during the commercial break. Consequently he or she may be more likely to assimilate some of the advertising message. Thus one might hypothesize that the effects of contextual involvement may be even greater in the case of print media. Although the two types of media have not been directly compared in the literature, Norris & Colman (1992) did find that subjects' involvement in magazine articles yielded a negative correlation with measures of recall, recognition, and global memory for the accompanying advertisements.

Measures of recall and recognition consist of cognitive responses that involve the generation of thoughts relevant to ad messages (i.e. ad cognitions). Since the direct causal impact of ad cognitions on Aad, and of Aad on Ab, have been well documented within the ad effects literature (Brown and Stayman 1992; MacKenzie, Lutz, and Belch 1986), we expect the negative influence of editorial context involvement to carry over to measures of ad and brand attitude. Therefore, we posit:

H1a: High editorial context involvement will result in less favorable Aad and Ab.

H1b: Low editorial context involvement will result in more favorable Aad and Ab.

MODERATING VARIABLES

Cognitive Priming

Research has demonstrated that the advertising context can prime or activate certain attributes to readers (viewers/listeners), and guide their interpretations of product information in the ad (Yi 1990; Wyer and Srull 1981; Higgins and King 1981). These interpretations may result in the formation or change of beliefs about the advertised brand, which will affect brand evaluations (Mitchell and Olson 1981). The process affects ad effectiveness primarily by increasing the accessibility of attributes from memory (e.g., "bringing the attribute to mind"). When the advertising context provides exposure to a certain attribute, the attribute becomes accessible and is subsequently more likely to be used in processing ad information and evaluating the advertised brand. If this attribute has positive implications for the evaluation of the advertised brand, overall brand evaluations should be enhanced. In contrast, if the primed attribute has negative implications for the advertised brand, overall brand evaluations should be diminished. Finally, if the primed attribute has evaluative implications that are unrelated to the product, overall brand evaluations should not be affected.

In a related test of this concept utilizing print advertisements, Yi (1990) found that after exposure to an ad emphasizing the large size of a car, subjects' (Ab) and purchase intention (PI) differed as a function of the attribute activated by the ad context. Specifically, Ab and PI were higher when the attribute of safety (as opposed to fuel economy) was made salient in the article preceding the ad.

It was hypothesized that while high program involvement may effectively activate attentional resources, it may hinder readers' ability to process an advertisement by directing those resources toward the contextual stimuli at the expense of a shift in attentional focus toward the new (advertising) message. But the priming of a related attribute should *enhance* subjects' ability to shift attentional focus, since the subject of that focus (i.e. the concept related to the advertising message) has already been accessed or activated from memory. Therefore an advertising context which primes attributes that are either positively *or* negatively associated with the advertised attribute, and have either positive *or* negative implications for the advertised brand (i.e. positive/negative priming) should serve to moderate (i.e. lessen) the negative relationship between context involvement and Aad. Positive and negative priming are *not* expected to have the same impact upon Ab, however, either in terms of direct (main) effects or interactions with context involvement. In this case, research has demonstrated that negative priming will have a deleterious influence upon brand evaluations (Yi 1990; 1993). The following hypotheses are proposed:

H2a: When context involvement is high, both positive and negative cognitive priming will result in more favorable ad evaluations (Aad) than neutral cognitive priming.

H2b: When context involvement is low, there will be no difference in ad evaluations (Aad) among the positive, negative, and/or neutral cognitive priming groups.

H2c: When context involvement is high, positive cognitive priming will result in more favorable brand evaluations (Ab), and negative cognitive priming will result in less favorable brand evaluations than neutral cognitive priming.

Program Induced Affect and the Affective Tone of the Ad

Advertising context can be negatively or positively valenced and can trigger affective reactions (e.g., feelings or moods). This overall affect generated by the context can be transferred to one's Aad, which can subsequently influence brand evaluations (Lutz

1985; MacKenzie, Lutz, and Belch 1986; Erdley and D'Agostino 1988). Many studies suggest that mood states influence evaluations and judgments in mood congruent directions (Isen and Shalker 1982; Veitch and Griffitt 1976). This would imply that, in most cases, commercials should be more effective if embedded in programs which are upbeat, positive, and happy. In a related study, Goldberg and Gorn (1987) found that, compared to commercials viewed in the context of a sad program, commercials viewed in the context of a happy television program resulted in a happier overall mood, more positive cognitive responses about the commercials, and greater perceived commercial effectiveness. In a study involving embedded print advertisements, Yi (1990) found that affective priming of the ad context (i.e., the affective tone of a magazine article) significantly influenced advertising effectiveness. Subjects' Aad and PI were higher when the affective tone of the article was positive, as opposed to when it was negative.

Other studies, however, have indicated that positive program induced affect may *not* always result in increased advertising effectiveness. For example, Murry, Lastovicka, and Singh (1992) found that program induced feelings were unrelated to Aad. Similarly, Lord and Burnkrandt (1993) found that program induced mood did not have an effect on cognitive ad processing. In addition, the popularity of programs eliciting negative feelings (e.g. a tragedy or soap opera), and the apparent success of various ads embedded within these programs, suggest that other factors must be taken into consideration in explaining the effects of program induced affect.

One such factor that has received attention in the literature is affective tone of the advertisement. In a recent study, happy commercials were found to be more favorably evaluated in the context of a happy program, whereas sad commercials were more effective in the context of a sad program (Kamins, Marks, and Skinner 1991). In attempting to explain this "consistency effect" within a broadcast media setting, researchers have suggested that compared to people in neutral moods, people who are in positive or negative (e.g. sad) moods tend to be more altruistic (Cialdini, Darby and Vincent 1973; Rogers, Miller, Mayer, and Duval 1982). It is postulated that people who are in a sad mood state have a drive to reduce their negative feelings, and that this may be accomplished by engaging in mood elevating behaviors such as altruistic behavior. Presumably the negative (e.g. sad) commercial allows the viewers to experience this altruistic response by vicariously participating in the assuagement of the negative condition that is portrayed. Thus when consumers feel sadness or empathy for other people, they may react positively to an advertisement that is consistent with their mood.

The Consistency Effects model implies that the "match" between affective tone of the program and ad will have a direct impact upon Aad, due to some type of empathic response (Kamins, Marks, and Skinner 1991). To our knowledge, this effect has not been demonstrated or examined within a print media setting. Indeed, it seems unlikely that the same level of empathic catharsis would occur while reading a magazine. However, in the latter case, it is possible that affective consistency may *in*directly influence ad attitudes. Bower (1981) has postulated that each distinct mood has a particular node available in memory which collects multiple aspects of the mood that are related (e.g. events or occurrences during which that feeling state was aroused). Nodes storing moods can be activated by a variety of stimuli (such as advertising context), which causes a spread of activation to other connected memory nodes. Once a mood state has been aroused, it influences perceptions and information processing. Thus people "attend to" and "learn more about" events (or stimuli) that match their mood state (Bower 1981). The implication is that a reader should react more positively toward a "consistent" ad (i.e. one that matches the affective tone of the editorial context) because attentional resources have previously been activated. Therefore, affective consistency may have the same moderating effect upon editorial involvement as cognitive priming, that is, it may enhance subjects' ability to shift attentional focus. The following hypotheses are proposed:

H3a: When editorial context involvement is high, a consistent affective condition will result in more favorable ad evaluations (Aad) than an inconsistent affective condition.

H3b: When editorial context involvement is low, there will be no difference in Aad between affective consistent and affective inconsistent treatment groups.

Ad Involvement

A third factor that may moderate the effects of editorial involvement on Aad is the consumer's motivation to process the advertisement (MacInnis, Moorman, and Jaworski 1991). A high level of ad processing motivation (i.e. involvement in the ad) may be situationally determined due to some specific task such as advertisement pretesting (Bloch, Ridgway, and Sherrell 1986), or internally generated as a result of inherent interest in the product (Bloch and Richins 1983), interest in the advertisement (Lutz, MacKenzie and Belch 1983), or some combination of these factors. This involvement may be expected to heighten and provide focus to the cognitive processing of the ad (Batra and Ray 1983). A reader who is highly involved in an advertising message presumably possesses sufficient processing motivation (and ability) to voluntarily divert at least some attentional resources from the context to the ad. Since the negative impact of program involvement on Aad results from the *inability* of highly involved readers to shift attentional focus, ad involvement should serve to moderate (i.e. lessen) this impact. We therefore propose:

H4a: When editorial context involvement is high, high ad involvement will result in more favorable ad evaluations (Aad) than low ad involvement.

H4b: When editorial context involvement is low, there will be no difference in Aad between high and low ad involvement groups.

As mentioned earlier, a high level of ad involvement may be either situationally determined or internally generated as a result of some inherent interest in the product. In the former case, ad *execution* involvement is said to be high (MacKenzie, Lutz, and Belch 1986). Since consumers devote most of their cognitive resources to ad evaluation, ad cognitions should be the dominant response to stimulus exposure (Lutz 1985), and these cognitions should have a significant impact upon Aad (Madden, Allen, and Twible 1988). On the other hand, when there is an inherent interest in the product, advertising *message* involvement is said to be high (MacKenzie, Lutz, and Belch 1986). In this case, because consumers tend to focus on product-related messages, brand cognitive responses will be strong (Madden, Allen, and Twible 1988; Mitchell and Olson 1981), and the influence of these brand cognitions on Ab should be increased (Hastak and Olson 1989; Muehling and Laczniak 1988). Since our hypotheses regarding advertising involvement deal with its impact on Aad, rather than Ab, the ad involvement processing instructions in Experiment 2 were designed to manipulate *execution* involvement.

METHODOLOGY

As stated earlier, we expect editorial involvement to influence advertising evaluations. In addition, positive and negative cognitive priming, affective consistency/inconsistency, and ad involvement are hypothesized to moderate the impact of editorial involvement on Aad and Ab. Although, Aad is posited to mediate the impact of editorial involvement on Ab, this relationship was not directly examined in our study.

Because available contextual stimuli precluded our use of one article to manipulate both cognitive priming and affective consistency, we conducted two experiments. Experiment 1 examined the effects of context involvement *(H1a/b)* and cognitive priming *(H2a/b/c)* on both dependent variables. Experiment 2 examined the effects of context involvement *(H1a/b)*, affective consistency *(H3a/b)*, and ad involvement *(H4a/b)* on Aad. Both experiments utilized print advertisements embedded within magazine articles. The ads, as well as the articles, varied across experiments.

Product Selection

Several criteria were used to select the product for these experiments: 1) the product needed to have several interrelated attributes so that both positive and negative priming effects could be examined, 2) subjects had to have some interest in the product in order to be able to process information in the ads, and 3) the product needed to be described in both cognitive and affective terms in order to assess both cognitive priming and affective consistency. Based upon these considerations and consonant with prior research in the area (Yi 1990; 1993), a new automobile was selected as the test product. Fictitious brand and company names were used to reduce any confounding or bias due to subject familiarity.

Stimuli Development

A pilot test was conducted utilizing a random sample of 50 undergraduate students in order to determine ad content and program context material. Participants were first asked to identify salient attributes of a new automobile. Then, for each attribute, associated attributes were solicited and the perceived relationship was assessed on a bipolar (-10 to +10) scale (John, Scott, and Bettman 1986). Results indicated that fuel efficiency, comfort/roominess, and driving pleasure are salient attributes of a new automobile.

Based on the pilot testing, four ads were constructed. Ad 1, used in the positive cognitive priming manipulation in Experiment 1, highlighted fuel efficiency as the focal attribute. Ad 2, used in the negative cognitive priming manipulation in Experiment 1, highlighted comfort and roominess. Ad 3, a neutral ad used in both Experiments 1 and 2, stressed simple driving pleasure. Ad 4, used in the affective consistent manipulation in Experiment 2, contained less informational copy, a larger illustration, and highlighted the emotional appeal of the product by emphasizing driving "excitement."

Two articles were selected in which to embed the ads. The cognitive priming article utilized for Experiment 1 involved a discussion of the importance of energy conservation amid dwindling global natural and environmental resources. It was assumed that this topic would be positively associated with fuel efficiency (the focal attribute of Ad 1), negatively associated with the comfort/roominess attribute of Ad 2 (i.e. due to the increased gas consumption inherent in operating a large luxury automobile), and unassociated with driving pleasure (the focal attribute of Ad 3).

A warm, humorous article regarding child-rearing was utilized to examine affective consistency in Experiment 2. It was assumed that greater affective consistency would occur when the emotional ad, as opposed to one of the more cognitively-oriented ads (i.e. Ad 3), was embedded within this context. While both the child rearing article and the emotional ad were "positive" in nature, they could be expected to elicit somewhat different emotional reactions (i.e. happiness vs. excitement). Therefore, the degree of affective consistency was assessed for all subjects across both conditions.

Both magazine articles were edited to contain approximately six pages of text. In each case, the appropriate full-page target ad was embedded after page four. The source of the articles did not appear on the stimuli.

EXPERIMENT 1

Design

To test H1 and H2, we conducted a 3 (cognitive priming: positive/negative/neutral) x 2 (context involvement: high/low) between-subjects experiment. A total of 120 undergraduate students at a major Northeastern university participated in the study. There were 20 subjects per cell.

Procedures

First, subjects were randomly assigned to one of the six treatment groups. Then, as part of the context involvement manipulation, subjects were given a set of instructions that varied depending upon treatment group. Subjects in the low context involvement manipulation were told that they were being asked to review an article for use in a subsequent marketing study. Subjects in the high context involvement condition were told that they were being asked to read the article because it had important implications for future class discussions, and that they would be asked questions germane to the topic.

After these initial instructions, subjects in all treatment conditions were required to examine the energy conservation article in which either the ad stressing fuel efficiency (positive priming) comfort/roominess (negative priming), or driving pleasure (neutral) had been embedded. Upon completion of this task, subjects filled out a questionnaire containing manipulation checks and dependent measures.

Measurement

Manipulation Checks. In order avoid influencing subjects' evaluations of the ads, manipulation checks were assessed subsequent to measurement of the dependent variable(s). Cognitive priming was evaluated by asking subjects to list any thoughts or ideas that came to mind when considering the advertisement or the product. Subjects in both the positive and negative cognitive priming conditions were expected to list the fuel efficiency attribute to a greater extent than subjects in the neutral condition. Further, the valence of this cognition was expected to vary depending upon condition (i.e. positive vs. negative priming).

Subjects provided ratings of their context involvement on three, 7-point semantic differential items adapted from Zaichkowsky's Personal Involvement Inventory (1985). The items were: 1) "paid attention to the article/did not pay attention to the article," 2) "felt it was important to pay attention to the article/did not feel that it was important," and 3) "was involved in reading the article/was not involved in reading the article." The scale formed by the unweighted sum of the three items had a Cronbach's alpha of 91.

Dependent Variables. Aad was measured using four, 7-point semantic differential items: favorable/unfavorable, positive/negative, bad/good, and liked a lot/no liking. The scale formed by an unweighted sum of the items had a Cronbach's alpha of .89. Ab was

measured by a similar set of four semantic differential items (Cronbach's alpha =.91) that had been reordered, restructured, and reverse-coded to minimize common methods variation.

Results

Manipulation Checks. The manipulation check for editorial involvement showed a significant main effect ($F=18.08$, $p<.001$) and no significant interactions. The mean in the high involvement condition was 4.87, compared to 2.88 in the low involvement condition.

The percentage of subjects listing fuel efficiency related cognitions was significantly higher in the positive ($\bar{x}=.93$) and negative ($\bar{x}=.82$) priming conditions than it was in the neutral ($\bar{x}=.16$) priming condition. ANOVA results indicated a main effect for priming ($F=23.03$, $p<.001$) and no two-way interactions. The percentage of negatively valenced focal attribute associations was significantly greater in the negative ($\bar{x}=.94$) as opposed to the positive and neutral priming groups ($\bar{x}=.07$ and $\bar{x}=.26$, respectively). Once again, ANOVA results indicated a significant main effect ($F=6.15$, $p<.01$) with no interactions.

Hypotheses Testing. H1 predicted that high editorial involvement would have a negative impact upon Aad and Ab. The ANOVA results indicated a significant main effect for context involvement on Aad ($F=25.33$, $p<.001$). The mean for the high context involvement condition was 3.33, compared to 5.15 in the low involvement condition. The correlation between context involvement and Aad was -.46. Therefore, H1 was confirmed for Aad. There was no significant main effect of context involvement on Ab.

H2 posited that the moderating impact of cognitive priming on the relationships examined above would vary by dependent measure. More specifically, when context involvement was high, *both* positive and negative cognitive priming were hypothesized to result in more favorable ad evaluations (Aad). However under high context involvement, these two types of priming were expected to have *opposite* effects on brand evaluations (Ab). Results indicated a nonsignificant context x priming interaction effect on Aad. However, the means for the positive priming/high involvement ($\bar{x}=3.87$), negative priming/high involvement ($\bar{x}=3.56$), and neutral/high involvement groups ($\bar{x}=2.14$) were in the predicted direction.

A significant two way interaction was observed between involvement and cognitive priming for Ab ($F=8.10$, $p<.01$). Under high context involvement, Ab was significantly greater for the positive cognitive priming condition ($\bar{x}=5.30$) than for the negative priming ($\bar{x}=2.52$) or neutral ($\bar{x}=3.08$) conditions. The means did not vary significantly under conditions of low involvement.

EXPERIMENT 2

Design

To test H1, H3 and H4, we conducted a 2 (affective consistency: high/low) x 2 (context involvement: high/low) x 2 (ad involvement: high/low) between subjects experiment. One hundred twenty undergraduate students at a major Northeastern university participated in the experiment. There were 15 subjects per cell.

Procedures

Subjects were randomly assigned to one of the eight treatment groups. Context involvement was manipulated using the same procedure as in Experiment 1. Then, as part of the ad involvement manipulation, subjects were given a set of instructions that varied depending upon treatment group. The instructions in the high ad (execution) involvement manipulation informed subjects that they would be asked to record their impressions of the embedded advertisements; instructions in the low ad involvement manipulation included no mention of the embedded ads. All subjects were then required to examine the child-rearing article in which either the emotional ad (Ad 4) or the neutral ad (Ad 3) had been embedded. The former combination represented the affective-consistent condition, whereas the latter combination represented the affective-inconsistent condition. After reading the article, subjects completed a questionnaire containing manipulation checks and dependent measures.

Measurement

Context involvement and Aad were measured using items and scales identical to those in Experiment 1. To assess the article/ad combinations for affective consistency, subjects indicated their affective reactions to the context and ads on ten 7-point Likert scale items: "happy," "elated," "pleased," "bored," "critical," "disgusted," "sad," "affectionate," "warmhearted," and "concerned" (Edell and Burke 1987; Batra and Ray 1986). Correlation coefficients were computed for each subject based upon these two sets of reactions. As mentioned earlier, it was assumed that affective consistency would be higher in treatment conditions where the emotional ad was embedded within the affective context. In order to insure that any observed effects were due to the *association* between context and ad, and not to some factor inherent in the ad *itself*, an independent convenience sample of 55 students provided ratings for both ads on the aforementioned Aad scale. Comparison of means for the two ads yielded no significant difference in attitude measures (t=1.39, p>.05).

Subjects provided ratings of their overall ad (execution) involvement on three, 7-point semantic differential items selected from Zaichkowsky's Personal Involvement Inventory (1985). The items were: 1) "paid attention to the ad/did not pay attention to the ad," 2) "felt it was important to pay attention to the ad/did not feel that it was important," and 3) "was involved in reading the advertisement/was not involved in reading the advertisement. The scale formed by the unweighted sum of the three items had a Cronbach's alpha of .91.

Results

Manipulation Checks. The manipulation check for context involvement showed a significant main effect (F=9.27, p<.01) and no interactions. The mean in the high involvement condition was 4.23 compared to 2.75 in the low involvement condition. The ad involvement manipulation also resulted in a significant main effect (F=17.62, p<.001), with no two or three way interactions present. High ad involvement subjects achieved a mean score of 5.79; low ad involvement subjects achieved a mean rating of 2.39. Finally, a check of affective consistency revealed a significant main effect (F=8.10, p<.01) and no two or three way interactions. The correlation for subjects in the consistent condition was .79 as opposed to -.04 in the inconsistent condition.

Hypotheses Testing. The ANOVA results indicated a significant main effect for context involvement on Aad (F=9.87, p<.01). The mean for the high context involvement condition was 3.27, compared to 5.10 in the low involvement condition. Therefore, as in Experiment 1, H1 is confirmed. H3a and H3b predicted that affective consistency/inconsistency would moderate the relationship between context involvement and Aad. More specifically, under conditions of high context involvement, a consistent affec-

tive condition was posited to result in more favorable ad evaluations than an inconsistent condition. Similarly, H4a and H4b predicted that under conditions of high context involvement, high *ad* involvement would result in more favorable ad evaluations than low ad involvement. Neither of these two-way interactions were significant. However, there was a significant three-way interaction (F=6.63, p<.05). Affective consistency resulted in more favorable ad evaluations when both context and ad involvement were high ($\bar{x}$ =6.02) than when both measures of involvement were low ($\bar{x}$ =4.07), or when levels were mixed ($\bar{x}$ =3.91 and $\bar{x}$ =3.84).

DISCUSSION

The impact of contextual factors on measures of advertising performance has been the focus of a considerable amount of research. The present study is important in that it attempts to specify the *conditions* under which these factors might influence ad effectiveness in terms of moderating variables. Results of Experiments 1 and 2 confirmed the general finding in the literature that contextual involvement may hinder advertising effectiveness (e.g. Norris and Colman 1992). The present study demonstrates that this negative impact may extend beyond measures of recall and recognition to include both ad and brand evaluations.

Both positive and negative cognitive priming have been demonstrated to have a direct effect on Ab (Yi 1990; 1993). This study examined the question of whether cognitive priming may have possible *indirect* effects as a result of its impact upon the context involvement/Ab or context involvement/Aad relationships. A significant interaction was observed in terms of the former, but not the latter. As expected, under conditions of high context involvement, positive cognitive priming was found to enhance subjects' attitudes toward the brand. Presumably, the priming of a related attribute that had positive implications for the advertised brand occurred to a greater extent when people were "focussing" upon the editorial material. Negative priming, on the other hand, was found to diminish subjects' brand evaluations, although this difference was not significant. Thus, the direction or valence of the priming (i.e. positive/negative) was found to be important.

Our initial hypotheses predicted that the direction of the priming would *not* be important in terms of its indirect effects upon Aad. Here it was postulated that the priming of a related attribute should enhance subjects' ability to shift attentional focus, since the subject of that focus had already been accessed from memory. This shifting of focus should have occurred regardless of whether the implications associated with that attribute were positive or negative. Although a comparison of means indicated that results were in the predicted direction, no significant interactions were found.

The implication of a significant finding (i.e. both positive and negative priming interacting with contextual involvement in a similar manner) might have been less of a need for concern (on the part of marketing practitioners) regarding the specific placement of any one particular ad within any one specific media vehicle. That is, when readers are "absorbed" with the editorial material, cutting through the clutter (by either positive or negative means) would be beneficial. The fact that this was *not* the case, however, seems to indicate that care must be taken in attempting to achieve the appropriate "match" between editorial content and advertising message.

In Experiment 2, affective consistency was found to positively impact Aad only when both editorial and ad involvement were high. Apparently (as hypothesized earlier) when context involvement is high, affective consistency may enhance subjects' ability to shift attentional focus. However, the lack of a two-way (context involvement x ad involvement) or (context involvement x affective consistency) interaction argues against the hypothesized interpretation that causing a shift in attentional focus *alone* is a sufficient condition for positively impacting Aad. Instead, it may be that some sort of processing goal must be present (MacInnis, Moorman, and Jaworski 1991). That is, the enhanced ability to shift attentional focus may result in more positive ad evaluations *only* if the motivation is present to form these evaluations "on-line," that is, with the goal of forming judgments about the ad (Lichtenstein and Srull 1985).

It appears that this on-line processing goal may have been induced by our instructions. In the high ad involvement manipulation, subjects were informed that they would be asked to record their impressions of the embedded advertisements. Perhaps results would have been different if we had only drawn subjects' attention to the ads, without an implied objective. Future research might examine the effects of other types of ad involvement manipulations upon these relationships.

The Elaboration Likelihood Model predicts that non-cognitive contextual influences should be stronger (i.e. they should serve as peripheral cues) when ads are processed in a low involvement manner (Petty, Cacioppo, and Schumann 1983). In contrast, processing goal theory suggests that context effects should be stronger when ads are actively processed, such that an evaluation is formed while the context is salient (Srull 1984). Our results not only agree with this latter theory, but they *also* seem to suggest that both a shift in attentional resources *and* a processing goal are required.

Limitations

Our measure of affective consistency is limited in that it only addresses the effects of a "positive" ad within a "positive" cognitive context. There are a wide variety of both positive and negative emotional responses that could have been investigated. Future research efforts might be directed toward an examination of additional affective combinations. In addition, a more extreme manipulation of affective consistency (i.e. utilizing, perhaps, a negatively valenced rather than a neutral ad) might have resulted in the manifestation of additional interaction effects.

Finally, available contextual stimuli precluded our examination of both cognitive priming and affective consistency within the same experimental setting. Although these two moderating variables were not hypothesized to interact, the construction of appropriate articles by the researcher would permit an investigation of this possibility.

REFERENCES

Batra, R., and Ray, M. L. (1986). "Affective Responses Mediating Acceptance of Advertising," *Journal of Consumer Research*, 13 (September), 234-249.

_____, (1983), "Operationalizing Involvement as Depth and Quality of Cognitive Response," in *Advances in Consumer Research*, Vol.X, Richard Bagozzi and Alice Tybout, eds., Ann Arbor, MI: Association for Consumer Research, 309-313.

Bloch, Peter H. (1981). "An Exploration into the Scaling of Consumers' Involvement with a Product Class," in *Advances in Consumer Research*, K. Monroe, ed. 8. Ann Arbor: Association for Consumer Research, 61-65.

_____, Peter H. & Marsha L. Richins (1983). "A Theoretical Model for the Study of Product Importance Perceptions," *Journal of Marketing*, 47 (Summer), 69-81.

Bower, Gordon H. (1981), "Mood and Memory," *American Psychologist*, 36 (February) 129-48.

Bryant, Jennings and Paul W. Comiskey (1978), "The Effect of Positioning a Message within Differentially Cognitively Involving Portions of a Television Segment on Recall of the Message," *Human Communication Research*, 5 (Fall) 63-75.

Cialdini, Robert B., Betty L. Darby and Joyce E. Vincent (1973), ""Transgression and Altruism: A Case for Hedonism," *Journal of Experimental Social Psychology*, 9 (November), 502-16.

Edell, Julie A., and Burke, M.C. (1987). "The Power of Feelings in Understanding Advertising Effects." *Journal of Consumer Research*, 14, 421-433.

Erdley, Cynthia A. and Paul R. D'Agostino (1988), "Cognitive and Affective Components of Automatic Priming Effects," *Journal of Personality and Social Psychology*, 54 (5), 741-747.

Goldberg, M.E. and Gorn, G.J. (1987). "Happy and Sad TV Programs: How they Affect Reactions to Commercials," *Journal of Consumer Research*, 14, 387-403.

Higgins, E.T. and G. King (1981), "Accessibility of Social Constructs: Information Processing Consequences of Individual and Contextual Variability," in *Personality, Cognition, and Social Interaction*, N.Cantor and J. Kihlstrom, eds. Hillsdale, NJ: Erlbaum, 69-122.

Isen, Alice M. and Thomas E. Shalker (1982), "The Effect of Feeling State on Evaluation of Positive, Neutral and Negative Stimuli: When You Accentuate the Positive, Do You Eliminate the Negative?," *Social Psychology Quarterly*, 45 (March), 58-63.

Kamins, Michael A., Lawrence J. Marks, and Deborah Skinner (1991), "Television Commercial Evaluation In The Context of Program Induced Mood: Congruency Versus Consistency Effects." *Journal of Advertising*, 20 (2), 1-14.

Lord, Kenneth R. and Robert E. Burnkrandt (1988), "Television Program Elaboration Effects on Commercial Processing," in *Advances in Consumer Research*, Vol. XV, Michael Houston, ed., Provo, UT: Association for Consumer Research, 213-218.

_____(1993), "Attention Versus Distraction: The Interactive Effect of Program Involvement And Attentional Devices on Commercial Processing," *Journal of Advertising*, 22 (March) 47-60.

Lichtenstein, Meryl and Thomas K. Srull (1985), "Conceptual and Methodological Issues in Examining the Relationship Between Consumer Memory and Judgment," in *Psychological Processes and Advertising Effects: Theory, Research, and Application*," eds. Linda F. Alwitt and Andrew A. Mitchell, Hillsdale, NJ: Lawrence Erlbaum, 113-128.

Lutz, Richard J. (1985), "Affective and Cognitive Antecedents of Attitude Toward the Ad: A Conceptual Framework," in *Psychological Processes and Advertising Effects*, Linda Alwitt and Andrew Mitchell, eds., Hillsdale, NJ: Erlbaum, 45-63.

MacKenzie, Scott B. and Richard J. Lutz (1989), "An Empirical Examination of the Structural Antecedents of Attitude toward the Ad in an Advertising Pretest Context," *Journal of Marketing*, 53 (April), 48-65.

MacInnis, Deborah T., Christine Moorman, and Bernard J. Jaworski (1991), "Enhancing and Measuring Consumers' Motivation, Opportunity, and Ability to Process Brand Information from Ads," *Journal of Marketing*, 55 (October), 32-53.

Murry, John P. Jr., John L. Lastovicka, and Surendra N. Singh, "Feeling and Liking Responses to Television Programs: An Examination of Two Explanations for Media-Context Effects," *Journal of Consumer Research*, 18, (March) 441-451.

Norris, Claire E., and Andrew M. Colman (1992), "Context effects on Recall and Recognition of Magazine Advertisements," *Journal of Advertising*, 21 (3), 37-46.

Schumann, David W. and Esther Thorson (1990), "The Influence of Viewing Context on Commercial Effectiveness: A Selection-Processing Model," *Current Issues and Research in Advertising*, 12 (1), 1-24.

Soldow, Gary F. and Victor Principe (1981), "Response to Commercials as a Function of Program Context," *Journal of Advertising Research*, 21 (2), 59-65.

Srull, Thomas K. (1984), "The Effect of Subjective Affective States on Memory and Judgment," *Advances in Consumer Research*, 11, 530-533.

_____Thomas K. and Robert S. Wyer (1980), "Category Accessibility and Social Perception: Some Implications for the Study of Person Memory and Interpersonal Judgements," *Journal of Personality and Social Psychology*, 38 (6), 841-856.

Yi, Youjae (1990), "Cognitive and Affective Priming Effects of the Context for Print Advertisements," *Journal of Advertising*, 19 (2), 40-48.

_____(1993), "Contextual Priming Effects in Print Advertisements: The Moderating Role of Prior Knowledge," *Journal of Advertising*, 22 (March) 1993.

Zaichkowsky, Judith Lynne (1985), "Measuring the Involvement Construct," *Journal of Consumer Research*, 12 (December), 341-352.

Please contact the first author for a complete reference list.

The Influence of Program Context and Order of Ad Presentation on Immediate and Delayed Responses to Television Advertisements

Valerie Starr, University of Connecticut
Charles A. Lowe, University of Connecticut

ABSTRACT

Differences in program context significantly influence the effectiveness of advertisements appearing at different points within the same program. Specifically, recall for brands and products advertised was found to be greater when a low-involvement point of the surrounding story was interrupted. Also within a relatively uninvolving program context, the first advertisement to appear in a series of advertisements had a significant advantage in recall over the second and third ads, perhaps because viewers became impatient for the program to resume and paid less attention to the ads. These results have implications for optimal placement of advertisements to enhance their effectiveness.

INTRODUCTION

Millions of dollars are spent annually on the creation and testing of television advertisements. Historically, marketers have assumed that audience attention to their message relied heavily, if not exclusively, upon the size and characteristics of the viewing audience. Specifically, the larger the audience and the greater the similarity of the audience to the target consumer, the more effective (at least potentially) the advertisement. Understandably, decisions of when and where to schedule television advertisements often have been based on estimates of audience size (e.g., Nielsen ratings) and audience characteristics (e.g., demographic or psychographic profiles) (Engel, Blackwell, & Miniard, 1990).

Recently, advertising researchers have begun to consider the context in which an advertisement appears, and the possible influence of this context on advertising effectiveness (Schultz, 1979). Those aspects of program context previously investigated include humor (Goldberg & Gorn, 1987), emotional content or mood (Pavelchak, Antil, & Munch, 1988; Schuman, 1986), similarity or congruence of the program and ad (Conard & Lowe, 1988), and the degree to which the program story line "involves" the audience (Soldow & Principe, 1981; Kennedy, 1971).

These several program context effects on advertising effectiveness should be of considerable interest to marketers concerned with promoting their products, since these effects suggest that size and similarity of the audience may not be of primary importance. Thus, the prevailing desire to have one's advertisements appear during popular (i.e., "prime-time") programs which have large audiences may be quite inappropriate even when these large audiences are dominated by the appropriate target consumers. For example, Pavelchak et al. (1988) found that emotionally involved viewers of Super Bowl XX could recall fewer advertisements shown during the game than did neutral viewers, even though the former watched more of the game and, presumably, saw more advertisements. The implication is that unless marketers consider program context effects, the financial costs of placing advertisements on specific television programs may be money spent unnecessarily.

Pavelchak et al. (1988) identified two competing predictions regarding the influence of program context on advertisement effectiveness. One prediction is that the experience of positive emotions would facilitate information processing because pleasant emotional states could be expected to increase the elaboration and activation of (more) cognitive categories than would unpleasant emotional states (Isen, 1984). This increased availability of cognitive categories would enable more encoding and recall of persuasive information (i.e., advertisements) presented while viewers are experiencing positive rather than negative emotions. In fact, some research has shown that viewers did exhibit better recall for advertisements which were presented during a "happy" program compared to a "sad" program (Goldberg & Gorn, 1987).

A second prediction is that emotional arousal should inhibit information processing because any "intense" feeling, regardless of its valence, would impair viewers' ability to attend to and/or to process information presented while these intense feelings are being experienced. Thus, advertisements presented during emotionally involving programs, regardless of the valence of the emotions elicited, would be screened out (Pavelchak et al., 1988). In short, any emotionally involving (e.g., very happy or very sad) program would impair viewers' ability to attend to and hence to recall advertisements that appear on the program.

Similar detrimental effects of arousal on recall have been predicted by Steiner (1963), who utilized the Gestalt principle of "need for closure." This principle, as applied to television programming, suggests that viewers experience a need for completion (or closure) when the plot of a program remains unresolved. Further, the more emotionally involving or suspenseful the story line, the greater viewers' need for closure. This need for closure regarding the story plot may cause the advertisements to be perceived as "noise," and as such, viewers may pay little attention to advertisements presented during an involving or suspenseful program (Kennedy, 1971). The net result of these advertising distractions would be lower recall for advertisements which interrupt a suspenseful program context.

Despite the intuitive appeal of this line of reasoning, Kennedy (1971) found little support for the prediction that advertisements presented during high-involvement programs would not be recalled as well as the same advertisements presented during low-involvement programs. Specifically, unaided brand recall showed a trend (p<.1) in the predicted direction, but aided brand recall, recall of product attributes, and recall of the advertising message did not differ as a function of the program context.

More recent research by Soldow and Principe (1981) investigated the effects of involvement on advertising effectiveness by presenting subjects with a series of three advertisements in the context of an involving or suspenseful program ("Baretta"), a non-involving or non-suspenseful program ("The Brady Bunch"), or in the absence of any program context (i.e., a control group). Their results revealed that compared to advertisements presented in isolation or in a low-involvement context, advertisements presented in a high-involvement context scored lower on several measures of advertising effectiveness including unaided brand recall, sales message recall, purchase interest, and positive attitude-toward-the-ad. Further, Soldow and Principe (1981) reported an interesting pattern of results due to ordinal position for this latter measure. While viewers of the high-involvement program reported less positive attitudes toward all advertisements than did viewers in the other two conditions, the high-involvement viewers exhibited more positive attitudes toward the first commercial compared to the second or third (last) commercials.

These differences in attitude-toward-the-ad were explained by the aforementioned principle of closure. According to Soldow and Principe (1981), their high-involvement condition created a greater need for closure, so that ads shown during the high-involvement program were more disruptive and disturbing than were the same ads shown during the less involving program. Further, Soldow and Principe suggested that the first ad in the sequence was accepted by viewers as an "inevitable" event, but that the subsequent ads served to increase viewers' annoyance because they prolonged viewers' need for closure with regard to the story line of the program.

Although the principle of closure provides an explanation which appears to account for the data, the order of presentation of the three commercials used by Soldow and Principe was not varied. Therefore, unique characteristics of the advertisement which always appeared in the first position, or properties of that ad which may have had a unique relationship to the high-involvement programs, cannot be eliminated as possible causes for the differences in audience response as a function of the ordinal position and program context.

The present study sought to determine the potential effects of program context and ordinal position of the advertisement on several measures of advertising effectiveness assessed at two different times. Several researchers have found that even within the same general type of program (e.g., situation comedy, suspense, etc.), different programs may not have the same influence on the effectiveness of the ads appearing within them (Yuspeh, 1979). To avoid such effects due to potential program differences, the present study manipulated context by presenting a series of three advertisements at either a relatively uninvolving or a relatively involving segment of the *same* program. To avoid the potential confounding of ordinal position with a particular advertisement and to lend generalizability across specific advertisements, each of three different advertisements was presented first, second, and third in a sequence of three advertisements. In addition, the present study included both "immediate" and day-after assessment of the advertisements' effectiveness. While most researchers have employed only immediate assessment, day-after assessment has become the standard measure by which marketing professionals evaluate the effectiveness of their advertisements (Haller, 1983).

Hypothesis 1: Drive for closure was expected to influence viewers' *affective reactions* to advertisements. Specifically, since drive for closure should be stronger during highly involving program segments than during less involving program segments, advertisements interrupting a highly involving program segment should be seen as more interfering, should create more annoyance, and should result in less positive attitudes toward the ad and in lower purchase interest in the product advertised than should advertisements interrupting a less involving program segment.

Hypothesis 2: Based on previous results demonstrating interference effects on *recall* of advertisements due to the emotional content of the program, it was expected that advertisements which interrupted highly involving program segments would be recalled less well (on each of several recall measures) than would advertisements which interrupted less involving program segments. In addition, all measures of recall were expected to be influenced by time of assessment such that viewers would show lower recall for day-after compared to immediate assessment.

Hypothesis 3: With regard to the ordinal position of advertisements, while viewers may have become conditioned to accept the inevitability of a "commercial break" (Soldow and Principe, 1981), lengthy commercial breaks which contain several advertisements should increase viewers' experienced need for closure regarding the program story line. Thus, we could expect that within a sequence of advertisements, ads which appear later would be seen as more annoying and as more interfering, and consequently, would be recalled less well and elicit fewer positive reactions (e.g., liking and purchase interest) than would ads which appear earlier.

METHOD

One hundred forty-eight students (84 females and 74 males) enrolled in an undergraduate psychology course at a large eastern university served as subjects in the actual experiment. An additional 48 students participated in the pretesting sessions. The study employed a mixed design, with two between groups variables—involvement (high vs. low) and time of recall (immediate vs. day-after), and one within groups variable—ordinal position of the advertisement (first vs. second vs. third).

To select the stimulus advertisements, twelve different advertisements which had been aired on television in the past two years to advertise a wide range of products relevant to college-age consumers were shown to 29 subjects. For each of these twelve advertisements, subjects indicated their liking [0=not at all, 6=very much] and the importance to them that they purchase a particular brand of the product advertised [0=not at all important, 6=very important]. Based on these responses (means are shown in Table 1), three advertisements were selected for the experiment (GE light bulbs, Hansen's fruit juice, and Aim toothpaste) because they did not differ in likability [F(2,26)=2.06, n.s.] or in brand importance [F(2,26)=2.16, n.s], were moderately likeable (M=2.64), and described products for which particular brands were moderately important (M=2.61).

To define the involvement manipulation, 19 subjects watched a videotaped episode of "Miami Vice" and rated the suspensefulness of the plot [0=boring, 6=very suspenseful] at four different points in the episode. Two of these points of interruption were selected for use in the experiment because they had different levels of suspense [M=3.11 vs. M=0.74, F(1,18)=49.93, p<.0001] and because they were separated by only 2.5 seconds of programming. Both points of interruption (i.e., high- and low-involvement points) were approximately 20 minutes into the "Miami Vice" episode.

Since the three advertisements could be arranged in six possible orders, twelve stimulus tapes were constructed by inserting the selected advertisements into either the low suspense or high suspense points of the "Miami Vice" episode. By employing twelve different tapes, each advertisement appeared an equal number of times in each ordinal position (first, second, or third) and in each sequential position relative to the other two advertisements. To conform to the cover story, the program was extended for approximately 12 minutes beyond the presentation of the three advertisements. Since the points of interruption for the high- and low-involvement conditions were separated by only 2.5 seconds, the "Miami Vice" segments which followed the advertisements were nearly identical in terms of total length and program content, included both suspenseful and non-suspenseful segments, and ended at precisely the same point.

Subjects were run in groups of 8 to 12 at staggered times throughout the day. The experimental room was arranged like a living room and contained couches, chairs, and a television monitor. The cover story informed subjects that as part of a study of "person perception," they would be shown a short program segment and would then be questioned about characters from the program. Each experimental group was then shown one of the twelve stimulus tapes containing the "Miami Vice" episode and the three advertisements. Both *involvement* (high or low) and *order of presentation* (first, second, and third) were manipulated by randomly assigning tapes to experimental sessions, with the restriction

TABLE 1
Ratings of Liking and Brand Importance for Ads Selected

Type of Rating	Hansen's Fruit Juice	GE Light Bulbs	Aim Toothpaste
Liking for Ad	2.24	2.76	2.92
Brand Importance	2.48	2.24	3.12

that each of the six orders had been presented to an equal number of subjects in each involvement condition.

Immediately following the conclusion of the "Miami Vice" episode, subjects attending each session were randomly assigned to one of two *time of assessment* conditions. "Day-after" assessment subjects were given a sealed envelope, told not to open the envelope until the next day (approximately 24 hours later), and dismissed. These envelopes contained the experimental questionnaire together with instructions for completing the questionnaire and returning it (sealed in the envelope provided) within 24 to 36 hours after the experimental session to a central location in the psychology building. Compliance was encouraged by making partial course credit contingent on following these instructions regarding when to open the envelope and how to complete and return the questionnaire. "Immediate" assessment subjects completed the experimental questionnaire once the "day-after" subjects had left the experimental room.

Measures: The experimental questionnaire included items which assessed the effectiveness of the involvement manipulation, subjects' reactions to the "Miami Vice" episode, and several dependent variables. As checks on the involvement manipulation, subjects were asked to indicate their perceived level of suspense at the point when the advertisements interrupted the show (0 to 6) and their experienced annoyance in response to this interruption (0 to 6). Assessment of the "Miami Vice" episode included asking subjects whether or not they had seen the particular episode before (0="no," 1="maybe," and 2="yes") and how much they had enjoyed the episode (0 to 6). The dependent variables included items which assessed (a) the perceived interference (0 to 6) of each advertisement, (b) liking (-3 through 0 to +3) for each advertisement and purchase interest in each product advertised (0 to 6), and (c) unaided recall of product type, brand name, message content and image content for each advertisement (open-ended responses). The open-ended responses for recall of product type and brand name were scored as either correct (0) or as incorrect (1), and the open-ended responses for message and image content were scored as no recall (0), partial recall (1) or total recall (2).

RESULTS

The data were analyzed using 3-way mixed-design ANOVAs which had involvement (high versus low) and time of assessment (immediate versus day-after) as between groups variables, and ordinal position (first, second, third) as the within groups variable. Minimal attrition occurred as a function of the time of assessment. Only 3% of the subjects in the day-after assessment conditions failed to return their completed questionnaires more than 24 hours or less than 36 hours from the initial viewing of the stimulus tape, and these early and late returns were not used in the analyses. Considerably more attrition occurred in responses to the liking and purchase interest questions, both of which offered subjects a "don't know" option. Overall, 44% of the subjects (42% in high involvement conditions and 46% in low involvement conditions) chose this

option, thus accounting for the reduced degrees of freedom reported for analyses on liking and purchase interest ratings.

Manipulation Checks

The only significant effect obtained for subjects' ratings of the level of suspense at the point of interruption was a main effect for involvement [$F(1,144)=15.53$, $p<.001$]. Specifically, subjects in the high-involvement conditions ($M=4.0$) judged the point at which the advertisements interrupted the program to be more interesting or suspenseful than did subjects in the low-involvement conditions ($M=3.6$).

Although 20% of the subjects reported that they "thought" they previously had seen the particular episode of "Miami Vice" used in the present study, this percentage, as well as subjects' ratings of enjoyment ($M=3.5$), remained constant across all experimental conditions. Thus, any effects due to possible previous exposure to the program or to the level of viewer enjoyment of the program were constant across experimental conditions.

Effects Due to Involvement

Affective Reactions: Hypothesis one predicted that viewers' drive for closure would be stronger when the advertisements interrupted a highly involving program segment, and that such advertisements would be seen as more interfering, as more annoying, as less likeable and would result in lower purchase interest compared to the same advertisements when they interrupted less involving program segments. These predictions were partially supported. Subjects felt that the three advertisements did interfere more with their enjoyment of the program [$M=3.1$ vs. $M=2.5$, $F(1,144)=5.42$, $p<.02$] and were marginally more annoying [$M=4.0$ vs. $M=3.6$, $F(1,144)=3.51$, $p<.06$] when the ads appeared during a more suspenseful rather than a less suspenseful point in the program. In addition, subjects experienced more interference with their enjoyment of the program as the advertisements continued (see ordinal position effects reported below). By contrast, subjects' liking for each of the three advertisements [$F(1,80)=1.62$, n.s.] and subjects' purchase interest in the products advertised [$F(1,80)<1$, n.s.] were not influenced by involvement.

Recall: Hypothesis two predicted that advertisements which interrupted highly involving program segments would be recalled less well on each of the several recall measures than would advertisements which had interrupted less involving program segments. Again these predictions were partially supported. Main effects due to involvement for both brand name recall [$F(1,144)=5.32$, $p<.02$] and product type recall [$F(1,144)=2.67$, $p<.1$] indicated that recall was lower for advertisements which interrupted the program episode at a highly involving point rather than at a less involving point, although this effect was marginal for recall of product type (for brand, $M=0.22$ vs. $M=0.34$; for product, $M=0.36$ vs. $M=0.45$). Differences due to involvement were not obtained for recall of the advertisements' message contents or image contents (F's<1.00 on both measures).

TABLE 2
Differences in Recall and Liking Over Time

Time of Assessment	Recall Measures				Affective Measure
	Product Type	Brand Name	Message Content	Image Content	Liking
Immediate	0.52	0.35	1.50	1.70	3.8
Day After	0.29	0.21	1.10	1.10	3.3

TABLE 3
Effects of Ordinal Position on Perceived Interference and Recall

Dependent Variable	Ordinal Position of Advertisement		
	First	Second	Third
Perceived Interference	2.6 b	2.7 b	3.1 a
Recall of Product Type	0.34 a	0.26 ab	0.24 b
Recall of Brand Name	0.47 a	0.39 ab	0.36 b

Note. Within each row, means not sharing the same subscript differ at p<.05 as indicated by specific comparisons.

Time of Assessment

As shown in Table 2, time of assessment had the expected effects on each of the four recall measures. Recall of product type [$F(1,144)=15.98$, $p<.001$], brand name [$F(1,144)=8.40$, $p<.01$], advertisement message [$F(1,144)=7.18$, $p<.01$] and advertisement images [$F(1,144)=8.01$, $p<.01$] were each lower when they were assessed the "day-after" rather than "immediately." In addition, liking for the advertisements was similarly influenced by time of assessment, with day-after assessment (M=3.4) showing significantly less liking [$F(1,80)=5.67$, $p<.01$] than "immediate" assessment (M=3.8). Although the means for purchase interested followed this same pattern (for day-after, M=3.3, for immediate, M=3.61), this difference did not reach statistical significance [$F(1,80)=2.19$, $p<.15$].

Effects of Ordinal Position

Hypothesis three predicted that advertisements which appeared later in a sequence would be seen as more annoying and more interfering, and consequently, would be recalled less well than would advertisements which appeared early in a sequence. The relevant means for which significant ordinal position effects were obtained are presented in Table 3, together with the results of specific comparisons conducted between the means for each dependent variable.

As expected, the perceived interference of the advertisements increased as the advertisements continued to appear [$F(2,288)=8.80$, $p<.001$]. As shown in Table 3, specific comparisons revealed that the third advertisement was seen as interfering significantly more ($p<.05$) with subjects' enjoyment of the program than either of the first two advertisements. Ordinal position did not influence recall of the advertisements' message contents [$F(2,288)=2.09$, $p<.13$] or image contents [$F(2,288)=1.14$, $p<.32$] but did influence recall of both product type [$F(2,288)=2.88$, $p<.06$] and brand name

[$F(2,288)=3.51$, $p<.03$]. Specific comparisons indicated that both product type and brand name were recalled better for the first advertisement shown than for the third advertisement shown. However, these results for brand recall were qualified by a marginally significant involvement by ordinal position interaction [$F(2,288)=2.45$, $p<.09$]. As shown in figure 1, the relative advantage of the first ad over the third ad occurred only under conditions of low involvement.

The results for the purchase interest measure are especially interesting, since two significant interactions involving ordinal position were obtained. First, a significant time of assessment by ordinal position interaction [$F(2,154)=5.20$, $p<.01$] revealed that the time of assessment effect held only for the first advertisement shown (see figure 2). For both the second and third advertisements, time of assessment had no effect on purchase interest. Second, a significant involvement by ordinal position interaction [$F(2,154)=3.18$, $p<.04$] indicated that involvement influenced purchase interest only for the second advertisement shown (see figure 3). Second or middle advertisements which interrupted low involvement program segments produced significantly more purchase interest ($p<.05$) than did (the same) advertisements when they interrupted highly involving program segments.

DISCUSSION

The results of the study suggest that when advertisements interrupt an involving or suspenseful part of a television program, viewers are annoyed and feel advertisements hinder enjoyment of the program more than when advertisements appear at a relatively uneventful point in the story. These reactions, or at least memories of these reactions, persist—when questioned the day after exposure to the ads, viewers remembered that the interruption had been unpleasant, even if they had forgotten the brands or products advertised.

FIGURE 1
The influence of ordinal position and involvement on brand recall

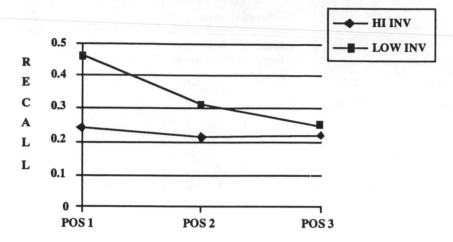

FIGURE 2
The influence of ordinal position and time of assessment on purchase interest

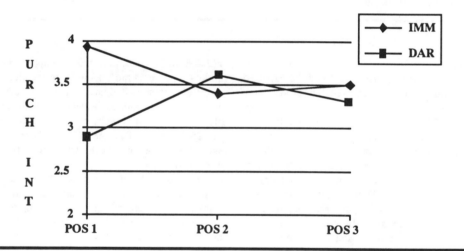

Perhaps more importantly, recall of the advertising message was similarly affected. Regardless of the specific ads used, brands and products advertised at a more involving point in the surrounding program are generally remembered less well than those advertised at a less suspenseful point--a disadvantage which again persists over time (i.e., day-after measures). The "need for closure" explanation proposed by Steiner (1963) would seem to explain this effect. Advertisements inserted at high suspense points create a greater need for closure than do the same advertisements when inserted at low suspense points in the story line. This heightened need for closure could lead to heightened arousal (i.e., feelings of annoyance and interference with enjoyment), which in turn could cause viewers to pay less attention to and thus remember less well the advertisements' messages.

Interestingly, while advertisements inserted at a suspenseful point in the program may "delay" closure, this delay did not affect viewers' overall enjoyment of the program. Viewers claimed to enjoy the program equally, regardless of when the advertisements

appeared. Thus, Isen's (1984) suggestion that differences in recall result from more efficient processing due to increased "positivity" of viewers' emotions does not account for the obtained results.

While the above discussion pertains to differences in an advertisement's effectiveness due to its insertion in the same program at points which differ in their level of suspense, the same could hold true for an advertisement inserted into different programs which differ in their overall level of suspense. Specifically, an advertisement presented during a highly suspenseful program might be *less* effective than the same advertisement presented during a less suspenseful program. To the extent that "suspenseful" programs attract larger audiences, the paradox arises that while advertisements shown during these programs would be seen by more people, viewers are likely to pay less attention to the advertising messages.

The ordinal position of an advertisement within a sequence of advertisements also seems to influence recall of the advertisement's message. Regardless of time of assessment, or the point of program

FIGURE 3
The influence of ordinal position and involvement on purchase interest

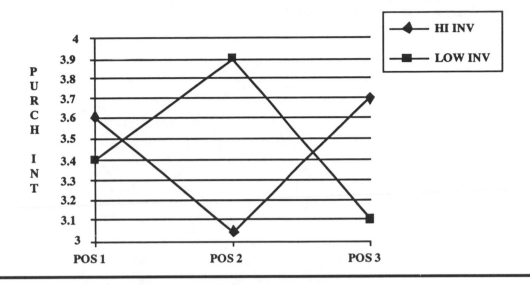

interruption, the first advertisement in a sequence achieved better recall for both product type and brand name than did either of the following ads. In addition to these recall differences, the results of the present study also suggest that ads appearing later in a commercial break may be perceived as "more interfering" with viewers' enjoyment. Again, the need for closure explanation would seem to account for these results. Viewers' need for closure could increase as the advertisements continue to appear and viewers see later ads as more interfering, which could cause viewers to pay less attention to and remember less well the advertising messages presented in ads appearing later in the sequence.

There was some indication that the influence of context may be more robust than the influence of ordinal position. While the context effects obtained on both affective and recall measures held true regardless of an advertisement's ordinal position, ordinal position effects did not generalize across context. For example, the advantage of the first ad over subsequent ads in brand recall disappeared under conditions of high involvement.

It should not be surprising that time of assessment had a substantial influence on viewers' reactions to the advertisements they were shown. Although viewers can recall several features of advertisements shown in sequence when they are asked to do so a short time later (e.g., approximately 20 minutes), their recall of these features, as well as their liking for the ads, is substantially reduced in as little as twenty-four hours. For example, in the present study, day-after recall across all four recall measures (type of product, brand name, message content, and image content) was reduced by an average of nearly 40%. It is not surprising, then, that marketers advocate the use of multiple exposures to reduce this effect, even when this strategy appears to have diminishing returns (Krugman, 1975).

To summarize, the results of the present study show that the effectiveness of an advertisement may be influenced by the point at which it is inserted into a program as well as its ordinal position vis-a-vis other advertisements. The implication of these findings is that decisions regarding the placement of advertising should not be based exclusively on the size and composition of the viewing audience, or on broad program categories. Ironically, the contexts

of the programs which typically attract advertisers may negate the benefits expected from strategic development and purposeful placement of advertising.

REFERENCES

Conard, M. & Lowe, C. (1988). The effectiveness of television advertising: Program context and advertising orientation. Paper presented at the annual convention of the American Psychological Association.

Engel, J.F., Blackwell, R.D., & Miniard, P. (1990). *Consumer Behavior (6th ed.)* Chicago: Drydon Press.

Goldberg, M.E. & Gorn, G.J. (1987). Happy and Sad T.V. Programs: How they affect reactions to commercials. *Journal of Consumer Research, 14*, 387-403.

Haller, T. (1983). *Danger: Marketing Researcher at Work.* Westport, CT: Quorum Books.

Krugman, Herbert E. (1975), What makes advertising effective. *Harvard Business Review*, March-April, 96-103.

Isen, Alice M. (1984). The Influence of Positive Affect on Decision-Making and Cognitive Organization. In T.C. Kinnear (Ed.), *Advances in Consumer Research*, Vol. 11. (pp. 534-537). Provo, UT: Association for Consumer Research.

Kennedy, J.R. (1971). How Program Environment Affects T.V. Commercials. *Journal of Advertising Research*, 11, 33-38.

Pavelchak, M.A., Antil, J.H., & Munch, J.M. (1988). The Super Bowl: An investigation into the relationship among program context, emotional experience, and ad recall. *Journal of Consumer Research*, 15, 360-367.

Schultz, D.E. (1979). Media research users want. *Journal of Advertising Research*, 19, 13-17.

Schumann, D.W. (1986). The influence of program contexts on commercial effectiveness: A review of the literature. Unpublished Manuscript, University of Tennessee College of Business Administration.

Soldow, G.F. & Principe, V. (1981). Response to commercials as a function of program context. *Journal of Advertising Research*, 21(2), 59-64.

Steiner, G.A. (1963). *The People Look at Television.* New
    York: Knopf.
Yuspeh, Sonia (1979). The Medium versus the Message. In
    George Hafter (Ed.), *Proceedings of the 10th National
    Attitude Research Conference*, (pp. 109-138). Chicago, IL:
    American Marketing Association.

Humor Mechanisms, Perceived Humor and Their Relationships to Various Executional Types in Advertising

Hyongoh Cho, University of Texas at Austin

ABSTRACT

This study investigates mechanisms underlying the formation of perceived humor in print ads and the relative effectiveness of various executional types in producing humor. Contemporary theories of humor are incorporated into an analysis of three humor mechanisms: cognitive, affective, and disparagement mechanisms. The cognitive mechanism is found to be the major determinant of perceived humor, whereas the other mechanisms have either minimal or negative impact on perceived humor.

A further analysis indicates that types of execution intended to produce humor may be grouped into six major categories, each of which tends to be a function of more than one humor mechanism. "Subtle complexity" is the most effective humorous device, followed by "slice-of-life." The most effective executional types are not necessarily those which are widely utilized by advertising practitioners.

Recent surveys estimate that 24 percent of TV commercials and 31 percent of radio commercials employ some form of humor (Weinberger and Campbell 1990). As a pleasant appeal widely used to enhance communication effect, humor is said to improve attitude toward the ad, attention and recall of simple messages, while its effect on persuasion tends to be complicated due to many moderating factors (Weinberger and Gulas 1992). While extensive research has investigated the *effect* of humorous executions on the communication outcomes, relatively little attention has been given to the analysis of the possible humor mechanisms and their relationship with various executional types utilized to elicit humor (Alden and Hoyer 1993; Speck 1991). An investigation into these issues may be particularly helpful to advertising practitioners who may then rely on theoretical guidelines rather than intuition or inspiration to design a humorous appeal. Toward this end, this study addresses three major issues: (1) the possible mechanisms underlying the formation of perceived humor in an advertising context; (2) the relationship between humor mechanisms and various executional types; and (3) the relative effectiveness of each executional type in generating humor. Here, mechanisms of perceived humor refer to the determinants of humor processing. Executional types simply describe various groups of executional elements purported to elicit humor. While a person may recognize the humorous intention behind various executional features in an ad (e.g., slapstick, ludicrousness, or play on words), mere recognition of such stimuli does not necessarily make one laugh. Perceived humor indicates one's humorous experience or appreciation of humor based on the evaluations of the executional features.

MECHANISMS OF PERCEIVED HUMOR

A review of contemporary humor theories indicates that these theories may be broadly categorized into three groups: cognitive, affective, and social/interpersonal approaches (Keith-Spiegel 1972; McGhee 1974; Speck 1991; Wicker et al. 1981; Wyer and Collins 1992). First, the cognitive approach emphasizes cognitive capacities and incongruity of events as main elements of perceived humor. Theories in this approach include incongruity (Nerhardt 1976), surprise (Descarte 1649, cited in Keith-Spiegel 1972), cognitive mastery (McGhee 1974), and incongruity-resolution theories (Suls 1972). While variants of incongruity theories (i.e., incongruity theory and surprise theory) emphasize the elements of unexpected-

ness, lack of consistency, and cognitive dissonance as a sufficient condition to produce humor, more complex cognitive theories (i.e., cognitive mastery theory and incongruity-resolution theory) suggest that individuals who recognize the perceptual incongruity of the incoming stimuli need to assimilate the discrepant events and resolve the incongruous parts in order to perceive them as humorous. According to the cognitive approach, the successful design of a humorous appeal needs to be based on an understanding of (1) the mental schema of the target audience; (2) consumers' problem-solving modes; and (3) fantasy-reality distinction. A humorous stimulus too discrepant with consumers' mental representations of reality may be difficult to be resolved, whereas a stimulus with little incongruity may not motivate consumers to engage in resolution of the incongruous parts. People may also engage in a form of problem solving using cognitive rules to reconcile incongruent stimulus with their mental schema (Suls 1972). Finally, expectancy violations may be perceived as being funny only when individuals have the capacity to distinguish between reality and fantasy (McGhee 1974). In this regard, a "play" cue (i.e., a cue signifying that the situation is not real and is to be taken playfully) may help the fluent transition from the problem-solving mode to perceptions of humorousness. Without a play cue, incongruity would lead to curiosity or puzzlement, and surprise may easily transform itself into fear or anxiety.

Second, the affective approach focuses on physiological arousal and thematic content (e.g., sex, aggression, and freedom) as the determinant of perceived humor. Theories in this approach include tension-release (Eastman 1936), arousal (Berlyne 1969), psychodynamic (Freud 1905/1960), and freedom theories (Mindess 1971). Tension-release and arousal theories mainly examine the physiological characteristics of humor by suggesting that the drive to regain homeostasis or an optimal arousal level is the driving force of humor. On the other hand, the psychodynamic theory suggests that humor enables people to disguise sexual drives or aggressiveness and thus escape briefly from strict regulation of affective expressions by social norms. Similarly, freedom theory indicates that humor occurs as a form of emotional release triggered by the sense of freedom through which we depart from the uniformity of social standards (Mindess 1971). In conjunction, advertisers may need to associate humor with subtle sexual themes and/or a sense of freedom in order to facilitate emotional release through a suitable form of humor. Also, a careful examination of the arousal level associated with perceived humor may allow practitioners to properly use either arousal-raising components (e.g., surprise, puzzlement), or arousal-relieving components (e.g., play cue, pleasant mood). When the program context or ad sequence creates a high arousal level such as excitement, fear and anger, a humorous message with arousal-relieving elements may be particularly effective because it reduces the tension level which is already high enough to produce an aversive reaction otherwise. On the other hand, a program context with a less emotional topic may need to be followed by a humorous ad with arousal-raising components to build up an optimal range of tension level.

Finally, the social/interpersonal approach attempts to explain humor in terms of social and interpersonal contexts within which humor is situated. Theories in this tradition include superiority (LaFave 1972), disparagement (Cantor and Zillmann 1973), and disposition theories (Zillmann et al. 1974). Central to superiority theory is a biased comparison of oneself with others so as to gratify ego-defensive needs. Similarly, disparagement theory contends that humor is a socially justified form of hostility and aggressiveness projected onto other individuals or groups without feelings of guilt. On the other hand, disposition theory takes a contingency approach by introducing the elements of group intimacy and its shared values as underlying dimensions of perceived humor. This theory suggests that perceived humor is an outcome of the interaction between the amount of disparagement and the strength of one's identification with the disparaged character. In the advertising context, the social/interpersonal approach would suggest that advertisers pay particular attention to values shared among the target audience and sublimated themes in their culture.

CHARACTERISTICS OF EXECUTIONAL TYPES

While there are numerous ways to describe executional features in an ad, this study limits the scope of executional types only to those widely utilized to produce humor. Humorous executional types have been classified by various criteria such as subject matter, form, motive type, and audience characteristics (Cattell and Luborsky 1947; Eysenck 1942; Fowler 1926). With many typologies proposed in previous humor studies, there have been recurrent themes. These themes include light-hearted mood, fantasy, word play, visual absurdity, nonsensical jokes, sarcasm, retaliative joke, and ludicrousness. While much theoretical work has been done on *humor mechanisms*, and many studies have examined various *executional types* pertaining to humor, few studies have attempted to explain how different humor mechanisms relate to uses of various executional types. It is unlikely that such a wide scope of executional features is explained by a single humor mechanism. For example, word play, visual absurdity and nonsensical jokes may activate cognitive processing by presenting logical paradoxes and perceptual incongruity. Sarcasm, ludicrousness, and retaliative jokes may facilitate negative social/interpersonal humor processing by eliciting feelings of superiority and disparagement. On the other hand, light-heartedness, fantasy, and sexual themes may constitute the primary components in the affective theories. By examining the relationship between various executional types and humor processing mechanisms, a more comprehensive understanding of how consumers process various executional types prior to humor appreciation may be acquired. This study reports an experiment conducted to assess the relationship among humor mechanisms, perceived humor and various executional types.

METHOD

One hundred and eleven student subjects were recruited from undergraduate courses at a large Southwestern university and given course credit for participation. Subjects were shown 27 full-size print advertisements that had been chosen to appear in "The One Show. Advertising's Best Print, Radio, TV"-an annual selection of the most creative ads in the United States- between 1981 and 1990. To select the stimuli for this experiment, three expert judges were asked separately to choose print ads in which the messages or visuals clearly showed the advertiser's humorous intention. By focusing on the presence of the humorous intention in an ad rather than on one's own perceived humor, a potential individual bias in the selection process was expected to be minimized (Madden and Weinberger 1982). From the print ads which were classified as having obvious humorous intention by all three judges, 27 ads covering various consumer and service goods were chosen for use in the study. The 27 print ads were transformed into slides and whenever necessary, an enlarged version of the body copy was also shown on the screen. Each subject viewed a different set of three

print ads in a small group of 11 to 15 subjects. After viewing each slide, subjects were asked to respond to questions measuring humor mechanisms, executional types, and perceived humor for each of the test ads. The subjects were then debriefed, and dismissed.

Measures

Mechanisms of Perceived Humor: An attempt was made to identify various theories underlying perceived humor. Because the tenets of each humor theory may not be easily reduced into single-sentence statements, a certain extent of conceptual transformation was inevitable in the scale development. The resulting 12 scales were intended to measure each of the cognitive, affective, and social/interpersonal theories. Five scales were directly borrowed from the study by Wicker et al. (1981). To conserve space, the scales are reported in Table 1. Subjects were asked to evaluate how closely each scale reflected their feelings on a 7-point scale anchored by "not at all" and "extremely."

Executional Types: Thirty-two scales were derived from studies that identified various techniques purported to produce humor (Andrews 1943; Cattell and Luborsky 1947; Eysenck 1942; Fowler 1926; Hassett and Houlihan 1979; Herzog and Larwin 1988; Kelly and Solomon 1975; Speck 1991). The scales reflect popular themes, situational components, personality factors, portrayals of action, complexity of verbal and visual elements, and social values (see Table 3). Subjects were asked to indicate the extent to which they agreed with each scale describing the ad on a 7-point scale anchored by "strongly disagree" and "strongly agree."

Perceived Humor: Perceived humor was measured by three 7-point semantic differential scales consisting of funny/not funny, humorous/not humorous, and amusing/not amusing (coefficient alpha=.96).

DATA ANALYSIS

Mechanisms of Perceived Humor

An exploratory factor analysis of the humor mechanisms revealed three principal components with an eigenvalue greater than 1.0, accounting for 55 percent of the variance in the mechanism scores. Loadings on the resulting dimensions using varimax-rotation appear in Table 1.

The dimensional structure of the humor mechanisms is fairly consistent with the three humor approaches previously discussed. The first dimension consists of novelty of ideas, surprise triggered by unexpectedness, resolution of incongruity, and sudden insight into the whole configuration. This dimension reflects a wide scope of incongruity and resolution theories and is referred to as the cognitive mechanism. The second dimension consists of tension-release, physiological arousal, fantasy, feelings of freedom, and sympathy. It is referred to as the affective mechanism because of the physiological and emotional elements commonly shared in this dimension. The scale of "sympathy" was initially conceived as a positive social/interpersonal context (i.e., disposition theory), but it loaded mainly on the affective dimension. This leaves the negative social/interpersonal scales as a separate, distinct dimension. The dimension of negative contexts is referred to as the disparagement mechanism. This dimension is characterized by hostility toward the disparaged characters or objects, superiority, and conflicting feelings. Interestingly, conflicting feelings or ambivalence were also rated as an indicant of the disparagement dimension. Conflicting feelings may be caused by the simultaneous experience of feeling superior and guilty against the disparaged in the ad. The coefficient alphas are .73 for the cognitive mechanism, .74 for the affective mechanism, and .61 for the disparagement mechanism.

TABLE 1
Loadings of Humor Mechanism Scales on Varimax-Rotated Principal Components

Humor Mechanism Scales	Cognitive	Affective	Disparagement
The ad was original and novel.	.75		
I was surprised by the punch line or some part of the ad.	.82		
When over surprise, the unexpected concept or situation in the ad made sense to me.	.69		
Parts of the ad initially perceived as unrelated suddenly fell into place.	.57		
Viewing the ad made me feel free, or 'above it all'.		.74	
I felt stimulated while viewing the ad.		.76	
Viewing the ad made me feel emotionally released.		.77	
The ad stimulated my imagery, fantasy, or daydreaming.		.70	
I felt sympathy or identification with a character or an object in the ad		.42	
I felt hostile toward a character or an object while viewing the ad.			.80
I felt superior to a character or an object in the ad.			.66
I experienced incompatible emotions or conflicting feelings at the same time.			.77

(N=311) After deleting 22 incomplete observations, 311 observations were used for the factor analysis by combining between subjects and within subjects variance.

The Relationship Between Humor Mechanisms and Perceived Humor

An initial regression analysis was conducted to examine the relationship between the three humor mechanisms and perceived humor. A total of 43 percent of the variance in perceived humor was explained by the three mechanisms (see Table 2). The additional impact of each mechanism on perceived humor was further examined by comparing a "full model" (containing all three mechanisms as determinants of perceived humor) with a "reduced model" (containing only two mechanisms as determinants of perceived humor). Each of the three mechanisms explained significant incremental variance of perceived humor beyond the other two mechanisms, with the cognitive mechanism accounting for the largest improvement in the variance of perceived humor (ΔR^2 =.15, p< .05), followed by the disparagement (ΔR^2 =.07, p< .05) and affective mechanisms (ΔR^2 =.04, p< .05). As a further step, a LISREL analysis (Jöreskog and Sörbom 1986) with maximum likelihood method was conducted. The structural model was based on the variance/covariance matrices with the measurement model. The model provides an acceptable "fit" to the data in terms of chi square value (X^2=70.4, p=.86) and goodness-of-fit index (GFI=.93). The resulting structural coefficients are consistent with the preceding regression analyses. Both the cognitive and disparagement mechanisms have substantial impact on perceived humor, whereas the effect of the affective mechanism is only marginal. Contrary to variants of disparagement theory, the effect of the disparagement dimension on perceived humor is strongly negative.

Characteristics of Executional Types

A principal components analysis was conducted to assess the structure of executional types in the print ads. The analysis produced nine distinct dimensions with eigenvalues greater than 1.0, far too many to use in the present analysis. A further analysis of the scree test indicated an "elbow" at the sixth dimension with diminishing returns. Accordingly, six principal components were retained, accounting for 52 percent of the variance in the scores of executional types. Loadings on the resulting varimax-rotated dimensions appear in Table 3. Twenty-four of 32 scales, or 75 percent of the scales, have primary loadings of greater than 0.45 on one of the six dimensions. Based on exploratory analysis of the individual items, these components are referred to as negativity (alpha=.77), slice-of-life (alpha=.76), ludicrousness (alpha=.72), subtle complexity (alpha=.71), perceptual interest (alpha=.71), and miniaturization (alpha=.52).

The scales for "negativity" consist of cynicism about morals, pessimistic attitudes, exchanges of retaliative jokes, and sarcasm. Exaggeration and underestimation are also perceived to represent negative sentiments, probably because distortion of reality often underlies depreciation or disparagement of the external reality and social norms. "Slice-of-life" involves ordinary people struggling with everyday predicaments, management of uncomfortable situations, and middle-class values. "Ludicrousness" indicates either adults behaving in an undignified, immature fashion, or people doing silly things. "Miniaturization" portrays children or animals struggling to get through seemingly complicated situations; it appeals to individual desire to regress into a childlike state or to empathize with those who are relatively powerless. "Subtle complexity" is characterized by various levels of complexity, metaphor, indirect situation, and tricky allusions in the message delivery. This type of execution tends to be subtle, inoffensive and sophisticated. "Perceptual interest" consists of contrast between verbal and visual elements, visual puns, and perceptual displacement.

The Relationship Between Humor Mechanisms and Executional Types

Several multiple regression analyses were conducted to examine the mechanisms underlying each type of execution. The results show that a majority of the executional types are determined by a

TABLE 2
Parameter Estimates for the Relationship between Humor Mechanisms and Perceived Humor

Regression Model	Predictors			R^2 (adj)	ΔR	F-change
	Cognitive	Affective	Disparage			
1	—a	.41*	-.32*	.27	.15*	29.0
					(model 4 over 1)	
2	.54*	—	-.26*	.39	.04*	6.8
					(model 4 over 2)	
3	.48*	.20*	—	.36	.07*	13.4
					(model 4 over 3)	
4	.44*	.21*	-.27*	.43		

LISREL Modeling	Path Coefficient
Cognitive→Humor	.56*
Affective→Humor	.07
Disparagement→Humor	-.30*
chi-square score	70.36
d.f.	84
GFI	.93
AGFI	.89
p=	.86

a — indicates that the predictor is excluded in the regression model.
* Significant at alpha < .05. (N=111: based on between subjects variance)

combination of the cognitive, disparagement and affective mechanisms (see Table 4). "Negativity" is primarily determined by the disparagement mechanism combined with the cognitive and affective mechanisms. Elements of ridicule and attack may characterize disparagement processing, whereas incongruity-resolution processing is stimulated by repetition, exaggeration, and irony (Speck 1991). "Ludicrousness" is exclusively determined by the disparagement mechanism. "Slice-of-life" is determined mainly by the affective mechanism augmented by the disparagement mechanism. Comically dramatized ordinary life may permit the audience an alternative point of view on daily episodes and bring them a momentary experience of freedom and emotional release. Similarly, "miniaturization" is affected by both affective and disparagement mechanisms. The audience may be tempted to mock at the ineptitude and gullibility of children and animals, and at the same time experience imaginary stimulation and sympathetic responses toward them. "Subtle complexity" is determined mainly by the cognitive mechanism augmented by the affective mechanism. It appears that intellectual stimulation and cognitive elaboration are often required in processing relatively complex form of humorous stimulus. "Perceptual interest" was initially expected to be affected by the cognitive mechanism. To our perplexity, it is strongly related to the disparagement and affective mechanisms. Confronting deformity of their perceptual worlds, audiences may defend their views of reality by projecting hostility or contempt toward the object instead of engaging in cognitive elaboration to reduce the perceptual incongruity. Nevertheless, the variance of perceptual interest explained by these mechanisms is only marginal, indicating that this type of appeal may not be well explained by the traditionally known humor mechanisms.

The Relationship Between Executional Types and Perceived Humor

As a further step, a partial correlation analysis was conducted to examine the relationship between executional types and per-

ceived humor. The results show that subtle complexity is most strongly related to perceived humor, followed by slice-of-life and perceptual interest (see Table 5). Negativity was initially found to have no significant relationship with perceived humor. After partialling out the impact of slice-of-life and subtle complexity on both negativity and perceived humor, negativity was significantly related to perceived humor. Ludicrousness and miniaturization are not significantly related to perceived humor. A close analysis indicates that certain executional types have complex interrelationships. For example, the relationship between negativity and perceived humor appears to be mediated by slice-of-life and subtle complexity. Similarly, subtle complexity tends to mediate the relationship between slice-of-life and perceived humor, but not vice versa, indicating that the effects of the affective mechanism on perceived humor may be mediated by the cognitive mechanism.

DISCUSSION

The investigation of the relationship between humor mechanisms and perceived humor indicates that perceived humor is mainly determined by the cognitive mechanism, while the effects of other mechanisms are either negative or minimal. Similarly, Alden et al. (1993) found that a majority of humorous advertising in various cultures contained incongruent cognitive structures, indicating that ads with incongruity-resolution principles may have the ability to generate humor in diverse cultures. Despite its marginal effect, the affective mechanism may underlie a major dimension of perceived humor through the mediation of the cognitive processing mechanism. Wicker et al. (1981) found that affective variables (e.g., anxiety, sympathy, emotional involvement) were a significant indicant of funniness to the extent that they induced incongruent responses to the messages. Contrary to the expectations of the disparagement theory, consumers' negative associations with the characters or objects in social/cultural context tend to be detrimental to the generation of humor. Consumers may recognize the humorous intention of the advertisers, but the nega-

TABLE 3

Loadings of Executional Type Scales on Varimax-Rotated Principal Components

Executional Type Scales	Highest Loadings
("Negativity" Dimension)	
Cynical about human progress or morals	.59
Retaliation in a trade-of-insult jokes	.47
Pessimistic attitude as opposed to optimism	.63
Exaggerated situations	.59
Representing something as less than is the case	.57
Sarcasm used to expose vice or folly	.70
("Slice-of-life" Dimension)	
Ordinary folk tries to overcome an everyday problem.	.77
Personal competence and ability to handle an uncomfortable situation	.65
Slice-of-life	.72
Predicament of the characters	.57
Empathy toward middle-class values	.56
("Ludicrousness" Dimension)	
Foolish adults behaving in an undignified or immature fashion	.79
People dressed up funny or doing silly things	.72
Something ludicrous	.62
("Subtle Complexity" Dimension)	
Subtle and sophisticated humorous mood	.76
Featuring complexity, metaphor or indirect situation	.51
Subtle humor with an element of the intellectual, tricky allusions	.76
Relatively complex, inoffensive form of humor .74	
("Perceptual Interest" Dimension)	
Verbal emphasis as opposed to visual imagery	- .81
Perceptual displacement or visual puns	.65
Emphasis on pictorial as opposed to verbal elements	.84
("Miniaturization" Dimension)	
Children or animal struggling to get through wordy and complicated copy	.66
Animation, imaginary creature or little people	.63
Individual desire to regress to a child-like state	.69

(N=311)

TABLE 4

The Effect of Humor Mechanisms on Executional types

Dependent Variables	Standardized coefficients			Adj R^2
	Cognitive	Affective	Disparagement	
Negativity	.14*	.13*	.48*	.25
Slice-of-life	.04	.41*	.16*	.19
Ludicrousness	.05	.03	.50*	.24
Subtle Complexity	.28*	.27*	-.05	.22
Perceptual Interest	.02	.13*	.14*	.03
Miniaturization	.01	.25*	.25*	.11

* Significant at alpha < .05. (N=111)

TABLE 5
Partial Correlation of Executional types with Perceived Humor

Execution Types	Partialling Out							
	Zero	Neg	SL	SC	Lud	PI	Min	All
Negativity (Neg)	.02	—	-.11	-.11	.03	.01	-.01	-.17*
Slice-of-life (SL)	.21*	.23*	—	.10	.22*	.21*	.20*	.21*
Subtle Complexity (SC)	.38*	.39*	.34*	—	.38*	.39	.37*	.37*
Ludicrousness (Lud)	-.03	-.03	-.08	.01	—	-.05	-.05	-.03
Perceptual Interest (PI)	.13*	.14*	.14*	.17*	.15*	—	.13*	.13*
Miniaturization (Min)	.07*	.08	.04	.03	.10	.06	—	.07

* Significant at alpha < .05. (N=111)

tive feelings or thoughts produced by the disparagement techniques may derail advertisers' humor intention and lead to indiscriminate antipathy toward both the endorser and the disparaged. Research indicates that extreme forms of disparagement hamper the resolution of the incongruity and produce an unexpected negative reaction from individuals because they may consider such brutal assaults as going beyond justifiable and legitimate levels (Wicker et al. 1980; Zillmann et al. 1974).

Consistent with the humor mechanisms, subjects are found to be most responsive to the executional components driven by the cognitive mechanism (i.e., subtle complexity), followed by those determined by the affective mechanism (i.e., slice-of-life). On the other hand, executional types driven by the disparagement mechanism (i.e., negativity, ludicrousness) show either an aversive or nonsignificant relationship with perceived humor. Considering that ludicrous humor is most frequently employed in the U.S and U.K, followed by satirical humor (Weinberger and Spotts 1989), the most effective executional types may not necessarily coincide with those widely utilized by advertising practitioners. These findings collectively suggest that advertising practitioners utilize the cognitive characteristics of a humorous scheme such as subtle complexity, metaphor and tricky allusions in the development of a humorous ad. The employment of a disparagement technique such as ludicrousness, satire, and retaliative jokes may be somewhat risky because of its tendency to induce negative reactions to the characters in the ad without much discrimination. These findings, however, should be taken with caution. A humorous ad often activates multiple processing mechanisms, complicating the understanding of the true force underlying consumers' ad processing. For example, a mild form of negativity may facilitate both disparagement and cognitive processing because consumers often perceive the public expression of the negative themes as incongruent from the regularities of social relationships. This form of humor may be effective as far as the positive reactions induced by the cognitive processing is strong enough to offset the negative effects of the disparagement processing.

Several limitations of the study undermine the generality of the findings. First, only print ads were included in the test, leaving other media unexamined. The configuration of executional types may vary across different media because media and audience factors may enable certain executional types to be more accessible and easier to execute. Second, only college students were recruited for the experiment. This sampling bias may have contributed to the salience of the cognitive mechanism as the explanation of humor appreciation because individuals show a wide range of intellectual

capacity which is central to the pursuit of cognitive humor processing. Third, the formal group environment with the instructor present may have sensitized subjects to the aspects of social desirability, biasing the subjects' evaluations against a socially discouraged form of humor. In an intimate group environment, subjects may feel securer and even encouraged to express a socially unacceptable form of humorous reactions. These factors merit further consideration when investigating the causal structure of perceived humor and the relative effectiveness of different executional types on attitudinal and behavioral consequences.

REFERENCES

Alden, Dana L. and Wayne D. Hoyer (1993), "An Examination of Cognitive Factors Related to Humorousness in Television Advertising," *Journal of Advertising*, 22 (2), June, 29-37.

_____, Wayne D. Hoyer, and Chol Lee (1993), "Identifying Global and Culture-Specific Dimensions of Humor in Advertising: A Multinational Analysis," *Journal of Marketing*, 57 (2), 64-75.

Andrews, T. Gaylord (1943), "A Factorial Analysis of Responses to the Comic as a Study of Personality," *Journal of General Psychology*, 28 (April), 209-224.

Berlyne, Daniel E. (1969), "Laughter, Humor, and Play," *Handbook of Social Psychology*, 3, 795-852.

Cantor, J.R. and Zillmann, D. (1973), "Resentment toward Victimized Protagonists and Severity of Misfortunes They Suffer as Factors in Humor Appreciation," *Journal of Experimental Research in Personality*, 6, 321-329.

Cattell, Raymond B. and Lester B. Luborsky (1947), "Personality Factors in Response to Humor," *Journal of Abnormal and Social Psychology*, 42 (4), October, 402-421.

Eastman, M. (1936), *Enjoyment of Laughter*. New York: Simon and Schuster.

Eysenck, H.J (1942), "The Appreciation of Humor: An Experimental and Theoretical Study," *British Journal of Psychology*, 32, 295-309.

Fowler, H.W. (1926), *A Dictionary of Modern English Usage*. London and New York: Oxford Univ. Press.

Freud. S. (1960), *Jokes and Their Relation to the Unconscious*. New York: Norton (First German ed., 1905).

Hassett, James and John Houlihan (1979), "Different Jokes for Different Folks," *Psychology Today*, January, 64-71.

Herzog, Thomas R. and David A. Larwin (1988), "The Appreciation of Humor in Captioned Cartoons," *The Journal of Psychology*, 122 (6), 597-607.

Jöreskog, Karl G. and Dag Sörbom (1986), *LISREL VI: Analysis of Linear Structural Relationships by the Method of Maximum Likelihood.* Mooresville, IN: Scientific Software, Inc.

Keith-Spiegel, Patricia (1972), "Early Conceptions of Humor: Varieties and Issues," in J.H Goldstein & P.E McGhee (Eds.), *Psychology of Humor*, New York: Academic Press, 3-39.

Kelly, Patrick J. and Paul J. Solomon (1975), "Humor in Television Advertising," *Journal of Advertising,* 4 (3), September, 31-35.

La Fave, L. (1972), "Humor Judgments as a Function of Reference Group and Identification Classes," In J.H. Goldstein & P.E. McGhee (Eds.), *Psychology of Humor.* New York: Academic Press.

Madden, Thomas J. and Marc G. Weinberger (1982), "The Effects of Humor on Attention in Magazine Advertising," *Journal of Advertising,* 11 (3), September, 8-14.

McGhee, Paul E. (1974), "Cognitive Mastery and Children's Humor," *Psychological Bulletin,* 81 (10), 721-730.

Mindess, H. (1971), *Laughter and Liberation.* Los Angeles: Nash.

Nerhardt, G. (1976), "Incongruity and Funniness: Towards a New Descriptive Model," A.J. Chapman & H. C. Foot (Eds.), *Humour and Laughter: Theory, Research, and Application;* London: Wiley, 55-62.

Speck, Paul (1991), "The Humorous Message Taxonomy: A Framework for the Study of Humorous Ads," in *Current Issues and Research in Advertising,* 13, 1-44.

Suls, Jerry M. (1972), "A Two-Stage Model for the Appreciation of Jokes and Cartoons: An Information-Processing Analysis," *The Psychology of Humor: Theoretical Perspectives and Empirical Issues.* J. H. Goldstein and P.E. McGhee, eds. New York: Academic Press, 81-100.

Weinberger, Marc G. and Leland Campbell (1991), "The Use and Impact of Humor in Radio Advertising," *Journal of Advertising Research,* 31 (December), 44-52.

_____and Charles S. Gulas (1992), "The Impact of Humor in Advertising: A Review," *Journal of Advertising,* 21 (4), December, 35-60.

_____and Harlan E. Spotts (1989), "Humor in U.S. versus U.K. TV Commercials: A Comparison," *Journal of Advertising,* 18 (2), June, 39-44.

Wicker, Frank W., William L. Barron III, and Amy C. Willis (1980), "Disparagement Humor: Dispositions and Resolutions," *Journal of Personality and Social Psychology,* 39 (4), 701-709.

_____, Irene M. Thorelli, William L. Barron, III, and Marguerite R. Ponder (1981), "Relationship among Affective and Cognitive Factors in Humor," *Journal of Research in Personality,* 15, 359-370.

Wyer, Robert S. and James E. Collins (1992), "A Theory of Humor Elicitation," *Psychological Review,* 99 (4), 663-688.

Zillmann, D., J. Bryant, and J. R. Cantor, (1974), "Brutality of Assault in Political Cartoons Affecting Humor Appreciation," *Journal of Research in Personality.,* 7, 334-356.

Assessing the Impact of Message Cues and Arguments in Persuasion: Conceptual and Methodological Issues

Charles S. Areni, Texas Tech University

K. Chris Cox, Nicholls State University

ABSTRACT

Postulates of the Elaboration Likelihood Model (ELM), the Heuristic–Systematic Model (HSM), and related models of persuasion in the marketing literature are compared and contrasted. Several recommendations are offered regarding directions for future research efforts. In general, these suggestions fall into the following categories: (1) propositions for future research efforts, (2) recommendations to enhance the quality of the tests of various aspects of the ELM and HSM, and (3) suggestions regarding more complete and practical conceptualizations of key constructs in each model.

Petty and Cacioppo's (1981a, 1986a) elaboration likelihood model (ELM) and Chaiken's (1980, Eagly & Chaiken, 1993) heuristic–systematic model (HSM) of persuasion have become quite influential in the marketing literature, due largely to their implications regarding the persuasive impact of various message elements commonly employed in advertising (cf. Petty, Cacioppo, & Schumann, 1983; MacKenzie, Lutz, & Belch, 1986; Munch & Swasy, 1988; Miniard et al. 1991).

Although the ELM and HSM initially posited relatively simple and distinct persuasive effects for the arguments and cues in a communication, as empirical research accumulated, the proposed relationships increased in complexity. Adding to this intricacy was the discovery that the impact of a given communication variable depended upon: (1) the mode in which it was presented (Chaiken & Eagly, 1983), (2) its *salience* within the communication (Pallak, 1983), (3) the *symbolic form* in which it was presented (Yalch & Elmore–Yalch, 1984), and most importantly, (4) the *manner* in which it was processed (Petty & Cacioppo, 1981b; Miniard et al. 1991). Finally, streams of research have emerged in the marketing literature that suggest even more complexity in the relationships among visually and verbally presented elements (MacKenzie & Spreng, 1992; Miniard, Bhatla, & Rose, 1990).

Despite these conceptual advances, however, the basic method of examining the ELM and HSM has evolved much more slowly. The diagnosticity of tests of the more intricate relationships in the model has been questioned (Stiff & Boster, 1987; Allen & Reynolds, 1993; Mongeau & Stiff, 1993). The following discussion addresses a number of conceptual and methodological issues relating to theories of persuasion in general, and the ELM and the HSM in particular. The issues discussed can be categorized as: (1) propositions for future research efforts,(2) recommendations to enhance the quality of the tests of various aspects of the ELM and HSM, and (3) suggestions regarding more complete and practical conceptualizations of key constructs in each model.

ARGUMENT-VERSUS CUE-BASED PERSUASION

Although numerous communication variables have been examined within the ELM, the HSM, and related streams of persuasion research, researchers have continually drawn the distinction between those that *comprise the fundamental message* and those that *create a setting for the message* (Chaiken, 1987; Petty & Cacioppo, 1986; Lutz, 1985). In the ELM, the former are termed *central arguments* and the latter *peripheral cues*, whereas in the HSM they are referred to as *persuasive arguments* and *heuristic cues*, respectively. For purposes of simplicity and clarity, we adopt

the term *argument* to refer to a communication element that constitutes part of the fundamental message, and *cues* to refer to a communication element that creates a setting for the message.[1]

Both the ELM and the HSM focus on the *amount of thought* the audience devotes to a communication as a primary moderator of the extent to which cues or arguments produce the strongest direct attitudinal effects. Specifically, they imply that when the amount of thought the audience devotes to the communication is high, consideration of *arguments* drives persuasion, via the central route and systematic processing, respectively. On the other hand, attitude shifts are directed by the consideration of *cues* when the amount of thought devoted to the communication is lower. In a typical test of this basic proposition, the valence of various communication elements and the amount of thought the audience devotes to the communication are manipulated. Those components that produce stronger attitudinal effects when an audience devotes little thought to the communication are termed peripheral or heuristic cues, whereas those that produce more pronounced effects when the audience devotes a great deal of thought to the communication are referred to as central or persuasive arguments.

HIERARCHICAL VERSUS ADDITIVE PERSUASION PROCESSES

The results of such tests imply a *hierarchical* relationship wherein the persuasive impact of cues are eclipsed by argument–based persuasion when the audience devotes more thought to the communication. Importantly, however, there are some differences in the status of the hierarchical persuasion postulate in the ELM, the HSM, and other theories of persuasion. For purposes of clarity, we will discuss these differences in terms of an equation introduced by MacKenzie and Spreng (1992). Their equation, however, is modified to reflect the terminology used in this discussion. As discussed above, the ELM and HSM imply:

$$\text{(EQ 1)} \qquad \text{Attitude} = \beta_0 + \beta_1 \text{ARG} + \beta_2 \text{CUE} + \in$$

where ARG is argument–related thought and CUE is cue–related thought. The hierarchical persuasion postulate implies that when the audience devotes a great amount of thought to a persuasive communication, the product $\beta_2 \text{CUE}$ approaches zero. However, some researchers have suggested that the ELM is unclear as to whether the coefficient, β_2, the variable, CUE, or both converge to zero (Stiff, 1986; Stiff & Boster, 1987). In other words, when an audience devotes a great deal of thought to a persuasive communication, does the *processing* of cues diminish (CUE $\Rightarrow$ 0), are *cues discounted* when the attitude is formed or changed ($\beta_2 \Rightarrow 0$), or, do *both* occur?

Due to this ostensible ambiguity, Stiff (1986) advanced Kahnemann's (1973) elastic capacity model (ECM) as an alternative to the ELM. He suggested that, unlike the ELM, the ECM

---

[1]It should be emphasized that the terms cue and argument do not refer to an element of the communication per se, but rather, to the audience member's *interpretation* of that communication element.

suggests that CUE approaches zero when an audience allocates a great deal of thought, or cognitive capacity, to a persuasive communication. Though this interpretation of the ECM offers some interesting possibilities, it is important to note that the model was intended to account for *attention* and *encoding* processes, not *persuasion* processes. There is some question as to whether it can be adapted to the latter context (Petty et al. 1987).

The ELM does not preclude that the *encoding* of message cues and arguments can coincide (Petty et al. 1987), despite Stiff's claims that it takes a single–channel, "either–or" approach to information processing. Rather, the ELM posits that when an audience allocates a great deal of thought to a persuasive communication, *attitude change* tends to be determined by the consideration of arguments rather than cues — β_2 approaches zero (Petty et al. 1993). MacKenzie and Spreng (1992) tested this postulate against the rival explanation that cue–related persuasion wanes at higher levels of elaboration likelihood because cue–related thought decreases (CUE approaches zero). In general, MacKenzie and Spreng's results were consistent with the ELM's strength of relationship predictions, but not the mean level predictions.

The HSM not only allows the *encoding* of message cues and arguments to coincide, but also posits that if the most salient cues are consistent with message arguments in terms of their evaluative implications, then the consideration of both will drive *persuasion* when an audience commits a great deal of thought to the communication. However, when cues and arguments are in conflict with respect to evaluative implications, the hierarchical persuasion postulate holds, and argument–based persuasion attenuates the impact of cue–based persuasion. Thus, rather than strictly adopting the hierarchical persuasion postulate, the HSM posits that argument– and cue–based persuasion can produce *additive* effects under certain conditions (i.e., when they are evaluatively congruent). If we let VAL_{cue} represent the evaluative implications of cue–related thought and VAL_{arg} represent the evaluative implications of argument–related thought, then the HSM posits that *when an audience devotes a substantial amount of thought to a persuasive communication*:[2]

(EQ 2)   Attitude $= \beta_0 + \beta_1 ARG + \beta_2 CUE + \in$
         when cor(VAL_{cue}, VAL_{arg}) is positive

(EQ 3)   Attitude $= \beta_0 + \beta_1 ARG + \in$
         when cor(VAL_{cue}, VAL_{arg}) is negative

The evidence for the additivity hypothesis is still emerging. However, it is difficult to assess in experiments that cross two levels of a cue with two levels of argument quality, because there is no "baseline" from which to assess each effect. If we were to find that when subjects devote a great deal of thought to a persuasive communication, the credible source/strong argument version of the communication results in more positive attitudes than the version in which subjects are exposed to the unreliable source/strong argument, we could be observing attenuation in the unreliable source/strong argument treatment and additivity in the credible source/strong argument treatment, as the HSM predicts. But, the difference might also be due to attenuation in the credible/strong condition and additivity in the unreliable/strong condition, or to additive effects in each condition.

In fact, most of the studies employing the aforementioned two level, fully crossed experimental design have found little or no persuasive influence of cues when an audience allocates a great deal of thought to a persuasive communication, suggesting that complete attenuation occurred. Maheswaran and Chaiken (1991) observed that when consistent in terms of valence, *both* cue– and argument–related thought are correlated with attitudes, but when they are inconsistent, only the argument–related thought is correlated with attitudes. However, they point to the need for a "message only" condition to provide a baseline for identifying additivity effects.

At least two variables would appear to moderate the likelihood of observing additive cue–and argument–based persuasion effects. Chaiken, Axsom, Liberman, & Wilson (1992) have discussed individual predispositions to use certain heuristics (i.e., experts are always right, length equals strength, etc.) as individual difference variables and as the results of learning via repeated use. "Chronically" accessible heuristics are likely to be associated with high levels of perceived reliability. Additivity would, therefore, appear to be more likely to occur when the communication contains a salient cue corresponding to a chronically accessible heuristic in memory.

The second moderating variable reflects an underresearched topic in the ELM and HSM programs of research, the temporal sequence of the presentation of cues and arguments. In tests of the ELM and HSM in advertising settings, the presentation of cues and arguments generally coincide; that is, both are presented as elements in a single communication. In some of the studies reporting additive cue–based persuasion, however, cues and arguments were presented in two distinct communications with the former preceding the latter (Maheswaran & Chaiken 1991). In the absence of more diagnostic information, the presentation of a simple cue may induce audience's to form an initial evaluation, even if motivation and ability to think about the focal topic are relatively high (Srull & Wyer 1989). The HSM suggests exactly this possibility. Chaiken et al. (1989) note that if highly motivated audience members cannot engage in systematic processing, then they will focus on a salient cue in the persuasion context and settle for an "insufficient" level of confidence in the judgment. An initial impression, once formed, might be expected to persist, even in the presence of subsequently presented communications containing conflicting information (Srull & Brand, 1983). Thus, prior presentation of a simple cue would appear to increase the likelihood of observing additive persuasion effects.

INDEPENDENCE VERSUS INTERDEPENDENCE

A second assumption implicit in the hierarchical persuasion postulate is that argument– and cue–based persuasion processes operate relatively *independently* in influencing attitude change. However, both the ELM and the HSM accommodate the notion that the processing of message cues can *bias* the processing of message arguments so as to make the latter consistent with the former in terms of valence.

Petty and Cacioppo (1986a) have described a number of variables that induce biased elaboration on a persuasive communication. They have found that: (1) pre–existing knowledge structures, (2) forewarnings of message content, (3) forewarnings regarding the persuasive intent of a message, (4) bogus personality feedback, (5) high levels of message repetition, and (6) audience

---

[2]It is important to note that the HSM conceptualizes heuristic and systematic processing as the endpoints of a persuasion continuum rather than as a strict dichotomy. The equations presented above, thus, represent extreme conditions where heuristic (i.e., cue–based) persuasion is either completely additive or completely attenuated.

expressions of approval or disapproval serve to bias the valence of argument–related thought and self generated argumentation.

The HSM has focused more on the biasing effects of cues that are elements of the persuasive communication itself. Chaiken and Maheswaran (1990) have examined the biasing impact of message cues on an audience's processing of message arguments. They manipulated the credibility of the source of a communication regarding a telephone answering machine, the ambiguity of the product claims in the communication, and subjects' motivation to process the communication. They observed that even when subjects' motivation was high, and product claims were ambiguous, the credibility of the source influenced their attitudes. Since they *measured* subjects' perceptions of source credibility and claim validity, they were able to demonstrate that the former influenced brand attitude indirectly via its biasing effect on the latter.

Several variables appear to moderate the extent to which the consideration of message cues biases the processing of message arguments. First, a cue–argument biasing effect is more likely when the arguments in the message are ambiguous with respect to the merits of the advocated position. Second, Lutz (1985) has noted that in an advertising pretest setting, subjects typically view an ad for a novel product, and are then asked to evaluate the product. Having little information on which to evaluate the unfamiliar product, an individual's thoughts about the product (argument–based thinking) are more likely to be biased by his or her assessment of the ad itself (cue–based thinking). MacKenzie et al. (1986) have provided evidence in support of Lutz's contention. Finally, it is important to note that the ambiguous arguments in Maheswaran and Chaiken's experiment were attributed to a (credible or unreliable) source that served as the most salient cue. This may be an important condition for observing a biasing effect. When the arguments in a message are not likely to be attributed to the most salient source, such as when celebrity endorsers appear in advertisements, or when there is no inherent relationship between the arguments and cues in a message, the biasing effect may be less likely to occur.

INFLUENCING THE ALLOCATION OF THOUGHT

The amount of thought devoted to a communication was initially conceptualized as an audience predisposition that was independent of the specific elements of the communication itself. However, recent evidence suggests that certain cues influence the amount of thought given to a persuasive communication by influencing an audience's motivation, ability, or opportunity process it (cf. Heesacker et al., 1983; Yalch & Elmore–Yalch, 1984; Swasy & Munch, 1985; Pechmann & Stewart, 1990). Petty and Cacioppo (1986a) have suggested that these effects tend to occur when the personal relevance of a communication is ambiguous and the audience is predisposed to allocate a moderate level of thought to it.

The HSM provides an interesting theoretical account regarding the conditions under which a communication element will enhance or decrease an audience's *motivation* to think about a persuasive communication. It posits that an audience member has a sufficiency threshold, or *desired* level of confidence, for every judgment task s/he faces. Thus, consideration of information relevant to a given judgment occurs until the audience's *perceived* level of confidence equals or exceeds their desired level. As an audience's motivation and ability to think about the focal topic increases, so too does its desired level of confidence.

According to the sufficiency principle, a communication variable or variables can enhance the amount of thought given to a persuasive communication by either increasing the audience's

desired level of confidence, or by undermining the audience's perceived confidence. A message presented by a prestigious, expert source increases the amount of thought devoted to a persuasive communication because it increases the audience's desired level of confidence. In other words, the appearance of the prestigious source suggests to the audience that the communication must be worthy of a great deal of thought. Conversely, a communication containing evaluatively inconsistent information undermines the audience's perceived confidence, making further consideration of relevant information necessary to attain a sufficient level of certainty (Maheswaran & Chaiken, 1991).

MacInnis, Moorman, and Jaworski (1991) have recently concluded that much more research is needed in the marketing literature regarding factors that enhance the amount of thought devoted to persuasive communications. Their framework identifies a number of communication elements that may influence an audience's ability, motivation, or opportunity to think about the information presented in an advertisement. The research propositions they offer represent potentially fruitful directions for future research efforts.

COMMUNICATION VARIABLES AND PERSUASION PROCESSES

Multiple Roles for Communication Variables

As empirical investigations of the HSM, and the ELM in particular, accumulated, researchers discovered that a given communication variable could take on multiple roles in the persuasion process depending on the audience's level of processing intensity. Investigators found, for example, that some *characteristics of the source* of a communication influence persuasion under conditions of high processing intensity as *arguments* rather than *cues* (Petty & Cacioppo, 1980; Kahle & Homer, 1985). Researchers also discovered that under conditions of low processing intensity, certain *message characteristics* persuade audiences as simple *cues* rather than *arguments* (Alba & Marmorstein, 1987). Further, several studies indicated that both source (Heesacker et al. 1983) and message (Swasy & Munch, 1985; Munch & Swasy, 1988) elements *influenced the amount of thought* devoted to persuasive communications; and, finally, source variables were found serve as *biasing influences* on an audience's processing of relevant arguments (Chaiken & Maheswaran, 1990).

The complexity that such findings add to theories of persuasion is obvious. A single variable, source credibility, has been shown to operate in three of the four roles described above: as a simple cue (Cacioppo et al., 1983), as a biasing influence (Chaiken & Maheswaran, 1990), or to enhance the amount of thought devoted to a persuasive communication (Heesacker et al., 1983). The discovery that specific communication variables can operate as cues in some situations and arguments in others suggests at least *three directions* for future research efforts. The *first* concerns the specification of the conditions under which a given variable will operate in a particular role. The *second* concerns the development of more rigorous conceptual definitions of some of the core constructs of the ELM and HSM. The *third* stems from methodological refinements of the standard ELM experiment. Each of these issues is discussed below.

Specifying Conditions Under Which a Variable Operates in a Given Role

Petty and Cacioppo (1986a) have suggested that communication variables operate: (1) as simple cues when an audience's elaboration is low, (2) as enhancers/inhibitors of issue–relevant thinking when an audience's elaboration is moderate, and (3) as arguments or biasing influences when an audience's elaboration is high. Although a great deal of evidence has accumulated establishing the first and last of these relationships, there is still some question as to whether the enhancer/inhibitor role requires *moderate* levels of elaboration. Many of the investigations reporting such effects have suggested that they occur under conditions of "low" elaboration (Swasy & Munch, 1985; Maheswaran & Chaiken, 1991). Of course, such a determination is difficult to make because examinations of the ELM typically manipulate elaboration at two levels for purposes of creating "high" and "low" conditions; it is difficult to determine where each condition falls along the elaboration continuum across studies. Perhaps many of the "low" elaboration conditions reported above actually fell closer to the midpoint of the continuum. Regardless, a more rigorous test of the points above would entail a manipulation that more clearly establishes distinct low, moderate, and high levels of elaboration.

Defining the Key Constructs

Argument Quality: Within the ELM, Petty and Cacioppo have adopted an empirical definition of argument quality. "Strong" arguments are those that elicit predominantly favorable cognitive responses, and "weak" arguments generate mostly unfavorable cognitive responses (Petty & Cacioppo, 1986a,b). Other researchers adopting empirically driven definitions of argument quality have focused on subjective perceptions of the arguments in a communication (Swasy & Munch, 1985), and changes in belief structures relevant to the principle assertions of the communication (Fishbein & Ajzen, 1975; Areni & Lutz, 1988; Eagly, 1991).

Defining strong and weak in terms of the cognitive responses they generate in pretest experiments constrains the utility of the ELM for at least two reasons. First, if strong (weak) arguments are "defined" as those generating primarily supporting (counter) arguments in a pretest, then the pretest has shown the arguments to operate via the central route *by definition*. Mongeau and Stiff (1993) have even suggested that this aspect of argument quality manipulations within the ELM render the model impossible to falsify. That is not the position adopted here. There is no reason why the empirical definition of argument quality necessitates the interaction between argument quality and elaboration demonstrated in so many tests of the ELM. However, the empirical definition does seem to guarantee that if elaboration likelihood is sufficiently high, then argument quality *must* persuade the audience via the central route.

This reasoning suggests a second major limitation of the empirical definition of argument quality. Tests of the ELM do not offer insights as to *why* a given argument is persuasive to an audience (Areni & Lutz, 1988). Petty and Cacioppo (1986b) have discussed need for a stronger conceptualization of the argument quality construct for exactly this reason. Research from a number of apparently unrelated disciplines suggests directions for the development of such a conceptual definition.

Perhaps the most obvious basis for conceptualizing argument quality is the area of formal logic. Indeed, Petty and Cacioppo described many of their strong arguments as being "logical." Much of the research of in this area has focused on the mental processes used in assessing the validity of the conclusions in logical syllogisms. Among the findings that have emerged are that individuals are more likely to accept conclusions associated with desirable outcomes and reject conclusions associated with undesirable outcomes (McGuire & McGuire, 1991), and that individuals weigh *objective correctness* more heavily than *logical validity* when evaluating the truth value of conclusions (Braine & Rumain, 1983). Unfortunately, the "formality" of formal logic makes it difficult to apply to the "natural language" of persuasive communica-

tions (Braine & Rumain, 1983). An interesting stream of research has emerged which attempts to link the rules of formal logic to arguments presented in natural language (Braine, 1980; Braine & Rumaine, 1983). While some research examining the logic of natural language arguments has emerged in psychology (Harris & Monaco, 1978) and marketing (Gardner, 1975; Burke et al., 1988), a more systematic incorporation of Braine's work into the literature on the ELM, HSM and other persuasion research is needed.

Research regarding the structural features of argument quality has focused on the strength of the supporting evidence for the principle assertions of a communication. Many models have proposed that persuasive arguments consistent solely of principle assertions and supporting arguments (Fishbein & Ajzen, 1975; Jaccard, 1981). However, more sophisticated models include additional elements. Boller, Swasy, and Munch (1990) have developed an interesting perspective based on Toulmin's (1958) model of argument structure. For purposes of understanding persuasive communications in an advertising setting, Boller et al. condense Toulmin's six argument elements into four dimensions: (a) claim assertions, (b) evidence (grounds), (c) authority (warrants and backing), and (d) probability (qualifiers and rebuttals). Boller et al. (1990) view persuasive arguments as consisting of various combinations of these four classes of statements.

A number of researchers have examined the impact of each of these components in persuasion, and have found that explicit statements of claim assertions are more effective when an audience is likely to devote little thought to a persuasive communication, whereas implicit statements are more effective for an audience willing to think more extensively (Kardes, 1988; Sawyer & Howard, 1991). The impact of supporting evidence and probability in terms of the ELM and HSM is less clear, although it has been suggested that the former operates via central or systematic processing (Areni & Lutz, 1988). In addition, the linguistics literature suggests that females may be more sensitive to the use of probability statements (Lakoff, 1975), and prefer supporting evidence based on the personal experiences of others rather than aggregate data (Tannen, 1990).

Elaboration Likelihood: Petty and Cacioppo's reference to persuasion's central route as entailing the *diligent* consideration of issue or object *relevant* information suggests that elaboration has two basic aspects: a level of *intensity*, which refers to the amount of cognitive capacity devoted to an information processing task, and *direction*, which refers to the nature of the information needed to attain specific processing objectives (Kahnemann, 1973).

The distinction between the intensity and directional components is central to the evaluation of empirical research because actual manipulations of elaboration have varied considerably regarding their impact on each dimension, and, as Wright (1980) notes, researchers have been slow to acknowledge the ramifications of these differences in the interpretation of persuasion outcomes. For example, a manipulation that requires one group of subjects to *evaluate an advertisement* for a fictitious new product (i.e., low brand elaboration) while a second group is asked to *evaluate the featured product* in the ad (i.e., high brand elaboration) would seem to be fundamentally different from a manipulation in which all subjects are given the latter task and the experimenters simply alter the economic incentive for completing the task successfully. In terms of the discussion above, the first manipulation primarily alters the direction component, whereas the second focuses predominantly on the intensity dimension. This distinction may be critical for evaluating the *mean difference* versus the *strength of relationship* hypotheses proposed by MacKenzie and Spreng (1992). A manipulation focusing on the direction component would almost certainly produce mean differences in the amount of thought given to arguments versus cues. However, the strength of relationship hypotheses may be more applicable for studies manipulating the intensity dimension of elaboration likelihood without influencing subjects' processing goals.

Explicitly Modelling the Constructs

Many of the investigations of the ELM, HSM, and related streams of research have relied on *inferring* the process by which various cues and arguments influence persuasion by observing the effect of experimental manipulations on subjects' attitudes. However, the review presented above suggests numerous processes by which a given communication variable can operate in the persuasion process. When two or more of these processes produce similar outcomes, the approach of inferring process from outcome may not allow a researcher to discriminate among them.

Consider an apparently straightforward experiment in which a researcher manipulates the physical attractiveness of the source of a communication, the valence of its arguments, and the audience's motivation to process its content. Suppose, as expected, only the source attractiveness manipulation influences subjects' attitudes when motivation is low. But, similar to Petty and Cacioppo (1981b), *both* the source attractiveness *and* the argument valence manipulation influence subjects' attitudes when motivation is high. Have we observed, in this instance, that the source manipulation operated as an argument rather than a cue in the high motivation condition as Petty and Cacioppo (1986a) have suggested? Or, have we produced evidence for Maheswaran and Chaiken's (1991) notion of additivity between argument– and cue–based persuasion? Even the inclusion of a "message only" control condition in the design would not eliminate this ambiguity (cf. Miniard et al. (1991).

Petty, Unnava, and Strathman (1991, p. 247) note that: "in most communication settings, a confluence of factors determines the nature of information processing rather than one variable acting in isolation. When multiple variables are involved, interaction effects are possible." It is obvious that communications in the "real world," particularly advertisements, are far more complex than those employed in previous ELM and HSM investigations. Researchers attempting to assess the impact of more realistic communications containing numerous elements may be faced with distinguishing among a multitude potential processes.

Now consider a magazine ad for a brand of toothpaste that contains the following components: (1) a photograph of an attractive model with a bright smile, (2) an endorsement by the American Dental Association (ADA), and (3) smaller copy regarding specific attributes of the toothpaste. The photograph of the model could influence persuasion as a cue, as a persuasive argument, or indirectly via its influence on the amount of thought given to the ad. Likewise, the endorsement of the ADA could operate as a cue, an influence on the amount of thought given to the ad, or a biasing influence on the audience's assessment of quality of the arguments in the copy. Further, the copy at the bottom of the page could serve as message arguments, or as a cue. Finally, if either the photograph or the ADA endorsement were perceived as incongruent with the copy of the ad, this evaluative inconsistency could further affect the amount of thought the audience devotes to the ad.

Suppose researchers were interested in examining the impact of this ad. The previous paragraph implies thirty–six [3 potential roles for the photograph X 3 potential roles for the ADA endorsement X 2 potential roles for the copy claims X 2 (presence versus absence of incongruity effects)] possibilities regarding its impact on an audience. Even if the audience's predisposition to think about the advertisement is taken into account, the possibilities are numerous. If our understanding of the persuasive impact of more complex, realistic advertisements is to progress, researchers must begin to accommodate and test the *simultaneous* effects of multiple communication variables. That is, we must begin assessing the *relative importance* of a communication element *given the presence of many others*. Hence, what is needed is a technique that explicitly models the causal relationships among the various latent constructs associated with the effects of source and message factors in persuasion (see also Mongeau & Stiff, 1993).

MacKenzie and Lutz (1989; MacKenzie et al., 1986) demonstrated the usefulness of applying structural equations modelling for assessing multiple potential advertising effects simultaneously representing an important deviation from the standard ELM and HSM experimental approach. As discussed above, ELM and HSM researchers have traditionally placed emphasis on assessing the impact of *experimental manipulations* on subjects' attitudes. But, the causal modelling approach places emphasis on *predicted relationships among measured latent constructs* rather than *predicted stimulus effects*. When causal models are used in conjunction with experimental design, the primary role of experimental manipulations is to create variance in the latent constructs hypothesized as antecedents to persuasion. Once experimental manipulations have influenced the appropriate latent antecedents, as assessed by an ANOVA, subjects can be pooled across treatments to create a single sample. Causal modelling may, in this manner, allow for tests of the persuasive effects of a communication containing a confluence of distinct elements.

CONCLUSION

The ELM and the HSM have yielded tremendous insights over the last fifteen years regarding the impact of various communication elements in persuasion. If these, and related theories of persuasion are to continue offering utility for understanding persuasion processes in more natural settings, several conceptual and methodological modifications will be facilitating. The present research has attempted to identify and discuss some of the most important of these issues in hopes of helping to initiate the next generation of research on persuasion processes.

REFERENCES
Available upon request from the first author.

New Directions in Behavioral Decision Theory: Implications for Consumer Choice

Ravi Dhar, Yale University

Most conceptions of rational choice assume that individual preferences are well defined and ordered. The field of *descriptive decision theory* has attempted to document evidence to define more precisely the bounds on human rationality. This viewpoint of consumers' decision making is also consistent with the emerging consensus among consumer decision researchers that preferences are often *fuzzy, unstable, and inconsistent* (Tversky, Sattah, and Slovic 1988; Payne, Bettman, and Johnson 1992). Consumers are depicted as *constructing* and expressing rankings with respect to possibilities that they have actually considered.

While the constructive view of individual decision making is becoming well established within consumer research, its focus has been somewhat narrow. Most of the previous research examines decision making within a cost-benefit framework trading off effort and accuracy in choice. The neglected role of other psychological variables on *constructive preferences* raises interesting questions. How do consumers value the processes that determine the outcomes of their decisions? Would these psychological processes imply a preference for a specific type of alternative? Such an approach to consumer behavior assumes that people are not just concerned with the objective consequences of decisions, but also with the affective consequences and psychological states that ameliorate or intensify these consequences.

A number of psychological variables that influence the construction process and are the focus of the present session. One set of problem depends on the *uncertainty of preferences*. Consumers often arrive at choice situations with no clear idea of their preferences finding it difficult to face multiple options. A second source of uncertainty arises when the choice situation involves self control that may threaten values that are important to consumers. The manner in which choices affected by such variables are resolved may result in systematic deviation from the normative standpoint. In such circumstances, the process of decision making is prone to various distortions and errors that can act as powerful barriers to rational thought.

The four papers in the session differ in their focus on the psychological variables that are examined. The first paper makes substantive contribution to our understanding of the manner in which preferences are constructed (Simonson and Tversky). Using the compromise effect as an illustration, the authors explore various influences on the magnitude of the context effects. They show that the magnitude of the compromise effect can be systematically influenced by the manipulations of the manner in which the choice sets are evaluated. The authors also examine the hypothesis that context effects can be obtained without providing any information about the absolute values of the alternatives. They argue that consumers can predict very accurately the likelihood whether or not they will choose a compromise option in a particular category.

The second paper (Sen and Johnson) explore the causes, effects, and the process underlying the mere ownership effect in consumer choice. Several different explanations have been suggested by social and cognitive psychologists, decision researchers, and economists. In a number of laboratory studies using simple choice sets, the authors find support for loss aversion as the key mechanism. They also obtain some evidence for a "gain-seeking" strategy, where consumers deviate from their endowment only if one of the remaining options provides a sufficiently positive incentive to do so.

The third paper (Wertenbroch) examines how consumer self-control influences the manner in which information is processed and its subsequent influence for marketing, an under researched area. The authors propose and test a framework for understanding these effects using data from laboratory tasks and scanner panel analysis. The results indicate that consumer price sensitivity depends, in part, on the degree to which package size can be instrumental for exercising self-control. The results suggest implications for segmentation, pricing, and packaging policies.

The fourth paper examines the effect of common and shared features among a set of alternatives under consideration on pre- and post-decisional processes (Dhar and Sherman). The authors proposed that the feature matching model of similarity (Tversky 1977) can be extended to understand how consumers decide among alternatives in a given choice context. In particular, they focus on the notion that features common to more than one alternative in the choice set are *canceled* or receive less weight. The authors conduct a series of experiments in order to specify both the causes, specific effects, and mediating processes that surround the changes in preference as function of the common and unique features. For example, the weighting of good and bad features can be systematically manipulated by the context that allows them to be seen as common or unique. The findings find strong support for the feature-matching model of preferences.

Given the diversity of the papers, the direction of the discussion was to arrive at a unifying force rather than a session summary. When taken as a group, the papers in the session helped to highlight some of the promising avenues that are emerging in the area of decision research.

Typicality as a Determinant of Affect in Retail Environments

John W. Barnes, University of Texas–El Paso
James C. Ward, Arizona State University

This paper explores the influence of retail environments on consumer moods and emotions. In particular, we focus on the influence of environmental prototypicality on measures of transient mood, emotion (P.A.D.), and attitude. The linkages among environment typicality, emotion, and mood have not been explored in the marketing literature. A path analysis of our measures shows that environmental typicality has strong direct effects on feelings of dominance, pleasure, and arousal; indirect effects on mood; and direct and indirect effects on attitude. Implications for theory and management are drawn.

The environments in which consumers shop, eat, and play arouse emotions and moods. These feelings can, in turn, influence consumer attitudes and behaviors. Although retailers have at least implicitly understood these relationships for decades, consumer researchers only recently began their systematic empirical study. Early studies showed that the emotion eliciting qualities of retail and service environments could be characterized in terms of Mehrabian and Russell's dimensions of pleasure, arousal, and dominance (Donovan and Rossiter 1982). Furthermore, these and later studies showed that the experience of these dimensions is linked to attitudes, intentions, and behaviors such as approach and avoidance (Donovan and Rossiter 1982), willingness to buy (Baker, Levy, and Grewal 1992), and unplanned spending (Donovan, Rossiter, and Nesdale 1993). Later research has begun to investigate the environmental qualities antecedent to the P.A.D. dimensions, that is, the characteristics of the environment that elicit emotion.

Hull and Harvey (1989) distinguish between micro characteristics of the environment and molar characteristics. Micro characteristics are the physical characteristics of the environment, the details such as color, light, and sound used to create a particular atmosphere. These are the characteristics that most research on the environment-emotion link in marketing has focused upon. For example, Bellizzi and Hite (1992) found a relationship between retail environment color and feelings. Baker, Levy, and Grewal (1992) found that lighting, music, and the number and friendliness of employees influenced shopper emotions.

Molar characteristics are "emergent properties" that result from the sum of such details. Although researchers in environmental psychology have shown an interest in affective reactions to more molar characteristics of environments such as their complexity, mystery, and coherence (Kaplan 1987), their naturalness (Kaplan and Kaplan 1982), and their schema consistency (Purcell 1986), the study of how such qualities arouse emotion and mood in consumption settings has been neglected. An exception to this neglect is a recently presented study by Smith and Sherman (1993) that demonstrated a link between broad dimensions of store image and transient mood. In this study, we will explore the relationship of an important molar characteristic of retail environments — their perceived prototypicality — to emotion and mood, a linkage of managerial significance and theoretical interest that has so far been neglected in our literature.

The question of how environmental typicality relates to emotion, mood, and attitude is theoretically interesting and managerially important. From a theoretical perspective, the expected relationship between environmental typicality and emotion is not at first obvious. A consumer in a highly typical environment might feel either positive or negative emotions, depending upon the kind of place he or she is seeking. A consumer seeking the familiar might feel good in a typical environment; a consumer seeking a novel experience might feel bored. However, these are speculations. The categorization literature has not examined the effect of typicality on emotion and mood, and neither has the environment literature in marketing.

The categorization literature suggests that the relationship between typicality and attitude is most often positive (Loken and Ward 1990), although this is not always the case. Ward and Loken (1987) found that consumers seeking variety, prestige, or scarcity negatively valued typicality. In the sole analysis of the effects of retail environment typicality on attitude, Ward, Bitner, and Barnes (1992) found a positive relationship. But their analysis did not attempt to assess emotional reactions to environmental typicality or their role in creating a positive typicality-attitude realtionship. The role of emotions in this linkage raises interesting questions.

What emotions do more typical environments evoke? For example, do consumers in a highly typical environment feel more or less arousal, more or less dominance, more or less pleasure than those in an atypical environment? How is the pattern of emotions evoked by more or less typical environments linked to attitude? For example, if a typical environment evokes little arousal, is this linked to a positive attitude toward the environment?

From a managerial perspective, the environmental typicality—emotion relationship should be of significant import to retailers and service providers. Retailers and service providers spend millions of dollars annually on the creation of environments designed to have positive effects on consumer emotions, attitudes, and behaviors. If environmental typicality provokes emotion, then it is an important, but largely unrecognized, aspect of store atmosphere. Both retailers and professional service providers sell the "intangible," some more than others. Both rely upon the environment as not only a tangible cue to their services, but also as a stimulus to favorable emotions likely to influence perception of both the seen and unseen aspects of their offerings. The typicality of their stores and offices is likely an important cue to consumers about the nature of these offerings, and also perhaps an important stimulus to the moods and emotions that can influence their perception.

In sum, our review suggests a need to investigate the links from environmental typicality to emotional qualities of the environment (pleasure, arousal, dominance) and from these to mood and attitude. Our study assesses these linkages via a path analysis of data from a field experiment in which pariciipants visited a set of fast food restaurants chosen to vary in typicality.

METHODS

Past studies of environmental effects on consumer behavior have often substituted laboratory pictures and/or scenarios for real environments. Although studies support the validity of such simulations (Bateson and Hui 1992), we believe that the power of environments to influence emotion as well as the nuances of these effects are ideally studied through actual experience. In this spirit, all of our subjects not only visited the restaurants in our study, they ordered food and ate there.

Participants

The participants were 86 students, mostly in their twenties, attending undergraduate marketing classes at a southwestern university. Since fast food restaurants consider young adults to be a

TABLE 1
Variable Means at Restaurant Level

Restaurant	Typ	Att	Ple	Ars	Dom	Mood
Arby's	5.02	6.14	4.77	5.11	5.72	3.86
Burger King	8.63	7.75	6.68	6.44	6.51	4.19
Carl's Jr.	6.35	4.65	5.45	5.25	5.12	3.25
Church's	5.00	4.57	4.57	5.05	4.91	3.31
Dairy Queen	4.98	6.12	4.23	5.15	4.81	3.57
Delectable Dog	2.67	2.33	3.31	3.21	3.07	2.21
El Pollo Asado	4.09	7.39	4.35	4.67	5.55	3.51
Jack in Box	6.93	4.33	5.35	5.21	4.72	3.65
Kentucky Fried	5.68	6.68	4.93	5.27	6.05	4.11
Long John Silv	3.10	4.69	5.05	5.21	4.35	3.05
McDonald's	9.33	6.25	5.53	5.01	5.19	4.15
Taco Bell	6.02	6.92	6.47	6.38	6.27	3.97
Ted's Hot Dogs	4.02	5.44	4.22	4.69	5.30	3.45
Whataburger	6.10	5.00	5.32	4.64	5.02	3.35
Wendy's	7.94	6.51	5.51	5.15	5.21	3.66

major target market, this group represented a significant segment of fast food consumers. The participants were given course credit for participation.

Cover Story

The cover story alleged the trips to the restaurants were for on-site taste tests. This story was employed to not only justify trips to the restaurants but also so the participants' attention would be on the usual focus of trips to fast food restaurants — food — instead of being unnaturally drawn to the restaurant's physical environments. The comments and questions of the participants throughout the trips indicated that they believed their purpose was taste-testing, not environmental research.

Trips

The students visited sets of restaurants in small groups supervised by a researcher. Fifteen fast-food restaurants (see Table 1 for names) were chosen as stimuli for the study by three criteria: Affiliation with a national or regional chain, within a 15 minute drive from campus, and primarily serving fast-food. Inspection of Table 1 suggests that these criteria resulted in a representative selection of restaurants including national chains specializing in a variety of food types, and some chains popular locally.

To simplify the logistics of the study, the students were divided into groups of five to eleven, and the fifteen restaurants were divided into sets of three. Visits by the entire group of 86 to each restaurant on a single trip were not possible due to transportation, time, and restaurant capacity constraints. Also, since each visit involved a taste test, the researchers did not wish to force participants to eat fast food at fifteen restaurants. Each group of students visited one set of three restaurants. Each set of three restaurants was visited by at least two groups of students totaling 14 to 19. Restaurants were assigned groups of students by a random selection without replacement procedure. Within each set of three restaurants, the order in which they were visited was counter-rotated for the two groups visiting each set.

The same researcher accompanied each group to the restaurants and administered all questionnaires. At each of the restaurant sites, participants were led through the front door of the restaurant so they could observe both its interior and exterior characteristics. The groups were seated at previously selected locations where they could observe as much as possible of the restaurant interior. To reinforce the cover story, participants taste tested an item of food at each restaurant. After the tasting, they responded to a questionnaire that asked them to rate the food's quality as well as its nutrient content. They also filled-out a short mood scale (described below) while inside the restaurant. The researcher explained the introduction of this scale by mentioning a need to control for any effect of participants' feelings on their ratings of the food.

Upon completion of the three site visits, each group returned to the university to fill out follow-up questionnaires. To continue the cover story, the first questionnaire asked for their nutritional beliefs and habits, how often they ate at fast food restaurants, and demographic information. Subsequent questionnaires contained the measure of typicality, the P.A.D. scale, the attitude scale, and other measures

Perceived Typicality

The participants were asked to rate their perceptions of the overall typicality of each restaurant they had visited on three zero to 10 scales with the following endpoints: very typical — very atypical; very good example — very poor example; very representative — very unrepresentative. These scales have been found in past research to correlate in theoretically expected ways with a variety of other measures of goodness of example as well as other measures (Loken and Ward 1990). The three scale items were summed and averaged for each respondent. The correlations of the three typicality measures with one another were all .93 or above. Overall their alpha was .94.

Attitude

Participants were asked to rate their overall attitude toward each restaurant they visited on three zero to 10 point scales with the following endpoints: low quality — high quality, bad — good; unsatisfactory — satisfactory. The three scale items were summed and averaged for each respondent. The correlations of the three attitude measures with one another were all .95 or above. Overall their alpha was .95.

TABLE 2
Correlation Matrix of Variables
N = 86

	Typ	Dom	Ars	Ple	Mod	Att
Typicality	1.0					
Dominance	.28	1.0				
Arousal	.53	.44	1.0			
Pleasure	.43	.25	.69	1.0		
Mood	.26	.78	.37	.37	1.0	
Attitude	.36	.46	.29	.23	.45	1.0

Mood

Mood was measured by the Peterson and Sauber (1983) MSF (Mood Short Form), a four-item scale that measures transitory mood. As noted, participants filled-out this scale while in the restaurants. The MSF asks respondents to describe "how you feel at the moment" by checking their agreement to four Likert statements: "Currently I am in a good mood;" "At this moment I feel 'edgy' or irritable;" "As I answer these questions I feel cheerful;" "For some reason I am not very comfortable right now." The second and fourth items are reverse scored. Data reported by Peterson and Sauber (1983) support the scales' validity. The scale's alpha was .71.

P.A.D.

Participants' emotional reactions to the fast food restaurant environments were measured by the Pleasure, Arousal, Dominance scale. This scale was specifically developed by Mehrabian and Russell (1974) to measure emotional reactions toward environments. The P.A.D. consists of three subscales. The pleasure scale measures peoples' general positive or negative affective reaction to the environment (i.e., their happiness, satisfaction, content, or lack thereof). The arousal scale measures the degree to which they feel awake, stimulated, and excited; or sleepy, relaxed, and calm. The dominance scale measures the extent to which they feel free to act in the situation (in control, influential) or constrained (controlled, influenced, submissive). Previous studies have validated the scale in retail environments (Donovan and Rossiter 1982). The alphas were .87 (P), .92 (A), and .89 (D).

RESULTS

A correlation matrix for the scales is shown in Table 2. The individual data for each measure was entered into a series of OLS regressions designed to estimate a path model. The path model treated typicality as an exogenous variable influencing emotions and through them such outcomes as mood and attitude. Conceptually, this path model was inspired by Bitner's (1992) conceptual model of the psychological effects of service environments. Like her model, our model begins with a physical characteristic of the service environment (typicality), assumes that this characteristic evokes emotional responses (pleasure, arousal, dominance), and then assumes that these emotional responses influence more cognitive appraisals such as attitude and mood, which has generally been defined as a more "cognitive" affective construct (Gardner 1985).

The figure shows the significant paths in the final model. The legend at the bottom indicates the significance level for each path. A summary of the results for the regressions used to estimate the direct effects and calculations for selected indirect effects are shown in Table 3. As we present the results, we will also interpret them and discuss their significance.

The figure shows that perceived typicality of the fast food environments was strongly related to emotions. The path from typicality to pleasure was .29, significant at alpha<.01. More typical environments elicited greater feelings of happiness, contentment, and satisfaction than less typical environments. We might speculate that typical fast food environments elicit more positive feelings because people desire these environments to be neither "too much nor too little." By "too much" we suggest that a fast food restaurant decorated in an opulent or unusual manner, like many trendy sit-down places, might be perceived as too expensive or too strange by many customers. By "too little" we suggest that a fast food restaurant decorated more cheaply or plainly than usual for national chains will be judged negatively, perhaps as to the quality of its food.

The path from typicality to arousal was .27, also significant at alpha<.01. Typical environments elicited greater feelings of wakefulness, stimulation, and excitement than less typical environments. The positive relationship between typicality and feelings of arousal might seem at first paradoxical, if we assume that the typical is boring. However, several explanations exist for this finding. First, part of the excitement of going to a fast food restaurant, or any restaurant, is anticipation and consumption of the food. Fast food patrons are likely to want standard fare in a standard place. To the extent the environment meets this expectation, they may feel more excited about picking up food or consuming it at the restaurant. Second, fast food restaurant environments that are less typical in a negative sense, that is, more plainly decorated than the typical place, are also likely to be perceived as less exciting. Third, environments less typical in other senses, that is, just different, or of higher than usual quality, might create feelings of disappointment, indifference, and boredom when viewed as fast food restaurants.

The path from typicality to dominance was .48, a strong relationship significant at alpha<.01. Dominance is intended to measure peoples' feeling that they are free to act in a situation versus being influenced, constrained, and controlled. In a typical environment, people may feel they know what to expect, where to

FIGURE
Typicality as a Determinant of Affect in the Retail Environment

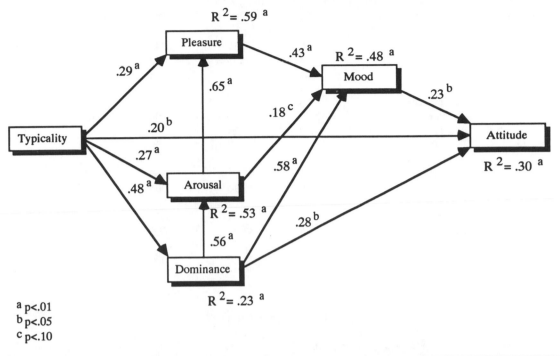

go, and what to do. In other words, they may feel more free to act than in a less typical, less familiar environment. Past studies showing strong correlations between ratings of familiarity and typicality provide some support for this suggestion.

Dominance is also related to feelings of arousal (.56, alpha<.01). Participants who felt more free to act reported greater feelings of arousal. Consumers may feel that they know what to do and what to expect in a typical environment. From another perspective, a typical environment does not confuse, disturb, or intimidate them. Therefore, they feel in control, free to act, and more excited about their trip for fast food. Consistent with the suggestion that typical environments evoke a pleasurable kind and degree of arousal, the path from arousal to pleasure is strongly significant (.65, alpha<.01).

The direct path from typicality to mood was only .11, not significant at alpha=.10. However, typicality is related to mood indirectly through dominance, pleasure, and arousal. We will examine the direct paths of these variables to mood first, and then the indirect effect of typicality on mood through them. The direct path from dominance to mood is .58, significant at alpha<.01. The direct path from pleasure to mood is .43, also significant at alpha<.01. Finally, the direct path from arousal to mood is .18, only marginally significant at alpha<.10. The indirect effects of typicality on mood through these variables are shown in Table 2. The strongest indirect effect of typicality on mood is directly through dominance, .29. The next strongest is through pleasure, .12. The other indirect effects are less than .10, but in sum suggest a substantial indirect effect of typicality on mood. Overall the antecedent variables yield a r-squared on mood of .48. The direct path from dominance to mood suggests feeling free to act is an antecedent to a good mood, a relationship that agrees with common sense, but has been rarely explored in the marketing literature. The borderline path from arousal to mood is not surprising, since most prior literature has described mood has a more cognitive than

arousal based construct (Gardner 1985). Overall, the idea that retail environments influence mood is intuitively appealing. Here we see that feeling dominant, in control of the service environment, is one of the strongest antecedents to a good mood. Many studies have shown that a good mood will in turn have a prevasive influence on perception of products and services (Gardner 1985).

Turning to attitude, we find that environmental typicality has a positive direct path to overall evaluation of the restaurants (.20, alpha<.05). This relationship was expected, since past studies of the typicality-attitude relationship have shown positive correlations between these constructs. Feelings of dominance also directly effect attitude (.28, alpha<.05) as does mood (.23, alpha<.05). Overall, the regressions on attitude yield a r-squared of .30, significant at alpha<.01. The indirect effects of typicality on attitude are interesting to examine. These occur through dominance (.13) and mood (total of indirect effects through mood, .14). These results suggest that at least part of the typicality-attitude relationship for fast food environments is due to the effect of typicality on feelings of dominance and mood.

DISCUSSION

We set out to explore the effect of a molar environmental characteristic, typicality, on emotion, mood, and attitude. We found that perceived typicality had strong direct effects on feelings of dominance, pleasure, and arousal; indirect effects on mood; and direct and indirect effects on attitude. Few studies have attempted to link typicality to emotion and mood, and none of the few efforts have been in the context of retail environments. Our findings are unique, and have theoretical and managerial implications we will discuss, but also have limitations. Our study was conducted in only one type of environment, fast food restaurants. The pattern of relations between typicality and emotion could be context dependent, and thus might change in other settings, such as upscale clothing boutiques, in which atypical environments might be val-

TABLE 3
Direct Effects Summary of Path Analysis Results

Dep. Variable	Ind. Variable	Beta	F	P	F(reg)	R2
Attitude	Typicality	.20	4.12	.046	11.81	.30
	Dominance	.28	6.55	.012	p=.00	
	Mood	.23	4.16	.045		
Mood	Dominance	.58	23.37	.000	18.66	.48
	Pleasure	.43	20.00	.000	p=.00	
	Arousal	.18	3.15	.079		
	Typicality	.11	1.67	.200		
Pleasure	Arousal	.65	81.71	.000	59.72	.59
	Typicalty	.29	16.10	.001	p=.00	
Arousal	Typicality	.27	9.69	.003	47.74	.53
	Dominance	.56	43.78	.000	p=.00	
Dominance	Typicality	.48	25.40	.000	25.40	.23
					p=.00	

Selected Indirect Effects

Indirect Effects of Typicality on Attitude

Through Mood
Mood-Pleasure-Typicality	.03
Mood-Arousal-Typicality	.01
Mood-Dominance-Typicality	.06
Mood-Pleasure-Arousal-Typicality	.02
Mood-Pleasure-Arousal-Dominace-Typicality	.02

Through Dominance
Domiance-Typicality	.13

Indirect Effects of Typicality on Mood

Dominance-Typicality	.29
Arousal-Typicality	.05
Pleasure-Typicality	.12
Pleasure-Arousal-Typicality	.08
Arousal-Dominance-Typicality	.05
Pleasure-Arousal-Dominance-Typicality	.08

ued. Research designed to assess the reliablity of our findings across a variety of environmental contexts is needed. Alternative explanations for the results exist, and also need to be ruled out by later studies. For example, Zajonc's mere exposure effect could have caused more typical, more familiar environments to evoke more favorable emotions.

Theoretically, the results raise some interesting issues for further research. We found positive direct relationships between typicality and dominance, and typicality and arousal. Although we speculated on the origins of these relations, further work should explicate the psychology of these links. The strong relationship of typicality to dominance, and dominance to mood and attitude, is particularly interesting.

In their pioneering work on the application of the P.A.D. framework to retail environments, Donovan and Rossiter (1982) dismissed the importance of dominance as an emotional reaction to retail environments. Although their dismissal was consistent with efforts to simplify the P.A.D. framework to only two dimensions, pleasure and arousal (Russell and Pratt 1980), dominance has emerged in several studies has strongly related to environmental preception and behavior (Hui and Bateson 1991). This study confirms its importance. More work is needed on its antecedents and consequences.

From a broad perspective, we feel that environments are among the more encompassing, multidimensional phenomena marketers study, and thus deserve to be studied from interdisciplinary perspectives. In this study, we made a modest effort in this direction by bringing together constructs previously used to study categorization, environmental psychology, and mood. Future studies should continue and further such efforts.

For managers the results reinforce the importance of perceived typicality as an aspect of the retail environment. Environmental typicality not only affects categorization and attitude, but also emotion. Thus, perceived typicality might be viewed as an important emergent or molar outcome of efforts to manipulate decor, lighting, music and so on to create a desired emotional atmosphere.

REFERENCES

Baker, Julie, Michael Levy, and Dhruv Grewal (1992), "An Experimental Approach to Making Retail Store Environmental Decisions," *Journal of Retailing,* 68 (4), 445-460.

Bateson, John E.G. and Michael K. Hui (1992), "The Ecological Validity of Photographic Slides and Videotapes in Simulating the Service Setting," *Journal of Consumer Research,* 19 (September), 271-284.

Bellizzi, Joseph and Robert Hite (1992), "Environmental Color, Consumer Feelings, and Purchase Likelihood," *Psychology and Marketing,* 9 (5), 347-363.

Bitner, Mary Jo (1992), "Servicescapes: The Impact of Physical Surroundings on Customers and Employees," *Journal of Marketing,* 56 (April), 57-71.

Donovan, Robert, John Rossiter, and Nesdale (1993), presented at special session on "The Influence of Environmental Factors on Consumer Behavior: A Decade Later," in *Advances in Consumer Research,* Vol. XX, Leigh McAlister and Michael L. Rothschild, eds., Association for Consumer Research, 630.

Gardner, Meryl (1985), "Mood States and Consumer Behavior: A Critical Review," *Journal of Consumer Research,* 12, 281-300.

Hull R. Bruce and Antony Harvey (1989), "Explaining the Emotion People Experience in Suburban Parks," *Environment and Behavior,* 21 (3), 322-345.

Kaplan, Stephen (1987), "Aesthetics, Affect, and Cognition," *Environment and Behavior,* 19(January), 3-32.

_____ and Rachel Kaplan (1982), *Cognition and Environment,* New York:Praeger Publishers.

Loken, Barbara and James Ward (1990), "Alternative Approaches to Understanding the Determinants of Typicality," *Journal of Consumer Research,* 17 (September), 111-26.

Mehrabian, A. and James A. Russell (1974), *An Approach to Environmental Psychology,* Cambridge, MA: MIT Press.

Peterson, Robert and Matthew Sauber (1983), "A Mood Scale for Survey Research," in *1983 AMA Educators' Proceedings,* eds. Patrick Murphy et al., Chicago, IL: American Marketing Association, 409-414.

Purcell, Allan T. (1986), "Environmental Perception and Affect: A Schema Discrepancy Model," *Environment and Behavior,* 18, 3-30.

Russell, James A. and G. Pratt (1980), "A Description of the Affective Quality Attributed to Environments," *Journal of Personality and Social Psychology,* 38 (August), 311-322.

Smith, Ruth Belk and Elaine Sherman (1993), "The Effects of Store Image and Mood on Consumer Behavior: A Theoretical and Empirical Analysis," in *Advances in Consumer Research,* Vol. XX, Leigh McAlister and Michael L. Rothschild, eds., Association for Consumer Research, 631.

Ward, James C., Mary Jo Bitner, and John Barnes (1992), "Measuring the Prototypicalityand Meaning of Retail Environments," *Journal of Retailing,* 68 (2), 194-219.

Ward, James C. and Barbara Loken (1987), "The Generality of Typicality Effects on Preference and Comparison: An Exploratory Test," in *Advances in Consumer Research,* Vol. XV, Michael Houston, eds., 55-61.

Effects of Schema Congruity and Involvement on Product Evaluations

Moonkyu Lee, University of Colorado at Denver

ABSTRACT

This study examined how consumer evaluations of products are influenced by two factors: the degree of congruity between products and their associated category schema and the level of consumers' involvement with the evaluation task. It was hypothesized that when product information is congruent with category schema, category-based processing occurs, resulting in assimilation effects; when it is incongruent, contrast or piecemeal processes are used, depending on the level of consumers' involvement. The results generally supported the prediction. Theoretical and managerial implications of the results are discussed.

INTRODUCTION

Assimilation-contrast theorists suggest that when people make an evaluative judgment of a social or a nonsocial object, they go through either one of two processes: sometimes they integrate the object into its associated category and make their evaluation on the basis of the category affect, while other times they contrast the object with the category and make their evaluation in the opposite direction from the category affect (Sherif and Hovland 1961; Sherif, Sherif, and Nebergall 1965). On the other hand, categorization researchers propose that sometimes people simply categorize the object and make their judgment on the basis of the likability of the category, while other times they piece together their judgment on the basis of the likability of the individual attributes of the object (Brewer 1988; Fiske 1982; Fiske and Pavelchak 1986; Fiske and Neuberg 1990; Pavelchak 1989).

Although these alternative modes of evaluation processes have been found and reported in numerous studies in the areas of social and cognitive psychology as well as consumer behavior, it is not yet clear when they occur and what types of judgmental consequences they produce. This research focuses on situations where consumers make their evaluative judgments of products, and predicts that the evaluation outcomes will be determined by the degree of congruity between products and their associated category schema, and the level of consumers' involvement with the evaluation task.

THEORETICAL BACKGROUND

Assimilation-Contrast Literature

Past research in psychology and consumer behavior has suggested that some judgments are very sensitive to the context in which they are made. Applied to the present research context, this means that the evaluation of a product is influenced not only by the overall configuration of the product information but also by the characteristics of the cognitive category accessible during the evaluation. The best known of such contextual phenomena are *assimilation* and *contrast* (Sherif and Hovland 1961; Sherif, Sherif, and Nebergall 1965). Assimilation takes place when the evaluation is made in a direction toward the current category; contrast occurs when it is made in a direction away from the category. Assimilation and contrast phenomena have been found in many empirical studies (e.g., Herr 1986, 1989; Herr, Sherman, and Fazio 1983; Martin 1986; Martin, Seta, and Crelia 1990; Wilson, Lisle, Kraft, and Wetzel 1989). As an example, Herr *et al.* (1983) found that assimilation took place when people considered a stimulus as a member of the primed category; otherwise, contrast occurred. They

assumed that the primed category served as a standard to which the stimulus was compared. However, this assimilation-contrast paradigm does not take into account the possible occurrence of a piecemeal-based evaluation process, which is described in the following section.

Categorization Literature

Categories are cognitive structures which contain instances or *category members* that are perceived similar or equivalent (Fiske and Pavelchak 1986; Smith and Medin 1981). Over time and through experience, people develop a number of categories of objects in an effort to organize and understand them. They also develop a set of expectations about the features of a typical category member with respect to a particular category (*category schema*), and an affective reaction to the category (*category affect*; Rosch 1978; Mervis and Rosch 1981; Smith and Medin 1981). When making an evaluative judgment of an object, they sometimes base their judgment on the affect associated with the category to which the object belong (*category-based process*), while other times they use their evaluations of individual attributes of the object (*piecemeal process*). Then, a question arises as to when people use a category-based and when they use a piecemeal process. This question can be answered by two conceptual models developed in the area, one by Fiske *et al.* (Fiske 1982; Fiske and Pavelchak 1986; Fiske and Neuberg 1990) and the other by Brewer (1988).

Fiske and her colleagues suggest that informational characteristics of a target stimulus determine which evaluation process is used; category-based processes are used when the stimulus information is descriptively congruent with the category schema, whereas piecemeal processes are used when the information is incongruent with it. Their conceptual model has gained a substantial amount of empirical support in psychology and consumer behavior (e.g., Boush and Loken 1991; Fiske, Neuberg, Beattie, and Milberg 1987; Meyers-Levy and Tybout 1989; Pavelchak 1989; Sujan 1985; Sujan and Bettman 1989). As an example, Sujan (1985) found that the alternative modes of processing occurred depending on the match or mismatch of a product to a category schema, with a match triggering category-based reactions and with a mismatch leading to piecemeal evaluations.

On the other hand, Brewer proposes that a perceiver's level of situational, task-oriented involvement is a primary determinant of different types of processing; category-based processing occurs under low involvement situations, whereas piecemeal processing takes place under high involvement situations. Her model also has been supported by many empirical studies (e.g., Borgida and Howard-Pitney 1983; Celsi and Olson 1988; Howard-Pitney, Borgida, and Omoto 1986; Omoto and Borgida 1988). For instance, Celsi and Olson (1988) found that highly involved consumers exerted more cognitive effort than low involved consumers in processing product information.

One limitation of these two models is that they place a lopsided emphasis upon either the informational or the motivational factor, when in fact, both factors might have a simultaneous influence on the evaluation process (see Wyer and Srull 1989, pp. 305-315, for a further discussion of these models).

In sum, the existing literature identifies different types of processes underlying product evaluations. It also indicates two important factors in determining which process is used: product-category schema congruity and situational involvement. In the next section, a conceptual model is developed along with some specific hypotheses.

A CONCEPTUAL MODEL OF PRODUCT EVALUATIONS

Initial Considerations

Suppose consumers, who are shopping for a color T.V. set, run across the following product: a *Zenith* color T.V. set with built-in stereo, multi-functional remote control, and automatic shut-off. If they find this product information sufficiently interesting and relevant to their goal, they will first try to categorize the product in an effort to make sense of it (Fiske and Neuberg 1990; Fiske and Pavelchak 1986). In this case, the most dominant cue will immediately bring to the consumers' mind an apparently appropriate category. In the product domain, it is believed that the most salient cues associated with basic level categories include brand name and price, since a substantial amount of research has demonstrated their dominant impact on product evaluations (Zeithaml 1988; Rao and Monroe 1989). These cues will serve as category labels which are used to organize and understand the remaining features of the product. When a category is accessed, the next step for the consumers would be to make a confirmation that the product is really a member of that category, by considering descriptive implications of the rest of the attribute information.

Successful Categorization

To the extent that the consumers perceive the attribute information to be congruent with the current category, regardless of their involvement levels, they will use the category affect as the basis for their overall evaluations, because this type of category-based process is much more efficient than any other types of processes from a cognitive economy standpoint (Fiske and Pavelchak 1986; Fiske and Neuberg 1990; Fiske and Taylor 1991). Even highly involved consumers would not feel the need to re-elaborate on the attribute information, unless they find anything different about the product. Category-based processing will result in assimilation effects; that is, the overall judgment will be made in a direction toward the category affect. Therefore, it is hypothesized that:

H1: Regardless of involvement levels, when the initial categorization is successful, category-based processing and assimilation effects will occur.

Unsuccessful Categorization

When the confirmation check reveals an incongruity between the product and the category expectations, consumers will react to the product information differently depending on their involvement levels.

Under Low Involvement Conditions. When the initial categorization is not successful due to the product-schema incongruity, and the consumers are not highly involved with the judgment task, a piecemeal elaboration upon product attributes is not likely to occur, which would require a considerable cognitive effort. Instead, a "contrast process" will be used; with the current category serving as a standard of comparison, the overall judgment will be made in the opposite direction from the category, simply because this type of process must be a much easier and faster way to reach a judgment than a piecemeal process. Contrast processing will lead to contrast effects, or the overall judgment negatively correlated with the category affect. Thus, it is predicted that:

H2: When the initial categorization is not successful and consumers are not highly involved with the judgment task, contrast processing and contrast effects will take place.

Under High Involvement Conditions. On the other hand, when the consumers are highly involved with the judgment task, they will not only notice the product-schema incongruity but also engage in piecemeal processing. In other words, they will evaluate the product in an attribute-by-attribute manner and integrate their attribute evaluations to reach a final judgment (Anderson 1974; Fishbein and Ajzen 1975; Fiske *et al.* 1987; Fiske and Pavelchak 1986; Pavelchak 1989; Sujan and Bettman 1989). Consequently, piecemeal processing will produce the overall judgment which is strongly correlated with the evaluations of individual product attributes (called *attribute effects*, hereafter), but not with the category affect. Therefore, it is predicted that:

H3: When the initial categorization is not successful but consumers are highly involved with the evaluation task, piecemeal processing and attribute effects will occur.

In this study, two types of correlations are used for testing the hypotheses: (1) correlations between overall judgments and category affect, and (2) those between overall judgments and attribute evaluations (cf. Fiske *et al.* 1987; Pavelchak 1989; Sujan and Bettman 1989). These correlations served as indicators of the different types of processing and judgmental effects proposed in the conceptual model. Specifically, it was predicted that assimilation effects resulting from category-based processing would be evidenced by a significant positive correlation between overall judgments and category affect, contrast effects from contrast processing would be detected by a significant negative correlation between overall judgements and category affect, and attribute effects from piecemeal processing would be indicated by a significant positive correlation between overall judgments and attribute evaluations. The expected pattern of results under the hypothesized conditions is summarized in Table 1.

METHOD

Pretests

A series of pretests was conducted to develop stimulus materials and to see if manipulations would work as intended.

Pretest 1. For a successful manipulation of product-schema congruity, it was very important to select a product category that the subject population was very familiar with. In other words, the product category had to be the one that was associated with a well-established schema. A pretest was conducted with sixty-two students enrolled in business courses at a midwestern university. They were asked to rate their familiarity with several product categories. The results indicated that they were most familiar with the fast-food category. Thus, this category was used for the experiment.

Pretest 2. The purpose of the second pretest was to select a brand name for stimulus materials. The selection criterion was basically the same as was used for selecting the product category: the brand name had to be the one that subjects were very familiar with. Pretest 2 was conducted to find out a brand name that met the criterion. In this pretest, names of fast-food restaurants were considered as brand names of fast-food. An unaided recall measure was used in the pretest, where 68 subjects participated and were asked to write down all the names of fast-food restaurants that they

TABLE 1
Expected Pattern of Results

Cognitive Processing	Judgmental Effect	Overall Judgment-Category Affect Correlation	Overall Judgment-Attribute Evaluation Correlation
category-based processing	assimilation effect	significant, positive	non-significant
contrast processing	contrast effect	significant, negative	non-significant
piecemeal processing	attribute effect	non-significant	significant, positive

were familiar with. *Burger King* was chosen for the study because it obtained almost 100% mentioning rate.

Pretest 3. The goal of the third pretest was twofold: to develop experimental stimuli for two schema congruity conditions (i.e., Congruent and Incongruent conditions) and involvement manipulation material for two involvement conditions (i.e., High and Low Involvement conditions), and to see if manipulations would work as expected.

Based on a focus group discussion, the congruity was operationalized in the following way. For the Congruent condition, a list of seven fast-food items was created that were typical of *Burger King* restaurants (e.g., cheese burger, broiler sandwich, French fries, apple pie, etc.). The list included the restaurant name. For the Incongruent condition, another list of seven food items were developed that were at odds with the *Burger King* image (e.g., personal pan pizza, stuffed pizza slice, garden salad, carrot cake, etc.). In addition, it was ensured that the descriptions within this condition were also varied so they were not suggestive of any particular type of restaurant.

For the involvement manipulation, a cash prize procedure was employed a la Celsi and Olson (1988). Specifically, for the High Involvement condition, subjects were told that they could win a $10 cash prize by answering a few questions correctly at the end of the pretest. Since they were also informed that the questions would be drawn from the main part of the pretest, they were expected to pay more attention to and become more involved with the test procedures.

The effectiveness of the stimulus materials and the involvement manipulation was tested through a 2 (schema congruity) X 2 (situational involvement) between-subjects, factorial design. Seventy nine students who were enrolled in marketing courses were randomly assigned to one of the four conditions. The effectiveness of the schema congruity manipulation was checked by subjects' ratings on 9-point scales on three questions: (1) "How typical are these food items of *Burger King*?" ("very atypical-very typical"), (2) "How similar are these items to those found in a usual *Burger King* menu?" ("very different-very similar"), and (3) "How likely will you find these items at *Burger King*?" ("very unlikely-very likely"). Since these three measures of perceived congruity obtained a high reliability (alpha=.80), simple average ratings on these items were used to check the success of the manipulation. These average ratings were analyzed in a two-way analysis of variance (ANOVA). As expected, schema congruity had a strong main effect on the average ratings of the three items (F(1,75)=538.99,

p<.001). The means of the average ratings differed significantly between the two congruity conditions (Ms=6.98 and 1.73 for the Congruent and Incongruent conditions, respectively; t(77)=17.03, p<.001). These results indicated that the manipulation of schema congruity worked as intended. Thus, the same materials were used in the main study.

Success of the involvement manipulation was examined by having subjects indicate how interested, how careful, and how attentive they were in reading the food list and evaluating the restaurant. Specifically, they were asked on 9-point scales: (1) "How interested were you when reading and evaluating the previous menu?" ("not-at-all interested-very interested"), (2) "How carefully did you read and evaluate the previous menu?" ("not-at-all carefully-very carefully"), and (3) "How attentive were you when reading and evaluating the previous menu?" ("not-at-all attentive-very attentive"). Since the ratings on these three items also showed a relatively high reliability (alpha=.81), simple average ratings on the measures were used again to check the success of the manipulation. These ratings were submitted to a two-way ANOVA. The results showed that the involvement manipulation had a significant main effect on the average ratings (F(1,75)=5.85, p<.01). The means of subjects' responses to those two questions differed significantly between the two involvement conditions (Ms=5.72 and 6.55 for the Low and High Involvement conditions, respectively; t(77)=2.34, p<.03). Thus, the manipulation of involvement was successful, and was used again in the main study.

Subjects and Design

One hundred and eleven students enrolled in business courses participated in the experiment for extra course credit. These subjects were randomly assigned to one of four treatment conditions in a 2 (schema congruity: Congruent vs. Incongruent) X 2 (situational involvement: High vs. Low) between-subjects, factorial design. Cell sizes ranged from 23 to 26.

Procedure

A computer laboratory was set up for the experiment. All the research instruments were provided on the computer screen and data were collected on-line. Upon arrival, subjects were randomly assigned to one of the treatment conditions and told that the purpose of the experiment was to help *Burger King* provide better service and higher quality food. They first provided their general impression of the restaurant by pressing a number on a 9-point bipolar scale on the screen, ranging from "very bad" (1) to "very good" (9).

Their ratings served as their original category affect. Then they were told that they would see a list of food items available at a *Burger King* restaurant and that they should read it with the purpose of forming an evaluation of this particular restaurant. At this point, the cash prize instruction was announced on the screen for the High Involvement conditions. Subjects then received one of the two stimuli that were developed in Pretest 3. They were asked to provide their overall evaluation of the restaurant by pressing a number on a 9-point scale shown on the screen, ranging from "very bad" (1) to "very good" (9). They also indicated their likings for the individual food items listed on the menu (i.e., their attribute evaluations) on 9-point scales from "strongly dislike" (1) to "strongly like" (9). They were then asked, "How important to you is the inclusion of the following food items to the menu of any fast-food restaurant in general (not necessarily *Burger King*)?" They provided their answers for all the seven food items on 9-point scales from "not-at-all important" (1) to "very important" (9). Then they filled in manipulation checks. The high involvement subjects completed the cash prize questionnaire at this point. Finally, subjects were debriefed and thanked.

RESULTS

Manipulation Checks

Schema Congruity. The same measures used in Pretest 3 were employed to check the effectiveness of the schema congruity manipulation. Since those measures showed a high reliability (alpha=.98), simple average ratings on these measures were used. Again, there was a significant main effect of congruity on the average ratings of the three items ($F(1,107)=471.26$, $p<.001$). Neither the main effect of involvement nor the congruity X involvement interaction was significant ($F(1,107)=2.75$, $p>.10$, and $F(1,107)=.38$, $p>.54$, respectively). Additionally, the means of the average ratings differed significantly between the two congruity conditions ($Ms=7.81$ and 2.16 for the Congruent and Incongruent conditions, respectively; $t(109)=21.61$, $p<.001$). Thus, the manipulation of congruity was successful.

Involvement. Again, the same measures used in Pretest 3 were employed to see if the involvement manipulation was successful. Simple average ratings on the three measures were used again to check the effectiveness of the manipulation, since the ratings on the items showed a high reliability (alpha=.77). Theses ratings were submitted to a two-way ANOVA. For the involvement manipulation, there was a significant main effect on the average ratings ($F(1,107)=12.86$, $p<.001$). The main effect for congruity and the congruity X involvement interaction were not significant ($F(1,107)=.08$, $p>.78$, and $F(1,107)=.00$, $p>.99$, respectively). The means of subjects' responses to those three questions differed significantly between the two involvement conditions ($Ms=6.23$ and 7.12 for the Low and High Involvement conditions, respectively; $t(109)=3.62$, $p<.001$). Thus, the manipulation of involvement was successful.

Judgment Correlations

As mentioned earlier, two sets of correlations were examined: correlations between overall judgments and category affect, and those between overall judgments and attribute evaluations. The use of such correlational measures is based upon the assumption that a high correlation of overall judgments with category affect or attribute evaluations should be indicative of utilization of either of these in arriving at the judgments.

Since category affect could be a function of attribute evaluations to a certain extent in reality, partial correlations were exam-

ined in the study. Specifically, they were correlations between overall judgments and category affect with the effects of attribute evaluations controlled for ($r_{j.ca}$), and those between overall judgments and attribute evaluations with the effects of category affect partialed out ($r_{j.att}$). Attribute evaluations were summarized using the simple average as well as weighted average rules. Since the attribute evaluations integrated by either of the rules were highly correlated ($r=.68$, $p < .01$), the results based on these rules were essentially similar. Thus, for the presentation purpose, only the results based on the weighted average rule will be described here (cf. Anderson 1965; Anderson and Birnbaum 1976).

The partial correlations, $r_{j.ca}$'s and $r_{j.att}$'s across the experimental conditions are shown in Table 2. H1 predicted that a successful initial categorization would bring about category-based processing and assimilation effects. This hypothesis was confirmed by strong positive $r_{j.ca}$'s ($r=.54$, $p=.003$, and $r=.43$, $p=.012$, for the Low and High Involvement conditions, respectively), and nonsignificant $r_{j.att}$ under the Congruent conditions ($r=.10$, $p=.324$, and $r=.31$, $p=.060$, for the Low and High Involvement conditions, respectively). H2 proposed that an unsuccessful categorization under a low involvement condition would result in contrast processing and contrast effects. This was directionally supported by the negative $r_{j.ca}$ under the Incongruent/Low Involvement condition ($r=-.10$, $p=.302$), which did not reach significance. A possible explanation for this nonsignificant $r_{j.ca}$ is that the relatively high category affect ($M=5.92$) might have had a ceiling effect on the overall judgments. The $r_{j.att}$ under the same condition was not significantly greater than zero, as expected ($r=.39$, $p=.021$). H3 predicted that an unsuccessful categorization under a high involvement condition would induce piecemeal processing and attribute effects. This hypothesis was confirmed by a significant positive $r_{j.att}$ ($r=.62$, $p=.000$) along with a nonsignificant $r_{j.ca}$ under the Incongruent/High Involvement condition ($r=-.24$, $p=.107$). Therefore, the correlational pattern generally supported the hypotheses.

DISCUSSION

The results of the study suggest that consumers engage in different types of information processing when evaluating products, depending on product-schema congruity and involvement levels. According to the results, consumers first check the congruity between incoming product information and their prior knowledge about the product. To the extent that they find a good match between these two, they do not go through an effortful piecemeal process; they simply use their evaluations of the product they formed before. Even when they do not find a good fit between the two, they do not use a piecemeal process unless they are highly motivated to do so. It is only when the information is incongruent with the category schema and they are highly involved with the evaluation situation that they engage in attribute-based piecemeal processing. The study findings have important theoretical and managerial implications, which are discussed below.

Theoretical Implications

First, the study results have an implication for the two categorization models discussed earlier, one by Fiske and her colleagues (Fiske 1982; Fiske and Pavelchak 1986; Fiske and Neuberg 1990) and the other by Brewer (1988). These models focus on *either* informational characteristics of a target stimulus *or* motivational aspects of a perceiver as a determinant of different types of cognitive processes underlying overall judgments of objects. The results of this study, however, suggest that *both* of these factors can influence the judgmental processes. For example, schema incon-

TABLE 2
Partial Correlations as a Function of Schema Congruity and Situational Involvement

Schema Congruity	Correlation between Judgments and Category Affect		Correlation between Judgments and Attribute Evaluations	
	Involvement		Involvement	
	Low	High	Low	High
Congruent	.54 **	.43 *	.10	.31
Incongruent	-.10	-.24	.39	.62 ***

* $p < .05$; ** $p < .01$; *** $p < .001$

gruity would not automatically elicit a piecemeal process unless it occurs under high involvement conditions. In addition, high involvement by itself would not induce a piecemeal process when the information is schema-congruent. In this sense, the study results provide a more integrative view on evaluation processes in comparison with the previous models.

Second, the results have implications for both categorization models and assimilation-contrast theory. Specifically, the possible occurrence of contrast has been overlooked in categorization models while that of piecemeal processes and attribute effects has been relatively neglected in the assimilation-contrast paradigm. The study results indicate that any of the processes and judgmental effects that these two groups of literature have proposed can occur, depending on the informational and motivational factors. In this light, the results suggest that the two groups of literature can be integrated to explain consumer information processing and judgments.

Finally, the findings also have an implication for the consumer behavior literature. One of the most controversial issues in consumer research has been when brand names affect product evaluations and when they do not (e.g., Jacoby, Szybillo, and Busato-Schach 1977; Maheswaran, Mackie, and Chaiken 1992; Peterson and Jolibert 1976). The research findings provide one possible answer to this research question; that is, brand names have a positive influence on product evaluations when product attribute information is congruent with brand category, while it may have a negative impact when attribute information is incongruent and consumers are not involved with the evaluation situation.

Managerial Implications

Marketers make a constant effort to change and improve their current products to survive competition. From a consumer's standpoint, such changes in product characteristics are perceived as "incongruities" with existing beliefs and expectations. Then, the marketers' goal is to shape the incongruities and position the products in their favor. The results of this study have some important strategic implications for the companies with this goal.

Companies launching a product with modified features should use a communication strategy that can elicit a high level of consumer involvement. At the same time, the advertising and promotional campaign should emphasize what has been changed about the product. The rationale underlying this strategy is that the increased level of involvement along with the perceived incongruity would

induce consumers to use piecemeal processes, instead of simply relying on some prejudgment or contrast processes.

In practice, however, it would be extremely costly for companies to utilize such massive advertising or promotion tools whenever they introduce a modified product. Thus, companies should take advantage of the image associated with the product before change. Specifically, if their existing product has been enjoying a favorable image, they should emphasize that the new, modified product belongs to the same category of the existing one, and thus minimize the perceived incongruity between the existing and the new one. The logic behind this strategy is that the minimized level of incongruity would trigger category-based processing, resulting in affect transfer from the existing to the modified product. On the other hand, if the current product does not have a good image, companies should make every effort to maximize the perceived incongruity between the current and the new product, encouraging contrast processing, or should try to elicit a high level of involvement, inducing piecemeal processing.

Limitations and Suggestions for Future Research

Interpretation of the results should be tempered by recognition of some limitations of the study. First, only one category and one brand name were examined in the analysis. Although the category and the brand name were selected based on a series of carefully designed pretests, future research should examine the generalizability of the current findings to other categories with different category labels and attributes. Second, only correlations were used as dependent measures in the study. Future studies should use process-oriented measures, in addition to outcome measures, to trace cognitive processes underlying judgmental effects. Third, the research framework was built upon an assumption that categorization would occur at the brand name level, when in reality, it can occur at any level of category (Pavelchak 1989). In other words, a product can be categorized into a number of different categories. For example, in the present study, the restaurant could have been categorized not only as a *Burger King* restaurant but also as a fast-food restaurant, a restaurant in general, and so forth. The assumption would have posed a problem in the study because, if the restaurant, *Burger King*, had been categorized into a higher level category, e.g., a fast-food restaurant category, the manipulation of schema congruity would not have been effective, and the expected piecemeal processes might not have occurred. Although the manipulation worked in this particular study, the assumption still remains restrictive on the generality of results. Future research should investigate what determines the level of categorization.

REFERENCES

Anderson, Norman H. (1965), "Averaging versus Adding as a Stimulus Combination Rule in Impression Formation," *Journal of Experimental Psychology*, 70, 394-400.

_____(1974), "Information Integration Theory: A Brief Summary," in *Contemporary Developments in Mathematical Psychology*, Vol.2, eds. David H. Krantz, R. Duncan Luce, Richard C. Atkinson, and Patrick Suppes, San Francisco: W. H. Freeman, 236-305.

_____and Michael H. Birnbaum (1976), "Test of an Additive Model of Social Inference," *Journal of Personality and Social Psychology*, 33, 655-662.

Borgida, Eugene and Beth Howard-Pitney (1983), "Personal Involvement and the Robustness of Perceptual Salience Effects," *Journal of Personality and Social Psychology*, 45, 560-570.

Boush, David M. and Barbara Loken (1991), "A Process-Tracing Study of Brand Extension Evaluation," *Journal of Marketing Research*, 28 (February), 16-28.

Brewer, Marilynn B. (1988), "A Dual-Process Model of Impression Formation," in *Advances in Social Cognition*, eds. Thomas K. Srull and Robert S. Wyer Jr., Hillsdale, NJ: Erlbaum, 1-36.

Celsi, Richard L. and Jerry C. Olson (1988), "The Role of Involvement in Attention and Comprehension Processes," *Journal of Consumer Research*, 15 (September), 210-224.

Fishbein, Martin and Icek Ajzen (1975), *Belief, Attitude, Intention and Behavior: An Introduction to Theory and Research*, Reading, MA: Addison-Wesley.

Fiske, Susan T. (1982), "Schema-triggered Affect: Applications to Social Perception," in *Affect and Cognition: The 17th Annual Carnegie Symposium on Cognition*, eds. Margaret S. Clark and Susan T. Fiske, Hillsdale, NJ: Erlbaum, 55-78.

_____and Steven L. Neuberg (1990), "A Continuum of Impression Formation, From Category-based to Individuating Processes: Influence of Information and Motivation on Attention and Interpretation," in *Advances in Experimental Social Psychology*, Vol. 23, eds. Mark P. Zanna, San Diego, CA: Academic Press, 1-74.

_____, Steven L. Neuberg, Ann E. Beattie, and Sandra J. Milberg (1987), "Category-based and Attribute-based Reactions to Others: Some Informational Conditions of Stereotyping and Individuating Process," *Journal of Experimental Social Psychology*, 23, 399-427.

_____and Mark A. Pavelchak (1986), "Category-based versus Piecemeal-based Affective Responses: Developments in Schema-Triggered Affect," in *The Handbook of Motivation and Cognition: Foundations of Social Behavior*, eds. Richard M. Sorrentino and E. Tory Higgins, New York: Guilford Press, 167-203.

_____and Shelly E. Taylor (1991), *Social Cognition*, Reading, MA: Addison-Wesley.

Herr, Paul M. (1986), "Consequences of Priming: Judgment and Behavior," *Journal of Personality and Social Psychology*, 51 (December), 1106-1115.

_____(1989), "Priming Price: Prior Knowledge and Context Effects," *Journal of Consumer Research*, 16 (June), 67-75.

_____, Steven J. Sherman, and Russell H. Fazio (1983), "On the Consequences of Priming: Assimilation and Contrast Effects," *The Journal of Experimental Social Psychology*, 19 (July), 323-340.

Howard-Pitney, Beth, Eugene Borgida, and Allen M. Omoto (1986), "Personal Involvement: An Examination of Processing Differences," *Social Cognition*, 4 (1), 39-57.

Jacoby, Jacob, Olson, Jerry C., and Busato-Schach, J. (1977), "Information Acquisition Behavior in Brand Choice Situations," *Journal of Consumer Research*, 3, 209-216.

Maheswaran, Durairaj, Diane M. Mackie, and Shelly Chaiken (1992), "Brand Name as a Heuristic Cue: The Effects of Task Importance and Expectancy Confirmation on Consumer Judgments," *Journal of Consumer Psychology*, 1 (4), 317-336.

Martin, Leonard L. (1986), "Set/Reset: Use and Disuse of Concepts in Impression Formation," *Journal of Personality and Social Psychology*," 51 (3), 493-504.

_____, John J. Seta, and Rick A. Crelia (1990), "Assimilation and Contrast as a Function of People's Willingness and Ability to Expend Effort in Forming an Impression," *Journal of Personality and Social Psychology*, 59 (1), 27-37.

Mervis, Carolyn B. and Eleanor Rosch (1981), "Categorization of Natural Objects," *Annual Review of Psychology*, 32, 89-115.

Meyers-Levy, Joan and Alice M. Tybout (1989), "Schema Congruity as a Basis for Product Evaluation," *Journal of Consumer Research*, 16 (June), 39-53.

Omoto, Allen M. and Eugene Borgida (1988), "Guess Who Might Be Coming to Dinner?: Personal Involvement and Racial Stereotyping," *Journal of Experimental Social Psychology*, 24, 571-593.

Pavelchak, Mark A. (1989), "Piecemeal and Category-based Evaluation: An Idiographic Analysis," *Journal of Personality and Social Psychology*, 56, 3, 354-363.

Peterson, Robert A., and Jolibert, Alain J. P. (1976), "A Cross-national Investigation of Price and Brand as Determinants of Product Quality," *Journal of Applied Psychology*, 61, 533-536.

Rao, Akshay R. and Kent B. Monroe (1989), "The Effect of Price, Brand Name, and Store Name on Buyers' Perceptions of Product Quality: An Integrative Review," *Journal of Marketing Research*, 26 (August), 351-357.

Rosch, Eleanor (1978), "Principles of Categorization," in *Cognition and Categorization*, eds. Eleanor Rosch and B. B. Lloyd, Hillsdale, NJ: Erlbaum, 27-48.

Sherif, Carolyn, Muzafur Sherif, and R. E. Nebergall (1965), *Attitude and Attitude Change: The Social Judgment-Involvement Approach*, Philadelphia, PA: Saunders.

Sherif, Muzafur, Carl D. Hovland (1961), *Social Judgment: Assimilation and Contrast Effects in Communication and Attitude Change*, New Haven, CT: Yale University Press.

Smith, Edward E. and Douglas L. Medin (1981), *Categories and Concepts*, Cambridge, MA: Harvard University Press.

Sujan, Mita (1985), "Consumer Knowledge: Effect on Evaluation Strategies Mediating Consumer Judgment," *Journal of Consumer Research*, 12 (June), 31-46.

_____and James Bettman (1989), "The Effect of Brand Positioning Strategies on Consumers' Brand and Category Perceptions: Some Insights from Schema Research," *Journal of Marketing Research*, 26 (November), 454-467.

_____, James Bettman, and Harish Sujan (1986), "Effects of Consumer Expectations on Information Processing in Selling Encounters," *Journal of Marketing Research*, 23 (November), 346-353.

Wilson, Timothy D., Douglas J. Lisle, Dolores Kraft, and Christopher G. Wetzel (1989), "Preferences as Expectation-Driven Inferences: Effects of Affective Experience," *Journal of Personality and Social Psychology*, 56, 4, 519-530.

Wyer, Robert S., Jr. and Thomas K. Srull (1989), *Memory and Cognition in Its Social Context*, Hillsdale, NJ: Lawrence Erlbaum Associates, Inc.

Zeithaml, Valarie A. (1988), "Consumer Perceptions of Price, Quality, and Value: A Means-End Model and Synthesis of Evidence," *Journal of Marketing*, 52 (July), 2-22.

Congruous and Incongruous Processes in Attitude Evaluation: Response Mode and Behavioral Intention

James R. Bailey, Rutgers University

ABSTRACT

Millar and Tesser (1986) propose that when attitude evaluation (i.e., cognitive vs. affective) and behavioral intention (i.e., instrumental vs. consumatory) are matched the attitude-behavior link is enhanced, whereas when mismatched the relationship suffers. The current study conceptually extends that model to attitude change, and uses a methodological technique that allows for an objective assessment of evaluation processes. Subjects either *judged* automobile alternatives (i.e., cognitive evaluation) or *chose* one (i.e., affective evaluation), and participated in either an *instrumental* or a *consumatory* behavioral condition. As anticipated, more attitude change occurred under conditions of a mismatch than a match. Implications for how consumer attitudes toward product alternatives change as a function of evaluative conditions are discussed.

ATTITUDE CHANGE AND THE MATCH-MISMATCH HYPOTHESIS

Millar and Tesser (1986) have tested a model in which attitude evaluation and behavioral intention interact to determine attitude-behavior correspondence (AB). They reasoned that behaviors performed for *instrumental* purposes (e.g., the development of a skill or knowledge) are driven by the *cognitive* attitude component, and behaviors engaged in for *consumatory* purposes (e.g., preferences) are driven by the *affective* attitude component. Hence, when attitudes are cognitively evaluated and behaviors are instrumental, or when attitudes are affectively evaluated and behaviors are consumatory, the AB relationship is enhanced because the component emphasized and the type of behavior are commensurate. Conversely, when cognitive evaluations are paired with consumatory tasks or affective evaluations with instrumental tasks, the AB relationship suffers because the component emphasized and behavior type are incommensurate. The former two conditions represent a match between evaluation and behavioral intention, whereas the latter two represent a mismatch.

Although Millar and Tesser's (1986) model provides a compelling account of the relation of attitude evaluation to subsequent behavior and effectively integrates several contradictory studies, they did not test the most likely operative causal mechanism: attitude change. Wilson (e.g., Wilson, Dunn, Kraft and Lisle, 1989) has maintained that cognitive evaluation disrupts the AB link by changing attitudes. Using a repeated measures design, Wilson, Kraft and Dunn (1989) compared analyzing reasons for an attitude—a cognitive focus—to a control group, where knowledge about the attitude object was included as a moderating variable. Results indicated that analytic evaluation did change attitudes, but only when subjects were unfamiliar with the attitude object.

Wilson, Kraft and Dunn's (1989) study represents the first direct test of the attitude change hypothesis, but it leaves a number of important questions unanswered. Their results support, at least provisionally, the idea that attitudes change as a function of evaluation, and are consistent with an emerging perspective in consumer research that mental representations are constructed by, among other things, task factors of the decision context (see Payne, Bettman and Johnson 1992 for a review; Upmeyer 1989). But because Wilson, Kraft and Dunn compared a cognitive focus only against a control condition, their study does not test how nonanalytic evaluation (i.e., affective focus) or behavioral intention (i.e., instru-

mental vs. consumatory) alters attitudes. The purpose of the current study, then, is to test the attitude change explanation within the complete theoretical framework of Millar and Tesser (1986). Attitude change should follow the same patterns as AB consistency: When attitude evaluation and behavioral intention are matched (cognitive-instrumental and affective-consumatory) there should be less attitude change than when mismatched (cognitive-consumatory and affective-instrumental).

Integrating Decision Research

One shortcoming of this line of research, though, has been a presumption that manipulations affect the nature and degree of evaluation differentially. Yet evidence for this claim is indirect, as these differences have only been inferred through outcome measures like coded written responses, thought listing or recall. One technique from the decision literature designed expressly to gauge deliberative process is the Information Display Board (IDB), which allows the careful charting of patterns of information acquisition, and shifts analytic focus from the residue of evaluative process (e.g., written responses) to process itself. Accordingly, the IDB appears optimal for representing attitude objects and observing the depth of evaluation directed toward them, and provides a methodological link between the decision making and attitude literatures (Upmeyer 1989).

Another beneficial meeting of attitude and decision research involves the manipulations themselves. Bailey and Billings (1994) and Billings and Scherer (1988) have evoked evaluative strategies similar to those evoked in the AB studies through *response mode*. Here, subjects who either *chose* one product alternative from many or *judged* each alternative represented on an IDB engaged in drastically different decision processes because of the different type of evaluation each induces. The choice mode is driven by the activation of preferences and a subsequent acquisition strategy geared toward identifying the alternative most harmonious with those preferences. In comparison, the judgment mode is compensatory in that features of each alternative are weighed and combined in relation to other alternatives as part of developing coherent representations. As a result, judgment is more analytical and thorough than choice.

The attitude focus manipulations employed by Millar and Tesser (1986) and the response mode manipulations employed by Bailey and Billings (1994) and Billings and Scherer (1988) are conceptually similar in important respects. Specifically, observing attitudes (an affective focus) reminds subjects of their attitudes, just as choice cues preferences, presumably driven by affective concerns (Zajonc and Markus 1982). These manipulations are similar in that subjects consider what they feel, not why they feel it, and result in an affective type of evaluation. Further, analyzing reasons for an attitude (a cognitive focus) and judgment both trigger a cognitive type of evaluation; the reasons focus by requesting an analysis of why, and the judgment mode by requiring subjects to render evaluative statements for each alternative.

Summary and Hypotheses

In summary, this study extends the research of Millar and Tesser (1986) and Wilson, Kraft and Dunn (1989) in three important ways. First, it directly examines the interactive effects of evaluation type and behavioral intention by measuring attitudes

Advances in Consumer Research
Volume 22, © 1995

before and after manipulations. Second, it employs the IDB methodology to verify the evaluation elicited by these manipulations. Third, it proposes that the judgment and choice distinction operates in a parallel manner to the cognitive and affective distinction. Formally stated, the hypothesis was: Under conditions where evaluation type and behavioral intention are matched (i.e., judgment-instrumental and choice-consumatory) there will be less attitude change than under conditions of mismatch (i.e., judgment-consumatory and choice-instrumental).

As a manipulation check based on previous research using response mode and the IDB methodology (Bailey and Billings 1994; Billings and Scherer 1988), we predict that the judgment conditions should result in more thorough evaluation (i.e., amount of information uncovered) than the choice conditions.

METHODS

Subjects and Overview

Subjects were 43 female and 42 male undergraduates at Rutgers University who were given course extra-credit for participating in a consumer study on automobiles, and completed a questionnaire regarding automobile characteristics (i.e., the pre-test attitude measure). Upon arrival for testing subjects were presented with the target IDB randomly assigned to one of four conditions defined by a 2 x 2 (Response Mode: Judgment vs. Choice x Behavioral Intention: Instrumental vs. Consumatory) factorial design. Once the task was completed, manipulation checks and the post-test attitude questionnaire were administered.

Stimulus Material

The IDB's consisted of eight used automobiles listed vertically and six dimensions listed horizontally, with values for each dimension recorded on cards contained in envelopes on the corresponding locations on the board. The dimensions and values were as follows: (a) make: Chrysler, Ford, GM, Volkswagen, Toyota, Honda, Nissan, Subaru; (b) type: sports, compact, mid-sized, full-sized; (c) mileage: 1,000-15,000; 15,000-30,000; 30,000-45,000; 45,000-60,000 (d) price: $2,500-5,000; $5,000-7,500; $7,500-10,000; $10,000-above; (e) features: stereo system, digital display instruments, air conditioning, none; and (f) color: red, blue, black, brown, green, white, orange, silver (the values under mileage, price, and features were each presented twice to cover all eight alternatives). This matrix yielded 48 pieces of information, 6 per alternative. To obtain information, subjects removed the cards from the envelopes and placed the cards back on the board so that the information was displayed. The configuration was randomized after each session to control for order effects.

Attitude Questionnaire

Studies that concentrated on the AB link (e.g., Millar and Tesser 1986) used only one item to measure attitudes, as did Wilson Kraft and Dunn (1989, Study 2) in their pre- and post-test design. Herein a more complete approach was adopted, using 38 items and assessing two dimensions. The *importance* of each dimension (e.g., make, mileage) was rated on a scale ranging from *extremely unimportant* (1) and *extremely important* (7), and the *desirability* of specific characteristics (e.g., Ford, Toyota) was rated on a scale ranging from *extremely undesirable* (1) to *extremely desirable* (7).

Prior to statistical analysis, component and composite measures of attitude change were calculated from the pre- and post-test questionnaires. The component measure was computed as the average absolute amount of change in the importance ratings added to the average absolute amount of change in the desirability rating

(both assessed from pre- to post-manipulation). This variable could assume values from 0 to 8.

The composite measure was computed as the difference between pre- and post-weighted attitude scores. These were calculated as the weighted average of the desirability ratings (D_i) for the pieces of information uncovered about an alternative during the task, where the weights were the importance ratings (I_i): $SI_i D_i/I_i$. For example, if four pieces of information about alternative A were uncovered, the score would be the weighted average of the four product scores, each product being an importance rating multiplied by a desirability rating. Separate scores were computed using the pre- and post-questionnaires, and the composite measure was computed as the average absolute difference between these weighted scores for each alternative, and could assume values from 0 to 25.

The rationale behind computing absolute amount of change in the component and composite measures was the absence of persuasive intent. Accordingly, change in either direction was considered. This was also the approach used by Wilson, Kraft and Dunn (1989).

Procedure

Once participants arrived at the laboratory (approximately one week later), the experimenter reiterated that this was a consumer study on automobiles, and in order to enhance experimental and mundane realism stressed the importance of consumer research and asked subjects to vividly image an automobile purchase. The IDB was then thoroughly explained, and participants were asked to practice on a sample IDB until comfortable with the task. When ready and after any questions were answered, participants were introduced to the test IDB, reminded of the nature of the study, and provided with one of two standardized sets of instructions to manipulate attitude focus and behavioral intention.

Choice versus judgment manipulation. Choice was manipulated by instructing subjects to choose one of the eight automobiles alternatives. Judgment was manipulated by instructing subjects to evaluate each alternative on a 7-point scale ranging from *very high quality* (1) to *very low quality* (7). These are the exact manipulations used in previous research on response mode (Bailey and Billings 1994; Billings and Scherer 1988).

Instrumental versus consumatory manipulation. The instrumental condition was manipulated by informing subjects that after completing the task, they would be given a test to measure their ability to discern automobile quality. Subjects in the consumatory condition were told that they would be given an unrelated test on social sensitivity following the task. These are the exact manipulations used by Millar and Tesser (1986).

RESULTS

Manipulation Checks

We used the *amount of information searched* (i.e., the total number of cards examined) as a meaningful variable sensitive to the thoroughness or depth of evaluation evoked by experimental conditions. Consistent with Bailey and Billings (1994) and Billings and Scherer (1988), subjects in the judgment condition searched more information (M=32.42) than subjects in the choice condition (M=22.02), F(1, 81)=28.05, p<.001, indicating the response mode manipulations were effective.

To test the effect of behavioral intention manipulations, responses on the post-task questionnaire indicated that subjects in the instrumental version expected to be tested on their ability to discern automobile quality to a greater degree (M=3.50) than did subjects in the consumatory version (M=2.60), F(1, 81)=5.84., p<.001. These results testify that the behavioral intention manipulations were effective.

FIGURE 1

Component Attitude Change as a Function of Response Mode and Behavioral Intention

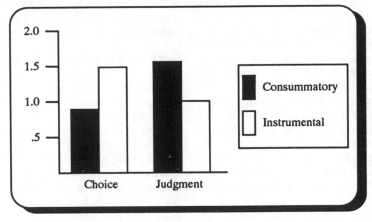

FIGURE 2

Composite Attitude Change as a Function of Response Mode and Behavioral Intention

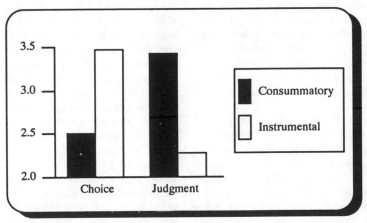

Attitude Change

Response mode and behavioral intention should interact to determine attitude change in an antagonistic pattern. Analysis of the component measure of attitude change indicated a significant interaction between response mode and behavioral intention, supporting this hypothesis, $F(1, 81)=26.38$, $p<.001$ (see Figure 1).

Analysis of the composite measure of attitude change yielded precisely the same pattern of results, $F(1,81)=6.4$, $p<.05$ (see Figure 2).

Additional Analysis

The possibility that the change reported above was due to polarization was tested by coding any change in extremity of evaluation (e.g., *undesirable* to *extremely undesirable*) as polarization. Consistent with the results of Wilson, Kraft and Dunn (1989), there were no effects of the condition on polarization (all $Fs<1.2$; $ps<.05$).

Analyses were also conducted to address the possibility of artifactual explanations. Wilson, Kraft and Dunn (1989) demonstrated that knowledge about an attitude object moderates the effects of a cognitive focus: Those unfamiliar with attitude objects were more affected by cognitive deliberations than those familiar with the objects. Hence, the post-experimental questionnaire queried subjects about experience assessing automobiles and their general level of interest about automobiles. Analyses indicated no significant main effects or interactions involving familiarity or interest (all $Fs<1.4$; $ps<.05$).

Finally, it is also possible that the amount of information uncovered on the IDB differentially affects attitudes and accounts for the interaction between response mode and behavioral intention. Hierarchical regression analyses were conducted on the component and composite measures of attitude change with amount of information searched (a continuous variable) entered as an additional independent variable along with response mode and behavioral intention. The interactions described previously were unchanged by this analysis, indicating that experimental conditions affected attitudes independent of amount of information searched.

DISCUSSION

This study demonstrated that the manner of evaluation and behavioral intention act in concert to influence attitudes. Although the framework put forth by Millar and Tesser (1986) was designed to explain attitude-behavior consistency, it appears to generalize to attitude change, and the current study is a more comprehensive test of the match-mismatch hypothesis than has been offered previously.

In those conditions where little attitude change occurred response mode elicited attitude evaluation that was congruous with the behavioral intention. The judgment-instrumental condition required an incorporation and organization of information into coherent wholes so that comparative judgments could be rendered about each alternative, and the expectation of a test of ability to discern automobile quality evokes a parallel process. Similarly, the requirements of the choice-consumatory condition are consonant; the individual preferences and desires cued by the instruction to choose among alternatives can be considered without concern for a test of discriminatory ability. In both cases, no attitude change occurs because the mental activity of the attitude focus and the behavior type are compatible.

By contrast, conditions resulting in a larger degree of attitude change represent a mismatch of evaluation and behavioral intention. In the choice-instrumental condition, subjects access their feelings regarding automobiles in order to choose, but their feelings are tempered by the simultaneous concern over an ability test. These incongruous purposes lead subjects to scrutinize feelings activated by the choice response mode in order to make them consistent with the concern over evaluation. The judgment-consumatory condition is more difficult to explain, but because the consumatory manipulation specifies no purpose, perhaps individual preferences were activated and subsequently reevaluated in the service of judgment. Attitude change occurs when evaluation and intention are mismatched because the mental activity involved with each is contradictory.

Two recent studies have tested hypotheses similar to those tested here. Millar and Millar (1990) and Edwards (1990) investigated attitude change as a function of attitude type (i.e., cognitive vs. affective) and means of persuasion (i.e., cognitive vs. affective). Like the results reported here, Millar and Millar find more attitude change when attitude type and means of persuasion were mismatched (e.g., cognitive and affective) than when they were matched (e.g., cognitive and cognitive). Edwards' results did not follow a mismatch-match pattern, but this may be due to subtle variations in procedure. There are differences among these studies, but all distinguish attitudes on a cognitive-affective dimension, and all suggest the utility of a matching principle for understanding attitude change.

Despite the similarity of our results to those obtained by Millar and Tesser (1986), it could be argued that response mode is mapping onto something entirely different than attitude evaluation. The reasoning against this criticism is strong. First, the results reported here support predictions generated from Millar and Tesser's (1986) model and Wilson's (e.g., Wilson, Kraft and Dunn 1989) attitude change hypothesis. Second, these results are precisely what would have been expected if manipulations like those of the above researchers had been employed. Finally, the processes are logically similar. The judgment mode, like analyzing reasons (a cognitive focus), requires an evaluative statement for each alternative, and results in a more complete and thorough search (Bailey and Billings 1994; Billings and Scherer 1987). By way of contrast, the choice mode, like observing attitudes (an affective focus), is guided by individual preferences and desires resulting in a less thorough information search. The focus here is clearly on one's feeling; what is wanted, not why it is wanted. Because of the truncated search, information that might call the prevailing attitude into question is never encountered. Similarly, when individuals focus on feelings,

they do not necessarily scrutinize these feelings. Although Johnson and Russo (1984) have argued that choice requires and optimal decision and is therefore more analytic than judgment, their point is that choice calls for the use of decision rules that promote a more detailed alignment with preferences.

Implications and Future Research

Marketing efforts have been largely concerned with changing consumer attitudes or preferences through persuasively styled messages. The presumption is that once changed these attitudes will extrapolate to consumer decisions. However, the current data suggest that attitudes, no matter how they may have been influenced by persuasive attempts, change as a function of the manner of evaluation engaged during the actual multi-alternative decision episode. Specifically, pre-decisional preferences may predict decisions under conditions where the underlying attitudes remain stable (e.g., judgment-instrumental and choice-consumatory), but the relationship may diminish when conditions promote reevaluation (e.g., judgment-consumatory and choice-instrumental). In general, any circumstances that influence the purpose of decision making may also influence attitude structure.

This effort is not without limitations. Perhaps the most prominent of these is that the instrumental behavioral intention manipulation—by posing the possibility of a test on analytic ability—seems removed from everyday consumer decision making. Nevertheless, to the extent that the instrumental condition furnished a type of *accountability* manipulation, it does have relevance for purchasing agents or other organizational operatives that are responsible for product evaluations. Second, the exclusive use of amount of information as a measure of evaluation is clearly a narrow index. Enlisting convergent, qualitative techniques such as thought-listing or verbal protocol techniques for corroborative evidence would improve confidence in this conjecture. Third, several small procedural variations could have significantly strengthened the study's design. Including a control group to gauge natural attitudinal fluctuations would have provided a sounder base for comparison. Also, collecting a measure of behavioral intention (as opposed to only manipulating it) would have allowed testing whether pre- or post-test attitudes better predict behaviors, and provided an additional test of Millar and Tesser's (1986) AB hypothesis.

Finally, although the congruency explanation evoked here is intuitively appealing, this study was not designed to test which model of attitude change applies. The results rule out polarization, but other models may apply. One interpretation pertains specifically to the type of evaluation elicited by manipulations. Judgment entails a careful and deliberative type of mental activity which directs attention to the merits of an attitude structure. On the other hand, choice is a preferential-based process where the concentration is on sentiment without concern for justification. These contrasting processes—judgment versus choice—bear significant resemblance to the dual process model of persuasion described by Petty and Cacioppo (e.g., 1986) and Chaiken, Liberman and Eagly (1989). Although there are significant differences between the approach employed herein and these two paradigms, the similarities warrant further exploration.

CONCLUSION

The current research was unique in that subjects evaluated their attitudes towards numerous objects simultaneously. Hence, in addition to the ostensible purpose of verifying differences in process, the IDB allowed for the presentation and consideration of attitude objects in a more realistic fashion. This research also extended inquiry on attitude evaluation to the decision making arena, because in most instances evaluation of product alternatives is in the service of making a consumer decision. There is mounting evidence that the underlying constellation of values or preferences that guide decisions are not stable, but rather are constructed by, among other things, the circumstances which require their use (Payne, Bettman and Johnson 1991; Upmeyer 1989). If different types of evaluation lead to differential changes in attitudes, this knowledge should facilitate speculation into what decisions consumers make, and more importantly, why they are made. A meeting of these two literatures could prove mutual profitable by furnishing an intelligible springboard for relating attitude change to actual purchasing decisions.

REFERENCES

Bailey, James. R. and Robert S. Billings (1994). "Sequential phases of judgment and the value representation of product alternatives," *Advances in Consumer Research, 21,* 437-441.

Billings, Robert S. and Lisa L. Scherer (1988), "The effects of response mode and importance on decision making strategies: Judgment versus choice," *Organizational Behavior and Human Decision Processes, 41,* 1-19.

Chaiken, Shelly, A. Liberman and Alice H. Eagly (1989). "Heuristic and systematic information processing within and beyond the persuasion context," in *Unintended thought,* ed. J. S. Uleman and J.A. Bargh, New York: Guilford Press.

Edwards, Karen. (1990). "The interplay of affect and cognition in attitude formation and change," *Journal of Personality and Social Psychology, 59,* 202-216.

Johnson, Eric, J. and J. Edward Russo (1984). "Product familiarity and learning new information," *Journal of Consumer Research, 11,* 542-550.

Millar, Murray. G. and Karen U. Millar (1990). "Attitude change as a function of attitude type and argument type," *Journal of Personality and Social Psychology, 59,* 217-228.

Millar, Murray. G. and Abraham Tesser (1986). "Effects of affective and cognitive focus on the attitude-behavior relation," *Journal of Personality and Social Psychology, 51,* 270-276.

Payne, John. W., James R. Bettman and Eric J. Johnson (1992), "Behavioral decision research: A constructive processing perspective," *Annual Review of Psychology, 43,* 87-131.

Petty, Richard. E. and John T. Cacioppo (1986). "The elaboration likelihood model of persuasion," in *Advances in experimental social psychology, Vol. 19,* ed. L. Berkowitz, New York: Academic Press.

Upmeyer, A. (Ed.) (1989). *Attitudes and behavioral decisions.* New York: Springer-Verlag.

Wilson, Timothy D., Dana. S. Dunn, Dolores Kraft and Douglas. J. Lisle (1989), "Introspection, attitude change, and attitude-behavior consistency: The disruptive effects of explaining why we feel the way we do," in *Advances in Experimental Social Psychology, Vol. 22,* ed. L. Berkowitz, New York: Academic Press.

Wilson, Timothy. D., Dolores Kraft, and Dana S. Dunn (1989). "The disruptive effects of explaining attitudes: The moderating effect of knowledge about the attitude object," *Journal of Experimental Social Psychology, 25,* 379-400.

Zajonc, Robert. B. and Hazel Markus (1982). "Affective and cognitive factors in preferences," *Journal of Consumer Research, 9,* 123-131.

Tell Me Again Why I Should Listen to You?: Source Effects Revisited

Nancy Artz, University of Southern Maine

The large number of source effects documented in the literature and the corresponding conceptual frameworks indicate that source plays a complex role in persuasion (cf. McGuire 1985; Wilson and Sherrell 1993). Early research examined how dimensions of source credibility such as expertise and trustworthiness influence attitudes through a process of internalization in which message arguments are accepted by the viewer. Researchers examining source attractiveness argued that attractiveness persuades through a process of identification (i.e., enhancement of viewer self–concept) rather than internalization of arguments. Involvement has been shown to be an important moderator of source effects. Source characteristics are thought to have a strong influence on attitudes when involvement is low because the viewer uses the source as a simple cue in deciding whether to accept or reject the message conclusion (Petty and Cacioppo 1984). Source variables can still have an effect in high involvement processing, but the extent and type of effect depends on message characteristics such as message strength and message ambiguity (Chaiken and Maheswaran 1994).

Each of the papers in this session explores the complexity of source effects from a different perspective. New mediating and moderating factors are identified (i.e., vocal characteristics, message format). The relationship between involvement and internalization/identification is examined further. Additional insight is gained into the way source variables affect cognitive processing. The extent to which source characteristics are considered by practitioners is uncovered. And, a conceptual model of the celebrity endorser selection process is offered that integrates the traditional dimensions of source credibility with the dimensions relevant in the celebrity endorsement context. All of the papers provide insight into when and why different sources are appropriate for different persuasive situations.

The paper by Claire Gélinas–Chebat and Jean–Charles Chebat, "Voice Intonation and Intensity as Antecedents of Source Credibility in the Advertising Context," examines source characteristics which have been previously ignored by consumer researchers. Specifically, the research focuses on the persuasive role of two major phonetic characteristics: voice intensity and voice intonation. An experiment was conducted to assess the effect of voice intensity (high or low), voice intonation (high or low), and involvement (high or low) on perceptions of source credibility and similarity/attractiveness. The results indicate that intensity and intonation play different roles as antecedents of credibility (i.e., internalization persuasion process) and similarity (i.e., identification persuasion process). Intonation has a main effect on perceived credibility while the effects of intensity on perceptions of credibility and similarity are moderated by involvement. Interestingly, intensity and intonation have an interactive effect on perceived credibility. Credibility is enhanced if both are low or both are high. The authors suggest explanations for the effects that are compatible with the common theoretical frameworks in the literature on internalization/identification and involvement. Again, this paper makes a contribution by identifying new antecedents of source effects.

The paper by Nancy Artz and Alice M. Tybout, "Source Expertise and Source Bias as Moderators of the Persuasive Effects of Numeric and Verbal Communications," examines the persuasive role of the traditional source credibility characteristics of expertise and bias. An experiment was conducted that manipulated message format (numeric/verbal), source expertise (expert/novice), and source bias (unbiased/biased). The results indicate that different types of sources are appropriate for numeric and verbal messages in that higher levels of source expertise can enhance the persuasiveness of numeric claims, but can be detrimental with verbal claims. This is argued to occur because consumers associate precise, numeric information with experts and associate imprecise, verbal information with novices. A source is thought to be most persuasive when the source's level of expertise is congruent with the level of expertise associated with the type of message. Interestingly, this effect of source–message congruence was only evident when the source was biased. Source bias appears to shift the focus of the processor's thoughts away from product attributes and toward other aspects of the communication (as opposed to increasing the total number of thoughts). The paper makes a contribution by providing additional insight into the process underlying source effects.

The paper by Alan R. Miciak and Carolyn L. Tripp, "Dimensions of Source Credibility in Celebrity Endorsement Situations," takes a fresh perspective by seeing whether the theoretical constructs found in the source effects literature are relevant to the actual selection of spokespersons by advertisers. Specifically, practitioners were surveyed to identify the criteria used when celebrity endorsers are selected. The results indicate that practitioners are highly sensitive to spokesperson credibility (expertise and trustworthiness) and attractiveness as well as to celebrity–audience congruence and celebrity–product congruence. Moreover, celebrity endorser selection is also driven by a number of practical concerns such as the size of the endorser's fees, the risk of negative publicity, whether the celebrity is currently endorsing other products, etc. An interesting line of future research would be to investigate the extent to which these practical concerns affect consumer perceptions of attractiveness and credibility. The authors propose a model of the selection process that highlights the importance of the communication context in the selection of celebrity endorsers. In other words, the model emphasizes that traditional source characteristics like credibility and attractiveness must be viewed in the context of the specific product endorsed, the target audience, and the specific creative execution. The authors also present a structural model of the relationship between attractiveness, trustworthiness, source–audience congruence, expertise, and source–product congruence.

As a group, the three papers in this session examine mediating and moderating factors underlying source effects. The paper by Gélinas–Chebat and Chebat explores vocal characteristics as antecedents of source credibility and attractiveness, and examines the moderating role of involvement. The paper by Artz and Tybout examines the interaction between source expertise and message format in influencing persuasion, and also explores the cognitive processes associated with the effect of source bias. The paper by Miciak and Tripp explores the extent to which practitioners are sensitive to mediating and moderating factors when they select celebrity endorsers, and proposes a conceptual model of the selection process that integrates the traditional dimensions of source credibility with the dimensions relevant in the celebrity endorsement context. In conclusion, the session focuses attention on the complex role of communication sources that results in different sources being appropriate for different persuasive situations. Future research should continue in the tradition of this session by exploring when and why source characteristics have the effects they do.

The discussant, Elizabeth J. Wilson, echoed these themes when she reviewed the contributions of each paper for theory development and management application. She encouraged researchers to continue to pursue a number of topics: 1) the role of self–monitoring in source effects which was discussed in the paper by Gélinas–Chebat and Chebat, but was not formally manipulated, 2) the managerial implications of the Artz and Tybout finding that novices can be more persuasive than experts in certain situations, and 3) a structural model using the Miciak and Tripp data to test traditional theorizing about separate roles for internalization and identification.

REFERENCES

Chaiken, Shelly and Durairaj Maheswaran (1994), "Heuristic Processing Can Bias Systematic Processing: Effects of Source Credibility, Argument Ambiguity, and Task Importance on Attitude Judgment," *Journal of Personality and Social Psychology*, 66 (3), 460–473.

McGuire, William J., (1985), "Attitudes and Attitude Change," *The Handbook of Social Psychology*, Vol. II, Gardner Lindzey and Elliot Aronson (Eds.), New York: Random House, pp. 233–346.

Petty, Richard E. and John T. Cacioppo (1984), "Source Factors and the Elaboration Likelihood Model of Persuasion," *Advances in Consumer Research*, Vol. 11, 668–672.

Wilson, Elizabeth J. and Daniel L. Sherrell (1993), "Source Effects in Communication and Persuasion Research: A Meta–Analysis of Effect Size," *Journal of the Academy of Marketing Science*, 21(Spring), 101–112.

Consumer Behavior in High Technology Markets

Rashi Glazer, University of California Berkeley

Among the most important business phenomena of our generation is the degree to which entire categories of products and services are based on technologies that did not even exist just a few years prior to their introduction. Recent surveys of executives across a wide range of industries suggest that an increasingly high proportion (as much as 80% in some cases) of both future sales and profits are expected to stem from such "high technology" products.

At the same time, most of our understanding of consumer behavior is, at best, "technology neutral" and, at worst, rooted in both theoretical and empirical work with product categories which have essentially remained unchanged for many years with respect to their underlying technologies. While there is no single agreement as to the precise definition of "high technology," theories of competitive strategy as well as actual business practice now explicitly recognize that there are important characteristics (rapidly changing life cycles, turbulence, information-intensity, etc.) which distinguish high technology from more traditional markets. Noticeably absent from the literature, however, has been systematic investigation into what might be assumed to be one of the most important defining characteristics of any market — the nature of its consumer behavior.

The special session was designed to address this under-researched — yet crucial — issue affecting a major and ever-growing sector of modern business activity. The premise of the session was that consumer behavior in high technology markets is not just "institutional" in nature (and therefore not worthy of serious academic inquiry), but rather may be fundamentally different than behavior in traditional environments and thus demands serious study. Indeed, the motivation for the session was derived from the fact that there are an increasing number of researchers — with interests in both traditional consumer behavior, industrial organization, and marketing/technology strategy — who are beginning to explore the dynamics of consumer behavior as they relate to high technology markets. The purpose of the session was to bring together a representative sample of this research within a single forum, so as to highlight the extent to which a variety of seemingly independent research streams are conceptually and formally related.

The three papers in the session dealt with a range of issues and phenomena and differed with respect to their theoretical/empirical orientation (although, in all cases, actual data are involved). In this regard, the papers reflect the fact that he session's general topic represents a meeting ground for researchers coming from a variety of orientations.

The first paper, *"A Consumer-Behavior Definition of High-Technology Markets"*, by Glazer and Stiving, attempts to derive a definition of "high technology" that is based less on producer-based characteristics than on consumer decision-making characteristics. After developing a conceptual framework for characterizing markets, the authors present data from a study suggesting that there is often more inter-product category variance than intra-product category variance with respect to the level of "technological intensity." Thus, for example, one company's soap offering may be deemed considerably more "high tech" by consumers than another company's computer.

The second paper, *"Metrics by Which Managers Evaluate R&D Groups,"* by Zettelmeyer and Hauser takes an expanded view of consumer behavior — by considering internal as well as external customers for new technologies. (This wider perspective on the meaning of a customer — and hence of consumer behavior — is in itself an important development that typifies much of the on-going research in the general area of marketing and technology.) The research focuses on the methods by which managers value R&D activity (or technology) and how these internal metrics, in turn, are related to external measures of customer satisfaction with new technologies.

The third paper, *"Consumer Behavior and Interactive Media"*, by Sultan and Winer, presents the initial findings of a rather broad research stream into the set of issues associated with emerging interactive media products and services (early efforts of the "information superhighway"). The authors present a number of hypotheses associated with consumer adoption of these new technologies that are rooted in the behavioral decision making literature. One of the features of the research is that the empirical component is based on a multi-firm panel survey of actual users of interactive media.

When taken as a group, the papers help improve our understanding not only of certain specific real-world marketing phenomena, but more generally, of the degree to which the insights about consumer decision making in high technology markets can provide the foundation for a richer (and perhaps more "realistic") consumer behavior theory.

The Moderating Effects of Learning Goals and the Acquisition of Product Information on the Limits of Price Acceptability

Rashmi Adaval, University of Illinois
Kent B. Monroe, University of Illinois

Consumers' perceptions of price acceptability can have an important influence on their transactions with sellers. Available evidence suggests that prices consumers find acceptable, may be influenced by several contextual variables (Monroe et al. 1977). Of particular importance is the relative knowledge that consumers have about the product category in general. Further, positive or negative information about a general product category (e.g., jeans) could affect consumers' willingness to pay a given amount of money for a specific product within this category (e.g., Levi's 505s). Positive or negative information about how manufacturers in a product category typically use high or low quality materials, or are noted for excellent or poor workmanship, can be conveyed either through word-of-mouth or through articles in the general press.

However, the effects of such information on price acceptability, may vary depending on consumers' prior knowledge of the range of prices that are typically paid for category exemplars and the conditions under which this price knowledge has been acquired. The research reported in this article, examined the impact of positive and negative product category information on consumers' judgments of price acceptability under conditions in which knowledge about the prices of particular products was acquired intentionally or incidentally.

WHAT MAKES A PRICE ACCEPTABLE?

The Concept of Acceptable Prices

Consumers normally do not have clearly defined point estimates of acceptable prices for a product. Instead, a range of prices are generally considered acceptable. The concept of an acceptable price range is rooted in social judgment theory and assimilation-contrast theory (Sherif 1963). Monroe (1971, 1973) offered theoretical arguments for the existence of reference prices, acceptable price ranges and a logarithmic psychological scale for price judgments.

Consumers' exposure to price variations in the marketplace results in a set of prices that they consider acceptable. Monroe (1990) defines this acceptable price range as *those prices that consumers are willing to pay for a good or service*. Each time a price stimulus is encountered in a purchase context, an implicit judgment is made regarding its acceptability for the product or service to which it pertains. The implicit judgment is made by comparing the price cue to either an internal referent stored in memory, an external referent at the point of judgment, or to an adapted referent based on these internal and external referents (Lichtenstein et al. 1988). However, it is important to note that these judgments of acceptability, which indicate a willingness to pay a certain price, may not always result in actual purchase behavior and transactions involving that amount of money. A decision not to purchase may occur because of lack of financial resources, or because of specific strong beliefs and attitudes that surface at the time of the actual purchase.

The acceptable price range is defined by the upper and lower price limits or endpoints (Gabor and Granger 1966). The upper limit identifies the price above which consumers would consider the product to be too expensive or belonging to a higher priced category. The lower price limit identifies the price below which

consumers would be suspicious of the quality or categorize it differently. Consumers differ not only in how wide a range of prices they find acceptable but also in whether this range includes predominantly higher market prices, predominantly lower prices, or a mix of higher and lower prices (Rao and Sieben 1992). It is likely that the prices consumers are willing to pay are included within both the actual market prices for products in the category, as well as the set that a consumer normally expects to see based on prior experience. However, not all of these actual or expected prices will be acceptable.

Cox (1986) contends that buyers do not bring rigidly formed price limits into a purchase situation and that the acceptable price range is influenced to some extent by the prices consumers encounter on a particular purchasing occasion. Numerous factors can affect the upper and lower limits of the acceptable price range, including brand name (Fouilhe 1970), market price knowledge (Kosenko and Rahtz 1988) and product involvement (Raju 1977).

The Relationship Between Perceived Value and Price Acceptability

A price's acceptability is likely to be influenced in part by the perceived value inferred from the transaction. Monroe (1984) proposed a conceptual model integrating the concepts of perceived quality and perceived value with the acceptable price range. Starting with Ahtola's (1984) conceptualization of "give" and "get", i.e., price is what the consumer has to *give* in order to *get* the product, Monroe noted the similarity to his conceptualization of perceived value (i.e., the perceived benefits relative to price). Although price influences the perceived sacrifice buyers must make to obtain a product (the "give" component), price also influences their perceptions of product quality (the "get" component). Buyers who focus on the "give" component are more likely to associate higher prices with greater sacrifices and are less likely to find higher prices acceptable to pay. In contrast, buyers who focus on the "get" component may associate higher prices with greater quality of the product, and are more likely to find higher prices acceptable. For lower prices, the reverse situation is likely to exist. That is, consumers who focus on the "give" component are more likely to find lower prices acceptable, but consumers who focus on the "get" component are less likely to find lower prices acceptable.

More generally, there is likely to be a tradeoff between the utility of the perceived sacrifice against the utility inferred from the perception of quality. If the positive utility inferred from the perception of quality is greater than the negative utility of the perceived sacrifice, then a positive perception of value results. As long as there is a positive perception of value, the prices will be considered acceptable.

Therefore, identifying when consumers are more likely to focus on the "get" component (i.e., infer positive quality from price) versus the "give" component (i.e., perceive price largely as a sacrifice) is important in understanding the phenomena. Previous research has demonstrated that consumers generally perceive that a price-quality relationship exists in the marketplace. However, consumers are more likely to infer positive quality from higher prices in some situations than others (Zeithaml 1988; Dodds, Monroe and Grewal 1991). Rao and Monroe (1988) found that consumers' use of extrinsic price cues and intrinsic product cues for

Advances in Consumer Research
Volume 22, © 1995

the assessment of product quality depends on their prior knowledge. Specifically, subjects who are either unfamiliar or highly familiar with a product category are more likely to perceive a strong price-quality relationship than those who are only moderately familiar with it. Consumers who do not have sufficient knowledge are more likely to use extrinsic cues like price in product quality assessments because they have relatively less developed schemas about how intrinsic information should be evaluated. However very knowledgeable consumers are also capable of using price as an indicator of quality *provided price has diagnostic value* (Rao and Monroe 1988). The differential use of price as an indicator of quality by people with differing knowledge levels implies that people may use price information in different ways to make quality inferences about the product. If these beliefs or quality inferences are reinforced or discredited (through positive or negative information about the general product category), perceptions of value would be affected leading to changes in prices considered acceptable.

The questions addressed by this research are: What makes a price acceptable and how does acceptability change when consumer market price knowledge is affected through different learning goals (intentional versus incidental) and different types of product category information (positive and negative)?

THE IMPACT OF POSITIVE AND NEGATIVE INFORMATION UNDER DIFFERENT LEARNING CONDITIONS

When consumers receive positive or negative information about the product category, their perceptions of quality may be influenced by this information. As argued above, these perceptions will influence overall perceptions of value and consequently, the acceptability of prices. However, the processing of positive or negative information may result in different kinds of inferences being drawn about quality. Recent work examining inferential processes has shown that consumers expand on given product information to form new beliefs (Ford and Smith 1987), or modify existing beliefs (Yi 1990a) about attributes that are either unknown or not mentioned in the communication. In addition, negative information may be effective in stimulating inferential thinking (Price 1992). Dick, Chakravarti and Biehal's (1990) work suggests that any factor that increases either the relevance, the accessibility, or the diagnosticity of an inferencing rule will increase the likelihood that inferential processing will occur.

Previous research suggests that consumer judgments are more influenced by negative than by positive information (Price 1992). Negative information about the product category in general, is likely to increase the perceived risk associated with the purchases of particular members of this category. Prices may be used to infer quality especially if the inferencing rule (drawing positive quality inferences from high price) is believed to be diagnostic. In general, if a positive price-quality relationship is observed in many product categories, it will lead to a highly accessible rule linking the two characteristics (Price 1992).

While negative information might enhance the use of this inferencing rule, nevertheless, an inference of high quality based on a high price might also depend on previous learning of price and product information. For example, prices of specific products that a consumer has previously encountered might be retrieved and reevaluated in light of new information about the product category in general. However, the ability to retrieve price information from memory obviously depends on how it was learned initially. Different processing goals at the time price information is encountered will lead to differences in the encoding of this information into

memory (Mazumdar and Monroe 1990). In some cases, buyers might learn price information *intentionally* because they expect to have to use it in performing some future task. However, people also encounter price information when they have other processing goals in mind for which the price information is not important. In such cases, the learning of the price information is only *incidental* (Mazumdar and Monroe 1990).

Intentional learning of price information should lead to greater knowledge about market prices than would incidental learning. Thus, consumers who have intentionally learned price information should be better able to integrate it with the positive or negative product category information they receive relative to consumers who learn about prices incidentally. Also, consumers who are knowledgeable about market prices for a product category are likely to use price cues in evaluations and choices differently than low price knowledge consumers.

When consumers are familiar with market prices for various brands and have a better overall understanding of the market, there are many pieces of information they can use. In the presence of these multiple pieces of information, they may be less likely to use price as a signal of quality (Dodds, Monroe and Grewal 1991). In addition, negative information about a product category also is likely to reduce the diagnosticity of price for making quality inferences. If so, these consumers will be more likely to focus on the price-perceived sacrifice relationship. As argued above, perceived value will therefore be less and a relatively high price that may have been initially considered acceptable might now be categorized as unacceptable.

However, consumers who have paid less attention to price and product information are likely to be less familiar with prevailing market prices. When negative information about the product category is encountered, because of insufficient knowledge, these consumers are more likely to perceive greater risk and to use price to infer product quality (Rao and Monroe 1988). Consequently, high prices will lead to positive perceptions of quality, leading to higher perceptions of value. Thus, prices that were initially considered too high (unacceptable) may now be categorized as acceptable.

As noted earlier, the attention devoted to examining and learning price information will determine how familiar a consumer is with market prices and, therefore, how this information may be used in subsequent purchase decisions. If intentional learning of price information, leads to high familiarity with prices, then consumers might use price as a diagnostic cue of quality. However, negative information about the product category, likely would diminish the use of price as an indicator of quality. In contrast, consumers who have only a cursory knowledge of market prices are less likely to question the use of price as a diagnostic cue of quality. This use of price as an indicator of quality might be more likely to occur when they believe that the quality of products in the category varies considerably. Thus, prices that might normally be considered unacceptable might now become acceptable. Thus, these consumers might consider higher prices to be more acceptable when they receive negative information about the product category as a whole than when they receive positive information about it. These changes in price acceptability can be determined by measuring the upper and lower limits of their acceptable price range. More specifically, it is hypothesized that:

H1: In conditions of intentional learning, subjects exposed to negative product information will have *lower* upper and lower price limits than when exposed to positive product information.

H2: In conditions of incidental learning, subjects exposed to negative product information will have *higher* upper and lower price limits than when exposed to positive product information.

METHOD

Subjects and Design

Fifty-two undergraduate students, enrolled in an introductory marketing course, participated in the experiment for extra course credit. Thirteen subjects were assigned randomly to each of the four conditions representing two learning goals (intentional versus incidental) and two types of product category information (positive versus negative).

Procedure

Upon arriving for the experiment, subjects were administered an initial questionnaire designed to assess their a priori perceptions of price acceptability and also their general product knowledge. This initial information was collected for three product categories (sneakers, jeans and 35mm compact cameras) of which jeans were the category of interest. The target category was chosen because (a) there was substantial variation in prices within the category, and (b) the category was one that subjects were familiar with and about which they had similar pre-experiment knowledge. The pre-measures of the acceptable price range were obtained using a price scale from $5 to $75. Subjects were asked to check all the prices that they found acceptable to pay for all three product categories. This was done in order to ensure that subjects did not remember what prices they had checked as 'acceptable' when the post measure was taken after experimental manipulations. No brand information was provided.

After subjects had indicated what prices they found acceptable, they were given a booklet containing (a) reviews of recent motion pictures, and (b) excerpts from *Consumer Reports* for several product categories. The excerpts on product categories were in the form of a table that listed brands, prices and performance with respect to various attributes. The prices were highlighted with markers. Subjects in the incidental learning condition were asked to skim through the entire booklet before focusing their attention on remembering information about the motion picture reviews for a memory test to be taken later. Subjects in the intentional learning condition were asked to focus on the product and price information table provided. Subjects in each condition were given 5-7 minutes to peruse the material.

After reading the booklet, subjects were asked to read another excerpt, ostensibly from *Consumer Reports*, pertaining to the product category of jeans. In the negative information condition, the report cast aspersions on the profit seeking motives of many industry giants, given the slim profits and intense competition. The report suggested that lately manufacturers had started using poor quality material in the jeans to cut down costs. Further, tests ostensibly conducted by *Consumer Reports* revealed problems with construction quality and tailoring of jeans. In the positive information condition, the same excerpt was modified to suggest that the industry was mature and that tests revealed that the quality of jeans was generally good.

Then, a second measure of the subjects' acceptable price ranges (the dependent variable) was taken via a sorting task. Subjects were asked to sort through numerous price tags ranging from $5 to $75 and to create piles that were acceptable and not acceptable. Finally a brief manipulation check was taken. The entire procedure took an hour to complete.

RESULTS AND ANALYSES

Manipulation Checks

To measure the effectiveness of the instructions and the information that was provided, two manipulation checks were performed. First, subjects indicated how much they concentrated on each type of information by reporting their agreement on a 7 point scale (1=agree, 7=disagree) in response to the following statements (a) "When I was given the booklet, I concentrated on the movie reviews," and (b) "When I was given the booklet, I concentrated on the product information." Subjects reported concentrating less on movie reviews under intentional price learning conditions than under incidental price learning conditions (3.7 vs. 2.7), $t(50)=1.86$, $p < 0.1$.

However, they did not differ significantly in the attention they reported paying to product information in the intentional condition relative to the incidental condition (4.2 vs. 4.3), $t(49)=0.22$, $p>0.1$. Although subjects in the intentional learning condition agreed that they paid more attention to the product information, the results should be interpreted cautiously since the manipulation check did not show a significant difference between groups. One factor to be kept in mind is that the time allocated for the task was the same for all subjects and if subjects differed in the amount of attention they devoted to the film reviews, it is likely that they had differed in the amount of attention or time they were able to spend on the product information.

The impact of different information types was confirmed by subjects' agreement with the statement, "After reading the excerpt, I felt that one has to be more careful when purchasing jeans." These judgments, along a scale from 1 (agree) to 7 (disagree), were greater when the information presented was negative (3.9) than when it was positive (5.0), $t(50)=-2.62$, $p<0.05$.

Effects on the Limits of the Acceptable Price Range

Analyses of subjects' pre-manipulation estimates of the upper and lower limits of the acceptable price range yielded no significant effects of either information type ($p<0.1$) or learning goals ($p<0.1$). Thus, subjects assigned to various experimental conditions did not systematically differ before being exposed to the manipulations. Consequently, only post-manipulation judgments were considered in the analyses.

Since a measure of prior knowledge was taken at the outset, it was treated as a covariate. The analysis of covariance revealed that it did not have a significant effect on the lower limit of the acceptable price range $F(1,51)=0.005$, $p>0.1$ or the upper limit of the acceptable price range $F(1,51)=1.809$, $p>0.1$. It was therefore dropped from the following analyses.

In intentional learning conditions, subjects exposed to negative product information, were not expected to use price as a diagnostic cue of quality and therefore would have *lower* upper and lower price limits than subjects exposed to positive product category information. In the incidental learning conditions, subjects exposed to negative product category information were expected to use higher prices to infer quality and therefore would have *higher* upper and lower price limits than subjects exposed to positive product category information. Table 1, which indicates the upper and lower limits of the acceptable price range under each condition, provides support for the hypotheses.

When subjects were explicitly instructed to pay attention to price, their highest and lowest acceptable prices were lower when negative information was conveyed about the general quality of jeans than when positive information was conveyed. In contrast, when subjects' attention was diverted to product-irrelevant aspects

TABLE 1
Upper and Lower Price Limits

| | Learning Goals | | | |
	Incidental	Intentional	Incidental	Intentional
Product Information	(upper limits)		(lower limits)	
Positive information	50.6	56.9	18.9	19.8
Negative information	57.4	50.4	22.3	17.0

of the information booklet (movie reviews), their upper and lower price limits were higher when they were provided with negative information. Although the interactive effects of information type (positive vs. negative) and learning goals (intentional vs. incidental) was significant only in the analyses of the upper limit (or the highest acceptable price), $F(1,51)=4.528$, $p<0.05$, the effects of these variables on the lower limit (or the lowest acceptable price) were similar in direction, $F(1,51)=1.619$, $p>0.1$. Moreover, an overall analysis of variance involving information type, learning goals and type of limits (upper vs. lower) yielded an interaction of the first two variables, $F(1,51)=4.396$, $p<0.05$, that was not contingent on the third, $F(1,51)=1.265$, $p>0.1$. Therefore, the hypothesized effects of these variables on perceptions of price acceptability were confirmed.

DISCUSSION

The results of this study suggest that the impact of pricing information is likely to depend on both the information subjects have available about the overall quality of the product (positive or negative) and the attention they have paid to the prices of the specific products they have encountered. When subjects were explicitly instructed to pay attention to the prices of specific products, the prices they considered acceptable decreased with negative product category information. Subjects in such conditions may have refrained from using the positive price-quality inference rule when the diagnosticity of this rule became suspect. These subjects might also have focused more on the perceived risk associated with purchasing the product at a high price. As a result, the prices they were willing to pay decreased.

In the incidental learning conditions, where prices were not the focus of subjects' attention at the time they perused the information booklet, subjects presumably did not extract information about specific brands and market prices leading to relatively low knowledge. When negative information was encountered about the overall product category, it may have led to the use of the positive price-quality inference rule. The diagnosticity of high price as a predictor of high quality was not questioned since knowledge levels were low. More specifically, when jeans were of inferior quality (as suggested by the negative information), subjects might be willing to accept higher prices in order to get a product of better quality.

Perhaps the most interesting aspect of this study surrounds the processing implications of contextual variables on the way in which people categorize prices as acceptable or not. The impact of positive and negative product category information on prices that consumers are willing to pay is important as is the identification of variables that could influence price acceptability. Consumers often

focus differentially on price information (depending of different learning goals). The limits of the acceptable price range may increase only under conditions when this increase in market price knowledge is accompanied by positive product information supporting consumers' beliefs about the positive price-quality relationship. However in the absence of any self-reported measures, the assumption that subjects make price-quality inferences was not tested. Nevertheless, the present study paves the way for future research that examines more directly the process by which the phenomena identified here might occur.

REFERENCES

Ahtola, Olli T. (1984), "Price as 'Give' Component in an Exchange Theoretic Multicomponent Model," *Advances in Consumer Research*, Vol. 11, ed. Thomas Kinnear, Ann Arbor, MI: Association for Consumer Research, 623-626.

Cox, Anthony D. (1986), "New Evidence Concerning Consumer Price Limits," in *Advances in Consumer Research*, Vol 13, ed. Richard Lutz, Provo, UT: Association for Consumer Research, 268-271.

Dick, Alan, Dipankar Chakravarti and Gabriel Biehal (1990), "Memory-based Inferences During Consumer Choice," *Journal of Consumer Research* 17(June), 82-93.

Dodds, William B., Kent B. Monroe and Dhruv Grewal (1991), "Effects of Price, Brand, and Store Information on Buyers' Product Evaluations," *Journal of Marketing Research*, 28(August), 307-319.

Ford, Gary T. and Ruth Ann Smith (1987), "Inferential Beliefs in Consumer Evaluations: An Assessment of Alternative Processing Strategies," Journal of Consumer Research, 14(December), 363-371.

Fouilhe, Pierre (1970), "The Subjective Evaluation of Price," in *Pricing Strategy*, eds. Bernard Taylor and Gordon Wells, Princeton, NJ: Brandon Systems Press, 89-97.

Gabor, Andre and Clive W. J. Granger (1966), "Price As an Indicator of Quality: Report On An Inquiry," *Economica*, 46(February), 43-70.

Kosenko, Rustan and Don Rahtz (1988), "Buyer Market Price Knowledge Influence on Acceptable Price Range and Price Limits," in *Advances in Consumer Research*, Vol 15, ed. Michael J. Houston, Provo, UT: Association for Consumer Research, 328-333.

Lichtenstein, Donald R., Peter H. Bloch, and William C. Black (1988), "Correlates of Price Acceptability," *Journal of Consumer Research*, 15(September), 243-252

Mazumdar, Tridib and Kent B. Monroe (1990), "The Effects of Buyers' Intentions to Learn Price Information on Price Encoding," *Journal of Retailing*, 66(Spring), 15-32.

Monroe, Kent B. (1971), "Measuring Price Thresholds by Psychophysics and Latitudes of Acceptance," *Journal of Marketing Research*, 8(November), 460-64.

_____(1973), "Buyers' Subjective Perceptions of Price," *Journal of Marketing Research*, 10(February), 70-80.

_____(1984), "Theoretical and Methodological Developments in Pricing," in *Advances in Consumer Research*, Vol. 11, ed. Thomas Kinnear, Ann Arbor, MI: Association for Consumer Research, 636-637.

_____Albert Della Bitta and Susan Downey (1977), "Contextual Influences on Subjective Price Perception," *Journal of Business Research*, 5(December), 277-291.

_____(1990), *Pricing: Making Profitable Decisions*, New York: McGraw Hill Publishing Co., 50-52.

Price, Lydia J. (1992), "The Effects of Message Valence on Inferential Processes," in *Advances in Consumer Research*, Vol. 19, eds. Michael Rothschild and Leigh McAlister, Provo, UT: Association for Consumer Research, 359-365.

Rao, Akshay R. and Kent B. Monroe (1988), "The Moderating Effect of Prior Knowledge on Cue Utilization in Product Evaluations," *Journal of Consumer Research*, 15(September), 253-264.

_____and Wanda A. Sieben (1992), "The Effect of Prior Knowledge on Price Acceptability and the Type of Information Examined," *Journal of Consumer Research*, 19(September), 256-270.

Raju, P.S. (1977), "Product Familiarity, Brand Familiarity and Price Influences on Product Evaluations," in *Advances in Consumer Research*, Vol 4, ed. William Perreault, Ann Arbor, MI: Association for Consumer Research, 64-71.

Sherif, Carolyn (1963), "Social Categorization as a Function of Latitude of Acceptance and Series Range," *Journal of Abnormal and Social Psychology*, 67(August), 148-56.

Yi, Youjae (1990a), "Direct and Indirect Approaches to Advertising Persuasion," *Journal of Business Research*, 20, 279-291.

Zeithaml, Valarie A, (1988), "Consumer Perceptions of Price, Quality and Value: A Means-End Model and Synthesis of Evidence," *Journal of Marketing*, 52 (July), 2-22.

Is There A Well-Defined Internal Reference Price?

Rajesh Chandrashekaran, Trenton State College
Harsharanjeet Jagpal, Rutgers University

ABSTRACT

This paper examines the impacts of multiple internal reference prices on consumers' evaluations of the offer. Our results show that although consumers use multiple internal reference prices in evaluating an offer, the effects of the reference prices are not mediated by the formation of a single, well-defined, unitized internal reference price (UIRP). Instead, the internal reference prices affect evaluations of the offer directly. Although the process by which internal reference prices affect the perceived offer-value is the same for the two product categories studied, internal reference price utilization is different.

INTRODUCTION

This paper examines the utilization of internal reference prices in evaluating the offer for two product categories. We first discuss the various definitions of internal reference price and review the literature. Then we propose two alternative models of consumer information-processing (unitization and non-unitization) and explain our data collection procedure. Finally, we discuss the empirical findings and suggest areas for future research.

DEFINING INTERNAL REFERENCE PRICE

Research on the formation and effects of internal reference prices has borrowed heavily from many psychological theories, particularly Adaptation Level Theory (Helson 1964). Considerable research supports the view that, from the consumer's perspective, price is a complex construct and is not merely the retail price (Kamen and Toman 1970; Monroe 1973; Winer 1986; Winer 1988; Jacobson and Obermiller 1990; Mayhew and Winer 1992; Rajendran and Tellis 1994). However, an extensive review of the literature reveals a wide variety of conceptual and operational definitions of internal reference price. Indeed, Winer (1988) points out that there are at least *five different* concepts that have been used as indicators of internal reference price.

Some studies have modeled consumers as "forward-looking." For example, Winer (1985) used "expected price" as a possible reference price for consumer durables. Jacobson and Obermiller (1990) also proposed that consumers form "expected future prices" which represent the prices consumers expect to see on their next purchase occasion which are used to decide whether to buy now or later. Based on the premise that consumers form expectations of future marketing activity from past exposure, and that these expectations are used to evaluate the current offering, Lattin and Bucklin (1989) also incorporated reference price effects in a multinomial logit model.

Other researchers view consumers as "backward-looking." A common conceptualization of reference price is as a summary of past prices (Kalwani, Kin Yim, Rinnie, and Sugita 1990; Mayhew and Winer 1992). Consistent with Adaptation Level Theory, Kalwani et al. (1990) use a weighted log-mean of the last five prices as an internal reference price. In addition to showing the reference effects of such a measure, the authors show that using a summary of past prices does not result in significantly better predictions than those obtained by simply using the price paid on the last purchase occasion.

Previous research has proposed other conceptually distinct definitions of reference price. For example, internal reference price has been studied according to consumers' perceptions of "fair price," which represents the price that consumers think is fair to charge for the product (Kamen and Toman 1970; Thaler 1985). As Emory (1970) points out, consumers' perceptions of a fair price need not correspond to any existing price. Therefore, this measure is conceptually different from a summary of past prices. Other commonly-used definitions of internal reference price include: reservation price (Scherer 1980), perceived price (Monroe 1973), recalled/evoked price (Rao and Gautschi 1982), lowest acceptable price (Stoetzel 1970), most-frequently encountered price (Olander 1970), and lowest market price (Biswas and Blair 1991).

As mentioned earlier, the literature on the definitions and effects of internal reference prices on consumer choice behavior is vast and cannot be dealt with in detail here due to space limitations. Interested readers are referred to some recent papers that provide excellent definitions and summaries of the effects of internal reference prices on consumers' purchase decisions (Klein and Oglethorpe 1987; Bearden, Kaicker, de Borrero, and Urbany 1992; Mayhew and Winer 1992; Rajendran and Tellis 1994).

Although the various definitions of internal reference price refer to constructs that are conceptually different, they all share the assumption that consumers use prices other than the retail price in relation to which the retail price is compared. As pointed out by Rajendran and Tellis (1994, p. 23), "empirical results generally support the inclusion of reference price in logit models of choice."

CRITIQUE OF THE LITERATURE

As discussed, there are numerous definitions and operationalizations of internal reference price. However, there has been no attempt to validate the different measures by incorporating them into a general model. As a result, three major issues must be addressed. First, most researchers have used *single* indicators of internal reference price (e.g., price last paid) and have implicitly treated these indicators as perfect measures of internal reference price. Because many research studies use internal reference price as an explanatory variable, this omission could be problematic and could lead to inconsistent parameter estimates (see Johnston 1984, pgs. 428-430). Second, previous studies have not incorporated multiple definitions of reference price in a single model to test whether the different measures capture the same underlying construct. That is, these studies have not attempted to test different theories of consumer information-processing. From a statistical viewpoint, omitting relevant price cues will lead to inconsistent parameter estimates if the omitted price cues are correlated to the included price cues (see Johnston 1984, pgs. 428-430). Third, most previous researchers have used scanner (single source) data and modeled internal reference price implicitly rather than explicitly (Mayhew and Winer 1992; Kalwani et. al 1990). As noted by Mayhew and Winer (1992, p. 64), such procedures require the strong "assumption that the specific reference price information and updating process used in the model *will yield reference prices similar to the consumer's true reference prices.*" (Emphasis added.)

INFORMATION-PROCESSING: UNITIZATION VERSUS NON-UNITIZATION

As suggested by previous researchers (Winer 1988; Klein and Oglethorpe 1987), we acknowledge that internal reference price is a multidimensional construct. Specifically, we measure various dimensions of internal reference price and incorporate these mul-

FIGURE 1
Unitized Model of Reference Price Effects

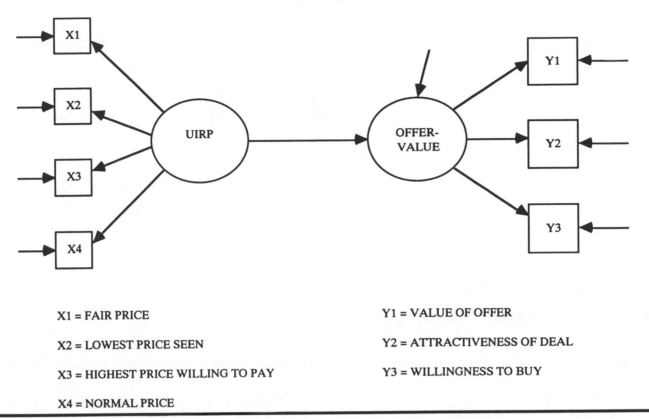

X1 = FAIR PRICE

X2 = LOWEST PRICE SEEN

X3 = HIGHEST PRICE WILLING TO PAY

X4 = NORMAL PRICE

Y1 = VALUE OF OFFER

Y2 = ATTRACTIVENESS OF DEAL

Y3 = WILLINGNESS TO BUY

tiple definitions into a single model which will enable us to validate the different measures and examine their relative importances in determining the final internal reference price and perceived offer-value.

We examine the behavioral process by which consumers integrate various internal reference prices and how these internal standards affect evaluations of the offer. After reviewing the literature (Thaler 1985; Winer 1988; Klein and Oglethorpe 1987; Bearden, Kaicker, de Borrero, and Urbany 1992), we selected four commonly-used measures of internal reference price: (i) fair price, (ii) reservation price (i.e., highest price willing to pay), (iii) normal (most frequently encountered) price, and (iv) lowest price seen. Although previously paid prices have been used as proxy measures of internal reference prices, such procedures assume that consumers can recall past prices accurately. There is evidence that, in general, consumers have difficulty in recalling past prices (Dickson and Sawyer 1990). Hence, we do not use previously paid price as an indicator of internal reference price.

Kosenko and Rahtz (1988, p. 332) suggest that "consumer market price knowledge should be a concern in future price threshold studies." Rajendran and Tellis (1994) also showed that consumers use contextual prices (i.e., the prices of other brands) as reference prices. Based on these findings, we measure consumers' perceptions of "normal market price" (price most frequently encountered) as a possible internal reference price.

Having acknowledged that consumers can have multiple reference prices, we need to examine three important questions. First, are the different internal references indicators of the same underlying construct? Do consumers combine the different internal reference prices to form an overall *unitized* internal reference price

(UIRP)? Third, what are the relative impacts of the internal prices on evaluations of the offer?

Figures 1 and 2 show two competing information-processing models by which internal reference prices can affect evaluations of the offer. The first model (see Figure 1) proposes that the different internal standards are integrated to form a single, well-defined internal reference price. We refer to this model as the "unitized" model. The second model (see Figure 2), in contrast, proposes that the various internal reference prices correspond to conceptually distinct constructs and that each affects evaluations of the offer directly. This model assumes that consumers compare incoming price cues against the internal cues independently. We refer to this information-processing strategy as the "non-unitized" model. The following section outlines the data collection procedure.

METHOD

Data were collected from 250 undergraduate student subjects. Each subject was exposed to two print ads: one for running shoes and the other for a compact disc stereo player. Consistent with retail/catalog ads in these categories, each ad contained a picture of the product, a small body of text describing key features of the product, and a retail price. The price cues were chosen to reflect the actual market prices for shoes ($34.95) and stereo players ($199) in surrounding retail stores. Approximately half the subjects first evaluated the ad for running shoes and then evaluated the ad for the stereo player, while the remaining subjects first saw the ad for the stereo player and were then exposed to the ad for running shoes. In this way, the order of presentation was counterbalanced. After viewing each ad, subjects responded to several questions pertaining to that product category.

FIGURE 2
Non-Unitized Model of Reference Price Effects

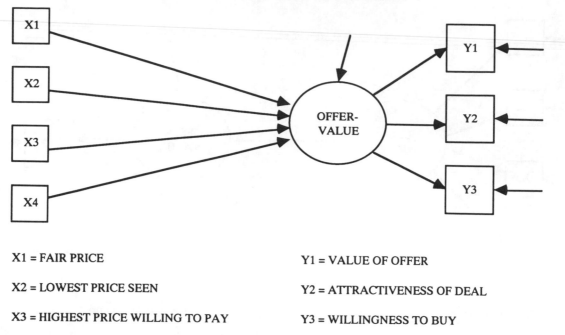

X1 = FAIR PRICE

X2 = LOWEST PRICE SEEN

X3 = HIGHEST PRICE WILLING TO PAY

X4 = NORMAL PRICE

Y1 = VALUE OF OFFER

Y2 = ATTRACTIVENESS OF DEAL

Y3 = WILLINGNESS TO BUY

Independent Variables

For each product category, subjects responded to the following questions that intended to measure their internal reference prices.

FAIR PRICE: I think a FAIR PRICE for the product shown would be $____.

LOWEST PRICE: The LOWEST PRICE I have seen this product for is $____.

HIGHEST PRICE: The HIGHEST PRICE I have seen this product for is $____.

NORMAL PRICE: I think the NORMAL (MOST FREQUENTLY ENCOUNTERED) PRICE for this product is $____.

Dependent Variables

The response of interest in this study is "perceived offer-value." Following Berkowitz and Walton (1980), we use three measures of offer-value:

VALUE FOR MONEY: I think the offered price represents a good value for my money.

ATTRACTIVENESS OF DEAL: I think the offered price represents a good deal.

WILLINGNESS TO BUY: I would be willing to purchase the item at the price indicated.

Each item was measured using a seven-point scale ranging from 1=disagree to 7=agree. Although all subjects responded to the same set of questions, the order of the questions was randomized across subjects to eliminate any position bias.

MODEL ESTIMATION AND EMPIRICAL RESULTS

In order to test the two information-processing models shown in figures 1 and 2 we used the structural equation methodology as implemented in LISREL 7 (Jöreskog and Sörbom 1988). Because the two models are not nested, we needed to choose statistical criteria for comparing non-nested models. Jöreskog and Sörbom (1993, p. 119) suggest the use of three criteria: AIC, CAIC, and ECVI, which are defined by:

$$AIC = \chi^2 + 2t$$
$$CAIC = \chi^2 + (1 + \ln N)t$$
$$ECVI = (\chi^2/N) + 2(t/N)$$

where "t" is the number of independent parameters being estimated and "N" is the sample size. All three statistics attempt to remove the bias in favor of over-parametrized models. Specifically, the models that yield the lowest values of AIC, CAIC, and ECVI are chosen.

For each product category, we first estimated the two information-processing models (see Figures 1 and 2). In the next step, we trimmed each model by eliminating non-significant paths. Finally, we compared the two trimmed models using the three model selection criteria: AIC, CAIC, and ECVI.

Table 1 shows the results for the stereo data. The results show that the unitized model does not provide a satisfactory fit. In contrast, the non-unitized model fits the data well (χ^2=6.75, d.f.=4, p=0.139) regardless of which model fit criterion is used. That is, the individual reference prices affect the perceived offer-value directly.

The estimated parameters of the model are shown in Figure 3. The standard errors are shown in parentheses and the non-significant paths are indicated by broken lines. As expected, all parameters are positive. Only two internal reference prices (FP and HP)

TABLE 1
Comparison of Competing Models for Stereos
(N = 235)

	Unitized Model	Non-Unitized Model
χ^2	32.46	6.75
d.f.	13	4
p	0.002	0.139
R^2	0.303	0.298
AIC	62.46	28.95
CAIC	129.40	78.01
ECVI	0.265	0.123

FIGURE 3
Non-Unitized Model of Reference Price Effects for Stereos

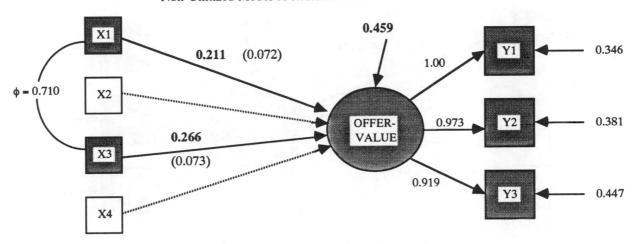

Chi-Square = 6.95, d.f. = 4, p = 0.139

X1 = FAIR PRICE

X2 = LOWEST PRICE SEEN

X3 = HIGHEST PRICE WILLING TO PAY

X4 = NORMAL PRICE

Y1 = VALUE OF OFFER

Y2 = ATTRACTIVENESS OF DEAL

Y3 = WILLINGNESS TO BUY

impact consumers' perceptions of offer-value for stereo players. These results are consistent with findings from earlier research (Kamen and Toman 1970; Thaler 1985), suggesting that consumers use some notion of "fair price" as a reference price. The use of "highest price willing to pay" (HP) lends support to the hypothesis that for such durable products as stereos, consumers use price to infer quality (within the acceptable range). In addition, the two price measures are significantly correlated ($\phi = 0.71$). Thus, using only one measure (either FP or HP) for reference price will result in inconsistent parameter estimates if internal reference price is used as an explanatory variable. Comparing the effects of the two internal reference prices on offer-value revealed no significant difference in the impacts of FP and HP on consumers' evaluations of the offer.

The results for shoes (see Table 2) are analogous to those obtained for stereos. The non-unitized model out-performs the unitized model regardless of the choice of model selection criterion (i.e., AIC, CAIC, or ECVI). Furthermore, the non-unitized model's fit is highly satisfactory ($\chi^2=7.92$, d.f.=4, p=0.095). Hence, the process by which internal reference prices affect perceived offer-value is similar across the product categories studied.

The estimated model parameters are shown in Figure 4 in which the standard errors are shown in parentheses and all non-significant paths are indicated by broken lines.

TABLE 2
Comparison of Competing Models for Running Shoes
(N = 226)

	Unitized Model	Non-Unitized Model
χ^2	50.15	7.92
d.f.	13	4
p	0.000	0.095
R^2	0.203	0.181
AIC	80.15	29.92
CAIC	146.45	78.55
ECVI	0.355	0.132

FIGURE 4
Non-Unitized Model of Reference Price Effects for Shoes

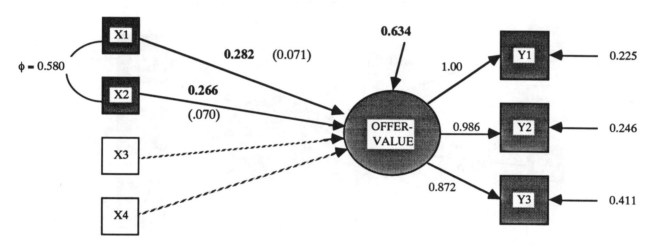

Chi-Square =7.92, d.f. = 4, p = 0.095

X1 = FAIR PRICE

X2 = LOWEST PRICE SEEN

X3 = HIGHEST PRICE WILLING TO PAY

X4 = NORMAL PRICE

Y1 = VALUE OF OFFER

Y2 = ATTRACTIVENESS OF DEAL

Y3 = WILLINGNESS TO BUY

FP is used as an internal reference price for running shoes. This result is similar to that obtained for stereo players. In addition, consumers also evaluate the retail price against the lowest price seen (LP). Furthermore, the two price cues are significantly correlated (ϕ=0.58). As with the previous product category, no significant difference in the impacts of the two internal reference prices on perceived offer-value was revealed.

Overall, the results strongly support the hypotheses that consumers possess multiple cognitive reference points. Comparing the results for shoes and stereos (Figures 3 and 4) reveals that, although the *process* by which internal reference prices affect consumers' evaluations is the same for the two product categories, there is a major difference in the *types* of price cues utilized.

Interestingly, fair price (FP) is used as an internal reference in both product categories. This finding has important implications: FP may serve as a reliable indicator of reference price. Thus, future studies should explicitly incorporate this measure in models dealing with the effects of reference prices on consumers' choices. In spite of this similarity in the results for both product categories, HP (which is used as an internal reference for stereos) is not used as a standard of comparison to evaluate the offer for shoes. Instead, consumers use their perceptions of the lowest market price (LP) to make judgments about offer-value. Thus, consumers' reservation prices are not always used as internal references against which retail prices are compared. These findings have important implications for how managers should convey price savings in retail ads.

DISCUSSION

In this paper, we presented some preliminary findings regarding how consumers utilize various internal reference prices and compared two information-processing models of how consumers evaluate prices. The results indicate that some IRP measures are more strongly associated with consumers' perceptions of "value" than others. Furthermore, consumers' use of internal reference prices is product specific. Consequently, it is inappropriate to use the same indicator of internal reference price for all products.

It is important to note that the results are preliminary and that the present study has some weaknesses that need to be addressed in future studies involving reference prices. First, estimates of internal reference prices were obtained after subjects were exposed to the advertised price. It is possible at least some subjects "internalized" the new information quickly and updated their internal standards. To be able to draw stronger conclusions, future studies must measure consumers' internal reference prices before and after presenting the advertised price. This will also enable researchers to understand how and when consumers accommodate new information into existing beliefs.

Future research should also replicate our study using other product categories, especially frequently-purchased products, and should allow for individual differences among consumers in level of knowledge, degree of product familiarity, and frequency of purchase.

REFERENCES

Bearden, William O., Ajit Kaicker, Melinda Smith de Borrero, and Joel E. Urbany (1992), "Examining Alternative Operational Measures of Internal Reference Prices," in John F. Sherry, Jr., and Brain Sternthal (eds.), *Advances in Consumer Research*, Vol. 19, Provo, UT: Association for Consumer Research, 629-635.

Biswas, Abhijit and Edward A. Blair (1991), "Contextual Effects of Reference Prices in Retail Advertisements," *Journal of Marketing*, 55 (July), 1-12.

Berkowitz, Eric N. and John R. Walton (1980), "Contextual Influences on Consumer Price Responses: An Experimental Analysis," *Journal of Marketing Research*, 17 (August), 349-358.

Dickson, P. and Alan G. Sawyer (1990), "The Price Knowledge and Search of Supermarket Shoppers," *Journal of Marketing*, 54 (July), 42-53.

Emory, Fred (1970), "Some Psychological Aspects of Price," in *Pricing Strategy*, eds. Bernard Taylor and Gordon Wills, Princeton, NJ: Brandon/Systems, 98-111.

Helson, Harry (1964), *Adaptation Level Theory*, New York: Harper and Row.Jacobson, Robert and Carl Obermiller (1990), "The Formation of Expected Future Price: A Reference Price for 'Forward-Looking' Consumers," *Journal of Consumer Research*, 16 (March), 420-432.

Johnston, Jack (1984), *Econometric Methods*, Mc-Graw Hill.Jöreskog, Carl, and Dag Sörbom (1988), LISREL 7: A Guide to the Program and Applications, Chicago: SPSS, Inc.

_____, _____(1993), *LISREL 8: Structural Equation Modeling with the SIMPLIS Command Language*, Hillsdale, NJ: Erlbaum.

Kalwani, Manohar U., Chi Kin Yim, Heikki J. Rinnie, and Yoshi Sugita (1990), "A Price Expectations Model of Customer Brand Choice," *Journal of Marketing Research*, 27 (August), 251-262.

Kamen, Joseph M. and Robert J. Toman (1970), "Psychophysics of Prices," *Journal of Marketing Research*, 7 (February), 27-35.

Klein, Noreen M.and Janet E. Oglethorpe (1987), "Cognitive Reference Points in Consumer Decision-Making," in Melanie Wallendorf and Paul Anderson (eds.), *Advances in Consumer Research*, Vol. 14, Provo, UT: Association for Consumer Research, 183-187.

Kosenko, Rustan and Don Rahtz (1988), "Buyer Market Price Knowledge Influence on Acceptable Price Range and Price Limits," in *Advances in Consumer Research*, Vol. 15, ed. Michael Houston, Provo, UT: Association for Consumer Research, 328-333.

Lattin, James M. and Randolf E. Bucklin (1989), "Reference Effects of Price and Promotion on Brand Choice Behavior," *Journal of Marketing Research*, 26 (August), 299-310.

Mayhew, Glenn E. and Russell S. Winer (1992), "An Empirical Analysis of Internal and External Reference Prices Using Scanner Data," *Journal of Consumer Research*, 19 (June), 62-70

Monroe, Kent B. (1973), "Buyers' Subjective Perceptions of Price," *Journal of Marketing Research*, 10 (February), 70-80.

Olander, Folke (1970), "The Influence of Price on the Consumer's Evaluation of Products and Purchases," in Bernard Taylor and Gordon Wills, eds., *Pricing Strategy*, Princeton, NJ: Brandon Systems Press, 50-69.

Rajendran K.N., and Gerard J. Tellis, (1994), "Contextual and Temporal Components of Reference Price," *Journal of Marketing*, 58 (January), 22-34.

Rao, Vithala, and David A. Gautschi (1982), "The Role of Price in Individual Utility Judgments: Development and Empirical Validation of Alternative Models," in *Research in Marketing*, ed. Leigh McAlister, Greenwich, CT: JAI Press.

Rosch, Eleanor (1975), "Cognitive Reference Points," *Cognitive Psychology*, 7 (October), 532-547.

Scherer, R. M. (1980), *Industrial Market Structure and Economic Performance*, Chicago, IL: Rand McNally.

Winer, Russell S. (1985), "A Price Vector Model of Demand for Consumer Durables: Preliminary developments," *Marketing Science*, 4 (Winter), 74-90.

_____(1986), "A Reference Price Model of Brand Choice for Frequently Purchased Products," *Journal of Consumer Research*, 13 (September), 250-256.

_____(1988), "Behavioral Perspective on Pricing: Buyers' Subjective Perceptions of Price Revisited," in *Issues in Pricing: Theory and Research*, ed. T. Devinney, Lexington, MA: Lexington, 35-57.

"Spending Power" and the Subjective Discretionary Income (SDI) Scale

John R. Rossiter, Australian Graduate School of Management

ABSTRACT

New measures of "spending power" from the economics literature are reviewed as alternatives to the total household income measure typically used in consumer research. The simplest of these, the Subjective Discretionary Income measure proposed by O'Guinn and Wells, is evaluated in a cross-national replication study with financial products. SDI appears to be a valid predictor of "investments," whereas total household income predicts "necessities." Lengthening of the SDI scale is suggested to increase its reliability.

INTRODUCTION

This paper has two purposes. The first purpose is to review the limitations of income as a measure of "spending power" in consumer behavior studies and to introduce consumer researchers to some alternative measures. The most important of these alternative measures of "spending power" come from economic research and may prove useful in consumer research. The second purpose is to provide a cross-national replication of one measure of "spending power" that has been used in consumer research—the Subjective Discretionary Income (SDI) measure proposed by O'Guinn and Wells (1989). To their credit, O'Guinn and Wells conducted extensive replications of the SDI measure in the U.S.A. However, with so many companies and advertising agencies now going "global," international replication of measures is of major importance. The opportunity arose to conduct a replication study of the SDI in Australia and the findings are reported in this paper.

MEASURES OF "SPENDING POWER"

Problems with Income as a Measure

Simply considered, consumer behavior is made possible by income. Yet there are severe problems with using income (usually measured as total household income) as an indicator of a household's current consumption capability or "spending power" (see also Lovell, Richardson, Travers and Wood 1990): (a) *Inaccurate reporting of income.* Consumer surveys may produce inaccurate reports of income. At the presumed top of the income scale, refusal rates on income questions are high, as indeed occurred in the survey reported the second part of the present study. At the presumed lower end, unreported income from "moonlighting" and from illegal businesses contributes a presumably large error, as does restricted-use income such as food stamps. (b) *Failure to add the value of household members' time not spent in income-earning employment.* The value of the full-time "houseperson's" time and the value of the time spent on household work by people working part-time and full-time is never figured in to household income. Nor is the value of tasks done by schoolchildren, such as washing the car or mowing the lawn. This "free" work effectively adds spending power in that the household is not having to use income to pay for the services thus provided. (c) *Payments received "in kind."* Similarly, value is received in many instances from employers, such as free gifts, free loans of equipment, and so forth; and, for some people, from the government, in the form of personal use of government equipment such as automobiles. Many of these "fringe benefits" are not recorded as income. (d) *Services received from ownership of household durables.* Products owned, such as housing itself, automobiles, vacuum cleaners, and the like, provide value which would otherwise have to be paid for each time, as in housing

or apartment rental, car rental, cleaning services, and so forth, at quite a high cost. Presumably, service value from these products exceeds in the long run the price paid for them and therefore is a form of income. (e) *Current income focus.* Most income surveys report only current income—a statistic that fails to take into account household or individual actions to "smooth" consumption over the family's or person's life cycle. A common occurrence of this is "borrowed" income in the form of housing or automobile loans. A long-term debt is incurred but the "spending power" is available "now," and therefore functionally is current income. Evidently, stated current income has many limitations as a measure of a household's actual capacity to engage in consumer behavior.

Alternative Measures

There have been a number of potential solutions proposed for getting around the limitations of income as a measure of the true "spending power" available to consumers. These include: Full Income, Equivalent Income, Resources, Objective Discretionary Income, and Subjective Discretionary Income (SDI). The first four are explained briefly below. The fifth measure, SDI, is explained in the empirical study that follows.

1. *Full Income* is a measure first proposed by Decker (1965) and operationalized recently by Richardson (1989). Full Income is the maximum income that could be received *if* the household devoted all of its human and financial resources solely to maximizing income. In particular, hours which could have been spent in paid work are treated as if they were in fact spent that way, and the after-tax income is imputed. Services received from consumer durables (which include owner-occupied houses) are valued for the after-tax return which would have been obtained had the money used for their purchase been invested in financial securities, less depreciation. The value of "payments in kind" is similarly imputed. Numerically, the value of non-market time and of an owner-occupied house are the major adjustment factors.

   Full Income is cumbersome to measure and compute in a standard consumer research survey. However, it is being seriously considered for government surveys in Australia as a measure for deciding social policy and in particular for defining the "poverty line" for consumer welfare payments (Harding 1994). The present measure, the "Henderson line," which is also used in the U.S., is based mainly on cash income and neglects the value of homes owned. By the Full Income measure, the emphasis shifts from retirees, who have low cash incomes but tend to be asset-rich, to blue-collar families, single parents, and unemployed youths, who are asset-poor as well as cash-poor.

2. *Equivalent Income* is a measure devised by Travers and Richardson (1990) which takes the after-tax, cash income of the household and divides it by an "equivalence" scale that rises proportionally with: the number of family members; children's ages, and thus their consumption costs; and the presence of a working spouse, who contributes additional household income not obtained if the spouse is present but not working. Each *adult* in the

Advances in Consumer Research
Volume 22, © 1995

household is then assumed to have the same "equivalent income"; that is, income is adjusted after accounting for "need" differences between households.

Equivalent Income is quite readily computable from measures typically included in consumer surveys and would appear to be worth investigating by consumer researchers. It is also relevant for social policy in the area of taxation. For instance, France uses a "pooled dependent" system (Garran 1994) whereby family income is combined for tax purposes and the tax threshold is varied according to the number of dependents, including a non-working spouse, live-in relatives and disabled family members.

3. *Resources* is a measure devised by Lovell, Richardson, Travers and Wood (1990) to measure *potentially available spending power* rather than current spending power. It attempts to assess the extent of "resources," including income, that the household has available to draw upon if necessary. These resources, combined with current income, are thought to reflect the household's "standard of living." Standard of living is a concept that is commonly acknowledged but not well measured. When standard of living has been investigated in previous research, it has been estimated with a single overall rating which is of doubtful validity (see, for example, Andrews and Withey 1976). The Resources measure begins with Equivalent Income as measured above and adds scale points for 13 other variables such as whether the house is owned outright, the value of the residence, ownership of a second dwelling, value of automobiles, durables, shareholdings and so forth as well as the more idiosyncratic characteristics of whether the household recently fell behind in payment of bills (reverse-scored), received material help from a welfare agency (also reverse-scored), and whether the household is able to raise $5,000 in a week in an emergency. As might be evident, this is more a measure of potentially available spending power than current spending power.

Resources requires measures to be added to a consumer survey (13 single-item variables in addition to the standard measures used to compute Equivalent Income) but is quite easy to calculate. As pointed out by a reviewer, Resources would provide an interesting economically-based alternative to demographically-based measures of *social class* (e.g., Coleman 1983). It might be the other side of the hyphen in the term "socio-economic status" in that Resources seems to reflect economic status without the social values implications. In today's material world, standard of living is perhaps more relevant than the historical concept of social class.

In an extremely important study, conducted only in Australia at present, Lovell et al. (1990) demonstrated that the population's "standard of living" (as indexed by the Resources measure above) is much more homogeneous than the population's income (Equivalent Income). Although 95% of Australians are spread, by definition, across nine and a half deciles in terms of income, they are located within the seventh and eighth deciles in terms of standard of living, which is only a 20% spread. It is the latter statistic that confirms the popular perception that Australia is a very egalitarian—and materially comfortable—society. Looked at another way, it should be of great interest to consumer researchers that after-tax equivalent income and, by implication, the usual total household income measure, is correlated extremely weakly (r=.05, d.f.=1,067, p=.08 but consider the large sample size) with the very effect—"standard of living"—that such income is purported to

produce! This suggests that "disposable" or "discretionary" income is being significantly overlooked when only total income is measured.

4. *Objective Discretionary Income*, or "Disposable Income," should, in theory, come closest to measuring "spending power." Discretionary Income (DI) is a widely-used concept for purposes of economic research. For example, the U.S. Bureau of the Census, working with the Consumer Research Center of the Conference Board, has developed a DI measure that begins with gross income and then subtracts the cost of housing, food, clothing, medical and other common household budget items as well as tax paid. These costs are assumed to be non-discretionary, that is, necessities.

Herein lies the major problem with "objective" measures that define spending power as what is left after money has been spent. The presumed "necessities" expenditures, for clothing, food and even the type of house that is purchased or rented, are obviously not 100% necessitated. The truth is that an unknown proportion of the "essential" expenditures is, for most individuals, discretionary.

The problem with Objective Discretionary Income is revealed in the following economic survey results. DI estimates for the U.S.A. for 1987 indicate that *over two-thirds* of households (71%) had *no* discretionary income after paying for so-called essentials (Bureau of the Census, 1989). Similarly, the present author's estimates for Australia, using data from the Australian Bureau of Statistics (1990), when cross-tabulated by gross income quintiles, produced the intuitively unacceptable result that, whereas the average DI per household in 1988-89 was approximately $3,500, this ranged from a *negative* $3,800 in the lowest income quintile; stayed negative in the second lowest income quintile; rose to marginally positive for the next two quintiles; and then reached a somewhat more credible $17,600 for *only* the uppermost income quintile. The negative DI for such an unbelievably large proportion of the population (well over 50% in the U.S.A. and 40% in Australia) is the problem: clearly, discretionary expenses are being misrepresented as necessary expenses.

5. *Subjective Discretionary Income* (SDI) stems from the work of Katona (1975) and his Index of Consumer Sentiment. O'Guinn and Wells (1989) trace the history of the SDI measure and it is their particular version of the measure that is examined in the present study. SDI is a measure of *perceived spending power*. As such, it should be a significant determinant of many types of consumer purchases. It is essentially a subjective measure of capacity to spend and in this sense is an "attitude" rather than an objective behavioral resource. (For a somewhat related approach to estimating spending power subjectively, see Wachtel and Blatt, 1990.) As in the O'Guinn and Wells (1989) study, the present study compares this subjective measure with the typical objective measure of total household income. The SDI measure is described in further detail next.

The SDI Measure

The O'Guinn and Wells (1989) measure of SDI has been employed in the advertising agency Needham Worldwide's Needham Lifestyle Survey for some years. It is composed of the sum of ratings on the following three items:

Item 1: No matter how fast our income goes up we never seem to get ahead (reverse-scored).

Item 2: We have more to spend on extras than most of our neighbors do (see modification below).

Item 3: Our family income is high enough to satisfy nearly all our important desires.

To better fit modern and more individualistic residential contexts, especially in urban areas, the wording of the second item was modified in the present study from "neighbors do" to "friends seem to."

In O'Guinn and Wells' studies, the three items were rated on 6-point scales ranging from definitely disagree (1) to definitely agree (6), with no neutral rating allowed. The present study employed a 5-point scale ranging from disagree strongly (1) to agree strongly (5), with a neutral point (3). As will be seen, this minor rating scale difference, which was insisted upon by the market research firm that collected the data, seemed to be more a matter of taste rather than substance. Total SDI scores on the O'Guinn and Wells scale thus can range from 3 to 18, whereas on the present SDI scale the scores can range from 3 to 15.

In the study reported here, the SDI was tested in an Australian context to examine its generalizability. Like O'Guinn and Wells' analysis, the present study analyzes the scale's reliability and its predictive validity.

THE STUDY

The data for the Australian study came from a sample of 1,427 households in one large and typical state, and were graciously made available for academic research by an Australian bank which wishes to remain anonymous. The door-to-door sampling method was as near random as is practically possible in commercial market research surveys. The present analysis is based on 1,187 households, constituting the 74% of the total sample in which respondents reported full financial data, including total household income. The 26% incidence of incomplete financial data is typical but apparently did not bias the final sample. Sex, age categories, and occupational categories estimated from the sample were within ±3% of population values reported from the Australian Bureau of Statistics census, and with a sample size of 1,000, sampling variance of 2 to 4% could be expected at the 95% confidence level due to sample size alone.

The Australian survey happened to duplicate one of the two applications investigated by O'Guinn and Wells (1989) in their U.S. surveys: namely consumers' financial behavior. The Australian survey measured, among many other variables, consumers' usage of personal loans, common stocks, mutual funds, and money market funds—variables that were examined for predictive validation purposes in the U.S. study. The Australian study also measured usage of several other financial products which clarify the contribution of SDI.

Reliability of the SDI Scale

International comparisons provide an extreme test of a scale's reliability in the sense of reliability as generalizability (Cronbach 1951). In the present study, the international comparison is probably less extreme because of the likely cultural similarities between the U.S.A. and Australia. In this section, comparisons between the SDI scale's psychometric properties in the U.S.A. and Australia are presented.

The distribution of scores on the SDI scale in the U.S.A. was shown by O'Guinn and Wells (1989, their Table 1) to be approximately normal with a slight leftward skew (lower frequencies to the right). Their quadrichotomized distribution exhibited the following percentage frequencies: Low (scores of 3-6), 20.4%; Medium-

Low (7-10), 35.2%; Medium-High (11-14), 32.9%; and High (15-18), 11.5%. Because the Australian version of the SDI scale had a different range of possible scores, it could not be identically subdivided and was instead trichotomized with 3-4-3 cutoffs, thus providing a slightly wider middle. The Australian data also exhibited a pronounced leftward skew while still being approximately normal. Percentage frequencies were as follows: Low (3-6), 28%; Medium (7-11), 66%; and High (12-15), 6%. The tendency for Australians' self-reports of SDI to cluster toward the middle is consistent with the homogeneity of the Resources measure of "standard of living" in Australia found by Lovell et al. (1990), as noted earlier.

The inter-item and item-total correlations in the two countries were highly consistent, as shown in Table 1. These results indicate that the SDI items "behave" in the same way in both nations.

The internal consistency of the SDI scale (Cronbach's coefficient alpha) was not calculated directly for the U.S. data by O'Guinn and Wells; instead, they stated that "the three items in the SDI scale...have always loaded on the same factor with factor loadings above .8" (1989, p. 35), implying a very high alpha. However, coefficient alpha for the Australian SDI scale was only .57, a level usually regarded as marginal if not unsatisfactory.

Despite the marginal internal-consistency reliability of the SDI scale in Australia, it was decided to proceed with it unchanged for the validity phase of the study to ensure comparability with the U.S. findings.

Validity of the SDI Scale

Two types of validity are of interest regarding the SDI scale: the discriminant validity of subjective discretionary income (SDI) and total family income (TFI) which should demonstrate that they are measuring different dimensions of spending power; and the predictive validity of SDI, especially in comparison with TFI, for consumers' financial behavior.

Discriminant Validity. In the U.S. data (for 1986), the correlation between SDI and TFI was $r=.34$ only. Though highly significant with the large sample size, the correlation suggests that SDI and TFI, in the U.S.A., have only 11.6% common variance. Using cross-tabulation, O'Guinn and Wells showed that this correlation allows wide variations in SDI at each level of total family income. In the Australian data, the correlation between SDI and TFI was lower still, at $r=.25$; even allowing for attentuation due to unreliability, the common variance of SDI and TFI, at 6.2%, is effectively zero. Most interestingly, the individual SDI scale item that was least correlated with TFI in the Australian data was the second, that "our family income is high enough to satisfy nearly all of our important desires," suggesting that high total income does *not* necessarily mean greater perceived spending power (see also the earlier result suggesting the homogeneity of "standard of living" in Australia). In any event, the lack of relationship between SDI and TFI in Australia makes their relative predictive capabilities all the more relevant.

Predictive Validity. O'Guinn and Wells compared the predictive validities of SDI and TFI by combining them in a *multivariate* equation and using logistic regression, an appropriate procedure given that the two predictor variables were somewhat correlated in the U.S. data. In the Australian data, however, SDI and TFI were effectively uncorrelated, so it is quite appropriate—and indeed practically realistic, as most market research managers use separate cross-tabs anyway—to compare their respective *univariate* predictions. O'Guinn and Wells reported Wald statistics, a form of maximum likelihood chi-square that indicates the strength of association of each predictor variable after adjusting for their joint effect

TABLE 1

SDI Inter-Item Correlations for the U.S.A.[1] (Below Diagonal) and Australia (Above Diagonal) and Item-Total Score Correlations

	Item 1	Item 2	Item 3	Total SDI Score U.S.A.	Total SDI Score Australia
Item 1		.23	.37	.62	.75
Item 2	.23		.31	.57	.66
Item 3	.35	.35		.69	.78

[1]U.S.A. data are from the 1986 survey results in O'Guinn and Wells (1989, their Table 2).

TABLE 2

Predictive Results for SDI and TFI for Financial Products[1] Common to the U.S. and Australian Surveys and for Australia Only (U.S. Results in Parentheses): Approximately Comparable χ^2 Values

	SDI	TFI
Mutual fund	59 (12)	12 (7)
Money market fund	56 (42)	10 (n.s.)
Common stock	35 (5)	50 (12)
Bank loan (personal)	n.s. $(7)^2$	61 (26)
Real estate	46	33
VISA card	13	29
Mastercard	7	30
First mortgage (own home)	3	75

[1]Patronage (0, 1) without regard to amount.
[2]Negative association.

---

in the regression. Therefore, the chi-square statistic was chosen for the Australian data also, though a simple χ^2, not an MLE-based adjusted χ^2. While not comparable precisely, χ^2 was a reasonably common statistic available for the two studies.

The predictive results are shown in Table 2. As the top half of the table indicates, the Australian predictive results for SDI and TFI were consistent with—but stronger than—the U.S. results for the four financial products included in both studies. Of the eight comparisons, the only inconsistencies involved two non-significant (p>.05) χ^2 values compared with significant but very small χ^2 values. Overall, SDI proved to be a much more important predictor variable in the Australian data than in the U.S. data for two of the products (mutual funds and common stocks), similarly highly predictive for a third (money market funds) and similarly unpredictive for the fourth (personal loans through a bank). Also, TFI proved to be a stronger predictor in the Australian data than in the U.S. data, directionally, for all four products and a much better predictor for two of these (common stocks and personal bank loans). Ignoring magnitude and focusing only on positive significance (p<.05), the U.S.-Australian results are consistent in six out of eight comparisons.

The results for the four other financial products measured only in the Australian survey, shown in the bottom half of the table, help to construct a fairly straightforward interpretation of the relative importance of SDI and TFI. SDI is evidently of major importance for discretionary *investments* (real estate, the stockmarket, and other high-return opportunities). TFI, on the other hand, is relatively more important for *necessities* (many would regard credit cards as necessities and TFI is clearly the single dominant predictor of personal loans and home loans). Again, it is important to observe that the "investment" types of financial products are not predicted well by total household income alone. Subjective discretionary income is therefore of considerable relevance to marketers of the more "high flying" financial products.

Future Research with SDI

The Australian findings suggest that whereas SDI is an important consumer variable, its measurement in an international or global context may suffer from marginal scale reliability if the O'Guinn and Wells SDI scale is used. The obvious solution to low reliability is to increase the number of items. However, scale *development* is recommended, based on theory and further research, rather than the mere extension of items "similar" to those in the 3-item scale at present.

Conceptually, items 2 and 3 seem to best capture what is meant by "subjective discretionary income," namely: "We have more to spend on *extras* than most of our friends seem to" and "Our family income is high enough to satisfy nearly all our important *desires*" (emphases added). In contrast, item 1 may have become too much of a cultural cliché, "...we never seem to get ahead," and it also makes the presumption that household income rises, "No matter how fast our income goes up...," which is not true for the majority of households in real terms. Also, item 2 seems to relate to discretionary expenditure on non-essential "luxuries" whereas item 3 allows for discretionary expenditure on better quality "necessities." These two items, which are correlated only about .3, might form the basis for two types of additional items. In any event, additional items reflecting degree of *choice* in how to spend income would appear to be conceptually appropriate.

SDI scale development would also be best pursued in several different countries, rather than in the two similar countries compared here, to develop a truly internationally applicable scale.

Predictive tests of SDI should also be extended to a broader range of products, as in the original O'Guinn and Wells' study, rather than being limited to financial products as investigated here.

SUMMARY

The typical practice of relying on simple reports of total household income in consumer behavior studies to represent the fundamental consumer concept of "spending power" reflects a limited perspective. A broader perspective—and deeper understanding —would be achieved in consumer research by using measures from economic research. *Full Income* (Becker 1965; Richardson 1989) appears to correct for the additional spending power released by household labor and products already acquired rather than having to be continually paid for and is relevant for social policy in the area of welfare payments. *Equivalent Income* (Travers and Richardson 1990) appears to be a useful "per capita" measure of spending power within the household and, since it corrects for the number and nature of dependents, it bears on taxation policy as well. *Resources* (Lovell et al. 1990) is a measure of *potentially available* spending power which appears to capture the important but surprisingly underinvestigated concept of "standard of living." *Objective Discretionary Income* (U.S. Bureau of Census) does *not* seem worth pursuing as it leads to an intuitively unrealistic distribution across the population by failing to acknowledge that much of the amount spent on "necessities" is in fact discretionary and, therefore, subjective. *Subjective Discretionary Income*, accordingly, appears to be a conceptually necessary aspect of "spending power" for consumer research.

Assuming that the traditional Total Household Income or total "family" income measure, TFI, continues to be used, then O'Guinn and Wells' (1989) Subjective Discretionary Income scale, SDI, appears to be a conceptually valid measure to use in addition. The dual use of TFI and SDI was shown in their U.S. study and in the present Australian replication to provide significant explanatory power for major financial products. TFI tends to predict "necessities" well, such as home loans and personal loans; SDI tends to predict "investments" well, such as mutual funds and money market funds; and *both* tend to be good predictors of credit card ownership, common stock ownership, and real estate investment

beyond one's own home. However, the SDI scale may require further development for international or global use. Its internal-consistency reliability was estimated to be only .6 in the Australian context and low reliability would necessarily limit its predictive validity when correlated with dependent variables (for all types of products and services). Improvement may be obtained by adding items tapping the "choice" aspect of subjective discretionary income.

Indeed, as the alternative income measures introduced in this article imply, having a *choice* of how to spend income appears to be the main concept missing when consumer researchers use "income" to mean "spending power." Amount of income matters, but so too does the extent to which the consumer is free to spend it.

REFERENCES

Andrews, F.M. and S.B. Withey (1976), *Social Indicators of Well-Being: Americans' Perceptions of Life Quality*, New York: Plenum.

Australian Bureau of Statistics (1990), ABS 1988-89 *Household Expenditure Survey*, Canberra, AS: Australian Government Printing Office.

Becker, G. (1965), "A Theory of the Allocation of Time," *The Economic Journal*, 75 (September), 493-517.

Bureau of the Census (1989), *A Marketer's Guide to Discretionary Income*, Washington DC: Government Printing Office.

Coleman, R.P. (1983), "The Continuing Significance of Social Class to Marketing," *Journal of Consumer Research*, 10 (December), 265-280.

Cronbach, L.J. (1951), "Coefficient Alpha and the Internal Structure of Tests," *Psychometrika*, 16 (September), 297-334.

Garran, R. (1994), "Howard Outlines Income Split Plan," *The Weekend Australian*, January 8-9, p. 8.

Harding, A. (1994), "Just Where Should We Draw the Poverty Line?" *The Australian*, August 9, p. 15.

Katona, G. (1975), *Psychological Economics*, New York: Elsevier.

Lovell, C.A.K., S. Richardson, P. Travers, and L. Wood (1990), "Resources and Functionings: A New View of Inequality in Australia," Working Paper no. 90-7, Department of Economics, University of Adelaide, South Australia 5001.

O'Guinn, T.C. and W.D. Wells (1989), "Subjective Discretionary Income," *Marketing Research*, 1 (March), 32-41.

Richardson, S. (1989), "Cash Income and Full Income: Does the Difference Matter," *Mimeo*, Department of Economics, University of Adelaide, South Australia 5001.

Travers, P. and S. Richardson (1990), "Measuring the Standard of Living," Working Paper no. 90-4, Department of Economics, University of Adelaide, South Australia 5001.

Wachtel, P.L. and S.J. Blatt (1990), "Perceptions of Economic Needs and of Anticipated Future Income," *Journal of Economic Psychology*, 11 (September), 403-415.

Framing Consumption as Play

Kent Grayson, London Business School
John Deighton, Harvard Business School

Despite the 1982 call for attention to play (Holbrook and Hirschman 1982) and one exploratory study (Holbrook, Chestnut, Oliva and Greenleaf 1984), consumer research has given little theoretical weight or empirical attention to play. This session brought together seven people whose research illuminates that an understanding of play and games is indispensable to understanding much of consumers' behavior. It was hoped that, by describing current work in play and games, the session could reflect the continued promise of this topic.

INTRODUCTION: PLAYING AND THE LOCUS OF RULES

Kent Grayson and John Deighton

Playing can be viewed as an agreement (or a social consensus) among two or more individuals to follow a unique set of rules; rules that the players consider to be different from those which govern their everyday lives. An important additional consideration for play is whether the agreements that make up the social consensus are (a) shared by the players alone or (b) shared also by the wider group or society in which the playing takes place (Deighton and Grayson, forthcoming). These basic distinctions are outlined in the table below:

	Playing	Gaming
Source of Rules	the players	precedent
Useful Skills	creativity flexibility	knowledge strategy

When the consensus is narrow (e.g., two people playing tennis "just for fun"), the players have significant latitude to alter the standard rules and to make up new ones. In this case, greater benefits are gleaned when the players are creative enough to devise new rules, and flexible enough to follow each other's lead in this regard. Alternatively, when two individuals are participating in a broader consensus (i.e., playing tennis in a professional match), the rules are set by precedent and are not under the control of the players. Thus, players increase their ability to glean benefits from the game by knowing the rules and by being able to work strategically within these rules.

Marketing has in the past been more game-like, with its focus on mass markets and on the building of broad social consensuses. However, as marketing becomes more targeted and interactive, both marketers and consumers will find themselves in more playful consumption situations, and will require new skills to glean benefits from it.

WHITE WATER FRAMED BY CANYON WALLS: PLAYING GAMES IN NATURE

Eric Arnould and Linda Price

Building from data collected from consumers and service providers during river rafting expeditions (see Arnould and Price 1993), this presentation presented a post-modern conception of play, which emphasizes the qualities of freedom, liberation, and protest against reason. The presentation also described consumers' post-modern perceptions of nature and how these two post-modern perspectives articulate with one another.

A key quality of post-modern play is that it pushes the boundaries between play and not-play. For example, post-modern play is set aside from life, yet it tells about life. Informants frequently noted that river rafting offered an escape from the everyday, while also reporting that their river rafting experiences taught them lessons that they carried into their everyday lives.

River rafting also pushes the boundaries between play and not-play by combining the sacred, the secular and the existential in a single activity. Its sacredness is reflected in the observation that consumers are often transformed by a river rafting experience, just as they are by rituals. Yet, participants often viewed their experience as hard work, which is inherently secular. And, river rafting is existential because of the real life-and-death dangers often associated with the activity.

This research also highlighted a post-modern conception of nature. Nature is viewed as an uncertain force that is divorced from the commercial relationships that govern the rest of life. It is thus seen as a locus for both authentication and an alternative way of life. Because nature governs rafting rules (and not the other way around), participants report primal experiences that do not follow the logic of reason. Thus, play in nature (i.e., post-modern play) is protected from rationalization.

SOUTH PACIFIC? TIC-TAC-TOE? NO? CONCEPTUALIZING CONSUMPTION AS PLAY

Douglas Holt

Drawing from an observational case study of spectators of professional baseball, this presentation cast play as one of the four key analytical categories used by Holt (forthcoming) to typologize consumer actions. Specifically, play references the interpersonal aspects of autotelic consumer actions. When consumers play, they use their engagement with the consumption object as a resource that they draw on to interact with other consumers. The interpersonal dimension distinguishes playing from other related concepts of autotelic consumption such as experiential consumption, flow, aesthetic experience, and sacred experience.

Different types of play can be delineated by looking at the differences in the implicit rules structuring the play. For example, baseball spectators engage in "arguing" (rule: taking contrary positions), "socializing" (rule: entertaining others, being witty), and "role playing" (rule: mimicking players, coaches and announcers). Overall, it was argued that playing is a central dimension of action in all consumption categories, not just those that are typically associated with play and games.

"GUESS WHAT I PAID FOR THIS" AND OTHER GAMES BARGAIN-HUNTERS PLAY

Robert M. Schindler

This presentation was a preliminary report of a series of depth interviews with deal-prone consumers. Two types of games were observed. The first is a solitary game, played against an impersonal seller. In "Wait," the consumer identifies a desired item, and then waits for the price to decrease substantially, hoping that this will occur before the item becomes unavailable. In "Radar," the player systematically scans for bargains by repeatedly carrying out a predetermined sequence of shopping activities. In "Stock Up," the player attempts to purchase enough of a discounted item so that repurchase is not necessary until the next time the item is discounted.

The second type of game is a social game, played against (and sometimes also in cooperation with) other consumers. In "Guess What I Paid For This," the consumer shows a second player a recent purchase and asks the second player to indicate what one would expect to pay for the item. In "Beat the Clock," the player takes sometimes extreme measures to purchase discounted merchandise before it can be purchased by other consumers. In "Santa Claus," the player purchases numerous items on deal for the purpose of giving them away, expecting to stimulate conversation about the source of this generosity.

It was observed that the informants usually believed that they would easily win most bargain-related games. However, it sometimes turned out that doing so was more difficult than the players had anticipated. On the other hand, it was also observed that bargain-related games enriched consumers' lives in many ways, including enjoying the camaraderie of bargain hunting with friends and experiencing the pleasures of obtaining a discount throughout consumption of the discounted product.

ALL THIS IS EXTREMELY WORTHWHILE, BUT...

Morris Holbrook

According to a typology offered by Holbrook (1994), play is self-oriented, active behavior that is intrinsically motivated (see table below). Although this session usefully addressed many issues related to play and consumption, each of the presentations drifted away from describing activities in the "play" cell below, and toward the discussion of activities that might better fit in other cells.

		Extrinsic	Intrinsic
Self-Oriented	*Active*	Efficiency (O/I ratio or convenience)	Play (fun)
	Reactive	Excellence (quality)	Esthetics (beauty)
Other-Oriented	*Active*	Politics (success)	Ethics (justice, virtue, or morality)
	Reactive	Esteem (reputation)	Spirituality (faith or ecstasy)

First, the rule orientation of Deighton and Grayson is too broad for a clear-cut definition of play, since their perspective might include rule-based consumption experiences other than games (e.g., starting one's car), as well as games that are not really playful (e.g., marketing warfare). Secondly, Arnould and Price include in their conception of play several other-oriented activities, which moves their focus from play into ethics and spirituality. Next,

because there is a difference between actually playing baseball and reactively watching baseball, Holt's conception includes various reactive aspects of consumption, which places his phenomena of interest at least partially in the esthetics area. Lastly, the bargain hunters described by Schindler seek various extrinsic benefits, including the self-oriented benefit of efficiency and the other-oriented benefits of success and esteem.

In sum, the presentations were valuable in highlighting the importance of play: they raised key issues related to the conceptualization of play, and suggested the complexity of the consumption experience. However, there are still inadequate answers regarding the nature of play *per se*, and regarding the types of play that might exist within the overall phenomenon of playful consumption.

REFERENCES

Arnould, Eric J. and Linda L. Price (1993), "River Magic: Extraordinary Experience and the Extended Service Encounter," *Journal of Consumer Research*, 20 (1), 24-45.

Deighton, John and Kent Grayson (forthcoming), "Marketing and Seduction: Managing Exchange Relationships by the Construction of Social Consensus," *Journal of Consumer Research*.

Holbrook, Morris B. (1994), "The Nature of Customer Value: An Axiology of Services in the Consumption Experience", in Roland Rust and Richard Oliver (eds.), *Service Quality: New Directions in Theory and Practice*, Thousand Oaks, CA: Sage Publications.

_____ , Robert B. Chestnut, Terence A. Oliva and Eric A. Greenleaf (1984), "Play as a Consumption Experience: The Roles of Emotions, Performance, and Personality in the Enjoyment of Games," *Journal of Consumer Research*, 11 (2), 728-739.

_____ and Elizabeth C. Hirschman (1982), "The Experiential Aspects of Consumption: Fantasies, Feelings and Fun," *Journal of Consumer Research*, 9 (2), 132-140.

Holt, Douglas (forthcoming), "How Consumers Consume: A Typology of Consumption Practices," *Journal of Consumer Research*.

Consumer Response to Four Categories of "Green" Television Commercials

Esther Thorson, University of Missouri-Columbia
Thomas Page, Michigan State University
Jeri Moore, CCS LTD, Tucson, Arizona

Although there is a significant research literature on what kinds of green messages exist in the media (e.g., see Weaver-Lariscy & Tinkham 1992; Frith 1992; Carlson, Kangun, and Grove 1992; and Cornwell and Schwepker 1992), there is much less research on how people respond to environmentally-based persuasive messages. To help fill that gap, this paper reports the results of an experiment that examined both consumer responses to four categories of greening commercials and some attitudinal antecedents of those responses.

Although there has been considerable coverage of green marketing issues in the popular press (e.g., Ottman, 1993), there has been little attention to the topic by academics. Indeed, there has been little or no research that looks at immediate consumer response to greening commercials.

Nevertheless there is a literature that focuses on identification of variables that predict which consumers will be "environmentally concerned." This literature was reviewed in detail by Schwepker and Cornwell (1991). A particularly relevant study in this literature is Balderjahn's (1988) conceptualization of how certain personality variables and attitudes about the environment are related to environmentally responsible patterns of consuming. Balderjahn showed that German consumers' attitudes toward pollution were related to their attitudes toward ecologically conscious living, and that, in turn, these attitudes served as predictors of energy conservation behavior, environmental concern, and recycling. In addition, consumers' belief in their own effectiveness and control was related to the same three variables. In a recent American replication and development of Balderjahn's work, Schwepker and Cornwell (1991) showed that consumers with a higher internal locus of control, who were concerned about litter, who believed there was a pollution problem, and who had a favorable attitude toward ecologically conscious living, were more inclined to report buying ecologically packaged products. Schwepker and Cornwell suggested that as people become more aware of the problem of solid waste, their attitudes and purchase intentions change correspondingly.

Another relevant area of research on greening advertising has been concerned with categorizing environmental ads. The first such study (Peterson, 1991) compared the percent of commercials that referred to environmental responsiblity in 1979 and 1989. The sample was identified from commercials appearing on the three networks, one local station and five cable companies on two randomly-chosen days of each month in two years, recorded between 8:00 a.m. and 12:00 p.m. Coders looked for commercials that directly advocated ecological responsibility, those that showed an ecologically responsible participant in a favorable light, and commercials that favorably illustrated a goal of an ecologically responsible issue. Commercials were identified as "directly or indirectly green," depending upon whether the ecological responsibility notion was there to sell goods, or was not related to the selling strategy. It also identified six categories of environmental concern: air, water, and noise pollution, depletion of resources, destruction of the landscape and population growth. The results indicated a change between 1979 and 1989 from 5.8% of ads being environmentally related to 6.9%. Although there was no change in the percentage of ads with direct ecology themes, all of the other categories were more frequently represented in 1989 than in 1979.

In a more recent study, Carlson, Grove, and Kangun (1993) sampled print ads from 18 popular press and environmental magazines, examining all issues from 1989 and 1990. Eventually, 100 ads were included in the study. The authors were interested in categorizing the ads in terms of (1) the type of environmental claim they made, and (2) "misleading/deceptive" categories of claims. Five types of claims were identified, including: product orientation, process orientation, image orientation, environmental fact (a statement ostensibly factual about the environment), and combinations of these categories. Four types of misleading categories were identified, including: vague/ambiguous ads, claims that omitted important information necessary to evaluate the ads' truthfulness, false ads, and ads that contained more than one misleading element.

The focus of the present study falls somewhere between the two approaches exemplified in the literature cited here. It is concerned with types of greening television commercials, but the central focus is on how consumers differentially respond to individual ads of various types, and secondarily, on what prior attitudes toward environmental issues are related to the responses to the ads. To provide a rationale for the approach, we turn next to a model of consumer processing that brings together attitudinal structure with a conception of how consumers deal with messages as they occur in their environment.

Consumer Attitudes and the Processing of Green Commercials

The core processing assumption made here is that prior attitudes guide information processing (Fazio 1989) and that the closer the specificity between attitudes and the target of the information processing, the more those attitudes will guide information processing (Ajzen & Fishbein 1977). In other words, attitudes about environmental issues in general should be predictive of the way that people evaluate green commercials and the companies that sponsor them. In this paper, then, we move back to a somewhat more general conception of what people bring to advertising, and adopt a functional view of attitudes (e.g., Shavitt 1989) as they are related to behaviors and processing of environmental stimuli.

A functional view of attitudes suggests that people hold attitudes to determine how to respond to their environment (Shavitt 1989). Therefore, if we know what attitudes relevant to particular stimuli are, we should be able to predict behaviors exhibited in response to those stimuli. Indeed, historically, the concept of attitude has commonly been defined in terms that emphasize its predictive relation to behavior. In one highly influential definition, for example, Allport (1937) refers to attitude as "a mental and neutral state of readiness . . exerting . . (an) influence upon the individual's response." Similarly, Campbell (1963) defined attitude as an "acquired behavioral disposition."

But in addition to prior attitudes, it is also clearly important to consider how messages themselves influence perceptions of the situation (Fazio 1989). As Carlson, Grove, and Kangun (1993) have shown, the way in which a brand or company is related to the environment in an advertisement clearly varies. And the way that consumer prior attitudes will be employed seems likely to depend upon just what the nature of that relationship is.

Although not posed specifically as a functional model, Lutz's work with antecedents of attitude toward the ad (Lutz, MacKenzie,

Advances in Consumer Research
Volume 22, © 1995

FIGURE 1
A Model of the Impact of Green Commercial Type and Attitudinal Antecedents on Liking For Green Ads and Their Sponsors

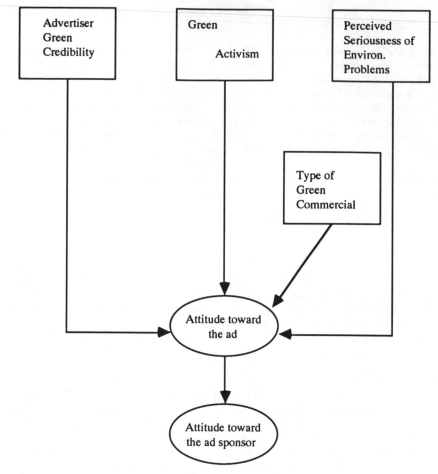

and Belch 1983; Lutz 1985; MacKenzie and Lutz 1989) can be treated as such, and is helpful in identifying and measuring attitudinal variables that are likely to predict how people will respond to green commercials. In a later form of the model, MacKenzie and Lutz (1989) suggested that four antecedents were important for predicting attitude toward the ad: prior attitudes toward advertising in general, prior attitudes toward the advertiser, mood during processing of the ad, and ad perceptions themselves. What MacKenzie and Lutz actually found was that *advertising* credibility in general influenced *advertiser* credibility, which in turn affected attitude toward the ad. But the strongest determinant of attitude toward the ad was *perception of the ad* itself. These results can be interpreted as indicating the most important determinant of consumer response to an ad will be the executional aspects of the ad itself, but that a secondary determinant will be prior attitudes about the advertiser, advertising in general, and other attitudes directly relevant to the domain of the advertising.

Using this general approach as a guide, we posited the model of processing green advertising shown in Figure 1. As can be seen, the model suggests that both the nature of the greening message and attitudinal orientations of consumers toward advertiser green credibility, toward the seriousness of environmental issues, and how "green" the consumers themselves actually are would predict two important consumer responses to green commercials: their attitudes toward the ads themselves, and their attitudes toward the sponsoring companies.

There were thus three attitudinal orientations that we thought would be predictive. The first was the orientation toward environmental activism. Here we were interested in the extent to which people perceived themselves as performing environmentally responsible activities such as recycling, using their cars less, supporting environmental groups and so on.

The second orientation concerned people's attitudes toward advertisers' credibility with respect to their environmental responsibilities. A recent national study (J. Walter Thompson Greenwatch) showed that only 17% of Americans thought business was doing an excellent or good job in their environmental responsbilities. Forty-one percent thought businesses were doing "only fair" and 38% rated them as poor. So we were interested in how well people thought businesses, i.e., advertisers, were doing in carrying out their own environmental responsiblities. A third attitudinal orientation was how serious a problem environmental issues were perceived to be. As noted above, Schwepker and Cornwell (1991) showed that perceived seriousness of the problem of solid waste disposal was signficantly related to intention to recycle. Because we were interested in more general issues than just solid waste, we asked consumers about such aspects of environmental concern as water pollution, oil spills, solid waste, vehicle exhaust, acid rain, and so on.

In addition to the attitudinal antecedents, our model also suggested that not all executional strategies would be equally effective. When we examined the popular press for case histories of how greening campaigns had fared, we found that two kinds of advertising had consistently created intense criticism from environmentalists. The first concerned *packaging*. For example, one of the best-known environmental marketing conflicts had concerned McDonald's use of styrofoam containers for its foods (Crown, 1990). The second area of problems concerned the environmental soundness of *products* themselves. Again, perhaps the most salient cases were, first, Hefty garbage bags, represented as biodegradable, but which in reality would not biodegrade when buried in landfills; and "biodegradable" diapers such as Bunnies, which actually were not biodegradable.

In contrast, two other kinds of messages appeared to be quite common on television, but seemed to attract much less negative press. The first was messages that were "instructional" in nature, that is, that suggested some behavior that we should all engaged in as environmentally conscious citizens. For example, Sea World and Anheuser Busch have long-running campaigns in which they say "let's teach our children about the oceans so they can take better care of them" or "let's recycle those aluminum cans." And a number of oil companies have been running campaigns that encourage "all of us to pitch in to reduce air pollution." We were unable to find any criticism in the popular press of these messages.

A second kind of message we found to receive little criticism was what we called "Look what we're doing" commercials. In these executions, the primary message was that the sponsoring company was doing something responsible about the environment. McDonald's was giving away trees for children to plant, Dow was recyling plastic into other consumer products, and Sea World was breeding endangered species. Of this kind of message, the only example of criticism we found was of Chevron's 10-year old campaign called "we do." In this series, Chevron claims that it is saving or restoring parts of its property so that various animals can survive. This campaign has received negative popular press coverage (Berry 1990), but the tracking data presented by Chevron (Winters 1991) clearly indicate that whenever the media weight for the commercials was increased, there was an immediate and positive response from consumers toward Chevron.

As we examined the ads of each category, however, it was clear that other influencing variables might be operating. For example, when we had a group of college students rate how "important" the environmental issue in each commercial was, it was clear that product and packaging were not seen as important, but that the issues in the instructional and look ads were. It was also clear that the product and packaging commercials emphasized product attributes, were more hard-sell, did not use image appeals, and seemed less emotional than the instructional and look commercials. Given the sparcity of greening commercials, however, it was not possible to examine the impact individually of all of these variables. We thus decided that an important first step was simply to use the four categories, which emphasized only the type of main selling point, and of necessity leave the finer differentiations of their executional structure to later research. It should also be noted that our catgories of television commercials were not perfectly consistent with the categorizations of Carlson et al (1993). The category of "product" was identical, but their categories of process, image and environmental fact did not correspond with our packaging, look, and instructional. We suspect that these differences are actual ones, and reflect the difference in what is advertised in the print medium, and how television advertising is structured.

Thus we were interested in four categories of greening commercials. For two of these categories (Packaging and Products), there was ample evidence of the likelihood of both consumer and environmental activist negative response. For the other two catego-

ries ("Look" and "Instructional") there was not this evidence, and indeed, in the one case where some consumer response data was available (Winters 1991) the response was very positive.

In general, the model of Figure 1 suggests that prior attitudes will interact with the nature of the greening message to produce consumer response. A number of testable hypotheses can be derived from the model.

A first hypothesis concerned the impact of the four different kinds of greening message. Based on the notion that the specific claims of packaging and product ads have often been met with criticism from environmentalists and consumers, we hypothesized that:

H1: Packaging and product commercials will produce less positive attitude toward the ad than look and instructional commercials.

Because of the extensive evidence that liking for ads is the best predictor of attitudes toward brands or sponsors of messages (e.g., Batra and Ray 1986; Gardner 1985; Mitchell and Olson 1981; MacKenzie and Lutz 1989)

H2: Attitude toward the ads will be positively correlated with attitudes toward the brands or sponsoring companies.

If indeed packaging and product commercials produce less positive attitude toward the ad than look and instructional commercials, then:

H3: Attitude toward the brands or sponsoring companies for packaging and product commercials will be less positive than for look and instructional commercials.

We turn next to a consideration of the relations of prior attitudes toward environmental issues and the role of business in the environment, to impact on processing the commercials. Both from an intuitive point of view and in terms of the general industry anxiety that there will be backlash toward green advertising, particularly by consumers who are more environmentally active (Briggs 1977; Gatten 1991), it seemed likely that the more active a consumer was in environmentally responsible behaviors, the more negative they would be toward green commercials. Thus:

H4: Environmental activism will be negatively related to attitude toward the greening commercials and their sponsoring companies.

Given MacKenzie and Lutz's finding that advertiser credibility was an important antecedent of attitude toward the ad and attitude toward the brand, it seemed likely that the credibility of advertisers specifically concerning the environment would also be a significant predictor of attitudes toward greening commercials and their sponsoring companies, and thus:

H5: Consumers who believe business is being credible in their response to environmental concerns will be more positive in their attitudes toward greening commercials and their sponsoring companies.

As noted above, Schwepker and Cornwell (1993) found a strong relationship between the belief that the solid waste problem is very serious, and intention to purchase environmentally packaged products. There is also clear evidence from at least one greening campaign (Chevron's "We do.", Winters 1990) that the more serious consumers think environmental problems are, the more positive they are about commercials linked to those enviornmental problems, and thus:

H6:   There will be a positive correlation between the belief that environmental problems in general are a serious problem and how positive people's attitude toward the ads and toward their sponsors are.

METHOD

Commercials

To determine what kinds of green messages are being brought to consumers, we first requested from Radio and TV Reports all the environmentally-related messages that were being shown on television in 1991. Radio and TV Reports essentially monitors all the commercials running on network programming, and can provide all the commercials running in various product and topic categories. Twenty-seven commercials were received and it appeared both from our own informal search and the report from Radio and TV Reports that this constituted the population of commercials with environmental themes that were running at that time.

In analyzing the 27 commercials we received, we identified four dominant types. The first type we labeled "Products." In these commercials, the featured goal was to sell products that had been positioned as being environmentally friendly. The second type we labeled "Green Packaging." Again, the salient feature of these commercials was to sell products, but to motivate the purchase by emphasizing that the packaging for the product was environmentally friendly.

A third type of green message we labeled "Look What We're Doing" (Look). Here the obvious intent was to improve the *image of the company* by telling consumers what environmentally friendly things the company was doing. The fourth type we labeled "Instructional." In Instructional commercials, the intent was also to improve company image, but to do so by associating the company with information about how the consumer could become more environmentally helpful, in other words, to provide instruction such as "let's all recycle," and here's how to do it.

Interestingly, there were few packaging and product commercials, and the instructional and look categories provided many more exemplars. We decided therefore to select for this test each commercial that clearly fit into each of our four categories. The result was the list of 12 commercials shown in Table 1.

To verify that each commercial did appropriately represent the category to which it had been assigned, we asked a group of eight college students to first read the definitions of the types of commercials, view each of our 12 ads, and then to determine to which category each commercial belonged. All the commercials were corectly classified, and interobserver agreement was 100%.

Subjects

A recruiting company provided 118 adult consumers between the ages of 21 and 65. Half of the subjects were recruited from a large metropolitan area and half were recruited from a middle-sized city in the upper midwest. Half of each sample were males. Subjects were paid $15 for their participation.

Dependent variables

To measure the environmental activity level of consumers, we used the Roper items (Roper Reports 1990) that have been em-

ployed for the last several years to measure over-time changes in American attitudes about participating in environmentally responsible behaviors (See Appendix 1). To measure advertiser "green credibility," consumers were asked whether advertisers were fully, fairly well, not too well or not at all well fulfilling three environmental responsibilities: (1) being good citizens of the communities in which they operate; (2) advertising honestly; and (3) cleaning up their own air and water pollution. To measure perceptions of the seriousness of environmental problems, we again used items developed by Roper (Roper Reports 1990) to monitor consumer attitudes toward the environment over time (See Appendix 2).

The items measuring attitude toward advertiser green credibility showed an unacceptably low Chronbach's alpha (.51), and its further use is therefore questionable. The other attitudinal scales showed acceptable although not high Chronbach values: consumer green activity (.79) and the seriousness of green problems (.66).

Attitude toward the ad was measured on a nine-point scale of +4 (like it a lot) to -4 (dislike it a lot). Attitude toward the sponsoring company was measured with the same nine-point scale in response to the question "How do you feel toward the [Company X]?" Although it is considered mandatory in the marketing literature to use multiple items to measure attitude toward ads and companies, asking a partipant virtually the same question three or more times was found to be irritating and tiresome to them. The advertising agency sponsoring the research was opposed to the possibility of irritating participants, and it was therefore necessary to use single-item measures. The potential for problems with this approach is considerably alleviated by the recent finding (Brown & Stayman 1992) in an extensive meta-analysis of attitude toward the ad studies, that "using multi- versus single-item scales to measure ad attitude had relatively minor effects on average correlations."

Procedure

Subjects in each city were tested individually by a single experimenter in a comfortable viewing room containing a 25-inch television. At the beginning of the session, the subject was welcomed, and then told that the intent of the study was to determine his or her responses to a series of television commercials of interest. Prior to the testing, the attitudinal items were administered. Thereafter, each subject viewed one of the three random orders of 10 of the green commercials. No subject saw more than one commercial for a single brand or company. Immediately after each commercial, the subject filled out the questionnaire for that commercial. After viewing the commercials, the subjects were thanked, paid, and excused.

RESULTS

The two samples

We examined each of the two samples (the large and small city) for differences in mean response to the ads and their sponsors, and mean scores on each of the five attitudinal scales. None of the comparisons were statistically significant (t-tests, p>.05), and therefore the two samples were combined for all subsequent analyses.

Overall pattern of responses to the commercials

Although it had not been specifically hypothesized, we were interested in whether the overall pattern of responses to the green commercials would indicate strong negativity ("backlash"). When we combined all of the messages, we found that the majority of evaluations of the commercials (62%) were positive, that is when we consider the scores of 2, 3, and 4 as positive. Most of the rest of the evaluations (30%) fell into the neutral category (1, 0, -1). Only 8% of the evaluations were essentially negative (scores of -2, -3, or

TABLE 1

Attitudes Toward Green Ads and Ad Sponsors and Their Intercorrelations for Each Commercial

Commercials	Att Toward Ad	Att Toward Sponsor	Correl.
Products			
Gasoline #1	1.28	.77	.67*
Disposable camera	.72	2.38	.21
Packaging			
Recyclable instant coffee jar	1.42	1.33	.29*
Refill packs for detergent	1.65	1.39	.44*
Look			
Gasoline #2 (we're saving animal habitats)	1.42	.78	.46*
Amusement park (we're breeding endangered animals)	2.36	2.12	.42*
Fast food restaurant (we're encouraging children to plant trees)	1.30	1.60	.73*
Chemical company (we're recycling plastics)	1.82	1.56	.57*
Instructional			
Amusement park (let's teach children about nature)	2.18	1.86	.56*
Aluminum company (let's recycle aluminum)	2.58	2.20	.43*
Gasoline #3 (let's use our car less often)	1.80	.46	.19
Gasoline #4 (let's clean up the air)	2.17	1.32	.44*

Significant at p < .01

-4). In response to the question about attitude toward the sponsoring companies, we found that over 50% of the responses were positive (score of 2, 3, or 4). It is clear, then, that there is a generally positive reaction to all of the greening messages that fell into the four categories we studied.

Tests of Hypotheses About the Impact of the Four Types of Commercials

Hypothesis 1 suggested that packaging and product commercials would show less positive attitude toward the ad than look and instructional commercials. Because there were differing numbers of commercials in each of the four groups, we first calculated the mean attitude toward the ad for each of the four types of commercials for each individual. (There was considerable consistency within each of the four groups in attitude toward the ad, and thus the combining of the commercials into a mean for each group was deemed appropriate. See Table 1.)

The means for each of the four groups were then used in a one-way, within-subject analysis of variance. This produced a significant F(3, 114)=8.49, p<.001. The means were as follows: Product=1.27, Packaging=1.54; Look=2.05; and Instructional=2.10.

We then compared the Look and Instructional means to the Product and Packaging means, and in support of Hypothesis 1, found that the former categories produced a signficantly higher mean (F(1, 114)=21.12, p<.001).

Hypothesis 2 suggested that attitude toward the ads would be positively correlated with attitudes toward the brands or sponsoring companies. To test the hypothesis, we correlated for each commercial, the attitude toward the ad and the attitude toward the sponsoring company. These correlations are shown in Table 1 and, as can be seen, all except the correlations for Arco and Kodak were significant. Thus there was clear support for Hypothesis 2.

Hypothesis 3 suggested that attitude toward the sponsoring companies for Packaging and Product commercials would be less positive than for Look and Instructional commercials. Again calculating a mean attitude toward the company for each subject for each of the four types of commercials allowed a one-way, within-subject analysis of variance to be run. Again, the hypothesis was supported (F(3, 114)=3.12, p<.05). The means for the four groups were: Product=1.04, Packaging=1.53; Look=1.89; and Instructional=1.69. Combining the Look and Instructional commercials and comparing their means to the combination of Packaging and

Product commercials, we again found the former category to be significantly more positively responded to $(F(1, 114)=6.25, p<.05)$. Thus Hypothesis 3 was also supported.

Tests of Hypotheses About the Impact of Prior Attitudes and Beliefs

To test these hypotheses, a regression analysis was carried out separately for each of the four types of commercials. This was done using first attitude toward the ad and then attitude toward the sponsoring company as the dependent variables, and with the hypothesized attitudes as independent variables.

Hypothesis 4 suggested that environmental activism would be negatively related to attitude toward the greening commercials and their sponsoring companies. Contrary to this prediction, environmental activism significantly negatively affected only the response to Instructional commercials $(B=-.26, t=-2.8, p=.006)$. There was no significant relationship between consumer activism and attitude toward the ad for the other three kinds of environmental commercials.

Hypothesis 5 suggested that consumers more positive about advertiser green credibility would be more positive in their attitude toward the greening commercials and their sponsoring companies. As indicated, the scale reliability of advertiser green credibility was not satisfactorily high. Interestingly, however, for each category of green ads except the Instructional commercials, advertiser green credibility produced significant positive beta weights for attitude toward the ad (Look: $B=.34, t=3.87, p=.0002$; Packaging: $B=.20, t=2.17, p=.03$: and Product: $B=.24, t=2.66, p=.009$). There was, however, no significant relationship between advertiser green credibility and attitude toward the sponsoring company. In spite, then, of the noise in this measure, these results can be seen as somewhat supportive of the hypothesis that when people find advertisers credible in their environmental activities, attitudes toward greening commercials are generally more positive. Again, however, there was no observable impact of advertiser green credibility on attitudes toward the sponsoring companies.

Hypothesis 6 suggested that there would be a positive correlation between the belief that environmental problems are a serious problem and how positive people's attitude toward the ads and toward their sponsors were. For attitude toward the ad, this hypothesis was supported for each of the commercial categories except Product: (Look: $B=.27, t=2.9, p=.004$; Packaging: $B=.21, t=2.26, p=.03$: and Instructional: $B=.28, t=-3.01, p=.003$). There was, however, no significant relationships between perceptions of the seriousness of environmental problems and attitude toward the sponsoring company. Thus Hypothesis 6 was supported only for attitude toward the ad.

DISCUSSION

The results of the present study provide clear evidence about how consumers respond to common categories of environmentally-based television commercials. First, most consumers are quite positive in their response to all green commercials. The majority of attitude toward the ad evaluations observed here were positive. This is particularly important because, first, it demonstrates that the oft-touted "backlash" of consumers toward green advertising (Briggs 1977; Gatten 1991) is not occurring, at least in their response to specific television commercials. Second, the positive response to the greening commercials is important because this response is significantly correlated with attitudes toward the sponsoring companies.

A second area of findings clearly demonstrated here is that two executional types of commercials are significantly superior in their impact to two others. When commercials say either "Look at all the good things we're doing for the environment" or "Let's all learn how to be better to our environment" there is a typically very positive response from consumers. The response to commercials that focus on a product or packaging is clearly not as positive as that to Look and Instructional commercials. It must, of course, be said that the four categories of green commercials identified here also vary along other dimensions than simply the main green message we have been concerned with, and it will be important to delve further into how these other executional characteristics also affect consumer response. At the present, however, there are probably not enough green television commercials to allow the kind of extensive crossing of these other executional variables with central green message to allow a complete analysis, but as advertisers move toward more green campaigns, this kind of study may eventually become possible.

A third result observed in the present study is that how "green" consumers are (i.e., as indexed by their green activism scores) does not affect responses to green commercials, except for the Instructional ones. This is surprising both in terms of what has been written in the popular press about the dangers of "green backlash" in response to green advertising (e.g., Briggs 1977; Gatten 1991). It has also proved surprising to many clients we have talked to about doing green advertising. Because there has been so much negative press about certain green campaigns (e.g., Hefty bags, Chevron, disposable diapers, etc.), many advertisers express fear of creating negative consumer response if they advertise "green." The present results strongly suggest that "green backlash" is probably not very likely. The only companies that received relatively negative evaluations in the present study were the oil companies, and even for these companies, if they used the "right" kind of green message, the response to their commercials was positive.

Finally, both the green credibility of advertisers in general and the seriousness with which people perceive environmental problems significantly affected attitudes toward green commercials. Those who were more positive about advertiser green credibility were more positive toward the commercials. Those who rated environmental problems are more serious also were more positive toward the commercials. Both of these findings are potentially important considerations for advertisers. For example, the more advertisers can build up positive attitudes in people about their response to the environment, the more positive they can expect the public's response to their advertising to be. And during times when the environment is of greater concern to people, advertisers can also expect that there will be more positive responses to their green advertising.

As with any study, there are weaknesses that most be observed and taken into consideration. Both attitude toward the ad and attitude toward the sponsor were measured with only a single item. The scale reliabilities were not as high as is preferable, and for advertiser green credibility, were unacceptably low. And of course, there was extraneous executional variation within the four categories of green commercials. Nevertheless, the strong patterning of the results and the fact that a large number of non-student adults were the subjects in the study provide considerable strength to the study and encourage our belief that it indeed provides reliable and useful information about how consumers are responding to green commercials.

REFERENCES

Ajzen, I., & Fishbein, Martin (1977). Attitude-behavior relations: A theoretical analysis and review of empirical research. *Psychological Bulletin*, 84, 888-918.

APPENDIX 1
Green Activism Items

Return beer or soda bottles for recycling
Use biodegradable paper products
Use emission control gasoline to help cut down on air pollution
Avoid using my car whenever possible
Contribute money to environmental groups such as Sierra Club, Audubon Society
Look for products made from or packaged in recycled paper or plastic
Separate glass, paper, tin cans, etc. for recycling
Not buy at restaurants that put take-out food in styrofoam containers
Do volunteer work for local environmental groups
Use household cleaners that are safe for the environment
Bundle up my newspapers for recycling

APPENDIX 2
Seriousness of Environmental Problems

Water pollution from industrial wastes
Accidental oil spills
Solid waste problems created by trash that people throw away
Outdoor air pollution from vehicle exhaust
Environmenal damage froma acid rain
Pollution caused by household cleaners and other chemicals used in homes
Solid waste problems created by packaging of food and goods
Global warming resulting from depletion of the ozone layer
Destruction of the rain forests

Allport, Gordon W. (1937). *Personality: A Psychological Interpretation.* New York: Henry Holt.

Balderjahn, Ingo (1988). Personality variables and environmental attitudes as predictors of ecologically responsible consumption patterns. *Journal of Business Research*, 17 (August), 51-56.

Batra, Rajeev, & Ray, Michael L. (1985). How advertising words at contact. In (Eds.) L. F. Alwitt and A, Mitchell, *Psychological Processes and Advertising Effects.* Hillsdale, NJ: Lawrence Erlbaum Associates, 13-43.

Berry, Jon (1990). Greens criticize Chevron image ads. *Adweek*, March 19, p. 31.

Briggs, Jean Al (1977). The price of environmentalism: The backlash begins. *Forbes*, June 15, 36-40.

Brown, Steven P. & Stayman, Douglas M. (1992). Antecedents and consequences of attitude toward the ad: A meta-analysis. *Journal of Consumer Research*, 19(1), 34-51.

Campbell, Donald T. (1963). Social attitudes and other acquired behavioral dispositions. In (Ed.), Sigmund Koch, *Psychology: A Study of a Science (Volume 6).* New York: MacGraw Hill.

Carlson, Les, Kangun, Norman, & Grove, Stephen (1992). A content analysis of environmental advertising claims. In (Ed.), Leonard Reid, *Proceedings of the 1992 Conference of the American Academy of Advertising.* Grady College of Journalism and Mass Communication, Athens, GA: University of Georgia.

Cornwell, T. Bettina, & Schwepker, Charles H., Jr. (1992). Attitudes and intentions regarding ecologically packaged products: Subcultural variations. In (Ed.), Leonard Reid, *Proceedings of the 1992 Conference of the American Academy of Advertising.* Grady College of Journalism and Mass Communication, Athens, GA: University of Georgia.

Crown, Judith (1990). McDonald's aims to recycle trash, image. *Crain's Chicago Business*, April 16, p. 3.

Fazio, Russell H. (1989). How do attitudes guide behavior? In (Eds.) R.M. Sorrentino and E.T. Higgins, *The Handbook of Motivation and Cognition: Foundations of Social Behavior.* New York: Guilford Press.

Frith, Katherine Toland (1992). The machine in the garden; Advertising and nature. In (Ed.), Leonard Reid, *Proceedings of the 1992 Conference of the American Academy of Advertising.* Grady College of Journalism and Mass Communication, Athens, GA: University of Georgia.

Gardner, Meryl P. (1985). Does attitude toward the ad affect brand attitude under a brand evaluation set? *Journal of Marketing Research*, 22(May), 192-198.

Gatten, Caroline (1991). Social issues guide consumer buying. *Marketing News*, December 9, p. 4.

J. Walter Thompson Greenwatch (1990). J. Walter Thompson, Chicago, IL.

Lutz, Richard J. (1985). Affective and cognitive antecedents of attitude toward the ad: A conceptual framework. In (Eds.) L. F. Alwitt and A, Mitchell, *Psychological Processes and Advertising Effects.* Hillsdale, NJ: Lawrence Erlbaum Associates, 13-43.

Lutz, Richard J., MacKenzie, Scott B., & Belch, George E. (1983). Attitude toward the ad as a mediator of advertising effectiveness: Determinanats and consequences. In (Eds) R.P. Bagozzi and A.M. Tybout, *Advances in Consumer Research, Volume 10*. Ann Arbor, MI: Association for Consumer Research, 532-539.

MacKenzie, Scott B., & Lutz, Richard J. (1989). An empirical examination of the structural antecedents of attitude toward the ad in an advertising pretesting context. *Journal of Marketing,* 53(April), 48-65.

Mehta, Abhilasha (1991). Consumers in the '90's: Impact of environmental concerns on consumer behavior: The Syracuse Report. Syracuse University, Department of Advertising.

Mitchell, Andrew A., & Olson, J.C. (1981). Are product attribute beliefs the only mediator of advertising effects on brand attitude? *Journal of Marketing Research*, 18(August), 318-332.

Ottman, Jacquelyn A. (1993). *Green Marketing*. Lincolnwood, IL: NTC Business Books.

Peterson, Robin T. (1991). Physical environment television advertisement themes: 1979 and 1989. *Journal of Business Ethics*, 10, 221-228.

Roper Reports. The Roper Organization, 1990.

Schwepker, Charles H., and Cornwell, T. Bettina (1991). An examination of ecologically concerned consumers and their intention to purchase ecologically packaged products. *Journal of Public Policy & Marketing,*,10(2), 1-25.

Shavitt, Sharon (1989). Operationalizing functional theories of attitude. In (Eds.) A. Pratkanis, S. Breckler, & A. Greenwald, *Attitude Structure and Function*. Hillsdale, NJ: Erlbaum, 311-337.

Weaver-Lariscy, Ruth Ann, & Tinkham, Spencer F. (1992). Knowledge and opinions as predictors of recycling behavior: Implications for environmental advertising strategy. In (Ed.), Leonard Reid, *Proceedings of the 1992 Conference of the American Academy of Advertising*. Grady College of Journalism and Mass Communication, Athens, GA: University of Georgia.

Winters, Lewis C. (1991). Copy research with hostile audiences during war and other trying times. In (Ed.) Joel S. Dubow, *Copy Research: The New Evidence*. Advertising Research Foundation Eighth Annual Copy Research Workshop, September 11, New York.

New Ways to Reach Non-recyclers: An Extension of the Model of Reasoned Action to Recycling Behaviors

Debra J. Dahab, University of Nebraska
James W. Gentry, University of Nebraska
Wanru Su, University of Nebraska[1]

ABSTRACT

Looking at recycling from a decision perspective enhances our understanding of how people translate attitudes and social considerations into behavioral intentions. This paper examines the role of prior behavior, the effects of perceived effort, and the role of social norms in the individual decision to recycle. While most recycling studies look just at product disposition behaviors, this study defines recycling to include product purchase and reuse behaviors and finds that people do organize disposition, reuse, and purchase under the same umbrella of recycling activities. The results of empirical testing suggest that initial trial is an important predictor of repeat behavior. Perceived effort is also an important attitudinal component in the decision process. This suggests that promotions should be designed to minimize the amount of perceived effort that is involved in product disposition and purchase and to encourage initial trial. The success of appeals to community values and social expectations may depend on the strength of community recycling norms.

INTRODUCTION

As reducing, recycling, and reusing become important public policies with respect to the consumption and disposition of consumer goods, marketers have the opportunity to use consumer behavior concepts to explain differences in behavior and offer insights into program development. This paper investigates recycling as a deliberative process using the model of reasoned action (Fishbein and Azjen 1975) to explain how attitudes and subjective norms affect the intent to engage in recycling activities and whether the motivational component of attitudes and norms is sufficient to energize intentions. Bagozzi and Dabholkar (1994) are the first to apply the model of reasoned action to a recycling context. However, the approach in this article is unique in several respects. First, "recycling" in this study is defined not only as an act of product disposition but also as a purchase activity. The study recognizes that recycling must include the remanufacture and purchase of a product made from recycled materials for recycling to occur. "Completing the recycling loop" includes consumption and disposition and reconsumption of the same materials in remanufactured form. The scales used in this study incorporate this important definition to test whether people perceive recycling as disposition only or as the full circle of recycling activities including purchase decisions.

Second, this study treats perceived effort as an antecedent in the model of reasoned action and as a construct distinct from attitudes. Finally, we suggest that prior behavior is important in a recycling decision and discuss how recycling incentives can be structured to encourage initial trial which may lead to repeat behavior. This paper explores hypothesized effects of community norms on recycling behavior and suggests why normative pressures may be inconsistent across communities. We test hypotheses relating to differences in recycling intentions based on variations in attitudes and community norms, perceived effort and costs in-

volved in recycling, and individual differences in action control. Implications for public policy and program development and promotions are discussed. Extended beyond recycling behavior, our findings contribute to the growing stream of work that enhances our understanding of the deliberative processes involved in arriving at behavioral intentions.

RECYCLING AS A REASONED ACTION

Distinguishing recyclers from non-recyclers on the basis of identifiable criteria has been the focus of psychologists, marketers, and environmental planners. However, as recycling behaviors diffuse throughout the population, it has become more useful to look at the individual decision making process to explain why some persons recycle and others do not, and what factors affect the recycling decision (Berger 1993; Jackson et al. 1992; Nelson 1993; Vining and Ebreo 1992). Viewing recycling within the context of decision making provides the opportunity to understand not only the specific behavior but to integrate and apply research from other studies of consumer behaviors to recycling and vice versa.

Subjective norms

The Fishbein and Azjen (1975) model of reasoned action, Ajzen's (1991) Theory of Planned Behavior, and Bagozzi and Warshaw's (1990) Theory of Trying hypothesize that behavior is a function of intentions which in turn are the result of a deliberative process that is affected by attitudes and social norms. The normative component of the model of reasoned action is the multiplicative result of the perceived social norm and the motivation to comply with the norm (Fishbein and Azjen 1975). Hopper and Nielsen (1991) examined the impact of a block leader program on social norms and recycling behaviors. While the relationship between behavior and norms is not clear in the Hopper and Nielson study since all groups showed distinct changes in behavior, the study does demonstrate that norms can be changed through persistent social contacts and through the perception that the individual is accountable to others for his or her actions. This may have important implications when the communication objective is to sustain behavioral changes rather than just to induce them.

Other writers have suggested that norms play a role in guiding recycling behavior (Jackson et al. 1992; Vining and Ebreo 1992). Dirksen and Gartrell (1993) compared the attitudes and recycling behaviors of individuals in two separate communities, one with a visible, highly publicized curbside recycling program and the other with minimal recycling opportunities. They found that persons with positive attitudes towards environmental concern will recycle if given the opportunity, but more importantly, their results also show that unconcerned individuals in the strong recycling community reported high levels of recycling. They conclude that "the social context alone was sufficient to produce the behavior" (p. 439). They suggest that "the highly visible, widespread, and socially desirable nature of the program meant that on a neighborhood basis, the norm for recycling was probably changed" (p. 440). As product disposition behaviors become more visible with the increased number of curbside recycling programs, one would expect the normative component of the recycling decision to become more important. Vining and Ebreo (1992) suggest that

[1]The authors would like to thank Doug Curry and Yasser Dahab for assisting in the data collection for this study.

changing to a curbside program may account for the increase in reported social norms in their longitudinal community study. The literature then clearly suggests the first hypothesis for this study:

H1:   Perceived social norms that support recycling will be positively related to the intent to recycle.

Attitudes and Individual Differences

The attitudinal component of the model of reasoned action is the multiplicative result of beliefs towards the behavior and the perceived effectiveness of engaging in the behavior. Support for the relationship between attitudes towards recycling and behavioral intentions has been mixed (Bagozzi and Dabholkar 1994; Balderjahn 1988; Kinnear, Thomas, and Taylor 1973; McCarty and Shrum 1993; Samdahl and Robertson 1989). The tenuous link between attitudes and intentions has led some researchers to examine the influence of other factors that may moderate the relationship. Berger and Corbin (1992) found that the level to which a person perceived his or her behavior to be effective in achieving the desired results moderated the relationship between attitudes and a variety of environmentally conscious consumer behaviors. Individual differences are also hypothesized to moderate the attitude-behavioral intention relationship in the reasoned action model. Fishbein and Azjen (1975) acknowledge that the relative importance of the normative and attitudinal components in the reasoned action model depends on individual characteristics.

Bagozzi, Baumgartner, and Yi (1992) note that:

the "theory says little about when favorable attitudes and subjective norms lead to intentions to act. Rather, the theory assumes that favorable attitudes and subjective norms inevitably lead to intentions. Self-regulatory processes constitute motivational mechanisms for energizing the linkages found in the theory of reasoned action " (p. 506).

They found that individuals who were action-oriented placed greater weight on attitudes in determining behavioral intentions relating to coupon use, while state-oriented individuals weighted subjective norms more in the behavioral intentions equation. Action-oriented individuals are more responsive to the personal rather than the social evaluation or consequences of the act. Differences in individual readiness to act, according to Bagozzi, Baumgartner, and Yi (1992), supply the motivation in the model of reasoned action. We suggest this explanation may be particularly useful in explaining recycling behaviors which the literature suggests may have both attitudinal and normative antecedents. The motivational component of recycling may also derive from the perceived effectiveness of the intended action (Pieters 1991). If the individual perceives that recycling will bring about the desired personal or social outcome, he or she will be more predisposed to act. In either case, action-oriented individuals are more secure in the belief that they control both the decision to act and the outcome of the action. State-oriented people, on the other hand, are more deliberative in their decisions and are, as a result, more attuned to the social normative consequences of their actions (Bagozzi, Baumgartner, and Yi 1992). Thus, while attitudes are hypothesized to be important in the recycling decision, individual differences in action orientation will moderate the relationship. Persons who are more state-oriented will be guided more by social norms in making their decisions regarding recycling. This leads to the following hypotheses:

H2:   Positive attitudes will be positively related to the intent to recycle.

H3:   Individual differences in action control will moderate the relationship between attitudes and intent to recycle and subjective norms and the intent to recycle as follows:

H3a: Action-oriented individuals will be guided more by attitudes than norms in arriving at behavioral intentions.

H3b: State-oriented individuals will be guided more by subjective norms than attitudes in arriving at behavioral intentions.

Perceived Effort and Its Relationship to Intent

Recycling is not without cost. In some communities individuals must make a special effort to take materials to drop-off sites. If recycling is voluntary, these costs are weighed against the benefits in the individual decision process. Bagozzi, Yi, and Baumgartner (1990) examined effort as a moderator of the relationship between attitudes, intent, and behavior in the reasoned action model. They found that when the behavior required substantial effort, intentions mediated the relationship between attitudes and behavior. However, when the effort required was low, the mediating role of intentions declined. This occurs because more deliberation is required as effort or perceived effort increases.

The effort required to recycle has been examined as part of the recycling decision process (Granzin and Olson 1991; Jackson et al. 1992; Pieters 1991). While perception of the effort required to engage in a behavior is the result of the positive or negative evaluation of a belief regarding an action, research has demonstrated that perceived effort is distinct from general attitudes toward recycling and is important in the recycling decision. This leads to the following hypothesis:

H4:   The lower the perceived effort or cost to recycle, the greater the intent to recycle.

Prior Behavior

Bagozzi, Baumgartner, and Yi (1992) and Bagozzi and Dabholkar (1994) argue that while the theory of reasoned action views attitudes and norms as sufficient to predict intentions, research has demonstrated that prior behavior may be an informational input to the reasoned action decision or it may activate a previously stored intention, subject to arousal associated with the presence of certain cues. In the case of recycling, prior behavior may break down some of the barriers to recycling caused by an inflated perception of effort or it may represent overcoming that initial resistance to changing old disposition patterns. Bagozzi and Dabholkar (1994) found that prior behavior is more effective than attitudes in predicting recycling intentions. We suggest that prior behavior should be related not only to positive intent, but also to more positive attitudes and a lower perception of effort as follows:

H5:   Self-reported prior recycling behavior will be a significant predictor of intent to recycle.

METHODOLOGY

Sample

Respondents were 111 residents of a medium-sized midwestern community. Fifty-six percent of the subjects were female; 44% were male. The community has an extensive drop-off system maintained by the city for collection of recyclables; curbside pickup is available on a private fee-for-service basis from haulers serving selected areas. A quota sampling procedure was used to obtain a sample that represented the demographics of the community. The city was divided into four quadrants using census tract information, and neighborhoods were identified within the quadrants based on demographic characteristics. Subjects were recruited by going door to door in identified neighborhoods. In most cases, the survey was left with the resident and picked up later in the day. Approximately 50% of the households agreed to participate; refusals were relatively uncommon as not-at-homes constituted the majority of the non-responses. Of those agreeing to participate, 70% completed the questionnaire. Compared to the demographics of the community as a whole, the sample underrepresented persons in the 35-44 age category and overrepresented persons in the highest and lowest income categories.

Measurement

New measures for recycling norms, attitudes, effort, intent, and prior behavior were developed for the study. The notion of recycling was expanded to include recovering product discards and depositing them in a collection program offered in the community, reusing them within the household, and purchasing products made from recycled materials. The measures of norm, attitude, and effort were five-point Likert scales with response choices ranging from "strongly agree" to "strongly disagree". "Recycling norm" in this study was defined as the extent to which an individual perceives an informal community rule that members ought to engage in recycling. The recycling norm scale consisted of nine items that asked if "people in this community" expect others to recycle specific materials. Sample items include "It seems that in this community a person is expected to recycle food containers made of steel or tin" and "Purchasing paper and paper products made from recycled materials is seen by people in my community as the appropriate thing to do."[2] The attitude measure consisted of nine statements about the personal and social value and importance of recycling in general. Sample items include "Recycling helps make the world a better place to live," "It doesn't pay us to recycle" and "Recycling is something I think I should do." The effort scale included eight items representing attitudes regarding the convenience, time involved, and general utility of recycling such as "Recycling requires too much household space" and "Recycling takes too much time". The intent scale consisted of a listing of recycling activities and asked respondents to indicate for each activity whether it was something they are currently doing, something they definitely intend to do, something they may do, or something they probably will not do. Prior behavior was self reported with the question, "Have you ever at any time done the following with household wastes or for household purchases?" A yes or no response for each item was possible. Action control was measured using Kuhl's (1985) state/action orientation scale.

Two items were eliminated from the original norm, prior behavior, and intent scales because of apparent confusion about the context. When asked about behaviors concerning the recycling of motor oil some respondents interpreted the question to include recycling by a service station providing oil changes while others responded in a more personal context. Similarly respondents were confused about what activities constitute yard waste recycling. Some respondents reported that they leave clippings on the lawn and did not know how to respond to the query within the given

---

[2] In developing the scale for recycling norms, it was assumed that the word "community" would be interpreted as "persons who are important" to the respondent.

parameters. A principal components analysis indicated that it was appropriate to view the remaining activities (minus yard waste and oil) as a single construct. This suggests that people do view recycling as all activities that "complete the loop." Similarly, the remaining scales all showed evidence of unidimensionality.

Item responses for each scale were summed to derive a single score for each subject for each scale with a higher score indicating a stronger norm, more favorable attitude, less perceived effort, stronger intentions, and more recycling experience. The results of the tests for inter-item reliability using Cronbach's alpha were .70 for the recycling norm, .94 for the effort, .88 for the intent, .63 for the prior behavior, and .79 for the state/action orientation scales.

Analysis

All of the variables were tested as continuous variables using multiple regression analysis, including the state/action orientation scale as recommended by Bagozzi, Baumgartner, and Yi (1992). Hypotheses 1 through 5 were tested in moderated regression models that included the interactions between action control and attitudes, norms, and prior behavior. The predictor variables were mean centered (Cronbach 1987; Yi 1989) to reduce multicollinearity in analyzing main effects and interactions using regression analysis. The regression equations were modeled after those used by Bagozzi, Baumgartner, and Yi (1992) in their coupon study:

$$BI = SAO + Effort + Rnorm + Att + SAO \times Rnorm + Att \times SAO \qquad (1)$$

$$BI = SAO + Effort + Rnorm + Att + Prior + SAO \times Rnorm + Att \times SAO + Prior \times SAO \qquad (2)$$

where   BI is behavioral intention,
           Att is attitude,
           Rnorm is recycling norm,
           SAO is action orientation,
           Effort is perceived effort, and
           Prior is prior recycling behavior.

The interaction terms treat action orientation as a moderator of the effects of attitude and norms on behavioral intentions. Hierarchical and stepwise models was also used; however, these techniques did not contribute beyond the results of the analysis of the moderated models shown in Table 1. Hypothesis 1 predicts that perceived social norms will be positively related to the intent to recycle. In the case of this community, the hypothesis was not supported. In both models recycling norms were not significant predictors of intent to engage in recycling behavior. Hypothesis 2 also was not supported in either model. Attitudes were not significantly related to intent to recycle.

Hypothesis 3 proposes that individual differences in action control will moderate the relationship between attitudes, subjective norms, and behavioral intentions. One would anticipate that as attitudes towards recycling became more positive and as action control increased, intent would increase. Thus, the interaction between action control and attitudes should be positive. Similarly, as the strength of the subjective norm increased, for persons scoring lower on the action control scale, intent would increase. This would result in a negative parameter for the SAO x Rnorm interaction. While the parameter for the attitude-action control interaction was in the right direction, the interaction was not significant for either model. The recycling norm-action control interaction was significant ($\beta=.17$, $t=2.27$, $p<.05$) for the model without prior behavior but the relationship was in a direction opposite to the one hypothesized.

TABLE 1
Standardized Coefficients for Recycling Models[a]

Variable	Model 1	Model 2
SAO (Action orientation)	**.17** **(2.37)***	.10 (1.48)
Effort (Perceived effort)	.60 (6.24)**	.39 (3.81)**
Rnorm (Recycling norm)	.08 (1.17)	.09 (1.37)
Att (Attitude)	.17 (1.77)	.13 (1.48)
SAOxRnorm (Interaction)	.17 (2.27)*	.07 (1.05)
SAOxAtt (Interaction)	.01 (.20)	.02 (.29)
Prior (Prior behavior)	--	.37 (4.27)**
SAOxPrior (Interaction)	--	.07 (.82)
R2	.60	.68
Adjusted R2	.57	.64

[a] Coefficients are standardized with t-values in parentheses. * $p<.05$, ** $p<.001$, N=87.

Hypothesis 4 suggests less perceived effort/costs leads to greater intent to recycle. This hypothesis was supported in both models. Effort was a significant predictor of intent in the model without prior behavior ($\beta=.60$, $t=6.24$, $p<.001$) and was also significant in the model with prior behavior ($\beta=.39$, $t=3.81$ $p<.001$).

Hypothesis 5 predicts that prior behavior will be a significant predictor of intent. The R^2 of the model with prior behavior increased to 0.68 from 0.60 in the model without prior behavior and the increase is significant ($F=7.9$, 8,78 df, $p=.01$). Thus, the addition of prior behavior to the model of reasoned action in this situation enhances the model's predictive value. In comparing the models with and without prior behavior as a predictor, it should be noted that action control was a significant predictor in the model without prior behavior ($\beta=.17$, $t=2.37$, $p<.05$). That is, persons who were more action-oriented were more likely to express positive recycling intentions. In the model with prior behavior, however, action control is no longer significant as a predictor ($\beta=.10$, $t=1.48$) while prior behavior was the primary predictor in the regression model ($\beta=.37$, $t=4.27$, $p<.001$). This suggests that there is an underlying overlap between prior behavior and action control which is confirmed by the significant correlation between SAO and Prior in Table 2 ($r=.27$, $p=.01$).

DISCUSSION

The results of this study show that, consistent with the findings of Bagozzi, Baumgartner, and Yi (1992), prior behavior enhances the predictive power of the model of reasoned action with regard to behavioral intentions. For individuals in certain communities where recycling norms are strong and where a sense of community is reinforced (Bagozzi 1992), prior behavior may provide the individual with social feedback that reinforces the community expectations of behavior. If norms develop by individual trial and community response, the positive consequences of prior behavior may serve to encourage future intent. Prior behavior may also provide the experience, or information, that lowers the perception of the effort required to engage in the behavior and improves attitudes toward the behavior (Bagozzi, Baumgartner, and Yi 1992). Our results show the perception of effort was strongly related to future intention to participate in all recycling activities (including product disposition, purchase, and reuse). The Bagozzi, Yi, and Baumgartner (1990) findings on the relationship between attitudes and effort may shed some light on the findings of this study. They demonstrate that perceived effort is a significant moderator of the attitude-intention relationship when the activity is perceived to require more effort. For reluctant non-recyclers who perceive recycling as a high effort activity, more deliberation may be necessary because perceived effort complicates the cost-benefit analysis. Attitudes in both models were not related to intentions. This may be explained by looking at the correlations between attitude, prior behavior, effort, and intent in Table 2. The correlations between all variable pairs are high; however in the models, effort and prior behavior account for more variation in behavioral intentions. Attitude may overlap with effort and prior behavior, and may move in the same direction, but attitudes alone do not account for a significant amount of variation in behavioral intentions. This may also explain the discrepancy between our results and the result of Bagozzi and Dabholkar (1994) regarding the role of attitudes in the recycling decisions. According to our results, attitudes may be

TABLE 2
Correlation Matrix for Scales Used in Recycling Study

Variable	SAO	Effort	Rnorm	Attitude	Prior	Intent
SAO (Action orientation)	1	.14	.06	.13	.27**	.29**
Effort (Perceived effort)		1	.26**	.61**	.52**	.66**
Rnorm (Recycling norm)			1	.22*	.21*	.36**
Attitude (Attitude towards recycling)				1	.49**	.60**
Prior (Prior recycling behavior)					1	.70**
Intent (Intent to recycle)						1

* p < .05
**p < .01

consistently high, but the key element appears to be attitude-behavior consistency, which appears to be moderated by perceptions of effort.

In this community, subjective norms appeared to have little influence on behavioral intentions. Fishbein et al. (1992) demonstrate that differences in levels of community cohesiveness can affect norm strength and subsequent behavioral intentions. Recycling in this particular community is not a visible activity as it might be in a community with a curbside program. This alone could account for the low level of perceived recycling norm. None of the neighborhoods surveyed had strong neighborhood recycling programs. Therefore, the descriptive norm or what appeared to be the community behavioral standard might have been difficult to identify, and the motivation to comply with the norm may have been particularly weak. The low visibility nature of recycling efforts throughout this community also supports the post hoc finding that recycling norms do not significantly differ among distinct neighborhoods within the community. We do not suggest, however, that the role of the community should be ignored in program promotions. In communities where programs are visible and where a strong sense of community exists, either in a neighborhood or on a broader level, the literature suggests that appeals that emphasize recycling as a community contribution or collective endeavor might be successful. This may be true particularly for individuals who have not yet internalized those higher order goals that Bagozzi and Dabholkar (1994) identified as antecedents to a reasoned action decision. In fact, such community pressure for these individuals may be important in stimulating individual goals depending on the community context.

Differences in action control only moderated the relationship between attitudes and intentions when prior behavior was not included in the model. However, contrary to our hypothesis, in the context of recycling action-oriented individuals were more likely to report higher social norms and related behavioral intentions. Again, this finding may be the result of the characteristics of this particular community where recycling is not a highly visible activity. When recycling norms are not developed, action-oriented persons may be leaders or innovators in terms of identifying and demonstrating

normative behavior. State-oriented persons, on the other hand, may not be guided by norms as predicted because the norms in this community were too difficult to identify. Attitudes in the context of this study, however, were easily ascertainable. Further, more action-oriented individuals did have stronger intentions to recycle, thus providing more support for the conclusion that inertia has to be overcome before people will participate in environmental efforts.

Future research should examine whether recycling norms differ among communities, whether differences in norms are related to the visibility of recycling behaviors, and whether these differences lead to differences in the role of norms in a reasoned action model. Moreover, future research should attempt to uncover how strong community norms evolve. Fully understanding the development and role of community norms offers the potential to design communications that recognize the normative component as part of a behavioral decision.

Attitudes play an important role in determining recycling intentions, but more important to communications strategists is the finding that perceived efforts outweigh general attitudes towards recycling and the environment in predicting behavioral intentions. Programs should be designed to minimize the perceived effort or costs required to recycle and strong incentives for initial trial are necessary. These could include discounts for initial pick-up of items or modest premiums to attract first time users to drop-off sites. Of course, the ensuing experience should be made as hassle-free as possible, through the consideration of such issues as convenience in selection of container types, cleanliness, and location of drop-offs and other customer service issues.

The role of marketing in recycling includes not only to understand how people make disposition decisions, but also to explore the relationship between disposition and purchase behaviors so people can be encouraged to complete the recycling loop. Our findings suggest that people do view both acquisition/consumption of recycled products and disposition of recyclables as recycling. This suggests that consumption and disposition decisions may be related. For some persons, buying a recycled product may be a decision that is impacted more by values, attitudes, and norms than by traditional price and product evaluations. Further research should examine the link between disposition and consumption decisions—do consumers recycle first and then become interested in purchases? How do costs and product evaluations fit into the purchase decisions? How do product promotions effect disposition behaviors? This paper integrates these two activities in a framework that offers the potential for understanding both consumption and disposition behaviors in terms of the model of reasoned action.

REFERENCES

Balderjahn, Ingo (1988), "Personality Variables and Environmental Attitudes as Predictors of Ecologically Responsible Consumption Patterns," *Journal of Business Research*, 17 (August), 51-56.

Bagozzi, Richard P. (1992), "The Self-Regulation of Attitudes, Intentions, and Behavior," *Social Psychology Quarterly*, 55 (No. 2), 178-204.

_____, Hans Baumgartner, and Youjae Yi (1992), "State versus Action Orientation and the Theory of Reasoned Action: An Application to Coupon Usage," *Journal of Consumer Research*, 18 (March), 505-518.

_____and Pratibha A. Dabholkar (1994), "Consumer Recycling Goals and Their Effect on Decisions to Recycle: A Means-End Chain Analysis," *Psychology and Marketing*, Forthcoming.

_____and Paul R. Warshaw (1990), "Trying to Consume," *Journal of Consumer Research*, 17 (September), 127-140.

_____Youjae Yi, and Johann Baumgartner (1990), "The Level of Effort Required for Behaviour as a Moderator of the Attitude-Behaviour Relationship," *European Journal of Social Psychology*, 20, 45-59.

Berger, Ida (1993), "A Framework for Understanding the Relationship between Environmental Attitudes and Consumer Behaviors," *Proceedings of the AMA Winter Educators' Conference*, Volume 4, 157-164.

_____and Ruth M. Corbin (1992), "Perceived Consumer Effectiveness and Faith in Others as Moderators of Environmentally Responsible Behaviors," *Journal of Public Policy and Marketing*, 11 (Fall), 79-89.

De Young, Raymond (1986), "Some Psychological Aspects of Recycling: The Structure of Conservation Satisfactions," *Environment and Behavior*, 18 (July), 435-449.

Derksen, Linda and John Gartrell (1993), "The Social Context of Recycling," *American Sociological Review*, 58 (June), 434-442.

Fishbein, Martin and Icek Ajzen (1975), *Belief, Attitude, Intention and Behavior*, Reading, MA: Addison-Wesley.

Fishbein, Martin, Darius K-S Chan, Kevin O'Reilly, Dan Schnell, Robert Wood, Carolyn Beeker, and David Cohn (1992), "Attitudinal and Normative Factors as Determinants of Gay Men's Intentions to Perform AIDS-Related Sexual Behaviors: A Multisite Analysis," *Journal of Applied Social Psychology*," 22 (13) 999-1011.

Granzin, Kent and Janeen E. Olson (1991), "Characterizing Participants in Activities Protecting the Environment: A Focus on Donating, Recycling and Conservation Behaviors," *Journal of Public Policy and Marketing*, 10 (Fall), 1-21.

Hopper, Joseph and Joyce McCarl Nielson (1991), "Recycling as Altruistic Behavior: Normative and Behavioral Strategies to Expand Participation in a Community Recycling Program," *Environment and Behavior*, 23 (March), 195-220.

Jackson, Anita L., Janeen E. Olson, Kent L. Granzin, and Alvin C. Burns (1992) "An Investigation of the Determinants of Recycling Consumer Behavior," Vol 20, *Advances in Consumer Research*, Leigh McAlister and Michael Rothschild (eds.), Salt Lake City, UT: Association for Consumer Research, 481-487.

Kinnear Thomas C., James R. Taylor, and Sadrudin A. Ahmed (1974), "Ecologically Concerned Consumers: Who Are They?" *Journal of Marketing*, 38 (April), 20-24.

Kuhl, Julius (1985), "Volitional Mediators of Cognition-Behavior Consistency: Self Regulatory Processes and Action Versus State Orientation," in *Action Control: From Cognition to Behavior*, Julius Kuhl and Jeurgen Beckmann, (eds.), New York: Springer, 101-128.

McCarty, John A. and L. J. Shrum (1993), "A Structural Equation Analysis of the Relationships of Personal Values, Attitudes and Beliefs About Recycling, and the Recycling of Solid Waste," *Advances in Consumer Research*, Vol 20, 641-646.

Nielsen, J.M. and B.L. Ellington (1983), "Social Processes and Resource Conservation," in N.R. Feimer and El S. Geller (eds.), *Environmental Psychology: Directions and Perspectives*, New York: Praeger, 288-312.

Pieters, Rik G. M. (1991), "Changing Garbage Disposal Patterns of Consumers: Motivation, Ability and Performance," *Journal of Public Policy and Marketing*, 10 (Fall), 59-76.

Samdahl, Diane M. and Robert Robertson (1989), "Social Determinants of Environmental Concern: Specification and Test of the Model," *Environment and Behavior*, 21 (January), 57-81.

Vining, Joanne and Angela Ebreo (1990), "What Makes a Recycler?: A Comparison of Recyclers and Nonrecyclers," *Environment and Behavior*, 22 (January), 55-73.

_____and _____(1992), "Predicting Recycling Behavior from Global and Specific Environmental Attitudes and Changes in Recycling Opportunities," *Journal of Applied Social Psychology*, 22 (20), 1580-1607.

Yi, Youjae (1989), "On the Evaluation of Main Effects in Multiplicative Regression Models," *Journal of the Market Research Society*, 31 (1), 134-138.

The Determinants of Consumers' Purchase Decisions for Recycled Products: An Application of Acquisition-Transaction Utility Theory

Lien-Ti Bei, Purdue University
Eithel M. Simpson, Purdue University

ABSTRACT

This study investigated the determinants of consumers' purchase probabilities toward eleven recycled products based on Thaler's (1983, 1985) *acquisition-transaction utility theory*, which suggested that consumers' purchase probabilities depended on the received value compared to the purchased cost. Consumers' psychological benefit from the purchase was added as part of the purchase utility in this study. The results showed that consumers who perceived more purchase utility from the purchase were more likely to buy the product. Purchase involvement was also positively related to the purchase probability. These results provided a consumers' viewpoint to aid in the development of marketing strategies for recycled products.

An environmental consciousness has been growing steadily over the past few years in the United States. The Roper Organization (1990) reports that public concern about environmental issues has grown faster than concern about any other national problem. According to the Capital Research Center in Washington, DC, the top ten environmental organizations in the United States have annual membership of almost eight million (Environmental Protection Agency 1991).

Manufacturers and marketers have responded to this environmental trend. The introduction of new "green" and "environmentally friendly" products has grown by more than 100% per year since 1985 (*Green Introductions* 1990). "Green" and "environmentally friendly" products are defined as those labeled or advertised with at least one of the following characteristics: 1) reducing water and air pollution, 2) reducing waste, 3) avoiding cruelty to animals, and 4) made of recycled material (Dagnoli 1991; *Green Introductions* 1990). However, the environmental consciousness-raising trend cannot ensure the success of the green market because consumers' purchase behaviors and attitudes have not changed as quickly as their environmental awareness (Larson 1990).

Promoting recycled products is the most difficult among those green products. Consumers have a common belief that recycled materials are inferior to virgin materials (Kashmanian et al. 1990). Recycled products are also believed to be more costly than virgin products, although these perceptions are oftentimes mistaken (Cude 1993). It has been a challenge to manufacturers and retailers to overcome these perceptions and educate consumers on the need of purchasing products and packaging made with recycled materials (Kashmanian et al. 1990).

The purpose of this study is to investigate the determinants of consumers' purchase probabilities on recycled products. Since consumers have different purchase involvement for different products (Zaichkowsky 1985), eleven representative recycled products are selected to test consumers' purchase decisions including purchase involvement.

To address these purposes, consumers' purchase behaviors are considered to be based on the *utility theory* (Thaler 1983). The theory assumes that consumers always try to maximize their purchase utility, which is the benefit received from the purchased good and the price when they make purchase decisions (Thaler 1985).

Consumers receive both quality benefits and psychological benefits by paying money and other cost, such as time and effort, for each purchase transaction (Lichtenstein, Netemeyer and Burton

1990). The quality benefit is the received quality from a product itself or life improvement through using a product. On the other hand, the psychological benefit is a positive feeling about the purchase, for example, self-image built from buying a special product or a feeling of getting a "deal" due to a low price.

Since consumers always try to maximize their purchase utility, it is assumed that if consumers choose to buy recycled products, they should perceive more purchase utility from the purchase of recycled products than from the purchase of ordinary ones. In other words, the sources of the extra utility of buying recycled products are the determinants of consumers' purchase decisions of recycled products.

CONCEPTUAL FRAMEWORK

While considerable research on the determinants of consumers' purchase decisions has been done, there was no such research especially focusing on the purchase of recycled products. The *acquisition-transaction utility theory* (Thaler 1983) was employed as a paradigm for examining the relationship between the purchase utility and the purchase decision of recycled products. However, because recycled products have a special attribute namely that they are made with recycled materials and good for the environment, the construction of this theory used in previous studies could not completely present the purchase utility of recycled products and had to be modified to provide a conceptual framework for this study.

Acquisition-Transaction Utility Theory

Thaler (1983, 1985) proposed that the total utility of a purchase was the sum of *acquisition utility* and *transaction utility*. According to Thaler's definition (1985), acquisition utility reflected the economic gain or loss from a purchase. It depended on the value of the good received compared to the cost (Thaler 1985). So, acquisition utility was a function of the utility of the purchased good determined by the inherent need-satisfying properties of the product (Lichtenstein et al. 1990; Thaler 1983). Lichtenstein et al. (1990) suggested that acquisition utility could be estimated by the utility of purchased good minus purchase price (shown as Equation [1]).

$$\text{Acquisition Utility} = \text{Utility of Purchased Good} - \text{Purchase Price} \quad [1]$$

There was an argument associated with the psychological part of acquisition utility. In previous studies, acquisition utility captured the results only from the "economic" point of view (Dickson and Sawyer. 1990; Lichtenstein et al. 1990; Thaler 1983), such as received quality of the product, but without the psychological part of acquisition utility. However, acquisition utility was defined as a function of the utility of the purchase good determined by the inherent need-satisfying properties of the products (Lichtenstein et al. 1990; Thaler 1983). Also, Thaler (1983) indicated that consumers' value of acquisition utility depended on their desire for the product. A recycled product has some unique attributes that it is made from recycled materials and good for the environment. Lancaster's (1966) *goods characteristics model* suggested that the attributes of goods could change consumers' purchase utilities and purchase decisions. For instance, a psychological feeling of contributing to the environment may be more significant than satisfaction with the product itself when consumers buy a recycled product. Therefore, the purchase utility related to recycled products' special attributes should be incorporated in the acquisition utility as the psychological utility. In this study, both received quality of the recycled product and psychological benefits from buying recycled products were included in the decision model as explanatory variables.

There were some studies suggesting several factors which associated with consumers' psychological feelings and contributed to their purchase behaviors for environmentally friendly products. Roper's (1990) survey concluded that environmental consciousness was associated with being a "green" consumer. Cude (1992) indicated that the high concern about the environmental issue and the positive attitude toward the green products could motivate behavior changes. Hence, the psychological benefit from buying recycled products was proposed to be based on consumers' environmental concern, attitude toward environmentally friendly products, and their feelings when purchasing recycled products.

Therefore, the utility of purchase good was captured as psychological benefit and believed quality by the consumer. This concept is illustrated as Equation [2].

Acquisition Utility
= Utility of Purchased Good - Purchase Price
= (Believed Quality + Psychological Benefit) -
Purchase Price   [2]

The second element of Thaler's theory, transaction utility, is the perceived merits of the "deal" (Thaler 1985). It is not only formed by the actual value of paying the price, but related to the expected price. For example, when consumers believe that a recycled product is more expensive than an ordinary one, they will expect the price of the recycled one to be higher than the price of the ordinary one, and tend not to buy the recycled product. However, once consumers find out the price of the recycled product is the same or even less than the price of the ordinary one with the same quality, they will feel that there is a "deal" for buying the recycled one and receive greater transaction utility from the purchase. Thaler (1983, 1985) suggested that transaction utility was a function of the difference between the purchase price and the expected price. During the purchase decision, the price that consumers expect to pay performed as an internal reference price (Dickson and Sawyer 1990; Lichtenstein and Bearden 1989; Lichtenstein et al. 1990; Monroe 1973). Lichtenstein et al. (1990) used Equation [3] to illustrate the definition of transaction utility.

Transaction utility =   Internal Reference Price -
           Purchase Price   [3]

The idea of the internal reference price implied the psychological part of the transaction utility. In this study, the price of an ordinary product was proposed as an internal reference price for a recycled product because consumers tended to compare a recycled product with an ordinary one. Therefore, the price difference of a recycled product from an ordinary one was hypothesized to have a positive relationship with transaction utility, as well as the probability to buy the recycled one.

Lichtenstein et al. (1990) used Equation [4] to explain the definition of total purchase utility. The purchase price can be held constant as to know the difference between consumers' purchase utility, because a product's actual price is not decided by consumers

and the prices for the same product are usually similar. Equation [5] presents the concept that total purchase utility is the function of believed quality, psychological benefit, and expected price, with the purchase price held constant in the present study. Consumers' purchase probability is, then, the function of their total purchase utility.

Total Purchase Utility
= Acquisition Utility + Transaction Utility
= Utility of Purchased Good - Purchase Price)
+(Internal Reference Price - Purchase Price)   [4]

Purchase Probability
= f(Total Purchase Utility)
= f(Believed Quality, Psychological Benefit,
Expected Price)   [5]
[with the purchase price held constant]

Based on Thaler's *acquisition-transaction utility theory*, the first hypothesis was developed: consumers who perceived more total purchase utility from the purchase of a particular recycled product were more likely to buy this particular recycled product. More purchase utility could be obtained either from *acquisition utility* (i.e., the received quality plus the psychological benefit minus the purchase price) or from *transaction utility* (i.e., the expected price minus the purchase price).

Purchase Involvement

Consumers' purchase decisions on recycled products in general might be different from decisions on a particular recycled product because consumers could be involved with products in different degrees due to product attributes (Cohen 1983; Zaichkowsky 1985). Also, Lancaster (1966) indicated that the attributes of goods could change consumers' purchase utilities and purchase decisions. Therefore, consumers' purchase decisions on particular recycled products with different attributes were investigated in this study.

When examining particular products or purchase decisions, many researchers suggested that low versus high involvement states were important (Clarke and Belk 1978; Cohen 1983; Zaichkowsky 1985). "Involvement" was defined as the importance of the product to the individual and to the individual's self-concept, values, and ego (Beatty, Kahle and Homer 1988; Zaichkowsky 1985). Involvement with purchases could lead consumers to search for more information and spend more time searching for the right selection (Clarke and Belk 1978). Consequently, purchase involvement was included in the study and was hypothesized to have a positive relationship with purchase behavior.

Two major factors were considered related to consumers' involvement of recycled products: 1) price (high or low), and 2) parts (the product itself or the package made of recycled materials). Hence, eleven recycled products were chosen according to these factors (shown in Table 1) by the panel of professors in consumer research and experts in material sciences. These representative products also included various categories of recycled products: paper, plastic, glass, metal, wool, and synthetic fiber. These eleven recycled products and packages were generally called "recycled products" in this study.

Zaichkowsky's (1985) Personal Involvement Inventory (PII) was employed to measure consumers' involvement or interest in the eleven recycled products in a pre-test. There were three reasons to select PII. First, the definition of involvement used in the PII scales was: "a person's perceived relevance of the object based on

TABLE 1
Tested Products and PII Scores

Made with Recycled Materials	Price	Parts	Categories	PII
Recycled-Paper Notebook	low	product	paper	106.74
Recycled Toilet Paper	low	product	paper	85.72
Recycled Baby Wipes	low	product	paper	84.02
Recycled Paper Coffee Filter	low	product	paper	91.40
Recycled Microwave Container	low	product	plastic	99.14
Recycled Trash Bag	low	product	plastic	109.84
Hamburger with Recycled Carton	low	package	paper	107.84
Cola in Recycled Pop Top Can	low	package	metal	109.16
Recycled Wool Sweater	high	product	wool	74.80
Recycled Polyester Area Rug	high	product	synthetic fiber	72.14
Perfume in Recycled Glass	high	package	glass	99.78

inherent needs, values, and interests" (Zaichkowsky 1985, p.342), which was consistent with the purpose of this study. Second, PII scales could be adopted to examine consumers' involvement with products, advertisements, or purchase decisions. In this study, purchase decisions were the basic concern. Third, the construct of the PII scale could focus on the product level to determine high or low involvement products (Zaichkowsky 1985).

PII scales were multi-item measures which had higher reliability than single-item measures (Zaichkowsky 1985). The reliability of the scale over time had a test-retest correlation of 0.90. Other internal scale reliabilities were an item-to-total score correlation of 0.50 or more, and a Cronbach alpha level of 0.95. The criterion-related validity and the construct validity (e.g., the test of the scale to theoretical propositions) were significant at the $a=.01$ level. PII score was ranged from a low of 20 to a high of 140, with a theoretical mean 80 (Zaichkowsky 1985).

Subjects in the pre-test included a convenience sample of 50 college students. Because the same recycled products and purchase decisions were used in the survey of the main study, subjects of this phase had to be different from respondents of the main study to avoid possible bias. The average PII score of each product is listed in Table 1. These scores were employed later as a variable "purchase involvement."

EMPIRICAL TESTS

Subjects

Data for the main study were collected from two Midwest cities. One was regularly used to test-market products. Its demographic characteristics are representative in particular categories: household size, age of household head, and annual family income. (*Indiana City* 1988). Five hundred random subjects were selected according to the city telephone directory. The other city was a college town. This group of subjects was 165 randomly selected residents and university students based on the resident and student telephone directories.

The instrument and the follow-up reminder postcard were mailed to each subject's address in Fall, 1992. The survey resulted in a total of 139 (21%) returns. Within them, 137 surveys were completed and used for the analysis, 59 cases from the representative city and 78 cases from the college-town. The proportion of the college-town sample had more students. However, no significant difference in their environmental concerns or purchase behaviors was found between the samples from the two cities.

Instruments

The entire questionnaire used for this study included three sections, each of which were developed from the instruments used in previous studies. The first and second sections came from the first two segments of the "Enviroshopping" questionnaire, as developed by the Extension Service, U.S. Department of Agriculture and the University of Florida (1991). The objective of these two sections was to assess consumers' degree of environmental responsibility concerning purchasing decisions and attitudes in general. There were four batteries of questions, which represented four concepts: reduce, recycled, reuse and reject, in each of these two segments. Reliability coefficients are 0.69, 0.86, 0.81 and 0.83 in the first segment, and 0.51, 0.79, 0.81, and 0.77 in the second segment for reduce, recycle, reuse and reject, respectively (The Extension Service 1991).

The third section was based on the related items in the instrument used in the Roper report (1990) to estimate consumers' purchase experience, believed quality and expected price of the eleven representative recycled products (as shown in Table 1). Respondents were asked to compare the quality and estimate the prices of recycled and virgin products.

Operational Definitions of Variables and Analysis

The dependent variable (Y) was consumers' actual purchase experiences of the eleven recycled products: have bought=1 and never bought=0. The independent variables were the psychological benefit (PSYCH), the believed quality (QUAL), the expected price difference (PRICE), and purchase involvement (PI) of each recycled product. The psychological benefit from the purchase of recycled products covered consumers' attitude and feeling about buying recycled products. The believed quality was based on the comparison of each pair of the recycled and ordinary products. The expected price difference was the percentage price difference of the recycled product from the ordinary one. Purchase involvement of each product, which was based on the product level, was captured in the pre-test by the PII scales.

Since the dependent variable, purchase experience for each recycled product, was a dichotomous categorical variable (i.e., have bought or have not bought), the multivariate logistic regression was considered an appropriate technique for this study. Equation [6] illustrates the concept of the logistic regression in this study (Aldrich and Nelson 1984).

$Y_{ij} = \{0, 1\}$,   1 = have bought , 0 = have not bought

$$P(Y_{ij} = 1) = \frac{\exp(\beta_0 + \beta_1 \, PSYCH_i + \beta_2 \, QUAL_{ij} + \beta_3 \, PRICE_{ij} + \beta_4 \, PI_j)}{1 + \exp(\beta_0 + \beta_1 \, PSYCH_i + \beta_2 \, QUAL_{ij} + \beta_3 \, PRICE_{ij} + \beta_4 \, PI_j)} \quad (6)$$

where *i* represents subjects and *j* denotes the eleven recycled products.

TABLE 2
The Logistic Regression Analysis for the Purchase Decision of the Eleven Recycled Products

Variable		Estimated Coefficient	Chi-Square
Intercept		-10.76**	164.12**
Psychological Benefit		0.38**	4.51*
Believed Quality			15.00**
	higher	0.35	15.38**
	same	—	—
	lower	-0.18	2.69
Expected Price		0.83	4.04*
Purchase Involvement		0.09	221.86**
Likelihood Ratio		Chi-Square =	1254.98

Note: ** denotes significant at the α =.01 level.
* denotes significant at the α =.05 level.

FINDINGS

Descriptive Results

Around two-fifths of the respondents (38%) answered that they seldom purchased products or packages made of recycled materials; one-third (32.4%) said sometimes. Only 5.1% of all respondents indicated that they always bought recycled products as available, and 0.7% have even paid more to buy those products for the sake of the environment.

Respondents' average attitudes toward recycled products and environmental issues were positive (mean=2.78; ranged 1 to 4), that most respondents agreed they should pay more attention to the environment, as well as make more effort to search for and to buy recycled products. Most respondents (89.1%) usually felt that they were saving the environment when they purchased some recycled products. Also, most believed that the quality (78.7%) and the price (67.4%) of a recycled product should be the same as an ordinary one. Only seven subjects believed that the quality of a recycled product should be higher than an ordinary one; and three subjects expected the price of a recycled product should be higher.

Purchase of Recycled Products

Consumers' purchase experiences varied with different recycled products. The most frequently bought products were hamburgers with recycled cartons (75.91%), recycled paper notebooks (72.26%), cola in recycled cans (62.04%), and recycled plastic trash bags (57.66%). Recycled products that few respondents bought were recycled polyester area rugs (5.11%), recycled baby wipes (5.15%), and recycled wool sweaters (9.49%).

The Determinants of Purchasing the Eleven Recycled Products

The results of the logistic regression for Equation [6] showed that the model fitted well (illustrated in Table 2). "Psychological benefit" from buying the recycled products was positively related to the probability of purchasing the products, with significance at the α=.05 level. "Believed quality" was also positively associated with the purchase behavior (α=.01). Especially, respondents who believed that the recycled products were superior to the ordinary ones in quality, were more likely to buy the recycled products than those who believed that the products were the same in quality (α=.01). Expected price difference was positively significant at the α=.05 level. This positive relationship meant that if consumers

expected a higher price for a recycled product compared with the ordinary one, they were more likely to buy the recycled product. The three utility variables were all consistent with the proposed relationship, which illustrated the function of the acquisition-transaction theory. "Purchase involvement" was also positively related to the purchase probability, with significance at the α=.01 level. This result supported the importance of the purchase involvement.

CONCLUSIONS AND IMPLICATIONS

The empirical findings of this study suggest that consumers' purchase behavior of recycled products can be explained well by Thaler's *acquisition-transaction utility theory* (1983 and 1985) if the psychological benefit is included as one kind of utility. The two components of the *acquisition-transaction utility theory* are fully supported by significant results of the psychological benefit, believed quality, and expected price. In addition, the product category itself provides different levels of involvement that is associated with consumers' purchase probabilities too.

Buying and using recycled products can stimulate the market of recycled materials, which is good for the environment. The results of this study suggest that consumers' willingness to buy recycled products can be motivated by emphasizing the importance of environmental issues, positive attitudes toward recycled products, and the feeling of contribution to the environment from the purchase of recycled products. According to the findings in this study, manufacturers, retailers, and marketers should promote recycled products by advertising the benefit to the environment through the purchase. By the influence of this kind of advertising, consumers would perceive more psychological benefits and may be more likely to buy recycled products.

Consumers also consider the price and quality of the recycled products. The price effect is actually from the perceived price difference between the recycled product and the ordinary one. This perceived difference, but not actual difference, affects consumers' willingness to buy the recycled products because the actual price is held constant in this study.

The quality of recycled products is another consideration to consumers. Recycled baby wipes and toilet paper are low-priced items, but consumers are not willing to buy these two products because of the believed poor quality of these products. So, manufacturers and marketers should emphasize and ensure that the quality of the recycled product is at least the same as the ordinary one. In addition, manufacturers should introduce more recycled packages that do not change the quality of the product itself.

Another implication is that manufacturers can use consumers' purchase involvement of recycled products to help determine if the product will succeed in the real market. Those recycled products, which can induce consumers' high purchase involvement, have more probability to success in the market, such as recycled plastic trash bags, cola in recycled cans, hamburgers with recycled paper cartons, and recycled paper notebooks.

The major limitation of the present study is the low response rate. This causes the difficulty in generalizing the results to non-respondents due to the possible self-selected bias.

This study is a special application of Thaler's *acquisition-transaction utility theory* by testing consumers' purchase behavior toward a particular category of products: recycled products. In this study, the psychological benefit of acquisition utility is further underlined, which was lacking in previous studies. It is suggested that researchers can use this study as a framework to examine the purchase utility of other "green" or "environmentally friendly" products. These terms are frequently used to describe the products in advertising and on labels without knowing why they can stimulate consumers' purchase behaviors. This study introduces a new direction of study for explaining how these terms can effect consumers' perceived psychological benefits of total purchase utility.

REFERENCES

Aldrich, John H. and Forrest D. Nelson (1984), *Linear Probability, Logit, and Probit Models*, California: Sage Publications.

Beatty, Sharon E., Lynn R. Kahle and Pamela Homer (1988), "The Involvement-Commitment Model: Theory and Implication," *Journal of Business Research*, 16 (March), 149-167.

Clarke, Keith and Russell W. Belk (1978), "The Effects of Products Involvement and Task Definition on Anticipated Consumer Effort," in *Advances in Consumer Research*, 5, H. Keith Hunt, ed., Ann Arbor, MI: Association for Consumer Research, 313-318.

Cohen, Joel B. (1983), "Involvement and You: 1000 Great Ideas," *Advances in Consumer Research*, 10, Richard Bagozzi and Alice Tybout, eds., Ann Arbor, MI: Association for Consumer Research, 325-328.

Cude, Brenda J. (1992), "Marketing Consumer Education "Green:" Issues and Approaches," *Proceedings: 38th Annual Conference of the American Council on Consumer Interests*, 187-193.

_____. (1993), "Does It Cost More to Buy 'Green'?" *Proceedings: 39th Annual Conference of the American Council on Consumer Interests*, 108-113.

Dagnoli, Judas (1991), "Whose Job Is It to Define Green?" *Advertising Age*, 4 February, 13.

Dickson, Peter R. and Alan G. Sawyer (1990). "The Price Knowledge and Search of Supermarket Shoppers," *Journal of Marketing*, 54 (July), 42-53.

Environmental Protection Agency (1991), *Assessing the Environmental Consumer Market*, Washington, DC: U.S. Environmental Protection Agency.

"'Green' Introductions Increase 100% a Year," (1990), *Supermarket News*, 6 August, 22.

Federal Register (1991), "Guidance for the Use of the Terms "Recycled" and "Recyclable" and the Recycling Emblem in Environmental Marketing Claims," *Federal Register*, 56, 191.

"Indiana City is Test-Marketing Hotspot" (1988), *Marketing News*, 22, 29 August, 46.

Kashmanian, Richard M., Trisha Ferrand, Karen Hurst, and Tapio L. Kuusinen (1990), "Let's Topple the Recycling Wall, Too," *Marketing News*, 24, 19 March, 20.

Lancaster, Kelvin J. (1966), "A New Approach to Consumer Theory," *Journal of Political Economy*, 74 (April), 132-157.

Larson, Melissa (1990), "Consumers Determine Package Success," *Packaging*, 35 (June), 38-42.

Lichtenstein, Donald R. and William O. Bearden (1989), "Contextual Influence on Perceptions of Merchant-Supplied Reference Price," *Journal of Consumer Research*, 16 (June), 55-66.

Lichtenstein, Donald R., Richard G. Netemeyer, and Scot Burton (1990), "Distinguishing Coupon Proneness from Value Consciousness: An Acquisition-Transaction Utility Theory Perspective," *Journal of Marketing*, 54 (July), 54-67.

Miller, Tom (1990), "Tomorrow's Green Market Consumer," *Mobius*, Fall, 33-37.

Monroe, Kent B. (1973), "Buyers' Subjective Perceptions of Price," *Journal of Marketing Research*, 10 (February), 70-80.

Thaler, Richard (1983), "Transaction Utility Theory," *Advances in Consumer Research*, 10, Richard P. Bagozzi and Alice M. Tybout, eds., Ann Arbor, MI: Association for Consumer Research, 229-232.

_____. (1985), "Mental Accounting and Consumer Choice," *Marketing Science*, 4 (Summer), 199-214.

The Cooperative Extension System National Initiative on Waste Management (1990), *Targeted Programs in the FY 1992-1995 Plan of Work CES National Initiative - Waste Management: Objectives and Indicators*, Washington, DC: U.S. Department of Agriculture.

The Extension Service, U.S. Department of Agriculture and University of Florida (1991), *Enviroshopping*, Florida: author, Enviroshopping Extension Education Module.

The Roper Organization (1990), *The Environment: Public Attitude and Individual Behavior*, A study conducted by The Roper Organization Inc., sponsored by S. C. Johnson & Son, Inc. New York: author.

Zaichkowsky, Judith L. (1985), "Measuring the Involvement Construct," *Journal of Consumer Research*, 12 (December), 341-352.

Environment-Impacting Consumer Behavior: An Operant Analysis

Gordon Robert Foxall, University of Birmingham

ABSTRACT

A model of purchase and consumption based on the principles of behavior analysis is applied to the understanding of social demarketing interventions aimed at environmental preservation. The explanatory framework of the Behavioral Perspective Model of purchase and consumption (BPM) is outlined. The findings of behavior analysts on resource conservation and pollution control are interpreted in terms of the classification of consumer behaviors and contingencies proposed by the model. These environmentally-impacting consumer behaviors are elucidated through discussion of both their consequences and the nature of intervention to ameliorate them. An appropriate social marketing mix for each class of consumer behavior is suggested.

Applied behavior analysis has contributed substantially to knowledge of economic consumption as it adversely affects the physical and social environment (Cone and Hayes 1980; Geller, Winett and Everett 1982). It rests critically and selectively on Skinner's (1953) behavior theory which stresses that the causes of behavior are found in its environmental consequences. The applied field experimentation that characterizes this approach has explored how antecedent and consequential stimuli influence such consumer behaviors as excessive use of private transportation, over-consumption of domestic energy, littering and waste generation, and consumption of scarce resources such as water. The ultimate purpose has been to ameliorate these ecologically deleterious outcomes through the modification of consumer behavior (Winkler and Winett 1982). Despite this theoretical underpinning and practical direction, the empirical findings produced by applied behavior analysts lack systematic organization and theory-based generalization. Despite comprehensive reviews and attempts to draw lessons from these findings (Cone and Hayes 1980; Geller 1989), behavior analysis lacks an integrative model of consumer behavior and the effects of intervention based on a critical evaluation of behavior theory.

Thus the field has tended to fall back on cognitive frameworks devised by consumer researchers (Schwartz 1991) or the basic social marketing models derived from rudimentary marketing (Geller 1989). Yet both of these approaches contain serious conceptual, methodological and practical difficulties. Social marketing programs have been criticised on the grounds that they consist largely of informational and exhortative campaigns which do not generally use the full integrated marketing mix but rely to a disproportionate extent on social advertising. Further, the effectiveness of campaigns intended to change behavior by modifying attitudes has been questioned. Nor are these conclusions the result of theoretical preference or speculation uninformed by empirical evidence. There is abundant support from the research of cognitive psychologists themselves that, to the extent that they rely heavily on the use of persuasive communications to change pre-behavioral attitudes and values, social information campaigns have had little impact on consumers' conservation behavior. Despite vast general public knowledge about the potentially catastrophic consequences of failing to conserve energy, researchers report an inability to identify the required relationship between attitudes toward energy use and conservation; even those maximally informed are no more likely to save energy; nor does specifically informing people about the personal costs of current energy use and the benefits of reducing consumption affect behavior (Costanzo, Archer, Aronson and Pettigrew 1986).

However, applied behavior analysis indicates that simply informing people of the consequences of their actions is unlikely to modify their behavior unless they have been systematically exposed to those consequences in the past. The causes of behavior cannot be found in variables inferred from the behavior itself such as attitudes and these inferences are not therefore legitimate targets for intervention. Social demarketing based on applied behavior analysis can be systematically related to marketing mix management by a model founded on the behavior theory that underpins that analysis, elucidating the nature of both environmentally-impacting consumer behavior and interventions designed to ameliorate its deleterious ecological effects. First, the model and applied behavior analysis are described. Second, general propositions which must be fulfilled if the model accurately synthesises the findings of the applied research of behavior analysts are derived. Third, the major target behaviors of this research - transportation, energy consumption, waste disposal, water use - are described in terms of the model; the model's capacity to encompass and explain the incentives and feedback that control each of these behaviors is a prime concern. Finally, the role of the marketing mix in influencing each class of environment-impacting consumer behavior is discussed.

THE BEHAVIORAL PERSPECTIVE MODEL

The Behavioral Perspective Model of purchase and consumption (BPM) provides an account of consumer choice based on the antecedent and consequent learning contingencies which have featured in applied behavior analytic studies: antecedent setting variables, and consequent reinforcement and punishment (Figure 1). The BPM also clarifies the role of marketing management in the control of consumer behavior. The provenance and structure of the model have been thoroughly described by Foxall (1993, 1994); the following account is a summary. At the theoretical level, the purpose of the model and its developmental research program is not to supplant these or other structural approaches but to further understanding of the role of contextual influences and consumers' learning histories on their current actions as buyers and users of economic resources. The central explanatory mechanism of the model is the synomorphic consumer situation, the meeting place of the consumer's history of reinforcement and punishment (representing the personal variables responsible for current behavior) and the setting in which purchase and consumption occur (representing the contextual influences on behavior). The former incorporates the consumer's prior experience of purchase and consumption and the effects of the consequences of these acts on the probability of their performing similar consumer behaviors in the present and future.

The settings in which consumer behavior occurs, such as a store, library, museum or passport office, can be described as relatively closed or relatively open. In sum, closed settings are those in which marketers or other providers exercise dominant control over what is available to the consumer, and are thus in a position to influence greatly his or her behavior; open settings are those in which the consumer has numerous choices, maximal discretion over what he or she will do (see Foxall 1993, 1994). Hence, closed behavior settings are those in which the setting is manipulated largely by persons or organizations other than the

FIGURE 1
Summary of the Behavioral Perspective Model

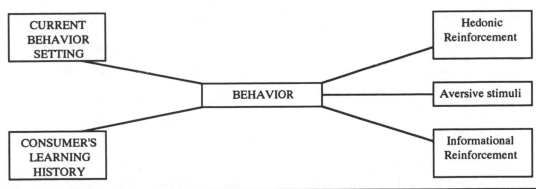

consumer and which encourage conformity to the behavior program ongoing in the setting. The physical and social surroundings which the consumer enters are particularly amenable to the achievement of such control. Banks, for instance, are arranged to maximize the orderly queuing by consumers and to minimize extraneous behavior patterns not connected with the efficient execution of current transactions. But a degree of closure may also be achieved symbolically as when a consumer feels under (benign) pressure to purchase a birthday present to repay a close relative's generosity; the source of closure here is the social rules which prescribe moral or material rewards for such reciprocity and, possibly, punishments for ignoring others' generosity. An open behavior setting is one from which such physical, social and verbal pressures are largely absent or in which their influence is less obviously traced and the customer is relatively free to determine his or her own rules for choosing among the products and brands on offer. An example is pre-purchase behavior for luxurious and innovative products: while social and other contextual influences are present, the consumer has discretion over which stores to visit, which products to examine and, if a purchase occurs, which particular product versions and brands to select. Behavior settings also perform the function of informing consumers of the consequences of their current behaviors - the reinforcing and/or punishing outcomes of purchase (or nonpurchase) and consumption.

Reinforcement takes two forms. In addition to the hedonic reinforcement customarily assumed by behavior analysis, which features the emotional and pleasurable consequences of behavior, the model incorporates informational reinforcement which is feedback on the level of performance of the consumer. Most significantly, it indicates the level of achievement or social status conferred by purchasing and consuming, and especially being seen to consume certain luxury and innovative products and services. Hedonic and informational reinforcements usually occur together but are conceptualized as independent influences on consumer choice; each can be high or low relative to the other or to itself at other times. When the consequences of behavior are remote from its performance, too small, too delayed or too improbable to affect it immediately and directly, verbal rules may act as discriminative stimuli, outlining the likely outcomes of behaving or failing to behave in specified ways, and providing motivation to act appropriately (Malott 1989). Antecedent (setting) and consequential stimuli (reinforcement and punishment), the rules that link them, and the consumer who brings a unique personal learning history to the setting combine to form the consumer situation.

The BPM proposes that consumer behavior can be described as Accomplishment, Pleasure, Accumulation or Maintenance de-

pending upon the pattern of its reinforcing consequences (Figure 2). Accomplishment is personal achievement that results in relatively high levels of both hedonic and informational reinforcement. In an open setting, it might take the form of conspicuous consumption; in a more closed setting, the completion of a commercial training course or of a personal development seminar such as est or Insight, or even of gambling in a casino. Pleasure is behavior usually reinforced by entertainment, which is maintained by a high level of hedonic reinforcement and level of informational reinforcement which, by comparison, is relatively low. In an open setting, it might be exemplified by watching popular TV programs; in a closed setting, watching an inescapable in-flight movie. Also in this category are behaviors reinforced negatively by the removal of an aversive stimulus, such as taking aspirin for a headache.

Accumulation is the collection of reinforcers which have some hedonic content but which are principally informational, where sustained collecting is itself further rewarded. In an open setting, collecting trading stamps, making the sequential purchases necessary to qualify for a special deal or final prize, and saving up to buy a major item all qualify; accumulation occurs also in closed settings such as token economies in therapeutic contexts. Finally, maintenance is routine behavior necessary to sustain one's physiological being (e.g. eating, sleeping) and to function as a member of a social group, to be a citizen in society (e.g. paying taxes for enforced consumption). Maintenance behaviors are controlled by levels of both hedonic and informational reinforcement which, though far from unimportant, are lower than those associated with the preceding classes of behavior; often they are controlled negatively by the removal of a threat. In an open setting, maintenance would include regular purchasing of food products; in a closed setting it is noticeable in the payment of taxes for the compulsory 'purchase' of streetlighting, community health schemes and the armed forces, and obtaining a passport in order to travel abroad. Each of these broad classes of behavior can be interpreted as being maintained on its own schedule of reinforcement: variable ratio in the case of accomplishment, variable interval for pleasure, fixed ratio for accumulation and fixed interval for maintenance. Figure 3 gives examples of consumer behaviors classified by operant class and closed-open behavior setting.

Each class of behavior is maintained by positive reinforcers, whether hedonic or informational, but each has a downside which often does not impinge directly upon the consumer. Social and public costs accrue to the community as a whole and not specifically to the individual consumer who is responsible for their being incurred. Consumer behaviors frequently take the form of behaviors that are damaging to the environment: e.g., seeking ever-

FIGURE 2
Operant Classes of Consumer Behavior

High Hedonic Reinforcement	ACCOMPLISHMENT	High Informational Reinforcement
High Hedonic Reinforcement	PLEASURE	low Informational Reinforcement
Low Hedonic Reinforcement	ACCUMULATION	High Informational Reinforcement
Low Hedonic Reinforcement	MAINTENANCE	low Informational Reinforcement

FIGURE 3
Consumer Behaviors belonging to Closed and Open Behavior Settings

	Closed	BEHAVIOR SETTING SCOPE	Open	
ACCOMPLISHMENT	CONTINGENCY CATEGORY 2	CONTINGENCY CATEGORY 1	HIGH HEDONIC	
	FULFILLMENT	STATUS GOODS	HIGH INFORMATIONAL	
PLEASURE	CONTINGENCY CATEGORY 4	CONTINGENCY CATEGORY 3	HIGH HEDONIC	
	INESCAPABLE ENTERTAINMENT	POPULAR ENTERTAINMENT	LOW INFORMATIONAL	
ACCUMULATION	CONTINGENCY CATEGORY 6	CONTINGENCY CATEGORY 5	LOW HEDONIC	
	TOKEN-BASED BUYING	SAVING AND COLLECTING	HIGH INFORMATIONAL	
MAINTENANCE	CONTINGENCY CATEGORY 8	CONTINGENCY CATEGORY 7	LOW HEDONIC	
	MANDATORY CONSUMPTION	ROUTINE PURCHASING	LOW INFORMATIONAL	

greater accomplishments that provide hedonic rewards and show forth one's status may result in the consumption of scarce and irreplaceable resources. Beyond a point, pleasure-seeking may also have a deleterious effect on the environment through indulgent energy consumption. Accumulation brings with it the concomitant need to dispose of packaging and, in an affluent societies marked by ever-shortening product life-cycles, the products themselves. And, finally, the consumption of the basic commodities of life themselves, such as water, now threatens further consumption by depleting stocks.

ENVIRONMENT-IMPACTING CONSUMER BEHAVIOR

Applied behavior analysis has been concerned for the most part to assess the extent to which contextual factors control the demand for products and services which have deleterious effects on the physical environment. Often, the unrestricted acquisition of short term reinforcements by a limited number of individuals leads to long term aversive consequences for all users. The hedonically reinforcing consequences of behavior are encountered quickly and directly after the action is performed, whereas the environmentally deleterious results of the behavior are encountered, if at all, indirectly and only after a period of time has elapsed. The immediate reinforcement of behavior with ultimately deleterious effects is so great, especially the hedonic, and the aversive outcomes so remote, that the longer-term consequences can sometimes only be reduced

or prevented through active self-management. The relatively open settings in which these behaviors typically take place and their maintenance by strongly hedonic reinforcers mean that some closure of the setting has been advocated in lieu of self-management in order to compel a degree of prosocial behavior.

Applied behavior analytic programs incorporate a variety of behavior-related antecedent and consequent stimuli. Antecedent stimuli have consisted of prompts, i.e. warnings, reasoned argument and facts, threats, pleas, etc. relating to the deleterious effects of actions that exploit or pollute the environment. Two varieties of consequential stimuli have been employed: feedback, i.e. information on the actual effects of individuals' actions, and incentives, i.e. financial bonuses, praise and encouragement. Antecedent prompts are intended to act as discriminative stimuli, signalling the aversive consequences of specific behaviors that impact the environment for ill. Feedback is essentially informational reinforcement, indicating the level of performance achieved by the consumer in, say, reducing his or her electricity consumption or private car mileage. Incentives are essentially hedonic reinforcers, rewarding consumers with additional consumption goods or the capacity to acquire them for their prosocial behaviors.

General Propositions

If the BPM interpretation of consumer behavior is accurate, then it should be possible to present a plausible interpretation of the consumer behaviors that have been the concerns of applied behavior analysis in terms derived from the model. (i) it should be possible to identify the contextual factors that control them in terms of hedonic and informational reinforcement and the setting variables that signal their availability. (ii) if specific classes of consumer behavior are maintained by defined patterns of high versus low hedonic and informational reinforcement and on schedules that can be consistently inferred, we would expect intervention to succeed when it either maintains current levels of reinforcement or increases the level of one source of reinforcement without reducing that of the other. (iii) for consumer behavior, we should expect hedonic reinforcement to play a broader role than informational and can predict that it would prove more effective in changing consumer behavior than either prompting or informational reinforcement alone. (iv) successful intervention should also feature changes in the nature of the behavior setting, opening or closing it further in order to make prosocial behaviors more probable. (v) an integrated program of antecedent and consequential stimuli should work best when rules that link behavior and its consequences with a degree of specificity (rather than through vague prompting) are provided and supported. These general propositions can be tested by reference to the literature on environmental intervention based on applied behavior analysis. Full references to the following literature survey can be found in Cone and Hayes (1980) and Geller et al. (1982). Space precludes full referencing.

Private Transportation as 'Accomplishment'

Of the environmentally-impacting consumer behaviors with which applied behavior analysts have been concerned, the use of private automobiles, often carrying a single individual to or from work, falls into this category. Such behavior is apparently maintained by high levels of both hedonic reinforcement - the fun of driving, control of one's journey - and informational reinforcement - speed, low and flexible journey times. In addition to these immediate sources of reinforcement, personal driving is powerfully maintained by intermittent reinforcements apparently available on a variable ratio schedule: social approval, personal safety, simplification of journey planning routines, all of which are contingent on the performance of a number of responses that varies among situations.

If this classification is correct, the research propositions developed above would lead to the following expectations with respect to successful strategies of behavior change. (i) since the current behaviors are maintained on high hedonic, high informational reinforcements, demarketing should attempt to replace the current behavior with alternatives similarly maintained, though hedonic reinforcement is likely to be the more effective. (ii) the use of aversive stimuli, punishing motorists through taxes, tolls and other uses of what essentially amounts to the price element of the marketing mix is likely to be counter productive since the high levels of both hedonic and informational reinforcement available from driving will compensate for attempts at punishment. (iii) the already open setting should be opened even further by the provision of effective competition to private driving: e.g. making buses more popular, comfortable and socially acceptable. (iv) general prompts alone are unlikely to work but discriminative stimuli, effectively linked to specific behaviors and their outcomes may be effective: these should stress the rewards for bus ridership in terms of the personal gratification this provides rather than vague predictions of a remote better environment.

Evidence for the classification of private motoring as accomplishment and for the efficacy of the above strategy in social demarketing is available from the findings of attempts to modify consumers' private transportation behavior which has been in-

tended to reduce fuel consumption, urban congestion, and pollution by discouraging unilateral use of private cars and promoting public transportation. The most successful interventions have offered hedonic reinforcement in the form of financial incentives: provision of small monetary rewards for riding the bus has, for example, increased the number of users of public travel services by 50-180% (Geller *et al.* 1982). The need for principally hedonic reinforcement, albeit coupled with informational reinforcement in the form of continuous and effective feedback, is indicated by the relatively unattractive pre-intervention pattern of consequences for bus ridership. Riding the bus and other strategies which avoid private transportation (such as walking, car pooling and cycling) are at best minimally reinforced hedonically by social contact and, eventually, feelings of fitness, and informationally by cost savings. But they are punished by aversive consequences: slowness, discomfort, danger, exposure, crowding, noise, inflexibility, unpredictability, and lack of control.

Discouragement of car travel has reduced mileage travelled by between 10 and 50% (Cone and Hayes 1980). The provision of informational reinforcement plays a strong role in reducing driving but only in combination with hedonic reinforcement; however, the two forms of reinforcement cannot in this case be effectively separated since each relies on the provision of the other. While feedback alone (on the number of miles travelled, operating costs, depreciation, social costs, etc.) had no effect on mileage travelled, performance feedback influences behavior by allowing the driver to monitor his or her behavior in order to achieve the incentives. Although hedonic reinforcement once again emerges as the most effective single means of modifying behavior, its use in tandem with informational reinforcement has a mutually strengthening effect and provides a cost effective form of intervention.

In the marketing of alternatives to private car use, notably transportation by bus which for many drivers is likely to prove highly disruptive of their journey routines, hedonic reinforcement has been used almost exclusively and has taken the form of cash payments for riding the bus and, more cost-effectively, of tokens redeemable at stores and for additional bus trips. The use in this context of a variable person schedule of reinforcement (VP) in which every nth passenger is rewarded rather than every passenger not only reduces the costs of the transit program but indicates the relevance of a kind of variable ratio schedule to the maintenance of behaviors in this category. The evidence is that this opening of the setting further by providing genuine competition to private motoring can be effective and that prompts alone are most ineffective.

Domestic Energy Consumption as 'Pleasure'

Among environmentally-impacting consumer behaviors, pleasure is exemplified by the over-consumption of domestic energy derived from fossil fuels, notably electricity for heating and lighting. The hedonic reinforcements are high and closely related temporally to the responses that produce them - convenience, comfort. While informational reinforcement is less obvious, social approval may follow generous use of these resources in the company of others (meanness will certainly lead to social disapproval and loss of status). Punishments are real and may be severe (e.g. having to pay one's electricity and gas bills) but are remote in time and place from the usage situation and may be mitigated by staged payments direct from a bank account. The long term consequences are remote: e.g. depletion of resources, social disapproval. Consumption behaviors are apparently controlled by a variable interval schedule: comfort and satisfaction depend upon employing the source of heat or light for a time that varies from occasion to occasion with the individual's task requirements and state variables (e.g. cold, hunger).

If this analysis and classification are correct, the following should be expected of a successful strategy of behavior change. (i) since the current behaviors are maintained by high hedonic and low informational reinforcement, any attempt to punish that behavior by introducing aversive stimuli (very high prices) or reducing hedonic consequences, without a corresponding increase in hedonic benefits, is likely to fail. (ii) social demarketing should concentrate on making the behavior (including avoidance) more involving, encouraging the avoidance of high bills and a feeling of self-gratification at saving energy and reducing pollution. (iii) if a sufficient level of hedonic benefit can be guaranteed, the setting could be closed by increasing the costs of energy. Support for the classification of domestic energy use as pleasure and for the efficacy of this strategy comes from the attempted modification of consumers' domestic energy consumption which has used antecedent prompting, feedback, and incentives, separately and in combination. Alone, information relating to the environmental effects of pollution caused by high consumption of electricity at peak periods had little if any effect on peak usage. Greater effect was achieved by consumer self-monitoring of current energy usage: peak consumption reduced by up to 30% of mean baseline levels. Overall energy usage (i.e. peak and non-peak consumption) has also proved sensitive to informational feedback, even at times of steep increases in the price of energy. Combined feedback and monetary incentives have reduced peaking by about 65% of baseline, confirming the efficacy of combined consequences.

In line with the basic principle of operant conditioning that reinforcement must immediately follow the performance of a response in order for learning to occur, it has been demonstrated that daily feedback on overall energy usage, especially when combined with group feedback and mild social commendation for 'prosocial' behavior can be effective. More practically, weekly or monthly feedback corresponding with normal billing periods is particularly efficacious. The combination of prompts and feedback with incentives (e.g. payments of up to $5 per week for reductions of gas/electricity consumption by 20% or more of baseline mean) is even more effective. Comparisons of the individual effects of the separate elements of persuasion (prompts, feedback and incentives) indicate, however, that only incentives have an appreciable effect on behavior.

Waste Disposal as a Problem of 'Accumulation'

Waste generation is a consequence of accumulation but it is actually a problem manifested in the opposite of accumulation: disposal. Indiscriminate waste disposal has relatively few hedonic benefits other than convenience but its informational outcomes are extensive if subtle: it confers status through the assumption that someone else will clear up, and it may also imply conspicuous consumption. Such behaviors are maintained seemingly on fixed ratio schedules. Their long term consequences are also remote: gradual spoliation of the physical environment, accruing social disapproval.

The general research propositions developed above indicate that if this analysis and classification are accurate, the following will apply. (i) given the assumed pattern of current behaviors being maintained by high informational and low hedonic reinforcement, behavior change is likely to be accomplished by increasing such hedonic consequences as aesthetic pleasure while not reducing informational feedback. (ii) the personal element in reinforce should be especially effective. (iii) the encouragement of prosocial behavior can be achieved by paying people to return/recycle waste

as long as the punishing consequence of doing so are moderate. (iv) closing the behavior setting by providing bins should be effective. (v) promotional appeals based on prompting in a general way would be ineffective but, modelling, showing the prosocial consequences of conformity would also be effective.

The findings of applied behavior analysis in this area do indeed confirm the analysis and classification. Attempts at reducing littering have relied heavily on the use of prompts. The results have been generally disappointing unless the prompts were accompanied by positive reinforcement, usually hedonic. Exhortations, lectures, and relevant general education have proved largely ineffective in this sphere. Even the attempt to reduce littering among children in a theatre by manipulating the physical environment (providing bags for waste) had little effect. Combined with messages pointing out the disadvantages of litter, the provision of bags had a moderate effect. However, when a reward of one dime was given for each bag of rubbish, the decrease in littering was massive. Another form of hedonic reward in the form of a ticket for a movie had a similarly substantial negative effect on littering. Similar results have been found in experimental studies of the reduction of littering in streets, and around and within buildings. Success is also apparent in the closure of the behavior setting, e.g. providing more litter bins and devising trash cans that are fun to use, and by ensuring the initial cleanliness and attractiveness of the environment; all of these strategies have had some effect by bringing behavior under stimulus control, but only the presentation of positive reinforcers in the form of payments has any dramatic effect on behavior. Prompts, used alone, have little if any effect, perhaps because of their reliance on punishment for unapproved behavior: the individual who litters nevertheless and avoids immediate punishment is actually likely to be reinforced for his or her littering. The relative effectiveness of prompts and incentives indicated by litter studies has been confirmed by experiments aimed at increasing consumers' willingness to conserve irreplaceable materials through recycling. Attempts at increasing consumers' purchases of returnable bottles are a typical example. The use of prompts informing customers of the savings to which such behavior would lead and that they would be contributing to the fight against pollution have had mixed effects. Giving consumers small financial rewards for the reuse of such items as egg cartons, milk containers and grocery bags, accompanied by in-store prompts and a pleasant and enthusiastic reaction by salespersons, has led to increases in custom.

Some attempts at increasing consumers' recycling behavior have had significant punishing consequences. The Bottle Laws enacted first in Oregon and subsequently adopted by several other states impose considerable transaction, inventory and time costs on retailers who pass them on to their customers (Guerts 1986). Both are penalized for their participation in the waste reduction campaign and, even though distributors are legally bound to comply, their consumers are in general unlikely to incur the costs involved in prepaying deposits and returning glass bottles unless they are adequately compensated for the punishing consequences of these prosocial endeavours. Experimental attempts to encourage the recovery of waste materials such as paper which can be recycled also indicate that prompts have minimal effects on behavior while the provision of hedonic and, to a smaller extent, informational reinforcers has a substantial reinforcing effect. Hence students offered prizes in contests and raffles are more likely to reduce wastage than those who are only exposed to educative prompting. The provision of convenient containers for the collection of recyclable waste is also significantly more effective than prompting on the promotion of appropriate prosocial behaviors perhaps because it achieves a degree of closure of the setting and the combination of prompts and suitable receptacles for the collection of waste has produced a combined effect on behavior greater than that expected from their individual contributions.

Domestic Water Consumption as 'Maintenance'

Maintenance is exemplified as an environmentally-impacting consumer behavior by the domestic over consumption of water. Both hedonic and informational reinforcements are low compared with those that control other the other classes of consumer behavior, though neither is absent: the luxury and status of having water continuously available on tap are easily taken for granted but being able to drink, clean, bathe and water the garden are indicative of comparative wealth and power; they are hedonic and informational benefits directly related to the consumer's state of deprivation. The consumption behaviors in question are apparently maintained on fixed interval ratios, most of the uses of water taking place at some time or other on most days or most weeks.

If accurate, this analysis and classification would suggest the following. (i) punishment, especially involving price would be especially efficacious in reducing consumption. (ii) metering, to provide general association between behavior and its contingent consequences and to provide accurate and quick feedback on the outcomes of consumption would be especially effective. (iii) closing the setting by reducing the time and place during which water can be consumed would be effective. There is less experimental evidence for the behavioral economics of water consumption and conservation than for the other commodities and products considered but the limited evidence suggests that this analysis and classification are correct. A study of the conservation of metered water in Perth, Australia (Geller *et al*. 1982) indicates that water consumption decreased by over 30% in both an experimental group provided with daily feedback on water use and a rebate proportionate to demand reduction, and a control group provided only with feedback, though change in climatic conditions may also have affected the results. The low elasticity of demand for water makes financial rebates less appropriate than for other classes of consumer behavior.

SOCIAL DEMARKETING

This survey indicates that the general propositions suggested above are accurate. The BPM provides a coherent and plausible model of the role of antecedent and consequential stimuli in the shaping and maintenance of environmentally-impacting consumer behavior. Hedonic reinforcement is, as expected, the single most important influence on such behavior but the three basic components of the model, used in optimal combination that varies depending on the class of behavior in question, exerts the greatest control. The most effective general strategy for behavior change indeed appears to be the maintenance of current levels of hedonic and/or informational reinforcement plus the enhancement of relatively low levels of reinforcement, plus the manipulation of behavior settings to signal the consequences of modified consumption. Finally, different marketing mix strategies can be extracted from the results of the applied behavior analyses for the four classes of environmentally-impacting consumer behavior identified and described by the BPM. The fulfillment of the specific propositions put forward for each of these consumer behavior classes suggests the following generalizations, each well-supported by empirical evidence and capable of serving as hypotheses for refinement and further testing.

Accomplishment

Modification of accomplishment behaviors, exemplified here by private motoring, requires the development of a radically more attractive product with strongly reinforcing hedonic and informational attributes: this may even necessitate the creation of a different product. Price may be important too, but only when the new or thoroughly revamped product has been successfully launched and established: the price of the original might then be raised to punish its use. Until this point is reached, however, such a price rise would have little overall effect on demand for the original product given the abundant hedonic and informational reinforcers it provides. Indeed, to the extent that private transportation is a prestige good, maintained by informational reinforcement that derives from conspicuous consumption, an increase in the costs associated with it might be counter-productive, encouraging rather than discouraging consumption. During the introductory phases of the new product, its price might be subsidized to ensure that consumers switched to its use: whether the price reduction has to be maintained indefinitely depends upon the effectiveness of the primary hedonic and informational reinforcers provided by the novel product. As far as promotion is concerned, prompts are unlikely to have a strong effect on demand, though coupled with effective consequential stimuli they provide a necessary informative and persuasive role. However, advertisements containing modelling of the prosocial behaviors advocated would probably both increase awareness of the campaign and encourage imitative responses. Finally, as far as place is concerned, the behavior setting should be opened further by increasing competition and making the new product widely and flexibly available.

Pleasure

Consumer behavior modification in the case of pleasure is more subtly changed through the provision of increased, relatively rapid and regular information on consumption. This information can be seen as part of the product provided by the utilities companies. The maintenance of hedonic reinforcement is important and, since the overall goal of the campaign is a reduction in energy use, this must be accomplished by the encouragement of personal and domestic arrangements which promote thermal savings (e.g. better insulation, the wearing of more heat-efficient clothing and the elimination of useless energy consumption such as the illumination of unoccupied rooms). These factors, which might be considered part of the place element of the marketing mix since they determine the location of consumption, contribute to the closure of the behavior setting. Price might also be used to deter over use of resources but, given the highly hedonic consequences of energy consumption, it is unlikely to have a strong independent effect on usage.

Accumulation

The single most cost-effective means of reducing littering is probably the closure of the behavior setting. Since litter is itself a discriminative stimulus for further littering, the provision of bins, bags and other containers that encourage disposal is likely to have a cumulative effect on behavior. Prompting alone also has some effect on litter disposal if it is directly related to the means of acting prosocially, e.g. by pointing out what to put, where to put it and when. The behavior setting for recycling can be closed by the provision of containers for bottles, plastics, papers, and so on in convenient positions for consumers to use. Hedonic reinforcement remains a strong influence on behavior though it will often be an expensive alternative: competitions and variable person schedules appear to be the most effective means of changing behavior, especially if coupled with promotional campaigns emphasizing modelled prosocial behavior. The costs involved in some prosocial behaviors presently punish the consumer - e.g. in the case of returning bottles and other packaging; either these costs must be reduced through the collection of waste materials or the financial recompense for their return must be expanded until behavior is economically controlled.

Maintenance

Finally, in the case of maintenance, exemplified by water consumption and conservation, it is important to control the behavior setting by installing water-conserving methods (e.g. smaller cisterns), by encouraging the use of rainwater for garden watering, and the opportunity to use water less expensive than fully-purified drinking water for some domestic purposes such as flushing toilets. The alternative place strategies (rationing, standpipes, etc.) are politically unacceptable and usually unnecessary except during emergencies, though metering is probably an essential prerequisite of most systems of behavior modification based on consequential stimuli whether informational or hedonic. Price might be used to overcome overuse, though again this would be politically acceptable only within close bounds.

REFERENCES

Cone, J. D. and Hayes, S. C., (1980) *Environmental Problems/ Behavioral Solutions*. Monterey, CA: Brooks/Cole.

Costanzo, M., Archer, D., Aronson, E. and Pettigrew, T. (1986) "Energy conservation behavior: the difficult path from information to action," *American Psychologist* 41: 521-528.

Foxall, G. R. (1993) "Situated Consumer Behavior," *Research in Consumer Behavior*, 6, 113-152.

_____(1994) "Behavior Analysis and Consumer Psychology," *Journal of Economic Psychology*, 15, 1-87.

Geller, E. S. (1989) "Applied behavior analysis and social marketing: an integration for environmental preservation," *Journal of Social Issues* 45: 17-36.

_____, R. A. Winett and P. B. Everett (1982) *Preserving the Environment*, Elmsford, N.Y: Pergamon.

Guerts, M. D. (1986) "The 'bottle bill' effect on grocery stores' costs," *International Journal of Retailing*, 1, 12-17.

Malott, R. W. (1989) "The achievement of evasive goals: control by rules describing contingencies that are not direct acting." In: Hayes, S. C. (ed.) 1989, *Rule-governed Behavior*, New York: Plenum.

Schwartz, I. S. (1991) "The study of consumer behavior and social validity: an essential partnership for applied behavior analysis," *Journal of Applied Behavior Analysis* 24: 241-4.

Skinner, B. F. (1953) *Science and Human Behavior*, NY: Macmillan.

Winkler, R. C. and Winett, R. A. (1982) "Behavioral interventions in resource conservation: a systems approach based on behavioral economics," *American Psychologist* 37: 421-435.

Session Summary
Understanding Consumer Decision Processes Using Verbalization Data: Substantive and Methodological Perspectives

Gabriel Biehal, University of Maryland
Dipankar Chakravarti, University of Arizona

Thought verbalization data are used extensively in consumer decision process research (Bettman and Park 1980; Bettman, Johnson and Payne 1990; Biehal and Chakravarti 1986) and researchers have developed various methods for collecting such data. Many researchers use retrospective protocols which require that subjects recount a prior decision episode verbally or in writing. Others ask subjects for introspective reports, i.e., verbalized thoughts about the reasons for current/past decisions. Still others use concurrent verbal protocols (verbalization simultaneous with task performance).

There is controversy about the validity of verbal protocol data. Since verbalization places demands on subjects' mental capabilities, it may distort underlying processes. Some psychologists (Nisbett and Wilson 1977) dismiss retrospective protocols as introspectional data of limited value. Others (e.g., Ericsson and Simon 1984) provide empirically-based rebuttals, mainly regarding the validity of concurrent protocols. Recent research shows that even concurrent verbalizing may subtly influence consumer decision processes (Biehal and Chakravarti 1989; Russo, Johnson and Stephens 1989). Hence, the strengths and weaknesses of various thought verbalization methodologies deserved more examination.

Session Overview

This session included three presentations that used different verbalization methods and contexts to study substantive consumer decision making issues. The first (Shah, Gilbert and Park) explored how introspection and concurrent verbalization may not only influence framing, processing and memory representations in the focal task, but also in subsequent tasks. In the second, Bhoovaraghava and Mitchell showed how retrospective and concurrent protocols along with process tracing data can provide converging evidence on base rate information use in consumer decisions. Kuusela, Ahtola and Chakravarti examined how self-perceived and actual knowledge influence decision framing and processing as well as choice times and outcomes. They showed how concurrent verbalization data can link task performance to process variables, noting that concurrent verbalization may create differential demand characteristics for low versus high knowledge (both actual and self-perceived) subjects. The discussant, Eric Johnson, provided a summary of the strengths and limitations of verbalization methods.

The Shah, Gilbert and Park Presentation

Reshma Shah, Robert Gilbert and C.W. Park (Pittsburgh) presented, "The Impact of Concurrent Verbal Protocols on Encoding and Retrieval." They reiterated the controversy about the validity of protocol data, noting recent research showing (a) that concurrent verbalization can interfere with information processing, memory and problem solving because it draws on limited attentional capacity (Biehal and Chakravarti 1989; Schooler and Schooler 1990; Schooler, Ohlsson and Brooks 1994); and (b) that introspection (through verbalization) can lower the quality of decisions and attenuate satisfaction with choices (Wilson and Schooler 1991; Wilson et al 1994). They also noted that verbal overshadowing (verbal disruption of non-verbal processes) may impair problem solving and learning (Fallshore and Schooler 1993).

The authors pointed out that whether concurrent verbal protocols facilitate or inhibit information processing may depend upon the task. Verbalization may induce more analytical processing relative to nonverbalizing conditions in which consumers may process more holistically. Due to greater analytical processing, verbalizing subjects should find technical, functional and utilitarian product attributes more salient and important in choice. Moreover, analytical processing should lower recall and recognition and also reduce liking and satisfaction with the task and the choice. In contrast, the absence of verbalization should generate more holistic processing. Hence, such subjects should deem artistic, aesthetic and luxurious product attributes as more salient and important. Moreover, recall and recognition should be facilitated and these subjects should exhibit greater liking and satisfaction with their choices and the task. Verbalization should also facilitate problem framing strategies and thus influence encoding/retrieval processes in subsequent tasks.

The empirical study considered the impact of concurrent verbalization instructions on consumer decision making in two sequential choice tasks. In Task 1, subjects made choices from among four homes, based upon pictures and descriptions of their location/surroundings and other features. Some subjects verbalized their choice process, whereas others did not. Following choice, measures were taken of recall, recognition, liking, satisfaction, attribute importance, and processing style. In Task 2, subjects once again chose from among a set of homes. Measures were taken to investigate the differential impact of verbalization on problem framing and subsequent decision making. The authors discussed the implications of the findings for the use of concurrent verbalization data in the study of consumer decisions.

The Bhoovaraghava and Mitchell Presentation

This presentation by Sriraman Bhoovaragava and Deborah Mitchell (Temple University) was entitled, "Point-of-view and Related Factors Affecting the Use of Base Rates: Verbalization Data as Converging Evidence on Decision Processes." The authors noted previous research showing that utilization of base rates and other information in decision-making is dependent both on the perceived relevance/diagnosticity of the information (Feldman and Lynch 1988) and on whether or not it conflicts with other environmental cues (Lynch and Ofir 1989). They then reported three studies examining how contextual variables and reference-dependence influence individuals' use of base rates in various decisions. A variable termed "point-of-view" (Kahneman and Lovallo 1993), as well as the reference point implicit in the valence of the potential decision outcome, directly affected base-rate utilization and predictive performance. Interestingly, decision makers' confidence in their predictions was negatively correlated with base-rate utilization and performance.

The three experiments manipulated 'point-of-view' (inside versus outside), outcome valence, and information consistency (Lynch and Ofir 1989). Consumers were asked to predict the likely outcome of service encounters, based on the information provided to them. Process data was collected in each study to investigate the cognitive processes underlying consumers' decision-making. In

Study 1, written retrospective protocols were collected and analyzed. In Study 2, consumers made decisions based on information acquired from a computer-based display (Mouselab). Finally, in Study 3 a small sample of consumers provided concurrent verbal protocols as part of their decision task.

All three studies demonstrated significant effects of 'point-of-view' as well as outcome valence on predictive performance. The findings replicated those of Lynch and Ofir (1989) regarding information consistency and base-rate utilization. Convergent process data collected in Studies 1-3 indicated the specific manner in which base rates were utilized. The presentation emphasized how different types of process data can be used for investigating biases in decision-making and the importance of convergent process evidence for a more complete understanding of consumer decision processes.

The Kuusela, Ahtola and Chakravarti Presentation

Hannu Kuusela (Tampere), Olli Ahtola (Helsinki School of Economics) and Dipankar Chakravarti (Arizona) presented, "The Effects of Self-Perceived and Actual Knowledge on Choice Processing: A Verbal Protocol Analysis. They began by noting prior research showing that the actual (objective) consumption relevant knowledge that consumers possess influences decision processes and outcomes (e.g., Bettman and Park 1980; Brucks 1985; Johnson and Russo 1984). They also noted the importance of self-perceived (subjective) knowledge (Park, Gardner and Thukral 1988) and argued that the effects may be motivational (influence task interest) or cognitive (influence information acquisition/use). Since self-perceived knowledge reflects a consumer's prior assessment of the decision task, it may influence problem-framing and guide processing. However, the correspondence between self-perceived and actual knowledge is often less than perfect and consumers must deal with unanticipated contingencies during choice. Consequently, the levels of, and correspondence between, self-perceived and actual knowledge should influence choice processes and outcomes.

Ecological correlations between self-perceived and actual knowledge make it difficult to study their separate and interactive effects (Brucks 1985). The authors reported a 2 x 2 randomized block experiment, manipulating the level of self-perceived knowledge (high/low) and blocking on actual knowledge (high/low). Sixty-four business student subjects from two Finnish universities chose among multi-attribute descriptions of alternative homeowners' insurance policies. The students varied in their actual knowledge of homeowners' policies and were blocked on this factor. Self-perceived knowledge was manipulated by asking subjects to take multiple choice tests that varied in difficulty and in the feedback provided. Verbal protocols and other relevant measures were collected during choice. The protocols were coded for evidence of problem framing, use of processing operations of different complexity (e.g., compensatory, pairwise comparison, holistic) and decision time.

The findings show that higher levels of both self-perceived and actual knowledge reduce explicit problem framing and lower both the number of elementary processing operations and decision time. Also, problem framing and elementary processing activities are highest when both self-perceived and actual knowledge are low. Decisions are made fastest when both self-perceived and actual knowledge are high. The protocol data in this study provide both process and outcome evidence regarding the effects of self-perceived and actual knowledge on choice. However, the collection and analysis of such data is not straightforward and the insights obtained vary by the level (macro or micro) of protocol coding and analysis (Biehal and Chakravarti 1986, 1989). The authors suggested useful rules of thumb for choosing coding schemes and the level of aggregation of code categories.

Discussant's Comments

Eric Johnson summarized the papers with an integrative analysis of the strengths and limitations of verbalization data, comparing such data with data from other process tracing methods such as Mouselab.

Special Session Summary
New Directions in Exploring the Interface of Consumer Cognition and Motivation

S. Ratneshwar, University of Florida

For the last two decades information-processing models have dominated the study of consumer decision-making. Correspondingly, interest in motivational factors and theories has tended to wane. Nevertheless, a "cold cognition" approach to consumer decision making has revealed numerous limitations. For example, while it is commonly acknowledged that consumer behavior is goal-directed, we know little about the overall structure of consumer goals and how these structures manifest themselves in day-to-day decision-making. Similarly, a broad class of individual, situational, and cultural factors related to consumer motivations are known to impact on consumer decisions, as proven by their relevance to key concepts such as market segmentation. Yet, we generally don't seem to consider these same factors when we study how consumers make choices. As a result, information-processing research has shed little light on the more molar, persistent, and contextually-grounded aspects of consumer motivation that drive much decision-making. Further, even though cognitive processes are known to be heavily influenced by emotional states as well as by the anticipated emotional consequences to the decision-maker, rarely has consumer research examined these relations.

Contrary to these trends, several investigators are now directing their research efforts at exploring the interface of consumer cognition and motivation. This special session brought together some of these researchers so as to stimulate the exchange of ideas about the potential value in these new research directions. A brief overview is provided below of the three papers presented at the session.

The paper by Sirsi, Reingen, and Ward presented an innovative theoretical and methodological perspective called microcultural analysis. A microculture is a group of people who identify with an overall belief-system or cause and have social contact with one another (e.g., members of a particular church group). The presentation focused on the study of causal reasoning structures: Why do consumers in different microcultures prefer and avoid different products, and how do their cognitive structures connect their beliefs to purchase and consumption behaviors?

In addressing this problem, Sirsi et al. argue that a complex set of individual, cultural, and social variables explain the sharing and variability in consumer belief system within a microculture. Within the individual, at the micro level, these reasoning structures link individual behavior to broader cultural motives and patterns of reasoning. At the macro level, the distribution of these reasoning structures across the interacting parties in a culture is a crucial aspect of the culture. Thus, their approach is concerned with not only the micro level of analysis, but also how the micro relates to the macro—the culture itself, its "group mind."

Sirsi et al. use the methods of interpretive ethnography to develop an emic perspective of the microculture. The results are an impressionistic picture of shared beliefs, and a broad understanding of the "pool" of cultural reasoning. Next, they turn to the perspectives and methods of ethnoscience and cognitive psychology to study the diversity of reasoning in the culture and develop more precise estimates of the sharing of specific concepts and paths of reasoning across people and consumption objects. Relying upon the ethnography, they create a pool of concepts relevant to reasoning about why products or services are consumed or avoided. Participants then use this pool to construct maps of the causal reasoning explaining their own behavior toward sets of products or services. Finally, the authors employ social network analysis to understand the pattern of social ties and structures in the microculture.

The paper by Luce, Bettman, and Payne presented a theoretical framework for understanding the motivational consequences of distressing decisions. Consumers are often faced with decisions where either the content of a decision (e.g., necessary attribute tradeoffs) or potential decision outcomes are very threatening. Consequently, consumers may be motivated to cope with or minimize anticipated and experienced negative emotions.

Luce et al. focus on how adaptive decision-making strategies might work to serve coping goals when people are faced with such inherently negative emotion-laden decisions. They propose a conceptual framework that includes: (1) a typology of various causes or types of decision-related emotion, (2) predictions regarding how the drive to cope with content-aroused emotion will influence one's decision strategy, and (3) an examination of how assessments of one's potential for coping with a decision influences emotional reactions to that decision.

Luce et al. consider two broad coping strategies. Problem-focused coping involves alleviating the environmental problem leading to emotion. Emotion-focused coping involves directly acting on emotion. Luce et al.'s conceptual framework develops the implications of consumers' motivations to use these two broad coping strategies. For instance, they reconcile the two strategies' seemingly inconsistent implications for decision-making processes by considering the specific aspects of processing upon which each coping strategy will operate most strongly. Thus, they argue that problem-focused coping motivations lead one towards more extensive processing at the same time that emotion-focused coping motivations lead one to process in a non-compensatory manner, avoiding explicit tradeoffs among attributes. This prediction that decision makers will simultaneously shift towards both more extensive and less compensatory processing is unique to the decision making literature.

Luce et al. suggest that coping is an important construct for understanding the generation of emotion, as well. Emotion generation and coping often operate iteratively; that is, emotional experience is altered by coping potential and efforts. The authors suggest how aspects of decision tasks, such as the presence of an easily justifiable status quo option, may moderate emotional reactions to task content by satisfying coping goals or providing coping mechanisms. Luce et al. also discuss how assessments of one's personal coping prospects or abilities to cope (e.g., assessments of one's decision-related expertise or knowledge) influence emotional reactions.

The paper by Huffman, Ratneshwar, and Mick proposed a hierarchical model for consumer goals. They view the consumer as a "motivated problem-solver" and suggest a conceptual framework wherein the evolution of consumer goals is a dynamic process that is a function of both person and situation. Their approach combines the stress on process issues that is epitomized by traditional consumer decision-making research with the structural, molar emphasis of means-end research. Thus, their research suggests how, in fact, consumer behavior can be purposive.

Drawing on a variety of source literatures, Huffman et al. propose a model with six levels of goal constructs that span the domains of being, doing, and having: (1) Life themes and values,

(2) life projects, (3) current concerns, (4) product purposes, (5) benefits sought, and (6) feature preferences.

Further, Huffman et al. examine the linkages between these different levels of goals as well as the dynamic processes involved in goal determination and goal change. They term the two main forces for goal determination as alignment and adaptation. Alignment is the process by which multiple goals are considered together and inconsistencies are reduced or eliminated. It may occur in a top-down as well as bottom-up manner. Incorporation is the process by which higher-level goals constrain, make coherent, and lend meaning to lower-level goals. Abstraction, on the other hand, refers to the manner in which lower-level goals are used for constructing or discovering higher-level goals. The second primary force for goal determination is adaptation, in which goals are shaped or constrained by contextual factors. Huffman et al. investigate these various processes of goal determination and suggest when each is likely to be salient. They also examine the dynamics of goal determination processes in relationship to consumer decision making and consumer learning mechanisms.

In sum, it is worth noting that in the last few years many social psychologists have come around to believe that cognition and motivation cannot be studied independent of each other because of their inherently synergistic relationship (Pervin 1989; Sorrentino and Higgins 1986). In the same vein, it might be speculated that in the future many consumer researchers also may find it fruitful to explore the relations between cognition and motivation. This session provided an opportunity for highlighting some of the important areas of current research and debating the pros and cons of various conceptual approaches.

The Interface of Consumer Cognition and Motivation
Desperately Seeking Susan (or *Anyone* Who Can Organize These Materials)

Jerome B. Kernan, George Mason University

If a discussant is lucky, s/he is confronted with a task not unlike that of an art teacher who visits a renowned gallery. It is tempting to dwell on the individual works, but one's professional responsibility demands that these be organized, related, or somehow connected to one another in a larger mosaic of expression. No one needs to proclaim that the work of Sirsi, Reingen and Ward, of Luce, Bettman and Payne, or of Huffman, Ratneshwar and Mick is first-rate; that much is obvious to any but the most uninformed consumer researcher. How these *relate* to one another, however, is not so obvious. They each speak to an interface between cognition and motivation, but from highly disparate perspectives and absent any apparent pattern. Yet this relational ambiguity is self-imposed; over the years we have allowed cognition and motivation to become disconnected by force of the differing ways each has been studied. So if the Israelis and Palestinians can sit down together without their weapons and if Ian Paisley can so much as utter the name Sinn Fein without cursing, it must be possible to find a rapprochement between psychology's long-lost relatives, cognition and motivation.

Over the years cognitive science has become the fair-haired child, while motivation has lost favor (Bolles 1974). This, in spite of the fact that the two are, ipso facto, inseparable (Ostrom 1994, Sorrentino & Higgins 1986). Cognition obviously is driven by some form of motivation (e.g., goals) and this produces consequences (e.g., goal modification). We might dress this up in all manner of trope (Soyland 1994), but the fact remains: people interpret and respond to information differently when their intentions are injected into processing tasks (Bandura 1989; Pervin 1989). Thus we must deal with matters of declarative vs. procedural knowledge (Smith 1994), automatic vs. conscious processing (Bargh 1994), and other slippery phenomena as people are portrayed with either machine-like or god-like metaphors (Weiner 1992).

And that's just in the laboratory. In the "real world," complications abound. Payne, Bettman and Johnson (1993) tell us that people decide *how to decide* their processing strategies according to complex goals. That's a machine-like rule, but who sets the machine? Luce, Bettman and Payne say the individual's emotions play a big part in all this, specifically how s/he *copes* with them. That smacks strongly of motivation. Simultaneously, Sirsi, Reingen and Ward point to the existence of microcultural reasoning structures—common understandings around which action is organized—much like Louis' (1983) culture-bearing milieux. We begin to see the mind/body dichotomy break down, as nurture interacts with nature. And the complexity comes to an idiosyncratic head in the work of Huffman, Ratneshwar and Mick, where we see not only goals, but *hierarchical* ones driving people's perceptions and behavior. Still more motivation.

What is to be made of all this? Since cognition lost motivation somewhere along the way as it developed into cognitive science, we seem to have acquiesced to a tacit assumption that what consumers process can be studied apart from why. Yet nobody believes this; *something* drives every human's information-handling strategies. What we need is "motivated" cognitive science; it introduces complexity, but it also adds realism to information-processing models. So with a bit of intellectual recklessness, here is one way—admittedly that of a tenderfoot—to organize cognition and motivation, to impose an organization on these interface papers.

If we use cognitive (representational) domination versus motivational (actional) domination of information processing as a horizontal axis and prescriptive (rule-laden) versus descriptive (goal-laden) accounts of how people interpret their environment as a vertical axis, a two-dimensional map emerges. Generally, the southern half of the map captures machine-like accounts of people, while the northern half reflects god-like metaphors. The western hemisphere is essentially nomothetic; the eastern one, idiographic. Thus, we place information-integration theory—with its how-to rules for representing environmental stimuli—in the southwestern quadrant. Luce, Bettman and Payne's work seems to fit best in the southeastern quadrant; it is based on rules, but motivated ones. Sirsi, Reingen and Ward's work belongs in the northwestern quadrant because it's mostly representational and culturally, not person-situated. Finally, Huffman, Ratneshwar and Mick's work occupies the northeastern quadrant, inasmuch as it is all-knowing and actional. Their information processer is a hermeneutic one (Packer 1985), engaged in Heidegger's "ready-to hand" mode of engagement.

This map reflects an ex post organization of cognition and motivation, so some interpretive liberty has been taken in order to fit the work of Sirsi, Reingen and Ward, of Luce, Bettman and Payne, and of Huffman, Ratneshwar and Mick (indeed, of Norman Anderson) to its dimensions. That is done with apologies to the authors. Similarly, while the map "advocates" a movement away from raw (or cold) cognition to motivated cognition (the northeastern quadrant), this should not be read as any sort of commentary on research not positioned there. Indeed, both the Sirsi, Reingen and Ward work and that of Luce, Bettman and Payne are labeled with arrows pointing to the northeastern quadrant, indicating that each of them contains strong shards of motivated cognition. The purpose of the map is merely to suggest that ecological validity seems better captured when information processers are adaptive rather than rigid in their reasoning and when motivation drives rather than is driven by their cognitions. It is not to suggest that any of the portrayed researchers do or should agree with this interpretation; they each have uniquely valid approaches to the cognition-motivation interface and that is as it should be.

It is not obvious that this map clarifies more than it confuses the relationship between cognition and motivation. Nor is it clear that it sensitizes us to the importance of the interface. Indeed, one might ask why we *should* care that consumer cognition and motivation be integrated. One can recite all the usual bromides about synergy and symbiosis, but it can be very comfortable to hide within the cocoons of our respective specialties. However, just as playing solitaire on a PC can become a crashing bore, so does the study of cognition eventually become empty unless it is infused with individuals' emotions, foibles, yearnings and deceits. We must never forget that consumers are real people.

REFERENCES

Bandura, Albert (1989), "Self-Regulation of Motivation and Action Through Internal Standards and Goal Systems," in *Goal Concepts in Personality and Social Psychology*, ed. Lawrence A. Pervin, Hillsdale, NJ: Erlbaum, 19-85.

FIGURE
Consumer Cognition and Motivation
A Tenderfoot's Map

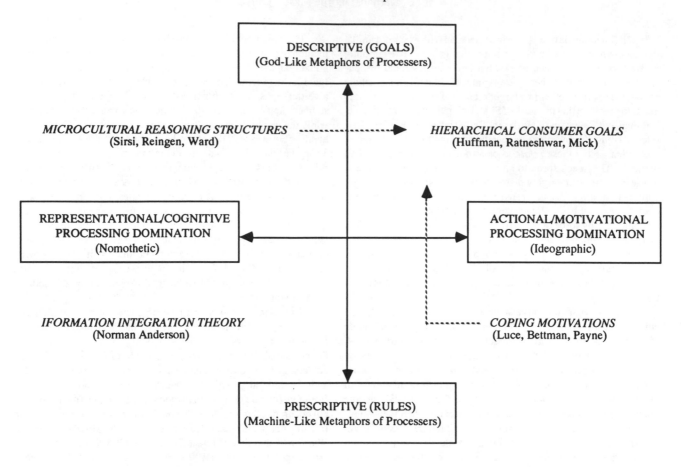

MICROCULTURAL REASONING STRUCTURES
(Sirsi, Reingen, Ward)

HIERARCHICAL CONSUMER GOALS
(Huffman, Ratneshwar, Mick)

DESCRIPTIVE (GOALS)
(God-Like Metaphors of Processers)

REPRESENTATIONAL/COGNITIVE
PROCESSING DOMINATION
(Nomothetic)

ACTIONAL/MOTIVATIONAL
PROCESSING DOMINATION
(Ideographic)

IFORMATION INTEGRATION THEORY
(Norman Anderson)

COPING MOTIVATIONS
(Luce, Bettman, Payne)

PRESCRIPTIVE (RULES)
(Machine-Like Metaphors of Processers)

Bargh, John A. (1994), "The Four Horsemen of Automaticity: Awareness, Intention, Efficiency, and Control in Social Cognition," in *Handbook of Social Cognition*, 2nd Ed. (Vol. 1), eds. Robert S. Wyer and Thomas K. Srull, Hillsdale, NJ: Erlbaum, 1-40.

Bolles, Robert C. (1974), "Cognition and Motivation: Some Historical Trends," in *Cognitive Views of Human Motivation*, ed. Bernard Weiner, New York: Academic Press, 1-20.

Louis, Meryl R. (1983), "Organizations as Culture-Bearing Milieux," in *Organizational Symbolism*, eds. Louis R. Pondy, Peter J. Frost, Gareth Morgan and Thomas C. Dandridge, Greenwich, CT: JAI Press, 39-54.

Ostrom, Thomas M. (1994), "Forward," in *Handbook of Social Cognition*, 2nd Ed. (Vol. 1), eds. Robert S. Wyer and Thomas K. Srull, Hillsdale, NJ: Erlbaum, vii-xii.

Packer, Martin J. (1985), "Hermeneutic Inquiry in the Study of Human Conduct," *American Psychologist*, 40 (October), 1081-1093.

Payne, John W., James R. Bettman and Eric J. Johnson (1993), *The Adaptive Decision Maker*, New York: Cambridge University Press.

Pervin, Lawrence A. (1989), "Goal Concepts in Personality and Social Psychology: A Historical Perspective," in *Goal Concepts in Personality and Social Psychology*, ed. Lawrence A. Pervin, Hillsdale, NJ: Erlbaum, 1-17.

Smith, Eliot R. (1994), "Procedural Knowledge and Processing Strategies in Social Cognition," in *Handbook of Social Cognition*, 2nd Ed. (Vol. 1), eds. Robert S. Wyer and Thomas K. Srull, Hillsdale, NJ: Erlbaum, 99-151.

Sorrentino, Richard M. and E. Tory Higgins (1986), "Motivation and Cognition: Warming Up to Synergism," in *Handbook of Motivation and Cognition: Foundations of Social Behavior*, eds. Richard M. Sorrentino and E. Tory Higgins, New York: Guilford Press, 3-19.

Soyland, A.J. (1994), *Psychology As Metaphor*, London: Sage.

Weiner, Bernard (1992), *Human Motivation: Metaphors, Theories, and Research*, Newbury Park, CA: Sage.

Anticipations and Consumer Decision Making

Michel Tuan Pham, Columbia University

THE NEGLECTED ROLE OF ANTICIPATIONS

Consumer decision making is often characterized as stimulus–based or memory–based (e.g., Lynch and Srull 1982), reflecting the field's emphasis on decisions based on information either *present* in the consumers' environment or *previously* memorized (e.g., Bettman, Johnson, and Payne 1991). For certain decisions, however, such information may be insufficient; and the consumer may attempt to *anticipate* what *will* (or may) happen. For instance, a consumer trying to make a decision about buying a dress may try to foresee the outcome of wearing it (e.g., receiving flattering comments, feeling proud). Similarly, decisions about magazine subscriptions would be facilitated if we could anticipate our future enjoyment of the magazine after several months of receiving it. Therefore, it is important that we better understand *how* and *when* consumers rely on such anticipations in making decisions.

This special session explored three sets of issues about anticipations and decision making: (1) What kinds of mental representations do consumers access or construct in their anticipations of future outcomes?; (2) How do consumers anticipate their future liking or hedonic responses?; and (3) How do they incorporate these considerations into their present decisions? These issues were examined from three theoretical perspectives—behavioral decision theory (Snell and Gibbs, this volume), affect and information processing (Pham 1994), and self concept (Phillips, Olson, and Baumgartner, this volume), with considerably different methodologies (scenario–based judgments, experiments; and depth interviews). The three papers and Andrew Mitchell's discussant comments are summarized below.

SUMMARY OF THE PAPERS

Jackie Snell and Brian Gibbs (see paper in this volume) address the following issue. Many products are either consumed over time (e.g., a magazine subscription) or purchased at one time and consumed at another (e.g., a vacation package). Decisions about such products therefore require expectations not only about future product performance, but also about one's *future* hedonic response to a delayed consumption of the product. The authors use a behavioral decision theory framework to discuss consumers' ability to predict their future hedonic responses to consumption.

They review evidence questioning the common assumption that people are able to predict how much they will enjoy an experience or a product when they make a choice. For instance, Kahneman and Snell (1992) asked subjects to predict their liking over time for various products (e.g., ice creams, yogurts, musical pieces) that they committed to consume every day. There was *no correlation* between predicted and actual changes in liking. This result suggests that it is important to study *how* consumers may predict changes in their hedonic responses over time.

They introduce the notion of *intuitive hedonics*, which they define as consumers' "common sense psychology regarding the dynamics of pleasure" (Snell and Gibbs, this volume). In a series of studies, they examine whether consumers' predictions about the hedonic outcome of various scenarios match predictions made by several psychological theories: classical conditioning, Weber's law, adaptation theory, opponent process theory, the mere exposure effect, and cognitive dissonance theory. While respondents' predictions were generally consistent with those of classical conditioning, Weber's law, and adaptation, they did not match predictions made by opponent process theory, mere exposure, and cognitive dissonance.

Adopting an information processing perspective, Michel Pham (1994) examines how consumers make decisions about future consumption episodes (e.g., going to a movie, having dinner at an exclusive restaurant). He argues that traditional consumer decision making models (e.g., expectancy–value) do not fully represent the processes underlying such decisions. Building on the postulate that affect is information (e.g., Schwartz 1990), he introduces the *affect recruitment heuristic*, which he suggests is a pervasive process through which consumers make decisions. This heuristic involves three steps: (1) a concrete mental representation of the consumption episode is accessed (e.g., the consumer "pictures" himself/herself at a movie); (2) an anticipatory affective response is instantiated *through this representation* (e.g., he/she experiences pleasant feelings in response to this "picture"); and (3) the anticipatory affective response is used as an informational input to the decision (e.g., he/she decides to go because it "feels good").

Pham (1994) further proposes that the use of these anticipatory affective responses obey accessibility and diagnosticity principles (e.g., Feldman and Lynch 1988). For example, anticipatory affective responses should be more accessible — and affect recruitment more influential — among consumers with high imagery abilities than among those with low imagery abilities. Also, anticipatory affective responses should be perceived as more diagnostic when consumption episodes are assessed for consummatory (or congenial) reasons than when they are assessed for instrumental reasons.

These propositions were tested in a series of five experiments, two of which were presented at the session. These two experiments relied on contextual mood as a means of manipulating anticipatory affective responses to an episode without altering its evaluative content. The first experiment suggests that consumers may regard feelings experienced during the decision process as having unique information value, and therefore incorporate these feelings into their decisions. The second experiment, which included process baseline conditions, suggests that the affect recruitment heuristic offers a plausible paramorphic description of how consumers with consummatory motives rely on their feelings to make decisions about consumption episodes. An expectancy–value model did not describe this process equally well.

Drawing on concepts from the self literature, Diane Phillips, Jerry Olson and Hans Baumgartner (see paper in this volume) describe a concept, called "Consumption Visions," that is consistent with the idea of affect recruitment. A consumption vision is "a visual image of of certain product–related behaviors and their consequences ... (they consist of) concrete and vivid mental images that enable consumers to vicariously experience the self–relevant consequences of product use" (Walker and Olson 1994, pp. 27,31). Phillips et al. discuss the concept of consumptions visions by exploring (1) their characteristics, (2) factors that influence them, and (3) their consequences on decision making. They illustrate their discussion with verbatim excerpts from unstructured depth interviews.

They speculate that consumptions visions have the following characteristics: (1) they may contain projections of "possible selves"; (2) they have a narrative form similar to that of miniature movies; (3) they have a visual representational format; (4) they may elicit affective responses; (5) they may provide tangible representations of consumers' goals. The authors further suggest that the likelihood of forming consumption visions depends on: (7) the level of involvement; (8) the consumer's propensity to process information visually; and (8) situational factors such as the presence of imagery–evoking stimuli in the consumer's environment. Finally, Phillips et al. propose that consumption visions may be used not only as inputs to decision making, but also as mood–management devices (e.g., fantasies).

DISCUSSION

Discussing Snell and Gibbs' paper, Andrew Mitchell suggested that in was not all that surprising that consumers are not very accurate when predicting their future hedonic responses. Rather than focusing on *whether* consumer consumer *can* make such predictions, research should assess *how* and *when* they *do* make such predictions. The studies conducted by Snell, Gibb, and Varey (1994) represent an important first step in that direction.

Mitchell then compared Pham's theoretical propositions with those of Phillips et al., noting that there was substantial overlap, although these two programs of research originated from different literatures. He observed that Pham's framework is defined more narrowly than Phillips et al.'s. Pham (1994) regards affect recruitment as a *decision heuristic*, whose use depends on (i.e. is restricted by) accessibility and diagnosticity principles. For instance, he predicts that affect recruitment would *not* be used when prior evaluations are highly accessible. Phillips et al. define consumption visions more broadly: the use of these visions is not limited to decision making. For instance, when they suggest that consumption visions may also serve mood–management functions, Phillips et al. implicitly include fantasies in the domain of consumption visions. Mitchell suggested that Phillips et al. be more precise about the boundaries of consumption visions as a theoretical construct. Is any kind of imagery a consumption vision? He also suggested that Pham's distinction between consummatory and instrumental motives be clarified. Finally, he stressed that future research needs to focus on *when* affect recruitment is likely to be used and consumption visions are likely to be formed.

The discussion was then opened to the audience, who engaged in a lively exchange with the speakers. For instance, the audience and the speakers debated on whether high consumer expertise in a product category would increase or decrease the likelihood of affect recruitment and the use of consumption visions. On the one hand, one could argue that unless a consumer has acquired sufficient experience with a product category, he or she would not be able to generate the concrete representations hypothesized by Pham and by Phillips et al. On the other hand, one could also speculate that those consumers who have extensive expertise already have well–formed attitudes about the product, hence would not need to engage in anticipation processes such as affect recruitment and consumption visions. This issue (as well as many others) is worthy of empirical examination.

REFERENCES

Bettman, James R., Eric J. Johnson, and John W. Payne (1991), "Consumer Decision Making," in *Handbook of Consumer Behavior*, eds. Thomas S. Robertson and Harold H. Kassarjian, Englewood Cliffs, NJ: Prentice–Hall, 50–84.

Feldman, Jack M. and John G. Lynch, Jr. (1988), "Self–Generated Validity and Other Effects of Measurement on Belief, Attitude, Intention, and Behavior," *Journal of Applied Psychology*, 73 (3), 421–435.

Lynch, John G. and Thomas K. Srull (1982), "Memory and Attentional Factors in Consumer Choice: Concepts and Research Methods," *Journal of Consumer Research*, 9 (June), 18–37.

Kahneman, Daniel and Jackie Snell (1992), "Predicting a Changing Taste: Do People Know What They Will Like?" *Journal of Behavioral Decision Making*, 5, 187-200.

Pham, Michel Tuan (1994), *Feeling Like Consuming: Affect as Information in Decisions about Consumption Episodes*, Doctoral Dissertation, University of Florida, Gainesville.

Phillips, Diane M., Jerry C. Olson, and Hans Baumgartner (1995), "Consumption Visions in Consumer Decision Making," in *Advances in Consumer Research*, Vol. 22, Frank Kardes and Mita Sujan (eds.), Association for Consumer Research: Provo, UT.

Schwarz, Norbert (1990), "Feelings as Information: Informational and Motivational Functions of Affective States," in *Handbook of Motivation and Cognition*, Vol. 2, eds. E. Torry Higgins and Richard M. Sorrentino, New York: Guilford Press, 527–561.

Snell, Jackie S., Brian J. Gibbs and Carol Varey (1994), "Intuitive hedonics: Consumer beliefs about the dynamics of liking," Paper submitted for publication.

Snell, Jackie S. and Brian J. Gibbs (1995), "Intuitive Hedonics: Do Consumers Know What They Will Like?" in *Advances in Consumer Research*, Vol. 22, Frank Kardes and Mita Sujan (eds.), Association for Consumer Research: Provo, UT.

Walker, Beth and Jerry C. Olson (1994), "The Activated Self in Consumer Behavior: A Cognitive Structure Perspective," Working Paper 184, The Pennsylvania State University, University Park, PA 16802.

Do Consumers Know What They Will Like?

Jackie Snell, San Jose State University
Brian J. Gibbs, Stanford University

Psychological hedonism is defined by Webster as "the theory that conduct is fundamentally motivated by the pursuit of pleasure or the avoidance of pain." Hedonism may not be the sole motivation, but most of us would agree that the pursuit of pleasure or avoidance of pain is, rightfully, an important aspect of product choice. We borrow the term "hedonics" from the Greek to refer very broadly to the study of pleasure and pain, liking and disliking, enjoyment, taste, disgust, and other such affective responses, and to specifically exclude social, moral, and ethical considerations in decision making.

Do people know how much they will enjoy an experience or product when they make a choice? Rational decision making requires that while I am shopping for groceries I can judge not only the objective attributes of the Grade A filet mignon but also can judge my own enjoyment of steak vs. chicken later in the week when it will be consumed (March 1978). How much I am willing to spend (in money or vacation time) to stay a second week in Hawaii will depend in part on my expectations about whether I will enjoy the second week of sailing and sunning more or less than the first. Marketers often study expectations about product attributes, but seldom do we study people's anticipation of their own responses to those attributes. Whenever tastes change or vary over time and choice is separated from consumption, then anticipation of our own liking or tastes and how they change as a function of experience, time, or the situation, is an important aspect of decision making.

DO PEOPLE KNOW THEIR OWN TASTES?

Our positivist heritage has lead us to use choice as a measure of utility: Whatever a person chooses reflects a maximization of his or her own utility function. We assume, rather than test, that people choose what is most enjoyable for them, that is, we assume people know their own tastes. But do they? Kahneman and Snell (1992) tested people's self-insight when predicting a changing taste. In a series of experiments participants were given a sample experience, a serving of ice cream or a taste of plain yogurt and a short musical piece, either self-chosen or experimenter-chosen. They were asked to commit to a week of daily repetition of the experience, to rate their current liking for the product(s) and to predict their own liking at the end of the week. The ice cream and unfamiliar music group came to the lab each day to participate, the yogurt and familiar music group committed to eat and listen at home, at the same time each day.

The norm among subjects was to predict satiation over the course of a week, and on average, for all the products except yogurt, satiation is what actually occurred. Yogurt provides the most interesting example, since most subjects were wrong in predicting even the direction of change. Most participants either predicted satiation as usual (50%) or no change (23%), though most (61%) liked plain yogurt more (or disliked it less) at the end of the week than at the beginning. Perhaps equally as surprising, most were substantially wrong in predicting their liking for their first serving (6 oz.) at home based on their liking for an initial taste (a teaspoon) in the lab (mean predicted =-0.62, mean actual =-2.13 on a 13 point scale).

For the other products, where on average satiation did occur, subjects displayed no self-insight regarding how much satiation would occur. Even the few individuals who did not experience actual satiation generally had predicted satiation. Correlations between the predicted and actual liking on day 8 for ice cream was -0.14 and for unfamiliar music was 0.24 (n=16, n.s. for both). As might be expected participants did show somewhat more self-insight when making predictions for listening to their own choice of favorite music at home for a week (r= .41, n=76, p<.01), but still expected more satiation than actually occurred (mean predicted change = -1.92, mean actual change = -0.79)

INTUITIVE HEDONICS

The preceding studies suggest that people do anticipate changing tastes, and perhaps suggest a bias toward expecting satiation. Snell, Gibbs and Varey (forthcoming) investigated individuals' intuitive knowledge regarding influences on taste, what we might loosely call lay theories of taste change. We use the term "intuitive hedonics" to focus on that part of common-sense psychology regarding the dynamics of pleasure. Using McCloskey's (1983) and diSessa's (1983, 1985) work in intuitive physics as a model, the approach we used was to infer the beliefs people use by analyzing their responses to hypothetical, every-day-life situations. We designed scenarios to describe situations that were natural yet similar to the experimental situations in six areas of psychology that bear on liking or enjoyment: classical conditioning, Weber's law, opponent processes, adaptation (also called habituation), mere exposure, and cognitive dissonance. We adopted this approach because we were more interested in the concepts that people *use* than those they simply espouse. For example, people may claim both "absence makes the heart grow fonder" and "out of sight out of mind", so that asking them to predict the outcome of several specific situations would tell more about their beliefs than asking directly for those beliefs.

In one set of surveys, respondents were asked which of two individuals, who were described as being identical in every way except those mentioned, felt more or less pleasure, was more or less irritated, etc. For example:

D. and J. both live close to a major highway. The noise from the highway is sufficient to be annoying to a weekend visitor, and the noise level is the same for D. and J. The section passing D.'s house was opened a year ago. The section passing J.'s house was opened last week. D. and J. are now each dining at home. Who is more annoyed by the noise?

In order to test for generality, at least three scenarios with different contexts were posed for each concept, and to test for robustness of the intuition, an alternate version of the questionnaire reversed the question, e.g. "Who is less annoyed by the noise?" (d'Arcais 1970).

Classical Conditioning and Weber's Law

In our scenarios designed to test intuitions of classical conditioning and Weber's Law, respondents generally responded consistently with those concepts. For example respondents believe a jingle associated with Saturday football games would be more liked than the same jingle associated with a disliked job (P=95%, n=43, p<.00001), and that a person with less money before the lottery would be happier at winning $100 (P=91%, n=43, p<.00001). For the Weber's Law questions respondents appear to use a number of mental accounts as the baseline for Weber's Law, rather than total wealth (see Kahneman and Tversky 1984; Thaler 1985).

Opponent Processes

Opponent process theory (Solomon 1980) states that the initial emotional response to a stimulus does not simply fade, but diminishes as the result of a counter-acting, or opponent, process. Adaptation occurs as, with repetition, the secondary process grows in size and duration so that it more effectively counteracts the initial process. In addition, as the secondary process grows and the primary process diminishes in effect, the secondary process itself becomes apparent ("rebound").

Our respondents clearly believe in adaptation of the primary process. Even for parachute jumping, the situation for which we expect our respondents to be least experienced, the expectation was for diminishing fear, the primary response, with increasing experience (P=97%, n=55, p<.00001). It is less clear whether they believe in a growing, and increasingly apparent secondary process. Our respondents thought an experienced individual would feel better or be happier in the afternoon, after morning exercise (P=74%, n=43, p<.001) or after an electric shock (P=93%, n=43, p<.00001), than would a novice. This is consistent with opponent process theory, and may well reflect belief in a specific opponent process for exercise, since release of endorphins with exercise has been a popular topic in general interest magazines. For electric shock this result is more surprising, and while it may reflect a belief in a secondary process, it may also reflect a belief that the novice is still suffering pain, or some other lingering primary response, to the shock. We are inclined to believe the later, since for a variety of other scenarios, including cold showers, hot saunas, and one version of the parachute scenario, respondents were evenly split over which character would be in a better mood later in the day. In a third version of the parachute question a majority of respondents *disagreed* with opponent process theory (P=90%, n=74, p<.00001).

Adaptation

Coombs and Avrunin (1977) suggest that we adapt to desirable outcomes, but that "bads escalate." Gibbs (1992) also found that subjects expected sensitization to a repeated aversive gustatory stimulus that they expected to actually taste. However, our survey results for scenarios involving a diminishing primary opponent process suggest that subjects expected adaptation even for unpleasant experiences. We were curious about the generality of beliefs in adaptation, and explored beliefs in adaptation further, especially in the realm of negative experiences. Our scenarios were inspired by research on adaptation to noise (Weinstein 1982), ice water (Hilgard et al. 1974), a low salt diet (Beauchamps, Bertino and Engelman 1983) and life as a lottery winner or paraplegic (Brickman, Coates, and Janoff-Bulman 1978). We were able to create scenarios for which people believed sensitization rather than adaptation to noise occurs, but generally people believed in more adaptation to noise, especially highway noise, than research suggests actually occurs. For example, even with a highway as close as 30 feet from one's window, 98% of respondents expressed a belief in adaptation (n=43, p<.00001). Weinstein (1982), whose subjects also expected adaptation, found that those subjects did not in fact adapt to highway noise. Our respondents were quite divided regarding whether one adapts to a low salt or low sugar diet, and were swayed one direction or the other by relatively small changes in the way the scenario or the question was worded. They did not know whether one adapts while having one's hand in ice water (one doesn't; put your hand in a bucket of ice water and see). However, they did not believe one adapts to life as a lottery winner or paraplegic (P=25% and 22%, n=74, p<.00001 for each). For more on beliefs about adaptation to extreme and/or bad events see Snell, Gibbs, and Varey (forthcoming) and Varey and Kahneman (1992). In summary,

though it is possible to describe situations in which people do not believe adaptation will occur, it seems that adaptation is a very broadly applied intuitive concept, and that people do not have a very clear sense of it's boundary conditions[1].

Exposure

It has been suggested that simple exposure, in and of itself, to a stimulus that is initially both novel and neutral, results in increasing liking. Zajonc (1968) labeled this effect "mere exposure". Most respondents appear to believe that liking increases with exposure for some stimuli or under some conditions, but not for others. Most responses for scenarios involving language or music were consistent with a mere exposure effect, e.g. for a scenario involving exposure to Thai music, 88% answered consistently with mere exposure theory (n=43, p< .00001) However, responses to questions involving abstract logos varied depending on the wording of the scenario or the question. Though some respondents may hold a generalized concept similar to mere exposure we speculate that other beliefs are at work here, perhaps involving inferences about learning, particularly for stimuli others are known to like (Schindler, Holbrook, and Greenleaf 1989).

Cognitive Dissonance

Cognitive Dissonance is the concept we feel most confident in asserting respondents did not use. The theory of cognitive dissonance (Festinger 1957) holds that inconsistency among cognitive elements (knowledge about one's world and self) creates a drive-like state of dissonance, which people are motivated to reduce. To accomplish this reduction, cognitive elements are modified to become more internally consistent. The standard method of operationalizing cognitive dissonance in the psychological literature is to manipulate justification, and our scenarios compared an individual who was paid or received course credit with one who did not. Respondents were evenly divided in their beliefs regarding whether a person being paid would be hungrier in a fast, or like to eat grasshoppers more, than a person not being paid. A majority did agree that (P=67%, n=41, p<.01) a student writing an essay justifying terrorism would be more likely to justify terrorism to friends outside of class if she or he did not receive a grade for the paper. Even this agreement was not robust, however: respondents were evenly divided in their beliefs on another version of the questionnaire which turned the question around to ask about which character was *less* likely to explain the terrorists point of view outside of class.

Summary

In summary, our respondents showed a consistent and robust use of concepts similar to classical conditioning and Weber's Law, and they probably use the concept of adaptation rather more liberally than is justified by experimental evidence, though in a few cases they don't apply it when probably they should. They probably do not believe in concepts of opponent processes and mere exposure, at least not as they are proposed in the academic literature. They do not use a concept of cognitive dissonance as it is defined by academics.

DISCUSSION

How do people predict their own liking in the future? We speculate that people may use current liking as a starting point, or anchor, and adjust the starting point according to relevant theories

---

[1]We might add that, after reviewing the literature, it is not clear to us whether researchers understand the boundaries either.

they hold about changes due to time, experience, or the situation. Other anchoring and adjustment studies have shown that people have difficulty accurately modifying the starting point (Tversky and Kahneman 1974; Wilson and Brekke 1994). Evidence consistent with a model of anchoring on current likes has also been found by Snell (1994) for self-prediction of liking. She shows that predictions for future liking of whole categories of foods can be influenced by satiation or temptation for a particular food in the same or a similar category, and that predictions for liking movies can be influenced by mood relevant, but product irrelevant, television ads.

How people predict their own future likes or tastes is an issue that deserves further study. If, as these preliminary studies suggest, people make predictable misjudgments, have ill formed theories of change, or don't understand when the theories apply, there may be much that we as academics or marketers could do to help. For example, it is likely that people would be more willing to change their diets if they fully believed they would shortly come to enjoy the new diet as much as their current one. On the other hand, there might be much greater neighborhood resistance to freeway construction if there were less expectation of adaptation to the noise.

REFERENCES

Beauchamp, Gary K., Mary Bertino, and Karl Engelman (1983), "Modification of Salt Taste," *Annals of Internal Medicine*, 98, 763-769.

Brickman, Phillip, Dan Coates, and Ronnie Janoff-Bulman (1978), "Lottery Winners and Accident Victims: Is Happiness Relative?" *Journal of Personality and Social Psychology*, 36, 917-927.

Coombs, Clyde H. and George S. Avrunin (1977), "Single Peaked Functions and the Theory of Preference," *Psychological Review*, 84, 216-230.

d'Arcais, Giovanni B. F. (1970), "Linguistic Structure and Focus of Comparison in Processing Comparative Sentences," in *Advances in Psycholinguistics* eds. Giovanni B. F. d'Arcais, et al. London: North-Holland, 307-321.

diSessa, Andrea A. (1983), "Phenomenology and the Evolution of Intuition," in *Mental Models*, eds. Dedre Gentner and Albert L. Stevens, Hillsdale, N.J.: Lawrence Erlbaum, 15-33.

diSessa, Andrea A. (1985), *Knowledge in Pieces*, address to the Fifteenth Annual Symposium of the Jean Piaget Society, Philadelphia, June.

Festinger, Leon (1957), *A Theory of Cognitive Dissonance*, Stanford, CA: Stanford University Press.

Gibbs, Brian J. (1992), *The Self-Manipulation of Tastes: Experiments on Expedient Utility*. Unpublished doctoral dissertation, Graduate School of Business, University of Chicago, 1101 E. 58th St., Chicago, IL, 60637.

Hilgard, Ernest, John C. Ruch, Arthur F. Lange, John R. Lenox, Arlene H. Morgan, and Lewis B. Sachs (1974), "The Psychophysics of Cold Pressor Pain and Its Modification through Hypnotic Suggestion," *American Journal of Psychology*, 87, 17-31.

Kahneman, Daniel and Jackie Snell (1992), "Predicting a Changing Taste: Do People Know What They Will Like?" *Journal of Behavioral Decision Making*, 5, 187-200.

Kahneman, Daniel and Amos Tversky (1984), "Choices, Values, and Frames," *American Psychologist*, 39, 341-350.

March, James (1978), "Bounded Rationality, Ambiguity, and the Engineering of Choice," *Bell Journal of Economics*, 9, 587-608.

McCloskey, Michael (1983), "Naive Theories of Motion," in *Mental Models* eds. Dedre Gentner and Albert L. Stevens, Hillsdale, N.J.: Lawrence Erlbaum, pp. 15-33.

Schindler, Robert M., Morris B. Holbrook and Eric A. Greenleaf (1989), "Using Connoisseurs to Predict Mass Tastes," *Marketing Letters*, 1, 47-54.

Snell, Jackie (1994), "Influencing Predictions of Taste: Do People Know what They Will Like?" Working Paper, Marketing Department, San Jose State University, San Jose, CA 95192-0069

Snell, Jackie, Brian J. Gibbs, and Carol Varey (forthcoming), "Intuitive Hedonics: Consumer Beliefs about the Dynamics of Liking," *Journal of Consumer Psychology*.

Solomon, Richard L. (1980), "The Opponent-Process Theory of Acquired Motivation: The Costs of Pleasure and the Benefits of Pain," *American Psychologist*, 35 (August), 691-712.

Thaler, Richard (1985), "Mental Accounting and Consumer Choice," *Marketing Science*, 4, 199-214.

Tversky, Amos, and Daniel Kahneman, (1974), "Judgment under Uncertainty: Heuristics and biases," *Science*, 185, 1124-1131.

Varey, Carol and Daniel Kahneman (1992), "Experiences Extended Across Time: Evaluation of Moments and Episodes," *Journal of Behavioral Decision Making*, 5, 169-185.

Weinstein, Neil D. (1982), "Community Noise Problems: Evidence Against Adaptation," *Journal of Environmental Psychology*, 2, 87-97.

Wilson, Timothy D. and Nancy Brekke (1994), "Mental Contamination and Mental Correction: Unwanted Influences on Judgments and Evaluations," *Psychological Bulletin*, 116, 117-142.

Zajonc, Robert B. (1968), "Attitudinal Effects of Mere Exposure," *Journal of Personality and Social Psychology Monograph Supplement*, 9 (#2 part 2).

Consumption Visions in Consumer Decision Making

Diane M. Phillips, Pennsylvania State University
Jerry C. Olson, Pennsylvania State University
Hans Baumgartner, Pennsylvania State University

ABSTRACT

We propose that consumers sometimes form mental images of future consumption situations and that these consumption visions influence their decision-making. A consumption vision is "a visual image of certain product-related behaviors and their consequences... (they consist of) concrete and vivid mental images that enable consumers to vicariously experience the self-relevant consequences of product use" (Walker and Olson 1994, pp. 27, 31). We describe some of the likely characteristics of consumption visions, propose several factors that may influence the formation of consumption visions, and discuss how consumer researchers can integrate consumption visions into decision-making research.

CONSUMPTION VISIONS AND CONSUMER DECISION MAKING

A 29-year-old bride-to-be is planning her wedding. She is trying to decide which of several options would be most appropriate—the country western wedding complete with cowboy boots and bluegrass band, the formal candlelight wedding with black tuxedos and caviar, or the garden wedding with climbing roses, fluffy pastries and a string quartet.

A 22-year-old woman is planning to take a vacation to celebrate her completion of college. The options under consideration are: touring Europe, relaxing on the beach of a tropical island, or hiking at a mountain retreat.

A 45-year-old male attorney is selecting a new sweater to wear skiing. He wants something sophisticated and elegant, yet sporty and functional.

According to traditional models of consumer decision-making (Bettman, Johnson and Payne 1991), these individuals will identify the relevant attributes of each option, evaluate the various attributes, and select the wedding, vacation, or sweater with the highest overall utility, based on a combination of their judgments about attribute values and importances. We contend that this process is not likely to occur in all decision-making situations. Traditional models of decision-making have worked fairly well for familiar, well-structured, and rational choices. However, these models may not describe how consumers make other types of decisions for which they have little experience, or where the problem is less well-defined, or where emotional considerations play an important role. When faced with such decisions, we propose that consumers form consumption visions to help them select an appropriate alternative.

WHAT ARE CONSUMPTION VISIONS?

A consumption vision is "a visual image of certain product-related behaviors and their consequences ... (they consist of) concrete and vivid mental images that enable consumers to vicariously experience the self-relevant consequences of product use" (Walker and Olson 1994, pp. 27, 31). For instance, the bride-to-be faces a difficult decision task in planning her wedding. She may have considerable uncertainty about the desirability of various choice alternatives. To help make this decision, she might create several consumption visions of possible weddings—the country western wedding, the formal candlelight wedding, or the garden wedding. Within each of these simulated consumption situations, the bride can imagine herself consuming various products and experiencing the consequences of this consumption with her friends and family. By imagining the likely outcomes, she is able to identify the salient characteristics of each decision alternative and develop beliefs about their outcomes. Also, she can experience affective reactions to the outcomes she imagines. In this way, the consumption vision allows her to form the cognitive and affective basis for her preferences. By constructing several consumption visions, she may be able to develop a preference for one of the wedding alternatives, for example, and the various products and services associated with that choice.

We believe consumers also form consumption visions when making purchase decisions less important than a wedding. For instance, the attorney might imagine wearing the new sweater while skiing or while eating in a resort restaurant. His decision to buy one sweater over another partly depends on the beliefs formed during such consumption visions and the affective reactions elicited by these anticipatory experiences.

The purpose of this paper is to discuss the concept of consumption visions and to explore its implications for consumer decision-making. We specify some of the conceptual characteristics of consumption visions, identify several factors which are likely to influence consumption visions, and describe some of the consequences of consumption visions. Because little work to date has examined consumption visions, much of our discussion is speculative. Our goal is to stimulate interest and future research in the phenomenon, not to present a fully-developed theory of consumption visions. To explore how people actually use consumption visions, we conducted unstructured, depth interviews with eight college students. These people described consumption visions they have had, discussed instances in which they did and did not use consumption visions, and speculated about how they typically use consumption visions in their decision making. To illustrate our discussion of consumption visions, we present verbatim excerpts from these interviews throughout the paper.

CHARACTERISTICS OF CONSUMPTION VISIONS

Although little direct research has been conducted on consumption visions, we can speculate about some of the likely characteristics of consumption visions that set them apart from other decision-making concepts. These include possible selves, narrative form, visual imagery, affective reactions, and goal representation.

Possible Selves

Consumers create consumption visions by projecting a "possible self" into a future consumption situation. Possible selves can represent what we would ideally like to be, what we probably will be, or what we are afraid of becoming (Markus and Nurius 1986). The depiction of a possible self in a consumption vision functions not only as a positive or negative incentive for future behavior, it also provides a standard for interpreting self-relevant consumption experiences.

Advances in Consumer Research
Volume 22, © 1995

Interestingly, subjects in our study described only consumption visions involving *positive* possible selves—for example, optimistic visions of being a wealthy business tycoon and more realistic visions of being a successful entrepreneur. One subject revealed a reason why people might have few consumption visions with negative possible selves:

"But there's no problem in my visions ... there are no problems for some reason ... I see mistakes and I change them right away. It's always perfect."

Narrative Form

We suggest that many consumption visions have a narrative form. That is, consumption visions have a character (the consumer's possible self), a plot (a series of events in which the character enacts behaviors and reacts to events) and a setting (an environment or context in which the action occurs). From a narrative perspective, consumption visions are "stories" created by the decision-making consumer. In constructing consumption visions, consumers project themselves into simulated consumption situations and observe the imaginary actions of the possible self in this context. The story-teller consumer also observes how the story "plays out," paying particular attention to the consequences that occur. The goals, motives and values associated with the projected possible self, combined with the features and context of the imaginary consumption situation, are the two main ingredients necessary for a consumption vision. We expect these narrative consumption visions to vary in complexity and elaboration. Some consumption narratives can be quite elaborate, much like a miniature play or movie, while others may have a simple form, similar to a sequence of static images or frames in a comic strip.

Consumers can construct (and view) a consumption vision narrative from different perspectives of the self (Nigro and Neisser 1983). Sometimes, consumers may see themselves from the "internal" perspective as if they were actually performing the actions themselves. Sometimes, they may experience a consumption vision from an "outside" perspective, as if they were observing the self performing the behaviors. For example, one subject contrasted these two perspectives in her consumption visions for an apartment and a new car:

"When I'm in the apartment, I see me ... I can see myself going to the apartment, going to the cabinet. I'll have everything in order ... I can see myself reaching for this and doing it and I'll know where it is and pouring whatever I have (a cup of coffee or tea) and going back and sitting on my couch ... and turning on the TV and I can see myself doing that."

"When I'm in the car, I see a body that looks like me ... I don't see myself in the car, holding the steering wheel, turning, making a left, looking out the mirrors, stuff like that ... I just see a body in there that looks like me going to work and coming back."

The internal perspective seems much more personal and realistic than the outside perspective. In our preliminary data, internal perspectives were reported in consumption visions of new apartments, new computers, and new suits, while outside perspectives were reported for exotic vacations, new sports cars, and dream houses. Perhaps consumers tend to use the internal perspective when viewing consumption visions involving their actual or current self, and tend to use the outside perspective when viewing consumption visions involving a possible or ideal self.

Visual Imagery

We suggest that consumers experience consumption visions as a series of visual images. Sometimes these images seem to be quite vivid, almost as if a tiny projector is presenting the action to the consumer's mind's eye. During the interviews, several subjects moved their hands and pointed while describing the placement of different objects in their consumption vision and to help illustrate to the interviewer "what it looks like." Apparently, one subject could "see" a detailed consumption vision of a new apartment and how the living room furniture would be positioned, as she moved her hands to describe that vision for the interviewer:

"You know, with a couch on one side, a couch on the other, and the TV right on the other wall, so that there would be three walls. Then maybe if I had a table or something, I'd put it on the other wall so that would kind of divide the living room and the dining room ... and then like a table in the middle of the two couches so that you could lay things on it or sit things on it. And a light, the lamps ... I'd have two end tables on each side of the couches; then I'd have the lamps there."

Although some consumption visions can be quite vivid, there are marked differences in level of elaboration and complexity. For example, one subject described his consumption vision for a new computer in simple terms with little visual imagery:

"Finances, budgeting, communicating with all kinds of different people. And a personal diary ... always updating my account and expenses for myself and the house and ... but, I don't know ... its just something I know I need someday. Its not a big issue. I just know I need it for business."

Other consumers seem to have very clear and detailed images of the different components of their consumption vision. For instance, after giving a detailed description of a consumption vision about vacationing on a tropical island, one subject gave a detailed description of a trip to an open-air market:

"There's a big market and everybody's walking with their own baskets to buy things fresh. I'd go to the seafood merchant and buy lobsters and oysters and crabs and then go to the fruit stand and get all these fresh vegetables and fruits like pine-apples and papayas and mangoes and strawberries (laughs). No meat really, just a lot of fish and seafood and fresh vegetables. And for some reason, Italian bread. I don't know why (laughs). Italian bread makes no sense, but Italian bread. And its just really busy. There are a lot of people and they're all screaming and yelling in their native language and me and my boyfriend are very fascinated and we just buy our stuff and walk around and we find that the people are really nice. If we don't know what something is, they explain it to us and if they have samples, they let us try it. And just carry on regular conversations with them about things. And I'd buy a lot of jewelry, beads and stuff."

The presence of vivid (Taylor and Thompson 1982) or complex (Markus and Nurius 1986) visual images in a consumption vision may have important decision-making implications. Vivid and complex consumption visions would contain numerous, visually elaborate images of the self performing a consumption activity. This type of depiction might motivate consumers to work harder to achieve these visions. However, these concrete and vivid images may also decrease consumers' openness to alternative consumption experiences and might contribute to dissatisfaction if actual experiences deviate from expectations.

Affective Reactions

We expect consumption visions to vary in their potential to elicit affective responses. Several subjects became obviously excited when describing their consumption visions—they became animated and tended to laugh and smile a lot. Some subjects reported it felt good to think about their consumption visions. This is consistent with previous research which found that people reported higher levels of positive affect when thinking about their life goals or when enacting behaviors to help them achieve their life goals (Emmons 1986). Consumers know it feels good to think of certain potential future situations. In fact, in some cases consumers may construct consumption visions as a temporary escape from stress, as a break from monotony, or as a quick "pick-me-up." For instance, one subject reported forming consumption visions:

"... usually when I'm very stressed or something. Or, I just can't take my environment any more so I just drift off and just see myself in this very happy state ... it makes me feel much better about myself afterwards. It kind of like relieves stress; it makes me relax. It makes me feel like there is something in the future to look forward to. Maybe this will actually happen to me sometime in the future."

Prior research has demonstrated the importance of hedonic motives in consumer behavior (Campbell 1989; Holbrook and Hirschman 1982). Apparently, consumers not only create consumption visions to help make decisions, they also purposely construct consumption visions to escape from the mundane aspects of life.

Goal Representation

By constructing consumption visions, consumers can form more tangible representations of their abstract goals, motives, and values. Consumption visions may represent realistic goals, or they may represent ideal goals that a consumer hopes to achieve someday. One subject described consumption visions as, "I can see it; it's something that I would like to aim for," whereas another said, "it is the ideal that you need to work toward." Previous literature has found evidence of both realistic and ideal visions of the future (Markus and Nurius 1986; Markus and Ruvolo 1989). Examples of realistic consumption visions from the interviews include wearing a new suit, using a new computer, and having a romantic dinner. Examples of ideal goals include owning a cruise line, living in a house like on the TV show Dallas, or driving a Mercedes Benz.

Consumption visions also give consumers a better idea of which actions are most likely to attain important goals. Further, consumption visions seem to provide motivation for consumers to work to attain the goals they create. One subject indicated that after forming a consumption vision, he allocated mental and financial resources to try to obtain the vision. Another individual described how she tried to achieve a match between her consumption vision and actual consumption:

"I know I'm going to...rent an apartment, so I start thinking ok, I want all this stuff in the apartment. Then that's what I go for. So like, you have this vision and you want to match that vision and you want to go and purchase those things that are in your vision. And along the way it might change, but more likely than not, you're going to keep most of what that vision is."

INFLUENCES ON CONSUMPTION VISIONS

A wide variety of factors may influence how and when consumers form consumption visions. We discuss three categories of factors that seem likely to affect consumption visions—the degree of personal relevance of, or consumers' involvement in, the purchase decision; individual differences such as previous experience and ability and/or preference to process information visually; and situational factors.

Personal Relevance or Involvement

Consumers form a consumption vision by projecting a possible self into an anticipated consumption situation. Therefore, we expect the degree of personal relevance of, or consumers' level of involvement in, the purchase decision to have a significant impact on the formation and use of consumption visions. Involvement will be high to the extent that products relate to important values and goals. This increased self-relevance should lead to more elaborate information processing (Celsi and Olson 1988), including the construction of more vivid and complex consumption visions. One subject illustrated the importance of self-relevance in the formation of consumption visions:

"Did you ever have ... kind of like when you decorate a room, for example, in the house. Have you ever had a corner and it needs something? You don't know what. So you sit down and think about it for a while. We could put a plant there or something, you know? I think it takes time to think about what I want to do to modify the home to make it more comfortable or look better or whatever...I would put time into thinking about that."

"We bought a washer and dryer when we first moved into the apartment because it had a washer/dryer hookup, but we didn't put a whole lot of thought into it, we just ... because we needed it, you know? Because we were tired of going to the laundromat every 2 or 3 days. And they were on sale so that was when we really ... It was a big ticket item that we didn't really put a lot of thought into. Plus we had credit at the furniture store where we bought it, so that helped."

This person formed a consumption vision for the more involving decision about filling an empty corner of a room, but he did not form a consumption vision for the purchase of a less relevant, although "big ticket" appliance. This example suggests that a high price does not always create the necessary involvement to generate a consumption vision. We suggest that consumers must perceive the consumption of a product to be at least somewhat relevant to the self before they are motivated to construct a consumption vision.

Individual Differences

We expect some consumers to be more likely than others to form consumption visions. Many individual differences, including demographics (gender, age, etc.) and trait variables (need for cognition, self-monitoring, etc.), are expected to influence whether individuals form consumption visions during decision making, how detailed these visions will be, and about which products consumption visions are formed.

Ability and/or preference to engage in visual processing of information seems to have particular potential as a predictor of the extent to which a consumer will form consumption visions. Researchers have developed several scales for measuring individual differences in imagery processing—one example is the Style of Processing scale of Childers, Houston, and Heckler (1985)—and we expect such individual differences in processing style to affect the incidence of using consumption visions for decision making.

Interestingly, one subject explicitly speculated about such individual differences in forming consumption visions:

"I think it depends on the person. It depends on their imagination. I know people who can't imagine themselves doing anything except what they're doing at the present..."

Situational Factors

A variety of stimuli in the immediate context are likely to influence the formation of a consumption vision. For example, information in an advertisement could encourage consumers to construct consumption visions. Stimuli such as an evocative picture, the use of concrete, imagery-eliciting words, or an explicit request to imagine a consumption situation may lead consumers to visualize future consumption situations (Lutz and Lutz 1978; MacInnis and Price 1987; Phillips 1994).

As another example, financial limitations might influence the construction of consumption visions—perhaps consumers are more likely to form consumption visions about choice alternatives they can reasonably afford to buy. In addition, as consumers get closer to the time of purchase, they may be more likely to create consumption visions. For instance, one subject described her consumption vision about an impending trip to Australia:

"My main vision right now is Australia because that's the next big thing in my life. So I envision that quite a bit. And I know in the Fall as it gets closer, I'm going to be envisioning it even more and as it gets to December, I'm going to be envisioning it a lot."

Note that by envisioning the people, the weather, and the tours she might encounter, this person could better prepare herself for actual consumption by bringing things she might need.

CONSEQUENCES OF CONSUMPTION VISIONS

In this section, we discuss several consequences of consumption visions for consumer decision making. We also briefly discuss some other outcomes of consumption visions.

Decision Making

Most traditional models of consumer decision making assume consumers integrate present-day beliefs and evaluations about product attributes to form attitudes toward purchasing a product. Few models of decision making discuss how consumers come to have these beliefs and evaluations. Very often, consumers must make decisions about choice alternatives for which they have little or no direct personal experience. For such decisions, consumers are likely to have few beliefs about product attributes or the personal consequences of product use upon which to base their decision.

We suggest that forming a consumption vision is one possible heuristic by which a consumer can decide among alternative courses of action. We discuss the possible effects of consumption visions on consumers' cognitive and affective reactions to products, intentions and behavior, and post-purchase evaluations.

Cognitive and affective reactions. The decision-making self may construct consumption visions to think about the attributes that characterize the product, to imagine the consequences resulting from using the product, and to predict the likelihood that consumption of the product will lead to the satisfaction of important values and goals. By mentally simulating a consumption event, a consumer can gain greater clarity about how product attributes relate to

the self via the consequences of product use. In addition, affective reactions to the imagined consumption experiences can influence the decision process. For example, Schwarz (1990) has suggested that people may ask themselves, "How do I feel about it?," and use these feelings to render a judgment. In sum, by visualizing future product use occasions in a consumption vision, consumers can form beliefs about their likely satisfaction with the product and imagine their affective reactions to these consumption experiences. They can use these cognitive and affective reactions to make more informed purchase decisions.

Intentions and Behavior. Research has shown that the mere act of imagining oneself performing certain behaviors can lead to changes in behavioral intentions to engage in these behaviors (e.g., Anderson 1983). In addition, visualizing a future event can enhance the performance of the actual behavior. For example, Gregory, Cialdini, and Carpenter (1982) showed that people who imagined themselves using and enjoying cable television subsequently subscribed to a cable TV service at a significantly higher rate than control subjects who were only told of the benefits of cable TV. These findings imply that the formation of consumption visions involving the self can increase consumers' intentions to follow a course of action and that consumption imagery may have a self-fulfilling effect on actual behavior.

Post-Purchase Evaluations. We might expect consumers to retrieve consumption visions after purchase to see how well actual use of the product corresponded with the imagined use of the product. Curiously, at least in our preliminary data, subjects did not report consulting their consumption visions after purchase. For instance, two subjects described what happened to the consumption vision for a new car and a new computer after purchase:

"I did all those things I envisioned I was going to do. After that, I don't remember doing anything else or thinking anything else, besides, 'I have a car' and that was it."

"With the computer, you're...always still consuming it. I don't know if there's a whole lot of re-evaluating, unless something goes wrong with it. So far, I'm pretty satisfied."

These examples are congruent with previous literature (Kahneman and Tversky 1982) that finds people tend to engage in complex mental manipulations only when something goes wrong. Thus, it would seem that consumption visions are likely to be reactivated and reconsidered only if the actual consumption experience is highly discrepant with expectations.

Other Outcomes

Aside from their use in decision making, consumption visions can also serve other purposes such as mood management or self-construction. Although many subjects reported experiencing positive affect when imagining positive outcomes of product use, other subjects mentioned using consumption visions for purely hedonic reasons. It simply feels good to imagine yourself in a happy future where certain goals have been fulfilled. With no intention of making a judgment about a specific consumption alternative, consumers may purposely evoke consumption visions to escape from the pressures of daily life and fantasize and daydream about positive possible selves and pleasurable consumption situations.

In addition to mood enhancement, consumption visions may also be used for self-construction. For example, the manner in which possible selves are depicted in consumption visions can help consumers define their roles in modern society. People's lives have become increasingly complex due to the demands of the multiple social roles of present-day life (Gergen 1991). Indeed, in one day an individual might enact the roles of spouse, parent, neighbor, doctor, and amateur musician, among others. Making purchase decisions in the context of these multiple roles/selves is complex and difficult. By constructing consumption visions based on the various perspectives, the consumer may be able to clarify the consumption situation and make more appropriate choices.

SUMMARY

There is currently a mismatch between our traditional models of consumer decision-making and the way consumers actually make decisions, at least for certain product choices. Multi-attribute models have been successful in modeling how consumers make decisions about mundane, frequently purchased products, where the problem is well-defined and decision making proceeds rationally. But these models cannot account for decisions in which less experience is available, where the problem is not well-structured, and where emotional reactions are important.

Whereas traditional models assume verbal and semantic processing, the consumption vision perspective focuses on visual and imaginal processing. The consumption vision approach explicitly acknowledges creative sense-making processes consumers use to anticipate the future. Consumption visions help consumers anticipate and make plans to navigate an uncertain future by providing concrete, vivid images of the self interacting with a product and experiencing the consequences of product use. Consumption visions allow consumers to vicariously participate in product consumption prior to purchase. By forming different consumption visions, consumers can mentally "try out" different choice alternatives and select the one that provides the greatest pleasure during consumption and leads to the satisfaction of important values and goals.

REFERENCES

Anderson, Craig A. (1983), "Imagination and Expectation: The Effect of Imagining Behavioral Scripts on Personal Intentions," *Journal of Personality and Social Psychology*, 45 (2), 293-305.

Bettman, James R., Eric J. Johnson, and John W. Payne (1991), "Consumer Decision Making," in *Handbook of Consumer Behavior*, eds. T.S. Robertson and H.H. Kassarjian, Englewood Cliffs, NJ: Prentice-Hall, 50-84.

Campbell, Colin (1989), *The Romantic Ethic and the Spirit of Modern Consumerism*, New York, NY: Basil Blackwell Inc.

Carroll, John S. (1978), "The Effect of Imagining an Event on Expectations for the Event: An Interpretation in Terms of the Availability Heuristic," *Journal of Experimental Social Psychology*, 14, 88-96.

Childers, Terry L., Michael J. Houston, and Susan E. Heckler (1985), "Measurement of Individual Differences in Visual Versus Verbal Information Processing," *Journal of Consumer Research*, 12 (September), 125-134.

Celsi, Richard L. and Jerry C. Olson (1988), "The Role of Involvement in Attention and Comprehension Processes," *Journal of Consumer Research*, 15 (September), 210-224.

Emmons, Robert A. (1986), "Personal Strivings: An Approach to Personality and Subjective Well-Being," *Journal of Personality and Social Psychology*, 51 (5), 1058-1068.

Gergen, Kenneth J. (1991), *The Saturated Self: Dilemmas of Identity in Contemporary Life*, New York, NY: Basic Books.

Gregory, W. Larry, Robert B. Cialdini, and Kathleen M. Carpenter (1982), "Self-Relevant Scenarios as Mediators of Likelihood Estimates and Compliance: Does Imagining Make It So?," *Journal of Personality and Social Psychology*, 43 (1), 89-99.

Holbrook, Morris B. and Elizabeth C. Hirschman (1982), "The Experiential Aspects of Consumption: Consumer Fantasies, Feelings, and Fun," *Journal of Consumer Research*, 9 (September), 132-140.

Kahneman, Daniel and Amos Tversky (1982), "The Simulation Heuristic" in *Judgment Under Uncertainty: Heuristics and Biases*, ed. D. Kahneman, P. Slovic, and A. Tversky, New York, NY: Cambridge University Press, 201-208

Markus, Hazel and Paula Nurius (1986), "Possible Selves," *American Psychologist*, 41 (9), 954-969.

Markus, Hazel and Ann Ruvolo (1989), "Possible Selves: Personalized Representations of Goals" in *Goal Concepts in Personality and Social Psychology*, ed. Lawrence A. Pervin. Hillsdale, NJ: Lawrence Erlbaum Associates, 211-241.

MacInnis, Deborah J. and Linda L. Price (1987), "The Role of Imagery in Information Processing: Review and Extensions," *Journal of Consumer Research*, 13 (March), 473-491.

Nigro, Georgia and Ulric Neisser (1983), "Point of View in Personal Memories," *Cognitive Psychology*, 15, 467-482.

Phillips, Diane M. (1994), "Anticipating the Future: Antecedents and Consequences of Consumption Vision Construction," working paper, The Pennsylvania State University, University Park, PA 16802.

Schwarz, Norbert (1990), "Feelings as Information: Informational and Motivational Functions of Affective States," in: *Handbook of Motivation and Cognition: Foundations of Social Behavior*, Vol. 2, eds. E. Tory Higgins and Richard M. Sorrentino, New York: Guilford, 527-561.

Taylor, Shelley E. and Suzanne C. Thompson (1982), "Stalking the Elusive 'Vividness' Effect," *Psychological Review*, 89 (2), 155-181.

Walker, Beth A. and Jerry C. Olson (1994), "The Activated Self in Consumer Behavior: A Cognitive Structure Perspective," working paper, The Pennsylvania State University, University Park, PA 16802.

The Relationship Between Context and Variety

Susan M. Broniarczyk, University of Texas at Austin
Leigh McAlister, University of Texas at Austin

Although there is a large body of consumer research on variety, it has focused on modeling varied behavior in consumer choice. The typical study infers variety-seeking behavior from brand switches in a consumer's purchase pattern in a product category. Empirical examination of scanner data has identified product categories in which variety-seeking occurs and the market structure implications for brand-switching. The purpose of this session was to move variety research the next step and examine actions that a manager can take to affect variety. The intent was to shed insight on the driving forces of consumer variety-seeking that existing models have taken as given. Specifically, the session addressed how changes in context affect consumer variety-seeking behavior and consumer assortment perceptions.

All three papers examined the effects of context on consumer variety, but examined different contexts and different measures of variety. The contexts examined ranged from the diversity offered in other product categories to category-specific characteristics such as sensory features and shelf display organization. The different measures of variety included consumer choice data, protocols for switching motivation, and perceptions of assortment offered within the category.

The first paper by Menon and Kahn discussed three experiments that tested the effect of the external context on variety chosen. The paper discussed how if the external consumption or purchase context is stimulating, it satisfies a consumer's internal need for stimulation, and thus reduces variety-seeking within a product category. For instance, consumers at a fast food restaurant may exhibit less variety in their hamburger choices if they have high variety in their accompanying soft drink choices. Overall, their results showed that variation across product categories or across consumption locations can reduce variety-seeking in a product category.

Van Trijp, Hoyer, and Inman presented a paper that examined the interactions between an individual's internal need for variety and product-specific factors in the external context on variety-seeking behavior. Using a Dutch household panel that provided underlying motives for brand switching, they distinguished between intrinsically and extrinsically motivated variety-seeking. Factors in the choice context such as product-level involvement, product differentiation, and sensory features of the product category were shown to extrinsically motivate variation in choice behavior. Furthermore, these product-specific factors interacted with individual factors on variety-seeking behavior.

The third paper by Broniarczyk and McAlister examined a different dimension of variety, namely consumer perceptions of the assortment offered by a retailer within a product category. Although consumer perceptions of assortment are an important determinant of store choice, this aspect of variety has not previously been examined in consumer research. An experiment examined the context effect of shelf display organization on consumer perceptions of assortment. Results showed that consumers had higher assortment perceptions when the shelf was organized congruent to their mental representation of the product category.

Wes Hutchinson served as the discussant and related the theme of the session, context effects in consumer variety decisions, to the broader framework of the role of focal information in the environment on consumer decision-making. This area has been relatively untapped area in variety research and has important implications for understanding consumer motivations for brand-switching and the actions managers can implement to modify consumer variety

The Effect of the Perception of Process Technology and Country-of-Manufacture (COM) Favorableness On Consumers' Overall Brand Evaluation

Dong-Jin Lee, Virginia Polytechnic Institute and State University
David Brinberg, Virginia Polytechnic Institute and State University

ABSTRACT

The objective of this paper is to examine the effect of the perception of process technology (hand-made vs. machine-made) and country-of-manufacture (COM) favorableness on consumers' evaluation of brands. Drawing from foreign direct investment (FDI) theory and country-of-origin literature, it is hypothesized that the effect of the perception of process technology would be greater in favorable COMs than in unfavorable COMs. This is due to the possibility that the derogation of brand evaluation would be greater for the hand-made brands than the machine-made brands as COM favorableness decreases. It was also hypothesized that the predictability of purchase intention from overall brand evaluation would be higher in the within-subjects design than in the between-subjects design because the addition of alternative attitudes in the within-subjects design can increase behavior predictions.

Results show that brand evaluation is a direct function of the perception of process technology and COM favorableness. Also, results show that, in the within-subjects design, the effect of perception of process technology on brand evaluation is significant under favorable COMs, but insignificant under unfavorable COMs. However, this result is not supported in the between-subjects design. In addition, the predictability of purchase intention from overall brand evaluation was higher in the within-subjects design than in the between-subjects design.

INTRODUCTION

The globalization of the marketplace has allowed the intertwining of international operations. Reflecting this trend, many of the products available in the market place have dual citizenship (Business Week 1991). Those products that are manufactured in one country and branded by a firm from another country are referred as "bi-national products" (Ettenson and Gaeth 1991; Chao 1993). Bi-national products are therefore associated with two countries: the Country-of-Origin (CO) and the Country-of-Manufacture (COM). The Country-of-Origin (CO) reflects the home country for a company, whereas the country-of-manufacture (COM) reflects the country where the actual manufacturing of the product takes place (Ozsomer and Cavusgil 1991; Chao 1993). The CO reflects the country that consumers infer from brand name, whereas the COM constitutes factual information regarding the final point of assembly, manifested in the made-in label.

Several studies have examined brand-COM interaction effects in relation to consumers' evaluation of bi-national brands (e.g., Johansson and Nebenzahl 1986; Han and Terpstra 1988; Wall, Liefeld, and Heslop 1991; Cordell 1992). Johansson and Nebenzahl (1986) argued that COM effects differ depending on brand image (e.g., brands with strong images are subject to less COM effect). The COM effect was found to be greater for brands with unfamiliar names than brands with familiar names (Wall, Liefeld, and Heslop 1991; Cordell 1992). This effect may occur because familiar brands have higher source credibility due to the maker's implied warranty. Therefore, when a product carries a known brand name, the impact of the COM cue on brand evaluation is diminished (Cordell 1992). Han and Terpstra (1988) have found that COM has a greater effect on brand evaluation than brand name and that COM effects are product dimension specific. For example, products dimensions

such as serviceability and workmanship are found to be more sensitive to COM than brand name stimuli.

Brands also can be classified in terms of their main process technology: hand-made brands and machine made brands (Abernathy and Utterback 1978). Many labor-intensive products (e.g., textile, shoe) still rely on the traditional hand-made skills of workers in their manufacturing process as well as the machine-made technology. These hand-made products are frequently considered for foreign manufacturing in order to utilize low labor cost in less-developed countries (Toyne and Walters 1989). If brands can be further classified in terms of their process technology (hand-made brands vs. machine-made brands), then the question remains: *Is there an interaction between the perception of process technology and COM favorableness on consumers' evaluations of brands?* This study posits that the effect of perception of process technology on brand evaluation is likely to be greater for brands with favorable COMs than brands with unfavorable COMs. This effect is posited to occur because the derogation of brand evaluation is likely to be greater for hand-made brands than for machine-made brands as COM favorableness decreases. If this interaction occurs, then manufacturers of hand-made products may need to consider more carefully foreign manufacturing decisions than manufacturers of machine-made products.

Another important aspect of a country of origin study that may effect the empirical results is the experimental design; i.e., between-subjects vs. within-subjects design (cf. Han and Terpstra 1988). In a within-subjects design, each subject is exposed to all treatments (e.g., several COMs), whereas, in a between-subjects design, each subject is exposed to one treatment only (e.g., one COM). Various factors need to be considered in choosing between the two designs (cf. Greenwald 1976; Pany and Reckers 1980; Adair, Spinner, Carlopio, and Lindsay 1983; Weber and Cook 1972; Kruglanski 1975; Shimp, Hyatt, and Snyder 1991). In a within-subjects design, respondents are aware of the range of alternatives when judging their purchase intention, whereas in a between-subjects design, purchase intention has no formal comparison of alternatives. This study posits that *predictability of purchase intention from overall brand evaluation would be higher in a within-subjects design than in a between-subjects design* because awareness of alternatives can increase behavior predictability (Wicker 1969; Triandis 1980; Davidson and Morrison 1983). By examining the design effect on the predictability of purchase intention, this study will provide researchers with a guideline in selecting an experimental design in country of origin studies.

Therefore, the purpose of this study is twofold: (1) to examine the perception of process technology and COM favorableness interaction effect in the evaluation of bi-national brands, and (2) to examine the experimental design effect (within vs. between) on predictability of purchase intention from brand evaluation.

CONCEPTUAL DEVELOPMENT

The Effect of the Perception of Process Technology on Overall Brand Evaluation

Technology refers to a set of principles and techniques useful for bringing about change toward desired ends (Taylor 1971).

Advances in Consumer Research
Volume 22, © 1995

Technology involves operations, material and equipment, and knowledge (Hunt 1970). Technology can be classified into two categories: product technology and process technology (Abernathy and Utterback 1978). Product technology refers to the ability to formulate and develop new products, whereas process technology deals with production methods. Since process technology deals with the production methods, one simple classification is hand-made process and machine-made process technology. Brands with hand-made process technology refer to those brands produced by using the workmanship or skill of workers, whereas brands with machine-made process technology refer to the brands are produced mainly using automatic assembly lines (Abernathy and Utterback 1978) .

Hand-made brands are likely to be evaluated higher than machine-made brands, ceteris paribus, since hand-made brands might imply great efforts, limited production, and exclusivity (Li and Monroe 1992). Therefore, it can be hypothesized that:

H1: Consumers' overall evaluation of a brand will be higher for hand-made brands than machine-made brands.

The Effect of COM Favorableness on Brand Evaluation

COM typically affects brand evaluation (Bilkey and Nes 1982; Morello 1984). In general, consumers' evaluation of a bi-national brand will increase as the favorableness of the COM increases (Bilkey and Nes 1982; Han 1989; Cordell 1992; Chao 1989). COM favorableness refers to consumers' beliefs about the degree to which the COM has a favorable or unfavorable image pertaining to a product it produces. COM favorableness may be related to the economic and technological development level of the country (Nagashima 1970). Therefore, we can hypothesize that:

H2: Consumers' overall evaluation of a brand will decrease as COM favorableness decreases.

The Interaction Effect of Process Technology Perception and COM Favorableness on Brand Evaluation

In an integrated approach to foreign direct investment (FDI) theory, Dunning (1980, 1981) discussed firm-specific advantages and country-specific advantages. Firm-specific advantages are mostly intangible in nature and involve technology, design, knowledge, management know-how, trademark, etc. Firm-specific advantages can be easily transferable to various locations of manufacture, usually at a minimum transfer cost. Country-specific advantages refer to the attractiveness of the country, including the market, labor (e.g., productivity and skill level of workers, workmanship), and raw materials. These country-specific attributes are inherently difficult to transfer to foreign manufacturing countries (COM).

Hand-made brands are more likely to rely on country-specific attributes (e.g. workmanship of the country's workers) which are relatively hard to transfer to foreign countries. On the other hand, machine-made brands rely on firm-specific attributes (e.g., the automatic assembly technology of the firm) that can easily be transferred to foreign manufacturing countries (Dunning 1980; Dunning 1981). Han and Terpstra (1988) also found that workmanship is a factor that is sensitive to changes in COMs. Therefore, as COM favorableness decreases, the derogation of brand evaluation is likely to be greater for hand-made brands than for machine-made brands. Thus, it can be postulated that the brand evaluation of hand-made brands are significantly higher than machine-made brands for the favorable COMs. The evaluation of hand-made brands is not likely to be significantly different from machine-made brands for unfavorable COMs. Therefore, we hypothesize that:

H3: COM favorableness moderates the perception of process technology - brand evaluation relationship. Specifically, for favorable COMs, the evaluation of a hand-made brand is significantly more positive than that of a machine-made brand. For unfavorable COMs, the evaluation of a hand-made brand is not significantly different from that of a machine-made brand.

Between-Subjects vs. Within-Subjects Experimental Design: Prediction of Purchase Intention from Brand Evaluation

In this section, we will discuss the two experimental designs in terms of their limitations and advantages, and will then compare behavioral predictability of each design.

Within-Subjects Design: The within-subject design may be susceptible to demand artifacts (Greenwald 1976; Pany and Reckers 1980; Adair, Spinner, Carlopio, and Lindsay 1983). For instance, the use of a within-subjects design is more likely to encourage subjects to form a hypothesis about the objective of the experiment and to bias their response than a between-subjects design.

Many studies, however, have challenged this notion and have concluded that demand artifacts are infrequent (Weber and Cook 1972; Kruglanski 1975; Shimp, Hyatt, and Snyder 1991), thus concern for the presence of demand artifacts should not be a reason to prefer a between-subjects design over a within-subjects design (Schepanski, Tubbs, Grimlund 1992).

Another concern in the use of a within-subjects design is related to cue salience, which can threaten the external validity of study findings (Schepanski et al 1992). Using a within-subjects design, however, can be justified if consumers are expected to evaluate multiple cues simultaneously in a real world setting (Han and Terpstra 1988; Monroe and Krishnan 1985). In other words, if the tasks and skills of everyday life are analogous to the within-subjects design, then the within-subjects design seems to be more appropriate (Anderson 1982). The within-subjects design also can improve the precision of the estimate of the treatment effects (Schepanski et al 1992).

Between-Subjects Design: The single stimulus in between-subjects design is likely to bring similar cases from the subjects' past experience to mind. This confounding of the stimulus with the context in which it is judged can weaken the power of the experiment (Schepanski et al 1992). The between-subjects design, however, can reduce the practice, sensitization, and carry-over effects for which the within-subjects design is often criticized (Greenwald 1976; Anderson 1982; Schepanski et al 1992).

Predictability of Behavioral Intention: Various factors need to be considered in choosing the between vs. within-subjects design. One important factor to be considered is the study purpose (Anderson 1982; Han and Terpstra 1988). If the purpose of the study is to predict behavior from the attitude, then the presentation of alternatives in addition to the attitude of interest can play an important role in behavior predictions (Wicker 1969; Triandis 1980; Davidson and Morrison 1983). For example, the within-subjects design provided more accurate predictions of contraceptive usage behaviors from attitudes (Davidson and Morrison 1983), since the between-subjects design may ignore important comparisons among alternatives.

This study posits that predictability of purchase intention from overall brand evaluation would be higher in the within-subjects design than in the between-subjects design because the addition of alternatives in the within-subjects design can increase the behavioral predictability (Wicker 1969; Triandis 1980; Davidson and Morrison 1983). Therefore,

TABLE 1

Selection of Brands and Countries

Products	Sweaters		Men's Shoes	
Process Technology	Hand-made	Machine-made	Hand-made	Machine-made
COM:				
Italy	Alpha Italy	Beta Italy	Kappa Italy	Zeta Italy
U.S.	Alpha U.S.	Beta U.S.	Kappa U.S.	Zeta U.S.
Philippines	Alpha Philippines	Beta Philippines	Kappa Philippines	Zeta Philippines

H4: The predictability of purchase intention from overall brand evaluation would be higher in the within-subjects design than in the between-subjects design.

METHOD

Research Design

Both a within-subjects design and a mixed mode design were employed for this study. For the mixed mode design, three COMs (Italy, U.S, Philippines) were between-subjects factors, and products (sweaters and men's shoes) and process technology (hand-made vs. machine made) were within-subjects factors. For the within-subjects design, COMs, products, and process technology were the within-subjects factors.

For each condition, subjects were presented a booklet containing descriptions of sweater and shoe brands and were asked to evaluate the assigned brands.

Subjects

Students enrolled in undergraduate marketing courses participated in this study as a partial requirement of the course. Out of the 138 students who participated in this study, 132 provided usable data (33, 33, 32 for each country condition in the between-subjects design; 34 in the within-subjects design).

Procedure

Subjects were first asked to evaluate the assigned brand after reading descriptions (intrinsic features as well as the COM information) of the assigned brand. Subjects then responded to measures of country favorableness, perception of the process technology of the brands, and demographics.

Selection of Products, Brands, and Countries

Two hypothetical brands were selected from each of two product categories: sweaters and men's shoes. The names for the sweater brands were Alpha (hand-made) and Beta (machine-made). The names for men's shoe brands were Kappa (hand-made) and Zeta (machine-made). The selection of sweater and shoe products was based on the following considerations: (1) both hand-made and machine-made process technologies are likely in the same product category (2) college students are likely to be familiar with both

products, (3) the products are important enough to college students for them to notice the COM information, (4) hypothetical brand names were used because this study focuses on brands with unfamiliar brand names, and (5) the same hypothetical Italian brands (CO) were used for all brands in order to hold the CO effect constant.

For each brand, three COMs were selected. The selected COMs were Italy (favorable), U.S. (moderate), and Philippines (unfavorable). COM favorableness for each country was measured as a manipulation check.

Reliability Analysis For Constructs

COM Favorableness: COM favorableness reflects subjects' beliefs about the degree to which each country has a favorable or unfavorable image as a manufacturing country. A 3-item 7-point semantic differential-like scales was used: unfavorable/favorable, bad/good, not developed/developed. The results of factor analysis indicated that the measure was unidimensional, and reliability analysis yielded high alpha coefficients of .95 (Italy/sweater), .95 (Italy/shoes), .93 (U.S./sweater), .96 (U.S./shoes), .95 (Philippines/sweater), and .95 (Philippines/shoes).

Perceptions of Process Technology: Perceptions of process technology reflects consumers' perceptions about the technology in the manufacturing process of the brands. A 3-item 7-point semantic differential-like scales was used: tailor-made/mass produced, hand-made/machine made, workmanship/automation. Based on the results of reliability and factor analyses, items yielded a unidimensional measure with reliability coefficients of .80 (hand-made/sweater), .88 (machine-made/sweater), .84 (hand-made/shoes), and .93 (machine-made/shoes).

Dependent Variables

Overall Brand Evaluation: A 3-item 7-point semantic differential scale was adapted from Mackenzie and Spreng (1992). The items included were bad/good, unfavorable/favorable, and poor/excellent. The measure was unidimensional with alpha coefficients of .91 (hand-made sweater), .92 (machine-made sweater), .94 (hand-made shoes), and .94 (machine-made shoes).

Purchase Intention: A 3-item 7-point semantic differential scales was used. The items included were: strongly not inclined to buy/strongly inclined to buy, most unlikely to buy/most likely to

TABLE 2
Comparisons of Hand-made vs. Machine-Made Brand Evaluation

	Between-Subjects Design			Within-Subjects Design		
-Italy						
	mean	t	p	mean	t	p
hand-sweater	5.0404	6.34	.000	5.3627	5.67	.000
machine-sweater	4.505			4.4020		
	mean	t	p	mean	t	p
hand-shoes	5.8384	5.80	.000	5.5196	6.17	.000
machine-shoes	4.8182			4.3529		
-U.S.						
	mean	t	p	mean	t	p
hand-sweater	5.2525	3.44	.002	5.0784	2.76	.009
machine-sweater	4.6869			4.5490		
	mean	t	p	mean	t	p
hand-shoes	5.4747	3.84	.000	5.0909	2.63	.013
machine-shoes	4.6768			4.5960		
-Philippines						
	mean	t	p	mean	t	p
hand-sweater	4.8542	4.36	.000	3.5490	1.47	.152
machine-sweater	4.0208			3.3039		
	mean	t	p	mean	t	p
hand-shoes	5.3125	4.08	.000	3.7559	.44	.660
machine-shoes	4.2292			3.6176		

buy, and strongly not motivated to buy/strongly motivated to buy. The measure resulted in one factor solution with alpha coefficients of .91 (hand-made sweater), .92 (machine-made sweater), .94 (hand-made shoes), and .94 (machine-made shoes).

RESULTS

Manipulation Checks

Manipulation checks were conducted for country favorableness and perception of process technology. Country favorableness was tested using ANOVA with repeated measures (country as a between-subjects factor and product as a within-subjects factor). There was a significant interaction between COM and product type (F=8.18, p=.001). This interaction can be attributed to the evaluation of Italy as a COM of sweaters (i.e., respondents evaluated Italy less favorably as a COM for sweaters than for shoes). For shoes, there was a significant difference between all three countries: Italy (6.27), U.S. (5.38), and Philippines (4.16). For sweaters, Italy (5.26) and U.S. (5.47) were significantly different than the Philippines (4.15), but Italy and U.S. were not significantly different.

Perception of process technology was tested using paired t-tests. Results show that Alpha was perceived as hand-made than Beta (t=23.93 p=.000). Also, Kappa was perceived as hand-made than Zeta (t=21.0, p=.000).

Hypothesis Testing

Process Technology Main Effect: Hypothesis one dealt with the main effect of process technology. We predicted that consumers' overall brand evaluation would be higher for hand-made brands than for machine-made brands, and in this study, consumers' overall evaluations of hand-made brands were significantly higher than those of machine-made brands. (See Table 2).

COM Favorableness Main Effect: In H2, we predicted that consumers' overall evaluation decreases as COM favorableness decreases. Analysis of variance (ANOVA) results provided support for the hypotheses for both sweaters and shoes. That is, sweater and shoes brands manufactured in Italy received significantly higher evaluations than those manufactured in U.S., and brands with U.S. COMs received significantly higher evaluations than those with Philippines COMs (F=3.92 p=.02).

Brand Prestige and Perceived Process Technology Interaction Effects: We predicted that the evaluations of hand-made brands would be higher than machine-made brands for favorable COMs, but not for unfavorable COMs (H3). Table 2 shows that, in the between-subjects design, the evaluations of hand-made brands are significantly higher than those of machine-made brands across COM favorableness conditions, thereby failing to support H3. However, in the within-subjects design, the evaluations of hand-made brands are significantly higher than those of machine-made brands only in favorable COMs. Under unfavorable COMs, the evaluations of hand-made brands do not significantly differ from those of machine-made brands, thereby supporting H3.

Within vs. Between-Subjects Design and Purchase Intention Prediction

We hypothesized that the within-subjects design would provide more accurate predictions of purchase intention from overall brand evaluation than the between-subjects design (H4). Results

TABLE 3
Predictions of Purchase Intention from Brand Evaluation and Experimental Design

	Between-Subjects		Within-Subjects
-Italy			
hand-made sweater	.2122	<	.5179*
machine-made sweater	.2833	<	.7329*
hand-made shoes	.3773*	<	.5041*
machine-made shoes	.3571	<	.6548*
-U.S.			
hand-made sweater	.6769*	>	.5167*
machine-made sweater	.6299*	<	.7064*
hand-made shoes	.7181*	>	.6104*
machine-made shoes	.7277*	<	.8063*
-Philippines			
hand-made sweater	.5894*	<	.6648*
machine-made sweater	.7677*	>	.7580*
hand-made shoes	.5693*	<	.7695*
machine-made shoes	.6272*	<	.7128*

(* significant at p=.05 level)

show that correlations between brand evaluation and purchase intention were higher for the within subject-designs in 9 predictions out of 12, generally supporting H4 (see Table 3).

DISCUSSION
This study focused on finding the effects of COM favorableness and the perception of process technology on consumers' evaluation of brands. We found that consumers' brand evaluation increases as a function of COM favorableness and the perception of process technology. The interaction effect of COM favorableness and perception of process technology was supported for the within-subjects design, but this result is not supported in the between-subjects design. In addition, the predictability of purchase intention for overall evaluation was higher in the within-subjects design than in the between-subjects design.

Because only one COM was given to subjects in the between-subjects design, subjects might think that the Philippines is a less-developed country, but still good at hand-made skills for textile products. That might lead to a difference in brand evaluation between hand-made vs. machine-made brands in the Philippines (no interaction effect). However, in the within-subjects design, subjects are aware of the entire range of countries, and Italy and US might be used as reference points in evaluating brands from the Philippines. Since there is a significant difference in COM favorableness between Italy/US and the Philippines, brands with Philippines COM might be perceived unfavorably regardless of the perception of process technology (interaction effect).

In the real world, people are expected to evaluate multiple cues simultaneously (Han and Terpstra 1988; Monroe and Krishnan 1985), therefore the interaction effect is more likely to happen in the real world. Though manufacturing of hand-made brands in less-developed countries may provide many benefits (e.g., low labor cost, accessibility to market), the benefits might have a trade-off with the greater derogation of the brand evaluation.

The study also examined the predictability of the two experimental designs. The within-subjects design was found to be more accurate than the between-subjects design in predicting purchase intention from brand evaluation. Many country of origin studies are conducted to predict the purchase intention for brands manufactured in foreign countries. Thus, this study provides another justification for using a within-subjects design in country of origin studies.

There are some limitations to this study. This study investigated only two product categories with student samples (cf. Albaum and Peterson 1984; Wall and Heslop 1986). Many country of origin studies found that country of origin effects are product specific (e.g., Etzel and Walker 1974; Cordell 1991), therefore the application of this study in more extended product contexts (e.g., real brands, different product category) and representative samples would be needed to assess the generalizability of our findings.

REFERENCES
Abernathy, W.J. and J. M. Utterback (1978), "Patterns of Industrial Innovation," *Technology Review*, June and July, 41-48.

Adair, J.G., B. Spinner, J. Carlopio and R. Lindsay (1983), "Where Is The Source of Artifact? Subject Roles or Hypothesis Learning," *Journal of Personality and Social Psychology*, 45, 1129-1131.

Albaum, Gerald and Robert A. Peterson (1984), "Empirical Research in International Marketing: 1976-1982," *Journal of International Business Studies*, 15 (Spring-Summer), 161-173.

Anderson, Norman H. (1982), *Methods of Information Integration Theory*, Academic Press, New York.

Bilkey, Warren J. and Erik Nes (1982), "Country-of Origin Effects on Product Evaluations," *Journal of International Business Studies*, 13 (Spring/Summer), 89-97.

Business Week (1991), Nov. 18.

Chao, Paul (1989), "Export and Reverse Investment: Strategic Implications for Newly Industrialized Countries," *Journal of International Business Studies*, 20 (Spring), 75-91.

Cordell, Victor V. (1991), "Competitive Context and Price as Moderators of Country of Origin Preferences," *Journal of the Academy of Marketing Science*, 19 (2), 123-128.

Cordell, Victor V. (1992), "Effects of Consumer Preference For Foreign Sourced Products," *Journal of International Business Studies*, 23 (Second Quarter), 251-269.

Davidson, Andrew R. and Diane M. Morrison (1983), "Prediction contraceptive Behavior From Attitudes: A Comparison of Within- Versus Across-Subjects Procedures," *Journal of Personality and Social Psychology*, 45, 5, 997-1009.

Dunning, J.H. (1980), "Toward an Eclectic Theory of International Production," *Journal of International Business Studies*, 11 (Spring/Summer), 10-12.

Dunning, J. H. (1981), *International Production and the Multinational Enterprise*, London: George Allen and Unwin 1981.

Etzel, MIchael J. and B. J. Walker (1974), "Advertising Strategy for Foreign Products," *Journal of Advertising Research*, 11 (September), 694-699.

Ettenson, Richard and Gary Gaeth (1991), "Consumer Perceptions of Hybrid (Bi-National) Products," *Journal of Consumer Marketing*, 8, 4 (Fall), 13-18.

Greenwald, Anthony G. (1976), "Within-Subjects Designs: To Use or Not To Use?" *Psychological Bulletin*, 83, 2, 314-320.

Han, C. Min and Vern Terpstra (1988), "Country-of-Origin Effects for Uni-National and Bi-National Products," *Journal of International Business Studies*, 19 (Summer), 235-255.

Han, C. Min (1989), "Country Image: Halo or Summary Construct?," *Journal of Marketing Research*, 26, May, 222-229.

Hunt, R.G. (1970), "Technology and Organization," *Academy of Management Journal*, September, 235-252.

Johansson, Johny K. and Israel D. Nebenzahl (1986), "Multinational Production: Effect on Brand Value," *Journal of International Business Studies*, 17 (Fall), 101-126.

Kruglanski, A. (1975), "The Human Subject in The Psychology Experiment: Fact and Artifact," *Advances in Experimental Social Psychology*, 8, 101-147.

Li, Wai-Kwan and Kent Monroe (1992), "The Role of Country of Origin Information on Buyers' Product Evaluation: An In-Depth Interview Approach," *AMA Educators Proceedings*, Summer, 274-280.

Mackenzie, Scott B. and Richard A. Spreng (1992), "How Does Motivation Moderate the Impact of Central and Peripheral Processing on Brand Attitudes and Intentions?" *Journal of Consumer Research*, 18, March, 519-529.

Monroe, Kent B. and R. Krishnan (1985), The Effect of Price on Subjective Product Evaluations, In J. Jacoby and J.C. Olson, eds., *Perceived Quality: How Consumers Views Stores and Merchandise*, Lexington Books.

Morello, Gabriele (1984), "The 'Made-in' Issue: A Comparative Research on the Image of Domestic and Foreign Products," *European Research*, January, 5-21.

Nagashima, Akira (1970), "A Comparison of Japanese and U.S. Attitudes toward Foreign Products," *Journal of Marketing*, 34(January), 68-74.

Ozsomer, Aysegul and S. Tamer Cavusgil (1991), "Country-of-Origin Effects on Product Evaluations: A Sequel to Bilkey and Nes Review," in *AMA Educators Proceedings*, Vol. 2, eds. Mary C. Gilly, F. Thomas Dwyer, Thomas W. Leigh, Alan J. Dubinsky, Marsha L. Richins, David Curry, Alladi Venkatesh,, Masaaki Kotabe, Ruby Roy Dholakia, Gerald E. Hills, Chicago, Il: American Marketing Association, 269-277.

Pany, K., and P. Reckers (1987), "Within-vs. Between-Subjects Experimental Designs," *Auditing: A Journal of Practice and Theory*, Fall, 39-53.

Schepanski, A., R.M. Tubbs and R.A. Grimlund (1992), "Issues of Concern Regarding Within and Between-subjects Designs in Behavioral Accounting Research," *Journal of Accounting Literature*, 11, 121-150.

Shimp, T., E. Hyatt, and D. Snyder (1991), "A Critical Appraisal of Demand Artifacts in Consumer Research," *Journal of Consumer Research*, December: 273-283.

Taylor, James C. (1971), *Technology and Plans For Organizational Change*, Institute for Social Research, The University of Michigan, Ann Arbor.

Toyne, Brian and Peter G. P. Walters (1989), *Global Marketing Management: A Strategic Perspective*, Needham, Massachusetts: Allyn and Bacon.

Triandis, H.C. (1980), Values, Attitudes and Interpersonal Behavior In H.E. Howe, Jr.(Ed.), *Nebraska Symposium on Motivation*, 27, Lincoln: University of Nebraska Press.

Wall, Marjorie and Louise A. Heslop (1986), "Consumer Attitude Toward Canadian-Made Versus Imported Products," *Journal of the Academy of Marketing Science*, 14 (2), 27-36.

Wall, Marjorie, John Liefeld, and Louis A. Heslop (1991), "Impact of Country-of-Origin Cues on Consumer Judgements in Multi-Cue Situations: a Covariance Analysis, *Journal of the Academy of Marketing Science*, 19 (2), 105-113.

Weber, S., and T. Cook (1972), "Subject Roles in Laboratory Research: An Examination of Subject Roles, Demand Characteristics, and Valid Inference." *Psychological Bulletin*, April, 273-295.

Wicker, A.W. (1969), "Attitudes Versus Actions: The Relationship of Verbal and Overt Behavioral Responses to Attitude objects," *Journal of Social Issues*, 25, 41-78.

Does Country of Origin Transfer Between Brands?

Vikas Mittal, Temple University
Michael Tsiros, Temple University[1]

ABSTRACT

Using theories of categorization and anchoring and adjustment, this article examines the effect of country of origin of one brand on another brand between contiguously presented brands. Results show moderate support for the effect of country of origin of a contiguously presented brand (reference brand) as an information cue about the target brand. In addition, the interaction between familiarity and country of origin was significant in predicting likelihood to buy the product.

INTRODUCTION

Technological advancement and diffusion has brought about numerous changes in the production and marketing of consumer and industrial goods. These changes have made possible the reduction of manufacturing and transaction costs. As a consequence global sourcing networks have attracted sufficient attention from both practitioners and academicians. The importance of country of origin (COO) as an information cue has rekindled the interest of marketing and international business researchers (Shimp, Samiee, and Madden 1993).

While COO has been extensively studied by researchers (see Baughn and Yaprak 1991 for an extensive review), few have taken a cognitive approach to studying its effect on consumer attitude formation and purchase intentions (see Hong and Wyer 1989; Han 1989 for notable exceptions). Generally, researchers have examined COO effects as they pertain to a single brand. Most consumer decisions, on the other hand, involve multiple brands. In such a situation, it is possible that the COO effects from one brand may "transfer" to another brand within the same choice set. The purpose of this paper is to examine the transfer of COO effects among contiguously displayed brands.

Using categorization theory and literature on anchoring and adjustment, propositions regarding COO effects in brand evaluation and purchasing are derived and tested. Results from an experiment show that while COO of a contiguously displayed brand (reference brand) does not influence attitudes toward the target brand, it may influence subject's likelihood to buy the brand. Furthermore, the influence of COO of the contiguously displayed brand on purchase likelihood of the target brand was moderated by the subject's familiarity with the product.

COUNTRY OF ORIGIN: LITERATURE REVIEW

Two works provide a comprehensive literature review of COO effects in a marketing context (Bilkey and Nes 1982; Baughn and Yaprak 1991); therefore, only a brief review is offered here.

Earlier studies investigating the role of demographic variables in explaining COO effects found that foreign products were more favorably evaluated by respondents who were female, older, and more educated (cf. Schooler 1971). Another group of researchers have investigated the effect of the level of economic development of a product's COO on consumer evaluations. The main finding from these studies has been that consumers not only perceive products manufactured in economically developed countries as having better quality but are also more likely to purchase them (cf. Krishnakumar 1974; Hampton 1977; Yaprak 1978).

Based on the notion of consumers' patriotic emotions and their effects on attitudes and purchase intentions, researchers have developed related constructs such as "consumer ethnocentrism" (eg. Shimp and Sharma 1987) and investigated their effect on consumer attitudes. Thus, studies have identified some degree of domestic product preference among French, West German, US, Japanese, Finnish, and Dutch consumers (see review by Hooley, Shipley, and Krieger 1988). Studies have also shown that US consumers, in the 1980's showed a significant preference for Japanese automobiles than domestic makes (cf. Johansson and Nebenzahl 1986).

More recently, researchers have examined COO from an information-processing perspective. Hong and Wyer (1989) suggested that COO activated thoughts about other product attitudes. The COO cue, therefore, may be related not only to specific beliefs about product attributes, but also to overall attitude toward the purchase. Han (1989) tested two alternative models: (1) the halo model, which posits that country image serves as halo on product evaluation and (2) the summary construct model which posits that country image functions as a summary construct. The halo construct model suggests that COO directly affects consumers' beliefs about product attributes and indirectly affects overall evaluation of products through those beliefs. The summary construct model suggests that COO directly affects consumers' attitude toward a brand rather than affecting it indirectly through product attribute ratings. Empirical results favored the halo construct model for products such as automobiles and the summary construct for products such as television sets. Han (1989) explained this finding based on the fact that automobiles are more complicated products with more product attributes than television sets.

COO TRANSFER BETWEEN CONTIGUOUS BRANDS

Starting from the literature on brand extensions, there has been considerable interest in exploring how perceptions of one brand (product) transfer to an associated brand (product). Using categorization theory (Rosch and Mervis 1975), Aaker and Keller (1990) demonstrated that brand image can transfer along several product dimensions. Similarly, Bickart, Buchanan, and Simmons (1993) showed that brand images do transfer between two brands that are displayed together in a retail catalog. The brand image transfer was particularly strong from an unfamiliar brand to a familiar brand. In particular, they found that the image of the familiar brand (Liz Claiborne) was negatively affected when it was displayed along with an unfamiliar brand. However, the reciprocal affect of the familiar brand on the unfamiliar brand was weak.

Following the definition of brand image transfer (Bickart, Buchanan, and Simmons 1993), we propose that COO transfer occurs between two brands in a choice set when the COO associations held in memory about one brand (say, Brand A) affect consumer judgments about another brand (say, Brand B). COO may transfer not only on an attribute level, but also on an overall basis. Furthermore, the "strength" of such a transfer is likely to vary based on contextual factors, such as consumer familiarity with the product, the degree of incongruity between the countries of origin and so forth.

[1]We would like to thank Kristine Gupta and Lena Tsiros for their invaluable support. We also acknowledge the help of Michael R. Gerhart in photographing the stimuli.

Empirical evidence shows that contextual information is required to interpret ambiguous stimuli (Neisser 1976). In a consumer decision-making setting, this information may come from sources such as other brands in the choice set or the physical setting of the decision task. One such source of contextual information is the COO of other brands in the choice set. Categorization theory and literature on adjustment and anchoring suggest that such contextual information is important as it influences consumer judgments and choices (Cohen and Basu 1987; Northcraft and Neale 1987).

Categorization

Categorization, considered a fundamental cognitive activity, has been extensively used to study consumer decision making (cf. Cohen and Basu 1987). The most frequently advanced models of categorization are the classical, the prototype, and the exemplar (Cohen and Basu 1987).

In the classical model, any object possessing the set of salient attributes is a member of the category, while any object lacking even one is not a member (Cohen and Basu 1987). In the prototype model, an object belongs to a category if there is a good fit between the object and the prototype, or the best example of the category (Rosch and Mervis 1975; Smith and Medin 1981). In the exemplar model, the object is compared with a specific example in the category. The exemplar, therefore must be accessible during the categorization process (Cohen and Basu 1987). Much empirical evidence suggests that when faced with an ambiguous stimuli, people try to classify it in existing categories in their memory (Ozanne, Brucks, and Grewal 1992).

Applied in this setting it may be argued that consumers, when faced with a brand for which they know little about, will try to classify it within an existing category. The cue for this categorization process may be provided by the COO of another brand in the choice set. This is particularly likely to occur when other brand attributes (eg. price) are non-diagnostic. Thus, when displayed along with a brand from Paris, a dress may be categorized as being more fashionable than if it were displayed alongside with another dress made in another country less known for its fashion industry.

Anchoring and adjustment

Norm theory suggests that in the absence of data people fill the missing links with "normal" values/events (Kahneman and Miller 1986). Thus, absent the information about reliability of a Japanese brand car, the customer will imbue it with the normal value of say "highly reliable." Related to norm theory, Kahneman (1992) defines anchoring effects as "cases in which a stimulus or a message that is clearly designated as irrelevant and uninformative nevertheless increases the normality of a possible outcome." (pp. 309) Stated differently, anchoring effects can drastically influence what will be considered as normal. For instance, Northcraft and Neale (1987) showed that the asking price of a house acted as a powerful anchor on people's estimates of the value of a house. Furthermore, they demonstrated that assessments of not only novices, but also of professionals were strongly influenced by an asking price that was considered completely uninformative by them. In another study, Urbany, Bearden, and Weilbaker (1988) showed that both plausible as well as exaggerated reference prices influenced consumers' perceptions of perceived offer value. Although believability of the ad significantly dropped for the case of the exaggerated reference price, a significant increase in perceived offer value was witnessed. Furthermore, evidence of estimates being assimilated to randomly produced anchors (eg., by spinning a fortune wheel) has also been documented. For instance, subjects were asked if the percentage of

African countries in the UN was higher or lower than a given number; the median estimates were 25 and 45 for groups that received 10 and 65 as the random number respectively (Slovic and Lichtenstein 1971). In the context of COO contiguously displayed brands can serve as powerful anchors for each other. For instance, an unknown brand of portable stereo displayed vis a vis a Sony (made in Japan) may be judged better, than if it were displayed along with an Weston (made in India).

Following the above arguments, it is expected that for contiguously displayed brands, the target brand evaluations will be biased toward the reference brand. According to categorization literature this may occur if consumers categorize the target brand in the same category as the reference brand. Predictions based on the anchoring and adjustment literature would be similar: the target brand would be anchored to the reference brand and the target brand's evaluation adjusted accordingly. Thus, for contiguously displayed brands the following hypotheses are proposed:

HYP 1: Evaluations of the target brand will be influenced by the presence of a reference brand with a different COO. When the COO of the reference brand is evaluated positively, evaluations will be higher. When the COO of the reference brand is evaluated negatively, evaluations will be lower.

HYP 2: Consumers' likelihood to buy the target brand will be influenced by the reference brand with a different COO. When the COO of the reference brand is evaluated positively, the likelihood to buy the target brand will be higher. When the COO of the reference brand is evaluated negatively, the likelihood to buy the target brand will be lower.

In addition, consumer experience with the product is expected to moderate the above effects. Prior work has shown that consumer familiarity with the product (Alba and Hutchinson 1987) influences their decision making. The diagnosticity of COO as a cue was expected to vary with a subject's experience with the product. However, no a priori predictions were made regarding this moderating effect.

METHOD

An experimental design using desk lamps as the product and students from a major university in the Northeast as subjects was conducted. Desk lamps were deemed appropriate because they enabled us to construct multi-cue stimuli and constitute an appropriate product for the student population.

Measures

Attitudes were measured via 14 semantic differential scales. These were constructed to tap 3 underlying dimensions of styling, quality and value. Likelihood to buy was measured via subject's response to the question "How likely would you be to buy the target brand of lamp?" on a 7-point scale anchored as "extremely likely to buy" and "not at all likely to buy." Product familiarity was measured via response to the question "Do you have a desk lamp that you use on a regular basis?" Subjects using the lamp in such a capacity then indicated the number of hours they used the lamp in an average week. In an average week, subjects reported using the lamp for 18 hours (std. dev.=14 hours). In addition, the usual demographic data were also collected.

Based on informal pretesting and a review of the past literature, the reference brands were manipulated as being made in Italy

TABLE 1
Descriptive Statistics

Attribute	Mean	Standard Deviation
Poor/Good Quality	5.07	1.16
Inferior/Superior Product	4.57	1.29
Won't/Will Last Long	4.93	1.26
Flimsy/Durable Construction	5.07	1.39
Very Poor/Very Good Material	5.19	1.17
Not/Very Stylish	4.43	1.71
Ugly/Beautiful Design	4.24	1.49
Old Fashioned/Contemporary	3.52	1.74
Not at al/Extremely Trendy	3.90	1.56
Poor/Good Value for the Money	5.10	1.28
Too Expensive/Reasonable Price	5.31	1.57

and Malaysia. These were chosen due to two reasons. First, several office products catalogs contain lamps manufactured in these countries. Second, students indicated that Italian lamps were, generally thought of being as better than Malaysian lamps. For the purpose of our study, the target brand was depicted as being made in Poland. This country was chosen as it had no brand connotation in reference to desk lamps.

Experiment

Subjects were 42 undergraduate students who were randomly assigned to the two reference brand conditions (Italy versus Malaysia). Due to missing values, data from two subjects were discarded. Thus, the final analysis is based on data from 40 respondents. Subjects were told that the study sought to gather their opinions regarding different desk lamps described on a pamphlet. The pamphlet described 2 lamps: the reference brand and the target brand. For each lamp, the pamphlet contained a picture of the lamp, wattage of the bulb, height, description of the lamp shade, material, country of origin, and the price. These dimensions were same for both reference brands. However, they varied slightly between the target and reference brand to avoid any salience bias that would have occurred had only the COO been different.

Subjects looked at the pamphlet and answered a series of questions regarding the different measures. Subjects took about 10 minutes to complete the questionnaire.

RESULTS

A factor analysis was conducted to see if the three attitudinal dimensions were being tapped. After discarding 3 ambiguous items, a 3-factor solution tapped the underlying dimensions of quality, value, and style. The descriptive statistics of the items comprising these factors are shown in Table 1. The rotated factors with their corresponding loadings are shown in Table 2. Additive scales were formed for subsequent analysis. The reliability alpha's for the scales are as follows: quality (alpha=.90), style (alpha=.78), and value (alpha=.74). These were used as dependent measures in the following analysis. The descriptive statistics for these scales are reported in Table 2.

An analysis of variance was conducted to ascertain the hypotheses. The effect of COO of the reference brand was not significant for quality, value, and style (p>.05). Thus, hypothesis 1 was not supported. Support, although marginal, for the second hypothesis was provided (p=.10) by the data. These results are shown in Table 3. Thus, a subject's likelihood to purchase the target brand is influenced by the presence of a reference brand with a different COO. In addition, consumers' likelihood to buy the target brand will be influenced by a reference brand with a different COO.

Although the main effect of familiarity was not significant (p>.1), the familiarity and COO interaction was significant (p<.05) for likelihood to buy (see Figure 1). For subjects who are more familiar with the product category, the likelihood to buy the target brand (made in Poland) increases when it is displayed along with the Italian reference brand. Familiarity has no influence when the COO of the reference brand is Malaysia. Thus, familiarity may moderate the buying decision when the COO is favorable.

DISCUSSION

The above pattern of results suggest that COO of reference brands in the choice set can indeed influence a consumer's likelihood to buy the target brand. COO of the reference brand has no influence on customer attitudes regarding quality, style or value of the target brand. Thus, while COO of reference brand does not influence attitudes, it appears to influence a consumer's likelihood to buy the product. This favors the findings of Han (1989) that COO may operate as a summary construct rather than a halo construct for less complicated products. That COO affects purchase likelihood and not perceptions of quality, style, and value may indicate that consumers in this setting may have used other product dimensions to arrive at their purchase decision. Further research is indicated to clarify this issue. These results also show that the COO of a reference brand can serve as a powerful anchor along which purchase likelihood of the target brand is adjusted. More interesting, data show that this anchoring and adjusting is mediated by consumer familiarity with the product category. Additionally, the familiarity effect is much stronger for the "positive" reference COO (i.e. Italy) than for the "negative" reference COO (Malaysia). Perhaps this is indicative of the "positive valence bias" that Meyer (1987) found in his studies. These findings have several implications for researchers and managers.

As researchers we first need to investigate the contextual effects on consumer judgment and choice that emanate from the diversity of the choice-set. COO differences are merely one of many such effects that should be investigated. Second, we need to better understand the cognitive mechanisms that underlie this effect. In particular, we need to establish conclusively whether COO affects attitudes for different products. Third, more conclusive and comprehensive evidence regarding the hypotheses suggested should be generated. More specifically, alternative hypoth-

TABLE 2
Rotated Factor Pattern

Attribute	Factor 1 (Quality)	Factor 2 (Style)	Factor 3 (Value)
Poor/Good Quality	.76	.11	.22
Inferior/Superior Product	.65	-.07	.53
Won't/Will Last Long	.90	.04	.08
Flimsy/Durable Construction	.61	.41	.37
Very Poor/Very Good Material	.58	.29	.57
Not/Very Stylish	.48	.68	-.03
Ugly/Beautiful Design	.31	.68	.36
Old Fashioned/Contemporary	-.10	.74	.17
Not at al/Extremely Trendy	-.01	.88	.10
Poor/Good Value for the Money	.41	-.04	.75
Too Expensive/Reasonable Price	.09	.03	.88
Eigenvalue	**3.76**	**2.51**	**2.38**
Mean	**4.95**	**4.02**	**5.20**
Standard Deviation	**1.04**	**1.26**	**1.28**

TABLE 3
Analysis of Variance for Likelihood to Buy

Source	DF	Sum of Squares	Mean Square	F-Value	p-value
Model	3	31.24	10.41	2.83	.05
COO	1	10.23	10.23	2.78	.10
Familiarity	1	6.07	6.07	1.65	.21
COO X Familiarity	1	14.95	14.95	4.07	.05
Error	36	132.36	3.68		
$R^2 = .19$					

FIGURE 1
COO x Familiarity Interaction

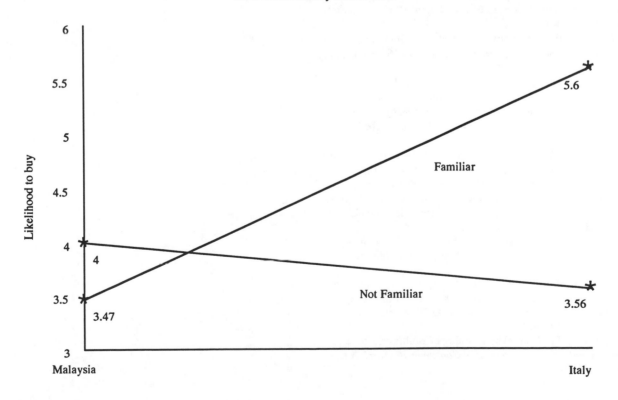

eses based on theories such as assimilation-contrast theory can be generated and evaluated against the hypotheses generated based on categorization and anchoring theory.

Managers need to be aware of the contextual effects introduced by COO of different brands in the choice set. This has implications for merchandise displays, catalog layouts, and so forth. For instance, in catalogs for office products COO of contiguously displayed brands may have a strong influence on the purchase intent of either brand. Managers may be able to significantly influence the sale of one brand by using the other brand as the cue. For example, are COO effects more salient than brand name effects of reference brands? Is there a COO by brand name interaction and what is the nature of the interaction?

These and other issues await further investigation. The need to attend to them becomes only more imperative as consumers are increasingly faced with global products.

REFERENCES

Alba Joseph W. and J. Wesley Hutchinson (1987), "Dimensions of Consumer Expertise," *Journal of Consumer Research*, 13 (March), 411-454.

Aaker, David A. and Kevin Lane Keller (1990), "Consumer Evaluations of Brand Extensions," *Journal of Marketing*, 54 (January, 27-41.

Baughn, Christopher C. and Attila Yaprak (1991), "Mapping Country-of-Origin Research: Recent Developments and Emerging Avenues," in *Product and Country Images* eds. Papadopoulos, Nicolas and Louise A. Heslop, 89-115.

Bickart, Barbara, Lauranne Buchanan, and Carolyn J. Simmons (1993), "Brand Image Transfer in a Retail Catalog," Working Paper.

Bilkey, Warren J. and Erik Nes (1982), "Country-of-Origin Effects on Product Evaluations," *Journal of International Business Studies*, 13, 89-99.

Cohen J. B. and K. Basu (1987)," Alternative models of categorization: Toward a contingent processing framework", *Journal of Consumer Research*, 13, 455-472.

Hampton, Gerry M. (1977), "Perceived Risk in Buying Products Made Abroad by American Firms," *Baylor Business Studies*, (October), 53-64.

Han, Min C. (1989), "Country Image: Halo or Summary Construct?" *Journal of Marketing Research*, 26 (May), 222-229.

Hong, Sung-Tai and Robert S. Wyer, Jr. (1989), "Effects of Country-of-Origin and Product-Attribute Information on Product Evaluation: An Information Processing Perspective," *Journal of Consumer Research*, 16 (September), 175-187.

Hooley, G. J., D. Shipley, and N. Krieger (1988), "A Method for Modelling Consumer Perceptions of Country of Origin," *International Marketing Review*, 6 (Autumn), 67-76.

Kahneman, Daniel (1992), "Reference Points, Anchors, Norms, and Mixed Feelings," *Organizational Behavior and Human Decision Processes*, 51, 296-312.

Kahneman, Daniel and Dale T. Miller (1986), "Norm Theory: Comparing Reality to Its Alternatives," *Psychological Review*, 93, 136-153.

Krishnakumar, Parameswar (1974), *An Exploratory Study of the Influence of Country of Origin on the Product Images of Persons from Selected Countries*, PhD Dissertation, The University of Florida.

Meyer, Robert. J (1987), "The Learning of Multiattribute Judgement Policies," *Journal of Consumer Research*, 14, Sep., 155-173.

Northcraft, Gregory B. and Margaret A. Neale (1987), "Experts, amateurs, and real estate. An anchoring-and adjustment perspective on property pricing decisions," *Organizational Behavior and Human Decision Processes*, 39(1), February, 84-97.

Neisser, U. (1976), *Cognition and Reality*. San Francisco: W.H. Freeman.

Ozanne, Julie L., Merrie Brucks, Dhruv Grewal (1992), " A study of information search behavior during the categorization of new products," *Journal of Consumer Research*, 18, March, 452-463.

Rosch, E. and C. B. Mervis(1975), "Family resemblances: Studies in the internal structure of categories", *Cognitive Psychology*, 7, 573-605.

Schooler, Robert D. (1971), "Bias Phenomena Attendant to the Marketing Foreign Goods in the U.S." *Journal of International Business Studies*, 2, 71-80.

Shimp, Terence A., Saeed Samiee, and Thomas J. Madden (1993), "Countries and Their Products: A Cognitive Structure Perspective," *Journal of the Academy of Marketing Science*, 21 (Fall), 323-330.

Shimp, Terence A. and Subhash Sharma (1987), "Consumer Ethnocentrism: Construction and Validation of the CETSCALE," *Journal of Marketing Research*, 24 (August), 280-289.

Slovic, Paul and Sarah Lichtenstein (1971), "Comparison of Bayesian and Regression Approaches to the Study of Information Processing in Judgment," *Organizational Behavior and Human Decision Processes*, 6, 649-744.

Smith, E. E. and D. L. Medin (1981), *Categories and concepts*, Cambridge, MA: Harvard University Press.

Urbany, Joel E., William Bearden, and Dan C. Weilbaker (1988), "The Effect of Plausible and Exaggerated Reference Prices on Consumer Perceptions and Price Search," *Journal of Consumer Research*, 15 (June), 95-110.

Yaprak, Attila (1978), *Formulating a Multinational Marketing Strategy: A Deductive, Cross-national Consumer Behavior Model*, PhD Dissertation, Georgia State University.

An Investigation of the Use of Price-Quality Schema by Urban Chinese Consumers

Ann Veeck, Louisiana State University
Alvin C. Burns, Louisiana State University

ABSTRACT

The strength of belief in a price-quality relationship has been found to differentiate groups of U.S. consumers and affect behavior in the marketplace. This study investigates the price-quality inferences of urban consumers in the burgeoning market economy of the People's Republic of China. While U.S. studies have found three or four distinct groups based on price-quality evaluations, two Chinese groups are found: (1) schematics who believe in a positive price-quality relationship and are likely to pay more for products, and (2) aschematics who are less trusting of a price-quality relationship and are likely to pay lower prices for products. Other comparisons between U.S. and urban Chinese consumers in price-quality beliefs are noted. It appears that urban Chinese consumers are either early in their price-quality experience and have not separated into price-perceived quality groups such as those found in the U.S., or fundamental differences underlie how the two cultures evaluate price-quality relationships.

INTRODUCTION

A consistent finding in recent price-perceived quality research is that notable differences exist among U.S. consumers in the degree to which they believe in a positive relationship between price and product quality. This phenomenon has alternately been called "reliance on price as a predictive cue" (Etgar and Malhotra 1981), belief in a positive relationship between price and quality (John, Scott, and Bettman 1986), a "price reliance schema" (Lichtenstein and Burton 1989), and a "price-quality schema" (Lichtenstein, Ridgway, and Netemeyer 1993). U.S. consumers who believe in a strong relationship between price and quality are believed to rely heavily on price as a cue in determining product preference (Etgar and Malhotra 1981; John, Scott, and Bettman 1986; Lichtenstein, Bloch, and Black 1988; Peterson and Wilson 1985).

A gap in our understanding of the price-perceived quality relationship is the lack of an international perspective. Literature reviews of international marketing have noted the paucity of pricing research, with calls for research that investigates the relationship between price and other marketing variables (Cavusgil and Nevin 1981; Douglas and Craig 1992; Li and Cavusgil 1991). An international perspective could be particularly useful in examining the price-quality perceptions of consumers, since it could highlight cultural differences in individuals' consumption experience. Toward this end, the objective of this study is to examine the use of price quality schema by consumers in the People's Republic of China. With its rapidly emerging market economy, China is a particularly appropriate nation in which to investigate this topic. Due to the newness of the nation's economic reforms, China's 1.2 billion consumers have only recently had a significant number of choices in brands and retailers. This situation leads to the question of the extent to which Chinese consumers are developing price-quality heuristics in their evaluation of products.

This paper investigates the presence of price-quality schema in Chinese consumers in two major cities in Eastern China. First, recent U.S. research that analyzes the price-quality schema is reviewed. Based on these U.S. studies and the post-Mao economic environment of China, hypotheses are developed. Then the results of an empirical study are reported and discussed, lending insight into the operation of price-quality schema in urban China.

THE PRICE-QUALITY SCHEMA

Zeithaml (1988, p.5) has defined perceived quality as "the consumer's judgement about the superiority or excellence of a product." The relationship between perceived quality and price has been investigated by economists and consumer researchers for years. Although the relationship between price and perceived quality has generally been found to be positive (Monroe and Krishnan 1985; Rao and Monroe 1989), this relationship is neither universal nor robust (Peterson and Wilson 1985; Zeithaml 1988). Recent research has noted the complexity of the price-quality relationship, with calls for research that investigates how variables moderate the relationship (Monroe and Dodds 1988; Monroe and Krishnan 1985; Olshavsky 1985; Peterson and Wilson 1985; Zeithaml 1988).

This study focuses on consumers' global assessments of the relationship between price and quality. Consumers view price as both an indicator of sacrifice and as an indicator of quality (Lichtenstein, Ridgway, and Netemeyer 1993; Monroe 1990). The degree to which consumers consider price as a surrogate for quality and/or sacrifice varies markedly by both the individual (e.g., Rao and Monroe 1988) and the product (e.g., Peterson and Wilson 1985). In particular, research has found a group of consumers that believes in and relies on a strong positive relationship between price and quality, regardless of the product type. Lichtenstein, Ridgway, and Netemeyer (1993, p.236) call this individual factor the "price-quality schema," defined as "the generalized belief across product categories that the level of the price cue is related positively to the quality level of the product." This definition will be used for the present study. A consumer who believes that "you get what you pay for" could be said to possess a price-quality schema. The consumer who has low trust in a relationship between price and product quality might be called "aschematic" (Lichtenstein and Burton 1988; Peterson and Wilson 1985).

U.S. studies that have classified individuals according to their price-quality perceptions have found distinct schematic groups (Etgar and Malhotra 1981; Lichtenstein and Burton 1989; Peterson and Wilson 1985). In addition, market behavior is affected by schema membership, with individuals who believe in a positive price-quality correspondence preferring higher-price products (John, Scott, and Bettman 1986); relying heavily on price as a cue to quality in relation to other cues (Etgar and Malhotra 1981; Peterson and Wilson 1985); demonstrating higher price acceptability levels (Lichtenstein, Bloch, and Black 1988); and exhibiting relatively lower ability to recall prices accurately (Lichtenstein, Ridgway, and Netemeyer 1993). However, virtually all price-quality schema research has been conducted with U.S. consumers, and our knowledge in this area remains culturally bound.

THE ECONOMIC ENVIRONMENT OF CHINA

The current economic transformation of China is unprecedented in size and speed: never before have so many people experienced economic change at such a breakneck rate. Since December, 1978, when the economic reforms championed by Deng Xiaoping were approved by the 11th Central Committee of the Communist Party, China's GNP has grown by almost 9% a year (*Beijing Review* 1993), reaching 13% in 1993 (Chen 1994). The economic reforms have brought an end to the exclusive control of the commercial sector by the state, resulting in sweeping changes under an economy officially defined as a "socialist market economy." Price constraints have been gradually lifted since 1978, with three-fourths of prices now set by the market (Jiang 1992; Li 1993). "Free markets," composed of independent vendors, and, more recently, private and collective stores, have begun providing alternatives to the state-run stores. Formerly without brands and not packaged, products are now produced by both private and state manufacturers, offering branded and advertised options for consumers.

In short, for the first time in forty years, urban Chinese consumers are experiencing choices in both price levels and product quality, and price-quality schema may be forming as a result. Unfortunately, along with expanded choice, market reforms have allowed inflation. Reports of annual inflation up to 20% in some cities in 1993 (*Beijing Review* 1994) suggest that price-quality beliefs of Chinese consumers will differ from those of U.S. consumers where prices are more stable. With no prior research on price-quality schema in Chinese consumers, one tact is to hypothesize patterns that are similar to those known for U.S. consumers. Empirical findings can then highlight cross-cultural similarities or dissimilarities. In sum, the newly-emerging market environment of China provides a dynamic setting to study the phenomenon of price-quality schema.

HYPOTHESES

U.S. studies have shown that the price-quality schema is a belief that guides the shopping behavior of some U.S. consumers across products and situations (Lichtenstein and Burton 1989; Peterson and Wilson 1985), and existing studies have not found demographic variables to account for this factor in consumers (Etgar and Malhotra 1980; Lichtenstein and Burton 1989). However, as Dickson and Sawyer (1990, p.51) state, "shoppers are very heterogeneous in terms of their attention and reaction to price and price promotions." Tellis and Gaeth (1990, p.36) suggest that consumers may exhibit this difference because, "their past experience may be consistent with a positive price-quality relationship, they might rationalize that the higher price results from firms spending more to supply quality, or they might trust the market..." Arguably, in the burgeoning market economy of China, operation of a price-quality schema should differentiate Chinese consumers. Therefore, just as distinct clusters of consumers based on the strength of the price-quality schema have been found in the U.S., so may distinct clusters of individuals exist in the China.

H1: Urban Chinese consumers can be meaningfully grouped based on the presence or absence of a price-quality schema.

U.S. studies have found that individuals with strong price-quality schema are more willing to pay a higher price for a product due to their belief that "you get what you pay for" (Lichtenstein, Bloch, and Black 1988; Peterson and Wilson 1985). Therefore, when asked what price they would most likely pay for a product, those with a stronger belief in a price-quality relationship should generally cite a higher price. This U.S. pattern leads to the second hypothesis:

H2: Urban Chinese consumers possessing a price-quality schema are likely to pay higher prices for products than those with a weak price-quality schema (assuming price-quality schema groups are found).

RESEARCH METHOD

Research Instrument

The development of the research instrument required an initial qualitative phase aimed at establishing construct equivalence (Berry 1980; Douglas and Craig 1983). A focus group of Chinese respondents who had recently arrived in the U.S. tested the appropriateness of constructs and stimuli. Since all participants in the focus group were bilingual, the discussion vacillated between Chinese and English. This qualitative phase confirmed that contemporary Chinese consumers did discern price and quality differences in products sold in China. At the same time, the focus group served to generate a list of products that were commonplace and exhibited price and quality variations in today's Chinese markets.

Consistent with Peterson and Wilson (1985) and Burton and Lichtenstein (1988), the research instrument asked respondents to evaluate a list of fourteen products on the statement "The higher the price, the higher the quality." Based on focus group findings, very few products from the Burton and Lichtenstein (1988) and Peterson and Wilson (1985) studies were included, since most of these products (i.e. suntan lotion, paper towels, frozen french fries, oil popcorn popper) were inappropriate for Chinese consumers. Fourteen durable and nondurable products available to urban Chinese consumers on the open market were identified and used as stimuli.

Additional information collected included the price respondents would be most likely to pay for each product, purchase experience, shopping preferences, and demographics. Following cross-cultural research guidelines, the questionnaire was written in English, translated into Chinese, then back-translated into English (Brislin, Lonner, and Thorndike 1973).

Data Collection

The questionnaires were administered by Chinese university faculty and graduate students to convenience samples of university students and adults consumers in two urban areas in China, Beijing (population 10.8 million) and Nanjing (population 2.8 million), in the summer of 1993. University students and adults consumers were surveyed to allow comparisons to U.S. studies involving both U.S. students (Etgar and Malhotra 1980; Lichtenstein and Burton 1989; Peterson and Wilson 1985) and adult consumers (Lichtenstein and Burton 1989).

A total of 290 questionnaires was collected: 72 Beijing university students; 75 Beijing adult consumers; 74 Nanjing university students; 69 Nanjing adult consumers. The overall adult consumer sample was 58% female, 60% in the 25-45 age bracket, and 75% university educated. Due to the nonrandom selection of the sample, a series of statistical tests (after scale refinement, described below) was conducted to determine if demographic factors would confound the findings. No significant differences were found in price-quality perceptions associated with education level or age in the adult consumer sample, and gender in both samples. Consequently, the internal validity of the study did not appear to be compromised by the sample composition.

Scale Refinement

The 14-product instrument was subjected to item analysis and purification, with a series of factor analyses and reliability assessments conducted on the central construct (Bearden, Netemeyer, and Mobley 1993; Churchill 1979). The final scale form was found to represent two separate dimensions: durable products and nondurable products. The durables price-perceived quality scale consisted of four products: 35 mm camera, man's watch, washing machine, and bicycle (Cronbach's alpha=.84). The nondurables

TABLE 1
Cluster Means and Standard Deviations for Price-Quality Perception*

Product	Product type (D= durable; N=non - durable)	Adult Consumers Cluster 1 "Schema - tics" (n=76)	Adult Consumers Cluster 2 "Aschema - tics" (n=68)	University Students Cluster 1 "Schema - tics (n=86)	University Students Cluster 2 "Aschema - tics" (n=60)
Durables scale	D	5.8 (0.6)	4.0 (1.3)	5.9 (0.6)	4.6 (1.3)
Non-durables scale	N	5.2 (0.8)	3.3 (1.0)	5.2 (0.7)	3.5 (1.0)
35mm camera	D	6.1 (0.8)	4.4 (1.8)	6.2 (0.7)	4.9 (1.5)
Washing machine	D	5.8 (0.9)	4.1 (1.5)	6.0 (0.8)	4.1 (1.4)
Men's watch	D	5.8 (1.2)	3.6 (1.7)	5.9 (1.1)	4.7 (1.5)
Bicycle	D	5.7 (1.0)	4.0 (1.7)	5.9 (1.1)	4.6 (1.5)
Roll of toilet paper	N	5.4 (1.3)	3.2 (1.4)	5.3 (1.3)	3.4 (1.4)
Laundry det- ergent	N	5.2 (1.2)	3.1 (1.3)	5.1 (1.3)	3.4 (1.4)
Ball point pen	N	5.1 (1.3)	3.6 (1.6)	5.3 (1.1)	3.6 (1.5)
Bottle of beer	N	5.2 (1.3)	3.6 (1.5)	5.2 (0.7)	3.7 (1.5)

Note: Based on ratings from 1 (strongly disagree) to 7 (strongly agree) on the statement "The higher the price, the higher the quality."
*All cluster means comparisons (Cluster 1: Cluster 2) are significantly different at $p<.001$

---

price-perceived quality scale also contained four products: toilet paper, beer, ball-point pen, and laundry detergent (Cronbach's alpha=.77). The items eliminated from the analysis included soap, cigarettes, soda, toothpaste, gold ring, and television. Most of the eliminated items have dual functions in China as products that are used every day and luxury items that can be presented as gifts, a characteristic that undoubtedly contributed to their weak factor loadings.

FINDINGS

Cluster Solution

Following a method parallel to U.S. studies (Lichtenstein and Burton 1988; Peterson and Wilson 1985), cluster analysis was conducted to determine if urban Chinese respondents could be grouped according to the presence or absence of a price-quality schema. The criterion variables used for the cluster analysis were the average price-quality perceptions for the four-product durables scale and the four-product nondurables scale. Adult consumers and university students were clustered independently using a two-stage procedure. First, a hierarchical method (Ward's method; squared Euclidean distances) was used to select a cluster solution and identify seed points. Then, a nonhierarchical cluster technique (parallel threshold procedure) was used to calibrate the results (Hair et al. 1992).

The cluster solutions were chosen based on uniformity of cluster sizes and change in agglomeration coefficients (Hair et al.

1992). A two-cluster solution provided the most interpretable results for both the adult consumer and university student sample (see Table 1). U.S. studies have found three- and four-cluster solutions (Etgar and Malhotra 1980; Lichtenstein and Burton 1988; Peterson and Wilson 1985), defining consumer segments along a continuum of price-quality perceptions. However, neither type of Chinese consumer group exhibited acceptable identification beyond two subgroups.

As can be seen in Table 1, in both samples, respondents in Cluster 1 reported significantly higher mean price-quality perceptions than did respondents in Cluster 2 for the durable products scale, the nondurable products scale, and all eight products taken individually ($p<.001$ for all cluster pairs). The mean response for "the higher the price, the higher the quality" for Cluster 1 of both samples corresponded to "agree" for the durables scale and "somewhat agree" for the nondurables scale. Cluster 2 of both samples, on the other hand, recorded a mean price-quality perception of "neither disagree nor agree" for durables and "somewhat disagree" for nondurables. Thus, the results support Hypothesis 1, and we have labeled the two clusters "schematics" and "aschematics" respectively.

While the mean responses for the schematic clusters of adult consumers and university students are similar, the number of university students classified as schematics is higher (see Table 1). Since the university students have significantly less purchase experience than the adult consumers ($p<.001$), this finding is consistent with U.S. studies finding that individuals with less

TABLE 2
MANOVA Results By Subsample and Product Group

Sample Group	Product Group	n	df	F-value
Adult consumers	Durables	108	4,106	2.30 [*]
Adult consumers	Nondurables	120	4,118	2.56 [**]
University students	Durables	115	4,113	2.52 [**]
University students	Nondurables	136	4,134	2.23 [*]

Note: MANOVA's were performed using log transformations to correct for heterogeneity of variance-covariance matrices found with raw price estimates
[*] $p < .10$
[**] $P < .05$

purchase experience are more likely to judge a product by its price (Rao and Monroe 1988; Rao and Sieben 1992).

To test Hypothesis 2, the mean price of the "price most likely to pay" for the durable and nondurable products defining the price-perceived quality scale was compared for the subgroups. The sample size decreased from 290 to 210 due to missing data. A MANOVA for each sample was conducted to compare the mean price differences of the cluster groups for the four durable products and the four nondurable products. To correct for abnormal distribution of values and heterogeneity of variance-covariance matrices, logarithm transformations were applied to all price variables (Hair et al. 1991). The responses exhibited large variances, perhaps due in part to the escalated inflation rates in urban China and the diverse reference products of respondents. Nevertheless, the MANOVA results showed evidence of significant differences for all group mean comparisons (see Table 2). Consistent with Hypothesis 2, schematics recorded a higher mean price than aschematics for all of the products investigated (see Table 3).

In an attempt to develop a fuller description of the clusters, statistical tests were conducted to discriminate the clusters on demographic variables (gender, age, income, education, city). No demographic variables were found to differentiate the consumers within their respective clusters. This result is consistent with U.S. studies that have been unable to define profiles for their U.S. clusters using demographic and socioeconomic variables (Etgar and Malhotra 1981; Lichtenstein and Burton 1988).

DISCUSSION

This study begins to explore the pervasiveness of price-quality schema in consumers by investigating its presence in urban Chinese consumers. China affords an interesting laboratory for the study of price-quality schema because its consumers are experiencing a transition from State-control where product prices and quality levels were set without the interplay of market forces to a market-driven economy. Only recently have urban Chinese been afforded an array of choices in products based on market price and product quality; however, the price-quality relationship is tenuous due to unstable markets and high inflation. Despite this turmoil in Chinese markets, the study's findings indicate that in China, as has been found in the U.S., a group of consumers tends to operate under the price-quality schema of "you get what you pay for."

Despite the apparent methodological limitations of this research, there are interesting similarities and departures apparent in this study from price-quality beliefs found in U.S. consumers. As for similarities, a definite price-quality schematic group exists in urban Chinese consumers, and the finding persists across university students and adult consumer populations as has been found in the

U.S. The schematic Chinese consumers are willing to pay more than aschematics for both durables and nondurables as has been documented in U.S. studies. Also as found in U.S. consumers, Chinese consumers with less purchase experience are more apt to possess a price-quality schema.

At this time, the major differences between the two cultures appear to be a matter of degree. Whereas U.S. studies have documented the existence of three or four distinct groups based on beliefs in a positive price-quality relationship, the Chinese sample in this study yielded only two groups: schematics and aschematics. One speculation for this difference is that Chinese markets are in flux, and Chinese consumers are early in their learning experience of whatever price-quality relationships underlie their market choices. The schematics may sense a general price-quality relationship, while the aschematics do not. On the other hand, Chinese consumers may be exhibiting a unique manifestation of price-quality evaluation. Certainly, these issues provide challenges for future research endeavors in cross-cultural price-quality schema.

REFERENCES

Bearden, William O., Richard G. Netemeyer, and Mary F. Mobley (1993), *Handbook of Marketing Scales*, Newbury Park, CA: Sage Publications Inc.

Beijing Review (1994), "10% GDP Growth Expected," 37 (January 10-16), 7.

Beijing Review (1993), "Comfortable Life Coming Soon to Cities," 36 (January 18), 4.

Berry J.W. (1980), "Introduction" to *Handbook of Cross-Cultural Psychology : Methodology*, Volume 2, Harry C. Triandis and John W. Berry, eds., Boston: Allyn and Bacon, Inc., 1-28.

Brislin, Richard W., Walter J. Lonner, and Robert M. Thorndike (1973), *Cross-Cultural Research Methods*, New York: John Wiley and Songs.

Cavusgil, S. Tamer and John R. Nevin (1981), "State-of-the-Art in International Marketing: An Assessment," in *Annual Review of Marketing* 1981, eds. B.M. Enis and K.J. Roering, Chicago: American Marketing Association, 195-216.

Chen, Kathy (1994a), "China's Premier Li Calls for Balance Between Economic Growth and Stability," *The Wall Street Journal*, (March 11), A8.

Churchill, Jr., Gilbert A. (1979), "A Paradigm for Developing Better Measures of Marketing Constructs," *Journal of Marketing Research*, 16 (February), 64-73.

Dickson, Peter R. and Alan G. Sawyer (1990), "The Price Knowledge and Search of Supermarket Shoppers," *Journal of Marketing*, 54 (July), 42-53.

TABLE 3

Cluster Means and Standard Deviations for "Price Most Likely to Pay"

(Price in *yuan*)

Product	Product type (D= durable; N=non - durable)	Adult Consumers Cluster 1 "Schema - tics" (n=56)	Adult Consumers Cluster 2 "Aschema - tics" (n=40)	University Students Cluster 1 "Schema - tics" (n=62)	University Students Cluster 2 "Aschema - tics" (n=52)
35mm camera	D	693.5 (547.9)	647.0 (613.9)	780.2 (1330.1)	477.1 (293.7)
Washing machine	D	959.1 (777.7)	703.7 (397.5)	736.4 (472.7)	622.3 (344.8)
Men's watch	D	234.7 [c] (359.7)	193.3 [c] (143.0)	261.4 [b] (252.6)	168.7 [b] (143.7)
Bicycle	D	376.1 (163.5)	365.0 (134.1)	394.4 [a] (229.7)	286.9 [a] (120.9)
Roll of toilet paper	N	0.97 [c] (.8)	0.70 [c] (.5)	1.19 (.6)	1.11 (.7)
Laundry detergent	N	2.55 [a] (1.5)	1.87 [a] (0.6)	2.00 (.4)	1.96 (.5)
Ball point pen	N	2.47 [b] (2.2)	1.54 [b] (1.6)	2.67 [a] (2.6)	1.60 [a] (1.1)
Bottle of beer	N	1.70 [c] (.8)	1.46 [c] (.5)	2.28 [c] (1.6)	1.82 [c] (.8)

Notes: 1) Based on the question "What is the price you would be most likely to pay for this product?"

2) Log transformations were performed on raw price estimates to correct for heterogeneity of variance-covariance matrices.

[a] $p < .01$.

[b] $p < .05$.

[c] $p < .10$.

Douglas, Susan P. and C. Samuel Craig (1992), "Advances in International Marketing," *International Journal of Research in Marketing*, 9, 291-318.

Douglas, Susan P. and C. Samuel Craig (1983), *International Marketing Research*. Englewood Cliffs: Prentice Hall, Inc.

Etgar, Michael and Naresh K. Malhotra (1981), "Determinants of Price Dependency: Personal and Perceptual Factors," *Journal of Consumer Research*, 8 (September), 217-222.

Hair, Jr., Joseph F., Rolph E. Anderson, Ronald L. Tatham, and William C. Black (1992), *Multivariate Data Analysis*, Third Edition, New York, NY: Macmillan Publishing Company.

Jiang, Zemin (1992), "Accelerating Reform and Opening Up" (text of the report delivered by Jiang to the 14th National Congress), *Beijing Review*, 35 (October 26), 10-33.

John, Deborah Roedder, Carol A. Scott, and James R. Bettman (1986), "Sampling Data for Covariation Assessment: The Effects of Prior Beliefs on Search Patterns," *Journal of Consumer Research*, 13 (June), 38-47.

Li, Rongxia (1993), "1992: Landmark of China's Economic Growth," *Beijing Review*, 36 (1), 15-19.

Li, Tiger and S. Tamer Cavusgil (1991), "International Marketing: A Reclassification of Research Streams and Assessment of Their Development since 1982," *Proceedings* of the American Marketing Association (Summer), 592-607.

Lichtenstein, Donald R., Peter H. Bloch, and William C. Black (1988), "Correlates of Price Acceptability," *Journal of Consumer Research*, 15 (September), 243-252.

Lichtenstein, Donald R. and Scot Burton (1989), "The Relationship Between Perceived and Objective Price-Quality," *Journal of Marketing Research*, 26 (November), 429-443.

Lichtenstein, Donald R., Nancy M. Ridgway, and Richard G. Netemeyer (1993), "Price Perceptions and Consumer Shopping Behavior: A Field Study," *Journal of Marketing Research*, 30 (May), 234-245.

Monroe, Kent B. (1990), *Pricing: Making Profitable Decisions*, Second Edition, New York: McGraw-Hill Book Company.

Monroe, Kent B. and William B. Dodds (1988), "A Research Program for Establishing the Validity of the Price-Quality Relationship," *Journal of the Academy of Marketing Science*, 16 (Spring), 151-168.

Monroe, Kent B. and R. Krishnan (1985), "The Effect of Price on Subjective Product Evaluations," in *Perceived Quality*, J. Jacoby and J. Olson, eds., Lexington, MA: D.C. Heath and Company, 209-232.

Olshavsky, Richard W. (1985), "Perceived Quality in Consumer Decision Making: An Integrated Theoretical Perspective," in *Perceived Quality*, eds., Jacob Jacoby and Jerry C. Olson, Lexington, MA: D.C. Heath and Company, 3-29.

Peterson and Wilson (1985), "Perceived Risk and Price Reliance Schema as Price-Perceived Quality Mediators," in *Perceived Quality: How Consumers View Stores and Merchandise*, Jacob Jacoby and Jerry C. Olson, eds., Lexington, MA: D.C. Heath and Company, 247-268.

Rao, Akshay R. and Kent B. Monroe (1989), "The Effect of Price, Brand Name, and Store Name on Buyers' Perceptions of Product Quality: An Integrative Review," *Journal of Marketing Research*, 26 (August), 351-357.

Rao, Akshay R. and Kent B. Monroe (1988), "The Moderating Effect of Prior Knowledge on Cue Utilization in Product Evaluations," *Journal of Consumer Research*, 15 (September), 253-264.

Rao, Akshay R. and Wanda A. Sieben (1992), "The Effect of Prior Knowledge on Price Acceptability and the Type of Information Examined," *Journal of Consumer Research*, 19 (September), 256-270.

Tellis, Gerard J. and Gary J. Gaeth, "Best Value, Price-Seeking, and Price Aversion: The Impact of Information and Learning on Consumer Choices," *Journal of Marketing*, 54 (April), 34-45.

Zeithaml, Valarie A. (1988), "Consumer Perceptions of Price, Quality and Value: A Means-End Model and Synthesis of Evidence," *Journal of Marketing*, 52 (July), 2-22.

Special Session Summary
The Odyssey Downunder: A Qualitative Study of Aboriginal Consumers

Ronald Groves, Edith Cowan University
Russell W. Belk, University of Utah

After months of planning and preparation a team of 5 marketing academics, 9 students (including two of Aboriginal descent), and a 3-person video crew, conducted intensive qualitative field research in Aboriginal communities in the far north of Western Australia during July of 1993. The Odyssey Downunder was inspired by the 1986 Consumer Behavior Odyssey in the United States. This session included a screening of a videotape produced from the project and three additional research papers that further explore substantive findings. We believe this to be the first major qualitative consumer behavior study in Australia and the first major consumer behavior study conducted in another culture (for the non-Australians) and among indigenous people (for the Australians). The project focused on the major consumption problems faced by contemporary Australian Aborigines, including the lures of consumer culture versus tribal tradition, severe alcoholism, gambling, and drug abuse, dependence on government welfare programs, desire to return to traditional and sacred lands, erosion of the sharing ethos on which prior survival depended, and consumption-related aspects of discrimination and prejudice by the dominant population. The session included a professionally produced video, slides, and participation by two observers of Aboriginal descent who monitored and facilitated the project. If consumer researchers are to begin to make the field of study truly global, we hope that this project will prove inspirational, instructive, substantively rich, and provocative.

Studies of culture contact and acculturation in consumer research have previously focused on immigrants' adaptation to a new culture. But in countries where locals have been overwhelmed and overpowered by the new arrivals, the greatest amount of change has been expected of and has occurred among the original inhabitants. This has been the case in countries in North and South America and in New Zealand and Australia. Because Australia is a large continent with fewer inhabitants than most European countries, there is the possibility that many Aboriginal Australians could either continue or regain a way of life closer to traditional lifestyles than to non-Aboriginal ways. Recent court action regarding native land claims (the Mabo decision) enlarges this possibility. But what do Aborigines themselves want? What are the attractions of traditional and nontraditional ways of life and specifically, what role does consumption play in these desires? How do Aborigines view the current consumption problems faced by their communities including poor health, dependence on government welfare programs, rampant alcoholism, widespread gambling, and, if it is a problem, the attractiveness of consumer culture? What is the historic and current role of politics, religion, education, employment possibilities, and discrimination in helping shape the consumer lifestyle choices now facing Aboriginal populations? What is the meaning of land to Aborigines and how does this differ from non-Aboriginal land meanings? These are the key issues addressed by the Odyssey Downunder.

The concept of the Odyssey Downunder was developed by Ron Groves and discussed with Russ Belk, a co-leader of the American Odyssey who visited during early 1992. Later that year Ron Groves began teaching an applied qualitative research class to a small group of hand picked students who became researchers in the Odyssey. Students and faculty participants also studied Ab-

original Australian culture and prior research in the region where we would work. Melanie Wallendorf, the other co-leader of the American Odyssey, conducted seminars with the students as well, and she, Russ Belk, and Ronald Hill critiqued their fieldwork, analysis, and research papers. Early in 1993, preliminary site visits were made by Ron Groves along with Kim Bridge, Noel Bridge, and Ernie Bridge (the first Aboriginal Minister in the Western Australian Parliament, who supported the project in a number of significant ways). Donations were obtained from firms including Quantas, Ansett Airlines, Shell Australia, and Nissan Australia and on July 1st the group set out from Perth for the 3500 kilometer journey north. Three four-wheel drive vehicles carried us to our research sites. In addition to the participants, these vehicles carried camera equipment, audio and video recording equipment, and camping equipment for the project. The group had previously been divided into three teams, each including an overseas professor experienced in naturalistic inquiry. To the extent possible, teams were balanced by age (21-51), gender (5 F; 12 M), and culture (1 HK Chinese; 2 Australians of Aboriginal descent; 11 other Australians, 2 Americans, 1 Dane) in order to enhance access and triangulation across potentially diverse perspectives. The sites were selected to provide contrast between communities. Three of the sites were on the Dampier Peninsula where the Bardi inhabitants have a close link with the sea. In contrast to this setting three additional communities were studied in a desert region within a day's drive of the coastal sites. The smallest of the communities has 60 inhabitants and all but one have populations of fewer than 600, with at least 80 percent being Aboriginal. The exception is a desert community of 3500 people, of whom approximately half are Aborigines.

As well be seen from the abstracts, two unique features of the research were the presence of a film (video) crew and the presence of two men of Aboriginal descent who observed the observers in process of conducting the research. This allowed us to present the key video produced from the project in the session (a total of 14 primarily instructional videos have been produced in total), as well as a final paper which examines biases of the research team and the effects of their presence. This is made possible because of the intimate familiarity of Kim and Noel Bridge with the areas studied. They were raised in one of the communities and one is a government liaison officer who frequently visits the other sites. Both men are well known in the three desert field sites. In February, 1994, Ron Groves and Martin McCarthy (a graduate student participant from the University of Western Australia) returned to the field sites, brought them copies of the videotape to be shown in the session, and obtained feedback from our informants before the final editing of this tape. The research continued later in 1994, but the results of this session do not include that work.

The videos produced from this project have been shown on Australian television. Because the Mabo land claims issue is politically volatile at this time, we hope that these videos contribute an Aboriginal voice to the critical public debate. For the ACR audience we hope to increase understanding of the complex consumer problems facing Aboriginal Australians and the cultural systems in which these problems are imbedded. Secondly, because naturalistic research methods are still new in consumer research, we hope to demonstrate their potential for investigating consumer groups and issues that are inaccessible in other ways. And thirdly, we hope to provide an assessment of the opportunities and problems of conducting research in another culture in this global age.

THE VIDEO AND PAPERS

From Dreamtime to Screentime: The Impact of Western Consumer Culture Upon Aboriginal Communities in the Kimberley
Ron Groves, Edith Cowan University
Russell W. Belk, University of Utah

Abstract

The video shown in the session begins with a brief contextualizing history of Australian Aborigines and the areas studied. The Aboriginal inhabitants of the Kimberley lived in harmony with their land as hunter gatherers for at least 40,000 years. Theirs was the oldest living culture known, based upon remembrance of the origin of life. Their land and the natural world it supported represented a symbolic footprint of the metaphysical ancestors responsible for creation during the Dreaming. They had no concept or word for either the passage of time or the accumulation of possessions. Despite centuries of contact with Asian traders, Aboriginal cultures remained little changed. Within twenty years of Western contact however, these cultures were under threat. A century later most traditional tribal lifestyles had perished, replaced by western consumer culture.

The video is a distillation of the naturalistic research conducted by the seventeen person research team and some of the emerging insights from this research. Three of these participants formed a video crew that captured both on-camera interviews and observations of everyday life and special events. After briefly introducing the project and its historic context, four descriptive findings are emphasized: the meanings of possessions and sharing, alcohol abuse problems, the meaning of the land, and attempts to revive parts of traditional Aboriginal culture. In addition three interpretive themes are discussed: tradition and change, consumerism, and freedom and control. In explicating these themes, the video shows portions of interviews with the members of the communities studied. In addition, observational footage, photographs from the research project, and some historical photographs are employed. By combining these "perspectives of action" with the interview material emphasizing "perspectives on action," a richer portrait emerges. Scenes of daily life, work, play, rituals, and environment help to contextualize and deepen the presentation. In the full length video (it was only possible to show a shortened version in the session) the titles and closing footage employ original music by one of the researchers, Noel Bridge. The result, we hope, is an intimate, scholarly, and empowering document.

Aboriginal Consumer Culture
Russell W. Belk, University of Utah
Ronald Groves, Edith Cowan University
Per Østergaard, Odense University

Abstract

After a 40,000 year history of self-sufficient living in harmony with the land, in the brief 200 years since contact with Westerners, Australian Aborigines have become dependent on the cash economy. A key dialectic tension that permeates contemporary Aboriginal culture is that between the consumer culture brought by the Westerners and the traditional cultures of Aboriginal people. This dialectic was a major focal point of the Odyssey Downunder. While this critical tension continues to create uncertainty regarding the future for Aborigines, we also found two systematic reactions: one is resistance and the other is selective adaptation. Both offer potential pathways to preserving Aboriginal values in the face of the growing attractiveness of the consumer lifestyles that typify the now dominant Australian culture. The resistance strategy is crystallized by an out station movement in which Aborigines are repatriating themselves to ancestral lands where they are able to gain access, thus separating themselves from the dominant culture as well as urban Aboriginal culture. This is a back to the land movement, but not one of voluntary simplicity. The other reactive strategy of selective adaptation seeks, on the production side, to develop Aboriginal industry and to acquire assets that will provide jobs and income. On the consumption side, selective adaptation involves embracing consumer culture but with a continued ethos of non-attached possession and sharing based on traditional cultural patterns once needed for survival. Although some of this ethos has eroded, it has by no means disappeared, nor is it likely to do so. We develop these perspectives using the voice of our informants in an effort to understand the role of consumption in contemporary and perhaps future Aboriginal culture. We conclude that both strategies are beneficial to Aborigines and that despite their mutual exclusivity they are simultaneously viable.

Australian Aborigines and the Dreaming: The Meaning of Land and Aboriginal Culture
Ronald Paul Hill, Villanova University

Abstract

The culture of Australian Aborigines is founded on the creation of life (Lawlor 1991). According to this ideology, their Creative Ancestors moved across an undifferentiated topography during the original "Dreaming," a time when they shaped a featureless world. Each night they would sleep and dream of their activities for the following day, which would then shift from dreams to actions. In this way, the Ancestors created all living things as well as structured the physical world. Wills (1982, p. 26) describes this epoch aptly, in an almost poetic way:

The Dreaming, this mystical, mythical core of Aboriginal culture is the land itself, the songs, the dances and the ceremonies; it is the ancestors who made the trees, the animals, the birds, who formed the mountains and the rivers, the bays and the inlets. The creation of life is the Dreaming.

As the world filled with vibrant life and physical beauty, the Ancestors tired and withdrew into every aspect of nature, "to reverberate like a potency within all they created" (Lawlor 1991, p. 15).

This creation myth has been passed from generation to generation, and has fundamentally the same assumptions across tribes and clans (Berndt and Berndt 1989; also see Partington 1985). The result is that Aborigines view land as a religious phenomenon, and believe that the relationship between themselves and the land originated with the Dreaming (Maddock 1972). For example, Aborigines often develop intimate ties to key ancestral sites in the land. Munn (1970, p. 147) states:

...in one instance, the rights of a particular patrilineal group to certain sites were explained by pointing out that the ancestors of the present owners had travelled there, singing as they went. To sing one's way from place to place implies that marks and names are being 'put' at each place—that is, that the site is being claimed. Thus group claims are based ultimately upon ancestral claims made through the marks of personal identification with which the ancestor imprints a place.

Given this perspective, Aborigines view rights to land as originating with the design of the world rather than with alienable legal title (Maddock 1972). As one Aborigine asserted, "[Europeans] look upon land as 'my land, I own that land'. Whereas Aborigines look at something as a part of the whole, a part of themselves, and they are part of that—the land. The land and they are one" (Bowden and Bunbury 1990, p. 54). Thus, land is seen as part of their "extended selves," something to be preserved and maintained (Belk 1988). Its loss or despoliation can result in a diminished sense of self, and, as the following Aborigine suggests, the possibility of damnation of their entire culture:

If we lose this land we lose our culture...What's under the earth, whether there's gold or riches, we don't want the riches. We want the land. We want our culture. This land has to stay as it is today (Wills 1982, p. 25).

The research presented as part of this session explored the relationship between the dreaming and deep spiritual ties to the land by Australian Aborigines based on naturalistic inquiry conducted in the Kimberley. The primary focus is on their relationship to traditional lands as well as the location of their current homes.

REFERENCES

Belk, Russell W. (1988), "Possessions and the Extended Self," *Journal of Consumer Research,* 15 (September), 139-150.

Berndt, Ronald M. and Catherine H. Berndt (1989), *The Speaking Land: Myth and Story in Aboriginal Australia,* Ringwood, Victoria: Penguin.

Bowden, Ros and Bill Bunbury (1990), *Being Aboriginal: Comments, Observations and Stories from Aboriginal Australians,* Maryborough, Victoria: Australian Broadcasting Corporation Enterprises.

Lawlor, Robert (1991), *Voices of the First Day: Awakening in the Aboriginal Dreamtime,* Rochester, VT: Inner Traditions International.

Maddock, Kenneth (1983), *Your Land Is Our Land: Aboriginal Land Rights,* Victoria: Penguin.

Munn, N. D. (1970), "The Transformation of Subjects into Objects in Walbiri and Pitjantjatjara Myth," in *Australian Aboriginal Anthropology: Modern Studies in the Social Anthropology of the Australian Aborigines,* ed. Ronald M. Berndt, Nedlands, Western Australia: University of Western Australia Press.

Partington, Geoffrey (1985), "The Australian Aborigines and the Human Past," *Mankind,* 15 (April), p. 26-40.

Wills, Nancy (1982), *Give Me Back My Dreaming: Background to the Australian Aboriginal Claim to Land Rights,* Lota, Australia: The Communist Arts Group.

Observers Observed: Researcher Behavior and Imagination on the Odyssey Downunder

Per Østergaard, Odense University, Denmark
Kim Bridge, Edith Cowan University, Australia
Noel Bridge, Edith Cowan University, Australia

Abstract

Results from a study conducted within The Odyssey Downunder are presented. Inspired by recent developments in anthropology (e.g., George W. Stocking, Jr. and James Clifford) the authors (two Aborigines and a Dane) observed how the other members of the Odyssey team (two Americans, eight Australians, and one Asian) coped with the Aboriginal culture.

The study draws on different data sources: 1) participant observation during the Odyssey, 2) interviews with participants during the Odyssey, 3) the transcribed interviews conducted by the participants on the Odyssey, and 4) the participants' fieldnotes. The methods used for interpretation of the data were derived from the above mentioned anthropologists.

The area for this study differs from traditional consumer research, because, until a few decades ago, the Aboriginal cultures studied were based on hunting and gathering and were not much influenced by a commodity consumption. This original culture seems to have allure for the researcher's imagination. Results indicate that very often the researchers seemed to look at this original culture as something good and the westernized commodity culture as something bad. Many Aborigines don't seem to have the same antagonistic impressions of the two different cultures. Another interesting aspect of our findings is how the researchers perceive the Aborigines. On the one hand they have sincere respect for these people. On the other hand it seems to be very difficult not to look upon the Aborigines as someone they (the Western researchers) have to help, since they cannot take care of themselves.

These results are interesting and shed light on the consumer researcher's own imagination as part of the Western culture and how this imagination biases the perception of the Aboriginal culture. It is shown how research results depend upon the researcher's own cultural background and the researcher's capability to be conscious of the "side-effects" of his/her westernized imagination. The objective is to understand the studied culture on its own premisses.

Fictional Subjects in Consumer Research

William D. Wells, University of Minnesota
Kendra L. Gale, University of Minnesota

ABSTRACT

This paper proposes a new source of data for consumer research. The source is network television. The data are the characters, events and artifacts in television programs. To illustrate the pros and cons of this approach, it "replicates" a previous study among real consumers.

INTRODUCTION

In the very first volume of *Advances in Consumer Research* a paper on "Consumer Perceptions of Product Warranties" noted that conclusions were "tentative" "due to its small sample size [and] the peculiar characteristics of the sample." (Lehmann and Ostlund 1974, 61-62). In the very first issue of the *Journal of Consumer Research* an article on "Marital Roles in Decision Processes" noted that conclusions were "limited" due to the "small body of data" (Davis and Rigaux, 1974, 59).

These perils are still with us. Despite warnings from methodologists (Jacoby 1976, Ferber 1977, Sears 1986, Monroe 1992), consumer researchers have continued to base "tentative" "limited" final comprehensive conclusions on MBA students and college sophomores.

This paper proposes a new source of data for consumer research. The source is network television. The new data are the characters, events, and artifacts in television programs. To illustrate the pros and cons of this approach, it "replicates" a recent *Journal of Consumer Research (JCR)* article.

Pros

As research subjects, television characters have much to recommend them. They use high involvement products and low involvement products, and a wide range of services. They appear in naturalistic settings. They do not know that they are being studied. Their behavior is public and permanent. Anyone can reexamine it.

Last but not least, they are economical. Compared with real respondents, they are substantially more accessible.

Cons

Of course these assets carry liabilities. Most important, television characters are not real people. We will discuss the implications of that fact later. For the moment we assert that—in certain ways and for certain purposes—they are "realer" than MBA students and college sophomores.

Researchers cannot ask them questions. One must infer knowledge, personality, attitudes and motives. This drawback leaves important information permanently in limbo.

Settings are not real either. They are created for effect, and cannot be considered typical. Obviously, fiction is not a perfect surrogate.

The end question is, do the pros outweigh the cons? Can television characters—and by extension characters in short stories, novels, theatrical productions and motion pictures— tell us anything about the real behavior of real consumers?

A FICTIONAL REPLICATION

To provide a partial answer to that question, we "replicated" a *JCR* article. The article is "Gift Selection for Easy and Difficult Recipients: A Social Roles Interpretation," by Cele Otnes, Tina M. Lowrey and Young Chan Kim (1993), *JCR* 20, (September) 229-244. Here (and again later) we emphasize that we are *not* critiquing that investigation. We are exploring the pros and cons of using television characters as research subjects. We selected the Otnes et al. report because it met the standards of a selective journal, and because gifts appear in many television narratives.

Data Sources

Otnes et al. (1993) recruited informants by placing ads in newspapers "in a midwestern city." The ads explained that the researchers "wished to conduct two in-depth interviews with each informant, accompany them on two Christmas shopping trips, and hold a brief follow-up interview in January" (Otnes et al. 1993, 230). The ads offered a $30 incentive.

After interviews and shopping trips with 15 informants, Otnes et al. transcribed the audio tapes and field notes. This procedure produced "almost 400 pages of text" (230).

Our procedure was of course quite different. In *TV Guide*, we found gift-content programs scheduled to appear on CBS, NBC, ABC and FOX during the 1993 Christmas season. Our frame included series and prime-time specials—not feature films, variety shows, news, or television tabloids.

The final sample included 41 programs. When edited to eliminate non-gift sequences, these programs provided five and one half hours of in-context gift exchanges. In these exchanges, 116 givers gave 200 gifts to 136 recipients.

Analysis

Using standard ethnographic concepts and methods, Otnes et al. "constructed" the meaning of their 400 pages. When disagreements surfaced, they "negotiated agreement" among individual interpretations (Otnes et al. 1993, 230).

Their analysis produced six "social roles:" the Pleaser, the Provider, the Compensator, the Socializer, the Acknowledger, and the Avoider. Each social role conveyed a role-specific message. Figure 1 (page 5) shows the roles and messages. The original article provides much more detailed information.

Otnes et al. described the gift-selection strategies associated with the roles, and classified recipients as "easy" or "difficult." One key finding was that gift-givers show "chameleon-like behavior:" they "change colors" to fit the gift occasion (Otnes et al. 1993, 231).

Our research questions were:

- Will the six roles in Figure 1 resurface in the TV stories?
- If so, will TV gift-givers use the same selection strategies?
- Will TV gift-givers show "chameleon-like" behavior?
- Can TV gift recipients be classified as "easy" or "difficult"?

Thus, we attempted a "fictional replication."

Our analysis paralleled Otnes et al. in some respects but not in others. Of course we started with entirely different data. Instead of 400 pages of text, we started with five and one-half hours of video tape. Instead of interviews and observations, we started with in-context gift exchanges.

On the first pass through the tape, we coded the gifts, the genders of the givers and the receivers, and the family (or other) relationships among them. We also assigned one of the six roles in

FIGURE 1
Gift-Giver's Social Roles
(from Otnes et al 1993, 232-239)

Role	Message
Pleaser	"I value you enough to get you something that I think you would enjoy." (232)
Provider	"I want to take care of your needs." (234)
Compensator	"I want to make it up to you" [even though I didn't cause your loss]. (235)
Socializer	"Here are some values or knowledge that I wish you to possess." (236)
Acknowledger	"I recognize that some relationship exists between us, and here is a token of that relationship." (236)
Avoider	"I do not wish to enter into a gift-exchange relationship with you," or "You are not worthy of being acknowledged at this time." (239)

Figure 1, and noted ideas for further investigation. In later passes through the tape, we added depth and nuance, and weighed the pros and cons of fictional consumers.

In conducting this analysis, we found our in-context record especially helpful. We did not depend on field notes. We returned again and again to the original. In early passes through the tape, we missed or (even worse) misperceived important implications. In later passes, we made corrections.

FINDINGS

In analyzing the gift exchanges, we were at the mercy of actors, script-writers and producers. We could not prescribe agendas, or make sure that topics were completely covered. We could not ask the characters why they did what they did, or stop the interview and probe for motives.

These data problems forced us to abandon one of our research objectives. Because we could not control content or ask direct questions, we could not classify recipients as "easy" or "difficult."

On the other hand, we easily confirmed Otnes et al.'s "chameleon" observation. In the Christmas episode of *Frasier*, for instance, Frasier was a Pleaser when he bought gifts for his son, an Acknowledger when he exchanged gifts with his co-workers, and an Avoider when he refused to celebrate with his father. In *Dave's World*, Sheldon was an Acknowledger when he bought gifts for his adult friends, and a Pleaser to his daughter, Carlie. In television stories, as in real life, gift-givers change colors to fit the situation.

The Six Roles

Our main question was, will the six roles in Figure 1 resurface in television fiction? The answer to that question was yes. All six roles were clearly evident. In *Dave's World*, for instance, Dave and Beth were Pleasers. They spent two episodes searching for a Cannibal Caveman, the only gift their son wanted. In *Grace Under Fire*, Grace was a Compensator for an Avoider father. In *Coach*, Hayden was a meta-Acknowledger. He recycled a "Karoke Junior" from Dauber into an impromptu gift for his boss, Howard. All six of Otnes et al.'s gift-giver roles advanced these tales in multiple manifestations.

Expanding the Definition of "Gift"

Our analysis led us to conclude that one common definition of "gift"—a physical object—invites researchers to ignore important gift exchanges. In the stories, many of the most salient gifts were ritual presentations of time, ideas, or achievements—a touching solo at a church service, a conferral of god motherhood, an announcement of a pregnancy, for instance. In two stories, givers offered themselves as "gifts" to be "unwrapped" by receivers.

Gifts of this sort were so poignant—and so clearly within the ordinary meaning of the word "gift"—that no study of gift exchanges should leave home without them. This observation agrees with similar comments by Belk and Coon (1993) and Sherry (1983).

Additional Social Roles

We also found that Otnes et al.'s six roles did not cover all of our "field data." To account for the TV gift exchanges, we needed new roles and additional subdivisions.

In part, this need to tamper with the constructs may have been personal. Roles can be partitioned indefinitely, and where one stops is ultimately one's own decision. But the range of gifts, gift-givers, and gift-giving situations was so great that (we believe) the original investigators would have found more roles if their data had been more heterogeneous. Here we emphasize again that we are *not* critiquing the Otnes et al. study. We are illustrating some possible advantages of TV stories as data sources.

The TV gift exchanges led us to divide Pleasers into "Agapic Pleasers" and "Utilitarian Pleasers." "Agapic Pleasers" are selfless givers. "Utilitarian Pleasers" have ulterior motives. We believe that this distinction is meaningful and important. Recent research supports this contention (Belk and Coon 1993).

The fictional exchanges encouraged further subdivision. For instance, we divided Agapic Pleasers into Effective and Inept. Effective Agapic Pleasers gave gifts that strengthened relationships. Inept Agapic Pleasers gave gifts that signaled innocent incompetence. One sent a "dribble glass" to a pen pal in a drought-stricken country. Another gave embarrassing "elf pajamas" to pre-adolescent grandchildren. This is not a trivial distinction. In the world of gift exchanges, it is not only the thought that counts. The consequences of being Effective and Inept are very different.

The stories also split Utilitarian Pleasers. The most important segments were: Self-givers, who gave gifts to themselves; Selfish Givers, who gave gifts they could co-enjoy; Apologizers, who tried to compensate for wrongs they had committed; and Bargainers, who intended to create obligations. At least one of those segments—Self-Givers—has been the subject of several recent gift-giving investigations (Mick and DeMoss 1990, Olshavsky and Lee 1993, Faure and Mick 1993).

These observations suggest that TV stories might serve as "20-20 foresight" in research with real consumers. Researchers who use TV stories as test sites can develop more incisive expectations.

Additional Strategies

Otnes et al. linked gift-giving roles with gift-giving strategies. In Otnes et al.'s terminology, a role is an intended message; a strategy is an enactment.

As was the case with roles, we needed new strategies. One of the most interesting new strategies embraced two roles, one in keeping with the season, the other more devious. In *Hearts Afire* for instance, Mavis gave her daughter a drum set to annoy her ex-husband. In *Fresh Prince*, Vivian conferred god motherhood on her butler to chastise her petty sisters. These duel strategies add new elements to Otnes' (1994) observations.

Another common and important strategy might be called "exchange in kind." In *Phenom*, for example, Angela heard that her boyfriend had visited three stores at the mall: Tiffany's, Eddie Bauer and Captain Jack's Novelty. Her conclusion was, "I'm either getting jewelry, a parka, or fake vomit." Her response was to purchase three gifts—an ID. bracelet, a Swiss Army knife, and a pair of Santa boxer shorts—so that her gift would match his in spirit. Other investigators (Belk 1979, Belk and Coon 1993, Wolfinbarger 1990) have also noted the decisive nature of expected balance.

Gender Differences

Because the fictional sample contained both males and females, we could examine gender differences. Like much previous research, the TV data suggest that women manage emotional relationships (Hochschild 1989). When the men in the stories went Christmas-shopping, women orchestrated much of the activity; and when situations were at all subtle, many of the men "just didn't get it." Moreover, almost all the self-givers were men. This observation parallels Fisher and Arnold (1990).

Prediction of Receiver Roles

Unlike Otnes et al.'s sample, the fictional sample included receivers as well as givers. This feature allowed us to predict the social roles that others will find when they focus on the receiver side of the gift exchange equation. We know we will be sorry we did this.

One reason we will be sorry is that the receiver data were thinner than the giver data. Because the TV stories were broadcast (and almost all set) in the few weeks before Christmas, they included more givers and preparations than receivers and consequences. As far as TV is concerned, when Christmas is over, it is over.

However, our data do suggest that receiver roles do not mirror giver roles, as we had at first expected. Instead, the receivers fell into two broad groups: receivers who accepted, and receivers who rejected, the givers' messages. For the most part, receivers who rejected the message rejected the gift. However, some receivers who rejected the message accepted the gift and ignored it, or accepted the gift and employed it for purposes not intended.

In the Christmas episode of *Roseanne*, for instance, Roseanne and Dan gave Becky money for college. Rejecting their Socializer message, Becky gave the money to her unapproved new husband. In gift exchanges, unaccepting acceptance parallels the distinction between sentiment and substance proposed by Sherry, McGrath and Levy (1992).

REALITY AND VALIDITY

The key question, of course, is: "Where do these observations represent, and where do they misrepresent, the real behavior of real consumers? This question applies to fictional data in the same way it applies to experiments, surveys, real-life ethnographic studies and other more traditional sources.

Although we do not have a complete answer to that question we do have some thoughts that may be useful. First and possibly most important, an investigator who uses fictional subjects must remember that the events in the stories are not real events, and the characters in the stories are not real people. If that is a trivial observation, it is an important trivial observation because the events

are familiar and the characters are vivid. In many cases the events are so familiar that they seem real, and the characters are so vivid that they seem to be personal acquaintances.

Our present thinking places fictional data on three levels: (1) Props, (2) Characters and Storylines, and (3) Myths. Each level has a different mode of contact with reality.

Props

Props (objects, dress, and environment) are pretty close to everyday experience. This is not to say they are exact duplicates. They're not. They are constructed artifacts, and probably oversample middle and upper class environments.

But props must conform to expectations. Viewers expect that a Christmas party hosted by wealthy Alex Halsey of *Sisters* will be more lavish in all respects than a Christmas party hosted by blue-collar Roseanne Conner. Something would seem very wrong if that did not happen. In comedy and drama, a sense of verisimilitude is an artistic and economic asset, and producers strive mightily to attain it (Barker 1988, Mayerle 1991).

So at the prop level—the level where consumer products are most common—artistic and economic considerations foster realism. Here, television stories are likely to include literal depictions of real objects (Solomon and Greenberg 1993), and reproduce real-world behavior.

Characters and Storylines

By contrast, characters are often stereotyped, and storylines are often formulaic exaggerations (Cantor 1992, Feuer 1992, Gerbner and Gross 1976, Vande Berg and Streckfuss 1992). There can be no doubt that television misrepresents at this level.

But, taken for what they are, even stereotypes and exaggerations can be informative. In the normal course of events, the interactions, customs and motives that govern everyday life are so implicit, so intricate, so common and so taken for granted that they are almost invisible. When caricatured for comedic or dramatic effect, they become a lot more evident (Hirschman 1988, McCracken 1988).

Myths

At the myth level, TV stories are visible idealizations of mainstream practices and values (Jhally and Lewis 1992; Hirschman 1988, 1992; Kottak 1991). Almost all the plots portrayed Christmas as a time for love and sharing, and resolved conflicts in favor of family togetherness. Even characters who were deeply cynical at the onset learned compassionate Christmas lessons by the time the play was over. In one guise or another, many of the sequences revived basic themes of Dickens' (1843) *Christmas Carol*.

So, at the prop level, TV stories are more or less accurate representations of the real world. At the character and storyline level, they are more or less inaccurate representations of the real world. At the myth level, they translate commonplace gestures and artifacts into idealized manifestations of dominant cultural phenomena.

SUMMARY AND EVALUATION

Our purpose was to explore the assets and liabilities of television stories as sources of consumer data. On the asset side we found that the huge variance among characters and situations, and the permanence and repeatability of the "original behavior," were especially valuable. Using these advantages, we replicated findings from several studies of real gift behavior.

We also found that the normal research definition of "gift" omits important intangibles, and that first-hand ethnographic methods are liable to underestimate the more devious aspects of gift exchanges. These findings suggest that TV stories can provide "20-20 foresight" in many kinds of research situations.

On the liability side we found that inability to control coverage or ask direct questions prevented us from meeting one of our research objectives. We also found that means and variances of personality traits, attitudes and strategies are virtually certain to be unrepresentative. This insidious hazard should not be underestimated.

We assume that further work along these lines will reveal more pros and more cons. However, we believe that the pros are valuable enough, and the cons controllable enough, to recommend fictional "informants." We extend this recommendation—and all of the accompanying cautions—to cross-cultural and historical consumer research, and to fictional informants from short stories, novels, theatrical productions and motion pictures (Goodwin 1992, Holbrook and Grayson 1986).

REFERENCES

Barker, David (1988), "'It's Been Real' : Forms of Television Representation," *Critical Studies in Mass Communication* 5, (March) 42-56.

Belk, Russell W. (1979), "Gift Giving Behavior," in *Research in Marketing*, Vol. 2, ed. Jagdish Sheth, Greenwich CT: JAI 95-126.

Belk, Russell W. and Gregory S. Coon (1993), "Gift Giving as Agapic Love: An Alternative to the Exchange Paradigm Based on Dating Experiences," *Journal of Consumer Research*, 20 (December), 393-417.

Cantor, Muriel G. (1992), "*Prime-Time Television: Content and Control*, Beverly Hills, CA and London: Sage Publications.

Davis, Harry, and Benny P. Rigaux (1974), "Perception of Marital Roles in Decision Processes," *Journal of Consumer Research*, 1 (June), 51-62.

Dickens, Charles (1843), "A Christmas Carol," in *Christmas Books*, London: Oxford University Press, 1968.

Dominick, Joseph and Gail Rauch (1972), "The Image of Women in Network TV Commercials," *Journal of Broadcasting*, 16 (Summer), 259-265.

Faure, Corinne and David Glen Mick (1993), "Self-Gifts Through the Lens of Attribution Theory," in *Advances in Consumer Research* Vol. 20, Leigh McAlister and Michael L. Rothschild eds, Provo, UT: Association for Consumer Research, 553-556.

Feuer, Jane (1992), "Genre Study and Television," in *Channels of Discourse, Reassembled*, Robert E. Allen ed., Chapel Hill NC: University of North Carolina Press.

Ferber, Robert (1977), "Research by Convenience," *Journal of Consumer Research*, 4 (June), 57-58.

Fisher, Eileen and Stephen J. Arnold (1990), "More than a labor of love: Gender Roles and Christmas Gift Shopping," *Journal of Consumer Research*, 17 (December), 333-345.

Gerbner, George and Larry Gross (1976), "Living with Television: the Violence Profile," *Journal of Communication*, 26 (Spring), 173-199.

Goodwin, Cathy (1992), "Good Guys Don't Wear Polyester: Consumption Ideology in a Detective Series," in *Advances in Consumer Research* Vol. 19, John F. Sherry, Jr. and Brian Sternthal eds., Provo, UT: Association for Consumer Research.

Hirschman, Elizabeth C. (1988), "The Ideology of Consumption: A Structural-Syntactical Analysis of '*Dallas*'," *Journal of Consumer Research*, 15 (December), 344-359.

_____(1992), "Using Consumption Imagery to Decode *Twin Peaks*," *American Journal of Semiotics* 9, (2-3), 185-218.

Hochschild, Arlie Russell (1989), *The Second Shift*, New York: Avon Books.

Holbrook, Morris B., and Mark W. Grayson (1986), "The Semiology of Cinematic Consumption: Symbolic Consumer Behavior in *Out of Africa*," *Journal of Consumer Research*, 13 (December), 374-381.

Jacoby, Jacob (1976), "Consumer Research: Telling It Like It Is," in *Advances in Consumer Research* Vol. 3, ed. Beverlee B. Anderson, Provo, UT: Association for Consumer Research, 1-11.

Jewett, Robert and John Lawrence (1977), *The American Monomyth*, New York: Doubleday.

Jhally, Sut and Justin Lewis (1992), *Enlightened Racism: The Cosby Show, Audiences, and the Myth of the American Dream*, Boulder, CO: Westview Press.

Kottak, Conrad P. (1991), *Prime Time Society: An Anthropological Analysis of American Television and Culture*, Belmont CA: Wadsworth Publishing.

Lehmann, Donald R., and Lyman E. Ostlund (1974), "Consumer Perceptions of Product Warranties: An Exploratory Study," in *Advances in Consumer Research*, Vol. 1, eds. Scott Ward and Peter Wright, Provo, UT: Association for Consumer Research, 51-65.

Mayerle, Judine (1991), "Roseanne — How did you get inside my house? A case study of a hit blue-collar situation comedy," *Journal of Popular Culture* 24 (Spring), 71-88.

Mick, David Glen and Michelle DeMoss (1990), "Self-Gifts: Phenomenological Insights from Four Contexts," *Journal of Consumer Research* 17 (December), 322-332.

Monroe, Kent (1992), "On Replication in Consumer Research: Part I," *Journal of Consumer Research*, 19 (June), i-ii.

Olshavsky, Richard W. and Dong Hwan Lee (1993), "Self-Gifts: A Metacognition Perspective" in *Advances in Consumer Research* Vol. 20, Leigh McAlister and Michael L. Rothschild eds., Provo, UT: Association for Consumer Research, 547-551.

Otnes, Cele (1994), "In-Laws and Outlaws: The Impact of Divorce and Remarriage Upon Christmas Gift Exchange," in *Advances in Consumer Research* Vol. 21, Chris T. Allen and Deborah Roedder John eds., Provo, UT: Association for Consumer Research, 25-29.

Otnes, Cele, Tina M. Lowrey and Young Chan Kim (1993), "Gift Selection for Easy and Difficult Recipients: A Social Roles Interpretation," *Journal of Consumer Research*, 20 (September), 229-244.

Sears, David O. (1986), "College Sophomores in the Laboratory: Influences of a Narrow Data Base on Social Psychology's View of Human Nature," *Journal of Personality and Social Psychology*, 51 (No. 3), 515-530.

Sherry, John F., Jr. (1983), "Gift Giving in Anthropological Perspective," *Journal of Consumer Research*, 20 (September), 157-168.

_____, Mary Ann McGrath and Sidney J. Levy (1992), "The Disposition of the Gift and Many Unhappy Returns," *Journal of Retailing*, 68 (Spring), 40-65.

Solomon, Michael R. and Lawrence Greenberg (1993), Setting the Stage: Collective Selection in the Stylistic Context of Commercials," *Journal of Consumer Research*, 22 (March), 11-23.

Vande Berg, Leah R. and Diane Streckfuss (1992), "Prime-time Portrayal of Women and the World of Work: A Demographic Profile," *Journal of Broadcasting and Electronic Media* 36 (Spring), 195-208.

Wolfinbarger, Mary Finley (1990), "Motivations and Symbolism in Gift-Giving Behavior," *Advances in Consumer Research* Vol. 17, ed. Marvin E. Goldberg, Gerald Gorn and Richard W. Pollay, Provo, UT: Association for Consumer Research, 699-706.

The Impact of Temporal Orientation on Higher Order Choices: A Phenomenological Investigation

Patricia Ann Walsh, University of Connecticut

ABSTRACT

I examine the influence of temporal orientation—the future–present dichotomy—on the higher order choices (spending–saving decisions) of five informants. Analysis of interview data reveals each informant's temporal orientation remains constant across the separate types of higher order choices. Analysis of spending and saving decisions explores similarities and differences in the strategies employed and consequences experienced. Further analysis yields a four fold table—recognition (or not) of present–future trade–offs by experiences of conflict (or not)—that captures the effect of temporal orientation on the higher order choices of these informants. Further investigation is encouraged.

For decades, economic research has examined many aggregate saving/spending issues. In the past decade, two ACR presidents (Andreasen 1993; Belk 1987) along with Wells (1993) call for consumer researchers to direct attention to broader issues including consumers' saving and spending decisions. Nonetheless, spending/saving decisions remain a virtually neglected, albeit important, consumer research area.

Recently Walsh and Spiggle (1993) turned their attention to the spending/saving issue. They identify temporal orientation—the present–future dichotomy—as one of four dimensions describing the spending decisions of their informants. This study builds on Walsh and Spiggle by examining spending, as well as saving, along the dimension of temporal orientation.

In contrast to the dearth of consumer research on the save/spend decision, time has received considerable attention including a special issue of the *Journal of Consumer Reserach* (March 1981). Some consumer researchers study time as a resource (c.f., Cherlow 1981; Holbrook and Lehmann 1981; Hunt and Kiker 1981; Kaufman, Lane, and Lindquist 1991; Mamorstein, Grewal, and Fishe 1992), others study time as a variable (c.f., Burke and Edell 1986; Olshavsky 1980; Richins and Bloch 1986). Bergadaa (1990) however, conceptualizes time as a perspective influencing consumer action. She terms this temporal orientation.

Bergadaa finds two primary temporal orientations—present and future. She finds present oriented individuals indicating a satisfaction with the present not planning to change. These individuals typically react to external events. On the other hand, she finds future oriented individuals anticipating changes in their presently experienced responsibilities. She characterizes them as wanting to construct their own lives. In other words, a future oriented individual is one who views the present from the vantage point or perspective of the future.

It is important to distinguish future oriented individuals from future oriented behaviors. Any individual, regardless of orientation, may engage in future oriented behaviors. A future oriented behavior is a behavior presently engaged in so as to prepare for the future. For example, one may save $100 a month in a college fund for a child. While this constitutes a future oriented behavior—planning for the future—it does not define the saver as a future oriented individual. A future oriented individual's behaviors reflect his/her anticipation of the future. It is this perspective that defines temporal orientation and subsequently motivates behaviors.

This study applies Bergadaa's conceptualization of temporal orientation to investigate higher order choices. Walsh and Spiggle coin higher order choices to capture the precursive nature of the spend–save decision—a decision that precedes, explicitly or implicitly, all purchase decisions.

DATA AND METHODS

Five single, young adult informants (age 21 to 27), each living with his/her parents, and paying neither room nor board participated in this research. Each informant comes from a working class background and represents their families' first generation to attend college. Four of the five informants work full–time; the fifth informant was working 20 to 30 hours per week and was to begin a full–time job the day after the interview. Table 1 presents their characteristics.

Each informant participated in a semi–structured, open–ended interview lasting from 33 to 1 hour and 26 minutes (average, 57 minutes)[1]. The interview guide focused on exploration of how each informant handled his/her money. Questions assessed each informant's method of saving, of spending, and the types of accounts each uses. In every case, probing for specific spending/saving examples followed the respondent's answers. Each interviews was tape–recorded and transcribed verbatim.

Analytic Procedures

The analysis began with open coding conducted during numerous readings of the transcripts. Next, a series of systematic tabulations revealed similarities and differences both across informants and across spending/saving incidents for a single informant (Spiggle forthcoming). This produced a set of provisional concepts and categories that were used to reexamine each transcript (c.f., Bergadaa 1990). This hermeneutic reexamination yielded denser categories—each more abstract and containing more concepts and properties than before.

Each interview transcript was decomposed and reassembled into several tabulations, providing a methodical way to analyze diverse spending/saving events across and within the informants. Each tabulation included illustrative quotes to retain context. Thus, while the analysis yields etic concepts—concepts not necessarily available to the informants (Wallendorf and Brucks 1993)—it remains grounded in the data.

The concepts generated in open coding aided in constructing the first tabulation. This tabulation itemized spending/saving incidents across informants and enabled systematic comparisons of each spending/saving event. It yielded more abstract categories that encompassing the concepts generated in open coding.

Next, the dimensions of each category's properties were delineated (Spiggle forthcoming; Strauss and Corbin 1990). The second tabulation identified strategies, conditions, and consequences of each spending/saving incident. Strategies, conditions, and consequences comprise axial coding, a process through which the "data are put back together in new ways...by making connections

---

[1]The interview schedule is available from the author upon request.

TABLE 1
Informant Characteristics

INFORMANT	(SEX)	AGE	OCCUPATION	EDUCATION
Terri	(F)	27	Accounting Clerk	Some Jr. College
Eileen	(F)	26	Merchandising Asst.	Two College Degrees
Carl	(M)	25	Trucking Dispatcher	College Graduate
Tom	(M)	23	Kitchen Worker	Some College
Michelle	(F)	21	Medical Records Clerk	Some College

between categories" (Strauss and Corbin 1990, p. 96). Axial coding thus enables the conceptual operations necessary to move from simple identification of emic–redundancies (Wallendorf and Brucks 1993) to the etic perspective[2]. Although presented linearly, the employment of these operations proceeded hermeneutically (Spiggle forthcoming).

An emic–perspective summary document was constructed (Wallendorf and Brucks 1993) for use as a member check (Lincoln and Guba 1985; Wallendorf and Belk 1989) for each informant. A thank you letter, the member check summary document, and a set of questions aimed at assessing the validity of that summary were mailed to, and returned by, each informant. All informants agreed with their higher order choice pattern summary, and surmised their description to be independent of the interviewer.

INFORMANT EXPERIENCES

The following sections provide evidence of how each informant's temporal orientation generates patterns of higher order choice strategies and consequences.

The Case of Spending

Present Orientation. Three informants, Eileen, Carl, and Terri, display a present–orientation toward spending. Eileen's present–orientation to spending manifests itself in her view of spending pattern stability. She routinely spends all available funds and anticipates no changes to this pattern. Eileen's spending patterns reveal two recurrent dimensions—(1) she focuses on immediate enjoyment and spends money to "keep a good feeling going" and (2) she characterizes many purchases as "spur of the moment." She explains what she spends money on:

> Personal things, those are feel betters. They are things that make me feel better...Because I like to play with the make–up and with my hair and when it all comes out great you feel great and if you have a bad hair day (giggle), then it's just a bad hair day (giggle).

Eileen demonstrates her present–focus to spending by references to feelings of self–entitlement and enjoyment. She grounds her spending decisions in terms of the present–day benefits and evaluates these benefits strictly from the vantage point of today. Further, Eileen gives no indication of anticipating future spending pattern alterations.

[2]Emic redundancies refer to surface level themes that recur across the interviews and are obvious to the informants themselves. Etic perspective refers to more abstract themes and concepts, not necessarily recognized by the informants but, available to the researcher through analysis.

Carl also possesses a present–orientation toward spending. He exhibits a very limited set of wants and agrees that his attitude toward spending is best characterized as apathetic.

> If I want it, I get it. If I don't, I don't. I mean, for me, there is not a big grey area. I know what I need and I know what I want.

Repeatedly, Carl indicated a general disinterest in spending by making statements like, "It [spending money] really doesn't phase me one way or the other."

Each week, Carl spends half his pay on immediate consumables—gas, drinks, and food—and deposits the other half to savings. Expenditures on immediate consumables encompass only one–half Carl's earnings; he saves the rest by default. Nevertheless, this accumulated "surplus" gives him the latitude to engage in unusual and lavish unplanned spending freedoms. In one such example, Carl described purchasing an extravagant gift—diamond earrings—for his girlfriend.

> I guess that I saved up before hand but...I didn't save it up for that particular reason...I had just been saving it and I said well, I'll get the earrings and I have the money, so I did.

Terri also exhibits a strong present orientation toward spending and routinely spends on immediate consumables. Unlike the other informants, Terri routinely uses credit cards for purchases she otherwise could not afford. Although she expressed both a desire to alleviate and a desire to expand her debt capacity, her spending examples illustrate a pattern of ever–mounting debt accumulations. Terri's present orientation evidences itself in her decisions to "buy now" and satisfy today's wants regardless of the financial pressures created.

> I usually go [to Fashion Bug] when I know that I can charge because that's the easiest way to do it. You know, charge now and worry about it later...When I go, I know that I *have to* get something and I know that it's going to be, you know, 50, 60 dollars and I just couldn't write a check for that because then it would leave me without for something else, to pay a bill or whatever. So, I usually try to charge it. If I can charge it, that's good.

Future Orientation. Tom and Michelle each possess a future spending orientation. Despite behavioral differences, the spending of each is motivated by the future orientation.

Tom describes regularly "blowing" the proceeds of each paycheck—typically on immediate consumables such as cigarettes, gasoline and beer—some time before receiving his next check. While these items parallel those described by Carl and Terri, closer reading reveals that Tom experiences spending differently.

FIGURE 1

SPENDING STRATEGIES & CONSEQUENCES		

		STRATEGY	
		BOUNDARY EXPANSION	STAYS WITHIN BOUNDARY
CONSEQUENCES	MINIMIZE UNSATISFIED WANTS	CARL TERRI	EILEEN
	MINIMIZE REGRETS	TOM	MICHELLE

Tom comments on how blowing his money makes him feel:

> It doesn't bother me. Right now. For the stage I'm in right now...[This stage is] uhm, something like, working in a grown–up world, living a child's life...I still think I'm a kid...I'm enjoying it. I'm going to be a kid for as long as I can...I'm sure that [my spending patterns] will change.

Tom views his "child's life" and his spending behaviors from a future–oriented perspective. Through an appreciation of the impermanence of his life–stage, Tom attains present–day spending freedoms while expecting to change these behaviors in the future. Despite expecting future spending restrictions, his plans for such change are abstract—another characteristic of future–oriented individuals (Bergadaa 1990).

Blowing all his money sometimes renders Tom unable to make necessary purchases. When this occurs, Tom often turns to his Mother for financial assistance. For example, when required to purchase a particular pair of shoes for work, Tom did not have the money—he already spent it all. A "gift" from his Mom enabled the purchase. This reliance on Mom reinforces Tom's child–like self–characterization.

Michelle saves about half of each paycheck much like Carl. With the other half, Michelle spends freely, particularly on self–indulgent goods and services "...that kind of like keep a good feeling going,"—extraordinarily similar to Eileen's "keep a good feeling going" rationale. However, unlike either Carl or Eileen, Michelle maintains a future orientation.

Michelle repeatedly spoke of spending as an attempt to avoid future regret attributable to forgone present consumption opportunities (Simonson 1992). It is this rationale—viewing spending from the perspective of the future—that classifies Michelle as future–oriented. She demonstrates this perspective in describing her indulgent visits to a tanning salon.

> I've been going to a tanning booth...It's kind of meaningless...You know, like, paying money to get tan. When you think about it, it's really kind of stupid...This is the time that I could do that, you know? I don't have to worry about anybody else and it's not like a joint account or anything. It's just my money. And I really might just as well do it while I have a chance. I can do whatever I want now so that I don't have to be like later, oh, you know, when I was growing up I couldn't go to the tanning booth and everybody went but I didn't want to spend the money. But I don't want that. So, I go.

She reinforces this future orientation later in the interview:

> I'm trying to do all of these things now, too, when I can buy what I want and not really have to do anything or get like any permission or approval or anything.

Other examples of Michelle's self–indulgent purchases including extra summer clothes, artificial finger nails, numerous pieces of gold jewelry, make–up, and a variety of hair salon services.

Spending Summary. Superficial analysis suggests that temporal orientation exerts little influence on the informant's spending behaviors and strategies. However, axial coding allows discernment of temporal orientation's impact on the informants' spending consequences. Figure 1 presents a four–fold space characterizing each informant according to the spending strategy employed and consequence experienced.

The spending strategy dichotomy—engages in boundary expansions and staying within boundaries—centers on the source of funds for spending and is independent of temporal orientation. Carl, Terri and Tom each engage in boundary expansions, although each uses a different method to fund this boundary expansion. Carl achieves spending boundary expansions via his nonpurposive savings; Terri expands her boundaries by using credit cards; and Tom relies on "parental donations" to expand his boundaries.

For the other two informants, Eileen and Michelle, spending remains within predefined ranges. For Eileen, this spending boundary includes all the proceeds of each pay and nothing more. Michelle, on the other hand, presets her spending boundary at one–half of each paycheck (the other half dedicated to savings). Neither informant expands their predefined spending boundaries.

The spending consequence dichotomy—minimize unsatisfied wants and minimize regret—align with each informant's spending temporal orientation. This dimension examines the motivation and the intended result for each informant's spending. Present– oriented spenders—Eileen, Carl, and Terri—reported spending so as to minimize presently unsatisfied wants. These three are motivated by the intent to minimize present regret despite differing funding sources. For each, attractive spending opportunities are met with consummated purchases.

The future oriented spenders, Tom and Michelle, reported spending money presently so as to minimize future regrets over forgone spending and consumption opportunities (Simonson 1992). Each regularly takes advantage of present spending opportunities, recognizing the fleeting nature of these opportunities.

The Case of Saving

For each informant, the temporal orientation influencing spending similarly influences saving. Eileen, Carl, and Terri each demonstrate present orientations toward spending and saving while Tom and Michelle each exhibit future orientations. As in the case of spending, the informants display different saving patterns and behaviors despite similar temporal orientations.

Present Orientation. Eileen saves money in a retirement account. This future oriented behavior coupled with her present–temporal orientation generates conflict. She attempts conflict reduction through two mechanisms; (1) she implements an external control agent to enable her savings (the payroll department), and (2) she frames the deposits as losses—reductions in her present– day consumption ability.

I took the 401–K plan at work...And I don't know if that was really voluntary either...Every single week it's coming out [of my pay] and I think, am I really sure that I want this out every single week? Is it really going to be worth it...I'm reaping no benefits from it now. Who knows if I'm going to need it then, but everybody puts something away for when they're old because they have to.

Throughout the interview Eileen expressed a widespread reluctance to deprive herself of immediately available rewards in favor of delayed future rewards (Hoch and Loewenstein 1991). She summarizes her feelings about saving:

It's not easy...To be saving—saving money. Because if you have the money and there is something out there that you want and that—you might just have made yourself think that there is something out there that you want—or whatever—or that you can afford, then there's a really good chance that you won't save your money or whatever. You know—like, there's always going to be something out there. You're always going to want something. Well for me, if I have the money, instead of wanting, I have to go out there and get it.

As previously mentioned, Carl deposits about one–half of each paycheck into a savings account. Despite this behavior, Carl, like Eileen, ignores present–future trade–offs. His savings is

nonpurposive; it is simply the amount of pay left over after spending on his limited set of wants and desires. It facilitates extraordinary purchase freedoms—it is not a savings devise for the future.

During a period of unemployment, Carl maintained his spending life–style through the funds available because of his pattern of nonpurposive saving accumulation. Like with spending, Carl remains apathetic toward all savings considerations.

Terri also embodies a present savings orientation. She saves money in a Christmas Club—a structured form of savings. These funds do not facilitate Terri's Christmas gift purchases. Instead, they serve as annual "lump sum" payments on her outstanding, and presently–pressing, credit card debt. Terri described her use of this account:

[At] Christmas time, I never have the cash. Well, I have a Christmas club but by the time that I get that, it's to pay on bills...I use [my Visa] a lot for cash advances which is bad because the interest on it is terrible...but, it's always convenient.

Terri repeatedly separates the acquisition of goods from payment. She recognizes this as a restriction on the use of her Christmas club savings and often restricts her ability to continue spending. Despite recognizing this, Terri consistently engages in these restrictive patterns.

Like Eileen, Terri also regularly deposits to another savings account via payroll deductions. For Terri, the external control over these deposits allows her to "forget" about the account and functions as a willpower strategy. As she stated:

I never seem to have extra money to save. Oh, I do, I'm sorry, I do have a savings account at the credit union at work. I have money taken right out of my pay so that's the only way that it ever really seems to work because it's too easy for me to go to a bank and say, OK, I want to take fifty out...That's the only way I can seem to save money is if it's taken right out of my check. That way, I can't get my hands on it. Now, I've been [working at this job] for six months and I do not know how to get the money out of the credit union. And that's, that's fine because as long as I don't know, I won't do it.

Terri's savings experiences suggest two themes: (1) Terri uses money initially intended as savings as payments for prior acquisitions; and (2) Terri exhibits an inability to save voluntarily and opts for external determination of the deposits.

Future Orientation. Like with spending, Michelle and Tom acknowledge impending future changes in their saving behaviors. Each plans to alter their saving patterns in the future.

Michelle routinely saves, depositing about one–half of each paycheck into her savings account, and indeed, her savings are dedicate for the future:

I don't have as many responsibilities...at this time in my life. Like, I don't have anything to keep me from spending it. Except for, maybe I want to save it, you know? ...Mostly, like, saving is just for the future. Not for any one thing, it's just for the future.

Michelle's future saving orientation is expressed through expectations of increasing future responsibilities and restrictions. In preparation for these approaching constraints, Michelle saves—an example of future oriented behavior by a future oriented individual.

FIGURE 2

SAVINGS
STRATEGIES & CONSEQUENCES

STRATEGY

	INTERNAL CONTROL	EXTERNAL CONTROL
CONFLICT	MICHELLE	EILEEN
FREEDOM	CARL TOM	TERRI

CONSEQUENCES

At one time, Michelle deposited more than half of each check to her savings account. Michelle experienced the dialectic of pleasure and discomfort from making these larger deposits.

> I was getting too greedy. I was seeing my bank account go up and up and I got greedy and put two hundred dollars in each pay...[I could be putting that much] in the bank but...without having the fun that I have. To have money in the bank, I'd have to give up spending money like that—on fun. And, that's something that I, hopefully, could start doing, you know?

The dialectic is expressed in the conflict over trading–off fun—present spending—for increased saving accumulations—future-based savings. Michelle's recognition of impending future demands simultaneously encourages her to save more now in preparation for the future, and to spend more now in light of the closing aperture of present–day freedoms.

Despite Tom's savings account balance of "two dollars and change," he also maintains a future savings orientation. Regardless of his present behaviors, he anticipates changes in the future. Tom described his feelings about saving.

> Right now, I guess I still have that immortality thing that little kids do. How they don't realize that life is only so long...So I don't worry about my future, my future with money. It'll be around.

Although Tom and Michelle each maintain saving future–orientations, Michelle's future is much nearer than Tom's. His self–characterization as a child evidences his far–off vision of the future. This vantage point allows Tom to presently feel financially at ease despite his lack of savings. Nonetheless, Tom repeatedly recognized a need to save when he gets nearer the future—nearer his "grown–up," more responsible time.

Saving Summary. Unlike with spending, no associations between temporal orientation and savings behaviors are uncovered for these informants. However, axial coding generates Figure 2 which characterizes the informants according to saving strategy (internal/external control) and consequence (conflict/freedom).

The saving strategy dichotomy focuses on who controls savings deposits—the informant (internal control) or someone else (external control). As Figure 2 depicts, Michelle, Carl, and Tom each control their saving contributions (Michelle and Carl deposit voluntarily, Tom voluntarily decides not to save). Eileen and Terri, on the other hand, employ external control—both employ "agents." This strategy ensures saving deposits.

The saving consequence dichotomy—conflict/freedom—focuses on the experienced result of saving. Despite differing temporal orientations and saving strategies, both Eileen and Michelle experience conflict over saving. For these two, conflict results from recognizing lost present–day consumption opportunities.

For Terri, Carl, and Tom, saving (or not) yields freedoms—although all three freedoms differ. For Terri freedom comes from freeing–up previously accumulated debt, Carl is able to free himself from dependence on a paycheck (he quit his job), and Tom frees himself from the constraint of saving, a constraint he anticipates in the future.

HIGHER ORDER CHOICES: AN INTEGRATION

This inquiry finds informants' temporal orientation influencing both types of higher order choices; those who exhibit a present (future) spending orientation also exhibit a present (future) saving orientation. Nonetheless, further analysis reveals variability across and within the informants in the strategies and consequences associated with spending and saving.

Only one of the four dimensions identified in this study—spending consequences (minimize unsatisfied wants–minimize regret)—aligns with temporal orientation. Spending strategies

FIGURE 3

		CONTEXT	
		RECOGNTION OF PRESENT–FUTURE TRADE-OFFS	NO RECOGNITION OF PRESENT–FUTURE TRADE-OFFS
OUTCOMES	EXPERIENCES CONFLICT	MICHELLE	EILEEN
	DOES NOT EXPERIENCE CONFLICT	TOM	CARL TERRI

HIGHER ORDER CHOICES CONTEXT AND OUTCOME

(boundary expansions–stay within boundaries), saving strategies (internal control–external control) and saving consequences (experiences of conflict–freedom) are all independent of temporal orientation. Despite this apparent weak association, temporal orientation does form the context within with each informant makes higher order choices.

Present oriented informants—Eileen, Carl, and Terri—do not expect future–imposed higher order choice alterations empowering each to spend freely in the present, to give minimal thought to saving, and to expect extending this pattern into the future. Although Tom and Michelle (future oriented informants) also spend freely, each gives substantial thought to saving. Their current higher order choices occur in response to an anticipated future—each anticipates future higher order choice pattern alterations due to portended responsibilities and subsequent restrictions. In other words, future oriented individuals recognize trade–offs between present and future higher order choices while present oriented individuals do not.

Higher order choice outcomes focus on the conflict or freedom the informants experience in spending and saving money. This dimension, however, is unrelated to the temporal orientation of the informants.

Figure 3 integrates the findings across higher order choices. The four–fold space merges the dichotomous higher order choice context (temporal orientation) with the dichotomous outcome of these choices. This representation captures each informant's dominant higher order choice experience and highlights their differences.

CONCLUSION

Consumer behavior theory and economic theory suggests that individuals who recognize present–future trade–offs in spending and saving will behave in certain ways. For example, Hoch and Loewenstein (1991) discuss transient alterations in tastes as time–inconsistent preferences. Similarly, Thaler and Shefrin (1981) theorize that the "doer" makes shortsighted decisions, acting more on impulse than the "planner"—the traditional "economic man." The future oriented informants, Tom and Michelle, contradict these theories. For them, doing (spending) occurs at the insistence of the planner and the planner voluntarily takes a back seat to the doer until the future arrives. In other words, the doer is not myopic but farsighted and functions so as to ameliorate the potential for future–based regret. Thus, what appears as time inconsistent preferences, are actually consistent within the framing of the future for future–oriented individuals.

Another interesting finding concerns the experience of conflict generated by higher order choices. Although conflict was most explicitly discussed in the savings context, Eileen and Michelle's experience of conflict transcends higher order choices. Conflict differentiates these two from the other informants who do not experience conflict over spending–saving trade–offs because they engage in boundary expansion strategies.

While Eileen and Michelle both experience conflict, the conflict type is different. In Lewin's framework (Gerard and Orive 1987), Michelle experiences approach–approach conflict. For her, conflict results from the forced choice between two desired activities—save or spend. Eileen's conflict, approach– avoidance conflict, includes the existence of two external barriers—(1) funds automatically removed from her paycheck and (2) deposited in an account unavailable to her until retirement— that prevent her from spending as she wants.

Future Directions

Subsequent higher order choice investigations might expand on at least two of the present findings. (1) The finding of conflict experienced only in the context of saving. (2) The contradictory tangle of the future oriented individuals' experiences of present–future trade–offs that do not correspond to the existing research representations of this trade–off. This may simply illustrate an anomaly or, alternatively, it may illustrate a previously neglected conceptualization that may pervade individuals' experiences. Further, investigations may study whether or not individuals are cognizant of present–future trade–offs and what underlying factors contribute to an individual's propensity to be future– or present–oriented.

Other obvious future directions include expanding this study to other age groups, other ethnic groups, and groups experiencing different types of daily–life financial demands (e.g., daily living expenses such as rent/mortgages, utilities, food, and so on). Another noticeable future direction involves incorporating the other three dimensions identified in Walsh and Spiggle (1993)—context dependence/independence, struggle/no struggle, and system of control/no system of control—and examining them separately across the two types of higher order choices.

This represents only a small sampling of potential future directions available to consumer researchers interested in this important, yet neglected, area.

KEY REFERENCES

Andreasen, Alan R. (1993), "The Future of the Association for Consumer Research: Backward to the Past," in *Advances in Consumer Research*, Vol. 20, eds., Provo, UT: Association for Consumer Research.

Bergadaa, Michelle M. (1990), "The Role of Time in the Action of the Consumer," *Journal of Consumer Research*, 17 (Dec.), 289–302.

Hoch, Stephen J. and George F. Loewenstein (1991), "Time–inconsistent Preferences and Consumer Self–Control," *Journal of Consumer Research*, 17 (March), 492–507.

Lincoln, Yvonna S. and Egon G. Guba (1985), *Naturalistic Inquiry*, Sage Publications, Newbury Park, CA.

Simonson, Itamar (1992), "The Influence of Anticipating Regret and Responsibility on Purchase Decisions," *Journal of Consumer Research*, 19 (June), 105–118.

Strauss, Anselm and Juliet Corbin (1990), *Basics of Qualitative Research: Grounded Theory, Procedures and Techniques*, Sage Publications, Newbury Park, CA.

Spiggle, Susan (forthcoming), "Analysis and Interpretation of Qualitative Data in Consumer Research," *Journal of Consumer Research*.

Thaler, Richard H. and H. M. Shefrin (1981), "An Economic Theory of Self–Control," *Journal of Political Economics*, 89 (2), 392–406.

Wallendorf, Melanie and Merrie Brucks (1993), "Introspection in Consumer Research: Implementation and Implications," *Journal of Consumer Research*, 20 (3), 339–359.

Walsh, Patricia Ann and Susan Spiggle (1994), "Consumer Spending Decisions: Dimensions and Dichotomies," in *Advances in Consumer Research*, Vol. 21, Provo: UT: Association for Consumer Research.

Wells, William D. (1993), "Discovery–oriented Consumer Research," *Journal of Consumer Research*, 19 (March), 489–504.

Please contact the author for a complete reference list.

Other-Than-Conscious Consumer Information Processing: Empirical Examinations of an Emerging and Controversial Topic

Susan E. Heckler, University of Arizona
Stewart Shapiro, University of Baltimore

While nonconscious processing has been an important topic in the psychology literature for decades, it has to date received relatively little attention in the marketing discipline. The goals of this double session were to (1) introduce some of the recent research being conducted on the topic, (2) provide empirical evidence that nonconscious processing does affect different aspects of consumer behavior, and (3) stimulate discussion and encourage future research in this important domain of study. The session provided a broad overview of "other-than-conscious" processing by investigating situations in which consciously encoded information was retrieved nonconsciously and those in which nonconscious encoding of stimulus characteristics or relational information occurs.

The first paper by Ronald C. Goodstein and Ajay Kalra investigated the controversial topic of subliminal advertising. Noting that those studies dismissing the effects of subliminal processing had examined cognitive responses to the stimuli, this paper investigated whether subliminal messages can, instead, influence affective responses. Their study compared affective reactions to print advertisements which either contained sexually-suggestive embeds (not consciously detected by subjects) versus no embeds. The results of the research showed that subliminal embeds significantly affected the levels of upbeat and negative feelings evoked from the ad and suggested that such opposing feelings may explain the results of previous studies which found no effect on attitude.

Luk Warlop and Chris Janiszewski investigated the mere exposure phenomenon which suggests that exposure to a stimulus can cause the stimulus to be more familiar during later judgments, and thus, bias such judgments toward the familiar object (when subjects are not consciously aware of the previous exposure.) Their study manipulated the level of ad exposure to determine if mere exposure could bias judgments of brand name memorability and attribute superiority when consumers did not consciously attempt to use brand familiarity as an input to brand judgment. Results indicated that subjects were more likely to judge a more frequently seen brand name as being more memorable and, additionally, to judge the brand as superior on an attribute which had not been previously advertised.

Carol Pluzinski and Shanker Krishnan presented a paper which extended research in the implicit memory literature by investigating whether nonconscious retrieval of consciously encoded brand information can affect actual choice behavior. Their study manipulated exposure to brand attribute information (exposure/no exposure) and brand prominence (dominant/weak) and measured the probability of choice and brand attribute memory. The results of the study suggest that under certain conditions prior exposure to marketing information can affect subsequent choice, without conscious recollection of the encoding episode.

The paper by Susan E. Heckler and Christopher P. Puto furthered research in the implicit learning literature by investigating whether subjects could nonconsciously process product covariation information, and further, whether this information would then be used when making attribute and preference judgments. Utilizing a methodology introduced in social cognition research, stimuli were presented which demonstrated relationships between physical characteristics (bottle shape) and product attributes not consciously identifiable by the subjects. Despite the subjects' inability to identify the relationships when consciously observing the stimuli, measures of memory and preference support the fact that the memory for the covariation had been developed nonconsciously.

Arthur S. Reber and Diane Zizak also focused on implicit learning. The purpose of their paper was to examine the robustness of implicit learning effects by using completely novel stimulus and by altering the stimulus set between study and test. Previous research has consistently shown that subjects can implicitly learn an artificial grammar of letter strings, use the implicitly learned rules in subsequent tasks and indicate a preference for the grammatically correct forms in subsequent judgments. Reber and Zizak showed that the robustness of these results depended upon the subjects being familiar with the characters in the string (e.g., letters of the alphabet). When totally unfamiliar Chinese characters were used, the grammar rules were learned implicitly, but preference judgments were not affected.

Finally, Stewart Shapiro, Deborah J. MacInnis and Susan E. Heckler examined the effect of nonconsciously encoded advertising information on consideration set formation. The study used a computer-based magazine to both occupy and track subjects' attentional resources while simultaneously exposing subjects to advertisements in their periphery. Results indicated that advertising information outside of the primary visual field can be processed nonconsciously and that the information can subsequently be used in the formation of consideration sets, despite the subjects having no conscious memory of seeing the ad.

Is More Exposure Always Better? Effects of Incidental Exposure to a Brand Name on Subsequent Processing of Advertising

John W. Pracejus, University of Florida[1]

ABSTRACT

This paper examines how repeated incidental exposures to an unfamiliar brand name interact with subsequent processing of an ad for the same brand. The two factors manipulated were the level of incidental preexposure and the argument strength of the ads. It was expected that preexposure would have a positive effect on brand evaluation. Preexposure was also expected to inflate the effect of the argument strength manipulation. Unexpectedly, preexposure was found to reduce the effect of argument strength upon brand evaluation. This unexpected finding may have implications for the role of product placement in an integrated marketing communications campaign.

INTRODUCTION

While a large part of the promotional budget for most brands is spent on traditional persuasion, an increasing amount of money is spent each year on simply exposing the consumer to the brand name. An increasing number of companies (e.g. Coca-Cola) are paying motion picture and television producers in exchange for simply placing their product in a movie or television show (Fahey and Lafayette, 1991). Advertisers also make substantial expenditures placing their brand names on posters in sports arenas (Welling 1986).

Nebenzahl and Hornik (1985) found that recall for brand names placed in sports arenas is limited. Pham (1992) examined some of the potential moderators (e.g. arousal) of the effectiveness of this type of brand exposure. There seems to be, however, no empirical evidence as to how other elements of the marketing mix (e.g. ads) might moderate the effects of these exposures. Given the current level of interest in integrated marketing communications, it seems that the interaction between simple brand exposures (e.g logo only billboards at televised sporting events) and subsequent ads for those brands should be examined.

BACKGROUND LITERATURE

The theory of mere exposure (Zajonc, 1968) suggests that increasing exposure to a stimulus generally increases preference for that stimulus. Mere exposure effects have been found for a variety of stimuli, including Chinese ideographs (Saegert and Jellison, 1970), nonsense words (Berryman, 1984) and line drawings of various complexity, (Stang and O'Connell 1974). Translated into a marketing context, these findings suggest that a brand manager should try to obtain as many exposures to the brand name as possible.

This strategy, however, assumes that brand names, as stimuli, do induce the mere exposure effect. It is important, therefore, to determine the properties of stimuli which lead to strong mere exposure effects. Several characteristics of logo-only billboards placed in televised sporting events need to be examined.

Known brand names are "meaningful words", which Bornstein (1989) found to be the stimulus category associated with the largest mere exposure effect. It should be noted that some brand names are better at conveying meaning than others. Robertson (1989) reviews brand name characteristics which are considered desirable.

Logos are often visually simple, as opposed to complex. Simple visual stimuli have been shown to lead to stronger mere exposure effects than complex stimuli (Zajonc, 1972). During a televised game, exposure to billboards is frequent, often with durations of one to six seconds. Higher frequencies have been shown to increase the mere exposure effect (Zajonc, 1974) and one to six seconds has been shown to be a good exposure duration for the effect (Bornstein, 1989). The findings of these studies lead to the following hypothesis:

H1: Repeated incidental exposures to an unfamiliar, relatively simple, brand name in a naturalistic setting, with exposure durations of one to six seconds have a positive effect on subject's subsequent ratings of attitude toward the brand and reported purchase intention.

In addition to the mere exposure effect, exposures to brand names could increase the likelihood of elaboration upon arguments made in subsequent advertisements, brochures or sales presentations for the product. If previous exposure increases subsequent elaboration upon the message argument, it's ultimate impact on persuasion will be moderated by the objective strength of these arguments (Petty and Cacioppo, 1986).

Petty and Cacioppo (1979) also find that arguments with high personal relevancy elicit greater argument scrutiny than do less personally relevant issues. A 2(message relevancy) by 2(argument strength) experiment found that the high involvement, high familiarity, groups showed a greater difference between strong and weak arguments, than did those in the low involvement, low familiarity groups.

Assuming that familiarity gained through mere exposure interacts in a manner similar to the familiarity/issue involvement construct proposed in the above studies leads to the following hypotheses:

H2: Subjects who have been repeatedly preexposed to a brand name are more affected by argument strength than are subjects who have not been preexposed.

METHOD

Overview

Subjects were either preexposed or not preexposed to an unfamiliar brand name. They were then allowed to view either a strong or weak argument for the brand. After incidental exposure to a brand name, and the opportunity to view an argument for this brand, the subjects were asked to evaluate the brand along several dimensions by filling out a questionnaire.

Subjects

Eighty-seven undergraduates at the University of Illinois participated in the study for course credit in Com 101, an introduction to mass communication. This course did not deal directly with advertising issues prior to the experiment.

[1]Completion of this research was facilitated by Leo Burnett USA, and the James Webb Young Fund. The author wishes to thank Tom O'Guinn, Sharon Shavitt, Bob Wyer, Al Muniz, Carl Kriegsman, The University of Illinois Social Cognition Group, Rich Lutz, John Lynch, Joel Cohen, Luk Warlop, Michel Pham and the three ACR reviewers for their helpful comments and encouragement.

Design

Subjects were randomly assigned to a 2(preexposure, no preexposure to the brand name) by 2(strong subsequent argument vs. weak subsequent argument for the brand) between subjects design.

Stimulus Material

The brand chosen was AGFA Film, a large seller in Europe, relatively unknown in the United States. The "film" product category was chosen because it is familiar to college students, and because it is a relatively inexpensive product which is unlikely to elicit extended information search. The brand AGFA is commonly seen on logo-only billboards appearing in the background of televised British soccer matches.

Preexposure manipulation

The first independent variable, preexposure to the brand name, was manipulated by selecting a portion of a soccer game in which the AGFA logo appeared frequently. Subjects in the preexposure group saw a portion of a soccer game where the AGFA logo was on the screen for a total of 39 seconds during 15 minutes of play. Each exposure duration was between one and ten seconds (mean duration=3.9 seconds; SD=2.77 seconds). The no preexposure group saw a 15 minute portion of a soccer game in which the stadium contained no advertising for AGFA. Both tapes were free from traditional television commercials.

Argument strength manipulation

Argument strength was manipulated by providing subjects with one of two ads for AGFA after viewing the soccer game. In one condition, the ad contained a strong and logical argument for the brand, in the other, the ad contained a weak and specious argument. The target ads (for AGFA) were embedded among 14 filler ads for actual goods and services typically purchased by students (e.g. jeans, exercise equipment). The fifteenth ad was the target (AGFA). Two versions of the target ad were produced. In the strong argument condition, the ad was constructed to make a good, logical argument (outstanding color reproduction, big seller worldwide, competitively priced). In the weak argument condition, the ad was constructed to make a poor, specious argument, expected to elicit counterarguing if closely examined ("It's a roll of fun", "when you see AGFA on the scene...things are about to get exciting").

Both of the ads were exactly the same size. They both used the same visual icon, a roll of film, which was placed in the lower right hand corner of each ad. Other visual elements such as font, and layout were identical in both ads.

Manipulation check

Twenty-six students from the same subject pool were presented with one of the two ads for AGFA, embedded in a group of filler ads. They were asked to rate the argument quality of the AGFA ad they saw (how "convincing" it was). Those who rated the weak ad gave it a mean rating of 2.8, while those who rated the strong argument ad gave it a mean rating of 4.8, both on a nine point scale. This difference is significant, ($F=5.58$, $p<.05$, $\omega^2=.15$) and in the predicted direction.

Cover Story

All subjects were told that they were participating in a study, conducted by the department of Kinesiology, on their perceptions of soccer. Before viewing the soccer tape, subjects were asked to fill out a four page questionnaire on their perceptions of soccer and other sports (e.g. rugby, Australian rules football). After watching the match, subjects were asked to fill out a questionnaire which asked some new questions about the game as well as repeating some of the perception questions from the initial questionnaire. Subjects were then told that a researcher from another department would be in shortly to administer an unrelated pilot study. A different researcher then entered and asked the subjects to view the packet of ads and then fill out the questionnaire which asked the brand perception and purchase intention questions about AGFA.

Dependent Variables

After looking through the packet of ads given to them by the second researcher, subjects filled out a questionnaire. This questionnaire asked for their evaluation of several of the advertised brands. The first brand to be evaluated was AGFA. Brand evaluation was measured through three, nine point semantic differential scales anchored by: good-bad, favorable-unfavorable, and desirable-undesirable ($\alpha=.935$). Subjects then reported probability of purchase, also on a nine point scale. Finally, subjects evaluated the ad for AGFA on three semantic differential scales anchored by: good-bad, favorable-unfavorable, and desirable-undesirable ($\alpha=.886$).

Check for Confounds and Bias

In order to insure that all subjects were starting from the same base of knowledge about the brand, subjects reported their prior familiarity with the brand AGFA. Six subjects reported some familiarity with AGFA. Their data were dropped from further analysis. Involvement with the product class was also measured by asking subjects how much photographic equipment they owned. Subjects who reported owning more than $500 worth of photographic equipment were to be eliminated as well. Subjects who fell into this category, however, had all previously been removed for being familiar with AGFA.

Overall, most subjects owned cameras (86.5%). To test whether the amount of camera equipment owned varied between cells, an analysis of variance was performed. This analysis revealed no difference between exposure groups ($F<1$), between argument manipulation groups ($F=1.32$, $p>.25$), or among the cells made up by their interaction ($F<1$).

RESULTS

The means for the three dependent measures are reported in table 1. Argument strength only had a significant main effect upon attitude toward the brand. ($F=10.77$, $p<.01$, $\omega^2=.10$). Contrary to H1, no significant main effects of preexposure were found. The interaction between preexposure and argument strength was significant for attitude toward the brand, ($F=5.13$, $p<.05$, $\omega^2=.05$) and for attitude toward the ad ($F=8.91$, $p<.01$, $\omega^2=.09$). The interaction effect upon purchase intention did not meet the traditional significance criteria of $p<.05$, but it was close. ($F=3.89$, $p<.052$, $\omega^2=.03$)

The interaction effects upon all of the dependent measures are in the direction opposite to what had been predicted by H2. Subjects in the preexposed groups were *less* influenced by argument strength (strong vs. weak) than were subjects who were not preexposed.

Simple effects follow-up tests revealed that in the not preexposed groups, argument quality significantly affected attitude toward the brand ($F=16.24$, $p<.01$, $\omega^2=.37$) attitude toward the ad ($F=8.69$, $p<.01$, $\omega^2=.56$) and purchase intention ($F=7.46$, $p<.05$, $\omega^2=.19$). Among the preexposed groups, however, argument strength did not significantly affect any of the dependent measures, even against a liberal $p<.15$ criterion.

DISCUSSION

It appears that rather than increasing scrutiny of the arguments, mere exposure to the brand name has, instead, decreased it.

TABLE 1

Mean Attitudes and Purchase Intentions as a Function of Argument Strength and Preexposure to the Brand Name

Dependent Variable	Preexposed		Not Preexposed	
	Strong Argument	Weak Argument	Strong Argument	Weak Argument
Attitude Toward Brand	16.11	14.15	19.50	12.00
Attitude Toward Ad	10.07	11.93	15.41	9.50
Purchase Intention	3.06	3.00	4.42	2.36

While these results do not match the predictions made previously, they do seem to indicate that prior, incidental exposures to a brand name can affect the processing of an ad for the brand. There are several possible explanations for these results.

Preexposure may be limiting the impact of argument strength upon brand evaluation through a process of curiosity reduction. Curiosity reduction could be the result of pairing of the brand name with the category (film) during preexposure. Curiosity reduction could also be the result of a feeling of familiarity.

Since the exposure stimulus in this study consisted of billboards which read "AGFA FILM", curiosity could have been satisfied by simply knowing that AGFA is a brand of film. This knowledge could have reduced curiosity among preexposed subjects enough to reduce argument scrutiny as well.

Another possibility is that preexposure caused some sort of feeling of familiarity (see Jacoby, 1989). Preexposed subjects might have felt that they knew about the brand without any cognitive basis for this feeling. This feeling of familiarity could have directly reduced curiosity about the brand and, therefore, reduced argument scrutiny.

FUTURE RESEARCH

Several issues need to be addressed in further research into the area of the current study. They include an examination of the mechanisms leading to the apparent reduction in argument scrutiny; looking at what the impact of incidental preexposure would be on subjects who were not shown a subsequent argument for the brand; the effect of different brand name characteristics upon the observed effect; and the impact of a longer span of time between preexposure and argument presentation.

The examination of the mechanisms leading to the apparent reduction in argument scrutiny could focus upon determining the impact of the pairing of the brand name with the product category during preexposure (in the current study the exposure stimuli read "AGFA Film", not just "AGFA"). This could easily be accomplished by manipulating whether or not the brand name was associated with its product category in the exposure stimuli (i.e AGFA with film). Finding no difference between groups exposed to the two types of preexposure stimuli (category associated or not) would argue against the "information about category leads to curiosity reduction" explanation for the findings of the current study.

It would also be interesting to look at the impact of preexposure on subjects who were not shown a subsequent argument for the brand. Finding evidence of different overall brand evaluation between preexposed groups and non preexposed groups, in the absence of subsequent persuasion, would be helpful for understanding the phenomenon.

Robertson (1989) suggests several characteristics of brand names which should effect encoding and retrieval. One characteristic is whether the word is a "real" word (eg. Budget rental car), a "morpheme combination" (eg. Lexus), or a completely meaning-less word (eg. Delco batteries). In the present study, the brand AGFA was probably in the third category. Perhaps argument strength and preexposure may impact differently upon brand names in the first two groups. An inclusion of brands from these first two categories would certainly be necessary in order to fully understand the observed phenomenon.

Examining the effect of more time between preexposure and argument presentation would help to determine whether the observed outcome of the current study increased, decreased, or completely changed over time. Whether the observed effect was extremely fleeting, or relatively long lasting would also have a significant effect upon its impact and application.

CONCLUSION

If the results of this study are reliable and replicable, they may point to a phenomenon with significant implications for people who buy and sell product placements. While the current study focuses only on an unfamiliar brand, there is no reason to rule out the possibility of similar findings for familiar brands as well. If the results of this study are found to be reliable across situations, they could have considerable impact on the way in which product placement and sports sponsorship are conducted.

REFERENCES

Berryman, J.C. (1984) Interest and liking: Further sequential effects". *Current Psychological Research and Review*, 3, 39-42.

Bornstein, R.F. (1989) "Exposure And Affect: Overview and Meta-Analysis of Research, 1968-1987". *Psychology Bulletin*, 106, 2, 265-286.

Fahey, A. and J. Lafayette (1991), "Coke Goes Hollywood." *Advertising Age*, Sept. 9,1991, 1.

Jacoby,L.L.,C.M. Kelly, J. Brown, and J. Jasechko (1989) "Becoming famous overnight: Limits on the ability to avoid unconscious influences of the past *Journal of Personality and Social Psychology*, 56, 326-338.

Nebenzahl, I. and J. Hornik (1985). "An experimental study of the effectiveness of commercial billboards in televised sports arenas". *International Journal of Advertising*, 4, 27-36

Petty, R.E. and J.T. Cacioppo (1986), "The elaboration likelihood model of persuasion". In Berkowitz (Ed.), *Advances in Experimental Social Psychology*, 19, 124-205. New York: Academic Press.

_____ (1979) "Issue involvement can increase or decrease persuasion by enhancing message-relevant cognitive responses". *Journal of Personality and Social Psychology*, 37, 1915-1926.

Pham, M. T. (1992) "Effects of involvement, arousal, and pleasure on the recognition of sponsorship stimuli" *Advances in Consumer Research*, 19, 85-93.

Robertson, K. (1989) "Strategically desirable brand name characteristics", *The Journal of Consumer Marketing*, 6, 4, 61-71.

Saegert, S.C., and J.M. Jellison (1970) "Effects of initial level of response competition and frequency of exposure on liking and exploratory behavior". *Journal of personality and social psychology*, 16, 553-558.

Stang, D.J., and E.J. O'Connell (1974) "The computer as experimenter in social psychology research". *Behavior Research Methods and Instrumentation*, 6, 223-231.

Welling B. (1986) "The biggest game on earth". *Business Week*, June 2, 20-22.

Zajonc, R.B. (1968), "Attitudinal effects of mere exposure." *Journal of Personality and Social Psychology Monographs*, 9(2, pt. 2), 1-27.

_____ , R. Crandall, R.V. Kail, and W. Swap (1974) "Effects of extreme exposure frequencies on different affective ratings of stimuli". *Perceptual and Motor Skills*, 38, 667-678.

_____ , P. Shaver, C. Tavris and D. Van Kreveld (1972) "Exposure, satiation, and stimulus discriminability". *Journal of Personality and Social Psychology*, 10, 248-263.

Altering Retrieval Sets: When will Contextual Cues make a Difference?

Elizabeth J. Cowley, University of Toronto
Sharmistha Law, University of Toronto

It is known that the retrieval of brand information is a necessary condition for choice. It is also known that retrieval is affected by cues present in the encoding and retrieval environment. This paper examines the role of prior knowledge as a moderator in the relationship between contextual cues and set formation. Results show that retrieval cues are influential in the formation of the retrieval set for the high knowledge consumers, while low knowledge consumers are unaffected by the retrieval cues. Not only are the retrieval sets of the high knowledge consumer altered across retrieval contexts, but the additions to the set are relevant to the new retrieval context.

INTRODUCTION

A great deal of attention has been paid to the advantage enjoyed by experts when solving a problem and making a decision. Experts have been found to more effectively use informal reasoning mechanisms (Voss, Blais, Means, Greene and Ahwesh 1986) and general principles (Chi, Feltovich and Glaser 1982; Larkin, McDermott, Simon and Simon 1980). In a marketing context, their improved performance has been attributed to an increased motivation to process attribute statements (Beattie 1983; Maheswaran and Sternthal 1990; Walker, Celsi and Olson 1987) and incongruent information (Sujan 1985); an ability to reorganize incoming information into a meaningful format (Hutchinson 1983; Srull 1983); or their efficiency in information search (Brucks 1985). Unfortunately, little attention has been paid to the ability of the expert to retrieve the most appropriate set of alternatives given a purchase objective (for an exception see Brucks 1985). This ability is critical in making optimal purchase decisions, as retrieval of the appropriate alternative is a necessary condition for its eventual choice. Sophisticated choice strategies are wasted if conducted on a suboptimal set of alternatives.

Recently, evidence has been offered supporting the idea that retrieval sets are dynamic, changing across choice occasions (Nedungadi 1990). These findings are counter to the previous assumption that retrieval sets are relatively static; that consumers generate and store the sets in order to simplify choice (Howard and Sheth 1969). In the *static model* of the retrieved set, the inclusion of a brand is decided on the basis of its assessed utility assigned during information search. In the *dynamic model* of the retrieved set, inclusion of a brand is influenced by the presence of a usage context, purchase objective or buying occasion at retrieval.

The *dynamic model* has essentially introduced flexibility into the retrieval process. It assumes that the consumer is able to recall different brands on various choice occasions. Given a set of information, people can recall different aspects of the information when presented with different cues (Anderson and Pichert 1978; Pichert and Anderson 1977). In a marketing setting, the ability to retrieve different details about a brands when the usage context varies has been related to the amount of prior knowledge held by the consumer (Cowley 1993). It is not clear however, that the ability to recover a richer description of brands in response to a variation in contextual cues will translate into relevant additions to the set of retrieved brands. A more appropriate retrieval set may result in more optimal decision making.

RETRIEVAL SETS AND CHOICE

In memory based choice, the formation of the retrieval set is a precursor to choice. According to Nedungadi (1990), choice is a two stage process. The first stage, the brand consideration stage, includes the retrieval of the set of alternatives. The second stage reduces the consideration set to a set of brands selected for further evaluation. Alba and Chattopadhyay (1985) distinguish the consideration set from the retrieved set conceptually, but use the retrieval set in their investigation of memory–based choice. The reasoning for the operationalization is 1] that retrieval is a necessary condition of choice and 2] that membership in the retrieval set is more stable. It is the retrieval set which is of interest here.

The issue critical to the thesis of this paper arises from the comparison of the *static model* and the *dynamic model* discussed above. Implicit in the *dynamic model* is the assumption that the consumer can access new information when the retrieval context changes. This ability may vary with the expertise held by the consumer in a given domain. In other words, prior knowledge may moderate the ability to alter the retrieval set in different contexts. Also, while few researchers would contest the importance of context in the formation of the set of alternatives, explicit attention has not been paid to the impact of the contextual cues existing at the time of encoding and their interaction with the cues present while retrieving, on the retrieval set. This paper addresses these gaps in the literature.

CONSUMER EXPERTISE

Retrieval

High knowledge consumers are better able to recall information relevant to a subject (Chiesi, Spilich and Voss 1979). Superior recall may result from a more effective memory search which requires the more elaborate knowledge structure associated with experts (Chi, Feltovich and Glaser 1982; Fiske, Kinder and Larter 1983; Mitchell, Dacin and Chi 1993).

Alba and Hutchinson (1987) suggest that the retrieval set for a higher knowledge consumer should include a superior group of brands. In this study, superiority of the set is assessed on the basis of its relevance to the decision context. If the mechanism influencing the formation of the retrieval set occurs when information is recalled, then brands most appropriate to the retrieval context would be present in the retrieval set independent of their appropriateness to the encoding context. In other words, the retrieval explanation predicts that the retrieval set of the consumer should be most appropriate to the retrieval context. It follows that as the retrieval context changes, so will the membership of the retrieved set: brands will be recovered which were inaccessible given a different retrieval context. Thus, the *dynamic model* will be upheld, and high knowledge consumers will recover new alternatives when the choice context varies.

Hypotheses

As predicted by the retrieval explanation, the elaborate knowledge structure of the high knowledge consumer results in flexible retrieval set, similar to the one modelled in the *dynamic* retrieval

Advances in Consumer Research
Volume 22, © 1995

DESIGN DIAGRAM

No Context Condition				Context Condition			
	ENCODING	RETRIEVAL			ENCODING	RETRIEVAL	
Knowledge level	encoding	recall session one	recall session two	Knowledge level	encoding	recall session one	recall session two
High		Context one	Context two	High		Context one	Context two
Low		Context one	Context two	Low		Context one	Context two

framework. The less developed knowledge structures of the low knowledge consumer however, will limit the ability of the decision maker to vary the retrieved set over choice occasions. When brand information is provided to consumers and later retrieved with various usage contexts:

H1: Consumers high in product knowledge will be more likely than consumers low in product knowledge to alter their retrieval sets given differences in retrieval contexts.

H2: Additions to the retrieval set or recovered brands, will be relevant to the new context.

Encoding

The accumulation of knowledge may occur over time and across different usage contexts. It is therefore, reasonable to expect that consumers' prior knowledge will impact their encoding of new information. In fact, the advantage of the expert at encoding is demonstrated by Johnson and Russo (1984) who report that knowledgeable consumers are able to concentrate on the information relevant to the task at hand (see also Spilich, Voss, Chiesi and Vesonder 1979). Alba and Hutchinson (1987) concur that the ability to interpret the attributes of a product on a task–relevant basis is a function of expertise within a product domain, and that high knowledge consumers are more able to identify relevant information (Alba 1983). The high knowledge consumer is thus more likely to guide their effort during encoding. It is predicted that high knowledge consumers will process the information relevant to the encoding context more selectively, and therefore find it more difficult to recover previously inaccessible information relevant to another context.

H3: The presence of a usage context at encoding will reduce the ability of the high knowledge consumer to recover brands when the usage context varies.

Summary

In summary, retrieval sets will vary over choice occasions for high knowledge consumers. Retrieval sets will vary less over purchase occasions for the low knowledge consumers when compared to high knowledge consumers. The presence of a context at encoding will affect the ability of the high knowledge consumer to recover different brands when compared to encoding without a usage context.

EMPIRICAL METHODS

Subjects and Design

Sixty six[1] undergraduate students of an eastern university participated in the study. All subjects participated in three sessions: encoding, recall session one and recall session two.

Encoding. During the encoding session subjects were randomly assigned to one of two conditions: *no encoding context* or *encoding context* (see the Design diagram). Subjects assigned to the *no encoding context* condition were simply asked to read the product information slowly and carefully. Subjects in the *encoding context* condition were given context one which was one of two usage contexts: *image* or *functional* (to be described later).

Recall One. During recall session one, subjects were asked to use context one (in the *encoding context* condition) or provided context one (in the *no encoding context* condition) when recalling information.

Recall Two. During recall session two, subjects were provided context two prior to retrieving the information.

The order of presentation of the retrieval contexts was counterbalanced across subjects to minimize any systematic bias due to differences in their content. The order of presentation of the contexts was not a significant factor in recovery performance (F=1.55, p>.22). This allays any concern that the content of the contexts drove the ability to recover brands.

Subjects were blocked as high or low in product knowledge on the basis of their subjective and objective knowledge in the domain, familiarity and experience scores. (see Design Diagram).

Stimulus

Brand information was presented as though the reader was taking a walk through a bicycle shop, looking at the merchandise on display. Ten bicycles were described with five bicycles suitable for each usage context: *image* or *functional*. Brand information was pretested to ensure that an equal amount of important information for each of the usage contexts. The *image* context was operationalized by instructing the subjects to imagine that they have recently joined a bicycle club, that the club meets for rides on weekend afternoons. They have been to one meeting, and they like the people in the club very much, but they noticed that everyone had a trendy, stylish bike. They are told that their bike is not trendy or stylish, so they are going

---

[1]Data for four of the subjects were excluded as they were unable to comprehend or complete the study.

TABLE ONE
Number of Recovered Brands

Knowledge Level	No Context Condition	Context Condition	Total Sample
High	1.11	.68	.81
Low	.2	.14	.16

shopping for a new bike. The *functional* usage context was operationalized by instructing the subjects to imagine that they have decided to ride a bicycle to school instead of taking the TTC or driving. They need a bicycle to get them from point A to point B. That they do not need anything fancy, they just something durable and reliable. They are also concerned for their safety on the street.

Bicycles were described with concrete attributes only. In other words, the attributes were quantified in terms of colour, size, durability, brand reputation and warranty specifications. A typical description was "the second mountain bike is blue, the brand name is well–known for quality and workmanship. The frame is plain and simple. The frame comes with a three year warranty."

Past research has demonstrated that the complexity of the information affects the influence of expertise on the amount recalled. Specifically, low knowledge consumers remembered at least as much of the simple information, but dramatically less of the complex information (Alba 1983). To avoid comprehension as an alternative explanation, terminology in the information was simple. Any less familiar terms were explained in nontechnical language. For instance, "the bike is an American brand, it has 26" wheels which is a size that is easy to handle".

As expected, the amount recalled, or in this case, the size of the retrieval set did not vary between high and low knowledge consumers (low knowledge=3.9, high knowledge=4.3, t=-0.7837, *p*>.44). The implication is that low knowledge subjects were able to understand the information as well as high knowledge subjects.

Measures of Expertise

To accurately capture the level of expertise, four measures were taken; experience, familiarity, subjective knowledge and objective knowledge. The experience measure was an indication of how often the subject rides a bicycle (*never – 0* and *very often – 10*). The familiarity measure was an indication of how familiar the subject felt they were with bicycles (*novice – 0* and *expert – 10*). The subjective measure of expertise was an indication of the amount of information the subject held with respect to bicycles (*novice – 0* and *expert – 10*). Finally, the objective measure of knowledge was a raw score on eight multiple choice questions, five definitions and the number of brandnames provided on an unaided test of recall.

The coefficient alpha for the sum of these four measure was .84. All of the correlation coefficients were significant (*p*<.0001). A median split of this score resulted in 31 high knowledge subjects and 31 low knowledge subjects.

Procedure

As described earlier, subjects were randomly assigned to one of the conditions: *no encoding context, encoding context*. Subjects in the *no encoding context* condition were not given a context prior to encoding, while subjects in the *encoding context* condition were

given context one before reading the brand information. All subjects read the stimulus information. The next twenty minutes were spent on an unrelated task.

During recall session one, subjects in the *no context* condition were given context one at retrieval. All subjects were using context one to retrieve the information. Subjects were instructed to write down the usage context and to list as many of the bicycles as they could possibly remember.

Following the first recall session one, subjects spent six minutes working at an additional unrelated task. Subjects were then told "that people can sometimes remember information that they thought they had forgotten if they were given a new perspective with which to think about the information". They were provided with usage context two. They were asked to provide the context and to list as many of the bicycles as possible.

Finally, subjects completed the expertise measures, were debriefed, thanked and awarded course credit.

The Dependent Measures

The retrieval sets provided by subjects were compared across the first and second recall sessions. When a new brand appeared in the second set which was not present in the first set, the change was captured as an instance of *recovery*. Thus, recovery is not just the inclusion of a detail not previously recalled, but remembering a brand not recalled in the first session. The greater the value of the *recovery* variable, the more substantial the change in the membership of the retrieval set over usage contexts. New members of the retrieval set were designated as *relevant* or *irrelevant* to the particular context on the basis of the pretest described earlier.

RESULTS

The Retrieval Explanation

Hypothesis One. The first hypothesis posits that high knowledge consumers would be more likely to *recover* brands when the retrieval context varies than would low knowledge consumers. This hypothesis was supported. There was a main effect for knowledge level on recovery of previously forgotten brands. A one way ANOVA of knowledge level on recovery found a main effect for prior knowledge(F=18.40, *p*<.0001). The result holds in each of the conditions: in the *no encoding context* condition (low knowledge=.20, high knowledge=1.11), and in the *encoding context* condition (low knowledge=.14, high knowledge=.68). (See Table One).

Hypothesis Two. Hypothesis two asserted that the recovered brands would be relevant to the new context. The hypothesis was supported. Relevance was based on the pretest mentioned in the procedure section. High knowledge consumers recovered brands relevant to the new context on 24 of the 26 recovery occasions (92%). There were only 5 instances amongst low knowledge subjects. The sample was too small to draw reliable statistical inferences.

Summary of Evidence for the Retrieval Explanation. The first two hypotheses support the retrieval explanation for the ability to alter the content of recall for high knowledge consumers. The cues present in the form of usage contexts at retrieval affect the content of the retrieval set for the high knowledge consumer. The same can not be said about the low knowledge consumer.

Hypothesis Three

The Influence of at Context at Encoding. Offering a usage context at encoding was expected to influence the ability to alter recall given a different retrieval context. High knowledge consumers were hypothesized to be less able to recover brands at retrieval in this condition. The demonstration of a significant interaction implies that the context present during encoding influences the *dynamic* nature of the retrieval set. An analysis of recovery performance indicated that the interaction between knowledge level and condition (presence or absence of a context at encoding) is significant($F=10.31$, $p<.0001$). High knowledge consumers were better able to alter their retrieval sets when they learn the information without a context (*encoding context*=.68, *no encoding context*=1.11).

DISCUSSION

The results of the study suggest that high knowledge consumers were able to alter their retrieval sets in the manner described in the *dynamic* set models. Low knowledge consumers were not able to recover brands. It is important to note that the changes in the retrieval set for high knowledge consumers, were relevant to the choice at hand. Hence, some of the advantage of the high knowledge consumer in choice may be explained by this ability to alter the retrieval set by recovering relevant brands.

The hypothesis of a positive correlation between the ability to recover brands when the purchase context varies and the ability to choose the most appropriate brand in a particular context is supported by an exploratory measure not reported in the results section. During both recall sessions, subjects were asked to indicate "which, if any, of the brands they had listed might consider purchasing". The measure was intended to investigate whether the recovered brands had a higher probability of membership in the consideration set than other brands. In total, subjects circled less than 20% of the listed brands. Of the recovered brands, 65% were circled by the subject as a brand which would be considered further. This suggests that the recovered brands were not only *objectively* relevant to the new context (pretest results indicate that they are appropriate given the purchase context), but that the brands were *subjectively* relevant (the subject indicates that the recovered brand is also a member of a subset of the retrieval set which will be further considered in choice).

It is also important to note that low knowledge consumers were not only less able to recover brands, but in statistic terms, their performance was not significantly different from zero. In each of the two conditions, the recovery performance of low knowledge consumers was not statistically significant: *no encoding context* (low knowledge consumers=.2, $t=1.5$, $p>.16$) and *encoding context* (low knowledge consumer=.14, $t=1.8$, $p>.085$).

Another interesting point is that while the provision of a usage context prior to encoding did not improve the probability of recovery for low knowledge consumers, it did result in an increase in the size of the retrieval set (*no encoding context*=3.1, *encoding context*=4.3, $t=1.97$, $p<.059$). It may be possible that the increase in the set size was a result of the providing a framework (in the form

of a usage context) which facilitated processing (Johnson and Bransford 1972). The provision of a context at encoding did not have the same effect on the retrieval set for high knowledge consumers.

What insights can marketing practioners glean from these results? First, it appears that providing a context for encoding is beneficial to low knowledge consumers. In order to facilitate consumer learning, marketers might therefore consider ways of framing product information in terms of usage situations. Second, the confirmation of the retrieval hypothesis suggests that while low knowledge consumers have static retrieval sets which are not responsive to changes in usage contexts, high knowledge consumers have *dynamic* sets. The results show that for high knowledge consumers, the recall of brands on a purchase occasion is influenced by the cues at retrieval. Relative to low knowledge consumers, high knowledge consumers are able to alter the composition of their retrieval sets such that they are more relevant to the choice at hand.

FUTURE WORK

The external validity of the empirical results presented here can be extended by the introduction of interfering information (relevant competing material). It is possible that the introduction of advertising clutter could differentially influence consumers of various knowledge levels. Interference may affect consumers of different knowledge levels differentially. Proactive interference may be more damaging to the formation of the retrieval set for low knowledge consumers, while retroactive interference should be more damaging for high knowledge consumers. Future work might investigate the extent to which interfering information influences the ability to alter membership in the retrieval set.

It would be valuable to investigate how the membership of the consideration set might be influenced when the choice occasion is not strictly memory–based, but incorporates brand information in the choice environment: a mixed choice task (see Lynch and Srull 1982).

REFERENCES

Alba, Joseph W. (1983), "The Effects of Brand Knowledge on the Comprehension, Retention, and Evaluation of Brand Information," in *Advances in Consumer Research*, Vol. 10, eds., Richard P. Bagozzi and Alice M. Tybout, Ann Arbor, MI: Association for Consumer Research, 577–580.

Alba, Joseph W. and Amitava Chattopadhyay, "The Effects of Context and Part–Category Cues on the Recall of Competing Brands," *Journal of Marketing Research*, 22: 340–349.

Alba, Joseph W. and J. Wesley Hutchinson (1987), "Dimensions of Consumer Expertise," *Journal of Consumer Research*, 13: 411–454.

Anderson, John R. (1983), "A Spreading Activation Theory of Memory," *Journal of Verbal Learning and Verbal Behavior*, 22: 261– 295.

Anderson, Richard C. and James W. Pichert (1978), "Recall of previously unrecallable information following a shift in perspective," *Journal of Verbal Learning and Verbal Behavior*, 17: 1–12.

Beattie, Ann E. (1982), "Brand Expertise and Advertising Persuasiveness," in *Advances in Consumer Research*, Vol. 9, ed. Andrew A. Mitchell, Ann Arbor, MI: Association for Consumer Research, 336–341.

Bransford, John D. and Marcia K. Johnson (1972), "Contextual Prerequisites for Understanding: Some Investigations of Comprehension and Recall," *Journal of Verbal Learning and Verbal Behavior*, 11: 717–726.

Brucks, Merrie (1985), "The Effects of Brand Class Knowledge on Search Behavior," *Journal of Consumer Research*, 12: 1–16.

Chi, Michelene T. H., Paul J. Feltovich and Robert Glaser (1981), "Categorization and Representation of Physics Problems by Experts and Novices," *Cognitive Science*, 5: 121–152.

Chiesi, Harry L., Spilich, George J. and Voss, James F. (1979), "Acquisition of Domain–Related Information in Relation to High and Low Domain Knowledge," *Journal of Verbal Learning and Verbal Behavior*, 18: 257–273.

Cowley, Elizabeth J. (1993), "Recovering Forgotten Information: A Study in Consumer Expertise," in *Advances in Consumer Research*, Vol. 21, eds. Chris T. Allen and Debra Roediger, Ann Arbor, MI: Association for Consumer Research, 336–341.

Fiske, Susan T., Kinder, Donald R. and Larter, Michael W. (1983), "The Novice and the Expert: Knowledge–Based Strategies in Political Cognition," *Journal of Experimental Social Psychology*, 19: 381–400.

Howard, John A. and Jagdish N. Sheth (1969), *The Theory of Buyer Behavior*, New York: Wiley.

Hutchinson, J. Wesley (1983), "Expertise and the Structure of Free Recall," in *Advances in Consumer Research*, Vol. 10, eds., Richard P. Bagozzi and Alice M. Tybout, Ann Arbor, MI: Association for Consumer Research, 585–589.

Johnson, Eric J. and J. Edward Russo (1984), "Brand Familiarity and Learning New Information," *Journal of Consumer Research*, 11: 542–550.

Larkin, Jill H., John McDermott, Dorthea P. Simon and Herbert A. Simon (1980), "Models of Competence in Solving Physics Problems," *Cognitive Science*, 4: 317–345.

Lynch, John G. Jr. and Thomas K. Srull (1982), "Memory and Attentional Factors in Consumer Choice: Concepts and Research Methods," *Journal of Consumer Research*, 9: 18–37.

Maheswaran, Durairaj and Brian Sternthal (1990), "The Effects of Knowledge, Motivation and Type of Message on ad Processing and Brand Judgements," *Journal of Consumer Research*, 17: 66–73.

Mitchell, Andrew A., Peter F. Dacin and Michelene T. H. Chi (1993), "Differences by Expertise in the Content and Organization of Knowledge for a Brand Class," Working Paper, University of Toronto.

Nedungadi, Prakash (1990), "Recall and Consideration Sets: Influencing Choice without Altering Brand Evaluations," *Journal of Consumer Research*, 17: 263–276.

Pichert, James W. and Richard C. Anderson (1977), "Taking Different Perspectives on a Story," *Journal of Educational Psychology*, 69: 309–315.

Spilich, George J., Gregg T. Vesonder, Harry L. Chiesi, and James F. Voss (1979), "Text Processing of Domain Related Information for Individuals with High and Low Domain Knowledge," *Journal of Verbal Learning and Verbal Behavior*, 18: 275–290.

Srull, Thomas K.(1983), "The Role of Prior Knowledge in the Acquisition, Retention, and Use of New Information," in *Advances in Consumer Research*, Vol. 10, eds. Richard P. Bagozzi and Alice M. Tybout, Ann Arbor, MI: Association for Consumer Research, 572–576.

Sujan, Mita (1985), "Consumer Knowledge: Effects on Evaluation Strategies Mediating Consumer Judgements," *Journal of Consumer Research*, 12: 31–46.

Voss, James F., Jeffrey Blais, Mary L. Means, Terry Greene and Ellen Ahwesh (1986), "Informal Reasoning and Subject Matter Knowledge in the Solving of Economics Problems by Naive and Novice Individuals," *Cognition and Instruction*, 3(4): 269–302.

Walker, Beth, Richard Celsi and Jerry Olson (1987), "Exploring the Structural Characteristics of Consumers' Knowledge," in *Advances in Consumer Research*, Vol. 14, eds. Melanie Wallendorf and Paul Anderson, Provo, UT: Association for Consumer Research, 17–21.

Asymmetric Choice Patterns Across Higher-Quality and Lower-Quality Brands

Subimal Chatterjee, State University of New York at Stony Brook
Timothy B. Heath, University of Pittsburgh

ABSTRACT

Existing research suggests that adding a dominated brand to a choice set benefits higher-quality brands more than lower-quality brands. For example, although adding a dominated brand to a choice set generally increases the choice share of the dominating or target brand (*attraction effect*; Huber, Payne, and Puto 1982), the added brand increases choice shares of higher-quality targets more than choice shares of lower-quality targets (Heath and Chatterjee 1993). We report an experiment that investigates choices and relative preferences between a higher quality (higher priced) brand and a lower quality (lower priced) brand. The results indicate that (1) subjects choosing the higher-quality brand prefer their brand more than subjects choosing the lower-quality brand prefer theirs, (2) adding a dominated brand increases the choice share of the higher-quality brand but not the lower-quality brand, and (3) adding a brand dominated by the lower-quality but not higher-quality brand can increase the higher-quality brand's choice share if that brand is obviously superior to the added brand.

Mounting evidence suggests that market interventions benefit higher-quality brands more than lower-quality brands. In real-world markets, price discounts move consumers from lower-quality to higher-quality brands more than from higher-quality to lower-quality brands (Allenby and Rossi 1991; Blattberg and Wisnewski 1989; Kamakura and Russell 1989). In experimental choice settings, brands of moderate price and quality (compromise brands) attract more consumers from lower quality (lower priced) brands than from higher quality (higher priced) brands (Simonson and Tversky 1992). Similarly, asymmetrically dominated brands increase choice probabilities of higher-quality brands more than choice probabilities of lower-quality brands (Heath and Chatterjee 1993). Consider the scenarios below where Scenarios 2 and 3 include a brand (C) dominated by one original brand but not by the other. Adding such brands generally increases the choice share of the dominating (target) brand, an effect dubbed the *attraction effect* (Huber, Payne, and Puto 1982). However, recent meta-analytic evidence shows that attraction effects are common with higher-quality targets (Scenario 2), but rare with lower-quality targets (Scenario 3; see Heath and Chatterjee 1993).

Scenario 1

Brand	Price	Quality
A	$4.95	75
B	$4.25	65

Scenario 2

Brand	Price	Quality
A	$4.95	75
B	$4.25	65
C	$4.95	72

Scenario 3

Brand	Price	Quality
A	$4.95	75
B	$4.25	65
C	$4.45	65

Using asymmetric dominance within experimental choice tasks, the current study extends evidence of differential preferences for higher-quality and lower-quality brands in three ways. First, it replicates evidence suggesting differential sensitivity to asymmetric dominance. Second, it tests the possibility that under certain circumstances, adding a brand dominated by the lower-quality but not higher-quality brand can increase the higher-quality brand's share. Third, it tests directly whether subjects choosing the higher-quality brand hold stronger relative preferences for their brand than subjects choosing the lower-quality brand hold for their brand. Relative preferences are operationalized as differences in attitudes toward higher-quality and lower-quality brands.

THEORY AND RESEARCH

Figure 1 illustrates the attraction effect. In Figure 1, Brands A and B are competitors and the entrants (S_1, S_2, and S_3) are added one at a time. Neither Brand A nor Brand B dominates the other since each is superior on one attribute. However, Brand S_1 is dominated by A but not by B (i.e., Brand S_1 is asymmetrically dominated). Attraction effects due to such brands have been reported across numerous product classes and studies (Huber, Payne, and Puto 1982; Huber and Puto 1983; Lehmann and Pan 1994; Mishra, Umesh, and Stem 1993; Pan and Lehmann 1993; Ratneshwar, Shocker and Stewart 1987; Simonson 1989; Wedell 1991). However, attraction effects vary across different types of target brands. Heath and Chatterjee (1993) reanalyzed data from thirty experimental choice sets and found that attraction to higher-quality brands occurred in nine of fourteen cases, but attraction to lower-quality brands occurred in only one of sixteen cases. The pattern parallels findings from real-world markets where it is easier to move consumers to higher-quality brands than to lower-quality brands. In one study, price discounts of frequently purchased grocery items attracted consumers from lower-quality to higher-quality brands in eight out of twelve cases, but attracted consumers from higher-quality to lower-quality brands in only three out of twenty-seven cases (Blattberg and Wisnewski 1989).

Researchers have proposed three explanations that may account for the observed asymmetric responses to price discounts. First discounting higher-quality brands results in favorable substitution and income effects, whereas discounting lower-quality brands results in favorable substitution effects but an unfavorable income effect (Allenby and Rossi 1991). The unfavorable income effect occurs because discounting the lower-quality brand increases discretionary income that enables consumers to buy higher-quality (higher priced) brands. Second, asymmetric price competition may be due to asymmetries in a property called *loss aversion*, the tendency for losses to be more unpleasant than gains of equal economic value are pleasant (Kahneman and Tversky 1979; Tversky and Kahneman 1991). Consumers may be more loss-averse for quality than price. Hardie, Johnson, and Fader (1993), for example, report loss-aversion coefficients that are greater for quality than price. Third, asymmetries in price competition may arise if consumers of higher-quality brands are more committed to quality than consumers of lower-quality brands are committed to non-quality attributes such as price (Blattberg and Wisnewski 1989).

In experimental choice settings, subjects do not actually buy brands or get an opportunity to trade one brand for the other. Thus,

FIGURE 1
Brand Configurations

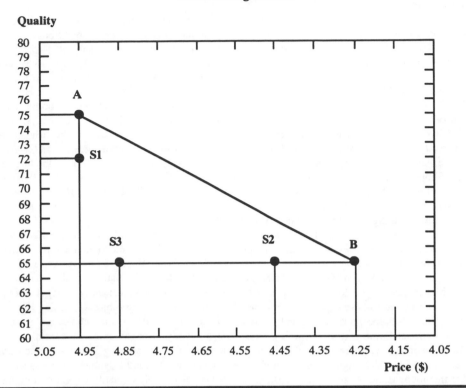

income or substitution effects are less likely to occur in experimental markets. Differential loss aversion and/or differential commitment to quality and price, on the other hand, can account for the asymmetries in choice patterns between higher and lower quality brands in experimental tasks (see Simonson and Tversky 1992)

Study Overview and Hypotheses

We tested three hypotheses investigating choices and relative preferences between a higher-quality and lower-quality brand in one experiment in which student subjects chose between two fictitious brands of beer, A and B (Figure 1). Brand A was the higher-quality, higher-priced brand (75-quality, $4.95 per six-pack). Brand B was the lower-quality, lower-priced brand (65-quality, $4.25 per six-pack). The control condition consisted of Brands A and B, whereas an out-of-stock brand was added in each of the three experimental conditions (Brands S_1, S_2, and S_3).

Based on prior research we expected that an asymmetrically dominated brand designed to make Brand A look more attractive (S1) would increase A's choice share and reduce B's, whereas an asymmetrically dominated entrant targeting Brand B (S2) would have no such effects.

H1: Introducing an asymmetrically dominated brand targeting the higher-quality brand (Brand S1 targeting Brand A) will increase the choice share of the higher-quality brand. Introducing an asymmetrically dominated brand targeting the lower-quality brand (Brand S2 targeting Brand B) will not increase the choice share of the lower-quality brand.

We extend prior research by testing the possibility that under certain circumstances, adding a brand dominated by the lower-

quality but not the higher-quality brand can increase the higher-quality brand's share. Consider Entrant S3 that is dominated by Brand B and not by Brand A (Figure 1). In addition to making Band B appear attractive through dominance, it may make Brand A appear attractive by being obviously inferior to A (Brand A offers 10 units more quality than S3 at a similar price). However, if people choosing higher-quality brands are less likely to switch than people choosing lower-quality brands, then S3 should increase Brand A's choice share by moving people off Brand B, even though A does not dominate it.[1]

H2: When asymmetrically dominated brands are obviously inferior to both lower-quality and higher-quality brands (e.g., S3), their effect will be to increase choice shares of the higher-quality brands.

Past research and Hypotheses 1 and 2 suggest that consumers of lower-quality brands are more likely to switch to higher-quality brands than consumers of higher-quality brands are likely to switch to lower-quality brands. The implication is that consumers preferring higher-quality brands prefer them more strongly over lower-quality brands, than consumers of lower-quality brands prefer their brands over higher-quality brands. Our third hypothesis is that the relative preferences of consumers of higher-quality brands are

---

[1]Past research has shown that people are less likely to prefer the cheapest alternative when they choose from a set of three brands (Simonson, Nowlis and Lemon 1993). This does not threaten our test since Brand S3 is kept out of stock and subjects always choose between two brands: A (highest price/quality) and B (lowest price/quality).

stronger than those of lower-quality brands, where relative preferences are operationalized as differences in attitudes toward higher-quality and lower-quality brands.

H3: Subjects choosing the higher-quality brand (A) will display stronger relative preferences than subjects choosing the lower-quality brand (B).

EXPERIMENT

Subjects and Procedure

Two-hundred-and-five business students from three large eastern universities served as subjects in a one-way between-subjects experiment consisting of one control group and three experimental groups. Subjects were told to imagine that they wished to buy a six-pack of beer. The control group was asked to choose from a choice set consisting of two brands: Brand A was priced at $4.95 and had a quality rating of 75 (1-100 scale). Brand B was priced at $4.25 and had a quality rating of 65. The three experimental groups chose between the same two brands, although an out-of-stock brand was included as well.

The brand configurations are shown in Figure 1. To assess differential effects on higher-quality and lower-quality brands, Brands S_1 and S_2 were configured to be equidistant from their respective target brands (i.e., S_1's proportional deviation from A's quality matched S_2's proportional deviation from B's price). Thus, S_1 had A's price but 4.0% lower quality, whereas S_2 had B's quality but 4.3% higher price. Brand S_3 was configured such that it was dominated by Brand B and not by Brand A, and yet made Brand A look attractive. Thus, S_3's quality was made equal to that of the lower-quality brand (B), and its price only slightly lower than A's (by 2%). Attraction effects to Brand A were expected with entrants S_1 and S_3. No attraction effects were expected to Brand B. After making their choices, subjects in all conditions rated each brand on a 1-20 like / dislike scale.

Analyses and Results

The data are analyzed in two stages. First, between-group differences in choice were assessed with Fisher's Exact Test of Independence. A separate 2 X 2 contingency table was formed for each pairwise comparison between control and experimental groups. Second, differences in relative preferences between subjects choosing Brand A and Brand B were assessed using ANOVAs.

Hypothesis 1 predicted that Brand S_1 would increase Brand A's share, whereas Brand S_2 would not increase Brand B's share. These effects were assessed by comparing target brands' shares between control and experimental conditions. Hypothesis 1 was supported. Brand S_1 significantly increased Brand A's share from 49.02% to 80.85% (p <.001). Brand S_2 did not significantly affect B's share ($B_{Control}$=50.98% vs. $B_{Experimental}$ =42.59%, p =.855).

Hypothesis 2 predicted that Brand S_3 would increase A's choice share rather than B's share, even though B, not A, dominated it. The hypothesis was supported. Brand S_3 increased A's share from 49.02% to 66.04% (p =.059).

Hypothesis 3 predicted that relative preferences would be stronger among subjects choosing the higher-quality brand (A) than subjects choosing the lower-quality brand (B). Relative preference was operationalized by taking the difference between the attitude towards the chosen brand and foregone brand.

Relative preference   = Liking$_{Brand A}$ - Liking$_{Brand B}$,
for subjects choosing Brand A,

= Liking$_{Brand B}$ - Liking$_{Brand A}$,
for subjects choosing Brand B.[2]

Relative preferences were tested separately in the control condition and experimental conditions. In the control condition, relative preferences were subjected to a one-way fixed-effects ANOVA: Choice (A vs. B). In the experimental conditions, relative preferences were subjected to a two-way fixed-effects ANOVA: Choice (A vs. B) and Added Brand (S_1 vs. S_2 vs. S_3).[3]

Hypothesis 3 was supported in both conditions. In the control condition, although there was a 50:50 split in choices, subjects choosing Brand A showed significantly stronger relative preferences than subjects choosing Brand B ($M_{Brand B}$=1.42, $M_{Brand A}$=4.13, $F_{(1,46)}$=6.38, p <.05). In the three experimental conditions, Brand A was favored by a 2:1 margin overall (67.53% for Brand A vs. 32.47% for Brand B) and subjects choosing Brand A showed significantly stronger relative preferences than subjects choosing Brand B ($M_{Brand B}$=4.62, $M_{Brand A}$=6.21, $F_{(1,144)}$=8.60, p <.01). However, the effect of the brand chosen was moderated by brand added (Interaction $F_{(2,144)}$=10.93, p <.01; see Table 1). When Brands S_1 or S_3 were added to the choice set, the pattern matched the pattern in the control condition. Relative preferences were significantly stronger among subjects choosing Brand A than among subjects choosing Brand B. However, when Brand S_2 was added to the choice set, relative preferences were significantly stronger among subjects choosing Brand B than among subjects choosing Brand A. Since Brand S_2 was clearly dominated by Brand B, subjects may have focused on the dominance relationship to justify a higher rating for Brand B.[4]

GENERAL DISCUSSION

Summary

Recent research suggests that asymmetrically dominated brands are more effective in improving choice shares of higher-quality than lower-quality target brands (Heath and Chatterjee 1993). The current study replicated and extended such asymmetries in three ways. We found that (1) asymmetrically dominated brands increased the share of the high-quality brand, but not the lower-quality brand, (2) adding a brand dominated by the lower-quality but not the higher-quality brand can increase the choice probability of the higher-quality brand if that brand is obviously superior to the new brand, and (3) relative preferences among subjects choosing the higher-quality brand were significantly greater than among subjects choosing the lower-quality brand. Thus, we replicated and extended prior asymmetries in choice patterns, and suggest and support an explanation for the asymmetries.

---

[2]To ensure uncontaminated choice processes, attitudes were measured only after choices were made. Although relative preferences may have been inflated to justify choices, such justification need not threaten our test since there is no *a priori* reason for expecting justification to vary across consumers of lower-quality and higher-quality brands.

[3]The control condition provides a pure test for differential preference strengths since it is not contaminated by perceptual biases arising from irrelevant alternatives.

[4]Although S_3 was dominated by Brand B, it was obviously inferior to both Brands A and B. Hence S_3 provides less reasons for justifying a higher rating for Brand B alone.

TABLE 1
Relative Preference Strengths Across Consumers of Higher-Quality (A) and Lower-Quality (B) Brands

Additional Brand	Subjects Choosing Brand A	Subjects Choosing Brand B	Tests
None (Control)	4.125 ($n = 24$)	1.417 ($n = 24$)	$F_{(1,46)} = 6.38$, $p < .05$
S_1	6.567 ($n = 37$)	1.444 ($n = 9$)	$F_{(1,44)} = 15.91$, $p < .001$
S_2	5.645 ($n = 31$)	8.285 ($n = 21$)	$F_{(1,50)} = 4.30$, $p < .05$
S_3	6.343 ($n = 35$)	1.765 ($n = 17$)	$F_{(1,50)} = 10.05$, $p < .005$

The current study suffers from three shortcomings that must be addressed. First, the experimental data were limited to a simple three-brand choice set where each brand was described on price and quality, and the added brand differed from targets only on one attribute. Such limitations are only partially mitigated by the fact that asymmetries in the attraction effect have been reported in a meta-analysis that used a wide variety of products and entrants that varied on two attributes compared to the targets (Heath and Chatterjee 1993). Future research needs to address scenarios that more closely approximate multiple-brand, multiple-attribute markets of the real world.

Second, difference measures were used to operationalize relative preferences. Difference scores may lead to a variety of potential problems including low reliability, false discriminant validity, spurious correlation, and variance restriction (see Peter, Churchill, and Brown 1993). One way of getting around these problems is to operationalize relative preferences more directly such that calculation of difference scores is unnecessary (Johns 1981). For example, a direct comparison measure of relative preferences may be operationalized in a question like "Overall how much do you prefer the brand chosen over the brand that was not chosen" that is scored on a scale anchored from "about the same" to "very much more than the brand not chosen."[5]

Third, we did not test the potential explanation of differential loss-aversion across higher-quality and lower-quality brands. Future research might do so with measures such as "Overall how much does an x% decrease in quality make you more unhappy than an x% increase in price," that is scored on a scale anchored from "about the same" to "very much more than an increase in price."

---

[5]However, direct comparison measures also suffer from measurement problems. For example, Dhar and Simonson (1992) found that in a judgement task involving a comparison between two options, focusing attention on one alternative (in this case the chosen option) tends to enhance its attractiveness.

REFERENCES

Allenby, Greg M. and Peter E. Rossi (1991), "Quality Perceptions and Asymmetric Switching Between Brands," *Marketing Science*, 10 (Summer), 185-204.

Blattberg, Robert C. and Kenneth J. Wisnewski (1989), "Price Induced Patterns of Competition," *Marketing Science*, 8 (Fall), 291-309.

Dhar, Ravi and Itamar Simonson (1992), "The Effect of Focus of Comparison on Consumer Preferences, " *Journal of Marketing Research*, 29 (November), 430-440.

Hardie, Bruce G. S,. Eric J. Johnson, and Peter S. Fader (1993), "Modeling Loss Aversion and Reference Dependence Effects on Brand Choice," *Marketing Science*, 12 (Fall), 378-394..

Heath, Timothy B. and Subimal Chatterjee (1993), "Attraction and Compromise Effects in Choice: Moderating Influences and Differential Loss Aversion to Quality and Nonquality Attributes," in *Advances in Consumer Research*, Vol. 20, Association for Consumer Research, 475.

Huber, Joel, John W. Payne, and Christopher Puto (1982), "Adding Asymmetrically Dominated Alternative: Violations of Regularity and the Similarity Hypothesis," *Journal of Consumer Research*, 9 (June), 90-98.

Huber, Joel and Christopher Puto (1983), "Market Boundaries and Product Choice: Illustrating Attraction and Substitution Effects," *Journal of Consumer Research*, 10 (June), 31-44.

Kahneman, Daniel and Amos Tversky (1979), "Prospect Theory: An Analysis of Decision Making Under Risk," *Economterica*, 47 (March), 263-291.

Lehmann, Donald R. and Yigang Pan (1994), "Context Effects, New Brand Entry, and Consideration Sets," *Journal of Marketing Research*, 30 (August), 331-349.

Mishra, Sanjay, U. N. Umesh, and Donald E. Stem, Jr. (1993), "Antecedents of the Attraction Effect, " *Journal of Marketing Research*, 30 (August), 331-349.

Pan, Yigang and Donald R. Lehmann (1993), "The Influence of New Brand Entry on Subjective Brand Judgments, " *Journal of Consumer Research*, 20 (June), 76-86.

Peter, J. Paul, Gilbert A. Churchill, Jr., and Tom J. Brown (1993), "Caution in the Use of Difference Scores in Consumer Research," *Journal of Consumer Research*, 19 (March), 655-662.

Johns, Gary (1981), "Difference Score Measures of Organizational Behavior Variables: A Critique, " *Organizational Behavior and Human Performance*, 27 (June), 443-463.

Ratneshwar, Srinivasan, Allan D. Shocker, and David W. Stewart (1987), "Toward Understanding the Attraction Effect: The Implications of Product Stimulus Meaningfulness and Familiarity, " *Journal of Consumer Research*, 13 (March), 520-533.

Simonson, Itamar (1989), "Choice Based on Reasons: The Case of Attraction and Compromise Effects," *Journal of Consumer Research*, 16 (September), 158-174.

Simonson, Itamar, Nowlis, Stephen, and Katherine Lemon (1993), "The Effect of Local Consideration sets on Global Choice Between Lower price and Higher Quality, " *Marketing Science*, 12 (Fall), 357-377.

Tversky, Amos and Daniel Kahneman (1991), " Loss Aversion in Riskless Choice: A Reference Dependent Model," *Quarterly Journal of Economics*, 106 (November), 1040-1061.

Wedell, Douglas H. (1991), "Distinguishing Among Models of Contextually Induced Preference Reversals," *Journal of Experimental Psychology: Learning, Memory, and Cognition*, 17 (4), 767-778.

Direct and Indirect Effects of Confidence on Purchase Intention

Michel Laroche, Concordia University
Chankon Kim, Concordia University
Lianxi Zhou, Concordia University

ABSTRACT

This study investigates two very different processes through which confidence toward a brand could affect intention to buy the same brand. The direct process describes the direct effect of confidence on intention. The indirect process represents the influence of confidence on brand attitude, which in turn affects intention. The empirical results from a structural equation analysis show that intention to buy a specific brand is both directly and indirectly affected by confidence toward that brand.

INTRODUCTION

The confidence construct was first proposed by Howard and Sheth (1969) as one of the determinants of purchase intentions. They postulate that confidence is positively related to intention. Similarly, Bennett and Harrell (1975) suggest that confidence plays a major role in predicting brand attitudes and intentions to buy. Despite some evidence of a positive relationship between confidence and intention (e.g., Bennett and Harrell 1975; Howard 1977; Laroche and Sadokierski 1994), the fundamental question as to how confidence affects intention has not been satisfactorily resolved. This is an issue of process which warrants more theoretical and empirical inquiry.

The existing literature provides two alternative explanations. In the first, confidence in brand evaluation is considered as one of the determinants of intention to buy. Thus, a direct relationship between confidence and intention is hypothesized. The second explanation posits that the influence of confidence on intention is through its influence on attitude toward the brand. In this view, an indirect relationship between confidence and intention is hypothesized, with attitude as an intermediate link.

To date, it is still not clear which explanation is more valid. One may also suspect a combination of direct and indirect processes. Therefore, the central question of interest in the present study is: Is the influence of confidence on purchase intention explained by a single process (i.e., a direct or an indirect effect) or by a multiple process (i.e., a combination of direct and indirect effects)? This question is examined in this paper under a multiple brand context, as it will be explained later.

The Confidence Construct

According to Howard (1989), confidence is the buyer's subjective certainty - his/her state of feeling sure - in making a judgment on the quality of a particular brand. In other words, confidence is the degree of certainty that one's evaluative judgment of the brand is correct (Howard 1989, p. 34). This definition has two theoretically different meanings. It may refer to the buyer's overall confidence in the brands, or alternatively, to the buyer's confidence in his ability to judge or evaluate attributes of the brands (Bennett and Harrell 1975). The latter meaning of the confidence construct is largely associated with the perception of risk underlying decision making. As Howard and Sheth (1969) postulated, confidence is the buyer's belief that s/he can estimate the payoff of purchasing a particular brand. In fact, Ostlund (1973) operationalized confidence as the degree of certainty regarding product performance risk and psychological risk. This postulation is also related to the term 'specific self-confidence' defined by Cox and Bauer (1964) as

"confidence in performing a specific task or in solving a specific problem."

In the psychological literature, the overall confidence in brand evaluations is often considered as one of the dimensions of the attitude construct. For example, Sample and Warland (1973) indicate that the certainty (or confidence) with which a person makes attitudinal judgments reflects the extent to which the person has actually formed an attitude toward a focal object. Fazio and Zanna (1981) further propose that confidence with which one's attitude is held represents one of the four qualitative dimensions of attitude - clarity, confidence, reliability, and accessibility. Moreover, based on a literature review, Raden (1985) summarizes several strength-related attitude properties in which the certainty or confidence toward an attitude object is also included.

However, Howard and Sheth (1969) and Howard (1989) do not agree with such a conceptualization. They argue that confidence is not a dimension of the attitude construct. Indeed, Day (1970) indicates that the confidence level may reflect uncertainty about the correctness of the brand judgment, or ambiguity as to the meaning of the attitude object. Accordingly, previous experience and familiarity with a particular brand are some of the determinants of one's confidence about that brand. Bennett and Harrell (1975) further note that the multiattribute attitude doesn't fully reflect the property of confidence. In fact, an individual's attitude toward an object, according to the multiattribute attitude model, is determined by the multiplicative summation of his/her subjective probabilities (i.e., beliefs) that the object possesses the considered attributes and his/her evaluations of these attributes. For the traditional attitude model, the certainties or probabilities apply to beliefs about the attitude object rather than to the evaluative attitude per se (Raden 1985).

Notwithstanding the probabilistic nature of beliefs in forming attitude, the overall certainty about the object has not been integrated into the attitude model (Bennett and Harrell 1975). Consequently, one tends to accept that overall confidence toward a brand is separate from the attitude toward the same brand.

This research has been designed to examine both these direct and indirect effects of confidence in brand judgments on purchase intention.

The Two Alternative Ways by which Confidence Affects Intention

The direct positive relationship between confidence and intention to buy was first proposed by Howard and Sheth (1969). Bennett and Harrell (1975) provide empirical evidence to support this argument. In a more recent study, Laroche and Sadokierski (1994) further show that intention to select an investment firm is a direct function of confidence in one's evaluations on the firm. They report that the effect of confidence on intention is much stronger than that of attitude toward the same brand. They also found that, in 14 out of 18 cases, attitude toward brand i is significantly related to intention toward the same brand *in addition* to the effect of confidence.

On the other hand, an argument may be made that confidence has a direct effect on attitude toward the brand, which in turn influences intention to buy, i.e., intention may be an indirect function of confidence. There is some evidence to support this argument. For example, Warland and Sample (1973) show that attitude toward student government is a better predictor of self-reported voting behavior in student elections for individuals with high certainty in their evaluative responses. Fazio and Zanna (1978a; 1978b) obtained similar results. Their studies demonstrate that certainty in judgments about the attitude object significantly enhances the prediction of behavior from attitude toward the object.

Given the above findings, it appears that the overall confidence toward a target brand can influence behavioral intention in two ways: it can have a direct effect on intention or it can indirectly affect intention through its effect on attitude toward the brand. Which explanation makes more sense, however, remains largely unclear in the existing literature. Furthermore, there exists yet another possibility; confidence may affect intention simultaneously in both direct and indirect ways.

Intuitively, the direct effect may be explained as follows: individuals who have higher certainty about their brand evaluations will be closer to some motivational equilibrium with respect to additional information search (Howard 1989). When individuals approach this level of equilibrium, they will need less product information, curtail their information search and thus, be more likely to be ready to act.

An explanation for the indirect effect, on the other hand, may come from the perspective of the consumer information search behavior. When consumers are not quite sure about their subjective brand judgments, they tend to search for more product-related information so as to reduce uncertainty (Urbany et al. 1989). Given limited information, consumers with higher levels of uncertainty are likely to be frustrated. As a result, the perceived attractiveness of the judged brand tends to be affected as a "compensation" for the uncertainty in brand evaluations, which, in turn, influences behavioral intention.

If both of these explanations are correct, there is finally the possibility that behavioral intention may be affected simultaneously by confidence both directly and indirectly.

The Competitive View of Intention Formation

Consumers are often faced with several brands or alternatives from which they have to choose. Most researchers acknowledge the influence of competing brands in explaining intentions and behavior. In their multi-brand model of intentions, Laroche and Brisoux (1989) formally postulate that consumers' intention to buy a specific brand is determined not only by the attitude toward the same brand but also by the attitudes toward other competing brands in the choice set (i.e., the distribution of attitudes toward all the brands in the choice set).

Similarly, Tyebjee (1979) suggests that an attitude should be considered in both absolute and relative senses. In the prediction of voting behavior, Jaccard (1981) shows that more variance is explained when attitudes toward other alternatives are included in the analysis. This conceptual position is also supported by several other studies (e.g., Malhotra 1986; Nantel 1986).

Using data on consumers' attitudes toward beers in a choice set, Laroche and Brisoux (1989) tested two different types of effects: a direct effect and a competitive effect. The direct effect suggests that intention to buy a brand is determined only by the attitude toward that brand. The competitive effect implies that attitudes toward other competing brands may affect intention toward a focal brand. According to the authors, the competitive effect, if it happens, tends to negatively influence intention to buy that specific brand. The expected direction of competition reflects the similarity effect (Tversky 1972), which suggests that choice

alternatives that are similar tend to draw shares from each other and are more competitive/substitutable than dissimilar alternatives (Kamakura and Srivastava 1984). Their findings show that the model specifying the multiple effects (combination of a direct effect and a competitive effect) is superior to the single effect model. More recently, Laroche and Sadokierski (1994) provided further evidence to support the competitive view of intention formation.

Alternative Models and Hypotheses

To incorporate the different views of the effects of confidence on intention into the multi-brand model of intentions (i.e., Laroche and Brisoux 1989), the present paper compared and tested three alternative models (see Figure 1).

The first model represents the direct link between confidence and intention. It is hypothesized that:

> *H1:* *Intention to buy a specific brand is directly affected by one's overall confidence toward that brand, independently of the effects of attitude toward the same brand.*

The second model postulates the indirect relationship between confidence and intention. The hypothesis is formulated as follows:

> *H2:* *Intention to buy a specific brand is indirectly affected by one's overall confidence toward that brand through attitude toward the same brand.*

The third model combines both the direct and indirect effects of confidence on intention. It is expected that:

> *H3:* *Intention to buy a specific brand is not only directly affected by one's overall confidence toward that brand but also indirectly affected through attitude toward the same brand.*

METHODOLOGY

Sample

The data used in this study came from a survey on the selection of cough/cold syrup medications. The four most popular brands (i.e., Dimetapp, Robitussin, Benylin, and Triaminic) were selected to test the alternative models. Many researchers (e.g., Lussier and Olshavsky 1979) have indicated that consumers tend to limit their final comparison to an average 4 to 7 brands since people have a tendency to reduce their information load and the cognitive complexity of the brand choice process. Therefore, a heavy competition among these four selected brands is expected. The respondents who had these four brands in their evoked sets were selected for analysis. Due to listwise deletions on some missing values, the sample sizes were respectively 107, 93, 118 and 95 for the four brands.

The population for this survey consisted in residents of the Ottawa and Hull census metropolitan areas. Area sampling was used due to convenience, and the lack of discriminating characteristics of cough/cold syrup consumers. Streets were randomly selected from a local street directory. An equal number of streets were chosen from each municipality. Streets were partitioned in two and delivery alternated between the mid-point and end or beginning of each street. Efforts were made to contact as many households on the selected streets as possible. The self-administered questionnaire was left with the consenting individuals to be picked up at a later time or mailed to the researcher (a stamped self-

FIGURE 1
The Three Alternative Models for Focal Brand A

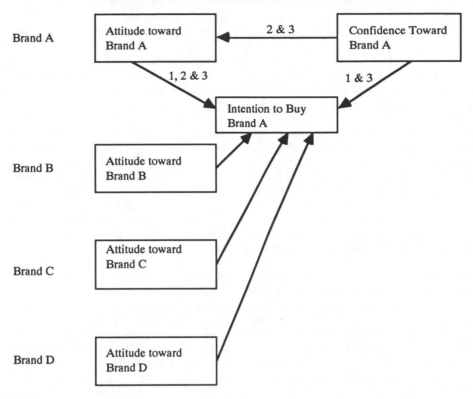

Notes:
1. Brand A is taken as the focal brand, while brand B, C, and D are considered as competing alternatives. A similar model is obtained when B, C and D are the focal brands.
2. In this diagram, Model 1 (direct effect only) is the model with the two lines marked 1, Model 2 (indirect effect only) is the model with the two lines marked 2, and Model 3 (combined effects model) is the model with the three lines marked 3. Lines without numbers are common to all three models.
3. Brand A = Dimetapp; Brand B = Robitussin; Brand C = Benylin; Brand D = Triaminic.

addressed envelope was provided). In total, 324 completed responses were obtained.

The sample's average age is between 30 and 39, the median level of education is junior college, and the median family income is between $60,000 and $69,000. Of those respondents, 28.7% are male and 71.3% are female. Overall, the sample seems to be skewed toward somewhat affluent families.

Measures

Confidence. The overall confidence toward the brand was measured by two 9-point semantic differential scales (Not confident at all/Very confident; Very uncertain/Very certain). The respondents were required to indicate how confident they were about their evaluation of each brand; and the extent to which they were certain about each brand. The reliabilities of the two measures were .84, .89, .84, and .81, respectively, for the concerned brands (i.e. Dimetapp, Robitussin, Benylin, and Triaminic).

Attitude. Four 9-point semantic differential scales (Very unfavourable/Very favourable, Dislike very much/Like very much, A very bad brand/A very good brand; Very unsatisfactory/Very satisfactory) were used in measuring attitudes toward the selected brands. The mean of these four scales was taken as the indicator of the attitude construct. The reliabilities of the four scales were .95, .93, .94, and .94, respectively, for the four brands.

Intention. Intention was measured by asking the respondent to indicate how many times s/he would buy a certain brand in the next ten purchase occasions. The measure was then divided by ten, thereby varying between 0 and 1. This measure has been used in the literature by Juster (1966) and Howard and Ostlund (1973).

ANALYSES AND RESULTS

In the present study, three different models were tested and compared in order to see the potential effects of confidence toward a brand on intention to buy the same brand. Model 1 represents the direct effect of confidence on purchase intention. Model 2 addresses the indirect effect, in which confidence in one's brand judgment directly affects attitude toward that brand which in turn influences purchase intention. Model 3 combines both the direct and indirect effects of confidence.

The structural equation analysis was used to test the alternative models. For each model, one of the four selected brands was taken as the focal brand and the other brands were considered as the competitors. Since Model 3 represents both direct and indirect effects, only the LISREL specifications for this model are given in Figure 2.

As summarized in Table 1, when Dimetapp was considered the focal brand and the other three were the competitors, Model 1 (hypothesizing a direct effect only) yielded a Chi-square value of

FIGURE 2
A LISREL Specification of the Combined Effects Model (Model 3)

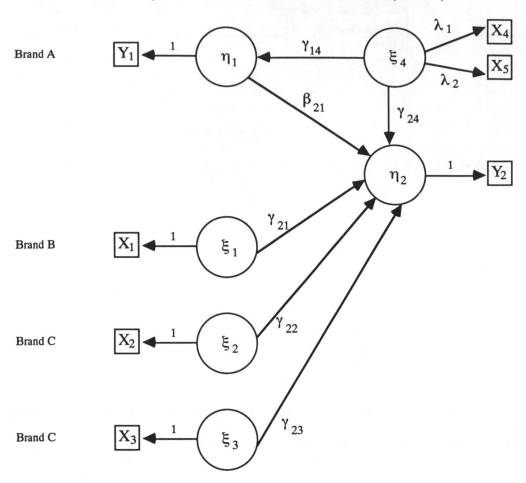

Legend:

The following specifications are for the model with focal brand A. A similar set of specifications is made when B, C and D are the focal brands, respectively.

X_1, X_2, X_3 =   The means of the four semantic differential scales of the global attitudes toward the non-focal brands B, C and D, respectively.

X_4, X_5 =   The two semantic differential scales of the overall confidence toward focal brand A.

Y_1 =   The mean of the four semantic differential scales of the global attitude toward focal brand A.

Y_2 =   The indicator of intention to buy focal brand A.

ξ_1, ξ_2, ξ_3 =   The global attitudes toward non-focal brands B, C and D, respectively.

ξ_4 =   The confidence in evaluating focal brand A.

η_1 =   The global attitude toward focal brand A.

η_2 =   The intention to buy focal brand A.

25.65 with 14 degrees of freedom, an adjusted goodness-of-fit index (AGFI) of .883, and a root mean square (RMSR) of .118. The probability level of the Chi-square value (p=.029) showed that the fit of the model was poor. Similar results were also obtained when any of the other three brands (Robitussin, Benylin, and Triaminic) was considered as the focal brand. Hence, none of these findings provides support for the direct effect model.

On the other hand, Model 2 (hypothesizing an indirect effect only), in all four situations involving a different focal brand, yielded a satisfactory goodness-of-fit indicators (i.e., Chi-square value, AGFI, and RMSR). Thus, hypothesis 2 was not rejected, i.e.,

intention to buy a specific brand was indirectly affected by one's confidence toward that brand through attitude toward the same brand.

The best fit indicators, however, were obtained for Model 3 in all four situations involving a different focal brand. These findings suggest that the influences of confidence on purchase intention are both direct and indirect. The Chi-square difference test (Table 2) showed that Model 3 was significantly better than both Model 1 and Model 2. Consequently, Model 3 was the best among the three alternative models. The squared multiple correlations for structural equations ranged from .12 to .44, and the total coefficient of

TABLE 1
Goodness-of-Fit Indicators for the Three Models

Model 1

| Indicators | *Focal Brand* | | | |
	A	B	C	D
χ^2	25.65	26.61	32.36	32.68
d.f.	14	14	14	14
p-value	.029	.022	.004	.003
AGFI	.883	.852	.863	.827
RMSR	.118	.136	.121	.146

Model 2

| Indicators | *Focal Brand* | | | |
	A	B	C	D
χ^2	17.98	11.77	18.92	15.48
d.f.	14	14	14	14
p-value	.208	.625	.168	.346
AGFI	.910	.931	.916	.912
RMSR	.078	.071	.074	.085

Model 3

| Indicators | *Focal Brand* | | | |
	A	B	C	D
χ^2	13.06	5.96	14.86	10.88
d.f.	13	13	13	13
p-value	.443	.948	.316	.621
AGFI	.928	.961	.929	.929
RMSR	.061	.060	.062	.076

TABLE 2
Chi-square Difference Tests for the Three Models

| Focal Brand | M3 - M1 | | | M3 - M2 | | |
	χ^2	d.f.	p-value	χ^2	d.f.	p-value
A	12.59	1	p<.001	4.92	1	p<.05
B	20.65	1	p<.001	5.81	1	p<.05
C	17.50	1	p<.001	4.06	1	p<.05
D	21.80	1	p<.001	4.60	1	p<.05

determination for structural equations ranged from .23 to .39 for the best model (i.e., Model 3) in all four situations involving a different focal brand.

Table 3 presents the estimates of the parameters and their corresponding t-values of the model 3. Table 4 provides the same results in a matrix format to a better visualize the results on the various paths. With respect to the path between confidence and intention, a significant positive relationship was found no matter which one of the four brands was used as the focal brand (see γ_{24}).

Similarly, the confidence-attitude link was also positive and highly significant for any of the four alternatives as the focal brand (see γ_{14}). Furthermore, a significant positive relationship between attitude toward the focal brand and intention to buy the same brand was found for each of the four brands (β_{21}). The significant negative influences of other competing brands on intention to buy the focal brand were observed in some cases (i.e., γ_{21} and γ_{23} for Dimetapp as the focal brand; γ_{21}, γ_{22} for Robitussin as the focal brand; γ_{21} and γ_{23} for Benylin as the focal brand). The influence of other

TABLE 3
Standardized Estimates For the Three Models
(Model 3)

Parameters (paths)		Focal Brand			
		A	B	C	D
		(N=107)	(N=93)	(N=118)	(N=95)
	NFB		NFB	NFB	NFB
λ_1		.929	.939	.831	.833
λ_2		.956(8.326) [a]	.860(7.245) [a]	.983(6.722) [a]	.793(5.473) [a]
γ_{24} (C→I)		.195(2.312) [b]	.234(2.406) [a]	.173(2.140) [b]	.266(2.229) [b]
γ_{14} (C→A)		.347(3.622) [a]	.473(4.443) [a]	.391(4.342) [a]	.525(4.482) [a]
β_{21} (A→I)		.482(5.913) [a]	.428(4.744) [a]	.487(6.140) [a]	.404(3.889) [a]
γ_{21} (A→I)	B / A / A / A	-.173(-2.282) [b]	-.233(-2.979) [a]	-.150(-2.078) [b]	-.046(-0.544)
γ_{22} (A→I)	C / C / B / B	-.088(-1.160)	-.209(-2.673) [a]	-.040(-0.549)	-.059(-0.702)
γ_{23} (A→I)	D / D / D / C	-.128(-1.689) [b]	-.119(-1.521) [c]	-.185(-2.555) [a]	-.045(-0.542)

[a] Significant at 0.01 (one-way).
[b] Significant at 0.05 (one-way).
[c] Significant at 0.10 (one-way).

Note: NFB indicates the names of the non-focal brands. Numbers inside the parentheses are the t-values of the estimates. Estimates without a t-value are the fixed parameters.

TABLE 4
Path Coefficients for Model 3 and Each Brand

Brand	C → I	Brand	C → A	Brand	A → I A	B	C	D
A	.195 [b]	A	.347 [a]	A	.482 [a]	-.233 [a]	-.150 [b]	-.046
B	.234 [a]	B	.473 [a]	B	-.173 [b]	.428 [a]	-.040	-.059
C	.173 [b]	C	.391 [a]	C	-.088	-.209 [a]	.487 [a]	-.045
D	.266 [b]	D	.525 [a]	D	-.128 [b]	-.119 [c]	-.185 [a]	.404 [a]

[a] Significant at 0.01 (one-way).
[b] Significant at 0.05 (one-way).
[c] Significant at 0.10 (one-way).

competitors on intention to buy a focal brand is consistent with the predictions of the multi-brand model of intentions (Laroche and Brisoux 1989), which suggests that intention to purchase the focal brand is negatively affected by the global attitude toward other competing brands.

In conclusion, of the three hypotheses, Hypothesis 3 was best supported by our data. Some support was shown for Hypothesis 2. Finally, Hypothesis 1 was rejected by the findings.

CONCLUSION AND DISCUSSION

This study has incorporated the confidence construct into the multi-brand model of intentions (Laroche and Brisoux 1989) and tested some alternative ways by which confidence toward a specific brand may affect intention to buy that brand. The findings show that

the combined effect model (Model 3) is the best one when compared to the other two models, suggesting that intention to buy a brand is not only directly affected by confidence toward the brand but also indirectly affected through one's attitude toward the same brand. This study also shows that intention to buy a specific brand is a positive (negative) function of attitudes toward the same brand (other competing brands), which is consistent with the earlier findings reported by Laroche and Brisoux (1989) and Laroche and Sadokierski (1994).

Given the above findings, it appears that individuals with different degrees of confidence toward a specific brand tend to have different perceptions and attitudinal judgments of the same brand, and are likely to have different levels of motivational equilibrium. The magnitudes of the parameter estimates indicate that the influence of confidence on attitude (γ_{14}) is significantly greater than the influence of confidence on intention (γ_{24}) for each of the four competing brands.

One major implication of the present study is that, in order to increase a consumer's intention to buy a specific brand, a marketer may try to enhance his/her confidence toward the brand. This can be realized by providing the consumer with more product-related information, or direct experience.

Future research may focus on whether the findings here can be replicated for other product classes. It is believed that the more important the product category is (i.e., the higher the level of involvement), the stronger the effects of confidence on intention will be found. In addition, there is also a need to incorporate cognitions into the proposed model. It is believed that the inclusion of cognition constructs will provide a more complete understanding of the influences of confidence on brand attitudes and purchase intentions.

REFERENCES

Bennett, Peter D. and Gilbert D. Harrell (1975), "The Role of Confidence in Understanding and Predicting Buyers' Attitudes and Purchase Intentions," *Journal of Consumer Research*, 2 (September), 110-117.

Cox, Donald F. and Raymond A. Bauer (1964), "Self-Confidence and Persuasibility in Women," *Public Opinion Quarterly*, 28 (Fall), 453-466.

Day, George S. (1970), *Buyer Attitudes and Brand Choice Behavior*, New York: The Free Press.

Fazio, Russell H. and Mark P. Zanna (1978a), "On the Predictive Validity of Attitudes: The Roles of Direct Experience and Confidence," *Journal of Personality*, 46, 228-243.

Fazio, Russell H. and Mark P. Zanna (1978b), "Attitudinal Qualities Relating to The Strength of The Attitude-Behavior Relationship," *Journal of Experimental Social Psychology*, 14, 398-408.

Fazio, Russell H. and Mark P. Zanna (1981), "Direct Experience and Attitude-Behavior Consistency," in *Advances in Experimental Social Psychology*, 14, ed. L. Berkowitz, New York: Academic Press, 161-202.

Howard, John A. (1973), "Confidence as a Validated Construct," in *Buyer Behavior: Theoretical and Empirical Foundations*, eds. John A. Howard and Lyman E. Ostlund, New York: Alfred A. Knopf, 426-433.

Howard, John A. (1977), *Consumer Behavior: Application of Theory*, New York: McGraw-Hill.

Howard, John A. (1989), *Consumer Behavior in Marketing Strategy*, Englewood Cliffs, NJ: Prentice Hall.

Howard, John A. and Lyman E. Ostlund (1973), "The Model: Current Status of Buying Behavior Theory," in *Buyer Behavior: Theoretical and Empirical Foundations*, eds. John A. Howard and Lyman E. Ostlund, New York: Alfred A. Knopf, 3-32.

Howard, John A. and Jagdish N. Sheth (1969), *The Theory of Buyer Behavior*, New York: John Wiley and Sons.

Jaccard, J. (1981), "Attitudes and Behavior: Implications of Attitudes Toward Behavioral Alternatives," *Journal of Experimental Social Psychology*, 17, 206-307.

Juster, F. T. (1966), "Consumer Buying Intentions and Purchase Probability: An Experiment in Survey Design," *Journal of the American Statistical Association*, 61, 659-696.

Kamakura, Wagner A. and Rajendra K. Srivastava (1984), "Predicting Choice Shares Under Conditions of Brand Interdependence," *Journal of Marketing Research*, 21 (November), 420-434.

Laroche, Michel and Jacques E. Brisoux (1989), "Incorporating Competition Into Consumer Behavior Models: The Case of the Attitude-Intention Relationship," *Journal of Economic Psychology*, 10 (September), 343-362.

Laroche, Michel and Robert Sadokierski (1994), "Role of Confidence in a Multi-Brand Model of Intentions for a High Involvement Service," *Journal of Business Research*, 29 (January), 1-12.

Lussier, Denis A. and Richard W. Olshavsky (1979), "Task Complexity and Contingent Processing in Brand Choice," *Journal of Consumer Research*, 6 (September), 154-165.

Malhotra, Naresh K. (1986), "An Approach to the Measurement of Consumer Preferences Using Limited Information," *Journal of Marketing Research*, 23 (February), 33-40.

Nantel, Jacques (1986), "Attitude-Behavior Consistency: Some Considerations Specific to Marketing Research," in *Marketing*, Vol. 7, ed. Thomas E. Muller, Montreal: Administrative Sciences Association of Canada, 271-279.

Ostlund, Lyman E. (1973), "Product Specific Self-Confidence Related to Buying Intentions," in *Buyer Behavior: Theoretical and Empirical Foundations*, eds. John A. Howard and Lyman E. Ostlund, New York: Alfred A. Knopf, 434-442.

Raden, D. (1985), "Strength-Related Attitude Dimensions," *Social Psychology Quarterly*, 48 (4), 312-330.

Sample, J. and R. H. Warland (1973), "Attitudes and The Prediction of Behavior," *Social Forces*, 51, 292-304.

Tversky, Amos (1972), "Elimination by Aspects: A Theory of Choice," *Psychological Review*, 79, 281-299.

Tyebjee, Tyzoon T. (1979), "Response Time, Conflict and Involvement in Brand Choice," *Journal of Consumer Research*, 6 (December), 295-303.

Urbany, Joel E., Peter R. Dickson, and William L. Wilkie (1989), "Buyer Uncertainty and Information Search," *Journal of Consumer Research*, 16 (September), 208-215.

Warland, R. H. and J. Sample (1973), "Response Certainty as a Moderator Variable in Attitude Measurement," *Rural Sociology*, 38, 174-186.

Self-Referencing: An Examination of Antecedents, Consequences, and Role in Message Processing

Jennifer Edson Escalas, Duke University
Parthasarathy Krishnamurthy, Pennsylvania State University

INTRODUCTION

Self-referencing as a mode of processing has attracted a great deal of research attention (e.g., Rogers, Kuiper, and Kirker 1977; Belleza 1984; Wagner 1984; Klein and Kihlstrom 1986; Burnkrant and Unnava 1989; Sujan, Bettman, and Baumgartner 1993). Defined as relating a stimulus to one's self related knowledge structures, self-referencing has been shown by many social cognition scholars to influence recall. The basic paradigm is that self-referencing enhances recall by increased elaboration and/or organization. Our special session was designed to highlight the advances in self-referencing being made in consumer research. In addition to addressing the consequences of self-referencing, the papers in this session consider its antecedents and its role as a process variable. Thus, the studies discussed in our session examine self-referencing as a dependent variable, a mediating variable, and an independent variable (see Figure).

THE ANTECEDENTS OF SELF-REFERENCING

Parthasarathy Krishnamurthy's paper addresses the question: Are there stimulus-related, subject-related, and contextual factors that systematically facilitate or inhibit self-referencing? In other words, the primary emphasis of his research is to understand the antecedents of spontaneous self-referencing. Thus he moves away from the traditional question of "what happens when self-referencing is induced?" and focuses on "when does self-referencing take place?" The paper presented focuses on the role of stimulus ambiguity in influencing spontaneous self-referencing. Krishnamurthy hypothesizes that stimulus ambiguity should enhance self-referencing because processing an ambiguous stimuli involves perceptual closure, which is an abstraction of meaning through a process of completing an otherwise incomplete stimulus (Snodgrass and Feenan 1991). Since people use available and/or accessible relevant knowledge structures to achieve this perceptual closure, and because self knowledge is known to be both available and accessible, an ambiguous stimulus is more likely to be perceptually closed using self related knowledge structures.

Krishnamurthy tests this proposition in a print advertising setting. His results for male subjects support the notion that ambiguous stimuli lead to more self referent processing. However, his results for female subjects are not in the hypothesized direction. In seeking an explanation for these counter-intuitive results, Krishnamurthy finds that ad liking is a significant mediator of the effect of ambiguous stimuli on self-referencing. The female subjects did not like the ambiguous stimulus and therefore did not engage in more self-referencing compared to the unambiguous stimulus. Krishnamurthy plans to examine the effects of stimulus ambiguity on self-referencing and the mediating effect of ad liking in future research, as well as examine other potential antecedents of self-referencing, such as message valence, input modality, and individual differences. Furthermore, he intends to develop and validate scale items for measuring self-referencing.

SELF-REFERENCING AS A MEDIATOR

In her research on mental simulation, Jennifer Edson Escalas finds self-referencing to be a mediating variable. Social psychologists have found that mental simulation leads to higher probability estimates for simulated events, positively affecting attitudes, behavioral intentions and actual behavior (e.g., Gregory, Chialdini, and Carpenter 1982). However, previous research into mental simulation does not provide an adequate explanation of why these outcomes occur. In two studies, Escalas, alone and with coauthor Linville, finds that subjects who mentally simulate using a running shoe have more favorable attitudes about the shoe and more favorable behavioral intentions towards trying on and/or purchasing the shoe. This occurs because self referencing focuses attention away from product features and onto the self, reducing counterarguing and/or source derogation which both negatively impact shoe attitudes. Furthermore, the self-referencing elicited in mental simulation generates positive affect that is transferred to the shoe, while those who do not self-reference either generate skeptical, disinterested emotions that negatively impact product attitudes or no significant feelings at all.

Escalas extends her self-referencing as mediating process from mental simulation to autobiographical memory retrieval. Using the data from Sujan, Bettman, and Baumgartner's second study (1993), she finds that subjects who were encouraged to retrieve autobiographical memories have more favorable attitudes towards the stimulus product than those who were not. More importantly, the self-referencing condition generates more positive affect and fewer counterarguments and product feature focused thoughts. The positive affect favorably impacts product attitudes while counterarguing lowers attitudes, replicating the self-referencing effects found for mental simulation.

SELF-REFERENCING AS AN INDEPENDENT VARIABLE THAT ENHANCES MESSAGE PROCESSING

It has been found in both consumer behavior research (e.g., Burnkrant and Unnava 1989) and psychology research (e.g., Rogers, Kuiper, and Kirker 1977; Belleza 1984; Brown, Keenan, and Potts 1986; Klein and Loftus 1988) that self-referencing increases elaboration, influences persuasion, and leads to higher recall of words or phrases. There are two arguments as to why this occurs. First, the motivation argument claims that information pertaining to the self is of intrinsic interest and therefore attracts more attention and leads to more cognitive effort. Second, the ability argument claims that self-referencing makes available a highly complex and integrated structure to which incoming information can be related. Thus, self-referencing could make it easier to process information.

Rohini Ahluwalia presented two studies, conducted with coauthors H. Rao Unnava and Robert E. Burnkrant, that examine these two arguments. In the first study, the authors use a secondary task method to assess cognitive effort under the assumption that if motivation is enhanced by self-referencing, then one should expect enhanced cognitive effort. Using a direct manipulation of self-referencing, they find that there is not a significant difference in cognitive effort between those subjects who self-reference and those who do not. Thus, it appears that if motivation leads to increased cognitive effort, then motivation to process is not enhanced by self-referencing.

In the second study, Unnava, Burnkrant, and Ahluwalia hypothesize that if the cognitive effort argument is correct, then the

FIGURE
Self-Referencing

	Independent Variable	Mediator	Dependent Variable
Krishnamurthy	Ambiguous Stimulus	Ad liking	SR
Escalas	Mental Simulation	SR Affect	Product Attitude
	Autobiographical Memory	SR Affect	Product Attitude
Unnava et.al.	SR		Message Elaboration

effects of ad copy induced self-referencing should be attenuated if the cognitive structure that it helps access is not rich or does not have strong associations. However, if the motivation argument is correct, then the effects of self-referencing should be attenuated for the people who are involved in the product category and thus are naturally motivated to process the information. Usage experience with the target product (contact lenses) was used to operationalize richness of cognitive structures and product category involvement. The results indicate that when ability is low to begin with (i.e., the self structure does not have rich experiences associated with it), self-referencing does not lead to enhanced elaboration. Overall, self-referencing appears to make rich cognitive structures more available, when they are present, and hence assists in elaboration of the target information.

DISCUSSION

Our discussant, Patricia Linville, summarized what these three papers tell us about self-referencing. First, we know self-referencing occurs with ambiguous stimuli and under conditions of mental simulation and activating autobiographical memory. We also know what happens when self-referencing occurs. Messages are elaborated, positive affect is generated, people are distracted from product feature evaluation, and attitudes towards products are improved. There are still some puzzles that exist. For example, the Unnava, Burnkrant, and Ahluwalia paper asserts that self-referencing leads to more cognitive elaboration, while the Escalas paper predicts simpler processing (distraction from product features, self focus, and increased role of affect).

For future research, Linville suggests that we consider multiple selves in addition to the unitary self we have focused on to date (e.g., Markus 1977; Linville 1985, 1987). Additionally, possible selves or future selves (Markus and Nurius 1986) might be interesting, particularly for mental simulation of future events. Recent work on chronically and automatically accessible self-constructs (e.g., Higgins, Bargh, and Lombardi 1985; Higgins, King, and Mavin 1982) might be directly relevant in testing the mechanisms underlying the increased elaboration found with self-referencing, particularly with respect to measures of cognitive effort. Another question is whether self-referencing leads to heuristic or systematic processing (e.g., Chaikin 1980). The studies presented here today lead to different conclusions. Linville also wonders what would be the result if subjects self-referenced a negative experience. And finally, there may be different types of self-knowledge that can be activated. For example, does activation of trait knowledge differ in its effects from activation of episodic memory? Overall, Linville found that the research presented in the session moves the self-referencing paradigm forward in ways that are creative, interesting, and relevant.

REFERENCES

Belleza, F.S. (1984), "The self as mnemonic device: The role of internal cues," *Journal of Personality and Social Psychology*, 47, 506-516.

Brown, Polly, Janice M. Keenan, and George R. Potts (1986), "The self-reference effect with imagery encoding," *Journal of Personality and Social Psychology*, 51 (November), 897-906.

Burnkrant, Robert E. and H. Rao Unnava (1989), "Self-referencing: A strategy for increasing processing of message content," *Personality and Social Psychology Bulletin*, 15 (December), 628-638.

Chaikin, S. (1980), "Heuristic versus systematic processing and the use of source versus message cues in persuasion," *Journal of Personality and Social Psychology*, 39, 752-766.

Gregory, W.L., R.B. Chialdini, and K.M. Carpenter (1982), "Self-relevant scenarios as mediators of likelihood estimates and compliance: Does imagining make it so?" *Journal of Personality and Social Psychology*, 43, 89-99.

Higgins E.T., J.A. Bargh, and W. Lombardi (1985), "The nature of priming effects on categorization," *Journal of Experimental Psychology: Learning, Memory and Cognition*, 11, 59-69.

Higgins E.T., G.A. King, and G.H. Mavin (1982), "Individual construct accessibility and subjective impression and recall," *Journal of Personality and Social Psychology*, 43, 35-47.

Klein, Stanley B., and John F. Kihlstrom (1986), "Elaboration, organization, and the self-reference effect in memory," *Journal of Experimental Psychology: General*, 115, 26-38.

Klein, S.B. and J. Loftus (1988), "The nature of self-referent encoding: The contributions of elaborative and organizational processes," *Journal of Personality and Social Psychology*, 55, 5-11.

Linville, Patricia W. (1985), "Self-complexity and affective extremity: Don't put all your eggs in one cognitive basket," *Social Cognition*, 3, 94-120.

Linville, Patricia W. (1987), "Self-complexity as a cognitive buffer against stress-related depression and illness," *Journal of Personality and Social Psychology*, 52, 663-676.

Markus, Hazel (1977), "Self-schemata and processing information about the self," *Journal of Personality and Social Psychology*, 35, 63-78.

Markus, Hazel and Paula Nurius (1986), "Possible selves," *American Psychologist*, 41, 954-969.

Rogers, T.B., N.A. Kuiper, and W.S. Kirker (1977), "Self-reference and the encoding of personal information," *Journal of Personality and Social Psychology*, 35 (September), 677-688.

Snodgrass, J. G. and K. Feenan (1991), "Priming effects in picture fragment completion: Support for the perceptual closure hypothesis," *Journal of Experimental Psychology: General*, 119 (3), 276-296.

Sujan, Mita, James R. Bettman, and Hans Baumgartner (1993), "Influencing judgements using autobiographical memories: A self-referencing perspective," *Journal of Marketing Research*, 30 (November), 422-436.

Wagner, Wolfgang (1984), "Recognition of own and others' utterances in a natural conversation," *Personality and Social Psychology Bulletin*, 10 (December), 596-604.

"I Saw the Sign": Current Trends in Marketing Signal Research

J. Jeffrey Inman, University of Wisconsin-Madison

The objective of this special session was to explore the role of associations among marketing phenomena in consumer choice heuristics. Unfortunately, the discussant, Terry Shimp, was unable to attend the conference due to an illness in the family.

The information processing literature is rife with evidence (see Bettman, Johnson, and Payne 1991 for a review) that consumers have limited processing capability (and motivation to utilize this capability). In many instances, therefore, consumers tend to use heuristics to reduce the amount of processing required. Heuristics such as lexicographic, elimination-by-aspects, and affect referral all serve to simplify the decision making process.

Consumers may also use associations between attributes to simplify the choice process, particularly in cases where one attribute is easily determined or processed and the other attribute is less observable or more difficult to process. The presence of the one attribute is used to "signal" the presence or level of the other attribute. The most often studied area of the association or "signal heuristic" is the literature on the price-quality relationship, where almost 100 studies have examined the relationship between price and consumers' perception of quality (see Zeithaml 1988 for a review). This research suggests that the strength of the price-perceived quality relationship is moderated by the availability of other information (e.g., brand names, advertising), individual factors (e.g., price awareness, expertise), and category factors (e.g., price variation, perceived quality variation).

Beyond the price-perceived quality literature, research on the use of signals by consumers is much more limited. Research in the scanner data modeling literature and consumer behavior literature led Inman, McAlister and Hoyer (1990) to hypothesize that consumers may associate the simple presence of a promotion signal (sign or marker attached to the brand display) with a price cut on the signed brand. Their experimental work and subsequent empirical work by Mayhew and Winer (1992) and Inman and McAlister (1993) support the notion that some consumers make this association.

The papers in this session extended the work on signals on three fronts. In the first paper, authored by Eric Greenleaf, the role of price signals was examined from the standpoint of the *seller*, as opposed to previous work which has focused primarily on signals from the buyer's perspective. The purpose of the paper is to observe how people set reserves in a particular type of auction, an open English auction where bidders have independent private values, and compare their behavior with normative predictions. Greenleaf does not expect that the sellers will set optimal reserves. Instead, based on some recent findings in consumer behavior, he hypothesized that when sellers set reserves in successive auctions and can learn from their experience, they will place too much emphasis on processing the signal of whether or not an object sells at auction (termed a "buy-in" if the object fails to sell), and too little emphasis on magnitude information (i.e., the price that the object brings if it does sell at auction, or the highest bid offered if it does not sell). Greenleaf noted that in almost all auction situations, sellers should expect buy-ins to occur occasionally even if they set the optimal reserve. Thus a buy-in does not necessarily indicate a faulty reserve strategy. Recent work in consumer behavior indicates that consumers tend to give more attention to discrete signals than to magnitude information when judging prices. There is also evidence that consumers attend more to frequency than to magnitude information when they examine a series of prices to judge the overall price of a market basket of goods at different stores (Alba, Broniarczyk,

Shimp, and Urbany 1993). He used this literature to make three predictions, which he then tested via experiment: sellers use a "buy-in" (i.e., failure of the item to sell) as a signal that the reserve is set too high, sellers set suboptimal buy-ins in cases where the probability of a buy-in at the optimal reserve is very high or very low, and sellers set lower, suboptimal reserves as the number of bidders decreases. These hypotheses were supported.

The second paper, by Kay Lemon and Deepak Gupta, focused on the multifaceted role of brand displays in consumer decision making and choice. Display provides multiple cues: availability, convenience, and price promotion; whereas price promotion merely signals a price advantage for the brand. Given that display signals an accompanying price cut (even when one is not present), the combination of price cut and display may serve to heighten the consumer's awareness of the price cut for brands which benefit from price promotion, and, therefore, increase the overall effectiveness of the promotion combination. Several hypotheses were tested with regard to the relative effectiveness of price promotion and display (See Figure 1). Evidence suggests that: (1) display will be more effective for low market share brands, (2) price promotion will be more effective for high price brands, and (3) simultaneous price promotion and display will be more effective for high price brands. The results of this research suggest that marketing managers may be over-promoting unnecessarily. A high market share, high price-tier national brand, for example, may be better off focusing on successive price promotions, rather than fighting for expensive end-of-aisle displays. High price-tier, niche brands, by comparison, may benefit by combining price promotions and displays in the same promotion. Private label brands may eschew price promotion entirely, and pursue a pure display promotion strategy. By understanding the position of the brand in the market, managers can begin to optimize their promotional strategies, choosing the combination of price promotion and display which will provide the strongest response from the consumer.

The third paper, co-authored by Jeff Inman and Anil Peter, examined the role of another type of signal, purchase quantity limits, on consumer choice. Scarcity theory (Lynn 1989) posits that when a product is made to appear scarce it becomes more desirable. This effect has been demonstrated even in instances of apparent scarcity. A limit sign effectively makes a brand more scarce and thus may act as a signal of scarcity. Consumers might infer that the price is attractive, so much so that the retailer wants to limit the quantity that can be purchased. The limit sign would thus represent a sign of a 'good deal'. Empirical work on promotional signals (Inman, McAlister and Hoyer 1990 and Inman and McAlister 1993) would suggest that such a signal would increase the likelihood of purchase. Inman and Peter predict that the impact of limit signs holds only for high need for cognition consumers. Experiment results show an effect for purchase quantity limits on choice and suggest that high need for cognition consumers account for this effect. Scanner panel data from a large grocery chain were also analyzed using 18 months of chain-level data. These data were for several different brands in various product categories that were promoted with a purchase limit on some occasions and with no purchase limitations on other occasions. Seemingly unrelated regression analysis was used to analyze individual brands and provided support for a limit effect on choice.

Much additional work remains to be done on the associations that consumers make between product attributes and between marketing phenomena. This session focused on research into this

Advances in Consumer Research
Volume 22, © 1995

FIGURE 1
Hypothesized Effects of Display and Price Promotion

Brand Position	High Familiarity	Low Familiarity
High Price-Tier	Strong Price Promotion Weak Display Positive Interaction	Strong Price Promotion Strong Display Positive Interaction
Low Price-Tier	Weak Price Promotion Weak Display Weak Interaction	Weak Price Promotion Strong Display Weak Interaction

important topic, one that has not received much attention at previous ACR conferences. Additional research to identify and assess the prevalence of such heuristics is greatly needed, as it opens the door for the incorporation of such heuristics into marketing strategy development, public policy generation, and consumer education. Savvy marketers can use associations, for example, to ensure that a promotion is always accompanied by a special display. Public policy makers should use research into these associations to ensure that unethical practices (e.g., attaching a promotion sign to a brand display with no price cut) that prey on consumers who use such heuristics are banned and that consumers are educated. The papers in this session represented a step in that direction.

REFERENCES

Alba, Joseph W., Susan M. Broniarczyk, Terence A. Shimp, and Joel E. Urbany (1993), "The Influence of Competing Cues on Consumer Perceptions of Comparative Prices," *Journal of Consumer Research*, in press.

Bettman, James R., Eric A. Johnson, and John W. Payne (1991), "Consumer Decision Making," in *Handbook of Consumer Behavior*, T. Robertson and H. Kassarjian (eds.). Prentice-Hall: Englewood Cliffs, NJ.

Inman, J. Jeffrey, Leigh McAlister, and Wayne D. Hoyer (1990), "Promotion Signal: Proxy for a Price Cut?" *Journal of Consumer Research*, 17 (March), 74-81.

_____ and Leigh McAlister (1993), "A Retailer Promotion Policy Model Considering Promotion Signal Sensitivity," *Marketing Science*, 12 (Fall), 339-356.

Mayhew, Glenn E. and Russell S. Winer (1992), "An Empirical Analysis of Internal and External Reference Prices Using Scanner Data," *Journal of Consumer Research*, 19 (June), 62-70.

Zeithaml, Valarie A. (1988), "Consumer Perceptions of Price Quality, and Value: A Means-End Model and Synthesis of Evidence," *Journal of Marketing*, 52 (July), 2-22.

What Causes Estimation Problems When Analyzing MTMM Data?

Joseph A. Cote, Washington State University

ABSTRACT

In recent years, there have been a plethora of alternative analytic techniques suggested for analyzing MTMM data. Previous research has compared alternative techniques without explicitly considering the possible reasons why some techniques encounter estimation problems (Bagozzi and Yi 1993, Marsh and Bailey 1991). This study attempts to identify what might be causing common estimation problems when using confirmatory factor analysis to models MTMM data. Five alternative factor analysis techniques (correlated errors—methods correlated, correlated uniqueness—methods uncorrelated, fixed errors, multiplicative, and the Rindskopf parameterization) were used to test for identification problems, multiplicative trait-method relationships, sampling error, true errors close to zero, or over-fitting. None of the recommended factor analysis techniques worked in most cases. It is suggested that a common cause of estimation problems is the quality of the data rather then the technique used to estimate parameters.

When designing measures, the assessment of validity is of utmost importance (Churchill 1979). The multitrait—multimethod (MTMM) matrix has become accepted as the preferred way to assess construct validity; and confirmatory factor analysis (CFA) is the most popular way to analyze MTMM data. CFA's elegance and power enticed researchers to quickly adopt the technique and develop specific guidelines for its application (Widaman 1985). Yet when these guidelines were applied, results were quite ambiguous. In most situations, models failed to converge, contained unreasonable or inconsistent estimates and/or failed to fit the data (Brannick and Spector 1990, Marsh 1989). Since 1985, researchers have jumped from technique to technique in order to solve estimation problems. This has lead to a "technique of the month" mentality. When any problems are encountered with a given estimation technique, a "new, improved" approach is suggested. Unfortunately, researchers have been less than systematic in identifying why a particular technique might be superior. For example, the direct products model was offered to deal with multiplicative models (Browne 1984), yet there was no attempt to determine if multiplicative relationships were common. Researchers have simply compared a set of alternative methods and then concluded that their suggested approach is best. When that "best" approach ultimately results in estimation problems, researchers simply move to the next "superior" approach. The purpose of this study is to take a more systematic look at potential causes of estimation problems when using confirmatory factor analysis to analyze MTMM data.

Numerous explanations for estimation problems have been proposed, but past discussion has centered around four possible explanations, error component close to boundary values, under identification, multiplicative models, and over fitting. Heywood cases and other boundary estimates are the most commonly encountered problems when estimation factor analysis models. Heywood cases were originally thought to be caused by true values close to the boundary combined with sampling fluctuations (Dillon, et al. 1987, van Driel 1978). Heywood cases were commonly dealt with by fixing the offending estimate (Cote and Buckley 1987). A more appropriate way to deal with true scores close to the boundary is to use Rindskopf's parameterization which eliminates the possibility of Heywood cases by fixing error variances (Rindskopf 1983, Rindskopf 1984). This leads to the first hypothesis:

H1 If estimation problems are caused by true values close to the boundary, then the Rindskopf parameterization should correct the problem.

The most recent explanation for estimation problems is under-identification (Brannick and Spector 1990, Kenny and Kashy 1992). Identification problems can occur in two ways, when there is less information than estimated parameters, and when sources of information duplicate each other (Bentler and Chou 1987). Bentler and Chou (1987) suggest that factors with only two loadings (e.g., two methods) are likely to be empirically under identified since the two items share too much information. They also point out that empirical under identification can occur if indicators are highly correlated (Kenny and Kashy 1992). When empirical under identification is encountered, it often results in Heywood cases and non-convergence. Under identification is often tricky to deal with, however, there have been several techniques recommended for solving this problem. The correlated uniqueness model is currently the most accepted way to deal with identification problems (Kenny and Kashy 1992, Marsh 1989). Unfortunately, the correlated uniqueness technique recommended by Marsh (1989) and tested in the literature (Bagozzi and Yi 1993, Kenny and Kashy 1992) do not account for correlated methods. Equality constraints can be used to allow for correlated methods (Cote and Greenberg 1990), although they increase the number of parameter estimates and impose different restrictive assumptions. Another suggestion for dealing with identification problems is to fix the error variance to estimated values (Marsh and Hocevar 1983). Fixing the error variance to estimated unique variance should help control empirical under identification problems since it reduces the number of parameter estimates. This leads to the next set of hypotheses:

H2 The correlated uniqueness model (methods uncorrelated) should be appropriate if empirical under identification is the cause of fitting problems.

H3 The correlated uniqueness model (correlated methods) should be appropriate if empirical under identification is the cause of fitting problems.

H4 If empirical under identification is causing fitting problems, then the fixed error variance models should be appropriate.

Another purported cause of estimation problems relates to Campbell and O'Connell's (1967, 1982) claim that traits and methods interact in a multiplicative rather than additive fashion. If multiplicative relationships exist, then traditional CFA models are misspecified, which would likely cause estimation problems (Bagozzi and Yi 1990, Bagozzi and Yi 1991, Lastovicka, et al. 1990). Browne (1990) developed the MUTMUM program for fitting direct product models to MTMM data. This technique assumes that trait and method effects are multiplicative rather than additive. Therefore,

H5 MUTMUM should effectively deal with estimation problems caused by multiplicative MTMM data.

A final cause of estimation problems is over-fitting (Bagozzi and Yi 1990). If a trait only model will fit the data, then it is

Advances in Consumer Research
Volume 22, © 1995

inappropriate to include method effects. By including method effects, the model is misspecified and as such will lead to estimation problems. This leads to the final hypothesis:

H6 If over-fitting is the cause of estimation problems, then a trait only model should adequately fit MTMM data.

Each of the hypotheses will be tested to determine if the commonly proposed explanations for estimation problems are truly causing the difficulties of analyzing MTMM data.

METHOD

Numerous MTMM matrices were screened on several criteria. First, as recommended by Brannick and Spector (1990) only MTMM matrices with more than two different traits and methods were included. Second, matrices were screened to ensure that traits were properly matched for each method. Third, matrices with low values on the validity diagonal (average < 0.4) were deleted since convergence was not demonstrated. Only data sets with sample sizes greater than (or very close to) 100 were selected (Boomsma 1985). Since we are interested in identifying the cause of estimation problems, matrices were screened out if they fit a traditional block diagonal model without problems. The Arora matrix was included even though the traditional block diagonal model fit since the factor loadings were inconsistent with (much higher than) the reliability estimates. In addition, if the trait only model was appropriate, the data set was dropped from further analysis, since over-fitting would occur if method effects were added (Bagozzi and Yi 1990, Bagozzi and Yi 1991). The trait only model was considered appropriate only when the CFA and Campbell and Fiske criteria agreed that no method effects exist (see Table 1 for studies considered for analysis).

EQS version 4.0 (Bentler 1992) was used to estimate all the additive models, and MUTMUM (Wothke and Browne 1990) was used to estimate the multiplicative models. Common factor analysis was used to generate unique variance estimates for the fixed errors model (if Heywood cases were encountered, principle components analysis was used). When fitting the models, there was no attempt to customize the model specification for any particular data set (Lehmann 1988 some data sets may necessitate alternative specifications). Automatic start values were used to fit the model and a maximum of 500 iterations was specified. Bagozzi and Yi (1990) outline several criteria that can be used to evaluate model appropriateness. Our analysis indicated only several of these were needed to identify estimation problems, the number of parameter estimates held at boundary values, the comparative fit index (RMSEA for MUTMUM), examination of residuals and assessing reasonableness of the estimates.

RESULTS

Despite carefully screening the matrices, estimating problems were common for all the models (see Table 2). Table 2 includes results from the traditional (block diagonal) model in order to show the types of estimation problems encountered. We can start by noting that a trait only model fit five of the 16 studies which met the screening criteria (Elbert, Flamer data set 1, Ostrom, Roberts, and Seymour). In addition to fitting a trait only model, these data sets also passed Campbell and Fiske's test for method effects. This would indicate that over-fitting might be a possible cause for estimation problems in some cases and provides partial support for hypothesis 6. These 5 data sets were eliminated from further study since adding method effects is inappropriate.

In general, there was little support for hypotheses 1 through 6 (see Table 3). The Rindskopf model failed to converge or had

boundary values (for factor correlations) for 10 of the 11 data sets which contain method effects. Only the estimation problems for the Arora data set seemed to be due to random error components close to boundary values (see table 2). This would indicate that boundary values do not seem to be a primary cause of estimation problems (H1 not supported).

The correlated errors model (methods correlated) resulted in Heywood cases for all 11 studies. The fixed errors model was appropriate for only three of the 11 data sets (Dunham, Flamer data set 2, and Marsh data set 2). Although it did not solve estimation problems for most cases, the correlated uniqueness model (methods uncorrelated) appears promising, fitting for four of the eleven data sets (Allen, Arora, Meier, and Shavelson). Unfortunately, further examination indicates other problems may exist. The correlated uniqueness model is unable to account for correlated methods, which may cause trait loadings to be inflated. For two data sets both the correlated uniqueness and another model fit the data. A comparison of these results indicate the correlated uniqueness model had consistently higher trait loadings than the other techniques (Arora $\lambda CU=0.819$, $\lambda rindskopf=0.656$; Meier $\lambda CU=0.815$, $\lambda direct\ products= 0.418$). This raises serious doubts about the appropriateness of assuming that methods are not correlated (Fiske and Campbell 1992). In sum, empirical under identification does not appear to be the primary source of estimation problems, although it may cause difficulty in some cases (H2, H3, and H4 marginally supported).

The direct products model seems appropriate only for the Meier data set. The Shavelson data set fit well, but the results seem inappropriate since random error is estimated to be zero, even though the average reliability is 0.76. Therefore, H5 must be rejected. It does not appear that multiplicative trait-method relationships were a common source of estimation problems.

DISCUSSION

In general, it appears that estimation problems in these data sets are not due to empirical under identification, multiplicative trait-method relationships, true errors close to zero, or sampling errors (although for any individual study these may be a problem). As such, there is no clear reason to assume that any given factor analysis technique is superior to another. The claims of previous researchers that the direct products model or correlated uniqueness model are superior to the block diagonal model (Bagozzi and Yi 1990, Bagozzi and Yi 1993, Marsh and Bailey 1991) are not supported by this study. The most surprising finding of this study is that in many cases, no models unambiguously fit the data. The results of this study beg the question, "what causes estimation problems when analyzing MTMM data?"

Multicollinearity

An often ignored problem in confirmatory factor analysis is multicollinearity. Multicollinearity can cause unstable estimates in analysis of covariance structures (Bentler and Chou 1987, Lehmann and Gupta 1989). With MTMM data, multicollinearity can exist among the traits or among the methods. For example, if the traits are highly correlated, then multicollinearity exists. Multicollinearity is commonly identified using three indicators, 1) change of estimates with minor changes in the model (such as dropping items or changing start values), 2) significance tests lead to conflicting conclusions, and 3) model coefficients have inappropriate signs (such as inconsistent patterns in the trait and method factor correlations). These conditions are commonly found when analyzing MTMM data (Bagozzi and Yi 1990). In fact, changing start values and dropping methods or traits are commonly used to beat MTMM data into submission. While there may be many other causes of

TABLE 1
Studies Considered for Analysis

Study	Average Validity Diagonal	Sample Size	Traits	Meth	Average Reliability
Allen	0.608	177	3	3	NA
Arora	0.669	96	3	3	0.761
Avison	0.409	148	3	3	NA
Bouchard	0.500	78	3	3	0.774
Brinberg	0.549	80	3	3	NA
Dickson	0.153	149	3	3	NA
Dunham	0.550	622	4	4	0.767
Elbert	0.734	250	4	3	0.661
Elig	0.259	252	7	3	0.837
Flamer 1	0.540	105	3	3	NA
Flamer 2	0.534	105	3	3	NA
Freedman	0.491	149	5	3	NA
Gingrich	0.111	297	3	4	0.563
Goodman	0.164	63	8	3	NA
Guillet	0.341	110	3	3	NA
Hicks	0.516	119	3	3	0.889
Humphrey	0.214	267	3	5	0.619
Jackson	0.355	155	6	5	NA
Jackson	0.368	137	4	4	NA
Johnstone	0.236	600	4	5	NA
Karst	0.488	80	3	3	NA
Koppel	0.414	62	4	3	NA
Kothandapani	0.481	100	3	4	0.890
Lamont 1	0.473	91	3	3	NA
Lamont 2	0.437	91	3	3	NA
Lawler	0.282	113	3	3	NA
Locke 1	0.331	81	5	4	NA
Locke 2	0.341	52	5	4	NA
Marsh1	0.601	286	5	3	NA
Marsh2	0.575	392	5	3	NA
Meier	0.664	320	3	3	0.876
Mitchell	0.130	105	3	3	0.484
Mosher	0.708	62	3	3	0.750
Ostrom	0.780	189	3	4	NA
Ritter	0.292	64	3	4	0.840
Roberts	0.737	120	3	3	0.839
Rose	0.486	75	4	4	NA
Roshal	0.290	610	3	3	NA
Schmitt	0.801	310	7	4	NA
Schneider	0.251	89	3	4	0.805
Seymour	0.732	132	4	3	NA
Shavelson	0.523	99	3	3	0.757
Smith 1	0.200	91	3	3	0.558
Smith 2	0.166	91	3	3	0.556
Stewart	0.767	24	4	3	NA
Tapp 1	0.150	122	4	4	NA
Tapp 2	0.176	105	4	4	NA
Teal	0.278	122	3	3	NA
Wanous	0.600	208	6	4	NA
Wirth	0.246	92	4	3	NA
Zuckerman	0.340	54	3	5	0.742

NOTE; Bold indicates those data sets that were included in the analysis. Avison was dropped since the three "methods" were different forms of behaviors. Dunham second trait was dropped since it was not identical for all methods. Schmitt and Wanous were dropped since they fit a traditonal model.

estimation problems, multicollinearity is a likely candidate. Mason and Perreault (Mason and Perreault 1991) note that multicollinearity is not a problem unless the sample size is small, overall R squared is low, and collinearity exceeds 0.65. While appropriate for regression analysis, these guidelines may understate the problem for confirmatory factor analysis of MTMM data, especially when both trait intercorrelations and method intercorrelations are high (Fiske and Campbell 1992). In such a case, a heterotrait-

TABLE 2
Confirmatory Factor Analysis Results

Trait Only Model		Chi Squared	df	Fit Index	Average residual	Largest residual	Boundary Estimates	No. of Sig. Error Loadings
1	Allen	205.6	24	0.827	0.059	0.178	0	7/9
1	Arora	107.6	24	0.844	0.054	0.243	0	9/9
2	Dunham	2843.8	98	0.738	0.055	0.314	0	16/16
*	Elbert	122.6	48	0.966	0.020	0.097	0	12/12
*	Flamer (data set 1)	23.3	24	1.000	0.038	0.221	0	8/9
	Flamer (data set 2)	31.1	24	0.981	0.035	0.193	1	6/9
	Freedman	575.8	80	0.655	0.880	0.326	1	15/15
	Hicks	138.1	24	0.759	0.054	0.498	3	6/9
	Kothandapani	387.3	51	0.545	0.089	0.432	1	10/12
	Marsh (data set 1)	1353.9	80	0.773	0.053	0.317	6	15/15
	Marsh (data set 2)	1250.5	80	0.813	0.071	0.364	4	15/15
2	Meier	759.3	24	0.686	0.034	0.260	0	9/9
*	Ostrom	135.5	51	0.953	0.025	0.117	0	12/12
*	Roberts	188.8	24	0.834	0.037	0.187	0	9/9
*	Seymour	259.4	48	0.870	0.035	0.138	0	12/12
2	Shavelson	122.8	24	0.779	0.061	0.181	0	9/9

*   Model fits and is appropriate.
1   Model fits, but Campbell and Fiske (1959) criteria indicate method effects exist.
2   Poor fit index indicates model does not fit.

Traditional Model		Chi Squared	df	Fit Index	Average residual	Largest residual	Boundary Estimates	No. of Sig. Error Loadings
	Allen	12.3	12	1.000	0.022	0.077	1	6/9
1	Arora	17.0	12	0.991	0.046	0.143	0	6/9
	Dunham	255.9	76	0.973	0.073	0.183	1	15/16
	Elbert	36.8	33	0.998	0.017	0.069	1	11/12
	Flamer (data set 1)	5.1	12	1.000	0.016	0.066	2	5/9
	Flamer (data set 2)	11.0	12	1.000	0.038	0.121	3	4/9
	Freedman	158.9	62	0.933	0.057	0.189	1	13/15
	Hicks	48.2	12	0.923	0.054	0.145	3	4/9
	Kothandapani	71.9	33	0.947	0.052	0.197	2	6/12
	Marsh (data set 1)	224.3	62	0.971	0.024	0.127	1	15/15
	Marsh (data set 2)	220.5	62	0.975	0.024	0.093	2	14/15
	Meier	109.1	12	0.958	0.048	0.199	3	6/9
	Ostrom	22.2	33	1.000	0.010	0.040	1	11/12
	Roberts	46.3	12	0.965	0.041	0.186	3	7/9
	Seymour	89.1	33	0.966	0.034	0.118	1	10/12
	Shavelson	5.6	12	1.000	0.020	0.058	1	6/9

1   Model fits, but results indicate items with low reliability have no estimated measurement error.

---

heteromethod correlation may be due to either correlated traits, correlated methods, or both. It therefore becomes very difficult to estimate the exact source of the correlation. To deal with the problem, researchers need to follow Campbell and Fiske's recommendation to use dissimilar traits and methods when collecting MTMM data.

Data Problems

Since the computation goal of confirmatory factor analysis is to replicate the target covariance matrix, any data problems that affect the nature of the covariance matrix will affect the results of

the factor analysis. Two possible causes of data problems are outliers and missing values. Bollen (1987) found that outliers can cause estimation problems. By dropping severe outliers he was able to eliminate Heywood cases. Bollen (1987) also discusses approaches for identifying and dealing with outliers. In addition, the treatment of missing values often can frustrate researchers. The method used to deal with missing data (e.g., pairwise versus listwise deletion) can affect the nature of the covariance matrix. For example, missing data in the Arora data set is a possible explanation for why the correlation between two items is greater than the reliability estimates of either (an inappropriate situation). Several

TABLE 2 (CONTINUED)
Confirmatory Factor Analysis Results

Correlated Errors Model (Correlated Methods)	Chi Squared	df	Fit Index	Average residual	Largest residual	Boundary Estimates	No. of Sig. Error Loadings
Allen	38.0	18	0.981	0.035	0.088	1	9/9
Arora	42.8	18	0.954	0.044	0.140	1	9/9
Dunham	453.5	88	0.945	0.062	0.182	1	16/16
Flamer (data set 2)	21.5	18	0.990	0.035	0.154	2	7/9
Freedman	207.7	74	0.907	0.135	0.406	1	13/15
Hicks	58.7	18	0.914	0.083	0.243	1	8/9
Kothandapani	113.3	41	0.902	0.079	0.382	1	8/12
Marsh (data set 1)	276.2	74	0.964	0.072	0.238	2	14/15
Marsh (data set 2)	337.3	74	0.958	0.074	0.303	1	14/15
Meier	503.6	18	0.792	0.168	0.440	1	9/9
Shavelson	20.9	18	0.993	0.048	0.192	2	9/9

	Correlated Uniqueness (Uncorrelated Methods)	Chi Squared	df	Fit Index	Average residual	Largest residual	Boundary Estimates	No. of Sig. Error Loadings
*	Allen	26.2	15	0.989	0.033	0.139	0	9/9
*	Arora	21.7	15	0.987	0.052	0.173	0	9/9
1	Dunham	753.6	61	0.896	0.075	0.421	0	16/16
	Flamer (data set 2)	12.2	15	1.000	0.044	0.121	1	6/9
	Freedman	180.1	50	0.909	0.087	0.390	3	12/15
	Hicks	25.7	15	0.977	0.052	0.185	2	6/9
1	Kothandapani	785.5	66	0.955	0.073	0.264	0	12/12
	Marsh (data set 1)	169.7	50	0.979	0.180	0.091	1	15/15
	Marsh (data set 2)	249.5	50	0.968	0.028	0.147	2	15/15
*	Meier	30.7	15	0.990	0.018	0.067	0	9/9
*	Shavelson	12.5	15	1.000	0.047	0.099	0	9/9

* Model fits and is appropriate.
1 Large residuals indicates model does not fit.

	Fixed Errors Model	Chi Squared	df	Fit Index	Average residual	Largest residual	Boundary Estimates	No. of Sig. Error Loadings
1	Allen	141.6	21	0.885	0.035	0.094	0	NA
	Arora	56.8	21	0.933	0.049	0.015	1	NA
*	Dunham	582.8	92	0.926	0.050	0.176	0	NA
*	Flamer (data set 2)	33.5	21	0.966	0.049	0.150	0	NA
	Freedman	185.9	77	0.924	0.090	0.206	1	NA
2	Hicks	86.2	21	0.862	0.067	0.238	0	NA
2	Kothandapani	148.7	45	0.860	0.064	0.206	0	NA
	Marsh (data set 1)	250.2	77	0.969	0.019	0.104	1	NA
*	Marsh (data set 2)	298.0	77	0.965	0.025	0.134	0	NA
	Meier	579.1	21	0.761	0.102	0.428	3	NA
	Shavelson	47.9	21	0.940	0.045	0.162	1	NA

* Model fits and is appropriate.
1 Model fits, but exceptional large standard errors exist for the trait correlcations.
2 Large residuals indicates model does not fit.

TABLE 2 (CONTINUED)
Confirmatory Factor Analysis Results

Direct Products Model	Chi Squared	df	Fit Index	Average residual	Largest residual	Boundary Estimates	No. of Sig. Error Loadings
Allen	62.9	21	0.106	0.049	0.203	3	6/9
Arora	46.9	21	0.114	0.083	0.293	6	1/9
Dunham	395.3	92	0.073	0.050	0.152	2	13/16
Flamer (data set 2)	25.6	21	0.046	0.057	0.188	3	2/9
Freedman	244.2	77	0.121	0.091	0.350	1	6/15
Hicks	85.8	21	0.162	0.103	0.309	6	0/9
Kothandapani	143.8	45	0.149	0.145	0.406	4	4/12
Marsh (data set 1)	324.4	77	0.106	0.043	0.127	1	15/15
Marsh (data set 2)	413.0	77	0.106	0.039	0.174	1	14/15
1 Meier	731.8	21	0.326	0.067	0.335	0	8/9
2 Shavelson	22.3	21	0.025	0.047	0.138	0	2/9

1 large RMSEA and residual indicates model does not fit.
2 Model fits, but results indicate items with low reliability have no measurement error.

Rindskopf Model	Chi Squared	df	Fit Index	Average residual	Largest residual	Boundary Estimates	No. of Sig. Error Loadings
* Arora	17.0	12	0.991	0.046	0.143	0	9/9
Freedman	158.9	62	0.933	0.057	0.190	1	15/15
Marsh (data set 1)	224.3	62	0.971	0.024	0.127	1	15/15

* Model fits and is appropriate. Data sets not reported in table did not converge.

---

techniques exist for dealing with missing data problems so that inappropriate or problem covariance matrices do not occur (Stewart 1982, Timm 1970). Lastly, Bagozzi and Yi (1993) suggest that estimation problems may arise if the reliability of the various items are drastically different.

Violation of Assumptions

Confirmatory factor analysis assumes that observations are identically distributed (Bentler and Chou 1987). In other words, each observation is assumed to have the same factor structure. It is quite possible that individuals may differ on their reactions to various methods. For example, some people may have a constant tendency bias for a particular scale while others may not. The extent to which this assumption complicates the analysis of MTMM data is unknown. It is also unclear how it might be tested for and corrected if it did exist. Clearly more research is needed on the nature of method effects if we are to address this possible problem.

Misspecification of the Model

Misspecification of MTMM models can occur in numerous ways. One of the most problematic is the specification of method effects themselves. It is generally assumed that systematic measurement error is captured by the different methods. However, this is not always the case (Brannick and Spector 1990, Marsh and Hocevar 1988). Systematic method effects may be represented by such things as halo effects or social desirability which can occur for some traits, but not others. Relatedly, the measurement error can occur at the item level rather than the measurement scale level as when bias is introduced by wording used in all the methods. In all these cases, the traditional specification of method effects would be

inaccurate. The best way to deal with these problems is to use a second order factor model (Gerbing and Anderson 1984, Marsh and Hocevar 1988). Because the exact nature of the method effects is not specified, the second order factor model can account of various types of method effects. In addition, it allows diagnostics at the item rather than the scale level (Gerbing and Anderson 1984, Marsh and Hocevar 1988).

CONCLUSIONS

There are a number of problems which may limit the applicability of confirmatory factor analysis for analyzing MTMM data. While some researchers have claimed there may be fundamental flaws with the application of additive confirmatory factor analysis (block diagonal model) to MTMM data (Bagozzi and Yi 1990, Bagozzi and Yi 1991), it is more likely that the specific data to which we apply the technique is the fundamental root of estimation problems. Confirmatory factor analysis of MTMM data is powerful when applied appropriately. But we cannot ask more of the procedure than it can realistically deliver.

There are some simple guidelines that researchers can follow that will minimize estimation problems. First, make certain that the correlation matrix appears reasonable. Start by calculating reliabilities and make certain the correlation between two variables don't exceed the reliabilities of those variables. This situation would indicate corrections should be made to the data before MTMM analysis begins. In addition, Campbell and Fiske's criteria for analyzing MTMM matrices can be used to identify potential problems (e.g., size of validity diagonal values relative to other values, lack of discrimination, etc.). The data sets should be examined for outliers using the techniques recommended by Bollen

TABLE 3
Summary of Model Appropriateness

	Trad.	Rindskopf	Correlated Errors	Correlated Uniqueness	Fixed Errors	Direct Product	PACM
Allen	boundary estimates (1)	did not converge	boundary estimates (1)	**model fit**	large std. error	boundary estimates (3)	**model fit**
Arora	inconsistent estimates	**model fit**	boundary estimates (1)	**model fit**	boundary estimates (1)	boundary estimates (6)	**model fit**
Dunham	boundary estimates (1)	did not converge	boundary estimates (1)	large residual	**model fit**	boundary estimates (2)	**model fit**
Flamer (data set 2)	boundary estimates (3)	did not converge	boundary estimates (2)	boundary estimate (1)	**model fit**	boundary estimates (3)	**model fit** no method effects
Freedman	boundary estimates (1)	boundary estimate (1)	boundary estimates (1)	boundary estimate (3)	boundary estimates (1)	boundary estimates (1)	low R^2
Hicks	boundary estimates (3)	did not converge	boundary estimates (1)	boundary estimate (2)	large residual	boundary estimates (6)	low R^2
Kothandapani	boundary estimates (1)	boundary estimate (1)	boundary estimates (1)	large residual	large residual	boundary estimates (5)	low R^2
Marsh (data set 1)	boundary estimates (1)	boundary estimate (1)	boundary estimates (2)	boundary estimate (1)	boundary estimates (1)	boundary estimates (1)	no discrim. validity
Marsh (data set 2)	boundary estimates (2)	did not converge	boundary estimates (1)	boundary estimate (2)	**model fit**	boundary estimates (1)	no discrim. validity
Meier	boundary estimates (2)	did not converge	boundary estimates (1)	**model fit**	boundary estimates (2)	**model fit**	no discrim. validity
Shavelson	boundary estimates (1)	did not converge	boundary estimates (2)	**model fit**	boundary estimates (1)	inconsistent estimates	**model fit**

Note: "Inconsistent estimates" indicate that items with low reliability had error loadings near zero.

(1987). Even a single outlier can cause severe estimation problems. When missing values exist, alternative methods for estimating covariance should be considered (Stewart 1982). Lastly, there may be a significant amount of multicollinearity present in the data which may result in instability of estimates when using confirmatory factor analysis. Campbell and Fiske's requirement of maximally dissimilar methods and discriminant traits appears to also hold true for confirmatory factor analysis (albeit to a lesser degree).

Researchers may also want to consider using second order factor analysis (Marsh and Hocevar 1988). This technique has not received wide application, and as such is untested. However, it does provide additional diagnostic information about each item in the analysis and has less restrictive assumptions about the nature of method effects. If a CFA model results in estimation problems, the second order factor model might provide the diagnostics to identify the cause of the problem.

Lastly, we clearly need to more carefully consider the nature of method effects. It is quite possible that our current view of the nature of method effects is flawed (Fiske and Campbell 1992). Either method effects do not exist as we currently view them, or the nature of the relationship between methods and traits is different than the additive or multiplicative models.

REFERENCES

Bagozzi, Richard P. and Youjae Yi (1990), "Assessing Method Variance in Multitrait-Multimethod Matrices: The Case of Self-Reported Affect and Perceptions at Work," *Journal of Applied Psychology*, 75 547-61.

Bagozzi, Richard P. and Youjae Yi (1991), "Multitrait-Multimethod Matrices in Consumer Research," *Journal of Consumer Research*, 17 (March), 426-39.

Bagozzi, Richard P. and Youjae Yi (1993), "Multitrait-Multimethod Matrices in Consumer Research: Critique and New Developments," *JCP*, 2 (2), 143-70.

Bentler, Peter M (1992), *EQS*, Los Angeles: BMDP Statistical Software, Inc.

Bentler, Peter M. and Chih-Ping Chou (1987), "Practical Issues in Structural Modeling," *Sociological Methods and Research*, 16 (August), 78-117.

Bollen, Kenneth A. (1987), "Outliers and Improper Solutions," *Sociological Methods and Research*, 15 (May), 375-84.

Boomsma, Anne (1985), "Nonconvergence Improper Solutions and Starting Values in LISREL Maximum Likelihood Estimation," *Psychometrika*, 50 (2), 229-42.

APPENDIX
Sources of Data

Allen, Jon G., and J. Herbert Hamsher (1974), "The Development and Validation of a Test of Emotional Styles", *Journal of Consulting and Clinical Psychology,* 42 (5), 663-8.

Arora, Raj (1982), "Validation of an S-O-R Model for Situation, Enduring and Response Components of Involvement", *Journal of Marketing Research,* 19 (November), 505-16.

Dunham, R., F. Smith, and R. Blackburn (1977), "Validation of the Index of Organizational Reactions with the JDI, MSQ, and the Faces Scales, "*Academy of Management Journal*, 20, 420-432.

Elbert, N. (1979), "Questionnaire Validation by Confirmatory Factor Analysis: An Improvement Over Multitrait-Multimethod Matrices, "*Decision Sciences,* 10 629-44.

Flamer, Stephen (1983), "Assessment of the MTMM Matrix Validity of LIkert Scales Via Confirmatory Factor Analysis, "*Multivariate Behavioral Research,* 18 (July), 275-308.

Freedman, Richard D., and Stephen A. Stumpf (1978), "Student Evaluations of Courses and Faculty Based on a Perceived Learning Criterion: Scale Construction, Validation, and Comparison of Results", *Applied Psychological Measurement,* 2 (Spring), 189-202.

Hicks, Jack M. (1067), "Comparative Validation of Attitude Measures by the Multitrait-Multimethod Matrix", *Educational and Psychological Measurement,* 27, 985-95.

Kothandapani, (1971), "Validation of Feeling, Belief, and Intention to Act as Three Components of Attitude and Their Contribution to Prediction of Contraceptive BEhavior," *Journal of Personality and Social Psychology*, 19 (September) 321-33.

Marsh, Herbert W. and Butler (1984), "Evaluating Reading Diagnostic Tests: An Application of Confirmatory Factor Analysis to MTMM Data," *Applied Psychological Measurement,* 8 (3), 307-20.

Meier. S. (1984), "The Construct Validity of Burnout," *Journal of Occupational Psychology,* 57, 211-219.

Ostrom, (1969), "The Relationship Betweent he Affective, Behavioral, and Cognitive Components of Attitude", *Journal of Applied Social Psychology,* 5, 12-30.

Roberts, Mary Ann, et al. (1981), "A Multitrait-Multimethod Analysis of Variance of Teachers' Ratings of Aggression, Hyperactivity, and Inattention", *Journal of Abnormal Child Psychology,* 9 (3), 371-80.

Seymour, Daniel and Greg Lessne (1984), "Spousal Conflict Arousal: Scale Development", *Journal of Consumer Research,* 11 (3), 810-21.

Shavelson, Richard J., and Roger Bolus (1982), "Self Concept: The Interplay of Theory and Methods, "*Journal of Educational Psychology,* 74 (1), 3-17.

Brannick, Michael T. and Paul E. Spector (1990), "Estimation Problems in the Block-Diagonal Model of the Multitrait-Multimethod Matrix," *Applied Psychological Measurement,* 14 (December), 325-339.

Browne, Michael W. (1984), "The Decomposition of Multitrait-Multimethod Matrices," *British Journal of Mathematical and Statistical Psychology,* 37 1-21.

Campbell, Donald T. and Edward J. O'Connell (1967), "Methods Factors in Multitrait-Multimethod Matrices: Multiplicative Rather than Additive?," *Multivariate Behavioral Research,* 2 (October), 409-26.

Campbell, Donald T. and Edward J. O'Connell (1982), "Methods as Diluting Trait Relationships Rather than Adding Irrelevant Systematic Variance," in D. B. a. L. H. Kidder (ed), *Forms of Validity Research*, San Francisco: Jossey Bass Inc., 93-110.

Churchill, Gilbert A. (1979), "A Paradigm for Developing Better Measures of Marketing Constructs," *Journal of Marketing Research,* 16 (February), 64-73.

Cote, Joseph A. and M. Ronald Buckley (1987), "Estimating Trait, Method, and Error Variance: Generalizing Across Seventy Construct Validation Studies," *JMR,* 26 (August), 315-9.

Cote, Joseph A. and Robert Greenberg (1990), "Systematic Measurement Error and Structural Equation Models," *ACR,* 17 426-33.

Dillon, William R., Ajith Kumar and Narandra Mulani (1987), "Offending Estimates in Covariance Structure Analysis: Comments on the Causes of and Solutions to Heywood Cases," *Psychological Bulletin,* 101 (January), 126-35.

Fiske, Donald W. and Donald T. Campbell (1992), "Citations Do Not Solve Problems," *Psych Bull,* 112 (3), 393-5.

Gerbing, David W. and James C. Anderson (1984), "On the Meaning of Within-Factor Correlated Measurement Errors," *Journal of Consumer Research,* 11 (June), 572-80.

Kenny, David A. and Deborah A. Kashy (1992), "Analysis of the Multitrait-Multimethod Matrix by Confirmatory Factor Analysis," *Psych Bull,* 112 (1), 165-72.

Lastovicka, John L., Jr. John P. Murry and Eric Joachimsthaler (1990), "Evaluating the Measurement Validity of Lifestyle Topologies With Qualitative Measures and Multiplicative Factoring," *Journal of Marketing Research*, 27 (February), 11-23.

Lehmann, Donald R. (1988), "An Alternative Procedure for Assessing Convergent and Discriminant Validity," *Applied Psychological Measurement*, 12 (December), 411-23.

Lehmann, Donald R. and Sunil Gupta (1989), "PACM: A Two Stage Procedure for Analyzing Structural Models," *Applied Psychological Measurement*, 13 (3), 301-21.

Marsh, Herbert and Michael Bailey (1991), "Confirmatory Factor Analysis of Multitrait-Multimethod Data: A Comparison of Alternative Models," *Applied Psychological Measurement*, 15 (March), 47-70.

Marsh, Herbert W. (1989), "Confirmatory Factor Analysis of Multitrait-Multimethod Data: Many Problems and a Few Solutions," *Applied Psychological Measurement*, 13 (December), 335-61.

Marsh, Herbert W. and Dennis Hocevar (1983), "Confirmatory Factor Analysis of Multitrait-Multimethod Matrices," *Journal of Educational Measurement*, 20 (Fall), 231-48.

Marsh, Herbert W. and Dennis Hocevar (1988), "A New More Powerful Approach to Multitrait-Multimethod Analyses: Application of Second-Order Confirmatory Factor Analysis," *Journal of Applied Psychology*, 73 (1), 107-17.

Mason, Charlotte H. and William D. Perreault (1991), "Collinearity Power and Interpertation of Multiple Regression Analysis," *Journal of Marketing Research*, 28 (August), 268-80.

Rindskopf, David (1983), "Parameterizing Inequality Constraints on Unique Variances in Linear Structural Models," *Psychometrika*, 48 73-83.

Rindskopf, David (1984), "Structural Equation Models: Empirical Identification Heywood Cases and Related Problems," *Sociological Methods and Research*, 13 (August), 109-19.

Stewart, David W. (1982), "Filling the Gaps: A Review of the Missing Data Problem," in W. O. B. Bruce J. Walker William R. Darden, Patrick W. Murphy, John R. Nevin, Jerry C. Olson and Barton A. Weitz (ed), *An Assessment of Marketing Thought and Practice*, Chicago: American Marketing Association, 395-9.

Timm, N. H. (1970), "The Estimation of Variance-Covariance and Correlation Matrices from Incomplete Data," *Psychometrika*, 35 (December), 417-37.

van Driel, Otto (1978), "On Various Causes of Improper Solutions in Maximum Likelihood Factor Analysis," *Psychometrika*, 43 (June), 225-43.

Widaman, Keith F. (1985), "Hierarchically Nested Covariance Structure Models for Multitrait-Multimethod Data," *Applied Psychological Measurement*, 9 (March), 1-26.

Wothke, Werner and Michael W. Browne (1990), "The Direct Product Model for the MTMM Matrix Parameterised as a Second Order Factor Analysis Model," *Psychometrika*, 55 (June), 255-62.

The Importance of Member Homogeneity to Focus Group Quality

Kim P. Corfman, New York University

An issue that is widely debated among those who provide and use focus group services is the importance of group member homogeneity to the quality of a group's output. The underlying thesis of this research is that the relative importance of homogeneity on each of two dimensions—*exogenous homogeneity* and *issue homogeneity*—depends on how the dimension relates to the focus group topic. Theory from social psychology on small group processes is used to support hypotheses concerning the impact of homogeneity on self-disclosure in focus groups. They are tested using data from 99 participants in 11 focus groups on a sensitive topic. Results suggest that homogeneity may not be as important as is commonly believed when the topic is of sufficient interest to the participants—even when the topic is potentially sensitive.

The last decade has produced a resurgence in the popularity of focus groups as a marketing tool. Despite their widespread use and an abundance of "how to" books and articles on the subject (e.g., Krueger 1988; Morgan 1988; Templeton 1987), little systematic research has been conducted on the theoretical foundations of the approach and little formal testing has been performed of the quality of output produced by various methods (Stewart and Shamdasani 1990).

An issue that is widely debated among those who provide and use focus group services is the importance of group member homogeneity to the quality of a group's output. As the following quotations illustrate, recommendations range from complete homogeneity to homogeneity on a subset (sometimes specified) of characteristics to an analysis of the trade-offs involved to a careful balancing of similarities and differences:

"Homogeneous groups....are generally more comfortable and open with each other, whereas mixed sex, ethnic, or socioeconomic groups make it more difficult to achieve a high degree of group interaction" (Keown 1983, p. 66)

"Mixing participants from distinct market segments into a single group is not recommended because each person's segment has different requirements" (Welch 1985, p. 247).

"The goal is homogeneity in background, not homogeneity in attitudes..." (Morgan 1988, p. 46).

"A number of individuals may be very different in national origin, religious beliefs, political persuasion, and the like; but if they share a common identity relevant to the discussion...., a group can form." (Goldman 1962, p. 62)

"Sometimes a varied group is wanted, for the interplay of diverse views on a topic that all can discuss.... However, sharp diversity or division in the group is hazardous." (Levy 1979, p. 30)

"....it is usually helpful to provide for both homogeneity and contrast within specific groups." (Wells 1974, p. 4)

Group member homogeneity can be defined on a number of dimensions. The underlying thesis of this research is that the importance of homogeneity on these dimensions depends on how the dimension relates to the focus group topic. Two forms of homogeneity are defined, *exogenous homogeneity* and *issue homogeneity*, and their influence on individual self-disclosure is examined in an exploratory study of focus groups on a sensitive topic.

BACKGROUND

Although experience with focus groups has led to a large body of popular wisdom on the subject, very little formal research has been conducted on factors affecting the productivity of focus groups, even less on the influence of group composition, and none on the effects of member homogeneity. Factors that have been investigated include acquaintanceship (Fern 1982; Nelson and Frontczak 1988), group size (Fern 1982), the importance of the moderator (Fern 1982), and moderator philosophy (McDonald 1992, 1993).

There is, however, a large literature in social psychology on small group processes and the influence of a variety of group member characteristics on interaction and group performance. The research that relates to our interests considers the effects of homogeneity in ability (Cartwright 1968; Goldman 1965; Laughlin, Branch and Johnson 1969), gender (Aries 1976; Reitan and Shaw 1964; Wyer and Malinowski 1972), age and education level (Cartwright 1968), race (Fenelon and Megargee 1971; Ruhe and Allen 1977), religion (Fiedler and Meuwese 1963), culture (Fiedler 1966), attitudes, opinions, and values (Cartwright 1968; Fisher 1980; Terborg, Castore and DeNinno 1976), and personality (Hoffman 1959; Triandis, Hall and Ewen 1965). In these studies the kinds of tasks employed are predominately more structured and clearly defined than the typical focus group "task," objective performance quality is much more easily determined, and the groups studied are far smaller (usually two to three members) than those normally assembled for focus groups. However, some of this work provides a useful foundation for theory building in the focus group context.

THEORY AND HYPOTHESES

Focus groups are used for a wide variety of purposes including generating hypotheses about behavior, brainstorming or testing ideas for new products, packaging, advertising, etc., gaining insight into how consumers view a brand or category and its users, what they want from it, and what associations they make among product attributes, learning about purchase and usage behavior, testing questionnaire language, observing the process of opinion formation, and explaining puzzling survey results. Calder (1977) proposes a taxonomy of focus group approaches with which the many uses of focus groups may be classified into three distinct groups: exploratory, phenomenological, and clinical. Although the demands placed on participants with these uses and approaches differ, in order to be successful, all rely on the willingness of participants to be open with their feelings, beliefs, ideas, behavior, etc. and to discuss them candidly with other group members. The factors that may influence the quality of a participant's involvement and willingness to self-disclose in a focus group include characteristics of the individual, the nature and sensitivity of the discussion topic, the composition of the group, moderator traits and style, and the physical environment. The focus of this study is the composition of the group, specifically, the degree of homogeneity among its members and how homogeneity affects self-disclosure in focus groups. As noted by Shaw (1981), "groups are homogeneous or heterogeneous with respect to specific characteristics, not all of which are relevant to the group's activities" (p. 238). Two types of homogeneity are considered here: *exogenous homogeneity* and *issue homogeneity*.

Exogenous Homogeneity

Exogenous homogeneity implies similarity in such characteristics as gender, ethnicity, social class, religion, personality, attitudes, values, and age when the factor is not highly correlated with response to the issue under investigation. Many have observed that exogenous homogeneity is important because consumers who differ greatly in social class and stage in the family life cycle have such different resources, problems, experiences, and perceptions that they may have difficulty communicating with each other (Krueger 1988; Merton, Fiske and Kendall 1990; Wells 1974). Researchers have explored the effects of homogeneity on such traits as ability (Goldberg et al. 1966; Goldman 1965; Laughlin, Branch and Johnson 1969; Shaw 1960), personality (Triandis, Hall and Ewen 1965; Hoffman 1959) and race (Fenelon and Megargee 1971; Ruhe and Allen 1977; Ruhe and Eatman 1977). Most of these studies indicate that heterogeneous groups outperform homogeneous groups on clearly defined intellective problem-solving tasks that are better accomplished by groups whose members have differing and complementary knowledge bases and experiences upon which to draw. These results have limited relevance to focus groups because most focus groups are designed to acquire information possessed by the group members about themselves and not to determine how well they solve artificial problems created by the researcher. (Exceptions may be the use of focus groups for more creative tasks such as brainstorming new product ideas.)

Research that is more closely related to the concerns of focus groups examines the effects of homogeneity on cohesiveness, which has been shown to enhance several aspects of group interaction. The evidence indicates that group members will be more attracted to each other and, thus, become more cohesive when they agree in their attitudes, have similar values, and have similar abilities and opinions (Cartwright 1968; Shaw 1981; Terborg et al. 1976). (A small amount of contradictory evidence comes from the context of work groups whose goals are such that some complementary differences in abilities might be valued and some similarities be judged irrelevant to the task, Gross 1956; Seashore 1954.) Cartwright (1968) and Shaw (1981) examine the effects of cohesiveness on group interaction and conclude that individuals in cohesive groups are likely to participate and communicate more (Back 1951; Lott and Lott 1961), feel greater self-esteem and less anxiety (Julian, Bishop and Fiedler 1966; Myers 1962; Seashore 1954), be more cooperative, accepting, and trusting of other members (Back 1951; Shaw and Shaw 1962), feel more secure (Pepitone and Reichling 1955), and be more effective in achieving the group goals (Goodacre 1951; Schacter et al. 1951; Shaw and Shaw 1962; Van Zelst 1952). The observation is also made that members of cohesive groups are more likely to conform to the norms of the group (Berkowitz 1954; Lott and Lott 1961; Schacter et al. 1951; Wyer 1966). This effect is expected to be weaker than the positive effects of cohesiveness; however, it can have negative consequences for focus groups if it leads to the repression of differing opinions and perspectives. In general, it seems reasonable to conclude that greater exogenous homogeneity will generally result in improved quality of interaction and increased self-disclosure in focus groups.

Issue Homogeneity

Issue homogeneity implies similarity in response to the focal issue, e.g., product usage, preference, attitude, motivation, etc. Lower levels of issue homogeneity are often better for provoking introspection through exposure to contrasting perspectives, revealing reasons behind differences in behavior and attitudes, and exposing the researcher to a broader range of consumer response (Krueger 1988; Wells 1974). However, very low levels may make productive discussion difficult because participants may be unable to understand each other's needs and behavior (Krueger 1988; Levy 1979). Due to the benefits of greater cohesiveness that result from homogeneity in attitudes, opinions, and values it seems reasonable to conclude that moderate levels of issue homogeneity will improve the quality of member interaction and encourage self-disclosure while allowing sufficient variation among members to stimulate insightful discussion.

It is important to note that the above arguments hold only for *benign* issue-related factors. When the topic is sensitive, it is important to have high levels of issue homogeneity. *Sensitive* issue-related factors affect willingness to discuss a particular issue openly (e.g., alcoholism when the topic is alcohol use, gender when the topic is contraception). When the use of a product or the need for it is a sensitive issue, only those who have similar needs and usage patterns may feel comfortable discussing it together (Levy 1979; Morgan 1988). Heterogeneity in ability to purchase a product or the impact of the purchase on an individual's budget can also create discomfort. Thus, income may be a sensitive factor for high ticket items. The presence of respected authority or someone who is superior in rank may also inhibit the open discussion (Cunninghis 1992).

Even when the topic is sensitive or there are sensitive issue-related factors, low levels of exogenous homogeneity may be less damaging to group interaction (and self-disclosure) when issue homogeneity is high. Morgan (1988) reports on work with groups of widows that were very mixed with regard to social class (exogenous heterogeneity), in which this factor had little impact because their bereavement created an important and fundamental similarity.

Hypotheses

In this study the focus is on the individual and how group composition influences his or her contributions to the discussion. At the individual level, heterogeneity determines a participant's feelings of uniqueness. From the discussion above, the following basic hypothesis is derived:

H1: Feelings of uniqueness on the part of focus group participants result in decreased self-disclosure.

Both exogenous and issue homogeneity are expected to encourage self-disclosure. However, when the topic is sensitive, homogeneity in sensitive issue-related factors is expected to be more important:

H2: When the discussion topic is sensitive, feeling unique in issue-related factors has a larger impact on self-disclosure than feeling unique in exogenous factors.

Although the focus of this study is the effects of uniqueness, other individual, relationship, and environmental factors that have been proposed as determinants of focus group quality are also examined.

METHOD

Topic and Subjects

The topic and subjects were selected to ensure that discussion would be both relevant and sensitive. A corporate sponsor was located who was interested in the results of focus groups conducted with college students on the subject of diet and weight loss products.

An undergraduate subject pool provided 99 participants. Pre-screening determined that none had participated in another focus group within the preceding six months or ever taken part in one on weight control, and that they were interested in the subject. Eleven groups were formed on the basis of the students' schedules, each containing from 7 to 12 members, with approximately equal representation of males and females. All sessions were conducted within a 22 day period. Subjects were asked not to discuss their experiences with anyone who might participate at a future date.

Data Collection

The sessions were held in a conference room equipped with a tape recorder, a video camera, and a table of refreshments. As they arrived, participants were given tents cards with their first names, offered refreshments, and invited to sit where they chose around an oblong conference table. Then they were asked to complete a three page prequestionnaire which requested information on the following exogenous factors—income, ethnicity, traditionalism, religiousness, social values, and their acquaintanceship with other members—and a variety of issue-related factors—height, weight, bone structure, desire to lose weight, diet habits, and use and harmfulness of exercise, weight loss programs, and diet pills.

The moderator for all 11 groups was a clinical psychologist, experienced in group therapy and a trained focus group moderator. He was thoroughly briefed on the topic and had input into the design of the discussion guide, but was not aware of the nature of the study. At the beginning of the session, he gave a standard focus group introduction and explained that the purpose of the group was to talk about "your feelings about eating and dieting, whether you are concerned about weight loss and why, and what you do about it if you are." After a warm up task, the discussion covered eating and exercise habits and use of weight loss products and programs. Of the 1.5 hour discussion, approximately a half hour at the end was devoted to discussion of two diet aids manufactured by the sponsor—one currently on the market and the other in testing.

At the conclusion of the discussion, participants were asked to complete a postquestionnaire which asked for self-reports on items relating to the focus group session: self-disclosure, group process (Open Group Process, Work Group Functioning Scale, Seashore et al. 1982), cohesiveness (Gross 1957), learning about themselves (insight), homogeneity (Group Homogeneity, Work Group Functioning Scale), interest and involvement in the discussion, and attitude toward the moderator. When they had completed this form they were given a final questionnaire and told that it was for an independent study on personality. (Subjects in this pool are accustomed to completing multiple independent experiments and surveys in a single session.) The personality questionnaire asked for self reports on items relating to adolescent self-esteem (Rosenberg 1965), interpersonal orientation (Swap & Rubin 1983), traditionalism (Corfman & Lehmann 1987), religiousness (Corfman & Lehmann 1987), and social values (Kahle's 1983 List of Values). The entire procedure lasted less than two hours.

ANALYSIS AND RESULTS

Variables and Indices

Items from the first postquestionnaire which relate to the focus group session were factor analyzed with varimax rotation. Seven factors were retained (using the eigenvalues greater than one criterion). Items loading at greater than .5 on a factor are examined. The factors are easily interpreted and where loadings are not consistent with expectations, they make sense in the context of the index. Indices were created by summing the relevant items. The

following are the resulting indices and their Cronbach alphas: Self-disclosure (α=.83), Interest/involvement (α=.83), Cohesiveness (α=.73), Insight (α=.77), Homogeneity (α=.64), and Comfort (α=.65). (These alpha levels are generally considered reasonable for exploratory research, Nunnally 1978.) The Comfort index is composed of a moderator item, a self-disclosure item, and a group process item, all of which relate to how comfortable the participant felt in the group. The eighth factor had two items relating to attitude toward the moderator, but their correlation was only .49, so the items were used separately.

Items from the second postquestionnaire relating to three personality traits were also factor analyzed. Four factors were retained, the first three of which are clearly the three traits: Self-esteem (α=.86), Traditionalism (α=.86), and Religiousness (r=.74). The fourth factor has only two items and is not easily interpreted.

The nine items in Kahle's List of Values (LOV) scale were factor analyzed and loaded on three factors: Self-Oriented (α=.74), Social (α=.75), and Stimulation (α=.45). Two dummy variables indicated to which of these categories the subject's most important value belonged.

Other variables were created as follows. The Interpersonal Orientation scale is the sum of 29 items and has a Cronbach alpha of .78. A Weight vs. Ideal variable was created by subtracting the subject's objective ideal weight (Bender 1973) from his or her actual weight. Negative scores were corrected to zero. (No one in the study was seriously underweight.) The uniqueness variables were created by calculating the proportion of the group that was the same as the subject on each factor. For example, for Diet Pill Harm, a subject who indicated in the prequestionnaire that he or she believed diet pills were harmful would have a uniqueness rating corresponding to the proportion of the group that believed they were harmful.

Regression

A regression was run using Self-disclosure as the dependent variable and four categories of independent variables: uniqueness dimensions, individual characteristics, relationship factors, and characteristics of the physical environment. The regression would have been run with a dummy variable for group membership as a control for the repeated measures design. However, group size served the same purpose as it was a linear combination of the group membership variables. Table 1 contains the variables and the results of the analysis. Comfort, Cohesiveness, and Insight were highly correlated. Thus, only one, Comfort, was included in the analysis. Gender uniqueness was omitted because there was virtually no variance; the numbers of men and women were close to equal in all groups. The R^2 for the regression is .68 (adjusted R^2=.42) and only six variables are significant.

The only uniqueness variable that is significant is exercise harm, indicating that those who felt they were more unique in their beliefs about the dangers associated with exercise were more reluctant to talk about themselves. Because few subjects felt exercise was harmful, the unique participants were those who felt it could be harmful. As the significance level is only $p<.10$ and the number of independent variables is large, the significance of this estimate may have been due to chance. (The single significant individual characteristic, the dummy variable associated with being from the West Indies, may safely be ignored, as there was only one individual in that category.) To check whether subjects' perceptions of homogeneity were related to the uniqueness variables examined here, correlations were examined. While Homogeneity is significantly correlated with four of the uniqueness variables (Traditionalism, Ethnicity, Weight vs. Ideal, and Diet Pill Use),

TABLE 1
Regression: Self-disclosure

		β
Individual Uniqueness		
Family income		.04
Ethnicity		-.07
Traditionalism		.08
Religiousness		.13
1st LOV value		-.07
Weight vs. ideal		.08
Exercise regularly		.06
Weight loss program use		.11
Diet pill use		.22
Exercise harm		-.19[c]
Weight loss program harm		.11
Diet pill harm		-.10
Individual		
Gender		-.06
Ethnicity:	African-American	-.01
	Asian	
	Caucasian	.07
	Latino	.10
	Middle Eastern	.01
	Native American	-.07
	West Indian	.37[b]
Self-esteem		.16
Interpersonal orientation		.08
Weight vs. ideal		.03
Exercise regularly		.07
Weight loss program use		-.01
Diet pill use		-.24
Exercise harm		.10
Weight loss program harm		-.12
Diet pill harm		.04
Relationship		
Acquaintanceship		-.12
Comfort in group		.45[a]
Interest in discussion		.23[c]
Moderator effectiveness		.16
Liking of moderator		-.23[b]
Physical environment		
Group size		.03
Distance from moderator		-.22[b]
Intercept		.00
R^2 (adjusted)		.65 (.45)[a]

[a]$p<.001$; [b]$p<.05$; [c]$p<.10$

again Homogeneity and Self-Disclosure are not significantly correlated.

Three relationship factors were significant. Those who felt more comfortable in the group and those who were interested and involved in the discussion were more like to self-disclose. The negative sign associated with Liking of Moderator is misleading and can be better understood through an examination of the rela-

tionship between the two moderator variables and Self-disclosure. While the moderator variables have a .49 correlation ($p<.001$), Effectiveness has a .29 ($p<.05$) correlation with Self-disclosure while Liking of Moderator is not significantly correlated with Self-disclosure. From this it appears that the regression signs are a result of estimate instability (due to collinearity) and perceptions of Moderator Effectiveness result in greater self-disclosure. One aspect of the physical environment has a significant effect. Participants who sat closer to the moderator disclosed more about themselves. Subjects chose where to sit and, it seems, those who were more comfortable sitting near the moderator were also those who were willing to talk about themselves.

CONCLUSIONS

In summary, the results of this exploratory study found that participants who were more unique in their beliefs that exercise was harmful may have disclosed less about themselves, although this finding was weak. Those who were comfortable, interested, felt the moderator was good at getting the group to talk, and sat closer to the moderator disclosed more. The weak findings for the importance of homogeneity suggest that homogeneity may not be as important as is commonly believed when the topic is of sufficient interest to the participants—even when the topic is potentially sensitive.

Some limitations of this study suggest stronger tests of the hypotheses. First, in this study the dependent variable, self-disclosure, is a self-rating. While one would hope that there is a relationship between perceived self-disclosure and objective self-disclosure, it is not clear how close that relationship is and the latter could be much more revealing. Transcripts of focus groups session could be content analyzed and varieties of self-disclosure identified and tallied. For example, it would be useful to distinguish among disclosure of past behavior, opinions, and reports of others' behavior and opinions, the latter being less personal and revealing. Another problem is the issue of accuracy of self-disclosure. Further, while subjects' disclosures were entirely plausible, this study could not discriminate true self-disclosure from inaccurate reports of behavior, feelings, etc. and it was not possible to tell who was withholding relevant information. It would be very interesting, although somewhat difficult, to design a study involving subjects about whom the researchers had confidential information. Second, there may have been insufficient variation in many of both the exogenous and issue-related factors to pick up the effects of heterogeneity on self-disclosure. Future studies could attempt to create heterogeneity on specific dimensions through selection of their members. Finally, it would also be useful to distinguish between kinds of uniqueness in a heterogeneous group. "Good" uniqueness, such as being the sole marathon runner in the group, may have a different effect on self-disclosure than "bad" uniqueness, such as being the sole diet pill taker.

Given the widespread use of the focus group technique in marketing practice, the almost complete absence of formal research on the subject is disturbing. A large number of generally accepted principles and practices have never been subjected to formal examination in an environment that controls for the many factors that interact to create a particular experience, nor have they been evaluated on the basis of more than intuitive assessments of session "quality." This study addresses commonly made untested recommendations which concern focus group composition. The results of this investigation provide some preliminary insight into the factors that influence self-disclosure in focus groups and should help users and providers of focus group services begin to design more effective studies.

REFERENCES

Aries, E. (1976), "Interaction Patterns and Themes of Male, Female, and Mixed Groups," *Small Group Behavior*, 7 (February), 7-18.

Back, K. W. (1951), "Influence through Social Communication," *Journal of Abnormal and Social Psychology*, 46, 9-23.

Bender, Arnold E. (1973), *Nutrition and Dietetic Foods*.

Berkowitz, Leonard (1954), "Group Standards, Cohesiveness, and Productivity," *Human Relations*, 4 (February), 509-519.

Calder, Bobby J. (1977), "Focus Groups and the Nature of Qualitative Marketing Research," *Journal of Marketing Research*, 14 (August), 353-364.

Cartwright, Dorwin (1968), "The Nature of Group Cohesiveness," in Dorwin Cartwright and Alvin Zander, eds., *Group Dynamics*, New York: Harper and Row, 91-109.

Corfman, Kim P. and Donald R. Lehmann (1987), "Models of Group Decision-Making and Relative Influence: An Experimental Investigation of Family Purchase Decisions," *Journal of Consumer Research*, 14 (June), 1-13.

Cunninghis, Burt (1992), lecture, Focus Group Moderators' Workshop, Consumer Sciences Inc., (November).

Fenelon, J. R. and E. I. Megargee (1971), "Influence of Race on the Manifestation of Leadership," *Journal of Applied Psychology*, 55, 353-358.

Fern, Edward F. (1982), "The Use of Focus Groups for Idea Generation: The Effects of Group Size, Acquaintanceship, and Moderator on Response Quantity and Quality," *Journal of Marketing Research*, 19 (February), 1-13.

Fiedler, F. E. (1966), "The Effect of Leadership and Cultural Heterogeneity on Group Performance: A Test of the Contingency Model," *Journal of Experimental Social Psychology*, 2, 237-264.

_____ and W. A. T. Meuwese (1963), "Leader's Contribution to Task Performance in Cohesive and Uncohesive Groups," *Journal of Abnormal and Social Psychology*, 67, 83-87.

Fisher, B. Aubrey (1980), *Small Group Decision Making*, New York: McGraw Hill.

Goldberg, M. L., A. H. Passow and J. Justman (1966), *The Effects of Ability Grouping*, New York: Teachers College Press.

Goldman, Alfred E. (1962), "The Group Depth Interview," *Journal of Marketing*, July, 61-68.

Goldman, M. (1965), "A Comparison of Individual and Group Performance for Varying Combinations of Initial Ability," *Journal of Personality and Social Psychology*, 1, 210-216.

Goodacre, D. M. (1951), "The Use of a Sociometric Test as a Predictor of Combat Unit Effectiveness," *Sociometry*, 14, 148-152.

Gross, E. (1956), "Symbiosis and Consensus as Integrative Factors in Small Groups," *American Sociological Review*, 21, 174-179.

Gross, E. F. (1957), "An Empirical Study of the Concepts of Cohesiveness and Compatibility," unpublished honors thesis, Harvard University, Department of Human Relations.

Hoffman, L. Richard (1959), "Homogeneity of Member Personality and its Effect on Group Problem-Solving," *Journal of Abnormal and Social Psychology*, 58, 27-32.

Julian, J. W., D. W. Bishop and F. E. Fiedler (1966), "Quasi-therapeutic Effects of Intergroup Competition," *Journal of Personality and Social Psychology*, 3, 321-327.

Kahle, Lynn R. (1983), *Social Values and Social Change*, New York: Praeger.

Keown, Charles (1983), "Focus Group Research: Tool for the Retailer," in Thomas J. Hayes and Carol B. Tathum, eds., *Focus Group Interviews: A Reader*, Chicago: American Marketing Association, 64-70.

Krueger, Richard A. (1988), *Focus Groups: A Practical Guide for Applied Research*, Beverly Hills, CA: Sage.

Laughlin, Patrick R., Laurence G. Branch and Homer H. Johnson (1969), "Individual Versus Triadic Performance on a Unidimensional Complementary Task as a Function of Initial Ability Level," *Journal of Personality and Social Psychology*, 12 (2), 144-150.

Levy, Sidney J. (1979), "Focus Group Interviewing," in James B. Higginbotham and Keith K. Cox, eds., *Focus Group Interviews: A Reader*, Chicago: American Marketing Association, 29-37.

Lott, A. J. and B. E. Lott (1961), "Group Cohesiveness, Communication Level, and Conformity," *Journal of Abnormal and Social Psychology*, 62, 408-412.

McDonald, William J. (1992), "The Influence of Moderator Philosophy on the Content of Focus Group Sessions: A Multivariate Analysis of Group Session Content," in Robert P. Leone and V. Kumar, eds., *Enhancing Knowledge Development in Marketing*, vol. 3, Summer, Chicago: American Marketing Association, 540-545.

_____ (1993), "Focus Group Research Dynamics and Reporting: An Examination of Research Objectives and Moderator Influences," *Journal of the Academy of Marketing Science*, forthcoming.

Merton, Robert K., Marjorie Fiske, and Patricia L. Kendall (1990), *The Focused Interview*, 2nd edition, New York: Free Press.

Morgan, David L. (1988), *Focus Groups as Qualitative Research*, Beverly Hills, CA: Sage.

Myers, A. E. (1962), "Team Competition, Success, and Adjustment of Group Members, *Journal of Abnormal and Social Psychology*, 65, 325-332.

Nelson, James E. and Nancy T. Frontczak (1988), "How Acquaintanceship and Analyst Can Influence Focus Group Results," *Journal of Advertising*, 17 (1), 41-48.

Nunnally, Jum C. (1978), *Psychometric Theory*, New York: McGraw-Hill.

Pepitone, A. and G. Reichling (1955), "Group Cohesiveness and the Expression of Hostility," *Human Relations*, 8, 327-337.

Reitan, Harold T. and Marvin E. Shaw (1964), "Group Membership, Sex-Composition of the Group, and Conformity Behavior," *Journal of Social Psychology*, 64 (October), 45-51.

Rosenberg, Morris (1965), *Society and the Adolescent Self-Image*, Princeton, NJ: Princeton University Press.

Ruhe, J. A. and W. R. Allen (1977), "Differences and Similarities between Black and White Leaders," in *Proceedings of the American Institute of Decision Sciences, Northeast Division*, April, 30-35.

_____ and J. Eatman (1977), "Effects of Racial Composition on Small Work Groups," *Small Group Behavior*, 8, 479-486.

Schacter, Stanley, Norris Ellertson, Dorothy McBride and Doris Gregory (1951), "An Experimental Study of Cohesiveness and Productivity," *Human Relations*, 4, 229-238.

Seashore, S. E. (1954), *Group Cohesiveness in the Industrial Work Group*, Ann Arbor, MI: University of Michigan Press.

_____ E. E. Lawler, P. Mirvis and C. Cammann (1982), eds., *Observing and Measuring Organizational Change: A guide to Field Practice*, NY: Wiley.

Shaw, Marvin E. (1960), "A Note Concerning Homogeneity of Membership and Group Problem Solving," *Journal of Abnormal and Social Psychology*, 60, 448-450.

_____ (1981), *Group Dynamics: The Psychology of Small Group Behavior*, New York: McGraw Hill.

_____ and Lilly May Shaw (1962), "Some Effects of Sociometric Grouping upon Learning in a Second Grade Classroom," *Journal of Social Psychology*, 57 (August), 453-458.

Stewart, David W. and Prem N. Shamdasani (1990), *Focus Groups: Theory and Practice*, Beverly Hills, CA: Sage.

Swap, Walter C. and Jeffrey Z. Rubin (1983), "Measurement of Interpersonal Orientation," *Journal of Personality and Social Psychology*, 44 (1), 208-219.

Templeton, J. F. (1987), *Focus Groups: A Guide for Marketing and Advertising Professionals*, Chicago: Probus.

Terborg, James R., Carl Castore and John A. DeNinno (1976), "A Longitudinal Field Investigation of the Impact of Group Composition on Group Performance and Cohesion," *Journal of Personality and Social Psychology*, 34 (November), 782-790.

Triandis, H. E., E. R. Hall and R. B. Ewen (1965), "Member Heterogeneity and Dyadic Creativity," *Human Relations*, 18, 33-55.

Welch, Joe L. (1985), "Researching Marketing Problems and Opportunities with Focus Groups," *Industrial Marketing Management*, 14 (November), 245-253.

Wells, William D. (1974), "Group Interviewing," in James B. Higginbotham and Keith K. Cox, eds., *Focus Group Interviews: A Reader*, Chicago: American Marketing Association, 2-12.

Wyer, R. S., Jr. (1966), "Effects of Incentive to Perform Well, Group Attraction, and Group Acceptance on Conformity in a Judgmental Task," *Journal of Personality and Social Psychology*, 4, 21-26.

_____ and C. Malinowski (1972), "Effects of Sex and Achievement Level upon Individualism and Competitiveness in Social Interaction," *Journal of Experimental Social Psychology*, 6, 255-263.

Van Zelst, Raymond H. (1952), "Validation of a Sociometric Regrouping Procedure," *Journal of Abnormal and Social Psychology*, 47 (April), 299-246.

Research Design Effects on the Reliability of Rating Scales in Marketing: An Update on Churchill and Peter

Elizabeth J. Wilson, Louisiana State University

ABSTRACT

A meta-analysis using the recently published *Handbook of Marketing Scales* is conducted to note similarities and differences in reliability estimate information as presented in a 1984 study by Gilbert Churchill and Paul Peter. A key research question is "how do research design characteristics affect the reliability (internal consistency) of a measurement scale?" Consistent with Churchill and Peter, we examine sampling characteristics, measure characteristics, and measure development characteristics to note whether any of these variables are systematically related to differences in the reliability of rating scales. Our results update and, to a large extent, reaffirm findings of Churchill and Peter even though almost ten years have past and very few of the scales included in the *Handbook* overlap with those included in their meta-analysis. In general, we found that rating scales used in marketing have an average reliability of 0.81; this indicates that researchers seem to be successfully meeting the challenges of developing measurement tools with a relatively high degree of psychometric rigor.

Churchill and Peter (1984) conducted a landmark study in which they used meta-analysis to determine whether particular research design variables (type of sample, type of subjects, use of reverse scoring, etc.) affected the overall reliability of rating scales in marketing. In other words, they studied the question, "what research design variables are likely to make one measurement scale more reliable than another?" If a researcher knows, for example, that a scale composed of semantic differential items with both numerical and verbal labels tends to have a higher reliability score, on average, than a scale using Likert-type items with labels on the polar points only, then that researcher can *build in* those aspects when designing a new measure.

The present study builds upon the work of Churchill and Peter (1984) to update and extend their findings. Bearden, Netemeyer, and Mobley's (1993) *Handbook of Marketing Scales* provides a set of scales and related developmental information for which a similar meta-analysis is conducted. Results of this study are compared to those from Churchill and Peter to note similarities and differences over time.

A meta-analytic review of Bearden et al. and comparison to findings of Churchill and Peter may be a useful contribution for three reasons. First, a programmatic update on this issue is needed since Churchill and Peter's findings are now almost ten years old. Second, new knowledge may be gained by this examination because there is relatively little overlap between the studies included in Churchill and Peter and Bearden et al.. Churchill and Peter examined 154 scales (from 107 studies) and Bearden et al. examined 122 scales—only 15 of the scales are common between the two. Third, Bearden et al. have a relatively wider domain compared to Churchill and Peter. Bearden et al. include scales from the psychology and organizational behavior literature because marketing scholars in particular areas tend to use these measures.

Next, a brief review of Churchill and Peter's findings is provided. The method used to conduct the meta-analysis is explained and findings are presented. Implications for measure development are offered along with concluding comments.

BACKGROUND

Churchill and Peter (1984; designated *CP* hereafter) studied effects of three general types of research design effects on the average reliability of 154 rating scale measures. Sampling characteristics, measure characteristics, and measure development procedures were examined to note whether particular characteristics and/or procedures tend to be related to higher levels of reliability (internal consistency) in rating scale measures. Each of these characteristics is discussed next. Interested readers are urged to refer to Tables 1-3 in CP for more detailed information.

Sampling Characteristics

Sampling characteristics are research design elements such as type of sample (nonprobability or probability), sample size, type of subjects (students, non-students), and method of data collection, to name a few. CP investigated these and other sampling characteristics; for some, formal hypotheses were stated. For example, CP expected college student samples to produce more reliable measures than samples using other types of respondents. The average reliability (expressed as coefficient alpha) of scales developed and tested using college students was $\alpha=0.81$ which is acceptable by psychometric standards (Nunnally 1978). However, this level of reliability was not significantly higher than the reliabilities computed from scales developed and tested using non-student samples (members of organizations ($\alpha=0.78$), head of household/housewife ($\alpha=0.75$), combination ($\alpha=0.71$), other ($\alpha=0.66$)). Thus, the hypothesis was not supported. In short, none of the sampling characteristic variables studied had a significant, predicted effect on a measure's reliability (the size of the validation sample had a significant negative effect on reliability and was not predicted *a priori*).

Measure Characteristics

Measure characteristics include number of items in the scale, number of dimensions, use of reverse scoring, and number of scale points, to name a few. CP found that two of nine measure characteristics had a significant effect on the level of reliability in a rating scale measure. First, a positive relationship between the number of items used and the reliability of the measure was proposed. This hypothesis was supported; the average number of items across 154 scales was 13.5. Since the hypothesis was examined via regression analysis, CP do not provide the average levels of reliability for measures having few compared to many items.

Second, a positive relationship was proposed to exist between the number of scale points (in the items) and the reliability of a measure (over a normal range). This hypothesis was supported based on 131 studies. The average number of scale points (per item) was 5.8; but again, CP do not report a breakdown of the average α value for measures containing items with many scale points compared to those items having few.

Hypotheses regarding the use of reverse scoring, dimensionality of scale measures, item difficulty, and extent of scale point description were not supported. No relationship was proposed *a priori*, nor found empirically, between measure reliability and type of item construction (Likert, semantic differential, etc.) or type of labels used on items (numerical, verbal, etc.).

Measure Development Procedures

Measure development procedure variables include the source of a scale (originally developed, borrowed-modified, borrowed-unmodified), procedures used to generate items (literature review, interviews, etc.), and whether the construct domain was defined, to name a few. None of CP's hypotheses pertaining to these elements of research design were supported. For example, scales borrowed from other domains did not have higher reliability scores than those that were newly developed specific to a marketing application. No relationship was proposed nor found regarding *a priori* specification of a measure's dimensionality or whether a measure was specifically investigated for dimensionality.

In summary, CP concluded that it was the characteristics of the measures themselves (the actual stimuli that subjects respond to) that accounted for differences in the reliability of rating scale measures. In other words, properties of the measures themselves were more influential in explaining differences in reliability compared to sampling characteristics or measure development procedures.

Method

In replicating and updating the CP study, their methodology was followed as closely as possible. A meta-analysis of the scale measures in Bearden et al. (1993; designated *BNM* hereafter) was conducted and data were analyzed in much the same way, with a few exceptions which are discussed in the Findings. Before providing the details of the method, a brief explanation is offered regarding the meta-analytic procedure.

Meta-Analysis

Meta-analysis is the statistical summary of findings across studies. In summarizing findings across many studies, researchers can better understand sources of variation about some phenomenon. Meta-analysis has been increasingly used in marketing; in some areas a quantitative cumulation or synthesis of findings may offer greater insight compared to another narrative literature review. Recent examples include Wilson and Sherrell (1993) and Brown and Stayman (1992).

To do a meta-analysis, a researcher gathers as many original studies as he/she can find on a topic. The findings of the individual studies, usually expressed as in terms of statistical effect-sizes or amount of explained variance (r^2, ω^2), become the dependent variables for the meta-analysis while other aspects of the studies (method characteristics and substantive characteristics) become independent variables. In this study, as in CP, the major dependent variable is the reported estimate of reliability. Independent variables are research design elements as discussed above. For those not familiar with meta-analysis, a few excellent sources of information are Rosenthal (1991); Hunter and Schmidt (1990); Houston, Peter, and Sawyer (1983); and Monroe and Krishnan (1983).

Procedure

We use BNM as our source of studies for the meta-analysis. They report scale development and testing information for 122 measures across six general areas that have been studied by marketing researchers (individual traits, values, involvement/information processing, advertising stimuli, attitudes about business, and sales/firm issues). A coding form was developed based on Tables 1-3 of CP; sampling, measure, and measure development characteristics were included so that results could be summarized and compared to those of CP. The variables included on the coding form are shown in Tables 3-5 of the present article.

Data were coded by two judges independently, following the same procedure as CP. After a set of studies was coded, the judges met to resolve any inconsistent evaluations. So, for each scale in BNM, we coded the reliability score and information regarding the sampling, measure, and measure development characteristics.

Additional information from subsequent research on measure reliability was sometimes included in BNM as supporting evidence. In these cases, an average reliability score was recorded for that particular scale. When multiple types of reliability were reported, those coefficients representing internal consistency were used first (coefficient alpha, reliability of the linear combination, composite reliability in structural equations (LISREL) applications) with other coefficients (split-half, Spearman-Brown, alternate forms, test-retest) used in the absence of internal consistency estimates. This was done to be consistent with CP.

Of the 122 measures presented in BNM, most could be included in the meta-analysis. Nine measures were not included since the original authors did not report quantitative estimates of reliability. In a few cases, missing information on some of the independent variables prevented a measure from being included in a particular analysis. So, the number of observations of reliability estimates generally ranges between 110-113 for the analyses and comparisons with CP. Sample size information for each statistical test is presented in Tables 3-5.

FINDINGS

Summary statistics for the reliability estimates are provided in Table 1. All reliability coefficients for the measures included in BNM were 0.60 or above. This is due to the fact that BNM's stated purpose was to compile multi-item, self-report measures developed and/or frequently used in marketing (BNM, 1993, p. 1). Many of the scales had been investigated by other researchers, in addition to the measure developers, to add further evidence as to the psychometric integrity of the particular measure. This is also reflected in the average reliability estimate (0.81) across studies.

In Table 2, the average reliability estimates are broken down into six groups according to the Chapters in BNM which represent general areas of marketing research. Measures of reactions to advertising stimuli and measures of sales/firm issues had the highest average reliability scores (0.84 and 0.83, respectively) while measures of individual traits and values had the lowest scores (0.78 and 0.77, respectively). The differences in the average reliability scores across the groups is significant.

Findings regarding reliability estimates and five sampling characteristics are shown in Table 3. We used the same type of analysis approach for each comparison (regression or ANOVA) as in CP for consistency. Comparisons of results to CP are shown in the right-most column of Table 3. In short, none of the sampling characteristics had a significant effect on the level of reliability of a rating scale measure. For example, there was no difference in reliability for measures using nonprobability samples compared to probability samples, no difference in reliability for studies using students compared to non-students, and so on. Results from BNM match those of CP except for one comparison. CP found, but did not hypothesize a priori, that measures developed using a smaller validation sample tended to be associated with higher average reliability estimates. We did not find this relationship to hold.

CP examined seven sampling characteristics while this study includes five. Insufficient information was available in BNM to do comparisons on "response rate" and "number of samples used to develop the measure."

TABLE 1
Summary Statistics for the Reliability of Scale Measures Across Studies

Range of Reliability Coefficient	Number of Estimates (%)	
0.00 to 0.59	0	(0)
0.60 to 0.64	4	(3)
0.65 to 0.69	6	(5)
0.70 to 0.74	15	(12)
0.75 to 0.79	16	(14)
0.80 to 0.84	33	(27)
0.85 to 0.89	21	(17)
0.90 to 0.94	16	(14)
0.95 to 0.99	2	(1)
Missing	9	(7)
Total	122	(100)
Mean reliability estimate	0.81	
Standard deviation	0.08	

TABLE 2
Average Reliability Estimates by Chapter in BNM

Chapter	Reliability		
	Mean	Std Dev	N of coef.
Individual Traits	0.78	0.09	25
Values	0.77	0.09	13
Involvement and Information Processing	0.83	0.07	24
Reactions to Advertising Stimuli	0.84	0.08	10
Attitudes towards Business Performance	0.82	0.08	12
Sales and Firm Issues	0.83	0.06	29

Note: F = 2.41, 5 and 107 d.f., $p \leq 0.04$; thus, the average reliability scores for measures differ significantly across general areas in marketing. In particular, the average reliability for scales measuring values is significantly different from the average reliability of scales measuring sales issues.

The effects of measure characteristics on reliability estimates are reported in Table 4. Eight of nine measure characteristics included in CP are included in the present analysis. Insufficient information was available to include "difficulty of items."

In six of eight comparisons, results from the meta-analysis of BNM match those of CP. Inconsistent results were found for "number of items in the final scale" and "number of scale points." CP obtained significant differences in reliability estimates for these two variables; however, no significant difference was obtained in the present analysis.

Finally, the impact of measure development procedures on reliability estimates is shown in Table 5. Data from BNM is consistent with CP in two of three comparisons. Reliability estimates differ significantly depending on the original source of the scale (F=4.96, 2 and 110 d.f., p<.009, developed scales have a higher reliability score, on average compared to borrowed-unmodified scales). However, as noted in the Table, this difference must be viewed with caution due to small cell sizes.

DISCUSSION

Results of the present meta-analysis reaffirm, to a large degree, the findings of CP. In a total of 16 comparisons, four comparisons were "misses" while 12 were "hits" in terms of matching of results. In other words, CP's results are confirmed in 75 percent of the comparisons to BNM. This result is robust (χ^2=26.00, 1 df, p<0.01) considering that almost ten years have past and that most of the scales do not overlap those included in CP's original study.

Implications for Research

Although our results largely mirror those of CP, what does this say about whether the reliabilities of rating scales can be affected by research design characteristics? For our results, significant differences in reliabilities were found for only one variable (source of scale). Thus, it seems that research design characteristics may have a minimal effect, at best, on levels of reliability in rating scales. To examine this issue further, we conducted an additional analysis using a subset of study characteristic variables.

The variables included in this post-hoc analysis are "nature of sample" (nonprobability, probability, other), "type of sample" (students, family members, organizational members), "type of research" (correlational, experimental), "respondent urgency" (forced choice, neutral point, other). These variables were chosen because they are salient study characteristics which may be more likely to influence the strength of manipulations and statistical effect sizes (Bearden, Netemeyer, and Mobley 1993; Calder, Phillips, and Tybout 1981; Peterson, Albaum, and Beltramini 1985) compared to other, more cursory characteristics (e.g., use of reverse scoring, type of label, etc.).

We entered all four variables (coded as effects) into the regression equation with average reliability as the dependent variable. Adjusted R^2 is .26 (F=4.13, p<.001) indicating that the average reliability of a rating scale does tend to change given different levels of these independent factors. Results of the model are shown in Table 6 and are explained next.

Scales which have a neutral point for respondents tend to be associated with higher levels of reliability compared to those that

TABLE 3
Impact of Sampling Characteristics on Reliability Estimates
(adapted from Churchill and Peter, 1984)

Sample Characteristics	Analysis Approach	Key Results				Conclusion and Comparison with CP*
Sample size	Regression analysis	$r^2 = .00$, $.025 \leq \beta \leq .027$, nss Mean sample size = 780 SD = 2450 Range = 12 to 26,000				No relationship; inconsistent with CP
Nature of sample	Analysis of variance	Sample Type:	N of coef.	Reliability Mean	SD	No relationship; consistent with CP
		Nonprob.	109	.81	.08	
		Probab.	2	.74	.13	
		Other	1	.72	.00	
Type of subjects	Analysis of variance	Subjects:	N of coef.	Reliability Mean	SD	No relationship; consistent with CP
		Students	27	.80	.09	
		Org.Members	32	.83	.07	
		Head HH	6	.82	.09	
		Combination	41	.80	.07	
		Other	7	.80	.08	
Method of data collection	Analysis of variance	Method:	N of coef.	Reliability Mean	SD	No relationship; consistent with CP
		Mail/Self	41	.81	.07	
		Inclass/Gp.	44	.80	.09	
		Tele/PI	9	.83	.07	
		Combination	13	.84	.07	
		Unknown	5	.79	.11	
Type of research	Analysis of variance	Research:	N of coef.	Reliability Mean	SD	No relationship; consistent with CP
		Experimental	5	.74	.13	
		Correlational	108	.81	.07	

*Churchill and Peter

use a forced choice or some other response mechanism (β=.25, p<.05). Scales which are borrowed from other literatures and unmodified for use in marketing studies tend to be associated with lower reliabilities, as one might expect, (β=-.33, p<.001). Scales used in correlational research, as opposed to experimental studies, tend to be associated with higher levels of reliability (β=.32, p<.01). This result must be viewed with some caution, however, since the number of observations is skewed. There were 108 correlational studies and only 5 experiments. The levels of the final variable, sample type, did not yield any significant differences in the average reliability of rating scales.

In sum, this analysis points out interesting trends. For example, in terms of increasing the reliability of a rating scale, including a neutral point in the type of response may be better than a forced choice, and use of a specially developed scale may be better than using a borrowed, unmodified scale. Calder et al. (1981) advocate the use of experiments in marketing over non-experimental formats because of enhanced control for stronger manipulations and statistical effects. The reliabilities of rating scales were not higher for the experimental studies, on average, although this may be due to the lack of a large number of observations on this comparison.

Limitations

One limitation of this analysis is the use of a "convenience sample" of scales in BNM to replicate CP's work. Although a very useful tool for researchers, the sample of observations regarding reliability of rating scales lacks much variance and consequently we do not find substantial differences in our comparisons. This finding may be because research design characteristics really don't have a substantial impact on scale reliabilities. In addition, this finding may be due to BNM's criteria for inclusion in the *Handbook*—only multi-item scales which tend to be used by marketing scholars. No single item measures nor infrequently used measures were included. Thus, BNM seem to have mostly "established" measures while CP may have had a larger proportion of less psychometrically sound measures. Indeed, they report a larger range of reliability estimates (0.26 to 0.99) whereas all of the measures in BNM had a reliability of *at least* 0.60. The average reliability score from measures included in BNM is higher than that from CP (0.81 compared to 0.75).

Bruner and Hensel (1992) also have a compilation of scales used in marketing. This information was not included in the meta-analysis as a database because it would have replicated information in BNM. In addition, BNM summarized scales which measure marketing-related "traits" while Bruner and Hensel's compilation

TABLE 4

Impact of Measure Characteristics on Reliability Estimates

Measure Characteristic	Analysis Approach	Key Results			Conclusion and Comparison with CP
Number of items in final scale	Regression analysis	$r^2 = .01$, $.104 \leq \beta \leq .188$, nss Number of scales = 112 Mean number of items = 22.6 Standard deviation = 17.5 Range = 3 to 121			No relationship; inconsistent with CP
Number of dimensions	Regression analysis	$r^2 = .00$, $-.435 \leq \beta \leq .338$, nss Number of scales = 112 Mean number of dimensions = 3.1 Standard deviation = 2.1 Range = 1 to 9			No relationship; consistent with CP
Reverse scoring	Analysis of variance	Reverse Yes No Unknown	N of coef. 60 44 9	Reliability Mean SD .81 .08 .83 .08 .76 .09	No relationship; consistent with CP
Type of scale	Analysis of variance	Scale Type Likert Semantic diff. Rating scale w/verbal anchor Forced choice Other	N of coef. 85 14 3 3 8	Reliability Mean SD .80 .08 .83 .09 .89 .07 .75 .05 .84 .10	No relationship; consistent with CP
Number of scale points	Regression analysis	$r^2 = .00$, $-.430 \leq \beta \leq .540$, nss Number of scales = 108 Mean number of scale points = 5.9 Standard deviation = 1.6 Range = 2 to 11			No relationship; inconsistent with CP
Type of labels	Analysis of variance	Labels Numerical and verbal labels Verbal only Other	N of coef. 78 29 6	Reliability Mean SD .81 .08 .81 .08 .78 .10	No relationship; consistent with CP
Extent of scale points description	Analysis of variance	Description All points Polar points Other	N of coef. 70 35 5	Reliability Mean SD .81 .08 .82 .08 .83 .06	No relationship; consistent with CP
Respondent uncertainty or ignorance	Analysis of variance	Uncertainty Forced choice Neutral point Other	N of coef. 21 84 7	Reliability Mean SD .78 .08 .82 .08 .78 .08	No relationship; consistent with CP

includes scales for general constructs such as general affect and satisfaction and more specific constructs such as cooking enjoyment and sales agent contact frequency. A future replication of the present study should include information from Bruner and Hensel (1992).

In conclusion, the status of the reliability of rating scale measures in marketing seems to be quite good and improving based on this comparison. Scales used to measure marketing traits are being developed with care and rigor; else, average reliability coefficients would not be at the levels found based on the information in CP and BNM.

REFERENCES

Bearden, William O., Richard G. Netemeyer, and Mary F. Mobley (1993), *Handbook of Marketing Scales*, Newbury Park, CA: Sage Publications.

Brown, Steven P. and Douglas M. Stayman (1992), "Antecedents and Consequences of Attitude toward the Ad," *Journal of Consumer Research* 19 (June): 34-51.

Bruner, Gordon C. and Paul J. Hensel (1992), *Marketing Scales Handbook*, Chicago, IL: American Marketing Association.

Calder, Bobby J., Lynn Phillips, and Alice M. Tybout (1981), "Designing Research for Application," *Journal of Consumer Research*, 8 (September), 197-207.

TABLE 5

Impact of Measure Development Procedures on Reliability Estimates

Measure Development Procedure	Analysis Approach	Key Results				Conclusion and Comparison with CP
Source of scale	Analysis of variance	Scale Status	N of coef.	Reliability Mean	SD	Relationship found;[**] inconsistent with CP
		Developed	103	.82	.08	
		Borrowed-unmodified	9	.74	.09	
		Borrowed-modified	1	.91	n/a	
Procedures used to generate items	Analysis of variance	Procedure	N of coef.	Reliability Mean	SD	No relationship; consistent with CP
		Lit Review	46	.81	.08	
		Interviews	13	.83	.08	
		Combination	32	.82	.08	
		Unknown	1	.60	n/a	
Investigated dimensionality empirically?	Analysis of variance	Investigated?	N of coef.	Reliability Mean	SD	No relationship;[**] consistent with CP
		Yes	111	.81	.08	
		No	1	.75	n/a	

[**] The average reliability of developed scales is significantly different from the average reliability of borrowed-unmodified scales. Results in this cell should be viewed with caution due to small cell sizes for the comparison.

TABLE 6

Modeling Results for a Subset of Independent Variables Using Effect Coding

Variables Entered	Beta	t-statistic	significance
Respondent Urgency -- Level 2	0.25	1.97	0.05
Source of Scale -- Level 2	-0.33	-2.93	0.001
Sample Type -- Level 2	0.03	0.26	0.79
Sample Type -- Level 1	-0.01	-0.51	0.96
Research Type	0.32	2.57	0.01
Nature of Sample -- Level 2	-0.01	-0.54	0.96
Respondent Urgency -- Level 1	0.03	0.24	0.81
Variables Not Entered			
Source of Scale -- Level 1			
Nature of Sample -- Level 1			

Adjusted R2 = .26

F = 4.13 (7,56 df), p < .001

Churchill, Gilbert A. and J. Paul Peter (1984), "Research Design Effects on the Reliability of Rating Scales: A Meta-Analysis," *Journal of Marketing Research* 21 (November) 360-375.

Houston, Michael J., J. Paul Peter, and Alan G. Sawyer (1983), "The Role of Meta-Analysis in Consumer Behavior Research," In *Advances in Consumer Research* 10 (Richard Bagozzi and Alice Tybout, eds.), Ann Arbor, MI: Association for Consumer Research, 497-502.

Hunter, John E. and Frank L. Schmidt (1990), *Meta-Analysis: Cumulating Research Findings Across Studies*, Beverly Hills, CA: Sage.

Monroe, Kent B. and R. Krishnan (1983), "A Procedure for Integrating Outcomes Across Studies," In *Advances in Consumer Research* 10 (Richard Bagozzi and Alice Tybout, eds.), Ann Arbor, MI: Association for Consumer Research, 503-508.

Nunnally, Jum (1978) *Psychometric Methods*, New York: McGraw Hill.

Peterson, Robert A., Gerald Albaum, and Richard Beltramini (1985), "A Meta-Analysis of Effect Sizes in Consumer Behavior Experiments," *Journal of Consumer Research*, 12 (June): 97-103.

Rosenthal, Robert (1991), *Meta-Analytic Procedures for Social Research*, Beverly Hills, CA: Sage.

Wilson, Elizabeth J. and Daniel L. Sherrell (1993), "Source Effects in Communication and Persuasion Research: A Meta-Analysis of Effect Size," *Journal of the Academy of Marketing Science* 21 (2): 101-112.

Special Session Summary
Marketing and the Poor
Linda F. Alwitt, DePaul University

Since the late 1970's, most marketers have paid a lot of attention to the affluent sector of society because therein lies much of their profit. The demographic profile of the U.S. has changed since the 1970's, and current stereotypes of the poor by marketers and other members of society are sometimes inaccurate. Identifying the poor and knowing how poor people manage within their economic constraints is essential to the development of appropriate actions by regulators, social service agents, and for–profit marketers. This special topic session examined problems of disadvantaged consumers and some implications for marketers and social policy makers.

Linda Alwitt summarized and gave examples of problems faced by poor American consumers, concluding that current problems are very similar to those described twenty years ago by Andreasen (1975). She also discussed problems faced by marketers when they enter into transactions with poor consumers, and proposed five classes of solutions based on a model of exchange which includes poor consumers, marketers and other components. The classes of solutions are: increase what the poor consumer has to exchange; increase the exchange power of poor consumers; decrease the exchange power of the marketer; alter what marketers have to exchange; reduce marketer risk.

The gradual process by which people become homeless, moving from self–sufficiency to living with other people to homelessness, was described in a paper by Renya Reed and Ronald Hill. This description of the process is supported by a re-analysis of 1988 New York City data on 1228 families using a continuous–time Markov chain model. The model also offers ways in which social service workers can predict the propensity for people to become homeless. They include: having ever been in a mental hospital; substance abuse; being a young black mother (and, due to shelter assignment rules at that time, also pregnant); having *fewer* children; having experienced dislocation from the family as a child; partner having lost a job; having worked *full–time* (rather than part–time). Indicators *negatively* associated with homelessness were: having worked part-time; ever had mental therapy; had a nervous problem in the past year.

Roger Baran reported that the wife is the key financial decision maker in low income families in which both husbands and wives are present. Baran's conclusions are based on a survey of a nation–wide sample of 641 low–income couples with annual incomes less than $15,000 from a marketing panel. The survey examined husband–wife involvement in various family decisions and tasks, in perceptions about who is the 'financial officer' (e.g., who decides how much money to save and how much to put in a checking account) and who performs financial tasks (e.g., who carries the checkbook or withdraws money from an account). Some public policy implications were discussed.

The fourth paper, by Anusree Mitra, Manoj Hastak, Gary T. Ford and Debra J. Ringold, was concerned with a specific public policy issue: can educationally disadvantaged consumers interpret nutrition information in the presence of a health claim? While the FDA perceives that health claims on food labels are potentially misleading and may undermine nutrition information, others suggest that health claims offer benefits such as making diet and health more salient. In an empirical study of 410 adults, the presence of health claims on a TV dinner package ("It does your heart good!")

and healthfulness based on nutrition information was varied in a forced viewing situation. Low levels of fat, cholesterol and sodium increased ratings of how good the product was for the heart. Moreover, education level of respondents did not interact with either the presence of the health claim or with nutrition information in evaluating the product as good for the heart. The authors conclude that consumers appear to be capable of making appropriate judgments about health claims in the presence of nutrition information — education notwithstanding.

Alan Mathios, formerly with the FTC and currently on the faculty of Consumer Economics at Cornell University, discussed the papers within the framework of the five classes of solutions discussed by Alwitt. The paper by Reed and Hill, which argues that financial assistance can be directed at high risk groups identified by their model, increases what the poor consumer has to exchange. Baran's conclusion has implications for increasing the exchange power of poor consumers. The Mitra *et al* paper examines issues related to limiting the exchange power of the marketer, increasing the exchange power of the poor, and changing what marketers have to offer. Mathios pointed out that this paper implies that less educated consumers do gain information from health claims as well as from nutrition information. This is important because the Nutrition Labeling and Education Act bans certain classes of claims, presuming that less educated consumers cannot evaluate them effectively. He also showed evidence that when health claims were permitted in advertising starting in 1985, there were declines in the ingestion of fat, saturated fat and cholesterol. Mathios also discussed the role that is and should be played by governmental agencies in protecting consumers, particularly those who are educationally disadvantaged.

The Influence of Employment-Status and Personal Values on Time Related Food Consumption Behavior and Opinion Leadership

Gregory M. Rose, University of Oregon
Lynn R. Kahle, University of Oregon
Aviv Shoham, Technion University

This study examines the attitudes and behavior of working and non-working women. As predicted, employment-status (full-time, part-time, or non-working), family income, number of children under 12, and personal values (the degree that a woman described herself as traditional and the importance she placed on self-fulfillment and belonging) were significantly related to the set of dependent variables in this study. The specific dependent variables examined were a woman's preference for convenience over price and ease of preparation in food, the frequency that she ate dinner away from home, and her areas of opinion leadership. Traditionalism and the number of children under 12 were especially important explanatory variables.

The increased labor force participation of women over the past decade has had a profound effect on American society. Changing demographics have led to a "splintering of the mass market" and a multiplicity of attitudes towards work, home, and family (Zeithaml 1985, p. 64).

Past studies have linked demographic variables, such as work status, number of children, and family income to family expenditure patterns (e.g. Bellante and Foster 1984; Bryant 1988; Rubin, Riney, and Molina 1990). These studies have produced mixed results. Some have found a direct relation between a woman's employment status (Bellante and Foster 1984) and family expenditures; others have found an indirect relation through income (Rubin, Riney, and Molina 1990).

Other studies have linked career aspirations to receptivity to career versus home-oriented advertisements (Barry, Gilly, and Doran 1985) and segmented women into 4 categories (stay at home, plan to work, just a job, and career) based on employment status and occupational aspirations (e.g., Bartos 1982). Although these studies underscore the importance of career aspirations, they have not examined the influence of more basic personal values, such as self-proclaimed traditionalism and the degree to which a woman values belonging or self-fulfillment.

This study examines the influence of a woman's employment, income, family size, and values on a variety of self-reported attitudes and behaviors. It is an attempt to place the demographics of expenditure studies in a more enlightening context with personal values. Three demographic variables (work status, number of children under 12, and family income) are included. These variables have been found to be of importance in several past studies (e.g. Bellante and Foster 1984; Rubin, Riney, and Molina 1990). Personal values are measured on three dimensions: 1) Self-fulfillment - the extent to which a woman is inner-directed and values self-fulfillment, sense of accomplishment, and self-respect, 2) Belonging - the extent to which she is outer-directed and values a sense of belonging, being respected by others, and having warm relationships with others, and 3) Traditionalism - the extent to which a woman perceives herself as traditional or modern. These constructs represent varying degrees of abstraction. Traditionalism is a relatively concrete value, specifically related to family role perceptions. Self-fulfillment and belonging are more abstract and provide a basic motivation for attitudes and behaviors. Past research has looked at the influence of career orientation. This study measures personal values on a more basic or broad level.

Expenditure studies have concentrated on the purchase of outside services or labor saving durables. The rationale behind these studies is that working will lead to increased time pressure, which will lead to the purchase of time saving goods and services (Becker 1965). Following this logic, three time-related dependent variables were included in this study. One focuses on the frequency with which a woman eats dinner away from home, and two focus on the importance she places on convenience in grocery products and ease of preparation in food products.

The second set of dependent variables examined perceived level of expertise and opinion leadership. Opinion leadership is product-category specific and directly related to enduring category involvement (Richins and Shaffer 1988). Empirically, personal values have been related to opinion leadership in fashion (Goldsmith, Heitmeyer, and Freiden 1991). Intuitively, opinion leaders should exhibit enduring involvement in categories that they find personally rewarding; that is, categories that match their personal values.

The specific areas of opinion leadership in this study were: raising children, cooking, business, and fashion. Each was selected for its relevance to women's roles at the home or office.

Expected Associations

Table 1 summarizes the expected relations in this study. The rationale underlying these expectations is that a woman's employment status and other demographic variables (number of children under 12 and family income) influence her attitudes and behavior. Demographics, however, provide only a partial explanation. Values - the importance a woman places on belonging and self-fulfillment, and the extent to which she defines herself as traditional - should provide additional explanatory power.

Full-time working women should emphasize time saving attributes and engage in time-saving behaviors (Becker 1965). Specifically, they will value convenience and ease of preparation, and will eat supper away from home more frequently than women devoting less time to employment.

Women with children at home will generally eat out less frequently, but having children at home will also place time pressure on women, which should lead to an emphasis on convenience, especially among working mothers.

Family income affords the resources to eat out and to purchase convenience products. This leads to the expectation that families with higher incomes will emphasize ease of preparation in purchasing food and convenience over price.

Traditional values should be associated with an emphasis on the family. Self-reported traditionals should eat dinner away from home less frequently and regard convenience as less important than women who describe themselves as modern.

Self-fulfillment should be associated with a tendency to find meaning away from the home and an emphasis on minimizing the time spent on household chores. Women with a high need for self-fulfillment, should place greater emphasis on convenience and ease of preparation, and eat dinner away from home more often than women with a lower need for self-fulfillment.

Women with a strong need for belonging will generally be other-oriented and place great value on their families eating to-

TABLE 1
Hypothesized Relationships

Independent Variable	Eat Out	Conveniene	Ease of Prep.	Child/ Baby	Clothing/ Fashion	Cooking	Business
Work-Status	+	+	+	−	+	−	+
Kids Under 12	−	+	+	+	−	+	−
Family Income	+	+	+	−	+	−	+
Traditionalism	−	−	−	+	−	+	−
Self-Fulfillment	+	+	+	−	+	−	+
Belonging	−	−	−	+	−	+	−

TABLE 2
Sample Characteristics

Age	% of Sample
18-29	8.9
30-44	16.1
45-59	58.4
60+	16.6
Education	
Some High school or less	9.1
High school Graduate	34.5
Some College	33.3
College Graduate	23.1
Family Income	
Under 20,000	14.8
$20,000 - $24,999	10.9
$25,000 - $34,999	19.5
$35,000 - $49,999	26.3
$50,000 - $74,999	20.5
Over $75,000	8.0

gether. They should eat with their family more frequently and eat dinner out less frequently than women with a low need for belonging.

Opinion Leadership. The rationale for the hypotheses on opinion leadership is straightforward. Opinion leadership on business and clothing should be associated with working outside of the home, a high family income, and valuing self-fulfillment. Both accomplishment and self-fulfillment are internal self-oriented values (Kahle 1983). In contrast, women with a high need for belonging and who describe themselves as traditional should be other-oriented and place great value on the home. Therefore, women that value belonging and self-described traditionals are expected to be opinion leaders on issues that involve the home (children and babies and cooking), but not on business and fashion.

In sum, the expected relations in this study represent three overall hypotheses. The dependent variables in this study should be influenced by a woman's work-status (Hypothesis 1), her family income and number of children at home (Hypothesis 2), and personal values - specifically, her degree of traditionalism and the importance she places on self-fulfillment and belonging (Hypothesis 3).

METHOD

Sampling Procedure

Fifteen monthly samples of approximately 100 women aged 18-65 were taken between May 1991 and August of 1992 from a midwestern city. Each sample was balanced to be nationally representative on income and education, see Table 2. The 15 individual samples were combined to form a total usable sample of 1,479 women. In several analyses, however, cases with missing values were excluded, reducing the sample size to 1,393. Both the mean values of the dependent variables and the residuals were plotted over time, and no pattern emerged. Combining the samples, therefore, appeared reasonable and all data were analyzed using the combined full sample.

Measurement – Dependent Variables

There were seven dependent variables in this study. The first three, which looked at time-related food consumption, were: (1) Eat Out - "During how many of the past 10 days did you eat supper away from your house?" (2) Convenience - "When you make decisions about grocery products, do you usually buy the item with the lowest price even if it is less convenient or the item with the greatest convenience even if it costs more?" (3) Ease of Preparation - "Speed and ease of preparation are most important when deciding what food to buy". All items were measured on an 11 point scale from 0 to 10.

The last four dependent variables measured areas of opinion leadership that were relevant to the home or workplace. All were measured by a single question with end-points from 0 (less likely) to 10 (more likely). The question utilized was: "Compared with most other adults you know, how likely are you to be asked for your ideas or advice on each of the following topics?: the latest clothing

TABLE 3

Multivariate Omnibus Tests of Significance

Independent Variable	DF Model	DF Error	Wilke's Lambda	F Value	P Value	Eta Squared
Work-Status	14	2766	.954	4.62	.001	.046
Children Under 12	14	2766	.817	21.05	.001	.183
Family Income	14	2766	.965	3.51	.001	.035
Traditional	21	3971	.925	5.17	.001	.075
Self-Fulfillment	7	1383	.981	3.84	.001	.019
Belonging	7	1383	.977	4.47	.001	.023
Work-Status by Children Under 12	28	4988	.962	1.94	.002	.038

and fashions, raising children and babies, cooking methods and recipes, and business issues".

Measurement – Independent Variables

The List of Values. Six values were utilized from the LOV (Kahle 1983): sense of accomplishment, self-respect, self-fulfillment, a sense of belonging, being well respected, and having warm relationships with others. Respondents were asked to rate each from 0 to 10, with 10 being the most important. A factor analysis confirmed the expected formation of an inner and other directed dimension; therefore, accomplishment, self-fulfillment, and self-respect were averaged to form a single scale and belonging, being well-respected, and warm relationships with others were averaged to form the second scale. The coefficient alpha for these scales was .68 for the belonging factor and .79 for the self-fulfillment factor. Both of these scales were converted into a high-low class variable by a median split.

Traditional versus Modern. The third predictor variable measured the extent to which a woman identified herself as modern or traditional. Respondents were asked to rate themselves on a 0 to 10 scale, with 0 representing traditional and 10 representing modern. Although only one item was used, it was directly related to the purpose of the study and it provided a relatively concrete measure that complimented the more abstract underlying measures from the LOV. An examination of the frequency distribution of this variable revealed four relatively equal and meaningful groups. From an original scale of 0 to 10, with 0 being modern and 10 being traditional, respondents were split into four groups: modern (<5), neutral (5), traditional (6-8), and very traditional (8+).

Demographic Variables. The final three predictor variables measured three key demographic characteristics: family income, the number of children at home under 12, and employment status. Single items were used to measure each of these variables. Family income was originally measured using ten levels which were collapsed into three categories (under $25,000, $25,000-$49,999, and $50,000 or over). Employment status was also collapsed to contain 3 levels: full-time, part-time, and non-working. These levels have generally been used in past studies and were operationalized in this study by the number of days a woman worked outside the home in the past week, with 5 or more being classified as full-time, 1-4 as part-time, and 0 as non-working. The term non-working refers only to the employee role and is used to mean not employed for pay outside of the home. Three categories were used for the number of children under 12: zero, one, and two or more. This seemed reasonable given the relatively few women with more than two children.

RESULTS

A six-factor MANOVA was used to test the hypothesized relations in this study. The impact of six independent variables (work status, family income, children under 12, traditionalism, self-fulfillment, and belonging) were assessed on seven dependent variables (eating out, convenience, ease of preparation; and opinion leadership on children and babies, clothing and fashion, cooking, and business issues). Initially, a model was ran to check for interactions between the variables. This model revealed one significant two-way interaction between work-status and children under 12, which was included in our final model.

Multivariate Analysis

A MANOVA was conducted to assess the multivariate significance of each independent variable and to protect against an inflated type one error rate. Table 3 summarizes the influence of each main effect and interaction on the set of dependent variables. All were significantly related to the set of dependent variables, p<.05, with effect sizes ranging from .183 for the number of children under 12 to .019 for self-fulfillment, see Table 3.

Univariate Analysis

The univariate analysis supported the MANOVA results. All overall Fs were statistically significant (p<.0001). Individual univariate F-tests were also conducted for each independent variable (both the main effects and the interaction) on each dependent variable. All variables were treated as if they were the last variable to enter the equation. Although somewhat conservative, this was done to control for the potential overlap between the independent variables and to insure that values contributed explanatory power even after controlling for the demographic variables. Table 4 summarizes the F-value for each of these tests.

Eating Out . Three main effects significantly influenced the frequency that a woman ate dinner away from home. First, the number of children a woman had at home was significantly related to the frequency that she ate dinner out (F=13.43; p<.01; 2,1389). An examination of the means revealed that women with two or more children were significantly less likely (p<.05) to eat dinner away from home than women with either one or no children under 12 at home. Table 5 presents the group means and post hoc comparison for all main effects. All test were conducted at p<.05.

The second significant main effect was for traditional (F=3.68; p<.05; 3,1389). Women who described themselves as modern were significantly more likely to eat dinner away from home than any of the other three groups (neutral, traditional, very traditional). Finally, belonging was significantly related to eating out, but contrary

TABLE 4
Univariate F Values

Independent Variable	Eat Out	Conv-eniene	Ease of Prep	Child/ Baby	Clothing/ Fashion	Cooking	Business
Work-Status	2.31	1.75	6.99a	5.35a	4.05b	4.83a	14.32a
Children Under 12	13.43a	13.64a	0.48	97.65a	2.91b	2.29	15.70a
Family Income	0.56	2.53	0.19	7.02a	0.91	2.84	13.13a
Traditionalism	3.68b	0.96	3.91a	7.68a	15.56a	11.61a	2.24
Self-Fulfillment	0.45	2.69	2.30	4.90	5.90a	6.09a	9.56a
Belonging	6.49a	5.45a	8.58a	0.28	1.55	1.98	7.26a
Work Status by Children Under 12	0.12	3.77b	1.80	3.38b	1.59	0.61	1.14

a p<.01
b p<.05

TABLE 5
Mean values and Student-Newman-Keuls Paired Contrasts*

Variable	Eat Out	Conv-eniene	Ease of Prep.	Child/ Baby	Clothing/ Fashion	Cooking	Business
Work Status							
Non- Working	2.28a	5.61a	4.87a	6.27a	4.38a	7.12a	3.82a
Part- Time	2.53ab	5.42a	4.95a	6.27a	4.45a	6.72ab	3.98a
Full Time	2.73b	5.78a	5.67b	5.49b	4.97b	6.42b	4.85b
Kids Under 12							
0	2.77a	5.99a	5.31a	4.92a	4.76a	6.79a	4.69a
1	2.53a	5.38b	5.44a	6.78b	4.85a	6.76a	4.05b
2 or more	1.99b	5.04b	5.02a	7.74c	4.33b	6.46a	3.64c
Family Income							
Under $25,000	2.56a	5.57a	5.31a	5.28a	4.81a	6.48a	3.96a
$25,000-$49,999	2.47a	5.58a	5.27a	6.04b	4.53a	6.78a	4.17a
Over $50,000	2.64a	5.83a	5.19a	6.28b	4.76a	6.82a	4.93b
Traditionalism							
Modern	2.86a	5.73a	5.53a	5.34a	5.48a	5.99a	4.68a
Neutral	2.52b	5.70a	5.60a	6.02b	4.83b	6.54b	4.25ab
Traditional	2.42b	5.56a	4.90b	6.02b	4.33c	6.92b	4.27ab
Very Traditional	2.39b	5.67a	5.17ab	6.29b	4.01c	7.56c	4.12b
Self- Fulfillment							
Low	2.61a	5.39a	4.97a	5.94a	4.39a	6.45a	4.09a
High	2.48a	5.91b	5.55b	5.87a	4.94b	6.97b	4.56b
Belonging							
Low	2.38a	5.38a	4.91a	5.98a	4.49a	6.44a	4.44a
High	2.67b	5.90b	5.56b	5.85a	4.83b	6.96b	4.24a

*Non-matching subscripts indicate a significant difference between means, p<.05.

to expectations, women that placed a high value on belonging were more likely to eat dinner away from home than women who placed less emphasis on this value. Perhaps, women with a high need for belonging have greater outside commitments, belong to more outside organizations, and therefore, eat dinner away from home relatively frequently.

Convenience. One interaction and two main effects were significantly related to convenience. First, woman with a high need for belonging placed great importance on convenience (F=5.45; p<.01; 1,1389). Second, both the main effect for children under 12 (F=13.64; p<.01; 2, 1389), and the interaction between work-status and children under 12 (F=3.77; p<.05; 4, 1389), were significantly related to the importance placed on convenience. Women without children were the most likely to purchase convenience items, irrespective of their level of employment, see table 5. For women with two or more children, however, there is an interaction between

TABLE 6
Observed Relationships

Independent Variable	Eat Out	Conv-enience	Ease of Prep.	Child/Baby	Clothing/Fashion	Cooking	Business
Work-Status			+	–	+	–	+
Kids Under 12	–	–a		+	–		–
Family Income				+a			+
Traditionalism	–		+	+	–	+	
Self–Fulfillment					+	+a	+
Belonging	+a	+a	+a				–
Work Status by Children Under 12		b		b			

a opposite the predicted direction.
b unexpected interaction

work status and convenience. As their commitment to work increases from non-working, to part-time, to full-time, women with two or more children, increasingly emphasize convenience.

In general, the value of convenience for non-working women was strongly influenced by the presence of children. Non-working women without children placed a higher value on convenience than women with 1, or 2, or more children. As women commit more time to outside employment, however, convenience becomes a higher priority for women with children. Thus, working women tend to emphasize convenience over price, while the relative preference for convenience for non-working women depends on the number of children present. The increased time pressure of working appears to lead to an increased emphasis on convenience for women with children, while convenience is highly valued by women without children regardless of their work status.

Ease of Preparation. Three main effects were statistically related to ease of preparation: (1) work status, ($F=6.99; p<.01; 2, 1389$), (2) traditional, ($F=3.91; p<.05; 3,1389$), and (3) belonging, ($F=8.58; p<.01; 1, 1389$).

Full-time working women placed greater emphasis on ease of preparation than either non-working or part-time working women, and women that described themselves as traditional were generally less likely to emphasize ease of preparation. Finally, women that valued belonging placed more emphasis on convenience. This finding was not predicted but was consistent with the finding for convenience. Women that value belonging appear to emphasize both convenience in purchasing grocery products and ease of preparation in preparing food.

Opinion Leadership on Children and Babies. The main effects for work-status ($F=5.35; p<.01; 2,1389$), children under 12 ($F=97.65; p<.01; 2,1389$), family income ($F=7.02; p<.01; 2, 1389$), and traditional ($F=7.68; p<.01; 3,1389$) were significant, as was the interaction between work-status and children under 12 ($F=3.38; p<.05; 4,1389$). Examining the work-status by children-under-12 interaction revealed some differences in slope but no dominant pattern; therefore, only the main effect was interpreted.

As expected, the less children a woman had the less she considered herself an opinion leader on children and babies. Work status, traditionalism, and family income were also significantly related to opinion leadership on children and babies; women with incomes below $25,000 and full-time working women were less likely to view themselves as opinion leaders than women with higher incomes or women that were less active in the workforce. More traditional women were also more likely to perceive themselves as opinion leaders on children and babies than self-described moderns.

Clothing and Fashion. Work status ($F=4.05; p<.05; 2,1389$), children under 12 ($F=2.91; p<.05; 2,1389$), and traditional ($F=15.56$;

$p<.01; 3,1389$), were significantly related to perceived opinion leadership on clothing and fashion. Full-time working women tended to perceive themselves as opinion leaders on clothing more than either part-time or non-working women, while women with 2 or more children, or that described themselves as traditional, were less likely to perceive themselves as opinion leaders in this area than either of their respective comparison groups, see Table 5.

Cooking. Three significant main effects were observed for opinion leadership on cooking. Traditional ($F=11.61; p<.01; 3,1389$) and self-fulfillment ($F=6.09; p<.01; 1,1389$) both increased the tendency of a woman to perceive herself as an opinion leader on cooking, while working decreased this tendency ($F=4.83; p<.01; 2,1389$). Non-working women were more likely to perceive themselves as opinion leaders on cooking than full-time working women.

Business. Work-status ($F=14.32; p<.01; 2,1389$), children under 12 ($F=15.70; p<.01; 2,1389$), family income ($F=13.13; p<.01; 2,1389$), self-fulfillment ($F=9.56; p<.01; 1,1389$), and belonging ($F=7.26; p<.01; 1,1389$) were all significantly related to opinion leadership on business issues. As expected, full-time working women were more likely to perceive themselves as opinion leaders on business issues than part-time or non-working women, as were women with incomes of over $50,000, and women without children. Women that valued self-fulfillment were more likely to perceive themselves as opinion leaders on business issues, while the post hoc contrast for belonging was not significant.

Overview. In summary, both the multivariate and univariate tests in this study generally supported the hypotheses. A woman's work status was related to the emphasis she placed on ease of preparation, and her opinion leadership on children and babies, cooking, clothing, and business issues. The frequency with which she ate dinner away from home and her emphasis on convenience, however, were unrelated to her work status. Thus, hypothesis one was partially supported. A woman's work status was an important explanatory variable for most of the dependent variables in this study.

Hypothesis two stated that other demographic variables, besides work status, would influence the dependent variables. This hypothesis was supported; the number of children at home and family income were both related to the set of dependent variables; as were traditionalism, self-fulfillment, and belonging (hypothesis three).

Overall, 26 statistically significant relations were found between the 6 predictor variables and the 7 dependent variables. Table 6 summarizes these relations. Eighteen of these relations were as predicted, 2 involved the unexpected interaction, and six were opposite the expected direction with 3 of these 6 involving the belonging factor.

DISCUSSION

The majority of relations were logically consistent and as expected. Work-status, family size, income, and values, were all important in explaining self-reported attitudes and behaviors.

Our results generally support a direct relation between a woman's employment and her attitudes and behavior (Bellante and Foster 1984). Work-status influenced five of the seven dependent variables even after the effects of income, family size, and values were statistically removed. Consistent with Reilly (1982), working appears to be associated with an emphasis on ease of preparation in food-related consumption. Women working full-time were more likely to emphasize ease of preparation when purchasing food. Working women were also more likely to perceive themselves as opinion leaders on clothing and business, and less likely to describe themselves as opinion leaders on cooking, and children/babies. All of these relations were as predicted.

Several other variables were also important in predicting self-reported attitudes and behaviors. The number of children at home under 12 was a particularly important explanatory variable. Generally, women with children under 12 ate dinner out less frequently, emphasized price instead of convenience, described themselves as opinion leader on children and babies, and reported low levels of opinion leadership on clothing and business. Moreover, an interaction was found between the number of children under 12 at home and work-status. Non-working women without children place a heavy emphasis on convenience, while non-working women with children emphasize price. As women with children increase their work force participation (from non-working, to working part-time, to working full-time), they increasingly emphasize convenience over price. Thus, for convenience, the presence of children at home moderates the influence of work-status.

Family income was a less important explanatory variable. In general, a preference for convenience appears to be driven more by necessity than income. Work-status was directly related to ease of preparation, while children under 12 was related to a preference for convenience. Income was not related to either of these variables. Thus, there does not appear to be an indirect relation between work-status and the dependent variables through income. Moreover, family income was not the most important variable in explaining the dependent variables in this study. Contrary to previous research (Bryant 1988; Rubin, Riney, and Molina 1990) which focused on expenditures and did not include psychographic variables, our study finds that the presence of children under 12 and the degree to which a woman identifies herself as traditional offer more predictive power than family income.

Traditional women were less likely to eat dinner away from home, and be opinion leaders on clothing and business, but were more likely to be opinion leaders on children (and babies) and cooking than women that described themselves as modern. Overall, traditionalism was an important variable that was significantly related to five of the seven dependent variables.

Self-fulfillment and belonging were also related to the dependent variables. Women pursue self-fulfillment in a variety of ways. As expected, self-fulfillment was positively related to opinion leaders on business and fashion. Self-fulfillment was also positively related to opinion leadership on cooking. Thus, self-fulfillment may be related to interest in a variety of content areas, with the particular content being specific to the individual.

Women that valued belonging, were more likely to eat dinner away from home, emphasize ease of preparation and convenience, and less likely to be opinion leaders on business issues. These relations were consistent and generally opposite expectations. Women with a high need for belonging do not appear to perceive the purchase of convenience products as indicative of a lack of commitment to their families. Instead, they may emphasize convenience and ease of preparation in order to increase their free-time for social interaction, both within and outside their families. The expectation of a negative relation between convenience and commitment to the family appears may be a 1950s notion whose time has passed.

In general, traditionalism provided a stronger influence on the dependent variables than either self-fulfillment or belonging. This is consistent with our expectations, because traditionalism is a more concrete and specific attitude than an overall valuing of self-fulfillment and belonging. These conclusions, however, should be regarded as preliminary because of the use of single-item measures for both traditionalism and the dependent measures in this study.

Despite these limitations, both demographic and psychographic variables were important in explaining the dependent variables in this study. Traditional values, employment status, family income, and children at home all provide important insights into the opinion leadership and food related behavior of working women. Although work-status is an important predictor of consumer behavior, its effect is influenced by other demographic and psychographic variables. Traditionalism and family size are particularly important.

REFERENCES

Barry, Thomas E., Mary C. Gilly, and Lindley E. Doran (1985), "Advertising to Women with Different Career Orientations," *Journal of Advertising Research*, 25 (April/May), 26-35.

Bartos, Rena (1982), *The Moving Target: What Every Marketer Should Know About Woman*, New York: The Free Press.

Becker, Gary S. (1965), "A Theory of the Allocation of Time," *Economic Journal*, 75 (September), 493-517.

Bellante, Don and Ann C. Foster (1984), "Working Wives and Expenditure on Services," *Journal of Consumer Research*, 11 (September), 700-707.

Bryant, Keith W. (1988), "Durables and Wives' Employment Yet Again," *Journal of Consumer Research*, 15 (June), 37-47.

Goldsmith, Ronald E., Jeanne R. Heitmeyer, and Jon B. Freiden (1991), "Social Values and Fashion Leadership," *Clothing and Textiles Research Journal*, 10 (Fall), 37-45.

Kahle, L. R. (1983), *Social Values and Social Change: Adaptations to Life in America*, New York: Praeger.

Reilly, Michael D. (1982), "Working Wives and Convenience Consumption," *Journal of Consumer Research*, (March), 407-418.

Richins, Marsha and Terri Root-Shaffer (1988), "The Role of Involvement and Opinion Leadership in Consumer Word-of-Mouth: An Implicit Model Made Explicit," in *Advances in Consumer Research*, 15, ed. Michael Houston (Provo UT: Association for Consumer Research), 32-36.

Rubin Rose M., Bobye J. Riney, and David J. Molina (1990), "Expenditure Pattern Differentials between One-Earner and Dual-Earner Households: 1972-1973 and 1984," *Journal of Consumer Research*, 17 (June), 43-52.

Zeithaml, Valarie A. (1985), "The New Demographics and Market Fragmentation," *Journal of Marketing*, 49 (summer), 64-75.

Personal Values and Shopping Behavior: A Structural Equation Test of the RVS in China

Zhengyuan Wang, University of Arkansas
C.P. Rao, Old Dominion University

INTRODUCTION

In recent years, one of the most dynamic areas of research in social science disciplines has been the measurement and functions of personal values (Kamakura and Mazzon 1991). Despite considerable empirical research on functions of values (Pitts and Woodside 1984), the measurement issue remains unresolved. There is disagreement among researchers concerning the conceptualization of values and the validity and reliability of various measures of values (e.g., Beatty et al. 1985; Miethe 1985; Munson 1984; Novak and MacEvoy 1990). Most previous research relies on exploratory factor analysis to assess the underlying dimensionality of values (e.g., Feather and Peay 1975; Maloney and Katz 1976; Munson and McQuarrie 1988; Valette-Florence and Jolibert 1990; Vinson et al. 1977). Many researchers regard values as consisting of independent dimensions which can be measured by single items (e.g., Rokeach 1973; Schopphoven 1991).

However, exploratory factor analysis and the use of single-item measures have shown to be inadequate in construct validation (Gerbing and Anderson 1988; Nunnally 1978). The present study attempts to overcome some of the weaknesses in previous research. Using confirmatory factor analysis via LISREL (Jöreskog and Sörbom 1988), it examined the dimensionality of the most widely used value instrument, the Rokeach Value Survey (RVS), in the context of Chinese culture. Although developed in Western countries, the Rokeach Value Survey has shown to be largely consistent with the Chinese Value Survey (Bond 1988; Ralston et al. 1992).

THEORETICAL BACKGROUND

Personal Values

Rokeach (1973) argues that values are separately organized into relatively enduring hierarchical structures of terminal and instrumental values. Terminal values are defined as a person's beliefs concerning desirable end-states of existence (ends) while instrumental values refer to a person's beliefs regarding desirable modes of conduct (means to achieve the ends). The Rokeach Value Survey (RVS) was developed by selecting 18 terminal and 18 instrumental values from a larger pool of several hundred values descriptors (Rokeach 1973). Earlier studies have provided some empirical evidence in support of the structure of terminal versus instrumental values (e.g., Feather and Peay 1975; Vinson et al. 1977).

The original version of the RVS consisted of 18 instrumental values and 18 terminal values that were rank ordered in terms of their importance as guiding principles of the respondent's life. The major limitations of the original RVS include: (1) subjects are forced to rank one value at the expense of another which may actually be equally important to them (Alwin and Krosnick 1985), (2) the presentation of the 36 value items may exceed the respondent's ability to accurately process information and thus distort the ranking procedure (Miller 1956), (3) the ranking nature of the data precludes the use of a wide variety of useful statistical analysis techniques that might otherwise be used (Rankin and Grube 1980).

To overcome these problems, researchers have modified the original RVS to yield an interval measure of value importance (Miethe 1985; Moore 1975; Munson and McIntyre 1979; Rankin and Grube 1980). Instead of ranking the values, respondents are required to assess the importance of each value item on a seven-point rating scale. Such a rating approach imposes fewer constraints on the data. Since the goal of value survey is to identify people's underlying value dimensions, the rating approach would seem to be preferred. The present study employed such a modified RVS. Since terminal and instrumental values are conceptually distinct constructs, the current study focused on instrumental values.

Structure of Instrumental Values

According to Rokeach (1973), both terminal and instrumental values are basically independent. In other words, each of the 36 value items represents a distinct personal value. Other researchers disagree with Rokeach and have sought to achieve a more parsimonious value structure (e.g., Beatty et al. 1985; McQuarrie and Langmeyer 1985; Munson and McQuarrie 1988; Prakash and Munson 1985). These researchers have noted that many of the Rokeach value items appeared to be largely irrelevant to consumption behavior. They argue that some value items can be dropped to make the measures of values more relevant to consumption. For example, Munson and McQuarrie (1988) developed their Value Instrumentality Inventory by retaining 24 value items out of the original 36 RVS items. One alternative measure of values, the List of Values (LOV), was developed by Kahle (1983) by modifying Rokeach's 18 terminal values into a smaller set of 9 values. In testing the causal model of value-attitude-behavior hierarchy, Homer and Kahle (1988) further reduced the nine values into three latent constructs: (1) individual internal values, (2) inter-personal internal values, and (3) external values.

A review of earlier studies that factor analyzed Rokeach's instrumental values suggests an internal versus external structure of instrumental values (Crosby et al. 1990; Feather and Peay 1975; Rokeach 1973; Vinson et al. 1977). Internal dimensions of Rokeach's instrumental values contain such value items as being ambitious, imaginative, independent, intellectual, etc. External dimensions reflect social conformity such as being forgiving, honest, polite or concern for others. The hypothesized structure of instrumental values is shown in Table 1. As noted by Crosby et al (1990), theoretical and empirical evidence of such internal and external dimensions can be found in a number of previous studies (e.g., Alwin and Jackson 1982; Lefcourt 1966; McGuire 1974).

The above theoretical arguments and empirical findings lead to the following two rival hypotheses:

H1: Rokeach instrumental values are independent with one another.

H2: Rokeach instrumental values contain two latent dimensions. One is internal and the other external.

Nomological Network of Instrumental Values

Previous research on RVS has called for further research that will examine the nomological network linking value dimensions to consumer behavior (e.g., Crosby et al. 1990). For a construct to have a real validity, it must be shown to be useful as an explanatory device. In other words, the construct must have nomological validity. The present study used two shopping behavior related constructs, shopping involvement and price sensitivity, to assess the nomological validity of instrumental values.

Earlier studies, both theoretical and empirical, have suggested linkages between instrumental values and shopping involvement and price sensitivity (e.g., Carman 1977; Darden et al. 1979; Petit

Advances in Consumer Research
Volume 22, © 1995

TABLE 1
Hypothesized Structure of Instrumental Values

Internal (Self-Direction)	External (Conformity)
Ambitious	Cheerful
Broadminded	Clean
Capable	Obedient
Courageous	Polite
Imaginative	Forgiving
Independent	Helpful
Intellectual	Honest
Logical	Loving
	Responsible
	Self-controlled

FIGURE 1
Nomological Network of Instrumental Values

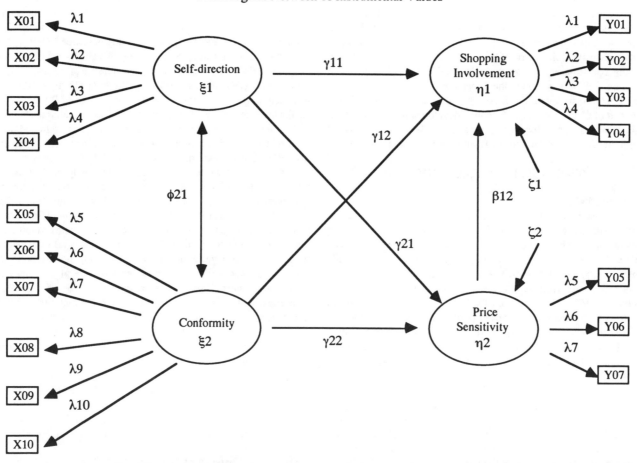

et al. 1985). Figure 1 presents the hypothesized nomological network of instrumental values. Chinese consumers with externally focused values (conformity dimension) are likely to be more involved in shopping than those with internally focused values (self-direction dimension). In China, the traditional doctrine of Confucianism, which is the foundation of the Chinese value system (Kluckhohn and Strodbeck 1961), teaches the values of diligence and frugality (Yau 1988). In addition, the propaganda of the Chinese Communist Party, China's ruling party over the past four decades, has also been extolling the virtue of thrifty and persuading people to resist the so-called "bourgeois" way of life. Capitalism has often been portrayed in China as encouraging a hedonic life style that is self-indulgent and wasteful. As a result, it is socially desirable to save money and be a meticulous shopper in China. Since consumers with internally focused values (self-direction dimension) are less prone to normative compliance, they are expected to be less involved in shopping and less sensitive to price.

TABLE 2
Chi-Square and Goodness of Fit Values for Rokeach Instrumental Value Models

Model	GFI	AGFI	χ^2	df	$\Delta\chi^2$	Δdf	p	Δ_1[a]	ρ_2[b]
1. Null	0.31	0.23	1907.25	153	-------	--	------	----	----
2. One-factor	0.43	0.28	1096.12	135	811.13	18	<0.001	0.43	0.38
3. Two-factor	0.87	0.83	279.88	134	1627.37	19	<0.001	0.85	0.91
4. Three-factor	0.88	0.84	256.38	132	1650.87	21	<0.001	0.87	0.92

[a] refers to Bentler & Bonett's (1980) normed index.
[b] refers to Bentler & Bonett's (1980) non-normed index, see also Tucker & Lewis (1973).

On the basis of the previous discussions, the following hypotheses are derived:

H3: There is a positive relationship between conformity dimension of instrumental values and the two constructs of shopping involvement and price sensitivity.

H4: There is a negative relationship between self-direction dimension of instrumental values and the two constructs of shopping involvement and price sensitivity.

METHOD

Research Design
The data used to test the research hypotheses resulted from personal interviews with pre-designed questionnaires. Data collection was undertaken respectively in two major Chinese cities: Beijing and Shanghai. No attempt was made to select the sample on a purely random basis. Rather, care was exercised in collecting a representative cross-section of the target population, which is defined in this study as the urban population in these two cities. Altogether 196 usable questionnaires were obtained in which 101 came from Beijing and 95 obtained from Shanghai. The demographic characteristics of the sample were similar to those of the target population.

The questionnaire was translated into Chinese by a doctoral student from China who was studying business administration at a Western university. The translated questionnaire was then back translated into English by another Chinese doctoral student. This process resulted in a number of modifications that were necessary to make the Chinese version of the questionnaire as less ambiguous as possible.

Operational Measures
Personal values measures. The construct of personal values was measured by asking respondents how important each of the 18 Rokeach instrumental values was to them on a seven-point importance rating scale. As will be discussed later, Rokeach instrumental values were found to comprise two latent dimensions: self-direction dimension and conformity dimension. The self-direction dimension consists of the following four items: (1) ambitious, (2) imaginative, (3) intellectual, and (4) logical while the conformity dimension consists of six items: (1) forgiving, (2) helpful, (3) honest, (4) cheerful, (5) responsible, and (6) self-controlled.

Shopping involvement and price sensitivity. Shopping involvement is defined as the self-relevance of shopping activities to the individual. It was measured on a 7-point Likert scale using four items adapted from the purchasing involvement scale developed by Slama and Tashchian (1985). They were: (1) "Before going shopping, I sit down and make out a complete shopping list;" (2) "I consult with friends and/or experts before making a major purchase;" (3) "I am an impulse buyer;" and (4) "I am a meticulous shopper." Note that item three above was reverse worded. Price sensitivity was measured with three items on a 7-point Likert scale: (1) "I like to bargain for most of the things I buy;" (2) "I shop a lot for specials;" and (3) "A store's own brand is usually a better buy than a nationally advertised brand."

RESULTS

Results of Testing Hypotheses 1 and 2
Hypotheses 1 and 2 are rival hypotheses regarding the structure of Rokeach instrumental values. The efforts to test H_1 and H_2 followed the recommended procedures for confirmatory factor analysis (Gerbing and Anderson 1988). Since H_1 states that Rokeach instrumental values are independent with one another, i.e., no factors underlie the observed Rokeach instrumental values, it constitutes the null or baseline model. Three hypothesized or comparison models were tested against the null model. To evaluate these competing models, chi-square differences and two incremental fit indices, namely, Bentler & Bonett's (1980) normed index, Δ_1, and Bentler & Bonett's (1980) non-normed index, ρ_2, were calculated. Table 2 presents values of chi-square and other goodness of fit indices for competing models of instrumental values.

As shown in Table 2, both the null model and one-factor model have very poor fit indices. The two- and three-factor models, on the other hand, have substantially improved fit indices. The hypothesized two-factor model, which corresponds to H_2, is shown in Table 1. Crosby et al. (1990) suggest that the external dimension of the two-factor model may contain two sub-dimensions: conformity and virtuousness. Conformity contains four items: (1) cheerful, (2) clean, (3) obedient, and (4) polite, while virtuousness consists of six items: (1) forgiving, (2) helpful, (3) honest, (4) loving, (5) responsible, and (6) self-controlled. So the three-factor model tested in the current study includes the following three factors: self-direction, conformity, and virtuousness.

Fit indices shown in Table 2 indicate that the three-factor model has a slightly better fit than the two-factor model. However, the inter-factor correlation between virtuousness and conformity, ϕ_{32}, is 0.88, indicating a lack of discriminant validity between conformity and virtuousness. In the two-factor model, the inter-factor correlation, ϕ_{21}, is -0.16, while the average factor loading is 0.71. These results provide support for H_2. It is also worth noting that

TABLE 3
Measurement Model Results for Instrumental Values

Construct /indicator	Parameter	Standardized coefficient	t-value	Average Variance Extracted
Self-direction (ξ_1)				0.56
Ambitious (x1)	λ_{11}	0.64	9.32	
Imaginative (x2)	λ_{21}	0.64	9.31	
Intellectual (x3)	λ_{31}	0.83	13.21	
Logical (x4)	λ_{41}	0.87	13.89	
Conformity (ξ_2)				0.53
Forgiving (x5)	λ_{52}	0.73	11.15	
Helpful (x6)	λ_{62}	0.77	12.13	
Honest (x7)	λ_{72}	0.81	12.98	
Cheerful (x8)	λ_{82}	0.70	10.63	
Responsible (x9)	λ_{92}	0.73	11.34	
Self-control (x10)	λ_{102}	0.60	8.80	
	ϕ_{21}	-0.17	-2.165	
	χ^2	51.40		
	df	34		
	p	0.028		
	GFI	0.953		
	AGFI	0.924		
	RMSR	0.035		

here that exploratory factor analysis using the criterion of eigenvalues greater than one also suggests a two-factor solution. The first two factors account for 57% of the total variance. Hence, it appears that Rokeach instrumental values contain two latent dimensions: internal and external values.

Results of Testing Hypotheses 3 and 4

Hypotheses 3 and 4 relate to the nomological network of instrumental values. As shown in Figure 1, two shopping behavior related constructs, shopping involvement and price sensitivity, were used to assess the nomological validity of instrumental values. Before a structural model assessing nomological validity is conducted, measurement models associated with instrumental values and shopping behaviors must first be examined (Anderson and Gerbing 1988). Following conventional scale development procedures (Nunnally 1978; Gerbing and Anderson 1988), the present study examined unidimensionality, reliability, convergent validity, and discriminant validity associated with each of the constructs shown in Figure 1.

Measurement Model for Instrumental Values. As recommended by Gerbing and Anderson (1988), confirmatory factor analysis was used to assess unidimensionality of instrumental values. As shown in Table 2, the initial two-factor confirmatory measurement model involving all 18 Rokeach instrumental value items resulted in a model fit that was not quite satisfactory (χ^2=279.88, df=134, p=0.000; GFI=0.869, AGFI=0.833, RMSR=0.074). An examination of corrected item-to-total correla-

tions as well as modification indices suggested the deletion of eight items. The practice of dropping some value items is consistent with previous research that attempted to modify existing measures of values (e.g., Kahle 1983; Munson and McQuarrie 1988).

As indicated in Table 3, a measurement model of the remaining ten items loading onto the two dimensions of instrumental values (self-direction and conformity) resulted in a model of acceptable fit (χ^2=51.40, df=34, p=0.028; GFI=0.953, AGFI=0.924, RMSR=0.035). These results seem to indicate that unidimensionality has been achieved.

Since the establishment of acceptable unidimensionality alone is not sufficient to ensure the usefulness of a scale, the reliability of the scale should then be assessed (Gerbing and Anderson 1988). Both Cronbach's (1951) coefficient alpha and Jöreskog's (1971) construct reliability are computed in this study. Both the coefficient alpha and construct reliability are 0.83 for self-direction dimension and 0.87 for conformity dimension. These results indicate that both the four-item self-direction measure and the six-item conformity measure seem to be quite reliable.

After unidimensionality and reliability have been acceptably established, the convergent and discriminant validity should be assessed (Anderson and Gerbing 1988). Two approaches were used to assess convergent validity. One approach recommended by Anderson and Gerbing (1988) is to examine whether each indicator's pattern coefficient (loading) from the measurement model is statistically significant. Another approach is recommended by Fornell and Larcker (1981). According to this approach, the average

TABLE 4
Measurement Model Results for Shopping Behavior Scales

Construct /indicator	Parameter	Standardized coefficient	t-value	Average Variance Extracted
Shopping involvement (ξ_1)				0.67
Y01	λ_{11}	0.87	14.69	
Y02	λ_{21}	0.82	13.41	
Y03	λ_{31}	0.70	10.75	
Y04	λ_{41}	0.88	15.16	
Price sensitivity (ξ_2)				0.75
Y05	λ_{52}	0.85	14.26	
Y06	λ_{62}	0.87	14.77	
Y07	λ_{72}	0.87	14.60	
	ϕ_{21}	0.27	3.67	
	χ^2	13.74		
	df	13		
	p	0.392		
	GFI	0.981		
	AGFI	0.959		
	RMSR	0.016		

variance extracted for each construct should be more than 0.5 in order to achieve convergent validity. As shown in Table 3, all the t tests for λ's are statistically significant and the average variance extracted for self-direction and conformity are 0.56 and 0.53 respectively. These results suggest that convergent validity for both measures is achieved.

There are also two approaches that can be used to assess discriminant validity. Anderson and Gerbing (1988) suggest that discriminant validity can be assessed by constraining the phi value for a pair of constructs to unity and then estimating the resulting measurement model. In the current study, the χ^2 value for the constrained model is 148.02 with 35 degrees of freedom. Because the χ^2 difference between the constrained and nonconstrained models is 96.62, which for 1 degree of freedom is highly significant, discriminant validity seems to be indicated. Fornell and Larcker (1981) present another approach to assess discriminant validity. According to them, for any pair of constructs to demonstrate discriminant validity, the average variance extracted for each construct should be greater than the squared structural link (derived by LISREL) between the pair. As shown in Table 3, the average variances extracted for self-direction and for conformity are far greater than ϕ_{21}^2, indicating that discriminant validity is achieved.

Measurement Model for Shopping Involvement and Price Sensitivity. Following the same procedures as those for the measurement model of instrumental values, unidimensionality, reliability, convergent and discriminant validity were assessed. As shown in Table 4, the measurement model for shopping involvement and price sensitivity has a very good fit, indicating that unidimensionality is achieved.

Both coefficient alpha and construct reliability are 0.89 for shopping involvement and 0.90 for price sensitivity. These results

indicate that both measures seem to be highly reliable. As shown in Table 4, all the t tests for λ's are statistically significant and the average variances extracted for both measures are greater than 0.5, suggesting that convergent validity is achieved. The χ^2 value for the constrained model is 71.61 with 14 degrees of freedom. Because the χ^2 difference between the constrained and nonconstrained models is 57.87, which for 1 degree of freedom is highly significant, discriminant validity seems to be indicated. In addition, the average variances extracted for shopping involvement and for price sensitivity, as shown in Table 4, are far greater than ϕ_{21}^2, indicating also that discriminant validity is achieved.

Structural Equation Model for the Nomological Network. Figure 1 presents the hypothesized nomological network of instrumental values. Table 5 displays the results of the full structural equation model that simultaneously models measurement and structural relations. As summarized in Table 5, all the goodness of fit indices demonstrate that the data provide a good fit for the overall model. The gamma coefficients linking two dimensions of instrumental values and two shopping behavior related constructs are in the expected direction and statistically significant at the 0.05 level for two of the four paths, namely, γ_{11} and γ_{12}. The path linking self-direction and price sensitivity (γ_{21}) is significant if tested with one-tail t test at the 0.10 level. These results provide some support to the hypothesized nomological network implied in H3 and H4.

DISCUSSION AND CONCLUSIONS

Research on personal values has been gaining momentum during the past few years. Although considerable empirical research has examined various functions of values, the issue of how to measure values accurately remains unresolved. Following the "two-step" approach recommended by Anderson and Gerbing

TABLE 5
Structural Equation Model Results for the Nomological Network

Parameter	Standardized coefficient	t-value
λ_{X11}	0.63	9.29
λ_{X21}	0.64	9.30
λ_{X31}	0.84	13.39
λ_{X41}	0.86	13.82
λ_{X52}	0.72	11.15
λ_{X62}	0.77	12.13
λ_{X72}	0.80	12.82
λ_{X82}	0.71	10.78
λ_{X92}	0.74	11.40
λ_{X102}	0.61	8.89
λ_{Y11}	0.87 [a]	
λ_{Y21}	0.82	14.01
λ_{Y31}	0.70	11.04
λ_{Y41}	0.88	15.61
λ_{Y52}	0.85 [a]	
λ_{Y62}	0.88	14.69
λ_{Y72}	0.87	14.56
γ_{11}	-.20	-2.62
γ_{21}	-.13	-1.60
γ_{12}	0.36	4.63
γ_{22}	0.05	0.51
β_{12}	0.22	2.50
ϕ_{21}	-.17	-2.18
ψ_{11}	0.80	7.15
ψ_{22}	0.91	7.04
χ^2	137.52	
df	113	
p	0.058	
GFI	0.927	
AGFI	0.901	
RMSR	0.042	

[a] The λ path was fixed at 1 to set the scale; therefore no t values are given.

(1988), the present study assessed unidimensionality, reliability, convergent validity, discriminant validity, and nomological validity of the Rokeach instrumental values.

Results suggest that the 18 Rokeach instrumental values are not independent with one another. Rather, there seem to be two latent dimensions measured by the RVS. One dimension identified in the current study was a four-item measure of self-direction and the other dimension was a six-item measure of conformity. Results of confirmatory factor analysis via LISREL provided support for the unidimensionality, reliability, convergent and discriminant validity associated with these two dimensions. Results of the full structural equation model that simultaneously models measurement and structural relations lend some support to the nomological network of instrumental values. Specifically, conformity dimension was found to be linked positively to shopping involvement while self-direction dimension had a negative relationship with shopping involvement. Although the relationships between price sensitivity and the two dimensions of instrumental values were not statistically significant at the 0.05 level, they were in the hypothesized direction.

Results of the study indicate an need for researchers to examine measures of personal values in a more rigorous manner. Structural equations with latent variables, as demonstrated in the current study, provide an appropriate way of assessing multi-item measurement scales. We believe research on personal values will benefit from further development of more valid and comprehensive value instruments.

Several limitations that could be explored in future studies are worth noting. First, the present study was based on a relatively small and nonprobability sample in China. Hence, caution must be exercised in generalizing the findings beyond the sample used. Second, a modified RVS instrument was used in the study that requires rating rather than ranking. Such scales have been found to be more susceptible to response styles and social desirability effects (Alwin and Krosnick 1985; Kamakura and Mazzon 1991; Rokeach 1973). Finally, this study has investigated only the Rokeach instrumental values. It would be interesting for future research to examine the Rokeach terminal values and other measures of personal values such as Kahle's (1983) List of Values (LOV).

REFERENCES

Alwin, Duane F. and Jon A. Krosnick (1985), "The Measurement of Values in Surveys: A Comparison of Ratings and Rankings," *Public Opinion Quarterly*, 49 (Winter), 535-552.

_____ and D.J. Jackson (1982), "The Statistical Analysis of Kohn's Measures of Parental Values," in K.G. Jöreskog and H. Wold, eds., *Systems Under Indirect Observation: Causality, Structure and Prediction*. Amsterdam: North-Holland, 197-223.

Anderson, James C. and David W. Gerbing (1988), "Structural Equation Modeling in Practice: A Review and Recommended Two-Step Approach," *Psychological Bulletin*, 103 (3), 411-423.

Beatty, Sharon E., Lynn R. Kahle, Pamela Homer, and Shekhar Misra (1985), "Alternative Measurement Approaches to Consumer Values: The List of Values and the Rokeach Value Survey," *Psychology and Marketing*, 2 (3), 181-200.

Bentler, P.M. and Douglas G. Bonett (1980), "Significance Test and Goodness of Fit in the Analysis of Covariance Structures," *Psychological Bulletin*, 88(3), 588-606.

Bond, Michael H. (1988), "Finding Universal Dimensions of Individual Variation in Multicultural Studies of Values: The Rokeach and Chinese Value Surveys," *Journal of Personality and Social Psychology*, 55 (6), 1009-1015.

Carman, J.M. (1977), "Values and Consumption Patterns: A Closed Loop," in H.K. Hunt, ed., *Advances in Consumer Research*, 5, 403-407.

Cronbach, Lee J. (1951), "Coefficient Alpha and the Internal Structure of Tests," *Psychometrika*, 16 (September), 297-334.

Crosby, Lawrence A., Mary Jo Bitner, James D. Gill (1990), "Organizational Structure of Values," *Journal of Business Research*, 20, 123-134.

Darden, W.R., O. Erdem, D.K. Darden, and T. Powell (1979), "Consumer Values and Shopping Orientations," in *Proceedings of the Southwestern Marketing Association*, San Antonio, TX.

Feather, N.T. and E.R. Peay (1975), "The Structure of Terminal and Instrumental Values: Dimensions and Clusters," *Australian Journal of Psychology*, 27, 151-164.

Fornell, Claes and David F. Larcker (1981), "Evaluating Structural Equation Models with Unobservable Variables and Measurement Error," *Journal of Marketing Research*, 18 (February), 39-50.

Gerbing, David W. and James C. Anderson (1988), "An Updated Paradigm for Scale Development Incorporating Unidimensionality and Its Assessment," *Journal of Marketing Research*, 25 (May), 186-192.

Grunert, Susanne C. and Gerhard Scherhorn (1990), "Consumer Values in West Germany: Underlying Dimensions and Cross-Cultural Comparison with North America," *Journal of Business Research*, 20, 97-107.

Homer, Pamela M. and Lynn R. Kahle (1988), "A Structural Equation Test of the Value-Attitude-Behavior Hierarchy," *Journal of Personality and Social Psychology*, 54 (4), 638-646.

Jöreskog, Karl G. (1971), "Statistical Analysis of Sets of Congeneric Tests," *Psychometrika*, 36 (June), 109-133.

_____ and Dag Sörbom (1988), *LISREL VII: Analysis of Linear Structural Relationships by Maximum Likelihood*. Mooresville, IN: Scientific Software.

Kahle, Lynn R. (1983), *Social Values and Social Change: Adaptation to Life in America*, New York: Praeger.

Kamakura, Wagner A. and Jose A. Mazzon (1991), "Value Segmentation: A Model for the Measurement of Values and Value Systems," *Journal of Consumer Research*, 18 (September), 208-218.

Kluckhohn, F.R. and Strodbeck, F.L. (1961), *Variations in Value Orientation*, IL: Row, Paterson and Co.

Lefcourt, H.M. (1966), "Internal Versus External Control of Reinforcement: A Review," *Psychological Bulletin*, 65, 206-220.

Maloney, J. and G.M. Katz (1976), "Value Structures and Orientations to Social Institutions," *Journal of Psychology*, 93, 203-211.

McGuire, William J. (1974), "Psychological Motives and Communication Gratification," in J.G. Blumler and C. Katz, eds., *The Use of Mass Communications*. Beverly Hills, CA: Sage Publications, 167-196.

McQuarrie, Edward F. and Daniel Langmeyer (1985), "Using Values to Measure Attitudes Toward Discontinuous Innovations," *Psychology & Marketing*, 2 (Winter), 239-252.

Miethe, Terance D. (1985), "The Validity and Reliability of Value Measurements," *Journal of Psychology*, 119 (5), 441-453.

Miller, George A. (1956), "The Magical Number Seven, Plus or Minus Two: Some Limits on Our Capacity for Processing Information," *Psychology Review* 63 (March), 81-97.

Moore, Michael (1975), "Rating vs. Ranking in the Rokeach Value Survey: An Israeli Comparison," *European Journal of Social Psychology*, 5 (3), 405-408.

Munson, J. Michael and Shelby H. McIntyre (1979), "Developing Practical Procedures for the Measurement of Personal Values in Cross-Cultural Marketing," *Journal of Marketing Research*, 16 (February), 55-60.

_____ (1984), "Personal Values: Considerations on Their Measurement and Application to Five Areas of Research Inquiry," in Pitts, Robert E. Jr. and Arch G. Woodside ed., *Personal Values and Consumer Psychology*, Mass.: Lexington Books.

_____ and Edward F. McQuarrie (1988), "Shortening the Rokeach Value Survey for Use in Consumer Research, *Advances in Consumer Research*, 15, 381-386.

Novak, Thomas P. and Bruce MacEvoy (1990), "On Comparing Alternative Segmentation Schemes: The List of Values (LOV) and Values and Life Styles (VALS)," *Journal of Consumer Research*, 17 (June), 105-109.

Nunnally, Jum C. (1978), *Psychometric Theory*. New York: McGraw-Hill Book Company.

Petit, Kathy L., Sonja L. Sawa, Ghazi H. Sawa (1985), "Frugality: A Cross National Moderator of the Price-Quality Relationship," *Psychology and Marketing*, 2, 253-266.

Pitts, Robert E., Jr. and Arch G. Woodside, eds. (1984), *Personal Values and Consumer Psychology*, M.A.: Lexington Books.

Prakash, Ved and J. Michael Munson (1985), "Values, Expectations from the Marketing System and Product Expectations," *Psychology & Marketing*, 2 (Winter), 279-296.

Ralston, D.A., D.J. Gustafson, P.M. Elsass, F. Cheung, R.H. Terpstra (1992), "Eastern Values: A Comparison of Managers in the United States, Hong Kong, and the People's Republic of China," *Journal of Applied Psychology*, 77(5), 664-671.

Rankin, William L. and Joel W. Grube (1980), "A Comparison of Ranking and Rating Procedures for Value System Measurement," *European Journal of Social Psychology*, 10 (3), 233-246.

Rokeach, Milton (1973), *The Nature of Human Values*. New York: Free Press.

Schopphoven, Iris (1991), "Values and Consumption Patterns: A Comparison between Rural and Urban Consumers in Western Germany," *European Journal of Marketing*, 25 (12), 20-35.

Slama, Mark E. and Armen Tashchian (1985), "Selected Socio-Economic and Demographic Characteristics Associated with Purchasing Involvement," *Journal of Marketing*, 49 (Winter), 72-82.

Tucker, L.R. and C. Lewis (1973), "A Reliability Coefficient for Maximum Likelihood Factor Analysis," *Psychometrika*, 38, 1-10.

Valette-Florence, P. and A. Jolibert (1990), "Social Values, A.I.O., and Consumption Patterns: Exploratory Findings," *Journal of Business Research*, 20, 109-122.

Vinson, D.E., J.D. Scott, and L.M. Lamont (1977), "The Role of Personal Values in Marketing and Consumer Behavior," *Journal of Marketing*, 41, 44-50.

Yau, Oliver H.M. (1988), "Chinese Cultural Values: Their Dimensions and Marketing Implications," *European Journal of Marketing*, 22 (5), 44-57.

Consumer Values, Product Benefits and Customer Value: A Consumption Behavior Approach

Albert Wenben Lai, University of Wisconsin-Madison

ABSTRACT

From the perspective of consumption behavior analysis, this paper constructs a framework of product valuation for consumers and its typology of product benefits. Then, the paper presents a comprehensive model of customer value for the consumer market integrating consumer values, product benefits, logistic benefits, and various costs of consumption. Finally, the implications of holistic consumption behavior analysis for marketing strategy are discussed.

"Everything we do starts with knowing a client's business inside out. That's the key— to anticipating their needs, to solving their problems, to bringing them opportunities they might not find on their own." — J. P. Morgan

INTRODUCTION

Most marketing strategists will agree that creating customer value is fundamental to both profit-seeking companies and non-profit organizations. Indeed, creating superior customer value is a necessary condition for a company securing a niche in a competitive environment, not to mention a leadership position in the market (Day 1990). According to Porter (1980), a company can follow two generic routes to compete in a market: differentiation and low-cost. Day (1990) maintains that both approaches have the same objective— to create superior customer value, because "regardless of which of these routes is emphasized, the effort will fail unless significant customer value is created" (Day 1990, p. 163).

Day (1990) addresses the issues in analyzing customer value and proposes that it can be expressed in a "value equation": "Customer's Perceived Benefits-Customer's Perceived Costs=Perceived Customer Value" (p. 142). Although Day's approach to customer value is basically sound, some details regarding consumer customers remain unclear. For example, the process by which consumers perceive product benefits is nebulous: Day particularly addresses product valuation by industrial customers in detail, but this is only in principle a part of a much more complex process of product valuation by consumers. Hence a theoretical framework which underlies the consumers' overall product valuation is still missing in the literature. Such a framework should address the issues of *how* consumers perceive the benefits and costs of products, as well as *what* possible benefits and costs consumers may perceive from products in the market. The current paper tries to fill these gaps.

In addition, the word "value" has discrepant meanings in the marketing literature, especially between its two areas: marketing strategy and consumer behavior. What marketing strategists mean by "customer value" is quite different from the meanings of the "consumer values" discussed in consumer behavior research (Clawson and Vinson 1978; Kahle 1977; Peter and Olson 1990; Sheth, Newman and Gross 1991; Vinson, Scott and Lamont 1977; Wilkie 1990). Generally speaking, "customer value" focuses on the buyers' evaluation of product purchase at the time of buying, while "consumer values" stress people's valuation on the consumption or possession of products. Actually, Day's approach to customer value (Day 1990), by emphasizing the customers' perceptions, indicates a direction in which the two different, but related, concepts of "value(s)" in marketing discipline might be integrated. The current paper helps accomplish this integration by suggesting a model of customer value for consumer markets.

This paper first reviews the literature on consumption behavior analysis relevant to marketing strategy. Next, a framework of product valuation for consumers and its typology of product benefit are proposed based on the consumption behavior analysis. After the process of product valuation for consumers has been made clear, the paper presents a comprehensive model of customer value for the consumer market integrating consumer values, product benefits, logistic benefits, and various costs of consumption. In the proposed model, product benefits, logistic benefits, and costs are defined in terms of consumers' perception in the activities of acquisition, consumption (or using) and maintenance, as well as consumers' expectation of personal values satisfaction before buying. Finally, the implications of consumption behavior analysis for marketing strategy are discussed.

CONSUMPTION BEHAVIOR ANALYSIS AND MARKETING STRATEGY

Many marketing researchers have maintained that detailed analyses of consumption behavior are the fundamental basis for creating superior customer value for consumers (Day 1990; Boyd and Levy 1963; Treacy and Wiersema 1993; Normann and Ramirez 1993). The importance of a comprehensive analysis of customers' consumption activities in planning effective marketing strategies was first pointed out by Boyd and Levy (1963). They maintain that marketing strategies should be planned and implemented in terms of the customer's needs and behavior patterns. Also, the core element of an effective marketing plan is to think in terms of the "consumption system" in which the product plays a part. Boyd and Levy defined a consumption system as "the way a purchaser of a product performs the total task ... that he or she is trying to accomplish when using the product — not baking a cake, but preparing a meal" (Boyd and Levy 1963, pp. 129-130).

Underlying this systematic view of consumption are at least two concepts critical to customer value analysis. First, this systematic view looks beyond the purchase behavior of buyers to the use behavior of consumers: "Whatever reasons people have for buying a particular product are rooted in how they use that product, and how well it serves the use to which they put it" (Boyd and Levy 1963, p. 130). Second, the systematic view emphasizes the dynamic interrelations between the products that comprise a consumption system: "The use behavior for a particular product is bound to be affected not only by ... the task to be performed with the use of that product but also by the related products and their use behaviors that make up the total consumption system" (Boyd and Levy 1963, p. 130).

Based on their observation of the holistic nature of customer judgment, Day et al. (1979) advocated the application of customer-oriented approaches to defining a product-market and then identifying its competitive structure. In particular, Day and his colleagues endorsed a usage-situation approach to defining a product-market (or competitive) structure. The usage-situation approach emphasizes that the anticipated use, the functions to be served, and the consumption context of a product ultimately influence consumers' choices among products/brands (Srivastava 1981). Although it takes a systematic view of consumption, the usage-situation

FIGURE 1
A Framework of Product Valuation for Consumers

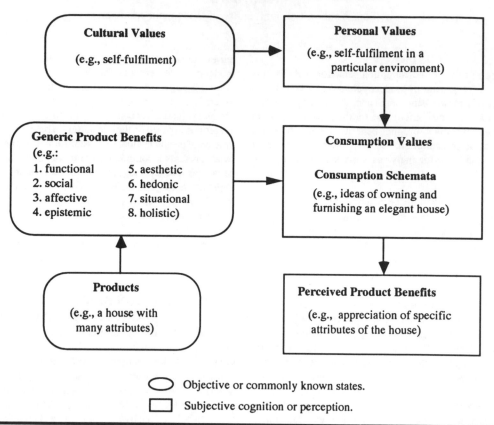

○ Objective or commonly known states.

□ Subjective cognition or perception.

approach stresses that the substitutability among products/brands in the usage-situation determines market structures (i.e., the competitive providers) of the product-type in question (Srivastava, Alpert and Shocker 1984). While the usage-situation approach is based on the holistic view of consumption behavior and is dubbed customer-oriented, it deals only with companies' need to define their product-market structures. It has nothing to do with the analysis of customer value and how this value can be expanded. As Solomon (1983) points out, conventional marketing research has paid much more attention to the substitutability of products than to their complementarity, and the usage-situation approach is no exception. In summary, the literature on consumption behavior analysis can proceed further to conceptualize the aspects of complementarity-in-use of products through which consumer may derive product benefits holistically in the product complement.

CONSUMER'S PRODUCT VALUATION AND TYPOLOGY OF PRODUCT BENEFITS

The questions of how and what consumers perceive from products in the market request the process and structure by which consumers value the products. Based on consumption behavior analysis, the current paper proposes a framework of product valuation for consumers and its typology of product benefits (see Figure 1). This model stresses that to investigate the consumer's product valuation, it is necessary to integrate cultural values, personal values, consumption values, and product benefits (Clawson and Vinson 1978).

Cultural Values

Cultural, social, and familial environments affect the formation and development of individual beliefs. In a socio-cultural environment, a set of values usually represents widely shared beliefs about what is desirable. These socio-cultural beliefs are called cultural values or "society core values" (Engel, Blackwell and Miniard 1990) and are implanted into individuals "naturally" through socialization and education, perhaps with some modification as personality and attitude moderate the learning process. For example, Kahle (1985) proposes a "List of Values" (LOV) generic to American culture in the 1980s, such as self-respect, security, self-fulfillment, fun and enjoyment in life, and warm relationships with others. These cultural values are seen by some social thinkers as "objective" (Frondizi 1963). This notion of being objective implies that they are commonly known to the members of a society. However, not all of the cultural values in a society will be adopted unanimously by its members. Some cultural values might be followed by only a small portion of the people, while other values might be accepted widely. In sum, cultural values are generic beliefs about what a society argues to be desirable and beneficial. These values are then freely adopted on an individual basis.

Personal Values

Personal values are the individuals' beliefs about what are desirable to themselves. They are self-centered; that is, personal values are closely linked to needs. Moreover, they are derived from, and modified through, personal, social, and cultural learning (Clawson and Vinson 1978). From a cognitive perspective, personal values are the mental representations of underlying needs after the modification, taking into account the realities of the world and reflecting the individual's personality (Wilkie 1990). For example, the cultural value of "self-fulfillment" might be manifested quite differently in the minds of two individuals with different familial and personal backgrounds.

According to Rokeach (1973), human values have two main types: terminal and instrumental. Terminal (or end-state) values are beliefs people have about the goals for which they strive (e.g., self-fulfillment, or enjoyment in life). Instrumental (or means) values are beliefs about desirable ways to attain these terminal values (e.g., owning an elegant house, or taking a vacation). Therefore, personal values generally correspond to terminal values, while values of desirable activities (to be discussed next) are comparable to instrumental values. Personal values are enduring beliefs which guide various actions and judgments across specific situations. Hence, personal values are more abstract and may be generalizable easier than values of actions. In other words, the concept of personal values is similar to the idea of "global values" (in the realm of a person's perception) proposed by Vinson et al. (1977); these are small in number (dozens) and considered to be at high levels of conceptualization.

Consumption Values

Consumption values refer to subjective beliefs about desirable ways to attain personal values. People achieve personal values (or goals) through actions or activities, such as social interaction, economic exchange, possession, and consumption (Sheth et al. 1991). According to *means-end chain models* of consumer product knowledge (Peter and Olson 1990), people may have ideas and preferences about various actions that can help them achieve personal values. Therefore, relative to personal values, consumption values are instrumental in nature. For example, owning an elegant house and acquiring a prestigious car are for some people desirable ways of achieving self-fulfillment. Attending football games (especially those of favorite teams) and taking a vacation trip are favorable activities which lead to personal fun and enjoyment. Furthermore, individuals may hold several personal values by which they direct or evaluate consumption activities. Therefore, the consumption values of these types of activities (or possessions) are sophisticated and do not simply satisfy one single personal value (Shet et al. 1991).

As we can observe in ourselves or others, consumption activities usually include an assortment of goods and services (Boyd and Levy 1963). For example, "owning an elegant house" requires house owners to acquire many goods and services in addition to the house itself, just as "taking a vacation trip" involves many other related acquisitions. Moreover, in a product constellation for a consumption activity, there may be some properties in common. McCracken (1988) observes that "the consumer goods in any complement are linked by some commonality or unity" (p. 119). From a social interaction perspective, Solomon (1983) maintains that consumers employ product constellations in "setting the stage" for the social roles they play. Product constellations occur, because individuals use entire complements of products to achieve personal values. The products unified in a constellation all carry the same information about individual values. Furthermore, Lai (1994) maintained that consumers may obtain satisfaction holistically from the related consumption activities and the constellation of products in use.

Consumption Schemata

Cognitive psychologists maintain that people may acquire knowledge structures to represent various consumption activities and product constellations (Abelson 1976; Crocker 1984). Lai (1994) uses the term *consumption schema* to refer to the cognitive structure which organizes and represents personal ideas and beliefs about the substance of a consumption activity, such as interrelationships among complementary products, the cultural value and social meanings of the commodities, and personal preferences and affec-

tive associations. Hence, a consumption schema represents a consumer's basic thoughts about a consumption activity, though peripheral adjustments may be needed to accommodate the specific situation in which the consumption takes place. In short, in consumption, or possession of products, people may acquire personal consumption schemata (or a particular planned pattern), including their anticipation of and requirements for a product (or a complement of products), reflecting their consumption values of that consumption or possession.

Typology of Product Benefits

From the customers' perspective, products are viewed as a bundle of benefits, not attributes (Day 1990; Peter and Olson 1990). In other words, "customers are less interested in the technical features of a product or service than in what benefits they get from buying, using or consuming the product." (Hooley and Saunders 1993, p. 17) In a competitive market, in addition to their basic benefits, products usually have many other attributes, such as features, styles, symbolism, durability, quality, and related services. By designing products with combinations of these attributes, marketers try to attract consumers with particular consumption values.

A comprehensive understanding of possible benefits that customers may seek in products is a fundamental basis for marketers to formulate sound marketing strategies, especially product differentiation or positioning (Peter 1990; Boyd and Levy 1968). Sheth et al. (1991) categorize five product benefits which influence the consumer's choice behavior: functional, social, emotional, epistemic and conditional. However, these benefits are only *generic*; that is, they are general, potential, and not yet applied to a specific consumption activity. Moreover, because Sheth et al.'s analysis is not grounded in a holistic approach to consumption behavior analysis, Sheth and his colleagues conflate product benefits with consumption values; that is, they do not distinguish "generic product benefits" from "consumption values," as the current paper does. Furthermore, their categorization ignores other important generic product benefits: e.g., hedonic benefits, aesthetic benefits, and holistic benefits.

Going beyond Sheth et al.'s original categorization of product benefits (Sheth et al. dubbed them as "consumption values"), the current paper proposes a typology of product benefits that a consumer may derive from possession or consumption. The typology includes eight generic product benefits: functional, social, affective, epistemic, aesthetic, hedonic, situational, and holistic. The definitions of these terms are discussed briefly in what follows:

(1) *Functional benefit* refers to a product's capacity for functional, utilitarian, or physical performance. Functional benefits are derived from the tangible and concrete attributes that a consumer may directly experience when using or consuming the product.

(2) *Social benefits* are the perceptual benefits acquired from a product's association with social class, social status, or a specific social group. Highly visible products (e.g., clothing, jewelry, and automobiles) often carry social benefits.

(3) *Affective benefit* refers to the perceptual benefit acquired from a product's capacity to arouse feelings or affective states. Affective benefits are often associated with cultural-ethnic meanings (e.g., Christmas trees, Thanksgiving turkeys) or personal, idiosyncratic meanings, tastes and memories (e.g., foods that arouse feelings of comfort through their association with childhood experiences, or cars with which consumers are said to have "love affairs").

(4) *Epistemic benefit* refers to the benefit acquired from a product's capacity to satisfy curiosity, provide novelty, and/or meet a desire for knowledge. Exploratory, novelty-seeking, and variety-

seeking consumption behaviors are examples of epistemic value pursuit. Also, a consumer's propensity to adopt new products is consistent with epistemic benefit (Sheth et al. 1991).

(5) *Aesthetic benefit* refers to the benefit acquired from a product's capacity to present a sense of beauty or to enhance personal expression. Aesthetic benefit usually is subjective and idiosyncratic. Style demands, product-appearance demands, art purchases, and fashion-following are examples of consumers' pursuing aesthetic benefits.

(6) *Hedonic benefit* refers to the benefit acquired from a product's capacity to meet a need of enjoyment, fun, pleasure, or distraction from work or anxiety. Olshavsky and Granbois (1979) claim that hedonic benefit is an important dimension of many products. People are not always looking for rational or "serious" benefits; they may want to relax or be distracted. Taking a vacation trip, going to bars, watching sports, comic movies or TV programs, or even buying funny trinkets to make fun of friends are examples of hedonic benefit pursuit.

(7) *Situational benefit* refers to the benefit acquired from a product's capacity to meet situational needs in specific circumstances. A product acquires situational value in the presence of antecedent physical or social contingencies that enhance its functional, social, or other benefits. Situational benefit is measured on the profile of a particular consumption situation.

(8) *Holistic benefit* refers to the perceptual benefit acquired from the complementarity, coherence, compatibility, and consistency in a product constellation as a whole. Holistic benefits are frequently required and perceived in clothes, furniture, and food consumption. Holistic product benefit is a result of "synergy" derived from a product combination. Its implications for marketing strategy will be discussed later in detail.

Different types of product benefits may be correlated and combined in particular consumption activities, or there may be trading off between them. In addition, a product may offer multiple generic benefits. For example,

"to a first-time home buyer, the purchase of a home might provide functional [benefit] (the home contains more space than the present apartment), social [benefit] (friends are also buying homes), emotional [benefit] (the consumer feels secure in owning a home), epistemic [benefit] (the novelty of purchasing a home is enjoyable), and situational [benefit] (starting a family)"[1] (Sheth et al. 1991; p. 163).

Perceived Product Benefits

Generic product benefits are intended benefits that manufacturers design into a product. However, these intended benefits may or may not be perceived or appreciated by particular consumers. A product has benefit to customers to the degree that they can perceive, appreciate and then use that product as anticipated consumption activities to achieve personal values. Normann and Ramirez (1993) recapitulate this concept well; "A company's offerings have values to the degree that customers can use them as inputs to leverage their own value creation. In this respect, then, companies don't profit from customers. They profit from customers' value-creating activities" (p. 74). In sum, consumers perceive and appreciate product benefits via their personal consumption values and consumption schemata; these product benefits are termed "*Perceived Product Benefits*" (Day 1990).

---

[1]The braces are the author's, to substitute the word "benefit" for the original word "value" and avoid confusion. The parentheses, however, are in the original passage.

In summary, the framework of consumers' product valuation delineates the relationship between "personal values", "generic product benefits", and "perceived product benefits" via "consumption values" and "consumption schemata" (see Figure 1). That is, it illuminates the structure of consumers' product valuation and how and what benefits consumers may perceive from products. With this framework of product valuation for consumers and its typology of product benefits in place, the current paper proceeds to investigate the concept of customer value.

A MODEL OF CUSTOMER VALUE FOR CONSUMER MARKETS

Customer Value and Consumer Values

Many marketing strategists and industrial-organization (I.O.) economists emphasize that creating superior "customer value" is a key element for companies' success (Day 1990, Porter 1980). However, what they mean by "customer value" is quite different from the meanings of the "consumer values" we have discussed above. "Value" to marketing strategists means a return for something in an exchange (e.g., the value of the dollar is variable). Therefore, the meaning of "customer value" is a level of return in the product benefits for certain amount of customer's money (i.e., the price) in a purchase exchange (e.g., to give the buyer good value at the right price). In addition, the concept of customer value has by nature a normative perspective, since it is a fundamental concept underlying the competitive analysis in the field of I.O., based on economic principles and the customer's choice in the market.

Consumer behavior researchers, on the other hand, generally use the word "values" to mean something desirable, useful, or important (Peter and Olson 1990). Our previous discussion also adopted this meaning. Consumer research usually is based on a descriptive-study perspective, such as in the fields of anthropology, sociology, and psychology. Therefore, "consumer values" refers to the important personal goals that consumers are seeking (Wilkie 1990). Furthermore, consumer behavior researchers emphasize that people can achieve some of their personal values through possession or consumption of products (Peter and Olson 1990; Sheth, et al. 1991).

In summary, "customer value" normatively focuses on a buyer's evaluation at the time of a product purchase, while "consumer values" descriptively stresses people's valuation of product consumption or possession. Consumer researchers will argue that consumers buy products not for the sake of its "transactional value" (a simple term for customer value) but for the product's benefits that will satisfy their needs or personal values. Our earlier discussions of the process of consumer valuation explored the domain of consumer benefits in product consumption or possession. However, in an exchange environment, product benefits alone do not completely explain consumers' product choice. Often, consumers may find products very desirable. Yet, in assuming that the consumer has adequate financial capacity, one must not equally assume that a purchase must follow. These cases imply that normative points of view are also necessary in consumer choice research. From an economics perspective, consumers may apply cost-and-benefit evaluation to a purchase decision, at least when the costs are "significant" to them (Olshavsky and Granbois 1979). Therefore, with respect to a sound customer value analysis for a consumer market, both the descriptive and normative aspects are essential (Boyd and Levy 1963; Day 1990).

The current paper proposes a comprehensive model of customer value for consumer markets (see Figure 2), based on Day's original idea of "value equation" and emphasizing customers'

FIGURE 2
A Model of Customer Value for Consumer Market

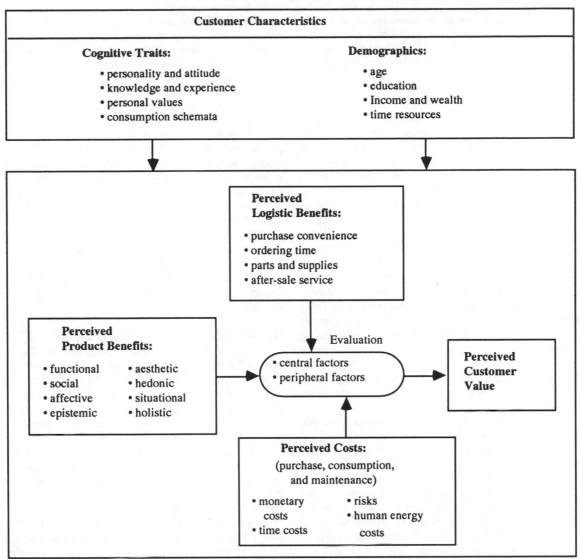

perception (Day 1990). This model integrates descriptive and normative points of view about consumer behavior, including the consumer values expectation before purchase, customer value evaluation at the time of buying, and value actualization in consumption or possession.

The Model

According to social psychologists, people's perception of objects and events is influenced by their *cognitive traits* (e.g., personality and attitude, personal values, and consumption schemata) and *demographics* (e.g., age, education, income and wealth, and time resources). As indicated in Figure 2, these factors of "Customer Characteristics" are the background of the customers' perception.

The buyers' evaluation of a product purchase begins from their perceived product benefits. The earlier discussions of consumers' product valuation have proposed a framework about how the customers perceive product benefits based on their terminal personal values and instrumental consumption values (or consumption

schemata). In addition, the discussion has suggested and illustrated a typology of generic product benefits with eight categories. As indicated in Figure 2, the model suggests that "Perceived Product Benefits" could be a single type or a combination of the eight categories of product benefits.

Nowadays, product benefits based on consumption or use of the product are not the sole benefits consumers can perceive (Day 1990). They may also derive benefits of a purchase from the buying activities per se and other consumption supporting features. Treacy and Wiersema (1993) claim that today's customers have "an expanded concept of value [purchase benefits] that includes convenience of purchase, [and] after-sale service" (p. 84), in addition to the traditional product benefits, such as quality and price. We conceptualize these new dimensions of purchase benefit and denote them as "logistic benefits." Logistic benefits of a product purchase are those benefits consumers can derive from the buying per se and other (after-purchase) consumption supporting features about the product. These include the purchase convenience, buying pleasure, variety of choice, short ordering time, availability of parts and supplies, warranty, and after-sale service. For the purpose of this discussion, the current paper does not probe the typology of logistic benefits. These logistic features, if designed by marketers in the product deal, are also subject to subjective consumers' perceptions to become desirable benefits for customers. Moreover, the perceptions of the customers are moderated by their personal values, consumption values, and other individual characteristics (see Figure 2).

As mentioned above, the costs of obtaining the perceived product and logistic benefits are usually the major concerns of buyers, since consumers may apply principles of costs-and-benefits to evaluate a purchase. The model proposes that the relevant costs of a purchase considered by consumer include monetary cost, time cost, risks, and human energy cost. Furthermore, every category of the costs may play a part in purchase, possession, consumption, and maintenance. The monetary cost refers simply to monetary payment. The time cost refers to the amount of time required for the relevant activities of acquisition or consumption. Consumers encounter risks when they face the uncertainty or potential negative consequences of consumer activities: being cheated, overcharged, or misled into buying an unnecessary product; while possessing or using certain products, such as unconventional clothes, may incur social costs which include being teased by colleagues. Maintenance risks include being overcharged for supplies and or suffering the possibility that they will be discontinued. Finally, the human energy cost refers to physical effort, difficulty of operation, and cognitive energy; these might be of great concern to elderly customers. Nevertheless, all of these costs, like the benefits, are also subject to consumers' perception. Since perceptions of time, money, risk, and human energy vary among people, these costs may be evaluated differently among customers.

According to the cost-and-benefit principle, customers evaluate the benefits against the costs and perceive the buying value of products. As indicated in Figure 2, the inputs of evaluation are the "perceived product benefits", "perceived logistic benefits", and "perceived costs". However, as suggested by many paradigms in consumer research, such as expectancy-value research (Fishbein and Ajzen 1975) and elimination-by-aspects analysis (Tversky, 1972), not all benefits and costs are equally evaluated. Some benefits and costs are considered central factors and are therefore weighted heavily, while others are perceived as peripheral factors and weighted less. This phenomenon concerning consumers' idiosyncratic patterns of weighting for the evaluating factors is also reflected in the model.

Finally, the model suggests that customer value is a consequence of subjective evaluation which in turn results from the summing up of the various perceived benefits and perceived costs, taking into account the differently weighted factors. In other words, the "perceived customer value" in the model is defined as the surplus (or the difference) between perceived benefits and perceived costs (Day 1990); that is, it refers to a level of subjective return for the customer perceived costs.

DISCUSSION: IMPLICATIONS FOR MARKETING STRATEGY

In the current model of consumer customer value, product benefits, logistic benefits, and costs are defined in terms of consumers' perception in the activities of acquisition, consumption (or using) and maintenance, as well as consumers' expectation of personal values satisfaction before buying. In other words, our consumption behavior approach is holistic analysis-oriented, going beyond traditional "customer-oriented" methods which usually focus on the buyers' economic evaluation at purchase.

As emphasized in the model, the importance of product benefits, logistic benefits, and costs vary among people due to their individual characteristics. These phenomena have led in marketing practice to benefit or cost segmentation— the process of dividing consumers into homogenous subgroups or segments based on their interest in particular product benefits. The benefits most important (central) to target customers is a fundamental issue in marketing strategies, such as product differentiation and positioning. For example, to succeed with a "value strategy" (also a high price strategy) a company needs to offer products with premium quality in the central benefits, such that their customers "correctly" perceive those benefits and are willing to pay the price premium (Treacy and Wiersema 1993). On the other hand, to make a "cost strategy" (or a low price strategy) profitable, a company must offer products with an acceptable level of quality in the central benefits and minimal quality in the peripheral factors, such that their customers will enjoy the product and perceive the purchase as a value (Normann and Ramfrez 1993).

The current paper's implications for market positioning are clear: its categorization of generic product and logistic benefits may help marketers identify their target consumers' central and peripheral benefits. Then, the typology could help companies design their products and related marketing programs, such as advertising and distribution.

Holistic Product Benefits and Marketing Strategy

One new category of product benefit introduced in the current paper is the "holistic product benefits" customers may perceive and appreciate in a product constellation. This type of product benefit has been largely ignored in the literature. Their implications for marketing practice will be discussed next.

In consumption settings where multiple products are needed, the product constellation forms a "consumption system" (Boyd and Levy 1963). A consumer may obtain utility holistically from the product constellation based on a personal consumption schema. When a consumer tries to combine a product constellation and to construct from it a meaningful combination, certain dimensions of compatibility and complementarity between products may be critical to perception of the products' benefits. These dimensions briefly described here (for a detail discussion and examples, please see Lai [1994]): (1) *"functional exhaustivity"* suggests that products are combined in a way that the required functions are completely fulfilled; (2) *"operational connectivity"* suggests that the operations (or the physical shapes and positions) of the products are smoothly connected. (3) *"aesthetic coherence"* relates to the sense of beauty or to personal expression in the product constellation; and, (4) *"meaning-role consistency"* refers to the perceived coherence between the cultural meanings of products and the social roles which the consumers assume (Solomon 1983).

The holistic product benefits may be a good basis for product positioning. As defined previously in the current paper, holistic product benefit refers to the perceptual benefits acquired from the complementarity, coherence, compatibility, and consistency in a product constellation as a whole. A company could set itself apart from the competition by identifying and promoting itself as the best provider of certain holistic benefits of a product constellation to satisfy consumer's needs. In pursuing a competitive positioning through holistic product benefits, the company may need to reshape its business scope or redefine its product lines, and consequently obtain its sustainable competitive advantage.

Organizations can design competitive marketing strategies based on meaningful and desirable combinations of product benefits for their customers. How to select a competitive strategy and the desirable benefits of the product will largely depend on the company's knowledge about the customers' consumption behavior. In addition, the relative defensibility of the strategy in the market is another problem in selecting a competitive strategy. The consumption behavior approach to the customer value would provide more strengths in strategy defensibility. For example, the positioning through holistic product benefits can enjoy the synergetic effects derived from a meaningful product combination that is developed from a comprehensive knowledge of customer consumption behavior. Furthermore, sometimes a company has to coordinate a complementary business group (also a synergy generating activity) to provide meaningful product combinations to customers (Normann and Ramirez 1993). In these situations, the defensibility of the competitive strategy would be even stronger because of the synergetic effects. Normann and Ramirez (1993) recapitulate this implication for marketing strategy well: "One of the chief strategic challenges of the new economy is to integrate [the consumption behavior] knowledge and [the interfirm] relationships— devise a good fit between [companies'] competencies and customers [(customers' needs or individual values)]..." (p. 74).

CONCLUSION

The consumption behavior approach to customer value can be an effective way of achieving more innovation, enhancing customer value, and obtaining greater marketing penetration and strategy sustainability. Consumption, like production, involves a constellation of goods and consumption values or desirable benefits. If marketers think of consumers as engaged in a constructive process by which they achieve their consumption values, it may be easy to see that a variety of holistic benefits are involved as customers use the products (Boyd and Levy 1963). Although the marketers may already plan and act in terms of consumer needs and behavior patterns, they can gain even more insight if they study consumer's consumption behaviors in which their products play a part. For knowledge of the customers' consumption behavior to be truly meaningful, much more would have to be known about the customers' personal values, feelings and thoughts, and consumption values. In other words, understanding the consumers' consumption behavior means that their activities should be analyzed thoroughly and holistically, from the expectation about consumption values at the prepurchase stage, to the purchase evaluation at the stage of selection and acquisition, to consumption values actualization in the stage of use, possession, and maintenance.

One caveat about customer value: greater customer value does not necessarily equal greater customer satisfaction. Customer value is defined as the difference (or surplus) between benefits and costs; it is a level of return for customer costs. From a cognitive perspective, according to expectation theory, satisfaction is the result of a comparison between what actually occurs and what is expected. Hence the customers' buying satisfaction depends on both their perceived value of the purchase and their knowledge of what a fair level of buying value should be. In short, customers will feel satisfied to the extent that the perceived value of their buying exceeds the standard they hold. From this point of view, exceeding value is the key for customer satisfaction, not customer value per se (a surplus value). This issue can be viewed as an avenue for further study.

REFERENCES

Abelson, Robert P. (1976), "Script Processing in Attitude Formation and Decision Making," in *Cognition and Social Behavior*, eds. John S. Carroll and John W. Payne, Hillsdale, NJ: Erlbaum, 33-45.

Boyd, Harper W. and Sidney J. Levy (1963), "New Dimensions in Consumer Analysis", *Harvard Business Review*, 41 (November-December), 129-140.

Clawson, C. Joseph and Donald E. Vinson (1978), "Human Values: A Historical and Interdisciplinary Analysis," in *Advances in Consumer Research*, Vol. 5, Provo, UT: Association for Consumer Research, 472-477.

Crocker, Jennifer (1984), "A Schematic Approach to Changing Consumers' Beliefs," in *Advances in Consumer Research*, Vol. 11, ed. Thomas C. Kinnear, Provo, UT: Association for Consumer Research, 472-477.

Day, George S. (1990), *Market Driven Strategy*, New York, NY: Free Press.

_____, Allan D. Shocker and Rajendra K. Srivastava (1979), "Customer-oriented Approaches to Identifying Product-Markets," *Journal of Marketing*, 43 (Fall), 8-19.

Engel, James F., Roger D. Blackwell and Paul W. Miniard (1990), *Consumer Behavior and Marketing Strategy, 6th ed.*, Chicago, IL: Dryden Press

Fishbein, Martin and Izek Ajzen (1975), *Belief, Attitude, Intention and Behavior.*, Reading, MA: Addison-Wesley.

Frondizi, Risieri (1971), *What is Value: An Introduction to Axiology, 2nd ed.*, Lasalle, IL: Open Court.

Hooley, Graham J. and John Saunders (1993), *Competitive Positioning: The Key to Marketing Strategy*, New York, NY: Prentice Hall.

Kahle, Lynn R. (1977), "Social Values in the Eighties: A Special Issue," *Psychology and Marketing*, 2 (December), 231-238.

Lai, Albert Wenben (1994), "Consumption Schemata: Their Effects on Consumer Decision Making," in *Advances in Consumer Research*, Vol. 21, Provo, UT: Association for Consumer Research, 489-494.

McCracken, Grant (1988), *Culture and Consumption: New Approaches to the Symbolic Character of Consumer Goods and Activities*, Bloomington, IN: Indiana University Press.

Normann, Richard and Rafael Ramirez (1993), "From Value Chain to Value Constellation: Designing Interactive Strategy", *Harvard Business Review*, 71 (July-August), 65-77.

Olshavsky, Richard W. and Donald H. Granbois (1979), "Consumer Decision Making—Fact or Fiction," *Journal of Consumer Research*, 6 (September), 93-100.

Peter, J. Paul and Jerry C. Olson (1990), *Consumer Behavior and Marketing Strategy, 2nd ed.*, Homewood, IL: Irwin

Porter, Michael E. (1980), *Competitive Strategy*, New York, NY: Free Press.

Rokeach, Milton (1973), *The Nature of Human Values*, New York, NY: Free Press

Sheth, Jagdish N., Bruce I. Newman and Barbara L. Gross (1991), "Why We Buy What We Buy: A Theory of Consumption Values," *Journal of Business Research*, 22, 159-170.

Solomon, Michael R. (1983), "The Role of Product as Social Stimuli: A Symbolic Interactionism Perspective," *Journal of Consumer Research*, 10 (December), 319-329.

Srivastava, Rajendra K. (1981), "Usage-Situational Influences on Perceptions of Product Markets: Theoretical and Empirical Issues," in *Advances in Consumer Research*, vol. 8, ed. Kent Monroe, Chicago: Association for Consumer Research, 106-111.

_____, Mark I. Alpert, and Allan D. Shocker (1984), "A Customer-oriented Approach for Determining Market Structure," *Journal of Marketing*, 48 (Spring), 32-45.

Treacy, Michael and Fred Wiersema (1993), "Customer Intimacy and Other Value Disciplines," *Harvard Business Review*, 41 (January-February), 84-93.

Tversky, Amos (1972), "Elimination by Aspects: A Theory of Choice," *Psychological Review*, 79, 281-299.

Vinson, Donald E., Jerome E. Scott and Lawrence M. Lamont (1977), "The Role of Personal Values in Marketing and Consumer Behavior," *Journal of Marketing*, 41 (April), 44-50.

Wilkie, William L. (1990), *Consumer Behavior, 2nd ed.*, New York, NY: John Wiley.

The Constructive Nature of Consumer Response to Differential Product Advantages

Ziv Carmon, Duke University
Stephen M. Nowlis, Washington State University

Most product and service categories include alternatives that differ in terms of the advantages they possess. Some offer higher quality (broadly defined to encompass such issues as reliability, durability, or unique features), and others, more attractive prices. The question of how consumers respond to differential advantages has become particularly relevant as markets are turning increasingly competitive. Not only do rapid technological improvements allow manufacturers to offer a wide variety of features, but there is also increased use of advertising to persuade consumers that one brand's advantages are more desirable than those of other brands.

It is widely believed that consumers' preferences are often constructed, and not merely revealed when assessments are required. As a result, they are sensitive to such things as the characteristics of the choice set (context) and the type of the evaluation (response mode) that is required. The constructive nature of consumer response to differential advantages was the focus of this session. Specifically, two of the papers in this session showed that commonly used methods for evaluating price-quality trade-offs that are normatively equivalent reveal very different preferences, attributing these differences to aspects of the constructive nature of these evaluations.

Carmon and Simonson examine the accuracy of consumers' assessments of the value of quality to them, using value-matching types of questions. In such questions consumers are asked about their willingness-to-pay for a brand given its description, as well as the description and price of a competing brand, which are provided as a reference. Carmon and Simonson find that value-matching responses systematically underestimate the value of quality. In other words, respondents systematically underestimated their willingness to pay for high quality alternatives and overestimated their willingness to pay for low quality ones, compared to the willingness displayed in choice. They explore several alternative psychological explanations for this effect, and show how awareness of this underestimation can be used by marketers to affect the choice among brands that differ in their price and quality.

Nowlis and Simonson propose that attributes differ in the degree to which they are diagnostic and can be meaningfully evaluated out of context based on their absolute values. In particular, evaluations of prices and product features are sensitive to the particular set of considered alternatives whereas perceived brand equity is usually less context sensitive. Building on these distinctions, they show that lower-price, lower-quality brands are more strongly preferred over higher-price, higher-quality brands when consumers make choices between brands rather than judge their likelihood of buying each brand. They also show that lower-quality brands with unique product features will be more strongly preferred over higher-quality brands that do not offer these features when consumers make choices rather than judgments.

The availability of a large number of brands, each claiming that its differential advantage is most important, complicates trading-off price and quality in many product categories. There are those who argue that the quality differences among brands are often largely minor. Advertising is commonly blamed for establishing distorted perceptions of the significance of various product and service features, thereby artificially decreasing consumers' price sensitivity. Mitra and Lynch show that in some decision environments differentiating advertising decreases price sensitivity by increasing the perceived differences among brands. They also show that advertising need not always have detrimental effects on consumer welfare, as in these contexts it allows customers to choose brands that are more in line with their personal tastes than in the absence of advertising.

The discussant, Bob Meyer, reviewed the papers and offered suggestions for future research.

Special Session Summary
Schema Incongruity: A Multidimensional Perspective Involving Advertising Schema, Self-Schema, and Product Schema

Kalpesh Kaushik Desai, University of Texas at Austin
Esra Gencturk, University of Texas at Austin

Schemas are generic knowledge structures of a stimulus domain stored in memory. Schema incongruity refers to any information about a stimulus that is not consistent with prior expectations. The concept of schema incongruity is important to marketers because the degree to which information is discrepant from schema expectations can affect a number of consumer judgments such as product evaluation and product typicality ratings. This special topic session considered issues related to the effects of schema incongruity in three different contexts: "advertising design"; "self-schema"; and "product schema." The first two contexts have not been researched in marketing to date and product schema incongruity was examined in novel contexts of brand extensions and multiple incongruities (i.e., incongruities involving more than one attribute and one brand).

The first paper by Kalpesh Kaushik Desai, Esra Gencturk, and Linda Rochford examined the influence of multiple incongruities (*MI*) on the changes in product category schema. MI was operationalized by manipulating two variables-*amount of incongruent information* (i.e., number of incongruent attributes) and *distribution of incongruent information* (i.e., a given number of incongruent attributes were either concentrated in few brands or dispersed across many brands). Two types of schema change were examined in this study: (1) an incongruent brand being rated more typical, and (2) in a brand classification task, an incongruent brand being not subtyped (i.e., it is sorted with other brands rather than alone). The experimental results revealed that incongruent brands were rated more typical when the incongruent attributes were dispersed (i.e., when the brands were moderately incongruent) whereas, fewer subtypes were created when the incongruent attributes were concentrated (i.e., when the brands were extremely incongruent). Hence, the results suggest that the way consumers classify brands into different subcategories is different from the way they rate the typicality of different brands. That is, though they rated extremely incongruent brands less typical than moderately incongruent brands, they still grouped the extremely incongruent brands with other brands in the same experimental condition.

The second paper by Joseph C. Nunes, Joan-Meyers Levy, and Laura Peracchio reported the findings of experiments that examined the influence of incongruity between the positioning of the product (achieved through ad copy) and its ad design as reflected in its *direction* (i.e., the placement of the product vertically, diagonally, or horizontally) and *symmetry* (i.e., whether the ad seems to be heavier on one side versus balanced) on product evaluations. The above relationships were examined for individuals who varied in their need for cognition (an indicator of an individual's motivation to process an ad). The results indicate that congruity between what is implied by ad layout and ad copy influences people's product evaluations when they are highly motivated to process an ad in detail, but this effect vanishes when the motivation is absent.

The third paper by Katryna Malafarina and Barbara Loken investigated the interactive effects of schema incongruities between endorser, product user, and target (self) schemas, on ad and brand evaluations. Specifically, they tested the moderating role of consumer's self-schema on the negative effects of a mismatch between the endorser and the product user image. In particular,

when a mismatch exists between the endorser and the user, the incongruity will be resolved by assimilating the information to one's self (leading to more positive affect toward the ad and brand) if the self-schema matches the endorser schema. In contrast, when the same endorser-user mismatch occurs and the self-schema does not match the endorser schema, accommodation will occur (leading to negative affect toward the ad and the brand). Analogous predictions are tested about the mismatches between the product-user schema and the self-schema, with the endorser schema moderating these effects. The above relationships were tested by manipulating the endorser and product-user schemas whereas, self-schema is derived as an individual difference variable.

The fourth paper by Eyal Moaz and Alice M. Tybout integrated schema incongruity theory and notions of task involvement to specifically test through two experiments (1) a positive, linear relationship between extension congruity (i.e., similarity with the parent brand concept) and positive extension evaluation under low consumer involvement condition, (2) an inverted U relationship, such that moderate extension incongruity is evaluated more favorably than either extension congruity or extreme incongruity under high consumer involvement condition, and (3) cognitive processes underlying the above relationships. The results of the experiments confirmed the first two relationships and found that indepth attribute processing took place only under high involvement condition and only for the congruent extension. Further, under this involvement condition, incongruity resolution processes were in evidence in the case of the moderately incongruent extension.

The findings from the above four studies establish the fact that consumers do operate with schemas in as diverse domains as ad design, self-schemas, and product schemas. Thus, the influence of schema incongruity should not be ignored by marketers.

A Brand as a Character, A Partner and a Person: Three Perspectives on the Question of Brand Personality

Jennifer Aaker, Stanford University
Susan Fournier, Harvard University

Introduction and Objective of Session

The idea of a brand personality is familiar and accepted by most advertising practitioners (e.g., Plummer 1985) and many marketing academics (e.g., Gardner and Levy 1955). For decades, researchers have argued that brand personality is an important topic of study because it can help to differentiate brands (e.g., Crask and Laskey 1990), develop the emotional aspects of a brand (e.g., Landon 1974) and augment the personal meaning of a brand to the consumer (e.g., Levy 1959). However, although brand personality is intuitively appealing and, as a result, has received considerable academic attention, it has been criticized on a number of dimensions; conceptual, methodological and substantive. First, at the conceptual level, there is still some ambiguity over what a brand personality *is*. How should it be defined and conceptualized? How (or when) is it different from brand image and/or user imagery? The answers to these questions have important implications for managers and academics interested in understanding the larger questions of why brand personality is important and how brand personality works.

Second, at the methodological level: how is brand personality best measured? While most researchers generally rely on qualitative methods, such as photo-sorts, free associations, psychodramatic exercises (cf. Levy 1985) these open-ended techniques are often dropped in the later stages of research as marketers look for more quantitative ways to detect and enumerate differences among their brands (Blackston 1993), the most common of which is the differential semantic scale (e.g. Birdwell 1968; Plummer 1985). However, studies using such scales are limited since the "right" way to compile the adjectives has not yet been determined.[1] Clearly, a brand personality research program should flow from the conceptual definition that guides it. Moreover, it would likely include both qualitative and quantitative methodologies in order to retain the advantages of both. However, what those methodologies are, and how they work together to articulate the conceptualization remain unclear.

Third, at the substantive level: what does personality do for a brand? What are the implications of having a brand personality? What marketing activities create or alter it? In the past, researchers have suggested that brand personality is most important when used as a research tool to identify personal meaning for the consumer (King 1989). Others assert that brand personality is needed as information for creatives when developing advertising (Lannon and Cooper 1983). Still others have suggested that brand personality should be seen as a more global construct: a key determinant of brand equity (Aaker 1991; Biel 1993). In brief, brand personality, as a construct, has multiple uses. However little systematic research has been conducted to understand or classify these uses. Is brand personality best used as a research tool, a clue for creatives or as a key element to brand equity? Or is the answer "D"?

The primary objective of this session is to address these three areas of ambiguity in brand personality research. As illustrated by the set-up of the session, our goal is not to converge on one definition, conceptualization and measurement tool for brand personality. Rather, we draw on diverse literatures such as narrative theory, social psychology and psychometric theory, and illuminate their potential contributions to the study of brand personality.

The secondary objective of this session is to provide a platform for future research on brand personalities and related topics. Upon reviewing the literature on brand personality, one gets the sense that each study does not receive the attention it may deserve—wheels are spinning yet brand personality research doesn't get very far. In order to give past, current and future studies some traction, solid theoretical frameworks and a sense of the topic's breadth are needed. By focusing on what brand personality is, how it can be measured and how it works, we hope to spur further research to take one of these three perspectives and address other issues of brand personality.[2]

Orientation of Session and Topics Covered

As outlined above, the goal of the proposed special session, "*A Brand as a Character, a Partner and a Person: Three Perspectives on the Question of Brand Personality*," is to serve as a forum to discuss current issues on brand personality and suggest areas for future research within the domain of brand personality. All three papers will address three fundamental questions involving brand personality via a particular behavioral perspective (a narrative, relationship and trait approach) and using a particular methodology (narrative analysis, depth interviews and multivariate analysis). Those questions are:

(1) What *is* brand personality?
(2) How can brand personality be *measured*?
(3) What are the *implications* of (a) having a brand personality, and (b) the advocated conceptualization of brand personality?

The first paper by Allen and Olson addresses these three questions by viewing brand personality from a "naive-psychological" (Heider 1958) and narrative (Bruner 1990) perspective. Brand personality is conceptualized based on the way that observers attribute personality characteristics to people during everyday interaction. Based on this conceptualization, the possibilities for using narrative theory as a profitable framework for understanding the processes by which consumers form personality impressions

---

[1] Some researchers have used adjectives extracted from personality inventories used for detecting emotional instability, schizophrenia or neuroticism (e.g., Maheshwari 1974). Others simply use attributes most related to the products being tested (e.g., Birdwell 1968; Schewe and Dillon 1978). Moreover, regardless of how the adjectives are selected, reliability and validity problems are generally not addressed. (See Sirgy 1982 for a more complete review of these and other measurement difficulties).

[2] Further areas of research might include; to what extent does a brand take on a personality before vs. after use? What roles do brand names, logos and symbols play in developing a brand personality? What impact does a brand personality have on loyalty? Under what situations is one brand personality preferred over another? What type of advertising (e.g. transformational vs. informational) is most effective in developing a brands with a strong personality? The three papers in this session will raise these and other ideas for future research.

(via brand characters and behaviors) are discussed. Viewing brand personality with a narrative perspective has direct implications for (a) the mode of thought used by consumers to derive personality meaning for brands, (b) the techniques used by advertisers to create brand personality and (c) how to measure consumers perceptions of brand personality. Finally, issues for future research on brand personality and the use of narrative theory are outlined.

The second paper by Fournier addresses the three questions by taking a relationship approach to brand personality research. Within Fournier's theoretical framework, the brand is treated as an active, contributing member of a relationship dyad that joins the consumer and the brand. It is suggested that consumers form trait inferences from the behaviors undertaken by the brand in its partnership role, and that these trait inferences then form the basis for consumer's evaluative conceptions of the brand. While previous work (cf., Allen and Olson 1994) suggests that consumers may draw inferences from the behaviors enacted by the brand or the brand character in advertising (e.g., the California Raisins, the Pillsbury Doughboy), Fournier suggests a broader source of behaviors from which trait inferences are made. Specifically, she proposes that all marketing mix activities and brand management decisions can be construed as "behaviors" enacted on the part of the brand, and applies act frequency theory (Buss and Craik 1983) to aid in understanding the personality implications of a range of observed brand behaviors. To illustrate the kinds of personality inferences consumers make based on brand behavior as well as the types of brand-consumer relationships, a series of depth interviews with consumers are described. In closing, the relationship-oriented view is compared to existing conceptualizations of brand personality. Measurement implications for articulating the character of a brand's personality, assessing brand personality strength, and tracking personality change over time are highlighted and discussed.

The third paper explores by Aaker the three questions by taking a trait approach to the study of brand personality. By drawing on personality measurement theory (e.g., Norman 1968; Osgood *et al.* 1957), Aaker operationalizes brand personality as the human characteristics of a brand. In order to identify the core factors which represent brand personality (much like the Big Five represent people personality), Aaker factor analyzes the individual ratings of 40 brands on 114 personality traits by 631 respondents recruited in the United States. The principal components factor analysis results in five significant factors. A second order factor analysis structures these five factors into fifteen sub-factors. Next, 45 personality traits that represent the Big-Five structure are identified via a clustering procedure (Nunnally 1967). In addition, the implications of this brand personality hierarchy (5 factors, 15 sub-factors and 45 traits) are discussed. Specifically, Aaker examines (1) what types of brands (and product categories) have particular personality profiles, (2) the relationship between self-concept and the personality of a chosen (and preferred) brand and (3) what types of brands have a different personality vs. user imagery, as well as what such a distinction means for the brand.

The discussant of the session will contribute in two ways: First, Keller will offer a global and critical perspective of brand personality by addressing questions such as: Does brand personality really exist? If it does, do all brands have personalities? When is it most helpful to think of brands in terms of "personalities"? Second, Keller will draw on his own research on brand equity to examine the relationship between brand personality and equity. Specifically, the discussant will address questions such as; Under what conditions do brand personality and brand equity positively correlate? Do they ever negatively correlate? Is it the strength, the favorability and/or uniqueness of the brand personality that leads to

brand equity? Alternatively, is there a certain type of personality that leads to greater equity?

Intended Audience

It is hoped that the session will appeal to marketing academics and practitioners interested in brand personality from both a *consumer* perspective (e.g. How do consumers see brands? When do consumers personify brands? How do they feel about brands?) and a *branding* perspective (e.g. What types of personal meanings are imbued in brands? What types of brands take on personalities? What does a personality do for a brand?). In addition, we hope to attract researchers interested using a variety of methodologies such as narrative analysis, depth interviews and multivariate analysis.

Statement of Contribution

The session has been designed so that its primary contribution will be to advance brand personality research at three levels: conceptual, methodological and substantive. However, in addition, we hope that, with the help of the discussant, a critical view of the topic is provided and areas for future research on brand personality are suggested.

CONCEPTUALIZING AND CREATING BRAND PERSONALITY: A NARRATIVE THEORY APPROACH

Douglas E. Allen and Jerry Olson, Penn State University

In this paper, we offer a conceptual analysis of the concept of brand personality and begin to develop a theory of brand personality. We show how this theory can guide research into the antecedents and consequences of brand personality. Narrative theory, which is especially useful in explaining how consumers interpret advertisers' attempts to create brand personality, is a key element in our approach. With this perspective we address a variety of questions, including: (a) What is brand personality? (b) How can brands have personalities? (c) How can marketers create a brand personality? (d) How can we measure brand personality? (e) What are the implications of having a brand personality?

Our definition of brand personality is based on an approach to understanding human interaction referred to as "naive psychology" (Heider 1958) or "folk psychology" (Bruner 1990). This perspective seeks to explain interpersonal relations by focusing on the way in which observers naturally attach meaning to everyday social situations. Thus, our conceptualization of personality is based on the process by which people attribute personality characteristics to other people. We define personality as the set of meanings constructed by an observer to describe the "inner" characteristics of another person. Personality meanings such as traits are created via inferences or attributions based on observations of another person's behavior. For example, an observer witnesses a person kick a dog and infers that the person is "mean". We emphasize that attributions about personality traits are based largely on observations of behavior (supposedly "caused" by the unobserved personality trait). Despite the circularity of this process, personality meanings have a useful function as they are abstract meanings that can be used to summarize complex behaviors and form expectations of future behaviors.

We use this same logic to conceptualize brand personality. Creating a brand personality literally involves the personification of a brand. Attributions of personality to a brand require that the brand performs intentional behaviors. To do so, the brand must be "alive" — the brand must be an action figure that intentionally does things. Based on the observed behaviors, consumers can make attributions about the brand's personality—"inner character," goals and values. In some marketing strategies, the brand is actually made to be "alive" and action-oriented ... as when the Raid can strides into a room and kills the bugs by itself or when the scrubbing brushes of Dow bathroom cleaner scurry around, joyously cleaning the tub. In other cases, the brand is personified in a character that is "alive" - Joe Camel represents Camel cigarettes, while the Jolly Green Giant personifies Green Giant vegetables. In sum, we define brand personality as the *specific set of meanings which describe the "inner" characteristics of a brand. These meanings are constructed by a consumer based on behaviors exhibited by personified brands or brand characters.*

The "folk psychological" perspective we use to explicate the concept of brand personality has several implications. For one, the mode of thought consumers use to derive personality meanings from brand behavior is likely to take on a narrative form. As opposed to a more scientific thought process used to form brand impressions, personality impressions formed in a folk-psychological manner involve a narrative thought process (Bruner 1986; 1990). As Bruner (1990) states, "its [folk psychology's] organizing principle is narrative..." (p. 35). Thus, Bruner argues that the primary way people make sense out of the behaviors of others (or fictional characters in a story) involves creating stories. Furthermore, Schank (1990) argues that all human knowledge is stored in the form of narratives. Thus, narrative thought plays an important role in constructing a brand personality.

The second implication of a narrative approach to brand personality is that marketers need to show the brand "doing things" in their advertising. In essence this involves portraying brands as characters in a story (Deighton, Romer and McQueen 1989). Thus, the Listerine bottle dons shield and sword and engages in combat with the plaque and gingivitis monster. The Raid can, wearing a military hat, strides into the room and kills the bugs by reaching up and squirting the nozzle under its hat. Such ads have a narrative form since the story shows the action sequence performed by the brand. Narratives or dramas provide more opportunities for portraying the intentional behaviors which are the bases for personality inferences.

Finally, a narrative perspective provides direction for measuring brand personality. For instance, by using an approach based on narrative theory (e.g., Tell me a story about brand X; What would brand X do in this circumstance?; If brand X were a person, how would it respond?) researchers may be able to identify which pattern of actions for a brand are most salient and meaningful. In addition to the successful use of stories as a projective technique, consumer stories may be also analyzed using literary or dramatic theory. For instance, Burke's pentad (Burke 1945) of Actor, Action, Goal, Scene and Instrument may be used to analyze consumer stories.

We conclude the paper by reviewing the key concepts in our vision of brand personality, identifying several issues for future research and suggesting several ways to address these issues.

THE BRAND-AS-RELATIONSHIP PARTNER: AN ALTERNATIVE VIEW OF BRAND PERSONALITY

Susan Fournier, Harvard Business School

Despite its acceptance in advertising and marketing practice, the brand personality construct has yet to receive dedicated theoretical attention in the consumer behavior literature. This paper uses interpersonal relationship theory to develop a conceptual framework for understanding and extending the notion of brand personality. Specifically, the brand is treated as *an active, contributing partner in the dyadic relationship that exists between the person and the brand,* a partner whose behaviors and actions

generate trait inferences that collectively summarize the consumer's perception of the brand's personality.

As a first step in the theory development, the legitimacy of considering the brand in a partnership role is debated. Can the brand be personalized as member of the relationship dyad? Do brands in fact reach out to customers on an individual basis, seeking to form one-on-one relationships with them? Can the brand be reasonably construed as an active contributor in the relationship? Through discussion, the "personalized," "dyadic," and "active" aspects of the brand are made salient. An important step in this argument is the author's proposal that, at a broad level of abstraction, all marketing mix activities and brand management decisions (e.g., a change in the brand's advertising campaign, a coupon drop, alteration of package size) can be construed as "behaviors" enacted on the part of the brand—behaviors that trigger attitudinal, cognitive, and/or behavioral responses on the part of the consumer. This exercise allows the audience to elevate the status of the brand from that of a passive object in one-sided marketing transactions to that of full-fledged relationship partner.

With this as a foundation, the author proposes a conceptual definition of the brand-as-partner (BAP) based on how the brand is evaluated in its role as member of the relationship dyad. The conceptualization goes beyond traditional concepts of brand personality to consider additional sources of identity and to specify the processes by which these sources are integrated into an evaluative conception of the brand. A framework depicting the component processes involved in the creation of the brand-as-partner notion embellishes this definition. A hierarchical set of identity themes and goals is first identified for the company and brand (see Mick and Buhl 1992 for a discussion of life themes and life projects). These goals constructs purposively generate a set of marketing actions and brand behaviors that unfold over time. Literature on the formation of person impressions (Srull and Wyer 1989) suggests that these behavioral acts are spontaneously translated into trait language, and that the trait inferences then form the basis for the evaluative concept of the brand.

In order to articulate the personality inferences that are stimulated by a range of common marketing actions, a series of depth interviews were conducted and are described. Next, the act frequency approach to personality (Buss and Craik 1983) is applied to aid in understanding how personality is inferred from a range of observed brand behaviors. An example for Colgate toothpaste is provided to illustrate the model. As a final exercise, the BAP notion is compared with existing conceptualizations of brand personality to highlight the explanatory power afforded by the relationship-oriented view. Implications for assessing the strength of a brand's personality within the role-theoretic framework are discussed, and the notion of brand personality is considered. Previously unrecognized outcome variables (such as commitment, satisfaction and involvement) that may be influenced by the strength and character of the BAP are also suggested. In closing, the implications and future ideas for BAP measurement are considered.

MEASURING THE HUMAN CHARACTERISTICS OF A BRAND: A BRAND PERSONALITY HIERARCHY

Jennifer Aaker, Stanford University

The idea that brands contain personal meaning for the consumer's self-conception has received a great deal of attention in the marketing and consumer behavior literatures in the last thirty years (see Sirgy 1982 for a review). Much of this research focuses on the idea that a brand can be thought of as having "personality,"[3] which is defined here as *the human characteristics associated with a brand.* For example, the brand personality of Levi's 501 jeans is American, western, ordinary, common, blue collar, hard working and traditional. By asking individuals to describe a brand as if it had come to life as a person, the meaning associated with a brand (as determined by factors such as brand attributes, benefits, price and product category; cf. Batra *et al.* 1993) can be identified.

Unfortunately, much of the research on brand personality has been limited due to the absence of a reliable and valid measurement tool that measures brand personalities across product categories. The primary purpose of this research was to develop a brand personality inventory (BPI) based on personality traits from psychology and marketing literatures that would capture the concept of brand personality. A factor analysis, based on the ratings of 114 personality traits on 40 brands in various product categories by 631 people, resulted in a highly stable five factor structure, termed here "The Big Five." A second level factor analysis (where each of the Big Five factors were individually factor analyzed) led to a secondary fifteen factor structure, termed here "The Little Fifteen." Finally, the personality traits which loaded into each of the Little Fifteen factors were cluster analyzed, resulting in the BPI, a 45 item inventory.

The BPI successfully met standards (Nunnally 1967) for internal reliability, test-retest reliability, content validity, nomological validity and construct validity. Tests of construct validity demonstrated that the traits which were positively related to a single factor had 1) high correlations with traits that measured the same factor and 2) low correlations with traits that measured other factors. Furthermore, although little theory exists to indicate what constructs brand personality predicts, attempts at illustrating predictive validity were made in two ways. First, the hypothesis that brands with strong personalities are associated with high levels of usage and preference (e.g. Biel 1993) was tested and supported. Second, the hypothesis that correlations between self-concept and brands used are higher than those between self-concept and brands not used (cf. Sirgy 1982) was tested and supported.

Finally, the theoretical implications of the existence of the Big Five factor structure as well as practical implications stemming from the 45 Item Inventory are discussed. Particular attention is given to the conceptual distinction between brand personality and user imagery. Specifically, we distinguish between the public vs. private nature of brand (i.e. to what extent the brand is bought/consumed by the consumer for him/her self vs. others), proposing that brand personality plays a greater role in consumer choice for private brands, while user imagery plays a greater role in consumer choice for public brands. In addition, however, we discuss what types of brands (and product categories) have particular personality profiles, and the relationship between self (actual and ideal) and brand preference and choice.

REFERENCES

Aaker, David A. (1991), *Managing Brand Equity,* New York: The Free Press.

Belch, George E. and E. Laird Landon, Jr. (1977), "Discriminant Validity of a Product-Anchored Self-Concept Measure," *Journal of Marketing Research*, 14 (May), 252-256.

Bellenger, Danny N., Earle Steinberg, and Wilbur W. Stanton (1976), "The Congruence of Store Image and Self Image," *Journal of Retailing*, 52 (Spring), 17-32.

Biel, Alexander (1993), "Converting Image into Equity", in *Advertising and Building Strong Brands*, eds. David A. Aaker and Alexander Biel, Hillsdale: NJ, Lawrence Erlbaum and Associates.

Birdwell, Al E. (1968), "A Study of Influence if Image Congruence on Consumer Choice," *Journal of Business*, 41 (January), 76-88.

Blackston, Max (1993), "Beyond Brand Personality: Building Brand Relationships," in *Brand Equity and Advertising*, eds. David A. Aaker and Alexander Biel, Hillsdale: NJ, Lawrence Erlbaum and Associates.

Bruner, Jerome (1986), *Actual Minds, Possible Words*. Cambridge, MA: Harvard University Press.

_____ (1990), *Acts of Meaning*. Cambridge, MA: Harvard University Press.

Burke, Kenneth (1945), *A Grammar of Motives*, New York, NY: Prentice Hall.

Buss, David M. and Kenneth H. Craik (1983), "The Act Frequency Approach to Personality," *Psychological Review*, 90 (2), 105-126.

Crask, Melvin R., and Henry A. Laskey (1990), "A Positioning-Based Decision Model for Selecting Advertising Messages," *Journal of Advertising Research*, (August/Sept.), 32-38.

Deighton, John, Daniel Romer and Josh McQueen (1989), "Using Drama to Persuade," *Journal of Consumer Research*, 16 (December), 335-343.

Gardner, Burleigh B. and Sidney J. Levy (1955), "The Product and the Brand," *Harvard Business Review*, 33 (April), 33-39.

Heider, Fritz (1958), *The Psychology of Interpersonal Relations*. New York, NY: Wiley.

King, Stephen (1989), "Branding Opportunities in Financial Services", in *Advertising and Marketing Financial Services Conference*.

Landon, E. Laird (1974), "Self-Concept, Ideal Self-Concept and Consumer Purchase Intentions," *Journal of Consumer Research*, 1 (September) 44-51.

Lannon, Judie and Peter Cooper (1983), "Humanistic Advertising: A Holistic Cultural Perspective", conference paper.

Levy, Sidney J. (1959), "Symbols for Sales," *Harvard Business Review*, 37 (4), 117-124.

_____ (1985), "Dreams, Fairy Tales, Animals and Cars," *Psychology and Marketing*, 2 (Summer), 67-81.

Meheshwari, Arun K. (1974), *Self-Product Image Congruence: A Macro-Level Analysis,* Ann Arbor, MI: University Microfilms International.

Mick, David Glen and Klaus Buhl (1992), "A Meaning-Based Model of Advertising Experiences," *Journal of Consumer Research*, 19 (3), 317-338.

Norman, Warren (1963), "Toward an Adequate Taxonomy of Personality Attributes," *Journal of Abnormal and Social Psychology*, 66 (6), 574-583.

---

[3]The term, personality, is used differently in the context of brands (consumer behavior) than in the context of persons (psychology). For example, while a person's personality is determined by multi-dimensional factors (e.g, appearance, traits and behavior), a brand, by its nature of being an inanimate object, has a personality that is determined by different factors (e.g, attributes, benefits, price, user imagery). The term, brand personality, is not being used here in a strict or literal sense, but as a metaphor. Like the person-as-a-computer metaphor in psychology, the brand-as-a-person has an element of truth in it; although brands are not people, they can be personified. In this paper, we address the questions of when and how brands are personified.

Nunnally, Jum C. (1967), *Psychometric Theory*, NY, New York: McGraw-Hill Book Company.

Osgood, C.E., George J. Suci and Percy M. Tannenbaum (1957), *The Measurement of Meaning*, Urbana: University of Illinois Press.

Plummer, Joseph T. (1985), "How Personality Makes a Difference," *Journal of Advertising Research*, 24 (December/January), 27-31.

Schewe, Charles D. and William R. Dillon (1978), "Marketing Information System Utilization: An Application of Self-Concept Theory," *Journal of Business Research*, 6 (January), 67-79.

Shank, Roger C. (1990), *Tell Me a Story*, New York, NY: Macmillan Press.

Sirgy, M. Joseph (1982), "Self-Concept in Consumer Behavior: A Critical Review," *Journal of Consumer Research*, 9 (December) 287-300.

Srull, Thomas K. and Robert S. Wyer (1989), "Person Memory and Judgment," *Psychological Review*, 96 (1), 58-83.

Interactive Marketing Technologies: Implications for Consumer Research

John Deighton, Harvard Business School

Chair: John Deighton, Harvard Business School

It has been speculated that interactive marketing technologies will transform the character of marketplace persuasion (Blattberg and Deighton 1991). If so, consumer behavior theories will change too. The aim of the session was to juxtapose talks about the practice of interactive marketing and talks about appropriate theoretical frameworks, to stimulate research at this frontier.

Christopher Meyer, Vice President, Mercer Management Consulting

Mr. Meyer is a consultant practicing in the information technology field.

He opened with a macroeconomic perspective, observing that economies have technology-driven life cycles. He identified four stages in a technology's influence on an economy: in the first there is basic science, in the second a technological infrastructure is built, in the third entrepreneurial businesses emerge, and in the last stage these enterprises coalesce into mature organizations. He suggested that the information economy's infrastructure had reached a critical mass, that the third phase was in place, and that recent mergers and alliances signalled tentative attempts to enter the fourth phase. He identified and discussed some critical aspects of the shift from a manufacturing economy to an information economy:

Smart products and services: he illustrated a retail catalog on CD-ROM known as En Passant, which compiled the offerings of some twenty catalog retailers to allow browsing by product type or price point across retailers' offerings. By storing the dates of gift-giving occasions, the service could make gift suggestions.

Computer simulation of consumer experience: Low-cost trial and testing was now possible. For example beauty consultants could illustrate the effects of cosmetics on digital images of customers' faces.

Electronic payment: The acquisition by Microsoft of Intuit, and the founding of First Virtual Holdings, offered the prospect of dependable on-line financial transfers.

He predicted in closing that the most significant consequence of interactive technologies will be, as is was for the telephone, not the content that the medium transmits but the sense of community that it creates.

Rishad Tobaccowala, Vice President and Director of Interactive Marketing, Leo Burnett Inc.

Mr Tobaccowala is charged with leading Leo Burnett's drive to compete in the field of interactive marketing communication.

He opened by defining interactive technologies as any two-way, real-time, addressable media with rich digital content. These media constituted a fourth communications revolution, after print, radio and television, with implications for distribution and selling as well.

By the end of 1995 there would be only 100,000 U. S. households with access to interactive television, but 10 million households using non-internet on-line services and 40 million with personal computers, as well as some 10 million kiosks, automatic tellers and other interactive devices. Differences between these communicators and those displaced will be:

They will advertise by invitation, not intrusion. Consumers can ask for advertising (or information) from Oldsmobile customer service representatives via on-line bulletin boards.

Expenditures on these media will be immediately and precisely linked to behavioral results - the media will be accountable.

Their audiences will be individuals, not segments. Marketing will shift from mass through targeted to relationship, as the content evolves from the form of a speech to that of a letter to a conversation.

Leo Burnett's programs for clients, which include McDonald's and Oldsmobile, have measured results with hard measures such as length of stay in the interaction, number of responses, and responses that result in sales, as well as soft measures such as content of consumer comments, navigability and consistency with brand values. He pointed to preliminary learning from interactive tests:

Brands are important to help consumers navigate on-line services.
The communication must invite true interaction, engaging the consumer to produce high involvement.
The sponsor must be responsive.
Control must be ceded to the audience.
Programs must be hybrids of interactive and conventional technologies.
Entertainment and sex have been two dependable draws in on-line services.

He identified issues that might be amenable to scholarly research:

Traditional advertising response models assume intrusion. Invitational advertising calls for entirely different conceptualization.

Crafting interactive persuasive messages uses different, poorly understood, psychological principles.

Management of the masses of data generated by interactive conversations calls for new decision support systems.

John Deighton, Associate Professor, Harvard Business School

This talk introduced the concept of "virtual relationships," patterns of interdependence between people and "smart" machines. A familiar example is the automated teller machine, which communicates customer-by-customer, tailoring the content of communication to each customer, taking into account the detailed history of past interactions just as human interaction takes account of history. This sensitivity to context is used to customize the product it delivers. For example, an ATM dispenses cash in response to a particular consumer's need, not to the average needs of consumers in a demographic or psychographic segment, and declines to advance cash when its memory of past interactions suggests the account is overdrawn. It can selectively deliver promotional messages when its memory of past interactions suggests they will be well received. As television shifts away from broadcast transmission and acquires the features of a client server computer network, so it too will be able to form one-to-one relationships with memory.

Theories that account for consumer *response* to broadcast media tend to emphasize *passivity*. Marketers are conceived of as acting on consumers, supplying the stimuli that consumers process and react to, often in states of low involvement. Theories to account for consumer *interaction* with responsive media emphasize *activity*, envisaging a consumer who initiates requests for information and advertising, co-produces what is consumed, and sustains relationships over time if the interactions are rewarding.

Interactive technologies permit the formation of virtual relationships. At best, these relationships are more than merely instrumental, and can elicit emotion from the consumers. To account for the expressive value of interactions with non-human sources, this presentation describes a theory of relationships formation and maintenance as the management of social context: essentially the machine "seduces" the consumer by inviting the consumer to co-create a lifelike context (Deighton and Grayson, forthcoming).

An exploratory study was described in which subjects discussed "continuing, evolving relationships between you and a machine, system, or entirely non-human object." The objects included software, computers, cars, voice mail, a calendar scheduling system, a mutual fund on-line system, America Online, the Internet, a negative option compact disk club, and a catalog. A content analysis of these descriptions identified such attributes as customization, responsiveness, anticipation, dependency, investment, exit costs, and domination and obedience. However, the emotional tonality of these relationships was unlike intimate personal relationships because there was no concern for the feelings of the other. These were essentially master-servant relationships. To illustrate that master-servant interactions are not culturally invariant, the story of Aladdin and his Magic Lamp was analyzed in three translations: from 1802, 1896 and 1970. The conclusion was that if the interactive marketer aspires to be the consumer's "obedient servant," the interface will have to be alert to the culture's conception of servanthood, and different interfaces may be required in different cultural settings.

Jonathan Frenzen, Visiting Assistant Professor of Marketing, University of Chicago.

Professor Frenzen was discussant and chaired the exchange between speakers and audience. He argued that while interactive technologies were new, the underlying market forces were not. Many familiar consumer theories would still apply. He pointed to Geertz's study of sellers searching for buyers and buyers for sellers in a peasant bazaar (Geertz 1973), and observed that modern methods of shopping, such as surfing the internet, had merely lowered search costs for buyers and sellers.

However pampering was a need that would endure, and one challenge to interactive marketers was to manage customer relationships artificially in a manner that emulated or evolved toward intimate human relationships. He suggested the Turing test to decide whether a virtual relationship was indistinguishable from the real thing or not. An important researchable issue would be the question of how to expand a relationship. He cited the work of the social psychologist Margaret Clark, who observes that as a relationship becomes deeper, the participants become less sensitive to the precise balance of indebtedness between them (Clark 1984). An-other feature of relationship expansion was each party's revealing of private information, the exchange of intimacies and confidences.

At a more macro level, he discussed the sociological concept of Blau spaces: when individuals are mapped into a space defined on demographic axes, the organizations to which they are affiliated and the markets in which they transact overlap. These patterns of overlap point to an exciting result for researchers interested in interactive marketing: as consumer researchers have long argued, individual brand purchases are an unnecessarily narrow research topic research, and overlap among markets and organizations is a fundamental attribute of markets that interactive marketers can pursue.

REFERENCES

Blattberg, Robert C. and John Deighton (1991), "Interactive Marketing: Exploiting the Age of Addressability," *Sloan Management Review*, Fall.

Clark, Margaret (1984), "Recordkeeping in two types of relationship," *Journal of Personality and Social Psychology*, 47 (September) 549-557.

Deighton, John and Kent Grayson (forthcoming), "Marketing and Seduction: Building Exchange Relationships by Managing Social Consensus," *Journal of Consumer Research*.

Geertz, Clifford (1973), *The Interpretation of Cultures*, New York: Basic Books.

A New Appraisal of the Belk Materialism Scale

Kathleen S. Micken, Old Dominion University

Belk has suggested that materialism is the most significant macro development in modern consumer behavior. Despite its importance, however, research about the construct is relatively new. As knowledge of the construct has advanced, and in response to reliability and validity problems, the Belk materialism scale has undergone several revisions. The most recent version has not yet been the subject of much test or study. This paper addresses the reliability and validity of the new scale via a study which employs an adult sample. It concludes with a discussion of content validity which may help explain some of the problems with the current scale as well as problems which have been reported for earlier versions.

The comedian George Carlin (1981) does a routine about our possessions, our "stuff." He pokes fun at the importance we attach to our possessions: we have special places for them, we may even move so that we have a larger house in which to accommodate them, and when we travel we carry some of them with us. This attachment to our "stuff" has been termed materialism and has become a focus of study in the social sciences (where it is sometimes also called "consumerism"). The focus is significant enough that Belk (1987) has labeled materialism the "dominant consumer ideology and the most significant macro development in modern consumer behavior" (p. 26). He is not alone. The importance of consumption in industrialized nations has been detailed by various writers (c.f. Horowitz 1985; McCracken 1988; Mason 1981; Nava 1992). Belk, however, has become one of materialism's most influential researchers. His seminal *Journal of Consumer Research* (1985) article on the subject is one of the most often cited articles from that journal (Cote, Leong, and Cote 1991). Further, Belk's (1984) definition of materialism seems to have been accepted in the marketing discipline.[1] He suggests that materialism might be thought of as seeking psychological well–being via consumption (Belk 1985, p. 265). More precisely,

> materialism reflects the importance a consumer attaches to worldly possessions. At the highest levels of materialism, such possessions assume a central place in a person's life and are believed to provide the greatest sources of satisfaction and dissatisfaction in life (Belk 1984, p. 291).

MEASURES OF MATERIALISM

While there is agreement on the definition of materialism, there is no clear agreement about how to measure the construct. Most acknowledge that materialism is a complex phenomenon, comprised of several dimensions. However, Belk (1984, 1985; Ger and Belk 1990, 1993) conceives of the dimensions as personality traits. Richins and Dawson (1990, 1992), on the other hand, have proposed that a value orientation is more accurate. Two scales to measure the construct have been developed. The Belk scale measures traits of possessiveness, envy, nongenerosity and preservation. The Richins and Dawson scale measures three domains: the centrality of acquisitions in one's life, whether acquisitions are used to define happiness, and whether they are used to define success. Because of its earlier appearance, the Belk scale has been more

widely used (see for example Dawson and Bamossy 1990; Ellis 1991; Hunt et al. 1990; Rudmin 1988; and Wallendorf and Arnould 1988). However, research which has investigated materialism using the two scales indicates that the Richins and Dawson scale is the more reliable (Cole et al. 1992; Othman 1989). Validity tests, usually correlations between the materialism scales and measures such as happiness and life satisfaction, have been less conclusive about the relative merits of the two scales (e.g., Belk 1985; Cole et al 1992; Dawson and Bamossy 1990; Hunt et al. 1990; Richins and Dawson 1992).

Thus, while materialism has been a topic of "report and discussion" for some years (Rudmin and Richins 1992), research is still in its relative infancy, as evidenced by the continuing scale development and testing. This article expands the understanding of materialism by moving forward the testing of the Belk materialism scale in four ways. First, the study employs the most recent, unpublished version of the scale (Ger and Belk 1993). Second, consistent with Ger and Belk's (1993) call for testing with adult, instead of student, samples this study employs a sample of adults. Third, the reliability of the scale is assessed. Finally, validity is addressed theoretically in a discussion of reasons why the Belk scale may not be measuring the materialism construct.

The paper begins with an assessment of the current state of the Belk scale. Next the study methodology is presented, followed by a discussion of the results. The paper concludes with a consideration of scale reliability and validity.

THE BELK SCALE

Initially, Belk (1984, 1985) proposed a multidimensional conceptualization of materialism, suggesting that it could be measured via three personality traits of possessiveness, nongenerosity, and envy. He reported (1984) coefficient alphas of .68, .72, and .80 for the subscales respectively. Belk has also suggested (1985) that materialism might be considered a single–factor construct which could be measured with the aggregation of the subscales. He (1985) reported alphas of .66 to .73 for the overall scale. In the 1985 study, Belk also conducted three tests of validity. He found that materialism was negatively, and significantly, correlated with happiness and life satisfaction. Second, blue collar workers had a higher mean materialism score than did students at a religious institute. In a three generation study of various attitudes and behaviors, however, no consistent patterns among materialism and the other measures could be ascertained.

Critiques and Tests of the Belk Scale by Other Researchers

Working with an early version of the Belk scale, Ellis (1992) analyzed responses to the scale using LISREL VII. He concluded that, with the then current state of the scale, it would be a mistake to take the aggregate of the three subscale scores as a measure of materialism. He did not suggest that the three–dimensional concept of materialism be thrown out, since there might be "enough positively correlated factors that might be capturing some aspects of this higher–order materialism construct" (p. 691).

Richins and Dawson (1992) also reviewed 12 separate data collections using the Belk scale. They found alphas of .09 to .81 for the individual subscales and alphas of .48 to .73 for the aggregate scale.

Cole et al. (1992) assessed both the reliability and validity of the scale. Their factor analysis resulted in nine (instead of three)

---

[1] While it is stated a bit differently, the definition employed by Richins and Dawson (1992) is consistent with Belk's: "materialism is a set of centrally held beliefs about the importance of possessions in one's life" (p. 308).

TABLE 1
Sample Demographics

Gender		Education	
Female	61.9%	Some High School	1.4%
Male	34.2	High School Grad	17.6%
No Answer	4.0	Some College	52.9%
		College Grad +	27.4%
Age		No Answer	0.7
18–34	54.3%		
35–49	32.4	**Occupation**	
50+	13.3	Blue Collar	11.2%
No Answer	1.1	White Collar	58.2
		Military	6.8
Household Income		Other	19.4
Less than $25k	31.7%	No Answer	4.4
$25–$34.9k	19.1		
$35–$49.9k	22.3	**Ethnic Background**	
$50k+	20.5	Black	14.7%
No Answer	6.5	White	76.3
		Other	8.3
		No Answer	1.8

initial factors accounting for 64.5 percent of the variance. Further, alphas for the three subscales were low.

Hendrickson and Morrisette (1992) employed the scale in a study focused on lifestyle analysis. Initial results indicated that materialism might not be an independent variable, but instead might be the result of a lifestyle choice. In analyzing the results, they found low alphas for the subscales. Consequently they, too, concluded that the Belk scale required additional refinement.

Revisions to the Belk Scale

Following the advice of such researchers, Belk has continued to refine the scale and to make it suitable for cross–cultural applications (Ger and Belk 1990, 1993). The research has incorporated qualitative as well as quantitative methods and has stretched over thirteen countries. In the process, some of the subscale items have changed and a new subscale has been added. Initially the new subscale was termed "tangibility"; most recently it is called "preservation." These changes have maintained the "moderately satisfactory alpha levels" for the scale and its subscales (Ger and Belk 1993, p. 17; see Table 2) and have addressed Ellis' concern that the subscales did not positively correlate with the overall scale. With these changes, the Belk scale has addressed some of the criticisms detailed above. The question is, however, has the refinement been sufficient? Finding an answer to that question is the purpose of this study.

METHODOLOGY

A questionnaire, with the materialism scale and demographic data questions, was administered to a stratified proportional random sample of the adult population in one of the fastest growing MSAs in the mid–Atlantic region. Respondents were selected so that the percentage from each city or county was equal to the proportion of residents living in the jurisdiction.

The sample size was selected according to a statistical power analysis approach, advocated by Cohen (1988). First, a significance level of .05 was employed. Second, since the materialism scales are still exploratory, detecting correlations as "low" as .20 would be desirable. Third, a power of 95 was selected to be consonant with the significance level of .05. With these decisions, a sample size of 266 was necessary.

Data for the study were collected via a questionnaire using the drop–off and pick–up methodology. Survey administrators were told to go only into neighborhoods which were considered "safe" and not to administer surveys after dark. To capture individuals who work outside the home during the week, surveys were administered on weekends as well as on week days.

To compute scale and subscale scores, responses to the items for each scale were summed, after adjusting for reverse scored items. Cronbach's alpha was computed as a measure of internal reliability. Correlations between demographics and the scales were computed. Finally, factor analysis was run to verify the factor structure.

RESULTS

Of the 280 surveys which were obtained, 278 were usable. Two contained so many unanswered items as to be useless. The Chi–square statistic of 3.537 (p=.316; df=3), which resulted from a comparison between the sample and actual population of the area, indicates that the desired proportional geographic stratification mentioned above was achieved. The demographic information about the sample is presented in Table 1.

While the drop–off and pick–up method did result in the desired proportional stratification, it may have also resulted in under– and over–representation in other areas. Women may have been more inclined to comply with a request to fill out the survey. They may also be the individual most likely to answer the door.

The high representation of "well educated" individuals may be accounted for because people with "some high school" may not have been willing to admit to not having a diploma (the drop–off and pick–up method may have compromised perceived anonymity). Additionally, those with less than a high school education or only a high school diploma tend to either be older and/or live in areas considered unsafe. The under representation of older people may have simultaneously led to an under representation of those without a high school degree.

Descriptive Statistics

After correcting the responses for the reverse scored items, scale means, standard deviations, and ranges were calculated.

TABLE 2
Comparison of Results
The Belk Scale
(Working Paper 1993—USA sample only)

Scale	Mean		Std. Dev.		Range		Alpha	
	Study	Belk	Study	Belk	Study	Belk	Study	Belk
Overall scale	56.8	61.1	8.6	NA	30–80	NA	.66	.62
Possessiveness	14.5	14.0	2.8	NA	6–20	NA	.38	.61
Nongenerosity	19.1	22.7	4.9	NA	9–32	NA	.64	.66
Envy	12.4	14.2	3.4	NA	5–21	NA	.50	.46
Preservation	10.8	10.1	2.9	NA	3–15	NA	.65	.55

These measures were then compared with those reported by Ger and Belk (1993), as reported in Table 2.

The other general assessment was to explore the relationships between demographics and materialism. Consistent with computations by Belk (1985) and Ger and Belk (1990, 1993), correlation analysis was run for the overall scale and subscales with education, age, gender, and household income. Significant correlations were found for gender, for age, and for income, as reported in Table 3. While neither Richins and Dawson (1992) nor Belk (1985; Ger and Belk 1990, 1993) has found a consistent relationship between materialism and gender, Ger and Belk (1993) did find some significant differences by gender for some of the subscales. In this study, the differences between men and women were on the traits of envy and nongenerosity as well as overall materialism. Additionally, age correlated with materialism. The statistically significant age correlations were with the overall scale and the envy subscale. These results are consistent with the findings reported by Richins and Dawson (1992). Finally, there was one other significant correlation of income with envy.

Reliability Assessment

The results of this study generally are consistent with those reported by Ger and Belk (1993, USA sample only), though, as reported in Table 2, there are some differences in the reliability scores. The more important issue is that for neither this study nor for the most recent work by Ger and Belk are the alphas within an acceptable range. Churchill (1979) has suggested that .60 is a minimal requirement for scale reliability; Nunnally (1978) has stated that .70 is the minimum acceptable level. Ger and Belk (1993) report that the reliability levels associated with the scale and subscales are "moderately satisfactory," but suggest that in using a single scale for international research there is a trade–off between reliability and cross–cultural adaptability.

It may be instructive to recall the inconsistencies reported above between Belk's findings and the results of those who have used his scale in other research. That this study also found inconsistent results, therefore, is not unusual. However, one must use caution when comparing across studies. At least four different versions of the Belk scale have been reported in the literature.

To determine if the reliability coefficients might be improved with the deletion of any of the scale items, item–to–total correla-

tions were calculated. Alphas for two subscales could be slightly improved, but not enough to reach the .70 level advocated by Nunnally. Alteration of the scale, therefore, does not seem to be warranted. Still, the use of the overall materialism scale or the subscales is problematic. Nunnally explains that scales with a coefficient alpha of less than .70 should be further examined because sufficient measurement error remains in the scale. The items may not be clearly written or they may not be sampling the content of the same construct (Nunnally 1978, p. 230). Both of these concerns are addressed later in the paper.

Factor Analysis

The main assumption of factor analysis, that the data are factorable, is not well met for the Belk scale. Evidence for this conclusion comes from a test for sampling adequacy as well as from examination of the correlation matrix. The Kaiser–Meyer–Olin (KMO) measure of sampling adequacy is an index for "comparing the magnitudes of the observed correlation coefficients [among the variables in the factor analysis] to the magnitudes of the partial correlation coefficients" (Norusis 1990, p. 162). If the variables have any factors in common, the partial correlation coefficients should be relatively small. Kaiser (1974) has devised an alliterative characterization for the measure. Results in the .90s are marvelous; those in the .80s are meritorious; measures in the .70s are middling; those in the .60s are mediocre; and those in the .50s are miserable. According to this progression, one could characterize the KMO measure for the Belk scale (.70875) as "middling."

Examination of the correlation matrix provides specific information about the problem. Tabachnick and Fidell (1989) caution that "factor analysis is exquisitely sensitive to the sizes of correlations" (p. 602) and that if no correlations exceed .30, the use of factor analysis is questionable. Examination of the matrix of correlations among the items for the Belk scale reveals that only five are .30 or better. With this information, one would expect the factor analysis to be a problem, and it is.

While Belk has suggested that four personality traits incline one toward materialism, factor analysis in this study did not yield the same conclusion. Instead, the scree plot and eigenvalues for the factors suggested that three through seven factors are possible. The four and six factor solutions are discussed, for reasons explained below.

TABLE 3
Correlations
The Belk Scale

	Educ.	Age	Gender*	Income
Overall Scale	–.0292	–.1221	.1913	–.0730
	(.633)	**(.045)**	**(.002)**	(.245)
Possessiveness	–.0108	–.0617	.0206	–.1014
	(.859)	(.310)	(.738)	(.103)
Nongenerosity	.0074	–.0740	.1903	–.0076
	(.903)	(.224)	**(.002)**	(.903)
Envy	–.0361	–.1950	.1923	–.1127
	(.553)	**(.001)**	**(.002)**	**(.071)**
Preservation	–.0956	.0695	–.0284	.0182
	(.114)	(.253)	(.645)	(.772)

* Point biserial correlations for gender; all others are Pearson product–moment correlations.

The four factor solution. Because the Belk scale is comprised of four subscales, factor analysis was run with four factors being specified. The resulting structure is presented in Table 4.

Consistent with Belk (1984, 1985; Ger and Belk 1990, 1993) nongenerosity was the first factor to emerge, indicating that it accounts for the greatest proportion of variation in the data. Since the nongenerosity subscale contains nine of the 21 items in the scale, this result is expected. Nunnally (1978) cautions against ascribing too much importance to the first factor if the scale is constructed so that more of its items measure factor one–type constructs. The only factor composed entirely of the original items is preservation, a not unsurprising result since the alpha for this subscale is the highest of the four. The envy and nongenerosity subscales are composed primarily of the "right" items, though there is some mix between the two (nongenerosity items loading on the envy subscale and vice versa). Again, knowledge of the internal consistency of these two subscales helps explain the results. Belk acknowledges that the nongenerosity subscale generally has been the "most internally consistent factor" (personal communication, May 7, 1993). The possessiveness subscale, however, is a mixture of possessiveness and nongenerosity items—again expected from reliability analysis.

What is to be made of the mix of items among the factors? Certainly factor analysis is not an exact analytical technique. The four factor solution, however, only accounts for 39.3 percent of the variation in the data, while other solutions explain more than 50 percent. In Ger and Belk's most recent cross–cultural study (1993), the four factors account for 28 percent of the variance for the overall sample, reflecting, perhaps, the cross–cultural research trade–off noted earlier. Second, factor analysis looks for commonalities. As noted above, the correlations among the items in the Belk scale are quite low, with only five being above .30. Thus there would appear to be too few commonalites among the items.

Belk may have consistently found four factors, in part at least, because he has consistently used homogeneous student samples to smooth out differences (Ger and Belk 1993). This study's design, however, sampled a more heterogeneous adult population. Nunnally (1978) issues a strong caution about sample composition. If a

scale's factors are to be interpreted solely for people with a particular characteristic, such as a given age range, then the sample *should* be homogeneous with respect to that characteristic. If the factors are intended to be generalized, however, then the sample should be similarly *heterogeneous*. Differences in age, sex, education, and the like can result in different factors emerging from the analysis. Thus, one should not expect that factors produced from student samples would be the same as those produced from an adult sample. Accordingly, the nine–factor solution reported by Cole et al. (1992) from a survey of adults in a large midwestern city is not surprising.

The six factor solution. Of the remaining possible solutions, the six factor structure (see Table 5), which explains 50.5 percent of the variation, is the most interpretable. This time, the nine nongenerosity items do not form a single factor, suggesting that nongenerosity may not be a single construct in people's minds. Nongenerosity is divided into three quite interpretable dimensions. The first deals with sharing with others (lending possessions, giving rides to those without transportation, and generally sharing what one has). The second face of nongenerosity seems to be selfishness, or a "me versus thee" mentality (not rejoicing in others' good fortunes, not donating to charity, and buying things for oneself instead of for others). Third, nongenerosity seems to manifest itself in an almost siege mentality (in not liking to have friends stay in one's home, not helping out the needy, and feeling that one generally doesn't get what one deserves from society).

The remaining three factors are quite separate from nongenerosity. Preservation remains intact. Two envy items load on the sixth factor (being envious, even jealous, of the wealthy and of people who seem to buy what they want). Finally, the possessiveness items load together. This last factor might be more accurately termed a "worry over loss of possessions" rather than the "desire to retain control or ownership of the possessions" as Belk (1985) defines it. This factor includes items which address emotional distress over actual and anticipated losses, as well as an item concerned with locking things up. The stray nongenerosity item which loads on this factor seems particularly relevant: "I worry about people taking my possessions." Thus, the six factor solution

TABLE 4
Four Factor Solution

	Factor			
	1	**2**	**3**	**4**
Nongenerosity				
I enjoy donating things for charity. * (NG)	.6433	.2104	.0694	−.1597
I enjoy sharing what I have. * (NG)	.6156	.1865	.1818	−.1487
I don't mind giving rides to those who don't have a car. * (NG)	.5521	−.0534	.2598	.0782
I enjoy having people I like stay in my home. * (NG)	.5128	−.1821	.1305	−.1007
If I have to choose between buying something for myself versus for someone I love, I would prefer buying for myself. (E)	.4376	.2309	.1530	−.0104
When friends do better than me in competition it usually makes me feel happy for them.* (NG)	.4375	.2334	−.1401	.0494
I do not enjoy donating things to the needy. (NG)	.4013	.1276	−.0535	.0405
Envy				
I am bothered when I see people who buy anything they want. (E)	.0222	.6016	.1527	.0229
There are certain people I would like to trade places with. (E)	.2830	.5920	−.1086	.1082
When friends have things I cannot afford, it bothers me. (NG)	.2230	.5567	.1269	−.0562
I don't seem to get what is coming to me. (E)	.2767	.5224	−.0895	−.0214
People who are very wealthy often feel they are too good to talk to average people. (E)	−.0606	.4765	.0756	−.0032
Possessiveness				
I don't like to lend things, even to good friends. (NG)	.3937	−.1326	.6168	.0458
I worry about people taking my possessions. (NG)	.1396	.2825	.5649	−.0177
I get very upset if something is stolen from me, even if it has little monetary value. (P)	−.2132	.3049	.5594	.1361
I am less likely than most people to lock things up. * (P)	.1013	−.1164	.5077	−.1780
I don't like to have anyone in my home when I'm not there. (P)	.2063	.0173	.5056	−.0577
I don't particularly get upset when I lose things. * (P)	−.2059	.1419	.3722	.2142
Preservation				
I like to collect things. (Pr)	−.0140	−.0529	−.1419	.8075
I have a lot of souvenirs. (Pr)	−.0311	−.0035	−.0439	.7728
I tend to hang on to things I should probably throw out. (Pr)	−.0372	.0604	.1357	.6784

* Reverse scored items.
(NG) Original Nongenerosity Subscale Item; (E) Original Envy Subscale Item
(P) Original Possessiveness Subscale Item; (Pr) Original Preservation Subscale Item

---

seems to better explain the variation in the personality traits which are being measured. Having said that, it should also be noted that the six factor solution is not as "clean" a solution, since nine items correlate at .30 or higher with more than one factor. The alphas for the six factors also attest to this situation, as noted in Table 5.

The pairing of nongenerosity and envy is worthy of an additional comment. Belk (1985) distinguishes between the two saying that nongenerosity is an unwillingness to give or share possessions with others, while envy is displeasure with another's superiority in happiness, success, reputation or possessions (Schoeck 1966, as quoted in Belk 1985). The pairing of items from these two subscales suggests that the distinction drawn in research may not be one made by people in everyday life. Alternatively, the items may not be written in a way that makes the distinction obvious. In either case it certainly can be imagined that one might be unwilling to share possessions because of not wanting to increase the success or good fortune of another. Hence nongenerosity and envy may be intertwined in people's perceptions. These are the concerns Nunnally (1978) had in mind when he spoke about the problems which might attend a scale with a low coefficient alpha, as noted above.

DISCUSSION

The reliability coefficients for the Belk scale are not as high as one might like. In this study, only two of the four subscales and the overall scale itself have coefficient alphas between .60 and .70. While these alphas might be judged by Churchill (1979) to be acceptable for basic research, they would not be for Nunnally (1978). Indeed, Ger and Belk (1993) refer to the alphas as "moderately acceptable." They suggests a willingness to trade some reliability for cross–cultural applicability. Whether this exchange is acceptable to the discipline, given the availability of a more reliable instrument (the Richins and Dawson scale), remains to be seen.

Reliability tests alone, however, are insufficient. A scale could reliably be measuring nonsense! Validity assessment helps to determine whether the scale is in fact measuring materialism.

The weakest form of validity is content or face validity which refers to a "rational appeal to the carefulness with which a domain of content has been sampled and placed in the form of a good test" (Nunnally 1978, p. 110). In making this assessment, it should first be noted that any scale is an indirect measure, since an idea, such as

TABLE 5
Six Factor Solution

	Factor					
	1	2	3	4	5	6
Factor 1 (Nongenerosity—not sharing) Alpha = .54						
I don't like to lend things, even to good friends. (NG)	.739	−.083	.037	.328	−.053	.101
I don't mind giving rides to those who don't have a car. * (NG)	.638	.227	.065	.049	.016	−.102
I enjoy sharing what I have. * (NG)	.615	.256	−.152	−.029	.228	.193
Factor 2 (Nongenerosity—selfishness) Alpha = .58						
When friends have things I cannot afford, it bothers me. (NG)	.081	.672	−.069	.152	−.037	.153
When friends do better than me in competition it usually makes me feel happy for them.* (NG)	.174	.657	.032	−.123	.021	−.249
There are certain people I would like to trade places with. (E)	−.087	.512	−.109	.016	.388	.249
I enjoy donating things for charity. * (NG)	.341	.448	−.170	.068	.404	−.119
If I have to choose between buying something for myself versus for someone I love, I would prefer buying for myself. (E)	.347	.365	−.019	.078	.149	.049
Factor 3 (Preservation) Alpha = .65						
I have a lot of souvenirs. (Pr)	−.004	−.084	.813	−.155	.018	.025
I like to collect things. (Pr)	.010	−.038	.776	−.059	−.028	.050
I tend to hang on to things I should probably throw out. (Pr)	−.046	.075	.674	.196	−.009	−.038
Factor 4 (Possessiveness—worry over loss) Alpha = .48						
I don't particularly get upset when I lose things. * (P)	−.302	.164	.202	.602	−.003	−.167
I don't like to have anyone in my home when I'm not there. (P)	.176	−.030	−.064	.548	.287	−.033
I get very upset if something is stolen from me, even if it has little monetary value. (P)	.039	.113	.129	.538	−.248	.313
I worry about people taking my possessions. (NG)	.258	.148	−.024	.511	.055	.264
I am less likely than most people to lock things up. * (P)	.205	−.102	−.186	.494	.071	−.098
Factor 5 (Nongenerosity—siege mentality) Alpha = .39						
I do not enjoy donating things to the needy. (NG)	.054	.017	.048	.040	.666	.051
I don't seem to get what is coming to me. (E)	−.081	.273	−.012	−.025	.561	.356
I enjoy having people I like stay in my home. * (NG)	.343	−.097	−.101	−.018	.499	−.169
Factor 6 (Envy—jealousy) Alpha = .32						
People who are very wealthy often feel they are too good to talk to average people. (E)	.042	−.065	.016	−.018	.164	.768
I am bothered when I see people who buy anything they want. (E)	.086	.451	.021	.085	−.152	.485

* Reverse scored items.
(NG) Original Nongenerosity Subscale Item; (E) Original Envy Subscale Item
(P) Original Possessiveness Subscale Item; (Pr) Original Preservation Subscale Item

---

materialism, is a theoretical construct (Bagozzi 1984). The Belk scale, however, is a doubly indirect measure. Not only does it indirectly assess four personality traits, but the scale is built on the assumption that people with these traits are more inclined to be materialistic. Thus, the Belk scale is an indirect measure of the construct itself and employs indirect measures of personality traits in the process.

Perhaps more importantly, the scale is not true to Belk's own definition of materialism—that at the highest levels of materialism, "possessions assume a central place in a person's life and are believed to provide the greatest sources of satisfaction and dissatisfaction" (Belk 1984, p. 291). While centrality of goods is implied by the personality measures, deriving happiness and satisfaction from goods are not. The scale focuses on whether there is a personality type that is more prone to materialism and concludes that people who are less generous, who are envious of others' possessions and possessive of their own, are materialistic. How-

ever, an envious person would not necessarily be a materialist, for one can envy "things" other than material possessions. Neither would a selfish person necessarily be materialistic. Further, the scale provides no means for assessing the role of possessions in one's life, which is what Belk's definition of materialism would seem to require. These concerns suggest two conclusions. First, to paraphrase Nunnally, the scale may need to be expanded to sample the entire domain of the materialism construct. Second, if personality traits are insufficient to measure materialism, then the idea that materialism is a manifestation of personality may need to be altered. The value conceptualization of Richins and Dawson suggests one alternative.

Materialism or Individualism?
The scale may be objected to on other, equally compelling grounds. Several scale items seem to be measures of individualism not materialism. In a cross-cultural study of individualism and

collectivism, Triandis et al. (1988) sought to develop an operational definition of individualism which was appropriate for the United States. Several of their findings are relevant here.

One of their primary determinations was that, paradoxically, people living in an individualistic culture, such as the U.S., had to be more attuned to the attitudes and behaviors of others. In collectivist cultures one is "born" a member of various ingroups, and need not work as hard at becoming accepted. A person in an individualist culture, on the other hand, generally is not born with many ingroup memberships and must become accepted into and retain ingroup membership. Further, because of the almost a priori ingroup acceptance in collectivist cultures, people have close ingroup relationships. In individualist cultures, on the other hand, the distance between the individual and ingroup is much greater. Finally, in collectivist cultures, ingroups may compete with outgroups, but people compete as ingroup members and not as individuals. In individualistic cultures, however, individuals compete with each other.

Three consequences relevant to the Belk materialism scale emerge from these ideas. First, in collectivist cultures individuals take pride in the achievements and successes of other ingroup members. In individualistic cultures, personal achievement and success as a result of competition with other individuals is prized. Second, in collectivist cultures not only are honor and success shared, but resources such as money, may be also. In fact, one way that Triandis et al. (1988) measure concern for an ingroup was with a "lending money to ingroup members" scenario. The third consequence is a repeat of the fact that in individualist cultures people often are emotionally detached from ingroups. The implication for the Belk scale is that all but three of the nongenerosity subscale items and one of the envy subscale items measure characteristics which would be expected of someone living in an individualist culture. Statements about sharing possessions and lending them to friends, about having people stay at one's home, about friends doing well, and about buying for oneself instead of a loved one, all seem to measure an individualistic orientation.

If these items are removed from the nongenerosity subscale, only three measures remain: two which address donating things to charity and one item which expresses concern over people taking one's possessions. None of these necessarily is connected to materialism. The charity items may be related more to measures of income, social class, or religion. Concern over theft of possessions may be related to where one lives and perceptions of the crime rate in society. Of course, these same concerns might be addressed to all the possessiveness subscale items which deal with loss of possessions.

These concerns raises the question of construct validity, specifically discriminant validity. What is being measured, individualism or materialism? Recent criticism of the individualism/collectivism model (c.f. Schwartz 1990) has suggested that focusing on the dichotomy has prevented investigation of the variations within individualism and within collectivism. While it may be that materialism offers one way to investigate differences among types of individualism, the current version of the scale would not seem sufficient to the task.

Limitations, Conclusions, and Future Research

Decisions about scale items and about the appropriate factor structure for the Belk scale, of course, cannot be based solely on the results of one study. Additional testing with adult samples is required. The results here, however, are consistent with the studies noted above which also reported reliability problems with the Belk scale. Thus, one conclusion is that, from the evidence in this study,

the new Belk scale has not resolved the reliability issue, at least for domestic research.

In terms of validity, this study advances the assessment of the scale by suggesting that some of the items measure individualism instead of materialism. Additional questions about the separation of the envy and nongenerosity traits have been raised. Finally, the scale itself is questioned because some concepts inherent in the definition of materialism (such as satisfaction in life) are not assessed by the scale.

If these issues can be resolved, then studies which address the validity of the scale by building the nomological network of associations between materialism and other consumer attitudes and behaviors is warranted.

REFERENCES

Bagozzi, Richard P. (1984), "A Prospectus for Theory Construction in Marketing," *Journal of Marketing*, 48 (Winter), 11 – 29.

Belk, Russell W. (1983), "Worldly Possessions: Issues and Criticisms," in *Advances in Consumer Research*, eds. R. P. Bagozzi and A. M. Tybout, Vol. 10, Ann Arbor, MI: Association for Consumer Research, 514-519.

_____(1984), "Three Scales to Measure Constructs of Materialism: Reliability, Validity, and Relationship to Measures of Happiness," in *Advances in Consumer Research*, ed. T. Kinnear, Vol. 11, Provo, UT: Association for Consumer Research, 291-297.

_____(1985), "Materialism: Trait Aspects of Living in the Material World," *Journal of Consumer Research*, 12 (December), 265 - 280.

_____(1987), "Material Values in the Comics: A Content Analysis of Comic Books Featuring Themes of Wealth," *Journal of Consumer Research*, 14 (June), 26-42.

Carlin, George (1981), "A Place for My Stuff," in *A Place for My Stuff!* , New York: Atlantic Recording Corp. (audio recording).

Churchill, Gilbert A., Jr. (1979), "Paradigm for Developing Better Measures of Marketing Constructs," *Journal of Marketing Research*, 16 (February), 64-73.

Cohen, Jacob (1988), *Statistical Power Analysis for the Behavioral Science*s (Second edition), New York: Academic Press.

Cole, Dennis, Newell D. Wright, M. Joseph Sirgy, R. Kosenko, Don Rahtz, and H. Lee Meadow (1992), "Testing the Reliability and Validity of Belk's and Richins' Materialism Scales," in *Developments in Marketing Science*, ed. V. L. Crittenden, Vol. 15, Coral Gables, FL: Academy of Marketing Science, 383-387.

Cote, Joseph A., Siew Meng Leong, and Jane Cote (1991), "Assessing the Influence of the Journal of Consumer Research," *Journal of Consumer Research*, 18 (December), 402 – 410.

Dawson, Scott and Gary Bamossy (1990), "Isolating the Effect of Non-Economic Factors on the Development of a Consumer Culture: A Comparison of Materialism in the Netherlands and the United States," in *Advances in Consumer Research*, eds. M. E. Goldberg, G. Gorn, and R. W. Pollay, Vol. 17, Provo, UT: Association for Consumer Research, 182 – 186.

Ellis, Seth R. (1992), "A Factor Analytic Investigation of Belk's Structure of the Materialism Construct," in *Advances in Consumer Research*, ed. Vol. 19, Provo, UT: Association for Consumer Research, 688 – 695.

Ger, Güliz and Russell W. Belk (1990), "Measuring and Comparing Materialism Cross-Culturally," in *Advances in Consumer Research*, eds. M. E. Goldberg, G. Gorn, and R. W. Pollay, Vol. 17, Provo, UT: Association for Consumer Research, 186–192.

_____and Russell W. Belk (1993), "Cross–Cultural Differences in Materialism," Working Paper , David Eccles School of Business, University of Utah, Salt Lake City, Utah 84112.

Hendrickson, Anthony and Hubert Morrisette (1992), "A Psychographic Approach to Materialism," in *Meaning, Measure and Morality of Materialism*, eds. F. W. Rudmin and M. Richins, Provo, UT: Association for Consumer Research, 128 – 139.

Horowitz, Daniel (1985), *Morality of Spending: Attitudes Toward the Consumer Society in America, 1875 – 1940*, Baltimore: Johns Hopkins University Press.

Hunt, James M., Jerome B. Kernan, Anindya Chatterjee, and Renee A. Florsheim (1990), "Locus of Control as a Personality Correlate of Materialism: An Empirical Note," *Psychological Reports*, 67, 1101 – 1102.

Kaiser, H. F. (1974), "An Index of Factorial Simplicity," *Psychometrika*, 39, 31 – 36.

McCracken, Grant (1988), *Culture and Consumption*, Bloomington, IN: Indiana University Press.

Mason, Roger S. (1981), *Conspicuous Consumption: A Study of Exceptional Consumer Behavior*, New York: St. Martin's Press.

Nava, Mica (1992), *Changing Cultures: Feminism, Youth and Consumerism*, London: Sage.

Norusis, Marija J. (1990), *SPSS Advanced Statistics Student Guide*, Chicago: IL.

Nunnally, Jum C. (1978), *Psychometric Theory*, New York: McGraw Hill.

Othman, Md. Nor (1988), *Materialism: Its Relationship to Some Selected Aspects of Consumer Behavior*, doctoral dissertation, Oklahoma State University.

Richins, Marsha L. and Scott Dawson (1990), "Measuring Material Values: A Preliminary Report of Scale Development," in *Advances in Consumer Research*, eds. M. E. Goldberg, G. J. Gorn, and R. W. Pollay, Vol. 17, Provo, UT: Association for Consumer Research, 169 – 175.

_____and Scott Dawson (1992), "A Consumer Values Orientation for Materialism and its Measurement: Scale Development and Validation," *Journal of Consumer Research*, 19 (December), 303 – 316.

Rudmin, Floyd W. (1988), *Ownership as Interpersonal Dominance: A History and Three Studies of the Social Psychology of Property*, Queen's University, Kingston, Ontario, Canada.

_____and Marsha Richins (1992), "Forward," in *Meaning, Measure, and Morality of Materialism*, eds. F. Rudmin and M. Richins, Provo, UT: Association for Consumer Research, ii.

Schoeck, Helmut (1966), *Envy: A Theory of Social Behavior*, trans. Michael Glennyard and Betty Ross, New York: Harcourt, Brace and World.

Schwartz, Shalom H. (1990), Individualism–Collectivism: Critique and Proposed Refinements, *Journal of Cross–Cultural Psychology*, 21 (2), 139 – 157.

Tabachnick, Barbara and Linda S. Fidell (1989), *Using Multivariate Statistics*, Second Edition, New York: Harper & Row, Publishers.

Triandis, Harry C., Robert Bontempo, M. J. Villareal, M. Asai, and N. Lucca (1988), "Individualism and Collectivism: Cross-Cultural Perspectives on Self-Ingroup Relationships," *Journal of Personality and Social Psychology*, 54 (February), 323 – 338.

Wallendorf, Melanie and Eric J. Arnould (1988), "My Favorite Things: A Cross-Cultural Inquiry into Object Attachment, Possessiveness, and Social Linkage," *Journal of Consumer Research*, 14, 531 – 547.

An Examination of Individual and Object-Specific Influences on the Extended Self and its Relation to Attachment and Satisfaction

Eugene Sivadas, University of Cincinnati
Ravi Venkatesh, University of Cincinnati

ABSTRACT

The extended self construct has been primarily examined in the post-positivist research tradition to study the relation between consumers possessions and their sense of self. We study this construct using "positivist" tools in order to foster critical pluralism within our field. We extend current research by examining whether individuals for whom possessions in general comprise the self to a greater degree are more likely to incorporate specific possessions in the extended self. We also examine the relation between object incorporation in the extended self and object attachment, and object incorporation and satisfaction in order to better specify the domain of the construct.

INTRODUCTION

Consumer researchers have not paid sufficient attention to post-consumption experiences (Wells 1993). Belk (1988, p. 139) suggests that "we cannot hope to understand consumer behavior without first gaining some understanding of the meanings that consumers attach to possessions." Belk's extended self construct examines the relation between consumers' possessions and their sense of self (Belk 1987; 1988;1990; 1991; 1992; Dawson and Bamossy 1991; Hirschman 1994; Mick and DeMoss 1990; Sanders 1990; Schultz, Kleine, and Kernan 1989; Sivadas and Machleit 1994).

The extended self consists of self plus possessions and is that part of self-identity which is defined by possessions including gifts, money, body-parts, monuments, and places (Belk 1988). The extended self construct builds upon the idea that consumers prefer products that are "congruent" with their selves (Belk 1988; Kleine, Kleine, and Kernan 1993; Sirgy 1982). The self provides a "sense of who and what we are" and possessions help support our sense of self because to a great extent we are what we have and possess (Belk 1988; James 1890; Kleine, Kleine, and Kernan 1993; Tuan 1980). The extended self construct has been developed and examined primarily from the post-positivist research tradition. The construct came in for criticism from Cohen (1989) and Solomon (1990) who suggested that it was not well-defined theoretically or operationally.

Cohen's primary concern was that the extended self construct did not adequately distinguish between possessions that were important to an individual and those that were part of the individual's extended self. Belk (1989) responded to these criticisms by providing some examples of how possessions that were important to him (e.g., the Nazi flag) were not part of his (Belk's) extended self. Belk (1989) further suggested that much of Cohen's (1989) criticisms emanated from a positivist point of view.

Recently, scholars have pointed to the need to bring about a rapprochement between what some see as a paradigmatic division within our field (Hunt 1991). Sivadas and Machleit (1994) developed a scale to measure the extent of possession incorporation in the extended self. They found strong support for Belk's (1988; 1989) assertion that possessions that were part of the extended self were empirically distinct from possessions that were important to the individual.

Belk (1989) reminds us that the extended self construct can be useful in both positivist and post-positivist research. Following Belk (1987) and Sivadas and Machleit (1994) we examine the extended self construct from a positivist standpoint, however we believe that our findings will be useful to researchers subscribing to either paradigm.

Our purpose is twofold. First, we examine to what degree is incorporation of possessions in the extended self an individual trait and to what degree is it the function of the possession being examined. Prior studies on the extended self have examined whether a particular possession or possessions are part of an individual's extended self (e.g., Belk 1990; Sanders 1990; Hirschman 1994). However, hardly any attention has been paid to whether some consumers are more likely to derive their identities from possessions than other consumers. Csikszentmihalyi and Rochberg-Halton (1981) have noted individual differences in importance attached to various possessions based on variables like age with older adults being more past-oriented. Culture has also been identified as influencing the role of possessions in "constructing and preserving identity" because the nature of the self varies across cultures (e.g., Belk 1984b; Mehta and Belk 1991).

However, individual variations in the incorporation of possessions in the extended self within the same age and cultural group has not been studied. Recent work on materialism suggests that materialism is an individual trait (Richins and Dawson 1992). We propose that the importance attached to possessions in providing a sense of self will vary across individuals and that individuals for whom possessions are important in general, will be more likely to incorporate a specific possession in their extended self.

We propose the following hypothesis,

H_1: The greater the extent to which possessions in general are part of an individual's extended self the more likely is the individual to incorporate any specific possession in his/her extended self.

Secondly, we empirically examine how the extended self is related to two constructs i.e., attachment, and satisfaction. The objective of doing so is to better specify the domain of this construct. As indicated earlier, the extended self construct has come in for criticism for being an all encompassing construct. For example, Solomon (1990, p. 68) commented "we run the risk of overextending the (extended self) construct and in so doing obviating its usefulness."

THE EXTENDED SELF AND ATTACHMENT

Attachment and extended self are treated as separate constructs in the literature (e.g., Ball and Tasaki 1992; Schultz, Kleine, and Kernan 1989). However, the boundaries of both these constructs remain unclear. In his criticism of the extended self construct, Cohen (1989, p. 126) inquired whether a "high degree" of attachment to a possession made it "self-defining." Belk (1989; 1992) responded by suggesting that attachment was implicated in the extended self construct. Attachment has been defined as the "degree of linkage perceived by an individual between him/her self and a particular possession" (Schultz, Kleine, and Kernan 1989, p. 360). Ball and Tasaki (1992, p. 158) offer another definition of attachment. They define attachment as "the extent to which an

FIGURE 1
Extended Self, Attachment, and Satisfaction

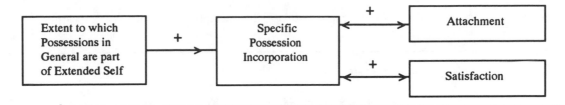

object which is owned, expected to be owned, or previously owned by an individual, is used by that individual to maintain his or her self-concept." Belk (1989), Schultz, Kleine, and Kernan (1989) and Sivadas and Machleit (1994) suggest that individuals are more likely to be attached to things that are part of their extended self.

The extended self refers to the "definition of self created by external objects with which one surrounds oneself" (Solomon 1994, p. 620). Cathecting objects into the self is a foundation for extended self and to some extent as Belk (1989) suggests, it appears that attachment is implicated in the extended self. However, keeping in mind the criticisms of Solomon (1990) and especially Cohen (1989, p. 126) who called the extended self construct "incredibly imprecise" and the fact that it is treated as a separate construct from attachment, it would be useful to empirically examine the boundaries of both these constructs. Also, in a cross-cultural study of favorite possessions, attachment has been successfully differentiated from the possessiveness component of materialism (Wallendorf and Arnould 1988).

Thus we posit that extended self and attachment are separate constructs, and consumers are more likely to be attached to possessions that are part of their extended self.

Therefore,

H_{2a}: Possession incorporation in the extended self is distinct from possession attachment.

H_{2b}: Possession attachment is positively correlated with possession incorporation in the extended self.

THE EXTENDED SELF AND SATISFACTION

Belk (1988) suggests that the extended self construct may provide a deeper understanding of consumption behavior than what is evidenced by merely looking at the satisfaction or dissatisfaction of consumers with products. Satisfaction or dissatisfaction is determined by the "overall feelings, or attitude, a person has about a product after it has been purchased" (Solomon 1990, p. 346). We examine the relationship between the degree of possession incorporation in the extended self and satisfaction of consumers with those very same possessions.

The following hypotheses are proposed,

H_{3a}: Possession incorporation in the extended self is distinct from satisfaction with possessions.

H_{3b}: Satisfaction with a possession is positively correlated with possession incorporation in the extended self.

Figure 1 provides a schematic representation of the relationship among the constructs being studied here.

METHOD

Procedure

Respondents were asked to complete a questionnaire consisting of various measures described in the next section. The four possessions used to measure the extent of possession incorporation in the extended self, attachment, and satisfaction were identified prior to the main study by asking 34 marketing undergraduates to list out their two most favorite possessions and two least favorite possessions. The possessions identified by most subjects as their most favorite were their car, music system, and pet. The extended self literature also suggests that these possessions are likely to form part of the extended self (Belk 1988, 1991; Hirschman 1994). The least favorite possession identified by the subjects showed considerable idiosyncratic variation. Hence, in the main study subjects were first asked to list their least favorite possession and then complete the three measures for their least favorite possession.

One hundred fifty-two undergraduate students at two large midwestern universities participated in the study, most for extra course credit. If a particular possession did not apply to them, for example if they did not own a pet, they were asked to skip that section. The order of presentation of the general scale was varied to control for possible order effects.

Measurement

The General Scale. Sivadas and Machleit (1994) have reported a scale development exercise for a measure to determine the extent of possession incorporation in the extended self. They first developed a generally phrased scale to determine the extent to which possessions in general comprise the self. They had then modified that scale to determine if a specific possession was incorporated in the extended self. The items were "The things I own help me achieve the identity I would like to have," "What I buy helps me narrow the gap between what I am and what I would like to be," "My possessions are part of what I am," "The things I own are central to my identity," "When something is stolen from me I feel as if my identity has been snatched from me," and "I derive some of my identity from the things I own." The fit values were evaluated using standard LISREL fit criteria. Consistent with Sivadas and Machleit, the fit values, except for the chi-squared which is significant, are acceptable (GFI=.88, AGFI=.72 and RMSR=.05) and the reliability is high (.899) leading us to conclude that the six-item measure is unidimensional, internally consistent, and reliable.

Possession Incorporation in the Extended Self. Specific-possession incorporation for the four possessions mentioned earlier i.e., car, music system, pet, and least favorite possession was measured using Sivadas and Machleit's (1994) six-item seven point likert-type scale. The items measuring possession incorporation in

TABLE 1
Confirmatory Factor Analyses Results

	Chi-Square	GFI	AGFI	RMSR	Coeff. Alpha
Possession Incorporation in the Extended Self					
Car	74.94, 9 d.f., p=.000	.87	.70	.048	.92
Music System	151.88, 9 d.f., p=.000	.77	.46	.065	.93
Pet	33.77, 9 d.f., p=.000	.88	.72	.026	.88
Least Favorite Possession	61.91, 9 d.f., p=.000	.87	.70	.052	.90
Possession Attachment					
Car	4.62, 2 d.f., p=.099	.98	.92	.028	.84
Music System	0.53, 2 d.f., p=.768	.99	.99	.014	.75
Pet	4.29, 2 d.f., p=.117	.98	.90	.023	.87
Least Favorite Possession	11.41, 2 d.f., p=.003	.98	.88	.076	.53

the extended self are phrased as follows: "My _____ helps me achieve the identity I want to have," "My _____ helps me narrow the gap between what I am and what I try to be," "My _____ is central to my identity," "My _____ is part of who I am," "If my _____ is stolen from me I will feel as if my identity has been snatched from me," and "I derive some of my identity from my _____." Sivadas and Machleit (1994) view this measure as an "alternate and not substitute" for the more time-consuming and cumbersome card-sorting procedure used by Belk (1987). The fit values are reported in Table 1 and given the acceptable fit and high reliabilities we conclude that the measure is unidimensional, internally consistent, and reliable.

Satisfaction. Satisfaction with possessions was assessed using Crosby and Stephens (1987) three-item seven point semantic differential scale. The satisfaction scale comprised of three semantic differential format items: satisfied/dissatisfied, pleased/displeased, and favorable/unfavorable. Since this was a three-item measure it was not possible to meaningfully evaluate the fit values from LISREL VI for this measure. However, the maximum likelihood factor loadings are significant and the measure is highly reliable (car=.95, music system=.96, pet=.95, and least favorite possession=.91).

Attachment. Schultz, Kleine, and Kernan (1989) suggest that attachment is a multidimensional concept which is made up of three fundamental dimensions "individuation, integration, and temporal orientation." Attachment was measured using the 3 attachment items used by Sivadas and Machleit (1994) plus 1 additional item was taken from Schultz's (1989) unpublished dissertation. These items were: "I have no feelings for my _____" (reverse coded), "I am emotionally attached to my _____," and "I am sentimental about my _____," and "My _____ reminds me of memories and experiences." The fit values reported in Table 1 are excellent and the measure appears to be unidimensional, and internally consistent.

Reliability values are high for car, music system, and pet but below acceptable levels for the least favorite possession. This measure thus appears to serve our purpose of examining whether the possession incorporation in the extended self is distinct from possession attachment, however researchers interested in gaining a deeper, more complete understanding of attachment may consider developing alternate measures of possession attachment.

RESULTS

Discriminant Validity

General Scale versus Possession-Specific Scale. We first examine whether individuals who in general derive greater identity from their possessions are more likely to incorporate specific possessions into their extended self. We assess the discriminant validity of the general scale with the possession incorporation in the extended self scale using the criterion set forth by Dillon and Goldstein (1984) and Fornell and Larcker (1981). First, as can be seen from Table 2, the average variance extracted is greater than the .50 rule of thumb which indicates that the variance in the measure accounted for by the construct exceeds that due to measurement error. These values are greater than the squared structural link between the general and possession specific measures in all four cases. This implies that the measures have more variance that is unique than common. This establishes discriminant validity between the two measures.

Having established the discriminant validity of the two measures we now test the hypothesis presented earlier that the greater the extent to which possessions in general are part of an individual's extended self the more likely is the individual to incorporate any specific possession in his/her extended self. Table 3 reports means of the extent to which each possession in our study was incorporated in the extended self.

TABLE 2
Discriminant Validity Assessment: Possession Incorporation Measure and Scale Measuring Degree to Which Possessions Comprise the Self

	Average Variance Extracted		Squared Structural Link
	Extended Self General Scale	Possession Incorporation in Extended Self	General/ Possession Incorporation
Car	.62	.68	.28
Music System	.60	.71	.31
Pet	.61	.79	.35
Least Favorite Possession	.58	.62	.06

TABLE 3
Mean Extent of Possession Incorporation in the Extended Self

	Means*	Std. Dev
Car	20.45	8.78
Music System	19.14	9.08
Pet	24.47	10.63
Least Favorite Possession	12.93	6.71

* Scores can range from 6 to 42, where a score of 42 indicates maximal incorporation in the extended self.

Linear regression models with possession incorporation as the dependent variable and scores on the extent to which possessions in general comprise an individual's self as the independent variable were employed to test this hypothesis that the greater the extent to which possessions in general comprise the self the more likely will it be for an individual to incorporate a specific possession in his/her extended self. This hypothesis was supported for car, music system, and pet at the .001 level (see Table 4). As can be inferred from the table, a substantial portion of the variance is explained by the extent to which possessions in general comprise an individual's self except in the case of least favorite possession.

Least Favorite Possession. Since prior work on the extended self has focused on most favorite possessions we decided to further explore the relation between the least favorite possession and sense of self. Scores on the extent to which possessions in general comprise an individual's self can range from 6 (indicating minimal contribution of possessions to providing sense of self) to 42 (indicating maximal contribution of possessions to providing a sense of self). In our study the scores of respondents ranged from the minimum possible score of 6 to 40. We performed a median split of the scores (median=28) and classified subjects into two groups:

those for whom possessions were very important in providing a sense of self and those for whom possessions in general are not very important in providing a sense of self.

Regression analysis with least favorite possession as the dependent variable indicated that the least favorite possession was less likely to be valued by consumers for whom possessions in general were important to their sense of self (b=-.085) than by consumers for whom possessions were not that important to their sense of self (b=.281). We interpret these findings as consistent with our theorizing that if possessions in general comprise the extended self to a greater degree then just as the most favorite possessions are valued more by people for whom possessions comprise the self to a greater degree, least favorite possessions should be valued less by these individuals as compared to individuals for whom possessions in general are less a part of their extended self.

Possession Incorporation and Attachment. Next, we examine the relation between possession incorporation in the extended self and possession attachment. The assessment of discriminant validity between possession incorporation in the extended self and possession attachment is presented below in Table 5. Our hypoth-

TABLE 4
Predicting Possession Incorporation in the Extended Self

	b	R-squared
Car	.52*	.27
Music System	.53*	.28
Pet	.56*	.31
Least Favorite Possession	.23**	.05

* Results are significant at .001.
** Result is significant at .01.

TABLE 5
Discriminant Validity Assessment: Possession Incorporation and Attachment

	Average Variance Extracted		Squared Structural Link
	Possession Attachment	Possession Incorporation in Extended Self	Attachment/ Possession Incorporation
Car	.59	.68	.60
Music System	.53	.71	.81
Pet	.68	.79	.36
Least Favorite Possession	.37	.62	.66

esis that attachment and possession incorporation are empirically distinct is supported only for pet but we do not have evidence for discriminant validity between possession attachment and possession incorporation in the extended self for car, music system, and least favorite possession.

We next test H2b, i.e., the more attached a consumer is to a possession the more that possession will be a part of the consumer's extended self. A correlational analysis was performed between attachment and possession incorporation in the extended self. The hypothesis was supported for all four possessions: car (r=.68; p=.000), music system (r=.76; p=.000), pet (r=.62; p=.000) and least favorite possession (r=.60; p=.000).

Possession Incorporation and Satisfaction. Table 6 shows the results of discriminant validity assessment between possessions incorporated in the extended self and satisfaction with possessions. Our hypothesis that incorporating possessions into the extended self is distinct from being satisfied with those possessions is supported for all four possessions considered in the study. We also find support for our hypothesis that consumers are more likely to be satisfied with possessions that are part of their extended self. This hypothesis was also supported for all four possessions: car (r=.52;

p=.000), music system (r=.52; p=.000), pet (r=.55; p=.000), and least favorite possession (r=.23; p=.003).

DISCUSSION AND CONCLUSION

Research on the extended self has examined whether specific possessions comprise the self. Our study extends this stream of research by suggesting that some individuals are more likely to incorporate possessions into the extended self than other individuals. This in turn impacts upon the degree to which individual possessions are incorporated into the self. A central research question that begs further empirical examination is why do individuals incorporate possessions into the extended self and why are some individuals more likely to do so than others.

Belk (1988) has suggested that the extended self construct may provide a deeper understanding of the consumption experience than what would be indicated by merely looking at consumers satisfaction with their possessions. Our study indicates that consumers are more likely to be satisfied with possessions that are part of their extended self. The relationship between satisfaction and self-extension merits further examination and theoretical development. For many consumption activities managers could go beyond look-

TABLE 6
Discriminant Validity Assessment: Possession Incorporation and Satisfaction

	Average Variance Extracted		Squared Structural Link
	Satisfaction	Possession Incorporation in Extended Self	Satisfaction/ Possession Incorporation
Car	.87	.68	.22
Music System	.90	.71	.12
Pet	.89	.79	.26
Least Favorite Possession	.79	.62	.10

ing at satisfaction of their consumers and see if their particular product or service is incorporated in the consumer's self. Ties of consumers with possessions that are part of their extended self may be more enduring than their ties with possessions with which they may be merely satisfied. For example, some consumers may be satisfied with the brands they are currently purchasing but for others consumers that brand may be part of their extended self. It is quite likely that consumers who incorporate a particular brand into their extended self may be more likely to stay loyal.

A potentially important stream of research would be the study of how do consumers form relationships with their possessions. The study of relationships i.e., relationship marketing is attracting increasing attention from marketing scholars. Most of the research within this stream has examined interorganizational relationships (e.g., Dwyer, Schurr, and Oh 1987). The relationships formed by individual consumers with companies and brands by being loyal to certain products or brands deserves closer examination. The extended self literature suggests that consumers cathect specific branded objects and not brands in general. There is thus a distinction between "my Toyota" and Toyotas in general. A greater understanding and empirical examination of this link may advance our understanding of constructs like brand loyalty and satisfaction.

The extended self literature looks at the positive contributions made to our individual identities by our possessions whereas the materialism literature has tended to focus on the negative consequences of drawing sustenance from possessions. For example, one stream of research within the materialism literature suggests that the "desire to possess and consume stems from insecurities or deeper dissatisfactions with one's self and one's life" (Richins and Dawson 1992, p. 313). Though we did not look at satisfaction with life in general, an interesting research question would be to compare the relationship of the extended self and materialism constructs. The extended self scale tested here makes such assessment possible.

We were not successful in discriminating between possession attachment and possession incorporation in the extended self except for pets. Here we must acknowledge that the measure of attachment we employed may have its limitations since it may not have done an adequate job of tapping into the domain of the attachment construct. Further research needs to be directed at studying the "boundaries" of both these constructs.

The extended self has primarily been examined by postpositivist researchers. Our study points to the contribution that positivist methods can make to this stream of research as well as the usefulness of the extended self construct in positivist research.

REFERENCES

Anderson, James C. and David W. Gerbing (1988), "Structural Equation Modeling in Practice: A Review and Recommended Two-Step Approach," *Psychological Bulletin*, 103(3), 411-423.

Ball, A. Dwayne and Lori H. Tasaki (1992), "The Role and Measurement of Attachment in Consumer Behavior," *Journal of Consumer Psychology*, 1(2), 155-172.

Belk, Russell W. (1984a), "Three Scales To Measure Construct Related to Materialism: Reliability, Validity, And Relationships To Measures of Happiness" in *Advances in Consumer Research*, Thomas C. Kinnear ed. Ann Arbor, MI: Association for Consumer Research, p. 291-297.

_____ (1984b), "Cultural and Historical Differences in the Concept of Self and Their Effects on Attitudes toward Having and Giving," in *Advances in Consumer Research*, Vol. 11, Thomas C. Kinnear ed. Ann Arbor, MI: Association for Consumer Research.

_____ (1987), "Identity and the Relevance of Market, Personal, and Community Possessions," in *Marketing and Semiotics:New Directions in the Study of Signs for Sale*, Jean Umiker-Sebeok, ed. Berlin, Germany: Mouton De Gruyter, 151-164.

_____ (1988), "Possessions and the Extended Self," *Journal of Consumer Research*, 15 (September), 139-168.

_____ (1989), "Extended Self and Extending Paradigmatic Perspective," *Journal of Consumer Research*, 16 (June), 129 132.

_____ (1990), "The Role of Possessions in Constructing and Maintaining A Sense of Past," in *Advances in Consumer Research*, Vol. 17, Marvin E. Goldberg, Gerald Gorn and Richard W. Pollay, eds. Provo, UT: Association for Consumer Research, 669-676.

_____ (1991), "The Ineluctable Mysteries of Possessions," *Journal of Social Behavior and Personality*, Vol. 6 (6), 17-55.

_____ (1992), "Attachment to Possessions," in *Place Attachment*, Irwin Altman and Setha M. Low, eds. New York: Plenum Press, 37-62.

Churchill, Gilbert A. Jr., and J. Paul Peter (1984), "Research Design Effects on the Reliability of Rating Scales: A Meta-Analysis," *Journal of Marketing Research*, 21 (November), 360-375.

Cohen, Joel B. (1989), "An Over-Extended Self," *Journal of Consumer Research*, 16 (June), 125-128.

Crosby, Lawrence A. and Nancy Stephens (1987), "Effects of Relationship Marketing on Satisfaction, Retention, and Prices in the Life Insurance Industry," *Journal of Marketing Research*, 24 (November), 404-411.

Csikszentmihalyi, Mihaly and Eugene Rochberg-Halton (1981), *The Meaning of Things: Domestic Symbols and the Self*, London: Cambridge University Press.

Dawson, Scott and Gary Bamossy (1991), "If "we are what we have," what are we when we don't have? An exploratory study of materialism among expatriate Americans," *Journal of Social Behavior and Personality*, Vol. 6 (6), 17-55.

Dillon, William R. and Matthew Goldstein (1984), *Multivariate Analysis: Methods and Applications*, New York: John Wiley & Sons, Inc.

Dwyer, F. Robert., Paul H. Schurr, and Sejo Oh (1987), "Developing Buyer-Seller Relationships," *Journal of Marketing*, 51 (April), 11-27.

Fornell, Claes and David F. Larcker (1981), "Evaluating Structural Equation Models with Unobservable Variables and Measurement Error," *Journal of Marketing Research*, 18 (February), 39-50.

Gerbing, David W. and James C. Anderson (1988), "An Updated Paradigm for Scale Development Incorporating Unidimensionality and Its Assessment," *Journal of Marketing Research*, 25 (May), 186-192.

Hirschman, Elizabeth C. (1994), "Consumers and Their Animal Companions," *Journal of Consumer Research*, 20 (March), 616-632.

Hunt, Shelby D. (1991), "Positivism and Paradigm Dominance in Consumer Research: Toward Critical Pluralism and Rapprochement," *Journal of Consumer Research*, 18 (June), 32-44.

James, William (1890), *The Principles of Psychology*, Vol.1, New York: Henry Holt.

Kleine, Robert E. III, Susan Schultz Kleine, and Jerome B. Kernan (1993), "Mundane Consumption and the Self: A Social-Identity Perspective," *Journal of Consumer Psychology*, 2(3), 209-235.

Mehta, Raj and Russell W. Belk (1991), "Artifacts, Identity, and Transition: Favorite Possessions of Indians and Indian Immigrants to the United States," *Journal of Consumer Research*, 17 (March), 398-411.

Mick, David Glen and Michelle DeMoss (1990), "To Me From Me: A Descriptive Phenomenology of Self-Gifts," in *Advances in Consumer Research*, Vol. 17, Marvin E. Goldberg, Gerald Gorn and Richard W. Pollay, eds. Provo, UT: Association for Consumer Research, 677-682.

Peter, J. Paul and Gilbert A. Churchill, Jr. (1986), "Relationships Among Research Design Choices and Psychometric Properties of Rating Scales: A Meta-Analysis," *Journal of Marketing Research*, 23 (February), 1-10.

Richins, Marsha L. and Scott Dawson (1992), "A Consumer Values Orientation for Materialism and Its Measurement: Scale Development and Validation," *Journal of Consumer Research*, 19 (December), 303-316.

Sanders, Clinton R. (1990), "The Animal `Other': Self Definition, Social Identity and Companion Animals," in *Advances in Consumer Research*, Vol. 17, Marvin E. Goldberg, Gerald Gorn and Richard W. Pollay eds. Provo, UT: Association for Consumer Research, 662-668.

Schultz, Susan E. (1989), "An Empirical Investigation of Person-Material Possession Attachment," *Unpublished PhD Dissertation*, University of Cincinnati.

_____ , Robert E. Kleine, III, and Jerome B. Kernan (1989), "'These Are A Few of My Favorite Things': Towards an Explication of Attachment as a Consumer Behavior Construct," in *Advances in Consumer Research*, Vol. 16, Thomas Srull, ed. Provo, UT: Association for Consumer Research, 359-366.

Sirgy, M. Joseph (1982), "Self-Concept in Consumer Behavior: A Critical Review," *Journal of Consumer Research*, 9 (December), 287-300.

Sivadas, Eugene and Karen A. Machleit (1994), "A Scale to Determine the Extent of Object Incorporation in the Extended Self," in *Marketing Theory and Applications*, Vol. 5, C. Whan Park and Daniel C. Smith, ed. Chicago, IL: American Marketing Association.

Solomon, Michael R. (1990), "The Imperial Self," in *Advances in Consumer Research*, Vol. 17, Marvin E. Goldberg, Gerald Gorn and Richard W. Pollay, eds. Provo, UT: Association for Consumer Research, 68-70.

_____ (1994), *Consumer Behavior*, 2nd edition, Needham Heights, MA: Allyn and Bacon.

Tuan, Yi-Fu (1978), "The Significance of the Artifact," *Geographical Review*, 70(4), 462-472.

Wallendorf, Melanie and Eric J. Arnould (1988), ""My Favorite Things:' A Cross-Cultural Inquiry into Object Attachment, Possessiveness, and Social Linkage," *Journal of Consumer Research*, 14 (March), 531-547.

Wells, William D. (1993), "Discovery-oriented Consumer Research," *Journal of Consumer Research*, 19 (March), 489-504.

The Role of Possessions in Creating, Maintaining, and Preserving One's Identity: Variation Over the Life Course

Jim Gentry, University of Nebraska
Stacey Menzel Baker, University of Nebraska-Lincoln
Frederic B. Kraft, Wichita State University

ABSTRACT

To determine the meaning of possessions to one's identity, three stages of the life course are investigated. Specifically, the role and nature of possessions as individuals seek to create (during youth), to maintain (during the mainstream years), and to preserve (during the elderly years) identity over time is examined. Comparisons are made between the stages to exemplify the different roles that possessions play across the life course. Following a discussion of how facing death forces individuals to resolve their identity and how individuals use possessions to make these resolutions at different life stages, the paper concludes by suggesting that marketers be more sensitive to the meanings which people attach to their possessions.

Possessions play a role in creating, maintaining, and preserving the identity of individuals (cf. Dittmar 1992; Solomon 1983). Over time, individuals develop a set of symbols which they believe represent the self-identity that they want to project (Hirschman 1980) as these material possessions are a part of one's identity (cf. Ball and Tasaki 1992; Belk 1988; Csikszentmihalyi and Rochberg-Halton 1981).

The symbolic role which possessions play in giving meaning to life is not a new concept in consumer research. However, recognizing the role that possessions play in different stages of the life course warrants more attention. The stages of the life course have been referred to as our years of learning, our years of earning, and our years of yearning (for immortality) (Neal 1989). Within each of these stages, individuals "use" possessions to enhance or maintain a positive identity over time. The salience of possessions to identity may be most noticeable as one realizes that death is imminent. With this realization, the identity of an individual becomes very central to one in one's remaining time.

The objective of this paper is to investigate the importance of possessions in creating, maintaining, and preserving one's identity over the life course. Particular attention is given to the role which possessions play in helping individuals to prepare for death. The paper begins by examining the roles that possessions play in this process. Next, the role of possessions over three trajectories in the life cycle (youth, mainstream, and elderly) are examined. Although it is realized that this trichotomy is a gross-oversimplification of the life course, the obvious variations within stages will be touched upon. In each stage, the roles which possessions play in facing death are explored. Finally, the implications of this research to marketers are offered.

IDENTITY AND POSSESSIONS

Through introspection, individuals achieve an understanding of their identity. Thus, a person's identity is said to be a function of how a person is viewed by himself/herself. One's identity is determined by examining the categories one uses to explain who s/he is in relation to past experiences, to others, and to the future. Thus, an individual's identity consists of the "personal and social characteristics of people as understood by themselves and others" (Dittmar 1992, p. 73). These personal and social characteristics are often expressed, to one's self and to others, through material possessions.

Dittmar (1991) notes the function of possessions for identity ranges from their functional (instrumental) roles to their symbolic roles by imbuing the possession with meaning. In their functional roles, possessions give the user control over an experience. In contrast, in their symbolic roles, possessions symbolize and reflect personal characteristics as well as group affiliation.

James (1890) suggested that a person will become whatever s/he can call his/her own. Pavia (1993) offered another perspective noting that identity may not only be a function of what one owns, but it may also be a function of one's ability to generate [and protect] what one owns. This process may vary over the life course since Pavia's perspective was derived from a group of informants in life's mainstream who were dying of AIDS.

The core self is composed of the ideas, talents, opinions, dreams, purposes, and commitments which provide the resources for creating, maintaining, and preserving one's identity over the life course (Nerken 1993). It may be that during certain times in the life course individuals draw more heavily on some of these resources than they do at other times in their lives. For instance, the young may focus on ideas and dreams of the future, the mainstream on talents and purpose, and the elderly more on dreams of the past and a yearning for a place in the future (immortality). In this paper, it is asserted that the contribution of possessions to self-identity differs across age groups as people in different stages are forced to prepare for an end to life.

THE ROLE OF POSSESSIONS OVER THE LIFE COURSE

Csikszentmihalyi and Rochberg-Halton (1981, p. 91) point out, "things tell us who we are, not in words but by embodying our intentions. In our everyday traffic of existence, we can also learn about ourselves from objects, almost as much as from people." Consumers use products to symbolize their identity to others (cf. Solomon 1983) as well as to define who they are to themselves (cf. Belk 1988). When consumers interact with or think about their possessions, a sense of identity is created, maintained, or preserved.

Life course research focuses on (1) the idea of a journey from beginning (birth) to an ending (death), and (2) the idea of seasons, or stages in this cycle, in that in one's life, one moves through a series of relatively stable segments within the total cycle (Levinson 1978). Transitions and trajectories over time are major elements in life course research. In transitions, changes in the life course are examined which are discrete and bounded in duration, with possible long-term consequences. In contrast, trajectories are long-term patterns of stability and change, often including multiple transitions, that can be reliably differentiated from alternative patterns. Adelman (1992), Belk (1992), and Gentry, et al. (Forthcoming), among others, have investigated possessions and their disposition during role transitions. In this paper, the focus is upon the role and meaning of possessions during life trajectories. Although there are most likely more than three stages in the life course (e.g., Levinson 1978), for the sake of simplicity, three broad stages (youth, mainstream, and elderly) are examined here. Within each trajectory, the role of possessions differs. Each stage will be examined in more detail in the following sections.

Youth

Individuals go through a normal process of "identification" through which, as children, they acquire social roles by consciously and unconsciously copying the behavior of significant others (Mowen 1993, p. 777). Psychologists have long been aware of the roles which parental figures and other people play in shaping and developing the selves of young children. Marketers have recognized that possessions acquire meaning during the socialization process (cf. Solomon 1983). However, the information which objects relay to the young is an important, and often neglected, aspect of learning about the self.

Strictly speaking, the young are seeking their own identity and trying to "separate" from their parents and from their peers to some extent to become their "own person." For example, when adolescent boys use such "macho" products as cars, clothes, and cologne, these possessions may bolster their developing and fragile masculine self-concepts (Solomon 1983). As adolescents struggle to create their own self identity, they may seek to acquire certain possessions (Belk 1988). These possessions may be used to plan for the future and to reflect ability, control, and power.

Ball and Tasaki (1992, p. 158) examined the role of attachment ("the extent to which an object which is owned, expected to be owned, or previously owned by an individual, is used by that individual to maintain his or her self-concept") to possessions. The authors found that attachment to products was higher prior to purchase than after purchase for 15-24 year olds, while attachment increased after purchase for older groups. Thus, the young may be more likely to dream of possessions and what those possessions will allow them to do, whereas their elders have the possessions which allow them to do the things of which the youth dream.

Possessions which reflect ability and control may be more important to youths. In a study of a group of Chicago residents between the ages of 8 and 30, Csikszentmihalyi and Rochberg-Halton (1981) found that this generation is more likely than its grandparents to give as examples of favorite possessions those that reflect ability or skills (e.g., athletic equipment) or those that they can manipulate or control (e.g., musical instruments, stereos).

The young are limited in that they do not have the privileges (nor the responsibilities) that adults have. They may want to be older and want to have the power and privileges which they perceive adults to have. Products sought by youths are often symbols of the power perceived to be held by adults. For instance, money may be seen as a source of power (Belk 1988; Ozanne, Hill, and Wright 1994). One informant of Ozanne, Hill, and Wright (1994)[1] noted:

> Money to me is power. That's how I think, money gives me power. Money gives me the okay to do anything I want to do, stand on my own two feet.

The meaning of possessions to the young may differ depending upon their outlook for the future. Some youths do not understand what it means "to become," instead they focus on the present and satisfying themselves. For example, a student who drops out of high school a month before graduation obviously does not have a

strong future orientation. Some do not foresee a future, instead they just act for now. Ozanne, Hill, and Wright (1994) provide a glimpse of these contrasting time orientations, as Mormon missionaries sacrifice an immediate, more "comfortable" lifestyle, whereas juvenile delinquents seek immediate gratification, power, and control, in part because some of the juvenile delinquents have trouble imagining being alive in five years.

Mainstream

The identities of mainstream adults (approximately ages 25-60) lie primarily in their roles; their identity comes from what they *do* (e.g. work, parenting, volunteering). In this stage, "identity" is based upon roles played, rather than on potential roles (promise) as with youths or roles once played (past) as with elderly. One's identity is a function of doing, being, and having. Possessions are important, but things are used to show who you are and to demonstrate your ability to generate them. They represent the "work identity" more than other sources of identity. The term "work" here is used broadly to include those tasks which constitute much of the individual's "flow experiences" (Csikszentmihalyi 1975); besides salaried or otherwise compensated activities, the term may include child care and home maintenance activities.

The mainstream years may encompass multiple transitions, including the bachelor, young married, early nest, full nest, and empty nest stages of the family life cycle. While one's identity changes across these stages, identity may have relatively more of a "current role" rather than "future role" or "past role" emphasis. However, of course, there are different time orientations in this stage. Thus, the role of possessions during this stage does vary perhaps more than in the other stages. For example, Olson (1985) found that younger couples give special objects which reflect future plans more importance, whereas older couples find objects which reflect past experiences to be more important to them. As this example illustrates, the mainstream years are the most difficult to make generalizations about because there is a great amount of variation. However, one thing that is clear is that products are used to set the stage for social roles (Solomon 1983).

Elderly

As one ages, death becomes more of a reality. As family roles diminish (due in part to the great mobility of our society), as friends die, as work roles are given up, and as one's physical condition deteriorates (making volunteer work harder), identity suffers. Identity for the elderly is redefined after the transition from the workplace due to retirement and, as one reaches the old-old stage, after the adjustment to a limited mobility status. Gramlich (1974, p. 65) notes that aging subjects individuals to more and more loss: loved ones are lost, health is lost, cherished goals are unrecognized and lost, cherished occupation and sources of pride and value are lost in the progress of time. "Every individual requires the ongoing validation of his world, including crucially the validation of his identity and place in others....Again, in the broad sense, all the actions of the significant others and even their simple presence serve this sustaining function" (Berger and Kellner 1964, pp. 4-5). As friends and family move or die, identity diminishes.

Heisley, Cours, and Wallendorf (1993) and Unruh (1983) found that elderly view the intergenerational disposition of possessions as a means of creating some immortality for themselves and as a means of strengthening family ties. Both motives of disposition aid in the preservation of identity. Unruh (1983, p. 340) notes that, before they die, people interpret and apportion cues to their personal identities for those who will survive. They hope to be remembered, for example, as good fathers, competent women, successful businesspersons, creative artists, or peacemakers. "What is being

---

[1] The quotes in this paper taken from Ozanne, Hill, and Wright (1994) were used with the authors' permission.

preserved after death is a self-concept which existed during life, was acknowledged by others, and had become a significant aspect of the dead person's self."

Belk (1991b, p. 120) discusses an elderly informant who has 20 cardboard boxes of mementos which she has placed in storage. She refuses to discard them, because it would be like throwing her life away. She hopes these will mean something to her heirs when they go through her possessions after her death, and that they will finally appreciate what an interesting life she had.

Often the things which are most stable and which will always be there are possessions. Thus, possessions may serve as a source of comfort. This perspective is similar to that presented by McCracken (1988), who suggests that we displace our hopes and ideals into possessions and places of the past or future. These values are seen as too fragile, unsafe, and easily challenged if left in the present. The elderly see the good as residing in a golden age of the past. In contrast, youths and those in the mainstream of life see the good as residing in a future yet to come; they may believe their lives will be or are wondrously transformed once they get the car or home of their dreams (Belk 1991a). Not only do possessions remain while spouses and friends die, but possessions may be used to filter out the negative experiences of the past and stimulate only positive memories. For example, Belk (1991a, p. 30) discusses the manner in which family photos are constructed and the editing out of any unappealing results. "In doing so, we fashion our pasts as we would like to remember them—without sickness, anger, pain, or death."

CONSIDERATIONS OF ONE'S DEATH: IMPLICATIONS FOR THE MEANING OF POSSESSIONS

Death and one's identity just preceding death are discussed with the assumption that, just prior to death, an individual's identity becomes very central to him/her. The acknowledgment that death will occur adds insight to the topic of "identity;" given this, it is somewhat surprising that death has received little attention in the consumer research area. Gorer (1965) asserts that death has become taboo, and that in the twentieth century it has replaced sex as the principal forbidden subject. To the extent possible, we will consider the meaning of possessions to those for whom death seems imminent.

Unruh (1983) distinguishes two categories of death: (1) those who have a physical condition likely to lead to death in a short or predictable period of time; and (2) those not medically defined as dying, but who have acquired an awareness that life will end in the not-too-distant future. One aspect which separates the life stages is that the first category of death may soon occur in all three stages, while the second category is restricted mainly to the elderly.

A variety of sources are used to support the logic contained in this paper. Examples from Adelman (1992) and Pavia (1993) who interviewed informants in the former category, and Heisley, Cours, and Wallendorf (1993) who investigated the meaning of possessions for those in the latter category are examined. The authors also have interviewed survivors in grief (Gentry, et al. Forthcoming) or Hospice counselors interacting with dying and survivors; these accounts deal with the deceased's processes while they were in the former category. In addition, examples which illustrate the role of possessions for the identity of juvenile delinquents and Mormon missionaries (Ozanne, Hill, and Wright 1994) are offered.

Preparation for Death in the Youth Years

Death in the youth years is rarely anticipated. However, some children face an untimely death because of terminal illness, while others are aware of their mortality because of the increasing violence in society. Increasing numbers of children have experienced the loss of close friends or witnessed violent crimes at school or at home. When asked what it was like to grow up where he did, one of Ozanne, Hill, and Wright's (1994) juvenile delinquent informants noted that:

It was tiring. I guess you could say "Man I want to get out of here!" Like you look around and there was a situation. You figure out who you should be with. You gonna look around now and be like "Where's so and so?" "He's dead." What about so and so?" "He's dead too. He got shot in the head." Somethin' like that.

The growth in the importance of possessions to the self concept of youths as they mature is described by Furnham and Jones (1987). However, this does not seem to occur with terminally ill children who become less interested in typical childhood possessions as they comprehend the finality of their illness and begin to exhibit disengaging behaviors. Some items in which they retain interest serve as tools for acting out and understanding the process of death and dying, e.g., boxes use for burying dolls, crayons for drawing graves, etc. (Bluebond-Langer 1989).

The third author has observed the use of possessions as a comforting mechanism for these children. One regional Hospice organization provides small toy bears for children under its care. These serve as a source of comfort and perhaps even as a personal confidant to whom the children can express their fears and whom they may even believe might accompany them past the time of death.

Part of the maturation process is the development of the ability to delay gratification. Children tend to be very present-time oriented but, with maturation, gradually acquire more of a future-time orientation. The violence present in the lives of many teenagers may add uncertainty to the process, converting doubts about "what will happen" to doubt about "future existence." Thus, societal cancer intensifies the "want it now" orientation already present as an age-graded function.

These youths who fear dying may seek instant gratification of the self, because they may think that there really is no future to which to look forward. An informant of Ozanne, Hill, and Wright (1994) explained this:

Like I can't walk through a mall you know and be like "Oh, I want to get that. I get that next week with my paycheck." or I'll get that, you know, when I get the money." You know I want that, I want to get that right now! I got to get that!

When depressing situations are faced everyday, some youths may know or think that death is imminent and that there is no way out. Thus, they may turn to acquiring possessions through nontraditional methods (e.g., killing for running shoes) using nontraditional possessions (e.g., guns other than for sport), and fantasizing about nontraditional possessions. In one of his commentaries, Donald Kaul (1993) has this tragic story to relate:

Something's wrong.
Recently the Washington Post carried a piece about John Wilson, the chairman of the D.C. council, who died earlier this month......In one of his last speeches, he offered this chilling anecdote:
He was seething over the fact his car had been stolen from in front of his house when he overheard some neighborhood boys talking about "different kinds of metal and stuff...colors...crushed velvet."

"I thought they were talking about cars," Wilson told his audience, "so I went over to talk to them and I said: 'Tell me something. What's the best kind of car to buy that nobody wants to steal.'"

The line is vintage Wilson. The boys broke into laughter and said: "We're not talking about cars, we're talking about caskets, what kind of caskets we want to be buried in."

The two extreme youth segments examined in Ozanne, Hill, and Wright (1994) represent two different perspectives toward the meaning of possessions. For some youths, such as the young Mormon missionaries, possessions symbolize future potential and the ability "to become." For others, such as the juvenile delinquents or the neighborhood boys which Kaul (1993) discusses, possessions symbolize undelayed self-gratification largely in part because of their frequent exposre to violence.

Preparation for Death in the Mainstream Years

In general, those in the mainstream, like youths, do not consider their deaths; instead they focus on their lives now. However, should one face one's own death during the mainstream years, one grieves the roles that must be given up.

Pavia (1993) discusses the meaning of possessions to those whose identity had already been lost in part, due to being in the last stages of AIDS. She re-interpreted the phrase "we are what we own" to be "we are what we own, *because* we are the ability to generate what we own." Weakened by AIDS and now homeless, some of her respondents were unable to protect their possessions from thieves and vandals. One of Pavia's[2] informants (who is in the mainstream stage of the life course) discusses how her identity has changed:

Jean [Female, 26]: That was my idea of who I was. So to have to find inside who I was, was really difficult. I had to introduce myself as "... this is what I do," and then all of the sudden it was,"Well, I stay at home. I am an ex-nurse."

For the dying, the loss of one's ability to fulfill one's self-identity may well threaten one's hopes of immortality. Survivors interviewed as part of a study of grief processes (Gentry, et al., Forthcoming) discuss the work and volunteer roles that were central to their deceased spouses' identities. Ann T. [Female, 48] notes that "for Mike, giving up teaching was the toughest thing. This was harder for him to accept than the cancer." David A. [Male, 47] says that his wife

kicked me out of the kitchen until she became bed-ridden in the last ten months. That bothered her greatly, as she was bothered when others were in *her* kitchen. Until the very end, she insisted on sending cards to congregation members [he is a minister with a congregation of 1200 members] for birthdays and anniversaries, though her left hand was paralyzed and her right one limited. She used crayolas. She died on a Wednesday, and some arrived on Thursday. I suggested that someone else could do this, but she was adamant. This gave her purpose.

For Pavia's mainstream informants who are dying of AIDS, the meaning of most possessions declines:

---

[2]The quotes from Pavia (1993) are used with her permission.

Arnold [Male, 25]: I told my parents and my sisters, and everybody in my life right now, "Don't get me anything for Christmas because I don't want anything; I don't need anything....I don't even own a comb. I do own a toothbrush, two of them, and I don't have a desire to [own] anymore.

Ivan [Male, 25]: I had an entire house worth of goods and I just left it all...I just left [my roommates] everything and started over.

Samantha [Female, 33]: I think that when [life] comes to an end, possessions should be an irrelevant matter.

These reactions are due, in part, to the forced nature of the dispossession process for the AIDS victims; the informants could not qualify for Medicaid until their financial resources were depleted. Those possessions which were kept did take on more meaning, in a process similar to that noted by Adelman (1992, p. 402) who discusses the desire for immortality among residents of a home for those dying of AIDS.

A long-term resident who entered the home with two bags of clothes, after two years and several close relationships with dying residents, her room is now filled with their possessions. She notes, 'I make this room for memories and good feelings.'

Our interpretation of the interviews conducted by Pavia (1993) with AIDS patients and of the ones which were conducted by Gentry, et al. (Forthcoming) with those who had lost a loved one in this Mainstream stage is that one's family roles and work roles are keys to one's identity. When death becomes a reality, although social networks are still in place for the most part, possessions become relatively less important. As Pavia (1993, p. 428) notes, "Loss of energy removed control over what they could do on a daily basis, and, ultimately, their ability to do the things that were integral to their perception of self." Thus, much of the meaning of possessions for those in this stage of life is associated with the ability to generate them.

Preparation for Death in the Elderly Years

To some extent, the elderly dying are isolated from others because of the inability of most in the U.S. society to deal with death (Schilling 1993). Elias (1985, p. 10) notes that we have an inability to give dying people the help and affection they are most in need of when parting from other human beings, just because another's death is a reminder of the possibility of one's own. He later concluded (p. 190), "Never before have people died as noiselessly and hygienically as today in these societies, and never in social conditions so much fostering solitude."

For those unable to maintain their "purpose," tangible objects may be even more important to the desire to be remembered. Unruh (1993, p. 343) suggests that the "accumulation of artifacts is a strategy by which the dying preserve identities over time and communicate their importance to survivors....For the elderly, these objects represent the last symbolic remnants of who and what they once were." Their desires to be remembered encourage the sanctification process observed in Gentry, et al. (Forthcoming). In the extreme, "a small number of objects become sanctified to such a degree that their loss would be as tragic for the survivors as was the death of the deceased" (Unruh 1993, p. 348).

Gentry, et al. (Forthcoming) interviewed Paula G. [Female, 35], who discusses her Aunt Leona's plans to dispose of her possessions prior to her death from cancer. Family had played a major role in Leona's identity. "Leona was the one who kept the family together. She always wrote and sent cards."

> In March, Leona started to make arrangements to have things allocated to our family. She had a will made up but there were the little things that needed to be taken care of. While Leona had some strength, she went room to room to see who gets what. Leona felt that each niece or nephew should choose; I felt that everyone would prefer that she decided who should get what. I felt that these things would mean a lot more to the recipient.
> Family heirlooms had to stay in the family. Leona decided the disposition according to the personality of the item and the receiver. Aunt Leona was very concerned that the "kids" would not like her choice. We only made it as far as the china cabinet. She died before we could finish all the possessions.

Leona's care in the selection of possessions to go to various family members indicates her continuing role as the conserver of family ties.

In some instances, possessions offer immortality. Viorst (1986, pp. 296-297) notes:

> It is easier to grow old if we are neither bored nor boring, if we have people and projects we care about....The process, begun in infancy, of loving and letting go can help prepare us for these final losses. But stripped—as age does strip us—of some of what we love in ourselves, we may find that a good old age demands a capacity for what is called "ego transcendence."....
> Ego transcendence allows us, while perceiving ourselves as finite, to connect to the future through people or through ideas, surpassing our personal limits by means of some legacy we can leave to the next generation. As grandparents, teachers, mentors, social reformers, collectors of art—or creators of art—we can touch those who will be there when we are gone. This endeavor to leave a trace—intellectual, spiritual, material, even physical—is a constructive way of dealing with the grief we are feeling over the loss of ourself.

For the elderly, who are well aware of their mortality, possessions take on different meanings than they do for their younger counterparts. Not only is immortality possible through the transference of possessions, but possessions may also help make sense of the past, and allow the elderly to figure out where they are now by putting them at ease with the present. For example, possessions may help the elderly accept the past by helping them to relive past experiences and emotions (e.g., through photographs). In addition, possessions may be a source of comfort for the elderly as they maintain their existence among the things which are familiar to them.

CONCLUSIONS

That people in different stages of life view the meaning of possessions in different ways is not a radical concept. However, we would assert that marketers (who are, for the most part, in the mainstream of life) in the past have tended to view possessions from their own frame of reference, and, in many cases, have failed to acknowledge the frames of reference for different life stages. An example of how differing frames of reference yield different meanings may be meaningful. Insurance companies are developing "grandparent policies" which would put funds in a trust for grandchildren to be paid out at critical times in their lives (e.g., going to college, getting married, etc.). Those in the mainstream years may see this as a greedy appeal to the elderly or a possible loss of degrees of freedom in terms of the use of the inheritance. On the other hand, we imagine that such policies will be very appealing to the elderly, as they offer some degree of immortality to the purchasers.

Marketers have argued for decades that firms do more than sell what they produce, that they produce what people want. Marketers, more than others, realize that products provide more than functional performance, that many have symbolic meaning that imbues them with value far in excess of what might be assessed from a utilitarian perspective. The stream of research stimulated by Belk (1988) certainly acknowledges the role that possessions play in one's identity. Kleine, Kleine, and Kernan (1993) point out that we know very little "about how individuals' access to identity-related products affects identity-related esteem and the trajectory of an identity's development." The purpose in this paper is to develop the notion that the roles played by possessions vary greatly across age groups.

We advocate greater sensitivity on the part of marketers toward the symbolic meaning of products. If products' meanings or if messages promoting the products contribute to violence or, on a more mundane level, to rebellion against family and "acceptable" culture, marketers should be proactive and attempt to change the product's image before social problems result or public backlash occurs.

This paper suggests that possessions have an even more important function during the elderly years. As other sources of identity are eliminated, possessions are likely to remain. Given the tendency to ignore one's own demise and aging processes if at all possible, it is difficult for marketers to present their products as objects that will take on greater and greater value to consumers as they age. Such efforts may violate cultural taboos and also be seen as presumptuous or offensive by consumers.

A recognition of the importance which the elderly, as well as the young and the mainstream, place on their possessions in helping to preserve their identity over time will facilitate their struggle to maintain their identity. As Fromm (1976, p. 76) asks, "If I am what I have and what I have is lost, who then am I?"

REFERENCES

Adelman, Mara (1992), "Rituals of Adversity and Remembering: The Role of Possessions for Persons and Community Living with AIDS," *Advances in Consumer Research*, 19, 401-403.

Ball, A. Dwayne and Lori H. Tasaki (1992), "The Role and Measurement of Attachment in Consumer Behavior," *Journal of Consumer Psychology*,1 (2), 155-172.

Belk, Russell W. (1988), "Possessions and the Extended Self," *Journal of Consumer Research*, 15, 139-168.

_____ (1991a), "The Ineluctable Mysteries of Possessions," in Floyd W. Rudmin (Ed.), *To Have Possessions: A Handbook of Ownership and Property*, Special Issue of the *Journal of Social Behavior and Personality*, 6 (No. 6), 17-55.

_____ (1991b), "Possessions and the Sense of Past," in Russell W. Belk (Ed.), *Highways and Buyways: Naturalistic Research from the Consumer Behavior Odyssey*, Provo, UT: Association for Consumer Research, 114-130.

_____ (1992), "Moving Possessions: An Analysis Based on Personal Documents from the 1847-1869 Mormon Migration," *Journal of Consumer Research*, 19, 339-361.

Berger, Peter and Hansfried Kellner (1964), "Marriage and the Construction of Reality," *Diogenes*, 46, 1-24.

Bluebond-Langer, Myra (1989), "Worlds of Dying Children and their Well Siblings," *Death Studies*, 13, 1-16.

Csikszentmihalyi, Mihaly (1975), "Play and Intrinsic Rewards," *Journal of Humanistic Psychology*, 15 (Summer), 41-63.

_____ and Eugene Rochberg-Halton (1981), *The Meaning of Things: Domestic Symbols of the Self*, Cambridge: Cambridge University Press.

Dittmar, Helga (1991), "Meanings of Material Possessions as Reflections of Identity: Gender and Social Material Position in Society," in Floyd W. Rudmin (Ed.), *To Have Possessions: A Handbook of Ownership and Property*, Special Issue of the *Journal of Social Behavior and Personality*, 6 (No. 6), 165-186.

_____ (1992), *The Social Psychology of Material Possessions: To Have is To Be*, New York: St. Martin's Press.

Elias, N. (1985), *The Loneliness of Dying*, Oxford: Basil Blackwell.

Fromm, Ethan (1976), *To Have or To Be*, New York: Harper and Row.

Furnham, Adrian and Steven Jones (1987), "Children's Views Regarding Possessions and their Theft," *Journal of Moral Education*, 16 (1), 18-30.

Gentry, James W., Patricia F. Kennedy, Catherine Paul, and Ronald Paul Hill (Forthcoming), "Family Transitions During Grief: Discontinuities in Household Consumption Patterns," *Journal of Business Research*.

Gorer, Geoffrey (1965), *Death, Grief, and Mourning in Contemporary Britain*, London: Cresset Press.

Gramlich, Edwin P. (1974), "Recognition and Management of Grief in Elderly Patients," in John Ellard, Vamik D. Volkan, and Norman L. Paul (Eds.), *Normal and Pathological Responses to Bereavement*, New York: MSS Information Corporation, 186-202.

Heisley, Deborah, Deborah Cours, and Melanie Wallendorf (1993), "Structural Dimensions of the Inter-generational Transfer of Possessions," *Proceedings*, Association for Consumer Research, Nashville.

Hirschman, Elizabeth C. (1980), "Comprehending Symbolic Consumptions," in *Symbolic Consumer Behavior: Proceedings of the Conference on Consumer Esthetics and Symbolic Consumption*, Elizabeth C. Hirschman and Morris B. Holbrook (Eds.), New York: Association for Consumer Research and Institute of Retail Management, New York University, 4-6.

James, William (1890), *The Principles of Psychology*, Vol. 1, New York: Henry Holt.

Kaul, Donald (1993), "Big-city Talk: Coffins, Not Cars," *Lincoln Journal-Star*, June 27, 4B.

Kleine, Robert E. III, Susan Schultz Kleine, and Jerome B. Kernan (1993), "Mundane Consumption and the Self: A Social-Identity Perspective," *Journal of Consumer Psychology*, 2 (No. 3), 209-235.

Levinson, Daniel J. (1978), *The Seasons of a Man's Life*, New York: Alfred A. Knopf.

McCracken, Grant (1988), *Culture and Consumption: New Approaches to the Symbolic Character of Consumer Goods and Activities*, Bloomington, IN: Indiana University Press.

Mowen, John C. (1993), *Consumer Behavior*, New York: Macmillan Publishing.

Neal, Joseph (1989), "The Prime of Life!", *The Excelerator*, July, 28-30.

Nerken, Ira R. (1993), "Grief and the Reflective Self: Toward a Clearer Model of Loss Resolution and Growth," *Death Studies*, 17, 1-27.

Olson, Clark D. (1984), "Materialism in the Home: The Impact of Artifacts on Dyadic Communication," in *Advances in Consumer Research*, Vol. 12, Elizabeth C. Hirschman and Morris B. Holbrook (Eds.), Provo, Utah: Association for Consumer Research, 388-393.

Ozanne, Julie L., Ronald Paul Hill, and Newell D. Wright (1994), "The Challenge of Adolescence and the Role of Consumer Behavior: A View from Two Contrasting Worlds," Working Paper.

Pavia, Theresa (1993), "Dispossessions and Perceptions of Self in Later Stage HIV Infection," *Advances in Consumer Research*, 20, 425-428.

Schilling, Chris (1993), *The Body and Social Theory*, London: Sage Publications.

Solomon, Michael R. (1983), "The Role of Products as Social Stimuli: A Symbolic Interactionism Perspective," *Journal of Consumer Research*, 10 (December), 319-329.

Unruh, David R. (1983), "Death and Personal History: Strategies of Identity Preservation," *Social Problems*, 30 (No. 3, February), 340-351.

Viorst, Judith (1986), *Necessary Losses*, New York: Simon and Schuster.

Comparing Scales to Measure Compulsive Buying: An Exploration of Their Dimensionality

Leslie Cole, Louisiana State University
Dan Sherrell, Louisiana State University

INTRODUCTION

Researchers have recently shown increased interest in understanding negative consumption behaviors, such as drug addiction (Hirschman 1992) and compulsive buying (Faber, O'Guinn and Krych 1987; Scherhorn, Raab and Reisch 1990). In particular, compulsive buying behavior has been examined from a phenomenological (O'Guinn and Faber 1989) as well as a conceptual (Valence, d'Astous and Fortier 1988) perspective.

At present, two research teams have focused on the development of instruments which appropriately tap the consumer's propensity to engage in compulsive buying behaviors (Valence, d'Astous and Fortier 1988; Faber and O'Guinn 1992). However, each group of researchers has taken a different approach to the task of scale development.

Valence et al. (1988) identified four conceptual dimensions associated with compulsive buying: a) tendency to spend; b) reactive aspect (i.e., presence of irresistible urge to buy); c) post-purchase guilt; and d) family environment. During refinement efforts, the fourth dimension of family environment was dropped from the scale development and subsequent analyses showed the other three dimensions to load together on one factor.

Faber and O'Guinn (1992) employed a phenomenological approach to the development of a scale designed to identify compulsive buyers in the general population. By examining in-depth interviews with self-reported compulsive buyers, Faber and O'Guinn (1992) constructed a screening scale to identify compulsive buyers. They suggest that various constructs such as self-esteem, materialism and credit usage are associated with compulsive buying, although their compulsive buying clinical screening scale is apparently based on the unidimensional compulsive buying construct.

The purpose of this paper is twofold: a) to empirically identify the various conceptual dimensions captured by each scale; and b) to compare the nomological and predictive validity exhibited by each scale. The evidence presented in pursuit of these two objectives should assist researchers interested in the topic of compulsive buying in deciding how best to measure the construct.

LITERATURE REVIEW

Defining Compulsive Buying

Negative consumption behaviors must be studied in order to more fully understand the effects of the consumption process on society and the well-being of others (Hirschman 1992; Wells 1993). One such negative consumption behavior is compulsive buying. A closely related consumption behavior without such negative consequences is impulsive buying (Rook and Hoch 1984). The presence of lack of volitional control and prepurchase planning present in impulsive purchasing is similar to that of compulsive buying. However, given the lack of negative consequences from impulsive buying in general, the focus of the present study is strictly on compulsive buying.

O'Guinn and Faber (1989) view compulsive buying as an addictive behavior with the following definition:

a response to an uncontrollable drive or desire to obtain, use or experience a feeling, substance, or activity that leads an individual to repetitively engage in a behavior that will ultimately cause harm to the individual and/or others (p. 148).

This definition is similar to that suggested by Valence et al. (1988), who identified three constructs associated with compulsive buying behavior: 1) a strong emotional activation (increase in psychological tension); 2) a high cognitive control (an acknowledgement that buying will reduce the tension); and 3) a high reactivity (looking for tension reduction, rather than ownership). It also should be noted that the O'Guinn and Faber (1989) definition is sufficiently general to allow for non-purchase consumption (e.g., anorexia/bulimia, or gambling). However, the objective of the study is to examine compulsive behavior as it relates to uncontrollable purchasing activity.

Conceptual Development of Valence et al. (1988) Scale

The first scale developed to tap the constructs underlying compulsive buying behavior was developed by Valence, d'Astous and Fortier (1988) and stems from early conceptual work done by Faber, O'Guinn, and Krych (1988). During the early stages of this scale's development there were four dimensions involved with this measure. The first dimension was identified as "tendency to spend", wherein a compulsive buyer should exhibit a higher propensity to spend than a noncompulsive buyer.

The second dimension, "reactive aspect", dealt with the individual's response to strong urges to purchase. Thus, an individual exhibiting compulsive buying behavior might feel that the motivations or urges to purchase are irresistible or beyond their control, while noncompulsive buyers would not view such motivations to purchase as uncontrollable.

The third dimension associated with compulsive buying by Valence et al. (1988) was post-purchase guilt. Researchers have reported evidence that individuals who engage in compulsive buying often felt remorse over their behaviors (Faber, O'Guinn and Krych 1987; O'Guinn and Faber 1989).

Finally, a fourth dimension was determined to be family environment, that is, the environment (which would include relationships among the family members) in which one grew up should suggest a predisposition to engage in negative consumption behaviors, such as compulsive buying (d'Astous, Maltais and Roberge 1990). However, in the final version of the Valence et al. (1988) scale, the dimension of family environment was dropped because of poor internal consistency.

The Valence et al. (1988) scale has been used in several studies. Scherhorn, Raab and Reisch (1990) employed the scale to study self-reported compulsive and "normal" German consumers. The scale exhibited a Cronbach's alpha of .92 across both samples, but produced different factor structures in the compulsive and normal consumer samples. The non-compulsive subjects' scale responses produced two factors, an irresistible urge to purchase and a certain amount of postpurchase guilt. The compulsive buyer group's scale answers resulted in three factors: a external urge to purchase and an internal urge to purchase, along with a third factor, noted to be postpurchase guilt, similar to the noncompulsive group. These results suggest that the Valence et al. (1988) scale strongly taps into a motivational construct related to compulsive buying.

D'Astous, Maltais and Roberge (1990) used the Valence et al. (1988) scale to study compulsive buying in adolescents. The scale displayed a Cronbach's alpha of .78 for the sample respondents. D'Astous, Maltais and Roberge (1990) found adolescents to exhibit a generalized urge to buy, influenced by their peers.

Faber and O'Guinn's (1992) Compulsive Buying Screening Scale

Building upon their earlier work, Faber and O'Guinn (1992) developed a scale intended to screen compulsive buyers out of the general population. Previously, the use of self-reported compulsive buyer samples had limited researchers in examining the phenomenon of compulsive buying behavior. In addition, some individuals may have difficulty in distinguishing *compulsive* buying from *impulsive* buying behavior. Nataraajan and Goff (1992) point out that distinct differences may exist between compulsive *shoppers* and compulsive *buyers*, much in the same way that shopping may be conducted for reasons that may differ from the motivation for purchasing. Consequently, a screening instrument for compulsive buying is badly needed.

Faber and O'Guinn (1992) conducted in-depth interviews of identified compulsive buyers to gather descriptions of the types of behaviors and feelings these individuals reported during compulsive buying activities. Additionally, items were included based upon prior research efforts and theoretical concerns and tended to focus on the behaviors associated with compulsive buying.

Currently, there are no published studies which use the Faber and O'Guinn clinical screening scale. However, work done by these authors has been crucial in calling attention to the problems associated with finding such a small segment within a given population.

Study Objectives

The purpose of this study is to empirically compare the Valence et al. (1988) and Faber and O'Guinn (1992) compulsive buying measures to assess their: a) dimensionality (both within and across scales) and b) relative performance in identifying compulsive buyers. Based on the discussion presented above, it is apparent that the two instruments were developed for slightly different purposes using different methodologies. While each scale has been developed from a different point, it is expected that each scale should tap into similar conceptual dimensions. The Valence et al. (1988) instrument seems more oriented toward measuring the degree of irresistible urge to purchase (or shop), while the Faber and O'Guinn (1992) measure is designed to capture behavioral and financial indicators of compulsive buying behavior.

The Faber and O'Guinn (1992) measure has norms associated with its use to identify compulsive buyers while the Valence et al. (1988) scale does not. Consequently, direct comparisons of performance are problematic. Comparisons of the groups of consumers identified by each scale across a common set of constructs suggested by the literature as associated with compulsive buying should enable some preliminary conclusions to be drawn.

METHODOLOGY

A study was conducted to identify the factor structures underlying the two compulsive buying scales, assess the level of nomological validity exhibited by each scale, and examine the predictive validity of the scales. Five separate constructs were identified from the compulsive buying literature as being closely associated with compulsive buying tendencies. These items were used to compare the nomological validity of the Valence et al. (1988) and Faber and O'Guinn (1992) scales.

The self-esteem construct has been central to much of the development of compulsive buying measures (Faber and O'Guinn 1989). Self-esteem was measured by a scale determined to tap an individual's state self-esteem (Heatherton and Polivy 1991). Low self-esteem has been shown to be related to compulsive buying in a number of previous studies (Faber and O'Guinn 1992, Scherhorn, Reisch and Raab 1990; d'Astous, Maltais and Roberge 1990).

Early work in this area suggested that compulsive individuals were strongly motivated to reduce tension and anxiety through the shopping process (Faber, O'Guinn and Krych 1988; O'Guinn and Faber 1989). Furthermore, it has been proposed that compulsive buyers have a greater need for the activity than do members of the general population (Faber, O'Guinn and Krych 1988). This need for shopping was operationalized as involvement with the shopping process and motivations to shop. The shopping involvement scale was a reduced form of the Zaichowsky (1986) involvement scale. Shopper motivations were measured with items which suggested shopping motivated by a need to escape (Attaway 1989).

In this study, the Richins and Dawson (1992) materialism scale was used. Developed as a measure of consumer values, rather than as a personality trait, this scale purports to measure three dimensions of materialism: success, happiness, and acquisition centrality. The first of these, materialism as a sign of success, suggests that individuals who wish to show their success materially are likely to engage in behavior which appears materialistic. Materialism as happiness is operationalized as acquisition which is important to overall happiness and life satisfaction. Finally, Richins and Dawson (1992) operationalize acquisition centrality as that type of materialism which represents consumption excess. Previous studies have used the Belk (1985) materialism scale, where materialism was inferred from measures of personality traits (O'Guinn and Faber 1989; Scherhorn 1990; Faber and O'Guinn 1992). The scale developed by Richins and Dawson conceptualizes materialism as a consumer value, allowing for more direct measure of the construct.

Previous studies indicated that consumers who engage in compulsive buying often experience credit card abuse (Faber and O'Guinn 1988b; d'Astous 1990). In another Faber and O'Guinn study, it was shown that compulsive buyers had a greater proportion of their monthly income going to service debt than did general consumers (Faber and O'Guinn 1992). In this study, credit card usage was operationalized with a multi-item measure focusing on credit card behaviors and developed by d'Astous (1990).

A questionnaire containing measures for each of the constructs described above as well as the two compulsive buying scales was administered during class time to a convenience sample of 337 college students from a large southern university, with 319 usable questionnaires being returned.

While there is debate over the use of student samples (Wells 1993), the college student population has some relevance to shopping and purchasing issues. For many college students, their college experience is one of the first opportunities to make shopping and purchase decisions in a fairly autonomous manner. This expectation was investigated through focus groups held with students similar to those used in the main sample. Themes which emerged from the focus groups showed that college students did, indeed, show some autonomy over their finances. Many students described their parents giving them lump sums of money for semester expenses. Further, many related that their parents had given them credit cards to use while they were at school. While individuals may not have formed stable purchase patterns at this stage in their life, they should still have a significant store of general purchase knowledge and experience. In addition, for purposes of scale comparison, the use of a homogeneous population would seem to be suggested (Calder, Phillips and Tybout 1981). Therefore, the use of a convenience sample of college students was deemed appropriate.

Measures

The Valence et al. (1988) scale is a multi-item measure using a five point Likert scale, ranging from (1) "strongly disagree" to (5) "strongly agree". The Faber and O'Guinn (1992) scale is also a multi-item instrument measured on a five point scale where the respondents are instructed to answer how often they have behaved in a certain manner. The scale endpoints range from (1) "never" to (5) "very often".

Self-esteem was measured using a scale designed to tap an individual's state self-esteem (Heatherton and Polivy 1991). Respondents were instructed to respond according to their degree of agreement with scale items, using (1) "not at all" to (5) "extremely". The shopping involvement scale was a reduced form of the Zaichowsky (1986) involvement scale. Using a seven point semantic differential scale, respondents were instructed to indicate their feelings about the shopping process. Shopper motivations were measured using a reduced form of a shopping motivation scale developed by Attaway (1989) and based on the functional, symbolic and experiential needs expressed by Park, Jaworski and MacInnis (1986). Using a five point Likert scale, respondents were asked to express their level of agreement with the statements provided.

Materialism was measured using a scale developed by Richins and Dawson (1992). Items reflecting each of the three dimensions of success, happiness and acquisition centrality was measured using a five point Likert scale, with responses ranging from (1) "strongly disagree" to (5) "strongly agree".

Credit card usage was measured with a scale developed by d'Astous (1990). The scale was a multi-item five point measure which asked how often the respondent engaged in the behavior, with responses ranging from (1) "never" to (5) "very often".

Scale Evaluation

Several steps were taken to compare the two compulsive buying scales. First, the Valence et al. (1988) (VDF) scale and the Faber and O'Guinn (1992) (FOG) scale were subjected to confirmatory factor analysis using the dimensions identified in previous studies. The VDF scale was hypothesized to based on three separate dimensions of tendency to spend, reactive aspect, and post-purchase guilt. The FOG scale has been presented as a unidimensional scale. Then, the two scales were combined in a confirmatory factor analysis to see if they revealed common dimensions in respondents' answers.

The nomological validity of the scales was investigated by correlating the summed scale responses with related constructs identified in the literature (i.e., self-esteem, shopping involvement, shopping motivation, materialism, and credit usage). Finally, the predictive validity of the two scales was examined in two stages. Each set of scale items was used in a cluster analysis to generate distinct groups of respondents. These respondent groups were then profiled on the set of five related constructs described above and the cluster solutions compared across the two compulsive scale groups. The second stage of predictive validity investigation involved building groups of compulsive and non-compulsive buyers based on the VDF scale and using the FOG scale items as predictive elements in a discriminant analysis. This analysis allowed the examination of the ability of the FOG scale to identify compulsive buyers in a specific population.

RESULTS

Scale Dimensionality

Valence et al. scale. The three dimensions identified by Valence et al. for their compulsive buying scale were used to develop a confirmatory factor model for analyzing the data from the respondents. Table 1 presents the factor loadings and fit statistics generated via LISREL VII (Jöreskog and Sörbom 1989). The goodness-of-fit (GFI) and the adjusted goodness-of-fit (AGFI)

indices exhibit respectable levels of fit (values in the mid .80s and higher have been suggested as evidence of acceptable fit (Bagozzi and Yi 1988)).

The internal consistency estimates of composite reliability for the three dimensions were .69, .86 and .61, respectively. The variance extracted estimates were moderate at best. Of the three dimensions, only one (reactive aspect) had a variance extracted estimate above .50.

Finally, the majority of the standardized residuals were below + 2.00, which is indicative of a reasonable model fit (Anderson and Gerbing 1988). The modification indices suggested that two of the scale items (one item from the tendency to spend dimension and one item from the postpurchase guilt dimension) should be correlated with each other across constructs. Therefore, the dimensions proposed by Valence et al. seem to be supported reasonably well by our data, although the amount of variance explained is not high. However, since the scale attempts to measure a type of consumption behavior that has been estimated to be present for only 10-15 percent of the population (Faber and O'Guinn 1992), the scale's performance is a reasonable one.

Faber and O'Guinn scale. Faber and O'Guinn posit a unidimensional scale with the behavioral construct of compulsive buying as the latent variable behind the scale items. A single factor confirmatory model was estimated using the sample data. The results of that analysis are reported in Table 2. The proposed single factor model does a reasonably good job of reproducing the observed correlation matrix, as evidenced by the fit statistics of GFI=.96 and AGFI=.91. The composite reliability is .76, while the average variance extracted is low (.33), but similar to the results for the Valence et al. scale. As was the case with the Valence et al. scale, there are two items with low factor loadings.

An additional model was run with the all the items from both scales. The confirmatory model was specified with the three factors from the Valence et al. scale, along with the single factor from Faber and O'Guinn scale. The results of this model test are presented in Table 3. As can be seen, the combined model did not represent the data as well as the separate models did. The goodness-of-fit indices were lower and the Chi-square statistic was noticeably higher. The combined model results suggested that the same two items from the Valence et al. scale wanted to load across the Valence constructs, while there were two Faber and O'Guinn scale items with low loadings. Interestingly, however, none of the separate scale items from the Valence et al. or the Faber and O'Guinn scale showed tendencies to load with the opposite scale. These results suggest that the two scales are measuring separate sets of constructs (or simply different dimensions of compulsive buying behavior).

Nomological Validity Comparisons

A correlation analysis was run between the summed scale scores for the Valence et al. scale, the Faber and O'Guinn scale, and the constructs of self-esteem, shopping involvement, shopping motivation, materialism, and credit card usage. These constructs had been identified earlier from the literature as conceptually linked to compulsive buying behavior. Table 4 shows the results of these comparisons.

All the validity constructs were significantly associated with both compulsive buying scales. Self-esteem was correlated negatively with both the Valence et al. scale (r=-.32) and the Faber and O'Guinn scale (r=-.28). Materialism was correlated more highly with the Valence et al. scale than the Faber and O'Guinn scale, although the difference was not large.

There were three validity constructs that showed large differences between scales were shopping involvement (VDF r=.38; FOG r=.23); shopping motivation (VDF r=.56; FOG r=.31); and

TABLE 1
Confirmatory Factor Analysis
Valence, d'Astous and Fortier Compulsive Buying Scale

Scale Items	Tendency to Spend	Reactive Aspect	Postpurchase Guilt
When I have money, I cannot help but spend part or the whole of it.	.65	---	---
I am often impulsive in my buying behavior.	.61	---	---
As soon as I enter a shopping center, I have an irresistible urge to go into a shop to buy something	.67	---	---
I am one of those people who often responds to direct mail offers (e.g., books or compact discs)	.22	---	---
I have often bought a product that I did not need, while knowing I had very little money left	.59	---	---
For me, shopping is a way of facing the stress of my daily life and of relaxing.	---	.71	---
I sometimes feel that something inside of me pushed me to go shopping.	---	.78	---
There are times when I have a strong urge to buy (clothing, compact discs, etc.).	---	.73	---
I often have an unexplainable urge, a sudden and spontaneous desire, to go and buy something in a store.	---	.69	---
At times, I have felt somewhat guilty after buying a product, because I seemed unreasonable.	---	---	.79
There are some things I buy that I do not show to anybody for fear of being perceived as irrational in my buying behavior.	---	---	.55
I have sometimes thought "If I had it to do over again, I would. . ." and felt sorry for something I have done or said.	---	---	.39
Composite Reliability:	.69	.86	.61
Average Variance Extracted:	.32	.53	.36

χ^2 (53 df): 184.69
GFI: .92
AGFI: .87
RMSQR: .06

TABLE 2
Confirmatory Factor Analysis
Faber and O'Guinn Compulsive Buying Scale

Scale Items	Compulsive Buying Behavior
If I have any money left at the end of the pay period, I just have to spend it	.67
I felt others would be horrified if they knew my spending habits	.65
I have bought things though I couldn't afford them	.72
I wrote a check when I knew I didn't have enough money in the bank to cover it	.44
I bought something in order to make myself feel better	.50
I felt anxious or nervous on days I didn't go shopping	.37
I made only the minimum payments on my credit cards	.56
Composite Reliability:	.76
Average Variance Extracted:	.33

χ^2 (14 df): 51.68
GFI: .96
AGFI: .91
RMSQR: .05

TABLE 3
Combined Confirmatory Factor Analysis
Valence, d'Astous and Fortier / Faber and O'Guinn Scales

Scale Items	Tendency to Spend	Reactive Aspect	Postpurchase Guilt	Faber & O'Guinn
When I have money, I cannot help but spend part or the whole of it.	.64	---	---	---
I am often impulsive in my buying behavior.	.58	---	---	---
As soon as I enter a shopping center, I have an irresistible urge to go into a shop to buy something	.65	---	---	---
I am one of those people who often responds to direct mail offers (e.g., books or compact discs)	.23	---	---	---
I have often bought a product that I did not need, while knowing I had very little money left	.65	---	---	---
For me, shopping is a way of facing the stress of my daily life and of relaxing.	---	.72	---	---
I sometimes feel that something inside of me pushed me to go shopping.	---	.79	---	---
There are times when I have a strong urge to buy (clothing, compact discs, etc.).	---	.73	---	---
I often have an unexplainable urge, a sudden and spontaneous desire, to go and buy something in a store.	---	.68	---	---
At times, I have felt somewhat guilty after buying a product, because I seemed unreasonable.	---	---	.76	---
There are some things I buy that I do not show to anybody for fear of being perceived as irrational in my buying behavior.	---	---	.57	---
I have sometimes thought "If I had it to do over again, I would. . ." and felt sorry for something I have done or said.	---	---	.40	---
If I have any money left at the end of the pay period, I just have to spend it	---	---	---	.72
I felt others would be horrified if they knew my spending habits	---	---	---	.62
I have bought things though I couldn't afford them	---	---	---	.67
I wrote a check when I knew I didn't have enough money in the bank to cover it	---	---	---	.42
I bought something in order to make myself feel better	---	---	---	.55
I felt anxious or nervous on days I didn't go shopping	---	---	---	.45
I made only the minimum payments on my credit cards	---	---	---	.49
Composite Reliability	.69	.82	.61	.76
Average Variance Extracted	.33	.53	.35	.32
χ_2 (146 df)	450.37			
GFI	.87			
RMSQR	.07			

credit card usage (VDF r=.36; FOG r=.71). Whereas the two items related to shopping (involvement and motivation) were correlated higher with the Valence et al. scale than the Faber and O'Guinn scale, the credit card usage item showed a much stronger relationship with the Faber and O'Guinn scale. This finding suggests that maybe the Valence et al. scale taps into a behavior more closely associated with shopping, while the Faber and O'Guinn scale measures compulsive *buying* behavior more closely.

Predictive Validity Comparisons

Cluster analysis. The first stage of the predictive analysis was an attempt to group respondents using both compulsive buying scales and to compare the identified groups. The results of these analyses are presented in Tables 5 and 6.

In determining the number of clusters to use as a solution, the percentage change criteria was used with the agglomeration schedule. In doing so, it appeared that for both scale analyses, there appeared to be a large jump in going from three to two clusters. There was some concern that using a two group solution would result in people who showed extreme levels of compulsive buying being grouped with individuals who reported some compulsive tendencies, but were not extreme across the whole range of scale items. For this reason, a three group solution was used for each scale analysis.

TABLE 4
Correlations Between Compulsive Buying Scales and Validity Constructs

	Self-Esteem	Shopping Involvement	Shopping Motivations	Materialism	Credit
VDF	-.32 [a]	.38 [a]	.56 [a]	.35 [a]	.36 [a]
FOG	-.28 [a]	.23 [a]	.31 [a]	.28 [a]	.71 [a]

[a] $p < .01$
Note: FOG items were reverse coded for clarity.

TABLE 5
Cluster Analysis Results: Valence et al. Scale Means[A]

Scale Items	Normal	Impulsive/ Guilty	Compulsive
When I have money, I cannot help but spend part or the whole of it.	1.82	2.68	3.74
I am often impulsive in my buying behavior.	1.81	2.92	3.27
As soon as I enter a shopping center, I have an irresistible urge to go into a shop to buy something	1.39	1.96	3.31
I am one of those people who often responds to direct mail offers (e.g., books or compact discs)	1.26	1.71	3.27
I have often bought a product that I did not need, while knowing I had very little money left	2.28	3.52	4.31
For me, shopping is a way of facing the stress of my daily life and of relaxing.	1.88	3.65	3.69
I sometimes feel that something inside of me pushed me to go shopping.	1.27	2.16	2.17
There are times when I have a strong urge to buy (clothing, compact discs, etc.).	1.33	2.27	3.36
I often have an unexplainable urge, a sudden and spontaneous desire, to go and buy something in a store.	1.24	1.65	2.61
At times, I have felt somewhat guilty after buying a product, because I seemed unreasonable.	1.39	1.66	1.62
There are some things I buy that I do not show to anybody for fear of being perceived as irrational in my buying behavior.	1.22	2.24	2.48
Nomological Validity Constructs			
Self-Esteem	3.48	3.32	3.19
Shopping Involvement	4.48	4.83	5.69
Shopping Motivation	2.78	3.28	3.97
Materialism	2.65	2.84	3.01
Credit Card Usage	1.90	2.30	2.52

[A] All item cluster means significantly different across groups ($p < .05$)

TABLE 6
Cluster Analysis Results: Faber and O'Guinn Scale Means[A]

Scale Items	Normal	Impulsive	Compulsive
If I have any money left at the end of the pay period, I just have to spend it	1.69	2.16	3.61
I felt others would be horrified if they knew my spending habits	1.55	2.18	3.26
I have bought things though I couldn't afford them	1.64	1.98	3.41
I wrote a check when I knew I didn't have enough money in the bank to cover it	1.34	1.69	2.44
I bought something in order to make myself feel better	2.74	2.71	3.72
I felt anxious or nervous on days I didn't go shopping	1.10	1.10	1.46
I made only the minimum payments on my credit cards	1.64	4.10	3.79
Nomological Validity Constructs			
Self-Esteem	3.38	3.32	3.06
Shopping Involvement	4.88	5.16	5.45
Shopping Motivation	3.27	3.24	3.76
Materialism	2.76	2.83	3.21
Credit Card Usage	1.80	2.81	3.46

[A] All item cluster means significantly different across groups (p < .05)

Following the decision to use a three group cluster solution for both scales, the means of the three groups for each scale were entered into separate, nonhierarchical cluster routines to generate respondent groups and profiles for the scale items.

Valence et al. Scale Cluster Profiles. In examining the profiles of the groups of respondents identified by the cluster analysis, it is apparent that the individuals in cluster three are more extreme on all but three of the scale items. Respondents in clusters two and three are similar on items relating to: a) "I feel guilty after buying a product"; (b) "..fear being perceived as irrational in my buying behavior"; and (c) "I often respond to direct mail offers". The groups identified by the cluster solution for the Valence et al. scale can be characterized as: cluster 1 - Normal Buyers; cluster 2 - Impulsive/Guilty Buyers; and cluster 3 - Compulsive Buyers. While the choice of labels is subjective, the scale clearly identifies respondents who differ in terms of being able to resist uncontrollable urges to shop or buy; feel guilty about unnecessary purchases; or view shopping/buying as a means of reducing stress. This is consistent with the conceptual taxonomy of buyers developed by Valence et al. 1

Faber and O'Guinn Scale Cluster Profiles. The profiles of the respondents grouped according to the Faber and O'Guinn scale also show clear demarcations between relatively normal buying behavior and compulsive buying patterns. Cluster 3 respondents again showed higher scores on all scale items except one: making the minimum payment on their credit cards. Respondents in cluster 2 were significantly different from the more "normal" subjects in cluster 1, in terms of being more motivated to spend money, buying things they couldn't afford, or worrying about what other people would think if they knew how much that person spent. However, respondents in cluster 2 showed some similarities to cluster 1 respondents in viewing buying as a way to feel better or being anxious/nervous if they didn't go shopping frequently. Cluster 1 could be labeled Normal Buyers; cluster 2 respondents could be called Impulsive Buyers; and cluster 3 subjects were clearly Compulsive Buyers. As with the Valence et al. scale results, the Faber

and O'Guinn group profiles are distinct with respect to buying behaviors and motivations.

Validity Construct Comparisons. Tables 5 and 6 also display the results of comparing the identified cluster groups across the five validity constructs. For both the Valence et al. scale and the Faber and O'Guinn scale, the groups labeled as compulsive score significantly lower on self-esteem matching reported evidence by Faber and O'Guinn 1992; and significantly higher on the remaining measures of shopping involvement, shopping motivation, materialism, and credit card usage.

Within scale comparisons showed that the impulsive and normal groups were not significantly different (p<.05) on self-esteem for each scale. For the Valence et al. scale, impulsive respondents were significantly different (p<.05) from compulsive subjects on shopping involvement and shopping motivation, but not significantly different from compulsives on materialism and credit card usage. For the Faber and O'Guinn groups, impulsive buyers were significantly different (p<.05) from compulsives on self-esteem, shopping motivation, materialism, and credit usage. Interestingly, compulsive buyers and impulsive buyers did not display significantly different ratings for shopping involvement.

Discriminant Analysis. It is difficult to directly compare the ability of the two compulsive buying scales to correctly identify compulsive buyers. The Faber and O'Guinn scale incorporates a scoring norm in its application, which typically results in around 10 percent of a group of individuals being identified as compulsive buyers. The Valence et al. scale contains no such norms or scoring to help group people. The end result of using the Valence et al. scale is simply the ability to array a set of subjects on a compulsive buying scale without knowing what cutoff points should be used to identify individuals as compulsive.

Given the characteristics of the two scales, it was decided to use subjects' scores on the Valence et al. scale as a means of grouping respondents and then using the Faber and O'Guinn scores as predictors. The samples' mean score on the Valence et al. scale was used as the cutoff point. Subjects falling two or more standard

TABLE 7
Discriminant Analysis Results:
Valence et al. Scale—Grouping Criteria; Faber & O'Guinn Scale—Predictors

Predictors	Std. Discriminant Coefficient	Wilks' Lambda	F=ratio [a]
"Just have to spend it"	0.44	0.46	68.59
"Have bought things I couldn't afford"	0.37	0.52	55.06
"Bought something to make me feel better"	0.50	0.48	61.98
"Feel nervous or anxious when I didn't shop"	0.21	0.67	28.59

Canonical Correlation   .79
Percent Correctly Classified:
     Analyzed Sample: 93.44%
     Holdout Sample: 89.66%

deviations away from the group mean were grouped into a compulsive and noncompulsive category, respectively. The resulting sample was then randomly split into halves to form a analysis and holdout sample. The results of the discriminant analysis are reported in Table 7.

Three items on the Faber and O'Guinn scale were significant predictors of compulsive buying group membership: a) "..have to spend any money left"; b) "..bought to make myself feel better" and c) ".. felt anxious when I didn't shop". These items correctly predicted group membership an average of 93.44 percent in the analysis sample and 89.66 percent in the holdout sample. The items in the Faber and O'Guinn scale do a good job of identifying individuals with compulsive buying tendencies, as measured by the Valence et al. scale.

DISCUSSION

The results of the analysis comparing the Valence et al. and Faber and O'Guinn scales suggest that both scales perform reasonably well and exhibit the dimensionality claimed for them by their authors. The Valence et al. scale taps compulsive buying *tendencies*, while the Faber and O'Guinn scale is able to identify the more extreme cases of compulsive buying *behavior*. The Valence et al. scale exhibited multiple dimensions in its confirmatory factor structure, while the Faber and O'Guinn scale showed only one. Additionally, attempts to combine the two sets of scale items proved ineffective, so there is the suggestion that each scale is measuring a different, but related underlying construct.

The cluster profiles exhibited by each scale were similar, but the Faber and O'Guinn respondent profiles were more differentiated than the Valence et al. profiles. Also, the credit usage of the compulsive buyer group from the Faber and O'Guinn scale analysis was more extreme than that of the compulsive buyer group from the Valence et al. scale analysis. Thus, the pattern of results suggest that the Faber and O'Guinn scale results in the identification of more extreme compulsive buyers, while the Valence et al. scale results in the measurement of a group of respondents' compulsive tendencies.

There is also a small amount of evidence suggesting that the Valence et al. scale leans more toward identifying compulsive shopping tendencies as opposed to compulsive buying tendencies. More of the Valence et al. scale items deal with the idea of shopping (six of 12 items mention or refer to shopping versus three of 13 items for the Faber and O'Guinn scale) than do the Faber and O'Guinn

scale. Shopping involvement and motivation were correlated more highly with the Valence et al. scale than with the Faber and O'Guinn scale. In sum, it would appear that the two scales are compatible, but distinct. Thus, researchers working in this area might consider using both scales to capture as much of the variance in the construct as possible.

Future research in this area should concentrate on exploring the extent and validity of our suggestion about the compulsive shopping orientation of the Valence et al. scale. The use of different subject groups, different types of shopping behaviors, and additional antecedent variables may help pinpoint the distinct differences between the two existing scales to measure compulsive consumption behavior. Another area of needed work concerns the development of norms for the Valence et al. scale, paralleling the norms for the Faber and O'Guinn scale. Such benchmarking activity would make the two scales more directly comparable.

BIBLIOGRAPHY

Anderson, James C. and David W. Gerbing (1988), "Structural Equation Modeling in Practice: A Review and Recommended Two-Step Approach," *Psychological Bulletin*, 103, 411-423.

Attaway, Jill (1989), *Influence of an Expanded Framework of Shopping Motivations and Inclusion of Non-Store Retailers on the Choice Set Formation Process*, unpublished dissertation, Baton Rouge, LA: Louisiana State University.

Bagozzi, Richard and Youjae Yi (1988), "On the Evaluation of Structural Equation Models," *Journal of the Academy of Marketing Science*, 16 (Spring) 74-94.

Belk, Russell, (1985), "Materialism Trait Aspects of Living in the Material World," *Journal of Consumer Research*, 12 (December), 265-280.

Calder, Phillips and Tybout (1981), "Designing Research for Application," *Journal of Consumer Research*, 8 (September)197-207.

d'Astous, Alain (1990), "An Inquiry into the Compulsive Side of "Normal" Consumers," *Journal of Consumer Policy*, 13 (March), 15-31.

d'Astous, Alain, Julie Maltais, and Caroline Roberge (1990), "Compulsive Buying Tendencies of Adolescent Consumers," in *Advances in Consumer Research*, Vol. 17, eds. Marvin Goldberg, Gerald Gorn, and Richard Pollay, Provo, UT: Association for Consumer Research, 306-312.

Faber, Ronald J. and Thomas C. O'Guinn (1992), "A Clinical Screener for Compulsive Buying," *Journal of Consumer Research*, 19 (December), 459-469.

_____ and _____ (1988b), "Compulsive Consumption and Credit Abuse," *Journal of Consumer Policy*, 11, 97-109.

_____ and _____ (1988a), "Dysfunctional Consumer Socialization: A Search for the Roots of Compulsive Buying," presented at the 13th International Association for Research in Economic Psychology Colloquium, Leuven, Belgium, September.

_____ and _____ (1989), "Classifying Compulsive Consumers: Advances in the Development of a Diagnostic Tool," in *Advances in Consumer Research*, Vol. 16, ed. Thomas K. Srull, Provo, UT: Association for Consumer Research, 745-748.

_____ , _____ and Raymond Krych (1988), "Compulsive Consumption," in *Advances in Consumer Research*, Vol. 14, eds. Melanie Wallendorf and Paul Anderson, Provo, UT: Association for Consumer Research, 132-135.

Heatherton, Todd F. and Janet Polivy (1991), "Development and Validation of a Scale for Measuring State Self-Esteem", *Journal of Personality and Social Psychology*, 60 (6), 895-910.

Hirschman, Elizabeth C. (1992), "The Consciousness of Addiction: Toward a General Theory of Compulsive Consumption," *Journal of Consumer Research*, 19 (September), 155-179.

Jöreskog, Karl G. and Dag Sörbom (1989), *LISREL 7: A Guide to the Program and Applications*, 2nd edition, Chicago: SPSS.

Nataraajan, Rajan and Brent G. Goff (1992), "Manifestations of Compulsiveness in the Consumer-Marketplace Domain," *Psychology and Marketing*, 9 (January), 31-44.

O'Guinn, Thomas C. and Ronald J. Faber (1989), "Compulsive Buying: A Phenomenological Exploration," *Journal of Consumer Research*, 16 (September), 147-157.

Park, C. Whan, Bernard J. Jaworski and Deborah J. MacInnis (1986), "Strategic Brand Concept-Image Management," *Journal of Marketing*, 50 (October), 135-145.

Richins, Marsha L. and Scott Dawson (1992), "A Consumer Values Orientation for Materialism and Its Measurement: Scale Development and Validation", *Journal of Consumer Research*, (December).

Rook, Dennis W. and Stephen J. Hoch (1984), "Consuming Impulses", *Advances in Consumer Research*, in *Advances in Consumer Research*, Vol. 12 eds. Elizabeth C. Hirschman and Morris B. Holbrook, Provo, UT: Association for Consumer Research, 36-40.

Scherhorn, Gerhard (1990), "The Addictive Trait in Buying Behaviour," *Journal of Consumer Policy*, 13 (March), 33-51.

Scherhorn, Gerhard, Lucia A. Reisch, and Gerhard Raab (1990), "Addictive Buying in West Germany, " *Journal of Consumer Policy*, 13 (December), 355-387.

Valence, Gilles, Alain d'Astous, and Louis Fortier (1988), "Compulsive Buying: Concept and Measurement," *Journal of Consumer Policy*, 11, 419-433.

Wells, William D. (1993), "Discovery-Oriented Consumer Research," *Journal of Consumer Research*, 19 (March), 489-504.

Zaichowsky, Judith (1986), "Measuring the Involvement Construct," *Journal of Consumer Research*, 12 (December), 341-352.

Styles of Thinking: A Bridge Between Personality and Cognition

Harish Sujan, Penn State University

Though questions concerning human intelligence have absorbed psychologists for a long time, this area of inquiry has received little attention in consumer research. Intelligence is likely to affect how consumers process information and arrive at decisions. Intelligence is likely to affect how marketers (advertisers, sales promoters, and salespeople) formulate persuasive schemes. Thus, a greater emphasis on researching intelligence in the consumer domain appears to be called for.

Robert J. Sternberg, a psychologist who is considered by many as the principal contributor in current times to research on intelligence, spoke first (for about half the session length) in this special sesssion. He spoke on his recent work on *styles of thinking*, a theory that concerns the use of intelligence. In earlier work, Sternberg (e.g., 1985) has theorized extensively on the nature of intelligence; proposing a broader and more malleable view of intelligence than traditional conceptualizations. Following Sternberg, *Stijn Van Osselaer*, University of Florida, described *an application of the theory of thinking styles to problem solving*. Then *I* spoke on *the matching of consumers' and salespeople's thinking styles*. Lastly, *Bart Weitz*, University of Florida, *discussed* the three presentations.

Robert J. Sternberg introduced his thinking styles as a preference in the use of one's abilities; often one failed to learn not because one lacked the ability but because the style of teaching was not a preferred one. For example, he had assumed that he lacked the ability to learn languages after being exposed to the mimic and memorize methods of instruction; when exposed to context based methods of language learning he found that he had the ability to learn languages after all. After reviewing some alternative theories of style, he presented his own which is based on the metaphor of government—it views intellectual or thinking styles in terms of mental self-government. Just as there are three functions of government, legislature, executive and judiciary, there are three functions of mental self-government. The legislative function of the mind is concerned with creating, formulating, imagining, and planning. The executive function is concerned with implementing and with doing. The judicial function is concerned with judging, evaluating, and comparing. To illustrate these styles he described three car salespeople he encountered. The legislative salesperson discussed with him how he would use the car, the executive salesperson focused on financing, and the judicial salesperson evaluated for him competitors' cars as inferior. He bought from the legislative salesperson since he, the customer, is legislative too.

Just as there are four forms of government, monarchic, hierarchic, oligarchic and anarchic, there are four parallel forms of mental self-government. The monarchic form is characterized by a preference for tasks and situations that allows focusing on one thing or aspect at a time and staying with that aspect until it is completed. The hierarchic form involves setting multiple goals, each of which have a different priority. The oligarchic form allows for multiple goals, all of which are equally important. Finally, the anarchic form is characterized by a preference for activities that lend themselves to great (sometimes too great) flexibility of approaches and to trying almost anything.

The level of mental self-government suggests that individuals vary in their degree of concern with detail. At the local level there is a preference for tasks, projects, and situations that require engagement with specific, concrete details. At the global level there is preference for problems that are general in nature and that require abstract thinking.

The scope of mental self-government can be either internal or external. On the one hand, the internal style refers to a preference for projects, tasks, or events that allow one to work independently from others. On the other hand, the external style refers to a preference for activities that allow working and interacting with others at different stages of progress.

The two leanings of government suggest that individuals vary in their degree of adherence to pre-existing rules or structures, that is, in their degree of mental liberalism and conservatism. The liberal intellectual style refers to a preference for tasks, projects, and situations that require going beyond existing rules and procedures and that allow substantial change. In contrast, the conservative intellectual style refers to a preference for tasks, projects, and situations that require adherence to existing rules and procedures.

He illustrated the measures he has developed to measure these styles by asking the audience to rate themselves on three statements each pertaining to legislative, executive and judicial styles. He presented data relating to the internal consistency of these measures—this data suggests acceptable consistency for all except the monarchic and anarchic forms.

He then presented the results of an investigation conducted with Elena Grigorenko. Study 1 revealed that at lower grades teachers are more legislative and less executive; that science teachers are more local and humanities teachers are more liberal; that older teachers are more executive, local and conservative; and that teachers' thinking styles matched the styles expressed in the school's ideology. Study 2, on the demographics of styles, revealed that the education level of the father, but not the mother, related negatively with judicial, local, conservative, and oligarchic styles. Younger siblings are more legislative, children of higher SES are less judicial, and students tend to match their teachers, though not the school in general, in style. Study 3 examined if students benefit if their styles match their teachers' styles. It was found that students are evaluated more positively by and receive better grades from teachers who match their styles than from those who do not. It was also found that teachers overestimate the extent to which their students match their own style. From these studies he concluded that intelligence is important, but no matter how broadly defined, it is not enough. We need to look at styles of thought too.

Lastly, he related thinking styles to methods of instruction and forms of assessment in the classroom. Illustratively, lecture methods of instruction tend to go with executive and hierarchical thinking styles while thought-based questioning go with judicial and legislative thinking styles. And, multiple choice tests that tap memory tend to go with executive and local thinking styles while projects that focus on creativity go with legislative thinking styles.

The theory of thinking styles is described in Sternberg (1988a; 1988b; 1994). Grigorenko and Sternberg (1994) details the investigations he described.

Stijn Van Osselaer, University of Florida, reported on research that related the legislative, judicial, and executive functions to stages in the Problem Solving Process. He identified six stages of problem-solving: problem definition, generation of possible solutions, comparison of possible solutions, deciding which solution to take, planning for execution, and execution. He hypothesized that people with a legislative thinking style, because of their focus on creating, are better at the first two stages (definition and generation of solutions), people with a judicial style of thinking, because of their focus on judging, are better at the next two stages (comparison of possible solutions and deciding which solution to take), and people with an executive thinking style, because of their focus on implementation, are better at the final two stages (planning for execution and execution itself). The data he used to test these hypotheses revealed only partial support. He suggested that an alternative way to relate thinking styles to the problem solving process is to look at preferences for problems, from a set of problems that systematically differ in the emphasis placed on the six stages. This data too revealed only partial support.

He suggested that preferences in the problem solving process could have an important bearing on consumer decision making. For example, preference for the generation of possible solutions might relate with the willingness to take additional brands into consideration, and preference for execution might relate with impulsive buying.

Following Stijn, *I* reported on research being conducted with Bob Sternberg on the matching of consumers' and salespeople's thinking styles. The first investigation used a negotiation exercise to test the hypothesis that dyads in which the buyer and the seller have similar thinking styles outperform dyads in which the buyer and the seller have different thinking styles. Correlating the absolute difference between buyer and seller thinking styles with the joint score in the negotiation, negative correlations—support for the matching hypothesis—were found for the three functions (judicial, legislative and executive), two levels (local and global) and the hierarchic form; there were no correlations for the monarchic form and the two scopes (internal and external). Reasoning that adaptable (Spiro and Weitz 1990) buyers and sellers would be able to deal with dissimilarity better, we compared the correlations for high (on average) and low adaptable dyads. With one exception, the executive thinking style, we found greater negative correlations—matching of thinking styles improves performance—with low adaptable dyads. A second investigation, with sales managers in a pharmaceutical firm, tested matching between thinking style and the nature of work. We found that jobs focused on either seeking orders from new customers or for new products were more likely to have legislative and monarchic sales managers and less likely to have internal sales managers.

A third investigation, also with sales managers in a pharmaceutical company, looked at the effect of thinking styles on job performance and psychological well-being. It was found that a legislative thinking style raises psychological well-being, as a result of increasing a customer orientation (Saxe and Weitz 1982); and an external thinking style raises job performance, again as a result of increasing a customer orientation.

In his discussion, Bart Weitz evaluated thinking styles against other conceptions of behavioral predispositions. He suggested that since little evidence has been found that people proceed systematically through stages of problem solving, it is more interesting to correlate thinking styles with preferences for different types of problems. He indicated that thinking style research had a good fit with questions concerning salespeople and sales managers.

The questions that followed focused on possible alternatives to this taxonomy for styles of thinking. In one question it was suggested that feeling styles may be needed to complement thinking styles.

REFERENCES

Grigorenko, Elena and Robert J. Sternberg (1994), "Thinking Styles in School Settings," Manuscript.

Saxe, Robert and Barton A. Weitz (1982), "The SOCO Scale: A Measure of the Customer Orientation of Salespeople," *Journal of Marketing Research*, 19 (August), 343-351.

Spiro, Rosann L. and Barton A. Weitz (1990), "Adaptive Selling: Conceptualization, Measurement, and Nomological Validity," *Journal of Marketing Research*, 27 (February), 61-69.

Sternberg, Robert J. (1985). *Beyond IQ: A Triarchic Theory of Human Intelligence*, New York: Cambridge University Press.

_____ (1988a), "Mental Self-Government: A Theory of Intellectual Styles and Their Development," *Human Development*, 31, 197-224.

_____ (1988b). *The Triarchic Mind: A New Theory of Human Intelligence*, New York: Viking.

_____ (1994), "Thinking Styles: Theory and Assessment at the Interface Between Intelligence and Personality," in *Personality and Intelligence* (eds. Robert J. Sternberg and Patricia Ruzgis), New York: Cambridge University Press, 169-187.

Seeing is Not Necessarily Believing: Interactions Between Prior Beliefs and New Information in Consumer Judgment and Choice

Cornelia Pechmann, University of California, Irvine

OVERVIEW OF SESSION

The three papers in this special session dealt with the same fundamental issue: How consumers integrate information from various sources, often conflicting, in forming brand evaluations and making brand choices. The specific focus is on understanding when and why consumers might rely on intuitive beliefs or naive theories, rather than other inputs, to infer a brand's rating on missing or ambiguous attributes. Thus the research grapples with decision-making in its real world complexity, a recurring but important theme in consumer research.

What makes the current research novel is that subjects could have relied on more reliable inputs, such as data available through information search. Thus the theoretical contributions of this special session lie in (a) examining how consumers weight prior beliefs or theories versus other inputs, and (b) identifying factors that determine which inputs will dominate. A unique methodological contribution is that the session brings together two previously disparate types of studies, on inference-making and information search. In terms of substantive contributions, the research addresses when and why advertising might be deceptive due to erroneous inference-making, and the potential impact of corrective advertising.

BRONIARCZYK AND ALBA PAPER

Broniarczyk and Alba's paper was entitled "Bases for Product Inference: Prior Beliefs and Data." In their research, subjects' intuitive beliefs or theories about attribute correlations conflicted with "data-based cues." Several experiments then examined: (a) the relative diagnosticity of prior beliefs vs. data-based cues in product inference, and (b) the influence of prior beliefs on the likelihood of product inference. Prior beliefs were operationalized as the intuitive relationship between warranty and durability. The data-based cues examined were the empirical correlation between the missing attribute and a presented attribute in a set of related brands, the overall ratings of the brand, and the average value of the missing attribute across the other brands.

A consistent finding was that prior beliefs (that a better warranty implies higher durability) were perceived as a more reliable basis for inference than data-based cues. Also, prior beliefs were shown to lead to a greater level of spontaneous inference than had been reported in previous studies even though the data supported an opposite basis for inference. In sum, prior theories dominated when pitted against the type of data-based cues discussed above. However, when subjects were provided with data about the company's prior reputation, that input was perceived as the most diagnostic and carried the most weight in consumer judgments.

JOHAR PAPER

Johar's paper was entitled "Do Consumers Update Prior Beliefs about Brands and Advertisers?: The Case of Corrective Advertising." It addressed when and why corrective advertising might inadvertently lower consumers' beliefs about the advertised brand on correlated claims that were not the target of the correction. The paper also examined the effects of corrective advertising on brand and advertiser evaluations.

The advertiser's prior reputation was again a critical variable, but rather than serving as an input to judgments it moderated subjects' reliance on other inputs. When subjects had a favorable prior evaluation of the advertiser, corrective (less favorable) information on the target attribute apparently was not perceived as diagnostic of the brand's rating on correlated attributes or brand evaluations. However, when subjects had an unfavorable prior evaluation of the advertiser, those exposed to corrective advertising tended to infer the advertised brand had a lower rating even on nontarget attributes and evaluated the brand less favorably. Further, corrective advertising lowered advertiser evaluations for companies with good reputations but actually increased advertiser evaluations for companies with poor reputations. This research addresses important issues about whether corrective advertising is a non-punitive remedy for deception.

PECHMANN PAPER

Pechmann talked about "When and How Extraneous Reference Prices Deter Choice of Competitors: Alternative Mediational Paths and Implications for Consumer Deception." In this research, subjects' favorable prior beliefs about the market leader were challenged by a competitor's advertising campaign. Reference prices were provided that either implied, or stated explicitly, that the competitor was substantially overpriced on certain services. These price comparisons were accurate but extraneous to the choice task in that they did not pertain to the class of service subjects required. The pertinent prices were omitted from the ads, and subjects could "call" the companies for accurate price data.

Instead, subjects tended to rely on the extraneous reference prices, particularly when the information was factual ("costs $3 more") vs. impressionistic ("costs more"), and when the targeted competitor was named vs. unnamed ("the competitor"). As predicted, these two message factors seemed to enhance the perceived diagnosticity and accessibility of the inference-related inputs. Reliance on inferences led subjects to (a) engage in less information search, (b) rate competitors lower on overall price, and (c) choose the more expensive advertised brand rather than a cheaper competitor—even though their most important decision criterion was low price.

In sum, consumers may make erroneous inferences about omitted product attributes without prompting, and these inferences may affect brand choice—even in situations when consumers could have engaged in information search. But it would be difficult to eradicate this type of miscomprehension because the government would have to ban direct, factual comparisons as these are most likely to be overgeneralized.

DISCUSSANT MAZIS' COMMENTS

The discussant, Mazis, focused on the contributions and potential limitations of the three papers. The papers were praised for consisting of high quality, theory-based, multiple-study research. More specific comments by the discussant are summarized below.

The Broniarczyk and Alba paper makes an important contribution because it contrasts two competing explanations of how consumers make inferences: by relying on prior beliefs vs. data-based cues. It has important public policy implications because it suggests that consumers often rely on incorrect beliefs (e.g., no cholesterol=no fat)even when faced with refutational evidence (e.g., nutritional information on the packaging). However, the low accessibility of the correlational data presented in the study may have contributed to subjects' reliance on prior beliefs or theories.

The Johar paper examines an important issue in corrective advertising—the role of the company's reputation—that has not received adequate attention in previous studies. Also, the research is timely in that we may see an increase in corrective advertising under the current FTC administration. The two studies were carefully conducted and manipulation checks were employed throughout. On the other hand, student subjects were used and the ads and reputation manipulation appeared to be somewhat contrived.

The Pechmann research devoted a great deal of attention to maximizing external validity. The two studies used real brands, a realistic cover story, and a sophisticated computer-simulated search task. It was found that naming competitors and factual claims were most effective at changing nontargeted beliefs, but not at changing targeted beliefs which would have been very predictable. One suggestion is to conduct follow-up analyses to examine the role of search directly and to examine the impact of the ads separated from the impact of search.

Overall, the studies were conducted carefully and make important contributions to the consumer inference-making literature.

Positive and Negative Effects of Brand Extension and Co-Branding

Allan D. Shocker, University of Minnesota

OBJECTIVES OF THE SESSION

Research on consumer behavior has had a strong history of important applications in arenas of managerial relevance. One substantial success has been that related to *brand equity*, where consumer research has provided virtually all the theoretical and empirical support for the benefits and risks of brand leveraging. An objective of this session was to encourage this research stream in new directions. It does this by demonstrating the relevance of psychological theory which has not previously been applied in marketing (the "concept combination" or "attribute inheritance" theory of Hampton [1987] and Smith, *et al.* [1988]). This theory is used to suggest how branded product concepts might combine to produce the concept for a co-branded product (*i.e.*, the placing of two (or more) brand names on a single product). It further suggests that the name of the product *category name* itself possesses properties similar to a brand and that this theoretical perspective may afford a means for helping managers make successful conventional brand extension decisions. Additionally, the theory and empirical research presented in the session is able to examine both positive and negative feedback effects from co-branding and brand extension.

FOUR PRESENTATIONS

Four papers comprised the session: 1. The first was *"On the Strategic Use of Branding Decisions for Inducing Positive Feedback Effects,"* by *C. Whan Park* (University of Pittsburgh, *Sung Youl Jun* (State University of New York at Binghampton), *and Allan D. Shocker* (University of Minnesota). The presentation began by noting that previous brand equity research has focused upon direct brand extensions (*e.g., Special-K waffles*), and primary attention has been paid to the *negative* effects of brand extensions upon the parent brand and its implications for managing brand equity. Negative feedback effects were found to be mainly due to either failure of the extension product or the lack of fit between the original and extension product categories (Keller and Aaker 1992; Loken and John 1993; Park, *et al.* 1992; Romeo 1991). Little attention has been paid to *positive* effects from strategic alliances, repositionings, and other possible branding strategies (Park, *et al.* 1994). Although the tasks of brand repositioning and enhancing brand equity usually have been attributed to advertising decisions, the authors postulated that creative branding strategies can also effectively contribute to such purpose. In the present study, they examined one specific cobranding strategy which uses an existing brand possessing complementary attribute associations to reposition an existing branded product (*e.g., Jaguar sedan by Toyota*). The study investigated whether this kind of co-branding enhanced the perceived attribute saliences and performance levels of the original or header brand concept (Jaguar sedan) and whether it had positive or negative effects upon the second or modifier brand (Toyota).

Pretests were used to identify an appropriate product class and brands; to generate an attribute set relevant to all brands; to verify complementarity of the brands chosen; to check the perceived fit between the brands and the sedan product; to verify that the description of the co-branded product resulted in the two brands conforming to roles sepcified for them by theory; and testing the believability, plausibility, and realism of the co-branded product. Subjects were 78 MBA students, randomly assigned to control and experimental groups in a "between-subjects" design. They rated

their familiarity with each of the brands [manipulation check], each branded concept's attribute salience and performance, the favorableness of their attitude and purchase intention toward each branded concept, the perceived fit between the constituent brands, and the degree of uniqueness and plausibility of the co-branded concept. In order to examine feedback effects experimental subjects responded to questions about one constituent brand concept (*i.e,* Jaguar sedan or Toyota sedan) after exposure to the co-branded concept. Control subjects responded to both constituent brand concepts in the absence of exposure to the co-branded concept.

Study hypotheses were suggested by concept combination theory. The empirical findings were as follows:

H1:   When an attribute is salient to at least one of the constituent brands, it will also be salient to the composite brand. *This hypothesis was supported.*

H2:   When either one of the constituent brands is perceived to perform well on an attribute, the perceived attribute performance level of the composite brand will also be high. *This hypothesis was also supported.*

H3:   When attitudes toward the modifier brand are favorable and the modifier is complementary to the header brand in attribute salience and performance levels, a composite branding strategy will lead to a more favorable evaluation of the composite brand than of the original header brand. *This hypothesis was also supported.*

The "Jaguar sedan by Toyota" concept had significantly higher evaluation in terms of attitude and purchase intention than did the Jaguar sedan alone.

H4:   When attitudes toward the modifier brand are favorable and the modifier is complementary to the header brand: (a) a composite branding strategy will lead to positive reciprocity effects on the header brand; and (b) a composite branding strategy will have neutral effects on the modifier brand. *This hypothesis was generally supported.*

The Jaguar sedan overall evaluations made after exposure to the co-branded concept were significantly higher than was the original Jaguar sedan evaluation. However, some attribute performance ratings were lower (*i.e.*, luxury, status symbol). The Toyota evaluations made after exposure to the co-branded concept were not significantly different than the original Toyota concept in overall evaluation, attribute salience, and attribute performance.

2. The second presentation was entitled, *"Attribute Inheritance: Its Role in Product Expectations and Competitive Evaluations of Brand Extensions,"* by Kalpesh Kaushik Desai, Wayne D. Hoyer, and Rajendra K. Srivastava (all of the University of Texas at Austin). Their study also contributes to the brand extension literature by shifting the focus of extant research from achieving favorable extension evaluation to ways of improving the extension's performance against competition in the new category. To succeed in the new category, the extension (EX) has to be evaluated favorably relative to the competition [*i.e.*, the "brands in consum-

ers' consideration sets" (CSB)]. This is possible when the EX is perceived as less similar to brands in the new category (i.e., it has something unique to offer) and the EX's performance on important attributes of the new category is better compared to that of the CSB. To determine the degree of perceived similarity of the EX with brands in the new category, we outline a methodology (Hampton 1987) that uncovers consumers' expectations about the EX (Pringles Pretzels) as comprised of attributes "inherited" from the parent product (Pringles) and the extension category (Pretzels). Limited inheritance of attributes from the extension category relative to the parent product will make the EX less similar to the brands in the extension category. The authors experimentally manipulate the degree of uniqueness of the parent product and the differentiation (variety) of the extension category—the two factors influencing the relative contribution of extension category and parent product to the nature of extension.

The hypotheses were tested across eight extensions in a 2 X 2 (uniqueness X differentiation) "between subjects" design. Results indicate that EXs of unique products are not only perceived as different from the brands in the extension category but their performance on the important attributes is also closer to that of the CSB. Also, though the extensions in less differentiated categories are not perceived as different from the brands in the extension category, their performance on the important attributes is closer to that of CSB. Despite the better performance on important attributes, the EXs of unique products and EXs in less differentiated categories were always evaluated less favorably (though quite close) compared to CSB. This demonstration suggested that EXs need to have more than unique features and better performance in the new category to overcome the equity advantage of the CSB. Also, knowing consumers' expectations about the precise nature of the EX might help the firm to develop the product and to emphasize appropriate features in its advertising.

3. The third presentation, *"Extensions of Strong and Weak Brands: Some Perils of Being Direct,"* was by Paul M. Herr and Ken Chapman (both of the University of Colorado at Boulder). Their work builds on Farquhar, Han, Herr, and Ijiri (1992). They presented the results of an experiment in which the method of brand extension and strength of brand in parent category prior to extension were manipulated. Consumers were exposed to print ads for three types of brand extensions; 1) direct extensions, in which the parent brand name was also the extension name (e.g., Nike Tennis Rackets), 2) indirect extensions, in which the parent brand endorsed the new product (e.g., The Avenger tennis racket by Nike), and 3) a new product introduced without benefit of brand extension (e.g., the Avenger tennis racket). Measures of liking for the extension, liking for the parent brand, and measures of the association following extension were collected. The results supported the authors' notion that different strategies should be employed for extending master brands than for extending weaker brands, and addressed the psychological basis for both category extensions and the appropriate strategies for managing them.

More specifically, the presence of a sub-brand (between the parent brand and the product name appears to have several interesting prophylactic effects on master brands. Although the commonly reported findings of superior affect transfer to close extensions by dominant brands (Aaker and Keller; 1990; Farquhar, Herr, and Fazio, 1990; and others) is replicated via sub-branding, subjects seem to be overtly unaware of the influence of the parent brand in the extension. Thus, a liked or disliked extension seemed to have no reciprocal impact on the liking of the parent brand at a later time. This was not the case when direct extensions were considered, i.e., no sub-brand intervened between the parent name and the extension

category. In those instances, the parent brand was tarnished or enhanced as a function of the subjects' liking of the extension. Overall, consumers' judgments of direct extensions were positively correlated with their subsequent judgments of the parent brand, while indirect extension judgments were uncorrelated with the parent. Measures of specific associations with the extensions suggested a number of processing models that may mediate these results.

4. The final paper, *"Spillover Effects of Brand Extensions: Can They Spread to a Firm's Established Products?"* was presented by Deborah Roedder John, Barbara Loken, and Christopher Joiner (all of the University of Minnesota-Twin Cities). They investigated the extent that consumer perceptions and reactions to brand extensions spill over to the parent company. And, if there is a spillover effect, they asked what are the potential risks or benefits to the parent company? To date, research addressing these issues (e.g., Loken and John 1993) has focused on whether spillover exists for *perceptions of the brand name*. Studies in this vein have measured whether consumer perceptions, beliefs, or overall affect toward the brand name are affected by the introduction of brand extensions. In contrast, their paper examined whether spillover exists for *perceptions of individual products* marketed under the brand name. The focus here was upon changes in consumer beliefs about individual products (e.g., Ivory shampoo, Ivory detergent) rather than changes in consumer beliefs about the brand name (e.g., Ivory), in general.

They considered several theoretical perspectives making different predictions about the types of products most likely subject to spillover effects. Based on ideas from categorization theory and attitude theory, these perspectives suggested that some individual products will be more affected than others, though they differ in predicting which products will be affected the most. The general prediction from the categorization perspective is that individual products that are most typical of the parent brand offerings will be subject to the greatest spillover effects. In contrast, the general prediction from the attitude strength literature is that individual products for whom consumer beliefs are the weakest will be subject to the greatest spillover effects.

These opposing predictions were tested in an experimental setting by examining changes in consumer beliefs about a variety of established products in the face of a brand extension (marketed under the same brand name) that either performed well (possible positive spillover) or poorly (possible negative spillover) on a particular attribute. The findings indicate that positive spillover effects are negligible, but that negative spillover effects are evident for some types of established products. Consistent with the attitude strength perspective, we found dilution effects for individual products when consumers had weak beliefs about the focal attribute. No support was found for the categorization prediction that dilution effects would be greatest for individual products higher in typicality.

CONCLUDING REMARKS

The favorable results reported by all authors indicate that co-branding and other strategic uses of brand names represent a fruitful area of additional inquiry. The presentations brought new theoretical insights to bear on this arena and demonstrated that they may provide a useful framework for prediction, and possibly explanation, of positive as well as negative effects on brand equity. At a minimum, the research provided evidence of consumers striving for cognitive consistency and that concept combination (attribute inheritance) and the other theories may capture the essence of the heuristics they use. Further research could more rigorously defend criteria of brand and product complementarity necessary for these theories to predict well. Much of the research was based upon complementary attributes and benefits; added research needs to examine what happens when conflicting, idiosyncratic, or irrelevant attributes are brought to the combination by different brand and product partners. Branding can be looked upon as a way of transfering meaning and preference across products; research to better understand what gets transferred and when and how is at the heart of the studies presented here and can generalize to other domains (*e.g.*, price-quality). The research results at best reflected consumer expectations; how these might be moderated by actual product experience seems worthy of further research. Concept combination theory has generally involved the combination of only two names. What happens when three or more are involved? Does the product category function similarly to a brand name in forming such combined concepts? These thoughts are suggestive of the richness of the arena and the session will hopefully stimulate much additional inquiry and insight.

REFERENCES

Aaker, David A. and Kevin Lane Keller (1990), "Consumer Evaluations of Brand Extensions," *Journal of Marketing*, 54 (February), 27-41.

Farquhar, Peter H., Paul M. Herr, and Russell H. Fazio (1990), "A Relational Model for Category Extensions of Brands," in Marvin E. Goldberg, Gerald Gorn, and Richard W. Pollay (eds.) *Advances in Consumer Research, Vol.17*, Provo UT: Association for Consumer Research, 856-860.

Farquhar, Peter H., Julia Y. Han, Paul M. Herr, and Yuji Ijiri (1992), "Strategies for Leveraging Master Brands," *Marketing Research*, 4, 32-43.

Hampton, James A. (1987), "Inheritance of Attributes in Natural Concept Conjunctions," *Memory & Cognition,* 15 (1), 55-71.

Keller, Kevin Lane and David A. Aaker (1992), "The Effects of Sequential Introduction of Brand Extensions," *Journal of Marketing Research*, 29 (February), 35-50.

Loken, Barbara and Deborah Roedder-John (1993), "Diluting Brand Beliefs: When do Brand Extensions Have a Negative Impact?" *Journal of Marketing*, 57 (July), 71-84.

Park, C. Whan, Michael S. McCarthy, and Sandra J. Milberg (1992), "The Effects of Direct and Associative Branding on the Evaluation and Reciprocity Effects of Brand Extensions," in Leigh McAlister and Michael Rothschild (eds.) *Advances in Consumer Research, Volume XX*, Provo, UT: Association of Consumer Research.

Park, C. Whan, Sung Youl Jun, and Allan D. Shocker (1994), "Composite Brand Extension: Its Process, Outcomes, and Promise," Working Paper, Minneapolis: Carlson School of Management, University of Minnesota.

Romeo, Jean B. (1991), "The Effect of Negative Information on the Evaluation of Brand Extensions and the Family Brand," in Rebecca H. Holman and Michael R. Solomon (eds.) *Advances in Consumer Research, Vol.18*, Provo UT: Association for Consumer Research, 399-406.

Smith, Edward E., Daniel N. Osherson, Lance J. Rips, and Margaret Keane (1988), "Combining Prototypes: A Selective Modification Model," *Cognitive Science*, 12, 485-527.

Effects of Involvement on On-line Brand Evaluations: A Stronger Test of the ELM

Jong-Won Park, Korea University
Manoj Hastak, American University

ABSTRACT

The Elaboration Likelihood Model predicts differences in the processes mediating persuasion effects for involved and uninvolved audiences — but only in those situations where persuasion occurs on-line, i.e., during message exposure. However, previous tests of the ELM have failed to provide compelling evidence for on-line persuasion, and hence have failed to create the strongest possible test for the ELM. Such a test was created in a pilot and a main study. Results from the pilot study showed that involvement influenced the response time for on-line brand evaluations and subsequent recall of product information. In the main experiment, typical ELM manipulations and procedures were replicated, but all subjects were instructed to evaluate the advertised brands while they were viewing the ads. The results were consistent with ELM predictions. Implication for future research on the ELM are discussed.

INTRODUCTION

The effects of issue involvement on the processes mediating issue evaluation are of interest to social psychologists as well as consumer researchers. A particularly well accepted model in this area is the Elaboration Likelihood Model (ELM) proposed by Petty and Cacioppo (1983, 1986). The ELM suggests that brand involvement (defined as degree of perceived personal relevance of the advertised brand) is one of the key determinants of the way in which audiences process an ad message for the brand. High brand involvement leads to a "central route" to persuasion in that the ad recipients carefully examine and process those ad message elements that they believe are central to a meaningful and logic evaluation of the brand (e.g., brand attribute information). By contrast, low brand involvement induces a "peripheral route" to persuasion whereby recipients evaluate the brand based on superficial analysis of readily available and salient cues in the ad regardless of whether these cues are meaningfully related to the brand (e.g., background music). These ELM predictions have received support in several studies (see Petty, Unnava, and Strathman 1991 for a review). Also, several models of advertising effects have suggested processing differences between high and low involvement audiences similar to the ELM (Batra and Ray 1985; Greenwald and Leavitt 1984; MacInnis and Jaworsky 1989; Mitchell 1986).

AN IMPLICIT ASSUMPTION IN THE ELM

Extensive critiques of the ELM on conceptual as well as methodological grounds have been reported in the persuasion literature (MacInnis and Jaworsky 1989; Areni and Lutz 1988; Miniard and Dickson 1988; Andrews 1988). However, one implicit but important assumption that forms the basis of the ELM framework has been virtually overlooked by researchers in this area. Specifically, it is assumed in the ELM that all audiences, be they involved or uninvolved with an advertised brand, form brand evaluations *on-line*, i.e., while they are exposed to the ad message. Stated differently, while the ELM hypothesizes different persuasion routes for involved versus uninvolved audiences, it implicitly assumes that persuasion occurs during ad exposure under both routes.

We should note here that we do not view the assumption of on-line persuasion as a general limitation of the ELM model. Rather, the assumption limits the persuasion contexts in which predictions based on the ELM can be reasonably expected to hold. The ELM says nothing about persuasion process that occur sometime after exposure to stimulus information, nor does it predict differences in on-line versus delayed (i.e., memory-based) persuasion. Predictions based on the ELM are only germane to situations where audiences form brand evaluations during exposure to advertising messages.

Implications for Empirical Tests of the ELM

The above discussion suggests that a compelling test of ELM predictions can only be conducted in contexts where on-line brand evaluation processes are occurring. This can be achieved in a laboratory study simply by giving subjects a brand-evaluation goal, i.e., requiring them to evaluate the advertised brand on-line. However, a careful examination of the processing goals and/or orienting instructions given to subjects in ELM studies shows that a brand evaluation goal is almost never explicitly given. Goals typically given subject include evaluating the sound quality of audio messages (Petty, Cacioppo and Goldman 1981; Petty and Cacioppo 1981), evaluating or forming an impression of the speaker (Chaiken 1980, experiment #2; Petty and Cacioppo 1984), evaluating the ad (Petty, Cacioppo, and Schumann 1983), viewing the ad in a natural manner (Celsi and Olson 1988), general comprehension (Chaiken 1980, experiment #1), evaluating the background program (Batra and Ray 1985) etc.. The intent of these instructions is likely to mask the true purpose of the study. However, an undesirable side effect of such instructions may be to inhibit or even discourage subjects from engaging in brand evaluation processing during message exposure. Furthermore, these studies do not even provide any (post-hoc) evidence to suggest that the obtained persuasion effects occurred on-line.

Failure to enforce a brand evaluation goal or otherwise provide evidence supporting on-line brand evaluation clearly opens the possibility that the quality of empirical tests of the ELM may be compromised. Furthermore, we believed that this may be a particularly serious problem for prediction concerning uninvolved audiences. An individual who is involved with an advertised brand will likely spontaneously evaluate the brand on-line because forming a brand evaluation is relevant to either his/her short-term goals or his/her enduring interest with the brand/product category. However, uninvolved audiences do not see the brand as personally relevant, and may therefore refrain from evaluating the brand because such an evaluation serves no objective. Indeed, there is considerable evidence in the literature on memory-based judgement and evaluation to show that individuals who do not have an evaluation objective when they are exposed to stimulus information do not spontaneously form evaluations on-line (Hastie and Park 1986; Lichtenstein and Srull 1985, 1987; Wyer and Srull 1989).

The preceding discussion suggests an alternative explanation for effects due to peripheral ad cues (e.g., an attractive source) on brand evaluation for uninvolved audiences that are obtained in empirical tests of the ELM. Rather than a peripheral cue serving as a low effort heuristic for brand evaluation on-line, the cue may influence brand evaluation later (when the evaluation is measured) in a memory-based manner. Since peripheral cues used in ELM studies are usually salient and vivid (e.g., pictures of celebrities in Petty, Cacioppo, and Schumann 1983), theses cues are likely more accessible in long term memory than are brand message arguments. As a consequence, peripheral cues could have strong effects on

435

uninvolved audiences regardless of whether these effects were on-line or memory based. Thus, peripheral cue effects for uninvolved audiences do not constitute a compelling test of the ELM since they potentially confound on-line and memory-based persuasion processes.

In sum, there is an implicit assumption in the ELM which needs to be empirically validated: persuasion occurs during ad message exposure regardless of which route (central or peripheral) is followed. We report on a pilot study and a main experiment which evaluated this critical assumption. In both studies subjects were explicitly instructed to evaluate the advertised brand during ad exposure. The pilot study examined the effect of involvement on response times for on-line brand evaluations and on recall. The main study attempted a replication of typical ELM tests to see if results found in previous studies could be obtained even when all subjects were given an explicit brand evaluation goal.

PILOT STUDY

As we noted earlier, The ELM suggests that involved audiences form evaluations that are carefully reasoned (central processing), whereas uninvolved audiences form evaluations that are relatively superficial (peripheral processing). Since central processing involves a more careful assessment of information in an ad, response times for generating brand evaluations should be longer for involved audiences than for uninvolved audiences. Also, involved audiences should recall ad information better than uninvolved audiences. These possibilities were examined in this study.

Procedure

Ball point pen was used as the target product. Print ads for fictitious brands of six different products including the target product were created for the study. The ad for the pen contained a simple headline, a picture of the product, and ten verbal product claims.

Fifty four subjects participated in the study. Upon arrival, subjects were seated in individual computer booths and were told that their task would be to evaluate each advertised product in the booklet they were about to receive. After a short computer practice session, they were assigned to either high or low involvement for the pen brand. Involvement was manipulated via two instructions given to subjects just before they examined the ads in the booklet. First, subjects were informed that during a subsequent session they would be asked to choose one of several brands of a product, and that an ad for one of these brands was in the booklet they were about to examine. Second, subjects were told that they would win a cash prize if their evaluation score for this same brand was similar to the overall rating given to the brand by *Consumer Reports*. The product for the choice task and the cash prize was varied: it was the ball point pen for the high involvement condition and a different product for the low involvement condition (see Celsi and Olson 1988; Maheswaran and Sternthal 1990 for a similar procedure).

Subjects examined the ads in the booklet one at a time at their own pace, and reported their brand evaluation on a 9-point scale (very poor-very good) by pressing the appropriate number on their keyboard. The computer automatically timed each evaluation. This procedure was carefully controlled to minimize any extraneous effects on the response times.

Next, after a five minute distraction task, subjects responded to three measures of "felt" involvement (Celsi and Olson 1988) on 9-point scales (not at all interested-very much interested in the product; not at all attentive-very much attentive to information; not at all concerned-very much concerned about the accuracy of the evaluation). Since these measures were highly inter-correlated (alpha=.82), the responses were averaged to construct a composite measure of felt involvement. Finally, subjects were asked to recall the original information for the pen brand. Recalled items were scored by two independent judges and the inter-judge agreement was 88.8%. Disagreements were resolved through discussion.

Results

Subjects in the high involvement conditions reported a higher level of felt involvement than those in the low involvement conditions (M=6.32 versus 5.19, F(1,53)=5.51, p<.05), indicating that the involvement manipulation was successful. An ANOVA on response times for evaluations revealed a significant effect for involvement (F=6.32, p<.05). As expected, involved subjects took longer to evaluate the brand than did uninvolved subjects (M=35.3 versus 26.7 seconds). Furthermore, involved subjects recalled more than did uninvolved subjects (M=3.41 versus 2.63, (F(1,26)=4.19, p<.10). In sum, the response time and recall data suggest that involved subjects processed product information more carefully in making on-line evaluations than uninvolved subjects.

MAIN STUDY

A key prediction of the ELM is that "central" message cues (e.g., message quality) have a stronger effect on involved audiences, while "peripheral" cues (e.g., source credibility) are more impactful on uninvolved audiences. We tested these predictions under conditions where subjects were clearly forming on-line brand evaluations. Results consistent with the ELM predictions should provide stronger support for the ELM than has been achieved in previous tests.

Method

Subjects and Design. A total of 144 male and female undergraduate students participated in the experiment for course credit. Of these, 138 provided usable responses. The design was a 2 (high/low involvement) by 2 (strong/weak ad message) by 2 (high/moderate source credibility) factorial.

Procedure. Upon arrival, subjects were randomly assigned to one of the eight experimental conditions. All subjects received a folder containing: (a) an introduction booklet, which described the general purpose of the study, experimental tasks, and lottery procedures designed to manipulate involvement, (b) an ad booklet, which contained eight mock ads including an ad for a running shoe brand (target ad), and (c) a dependent measure booklet.

The introduction booklet informed subjects that their task was to examine several product ads at their own pace, and to form an overall evaluation of each of the advertised brands. In addition, subjects were asked to indicate this overall evaluation on response scales that were provided on a separate sheet. Thus, all subjects were given a brand evaluation goal, and these evaluations were measured on-line, i.e., while the pertinent ads were in front of the subjects. Next, after a brief distracting task, subjects were asked to complete the dependent measure booklet. The entire experimental procedure took about 30 minutes, and concluded with a debriefing of subjects.

Manipulation of Involvement. Involvement was manipulated through the use of lotteries. The introduction booklet informed subjects that several lotteries, each for a different product category, would be run as a compensation for their participation, and that they had been randomly assigned to one of these lotteries. Subjects in the high involvement condition were told that they would participate in a lottery for the target product (running shoes). In contrast, subjects in the low involvement condition were informed that they would participate in a lottery for another product (boombox). All subjects were told that lottery winners would be chosen at random after the experiment, and would be allowed to select their preferred brand from among those available within the product category. To bolster the involvement manipulation, subjects were told that they would see an ad for one brand of the lottery product during the study, and that this brand would be one of those available in the lottery.

Manipulation of Message Quality. A variety of message arguments for running shoes were pretested in terms of their convincingness and persuasive strength. The results of the pretest were used to create a strong and a weak version of the running shoe ad. Both versions contained eight arguments, and were approximately equal in length. However, the strong ad version contained relatively compelling and persuasive claims about the advertised brand, while the weak ad version contained relatively uncompelling and vacuous brand claims.

Manipulation of Source Credibility. The running shoe ad contained a headline featuring a personal testimonial for the advertised brand. In the high credibility condition, the endorser was described as a special columnist for the *Runner's World* magazine. In the moderate credibility condition, the endorser was introduced as a political consultant.

Dependent Measures. Subjects' evaluation of the running shoe brand was measured on two 9-point scales (not at all-very likable; very unsatisfactory-very satisfactory). Since the two measures were highly intercorrelated (r=.81), responses were averaged to construct a composite measure. Other dependent variables included subjects' ratings of message argument quality and source credibility, unaided recall of ad message content, self-reported levels of felt involvement with the advertised brand, and (enduring) product category involvement. As an instruction check, subjects were asked to recall the product lottery to which they had been assigned.

Results

Manipulation Checks. To assess the effectiveness of the message quality manipulation, subjects were asked to rate the brand information in the running shoe ad on two 9-point scales (not at all-very convincing; very weak-very strong). A three-way ANOVA on the average of these ratings (which were highly correlated, r=.86) yielded only a significant main effect for the message quality manipulation (F=44.82, p<.001). As expected, subjects who had received the strong version of the ad rated the message quality stronger (M=5.79) than those who had received the weak version (M=3.46).

As a check on the source credibility manipulation, subjects were asked to rate the person who recommended the running shoe brand on two 9-point scales (not at all-very credible; not at all-very knowledgeable). A three-way ANOVA on the average of these ratings (which were highly correlated, r=.87) yielded significant main effects for the source credibility manipulation (F=72.92, p<.001) as well as the message quality manipulation (F=10.17, p<.01). As expected, subjects in the high credibility condition rated the source as more credible than did subjects in the low credibility condition (M=5.79 versus M=3.50). Also, subjects who had received the strong version of the ad rated the source as more credible than did subjects who had received the weak version (M=5.34 versus M=4.30). Importantly, none of the interactions were significant (F<1). In short, the source credibility manipulation was successful.

The effectiveness of the involvement manipulation was assessed in two ways. First, we examined whether or not subjects correctly recalled the product lottery to which they had been assigned. Only one subject incorrectly recalled the lottery. This suggests that the lottery manipulation successfully influenced personal relevance (i.e., subjects know whether or not they would be making a short term decision regarding the running shoe brand). Note, however, that the ultimate goal of this manipulation was to influence the degree to which subjects actually felt involved with the brand message during exposure to the ad. Therefore, as a more direct check, we examined the effects of the lottery manipulation on three 9-point scales designed to measure how involved subjects actually felt, and how attentively and carefully subjects processed the running shoe brand message (paying a little-paying a lot of attention; not at all carefully-very carefully read; not at all-very involved). A three-way ANOVA on the average of these scales (average r=.66) did not yield any significant main or interactive effects. Contrary to expectations, the main effect due to the involvement manipulation was not significant (M=5.63 versus M=5.23, F=2.04, p>.10), although the means were in the expected direction. Thus, subjects in the high involvement condition did seem to recognize the personal relevance of the advertised running shoe, but did not actually feel more involved, or process brand message information more intensely than did subjects in the low involvement conditions.

Tests of the ELM. Failure to successfully manipulate involvement limits our ability to conduct strong tests of the ELM. Since subjects in the high/low involvement conditions did not differ on intensity and degree of brand message processing, we would not expect differential effects of the message quality and source credibility manipulations on these subjects. This proved to be the case. A three-way ANOVA (involvement by message quality by source credibility) on overall evaluations revealed significant main effects due to the source credibility manipulation (F=8.16, p<.01) and the message quality manipulation (F=52.71, p<.001), but no significant interactions. The high credibility source led to more positive evaluations than the moderate credibility source (M=5.47 versus 4.59), while the strong quality message led to more positive evaluations than the weak quality message (M=6.19 versus 3.89). Importantly, neither the involvement by source credibility interaction nor the involvement by message quality interaction was significant (F=1.73, p<.19, and F<1, respectively). Note that while these results are consistent with the ELM, they do not provide compelling support since they require acceptance of null hypotheses.

Two sets of analysis were done in an attempt to create somewhat stronger tests for the ELM than those reported above. First, a median split on our measure of felt involvement (based on the involvement manipulation check measures) was used to create two groups that differed significantly on actual levels of involvement experienced during the ad viewing episode, and all analyses were conducted using this blocking factor. Second, a median split on our measure of product class involvement (i.e., involvement with running shoes in general) was used in all analyses. These two approaches generated similar results. To conserve space, we report only on the results based on the felt involvement blocking factor. As a result of the median split, 69 (68) subjects were assigned to the high (low) felt involvement conditions. These groups differed significantly on reported felt involvement (M=6.75 versus 3.98, F=323.99, p<.0001).

A three-way ANOVA on overall evaluations as a function of felt involvement (blocking factor), message quality, and source credibility revealed significant main effects for the source credibility and message quality manipulations (F=8.99, p<.005; F=55.45, p<.0001, respectively). More importantly, and as hypothesized in the ELM, these effects were qualified by significant involvement by source credibility and involvement by message quality interac-

TABLE 1
Brand Evaluations as a Function of Involvement and Credibility

	Felt Involvement	
	Low	High
Source Credibility		
Moderate	4.19 (n=35)	4.99 (n=36)
High	6.03 (n=33)	4.91 (n=33)

TABLE 2
Brand Evaluations as a Function of Involvement and Message Quality

	Felt Involvement	
	Low	High
Message Quality		
Weak	4.27 (n=35)	3.57 (n=36)
Strong	5.81 (n=33)	6.65 (n=33)

tions. The involvement by source credibility interaction (F=7.76, p<.01) indicated that source credibility effects on evaluations were different for high versus low involvement conditions (see Table 1).

Planned comparisons revealed that the highly credible source produced more positive evaluations than did the source of moderate credibility when felt involvement was low (F=20.89, p<.001) but not when it was high (F<1). This result is consistent with the ELM.

The involvement x message quality interaction (F=6.14, p<.02) indicated that message quality effects on evaluations also differed across the two involvement conditions (see Table 2).

Planned comparisons revealed that although message quality affected evaluations under both high involvement (F=41.56, p<.001) and low involvement (F= 15.29, p<.001), the impact of message quality was much greater in the high involvement conditions (R^2=.39) than in the low involvement conditions (R^2=.15). This result is also consistent with the ELM.

DISCUSSION

The ELM predicts the process mediators of persuasion only in on-line persuasion contexts. Unfortunately, previous tests have failed to provide compelling evidence for on-line persuasion, and hence have not generated the strongest possible tests of the ELM. We sought to achieve such a test by giving all our subjects clear instructions to engage in on-line brand evaluations. Also, we measured these evaluations as they were formed (rather than after subjects had viewed all our ads) to ensure that subjects followed our instructions. Results from our two studies provide support for the ELM. Specifically, reaction times for evaluations and recall of information were greater for involved subjects than for uninvolved subjects. Also, message quality had a stronger effect on brand attitude for involved subjects while source credibility had a stronger effect on brand attitudes for uninvolved subjects.

There is, of course, one important caveat to our results, and that concerns our failure to manipulate involvement in the main study. We used a (lottery) procedure similar to one that has been successfully used in past research (Celsi and Olson 1988). Our subjects seemed to recognize the implications of the lottery, but did not process product information with differential intensities as a result.

One possibility for why the involvement manipulation failed may be that subjects' involvement with the product class (running shoes) had a strong impact on how involved they felt with the running shoe ad (felt involvement), and this overpowered our lottery manipulation. This argument is bolstered by the fact that our measures of product class involvement and felt involvement were significantly correlated (r=.45), and both measures yielded similar results when introduced as blocking variables in our analyses. Interestingly, Celsi and Olson (1988) also found that the lottery manipulation produced much weaker (although significant) effects on felt involvement than did product class involvement in their study.

In sum, while our results are consistent with the ELM, they do not provide unambiguous evidence for the casual influence of involvement on on-line evaluation processes. Constructive replications that create successful manipulations of involvement are needed to produce such evidence. Also, future research should examine the effects of brand involvement on the processing goals that subjects adopt during ad exposure. Finally, the effects of "central" and "peripheral" cues on persuasion that is on-line versus memory-based, and mediators of these effects are important and unresolved issues that should be investigated.

REFERENCES

Andrews, J. C. (1988), "Motivation, Ability, and Opportunity to Process Information: Conceptual and Experimental Manipulation Issues," in *Advances in Consumer Research*, 15, M. J. Houston, ed., Association for Consumer Research, 197-203.

Areni, C. S. and R. J. Lutz (1988), "The Role of Argument Quality in the Elaboration Likelihood Model," in *Advances in Consumer Research*, 15, M.J. Houston, ed., Association for Consumer Research, 197-203.

Batra, R and M. L. Ray (1985), "How Advertising Works at Contact," in *Psychological processes and Advertising Effects: Theory, Research, and Applications*, eds., L. Alwitt and A. A. Mitchell, Hillsdale, NJ: Lawrence Erlbaum, 13-43.

Celsi, R. L. and J. C. Olson (1988), "The Role of Involvement in Attention and Comprehension Processes," *Journal of Consumer Research*, 15 (2), 210-224.

Chaiken, S. (1980), "Heuristic versus Systematic Information processing and the Use of Source versus Message Cues in Persuasion," *Journal of Personality and Social Psychology*, 39 (5), 752-766.

Greenwald, A. and C. Leavitt (1984), "Audience Involvement in Advertising: Four Levels," *Journal of Consumer Research*, 11 (June), 581-592.

Hastie, R. and B. Park (1986), "The Relationship Between Memory and Judgment Depends on Whether the Judgment Task is Memory-Based or On-Line," *Psychological Review*, 93 (July), 258-268.

Lichtenstein, M. and T. K. Srull (1985), "Conceptual and Methodological Issues in Examining the Relationship Between Consumer Memory and Judgment," in *Psychological Processes and Advertising Effects: Theory, Research and Applications*, eds., L. Alwitt and A. A. Mitchell, Hillsdale, NJ: Lawrence Earlbaum, 113-128.

_____ and _____ (1987), "Processing Objectives as a Determinant of the Relationship Between Recall and Judgment," *Journal of Experimental Social Psychology*, 23 (March), 93-118.

MacInnis, D. J. and B. J. Jawroski (1989), "Information Processing from Advertisements: Toward an Integrative Framework," *Journal of Marketing*, 53 (October), 1-23.

Maheswaran, D. and B. Sternthal (1990), "The Effects of Knowledge, Motivation, and Type of Message on Ad Processing and Product Judgments," *Journal of Consumer Research*, 17 (June), 66-73.

Miniard, P. W., P. R. Dickson, and K. R. Lord (1988), "Some Central and Peripheral Thoughts on Routes to Persuasion," in *Advances in Consumer Research*, 15, M. J. Houston, ed., Association for Consumer Research, 197-203.

Mitchell, A. A. (1986), "Theoretical and Methodological Issues in Developing an Individual- Level Model of Advertising Effects," in *Advertising and Consumer Psychology*, eds., J. C. Olson and K. Sentis, 3, 172-196.

Petty, R. E. and J. T. Cacioppo (1981), "Issue Involvement as a Moderator of the Effects on Attitude of Advertising Content and Context," in *Advances in Consumer Research*, 8, K. B. Monroe, ed., Association for Consumer Research, 20-24.

_____ and _____ (1983), "Central and Peripheral Routes to Persuasion: Application to Advertising," in *Advertising and Consumer Psychology*, L. Percy and A. Woodside, eds., Lexington, MA: Heath, 3-23.

_____ and _____ (1986), "The Elaboration Likelihood Model of Persuasion," in *Advances in Experimental Social Psychology*, ed., L. Berkowitz, 19, Orlando, FL: Academic Press, 123-205.

_____ , _____ , and R. Goldman (1981), "Personal Involvement as a Determinant of Argument-Based Persuasion," *Journal of Personality and Social Psychology*, 41, 847-855.

_____ , _____ , and D. M. Schumann (1983), "Central and Peripheral Routes to Advertising Effectiveness: The Moderating Role of Involvement," *Journal of Consumer Research*, 10 (September), 135-146.

_____ , R. Unnava, and A. J. Strathman (1991), in *Handbook of Consumer Behavior*, eds., T. S. Robertson and H. H. Kassarjian, Englewood Cliffs, NJ: Prentice-Hall, 1-49.

Wyer, R. S. Jr. and T. K. Srull (1989), *Memory and Cognition in Its Social Context*, Hillsdale, NJ: Erlbaum.

Conceptualizing and Operationalizing Affect, Reason, and Involvement in Persuasion: The ARI Model and the CASC Scale

Ross Buck, University of Connecticut
Arjun Chaudhuri, Fairfield University
Mats Georgson, University of Connecticut
Srinivas Kowta, University of Connecticut

ABSTRACT

Two of the traditional problems in studying emotion in persuasion research have been (1) how to conceptualize emotion and its relationship with the "cold" cognitive processing typically associated with reason and (2) how to operationalize emotion. This paper addresses these issues in a fundamentally new way. The *ARI Model (Affect-Reason-Involvement Model)* defines and describes the relationships between affect, reason, and involvement; arguing that both affective and rational involvement are important in persuasion. These involve *syncretic* and *analytic* cognition, respectively associated with right and left hemisphere processing. The *CASC Scale (Communication via Syncretic and Analytic Cognition Scale* is a developing instrument designed to operationalize affective and rational responses to advertising and to commercial products. It is based upon a new conceptualization of the affects that recognizes reptilian, individualistic-limbic, prosocial-limbic, social, cognitive, and moral emotions.

INTRODUCTION

This paper presents a new conceptualization of emotion and reason and their relationships with involvement, and a new scale designed to capture both analytic rational knowledge and the many varieties of emotional knowledge.

Affect and Persuasion.

Emotion is a "hot topic" in the social and behavioral sciences, due in part to new capabilities to observe and measure emotional phenomena. It is now possible to capture subtle nuances of expressive behavior using inexpensive videotape technology, and we have powerful new methods of observing and manipulating biological phenomena associated with emotion—from brain scans, to new methods of following the course of neurochemical systems within the brain, to new psychoactive drugs such as Prozac.

The primacy of emotion vs. cognition. The question of the "primacy" of affect and reason in persuasion was the focus of the debate between Robert Zajonc (1980;1984) and Richard Lazarus (1982;1984). Zajonc argued that emotion could occur prior to, and independently of, cognition; while Lazarus replied that cognition was necessary for emotion. The issue arguably represented a difference in how the protagonists defined "cognition:" as involving direct acquaintance (knowledge by acquaintance or *syncretic cognition*) as opposed to information processing (knowledge by description or *analytic cognition*. See Buck, 1990; Buck & Chaudhuri, in press; Chaudhuri & Buck, in press; Tucker, 1981). The controversy was resolved by new evidence from LeDoux and his colleagues demonstrating conclusively that emotion-related structures in the limbic system receive early and independent input about events (LeDoux, 1986). Lazarus (1991) has acknowledged that LeDoux's findings and the distinction between analytic and syncretic knowledge effectively demonstrates that raw affect indeed constitutes a kind of knowledge that can precede, and indeed contribute to, analytic knowledge.

The distinction between analytic and syncretic cognition in analogous in some respects to distinctions between systematic and heuristic processing (Chaiken 1980) and between central vs. peripheral routes to persuasion (Petty & Cacioppo 1986). It also relates to differences in how print and electronic media are processed. It is generally accepted that electronic media are more "emotional" than print, and indeed Chaudhuri and Buck (in press) showed that televised ads elicit more syncretic processing, and print ads more analytic processing, even after relevant product category and ad strategy variables are controlled.

Affect in political perception. One of the clearest applications of the role of syncretic vs. analytic cognition to persuasion is in the area of politics. The 1960 Presidential debates, in which radio listeners thought Nixon won, while TV viewers thought Kennedy won, are celebrated (or mourned) as a watershed in American politics. Abelson and his colleagues (1982) demonstrated that surveys could predict political preferences better from asking respondents their feelings about candidate than by more "semantically filtered" judgments of candidates' traits. McHugo and his colleagues (1985) showed viewers segments from the 1984 Presidential debates between Walter Mondale and Ronald Reagan. They found using facial EMG that viewing Reagan smiling induced invisible tendencies to smile on the part of viewers, while viewing Reagan frowning induced tendencies to frown. This effect was unrelated to the viewer's prior attitudes toward Reagan. Mondale's expressions did not have this effect on viewers. This ability to induce emotional reactions in viewers may be the basis of Reagan's celebrated "teflon factor" and, more generally, of charisma.

Implications. These findings imply that emotion is central to the persuasion process, particularly in a world increasingly dominated by electronic media. But while much theory and research have been directed to understanding the role of reason, or systematic processing, in the "central route " to persuasion, relatively less attention has been directed to emotion, or its relationship with reason. The conceptualization of affect, reason, and their relationship is the goal of the ARI model, and the measurement of syncretic (affective) and analytic (rational) cognition the goal of the CASC scale.

CONCEPTUALIZATION: THE ARI MODEL

The nature of affect, reason, and their relationship with one another and with the construct of involvement are the subject matter of the ARI (Affect-Reason-Involvement) model (Buck & Chaudhuri, in press). This section describes the model and summarizes initial empirical studies based upon it.

The relationship of affect and reason. Affect and reason are often considered to be at ends of a continuum, but we consider them to be qualitatively different kinds of systems which interact with one another (Buck, 1985; 1988). Affect is based upon biologically-structured special-purpose processing systems (SPPSs) which are innate, that is, are phylogenetic adaptations. Reason is based upon general-purpose processing systems (GPPSs) which are structured by the organism's experience over the course of individual development: that is, structured during ontogeny. Both affect and reason are held to be "cognition" since both support knowledge. Reason involves analytic cognition which is sequential, analytic, and asso-

FIGURE 1
The relationship between affect (syncretic cognition) and reason (analytic cognition)

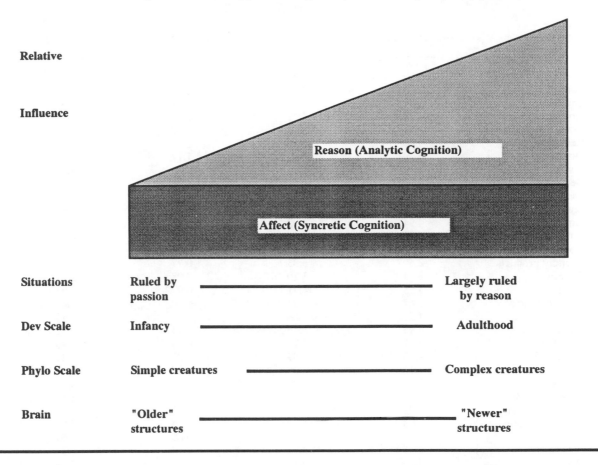

ciated with left cerebral hemisphere functioning in most human beings. Affect is syncretic cognition which is holistic and synthetic and associated with the functioning of the right hemisphere (Tucker, 1981). We define affect formally as the syncretic knowledge-by-acquaintance of feelings and desires.

The relationship between affect and reason is expressed by *Figure 1*. The continuum at the base of Figure 1 describes the mix of affect and reason, and is termed the affect/reason continuum (*A/R Continuum*). On the extreme left of the continuum, the influence of affect is total: reason has no influence. As one goes to the right, reason exerts an increasing influence relative to affect, but the influence of affect never falls to zero.

One way to interpret the A/R Continuum is by situations in which the relative influence of affect and reason vary. We assume that affect has a role in all situations, while the influence of reason varies from zero (in situations ruled wholly by passion) to high levels (in situations where "mindful" systematic analysis is paramount). However, even in the latter, highly mindful situation, affect retains influence: thus the relative influence of affect never falls to zero. Another way the A/R continuum can be interpreted is as a developmental scale, with the newborn at the left functioning virtually wholly according to innate affective control systems, with the influence of reason increasing with age. The A/R continuum also can reflect the brain structures that support affect and reason: the phylogenetically older subcortical and limbic system structures supporting affect are always functioning in all situations, and are present in simple creatures; while the phylogenetically newer

neocortical structures supporting increasingly complex analytic-rational controls may or may not be activated depending upon situational demands, and they evolved gradually to reach their greatest volume relative to the older structures in the mammals and, particularly, human beings.

The A/R Continuum in consumer research. Both advertisements and products can be placed on the A/R continuum, reflecting the ratio of affect to reason in the appeal used by the advertisement, or in the possession and use of that product (Chaudhuri & Buck, 1993). Thus, an affectively loaded advertisement or product has a high A/R ration, while an ad or product to be dealt with "mindfully" has a low A/R ratio. The A/R ratio of 30 common products is given in *Table 1* (Chaudhuri, 1992). It was operationalized by asking 104 raters to evaluate each product on two three-item scales derived from "pleasure" and "risk" scales of the Revised Personal Involvement Inventory (McQuarrie & Munson, 1987). In a second study Chaudhuri (1993) assessed the A/R ratio of 76 common products by single-item scales asking 216 undergraduate subjects about the amount of pleasure that can be derived from the product (affect), and the degree to which brands of the product can be differentiated (reason). Both studies showed that products such as candy and snack foods have high A/R ratios, automobiles and airline services are relatively balanced in A/R scores, and appliances and laundry products have low A/R ratios.

Level of Involvement (LI). We define *involvement* following Batra and Ray (1983) as the "depth and quality of cognitive response" (p. 309), but we suggest that both affective and rational

TABLE 1
A/R Ratio and LI data for 30 common products
Data from Chaudhuri (1992)

Product	Affect mean	Reason mean	A/R ratio	(R + A) / 2
Autos	6.20	5.25	1.18	5.73
Candy	4.60	3.37	1.36	3.99
Sneakers	5.44	3.92	1.38	4.68
Appliances	2.78	4.71	0.59	3.75
Coffee	2.71	3.45	0.79	3.08
Cereal	4.60	3.20	1.44	3.90
Diamonds	5.40	4.62	1.17	5.01
Insurance	2.45	5.54	0.44	4.00
Beer	4.99	4.04	1.24	4.52
Dental hygiene	3.52	3.12	1.13	3.32
Soft drinks	4.81	2.92	1.65	3.87
Airlines	4.94	4.92	1.00	4.93
Long dist phone	3.83	4.57	0.84	4.20
House. cleaners	2.23	3.14	0.71	2.69
Laundry products	2.59	3.35	0.77	2.97
Batteries	3.13	3.19	0.98	3.16
Wine	4.55	4.71	0.97	4.63
Paper products	2.47	2.73	0.90	2.60
Fast food	4.53	3.68	1.23	4.11
Snack foods	4.95	3.46	1.43	4.21
Credit cards	4.71	5.24	0.89	4.98
Camera film	4.73	3.89	1.22	4.31
Deodorants	3.12	3.20	0.98	3.16
Bath soap	3.28	2.78	1.18	3.03
Greeting cards	5.46	3.87	1.41	4.67
Pharmaceuticals	2.92	4.67	0.62	3.80
Pers. computers	5.03	4.87	1.03	4.95
Express mail	3.24	4.06	0.80	3.65
Pet foods	2.35	3.27	0.70	2.81
Watches	5.16	4.12	1.25	4.64

Note: Reason measured by three "risk" items from McQuarrie & Munson (1987):
        No risk vs. risky; Easy to go wrong vs. hard to go wrong;
        Hard to pick vs. easy to choose.
        Affect measured by three "hedonic" items from McQuarrie & Munson (1987):
        Appealing vs. unappealing; Unexciting vs. exciting; Fun vs. not fun.

involvement are possible, involving the depth and quality of syncretic and analytic cognitive responding, respectively (Chaudhuri & Buck, 1993). Given this definition, we suggest that the *Level of Involvement (LI)* can be defined simply as the average of affective and rational involvement: that is, $LI=(A+R)/2$. The appropriate figures for involvement are given in *Table 1*. Studies are continuing to assess the reliability and validity of the ARI model and the stability of the A/R and LI measures (Georgson, 1993; Kowta, 1993).

The ARI solid. The *ARI Solid* is a 3D figure bounded on one side by a low-high LI dimension and on the other by the A/R continuum (See *Figure 2*). The relative influence of affect and reason at any point on the A/R continuum is represented by an *ARI Slice* in which the relative influence of affect and reason remains constant as involvement increases. The specific ARI slice is known by the A/R ratio.

The "floor" of the ARI Solid is a two-dimensional space with an involvement dimension on the Y-axis and the A/R Continuum on the X-axis (See *Figure 3*, top). The position of an object on this floor is represented by LI and the A/R Ratio. It is similar in some respects to the FCB Grid shown at the bottom of *Figure 3*, which contrasts high and low involvement with "think" and "feel" categories (Vaughan, 1980; 1986). Indeed, although developed independently the ARI Model could be considered an extension of the basic conceptualization underlying the FCB grid. Unlike the earlier conceptualization, the ARI Model allows us to describe and measure mixtures of affective and rational processing, and to use these same data to measure involvement, vis a vis both advertisements and products.

Evaluation and the ARI Model. The ARI model helps us to conceptualize and measure how objects—advertisements and products —are cognitively processed, and the level of involvement as defined by the depth and quality of this processing: it provides a representation of the depth of thought and feeling about an object. However, the ARI Model does not in itself represent evaluation: whether the object is liked or disliked, approached or avoided, loved or loathed. Evaluation may be represented as a dimension perpendicular to the floor of the ARI solid, and measured using standard

FIGURE 2
The ARI (affect-reason-involvement) solid

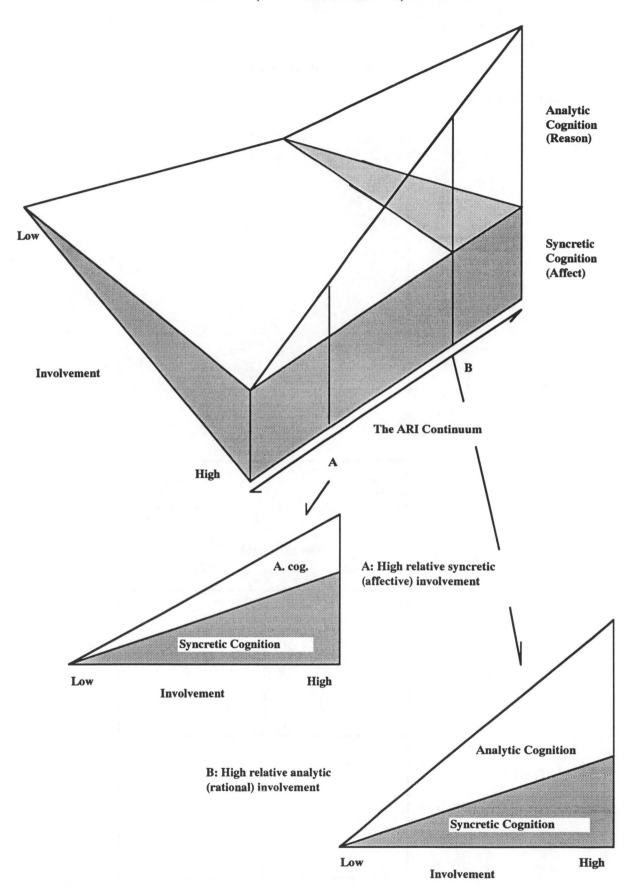

FIGURE 3
The floor of the ARI solid compared with the FCB Grid

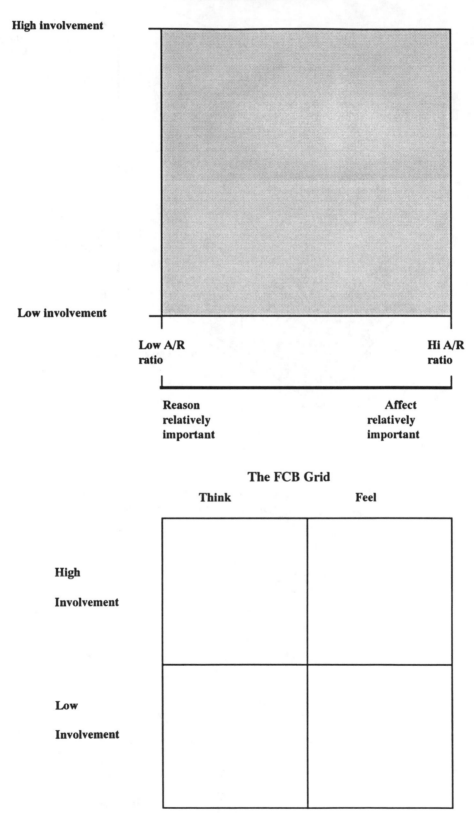

TABLE 2
Principal Components Solutions of Three Administrations of the CASC Scale (Version 1)
(Chaudhuri & Buck, in preparation)

Item	Factor 1 S1	S2	S3	Factor 2 S1	S2	S3	Factor 3 S1	S2	S3	Factor 4 S1	S2	S3	Factor 5 S1	S2	S3
ANALYT.															
Diff comp.	.80	.73	.84												
Pros & cons	.87	.84	.88												
Arguments	.85	.77	.86												
Think facts	.84	.85	.86												
PROSOC.															
Happy				.61	.65	.68									
Proud				.79	.75	.62					.56				
Hope				.60	.68	.58									
Affiliation				.68	.80	.70									
INDIVIST.															
Fear														.93	.95
Anger							.85	.87	.88						
Disgust							.60	.68	.58						
Irritated							.84	.79	.76						
REPTIL.															
Envy						.71				.58	.74				
Aggressive				.66							.70	.81			
Sexy										.70	.68	.76			
Power				.85							.67	.65			
% VAR. (rounded)	19	25	24	24	17	20	15	15	15	7	7	7		6	6

Note: Subjects rated thoughts and feelings toward five television and five magazine advertisements. Three independent samples responded: S1 = 30; S2 = 37, S3 = 24 individuals. Principal components factor analysis (varimax rotation) was used to analyze all three samples: only positive loadings above .50 are shown. *Analyt.* = Analytic-cognitive items; *Prosoc.* = Prosocial-limbic items; *Indivist.* = Individualistic-limbic items; *Reptil.* = Reptilian items.

---

scales of liking or acceptance. In particular, Cacioppo and Berntson's (1994) application of the approach-avoidance conflict to assess independent positive and negative processes in persuasion can be used to measure evaluation. The position of an object—ad or product—at any point in time may thus be described in three dimensions: LI, A/R Ratio, and evaluation.

Present status. Work on the ARI Model has turned to developing reliable and valid operational measures of A and R: affect and reason, respectively. This is the CASC scale (Chaudhuri & Buck, 1994). Before discussing this scale, we describe our conceptualization of affect in greater detail.

OPERATIONALIZATION: THE CASC SCALE

Emotion has usually been thought of as undifferentiated relative to reason, and although different theories have been offered, there seems to be consensus that there are at least two dimensions of emotion: an evaluative good-bad or pleasant-

unpleasant dimension and a strong-weak dimension (Schlosberg, 1952; Russell, 1991). More controversial is the notion based upon the theorizing of Silvan Tomkins (1962; 1963) that there are a fixed number of biologically-based "primary affects" associated with universally-recognized facial displays of happiness, sadness, fear, anger, etc. (see the spirited discussion by Ekman [1994] and Izard [1994] versus Russell, 1994). We suggest that *both* of these views *are in fact correct* , and that in fact many apparently competing theories of emotion are actually considering different portions of the complex hierarchically-organized emotion systems of the brain (Buck, 1985).

A Typology of Emotion. Specifically, Buck (1988) pointed out that basic *approach-avoidance* and *arousal* systems are characteristic of virtually all animate life forms, and are represented in the human brain in brainstem mechanisms. These are the pleasant-unpleasant and strong-weak dimensions. However, more complex emotions have evolved with more complex creatures, and are associated with more recently evolved parts of the brain. Drawing upon P. D. MacLean's (1990) Triune Theory of the brain, Buck (1988) argued that there are *Reptilian* emotions involving "raw" sex and aggression, *Individualistic-Limbic* emotions involving self-preservation (anger, fear); and *Prosocial-Limbic* emotions involving species preservation (attachment). All of the foregoing emotions are biologically-based. Attachment serves as the biological basis of a range of *Social Emotions* (love, pride, guilt, shame, envy, jealousy, pity, scorn). There are also *Cognitive Emotions* underlying White's (1959) effectance motives involved in the structuring of the cognitive system (curiosity, surprise, interest, boredom, etc.) and *Moral Emotions* that reflect both social experience and cognitive functioning (i.e., feelings of distributive and retributive justice).

It is important to note that these emotions are not logically organized; rather, they are biologically organized. Linguistic self-reports are of little use in getting at the fundamental structure of emotion, but that structure is revealed in the organization of the brain (Buck, 1988).

The CASC Scale. Chaudhuri (1993) and Chaudhuri and Buck (1993; Submitted) have found evidence that these different emotions are indeed aroused in advertisements, and began the construction of the *Communication via Analytic and Syncretic Cognition (CASC)* Scale (Chaudhuri & Buck, 1994). In the process, it was found that it is relatively easy reliably to measure rational (analytic-cognitive) responses to a wide variety of advertisements by a 4 item subscale, and that 4-item reptilian, individualistic, and prosocial subscales hang together well (although fear may load on a factor of its own. See *Table 2*).

The number of emotions potentially evoked by advertisements is very large, and some advertisements are clearly relevant to some emotions, and not others. Consider two advertisements, each of which shows a photograph of an embrace. A Calvin Klein ad shows a passionate embrace between a man naked from the waist up, and a woman naked from the waist down. In comparison, an AT&T ad shows a warm embrace between a man in a military uniform and a little girl. First, it is clear that we could ask if either made one feel good or bad, and strong or weak; but the value of such general information is questionable. Also, we could ask if the ad aroused feelings of raw sexual power. That would be clearly relevant to the Calvin Klein ad, but ridiculous and, indeed, inappropriate when applied to the other. Only relatively few ads appeal to the raw reptilian emotions of sex and power: Calvin Klein ads and ads for quite a few brands of beer among them. Questions relating to reptilian emotions would only be relevant when the ad in question is appealing to reptilian emotions: the same is true of each of the sorts of emotion mentioned above: Individualistic-Limbic, Prosocial-Limbic, Social, Cognitive, and Moral. For this reason, the developing CASC Scale has one brief Analytic Cognition scale, but a number of different Syncretic Cognition scales: affect turns out to be much more complex and differentiated than reason!

DISCUSSION

The ARI Model has the potential to serve as an integrative viewpoint which will clarify the role of affect and reason in persuasion. The CASC scale represents a new way to conceptualize and operationalize affect in the context of persuasion research. We submit that the ARI Model and CASC scale can have a significant theoretical and empirical impact upon the field.

More specifically, we see the usefulness of the affective segmenting of the audience: are they hopeful, fearful, angry, sad, complacent? In a highly emotionally-charged issue like the health care debate, the relevant feelings of the audience are critical in determining the persuasive impact of a message: the well-known

Harry and Louise ads in particular have been highly effective in frightening the audience, and in undermining hope and trust in the government where health care is concerned.

In addition, it is apparent that emotions themselves can be considered a product. The buyer will pay a premium for the right feelings, and reptilian emotions are particularly powerful in this regard. For example, macho feelings might be associated with a Humvee vehicle, or feelings of women's liberation with Virginia Slim cigarettes. Entertainment programming is successful if it elicits the right feelings, as is music, literature, and indeed all of the arts. Note that the right feelings are not necessarily positive feelings. Audiences are strongly motivated to experience in moderation "negative" affects as well: witness the popularity of violent programming, horror shows, and "tearjerkers" (Buck, 1988b). The understanding of the nature of the feelings in the audience, and how to effectively elicit feelings, have always been central to the creative process in advertising, but have not usually been the focus of advertising research.

Our conception is quite unlike traditional cognitive models of persuasion. However, it is compatible with the new evidence of the importance of emotion in persuasion, and may serve to aid in its conceptualization and measurement in advertising research.

CITATIONS

Abelson, R. P., Kinder, D. R., Peters, M. D., & Fiske, S. T. (1982). Affective and semantic components in political person perception. *Journal of Personality and Social Psychology. 42*(4), 619-630.

Batra, R., & Ray, M. L. (1983). Conceptualizing involvement as depth and quality of cognitive response. In R. P. Bagozzi and A. M. Tybout (Eds.), *Advances in Consumer research*. Vol. 10. (pp. 309-313). Ann Arbor, MI: Association for Consumer Research.

Buck, R. (1985). Prime theory: An integrated view of motivation and emotion. *Psychological Review, 92*, 389-413.

Buck, R. (1988a). *Human motivation and emotion*. New York: Wiley.

Buck, R. (1988b). Emotional education and mass media: A new view of the global village. In R. P. Hawkins, J. M. Weimann, & S. Pingree (Eds.), *Advancing communication science: Merging mass and interpersonal perspectives*. Beverly Hills, CA: Sage Publications.

Buck, R. (1990) William James and current issues in emotion, cognition, and communication. *Personality and Social Psychology Bulletin. 16*(4), 612-625.

Buck, R., & Chaudhuri, A. (In press). Affect, reason, and involvement in persuasion: the ARI model. In P. Weinberg (Ed.), *Konsumentenforschung*.

Cacioppo, J. T., & Petty, G. G. (1994). Relationship between attitudes and evaluative space: A critical review, with emphasis on the separability of positive and negative substrates. *Psychological Bulletin, 115*(3), 401-423.

Chaiken, S. (1980).Heuristic versus systematic information processing and the use of source versus message cues in persuasion. *Journal of Personality and Social Psychology. 39*(5), 752-766.

Chaudhuri, A. (1992). Unpublished data, University of Connecticut.

Chaudhuri, A. (1993). Advertising implications of the pleasure principle in the classification of products. In W. F. van Raaij and G. J. Bamossy (Eds.), *European Advances in consumer research*, Vol. 1. (pp. 154-159). Provo, Utah: Association for Consumer Research.

Chaudhuri, A., & Buck, R. (1992). Advertising variables that predict consumer responses, in *Enhancing knowledge development in marketing.* Proceedings of the 1992 Summer Marketing Educator's Conference, Chicago, IL: American Marketing Association.

Chaudhuri, A., & Buck, R. (1993). The relationship of advertising variables to analytic and syncretic cognitions. In R. Varadarajan and B. Jaworski (Eds.), *Marketing theory and applications*, Vol. 4. (pp. 193-198). Chicago, IL: American Marketing Association.

Chaudhuri, A., & Buck, R. (1994). Are advertisers using brain theory? Introducing the CASC Scale. In C. W. Park & D. Smith (Eds.), *Marketing Theory and Applications.* Vol. 5. (pp. 161-162) Chicago, IL.: American Marketing Association.

Chaudhuri, A., & Buck, R. (in press). Media differences in rational and emotional responses to advertising. *Journal of Broadcasting and Electronic Media.*

Chaudhuri, A., & Buck, R. (Submitted). Affect, reason, and persuasion: Advertising variables that predict affective and analytic-cognitive responses.

Ekman, P. (1994). Strong evidence for universals in facial expression: A reply to Russell's mistaken critique. *Psychological Bulletin. 115*(2), 268-287.

Georgson, M. (1993). Affect and reason in product perceptions. Unpublished paper, University of Connecticut.

Izard (1994). Innate and universal facial expressions: Evidence from developmental and cross-cultural research. *Psychological Bulletin. 115*(2), 288-299.

Kowta, S. (1993). Unpublished data, University of Connecticut.

Lazarus, R. S. (1982). Thoughts on the relations between affect and cognition. *American Psychologist, 37,* 1019-1024.

Lazarus, R. S. (1982). On the primacy of cognition. *American Psychologist, 39,* 124-129.

LeDoux, J. E. (1986). A neurobiological view of the psychology of emotion. In J. LeDoux and W. F. Hirst (Eds.), *Mind and brain: Dialogues between cognitive psychology and neuroscience.* New York: Cambridge University Press.

McHugo, G. J., Lanzetta, J. T., Sullivan, D. G., Masters, R. D., & Englis, B. G. (1985). Emotional reactions to a political leader's expressive displays. *Journal of Personality and Social Psychology. 49*(6), 1513-1529.

MacLean, P. D. (1990). *The triune brain in evolution: Role in paleocerebral functions.* New York: Plenum Press.

McQuarrie, E. F., & Munson, J. M. (1987). The Zaichkowsky Personal Involvement Inventory: Modification and extension. *Advances in Consumer Research, Vol. 14,* Ann Arbor: Association for Consumer Research, 36-40.

Petty, R. E., & Cacioppo, J. T. (1986). *Communication and persuasion: Central and peripheral routes to attitude change.* New York: Springer Verlag.

Russell, J. A. (1991). Culture and the categorization of emotion. *Psychological Bulletin. 110,* 426-450.

Russell, J. A. (1994). Is there universal recognition of emotion from facial expression? A review of the cross-cultural studies. *Psychological Bulletin. 115*(1), 102-141.

Schlosberg, H. (1952). The description of facial expression in terms of two dimensions. *Journal of Experimental Psychology, 44,* 81-88.

Tomkins, S. S. (1962-1963). *Affect, imagery, consciousness.* (Volumes 1 and 2). New York: Springer.

Tucker, D. (1981). Lateral brain function, emotion, and conceptualization. *Psychological Bulletin. 89.* 19-46.

Vaughn, R. (1980). How advertising works: A planning model. *Journal of Advertising Research. 20*(5). 27-33.

Vaughn, R. (1986). How advertising works: A planning model revised. *Journal of Advertising Research. 26*(1). 57-66.

White, R. W. (1959). Motivation reconsidered: The concept of competence. *Psychological Review, 66,* 297-333.

Zajonc, R. (1980). Feeling and thinking: Preferences need no inferences. *American Psychologist, 35,* 117-123.

Zajonc, R. (1984). On the primacy of affect. *American Psychologist, 39,* 117-123.

Do We Need Involvement to Understand Consumer Behavior?

Theo B.C. Poiesz, Tilburg University, the Netherlands
Cees, J.P.M. de Bont, Tilburg University, the Netherlands

ABSTRACT

In this paper the literature on the involvement concept is reviewed. One of the conclusions is that the cumulation of knowledge on involvement is hampered by the lack of conceptual clarity, the seemingly uncontrolled application, the overlap with presumed antecedents and consequences, and the unavoidable lack of consistent operationalisations. An alternative, more restricted, conceptualization is proposed.

INTRODUCTION

The concept of involvement has a long history in the consumer behavior literature. Generally, involvement is rather crudely defined as personal relevance or *perceived* personal relevance of a stimulus or situation. For several reasons it is a noteworthy concept. First, it receives an impressive amount of attention in the literature. Second, it addresses our way of thinking about consumer behavior; involvement is not just another determinant, but has paradigmatic implications as well. Third, involvement can be easily 'attached' to already existing concepts and theories. As such it fosters the (re)interpretation of available knowledge and stimulates research. Finally, involvement addresses the issue of external validity.

Popularity has its price, however. The rapid growth of attention for the concept resulted in a fragmentation of involvement research. Even though there are some more or less generally accepted aspects of involvement (see later), there are still too many loose conceptual and operational ends. Obviously, the absence of a single unequivocal definition hampers comparisons between studies, and prevents efficient cumulation of knowledge. These observations leave us with a dilemma: on the one hand the concept is more or less generally viewed to be relevant for the study of consumer behavior; on the other hand, there is uncertainty with regard to its exact position in de field. This calls for a critical assessment of the following issues: 1. Conceptualisations of involvement; 2. Operationalisations of involvement; and 3. Antecedents and consequences of involvement. Each of these sections will be concluded by a provisional discussion, which will be combined in a general discussion.

CONCEPTUALISATIONS OF INVOLVEMENT

Because the involvement literature is reviewed extensively in several publications (e.g. Andrews et al., 1990), the present review will focus on some major conceptualisations only.

Sherif and Cantril (1947) introduced ego-involvement to refer to the linkage of new information with central, or ego-involved, attitudes. In the consumer behavior literature, Krugman (1965) viewed involvement as the number of bridging experiences, connections or personal references, between an individual and a product or issue per minute. Mitchell (1979; 1981), Bloch (1982), and Andrews et al. (1990) refer to involvement as an internal state variable that indicates the amount of arousal, interest, or drive invoked by a particular stimulus or situation. For many researchers involvement is equivalent to motivation to process information (e.g. Bloch and Richins, 1983; Burnkrant and Sawyer, 1983; Cohen, 1983; Greenwald and Leavitt, 1984; Bloch, Sherell, and Ridgway, 1986). Greenwald and Leavitt (1984) distinguish four levels of audience involvement: preattention, focal attention, comprehension, and elaboration. For several authors involvement stands for perceived personal relevance (e.g. Petty and Cacioppo,

1981; Zaichkowksy, 1985; Richins and Bloch, 1986; Celsi and Olson, 1988). Zaichkowsky (1985) defines involvement as a person's perceived relevance of an object based on inherent needs, values and interests.

By using the term 'felt involvement' some authors emphasize the experiential, phenomenological nature of the concept. According to Celsi and Olson (1988) concepts like: message-processing involvement (Petty and Cacioppo, 1981), audience involvement (Greenwald and Leavitt, 1984), and response involvement (Houston and Rothschild, 1978) can be regarded as effects of felt involvement.

Involvement has been conceptually related to objects or issues such as: product involvement, (Cohen, 1983; Mitchell, 1979), ad involvement (Lord and Burnkrant, 1993), program involvement (Lord and Burnkrant, 1993), message involvement (Mitchell, 1979; Laczniak and Muehling, 1990), and issue involvement (Laurent and Kapferer, 1985; Maheswaran and Meyers-Levy 1990). Sometimes the involvement construct is related to behaviors: e.g. purchase involvement (Antil, 1984; Mittal and Lee, 1989) and response involvement (Zimbardo, 1960; Bloch and Richins, 1983; Houston and Rothschild, 1978). Obviously, in situational involvement the construct is linked to the individual context (Bloch and Richins, 1983; Houston and Rothschild, 1978). Enduring involvement (Bloch and Richins, 1983; Houston and Rothschild, 1978) and outcome-relevant involvement (Johnson and Eagly, 1989) stress the interaction between a person and an object. Finally, some miscellaneous types of involvement can be found: e.g. value-relevant involvement (Ostrom and Brock, 1968; Johnson and Eagly, 1989) and impression-relevant involvement (Johnson and Eagly, 1989).

Conceptualisation: provisional discussion

Even though there seems to be a general agreement that involvement does relate to personal relevance, it remains unclear whether involvement should be interpreted as its synonym, as its conceptual equivalent, as something more general (or more specific) than personal relevance. Over time, in the consumer behavior literature, the concept seems to have changed its meaning to personal relevance. The problem of involvement may be located in its inherent plausibility or conceptual self-evidence which prevents the user from explicitly considering the question of its unique status and contribution. This renders it difficult, if not impossible, to distinguish involvement from competing, but closely related concepts in the psychological and consumer behavior literature such as need, value, interest, drive, arousal, and motivation. Rather than focusing on the very conceptualization of involvement itself, the literature presents an inventory of different *levels* of involvement (preattention, focal attention, etc.), different *types* of involvement (enduring involvement, response involvement, etc.), different *properties* of involvement (intensity, direction, and persistence), different *sources* of involvement (personal, physical, situational), and different *objects* and *issues* to which the concept may be applied (message involvement, ad involvement, program involvement, product involvement, etc.). We do not seem to know what involvement is, but we do manage to produce all kinds of differentiations. By result, the involvement concept emerges as a loose conglomerate of various underlying notions, explicit or otherwise, whose core meaning and mutual relationships remain obscure. By simultaneously representing several more or less equivalent concepts, involvement-not surprisingly-is viewed as making a significant contribution to the explanation of behavior variance. However, it remains unclear whether and to what extent the explained variance can be attributed to the involvement concept *per se*.

Over the years, several authors have expressed criticism with respect to conceptualisations and operationalisations of involvement (e.g. Cohen, 1983; Zaichkowsky, 1985; Andrews et al., 1990), and with regard to the (lack of) direction that involvement research is taking (Rothschild, 1984). The general uneasiness with the concept seems reflected in concepts such as 'felt involvement'. Even though many existing psychological concepts relate to feelings, their conceptual clarity does not require this to be specified. For example, it is not necessary to refer to 'felt attitudes', 'felt motivation', 'felt ability', 'felt attention', etc. Then why would we need 'felt' involvement?

OPERATIONALISATIONS OF INVOLVEMENT

Unavoidably, conceptual problems or questions are reflected in manipulations and operationalisations. Often, involvement is manipulated by referring to the seriousness of the consequence of an issue, which, in turn, may be varied on the basis of distance from a person (geographical and time). Examples are provided in studies by Petty and Cacioppo (1981), Maheswaran and Meyers-Levy (1990), MacInnis and Park (1991), Chen et al. (1992), and Swinyard (1993). In other studies involvement is manipulated by varying consequences for the self (Celsi and Olson, 1988; Miniard et al., 1991). Sometimes manipulations do not seem to allow for a distinction between causes and effects of involvement. In a study by Mano and Oliver (1993) subjects were asked to consider either a product requiring little deliberation or a product requiring much deliberation. Thus, involvement was manipulated by referring to its presumed consequences. Similarly, Buchholz and Smith (1991) instructed subjects in the high involvement condition to maximize attention to the ad and the amount of brand processing.

Many researchers use multiple-item scales to measure involvement. For a review of involvement measures in advertising and consumer research see Andrews et al. (1990). Here we only mention that multiple-item scales have been developed by Lastovicka and Gardner (1979), by Laurent and Kapferer (1985), and by Zaichkowsky (1985; 1987). In the development of the measurement scales, different conceptual perspectives resulted in different multi-item scales. Other researchers use 2-item scales (Celsi and Olson, 1988), or even a single-item scale (Donthu et al., 1993) to measure involvement.

Finally, some alternative types of operationalisations do not use measurement scales at all. In Lord and Burnkrant (1993) program involvement was assessed by measuring the response (attention) time in a concurrent task. Longer response times were assumed to indicate that more attention is paid to the primary task (viewing the program). In Laczniak and Muehling (1990) cognitive response elicitation was used to distinguish between more involved and less involved subjects. The subjects having only one or fewer message-related responses (as opposed to ad-and product related thoughts) were assigned to the low-involvement group.

Operationalisation: provisional discussion

The first conclusion is that inter-study comparisons are hampered by the lack of a standardized (set of) measurement instrument(s). In their attempts to manipulate involvement, some authors went so far as to reverse cause and effect. Apparently, the reasoning was that if an increase in involvement causes a higher level of elaboration or attention, then a request to engage in more elaboration or to pay close attention can serve as a manipulation of involvement.

In more general terms, manipulations of involvement seem to concentrate on the size of the effect and/or its probability, distance, or relevance. A critical question is whether the instructions manipulated involvement exclusively, or had other, unspecified psychological, effects as well. Unfortunately, without a very clear notion of the exact nature of involvement and of its relationships to other psychological variables, this question can not be answered. The lack of conceptual clarity does not only prevent us from distinguishing between involvement and seemingly equivalent or neighbouring concepts, but may also prevent us from making a clear distinction between involvement, its antecedents, and its consequences. This is demonstrated by the types of manipulations of involvement reported in the literature. For some of these, it is not clear whether an antecedent, a consequence, or involvement itself is manipulated.

ANTECEDENTS AND CONSEQUENCES OF INVOLVEMENT

The need to distinguish between involvement and its effects on cognitive processing and its causal antecedents has been stressed by Cohen (1983), Greenwald and Leavitt (1984), Celsi and Olson (1988), Mittal and Lee (1989), and Andrews et al. (1990). The following antecedents are mentioned in literature:

- Physical and social aspects of the immediate environment (Celsi and Olson, 1988);
- Intrinsic characteristics of the individual (Houston and Rothschild, 1978; Zaichkowsky, 1985; Richins and Bloch, 1986);
- Products with salient distinguishing attributes (Hupfer and Gardner, 1971; Robertson, 1976; Lastovicka and Gardner, 1979).

Mostly, consequences of involvement are proposed in the field of information processing. Suggested consequences are attention and comprehension processes, and levels of processing (Celsi and Olson, 1988; Maheswaran and Meyers-Levy, 1990; Miniard et al., 1991; Lord and Burnkrant, 1993), motivation to process information (Burnkrant and Sawyer, 1983; Bloch et al., 1986), amount of counterargumentation (Chen et al., 1992), and type of processing (Mittal, 1988). Other consequences of involvement can be viewed as the outcomes of information processing: attitudes, persuasion (Sherif and Hovland, 1961; Petty et al., 1983; Laczniak and Muehling, 1990; Maheswaran and Meyers-levy, 1990; MacInnis and Park, 1991; Miniard et al., 1991; Chen et al., 1992), and behavioral intention (Swinyard, 1993). Some consequences of involvement are suggested in the domain of purchase and consumption: frequency of product usage (Mittal and Lee, 1989), brand loyalty, post purchase satisfaction (Richins and Bloch, 1991), adoption of new products (Foxall and Bhate, 1993), and voting behavior (Burton and Netemeyer, 1992). In some studies the consequences consist of experiences: shopping enjoyment (Mittal and Lee, 1989), brand commitment (Mittal and Lee, 1989), and consumption experience (Mano and Oliver, 1993). Consequences that can not be attributed to the mentioned categories are: arousal (Mitchell, 1981), extensiveness of decision process (Mittal and Lee, 1989), interest in advertising (Mittal and Lee, 1989), differences in advertising effectiveness of radio and television (Buchholz and Smith, 1991), and perceived argument truth (Hawkins and Hoch, 1992).

Antecedents and consequences: provisional discussion

The inventory of antecedents and consequences does not present clear clues on the possible solution of the conceptual problem of involvement. The observed statistical covariation is attributed to cause-effect relationships, but could also be interpreted as reflecting common psychological elements and meanings. To add to the confusion, some of the antecedents and consequences would not be out of place in a multi-item involvement inventory. Stated differently: if we were to dismantle the involvement concept and would exclude synonyms, antecedents, and consequences from its conceptualization, what would be the residue, if any? Is there something like a core meaning of involvement, or is involvement nothing but a conceptual and statistical artefact?

GENERAL DISCUSSION

Originally, involvement was meant to express the intensity of mental or cognitive elaboration (see Krugman, 1965). In the provisional discussions we concluded that involvement shows a tendency to be confused with other concepts and with its antecedents and consequences. If involvement implicitly claims to be an integral aspect of just about everything, without having idiosyncratic characteristics of its own, then the inevitable question is whether we need the concept at all in theory development and application. We will address the potential legitimacy of both a negative and a positive answer to this question in the light of the previous provisional discussions.

For reasons of conceptual clarity and parsimony, we propose that the answer may be *negative* to the extent that involvement only adds to the confusion by merely claiming the role already played by other well-known theoretical concepts such as, for example, personal relevance and motivation. The answer may only be *positive* if it can be shown that there is a need for a motivational concept that is more than a mere conceptual substitute and that has explanatory value of its own.

For reasons to be explained shortly we propose to conceive of involvement as referring to the momentary mobilisation of behavioral resources for the achievement of a personally relevant goal. Behavioral resources comprise physical (sensory and physiological) capacity, mental capacity, and energy (arousal). It is assumed that behavioral resources will be mobilized to the extent that three conditions are met simultaneously: the goal is subjectively relevant, and the perceived ability and perceived opportunity to achieve that goal are favorable. (Compare Petty and Cacioppo, e.g. 1981, who refer to involvement as the combination of motivation and ability, where opportunity is subsumed under ability). This notion of involvement differs from personal relevance (or motivation) by the specification of two additional conditions, which implies that *high* personal relevance may be associated with *low* involvement. For example, if an unpolluted environment is highly personally relevant, and perceived ability and/or opportunity to contribute to a clean environment are low, no behavioral resources are mobilized (involvement is low). When personal relevance is held constant (or even reduced slightly), the level of involvement may be increased by increasing perceived ability and/or opportunity. These examples show that there is a loose relationship between personal relevance and involvement. Therefore, it is proposed to consistently conceive of involvement as the consequence of the combined subjective assessments of motivation and ability and opportunity, and *not* to take involvement as the mere equivalent of personal relevance. If, in the literature, involvement is conceptually and operationally defined as personal relevance, while involvement is meant to represent behavioral resource mobilization, considerable conceptual confusion will occur. We assume

that this confusion remains largely unnoticed, however, due to the fact that in many involvement studies reported in the literature subjects are exposed to favorable ability and opportunity conditions only, thus allowing only personal relevance to vary. This seems to explain why, in these studies, personal relevance could be (but should not have been) simply equated-or confused-with involvement.

Involvement, in the present interpretation of mobilization of behavioral resources, may be considered a determinant or antecedent to behavioral phenomena such as behavior persistence and behavior intensity. The conceptualization (re-)proposed here implies that involvement is different from motivation, personal relevance, and arousal. It allows for a distinction between involvement and its antecedents and consequences in a conceptual, methodological, and operational sense. Of course, to the extent that ability and opportunity conditions become more favorable, the difference between personal relevance and involvement becomes smaller.

For the present conceptualization of involvement-the mobilization of behavioral resources-no operationalization is readily available. At least two operationalization possibilities present themselves. The first is to develop a scale for the subjective assessment of the degree to which behavioral resources are mobilized. The problem inherent to this option is that the mobilization of resources may not be accessible to conscious assessment, and the very assessment may even interfere with the very phenomenon. The second option is to regard involvement as a phenomenon that can not be measured directly and to resort an operational definition in the form of the measurement of the three antecedent psychological conditions suggested in this paper. In the latter option involvement is taken as some combination (comparable to, for example, a latent construct in LISREL terms) of the subjective assessments of motivation, ability, and opportunity. According to the view presented here, involvement can be manipulated by changing the levels of either one or a combination of the three mentioned conditions. This implies that involvement may be manipulated by changing other conditions than motivation or personal relevance alone.

In the present interpretation, concepts such as product involvement, message involvement, enduring involvement, and situational involvement would acquire a different meaning than suggested in the literature. Product involvement, for example, would not be taken as the conceptual equivalent of product interest, but as the mobilization of behavioral resources with respect to a particular product at a particular moment and in a particular situation. Involvement should *not* be uniquely associated with a person, an object, or a situation. The same object may invoke high levels of involvement in one situation, and low levels of involvement in another. The suggestion of involvement types (e.g. Krugman, 1965-high and low involving media) prompted consumer behavior researchers to produce endless differentiations. Although these may have contributed to a rich description of consumer behavior, they do not seem to have really contributed to a consistent and parsimonious understanding of that behavior. (By comparison, it would not be useful nor efficient to distinguish between different types of health such as genetic health, stress health, exercise health, eating health, and drinking health. Of course, by statistical analyses the effects of different health factors might be partialled out, but this would not legitimize a distinction of different types of health). Similarly, personal involvement, object or issue involvement, and situational involvement are not different *types* of involvement; they merely refer to different *aspects* of the same phenomenon from which a particular level of involvement emerges. The assumption of different types of involvement holds the risk that the same involvement is attributed to the *person* by researcher 1, to the *object* by researcher 2, and to the *situation* by researcher 3, merely depending upon what happens to be the particular interest of the individual researcher. In the present reasoning, involvement is dependent upon the combination of characteristics of the person, the object/ issue, and the situation. These characteristics, *in themselves*, should not be taken as more or less involving.

In conclusion, the traditional conceptualizations of involvement do not allow a description of its scope which is due, to a large extent, to the absence of boundaries of the concept itself. As the scope is endless, so is research on involvement-the concept may continue to grow rank forever. That involvement does explain behavior variance is not a critical issue here. What is critical is whether the variance is correctly or incorrectly attributed to personal relevance.

To return to the title: involvement is a necessary concept indeed, but its conceptualisation needs adaptation to avoid confusion, to allow for operationalisation and integration, to avoid uncontrolled growth and unwarranted application, and to fully exploit its basic, inherent meaning.

REFERENCES

Andrews, J.Craig, Srinivas Durvasula and Syed H. Akhter (1990), "A framework for conceptualizing and measuring the involvement construct in advertising research," *Journal of Advertising*, 19, 27-40.

Antil, John (1984), "Conceptualization and operationalisation of involvement," in *Advances in Consumer Research*, Vol. 11, ed. T. Kinnear, Provo, UT: Association for Consumer Research, 203-209.

Bloch, Peter H. (1982), "Involvement beyond the purchase process: conceptual issues and empirical investigation," in *Advances of Consumer Research*, Vol. 9, ed. Andrew A. Mitchell, Ann Arbor, MI: Association for Consumer Research, 413-417.

Bloch, Peter H. and Marsha L. Richins (1983), "A theoretical model for the study of product importance perceptions," *Journal of Marketing*, 47 (Summer), 69-81.

Bloch, Peter H., Daniel L. Sherrell and Nancy M. Ridgway (1986), "Consumer search: An extended framework," *Journal of Consumer Research*, 13 (June), 119-126.

Buchholz, Laura M. and Robert E. Smith (1991), "The role of consumer involvement in determining cognitive response to broadcast advertising," *Journal of Advertising*, 20, 4-17.

Burnkrant, Robert E. and Allan G. Sawyer, (1983), "Effects of involvement and message content of information-processing intensity," in *Information Processing Research in Advertising*, ed. Richard J. Harris, Hillsdale, NJ: Lawrence Erlbaum Association, 46-64.

Burton, Scot and Richard G. Netemeyer (1992), "The effect of enduring, situational, and response involvement on preference stability in the context of voting behavior," *Psychology and Marketing*, 9 (March/April), 143-156.

Celsi, Richard L. and Jerry C. Olson (1988), "The role of involvement in attention and comprehension processes," *Journal of Consumer Research*, 15 (September), 210-24.

Chen, Hong Chyi, Richard Reardon, Cornelia Rea and David J. Moore (1992), "Forewarning of content and involvement: consequences for persuasion and resistance to persuasion," *Journal of Experimental Social Psychology*, 28, 523-541.

Cohen, Joel B. (1983), "Involvement and you: 1000 great ideas". in *Advances in Consumer Research*, Vol. 10, eds. Richard Bagozzi and Alice Tybout, Ann Arbor, MI: Association for Consumer Research, 325-328.

Donthu, Naveen, Joseph Cherian and Mukesh Bhargava (1993), "Factors influencing recall of outdoor advertising," *Journal of Advertising Research*, May/June, 64-72.

Foxall, Gordon R. and Seema Bhate (1993), "Cognitive styles and personal involvement of market initiators for 'healthy' food brands: implications for adoption theory," *Journal of Economic Psychology*, 14, 33-56.

Greenwald, Anthony G. and Clark Leavitt (1984), "Audience involvement in advertising: four levels," *Journal of Consumer Research*, 11 (June), 581-92.

Hawkins, Scott A. and Stephen J. Hoch (1992), "Low involvement learning: memory without evaluation," *Journal of Consumer Research*, 19 (September), 212-25.

Houston, Michael J. and Michael L. Rothschild (1978), "Conceptual and methodological perspectives on involvement," in *Research frontiers in marketing: dialogues and directions*, ed. S. Jain, Chicago: American Marketing Association, 184-187.

Hupfer, Nancy T. and David M. Gardner (1971), "Differential involvement with products and issues: An exploratory study," in *Advances in Consumer Research*, ed. David M. Gardner, College Park, MD: Association for consumer research, 262-269.

Johnson, Blair T. and Alice H. Eagly (1989), "Effects of involvement on persuasion: a meta-analysis," *Psychological Bulletin*, 106, 290-314.

Krugman, Herbert E. (1965), "The impact of television advertising: learning without involvement," *Public Opinion Quarterly*, 29 (Fall), 349-356.

Krugman, Herbert E. (1965), "The measurement of advertising involvement," *Public Opinion Quarterly*, 30 (Winter), 583-596.

Laczniak, Russell N. and Darrel D. Muehling (1990), "Delayed effects of advertising moderated by involvement," *Journal of Business Research*, 20, 263-277.

Lastovicka, John L. and David M. Gardner (1979), "Components of involvement," in *Attitude research plays for high stakes*, eds. John C. Maloney and Bernard Silverman, Chicago: American Marketing Association, 53-73.

Laurent, Gilles and Jean-Noel Kapferer (1985), "Measuring consumer involvement profiles," *Journal of Marketing Research*, 22, 41-53.

Lord, Kenneth R. and Robert E. Burnkrant (1993), "Attention versus distraction: the interactive effect of program involvement and attentional devices on commercial processing," *Journal of Advertising*, 22 (March), 47-60.

MacInnis, Deborah J. and C. Whan Park (1991), "The differential role of characteristics of music on high- and low-involvement consumers' processing of ads," *Journal of Consumer Research*, 18 (September), 161-173.

Maheswaran, Durairaj and Joan Meyers-Levy (1990), "The influence of message framing and issue involvement," *Journal of Marketing Research*, 27 (August), 361-367.

Mano, Haim and Richard L. Oliver (1993), "Assessing the dimensionality and structure of the consumption experience: evaluation, feeling, and satisfaction," *Journal of Consumer Research*, 20 (December), 451-466.

Miniard, Paul W., Sunil Bhatla, Kenneth R. Lord, Peter R. Dickson and H. Rao Unnava (1991), "Picture-based persuasion processes and the moderating role of involvement," *Journal of Consumer Research*, 18 (June), 92-107.

Mitchell, Andrew A. (1979), "Involvement: a potentially important mediator of consumer behavior," in *Advances in Consumer Research*, Vol. 6, ed. William L. Wilke, Ann Arbor, MI: Association for Consumer Research, 191-196.

Mitchell, Andrew A. (1981), "The dimensions of advertising involvement," in *Advances for Consumer Research*, Vol 8, ed. Kent Monroe, Ann Arbor (MI.): Association for Consumer Research, 25-30.

Mittal, Banwari (1988), "The role of affective choice mode in the consumer purchase of expressive products," *Journal of Economic Psychology*, 9, 499-524.

Mittal, Banwari and Myung-Soo Lee (1989), "A causal model of consumer involvement," *Journal of Economic Psychology*, 10, 363-389.

Ostrom Thomas M. and Timothy C. Brock (1968), "A cognitive model of attitudinal involvement," in *Theories of cognitive consistency: a sourcebook*, eds. Robert P. Abelson et al.,Chicago: Rand-McNally, 373-83.

Petty, Richard E. and John T. Cacioppo (1981), "Issue involvement as moderator of the effects on attitude of advertising content and context," in *Advances of Consumer Research*, Vol. 8, ed. Kent B. Monroe, Ann Arbor, MI: Association for Consumer Research, 20-24.

Petty, Richard E., John T. Cacioppo and David Schumann (1983), "Central and peripheral routes to advertising effectiveness: The moderating role of involvement," *Journal of Consumer Research*, 10, 135-146.

Richins, Marsha L. and Peter H. Bloch (1986), "After the new wears off: The temporal context of product involvement," *Journal of Consumer Research*, 13, 280-285.

Richins, Marsha L. and Peter H. Bloch (1991), "Post-purchase product satisfaction: incorporating the effects of involvement and time," *Journal of Business Research*, 23, 145-158.

Robertson, Thomas S. (1976), "Low commitment consumer behavior," *Journal of Advertising Research*, 16, 619-627.

Rothschild, Michael L. (1984), "Perspectives on involvement: current problems and future directions," in *Advances in Consumer Research*, Vol. 11, ed. Thomas Kinnear, Ann Arbor, MI: Association for Consumer Research, 216-227.

Sherif, Muzafer and Hadley Cantril (1947), *The psychology of ego involvements: social attitudes and identifications*. New-York: Wiley.

Sherif, Muzafer and C.I. Hovland (1961), *Social judgment: assimilation and contrast effects in communication and attitude change*. New Haven, C.T.: Yale University Press.

Swinyard, William R. (1993), "The effects of mood, involvement, and quality of store experience on shopping intentions," *Journal of Consumer Research*, 20 (September), 271-280.

Zaichkowski, Judith L. (1985), "Measuring the involvement construct," *Journal of Consumer Research*, 12 (December), 341-352.

Zaichkowski, Judith L. (1987), *The personal involvement inventory: reduction, revision and application to advertising*, Discussion Paper #87-08-08, Simon Fraser University, Faculty of Business Administration.

Zimbardo, Philip G. (1960), "Involvement and communication discrepancy as determinants of opinion conformity," *Journal of Abnormal and Social Psychology*, 60, 86-94.

New Directions in Affect and Consumer Satisfaction

Richard A. Spreng, Michigan State University

Recently satisfaction researchers have been broadening the scope of post consumption processes to include investigating affective responses to consumption. The session was intended to explore new directions in consumer satisfaction research. All three papers went beyond the dominant paradigm in consumer satisfaction research, and suggested new models that provide richer frameworks for studying post-consumption phenomena. The three papers differed from each other in various ways. Each proposed new models to the consumer satisfaction research literature. Each paper differed in the kind of product/service examined: Spreng and Mackoy examined a service, Krishnan and Olshavsky looked at experiences that are characterized by hedonic attributes, and Mick and Fournier explored high technology products. Finally, the papers differed in the methodology employed, with Spreng and Mackoy using a field experiment, Krishnan and Olshavsky using focus groups and a laboratory experiment, and Mick and Fournier using a naturalistic, phenomenological, and longitudinal approach. Robert Woodruff acted as the discussant for the session, making comments on each paper and moderating discussion.

The Spreng and Mackoy paper argued that while researchers and managers agree that there may be important differences among certain post-purchase concepts such as satisfaction and affect, there is a great need for clarifying these various post-purchase constructs and integrating theories and concepts dealing with post purchase evaluation. A conceptual model, based on Cohen and Areni's (1991) model, was presented to provide a hypothesized causal sequence of post-purchase constructs. Results of a field experiment were presented that examined the empirical relationships among various post-purchase constructs. While past research has generally included only positive and negative affect in satisfaction models, Spreng and Mackoy's results indicated support for four distinct constructs of affect: low arousal positive affect (e.g., "pleased"), high arousal positive affect (e.g., "delighted"), low arousal negative affect (e.g., "displeased"), and high arousal negative affect (e.g., "angry"). Also, these four affects were distinct from satisfaction, and were differentially influenced by antecedents such as surprise, expectations disconfirmation, and desires congruency. For example, they found that while the low arousal affects were more strongly related to satisfaction, the high arousal affects were more strongly influenced by surprise. Thus, the results provide preliminary evidence regarding the creation of high arousal affective responses such as "delight." Woodruff pointed out that results such as these, showing that satisfaction is a low arousal construct, may call into question the standard assumption that "satisfaction" is really very motivating in terms of subsequent behavior.

Krishnan and Olshavsky presented a model that incorporated two distinct emotion outcomes. First, they argued that some products are chosen because of their emotion producing characteristics. For example, while fear is generally considered a negative emotion, some products, such as horror movies or bunggie jumping, are consumed for the explicit purpose of producing fear. These emotions are described as emotions that are "experienced directly during the consumption episode." Second, emotions can be elicited as a consumer evaluates the "directly experienced emotions." For example, a consumer may be scared by an amusement park ride, but have a positive emotion such as joy as the experience is evaluated. The results of two exploratory studies indicated support for the proposed model. The full paper is included in this volume.

Woodruff commented that the results support the view that emotions are complex.

Mick and Fournier argued that the dominant disconfirmation of expectations model has led to "paradigm sedimentation," and used multiple qualitative methods to investigate what consumer satisfaction means from the consumers' perspective. They used a "combination of naturalistic, phenomenological, and longitudinal research" methods, and presented a number of cases that indicated that sometimes consumers do not have pre-use expectations or their expectations change during consumption, and that satisfaction is often not the "rational, conscious, formulaic, and instrumental phenomenon" assumed by the disconfirmation paradigm. By defining satisfaction as "a meaning-based, multidimensional subjective process that evolves over the full course of pre-consumption, consumption, and disposition," they argued that qualitative methods can be of great value in understanding satisfaction. Mick and Fournier cautioned against searching for a single, all encompassing satisfaction model, and found evidence of different satisfaction models. Some of these models had not been previously identified, and they may operate simultaneously or in sequence. For example, they identified a number of modes of satisfaction (adding to Oliver's 1989 five modes) such as satisfaction as awe, as relief, as helplessness, or as love. Woodruff agreed that instead of searching for one, monolithic model of consumer satisfaction, perhaps we should seek to understand the meaning that consumers bring to consumption.

The Dual Role of Emotions in Consumer Satisfaction/Dissatisfaction

H. Shanker Krishnan, Indiana University
Richard W. Olshavsky, Indiana University

ABSTRACT

Prior studies on consumption emotions have not made a distinction between emotions experienced directly during consumption and emotions evoked during the evaluation of these directly experienced emotions. This distinction is particularly relevant since a negative emotion (e.g., fear) directly experienced during consumption can evoke a positive emotion (e.g., joy) if a negative emotion was desired (e.g., for horror movies, rollercoaster rides). We present a model that attempts to capture this dual role of emotions on satisfaction. Results from two exploratory studies (a focus group and a lab experiment) provide initial support for the model.

INTRODUCTION

Current models of satisfaction have explicitly considered the role of "consumption emotion" patterns as predictors of satisfaction (e.g., Mano and Oliver 1993; Oliver 1993; Oliver and Westbrook 1993; Westbrook 1987). "Consumption emotion refers to the set of emotional responses elicited specifically during product usage or consumption experiences, as described either by the distinctive categories of emotional experience and expression (e.g., joy, anger, and fear) or by the structural dimensions underlying emotional categories, such as pleasantness/unpleasantness, relaxation/action, or calmness/excitement" (Westbrook and Oliver, 1991, p. 85). The general finding is that distinct patterns of affective experiences are systematically related to different levels of a unidimensional satisfaction response. Also, Oliver (1993) found that attribute satisfaction affects both emotions and overall satisfaction.

These studies make an important contribution to our understanding of the role of emotions in satisfaction. However, a distinction has not been made between emotions experienced directly during the consumption episode, and emotions evoked during the evaluation of this directly experienced emotion. Making a distinction between these two types of emotions is particularly relevant for hedonic attributes (Holbrook and Hirschman 1982). Whereas utilitarian attributes seem to be based on relatively objective product features such as fluoride content and miles per gallon, hedonic attributes, by definition, imply a direct affective experience. For example, consumers may experience excitement and interest during a music concert, and evaluate the experience as "joyful." Moreover, the valence of these two types of affect may be different. For instance, consumers may be extremely frightened (a negative emotion) during a rollercoaster ride but their evaluation of this experience may be joyful (a positive emotion), since they wanted to be frightened. These direct affective experiences may provide particularly strong influences on overall satisfaction for products/services that are primarily hedonic in nature.

The purpose of our paper is to further explore these two distinct types of emotions that occur at consumption and to examine their specific roles in understanding overall satisfaction. First we present a model that explicates the dual role of emotions in consumption and their separate effects on satisfaction responses. Then we present exploratory data from two studies that provide some initial support for these two separate roles of emotions for hedonic products. Finally, we discuss implications for future research in this area.

THE DUAL ROLE MODEL

Building on the constructs expressed in Westbrook and Oliver (1991), overall satisfaction is viewed as the postchoice evaluation judgment concerning the purchase of a specific product or service. Overall satisfaction is modeled as a unidimensional affective concept. As shown in the Figure, following Oliver (1993), overall satisfaction is determined by the cumulative impact of satisfaction experienced on each of the salient attributes (possibly in proportion to their importance weights). Although not depicted in the Figure, overall satisfaction may also be determined, in part, by preexisting or concurrent affective states such as mood.

Consistent with prior research, we suggest that consumers approach consumption experiences with desires (D_i) and expectations (E_i) pertaining to each attribute. For hedonic attributes, consumers may describe both desires and expectations in terms of specific emotions ("I want to see an *exciting* movie") and the corresponding level ("I think this concert will be *extremely* boring"). Expectation is assumed to influence perceived performance (only). Perceived performance (PP_i) refers to the individual's perceptions of how the product performed on that attribute. Whenever the performance of a hedonic attribute is "perceived," one or more emotions (EM^1) are automatically evoked (Mano and Oliver 1993). Individual attributions (A^1) on the origin of these emotions moderate the specific types of emotions experienced, and also moderate the effects of these emotions on satisfaction. For example, if a rollercoaster ride operator fails to secure the safety restraint then PP may be negative and other-oriented, with emotions of anger, disgust, or contempt experienced; if fastening the safety restraint was your responsibility, then PP may be negative and self-oriented with emotions of shame and guilt evoked (following Oliver 1993). These moderated emotions represent the first of the two hypothesized roles of emotions in determining satisfaction.

After experiencing a product, a comparison process takes place between desire and perceived performance (Olshavsky and Spreng 1989; Spreng and Olshavsky 1993; see Woodruff et al, 1983 for other comparison standards). This comparison process is cognitive in nature and is labeled evaluated performance (EP_i);[1] it essentially tells the individual whether they "got what they wanted." For hedonic attributes, the comparison process leads to a second emotion (EM^2) based on the individual's evaluation of the (earlier) directly experienced emotion; evoked emotions may be positive, negative or of mixed valence. Again, individual attributions (A^2) moderate the type of emotions experienced, and also moderate the effects of these emotions on satisfaction. Note that these second emotions and the corresponding attributions are distinct from those that occur directly during consumption. This second role of emotions in determining satisfaction appears consistent with prior treatments of this concept.[2]

---

[1] Spreng and Olshavsky (1993) refer to this as "desires congruency."

[2] Cognitive responses to utilitarian and hedonic attributes are also expected to occur and to impact satisfaction, but these influences are not addressed in this paper.

FIGURE
A Model of the Dual Role of Emotions in Consumer S/DS

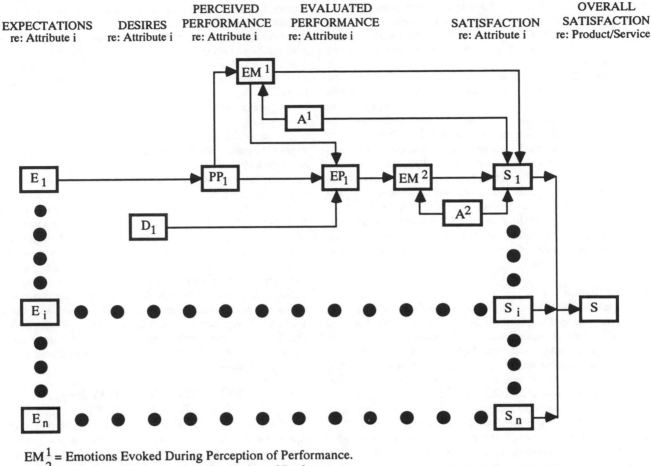

EXPECTATIONS re: Attribute i | DESIRES re: Attribute i | PERCEIVED PERFORMANCE re: Attribute i | EVALUATED PERFORMANCE re: Attribute i | SATISFACTION re: Attribute i | OVERALL SATISFACTION re: Product/Service

EM^1 = Emotions Evoked During Perception of Performance.
EM^2 = Emotions Evoked During Evaluation of Performance.
A^1 = Attributions for EM^1.
A^2 = Attributions for EM^2.

Satisfaction at the level of each attribute (S_i) is thus determined by the moderated emotions that are generated directly from consumption (i.e., EM^1) *and* by the moderated emotions that are evoked following the evaluation of the directly generated emotions (i.e., EM_2). As noted earlier, the emotion directly experienced and the emotion evoked during the evaluation of performance may be different in type and even opposite in valence. For example, some consumers are extremely frightened while flying. While most of these consumers will have a negative emotional response to this frightening experience, some consumers may have a positive emotional response to this frightening experience (because they desire to be frightened). Also, many consumers seem to greatly enjoy fearful experiences such as horror movies, some types of amusement park rides, and bungee jumping.

As one source of complexity, some consumption experiences may lead to such strong direct emotions (EM^1) that these emotions overwhelm the emotions that arise from the comparison process (EM^2) on one or more of the other attributes (hedonic or utilitarian). For example, the tremendous fear that some consumers experience (EM^1) while flying could overwhelm any other emotions elicited by the comparison process (EM^2) on attributes such as staff friendliness, food quality, and meeting flight schedule times. Re-

sults of a study reported in the *Marketing News* (Vol. 28, No. 17, August 15, 1994) illustrate the above idea; results show that among shoppers in an upscale, enclosed mall in Miami the group that felt "unsafe...appeared so concerned about its safety that only 27.9% liked the atmosphere/decor of the mall. In contrast, 43.4% of the safe group liked the atmosphere."

An important aspect of our model is that we explicitly suggest that perceptions of product performance and comparisons of product performance to desires are based on salient product attributes (Oliver 1993), and that these attributes can be categorized as either utilitarian or hedonic, or a mix of the two types (Holbrook and Hirschman 1982; Mano and Oliver 1993). Recognition of the dual emotional responses to hedonic attributes is crucial to our model. But, note that if all of the attributes are utilitarian in nature, the only emotions that will impact satisfaction are those evoked in response to evaluations of the utilitarian attributes (EM^2).

EXPLORATORY STUDY 1 — FOCUS GROUPS

Study 1 had two goals: first, to determine whether consumers are able to identify their emotions at various stages of the consumption experience, and second, whether experienced emotions are different from evaluated emotions in terms of valence. In order to explore how consumers evaluate emotions from hedonic products, two focus groups were conducted (with seven and ten students). Undergraduate students recruited from marketing classes were offered course credit for participation. The moderator was a graduate student with prior experience in conducting depth interviews. Two relevant experiential services (rollercoaster rides and horror movies) and a set of questions were deemed satisfactory based on a pre-test.

After a general introduction in which the session was described as a discussion of consumption experiences with products/ services, each session was broken up into two parts so that the discussion would focus on each of the two experiential categories in turn. In order to make a specific experience highly salient, the moderator asked each participant to name the "scariest" rollercoaster ride (horror movie) they had experienced. Participants were instructed to answer subsequent questions using this particular experience episode. Initial discussion focused on when they participated in these activities. Subsequently the focus turned to the participants' thoughts/feelings during the consumption experience. The discussion was structured around the following areas: expectations, desires, perceived performance, evaluated performance, and overall satisfaction.

Study 1 Results

The focus group results indicated that participants were able to relate their thoughts and feelings about all of the areas of inquiry. Although the experiences were sometimes a few months old (or more in some cases), participants had vivid memories, since the experiences had prompted intense feelings. Participants described their *expectations* based on their own earlier experiences with the same or similar activities and based on observations of other consumers engaging in these activities (e.g., "I think I was expecting to feel sick and just terrified."). Participants described their *desires* relevant to engaging in these activities in terms of emotions such as fear, thrills, arousal, and excitement (e.g., "I wanted to feel scared and out of control because the roller coaster, you really can't — it's not like you can tell them to stop and you get off...").

Importantly, participants were also able to describe the specific emotions they felt *during* the consumption experience (i.e., *perceived performance*). Illustrative comments are presented in Table 1. In general, participants' experienced emotions corresponded most closely with the fear, joy, and interest emotions from Izard's affect taxonomy (1977). Unexpected events led to the emergence of surprise as another emotional element. The intensity of the emotion varied during the experience episode, and seemed to depend partly on believability. Compared to horror movies, the rides seemed to be more "real" in terms of their potential to induce intense emotions.

Participants were also able to describe their emotions as they *evaluated* the consumption experience (i.e., *evaluated performance*). They evaluated the movie in terms of their desires (e.g., "it wasn't scary enough"). Illustrative comments are shown in Table 1. An outcome relevant to our theoretical perspective, was that participants evaluated felt negative emotions in positive terms. The rollercoaster ride may have been intensely scary, but participants walked out of it with the evaluation that it was fun (joyful). It is important to note that these are not akin to mixed emotions which generally refer to distinct emotions that are experienced concurrently. Rather, participants seemed to be referring to one set of emotions during consumption that gave rise to other emotions during evaluation.

Finally, participants were able to describe their satisfaction levels (see Table 1). Satisfaction seemed to depend upon evaluated performance (i.e., whether or not the ride or movie was as scary as was desired). In most cases, participants indicated considerable satisfaction; in some cases they were willing to stand in line (again) for two hours or more to repeat the experience or to rent other movies that were sequels to the original horror film. But, if the movie (or ride) was not scary enough, the dissatisfaction with these attributes would lead to overall negative evaluations of the movie (ride). Finally, of considerable interest, the direct emotions experienced by some of our participants were so negative and intense (i.e., the effects were strong and enduring) that they never wanted to see another horror movie or go on another amusement park ride.

The first study generally supported the notion that consumers can, when specifically asked to do so, describe emotions at various stages of a consumption experience. Specifically, participants were able to articulate desires and expectations with respect to emotions (antecedents of consumption emotions), the actual experienced emotion itself, and their evaluation of this emotion in terms of other emotions and satisfaction levels. Although these were experiences that they were asked to relate from memory, participants were able to describe their feelings before, during, and after the experience. Given that our procedure focused on a memory based "re-experiencing" of the original consumption, other studies that focus on concurrent evaluations are needed to corroborate this finding. The second goal of our study was also achieved since consumers' evaluations of the negative emotions directly experienced during consumption were positive, and thus opposite in valence. Both of these findings however provide only initial support for our model; the demand effects inherent in using focus groups lead us to a second exploratory study.

EXPLORATORY STUDY 2 — A LAB EXPERIMENT

The second exploratory study used a lab experiment to further explore the notion of the dual role of emotions in experiential aspects of consumption. Specifically we wished to explore whether experienced negative emotions, if desired, could lead to favorable satisfaction responses. Whereas in Study 1 we explored actual emotions experienced during a prior consumption episode, in the second study we asked for consumer reactions to scenarios. Manipulations of desired positive and negative emotions were embedded in these scenarios and participants were asked for their reactions to these scenarios.

Study Design

Ninety eight undergraduate students at the School of Business, Indiana University participated in this study for course credit. A 2 (desires: joy vs. fear) x 2 (expectations: low vs. high) x 2 (perceived performance: low vs. high) factorial design was used to explore the impact of these factors on satisfaction and other post-consumption responses. A basketball game and a horror movie were chosen as consumption experiences for positive (joy) and negative (fear) emotions respectively. Desires were manipulated with a statement that focused on the corresponding emotion. For example, for movies, the statement "you have just managed to get first show tickets for a new horror movie that you hope will be as scary as the last one from this producer" was used to make the desire for a negative emotion (i.e., fear) particularly salient. Expectations were manipulated with a statement attributed to an independent newspaper review that the movie "is guaranteed to chill your spine" (high expectations) or that it "has been hyped up and is not very scary" (low expectations). Finally, perceived performance was manipulated by focusing on how predictable the movie was and hence not scary (low perceived performance) or that it kept you "on the edge

TABLE 1
Selected Focus Group Comments

Product/Service 1: Roller coaster rides

Perceived Performance

And when it falls down, honestly, I can't breathe. I feel the feeling that people jump out from a high building, and it makes me very excited.

I was nervous before and then once I was actually on it, I was more nervous. The excitement before was just anticipating what was going to happen because you really didn't know what it was going to be like. You just don't know where your heart is after it goes down.

Fear, excitement, adrenalin rush!

Usually I can't believe I am going on this ride. I t drives me nuts.

Evaluated Performance

It's just fun. I don't like the part when you're winding your way around because you know what's coming up, but actually going down I like that part.

My stomach would get tighter and tighter, finally at the very top, it just released you. The part where you drop, it was kind of what you wanted.

...it's so dark and you can't see anything. You took a ride up and down but you don't know your direction. That scares me but it was thrilling and exciting.

I guess you tend to like just the big rides—the rides that scare you the most.

I am the one screaming with my hands in the air. There is like the physical side where your stomach drops and it's like, it's fun. It's exciting.

Satisfaction

Because, you know, I did get excited, and it was fun, and it was pretty long. I mean, I'm satisfied enough where I would go on it again. I would wait and go on it again.

Yes, since I wanted to know how would I feel if I fall down from a building. I never tried it and I tried the best. I was satisfied.

I was satisfied although I thought it should have lasted longer. It was short.

Yes, I was satisfied because I was thrilled, but I was hoping that the ride was longer. You actually waited a long time for a 30 second ride.

Product/Service 2: Scary movies

Perceived Performance

Fear and tension. The scary movie would start playing and your stomach knots up and you know something is going to come around the corner. It's kind of fear and tension, so your body tenses.

You kind of go through stages when you're watching it, like you're excited in a stage, some of it—nothing's happening and you're just sitting there and not excited, just kind of watching. And then you get excited again in a scary part like if someone falls asleep and Freddy comes to the dream.

...like in Misery, you are sitting on the edge of your seat wondering what she's going to do next.

It scared me out of my pants.

...you're excited during it, you know your heart's pounding faster, you're really like engrossed in the movie, and if you're watching a romantic movie you're kind of relaxed and just like going with it.

Basically, it was just some fear, throughout the whole thing I was biting my nails off.

Evaluated Performance

It was kind of unbelievable, but I was still scared and I liked it.

The first movies, I liked those a lot. Yes, they scared me but that's what I wanted.

I just wanted it to end as soon as it can and just get out of there.

Satisfaction

I saw Children of the Corn when I was a lot younger so afterwards I was scared to go anywhere near a cornfield.

I can say when I saw the movie Aliens, it made me sick, really sick. Well, when I saw the movie I just wanted to have the end very quickly. I lose my appetite afterwards for the whole day.

I remember after watching that movie I couldn't really sleep at night.

I was at home going to the bathroom, I had problems. I couldn't even sleep alone at night.

I guess I was satisfied because the movie stuck with me for a while.

TABLE 2
Mean Values for Manipulation Checks in Study 2*

Conditions		Expectations		Anticipations		Desires Enjoy		Desires - Excite		Desires - Scary	
Expectations	Performance	Game	Movie	Game	Movie	Game	Movie	Game	Movie	Game	Movie
Low	Low	2.80	3.76	3.76	4.20	5.76	5.88	5.24	5.58	1.88	5.72
Low	High	2.79	2.88	3.83	3.92	5.75	5.59	5.17	6.26	2.13	6.22
High	Low	6.54	6.08	6.54	6.08	6.50	5.96	6.58	6.26	2.21	6.17
High	High	6.04	5.84	6.28	6.12	6.46	5.92	6.64	6.24	2.58	6.24

* Since the basketball game and the horror movie represent two different consumption experiences, the means cannot be directly compared across columns.

of your seat the whole time and was very scary" (high perceived performance).

To reduce the demand effects inherent in a complete within-subjects design, each subject was asked to react to only two scenarios, one for the basketball game and one for the horror movie (desires manipulation). Moreover, the two scenarios to which each subject was exposed were in diagonally opposite cells for expectations and perceived performance. For example, if a particular subject was in the low expectations, low perceived performance cell for the horror movie, they would be placed in the high expectations, high perceived performance cell for the basketball game.

After reading each of the two scenarios, subjects were asked to evaluate how satisfied they would be in this situation, and to indicate the likelihood of other post-consumption behaviors such as positive word-of-mouth, complaining, and loyalty. To investigate the efficacy of the scenarios in manipulating expectations and desires, subjects were exposed to two additional scenarios (one for each consumption experience) that represented a different cell in the design. This time, their reactions to these scenarios focused on measuring their expectations and desires for enjoyable or scary experiences. The perceived performance manipulation was fairly direct and hence not conducive to a specific check.

Study 2 Results

Table 2 reports the mean values on the manipulation checks for desires and expectations used in the study. Separate 2 (expectations) x 2 (perceived performance) ANOVA models (one for each of the two desire conditions) were used to test the efficacy of the expectations manipulations. The expectations manipulation was successful as evident from a comparison of mean scores of expectations across the cells in the study. Compared to the low expectations condition, expectations for the basketball game $(F(1,94)=278.75, p<.001)$ and the horror movie $(F(1,94)=87.29, p<.001)$ were significantly higher in the high expectations condition. Similarly, anticipations were also higher in the high expectations condition for the basketball game $(F(1,94)=147.18, p<.001)$ and the horror movie $(F(1,94)=78.59, p<.001)$. Since the pattern of these expectations did not differ between the two consumption experiences (desires conditions), the expectations manipulation was successful.

Since desire was manipulated using scenarios involving experiences that differed in many, unknown ways (basketball game vs. horror movie), their differences cannot be directly tested. Rather, across the two desires conditions, we compare patterns of levels of desired emotions to assess the efficacy of the desires manipulation. Most importantly, the basketball game scenarios scored substantially lower (mean=2.20) than the horror movie (mean=6.09) on the scariness measure. On the other hand, subjects indicated that they desired more enjoyment from the basketball game (mean=6.12) compared to the horror movie (mean=5.84). Finally, desired excitement scores were equal for the basketball game and horror movie scenarios, which reflects arousal and/or the interest emotion. In summary, although we cannot test for statistical significance, the desires manipulation appears to be successful as indicated by these mean scores.

To test the effects of expectation and perceived performance on satisfaction, separate 2 x 2 ANOVA models were used for each of the two desire conditions. Table 3 reports mean values on satisfaction, positive word-of-mouth, complaining, and loyalty measures across the eight study cells. As expected, for desires relating to positive experiences (joy from the basketball game), high levels of perceived performance led to high levels of satisfaction $(F(1,94)=109.96, p<.001)$. Moreover, expectations about the game did not have any effect on satisfaction $(F<1)$. Hence, perceived performance appears to be more diagnostic in understanding satisfaction than expectations; this result is consistent with our model. Perceived performance also has a positive association with positive word-of-mouth and loyalty and a negative relationship with complaining behavior.

A similar pattern is evident for the horror movie in spite of the fact that the desires for this experience were characterized by a negative emotion, namely fear. The means in Table 3 show that when the horror movie was perceived as extremely scary, subjects were more satisfied (than when the horror movie was less scary, $F(1,94)=398.58, p<.001)$. Moreover, lower expectations led to higher levels of satisfaction $(F(1,94)=7.82, p<.01)$. Finally, similar to the basketball game patterns, higher perceived performance led to higher loyalty and positive word-of-mouth, and lower levels of complaining behavior. The only interaction that was observed was for complaining behavior, with results indicating that subjects are more likely to complain after a low level of perceived performance when expectations are high than when expectations are low.

In summary, in this second study subjects reacted to consumption context descriptions regarding performance on hedonic attributes, and evaluated how they would feel in these situations.[3] The results show that subjects may experience a negative emotion (fear) during consumption, but if this is the desired emotion (as for horror movies), this leads to higher levels of satisfaction. This

[3]Only the direct effect of perceived performance on satisfaction is examined in this study. As depicted in the Figure, the effect of perceived performance on satisfaction can also be partly mediated by evaluated performance.

TABLE 3
Mean Values for Study 2 Dependent Measures*

Conditions		Satisfaction		Positive WOM		Complaining		Loyalty	
Expectations	Performance	Game	Movie	Game	Movie	Game	Movie	Game	Movie
Low	Low	3.40	2.80	2.40	2.20	4.24	5.28	4.48	3.36
Low	High	6.16	6.67	4.96	5.46	2.13	2.33	4.71	5.96
High	Low	3.71	2.00	2.71	1.71	4.17	6.04	4.79	3.38
High	High	6.48	6.32	5.20	5.44	2.44	1.72	5.36	5.64

* Since the basketball game and the horror movie represent two different consumption experiences, the means cannot be directly compared across columns.

result contrasts with Westbrook's (1987) finding that consumption-based negative affect leads to dissatisfaction. Our Study Two results generally parallel the comments in our focus groups and hence, the dual role of emotions is substantiated in both studies. We should note here that the scenarios made only one attribute/emotion salient, and hence, attribute and overall satisfaction may not differ very much. When multiple attributes/emotions are involved, the overall satisfaction may be modeled as a complex function of satisfaction with individual attributes (Oliver 1993).

GENERAL DISCUSSION

Our model and preliminary empirical results suggest that the relationship between emotions and satisfaction is considerably complex for products that are primarily hedonic in nature. Specifically, we have suggested that expectations and desires for hedonic attributes center on the specific emotions that form an integral part of that consumption experience. Moreover these pre-consumption standards may be formulated not only in terms of the type of emotion (fear, joy), but also the degree of emotion (extremely scared or very joyful). This idea is an extension of Oliver's (1993) notion of an attribute basis for satisfaction, except that the attributes are hedonic in nature.

Second, our model and exploratory research alerts researchers to the possibility that the emotion experienced during consumption is conceptually different from evaluations of this emotion. This distinction is critical for hedonic bases of consumption where the emotion *is* the consumption experience itself. Moreover, the separation of these two as distinct emotions raises the possibility that they may be quite different in valence. As demonstrated in our preliminary studies, positive emotions (joy) may be evoked in response to evaluations of negative emotions (fear). It is also possible that negative emotions could be experienced in response to positive emotions; for example, even pleasant stimuli (such as music) may, in certain conditions (e.g., when one is trying to concentrate on one's work), evoke negative emotions. Further explorations of these dual emotions is necessary for a complete understanding of these phenomena.

Finally, the relationships of these emotions to satisfaction is an important topic. Given that these consumption emotions may have strong direct effects (Westbrook 1987) or moderate effects of other variables on satisfaction, the separate role of these two types of emotions needs to be subjected to greater scrutiny. This implies that to correctly understand the nature of the relationship between emotions and satisfaction, future studies should have separate measures of those emotions that result directly from the hedonic experience and those that result indirectly from a comparison process.

Limitations

Two separate studies offer initial support for the notion of dual role of emotions; however, these findings are exploratory. First, the focus group results are fairly tentative given the small sample and directive nature of the discussion. Hence, since no deception was involved, the possibility of demand effects and "artificial results" should not be ruled out. The second study used a different approach with manipulation of key concepts using scenarios, and hence does not suffer the same problems. However, even here, some limitations are present. First, the scenarios may be so directive that there was no possibility for other responses. Hence, once again demand effects may color the subjects' responses. Second, the desires manipulation is confounded with the nature of the service (the basketball game vs. the horror movie). Hence, future research needs to disentangle product effects. Third, these scenarios attempt to place students in various consumption contexts and assess their emotions. Since we want to investigate experiential aspects of consumption, it may be more instructive to assess emotions from actual experiences as they occur. Even though the first study focused on actual experiences, these consumption contexts were months and sometimes years in the past. Finally, although both studies offer support for parts of the dual emotions model, they do not test the entire model or compare this model with other models.

In conclusion, we have proposed and partially tested a model of satisfaction that parses emotions into consumption-based and evaluation-based responses. Our exploratory research offers evidence in support of these distinctions. Given the limitations discussed above, we call for a more systematic exploration of this topic.

REFERENCES

Holbrook, Morris B. and Elizabeth C. Hirschman (1982), "The Experiential Aspects of Consumption: Consumer Fantasies, Feelings, and Fun," *Journal of Consumer Research*, 9 (September), 132-140.

Izard, Carroll E. (1977), *Human Emotion*. New York: Plenum Press.

Mano, Haim and Richard L. Oliver (1993), "Assessing the Dimensionality and Structure of the Emotion Experience: Evaluation, Feeling, and Satisfaction," *Journal of Consumer Research*, 20(December),451-66.

Oliver, Richard L. (1993), "Cognitive, Affective, and Attribute Bases of the Satisfaction Response," *Journal of Consumer Research*, 20 (December), 418-430.

Oliver, Richard L. and Robert A. Westbrook (1993), "Profiles of Consumer Emotions and Satisfaction in Ownership and Usage," *Journal of Consumer Satisfaction, Dissatisfaction and Complaining Behavior*, Vol. 6, 12-27.

Olshavsky, Richard W. and Richard A. Spreng (1989), "A Desires as Standard Model of Consumer Satisfaction," *Journal of Consumer Satisfaction, Dissatisfaction and Complaining Behavior*," 2,49-54.

Spreng, Richard A. and Richard W. Olshavsky (1993), "A Desires Congruency Model of Consumer Satisfaction," *Journal of the Academy of Marketing Sciences*, 21, No. 3, 169-177.

Westbrook, Robert A. (1987), "Product/Consumption-Based Affective Responses and Postpurchase Processes," *Journal of Marketing Research*, 24 (August), 258-70.

Westbrook, Robert A. and Richard L. Oliver (1991), "The Dimensionality of Consumption Emotion Patterns and Consumer Satisfaction," *Journal of Consumer Research*, 18 (June), 84-91.

Cross-cultural Consumer Research: A Twenty-Year Review

Jane Z. Sojka, Washington State University
Patriya S. Tansuhaj, Washington State University[1]

ABSTRACT

We examined cross-cultural consumer behavior publications which have appeared in four major marketing journals and proceedings, *Journal of Consumer Research, Journal of Marketing, Journal of Marketing Research,* and *Advances in Consumer Research* over a twenty-year period ranging from 1970-1990. The review and analysis are organized by chronological order, by geographic order, and by cultural variables—language, artifacts, and values. Publication trends, cross-cultural similarities across seemingly diverse cultures, are discussed. Suggestions for future research and a more complete conceptual definition of culture are then provided.

INTRODUCTION

The diversity and overwhelming scope of cross-cultural consumer behavior research necessitates an integrative review of pertinent research appearing in marketing journals if the field is to progress in a systematic fashion. There have been numerous literature reviews of consumer behavior topics which have relevance to cross-cultural studies (cf., Folkes 1988; Helegeson, Kluge, Mager and Taylor 1984; McAlister and Pessemier 1982; Sheppard, Hartwick and Warshaw 1988; Sirgy 1982). These reviews, however, focus on a particular consumer topic as opposed to the international focus presented in this paper. The purpose of this literature review is to review systematically cross-cultural consumer research over a twenty-year period. An examination of twenty years' worth of diverse research in this discipline allows for identification of shifts and changes in a longitudinal manner.

The comprehensive literature review of cross-cultural consumer behavior research undertaken in this paper could advance the consumer behavior discipline in several ways. First, it identifies areas needing additional research. Second, an agreed upon set of terminology and definitions are desirable to advance the field of cross-cultural consumer behavior research. Finally, an added benefit of exploring consumer behavior in other cultures is that it frequently offers additional insight into future subcultural consumer behavior both in the United States and other countries (van Raaij 1978).

REVIEW METHOD

Article Selection

The all-encompassing nature of culture made the selection of research to be studied a crucial point in conducting a systematic literature review. First, consumer behavior research that dealt with a country other than the U.S. was cited as cross-cultural. The second criterion was the inclusion of the term "culture" in the article title. Articles dealing with a subculture, ethnic group, or group of people with minority status were also included in the literature review. The final criterion used for selecting articles appropriate for this literature review is the requirement that the research deal with consumers and consumer behavior.

---

[1]The authors gratefully acknowledge valuable comments from Jim Gentry and three anonymous reviewers, and the editorial and graphic assistance from Kris Kilgore.

With the focus of cultural implications on marketing and consumer behavior, the research scope was limited to major marketing publications: *Journal of Consumer Research, Journal of Marketing Research, Advances in Consumer Research,* and *The Journal of Marketing.* To be certain that these are representative sources for the majority of cross-cultural consumer research, a manual and computerized search of the Social Science Citation Index from 1970-1990 was undertaken. While this search yielded a total of 25 additional cross-cultural articles, virtually all of the citations were from different journals; hence it is reasonable to assume that the four journals surveyed adequately represent the concentration of cross-cultural consumer research. A twenty-year time frame, 1970 to 1990, was determined to be appropriate for a longitudinal analysis. In using the aforementioned selection criteria, a total of 118 articles are included in this review.

Framework for Review

After examining the published research as our data, it became apparent that cross-cultural consumer behavior researchers operationalized "culture" in three primary classifications. We categorized the various operationalizations and grouped them as occurring (1) through language, (2) through material goods or artifacts, and (3) through beliefs or value systems.

RESULTS

Publication Trends

Cross-cultural research has been steadily increasing since 1970, both in terms of the number of studies published (see Figure 1) and with respect to the countries explored (see Figures 3 - 5). A frequency count of published research reveals that France was the most studied country followed by England and Japan. The publication trend corresponds with the increased number of anthropological citations as noted by Leong (1989) in his examinations of the *Journal of Consumer Research* from 1974-1988. Both findings reiterate the rising interest and importance of cross-cultural consumer behavior research.

U.S. Subcultural Research Trends

Over time, not only has the number of subcultural studies increased, but the cultures being investigated have broadened in scope. Figure 2 illustrates the diversity of American subcultures examined by consumer behavior researchers. Each subculture is presented as a box. In 1970, for example, the African American subculture was studied twice (as indicated by the letter "A"). The trend shifted away from studying the African-American subculture to studies of the Hispanic subculture in the mid-1980s.

Reflecting the social influences of the 1960s, most subcultural studies published between 1970-1975 dealt with the African-American subculture—frequently referred to as "negroes" (Bush, Gwinner, and Solomon 1974; Cohen 1970; Gensch, and Staelin 1972; Gould, Sigband, and Zoerner 1970; Pruden and Longman 1972; Sexton 1971a, 1971b, 1972). The research produced was largely descriptive. Once researchers began holding income constant, racial differences seemed to disappear as well as publication opportunities. Only one study prior to 1975 (Pruden and Longman 1972) examined more than one subculture simultaneously. In an initial attempt to examine race, alienation and consumerism, Pruden

FIGURE 1
Publication Trends (Number of Articles per Year)

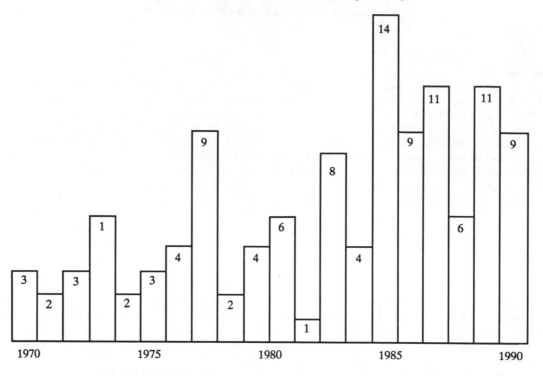

and Longman (1972) contrasted high-income Anglo-Americans with low-income Mexican-Americans and African-American consumers. Researchers investigating topics such as food purchasing behavior, black/white reaction to integrated advertisements, and African-American shopping behavior, for example, noted similarities and differences between the two ethnic groups, but neglected to take the next step in explaining the behavior they cited. Indeed, the term "culture" was scarcely seen in the literature until 1974 when the consumer behavior field came into its own journal and conference.

Expanding Beyond the African-American Subculture

From 1975 to 1985, cross-cultural research continued to expand both in terms of the number of articles published and the diversity of subcultures investigated. Following on the heels of the 1975-85 expansion, during the 1986-1990 period, only 7 of the 37 articles published examined subcultures (as opposed to cultures outside the United States). Yet, even the subcultures studied reflect the discipline's increasing range. As reflected in demographic and sociological changes within the U.S., the Hispanic subculture was frequently topic for research as shown in Figure 2. Subcultural research has become increasingly sophisticated with comparison of more diverse groups. Hirschman (1985), for example, examined similarities of the consumption patterns of U.S. Blacks, Italians, WASPs, and Jews with those of non-industrialized cultures. If the U.S. continues the trend toward "ethnic upsurges" as noted by Schlesinger (1991) in his book, *The Disuniting of America*, continued research with additional subcultures represented is warranted. After 1986, only one article examined the African-American subculture and that was in conjunction with the Hispanic and Polish subcultures (Reilly and Wallendorf 1987).

Cross-cultural Consumer Research Trends: Beyond U.S. Subcultures

In reviewing the countries and cultures studied by consumer researchers during the last two decades, a diverse and substantial number of cultures have been investigated. Classifying research by country, as straightforward as it sounds, proved challenging in some cases such as in studies of ethnicity where ethnic values (such as Chineseness) were examined not in China, but in Singapore (McCullough 1986; Tan and McCullough 1985). In such cases, the articles were classified by where the sample was taken. Also, since some researchers examined more than one country or culture at a time, a single article may be cross-listed under several countries.

The level of investigation of cross-cultural research has become more sophisticated over the years with researchers comparing and contrasting two or more cultures simultaneously. Green et al. (1983), for example, examined family purchases in the U.S., France, Holland, Gabon, and Venezuela, while Kim, Laroche and Joy (1990) examined the French and English subcultures in Canada. Prior to 1975, cross-cultural research focused on comparing a single culture with the U.S. Clearly the 1975-85 decade saw cross-cultural researchers expanding the scope of their research to include more diverse cultures and subcultures in a simultaneous examination.

Cultures Studied. The majority of cultures or countries investigated are located in the Pacific Rim or Europe. Figures 3-5 summarize published research by country in diverse geographic regions of the world. Under each country heading, the name of the first author and date of publication are noted in a "box." Consistent with the previous Figure, an "*" signifies that more than one country/culture was studied. For example, the boxes containing "Cote 1989" have an asterisk and are therefore listed under coun-

FIGURE 2
Number of U.S. Subcultures Studied

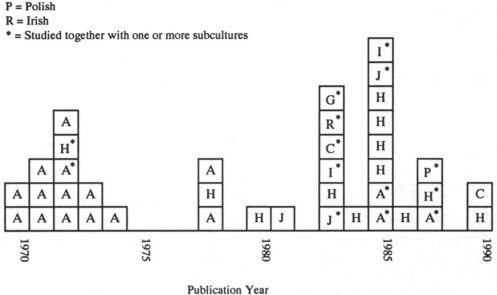

A = African American
C = Chinese
G = Greek
H = Hispanic
I = Italian
J = Jewish
P = Polish
R = Irish
* = Studied together with one or more subcultures

Publication Year

tries studied in that article: Jordan and Thailand (see Figures 3 and 5). Finally, while most of the cross-cultural research dealt with industrialized cultures, articles that explicitly examined primitive (meaning non-industrialized cultures indigenous to the geographical region) cultures are marked with "P" and will be discussed in a separate section.

In reviewing the literature, we attempted to distinguish studies of cross-national nature from those examining more specific cultural elements in the consumer behavior context. Consumer behavior researchers have done an admirable job in the initial step of studying a large number of countries; nonetheless, a cross-national study (noted as a letter "N" in Figures 3-5) does not always translate into a cross-cultural analysis (indicated by the letter "C" in the Figures). For instance, Douglas' (1976, 1979) descriptive study of family decision-making or women's life-styles in different countries without explaining results on the basis of cultural differences is an example of a cross-national analysis examining the differences between two countries. Since the research compared France with the U.S., these articles are listed in Figure 3 under France with an "N" signifying a cross-national study. Culture, on the other hand, is not bound by national or state borders. A cross-cultural study, therefore, examines data and explains results on the basis of cultural meaning, not national boundaries.

Differences between European and Asian Studies. The majority of research on the Asian countries was culturally oriented, specific cultural elements were examined more closely. Researchers seem fascinated with understanding differences between Eastern and Western values, language, and artifacts as exemplified by the number of cross-cultural studies (noted with a "C" in Figure 5). In contrast, studies of Europe are more likely to be cross-national

(i.e., comparing consumer behavior in the U.S. with that of a Western European country, as noted with an "N" in Figure 3). The difference in research focus may imply that American researchers assume more cultural similarities with Western culture counterparts than Oriental countries. Furthermore, cultures of Eastern Europe were not examined during the twenty-year period of this review.

Investigating Cultural Elements

Language and Culture. To each culture, language offers an interpretative code or schema for organizing and presenting the world. Hence, language serves various functions in a cultural context. Socio-linguists postulate that language is important in the formation of thought patterns and behavioral responses (Douglas 1979). As Mick (1986) notes, meaning is not an individual enterprise, but rather "a social procedure for defining objects to achieve a practical effect" (p. 204). Thus, language represents one aspect of an emic (defined as the articulation of native understanding as they see them) view of the external cultural environment.

When dealing with a subculture speaking a language distinct from the dominant culture (e.g., Hispanics in the U.S.) or as in bilingual countries (e.g., Canada) language was often used as a segmentation variable or measure of ethnicity.

Not surprisingly, it appears, that language is a poor indicator of ethnicity. Conflicting reports on hispanic brand loyalty and English/French Canadian purchase patterns represent a need to more clearly isolate subpopulations on a variable other than language (O'Guinn and Faber 1985; Saegert Hoover and Hilger 1985; Schaninger, Bourgeois, and Buss 1985; Valencia 1985). Indeed, three separate studies comparing three distinct cultures/subcul-

FIGURE 3
Cross-cultural Studies of Europe and Middle East

C = Cultural study
N = National study
* = More than one culture/country discussed

	Green* 1974 N									
	Green 1975 N									
	Douglas 1976 N									
	Douglas 1979 N									
Hempel 1974 N	Douglas 1980 N									
Douglas* 1977 C	Davis 1981 N									
Douglas* 1979 C	Joilbert* 1981 C									
Davis* 1981 N	Green* 1983 N									
Arnold* 1983 N	Jolibert 1983 C	Engledow 1975 N								
O'Conner 1985 C	O'Conner 1985 C	Anderson 1977 N	Tigert* 1980 N							
Wiley* 1974 N	Wiley* 1974 N	Leeflang 1974 N	Arnold* 1974 N							
Weitenberger 1989 N	Douglas* 1987 C	Wiley* 1985 N	Green* 1983 N	Douglas* 1979 C						
Ward* 1986 N	Meyer 1987 N	Ger* 1990 C	Wiley 1985 C	O'Conner* 1985 C	Costa 1989 C	Douglas* 1979 C				
Ger 1990 C	Ger 1990 C	Rudmin 1990 C	Dawson 1990 C	Wiley 1985 N	Costa 1990 C	O'Conner 1985 C	Ger 1990 C	Arndt 1981 C	Jaffe* 1984 N	Cote* 1989 C

England   France   Germany   Netherlands   Denmark   Greece   Sweden   Turkey   Norway   Israel   Jordan

tures—Hispanics in the U.S. (Deshpande, Hoyer, and Donthu 1986), French and English speaking Canadians (Kim, Larouche, and Joy 1990), and Mexicans, Australians, and Americans (Gilly 1988)—all concluded that language alone could not accurately predict or explain differences found between subcultures and cultures.

As opposed to using language as a subcultural identifier, Hirschman (1981) proposes using an emic measure of ethnicity which permits the individual to ascribe religious and cultural identity to him/herself. While Hirschman's work on ethnicity was initially tested on the Jewish subculture, it appears to have promise in cross-cultural and subcultural contexts (Ellis, Wallendorf, and Tan 1985; Hirschman 1983; Laroche, Joy, Hui, and Kim 1991; McCullough, Tan, and Wong 1986). The self-identification measure proposed by Hirschman avoids ethnocentric bias of the researcher as might be present in determining subpopulations on the basis of language alone. Although language may prove to be a poor segmentation variable, language preference is still the predominant determinant of acculturation in cross-cultural psychology literature

and research suggests it may be instrumental in anticipating and encouraging diffusion of innovations among different cultures (Takada and Jain 1991).

Artifacts as Cultural Representations. Material possessions and tangible goods, including food, represented another avenue pursued by consumer researchers to make operational definitions of the abstract culture concept more concrete. Goods carry and communicate visible evidence of cultural meaning (Lee 1989; McCracken 1986; Mick 1986), and in some cultures offer evidence of social success (Belk 1984). The study of goods and material possessions is closely linked to the concept of materialism proposed by Belk and Bryce (1986) as "the tendency to view possessions as the primary sources of satisfaction and dissatisfaction" (p. 568). While materialism is an internalized value, it outwardly results in possessions obtained to enhance that materialistic value.

Figure 7 notes an array of cultural artifacts examined in a cross-cultural context. Types of goods or artifacts studied are obviously broad categories. The "general" category (as noted in Arnould 1989) is used when the researcher examined artifacts in

FIGURE 4
Cross-cultural Consumer Studies of the Americas (Excluding U.S.) and Africa

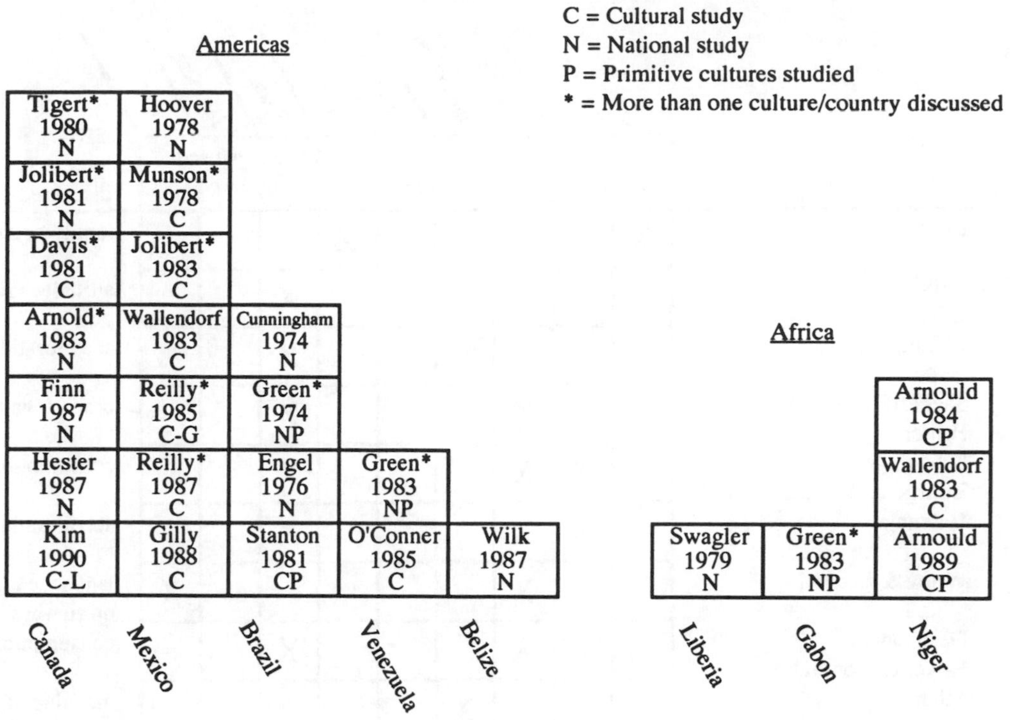

C = Cultural study
N = National study
P = Primitive cultures studied
* = More than one culture/country discussed

Americas

Africa

Tigert* 1980 N	Hoover 1978 N			
Jolibert* 1981 N	Munson* 1978 C			
Davis* 1981 C	Jolibert* 1983 C			
Arnold* 1983 N	Wallendorf 1983 C	Cunningham 1974 N		
Finn 1987 N	Reilly* 1985 C-G	Green* 1974 NP		
Hester 1987 N	Reilly* 1987 C	Engel 1976 N	Green* 1983 NP	
Kim 1990 C-L	Gilly 1988 C	Stanton 1981 CP	O'Conner 1985 C	Wilk 1987 N

Canada   Mexico   Brazil   Venezuela   Belize

	Arnould 1984 CP
	Wallendorf 1983 C
Swagler 1979 N	Green* 1983 NP	Arnould 1989 CP

Liberia   Gabon   Niger

FIGURE 5
Cross-cultural Consumer Behavior Research Asia and Australia

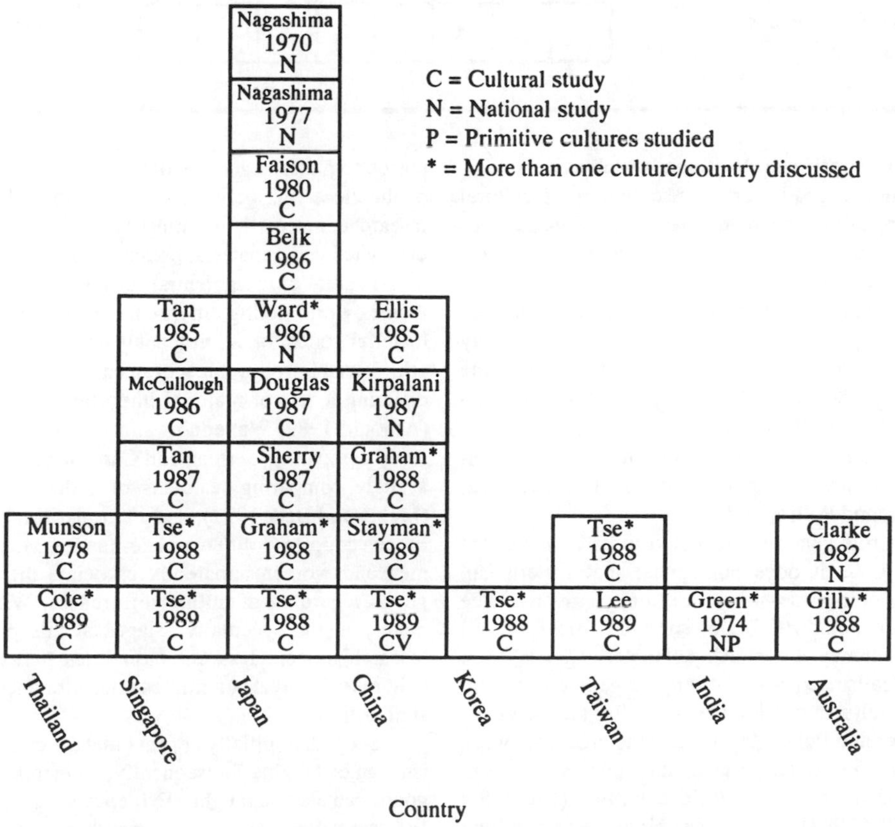

	Nagashima 1970 N						
	Nagashima 1977 N						
	Faison 1980 C						
	Belk 1986 C						
Tan 1985 C	Ward* 1986 N	Ellis 1985 C					
McCullough 1986 C	Douglas 1987 C	Kirpalani 1987 N					
Tan 1987 C	Sherry 1987 C	Graham* 1988 C					

C = Cultural study
N = National study
P = Primitive cultures studied
* = More than one culture/country discussed

| Munson 1978 C | Tse* 1988 C | Graham* 1988 C | Stayman* 1989 C | | Tse* 1988 C | | Clarke 1982 N |
| Cote* 1989 C | Tse* 1989 C | Tse* 1988 C | Tse* 1989 CV | Tse* 1988 C | Lee 1989 C | Green* 1974 NP | Gilly* 1988 C |

Thailand   Singapore   Japan   China   Korea   Taiwan   India   Australia

Country

FIGURE 6
Operationalization of Culture: Language

Year	Author	Research Setting (cultural)	Research Setting (sub-cultural)	Research Method (empirical)	Research Method (theoretical)	Research Method (naturalistic)	Language used in research (French)	Language used in research (Spanish)	Language used in research (Japanese)	Language used in research (other)	CB topic discussed
1979	Douglas	X		X			X				family decisions
1984	Belk			X				X			attitudes towards gifts
1985	O'Guinn & Faber		X	X				X			acculturation
1985	Saegert, Hoover & Hilger		X	X				X			brand loyalty
1985	Schaninger, Bourgeois & Buss		X	X				X			consumption
1985	Valencia		X	X				X			acculturation
1985	Wiley & Bechtel	X		X						X	language effects on surveys
1986	Deshpande, Hoyer & Donthul		X	X				X			consumption
1986	Mick				X						meaning of goods
1987	Sherry & Camargo	X			X				X		product labels
1988	Gilly	X		X				X			advertising
1989	Penazola				X						consumer acculturation
1990	Kim, Laroche & Joy		X	X			X				ethnicity

general as opposed to a specific class of goods such as durables.

Substituting tangible goods for representations of cultural values is intuitively appealing and overcomes many of the methodological challenges of accessing and evaluating consumers' internal beliefs and values which become further convoluted by cross-cultural analysis. And yet, it is crucial in a cross-cultural analysis to remember that meanings assigned to goods by the researcher may or may not accurately represent the meanings understood by the host culture. Hence, a phenomenological approach—where description exists at the level of the respondent—or a hermeneutical approach—in which cultural artifacts are examined as an embodiment of cultural values—would both be appropriate (Dilthey 1972; Thompson, Locander, and Pollio 1989).

While materialism is generally accepted to be an important cultural trait in the U.S., it does not appear that materialism expressed through tangible possessions is culturally universal (Lee 1989; Wallendorf and Arnould 1988). Dawson and Bamossy (1990) found the "increased saliency of ownership of material goods" to be related to Calvinist idealism expressed through organized religion; thus including many cultures outside the U.S.. Regardless of the dominant religion, Ger and Belk (1990) found the protestant work ethic and the subsequent increased value of material possessions to be surprisingly prevalent in Third World countries (Lee 1989; Wallendorf and Arnould 1987). The degree of importance a culture places on material goods still is open to debate. However, because of the close link between materialism and tangible goods, U.S. researchers in particular must be aware of potential ethnocentric bias when using material possessions as cultural measures.

In spite of the potential for ethnocentric bias, however, two themes worth noting emerge from the current literature utilizing material goods for cultural analysis. Sex differences, as a moderating variable, may represent an underlying variable accounting for differing levels of material importance on a cross-cultural basis (Arnould 1989; Wallendorf and Arnould 1988). For example, a study comparing German and Canadian students (Rudman 1990), a study comparing residents of India with Indian immigrants (Mehta and Belk 1991), and a comparison between Mexican and French couples (Jolibert and Fernandez-Moreno 1983), found that men and women apparently associate different meanings with goods, regardless of cultural differences. While this observation is merely in the speculative stages at this point of cross-cultural research, nonetheless commonalities between the sexes across cultures offer great potential as a basis for uncovering cross-cultural similarities.

Second, it initially appears that the cultural value of materialism can be taught. Subsequently, an increased value and need for goods can also be taught. Evidence suggests that the diffusion of Western values and goods, currently occurring in the Pacific Rim,

FIGURE 7
Operationalization of Culture: Artifacts

Year	Author	Research Method (empirical)	Research Method (theoretical)	Research Method (naturalistic)	general	durable goods	small appliances	clothing	toys	autos	recreational equip	food	toiletries	CB Topic
1980	Tigert, King & Ring	X						X						diffusion adoption
1981	Arnat, et al.	X							X					decision process
1982	Clarke & Souter					X	X							consumption
1983	Jolibert & Fernandez-Moreno	X						X	X					gift-giving
1983	Wallendorf & Reilly	X										X		consumption
1984	Belk		X		X									gift-giving
1985	Mick		X		X									semiotics
1985	Tan & McCullough	X				X	X			X		X	X	consumption
1986	McCracken		X		X									advertising
1988	Roth & Moorman		X		X									decision process
1988	Tse, Wong & Tan						X	X			X			relation between goods & selfconcept
1988	Wallendorf & Arnould	X			X									product attributes
1989	Arnould			X	X									diffusion
1989	Lee	X						X		X	X			consumption
1989	McCracken		X		X									advertising
1990	Ger & Belk		X		X									materialism

is a result of language similarity and other variables which communicate materialistic values through advertising and other communication mechanisms (Takada and Jain 1991; Tse, Belk, and Zhou 1989). Clearly the study of archaeology holds promise for future investigation in consumer research.

Beliefs and Values as Indicants of Culture. The third set of variables used frequently by researchers studying cross-cultural consumer behavior reflect the belief and value systems inherent in each cultural setting (see Figure 8). Judging by the number of articles utilizing values and beliefs as operational definitions of culture, many researchers feel that the knowledge of value and belief systems is instrumental in understanding and predicting consumer behavior in cross-cultural settings (Henry 1976; Munson and McIntyre 1978; O'Guinn, Lee, and Faber 1986; Roth and Moorman 1988).

In addition to materialism previously discussed, two key values—fate orientation and relationship to others (including individual determinism)—received sufficient attention in the reviewed literature to warrant comparisons across cultures. Fate orientation, or fatalism, may be defined as "the belief that all events are predetermined by fate and therefore unalterable by man" (Gentry, Tansuhaj, Manzer, and John 1988). Literature examining fatalistic beliefs cuts across a diverse cross-section of world culture—including Mexico, India, Jordan, and geographic regions of the U.S. and Brazil, for example—that at first glance would have seemingly little in common. Yet initial findings suggest that cross-culturally, a fatalistic approach to life may affect behavioral intentions which in turn influence attitudes towards brand loyalty and perceived risk

FIGURE 8
Operationalization of Culture: Beliefs and Values

Year	Author	Research Method			Beliefs or value system								CB Topic
		empirical	theoretical	naturalistic	relationship to nature	family roles	fatalism	relations to others	asthetics	materialism	time dimension	personal perception	
1976	Henry	X			X			X			X		product choice (Auto)
1977	Douglas & Urban	X				X							segmentation
1978	Kanter		X				X			X	X		advertising
1978	Munson & McIntyre	X				X							Rokeach value scale
1980	Faison	X					X						product choice (food, etc.)
1981	Stanton, Lowenhar & Chandran		X				X						consumption
1984	Belk		X					X					gift-giving
1985	Hirshman		X	X		X							consumption
1985	Saegert, Hoover & Hilger	X					X						brand loyalty
1985	Imperia, O'Guinn & McAdams	X				X							decision process
1986	Belk & Bryce	X								X			advertising
1986	Kahle	X						X				X	segmentation
1986	McCullough, Tan & Wong	X			X	X		X				X	Chineseness scale
1986	O'Guinn, Lee & Faber		X							X			advertising
1987	Douglas		X									X	consumer markets
1987	Sherry & Camargo			X	X								brand loyalty packaging
1987	Wilk					X							decision process
1988	Gentry, Tansuhaj, Manzer & John	X					X						consumption
1988	Graham, Kim, Lin & Robinson	X						X	X				sales
1988	Tse, Wong & Tan	X						X	X				product attributes
1988	Wallendorf & Arnould	X								X			relation between goods and self-concept
1989	Cote & Tansuhaj	X					X				X		behavior-intention models
1990	Rudmin	X								X			gender differences
1990	Dawson & Bamossy	X								X			scale test

(Cote and Tansuhaj 1989; Gentry, Tansuhaj, Manzer, and John 1988; Mehta and Belk 1991; Saegert, Hoover, and Tharp 1985; Stanton, Chandran, and Lowenhar 1981). Contradictory research exists to question the validity of using potentially stereotypical values to explain and predict consumer behavior. The dynamic nature of culture means changing cultural values over time. In his study of the Europeanizing of America, Kanter (1978) proposes that as a result of external conditions, Americans are becoming more fatalistic in their approach to life. Douglas (1987) reports a similar Japanese phenomenon where in certain areas of their lives, the Japanese are placing a growing emphasis on personal goals and achievement as opposed to group objectives.

Furthermore, because values are internalized, the danger of ethnocentrism and overly broad generalizations distorting perceptions is quite probable. Clarke and Soutar (1982) cite a "greater orientation to convenience and labor-saving devices in North America" (p. 459). Most Americans might argue that laziness is not an American value and is certainly not a value held by our North American neighbors. Although measures of values may be culturally bound, and hence, somewhat limited in their predictive abilities, researchers have continued to study values in different cultural contexts.

Consumer Behavior Topics under Cross-Cultural Examination

As illustrated in Figures 6-8, a variety of consumer behavior topics are discussed in a cross-cultural context. As might be surmised, the topics of consumer acculturation, adoption, decision processes and diffusion are frequently examined. Other topics discussed in more than one article include advertising, gift-giving, family decision-making, brand loyalty, and information processing. Another group of cross-cultural studies was focused on validating various value scales used in the consumer behavior discipline.

DISCUSSION AND SUGGESTIONS FOR FUTURE RESEARCH

While cross-cultural consumer behavior research has certainly progressed as a field throughout the twenty years of work examined in this review, there nonetheless are aspects of this research which warrant further attention if the field is to contribute to our understanding of consumer behavior. Issues of particular concern include: definition of cultural concepts, re-visiting early cross-cultural research, critical assessment of cross-cultural methods, focus on commonalities among cultures, and increased emphasis on theoretical underpinnings of cross-cultural consumer behavior.

Much of the reviewed cross-cultural did not mention which definition of the term 'culture' was adopted. The large number of definitions and the fact that the term is used frequently in common conversation (with no apparent communication confusion) does not excuse scientific researchers from providing readers with a theoretical and/or operational definition of the construct under investigation. To this end, we propose that culture be conceptually defined as *a dynamic set of socially acquired behavior patterns and meanings common to the members of a particular society or human group, including the key elements of language, artifacts, beliefs, and values.* Other terms used in cross-cultural research such as socio-culture, assimilation, acculturation, and socialization need to be explicitly defined by the researcher to avoid the terminology confusion that now exists.

A second criticism of the cross-cultural consumer behavior field is the need to re-visit early topics of research: most notably consumer research on the African-American culture. While the early research was fundamental in sparking the interest on cross-cultural topics, as a society and discipline we have moved beyond "negro" perceptions to a broader-based African-American culture. Examinations of the Hispanic subculture has produced a number of theoretical observations on the assimilation and acculturation of Hispanic consumer behavior; likewise, it is time to re-examine the consumer behavior of the African-American culture with a fresh perspective. In addition, the Asian or Oriental subculture deserves more attention.

While a discussion on cross-cultural methods is beyond the scope of this paper, it nonetheless, needs to be addressed if the field is to move beyond the descriptive research stage. Briefly stated, cross-cultural research is a field ripe for post-positivist inquiry.

To advance this area further, there needs to be a greater emphasis on seeking out commonalities among cultures. Hirschman (1985), for example, found similar consumption patterns among primitive cultures and U.S. subcultures. From a preliminary overview, several topics such as materialism, consumption patterns between same sexed individuals, and family structure similarities offer commonalities between unique cultures that need further investigation.

Another criticism of the cross-cultural field is the relatively large number of descriptive research articles and the relatively small number of articles offering theoretical explanations. The descriptive research was necessary for the beginning rudimentary exploration; yet theoretical explanations of the phenomenon described must be included in the analysis.

CONCLUSION

The articles examined in this study attest to the fact that consumer researchers have expanded their research horizons to include cultures other than their own. However, the field remains ripe for additional research on explanations of cultural phenomena and impacts upon consumer behavior. In addition, the real challenge for consumer researchers is to look further for similarities among people of the world, as opposed to differences. The focus on cultural similarities and theoretical explanations may ultimately transform the culturally bound theories in consumer behavior to a field with generalizable theories. Hence, the future holds promise for building additional sources of cross-cultural knowledge rooted in the foundations already established.

REFERENCES

Alexander, Katherine and James McCullough (1980), "Cultural Differences in Preventative Health Care Choice: A Study of Participation in a Cervical Cancer Screening Program Among Mexican-Americans" in *Advances in Consumer Research*, Vol. 7, ed. J.C. Olson, Ann Arbor, MI: Association for Consumer Research 617-621.

Anderson, Ronald and Jack Engledow (1977), "A Factor Analytic Comparison of U.S. and German Information Seekers," *Journal of Consumer Research*, 3 (March), 185-196.

Andreasen, Alan R. (1990), "Cultural Interpenetration: A Critical Consumer Research Issue for the 1990s," in *Advances in Consumer Research*, Vol. 17, eds. Marvin Goldberg, Gerald Gorn and Richard W. Pollay, Provo, UT: Association for Consumer Research, 847-849.

_____ and Jean M. Manning, (1980), "Conducting Cross-National Consumer Policy Research," in *Advances in Consumer Research*, Vol. 7, ed. J.C.Olson, Ann Arbor, MI: Association for Consumer Research, 77-82.

Arndt Johan, Kjell Gronhang, Richard E. Homans, R. Neil Maddox, and Frederick E. May (1981), "Toward a Replication Tradition in Consumer Behavior: Cross-Cultural Replication of Bennett and Mandell's Study of the Learning-Information Seeking Hypothesis," in *Advances in Consumer Research*, Vol 8, ed. Kent Monroe, Ann Arbor, MI: Association for Consumer Research, 564-567.

Arnold, Stephen J., Tae H. Oum, and Douglas J. Tigert (1983), "Determinant Attributes in Retail Patronage: Seasonal, Temporal, Regional, and International Comparisons," *Journal of Marketing Research*, 20 (May), 149-157.

Arnould, Eric J. (1983), "Fancies and Glimmers: Culture and Consumer Behavior," in *Advances in Consumer Research*, Vol. 10, eds. R. Bagozzi and A. Tybout, Ann Arbor, MI: Association for Consumer Research, 702-704.

_____(1989), "Toward a Broadened Theory of Preference Formation and the Diffusion of Innovations: Cases from Zinder Province, Niger Republic," *Journal of Consumer Research*, 16 (September) 239-267.

_____and Richard R. Wilk (1984), "Why Do the Natives Wear Adidas?" in *Advances in Consumer Research*, Vol. 11, ed. Thomas Kinnear, Provo, UT: Association for Consumer Research 748-752.

Baumgartner, Gary and Alain Jolibert (1978), "The Perception of Foreign Products in France," in *Advances in Consumer Research*, Vol. 5, ed. H.K. Hunt, Ann Arbor, MI: Association for Consumer Research, 603-605.

Belk, Russell W., (1984), "Cultural and Historical Differences in Concepts of Self and Their Effects on Attitudes Toward Having and Giving," in *Advances in Consumer Research*, Vol. 11, ed. Thomas Kinnear, Provo, UT: Association for Consumer Research 753-760.

_____and Wendy J. Bryce (1986), "Materialism and Individual Determinism in U.S. and Japanese Print and Television Advertising," in *Advances in Consumer Research*, Vol. 13, ed. Richard Lutz, Provo, UT: Association for Consumer Research, 568-572.

Brislin, Richard W. (1970), "Back-Translation for Cross-Cultural Research," *Journal of Cross-Cultural Psychology*, 1 (3), 185-216.

Bush, Ronald F., Robert F. Gwinner, and Paul J. Solomon (1974), "White Consumer Sales Response to Black Models," *Journal of Marketing*, 38 (April), 25-29.

Clarke, Yvonne and Geoffrey N. Soutar (1982), "Consumer Acquisition Patterns for Durable Goods: Australian Evidence," *Journal of Consumer Research*, 8 (March), 456-460.

Cohen, Dorothy (1970), "Advertising and the Black Community," *Journal of Marketing*, 34 (October), 3-11.

Costa, Janeen Arnold (1989), "On Display: Social and Cultural Dimensions of Consumer Behavior in the Greek Saloni," in *Advances in Consumer Research*, Vol. 16, ed. Thomas K. Srull, Provo, UT: Association for Consumer Research, 562-566.

_____(1990), "Toward an Understanding of Social and World Systemic Processes in the Spread of Consumer Culture: An Anthropological Case Study," in *Advances in Consumer Research*, Vol. 17, eds. Marvin Goldberg, Gerald Gorn and Richard W. Pollay, Provo, UT: Association for Consumer Research, 826-832.

Cote, Joseph and Patriya S. Tansuhaj (1989), "Culture Bound Assumptions in Behavior Intention Models," in *Advances in Consumer Research*, Vol. 16, ed. Thomas K. Srull, Provo, UT: Association for Consumer Research, 105-110.

Cunningham, William H., Russell M. Moore, and Isabella C. M. Cunningham (1974), "Urban Markets in Industrializing Countries: The Sao Paulo Experience," *Journal of Marketing*, 38 (April), 2-12.

Davis, Harry L., Susan P. Douglas, and Alvin J. Silk (1981), "Measure Unreliability: A Hidden Threat to Cross-National Marketing Research?" *Journal of Marketing*, 45 (Spring), 98-109.

Dawson, Scott and Gary Bamossy (1990), "Isolating the Effect of Non-Economic Factors on the Development of a Consumer Culture: A Comparison of Materialism in the Netherlands and the United States," in *Advances in Consumer Research*, Vol. 17, eds. Marvin Goldberg, Gerald Gorn and Richard W. Pollay, Provo, UT: Association for Consumer Research, 182-185.

Deshpande, Rohit, Wayne D. Hoyer and Naveen Donthu (1986), "The Intensity of Ethnic Affiliation: A Study of the Sociology of Hispanic Consumption," *Journal of Consumer Research*, 13 (September), 214-220.

Dilthey, Wilhelm (1972), "The Rise of Hermeneutics," trans. Fredric Jameson, *New Literary History*, 3 (Spring), 229-244.

Donohue, Thomas R., Timothy P. Meyer, and Lucy Henke (1978), "Black and While Children: Perceptions of TV Commercials," *Journal of Marketing*, 42 (October) 34-40.

Douglas, Susan P. (1976), "Cross-National Comparisons and Consumer Stereotypes: A Case Study of Working and Non-Working Wives in the U.S. and France," *Journal of Consumer Research*, 3 (June), 12-20.

Douglas, Susan P., (1979), "A Cross-National Exploration of Husband-Wife Involvement in Selected Household Activities," in *Advances in Consumer Research*, Vol. 6, ed. W.L. Wilkie, Ann Arbor, MI: Association for Consumer Research, 364-371.

_____(1980), "On the Use of Verbal Protocols in Cross-Cultural and Cross-National Consumer Research," in *Advances in Consumer Research*, Vol. 7, ed. J.C. Olson, Ann Arbor, MI: Association for Consumer Research, 684-687.

_____(1987), "Emerging Consumer Markets in Japan," in *Advances in Consumer Research*, Vol. 14, eds. M. Wallendorf and P. Anderson, Provo, UT: Association for Consumer Research, 392-393.

_____and Christine D. Urban (1977), "Life-Style Analysis to Profile Women in International Markets," *Journal of Marketing*, 41 (July), 46-54.

Ellis, Seth, James McCullough, Melanie Wallendorf, and Chin Tion Tan (1985), "Cultural Values and Behavior: Chineseness within Geographic Boundaries," in *Advances in Consumer Research*, Vol.12, eds. Elizabeth C. Hirschman and Morris B. Holbrook, Provo, UT: Association for Consumer Research, 126-128.

Engel, James F. (1976), "Psychographic Research in a Cross-Cultural Nonproduct Setting," in *Advances in Consumer Research*, Vol. 3 ed. B. B. Anderson, Cincinnati OH: Association for Consumer Research, 98-101.

Engledow, Jack L., Hans B. Thorelli, and Helmut Beck (1975), "The Information Seekers—A Cross-Cultural Consumer Elite," in *Advances in Consumer Research*, Vol. 2 ed. Mary Jaone Schlinger, Chicago, IL: Association for Consumer Research, 141-155.

Fairchild, Henry P. (1970), *Dictionary of Sociology*, Totowa, NJ: Littlefield & Adams.

Faison, Edmund W.J. (1980), "Cultural Comparisons of Variety-Seeking Behavior," in *Advances in Consumer Research*, Vol. 7, ed. J.C. Olson, Ann Arbor, MI: Association for Consumer Research, 255-257.

Farris, Buford E. and Norval D. Glenn (1976), "Fatalism and Familism among Anglos and Mexican Americans in San Antonio," *Sociology and Social Research*, 60 (No. 4, July), 393-402.

Finn, Albert (1987), "The Sensitivity of Canadian Consumer Product Market Segments to Changes in Macroeconomic Conditions," in *Advances in Consumer Research*, Vol. 14, eds. M. Wallendorf and P. Anderson, Provo, UT: Association for Consumer Research, 562.

Folkes, Valerie S. (1988), "Recent Attribution Research in Consumer Behavior: A Review and New Directions," *Journal of Consumer Research*, 14 (March), 548-565.

Gentry, James W., Patriya Tansuhaj, L. Lee Manzer, and Joby John (1988), "Do Geographic Subcultures Vary Culturally?" in *Advances in Consumer Research*, Vol 15, ed. Michael J. Houston, Provo, UT: Association for Consumer Research, 411-417.

Ger, Guliz and Russell W. Belk (1990), "Measuring and Comparing Materialism Cross-Culturally," in *Advances in Consumer Research*, Vol. 17, eds. Marvin Goldberg, Gerald Gorn and Richard W. Pollay, Provo, UT: Association for Consumer Research, 186-192.

Gensch, Dennis H. and Richard Staelin (1972), "The Appeal of Buying Black," *Journal of Marketing Research*, 9 (May), 141-148.

Gilly, Mary C. (1988), "Sex Roles in Advertising: A Comparison of Television Advertisements in Australia, Mexico, and the United States," *Journal of Marketing*, 52 (April), 75-85.

Glaser, Barney G. and Anselm Strauss (1967), *The Discovery of Grounded Theory*, Chicago, IL: Aldine.

Goldman, Arieh (1974), "Outreach of Consumers and the Modernization of Urban Food Retailing in Developing Countries," *Journal of Marketing*, 38 (October), 8-16.

Gould, John W., Norman B. Sigband, and Cyril E. Zoerner Jr., (1970), "Black Consumer Reactions to `Integrated' Advertising: An Exploratory Study," *Journal of Marketing*, 34 (July), 20-26.

Graham, John L., Dong Ki Kim, Chi-Yuan Lin, and Michael Robinson (1988), "Buyer-Seller Negotiations around the Pacific Rim: Differences in Fundamental Exchange Processes," *Journal of Consumer Research*, 15 (June), 48-54.

Green, Robert T. and Philip D. White (1976), "Methodological Considerations in Cross-National Research," *Journal of International Business Studies*, 7 (Fall/Winter), 81-88.

_____, Isabella, C. M. Cunningham, and William H. Cunningham (1974), "Cross-Cultural Consumer Profiles: An Exploratory Investigation," in *Advances in Consumer Research*, Vol. 1, eds. Scott Ward and Peter Wright, Urbana, IL: Association for Consumer Research, 136-144.

_____and Eric Langeard (1975), "A Cross-National Comparison of Consumer Habits and Innovator Characteristics," *Journal of Marketing*, 39 (July), 34-41.

_____, Jean-Paul Leonardi, Jean-Louis Chandon, Isabella C.M. Cunningham, Bronis Verhage, and Alain Strazzieri (1983), "Societal Development and Family Purchasing Roles: A Cross-National Study," *Journal of Consumer Research*, 9 (March), 436-442.

Haaland, Gordon A., (1974), "The Context of Social, Cultural, and Consumer Behavior," in *Advances in Consumer Research*, Vol.1. eds. Scott Ward and Peter Wright, Urbana, IL: Association for Consumer Research, 145-153.

Hall, Edward T. and Mildred Reed Hall (1989), *Understanding Cultural Differences*, Yarmouth, MA: International Press.

Hawes, Douglass K., Sigmund Gronmo, and John Arndt (1978), "Shopping and Leisure Time: Some Preliminary Cross-Cultural Comparisons of Time-Budget Expenditures," in *Advances in Consumer Research*, Vol. 5, ed. H.K. Hunt, Ann Arbor, MI: Association for Consumer Research, 151-159.

Hawkins, Del I., Don Roupe and Kenneth A. Coney (1981), "The Influence of Geographic Subcultures in the United States," in *Advances in Consumer Research*, Vol 8, ed. Kent Monroe, Ann Arbor, MI: Association for Consumer Research, 713-717.

Helgeson, James G., E. Alan Kluge, John Mager, and Cheri Taylor (1984), "Trends in Consumer Behavior Literature: A Content Analysis," *Journal of Consumer Research*, 10 (March), 449-454.

Hempel, Donald J. (1974), "Family Buying Decisions: A Cross-Cultural Perspective," *Journal of Marketing Research*, 11 (August), 295-302.

Henry, Walter A. (1976), "Cultural Values Do Correlate With Consumer Behavior," *Journal of Marketing Research*, 13 (May), 121-127.

Hester, Susan B. and Mary Yeun (1987), "The Influence of Country of Origin on Consumer Attitude and Buying Behavior in the United States and Canada," in *Advances in Consumer Research*, Vol. 14, eds. M. Wallendorf and P. Anderson, Provo, UT: Association for Consumer Research, 538-542.

Hills, Gerald E., Donald H. Granbois, and James M. Patterson (1973), "Black Consumer Perceptions of Food Store Attributes," *Journal of Marketing*, 37 (April), 47-57.

Hirschman, Elizabeth C. (1981), "American Jewish Ethnicity: Its Relationship to Some Selected Aspects of Consumer Behavior," *Journal of Marketing*, 45 (Summer), 102-110.

_____(1983), "Cognitive Structure Across Consumer Ethnic Subcultures: A Comparative Analysis," in *Advances in Consumer Research*, Vol. 10, ed. R. Bagozzi and A. Tybout, Ann Arbor, MI: Association for Consumer Research, 197-202.

_____(1985), "Primitive Aspects of Consumption in Modern American Society," *Journal of Consumer Research*, 12 (September), 142-154.

_____and Michael R. Solomon (1983), "The Relationship of Age and Gender Subcultures to the Consumption of Rational and Arational Experiences," in *Advances in Consumer Research*, Vol. 10, eds. R. Bagozzi and A. Tybout, Ann Arbor, MI: Association for Consumer Research, 334-338.

Hoover, Robert J., Robert T. Green, and Joel Saegert (1978), "A Cross-National Study of Perceived Risk," *Journal of Marketing*, 42 (July), 102-108.

Imperia, Giovanna, Thomas C. O'Guinn, and Elizabeth A. MacAdams (1985), "Family Decision Making Role Perceptions Among Mexican-Americans and Anglo Wives: A Cross Cultural Comparison," in *Advances in Consumer Research*, Vol. 12, eds. Elizabeth C. Hirschman and Morris B. Holbrook, Provo, UT: Association for Consumer Research, 71-74.

Jaffe, Eugene D. and Israel D. Nebenzahl (1984), "Alternative Questionnaire Formats For Country Image Studies," *Journal of Marketing Research*, 21 (November), 463-471.

Jolibert, Alain J.P. and Gary Baumgartner (1981), "Toward a Definition of the Consumerist Segment in France," *Journal of Consumer Research*, 8 (June), 114-117.

_____and Carlos Fernandez-Moreno (1983), "A Comparison of French and Mexican Gift Giving Practices," in *Advances in Consumer Research*, Vol. 10, eds. R. Bagozzi and A. Tybout, Ann Arbor, MI: Association for Consumer Research, 191-196.

Kahle, Lynn R., (1986), "The Nine Nations of North America and the Value Basis of Geographic Segmentation," *Journal of Marketing*, 50 (April), 37-47.

Kanter, Donald L. (1978), "The Europeanizing of America: A Study in Changing Values," in *Advances in Consumer Research*, Vol. 5, ed. H.K. Hunt, Ann Arbor, MI: Association for Consumer Research, 408-410.

Kelly, Robert F., (1987), "Culture as Commodity: The Marketing of Cultural Objects and Cultural Experiences," in *Advances in Consumer Research*, Vol. 14, eds. M. Wallendorf and P. Anderson, Provo, UT: Association for Consumer Research, 347-351.

Kim, Chankon, Michael Laroche, and Annamma Joy (1990), "An Empirical Study of the Effects of Ethnicity on Consumption Patterns in a Bi-Cultural Environment," in *Advances in Consumer Research*, Vol. 17, eds. Marvin Goldberg, Gerald Gorn, and Richard W. Pollay, Provo, UT: Association for Consumer Research, 839-846.

Kirpalani, V.H. and Xu Kuan, (1987), "Effective International Market Potential Assessment: China," in *Advances in Consumer Research*, Vol. 14, eds. M. Wallendorf and P. Anderson, Provo, UT: Association for Consumer Research, 398-402.

Langeard, E., M. Crousillat, and R. Weisz (1978), "Exposure to Cultural Activities and Opinion Leadership," in *Advances in Consumer Research*, Vol. 5, ed. H. K. Hunt, Ann Arbor, MI: Association for Consumer Research, 606-610.

Lee, Wei-Na (1989), "The Mass-Mediated Consumption Realities of Three Cultural Groups," in *Advances in Consumer Research*, Vol. 16, ed. Thomas K. Srull, Provo, UT: Association for Consumer Research, 771-778.

Leeflang, Peter S.H. and Jan C. Reuijl (1985), "Advertising and Industry Sales: An Empirical Study of the West German Cigarette Market," *Journal of Marketing*, 49 (Fall), 92-98.

Leong, Siew Meng (1989), "A Citation Analysis of the Journal of Consumer Research," *Journal of Consumer Research*, 15 (March), 492-497.

Lumpkin, James R. (1985), "Validity of a Brief Locus of Control Scale for Survey Research," *Psychological Reports*, 57, 655-659.

McAlister, Leigh and Edgar Pessemier (1982), "Variety Seeking Behavior: An Interdisciplinary Review," *Journal of Consumer Research*, 9 (December), 311-322.

McCarty, John A. (1989), "Current Theory and Research on Cross-Cultural Factors in Consumer Behavior," in *Advances in Consumer Research*, Vol. 16, ed. Thomas K. Srull, Provo, UT: Association for Consumer Research, 127-129.

McCracken, Grant (1986), "Culture and Consumption: A Theoretical Account of the Structure and Movement of the Cultural Meaning of Consumer Goods," *Journal of Consumer Research*, 13 (June), 71-84.

_____(1989), "Who is the Celebrity Endorser? Cultural Foundations of the Endorsement Process," *Journal of Consumer Research*, 16 (December), 310-321.

McCullough, James, Chin Tiong Tan, and John Wong (1986), "Effects of Stereotyping in Cross Cultural Research: Are the Chinese Really Chinese?" in *Advances in Consumer Behavior*, Vol. 13, ed. Richard Lutz, Provo, UT: Association for Consumer Research, 576-578.

Mayer, Robert N. (1987), "Consumer Use of Videotex Services in France," in *Advances in Consumer Research*, Vol. 14, eds. M. Wallendorf and P. Anderson, Provo, UT: Association for Consumer Research, 574.

Mick, David Glen (1986), "Consumer Research and Semiotics: Exploring the Morphology of Signs, Symbols, and Significance," *Journal of Consumer Research*, 13 (September), 196-213.

Munson, J. Michael and Shelby McIntyre (1978), "Personal Values: A Cross Cultural Assessment of Self Values and Values Attributed to a Distant Cultural Stereotype," in *Advances in Consumer Research*, Vol.5, ed. H.K. Hunt, Ann Arbor, Mi: Association for Consumer Research, 160-166.

Munson, J. Michael and Shelby H. McIntyre (1979), "Developing Practical Procedures for the Measurement of Personal Values in Cross-Cultural Marketing," *Journal of Marketing Research*, 16 (February), 48-52.

Murphy, Patrick E., Norman Kangun, and William B. Locander (1978), "Environmentally Concerned Consumers-Racial Variations," *Journal of Marketing*, 42 (October), 61-66.

Nagashima, Akira (1970), "A Comparison of Japanese and U.S. Attitudes Toward Foreign Products," *Journal of Marketing*, 34 (January), 68-74.

_____(1977), "A Comparative `Made in' Product Image Survey Among Japanese Businessmen," *Journal of Marketing*, 41 (July), 95-100.

O'Connor, P.J., Gary L. Sullivan, and Dana A. Pogorzelski (1985), "Cross Cultural Family Purchasing Decisions: A Literature Review," in *Advances in Consumer Research*, Vol. 12, eds. Elizabeth C. Hirschman and Morris B. Holbrook, Provo, UT: Association for Consumer Research, 59-64.

O'Guinn, Thomas C. and Ronald J.Faber (1985), "New Perspectives on Acculturation: The Relationship of General and Role Specific Acculturation with Hispanics' Consumer Attitudes," in *Advances in Consumer Research*, Vol. 12, eds. Elizabeth C. Hirschman and Morris B. Holbrook, Provo, UT: Association for Consumer Research, 113-117.

_____, Wei-Na Lee, and Ronald J. Faber (1986), "Acculturation: The Impact of Divergent Paths on Buyer Behavior," in *Advances in Consumer Behavior*, Vol. 13, ed. Richard Lutz, Provo, UT: Association for Consumer Research, 579-583.

Penaloza, Lisa N. (1989), "Immigrant Consumer Acculturation," in *Advances in Consumer Research*, Vol. 16, ed. Thomas K. Srull, Provo, UT: Association for Consumer Research, 110-118.

Pruden, Henry O. and Douglas S. Longman (1972), "Race, Alienation and Consumerism," *Journal of Marketing*, 36 (July), 58-63.

Reilly, Michael and Melanie Wallendorf (1984), "A Longitudinal Study of Mexican-American Assimilation," in *Advances in Consumer Behavior*, Vol. 11, ed. Thomas Kinnear, Provo, UT: Association for Consumer Research, 735-740.

_____, and William L. Rathje (1985), "Consumption and Status Across Cultural Boundaries: Nonreactive Evidence," in *Advances in Consumer Research*, Vol. 12, eds. Elizabeth C. Hirschman and Morris B. Holbrook, Provo, UT: Association for Consumer Research, 129-132.

_____, and Melanie Wallendorf (1987), "A Comparison of Group Differences in Food Consumption Using Household Refuse," *Journal of Consumer Research*, 14 (September), 289-294.

Richins, Marsha L. and Scott Dawson (1990), "Measuring Material Values: A Preliminary Report of Scale Development," in *Advances in Consumer Research*, Vol. 17, eds. Marvin Goldberg, Gerald Gorn and Richard W. Pollay, Provo, UT: Association for Consumer Research, 169-175.

Roth, Martin S. and Christine Moorman (1988), "The Cultural Content of Cognition and the Cognitive Content of Culture: Implications for Consumer Research," in *Advances in Consumer Research*, Vol 15, ed. Michael J. Houston, Provo, UT:Association for Consumer Research, 403-410.

Rudmin, Floyd W. (1990), "German and Canadian Data on Motivations for Ownership: Was Pythagoras Right?" in *Advances in Consumer Research*, Vol. 17, eds. Marvin Goldberg, Gerald Gorn and Richard W. Pollay, Provo, UT: Association for Consumer Research, 176-181.

Saegert, Joel, Eleanor Young, and Merry Mayne Saegert (1978), "Fad Food Use Among Anglo- and Mexican-Americans: An Example of Research in Consumer Behavior and Home Economics," in *Advances in Consumer Research*, Vol.5, ed. H.K. Hunt, Ann Arbor, MI: Association for Consumer Research, 730-733.

_____, Robert J. Hoover, and Marye Tharp Hilger (1985), "Characteristics of Mexican American Consumers," *Journal of Consumer Research*, 12 (June), 104-109.

Schaninger, Charles M., Jacques C. Bourgeois, and Christian Buss, (1985), "French-English Canadian Subcultural Consumption Differences," *Journal of Marketing*, 49 (Spring), 82-92.

Schlesinger, Arthur M. Jr. (1991) *The Disuniting of America*, Nashville, TN: White Direct Books.

Sexton, Donald E. (1971), "Comparing the Cost of Food to Blacks and to Whites—A Survey," *Journal of Marketing*, 35 (July), 40-46.

_____(1971), "Do Blacks Pay More?", *Journal of Marketing Research*, 8 (November), 420-426.

_____(1972), "Black Buyer Behavior," *Journal of Marketing*, 36 (October), 36-39.

Sheppard, Blair H., Jon Hartwick, and Paul R. Warshaw (1988), "The Theory of Reasoned Action: A Meta-Analysis of Past Research with Recommendations for Modifications and Future Research," *Journal of Consumer Research*, 15 (December), 325-343.

Sherry, John F. Jr. (1986), "The Cultural Perspective in Consumer Research," in *Advances in Consumer Research*, Vol. 13, ed. Richard Lutz, Provo, UT: Association for Consumer Research, 573-575.

_____(1989), "Observations on Marketing and Consumption: An Anthropological Note," in *Advances in Consumer Research*, Vol. 16, ed. Thomas K. Srull, Provo, UT: Association for Consumer Research, 555-561.

_____(1990), "A Sociocultural Analysis of a Midwestern American Flea Market," *Journal of Consumer Research*, 17 (June), 13-30.

_____, and Eduardo G. Camargo (1987), "`May Your Life Be Marvelous:' English Language Labelling and the Semiotics of Japanese Promotion," *Journal of Consumer Research*, 14 (September), 174-188.

Shimp, Terence A. and Subhash Sharma (1987), "Consumer Ethnocentrism: Construction and Validation of the CETSCALE," *Journal of Marketing Research*, 24 (August), 280-289.

Sirgy, M. Joseph (1982), "Self-Concept in Consumer Behavior: A Critical Review," *Journal of Consumer Research*, 9 (December), 287-300.

Stanton, John, Rajan Chandran, and Jeffrey Lowenhar (1981), "Consumerism in Developing Countries—The Brazilian Experience," in *Advances in Consumer Research*, Vol 8, ed. Kent Monroe, Ann Arbor, MI: Association for Consumer Research, 718-722.

Stayman, Douglas M. and Rohit Deshpande (1989), "Situational Ethnicity and Consumer Behavior," *Journal of Consumer Research*, 16 (September), 361-371.

Sudman, Seymour (1985), "Efficient Screening Methods for the Sampling of Geographically Clustered Populations," *Journal of Marketing Research*, 22 (February), 20-29.

Swagler, Roger M. (1977), "Information Patterns in Indigenous African Markets: A Lesson in Consumer Performance," in *Advances in Consumer Research*, Vol. 4, ed. William D. Perreault, Atlanta, GA: Association for Consumer Research, 297-301.

Tan, Chin Tiong and James McCullough (1985), "Relating Ethnic Attitudes and Consumption Values in an Asian Context," in *Advances in Consumer Research*, Vol. 12, eds. Elizabeth C. Hirschman and Morris B. Holbrook, Provo, UT: Association for Consumer Research, 122-126.

_____, Jim McCullough, and Jeannie Teoh (1987), "An Individual Analysis Approach to Cross Cultural Research," in *Advances in Consumer Research*, Vol. 14, eds. M. Wallendorf and P. Anderson, Provo, UT: Association for Consumer Research, 394-397.

_____and John U. Farley (1987), "The Impact of Cultural Patterns on Cognition and Intention in Singapore," *Journal of Consumer Research*, 13 (March), 540-544.

Tigert, D.J., C.W. King, and L. Ring (1980), "Fashion Involvement: A Cross-Cultural Comparative Analysis," in *Advances in Consumer Research*, Vol. 7, ed. J.C. Olson, Ann Arbor, MI: Association for Consumer Research, 17-21.

Thompson, Craig J., William B. Locander, and Howard B. Pollio (1989), "Putting Consumer Experience Back into Consumer Research: The Philosophy and Method of Existential-Phenomenology," *Journal of Consumer Research*, 16 (September) 133-146.

Tse David K., John K. Wong, and Chin Tiong Tan (1988), "Towards Some Standardized Cross-Cultural Consumption Values," in *Advances in Consumer Research*, Vol 15, ed. Michael J. Houston, Provo, UT: Association for Consumer Research, 387-394.

_____, Russell W. Belk, and Nan Zhou (1989), "Becoming a Consumer Society: A Longitudinal and Cross-Cultural Content Analysis of Print Ads from Hong Kong, the People's Republic of China, and Taiwan," *Journal of Consumer Research*, 15 (March), 457-472.

Valencia, Humberto (1985), "Developing an Index to Measure `Hispanicness'," in *Advances in Consumer Research*, Vol.12, eds. Elizabeth C. Hirschman and Morris B. Holbrook, Provo, UT: Association for Consumer Research, 118-122.

van Raaij, W. Fred (1978), "Cross-Cultural Research Methodology as a Case of Construct Validity," in *Advances in Consumer Research*, Vol. 5, ed. H.K. Hunt, Ann Arbor, MI: Association for Consumer Research, 693-701.

Wallendorf, Melanie and Michael D. Reilly (1983a), "Distinguishing Culture of Origin from Culture of Residence," in *Advances in Consumer Research*,Vol. 10, eds. R. Bagozzi and A. Tybout, Ann Arbor, MI: Association for Consumer Research, 699-701.

_____and Michael D. Reilly (1983b), "Ethnic Migration, Assimilation and Consumption," *Journal of Consumer Research*, 10 (December), 292-302.

_____, and Eric J. Arnould (1988), "'My Favorite Things': A Cross-Cultural Inquiry into Object Attachment, Possessiveness, and Social Linkage," *Journal of Consumer Research*, 14 (March), 531-547.

Ward, Scott, Thomas S. Robertson, Donna M. Klees, and Hubert Gatignon (1986), "Children's Purchase Requests and Parental Yielding: A Cross-National Study," in *Advances in Consumer Research*, Vol. 13, ed. Richard J. Lutz. Provo, UT: Association for Consumer Research, 629-632.

Weinberger, Marc G. and Harlan E. Spotts (1989), "A Situational View of Information Content in TV Advertising in the US and UK," *Journal of Marketing*, 53 (January), 89-94.

Wiley, James B. and Gordon G. Bechtel (1985), "Scaling of Cross-National Survey Data," in *Advances in Consumer Research*, Vol. 12, eds. Elizabeth C. Hirschman and Morris B. Holbrook, Provo, UT: Association for Consumer Research, 215-219.

Wilk, Richard R. (1987), "House, Home, and Consumer Decision Making in Two Cultures," in *Advances in Consumer Research*, Vol. 14, eds. M. Wallendorf and P. Anderson, Provo, UT: Association for Consumer Research, 303-307.

Wilkes, Robert E. and Humberto Valencia, (1985), "A Note on Generic Purchaser Generalizations and Subcultural Variations," *Journal of Marketing*, 49 (Summer), 114-120.

Development and Testing of a Cross-Culturally Valid Instrument: Food-Related Life Style

Karen Brunsø, The Aarhus School of Business
Klaus G. Grunert, The Aarhus School of Business

ABSTRACT

Based on a cognitive perspective, we propose to make life style specific to certain areas of consumption. The specific area of consumption studied here is food, resulting in a concept of *food-related life style*. We have developed an instrument that can measure food-related life style in a cross-culturally valid way. To this end we have developed a pool of 202 items, collected data in three countries, and have constructed scales based on cross-culturally stable factor patterns. We have then applied the set of scales to a fourth country, in order to further test the cross-cultural validity of the instrument.

PROBLEMS WITH LIFE STYLE INSTRUMENTS IN MARKET SURVEILLANCE

In the market surveillance of consumers, life-style instruments have been used in order to detect major trends over time and/or in order to analyse differences and similarities across markets in the search of global or, eg, pan-European segments. Most life style studies, commercial and academic, follow a common pattern. They are based on a large battery of AIO items that are reduced analytically to few, usually only two, dimensions. The resulting space, sometimes called an attitude map or a value map, is then used to classify consumers on the remaining dimensions, which leads to life style segments. This type of life style research has been criticized on several grounds (eg, Anderson and Golden 1984; Askegaard 1993; Banning 1987; Lastovicka 1982; Roos 1986). Apart from the general terminological confusion about the term life style (Anderson and Golden 1984), it has been criticized that the instruments are not guided by theory. Life style types come about based on dimensions derived by exploratory data analysis techniques like factor analysis or correspondence analysis. These techniques are applied to sets of items, the generation of which is not theoretically guided either, but is very much based on common sense reasoning and implicit experience in carrying out market research. While such a research procedure may be appropriate in the early phase of the life cycle of a research technique, one should hope that, based on such exploratory analysis, theory should develop, which could then guide the analysis of new and better measurement instruments. Also, many feel that consumer behaviour is such a well-researched area that it should be possible to obtain some theoretical input from there that could enrich life style research. Another major criticism, and one we explicitly will take up in this paper, is that the cross-cultural validity of the international life style instruments remains to be demonstrated. The larger pan-European life style studies like RISC and CCA[1] provide data which aim at identifying similar life style segments across borders, and numerous other life style studies have tried to identify cultural differences in life style (eg, Douglas and Urban, 1977; Hui, Joy, Kim and Laroche 1990; Laroche et al. 1990; Linton and Broadbent 1975). Collecting data in different cultures with the aim of obtaining comparative results requires that the measurement intrument has cross-cultural validity, ie, that *translation* and *measurement*

equivalence are ensured or at least tested (cp. Chandran and Wiley 1987; Green and White 1976; Sekaran 1983). For the kind of data involved in life style studies, *factor invariance* is a good criterion for investigating the degree of translation and measurement equivalence actually achieved. Various degrees of factor invariance can be distinguished, corresponding to various degrees of cultural comparability (S.C. Grunert, K.G. Grunert, and Kristensen 1992). However, such investigations have not yet been reported for life style data.

We have tried to develop a life style instrument that makes progress with these problems. We will briefly present a theoretical framework that can guide us in the formulation of candidates for life style items, show how we have selected items that are cross-culturally valid, based on an extended factor congruence criterion, and test the selected items in a new cultural setting for further cross-cultural validation.

A COGNITIVE APPROACH TO LIFE STYLE

We regard life style as a mental construct which explains, but is not identical with, actual behaviour, and define life style as *the system of cognitive categories, scripts, and their associations, which relate a set of products to a set of values*. This proposed definition warrants a number of comments.

(i) It makes life style distinct from values, since values are self-relevant and provide motivation, while life style links products to self-relevant consequences, ie, values.

(ii) Life styles transcend individual brands or products, but may be specific to a product class. Thus, it makes sense to talk about a food-related life style, or a housing-related life style.

(iii) Life styles are clearly placed in a hierarchy of constructs of different levels of abstraction, where life styles have an intermediate place between values and product/brand perceptions or attitudes.

STUDY I: DEVELOPING A CROSS-CULTURALLY VALID INSTRUMENT TO MEASURE FOOD-RELATED LIFE STYLE

We have argued that life style may be specific to a product class. The product class we have chosen for the current project is food products. Hence, we aim to develop a cross-culturally valid instrument to measure food-related life style (FRL). How are food products related to values in consumers' cognitive structure? It may be possible to distinguish relevant parts or aspects of cognitive structure, which may then be the starting point for item formulation. In figure 1, an attempt is made to delineate relevant parts of cognitive structure, and how they contribute to linking food products to values. The boxes indicate groups of cognitive categories, and the lines associations between them.

Shopping scripts. How do people shop for food products? Is their decision-making characterized by impulse buying, or by extensive deliberation? Do they read labels and other product information, or do they rely on the advice of experts, like friends or sales personnel? In which shops - one-stop shopping versus speciality food shops?

Meal preparation scripts. How are the products purchased transformed into meals? How much time is used for preparation? Is preparation characterized by efficiency, or by indulgence? Is it a

---

[1]RISC: Research Institute of Social Change; CCA: Centre de Communication Avancé

Advances in Consumer Research
Volume 22, © 1995

FIGURE 1
A cognitive structure model for food-related life style

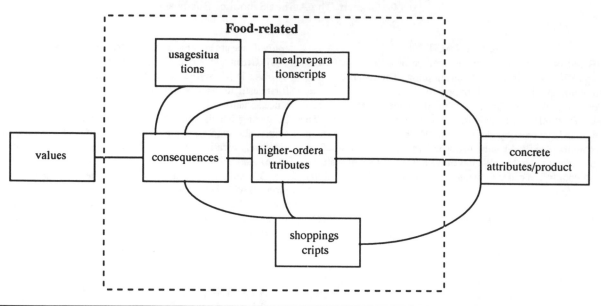

social activity, or one characterized by family division of labour? To which extent is it planned or spontaneous?

Desired higher-order product attributes. This refers not to concrete attributes of individual products, but to attributes which may apply to food products in general. Examples may be healthy, nutritious, natural, convenient.

Usage situations. What are "the" meals? How are they spread over the day? Is a meal perceived differently when eaten alone, rather then with the family?

Desired consequences. What is expected from a meal, and what is the relative importance of these various consequences? How important is nutrition compared to the social event? How important is hedonism (cf. S.C. Grunert 1993).

We have then developed a survey instrument by applying the following procedure:

- Generation of a pool of items covering the five elements of food-related life styles based on the theoretical foundation.
- Collection of data, using the item pool, in three European countries.
- Exploratory factor analysis, within each of the five elements, and separately for each country.
- Search for factors which seem to be stable across the three samples.
- Construction of scales for each of the remaining factors. Analysis of scale reliability across and within samples. Modification of scales with the aim to retain three items per scale.
- Testing the set of cross-cultural factors by confirmatory factor analysis.

We have then applied the instrument obtained in a fourth country for further cross-cultural validation. This will be addressed in the next section.

Generation of item pool

202 Likert-type items were constructed which covered the five constructs of food-related life style defined above (Shopping scripts,

desired higher-order product attributes, meal preparation scripts, usage situations, and desired consequences). Inspiration for formulating these items was drawn from the food choice literature, food journals, women's magazines, and earlier life style studies like RISC. Agreement with the items had to be rated on a five-point scale. The items were originally formulated in English and subsequently translated into Danish and French. Items were arranged by the five constructs in the questionnaire; the sequence in which the five constructs appeared was varied at random in the questionnaire.

Data collection

Data were collected in Denmark, England, and France. Given the nature of this study, sampling was done not with respect to representativeness, but with respect to obtaining three samples which would be as homogeneous as possible. The target population was defined as married women with children at school age living in metropolitan areas. In each country, one metropolitan area was selected, viz. Copenhagen, London, and Paris. In each of these areas schools were selected (2 in Copenhagen, 4 in London, 3 in Paris), with the aim of soliciting the co-operation of teachers in asking school children to take a questionnaire home to their mothers. In each country, 300 questionnaires were distributed in this way. The response rates were 78% in Denmark, 47% in England, and 32% in France, resulting in sample sizes of 233, 139, and 94.

Exploratory factor analysis and construction of scales

For each sample and for the five groups of items, separate exploratory factor analyses (principal component analysis, varimax rotation) were carried out. The aim of this procedure was to check whether items would tend to group together in similar factors across the three samples. Factor congruence across cultures is a major indicator of a cross-culturally similar interpretation of the items (S.C. Grunert et al. 1992). 21 factors were identified which seem to appear across the three samples. They were:

- shopping scripts: importance of product information, attitude towards advertising, joy of shopping, speciality shops, price criterion, shopping list

- higher-order product attributes: health, price-quality-relation, novelty, organic products
- meal preparation scripts: involvement with cooking, looking for new ways, convenience, whole family, spontaneity, women's task
- usage situations: snacks versus meals, social event
- desired consequences: self-fulfilment in food, security, social relationships.

Items with high loadings on these factors in at least two of the three samples were combined into scales. Scale reliabilities (Cronbach's alpha) were computed, and where scales contained more than three items, the items which gave the highest reliability for the pooled data were retained. Subsequently, the reliabilities were checked also for the three samples separately. Results from these analysis can be found in Grunert, Brunsø and Bisp (forthcoming). Not all the resulting scales were satisfactory. In a number of cases, only two suitable items were found for a scale. This has lead to some modifications in the study described in the next section.[2]

Confirmatory factor analysis

Confirmatory factor analysis can be used to find out whether a set of data is compatible with a pre-specified factor structure. It can also be applied to multiple samples and can then be used to check whether the data are compatible with the assumption that the factor structure in the samples is the same. Factor invariance has often been suggested as a validation instrument in cross-cultural research. S.C. Grunert et al. (1992) have recently suggested that several levels of factor congruence may be distinguished and have related these levels to different degrees of cultural compatibility based on a cognitive view of cultural differences. The basic argument is as follows: If we have a vector of measures which, like in the present study, is taken as indicators of a smaller set of underlying latent variables, then we have, in LISREL notation,

$$X=\Lambda\xi+\delta$$
and
$$\Sigma=\Lambda\Phi\Lambda'+\Theta_\delta$$

with X a vector of measured values, Λ a matrix of factor loadings, ξ a vector of factor scores, δ a vector of error terms, Σ the covariance matrix of the measured values, Φ the covariance matrix of the factor scores, and Θ_δ the covariance matrix of the error terms. When discussing factor congruence, the common interpretation is that the matrix of loadings in two samples has the same pattern, ie, the same non-zero elements. However, this is obviously only the weakest form of comparability between two sets of data. A stronger form of comparability would exist when the matrix of loadings were in fact identical, since this seems to indicate that the way in which the measurement items relate to underlying constructs was in fact the same across samples. This would still allow, however, differences in how the factors are correlated in the two samples, and differences in error, ie, in the reliabilities of the individual items. Identical correlations between the factors would strengthen our confidence in that the factors do in fact tap the same sets of meanings in different cultures, whereas identical item reliabilities would strengthen our belief in that the individual items in fact were perceived (cognitively processed) in the same way. In cross-cultural research, which

---

[2]The complete set of scales can be obtained from Karen Brunsø - fax +45 86 15 39 88 or e-mail kab@hdc.hha.dk

usually involves translation and therefore mapping questionnaire items from one set of cognitive categories into another, we would not usually expect item reliabilities to be the same. Thus, four levels of cross-cultural comparability can be distinguished (S.C. Grunert et al. 1992):

- Λ_i and Λ_j have the same pattern: *minimal cultural comparability*
- $\Lambda_i=\Lambda_j$: *weak cultural comparability*
- $\Lambda_i=\Lambda_j$, and $\Phi_i=\Phi_j$: *strong cultural comparability*
- $\Lambda_i=\Lambda_j$, $\Phi_i=\Phi_j$, and $\Theta_{\delta i}=\Theta_{\delta j}$:*weak cultural identity*

The strongest condition is called weak cultural identity, because the only way in which the samples can differ is in the level of endorsement of the various items, while everything else - their complete meaning structure, including item reliabilities - is the same. When also the levels of endorsement are the same, one would talk *about strong cultural identity*. For each of the five areas of food-related life style, the items retained were entered into confirmatory factor analyses corresponding to the four levels of cultural comparability described above. The results can be seen in table 1. Several measures of fit are given: for each sample, the goodness of fit index GFI and the root mean square residuals RMR, and for the set of three samples the χ^2 value and the degrees of freedom. Since the χ^2 value is vulnerable to sample size, a rule of thumb is to look at the size of χ^2 relative to the degrees of freedom eg, by dividing χ^2 with degrees of freedom. The GFI measure indicates the relative amount of variances and covariances accounted for by the model, a value of .9 or more indicates that the model fits the data well (Bagozzi and Yi 1988). Furthermore, the GFI measure is independent of sample size, and can be used for comparison of different models on the same data and on different data. The third measure, RMR, is a measure of the average of the fitted residuals, and can be used for comparison of different models on the same data. RMR should below (Bagozzi and Yi 1988).

The results from the analysis can also be used to detect weak items. This can be done by inspecting the estimated loadings, the item reliabilities, and the modifications indices for loadings forced to be zero. The following results emerged:

Shopping scripts. The tests yield results which indicate that the criteria of minimum and weak cultural comparability can be accepted at least for the Copenhagen and Paris samples. The values for the London sample are worse, and a number of problematic items were identified.

Higher-order product attributes. All four tests show a reasonably good fit, but weak cultural comparability seems again to be the best description across the three samples, considering especially the behaviour of the RMR in the Paris sample.

Meal preparation scripts. The fit is not as good as for the other aspects of FRL, and the fit for the Danish sample is notably better than for the other two. A main problem seems to reside in the *convenience* scale, and some items were correspondingly changed for the next study.

Usage situations. The data have generally a high degree of comparability. All datasets fulfil the conditions of weak cultural comparability, and even for the two more stringent criteria the fit indices are still rather acceptable.

Desired consequences. As for *usage situations,* the data have generally a high degree of comparability. All datasets fulfil the conditions of weak cultural comparability, and even for the two more stringent criteria the fit indices are still rather acceptable.

TABLE 1
Confirmatory factor analysis, study I

FRL area	Copenhagen		London		Paris		χ^2/df
	GFI	RMR	GFI	RMR	GFI	RMR	
Shopping scripts							
minimum cultural comparability	.907	.093	.850	.154	.898	.102	1.683
weak cultural comparability	.901	.096	.832	.144	.887	.107	1.711
strong cultural comparability	.894	.110	.822	.176	.869	.135	1.657
weak cultural identity	.877	.118	.799	.178	.854	.134	1.724
Higher-order product attributes							
minimum cultural comparability	.969	.046	.978	.049	.954	.067	1.467
weak cultural comparability	.967	.049	.976	.056	.951	.083	1.324
strong cultural comparability	.959	.071	.958	.087	.924	.119	1.418
weak cultural identity	.945	.082	.944	.093	.905	.144	1.530
Meal preparation scripts							
minimum cultural comparability	.945	.071	.888	.130	.864	.111	1.451
weak cultural comparability	.941	.077	.874	.137	.861	.119	1.430
strong cultural comparability	.926	.103	.859	.163	.814	.165	1.558
weak cultural identity	.898	.122	.828	.185	.792	.178	1.813
Usage situations							
minimum cultural comparability	.964	.082	.984	.061	.982	.051	1.584
weak cultural comparability	.961	.086	.981	.069	.977	.066	1.345
strong cultural comparability	.955	.101	.972	.101	.978	.067	1.551
weak cultural identity	.952	.097	.956	.124	.951	.104	1.354
Desired consequences							
minimum cultural comparability	.976	.067	.972	.079	.975	.056	1.337
weak cultural comparability	.972	.070	.972	.076	.964	.073	1.229
strong cultural comparability	.970	.075	.959	.113	.945	.104	1.109
weak cultural identity	.954	.101	.943	.145	.933	.118	1.210

In general, the results of the confirmatory factor analysis show that the scales developed are a promising starting point for the development of a cross-culturally valid instrument to measure food-related life styles. For all five elements of food-related life style, at least the level of weak cultural comparability was obtained. However, the analysis also pointed at certain scale items which had to be improved.

STUDY II: CROSS-CULTURAL VALIDATION IN A NEW CULTURAL SETTING

The first study allowed us to identify 21 cross-culturally valid scales. We then improved the items based on the results of the previous analysis and filled up with new items so that all 21 scales had 3 items. In addition, discussions with users of the instrument led us to include two additional scales for abstract product attributes, namely *freshness* and *tastiness*. We then went into the first full-scale application of the instrument, ie its application with a representative random sample. We chose to carry out this application in a fourth cultural setting, Germany, in order to find out whether the data are compatible with the structure emanating from study I.

Sample and data collection

The population was defined as persons of age 16 and above who have the main responsibility for buying food and preparing meals in the household. A representative sample of 1000 respondents was obtained by a random-route procedure. Data collection was carried out by personal interviews.

Confirmatory factor analysis

In order to test to what degree the structure in the German data is comparable with the structure in the data from the first study,

confirmatory factor analysis was conducted with the new data. For minimum cultural comparability, this was done by imposing the pattern of factor loadings corresponding to the factor pattern resulting from study I. For the higher levels of cultural comparability, this was done by fixing the respective parameters (factor loadings, factor correlations, and item reliabilities) to the values estimated in study I for these parameters at the respective level of comparability.

The results can be seen in table 2. It can be seen that the RMR values are higher compared to the first study, which may be explained by the fact that the measurement scale used in the second study was extended from a 5 to a 7-point scale. The size of the residuals vary with the scale of the variables; changing the unit of measurement of a variable will change the variances and covariances, and thus the size of the residuals. For this reason, RMR will only be evaluated if it is considerably higher than average for a construct given the level of cultural comparability, or if it makes a jump in value (cf. Bagozzi and Yi 1988).

Except for the construct *usage situations* it has not been possible to impose a complete data structure on the new data, because new items were developed for the German sample. For the new items, only the loading pattern could be specified. The following results can be obtained from the cross-cultural comparability analysis:

Shopping scripts. The model fit is acceptable for both minimum and weak cultural comparability, after which there is a drop for all three measures of fit. One item has been added to this construct compared to study I; analysis of model fit without this item does not change the result.

Higher-order product attributes. Again both minimum and weak cultural comparability can be accepted. From this level, the model fit drops dramatically, and RMR can not be computed due to

TABLE 2
Confirmatory factor analysis, study II

	GFI	RMR	χ^2/df
Shopping scripts			
minimum cultural comparability	.967	.18	2.535
weak cultural comparability	.934	.226	4.412
strong cultural comparability	.834	.477	10.092
weak cultural identity	.462	.911	108.893
Higher-order product attributes			
minimum cultural comparability			
weak cultural comparability	.933	.187	5.232
strong cultural comparability	.927	.198	5.440
weak cultural identity	.871	—	83.849
	.59	—	60.58
Meal preparation scripts			
minimum cultural comparability	.947	.252	4.260
weak cultural comparability	.929	.326	5.433
strong cultural comparability	.737	—	16.462
weak cultural identity	.395	1.143	117.669
Usage situations			
minimum cultural comparability	.989	.147	4.006
weak cultural comparability	.983	.203	4.307
strong cultural comparability	.922	.467	15.301
weak cultural identity	.539	1.421	256.599
Desired consequences			
minimum cultural comparability	.971	.180	5.750
weak cultural comparability	.919	.389	14.482
strong cultural comparability	.899	.440	14.407
weak cultural identity	—	—	—

(dashes indicate that fit could not be estimated)

failed admissibility test. For this construct 10 new items were developed, and deletion of some of these can improve model fit.

Meal preparation scripts. Here the values of RMR are somewhat higher than for the two previous constructs, while the two other measures are about the same. Based on the measures of χ^2 and GFI, this construct also fulfill the criteria for minimum and weak cultural comparability.

Usage situations. This construct has the best model fit at the minimum and weak cultural comparability levels with respect to GFI, and also with respect to χ^2 at the weak cultural comparability level. This is, as mentioned, the only construct which is completely identical to the first study.

Desired consequences. The results suggest that only minimum cultural comparability can be accepted here, due to a considerable drop/jump in both χ^2 and RMR after this level.

When comparing the results from tables 1 and 2, it has to be kept in mind that table 2 represents a much stronger test. In table 1, the data were tested against a structure developed on the same data, and all parameters, even when forced to be equal across samples, were estimated for optimal fit. In table 2, the same structure is applied to new data, and the fit is estimated based on parameter estimates from the first study.

Generally, none of the factors can be said to be culturally identical or to be strongly culturally comparable. On the other hand, most of the constructs can be said to meet the criteria for minimum and weak cultural comparability. This result supports that the items have been interpreted in a similar way in Germany compared to the first study, and yield support for the instrument as being cross-cultural valid. Further validation should take place though, with adjustments of the instrument, in a new cultural setting.

CONCLUSIONS

Starting from the need to develop an efficient instrument for the surveillance of consumers on export markets, we have attempted to present a new view of life style, based on a cognitive perspective, which makes life style specific to certain areas of consumption. The specific area of consumption studied here is food, resulting in a concept of *food-related life style.* We have tried to develop an instrument that can measure food-related life style in a cross-culturally valid way. To this end, we have collected a pool of 202 items, collected data in three countries, and have constructed scales based on cross-culturally stable factor patterns. These scales have then been subjected to a number of tests of reliability and validity.

We have then applied the set of scales to a fourth country, Germany, based on a representative sample of 1000 respondents.

When imposing the data structure obtained from the first study on the new data by confirmatory factor analysis, it was found that at least minimum cultural comparability exists for all scales.

The present research would benefit from more replications in additional countries, leading to more evidence for the cross-cultural validity of the scales developed. In addition, research relating these scales to behavioural variables, thus providing some evidence for its applicability in terms of prognostic validity, is clearly called for.

REFERENCES

Anderson, Thomas W. and Linda L. Golden (1984),"Life style and psychographics: A critical review and recommendation," in *Advances in Consumer Research*, ed. T.C. Kinnear Vol. 11, pp. 405-411. Provo, UT: Association for Consumer Research.

Askegaard, Søren (1993),"Livsstilsbegrebet: Problemer og muligheder," *Ledelse og Erhvervsøkonomi*, 57, 91-102.

Bagozzi, Richard and Youjae Yi (1988),"On the Evaluation of Structural Equation Models," *Journal of the Academy of Marketing Science*, 16 (1), 74-94.

Banning, T.E. (1987), *Lebensstilorientierte Marketing Theorie*, Heidelberg: Physica.

Chandran, Rajan and James B. Wiley (1987),"Instrument equivalence in cross-cultural research," in *Proceedings of the Second Symposium on Cross-cultural Consumer and Business Studies*, eds. C.F. Keown & A.G. Woodside, pp. 108-112. Honolulu, HA: University of Hawaii.

Douglas, Susan P. and Christine D. Urban (1977),"Life-style analysis to profile women in international markets," *Journal of Marketing*, 41(3), 46-54.

Green, R. D. and White, P. (1976),"Methodological considerations in cross-national consumer research," *Journal of International Business Studies*, 7, 81-87.

Grunert, Klaus G., Karen Brunsø and Søren Bisp (forthcomming),"Food-related life style: Development of a cross-culturally valid instrument for market surveillance," in: L. Kahle & C. Chiagouris (Eds.), *Values, lifestyles, and psychographics*. Hillsdale, NJ: Erlbaum.

Grunert, Suzanne C. (1993), *Essen und Emotionen. Weinheim*, PVU.

Grunert, Suzanne C., Klaus G. Grunert and Kai Kristensen (1992),"The cross-cultural validity of the List of Values LOV: A comparison of nine samples from five countries," in *Developments and applications in structural equation modelling*, eds. J.J.G. Schmeets, M.E.P. Odekerken & F.J.R. van de Pol, pp. 89-99. Amsterdam: Sociometric Research Foundation.

Hui, Michael, Annamma Joy, Chankon Kim and Michel Laroche (1990),"Differences in lifestyle among four major subcultures in a bi-cultural environment," in *Proceedings of the Third Symposium on Cross-cultural Consumer and Business Studies*, eds. C. F. Keown et al., pp. 139-150. Honolulu, HA: University of Hawaii.

Laroche, Michel, Ron McTavish, Lester Johnson, Annamma Joy, Chankon Kim and Susan Rankine (1990),"Consumption patterns and lifestyle differences betweeen English-French Canadian and Australian consumers," in *Procedings of the Third Symposium on Cross-cultural Consumer and Business Studies*, eds. C. F. Keown et al., pp 151-160. Honolulu, HA: University of Hawaii.

Lastovicka, John L. (1982),"On the validation of life style traits," *Journal of Marketing Research*, 19, 126-138.

Linton, Anna and Simon Broadbent (1975),"International life style comparisons: An aid to marketers,"*Advertising Quarterly* (Summer), 15-18.

Roos, J.P. (1986),"On way of life typologies," in *Environmental impact of consumption patterns*, ed. Liisa Uusitalo, pp. 38-55. Aldershot: Gower.

Sekaran, Uma (1983),"Methodological and theoretical issues and advancements in cross-cultural research," *Journal of International Business Studies*, 14(3), 61-73.

Consuming Rastafari: Ethnographic Research in Context and Meaning

Barbara Olsen, SUNY/Old Westbury

ABSTRACT

This paper explores how a religious orientation intersects with consumer behavior within the broadened perspective of consumption activities. Research is based on ethnographic fieldwork spanning twenty years with six individuals from a small Jamaican fishing village that evolved into a tourist town. Jamaican socioeconomic history provides a cultural explanation for the particular visible expressions of Rastafarian symbolic forms that have been adopted and are consumed in sacred and secular contexts. By using the theory of extended self, the local logic that informs an identification with Rastafari is applied to individual strategies for survival.

INTRODUCTION

Rastafari is a cultural, religious movement that began in Jamaica in the 1930s. Its adherents are known as Rastafarians, Rastas or Dreads. Cosmologically loaded goods and behaviors are consumed by Rastafarians through an ideology that is informed by Biblical scripture and Ethiopian history. Using the concept of "extended self" (Belk 1988), the Rastas have borrowed cultural practices and symbols from history to identify with the Rastafari movement. This visible expression of a Rasta culture has contributed to various lifestyles that evolved among the informants to help them manipulate their fortunes during a time of great social and economic change in Jamaica.

Consumer research is beginning to investigate a broadened perspective of consumption activities linking identity to different aspects of culture. These forays include the spiritual dimension (Belk, Wallendorf and Sherry 1989; Hirschman 1985; O'Guinn and Belk 1989), ritual behavior and symbolic consumption (Rook 1984; Rook and Levy 1983), and the interconnection between objects, styles and extended selves (Belk 1988; Hirschman and LaBarbera 1990).

For sixty years Rastafari has been a religion of an alienated subculture whose critique of history and ridicule of British cultural norms still threatens the social elite. By the 1970s Rastafari expression was popularized by reggae music and co-opted by politicians who used dread talk and wore the colors to capture votes (Waters 1985). It continues as a religious and cultural force influencing popular fashion and lifestyle alternatives described by the use of an Ital diet, Iyaric language, symbolic hairstyle, clothing, colors and adornment. These characteristics have become globally recognized symbolic markers of Rastafari. Using ethnography based on research conducted in Negril, Jamaica, for over two decades, the methodology employs a life history approach to interpret what Rastafari means in the lives of six individuals who identify to varying degrees with its ideology. Life history is a methodology that utilizes the emic (insider) viewpoint and thus allows an individual to contribute his/her recollected life story for interpretation and analysis. The respondents represent a demographic spread of age, gender, single-married and various household typologies. I also chose people I had known the longest, who felt comfortable contributing their stories. Our familiarity with each other helped erase the cultural barrier between us.

These lives touched by Rastafari intersect with consumer research. Belk, Wallendorf and Sherry's (1989) analysis of the sacred-profane continuum regarding persons, places, experiences, times, tangible and intangible things, applies in the consumption of Rastafari. The emergence of Rastafari as a religion began in 1930 with the coronation of Ras Tafari, later known as Haile Selassie, the Emperor of Ethiopia. Jamaican preachers looking for the second coming of Christ identified Selassie as the returned messiah. For the disenfranchised black Jamaican living in an English colony, Africa became the promised land. In reclaiming ancestral history, African cultural patterns and symbols became sacralized by the Rastas and secularized by Rasta impostors.

Belk notes that the constellation from which we choose possessions to identify with our extended selves includes the "...body, internal processes, ideas and experiences, and those persons, places and things to which one feels attached" (1988: 141). The more strongly we connect with, control or are controlled by these extensions, the more they become part of self. Belk's (1988) notion that "abstract ideas" are consumable, is applied by Abelson (1986) and Hirschman and LaBarbera (1990) to consider religious beliefs as possession objects. According to Abelson, beliefs are free commodities which can be inherited or adopted. They are displayed, defended, suffered for, accumulated and are valuable. Beliefs are also difficult to change except to refashion an identity (1986: 231). In the Jamaican context, the Rastafarian movement is most significantly linked with identity reconstruction. Africans of the West Indies arrived during the forced migration of the diaspora when European slave holders tried to remove all vestiges of tribal culture. Contemporary African-based religions of the Caribbean are a possession that incorporate an African identity in the extended self.

BACKGROUND: HISTORICAL ROOTS OF THE RASTAFARI MOVEMENT

The Rastafari movement emerged during the 1930s as a cultural response to severe social and economic oppression in Jamaica where ninety-five percent of the African-Jamaican population has traditionally been controlled by the five percent British-focused white and brown elite. The African folk culture, including kinship, mating practices, matrilineal decent, music and religion were expressions that those of the diaspora in the new world could control.

Most Jamaican slaves originated along the African west coast area now known as Nigeria. Although the Ashanti tribe comprised about fifteen percent of the slave population, it is believed that their cosmology (religion and mythology) predominated. The Ashanti brought the religious practices of obeah and myalism, both known for spirit possession and curing. Obeah and myal evolved into the Jamaican Myal, Kumina and Revival religious sects. All three sects include African traditions that helped preserve African identity long after the abolition of slavery in 1838. Freedom had very little affect on alleviating harsh social and economic conditions and these sects empowered the weak to subvert the master class in the struggle for a better future. Blacks, discouraged from worshipping in established churches, also joined Native Baptist which condoned dancing, drumming, glossolalia and possession. Revival movements emerge during economic crises and appeared around the world and in Jamaica in the 1840s, 1860s and 1930s.

Rastafari emerged in the urban ghetto as a religion of the oppressed in response to climatic disaster and economic depression. Inspiration drew from several leaders with ties to Revival sects whose members had also worked as migrants throughout the Caribbean under colonialism. Leonard Howell, considered the founder of Rastafari, also fought in the 1896 Ashanti War for the British in the West Indian Regiment. Howell's ideology was fortified by Marcus Garvey and his Universal Negro Improvement Association founded in 1914 to promote African pride, socio-political justice and repatriation to Africa.

By the 1920s the small cadre of Rasta preachers praised Africa, freedom and liberation (Barrett 1974: 159; Smith et al. 1960: 6-7). The preachers adapted Biblical prophesy to their context of British domination. The Bible predicted a new Messiah would deliver the faithful from the merchant class (Revelations 17-19). The preachers believed Babylon (white, western civilization) would fall in the Apocalypse. The Bible also said, "Princes shall come out of Egypt; Ethiopia shall soon stretch out her hands unto God" (Psalms 68:31; see also Isaiah 11:1-2; Revelation 5:5,19).

Thus, when Ras (Duke) Tafari, a direct descendent of Solomon and Queen Makeda of Sheba, was crowned the 225th Emperor of Ethiopia in 1930, he became the prophesied Messiah. During his coronation Ras Tafari was renamed Haile Selassie, (power of the Trinity), and adopted the title "King of Kings, Lord of Lords, His Imperial Majesty of the Conquering Lion of the Tribe of Judah, Elect of God." To the preachers Selassie was Jahweh, the living God. Selassie's deposition in 1974 and mysterious death in 1975 reinforced belief of his divinity among the faithful. However, other Rastafarians doubt his role in the future of the movement (Simpson 1985: 287).

Chevannes claims that initially both sexes were equal members of this acephalous, fragmented, nondenominational faith, but after the 1950s it evolved into a patriarchal society of brethren with "spouses" related through men (1989b). Adherents often display the Emperor's picture, fly the Ethiopian flag of red, green and gold surrounding a standing lion symbolizing the Solomonic lineage, use the colors in their dress and wear the star of David. Nyabingi (named for an Order established in 1935 in the Congo and Ethiopia with Selassie as figurehead) festivals, called "grounations" or "I-ssembles" are celebrated with drumming, chanting and dancing on Ethiopian Christmas, January 7; New Year's day, September 11; Selassie's birthday, July 23; his coronation, November 2; his visit to Jamaica, April 21 (1966); and African Liberation Day when the OAU was founded on May 26 (1963) (Homiak 1985: 361).

A Rasta's most valued possession is an agile mind honed during meetings for spiritual understanding called "reasoning" sessions where copious amounts of ganja (marijuana) are smoked. The holy herb, sanctioned by the Bible (Genesis 8; Psalm 18, 104; Revelations 22) is blessed before each inhalation. Revelations 17-20 and Leviticus prescribe a strict, natural (vital/Ital) diet: avoiding meat (particularly pork), salt, processed foods, alcohol and tobacco.

Women wear long skirts and always keep their heads covered. They stay in their yards with the children. Birth control is prohibited. Women are considered dangerous during menses so avoid touching crops and cooking during these times. Rasta fathers take active domestic roles caring for their children, especially sons (see Chevannes 1989a, 1989b, 1990; Barrett 1974, 1977; Campbell 1985; Homiak 1985; Owens 1976; Smith et al 1960).

Hair Culture

Hair, the most visible extension of self, is connected in Jamaica with social values. Good and bad hair is situated, respectively, within the elite/white and peasant/black power structure (Chevannes 1989b: 11). In the 1930s, facial hair was taboo, so "beardmen" grew beards to set themselves apart. In 1949 the Youth Black Faith separated from older Revival Rastas by adopting the Nazarite vow to grow locks (Numbers 6:5) which, like Samson's, (Judges 16:17) conserves strength. They copied Selassie's beard from *National Geographic* photos. "Locksmen" of the 1950s

ridiculed society by growing hair like derelicts in matted "dreadlocks" (Chevannes 1990: 69; 1989b: 2).

Others attribute dreadlocks to Ethiopian hairstyles worn among the Gallah, Maasai and Somali and say that they were adopted by Rastas in the 1950s because a fierce look would protect them from abuse (Barrett 1977; Smith, et al. 1960). Campbell links locks to sympathy with the 1950s Mau-Mau movement and hair seen in newsreels (1985: 98, 100). Due to bad associations with locks, colored woven tams were adopted in the 1960s to hide hair in public and avoid harassment. Chevannes also situates Rasta hair culture and male domination as role reversals within the historical gender power struggle experienced by Jamaican males in a matri-archal society (1989b).

Dread Talk

Rastas transgressed social norms. Their use of ganja with a pro-Africa, anti-British, anti-capitalist, anti-establishment philosophy made them the focus of persecution until the 1970s. The 1950s and 60s were repressive. Rastas were brutalized and arrested on the slightest provocation. Many of their squatter communities were razed. In 1958, a Rasta compound called Back-O-Wall, under the leadership of a preacher named Prince Edward Emanuel, was destroyed by the police. This group's dissolution scattered many Rastas to the hinterlands and established preacher Emanuel's fame throughout the island. Such altercations with police also nurtured Rastas' desire for repatriation to Africa and popularized the phrase "better must come" among those who anticipate political and economic change at home in Jamaica.

The evolution of an I-argot as a language of resistance in the 1960s represented the power of secret communication similar to Chinese and East Indians speaking in the presence of African Jamaicans (Chevannes 1989b: 5). Dread talk called the "Iyaric language" is purged of negative associations. For instance, sincerely is corrected as Icerely or Incerely, dedicate is livicate, deadline becomes lifeline and understand is overstand (see Owens 1976; Pollard 1980; Simpson 1985). It also symbolizes a heightened self-perception in which "me" the object is replaced with "I" as subject.

Vocal protest also found expression in music. Rasta drummers were connected to Revival Kumina "burra" drumming and influenced reggae songs written and performed by Rastas in the late 1960s (White 1967). Rastas also became poets, sculptors and painters.

Copying and Co-opting

The symbolic manifestation of the movement was adopted by dissidents and those identifying with the counter culture of the 1970s. The Rasta population was estimated at over 80,000 out of two million by the 1970s and society began accepting their style while rejecting the religious, revolutionary philosophy. Politicians defused the Rasta movement's sociological potential by co-opting its symbols and fostered assimilation by the middle class who grew locks and wore Rasta fashions.

"Rude boys" grew dreadlocks, wore the colors and spoke dread talk to identify with the music culture. As tourism grew in the 1980s foreigners filtered onto the beaches and male youths found Rasta identity an asset attracting foreign women who sought their company during holidays. By the mid-1980s this was a trend in Negril where Rasta males were called "Rentals" as in "Rent-a-Dread" (see Spencer 1988) and became known locally as "Rastatutes" who traded sex for favors. Consequently, it is very difficult to distinguish between the sacred and secular use of Rastafarian symbols as their use migrates from the faithful to faddists.

ETHNOGRAPHIC METHODOLOGY

The analysis that follows is based on ethnographic fieldwork using participant observation and in-depth interviews conducted for a twenty-year period in the same community. Individuals in different social contexts appear to selectively choose ideological elements from the Rasta culture that suit their own personal agendas. For some, it is a religion of deep spiritual meaning that reinforces one's physical and emotional survival. For others, it is a cult of convenience from which stylistic markers are utilized to identify with popular culture. Ethnography is a tool to understand this contextual expression through "... words, images, institutions, behaviors - in terms of which, in each place, people actually represented themselves to themselves and to one another" (Geertz 1983: 58).

Hill (1993) sees a need for cross-disciplinary borrowing in qualitative consumer research and offers guidelines for using ethnography. Qualitative data relies on an emic understanding of the world experienced by the informant. We try to see from the "native" perspective filtered by our own etic interpretation informed by social science. He says, "If the emic perspective is the 'heart' and the etic perspective is the 'brain' of ethnographic inquiry, then field work is the 'soul'" (1993: 59).

This paper results from longitudinal research (Olsen 1989) on the impact of the development of tourism during a period of intense social transformation in Negril. Fieldwork from 1971 through 1993 involved two years' residence, community participant-observation and in-depth interviews conducted among several families with continuous repeat visits and letter communication.

FINDINGS: LIVES TOUCHED BY RASTAFARI

This paper considers how six individuals (whose identities have been altered) relate to and through Rastafari. Jimbo and Kay are in their thirties, and Grace and Gordon are a couple in their forties. Scribe is an artist of fifty and Gladstone, in his seventies, considers himself the eldest Rasta in the western parishes. All have chosen to identify with Rastafari for personal reasons within the social context of their own lives.

Gladstone

Gladstone was nine when Selassie was crowned so he believes he grew up in the movement. Historical events that shaped the movement reinforced his faith. In 1958 he was living in the Rasta camp Back-O-Wall. The police raided the camp and smashed everything and everyone in sight (see Barrett 1974: 167; Smith et al. 1960: 19). He said he just "stood fast" when the police hit him on the head with a gun and baton. They beat his back and broke his arm. All were taken to the hospital where their locks were shorn and their beards were shaved. The scars on his head and a twisted arm are testaments to defending his faith. The value of our belief as a possession increases when we suffer for it (Abelson 1986). Gladstone is constantly aware of the sacrifice he paid to possess his faith. Gladstone says that in those days Rastas could not buy goods from a shop or even walk along the roads without being harassed. People threw stones at them and they were arrested for no reason.

For Gladstone, knowledge is power. His most valued possessions, besides faith, Bible, son and scars, are audio tapes recorded from the radio of Prince Edward Emanuel giving sermons and answers to letters from as far away as Ghana. When he played them for me he leaned into the speaker to catch every word, responding to the voice on the tape "Yes, yes, sure, sure," and "praise Jah Rastafari for giving I-n-I the good life."

Today he lives a spiritual life with his son, Tone, now a teen. Gladstone said, "I-n-I took Tone from the mother at age two and raised him as a Rasta." They live a spartan life with the barest essentials in a red, green and gold painted two room house on "captured land." A garden of fruit and vegetables, including yam, cassava, paw paw and comfrey (the "medicine" plant), provides for their modified Ital diet. They also eat the chickens and eggs they raise on their land. A strict Ital diet prohibits salt, sugar, white flour, tinned (canned) and processed foods and all flesh, except for fish (with scales) under twelve inches long.

Over the twenty-four years I have known Gladstone, he was removed from several properties on which he squatted when land was reclaimed to sell to foreigners. Today, he makes extra cash from coconut pins he and Tone design and paint (red, green and gold) with images of Haile Selassie, the Lion of Judah and the star of David and sell to tourists in town. He is saving for when the government comes to reclaim his land and he can offer to buy it. In the back of his mind he still hopes one day to fly to Africa where he will meet all the true Rastas again. As the oldest Rasta with the longest membership, Gladstone's belief is firm. He awaits repatriation and the Apocalypse and lives through complete identification with Jah Rastafari.

Grace and Gordon

Grace and Gordon became Rastas after leaving the "rat race" in the 1970s to pioneer in Negril adopting Rastafari for guidance. They raised a second set of children in the spirit of Jah. By the mid-1980s, faith faded into fad. They reentered society to survive in a tourist sector they could not avoid.

The first year in Negril they ate meat, smoked cigarettes, drank alcohol and used birth control all of which Rastas associate with Babylon. By 1975 Rastafari penetrated their social network and old habits transformed to a new lifestyle. They avoided birth control because it was "genocide against the black race," became vegetarians, read the Bible and prepared for when "Babylon will burn in the Apocalypse and only the righteous will survive." The Bible explained why the Israelites were black and Jah Rastafari the true God.

Grace's Ital diet was spiritual. In one letter she wrote, "Sister try to eat well, it's the true and only answer to life - if you feed your body right your mind will be very clear, like crystal and you will see your path clearly - believe me - No tin food, frozen food, flesh or chemicals - try and you will feel the positive flow - No salt." They wore the colors, grew locks (often concealed under colorful tams), smoked the holy herb and reasoned with brethren who passed in and out of their yard.

Grace had five more children at home; Wisdom, Zion, Star, Iman and Iver, commemorating Rastafari. The years were hard. Home schooling was inadequate. They rented cottages that Gordon built by hand and painted Rasta colors. The urban amenities crept back in. By 1985, their lives were no longer defined by Rastafari. They cut their locks, but still believed in the divinity of Jah.

So many impostors had taken on the look of Rastafari that the symbols had lost their meaning. They were cosmopolitan again rather than provincial. Gordon drinks beer and Grace cooks with salt and dairy products, eggs, sugar and even lobster, but they do not eat meat. Both wear the colors but the spirit is gone. They are entrepreneurs living a fast life packed with luxuries. Grace admits they "moved beyond Rasta."

Considering belief as a commodity that can be borrowed, invested in, valued and disposed of (Abelson 1986), Grace and Gordon eased into the faith making a public commitment to Rastafari that was irrevocable at least in the names of their children. To urban friends and family, for ten years they were the embodiment of Rastafari. Rasta identity had become part of their extended selves (Belk 1988). When Rastafari became secularized (Belk, Wallendorf and Sherry 1989), the pristine lifestyle lost its potency.

Its value that set Rastas apart from others was diminished and this socially aware couple, very conscious of public opinion, returned to a middle class lifestyle.

Scribe

Scribe, an artist and poet came to Negril in the early 1970s to establish a gallery that earned him national recognition. The traffic through his business slowly turned from procurers of paintings to procurers of ganja and cocaine. Now fifty with grey locks framing a wizened face creased with furrows, Scribe uses the spirit of Jah to keep him clean and save his life.

In the late 1980s our conversations centered on the destructive power of crack cocaine. In recovery, he mourns those he introduced to crack and turns to his Bible and ganja for relief. He married Mia, a foreigner, in 1980 and they have three children. She told me the nurse at the clinic treats them as pariahs. Mia avoids dealing with society and yearns to take the family to her homeland. Scribe wanted justice in Jamaica. His understanding of the system from a dealers' perspective confirmed my observations. Jamaica is a trans-shipment center for cocaine which is regularly dropped from airplanes in large black plastic garbage bags and available everywhere. It is cheap and impure. Prostitutes hustle to get $10 bags of crack and users develop skin lesions from its toxicity. The government however, prosecutes the ganja users. Scribe did not understand the vendetta against the holy herb. Of the crack, he said, "I could not take it no more. Yes man, I quit. I stopped about a dozen people from doin' it because I could share my experience with dem and it helps. I am a humanitarian and I love people, never was my intention to use people for my material gains." While crediting Ital food and Jah for saving his life, Scribe described how cocaine had consumed his life. In 1992 the land on which he lived in Negril was sold and Scribe moved to the city.

Kay

Kay was fifteen when I met her in 1971. She is now in her mid-thirties with two teens and two toddlers living in a two room cottage on land inherited from her father. She is a dignified Rastawoman and always wears long skirts and a tam over her long locks that fall around her shoulders.

She became a Rasta in 1977 when diagnosed with a uterine tumor and refused to have a hysterectomy because in Jamaica, "Men do not want a mule, a sterile woman." She wanted more children. After being cured by Bongo-Hu-I, a Rasta doctor (see Jerome 1981), she turned her life over to Jah. The doctor prescribed herbs and told her to change her diet. She gave up meat, shell fish, salt, tinned food, beer and soft drinks. After a year the bleeding stopped. She eats an Ital diet and worships Jah Rastafari who she credits for saving her life.

As fewer single women adopt Rastafari, Kay's identification with the faith has set her apart from her classmates living on the road. In a town of limited opportunities, she assumed a Rasta persona as much to rebel against traditional society as to control her own life. Four years ago Kay met her current lover, a Rasta musician, and had the toddlers by him. He visits every five months and she fears he will give her aids because he has other lovers. She exclaimed her body is her temple. She can control the diet but men control sex. On another level, she is conscious of historical oppression and recently, of the degradation that accompanied cocaine into Negril. It claimed the life of her brother.

Kay marginally supports her family from her restaurant but is not a hustler. Her quiet faith trusts "Jah will provide" and she tries to be a model for the youths who gather at her shop.

Jimbo

Jimbo was a school boy of ten when I met him in 1971 and at our last interview was over thirty. He lives at home with his parents and what remains of his twelve siblings. Jimbo grew up on the road. He learned the trade of a mason and was currently building octagons on family land to rent to tourists. His desires were influenced by tourists and foreign residents. Jimbo confided that he prefers cultivating ganja and escorting female tourists around on his motorcycle.

Jimbo became a Rasta in 1984 after a motorcycle accident. When asked what being a Rasta meant he responded, "Well, me no follow it. Me just grow me dreads and live. None of dat Selassie business. Selassie a man like me, not a god. Baldhead comb made me crazy. Hair make me feel like a king." Regarding diet, Jimbo responded "Me eat meat same way, man. Drink Heineken beer. ... But, I not a Dread! I a Rasta." His distinction between Rasta and Dread was that a Dread was a man who, because of cocaine use, became impotent. From his perspective, "half of Jamaica, baldhead and Dread were affected by cocaine." Jimbo's interest is romancing tourist women. He carries them around on the back of his bike and they take him to dinner, disco and concerts on the beach. His Rasta identity has made him accessible to those tourists, especially women, who want a more ethnic experience during vacation.

DISCUSSION

Belk says that our possessions become tools or weapons that symbolically extend our selves by allowing us to become different (1988: 145). Rastafari belief as a possession object (Abelson 1986) facilitated a transformation in identity for these six individuals. The most obvious means was by changing the externals and adopting Rasta fashion and lifestyle symbols. Lewis (1993) notes that for a Rasta the body becomes a social text and ritualized grooming symbolizes rituals of reversal forming a new identity. Each Rasta adopted a new persona through which each could take control of their life when so many around them are losing control. They redefine a healthier lifestyle, chose symbolic artifacts and style for identity, affiliate with the Spirit of Africa and socially network for positions of power that the identity will obtain.

If we interpret Rastafari as a brand of religion we can apply Rook and Levy's (1983) analysis of consumer myths and brand use cultivated through ritual systems of behavior in which grooming is associated with healing or magical transformation into states of being that enable one to perform more powerfully in social contexts. Rastafarian cultural artifacts; such as hair style, language, color association and symbolic icons also confirm and dramatize historicized myths (Douglas 1970; Rook 1984). These symbolic markers are sacralized when used to reinforce one's faith. Gladstone's impoverished life is enriched through transcendence in Rastafari. Scribe and Kay recognize the social value of being role models for their peers. Grace and Gordon used Rasta to simplify their life and join a counterculture. In the process, they became controlled by the ideology producing five more children in the name of Jah. Their struggle to survive lost its significance when the symbols of Rastafari diffused into popular culture. Being a Rasta lost its value. Jimbo admittedly has adopted the fad without faith. He controls the symbols which empower him to attract attention.

Ethnography uses thick description to understand people living in historical moments of their own creation. The evolution of the development of Rasta style is best understood in the context of Jamaican political history and particularly of Negril's transformation into a tourist town. Douglas states "..the human body is always treated as an image of society ...bodily control is an expression of social control - abandonment of bodily control in ritual responds to the requirements of a social experience which is being expressed." "Bodily style" is local and limited to a social context within a cultural experience (1970: 66-71). In the rigid colonial social structure of Jamaica in the 1930s, Rastafari role reversals inverted British social norms. Rastas are African focused, often polygamous, lion haired, anti-capitalist, anti-establishment and anti-modern. In the 1970s and 1980s, Negril was developing for tourism and Rastas had become role models for self determination in a changing economic landscape.

CONCLUSION

Religious movements come into existence at particular moments in history to service communal needs during contests of social disruption. Today, it is not a coincidence that Rastafari symbols are more observable among male subcultures of tourist towns along the coastal corridor where the two worlds clash most immediately. The sacred-profane continuum portrayed by Rastafari in Negril, reflects the impact of tourism. The six individuals whose lives were touched by Rastafari are situated along this continuum and use the ideology to accommodate their lifestyles. Gladstone, the eldest, represents the most spiritual and Jimbo the most secular. Kay and Scribe find God in Jah and health in an Ital diet. The lives of Gordon and Grace reflect the historical progression of the movement from a spiritual reaction to Babylon to its co-optation as a fashion trend.

The symbols we adopt speak for us. Considering extended self, the identification of hair with a lion's mane suggests Turner's notion of the "man-lion monster" metaphor positioned as a social lesson. Symbols are chosen to make audiences think (1967: 105). In the Jamaican context, Eurocentric society is forced to rethink the status quo as Rastafari offers an alternative. Dreadlocks have different meanings for each context. Gladstone in his heart is an African, but popular culture has adopted symbol without historic content and we are left questioning the icons. For the Rastas portrayed in this analysis, all communicated through its symbols. Locks define identity to the audience, diet defines one's health, while worshipping Selassie and yearning for Africa represent complete emersion in the belief. Rastafari is individually interpreted according to the social context of each person adopting symbol and sentiment. For some, it is a religious belief system controlling daily life, for others it is a fashion style used to control one's status in the social community.

Extending research with these and other informants will track the value of Rastafari to them over time as they continue to react to development for tourism and increasing consumption opportunities. Future research would also benefit from cross-cultural comparative analysis of the sacred and secular uses of Rastafari to determine how these loaded symbols are used as the extension of self.

REFERENCES

Abelson, Robert P. (1986), "Beliefs are Like Possessions," *Journal for the Theory of Social Behavior,* 16 (3), 223-250.

Barrett, Leonard (1974), *Soul-Force,* NY: Anchor Books.

_____ (1977), *The Rastafarians: The Dreadlocks of Jamaica,* London: Heinemann Educational Books.

Belk, Russell W. (1988), "Possessions and the Extended Self," *Journal of Consumer Research,* Vol. 15, 139-168.

_____, Melanie Wallendorf and John F. Sherry, Jr. (1989), "The Sacred and the Profane in Consumer Behavior: Theodicy on the Odyssey," *Journal of Consumer Research,* Vol. 16, 1-38.

Campbell, Horace (1985), *Rasta and Resistance,* London: Hansib.

Chevannes, Barry (1990), "Rastafari: Towards a New Approach," *New West IndianGuide,* 64 (3&4), 127-148.

_____, (1989a), "The Origin of the Dreadlocks," Institute of Social Studies, Den Haag, June.

_____, (1989b), "The Phallus and the Outcast: Symbolism of the Dreadlocks in Jamaica," Institute for the Study of Man.

Douglas, Mary (1970), *Natural Symbols,* NY: Pantheon Books.

Geertz, Clifford (1983), *Local Knowledge,* NY: Basic Books.

Hill, Ronald Paul (1993), "A Primer for Ethnographic Research with a Focus on Social Policy Issues Involving Consumer Behavior," in *Advances in Consumer Research,* Vol. 20, Provo, Utah: Association for Consumer Research, 59-62.

Hirschman, Elizabeth C. (1985), "Primitive Aspects of Consumption in Modern American Society," *Journal of Consumer Research,* Vol. 12, 142-153.

_____ and Priscilla A. LaBarbera (1990), "Dimensions of Possession Importance," *Psychology & Marketing,* 7(3), 215-33.

Homiak, John Paul (1985), "The 'Ancients of Days' Seated Black; Eldership, Oral Tradition, and Ritual in Rastafari Culture," Ph.D. Thesis, Brandeis University, Ann Arbor: Microfilms.

Jerome, Julius (1981), "Rasta Doctor and a Unique Medical Clinic in Jamaica, West Indies: The Divine Theocratic Government of Ras Tafari Selassie I," AB Thesis, SUNY Purchase.

Lewis, William F. (1993), *Soul Rebels,* IL: Waveland Press.

O'Guinn, Thomas C. and Russell W. Belk (1989), "Heaven on Earth: Consumption at Heritage Village USA," *Journal of Consumer Research,* 16 (2), 227-238.

Olsen, Barbara (1989), "The Personal and Social Costs of Development in Negril, Jamaica, West Indies; 1971-1988," Ph.D. Thesis, Graduate Faculty of the New School for Social Research.

Owens, Joseph V. (1976), *Dread: The Rastafarians of Jamaica,* JA: Sangster.

Pollard, Velma (1980), "Dread Talk-The Speech of the Rastafarian in Jamaica," *Caribbean Quarterly* 26 (4), 32-41.

Rook, Dennis W. (1984), "Ritual Behavior and Consumer Symbolism," in *Advances in Consumer Research,* Vol. 11, ed. Thomas C. Kinnear, Provo, UT: Assoc. for Consumer Research, 279-284.

_____, and Sidney J. Levy (1983), "Psychological Themes in Consumer Grooming Rituals," in *Advances in Consumer Research,* Vol. 10, Assoc. for Consumer Research, 329-333.

Simpson, George (1985), "Some Reflections on the Rastafari Movement," *Phylon,* 46 (4): 286-291).

Smith, M.G., Roy Augier and Rex Nettleford (1960), *The Rastafari Movement in Kingston, Jamaica,* ISER, UWI Mona, JA.

Spencer, Ian (1988), "Rent-A-Dread is Big Business," *The Jamaican Daily Gleaner,* (August).

Turner, Victor (1967), *The Forest of Symbols,* Ithaca, NY: Cornell.

Waters, Anita M. (1985), *Race, Class and Political Symbols,* NJ: Transaction.

White, Garth (1967), "Rudie, Oh Rudie!" *Caribbean Quarterly,* 13 (3): 39-44.

Notes on *The Journal of Consumer Research*: The Unexpected Challenges of a Start-up

Ronald E. Frank, Emory University

JCR's Existence!

In the late 1950s and early '60s, considerable emphasis was placed on the development of scholarly inquiry in the field of business education. Largely as a result of the funding initiatives of the Ford and Carnegie Foundations, much was done to enhance scholarship across all business disciplines.

One of the first results was the rapid emergence of interest in methodology under the rubric of marketing research, which in turn resulted in the initiation of the *Journal of Marketing Research* in 1964. At that time, data analysis was a hot topic; hence, much of *JMR*'s initial focus was either on data analysis and/or research methodology.

As the decade of the '60s progressed, two other foci developed in the field, both of which had strong methodological underpinnings. In spirit, if not in detail, they overlapped the focus of *JMR*. They were consumer behavior and management science applications in marketing.

As a result of this, an effort was made to broaden the aegis of the *Journal of Marketing Research*. At that time both Bob Ferber and I had executive roles in the American Marketing Association. At one point we and others met with the then-editor of the *Journal of Marketing Research*. The purpose of the meeting was to consider the possibility of broadening *JMR*'s scope. One thought would have been to go to a section format, of which one would have been marketing research and others most likely would have been consumer behavior and management science. Along with a change to sections, there would have been an increase in frequency of publication. At that point the then-editor felt our proposal would neither work logistically nor fit in terms of the AMA/*JMR* objectives.

At about the same time, the idea for a new journal was born. It was Bob Ferber's vision. The then-Board of Directors of the American Marketing Association (by chance both Bob and I were on the Board at the time) met and, after an extended discussion, decided to provide $50,000 in working capital to initiate the *Journal of Consumer Research*. They did this in spite of the fact that at that point none of the other nine co-sponsors were willing to provide financial support.

In addition, the American Marketing Association initially handled the subscription servicing for the journal and did some advertising to help us get it established. However, it was not willing to have the journal be an AMA journal nor, to my memory, was it the interest of *JCR* which represented ten different disciplinary organizations.

At that stage in the AMA's history its leadership was finding it increasingly difficult to support the increased specialization of research that was occurring within its academic membership. The language of practice and scholarship was diverging as were the issues of interest. The ratio of symbols to words was increasing in scholarly journals. More constructs associated with terms unfamiliar to many practitioners became part of the body of scholarly inquiry. Along with this specialization in language and focus was an increased resistance by a number of persons, who were among the leaders in the practice of marketing research, to fostering any further "academic journals." Had the AMA been more responsive, it's quite possible that the *JCR* and the journal *Marketing Science* would not exist. Instead the world might well have had a *JMR* which was sectioned and published more frequently.

The house of intellect is like the Mississippi River in flood stage. Given that the AMA did not respond in a fashion that kept up with these developments in the field, these journals came into existence under other auspices.

With the loan in hand, the board, which Bob Ferber chaired, asked me to serve as editor. Little did any of us know the potentially perilous venture we were undertaking.

Forming an editorial board, working with the associations and getting the journal in print turned out to be the easy part.

Would you believe that two weeks before the first edition of the journal was to be mailed, had a three-vote margin been different, the journal would have closed its doors?

Two weeks before the first issue was to hit print Bob Ferber was out of the country and out of touch. I received a call from someone in the leadership at the American Marketing Association telling me that at a Board meeting a few days from the time of the call, the AMA board was going to vote against continuing the $50,000 loan to the journal. The then-board regretted making the loan. It was not interested in an academic journal.

I requested to attend the board meeting. Initially, my request was refused. After an extended discussion it was agreed that I could have "permission" to meet with the executive committee of the association the night before the board meeting in Chicago.

I went to Chicago and met with that group. Once more an extended conversation ensued. They primarily were there to deliver a message that their largesse was at an end. I insisted that I be given the right to attend the board meeting. Their initial response was no as I was not a board member.

After another extended discussion I was given 10 minutes of board time. I made the case during those ten minutes as to the singular inappropriateness of withdrawing the loan at this particular point, irrespective of what the board felt. I did point out to them that the past board, acting in good faith on behalf of the AMA, had approved the venture. I was told after the board meeting that *only* by a three-vote margin did the board vote to continue to support the loan. Had they rescinded the loan, maybe we would have bailed it out. We'll never know. Fortunately, we never had to find out.

About a year later at a *JCR* board meeting the then-President of the American Marketing Association came with the intent to demand that the AMA be repaid as soon as possible—or else!

There is an unheralded hero in this story—a man by the name of Wayne Lumberg, who was then Executive Director of the American Marketing Association. As I've indicated, the Association—in effect Wayne—took responsibility for handling the processing of subscription payments and the like. One of the things Wayne did, on his own recognizance, was bill for the entire first year irrespective of when a subscriber signed up. Hence, if you subscribed for the fourth issue of year one you would be sent the first three issues and a bill for the entire year. It turns out that so doing together with the growth in subscriptions of the journal put us in a position to be able to pay off the loan at the end of the first year of publication. Little did the President know, when he walked into the *JCR* board meeting, that he would be informed that we were prepared to pay off the American Marketing Association and would proceed unencumbered by the loan. Thus ended the first year of *JCR*s existence.

JCR's Focus!

When *JCR* started it was the clear desire of all involved to see it as the preeminent interdisciplinary journal in consumer behavior.

Advances in Consumer Research
Volume 22, © 1995

The word interdisciplinary was and still is somewhat nebulous. There were five different types of articles that we had in mind when it came to publication in *JCR*. The first were articles drawing on knowledge in more than one discipline to pursue scholarly inquiry on some issue related to consumer behavior. Next were articles that would be based on knowledge from a single discipline but wherein the conclusions were well developed with respect to implications for research in other disciplines. Third were those that would attempt to summarize knowledge across many disciplines and, by so doing, arrive at insights (hopefully contributions to knowledge) that added value to what was already known. Fourth was *JCR*'s willingness to publish work from a variety of disciplines wherein the author's purpose was to communicate knowledge about consumer behavior based on one discipline to scholars in others. The last, and far from least, was to foster a place for the publication of inquiries involving the talents of individuals from more than one discipline. We thought this type of article would most likely deal with key public policy or corporate policy issues which frequently demand by their very nature understandings gleaned from a broad spectrum of disciplines.

I believe that the first two of these *JCR* did a reasonable job of delivering—that is, serving as a forum for work involving constructs from more than one discipline as well as taking work from a single discipline and drawing out implications for others. During the first several years, we did publish a few review articles. I think in the main they were helpful but did not go as far as we all hoped in providing added value beyond summarizing knowledge across disciplines.

With regard to the last two types of articles we contributed relatively little. It proved quite difficult to attract articles from scholars in disciplines other than marketing and the Association for Consumer Research to this new forum. Every member of the board and I tried for an extended period of time. Often I would get an article from a "statesman" in another discipline who had given a speech that he was willing to have us publish but which would not find a home in the disciplinary journals with which his work was primarily associated. That isn't what we had in mind when we started the journal, nor is it now.

To date, we have relatively few examples of teams which have done interdisciplinary work on key strategic issues let alone contributed to our scholarly literature in consumer behavior. I would like to have seen *JCR* be more of a change agent in redefining professional boundaries, but it may be a bit much to expect. Journals are more apt to reflect underlying trends in the "sociology" of the professions than create them.

Even though we did not accomplish all of our goals, one thing is clear—*JCR* played, and continues to play, a very important role in providing a vehicle for scholars interested in consumer behavior to have an archival journal to facilitate building on each other's work and hence helping serve as a catalyst/an accelerator in the evolution of scholarly inquiry in consumer behavior.

My belief is that if *JCR* had not existed, something else would have fulfilled the same function. It might have taken a bit longer and taken a different form—but there would have been an effective communication vehicle among serious scholars of consumer behavior, if for no other reason than the then and future leadership of ACR would not have let the need for such a journal remain unattended.

Framing a Rainbow, Focusing the Light: *JCR*'s First Twenty Years

Jerome B. Kernan, George Mason University[1]

ABSTRACT

This paper commemorates the initial years of the *Journal of Consumer Research*, from the inception of its idea in 1970 through its first twenty years of publication (1974-1994). An unofficial history is recounted—from the perspective of *JCR*'s founding advocates, from that of its policy board, and through the reflections of its first six editors. The journal's unique mission among social-science periodicals is seen as the source of both its developmental problems and its unparalleled success.

The *Journal of Consumer Research* is the only academic serial devoted exclusively to the field of consumer behavior, broadly construed. Its preeminent status among social-sciences journals is due most apparently to the state-of-the-art papers it publishes, but that success also is attributable to the philosophy which has always underpinned its day-to-day operation, namely that consumer behavior cannot be understood fully except through interdisciplinary research. *JCR* was conceived and chartered as an outlet which welcomes varying perspectives on what constitutes consumer behavior and of how it should be investigated and that inclusive philosophy has remained intact throughout its 20-year history, guiding the choice of editors (always active researchers themselves) and the implementation of reviewing policy (uncommonly timely, rigorous, and constructive). The journal has benefited from an unbroken series of renowned and devoted editors, who with their staffs have worked in partnership with talented, caring reviewers to polish contributing authors' ideas (already the best contemporary scholarship) into a corpus that has defined consumer behavior as a recognized, independent discipline. *JCR* also has been sustained from the outset by its policy board, which selects its editors, establishes broad operating guidelines, and oversees financial matters. Since this board (*JCR*, Inc.) is composed of representatives of the journal's sponsoring associations, the preservation of multidisciplinary editorial foci has never been in jeopardy.

JCR was launched as and has remained an interdisciplinary enterprise because of a steadfast conviction that understanding from a single perspective (or a few) is inherently limited. Imagine *JCR* as a rainbow. Just as the white light of understanding is dispersed into the spectrum of colors, each perspective on con-

sumer behavior represents only a small portion of the spectrum's frequencies. We can add or subtract these portions, reflect or refract them, but white light—true understanding—requires that we perceive *all* the frequencies. We might mix the red light of economics with the green light of psychology to produce the yellow of economic psychology, for example, but even this combination will leave the rest of the spectrum (the remaining antecedents of behavior) invisible to us and our understanding of consumers will be limited. The object of our study—consumer behavior—is inherently combinatorial; that is an ontological fact and it is our challenge. We can ignore this, myopic in the comfort of our respective specialties, but only at the risk of a blurred vision of the consumer, who is not just an anthropological being, a psychological being, or a sociological being, but all these and more. The consumer thinks, feels, and does, and each of these must be seen in its naturally-occurring context. Living is more than TV commercials and brands picked off a supermarket shelf; we consume all manner of material and nonmaterial, commercial and noncommercial entities and all this must be portrayed within the panorama of everyday life. As individual researchers each of us is free to focus on a favorite perspective ("color me purple"), but as a community we must accept the collective responsibility of encouraging all perspectives and integrating them.

JCR has functioned as the nexus for this collective responsibility; it has advocated multidisciplinary perspectives (captured all the hues of the rainbow) and wherever possible fused them into interdisciplinary ones (refracted them into the prism of white light). Every *JCR* editor has suffered the policy board's pleas for diversity; every author has struggled to articulate ideas for the non-specialist reader. The result has been a catholicity rare among social-science journals and unmatched by any devoted to consumer research. It has not been easy—editors have been obliged to compensate for underrepresented perspectives and have presided reluctantly over internecine squabbles, as one or another perspective has imagined inequitable treatment—but the ideal of an interdisciplinary journal has never been abandoned. This steadfast pursuit of "the rainbow" has been the journal's greatest liability—many authors prefer to publish their best research in discipline-specific outlets (one of the colors) and an interdisciplinary journal is considerably more difficult to manage. But diversity has been the journal's greatest asset too—its contents represent the corpus of consumer research as a discipline; to the scientific community, consumer behavior *is* what *JCR* prints. This reality played a significant role in the University of Chicago Press' decision to become our publisher, beginning in 1990 with Volume 17.

BEGINNINGS

The *JCR* we recognize today grew out of a particular set of circumstances that prevailed in the United States during the 1960s, particularly as they converged on America's business schools. These forces prompted the founding of the Association for Consumer Research, and a journal "for" ACR seemed a natural concomitant (see Kernan 1995 for an elaboration). The organization and the journal in this sense being so inextricably intertwined has given rise to a persistent error that ACR owns *JCR*. It does not. ACR is a nonprofit organization registered in the state of Georgia. *JCR*, Inc. is a nonprofit corporation registered in the state of California, which is owned by its sponsoring-association members (one of which is the Association for Consumer Research) and

---

[1]The author is ACR's representative to the *JCR* Policy Board. He thanks Valerie Folkes for suggesting this commemoration, for spearheading the Board's approval of it, and for supporting its implementation in nonpareil fashion. Frank Kardes and Mita Sujan were most accommodating and their encouragement is much appreciated too. Finally, sincere gratitude is expressed to *JCR*'s editors—to Jim Bettman, Ron Frank, Rich Lutz, Kent Monroe, Brian Sternthal and, in particular, to Hal Kassarjian—for the splendid cooperation which made this commemoration possible. This paper reflects the author's own views; it should not be construed to represent the official position or any policies of the Association for Consumer Research, the *Journal of Consumer Research* or any of its editors, the *JCR* Policy Board, *JCR*, Inc., or the University of Chicago Press. All errors of fact or interpretation are the sole responsibility of the author who, with all the parties involved, wishes that Bob Ferber were here to lend this wisdom and class to this commemoration.

governed by a policy board of those members. (At this writing, *JCR*'s CEO is Valerie Folkes, who sits on the policy board as the representative of APA's Division 8, one of *JCR*'s twelve sponsoring associations.) Legal distinctions notwithstanding, however, it is difficult to dissuade most ACR people (as well as some others, it seems) from the association's proprietary claim on *JCR*. (It is ACR, not any other of the journal's sponsoring associations, which commemorates this twentieth anniversary.) Indeed, the idea for a journal devoted exclusively to consumer behavior was an integral part of the thinking that led to the formation of an association devoted exclusively to consumer behavior.

American business schools were overhauled during the early 1960s (Kernan 1995), with the result that quantitative analysis, the behavioral sciences, and theory (cf. simple description) came to be idolized. Research supplanted teaching as the de rigueur faculty activity, as the professional-school mentality gave way to one associated with the familiar arts-and-sciences model. Burgeoning enrollments were driving haphazard expansion, but messianic faculties were interested only in their developing doctoral programs and research grants. Marketing departments were being influenced by professors not, or only tangentially, trained in the discipline (e. g., Alderson, Bauer, Britt, Engel, Green, Howard, Kassarjian, Kernan, Kotler, Nicosia, Tucker) and the best marketing literature often came from "outside" sources (e. g., Banks, Ferber, Jacoby, Katona, Levy, Ramond, Rogers, Wells). Compared with the immediately-preceding period, there was a groundswell of papers being written but relatively few apposite outlets in which to publish the work. Fortunately, "scientific marketing" came along as an umbrella under which most anything nontraditional could be justified, hence published, particularly if it could be made to appear mathematical. AMA capitalized on this surfeit when it launched the *Journal of Marketing Research*, in Febrary 1964, with Bob Ferber as editor. *JMR* was an instant success, partly because it inherited a ready market of readers and contributors, but also because of Ferber's acumen as an editor. (He had an uncanny ability to tease the very best out of each author, to make every published article as potent as possible, even though many of us did not understand the metamorphosis as he shaped it.) That outlet quickly became the journal of choice for consumer researchers and a perusal of its early volumes testifies to the success we had in getting our work published there. Indeed, there were some complaints after a few years that *JMR* had become too "behaviorally oriented."

The founders of ACR were aware that *JMR* was under some pressure to resist our "takeover" when we convened in 1969 at Ohio State. It was by no means just to outflank the *JMR* problem, however, that the idea of "our own" journal was broached. That notion had been alive for some time, for reasons quite apart from *JMR* (which editorship had just passed from Ferber, who had been elected AMA President, to Ralph Day, who was hardly an enemy of behavioral research). The problem with any existing journal was twofold: control and focus. We wanted to maintain the former and direct the latter, and no established journal was likely to yield on either point. A new journal was the obvious, and only, solution. Starting one, however, was another matter and we all realized it. So the idea remained a goal (but see Engel 1994) until our next annual meeting, in 1970, at Amherst, where a committee of Joel Cohen, Jack Jacoby and Bill Wells was appointed to investigate the particulars of inaugurating what was four years hence to be called the *Journal of Consumer Research*.

Good ideas are difficult to conceal and it turns out that ACR was not alone in its perception of the need for a consumer-behavior journal. Over the next year several expressions of interest occurred (likely reflecting as many motivations) and, shortly after the ACR

conference at College Park, a group of organizers was convened in Chicago at the O'Hare Hilton (see Kassarjian 1991). This October 23 meeting was organized by Bob Ferber, since AMA now supported the idea of a new journal. Among the attendees were Jack Jacoby, nominally representing Division 23 of the American Psychological Association (which also by now had declared its interest), and Cohen, Kassarjian and Wells, officially representing ACR. The essential characteristics of the new journal were established at that meeting—its concentration on consumer behavior, broadly construed, its interdisciplinary perspective, and its governance by a policy board composed of the representatives of its sponsoring associations—although the details would require some months to clarify. The main title originally was *Research on Consumer Behavior* (changed for some tangled reasons to the *Journal of Consumer Research* before the inaugural issue), but the subtitle has always been *An Interdisciplinary Quarterly*. Ferber used his AMA clout to get that organization to handle the business end of the new operation and to pony up a $50,000 loan to cover its operating expenses. (ACR and APA Division 23 also made nominal pledges.) In due course, the initial policy board was formed, representing the American Association for Public Opinion Research (AAPOR), the American Council on Consumer Interests (ACCI), the American Economic Association (AEA), the American Home Economics Association (AHEA), AMA (Ferber, acting as chair), APA 23 (Jacoby), the American Sociological Association (ASocA), the American Statistical Association (AStatA), ACR (Wells), and The Institute of Management Sciences (TIMS). Ron Frank at the Wharton School was named Editor, and a 25-person editorial review board was appointed (including people well-known in ACR circles, such as Jim Bettman, Marty Fishbein, Monty Friedman, Paul Green, Marsh Greenberg, Jack Jacoby, Hal Kassarjian, Mike Ray, Bill Wells, Bill Wilkie, and Peter Wright). As we know, Volume 1, Number 1 was issued in June 1974, with a lead article by George Katona. The annual subscription rate for an ACR member was $12.50.

Although the AMA loan was repaid within a year and the journal has never missed publishing an issue on time, no one should get the impression that *JCR*'s success has come easily, that the road has been smooth, or that a whole series of obstacles did not threaten its very existence over the years (see Kassarjian and Bettman 1984). Any of its editors can relate a gaggle of horror stories and the policy board has winced more than occasionally. As an example, Ron Frank was obliged to confront a wavering AMA board at the eleventh hour of *JCR*'s birth—as Volume 1, Number 1 was about to go to press. With the aid of some accounting wizardry by Wayne Lemburg (AMA's executive editor), he was able to sustain the financial backing for the new journal, but only by the narrowest of margins. So dedication and luck have somehow seen us through our problems. Yet the question remains: did ACR strike a good bargain when it cast its lot with *JCR*? Was there a better option? We cannot ignore the historical backdrop out of which ACR aligned itself with *JCR*.

THE ACR/*JCR* ALLIANCE

There was little question at the time that consumer research could support, and in that sense needed, a journal. But the form this might take was anything but clear. We in ACR were the most vociferous advocates of the idea, but others claimed an interest too. And there was the additional complication of means—among the would-be sponsors, only AMA had the wherewithal to launch such a serial. ACR's realistic option, then, was to forge ahead on its own—to gamble that we might eventually produce a satisfactory journal—or to seek support from other parties interested in forming a coalition which could begin publishing in the immediate future. The first option afforded both the control and focus we wanted, but it required money that we did not have. The second one was risky (our interests might be coopted by a coalition), but it seemed workable—worth the risk, as it were. And there was another factor no one could ignore as this decision was framed. We had no assurance that AMA would not strike preemptively. Ron Frank has made the astute observation that, had AMA's leadership chosen to keep pace with developments in marketing at the time, it could easily have launched its own journals (or expanded *JMR* into a sectioned monthly, after the fashion of *JPSP*), and thereby forestalled serials such as *JCR* and *Marketing Science*. Fortunately for us, the practitioner faction of AMA (then as now) was not interested in sponsoring "yet another academic journal," and the opportunity for *JCR* remained open.

This is hindsight, however; none of the parties to *JCR*'s formation dared assume that AMA would be satisfied with a passive stake in the new journal. So when Bob Ferber outlined AMA's offer in 1971 we perceived it with a minimum of skepticism; it provided the needed start-up money, it came without an egregious demand for control, and it signaled that AMA was not interested in competing head-on with the new journal. (Some numbers help to underscore the seriousness with which an AMA threat had to be taken. As we convened in Columbus for the initial ACR gathering, *JMR* already had a circulation of some 12,000. That is to be contrasted with *JCR*'s current circulation of some 3,000.) Only time will determine whether ACR made the best choice in 1971. To suggest that aligning ourselves with several other organizations amounted to a Faustian bargain, however, is to ignore the reality within which that decision was made.

TO BE UNIQUE

JCR's founding coalition reflected more than expediency, although that certainly was a consideration. The group of sponsoring organizations served a defensive purpose for ACR, to be sure, but it also facilitated two very positive goals, neither of which was within our immediate reach were we to strike out with our own journal. Most obviously, the affiliation conferred a professional credibility on the discipline we were spearheading—if all these established organizations recognized consumer behavior, there must be something to it and to this new journal. But more importantly, each of these sponsoring organizations represented a separate discipline, a particular way of studying consumer behavior, and that idea was at the core of ACR's founding philosophy. Consumer research was not marketing research, or public-opinion research, or psychological research, or sociological research, but all of these—and more. It was not a discipline only of discovery, but of application as well—in both the private and public sectors, for the benefit of both buyers and sellers. ACR's founders welcomed all these perspectives, but we were not so naive as to assume that our ranks would or could produce the variegated approaches we knew were essential to the discipline's development. Thus the founding premise of *JCR* was very much akin to that of ACR; both entities grew out of a multidisciplinary (if not interdisciplinary) imperative. And because of this identity (at least harmony) of interests it is not clear how "an ACR journal" would differ in any substantive way from *JCR*.

The steadfast pursuit of an interdisciplinary goal has distinguished *JCR* from virtually every social-science journal, just as ACR's inclusive membership criteria (some would argue whether there are criteria) set it apart from otherwise-comparable professional organizations. Being interdisciplinary "isn't easy," as every *JCR* editor and every ACR president has discovered. Specialization (the more, the better) makes the world tidy and comfortable, whereas its opposite breeds unruliness and a collective angst. Yet there has never been a suggestion from any serious quarter of either ACR's or *JCR*'s constituency that the interdisciplinary imperative be abandoned as a hopeless ideal. Perhaps we've been pig-headed, but the pursuit of this unique identity has persisted, in spite of all the baggage it packs.

THE VENTURE COMMENCES—VOLUMES 1-3

Ron Frank was charged with the initial responsibility of making the journal's lofty ideals happen and his inaugural editorial (Frank 1974) indicates that he understood the challenge. Referring to *JCR* as an anomaly in the house of intellect, he outlined its unusual, integrative objectives and compared these to the imperatives which drive individual disciplines. He was quite aware that specialists were wont to publish their best work in their respective disciplines' journals, yet he urged researchers to address a larger audience in the interest of interdisciplinary understanding.

Easier said than done, of course, but *JCR*'s first three volumes do contain some unmistakable shards of interdisciplinary content. (Ron would suggest a less sanguine interpretation, but he is notoriously self-critical.) Those initial volumes hardly reflect the sort of interdisciplinary content found in, say, *Behavioral Science*, but they established a policy that has remained in place since—namely, that research in one discipline must be intelligible to investigators in other disciplines. So while *JCR* did not (and still does not) attract truly interdisciplinary research, it positioned itself firmly as *the* venue for multidisciplinary attention to and understanding of consumer behavior. (See Ferber 1976a for an excellent example.) Less obviously, yet perhaps more importantly, this period saw the establishment of the journal as the principal archive for consumer-behavior research—as we have come to agree, consumer research *is* what *JCR* publishes.

THE FERBER YEARS—VOLUMES 4-8

As Ron's term as editor came to a close the policy board was forced to assess the flegling journal's accomplishments. Unfortunately, three years of hoping did not prove sufficient; the interdisciplinary goal remained a long way off, in spite of a sound beginning. Accordingly, a nine-point action plan was enunciated and Bob Ferber (who had just completed a stint as editor of *JASA*) was given the editorial reins of *JCR*. This plan (see Wind 1977) sought to implement specific steps designed to move the journal toward its interdisciplinary goal. (One of them was what is now called the Ferber award, for interdisciplinary research based on a doctoral dissertation.) The board was concerned that *JCR* was too oriented toward marketing and social psychology, that other perspectives of consumer behavior were underrepresented in its pages. The new editor and the board agreed to solicit manuscripts from scholars outside these disciplines, to encourage comments on articles written in one discipline from researchers in another, to sponsor topical issues of the journal (e. g., on decision making) which were likely to attract and could profit by an interdisciplinary focus, etc. The initial experience of *JCR* had made it abundantly clear that one could not simply will that a journal be interdisciplinary; one had to do something to counteract the entrenched ethos of the social sciences.

The new editor used his considerable influence to implement the policy board's marching orders (see Ferber 1976b). This was the period during which *JCR* published several special-topic issues and in which we were treated to Bob's seductive homilies (Ferber 1977a, 1977b, 1979, 1981). His skill as an editor is legendary and need not be repeated here, except to note that *JCR*'s growth, development, its indelible position among social-science journals owes much to him. One wonders how he accomplished so much without apparent effort. One wonders how many clickety-clacks punctuated the Illinois-Central commutes between his Champaign-Urbana and Chicago offices. Whatever was the case, there is little question that *JCR* established its foothold under Bob Ferber's editorship—henceforth, the journal was here to stay.

The unthinkable happened on September 8, 1981, when Bob died unexpectedly at the age of 59. He left a vast legacy, but it would take some time for everyone to realize its dimensions (see Kassarjian 1981, 1991). At the moment, we were just paralyzed by the shock of his passing. Then it occurred to us that *JCR* needed immediate attention. Fortunately, Audrey Young (Bob's managing editor) kept a cool head throughout the turmoil and a transition team was put into place to keep the journal running until a permanent editorial office could be reestablished. Seymour Sudman stepped forward and agreed to edit the remaining two issues of Volume 8, which went to press essentially on time. He carried out this responsibility with characteristic grace and effectiveness, without the remotest concern for recognition or thanks. But that is Seymour, whose many contributions to *JCR* have gone largely unheralded over the years. Meanwhile, the policy board was busy picking up the pieces, getting the journal back to "normal." Ferber's successor was to be a team—Hal Kassarjian and Jim Bettman—effective January 1, 1982.

THE UCLA CONNECTION—VOLUMES 9-14

The *JCR* inherited by Hal and Jim was an established journal, but it arrived at its new home in Los Angeles with many loose ends. There was the ordinary confusion that accompanies any editorial transition, but now there was much more. This was no ordinary transition. It had not been planned. In a flash, the journal had lost its famous helmsman. Bob Ferber was a hard act to follow under the best of circumstances and these were hardly the best. There was concern that public confidence in *JCR* might erode. Kassarjian and Bettman were highly-respected researchers, but could they sustain the journal at the level Bob had achieved for it? This was a scary juncture in the life of *JCR*.

Happily, the fears were unfounded. With characteristic aplomb (and endless hours of ad hoc learning), Hal and Jim set about the task of calming *JCR*'s many constituencies. (Bettman's imminent move across the country to the Fuqua School was accommodated alongside all the other start-up details.) Quietly, but firmly, these co-editors trotted out administrative and leadership talents that few of us imagined they possessed. More reviewers were enlisted and authors were figuratively caressed as the volume of submitted papers increased dramatically. *JCR* was not only to be safe in its new hands, it was to grow. We had survived the trauma of Bob's loss. The journal was moving forward in a post-Ferber era.

The Kassarjian-Bettman team set out to make *JCR* still better, yet not to forego its interdisciplinary goal. Toward this end, they initiated many changes—the appointment of seven advisory editors, a great expansion of the editorial board, and a double-blind manuscript-review process—all of which were announced in the first issue under their watch (see Kassarjian and Bettman 1982). With the exception of an advisory-editor scheme (abandoned by 1985), these new mechanisms worked well (see Kassarjian and Bettman 1988) and the increasingly large flow of manuscripts received prompt and thorough reviews. (It was during the UCLA period that *JCR*'s manuscript submission totals first crossed the 200-per-year level. Subsequent editors have been pleased to maintain that stability.) This was also the period during which the interpretivist (aka postmodern) paradigm began to challenge the dominant positivist thinking in *JCR* circles, and it would be remiss to ignore the risk assumed by Hal and Jim as they encouraged every plausible attempt by submitting authors to breathe fresh air into the discipline. The pluralism we now take for granted was hotly contested during those years and it is fortunate that the journal was being run by editors with an eye to the future, yet an ear to the ground. These were heady times; we were feeling our oats, as it were, convinced that the discipline was robust enough to sustain internecine squabbles.

Overall, the Kassarjian-Bettman period in the journal's history was marked by a good deal of growth—issues were becoming thicker and their contents reflected increasing diversity. We were not seeing the sort of interdisciplinary work the founders had envisioned (contents then, as now, were driven from the bottom up, by submissions), but authorial voices were not in unison either. We were not without problems (and Hal and Jim were by now exhausted), but the outlook for the discipline and the journal was decidedly optimistic. The immediate problem confronting Rich Lutz, as he assumed the editorship in 1988, was to build on these strengths and, as always, to move us a bit more toward that evasive interdisciplinary goal.

COMING OF AGE IN GAINESVILLE—VOLUMES 15-17

If *JCR* began under Ron Frank, established its foothold under Bob Ferber, and stabilized under Hal Kassarjian and Jim Bettman, it came of age under the editorship of Rich Lutz at the University of Florida, beginning in 1988. In part, Rich (as have all the journal's editors) benefited from the gains of his predecessors, which needed merely to be consolidated. Beyond that, however, he initiated several things that mark the *JCR* we recognize today. With characteristic vigor, Rich outlined many of these in an editorial at the outset of his watch (Lutz 1988)—an expanded editorial board (particularly to include postpositivist expertise), the reinstitution of an advisory-editor system, and the now-famous statement of editorial philosophy (complete with a revised style sheet). All these changes were designed to ensure *JCR*'s impact on the discipline, particularly its growing position as the interdisciplinary repository of consumer-behavior research, and by virtually any standard they proved very (some would suggest wildly) effective. "Those amazing *JCR* reviews" can be traced to this period simply because Rich rode such close herd on the editorial board (whose best were now being recognized with annual awards), on the ad hoc reviewers and, most of all, on himself. We were publishing more pages and these reflected increasing diversity. (On the latter point, it is reasonable to characterize this period as the inflection during which "postmodern" perspectives shed their weird-science connotation within *JCR* circles. Lutz would not tolerate intellectual arrogance; he insisted on paradigmatic diversity.) The journal was approaching the point where it had no real competition for first place among consumer-behavior scholars and it was beginning to show up respectably in citation indices. None of this satisfied Rich's never-enough standards, of course (see Lutz 1991), but a fair reading of this period would conclude that it was virtually all positive.

This was also the period during which *JCR* came of age in a business-operations sense. For some years it had been clear that our editors and their staffs were spending altogether too much time on non-editorial, yet essential, matters. Good editors may have no taste or talent for things such as subscription fulfillment and printing contracts, yet these matters require careful attention if a journal is to survive, let alone prosper, and they become more complicated with growth. Although Keith Hunt had served us well during a previous period of near chaos, it was becoming clear that even he could no longer manage everything our large operation required.

Perversely, however, our problems constituted a bargaining strength, as commercial publishers began to court us. The highly successful *JCR* had become a valuable asset, a takeover target of sorts. Over the ensuing months a flurry of negotiating with several publishers occurred, with the result that we struck an agreement with the University of Chicago Press, which began publishing *JCR* with Volume 17, in June, 1990. Essentially, this agreement (since renewed) calls for UCP to fund the operating costs of the journal in return for a share of any profits. *JCR* is guaranteed a percentage of subscription revenue, controls subscription rates, and is freed from all responsibility except that of editorial content. (Which is to say it benefits from the long-established facilities and reputation of UCP.) The arrangement has unshackled our editorial office from some onerous responsibilities (placing those in highly-experienced hands) and thereby cleared the desk, properly, for matters of editorial policy. In addition, the contract has provided a degree of financial stability to the journal, which would be unavailable to us were we to have remained the sole venture capitalist. Hence Rich Lutz should be recognized not only for the editorial achievements accrued during his stint but also for bringing *JCR* into "the big time" in a business sense.

On that score, it would be remiss if we failed to acknowledge the singular effort of Michelle Miller Harmon who, in addition to her other *JCR* duties, spearheaded the initial negotiating with UCP, in all its laborious detail. (As policy-board president during that period, this writer observed her skill and dedication firsthand.) We take nothing away from Rich when we affirm that *JCR*'s deal with UCP would not be so swell were it not for Michelle's incredible enthusiasm and persistence. She is an extraordinary professional, yet another in the long line of staff people who have refused to regard their *JCR* responsibilities as merely a job. As we concluded Volume 17, then, the journal was something of a high-flying enterprise. It had developed on a variety of fronts and these gains needed to be consolidated. Its next editor would need a steady hand. Since no one manifests this quality better than Kent Monroe, he was appointed by the policy board.

NUDGING DIVERSITY AMIDST ABUNDANCE— VOLUMES 18-20

More than any of his predecessors, Kent Monroe inherited a successful *JCR* in 1991. Lest it be inferred that he was handed a piece of cake, however, we should recognize that his assignment was fraught with downside risk—we had a lot to lose were the journal to be mismanaged. Based on his presentation to the policy board in 1989 (see Monroe 1990, 1991), it was apparent that Kent realized this. Moreover, his suggested strategy of "nudging *JCR* along" seemed just the delicate hand required for the time. He would need extraordinary patience because, in addition to the usual turmoil accompanying the editorial-office transition (Gainesville to Blacksburg), the business-operations transition to the University of Chicago Press had yet to be completed. That would seem to be a very full plate, yet still another complication intervened as he decided to move to the University of Illinois only months after his editorial stint began. (We began to wonder about the possibility of a Bettman bacterium.)

Kent was very sensitive to *JCR*'s original interdisciplinary objective and to the limited success experienced in attaining it. After the sort of careful analysis one associates with him, he concluded that the journal was very (too?) full of empiricism, bred largely out of psychological theory. We were not publishing many review papers and, in general, there was little that could be called

theory development. Our ideas and methodologies were essentially borrowed ones and we were not really defining, describing, or explaining consumer behavior as an entity unto itself. Too many of us were taking an expedient, "cherry-picking" approach to research, rather than grounding our work in its proper (but developmentally difficult) perspective. Kent sought to correct all this with several gentle moves, using some principles of signaling theory. He expanded the editorial board, particularly to include more female scholars and those constituencies historically underrepresented. He commissioned think pieces by some of our senior scholars (e. g., Wells 1993) in an effort to sensitize everyone to our heritage and legacy. And he encouraged papers (both theoretical and applications-oriented) whose conceptual underpinnings differed from the usual. All these moves were in the cause of promoting greater diversity, with the hope that, ultimately, they would encourage interdisciplinary thinking.

That goal was not realized (see Monroe 1993a, 1993b), but neither was it thwarted. *JCR* reached new heights of pluralism under Kent's watch and it continued to grow—the quarterly issues expanded to whatever size necessary to accommodate all the acceptable manuscripts (with some spillover for his successor). Kent would be the first to admit to an unfulfilled agenda (see Monroe 1994), but there can be no question that he accomplished all that was expected of him and more. The *JCR* he passed on had all the momentum of and more diversity than the journal he inherited. As Brian Sternthal prepared to chart a course for the future, therefore, any question of the journal's credibility was moot. The new editor's attention, perhaps for the first time in *JCR*'s short history, could focus on issues at the forefront of consumer research.

CHARTING *JCR*'S COURSE—VOLUMES 21ff.

Although it would be rash to characterize *JCR*'s first twenty years as an unqualified success, it is fair to say that most academic journals envy our position. As Brian Sternthal took the helm of *JCR* in 1994, he had the luxury of options largely unknown to his predecessors. Brian's problem is not a struggle to achieve respectability, but the slippery challenge of staying on top, of keeping intact *JCR*'s preeminent position among social-science journals, of satisfying the strict expectations associated with a leader. Since he deals from a position of strength he can afford to take certain chances, but a poor choice—because we are so conspicuous in the research community—can bear severe consequences.

Brian realizes all this, and has been astute enough to surround himself with a cadre of associate editors with whom he can pool his judgment. The collective wisdom of Brian, Joe Alba, John Lynch, Bob Meyer, Marsha Richins, Debbie Roedder John, John Sherry, and Russ Winer is not likely to be led astray, so we should not fear being run aground by *JCR*'s new crew. Only time will tell where and how far we will be taken, of course, but it is already clear that they plan to run a tight ship (see Sternthal 1994). A smart guess would be to expect diversity, a genuine concern for conceptual and methodological rigor, and no tolerance for indolence in any form— things *JCR* has always stood for, only more so, since the whole world now has a spyglass trained on us. Will this mean impossible acceptance standards for contributing authors? Tougher ones, to be sure; but certainly not anything beyond our potential. And that, after all, is what the journal has always sought to squeeze out of each one of us.

LOOKING BACK—TO THE FUTURE

JCR's unarguable success over these twenty years, like that of any journal, is due most palpably to the papers it has published. Of course those state-of-the-art pieces would not have appeared under its imprint had not their authors been convinced that the journal was the most suitable and prestigious outlet for their work. That so many consumer reaearchers have regarded *JCR* as *the* place to publish might be dismissed as luck or attributed to matters of happy circumstance (being in the right place at the right time), but it more likely reflects how the journal has operated. Specifically, a tripartite harmony of editors (and their staffs), the editorial board, and the policy board has always resonated a welcome theme to contributors—*JCR* welcomes your work (even if it is "different"), our review process is aimed at heightening its impact and, if it meets our standards, it will be published without unreasonable delay—and there is no reason to suppose that this chant will not continue into the forseeable future. Achieving this harmony has not been easy and there is nothing automatic about maintaining it. Since it has been the key to *JCR*'s success, however, it would be foolish to change things—we should look to the journal's past to anticipate its future.

A contour of *JCR*'s contents has been the subject of several analyses (see Cote, Leong and Cote 1991, Hoffman and Holbrook 1993, Leong 1989, Zinkhan, Roth and Saxton 1992). While there are many ways to interpret these findings, a fair conclusion would be that the journal cites, more than it is cited by, comparable social-science serials. That *JCR* has a surplus of such outdegree likely reflects its historical subject-concentration on marketing and psychology. It has published comparatively few papers of the sort most likely to be cited by cognate disciplines (e. g., integrative reviews, novel methodologies, unique conceptualizations) and this relative dearth—along with "the interdisciplinary tightrope"—has been a source of concern for many years. (Everyone recognizes the situation and its antecedents. The problem, notwithstanding some attenuation in recent years, is what to *do* about it.) Recognizing the inherent limitations in such a tack, we have traditionally dumped this imbalance in the already-overloaded lap of *JCR*'s editors, whom we expect to be superhuman.

JCR's Editors—Only the Best Need Apply

Since *JCR*'s editor plays such a pivotal role in the journal's well-being, a great deal of care has marked the editor-selection process. Editors are appointed for three-year terms, beginning with the calendar year, but their editorial responsibility begins with the volume year (in June). For example, Brian Sternthal's first issue was Volume 21, Number 1 (June 1994), even though his term of office dates from January 1, 1994. Choosing a new editor takes almost two years' lead time. (The search which culminated in Brian's selection began in the Spring of 1992; he was appointed on December 13 of that year and, with Kent, spent all of 1993 effecting an orderly, Champaign-Urbana-to-Evanston transition.) The policy board advertises the position widely and consults with *JCR*'s editorial board. The received applications are evaluated and a few (usually three) finalist-candidates are invited to prepare presentations for the board. Each finalist submits an extensive written document, which the board studies for some weeks and uses as the basis for discussion when each finalist appears personally before the board. The presentations afford candidates the opportunity to demonstrate their knowledge of *JCR*, as well as their aptitude for achieving its goals. (Until recently, each candidate also was required to bring institutional support to the office, but that issue is no longer a significant consideration.) The would-be editor must be smart, but not arrogant. S/he (thus far, every editor has been "he") must have a respectable bibliography, for reasons of credibility and to assure empathy for contributing authors' concerns. Knowledge of the discipline—past, present, and likely future—is essential,

otherwise there is little to guide the selection of acceptable manuscripts. An editor must have interpersonal skills, because most of what s/he must tell people is bad news. Perhaps most of all, however, a successful editor must *want* the job and be willing to give it the enormous time and energy it requires. (It is a rule—every editor's personal life and private ambitions suffer during the term of office.)

Given these stringent criteria, it is a wonder that *JCR* has been able to corral such an unbroken string of wise and dedicated editors. We must assume that these people, apart from their obvious qualities, are researchers who care not only about their own work, but also about the discipline, per se, and who have perceived the latter concern as a responsibility. If there is such a thing as professional noblesse oblige, all *JCR*'s editors have demonstrated it and we all have benefited. For their part, each of our editors would insist that, while a contribution has been made, much also has been received. Indeed, the most consistent theme shared by former editors is how much they learned, how much they grew as a consequence of editing *JCR*. Every one of them experienced some disappointment and frustration but, in retrospect, these pale in comparison with the accrued personal development. All of them allow that they did not publish as broad a variety of papers as they would have liked and that they never enjoyed the luxury of a top-down editorial strategy, but each of them just as quickly admits how his understanding of and appreciation for the discipline grew as a result of the editorship experience.

The Editorial Review Process—*JCR*'s Guiding Light

A similar chorus of hosannas is due *JCR*'s editorial review board which, over the past twenty years, has been an exemplar of expertise, efficiency, and civility. (If there is a more constructive, more dedicated set of reviewers, this writer would like to be introduced to them.) The exceptional thing about a *JCR* review is not that it is thorough, not that it is timely, not that it is professionally helpful, or not that it is written in a constructive fashion, but that it is all of these. The quality of *JCR* reviews is legendary, as are the skill and dedication of those responsible for them. None of this is by chance; reviewers are selected with great care, they are widely experienced, and each agrees to abide by *JCR*'s editorial philosophy. Submitting authors therefore do not encounter a bunch of hired guns, eager to find every conceivable error in a manuscript, relishing the prospect of embarrassing yet another would-be researcher. Rather, manuscripts are treated with respect and, when possible, improved cooperatively to the point where they satisfy *JCR*'s acceptance standards. Although most manuscripts do not have the potential to meet these standards (over the years, about 85 percent of all submissions have been rejected), their authors are not dismissed as incompetent. Instead, the good in each paper is highlighted and suggestions are made for developing it.

This policy places a significant burden on our reviewers and editors (truly spectacular papers are the easiest to review), but it has remained in place for some time. As a consequence, a number of papers is published every year in other journals, based on what their authors learned in the process of being rejected by *JCR*. This is good human relations, of course, but it also has proved to be smart editorial policy—many successful *JCR* contributors learned how to do and present acceptable work as a result of previous, unsuccessful attempts. No author likes rejection letters, but one from *JCR* always manages to convey a tone of hope, the sense that one should not be discouraged, a challenge to persevere. Because these rejections are always devoid of enmity, they commonly are received—after the initial shock—in the constructive spirit in which they are sent. More than one researcher's career has been salvaged by this policy and the discipline has benefited as a consequence. All this because our ad hoc reviewers, our editorial board, and our editors have regarded manuscript assessment as an act of stewardship, a process where the scarce resource of ideas must be handled with utmost care. Surely mistakes have been made, but *JCR* has not come by its enviable reputation among authors because it treats them badly. Perhaps John Sherry best captures the spirit of it all when he asserts *JCR*'s reviewing process to be an integral part of the gift economy that sustains our academic enterprise.

The Policy Board—*JCR*'s Invisible Hand

The policy board is the remaining element that contributes to *JCR*'s successful operation. Few people understand what this "board of directors" actually does, but its functions impinge directly on how and how well the journal satisfies its authors and audience. Most obviously, this board selects *JCR*'s editors. It also promulgates broad editorial policy. Beyond diversity and the interdisciplinary imperative, however, what the journal publishes is left to the discretion of the editor; the board has never been interested in micromanagement. Editors serve at the pleasure of the board and it has questioned them frequently, but such queries are more in the nature of explanations than confrontations. In turn, editors often have asked the board for counsel on problems they encounter or ideas they are considering. The board thinks of the editor as the journal's chief operating officer—someone to be selected with great care, to be supported, but to be left free to do the job, unencumbered by a group of doting overseers.

Board members are appointed by their respective organizations (*JCR*'s sponsoring associations), typically for three-year terms. Presently, the board consists of twelve members—one each for the original ten sponsors (less ACCI, which dropped its affiliation, but which was replaced by ICA) plus two others, representing APA Division 8 and AAA, which associations since have become sponsors. (At this writing, three other associations have petitioned for sponsorship.) These members, like *JCR*'s editors, serve without remuneration or apparent perquisites. (They pay the same subscription rates, receive their copies of the journal in the same mail, and are otherwise treated identically to other *JCR* subscribers. As authors, they receive the same rejection letters as everyone else.)

From the perspective of ACR, the board's diversity is both good and bad. Good because it naturally brings a wide range of perspective to the table, and that keeps *JCR* on its toes, so to speak. But bad because ACR gets just one of twelve votes when ballots are cast. Before anyone gets the impression that ACR's (or any other sponsor's) interests have been sacrificed on an altar of diversity, however, it is instructive to look at an issue of the journal to see just how alien these eleven votes are likely to be. The majority of policy board members are not strangers to ACR and they don't vote as enemies. Indeed, the board has a tradition of doing what is best for *JCR* and, since its and ACR's interests have always been virtually identical, we have been well served. (Having observed board behavior for some years, it is not clear to this writer how an all-ACR board might have acted differently.) One should not get the impression from any of this that the board has no internal problems, however. Any group of twelve will find some things on which disagreement is inevitable. But in fairness, nothing in this writer's recollection has ever been such a bone of contention that the journal suffered as a consequence of gridlock. The board's most difficult problem over the years has been the dedication (more explicitly, lack of it) of some very few of its members. To ACR people, this may seem strange. After all, the board's principal meeting is held in conjunction with the annual ACR conference. What seems so convenient to us, however, is not so to those very few board members who are not active in ACR. Their attendance represents a real chore. Although we have taken several steps to alleviate this problem, it is not yet resolved and we continue to wrestle with it.

Subscription rates are a board decision; so was the agreement with the University of Chicago Press. And so is a myriad of details that affects the journal's solvency and liquidity. We are a not-for-profit organization with a conservative bent. By almost any reasonable comparison, *JCR*'s subscription rates are low. That is by design. Our financial position is very solid—to the point where we felt it prudent to place our investments in the hands of a longstanding financial-management house. That is boring stuff until one realizes that, because of the board's careful policies, *JCR*'s editors have been free to publish *all* the acceptable papers they get. (Those fat issues are *very* expensive.) Similarly, we have been confronting the dawn of electronic publishing. Everyone comments when the appearance of the journal changes, but we must consider the possibility that journals as we know them may soon become an anachronism. It is already easier and cheaper to retrieve an article through a computer bulletin board than to buy a reprint. The first twenty of *JCR*'s volumes take up some 2,400 cubic inches of shelf space (more if they are bound), yet these contents would fit easily on a single 5-inch CD/ROM—which can be indexed better and doesn't fall prey to the razor blades of selfish library patrons.

Finally, the board is just as aware as everyone else that *JCR* is not as user-friendly as it might be, particularly to people whose jobs require the *use* of consumer research. Toward this end, we are examining ways by which we might give practitioners better access to the journal's contents. Around most commercial research departments, for example, *JCR* is called a top-of-the-shelf journal—not for its prestige but for where it is housed—and it would help our cause if we deciphered some of the journal's arcana for such would-be users. (Talking to ourselves may be fun, but it isn't the only way to develop the discipline.) Overall, the policy board is continuing the long tradition of supporting the public aspects of *JCR*. That most people do not "see" the board's actions does not matter, so long as the consequences are apparent. Like *JCR*'s editors and reviewers, the policy board has a history of dedication to the journal's goals and well-being. Indeed, for those wont to diminish the board's significance, it is well to remember that it came first.

WHITHER *JCR*?

Although this commemoration has been written from an ACR perspective, anyone remotely familiar with *JCR* would conclude that—in spite of all its successes—it has thus far failed to achieve its goal of being a truly interdisciplinary journal. Its contents have been very lopsided in favor of experimentation, inspired by psychology and housed in a marketing-like context. We have seen very few conceptual or methodological breakthroughs and we still are waiting for the long-sought theory of consumer behavior—the one not pieced together from other disciplines. We have rarely paused sufficiently to summarize what we do know about various facets of consumer behavior and to integrate this information. It is as though we haven't had a master plan for accumulating a corpus of knowledge, much less one for applying it to the world's problems. Among our ranks we have some perfectly brilliant thinkers; yet even they seem to have been more concerned with specialized research than with the orderly development of disciplinary understanding. Distressing. Frustrating.

Before we leap to weary forecasts that *JCR* and the discipline are doomed to a desultory future, it is useful to consider these problems in perspective. It is altogether possible that our close proximity to these disappointments jades our perception of them.

We have become our worst critics. Our impatience has clouded our ability to judge progress objectively. *JCR* has existed for twenty years and we fret that its every issue is not replete with the quantum-leap chapters of consumer behavior's history. In our frustration, we fail to recognize two critical things. First, the horizon involved is but a speck of time; no discipline evolves, much less matures, in so few years. Second, no epic unfolds recursively; there are always false starts, excessive considerations of trivialities, and ontological bickerings. So instead of flagellating ourselves over the paltry accomplishments of the past, we should focus on the future—on our ability to recognize the myriad facets of the consumer-behavior mosaic and to weave them into the epic story everyone will understand. That raincheck is what all *JCR*'s editors have issued to us. That promissory note is what influences their behavior—how they evaluate submitted papers, why they commission invited ones, and when they promulgate those oh-so-carefully-worded editorials. Their job is to accumulate all the pieces of the story that one day (but not prematurely) will be composed. To belabor the cliche, they truly must be able to see the forest for the trees.

Like all journals, *JCR* has been a product of its time. It has reflected the currents within consumer research, even as it has given shape to them. It captured a dramatic upheaval and legitimized it, proclaiming an editorial mandate for the emerging discipline of consumer behavior. It provided a forum for this scholary tradition, giving voice to new ideas and approaches, but never priveleging one perspective over others. Ontological roots have been planted and a corpus of knowledge has emerged. But we delude ourselves if we regard all this as anything more than a beginning. We are still in a groping stage, trying to sort the wheat from the chaff and struggling to overcome our insular way of thinking (that unwritten rhetorical calculus which we deny publically, but which conspires against fresh, integrative contemplation). Most of us are adept at (and happier) doing studies within the inner sanctum of a specialty, no matter how arcane, how tortured the connection with sensible theory, or how removed the apposition to consumers' everyday lives. Not to worry, however, for the safety of such cocoons is under increasing threat. With every passing day, our review process insists—beyond facts stated articulately—that *JCR* papers make a significant contribution, that they add something worthwhile to the corpus of consumer-behavior literature. But this ratcheting takes time; we must be patient while it takes effect. We cannot expect *JCR* miraculously to transcend the era of which it is but a product.

As we consider the development of consumer behavior, it seems reasonable that (like all disciplines) it should follow the familiar Hegelian pattern of thesis-antithesis-synthesis. Thus far, *JCR*'s pages have been skewed toward thesis, with some incidence of antithesis. All this has been in the cause of assembling the facets of the consumer-behavior mosaic, while analyzing them for authenticity. There have been few attempts actually to construct the mosaic for the sensible reason that neither its components nor their pattern of fit is sufficently clear. Eventually that blueprint will be revealed but, until it is, we must remain watchful.

On the occasion of *JCR*'s tenth anniversary, its editors lamented the mix of papers that had been published, expressing a particular concern for the specialized direction in which the journal then seemed to be headed (see Kassarjian and Bettman 1984). Although they did not use the term, Hal and Jim were distressed that *JCR* had been able to feature so little synthesis over the course of ten volumes. While we can identify with their chagrin, it seems unwarranted historically—there was very little *to* synthesize. Indeed the early "integrative" papers in *JCR* and the molar problems they addressed reflect more an agenda for the discipline and journal than a synthesis of consumer-behavior knowledge. That agenda is

what attracted so many researchers and it has never been abandoned although, to the consternation of everyone, we seem to be taking forever getting through it. The synthesis (or syntheses) will happen in due course, but we must not let impetuosity distract or dissuade us from our original goal. No one has ever demonstrated (even claimed) that an interdisciplinary approach to consumer behavior is wrong-headed. Difficult, to be sure, but not stupid. We have had many opportunities over the years to abandon that goal, to take an easier path. Yet we have never succumbed to the temptation. Perhaps that is because the journal was founded on a note of optimism and we have continued tilting at windmills. Call us incorrigible romantics, but we believe in happy endings. So while our critics chuckle, we will stay busy—framing *JCR*'s multidisciplinary rainbow, focusing its interdisciplinary light.

REFERENCES

Cote, Joseph A., Siew Meng Leong and Jane Cote (1991), "Assessing the Influence of the *Journal of Consumer Research*: A Citation Analysis," *Journal of Consumer Research*, 18 (December), 402-410.

Engel, James F. (1994), "ACR's 25th Anniversary—How It All Began," *ACR Newsletter*, 25 (June), 3-5.

Ferber, Robert F. (1976a), "Guest Editor's Introduction," *Journal of Consumer Research*, 2 (March), vi-vii.

_____ (1976b), "Statement of Objectives and Future Goals of JCR," *Journal of Consumer Research*, 3 (September), vi.

_____ (1977a), "Research by Convenience," *Journal of Consumer Research*, 4 (June), 57-58.

_____ (1977b), "Can Consumer Research be Interdisciplinary?," *Journal of Consumer Research*, 4 (December), 189-192.

_____ (1979), "How Not to Write a Prize-Winning Article," *Journal of Consumer Research*, 5 (March), 303-305.

_____ (1981), "Where Two Heads Are Better Than One," *Journal of Consumer Research*, 7 (March), 425-426.

Frank, Ronald E. (1974), "*The Journal of Consumer Research*: An Introduction," *Journal of Consumer Research*, 1 (June), iv-v.

Hoffman, Donna L. and Morris B. Holbrook (1993), "The Intellectual Structure of Consumer Research: A Bibliometric Study of Author Cocitations in the First 15 Years of the *Journal of Consumer Research*, *Journal of Consumer Research*, 19 (March), 505-517.

Kassarjian, Harold H. (1981), "In Memoriam," *Journal of Consumer Research*, 8 (December), vi-viii.

_____ (1991), "Robert Ferber and the Robert Ferber Award," *Journal of Consumer Research*, 18 (June), v-viii.

_____ and James R. Bettman (1982), "Editorial," *Journal of Consumer Research*, 9 (June), 1-3.

_____ and _____ (1984), "Tenth Anniversary Editorial," *Journal of Consumer Research*, 10 (March), iii-iv.

_____ and _____ (1988), "Editorial," *Journal of Consumer Research*. 14 (March), vi.

Kernan, Jerome B. (1995), "Declaring A Discipline: Reflections on ACR's Silver Anniversary," this volume.

Leong, Siew Meng (1989), "A Citation Analysis of the *Journal of Consumer Research*," *Journal of Consumer Research*, 15 (March), 492-497.

Lutz, Richard J. (1988), "Editorial," *Journal of Consumer Research*, 15 (June), ii-iii.

_____ (1991), "Editorial, "*Journal of Consumer Research*, 17 (March), vii-xiii.

Monroe, Kent B. (1990), "From the Editor-Elect," *Journal of Consumer Research*, 16 (March), vii-viii.

_____ (1991), "Editorial," *Journal of Consumer Research*, 18 (June), iii-iv.

_____ (1993a), "Editorial," *Journal of Consumer Research*, 19 (March), v.

_____ (1993b), "Editorial," *Journal of Consumer Research*, 20 (December), iii-v.

_____ (1994), "Editorial," *Journal of Consumer Research*, 20 (March), v-viii.

Sternthal, Brian (1994), "Editorial," *Journal of Consumer Research*, 21 (June), iii-v.

Wells, William D. (1993), "Discovery-Oriented Consumer Research," *Journal of Consumer Research*, 19 (March), 489-504.

Wind, Jerry (1977), "New Directions for *JCR*," *Journal of Consumer Research*, 4 (June), 59-60.

Zinkhan, George, M., Martin S. Roth and Mary Jane Saxton (1992), "Knowledge Development and Scientific Status in Consumer-Behavior Research: A Social Exchange Perspective," *Journal of Consumer Research*, 19 (September), 282-291.

Special Session Summary
Experiments with Social Networks and Social Boundaries

Jonathan Frenzen, University of Chicago

The goal of this session was to demonstrate how social network studies can be usefully conducted *in vivo*—within the naturalistic context of social networks and *in vitro*—within the controlled environment of the laboratory. The three speakers, Dawn Iacobucci, John Pantzalis, and Jonathan Frenzen, offered three approaches.

Dawn Iacobucci described a statistical method for comparing experimental data gathered from separate social networks formed experimentally or naturalistically. Prior to the publication of this work (Iacobucci and Hopkins 1994) researchers were limited to the comparison of one network to hypothesized population parameters (analogous to a one-sample t-test), or the comparison of multiple relational structures (e.g. frequency of contact vs. tie strength) measured on the same group of actors (analogous to a correlation coefficient). The new techniques permit researchers to compare network structures that arise in response, for example, to different incentives used in coalition experiments among different sets of actors (analogous to two sample t-tests or between-subject analyses of variance). Coalition data reported in Komorita and Tumonis (1980) were used to demonstrate the techniques.

Jonathan Frenzen described a new technique for testing an extension of Granovetter's "Strength of Weak Ties" theory proposed in Frenzen and Nakamoto 1993. The technique uses real social networks as "living laboratories". Exchange objects are introduced into a network to generate a real-time trace as the exchange objects flowed through two different social networks. One network was a sorority (n=55) at a Southwestern university and the second contained the members of an executive training program (n=77) at a Midwestern university. Frenzen showed how the experiments conducted within these real networks supported the hypotheses posed in the 1993 article. Frenzen briefly considered the advantages of quasi-experiments conducted in the context of real social networks, and proposed several applications of the network tracing techniques developed in the studies to marketing problems.

John Pantzalis proposed a theory and described an experiment for studying the simultaneous diffusion of exclusive brands across social class boundaries. Here the groups under study were defined demographically rather than relationally. Pantzalis looked at two social groups, a high income group H and a lower income group L for which H functions as an aspirational group. He claimed, following Veblen, that brand ownership restricted by high prices to the aspiration group H creates exclusivity and turns the brand into a status symbol. As the brand is adopted by H it becomes a symbol of membership in H and increases its desirability among members of L. However, as L begins to adopt the brand, its exclusivity declines, the brand loses its ability to differentiate L and H, and loses its attraction to H. Pantzalis hypothesized the interdependence of demand between H and L was a function of the social distance between the two groups. He described an experiment designed to test his hypotheses and proposed several approaches to testing the hypotheses in a naturalistic setting.

REFERENCES

Iacobucci, Dawn and Nigel Hopkins (1994), "Detection of Experimental Effects in Social Network Analysis," *Social Networks*, v16, 1, January, p1-42.

Frenzen, Jonathan and Kent Nakamoto (1993), "Structure, Cooperation, and the Flow of Market Information," *Journal of Consumer Research*, 20 (December), p 360-375.

Komorita, S. and T. Tumonis (1980), "Extensions and Tests of Some Descriptive Theories of Coalition Formation," *Journal of Personality and Social Psychology* 39 (3), 421-431.

Adolescent Compulsive Consumption: Issues in Motivation, Identification and Prevention

Joan Scattone, New York University
Durairaj Maheswaran, New York University

Compulsive consumption involves behaviors that are very difficult to control through reason and willpower and are often associated with negative consequences (Hirschman 1992). Studies have reported that there has been a considerable increase in drug, alcohol and cigarette consumption during the last decade and more important, such consumption is growing among adolescents. For example, a recent survey conducted by the Center for Disease Control found that smoking is on the increase among high school and college students whereas it has remained stagnant among the older segments of the population. In addition, a study of 212,802 students in 1,588 schools and 34 states revealed that the use of drugs increased during the 1991-92 school year after a three year plateau (PRIDE 1992). Fifty-six percent of high school students and thirty percent of students in grades 6-8 reported using at least one of the three primary "gateway" drugs: liquor, beer, or marijuana. These figures highlight the continuing importance of research intended to enhance our understanding of the factors that influence the consumption of illicit substances by young people.

In order to effectively combat the prevalence of such behaviors and design effective communication strategies and successful intervention programs, it is important to understand the *whys* of such behaviors. While some consumer research has addressed the importance of such addictive consumption among adults (Hirschman 1992), relatively little systematic empirical research has addressed the issues related to compulsive consumption among adolescents (Rose, Bearden and Teel 1992). The objectives of this special session were threefold. First it attempted to create awareness among consumer researchers of this important social issue by sharing three relevant papers in a discussion format. Second, it examined the underlying psychological processes, motivations and factors that influence adolescent compulsive consumption. Finally, implications for prevention strategies (e.g. public service advertising) based on the findings of these studies were discussed.

The first presentation, "Factors Influencing Adolescent Drug Use: An Attributional Analysis" by F. Robert Shoaf, Joan Scattone, Durairaj Maheswaran and Maureen Morrin, examined the impact of gender and education on conforming behavior using an attribution theory framework. In general, the study confirmed the results of Rose et.al. (1992) relating attributional thought, particularly that of an external nature, to a decline in intentions to conform with a group's marijuana use. Gender-based differences were found in intentions to conform and the nature (i.e. locus) of attributional thought. Females' weaker intentions to conform were viewed partly as a function of their tendency to be less likely to make internal attributions and more likely to make external attributions for their friends' drug use than males. However, gender based differences persisted only through high school and undergraduate levels of education. At the graduate level, males and females displayed no differences in their intentions to conform or the nature of their attributional thought. Both genders displayed an increasing tendency to make internal attributions and a decreasing tendency to make external attributions as education increased.

The second presentation, "Conformity in Illicit Consumption: the Effects of Attitude, Attribution and Group Attractiveness", by Randall Rose, William Bearden and Kenneth Manning further examined the relationship between attributions and conformity. While the association between attributional thinking and conformity intentions was found to be robust in the Rose et al. (1992)

studies, the mechanisms underlying the observed relationships had not been studied. The current research provided information regarding why a program based on introducing biases toward external attributions for illicit consumption may work to reduce conformity. This is a meaningful contribution because it has been noted elsewhere that intervention programs tend to be complex and multifaceted. Consequently, it is not always clear what components of a given program are effective or ineffective in reducing illicit consumption (Beisecker 1991). Therefore, in order to design more efficient and effective intervention programs, research is needed that addresses fundamental process issues. This presentation described three studies designed to identify the processes underlying the associations between attributions and conformity observed in prior research. Results from Study 1 indicated that attitude toward marijuana use and reported marijuana usage affect the explanations made to account for a peer group's illicit consumption. In Studies 2 and 3, support was obtained for group attractiveness as a mediator of the effects of external attributions on conformity intentions. The implications of these findings for theory, insights regarding intervention programs, and suggestions for future research were also discussed.

The third presentation, by Cornelia Pechmann and Susan Knight, discussed their research on "Identifying and Classifying Adolescent Smoker Attributes Using a Modification of the Zaltman Metaphor Elicitation Technique (ZMET)." They examined youths' positive and negative perceptions of teenage smokers. Their goal was to create a better perceptual measure of smoking and anti-smoking ad effects. Earlier measures were incomplete, lacked uniformity and dimensionality, and used biased, adult-oriented wording. To determine smoker traits, Pechmann and Knight used a ZMET modification (Zaltman and Higie 1993). Youths aged 13-15 made individual collages and discussed these in focus groups. The data (collages, audiotaped discussions, and research observations) were analyzed using HyperQual software. Six underlying construct categories (plus one Global category) were identified: Social Facility, Self-Governance, Internal Welfare (Spranger 1955), Sex Appeal (Erikson 1950), Material Welfare (Havighurst 1951), and Health. Several differences were noted due to gender and smoking orientation (Never Smokers, Vulnerables, and Smokers). The underlying theory involves impression management (Schlenker 1980) and attributions due to correspondent inferences (Jones and Davis 1965). The final measure, consisting of 26 semantic differential items, is being tested for reliability and validity.

Among the three presentations there was convergent evidence for the differential impact of external and internal attributions on adolescents' tendencies to consume drugs such as tobacco and marijuana. The Rose et.al. and Pechmann and Knight papers shed some light on the mediating impact of group attractiveness. Shoaf et.al. and Pechmann and Knight provided evidence of gender-based differences in motivations for engaging in compulsive consumption among adolescents.

The discussant, Manoj Hastak, gave credence to the importance of this research topic, the paucity of research and the particular difficulty associated with data collection in this area. He pointed out that this session focused specifically on preventing the initiation of addictive behaviors and explaining the onset of such behaviors with respect to social influence and underlying cognitive mechanisms. Several mediation and measurement issues were discussed as potential sources for additional research. These included examining the impact of prior attitudes and the sequence of attributional thoughts, assessing whether attributional effects differ for individuals who are neutral or undecided and comparing cognitive responses to belief ratings in evaluating the underlying cognitive processes.

REFERENCES

Beisecker, Analee E. (1991), "Interpersonal Approaches to Drug Abuse Prevention," in *Persuasive Communication and Drug Abuse Prevention*, eds. Lewis Donohew, Howard E. Sypher, and William J. Bukoski, Hilldale, NJ: Lawrence Earlbaum Associates, 229-238.

Erikson, E. H. (1950), *Childhood and Society*, New York: W.W. Norton.

Havighurst, R. J. (1951), *Developmental Tasks and Education*, New York: Longmans, Green.

Hirschman, E. (1992) "The Consciousness of Addiction: Toward a General Theory of Compulsive Consumption", *Journal of Consumer Research*, 19 (September), 155-179.

Jones, E. E., and K. E. Davis (1965), "From Acts to Dispositions: The Attribution Process in Person Perception," in L. Berkowitz (Ed.), *Advances in Experimental Social Psychology*, 2, 219-266, San Diego, CA: Academic Press.

PRIDE Survey of Alcohol and Other Drug Use (1992), National Parents' Resource Institute for Drug Education, Atlanta, Georgia, 30303.

Rose, Randall L., Bearden, William O. and Teel, Jesse E. (1992) "An Attributional Analysis of Resistance to Group Pressure Regarding Illicit Drug and Alcohol Consumption", *Journal of Consumer Research*, 19 (September), 1-13.

Schlenker, Barry R. (1980), *Impression Management: the Self-Concept, Social Identity, and Interpersonal Relations*, Monterey, CA: Brooks/Cole.

Spranger, E. (1955), *Psychologie des Jugendalters*, 24 ed., Heidelberg: Quelle and Meyer.

Zaltman, Gerald, and Robin A. Higie (1993), "Seeing the Voice of the Customer: The Zaltman Metaphor Elicitation Technique," Marketing Science Institute working paper.

Gender Differences in Adolescent Compulsive Consumption

F. Robert Shoaf, New York University
Joan Scattone, New York University
Maureen Morrin, Boston University
Durairaj Maheswaran, New York University

ADOLESCENT COMPULSIVE CONSUMPTION

Compulsive consumption involves behaviors that are very difficult to control through reason and willpower and are often associated with negative consequences (Hirschman 1992). Several types of compulsive consumption, such as smoking, drinking, and drug use, begin during the adolescent years. For example, the average age when smoking begins is 14.5 years (Roberts and Watson 1994). Yet, relatively little empirical research has addressed the issue of compulsive consumption among adolescents.

A considerable amount of research in the field of health psychology has been devoted to uncovering various "risk factors" associated with the onset of adolescent use of "gateway" drugs such as tobacco and alcohol as well as illicit drugs such as marijuana. These studies generally assess the degree of correlation between drug use and such developmental factors as attachment to parents or exposure to the behaviors of peers (Bailey and Hubbard 1990, 1991).

Social influences such as peer pressure have long been considered key factors in models of adolescent substance use (Graham, Marks, and Hansen 1991). Brown, Clasen and Eicher (1986) suggest that an individual manifests his or her need for affiliation with peers by conforming to group norms and that a group is actually strengthened when conformity pressures are exerted. While researchers have attempted to uncover various risk factors associated with drug use among adolescents, such as peer pressure, little research has been devoted to examining the cognitive processes underlying adolescents' decisions to conform with their peers. Investigation in this area would likely aid our understanding of why some adolescents succumb to peer pressure while others do not, and, perhaps more importantly, provide direction regarding how to develop more effective communication strategies to "demarket" the use of drugs.

GROUP CONFORMITY AND ATTRIBUTION THEORY

Attribution theory deals with how people arrive at explanations or make causal inferences for various behaviors and attitudes (see Folkes 1988 for a review). In the context of group behavior, attribution theory suggests that individuals attempt to explain differences between their behavior or opinions and those demonstrated by their peer group. An individual's decision regarding whether or not to conform to group behavior is partly based on his or her ability to generate plausible explanations for the group's behavior.

Rose, Bearden and Teel (1992) examined the relationship between adolescents' attributional processing styles and their willingness to conform to group pressure to smoke marijuana. They investigated the types of causal reasoning adolescents tended to engage in after being exposed to a hypothetical situation involving marijuana use by their peers. The authors found that adolescents who exhibited a higher level of attributional thinking were less likely to conform to group behavior.

The researchers also examined the types of attributions that adolescents were likely to make in such a situation. They grouped attributions into two types: those based on an internal locus of causality and those based on an external locus of causality. Internal

locus of causality attributions focused on personal characteristics and included: No fear of the law, Desire to get high, and No health concerns. External locus of causality attributions focused on situational factors and included: Peer pressure, Desire to look cool, and Desire to fit in. Rose et al. found that locus of causality was indeed correlated with intention to conform. Specifically, adolescents who were more likely to attribute drug use to situational causes, that is, exhibited an external locus of causality, were less likely to state they would conform with the group's marijuana smoking behavior. Rose et al.(1992) speculated that adolescents exhibiting an internal locus of causality may be more likely to conform as a result of perceived group attractiveness. Internal (vs external) attributions may be perceived more favorably, which, in turn, enhances a group's attractiveness resulting in higher levels of conformity.

The present study extends the findings of Rose et al. by examining an additional factor believed to provide added insight into the types of attributional thinking engaged in by adolescents, namely, the effect of gender on cognitive processing style.

GENDER EFFECTS ON PROCESSING STYLE

Prior consumer research has shown that males and females process information differently (Meyers-Levy 1989). Whereas females tend to engage in a fairly high level of elaboration of messages, males' cognitive processing style is more schematic or thematic (Meyers-Levy and Maheswaran 1991). One extension of this finding is whether males and females are also likely to differ in their attributional thinking. It is likely that females who have been found to cognitively process messages to a greater extent than males, may engage in higher levels of attributional thinking when confronted with a group conformity situation.

Research has also shown that males and females tend to pursue different types of goals according to their sex roles (Meyers-Levy 1988; Bakan 1966; Carlson 1971, 1972). Males tend to pursue goals that have personal consequences: a "self" focus. Females tend to pursue goals related to both themselves and to others: a "self and other" focus. We examined whether a similar difference between the sexes would emerge in terms of locus of causality of attributional thoughts. Since females have been found to focus on both "self and other" (vs. only "self"), we suggest that female adolescents may exhibit a higher tendency to engage in attributional thinking with an external locus of causality, that is, which takes into account situational influences such as the opinions of others, more than male adolescents.

HYPOTHESES

Based on the above discussion, we examined the possibility that gender differences in cognitive processing styles would emerge in the context of adolescent attributional thinking in a group conformity situation. The following hypotheses were investigated in the present research. Based on research in gender differences, H1 and H2 are proposed.

H1: Female adolescents will exhibit a higher tendency to engage in attributional thinking than male adolescents.

H2: The impact of attributional thinking (with either an

TABLE 1
Attributions and their Effects on Conformity

	Correlation with Conformity	Mean	Standard deviation
Attributions:			
Peer pressure	-.197*	6.17	2.54
Looking cool	-.236**	6.43	2.69
Fitting in	-.060	6.91	2.22
No health concerns	.158	4.28	2.37
No fear of the law	-.018	4.63	2.44
Getting high	.095	6.75	2.17
Effects of attributions on intended conformity:			
Effect of peer pressure	.132	3.16	2.01
Effect of looking cool	.072	3.01	2.05
Effect of fitting in	.207*	3.23	2.13
Effect of no health concerns	.303**	2.80	1.86
Effect of no fear of the law	.329**	2.92	2.16
Effect of getting high	.569**	3.81	2.53

Note: * p<.05, ** p<.01

All measures are based on 9-point rating scales (attributions: 1=extremely unlikely, 9=extremely likely; effect of attributions: 1=less likely, 9=more likely).

external or internal locus of causality) on intentions to conform with group behavior will be higher for females than for males.

Next, given the results of Rose et al. (1992), which suggest that intention to conform is negatively correlated with the level of attributional thinking, H3, H4 and H5 are predicted.

H3: Female adolescents will exhibit a lower intention to conform with group behavior than male adolescents.

Given the tendency of females to be motivated by a "self and other" focus, compared to males' tendency to focus on "self" goals, we predict:

H4: Female adolescents will exhibit a higher tendency to exhibit attributional thinking involving an external locus of control than male adolescents.

H5: Female adolescents will exhibit a lower tendency to exhibit attributional thinking involving an internal locus of control than male adolescents.

METHOD

One hundred and thirty-five high school students (75 males and 60 females) participated in the study in a familiar classroom setting. The procedure and dependent measures were identical to the Rose et al. (1992) study. Subjects were given a booklet in which they were instructed to imagine that they were at a party where they were offered marijuana by three of their friends who were smoking. After reading the scenario, subjects completed a thought-listing task and responded to a series of questions regarding the likelihood that they would smoke the marijuana and the plausibility of various potential reasons for their friends' drug use.

Three internal locus of causality and three external locus of causality reasons for the group's behavior were provided. The internal explanations were: "Your friends are smoking marijuana because they do not mind damaging their health", "Your friends are smoking marijuana because they want to get high", and "Your friends are smoking marijuana because they aren't afraid of getting

in trouble with the law". The external explanations were: "Your friends are smoking marijuana because they feel pressure from their friends", "Your friends are smoking marijuana because they want to look "cool" to impress their friends", "Your friends are smoking marijuana because they want to "fit in" with their friends". Subjects judged the plausibility of these explanations by indicating the likelihood, on a nine-point scale anchored by extremely unlikely and extremely likely, that the group's behavior resulted from each of the six causes. They also reported the effect each of these attributions would have on their own conformity by indicating the degree to which each explanation would make them more or less likely to smoke marijuana. Finally, subjects were asked to judge the locus of causality for the group's behavior by indicating the extent to which the reason(s) for their friend's smoking was "completely internal" versus "completely external".

RESULTS

We examined the parallel between our findings and Rose et al. (1992) results. Our major findings converged. Rose et al. (1992) found that the three external attribution explanations provided were negatively correlated with intentions. We found similar significant negative relationships for two of the three external attributions (peer pressure and look cool) and directional support for the third (fit in). These findings suggest that when external attributions were likely, they diminished the intention to smoke marijuana. We also replicated the positive correlations with intentions for the two internal attributions, health concerns and getting high. However, these correlations were not significant. Finally, the findings were inconclusive on the third internal attribution, no fear of the law, with a correlation of -.018 for our study and a correlation of .056 for the Rose et al (1992) study. In both the studies these correlations were not significant.

In addition, consistent with the results found by Rose et al. (1992), subjects reported a lower likelihood to conform when different types of attributions were presented as a potential reason for their friends' drug use. In other words, any explanation for the group's behavior had the effect of diminishing intended conformity (Table 1). Also, we found directional but non-significant support for the negative correlation between subjects' perceived locus of

TABLE 2
Comparison of Attributions by Males and Females in Public High School

	Males (n=75)	Females (n=60)
Conformity **	3.04	2.15
Locus of causality	5.46	5.39
External	6.32	6.77
Peer pressure *	5.88	6.61
Looking cool	6.32	6.63
Fitting in	6.77	7.07
Internal **	4.76	3.95
No health concerns	4.40	4.14
No fear of the law ***	5.23	3.84
Getting high	6.82	6.65
Effect of External **	3.42	2.77
Effect of peer pressure	3.39	2.88
Effect of looking cool**	3.36	2.56
Effect of fitting in *	3.51	2.88
Effect of Internal***	3.23	2.35
Effect of no health concerns ***	3.21	2.27
Effect of no fear of the law **	3.29	2.43
Effect of getting high	3.97	3.60

Notes: * $p<.10$, ** $p<.05$, *** $p<.01$.
Likelihood to conform is based on an 11-point scale; all other measures are based on 9-point scales. "External" is an average of the scores for peer pressure, looking cool and fitting in. "Internal" is an average of the scores for no health concerns and no fear of the law. "Effect of External" is an average of the scores for the effects of peer pressure, looking cool and fitting in. "Effect of Internal" is an average of the scores for the effects of no health concerns and no fear of the law.

---

causality for the group's behavior and their intentions to conform with the group, suggesting an inverse relationship between intentions and the tendency to make *external* attributions (r=-.08).

GENDER DIFFERENCES

To test our gender related hypotheses, we examined the subjects' attributional thinking and their relationships with intentions to conform by gender. As stated in our first hypothesis, we expected females to display a higher tendency to engage in attributional thinking than males. We examined females' and males' self reports of their tendency to engage in attributional thinking and did not find evidence of gender differences (Ms= 4.98 and 4.49, respectively). Thus, H1 was not supported.

H2 posited that the presence of attributional thinking would have a greater impact on intentions to conform for females than males and this should hold for both internal and external attributions. In accord, females expressed a greater reduction in conformity than did males when presented with any of the six attributions. A comparison of values for the Effect of Internal (a composite score of the effects of no health concerns and no fear of the law) indicated that females experienced a greater reduction in intended conformity when confronted with attributions that were internal in nature than did males (t=2.81, p <.01)[1]. Similarly, females reported a greater reduction in intentions to conform when presented with attributions that were external (a composite score of the effect of the three external attributions) in nature (t=2.06, p<.05). Specifically, the effects on conformity of "looking cool", "no concerns about health" and "no fear of legal trouble" were significantly higher for females than males (t= 2.25, 2.92, 2.31, respectively; ps<.05). Gender differences in the effect of "fitting in" approached significance (t=1.70, p<.10), whereas differences yielded by "peer pressure" and "desire to get high" were directionally consistent (Table 2).

H3 posited that females would exhibit lower intentions to conform than males. In accord, females' self-reports of intentions to conform were weaker than males' (Ms=2.15 vs. 3.04; t=1.98, p<.05). This is consistent with other research that has found females less willing to accede to antisocial peer pressures (Berndt 1979; Brown, Clasen and Eicher 1986).

Rose et al. (1992) contend that the type, as well as the extent, of attributional thinking may impact intentions to conform with the group's drug use. Although the extent of attributional thinking did not differ for our male and female subjects, their intentions to conform were different. H4 and H5 examined the possibility that the type of attributions (external vs. internal) that females make may contribute to the differences in intention to conform.

H4 suggested that the weaker intentions to conform reported by females may be attributed to a slightly *greater* likelihood to make *external* attributions for the group's behavior. A comparison of their scores on External[2] indicated that females' perceptions of external attributions as plausible explanations for the group's drug use were somewhat stronger than males' (means=6.77 and 6.32, respectively). However, this difference was not statistically significant, thus lends only directional support for H4. Specifically, the effects on the likelihood to attribute the group's behavior to peer pressure approached significance (Ms=6.61 vs. 5.88, t=-1.66, p<.10). While females were more likely than males to attribute the drug use to a desire to look cool (Ms= 6.63 vs. 6.32) or a desire to fit in with the group (Ms.= 7.07 vs. 6.77), these differences were not statistically significant (Table 2).

H5 suggested that females' lower level of intended conformity may also be explained by their tendency to be *less* likely than males to attribute the group's behavior to *internal* factors. A comparison

---

[1]Degrees of freedom = (1, 133) for all t-tests on gender.

[2]External is a composite average of subjects' ratings of the plausibility of the three external attributions.

of the scores for Internal[3] indicated females were less likely to view internal attributions as plausible explanations (t=2.37, p<.05), thus providing support for H5. Specifically, females were significantly *less* likely to attribute the group's behavior to a lack of concern about getting into trouble with the law (t=3.35, p <.001). However, both females and males perceived the desire to get high as a strong potential motivator of the group's behavior (Ms=6.65 vs. 6.82), and the lack of concern for their health (Ms=4.14 vs. 4.40) as a relatively weak explanation for their friends' behavior.

We also found that females were *less* likely than males to think their friends outside the group would approve of their smoking the marijuana (t=2.69, p<.01). In addition, a positive correlation (r=.30, p=.05) was found between females' perceptions of whether their friends outside the group would approve and their own intentions to conform. No correlation was found between these measures for males.

DISCUSSION

Our findings revealed an interesting pattern of differences in the attributional thinking based on gender. While males and females do not differ in the amount of attributional thinking, they do considerably differ in their locus of attributional thinking. We also found that women in general are more externally focused whereas males are internally focused.

Our female subjects' heightened sensitivity to the opinions of their friends is consistent with other findings that adolescent females are more concerned with maintaining friendships than are adolescent males (Douvan and Adelson 1969). Similarly, teenage females are more likely to cite peer approval or friendship issues as likely causes for acquiescence with another teen's request to engage in misconduct, and are more likely to predict peer disapproval and negative consequences to the friendship upon refusing another teen's request to engage in misconduct (Pearl, Bryan and Hersog 1990).

Perhaps females' greater proclivity toward maintaining friendships and their perceptions regarding the impact of peer approval and disapproval on these friendships leads to their development of a more external orientation regarding the motivations for their own behavior and that of their peers. Such a tendency to view conforming behavior as externally motivated may be manifested in a stronger tendency to exhibit external attributions and a weaker tendency to exhibit internal attributions for such behavior. As evidenced by our own results and those found by Rose et al. (1992), external attributions tend to have a greater diminishing impact on intentions to conform with a group's illicit drug use. Females' greater tendency to exhibit external locus of causality attributions may in turn lead to their weaker intentions to conform.

Males and females have shown differences in their likelihood to conform with a group's use of drugs and the types of attributions they make to explain the group's behavior. Understanding these differences is important as there may be implications for the type of anti-drug campaigns that may be most effective for each of the genders. For instance, a campaign targeted at teenage girls might focus on peer approval of saying no to drugs and peer disapproval of drug use. A more effective campaign for males might stress the importance of being an individual by not succumbing to peer pressure and point out that using drugs is not "cool". Also, male adolescents, for example, might be less likely to engage in detailed

processing of anti-drug advertising messages (unless elements such as incongruent information are included to induce such processing; see Meyers-Levy and Maheswaran 1991). Additional research is needed to further explore these issues and implications for preventive and intervention programs.

REFERENCES

Bailey, Susan L. and Robert L. Hubbard (1990), "Developmental Variation in the Context of Marijuana Initiation Among Adolescents", *Journal of Health and Social Behavior*, 31(1), 58-70.

Bailey, Susan L. and Robert L. Hubbard (1991), "Developmental Changes in Peer Factors and the Influence on Marijuana Initiation Among Secondary School Students", *Journal of Youth and Adolescence*, 20(3), 339-360.

Bakan, David (1966), *The Duality of Human Existence*, Boston: Beacon Press.

Beck, Kenneth H. and Terry G. Summons (1987), "Adolescent Gender Differences in Alcohol Beliefs and Behaviors", *Journal of Alcohol and Drug Addiction*, 33(1), 31-44.

Berndt, Thomas J. (1979), "Developmental Changes in Conformity to Peers and Parents", *Developmental Psychology*, 15, 606-616.

Brown, B. Bradford, Donna R. Clasen and Sue Ann Eicher (1986), "Perceptions of Peer Pressure, Peer Conformity Dispositions, and Self-reported Behavior Among Adolescents", *Developmental Psychology*, 22, 521-530.

Carlson, Rae (1971), "Sex Differences in Ego Functioning: Exploratory Studies of Agency and Communion", *Journal of Consulting and Clinical Psychology*, 37 (October), 267-277.

Carlson, Rae (1972), "Understanding Women: Implications for Personality Theory and Research", *Journal of Social Issues*, 28(2), 17-32.

Carman, Roderick and Charles Holmgren (1986), "Gender Differences in the Relationship of Drinking Motivations and Outcomes", *Journal of Psychology*, 120(4), 375-378.

Dielman, T.E., Pamela C. Campanelli, Jean T. Shope and Amy T. Butchart (1987), "Susceptibility to Peer Pressure, Self-esteem, and Health Locus of Control as Correlates of Adolescent Substance Abuse", *Health Education Quarterly*, 14(2), 207-221.

Douvan, Elizabeth and Joseph Adelson (1966), *The Adolescent Experience*, NY: Wiley.

Eiser, J. Richard, Christine Eiser, Philip Gammage and Michelle Morgan (1989), *British Journal of Addiction*, 84(9), 1059-1065.

Fitzgerald, J.L. and H.A. Mulford (1987), "Self-report Validity Issues", *Journal of Studies on Alcohol*, 48(3), 207-211.

Folkes, Valerie S. (1984), Recent Attribution Research in Consumer Behavior: A Review and New Directions", *Journal of Consumer Research*, 14 (March), 548-565.

Graham, John W., Gary Marks and William B. Hansen (1991), "Social Influence Processes Affecting Adolescent Substance Use", *Journal of Applied Psychology*, 76(2), 291-298.

Gritz, Ellen R. (1986), "Gender and the Teenage Smoker", *National Institute on Drug Abuse Research Monograph Series*, Mono 65, 70-79, Jonsson Comprehensive Cancer Center, Division of Cancer Control, Los Angeles, CA.

Hirschman, Elizabeth C. (1992), "The Consciousness of Addiction: Toward a General Theory of Compulsive Consumption", *Journal of Consumer Research*, 19(2), 155-179.

---

[3]Internal is a composite average of subjects' ratings of the plausibility of two of the three internal attributions: no concerns about one's health and no fear of getting into legal trouble.

Hover, Susan J. and Lisa R. Gaffney (1988), "Factors Associated with Smoking Behavior in Adolescent Girls", *Addictive Behaviors*, 13(2), 139-145.

Huselid, Rebecca F. and M. Lynne Cooper (1992), "Gender Roles as Mediators of Sex Differences in Adolescent Alcohol Use and Abuse", *Journal of Health and Social Behavior*, 33(4), 348-362.

McInman, Adrian D. and J. Robert Grove (1991), "Multidimensional Self-concept, Cigarette Smoking, and Intentions to Smoke in Adolescents", *Australian Psychologist*, 26(3), 192-196.

Meyers-Levy, Joan (1988), "The Influence of Sex Roles on Judgment", *Journal of Consumer Research*, 14 (March), 522-530.

Meyers-Levy, Joan (1989), "Gender Differences in Information Processing: a Selectivity Interpretation", in *Cognitive and Affective Responses to Advertising*, eds. Patricia Cafferata and Alice Tybout, Lexington, MA: Lexington.

Meyers-Levy, Joan and Durairaj Maheswaran (1991), "Exploring Differences in Males' and Females' Processing Strategies", *Journal of Consumer Research*, 18, June, 63-70.

Pearl, Ruth; Tanis Bryan and Allen Hersog (1990), "Resisting or Acquiescing to Peer Pressure to Engage in Misconduct: Adolescents' Expectations of Probable Consequences", *Journal of Youth and Adolescence*, 19, 43-55.

Roberts, Steven V. and Traci Watson (1994), "Teens on Tobacco: Kids Smoke for Reasons All Their Own", *U.S. News and World Report*, April 18, 38-43.

Rose, Randall L., William O. Bearden and Jesse E. Teel (1992), "An Attributional Analysis of Resistance to Group Pressure Regarding Illicit Drug and Alcohol Consumption", *Journal of Consumer Research*, 19, 1-13.

Van Roosmalen, Erica H., and Susan A. McDaniel (1992), "Adolescent Smoking Intentions: Gender Differences in Peer Context", *Adolescence*, 27(105), 87-105.

Session Overview
Consumer Acculturation: Immigrants, Migrants and Expatriates

Mary C. Gilly, University of California, Irvine

In our contemporary global economy, there is continuous movement of people, products and companies across national boundaries. While tourism is the way most people see and experience other countries, an increasing number of individuals and families are spending extended periods of time living in countries other than their country of birth. When living in another country on a long term basis, it is necessary to engage in various consumer behaviors in order to conduct everyday life. Often, the marketplace is very different from that which was left behind, both in terms of the products available and the way of conducting transactions. Thus emigration entails daily cross-cultural consumer experiences which present special challenges to all involved.

Two aspects of the cross-cultural living experience are of particular interest here. First, the ways in which consumers adapt to and adopt their new culture's products and behaviors, and perhaps values, is of interest to consumer researchers. Consumer acculturation has been defined as "the process of adaptation to the cultural consumption values and behaviors of one cultural group by members of another cultural group" (Penaloza 1989). Hall (1959) maintained that the study of culture is important not because of what is learned about another's way of doing things, but because of what it reveals about ourselves. More recently, Hofstede (1991) argued similarly for the study of other cultures. Thus, by studying people who have had to adapt to being consumers in a different culture, we can gain insights into our own.

Second, the study of people who have left their country of birth enables consumer researchers to examine the meaning of possessions in a different light. When home is left behind, both possessions and familiar products are left behind and may take on new meanings for the emigrant (Belk 1992; Mehta and Belk 1991; Wallendorf and Arnould 1988). Adaptation to new products, and attempts to obtain familiar ones, offer insights into consumer behaviors which have received little research attention.

The objective of the special session was to examine the topic of consumer acculturation by discussing three very different types of people who have emigrated. Immigrants come to a foreign country to take up residence on a relatively permanent basis. Migrants also come to a foreign country to take up residence, but they do not settle in one place permanently. Expatriates are sent to foreign countries by their employers for temporary assignments, lasting on average four years (Black and Stephens 1989). For this special session, the immigrant and migrant groups were Mexicans coming to the U.S. while the expatriates were U.S. citizens residing in Spain.

The first paper presented was "Marketers as Agents of Immigrant Consumer Acculturation," by Lisa Penaloza, University of Illinois. Penaloza pointed out that retailers' influence on immigrant consumer acculturation has been less studied than the influence of family, peers, media, etc. Reporting on interviews conducted with retailers serving an area with a large Mexican immigrant population, she identified a number of ways in which marketers serve to introduce immigrant consumers to the norms of consumer behavior in the U.S.

The next paper was presented by John Schouten, University of Portland, "Peonage or Pioneering: Mexican Migration in the Pacific Northwest," co-authored with Alexandra Velasquez, University of Portland. Studying a Mexican migrant worker population in Cornelius, OR, they found that consumer acculturation mirrored other aspects of acculturation. Schouten identified three levels of acculturation: instrumental (migrants who make minimal adjustments to the U.S. marketplace and who maintain loyalty to Mexico), marginalization (migrants who have failed to achieve their goals in the U.S. and who have no affiliation with the U.S. or with Mexico), and terminal (migrants who have acculturated to the U.S. environment and plan to remain as immigrants).

The final presentation was by Mary Gilly, University of California, Irvine, "The Consumer Acculturation of Expatriate Americans." Reporting on in-depth interviews with expatriate American women in Spain and participant observation, Gilly discussed the topics of the meaning of possessions (e.g., leaving possessions behind and dealing with the unavailability of U.S. products) and the learning about a new consumer environment.

Thomas O'Guinn, University of Illinois led the discussion of the papers. He made the observation that most models of acculturation assume there is a culture to which one aspires. In a consumer context, as these papers illustrate, it may be that individuals living in a country other than their country of birth adapt and adjust to the consumer environment, rather than outright adoption of the host country's norms. O'Guinn pointed out the need to study how these groups socially construct the culture they are encountering. Members of the audience shared their own experiences living in other countries, and observed the similarities across the diverse groups of immigrants, migrants and expatriates in terms of their consumer acculturation.

REFERENCES

Belk, Russell W. (1992), "Moving Possessions: An Analysis Based on Personal Documents from the 1847-1869 Mormon Migration," *Journal of Consumer Research*, 19 (December), 339-361.

Black, J. Stewart and Gregory K. Stephens (1989), "The Influence of the Spouse on American Expatriate Adjustment and Intent to Stay in Pacific Rim Overseas Assignments," *Journal of Management*, 15, 4, 529-544.

Hall, Edward t. (1959), *The Silent Language*, Garden City, NY: Anchor Press/Doubleday.

Hofstede, Geert (1991), *Cultures and Organizations. —Software of the Mind*, London: McGraw-Hill.

Mehta, Raj and Russell W. Belk (1991), "Artifacts, Identity, and Transition: Favorite Possessions of Indians and Indian Immigrants to the United States," *Journal of Consumer Research*, 17 (March), 398-411.

Penaloza, Lisa (1989), "An Empirical Exploration of the Hispanic Immigrant Family," Doctoral Dissertation, University of California, Irvine.

Wallendorf, Melanie and Eric J. Arnould (1988), "'My Favorite Things': A Cross-Cultural Inquiry into Object Attachment, Possessiveness, and Social Linkage," *Journal of Consumer Research*, 14, 531-547.

The Consumer Acculturation of Expatriate Americans

Mary C. Gilly, University of California, Irvine

ABSTRACT

As U.S. business expands overseas, more Americans are experiencing the role of expatriate. Research in the field of management suggests that the adjustment to a new cultural environment is difficult for both expatriates and their families. Consumer researchers have examined the adjustment of immigrants (cf. Belk 1992) but not the experience of expatriates. Expatriates offer the unique opportunity to examine two issues of interest to consumer researchers: consumer learning and the meaning of possessions. The qualitative research reported here examines the expatriate consumer experience from the perspective of American women living in Madrid, Spain.

INTRODUCTION

One area of cross-cultural consumer research which has been virtually ignored in the marketing and consumer behavior literature is the consumer experiences of American expatriates (for an exception, see Dawson and Bamossy 1991). In the organizational behavior literature, a body of research on expatriate managers has recently emerged (cf. Black 1988; Black, Mendenhall and Oddou 1991; Mendenhall and Oddou 1985). Research specifically on the spouses of expatriate managers suggests that adjustment to living conditions (housing, food, shopping, transportation, entertainment/recreation, and health care) facilitates cultural adjustment, and is correlated with the expatriate's intent to stay with the assignment (Black and Gregersen 1991; Black and Stephens 1989). Belk (1992) suggests that "the meaning of possessions should be studied among contemporary movers (including moves precipitated by...migration between cultures)" (p. 358).

Examining expatriate consumer experiences offers several benefits. First, expatriates enter a new consumer environment, most likely far different from simply moving within the increasingly homogenous U.S. Thus, consumer learning must take place, providing the opportunity to study the consumer learning of adults, rather than children, which is the usual sample unit.

Second, a sample of expatriates provides the opportunity to study the meaning of possessions in a new and potentially insightful way. It has been suggested that the U.S. consumer culture encourages the salience of material items in the definition of self (Dawson and Bamossy 1991). It is thus important to explore what U.S. products and possessions are missed most by expatriates, and why.

The purpose of this paper is to examine the consumer experiences of expatriate Americans. First, the relevant literature is briefly reviewed. Then, a study involving participant observation and in-depth interviews of American women living in Madrid, Spain is described and the results presented. Finally, implications for consumer learning, the meaning of possessions and cross-cultural research are explored.

LITERATURE REVIEW

As the international activities of U.S. firms increase, more American employees are sent overseas on temporary assignments (Gregersen and Black 1992). While Belk (1992) claims that contemporary geographical moves within the developed world are relatively "unproblematic," he acknowledges that "challenges remain in such moves as...leaving country of birth,...and going to a very new and unfamiliar environment" (p. 358). Expatriate employees and their families typically face difficult adjustments to

living in a foreign culture. Between 16 and 40 percent of American employees sent abroad return from their work assignments early (Black, Mendenhall and Oddou 1991). The primary reason given by American firms for these premature returns is the failure of the expatriate's spouse to successfully adapt to the foreign culture. A secondary reason is the failure of the expatriate him/herself to adapt to both living and working in a different culture (Tung 1981).

From a non-job standpoint, expatriation represents a difficult adjustment for a number of reasons. First, such a move often necessitates the disposition of objects which have important meanings for the expatriate. Because the average expected length of time in the overseas assignment is four years (Black and Stephens 1989), such disposition may be temporary (e.g., storing furniture, renting the home) or permanent (e.g., selling the car, giving away clothes). Wallendorf and Arnould (1988) suggest that, because objects carry meaning related to self-concept, "losing or severing our connection to objects non voluntarily can change the meaning of life for individuals" (p. 532). Even when an expatriate has eagerly pursued an overseas assignment, there are aspects of the move which are "non voluntary." Expense or lack of space may preclude bringing along treasured objects.

There is some anecdotal evidence that expatriates also miss goods which are unavailable in their host country.

> For 24 years I have seen expatriate spouses come and go; many would fail or be miserable because they didn't have the split level home on a dead end street, the Jell-O, the cotton bread, the prepared foods, etc. (An American HRM executive quoted in Black and Gregersen (1991)).

Chatwin (1990) interviewed American expatriates in Lausanne, Switzerland and found that adaptation to a new culture could be detected through the pattern of adjustment of food-related behaviors. She found four main periods of adjustment: 1) euphoria, where new arrivals are open to new sights, sounds and tastes, 2) skepticism, where the newness becomes threatening, 3) integration, where guilt feelings emerge (because Americans place value in learning new ways) so that some effort is made to obtain some ingredients for favorite dishes from local sources, and 4) adaptation, where ingredients are consciously substituted and foods from home are combined with foods from the host country, with the expatriate again willing to try completely new foods. Thus, food can be an intensely personal and self-defining consumer product for expatriates (as the quotation above suggests).

Conversely, Dawson and Bamossy (1991) suggest that, "being thrust into a foreign cultural environment without one's worldly possessions is likely to cause an expatriate to view having possessions from an entirely different perspective, and to focus more on concerns of doing and being" (p. 367). In their study of expatriate Americans living in the Netherlands, they found that the expatriates had consistently lower materialism scores (using Belk's measures) than either the Dutch or the American samples. Thus, the "doing without" of familiar possessions and products can be either a miserable or a liberating experience.

A second reason expatriates face difficulties is the general problem of adjusting to a new and different culture. A great deal of time and energy must be invested to adjust to such new aspects of the culture as transportation systems, housing arrangements, health care providers, and types of food and their preparation (Gregersen and Black 1992). In the consumer behavior literature, the problem has been studied within the context of acculturation, defined as the "adoption of the dominant society's attitudes, values and behaviors" (O'Guinn, Lee and Faber 1986, p. 579). Acculturation is a term typically used in reference to immigrants who plan to stay permanently in their adopted country. While it can also be applied to the temporary adoption of the new culture's norms of behavior, a related but more relevant stream of research might be that on culture shock (Gullahorn and Gullahorn 1962; Oberg 1960; Torbiorn 1982). Culture shock scholars suggest that people face uncertainty about what behavior is acceptable when they enter a new culture. Over time, they discover differences in cultural norms so that they are no longer certain what behaviors are acceptable and what are offensive. Many of the symptoms of culture shock (e.g., anxiety, confusion, apathy (Torbiorn 1982)) result from the stress of uncertainty concerning behavioral expectations. Therefore, the process of cross-cultural adjustment involves uncertainty reduction by learning whether behaviors are appropriate or not in the new culture (Black and Gregersen 1991).

The qualitative research reported here was designed to complement the survey research conducted on expatriate spouses and their adjustment to a new culture (e.g., Black and Stephens 1989). Specifically, the research focuses on expatriate spouses' adjustment to leaving behind possessions, to the unavailability of certain American products, and to learning new ways of shopping for goods and obtaining services.

RESEARCH DESIGN

Because of the dearth of research on the consumer experiences of expatriate Americans, a qualitative approach is appropriate. It was important that informants be chosen who would have had significant experience shopping in Spain. Thus, women were targeted because of previous research which indicates that the great majority of expatriates are men and that 80% of expatriate spouses do not work outside of the home (Stephens and Black 1988). Belk (1992) suggests that, "gender should be an important consideration in analyzing the uses and meanings of possessions during geographic movements" (p. 358). Further, most day-to-day consumer experiences revolve around the purchase and preparation of food, typically the domain of women (cf. Levy 1981; Thompson, Locander and Pollio 1990). The researcher conducting the interviews is a woman, obviating some of the concerns of Bristor and Fischer (1993).

Twelve expatriate American women agreed to be interviewed. Contacts were made through personal contact with the researcher, referrals from other informants, and through the cooperation of the American Women's Club in Madrid, Spain. All of the informants had been in Spain for a minimum of six months. Informants were chosen such that the sample would represent a range of ages, household compositions, and backgrounds. In addition, the researcher engaged in participant observation, living as an expatriate for a year in Madrid. Shopping experiences were noted, and photographs taken. The in-depth interview tapes were transcribed and analyzed as outlined by McCracken (1988). The Table gives characteristics of the twelve informants (excluding the researcher).

In reporting results, all informants have been given names other than their own. Following an informant's pseudonym, the informant's age is indicated, followed by her length of time in Spain as of the date of the interview. A great deal of research supports the idea that adaptation to the new culture changes over time for expatriates (cf. Black et al. 1991; Gullahorn and Gullahorn 1962; Torbiorn 1982).

RESULTS

Disposition of Possessions

When employees take overseas assignments, they may bring all of their household and personal possessions, or they can take the bare minimum to the new country. Only three of the twelve informants brought virtually all of their possessions. Ellen (40; 6 mos.) expects to be in Spain for 10 years, and thus brought her entire household contents. The only other informants who brought "everything" were Monica (43; 7 mos.) and Toni (48; 2.5 yrs.). They plan to stay 2.5 years and 5 years respectively, but because the employers paid for moving the household, these two women chose to bring all of their possessions. However, even these three women had to leave possessions behind because of the difference in voltage, or because the object did not "fit" in terms of size or aesthetics.

All of the other informants brought limited amounts of goods, moving into furnished apartments in Madrid. Most of these informants mentioned bringing clothing and books, as well as personal items such as photographs and jewelry. Three informants brought their dogs. Interestingly, several informants chose to bring housewares, such as linens, pots and pans, and Tupperware, despite the fact that they were provided with furnished apartments and comparable items are available in Madrid.

All of the expatriate informants had possessions they had left behind. These objects were donated (antique furniture), rented or sold (houses), given to friends to use (110 volt appliances), or put in storage (bikes, vacuum, garden equipment). Most of the informants who had brought very little to Madrid left an entire furnished house (to rent or for a family member to use) and left other possessions in storage. Marilyn (29; 1.5 yrs.) sold furniture, car, condo, "everything." She did leave behind some clothes, books and "sentimental things that I wouldn't sell." This was the one unmarried informant.

The attitudes of the informants toward disposing of possessions varied widely, from Ellen (40; 6 mos.) who described the process as being very difficult and painful to Marty (56; 3 yrs.) who disposed of much of her furniture (by giving it to her children or selling it) because the tenants wanted the house unfurnished and "I didn't have antiques so I figured whatever I had I could replace." The strength of feelings seems to be related to how well they were adjusting. Ellen was having a difficult time adjusting to Spain, despite her extensive prior expatriate experiences and her fluency in Spanish. Conversely, Marty saw her time in Spain as an "adventure," saying, "I don't want to go back to the U.S. I want to experience new things." This latter attitude is consistent with Dawson and Bamossy's (1991) survey findings that expatriates become less materialistic and become more interested in activities. The remaining informants expressed attitudes between these two extremes, expressing ambivalence about leaving their possessions but enjoying their new experiences.

When informants were asked what they missed most about living in the U.S., interestingly, "things" were not mentioned frequently. Rather, answers focused on having familiarity with how things work. This theme was expressed in a number of ways, such as missing "the ability to communicate" (Nora, 60; 7 mos.), "being able to rush out and get something and I know exactly where it is, it's fairly close and they have a good selection of what I need" (Deborah, 30; 9 mos.), "independence" (Toni, 48; 2.5 yrs), "knowing where to go; knowing what to pay; I miss the sense of mastery of the situation you have in the U.S." (Ruth, 51; 1 yr). These statements are consistent with the literature on culture shock which suggests that it is stressful not knowing what behaviors are accept-

TABLE
Characteristics of Informants

Informant	Age	Time in Spain	Expected Total Time in Spain	Previous International Experience	Spanish Fluency on Arrival	Cross-Cultural Training
Deborah	30	9 mos.	9 mos.	3 yrs.	None	No
Diane	37	1 yr.	1 yr.	0	None	No
Ellen	40	6 mos.	10 yrs.	25 yrs.	Fluent	No
Emily	50	1.5 yrs.	3 yrs.	0	None	Yes
Marilyn	29	1.5 yrs.	3 yrs.	1 yr.	Mediocre	No
Marty	56	3 yrs.	4 yrs.	0	Minimal	No
Mary Ellen	55	2.5 yrs.	4 yrs.	20 yrs.	Fluent	No
Monica	43	7 mos.	2.5 yrs.	0	Some	No
Nora	60	1.5 yrs.	4 yrs.	0	None	No
Ruth	51	1 yr.	2 yrs.	2 yrs.	Low	No
Sharon	58	1.5 yrs.	1.5 yrs.	9 yrs.	Poor	No
Toni	48	2.5 yrs.	5 yrs.	6 yrs.	Some	Yes
mean	46.4 yrs.	1.5 yrs.	3.4 yrs.	5.5 yrs.		

able in the new culture. Thus, it is "easy" to live in the U.S. where the expatriates know how things work, while it is "difficult" to live in Spain, where they face a learning situation because they don't know were to go, how to make purchases, and often do not have the language skills to learn this information easily.

Missing American Products

All of the informants had "sources" of U.S. products, typically friends and family coming to visit, or their own trips back to the U.S. The list of products missed and sought out reflected an interesting variety of products. Ellen (40; 6 mos.) had not been able to find cottage cheese and peanut butter. She was considering doing an import/export business on her own, targeting the American expatriate community. Deborah (30; 9 mos.) and Diane (37; 1 yr.) both had people bring them over-the-counter medications, suggesting a lack of trust in Spanish medications. Monica (43; 7 mos.) had people bring her Charmin toilet paper. She said she hadn't even tried to find anything comparable because she kept having visitors from the U.S.! Nora (60; 1.5 yrs.) brought back Crisco shortening, corn meal and Jell-O from the U.S. at Christmas. Mary Ellen (55; 2.5 yrs.) freezes corn tortillas and brings them back in her suitcase. Bisquick, microwave popcorn, pancake syrup and sour cream were other products missed by these expatriates. The American Women's Club of Madrid has a "bring and buy" sale regularly, where members bring things to sell, and the American products brought back from the States are always popular. The prominence of food in the list of products missed supports Chatwin's (1990) findings regarding the importance of familiar foods to expatriates.

Learning About A New Consumer Environment

Two product categories were chosen for more in-depth questioning. Informants were asked about differences they had observed in purchasing grocery products and health care products and services. Because of the frequent need for grocery shopping, this was the area which received the more complete response.

Informants all observed that grocery shopping must be done more frequently in Spain than in the U.S. This is due to several factors. First, packaged goods are less available in Spain; therefore,

these expatriate women found themselves preparing more fresh (and therefore perishable) foods than in the U.S. Further, many of the informants did not have automobiles in Madrid (because of fears of driving in a foreign country and lack of parking, as well as the availability of good public transportation) and were constrained by the amount they could carry home by foot or on the bus. Thus, they had to make smaller trips more frequently. Third, shopping is done more frequently by these expatriates because of a lack of space for storing products in the home. Madrid is a city of apartments (pisos) which, while spacious, tend to be smaller than the suburban homes these women had left in the U.S. This increased frequency of shopping was a major adjustment problem for the informants. As Ellen (40; 6 mos.) put it, "Grocery shopping is something I hate to do and now I have to do it more frequently!"

Another theme which emerged was a perception that Spain offered less variety of goods. But when looking at the specific products mentioned by informants, the variety appears to be lacking in products which Americans purchase frequently but Spaniards do not. Examples informants gave were product categories such as frozen foods, canned goods, cake mixes, canned soup ("Two different types of Campbell's and that's it," said Nora, 60; 1.5 yrs.), and, of course, Jell-O ("Just orange and strawberry," said Emily, 50; 1.5 yrs.). My own observations of selection reveal that a typical Spanish store will devote an entire aisle to varieties of olive oil (vs. one or two brands in the U.S.), and almost that much space to all kinds of jars and cans of asparagus. These are two product categories consumed more in Spain than in the U.S. Thus, the expatriates tend to attribute the problem to supply (i.e., the stores do not offer variety) while it is more likely one of demand (i.e., the expatriates do not purchase the products for which there is variety).

Related to the theme of frustration over not being in control mentioned previously is the observations made by several informants about the lack of self-service in the Spanish markets. In almost all Spanish stores, consumers are not allowed to choose their own produce, but must rely on the grocer to give them six apples, four tomatoes, or whatever (as Sharon (58; 1.5 yrs.) said, "You can't touch the fruits or vegetables; they just about smack your hand if you do"). Ruth (51; 1 yr.) expressed the sentiments of many of the informants when she said, "In the U.S. I feel more in control because of self-service. More personal contact cuts both ways—you have a person smiling at you as they're putting rotten tomatoes in your bag."

Many expatriates express concern about hygiene and cleanliness in the new country (Torbiorn 1982). This concern emerged in the interviews about both grocery products and health care services. Two of the informants focused on the display of meat products in Spain. As Deborah (30; 9 mos.) said, "Meat is packaged in the U.S. and in Spain it's less sanitary. We have ours in packaging and they have theirs kind of hanging out there with the heads on and the arms and the eyes on the fish looking at you." This sentiment was echoed by Marty (56; 3 yrs.): "They have rabbits and chickens hanging up, looking at you." However, this concern for "sanitation" may simply be an American aversion to seeing food as it was when it was alive. Spaniards, like many Europeans, display whole fish, rabbits, pigs, etc. in restaurants to suggest freshness.

Several of the other informants expressed concern about hygiene and safety regarding health care products. The common adjective used to describe health care services was "scary." Diane (37; 1 yr.) said, "I view the pharmacies as almost scary—there's not enough regulation on the pharmacy." Nora (60; 1.5 yrs.) said, "It's scary thinking about going to a doctor here because it would have to be someone English-speaking or I wouldn't feel comfortable or confident." Marilyn (29; 1.5 yrs.) echoed this sentiment, "I'm scared of it [health care]. If something serious happens to me, my roommates know they should drive me to the airport and put me on a plane to the U.S.!"

This fear of Spanish health care is countered by the informants who had actually used it. Their experiences (ranging from 27 stitches in Ellen's (40; 6 mos.) daughter's hand to Toni's (48; 2.5 yrs.) root canal) were generally quite positive. Thus, it appears that it is the "fear of the unknown" that is driving the non-users' opinions of Spanish health care services.

Informants were asked who they ask for advice on where to go for a product or service. All of the expatriates said that they ask other Americans who have been in Spain longer for product advice. The American Women's Club of Madrid keeps a file of members' suggestions and publishes a book, *Bear Facts*, with advice for American expatriates in Madrid. Other sources of information included Spaniards at the husband's workplace, Spanish neighbors or the portero. (Each apartment building has a portero who has a desk in the lobby and is in charge of the building.) But the overwhelming tendency was to rely on fellow expatriates. This theme suggests the importance of perceived homophily (i.e., shared needs) in word-of-mouth seeking for expatriates, rather than expertise (which Spaniards would more likely have).

Informants were asked what changes they had noticed in themselves as consumers since coming to Spain. The common theme here was a decrease in materialism. Monica (43; 7 mos.) said, "I'm spending less money; not shopping as much," while Ruth (51; 1 yr.) said, "I wait longer to buy something," and Marilyn (29; 1.5 yrs.) summed it up when she said, "I'm less materialistic. I have less money and everything is more expensive. I'm out of the habit of shopping just for shopping sake." These statements, again, support the Dawson and Bamossy (1991) survey findings of less materialism among American expatriates living in the Netherlands.

CONCLUSIONS

The interviews with American expatriates in Spain, and the expatriate experiences of the researcher, confirm the difficulty involved in leaving the U.S. and adjusting to a new consumer environment. Most expatriates leave behind most of their possessions, only bringing clothing, books, and perhaps a few personal items such as photographs or jewelry. Belk (1992) says that, "During geographic transitions we move those possessions that are most apt to move us" (p. 339). However, it is interesting to note that none of the women mentioned bringing a particular special possession nor were special possessions typically mentioned when informants were asked what they missed. It may be that people who are willing to take overseas assignments are generally less attached to their possessions than people who do not choose to go overseas. When I was preparing to leave for my expatriate experience in Spain, many people reacted to the news with comments such as, "How could you stand to leave all your things with strangers?" It may be that there is an expatriate "personality" which enables people to leave possessions behind in favor of new experiences. This issue deserves further study.

The one thing expatriates missed most was being familiar with the "way things work," particularly as consumers. Thus, they learned to rely on other American expatriates for product and shopping advice because these information sources have already "conquered" the unknown. Still, informants admitted to consumer learning by trial and error, observation and "fumbling around."

Similar to the findings of Dawson and Bamossy (1991), the informants became less materialistic as they learned to "do without" their possessions. However, there were certain American products, particularly food, which seemed to symbolize home. These products were sought out and obtained at great expense and effort. Belk (1992) observes that people may gain a feeling of security from familiar things which symbolize connections to past life and home. Thus, while possessions seemed to lose their importance overall, certain products retained (or perhaps gained) significance for these expatriates.

Further research is needed to gain a full understanding of the expatriate consumer experience. The informants in this study felt frustration because they did not understand how things worked in the new culture. Is this frustration felt because of the language barrier or would American expatriates in English-speaking countries have similar experiences? Research on other American expatriates would help to answer this question.

The consumer experiences of expatriates represent an opportunity for a unique perspective on other cultures, as well as our own. Further research on expatriate consumers would contribute to the literature on consumer learning, the meaning of possessions, and cross-cultural understanding.

REFERENCES

Belk, Russell W. (1992), "Moving Possessions: An Analysis Based on Personal Documents from the 1847-1869 Mormon Migration," *Journal of Consumer Research*, 19 (December), 339-361.

Black, J. Stewart (1988), "Workrole Transitions: A Study of American Expatriate Managers in Japan," *Journal of International Business Studies*, 19, 277-94.

Black, J. Stewart and Hal B. Gregersen (1991), "The Other Half of the Picture: Antecedents of Spouse Cross-Cultural Adjustment," *Journal of International Business Studies*, 22, 3, 461-477.

Black, J. Stewart, Mark Mendenhall and Gary Oddou (1991), "Toward a Comprehensive Model of International Adjustment: An Integration of Multiple Theoretical Perspectives," *Academy of Management Review*, 16, 2, 291-317.

Black J. Stewart and Gregory K. Stephens (1989), "The Influence of the Spouse on American Expatriate Adjustment and Intent to Stay in Pacific Rim Overseas Assignments," *Journal of Management*, 15, 4, 529-544.

Bristor, Julia M. and Eileen Fischer (1993), "Feminist Thought: Implications for Consumer Research," *Journal of Consumer Research*, 19 (March), 518-536.

Chatwin, Mary Ellen (1991), "Nostalgia, Loneliness and Culture Shock: Perspectives for the Socio-Cultural Study of Feelings in Transition," Working Paper, Anthropology Department, Webster University, Geneva.

Dawson, Scott and Gary Bamossy (1991), "If 'We Are What We Have,' What Are We When We Don't Have?: An Exploratory Study of Materialism Among Expatriate Americans," in Rudmin, F. W. (ed.), *To Have Possessions: A Handbook on Ownership and Property* (Special Issue of *Journal of Social Behavior and Personality*), 66, 363-384.

Gullahorn, John R. and J. E. Gullahorn (1962), "An Extension of the U-Curve Hypothesis," *Journal of Social Issues*, 3, 33-47.

Gregersen, Hal B. and J. Stewart Black (1992), "Antecedents to Commitment to a Parent Company and a Foreign Operation," *Academy of Management Journal*, 35, 1, 1-26.

Levy, Sidney J. (1981), "Interpreting Consumer Mythology: A Structural Approach to Consumer Behavior," *Journal of Marketing*, 45, 49-61.

McCracken, Grant (1988), *The Long Interview*, Newbury Park: Sage Publications.

Oberg, K. (1960), "Culture Shock: Adjusting to a New Cultural Environment," *Practical Anthropologist*, 7, 177-182.

O'Guinn, Thomas C., Wei-Na Lee and Ronald J. Faber (1986), "Acculturation: The Impact of Divergent Paths on Buyer Behavior," in Richard J. Lutz (ed.), *Advances in Consumer Research*, 13, 579-583.

Stephens, Gregory K. and J. Stewart Black (1988), "International Transfers and Dual-Career Couples," Paper presented at the Annual Academy of Management Meetings, Anaheim, CA.

Thompson, Craig J., William B. Locander and Howard R. Pollio (1990), "The Lived Meaning of Free Choice: An Existential-Phenomenological Description of Everyday Consumer Experiences of Contemporary Married Women," *Journal of Consumer Research*, 17, 346-361.

Torbiorn, Igamar (1982), *Living Abroad*, New York: Wiley.

Tung, R. (1981), "Selecting and Training of Personnel for Overseas Assignments," *Columbia Journal of World Business*, 16, 68-78.

Wallendorf, Melanie and Eric J. Arnould (1988), "'My Favorite Things': A Cross-Cultural Inquiry into Object Attachment, Possessiveness, and Social Linkage," *Journal of Consumer Research*, 14, 531-547.

Peripheral Cues as Sources of Market Inefficiencies in the U.S. and Russia

Timothy B. Heath, University of Pittsburgh
David L. Mothersbaugh, University of Pittsburgh
Michael S. McCarthy, Miami University
Gangseog Ryu, University of Pittsburgh[1]

While the consumer welfare implications of advertising have been debated extensively, little experimental research has assessed advertising's ability to damage markets by leading consumers to choose objectively inferior brands. The current study examines this issue by assessing the possibility that nonoptimal choices arise from advertising's peripheral cues (e.g., spokesperson fame and liking). Given the expansion of free markets in the Eastern Block, we assessed these effects on both U.S. (Experiment 1) and Russian (Experiment 2) consumers. The results show that in both the U.S. and Russia, well-liked peripheral cues increase the probability of choosing objectively inferior brands even when consumers think hard about their decisions. It appears that consumers are willing to give up certain product features for stronger peripheral cues. These results suggest that peripheral cues can serve as sources of market inefficiencies in various cultures.

The moral and economic implications of advertising have been the subject of protracted debate. Some people credit advertising with improving markets by supplying information and stimulating competition (e.g., Stigler 1961). Others believe advertising damages markets by erecting barriers to entry, providing no information or misinformation, and promoting competition on nonsubstantive features such as an ad's humor (e.g., Norris 1984; Shimp and Gresham 1983). However, little research has experimentally assessed advertising's ability to yield nonoptimal choices. Instead, research typically tests advertising's effects on potential mediators such as beliefs and attitudes. Better ads (Kirmani 1990) and higher prices (Monroe 1973) increase perceived quality, and popular advertising techniques easily mislead consumers (Gaeth and Heath 1987). The current study extends this research by testing advertising's ability to directly bias choice toward nonoptimal brands.

We assess the influence of advertising's *peripheral* or *heuristic cues*, nonproduct features such as a spokesperson's fame and liking (Chaiken 1980; Petty and Cacioppo 1986). It is generally believed that central cues (e.g., product features) dominate and peripheral cues wield little influence when consumers think hard about their evaluations (i.e., engage in issue-relevant thinking). However, this belief stems largely from research in noncompetitive settings where only a single brand or issue is evaluated. In the context of competition, recent research shows that peripheral cues can alter attitudes and choices when product attributes are either traded-off or constant across brands, regardless of issue-relevant thinking (Heath, McCarthy, and Mothersbaugh 1994; Miniard, Sirdeshmukh, and Innis 1992). Although these effects extend popular multi-process theories of persuasion, they need not reflect detrimental advertising effects since chosen brands were not necessarily inferior to unchosen brands. The current study extends this research by testing the ability of peripheral cues to damage consumer welfare by generating choices of brands inferior on some attributes but superior on none (dominated or objectively inferior brands).

At least three definitions or indicators of market inefficiency exist: (1) the existence of dominated brands, (2) prices higher than the point where marginal cost equals marginal revenue (supernormal profits), and (3) lower price-quality correlations. Each indicator faces validity questions. Characterizing brands as dominating or dominated requires precise information on objective product attributes and assumes that consumers weight the attributes on which the dominated brand is inferior. Whether profits are considered supernormal can depend on the accounting methods used. And price-quality correlations assume that quality is unidimensional and can be measured exactly, assumptions that have been criticized as untenable (see Curry and Faulds 1986; Hjorth-Anderson 1984). The current study uses a modified version of the dominance definition. We operationalize inefficiency as the probability of choosing a brand dominated on objective product features within experimental choice sets. This definition is easily operationalized and reflects what would be considered damaged consumer welfare in real-world markets. We tested peripheral-cue effects on inefficiencies with both U.S. (Experiment 1) and Russian (Experiment 2) consumers. Since persuasive product advertising is relatively new in the former Eastern Block countries, consumers from those countries may be more or less susceptible to advertising's influence relative to Western consumers.

EXPERIMENT 1

Experiment 1 tests the impact of consumers' evaluations of peripheral cues on choice. When a famous spokesperson or vivid ad copy is used by a dominated brand, consumers who like that particular person or copy are expected to choose the dominated brand more than those who do not. The implication is that liked peripheral cues can make up for deficits on objective product features (i.e., a compensatory model with peripheral and central cues).

Moreover, this effect should become stronger as information on other product attributes on which the brands are comparable is added, because consumer perceptions of the relative superiority of the dominating brand should decrease. This is because the relative influence of an attribute is typically reduced as others are added. For example, the relationship between price and perceived quality erodes as information on other product features is added (Monroe 1973). Therefore, two information environments were tested: one in which an overall quality rating was not supplied and one in which it was. The two target brands, one dominating the other, were equated on the overall quality rating when it was supplied. Experiment 1 tests the following hypotheses:

H1: Positive evaluations of a dominated brand's peripheral cues will (a) increase the probability that the dominated brand is chosen (increasing inefficiencies), and (b) improve attitudes toward the dominated brand.

H2: Hypothesis 1's peripheral-cue effects on (a) choices of dominated brands and (b) attitudes toward dominated brands will be stronger when dominated

[1]The authors wish to thank Olga A. Tretjak, Vladimir Tretjak, and Serqey V. Shkurnikov for their help in data collection in Russia.

and dominating brands are said to be of equal overall quality.

Method

Subjects, Stimuli, and Design. Fifty-six undergraduate marketing students participated in the experiment as part of an in-class exercise for which they received extra-credit points. Subjects were randomly assigned to experimental conditions. Stimuli are presented in the appendices. Two product classes (cameras and cruises) and two types of peripheral cue (spokesperson and ad copy) were tested to enhance generalizability. Pretests indicated that Jay Leno (talk-show host) and Michael J. Fox (actor) were more famous and better liked than other fictitious spokespeople such as Alex Tyler. Pretests also indicated that ad copies were rated as more exciting and more liked when they used slightly more vivid language (e.g., "stroll" vs. "walk"; see Heath et al. 1994).

Four brands were presented within a given choice set. Fictitious brand names were used to eliminate effects of brand familiarity and liking (Brands J, L, N, P). Brands L and N dominated Brands J and P. The latter were inferior on multiple dimensions and superior on none, and were included to reduce experimental demand. Only Brands L and N, the target brands, were expected to be chosen (and, in fact, were the only ones chosen). Within the target brands, Brand N dominated Brand L. Brand N was comparable to Brand L on all dimensions except one. In cruises, Brand N's cabin was 185 square feet whereas Brand L's was 140 square feet. In cameras, Brand N's zoom ratio was 4 to 1 whereas Brand L's was 3 to 1 (see Appendix B).

Experiment 1 manipulated peripheral-cue strength and product dominance within subjects, and presence of overall quality ratings (absent vs. present) between subjects. Type of peripheral cue (spokesperson fame vs. ad-copy vividness) and product class (cameras vs. cruises) were counterbalanced between subjects. There was no spokesperson indicated in the ads testing vividness, and no vividness manipulation in the ads testing spokesperson fame. Brand L, the dominated target brand, always had vivid ad copy or the famous spokesperson (Jay Leno), whereas Brand N had less vivid ad copy or a nonfamous spokesperson (Alex Tyler). To reduce demand, peripheral cues were varied across nontarget brands as well (J and P), where Michael J. Fox served as the famous spokesperson.

Procedure. Each subject received a booklet containing ads for each of four fictitious brands, brand information, and dependent measures. Ads consisted of scripts for radio ads to reduce confounding influences from typical advertising features (e.g., layouts, music, etc.). Brand information was summarized in a table following the four ads (see Appendix B). After making their choices, subjects responded to a series of questions. Subjects were asked to indicate (1) their attitudes toward each of the brands on nine-point bad/good and unfavorable/favorable scales, (2) how much they liked Brand L's famous spokesperson on a nine-point dislike/like scale, or how much they liked Brand L's more vivid text on nine-point dull/exciting and dislike/like scales, (3) the importance of price, quality, and cabin size (cruise conditions) or zoom ratio (camera conditions) on nine-point unimportant/important scales, and (4) their degree of issue-relevant thinking.

Results

The data were collapsed across counterbalanced variables (product class and type of peripheral cue) since these variables yielded no effects. The two scales measuring liking for the dominated brand's ad copy were averaged due to their high correlation (r=0.90). Median splits on this average as well as on

spokesperson liking divided subjects into those who liked the dominated brands' peripheral cues more and those who liked them less. Even after collapsing across counterbalanced variables, a two-way LOGIT based on peripheral-cue liking and presence of overall quality ratings was not estimable due to small n's when the two main effects and interaction were included. Therefore, two models were run separately: one with the main effects of peripheral-cue liking and presence of quality ratings, and the other with the main effect of peripheral-cue liking and the interaction between peripheral-cue liking and presence of quality ratings. The probability of choosing dominated brands across experimental conditions is summarized in Table 1.

Hypothesis 1a predicted that peripheral-cue liking would increase choice probabilities of dominated brands. Hypothesis 1a was supported. Peripheral-cue liking generated greater shares for dominated brands (36% vs. 3%; $\chi^2_{(1)}$= 6.80, p <.01).[2]

Hypothesis 2a predicted that reporting equivalent overall quality across the dominated and dominating brands would increase the peripheral-cue effect on choices of the dominated brand. Hypothesis 2a was not supported. The interaction between peripheral-cue liking and presence of quality ratings was not statistically significant ($\chi^2_{(1)}$= 0.02); nor was the main effect of presence of quality ratings ($\chi^2_{(1)}$= 0.79).

Hypotheses 1b and 2b were tested by subjecting attitudes toward dominated brands to a two-way between-subjects ANOVA: peripheral-cue liking by presence of quality ratings. The two attitude scales were combined due to their high correlation (r=0.92). Hypothesis 1b predicted that peripheral-cue liking would increase attitudes toward dominated brands. The significant main effect of peripheral-cue liking supported Hypothesis 1b ($F_{(1,51)}$= 8.42, p <.01). Attitudes toward dominated brands were higher when peripheral cues were more liked (M=7.62) than when they were less liked (M=6.83).

Hypothesis 2b predicted that the peripheral-cue effect would be stronger when the two brands were said to have the same overall quality. Hypothesis 2b was not supported. The interaction between peripheral-cue liking and presence of quality ratings was not significant ($F_{(1,51)}$= 1.61); nor was the main effect of presence of quality ratings ($F_{(1,51)}$< 1.00).

Discussion

The results of Experiment 1 demonstrate that peripheral cues can lead consumers to choose objectively inferior brands. Liking for peripheral cues led over 30% of the people to choose a brand dominated on objective product features. Although it is possible that subjects did not recognize Brand N's superiority over Brand L, this seems unlikely for three reasons. First, the attribute information was clearly presented in table form so that cross-brand differences were quite salient. Second, Brand N commanded a large share which it would not have commanded had subjects been unaware of its superiority. Third, two items measuring issue-relevant thinking suggest that the subjects considered their decisions carefully. The first measured how carefully subjects evaluated the experimental brands relative to how carefully they evaluate household products such as paper towels, laundry detergents, and cleansers. The second measured how carefully subjects evaluated the experimental brands relative to how carefully they evaluate

---

[2]This is the χ^2 from the main effects model and is virtually identical to that from the model in which the other term was the interaction of peripheral-cue liking with quality rating ($\chi^2_{(1)}$ = 6.62).

TABLE 1
Probability of Choosing the Dominated Brand in Experiment 1

	Less Liking for Peripheral Cues	More Liking for Peripheral Cues
Quality Rating Absent	0.0%	30.7%
	(*n*=15)	(*n*=13)
Quality Rating Present	6.2%	41.7%
	(*n*=16)	(*n*=12)

consumer electronics products such as televisions, stereo equipment, and microwave ovens. The two scales ranged from -8 (much less carefully) to +8 (much more carefully). Subjects reported evaluating experimental brands more carefully than household products (M=4.14; $t_{(55)}$= 9.07, p <.01) and about as carefully as consumer electronics products (M=-0.64; $t_{(55)}$= 1.71, *ns*). Therefore, it appears that subjects were cognizant of Brand N's objective superiority, and that some were willing to trade that superiority for stronger advertising features such as vivid copy or famous spokespeople.

The findings are subject to three alternative explanations. First, subjects may have chosen the dominated brand because they did not consider the attribute on which it was inferior to be important (cabin size or zoom ratio). This explanation can be tested by examining reported attribute weights of subjects choosing Brand L. If subjects choosing dominated brands did not weight cabin size or zoom ratio, then their reported importances for these attributes should be near 1 on the 1-9 scales. However, this test is conservative because attribute weights were measured after choice and, therefore, may be deflated by the desire to justify their decision and/or reduce dissonance. Despite this downward bias, people choosing dominated brands rated the importance of cabin size and zoom ratios significantly higher than 1.0 (M=4.30; $t_{(9)}$= 5.36, p <.01) and not significantly lower than the scale's mid-point of 5.0 ($t_{(9)}$= -1.13, *ns*). It appears, therefore, that Brand N dominated Brand L on objective attributes even in the eyes of those choosing Brand L. These consumers, however, were willing to trade off objective inferiority for stronger peripheral cues.

Second, and relatedly, consumers may generally regard the difference between Brands N and L to not matter. However, this explanation is untenable since it implies that consumers would be perfectly indifferent between, for example, cruise cabins of 140 sq. ft. and 185 sq. ft. (in the absence of peripheral cues). A modified version of this explanation, however, is plausible, although it is consistent with the conclusion that peripheral cues led consumers to nonoptimal choices. Peripheral cues may have signalled that the attribute deficits were not important. For example, consumers may have reasoned that if the smaller cabin was large enough for a given spokesperson, then it was large enough for them. Although the current study did not assess such effects, they seem far less probable when vivid text served as the peripheral cue. Therefore, it is likely that Brand L's weaknesses mattered to consumers in the absence of peripheral cues, although in the context of peripheral cues some consumers (1) were willing to trade off stronger peripheral cues for weaker product features, and/or (2) assumed that the weaknesses were inconsequential when associated with stronger peripheral cues. Both effects reflect the ability of peripheral cues to lead consumers to choose objectively inferior brands.

Third, it might be argued that the peripheral cues conveyed product information which then eliminated dominance. However, this is unlikely since, in an earlier study (Heath et al. 1994), comparable cues had no effect on brand attitudes when subjects thought hard about their evaluations and (1) evaluated a single product (Experiment 1) or (2) evaluated multiple products with small trade-offs across attributes (Experiment 3). Therefore, it appears that consumers make decisions in part on the basis of persuasive marketing messages that then lead them to choose objectively inferior brands, brands they would not choose otherwise. This effect may help to account for the existence of dominated brands in the marketplace (see Hjorth-Anderson 1984).

The peripheral-cue effects reported here run counter to multiprocess theories claiming that peripheral cues are ineffective in the context of issue-relevant thinking (see Petty and Cacioppo 1986; Chaiken 1980). However, the results are consistent with recent demonstrations that peripheral cues wield considerable influence in competitive settings despite issue-relevant thinking (cf. Heath et al. 1994; Miniard et al. 1992). They extend these findings by showing that the effects are not limited to situations in which trade-offs exist across brands.

Contrary to Hypothesis 2, the peripheral-cue effect on choices of dominated brands was not moderated by additional information on the brands. One potential explanation is that there was enough comparable information across the two target brands that adding one more piece of information was relatively unimportant.

EXPERIMENT 2

Experiment 2 tests the impact of peripheral cues on choices of dominated brands by Russian consumers. Russian markets are increasingly open to Western goods and advertising is increasing rapidly. However, it is not clear whether Russians will react to persuasive advertising messages in the same way Americans do. For example, Russia's anti-capitalistic heritage might leave Russians less susceptible to advertising's persuasive efforts. Therefore, Experiment 2 reassesses Hypotheses 1 on Russian consumers.

Since the presence of overall quality ratings had no effect in Experiment 1, it was excluded from Experiment 2. Instead, we assessed two other variables that might moderate the effects of peripheral cues on inefficiencies: (1) the importance of the product attribute on which the dominated brand is inferior relative to the dominating brand, and (2) the size of the difference on that attribute between dominated and dominating brands. Experiment 2, therefore, also tests the following hypothesis:

H3: The positive effects of peripheral-cue liking on (a) choice probabilities and (b) brand attitudes will increase as the dominated attributes become less important and/or the discrepancy between dominating and dominated brands decreases.

Method

Subjects consisted of 134 students at Russia's Railway Institute in St. Petersburg who were paid $2 (U.S.) for their participation (the institute is similar to an engineering college in the U.S.). Three native Russians briefed us on various facets of Russian culture prior

TABLE 2
Probability of Choosing the Dominated Brand in Experiment 2

		Less Liking for Peripheral Cues	More Liking for Peripheral Cues
Weakness on Rewind Speed	Small Weakness	20.0% (n=20)	25.0% (n=16)
	Large Weakness	10.5% (n=19)	20.0% (n=15)
Weakness on Overall Quality	Small Weakness	0.0% (n=18)	38.5% (n=13)
	Large Weakness	11.1% (n=18)	13.3% (n=15)

to the experiment's design. Based on their recommendations, Experiment 2 excluded the vividness manipulation due to translation problems, and excluded cruises due to their limited exposure among most Russians. Our consultants assured us that Russians were knowledgeable about automatic focus cameras and that they had various cultural heros that could serve as spokespeople. Therefore, Experiment 2 assessed cameras and the impact of Vladislav Tretjak as a spokesperson. Tretjak was a famous goalie on the Russian hockey team for many years. The camera ads from Experiment 1's spokesperson conditions were translated into Russian. To reduce demand, one of the nontarget brands used a famous spokesperson (Yuri Senkevich) while the other did not.

The structure of Experiment 2's brand attributes was comparable to that of Experiment 1's camera conditions with quality-ratings except that two attributes were dropped (weight and zoom ratio) and one was added (rewind speed; see Appendix C). As seen in Appendix C, Brand L was inferior to Brand N on either an unimportant attribute (rewind speed) or an important attribute (overall quality). Moreover, Brand L's weakness was relatively small or relatively large. The dominated attribute and the size of the dominance were varied between subjects. The procedure was comparable to that of Experiment 1.

Results and Discussion

A median split on subjects' reported liking of the spokesperson was performed and then this variable plus the dominance attribute (less important rewind speed vs. more important overall quality) and dominance size (small vs. large) were submitted to LOGITs. However, the higher-order interactions were not estimable due to small n's. Interactions added one at a time proved to be nonsignificant. Therefore, we report results from the main effects model. Choice probabilities across experimental conditions are summarized in Table 2.

Hypothesis 1a predicted that peripheral-cue liking would increase choice probabilities of dominated brands. Hypothesis 1a was supported. Subjects rating the spokesperson more positively were more likely to choose the dominated brand (23.7%) than those who rated him less positively (10.7%; $\chi^2_{(1)}$= 4.00, p <.05). Hypothesis 3a predicted that this effect would depend on (1) the importance of the attribute on which the dominated brand was inferior and (2) the size of the dominated brand's deficiency. However, Hypothesis 3a was not supported. The only significant effect on choice was that of spokesperson liking. As in Experiment 1, this effect cannot be attributed to no weight being placed on the attributes on which the dominated brand was inferior. Subjects choosing the dominated brand rated the importance of quality and rewind speed significantly above the scale's mid-point (M=7.45; $t(21)$= 5.24, p <.01). Therefore, it appears that they were willing to

trade off quality or rewind speed for a spokesperson's recommendation.

Hypothesis 1b predicted that peripheral-cue liking would increase attitudes toward the dominated brand. The two measures of attitudes toward the dominating brand were averaged due to their high correlation (r=.79). A three-way ANOVA on these measures failed to support Hypothesis 1b. Peripheral-cue liking had no effect on attitudes toward the dominated brand. The only significant effect was the main effect of the attribute on which dominance occurred ($F_{(1, 90)}$= 5.52, p <.05). The dominated brand was rated lower when it was inferior on overall quality (M=2.07) than when it was inferior on rewind speed (M=2.68).

Issue-relevant thinking was again prevalent. Subjects reported evaluating experimental brands more carefully than household products (M=4.91; $t_{(134)}$= 16.56, p <.01) but about as carefully as consumer electronics products (M=1.74; $t_{(134)}$= 1.74, ns). As in Experiment 1, therefore, the peripheral-cue effects reported here run counter to the popular belief that peripheral cues yield little influence in the context of issue-relevant thinking (see Petty and Cacioppo 1986; Chaiken 1980).

GENERAL DISCUSSION

Prior experimental research shows that advertising has the potential to bias consumer beliefs and alter choice probabilities when trade-offs exist across brands, even when consumers engage in issue-relevant thinking (e.g., Heath et al. 1994). The current study extends this research by showing that peripheral cues can lead consumers to choose objectively inferior brands. Despite careful evaluations, consumers are willing to trade off certain product features for strong advertising cues such as famous spokespeople or more vivid copy. This effect occurred in both U.S. and Russian consumers. The implication is that peripheral cues can generate market inefficiencies and potentially damage consumer welfare. Although it is sometimes argued that an advertiser can get a consumer to purchase an inferior product only once, the evidence suggests otherwise (see Norris 1984). Consumers often have limited information on other brands, and product experiences are often ambiguous and subject to advertising-based biases. For example, Levin and Gaeth (1988) found that ground beef tasted better when consumers were told beforehand that it was 85% lean than 15% fat.

As markets open in the former Eastern Block, governments, marketers, and consumers should be sensitive to the costs and benefits of advertising. The current study suggests that consumers in these countries are just as susceptible to advertising-generated biases as consumers in the West. The implication is that markets and advertising should be carefully monitored and, if need be, regulated as they evolve, rather than waiting until advertisers have

APPENDIX A
Advertising Copy

Spokesperson Conditions	Vividness Conditions
Camera Copy: Version 1 - If you're thinking about buying a new compact 35mm camera, you're not alone. More and more people are buying compact 35mm cameras ever year. That's why you should consider a new (camera name) camera. I recently purchased one and found everything about it to be great. Taking pictures with (camera name) is simple. Its automatic features make it easy to use. It's small, so you can take it wherever you're going. You'll find its price to be low as well. When it's time for you to go ahead and buy a compact 35mm camera, give (camera name) a look. I'm sure glad I did.	*Vivid Copy: Cameras -* If you're thinking about buying a new compact 35mm camera, you're not alone. More and more folks are buying compact 35mm cameras every year. That's why you should consider a new (camera name) camera. I recently purchased one and found everything about it to be great. Taking pictures with (camera name) is not only fun, it's easy. Its automatic features make it a pleasure to use and its small size lets you take it everywhere. You'll find its price easy to take as well. When it's time for you to take the plunge and buy a compact 35mm camera, give (camera name) a look. I'm sure glad I did.
Camera Copy: Version 2 - More people than ever before are buying compact 35mm cameras. And for a lot of good reasons. So, maybe it's time for you to give some serious thought to buying a (camera name) camera. I just purchased a new (camera name) camera and found that it offers me a wide variety of niceties. It's small in size even though it has several automatic features. And its got an affordable price. So if you're thinking that buying a compact 35mm camera might be nice look at a new (camera name) today. I'm happy I did.	*Nonvivid Copy: Cameras -* More people than ever before are buying compact 35mm cameras. And for a lot of good reasons. So, maybe it's time for you to give some serious thought to buying a (camera name) camera. I just purchased a new (camera name) camera and found that it offers me a wide variety of niceties. It's small in size even though it has several automatic features. And its got an affordable price. So if you're thinking that buying a compact 35mm camera might be nice look at a new (camera name) today. I'm happy I did.
Cruise Copy: Version 1 - If you're thinking about taking a cruise, you're not alone. More and more folks are taking their vacations on cruises every year. In fact, I recently took my vacation on a (cruise name) cruiseship. Aboard a (cruise name) cruise, you can enjoy yourself in many ways. After participating in one of the many sports and activities, you can just hang around the pool. At night, you can enjoy fine dining, entertainment, and a walk around the deck. When it's time for you to go ahead and take the cruise you deserve, give (cruise name) cruises a call. I'm glad I did.	*Vivid Copy: Cruises -* If you're thinking about taking a cruise, you're not alone. More and more folks are taking their vacations on cruises every year. In fact, I recently took my vacation on a (cruise name) cruiseship. Aboard a (cruise name) cruise, you can indulge yourself in many ways. After enjoying your favorite sport, you can unwind and soak up the sun around the pool. A quick change in your state room and you're off to an evening of fabulous dining, entertainment, and a leisurely stroll around the deck. When it's time for you to go ahead and take the cruise you deserve, give (cruise name) cruises a call. I'm glad I did.
Cruise Copy: Version 2 - More people than ever before are taking their vacations aboard a cruise ship. And for a lot of good reasons. So, maybe it's time for you to do what I did and take a cruise aboard (cruise name) cruises. (Cruise name) cruises offer you a wide variety of fun and exciting sports and activities, You can enjoy the sun while walking the deck or sitting by the pool. In addition to the great state rooms you'll find the dining and entertainment to be wonderful. So if you're thinking about taking your next vacation aboard a cruise, give (Cruise name) cruises a call today. I'm happy I did.	*Nonvivid Copy: Cruises -* More people than ever before are taking their vacations aboard a cruise ship. And for a lot of good reasons. So, maybe it's time for you to do what I did and take a cruse aboard (cruise name) cruises. (cruise name) cruises offer you a wide variety of fun and exciting sports and activities. You can enjoy the sum while walking the deck or sitting by the pool. In addition to the great state rooms you'll find the dining and entertainment to be wonderful. So if you're thinking about taking your next vacation aboard a cruise, give (cruise name) cruises a call today. I'm happy I did.

the chance to establish entrenched beliefs that are not easily changed after the fact. For example, consumers continued to purchase *Listerine* for its purported cold-prevention properties even after a corrective advertising campaign had been run (see Norris 1984; Wilkie, McNeill, and Mazis 1984).

In the current study, the effects of peripheral cues were such that they persuaded a consumer to try choose one brand rather than another. However, more insidious effects are possible when we consider choices to engage in a given behavior or not (e.g., smoking). The findings of the current study suggest that relatively innocuous advertising stimuli such as a spokesperson or vivid text might be enough to draw a consumer into detrimental behaviors when s/he is relatively undecided (e.g., *Joe Camel*). The results support restrictions on advertisements for potentially harmful products.

REFERENCES

Chaiken, Shelly (1980), "Heuristic Versus Systematic Information Processing and the Use of Source Versus Message Cues in Persuasion," *Journal of Personality and Social Psychology*, 39 (November), 752-766.

Curry, David J. and David J. Faulds (1986), "Indexing Product Quality: Issues, Theory, and Results," *Journal of Consumer Research*, 13 (June), 134-145.

APPENDIX B
Product Information for Experiment 1

Cruises: Quality Absent

Cruise	Price	Days	Islands	Room Size	Olympic Pool	Athletic Activities	Night Club
J	$1,025	6	3	120 sq. ft.	Yes	Yes	Yes
L	$795	7	5	140 sq. ft.	Yes	Yes	Yes
N	$795	7	5	185 sq. ft.	Yes	Yes	Yes
P	$1,095	6	4	125 sq. ft.	Yes	Yes	Yes

Cruises: Quality Present

Cruise	Price	Overall Quality	Days	Islands	Room Size	Olympic Pool	Athletic Activities	Night Club
J	$1,025	2.75	6	3	120 sq. ft.	Yes	Yes	Yes
L	$795	3.00	7	5	140 sq. ft.	Yes	Yes	Yes
N	$795	3.00	7	5	185 sq. ft.	Yes	Yes	Yes
P	$1,095	2.50	6	4	125 sq. ft.	Yes	Yes	Yes

Cameras: Quality Absent

Camera	Price	Weight	Zoom Ratio	Auto Film Loading	Auto Flash	Auto Focus	Auto Film Advance
J	$350	12 oz.	2.2 to 1	Yes	Yes	Yes	Yes
L	$310	10 oz.	3.0 to 1	Yes	Yes	Yes	Yes
N	$310	10 oz.	4.0 to 1	Yes	Yes	Yes	Yes
P	$375	13 oz.	2.1 to 1	Yes	Yes	Yes	Yes

Cameras: Quality Present

Camera	Price	Overall Quality	Weight	Zoom Ratio	Auto Film Loading	Auto Flash	Auto Focus	Auto Film Advance
J	$350	2.75	12 oz.	2.2 to 1	Yes	Yes	Yes	Yes
L	$310	3.00	10 oz.	3.0 to 1	Yes	Yes	Yes	Yes
N	$310	3.00	10 oz.	4.0 to 1	Yes	Yes	Yes	Yes
P	$375	2.50	13 oz.	2.1 to 1	Yes	Yes	Yes	Yes

Gaeth, Gary J. and Timothy B. Heath (1987), "The Cognitive Processing of Misleading Advertising in Young and Old Adults," *Journal of Consumer Research*, 14 (June), 43-54.

Heath, Timothy B., Michael S. McCarthy, and David L. Mothersbaugh (1994), "Spokesperson Fame and Vividness Effects in the Context of Issue-Relevant Thinking: The Moderating Role of Competitive Setting," *Journal of Consumer Research*, 20 (March), 520-534.

Hjorth-Anderson, Chr. (1984), "The Concept of Quality and the Efficiency of Markets for Consumer Products," *Journal of Consumer Research*, 11 (September), 708-718.

Kirmani, Amna (1990), "The Effect of Perceived Advertising Costs on Brand Perceptions," *Journal of Consumer Research*, 17 (September), 160-171.

Levin, Irwin P. and Gary J. Gaeth (1988), "How Consumers are Affected by the Framing of Attribute Information Before and After Consuming the Product," *Journal of Consumer Research*, 15 (December), 374-378.

Miniard, Paul W., Deepak Sirdeshmukh, and Daniel E. Innis (1992), "Peripheral Persuasion and Brand Choice," *Journal of Consumer Research*, 19 (September), 226-239.

Monroe, Kent (1973), "Buyers' Subjective Perceptions of Price," *Journal of Marketing Research*, 10 (February), 70-80.

Norris, Vincent P. (1984), "The Economic Effects of Advertising: A Review of the Literature," in *Current Issues and Research in Advertising, Vol. 2*, eds. James H. Leigh and Claude R. Martin, Jr., Ann Arbor: University of Michigan, 39-134.

Petty, Richard E. and John T. Cacioppo (1986), *Communication and Persuasion: Central and Peripheral Routes to Attitude Change*, New York, Springer.

Shimp, Terence A. and Larry Gresham (1983), "An Information Processing Perspective on Recent Advertising Literature," in *Current Issues and Research in Advertising*, eds. James H. Leigh and Claude R. Martin, Jr., Ann Arbor: University of Michigan, 39-76.

Stigler, George J. (1961), "The Economics of Information," *Journal of Political Economy*, 69 (June), 213-225.

Wilkie, William L., Dennis L. McNeill, and Michael B. Mazis (1984), "Marketing's 'Scarlet Letter': The Theory and Practice of Corrective Advertising," *Journal of Marketing*, 48 (Spring), 11-31.

APPENDIX C
Product Information for Experiment 2

Small Dominance On Quality

Camera	Price*	Overall Quality	Rewind Speed	Auto Film Loading	Auto Focus	Auto Film Advance
J	4500	2.75	12 sec.	Yes	Yes	Yes
L	4000	3.70	8 sec.	Yes	Yes	Yes
N	4000	3.75	8 sec.	Yes	Yes	Yes
P	4750	2.50	13 sec.	Yes	Yes	Yes

Large Dominance On Quality

Camera	Price	Overall Quality	Rewind Speed	Auto Film Loading	Auto Focus	Auto Film Advance
J	4500	2.75	12 sec.	Yes	Yes	Yes
L	4000	3.00	8 sec.	Yes	Yes	Yes
N	4000	3.75	8 sec.	Yes	Yes	Yes
P	4750	2.50	13 sec.	Yes	Yes	Yes

Small Dominance On Rewind Speed

Camera	Price	Overall Quality	Rewind Speed	Auto Film Loading	Auto Focus	Auto Film Advance
J	4500	2.75	12 sec.	Yes	Yes	Yes
L	4000	3.75	8.1 sec.	Yes	Yes	Yes
N	4000	3.75	8.0 sec.	Yes	Yes	Yes
P	4750	2.50	13 sec.	Yes	Yes	Yes

Large Dominance On Rewind Speed

Camera	Price	Overall Quality	Rewind Speed	Auto Film Loading	Auto Focus	Auto Film Advance
J	4500	2.75	12 sec.	Yes	Yes	Yes
L	4000	3.75	9.6 sec.	Yes	Yes	Yes
N	4000	3.75	8.0 sec.	Yes	Yes	Yes
P	4750	2.50	13 sec.	Yes	Yes	Yes

*All prices are in 1992 Rubles.

A Model of the Determinants of Retail Search

Jeffrey G. Blodgett, University of Mississippi
Donna J. Hill, Bradley University
George Stone, University of Mississippi

ABSTRACT

The purpose of this study was to develop a model of the information search process that better reflects consumers' search strategies. In this model, the amount of retail search undertaken, and the extent to which a consumer relies on interpersonal and neutral sources, are hypothesized to be dependent upon the importance of the product, time availability, perceived risk, subjective knowledge, and enjoyment. Building upon previous research, the authors hypothesize that consumers who rely upon interpersonal advice or neutral sources will, in turn, undertake less retail search. The structural model was tested using LISREL VII, with a sample of 172 consumers who had recently made a major household purchase. The authors suggest that the low explanatory power of the model may be due to the changing retail environment (e.g., new types of stores, changing socio-demographics, technological advancements, etc.), and provide directions for future research.

INTRODUCTION

A considerable amount of research in consumer behavior has attempted to explain why some consumers search for a great deal of information prior to making a purchase while others search very little, if at all (Beatty and Smith 1987; Bloch, Sherrel, and Ridgway 1986; Furse, Punj, and Stewart 1984; Punj and Staelin 1983; Duncan and Olshavsky 1982; Kiel and Layton 1981; Moore and Lehmann 1980; Westbrook and Fornell 1979; Jacoby, Chestnut, and Fisher 1978; Newman 1977; Claxton, Fry, and Portis 1974; Newman and Staelin 1972). One of the underlying goals of this research has been to explain why different individuals rely on different search strategies; that is, why some consumers reference several consumer rating guides (such as *Consumer Reports*), or spend a considerable amount of time visiting several retail stores and evaluating several brands, while other consumers visit only one retail store and rely mainly on the advice of a friend or a salesperson when deciding which brand to buy. Although these studies have increased our general understanding of the information search process, researchers have yet to explain much of its variance.

Blodgett and Hill (1991) suggested that one reason for the low explanatory power of current models of information search has to do with the conceptualization and measurement of the various dimensions of search (in particular, interpersonal search and neutral sources search). Traditionally, researchers have measured these two dimensions of information search by asking consumers how many times each particular search behavior was undertaken; for example, how many people they talked to, how many magazines or consumer guides they read, etc. (Kiel and Layton 1981; Duncan and Olshavsky 1982; Furse et al. 1984). A serious limitation of these measures is that they do not indicate how much the consumer *relied* on each particular type of information source when making the purchase decision. To overcome the deficiencies of these amount-of-search measures Blodgett and Hill (1991) suggested the use of "instrumentality" measures. These measures focus on the extent to which a consumer relied on a particular information source when making a purchase decision. As such, these instrumentality (or reliance) measures have the potential to provide greater insight into consumers' search strategies. Using these reliance measures, Blodgett and Hill (1991) provided evidence that interpersonal and

neutral sources can serve as substitutes for retail search. These findings are consistent with those of previous researchers (e.g., Furse et al. 1984; Kiel and Layton 1981) who have created profiles of consumers' search strategies. The purpose of this paper is to present a causal model of the information search process, one that better reflects consumer's search strategies. In doing so, this research builds upon, and complements the work of Beatty and Smith (1987) and other researchers (Bloch et al. 1986; Furse et al. 1984; Punj and Staelin 1983; Duncan and Olshavsky 1982; Kiel and Layton 1981; Moore and Lehmann 1980; Westbrook and Fornell 1979; Jacoby et al. 1978; Claxton et al. 1974), and takes into account the suggestions of Blodgett and Hill (1991). In this model, the amount of retail search undertaken, and the extent to which a consumer relies on interpersonal and neutral sources, are hypothesized to be dependent upon the importance of the product, time availability, perceived risk, subjective knowledge, and enjoyment. Building upon previous research, we hypothesize that consumers who rely upon interpersonal advice or neutral sources will, in turn, undertake less retail search. In doing so, we model information search as a *dynamic* process, thus (potentially) providing greater insight into consumers' search strategies. (See Figure 1 for the hypothesized causal model.)

HYPOTHESES

Since previous studies (e.g., Bloch et al. 1986; Punj and Stewart 1983), and consumer behavior textbooks (e.g., Engel and Blackwell 1982) have more than adequately discussed the underlying theory of information search we will focus directly on the hypothesized model. As previously mentioned, the explanatory variables included in the model are product importance, subjective knowledge, perceived risk, time availability, and pleasure. We do not claim to have included all possible explanatory variables in this study. We recognize that other authors have investigated other possible determinants (e.g., perceived variance among alternatives, satisfaction with prior purchase, ego involvement, etc.); however, based on a search of the literature this subset appears to represent most of the major explanatory variables. Another reason for including this particular set of variables is that we have tried to closely mirror the Beatty and Smith (1987) study so that we can assess the explanatory power of the proposed model in relation to their findings. In the following section we will elaborate on these variables, discuss previous empirical findings, and present our hypotheses.

Time Availability. Time availability refers to the amount of time consumers have to educate themselves about the product category and the alternatives that are available, prior to making a purchase decision. As such, time availability encompasses both the time it takes to physically search for information, and the time it takes to mentally process that information. All things being equal, increased amounts of time allows one to conduct greater amounts of external search, and to adequately process that information prior to making the purchase decision.

The empirical evidence regarding the effect of time availability on retail search is mixed. Although Moore and Lehmann (1980) and Beatty and Smith (1987) found that time availability leads to increased levels of retail search, Kiel and Layton (1981) and

Advances in Consumer Research
Volume 22, © 1995

FIGURE 1
A Model of the Determinants of Information Search

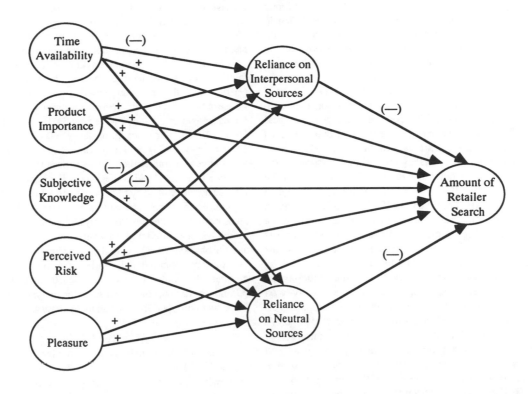

Newman and Staelin (1972) both found no relationship between perceived urgency of purchase and retail search. Other researchers have found that consumers who have sufficient amounts of time are more likely to consult neutral sources (Beatty and Smith 1987), while consumers who are under time constraints are more apt to rely on a simple heuristic, such as asking for advice from a more knowledgeable friend (i.e., a purchase pal) when making the purchase decision (Furse et al. 1984). Based on this research, we hypothesize that consumers who have sufficient amounts of time to search for information will undertake greater amounts of retail search, and are more likely to rely on neutral sources when making their purchase decisions, while consumers who have little time in which to search will rely more heavily on interpersonal sources.

Subjective Knowledge. Subjective knowledge is a global self-assessment of how much one knows about a product class, vis-a-vis other consumers, and is an indication of one's self-confidence regarding a particular product category (Brucks 1985; Park and Lessig 1981).

Park and Lessig (1981) and Selnes and Gronhaug (1986) state that subjective knowledge is strongly related to the use of different *types* of information. Consumers who perceive themselves as being highly knowledgeable about a product category have been found to undertake less external search (Beatty and Smith 1987), to seek less advice from friends (Beatty and Smith 1987), to seek more information from neutral sources (Selnes and Gronhaug 1986; Kiel and Layton 1981), and to rely less on dealer evaluations (Brucks 1985). On the other hand, those consumers who perceive themselves as having little knowledge about a product class have been found to undertake the greatest amount of search activity (Kiel and Layton 1981; Furse et al. 1984), and to be more apt to ask for advice from

a friend (i.e., a purchase pal) when making the purchase decision (Beatty and Smith 1987; Furse et al. 1984; Duncan and Olshavsky 1982). Based on this research, we hypothesize that consumers who perceive themselves as being highly knowledgeable about a particular product category will undertake lessor amounts of retail search, and will rely more heavily on neutral sources, while consumers who perceive themselves as less knowledgeable about a product category will undertake greater amounts of retail search and will rely more heavily on interpersonal information.

Product Importance. The concept of product importance recognizes that consumers attach more "worth" to some products than to others (Bloch and Richins 1983). When the product is perceived as being important consumers will conduct a more extensive search process in order to make a good decision (Beatty and Smith 1987; Jacoby, Chestnut, and Fisher 1978; Newman 1977). When a product is perceived as being important consumers are also more likely to seek out information from friends and relatives (Beatty and Smith 1987), and should be more willing to consult neutral sources. Based on this research, we hypothesize that when the product is perceived as being important consumers will undertake greater amounts of retail search, and will also rely more heavily on both interpersonal and neutral sources.

Pleasure. Pleasure refers to the level of enjoyment that consumers experience with a certain product category (Bellenger and Korgoankar 1980; McQuarrie and Munson 1987). Some people (e.g., car enthusiasts, camera buffs) inherently derive pleasure out of certain product categories while other people view the same product category strictly in functional terms.

Consumers who inherently derive pleasure from a certain product category have been found to conduct greater amounts of external search (Bloch et al. 1986). People who experience greater amounts of pleasure with a product category should also be more apt to read hobbyist magazines and articles in consumer rating guides regarding that product category. Indeed, Beatty and Smith (1987) found that a similar variable, ego involvement, led to increased neutral source search. Based on this research, we hypothesize that consumers who inherently derive pleasure from a certain product category will undertake greater amounts of retail search, and will rely more heavily on neutral sources of information.

Perceived Risk. Perceived risk refers to the perceived costs of making a poor purchase decision. These costs (or on the other hand, perceived benefits) can be both economic and psychological (Newman 1977). Several researchers have found that perceived risk leads to greater depth of external search (Swan 1972; Capon and Burke 1980; Duncan and Olshavsky 1982). Consumers who perceive a high degree of risk are also more likely to seek advice from friends and relatives (Cox 1967; Lutz and Reilly 1974) and to consult neutral sources (Clarke and Belk 1979; Moore and Lehmann 1980; Newman 1977). Therefore, we hypothesize that when consumers perceive a high degree of risk they will conduct greater amounts of retail search, and will rely to a greater extent on the advice of friends and relatives, and on neutral sources.

Reliance on Interpersonal Sources. Rather than undertake an extensive search process, some consumers rely more heavily on advice from friends and relatives when making the purchase decision (see Kiel and Layton 1981; Westbrook and Fornell 1979). We explicitly recognize the dynamic nature of the information search process by hypothesizing that consumers who rely more heavily on interpersonal sources will, in turn, undertake less retail search. Support for this hypothesis also comes from Bloch et al. (1986) who pointed out that discussions with friends can serve the same purpose as browsing through a store, and by Blodgett and Hill (1991), who found a negative relationship between reliance on interpersonal sources and reliance on retail search.

Reliance on Neutral Sources. The extent to which consumers rely on neutral sources can also affect the amount of retail search undertaken. Rather than personally inspect and compare brands, or rely on a salesperson to explain the features and benefits of a product, oftentimes consumers instead will turn to hobbyist magazines or consumer rating guides. This type of information search, in effect, helps consumers to narrow their "evoked set" so that less retail search is needed. Therefore, we hypothesize that consumers who rely more heavily on neutral sources will undertake less retail search.

METHOD

The data were collected via a self-report questionnaire administered to staff members at a large midwestern public university, and from evening MBA students at a private midwestern university. A total of 172 useable questionnaires were collected. Respondents were asked to report on their last major household purchase (excluding an automobile) within the last twelve months, and were given $3 in exchange for their participation. Focal products included televisions, microwave ovens, VCR's, cameras, camcorders, stereos, refrigerators, and other major appliances (this group of products is similar to that used by Beatty and Smith 1987). The average cost of the focal product was $684 (s.d.=$809). Respondents, on average, visited 3.11 stores and considered 2.88 brands. They asked for advice from 2.19 friends, and obtained information from .62 neutral sources.

Approximately fifty-seven percent of the respondents were female, while 43% were male. Fifty percent were married or divorced, while 50% were single. Sixty-eight percent of the respondents were university staff members (mainly secretaries and

clerks), while 32% were professional employees enrolled in an evening MBA program. Forty-nine percent were college graduates, 36% had attended some college, while 15% reported that their highest educational level was high school. Approximately 51% of respondents stated that they were making a "first time" purchase, 25% had purchased a similar product once previously, while 21% had purchased a similar product more than once previously.

Measures. After first specifying the domain of each construct multiple item scales were developed, as suggested by Churchill (1979). All of the items were based on previous research, and were measured on seven-point scales. In order to minimize response biases several of the items were negatively worded (Feldman and Lynch 1988). Product importance was based on scales by Zaichkowsky (1985) and Laurent and Kapferer (1985). Subjective knowledge and time availability were based on items developed by Beatty and Smith (1987). Pleasure and perceived risk were taken from scales developed by McQuarrie and Munson (1987). Reliance on interpersonal sources and reliance on neutral sources were measured with scales developed by Blodgett and Hill (1991). Retail search was measured with a two-item scale developed by Duncan and Olshavsky (1982). One item measured the number of stores that the consumer visited, while the second one measured the number of brands considered. Based on statistical analyses (Cronbach's alpha, confirmatory factor analysis) a few of the initial items were dropped from subsequent analyses.

RESULTS

The structural model was analyzed using LISREL VII (Joreskog and Sorbom 1990). The original model provided a poor fit to the data, with many of the hypothesized relationships being non-significant. Therefore, all of the hypothesized paths that were found to be non-significant (at the .05 level) were fixed to zero, one at a time. This model trimming process continued until only those paths that were significant at the $p=.05$ level remained. The final model fit the data quite well, producing a non-significant chi-square ($X^2_{156}=174.59$, $p=.147$), a goodness-of-fit (GFI) index of .906, and a Tucker-Lewis index of .987. Although the final model fit the data quite well, the overall explanatory power was quite low. (See Table 1 for a summary of the structural coefficients and the fit indices.)

Surprisingly, very few of the hypothesized paths were found to be significant. As hypothesized, time availability had a positive effect (.240) on retail search; however, time availability had no effect on consumers' reliance on interpersonal sources or on neutral sources. Subjective knowledge had a significant effect (.140) on consumers' reliance on neutral sources, but it had no effect on retail search or on consumers' reliance on interpersonal sources. Although pleasure had no significant effect on retail search, it did have a positive effect (.216) on consumers' reliance on neutral sources, as was hypothesized. Contrary to expectations, product importance and perceived risk had no effects on search whatsoever (i.e., retail, interpersonal, or neutral). In addition, we had hypothesized that consumers who relied more heavily on interpersonal or neutral sources would undertake lessor amounts of retail search. However, reliance on interpersonal sources had no effect on retail search, while the effect of reliance on neutral sources on retail search was in the opposite direction of what we had anticipated. Rather than having a negative effect, reliance on neutral sources had a significant, positive effect (.192) on retail search.

DISCUSSION

The purpose of this research was to build a model of the information search process that more accurately depicted consumers' search strategies. In doing so, we had hoped to explain a greater

TABLE 1
Structural Model

From → To	Standardized Effect
Time → Retailer	.240
Time → Interpersonal	*n.s.*
Time → Neutral	*n.s.*
S.Know → Retailer	*n.s.*
S.Know → Interpersonal	*n.s.*
S.Know → Neutral	.140
P.Imp → Retailer	*n.s.*
P.Imp → Interpersonal	*n.s.*
P.Imp → Neutral	*n.s.*
Plsr → Retailer	*n.s.*
Plsr → Neutral	.216
P.Risk → Retailer	*n.s.*
P.Risk → Interpersonal	*n.s.*
P.Risk → Neutral	*n.s.*
Interpersonal → Retailer	*n.s.*
Neutral → Retailer	.192 [1]

$X^2_{156} = 174.59$, $p = .147$	SMC (Retailer) = 9.9%
GFI = .906	SMC (Interpersonal) = 0%
Tucker-Lewis = .987	SMC (Neutral) = 8.4%

[1] This coefficient was in the opposite direction of that hypothesized

percentage of the variation of information search than had previous studies. However, whereas Beatty and Smith (1987) were able to explain 29% of the variance of retail search, the current model explained only 9.9% of the variance of retail search. This result is very surprising, especially since we used essentially the same set of explanatory variables as did Beatty and Smith (1987). Given the seemingly logical premise that interpersonal search and neutral sources can serve as substitutes for retail search, we had expected that the addition of the reliance measures would greatly enhance the explanatory power of the model. Based on previous research (Bloch et al. 1986; Furse et al. 1984; Kiel and Layton 1981; Blodgett and Hill 1991) we had expected that consumers who relied on interpersonal sources would undertake less retail search; however, we found reliance on interpersonal sources to have no effect on retail search. We also expected that those consumers who relied on neutral sources would undertake less retail search; however, reliance on neutral sources actually had a positive effect on retail search. In retrospect, this finding is actually consistent with Westbrook and Fornell (1979), who found that one group of shoppers who relied heavily on neutral information sources visited several retail stores. Apparently, at least for some people, neutral sources supplement, facilitate, and enhance retail search. This latter finding implies that retailers could use neutral sources of information to their advantage. Indeed, many retailers have installed electronic displays that provide neutral information in a *Consumer Reports* type of format (King and Hill 1994). For example, in many of its stores, K-Mart has installed "walk-up information centers" (Fox 1992) which provide comparative information on K-Mart's selection of large-screen TV's, camcorders,

and cameras, etc. Neutral information presented in this type of format might cause consumers to consider certain retail stores and compare certain brands that they might not otherwise have included in their evoked set.

Another surprising finding is that none of the explanatory variables included in the model (time availability, product importance, subjective knowledge, perceived risk) had a significant effect on consumers' reliance on interpersonal sources. We had expected that consumers who perceived themselves as having little knowledge about the product class, who were purchasing a product that they considered to be important, who perceived the financial or psychological risk of making a poor decision to be high, or who had little time in which to visit several retailers and compare different brands would instead rely on the advice of a friend (i.e., a purchase pal). Previous research (Beatty and Smith 1987; Furse et al. 1984; Duncan and Olshavsky 1982; Kiel and Layton 1981; Moore and Lehmann 1980; Jacoby et al. 1978) had found these four variables to affect the *amount* of interpersonal search undertaken by consumers. Given the limitations of traditional, amount-of-search measures, we had anticipated that these four explanatory variables would be even more strongly related to the reliance measure.

The low explanatory power of the model suggests that there are a number of unmodeled antecedents of retail search. Previous research has indicated that retail search is influenced by a number of factors, not all of which were included in our study. Specifically, such factors as the perceived variance among brands (Duncan and Olshavsky 1982), the stability of product categories (Urbany and Dickson 1987), and the retail environment (Urbany 1986) were not included in our model. Since most of these variables are market related, failure to include these variables would be especially problematic if the retail marketplace had changed significantly over the last several years. Indeed, the retail industry has undergone dramatic structural changes since the 1980's, as evidenced by the emergence of new and different types of retailers. Category killers (e.g., Toys 'R' Us, Circuit City, Best Buy, Home Depot), for example, now dominate specific product categories with a wide variety of brand names at guaranteed low prices. Warehouse clubs (e.g., Sam's Wholesale Club, Price Club) and superstores, which were in their infancy several years ago, have emerged as major players, while discount stores (e.g., Wal-Mart) have continued to thrive and expand, thus creating fierce price competition among the various retailers (Mason, Mayer, and Wilkinson 1993). In order to compete more effectively against these new rivals the large mass retailers (e.g., Sears and Montgomery Ward) have expanded their product selection to include a variety of name brands, and have instituted "everyday low prices." With most of these retailers now guaranteeing "Satisfaction or your money back!", consumers know they can return any item that does not live up to their expectations. With so many retailers carrying similar brands, guaranteeing low prices and "Satisfaction or your money back!", the risk of making a poor purchase decision is less today than what it was just five years ago. Hence, consumers today may not feel the need to visit several different retailers to compare prices and product selection. Likewise, consumers may also feel less need to seek the advice of friends or to consult neutral sources. Because of the many changes in the retail environment, it may be that current models of information search are outdated, and that a new paradigm is needed. In order to better reflect today's retail environment, we suggest that researchers incorporate market structure variables (e.g., product differentiation, stability of product category, retail environment) into future models of information search.

Sociodemographic changes have also affected the retailing industry. With the increase in two-wage earner families since the late 1970's (Mason et al. 1993) consumers have come to place increased importance on time. With all of the demands placed on their time consumers are less willing to spend their free time shopping around. As a result, consumers today may actually do very little comparison shopping. With many stores offering wide product selections at everyday low prices and "Satisfaction or your money back" time-pressed consumers may feel comfortable visiting only a single store, especially if they perceive little variation among the brands (Duncan and Olshavsky 1982) carried by the various retailers, and are satisfied with a previous purchase (Kiel and Layton 1981). Olshavsky and Granbois' (1979) contention, that very little search occurs prior to most purchases, may ring even more true today. Again, it appears that the changing retail environment may play an increasingly important role in the information search process.

The concept of ongoing search (Bloch et al. 1986) also deserves greater attention. Bloch et al. (1986) stated that one of the primary motivations of ongoing search is pleasure. Some consumers actually enjoy casually browsing among various stores to learn more about certain products — despite having no immediate purchase intentions. Although they might not currently be in the market for such a product, these consumers may be preparing themselves for a future purchase. The cumulative effect of this ongoing search is that the final purchase decision requires little additional retail search. Hence, when researchers ask consumers how many stores they visited and how many brands they considered the amount of retail search is underreported because ongoing retail search is not adequately taken into consideration; the same may be true for interpersonal and neutral search also. Although ongoing

search, and its effects, are somewhat reflected (albeit poorly) in the present model (through pleasure and subjective knowledge), we suggest that this concept needs to be more fully developed and integrated into the information search model.

Finally, another reason for the low explanatory power of the model may have to do with our measure of retail search. Our measure of retail search consisted of two items, one measuring the number of stores visited and the other measuring the number of brands considered (per Duncan and Olshavsky 1982). Some researchers (Beatty and Smith 1987; Kiel and Layton 1981) have used a somewhat broader measure of retail search, one that reflects how much time was spent at the retailer, and how many phone calls were made to various retailers. It could be that this broader measure more accurately reflects retail search, and that our narrower measure limited the explanatory power of our model.

SUMMARY AND DIRECTIONS FOR FUTURE RESEARCH

This study suggests several fertile directions for future research. First, the concept of reliance on different information sources needs to be further investigated. Conceptually, the amount of a particular type of information search, and the level of reliance placed on that information source, are two distinct constructs (Blodgett and Hill 1991; Engel, Kollat, and Blackwell 1968). It is unclear, however, as to which specific factors cause consumers to rely on different sources of information, and how the level of reliance on each information source affects the retail search process.

Second, it would be of interest to both managers and researchers to explore the effects of relatively recent changes in the retail environment on search behavior. These changes include new types of retail institutions (e.g., category killers, superstores, etc.), new technological developments (e.g., electronic catalogs, computerized information services such as Prodigy, etc.), and changes in economic and family structure (e.g., two-wage earner families with less time to shop).

In summary, the investigation of the consumer search process is crucial to marketers since such knowledge can influence both manufacturers' and retailers' marketing strategies. As this research indicates, there is great potential for developing more sophisticated models of the information search process. By building on the substantial search literature already available and by incorporating such variables as market structure, etc., our understanding and ability to use the search process to provide valuable insights into consumer decision making will be greatly enhanced.

REFERENCE LIST

Beatty, S.E. & Smith, S.M. (1987). "External Search Effort: An Investigation Across Several Product Categories," *Journal of Consumer Research*, 14 (June), 83-95.

Bellenger, D. N. & Korgoankar, P. (1980). "Profiling the Recreational Shopper," *Journal of Retailing*, 58 (Spring), 58-81.

Bloch, P.H. & Richins, M.L. (1983). "Shopping Without Purchase: An Investigation of Consumer Browsing Behavior," in *Advances in Consumer Research*, vol. 10, eds. Richard P. Bagozzi and Alice M. Tybout, Ann Arbor, MI: Association for Consumer Research, 389-393.

Bloch, P.H., Sherrel, D.L. & Ridgway, N.M. (1986). "Consumer Search: An Extended Framework," *Journal of Consumer Research*, 13 (June), 119-126.

Blodgett, J. & Hill, D. (1991). "An Exploratory Study Comparing Amount of Search Measures to Consumers' Reliance on Each Source of Information," in *Advances in Consumer Research*, vol. 18, Provo, Utah: Association for Consumer Research. 773-779.

Brucks, M. (1985). "The Effects of Product Class Knowledge on Information Search Behavior", *Journal of Consumer Research*, 12 (June), 1-16.

Capon, N. & Burke, M. (1980). "Individual, Product Class, and Task Related Factors in Consumer Information Processing," *Journal of Consumer Research*, 7 (December), 314-326.

Churchill, G. (1979). "A Paradigm for Developing Better Measures of Marketing Constructs," *Journal of Marketing Research*, 16 (February), 64-73.

Clarke, K. & Belk, R.W. (1979). "The Effects of Product Involvement and Task Definition on Anticipated Consumer Effort," in *Advances in Consumer Research*, vol.6, ed. William L. Wilkie, Ann Arbor, MI: Association for Consumer Research, 313-318.

Claxton, J.D., Fry, J.N. & Portis, B.P. (1974). "A Taxonomy of Prepurchase Information Gathering Patterns," *Journal of Consumer Research*, 1 (December), 35-42.

Cox, D.F. (1967). *Risk Taking and Information Handling in Consumer Behavior*, Cambridge, MA: Harvard Business School.

Duncan, C.P. & Olshavsky, R.W. (1982). "External Search: The Role of Consumer Beliefs," *Journal of Marketing Research*, 19 (February), 32-43.

Engel. J.F., & Blackwell, R.D. (1982). *Consumer Behavior*, Chicago, Il.: The Dryden Press.

Engel. J.F., Kollat, & Blackwell, R.D. (1968). *Consumer Behavior*, Chicago, Il.: Holt, Rinehart, and Winston, Inc.

Feldman, J.M. & Lynch, J.G. (1988). "Self-Generated Validity and Other Effects of Measurement on Belief, Attitude, Intention, and Behavior," *Journal of Applied Psychology*, 73, no.3, 421-435.

Fox, B. (1992). "Retailers Turn to Kiosks," *Chain Store Age Executive*, March, 35-36.

Furse, D.H., Punj, G.N. & Stewart, D.W. (1984). "A Typology of Individual Search Strategies Among Purchasers of New Automobiles," *Journal of Consumer Research*, 10 (March), 417-31.

Jacoby, J., Chestnut, R.W. & Fisher, W.A. (1978). "A Behavioral Process Approach to Information Acquisition in Nondurable Purchasing," *Journal of Marketing Research*, 15 (November), 532-44.

Joreskog & Sorbom (1990). *LISREL VII: Analysis of Linear Structural Relationships by the Method of Maximum Likelihood: User's Guide*, Mooresville, IN: Scientific Software, Inc.

Kiel, G.C. & Layton, R.A. (1981). "Dimensions of Consumer Information Seeking Behavior," *Journal of Marketing Research*, 18 (May), 233-39.

King, M. & Hill, D.J. (1994). "Electronic Decision Aids: Integration of a Consumer Perspective," *Journal of Public Policy*, 17, 181-202.

Laurent, G. & Kapferer, J.N. (1985). "Measuring Consumer Involvement Profiles," *Journal of Marketing Research*, 22 (February), 41-53.

Lutz, R.J. & Reilly, P.J. (1973). "An Exploration of the Effects of Perceived Social and Performance Risk on Consumer Information Acquisition," in *Advances in Consumer Research*, vol. 1, eds. Scott Ward and Peter Wright, Urbana, IL: Association for Consumer Research, 393-405.

McQuarrie, E.F. & Munson, J.M. (1987). "The Zaichkowsky Personal Involvement Inventory: Modification and Extension," in *Advances in Consumer Research*, 14, M. Wallendorf and P. Anderson, eds., Association for Consumer Research, 36-40.

Mason, J.B. & Mayer, M.L. (1993). *Modern Retailing and Practice*, Homewood, IL: Irwin.

Moore, W.L. & Lehmann, D.R. (1980). "Individual Differences in Search Behavior for a Nondurable," *Journal of Consumer Research*, 7 (December), 296-307.

Newman, J.W. (1977). "Consumer External Search: Amount and Determinants," in *Consumer and Industrial Buying Behavior*, eds. Arch Woodside, Jagdish Sheth, and Peter Bennett, New York: North-Holland.

Newman, J.W. & Staelin, R. (1971). "Multivariate Analysis of Differences in Buyer Decision Time," *Journal of Marketing Research*, 8 (May), 192-198.

Olshavsky, R.W. & Granbois, D.H. (1979). "Consumer Decision Making — Fact or Fiction," *Journal of Consumer Research*, 6 (September), 93-100.

Park, C.W. & Lessig, V.P. (1981). "Familiarity and its Impact on Consumer Decision Biases and Heuristics," *Journal of Consumer Research*, 8 (September), 223-230.

Punj, G.N. & Staelin, R. (1983). "A Model of Consumer Information Search Behavior for New Automobiles," *Journal of Consumer Research*, 9 (March), 366-380.

Punj, G.N. & Stewart, D.W. (1983). "An Interaction Framework of Consumer Information Acquisition," *Journal of Consumer Research*, 10 (September), 208-216.

Selnes, F. & Gronhaug, K. (1986). "Subjective and Objective Measures of Product Knowledge Contrasted," in R. Lutz (ed.), *Advances in Consumer Research*, 13, Provo, Utah: ACR, 67-71.

Swan, J.E. (1972). "Search Behavior Related to Expectations Concerning Brand Performance," *Journal of Applied Psychology*, 56 (August), 332-335.

Urbany, J.E. (1986). "An Experimental Examination of the Economics of Information," *Journal of Consumer Research*, 13 (September), 257-271.

Urbany, J.E. & Dickson, P.R. (1987). "Information Search in the Retail Grocery Market," working paper, The Ohio State University.

Westbrook, R.A. & Fornell, C. (1979). "Patterns of Information Source Useage Among Durable Goods Buyers," *Journal of Marketing Research*, 16 (August), 303-312.

Zaichkowsky, J.L. (1985). "Measuring the Involvement Construct," *Journal of Consumer Research*, 12 (December), 341-352.

New Research on Limited Cognitive Capacity: Effects of Arousal, Mood and Modality

Nader T. Tavassoli, University of Minnesota

Consider a "normal" exposure to an advertisement. Even if the advertisement captures the audience's attention that audience may not be *willing or able* to fully process its content. Indeed most advertisement exposures are characterized by the availability of low cognitive capacity, such as, low involvement or contextual distractions (e.g., Hawkins and Hoch 1992). The session addressed three different variables which may limit cognitive capacity: arousal, positive mood and presentation modality. Moreover, in a combined seven studies the presenters focused on a variety of effects of limited capacity in the realm of persuasion, memory, and inference-making. Dipankar Chakravarti of the University of Arizona commented on the three presentations and moderated the ensuing discussion.

Arousal

The first presentation by Michel Tuan Pham of Columbia University examined how cognitive capacity is influenced by arousal as generated by intense emotions or physical exercise (e.g., Sanbonmatsu and Kardes 1988). Three studies provide a clever test of processing strategies people employ when cognitive capacity is limited. The results of these studies provide coherent and convincing evidence that there are two distinct effects of limited capacity on persuasion. First, a *representation* effect causes information which requires at least moderate cognitive effort to process to be superficially encoded or to be misrepresented. This notion is similar to an increased impact of easy-to-process peripheral cues and a decreased impact of capacity-demanding central claims under low motivation or low ability to process information in the Elaboration Likelihood Model (Petty and Cacioppo 1986).

A second effect qualifies this logic, however. A *selection* effect will increase the impact of diagnostic cues on the persuasion process regardless of their capacity demands. Using a creative design, Pham demonstrated that easy-to-process non-diagnostic cues have a lower influence, and capacity-demanding but diagnostic claims have a higher influence when capacity is constrained by arousal. Pham's work should be of particular interest to persuasion researchers and for the use of peripheral cues (e.g., attractive endorsers or spokespersons) in advertising practice.

Mood

The second presentation by Angela Lee of Toronto University tested the moderating role of positive mood on information processing. Lee contrasted two popular views. The first view proposes that positive mood decreases cognitive capacity available for elaboration by (a) decreasing the motivation to engage in extensive processing (i.e., mood protection), or (b) by activating and retrieving mood-congruent materials which occupy capacity in short-term memory (e.g., Mackie and Worth 1989). The second view proposes that the activation of mood-congruent material increases its accessibility but does not occupy capacity in short-term memory (i.e., the information is not retrieved). Instead, the increased activation may aide elaborative processes such as categorization and inferencing. This should have a positive effect on memory.

In addition Lee examined the differential effect of cognitive capacity limitations on explicit memory—typical ad-copy measures like free recall—versus implicit memory—an emerging area in consumer research which relates to consideration-set formation and stimulus-based factors that affect low-involvement choice. Preliminary results of an experiment favor the second view, namely that positive mood facilitates elaboration and does not decrease available mental capacity. Both explicit memory (recall of brand names) and conceptual priming benefited from a positive versus a neutral mood state. Perceptual priming, which is less sensitive to differences in elaboration, remained unaffected by the mood manipulation. In addition to providing new insights on the moderating role of positive mood on types of memory, Lee's research should have special appeal to the measurement of ad-copy effectiveness which primarily relies on explicit measures of memory.

Modality

The third presentation by Nader Tavassoli of the University of Minnesota focused on the presentation format of verbal information (i.e., spoken and written). In the print media it is written, on the radio it is spoken, and on television it is either spoken, written, alternating between the two modes (or it is bi-modal). A dominant view is that the presentational features of a message are shallowly processed and that semantic features are deeply processed (Craik and Lockhart 1979). Tavassoli argued that depth-of-processing is *dependent* on the format of presentation, for example, via differences in available cognitive capacity. Two types of processing were explored in three studies: item-specific and relational (Meyers-Levy 1991). For example, an item-specific elaboration on "compact car" could be the thought "parking would be easy." A relational elaboration is one that integrates claims such as "compact car" and "fast acceleration" and may prompt the bridging thought "I wonder if it's safe."

Based on the notion of separate mental channels for the processing of spoken versus written information (Penney 1989), cognitive capacity available for elaboration should be maximized within each channel by alternating the presentation of verbal information between the spoken and written modality. Compared to a uni-modal presentation there should be *less* interference between successive advertising claims if these are alternating spoken and written. In other words, the level of *item-specific* elaboration should be *higher* in the alternating mode than in uni-modal presentations. Conversely, the mechanism that maximizes item-specific elaborations, that is, separate channels, should also *decrease relational* elaboration between successive items of information compared to a uni-modal presentation. More simply stated, there should be less relational elaboration (integration) between information in different modalities compared to in the same modality. The first two studies found overall support for item-specific and relational memory. The third study extended the notion of separate channels to deep levels of elaboration, that is, to item-specific and relational inferences using a response latency approach. Besides theoretical contributions, Tavassoli's findings have implications for ad-copy design, public policy issues (memory for warning labels versus integration with brand information) and the selective interference of advertising context.

REFERENCES

Craik, F.I.M. & Lockhart, R.S. (1972). Levels of Processing: A Framework for Memory Research. *Journal of Verbal Learning and Verbal Behavior*, 11, 671-84.

Hawkins, S.A., & Hoch, S.J. (1992). Low-involvement Learning: Memory without evaluation. *Journal of Consumer Research*, 19, 212-225.

Mackie, D.M., & Worth, L.T. (1989). Processing Deficits and the Mediation of Positive Affect in Persuasion. *Journal of Personality and Social Psychology*, 57, 27-40.

Meyers-Levy, J. (1991). Elaborating on Elaboration: The Distinction between Relational and Item-specific Elaboration. *Journal of Consumer Research*, 358-67.

Penney, C.G. (1989). Modality Effects and the Structure of Short-term Verbal Memory. *Memory & Cognition*, 398-422.

Petty, R. E. & Cacioppo, J.T. (1986). *Communication and Persuasion*. NY: Springer.

Sanbonmatsu, D.M. & Kardes, F.R. (1988). The Effects of Physiological Arousal on Information Processing and Persuasion. *Journal of Consumer Research*, 15, 379-85.

Worth, L.T., & Mackie, D.M. (1987). Cognitive Mediation of Positive Affect in Persuasion. *Social Cognition*, 5, 76-94.

Exploring Consumers' Interpretations of a Product Related Illness

Zeynep Gürhan, New York University
Elizabeth H. Creyer, University of Iowa

ABSTRACT

Two studies explored the role of counterfactual processing on consumers' assignments of blame when evaluating a product related illness. The first study underscored the importance of counterfactual processing in consumers' willingness to award money to the injured party. We found that the willingness to award money is partly determined by the blame assigned to the manufacturer, the manufacturer's market share, event foreseeability, and the number of counterfactual alternatives generated related to the manufacturer and to the store where the product was purchased. In the second study, we determined that whether or not the product was being promoted also influenced the assignment of blame.

After an event or incident has occurred, people often evaluate its outcome by constructing alternative outcomes (Kahneman and Miller 1986). Consider the following scenario about a hypothetical consumer.

Mrs. Watson had a severe headache when she was working at the office. Because an important meeting was scheduled for the next day, she was not able to go home. She went to the nearest store but she could not find her regular brand of pain reliever. Since she did not have time to visit another store, she decided to buy a new brand that was currently being promoted. Unfortunately, after taking the medicine, she became ill and was rushed to the hospital. Doctors determined that she had an allergic reaction to one of the ingredients.

After reading such a story it is possible to imagine a number of "what ifs..." "If Mrs. Watson had found her regular brand of pain reliever..." "If the new brand was not on promotion..." "If she had time to look for another store..." Thus, our interpretation of the event is guided by not only what happened, but also by what might have happened. That is, behaviors, thoughts, and feelings are determined by both reality and imagined alternatives to reality, which are known as counterfactuals (Wells and Gavanski 1989). Counterfactual processing has been identified as playing a possible role in the assessment of causality (Wells and Gavanski 1989), victim compensation (Miller and McFarland 1986), attribution of responsibility (Miller and Gunasegaram 1990), and feelings of happiness and regret (Creyer and Gürhan 1994; Kahneman and Tversky 1982).

Therefore a better understanding of counterfactual processes should improve our understanding of consumer behavior. Specifically, the purpose of this research is to explore the role counterfactual processing plays in consumers' assignments of blame when evaluating a product related illness. Blame assignment for product related injuries and illnesses seems to be an important concern to marketers, consumers, and policy makers (Griffin et al. 1992; McGill 1990) and offers an interesting context in which to analyze counterfactual processes.

THEORETICAL BACKGROUND

How people create imagined alternatives (that is, counterfactuals) has long been a topic of interest among psychologists and philosophers alike (Johnson 1986; Kahneman and Varey 1990). Extensive prior research has demonstrated that the extent to which an event is judged to play a causal role in an outcome depends on the extent to which a change, or mutation, to that event would undo the outcome (Kahneman and Tversky 1982; Wells and Gavanski 1989). As Wells and Gavanski point out, events are neither mutable nor immutable, but instead vary in terms of their mutability. Not surprisingly, substantial research has explored those factors influencing the mutability of events.

Kahneman and Miller (1986) hypothesize that easy to visualize alternatives are more mutable than alternatives that are more difficult to imagine. For example, exceptional events are clearly more mutable than unexceptional events (Kahneman and Miller 1986; Kahneman and Tversky 1982). Kahneman and Tversky (1982) asked people to consider the fate of a passenger killed in a crash of a commercial airliner; one of the passengers of the ill-fated flight switched planes just moments before the flight took off. The results indicate that people perceive the fate of this passenger to be more tragic than the fate of other passengers who were booked on the flight weeks in advance.

Theorists (Kahneman and Miller 1986; Kahneman and Tversky 1982; Miller, Turnbull, and McFarland 1990; Wells, Taylor, and Turtle 1987) suggest that this is because the counterfactual alternative of "not dying in a plane crash" is somehow closer to reality in the case of the passenger who switched flights than in the case of passengers who were booked weeks in advance. The mutability of an event also seems to be influenced by the number of alternative behaviors which are available to the main, or focal, actor in the event. Wells and Gavanski (1989) demonstrated that the greater the number of options which were available to the actor, the more likely observers are to imagine an alternative to the outcome. Counterfactual processing has also been found to influence the victim who had experienced a more common fate. Observers offered greater compensation for the same injury which occurred in the exceptional context. Greater compensation for the victim injured in the exceptional case may imply that the victim injured in the exceptional case is blamed less for his injuries than the victim in the common case.

We draw upon prior research to explore how consumers' interpretations of a product related illness are influenced by counterfactual processes. Two studies in which a short vignette describing the circumstances surrounding the illness of a hypothetical consumer were presented to subjects. The first study examined whether the extent to which the consumer, the manufacturer, and the store are blamed for the consumer's illness is influenced by time pressure, the consumer's level of experience with other brands, the product's market share, the number of counterfactual alternatives generated, and the foreseeability of the event. In the second study, we explored whether assignments of blame were also influenced by whether or not the product causing the illness was on promotion.

STUDY 1

Prior research has found that as the exceptionality of the event increases, people are more likely to engage in counterfactual processing (Kahneman and Miller 1986; Wells and Gavanski 1989). The amount of counterfactual processing that occurs, in turn, influences observers' reactions towards the victim; subjects offered greater compensation for a victim injured in an exceptional circumstance compared to a victim injured in an unexceptional circumstance (Miller and McFarland 1989).

We therefore suggest that when consumers evaluate a product related illness, their assignments of blame and their willingness to award money to the injured party will be influenced by the exceptionality of the circumstance. Usually there are a number of factors involved in a product related illness. One factor likely to influence the exceptionality of the circumstance surrounding a product related illness is the market share of the product, which in this case, is an over-the-counter pain reliever. It is proposed that when a high-share brand fails, it is considered to be more exceptional as compared to the case when a low-share brand fails. This is because high-share brands presumably enjoy higher reputations with respect to their quality. Hence, subjects are more likely to perceive a high-share brand's failure as an exceptional event. Therefore, we hypothesize that they will be more likely to blame the manufacturer and award money to Mrs. Watson when she buys a high-share brand.

Another factor likely to influence the exceptionality of the event is whether or not the victim had previous experience with other brands of pain reliever. If the victim had only used one brand of pain reliever, then becoming ill after trying a new brand is not likely to be perceived as being particularly surprising—the victim may have had similar reactions to the other brands. However, if the victim had used different brands of pain reliever in the past, then becoming ill after using the new brand would seem to be more unlikely, and thus, more exceptional.

Furthermore, we suggest that whether or not the choice of pain reliever was made under time pressure will influence subjects' perceptions of the exceptionality of the circumstance. When the consumer only had a short time to purchase a pain reliever, the choices available were limited. However, when a purchase was not made under time pressure, then the choices available to the consumer were not as limited (e.g., the consumer could have visited another store). Consequently, subjects are expected to generate a greater number of alternative courses of action that could have been taken by the consumer when there was a lack of time pressure. This in turn, implies that subjects will be more likely to place greater blame on the manufacturer, and less blame on the victim, when the purchase was made under time pressure.

Previous research also suggests that the order of the mutation has an impact on causal attributions (Wells and Gavanski 1989). Wells and Gavanski define a mutation as "a deletion, substitution, or other distortion of an event" (p. 161). In their experiments, subjects were asked to list four things that could have been different in the story to prevent the freak events. They found that the influence of counterfactual processing was greater when subjects engaged in the mutation task prior to causal attributions; they awarded more money to the focal individual as a result of his/her injuries. Therefore, we also expect that subjects will blame Mrs. Watson less when they perform the mutation task first.

Event foreseeability is another variable which is likely to influence the blame assignment and willingness to award money (Miller et al. 1990). Foreseeable fates are more easily imagined than unforeseeable fates. Subjects should be less likely to award money to Mrs. Watson when they believe that she could have easily foreseen this event. The above discussion leads to the following hypothesis.

H1:   Subjects are more likely to blame the manufacturer and award money to Mrs. Watson when the product's market share is high, when she has previous experience with the other brands, when she is under time pressure, when subjects perform the mutation task prior to the blame assignment and when they think that Mrs. Watson could not have foreseen this freak event.

Previous research also indicates that mutability mediates perceived causality (Wells and Gavanski 1989). Thus, it may be possible to argue that as the number of counterfactuals related to the accused party (manufacturer) increases, perceivers are more likely to assign a causal role to the accused party. Therefore, the greater the number of counterfactuals generated related to the manufacturer, the greater the blame assigned to the manufacturer.

H2:   Subjects are more likely to blame the manufacturer and award money to Mrs. Watson when the number of counterfactuals related to the manufacturer is high.

Whereas prior research (Wells and Gavanski 1989) has suggested that the greater the mutability of an event, the greater its causal role, it has not examined whether the causal role of one contributing factor increases as the causal role of another factor decreases. We examine whether the blame assigned to the manufacturer varies with the blame assigned to Mrs. Watson, to the store, and to fate. It is intuitive to expect that the blame assigned to the manufacturer is inversely related to the blame assigned to the focal actor, Mrs. Watson. However, it is more interesting to investigate whether the blame assigned to the manufacturer will vary with the blame assigned to fate and to the store. Kahneman and Miller (1986) have suggested that options which are easier to visualize are more mutable than options which are harder to imagine. This may indicate that if people are more likely to assign blame to the tangible features of an event (e.g., manufacturer), they may be less likely to assign blame to intangible features such as fate or bad luck. Thus, we expect an inverse relationship between the blame assigned to the manufacturer and to fate. We expect to observe a positive relationship between the blame assigned to the manufacturer and to the store because as less blame is assigned to the victim, more blame should be assigned to the other, tangible aspects of the event.

H3:   Blame assigned to the manufacturer will be negatively related to the blame assigned to Mrs. Watson and fate and positively related to the blame assigned to the store.

Method

Subjects. One hundred thirty-nine undergraduates enrolled in introductory marketing and economics classes at two large northeastern universities served as subjects. In the vignette, we did not specifically mention that the ingredients were listed on the package; a pretest indicated that the students were generally aware that manufacturers are required to list the ingredients on the package. However, an analysis of the subjects' written responses revealed that 11 subjects incorrectly assumed that the ingredients were not listed on the package; data from these subjects were therefore not included in the analysis. Additionally, data from five other subjects were deleted because they did not complete the tasks.

Stimuli and Design. This study is a 2 (high or low market share) X 2 (absence or presence of previous experience) X 2 (absence or presence of time pressure) X 2 (order of the mutation task: before or after the blame assignment) between subjects factorial design. Subjects were presented a short vignette describing a product related illness. A hypothetical consumer identified as Mrs. Watson, was at work when she suddenly got a headache. Unfortunately, she was not able to go home to rest because she needed to prepare for an important meeting the next day. She went to a store to buy a pain reliever and decided to try a new brand, called *Bomex, which was on promotion.* Shortly after taking *Bomex*, she became very ill and was rushed to the hospital where doctors determined that she was allergic to one of the ingredients. Mrs. Watson is now asking for monetary compensation from the drug manufacturer. Subjects' tasks were to assign blame to the different parties involved in this situation, generate counterfactual thoughts identifying how the illness might *not* have occurred, and determine whether Mrs. Watson should receive money from the drug manufacturer.

Several different factors in the situation were varied. Market share of the hypothetical drug was either high or low. Information presented about the drug stated the following: "According to the results of a recent market survey, 70% (30%) of consumers use Bomex when they have a headache." Time pressure was also manipulated. In the high time pressure condition, subjects were told that the first store Mrs. Watson visited did not have her regular brand of pain reliever; since she didn't have time to go to another store she purchased *Bomex,* a brand heavily promoted. In the low time pressure condition, Mrs. Watson had the time to look for her regular brand in another store but still chose to buy *Bomex,* which was on promotion. The prior experience of Mrs. Watson also varied. In the high experience condition, subjects were informed that Mrs. Watson had tried other brands of pain reliever in the past. In the low experience condition, subjects were told that Mrs. Watson had only used her favorite brand of pain reliever.

Finally, the order of the mutation task differentiated the conditions. Half the subjects read the vignette and then listed ways that the outcome could have been avoided. The other subjects completed the other tasks first.

Procedure

Subjects, randomly assigned to one of the conditions, were run in groups of approximately 25 during a normal class period. At the beginning of class booklets containing the vignette and dependent measures were handed out to subjects. Subjects completed the task at their own pace. After completing the tasks, which took approximately 10 to 15 minutes, subjects were thanked and debriefed.

Dependent Measures

Blame assigned to the manufacturer was assessed by two different measures. The first measure asked whether they would be likely to award Mrs. Watson monetary compensation (yes or no) and its amount. Blame assigned to the manufacturer was also measured on two 7 point items ranging from 1 (very little) to 7 (a great deal). The first item asked subjects to indicate "To what extent is the drug manufacturer to blame for this situation?" The second inquired "To what extent can Mrs. Watson's sickness be attributed to the drug manufacturer?" The higher the value, the greater the blame assigned to the manufacturer. These items were highly correlated (r=.64) and averaged to form an overall index for blame assigned to the drug manufacturer. Blame assigned to fate, the store, and to Mrs. Watson were each measured by an item which assessed the blame assignment on a 7 point scale anchored by "very little" and "a great deal".

Additionally, subjects indicated their agreement with two items which stated "Mrs. Watson could not have done anything to avoid this event" and "Mrs. Watson had no way of knowing that she could have an allergic reaction." These items were averaged (r=.56) to form an index for event foreseeability; lower values indicate that Mrs. Watson could not have foreseen this freak event.

Results and Discussion

First, we examined the effect of counterfactual processing and experimental manipulations on the willingness to award money to Mrs. Watson. Next, we explored how the blame assigned to the manufacturer varied with the blame assigned to the other factors.

Subjects' counterfactual thoughts were coded into four categories: counterfactuals related to Mrs. Watson (e.g., "Mrs. Watson could have gone to another store"; "Mrs. Watson could have asked her doctor"), counterfactuals related to the drug manufacturer (e.g., "If the manufacturer did not promote the product..."; "If the manufacturer used another ingredient..."), counterfactuals related to the store (e.g., "If Mrs. Watson's regular brand was in stock..."; "If the store was closed..."), and counterfactuals related to fate (e.g., "If Mrs. Watson never got a headache..."; "If there was no meeting the next day...").

A logistic regression was conducted to explore the impact of counterfactual processing and experimental manipulations on the willingness to award money to Mrs. Watson. The willingness to award money (binary outcome) served as the dependent variable and the experimental manipulations, assignments of blame, event foreseeability, and the number of counterfactuals generated served as independent variables. The four experimental manipulations have been recorded as dummy variables.

The chi square value is 119.44, the value of -2 Log Likelihood for this model. The observed significance level (p=.18) indicates that this model does not differ significantly from the perfect model. The goodness of fit statistic (chi-square=107.44, p=.43) also leads to a similar conclusion. The logistic regression coefficients and associated statistics are presented in Table 1.

As Table 1 reveals, market share of the manufacturer, blame assigned to the manufacturer, event foreseeability, and the number of manufacturer and store related counterfactual thoughts significantly influenced the willingness to award money. Specifically, subjects were more likely to award money to Mrs. Watson when (1) the manufacturer's market share was high, (2) greater blame was assigned to the manufacturer, (3) they believed that Mrs. Watson could not have foreseen this freak event, (4) a high number of counterfactual alternatives involving the manufacturer were generated, and (5) a high number of counterfactual alternatives involving the store were generated.

The finding that subjects were more likely to award money when they believed the consumer could not have foreseen the event and when the manufacturer was assigned a large portion of the blame for the illness are intuitive. More interesting are the findings regarding the market share and the number of counterfactuals generated related to both the manufacturer and the store. The manufacturer of the low-share brand was blamed less for the consumer's illness compared to the manufacturer of the high-share brand. This may be explained by the fact that an illness as a result of a product failure is considered to be more exceptional when the product is used by many consumers and enjoys a higher-share. Therefore, subjects were more sympathetic towards Mrs. Watson when she met with an exceptional fate (injury as a result of using a high-share brand), as compared to the situation when she used the low-share brand (Miller and McFarland 1986). These findings give partial support to the first and second hypotheses. Our expectations regarding the impact of market share, event foreseeability, and the number of manufacturer related counterfactuals were confirmed. Although it was not hypothesized, the results also suggest that the number of store related counterfactuals has an impact on subjects' willingness to award money. However, our data did not provide enough evidence to suggest that the order of the mutation task, time pressure, and previous experience with the product category influence the subjects' willingness to award money.

A regression analysis which included the blame assigned to the manufacturer as the dependent variable was used to analyze how the blame assigned to the manufacturer varies with the blame assigned to the other factors. Dummy coded experimental manipulations and the blame assigned to Mrs. Watson, to fate, and to the store served as independent variables. The overall model was significant (F(7,114)=5.45, p<.001) and accounted for 25% of the

TABLE 1
Logistic Regression Results for the Willingness to Award Money

Independent Variables	B	S.E.	Wald	df	Sig.
Market Share (1=Low; O=High)	-.86	.49	3.09	1	.08
Prev. Exper. (1=Yes; O=No)	-.45	.47	.92	1	.34
Time Pressure (1=Yes; O=No)	.00	.48	.00	1	.99
Order of Mutation (1=First)	.20	.52	.15	1	.70
Blame (Mrs. Watson)	-.17	.14	1.63	1	.20
Blame (manufacturer)	.31	.16	3.89	1	.05
Blame (store)	.16	.18	.82	1	.37
Blame (fate)	-.02	.11	.02	1	.88
Foreseeability	-.31	.14	4.72	1	.03
Number of cf's-Mrs. Watson	.20	.19	1.17	1	.28
Number of cf's-manufacturer	.61	.32	3.66	1	.06
Number of cf's-store	.89	.49	3.28	1	.07
Number of cf's-fate	-.06	.25	.06	1	.81
Constant	-.10	1.45	.01	1	.94

variation. The analysis suggests that the blame assigned to the manufacturer is significantly related to the blame assigned to Mrs. Watson (beta=-.41, t=-4.91, p<.001), the blame assigned to the store (beta=.24, t=2.88, p<.005), and the blame assigned to fate (beta=-.26, t=-3.21, p<.001).

The results of the first study underscored the importance of counterfactual processing and market share of the manufacturer in subjects' willingness to award money to the victim. Additionally, we showed that the blame assigned to the manufacturer was positively related to the blame assigned to the store and negatively related to the blame assigned to Mrs. Watson and fate. Furthermore, an informal analysis of the mutation task revealed that some of the subjects generated counterfactuals which referred to the fact that the brand was on promotion. However, since the presence of promotion was not manipulated in the first study, we could not directly test its impact. We address this issue in the second experiment.

STUDY 2

Hypotheses

In the second study, we explored the impact of market share and promotion on the assignment of blame within the same context of product related illness. Based on the previous research and the results of the first study, we expect to replicate the findings regarding the impact of market share on the assignment of blame to the manufacturer. It has been suggested that when the market share is high, subjects are more likely to blame the manufacturer because they have more sympathy towards the victim in an exceptional circumstance. Additionally, we propose that buying the product on promotion increases the perceived mutability of the outcome. Thus, subjects are more likely to engage in counterfactual processing when the product is bought on promotion. Furthermore, when the product is bought on a promotion, subjects will be more likely to attribute the purchase to the promotion as opposed to internal factors (Scott 1976). Therefore, they will blame Mrs. Watson less when the product is on promotion. We again propose that blame assignments will be affected by the order of the mutation task. Greater blame will be assigned to the manufacturer when subjects perform the mutation task prior to the blame assignment.

H4a: Blame assigned to the manufacturer (Mrs. Watson) will increase when the market share of the product is high (low).

H4b: Blame assigned to the manufacturer (Mrs. Watson) will increase (decrease) when the product is bought on a promotion.

H4c: Blame assigned to the manufacturer (Mrs. Watson) will increase (decrease) when the subjects perform the mutation task prior to the blame assignment.

Method

Subjects. One-hundred two undergraduates in a large northeastern university volunteered to participate in the study.

Stimuli and Design. The same vignette used in study 1 was again used in study 2 with the following exceptions. The levels of market share used to define the manufacturer differed slightly and whether the product was or was not promoted was varied. In the high market share condition, subjects were told the following: "According to the results of a recent market survey, Bomex is the best selling brand of all pain relievers and more than half of the consumers use Bomex when they have a headache." In the low market share condition, subjects were presented the following sentence: "The results of a recent market survey revealed that Bomex has a low market share. Only 10% of the consumers use Bomex when they have a headache." To manipulate promotion, half of the subjects were told that she saw Bomex on promotion and its price was reduced by 25%. The other half were not given any information about the promotion or the price.

Subjects filled out a questionnaire containing the market share information, the hypothetical scenario, and the dependent measures which took approximately 10 minutes.

Dependent Measures

Blame assigned to the manufacturer was measured on two 7 point items ranging from 1 (very little) to 7 (a great deal). The higher the value, the greater the blame assigned to the manufacturer. As these items were highly correlated (r=.71) they were averaged to form an overall index for blame assigned to the drug manufacturer. Blame assigned to fate, to the store, and to Mrs. Watson were each measured by an item which assessed the blame assignment on a 7 point scale anchored by "very little" and "a great deal."

TABLE 2
Blame Assigned to Mrs. Watson as a Function of Market Share, Promotion, and Order of the Mutation Task

	Promotion			
	Absent		Present	
	Order of the Mutation Task			
	First	Last	First	Last
High Market Share	3.57	3.09	3.72	3.07
Low Market Share	4.77	2.92	3.84	5.33

Results and Discussion

The data were analyzed as a 2 (high or low market share) X 2 (presence or absence of promotion) x 2 (order of the mutation task: before or after the blame assignment) between-subjects factorial design.

An ANOVA model which included the blame assigned to the manufacturer was significant ($F(7,74)=2.53$, $p<.02$). As expected, greater blame was reported when the product was on promotion ($F(1,94)=2.79$, $p<.05$ (one-tailed), Ms=2.86 vs. 3.37). Moreover, subjects assigned greater blame when they performed the mutation task prior to the blame assignments ($F(1,94)=8.84$, $p<.004$, Ms=3.61 vs. 2.63). However, the effect of the market share was insignificant ($p=.28$).

Another model which included the blame assigned to Mrs. Watson was marginally significant ($F(7,93)=1.98$, $p<.07$). As expected, blame assigned to Mrs. Watson was greater when the market share is low ($F(1,93)=3.93$, $p<.05$, Ms=4.22 vs. 3.67). Additionally, the results suggest a significant two-way interaction between promotion and the order of the mutation task ($F(1,93)=3.37$, $p<.07$) and a three-way interaction among market share, promotion, and the order of the mutation task ($F(1,93)=4.16$, $p<.04$). The means of the model are presented in Table 2.

In order to explore the three-way interaction, we analyzed the data separately for the promotion absent and promotion present conditions. In the no promotion condition, Mrs. Watson was blamed more when she bought the low-share brand and when the mutation task was performed before the blame assignment as compared to when the mutation task was performed after the blame assignment. A series of planned contrasts revealed a significant difference only for these two cells ($t=2.19$, df=93, $p<.03$). In this case, blame assigned to Mrs. Watson is significantly correlated with the number of counterfactual thoughts related to Mrs. Watson ($r=.70$) and fate ($r=-.58$). However, when Mrs. Watson bought Bomex on promotion, we observed a reverse pattern. She was blamed more when she bought the low-share brand on promotion and when the mutation task was performed after the blame assignment. In this case, the order of the mutation task influenced the blame assigned to Mrs. Watson in the expected way; subjects blamed Mrs. Watson less when they performed the mutation task prior to the blame assignment.

An ANOVA model which included the blame assigned to the store was also significant ($F(7,94)=2.41$, $p<.03$). There are three significant main effects. The store is blamed more for selling a low-share brand as opposed to a high-share brand ($F(1,94)=4.96$, $p<.03$, Ms=1.75 vs. 1.28). Additionally, subjects blamed the store more when the product was on promotion ($F(1,94)=3.05$, $p<.05$, Ms=1.34 vs. 1.69) and when the mutation task was performed before the blame assignment ($F(1,94)=3.11$, $p<.05$ (one-tailed), Ms=1.69 vs. 1.34).

GENERAL DISCUSSION

These two experiments suggest that counterfactual processing can influence how blame is assigned when evaluating a product related illness or injury. The first study underscored the importance of counterfactual processing in consumers' willingness to award money to the injured party. We found that willingness to award money is partly determined by the blame assigned to the manufacturer, the manufacturer's market share, event foreseeability, and the number of counterfactuals generated related to the manufacturer and to the store. Subjects are more likely to award money to the injured party when the manufacturer's market share is high, when greater blame is assigned to the manufacturer, when they think that Mrs. Watson could not have foreseen this freak event, and when the number of counterfactual alternatives related to the manufacturer and to the store is higher. Additionally, we showed that blame assigned to the manufacturer is negatively related to the blame assigned to Mrs. Watson and to "fate" and positively related to the blame assigned to the store.

In the second study, we determined that in addition to market share and counterfactual processing, whether or not the product was being promoted also influenced the assignment of blame. The manufacturer was blamed more when the product was on promotion.

Our data did not support the hypotheses about the impact of previous experience with the product category and time pressure on counterfactual processing and assignment of blame. One explanation for these insignificant results might be that our experimental manipulations were not strong enough to reveal the hypothesized effects, therefore, a larger sample size might be required to observe any effect. Still another explanation might be that previous experience and time pressure do not influence the exceptionality of the situation and do not lead to counterfactual processing. We tend to favor the former explanation because there are theoretical reasons to expect these hypothesized effects. An important task for future studies can be exploring the robustness of these effects.

The present research suffers from the usual shortcomings of laboratory research. However, these shortcomings provide us with an opportunity for future research. More realistic stimuli, such as videotapes of actual product related accidents or injuries and more detailed descriptions of the accidents could improve the external validity of the research. Additionally, we only collected outcome measures which made it neccessary for us to conjecture how people assessed the product related illness. Future studies should employ cognitive process measures to inquire mediating variables that might affect blame assignments.

The current findings suggest that counterfactual processing seem to influence consumers' blame assignments in a product failure. It is likely that counterfactual processing might play a significant role in explaining consumers' reactions to various other stimuli in different contexts. For example, a consumer's attitude toward a product might be more favorable if the product performs very well in a situation where the counterfactual alternative related to its malfunctioning is highly available. Future research should also explore the impact of counterfactual processing in these different contexts.

REFERENCES

Creyer, Elizabeth H. and Zeynep Gürhan (1994), "Who's to Blame?: Counterfactual Reasoning and the Development of Regret," unpublished manuscript.

Griffin, Mitch, Barry J. Babin, and William R. Darden (1992), "Consumer Assessments of Responsibility for Product Related Injuries: The Impact of Regulations, Warnings, and Promotional Policies," in *Advances in Consumer Research*, John F. Sherry Jr. and Brian Sternthal (eds.), 19, 870-877.

Johnson, Joel T. (1986), "The Knowledge of What Might Have Been: Affective and Attributional Consequences of Near Outcomes," *Personality and Social Psychology Bulletin*, 12 (1), 551-562.

Kahneman, Daniel and Dale T. Miller (1986), "Norm Theory: Comparing Reality to its Alternatives," *Psychological Review*, 93 (2), 136-153.

Kahneman, Daniel and Amos Tversky (1982), "The Simulation Heuristic," in *Judgment under Uncertainty: Heuristics and Biases*, D. Kahneman, P. Slovic, and A. Tversky (eds.), New York: Cambridge University Press, 201-208.

Kahneman, Daniel and Carol A. Varey (1990), "Propensities and Counterfactuals: The Loser That Almost Won," *Journal of Personality and Social Psychology*, 59 (6), 1101-1110.

McGill, Ann L. (1990), "Predicting Consumers' Reactions to Product Failure: Do Responsibility Judgments Follow from Consumers' Causal Explanations?" *Marketing Letters*, 2 (1), 59-70.

Miller, Dale T. and Saku Gunesagaram (1990), "Temporal Order and Perceived Mutability of Events: Implications for Blame Assignment," *Journal of Personality and Social Psychology*, 59 (6), 1111-1118.

Miller, Dale T. and Cathy McFarland (1986), "Counterfactual Thinking and Victim Compensation: A Test of Norm Theory," *Personality and Social Psychology Bulletin*, 12 (4), 513-519.

Miller, Dale T., William Turnbull, and Cathy McFarland (1990), "Counterfactual Thinking and Social Perception: Thinking About What Might Have Been," in *Advances in Experimental Social Psychology*, ed. Mark P. Zanna, San Diego, CA: Academic Press, 305-331.

Scott, Carol A. (1976), "The Effects of Trial and Incentives on Repeat Purchase Behavior," *Journal of Marketing Research*, 13 (August), 263-269.

Wells, Gary L., Brian R. Taylor, and John W. Turtle (1987), "The Undoing of Scenarios," *Journal of Personality and Social Psychology*, 53 (3), 421-430.

Wells, Gary L. and Igor Gavanski (1989), "Mental Simulation of Causality," *Journal of Personality and Social Psychology*, 56, 161-169.

Postconsumption Competition: The Effects of Choice and Non-Choice Alternatives on Satisfaction Formation

Cornelia Dröge, Michigan State University
Robert D. Mackoy, Butler University

ABSTRACT

Current models of satisfaction formation focus on the single product or service chosen; this paper proposes that, in a competitive environment, alternative products or services *not* chosen can also impact satisfaction formation. Five propositions regarding a revised conceptualization of satisfaction formation processes are offered. The first is a general proposition stating that *multiple* prechoice alternatives can remain relevant in the ultimate satisfaction formation process. The second proposition states that multiple paths of satisfaction processing are interrelated. The remaining propositions specify three conditions under which this reconceptualized process of satisfaction formation is likely to hold.

INTRODUCTION

The vast literature on consumer choice behavior addresses the question of how consumers decide which of multiple competing alternatives to purchase. The notion of competition is an integral element of the choice process. Yet postchoice processes, such as satisfaction formation, are modeled in a manner inconsistent with the competitive reality in which they, too, occur. Current models of satisfaction formation focus exclusively on the single, chosen product while assuming that evaluations of competing products are no longer salient.

We contend that in many situations competing alternatives remain salient in postconsumption satisfaction formation processes. We propose a satisfaction formation model which explicitly considers how the ongoing evaluation of competitive alternatives affects satisfaction with the consumption experience. The traditional model of satisfaction formation is a special case of the proposed model.

In this paper, the current conceptualization of satisfaction formation, referred to as the traditional model, is summarized briefly. Then, five propositions are presented which jointly offer a revised conceptualization of the satisfaction formation processes. The first and second propositions provide an overview of the new model specifying the primary structural components of the new conceptualization. The remaining three propositions indicate three conditions under which this expanded conceptualization is likely to hold. Finally, conceptual and managerial implications are presented.

CURRENT MODELS OF SATISFACTION FORMATION

Study of consumer satisfaction is one topic which resides primarily in the post-decision, consuming realm of consumer behavior. Traditional models of satisfaction formation typically regard consumer choice as a given and specify satisfaction to be a function of antecedents such as expectation, desire, attitude, perceived performance, and disconfirmation relative to the *one* choice already made. Thus, most satisfaction models have been structured and tested in a manner consistent with Alderson's (1957) distinctions, that is, with consumption as totally separate from the "buying" process.

However, should the fact that it is possible to distinguish between the purchase decision and consumption imply that it is desirable to study each as if they were unrelated? Consider the implications of the current literature as illustrated in Figure 1. The consumer considers purchasing one of three alternative products or services. Numerous models of how the choice is made have been proposed, tested and supported (e.g., Bettman, Johnson and Payne 1991). Often such choice processes include intensive information manipulation on an attribute-by-attribute basis, comparing expected characteristics or performance levels. Such comparisons are made with the consumer's internal ideal standards and/or with the characteristics and performance levels of the other alternatives. The end result of this "choosing" or "buying" process is a selected alternative, in this case, Alternative B (see Figure 1).

Consumer satisfaction, as part of the "consuming process," is modeled as a response or a judgment of the consumption experience related *only* to Alternative B. Expectations, desires, attitudes, perceived performance, and disconfirmation related to Alternative B are considered sufficient to understand satisfaction with the consumption experience.

Thus when we compare the prechoice decision models with the postchoice satisfaction models, we note three important contrasts. *First*, all alternatives in the choice set are salient prechoice, but only the chosen alternative remains salient in satisfaction formation postchoice. *Second*, prechoice models typically offer some explanation as to how the alternatives are compared to one another, while postchoice satisfaction models typically offer no explanation as to how the alternatives *not* chosen potentially interact or impact overall satisfaction. *Third*, prechoice models often incorporate moderating factors such as involvement into explanations of alternative processing while postchoice satisfaction models assume that no moderating factor can make alternatives *not* chosen salient.

In summary, satisfaction is conceptualized as a single process related to a single target (see Figure 1). *When one considers the intensive prechoice processing which involved Alternatives A and C in addition to B, it seems unreasonable to assume that thoughts or feelings about alternatives not selected become totally irrelevant to postchoice satisfaction formation processes.* Expectations, desires and attitudes regarding the chosen Alternative B evolved in relation to expectations, desires and attitudes regarding the two other alternatives. Likewise, in some usage contexts, the perceived performance of Alternatives A and C may influence the consumer's interpretation of the consumption experience related to Alternative B. Given that many consumer decisions of interest to marketers occur in a competitive context — one in which alternatives exist, information (including trial) is available, processing is encouraged, and risk is involved — it becomes clear that the satisfaction literature has not developed a satisfaction model which explicitly considers the comprehensiveness of the processing of competitive alternatives. Figure 2 depicts a model proposed to address these issues. The basic propositions related to Figure 2 are delineated below. Throughout the subsequent discussion the chosen alternative will be called the "choice" while the non-chosen alternative(s) that was (were) in the consumer's original choice set will be called the "nonchoice(s)."

Proposition 1: Those alternatives salient pre-decision can remain salient post-decision. The evaluation of both the choice and the nonchoices can impact ultimate satisfaction with the consumption experience.

FIGURE 1
Pre-Decision Versus Post-Decision Models

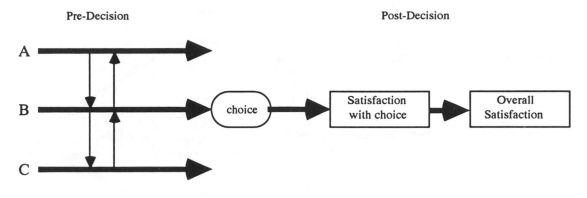

Pre-Decision   Post-Decision

Choice Models:

Alternatives A, B, and C are
considered and comparatively
evaluated. Expectations and
desires are formed relative to
all three alternatives.

Traditional
Satisfaction Models:

Only the antecedent constructs in relation
to the choice (here, alternative B) are
considered relevant.

Support for Proposition 1 comes from a number of sources. First, in *A Theory of Cognitive Dissonance*, Festinger (1957) explicitly recognizes that dissonance can be created by the simple act of choosing one alternative while rejecting others. He states:

"....There will be some cognitive elements corresponding to the positive aspects of the unchosen alternative and some elements corresponding to the negative aspects of the chosen alternative which will be dissonant with the cognition of having chosen one particular alternative...." (p. 36).

Thus, Festinger provides some support for hypothesizing that nonchoices may continue to have an impact on consumers' postchoice experiences, at the very least in the period immediately following the act of choosing.

Second, theoretical support may also be found in economic regret theory. Loomes and Sugden (1982) state that ultimate utility derived from the choice is not

"....independent of the nature and combination of actions simultaneously rejected...." (p. 82).

In their theory, the anticipation of regret (and/or "rejoicing") related to the nonchoices is combined with factors derived from conventional utility theory. The entire constellation of alternatives in the choice set is evaluated in terms of expectations following the decision. For our purposes, the important point is that consumers develop expectations regarding their potential future responses of regret or rejoicing to both choice and nonchoice alternatives, and the degree to which these responses to both choice and nonchoices are realized determines ultimate utility (i.e., satisfaction).

We propose that nonchoices be incorporated in the satisfaction formation process through their direct impact on overall satisfaction; i.e., that "satisfaction" with nonchoices as well as satisfaction with the choice can determine overall satisfaction (see Figure 2). Two issues need to be addressed. First, what is overall satisfaction? Satisfaction scholars appear to be moving toward broadly defined

targets of satisfaction (e.g., Bitner and Hubbert 1993). There seems to be a transition from focusing on a single, specific target of satisfaction (e.g., the product chosen) to focusing on an overall target (e.g., the consumption experience). Some studies have included both specific and general targets (e.g., Bitner 1990). Thus we conceptualize satisfaction to be realized at two levels: satisfaction with each of multiple targets (one of which is the choice) and satisfaction overall.

Second, what is the meaning of "satisfaction" with nonchoices? As stated by Houston, Sherman and Baker (1991):

"....we can and do encounter alternatives we rejected when visiting another university that we had considered attending or seeing someone driving another car we considered. At such times the focus for feelings of satisfaction or regret may be the rejected alternatives...." (p. 425).

The authors demonstrate, as proposed by Festinger (1957), that continued processing of information about the nonchoices could have an impact on overall satisfaction formation. Partial experiences (visiting the nonchoice university) or vicarious experiences (seeing someone driving the nonchoice car) may provide the necessary points of reference ("target") in this process. Remembered satisfaction with alternatives not chosen at a particular time, but previously chosen, could also impact overall satisfaction. For example, consider someone who has chosen to dine at restaurant B instead of restaurant A on a given night, where both restaurants have been frequented in the past. On this particular evening, a long wait is experienced. After 45 minutes, the consumer is poignantly aware that the restaurant A wait was never longer than half an hour. After an hour, images of restaurant A's dessert exasperate a growing hunger and impatience. Remembered satisfaction with restaurant A has an impact on the growing dissatisfaction with restaurant B.

Proposition 2: The paths of satisfaction formation processing leading to satisfaction with both choice and nonchoice targets are interrelated.

FIGURE 2
Pre-Decision Versus Post-Decision Proposed Model

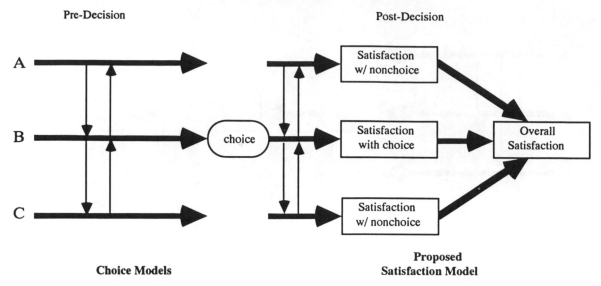

Constructs relevant to both choice ("B") and nonchoice
("A" and "C") alternatives affect post-choice satisfaction
processes and overall satisfaction.

If satisfaction with the choice and satisfaction with the nonchoices both contribute to overall satisfaction (see Figure 2), it is reasonable ask what processes lead to satisfaction with each target. In addition to assuming a single target of satisfaction (i.e., the choice), the traditional model posits that all relevant antecedents of satisfaction also have a single target (though possibly consisting of multiple relevant attributes). For example, common antecedents of satisfaction are expectations and disconfirmation. The traditional satisfaction literature has investigated in great detail the standards of comparison to which the *one* target is compared, but such standards are assumed to be incorporated in disconfirmation (or possibly expectations). For example, when Cadotte, Woodruff and Jenkins (1987) talk about "best brand norms" or when Tse and Wilton (1988) talk about "ideal standards," they are referring to a set standard against which the person judges the target's performance.

In contrast we propose, as indicated in Figure 2, that it is likely that the processes themselves are interrelated. Expectations, desires, and attitudes formed prior to the act of choice continue to be updated and compared in the processing following choice. For example, actual prechoice expectations can be different from postchoice memory of prechoice expectations. In addition, disconfirmation related to nonchoice targets may directly impact satisfaction with the choice target.

CONTEXTS FAVORABLE TO THE NEW MODEL

The model that we propose is more comprehensive than the traditional model of satisfaction formation. We do not state that nonchoices are *always* salient in postchoice processing; indeed the seminal model with one target is a special subset of our model that probably adequately describes many consumption experiences. Thus the question arises of when it becomes more likely that the traditional model's explanatory power falls short. The remaining three propositions focus on factors which may influence the degree

to which nonchoices affect satisfaction formation: dissatisfaction with the choice, involvement, and the number of close competitors.

Proposition 3: The higher the level of dissatisfaction with the choice, the more likely that nonchoices are salient postchoice.

Consumers who are dissatisfied may process differently than consumers who are satisfied. Satisfied consumers do not feel the need to rethink or reanalyze the factors which are responsible for their largely positive state, perhaps because there has been closure on the process. On the other hand, consistent with cognitive dissonance theory, dissatisfied consumers do not reach closure as easily. They experience "psychological discomfort" (Festinger 1957) and become motivated to reduce this dissonance. Empirical evidence is consistent with this explanation. For example, Maddox (1981) hypothesized that dissatisfied consumers need to rationalize their negative feelings. Westbrook and Newman (1978) hypothesized that dissatisfied consumers experience an "amplified sensitivity" to the satisfaction formation process. Dröge and Halstead (1991) found strong empirical evidence of differential processing among dissatisfied consumers; they hypothesized that dissatisfied consumers engaged in greater cognitive processing.

If dissatisfied consumers process more extensively, it is reasonable to propose that this processing encompasses nonchoices. Some of the additional processing likely involves reexamining expectations and desires with regard to the choice. However, in addition, the "...positive aspects of the unchosen alternative...." described by Festinger (1957) will likely be recalled during this processing, as the dissatisfied consumers experience the actualized regret described by Loomes and Sugden (1982). By contemplating the now relatively more attractive nonchoices, consumers may lay the groundwork to avoid being dissatisfied in the future (Westbrook and Newman 1978), or they may simply be trying to come to terms with their dissatisfaction.

Proposition 4: The higher the level of involvement, the more likely that nonchoices are salient postchoice.

Involvement may be thought of as a person's degree of interest or level of arousal with a product or service due to its personal relevance. Although different kinds of involvement have been identified (e.g., Richins and Bloch 1986), there appears to be agreement that involvement usually results in higher levels of attention to and search for information (Houston and Rothschild 1978; Tigert, Ring and King 1976), in increased processing of information (Petty, Cacioppo and Schumann 1983), and a narrower "latitude of acceptance" (Rothschild and Houston 1977).

The increased level of information search and processing coupled with the more stringent acceptance criteria of highly involved consumers logically implies an intensive comparison process among the members of the choice set. The intensive comparison process results in heightened awareness of desires, expectations and attitudes with regard to *each* of the choice set members. For high involvement consumers, it is unlikely that nonchoice alternatives will suddenly become irrelevant in postchoice processing. Conversely, for low involvement consumers, wider latitudes of acceptance and reduced information processing make it less likely that nonchoice alternatives will continue to have much salience postchoice. Festinger (1957) stated that favorable attributes of nonchoices and unfavorable attributes of the choice produce postchoice dissonance. The larger the number of salient attributes and the more intensive the processing, the greater the likelihood that postchoice dissonance will result. The greater the dissonance, the greater the motivation to reduce the dissonance, and hence, the more likely it is that nonchoices will remain salient during post-consumption satisfaction formation.

Proposition 5: The more difficult the tradeoffs among competing alternatives, the more likely that nonchoices are salient postchoice.

If products and services are conceived of as bundles of attributes, then closely competing products/services ("close competitors") would be those which possess both similar attributes, and similar amounts of each attribute. Choosing between close competitors may require more extensive processing than does choosing between competitors which are not perceived as close. The additional processing may be required because no matter which type of decision strategy is being used (e.g., compensatory, lexicographic, elimination by aspects, etc.), similar ratings of the attributes of each alternative complicates the decision process. Even if competitors are not "close" in this sense, more extensive processing may be necessary if the tradeoffs between the alternatives are difficult. The increased processing due to similarity between alternatives or due to the difficulty of making tradeoffs has the same consequences as the increased processing due to involvement: it can result in the formation of highly refined expectations and attitudes regarding multiple alternatives and/or in postchoice cognitive dissonance. In short, nonchoices are more likely to remain salient in the postchoice formation of overall satisfaction.

DISCUSSION

We have presented a comprehensive model of satisfaction formation which builds on the traditional model by including the potential incorporation of competitive factors postchoice. Postchoice competition exists when nonchoices remain salient in the satisfaction process. When this occurs, parallel yet interrelated processing paths (associated with the choice and each of the salient nonchoices)

are proposed to lead to satisfaction with each target, and hence to satisfaction overall. When nonchoices are *not* salient postchoice, the model reduces to a single path model identical to the traditional model. This is the sense in which the traditional model is a special case of the competitive satisfaction model.

The traditional models' focus solely on the choice has been critical to the development of satisfaction formation constructs and to the specification of fundamental relationships. To address critical issues of internal validity, seminal works in developing the current disconfirmation-based models of satisfaction formation have utilized experimental methods in which subjects were exposed to a single product in a non-competitive context (e.g., Churchill and Surprenant 1982; Tse and Wilton 1988; Spreng and Olshavsky 1993). While useful for construct and model development, single product empirical tests artificially remove examination of the satisfaction process from the competitive environment in which it actually occurs. Although some questions remain regarding the conceptualization of and relationship between key constructs (e.g., Yi 1990), we believe that theoretical breakthroughs are unlikely to occur unless the reality of continuing competition is incorporated explicitly into a more generalizable model.

We contend that satisfaction research may advance more rapidly in the context of the comprehensive, competitive model. There are three reasons for this. First, explicitly incorporating competitive elements in the satisfaction formation model will make it more consistent with current choice models. The traditional model of satisfaction formation lacks theoretical links to the rich choice literature; the competitive model offers the framework for potentially becoming theoretically integrated with this literature. Second, the competitive model offers the potential to explain exactly how satisfaction relates to intentions and future behaviors. For example, the traditional model inadequately explains why many consumers do not repurchase even when they are highly satisfied with their choice. The competitive model provides a more reasonable context for addressing this issue. Third, the generalizability of the competitive model should contribute to its managerial relevance, and the model fits well with the strategic objective of developing long-term competitive advantage.

The proposed competitive model needs to be developed empirically and theoretically. Empirically, the next step is to determine whether there is initial support for the competitive model by showing cases in which nonchoices are salient postchoice. A logical context in which to test the model would be one in which the conditions presented in Propositions 3, 4, and/or 5 applied; i.e., a situation in which there is expected to be widespread dissatisfaction, and/or high involvement, and/or product similarity. Once support for the model is demonstrated, other specific conditions under which the model applies can be explored, and the paths tentatively identified here can be empirically tested.

Opportunities for theoretical development occur on several fronts. First, work needs to be done to determine other conditions under which one can expect a priori that the nonchoices remain salient postchoice. In this paper, one product-related factor (product similarity) and two consumer-related factors (level of dissatisfaction and involvement) are proposed to be criteria affecting nonchoice salience. Second, what specific elements of choice models apply to postchoice satisfaction formation? For example, does the choice heuristic utilized affect whether nonchoices remain salient postchoice? Third, exactly how does the proposed model relate to the consumer's consideration set? Might the continuing salience of nonchoices in postchoice processes provide empirical evidence of which specific elements comprised the consideration set? Fourth, if nonchoices remain salient, what effect do they have on future choices? For example, are such effects mediated by satisfaction or are there also direct effects?

Two major managerial implications should also result from development of the propositions. First, if the model is supported, it will provide clear evidence that competition continues postchoice. Most marketing effort is directed towards attracting customers by focusing on prechoice competition. The model implies that one's competitors can affect the satisfaction formation of one's own customers, and vice versa. *This opens explicit consideration of a new competitive arena requiring new strategies and tactics.* Defensively, managers may have to alter their strategies for increasing/ maintaining consumer satisfaction and preventing dissatisfaction. Offensively, managers can develop methods for affecting the satisfaction formation of their competitors' customers. Second, managers may have to alter the way they monitor customer satisfaction. Not only should process variables relevant to one's own product/service be monitored, but the monitoring system should also be expanded to include relevant process variables pertaining to the products/services of one's major competitors. By doing so, managers can gain insights into potentially exploitable causes of dissatisfaction with competing products, while also monitoring the effects of competitors' actions on one's own customers. Specifically, for one's own customers, managers can determine a) what specific factors affect satisfaction and dissatisfaction, and b) if the satisfaction processes of one's own customers are affected postchoice by one's competitors. For the customers of one's competitors, managers can determine a) what specific factors affect their satisfaction and dissatisfaction, and b) if one's own products remain salient to competitors' customers postchoice. This information can be used to develop strategies to exploit advantages and minimize the consequences of the firm's weaknesses.

In summary, we propose that it is essential for satisfaction researchers to include competitive alternatives in the analysis of postchoice satisfaction not because these nonchoices are *always* relevant but because a determination of *when* and *how* they remain salient has major theoretical and managerial implications.

REFERENCES

Alderson, Wroe (1957), *Marketing Behavior and Executive Action*, Homewood, IL: Richard D. Irwin.

Bettman, James R., Eric J. Johnson, and John W. Payne (1991), "Consumer Decision Making," in *Handbook of Consumer Behavior*, Thomas S. Robertson and Harold Kassarjian, eds. Englewood Cliffs, NJ: Prentice-Hall, 50-84.

Bitner, Mary Jo (1990), "Evaluating Service Encounters: The Effect of Physical Surroundings and Employee Responses," *Journal of Marketing*, 54 (April): 69-82.

Bitner, Mary Jo, and Amy R. Hubbert (1993), "Encounter Satisfaction Versus Overall Satisfaction Versus Quality," in *Service Quality: New Directions in Theory and Practice*, Roland T. Rust and Richard L. Oliver, eds. Thousand Oaks, CA: Sage Publications, Inc., 72-94.

Cadotte, Ernest R., Robert B. Woodruff, Roger L. Jenkins (1987), "Expectations and Norms in Models of Consumer Satisfaction," *Journal of Marketing Research*, 24:3, 305-314.

Churchill, Gilbert A., Jr., and Carol Surprenant (1982), "An Investigation into the Determinants of Consumer Satisfaction," *Journal of Marketing Research*, 19:4 (November), 491-504.

Dröge, Cornelia, and Diane Halstead (1991), "Postpurchase Hierarchies of Effects: The Antecedents and Consequences of Satisfaction for Complainers versus Non-complainers," *International Journal of Research in Marketing*, 8:4, 315-328.

Festinger, Leon (1957), *A Theory of Cognitive Dissonance*, Stanford, CA: Stanford University Press.

Houston, Michael J. and Michael L. Rothschild (1978), "Conceptual and Methodological Perspectives on Involvement," in *1978 AMA Educators' Proceedings*, Subhash C. Jain, ed. Chicago, IL: American Marketing Association, 184-187.

Houston, David A., Steven J. Sherman, and Sara M. Baker (1991), "Feature Matching, Unique Features, and the Dynamics of the Choice Process: Predecision Conflict and Postdecision Satisfaction," *Journal of Experimental Social Psychology*, 27:5, 411-430.

Loomes, Graham, and Robert Sugden (1982), "Regret Theory: An Alternative Theory of Rational Choice Under Uncertainty," *The Economic Journal*, 92 (December), 805-824.

Maddox, R. Neil (1981), "Two-Factor Theory and Consumer Satisfaction: Replication and Extension," *Journal of Consumer Research*, 8:1, 97-102.

Petty, Richard E., John T. Cacioppo, and David Schumann (1983), "Central and Peripheral Routes to Advertising Effectiveness: The Moderating Role of Involvement," *Journal of Consumer Research*, 10:2, 135-144.

Richins, Marsha L. and Peter H. Bloch (1991), "Post-Purchase Product Satisfaction: Incorporating the Effects of Involvement and Time," *Journal of Business Research*, 23:2, 145-158.

Rothschild, Michael L., and Michael J. Houston (1977), "The Consumer Involvement Matrix: Some Preliminary Findings," in *Proceedings: AMA Educators' Conference*, Barnett A. Greenberg and Danny N. Ballinger, eds. Chicago, IL: American Marketing Association.

Spreng, Richard A., and Richard W. Olshavsky (1993), "A Desires Congruency Model of Consumer Satisfaction," *Journal of the Academy of Marketing Science*, 21:3, 169-178.

Tigert, Douglas J., Lawrence J. Ring, and Charles W. King (1976), "Fashion Involvement and Buying Behavior," in *Advances in Consumer Research*, Vol. 3, Beverlee B. Anderson, ed. Ann Arbor, MI: Association for Consumer Research, 46-52.

Tse, David K. and Peter C. Wilton (1988), "Models of Consumer Satisfaction Formation: An Extension," *Journal of Marketing Research*, 25:2 (May), 204-212.

Westbrook, Robert A. and Joseph W. Newman (1978), "An Analysis of Shopper Dissatisfaction for Major Household Appliances," *Journal of Marketing Research*, 15:3, 456-466.

Yi, Youjae (1990), "A Critical Review of Consumer Satisfaction," in *Review of Marketing 1990*, Valarie A. Zeithaml, ed. Chicago, IL: American Marketing Association.

Do Consumers Seek Emotional Situations: The Need For Emotion Scale

Niranjan V. Raman, University of Texas at Austin
Prithviraj Chattopadhyay, University of Texas at Austin
Wayne D. Hoyer, University of Texas at Austin

ABSTRACT

Although it has been suggested that individuals differ in their need to seek out emotional stimuli, no construct has been developed to measure this tendency. This research focuses on the development of the concept of Need for Emotion, and describes the construction of a scale designed to capture individual differences on this dimension. The twelve item scale was found to meet reliability and validity tests.

The construct of need for cognition (NFC), which captures the "differences among individuals in their tendency to engage in and enjoy thinking" (Cacioppo and Petty 1982), has been well established in communication and persuasion literature. Defined as an individual's tendency to think about and elaborate on events in searching for reality, the 18-item NFC scale (Cacioppo, Petty, and Kao 1984) has been tested and found to meet standards of reliability and validity (Osberg 1987; Sadowski and Gulgoz 1992; Tolentino, Curry and Leak 1990). More importantly, the construct has found useful applications in empirical research dealing with, for example, whether individuals will process persuasive communication along the central or peripheral route to persuasion (Batra and Stayman 1990).

However, cognition represents only one mode of information processing. Individuals may also differ in their tendencies to process affective or emotional stimuli. Similar to "thinkers" who find it "fun to think" (Murphy 1947), it is possible to conceive of "experiencers" or "feelers" who enjoy "experiencing emotion". Thus a "Need for Emotion" (NFE) might be conceived of as a construct that taps into a tendency to seek out and enjoy emotional situations and as a preference to behave in a particular way (Jung 1970).

The importance of such a construct stems from the fact that many situations of interest in the field of consumer behavior may potentially be impacted by an individual's need for emotion, giving rise to a variety of important questions. For example, if certain television viewers are more likely to prefer affective stimuli, would the type of commercial (informative or emotional) have an impact on persuasion? Does product packaging have to be more affective or informational to catch consumers' attention and influence purchase? Are early adopters high or low in terms of preference for emotional stimuli, and what impact does this have on the introduction of new products? These and other questions may be better addressed through an understanding of individual differences in the need for emotion.

The aim of this paper is to introduce a scale which attempts to assess individual differences in the way people deal with emotion in a fashion analogous to the NFC scale. The definition of the NFE construct, and its distinction from existing concepts and constructs in the literature are discussed. This is followed by a description of the development of the scale, and its subsequent testing for reliability and validity. Applications and directions for future research are also suggested.

CONCEPT DEVELOPMENT

Although extensive studies have demonstrated the importance of effects of affect and moods on consumers' memories, evaluations, judgment and behavior (e.g. Edell and Burke 1987; Gardner 1985), most research in consumer behavior has focused on affective components of ads (Aaker and Bruzzone 1985; Mitchell 1986) or affective responses to ads (Holbrook and Batra 1987; Stout and Leckenby 1986). Alternatively, many studies in this area have induced a specific emotion in subjects artificially, and then examined the effects of this affect for all subjects in that condition taken together (Booth-Butterfield and Booth-Butterfield 1990). Differences across individuals regarding a need for seeking out and experiencing emotion have, for the most part, been ignored (with the exception of Allen and Hamsher 1974). This omission is surprising, given the potential for such a construct.

This research centers on the operating hypothesis that individuals vary in the degree that emotion is sought, and furthermore, that this individuality is relevant to the buyer behavior context. The rationale for this stems from two points. First, it has been established that individuals may differ in expressiveness, orientation, and intensity of experience of emotion (e.g. Allen and Hamsher 1974; Booth-Butterfield and Booth-Butterfield 1990). Based on these differences, researchers have speculated that individuals may also differ in their need to seek out emotional stimuli (Harris and Moore 1990; Larsen and Diener 1987). Second, as indicated earlier, many situations in buyer behavior such as information processing, decision-making, and impulse-buying, may be better understood by taking into account individual differences in dealing with emotions and emotional situations.

Need for Emotion

The need for emotion (NFE) is defined as the tendency or propensity for individuals to seek out emotional situations, enjoy emotional stimuli, and exhibit a preference to use emotion in interacting with the world. Emotions have been differentiated from longer affective states like moods as being more intense, attention-getting and associated with specific objects or events (Clark and Isen 1982). Individuals are usually aware of their emotions while longer emotional states such as moods are more general, less intensive, and may operate without an individual's consciousness (Gardner 1985). Since the NFE construct would mainly tap into individuals' tendencies to seek out and enjoy emotional situations which are specific events or objects, we suggest that the NFE taps mainly into short term emotion, rather than longer emotional states. However, in as much as the NFE taps into a stable tendency to seek and enjoy emotion, and process affective information, the construct should help to explain stable patterns of individual behavior. It is important to note that the NFE is conceptualized to be independent from the NFC, so that a person may be high on either, or on both affective and cognitive dimensions.

Previous research has linked cognition to masculinity, and emotions to femininity (Greenblatt, Hasenauer, and Freimuth 1980), thus suggesting an inverse correlation between the modes of processing. However, Bem (1985) suggests that the relationship is not that straightforward. She brings up the idea that although many men and women may differ along these dimensions, some people may be androgynous, or high on both the relevant dimensions. Therefore, on a cautious note, it is suggested that NFE and NFC may be independent to some degree. Nevertheless, since significant gender differences have been found in affective intensity (Flett et al. 1986a), and women have also been found to be more affectively oriented than men (Booth-Butterfield and Booth-Butterfield 1990), women are expected to have higher scores on NFE than men.

It is also important to note that NFE differs from a few constructs in this area of research that have been already examined in previous work. These constructs include affect intensity, emotional styles, and affective orientation. While these constructs are related to NFE, there are clear differences between these constructs and NFE, both theoretically, and in the way that they have been measured.

Affect Intensity

Individuals have been found to differ in the intensity with which they experience affect (Larsen and Diener 1987). Affect intensity can be described as the individual difference in the intensity of emotional response to a given level of affect stimulus (Diener, Larsen, Levine and Emmons 1985). A 40-item Affect Intensity Measure (AIM) was developed by Larsen (1984) and has been useful in separating subjects who respond more strongly to affective stimuli than those who respond less strongly. The measure includes items such as " My happy moods are so strong that I feel like I'm in heaven," as well as reverse-scored items like " Calm and cool could easily describe me." The scale has been tested for reliability and validity, and proven to be acceptable on both counts (Flett et al. 1986b; Larsen 1984; Larsen and Diener 1985).

Larsen, Diener and Emmons (1986) suggest that affect intensity is considered to be a stable individual difference factor and is presumed to be reflected in the responses of certain individuals who modulate the intensity of the stimulus such that they consistently exhibit stronger emotional reactions relative to other individuals. In support, high-intense subjects' responses to actual and hypothetical life events were found to be stronger in affect intensity than low-intense subjects' responses to the same events (Larsen, Diener and Emmons 1986). This difference was independent of positive or negative emotion inducing events.

Larsen and Diener (1987) have suggested that individuals differ in their emotional responses to situations, and attempt to maintain consistency in their emotional responses by engaging in appropriate activities. In particular, individuals high on the affect intensity dimension have been presumed to seek out and prefer emotional stimuli, and enjoy their stimulation. However, Larsen and Diener (1987) do not test this assertion, although work by Moore, Harris and Chen (1994) gives some support to this contention. In any case, the two constructs are different conceptually. AIM measures the intensity with which an individual responds to an affective stimulus while the NFE is designed to tap into an individual's tendency to seek out affective stimuli and enjoy these emotional situations. There is also the possibility that a high AIM person may be a low NFE person and vice versa for the following reasons. Because a high AIM person responds very strongly to emotional stimulus, he or she may seek to avoid emotional situations altogether. Thus, this individual may be a low NFE person. But it is also possible that another individual may seek out, enjoy, and respond strongly to emotional stimuli and hence be a high NFE as well as a high AIM person. Conversely, there may be low AIM individuals who are high NFE persons because they can't experience the affective intensity that they desire in reaction to an emotional stimulus. Thus response to emotions (AIM) and seeking out or enjoying emotions (NFE) may be both positively or negatively correlated and this would need to be empirically tested.

Test of Emotional Styles

Allen and Hamsher (1974) developed and validated a Test of Emotional Styles (TES) that included a dimension of emotional orientation. Orientation refers to "attitudes toward emotional experiences and expressions," where a positive orientation refers to a tendency to seek emotional experiences and find comfort in them while a negative orientation refers to avoidance of such situations. However, while this dimension is conceptually identical to NFE, the TES scale has some serious shortcomings. The orientation dimension of the TES scale has 30 paired items to which responses are dichotomous (i.e., true/false, or desirable/not desirable)[1]. With such binary responses, each item can only have minimal variability (Comrey 1988, DeVellis 1991) and the scale would be restricted in its ability to adequately discriminate the degree to which individuals differ on this dimension. Furthermore, Comrey (1988) argues that with such items a phi (point-biserial) coefficient is used, and there is a likelihood of phi coefficients being quite high when there is little variance in the data set. This may happen if just one individual responded "no" to two items to which all the remaining responses were "yes", and may lead to correlational distortions (Comrey 1988). As evidence, an empirical study which used this scale (Woods, Cole and Ferrandez 1977) concluded that there was doubt as to the construct validity of the subscales of TES. Hence there is a need for a different scale which enables stronger reliability and validity (Comrey 1988).

Affective Orientation

Booth-Butterfield and Booth-Butterfield (1990) pointed out that certain individuals have a tendency to use affect as information and rely on their feelings to make decisions. Affective orientation was defined by these authors as the degree to which individuals are conscious of affective cues and use these cues to guide decision-making processes. Affectively oriented persons are considered to be persons who recognize emotional feelings and consider such emotions valuable in their decision making. On the other hand, non-affectively oriented people are those who are more focused on logic and objective facts and for whom affect is superfluous to decisions and has little to contribute to the decision process. The Affective Orientation Scale (AOS) (Booth-Butterfield and Booth-Butterfield 1990, Study 1) is designed to measure this tendency and consists of 20 items such as "I listen to what my "gut" or "heart" says in many situations" and "I try not to let my feelings guide my actions" (reverse scored).

Although the conceptual definition of affective orientation suggests a negative correlation with the NFC construct, the AOS was found to be uncorrelated with NFC (Booth-Butterfield and Booth-Butterfield 1990, Study 2), indicating independence of these constructs. In contrast, NFE is a broader measure which goes beyond the use of affect in decision making and indicates a preference to seek out and enjoy affective situations. Nevertheless since need-for-emotion and affective orientation both deal with individual differences regarding affect and emotion, we expect a strong correlation between AOS and NFE.

Summary of purpose

To summarize, we feel that the Need for Emotion represents a potentially valuable construct which can provide important insights regarding how individuals seek out situations of varying emotional intensity, process information from communications and engage in decision making. The aim of this research is to construct a scale to measure individual NFE, and test it for reliability and validity by relating it to other important constructs. Specifi-

---

[1]The entire scale is a 75-item forced-choice measure.

cally, we expect a positive correlation between NFE and AOS, but no correlation between NFE and NFC. Finally, we expect women to have higher NFE scores than men.

METHODOLOGY

A pool of 48 items was generated for development of the scale. These items were developed keeping the conceptual definition of the NFE in mind. Previous research into related concepts and their attendant scales (e.g. Booth-Butterfield and Booth-Butterfield 1990; Larsen and Diener 1987), as well as the distinctions between them, served as a guide in generating these items. Thus, these items focus on (1) whether a person seeks to be involved in situations where there is a potential for emotion laden stimuli to be present; (2) whether a person is comfortable with and even enjoys experiencing such situations; (3) whether a person prefers to process emotional information; (4) on preferences and general behaviors across situations; (5) on emotion as a single dimension, rather than on various emotional sub-dimensions. None of the NFE items were imported from previous scales. To control for response bias, 23 of the 48 items were reverse-keyed.

Following this, the measure was administered to a sample of 203 undergraduate students at a large southwestern university. The sample consisted of an almost equal number of males and females. More importantly, in order to generate variation in the NFE of the developmental sample, subjects having different majors including business, advertising, engineering and liberal arts, were included in this sample.

Procedure

Subjects' responses to the NFE, NFC and the AOS were recorded concurrently on a 5-interval Likert scale ranging from Strongly Disagree to Strongly Agree. To control for response bias, all the items from these three scales and a few dummy items such as "I always use coupons" were mixed together. These were then interspersed evenly and care taken that no two items that could be perceived to be similar, appeared consecutively.

Six subjects did not complete a large part of the instrument (fifteen items or more), or did so in a manner that suggested that responses were not true (for example, marking the same response for ten or more items, some of which were reversed). Hence, these were dropped out of the analyses and the final sample consisted of 197 valid responses.

RESULTS

Responses to the 48 items under consideration were factor-analyzed by a principal components analysis in order to determine the number of underlying factors. Thirteen factors with eigenvalues values greater than one were extracted but a scree plot indicated that only the first two factors accounted for most of the variation. Hence, in accordance with applications of factor analysis in scale development (Comrey 1988; DeVellis 1991), the factor analysis was rerun specifying two factors with a varimax rotation.

The first factor (Eigenvalue 12.33) accounted for 25.7 per cent of the total variance while the second factor (Eigenvalue 3.51) accounted for 7.3 per cent of the total variance. A total of 20 items with factor loadings greater than .40 loaded on the first factor. These items such as "I look forward to situations that I know are less emotionally involving" (reverse-keyed), related to individual's desires to look forward to emotional situations. This suggested that the first factor was the need for emotion factor. Ten items with loadings greater than .40 loaded on the second factor, and these items related to generation of emotions. Items that loaded on both factors were dropped for obvious reasons.

Scale reliability

The 20 items that had strong loadings on the first factor were then subjected to reliability analyses. Item-whole correlations and alphas for the scale excluding each item successively were examined. Six items were found to have low item-whole correlations and found to reduce alpha of the overall scale. Hence these items were dropped and the remaining fourteen items were factor analyzed again. All but two items had strong loadings on the first factor. Thus the final scale consists of 12 items. Table 1 displays the need for emotion scale along with the item-whole correlations. The overall alpha for the scale was found to be .87. Unexpectedly, all the 12 items in the scale are reverse-scaled. This finding is discussed in a later section.

Scale validity

The next step of the development of this scale was to examine convergence with related constructs and discriminant validity. As mentioned previously, NFE was expected to have a high correlation with the AOS, and a low or no correlation with the NFC. A negative NFE-NFC correlation would indicate that NFE was simply measuring the opposite of NFC (Booth-Butterfield and Booth-Butterfield 1990).

Results of correlation analysis performed on the three scales are displayed in Table 2. Alphas for the three scales are also reported. As expected, a strong correlation with AOS was found. However, a moderate correlation with NFC was found which suggested that the two constructs were related.

It can be argued that the .69 correlation found between the scales is too high and may suggest conceptual redundancy. However, the two constructs are conceptualized differently and different measures developed accordingly for each. Nevertheless, to examine this issue further, the 20 items of the AOS and the 12 items of the NFE scale were subjected jointly to factor analysis. Since these two constructs are, by definition related, two factors and an oblique rotation were specified. Factor I clearly represented the affective orientation factor, with 14 items from the 20-item AOS having strong loadings on this factor. Factor II or the second factor, was found to be the NFE factor with 11 items from the 12-item NFE scale having strong loadings on this factor. Although five items from the AOS were also found to load on the second factor, the loadings of these AOS items were considerably lower than almost all of the NFE items. Hence, the two scales do appear to measure related constructs that are different from each other.

A t-test was performed to test the gender difference on NFE scores. As hypothesized, female subjects had a higher mean NFE score (Mf=46.62, S.D.=8.97) than male subjects (Mm=43.83, S.D.=8.54), and this difference was found to be statistically significant (t=2.23, p<.05, df=195).

To lend additional support to these findings, we replicated part of our study with a holdout sample (N=212) with similar characteristics as the original sample. Factor analysis and reliability analysis indicated that 10 of the original 12 items of the NFE scale loaded on a single factor. We then subjected these 10 items to a factor analysis with the AOS items to support the idea that they are two distinct measures. An inspection of the eigenvalues and the interpretability of the factors indicated that there were four factors in the solution. Hence the factor analysis was rerun specifying four factors with an oblique rotation. Similar to the initial study, we found that 9 of the 10 NFE items loaded on one factor, along with 1 item of the AOS. The remaining factors were made up of the remaining AOS items. This lends further support to our suggestion that NFE is a unidimensional construct distinct from AOS. The reliability of the scale using the holdout sample data was .84. Correlation with AOS was .67 and with NFC was .31 (p<.01).

TABLE 1
The Need for Emotion Scale

Scale Item	Item-Whole Correlation
1. I try to anticipate and avoid situations where there is a likely chance of my getting emotionally involved.	.61
2. Experiencing strong emotions is not something I enjoy very much.	.58
3. I would rather be in a situation in which I experience little emotion than one which is sure to get me emotionally involved.	.66
4. I don't look forward to being in situations that others have found to be emotional.	.61
5. I look forward to situations that I know are less emotionally involving.	.59
6. I like to be unemotional in emotional situations.	.63
7. I find little satisfaction in experiencing strong emotions.	.56
8. I prefer to keep my feelings under check.	.48
9. I feel relief rather than fulfilled after experiencing a situation that was very emotional.	.48
10. I prefer to ignore the emotional aspects of situations rather than getting involved in them.	.50
11. More often than not, making decisions based on emotions just leads to more errors.	.46
12. I don't like to have the responsibility of handling a situation that is emotional in nature.	.60

TABLE 2
Correlation between NFE, NFC and AOS

Correlation Matrix

	NFE	NFC	AOS
NFE	—	.46*	.69*
NFC		—	.26*
AOS			—

* All correlations significant at p < .01 (2-tailed)
Note: The alphas for NFE, NFC and AOS were .88, .83 and .90 respectively.

DISCUSSION

Although previous research has indicated that individuals differ in their preferences and responses toward emotional stimuli, most information-processing models do not account for this individual variability. A construct analogous to the need-for-cognition was proposed and its importance and relevance to the consumer behavior literature pointed out.

A scale to measure need-for-emotion was developed and this twelve-item scale was found to possess high reliability. Further, a test for convergence with the related concepts of affective orientation and gender, was performed. As hypothesized, the AOS was positively correlated with NFE, and females were found to be higher in need-for-emotion than males. Replication with a holdout sample supported our initial findings.

In terms of discriminant validity, while NFE and NFC were hypothesized to be independent constructs, a moderate correlation between these two constructs was found. We offer the following explanation for this finding. Cognition and affective systems are considered to interact with each other (Arnold 1960; Izard 1977) and not function in isolation. Although, the issue of acquisition of affect has been a controversial one in the literature (e.g. Lazarus 1982; Zajonc 1980; Zajonc and Markus 1982), the strong correlation between NFC and NFE supports the viewpoint that cognition and emotion are indeed related. Besides, both these constructs describe a tendency to "seek out stimuli", albeit different types of stimuli. Therefore, it is possible that both NFC and NFE tap into a higher order construct of need for more intensive processing. Evidently, additional research is required to make stronger inferences.

An unexpected finding of this research was that the entire NFE scale consisted of reverse-keyed items. This leads us to speculate that individuals may actually differ in their need to avoid emotional situations rather than differ in their need to seek out emotional situations. An alternative explanation focuses on the wording of the items in the scale. The word "emotion" or "emotional situation" appears frequently in the scale and there is a possibility that subjects may have interpreted these terms to connote negative emotions. This may be another reason why we found differences among individuals in their need to avoid emotional situations rather than differences in their need to actively seek out emotional situations. Evidently, the NFE construct needs to be refined further. More specifically, some items need to be rephrased to suggest emotions without suggesting a negative feeling, and the scale tested again with these modifications.

LIMITATIONS

Individuals' needs or preferences for specific emotions have not been examined in this research. For example, people may vary in their needs to feel various emotions like joy and anger, or positive versus negative affect. Our first attempt was to establish a generalized, more global need for emotion. Future studies should be conducted on specific emotions to examine these issues.

As with any research dealing with emotion, the limitations of attempting to measure emotion through cognitive means (i.e., via a questionnaire) are obvious. However, current alternative measures of emotion (i.e., physiological measures) have their own limitations such as low levels of reliability and validity. The NFE scale also asks subjects for self reports of behaviors or preferences and examines whether certain groups of subjects have consistently higher needs for emotion. This may capture stereotypical images subjects have of themselves, rather than their actual need for emotion. For example, men may be socialized into the idea that they have a lower need for emotion than women and this may show up as consistently lower scores for men on this scale. However, consistent differences obtained in the hypothesized directions on this scale between the various populations will enable a higher degree of confidence in the validity of this scale. Also, to the extent that consumers internalize a stereotypical image and behave accordingly, the predictive validity of NFE will not be affected.

Notwithstanding these limitations, the findings of this study are promising, and suggest that there is a latent construct which we label NFE, that has not been identified in previous research. However, the scale need to be refined, and more rigorous methods such as confirmatory factor analysis should be used, before any definitive conclusions can be drawn regarding this construct. Future work will address these concerns.

REFERENCES

Aaker, David A. and Donald E. Bruzzone (1985), "Causes of Irritation in Advertising," *Journal of Marketing*, 49 (Spring), 47-57.

Allen, Jon G. and J. Herbert Hamsher (1974), "The Development and Validation of a Test of Emotional Styles," *Journal of Consulting and Clinical Psychology*, 42 (5), 663-668.

Arnold, Magda B. (1960). *Emotion and Personality*, Vol. 1. New York: Columbia University Press.

Batra, Rajeev and Douglas M. Stayman (1990), "The Role of Mood in Advertising Effectiveness," *Journal of Consumer Research*, 17 (September), 203-214.

Bem, Sandra L. (1985), "Androgyny and Gender Schema Theory: A Conceptual and Empirical Integration," in T.B. Sondereggen (Ed.) *Nebraska Symposium on Motivation, Psychology and Gender*, Lincoln: University of Nebraska Press.

Booth-Butterfield, Melanie and Steve Booth-Butterfield (1990), "Conceptualizing Affect as Information in Communication Production," *Human Communication Research*, 16 (4), 451-476.

Cacioppo, John T. and Richard E. Petty (1982), "The Need for Cognition," *Journal of Personality and Social Psychology*, 42 (1), 116-131.

Cacioppo, John T., Richard E. Petty and Chuan Feng Kao (1984), "The Efficient Assessment of Need for Cognition," *Journal of Personality Assessment*, 48 (3), 306-307.

Clark, Margaret and Alice Isen (1982), "Toward Understanding the Relationship Between Feeling States and Social Behavior," in *Cognitive Social Psychology*, Eds. Albert Hastorf and Alice Isen, New York: Elsevier/North-Holland, 73-108.

Comrey, Andrew L. (1988), "Factor-Analytic Methods of Scale Development in Personality and Clinical Psychology," *Journal of Consulting and Clinical Psychology*, 56 (5), 754-761.

DeVellis, Robert F. (1991). *Scale Development: Theory and Applications*. Newbury Park: Sage Publications.

Diener, Ed, Randy J. Larsen, S. Levine and Robert A. Emmons (1985), "Frequency and Intensity: The Underlying Dimensions of Affect," *Journal of Personality and Social Psychology*, 48, 1253-1265.

Edell, Julie A. and Marian Chapman Burke (1987), "The Power of Feelings in Understanding Advertising Effects," *Journal of Consumer Research*, 14 (December), 421-433.

Flett, Gordon L., Paul Boase, Mary P. McAndrews, Kirk R. Blankstein and Patricia Pliner (1986a), "Affect Intensity and Self-Consciousness in College Students," *Psychological Reports*, 58, 148-150.

_____, Paul Boase, Mary P. McAndrews, Patricia Pliner and Kirk R. Blankstein (1986b), "Affect Intensity and the Appraisal of Emotion," *Journal of Research in Personality*, 20, 447-459.

Gardner, Meryl P. (1985), "Mood States and Consumer Behavior: A Critical Review," *Journal of Consumer Research*, 12 (December), 281-300.

Greenblatt, L., J. Hasenauer and V. Freimuth (1980), "Psychological Sex Type and Androgeny in the Study of Communication Variables: Self-Disclosure and Communication Apprehension," *Human Communication Research*, 6, 117-129.

Harris, William D. and David J. Moore (1990), "Affect Intensity as an Individual Difference Variable in Consumer Response to Advertising Appeals," in Marvin E. Goldberg, Gerald Gorn and Richard W. Pollay (Eds.) *Advances in Consumer Research*, 17, 792-797.

Holbrook, Michael B. and Rajeev Batra (1987), "Assessing the Role of Emotions as Mediators of Consumer Responses to Advertising," *Journal of Consumer Research*, 14, 404-420.

Izard, Carroll E. (1977). *Human Emotions*. New York: Plenum Press.

Jung, Carl G. (1970). *The Development of Personality*. Princeton, New Jersey: Princeton University Press.

Larsen, Randy J. (1984), "Theory and Measurement of Affect Intensity as an Individual Difference Characteristic, " *Dissertation Abstracts International*, 85, 2297B. (University Microfilms No. 84-22112).

_____ and Ed Diener (1985), " A Multitrait-Multimethod Examination of Affect Structure: Hedonic Level and Emotional Intensity," *Personality and Individual Differences*, 6, 631-636.

_____ and, (1987), "Affect Intensity as an Individual Difference Characteristic: A Review," *Journal of Research in Personality*, 21, 1-39.

_____ , Ed Diener and Robert A. Emmons (1986), "Affect Intensity and Reactions to Daily Life Events, " *Journal of Personality and Social Psychology*, 51, 803-814.

Lazarus, Richard S. (1982), "Thoughts on the relations between emotion and cognition, " *American Psychologist*, 35, 1019-1024.

Moore, David J., William D. Harris and Hong C. Chen (1994), "Exploring the Role of Individual Differences in Affect Intensity on the Consumer's Response to Advertising Appeals," in Chris T. Allen and Deborah Roedder John (Eds.) *Advances in Consumer Research*, 21, 181-187.

Mitchell, Andrew A. (1986), "The Effect of Verbal and Visual Components of Advertising on Brand Attitudes and Attitude toward Advertisement," *Journal of Consumer Research*, 13, 12-24.

Murphy, G. (1947). *Personality: A Biosocial Approach to Origins and Structure*. New York: Harper.

Osberg, Timothy M. (1987), "The Convergent and Discriminant Validity of the Need for Cognition Scale," *Journal of Personality Assessment*, 51 (3), 441-450.

Russell, J. A. (1980), " A Circumplex Model of Affect," *Journal of Personality and Social Psychology*, 39, 1161-1178.

Sadowski, Cyril J. and Sami Gulgoz (1992), "Internal Consistency and Test-Retest Reliability of the Need for Cognition Scale," *Perceptual and Motor Skills*, 74 (2), 610.

Stout, Patricia A. and John D. Leckenby (1986), "Measuring Emotional Response to Advertising," *Journal of Advertising*, 15 (4), 35-42.

Tolentino, Eugenia, Lisa Curry and Gary Leak (1990), "Further Validation of the Short Form of the Need for Cognition Scale," *Psychological Reports*, 66 (1), 321-322.

Woods, Donald J., Sandra Cole and George Ferrandez (1977), "Dream Reports and the Test of Emotional Styles: A Convergent-Discriminant Validity Study," *Journal of Clinical Psychology*, 33 (4), 1021-1022.

Zajonc, Robert B. (1980), "Feeling and Thinking: Preferences Need no Inferences," *American Psychologist*, 35, 151-175.

Zajonc Robert B. and Hazel Markus (1982), "Affective and Cognitive Factors in Preferences," *Journal of Consumer Research*, 9, 123-131.

Consumer Satisfaction: Cognitive and Affective Dimensions

Narasimhan (Han) Srinivasan, University of Connecticut

Overall, I liked the papers and the creativity and rigor of thinking apparent in each of the papers. First, let me deal with how the three papers appear to fit in the same session. Then, the papers will be commented upon individually.

Droge and Mackoy's paper, "Postconsumption Competition: The Effects of Choice and Non-Choice Alternatives on Satisfaction Formation," sets an appropriately broad framework, removing the isolation of the chosen brand to measure satisfaction, after any decision-making context. Rightly, it has been recognized that the literature has touched upon this aspect previously: for example, cognitive dissonance theory and regret theory talk about non-chosen alternatives impacting the chosen alternative. An example of neutralizing dissonance is the wide use of accepting competitor's promotional incentives, such as doubling/tripling coupons and other special deals. Where trial is not costly, e.g. a store having a return policy with no questions asked, perhaps, no decision is ever final and it is always possible to return the chosen alternative in favor of a non-chosen alternative.

Gurhan and Creyer's work, "Exploring Consumers' Interpretations of a Product Related Illness," fits well in this broad framework in the sense that possible courses of action that a consumer could have followed is considered in evaluating the degree of responsibility/blame for the consequences of the decision an individual makes. Had a different course of action been followed (i.e. a different alternative chosen), there would be less cognitive dissonance and no regret, perhaps. Re-evaluating the wisdom of one's choice with hindsight happens commonly, particularly when there are potential legal consequences of product liability. e.g. smoking, toy guns, etc.

Raman, Chattopadhyay and Hoyer's manuscript, "Do Consumers Seek Emotional Situations: The Need for Emotion Scale," adds to this big picture in expanding the decision making context itself from its cognitive orientation bias. There are additional dimensions of choice that have not been as heavily researched as cognition, such as emotions. These could be momentary, being salient only at the time of decision making, or may linger for long because the product has a lot of emotional overtones. e.g. decision-making process involving the choice of a potential spouse. Do the emotional overtones associated with non-chosen alternatives (assuming that they exist, of course) remain time-capsuled (or get etched in memory after cognitive distortion), so that an "old flame" never dies? Sometimes, people remarry the same person, like Elizabeth Taylor; sometimes, the intensity of emotion may not diminish but the valence may change, particularly in hotly contested separations/divorces. In the above examples, strong emotions are aroused and could dominate the cognitive dimension.

In the three papers, we are essentially dealing with the conceptual complexity of satisfaction. Is it stationary, due to the constraints of operational definition? Is it dynamic? For instance, what happens to my satisfaction when I buy a personal computer and better models at cheaper prices keep appearing on the market? When I spend a lot of time learning how to operate certain software and then something else comes along, do I feel less satisfied with my own learning? How much of it is attributable to one's self or to the external environment? Can satisfaction be sub-divided into several components: fit with the current need, sense of accomplishment in solving a complex task, length of usefulness of chosen alternative given uncertainty. When does something become "sour grapes" and remain so? Under what conditions do "failures become stepping stones to success?" i.e. present dissatisfaction turns out to have been a good thing to happen because we learnt tremendously from the situation.

Now, let me take the papers individually:
1) The Gurhan and Creyer paper is interesting and particularly useful for trial lawyers perhaps. It found that there is a variation in (1) the willingness to award money to victims and (2) the amount of blame attributed to firms for product liability.

Perhaps because I just talked to a friend of mine, who testified in federal court recently about monopolistic competition in a seemingly fragmented market, I don't understand fully the manipulation of market share: 70% versus 30% for high and low market share respectively. Does it not depend upon market structure? In a very competitive market, 30% could be the share of the market leader. It is possible that nobody else in the market has more than 30% individually because the concentration ratio is very low. On the other hand, 70% denotes market domination, of course. Perhaps, you had pre-tested these levels and have not provided the figures in the manuscript. How many people could have made (in)correct assumptions about the relevant market, in terms of its structure? Vignettes are useful, I agree, but when the cognitive processing of information may be different due to differential comprehension of the stimuli, then some error could creep in.

If Mrs. Watson had the time to look for her regular brand in another store but still chose to buy *Bomex*, which was on promotion, what about the possible interaction due to promotion? What if Mrs. Watson did not have the energy or the inclination or did not want to make the effort and is just plain lazy, as is being assumed? How far is the other store? Round the block or across town? Time alone is not the only relevant cost.

Both the items tapping at the blame assignment relating to the manufacturer appear to have face validity. However, it is surprising that the correlation of the two items is only 0.64. The index for event foreseeability, on the other hand, does not appear to have face validity and it is not surprising that the correlation is only 0.56. Under high time pressure particularly, when the regular brand is not available, it appears quite rational to buy an alternative on promotion. What does this have to do with foreseeability of allergic reaction?

The significant impact (p<0.10) of market share could have an alternate explanation. High market share brands generally come from very reputable companies, which are usually large and hence can afford to make large payments in damages. Suppose there is environmental damage caused by oil spills and the company involved is not Exxon, but a very small company. Wouldn't the damages being awarded change? Exceptionality of occurrence aside, ability to pay also figures in the respondent's intuitive thinking and judgment, I feel.

In the second experiment, where the manipulation of market share has been improved, the significance vanishes when examining the blame assigned to the manufacturer! The culprit is guilty, whether rich or poor. On the other hand, when examining the blame assigned to Mrs. Watson, market share becomes significant and the expected interaction with promotion shows up.

I'm just curious that there is no analysis or even mention of the amount of money that Mrs. Watson seemed to merit under different scenarios. You have the opportunity to use a ratio level dependent variable instead of just nominal data.

2) The Droge and Mackoy paper is a conceptual paper, having a lot of merit in that it brings in greater realism to the context under investigation. I believe that the context can even be enhanced when we consider "new" alternatives not currently available in the market but which are expected. When decisions can be reversed, such as product returns, alternatives will continue to exert competitive pressure. For example, when deciding to purchase a personal computer and/or software, would not the market entry of better and cheaper alternatives impact the (dis)satisfaction with my purchase? I'd like to see some empirical follow-up because it is an exciting new avenue.

3) The Raman, Chattopadhyay and Hoyer paper reveals a good awareness of the related literature. The methodology for scale refinement is pretty standard and appears to have been followed. The potential applicability of the scale in terms of predictive validity remains to be shown.

The conceptual definition of the Need for Emotion (NFE) scale is given as "the tendency or propensity for individuals to seek out emotional situations, enjoy emotional stimuli and exhibit a preference to use emotion in interacting with the world." In hindsight, it appears that this has not been accomplished, though an avoidance of emotion is being tapped.

Supposedly, NFE taps mainly into short term emotion. How "short" is short-term? What is its stability? One of the examples cited in the Droge and Mackoy paper is visiting a university which we rejected attending or seeing someone driving another car we considered. Residual emotions are a factor to contend with and perhaps the emotion scale may help in measuring the declining intensity over time.

The authors do a splendid job of spelling out that there are affect intensity differences across individuals and show awareness of different scales which are available in the literature: Larsen's Affect Intensity Measure (AIM), Allen and Hamsher's Test of Emotional Styles (TES) and Booth-Butterfield and Booth-Butterfield (1990)'s Affective Orientation Scale (AOS). However, the use of the literature could have been better.

The conceptual distinction between Larsen's Affect Intensity Measure (AIM) and the NFE is given as follows: While AIM measures the intensity of response to an affective stimulus, NFE taps the "tendency to seek out affective stimuli and enjoy these emotional situations." On the surface, it appears that AIM would be applicable widely, whereas the NFE would try to isolate the self-selection behavior of individuals who *seek out and enjoy* emotional stimuli. Under what conditions would one wish to use the NFE? Hopefully, when further work is done on criterion validity, such questions would be answered. Also, the persuasiveness is less than strong when it is stated that low AIM individuals could have high NFE scores and vice versa. Why wasn't AIM used in the study? An empirical testing could have answered this speculation.

As the authors recognize, another scale in the literature called the Test of Emotional Styles (TES) is very close conceptually because it includes "attitudes toward emotional experiences and expressions." Actually, the paper states that it is "conceptually identical to NFE." Unfortunately, while re-inventing the wheel, "none of the NFE items were imported from previous scales." Why not in this case, if there is conceptual identity? While there could be methodological deficiencies, isn't it possible to convert the scaling procedure to being Likert-type? I'd suggest that reworking the response format of TES could be a worthwhile exercise.

The Affective Orientation Scale which taps the "degree to which individuals are conscious of affective cues and use these cues to guide decision-making processes" is used in this study, though this scale appears to have a cognitive bias commonly found in consumer decision-making models. Yet, the correlation of the AOS and NFE was 0.69, consistent with a moderate correlation between NFE and NFC (0.46 and 0.31 in the first and second samples respectively). The use of a cognitive oriented measuring instrument could have made a contribution, I suppose.

Some questions on the analysis:

The first factor (the general factor) appeared to be the "need for emotion" dimension, whereas the second factor appeared to reflect a "generation of emotions" dimension. What exactly is this second factor and why was it discarded? Is it possible to isolate those items which loaded on both factors (48 items-20 items for first factor-10 items for second factor = 18 items?) and use these to form a scale which includes the need and generation of emotions, because it is these items which appear to correspond to the seeking out and enjoyment of emotions? Being a full information analysis, the number of factors in a factor analysis depends on the type and number of items you throw in. Hence, it is possible that the common items, when a factor analysis is done just with these items, will all load on a single factor and the Cronbach alpha will be high.

In the second analysis, the NFE and AOS items were factor analyzed and four factors emerged. Was this as expected? What is the correlation between NFE and AOS in the second sample? How were the four dimensions related in the oblique rotation? Information is missing about the relationship of NFE with the other three factors.

It was found that all the items of NFE were reverse coded items i.e. subjects indicated avoidance of emotional situations. If this denotes a tendency to self-proclaim being non-emotive on the part of the respondents, perhaps it would be useful to test the scale for social desirability bias in future research. The gender difference found in NFE could just be a reflection of social values.

REFERENCES

Droge, Cornelia and Robert D. Mackoy (1994), "Postconsumption Competition: The Effects of Choice and Non-Choice Alternatives on Satisfaction Formation," ACR, Boston.

Gurhan, Zeynep and Elizabeth H. Creyer (1994), "Exploring Consumers' Interpretations of a Product Related Illness," ACR, Boston.

Raman, Niranjan V., Prithviraj Chattopadhyay and Wayne D. Hoyer (1994), "Do Consumers Seek Emotional Situations: The Need for Emotion Scale," ACR, Boston.

Abbott and Costello Meet Frankenstein: An ACR Retrospective

Joel B. Cohen, University of Florida

As I thought about whether to accept Jerry Kernan's invitation to write and deliver this paper at a session to commemorate the twenty-fifth anniversary of ACR's founding, my first reaction was "Who the hell wants to hear any of this?" I mean, we weren't exactly the Continental Congress coming together to build a new nation.

Coincidentally, I had recently been drafted to serve on and then to chair a committee asked to take stock of ACR: had it been faithful to its original agenda; had it become too much like the organizations from which it originally sought to distance itself; had it simply become an outlet for not-quite-ready-for-prime-time papers, thereby putting advancement of members' careers ahead of larger disciplinary objectives? Frankly, the only enthusiasm I observed for a penetrating analysis of such issues was among a small core of "old guard" members, some of whose views you are hearing today, as well as in some previous presidential addresses and other writings. A far more mainstream voice came through loud and clear: "If it ain't broke, don't fix it."

Several productive members of the field went out of their way to tell me that it "ain't broke." They can make a good case. Just look at how many people are coming to the conference and appearing on the program. No longer dominated by a core of behaviorally-focused academic departments and their Ph.D. programs, ACR has opened its doors wide, so much so in fact that even seven concurrent sessions are not enough. We have now added a "research notes"/poster session format to accommodate the many people wishing to give papers. In fact, I think that the Program Committee itself has more people on it than the number presenting papers at the early conferences. Bill Wilkie, in the third edition of his Consumer Behavior text, points out that ACR has now grown to some 1,500 members from 30 nations. Change ACR? Hell, it would make more sense to sell stock in it!

Accordingly, I advised our current President that an assessment dominated by a contingent of "founding fathers" would probably not represent the larger ACR membership. If such an assessment is to be carried out, either the elected leadership should do it, or a much more broadly representative committee should be appointed.

But, as I thought about Jerry's invitation, I decided that this was probably the appropriate forum to present some personal views about ACR. Okay, but no dusty scrapbooks or photograph albums. No tape of Barbra Streisand singing "Memories." People start looking at their watches and contemplating other places to be when they are subjected to one person's nostalgia. Spice it up a bit. I need a script—perhaps a movie plot will do.

Do you remember those old Abbott and Costello flicks? They're sort of lovable guys who mistakenly think they're in control of their own destiny and bumble their way into situations they hadn't foreseen. But they mean well, and sure enough things sort of work out. Oh, not the way they intended, of course, but pretty well.

A lot of people are doing Frankenstein these days, but nothing like *Abbott and Costello Meet Frankenstein*. In serious renditions, Dr. Frankenstein is assigned some transcendent symbolic significance—egotistical man challenging the forces of nature. You know, like *Jurassic Park*. And, of course, the monster can represent all sorts of profound things. But in simpler Abbott and Costello times, he was just some big, overgrown galoot who, devoid of purpose and out of control, wandered over the landscape.

Nah, I can't see the tie-in to ACR either. Still, if we go back twenty-five years, maybe we *were* Abbott and Costello. Be my guest if you want to cast the movie. I can assure you I had no one in mind for any role. So let's think of them as symbolic stand-ins for a small contingent of actually quite disparate characters.

The movie opens. Here we are, thinking great thoughts, in Columbus, Ohio. Cut: boring. Next scene. The members of our merry band, a.k.a. Abbott and Costello, have found that they agree on a few important things. First, and most important, they were convinced that the scholarly study of consumer behavior was worthwhile, per se, and *not* because therein lies marketing success. More effective marketing, just like better medical practice or more effective applications in general, typically results from the gains that science makes in understanding the factors and processes at work. But increases in brand shares could not be the sine qua non used to justify research on consumer behavior—of that we were clearly in agreement.

Lest some of the younger members of the field think this view is roughly equivalent to a cultural truism, I can recall that the expression of this position in a public forum led a widely respected senior colleague to respond that people who took that view did not belong in marketing departments. Moreover, this response was not particularly surprising at the time. A cursory review of the *current* marketing literature will amply testify to the importance of the brand manager's perspective in determining what problems marketing academics see as important. So make no mistake about it: ACR has always been a rather exotic enterprise, deigning to believe that an activity producing two-thirds of our annual GNP might be worth studying in its own right.

PREMISES AND PROMISES

A key premise was that consumer behavior was indeed a unique domain for study, whose scope implied that it should be approached from a variety of perspectives and orientations. We thought the discipline could be built on a combination of good descriptive research together with judicious use of theory and research from the larger social and behavioral sciences. This view implicitly made the careful choice and conceptualization of the behavioral context—and hence its representation in research studies—pivotal factors in evaluating that research. Needless to say, we also agreed that the discipline would be significantly advanced if there were a regular forum for presenting and discussing such research.

We were hardly of one mind as to the types of knowledge we wished to contribute by studying consumer behavior, but by and large we respected the disagreements we knew existed. Many clearly wanted to learn more about how consumers responded to various activities of the marketing system, some because of an implicit interest in changing attitudes and behavior, some to improve marketing practice, and a few to better evaluate the system's overall performance. Others thought about consumer behavior as a prototypical representation of mainstream human experience. Hence, the study of consumer behavior might be a way to examine many of the important theoretical issues that behavioral scientists (particularly social psychologists) were grappling with at the time. Others were just plain fascinated with what it was consumers did and wanted to carry out the kinds of empirical work that would more adequately describe such behavior. Still others saw the systematic study of consumer behavior as a way of injecting far greater realism into public policy discussions, which have always been dominated by the premises and assumptions of economic theory. All told, this was quite an agenda, and we hoped to learn from each other as we went along.

Cut to scene of fledgling monster on scaffolding being hoisted by pulleys to the roof of a castle. The prospect of giving life to this, our creation, became quite compelling. And since we're Abbott and Costello, we giddily charge ahead. Someone says, "Hey, why don't we . . .?" A brief pause to order another pitcher of beer and then "Yeah, let's do it!" We believe the slogan, "If you build it, they will come," so why not schedule a conference and guarantee an entire block of rooms using a personal credit card? We hatch a vaguely conceived plan to give the AMA an incentive to support our efforts rather than risk the emerging behavioral wing of the field breaking away. At the same time, we reach out to other disciplines and government officials because we know we must establish our own identity: we cannot remain in AMA's orbit and achieve our broader substantive agenda. So we put the "plan" into action, really just making it up as we go along.

Someone hatches a scheme that sounds a bit like a John Le Carré spy novel. New journals are emerging everywhere: the horn of plenty holds sway for the moment in academia. So we allow word to leak out that suggests we may be talking to publishers about starting our own journal—something we know we can't afford to get off the ground on our own. We make subtle inquiries through AMA editorial offices about break-even levels, the number of subscribing libraries, manuscript flow necessary to support a high quality journal, etc. We casually wonder if a new behavioral journal would have much of an impact on the *Journal of Marketing Research*, itself still an infant. When asked directly about our plans, we are evasive, almost secretive. AMA officials hold meetings and move quickly to preempt plans we do *not* have to start our own journal. They offer the needed financial support in return for keeping us within the fold and for what they perceive (correctly, it turns out) to be the potential of such a journal.

But having seen Abbott and Costello movies, you know that the journal caper has some twists and turns that our bumbling heroes have not thought through. "Hey, isn't it nice that AMA agrees with us that readership could be expanded if other disciplines were formally invited aboard?" Don't worry about the details. So ACR becomes undoubtedly the only association whose members contribute 80% of the articles and a comparable proportion of individual subscriptions in return for a 8% voice in the running of the journal. "Hey, Abbotttt!" is what Lou used to say when he figured out that he messed up.

And now the monster was afoot. We had set it loose. It was clearly hungry and quite rambunctious. It needed directors and emissaries and special committees. We respectfully watched it grow. And it continued to grow, becoming a seven concurrent session monster with odd-looking appendages. Its appetite had become prodigious, and so it went in search of more exotic fare, including special conferences and publication opportunities. And people were honored when it praised them and gave them awards.

But all this begs the question, "Is the monster running amok and in need of collaring or has he simply had the ups and downs of most adolescents, but now is on track to becoming a model citizen, albeit somewhat different in temperament and behavior than originally envisioned?" And if by chance it is the former, who's going to walk up to him and get him to shape up?

ASSESSING THE NATURE OF THE BEAST

There seems little question that ACR—over the past twenty-five years—has been a vital force in putting the study of consumer

behavior on the academic map. Contributions from a variety of disciplines are easily found, the infusion of each stemming from the field's long-standing interests (e.g., attitude formation and change, judgement and decision making), but also benefitting from marketing academics' sojourns across campus and the willingness of some academic departments to step up to the plate in pursuit of this objective.

Still, some would argue that the field seems embarked on a quest to learn more and more about less and less. Another spin on this complaint is that we have developed few broadly comprehensive models or middle-range theories, and beyond extensive borrowing of concepts and methods, we have not really looked at consumer behavior with much originality of purpose. These and related criticisms have been voiced many times over our brief history.

At a less abstract level, I can vividly recall the questions I asked virtually all prospective faculty members until some time in the late '70s, when I became so discouraged by the answers that I simply gave up. I asked simply, "What are you personally interested in learning about? How will this project increase your understanding of that topic/issue?" I thought of these as essentially batting practice questions and a good way of getting started. But, by the late '70s, instead of being hit out of the ball park, these questions stopped people dead in their tracks. What I usually heard was, "Well, I don't exactly know what you are asking, but let me describe my 2x3x3 factorial with 2 covariates." When this first began to happen, I usually interrupted and said that I would be happy to hear about the operational aspects of the research later, then I repeated the question. At this point, I usually heard something like, "Oh, I see what you are getting at." Then they would proceed to tell me that they were interested in such and such interaction or the impact of a particular moderator, that sort of thing. Early on, I had the energy to be relentless. So I often said, "Suppose things came out exactly as you predicted. What would you have learned that you regard as worthwhile?" At that point, there was often a painful silence.

Here is what I believe I have learned about progress in our field from these and related experiences (e.g. writing the *Annual Review of Psychology* chapter, journal and conference reviewing). The *science* of doing consumer research has dramatically improved over the years: indeed, it has become a fixation in our stronger Ph.D. programs. That, of course, is good news: research rigor has grown by leaps and bounds since ACR first started holding conferences. At the same time, our field has fragmented—in keeping with mature disciplines—and so researchers often start their inquiries by zooming in on previously circumscribed relationships. Understandable, perhaps unavoidable, but there is a risk of losing contact with the issues that spawned the research in the first place.

It might be appropriate to question whether the discipline has achieved the assumed degree of maturity. Perhaps we are largely kidding ourselves when, with minor variations, we do the same study which might have been done in a field that gave no consideration whatever to what consumers do and how they do it. In other cases, researchers almost seem to have gone out of their way to find projects that are at best tangential to consumers' experiences and settings, as if to demonstrate greater vision and the value of creative self-expression.

Then too, our field has proven to be a particularly fertile ground for the research equivalent of "one-night stands" and what I shall call "peacock displays." Permit me to describe two types of one-night stands. The "grab them while they're hot" types of papers show an entrepreneurial talent for scooping other people when something that seems particularly clever appears in a respected discipline. Unfortunately, the researcher hasn't seemed to take the time to figure out what level of contribution, if any, is likely. So, once the scoop has occurred, it's back to keeping one's eyes and ears open for the next opportunity. The second type of one-night stand follows from reading a study carried out elsewhere and thinking, "I can do that." So you do, with a twist or two, of course. Another line on the résumé. The opposite of "one-night stands" is programmatic research, of which not enough good things can possibly be said.

"Peacock displays" are somewhat different. All through the animal kingdom, species strut, dance, display prominent coloring and emit sounds in order to signal their special qualities to others. But we've really had too much of that over our twenty-five years. Okay, your paper demonstrated a reading acquaintance with ancient Sanskrit; or perhaps you have an uncanny ability to observe Jungian archetypes in your colleagues; or perhaps you are prepared to resist all logical arguments and empirical evidence that you do, in fact, exist. Please! If a mastery of Sanskrit or the Heisenberg Uncertainty Principle would somehow be useful to our field, rather than substituting the trappings of knowledge for genuine insight, let's seek the depth of a real expert, someone who has made this their life's work. If you truly think some perspective, some approach, some research method has value in our quest to better understand consumer behavior, others are more likely to agree with you if you translate this conviction into a substantive contribution. In today's vernacular, don't just "talk the talk, walk the walk." Flagellating ourselves in public because in our heart of hearts it doesn't seem possible to know anything for certain is an utterly useless activity. And it's a transparently self-serving basis for asking others to accept whatever opinion you woke up with today.

I think it would be worthwhile for those seriously interested in the development of this field to think about how it has been evolving and where it might be headed. To that end, let me return to what it is we hoped to learn about and contribute by coming together under the auspices of the Association for Consumer Research. We might ask, for example, "How have we done in understanding consumers' responses to various activities of the marketing system?" It is not my intention to try to provide any type of definitive answer to such a broad question in these few pages, and I well understand that other people may have a different impression. As a start, however, my sense is that we have pretty much operationalized marketing variables and response contexts in ways that are much more convenient but which sacrifice essential elements of reality. Some limitations are often duly noted but not addressed in follow-up studies.

How about what I would term the "basic behavioral science orientation," which looked at consumer behavior as possibly the ideal "laboratory" for carrying out behavioral research? Well, one problem here is that we have too often been content to settle for consumer behavior "cover stories" rather than submitting such theory to the more searching, severe examination that real-life dilemmas and settings would allow. All too often, we do not clearly decide whether particular research is intended to: (1) provide a better or more complete explanation of a particular action or outcome important in our discipline; or (2) help us understand or qualify a relationship among a set of theoretically important constructs. In the former case, we cannot sensibly avoid assessing conceptual relevance to the behavioral episode we are trying to understand. In the latter, we have an obligation, first, to act consistent with the recognition that all theories are naturally situated in particular contexts, and, second, to determine if particular behaviors of consumers would provide a meaningful opportunity for furthering understanding. Accordingly, setting out to run a study as a "test" of a theory (in an "up" or "down" sense) is a quixotic enterprise. Instead, a series of studies should be seen as an opportunity to more fully explicate a theory's internal structure and the factors that qualify and moderate its role in a larger theoretical network. I do not believe that our discipline's report card on these fundamental research decisions is particularly impressive.

I think few would disagree with a negative assessment of our field's efforts to describe the behaviors of consuming units and to evaluate system-wide performance. Large-scale field projects are time-consuming and often costly, but even beyond that, there has not been much attention to the use of secondary data. A recent infusion of interest in rich, descriptive research might help remedy this state of affairs, but that depends largely on the criteria used to select behaviors for study. To this point, I can see little to be overly optimistic about in that regard.

Finally, mainstream consumer behavior researchers have tended to shy away from public policy issues unless these could be fairly closely wedded to traditional research paradigms. While this has allowed us to sidestep the burden of grappling with complex and subtle questions, our framing of such issues has tended to place our research on the periphery of meaningful public policy topics and discussions.

WHAT ROLE FOR ACR?

This brief overview of the field's performance against knowledge goals that were important to us when ACR was established was not presented as or meant to be an indictment of ACR. Professional associations tend to be responsive to the wishes of their members. The question then becomes, "To what degree should ACR explicitly adopt a leadership role and try to influence the type of research in the field?"

I am by no means convinced that ACR could have a strong impact on individual researchers' decisions, even if it wished to. Still, I will end this paper by making the point that I think it is important to take stock of where we have been and where we appear to be going. There are many who feel, perhaps vaguely, that the study of consumer behavior has been losing momentum and vitality. If enough of a consensus is reached that we can be and should be doing better, then it is up to us, both as individuals and as a professional organization, to raise our sights and think more in terms of contributions to the field than simply conference papers and publications.

Beyond that, I've had a lot of fun bumbling along with a cast of characters whose enthusiasm, optimism, and selfless pursuit of the common good got this show on the road.

ACR'S 25TH ANNIVERSARY
How it All Began
James F. Engel, Eastern College

"Wow—a review of our history. Just what I've been waiting for." I can hear your voices now! But, seriously, it's kind of interesting how, to use Kassarjian's favorite phrase, a "bunch of old farts pulled it off 25 years ago." So, as the leader of that bunch, I guess I'm nominated to set it all straight.

I'll bet very few remember that the American Marketing Association gave birth to ACR, a fact that some in those ranks soon began to regret. But more about that later. I have one of the few copies of a brown notebook with these immortal words on the cover: *The American Marketing Association Consumer Behavior Research Workshop* presented by Continuing Education Division, College of Administrative Science, Ohio State University, August 21-23, 1969. There are those voices again—*"I've got to have one of those."*

Anyway, Dick Cardozo from Minnesota somehow got himself in the position of power as head of an AMA Task Force on Marketing Methodology that was mandated to get smaller groups of specialists together to wrestle with latest developments. As head of the now legendary consumer behavior group at Ohio State (Engel, Kollat, Blackwell, and Talarzyk), I got Cardozo on the phone and said in my quiet and gentle way, "It's about time you had a good idea, and such a deal we have for you!" The upshot was that we were given the opportunity to host the first real professional gathering of consumer research types without the contamination of the marketing old guard.

What would you do if you were given that kind of ball? Of course—invite your cronies. And so we did, but we had a more serious purpose. We tried to identify those whom we felt were making the greatest contribution to the field and to give a platform to present what currently was most exciting to them. So, 12 outside presenters were recruited, and the four of us made 16. That left room for 23 others, some of whom we invited from business and related fields. The remaining slots in this opportunity to make history went to the first of the vast multitude who responded to an open AMA invitation.

Now I will reveal for the first time in decades just who those presenters were and the titles of their papers. Are you ready for this? Here goes:

Tom Robertson (with Jim Myers), "Dimensions of Opinion Leadership."

Doug Tigert, "A Psychographic Profile of Magazine Audiences: An Investigation of a Medium's Climate."

Hal Kassarjian, "The Negro and Mass Media: A Preliminary Analysis of 1969 Magazine Advertisements."

Paul Green (with Tom Morris), "Individual Difference Models in Multidimensional Scaling: An Empirical Comparison."

Don Granbois (with Ron Willett), "Correlates of Fulfillment of Brand and Store Intentions for Durable Goods."

Ven Venkatesan (with Jag Sheth), "Risk-Reduction Processes in Repetitive Consumer Behavior: A Further Experiment"

Jag Sheth, "Attitudes as a Function of Evaluative Beliefs."

Joel Cohen (with Marv Goldberg), "The Effects of Brand Familiarity and Performance Upon Post-Decision Product Evaluation."

Jim Stafford (with Al Birdwell and Charles Van Tassel), "Verbal versus Non-Verbal Measures of Attitudes: Use of the Pupillograph."

Al Martin (with Jim Engel and Larry Light), "An Exponential Model for Predicting Trial of a New Consumer Product."

Dick Cardozo, "The Buying Game: A Simulation of Industrial Purchasing Behavior."

Dave Kollat (with Jim Engel and Roger Blackwell), "Current Problems in Consumer Behavior Research." [you wouldn't expect us to exclude ourselves would you?]

But I have saved the most interesting paper for last. You won't believe this: Bill Wells, "It Is Very Important for People to Wash Their Hands Before Eating Each Meal." And wouldn't you know that this was the only one to get mentioned in the press?

Catch these words by Paul Swinehart in the *Columbus Dispatch*: "A University of Chicago researcher in consumer behavior warned advertisers that their emphasis on psychedelic art and rock music may not appeal to the customers who buy most of their products. 'Our findings confirm and define a wide gap between the bearded swinging youth and the mass market,' Dr. Wells said. The survey indicates that the typical consumer 'doesn't want to think that he or she is a bit of a swinger, places a high value on home and family life, thinks that all men should be clean shaven every day, and thinks that hippies should be drafted,' he said." How's that for a slice of history?

Okay, I've had some fun in describing the event so far, but those of us who were there still talk about this as a genuine highlight of our professional lives. First of all, realize that this was one of the very first times in which competent researchers in our field were gathered in one place for serious dialog. We had these papers in advance and were prepared to critique in a constructive way. And, even more amazing, everybody went to every session and contributed. The net result was professionalism at its very best.

When we were planning this whole thing, Dave Kollat had an idea which intrigued us. Occasionally I let him speak at meetings but not often. This time I'm glad I did, because he was the one who suggested that we present the idea of forming our own professional association. Okay, the truth is finally out. I've been taking credit for this all along, and now my conscience is clear. Kollat is the real "father of our field," not me.

Actually we didn't even need to plant this suggestion, because there was real unanimity that we all longed for this kind of high-level professional interchange to continue in the future. Frankly we weren't getting this kind of benefit from AMA at that point; most of us went to AMA sessions only for personal visibility and to fish in the slave market for young faculty. Furthermore, we were being strangled by a lack of avenues for publication.

Somehow the notion of an Association for Consumer Research made it to the floor.

There was such strong support that the following things happened:

- We agreed to set up a steering group with me as chair along with Kassarjian and Cohen. Little did they know what they were unleashing when they made us into a troika with such power.

- The group expressed such confidence in us that they passed the hat and raised a kitty of about $500 for our treasury. Would you still express such confidence us? I don't think I would.

• We agreed to meet in 1970 at U. Mass immediately prior to AMA meetings in Boston with invitations extended to a much wider group.

So the baby was conceived and most of us left for the AMA meetings in Cincinnati with a notable lack of enthusiasm. Somehow Kassarjian, Cohen, and I found strength to have dinner on Sunday night to discuss this whole thing. As I remember, the only place we could get a drink was in Kentucky, and we went to the only joint we could find open.

Through some miracle the three of us managed to stop dominating and interrupting each other long enough to come up with the rough structure of what was to emerge a year later as ACR. Here were some of the main building blocks:

• *A platform for those who are engaged in consumer research from a variety of applied perspectives*—government, business, home economics and consumer interests, consumer psychology. No postmodern stuff at that point. If I remember right, Holbrook and Hirschmann might still have been in diapers (or graduate school—what's the difference?)

• *A commitment to build a high level of conceptual and methodological professionalism in a field which still was pretty much in its infancy.* We particularly wanted to see an end to the "theory of the month club" in which poorly conceptualized borrowing from behavioral sciences was creeping into our discipline.

• *Pursuit of diverse avenues of research in which there is genuine theoretical and practical relevance.*

So we divvied up the assignments. I took on creation of a constitution. This was done by borrowing what seemed to be good from AAPOR and other organizations. There were a few unique wrinkles such as formation of an Advisory Council as a means of accountability beyond our own ranks. This was finally ratified at the 1971 meeting at University of Maryland in a meeting I chaired. Inspite of some grumbling and discontent, it managed to pass pretty much intact. By the way, does that constitution still exist? I haven't seen or heard anything of it since that time.

Cohen more or less took on the assignment of building the membership. I don't remember what Kassarjian did. Does he ever do anything?

Back to my narrative—the best story of all about ACR really demonstrates the uniqueness of Joel. Maybe you've heard it before, but here at the facts.

It seems that Bob Ferber and the old guard at AMA got mighty scared when they heard that we were forming our own association. Gasp! Competition for the mighty AMA. Joel called Hal and me up and suggested the darndest bluff you have every heard, and of course we went along. He suggested that we float the rumor that we were about to start our own publication—*The Journal of Consumer Research*. That was about as likely given our treasury as Hal Kassarjian becoming an introvert.

But Joel demonstrated how to manipulate the opinion leadership channels, and Chicago erupted. How dare we? So they conceived the counter strategy of starting this journal themselves and asking other associations such as ACR to join as partners. Of course that's what we wanted all along. AMA took the bait and we got our own professional journal in 1974 without having to bankroll it.

We held our next meeting at U. Mass in 1970 with at least a 500% increase in our numbers. This meeting, of course, was the real launch of ACR as we know it. As yet we were not a formal association, so an operating committee continued to govern until the 1971 meeting when the constitution was ratified. Bob Perloff succeeded me as chair, and the baby began to take the form of a reasonably healthy, somewhat unruly infant. And on the story goes, but I'll let others fill in the rest.

It has been enormously gratifying to me to see this dream come true, and I'm grateful to have had some role in helping that to happen. No one ever could have envisioned in 1969 how important our professional field would become. And I always have considered it to be a real honor to have been elected as one of the first two Fellows in Consumer Research along with John Howard. That really makes it all worthwhile.

I have teased my two colleagues, Joel Cohen and Hal Kassarjian, somewhat unmercifully here. I fully expect retaliation, but always remember that I alone have given you the unbiased, genuine truth. Seriously, we worked together very well as a team, and I will always respect them as genuine pioneers, true professionals, and great friends.

Some Recollections from a Quarter Century Ago

Harold H. Kassarjian, UCLA[1]

It was a different world ... 25 years ago. In Spring 1970, Professor Venkatesan sent out the preliminary schedule of the first true Association for Consumer Research meeting in Amherst. Not unlike today, it was to start Friday morning and go through Sunday noon. Ven wrote:

The total cost of the sessions will be $65.00. This includes transportation from and to Bradley Airport (in Hartford-Springfield), two nights (lodging) in Amherst, all meals starting from lunch on Friday through lunch on Sunday (as well as refreshments and other conference materials.)

A year later, for the 1971 meetings the registration fee was reduced to $45.00. From the first volume of the Newsletter we see:

The registration fee of $45.00 includes all meals (breakfast, lunch and dinners for the three days as well as coffee breaks), registration materials, and a copy of the conference proceedings.

However it did not include the "hotel" charges. Room rates were $8.00 for a single and $12.00 for double occupancy. The following year in Chicago the registration including lunches and dinners stayed the same $45.00 but room rates jumped to $9.50 per person per night, and for those who came by car, parking was an exorbitant fifty cents per entry.

Indeed, it was a different time. It academia, the cognitive revolution had started in psychology. Universities were in a growth spurt and we were headed for the moon to everyone's disbelief and amazement. The Ford and Carnegie reports criticizing the state of business schools was beginning to have an effect.

Little by little, thinking and ideas from scientific disciplines began to infiltrate into marketing. New names had appeared and were making an impact: Bob Ferber, Paul Green, Al Kuehn, Al Silk, Everett Rogers, Bob Holloway, Jag Sheth, and of course, Joel Cohen, Bill Wells and Jerry Kernan. New ideas and weird approaches were being introduced to marketing: laboratory research, mathematical models, empiricism, simulation, and positivism ... the era of data analysis had arrived.

---

[1]Portions of this paper were written while the author was a Visiting Professor and Interim Dean at the American University of Armenia in Yerevan, Armenia. For more a more complete presentation of this material, see Harold H. Kassarjian, "Scholarly Traditions and European Roots of American Consumer Behavior," In G. Laurent, G. L. Lilien, and B. Pras (eds.), *Research Traditions in Marketing*, Boston: Klewer, 1994, pp. 265-279; Harold H. Kassarjian and James R. Bettman, "Tenth Anniversary Editorial," *Journal of Consumer Research*, 10, March 1984, v-vi; Harold H. Kassarjian, "In Memoriam: Robert Ferber, *Journal of Consumer Research*, 8 (December 1981), vi-viii [Reprinted from A. Mitchell (ed.), *Advances in Consumer Research*, Vol IX, iii-iv]. Obviously the interested reader should turn to the papers presented in this session by Jerry Kernan, Bill Wells and Joel Cohen, as well as Kernan's paper presented in the session on the 20th Anniversary of the Journal of Consumer Research also found in this volume. Jim Engel presents his recollections in a engaging article presented in the June 1994 *ACR Newsletter*.

But it was also a difficult time in academia. The country soon found itself in another war. Campuses, at times, looked more like a war zone with helmeted troops, rifles, and tear gas, rather than a quiet sanctuary. Marketing was perceived as the hand maiden of the military-industrial complex. Enrollment in classes dropped precipitously. Academic jobs dried up. The Young Turks-today's old-geezers-vainly tried to distance themselves from the establishment. Led by the likes of Kotler and Levy we broadened the marketing concept to include not only sellers of coffee and tooth paste, but also hospitals, charities, universities, social causes, and of course, the government with the help of the likes of Mary Gardner Jones and the Federal Trade Commission. Many of us were loudly proclaiming that consumer research could be used for the good as well as the evils of trade-that we could be relevant to the protection of consumers as well as their exploitation. We proclaimed that we are not the hand-maidens of industry.

In those days, some of us were in academia, for example, Bill Wells; others stayed in industry, for example, Joel Cohen; and still others of us went to Washington behind Bill Wilkie and Dave Gardner to work for the government: The Federal Trade Commission, the White House, The Postal Commission, and the Food and Drug Administration. It was exciting times, and our goals were more or less similar, modeler and behaviorist alike, academic, industry and government types alike. And so, the Association for Consumer Research emerged, an interdisciplinary group of ragtag psychologists, home economists, government regulators, advertising and marketing practitioners, operations researchers, marketing professors, and assorted others interested in the behavior of the consumer.

By the late 1960's there were more and more consumer behavior types coming into the field. Some were newly minted doctoral students and others were stepping over from sister disciplines. The *Journal of Marketing Research*, edited by Ferber, had recently begun publication was being overwhelmed by behavioral articles. For us, who were doing the research, it was getting harder and harder to find outlets for our work. In addition, the American Marketing Association in its usual conservative ways had been preventing too many behavioral articles from appearing in their program, in their proceedings, and in the *Journal of Marketing Research*. We had started to overwhelm the traditional marketing type articles of the era-a condition that the establishment at AMA considered unacceptable. Where ever behavioral types got together, there was talk of a new association and a new journal. Both were needed.

As you have heard over and over again, some time in early 1969, Jim Engel and the Ohio State Consumer Behavior group got a small seed grant, ironically from the AMA, for a workshop to be held at Ohio State. I don't know how the list of participants was selected but it included most everyone at the time in the field of consumer behavior. From bits and pieces and from failing memory, I recall a few events.

I had presented my study on the role of Blacks in Advertising. I shall never forget it. That Summer I was taking a trip to the Soviet Union. I had not finished the data processing or writing up the paper for the meeting so I took along computer output, and one day sat in a hotel and tried to finish writing the paper. It was mostly done that day except and I put all my handwritten yellow sheets of paper, tables, computer output, and scribblings in my new Samsonite brief case. A few days later when I was leaving, problems started. It was the time of the cold war, the Berlin wall, sabre rattling, Cuba, and both sides wary of the other.

So along comes Kassarjian trying to get out of the Soviet Union with a brief case crammed with numbers on computer paper, tables about Negroes (it was Negroes then, and not yet Blacks or African-Americans), and Jews and Mexicans and Chinese, and who knows what else. I had tables and tables of numbers. I had a hellova time explaining to Soviet officials in English what my notes on yellow pads were about. And what all the numbers meant. I feebly tried to explain that it was the percentages of blacks in ads in *Goodhousekeeping* and *TIME* and had absolutely nothing to do with the Soviet Union. I don't remember much anymore, I don't remember what was said and what stupid answers I gave, but I do remember being put into a car in a most unfriendly manner, taken to the plane that was awaiting me on the field, assured my baggage would arrive, wished a good trip and an invitation to return to Mother Russia.

Upon landing in Germany my next task was to get the paper typed up. A day more of writing, and the two days of typing with the help of my wife, Traute, on an ancient typewriter with a German Keyboard led to the final paper. Next a trip to the Post Office and my paper was off to Ohio State. A few days later (maybe it was a week or more), I was off to Ohio State. The conference papers had been duplicated and distributed, mine with all the typing errors and German characters.

All of the materials at the conference had on them the ACR logo. Ever wonder where that logo came from? It was created and designed by one of the staff people at the Ohio State extension programs to fill white space on the program. It has stayed substantially the same since. In a way the creation of that logo neatly represents ACR, in my opinion. Unlike other organizations, we did not spend hundreds of thousands of dollars designing a logo, ... it just sort of happened.

Housing at Ohio State was on campus. It may have been in executive program housing. I don't remember. But I do remember that it had a charm to it. There was more of a comraderie than one can find at a Marriott Palace or a Hilton Castle. Most of our meals were on campus, the student union or the faculty club or something. There was a bus from the meeting room to the dorms, but it was within walking distance. I remember walking back one late afternoon with several others: Stu Bither from Penn State for sure, perhaps Venkatesan and Joel Cohen, and perhaps Jerry Kernan. It was a hot day and we stopped at a little cafe for a beer, sitting at a creaky old table in front. The reaction of all of us was that this was a wonderful fantastic, fabulous meeting and that this we simply must continue. We must meet again. There was an electricity in the air. Consumer Researchers had met together and talked for three days about studies and about research and about each-other's work.

That topic of conversation was being held in other places and that evening it was the common belief that we would continue. The next day, Saturday, we listened to more papers and that afternoon, one of the session was entitled something like, " a wrap-up" or "summary" or "future". Engel, I thought, but maybe it was Kollat, suggested at that session that we organize into a new organization. When it was over, I remember seeing Jim smile. His eyes proclaimed, we pulled it off, a great conference, and now a new association has been formed. I figured that Jim and his associates had the same idea that other clumps of attendees had. That we wanted it to continue. I remember saying that we needed money for mailings and to get started. Jim passed a hat around. I think it was Flemming Hansen who suggested that faculty should toss in $10 and students $5. ACR dues stayed at that level for many years. We all went away from that session very excited and that evening at cocktails and dinner the one consistent topic of conversation was

the new association, the next meeting, a chair for the following year, and those sorts of issues. Jim Engel agreed to be the chairman of the new group until the following year when we could organize with a constitution and all those sorts of finery.

I don't remember much about the papers that were presented. On my session I think Tom Robertson and Jim Myers presented their stuff on diffusion. Doug Tigert introduced his work on psychographics.

Paul Green had a paper on multidimensional scaling. He was hot on that topic at that time. Ven was doing a lot of experimental work running subjects and he was on the program. It was here that Cohen and Goldberg presented their paper on instant coffee and cognitive dissonance that we had all worked on in 1968 at Illinois. Wells presented his paper on life style with the irreverent title, "It's Very Important for People to Wash Their Hands Before Eating Each Meal." Jim Engel, in his endearing article in the June 1994 ACR Newsletter presents more detail on what really happened, or at least what he thinks really happened.

During the rest of that year there was lots of phone calls and letters written back and forth. The next meeting was to be in 1970 at the University of Massachusetts, partially because Venkatesan was there and he agreed to be in charge of arrangements. The program chairman was Joel Cohen. I do know that Cohen had to pledge his soul, or at least a large amount of money to the "hotel" or to somebody, since the association did not have a track record and there was no reason why it should be believed that we could pay our bills. What gall Cohen had in those days.

I remember that Bettman was at Amherst at that first true ACR meeting, as was Bill Wilkie. Bob Ferber was there, Also, Jerry Kernan, Bill Wells, and I think Flemming Hansen-program chair of the 1995 ACR Europe conference. Jim Engel was there. Wilkie has a wonderful story on how the program chair for the following year was selected. Please ask him about it. It is hilarious and sort of true, although I think it must have been embellished a bit making it even funnier.

I had volunteered to be the editor of the Newsletter. In the first issue of the Newsletter (January 1971) I wrote:

"The first meeting of the Association for Consumer Research was held in Amherst, at the University of Massachusetts, on August 28-30, 1970. A great deal of enthusiasm, along with (some) hesitation, lead to the formation of the Association. About 120 people attended the first meeting under the directorship of M. Venkatesan. The university types were from Marketing, Psychology, Home Economics, Sociology, Agricultural Economics, and assorted others.

Since the meetings were held just prior to the American Marketing Association meetings in Boston, naturally the greatest representation came from marketing departments, although the response from other (academic departments), government and industry was not insignificant.

At the various formal and informal business meetings, the purposes of the organization began to emerge. Clearly, the overwhelming desire was to make the membership interdisciplinary. Hence we decided that the 1971 meetings would be held just before the American Psychological Association Convention in Washington. It was planned that in future years, we will meet in proximity to other associations, to make it convenient for all of us.

The Newsletter continues,

A new journal to be published on a quarterly basis is also now much more than merely a vision to be argued about. At a spontaneous advisory board meeting held in December, Joel

Cohen was railroaded into investigating the possibility of housing the journal at the University of Illinois. He has been furiously gathering information, cost figures, negotiating with commercial publishers and such. At the 1971 meetings he will present a report and request approval of our amazing publishing venture. It is quite possible that the first issue of a new journal can emerge by early 1972. Full details will be presented at the 1971 meetings ... .

It was, indeed, a different time. We had formed a new association-an interdisciplinary group that was not beholden to the establishment or the military-industrial complex so maligned at that time. It was fun, the conferences tended toward the irreverent and people worked together to get things done because it was fun. I remember in 1977 our conference hotel, just shortly before we were to meet, pushed us out because they had a larger group with more clout that wanted the hotel that weekend. Keith Hunt and I, as program chair and president, flew to Chicago and that afternoon selected a new hotel, the O'Hare Hilton. In just days, everything was reorganized and changed to fit the new venue. Well, almost everything. Disaster struck when we realized that Hunt had forgotten to bring the ACR football for the annual ACR football game. Keith Hunt, as only Keith Hunt can do, managed to persuade the hotel manager to run from O'Hare to downtown Chicago to buy us a football. Somehow, playing football in front of the O'Hare Airport with planes landing and taking off, traffic, noise, and amazed travelers looking on, has to be a major highlight of that year.

There are many other highlights that you have heard about and will hear more about in these three days. To me, the most exciting of all those events was first, the start of this organization. And second, the start of our amazing publishing venture-the birth of the *Journal of Consumer Research*. But that is another story to be told at another time-in fact, tomorrow evening.

We, ... well at least I, will not be here twenty-five years from now for the celebration of our 50th Anniversary. Others will take our place on this podium to talk about the previous 25 years. I hope they will be able to tell a generation of consumer researchers who are today yet in diapers, that they too had fun. I hope they will say that at the end of the twentieth century and beginning of the twenty-first century consumer research continued to be as exciting and as interesting as ever, but most of all, it continued to be irreverent and fun!

Declaring A Discipline: Reflections on ACR's Silver Anniversary

Jerome B. Kernan, George Mason University

ABSTRACT

This paper reflects on ACR's formative years, on the conditions and people surrounding the association's establishment in 1969. The events which conspired to produce consumer behavior as a discipline are recounted and traced to the ACR ethos which developed over the subsequent 25-year period.

As we pause to commemorate—indeed, celebrate—the Association for Consumer Research's first twenty-five years, it is useful to reflect on our beginnings. Any worthwhile organization respects its history, for therein lies its heritage and legacy. The origins of this association, which has served as the nexus for so many of our careers, can be traced to a cadre of people who seized the opportunity to declare a new discipline—what we now call consumer research. As one of the surviving dinosaurs of ACR's pre-history, I have been asked to reflect on these early years—to offer some perspective on what happened and why—in an attempt to explain the events that shaped the organization's evolution. It is a privilege to do this, but I must begin with a huge caveat. Several recollections of ACR's origins have been spawned by this period of celebration (e.g., Cohen 1995, Engel 1994, Kassarjian 1995, Wells 1995) which, because they are recollections, do not agree in every detail. Conceivably, these emic versions of the organization's history might yield to a satisfactorily etic amalgamation (to the "truth," in a positivist sense), but we who have offered them are content that they be regarded in the postmodern sense of experienced reality—what that period represented uniquely to each of us.[1] My reflections do not constitute a history of ACR. Owing to my longevity, a benevolent request to reminisce about the organization's formative period was extended and I acceded. My comments might be dangerously effete, of course, and readers should recognize this limitation.

A FACILITATING AMBIENCE

Much as we would like to take all the credit, ACR's founders were helped immeasurably by a heady atmosphere that drove higher education, beginning in the early 1960s. (The political turmoil later in that decade did not seriously disrupt most American business schools, although it had a profound effect on other sectors of higher education.) Prior to that, business schools focused on vocational training. In marketing, for example, one learned about "functions," a euphemism for what practitioners did on a day-to-day basis. Charitably, this was a descriptive approach to the discipline, and students used more picturesque designations. The closest one got to consumer behavior were two functions, "buying" and "selling." Business-school graduates learned in spite of their training, corporate employers became disillusioned with the educa-

tional process, and eventually the problem was dumped in the laps of foundations for study. Three major reports emerged—Dahl, Haire and Lazarsfeld (1959) and Gordon and Howell (1959), both sponsored by the Ford Foundation, and Pierson et al. (1959), sponsored by the Carnegie Foundation. Although done independently, each of these reports recommended essentially the same cure for America's business schools—stop teaching descriptive material and start emphasizing theory and research. In particular, they urged that the curriculum and faculty attention be infused with the mathematical and behavioral-science foundations underlying the decision-making process. The charge of these reports to business schools was clear and adamant: Get respectable!

In response, deans tripped over one another in the rush to perform their institutional penance. Curricula were revised and faculties were transformed, largely by bolstering them with people trained in mathematics, statistics, and the behavioral sciences. The schools were forever changed, for these new people thought and behaved according to an arts-and-science ethos, including the preoccupation with research as the nexus of faculty life. The new faculty took on an elite status, owing to their special skills, short supply, and privileged terms of employment, so there was some resentment; but given the times, there was little dispute about who was wearing the white hats—every dean was happy to parade his bevy of stars before anyone who questioned his leadership. These halcyon days were further enabled by historically-unprecedented large budgets; economic times were good, the mood of the country was positive, benefactors and legislatures were generous, and there was a crop of baby-boom students clamoring for admission to college. And to business programs in particular, as this campus venue (with engineering) was seen as the launching pad to the American dream, even for women. This was a great period of expansion for America's business schools—in budgets, in physical construction, and in enrollments. It also provided the impetus for the phenomenal growth in our Ph.D. programs during the ensuing years.

In large part, the people who started ACR came from this privileged faculty pool. It is wrong to imply that pockets of support for the idea did not exist outside business schools (in psychology departments, in government agencies, and in industry), but the formal move to inaugurate a fledgling organization was made essentially by marketing professors, who shared an out-of-step objection to the managerial cadence of that period. This was the era of 4P-time; Jerry McCarthy was its Sousa and the AMA sought to enforce the credo that marketing is what marketing managers do. All this seemed alien to us, since we wanted to study how and why consumers behave as they do. We had little interest in using that knowledge to increase market share; the challenge—the fun part— was in figuring out how the world works, not in making the world work better. (To the extent that this distinction perseveres today, it explains why appeals to critical theory—e. g., Murray and Ozanne's 1991 *JCR* piece—have not been embraced by large numbers of ACR members.) We felt the need for a professional association that focused on what we cared about and did. AMA, with all its formality, its increasingly unforgiving size, its unholy alliance with textbook publishers, and its hiring-hall emphasis on recruiting and teaching, was avoiding everything we deemed central. Its conference papers were awful. Even when AMA broke from the Allied Social Sciences (where some 5,000 conferees would fight over hotel space, usually during the Christmas holidays, in some dread-

[1] I want to express my appreciation to Frank Kardes and Mita Sujan for creating this opportunity to reflect on ACR's early years and to Joel Cohen, Hal Kassarjian, and Bill Wells for acting as a sounding board for my unreliable memory. Keith Hunt, as always, served as an additional reality check. However, none of these people should be blamed for any errors in this paper; these are my exclusive responsibility. Finally, I trust that no one mentioned here takes offense at my characterizations, which are well-intentioned and meant to be interpreted in the most charitable sense.

ful midwestern venue), to establish the Summer Educators Conference, things got no better. The problem (if not the solution) seemed simple: We didn't want a conference for educators; we needed one for researchers. And that's why we insisted that the term "research" be featured prominently in the new organization's name.

No one should infer that ACR's founding group—ragtag as we were in many ways—was not aware of its contemporary leverage. We were very active people, publishing in the best journals available. We were prominent (if not always beloved) at our universities and had that degree of self-sufficiency which only youth and naiveté can bestow. It is not boasting to say that we were very much full of ourselves, but it is equally true that none of us took himself all that seriously. We were embarking on a lark, which probably would work. But if it didn't, there was a whole life of tomorrows when we could try again. The immediate problem was to stake our claim, quickly and with sufficient credibility to make it stick. The solution resided in AMA. The plan, concocted over some months, was to get its blessing (and some of its money) under the rubric of "a workshop on experimental research in consumer behavior" to be held at Ohio State University in August, 1969. That workshop, shepherded by Jim Engel, has come to be designated as the first meeting of the organization now called ACR. Our cover story to AMA was that certain advanced methodologies were becoming available to consumer researchers and that these were worth investigating in a workshop setting. AMA (although Dick Cardozo may have seen through our scheme entirely) took a paternalistic stance and conferred its imprimatur almost without hesitating. So we were hatched out of AMA—its quasi-bastard child. Yet ACR got the legitimacy it needed and AMA got rid of some noisy complainers. Neither party to this birth is likely to have behaved so cavalierly, however, were it not for the heady times, the unbounded optimism, the prevailing Zeitgeist.

THE LONG ROAD FROM AMA TO ACR

ACR grew out of AMA, but the fledgling organization hardly emerged overnight. We were neither prescient enough nor bold enough simply to plunge our banner into the intellectual terrain. Instead, we took a pragmatic path toward independence, what was then called scientific marketing. By contemporary standards, this may seem desultory, even cowardly, but it seemed efficacious at the time. "Respectability" was reckoned in accordance with logical positivism (the hypothetico-deductive model of science) and marketing was being nominated for scientific status within this context. Since consumer behavior—particularly if it could be quantified—contributed to marketing's ability to predict, our work took on an importance it otherwise lacked and this participation gave us a foot in the door.

A review of contemporary marketing books—e.g., Alderson 1957, Banks 1965, Bliss 1965, Boyd and Levy 1967, Ferber 1949, Frank and Green 1967, Frank, Kuehn and Massy 1962, Frank, Massy and Wind 1972, Green and Rao 1972, Green and Tull 1966, Green and Wind 1973, Howard 1963, 1965, Oxenfeldt, Miller, Schuchman and Winick 1961, Robertson 1971, Wells 1974, Zaltman 1965—reveals that the overwhelming majority of them had a quantitative bent, in keeping with the "scientific" imperative of the time. Recall that this was the period during which Scott Paper's Tom McCabe engineered the establishment of the Marketing Science Institute (1962 at the Wharton School, later moved to Cambridge) and throughout which there was a serious debate over marketing's scientific status. In retrospect, that argument contained more rhetoric than reason, but its mere existence testifies to the tone of the times. The prevalent feeling among ACR's organizers was that we should move systematically, yet gradually, away

from marketing toward our distinct identity. We wanted our own home but saw little profit in burning bridges along the way. This sentiment was especially strong among those from business and government, whose future with ACR depended on a marketing connection.

Those of us in university posts brought plenty of raw material to our marketing jobs—e.g., Berelson and Steiner 1964, Edwards 1957, Festinger 1957, Fishbein 1967, Handy and Kurtz 1964, Heider 1958, Karlins and Abelson 1959, Katona 1951, Katz and Lazarsfeld 1955, Kuhn 1963, Mills 1959, Osgood, Suci and Tannenbaum 1957, Rogers 1962, Shannon and Weaver 1949, Thurstone 1959—and we sought to infuse our work with these foundations. In addition, we had some prototypical consumer-behavior sources available, thanks largely to marketing practitioners—e.g., Dichter 1964, Ferber and Wales 1958, Foote 1961, Katona 1961, Newman 1957, Smith 1954, Wulfeck and Bennett 1954. Out of this conglomeration the early library of consumer behavior emerged—e.g., Arndt 1968, Bennett and Kassarjian 1972, Britt 1966, 1970a, 1970b, Cohen 1972, Cox 1967, Engel 1968, Farley, Howard and Ring 1974, Ferber 1977, Hansen 1972, Kassarjian and Robertson 1968, McNeal 1965, Myers and Reynolds 1967, Newman 1966, Nicosia 1966, Sheth 1974, Sommers and Kernan 1967, Tucker 1967, Ward and Robertson 1973, Zaltman, Pinson and Angelmar 1973. This array includes genuine textbooks, compilations of previously-published journal articles, and proceedings of workshops on various topics. The books everyone remembers from this period are Howard and Sheth (1969) and Engel, Kollat and Blackwell (1968)—the former because it represented the first comprehensive theory of consumer behavior that had been subjected to systematic empirical testing and the latter, accompanied by Blackwell, Engel and Kollat (1969) and Kollat, Blackwell, and Engel (1970), because it obviated what had been a pedagogical nightmare for us. We complained about the marketing orientation to consumer behavior but did little to change it. In the manner of spoiled children, most of us took from our host discipline while we cursed it. Similarly, some of us were aware of metaphysical alternatives to the received view of knowledge, yet we played along with the epistemological dicta of modernism in our teaching, research, and reviewing. This was disingenuous, but scientific marketing afforded us a bridge to the disciplinary turf where ultimately we could proclaim a new, realistic set of rules. We are only now coming to that realization and we may never have got here were it not for the courage of some people *not* among us at the outset. The most we "founders"can claim is the good sense not to have suffocated these people as they pleaded for realism in our discipline.

HIDDEN COLLEGES, FALSE STARTS, AND PREMONITIONS OF OHIO STATE

The 1969 workshop at Ohio State was a signal event in ACR's history, but it is wrong to imagine that this enterprise emerged out of nothing. Prior to our convening in Columbus there was no formal organization of consumer researchers, but there was a good deal of informal contact among us. As with most disciplines, we had hidden colleges; everyone knew who was doing what, who had the best ideas, who was a good sounding board. Indeed, several workshops occurred prior to the gathering arranged by Jim Engel. For example, NYU had hosted seminars since the early 1950s (Clark 1954, 1955, 1958); Joe Newman drew an impressive group together at Stanford in 1964 (Newman 1966); and Monty Sommers and I hosted a similar workshop at Austin in 1966 (Sommers and Kernan 1967). The following year saw the first of the Columbia conferences on buyer behavior (Arndt 1968) and John Howard's group followed this with another one in 1969 (Sheth 1974). In addition, people like the late Ray Bauer at Harvard (the only person I've ever encountered who could write finished manuscripts while watching NFL telecasts), after having stunned the 1960 AMA conference with his "Consumer Behavior as Risk Taking" paper, had placed many of his perceived-risk doctoral students in a network around the country—e.g., Johny Arndt at Columbia, Jeff Barach at Tulane, Don Cox at Coca Cola, Charlie King at the Krannert School, Stu Rich at Oregon, and Larry Wortzel at BU (see Cox 1967). This backdrop should suggest that there was nothing revolutionary about the Ohio State meeting; indeed, Jim and his colleagues faced no mystery about whom to invite—it was an evolutionary event for which they had merely to "round up the usual suspects." None of this is to detract from the importance of that gathering in August 1969, however, for it differed from all the previous ones in a most fundamental way. After all the casual alliances, all the ad hoc get-togethers, and all the ruminations about our confused professional identity, the Columbus enclave resolved to change things, and to do so with permanence. No one knew exactly what this meant (it was as much aspiration as understanding), but we were resolved to strike out on our own, to run up our flag, to declare consumer behavior as a discipline unto itself. Much remained to be done, but that *commitment* in 1969 is what makes the Ohio State meeting the de facto beginning of ACR. And what a time to begin! No one had yet proclaimed the world postmodern, but we converged on Columbus amidst a bewildering array of contemporaneous events—the country was abuzz about Ted Kennedy's account of his weekend at Chappaquiddick, everyone was celebrating Neil Armstrong's Apollo walk on the moon, hurricane Camille had just killed hundreds of Gulf-Coast residents, gay activists at the Stonewall Cafe alerted us to the future as they refused to accept the brutality of "New York's finest" passively, and there was this happening called Woodstock. That we were able to focus on consumer research within this cacophony says something about us, but whatever that may be is not clear even to this day. What is clear from the shards of August 1969 (now something of a collectors' item) is that Jim's group was thinking presciently, for there—big as life and exactly as we know it today—was the ACR logo, emblazoned on our workshop binders.

OHIO STATE—1969

I suppose there are as many versions of that gathering in Columbus (also, perhaps, of its antecedents) as there were people in attendance. My own recollection is not all that clear (Bill Wells, to no one's surprise, gave the most interesting paper), but I am struck by how it seems, in retrospect, to age us. Can you imagine Marvin Goldberg as a graduate student? How about Cohen as an untenured assistant professor? Such reflections make those of us whose status hasn't changed since then feel positively ancient. The important part of that meeting, however, occurred just before we dispersed (many to the AMA meetings in Cincinnati). Beginning only half seriously, but eventually in a most considered context (we each pitched in some money), it was decided to move ahead with the idea of a new professional association. Jim, Joel, and Hal Kassarjian took the money and ran—ostensibly to cover their expenses while they investigated what needed to be done (at the now famous bar in Newport, Kentucky). Jim (see Engel 1994) would have you believe that only the three of them crossed the Ohio River that fateful night in the service of ACR's higher objectives, but those of us chasing our money—in familiar territory, no less—know better. In any case, out of that and numerous subsequent conversations evolved a set of initial objectives for our new organization and these were reported formally at our next gathering, Amherst, in 1970.

AMHERST—1970

The 1970 AMA meetings were in Boston and UMASS had recently completed a new student center/conference facility, so Ven Venkatesan was prevailed upon to host the soon-to-be ACR gathering at Amherst. If you are familiar with New England, you realize that it is not the most convenient place to fly. Commonly, the airlines (the real ones) serve Boston and "other." The most convenient other for Amherst was Hartford/Springfield, accompanied by a forever van ride through western Massachusetts. I relate this because it punctuates our contemporary mentality about conference sites; these were the times before Keith Hunt roamed the globe in search of the most sybaritic venue available. We were not just cheap. Indeed, part of our reasoning was that a dreadful site would encourage people to concentrate on the conference business at hand. (What else was there?) Another objective of our fledgling organization that emerged at this conference was that paper sessions were to be true dialogues—not the numbing lectures we seem to have backslid into in recent years. All our sessions were full, the halls were empty, and we yelled at one another during presentations. And we learned. Like other organizations, we probably put too much emphasis on conferences, but that seemed important at the time. We were especially concerned that the dialogue be informed by other-than-academic-marketing considerations so we welcomed people different from ourselves to the sessions. (In fact, a perusal of ACR's membership or conference attendance during the early years will show that we attracted substantial numbers of nonmarketing academics and of people from both the business and public sectors. Somehow, we have lost much of this support in the intervening years.) These dialogues were variegated, but always lively and constructive—from a concern for content (mostly from business and government people) to one of methodology. (One recalls Joel's favorite comment: "This is awful!") We were reminded more than occasionally that our theories were either bankrupt or the product of larceny. And we resolved to correct all these shortcomings by devising Ph.D. programs for our progeny that would package for them the intellectual foundations we had been obliged to ferret out on our own. Moreover, these students would be brought on board as soon as they were ready, meaning that doctoral candidates would be welcomed at conferences, where they could benefit from the largest possible sounding board for their work. (From time to time, it has been suggested that ACR sponsor a doctoral consortium, after the fashion of AMA, but this idea has never come to fruition.) One more thing emerged concerning these students. It was decided—rather adamantly—that ACR conferences would not feature displays by textbook publishers and that we would not encourage them to sponsor cocktail parties, both in reaction to the hated AMA practices of the sort. In addition, there was to be no hiring-hall recruiting at our conferences; if students were to be interviewed, it was to be on an informal basis—a practice which prevails even to this day. In retrospect, these policies reflect our objective to distance ACR from the teaching-dominated tone of AMA and its conferences. In our organization, *research* was to be the focus—even to the point of including that word in the association's name. Regarding the name, incidentally, the A was never intended to stand for American. We were aware from the outset that our colleagues around the world had ideas from which everyone could benefit. It is therefore unfortunate, in spite of the long-term prodding of members like Fred van Raaij, that we waited until 1985 to sponsor a conference in Singapore (Tan and Sheth 1985), and until 1992 to sponsor one on the European continent (van Raaij and Bamossy 1993).

All these objectives emerged, more or less formally, at the Amherst conference. But ACR did not yet exist as an entity. That detail had to await our next conference, at College Park, a year hence. In the meantime, we were moving along at the behest of a committee, with Jim Engel serving as chair. So Ven arranged for the site, Joel handled the program (no proceedings), and everyone just pitched in, doing whatever needed doing. That operating mode pretty much characterized our early years, and it likely is the source of the organization's initial success. (Dumb luck also deserves a healthy share of the credit.) Those who wonder how we survived financially should not look askance at our paltry dues. Instead, they should realize that we took very much a proprietary interest in this association (there is no other word to describe it). It was common-place, for example, to pay for things out of one's own funds, rather than charge the association. (At the extreme, Joel once pledged a goodly portion of his annual salary in order to secure our conference facilities.) Many others carried the organization in similar ways. For instance, the practice of program chairs billing the association for their expenses is something that never occurred to us during the early years. We did not regard ACR as a faceless entity, something with which we struck a bookkeeping balance. Rather, it was an extension of ourselves—to be nurtured, to be supported, to be celebrated. So we left Amherst—I in an ambulance, because it was the only conveyance available to connect with my flight out of Hartford—encouraged that things were falling into place. In a year, we would be official.

COLLEGE PARK—1971

Both AMA and APA met in Washington in 1971, so we decided to sandwich our conference between them, on September 1, 2, and 3, at the College Park campus of the University of Maryland. (We were still deferential to other organizations and to site costs.) Phil Kuehl did the arrangements, Dave Gardner handled the program, and Bob Perloff succeeded Jim Engel as our chair (subsequently to be called president). This conference was distinctive in at least two respects. First, it was the occasion for the approval of the constitution that had been being crafted for the past year or so—the instrument that officially designated us as the Association for Consumer Research. Second, this was the meeting out of which our first volume of proceedings emerged (Gardner 1971) and that publication made a reality of one of our initial objectives—to *disseminate* research about consumer behavior.

Jim's modesty is showing when he suggests that our constitution and by-laws were just lifted from those of AAPOR (see Engel 1994). In fact, he (and others) poured over a lot of sources and tailored the conglomeration to our unique requirements and circumstances. The "ratification" was anything but perfunctory, but Jim managed to steer the document through all our objections with a minimum of shouting, convincing people of the need for an advisory council, for instance. So ACR became a de jure entity in 1971, even though it would be 1976 before Ken Bernhardt engineered our incorporation as a nonprofit organization (in Georgia). Our tax-exempt status from the IRS was received the following year, in 1977.

Those new to ACR might be surprised at the catholicity of topics addressed at this conference (at all the early ones, for that matter). We were much more than a group of academics looking for yet another line-item to add to our CVs; there was overt attention to theory development, research standards and ethics, and to the *use* of research findings—for both the public and private interest. There were several rap sessions scheduled as a part of the College Park conference and one of them turned out to have profound consequences. Mary Gardiner Jones, an FTC commissioner, spoke to us about the need of the Commission for valid social-science research in its deliberations and rule-making. You might imagine how aghast we were as she matter-of-factly told us of the "ammunition" needed to set public policy properly. This advocacy mentality seemed to fly in the face of everything we had come to believe about science and the search for truth and she had to field some very hostile questions. Over the next several months, however, both she and we came to understand one another's position and a rapprochement set in. The story is a long one but its upshot is that, as a result of this rap session, a whole string of ACR researchers—Alan Andreasen, Ken Bernhardt, Joel Cohen, Gary Ford, Dave Gardner, Keith Hunt, Jack Jacoby, Hal Kassarjian, Mike Mazis, Dick Mizerski, Kent Monroe, Ivan Preston, Debbie Roedder-John, Terry Shimp, Scott Ward, and Bill Wilkie, to name just those who spring to mind—came into contact with the federal regulatory system. As a consequence of their work (and surely that of others, whose contributions regrettably are not salient as I write this), laws affecting consumers no longer are influenced just by economists and lawyers. ACR truly has made a difference in this context and it is a pity that this contribution is not recognized more widely.

We have never been a tidy group and it is perhaps fitting that our proceedings volumes reflect this disdain for order. For the uninitiated, ACR's first volume of proceedings (Gardner 1971) contains papers from our *second* annual conference. Our first annual conference (Amherst, 1970) had no proceedings and it wasn't really our first conference (Ohio State in 1969 was; otherwise, 1994 doesn't add up to a silver anniversary). And that is just the beginning of the adventure in the numbering of ACR's proceedings volumes, more about which below.

CHICAGO—1972

Our next conference was in Chicago. It is easy for me to remember because, as a member of the program committee, I was obliged to visit the site—the continuing education center at the University of Chicago—in January of 1972. With Bill Wells as our host, we surveyed the meeting place until about dusk and then proceeded across the Midway to the university campus where, as a faculty member (prior to his agency days), Bill had his office. We were on foot. Never joke about Chicago being the "windy" city. Both my ears were frostbitten in a matter of ten minutes.

We convened on November 3-5, presumably to benefit from Chicago's balmy autumn climate. Some of us went to the site two days early, however, to participate in a workshop devoted to information processing. (Yes, the topic was popular even then.) This affair was organized by George Haines, Dave Hughes, and Mike Ray and it resulted in a book (Hughes and Ray 1974)—the first of many publications (excluding our conference proceedings volumes) spawned by an ACR gathering. Joel (by now working for National Analysts with Marsh Greenberg) was then our president— the first, since his pre-constitution predecessors were called chairmen—and he scolded us all (appropriately) in his presidential address. Unfortunately, his remarks do not appear in that conference's proceedings volume (Ventakesan 1972). My other recollection of this conference is the insight offered us by NSF's George Brosseau, who served during the early years as ACR's "man in Washington," regarding federal research funding possibilities.

BOSTON—1973

Our fifth conference represented a watershed in many ways; it was the inflection, from finding-our-way gatherings to the annual-conference model we recognize today. To meet in Boston was an act of maturation; we could now afford a big city and a real hotel. People talked about diversions like the Combat Zone. Bob Pratt (then of General Electric) was already reflecting on ACR's past and future in his presidential address. Everyone referred to the organization as though it had always existed. (And our west-coast contingent was complaining about the inequity of having to "fly the hump.") The conference program was quite good but, except for a knock-em-dead talk by Dan Yankelovich, it already showed unmistakable signs of a drift into papers by professors. Jerry Zaltman chaired an excellent session about broadening the concept of consumer behavior and this led eventually to yet another ACR publication (Zaltman and Sternthal 1975). Of perhaps greatest historical significance, however, is that Scott Ward and Peter Wright decided to designate the conference proceedings *Advances in Consumer Research*, which became volume one of the series people know today (Ward and Wright 1974). Keep in mind that Boston was the fifth of our conferences and the third for which a proceedings volume was issued. (Perhaps we should have a Julian/Gregorian face-off, so that everyone can count from the same origin.) It would take ten more years for these volumes to bear the Provo, UT designation (Kinnear 1984).

CHICAGO(AGAIN)/CINCINNATI/ATLANTA— 1974, 1975, 1976

From an historical perspective there is nothing especially noteworthy about the next three conferences; the organization clearly had a foothold, it was becoming more popular, and we were sliding into patterns (some of which exist even to this day). Only personal memories of these gatherings prompt me to allude to them briefly. We returned to Chicago in 1974, this time to the O'Hare Inn (not to be confused with the O'Hare Hilton). If such a quick return to that city seems strange, one needs to realize the players involved—a group some of us regarded as the Chicago Mafia. Bill Wells (now at work at Needham) was our president, and the conference was chaired by Joe Plummer (then at Burnett) and our sorely-missed Mary Jane Schlinger—assisted by what appeared to be a goodly portion of Burnett's Chicago office staff. That we do not have a record of Bill's presidential address (which to this day stands unchallenged for its brevity) testifies to the no-paper-trail modus operandi of this group.

Cincinnati was next and is memorable for several reasons. Stan Shores (of Procter and Gamble) and I ran the program (which is to say our secretaries ran it), Bev Anderson edited the proceedings volume, and Jack Jacoby was ACR's president. There were several notables on the program—e.g., Leo Bogart, Martin Lipset, Nate Maccoby—and this was the occasion of Jack's famous "telling it like it is" presidential address (Jacoby 1976). As past-president, it was Wells' duty to introduce Jack, and Bill prepared for this task by conducting some interesting man-on-the-street interviews. (He would be delighted to elaborate, given the appropriate incentive.) Another highlight of this conference—albeit one appreciated only by certain victims—was the beginning of an elaborate manual on how to run a conference. We decided that, for purposes of both arrangements and programs, it was foolish to reinvent the wheel each year. But *the* highlight of Cincinnati was the first ACR football game, otherwise known as the mud bowl, played in a rain-soaked Nippert Stadium. As reported contemporaneously by Messrs. Bettman and Lehmann, the stars of this Saturday afternoon contest were Jim Bettman and Don Lehmann. (I still have the official game ball.)

The following year we went to Atlanta, where Doug Egan arranged for us to bunk at Dunfey's (?) something-or-other hotel (on Peachtree Street, of course, but a zillion miles from the city center). Dave Gardner was president, the late Fred Reynolds and Roy Stout (Coca Cola) chaired the conference, and Bill Perrault edited the proceedings. But that's not the memorable part. There

was another football game. A bunch of us vs. a bunch of us at Grant Park. On my team, Rick Staelin (he of the collegiate fame) was the quarterback and I was a wideout. (Everyone except Bill Wilkie was a wideout. Wilkie blocked.) I headed for a zone defended by Brian Sternthal. "Easy pickings," I reassured myself. I made my cut according to the elaborate play Rick had called ("Everybody go out"), just as he threw the perfect spiral. I jumped. Brian jumped. The pass tipped past both of us. Brian leaped either higher or sooner than I because he broke his fall on me—specifically, his elbow made a lasting impression on my rib cage. So there we lay, a couple of bruised and empty-handed guys. What else to do except get up and try again? Which we did, but my how it hurt! After another 30 minutes or so everyone was tired or bored so we took a city bus back to the conference hotel, where the evening reception was already in full swing. A quick shower—still very sore—and on to the drinks. I checked with Brian, because I felt miserable. He was fine. Fred assured me that I just needed a few more drinks. I accommodated. It didn't help. To bed by 1:00 and up by 7:00, but no sleep worth counting. This was really stupid. Off to the nearest hospital. Three broken ribs; one punctured lung. There is nothing easy about Sternthal. Be a blocker. (For the remaining ACR football excursions, I contented myself with scorekeeping.)

THE ACR ETHOS

There is little I can add to the common knowledge of our history beyond these recollections of the very early days. It should be clear from my musings, however, that ACR has developed a distinct ethos that sets it apart from other professional organizations. We have benefited from externalities, we have been very lucky, and many people have worked hard to bring about the association's unarguable success. Absent our distinct raison d'être and modus operandi, however, none of these factors could have produced the preeminence ACR enjoys today. Our organizational character was palpable at the association's inception and we have nurtured it ever since.

ACR is, and has always been, about consumer research—its discovery, dissemination, and application. Individual members may emphasize one or another of these facets, they might believe passionately in this or that metaphysic, and they often represent differing constituencies. Whether one thinks of us as interdisciplinary, plural, or variegated, however, we have always had the durable nexus of research to bind everyone together. Dialogue has been our hallmark. Not dialogue as one experiences in many professional associations (e. g., networking), but exchanges focused on ideas. For this reason, ACR is perhaps the least status-conscious group about; it is as close to a meritocracy as one is likely to find. (Consider our membership qualifications: we are concerned with people's interests and what they know, not with their pedigree. Ignore the occasional fop; notice how accessible most ACR people are.) This commerce of ideas—not restricted to an elite plutocracy—has kept the organization vibrant, insulating it from the malignancy of self-importance and irrelevance.

Our single-minded concern for research has made us very much a task-oriented association. (There are emerging signs of group-maintenance concerns, but these are a natural development.) That there still are some founding members around to remind everyone of our inauspicious beginnings also has helped to focus us on "getting the job done." We began ACR with a cottage-industry mentality; we could not afford to waste money or time. Unlike today, the association, per se, had no budget. Volunteerism abounded, for this was *our* association; people were concerned with how much they could give. There was no ceremony about it because ours was not a faceless bureaucracy which needed to "recognize" its benefactors. And that tradition continues to this day—in spite of our large budgets, arrangements with outside publishers, and other trappings of commercial success, ACR members are at least willing, and generally eager, to do the organization's business, all without fanfare. (My sense is that Keith Hunt's gentle demeanor is largely responsible for sustaining the family atmosphere which encourages this spirit.) We have never been a group which pontificates; instead, we just go about our business—quietly but effectively.

This relaxed spirit of cooperation is evident even in the case of ACR's office holders. We have been blessed over the years with excellent election slates and the organization's officers have done our bidding well. Everyone knows the list of presidents and conference chairs, but many others have sustained us —often at considerable personal sacrifice—over the years. We are particularly indebted to our executive secretaries—Phil Kuehl, Jim Taylor, Ken Bernhardt, Tom Kinnear, and (ACR's soul) Keith Hunt—who have constituted our only headquarters, dealt with everyone's grief, and answered all the bizarre inquiries. And to the editors of the *Newsletter*—Hal Kassarjian (beginning in 1971 with a 7-page mimeographed piece, replete with the sort of understatement we've come to associate with him), Jack Jacoby, Jerry Olson, Bob Witt, Rich Lutz, Bill Locander, Laird Landon, Dick Reizenstein (our resident oenologist), Mickey Belch, Rich Yalch (he of the infamous "lists"), Valerie Zeithaml, and the tower twins, Peter Bloch and Jim Muncy—who in many ways *are* the voice of ACR between conferences. Whatever cohesion we have experienced over the years is due in large part to the effective and amiable efforts of these people. An abiding focus on research may have made everyone's job easier, but a determination to advance the organization's goals still was necessary.

LEGACIES AND HOPES

I do not mean to give the impression that ACR has meandered along for these twenty-five years, unscathed and never touched by controversy. We have had our squabbles but, in the large scheme of things, they have been constructive and reasonably civil. In 1978, for example, we were asked to boycott our conference hotel in Miami Beach in an effort to pressure the Florida legislature to ratify the equal-rights amendment. (We didn't, because the wrong people—innocent hotel workers—would have been adversely affected.) Several of us have used the occasion of our presidential addresses to scold or encourage the membership (see Spiggle and Goodwin 1988), much as Bill Wells did in his *JCR* sermonette (Wells 1993). And one would need to have been on another planet to have missed the exchanges associated with the paradigm-shift phenomenon during the 1980s (e. g., Belk 1986, 1987, Hirschman 1986, Holbrook 1986). Compared with the disputes in other social-science disciplines, however, these rifts were mild and their resolution generally has been a constructive accommodation. Moreover, even at the height of the "battle," there were no ad hominem attacks. We diced over ideas, but never over the integrity or sincerity of their champions.

All told, then, while ACR has not fulfilled everyone's hopes, it can hardly be characterized as a failure—even a disappointment. Indeed, it has given us a legacy, if only in the form of a professional identity. Those of us interested in consumer behavior—for whatever reason, from whatever perspective—now have a credible label under which to pursue our activities, without fear of misunderstanding or ridicule. To those who want, ACR provides aid and comfort; yet it is not a demanding mistress—it is rather like a resident program on our personal-computing systems, on call. When we choose to wear the ACR label we can expect a tolerance for our ideas, however unpopular they may be. And we will find a respect for the history of ideas. (Truly, are there any new ones?) All this because ACR people have always chased the same elusive thing—an independent explanation of that large part of daily life having to do with consumption. Anyone who can contribute to the attainment of this goal has been welcome.

Only a few of us lived through the difficult years as the ACR identity was established and perhaps only we realize its tenuous nature. Do not imagine us to be alarmists, then, when we admonish you that the organization—the discipline—must be nurtured. The consumer-research identity may be a fait accompli, but its credibility is not immune from natural advances in the arts and sciences. We have a beginning, but no more. This seed must be nourished so that future generations of researchers can bring it into full bloom, so that ACR's original aspirations can be brought to fruition. We will not live to see that culmination, and we envy the excitement you will experience. Yet we have a trove of memories, amassed along the rocky road of the association's first twenty-five years.

Our first membership directory in 1973, the first Ferber award (Bob's name not then attached) to Leigh McAlister in 1978, and our initial selection of Jim Engel and John Howard as ACR Fellows in 1979 each represent a milestone in ACR's history, even though their significance may seem incidental except to those who were there at the time. Similarly, if you've only heard about the roast of Jim Bettman and Hal Kassarjian at the Cambridge conference in 1987, as they retired from a six-year watch as *JCR* editors, you don't have a flavor of that event. And speaking of *JCR*, which is not owned by ACR (see Kernan 1995), you know little if your sense is that it's merely a journal started in 1974. To understand the fabric of this association one needs to have experienced the "little things" as we developed—Mike Ray insisting on his "microtheoretical notions," Jack Jacoby's perennial response ("that's not what our study says; read it again"), Jag Sheth's musings ("but if you multiply by the importance weights"), Rob Settle's dismissive "it's all attribution theory," or Russ Belk's famous "dogfood" characterization. One needs to have seen Alan Sawyer looking for his shoes, or Kernan complaining about the ever-present chicken at conference lunches, or Kassarjian writing his discussion paper on a plane headed for Freeport, or Wilkie in tube socks at the Doral Country Club, or Alice Tybout desperately distributing the last of the champagne bottles in San Francisco, or Jerry Zaltman's familiar I-know-something-you-don't-know expression, because these incidents speak of us as people, rather than just researchers with extensive bibliographies. (ACR was not founded by individuals who subscribe to the dictum "I attach no importance to what I have written—so long as it is published.") Occasionally, some of us think ACR has become too big, too complex, and too officious—it has evolved into the very sort of bureaucratic monster against which we rebelled originally (see Cohen 1995)—and that it is time for us to start a new rump group. Such lapses into wistfulness are not driven by our desire to maintain control of the organization, however. Rather, they ensue from a nostalgic past when conference nametags were superfluous. (Younger members of ACR might ponder the fact that we elders don't know "all these people" either.)

Developing the consumer-behavior discipline has been a great adventure and I am grateful for the opportunity to reflect upon it (and for your indulgence of my informal style). I have come to know a host of bright colleagues and it has been my privilege to help, but mostly to be helped by, them. In addition to these professional benefits, ACR has been the source of many dear friendships. So I can only hope that your experience with the association will be as rewarding as has been mine and that you will keep in mind one other thing. Fun. We always had fun.

REFERENCES

Alderson, Wroe (1957), *Marketing Behavior and Executive Action: A Functionalist Approach to Marketing Theory*, Homewood, IL: Irwin.

Arndt, Johan, ed. (1968), *Insights into Consumer Behavior*, Boston: Allyn & Bacon.

Banks, Seymour (1965), *Experimentation in Marketing*, New York: McGraw-Hill.

Belk, Russell W. (1986), "What Should ACR Want to Be When It Grows Up?," *Advances in Consumer Research*, Vol. 13, Richard J. Lutz, ed., Provo, UT: Association for Consumer Research, 423-424.

_____ (1987), "ACR Presidential Address: Happy Thought," *Advances in Consumer Research*, Vol. 14, Melanie Wallendorf and Paul F. Anderson, eds., Provo, UT: Association for Consumer Research, 1-4.

Bennett, Peter D. and Harold H. Kassarjian (1972), *Consumer Behavior*, Englewood Cliffs, NJ: Prentice-Hall.

Berelson, Bernard and Gary A. Steiner (1964), *Human Behavior: An Inventory of Scientific Findings*, New York: Harcourt, Brace.

Blackwell, Roger D., James F. Engel and David T. Kollat (1969), *Cases in Consumer Behavior*, New York: Holt, Rinehart and Winston.

Bliss, Perry, ed. (1965), *Marketing and the Behavioral Sciences*, Boston: Allyn & Bacon.

Boyd, Harper W., Jr. and Sidney J. Levy (1967), *Promotion: A Behavioral View*, Englewood Cliffs, NJ: Prentice-Hall.

Britt, Stuart Henderson, ed. (1966), *Consumer Behavior and the Behavioral Sciences: Theories and Applications*, New York: Wiley.

_____ (1970a), *Consumer Behavior in Theory and in Action*, New York: Wiley.

_____ (1970b), *Psychological Experiments in Consumer Behavior*, New York: Wiley.

Clark, Lincoln H., ed. (1954), *Consumer Behavior, Vol. I*, New York: New York University Press.

_____ (1955), *Consumer Behavior, Vol. II*, New York: New York University Press.

_____ (1958), *Consumer Behavior, Vol. III*, New York: New York University Press.

Cohen, Joel B., ed. (1972), *Behavioral Science Foundations of Consumer Behavior*, New York: Free Press.

_____ (1995), "Abbott and Costello Meet Frankenstein: An ACR Retrospective," this volume.

Cox, Donald F., ed. (1967), *Risk Taking and Information Handling in Consumer Behavior*, Boston: Harvard Business School.

Dahl, Robert A., Mason Haire and Paul F. Lazarsfeld (1959), *Social Science Research on Business: Product and Potential*, New York: Columbia University Press.

Dichter, Ernest (1964), *Handbook of Consumer Motivations*, New York: McGraw-Hill.

Edwards, Allen L. (1957), *Techniques of Attitude Scale Construction*, New York: Appleton-Century-Crofts.

Engel, James F., ed. (1968), *Consumer Behavior: Selected Readings*, Homewood, IL: Irwin.

_____ (1994), "ACR's 25th Anniversary—How It All Began," *ACR Newsletter*, 25 (June), 3-5.

_____ , David T. Kollat and Roger D. Blackwell (1968), *Consumer Behavior*, New York: Holt, Rinehart and Winston.

Farley, John U., John A. Howard and L. Winston Ring, eds. (1974), *Consumer Behavior: Theory and Application*, Boston: Allyn & Bacon.

Ferber, Robert (1949), *Statistical Techniques in Market Research*, New York: McGraw-Hill.

_____ , ed. (1977), *Selected Aspects of Consumer Behavior: A Summary from the Perspective of Different Disciplines*, Washington: U. S. Government Printing Office.

_____ and Hugh G. Wales, eds. (1958), *Motivation and Market Behavior*, Homewood, IL: Irwin.

Festinger, Leon (1957), *A Theory of Cognitive Dissonance*, Palo Alto, CA: Stanford University Press.

Fishbein, Martin, ed. (1967), *Readings in Attitude Theory and Measurement*, New York: Wiley.

Foote, Nelson N., ed. (1961), *Household Decision Making*, New York: New York University Press.

Frank, Ronald E. and Paul E. Green (1967), *Quantitative Methods in Marketing*, Englewood Cliffs, NJ: Prentice-Hall.

_____ , Alfred A. Kuehn and William F. Massy (1962), *Quantitative Techniques in Marketing Analysis*, Homewood, IL: Irwin.

_____ , William F. Massy and Yoram Wind (1972), *Market Segmentation*, Englewood Cliffs, NJ: Prentice-Hall.

Gardner, David M., ed. (1971), *Proceedings: 2nd Annual Conference*, College Park, MD: Association for Consumer Research.

Gordon, Robert A. and James E. Howell (1959), *Higher Education for Business*, New York: Columbia University Press.

Green, Paul E. and Vithala P. Rao (1972), *Applied Multidimensional Scaling*, New York: Holt, Rinehart and Winston.

_____ and Donald S. Tull (1966), *Research for Marketing Decisions*, Englewood Cliffs, NJ: Prentice-Hall.

_____ and Yoram Wind (1973), *Multiattribute Decisions in Marketing*, New York: Holt, Rinehart and Winston.

Handy, Rollo and Paul Kurtz (1964), *A Current Appraisal of the Behavioral Sciences*, Great Barrinton, MA: Behavioral Research Council.

Hansen, Fleming (1972), *Consumer Choice Behavior*, New York: Free Press.

Heider, Fritz (1958), *The Psychology of Interpersonal Relations*, New York: Wiley.

Hirschman, Elizabeth C. (1986), "Marketing, Intellectual Creativity, and Consumer Research," *Advances in Consumer Research*, Vol. 13, Richard J. Lutz, ed., Provo, UT: Association for Consumer Research, 433-435.

Holbrook, Morris B. (1986), "Whither ACR? Some Pastoral Reflections on Bears, Baltimore, Baseball, and Resurrecting Consumer Research," *Advances in Consumer Research*, Vol. 13, Richard J. Lutz, ed., Provo, UT: Association for Consumer Research, 436-441.

Howard, John A. (1963), *Marketing: Executive and Buyer Behavior*, New York: Columbia University Press.

_____ (1965), *Marketing Theory*, Boston: Allyn & Bacon.

_____ and Jagdish N. Sheth (1969), *The Theory of Buyer Behavior*, New York: Wiley.

Hughes, G. David and Michael L. Ray, eds. (1974), *Buyer/Consumer Information Processing*, Chapel Hill: University of North Carolina Press.

Jacoby, Jacob (1976), "Consumer Research: Telling It Like It Is," *Advances in Consumer Research*, Vol. 3, Beverlee B. Anderson, ed., Atlanta: Association for Consumer Research, 1-11.

Karlins, Marvin and Herbert I. Abelson (1959), *Persuasion*, New York: Springer.

Kassarjian, Harold H. (1995), "Some Recollections from A Quarter Century Ago," this volume.

_____ , and Thomas S. Robertson, eds. (1968), *Perspectives in Consumer Behavior*, Glenview, IL: Scott, Foresman.

Katona, George (1951), *Psychological Analysis of Economic Behavior*, New York: McGraw-Hill.

Katz, Elihu and Paul Lazarsfeld (1955), *Personal Influence*, New York: Free Press.

Kernan, Jerome B. (1995), "Framing A Rainbow, Focusing the Light: *JCR*'s First Twenty Years ," this volume.

Kinnear, Thomas C., ed. (1984), *Advances in Consumer Research*, Vol. 11, Provo, UT: Association for Consumer Research.

Kollat, David T., Roger D. Blackwell and James F. Engel, eds. (1970), *Research in Consumer Behavior*, New York: Holt, Rinehart and Winston.

Kuhn, Alfred (1963), *The Study of Society: A Unified Approach*, Homewood, IL: Dorsey Press.

McNeal, James U., ed. (1965), *Dimensions of Consumer Behavior*, New York: Appleton-Century-Crofts.

Mills, C. Wright (1959), *The Sociological Imagination*, New York: Oxford University Press.

Murray, Jeff B. and Julie L. Ozanne (1991), "The Critical Imagination: Emancipatory Interests in Consumer Research," *Journal of Consumer Research*, 18 (September), 129-144.

Myers, James H. and William H. Reynolds (1967), *Consumer Behavior and Marketing Management*, Boston: Houghton-Mifflin.

Newman, Joseph W. (1957), *Motivation Research and Marketing Management*, Boston: Harvard Business School.

_____ , ed. (1966), *On Knowing the Consumer*, New York: Wiley.

Nicosia, Francesco M. (1966), *Consumer Decision Processes: Marketing and Advertising Implications*, Englewood Cliffs, NJ: Prentice-Hall.

Osgood, Charles E., George J. Suci and Percy H. Tannenbaum (1957), *The Measurement of Meaning*, Urbana: University of Illinois Press.

Oxenfeldt, Alfred, David Miller, Abraham Shuchman and Charles Winick (1961), *Insights into Pricing from Operations Research and Behavioral Science*, Belmont, CA: Wadsworth.

Pierson, Frank C. et al. (1959), *The Education of American Businessmen*, New York: McGraw-Hill.

Robertson, Thomas S. (1971), *Innovative Behavior and Communication*, New York: Holt, Rinehart and Winston.

Rogers, Everett M. (1962), *Diffusion of Innovations*, New York: Free Press.

Shannon, Claude E. and Warren Weaver (1949), *The Mathematical Theory of Communication*, Urbana: University of Illinois Press.

Sheth, Jagdish N., ed. (1974), *Models of Buyer Behavior: Conceptual, Quantitative & Empirical*, New York: Harper & Row.

Smith, George Horsley (1954), *Motivation Research in Advertising and Marketing*, New York: McGraw-Hill.

Sommers, Montrose S. and Jerome B. Kernan, eds. (1967), *Explorations in Consumer Behavior*, Austin: University of Texas Press.

Spiggle, Susan and Cathy Goodwin (1988), "Values and Issues in the Field of Consumer Research: A Content Analysis of ACR Presidential Addresses." *Advances in Consumer Research*, Vol. 15, Michael J. Houston, ed., Provo, UT: Association for Consumer Research, 5-12.

Tan, Chin Tiong and Jagdish N. Sheth, eds. (1985), *Historical Perspective in Consumer Research: National and International Perspectives*, Provo, UT: Association for Consumer Research.

Thurstone, L.L. (1959), *The Measurement of Values*, Chicago: University of Chicago Press.

Tucker, W.T. (1967), *Foundations for A Theory of Consumer Behavior*, New York: Holt, Rinehart and Winston.

van Raaij, W. Fred and Gary J. Bamossy, eds. (1993), *European Advances in Consumer Research*, Vol. 1, Provo, UT: Association for Consumer Research.

Venkatesan, M., ed. (1972), *Proceedings: 3rd Annual Conference*, College Park, MD: Association for Consumer Research.

Ward, Scott and Thomas S. Robertson, eds. (1973), *Consumer Behavior: Theoretical Sources*, Englewood Cliffs, NJ: Prentice-Hall.

_____ and Peter Wright, eds. (1974), *Advances in Consumer Research*, Vol. 1, Urbana, IL: Association for Consumer Research.

Wells, William D., ed. (1974), *Life Style and Psychographics*, Chicago: American Marketing Association.

_____ (1993), "Discovery-Oriented Consumer Research," *Journal of Consumer Research*, 19 (March), 489-504.

_____ (1995), "What Do We Want to Be When We Grow Up?," this volume.

Wulfeck, Joseph W. and Edward M. Bennett (1954), *The Language of Dynamic Psychology as Related to Motivation Research*, New York: McGraw-Hill.

Zaltman, Gerald (1965), *Marketing: Contributions from the Behavioral Sciences*, New York: Harcourt, Brace.

_____ , Christian R. A. Pinson and Reinard Angelmar (1973), *Metatheory and Consumer Research*, New York: Holt Rinehart and Winston.

_____ and Brian Sternthal, eds. (1975), *Broadening the Concept of Consumer Behavior*, Ann Arbor, MI: Association for Consumer Research.

Anniversary Session
What Do We Want To Be When We Grow Up?

William D. Wells, University of Minnesota

Good evening. It is indeed a pleasure to be here. Just being present at this Geezerfest is an uncommon privilege.

This is going to be about Yesterday, Today and Tomorrow. Yesterday refers to 1969 and the decade before and after. Today refers to—well, today: where we are and where we might be heading. Tomorrow is about effectiveness and independence.

Being a twenty-fifth, this birthday begs for tokens of longevity. To honor this tradition, I will confer some tastefully appropriate, expensively framed certificates upon a few distinguished persons.

YESTERDAY

To start with yesterday, I'd like to tell you how I first met Hal Kassarjian. It was at an American Association for Public Opinion Research conference at the Hotel Sagamore on Lake George about a decade before the Ohio State workshop. While waiting for the opening reception, I wandered along the lake shore, basking in the warm Spring weather.

At the end of the hotel pier sat Hal Kassarjian, dangling a string into the Lake George water. Noting he had not caught any fish, I asked him what he used for bait. He raised the string to show no bait, and no hook—just a string. A little surprised at this, I asked, "How are you going to catch a fish without a hook?" His response was classic Kassarjian: "What the hell would I do with a fish if I caught one?"

Scott Armstrong says we can't predict anything (Armstrong 1991). I say we can. I could have predicted Hal's advice to graduate students, and his judgments as *JCR* co-editor.

Still dwelling on the past, we fast-forward to the Ohio State workshop. In the spirit of prediction, let's ask why that event was so propitious. Why did that specific conference—and the two or three years that followed—create the moment we are celebrating?

Certainly, the time was right. Within the business world, advertisers and agencies had built productive research factories. Within government, a reinvigorated FTC had launched a new crusade against deceptive marketing communication. Within academia, marketing departments had expanded rapidly. Within marketing, consumer behavior had attracted new research attention.

Engel, Kollat and Blackwell—the conference hosts—had just published their encyclopedia (1968). Nicosia (1966) and Howard and Sheth (1969) had just presented general theories. In Howard and Sheth's case, it was not just your ordinary inventory. It was "The Theory of Buyer Behavior." So, consumer research was in the air, along with tendencies to overestimate and motivating feelings that this new discipline was important.

But there was more to it than that. Throughout the Ohio State workshop, Engel, Kollat and Blackwell, and Kassarjian, Kernan and Cohen, and everyone else, maintained that this new enterprise had reached new competence. It was more than just an academic curiosity. It was ready to face reality and contribute to important real decisions.

So the Constitution promised that ACR would "provide a forum for exchange of ideas among those interested in consumer behavior research in academic disciplines, in government at all levels from local through national, in private business, and in other sectors such as nonprofit organizations and foundations." The Constitution also promised that ACR would focus on "a better understanding of consumer behavior from a variety of perspectives" (Pratt 1974).

Based on those pattern-breaking promises, ACR's Second Annual Conference attracted presenters and discussants from the American Institute for Architects, Consumers Union, the Consumer Research Institute, E. I. Du Pont, GTE Sylvania, the Federal Trade Commission, the National Bureau of Standards, the U. S. Department of Commerce, and the Commerce Committee of the U. S. Senate (Gardner 1971).

At that conference, Mary Gardner Jones, an FTC Commissioner, summarized the real-world perspective (Jones 1971). In describing "The FTC's Need for Social Science Research," Commissioner Jones told us that the FTC needed to be certain that its "always meager resources are used with maximal effectiveness, both in determining areas in which the Commission's resources should be applied and in insuring that the actions which it does decide to take will, in fact, achieve the end result sought to be obtained" (Jones 1971, 2). She went on to call for "precise knowledge of the actuality of consumer behavior" and valid means for "measuring the effectiveness of programs or actions" (Jones 1971, 4).

Although Commissioner Jones spoke for government and not for industry, her wish list was fully general. Then—as now—both government and industry needed to leverage their limited resources. Then—as now—they needed precise knowledge of actuality and valid means for measuring programs or actions.

Accordingly, the Third Annual Conference attracted even more real-world attention. The Third Conference featured presenters and discussants from Air Canada, AT & T, Bozell & Jacobs, the Bureau of the Census, the Consumer Research Institute, Elrick & Lavidge, the Federal Trade Commission, the Food and Drug Administration, the Ford Motor Company, General Electric, the Leo Burnett Company, Management Horizons, Market Facts, National Analysts, the National Science Foundation, Procter & Gamble, the Standard Oil Company, Westat Research, and the U. S. Department of Agriculture (Venkatesan 1972).

Like Commissioner Jones the year before, these outsiders all asked for help. One after another, they reaffirmed a healthy need for valid substance and effective method.

This is not to say they came empty-handed. They brought models and methods, insight and encouragement, new ideas and novel ways of looking at familiar situations. Many told about important first-hand experiences. Some offered collaboration and co-authorship, and previously inaccessible real-world data. These contributions made our conference more auspicious for the academicians who were present.

During that conference, Jagdish Sheth upped the ante. Sheth said, "Within a very short period of time, we seem to have firmly laid the foundation for building a distinct discipline of buyer behavior which will neither be a subsystem of marketing nor that of any of the other older social sciences" (Sheth 1972, 565). He went on to predict that consumer research would produce method and substance that would alter the course of psychology, sociology and economics, and that consumer researchers would work with "researchers from hard sciences such as physics, mechanics and biochemistry in search for solution of social and environmental problems" (Sheth 1972, 571). Remember, optimism was rampant, and overestimation was not uncommon.

561

Although Sheth's bet might seem far-fetched, it followed from the founding promise. Then, as now, academic researchers had incentive and occasion to abandon isolation. Then, as now, they had reason to unravel the complexities of real transactions. In Sheth's view (and in my view) then and now, a sharp focus on reality would immunize us from the "crisis of relevance" that had impoverished the other older disciplines (Sheth 1972, 565-573; Wells 1993).

Thus, from both inside and outside, the great hope for ACR was that it would turn out to be more than just one more string dangling in the academic water. The great hope was that consumer research in general, and ACR in particular, would fish for real fish. The criterion was to be external credibility, and the venue was to be the real behavior of real consumers.

Joel Cohen reiterated independence as ACR's first president. Like Sheth, Cohen predicted that consumer research would become "a distinct field of inquiry, and not merely a branch of marketing, psychology, economics or any other social science" (Cohen 1973). This may have been the first and last time Cohen and Sheth agreed on anything.

Jerry Kernan reinforced tripartite distinctiveness five years later. In discussing "Consumer Research and the Public Purpose," Kernan (1979) positioned ACR as the enterprise that would "orchestrate the natural talents of academia, government and industry so as to enhance consumer welfare" (Kernan 1979, 1).

The bottom line (a fresh cliché back then) was that consumer research in general and ACR in particular would be different from, more realistic than, and more effective than their predecessors. Unlike the older other disciplines, consumer research would solve real problems. Unlike the older other professional associations, ACR would reap the benefits of cross-cultural collaboration.

TODAY

We now fast-forward to the present celebration.

One benefit of senior citizenship is you are expected to get crotchety. Maybe I shouldn't say "senior citizenship." It's Politically Incorrect, and present company might be prematurely sensitive.

Hal Kassarjian prefers "old fart," but that's not quite right either. Would you call Alice Tybout an "old fart" even if you were not one of her graduate students? Even if you would call Alice an old fart, how about Frank Kardes and Mita Sujan? Think about that for a moment. We'll come back to it.

One benefit of reaching the state of having become chronologically advantaged is that you are expected to get crotchety. I will therefore spend the next few minutes asking whether we have met our founding forecasts: Twenty-five years into the mission (another fresh cliché back then) is ACR different from, more realistic than, and more effective than its academic predecessors?

Maybe that's not even the right question. The Ohio State workshop listed 13 papers (Engel 1994). This year's program listed 320 papers, research notes, discussions and addresses. It would have listed even more if Mita Sujan had not fled the country. We're clearly doing something right. ACR is alive and thriving.

Yet, when laid against the founding promise, several vacancies are obvious. For one thing, we're not as different we used to be. Whatever happened to *ACR Live* with Rich Lutz as Dan Aykroyd and Jim Bettman as Steve Martin? Whatever happened to the ACR football game?

I thought the football game was permanent . One year—this was before e-mail—no one brought a football. That didn't stop our athletes. They played the game without one.

Scott Armstrong says we can't predict anything. I say we can. I say that anyone who saw that game could have predicted that

researchers would regret the ambiguity of memory-based inferences (Cohen and Basu 1987; Mizerski, Golden and Kernan 1979).

Whatever happened to real transactions and naturalistic settings? Although we have avoided white rats, we have not avoided MBA candidates and college sophomores. Although we have avoided *Econometrica*, we have not avoided a crisis of relevance. We're astonishingly willing to settle for virtual research—student subjects, fictional products, artificial stimuli and a litany of "limitations." We still suffer from the ravages of physics envy and the LISREL complex. We still have trouble with the difference between rigor and *rigor mortis*.

Whatever happened to multiple perspectives and multidisciplinarity? Where are the reports from the American Institute for Architects, the Department of Agriculture, the Department of Commerce, the Food and Drug Administration, Du Pont, General Electric, Procter & Gamble, the television networks, airlines, advertising agencies? Where is Mary Gardner Jones now that we need her to tell us that real-world decision makers pine for precise knowledge of actuality and valid means for measuring programs or actions?

Whatever happened to independence? Where are the constructs and methods that other disciplines line up to borrow?

TOMORROW

A first move toward becoming different from, more realistic than and more effective than our predecessors would be to get outsiders back into this now insular association. They would bring models and methods, insight and encouragement, interesting ideas and novel ways of looking at familiar situations. They would recount important first-hand experiences. They would offer collaboration and co-authorship, and previously inaccessible real-world data. They would make our conferences more auspicious for the academicians who are present.

Of course they would tell us we're too academic. That's a given. Of course they would scoff at theories based on college students. Of course they would deny that p<.05 is the answer to a research question. They would puncture academic myths, demand external credibility, and push us hard toward useful outcomes.

They would not be 100 percent right. But they would not be 100 percent wrong either. Like consultants who help firms reconstitute, they would force us to revise our self-deceptions.

Scott Armstrong says we can't predict anything. I say we can. I say if we readmit outsiders we will have reason and occasion to unravel the complexities of real transactions. If we fish for real fish with real bait and real hooks we will catch precise knowledge of actuality and valid means for measuring programs or actions.

If we do that we will be different from, more realistic than and more effective than our predecessors. We will have grown up. We will have become a distinct and honored discipline that is not a mere subsystem of any of the other older social sciences.

That was a motivating promise yesterday. It's a viable option today. It could revalidate our enterprise tomorrow.

AWARDS AND CITATIONS

I almost forgot the certificates. After thinking about this for a while, I finally decided that "old fart" isn't so insensitive after all. In addition to being P. C.—physiologically correct—it captures an irreverence that is one of our most valuable traditions.

In preparing these awards, I considered the professorial dignity of the recipients. Instead of calling them just plain old farts, I followed the academic custom of illuminating the honor with archaic script and really bad spelling. So, on the occasion of ACR's twenty-fifth birthday, here are Olde Farte diplomas, *honoris causa*—

for Hal Kassarjian, Joel Cohen and Jerry Kernan—with all the rights, privileges and immunities thereunto appertaining.

That still leaves the problem of President Tybout and Co-chairs Kardes and Sujan. I must confess I've not solved that dilemma. Perhaps someone else will solve it. Or perhaps time will solve it, and Alice, Frank and Mita can become Olde Fartes on the fiftieth.

REFERENCES

Armstrong, J. Scott (1991), "Prediction of Consumer Behavior by Experts and Novices," *Journal of Consumer Research*, 18 (September), 251-256.

Cohen, Joel B. (1973), "Outgoing President Joel B. Cohen's Presidential Address," *Association for Consumer Research Newsletter*, 3, (January), 3-5.

_____ and Kunal Basu (1987). "Alternative Models of Categorization: Toward a Contingent Processing Framework," *Journal of Consumer Research* 13 (March) 455-472.

Engel, James F. (1994), "ACR's 25th Anniversary—How It All Began," *ACR Newsletter*, (June), 3-5.

_____, David T. Kollat and Roger D. Blackwell (1968), *Consumer Behavior*, New York: Holt, Rinehart & Winston.

Gardner, David M. (1971), ed. *Proceedings, 2nd Annual Conference*, College Park, MD: Association for Consumer Research.

Howard, John A. and Jagdish N. Sheth (1969), *The Theory of Buyer Behavior*, New York: Wiley.

Jones, Mary Gardner (1971), "The FTC's Need for Social Science Research," in *Proceedings, 2nd Annual Conference*, ed. David M. Gardner, College Park, MD: Association for Consumer Research, 1-9.

Kernan, Jerome B. (1979), "Presidential Address: Consumer Research and the Public Purpose," in *Advances in Consumer Research* Vol. 6, ed. William L. Wilkie, Ann Arbor, MI: Association for Consumer Research, 1-2.

Mizerski, Richard W., Linda L. Golden, and Jerome B. Kernan (1979), "The Attribution Process in Consumer Decision Making," *Journal of Consumer Research* 6 (September), 123-140.

Nicosia, Franco M. (1966), *Consumer Decision Processes.*, Englewood Cliffs, NJ: Prentice Hall.

Pratt, Robert W. Jr. (1974), "ACR: A Perspective," in *Association for Consumer Research 1973 Proceedings*, ed. Scott Ward and Peter Wright, Urbana, IL: Association for Consumer Research, 1-8.

Sheth, Jagdish N. (1972), "The Future of Buyer Behavior Theory," in *Proceedings 3rd Annual Conference 1972*, ed. M. Venkatesan, College Park, MD: Association for Consumer Research, 562-575.

Venkatesan, M. (1972) ed. *Proceedings, 3rd Annual Conference 1972*, College Park, MD: Association for Consumer Research.

Wells, William D. (1993), "Discovery-oriented Consumer Research," *Journal of Consumer Research*, 19 (March), 489-504.

Session Summary
Divergent Perspectives on the Role of Prior Knowledge in Consumer Information Search and Processing

Christine Moorman, University of Wisconsin-Madison
Aric Rindfleisch, University of Wisconsin-Madison

SESSION OVERVIEW

This double session examined the effect of prior knowledge on consumer information search and processing. The session included seven presentations and discussant comments. The papers presented in the session were very broad in both their theoretical and methodological orientations. Theoretically, these papers contained perspectives from both economic theory, as well as an array of psychological theories involving cognitive structure, affect, motivation, and the impact of various environmental factors. This group of papers also displayed a considerable amount of methodological breadth, and included experiments, survey research, and qualitative interviews. Despite this diversity, the seven papers were tied together by four central themes: (1) divergent perspectives of the relationship between search and prior knowledge; (2) the nature of consumer information search processes; (3) the nature of prior knowledge; and (4) managerial and public policy implications.

SUMMARY OF INDIVIDUAL PAPERS

"Exploring the Search Process for Durables"
Carol A. Fiske, University of South Carolina
Lisa A. Luebbenhussen, University of South Carolina
Anthony Miyazaki, University of South Carolina
Joel E. Urbany, University of Notre Dame

This paper attempted to clarify the form of the knowledge-search relationship via a set of exploratory interviews of consumers faced with the purchase of a personal computer. Based on these interviews, the authors suggested that this purchase is a complex task involving multiple decisions. Consumers make this process more tractable by first searching in order to specify a preferred feature set (PFS) and then searching to match it. This study indicated that, although experts and novices can be described using the same general model, they differ in their specification of PFS. Experts put greater emphasis on higher-order considerations (e.g., technological obsolescence) and were more capable of translating application needs into specific product features. Novices tended to rely heavily upon experts or informed others to assist them in determining their PFS. As suggested by their earlier work (Fiske et al. 1994), these authors maintain that the exact form of the knowledge-search relationship is highly dependent upon characteristics of the task environment. For example, experts are more likely to search more than novices only when they are sufficiently motivated by elements of the task environment.

"Examining the Sequential Nature of Search"
Narasimhan Srinivasan, University of Connecticut
Girish N. Punj, University of Connecticut

Srinivasan and Punj examined the sequence of information search activities in the context of purchasing a new car. In specific, they focused on the sequential nature of dealer visits using the Punj and Staelin (1983) database of new car buyers. Srinivasan and Punj explored these dealer visits in great detail (with variance in the number of dealer visits as the key dependent variable), employed multiple measures of prior knowledge, and included sociodemographic variables such as age, income, and household

size as control variables. Although their findings at the time of presentation were still exploratory, Srinivasan and Punj's initial analysis appeared to uncover a number of interesting results. For example, they noted that as the number of dealers visited increases, incremental purchase probability decreases and sociodemographic distinctions between new car buyers become less pronounced.

"The Economics of Consumer Knowledge"
Brian T. Ratchford, State University of New York at Buffalo

Ratchford presented a summary of human capital theory and demonstrated its relevance to consumer information search activities. According to human capital theory, prior "investments" in product or brand usage make current consumption more productive or less costly. For example, prior knowledge of classical music makes a concert more enjoyable for an aficionado compared to a neophyte. In fact, Ratchford noted that some strident supporters of the human capital theory suggest that consumer preferences are wholly determined by their past investments in human capital (Stigler and Becker 1977). In addition to outlining the tenets of human capital theory, Ratchford also presented a number of potential applications of this theory in order to understand and analyze both consumer search and decision making. For example, to the extent that consumers find it more cost effective to engage in consumption related to their expertise, both search and consumption may be confined to areas in which consumers have extensive knowledge.

"The Role of Prior Knowledge in the Acquisition of Product Information: A Test of Four Models"
Christine Moorman, University of Wisconsin-Madison
Aric Rindfleisch, University of Wisconsin-Madison

Moorman and Rindfleisch presented an empirical examination of four models of the knowledge-search relationship. These four models include: (1) the Enrichment model; (2) the Inverted-U model (3) the Cost-Benefit model; and (4) the Motivation as a Moderator model. These four models were tested in a computerized search experiment across four different product/service categories. Although Moorman and Rindfleisch measured both subjective and objective knowledge as well as a number of search outcomes, their presentation focused solely on objective knowledge and degree of search. Their results call into question the generalizability of the cost-benefit model and indicate that the enrichment model should be supplanted with a concave curvilinear model. The success of both the curvilinear model and the Motivation as a Moderator model suggest that low motivation may produce a curvilinear knowledge-search relationship while high motivation may lead to a linear knowledge-search relationship.

"Affect-Driven Distortion of Product Information in Consumer Information Search and Processing Activities"
J. Edward Russo, Cornell University
Victoria Husted Medvec, Cornell University

Russo and Medvec introduced the moderating role of affect in the knowledge-search relationship. These authors conducted an experiment designed to test the impact of prior positive affect on:

Advances in Consumer Research
Volume 22, © 1995

(1) the interpretation of product information; (2) the extent of pre-purchase information search; and (3) the choice itself. In this experiment, subjects were asked to choose between two restaurants; one restaurant was manipulated to engender positive affect. As expected, this initial endowment of positive affect significantly influenced both information search and consumer choice. In specific, subjects who strongly accepted the affect manipulation searched less and were more likely to select the affect-endowed restaurant compared to subjects whose acceptance was weaker. Furthermore, evaluative ratings of product information showed affect-based distortion. Relative to the control group, affectively-endowed subjects interpreted information as more favorable for the endowed restaurant.

"The Moderating Effects of Information Search Environment Characteristics on Expert Judgment"
Mark T. Spence, Southern Connecticut State University
Merrie Brucks, University of Arizona

Spence and Brucks investigated why experts' enhanced cognitive structures and processes do not necessarily lead to improved decision making or superior judgment. These authors suggested that since experts and novices differ in their ability to form representations of a decision task, a highly structured information environment may mask the benefits of expertise. Using a laboratory experiment in which experts (real estate professionals) and novices (students) were asked to appraise a piece of property, Spence and Brucks found that when given a decision aid, experts made more accurate and tightly clustered decisions and were more confident in their decisions compared to novices. Furthermore, when this decision aid was removed, novices' decision quality degraded considerably and they were more prone to error. Experts, in contrast, were less affected by the presence or absence of a decision aid.

"Subjective and Objective Knowledge and their Consequences: Limits of Experimental Approaches"
David L. Mothersbaugh, University of Pittsburgh
Lawrence F. Feick, University of Pittsburgh
C. Whan Park, University of Pittsburgh

In this final paper, the authors noted that subjective knowledge (SK) and objective knowledge (OK) covary naturally, making it difficult to distinguish their effects on search. They suggested that an orthogonal manipulation would help distinguish their effects. However, a number of conceptual and methodological issues, such as resistance to feedback, external attributions, and subject sensitization make knowledge manipulations difficult. After outlining a number of ways to operationalize such a manipulation, Mothersbaugh, Feick, and Park illustrated one of the options by attempting to manipulate SK in a group of 48 subjects by measuring OK (time 1) and then providing feedback to manipulate SK (time 2). Although their results suggest that feedback influenced SK, the manipulation was not orthogonal since OK also influenced SK. Considering the dynamic relationship between knowledge and search, these authors suggested that rather than trying to manipulate either subjective or objective knowledge, it may be more useful to examine the effects of both types of knowledge in their natural covarying states, with a greater focus on the metacognitive skills that guide search.

Discussant
J. Wesley Hutchinson, University of Pennsylvania

Wes Hutchinson commented on the importance of this area of research and noted that all seven papers bring valuable and novel approaches to the knowledge-search literature. He also suggested that these diverse approaches provide a coherent fit and can be conceptually linked among a number of dimensions. For example, he noted that the Fiske et al., Srinivasan and Punj, Ratchford, Moorman and Rindfleisch, and Russo and Medvec papers all deal in one manner or another with the costs of search. Wes also pointed out a number of interesting avenues for future research in this area, such as the impact of the cumulative effects of prior knowledge upon future search, and the important distinction between focal (i.e., repeated) and novel consumer search activities.

The session was chaired by Christine Moorman.

REFERENCES
Fiske, Carol A., Lisa A. Luebbenhussen, Anthony D. Miyazaki, and Joel Urbany (1994), "The Knowledge-Search Relationship: It Depends," in *Advances in Consumer Research*, 22, Chris T. Allen and Deborah Roedder John, eds., Provo, UT: Association for Consumer Research, 43-50.
Punj, Girish N. and Richard Staelin (1983), "A Model of Consumer Information Search Behavior for New Automobiles," *Journal of Consumer Research*, 9 (March), 366-380.
Stigler, George and Gary S. Becker (1977), "De Gustibus Non Est Disputandum," *American Economic Review*, 67, 76-90.

Consumer Use Innovative Behavior: An Approach Toward Its Causes

Kyungae Park, University of Wisconsin-Stevens Point
Carl L. Dyer, The University of Tennessee

ABSTRACT

This study attempts to understand innovative product usage behavior by investigating the causes of this behavior. Use and purchase in innovative behavior are compared to each other in terms of the causes of these behaviors. The conceptual model of use innovative behavior is tested for the clothing product. The model supports a causal link of innovativeness trait, interest toward the specific product category, communicated experience and innovative behavior (use and purchase). While use and purchase are related to each other, product attribute evaluation and spending on products appear to be the major antecedents of whether to use old products or to buy a new product.

Criticism of innovativeness research focused on initial purchase behaviors of new products has inevitably led to product usage behavior in the post-adoption process as a research area of concern to consumer researchers. Product usage behavior broadly affects consumer behavior such as consumer satisfaction, repurchase, brand or store loyalty and word-of-mouth. Hence, understanding a commitment to the product helps marketers pursue a long-term relationship with their customers and helps researchers understand the complete diffusion process. Especially for visible products such as clothing fashion, the effects of usage behavior on other consumers and the diffusion are conspicuous. Consumers are continuously exposed to new products and wearing clothes (usage behavior) mostly requires combinations of multiple items. In clothing products, taste and discrimination of relative beauty (benefits) depend on perceptions rather than do objective criteria (Petrosky 1991). Creative consumers frequently adopt new fashion by new coordination of existing clothes as well as by purchase of a new product. Such unique and creative use by consumers can be a source of new clothing fashion for apparel manufacturers who regularly observe street fashions for new inspiration. That is, fashion innovations can start from consumers as well as from industry (Sproles 1979, p.100).

Use innovativeness, since the introduction of the concept by Hirschman (1980), has acquired attention by recent consumer innovativeness and product usage researchers. Use innovativeness is innovative product usage behavior of a previously adopted product in a novel way and in a variety of ways (Price and Ridgway, 1983). That is, use innovativeness is innovative behavior relative to the product usage process while purchase innovativeness relates to the product purchase process. These two innovative behaviors need to be separated as "a consumer may purchase a product or instead not to purchase-stretching a currently owned product to additional uses....this decision to buy or not to buy represents nearly dichotomous manifestations of high stimulation needs" (Price and Ridgway 1982, p.57). However, "the highly creative consumers will be more adept at both types" of innovative behaviors (Hirschman 1980, p.289). Creative consumers, who have problem-solving capabilities in consumption situations, are competent to new product evaluation (Hirschman 1980). They may adopt the idea of the innovation but do not necessarily purchase a new product. Instead they may decide to utilize existing products in a new way. Such creative and innovative use by consumers can be a source of an innovation that generates a secondary diffusion. Furthermore, it can be an alternative behavior to purchase that generates a secondary adoption.

Faced with a new product, when do consumers decide to purchase and when to use? What affects such decision-making? That is, what are the causes of use innovative behavior and how are its causes different from those of purchase innovative behavior?

RESEARCH PURPOSES

The objective of the study is to understand consumer use innovative behavior by identifying the causes of use innovative behavior and examining its causes along with those of purchase innovative behavior. There has been no approach to investigate use innovative behavior parallel to purchase innovative behavior in that use can be an alternative to purchase (another way of adoption) in the consumer purchase decision-making process. Examination of the predictors for innovativeness (adoption/purchase) has a well-established research background. The approach of this study in investigating the causes of use innovativeness is to follow this rich innovativeness framework from which the relevant variables for this study are borrowed. Such an approach appears to be reasonable in understanding both innovative behaviors as well as use innovative behavior.

RESEARCH BACKGROUND

Innovative Behavior: Its Causes

One of the major contributions in innovativeness research provided by recent researchers (Carlson and Grossbart 1985; Foxall 1989; Kirton 1989; Mudd 1990; Goldsmith and Hofaker 1991; Goldsmith and Flynn 1992; Midgley and Dowling 1993) is the conceptualization that regards innovativeness as an individual's latent trait for new and different experiences and distinguishes this trait from an actual adoption behavior. This conceptualization began with Midgley and Dowling (1978). They argue that psychological and sociological traits interact with the innovativeness trait and that between an individual's innovativeness (predisposition to acquire new products across product categories) and an observed adoption behavior exist intervening variables which include interest toward the specific product category, communicated experience and various situational effects (Midgley and Dowling 1978). They argue that situational effects imply a variety of situation-specific and person-specific factors like financial resources or a latent need for the innovation's perceived benefits. Therefore, for a new product, the observed behavior of adoption is a complex function of the innovativeness trait, product category interest, a network of information influence, an individual's situations and personal characteristics.

A number of researchers have sought variables to better understand and predict consumer innovative behavior. Innovative behavior has been related to higher income or higher spending on products (Mason and Bellenger 1973-4; Baumgarten 1975; Forsythe et al. 1991; Goldsmith and Flynn 1992); higher product interest (Schrank and Gilmore 1973; Mason and Bellenger 1973-4; Reynolds and Darden 1973, 1974; Goldsmith et al. 1987); higher communicated experience (Mason and Bellenger 1973-4; Reynolds and Darden 1973, 1974; Painter and Granzin 1976; Goldsmith and Flynn 1992); and higher perceptions of innovation attributes (Labay and Kinnear 1981; Holak 1988; Holak and Lehmann 1990). Therefore, in terms of the interacted effects of the innovativeness trait and the intervening variables on an adoption behavior, the relationships between each of these intervening variables and innovative behavior have been verified by previous research.

Use Innovative Behavior: The Concept and Research

Hirschman (1980) made a subtle distinction between components of innovative behavior: the actual adoption of a new product (purchase innovativeness); the acquisition of new product information (vicarious innovativeness); and the adaptive use of old products (use innovativeness). Through vicarious innovativeness, consumers can adopt the product concept without adopting the product itself so that they avoid the risk and expense relative to the adoption. Further, Hirschman (1980) explained use innovativeness with problem-solving capabilities of creative consumers who could construct alternatives when confronted by a new product. That is, innovative consumers are competent in product evaluation. Based on their decisions regarding whether actual purchase is desirable, consumers may take one of two actions: to purchase a new product that is perceived to be better for solving the new consumption problem or to utilize a previously adopted product in an innovative way (Hirschman 1980). Whether they decide to purchase or to use, consumers have presumably considered and adopted the concept of the innovation.

Price and Ridgway (1983) specified use innovativeness as two levels of product consumption behavior: novel uses and a variety of uses. Empirical research has examined use innovativeness as a product consumption behavior in post-adoption process and attempted to relate it with product usage variables such as use patterns, use frequency and use variety toward multi-functional consumer durables (Price and Ridgway 1983, 1984; Anderson and Ortinau 1988; Ram and Jung 1989; Foxall and Bhate 1991).

Innovative Behavior: Purchase Versus Use

Purchase innovativeness refers to buying a new product while use innovativeness refers to using a product (an old or a new product) in a new way. Price and Ridgway (1982) found that use innovativeness was not correlated with exploratory purchase behavior. They concluded that use innovativeness is expected to be separated from purchase behavior since a decision to buy or not to buy leads to two different behaviors. On the other hand, Hirschman (1980) implied a positive relationship for use and purchase when she mentioned that the innovative behaviors do originate from the same trait of novelty seeking, and creative consumers may exhibit both innovative behaviors on occasion. The question is: when do consumers decide to use old products rather than to buy a new product, and what affects such a decision-making? Clearly, creative consumers who engage in active product evaluations may decide it is not necessary to purchase a new product as they can adapt old products to adopt the concept of the innovation. Consumers involved in this way can logically be expected to be committed to products in the after-purchase process and to continuously try new ways to utilize products. Conversely, consumers who have higher financial resources (income or spending) will purchase new products on more occasions than they will adapt an old product regardless of the evaluation of the new product attributes. These tend to be heavy buyers (Gatignon and Robertson 1985). Therefore, while the innovativeness trait can be actualized into both types of innovative behaviors, financial resources and product attribute evaluation can explain either of the innovative behaviors: use or purchase.

CONCEPTUAL MODEL

Based on the review above, this study proposes a conceptual model of use innovative behavior (Figure 1). Innovativeness trait is an individual's predisposition to innovate (by acquiring new products) across product classes. The general innovativeness trait itself is not expected to have a strong relationship to the specific innovative behavior. Through interactions with some intervening variables, this trait is translated to an actual innovative behavior in a specific product category. Interest in the specific product categories (i.e., clothing, automobile, computers, etc.) leads to information seeking toward new products (communicated experience). When innovative consumers acquire information of a new product, they evaluate new product attributes to decide whether to buy or not. Innovative consumers who have higher financial resources and who tend to be heavy buyers do not necessarily engage in an extensive evaluation process while innovative consumers who have higher commitment to the products do not necessarily spend to buy a new product. Therefore, spending on products along with product attribute evaluation is assumed to differentiate use innovative behavior from purchase innovative behavior.

This model has some limitations: 1) While the innovativeness trait is not expected to have a strong direct relationship to innovative behaviors, the simplified model does not consider other person-specific variables such as psychological or sociological traits; 2) The relationship between purchase innovative behavior and use innovative behavior is not considered in the model; 3) The causal relationships of the intervening variables are constrained based on consumer decision-making process. A different direction of a causal relationship or an interaction between the variables might be suggested. However, the major goal of this study is to understand use innovativeness based on the limited research background. If this exploratory study finds support for this simplified test, more elaborate models considering the simultaneous relationship between purchase and use behavior may be developed in the future.

METHODOLOGY

Research Design

Clothing products were used to test the conceptual model. Survey by self-administered questionnaire was used to gather data. The questionnaire was revised through the following steps: 1) Six graduate students participated in the focus group interview to evaluate the scales; 2) The revised questionnaire was pretested with 66 undergraduate students who were enrolled in a marketing class and six of them participated in the focus group interview. The pretest was statistically analyzed for reliability and validity; 3) The final questionnaire was revised based on the pretest and the focus group interview.

College students of a southeastern university were the subjects. Based on student demographics, seven classes were judged to represent the student population best. Data was collected during regular class meetings. The total number of responses collected was 586. Except unusable ones, 539 responses were used for the data analysis.

Variable Measurement

Hirschman (1984)'s Novelty Seeking scale was adapted to measure the innovativeness trait. The scale asked how willing the individual was to seek information that was new and different pertinent to 13 consumption areas with a 7-point scale. Schrank (1973)'s Clothing Interest Inventory was adapted to measure the product interest. It consisted of 5 items indicating agreement on a five-point scale on the extent to which the respondent was interested in clothing. The communicated experience scale developed, based on past research, consisted of three items representing information

FIGURE 1
Conceptual Model for Use Innovative Behavior

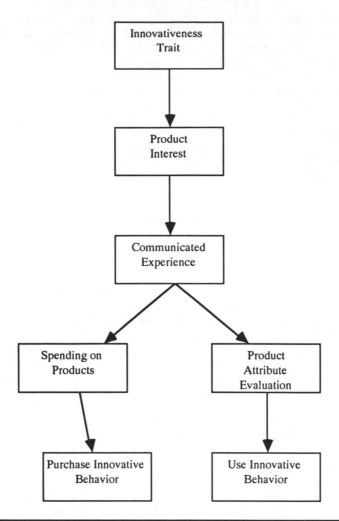

sources including print media readership, store display observation and personal discussion on a five-point scale by exposure hours to these sources. To measure the product attribute evaluation, the 16 item attribute inventory of the clothing product (price; quality; fashion; pretty/good looking; ease of care; comfort; sale item; versatility; looking attractive; matching other styles; fitting with physical appearance; fitting with image; appropriate for occasion; socially acceptable style; acceptable to others; and not getting bored) was developed based on past research. The respondent was asked to indicate how important each attribute was in purchasing and using a product on a 5-point scale. The one-item spending on products asked the extent of spending on wardrobe the last year. The purchase innovative behavior scale was developed based on the cross-sectional method. It asked the respondents: 1) to list the clothing items they had purchased in the last two months (Clothing type categories were provided to help the respondents remember their past purchases.); and 2) to evaluate the degree of novelty, on a five-point scale, for each item they listed. The number of actual purchases and the degree of novelty were multiplied. According to Rogers (1983, p.19), an innovation depends on the consumer's perception. That is, "the innovation need not to be new in an absolute sense. What is important is individual's perception of an object as new..." (Sproles 1979, p.99). Although similar measure-

ments have been used, this method makes the respondent define an innovation as a style perceived as new. The use innovative behavior scale was developed based on the guideline by Hirschman (1980) and on the specific usage behavior and use pattern questions by Price and Ridgway (1983). The scale asked the respondents the extent to which they had used clothing in new ways and in a variety of ways in the last two seasons. It consisted of seven items on a seven-point scale. Again, the respondent defined what was a new way and what was a different way.

ANALYSIS AND RESULTS

For reliability tests, Cronbach's alpha and item-to-total correlation were used. Alpha scores of all the multi-item scales were in the range of .80 and .93. Innovativeness trait had small positive correlations with innovative behaviors (r=.17, p<.01 for use, r=.14, p<.01 for purchase) as hypothesized. That is, a general trait to innovate by itself is not enough to predict an innovative behavior of a specific product class. Purchase and use behaviors were correlated (r=.32, p<.01). It indicates that a consumer who has a higher trait to innovate can exhibit both innovative behaviors depending on the occasion. To investigate the effects of the intervening variables on innovative behaviors, path coefficients were estimated for the following equations:

Product Interest= f(Innovativeness Trait)

Communicated Experience= f(Innovativeness Trait, Product Interest)

Product Attribute Evaluation= f(Innovativeness Trait, Product Interest, Communicated Experience)

Spending on Products= f(Innovativeness Trait, Product Interest, Communicated Experience)

Use Innovative Behavior= f(Innovativeness Trait, Product Interest, Communicated Experience, Product Attribute Evaluation, Spending on Products)

Purchase Innovative Behavior= f(Innovativeness Trait, Product Interest, Communicated Experience, Product Attribute Evaluation, Spending on Products)

A potential limitation is probable multicollinearity of the variables. Significant correlations between the variables may render path coefficients unstable. See Table 1. Table 2 shows the results obtained. The causal relationship of innovativeness trait → product interest → communicated experience was supported as hypothesized. Product attribute evaluation was a consequence of product interest, not of communicated experience. Consumers who were interested in the product category evaluated the attributes of a new product to decide to buy or to utilize. Such a commitment was observed regardless of information seeking. Spending on products was affected by product interest and communicated experience. All these preceding variables except spending on products were the antecedents of use innovative behavior. On the other hand, purchase innovative behavior was a consequence of communicated experience and spending on products. These consumers tend to make a quick decision in buying a new product when they are aware of a new product. Figure 2 shows the empirical model supported by the analysis.

DISCUSSION

The results indicate that the general predisposition toward innovation across product categories does not necessarily predict an innovative behavior of a specific product category. Through intervening variables, this trait is actualized to an observed innovative behavior within the specific product category. However, a small direct impact of innovativeness trait on use innovative behavior indicates that use innovativeness may be an exhibition of a genuine innovativeness. Innovative usage behavior requires an individual's involvement to products, higher creativity and problem-solving capability. Therefore, use innovative consumers have a higher intention to try something new and different with various product categories, which provides different experiences from which probably lead to innovative usage in a specific product.

However, these two innovative behaviors are not mutually exclusive. A positive relationship between purchase and use innovative behaviors implies that these two innovative behaviors do originate from the same personality trait of a higher order but differ due to the results of different effects of intervening factors. That is, innovative consumers may decide upon either action depending on the occasions they face.

The results show a causal link of innovativeness trait, product interest, communicated experience and innovative behaviors. The direct impact of product attribute evaluation on use innovativeness

indicates that use innovative consumers, who are willing to innovate and are interested in a specific product category, tend to be more active in solving consumption problems. Using old products or adapting products instead of buying new ones requires higher involvement, not necessarily higher spending. Low importance of product attributes combined with impact of spending on products on purchase innovativeness indicate that purchase innovative consumers do not necessarily engage in product evaluation. They probably are impulsive heavy buyers.

Generally, the predictabilities of the model for both innovative behaviors are low. This can be explained: 1) Though an innovative behavior is a function of person-specific, situation-specific and product-specific variables, individual characteristics such as psychological and sociological traits are not included in the model; 2) Use-specific variables such as product involvement or usage patterns are not included to explain use innovativeness as a post-adoption behavior.

A major limitation of the study is the limited sampling. College students from a southeastern university cannot represent general consumer groups. Consequently, the results may not be generalized beyond the clothing product category for a subset of the student population. Nevertheless, this study partially supports the conceptual model and provides a valuable first step toward understanding use innovativeness in conjunction with purchase innovativeness. Specifically, this study contributes to the following: 1) While a general innovativeness trait appears to cause use innovative behavior, purchase innovative behavior appears to be more product-specific; 2) Use and purchase innovative behavior are related each other; 3) The consumer decision-making process toward innovative behavior, innovativeness trait → product interest → communicated experience → innovative behavior is supported; 4) The impacts of spending on products along with product attribute evaluation on the distinction between innovative behaviors are supported.

Based on the results and discussions, the following implications are suggested for future studies: 1) Testing the model using several product categories will provide a closer examination of the model; 2) The stability of the model would be observed by comparing the model across several sampling groups; 3) The relationships of the variables incorporated into the model need to be more fully specified; 4) Use specific variables including knowledge, use experience and use patterns need to be included; and 5) Different analyses, such as discriminant analysis, considering the positive relationship of purchase and use behaviors would be more appropriate in investigating the relationships of the innovativeness trait, intervening variables and the two innovative behaviors.

REFERENCES

Anderson, R. L. and Ortinau, D. J. (1988), "Exploring Consumers' Post-adoption Attitudes and Use Behaviors in Monitoring the Diffusion of a Technology-Based Discontinuous Innovation," *Journal of Business Research* 17, 283-298.

Baumgarten, S. A. (1975), "The Innovative Communicator in the Diffusion Process," *Journal of Marketing Research* 12, 12-17.

Carlson, L. and Grossbart, S. L. (1985), "Towards a Better Understanding of Inherent Innovativeness," in *American Marketing Association Educators' Proceedings,* Vol 50, Belk et al., eds., American Marketing association, Chicago, 88-91.

Foxall, G. R. (1989), "Adaptive and Innovative Cognitive Styles of Market Initiators," in M. J. Kirton (ed.), *Adaptors and Innovators: Styles of creativity and problem-solving,* Routledge, London and New York.

TABLE 1
Correlation Matrix

	Z_1: Trait	Z_2: Interest	Z_3: Comm	Z_4: Eval	Z_5: Spend	Z_6: UIB	Z_7: PIB
Z_1	--						
Z_2	.1989						
Z_3	.1530	.5889					
Z_4	.1432	.3318	.2287				
Z_5	.1190	.4449	.4057	.0375 [a]			
Z_6	.1687	.3548	.3773	.2162	.1518		
Z_7	.1430	.3833	.4504	.1464	.4387	.3245	--

[a] $p > .05$
$p < .01$ for all other entries

TABLE 2
Path Coefficients

Variables	Equations	R^2
Z_1: Trait	—	
Z_2: Interest	$.20Z_1{}^{a}$	.04
Z_3: Comm	$.04Z_1 + .58Z_2{}^{a}$	.35
Z_4: Eval	$.08Z_1 + .29Z_2{}^{a} + .05Z_3$	.12
Z_5: Spend	$.03Z_1 + .39Z_2{}^{a} + .12Z_3{}^{d}$	.23
Z_6: UIB		.19
Z_7: PIB	$.09Z_1{}^{d} + .20Z_2{}^{b} + .28Z_3{}^{a} + .09Z_4{}^{d} - .07Z_5$	.27
	$.05Z_1 + .07Z_2 + .31Z_3{}^{a} + .03Z_4 + .24Z_6{}^{a}$	

[a] $p < .0001$
[b] $p < .001$
[c] $p < .01$
[d] $p < .05$

Foxall, G. R. and Bhate, S. (1991), "Cognitive Style, Personal Involvement and Situation as Determinants of Computer Use," *Technovation* 11:3, 183-199.

Gatignon, H. and Robertson, T. S. (1985), "A Propositional Inventory for New Diffusion Research," *Journal of Consumer Research* 11(March), 849-867.

Goldsmith, R. E., and Flynn, L. R. (1992), "Identifying Innovators in Consumer Product Markets," *European Journal of Marketing*, 26:12, 42-55.

Goldsmith, R. E., and Hofacker, C. F. (1991), "Measuring Consumer Innovativeness," *Journal of the Academy of Marketing Science*, 19:3 (Summer), 209-221.

Goldsmith, R. E., Stith, M. T., and White, J. D. (1987), "Race and Sex Differences in Self-identified Innovativeness and Opinion Leadership," *Journal of Retailing*, 63:4, 411-425.

Hirschman, E. (1980), "Innovativeness, Novelty Seeking, and Consumer Creativity," *Journal of Consumer Research* 7(Dec), 283-295.

Hirschman, E. (1984), "Experience Seeking: A Subjectivist Perspective of Consumption," *Journal of Business Research* 12, 115-136.

Holak, Susan L. (1988), "Determinants of Innovative Durables Adoption: An Empirical Study with Implications for Early Product Screening," *Journal of Product Innovation Management*, 5, 50-69.

Holak, Susan L. and Lehmann, D. R. (1990), "Purchase Intentions and the Dimensions of Innovation: An Exploratory Model," *Journal of Product Innovation Management*, 7, 59-73.

FIGURE 2
Empirical Model for Use Innovative Behavior

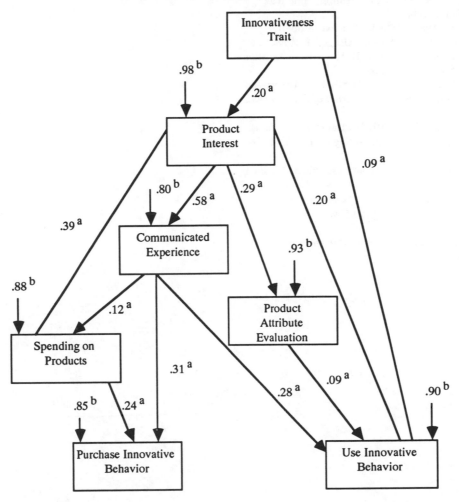

a Significant Path Coefficient

b Residual Path Coefficient

Kirton, M. J. (1989), "Adaptors and Innovators at Work," in M.J. Kirton (ed.), *Adaptors and Innovators: Styles of creativity and problem-solving*, Routledge, London and New York.

Labay, D. G. and Kinnear, T. C. (1981), "Exploring the Consumer Decision Process in the Adoption of Solar Energy Systems," *Journal of Consumer Research*, 8 (December), 271-278.

Mason, J. B. and Bellenger, D (1973/4), "Analyzing High Fashion Acceptance," *Journal of Retailing*, 49:4, 79-88.

Midgley, D. F. and Dowling, G. R. (1978), "Innovativeness: The Concept and Its Measurement," *Journal of Consumer Research* 4, 229-242.

Midgley, D. F. and Dowling, G. R. (1993), "A Longitudinal Study of Product Form Innovation: The Interaction between Predispositions and Social Messages," *Journal of Consumer Research*, 19 (March), 611-625.

Mudd, S. (1990), "The Place of Innovativeness in Models of the Adoption Process: An Integrative Review," *Technovation*, 10:2, 119-136.

Painter, J. J. and Granzin, L. L. (1976), "Profiling the Male Fashion Innovator-Another Step," in *Advances in Consumer Research*, 3, 40-45.

Painter, J. J. and Pinegar, M. L. (1971), "Post High-teens and Fashion Innovation," *Journal of Marketing Research* 8, 368-369.

Petrosky, A. R. (1991), "Extending Innovation Characteristic Perception to Diffusion Channel Intermediaries and Aesthetic Products," in *Advances in Consumer Research* 18, 627-634.

Price, L. L. and Ridgway, N. M. (1982), "Use Innovativeness, Vicarious Exploration and Purchase Exploration: Three Facets of Consumer Varied Behavior," in *American Marketing Association Educators' Conference Proceedings*, B. Walker, ed., Chicago: AMA, 56-60.

Price, L. L. and Ridgway, N. M. (1983), "Development of a Scale to Measure Use Innovativeness," in *Advances in Consumer Research*, eds., Bagozzi, R. P. and Tybout, A. M., Ann Arbor, MI: Association for Consumer Research 10, 679-684.

Price, L. L. and Ridgway, N. M. (1984), "Use Innovativeness and Technology Integration: An Exploration of Personal Computers," in *AMA Educators' Proceedings,* American Marketing Association, 83-87.

Ram, S. and Jung, H. S. (1989), "The Link between Involvement, Use Innovativeness and Product Usage," in *Advances in Consumer Research,* ed., Sruel, T. K. Hawaii: Association for Consumer Research 16, 160-166.

Reynolds, F. D. and Darden, W. R. (1973), "Fashion Theory and Pragmatics: The Case of the Midi," *Journal of Retailing* 49, 51-62.

Reynolds, F. D. and Darden, W. R.(1974), "Backward Profiling of Male Innovators," *Journal of Marketing Research* 11, 79-85.

Rogers, E. M. (1983), *Diffusion of Innovations*, 3rd ed. The Free Press, New York.

Schrank, H. L. and Gilmore, D. L. (1973), "Correlates of Fashion Leadership," *The Sociological Quarterly* 14, 534-543.

Sproles, G. B. (1979), *Fashion: Consumer Behavior toward Dress,* Minneapolis: Burgess.

Consumer Factors Influencing the Use of Nutrition Information Sources

Guijing Wang, University of Georgia
Stanley M. Fletcher, University of Georgia
Dale H. Carley, University of Georgia[1]

ABSTRACT

Consumer usage of nutrition information sources is investigated in a cost-benefit framework using the 1987-88 Nationwide Food Consumption Survey data. Results show that food expenditure, family size, age, education and enduring importance of nutrition are major predictors in positive direction in the usage for all sources. Income has a significant effect on the usage in varied directions across the sources. The sources consumers used and preferred may be different. Hence, consumers may be willing to pay for but unwilling to use obtained nutrition information. These findings have important implications for the design of nutrition information programs.

In the past several decades, much research has been conducted on consumer usage of nutrition information. As early as 1970's, Jacoby, Chestnut, and Silberman (1977) pointed out that majority of consumers claimed they wanted and were willing to pay for nutrition information. However, they found that most consumers neither acquired nutrition information when making purchase decisions nor comprehended most information they received. Up to 1990's, Moorman (1990) reported that 20 years research indicated that adequate nutrition information and its use were far from satisfactory. In order to enhance the efficiency of nutrition information, it is necessary to understand how consumers perceive and use such information (Lenahan, et al. 1973).

Feick, Herrmann, and Warland (1986) conducted a probit analysis of consumer usage of different nutrition information sources in a cost-benefit framework. Based on their data obtained from telephone interviews with 1,265 women between the ages of 20 and 59, they found some variables such as concerns on future health and experience on reading food advertisement had consistent effect on the usage across six information sources. Other variables such as present health, age, and education had varied effects on the usage across information sources.

Moorman (1990) investigated the effects of consumer characteristics such as nutrient familiarity, education, age, and stimulus characteristics such as information format and content on the utilization of nutrition information. She pointed out that effectively designed nutrition disclosures facilitate information utilization. Bass (1991) conducted a study on consumer use and satisfaction of food labels. She found that food labels, the most used source of nutrition information (Navder 1993), was indeed used for various reasons with various satisfaction levels. Burton and Biswas (1993) examined the effects of changes in labels required by the nutrition labeling and education act of 1990 (NLEA) on nonstudents aged 18 years or older. Their survey results showed consumer attitude and perception of nutrition likelihood were strongly related to nutrition information recommended by the NLEA.

Cole and Balasubramanian (1993) provided some insights about nutritional information usage and age differences in consumer search for and use of the information. They concluded that

---

[1]The authors wish to thank two anonymous referees for comments and suggestions that led to improvements of an earlier version of this manuscript.

elderly adults tended to search less intensely and less accurately than young adults. This finding appears in conflict with that of Moorman (1990) who found that age is positively related to information processing and comprehension accuracy. Moorman and Matulich (1993) examined the effects of various consumer characteristics on health information acquisition behaviors. Their results showed that consumer health motivation and ability characteristics are not always critical precursors of the information acquisition behaviors. Jensen and Kesavan (1993) analyzed the relationship between the sources of information, consumer attitudes on nutrition, and consumption of dairy products. They found that nutrition massages related to calcium affected demand for dairy products.

The above mentioned studies are among the most significant attempts in exploring consumer usage of nutrition information. However, some of them only focused on the usage of nutrition information sources of a specific population group (Feick, Herrmann and Warland 1986, Burton and Biswas 1993, Cole and Balasubramanian 1993). Others typically investigated a specific information source such as food labeling or the relationship between nutrition information and food consumption (Bass 1991, and Jensen and Kesavan 1993).

This study adds to the literature in that determinants of consumer usage of various nutrition information sources and whether consumers obtain nutrition information from their preferred sources are investigated. In the next section, the current usage levels of nutrition information sources and factors which may affect consumer benefits and costs of information search are discussed. Then a model is specified for analyzing whether consumers use these information sources and whether the source used is their preferred. The model is applied into the 1987-88 Nationwide Food Consumption Survey (NFCS), the most recent and complete household food practice data source available. The estimation results and their possible implications are discussed. Finally, a conclusion of this research is provided.

INFORMATION SOURCES AND FACTORS AFFECTING CONSUMER USAGE

In the 1987-88 Nationwide Food Consumption Survey (NFCS), consumers were asked whether they obtained nutrition information from any of eight sources during the last year and which source is their most preferred. The eight sources and their current usage levels are highlighted in table 1.

The table 1 shows that newspapers, magazines or books, and food packages or labels are the most often used sources. More than 45 percent of consumers used them. This is followed by the sources of a doctor, nurse or health professional, and radio or television which are used by more than one third consumers. The sources of food company publications, government or health organization publications, a nutritionist, dietitian, home economist, or extension agent, and relatives or friends are rarely used as nutrition information sources by consumers (less than a quarter consumers).

Another set of question in the NFCS is to ask what is consumers' most preferred information source on nutrition. The survey results are also reported in table 1. These results show that a doctor, nurse or other health professional is most likely to be a consumer's

TABLE 1
Nutrition Information Sources and Their Current Usage Levels

Information Sources	Usage (%)[a] (N=4250)	Success of usage (%)[b]
1) Doctor, nurse, or other health professional	35.5	34.6 (1492) [c]
2) Nutritionist, dietitian, home economist or extension agent	17.1	13.6 (746)
3) Relatives or friends	24.1	3.6 (1013)
4) Radio or television	33.2	4.7 (1385)
5) Newspapers, magazines, or books	47.4	18.5 (1986)
6) Government or health organization publications	14.1	2.8 (590)
7) Food company publications	12.8	0.7 (534)
8) Food packages or labels	45.0	10.9 (1890)

[a] $\dfrac{\text{Number of consumers who use an information source}}{\text{Total number of consumers}}$

[b] $\dfrac{\text{Number of consumers who use an information source which is the preferred source}}{\text{Number of consumers who use an information source}}$

[c] Number in parenthesis is sample size.

most preferred information sources if he/she uses them. The proportions of consumers who prefer food company publications, government or health organization publications, relatives or friends, radio or television, and food packages or labels are very low. These facts may indicate the credibility of these sources.

In order to comprehend the consumer usage of these information sources, it is necessary to investigate the factors affecting consumer information search. Russo and Leclerc (1991) conducted a research in the success of product information programs using a cost-benefit analysis. They claimed that from the consumer's perspective the cost-benefit framework is a useful guide to program design. According to Stigler's cost-benefit approach, consumers obtain the amount of information up to the point at which the anticipated marginal benefits equal marginal costs of information search. Feick, Herrmann, and Warland (1986) provided a detailed discussion of possible benefits and costs of information search. Following their procedure, the perceived benefits of search for nutrition information are affected by the enduring importance of nutrition to the individual and his enduring interest in nutrition.

They used the self-reported individual's present health such as poor and excellent as the measurement of the importance of and interest in nutrition. In this study, the consumption level of fat and cholesterol are used to capture the effect of enduring importance of nutrition.

In the last several decades, consumers have become increasingly aware of health and food nutrients. Fat and cholesterol are probably the most well known nutrients which affect consumer food purchase decisions in the United States. Consumers who consume more fat and cholesterol can be assumed to be less concerns about the importance of nutrition. Hence, they may also be less likely to search and use more nutrition information. One of the hypothesis is that the amount of consumer search for nutrition information depends on the enduring importance of nutrition.

Feick, Herrmann, and Warland also discussed the appropriateness of age, married status of individuals, and involvement of children as major factors influencing the benefits of nutrition information. Besides the age, household head status and household size are used as the factors affecting consumer information search instead of the married status and involvement of children in this study. The household head status means whether or not a household is headed by both male and female.

Costs of information search are mainly determined by opportunity cost of time and efficiency of search. Feick, Herrmann, and Warland explained the appropriateness of marginal wage (income) and household size as measures of the opportunity cost. The efficiency of search are determined by education and experience (age).

In addition to the above factors, food cost at-home consumption, region and urbanization of a consumer resides, and race are used as explanatory variables in this study. These variables have not been addressed properly in the literature, partially because of data limitations. Food expenditure is hypothesized to affect consumer information search in a positive direction. Urbanization and region a consumer resides may be associated with the availability and accessibility of various information sources. Moreover, consumers in different areas may use nutrition information differently based on beliefs or traditional food consumption behaviors. Thus the benefits and costs of information search are expected to be different among residence areas. Race is postulated to affect consumer information search because the value, attitude, and perception of nutrition information may differ among racial groups.

In summary, the above factors which affect the benefits and costs of information search should be included in studying the determinants of consumer usage of nutrition information. Feick, Herrmann, and Warland also explained different effects of these factors on the extent of information search from various sources are present. For example, reading books is time consuming. The opportunity cost of time should be more important in analyzing the information search from this source. Listening radio or watching television may be a kind of entertainment. The effect of opportunity cost of time on obtaining nutrition information from this source may be negligible. In spite of this fact, the same set of explanatory variable are used for all the information sources for the comparability across these sources. In addition, utilizing different sets of explanatory variables for each information source requires a number of assumptions about the source and the information available from them (Feick, Herrmann and Warland 1986).

THE MODEL

Consumers maximize their utility derived from various nutrition information sources. The amount of information searched is optimized according to the rule of Stigler's marginal benefits and costs of information search (1961). Consumers, the utility maximizers, make decisions on whether they search nutrition information based on the utility derived from various alternatives. The utility level derived from an alternative depends on consumers' socio-economic and demographic characteristics such as their education, race, age, family size, and income which associate with consumer benefits and costs of information search.

Assume that the utilities derived from the two choices of an individual who uses and does not use a nutrition information source are U_{i0} and U_{i1}, respectively. They can be expressed as:

$$U_{i0} = \overline{U}_{i0} + e_{i0} ,$$
$$U_{i1} = \overline{U}_{i1} + e_{i1} , \qquad (1)$$

where $\overline{U}_{i0}$ and $\overline{U}_{i1}$ are average utilities from the two choices, respectively, e_{i0} and e_{i1} are random errors. The average utilities are used since the individual's socio-economic characteristics do not vary across alternatives.

The utilities, U_{i0} and U_{i1}, are random variables. The consumer i will use this source only if $U_{i0} > U_{i1}$. Define a latent random variable as $Y^* = U_{i0} - U_{i1} > 0$, a linear statistical model can be expressed as:

$$Y_i^* = x'_i \beta + e_i^* , \, i = 1, \ldots , T \qquad (2)$$

where Y^* is consumer usage of this source, x is a vector of explanatory variables, ß is a vector of coefficients to be estimated, and e^* is the error term. The dependent variable, Y^*, is unobservable. The observable variable, Y, is a discrete (binary) choice variable and is defined as:

$$Y_i = \begin{cases} 1, & \text{if household } i \text{ uses the nutrition} \\ & \quad \text{information source,} \\ 0, & \text{otherwise} \end{cases}$$

The values of Y_i are determined by the following relationship:

$$Y_i = \begin{cases} 1, & \text{if } Y^* > 0 , \\ 0, & \text{if } Y^* \leq 0 , \end{cases}$$

Due to the difficulties of the standard regression technique for the discrete choice model, several alternative procedures such as probit and logit models are proposed (Maddala 1983). The logit model is utilized in this study.

In the logit model, the interest is in the probability of Y_i (a random variable) taking a value of 1 or 0 and what factors affect this probability. The probability for $Y_i = 1$ is given by:

$$P_i = Pr[Y_i = 1] = Pr[Y^* > 0] = Pr[e_i^* > -x_i' \beta] \qquad (3)$$

The probability distribution of e_i^* is assumed to be determined by a logistic distribution and the P_i can be estimated by:

$$P_i = \frac{1}{1 + e^{-x_i' \beta}} , \qquad (4)$$

where x is a vector of independent variables with ß as the corresponding regression coefficients to be estimated. Its log likelihood function is expressed as:

$$\ln L = \sum_{i=1}^{T} Y_i \ln(P_i) + \sum_{i=1}^{T} 1 - Y_i \ln(1 - P_i) , \qquad (5)$$

where T is the number of households.

The utility derived from an individual's preferred nutrition information source should be different from the utility derived from a source which is not his/her preferred source. For an information source used by the individual, two possibilities exist. They are 1) he/she uses the source which is his/her preferred source, and 2) he/she uses the source but it is not the preferred source. Whether the information source used by the consumer is his/her preferred source is a measure of success of consumer information search.

The success can be modeled and estimated in the exact same way as the logit procedure described above by the following assumptions. Assume that the utilities derived from the two possibilities of an information source used by a consumer i is his/

her preferred source and not his/her preferred source are U_{i0} and U_{i1}, respectively. The observable variable, Y, is a discrete (binary) choice variable and is defined as:

$$Y_i = \begin{cases} 1, & \text{if an information source used is the} \\ & \text{consumer's preferred} \\ 0, & \text{otherwise.} \end{cases}$$

DATA SOURCE

The data source used in this study is the 1987-88 Nationwide Food Consumption Survey (NFCS) which was conducted between April 1987 and August 1988 sponsored by the United States Department of Agriculture. The survey is a self-weighing, multi-stage, stratified, area probability sample representative of the households in the 48 conterminous States of the United States. There are 4,250 housekeeping households which are used for this study. The housekeeping households are defined as at least one member had ten or more meals from household food supply during the survey week.

Consumer usage and preference of nutrition information from eight popular sources has been discussed previously. The survey contains many important economic and socio-demographic variables. These variables are important determinants of consumer benefits and costs of information search. They are used as explanatory variables in the logit analysis. The variable definitions and selected sample statistics are presented in table 2.

RESULTS

The logit model was used to estimate the determinants of consumer search for four nutrition information sources[2]. The estimation results are presented in table 3. The majority of the estimated parameters are statistically significant at the 0.05 significance level for all the four information sources. The likelihood ratio chi-square statistics suggest the overall significance of the models. Within the sample, more than 62 percent of the observations are correctly predicted for all the information sources.

The estimated coefficient of food expenditure at-home is statistically significant and positive in all equations. This is expected because the more food a household consumes at-home, the more it searches for nutrition information in order to make better food choice. Because no previous studies incorporated food expenditure as an explanatory variable, no comparison can be made for this finding. The coefficient of income, a major component of opportunity cost of time, presents an interesting pattern. When incomes increase, the probability of obtaining nutrition information from a doctor, nurse or other health professional decreases. The opposite is held for the equations of books and labels, respectively. This pattern suggests that high income consumers may visit doctors and health professionals less often than low income consumers. In addition, they may be more accessible to the sources of newspapers, magazines, and books, and understanding the nutrition information provided in food packages and labels better than do the others. Inconsistent results were found by Feick, Herrmann, and Warland (1986). They reported that income was not a major determinant for the use of all information sources.

Family size is not a significant predictor of information search from doctor and television while it is a significant predictor in

---

[2]The other four sources were not analyzed by the logit procedure because there were not sufficient consumers using them (table 1).

positive direction in the equations of books and labels. These findings are consistent with those of Feick, Herrmann, and Warland. Their results suggested that number of children is a significant and positive determinants of usage of labels. The coefficient of age is statistically significant and positive in equations of doctors and books. For elderly households, they may visit doctors more often than young households. Therefore, they are more likely to obtain nutrition information from doctors than the latter. Additionally, elderly households may own high human capital and more readily access to newspapers, magazines, and books.

The age effect on information search is consistent with Feick, Herrmann, and Warland's find. They found that age was a significant and positive predictor of information search from magazines and newspapers, and books and pamphlets. Moorman (1990) also found that age is positively related to ability to process and comprehension accuracy of nutrition information. Different finding about the age effect was found by Cole and Balasubramanian (1993). They reported older consumers had difficulties in using nutrition information. They interpreted this conflict as the results of greatly different age subjects used in different studies. In addition, their small sample (79 consumers), interview methods, and grouping of consumers (younger consumer aged between 20 and 59 years and older consumer aged between 60 to 89 years) may be responsible to this contradiction. The controversial conclusion was also obtained by Moorman and Matulich (1993). They pointed out that age has a negative main effect on information acquisition.

Education increases the amount of nutrition information search from every sources. This is consistent with the finding of Feick, Herrmann, and Warland. They interpreted this finding as nutrition information was too technical or confusing to many consumers. Because previous research suggested that effectively designed nutrition disclosures facilitate information utilization (Moorman 1986), the information format and disclosures need to be improved. Consumer education program in improving comprehension of nutrition information may be necessitated.

Race is not a significant determinants for information search from doctors, but it is from the sources of television, books, and labels. The probabilities of obtaining nutrition information from television, books, and labels are higher for white households than for other racial groups. Both male and female headed households search more nutrition information from all sources than single headed households. This is a different finding from Feick, Herrmann, and Warland. They reported that marital status was not a significant predictor of information search from any source.

Consumer resident areas are also influencing consumer search for nutrition information from some sources. Compared with suburban residents, central city and non-metro consumers search more information from the sources of radio or television, and newspapers, magazines, or books. Non-metro households obtain nutrition information from food packages and labels more often than others. Compared with west region, households in northeast search information less often from the sources of radio or television, newspapers, magazines, or books, and food packages or labels. Midwest residents are more likely to obtain information from a doctor, nurse, or other health professional, and food packages or labels, but less likely to use the sources of radio or television, and newspapers, magazines, or books. Because most previous studies used regional survey data, no comparison can be made on these findings. The regional differences in information usage may indicate that consumer's accessibility or believes on information vary across regions.

Another plausible finding is that enduring importance of nutrition is a significant predictor in positive direction for all

TABLE 2
Variable Definition and Selected Sample Statistics (N = 4250)

Variables	Definitions	Means
Y($)	per capita annual income	13976 (15098) [a]
FE($)	weekly per capita at-home food expenditure	27.38 (13.39)
SFS	standard family size (21 meal equivalent person)	2.42 (1.34)
AGE(year)	age of household head	46.71 (17.29)
FAT(g)	weekly per capita at-home fat consumption	908.57 (482.45)
CHL(mg)	weekly per capita at-home cholesterol consumption	2933.5 (1640.9)
ED1	1 if household head completed less than 9 years of school, 0 otherwise	0.14
ED2	1 if household head completed at least 9 years but less than one year college, 0 otherwise	0.48
ED3	1 if household head completed 1-4 years of college, 0 otherwise	0.31
ED4	1 if household head completed more than 4 years of college, 0 otherwise	0.07
RA1	1 if household head is white, 0 otherwise	0.85
RA2	1 if household head is black, 0 otherwise	0.12
RA3	1 if household head is not white or black, 0 otherwise	0.03
BMF	1 if household headed by both male and female, 0 otherwise	0.75
NBMF	1 if household is not BMF, 0 otherwise	0.25
RS	1 if household currently receive food stamps, 0 otherwise	0.07
NRS	1 if household currently not receive food stamps, 0 otherwise	0.93
UB1	1 if household lives in central city, 0 otherwise	0.23
UB2	1 if household lives in suburban, 0 otherwise	0.47
UB3	1 if household lives in non-metro area, 0 otherwise.	0.30
RE1	1 if northeast region resident, 0 otherwise	0.20
RE2	1 if midwest region resident, 0 otherwise	0.26
RE3	1 if south region resident, 0 otherwise	0.35
RE4	1 if west region resident, 0 otherwise	0.19

[a] Number in parenthesis is standard deviation.

TABLE 3
Estimated Results of Consumer Information Usage (N = 4192a)

Variable	Doctor, nurse or other health professional	Radio or television	Newspaper, magazines or books	Food packages or labels
Ln(FE)	0.662**	0.441**	0.645**	0.930**
	(6.14)[b]	(4.06)	(5.97)	(8.55)
Ln(Y)	-0.169**	0.031	0.105**	0.058*
	(-5.07)	(0.91)	(3.04)	(1.74)
Ln(SFS)	-0.097	0.076	0.246**	0.234**
	(-1.20)	(0.93)	(3.25)	(2.89)
Ln(AGE)	0.279**	0.100	0.249**	0.020
	(2.95)	(1.05)	(2.65)	(0.22)
ED1	0.104	-0.365**	-0.659**	-0.204*
	(0.97)	(-3.14)	(-5.78)	(-1.84)
ED2	0.117	0.210**	0.498**	0.461**
	(1.48)	(2.68)	(6.46)	(5.96)
ED3	0.361**	0.056	0.621**	0.508**
	(2.80)	(0.42)	(4.70)	(3.89)
RA1	-0.025	0.177*	0.548**	0.492**
	(-0.25)	(1.67)	(5.20)	(4.68)
BMF	0.332**	0.126	0.167*	0.198**
	(3.66)	(1.37)	(1.85)	(2.20)
UB1	0.070	0.236**	0.211**	-0.058
	(0.81)	(2.67)	(2.42)	(-0.66)
UB3	0.020	0.428**	0.387**	0.322**
	(0.25)	(5.21)	(4.77)	(4.00)
RE1	-0.075	-0.397**	-0.846**	-0.760**
	(-0.70)	(-3.66)	(-7.94)	(-7.10)
RE2	0.222**	-0.216**	-0.333**	0.246**
	(2.22)	(-2.15)	(-3.34)	(2.50)
RE3	0.117	-0.087	-0.465**	-0.043
	(1.20)	(-0.89)	(-4.79)	(-0.44)
FAT	-0.001**	-0.0002**	-0.001**	-0.001**
	(-6.00)	(-2.35)	(-5.05)	(-6.76)
CONT	-2.023**	-2.917**	-4.263**	-4.057**
	(-3.76)	(-5.33)	(-7.83)	(-7.52)
L-Final	-2677.9	-2605.8	-2678.8	-2687.1
L-Initial	-2729.1	-2659.6	-2899.9	-2885.4
Chi-Square	102.5	107.6	442.1	396.6
%-Correct	64.9	66.7	62.8	63.6
One	1492	1385	1986	1890
Zero	2700	2807	2206	2302

[a] Fifty eight observations are deleted owing to incomplete information for the logit analysis.

[b] Figures in parentheses are asymptotic t-ratios.

** and * denote statistically significance at the 0.01 and 0.05 significant levels, respectively.

---

information sources[3]. Consumers with low level of enduring importance of nutrition search less information from all sources than do the other consumers. This is consistent with previous studies. Feick, Herrmann, and Warland (1986) found that the importance of food consumption on future health was a significant predictor on nutrition information search from every sources in positive direction. Moorman and Matulich (1993) concluded that health motivation increases the amount of health information usage. Burton and Biswas (1993) also reported that the information about cholesterol and fat are major determinants of consumer perception of nutrition information. This finding is useful in consumer education program. For example, efforts in educating consumers about the effects of food consumption on future health will improve consumer usage of nutrition information.

[3]Only fat consumption is included in logit analysis since cholesterol consumption is highly correlated with the fat consumption.

TABLE 4
Estimated Results of the Success of Information Usage (N=4192a)

Variable	Doctor, nurse or other health professional	Radio or television	Newspaper, magazines or books	Food packages or labels
Ln(FE)	-0.312*	-0.835**	-0.046	0.201
	(-1.76)[b]	(-3.09)	(-0.29)	(1.04)
Ln(Y)	-0.033	-0.034	0.070	0.107
	(-0.72)	(-0.39)	(1.26)	(1.57)
Ln(SFS)	-0.109	-0.008	0.103	0.165
	(-0.80)	(-0.04)	(0.86)	(1.14)
Ln(AGE)	0.132	-0.375	-0.080	-0.564**
	(0.86)	(-1.54)	(-0.57)	(3.35)
ED1	0.289	0.175	-0.056	0.357*
	(1.55)	(0.61)	(-0.27)	(1.69)
ED2	-0.319**	-0.335*	0.187*	-0.261*
	(-2.52)	(-1.66)	(1.70)	(-1.95)
ED3	-0.692**	-0.662*	0.498**	-0.421*
	(-3.44)	(-1.68)	(2.95)	(-1.89)
RA1	-0.279*	-0.170	0.273	0.513**
	(-1.63)	(-0.67)	(1.53)	(2.21)
BMF	-0.161	-0.055	-0.142	-0.128
	(-1.04)	(-0.24)	(-1.07)	(-0.80)
UB1	-0.063	-0.057	0.116	-0.411**
	(-0.45)	(-0.26)	(0.93)	(-2.55)
UB3	0.222*	-0.394*	-0.015	-0.210
	(1.62)	(-1.85)	(-0.13)	(-1.52)
RE1	0.552**	0.181	-0.078	0.144
	(3.12)	(0.72)	(-0.53)	(0.73)
RE2	0.249	-0.516**	-0.419**	0.102
	(1.54)	(-2.04)	(-3.13)	(0.60)
RE3	0.327**	-0.353	-0.322**	0.227
	(2.04)	(-1.50)	(-2.45)	(1.35)
FAT	0.0002	0.001**	0.000004	-0.0001
	(1.25)	(2.36)	(0.023)	(-0.58)
CONT	1.218	2.550*	-0.977	-1.148
	(1.40)	(1.85)	(-1.19)	(-1.17)
L-Final	-972.2	-486.1	-1262.6	-956.5
L-Initial	-1010.3	-503.8	-1281.4	-975.5
Chi-Square	76.4	35.4	37.5	38.0
%-Correct	60.7	88.2	65.5	78.8
One	879	162	688	400
Zero	613	1221	1298	1490
Total sample 1492	1385	1986	1890	

[a] Fifty eight observations are deleted owing to incomplete information for the logit analysis.

[b] Figures in parentheses are asymptotic t-ratios.

** and * denote statistically significance at the 0.01 and 0.05 significant levels, respectively.

Turning to the question of whether consumers achieve their preferred information sources, the logit model was estimated again to analyze the determinants of success of information usage. The estimation results are presented in table 4. Generally, the models are not fitted as well as those of determinants of consumer usage. Out of a sample of 1385 households who search nutrition information from the source of radio and television, there are only 162, below 12%, households used their preferred information source. These facts suggest that nutrition information appeared in food advertisement in radio and television programs may not help food promotions for the food industry. Including nutrition information in television and radio programs may not be an effective way in educating consumers to make right food choices because they are more likely to ignore the information from this source.

The relatively poorer estimation results of the success equations suggest that majority consumer socio-economic and demographic characteristics such as income, family size, age, and household head status are not significant determinants in the success of consumer search for nutrition information. Although consumers do obtain nutrition information from various sources, it is far from the satisfactory of using them. This finding may imply that consumers have a difficulty time in finding their preferred information sources. This may be a major reason why consumers want and are willing to pay for nutrition information but neither acquire such information when making purchase decisions or comprehend most nutrition information once they receive it (Jacoby, Chestnut, and Silberma 1977). If consumers did not obtain nutrition information from their preferred sources, the usefulness of nutrition information they obtained and the benefits of searching nutrition information may be severely limited. For example, they may simply do not believe or understand the information they obtained so that they do not use the information in making food purchase decisions.

CONCLUSIONS

The current levels of consumer usage of nutrition information and factors related to the usage were discussed. Then the determinants of consumer usage of nutrition information were investigated by a qualitative response model. Data from a national survey, the 1987-88 Nationwide Food Consumption Survey (NFCS), was analyzed. Majority results are consistent with previous studies such as Feick, Herrmann, and Warland (1986), and Moorman (1990). Compared with previous studies, this study has several unique features. First, a more comprehensive data, the most recent and complete national survey, serves as the database while most previous studies used rather limited regional survey data. This makes the inclusion of food expenditure and regions of residence as explanatory variables possible.

Second, the consumption of fat and cholesterol is used to capture the effect of enduring importance of nutrition on information usage. In the literature, self-reporting health conditions and information index were often used and biased research results might be obtained. For example, self-reporting health condition is greatly affected by consumer characteristics. Some consumers may like to overstate while others may like to understate their health conditions. Finally, factors influencing consumer behavior in information search are thoroughly investigated. After estimating the determinants of consumer usage of nutrition information, this study further verifies whether consumers use their preferred sources.

The factors influencing consumer usage of nutrition information are identified successfully by the logit model. Food expenditure at-home, family size, age, education, household head status, and importance of nutrition are major predictors in positive direction in consumer information usage for all information sources. Income has a significant effects on information search but that varies across the sources. For example, high income consumers are more likely to use the source of newspapers, magazines, or books, and food packages or labels while they are less likely to use the source of a doctor, nurse, home economist or extension agent than do the low income consumers. The results also indicate that consumer information usage varies across urbanization areas and regions. These findings are useful for consumer education programs such as identifying the targets of consumer education programs and the design of information disclosures.

The results suggest that factors influencing consumer decision on information usage are not necessary to be significant determinants of the success of consumer information search. Consumers may not be able to find their preferred information sources. This finding reinforces the results of previous studies such as consumers' willingness to pay for nutrition information but unwilling to use it when making purchase decisions (Jacoby, Chestnut, and Silberman 1977, and Feick, Herrmann, and Warland 1986). Thus there is

much need in improving nutrition information disclosures to facilitate consumer information utilization.

REFERENCES

Amemiya, T. (1981), "Qualitative Response Models: A Survey," *Journal of Economic Literature*, 19:1483-1536.

Arabsheibani, G.R. (1993), "The Determinants of Success in Educational Choice," *Economics Letter*, 42:411-417.

Bass, V.F. (1991), "Food Labeling and Consumer Satisfaction," *Journal of Home Economics*, 83(Spring):2-5.

Burton, S. and A. Biswas (1993), "Preliminary Assessment of Changes in Labels Required by the Nutrition Labeling and Education Act of 1990," *The Journal of Consumer Affairs*, 27(Summer):127-145.

Cole, C.A. and S.K. Balasubramanian (1993), "Age Differences in Consumers' Search for Information: Public Policy Implications," *Journal of Consumer Research*, 20(June):157-169.

Cole, C.A. and G.J. Gaeth (1990), "Cognitive and Age-Related Differences in the Ability to Use Nutritional Information in a Complex Environment," *Journal of Marketing Research*, XXVII(May):175-84.

Cramer, J.S. (1991), *The Logit Model: An Introduction for Economists.* Edward Arnold, A Division of Hodder and Stoughton Limited.

Daly, P. (1976), "The Response of Consumers to Nutrition Labeling," *The Journal of Consumer Affairs*, 10(Winter):170-178.

Feick, L.F., R.O. Herrmann and R.H. Warland (1986), "Search for Nutrition Information: A Probit Analysis of the Use of Different Information Sources," *The Journal of Consumer Affairs*,20(Winter):173-192.

Hauser, J.R., G.L. Urban and B.D. Weinberg (1993), "How Consumers Allocate Their Time When Searching for Information," *Journal of Marketing Research*, XXX(November):452-66.

Jacoby, J., R.W. Chestnut and W. Silberman (1977),"Consumer Use and Comprehension of Nutrition Information," *Journal of Consumer Research*, 4:119-128.

Jensen, H.H. and T. Kesavan (1993), "Sources of Information, Consumer Attitudes on Nutrition, and Consumption of Dairy Products," *The Journal of Consumer Affairs*, 27(Winter):357-76.

Lambert-Lagace, L. (1983), "Media, Nutrition Information, and Consumer Reactions," *Journal of Nutrition Education*, 15:6-7.

Lenahan, R.J., J.A. Thomas, D.A. Taylor, D.L. Call and D.I. Padberg (1973), "Consumer Reaction to Nutritional Labels on Food Products," *The Journal of Consumer Affairs*, 7(Summer):1-12.

Levy, A.S., O. Matthews, M. Stephenson, J. E. Tenney and R.E. Shuker (1985), "The Impact of a Nutrition Information Program on Food Purchases," *Journal of Public Policy and Marketing*, 4:1-13.

Maddala, G.S. (1983), *Limited-dependent and qualitative variables in econometrics*, Cambridge University Press, New York, NY.

Moorman, C. (1990), "The Effects of Stimulus and Consumer Characteristics on the Utilization of Nutrition Information," *Journal of Consumer Research*, 17(December):362-74.

Moorman, C. and E. Matulich (1993), "A Model of Consumers' Preventive Health Behaviors: The Role of Health Motivation and Health Ability," *Journal of Consumer Research*, 20(September):208-228.

Navder, K.P. (1993), "Food and Nutrition Labeling: Past, Present and Future," *Journal of Home Economics*, 85(Summer):43-50.

Russo, J.E., R. Staelin, C.A. Nolan, G.J. Rusell and B.L. Metcalf (1984), "Nutrition Information in the Supermarket," *Journal of Consumer Research*, 13(June):48-70.

Russo, J.E. and F. Leclerc (1991), "Characteristics of Successful Product Information Programs," *Journal of Social Issues*, 47(1):73-92.

Stigler, G.J. (1961), "The Economics of Information," *The Journal of Political Economy*, 69(June):213-225.

Urbany, J.E. (1986), "An Experimental Examination of the Economics of Information," *Journal of Consumer Research*, 13(September):257-271.

The Case of the Dusty Stair Climber: A Taxonomy and Exploratory Study of Product Nonuse

Amanda B. Bower, University of South Carolina
David E. Sprott, University of South Carolina

The current research is concerned with product nonuse. Specifically, the research asks why a consumer would actively obtain products that are either never used or perhaps are used on a single occasion. A taxonomy of product nonuse is developed which is based broadly on whether the driving force behind the nonuse is primarily due to forces external to or influences from within the individual consumer. The research includes exploratory data that provides support for the developed taxonomy.

PRODUCT NONUSE

Who among us has not bought a sack of potatoes that went bad and unused in the cupboard or bought a stationary bike that sat in the corner of the bedroom, only to become an overpriced clothes hanger? Consumer experiences such as these are examples of product nonuse. Product nonuse can be observed in a variety of product categories, from perishables (e.g., potatoes, lettuce, yogurt) to durables (e.g., exercise equipment). The phenomenon may also be observed in soft goods categories (e.g., clothes, shoes) and services (e.g., gym memberships).

Product nonuse is broadly defined to occur when the consumption of a product fails to occur after it is obtained. Implicit in this definition are a number of assumptions and terms that need further clarification. First, the preceding definition implicitly assumes that at the time of purchase the buyer does have the intention of consuming the product. This self-evident assumption is provided only to clarify the domain of inquiry. Second, by nonuse we mean that the product is not being used as intended at the time of purchase (e.g., the stationary bike that was purchased to be ridden but is draped in clothes).

Does nonuse of a product necessarily have to be defined as *never* having used the product? It is unnecessarily restrictive to conceptualize nonuse in such extreme terms. For example, assume the exercise bike was used twice a week for a month (or less) until the consumer ceased to ride the bike at all for an extended period, say a year or more. Such a pattern of use would not fall within the preceding zero-use definition, although such an occurrence would be considered as product nonuse. Therefore, we adopt a somewhat less restrictive definition of nonuse.

A product is considered to be nonused if it has not been used at all, or if it has been used a few times, whereby the period of use is followed by nonuse. The first condition is clear and needs no further explanation. The second condition considers both the amount and pattern of use of a product. That is, product nonuse is also conceptualized as a discontinuous function with product use being confined to a finite and limited length of time, which is then proceeded by a period of nonuse. Whereas, a product that is used continuously (although less than expected) for an extended period of time is not, according to our conceptualization, a nonused product.

Consider the following example illustrating these distinctions between product use and product nonuse. Three different purchasers each obtained an exercise bike. All three purchased the bike with the expectation of riding it five times a week. Assuming 6 months of ownership, Purchaser 1 has ridden the product about two times every week. On the other hand, the bike belonging to Purchaser 2 has been entirely neglected, while Purchaser 3 rode the bike for the first two weeks (at 5 times per week) and then stopped riding the bike entirely. Product nonuse is considered to have occurred in regard to Purchasers 2 and 3, but not Purchaser 1.

To further clarify the domain of inquiry, several additional points about what is and is not considered to be a nonused product need to be addressed. First, it is recognized that many products are characterized by a declining amount of use, or are used until the person, for example, changes life stages. A child will probably ride his bike less as he gets older. Because that bike is not used now does not mean it was not well used *before*. The difference between used and nonused products is that in the latter, any use will occur within a limited amount of time after obtainment, and then that use rapidly declines.

Second, this conceptualization of product nonuse does not include those products that can be reused but are purchased with the intention of a single consumption occasion. For example, prom dresses are expensive, non-perishable, and can be used multiple times, but are bought with only one use in mind.

Third, we are not concerned here with those products that were involuntarily obtained by the consumer (i.e., unrequested gifts). The only types of gifts included in our conceptualization are those that are actively sought. Our respondents are undergraduate students who are still primarily dependent on their parents. Therefore, when asking for a gift for Christmas, birthday, etc. we are assuming that they recognize that they are actively guiding the choice of the product.

Finally, we do not mean to imply that there is single, identifiable point at which a product is used or nonused. Our conceptualization of product nonuse is meant to provide a guideline for identifying those characteristics which are indicative of nonuse. It is recognized that there may be cases where determining the existence of nonuse may be difficult.

METHODOLOGY

Taxonomic Development

Prior to data collection, a classification of nonuse was generated from researcher introspection in order to aid in the interpretation of the data. The proposed taxonomy is based broadly on whether or not the reasons for nonuse are beyond the control of the consumer, *environmental factors*, or within the control of the consumer, *decision factors*. Because the goal of creating this classification was to better understand the domain of inquiry, these categories were not meant to be either mutually exclusive or all encompassing.

The data are congruent with the initial categories. Responses were judged individually by the two researchers, and any conflict in categorization was resolved by discussion. Further, the data not only provided a better understanding of major categories but also suggested subcategories.

Respondents and Procedure

The sample consisted of 68 undergraduate business students. One questionnaire was illegible and dropped from further consideration. Respondents were informed that the purpose of the research was to explore why people purchase products that they never use. Further, they were told that if they were unable to think of a case of their own product nonuse, then they need not feel obligated to complete the questionnaire. All students were given class credit regardless of their ability to respond. Three examples of product nonuse involving clothing (shoes), food (lettuce), and fitness equipment (club membership) were provided to clarify the respondents' task.

Measures

Following the nonuse examples, the respondents were presented with a series of open-ended questions. These asked for a product description, when it was purchased, the price, the amount of any price reductions, the extent of use, why it was bought, why it wasn't used, and what happened to it. Following these questions were two Likert-type items (7 to 1 scale). These are: "If you had to make this purchase again, would you do so?" (definitely yes/ definitely no), and "How satisfied were you with this purchase?" (very satisfied/ very unsatisfied). The next two questions were dichotomous and referred to the unused product described in the open-ended portion of the questionnaire. The first asked if they had ever purchased other items related to that product, while the second asked if those products had also been nonused. The final two questions requested the respondent's age and gender.

Sample Characteristics

Sixty-seven percent of the 67 respondents were male (n=45) and 33% (n=22) were female, with an average age of 22.6 years. The wide variety of reported products were separated into one of 7 categories: (1.) *clothing* (46.3%, n=31, e.g.; shoes, dresses, ties); (2.) *exercise equipment or services* (9%, n=6, e.g.; weight machines, fitness club memberships); (3.) *sporting goods* (10.4%, n=7, e.g.; bat, bicycle); (4.) *music related products* (4.5%, n=3; CDs); (5.) *food related products* (6%, n=4, e.g.; yogurt, lettuce); (6.) *technological products* (6.0%, n=4, e.g.; television, computer equipment); and (7.) *miscellaneous products* (17.9%, n=12, e.g.; contact lenses, walkie talkies).[1] The average price of the products purchased was $72.67, the minimum price paid was $0.10 for lettuce and a maximum of $870.00 for an exercise machine.

Before nonuse occurred, the products were used an average of 3.5 times. Respondents using the product two or less times accounted for 63.5% (n=40) of the sample. Specifically, 20.9% (n=14) did *not* use the product at all, 19.4% (n=13) used the product once and 19.4% (n=13) used the product twice. The maximum amount of usage was 20 times for a bicycle, a CD, and a pair of contact lenses. Since they exhibited the discussed pattern of nonuse these products will be included in the data analyses.

Almost 84% (n=56) of the products were kept by the respondent. This is interesting considering the average product was purchased 76 weeks ago. The remaining respondents either sold the product, threw it out, gave it away, or it expired.

Respondents, on average, would not make the purchase again (mean=2.3, s.d.=1.9) and were unsatisfied with the purchase (mean=2.7, s.d.=1.7). Sixty-one percent of the respondents (n=41) purchased items related to the nonused product, of whom 75.6% (n=31) felt that they did not adequately use them.

A TAXONOMY OF PRODUCT NONUSE

Environmental Factors

There exist situational forces that can be responsible for product nonuse and are outside of the consumer's control. These

---

[1]Because the examples provided may have primed related instances in the respondents' memories, this may have artificially increased the number of cases in the categories of clothing, food, and fitness equipment.

situational forces can be either external or directly related to the product.

Sources external to the product. These situational influences are related to changes in the external environment that prevented the purchaser from using the product in the intended environment. For example, if a woman buys a non-refundable airline ticket but becomes ill and is unable to use the ticket to go on vacation, the ticket is considered nonused.

Approximately 7% (n=5) of the respondents provided information on products that fell into disuse due to sources external to the product and not within the control of the respondent. The environment physically altered two of these products so that they could no longer function. For example:

Male, 22, tennis shoes: I recently purchased a pair of running shoes because my old pair were worn out and looked terrible. I played golf in the rain in them one day and after that they smell and if I ever wear them again they will make my feet stink.

The remaining products (n=3) became unusable due to environmental changes such that the product would no longer have a context in which to be utilized. For example, one respondent asked for and received a 10 speed bicycle for his 15th birthday. However:

Male, 21, bicycle: We stopped using bikes because it was too cold to ride around in the winter, and when spring rolled around my friends had their drivers license, and we no longer needed bikes.

Sources related to the product. Nonuse may also be due to some failure of the product. For example a product may break very shortly after purchase. Even if the consumer has the opportunity to replace that product with another, the first product remains unused.

Thirteen percent (n=9) of the sample provided nonuse experiences related to product factors. There were a variety of products in this category (e.g., hair conditioner and computer equipment).

Male, 22, yogurt: I usually buy [brand A] blended yogurt, but decided to try the [brand B yogurt] for the different flavors. I like yogurt so I purchased [brand B]. . . The product had to be mixed and the fruit was hard and not blended like [brand A]. The date expired and I threw it away.

Decision Factors

There may be situations where there is a conflict between the decisions to purchase and to consume, and that conflict is due to some inconsistency within the consumer. Why would a person purchase a product and then later decide against using it? The literature suggests the potential of preference fluctuations between the purchase and the consumption of the product. As Simonson (1990) states, the consumption of a product often occurs at a different time than the decision to purchase. Therefore, a person must try to predict their preferences at the time of consumption (Kahneman and Snell 1990). Ironically, Kahneman and Snell found that people are very bad at determining what their future preferences will be. Similarly, Simonson (1990) concludes that people are aware that they are unsure of their future preferences, and have some doubt in determining what those future preferences might be. The fact that future preferences could be somehow different than the ones currently held is the basis of this article. The decisions to purchase and to consume are two different behaviors with each potentially having two different sets of motivations. Nonuse can stem from a consumer's failure to either correctly evaluate the product prior to purchase or due to some desire based on misevaluated goals.

Two categories of nonuse due to decision factors were identified. The first includes those situations where the consumer began the decision making process based on a direct encounter with the purchase situation (e.g., a major price reduction). The second category contains all of those purchases that were intended to satisfy some (possibly enduring) goal. The primary difference between the two is that in the latter there is some specific need or want driving the search and evaluation of the product.

Specific to Purchase. This category refers to those situations where the person made the decision to purchase as a result of factors contained within the purchase situation. An example of this type of nonuse situation is a woman's decision to buy a pair of shoes due to her friend's encouragement at the point of purchase.

As previously stated, the decision to purchase and the decision to consume may be two different decisions with different sets of decision criteria. An inconsistent evaluation of a product may occur when those decision criteria of consumption are either not present or underweighed in the decision to purchase. Additionally, those decision criteria that motivated the purchase may not be present or are underweighed at the time of consumption.

Hoch and Loewenstein (1991) explored time-inconsistent preferences; that is a person's short term preferences can conflict with preferences that are consistent with long term goals. They identified that people do engage in behavior that is often regretted after the fact and that would have been rejected if they had thought about it more objectively.

The following are some of the reasons why the weighting of decision criteria may be inconsistent between prepurchase and post purchase of the product.

1. Social Influence. This influence refers to any effect that people such as friends or sales associates can have on the consumer's decision to purchase a product. Six percent (n=4) of the respondents provided a product nonuse experience related to social influence at the time of purchase.

Each of these respondents indicated a form of reference group pressure as a potential reason for the subsequent nonuse. There is evidence that reference groups can influence consumer purchase behavior (cf. Bearden and Etzel 1982). Consider the following discussions of two different coats.

Male, 22, coat: When I got it, every one had one and so I got it because of that. . I really hated I bought that damn coat. It matched nothing I already had and the brown was like a rust color...When the style left my coat went along with it.

Male, 21, 'Michael Jackson Jacket': In grade school I bought a jacket...I thought it was the coolest thing at the time. I guess I thought other kids would like it too. I was ridiculed by kids. They obviously did not have the same ideas about Michael Jackson I did. It was put into my closet and I have never seen it since. My mom actually bought it. I begged her. We even left the store and came back to get it.

Nonuse appears to manifest itself when social pressure is the opposite of personal preference and the salience of each changes between the time of purchase and the time of consumption. This can occur in two different ways. First, when social pressure is more salient at the time of purchase and favors the product, then purchase will occur. However, if personal preference is then more salient at the time of consumption and does not favor the product, then consumption will not occur (e.g., the brown jacket). Similarly, if it

is personal preference that is more salient at the time of purchase and is favorable to purchase, but social pressure is more salient at the time of consumption and contrary to that evaluation then consumption will not occur (e.g., 'Michael Jackson' jacket).

2. Price Savings Influence. This category includes those purchases where a primary motivation for the purchase was the prospect of saving money. Schindler (1989) calls this influence "smart-shopper" feelings. "The term 'smart-shopper' feelings will be used to refer to the ego-related affect which may be generated in a consumer by a price" (p.448). These feelings can cause the buyer to alter his or her perception of other attributes in order to rationalize the purchase. They may also distract the consumer from the consideration of other attributes (Gardner and Strang 1984).

The strongest support for any of the categories was provided for the price-related influences. Almost 27% (n=18) indicated that the nonused product was purchased at a discounted price, and many indicated that this was a primary reason for purchase.

Female, 28, shoes: I purchased the product because it was on sale and I thought it was something that I could always use sometime or later. I stopped [using the product] because they were high heels and I usually wear flats everyday.

Female, 21, skirt: I thought I needed a skirt like that, also it was only $7.00 and I just bought it. I got home and decided that I didn't really like it. It is in my closet with the tags still on it.

Female, 20, jacket: I just wanted to buy it. It was on sale and I thought it would look good with jeans. It looked stupid. The color was totally wrong and it was too short.

The preceding examples supports the contention of Schindler (1989), because it appears that the opportunity of a good deal somehow impacted the respondents' judgment of other product attributes. Each of the respondents purchased the product for a specific set of reasons (including a price reduction and other attributes), but when the person's failure to use the product was considered, the only reason that could still justify the purchase was the reduced price.

3. Potential Loss of Opportunity. A consumer may make a purchase that is primarily driven by the perceived limited availability of the product. For example, if the store is almost out of the product, the consumer may recognize the limited opportunity of owning this product. As in the case of the smart-shopper, the consumer's "judgment" of other product features (e.g., fit, style) may be lessened.

Male, 20, hammock: While in Mexico, I was on a mission trip, and we slept in hammocks. I thought it was unique as well as comfortable; so I bought one...∑and planned on using it in my room or hanging it in the yard. I guess because of two different cultures, there you need it and here it's just something extra.

4. Other Influences. Six responses could be broadly classified as related to decision factors; however, there was not enough information in their responses to provide any deeper insights into the potential cause of the nonuse.

Purchase Inspired by Consumer Goals. In the previous category, purchase of the nonused product was a direct result of an encounter with the purchase situation and no forethought went into the purchase. Purchases of nonused products in this category, however, are inspired by some goal of the individual.

There appear to be two different types of goals in the data. The first type were product-specific, *narrow goals* (n=5). By this we mean, purchase of this specific product would solve a specific need.

Female, Age 21, jacket: Coming down [South] I needed a jacket that was lighter than a leather jacket but was warm enough for [the South's] winter.

She discovered she had a need for a specific product, and had the goal of satisfying that need. The importance of separating this type of purchase from the previous category is the recognition of the difference between a planned and an unplanned purchase.

The other, more predominant type of goal that motivated product purchase were *general goals*. General goals could be satisfied by any number of products, and the purchase of this product was an attempt to reach that goal. Very often (n=11) that goal was related to weight loss or getting into shape.

Female, 20, gym membership: I wanted to get in shape, lose weight, be healthy.

Many of these goals appear to stem from a perceived possible self. According to Morgan (1993) an individual can attribute certain consumption behaviors to the attempt to achieve a positive, possible self. A possible self is one that represents, "...what we could become, what we would like to become and, most importantly, what we are afraid of becoming" (Markus and Nurius 1986, p. 954). Possible selves are drawn from past experiences, present activities, and the envisioned self in the future. Therefore, as Morgan (1993) proposes, certain consumption behaviors are related to our attempt to achieve those positive selves that we prefer to become, as well as avoid undesirable selves that we could become. Therefore, the purchase of exercise equipment might bring a woman closer to her positive possible self because of its perceived potential. It is this "hoped-for result" that motivated several of these purchases.

Male, 21, Gym membership: To get fit and get a little bigger and stronger. It would make me feel good about myself in the way I look and feel.

There appear to be two major reasons that purchases intended to satisfy goals fell into nonuse. (In the case of some responses, the cause of nonuse could not be determined.)

1. Product Dissatisfaction. The product did not fail or break, and the product is still able to perform the task it was intended to perform. However, in the evaluation of the product at purchase, the consumer somehow failed to correctly select a product s/he would be happy with.

Female, 21, jacket: Everyone seems to own this jacket and I feel I bought it too big...The main reason is that I don't care for the way the product looks on me anymore.

Female, 23, jeans: I wanted a pair of jeans that were 'fitted'- (not to look tight). My boyfriend was a big influence for owning this product ('sexy'). I thought the jeans would make my 'backside' look good, but instead the front (stride) looked long. [I stopped wearing them] because of the way they made me look long and straight from the front.

Female, 21, beach cruiser: I bought it and about 3 months later I found a bike that I liked better. This happened all the time. It was too trendy & I became bored with it quickly.

2. Goal Motivation. When products were purchased to achieve a goal, the motivation to achieve that goal seemed to be a crucial element in the motivation required to use the product.

Female, 22, wok: I wanted to try and cook stirfry [but I] didn't take time out to use it.

In some cases the product was purchased as a means to achieve that goal, and in others it was purchased as an incentive. For example, eight people purchased some sort of equipment that they felt would help them to lose weight or get into shape. Price ranged from $10 up to $870, with an average price of $230. Given reasons for nonuse varied little.

Female, 23, exercise video and weights: I got lazy and busy.

Female, 21, step-climber: Didn't like it. Too much work.

Male, 22, fitness club membership: Didn't have time or was lazy.

Male, 21, gym membership: Couldn't get in the groove to lift.

Obviously people are not going to spend an average of $230 and then neglect it if they were aware that they would be "lazy and busy." In many cases, the respondents cited their busyness as a primary reason for the nonuse of the product. However, based on reported products that were bought as incentives for achieving the goal, that busyness seems to indicate a lack of motivation and a lack of determination to achieve the goal.

Three females bought clothes with the intention of providing themselves with that determination to achieve their goal.

Female, 20, jeans: I purchased a pair of jeans- a little snug. The intention was to lose weight to fit into them... I guess it was to satisfy reaching a goal. It was an inspiration to work out.

Female, 20, dress: Purchased a size too small b/c I wanted to lose weight & never did...thought it would give me that incentive to lose the weight.

Female, 20, skirt: My ingenious idea was that I'd lose a few pounds and fit into the size 4 rather than gain a few and fit into the size 6. Obviously, I never lost the weight so the skirt was snug.

Not only did these women provide themselves with a conceptual possible self to eventually fit into, they bought physical molds to measure that fit. These articles of clothes were to inspire them to achieve a goal. Unfortunately, they lacked the motivation or determination to achieve that goal, and because the product did not fit, it went nonused.

DISCUSSION

All respondents (n=67) recounted an incident of product nonuse indicating that the phenomenon is fairly widespread. The fact that the students were informed that they were not obligated to invent an example if they were unable to think of one provides further support for the robustness of this phenomenon.

There is some evidence in the data that tends to suggest that nonuse behavior may be a common tendency among the respondents. Nearly half of the respondents indicated that they have nonused products related to the focal product.

Female, 39, mail-order blouse: I purchased many items the same way (mail order) before and I was happy with them. This time I was satisfied with the product (quality, color, etc.) but I just never wanted to wear it; somehow it didn't agree with my style, personality? It happened to me before with some other items (clothing) both purchased by mail, telephone or in the stores and all that I can say is that while being attracted to them in the very beginning, I lost interest in them after wearing them once. Again, they didn't agree with me or vice versa!

The current research indicates a number of possible reasons for product nonuse to occur. Each of these potential sources of product nonuse have a number of interesting implications. None so striking, perhaps, as the case of the effects of discount pricing on subsequent product nonuse. As a field, marketers, at times, tend to concentrate on the effect of price discounts on the sales of products. However, the current research expands that perspective, that is, what is the continuing effect of these pricing discounts on the consumer. Apparently some individuals may fail to use sale items once they are brought home.

Similarly, there are a number of interesting implications with regard to the product nonuse associated with exercise related products. For example, consider the apparent success of those January advertising campaigns that attempt to persuade consumers to purchase exercise products to lose those extra holiday pounds. Most of these persuasion attempts rely on appealing to the consumer's desire of an ideal self. However, it appears that consumers in such situations may not only fail to attain the possible self, but fail to use the product as well.

There are two limitations in this current investigation of product nonuse. The restricted sample, college age students, utilized by the current research may limit the generalizability of these findings. However, due to the exploratory nature of the research, the implied directions for future work are still significant and provide a good starting point for future research. Further, although the results suggest some possible mechanisms of product nonuse, this is not a complete listing of all potential causes.

There are number of future opportunities related to product nonuse. Qualitative research should explore the breadth of the phenomenon to gain a better understanding of possible underlying causes as well as underlying dimensions of the taxonomy.

We have discussed the conceptualization of "limited amount of time" as a continuum from limited to extended. While we fail here to provide an objective criteria, future research may explore people's perceptions of what amount of product use time must pass before they do not feel that the product has been neglected. Further, it would be useful to relate that to the cost of the product, the expectations of the product at the time of purchase, as well as product obtrusiveness (i.e., it is easier to hide and ignore unworn shoes than it is a stationary bike).

REFERENCES

Bearden, William O. and Michael J. Etzel (1982), "Reference Group Influence on Product and Brand Purchase Decisions," *Journal of Consumer Research*, 9 (September), 183-194 .

Gardner, Meryl P. and Roger A. Strang (1984), "Consumer Responses to Promotions: Some New Perspectives," in *Advances in Consumer Research*, Vol. 11, ed. Thomas C. Kinnear, Ann Arbor, MI: Association for Consumer Research, 420-425.

Hoch, Stephen J. and George F. Loewenstein (1991), "Time-Inconsistent Preferences and Consumer Self-Control," *Journal of Consumer Research*, 17 (March), 492-507.

Kahneman, Daniel and Jackie Snell (1990), "Predicting Utility," in *Insights in Decision Making*, ed. Robin M. Hogarth, Chicago: The University of Chicago Press.

Markus, Hazel and Paula Nurius (1986), "Possible Selves," *American Psychologist*, 41 (9), 954-969.

Morgan, Amy J. (1993), "The Evolving Self in Consumer Behavior: Exploring Possible Selves," in *Advances in Consumer Research* Vol. 20, eds. Leigh McAlister and Michael L. Rothschild, Provo, UT: Association for Consumer Research, 429-432.

Schindler, Robert M. (1989), "The Excitement of Getting a Bargain: Some Hypotheses Concerning the Origins and Effects of Smart-Shopper Feelings," in *Advances in Consumer Research*, Vol. 16, ed. Thomas K. Srull, Provo, UT: Association for Consumer Research, 447-453.

Simonson, Itamar (1990), "The Effect of Purchase Quantity and Timing on Variety-Seeking Behavior," *Journal of Marketing Research*, 27 (May), 150-162.

Special Session Summary
Emerging Issues In Product Bundling

Michal Ann Strahilevitz, University of Illinois at Urbana-Champaign

Product bundling has become a very common phenomenon in the marketplace. The variety of bundling strategies appears almost endless. These include offering "more of the same" (e.g., buy three, get one free), bundling the product with a complementary item (e.g., free film with the purchase of a camera), offering something totally unrelated (e.g., a promised donation to the March of Dimes with the purchase of a submarine sandwich) and bundling transactions together (e.g., trading in an old car for a new one). The purpose of this session was to offer new insights into how consumers go about evaluating various types of product bundles. The papers presented draw on previous work from several areas of research including behavioral decision theory, information processing, and the role of affect in consumer behavior. While each of the papers presented was grounded in theory, each presentation concluded with a discussion of implications for marketers interested in optimizing their product bundling strategies.

The first paper by Rajneesh Suri and Kent Monroe examined how consumers' perceptions of bundle savings are influenced by their purchase plans. More specifically, consumers may plan to buy none, one, or more than one item in a product bundle prior to being aware of the bundle offer. The research presented used a 3 (purchase plans) x 3 (bundle price) x 3 (savings on unplanned purchase) between subjects design. The results suggest that purchase plans do influence the perception of savings on bundle offers. Furthermore, the results suggest that the perception of savings and the process used to evaluate the savings on the bundle may be moderated by the relative price of the planned purchase vis-a-vis the unplanned purchase.

The second paper by Michal Strahilevitz and John Myers focused on the bundling of products with promised contributions to charity. The research presented consisted of three lab experiments and one field study. The studies investigated how the nature of the product being promoted and the magnitude of the promised donation to charity relative to the product's price interact to determine the effectiveness that a given donation to charity incentive will have in adding value to a given product. Dependent measures taken included both stated preference and actual purchase behavior. The results suggest that charity incentives will be relatively more effective in promoting products perceived as "frivolous luxuries" (e.g., a hot fudge sundae), than in promoting products perceived as "practical necessities" (e.g., a box of laundry detergent). The data also indicate that the effectiveness of altruistic incentives may be much less sensitive to magnitude (i.e., how much was being contributed) than are monetary incentives (i.e., how large was the rebate). Finally, the results suggest an interaction between product type (i.e., "frivolous" or "practical") and percentage of price being contributed to charity (e.g., 5% or 50%).

The third paper by Irwin Levin, Gary Gaeth, and Larry Menke focused on how consumers process information leading to judgments about product bundles. The research used a variety of response measures, comparing responses to individual products with responses to bundles consisting of specific combinations of these individual products. The results suggest that judgments of the monetary worth of product bundles are governed by an adding process; with the judged overall worth of a bundle being a function of the sum of the judged worths of its component parts. In contrast, evaluations of product bundle quality appear to be governed by an averaging process; with the relative impact of a tie-in product on quality perception often being far greater than its monetary value would suggest. This last result was especially pronounced for product classes with which the subjects were unfamiliar.

The fourth paper by Dipankar Chakravarti, Rajan Krish, Pallab Paul, and Joydeep Srivastava explored how bundled versus unbundled transactions with differentially priced component transactions can influence consumers' perceptions of transaction fairness, judged desirability, and choice. The authors used a scenario involving the purchase of a new car along with the trade-in of an old car. These component transactions were either presented as a bundle with a single net price tag for the transaction, or as segregated propositions with four different sets of separate prices for the new car and the trade-in (same net price as the bundle). These five presentations were crossed with a factor involving the absence/presence of reference prices for the component transactions (i.e. the new and the old cars). The price levels were chosen so that the reference price comparisons would result in the component transactions being coded as gains, losses or neutral. The findings showed systematic and theoretically consistent variations in fairness perceptions, desirability judgments, and choice of a target option as a function of how the transactions were presented (bundled/unbundled) and priced.

While there was no formal discussant for this special session, it ended with a lively discussion which focused not only on the content of the papers presented, but on directions for future research as well.

Effect of Consumers' Purchase Plans on the Evaluation of Bundle Offers

Rajneesh Suri, University of Illinois, Urbana-Champaign
Kent B. Monroe, University of Illinois, Urbana-Champaign

Bundling of more than one product has been a strategy used by retailers and manufacturers for decades in both consumer and industrial markets (Nagle 1984). The hardware and software packages offered by computer manufacturers, vacation packages offered by the various travel agencies, a shaving foam sold along with razors are a few commercial examples of bundling. There are two main forms of bundling -pure bundling (where the products or services are available only in bundle form) and mixed bundling (where the consumer has an option to purchase the products or services individually or as a bundle). However, mixed bundling, has been a popular strategy followed by marketers and is the focus of this study.

Despite the widespread use of bundling in marketing, most investigations in this area have been based on the economics literature, focussing on issues such as sellers' incentive to bundle, consumer welfare, and the effect on competition (Adams and Yellen 1976; Dansby and Conrad 1984; Schmalensee 1984; Stigler 1961). There have been very few studies exploring the individual's behavior in response to bundling. The three recent behavioral studies in this area are the studies by Gaeth et al. (1990), Yadav and Monroe (1993) and Chakravarti et al. (1994). Gaeth et al. (1990) showed how the overall evaluation of the bundle is affected by the individual items in the bundle, while the study by Yadav and Monroe (1993) explored how buyers perceived the savings when evaluating bundle offers. Chakravarti et al. (1994) explored the effects of segregation of information about the bundle item on the evaluation of the bundle. In this study we extend the behavioral research on bundling by exploring how consumers' perceptions of the savings on the bundle offers is influenced by their *purchase plans*, a contextual variable. Previous research has implicitly assumed that consumers are willing or planning to purchase individual items of the bundles. Such a scenario, however, might be only one of the possible options.

CONCEPTUAL DEVELOPMENT

Behavioral research on bundling has explored how sellers should present price information to buyers to promote bundle offers. Buyers' perceptions of savings on the bundle has been shown to be the sum of the perceived savings on the individual items if purchased separately and the additional savings when the items are bought together as a bundle (Yadav and Monroe 1993). This finding is consistent with Thaler's (1985) argument that segregation of multiple gains, instead of integration, leads to higher perceptions of overall gains. Hence, the segregation of gains (vis a vis integration) should be a preferred method of framing multiple gains. Also Thaler (1985) proposed that the overall utility of single item transactions could be decomposed into acquisition utility and transaction utility. (Even though Thaler developed the construct of transaction and acquisition utility for single item transactions, it can be extended to bundle offers as well.) Though both these utilities affect the formation of the overall utility of a bundle, we limit our focus to the influence of the purchase plans on the transaction utility of the bundle offers, i.e., the perceived savings on the bundle offer.

More often than not, consumers do carry with them a mental or a physical note of what they plan to buy during their trips to the stores. Undoubtedly for items like tours/ travel packages or for a purchase of a "high ticket item" like computers or any white or brown goods (e.g., TV or an Audio system), consumers do have a plan to purchase a particular product or service. However, consumers may then be confronted with a situation where at least one (or none!) of the items of a bundle offer is the product or service planned for purchase.

Consider a simple scenario of a bundle containing two items A and B. Consumers then may have either of the following possible purchase plans:

(a) *Plan 1*: purchase product A only.
(b) *Plan 2*: purchase product B only.
(c) *Plan 3*: purchase neither product A nor B.
(d) *Plan 4*: purchase both product A and B.

The item (service or product) which a consumer has planned to purchase will be termed the "planned purchase" while the item for which no purchase plan exists will be the "unplanned purchase". For example, in purchase plan 1, item A is the planned purchase while B is an unplanned purchase. *The research issue now is, how do these purchase plans affect the consumers' perceptions of savings on the bundle offers?*

Past research (Yadav and Monroe 1993; Chakravarti et al. 1994) has shown that a target bundle was evaluated more favorably and chosen more often when its components were presented in segregated (separate price tags) versus consolidated (single, equivalent tag) fashion, a notion consistent with mental accounting predictions (Thaler 1985) based on prospect theory (Kahneman and Tversky 1976).

Chakravarti et al. (1994) further argued that, segregation changes the locus of consumers' attention and influences the salience of bundle features. For instance, savings on the focal products may anchor the bundle evaluation (Gaeth et al. 1991; Yadav and Monroe 1993) and may even influence the perceived value of the components (Kaicker, Bearden, and Urbany 1993). Similarly consumers' predetermined plan (purchase plan) to buy a particular item during their visit to a store (or a service provider), may also provide a context which causes a shift in the locus of attention to the planned purchase in the bundle. In the following sections we will elaborate on our propositions under each purchase plan.

When Purchase of Only One Item in the Bundle Had Been Planned (i.e., Plan 1 or Plan 2)

Yadav (1990) proposed that in order to evaluate a bundle, the buyer will follow a sequential "step by step" structure using the anchoring and adjustment heuristic (Tversky and Kahneman 1974). "Anchoring and adjustment" heuristic suggests that (a) an arbitrarily chosen reference point (anchor) will significantly influence value estimates, and (b) value estimates will be insufficiently adjusted away from the reference point towards the value of the object of estimation. Tversky and Kahneman (1974) suggested that the anchoring and adjustment process occurs even if someone is not supplied an anchoring value, and people implicitly generate and use an anchoring value at the start of an estimation process, even if the task does not explicitly require one.

Given that the buyer has a plan to buy a particular item, that item would become salient and hence would act as an anchor in the evaluation of the bundle. The perception of savings on the bundle is based on the amount needed to purchase (i.e., sale price) the items (of a bundle) separately, which then acts as a reference price for evaluating the bundle price and the regular prices of individual items in the bundle (Yadav and Monroe 1993). Also since consumers are more likely to attend to the savings on the bundle first and then the savings on the individual items (Yadav and Monroe 1993), it can be argued that consumers first anchor on the sale price (or the sum of the sale prices) of the individual items to evaluate the bundle price, to be followed by the evaluation of the regular price (or the sum of the regular prices) of each item. Thus, in a situation where the consumer has a plan to buy only one item in the bundle, the sale price of the planned purchase would act as a reference (anchor) to evaluate the bundle price. The difference between the sale price of planned purchase and the bundle price would then be used as a reference to evaluate the price of the unplanned purchase. Thus:

Hypothesis 1(a): Given that the consumer has planned to purchase only one item (i.e., purchase plan 1 or 2) in the bundle, the perceived savings on the bundle offer would be evaluated as a comparison of sale price of the unplanned purchase with the additional amount one pays (over and above the sale price of the planned purchase) to buy the bundle.

Thus the difference between the sale price of the planned purchase and the bundle price would be used as a reference (or anchor) to evaluate the savings on the unplanned purchase. Following the "anchoring and adjustment" heuristic (Tversky and Kahneman 1974), this subsequent evaluation of the unplanned purchase item would lead to an adjustment of the evaluation of the anchor (planned purchase), resulting in an adjustment in the evaluation of the bundle itself. Thus, if the evaluation of the second, unplanned item, is more (less) favorable than the evaluation of the planned anchor item, then the evaluation for the bundle would be more (less) favorable than the evaluation of the anchor (Chakravarti et al. 1994; Yadav 1994).

Hypothesis 1(b): Given that the consumer has planned to purchase only one item of the bundle, the consumer's perception of the deal would be directly related to the savings on the unplanned purchase.

Tversky and Kahneman (1974) also argued that the adjustment under the "anchoring and adjustment" heuristic tends to be insufficient, and the final evaluation is biased in the direction of the initial anchor evaluation. Empirical support for this argument has been observed in spouse's evaluations of new products (Davis et al. 1986), realtors' determination of fair market value of residential properties (Northcraft and Neale 1987), and in auditors' evaluations of fraud estimates (Joyce and Biddle 1981). Recently, Yadav (1994) found that subjects readily adjusted the bundle evaluation downwards when faced with an excellent anchor and a moderate add on while the tendency to adjust upwards was considerably less.

Thus the impact of the savings on the unplanned purchase on the perception of savings of the bundle offers would be greater when the price of the planned purchase is lower than the price of the unplanned purchase. Thus:

Hypothesis 1(c): Given that the consumer has planned to purchase only one item in the bundle, the unplanned purchase will influence the consumer's perception of the savings on the bundle, more when the planned purchase price is lower than when it is higher than the unplanned purchase.

When Both Items in the Bundle Are Unplanned Purchases

Yadav and Monroe (1993) observed that buyers who intend to purchase the bundle may first attend to savings offered directly on the bundle itself and subsequently notice the savings on the individual items. However, under a scenario where there is no plan to buy either item in the bundle (i.e., purchase plan 3), the consumers while attempting to evaluate the savings on the bundle will try to minimize their cognitive effort (Beach and Mitchell 1978; Payne, Bettman and Johnson 1988). Thus we propose that the transaction value or the savings on the bundle would be evaluated by anchoring on the sum of the sale prices of individual items, which is then compared with the bundle price.

Hypothesis 2: Given that the consumer has not planned to purchase either of the items in the bundle (i.e., Purchase Plan 3), the consumer's evaluation of the savings on the bundle would be influenced by the comparison of the bundle price with the sum of the sale prices of the items if bought separately.

When Both Items in the Bundle Are Planned Purchases

Yadav and Monroe's (1993) study implicitly assumed that the buyers had plans to purchase both items in the bundle (i.e., Purchase Plan 4), and hence showed that the bundle' transaction utility would be the sum of the perceived savings on the individual items if bought separately and the additional savings when the items are bought as a bundle. Since we do not examine the evaluations of bundle offers within the context of purchase plan 4, we do not provide specific hypothesis.

RESEARCH METHOD

To examine the effects of the three purchase plans, 205 undergraduate students at a state university in the mid-west participated in a laboratory experiment for extra credit. As in the study by Yadav and Monroe (1993), two luggage items (garment bag and a duffle bag) were selected as the product stimuli. These items were selected because subjects are reasonably knowledgeable about the products as well as their prices (Yadav and Monroe 1993). In this study the regular price of the garment bag and duffle bag were $120 and $60 respectively.

Design

A 2 (savings on unplanned purchase) x 3 (purchase plans) x 3 (bundle price) between subjects design was used to create the alternative price scenarios for understanding the impact of the purchase plans. The two levels of savings on the unplanned purchase were $0 and $10, while the bundle prices were $120, $130 and $140. Three different vignettes were used to create the manipulation for the three purchase plans.

Procedure

Each response booklet introduced the subject to a vignette which was basically a manipulation for the purchase plan. Then, the subjects examined a print advertisement featuring the garment bag and the duffle bag along with their retail and sale prices and also a price (bundle price) if both items were bought together as a bundle. After examining the advertisement, subjects responded to 11 scales focussing on perceptions of the two savings in the bundle offer:

Item Transaction Value (4 items): The perception of savings associated with purchasing all bundle items separately.
Total Transaction Value (7 items): The perception of overall savings associated with purchasing the bundle of items as a set.

TABLE 1
Impact of Different Savings on the Total Transaction Value

Independent	Plan 1	Plan 2	Plan 3
Intercept	3.76	2.47	3.08
	(2.033) [a]	(4.40) [b]	(3.34) [b]
Additional	0.454	0.59	0.43
Savings on Bundle	(3.45) [b]	(4.72) [b]	(2.30) [a]
Saving on A	-0.003	0.217	.
	(-0.024)	(1.74) [c]	
Saving on B	0.194	.	0.28
	(1.467)		(1.48)
Model R^2	0.115	0.243	0.049

Note: Values in the parenthesis are t-statistics. a=$p<0.05$; b=$p<0.01$; c=$p<0.10$

TABLE 2
Bundle Price Scenario

Item	Price or Savings on Items if Bought Separately		
	Regular Price	Sale Price	Perceived Savings
A	$120	$110	$10
B	$60	$50	$10
Total	$180	$160	$20

OR Buy A and B as a set for $140
where, A = Garment Bag; B = Duffle Bag

Subjects were then asked to give thought listings about the process they followed to evaluate the (1) overall savings on the bundle, (2) savings on the garment bag, and (3) savings on the duffle bag. Finally in the last section, classification information (age, sex) and the respondents' estimates of the actual monetary savings on the bundle were obtained. Also the subjects were asked an open-ended question about their perceptions regarding the purpose of the study.

RESULTS

Factor Analysis

The 11 items used in the study were classified into two factors accounting for 73% of the variance (item transaction value 43%; total transaction value 31%). The item loadings varied from .69 to .95 and the Cronbach's alpha (n=205) for the two constructs was >0.80 [item transaction value (0.88); total transaction value (0.908)].

Manipulation Checks

With item transaction value as the dependent variable in the analysis of variance, all levels of the three factors showed significant differences: bundle price ($F_{2,204}=3.79$, $p<0.024$, $eta^2=0.039$);

purchase plan ($F_{2,204}=80.85$, $p<0.00$, $eta^2=0.464$); savings on unplanned purchase ($F_{2,204}=3.35$, $p<0.069$, $eta^2=0.018$). Using item transaction value, there was also a significant interaction effect between purchase plan and the savings on unplanned purchase ($F_{2,204}=28.19$, $p<0.00$, $eta^2=0.232$).

With total transaction value as the dependent variable in the analysis of variance, only bundle price showed significant differences: bundle price ($F_{2,204}=18.22$, $p<0.00$, $eta^2=0.163$); purchase plan ($F_{2,204}=0.33$, $p<0.72$, $eta^2=0.004$); savings on unplanned purchase ($F_{2,204}=0.86$, $p<0.356$, $eta^2 = 0.005$).

Effect of Different Types of Savings on Total Transaction Value

To determine the impact of the various types of savings i.e., additional savings on the bundle, savings on item A, and savings on item B, we conducted a regression analysis (Table 1).

Open Ended Questions

The three open-ended questions, provided information on the process used by the respondents while determining the savings on the bundle and the individual items. The responses were coded by a single judge, and were categorized into one of the fourteen different frames or processes used by the respondents to evaluate

TABLE 3
Summary of the Responses to Open-ended Questions

P.Plan	Frames								Un-Codable	Total
	1	**2**	**3**	**5**	**6**	**7**	**8**	**X**		
Plan1	6	2	13	1	10	5	-	5	22	64
Plan2	14	4	6	6	6	1	6	1	20	64
Plan3	6	11	11	8	-	5	-	2	23	66

X = Others (Miscellaneous)

the savings. Of the fourteen frames the seven frames given below were used most often (The frames are in reference to the manipulation shown in Table 2).

Frame 1: Total transaction value is the additional savings on the bundle only ($160 - $140=$20)

Frame 2: Total transaction value is perceived as a comparison of the individual items' regular prices to the bundle price ($180 - $140=$40).

Frame 3: Total transaction value is the combination of the perceived additional savings on the bundle and the perceived savings on both items if bought separately ($20 + $10 +$10=$40).

Frame 5: Total transaction value is perceived as a comparison of B's regular price($60) with the additional amount one pays to buy the bundle over and above the sale price of A ($140- $110=$30) (total transaction value=$60 - $30=$30).

Frame 6: Total transaction value is perceived as a comparison of B's sale price ($50) with the additional amount one pays to buy the bundle over and above the sale price of A ($140 - $110 =$30) (total transaction value=$50 - $30=$20).

Frame 7: Total transaction value is the combination of the perceived additional savings on the bundle and the comparison of B's sale price ($50) with the additional amount one pays to buy the bundle over and above the sale price of A ($140 - $110=$30) (total transaction value=$20 + ($50 - $30)=$40).

Frame 8: Total transaction value is perceived as a comparison of A's sale price($110) with the additional amount one pays to buy the bundle over and above the sale price of B ($140 - $50 =$90) (total transaction value=$110 - $90=$20).

It should be noted that frames 1,6 and 8 lead to a response that $20 would be saved, while frames 2,3 and 7 lead to a response that $40 would be saved. Frame 5 leads to a judged savings of $30. It is clear that different ways of processing the information could lead to *similar* judgements. The number of open ended responses corresponding to these seven frames (for each of the purchase plans) have been summarized in Table 3.

DISCUSSION

The regression coefficient for the various types of savings in Table 1, indicates that the savings on the unplanned purchase (i.e., savings on item A for Plan 2 and savings on item B for plan 1) significantly influences the total savings on the bundle for plan 2 only (beta for savings on A is 0.217; $p<0.10$). The impact of the savings on the unplanned purchase on the total savings was not significant for purchase plan 1 (beta for savings on B is 0.194; $p<0.23$). This result indicates support for hypothesis 1(b) for purchase plan 2 only, i.e., when there was a prior intention to purchase an item which had the lower price of the two items in the bundle. This result could be because of an insufficient adjustment

by the subsequent evaluation of the low-priced unplanned purchase on the planned purchase, i.e., a high price item (i.e., A), in case of purchase plan 1. On the other hand the evaluation of a low price anchor (i.e., item B in plan 2) is influenced by the subsequent evaluation of the high-priced unplanned item (i.e., A) in case of plan 2, supporting hypothesis 1(c). Overall we observed a significant effect ($p<0.05$) of the additional savings on the bundle on the evaluation of savings on the bundle (see beta coefficients in Table 1). This finding is consistent with Yadav and Monroe's (1993) argument that, when consumers evaluate the overall savings on bundle offers, the savings on the bundle has a greater effect than the savings on the individual items. Additionally, this study has also shown that the saving on the unplanned purchase has a significant impact on the evaluation of the savings on bundle offers while the saving on the planned purchase item does not (beta coefficients for savings on A under purchase plan 1 and savings on B under purchase plan 2 were not significant).

From Table 3 we conclude that when consumers have an intention to buy only one item in the bundle, they may anchor on the sale price of the planned purchase item to evaluate the bundle price and then evaluate the savings on the unplanned purchase. However, support for such a process mechanism was found only when there was a plan to purchase the higher-priced item of the two item bundle, i.e., purchase plan 1. When the planned purchase was the lower-priced item of the two item bundle i.e., purchase plan 2, there was a greater tendency to evaluate the additional savings on the bundle.

In purchase situations where there was no plan to buy either item in the bundle, the perception of the total savings on the bundle was affected significantly by the additional savings on the bundle (beta=0.43; $p< 0.05$). The effect of the savings on individual items was not significant. This finding is consistent with the notion that consumers first evaluate the additional savings on the bundle and then look at the savings on individual items in the bundle (Yadav and Monroe 1993). Thus, when there is no plan to buy either item in the bundle, consumers would evaluate the savings on the bundle offers by looking at the additional savings on the bundle, thereby avoiding further processing of savings on the individual items.

In essence our study has shown that prior intentions to purchase an item (i.e., a purchase plan) significantly influences the perception of savings on bundle offerings. Furthermore, the perception of savings and the process used to evaluate the savings on the bundle is further moderated by the price of the planned purchase vis-a-vis the unplanned purchase.

Future Research

The dependent measures used in this study need to be further developed so as to account for all three transaction values indicated

APPENDIX

Frames Used to Evaluate the Savings on the Bundle

<u>Frame 1</u>: Total transaction value is the additional savings on the bundle only

<u>Frame 2</u>: Total transaction value is perceived as a comparison of the individual items' regular prices to the bundle price.

<u>Frame 3</u>: Total transaction value is the combination of the perceived additional savings on the bundle and the perceived savings on both items if bought separately.

<u>Frame 4</u>: Total transaction value is perceived as a comparison of B's regular price with the additional amount one pays to buy the bundle over and above the regular price of A.

<u>Frame 5</u>: Total transaction value is perceived as a comparison of B's regular price with the additional amount one pays to buy the bundle over and above the sale price of A.

<u>Frame 6</u>: Total transaction value is perceived as a comparison of B's sale price with the additional amount one pays to buy the bundle over and above the sale price of A.

<u>Frame 7</u>: Total transaction value is the combination of the perceived additional savings on the bundle and the comparison of B's sale price with the additional amount one pays to buy the bundle over and above the sale price of A.

<u>Frame 8</u>: Total transaction value is perceived as a comparison of A's sale price with the additional amount one pays to buy the bundle over and above the sale price of B.

<u>Frame 9</u>: Total transaction value is perceived as a comparison of the individual items' regular prices to their sale prices.

<u>Frame 10</u>: Total transaction value is perceived as a comparison of A's regular price with the additional amount one pays to buy the bundle over and above the sale price of B.

<u>Frame 11</u>: Total transaction value is a combination of the perceived additional savings on the bundle and the perceived savings on item A only.

<u>Frame 12</u>: Total transaction value is the combination of the perceived additional savings on the bundle and the perceived savings on item B only.

<u>Frame 13</u>: Total transaction value is perceived as a comparison of B's sale price with the additional amount one pays to buy the bundle over and above the regular price of A.

<u>Frame 14</u>: Total transaction value is perceived as a comparison of B's sale price with the additional amount one pays to buy the bundle over and above the sale price of A.

Open-ended questions

(A) Please elaborate on and write down the steps you followed while evaluating this offer (i.e., with both the garment bag and the tote bag).

(B) Please elaborate on and write down the steps you followed while evaluating the savings on the *Garment bag*.

(C) Please elaborate on the steps you followed while evaluating the savings on the *Duffle bag*.

---

in the study by Yadav and Monroe (1993), i.e., bundle transaction value, item transaction value and total transaction value. Despite having borrowed the measures from Yadav and Monroe study, the present study could find only two factors that could explain the item and total transaction value. Furthermore the coding of the results of the open ended questions indicate that the respondents' prior purchase of one of the bundle items or the relevance of the items (stimuli) to the respondents did influence their evaluations of the bundle offers. This suggests a future research possibility of determining the effects of prior experience with the purchase of a product or prior knowledge about an item in the bundle on the evaluation of the bundle offer.

REFERENCES

Adams, W. J. and J.L.Yellen (1976), "Commodity Bundling and the Burden of Monopoly," *Quarterly Journal Of Economics*, 90(August), 475-98.

Anderson, Norman H.(1981), *Foundations of Information Integration Theory*, New York: Academic Press.

Beach, L. R. and T. R. Mitchell (1978),"A Contingency Model for the Selection of Decision Strategies," *Academy of Management Review* (3), 439-449.

Chakravarti, Dipankar, Rajan Krish, Pallab Paul and Joydeep Srivastava (1994),"Segregated and Consolidated Presentation and Pricing of Product Bundles: Influences on Evaluation and Choice," Working Paper, University of Arizona, Tucson, Arizona 85721.

Dansby, Robert E. and Cecilia Conrad (1984),"Commodity Bundling," *American Economic Review*, 74(May), 377-381.

Davis, Harry L., Stephen J. Hoch, and E. K. Easton Ragsdale (1986), "An Anchoring and Adjustment Model of Spousal Predictions," *Journal of Consumer Research*, 13(June), 25-37.

Gaeth, Gary J., Irwin P. Lewin, Goutam Chakraborty, and Aron M. Levin (1990), "Consumer Evaluation of Multi-Product Bundles: An Information Integration Analysis," *Marketing Letters*, 2(January), 42-57.

Joyce, Edward and Gary C. Biddle (1981), "Anchoring and Adjustment in Probabilistic Inference in Auditing," *Journal of Accounting Research*, 19(Spring), 120-145.

Kahneman, Daniel and Amos Tversky (1974),"Prospect Theory; An Analysis of Decision Under Risk," *Econometrica*, 47 (March), 263-91.

Kaicker, Ajit, William O. Bearden and Joel E. Urbany (1993),"The Effects of Incremental Savings, Perceived Quality and Perceived Sacrifice on Evaluations of Focal and Add-On Products Used to Form Product Bundles," Working Paper, University of South Carolina, Columbia, SC.

Nagle, Thomas (1984),"Economic Foundations of Pricing," *Journal of Business Research*, 57 (No. 1, Part 2), 3-26.

Northcraft, Gregory B. and Margaret A. Neale (1987),"Experts, Amateurs, and Real Estate: An Anchoring and Adjustment Perspective on Property Pricing Decisions," *Organizational Behavior and Human Decision Processes*, 39(February), 84-97.

Payne, John. W., James. R. Bettman and Eric. J. Johnson (1988),"Adaptive Strategy Selection in Decision Making," *Journal of Experimental Psychology: Learning, Memory and Cognition* (14), 534-552.

Schmalensee, Richard A.(1984)," Commodity Bundling by Single Product Monopolies," *Journal of Law and Economics*, 25 (April), 67-72.

Stigler, George J.(1961),"The Economics of Information," *Journal of Political Economy*, 69 (June), 213-25.

Thaler, Richard (1985), "Mental Accounting and Consumer Choice," *Marketing Science*, 4 (Summer), 199-214.

Tversky, Amos and Daniel Kahneman (1974),"Judgement under Uncertainty: Heuristics and Biases," *Science*, 185 (September), 1124-1131.

Yadav, Manjit S. and Kent B. Monroe (1993),"How Buyers Perceive Savings in a Bundle Price: An Examination of Bundle's Transaction Value," *Journal of Marketing Research*,30 (August), 350-358.

Yadav, Manjit (1994),"How Buyers Evaluate Product Bundles: A Model of Anchoring and Adjustment," *Journal of Consumer Research*, 21 (September), 342-353.

Yadav, Manjit (1990),"An Examination of How Buyers Subjectively Perceive and Evaluate Product Bundles," Unpublished Doctoral Dissertation, Department of Marketing, Virginia Polytechnic Institute and State University, Blacksburg, VA 24061.

Customer Relationships with Retail Salespeople: A Conceptual Model and Propositions

Kristy L. Ellis, University of Alabama
Sharon E. Beatty, University of Alabama

ABSTRACT

The concept of relationship marketing has assumed a significant role in the practice and study of marketing. Relationship marketing has been studied in several contexts. However, the state of knowledge in the area of long-term customer relationships with retail salespeople is very limited. This paper proposes a model of the relationship seeking/maintaining process. In addition, a relationship classification schema, which uses personal needs to classify customers in terms of the types of relationships they have with salespeople in a department store setting, is presented. Research propositions are also offered.

INTRODUCTION

The emergence of the concept of relationship marketing has had an enormous impact on business practitioners and academicians alike. Under a relationship orientation, the emphasis is on the maintenance of long-term exchange relationships with customers. This implies that firms must consider how their actions, policies, and training procedures will best facilitate long-term relationship development and maintenance with their customers (Czepiel 1990a). In this respect, managing salesperson-customer relationships is vital for retailing and service firms, in that the salesperson *is* often the company in the customer's eyes, and can significantly add value to the product with the provision of psychological and social utilities (Gummesson 1987; Czepiel 1990a). Thus, how the customer-salesperson relationship should be managed is of utmost importance. In order to do this, managers need more information regarding the customer's view of the customer-salesperson relationship. Thus, our focus in this paper is on the nature and types of customer-salesperson relationships and the reasons for relationships, from a customer perspective.

This issue—how companies can more effectively encourage the development and maintenance of long-term relationships with retail customers—has received some attention (cf. Berry and Gresham 1986). Relationship building processes in the services marketing, channels, and industrial marketing areas have been discussed (cf. Congram 1987; Dwyer, Schurr, and Oh 1987; Gummesson 1987; Hakansson 1982). Although there is a considerable amount of overlap in terms of critical variables, and the issue is controversial, (see, for example, Fern and Brown (1984)), we feel that there are important differences between industrial and channel settings/relationships and consumer settings/relationships. Heavily studied relationship marketing contexts (industrial markets and channels) share several commonalties, such as the complexity of exchanged assets, a limited number of partners, high switching costs, and contractual arrangements (Hakansson 1982). These structural characteristics do not necessarily apply to retail contexts and other consumer marketing areas.

While the importance of building long-term relationships and relationship strategies and processes have received some attention in consumer marketing contexts, other aspects of long-term buyer-seller relationships have been ignored. The long-term relationship between salespeople and customers in a retail setting as viewed from the customer's perspective is one such area. Several authors have discussed the nature and types of customer expectations in service relationships and how the organization should respond to these expectations (cf. Parasuraman, Zeithaml, and Berry 1991;

Webster 1991; Zeithaml, Berry, and Parasuraman 1993). In addition, it has been suggested that customers want relationships with retail sales personnel (Beatty et al. 1993; Parasuraman et al. 1991). For example, Berry and Parasuraman (1991) found that customers want ongoing, close relationships with the salespeople with whom they deal.

Further, the increasing time-related demands felt by the customer of the 1990s and the growing adversity to shopping will likely make relationships with salespeople very popular due to time saving and other benefits they can provide (Solomon 1987; Meyer 1990). Yet, no one has examined customers' reasons for engaging in relationships with sales personnel, the nature of these relationships, or their consequences (Ellis, Lee, and Beatty 1993).

Evidence of distinct types of relationships between customers and retail salespeople exists. Beatty et al. (1993) examined long-term relationships between customers and salespeople in a high-service department store setting using naturalistic inquiry. These researchers discovered that some relationships were mainly functional or economic in nature—the customer valued convenience, time savings, the salesperson's product knowledge, etc.

Other customers, while recognizing the functional benefits of the relationships, valued the social aspects of the relationships more highly. That is, these customers benefited immensely from the friendship, conversation, company, and other social interactions with the salesperson. A third group of customers revealed that they benefited from both the functional and the social aspects of their relationships. A series of additional depth interviews with "relationship" customers of the same department store verified these functional, social, and combination functional-social types of relationships. Others have suggested similar relationship types (Turnbull and Wilson 1989; Czepiel 1990a; 1990b; Mummalaneni and Wilson 1991).

Further, there is a vast array of literature in the shopping/patronage motivations area, in which researchers have sought to identify customers' motivations for shopping and to categorize customers in terms of their shopping orientations. Although comparability of studies in this area is difficult, both economically and socially motivated shopper types have consistently appeared (cf. Stone 1954; Darden and Reynolds 1971; Moschis 1976; Bellenger and Korgaonkar 1980; Westbrook and Black 1985). Although the area of shopping motivations provides an excellent starting point to begin analyzing customers' needs and reasons for relationships, this literature base does not address these ideas from a relationship perspective. Further, shopping motives are not equivalent to relationship motives. However, research in the shopping/patronage motivations area has addressed other issues, including personal characteristics of shoppers, such as demographics, lifestyles, and psychographics, as correlates of different patterns of store patronage (Sheth 1983). Obviously, an important question is, "What personal characteristics or needs cause customers to seek/maintain long-term relationships with salespeople or service providers?" Further, how do these characteristics/needs affect the nature of the relationship established? And, can these relationships be defined by their functional and social dimensions, as suggested by Beatty et al. (1993)?

We are also interested in the extent to which relationships occur across retail/service settings, as well as the potential outcomes of these relationships. Thus, the first objective of this paper is to provide an initial conceptual model of the relationship seeking/ maintaining process. Then, a relationship classification schema, which categorizes customers in terms of the types of salesperson relationships they are most likely to have, is offered. In addition, a series of propositions related to the model and schema are provided. Because the various constructs included in the model and schema emerged from exploratory work conducted in a fashion department store, our interests here are focused primarily on fashion issues, i.e., clothing and accessories. Some driving needs identified may be context specific, but most are likely to be generalizable across broader contexts.

A customer-salesperson relationship exists when there is an ongoing series of interactions between a customer and a salesperson. The parties know each other, trust each other, and the interactions have occurred in the past, are presently occurring, and are expected to occur over an extended period of time in the future, barring unavoidable circumstances. A relationship may vary on such factors as the degree of closeness, the length and frequency of contact, and the amount of commitment, depending on the preferences and situations of the individuals involved.

We are interested in this relationship seeking/maintaining customer segment and use the terms "seeking/maintaining" or "engaging in" relationships to describe what is happening. "Maintaining" is used because many customers currently have relationships with retail salespeople. "Seeking" also applies because customers may also look for relationships in other settings, but may or may not be able to find them. "Engaging in" encompasses both seeking and maintaining.

The following section describes the overall conceptual model— the relationship seeking/maintaining process. Next, a relationship classification schema, which depicts relationship types (social, functional, and combination social-functional) in terms of their connection to the personal need variables, is described. Research propositions are also presented within the discussion.

CONCEPTUAL FRAMEWORK

Conceptual Model: The Relationship Seeking/Maintaining Process

The relationship seeking/maintaining process is presented in Figure 1.1. Someone who seeks/maintains relationships with salespeople is likely to be a heavy apparel purchaser (HAP) or there will be little value in maintaining a relationship from either the salesperson's or the customer's perspective. HAPs are likely to spend money on clothing/accessories in three ways: (1) traditional shopping in retail outlets (such as department stores or specialty stores) or outlet stores/malls; (2) shopping through "direct" retail outlets, such as mail order catalogs or television home shopping; and/or (3) buying products through their relationships with salespeople. The customer of interest in this paper is of the third type. This individual acquires a significant portion of his/her clothing/ accessories through relationship(s) with retail sales associates.

Next, several personal needs, categorized as functional and/or social, encourage a HAP to engage in relationships with salespeople or service providers. The different personal needs translate into different perceived benefits and lead to the varying types of relationships. The actual relationship and/or relationship benefits may lead to relationship seeking/maintaining in other settings. Personal needs may also lead to seeking/maintaining other relationships.

Results of having an ongoing relationship with a salesperson are likely to be satisfaction with the relationship, which leads to greater sales person/store loyalty, and behavioral outcomes, such as positive word of mouth and higher levels of purchasing (Berry and Parasuraman 1991). Finally, satisfaction with the current relationship may also lead to customers seeking relationships in other settings.

Relationships and Personal Needs

A relationship classification schema is presented in Figure 1.2. Heavy apparel purchasing is not part of the model in terms of the four cells. Instead, a customer must initially be a heavy apparel purchaser (HAP) to be a potential "relationship customer."

To fully understand why some HAPs choose to engage in relationships to obtain much of their apparel and accessories, we need to examine their personal needs. It is likely that HAPs with different needs will seek different benefits from relationships with salespeople or service providers. We believe four personal needs drive HAPs to value and engage in relationships, and determine the benefits valued and the corresponding nature of the relationship. These variables are now described.

Perception of Time/Role Overload. Many factors have contributed to the rise in the perception of time scarcity among consumers. For example, the increased number of working wives and single parent households has been cited as a possible cause contributing to the perception of time scarcity. Whatever the cause, perceived time shortage is believed to result in perceived role overload (RO), which "occurs when the total prescribed activities of one or more roles are greater than individuals can handle adequately or comfortably" (Voydanoff and Kelly 1984, p. 881). Reilly (1982) describes RO as "conflict that occurs when the sheer volume of behavior demanded...exceeds available time and energy" (p. 408).

Shopping Enjoyment. Solomon (1987) studied surrogate consumers, or wardrobe consultants, in the apparel area. These individuals serve in roles that are similar to some of the roles fulfilled by sales associates engaging in customer relationships. Solomon (1987) verified that some consumers use a wardrobe consultant primarily because they do not like to shop. Likewise, Forsythe et al. (1990) found that nonusers of professional shoppers enjoy shopping more than users. Thus, the surrogate provides customers the functional benefits of engaging or aiding in the search and selection process, which are greatly valued by individuals who do not enjoy shopping.

Shopping Confidence. Solomon (1986, 1987) also discusses the symbolic benefits that are part of the professional shopper's product offering. Symbolically, a surrogate can offer "such subjective benefits as stylistic guidance, reassurance, or status" (Solomon 1987, p.113). These consumers may feel that they lack the expertise to shop wisely for clothing. Therefore, lacking confidence in their shopping capabilities, they consequently turn to a salesperson for guidance and support.

Sociability. It is useful to examine whether variables that affect a person's interpersonal relationships in general also affect a person's relationships with salespeople. One personal need that may affect the nature of a customer-salesperson relationship is sociability. According to Buss and Plomin (1975), the highly sociable person, by definition, seeks relationships. This "temperament...has a directional component: seeking other persons, preferring their presence, and responding to them" (p. 88). Highly sociable people tend to appreciate friendships and opportunities to engage in relationships.

Description of Cell Members. These needs may be used to classify HAPs in terms of the types of relationships they tend to have: social, functional, and a combination of social and functional.

FIGURE 1.1
Overall Conceptual Model
The Relationship Seeking/Maintaining Process

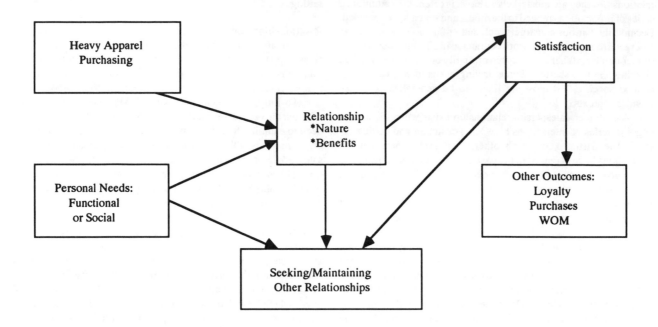

FIGURE 1.2
Relationship Classification Schema

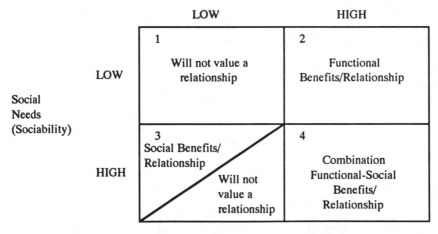

Role overload (RO), lack of shopping enjoyment, and lack of shopping confidence may be translated into functional needs. That is, an individual who is high on one or more of these functional variables is said to have high functional needs for a relationship. Social needs pertain to an individual's level of sociability. Someone who is high on sociability has high social needs. Each cell of the schema is now described as it relates to the personal needs.

Cell 1 describes HAPs who are low on both social and functional needs. They enjoy shopping, are confident in their own

shopping, do not feel that they are significantly pressed for time (that is, do not perceive high RO), and are not highly sociable. This group of customers tends to not engage in relationships because there is no strong need for such relationships.

Cell 2 consists of HAPs who don't like to shop, do not have confidence in their ability to shop, and/or perceive a high amount of RO, but are not highly sociable. Having high functional needs and low social needs, these customers tend to value and seek relationships which are functionally based. Thus, these customers value such services as merchandise selection and coordination, and having merchandise ready for pick up.

Cell 3 is split because social needs alone are not a sufficient antecedent to seeking relationships. The upper half of Cell 3 contains the HAP with high social needs and low functional needs. This person is highly sociable and enjoys shopping, is confident is his/her own shopping, and does not perceive high RO. Although this individual may benefit functionally from the services provided, it is mainly the social aspects of the relationships that s/he values when s/he chooses to engage in a relationship. There are also HAPs in this cell who do not engage in relationships because they have low functional needs (i.e., they like to shop, are confident in their shopping, and do not perceive high RO). These individuals tend to value shopping for themselves more than the social benefits provided by a relationship.

HAPs who are highly sociable and also do not enjoy shopping, are not confident in their shopping abilities, and/or perceive RO fall into *Cell 4.* These individuals need the functional services provided by salespeople, but also need and desire the social aspects of their relationships.

The following research propositions relate to the schema previously discussed.

H1: *HAPs who score low on both functional and social needs:*
   a) are least likely of all groups to have relationships:
   b) do not tend to value relationship benefits; and
   c) do not tend to seek additional relationships.

H2: *HAPs who score high on functional needs and low on social needs:*
   a) are most likely of all groups to have functional relationships;
   b) value functional benefits more than social benefits;
   c) tend to have functional relationships more so than social relationships; and
   d) seek additional functional relationships more so than social relationships.

H3: *Relationship customers who score high on social needs and low on functional needs:*
   a) are most likely of all groups to have social relationships;
   b) value social benefits more than functional benefits;
   c) have social relationships more so than functional relationships; and
   d) seek additional social relationships more so than functional relationships.

H4: *HAPs who score high on both functional and social needs:*
   a) are most likely of all groups to have combination functional and social relationships;
   b) value both functional and social benefits;
   c) have combination functional and social relationships; and
   d) seek additional combination relationships.

Relationship Consequences

According to several authors, both the economic and social needs of the exchange partners may be met in buyer-seller relationships (Dwyer et al. 1987; Turnbull and Wilson 1989; Czepiel 1990a; 1990b; Mummalaneni and Wilson 1991). These types of customer-salesperson relationships tend to be very close, with high levels of trust existing between the parties (Beatty et al. 1993). This closeness and trust allow customers' needs, both functional and social, to be met exceedingly well. Thus, satisfaction and loyalty are likely to result (Dwyer et al. 1987; Berry et al. 1991; Parasuraman et al. 1991). Finally, additional outcomes may follow from satisfaction and loyalty, namely positive word-of-mouth and purchases (Berry et al. 1991). In addition, because of the satisfaction that is likely to result when relationship customers' needs are met, these individuals are likely to seek/maintain relationships with salespeople/service providers in other settings (Beatty et al. 1993). The above discussion leads to the following research propositions.

H5: *HAPs who engage in relationships:*
   a) are more satisfied with the company than are those who do not engage in relationships.
   b) are more loyal to the company than those who do not engage in relationships.
   c) have higher purchase levels with the company than those who do not engage in relationships.
   d) are more likely to exhibit word of mouth about the company than are those who do not engage in relationships.

H6: *Relationship benefits lead to:*
   a) satisfaction with the relationship/salesperson;
   b) satisfaction with the company; and
   c) similar relationship seeking/maintaining in other settings.

H7: *Relationship/salesperson satisfaction leads to:*
   a) satisfaction with the company;
   b) salesperson loyalty;
   c) company loyalty;
   d) higher levels of purchasing with the salesperson;
   e) higher levels of purchasing with the company;
   f) positive word of mouth about the salesperson;
   g) positive word of mouth about the company;
   h) similar relationship seeking/maintaining in other settings.

CONCLUSION

In conclusion, relationship marketing has been studied in several areas of marketing. However, research involving the customer-salesperson relationship in retail settings, particularly from a customer perspective, is severely lacking. Studying these types of relationships has several practical and theoretical implications.

First, from a managerial viewpoint, knowing why some customers have relationships and what benefits they value is important. This would allow managers to specifically target the different types of relationship customers. In this era of intense competition between retailers, creating a competitive advantage is essential to survival of retailing firms. Berry and his colleagues talk about creating customer delight and exceeding customer expectations. One way to accomplish this, we believe, is by developing and maintaining customer-salesperson relationships. Since loyalty and satisfaction are likely results of these relationships, retailers should find the practice of relationship development and maintenance an attractive alternative to competing in the marketplace. Studying this issue would enhance our ability to do this.

Finally, theory in this area of marketing is almost non-existent. Hopefully this paper will serve as a beginning in the theory building process and in the study of customer-salesperson relationships in other retail/service settings.

REFERENCES

Beatty, Sharon E., Morris L. Mayer, James E. Coleman, Kristy L. Ellis, and Jungki Lee (1993), "Long-Term Buyer-Seller Relationships in a Retail Context: A Naturalistic Inquiry," Working Paper, The University of Alabama.

Bellenger, Danny N. and Pradeep K. Korgaonkar (1980), "Profiling the Recreational Shopper," *Journal of Retailing*, 56 (Fall), 77-91.

Berry, Leonard L. and Larry G. Gresham (1986), "Relationship Retailing: Transforming Customers into Clients," *Business Horizons*, November-December, 43-7.

_____ and A. Parasuraman (1991), *Marketing Services: Competing Through Quality*, New York: The Free Press.

Buss, Arnold H. and Robert Plomin (1975), *A Temperament Theory of Personality Development*, New York: John Wiley and Sons.

Congram, Carole A. (1987), "Managing Long-Term Relationships," in *The Services Challenge: Integrating for Competitive Advantage*, John A. Czepiel, Carole A. Congram, and James Shanahan, eds. Chicago: American Marketing Association, 95-96.

Czepiel, John A. (1990a), "Service Encounters and Service Relationships: Implications for Research," *Journal of Business Research*, 20, 13-21.

_____ (1990b), "Managing Relationships with Customers: A Differentiating Philosophy of Marketing," in *Service Management Effectiveness: Balancing Strategy, Organization and Human Resources, Operations and Marketing*, David E. Bowen, Richard B. Chase, and Thomas E. Cummings and Associates, eds. San Francisco: Jossey-Bass, 299-323.

Darden, William R. and Fred D. Reynolds (1971), "Shopping Orientations and Product Usage Roles," *Journal of Marketing Research*, 8 (November), 505-508.

Dwyer, Robert F., Paul H. Schurr, and Sejo Oh (1987), "Developing Buyer-Seller Relationships," *Journal of Marketing*, 51 (April), 11-27.

Ellis, Kristy L., Jungki Lee, and Sharon E. Beatty (1993), "Relationships in Consumer Marketing: Directions for Future Research," in *Enhancing Knowledge Development in Marketing*, Vol. 4, David W. Cravens and Peter R. Dickson, eds. Chicago: American Marketing Association, 225-230.

Fern, Edward F. And James R. Brown (1984), "The Industrial/Consumer Marketing Dichotomy: A Case of Insufficient Justification," *Journal of Marketing*, 48 (Spring), 68-77.

Forsythe, Sandra, Sara Butler, and Robert Schaefer (1990), "Surrogate Usage in the Acquisition of Women's Business Apparel," *Journal of Retailing*, 66 (Winter), 446-69.

Gummesson, Evert (1987), "The New Marketing—Developing Long-Term Interactive Relationships," *Long Range Planning*, 20 (4), 10-20.

Hakansson, Hakan (1982), *International Marketing and Purchasing of Industrial Goods: An Interaction Approach*, New York, NY: John Wiley and Sons.

Meyer, Edward H. (1990), "Retail on the Rebound," *Direct Marketing* (May), 53.

Moschis, George P. (1976), "Shopping Orientations and Consumer Uses of Information," *Journal of Retailing*, 52 (Summer) 61-70.

Mummalaneni, Venkatapparao and David T. Wilson (1991), "The Influence of a Close Personal Relationship Between a Buyer and a Seller on the Continued Stability of Their Role Relationship," ISBM Report 4-1991, College of Business Administration, Penn State University.

Parasuraman, A., Leonard L. Berry, and Valerie A. Zeithaml (1991), "Understanding Customer Expectations of Service," *Sloan Management Review*, Spring, 39-48.

Reilly, Michael D. (1982), "Working Wives and Convenience Consumption," *Journal of Consumer Research*, 8 (March), 407-418.

Sheth, Jagdish N. (1983), "An Integrative Theory of Patronage Preference and Behavior," in *Patronage Behavior and Retail Management*, William R. Darden and Robert F. Lusch, eds. New York: North-Holland, 8-28.

Solomon, Michael (1986), "The Missing Link: Surrogate Consumers in the Marketing Chain," *Journal of Marketing*, 50 (October), 208-218.

_____ (1987), "The Wardrobe Consultant: Exploring the Role of a New Retailing Partner," *Journal of Retailing*, 63 (Summer), 110-128.

Stone, Gregory P. (1954), "City Shoppers and Urban Identification: Observation on the Social Psychology of City Life," *American Journal of Sociology*, 60 (July), 36-45.

Turnbull, Peter W. And David T. Wilson (1989), "Developing and Protecting Profitable Customer Relationships, *Industrial Marketing Management*, 18 (August), 233-238.

Voydanoff, Patricia and Robert F. Kelly (1984), Determinants of Work-Related Family Problems Among Employed Parents," *Journal of Marriage and the Family*, 46 (November), 881-892.

Webster, Cynthia (1991), "Influences Upon Consumer Expectations of Services," *Journal of Services Marketing*, 5 (Winter), 5-17.

Westbrook, Robert A. and William C. Black (1985), "A Motivation-Based Shopper Typology," *Journal of Retailing*, 61 (Spring), 78-103.

Zeithaml, Valerie A., Leonard L. Berry, and A. Parasuraman (1993), "The Nature and Determinants of Customer Expectations of Service," *Journal of the Academy of Marketing Science*, 21 (Winter), 1-12.

Assessing Actual Service Performance:
Incongruities Between Expectation and Evaluation Criteria

Valerie A. Taylor, University of South Carolina
Anthony D. Miyazaki, University of South Carolina[1]

ABSTRACT

A key link in both service quality and service satisfaction models is the link between the actual service and the perceived service. However, this link, which is particularly critical for services that are high in credence qualities, is often weak and has received limited attention in the marketing and consumer behavior literature. The processes involved in forming expectations and evaluations for such services are considered in this paper and particular incongruities are illustrated. The authors then present propositions which examine the process by which consumers may evaluate services high in credence attributes and discuss consumer and marketer implications of the discussed incongruities.

INTRODUCTION

Significant advances are being made concerning satisfaction and quality perceptions for services. However, a key link in the service quality model has received limited attention: the link between the actual service and the perceived service, particularly regarding services high in credence attributes (i.e., those that cannot be easily evaluated by consumers without consulting expert opinion [Steenkamp 1990]). Because many consumers are not able to appropriately evaluate services high in credence attributes (e.g., auto repair, technical services, medical procedures), there are concerns regarding consumer fraud. Specifically, the opportunity exists for service providers to misrepresent services that are needed or performed, which ultimately might result in monetary and other types of losses to consumers and loss of consumer confidence toward the companies or industries involved. (Additionally, consumer inability to appropriately evaluate services high in credence attributes might alternatively work *against* the service provider. In this situation, rather than consumer fraud, the concern is that consumers may perceive the service more negatively than deserved.)

Consequently, an understanding of the processes involved in consumer evaluations of services high in credence attributes would make an important contribution from both public policy and management perspectives. In this paper we explore a portion of the decision making process that consumers face in making judgments about service quality. Specifically, we address the attribute incongruities between expectations and evaluations and the role of ambiguity in the consumer satisfaction process for services high in credence attributes (cf. Bolton and Drew 1991; Parasuraman, Zeithaml, and Berry 1985; Spreng and Olshavsky 1993).

The "Sixth Gap"

In their conceptual model of service quality Parasuraman et al. (1985) illustrate five discrepancies or gaps "regarding executive perceptions of service quality and the tasks associated with service delivery to consumers" (p. 44). The five identified gaps are (1) consumer expectation—management perception, (2) management perception—service quality specification, (3) service quality specifications—service delivery, (4) service delivery—external communications, and (5) expected service—perceived service.

Our research concerns services which are high in credence attributes, and are therefore difficult, if not impossible, for consumers to evaluate. In essence a sixth gap is indicated for services in which technical (actual) performance cannot be reasonably assessed. This sixth gap is a critical discrepancy between service delivery (the actual service) and service perception (on which consumer evaluations must be based). Although the Parasuraman et al. (1985) model indicates an essential connection between service delivery and service perception, Zeithaml (1988) illustrates the lack of correspondence often found between objective quality (actual service delivery) and subjective quality (based on the service perception). When a consumer is unable to form a reasonably accurate perception of the service being rendered, whether due to lack of knowledge on the consumer's part or due to the nature of the service (i.e., key attributes take the form of credence properties), the consumer will undoubtedly experience difficulties in forming an accurate or unbiased evaluation of service quality (cf. Klein and Oglethorpe 1987). Unfortunately, the inadequacy in the evaluation may not be known to the consumer (a critical issue with both managerial and public policy concerns, and one that we consider in the following discussion). It is noted that the examination of the sixth gap is important to researchers of service satisfaction as well as service quality, since both rely on a service perception that should reasonably reflect the actual service delivery.

Service Satisfaction and Service Quality

Much of the recent service satisfaction and service quality literature has focused on a disconfirmation model, in which consumers compare their perceptions of the service with some comparison standard, resulting in a feeling of satisfaction or dissatisfaction, or a judgment of service quality (Bearden and Teel 1983; Hill 1986; Parasuraman et al. 1985). Service perception has also been referred to as an evaluation or perception of service performance. However, it is important to note that this evaluation is *not* equivalent to an estimation of service quality. In fact, this evaluation (or perhaps, more clearly stated, "service perception") has been proposed to be an antecedent to the development of a service quality assessment (Bolton and Drew 1991; Cronin and Taylor 1992; Parasuraman et al. 1985, 1988).[2] Several variants of the disconfirmation model also exist for service satisfaction, yet all depend on service perception in order to form the satisfaction judgment (see, e.g., McGill and Iacobucci 1992; Spreng and Olshavsky 1993; Yi 1993).

Although there is currently conflict regarding the particular processes that lead to satisfaction and quality judgments, one

---

[1]The authors thank Bill Bearden, Joe Urbany, and three anonymous reviewers for their insightful suggestions.

[2]Although some controversy exists concerning the use of the disconfirmation model for service quality measurement, both the Cronin and Taylor (1992) SERVPERF measure and the Parasuraman et al. (1988) SERVQUAL measure use service perception (i.e., service "performance" perception) as a key determinant in assessing service quality. Thus, the formation of an accurate service perception is critical to the consumer's construction of a quality assessment in either model.

common premise in the literature is that the consumer is able to somewhat accurately assess the performance of the actual service. Considering that some core benefit is initially sought by consumers when soliciting a service, this core benefit would appear to be the most important factor from an overall economic perspective. (That is, the core benefit should be key to decisions involving satisfaction, quality judgments, willingness to pay, and desire for repeat purchases.) Thus, to make meaningful satisfaction judgments and tenable estimations of quality, one must first be able to make a reasonably accurate evaluation of the service performance in question, that is, the core benefit. In light of this necessity, it is essential to understand the estimation and evaluation processes that are based on what often is a misconstrued perception of "true" service performance.

PERCEIVING AND EVALUATING SERVICE ENCOUNTERS

Credence Nature of Many Services. People often purchase and consume services that are high in credence attributes, which Darby and Karni (1973) define as "those [attributes] which, although worthwhile, cannot be evaluated in normal use" (p. 68).[3] This is the case when consumers are unfamiliar with the intricacies of a particular service, and thus must purchase diagnostic information at an additional cost (often from the same service provider). Darby and Karni propose that the line between experience attributes and credence attributes is sometimes fuzzy, in that some credence attributes may become discernable after the passage of time. For example, treatment received by a doctor for back pain might not be assessable directly following the initial service visit or prescription of medication, but over time, the continuation or cessation of pain provides evidence of the effectiveness (or lack thereof) of the doctor's care.

The credence nature of many services creates a dilemma for consumer evaluation of these services. Darby and Karni (1973) suggest that the implications surrounding this dilemma are potentially severe, and that opportunities exist for service providers to fraudulently misdiagnose and/or mismanage service encounters (see, e.g., Yin 1992).

Core benefits and peripheral benefits. When a service is purchased, buyers are presumably in need of, or desire, some "core benefit" in exchange for their funds. Although other benefits may also be both expected and included in the final service package, the core benefit presumably drives the buyer to seek out a service provider. Peripheral benefits, however, may be either added benefits that carry obvious monetary or convenience value (e.g., a "loaner" car or shuttle service while one's car is being repaired) or marketer-controlled environmental factors that enhance the pleasure or comfort (or reduce the discomfort) associated with the service encounter, (e.g., a clean and pleasant waiting area or the availability of fresh coffee while waiting).[4] Thus, core service

benefits are those central to the solicitation of the service, and result from the actual performance of the core service. Peripheral service benefits include all other benefits, such as those resulting from the marketer-controlled service environment, the manner of delivery of the core service, and buyer-seller interactions.

Consider the previous example of going to a physician for the treatment of back pain. The core benefit of soliciting the physician's services would be to relieve oneself of the back pain. Peripheral benefits that carry monetary or convenience value might include receiving training or instruction on how to prevent back pain, and perhaps home remedies for dealing with future pain. Peripheral benefits that enhance the comfort of the service encounter might include friendly staff, a pleasant waiting area, and the appearance of professional treatment. Other peripheral benefits may fall into both categories, such as a timely appointment, a short waiting time, and convenient parking.

The literature is replete with examples of how different "peripheral" benefits may be important in determining satisfaction, perceived quality, and in deciding which service provider to choose (see, e.g., Bearden and Teel 1983; Bitner 1990, 1991; Bitner, Booms, and Tetreault 1990; Churchill and Surprenant 1982; Crosby and Stephens 1987; McGill and Iacobucci 1992; Parasuraman et al. 1985, 1988). Unfortunately, little focus has been given to the role that the "core" service benefit plays in determining these outcomes, particularly in cases where the core benefit is high in credence attributes.

The Table presents several marketplace examples of services high in credence attributes with each core benefit and set of peripheral benefits. A delineation is made between the core and peripheral benefits sought. Further, a distinction is made between expectation and evaluation attributes. As is evident from the Table, in each instance there is clearly an expectation for the core attribute. However, unless a consumer is an expert in the particular service category, there is no way to evaluate this attribute directly. For instance, in the case of the oil change service, unless consumers are sufficiently knowledgeable, they have no way to evaluate that the oil in their vehicle was changed correctly (or even changed at all), although this expectation surely exists. Therefore, the inability to objectively evaluate a service, or (in many cases) to even determine whether it was performed, may bias or obstruct the processes of satisfaction judgment and service quality perception that are discussed in the literature. In other words, if consumers are not able to directly evaluate the performance of a particular service, they may base their judgments of service quality on the "wrong reasons" (i.e., not on the core service benefit). This may then result in the consumer forming satisfaction judgments based on the evaluation of peripheral service benefits rather than core service benefits, and hence interject bias into the evaluation of the core service benefits. Thus, if consumers cannot "accurately" determine the performance of a particular service with respect to the core service benefit, they cannot form either satisfaction judgments or perceptions of service quality that accurately reflect the performance of that core service benefit. We now explain the impact of this phenomenon in more detail and offer several propositions.

PROPOSITIONS
To this point we have illustrated the importance of understanding how consumers and marketers deal with the dilemma identified in "the sixth gap": the disparity which often occurs between service delivery and perceived service performance. We now present a conceptualization of the evaluation process surrounding the sixth gap, which is discussed within the framework of the disconfirmation paradigm, wherein expectations are compared to perceived performance in making satisfaction judgments.

---

[3]Nelson (1970) delineates between "search" qualities (those which can be known before purchase) and "experience" qualities (those which can be known only after purchase). Darby and Karni (1973) further specify that experience attributes can be known costlessly after purchase, while credence attributes "are expensive to judge even after purchase" (p. 69).

[4]The "service encounter" encompasses the period of time in which the buyer experiences the service (Bitner, Booms, and Tetreault 1990; Shostack 1985). Most models assume that the consumer can use both quality cues and quality attributes (cf. Steenkamp 1990) to make evaluative judgments concerning the service encounter.

TABLE
Marketplace Examples of Services High in Credence Attributes

<u>Typical Expectation Attributes</u>	<u>Typical Evaluation Attributes</u>
1. A routine physical examination by a physician.	
Core Benefit:	
valid & complete diagnosis	—
Peripheral Benefits:	
treated w/ compassion	"bedside manner"
short waiting time	waiting time
have questions answered	answers to questions
	filing for insurance
2. Optometrist	
Core:	
accurate prescription	—
Peripheral:	
Waiting time	waiting time
	time spent diagnosing prescription
	"chairside manner"
3. Oil change	
Core:	
Oil changed correctly	—
(longer engine life)	
Peripheral:	
Waiting time	waiting time
Pleasant environment	environment
	friendliness of staff
	waiting room
4. Electrician/Plumber	
Core:	
Proper work done	—
Peripheral:	
Doesn't make a big mess	Level of cleanliness
5. Auto repair	
Core:	
Have car fixed correctly	—
Peripheral:	
Not get "ripped off"	—
Comfortable waiting area	Evaluate waiting area
	Friendliness of service
	Cleanliness of shop
	Explanations offered

6. Other Examples
- Pest control (termites)
- Full service brokerage
- Real estate agents
- Technical maintenance and repair (eg. computers, televisions, business equipment, heating / air conditioning).

Incongruity Between Expectations and Evaluations of Service Benefits

Before seeking out a service, consumers are assumed to have a need, and therefore, are assumed to have certain expectations as to what they anticipate the service will offer (in terms of levels of service benefits) or expectations as to what they desire in order to meet their needs (Spreng and Olshavsky 1993).[5] The important point is to note that some expectation is present concerning the core service benefit. Although this expectation may be limited to only an assumption that the core service will be provided, many consumers are likely to expect, at the very least, a satisfactory level of performance (whatever that is for the particular service) or even a superior level of performance in reference to the particular cost (if an optimizing strategy is assumed). Although some peripheral benefits may be considered in selecting a particular service provider, because they are relatively less important in solving the core need, fewer of the peripheral service benefits would presumably be considered (and thus fewer pre-encounter expectations would be formed concerning them) in relation to the number that are later evaluated.

---

[5]The services referred to in this section are those which have core service benefits high in credence attributes.

After selecting a service provider and making an agreement to purchase the desired core service, actual service delivery takes place. This consists of the delivery of the core service benefit(s) and the peripheral service benefits. However, because of the credence nature of the core service benefit, the consumer is not able to determine (by definition) that the service was performed correctly, and may even be unable to determine if the service was performed at all. For example, although you might watch the mechanic lift up the hood and hook your car up to some type of technical device in the process of performing a routine diagnostic check of your car engine, unless you were knowledgeable about the service being performed, you would not be able to determine the accuracy or appropriateness of the diagnosis of the vehicle's condition. However, many of the peripheral service benefits would be directly observable (e.g., the pleasant decor of the waiting area, the shuttle service, the clean work area).

McGill and Iacobucci (1992) propose the possibility of an incongruency between the attributes used for expectations (comparison standards) and evaluations. Specifically, they propose that consumers who lack experience with a particular service have pre-experience expectations that are relatively incomplete, while post-experience evaluations are based on a more thorough set of attributes (thus post-experience comparison standards are often formed).

We conceptualize this incongruency from another perspective: that when consumers are unable to directly evaluate the core service, their pre-encounter *expectations* are likely to be based on the core service benefit(s), whereas their post-encounter *evaluations* likely are focused on peripheral service benefits. For example, a consumer evaluating an oil change would likely have expectations on both core and peripheral service benefits (i.e., core benefit: that the oil is changed correctly; and peripheral benefits: that there is a pleasant environment in which to wait and there is a short waiting period). However, it is likely that only the peripheral benefits will actually be evaluated since there is no way for the non-expert consumer to evaluate the core service benefit(s) directly. Thus, with respect to perception of overall service performance, peripheral service benefits are likely to be included with (and even take the place of) the initial core benefit expectations in this evaluation, as compared to the formation of the pre-encounter overall service performance expectation where core service benefits were the primary focus.

Thus, there is an incongruency between the criteria on which the service expectation is formed and the criteria that the consumer is able to actually evaluate. Specifically, for service situations that have core service benefits that are high in credence attributes, a lack of congruency will exist between the criteria used in forming an *expectation* of overall service performance and the criteria used in forming an *evaluation* of the overall service performance. Expectations of service performance will be based on criteria pertaining to both core service benefits and some peripheral service benefits, whereas evaluations of service performance (i.e., perceived overall performance) will be based only on peripheral service benefits. This creates the aforementioned dilemma for consumers in evaluating service performance levels, which further extends to the formation of future judgments of service quality. This incongruency between the criteria used to develop expectations and those used to evaluate service performance leads to our first set of propositions.

P1: As the number and degree of credence attributes in the service increases, the degree of incongruity between the expectation and evaluation criteria that consumers use in assessing that service will increase.

Specifically, concerning the core and peripheral service benefits:

P2a: In forming judgments concerning the core service benefit for services high in core credence attributes, the number of expectation criteria will be greater than the number of evaluation criteria used in the assessment.

P2b: In forming judgments concerning the peripheral service benefits for services high in core credence attributes, the number of expectation criteria will be less than the number of evaluation criteria used in the assessment.

P2c: For services high in core credence attributes, expectation criteria will exist for both core and peripheral service benefits; evaluation criteria will exist primarily for peripheral service benefits. Whereas for services low in core credence attributes, there will be more congruity between expectation criteria and evaluation criteria.

The next section considers whether some consumers make inferences about core performance although only the peripheral benefits can be evaluated.

Alternate Processes—Oblivious Vs. Cognizant Consumers

The question remains as to whether consumers will form *any* type of evaluation concerning the core service benefits. It seems plausible that consumers have a need to manage their service provider choices by making inferences about overall service quality. An individual difference variable can be conceived which suggests alternate processes in the formation of overall performance evaluation (i.e., the perceived performance for the service encounter as a whole). We suggest that there is a continuum of consumer awareness of the inability to evaluate the high credence attribute core service benefits. This continuum ranges from a low end, where consumers are oblivious to their inability to make objective evaluations, to a high end, where consumers are quite cognizant of this dilemma.[6] We suggest that how a consumer evaluates core service performance and overall service performance depends to some degree on his or her level of awareness.

Consumers low in awareness may be inclined to infer a certain level of performance about the core service benefit (basing these inferences on evaluations of peripheral service benefits). These "oblivious" consumers may think that all is well as far as their ability to evaluate overall service. In fact, they may believe (falsely) that their ability to evaluate the core service performance is unrestricted. They necessarily use peripheral service benefits as cues (whether appropriate or not) to infer core performance, resulting in a relatively confident belief about their ability to evaluate core service performance. They then base their overall evaluations of service performance on some combination of their peripheral benefit evaluations and their (necessarily inferred) core service evaluations.

Conversely, consumers high in awareness are unlikely to form a perception of core service performance and likely to proceed

---

[6]Some determinants as to a consumer's position on this continuum are likely consumer education, experience with the particular service, and/or need-for-cognition (NFC). Specifically, those consumers who have more knowledge and experience regarding the service and are high in NFC would be more "cognizant" than those who have less education or experience and are lower in NFC.

directly to the formation of some overall service performance evaluation. These "cognizant" consumers know that they cannot directly perceive the core service performance. As a consequence, several outcomes may result. Cognizant consumers may (1) delay core performance evaluation until they can somehow directly evaluate it by either (a) learning how to evaluate core service benefits (if that is possible) or (b) using a trusted (perhaps hired) source to evaluate performance for them; (2) accept that they cannot evaluate it and purchase insurance (i.e., actual insurance, service contracts, warranties, etc.) as protection against potentially bad performance; (3) grudgingly base the core service benefit performance evaluation on "rational" or "sensible" cues (particularly if they are high need-for-cognition); (4) remain frustrated; (5) accept the ambiguity as part of the purchase/consumption process.

In all cases except (3) above, the cognizant consumer will likely neglect to form an evaluation of the core service benefit performance, and will purposefully base overall service performance on some of the peripheral service benefit evaluations. It is important to note that in either case (i.e., making an inference about core service performance or neglecting to do so), the consumer still does not necessarily form an unbiased or reasonably accurate perception of the core service performance, and thus may not form an accurate perception of overall service performance.

Concerning case (5) above, in which the consumer accepts ambiguity as a part of the purchase process, is it reasonable to presume that consumers will be content in forming performance perceptions when they know that diagnostic information concerning the core service benefit is missing? Yalch (1992), commenting on Sirdeshmukh and Unnava (1992), suggests that evaluations may "tend to be based only on a limited amount of information even when much information is provided" (p. 278). This may explain some consumers' complacency in not being able to evaluate the core service benefit, particularly if it is felt that certain peripheral service benefits reliably predict core benefit performance.

Role of Perceived Ambiguity

Yi (1993), addressing the role of ambiguity in consumer satisfaction processes, found that expectations for an ambiguous product (one that was difficult to evaluate) drove satisfaction, whereas performance drove satisfaction for an unambiguous product (that was easier to evaluate). We conceptualize ambiguity with respect to how diagnostic consumers perceive the peripheral service benefits to be in predicting core service benefit performance. Thus, cognizant consumers, because they tend to perceive high ambiguity concerning the ability of the peripheral service benefits to predict core service performance, will be less likely than oblivious consumers to make an inference concerning core service performance. Conversely, because oblivious consumers do not tend to perceive the ambiguity, they are more likely to be unaware of their incapacity to evaluate the core service benefit(s). Hence, they are more likely to make inferences about the performance of the core service based on the peripheral benefits even in the face of ambiguity between the peripheral and core service benefits. This leads to the following two propositions:

P3: The more (less) perceived ambiguity concerning the relationship between the performance of a particular peripheral service benefit cue and the performance of the core service, the less (more) likely that cue will be used in forming a performance inference regarding the core service.

P4: "Cognizant" consumers are less likely to form inferences about the core service benefit than are "oblivious" consumers.

Ambiguity and Confidence in the Perception of Performance

We propose that consumer inability to form evaluations concerning the core service benefit will result in consumers holding their overall service performance evaluation with a low degree of confidence. Other researchers have similarity proposed that ambiguity affects the degree of confidence of a judgment. For example, in a discussion of reference pricing, Klein and Oglethorpe (1987) propose that "the greater the ambiguity of a stimulus being evaluated, the harder it should be to confidently establish a fair price" (p. 186). Further, they suggest that expectations should be held with more confidence and used more frequently when the stimulus is unambiguous. We propose a similar line of thinking.

P5: The more (less) perceived ambiguity concerning the relationship between the performance of the group of peripheral service benefits (as a whole) and the performance of the core service, the less (more) confidence will be held in (a) the perception of core service benefit performance and (b) the perception of overall service performance.

MARKETER (SERVICE PROVIDER) IMPLICATIONS

To this point, we have presented a situation in which consumers, because of the credence nature of the core service attributes, are largely unable to evaluate core service performance. We have also developed the consumer implications of this dilemma. We now discuss five potential actions or reactions of marketers to consumers' inabilities to evaluate core service performance.

First, there is evidence supporting the idea that some marketers provide or emphasize key attributes that are easier for consumers to evaluate (McGill and Iacobucci 1992). This marketing action may lead consumers to have less concern for the core service benefit even when expectations are being formed. Presumably, this would result in consumers having a stronger degree of confidence in their evaluations, since they are based on concrete evidence for the cues included in the evaluation model. That is, if consumers focus expectations on peripheral service benefits, and then because of the credence nature of the core service benefit focus evaluations on peripheral service benefits, there is much congruity between expectation and evaluation criteria.

Second, service providers may expand both employees' and customers' perceptions of the service package that is sold. Here the marketer's message might be that it offers much more than the core service, giving consumers alternate "core" service benefits (previously considered peripheral benefits by cognizant consumers) upon which consumers could form evaluations of overall performance. Unfortunately, this also dilutes or diffuses the focus that should be on the core service. For instance, certain oil change services have successfully expanded their marketplace images to be more than just an oil change service. Their customers likely think about the peripheral service benefits as much, if not more than, the core service(s) when they think about what these companies offer. As another marketplace example, a particular muffler repair company provides consumers with peripheral service benefits that can be "objectively" evaluated (e.g., written estimates and a promise to take customers into the garage for explanations of the recommended repairs). Thus, their consumers likely focus their evaluations on these peripheral service benefits rather than the core service benefit which they may be unable to evaluate.

Third, the service provider may also try to emphasize credibility and build trust. This can be done through recommendations, seals of approval, capitalizing on the number of years in business, and making certifiable credentials (such as degrees, certificates of training, membership in trade organizations, and government licenses) known to consumers.

A fourth alternative is that service providers (or industry representatives) may choose to train consumers in how to evaluate the core service performance. Presumably, with training, previously "oblivious" consumers would become more cognizant of their inabilities to evaluate core service performance. In addition, in some instances, consumers might be educated such that they actually could directly evaluate the core service performance. As such, this appears to be the best option from a public policy perspective.

Finally, if a large number of consumers are found to be oblivious of their inability to evaluate performance, service providers may choose to ignore the issue and let things continue as they are.

In effect, the first two strategies increase the importance of the peripheral service benefits and lessen the concern about core service benefits. Thus, these strategies dilute the ambiguity for the consumers attempting to make evaluations by giving them more concrete attributes on which to focus. Hence, there would be more congruity between their expectation and evaluation criteria. An important public policy issue arises if consumers are led astray by this marketer action and are persuaded to focus on cues that may not reflect true performance in the core service (and thus lead to long-term dissatisfaction if the performance level is overestimated). This state of affairs would be particularly troubling since many consumers still would not have recognized their inability to evaluate the core service benefit.

CONCLUSIONS

Given the difficulty of accurately perceiving core service benefits when the core service is high in credence attributes, and the importance of perceived service performance in the construction of satisfaction judgments and service quality assessments, this area of research is of particular importance to both academia and marketing management. The significance of this marketplace phenomenon is highlighted when one considers the impact of the growing service sector, and the increasing managerial focus on customer service elements of the product offering. Further, this research identifies a sixth gap in the service satisfaction model and explores the processes by which consumers cope with the nuances created by this sixth gap.

REFERENCES

Bearden, William O. and Jesse E. Teel (1983), "Selected Determinants of Consumer Satisfaction and Complaint Reports," *Journal of Marketing Research*, 20 (February), 21-28.

Bitner, Mary Jo (1990), "Evaluating Service Encounters: The Effects of Physical Surroundings and Employee Responses," *Journal of Marketing*, 54 (April), 69-82.

Bitner, Mary Jo (1991), "The Evolution of the Services Marketing Mix and Its Relationship to Service Quality," in *Service Quality: Multidisciplinary and Multinational Perspectives*, eds., Stephen W. Brown, Evert Gummesson, Bo Edvardsson, and BengtOve Gustavsson, Lexington, MA: D.C. Heath and Co., 23-37.

Bitner, Mary Jo, Bernard H. Booms, and Mary Stanfield Tetreault (1990), "The Service Encounter: Diagnosing Favorable and Unfavorable Incidents," *Journal of Marketing*, 54 (January), 71-84.

Bolton, Ruth N. and James H. Drew (1991), "A Multistage Model of Customers' Assessments of Service Quality and Value," *Journal of Consumer Research*, 17 (March), 375-384.

Churchill, Gilbert A., Jr. and Carol Surprenant (1982), "An Investigation Into the Determinants of Customer Satisfaction," *Journal of Marketing Research*, 19 (November), 491-504.

Cronin, J. Joseph, Jr. and Steven A. Taylor (1992), "Measuring Service Quality: A Reexamination and Extension," *Journal of Marketing*, 56 (July), 55-68.

Crosby, Lawrence A. and Nancy Stephens (1987), "Effects of Relationship Marketing on Satisfaction, Retention, and Prices in the Life Insurance Industry," *Journal of Marketing Research*, 24 (November), 404-411.

Darby, Michael R. and Edi Karni (1973), "Free Competition and the Optimal Amount of Fraud," *Journal of Law and Economics*, 16 (April), 67-88.

Hill, Donna J. (1986), "Satisfaction and Consumer Services," in *Advances in Consumer Research*, Vol. 13, Richard J. Lutz, ed., Provo, UT: Association of Consumer Research, 311-315.

Klein, Noreen M. and Janet E. Oglethorpe (1986), "Cognitive Reference Points in Consumer Decision Making," in *Advances in Consumer Research*, Vol. 14, Melanie Wallendorf and Paul Anderson, eds., Provo, UT: Association of Consumer Research, 183-187.

McGill, Ann L. and Dawn Iacobucci (1992), "The Role of Post-Experience Comparison Standards in the Evaluation of Unfamiliar Services," in *Advances in Consumer Research*, Vol. 19, John F. Sherry, Jr. and Brian Sternthal, eds., Provo, UT: Association of Consumer Research, 570-578.

Nelson, Phillip (1970), "Information and Consumer Behavior," *Journal of Political Economy*, 78 (March/April), 311-329.

Parasuraman, A., Valarie A. Zeithaml, and Leonard L. Berry (1985), "A Conceptual Model of Service Quality and Its Implications for Future Research," *Journal of Marketing*, 49 (4), 41-50.

Parasuraman, A., Valarie A. Zeithaml, and Leonard L. Berry (1988), "SERVQUAL: A Multiple Item Scale for Measuring Consumer Perceptions of Service Quality," *Journal of Retailing*, 64 (1), 12-37.

Shostack, G. Lynn (1985), "Planning the Service Encounter," in *The Service Encounter*, John A. Czepiel, Michael R. Solomon, and Carol F. Surprenant, eds., Lexington, MA: Lexington Books, 243-254.

Sirdeshmukh, Deepak and H. Rao Unnava (1992), "The Effects of Missing Information on Consumer Product Evaluations," in *Advances in Consumer Research*, Vol. 19, John F. Sherry, Jr. and Brian Sternthal, eds., Provo, UT: Association for Consumer Research, 284-289.

Spreng, Richard A. and Richard W. Olshavsky (1993), "A Desires Congruency Model of Consumer Satisfaction," *Journal of the Academy of Marketing Science*, 21, 169-177.

Steenkamp, Jan-Benedict E.M. (1990), "Conceptual Model of the Quality Perception Process," *Journal of Business Research*, 21, 309-333.

Yalch, Richard (1992), "Comment on Factors Affecting Evaluations," in *Advances in Consumer Research*, Vol. 19, John F. Sherry, Jr. and Brian Sternthal, eds., Provo, UT: Association for Consumer Research, 276-278.

Yi, Youjae (1993), "The Determinants of Consumer Satisfaction: The Moderating Role of Ambiguity," in *Advances in Consumer Research*, Vol. 20, Leigh McAlister and Michael L. Rothschild, eds., Provo, UT: Association for Consumer Research, 502-6.

Yin, Tung (1992), "Retailing: Sears Is Accused of Billing Fraud at Auto Centers," *Wall Street Journal*, June 12, B1.

Zeithaml, Valarie A. (1988), "Consumer Perceptions of Price, Quality, and Value: A Means-End Model and Synthesis of Evidence," *Journal of Marketing*, 52 (July), 2-22.

Cold Call Sales Effectiveness: An Investigation of Source Perceptions and Gender Differences

Sharon R. Lundgren, Texas A&M University

ABSTRACT

People approached in a cold call influence situation quickly seek source information to help determine if they will attend to or comply with the appeal. Those approached rely on source perceptions, and in ambiguous situations, sex characteristics, to shape their perceptions. 190 male and female introductory psychology students were individually approached in the first experiment during an ongoing experiment by a male or female solicitor attempting to sell inexpensive raffle tickets. Subjects were approached by the solicitor using either a friendly, dominant, competent, or neutral style. In the second experiment, 134 subjects were approached in either the friendly, dominant, or neutral style by a solicitor selling more expensive booklets. In both studies, subjects did not rely on sex characteristics. Solicitors selling the inexpensive ticket in Experiment 1 who were perceived as dominant had the highest overall influence rates, whereas solicitors selling the more expensive item in Experiment 2 who were perceived to be friendly had the highest overall influence rates. Additionally, males in Experiment 2 had greater overall sales rates. These findings and are discussed in light of the relevant literature.

Consumers today are often distrustful of any salesperson who approaches them. It is difficult for salespeople to break through the defensive barriers installed by the wary consumer. Salespeople have evolved tactics to catch the consumer off guard, such as calling potential customers unexpectedly and surprising them with an influence appeal. This is termed a "cold-call" approach. Salespeople can catch the consumer before the consumer can marshal resistance to the appeal. Cold-call selling is still preferred to other forewarned methods by many sellers today; consider the high priced vacuum salespersons, newspaper subscription peddlers and even cookie-weilding girl scouts. This type of selling is a two stage process of influence: First, the consumer must attend to and comprehend the appeal, and second, the consumer must yield to the appeal. These are two separate processes, as a consumer who listens to the appeal may not necessarily yield.

Little research has been conducted on actual cold-call selling; it is a discrete phenomena from those types of influence attempts in which the subject has previous knowledge of the appeal. Forewarning subjects of an impending influence attempt has been found to increase subjects' motivation to defend their beliefs on certain issues, and it increases their resistance to persuasion (McGuire, 1964; Lundgren & Wood, 1994). An audience that has been distracted or not forewarned of the appeal has a harder time building counterarguements to the appeal, and is easier to influence (Hass & Grady, 1975). Salespeople similarly believe that an approach without forewarning will have these desirable effects. Cold-call selling thus provides a rich context for laboratory study of the processes of attention, comprehension and yielding. Subjects who are unaware of the impending salespitch should be more willing to attend to and comprehend the appeal and should not be predisposed to resist yielding to the appeal.

Whereas much social psychological research has examined important characteristics of the communicators in influence settings, (e.g., a communicator's expertise, Eagly, 1983; Hass, 1981; and credibility of the communicator, Hovland & Weiss, 1952), there has been little attention to the importance of characteristics of the communicators in cold-call settings. Thus not much is known about the psychological processes involved in these settings. To help illuminate these processes, the present research will examine whether the consumers' willingness to listen and decision to yield in a cold-call setting are affected by the sex and the behavior of the salesperson. These characteristics are important to understanding cold-call influence because they potentially could affect the apparent perception of the salesperson, the amount of reactance evoked within the consumer by the influence appeal, and the consumer's liking for the salesperson. All of these processes plausibly affect attention, yielding, and opinion change to cold-call appeals.

Effects of Influence Style

Direct empirical observations of men and women influencing others in group contexts have revealed that style is indeed important. Often, who attracts attention in a group is determined by the behavioral style of the speakers. In general, research suggests that styles which enhance the source's apparent competence have the effect of attracting attention of others and increasing influence. For example, a confederate exhibiting dominant behavior in one study was not perceived as competent, and was not influential (Ridgeway, 1987). However, a confederate adopting a dominant style in another study was perceived as competent and the style enhanced influence (Shackelford, Wood, and Worchel, 1990). Although dominant influence agents are uniformly disliked (Ridgeway & Diekema, 1989; Shackelford, Wood, and Worchel, 1990), they can be influential if dominance is linked to competence.

In the present research I am interested in cold-call selling, which is typically a one-on-one interaction. It is thus less important than in group contexts for the agent to attract attention away from other possible sources. However, a dominant approach may be helpful in attracting a target's initial attention even in cold-call selling.

Highly competent sources or dominant styles generate reactance. According to reactance theory (Brehm & Cohen, 1962; Brehm, 1966), the person influenced must feel that he she has the freedom to turn the solicitor away at any point, or be able to turn down the request after hearing the solicitor's pitch. If the solicitor threatens or limits this freedom, the target should feel aroused (Brehm and Cohen, 1962; Brehm, 1966).

In the cold-call scenario, this might occur when a high-pressure solicitor is perceived by the target as overpowering or pushy. The client may then feel the need to react defensively or to stop listening to the solicitor altogether. How much reactance the target experiences depends upon several factors, such as how the message relates to that individual's value-system, or the unfavorable consequences that might result from the interaction with the solicitor. The receiver who feels threatened should not take the advocated position of the communicator but rather maintain his or her own position with increased confidence in order to reduce the arousal level.

Likable sources are influential. We tend to be influenced by those we like (Cialdini, 1988). This has implications for professional salespeople; they can attempt to behave in a likable manner. This should keep the customer from reacting defensively towards the agent and refusing to listen or terminating the pitch early. According to Cialdini, we like people who are nice or act decently; also, we will be attracted to those who display positive rather than negative traits or habits (Kaplan & Anderson, 1973). People we like also tend to be people we trust, and trust has been shown to have a favorable influence on dyadic interactions (Schurr & Ozanne, 1985).

Gender Effects

There is also reason to suspect that there are sex differences in the effectiveness of cold-call selling. Until more recently, women did not assume sales positions. Their competence was particularly suspect in those positions dealing with typically male-oriented or high technology products (Skolnik, 1985). Although some marketers studying sales techniques indicate women can be more influential than men (Boyan, 1989a, Boyan, 1989b; Skolnik, 1985), social psychological research findings have not suppported that claim. A recent meta-analytic review of research on mixed sex task groups revealed greater influence of males than females (Lockheed, 1985). Indeed, a number of individual studies have shown adult males to have greater influence on others than do women in group settings (Nemeth, Endicott, & Wachtler 1976, and Pugh & Wahrmann, 1985). When no information is available to identify who is expected to be the most competent, such as in a condition in which no predominant behavioral style is evident, socially important attributes, such as gender, should come into focus. In our society, a higher value is attached to traditionally masculine characteristics than traditionally feminine ones. In this view, men are more influential because males possess the "superior" features associated with their sex, such as being stronger, more competent, and more knowledgeable. From this perspective, then, males should be more influential than females at both stages of cold-call selling when no predominant behavioral style is evident.

Males and females as consumers, however, should not tend to vary much in their influenceability. A recent meta-analytical review showed women to be only slightly more influenceable then men (Eagly & Carli, 1981). Since the effect was so small, sex differences in influenceability would not be expected here.

Present Research

The present research was designed to examine behavior and sex differences in cold-call sales effectiveness. These two experiments are simulations of cold-call selling in the laboratory. Both studies manipulated the behavioral style of the solicitor interrupting an experiment. Behavior styles were operationalized so that both male and female confederates evoked the same mannerisms and body language for each of the styles, to guarantee that perceptions of each style would not vary across the confederates. The threatening manner was portrayed by the confederate acting in a pushy, persistent, overbearing manner; the confederate spoke in a loud voice and attempted to push his or her way into the room. The friendly manner was portrayed by the confederate acting polite, smiling frequently, and approaching the subject in a friendly manner. The competent style was displayed by the confederate standing in an upright posture, with self-assured gestures and speech. The speech contained larger vocabulary, and the confederate additionally dressed in a blazer. The neutral confederate was portrayed by the confederate acting in a casual, matter-of-fact manner without appearing to be particularly friendly, pushy, or particularly knowledgeable. In addition to this training, each confederate demonstrated the four styles via videotape for the pilot test of the styles. 233 Introductory Psychology students rated the videos on the impressions questionnaire, and found the confederates using the competent style to be perceived as more competent than the those using other styles, the confederates using the friendly style to be more friendly than those using other styles, and the confederates using the dominant style to be more dominant than those using other styles (all p's <.001). One of four confederates, two male and two female, selected to be average in physical attractiveness, served in the experiments. Confederates were trained to follow standard style patterns when delivering the influ-

ence appeal. Extensive pretesting was conducted to ensure that none of the confederates differed from the others in their portrayals of the four styles; therefore, subjects perceived both male and female confederates similarly on their operationalization of the styles.

H1: Salespersons using the dominant style should be more effective in garnering agreement to listen from the subjects, and should also keep the subjects listening to the sales pitch for a longer amount of time than when they are using the friendly, competent or neutral styles.

H2: The salespersons using the competent and friendly styles should sell more frequently than when using the dominant or neutral styles.

H3: Due to the ambiguous perceptions of the salespersons using the neutral style, subjects should instead rely on quick judgments of other status characteristics, particularly expectations based upon gender. Salesmen should be the most effective at procuring listening, comprehension, and yielding from the subject in the neutral style condition.

Experiment 1

Naive male and female subjects worked on a timed IQ test and were interrupted by a solicitor asking them to purchase a 50 cent raffle ticket for a psychology club. The solicitor was either male or female, and furthermore, adopted a dominant, pushy style, a friendly, warm style, a competent, knowledgeable style, or a neutral style.

METHOD

Subjects

Subjects were 190 male and female Introductory Psychology undergraduates at Texas A&M University. They were run individually.

Design and Procedure

A Sex of Confederate (Male vs Female), x Sex of Subject (Male vs Female) x Influence Style (Dominant vs Friendly vs Competent vs Neutral) between subjects factorial design was employed. Subjects were told that the experiment concerned intelligence testing in word games. The subjects were isolated into individual rooms and were encouraged to find as many words as possible in the time limit given. Subjects were instructed via intercom to begin the word game. Approximately ten minutes into the word game, a confederate knocked on the subject's door. The confederate identified himself or herself as a member of Psi Chi, the Psychology Honors Club, and requested the subject to listen. If the subject did not agree to listen, the confederate requested the subject listen for just 30 or so seconds. If the subject refused to listen after the second request, the confederate left the subject's room. If the subject agreed to listen, the solicitor told the subject that Psi Chi was having a raffle to raise money to send students, including the confederate, to a professional convention where research papers could be presented. The tickets were 50 cents each, and there were supposedly two chances to win $40.00 in the upcoming raffle. The confederate then asked the subject if he or she would be interested in purchasing one of these tickets, and then either completed the sale, or left with "no."

The experimenter terminated the experiment shortly after subjects had approached by the confederate. The experimenter explained that the solicitor was part of the experiment and had the subjects fill out their impression of the confederate on a questionnaire. Once this was done, the experimenter discussed the confederate's style and other information relevant to the debriefing.

RESULTS

Influence of Source

Influence of the source was measured in several different ways. Whether the subject attempted to terminate the salespitch or listened to the whole pitch was labeled "listening," and the number of seconds the subjects listened to the salespitch was labeled "comprehension time." The third influence measure assessed whether the subject purchased the ticker or not and was labeled "sales." The total sales variable included not only money exchanges, but I.O.U.'s for the subjects who agreed to purchase but did not have the money available.

Listening and comprehension time. Analysis of variance revealed a significant main effect for confederates' style on the frequency with which subjects listened to the salespitch, $F(3,174)=3.66, p<.02$. Subjects were less likely to terminate sales pitches with either the friendly style ($M=.89$), the competent style ($M=.90$), or the dominant style ($M=.90$) than they were with the neutral style control ($M=.70$, all p's<.03). This finding appears to reflect a overall positivity effect, in that either dominance, competence, or liking enhanced willingness to listen, compared with neutral style. A significant main effect occurred also for style in the number of seconds the subject allowed the confederate to speak, $F(3,174)=8.343, p<.001$, in that the neutral style control pitch was allowed the least amount of time ($M=25.96$) compared with each of the other three styles, the friendly style ($M=40.70$), the competent style ($M=38.50$), and the dominant style ($M=34.69$, all p's<.01). The dominant style thus was not found to garner more listening or comprehension time than the other styles, as was predicted.

Sales. Analysis of variance revealed a significant main effect for style in the amount of overall sales, $F(3,174)=5.017, p<.002$. Surprisingly, planned comparisons showed that the confederate using the dominant style ($M=.65$) sold significantly more tickets than either the competent or friendly styles(M's=.48) or the neutral style ($M=.26$), $t(186)=2.95$ p <.005. The dominant style thus proved to be the most effective sales style. No other main effects or interactions were found.

Subject's Perceptions of Source Mediate Influence

The likelihood of the subject listening to the entire pitch increased with greater perceived dominance of the confederate, $r=.13, p<.05$, and marginally with greater perceived competence, $r=.11, p<.07$. Dominance commanded attention from the subjects and competence garnered it. All three perceptions also correlated with the length of time spent listening to the pitch: Subjects who perceived the confederate to be more dominant listened longer, $r=.12, p<.06$ (although marginal), competent, $r=.24, p<.001$, and friendly, $r=.19, p<.01$. Finally, the more dominant subjects perceived the confederate to be, the greater the likelihood of the confederate making a sale, $r=.22, p<.01$. Surprisingly, then, across the three influence measures, the perception of dominance was the best predictor of influence success.

Gender Differences

As would be exppected, no effects for confederate sex emerged across the styles. However, the expected effect in the neutral style did not emerge, either. Finally, no gender effects were observed in influenceability of the subject.

Experiment 2

It is surprising that no gender effects was obtained in the neutral style. One possible explanation for the lack of sex effects is that the paradigm may not have clearly represented a sales or influence paradigm. The supposed purpose of the raffle sale was to send undergraduates to a research convention, and the subjects who bought a ticket were not guaranteed to win the prize. Hence, the subjects did not directly receive anything for their purchase. For this reason, many subjects may have viewed the request as a request for assistance or a donation, which would generate helping behavior instead of a sales interaction, and perhaps not necessitating any judgments of competence from the subject. To investigate this, the persuasion appeal needed to clearly involve a direct sale instead of a request for help or a donation. Therefore the nature of the appeal was changed from a fund-raising project to a direct sales project for Experiment 2. The solicitor in Experiment 2 sold $5.00 booklets on professors' course grades, a motive clearly for the solicitor's profit. Additionally, the competent condition was dropped for Experiment 2, because of the inherent difficulty of being competent and knowledgeable of such items as raffle tickets or booklets. Experimental focus instead turned to the more behavioral styles, such as the friendly, dominant and neutral style.

METHOD

Subjects

Subjects were 134 male and female Introductory Psychology undergraduates at Texas A&M University. They were run individually.

Procedure

The procedure was identical to the first experiment except that these solicitors adopted a dominant, friendly, or neutral style only. Additionally, the solicitor attempted to sell a $5.00 booklet. The booklets identified the average grades earned in various courses taught by different professors at the university.

RESULTS

Influence

Listening and comprehension time. Analysis of variance revealed a significant main effect for confederates' style on the frequency with which subjects listened to the salespitch, $F(2,132)=13.74, p<.001$. Subjects were more likely to terminate sales pitches with the neutral style ($M=0.73$) than with the dominant style ($M=0.97$), or the friendly style ($M=1.00$). This finding appears to reflect a overall positivity effect similar to that found in Experiment 1, in that either dominance or liking enhanced willingness to listen, compared to the neutral style. However, the the dominant style did not garner more listening than the friendly style as predicted. Analysis of variance again revealed a significant main effect for style in the number of seconds the subject allowed the confederate to speak, $F(2,132)=17.36, p<.001$. As expected, the dominant style was listened to marginally longer ($M=62.68$) compared with the other styles, the friendly style ($M=44.57$) and the neutral style ($M=32.45$), $F(1,132)=3.60, p<.06$.

Sales. Analysis of variance revealed a marginal main effect for style in the amount of overall sales, $F(2,132)=2.89$ $p<.06$. The confederates using the friendly style sold more ($M=0.32$) than confederates using either the dominant style ($M=0.17$), or neutral style ($M=0.14$). As predicted, the friendly style thus proved to be the most effective sales style in garnering the actual sale.

Confederate Sex Differences

On overall measures, the sex of the confederates did not have a significant effect on listening or the length of time subjects listened to the salespitch, but males (M=0.30) sold significantly more booklets than females (M=0.13), $F(2,132)$=5.28 p<.03. The predicted gender effects on the neutral style again did not occur. Finally, there were no gender effects on influenceability of subjects.

DISCUSSION

Surprisingly, when the cost was low, a dominant approach garnered the most influence. Shackelford, Wood and Worchel (1990) noted that when a source using a dominant style is perceived as competent, targets listened, comprehended, and complied to the influence appeal. This finding is supported by the specific perceptions of the confederate that were related to successful influence of raffle tickets. In the correlations, perceptions of dominance appeared to be the critical factor generating influence for the styles manipulated in the low-cost purchase: Of the three source perceptions evaluated, only dominance predicted all three influence measures. Perhaps subjects decided that 50 cents was too cheap to bother exerting effort in order to terminate a pushy solicitor. In other words, it was easier to pay the solicitor to terminate the pitch. Influence on higher priced items can often increase reactance in consumers (Clee & Wicklund, 1980); perhaps the menial cost of the ticket did not add to any reactance already prompted by the dominant style, and therefore, the amount of reactance alone was not enough to refuse the sale. Further, the small sum could be legitimized as a donation to help others (Brockner, Guzzi, Kane, Levine, & Shaper, 1984), regardless of the solicitor's demeanor.

However, when the price increased, and the sale became less philanthropic, the friendly solicitor was the most influential. Although a positivity effect for dominance occurred with the likelihood of listening and the time spent listening, subjects did not purchase as much from dominant solicitors as from friendly solicitors with the higher priced item. Caution does need to be taken in interpreting price comparisons as the prices and products were not carefully pretested. On the whole, though, these results indicate that style is important in garnering listening and yielding, but that effective styles may vary with the cost and the nature of the product sold.

As predicted, there were no gender differences in any of the standardized styles. Male and female sources were expected to be perceived similarly when adopting the friendly, the dominant, or the competent style, because the sources received extensive training to ensure that men and women delivered the pitch in the same way. The perception ratings of confederates from subjects in the study revealed few effects for the styles. Thus, for all sources, the dominant style was perceived as especially dominant, the competent as especially competent, and the friendly style as particularly friendly. Given these clear style patterns, there was no need for subjects to rely on source gender to form perceptions of the source. It is surprising, however, that sex did not have any effect in the neutral style, as had been hypothesized. All of the styles, including the neutral style, were pretested so that they were carried out the same by all of the confederates, regardless of sex; because emphasis was placed on standardizing the neutral style, male and female solicitors did not differ in their delivery of this style. Perhaps the neutral style was not interpreted as ambiguously as predicted and therefore, gender status was not necessary; due to the standardization, this neutral style may have become a type of style of it's own, so subjects did not need to refer to other status characteristics, such as gender.

A sex effect was found overall in Experiment 2, in that males were found to sell more. Interestingly, in Experiment 1, there was no overall gender effect on the less expensive tickets. When the financial risks increased, subjects may have looked toward diffuse status characteristics, such as gender, to determine the positivity of the sales encounter. In other words, subjects may have needed more information in the higher priced interaction and thus turned to gender. Attributions of knowledgeability or competence, which are usually attributed to males, may have allowed the males to sell more of the booklets.

Whether the behavior and gender effects observed in this study are similar to the sex and behavior effects so often observed in the real world is an interesting question. The confederates did not differentiate styles according to their sex, as might typically be the case in natural settings. The influence styles established in the present research were identical for males and females. Were the confederates allowed to adopt more natural styles, males might have adopted a dominant and assertive sales role whereas females might have been friendlier. It would be of interest to design a study in which sources do not adopt a standardized style but rather are allowed to adopt their own personal style. It should be the case that solicitors would adopt a variety of styles, but females should tend to take on a style that would be perceived as more friendly overall and males a style perceived as more dominant. Then sex differences related to not only subjects' perceptions of the confederates, but to influence as well, might be seen. After proper pretesting on pricing and product, this experiment could also be taken to the field as well as conducted in the laboratory, as it would be interesting to determine what styles and gender are most effectively on the consumer's turf, when consumers are busy with their own routines.

The behavioral styles that occur naturally in the real world are likely combinations of these styles, rather than a style such as dominant behavior in isolation from friendliness or competence. It would thus be interesting to determine the combinations of behaviors of styles that are more frequently used in less constricted settings. Also, do the style and gender effects differ in cold-call vs. forewarned sales attempts? Finally, what are the implications for sales settings other than face-to-face cold call sales? These experimental findings should be relevant to telemarketers who solicit unwary consumers over the phone, and other salespersons who attempt to influence consumers unaware of the impending salespitch.

REFERENCES

Boyan, L. (1989a). Who's more productive? *American Salesman, 34*, 16-19.

Boyan, L. (1989b). What salespeople can learn from each other. *American Salesman, 34*, 13-15.

Brehm, J. W. (1966). *A theory of psychological reactance.* New York: Academic Press.

Brehm, J. and Cohen, A. (1962). *Explorations in cognitive dissonance.* New York: John Wiley and Sons, Inc.

Brockner, J., Buzzi, B., Kane, J., Levine, E., & Shaplen, K. (1984). Organizational fundraising: Further evidence of the effect of legitimizing small donations. *Journal of Consumer Research, 11,* 611-614.

Cialdini, R. B. (1988). *Influence: Science and practice.* Glenville, IL: Scott, Foresman, and Company.

Clee, M.A., & Wicklund, R.A. (1980). Consumer behavior and psychological reactance. *Journal of Consumer Research, 6,* 389-405.

Eagly, A. H. (1983). Gender and social influence: A social psychological analysis. *American Psychologist, 38,* 971-981.

Eagly, A. H., & Carli, L.L. (1981). Sex of researchers and sex-typed communications as determinants of sex differences in influenceability: A meta-analysis of social influence studies. *Psychological Bulletin 90,* 1-20.

Hass, R. G. (1981). Effects of source characteristics on cognitive responses and persuasion. In R. E. Petty, T. M. Ostrom, & T. C. Brock (Eds.), *Cognitive responses in persuasion* (pp. 141-172). Hillsdale, NJ: Erlbaum.

Hass, R. G., & Grady, K. (1975). Temporal delay, type of forewarning, and resistance to influence. *Journal of Experimental Social Psychology, 11,* 459-469.

Kaplan, M., & Anderson, H. (1973). Information integration theory and reinforcement theory as approaches to interpersonal attraction. *Journal of Personality and Social Psychology, 28,* 301-312.

Lockheed, M. (1985). Sex and social influence: A meta-analysis guided by theory. In J. Berger, and Zelditch, Jr. (Eds.) *Status, reward and influence: How Expectations Organize Behavior.* (pp. 406-429). San Francisco: Jossey-Bass Inc.

Lundgren, S., & Wood, W. (1994). *A meta-analytic review of forewarnings of persuasive appeals.* Paper presented at the Society of Consumer Psychology Annual conference, St. Petersberg, FL.

McGuire, W. J. (1964). Inducing resistance to persuasion: Some contemporary approaches. In L. Berkowicz (Ed.), *Advances in Experimental Social Psychology* (Vol. 1). New York: Academic Press.

Nemeth, C., Endicott, J., & Wachtler, J. (1976). From the 50's to the 70's: Women in jury deliberations. *Sociometry, 39,* 293-304.

Pugh, M., & Wahrmann, R. (1971). Sex, non-conformity and influence. *Sociometry, 37,* 137-147.

Ridgeway, C.L. (1987). Nonverbal behavior, dominance, and the basis of status in task groups. *American Sociological Review, 52,* 683-694.

Ridgeway, C., & Diekema, D. (1989). Dominance and collective hierarchy formation in male and female task groups. *American Sociological Review, 54,* 79-93.

Schurr, P. H., & Ozanne, J.L. (1985). Influences on exchange processes: Buyer's preconceptions of a seller's trustworthiness and bargaining toughness. *Journal of Consumer Research, 11* 939-953.

Shackelford, S., Wood, W., and Worchel, S. (1990). *Low status group members influence others: The importance of behavioral style.* Unpublished masters thesis, Texas A & M University.

Skolnik, R. (1985). A woman's place is on the sales force. *Sales and Marketing Management, 134,* 34-37.

"Professors", "Get-Me-Dones", and "Moochers": How Car Salespeople Experience Their Customers

Marla Felcher, Northwestern University

ABSTRACT

Through participant observation and interviews, it was found that car salespeople oftentimes view sales encounters as a struggle between themselves and their customers, with more on the line than commissions. In addition to monetary rewards, the salespeople also strive to control the sales encounter. This quest for control may conflict with both the needs of the organization and those of the customer. A by-product of this conflict is customer-directed hostility, oftentimes based on customers' ethnicity. Implications for consumers' perceptions of service quality in light of these findings are addressed.

In her recent book documenting the experiences of McDonald's counter workers and Combined Insurance salesmen, Leidner (1993) argues that in doing their jobs, interactive service workers must successfully align the interests of three parties: customers, management and themselves. Specifically, these front-line workers must learn to satisfy customer demands, adhere to management edicts, and "minimize their own discomfort" (p. 7). While the interests of both customers and managers have been addressed by marketing, consumer behavior and management researchers, outside of the sociology of work literature, surprisingly little attention has been paid to the feelings and experiences of *service providers*.

In this study I focus on one type of service provider, car salespeople. From data gleaned through participant observation and interviews within a car dealership, I argue that a comprehensive examination of the sales process must take into account the experiential aspects of the service encounter from the salesperson's perspective, for the extent to which his/her experiences, interests, and goals align with those of the organization's customers and management will effect customers' perceptions of overall service quality. Just as highly routinized service scripts such as those at McDonald's may lead customers to experience service workers as unresponsive, stupid or robot-like (Leidner 1993), salepersons' perceptions of customer demands as being unreasonable may lead customers to experience service workers as unresponsive, insolent, or elusive.

Selling cars is a highly interactive type of service work, idiosyncratic in a few respects. First, in many dealerships, as in the one studied, the salespeople received no base pay, only commissions based on the profitability of cars sold. Second, car salespeople work in a relatively low status job, oftentimes perceived quite negatively by the public. The job provides no "status shield" (Hochschild 1983); many customers who would ordinarily treat higher-status workers with respect are quite ready to express anger or contempt toward car salespeople. It is up to the salespeople to figure out a way to defend themselves from demeaning treatment by customers; to maintain a positive self-concept they need to learn ways to accept poor treatment without taking it personally (Leidner 1993).

In the following sections I expand on the themes which emerged from my study of these service workers; namely, an overall perceived lack of control over the work environment, and the various methods the salespeople grew to rely on in an attempt to increase their control. Many attitudes and behaviors expressed by the salespeople suggested that within their personal objective functions, ontological control played a role equal to if not greater than earnings maximization.

METHOD

A grounded theory approach was taken to study the salesperson-customer relationship (Strauss and Corbin 1990). Therefore no a priori theories were specified and tested, rather, a theory was inductively derived from the fieldwork experience. A grounded theory is:

> ... discovered, developed, and provisionally verified through systematic data collection and analysis of data pertaining to that phenomenon. Therefore, data collection, analysis, and theory stand in reciprocal relationship with each other. One does not begin with a theory, then prove it. Rather, one begins with an area of study and what is relevant to that area is allowed to emerge (Strauss and Corbin 1990; p. 23).

A grounded theory is developed around a research question which specifies the area of study. The current research began with the question, "What is the nature of the car salesperson-customer relationship, from the perspective of the salesperson, where the monetary reward system is based exclusively on commissions?".

Two types of data were collected to address this question: the researcher's participant-observation among the salespeople, and non-directive interviews with the salespeople. The data were collected across eight consecutive weeks, during the approximately 40 hours the researcher spent within a foreign car dealership. The dealership was located in an affluent suburb of Chicago. All observations and interviews, except one, took place in the center of the dealership where the salespeople congregated when not interacting with customers. The interview with the General Manager of the dealership took place in his private office, which was adjacent to the selling floor. The salespeople were told the researcher was collecting data for a paper on "customer-salespeople interactions".

All of the dealership's salespeople, eight white males between the ages of 35 and 65, were interviewed and observed. The youngest salesperson had been selling cars for less than one year. The other salespeople had been selling cars for between eight and thirty years, most working at this dealership for over ten years.

The commission system was based on the profit generated from selling a car. Salespeople were paid a 20% commission on profits up to $900, and 25% on profits over $900. A fixed overhead of $150 was subtracted from all commissions on the sale of a car, which went the dealer. If, for example, a profit on a car was $1,050, the salesperson's commission was $112.50 (($1,050 x .25)-$150).

Unlike many dealerships, there was a fixed order in which the salespeople took turns waiting on customers. When each salesperson arrived at the dealership each morning, he signed his name on a list. The list specified the order in which the salespeople waited on customers. When a customer either walked into the showroom or called on the phone, the salesperson whose name was at the top of the list was responsible for waiting on or talking with that customer. If a salesperson "missed" his turn either by being on a break, or by not wanting to wait on a specific customer, his name was placed at the bottom of the list.

EMERGENT THEMES

Perceived Lack of Environmental Control

Overall, the salespeople perceived they had little control over their work environment, where there was only a tenuous connection between their actions and the outcome of a specific sales encounter. They were operating within a highly competitive market, and selling a car is typically a long, multi-stage transaction where the deal can fall through at any point, with little financial risk to the consumer. When questioned about the monthly range of number of cars sold, the salespeople generally agreed it was quite narrow, falling between 17 in a bad month and 20 in a good one. Only two salespeople reported the range to be wider; both attributed the variance to factors they didn't understand, or were outside of their control:

It's been as good as 38 (cars); we had less salesmen then though, we used to have only 3 and now we have 8 ... the worst I ever did was 7 in a month ...The real difference between a good and bad month is traffic. I don't think I do anything different. And you know what they say, you can't sell a ghost. (Mike)

Well, yesterday there certainly was enough traffic in here, but not the right kind. The quality just wasn't good. We can't control that though, it's completely out of our control. I would rather have fewer people, but better quality. (Hank)

The competitive environment within which these men worked contributed to this perceived lack of control. The manufacturer operated five additional dealerships within ten miles. Three competitors operated dealerships within one quarter of a mile. The surrounding neighborhoods were quite affluent, where buyers tended to be well-educated and sophisticated, engaging in extensive pre-search behaviors such as collecting dealer invoice information and reading *Consumer Reports*. The General Manager described the environment this way:

It used to be that customers were at the mercy of the salesmen, and now the salesmen are totally at the mercy of the customers. People are more sophisticated now, they know more and shop around. It used to be they bought out of loyalty, loyalty to a manufacturer and to a salesman. There's none of that anymore...In the old days salesmen made a lot more money on each sale. People weren't as sophisticated, they didn't shop around and know you could discount shop. (Larry)

Another factor contributing toward this perceived lack of control is the relatively long and complex sales cycle. Customers typically make multiple visits to a dealership before they buy a car. From the salesperson's perspective, many things can "go wrong" between the initial contact with a customer and a car purchase. A customer may spend multiple hours with a salesperson then fail to ask for him on subsequent visits. Or a customer may come back to buy on a salesperson's day off. In either case, it is up to the salespeople involved to "work something out", in terms of splitting commissions. However, this doesn't always occur.

Well, it was too bad. Mark should have had 50% of that (commission). You know he did all the ground work. The car was sold when those people left here after talking to him that first night. But when they came back they didn't ask for him,

so he doesn't get the commission ... Probably Mark wasn't too happy about it, but he'll get over it. Those things just happen. (Hank)

Sometimes a customer makes a deal with a salesperson, leaves a check as a deposit, then goes to another dealership and buys a car. If this occurs within 48 hours, legally the check hasn't bound the customer to the sale, and it must be returned.

Financing is another hurdle a salesperson must jump; he can strike a deal with a customer who is turned down for credit. Again, in this situation there is little he can do.

Poor Hank. This girl gives him $1000 cash, in his hand, for a Camry. He asks Rich to run a credit check on her and finds out she's bankrupt, and he gives it right back to her. (Jim)

This highly competitive environment suggests car buyers have a large number of alternatives from which to choose; they have multiple places to buy one of multiple kinds of cars, typically over an extended period of time. Emerson's (1962) theory of power-dependence relations predicts that this unilateral proliferation of alternatives will increase the dependence of salespeople on customers, increasing the power of customers, and lowering that of the salesperson. This low power base diminishes the salespersons' status vis-a-vis their customers. Within any relationship, the lower status participant contributes more to the relationship than the higher status one (Hochschild 1983). Furthermore, within our culture the job of selling cars is a relatively low status one; many customers have quite negative a priori attitudes about car salespeople before the sales encounter begins. This is clearly the perception of the salesperson: customers are not to be trusted, for they routinely break deals, lie, and in general, treat them with little respect.

I spent over 2 hours with them last week and they come in here and treat you like you're a clerk at Montgomery Ward making $3.65 an hour. They have no regard for you at all. (Mark)

You know, customers think that car salesmen are the slime of the earth. You can't believe the abuse, what they'll ask us to do they wouldn't ask a clerk at Woolworth's to do. They'll get us to move out cars; I wanna drive this one, I wanna drive that one, and we'll do it cause we have to! (Bob)

Look at them, I'd like to throw them out of here. The guy says to her, "Look at this piece of junk, they just put convertable tops on this crap. Park this in front of your house and watch your property values fall". They haven't even looked at me yet. They won't even look at me. (Rob)

Customer behaviors such as these magnify customer-salesperson status differentials. Asking to test drive multiple cars, failing to maintain eye contact, harshly criticizing cars, breaking deals, and lying to the salespeople about prices quoted at competitive dealerships are customer behaviors which they view as at best annoying, and at worst, unfair attempts to usurp control. Customers would not act this way, they feel, if they viewed the salesperson as being of equal status.

SALESPERSON ATTEMPTS TO USURP CONTROL

"Getting the Jump" on Customers

To the extent that a salesperson's primary objective is to maximize his earnings, we would expect him to acquiesce to these customer demands, simply ignoring demeaning comments and behaviors. His goal should be to satisfy the customer, in order to maximize the liklihood of a sale. This is not always what occurs. Rather, in many cases the salespeople come to view the sales encounter as a struggle to maintain control over the customer. Making a sale becomes a goal subordinate to the higher-order goal of maintaining control. This struggle was best described by the General Manager:

> You know, customers can't make a floormat out of me, they can't use me to wipe their feet on. You've got to lead them; they can't lead you. If a customer takes the lead I stop and come into my office. I leave them right on the floor, in front of a car. Then I motion for them to come into my office; I make them come to me. It's a psychological power thing. And when they start to chisel I say, "look, for the amount of money you want to pay you can't buy this car". They can buy a used car, or another model, but not this one. You have to keep the lead. (Larry)

The salespeople talked extensively among themselves about specific situations in which a customer tried to maintain control during the encounter, but the salesperson ultimately "won". While winning typically entailed a customer buying at the salesperson's price, it certainly was not limited to this behavior. A salesperson could also gain control by "letting a customer walk", refusing to let someone test drive a car, and simply refusing to negotiate at all.

> Like yesterday a man and his son come in here. The son was ready to walk from the beginning. But I got the father to listen for about 20 minutes. They didn't buy though, they thought they could get a better price. So I let them walk. (Jim)

> Get them out of here, I mean it. What the hell are they doing? They are deciding between a coup and a four-door; two totally different cars. A decision like that they can't be serious about buying; either you have a family and need a four-door or you don't. They can't possibly be making that kind of decision. I don't want them in here causing trouble, walking around just creating traffic. I want to get them out of here. (Larry)

> He told you he won't be able to buy a car until next month and you let him test drive? I wouldn't let him touch a car with a story like that. (Bob)

The struggle between service providers and customers has been documented across many types of occupations including waiters (Mars and Nicod 1984), jazz musicians (Becker 1951), domestic car salespeople (Miller 1964), bus drivers (Richman 1969), strippers (Boles and Garbin 1974) and cocktail waitresses (Spradley and Mann 1975). Leidner (1993) describes the Combined Insurance salesperson training program, which explicitly recognizes the need for salespeople to control customers, who are "raw materials to be manipulated, not superiors to be obeyed" (p. 122). Whyte (1946) in his study of restaurants notes,

> The first point that stands out is that the well-adjusted waitress does not simply respond to her customers. She acts with some

skill to control their behavior. The first question to ask when we look at the customer relationship is, "Does the waitress get the jump on the customer, or does the customer get the jump on the waitress?" (p. 109)

From a service provider's perspective, virtually any kind of behavior can signal an attempt on behalf of a customer to control the service encounter. From the customer's perspective, as well as the perspective of the organization, these behaviors are likely to be viewed as totally appropriate. For example, bus drivers resent when passengers flag them down by waving instruments such as umbrellas rather than their arms (Richman 1969), and jazz musicians resent when audiences request certain types of songs (Becker 1951). Vendors become especially annoyed when shoppers are careless with merchandise, require high levels of assistance during busy times, seem impatient, and exhibit "difficult" dispositions (Prus 1989). McDonalds' counter workers prefer customers who "know how to play their part", and resent those who seem to disregard the workers' concern for speed (Leidner 1993). In the current study, the car salespeople strongly resented being asked to test drive multiple cars, and customers who brought other dealers' advertisements with them into the showroom.

Regardless of customers' motives for engaging in these behaviors, service providers perceive each as being inappropriate attempts by the customer to maintain control of the sales encounter. However, given their occupational role, they feel they have no alternative but to acquiesce. As Hochschild (1983) notes:

> ... in the public world of work, it is often part of an individual's job to accept uneven exchanges, to be treated with disrespect or anger by a client ... where the customer is king, unequal exchanges are normal, and from the beginning customer and client assume different rights ... the ledger is supposedly evened by a wage (p. 85).

Customer Taxonomies

For a salesperson to maintain control and in general, to feel effective within his work environment, it becomes extremely important for him to be able to identify early-on in the sales process those customers who are most likely to allow him to do so. The question becomes, which customers are most likely to allow him to "get the jump"? Which person will actually buy a car? This prediction is an extremely difficult if not impossible one. In an effort to bring order to this uncertain, ambiguous work environment, the salespeople developed an elaborate customer taxonomy. The function of this taxonomy is to provide causal explanations of customer behavior, increasing the perceived predictability of their work environment (Davis 1959).

The taxonomy is based on two types of customer cues. First, customers are classifed as soon as they walk through the showroom door, before engaging in any conversation whatsoever. This initial classification is, by necessity, based on purely physical attributes such as gender, dress, age, and most often, ethnicity. Cues such as these have been labelled by previous reseachers as primary and secondary traits (Mars and Nicod 1984), transaction-defining cues (Rafaeli and Sutton 1989), and "body gloss" (Goffman 1971). For the car salespeople, the most commonly used physically-based categories were "hindus" and "dots" (Asian Indians), "chinks" (Orientals, typically Koreans), "blacks", "homosexuals", Russian Jews, and "professors". "Professors" are customers who visibly carry information with them, typically *Consumer Reports* and various newspaper ads. The behaviors associated with these categories are derived from pre-existing cultural stereotypes, as well as the stories, myths, and folklore of fellow salespeople.

"Chinks" are seen as tough negotiators, outdone only by "hindus". Russian Jews are aggressive and argumentative, and shop around. "Blacks" are bad credit risks, while "homosexuals" are good ones, trading in "clean cars in good condition".

Once the salesperson begins interacting with a customer, he is able to adjust his initial physically-based classification, making finer distinctions based on idiosyncratic customer behaviors. Thus, the second phase of the customer classification process is based on cues derived from the customer-salesperson interaction. Customer categories derived this way are "moochers", who take a lot of the salesperson's time, "get-me-dones", who had been denied credit at multiple dealers and simply want to buy a car with guaranteed credit and low monthly payments — with little or no regard for the ultimate price of the car, "know-it-alls", who do extensive research before reaching the dealer and let the salesperson know it, and "tire kickers", who physically bang the cars around and ask a lot of questions. "Moochers", "know-it-alls", and "tire kickers" are represented across all physcially-based categories; e.g., a "moocher" is just as likely to be a Russian Jew as he is to be a "chink". The only exception is "get-me-dones", most often "blacks from the South Side".

One of the most compelling aspects of this taxonomy is that while the salespeople quite explicitly spoke of it amongst themselves, when posed with the questions, "How can you tell a good prospect from a bad one?", or "How can you tell whether or not a customer will buy a car?" the answer was always, without exception, "You never can tell". Any salesperson who thought he could infer a customer's behavior based on one of these categories, they explained, would be ineffectual, and wouldn't last in the business very long. Every salesperson had a repertoire of stories, replete with examples of situations in which he had misjudged a customer. The theme of every story was, "people who look like they won't/can't buy a car sometimes do". The following is prototypic of the stories they told:

... one day this big guy comes in wearing this really wrinkled, dirty pinstripe suit. He was a mess. He says he wants to see an Electra. Now this was a *really* expensive car. So I think to myself, if this guy can afford an Electra, I can afford the Sears Tower. So I ask him if he has a trade-in ... (it's) a Cadillac with 600 miles... we had to give *him* money on the deal, figuring the trade-in and all. You just never know. (Jim)

Mars and Nicod (1984) in their study of waiters also comment on the prevalence of these types of stories among restaurant waiters:

There is a wealth of folklore in the industry about eccentrics who have none of the defining traits — either primary or secondary — that is appropriate to their particularly high status. Stories are told of well-known lords, politicians and actors who appear in restaurants ragged, dirty, drunk or using crude language. These, which are impossible to authenticate, point up the anxiety that waiters experience in making their assessments on relatively little evidence (p. 61).

It seems that instead of updating or even abandoning their classifications in the face of contradictory evidence, service providers tend to rely on "... posterioir reconstructions and rationalizations" that conform with their preconceived stereotypes (Davis 1959, p. 163).

Salespeople classify customers, rightly or wrongly, to bring order and structure into an otherwise uncertain environment. Specifically, classification allows a salesperson "... to identify who

people are, anticipate their behavior, and plan strategies for performing (his) role" (Spradley and Mann 1975, p. 63). Each customer category has associated with it specific customer behaviors; taxonomies help the salespeople choose appropriate selling strategies to match these behaviors. "Hindus" and "get-me-dones" both signal to the salesperson that he should start with a high asking price, while Russian Jews, "professors", and "know-it-alls" signal lower, more competitive ones. It is "worth it" for a salesperson to spend a lot of time with a "get-me-done" or "homosexual", because there is likely to be a high payoff; however, a salesperson only wastes time trying to sell to a "moocher".

During the course of the fieldwork, multiple salespeople were observed refusing to wait on customers, by "passing" on their turn. In all cases, the salespeople made this decision based on purely physically-based cues, before any interaction had taken place at all. Instead of waiting on these customers they preferred to watch television. Jim's reaction was prototypic of this scenario: when an Indian man and woman walked into the dealership he looked at them and said, "I don't want anymore; I give up". When questioned about this behavior the salespeople in all cases reported that the customer would only "waste my time". The categories into which they had classified the customers suggested that regardless of the selling strategy chosen, a car would not be sold. Watching television would, in their eyes, have a higher payoff.

Customer-Directed Hostility

The emic terms used to categorize customers by the car salespeople as well as by service providers within other occupations are typically quite derogatory. Negative terms such as "chink", "know-it-all" and "moocher" were used by the car salespeople to describe their customers. Waitresses refer to bar patrons as "hands" and "bitches" (Spradley and Mann 1975), jazz musicians refer to audience members as "squares" (Becker 1951), bus riders are called "briefcase and jam-butty men" by drivers (Richman 1969), airline passengers are known as "irates" and "discount people" to flight attendants (Hochschild 1983), waiters refer to restaurant patrons as "punters" and "prostitutes" (Mars and Nicod 1984), taxi riders call their fares "slobs" and "yokels" (Davis 1959), and Disneyland ride operators label demanding patrons "ducks" (Van Maanen and Kunda 1989). Van Maanen (1978) theorizes that in order to be deserving of such negative labels, the customer has to have violated a norm "sacred in the occupational culture"; he terms these types of customers "assholes".

Classifying customers into derogatory groups (known only to the salespeople) represents one level of customer-directed hostility. Hostility takes another form when it is more explicitly manifest within a sales encounter:

Did you smell those Nigerians? Man, every time they got close to me I had to move away. Maybe they think B.O. smells good or something. And he's a doctor! I wouldn't let him get near me with than smell, man! (Jim)

Look at those two. They make me sick. I'm doing her a favor by the size of that rear end. (He had taken away a box of cookies, intended for the salesmen, which the customer had started eating) ... If that man was on fire I wouldn't piss on him to put it out. Look at him with his crazy wife; typical Midwesterners, crackpots both of them. (Mark)

Not too many "dots" today. You know, Hitler had the wrong idea with the Jews. He should have left the Jews alone, they're OK. He should have gotten rid of all the "dots"... they're the only ones I can't take. I was the only person who stood up and cheered when Ghandi died in that movie. They come in here and are $2-3,000 off everytime...I just won't wait on them. (Steve)

Referring to a customer as a "dot" or "chink" to a fellow worker is one thing; moving away from them because they "smell bad", jerking cookies away because "her rear end is too big", or simply refusing to wait on a customer is quite another. In the first two scenarios, the salesperson explicitly acted on his hostility in a manner that was potentially perceptable to the customer. In the third scenario, the hostility is so great, that the type of service this salesperson would give any Indian walking into the dealership could be questioned. Had these customers been asked to assess these service encounters, it is likely that they would have judged the attitudes of the salespeople to be less than satisfactory. This is key, given the findings of Bitner, Booms and Tetreault (1990):

... it is not the quality of the core service or failure to address a special need or request that causes dissatisfaction, but rather the assessed character or attitude of the service employee (p. 81).

The hostility exhibited by the salespeople toward their customers is a typical reaction to situations in which a person is prevented from obtaining a desired outcome (Wortman and Brehm 1975). From the salesperson's perspective, customers serve as obstacles to multiple desired outcomes: money, self-efficacy and control. Derogatory customer-labelling and hostile behaviors are further attempts by the salespeople to exert control within their work environment.

DISCUSSION

This research takes a descriptive approach to understanding sales encounters. The findings suggest that a comprehensive examination of the sales process must take into account the intrinsic, experiential aspects of the sales encounter — from the salesperson's perspective. Salespeople are not exclusively motivated to maximize their earnings, but also to improve the quality of their sales and work experiences. A salesperson realizes important non-pecuniary rewards when he "passes" on a customer and opts instead to watch television, sells at "my price", "allows" a customer to leave the showroom, and labels someone a "moocher".

It is the salesperson's attempt to realize these non-pecuniary rewards that can lead to the discrepancy between an organization's service specifications and its ultimate delivery. The dealership's 100% commission system is unable to squelch a salesperson's intrinsic need to maintain control and to feel effective within his work environment. At times, these needs conflict with those of the organization and the customer (Leidner 1993). A by-product of this conflict is negative, customer-directed hostility. It is at this point that the potential is greatest for a customer to experience a quite negative sales encounter.

There is ample evidence that service providers' negative feelings toward customers "leak out" both intentionally and by mistake (Hochschild 1983; Leidner 1993; Sutton 1991). Negative feelings can be expressed in a multitude of ways, some barely perceptable by customers, and others quite explicit. Flight attendants report they are most likely to let their true (negative) feelings surface when flights are crowded with demanding passengers, and they are required "... to make personal human contact at an inhuman speed" (Hochschild 1983, p. 126). A refusal to smile or a curt reply to a customer request can signal a negative emotion, as can "accidentally" spilling a drink on a particularly demeaning passenger.

Disneyland employees report using tactics such as the "seatbelt squeeze", "a rapid cinching up of required seatbelt such that the passenger is doubled over at the point of departure and left gasping for the duration of the ride", and the "seatbelt slap", "an equally distinguished gesture by which an offending customer receives a sharp, quick snap of a hard plastic belt across the face" (Van Maanen and Kunda 1989; p. 67). Both taxi drivers (Davis 1959) and bus drivers (Richman 1969) report intentionally "missing" customers they don't like, or making them "run for it".

The display of negative emotions by service providers can have profound effects on customers' assessments of service quality. Customers were not interviewed as part of this project, therefore, we do not know their perceptions of specific sales encounters. However, we are able to do some speculation. It is not likely that, if questioned, the Nigerians would report they didn't buy a car from Jim because he had unusually high requirements for interpersonal space maintenance, or that the "Midwesterners" would report not buying because Mark jerked the cookies away from them. It is possible, however, that they would report not buying because they just didn't feel comfortable with or trust the salesperson; attitudes formed by the salespersons' behaviors.

Though the current study focused on a sales organization, there are implications for all organizations that employ high-contact workers. During the Industrial Revolution organizations realized the importance of product standardization, learning how to design manufacturing processes to reach this goal. A service-based economy, however, creates a new set of demands: the standardization of human interaction (Leidner 1993). Despite organizations' attempts to control employees' behaviors, they sometimes choose to act in "unstandardized" ways. It is ultimately the service provider's decision whether or not to act pleasant, indifferent, or even hostile toward a customer.

The standardization of highly interactive service work can have both positive and negative effects on employees' attitudes and behaviors. Hochschild (1983) points out the largely negative consequences of such standardization, such as workers losing control of their "real" emotions and feelings. Leidner (1993) notes, however, that for McDonald's counter workers, the memorized scripts they were instructed to use with customers "... apparently seemed a lifeline rather than a constraint" (p. 116). Likewise, the scripts and "feeling rules" Combined Insurance salespeople memorized as part of their intensive Positive Mental Attitude training helped to shield them from personalizing customer insults and rejection.

In order to provide high levels of service in an efficient, effective way, an organization must first identify all interactions, no matter how fleeting, a customer may have with contact personnel (Olivia, Oliver and MacMillan 1992). The next step is to determine the role each encounter plays in influencing customers' judgments of service quality. To the extent that a particular service encounter is deemed important, employees occupying that contact position need to be selected and trained accordingly. The most important finding to come out of this research is that organizations need to explicitly acknowledge the inherent, very human conflict between employees and customers. Specifically, they need to recognize that the needs of their employees may not always be congruent with a "customer is king" mentality. Future research needs to address exactly how, and in what form this recognition should occur.

REFERENCES

Becker, Howard S. (1951), "The Professional Dance Musician and His Audience," *The American Journal of Sociology,* LVII, (September), 158-165.

Bitner, Mary Jo, Bernard M. Booms and Mary Stanfield Tetreault (1990), "The Service Encounter: Diagnosing Favorable and Unfavorable Incidents," *Journal of Marketing* (January), 71-84.

Boles, Jacqueline and Albeno P. Garbin (1974), "The Strip Club and Stripper-Customer Patterns of Interaction," *Sociology and Social Research*, 58 (January), 136-144.

Davis, Fred (1959), "The Cabdriver and His Fare: Facets of a Fleeting Relationship, "*The American Journal of Sociology*, LXV (September), 158-165.

Emerson, Richard M. (1962), "Power-Dependence Relations," *American Sociological Review*, 27 (February), 32-33.

Goffman, Erving (1971), *Relations in Public*, New York: Harper & Row.

Hochschild, Arlie Russell (1983), *The Managed Heart*, Berkeley: University of California Press, Ltd.

Leidner, Robin (1993), *Fast Food, Fast Talk: Service Work and the Routinization of Everyday Life*, Berkeley: University of California Press, Ltd.

Mars, Gerald and Michael Nicod (1984), *The World of Waiters*, Boston: George Allen & Unwin.

Miller, Stephen (1964), "The Social Base of Sales Behavior," *Social Problems*, 12 (Summer), 15-24.

Oliva, Terence A., Richard L. Oliver, and Ian C. MacMillan (1992), "A Catastrophe Model for Developing Service Satisfaction Strategies," *Journal of Marketing*, 56 (July), 83-95.

Prus, Robert C. (1989), *Making Sales: Influence as Interpersonal Accomplishment*, Newbury Park: Sage Publications.

Rafaeli, Anat and Robert I. Sutton (1989), "The Expression of Emotion in Organizational Life," in *Research in Organizational Behavior*, L.L. Cummings and Barry M. Staw, eds. Greenwich: JAI Press, Inc.

Richman, Joel (1964), "Busmen V. The Public," *New Society*, (August 14), 243-244.

Spradley, James P. and Brenda J. Mann (1975), *The Cocktail Waitress*, New York: John Wiley & Sons, Inc.

Strauss, Anselm and Juliet Corbin (1990), *Basics of Qualitative Research*, Newbury Park: Sage Publications.

Sutton, Robert I. (1991) "Maintaining Norms About Expressed Emotions: The Case of Bill Collectors," *Administrative Science Quarterly*, 36 (June), 245-268.

Van Maanen, John (1978), "The Asshole," in *Policing*, P.K. Manning and John Van Maanen, eds., Santa Monica: Goodyear Press.

_____ and Gideon Kunda (1989), "Real Feelings: Emotional Expression and Organizational Culture," in *Research in Organizational Behavior*, L.L. Cummings and Barry M. Staw, eds. Greenwich: JAI Press Inc.

Whyte, William Foote (1948), *Human Relations in the Restaurant Industry*, New York: McGaw-Hill Book Company, Inc.

Wortman, Camille and Jack Brehm (1975), "Response to Uncontrollable Outcomes: An Integration of Reactance Theory and The Learned Helplessness Model," in *Advances in Experimental Social Psychology*, L. Berkowitz, ed. New York: Academic Press.

Quantitative and Qualitative Differences in Older and Younger Consumers' Recall of Radio Advertising

Catherine A. Cole, University of Iowa
Nadine M. Castellano, University of Iowa[1]
Donald Schum, University of Iowa

ABSTRACT

In this experiment consumers listened to a radio program with either one or three repetitions of three embedded test commercials. In the commercials, we manipulated either the level of background noise or the presence of a disclaimer or the level of within message claim repetitions. Older adults had lower recall for claims made in advertising than younger adults. In addition, the format of the test commercials improved younger adults recall more than older adults recall. We also found preliminary evidence that older adults tended to recall advertising in different ways than younger adults.

Prior literature has unveiled age differences in responses to advertising in a variety of media(Cole and Houston 1987, Gorn et al 1991, Stephens and Warrens 1983/1984). In this experiment, we examine how three advertising characteristics (level of background noise, presence of disclaimer and level of within message repetitions) affect older and younger consumers' recall of radio advertising. The first two factors have been unstudied with respect to older adults. Although message repetitions have been studied, within message repetitions of the same claims have not. These factors may differentially affect elderly adult's recall when compared to that of younger adults. Consequently, the first major contribution of this research is to investigate age differences in learning under three specific advertising formats.

We focus on one medium, the radio. Researchers have not studied radio advertising as much as they have studied television and print advertising. Interestingly, because radio is only an audio medium, theories developed to understand how television and print advertising work may not generalize to radio advertising. Consequently, an additional contribution of this research is to enhance our understanding of how radio advertising works.

Much of the previous research investigating age differences in advertising focuses on quantitative differences in recall. Qualitative difference, however, may reveal additional insights into how the elderly process information contained in advertisements. Following Adams, et al (1990) recall protocols are analyzed for differences in recall content. Analysis of the data from this experiment is thus both quantitative and qualitative, fulfilling our final objective of expanding the way we measure age differences in recall.

BACKGROUND AND HYPOTHESES

In order to study the three advertising factors of background noise, within message repetitions and disclaimer presence, we must first investigate the process by which adults recall aurally presented information. Current models of speech processing recognize that speech must be processed "on-line" as it is presented, thus requiring continuous processing in working memory; (Stine and Wingfield 1987). Even though working memory is partially cleared so that sentences can be processed, some information must be retained to determine the coherence of the speech. (Baddeley, Lodge, Nimmo-Smith and Bereton 1985). The listener uses linguistic context and world knowledge to frame and interpret auditory input.

In summary, when decoding speech, we first interpret relatively small chunks of information. Then we integrate each chunk with previously processed information (Stine and Wingfield 1987). Impairments of prose comprehension result whenever the capacity of the working memory buffer is exceeded. Researchers have documented age differences in this process. They often attribute such age differences to age-related declines in working memory speed (Light and Burke 1988). In our research, we ask about conditions that might affect age differences in processing of radio advertising.

Previous work suggests that age differences in performance on speech perception tests tend to be greater in noisy conditions than in less noisy conditions (Hutchinson 1989). Hutchinson speculates that this may occur because background babble has a masking effect on acoustic cues that aid in understanding. Gorn et al (1991) extend this research by predicting that background music in television commercials may impair learning among elderly consumers. They argue and find that music distracts the elderly from attending to and processing relevant information. Recall of product claims was lower for elderly exposed to the commercial with background music than when compared to elderly exposed to the same commercial without background music.

Based on this literature, we predict:

H1: Older adults will recall more from a message without background music than from a message with background music, but the presence or absence of background music will not affect younger adults' recall levels.

Another important variable is repetition level. The relationship between repetitions and learning has been well established through years of research in verbal learning and in studies on advertising effects. Consequently, we expect that as commercial repetitions go from low to moderate consumers will recall more about the commercials. Although one would expect this to be true of both younger and older adults, one would expect that age differences might diminish at moderate levels of repetition because older adults, starting from a lower recall level, would experience a disproportionately high increase in learning. The aging studies literature indicates that increasing repetitions of word pair associates reduces age differences in recall (Kausler 1982). Thus we hypothesize:

H2: Both older and younger consumers will recall more as commercial repetitions increase, but older consumers will benefit more than younger consumers from the increased repetitions.

A related, but not as well studied, issue is whether increasing the number of within message repetitions of key claims affects learning. Sewall and Sarel (1986) find that as the number of brand name mentions increases, the level of brand name recall increases in a population of varying ages. Thus, not only do we predict that

[1]Acknowledgements: Nadine Catellano is supported by the University of Iowa Center on Aging through NIA Grant #AG00214. The subject money was supported by a grant from the Marketing Science Institute.

increasing the number of within message repetitions of key claims will increase learning, but we also predict that it will differentially benefit older consumers:

> *H3: As the number of within message repetitions of key claims increases, both older and younger consumers will recall more, but older consumers will benefit more from the increased repetitions.*

A final factor we looked at was the presence or absence of a disclaimer at the end of a commercial. In order to correct a misleading commercial, the Federal Trade Commission requires the advertiser to produce subsequent commercials with explicit warning messages. In this article, we are interested in whether the presence or absence of a disclaimer affects older and younger adult's recall of the commercial. Generally the disclaimer will add to the amount of information in the commercial because the advertiser generally wants to communicate specific claims, whether or not a disclaimer is present. We hypothesize that younger adults will recall more when more information is present. Thus we hypothesize the following:

> *H4: A disclaimer at the end of a commercial will increase younger adults, but not older adults, claim recall.*

Age Differences in Content of Recall

The first four hypotheses concentrate on whether or not the amount of recall differs between older and younger subjects. An important question is does the content of recall vary by age. The marketing literature abounds with studies which assess advertising effectiveness by awarding points for every claim recalled by the subject (e.g., Cole and Houston 1987, Singh, Rothschild and Churchill 1988, Unnava and Burnkrant 1991). However, in the gerontology literature Adams and her colleagues (Adams, Labouvie-Vief, Hobart and Dorosz 1990) suggest that traditional measures of recall emphasize ability to reproduce propositions contained in text, while devaluing text evaluation and interpretive processes. Thus, these traditional measures favor younger adults whose main developmental task is to acquire and store the information and knowledge systems of their culture. (See Adams et al. 1990.) In contrast, older adults may take text based information and encode it into more integrative units of meaning. Such an encoding style would be consistent with the older cohorts developmental task, which is to find efficient means of storing information and for transmitting cultural knowledge.

> *H5: Older adults recall protocols will include smaller percentages of exact or gist listings of claims and larger percentages of integrative ideas than younger adults' recall protocols.*

METHOD

Experimental Design

The research design was a 2 age group (21-64, 65-88) x 2 repetition level(1 or 3 repetitions) x 2 format between subject design. Each subject heard 45 minutes of programming with three embedded test commercials and two embedded filler commercials.

Procedures

We tested subjects in groups of five to twenty persons each. First, a pure-tone hearing screening was completed on each subject under earphones in a quiet room. Hearing was screened at 30 Db HL at the octave frequencies from 250 through 4000 HZ. In order to be included in the study, each subject needed to pass the hearing screening at all frequencies in at least one ear. The use of a screening level of 30 Db HL in combination with the presentation level for the speech material of 75 Db SPL insured that the signal from the recorded broadcast was fully audible in at least one ear of each listener.

If the subject failed the hearing test she was still allowed to participate in the experiment, but her questionnaire was marked for removal from the actual analysis. After every subject had completed the hearing test, she learned that we wanted consumers to evaluate two different radio programs. We then played the tape version dictated by the randomization procedure. After listening to the tape, subjects completed the questionnaires. They were paid ($7.00 per person) and then were free to leave. It took about one and a half hours for subjects to complete the study.

Subjects

We recruited 170 consumers from parents groups and senior centers, but included in the analysis only the 157 who passed the hearing screening test. We conducted our analysis by comparing two age groups of consumers: those under the age of 65 and those 65 and over. The average age for the younger subjects was 40 (S.D.=8.8 years); the average age for the older subjects was 74 (S.D.=6.6). The younger consumers had more education than the older consumers (t=3.17, df=144, p<.05). Both groups were equally likely to have radios in their houses; both estimated that they listened to the radio about 14 hours a week.

Stimulus Material and Radio Programming

From two radio stations outside the test market, we obtained tapes of regular morning drive talk shows. We then edited the programs to insert our own music and advertisements. The first show included an opening and then an interview with a representative from Sea World and Bush Garden. The second show also had an opening and then played music. To make sure that the music would appeal to subjects of all ages we edited in 3 top hits from 1992, 1936 and 1946. We prepared different versions of our radio show tape by embedding three test and two filler commercials. The format and repetition level of the commercials varied across versions.

To select commercials we acquired tapes of commercials from ad agencies. One format manipulation was the *number of within message repetitions of key claims*. We had a bank cash card ad that made 3 claims during the 30 second commercial. We professionally added a tag line at the end of the ad in which the announcer said "Remember folks...." and then repeated the claims. Another format manipulation involved the *subtraction of background noise*. We had an ad for a business pages book that had a persistent scratchy violin in the background throughout the 30 second commercial. In our tape editing facilities, we hired actors to redo the ad without the scratchy violin as background noise. Another format manipulation involved the creation of a new commercial. We perused the FTC records for cases of deceptive advertising and found one for a product that starts cars with dead batteries. We then created two versions of a commercial for this product, one with and one without *a disclaimer* required by the FTC.

Dependent Variables

1. Claim Recall. To obtain recall measures we asked participants to write down what was said about a specific product in each commercial. Following the traditional means of measuring recall, we compared this response against an actual list of claims in the

TABLE 1
Claim Recall
(Means and Standard Deviations)

| | Younger Adults | | | | Older Adults | | | |
| | Format A | | Format B | | Format A | | Format B | |
	R = 1	R = 3	R = 1	R = 3	R = 1	R = 3	R = 1	R = 3
Car Starter[1]	.71 (.59)	1.25 (.79)	1.71 (1.16)	1.96 (1.33)	.44 (.65)	.63 (.68)	.44 (.70)	.75 (.93)
Bank Card[1]	.17 (.53)	.65 (1.04)	.35 (.70)	1.39 (1.33)	.0	.05 (.23)	.11 (.32)	.50 (.73)
Business Pages[1]	.41 (.51)	.75 (.72)	.41 (.62)	.57 (.73)	0	0	.06 (.23)	.19 (.40)
N	22	23	20	21	18	18	17	18

[1]For the Car Starter ad, Format A had do disclaimer, Format B did.
  For the Bank Card ad, Format B repeated the three main claims at the end of the commercial.
  For the Business Pages ad, Format B had background noise.

commercial. Two separate coders recorded the number of claims recalled (either gist or verbatim recall was acceptable). They agreed on 96% of their counts. We arbitrarily selected the first coder's count in the cases of disagreement.

2. Content Analysis of Recall Protocols. We also analyzed these responses according to a classification scheme specified by Adams, et al. (1990). First, we divided each recall protocol into separate idea units. An idea unit is "a combination of words in the text that conveyed a single complete idea" (Adams et al. 1990). Using an example from a Swiss Airlines commercial, if the subject stated that "There was a man asking a passenger at Heathrow airport which airline flew the most often to Switzerland, but the passenger couldn't get it." Four idea units would be identified. These idea units consist of (1) the concept of a man asking a passenger questions, (2) the fact that it took place at Heathrow airport, (3) the concept that the question was which airline flew most often to Switzerland, and (4) the passenger didn't understand. Each identified idea unit was assigned to one of the following four response categories (again following Adams, et al. 1990): (a) Text-based listings, (b) Addition listing, (c) Integration listing, and (d) Interpretation of story. Statements not falling in these categories (false and irrelevant statements) were ignored. We coded an idea unit as a *text-based listing* if it was a basic repeating of the text in the ad. (For example, see the first three idea units in the Swiss Airlines example above.) An *addition listing* would incorporate a single idea from outside the actual advertisement. We coded an idea unit as an *integration listing* if it condensed and summarized the information in the advertisement. (See the fourth idea unit in the Swiss Airlines example above.) An *interpretation* would occur if the coder could not tie the response directly to any aspect of the advertisement per se, but found it relevant to the story as a whole. In addition, interpretations included some type of personal judgment or opinion. There was very high agreement between the independent coders (95%) about how to classify each idea unit.

RESULTS

Claim Recall

Table 1 contains the mean and standard deviations for claim recall scores; Table 2 contains the individual ANOVA results for each advertisement.

1. Car Starter Ad. Elderly adults recalled significantly fewer claims from the Car Starter ad than younger adults (F(1,147)=33.25, p<.01). Also, all adults recalled more claims after hearing the message three times than after hearing it once (F(1,147)=4.94, p<.02). Although this finding is partially consistent with hypothesis H2, which notes that as repetitions increase claim recall should increase, it is inconsistent with the notion that older adults should differentially benefit from increasing repetitions when compared to younger adults.

The significant format effect is qualified by the age by format interaction. After young adults heard the message with the disclaimer, they recalled significantly more claims than after hearing the message without the warning (p<.06), but message format did not affect how much older adults recalled (p<.24). This result is consistent with Hypothesis H4 which suggested that a disclaimer would differentially increase the recall of younger consumers.

2. Bank Card Ad. The significant main effects for claim recall for the Bank Card ad are qualified by significant two way interactions: the age by repetition interaction (F(1,154)=4.8, p<.03) and the significant repetition by format interaction (F=3.4, p<.06). There were no significant age differences in claim recall when listeners heard the message only once (p<.23), but when repetitions increased to 3, younger adults recalled more claims (p<.01), while older adults did not recall significantly more claims (p<.20). This pattern meant that at three repetitions a significant age difference in recall emerged (p<.01). Contrary to H2, younger adults, not older adults, were differentially benefited by increasing repetitions.

The repetition by format interaction is interesting from an advertising perspective. At one repetition, there was no difference in recall levels between the messages with and without repetitions of key claims (p<.41), at 3 repetitions, the commercial with more

TABLE 2
ANOVA Results

	Car Starter Ad		Bank Card Ad		Business Pages Ad	
	Claim Recall		Claim Recall		Claim Recall	
	F	P	F	P	F	P
Age (A)	33.25	.01	15.25	.01	35.76	.01
Repetition (R)	4.94	.02	16.00	.01	3.87	.05
Format (F)	9.90	.01	9.14	.00	<1	
A x R	<1		4.80	.03	1.25	.25
A x F	7.42	.01	<1		1.82	.17
R x F	<1		3.4	.06	<1	
A x R x F	<1		<1		1.0	.31

TABLE 3
Content Analysis of Recall Protocols: Types of Idea Units as a Percentage of Total Idea Units

	Car Starter Ad		Bank Card Ad		Business Pages Ad	
	Younger Adults	Older Adults	Younger Adults	Older Adults	Younger Adults	Older Adults
Listings	.91	.82	.56	.44	.74	.67
Additions	.004	.00	.01	.00	.02	.00
Integrations	.08	.13	.43	.49	.24	.19
Interpretations	.01	.05	.00	.07	.00	.14

repetitions generated significantly stronger recall levels (p<.01) for both age groups. This offers partial support for Hypothesis H3 which predicts that as within message repetitions increases, recall should increase.

3. Business Pages Ad. There were two significant main effects and no interactions. Older adults recalled significantly less than younger adults and repetitions increased recall. Thus, we have no support for hypothesis H1 predicting that background music would differentially affect older adults. This results offers partial support for H2 which predicts that recall increases as repetitions increase.

Content Analysis of Recall

We next analyzed the recall protocols of our consumers. The percentages of idea units that fell into each thought category for each advertisement for each age group are shown in Table 3. It appears that older adults (when compared to younger adults) tend to produce a smaller percentage of listings and a larger percentage of integrations and interpretations in their recall protocols. However no differences were statistically significant. Thus we have weak support for hypothesis H5 which predicts age differences in the content of recall.

CONCLUSIONS

At the outset, we stated that we wanted to develop a better understanding of how radio advertising works. We found that increasing the number of repetitions of a commercial from low to moderate increases claim recall, regardless of commercial format. (For the Car Starter and the Business Pages Ads increasing repetitions improved claim recall for both age groups, for the Bank Card Ad increasing repetitions improved claim recall only for the younger consumers.)

We expected to find and found that older consumers recall less from radio advertising than younger consumers. We had also expected that our format manipulations (designed to facilitate processing) would differentially benefit older adults. Instead, we found that either both age groups benefited equally or that younger adults benefited more. For example, increasing repetitions of the bank card ad improved commercial recall for younger adults, but not older adults.

We also investigated whether the emphasis on literal or gist recall overstated the size of age differences in recall by content analyzing older and younger adult's recall protocols. We found no significant differences in percentages of types of thought. However, we found trends suggesting that elderly adults tend to generate more integrative and interpretive idea units than younger adults. We can speculate that at higher levels of repetition, where more elderly consumers recall the commercials, more differences in the content of recall protocols may emerge.

We were concerned that an alternative explanation for our results may be that older adults were less interested or involved with the test products than younger adults. At the end of the questionnaire, we collected involvement measures for the three product classes for the test items. We tested for age differences in level of involvement with the three product classes and found one: older adults were more interested in a new way to start a disabled car (the car starter product) than younger adults (t=2.05, p<.04). Notice, however, that if involvement affects recall levels, the involvement results bias our data toward not finding age differences in recall.

This research provides insight into how radio advertising in remembered. It follows up on Sewall and Sarrel's (1986) by manipulating radio commercial format factors and evaluating impact on recall. In addition, Adams's method for measuring recall seem to indicate that traditional claim recall measures may not capture all the information that older adult's remember.

REFERENCES

Adams, C., G. Labouvie-Vief, C. Hobart and M. Dorosz (1990), "Adult Age Group Differences in Story Recall Style," *Journal of Gerontology: Psychological Sciences*, 45(1),P17-P27.

Baddeley, A. Logie, R. Nimmo-Smith, I & Brereton, N. (1985) "Components of fluent reading." *Journal of Memory and Language*, 24, 119-131

Bruner, G. (1990) "Music, Mood and Marketing" *Journal of Marketing*, 54(October): 94-104.

Cole, C. and M. Houston (1987), "Encoding and Media Effects on Consumer Learning Deficiencies in the Elderly," *Journal of Marketing Research*, 24 (February):55-63.

Cohen,G.(1988) " Age Differences in Memory for Texts: Production Deficiencies or Processing Limitations?" in *Language, Memory and Aging*, eds. L. Light and D. Burke, New York: Cambridge University Press, 171-190.

Gorn, G. M. Goldberg, A. Chattopadhyay and D. Litvack (1991), "Music and Information in Commercials: Their Effects with an Elderly Sample, *Journal of Advertising Research*, 31(Oct/Nov),23-32.

Hutchinson, K.(1989) "Influence of Sentence Context on Speech Perception in Young and Older Adults" *Journal of Gerontology: Psychological Sciences*, 44(2):P36-44.

Kausler,D.(1982) *Experimental Psychology and Human Aging*, New York:John Wiley & Sons.

Sewall, M. and D. Sarel (1986), "Characteristics of Radio Commercials and Their Recall Effectiveness," *Journal of Marketing*, 50(January):52-59.

Singh, S., M. Rothschild, and G. Churchill, Jr. (1988), "Recognition Versus Recall as Measures of Television Commercial Forgetting," *Journal of Marketing Research*, 25, (February), 72-80.

Stephens, N. and R. Warrens (1983/1984), "Advertising Frequency Requirements for Older Adults," *Journal of Advertising Research*, 23(December/January):23-32.

Stine, E. and A. Wingfield (1987) "Process and Strategy in Memory for Speech Among Younger and Older Adults" *Psychology and Aging* 2(3):272-279.

Unnava, H. Rao and Robert E. Burnkrant, (1991), "Effects of Repeating Varied Ad Executions of Brand Name Memory," *Journal of Marketing Research*, 28, (November), 406-416.

Zelinksi, E. and M. Gilewski (1988) "Integrating Information from Discourse: Do Older Adults Show Deficits?" in *Language, Memory and Aging* op cit

The Children's Birthday Party: A Study of Mothers as Socialization Agents

Cele Otnes, University of Illinois at Urbana-Champaign
Michelle Nelson, University of Illinois at Urbana-Champaign
Mary Ann McGrath, Loyola University-Chicago

ABSTRACT

Recently, studies of symbolic consumption have examined how consumers acquire and use goods in ritual contexts. Yet the processes involved as consumers learn to participate in these contexts have been virtually ignored. Using Rook's (1985) framework for understanding consumption rituals, this paper employs interpretive methodology to examine how mothers act as socialization agents, and teach their children to participate in various aspects of the birthday party. Our findings suggest mothers use ritual artifacts, scripts, performance roles and the ritual audience to teach children both general knowledge and values, and specific behaviors necessary for successful participation in this ritual. Research implications are discussed.

Recently, researchers interested in symbolic consumption have begun to focus upon how consumers acquire and use goods and services in ritual contexts (e.g., Lowrey and Otnes 1994; Otnes, Lowrey and Kim 1993; Rook 1985; Wallendorf and Arnould 1991). However, one issue that remains underexplored is how consumers are socialized to participate in these occasions, although Ward (1974) has observed that understanding how people learn to consume should be a salient research issue.

Belk (1979) has observed that parents act as socialization agents by typically giving their children sex-typed toys at Christmas. More recently, Otnes and McGrath explored how socialization contributed to gender differences among children celebrating birthday parties. They define ritual socialization as: "The processes by which individuals acquire the abilities, interests and information necessary for them to participate in rituals, and to master the use and understanding of specific goods and services used by themselves and others in a ritual setting" (1994, p. 74-75). While both papers make inferences about socialization within ritual contexts, the influence of "socialization agents" within these contexts has only been indirectly studied. This paper extends the research in this area, by exploring how mothers socialize their children to participate in birthday parties. We focus on mothers because women are typically the caretakers of ritual in American culture (e.g., Caplow 1982; Cheal 1987; Sherry and McGrath 1989). Moreover, birthday parties are pervasive events, but have received minimal attention by researchers. Indeed, all studies except Otnes and McGrath's have focused upon these events as they have occurred in kindergartens only, and only in cultures other than the U.S. (Doleve and Gandelman 1980; Handelman and Handelman 1991; Haskina 1941; Katerbursky 1962; Weil 1986).

The framework for this research is the typology of ritual elements described by Rook (1985). We explore the following research question: What socialization functions do the ritual artifacts, scripts, performance roles and the ritual audience of the birthday party serve for mothers of children participating in these parties? We examine each element of this question separately.

METHOD

To capture a phenomenological understanding of children's birthday parties, we recruited thirteen mothers of children ages three to five who were enrolled at a daycare center affiliated with a state university in the Midwest. Interviews were conducted between June and August, 1992. All informants were middle-class and employed. Most were Caucasian and married, and most had two children.

Interviews were conducted by two of the authors, and by an undergraduate trained in qualitative interviewing techniques while participating in an intensive research program. Each mother was interviewed once, then provided with a projective instrument to complete at home.

Mothers were asked to react to three sets of projective stimuli or drawings of children engaged in activities at birthday parties. These included drawings of: (1) children playing "Pin the Tail on the Donkey"; (2) a child opening a birthday present; and (3) an adult of undiscernible gender presenting a birthday cake to children at a table. Mothers also completed a series of sentence stems, such as "Children's birthday parties are..." and "The older I get, children's birthday parties..." Finally, mothers were asked to describe a dream they might have had about their child's birthday party.

Interviews were conducted at either the childcare center or at the mother's place of employment. We followed a structured interview schedule such as that recommended by McCracken (1988), but encouraged our informants to discuss any birthday-related topics they desired. Interviews typically lasted from between 45 minutes to one hour. All interviews were audiotaped and transcribed, yielding over 150 pages of text. In interpreting this material, we employed the "constant comparative" method discussed by Lincoln and Guba (1985). That is, we read, reread and interpreted the text until we reached a common understanding of what we believed it to represent. In addition, the second author was not involved in data collection, and therefore acted as an external auditor for interpretation, thus enhancing the validity of the interpretation. In the following sections, informant names have been changed to assure their anonymity.

This paper does not address the issue of gender differences in socialization among participants. Researchers interested in such questions should consult a recent study by Otnes and McGrath (1994), which specifically examines gender differences in the ritual socialization of children's birthday parties.

Socialization Through Ritual Artifacts

Admittedly, it is difficult to discuss ritual artifacts separately from the ritual scripts that govern their use. We have approached this problem by discussing "themed" artifacts with no particular scripts associated with them below, and by discussing artifacts with highly prescribed uses in the next section.

The Theme As Participatory Planning Tool. While "themed" parties may carry negative connotations of commercialization, our mothers used themed decorations, party favors, and cake for two primary purposes: 1) to instruct children how to plan parties; and 2) to indicate approval or disapproval of commercial elements aimed at children. Among the themes mentioned were Barbie, Beauty and the Beast, Ninja Turtles, and "pirates." That mothers use artifacts for socialization is not surprising, given that "such artifacts often communicate specific symbolic messages that are integral to the meaning of the total experience" (Douglas and Isherwood 1979, quoted in Rook 1985, p. 253).

Mothers made theme planning a learning experience by discussing potential themes with their children and taking them shopping for artifacts. For example, although Christine paid to have her son's party at a children's gym, he selected the superhero motif and the flavor and design of the cake. Likewise, Pam described her child's role in planning:

> She was involved in choosing some of the little prizes and the cake. We took her with us when we went to the store...that has a bakery and they make these birthday cakes on various themes...she was allowed to choose which one...she chose Cinderella.

In Mary's case, her son not only selected the theme, but actively helped her to create it:

> He was pretty involved, at this age...he knew what he wanted on his cake...I knew that if I just went and got something and he knew how he wanted it, it just did not work. So we did a lot together.

The Theme as Opportunity for Approval/Disapproval. Mothers also often indicated the parameters of appropriate theme choices by approving or disapproving their child's selection. Most themes appeared to be "learned" by the children from movies or television, and less from mothers' own suggestions. Thus, it appeared important that mothers placed "boundaries" on their children's choices. Christine said her daughter "had seen [101 Dalmatians]...in the movie theater the year before, and then she knew she was gonna get the video...Because I liked it. And we figured out games [for the party] that were all dog-related."

When mothers did not agree with their child's theme selection, they pointed this fact out to the child. For example, despite the popularity of "Ninja Turtles" in our culture, this theme was mentioned by at least three informants as one of which they disapproved. Darlene stated pointedly: "We don't encourage [Jake] to be into Ninja Turtles...In fact, we discourage him." When her son wanted to employ that theme for his third birthday party, "I was fighting it all the way...I think I gave him some other options. I think they are too aggressive."

Likewise, Mary told how she used the absence of "commercial" themes at her son's parties to teach him other values. When asked if parties were too commercialized, she replied:

> It is not so much the money, but the values I have about it and people have different values and that is fine, but I *have to explain to Carl* that we have decided to do it this way because we think birthdays are very special, but we celebrate them differently than other people...that's what we think is important that is *the lesson we try to show* (emphasis added).

In summary, the party "theme" appeared to be a vehicle that helped mothers teach children how to plan for parties, as well as provide mothers with an opportunity to voice their approval or disapproval of certain commercial elements aimed at children.

Socialization Through Ritual Scripts

Everyone's a Winner in This Game. Traditionally, games at birthday parties represented a "symbolic wiping out of the past year and the starting of the new year ahead." Certain games that exemplified skill or strength were thus employed as a sort of "growth chart" to "show how much progress the birthday child had made in the past year" (Rinkoff 1967, p. 5). These games were thus used to measure *individual* growth and progress of the child from year to year. Games or activities were mentioned as important elements of birthday parties by eleven mothers. As Lisa explained, "you need

some games, so that kids can be active, you can't really have them just sit down the whole time."

Our informants appeared apprehensive about introducing competitive games that stressed "child against child" and could result in hurt feelings. Pam described the difficulty of this scenario in her response to the "Pin-the-Tail-on-the-Donkey" projective picture and offered a way to re-create the conventional script, which calls for only one "winner":

> The mom and dad nervously try to patch up some of the hurt feelings by ensuring each child a 'prize.' They dance around the winner issue with some success (Good for them). They quickly 'can' the other competitive games and turn the kids loose....

When asked what kinds of activities she would plan, Diane responded, "Outdoor games...something where everybody wins." In fact, she planned a treasure hunt where: "They all got in like one big cohort, and they all helped each other...It was really nice, they really liked it, and everybody got a prize at the end."

In this way, our informants seem to encourage their children to participate in games for the *intangible* feelings of "fun" and "self-confidence," rather than for *material* benefits. Barb related how she handled the situation: "It's difficult to select only one 'winner,' therefore, it's a good idea for everyone to receive a prize or party favor at the end of the party."

By downplaying competitiveness, mothers also help eliminate children's anxiety at birthday parties. For not only are the mom and dad "nervous," but as Diane noted: "The children are...a little anxious about who is going to win, until it is *explained* to them that everyone gets a prize." By including the "participating is winning" script, mothers attempt to instill good sportsmanship in children, to alleviate competitiveness within this ritual context, and to teach children that not all games have just one winner.

Cake Presentation and Learning to Feel Special. Cake presentation is the most widely recognized ritual script enacted at the birthday party, for this is the time when the spotlight is on the birthday child (Kraus 1983; Wolfsohn 1979). Indeed, for many children "the cake is the party" (Wolfsohn 1979, p.88). According to Carla, "if you say *birthday*, [her son] talks about what *flavor*." Although the cake itself might not be the nutritious food mothers generally advocate for their children, cake was specifically mentioned more than 60 times, as the single most common required element for a successful birthday party. Other standard elements of the cake presentation script—e.g., blowing out the candles; the wish and singing the birthday song were all mentioned by our informants.

In terms of socializing children via cake presentation, mothers again often emphasized the *intangible rewards* of feeling special for the birthday boy or girl. Natalie recounted: "There has to be some point, for almost any child...where that child feels they are the center of the birthday universe...where you bring the cake." This action has the effect of helping the birthday child realize he or she has been "singularized," and that the ritual is not just a collective event, but is truly *for* him or her (Handelman and Handelman 1991; Otnes and McGrath 1994).

Therefore, this ritual script dictates this is the "child's day," in which "he can eat what he wants, he can do what he wants, if he wants cake in the morning, he just knows that one day of the year he can do what he feels like doing. I guess we all need a day like that," commented Mary. Natalie also described the maternal benefits of singularization: "It's the one time you can indulge your child and nobody will yell at you for it." For in our society, highly permissive child-rearing practices are not considered good parenting, and may lead to undesirable behaviors (Baumrind 1971; Maccoby & Martin 1983).

The cake presentation therefore becomes a symbol of love and indulgence that mothers use to show the child that he or she is special. But it also teaches children that particular foods are reserved for special occasions. As Natalie wrote in her projective exercise: "The cake is a two layer, double fudge with chocolate icing, his favorite. It's a special deal because his folks don't have sugar in the house much." Likewise, Christine, said: "the mother has purchased much too large of a cake. The children are excited to see the beautiful cake."

Gifts As Lessons In Graciousness. While mothers will "spotlight" their children with cake, they are somewhat wary when it comes to the gift-opening script. Materialism and selfishness are viewed as two vices in our culture, and our informants worried about their children expressing egocentrism. When describing what she liked least about birthday parties, Mary said: "When it gets, gimme, gimme, gimme and open up the next thing and not appreciating what you got...I guess I dislike the focus on the material stuff." Similarly, a dream party for Paula would involve "a lot less emphasis on presents. If we could do almost without the presents, I would be happiest. Because I think it encourages greed."

While many children enjoy unwrapping gifts (Otnes and McGrath 1994), mothers believe gift-giving scripts should teach the child how to *accept* gifts as well. According to Paula, the child should, "learn how to feel special, how to allow themselves to be given to, and take it graciously." In one projective description, one informant explained the difficulty in imparting this lesson: "Hopefully Mom and Dad can explain that the gift was meant to celebrate completing another year of growth and achievement and not just as a way to collect loot."

Parents are often nervous about their child's reaction to gifts, however, as demonstrated by Christine's story:

I'm petrified they are going to say something like, 'Hey, I already have this.' My eight-year-old would never do this because he knows I'll take all his toys and give them to the Salvation Army if I find out...With the four-year-old, I worry...[but] his last party this little boy brought this koala bear and I thought it was the coolest thing and as he opened it, I thought, 'He is going to say that I'm too old to play with stuffed animals,' but he didn't...and I felt a lot of stress...because kids are all watching as you open your present and they all want the kids to be thoroughly thrilled with your present.

Sherry, et al. (1993) observe that many recounts of failed gift exchanges were accompanied by comments that indicate disappointment or resentment, and by facial expressions that reveal such emotions. Cognizant of that fact, Christine and other mothers seemed intent upon teaching their children to omit such negative cues during gift receipt.

Related to this issue is that of teaching the child that he or she actually *deserves* presents. In this manner, gifts perform a similar singularizing function as birthday cakes. Paula remarked that children should learn, "How to feel special, how to allow themselves to be given to, and to take it graciously...Somehow, if they could learn that by virtue of being born, you deserve some love and attention from family and friends." Further evidence that gift-giving is used to teach children specific skills is provided in our discussion of the ritual audience.

Socialization and Ritual Performance Roles

Otnes and McGrath (1994) observe that children can express various roles at birthday parties, such as the "birthday boy/girl," and the planner/helper. In addition, our informants discussed an additional role—that of teaching their child to be a good host or hostess. Given these children's ages, we were a bit surprised at the salience of this role.

Host/Hostess Roles. Two themes consistently emerged when mothers elaborated upon their child's role as host or hostess. First, mothers wanted their children to learn to be gracious. Barb stressed the importance of this skill:

I think [birthday parties] should teach them to be good...I've always emphasized the importance of Thank-You notes. They always have to write hand-written, whether it's just one sentence, but at least some acknowledgement to thank people for coming and thinking of them.

The importance of Thank-You notes was mentioned by four of our thirteen mothers. These young children could not write these notes by themselves; rather, mothers typically wrote them and instructed their children to sign or scribble on them. Interestingly, only one mother insistent upon this practice had a male child. This finding is consistent with evidence that boys and girls are socialized differently with regard to expressing politeness in ritual contexts (Otnes, Kim and Kim 1994a; Otnes, Kim and Kim 1994b; Otnes and McGrath 1994).

The second aspect of the host/hostess role stressed by mothers was that their children learn to include others in the celebration. Darlene noted that her son "helped the other children, like with the pot game, told them how to do it. In other words, *we let him cooperate*." Barb offered a more pointed discussion of this issue:

[Her daughter] has a class with nine or ten girls and I made it very clear to her that if it was a big group, we'd invite all of the girls even if we had to sacrifice. Rather than exclude three or four. It has been very hurtful to her in the last year where, you know, the majority is invited and a few are excluded.

Thus, these mothers were concerned that their children learn that one role of the host or hostess is to make others feel welcome and avoid snobbery.

Planners/Helpers. Almost all mothers described how their children helped with party preparations. One main reason for this activity is to allow parents and children to enjoy quality creative, cooperative and productive time together. Yet as noted earlier, mothers also used the planning stage to educate their children with respect to values they believe are important. For instance, many apparently wanted to instill the belief that planning is part of the fun of the party. Paula noted that making invitations was a way she could, "Bring Dean in. Because you've got to color, and you've got to write the names on them. He was excited and that was an activity we could do while others were doing other things." Likewise, Mary noted it was important she and her son make planning "a project rather than 'Oh God, we have to do this,' but starting with a theme and enough in advance so we can...make the boat or castle or whatever." In particular, those mothers whose parties were not conducted by "party professionals" seemed intent upon instilling the belief that the birthday party is a process, rather than an event.

A second educational function of planning for mothers appeared to be to familiarize children with ritual traditions. Caplow (1982) observed that the Christmas celebration in "Middletown" was governed by certain unwritten rules about the ways it should proceed. Our study reveals mothers apparently begin to instill such rules related to birthday parties in very young children. For example, Janet (who is Brazilian) observed her daughter liked to help make special candies for her birthday party, then said: "It is a special candy...it is not a birthday party without this candy."

In summary, the various ritual performance roles that children can express offer mothers many opportunities to instill values and knowledge relevant to the birthday party context in their children.

Socialization and the Ritual Audience

Children who are guests at birthday parties comprise the ritual audience for the event. Many mothers apparently expected their children to master several aspects of this role, namely: 1) to behave in a polite and controlled manner; 2) to be grateful for inclusion in the special context and 3) to celebrate someone else's special day. Part of this last lesson includes planning and delivering a birthday gift to another child.

Learning Good Behavior. Completions to the projective exercise "When I take my child to another child's party..." indicate the mother's behavioral expectations for guests. These completions included: "I stress the importance of being a good and well-mannered guest;" "I hope he will behave civilly, share and cooperate;" and "[I] instruct him on various party etiquettes."

Thus, children are expected to understand that at certain times, impression management is appropriate; in other words, their mothers expect them to act *better* than usual. This distinction, is sometimes communicated through the use of special clothing at birthday parties. Notably, girls' use of special items such as "party shoes" and tights may help communicate this lesson. Absent these cues, mothers take a more direct approach and specifically instruct their children to be well-behaved and polite.

Learning Gratitude for Inclusion. As guests, children are expected to express gratitude in the ritual celebration of another. Barb discussed the feelings of her daughter Edie: "She felt so special that they would call and ask her. I mean, kids really feel like it's the big thing to be invited to a party...Being included. It is just fun to help someone celebrate a birthday." Darlene mentioned that by going to birthday parties, "They feel loved and they know they have friends." In contrast, threats of exclusion can serve as powerful verbal weapons. Darlene noted that, especially among the girls, "they're saying 'If you're not nice to me, you can't come to my birthday party.'"

Inclusion in the birthday party of a friend may be the first opportunity children have to participate in a ritual celebration outside of their immediate kinship network. The children are given both symbolic and tangible access to a larger world through the homes, traditions and lifestyles of other families. They are exposed to a different set of practices and learn to appreciate "other people's lifestyles" and the fact that not every acts the same.

Learning to Celebrate for Another. The audience is also socialized to give, rather than to receive. This includes giving presents, but also giving center-stage attention to the birthday child:

> There are some special moments in life that are marked. That the people you care about, you have these little traditions with them to honor them and that a lot of care and thoughtfulness goes into that to make the place festive or choose a gift thoughtfully to want to give to someone. I think that's very important and I'm very pleased my kids spontaneously do that. [Pam]

Paula wants her son Dean to learn "that these kids have special days, and these presents are not for you." In a more direct way, Sandra allows her twin daughters to choose separate gifts for friends whose parties they attending. Christine also allows her children to choose gifts for others' birthdays: "We go to the store and they help pick out presents." Indeed, little girls appear much more directly socialized to understand gift-buying at an early age (Otnes and McGrath 1994). Pam discusses her daughter's early involvement in gift-giving in general:

> I think it's a way of honoring the person...to spend a little time thinking about what would be an appropriate present for that child...And sometimes she wants to do presents that are not necessarily associated with birthdays...and I think that's great. So I don't discourage that.

Thus, some mothers expect their children not only to want to give, but also to give something that the birthday boy or girl would like.

The birthday child is certainly socialized to act according to various scripts when opening the gifts. Yet guests also learn to follow scripts *during* the gift-opening as well, for this event is "important to the children who have given gifts, for this is an opportunity for recognition for them, too" (Wolfsohn 1979, p. 90). Indeed, participating in the gift-giving process is emphasized by mothers more than the material artifact of the present itself. Gift-giving is seen as a way to show the child how to give graciously and how not to be selfish. When asked how much she spends on gifts for other children, Barb replied," They're little things but it doesn't matter if it's a $2 gift or a $10 gift, *it's just the gift giving and the child participating that's important and it makes it a lot of fun.*"

In fact, many children are eager to participate in this ritual script, with each vying for attention of the birthday child to open his/her present next. Responses from the "gift-giving" projective reflect the mothers' assessment of this script. Barb observed, "guests are also interested in the gifts and perhaps look forward to sharing the toy, book, etc." Darlene related in a projective story, "Meanwhile the other children are waiting for him (the birthday boy) to open *their* gift."

Just Having Fun. Interestingly, mothers also often expressed hope that their children simply enjoy parties. The noun "party" is transformed into a verb, as the children are presented with a variety of activities and foods for their enjoyment. Four of the thirteen completions to the sentence stem "When I take my child to another child's party..." indicate hope that the child will enjoy him/herself. Much of the party presentation is with the needs of the ritual audience in mind. For example, Sandra ordered pizzas with various toppings to cater to the vegetarian guests. Faces are painted, treasure hunts are conducted and games are played with the express purpose of amusing the ritual audience. Yet often, those same mothers who hope their children just have fun have also provided indirect cues that related to expected attitudes or behavior.

SUMMARY AND CONCLUSIONS

Our study is one of the first to consider how consumers are socialized to participate in various rituals. By examining children's birthday parties, we could shed light upon the early stages of ritual socialization. We have demonstrated that through interactions and discussions, mothers teach their children how to use and understand specific goods and services in this setting.

Table 1 summarizes the socialization themes that emerged when each element of Rook's framework was examined. This table reveals that a few emerged across elements—namely, the need to educate children in party planning and gracious behavior. However, others were more specific to one particular element—e.g., the need to instill good sportsmanship in children through game-

TABLE 1
Socialization Functions of Birthday Parties

Ritual Elements	What Children Should Learn
Artifacts:	How to Plan Parties
Themed Elements	Mothers' Approval/Disapproval of Commercial Elements
Scripts:	
Games/Planned Activities	Good Sportsmanship
	To Downplay Competitiveness
Cake Presentation	Birthday Child is Singularized
	Birthdays (and cake) are special
Gift Opening	Gracious Acceptance of Gifts
Roles:	
Host/Hostess	Graciousness by Including Guests
	Gratitude Toward Guests For Sharing in the Celebration
Planner/Helper	Party Planning is Part of the Fun
	Family/Subcultural Traditions
Audience:	Good Behavior at Parties
	Gratitude for Inclusion
	How to Celebrate for Another
	Birthday Parties are Fun

playing. Overall, the range of instructional functions reveals that mothers take advantage of the multifaceted nature of birthday parties and use these contexts to impart a variety of lessons both inherent in, and generalizable beyond, the ritual itself. Yet the complex nature of these occasions also means that some of the lessons children receive are contradictory. For example, many children were expected to master both the ability to include others in their celebration and the ability to allow themselves to be singularized through cake and gifts. That some mothers expressed anxiety over their children's potential behavior—and mentioned their children's initial anxiety at parties as well—could reflect the difficulty in resolving such ambiguous lessons when learning how to be a ritual participant.

Future Research

This study examined children who were just beginning to understand the meaning of birthday parties. It would thus be of interest to follow children throughout subsequent birthdays to discern changes in their ritual participation. A longitudinal case study of a subset of "birthday children" or a concurrent look at how various age groups celebrate birthdays could accomplish this objective. Obviously, the needs and wants of a three-year-old are very different from those of a teenager. Even adults celebrate birthdays, although in much different ways. Given the expenditures devoted to birthdays in this culture, examining different age groups would enable marketers and retailers to define their needs and desires in a more comprehensive manner.

Similarly, the findings in this study can be related to more general issues of how children are socialized to become consumers. For example, exploring how children learn to plan purchases (such as a friend's gift or cake), how they learn to exchange goods, and how they gain consumer values (such as materialism or anti-materialism) could be included in future research.

Furthermore, this study interviewed middle-class mothers as socialization agents, which raises questions about a potential social response bias. Mothers who are well-read and working (like those of our sample) are typically aware of socially-dictated behaviors for themselves and their children, and thus their responses may reflect such a desire to have their children thought of as well-behaved. However, actual behavior at birthday parties may be somewhat different than reported. Future research could thus involve examining the expectations of parents and children before parties with actual behavior at parties, and with follow-up reflections about parties.

Finally, as "traditional families" continue to change, undoubtedly so will the roles and identities of these socialization agents. Such questions arise as: Will "family" parties become an old-fashioned memory of the past? Will fathers, grandmothers, or hired "party planners," play a greater role in the party planning and socialization process? For while some traditional scripts of birthday parties are still practiced, more mothers have nontraditional roles outside of the home, and may find it necessary or desirable to hire someone to plan their children's parties for them. Likewise, there were allusions in our text to mothers who throw elaborate parties for their children to alleviate their guilt over not spending quality time with them. Certainly, these issues are worthy of further exploration in the face of dramatic sociological changes in our culture.

By studying consumers as they are socialized to participate in rituals, we gain a better understanding of how they master artifacts, scripts, performance roles and expectations of the audience. Moreover, given the pervasive nature of rituals in all cultures, continued study in this area is essential in order to achieve a holistic understanding of how consumers participate in symbolic consumption. Finally, marketers and retailers would benefit from gaining an understanding of the ways artifacts (and scripts for their use) are employed as tools for education and socialization as well.

REFERENCES

Baumrind, D. (1971), "Current Patterns of Parental Authority," *Developmental Psychology Monographs*, 4 (1, Part 2).

Belk, Russell W. (1979), "Gift Giving Behavior," in *Research in Marketing*, ed. Jagdish N. Sheth, Greenwich, CT: JAI Press, 95-126.

Belk, Russell W. and Gregory S. Coon (1993), "Gift Giving as Agapic Love: An Alternative to the Exchange Paradigm Based on Dating Experiences," *Journal of Consumer Research*, 20, (December), 393-417.

Belk, Russell W., Melanie Wallendorf and John F. Sherry, Jr. (1989), "The Sacred and Profane in Consumer Behavior: Theodicy on the Odyssey," *Journal of Consumer Research* 16 (June), 1-38.

Caplow, Theodore (1982), "Christmas Gifts and Kin Networks," *American Sociological Review*, 48 (6), 383-392. Discussion 48 (12) 874-876.

Cheal, David (1987), "Showing Them You Love Them: Gift-Giving and the Dialectic of Intimacy," *The Sociological Review*, 35 (1), 150-169.

Doleve-Gandelman, Taili (1980), "Ceremonie d'anniversaire at identite sociale en Israel."Paper presented to a Colloquium on Production et maintien de l'identite. Toulouse.

Douglas, Mary and Baron Isherwood (1979), *The World of Goods: Toward an Anthropology of Consumption*, New York: Basic Books.

Handelman, Lea Shamgar and Don Handelman (1991), "Celebrations of Bureaucracy: Birthday Parties in Israeli Kindergartens," *Ethnology*, 30 (October), 293-312.

Haskina, T. (1941), "Birthday Party in the Kindergarten," *Hed HaGan*, 5:34-37 (in Hebrew).

Katerbursky, Z. (1962), *The Ways of the Garden*, Tel Aviv (in Hebrew)

Kraus, Charles and Linda (1983) *Charles the Clown's Guide to Birthday Parties*, California: Jalmar Press.

Lincoln, Yvonna S. and Egon G. Guba (1985), *Naturalistic Inquiry*, Newbury Park, CA: Sage.

Lowrey, Tina M. and Cele Otnes (1994), "Construction of a Meaningful Wedding: Differences Between the Priorities of Brides and Grooms," in *Gender and Consumer Behavior*, ed. Janeen Costa, Beverly Hills: Sage, 164-183.

Maccoby, E. E. and J. A. Martin (1983), "Socialization in the Context of the Family: Parent-Child Interaction." in *Handbook of Child Psychology*, Vol 4, *Socialization, Personality, and Social Behavior*, ed. P. H. Mussen New York: Wiley.

McCracken, Grant (1988), *The Long Interview*, Newbury Park, CA: Sage.

Otnes, Cele, Tina M. Lowrey and Young Chan Kim (1993), "Gift Selection for 'Easy' and 'Difficult' Recipients: A Social Roles Interpretation," *Journal of Consumer Research*, 20, (September), 229-244.

Otnes, Cele and Mary Ann McGrath (1994), "Ritual Socialization and the Children's Birthday Party: The Early Emergence of Gender Differences," *Journal of Ritual Studies*, (Winter), 73-93.

Otnes, Cele, Young Chan Kim and Kyungseung Kim (1994a), "All I Want for Christmas: An Analysis of Children's Brand Requests to Santa Claus," *Journal of Popular Culture*, (Forthcoming, Summer).

Otnes, Cele, Kyungseung Kim, and Young Chan Kim (1994b), "Yes, Virginia, There is a Gender Difference: Analyzing Children's Requests to Santa Claus," *Journal of Popular Culture*, (Forthcoming, Fall).

Rinkoff, Barbara (1967), *Birthday Parties Around the World*, New York: M. Barrows and Company, Inc.

Rook, Dennis W. (1985), "The Ritual Dimension of Consumer Behavior," *Journal of Consumer Research*, 12, (December), 251-264.

Sherry, John F., Jr. and Mary Ann McGrath (1989), "Unpacking the Holiday Presence: A Comparative Ethnography of Two Gift Stores," in *Interpretive Consumer Research*, ed. Elizabeth C. Hirschman, Provo, UT: Association for Consumer Research, 148-167.

Sherry, John F., Mary Ann McGrath and Sidney Levy (1993), "The Dark Side of the Gift," *Journal of Business Research*, 28, (November), 225-245.

Wallendorf, Melanie and Eric J. Arnold (1991), "We Gather Together: Consumption Rituals of Thanksgiving Day," *Journal of Consumer Research*, 18 (June), 13-31.

Ward, Scott (1974), "Consumer Socialization," *Journal of Consumer Research*, 1, (September), 1-16.

Weil, Shalva (1986), "The Language and Ritual of Socialization: Birthday Parties in a Kindergarten Context," *Man*, 21, (June), 329-341.

Wolfsohn, Reeta Bochner (1979), *Successful Children's Parties*, New York: Arco Publishing, Inc.

Parents' Perception Regarding Children's Use of Clothing Evaluative Criteria: An Exploratory Study From the Consumer Socialization Process Perspective

Soyeon Shim, University of Arizona
Lisa Snyder, University of Arizona
Kenneth C. Gehrt, University of Arizona

ABSTRACT

This exploratory study found that parental socialization variables were significantly related to children's social-structural and developmental variables (e.g., child's age, birth order, and parent's marital status). However, a limited number of social-structural and developmental variables (age and social class only) were found to be directly linked with parents' perception of children's use of clothing evaluative criteria.

This exploratory research was interested in learning about parents' perception of the process by which children become conscious of clothing evaluation. Clothing products were of interest because of the increasing value of the children's clothing market as well as clothing's important role in children's socialization process as evident in many previous studies (e.g., Kaiser 1990). According to Moschis (1987), antecedent variables such as social-structural and developmental variables affect socialization processes via socialization agents. Along with antecedent variables, socialization processes, in turn, influence consumer learning properties, which are termed socialization outcomes. Based on these three elements of the consumer socialization model, the objective of this study was to examine relationships among parents' perception regarding children's use of clothing evaluative criteria, antecedent variables, and parental socialization variables.

Children observe parents judging products using evaluative criteria and may store and use those evaluative criteria later for product choices of their own, such as toys, snacks and clothing (Davis 1976). Because children develop simple consumer orientation first before developing complex orientation (Moschis, 1987), it was assumed in this study that basic criteria such as price, brand name, peer influence, style, and color were used by children in judging clothing.

While *price* is a theoretically important matter to children, research showed, however, that they may not be very knowledgeable about price of products (Stephens and Moore 1975). *Brand name* has a high significance to children in that they hold a large number of brands in their mind, termed the brand repertoire (McNeal, McDaniel and Smart 1983). Another important factor is *peer influence* in clothing selection among children and adolescents because of conformity and acceptance to groups (e.g., Davis 1984; Kaiser 1990). Both *style* and *color* are also important aspects to children in clothing selection, respectively, because children not only are concerned with the physical attributes of the products, but also are highly visual-oriented in choosing products (e.g., McNeal 1987). Using parents' perception regarding children's use of those five evaluative criteria as an outcome of the consumer socialization, three hypotheses were developed in the following manner.

Development of Hypothesis 1

Considerable evidence exists that parents are the most significant agent in young children's consumer socialization processes and are instrumental in influencing young children about consumer decisions such as evaluative criteria (e.g., Haynes, Burts, Dukes and Cloud 1993). Previous research indicated that parental influence on children's understanding of money (e.g., money education, allowance) was one of the most important aspects of the children's

learning process in becoming consumers (Furth 1980; Moschis 1987). Parental restriction and children's television product requests have also been important in children's socialization processes because television viewing was associated with the acquisition of a wide variety of both desirable and undesirable consumer orientations (Moshis 1987). Ward and Wackman (1972) found that the more restrictions parents place on a child's television viewing, the less parents yield to the child's purchase requests.

Moschis, Moore and Stephens (1977) indicated that parent-child interactions within the retail setting help children and adolescents learn shopping attitudes and behavior, especially for consumer goods such as clothing. Francis and Burns (1992) also found that mothers were effective long-term consumer socialization agents for adolescent girls' clothing shopping behavior and attitudes, imparting especially the means of clothing acquisition and overall clothing satisfaction. In terms of children's actual shopping participation, it is the parents who first introduce their children to the retail store and buying procedure. Therefore, parental socialization variables were hypothesized to be important in children's use of clothing criteria.

[H1] Parents' perception regarding children's use of clothing evaluative criteria is associated with the following parental socialization variables: (a) money education; (b) shopping participation; (c) television restriction; (d) television products requested by children; (e) total amount of allowance; (f) parents' emphasis on brand name; (g) parents' emphasis on price; (h) parents' emphasis on color; (i) parents' emphasis on peer influence; and (j) parents' emphasis on style.

Development of Hypotheses 2 and 3

In the consumption of clothing, girls, as compared to boys, become more aware of and interested in clothing (e.g., Haynes et al. 1993); are more brand conscious but less price conscious (e.g., Moschis and Moore 1979); and rely more on parents for product information (Moschis 1987). Social class also significantly influences children's socialization (e.g., Moschis and Moore 1978). Focusing on preschoolers, Haynes et al. (1993) found that mothers with a lower income, as compared to those with a higher income, were more likely to report that their children were brand conscious.

Ethnic differences in consumer awareness seem evident early in life. For instance, white children had a higher interaction with parents about consumption and greater knowledge of economic concepts and the consumer role than did black children (Moschis and Moore 1985). Family characteristics such as parent's marital status and the number of siblings were also deemed influential in children's socialization process. For instance, single-parent households tend to be headed by single mothers who may have lower family incomes than do both-parent households (Lino 1991). Consequently, single parents might have limited money and time resources available for their children, a situation which may reduce their level of interaction with children. Finally, while a greater number of siblings may provide more interaction among siblings, it may limit the degree of a parent's interaction with each child.

As compared to younger children, older children tended to express greater interest in clothing purchases; to become more independent of parents in consumer decision-making; to use more mass media; and to request products seen on television less frequently but to receive mothers' yielding on their purchase request (e.g. Haynes et al. 1993). This tendency may reflect a perceived increase in the competence of older children in their decision-making process.

The birth order of a child plays a significant role in how a child acquires consumer skills. As compared to later-borns, first-borns were more likely to acquire consumer skills earlier, have positive orientations toward commercial stimuli, and interact with their parents in consumption decisions (Moschis 1987). Therefore, the following hypotheses were developed.

[H2] Parents' perception regarding children's use of clothing evaluative criteria and [H3] parental socialization variables are associated with the following antecedents: (a) gender; (b) social class; (c) ethnicity; (d) parent's marital status; (e) the number of other siblings; (f) age and (g) birth order.

METHODS

Instrument Development

Prior to the development of the instrument, eight children were interviewed for better understanding of their clothing consumption behavior. Brand, price, peer influence, style, and color were most frequently mentioned as criteria to look for or talk about with their parents when buying clothes.

A total of 21 Likert-type statements (1=strongly disagree to 5=strongly agree) were developed by researchers measuring parents' perception regarding children's use of price, color, brand name, peer influence, and style when buying clothes. A principal factor analysis with varimax rotation, using the minimum eigenvalue of one as the criterion, revealed five factors. Only items loading more than .50 on a single factor were included, retaining 20 statements. Factors were labeled (a) Brand Conscious (e.g., My child often asks me for certain brand names); (b) Price Conscious (e.g., My child considers price an important factor when purchasing clothing); (c) Color Conscious (e.g., Color is the most important factor to my child when purchasing clothing); (d) Peer Conscious (e.g., My child makes his/her own clothing purchase decisions, independent of his/her friends); and (e) Style Conscious (e.g., My child buys strictly for the style of the outfit). The total variance explained was 64.8%, and factor loadings ranged from .54 to .89, with standardized alpha coefficients ranging from .67 to .88.

A total of 18 statements were developed by researchers to measure part of the parental socialization variables (e.g., parents' belief about their money education). Factor analysis revealed four factors, retaining 11 statements: (a) Money Education (e.g., I make a concerted effort to teach my child how to budget money); (b) Shopping Participation (e.g., Whenever possible, I try to take my child shopping); (c) Television Restriction (e.g., I often place restrictions on my child's television viewing); and (d) Television Products Requested (e.g., My child often asks me for products that he/she sees on TV). The total percent of variance explained was 60.4%, with factor loading ranging from .50 to .87. Standardized alpha coefficients ranged from .64 to .75.

The total amount of allowance given to the child was determined by asking how much was provided for each month. The parent's own emphasis on clothing evaluative criteria (e.g., price, color) was measured by asking respondents to indicate how important each criterion was to them in shopping for their own clothes (1=very unimportant to 5=very important). To minimize a priming effect (Fiske and Taylor 1984, p. 231), the questions and scales

measuring the parent's own emphasis were differently formatted than those measuring the parent's perception regarding children's usage of evaluative criteria. Social-structural (e.g., social class) and developmental (e.g., age) variables were requested by using a categorical format.

Sampling and Data Collection

A pretested questionnaire was sent to a total of 500 parents of children in the first through sixth grade who were selected from the Directory of a school district located in a southwestern city. Parents were instructed to identify one child in the family who is in the first through sixth grade and keep that child in mind while responding to the questionnaire. Of those delivered (n=468), a total of 196 questionnaires were returned, resulting in a 39% response rate. One hundred eighty-nine usable questionnaires were included in the analysis.

RESULTS

Respondents' Characteristics

Parents of almost an equal number of boys and girls were represented, with an approximately normal distribution of age between 6 and 12. About 61.3% were first-borns, while 11% were the only child. The majority of the parents who responded to the survey were mothers (83.5%), married (88.4%), white (92.1%), and in an income category of $50,000 and above (81.1%). More than 46% of the respondents and 70% of their spouses were in the upper level of professional occupation categories. A high percentage of respondents (71%) and their spouses (81%) reported having earned a Bachelor's degree and above. While representing similar socio-economic characteristics to the profile of the school district in this study, respondents represented a more affluent and highly educated group of people than the U.S. demographic profile (*U.S. Bureau of Census*, 1989), Therefore, these characteristics should be kept in mind in interpreting the results of the study.

Testing Hypothesis 1

To overcome the limitation regarding high correlations among the independent variables, a possible multicollinearity problem was first detected by examining the correlation matrix among the predictor variables. None of the correlation coefficients was very large.

As a result of a series of stepwise multiple regression analyses, *Brand Conscious* was predicted by five predictors (R^2=.22, F=6.81, p <.001). Included were Shopping Participation (β=.27, p <.001), Television Restriction (β=-.23, p<.001), parent's own emphasis on brand (β=.22, p<.01), total allowance (β=.19, p<.05), and Television Products Requested (β=.17, p <.01). Four predictors were entered in explaining *Price Conscious* (R^2=.23, F=9.16, p <.001): Shopping Participation (β=.26, p <.01), Television Products Requested (β=-.19, p<.05), total allowance (β=.19, p<.01), and parent's own emphasis on price (β=.18, p<.01). Predictors of *Color Conscious* had an R^2 value of .15 (F=7.17, p <.001) and included three predictors: Shopping Participation (β=.27, p<.5), parent's own emphasis on color (β=.21, p<.0), and Television Products Requested (β=.18, p <.05). *Peer Conscious* had an R^2 value of .17 (F=8.81, p <.001) and was influenced by Television Products Requested (β=.35, p <.001), the parent's own emphasis on brand (β=.17, p<.05), and Shopping Participation (β=.23, p<.01). Finally, *Style Conscious* had an R^2 value of .17 (F=6.48, p <.001) and included parent's own emphasis on style of clothing (β=.29, p<.001), Television Restrictions (β=-.22, p<.01), Television Products Requested (β=.21, p<.01), and Shopping Participation (β=.18, p<.05).

Overall, most predictors were significant in explaining parents' perception of children's consciousness of evaluative criteria, except for Money Education. Therefore, Hypothesis 1 was accepted, with the exception H1-a (Money Education).

Testing Hypotheses 2 and 3

As a result of stepwise regression analyses, *Brand Conscious* was predicted by two variables and had an R^2 value of .18 (F=10.01, p<.001). Included were the child's age (β =.38, p<.001) and social class (β=-.14, p <.01). *Price Conscious* (R^2=.16, F=9.76, p<.001) was predicted by one variable, the child's age (β=.40, p <.001). Therefore, only Hypotheses 2-b (age) and 2-f (social class) were accepted. *Money Education* was predicted by two variables and had an R^2 value of .05 (F=4.88, p<.001). Included were the number of other children in the family (β=-.21, p<.05) and the birth order of the child (β=-.27, p<.05). Shopping Participation had an R^2 value of .07 (F=6.91, p <.001) and was influenced by age of the child (β=.19, p<.001) and the number of other children who were in the family (β=-.18, p<.01). *Television Restrictions* had an R^2 value of .11 (F=11.18, p <.001) and was influenced by the parent's marital status (β=-.24, p<.001) and child's age (β=-.22, p<.001). Age (β=-.31, p <.001) was also entered in explaining Television Products Requested (R^2=.10, F=19.59, p <.001). *Total allowance* had an R^2 value of .08 and was influenced by the child's age (β=.25, p<.01) and by ethnicity (β=-.20, p<.01). The child's gender and social class did not explain any of the parental socialization variables. Therefore, only Hypotheses 3-c through 3-g (ethnicity, marital status, number of other siblings, age, and birth order) were accepted.

DISCUSSION

Several antecedent variables appeared to have direct relationships with parental socialization variables. Many of the parental socialization variables, in turn, demonstrated a significant relationship with parents' perception regarding children's use of clothing evaluative criteria. Theoretically, these results are consistent with Moschis' consumer socialization model (1987). However, antecedent variables had little connection with parents' perception regarding children's use of evaluative criteria. This finding is somewhat consistent with the results of Haynes et al. (1993) in that family demographics were not highly significant in explaining children's clothing consumption behavior. One reason for the lack of association of antecedent variables with consumer outcome in this study may lie in the children's age group investigated. It may be that, for the age group of 6 to 12 years, parental socialization variables play more significant roles in parents' perception of children's consumer socialization than do children's social-structural or developmental variables, except for age itself.

It should be noted, however, that children's social-structural and developmental variables appeared to have significant relationships with parental socialization variables, implying the importance of children's antecedent variables as an indirect factor for the socialization outcome. As children get older, entering an early adolescent period, their other background then may have a more direct link with their socialization outcome. Further research is warranted including a wide range of age groups to determine the direct effects of other antecedent variables on the socialization process.

Relationships of Parental Socialization Variables with Parents' Perception regarding Children's Use of Clothing Evaluative Criteria

Parents' involving the children in shopping and parents' own emphasis of evaluative criteria were of significant value in predicting parents' perception of their children becoming highly conscious of several clothing evaluative criteria. For instance, the more frequently the parents took the children shopping, the more conscious the children were reported being of brand, price, color, peers, and style in buying clothes.

Parents' own emphasis on a particular evaluative criterion had a positive relationship with parents' perception of children's consciousness of that criterion. It may be that children often observe the way in which parents discuss making a consumption decision and learn to do the same thing. If this interpretation is indeed true, this finding supports many previous studies regarding the impact of parents' direct interaction with children in a retail setting (e.g., Francis and Burns 1992). Relationships between parents' evaluative criteria and parents' perception regarding children's criteria, however, should be interpreted with caution because of a possible priming effect.

Children's television product requests and parents' restriction on television viewing were significantly related to parents' perception regarding children's use of evaluative criteria. For instance, the more frequently children asked for products that they saw on television, the more conscious children were reported being of brand, color, peers, and style. However, those who frequently requested television products were reported as being less conscious of price; this finding may be because prices are hardly mentioned in advertising to children (McNeal 1987), or they may not realize price of the product as a limiting factor for much consumption. Children who received more parental restriction regarding television viewing tended to be less conscious of brand name and style of clothing than did their counterparts with little restriction. This finding supports previous researchers (e.g., Moschis 1987) in that television viewing is associated with both desirable (e.g., knowledge of brand or style) and undesirable (e.g., lack of awareness of price) consumer orientation in this study.

The total amount of allowance given to children was a significant factor for parents' perception regarding children's being brand and price conscious, while parents' money education at home was not significant for any of the evaluative criteria. One reason for the lack of the money education relationship may be explained by a problem derived from "social desirability," i.e., the tendency of people to select the "nicer" or more flattering answers (Crowne and Marlow 1960). The examination of descriptive analysis of this scale indeed revealed that the majority of the parents responded favorably to the questions measuring their concerted efforts of educating their children about money. On the other hand, the outcome about the actual allowance practice reinforces importance of allowance as part of consumer education, and is consistent with previous findings that the more opportunities children have to manage money, the more skills they acquire in consumer behavior (McNeal 1987). An implication here is that parents need actually to give some money to children for them to manage, if they wish to educate their children about how to become conscious consumers.

Parents can teach their children to become conscious consumers by allowing them to manage their own money and take part in shopping activities, and by paying attention to what their children watch on television and how to react to their purchase requests. Also, parents need to be made aware of their own consumption behavior because children learn from observing their parents. Knowing that children's consumer behavior is a learned behavior from parents, retailers may benefit by targeting parents first so that parent consumers first develop loyalty to the brand name or store, an allegiance which, in turn, may be transmitted to children consumers later in their lives.

Relationships of Antecedent Variables with Parental Socialization Variables and with Parents' Perception Regarding Children's Use of Evaluative Criteria

Children's age was a significant variable in explaining many of the parental socialization variables. The older the children were, the greater shopping participation with parents took place, supporting a previous research finding that as children's ages increased, so did the purchasing decisions the children became involved in (McNeal 1987). Older children were reported as receiving less television restriction from their parents and as less frequently requesting products that they saw on television than were younger children. One reason for this finding may be that older children are more self-disciplined about watching television than are younger children, and have outgrown the "I want" stage of their lives. Also, older children may be able to distinguish between actually needing the product and wanting the product.

Children's age had a positive relationship with parents' perception regarding children's brand and price consciousness, meaning that older children were more brand and price conscious than were younger children. However, social class had a negative relationship with parents' perception regarding children's brand consciousness, meaning that the higher the social class, the less conscious of brand name children were reported as being. This finding supports those of the Haynes et al. (1993) study in that children from lower-income families showed more preference for brand-name clothing than did children from higher income families. Parents from a high social class may not necessarily emphasize brand name as much as do parents from lower classes, supporting literature that portrays upper-class consumers as placing less importance on brand name or prestige than do lower classes (Engel, Blackwell and Miniard 1993).

Ethnicity, parent's marital status, number of other siblings, and the child's birth order had relationships with various parental socialization variables. For instance, whites tended to give more allowance to children than did other ethnic groups; this finding might explain why white children were more knowledgeable about economics and their role as a consumer, as was found in a previous study (Moschis and Moore 1979). Single parents tended to place less restriction on children's television viewing than did married parents. Single parents might have limited time resources or attention available for their children, as compared to married parents. Not surprisingly, the greater number of children in the family, the less shopping participation occurred. Of course, it is much easier for parents to shop accompanied by no children or a smaller number of children than a larger number of children.

Parents' belief about money education at home appeared to depend on two variables—the number of children in the family and the birth order of the child. The more children the parents had, the less money education occurred. The greater number of siblings in a family may mean that less time is available for the parents to spend interacting with children about money. First-borns tended to receive more money education than did later-borns, an outcome supporting Moschis' (1987) statement that first-born children acquire better consumer skills than later-born children.

It seems surprising that children's gender was a significant predictor of neither any parental socialization variables nor parents' perception regarding children's use of evaluative criteria. This finding does not support many previous studies, indicating that boys and girls develop a different orientation toward clothing and consumption in general (e.g., Haynes et al. 1993; Moschis and Moore 1978, 1979) and that they are treated differently by parents (McNeal 1969; Moschis 1987). Perhaps parents believe that boys today, at least among the age group of 6 to 12, may be as conscious of clothing as girls are. Further research is warranted, however, regarding gender effects on younger children's clothing consumption in general.

LIMITATIONS AND FUTURE STUDIES

In this study parents were assumed to be knowledgeable about their children's consumer behavior and were asked to respond to the questionnaire. While self-reporting, a technique depending on the subject's memory, is a problem with all survey research (Kraut and Lewis 1982), our rationale was that parents' responses about their children may be more accurate than children's own reports, especially among young children. For future study, a dyadic approach is recommended by developing a simple questionnaire or an interview schedule for children and having their parents respond to questions pertaining to parental interaction and social-structural variables.

Another limitation was the fact that five criterion variables (e.g., Brand Conscious)—identified by principal component factor analysis—were assumed to be independent of one another. For future studies, the use of the LISREL program, which takes relationships among the dependent variables into consideration in estimating parameters, would be desirable.

The respondents in the study were selected from only one school district, an area which represented fairly affluent families. The sample size was also relatively small for running the stepwise regression analysis in estimating several parameters. Therefore, a larger size of sample, including a wide range of socio-economic groups, should be investigated to learn more about effects of social-structural variables on children's consumer socialization processes.

Finally, the current study focused on parents as socialization agents for children, and the majority of respondents were mothers. Therefore, other socialization agents need to be examined, including fathers, teachers and school, businesses, friends, and other, especially younger, siblings in the family.

REFERENCES

Crowne, D. and D. Marlowe (1960), "A New Scale of Social Desirability Independent of Pathology," *Journal of Consulting Psychology*, 24, 349-354.

Davis, H. L. (1976), "Decision Making Within the Household," *Journal of Consumer Research*, 2, 241-260.

Davis, L. L. (1984), Judgment Ambiguity, Self-Consciousness, and Conformity in Judgments of Fashionability. *Psychological Reports*, 54, 671-675.

Engel, J. F., Blackwell, R. D. and Miniard, P. (1990), *Consumer Behavior*, (6th ed.). Orlando: Dryden Press.

Furth, H. G. (1980), *The World of Grown-Ups*, New York: Elsevier.

Fiske, S. T. and S. E. Taylor (1984), *Social Cognition*, New York: Random House.

Francis, S. and L. D. Burns (1992), "Effect of Consumer Socialization on Clothing Shopping Attitudes, Clothing Acquisition, and Clothing Satisfaction," *Clothing and Textiles Research Journal*, 10, 35-39.

Haynes, J. L., D. C. Burts, A. Dukes and R. Cloud (1993), "Consumer Socialization of Preschoolers and Kindergartners as Related to Clothing Consumption," *Psychology and Marketing*, 10, 151-166.

Kaiser, S. B. (1990), *The Social Psychology of Clothing* (2nd ed.), New York: Macmillan.

Kraut, R. E. and S. H. Lewis (1982), "Person Perception and Self-Awareness: Knowledge of Influences on One's Own Judgments," *Journal of Personality and Social Psychology*, 42, 448-460.

Lino, M. (1991), "Expenditures on a Child by Single-Parent Families," *Family Economic Review,* 4, 2-7.

McNeal, J. U. (1969), "The Child Consumer: A New Market," *Journal of Retailing,* 45, 15-22.

_____(1987), *Children as Consumers,* Lexington: D. C. Heath.

_____S. W. McDaniel and D. Smart (1983), The Brand repertoire: Its content and organization. In Murphy, P., et al (Eds.) *AMA Educators Conference Proceedings,* (pp. 92-96) Chicago: American Marketing Association.

Moschis, G. P. (1987), *Consumer Socialization: A Life-Cycle Perspective.* Lexington: D. C. Heath.

_____and R. L. Moore (1978), "An Analysis of the Acquisition of Some Consumer Competencies among Adolescents," *Journal of Consumer Affairs,* 12, 277-291.

_____(1979), "Decision Making among the Young: A Socialization Perspective," *Journal of Consumer Research,* 6, 101-112.

_____(1985), "Racial and Socioeconomic Influence on the Development of Consumer Behavior," In E. Hirshman and M. Holbrook (eds.) *Advances in Consumer Research,* Provo, UT: Association for Consumer Research, 525-531.

Stephens, L. F. and R. L. Moore (1975). Price accuracy as a consumer skill. *Journal of Advertising Research,* *15*(4), 27-34.

U. S. Bureau of Census (1989), *Statistical Abstract of the United States* (109th ed.), Washington, D C: U. S. Government Printing Office.

Ward, S. and D. B. Wackman (1972), "Children's Purchase Influence Attempts and Parental Yielding," *Journal of Marketing Research,* 9, 316-319.

Experiential Aspects of Elementary School Choice for Upper-Middle Class Urban Americans: How Tough Choices Can Lead Down the Path to "Power Kindergarten"

Kathryn A. Fitzgerald, University of California Los Angeles

ABSTRACT

Growing numbers of middle class Americans in urban areas are considering significant expenditures on private schooling. This project examines the experience of members of this new segment in making difficult, philosophically uncomfortable decisions. In-depth interviews confirmed that this is an involving and emotionally charged issue entailing a variety of conflicts, compromises, and sacrifices. Their accounts form the basis for interpretive themes relating this choice to the self and exploring the meaning of "public" and "private" education.

A generation that viewed itself as open-minded and socially committed suffers a humbling showdown with conscience as it abandons the public school system. [Elizabeth Shogren, LA Times]

Anyone who reads newspapers or news magazines regularly has likely encountered several accounts of the growing numbers of Americans exploring private school options, particularly in urban areas. It seems what was once the province of the wealthy or religiously devout is now a serious consideration for a growing number of families.

Spurred by a barrage of news stories about violence and poor academic performance, many parents who are themselves the products of public schooling no longer feel comfortable using public education for their own children. For example, in Los Angeles County 18% of all students now attend private schools, and 52% of the remaining students who are enrolled in public schools come from families with incomes low enough to qualify for subsidized lunches (Shogren, 1993). Thus, families who never expected to be in the market for private education are now facing the prospect of devoting significant amounts of money to it over a number of years. Moreover, this annual expenditure of several thousand dollars per child is more burdensome than that for college education because it begins at a point in the family life cycle where savings have not had much time to accumulate.

This project examines the experience of upper-middle class families in making elementary school educational choices for their children. Investigation of the use of private schools stems from a desire to explore a timely, impactful aspect of consumption that has life-altering effects on those involved and answers calls to move beyond research concerned with low involvement items and early stages of consumption processes (Arndt, 1976; Wells, 1993). Focus was restricted to the elementary level since it is the first time a decision between public and private schooling can potentially arise. Information was gathered through in-depth interviews conducted with mothers either currently seeking entrance or already having their children enrolled in elementary school. The data gathered to date indicate that this issue may emerge long before the eldest child approaches entry into kindergarten, possibly as early as the age of one, and may influence decisions about preschool training as well. If parents do ultimately decide to pursue private elementary education, the information acquisition and application process begins in earnest around September of the year before the child is to begin kindergarten. This issue is so involving and emotionally charged that in some cases it dominates much of family life over the long months until admissions decisions are announced in the spring.

Some of the quotations included may seem a bit extreme and are (hopefully) quite entertaining, but the reader should bear in mind that the participants themselves were quite aware of the irony of devoting so much "blood, sweat, and tears" to the education of five-year-olds and were able to see some humor in the situation. Despite occasional commentary with critical overtones, the author empathizes with the dilemma that led these women down the paths they chose and considers it to be a decision she herself may one day face.

In sum, choice of an elementary school can rightfully be considered one of the more important consumption decisions that will be encountered, by virtue of the fact that it involves a very large expenditure of money, is an issue for a growing number of families, is highly emotionally charged, takes place over an extended period of time, and has broader societal implications. It is truly an involving purchase in the most meaningful sense of the word.

Discussion in this paper is structured as follows: the methodological approach is presented first, followed by a description of issues from each participant's individual experience, presentation of interpretive themes focussing on relations to the self and the meaning of public and private education, and, finally, concluding comments linking this domain to other consumption areas.

METHODOLOGY

This project represents a blend of the methodological approaches advocated in the consumer research literature by Craig Thompson (Thompson et al., 1989) and Grant McCracken (1988). Because the experiential nature of school choice was of most interest, an existential-phenomenological approach was used to structure interview questions. The author initiated the interview with a very general, open-ended question about how the decision was experienced. While some issues of *a priori* interest were explored, participants were largely responsible for guiding the direction of discussion to those aspects that were most personally compelling. The majority of questions were a conversational response to participant discussion rather than part of a structured questionnaire or checklist. All spoke at length about their experiences and feelings with very little prompting required on the part of the interviewer.

However, the research was done in a very iterative manner in which review of relevant literature was interspersed between each interview. Thus, some specific questions did become of more interest as the project progressed. In terms of analysis, an iterative hermeneutic approach was adopted to identify common thematic patterns. This approach involves back-and-forth alternation between the idiographic coding and interpretation of each individual interview transcript and the collective analysis of multiple transcripts and journal notes. Finally, the author also was cognizant of the goals of the constant comparative method proposed by Glaser & Strauss (1967) throughout the course of the project

Some sampling issues particular to this study deserve special mention. It was initiated and completed as a project for a ten-week doctoral seminar and, thus, utilized only a restricted sample size. Therefore, the findings should be regarded as somewhat preliminary in nature. The data is based on in-depth interviews conducted by the author with three married women in the Los Angeles area. Each interview lasted from one to one-and-a-half hours and was recorded on audio tape.

Participants were identified by referral from an initial set of four women known to be going through the application process. These original names were supplied by the author's advisor, who herself was personally immersed in the school choice process. One of the original four women contacted, Veronica, was very eager to talk about the issue herself and, consequently, was included as the first interviewee. While she was quite forthcoming on a variety of areas, the possibility of a biasing influence from her personal connection cannot be entirely eliminated. The second interviewee, Rachel, was identified by one of the other original four women and does not know Veronica socially. She actually went through this process for the first time with her eldest child five years ago, so her discussion of some issues was retrospective in nature. Rachel in turn supplied the referral for the final interviewee, Mary. Mary also went through the decision process for the first time five years ago but has recently returned her children to public schooling for financial reasons and is, thus, still currently immersed in the issue. Both Rachel and Mary supplied information about the actual consumption experience of private schooling in addition to information about the initial decision process.

All of the women live in the same suburb of Los Angeles and all are Jewish. Therefore, some issues raised relating to parochial schools may not be a factor for all families. All three came from middle class backgrounds, as did their spouses. However, there was quite a range in the education level of the interviewees' parents, from no high school diploma to college professor. They are all themselves products of public schools and appear to have risen about one social class level above that of their parents. While well-educated and qualified for professional positions, none have a strong "career orientation" at this point.

Because this topic is inherently value-laden, the issue of self-presentational bias cannot be entirely avoided, and this fact was kept in mind throughout the data collection and analysis process. However, the author did also make a concerted effort to minimize such bias by trying seem as empathetic and similar to the participants as possible. While there certainly were "politically correct" statements made, as the interviews progressed they became fewer and, on balance, the participants seemed to be expressing their true views.

In no way do the participants represent all or even most parents in urban areas. While not wealthy, even by Los Angeles standards, their gross family incomes are above average. Gross family income was the one issue that caused visible discomfort, with participants giving only a range or "six figures" as a response. However, all three appear to fall within $75,000—$250,000. Thus, the educational choices considered by these women are not intended to be representative of the full spectrum of options faced by contemporary parents. Rather, the study provides an initial rich, deep plumbing of a *particular* segment in a particular urban area.

THE INDIVIDUAL EXPERIENCES

This section presents some of the issues that were of most import to each of the women interviewed. These emergent issues form the basis for the interpretive themes developed in the subsequent section.

Veronica

The bulk of her discussion centered on the issues of monetary sacrifice and problems with the quality of life in Los Angeles. She spoke *at length* about what she considers to be the good life to which an established physician's family should be entitled, and the income level required to live it in Los Angeles today.

You have to really be above $400,00 as far as I'm concerned to really have the Mercedes and the big house and the private schools and the traveling...So you don't have as much fun because every time you go to the theater and it's $100, you say, "Oh, this is $100 night, and if..." So I think it's really your people in the middle that are just really struggling. Because there's enough money for it to be a crisis. If we were broke, it wouldn't be an issue. They'd go to public school and that would be it. It's that torment that we can afford more if we give up everything else.

However, she does also genuinely fear that expenditures on education for grades K-12 will erode their ability to provide for upper education.

I really feel that we have a responsibility to provide for their college education, professional school as indicated, and for them to transition into adult life.

She also notes that both she and her husband are the products of public schools and find the idea of private elementary tuition shocking. She further indicates that the situation is uniquely volatile for her family because they have twins and have to adjust to paying double tuition at once and because her husband sacrificed many years as a physician and is now seeing his reward for that sacrifice lost to elementary school.

For us, the idea of devoting all of our discretionary resources just for education is just mind boggling, especially for kindergarten. So it's a touchy subject for us, maybe more so than for some other people. We've had more fights this year than in the ten years we've known each other. We've had more arguing, and we've been under more tension, because it becomes a real battle over how we're going to meet everybody's priorities if all of our discretionary income is gonna go for elementary school. And it's been VERY difficult for my husband as a 47 year-old physician to have all that delayed gratification in his teens and twenties as he struggled through medical school and residency...

Veronica does not want to return to the workforce despite the above concerns with the financial strain of private school. She views her role in handling all domestic responsibilities and an exaggerated account of the cost of child care[1] as reasons for it being either impossible or at least not worth the sacrifice for her to do so. She also considers it to be a sign of social status for a family to have the wife at home.

I'm not going to work full time unless I'm in a place where the children are close and have child care and so forth. I cannot

---

[1]While Veronica cites the cost of child care at $400 per week, a local agency puts the figure at about $300-350 for an experienced, full-time, English-speaking child care provider to work in the home. Veronica would only need after-school care since kindergarten is full-day at most of these private schools. Also, she already has part-time help so that the marginal increase in cost would not be that great.

imagine doing a 50 hour-a-week job and generating enough capital to pay somebody $400 a week, which is what you have to spend...Our dilemma is, do we just put them in a public school and have me at home? Or do we hire a Third World country nanny, and I'll have a ridiculous job where I'm gone 60 hours a week? I really think that a five-year-old needs some parental figure, and if I go to work, they're not gonna have any... The less expensive [private] schools are the ones that offer child care because they have to appeal to more middle class households where both parents are working and cannot afford a nanny as well as a private school.

While she speaks of desiring diversity, she also fears the consequences for her children of any real diversity. Veronica several times indicated that she values assimilation and fitting in more than diversity and desires to have the income to be able to insulate her family from what she perceives as the problems of urban life.

We would like them to grow up in an environment with an exposure to all kinds of people. The minorities that are there [in private schools] are so affluent that they're not representative of the real world...Our concern with the public schools is really the safety issue. I have blond-haired, blue-eyed children who are not very physical and not very aggressive, and I worry about interactions on playgrounds...In Beverly Hills you have a lot of cultural tensions, which concerns me. There was a large influx in the 70's and 80's of Iranians who don't assimilate easily with the native population, you know, the American population, so that creates a whole kind of divisive thing.

Thus, Veronica particularly feels conflicts between the desire to provide for her children and the pull of her own and her husband's interests. She is also both attracted to prestige and interested in positive peer influence for her children and repulsed by the possibility of elitism.

Mary

Mary is very connected to her three children and spoke of not being able to let go in other areas, such as letting them ride their bikes around the neighborhood. She has had her children in two different public schools and in a private school. Most, recently, she was forced for financial reasons to withdraw her two eldest children from the private Jewish school they attended. She seems quite uncertain about her own judgment and seeks reassurance and consensus from other parents, despite the fact that she objectively has the most knowledge about education of any of the three participants. She is currently taking classes to enable herself to return to work next year as a math teacher. Mary relied heavily on word-of-mouth advice when she originally made choices about education for her eldest son five years ago. "Meeting other mothers, that was...Word of mouth, friends, that was definitely my biggest resource."

Her major concern with the current situation is that she isn't confident in the public schools. She feels she has to continually monitor them and can't relax and be satisfied that her children are getting what they need from the school. She has even formulated four alternative strategies in case she becomes convinced that the public school her children are currently attending is not adequate. All of this concern comes in spite of the fact that they are in one of the best public elementary schools in the Los Angeles area, the same one that Veronica would like to be able to permit into using special

rules of the LA school district.

Well, I go back and forth. If it wasn't a matter of finances, my kids would be in private school because to me, although they get a different...(sigh) although they get a different experience at public school, and its' a good experience, I feel safe at private school. I know that my child is being looked after well. At public school I always have my doubts, and that's my biggest fear. It's just, I'm just not completely confident there.

Mary also places a very high value on being informed about what is taking place in the classroom and about teachers' assessments of her children's strengths and weaknesses. She wants to know exactly what needs improvement so that she can give them extra help. In comparing public and private schools, she was quite upset about the lack of communication from the public schools. She does not like the fact that there are no regularly scheduled conferences or that homework comes home with only letter grades and no comments or suggestions for improvement.

I have a lot of my daughter's last year's work [from private school] at home so I can track—I'm trying to make some comparisons...I'll talk to my friends whose kids are still at Stephen Weiss, and ask what their kids are doing. My son is just starting multiplication, and those kids are up to their sixes in the times tables. So, I know my kids are behind, and maybe it's not a big deal, but it bothers me.

Finally, Mary also shows a reluctance to let go of her children in that she seeks to gain social ties and stimulation from the school they attend. She was very attached to the private school her children attended for several years, and she described actual grief at having to pull them out.

I cried when I took them out of Stephen Weiss. I cried for three days. It was almost like when my father died.

In addition, one thing she mentioned *repeatedly* throughout the interview was the number of things constantly "going on" at Stephen Weiss, which is a Jewish temple as well as a school. She hopes that her children will be able to return at some point and has retained her membership at the temple.

It's *amazing* all the things that that place has gong on! It impresses me—to no end. There's always something, support groups. They've even got a class for women to bring their housekeepers—they give a Red Cross class in Spanish. They've got [charity] projects going on in class. It's nice. I've come in and helped with that. It's very nice. They've *always* got things going on. A lot of stimulation—for the kids.

The only negative thing she expressed about Stephen Weiss, other than being angry that it costs so much more than Catholic schools, was the reaction of some of the mothers after she put her children in public school.

I felt like after I left, that maybe I thought they were my friends and they were, but I didn't get as many calls—you know what I'm saying? My kids weren't there anymore so I, you know, I was non-existent. There are some very wealthy people up there, and they have a reputation of being very snobby at that school. But I did meet some very nice, down-to-earth people, and that's who I've remained friends with.

Thus, Mary strongly exhibits reliance on peer group, competition, and budgetary adjustment. She also particularly feels the conflict between providing both for current education and for later education and conflict between the desire for positive peer influence and a distaste for snobbishness and social comparison.

Rachel

Rachel is driven primarily by her values. She seemed to be the most concerned about diversity and exposing her children to the "real world." However, she also did not feel that the public schools serve children from families like her own. She concluded that their mission is to serve those with special problems and reluctantly abandoned the public schools, although she still monitors what is happening there.

> I remember thinking at the time that if my housekeeper's child was going to go to school, this is the school I would want for that child because they would do their best to teach him English and bring him up and integrate him into society...And I will never forget that I asked the question, "What if your child speaks English well, he comes out of a good nursery school, and he has good self esteem, what do you do for him?" And the principal said, "Nothing. They have no problems, we don't have to worry about it."

Rachel considered the values held by private schools as an explicit choice criteria on which she judged them. She asked all the schools what kinds of community service programs they had for the children to be involved with. However, her well-intentioned concern did have a patronizing edge at times.

> One of my son's kindergarten classes adopted an animal at the zoo, and it was their job to take care of it. And every Friday they have to bring food for the poor people.

Another of the school's programs, having the children become pen pals with Head Start children, serves to create a demarcation between "us" and "them" in addition to the positive function it may serve.

> And my other son went down to visit Head Start programs and had a pen pal there for a whole year that, you know, he would talk to and he would deal—you know it brings up issues that maybe I don't want to deal with, but I think it's good for the children to be aware of what's going on. My second grade son came home and said Alex had burn marks all over him because his mother got mad at him and hit him with an iron. And, you know, that was incomprehensible to my son, that parents could do something like that. But I think that's OK. They have to realize there's other types of people in the world.

Costa & Belk (1990) note that the nouveaux riches often use purchases of art and philanthropic donations as a means of symbolically "cleansing" their new money, which possesses a lingering taint from the historical disdain of Western aristocracy for trade. One might posit that Rachel derives a similar type of symbolic cleansing from the self-selection and homogeneity of the private school by pointing to the community service activities undertaken there.

The foregoing descriptions demonstrate that each of these mothers, although quite similar in characteristics such as religion, suburban geographic residence, consideration set, and general income level, experienced this issue quite differently. From their individual experiences the first brushstrokes of an interpretive picture can begin to be painted.

INTERPRETIVE THEMES

Three major self-related processes can be detected from the participants' experience with the school choice situation: the investment of extended self, the demarcation of the self vs. the other, and the commoditization of the self. The dynamics of these thematic processes also provide the basis for an analysis of the meaning of "public" vs. "private" in education.

Investment of the Extended Self

Once local public school options have been judged to be inadequate, the extended self as described by Belk (1988) becomes closely intertwined in the decision process. In that seminal piece, Belk presented Sartre's theory about three processes through which individuals incorporate objects into their extended selves: knowing, controlling, and/or creating the object. The private school appears to be incorporated into the participants' extended selves primarily through knowing and controlling, but creating through paying the high tuition may apply as well.

Briefly, Sartre maintains that knowing an object comes about through a carnal and sexual desire to have the object. There seems to be little doubt that visiting the prestigious, exclusive schools considered by these women did plant the seeds of desire and wanting. Consider some statements about the schools:

> It was very difficult leaving Stephen Weiss because it was like a perfect world up there, and everything just was nice and everybody was really—had their child's best interests in mind, and—just even the artistic materials that they used. Everything was so wonderful there, and public school just couldn't compare...It's a very strong place. I just think it's a good place to be affiliated with. I really can't say enough about it. —Mary

> Sue (her daughter), who went with me to submit the application, just fell in love with the place because it's on top, like by Mulholland, with beautiful rolling lawns, brand new gorgeous facility, and she hasn't stopped talking about how she wants to go to Stephen Weiss for school. So even a four-year-old can discern the differences. She was very impressed with the lawns and the playgrounds. —Veronica

The above quotations illustrate wanting and a projection of ideal selves into the school environment. All respondents described the overall "feel" as being the essence of a decision to favor a particular school. However, they were also sensitive to a feeling of fitting in or feeling comfortable with the educational philosophy and the type of parents sending their children to a school as well.

> One thing I considered that maybe doesn't sound that important is how comfortable I would be at the school. You know, when I look at the other mothers and I saw the cars they drove, and I saw the way they dressed...I personally am not comfortable at a school where women wear leather outfits to go pick up their children in carpool. I wanted a school where I feel comfortable because I felt that if I didn't feel comfortable, I didn't think my children would feel comfortable. —Rachel

Sartre describes controlling as overcoming, conquering, or mastering. Gaining admission can be seen as a form of conquering and having successfully mastered the intricacies of the kindergarten placement process on the part of these mothers. While they all hate this process, resent having to go through it, and have a sense of the ludicrousness involved, they do become caught up in it.

> You had to write about your child. "Tell us about your child." "Tell us why you think this school is appropriate for your child." "What are your most important goals for the schooling of your child." They were as tough as when I was trying to get into graduate school...While I was going through it, I really, truly felt it was the most important decision I would ever make, and I was panic-stricken. It was really hard. —Rachel

Costa & Belk's (1990) analysis is again germaine to the present discussion. They applied the analogy of the geographic immigrant to the experience of the nouveaux riches entering an alien social world in which they must "learn" how to be wealthy. While the participants in this study likely do not meet the net worth criteria employed by Costa & Belk, this experience of learning to navigate the terrain of the exclusive private elementary school is actually quite similar in some respects.

Because of the dearth of clear measurable criteria and the lack of participant experience, the power wielded by school reputations passed on through the social networks of mothers was quite striking. All of the women had belonged to organized baby groups, such as Mommy & Me, a practice quite common among this socio-economic group in Los Angeles. They all described a highly stable consensus among their peers as to the nature of the hierarchical quality tiers of private schools. While participants were much less certain about the specific reasons for these reputations, they placed a great deal of faith in these groupings. Thus, the peer group almost entirely defined a set of schools from within which individual preference for dimensions such as parochial vs. secular, traditional vs. liberal, selective vs. (more) egalitarian could be used to make final choices.

The Self vs. The Other

Thorstein Veblen's (1899) classic *The Theory of the Leisure Class* provides a framework for understanding dual processes underlying the mixed feelings about the exclusiveness and sheltering atmosphere of top tier private schools. According to this theory, the primary force driving wealth accumulation is a motive for social comparison rather than for consumption per se. Thus, the goal being sought is favorable comparison with the rest of the community. In a modern urban setting, the community can be thought of as various reference groups, such as neighbors, business associates, and other parents. By sending their children to exclusive private schools, these parents are initiating two new types of self-other processes. First, they are distinguishing themselves from lower classes who must settle for whatever the current state of public education might be. Second, they are entering a new higher-status reference group comprised of the other parents at the private schools.

Separation from the Lower Classes. Demarcation of the family unit from the less fortunate other is apparent in Rachel's comments about public school being a place for her housekeeper's son and in her story about the Head Start boy showing her son "other types of people". Similarly, Veronica's comment about worries for blue-eyed blonde children in a public playground and other comments about desiring insulation from urban problems demonstrate this urge toward separation. At the same time, these urges to distance self from others run counter to their views that they should be open, accepting, and egalitarian towards others. In a sense, by withdrawing from the more pressing problems with public school, they are also withdrawing from their own roots. Thus, the psycho-logical conflict between desires for safety and security and for diversity.

Comparison to the Typical Private School Family. Conversely, all of these mothers were well aware that their families are among the bottom level of wealth within the set of families sending their children to the prestigious elementary schools. While Veblen would state that individuals are always looking to the class above them as a goal, initiating frequent contact with such a class prematurely is an action in opposition to the goal of positive comparison. Participants were all quite uneasy and anxious about the impact of the inevitable comparitive shortcomings, both upon themselves and their children.

> And the wealth of these kids is just mind boggling. You put them in an environment in which we cannot compete, nor do we WANT them to compete and have those kinds of values. I don't want them to come home and say, "Why don't we live in a ten bedroom house?" —Veronica

Even Mary, who was highly attached to the social bonds she established through her children's private school, was sensitive to this issue. Her comments about her fall from grace after withdrawing her children highlight this clearly. She also commented about the extreme affluence and conspicuous consumption of families at Stephen Weiss:

> They have nothing better to do than spend $75,000 on a Bar or Bat Mitzvah. I'm not kidding. I have heard stories that some of them went to the extent of renting the Trojan horse (the one ridden by the USC mascot) and having their child make her entrance on the Trojan horse.

The Commoditization of the Self

Arjun Appadurai (1986) defines a commodity as a thing that, at a certain phase of its social career and in a certain context, meet the symbolic, classificatory, and moral requirements of exchangeability. In all social systems, culture *constructs* these requirements in order to set some bounds on the natural tendency for technology the expand the domain of what is readily seen as an allowable commodity. In his view, human beings are the most prominant class of things exempted from commodity status.

During the school application process, a very young child and his or her family are, in a sense, being commoditized. They perceive of themselves as being judged to have a particular exchange value to the school. Generally, this entails value in terms of the child's intelligence and social skills/ability to conform to the classroom structure and the parent's income, stability and social standing. This is a highly uncomfortable feeling that creates a great deal of anger and hostility in the participants.

> Oh, it was awful. I didn't really want to put my child through a whole evaluation process that's gonna decide his life at four years old. I felt like if all they care about is my financial statement, then they should just ask and not make my child go through all of this. —Rachel

The Meaning of Public and Private

Second perhaps to safety, the perception that the middle class is disappearing is the central force in leading the participants to favor private education. All seemed to share some feeling that America is moving toward a two-class society, the future composition of which will largely be determined by quality of education. Quality of education is in turn viewed as largely based on the public/

private distinction. This view spurs the commitment to make a sacrifice to ensure that their children are among the "haves."

Personally, I think we're moving to a more class society where there's those that have it and those who don't have it, and that's very scary. At least in education because you've got those going to private schools and those who don't, and there doesn't seem to be...a level of equality. We made a trade-off saying that I have to go back to work and basically my income goes to keeping those kids in private schools. It doesn't go to having a fur coat or new cars or taking family vacations or worrying about retirement. —Rachel

At the same time, recognizing and perhaps contributing to the demise of quality public education is an affront on a sacred institution that has been viewed as the central vehicle for upward mobility since its inception. It is a symbol for the notion that the American Dream is open to all of its citizens, so long as they apply themselves diligently.

I think it's sad. It's really upsetting that parents have to go through it, that we can't use the public school system and feel comfortable with it. It would be nice to just have a neighborhood school and let your kids be able to walk to school and play with their friends. —Rachel

One can also see the same public/private distinction in the domain of healthcare. The current political debate over universal healthcare is essentially an attempt by supporters to decommoditize it and view it as a right rather than a good, and an attempt by opponents to raise quality concerns by means of drawing a public vs. private distinction. Veronica provided a fascinating glimpse of the meaning of "public" and "private" education by drawing a direct parallel between the generic, public HMO medicine practiced by her husband and her perception of the mundane learning offered by public schools.

It's a different kind of feel [in public schools]. You know, it's like the difference between private medicine and Californiacare. Californiacare is like herd mentality. Factory medicine, you know, as opposed to going to a private doctor in Beverly Hills who's got original art on the wall. It's a different kind of feel...

Part of what this different "feel" means is also security and peace of mind, as illustrated by Mary's comments. This is the intangible quality that comes along with the aesthetically pleasing physical facility and the involved, well-mannered parents.

CONCLUSION

This project illuminated an intensely emotional and stressful consumption process. Participants were eager to discuss their dilemma and seemed to find it cathartic. It provides an initial peek at how individuals deal with tough consumption decisions that strike close to home. The data gathered to date also provide a great deal of information not included within the scope of this paper. For instance, insights about some of the major factors contributing to the perceptions of inadequacy formed by these new refugees from the public system may be instructive for policy use by public school officials in attempts to overcome the highly publicized "crisis of confidence". Briefly, in addition to safety, they include: class size, perceived commitment to "normal" or non-challenged students, the perceived competence of the principal, his or her presence at school functions, and parent involvement.

Much more investigation remains to be done to gain a full understanding of the educational choice process, including study of its impact on marital dynamics and on friendships among parents in the wake of acceptances and rejections. The experiences of fathers is also open to exploration, as well as the impact of the process on the child's self esteem. Finally, the sampling frame should be substantially expanded since educational choice among families of lower income is likely to be experienced quite differently.

Some issues raised during this project can also be explored in other consumption contexts. The emotional strain of making critical choices for family members naturally extends to choices about retirement homes for aging parents. In some cases, the same agonizing financial decisions may also be involved. Conflict between societal welfare and individual wants may also be present in less impactful but more frequent product decisions relating to environmental issues, such as recycling and/or purchasing more expensive recycled products. The application of the private/public distinction to healthcare also warrants further study. Finally, the public vs. private and self vs. the other themes can be detected in some of the current controversies over how the Internet should adapt to mass usage. Now that it is being pushed for use in schools, debates wage about the desirability and feasibility of limiting the totally unregulated status that has attracted pornographers. A San Francisco group has already created the first "gated community" on the Internet which requires a password for entry. The social process has been likened to earlier physical migration to suburbs (*Time Magazine*, 1994). It also has many of the elements of the forces that are leading parents, even in some suburbs, to withdraw from public education.

REFERENCES

Ansberry, Clare (1993), "To Get Kids into Preschool, Parents Collar VIPs to Pen High-Sounding References," *Wall Street Journal,* December 20, A1, A8.

Appadurai, Arjun (1986), *The Social Life of Things: Commodities in Cultural Perspective,* Cambridge, England: University of Cambridge Press.

Arndt, Johan (1976), "Reflections on Research in Consumer Behavior," *Advances in Consumer Research,* Vol. 3, ed. Beverlee B. Anderson, Ann Arbor, MI: Association for Consumer Research, 213-221.

Belk, Russell W. (1988), "Possessions and the Extended Self," *Journal of Consumer Research,* 15(Sept), 139-168.

Coleman, James S. (1988), "'Social Capital' and Schools," *The Education Digest,* (April), 6-9.

Costa, Janeen A. and Russell W. Belk (1990), "Nouveaux Riches as Quintessential Americans: Case Studies of Consumption in an Extended Family," *Advances in Nonprofit Marketing,* vol. 3, 83-140.

Gardner, Ralph (1994), "You'll Never Eat School Lunch in This Town Again," *Spy Magazine,* February, 46-50.

Glazer, Barney and Anselm L. Strauss (1967), "The Constant Comparative Method of Qualitative Analysis," in *The Discovery of Grounded Theory: Strategies for Qualitative Research,* New York: Aldine De Gruyter, Chapter 5, 101-115.

McCracken, Grant (1988), *The Long Interview,* London: Sage Publications, Inc.

Shogren, Elizabeth (1993), "A Private Dilemma for Parents: A Generation that Viewed Itself as Open-Minded Suffers a Humbling Showdown with Conscience," *Los Angeles Times,* January 26, A1, A14, A15.

Solomon, Michael R. (1983), "The Role of Products as Social Stimuli: A Symbolic Interactionism Perspective," *Journal of Consumer Research,* 10(Dec), 319-329.

Thompson, Craig, William Locander, and Howard Pollio (1989), "Putting the Experience Back into Consumer Research: The Philosophy and Method of Existential-Phenomenology," *Journal of Consumer Research,* 16(Sept), 133-146.

Time Magazine (1994), "Battle for the Soul of the Internet," July 25.

Toch, Thomas (1991), "The Exodus," *U. S. News & World Report,* December 9, 66-77.

Veblen, Thorstein (1899), *The Theory of the Leisure Class,* New York, NY: Macmillan.

Wells, William (1993), "Discovery-Oriented Consumer Research," *Journal of Consumer Research,* 19(March), 489-504.

Product Design, Aesthetics, and Consumer Research

Robert W. Veryzer, Jr., Rensselaer Polytechnic Institute

Product design and aesthetics are important determinants of consumers' preferences and choices. Design and aesthetics are increasingly being used by companies as a way of differentiating products in order to successfully compete in a marketplace filled with products from around the world. The resurgence of product design and aesthetics as elements that are being employed to produce products which more fully satisfy consumer needs and provide a competitive advantage represents a return to a focus on the product component of the marketing mix. However, there is still much that is not understood concerning the relationship between design (inclusive of aesthetics) and consumers' responses to products (e.g., preference, choice, consideration set formation, fashion trends, etc.). Product design and aesthetics research is still in its infancy even though it has periodically received attention from consumer researchers as well as researchers in other disciplines. As yet, the scope and direction of this stream of research and its relationship to consumer research have not been clearly defined. The purpose of this special session was to explore the place of product design and aesthetics research in consumer research. Toward that end, papers were presented that covered a variety of product design and aesthetics topics and demonstrated different conceptual and methodological approaches to studying the influence of product design on consumer behavior. The session also provided a forum for critical evaluation and constructive thinking concerning design and aesthetics research.

This special session began with an introduction by Robert W. Veryzer, Jr., which provided a context and structure for the session. Many of his remarks were drawn from the paper "The Place of Product Design and Aesthetics in Consumer Research," which discusses the relationships between design, aesthetics, and consumer research and why the discipline of consumer research is uniquely suited for the study of these relationships. In the paper, a conceptualization of design that distinguishes between the different roles that design may play in the interaction between consumer and product is discussed. A framework for understanding and classifying objects (i.e., products) with respect to design and aesthetics is also presented and discussed.

In the second paper, "Aesthetic Aspects of the Consumption of Fashion Design: the Conceptual and Empirical Challenge," Molly Eckman and Janet Wagner review conceptual and empirical work on the aesthetics of fashion design. The authors then address some of the conceptual and methodological challenges facing consumer researchers. In addition, they identify factors that discourage research on fashion design such as cultural values, misunderstanding of fashion change, and the complexity of the relationship between fashion goods and the consumer. The authors conclude with suggestions for future research.

In the third paper, "Why Some Products 'Just Feel Right' or, the Phenomenology of Product Rightness" by Jeff Durgee and Gina Colarelli O'Conner, the possibility that there is a set of products that inspire a special feeling of "rightness" in consumers is explored using a phenomenological approach. The authors discuss their findings from interviews in which consumers were asked to respond to the question "What products feel right?" The authors report that product "rightness" seems to be associated with high functional value, versatility, prototypic life experiences, self-expressiveness, and instant satisfaction.

The final paper of the session, "The Role of Package Appearance in Choice" by Lawrence L. Garber, Jr., proposes a staged model of choice that explicitly considers the role of package appearance in the formation of the consideration set at the point of purchase. The model suggests that the formation of a visually oriented preattention/attention set precedes and affects formation of a subsequent product-benefits-oriented consideration set. The paper also discusses a series of proposed experiments utilizing computer-simulated shopping trips that will be used to test the model. Some preliminary data and results were presented and discussed in the session.

The discussant for this special session was Morris B. Holbrook, who offered a number of insightful comments to the presenters concerning their research. He also raised several important questions concerning the nature of (profound) aesthetic experience and the "products" to which such experience most applies. Some of the other issues that were discussed concerned whether or not there is anything "aesthetically" consistent across the product choices that people make and whether or not the study of aesthetics is, or should be, elitist.

The papers that were presented and discussed in this special session offer a number of interesting ideas and research insights. The authors of these papers committed to publishing in *Advances in Consumer Research* because these proceedings play an extremely important role in the dissemination of knowledge in our field. The proceedings provide an opportunity for researchers to present some of their emerging research ideas. These ideas represent new and often unexplored directions in consumer (or any other) research. It is hoped that the papers published here will promote a better understanding of product design and aesthetics and that they will serve to further stimulate research in these areas.

The Place of Product Design and Aesthetics in Consumer Research

Robert W. Veryzer, Jr., Rensselaer Polytechnic Institute

ABSTRACT

Product design and aesthetics research is still in its infancy even though it has periodically received attention from consumer researchers as well as researchers in other disciplines. The scope and direction of this stream of research has yet to be clearly defined, and the stream's relationship to consumer research continues to be rather vague. This paper examines the place of product design and aesthetics research in consumer research. The paper begins by discussing design and aesthetics and provides some background concerning the study of these topics. The efforts of consumer researchers in these areas and the unique suitability of the discipline of consumer research for studying product design and aesthetics are then discussed. Finally, recommendations are presented concerning the significant research questions and issues that need to be addressed if this area is to become a viable stream in consumer research.

INTRODUCTION

There is a growing recognition that product design is emerging as a key marketing element (Kotler and Rath 1984; Holbrook and Zirlin 1985; Wallendorf 1980). This is especially true of the portions of product design that involve construction for human interaction and aesthetics. Design, which refers to the organization of elements of an object, and aesthetics are inherently linked since the design or physical form of a product encompasses aesthetic aspects of the product (e.g., shape, color, texture, etc.). The importance of product design as a determinant of consumer behavior is increasing as the technology gaps between companies become smaller and companies are able to produce products that are similar with respect to features, quality, and costs (i.e., price).

Despite the growing awareness of the influence that product design can have on product preferences, surprisingly little in the way of design or aesthetic theory has been advanced that aids in our understanding of how people respond to design or how aesthetic responses are formed (Berlyne 1974, p. 5; Gorski 1987, p. 68). Disciplines such as industrial (product) design[1] are looking to the psychological sciences to address the lack of design theory (Gorski 1987). The progress of consumer researchers in this area has been limited and sporadic. As a result of the absence of theory, there continues to be a great deal of unease when it comes to making decisions about design and managing design projects. This is particularly problematic for managers charged with transferring new technology out of the laboratory and into the market. It is at this point that design and aesthetics play a crucial role in communicating a product's identity and use to consumers.

DESIGN AND AESTHETICS

The term "design" may be used to refer to a process or to a particular (product) composition. For the development of consumer and industrial products this process typically involves collaboration among industrial (product) designers, engineers, marketing experts, scientists, technicians, as well as others (Izzi and Caplan 1972). The objective of the design process is to produce a product "design." "Design" as it is used to refer to a particular product configuration (i.e., arrangement of elements or parts) may be viewed as involving a number of important considerations. A successful (i.e., "good," optimal) design is one that performs its intended function(s) well, is economical (i.e., profitable for the manufacturer and a good value for the consumer), and is pleasant to behold. In addition, product design (i.e., configuration) plays a crucial role in communicating a product's use (i.e., function) and operating procedure to the consumer (e.g., Norman 1988). The ability of a design to communicate a product's function and use to the consumer through its form is paramount since part of the role of a product's design is to interpret technology. This facet of design is growing in importance as the products that we interact with on a daily basis are increasingly becoming more complex. Thus, from a functional or operational point of view a key design issue is how to structure a product so as to promote or maximize (product) interpretation, understanding, and use (e.g., performance, safety).

Product design (i.e., industrial design) is perhaps most associated with aesthetic considerations (Bel Geddes 1934, pp. 222-241). While aesthetic considerations (e.g., shape, symmetry, texture, etc.) usually pertain to the external surface(s) which house or protect the inner workings (e.g., mechanical or electrical components) of a product, these considerations are not entirely independent of other design concerns. For example, aesthetic considerations are influenced by (product) structure (i.e., mechanisms and components that allow the product to perform a particular function). This is especially true of designs that strive to communicate the function of a product rather than to conceal it. In such cases, many elements of a product design that are thought of as being "aesthetic" (e.g., shape) are, in fact, frequently the principal means by which the purpose and use of the object are communicated. This is particularly true today since computer chip technology has freed many products from having to assume forms determined by the larger mechanical components used in the past. Thus, aesthetic considerations in product design can be quite complex and broad in scope since aesthetics (i.e., form, configuration) often plays a central role in object perception, recognition, interpretation, understanding, and use.

Product aesthetics (i.e., design) can exert a significant influence on consumer behavior (e.g., Veryzer 1993). Enhanced product appearance can certainly be advantageous in a commercial sense, even for utilitarian products. Although product aesthetics is central to product design, it is this facet that is least well understood. Despite the relatively long duration of aesthetics study in disciplines such as philosophy, art criticism, art history, psychology, anthropology, experimental aesthetics, industrial design, (and more recently consumer research), there has been a striking inability to formulate a coherent theory with respect to the aesthetic aspect of design. Progress in this area has been inhibited by two unresolved issues that are fundamental to aesthetics research. The first issue concerns the locus of aesthetic experience. The crucial question is whether aesthetic experience emanates from the object or is generated by the perceiver of the object. This issue is apparent in a number of ongoing debates such as whether or not beauty is governed by rules and whether or not aesthetic response is subjective. A second issue concerns the nature of the aesthetic value of an object. Some aestheticians (e.g., Bullough 1912, pp. 783-785)

---

[1]The phrase "industrial design," which is a holdover from the days of the industrial revolution, has served to obscure the profession charged with shaping most of the products that are produced and sold. Industrial designers (e.g., Henry Dreyfuss, Raymond Loewy, etc.) are concerned with enhancing the appearance of manufactured products as well as improving their utility.

maintain that "aesthetic objects" belong to a special class of objects consisting chiefly of works of fine art and natural phenomena (e.g., the human body, landscapes). Furthermore, it is often held that aesthetic appreciation (i.e., experience) can only take place when the object is viewed without attention to any practical or utilitarian consideration (e.g., Bullough 1912). This view, which has resulted in a "philosophy of art" definition being associated with the term "aesthetics," is divergent from the classical roots of aesthetics (e.g., Plato, *The Republic*) as well as the view of aestheticians who hold a wider conception of aesthetics (e.g., Berlyne 1974, p.1).

Even though design and aesthetics have been studied for quite some time, there continues to be a great deal of uncertainty and ambiguity concerning them. This is due primarily to the absence of theory which encourages the impression that "good" design is a rather arbitrary affair (Finn 1990). While the person—product relationship which *is* design is a complex one, it is likely to seem less arbitrary as we learn to better identify and differentiate its essential parts and the factors that influence responses to it.

PRODUCT DESIGN AND AESTHETICS IN CONSUMER RESEARCH

Since design and aesthetics are potentially important factors in the selection of many, if not most, products, it is not surprising that consumer researchers have found them worthwhile to study. Consumer researchers have tended to focus on the aesthetic aspect of product design. This is not surprising since this is a central concern of design and most person—product relationships (i.e., interactions) begin with (the perception of) a product's appearance (Izzi and Caplan 1972).

Beginning with some early explorations in the mid-1970s and early 1980s (e.g., Holbrook 1980; Olson 1981; Sewall 1978; Wallendorf 1980) a "slender stream of research in consumer aesthetics" began to flow (Holbrook and Zirlin 1985, p. 2). Consumer researchers began to grapple with some of the significant questions concerning aesthetic responses such as: "What is an aesthetic response?" and "How are aesthetic responses formed?" (e.g., Holbrook 1980; Olson 1981). Much of this early work was concerned with determining what the aesthetic aspect of consumption is and how aesthetic phenomena could be researched. Consumer researchers debated the definition and scope of consumer aesthetics - with some in the field preferring to apply aesthetic experience only to so called "artistic" or "cultural products" (Holbrook 1980), while others acknowledged that virtually any product has an aesthetic component (Holbrook and Zirlin 1985; Olson 1981). Although this latter view, which is consistent with an industrial design perspective, seems to have gained general acceptance among consumer researchers, the tendencies to associate aesthetics with "art" and "emotion," to discount its systematic influence, and to discuss "aesthetic objects" are still present within the consumer research discipline.

Even though the aesthetic aspect of product design has been introduced into the field of consumer research, our understanding of the phenomenon has not advanced much beyond that which we inherited from other disciplines. There are a number of reasons that the discipline of consumer research has not made more progress in the areas of product design and aesthetics. Perhaps the most important reasons for the slow rate of progress are that the relevance of product design for consumer research and design's applicability to a broad range of products have been largely overlooked. Part of the reason for this may be due to conceptions of design and aesthetics as being essentially superficial styling or as pertaining primarily to works of art. Such views cast the influence and scope of design and aesthetics in very narrow terms. This tends to minimize design's importance (i.e., relevance to most product purchase situations) and obscure its relationship to other areas that are of interest to consumer researchers (e.g., attitude, involvement, diffusion of innovations, etc.). Many of the obstacles that have limited consumer researchers progress in the areas of design and aesthetics are the same fundamental issues that have impeded researchers in other disciplines that have studied these topics. The fundamental design issue concerns how to best configure a product. This issue is extremely complex because peoples' interactions with product designs involve multiple design considerations (e.g., function, communication/interpretation, aesthetics) that affect a number of different reactions (e.g., understanding, aesthetic response) to the product (design). Issues such as the locus of aesthetic experience and the nature of an "aesthetic object" (i.e., what constitutes an aesthetic object) continue to stir debate and cloud aesthetic research (Holbrook and Zirlin 1985). These fundamental issues must be addressed if design and aesthetics research is to become a viable stream in consumer research.

Although there are a number of obstacles that must be overcome, there is perhaps no discipline more ideally suited for the study of product design than that of consumer research. This discipline offers the unique combination of scientific research methods and a tangible research context (i.e., marketing, consumer/product focus). The consumer/product context (as opposed to an "art" context) is extremely helpful for investigating design and aesthetics questions because it allows philosophical questions to be recast in a more concrete form. This can be done because "successful" or "good" design in a marketing context is more easily defined (i.e., more objective) than it is in an "art" context. This is not to say that "good" design should be defined solely in terms of success in the marketplace or that it will always result in high sales or increased market share. Rather, this context provides a means for assessing the effects of a design because they are manifest in observable behavior (e.g., product purchase) which is not shrouded in the subtleties of "artistic appreciation." Consumer research offers a more direct, concrete context in which to investigate the influence of design and the factors that underlie peoples' responses to it (e.g., cultural influences, psychological influences, visual organization principles, etc.).

If consumer researchers are to make a genuine contribution to our understanding of design and aesthetics beyond those made by other disciplines, the unique research context that our field offers must be embraced. This means that the applied consumer/product context of consumer research must be evident in the view of design that the discipline adopts and the products on which it focuses.

RECOMMENDATIONS FOR CONSUMER RESEARCH

In order for design and aesthetics research to progress researchers must address the fundamental issues that have inhibited the development of theory. Moreover, consumer researchers need to develop new ways of thinking about design and aesthetics that reflect an applied consumer/product context.

It is important for consumer researchers to adopt a conceptualization of design that acknowledges the different aspects of product design (i.e., functional, communicative, and aesthetic) and the relationships and trade-offs among them. These aspects represent different roles that the design of a product can play. The roles are the different but often interrelated bases for the interaction between person and object (i.e., consumer and product). The various aspects of product design play a vital role in the interaction between consumer and product and thus may affect consumer behavior (e.g., comprehension, categorization, aesthetic response, preference, choice, use/performance, etc.).

In addition to adopting a conceptualization that reflects the various roles that design plays in a consumer behavior context, a more complete understanding of each design aspect is needed. The functional aspect of product design would seem to be relatively straight forward. This aspect of a product's design is often thought to fall almost entirely within the domain of engineering design. However, when considered in terms of the consumer—product interaction a broader view of the functional aspect of design emerges. For example, a screwdriver may be used to turn screws or pry things open; shoes may be worn on feet or used to hammer tacks into a wall. An object's form or configuration determines what one can use the object to do.[2] While there is a certain truth to the maxim "form follows function" this saying tends to obscure the fact that function follows (i.e., is determined by) form. The form/function distinction is somewhat misleading because the form (i.e., configuration) of a product determines both how the product looks (i.e., aesthetics) and how it might be used (i.e., function).

The communicative aspect or role of design (e.g., product semantics) needs to be explicitly differentiated from other design considerations and studied. This aspect involves visual and iconic cues that help people to interpret what an object does and how it is operated or used (e.g., the environmental controls in most recent automobiles use the color red to indicate warm air and blue to indicate cool air). The ability of a product (design) to effectively communicate its function and how it may be properly operated can greatly facilitate successful person—product interaction. Thus, the communicative aspect of design may affect how consumers perceive and categorize a product (e.g., product class, complexity level/technological sophistication), influence their attitude toward its use (e.g., difficult to use), and shape their perception of the risks involved in purchasing the product (e.g., afraid they will never use it because it is too difficult to figure out). Design which makes a product more intelligible assists interpretation and enhances person—product interaction. Ultimately, the communicative aspect of a design can make a product easier to use and thereby increase the utility of the product.

Progress in the area of the aesthetic aspect of design will depend on consumer researchers' willingness to adopt (maintain) a more practical view of aesthetics than has been adopted by other disciplines (except industrial design). The view of aesthetics as pertaining only to art objects is too limited for consumer aesthetics and, as was pointed out earlier, is not completely true to the classical roots of aesthetic inquiry (e.g., Plato, *The Republic*). Consumer researchers should embrace a more inclusive view of aesthetic experience. An aesthetic response has been defined as a response arising from the interaction between an object's appearance (i.e., characteristics and configuration) and the perceiver of the object (Berlyne 1974; Veryzer 1993).[3] This definition allows for the possibility that virtually any product can be appreciated in an aesthetic sense (Berlyne 1974; Wallendorf 1980). Although this definition recognizes that all product designs involve an aesthetic component, is does not suggest that aesthetic response plays a significant role in the purchase of every product. Another feature of this definition is that it clearly acknowledges the interaction

between the perceiver and the object (i.e., product) in the formation of an aesthetic response.

Consumer researchers must also address questions concerning a product's "nature" (i.e., aesthetic vs. utilitarian). Distinctions are often made between "aesthetic" and "utilitarian" objects (e.g., Holbrook 1980; Holbrook and Zirlin 1985). Clear distinctions such as these can be difficult to make because all objects have an aesthetic component in that they have a physical form or appearance that can be perceived and thus give rise to an aesthetic response (Berlyne 1974, p. 1; Holbrook and Zirlin 1985; Wallendorf 1980). Likewise, one can argue that every object, even "art" objects, may serve a utilitarian purpose or function (e.g., plays, music, novels, and movies can be used to entertain; paintings and sculpture can be used to establish a mood in a living or work space). Furthermore, distinctions concerning the "aestheticness" (i.e., aesthetic or utilitarian nature) of an object imply that aesthetic experience emanates from the object. While the aesthetic vs. utilitarian distinction may possibly be made with respect to how a particular object is viewed or used (i.e., consumed) by a particular person on a particular occasion, such a distinction is person and situation specific (i.e., dependent). For example, consider the use of "utilitarian" objects such as railroad paraphernalia (e.g., lanterns, railroad track, railroad cars, crossing gates, etc.) to decorate the interior of a restaurant. In such instances there is an inversion of a product's apparent nature from utilitarian to aesthetic because of circumstances particular to the perceiver or as in this case the situation. Thus, the aesthetic vs. utilitarian distinction is not intrinsic to an object. Although some objects may be more likely to be appreciated primarily in either an aesthetic or utilitarian sense within the context of a particular culture (i.e., situation), how the object is ultimately perceived is determined in large measure by the perceiver and the underlying factors that affect his or her perception (e.g., culture, psychological characteristics, etc.).

A more useful way of classifying products may be to focus on the aesthetic and/or utilitarian *intention* (i.e., the purpose or aim of the interest in the object) of the perceiver. This approach acknowledges the role of the perceiver as well as the situational factors in determining the "nature" (aesthetic or utilitarian) of an object. For example, an antique clock could potentially be appreciated for primarily aesthetic or utilitarian reasons. The degree to which it is appreciated for either one or both of these things is not fixed by the object (e.g., clock) itself but rather can vary depending on the "intention" (i.e., reason for examining the object) of the perceiver of the object on a particular occasion. Clearly, there may be factors such as culture or situation specific influences (e.g., peer group, economic circumstances) that encourage a tendency to appreciate a product in a particular manner (i.e., aesthetic or utilitarian). Thus, to some degree intention may be "fixed" (i.e., determined) by factors external to the product (e.g., in one culture a play may be a way of imparting history or values while in another culture the play may be viewed as entertainment).

Another way of looking at products involves the sentient nature of (a response to) an object. *"Sentientality"* refers to the degree to which the design of a product consistently promotes a particular sensation or feeling (e.g., aesthetic response) across perceivers of the product. Sentientality is concerned with the *consistency* of the response to the product rather than whether the response is positive or negative. Therefore, high-sentientality can refer to either a consistently positive or consistently negative (or consistently neutral) response. In the case of products exhibiting high-sentientality, it is likely that the consistent (i.e., systematic) response is due to underlying factors that consciously or unconsciously influence peoples reactions to the object (e.g., visual

---

[2]This view of the functional aspect of design raises some interesting questions concerning design to guard against product misuse as well as other safety issues.

[3]This definition reflects a visual orientation but may be adapted to reflect other orientations (e.g., auditory, tactile, etc.).

FIGURE 1
Product Design Disposition Grid

Intention

	Utilitarian	Aesthetic
Low (Consistency)	utilitarian appreciation/ inconsistent response	aesthetic appreciation/ inconsistent response
High (Consistency)	utilitarian appreciation/ consistent response	aesthetic appreciation/ consistent response

Sentientality

organization principles - unity, proportion, etc.).[4] Products that do not foster consistent responses across perceivers can be said to exhibit low-sentientality. In such cases, responses to product design are likely to reflect primarily idiosyncratic influences (e.g., person specific experiences). Sentientality acknowledges the role of the product in forming responses to design. However, it is likely to be dependent, in part, on things such as internalized visual organization principles and prevalent aesthetic associations (i.e., association between an element or characteristic of an object and a previously encountered object or situation) that the perceiver has developed. Thus, the sentientality exhibited by a product is not necessarily intrinsic to the product itself (e.g., products that display the colors associated with a particular school may be prized in the region near the school but treated indifferently outside of that region).

These two dimensions (i.e., continuums), perceiver intention and product sentientality, can be combined to form a grid that can be used to "classify" products according to the perceiver's intention toward the product (i.e., aesthetic and/or utilitarian interest) and the degree to which the product fosters a systematic response when perceived. In Figure 1, the four panels of the grid represent different product "natures" or dispositions with respect to consumer response to product design. A consumer's response may reflect a utilitarian or aesthetic intention or possibly both. For products where the perceiver's current intention is utilitarian the response would involve a reaction to the product's abilities (or suitability) to perform a given task (e.g., frustration because a product is difficult to operate). For products where the perceiver's current intention involved aesthetic appreciation the reaction would be an aesthetic response. In cases where the perceiver's intention concerns both utilitarian and aesthetic appreciation both types of responses would be involved. Sentientality refers to the consistency of these "intention-based" responses. That is, the degree to which a product promotes a consistent response with respect to aesthetic- and/or utilitarian-based responses. For example, consumers may consis-

tently appreciate the accuracy of a particular digital wristwatch in keeping time (i.e., high-sentientality of utilitarian-based intention). However, consumers may have a wide variety of reactions to the watch's appearance (i.e., low-sentientality of aesthetic-based intention). In the event forces external to the product shift, the "disposition" of the product may change (e.g., new technology could make the watch obsolete; a "back-to-basics" trend could lead consumers to view the high-tech. look of digital watches negatively).

The product design disposition grid is one approach to understanding product responses to design and the mutable nature of products. The approach acknowledges the roles of both the product and the perceiver in forming a response to a (product) design. An approach such as this would seem to offer a perspective that is less problematic with respect to the changeable nature of products than the traditional aesthetic vs. utilitarian distinction.

In addition to the areas that relate directly to the fundamental issues of design and aesthetics, there are a number of other important research questions that need to be investigated. More research is needed to identify factors that influence peoples' responses to product designs (e.g., psychological factors, culture, socio-economic factors, gender, visual organization principles, prototypicality, etc.). Another area that requires further study concerns the relationship between product "disposition" and fashion cycles. Changes in product preference patterns suggest that a disruption or shift in a product's sentientality may have occurred. A better understanding of the process by which such shifts occur could lead to a more complete understanding of fashion as it pertains to product design. The development of methods for studying the consumer—product interaction should also receive more attention. Ultimately, methods are needed that can guide decisions concerning product configuration. Finally, the relationships between design and other streams in consumer research need to be explored. The often subtle and unconscious influence of design and aesthetics on consumers' product perceptions may have an indirect affect on a broad range of behaviors. Design and aesthetics may be a factor in areas of interest to consumer researchers such as attitude formation, brand choice, categorization, involvement, symbolic consumption, etc.

[4]See Veryzer 1993 for a discussion of the Design Principle Algorithm explanation of aesthetic response.

CONCLUSION

Design is an important variable that can have a significant impact on consumers' responses to products. As such, it is a legitimate marketing interest that merits the attention of consumer researchers. The discipline of consumer research is well suited for studying product design and aesthetics because of its research methods and its applied consumer/product context. The ability to make new and meaningful contributions to our knowledge of design and aesthetics will depend on utilization of this context in order to address the issues that continue to inhibit progress in these areas. If this stream is to become viable, the ambiguities surrounding conceptions of design and aesthetics as well as the questions concerning the products suitable for study must be addressed. Although the discipline of consumer research has not rushed to investigate or embrace the study of design and aesthetics, it has in the past clearly shown that it is open to exploring areas such as these. However, the burden falls, as it should, on the researchers investigating these topics to demonstrate that design and aesthetic considerations are important and relevant to consumer research. In order to do this consumer researchers must be willing to approach design and aesthetics from their own perspective and formulate new ways of thinking about these topics that reflect the unique perspective of the consumer research discipline.

REFERENCES

Berlyne, D. E. (1974), *Studies in the New Experimental Aesthetics,* New York: John Wiley and Sons.

Bel Geddes, Norman (1934), *Horizons*, John Lane, The Bodley Head.

Bullough, Edward (1912), "'Psychical Distance' as a Factor in Art and an Aesthetic Principle," *British Journal of Psychology*, Vol. 5: pp. 87-98.

Finn, David (1990), "Good Design is Good Business," *Marketing News*, November 26, 1990, p. 9.

Gorski, D. (1987), *The Cognitive Condition of Design*, ed. Brian Zaff, Symposium Proceedings (March) 1987.

Holbrook, Morris B. (1980), "Some Preliminary Notes on Research in Consumer Esthetics," in *Advances in Consumer Research*, ed., Jerry C. Olson, Ann Arbor, MI: Association for Consumer Research, Vol. 7, pp. 104-108.

_____, and Robert B. Zirlin (1985), "Artistic Creation, Artworks, and Aesthetic Appreciation: Some Philosophical Contributions to Nonprofit Marketing," *Advances in Nonprofit Marketing*, Vol. 1, pp. 1-54.

Izzi, Ed and Ralph Caplan (1972), "Illustrated Answers to the Ten Most Common Questions About Industrial Design," *Westinghouse ENGINEER,* Westinghouse Electric Corporation, (July).

Kotler, Philip and G. Alexander Rath (1984), "Design: A Powerful But Neglected Strategic Tool," *The Journal of Business Strategy*, Vol. 5 (Fall), pp. 16-21.

Norman, Donald A. (1988), *The Design of Everyday Things*, New York, Basic Books, Inc.

Olson, Jerry C. (1981), "What is an Esthetic Response?" *Symbolic Consumer Behavior*, eds. Elizabeth C. Hirschman and Morris B. Holbrook, Ann Arbor, MI: Association for Consumer Research, pp. 71-74.

Plato, *The Republic*, tr. by Francis M Cornford, New York: Oxford University Press, 1945.

Sewall, Murphy A. (1978), "Nonmetric Unidimensional Scaling of Consumer Preferences for Proposed Product Designs," in *Advances in Consumer Research*, ed. H. Keith Hunt, Ann Arbor, MI: Association for Consumer Research, Vol. 5, pp. 22-25.

Veryzer, Robert W. (1993), "Aesthetic Response and the Influence of Design Principles on Product Preferences," in *Advances in Consumer Research*, eds., Leigh McAlister and Michael L. Rothschild, Provo, UT: Association for Consumer Research, Vol. 20, pp. 224-228.

Wallendorf, Melanie (1980), "The Formation of Aesthetic Criteria Through Social Structures and Social Institutions," in *Advances in Consumer Research*, ed., Jerry C. Olson, Ann Arbor, MI: Association for Consumer Research, Vol. 7, pp. 3-6.

Aesthetic Aspects of the Consumption of Fashion Design: The Conceptual and Empirical Challenge

Molly Eckman, Colorado State University
Janet Wagner, University of Maryland

"...America is distrustful of aesthetics, considering them false and of no value. This is a national failing and, in some ways, the worse sort of reverse snobbism.." (Cohen 1993).

Aesthetics is a branch of philosophy dating to Plato and Aristotle. Prior to the nineteenth century, aesthetics had two goals, to analyze the creative process and establish rules for judging beauty and taste in the fine arts. In the late nineteenth century, two developments changed that direction. First, as psychology developed an epistemology, aestheticians began to apply its theory and methods to the study of aesthetic judgments. Second, as standards of living rose, consumers began to demand products that were both functional and attractive. In response, aestheticians broadened their scope to include the design of everyday objects. Today, the term "aesthetics" is construed to mean the study of both the fine and applied arts.

In the broadest sense, art includes objects and endeavors designed to appeal to any sense. However, in common usage, the fine arts are often taken to mean the visual arts, particularly painting and sculpture. According to aestheticians, the purpose of the visual arts is to create "significant form"—a beautiful object that conveys meaning (Bell 1914). Individuals consume art to meet higher order needs—pleasure in perceiving beauty and emotion in grasping the meaning of symbols. In the "aesthetic experience", beauty and expression are inextricably linked.

The applied arts refer to the design of household objects, such as consumer products, furniture, appliances and clothing. Compared to painting and sculpture, the applied arts meet a broader set of needs. To achieve significant form, applied art must meet utilitarian as well as aesthetic needs. Examples of significant form in the design of household objects include the Norelco shaver, the Black & Decker drill, the Bentwood rocker, and the Chanel suit. While most household objects are not such fine examples of significant form, in a society where most products meet utilitarian needs, aesthetic attributes may be determining factors in consumer choice.

More than a decade ago, Holbrook (1981) challenged consumer researchers to shift their focus from utilitarian to aesthetic attributes of products. Despite sporadic attempts to rise to Holbrook's challenge, we continue to neglect the aesthetic aspects of consumption. Nowhere is this more apparent than in the design of fashion goods.

Fashion is a pervasive phenomenon of our culture. While fashion affects the design and consumption of many products, clothing is the classic example. In fact, the effect of fashion on the way we dress is so profound that the design, production and marketing of clothing, which encompasses many industries, is collectively known as "the fashion industry." Given the status of fashion as a multibillion dollar industry and the ability of "significant form" to meet a broad spectrum of consumer needs, the aesthetic aspects of fashion are a compelling area for future research.

The purpose of this paper is to stimulate more research on the aesthetic aspects of fashion design, focusing on clothing. To that end, we will begin by reviewing conceptual and empirical work on the aesthetics of fashion, a small body of scholarship that is primarily the domain of disciplines other than consumer behavior.

We will then identify factors discouraging research on fashion design and suggest ideas for future research.

CONCEPTUAL AND EMPIRICAL WORK ON THE AESTHETICS OF FASHION

Sproles (1979) proposed a model of fashion-oriented consumer behavior.[1] While similar in many respects to conventional consumer behavior models, the Sproles model is based on the assumption that the aesthetic attributes of fashion goods "overwhelm" the utilitarian attributes. Although the model suffers from some misspecification, particularly in the decision-making stages, Sproles offers three insights into the role of aesthetics in fashion. First, the elements of design—silhouette, color, detail, and texture—are explicit inputs to the decision-making process. Second, the primary unit of analysis for fashion-oriented decisions is style, not brand. Finally, the interaction of style and the consumer's physical characteristics—body type and coloring—is a unique aspect of the aesthetics of fashion. Unlike other art forms, the aesthetic significance of a fashion object depends on how it appears on the human body.

Like conventional models of consumer behavior, the Sproles (1979) model is based on the information-processing paradigm of cognitive psychology. As such, the Sproles model assumes an individual consumer evaluating products for his own use. The focus of most research on the aesthetics of fashion has been the evaluation of clothing worn by others, with an emphasis on expressiveness, rather than attractiveness. The results of such research provide valuable information on one set of inputs to the decision-making process, but tell little about how consumers process information on fashion objects for their own use. Moreover, the results of such research offer little insight into how consumers evaluate attractiveness. In the following discussion, we will review research on how individual consumers evaluate fashion goods for their own use. The focus will be judgments of attractiveness, rather than expressiveness.

The results of research on judgments of attractiveness are useful in building the Sproles (1979) model. The relationship between attractiveness and expressiveness was explored by Morganosky and Postlewait (1989). In mall intercepts, shoppers evaluated the aesthetic quality of 16 styles of men's and women's clothing. Attractiveness of form was rated as more important than expressiveness. Support for the assumption that aesthetic attributes dominate utilitarian attributes was offered by Eckman, Damhorst and Kadolph (1990). In a point of purchase study, female shoppers were asked to recall attributes considered in purchasing fashion items. The aesthetic attributes of color, pattern, style, and fabric were recalled more often than utilitarian attributes.

Although Sproles (1979,1981) argues that consumers process information by style, not brand, he ignores the issue of specific information-processing strategies. Holbrook and Moore (1981 tested the notion that information on visual attributes is processed

---

[1]Published in book form, the Sproles (1979) L model has had relatively little exposure. Two exceptions are the research of Eckman and Wagner (1994) and Wagner, Anderson and Ettenson (1990).

configurationally. Consumers evaluated a set of line drawings of sweaters, developed from a conjoint model with interaction terms. The results of the analysis showed interaction terms to be significant, confirming that visual information is processed configurationally.

Eckman and Wagner (1994) also used a conjoint model with interaction terms to explore the processing of visual information by asking consumers to evaluate the attractiveness of men's suits. Numerous main effects were observed for individual design elements; however, evaluations of attractiveness were dominated by the interaction of jacket silhouette and color.

Sproles (1979) suggests that judgments of attractiveness may be affected by consumer characteristics, such as gender, age and personality, and external factors, such as culture. The effect of gender on judgments of style remains controversial. Holbrook (1986) studied M.B.A. student evaluations of men's tailored clothing, and found that men and women seemed to differ in their preferences for design elements. The results of other research (e.g., Lubner-Rupert and Winakor 1985; Minshall, Winakor and Swiney 1982; Morganosky and Postlewaite 1989) suggest that gender has no effect on aesthetic judgments. Eckman and Wagner (1994) found no difference in the processing of information by gender; however, differences were observed between older and younger consumers. Holbrook (1986) reported differences in evaluations of style by personality. Among women, the preferences of visually-oriented women differed from the preferences of verbally-oriented women. However, no differences were observed by personality among men.

In a cross-cultural study, Wagner, Anderson and Ettenson (1990) compared judgments of the attractiveness of women's suits by Chinese and American consumers. The results showed differences in preferences by culture, with the Chinese preferring longer jackets and the Americans preferring solid slacks.

FACTORS DISCOURAGING RESEARCH ON THE AESTHETICS OF FASHION

Given the pervasive effect of fashion on goods and services marketed in the U.S. and around the world, and the array of research techniques at our disposal, researchers' neglect of the aesthetics of fashion is somewhat puzzling. This neglect stems from four sources—cultural values, misunderstanding of fashion change, the complexity of the relationship between fashion goods and the consumer, and a variety of methodological challenges.

Cultural Values

Certain values of American culture may inhibit research on the aesthetics of fashion. Such values include faith in capitalism, belief in democracy, and the association of fashion with femininity. Many Americans have a streak of philistinism, stemming from our capitalistic and democratic traditions. As consumer researchers, we are no exception. Given the narrowness and ideological bent of our business school backgrounds, many of us lack appreciation of the arts. Others of us are simultaneously uncomfortable with and attracted by the notion of status. As we assiduously avoid fashion in dress, we actively follow fashion in other types of behavior, ranging from the consumption of other products to our choice of research topics.

Research on the aesthetics of fashion may also be inhibited by the association of fashion with femininity (Davis 1992). To the extent that marketing has been, until recently, a male-dominated field, the association of fashion with femininity (and weakness) may have made research in this area less appealing. The historical record shows that before the industrial revolution, men and women were equally concerned with fashion. As labor became disengaged from the home, men adopted more conservative dress. According to Veblen's (1899) classic work on conspicuous consumption, women became the vehicle for displaying household status through their appearances. The "Peacock Revolution" of the 1960's is often cited as the twentieth century revival of interest in men's fashion. However, this appears to have done little to reduce the perception that fashion is a female preoccupation.

Misunderstanding of Fashion Change

Despite recent research on the fashion process, fashion change is widely misunderstood. The popular stereotype is one of rapid and unpredictable changes in aesthetic standards, making fashion a frivolous topic unworthy of rigorous research. The results of research on fashion change challenge this stereotype. In a time series analysis of changes in the aesthetic attributes of evening dress, Lowe and Lowe (1985) reported that the rate of fashion change is quite constant. While the amount of change in a given attribute may be erratic, the average amount of change over time is constant, and evolves in a consistent direction. The Lowes suggest that design principles govern the relationship among aesthetic attributes and serve as "brakes" on the rate of fashion change.

The Consumer's Relationship to the Fashion Object

Another deterrent to research on the aesthetics of fashion is the complex relationship between the consumer and the fashion object. This relationship has both physical and psychological dimensions. As physical entities, painting, sculpture and other visual art forms can be judged as stand alone objects. However, the aesthetic quality of a fashion object is best judged when worn on the human body. When a fashion object is worn, the elements of design (silhouette, color and texture) interact with the physical characteristics of the consumer (body type and coloring) to create form (DeLong 1987; Sproles 1979)[2]. The entire form is then evaluated in terms of how closely it fits the "cultural ideal" of attractiveness. The complexity of the relationship between the design elements and the physical characteristics of the consumer renders the construction of valid research instruments difficult, but not impossible.

The relationship of fashion to the consumer's psychological state is also complex. While multiple motives have been ascribed to fashionable dressing, Sproles (1979, 1981) argues that aesthetic motives may dominate, or even overwhelm, utilitarian motives. The archaeological record indicates that among prehistoric people the primary motive for dress was to beautify the body. Contemporary scholars concur that among modern consumers the desire to enhance physical attractiveness continues to motivate the consumption of fashion goods. However, the pursuit of beauty is not the only aesthetic motive. A second aesthetic motive is expressiveness—the need to convey meaning. In fact, perceptions of meaning in dress may be the most actively studied topic with respect to fashion.

Research suggests that consumers infer numerous personal characteristics, including intelligence (Behling and Williams 1991), status (Damhorst 1985), and personality (Gordon, Infante and Braun 1985; Sweat and Zentner 1985) from the dress of others. It tells us nothing, however, about the meaning consumers ascribe to

---

[2]In fact, physical characteristics such as body type and coloring have their own fashion cycles. As documented by the fashion press and our own observations, the fashionable body of the twentieth century has evolved from plump and pale to thin and bronzed.

their own clothing. This is a particularly intriguing topic, because in buying and using fashion goods, individuals are not just consumers; they are also designers. In shopping for fashion goods, the consumer is engaged in a creative process of collecting aesthetic objects to enhance the "constellation" of fashion goods[3] that is his wardrobe. The creative process continues in the daily dressing ritual[4], as the consumer combines fashion items with his own physical characteristics in attractive (he hopes) and expressive forms. As consumer researchers, we are beginning to explore aesthetic judgments of fashion goods. However, we persist in ignoring the creative process, which is an integral part of the consumption of fashion. The emerging experiential paradigm may lend itself well to research on the creative process.

Methodological Challenges

Holbrook (1981) noted that in using the information processing paradigm, most of us rely on the verbal/additive model. In this model, it is assumed that information is processed in a linear manner. While the verbal/additive model is useful in analyzing the processing of utilitarian attributes, which are easily presented in verbal protocols, it is not well-suited to analyzing aesthetic attributes. Because visual information is processed configurationally, aesthetic attributes are presented more effectively in pictures.

To accommodate the configurational processing of aesthetic attributes, the conventional conjoint model can be extended to include interaction terms, an approach used by Holbrook and Moore (1981), Wagner, Anderson and Ettenson (1990), and Eckman and Wagner (1994) in analyzing aesthetic judgments. In using conjoint models with interaction terms, the number of variables and interaction terms mst be limited, to keep the number of stimuli manageable. Limiting the number of variables and interaction terms also means that visual images may have to be kept simple. Fortunately, pictorial information is more easily processed than verbal information, so respondents should be able to evaluate a large number of reasonable complicated images without tiring.

Another methodological problem of research on aesthetics is developing valid instruments. The ideal stimuli would be real fashion objects (Holbrook 1986; Sproles 1981), evaluated as worn by the consumer. However, locating or developing stimuli with the appropriate set of aesthetic attributes is impractical. Researchers have compromised by using photographs (e.g., Morganosky and Postlewait 1989) or line drawings (e.g., Eckman and Wagner 1994; Holbrook 1986; Wagner, Anderson and Ettenson 1990). Photographs produce realistic images; however, unless carefully controlled, confounding variables may bias subjects' judgments. Confounding variables are more easily controlled through line drawings. When drawn for a specific research problem, line drawings offer the advantage of experimental control over the manipulation of aesthetic attributes. However, line drawings make it difficult to present aesthetic attributes such as color and texture (Holbrook 1986). While presenting texture may be impossible, color can be easily added to line drawings, which can then be photographed and shown as slides (see Eckman and Wagner 1994). Line drawings have been criticized for being less realistic than photographs. Whisney, Winakor and Wolins (1979) compared consumer evaluations of attractiveness from line drawings and photographs, and found no difference.

---

[3]See Solomon and Assael (1987) for a discussion of the "consumption constellation."

[4]See Rook (1985) for a discussion of consumer rituals, including the grooming ritual.

The next best thing to real stimuli may be virtual reality. In recent research at Harvard, consumer shopping behavior was studied by simulating a store environment (Burke 1994). Retailers are speculating that there will soon be programs allowing consumers to see images of themselves wearing different fashion items. Such technology would be well-suited to research on aesthetic judgments.

FUTURE RESEARCH ON THE AESTHETICS OF FASHION

Research on aesthetics in general, and fashion, in particular, is in a position similar to that of gift-giving research ten years ago. Numerous questions present themselves. Some will need to be answered by research in the information processing tradtion; others will be more amenable to research in the experiential paradigm. Our review and assessment of research on the aesthetics of fashion design suggests the following questions for future research.

Research Questions in the Information Processing Paradigm

1. What is the relative importance of function and aesthetics in judgments of fashion goods? Does this differ by situation—gift or personal use?

2. What combination or combinations of aesthetic attributes is favored? Are there certain "aesthetic rules" that govern preferences for fashion?

3. What information processing strategies are used in aesthetic judgments? How do individual differences—experience, innovativeness and involvement—affect judgment strategies?

4. How does the fashion object interact with body type and personality to affect aesthetic judgments?

Research Questions in the Experiential Paradigm

1. What meaning do consumers attach to their own fashion objects? Why do some fashion objects "feel right" when worn? Why do others "feel wrong" and are never worn? What meaning do consumers assign to the aesthetic attributes, such as silhouette, color and texture?

2. What is the relationship of dressing to mood and emotion?

3. What is the creative process involved in shopping and building a wardrobe? What role does collecting play in acquiring fashion objects? What is the creative process involved in the dressing ritual?

CONCLUSION

In this paper, we have discussed the role of aesthetics in fashion-oriented consumer behavior. We have reviewed the limited body of conceptual and empirical work on the aesthetics of fashion, and presented cultural, conceptual and methodological factors that may have discouraged scholarship on fashion. Finally, we have proposed questions for future research, arguing that research on the aesthetics of fashion presents a wealth of opportunities and challenges for consumer researchers.

REFERENCES

Behling, Dorothy U. (1991), "Influence of Dress on Perceptions of Intelligence and Expectations of Scholastic Achievements," *Clothing and Textiles Research Journal*, 9 (4), 1-7.

Bell, Clive (1914), "Art as Significant Form," in *Aesthetics* (1989), eds. George Dickie, Richard Scalafani and Ronald Robin, NY: St. Martins Press.

Burke, Raymond R. (1994) "The Virtual Store: A New Tool for Consumer Research," In Retailing Review, *Stores*, 76 (August), RRI-RR3.

Cohen, Richard (1993), "The Columnist's Old Clothes," *The Washington Post Magazine*, (October 17), 5.

Damhorst, Mary Lynn (1985), "Meanings of Social Cues in Social Context," *Clothing and Textiles Research Journal*, 3 (2), 39-48.

Davis, Fred (1992), *Fashion, Culture and Identity*, Chicago: The University of Chicago Press.

DeLong, Marilyn Revell (1987), *The Way We Look*, Ames, IA: Iowa State University Press.

Eckman, Molly, Mary Lynn Damhorst and Sara J. Kadolph (1990), "Toward a Model of the In-Store Purchase Decision Process: Consumer Use of Criteria for Evaluating Women's Apparel," *Clothing and Textiles Research Journal*, 8 (2), 13-22.

_____ and Janet Wagner (1994), "Judging the Attractiveness of Product Design: The Effect of Visual Attributes and Consumer Characteristics," in ed. Chris T. Allen and Deborah Roedder John, *Advances in Consumer Research*, XXI, Provo, UT: Association for Consumer Research, 560-564.

Gordon, William I., Dominic A. Infante and Audrey A. Braun (1985), "Communicator Style and Fashion Innovativeness," in ed . Michael R. Solomon, *The Psychology of Fashion*, Lexington, MA: D.C. Heath and Company, 161-176.

Holbrook, Morris (1981), "The Esthetic Imperative in Consumer Research," in eds. Elizabeth C. Hirschman and Morris B. Holbrook, *Symbolic Consumer Behavior*, Provo, UT: Association for Consumer Research, 36-37.

_____ (1986), "Aims, Concepts and Methods for the Representation of Individual Differences in Esthetic Responses to Design Features," *Journal of Consumer Research*, 13 (3).

_____ and William B. Moore (1981), "Feature Interactions in Consumer Judgments of Verbal Versus Pictorial Presentations," in *Journal of Consumer Research*, 8 (2), 103-113.

Lowe, Elizabeth D. and John W.G. Lowe (1985), "Quantitative Analysis of Women's Dress," in ed. Michael R. Solomon, *The Psychology of Fashion*, Lexington, MA: D.C. Heath and Company, 193-206.

Lubner-Rupert, Jacqueline and Geitel Winakor (1985), "Male and Female Style Preference and Perceived Fashion Risk," *Home Economics Research Journal*, 13 (March), 256-266.

Minshall, Bettie, Geitel Winakor and Jane L. Swiney (1982), "Fashion Preferences of Males and Females, Risks Perceived, and Temporal Quality of Styles," *Home Economics Research Journal*, 10 (June), 369-379.

Morganosky, Michelle A. and Deborah S. Postlewait (1989), "Consumers' Evaluations of Apparel Form, Expression and Aesthetic Quality," *Clothing and Textiles Research Journal*, 7 (2), 11-15.

Rook, Dennis W. (1985), "The Ritual Dimension of Consumer Behavior, "*Journal of Consumer Research*, 12 (3),251-264.

Solomon, Michael R. and Henry Assael (1987), "The Forest and the Trees: A Gestalt Approach to Symbolic Consumption," in *Semiotics: New Directions in the Study of Signs for Sale*," ed. Jean Umiker-Sebeck, Berlin: Mouton de Gruyter, 189-218.

Sproles, George B. (1979), *Fashion*, Burgess Publishing Company, Minneapolis, MN.

_____ (1981), "The Role of Aesthetics in Fashion-Oriented Consumer Behavior," in ed. George B. Sproles *Perspectives of Fashion*, Burgess Publishing Company, Minneapolis, MN., 120-126.

Sweat, Sarah J. and Mary Ann Zentner (1985), "Attributions Toward Female Appearance Styles," in ed. Michael R. Solomon, *The Psychology of Fashion*, Lexington, MA: D.C. Heath and Company, 321-336.

Veblen, Thorstein (1899), *The Theory of the Leisure Class*, New York: MacMillan.

Wagner, Janet, Clarita Anderson and Richard Ettenson (1990), "Evaluating Attractiveness in Apparel Design: A Comparison of Chinese and American Consumers," in ed. Patricia A. Horridge, *ACPTC Proceedings*, Monument, CO: Association of College Professors of Textiles and Clothing, 97.

Whisney, Anita J., Geitel Winakor and Leroy Wolins (1979), "Fashion Preference: Drawings versus Photographs," *Home Economics Research Journal*, 8 (November), 138-150.

Why Some Products "Just Feel Right", Or, The Phenomenology of Product Rightness

Jeffrey F. Durgee, Rensselaer Polytechnic Institute
Gina Colarelli O'Connor, Rensselaer Polytechnic Institute

ABSTRACT

The purpose of this paper is to explore the possibility that there is a set of products which have a special feeling of rightness to consumers. In one-on-one, nondirective interviews (only question: "What items feel right to you?"), 24 respondents describe 40 everyday products. It appears that product "rightness" is associated with high functional value, versatility, prototypic life experiences, self-expressiveness, instant satisfaction, and surprisingly many flaws. Elements not closely associated with rightness include price and brand name.

INTRODUCTION

In their efforts to understand the person-product relationship, researchers, product planners and designers have taken many different approaches. Some seek to understand how product attributes are matched point for point with buyer wants (Hauser and Clausing 1998). Some seek product designs which will satisfy (Griffin 1993), delight or surprise buyers. Others focus on identifying buyer problems (Crawford 1991).

We propose a new approach. Specifically, we make the assumption that out of the thousands of products on the market, there is a subset which are perceived as having a special quality or feeling of rightness to consumers. Among certain individual consumers, these products strike a responsive chord. Whether for functional reasons, aesthetic reasons or both, they inspire special feelings of appropriateness and personal connectedness. They range from small items such as Soft Scrub cleanser to Mercedes automobiles and banquet halls.

This report summarizes initial, topline findings from an exploratory study of "right" items. While we eventually hope to interview over 100 people, this report summarizes results from 24 interviews. Our goal here is to raise issues and explore directions for subsequent research.

PRODUCT RIGHTNESS

Advertisers have been claiming that their products are more right than others for some time. Ads claim that "It just feels right" (Mazda) and "It's the right beer now" (Coors Light). But what does rightness mean? We suggest that certain products are felt by certain individuals to be right insofar as they have a personal, intriguing, aesthetic quality. Consumers feel warm about them and are in awe of the designer's ingenuity. The goal of all products is to enhance life, and these products seem to have a small, special advantage in this regard. The designer Milton Glazer says that good art makes people feel better about life in general. Products that are felt to be right might also have this capability. When a product design truly touches people and makes them feel this good, this is the designer's highest calling. As Read (1931) suggests, in early civilizations, art and tools were fused together. An earthen pot was art as well as being a pot. We suggest that certain products today might have this quality of total functional and aesthetic rightness.

While designers are aware of the importance of rightness, their focus is on internal rightness or integration within the product design. New design approaches (Clark and Fujimoto 1990) call for close integration of all aspects of the product including function, form and all subcomponents. Apparently, the success of the Honda Accord was due to the fact that everything in this car was designed around a common theme: "man maximum-machine minimum." We are interested in internal design issues although we are also interested in the larger gestalt including design rightness in the total life context of the individual.

Note that right products do not necessarily refer to:

- high sales volume products (Cleary 1981)
- products on lists of industrial design competition winners
- hobby or enthusiast products
- heirlooms, gifts (Csikszentmihalyi and Rochberg-Halton 1981)
- products which critics judge to be archetypal examples of their category (Cornfield and Edwards 1983)
- products which people label "my favorite things" (Wallendorf and Arnold 1988)
- firsts to market in their categories

Rather, products which are felt to be right might actually be low volume products, design competition losers, everyday (nonhobby) products, purchased items, second (or later) to market, and not particularly cherished items. They just happen to feel right to certain individuals.

METHOD

Twenty-four respondents were randomly selected and individually interviewed for 20 minutes to an hour. Respondents were half male, half female and included people ages 23 to 67. Throughout the interviewing, the approach was phenomenological (Thompson, Locander and Pollio 1989). The goal in each interview was simply a first person account of some product which is felt to be right. The respondents determined the directions and contents of the interview. Respondents were simply asked to give long, detailed answers to this question:

> Of all the products and things in your life, which one or two products feel the most right or give you the greatest feeling of rightness?

RESULTS

Interestingly, most of the people answered very quickly and gave long, detailed answers. The low response latency suggests that right products actually exist, that is, that respondents did not invent answers to please the interviewers. While people obviously do not spend much time each day thinking about products such as cleanser and teflon pans, they nevertheless carry with them enough of a sense of appreciation of these items and the roles they play in their daily lives that they are ready and quick to talk about them. Moreover, they were generally very enthusiastic. Any product designer would beam with pride if he or she could hear how much their products pleased these people.

(It is interesting that the Saturn division of General Motors now sponsors a group of Saturn owner enthusiasts who get together for picnics, reunions and other opportunities to share their enthusiasm for this car.)

First, second and third-mentioned products which were felt to be right include the following:

Big Bertha golf clubs
Movado watch
Lands End barn coat
stereo
ergonomic chair
TV remote control
Soft Scrub cleanser
bottled taco sauce
teflon pan
Mazda MX6
Singer sewing machine
vacuum cleaner
Electric razor
Pierre Cardin silk blouse
leather beach volleyball
Saab
Swiss Army knife
Nikon camera
Mistral sailboard
old leather briefcase

Mercedes Benz 300 sedan
JVC CD player
Macintosh computer
Toyota Camry
banquet room
runners watch
Post-it notes
greeting cards
Ivory Snow detergent
PRE skis
wicker shelf and cabinet
Timberland shoe boots
black leather bag
Sam Adams beer
Honda Accord
chop saw
Thunderbird automobile
Honda rototiller
leather recliner chair
Tide soap return-to-bottle cap

As the list indicates, the products tend to be basic, everyday things. People use them on a regular basis. They are literally part of daily life, so the rightness feeling would be very immediate and familiar. Absent from the list are high tech items such as microwave ovens and miracle drugs. An item such as a microwave oven represents very complex technology. As we will see below, people like to see how things work; they like to be able to appreciate the designer's ingenuity. Items such as miracle drugs, formal dresswear, mouse-traps and Christmas decorations are used so infrequently that they probably fall out of consciousness very easily.

Note that most of the items are tools. They are used for instrumental reasons, that is, for achieving some external goal or change. Not included in the list were expressive items (valued for their own sake) such as paintings, jewelry or family photographs. The Honda rototiller was valued for how it tills the ground, the Saab, for how it gets its owner to work, and the black leather bag, for how it holds many things (clothes, school books, purse items).

In fact, a major attribute that many respondents valued in these items was versatility. Obviously, the Swiss Army Knife does many different things. The runner's watch was valued because it not only keeps time, but also tells time in other time zones, gives lap times, records telephone numbers, and works as an alarm clock. Respondents noted how Soft Scrub washes any surface, the chop saw does many different kinds of wood cuts, the teflon pan cooks practically anything, and the silk blouse and shoe boots can be worn with anything.

Not only is product functionality important in rightness but it also seems to be important that the function is achieved in an ingenious, parsimonious manner, or, what mathematicians would call an elegant solution. As Arnheim (1966) says regarding the function of art, "the number of units employed should not be larger than that needed to attain the effect..." (p. 172). The Macintosh computer owner valued its simplicity, the owner of the Big Bertha golf clubs noted how effective their oversized heads were, and the respondent who liked the Tide return-to-bottle cap noted how it represented such a clean, simple solution to such a messy, sticky problem. The woman who liked the Eureka vacuum cleaner admired its ingenuity insofar as it runs the dirt through a clear pan of water which collects it. Interestingly, this pan is clearly visible using the product. The user can really appreciate the cleverness of the design. In fact, the message for designers here is clear: if you have an ingenious solution to a common user problem, make the

solution clearly visible. While this breaks an old rule in design - "design from the inside out"-it might be that people occasionally like to see the workings, particularly if they represent clever design solutions.

Women especially appreciate right products' functionality. The owners of the Macintosh, the Thunderbird automobile, and the Honda rototiller enjoyed the fact that they could operate these things themselves. They did not need to ask a man how to operate them.

Some other findings regarding right items include:

1. Few mentions of price.
Price does not seem play a major role in right products. In fact, one respondent, a young male, indicated his "right" car is a Nissan Pathfinder - although he "couldn't afford one." While a few respondents noted how happy they were that they got a high end item for a good price (silk blouse, Saab, Movado watch, Mazda, stereo, Big Bertha golf clubs, Mercedes 300), price was not mentioned until fairly late in each interview. Again, the message here is clear for marketers: If your product is felt to be right, charge a high price.

2. Brand names are not at top of mind.
It appears that when people think of right products, they think of the category first, and the brand name later. Asked for a "right" product, a respondent might answer, "my sewing machine" or "my skis" and then talk for a while about how these function or look. Only later in the interviews would they mention brand name. This reflects the basic concern noted above with product function.

3. Many flaws.
There is an old saying that a jewel or painting is not truly beautiful unless it has a minor flaw. The same appears to be true with right items. In spite of all the manufacturers' desires to achieve total quality, products which are felt to be right have many things wrong. The Mercedes 300 rides too hard, the Movado watch stops, the runner's watch is ugly, and the Mazda lacks headroom. In spite of these flaws-or perhaps because of them-the owners are strongly attached to them.

4. Prototypical
Particularly among the women respondents, items were felt to be right insofar as they reflected earlier, childhood experiences. The woman who loved the Big Bertha golf clubs because they had oversized heads spoke late in the interview about learning to play golf with her late (and dearly loved) father's clubs-which had oversized heads. The woman who liked the teflon pan spoke of how it brought back warm memories of cooking alongside her grandmother on Sunday mornings. The woman who liked the wicker shelf and cabinet said it reminded her of weekends at her aunt and uncle's farm. New product designers who are developing new designs for products aimed at women might consider exploring childhood memories of items which are close to the category.

5. Reflect personality, self
Many writers (e.g., Moncrieff 1978) note how people feel a sense of oneness with aesthetic objects. As Read (1931) writes, "The work of art is in some sense a liberation of the personality....We contemplate a work of art, and immediately there is a release" (p. 39). There were many instances of felt

connections between respondents and items. In many cases, this was physical. The skier, for example, in describing his skis said, (They) .." are so responsive...in the way they turned...that I could almost think about the turn.. and (then) the ski initiated the turn." The woman describing her golf clubs called them, "an extension of myself." Right products, people often claimed, feel like they were built "just for me." The Macintosh computer and Movado watch make their owners feel "comfortable" and "secure."

However, personalities are also expressed in right products in other ways. The owner of the old leather briefcase seemed to have a rather perverse personality, and valued the briefcase because of "its reverse snob appeal." The Big Bertha golf clubs have a striking appearance, and the owner is a person who lives alone and uses things to get attention and meet new people. The Macintosh owner described herself as "more artistic and creative" and "less analytic" than IBM users. The shoeboots owner said of them that "They fit my personality better; they're not ugly, like work boots, but they're not necessarily dress shoes.."

In fact, if there is any one personality trait common across all right items, it is a type of quirkiness or oddness. Perhaps because many of the respondents were drawn from a convenience sample on a college campus, many of the items have an offbeat character. Macintosh is a different computer from a more mainstream IBM product, runners watches are different from regular watches, and the Swiss Army knife is a nontypical jackknife. As indicated above, none of the products were really first to market in their respective categories. Rather, they seemed to be relative latecomers, but with some appealing point of difference. The shoeboots are a novel kind of shoe, and the Movado watch represents a novel design.

6. Love at First Sight, Continued Satisfaction
In describing a banquet room, one respondent told this story:

> "I'm getting married, and we were looking for a place to have the wedding and we had been to about 5 or 6 places...this was not quite right...and this other place was not quite right...but then we went to a place called The Highlander in Glens Falls. I went in the lobby and I knew immediately that this was right. It was immaculately clean, the floor was not just marble but inlaid different types of patterns on the floor. (In) it's restaurant, the doors were lead and glass and you just knew that this was right....You go in there and sure enough they had a wedding coordinator.."

As if they were falling in love, respondents seem to know immediately that a product is right for them. There appears to be little post-purchase dissonance, and these products are a continued source of satisfaction. Owners of the Saab and mazda automobiles report sustained feelings of happiness, the Saab owner reporting that, "It just keeps running and running."

CONCLUSION

There appears to be a set of products on the market which consumers feel are especially "right." These products are valued mainly for their functional properties, especially their multi-functionality or versatility and the extent to which they represent ingenious design solutions to user problems. These products seem to reflect or express user personalities, and, in the case of women,

sometimes reflect positive, prototypic, childhood experiences. They also have a surprising number of flaws (in an era which stresses total quality management), and do not seem to be have a lot to do with price or brand name.

There is an old saying in marketing that "you sell to one person at a time." Given new manufacturing capabilities such as flexible manufacturing, it may become possible in the future to design and produce specifically individual products for individual consumers. Short of that, designers might consider factors that account for "right" products, and attempt to incorporate these in the planning and design process.

Future research on product rightness will attempt to broaden the sample of consumers and variety of product types. We will be looking for novel ways to understand the experience of rightness and see if there are further differences in ways that different groups share this experience.

REFERENCES

Arnheim, R. (1966) *Toward a Psychology of Art.* Berkeley: University of California Press.

Cleary, D.P. (1981) *Great American Brands.* USA: Fairchild Publications.

Cornfield, B. and O. Edwards (1983), *Quintessence: The Quality of Having It.* New York, Crown Publishers, Inc.

Crawford, C.M. (1991) *New Products Management.* Boston: Irwin.

Clark, K. and T. Fujimoto, (1990), "The Power of Product Integrity", *Harvard Business Review.* Nov.-Dec., 107-118.

Csikszentmihalyi, M. and E. Rochberg-Halton (1981), *The Meaning of Things: Domestic Symbols and the Self,* Cambridge, MA: Cambridge University Press.

Griffin, A.J. (1993) "The Voice of the Customer", *Marketing Science.* 12 (1).

Hauser, J.R. and D. Clausing (1988) "The House of Quality," *Harvard Business Review.* May-June, pp 63-73.

Moncrieff, D. (1978) "Aesthetic Consciousness" in *Existential-Phenumenological Alternatives for Psychology.* R. Valle and M. King, eds. New York: Oxford University Press.

Read, H. (1931) *The Meaning of Art.* London: Faber and Faber.

Thompson, C., Locander, W. and H. Pollio (1989) "Putting Consumer Experience Back Into Consumer Research: The Philosophy and Method of Existential Phenomenology," *Journal of Consumer Research.* Vol. 16, Sept. pp. 133-146.

Wallendorf, M. and E.J. Arnould (1988) "My Favorite Things': A Cross-Cultural Inquiry into Object Attachment, Possessiveness, and Social Linkage" *Journal of Consumer Research.* Vol. 14, pp. 531-547.

The Package Appearance in Choice

Lawrence L. Garber, Jr., University of North Carolina at Chapel Hill[1]

Though we all know and accept the notion that the visual and graphical aspects of the product or service have an impact on consumer choice at the point of purchase, little is known or understood about how it has its effect. This research proposes a theoretical framework to account for this effect, and some empirical methods for its test. Viewing consumer decision-making as based upon a nested set of alternatives, this paper proposes a staged model of choice that explicitly considers the role of visual perception and package appearance in formation of the consideration set at the point of purchase. More specifically, the formation of a visually oriented preattention/attention set is conceived to precede and affect formation of a subsequent product-benefits-oriented consideration set.

The empirical test of this model incorporates experiments in which subjects undertake a series of six computer-simulated shopping trips across four supermarket categories: flour, raisins, spaghetti and dry cereal. The computer simulation employed is a virtual-reality supermarket representation developed and validated by Professor Raymond Burke. By this simulation, the subject is able to browse a set of supermarket facings, pull brands of interest from the shelf, turn and read the packages, and select them for purchase. Manipulations consist of the alteration of a certain few of the of the existing packages in the display. These changes are calibrated through pretesting to represent varying degrees of typicality, novelty and appropriateness for the category, while maintaining prior levels of brand identifiability. It is hypothesized that consumers will more likely attend to those new packages which are sufficiently novel or typical, and are more likely to consider those novel brands that are appropriate to the category.

SCENARIO

George hurries into the supermarket needing a couple of items, a bottle of cola and and some dishwashing detergent. He always drinks the same cola and, knowing his mind on this product, goes to the soft drink aisle first. George quickly scans the facings, catches sight of the characteristic red color and the distinctive wavy design that identify his preferred brand, and grabs it on sight before rushing to the detergent aisle.

By contrast, George is uncertain about which dishwashing detergent to buy. Unconcerned about small differences in price and believing that any brand will "do the job", he turns into the detergent aisle intending to both see what is available and make a quick purchase decision.

George has (varying degrees of) prior knowledge about some but not all of the relatively large number of brands available in the detergent category, though no particular preferences beyond the fact that he usually buys a lemon detergent. He is already scanning the category facings as he turns the corner and heads to the yellow section of the aisle, knowing that this color typically denotes the lemon detergents.

As George searches out and attends to the brands that he remembers from past purchase occasions or from television advertising, and from which he intends to select his purchase, there are a few others that catch his eye. Some unknown brands draw his attention because they appear similar to his remembered brands; others because their appearance is so very different.

Those brands similar in appearance have bottle shapes and liquid contents virtually identical in form, consistency and yellow color. George wonders if their like appearance means that he can expect like performance.

George is also distracted by a few brands made distinctive by an appearance that departs from George's sense of what is typical for the category. There is one brand, for instance, whose bottle is opaque rather than transparent, and whose pastel yellow surface looks soft relative to the sharp, translucent yellow liquids seen through the bottles of its competitor brands. George wonders if this brand might not be a little milder and questions its cleaning ability. Another brand catches George's eye because of its distinctive barbell shape, a bulky cylinder with larger drum shapes at either end; George in this case wonders if this brand is perhaps more powerful, but thinks the bottle is ugly. A third brand stands out to George because its liquid is a contrasting yellow-green in color, and he notes that it is a lemon-lime detergent.

George is in a quandary because, with the unanticipated addition of several relatively unknown brands to his consideration set, he is no longer certain how he should decide between the brands that he is considering. Now caught up in his detergent choice but still feeling the need to hurry, George finally concludes that he is in the mood to try something different and picks the lemon-lime for its attractive and distinctive appearance, having also decided that he expects it will do a good job. George tosses the bottle into his basket and heads to the checkout.

INTRODUCTION

This paper is about how consideration sets are formed, and how the appearance of brands in their packages plays a role in their formation at the point of purchase. There has been very little in the marketing literature on either topic.

Though there has been considerable evidence offered of the existence of staged models of choice (for a review, see Shocker et al. 1991), there has been less written concerning how these sets are formed at each stage. As to package appearance, it is generally accepted that the visual aspects of a product or its package have an important effect on consumer choice at the point of purchase. However, there is virtually nothing in the academic literature on the

[1]The author gratefully acknowledges the invaluable guidance of Morgan Jones, Ray Burke, Joel Huber, Charlotte Mason, Bill Perreault and Jim Bettman through every stage of this dissertation research; the helpful comments of Rick Starr, Rick Staelin, Don Lehmann and two anonymous MSI reviewers, Darius Sabavala, Paul Bloom, Gary Armstrong, George Milne, Sharon Hodge and Tom Boyd; and the financial assistance of the Marketing Science Institute.

topic. I will argue in the following that appearance affects choice indirectly through its influence on which brands, and how many, enter the individual consumer's consideration set.

The purpose of this dissertation is to propose and test a model of choice that explicitly considers the role that visual perception plays in formation of the consideration set. A key feature of this model is the formation of a prior set, conceived as visual in nature, in which the consideration set is nested, and from which all the members of the consideration set are drawn. It will be called the attention set.

VISUAL PERCEPTION AND PACKAGE APPEARANCE

George's two purchases in the above scenario illustrate plausible ways in which brand or package appearance may influence choice. But in only one instance, the detergent choice, does George make a considered decision. It is the considered decision that is the subject of this paper.

In the cola example, George is predisposed to his preferred brand and grabs it on sight, without reference to other brands in the category. Package appearance in this instance serves primarily to expedite search and identification. In the contrasting detergent example, in which George scans the category facings and attends to several previously unknown or unnoticed brands that catch his eye, package appearance may also serve to alter or interrupt search (Bettman 1979), and in so doing plays a central role in (re)shaping the choice process itself. In this case, brand packages as visual stimuli play a role in differentiating between brands considered for purchase.

And yet, as important as package appearance is, there is no comprehensive theory available to account for its influence on consideration at the point of purchase. A reason for this may be the traditional tendency to treat the consumer decision process as rational, in which the decision is based upon deriving some optimal combination of performance attributes and levels. Implicit in a multiattributed approach to choice modeling, in which products are defined as some bundled combination of attributes and levels, is that consumers can only differentiate brands on the basis of these features. But what if for some reason the consumer cannot differentiate brands on the basis of performance attributes? Would all the brands then fall into the center of this consumer's perceptual map? Would he or she be unable to make a choice decision? In reality, we know that the consumer is more flexible than this. If he or she is unable to differentiate brands on the basis of one set of criteria, then the consumer can simply differentiate brands on some other basis. Our conclusion, then, is that choice decisions, given imperfect brand knowledge and brand sets which may be at parity on important dimensions, are context dependent, and many kinds of criteria may be applied, including information supplied at the point of purchase such as the text and visuals available on a brand's package, in order to differentiate brands and come to a purchase decision.

The purpose of this paper is to propose a theoretical framework that accounts for these effects, and to test three hypotheses on fundamental aspects of this model.

THEORETICAL FRAMEWORK

To encompass the several diverse roles that package appearance is hypothesized to play in consideration and choice, a theoretical framework by Roberts (1989) is adopted and extended. As shown in *Figure I*, Roberts casts choice as a phased process comprising three stages in time (pg. 749): "The probability of brand choice, given category purchase, can be thought to have three elements: the probability of being aware of brand j; the probability

of considering brand j, given awareness of it; and the probability of choosing brand j, given awareness and consideration." This framework forms the backbone of the extended model shown in *Figure II*, which explicitly considers the effects of different kinds of visual stimulus on those stages of choice where they are hypothesized to play a role.

Stage O concerns the likelihood that a given consumer will attend to a given product category motivated by a pragmatic set of needs-satisfying goals, such as, "I am thirsty," or "I am out of detergent." These pragmatic goals are thought to predispose the consumer to those brands that he or she expects will provide those performance benefits. These brands are called typical for the category. Visually typical brand alternatives are more likely to be noticed and preferred by the consumer (Loken and Ward 1990), and will likely be chosen for purchase unless some distracting stimulus or event interrupts and changes the decision process. Those brands which succeed in distracting the consumer are called visually novel.

It will be argued in the following that package appearance can play important roles in defining the perceived visual typicality or novelty of brands, particularly the latter.

Stages I and II concern the formation of two brand sets that are monotonically related: first, an awareness/ attention set (hereafter called attention set), in which brands in a supermarket facing are first seen from some distance and attended to on the basis of (relative) appearance; and second, a consideration set, in which some members of the Stage I attention set are evaluated and considered for purchase. It is these two stages which are the subject of the three hypotheses.

Stage I defines a visual scanning process that begins as soon as the category facings are in sight, which is to say at some distance. This search of the facings continues as the consumer moves closer. If the number of brand alternatives is sufficiently large (Bettman 1979) — a number which may not be very large at all (Roberts and Lattin 1991) — the consumer will not likely attend to all of them, but only to those that stand out according to the sufficiency of their visually typical or novel appearance.

Where Stage I is conceived as a process of arousal and motivation, Stage II is more evaluative in nature, as the consumer studies the brands more closely, picking up and reading the packages, checking the price and so on. Consumers will tend to consider visually typical brands that pass into their consideration sets because they expect that they will perform well (Nedungadi 1990). However, consumers have no such expectations of visually novel brands. Therefore, for a novel brand to graduate from the attention set to the consideration set, it must pass an appropriateness screen. That is to say, it must be judged as appropriate for the category, or concordant with performance needs and goals.

Choice of a brand from the consideration set is accomplished by a final decision step.

HYPOTHESES

Three hypotheses are developed. They concern the conjunctive screens related to the formation of the respective brand sets of Stages II and III shown in Figure II. The first two hypotheses concern the visual typicality and novelty criteria associated with Stage I attention sets. Hypothesis III concerns the appropriateness criterion associated with Stage III consideration sets.

Hypotheses 1 and 2: Formation of the Attention Set

This paper concerns itself with the relative role of package appearance. In a competitive environment such as a supermarket aisle, brands are seen in the context of their competitors in contiguous category facings such as those shown in *Figure III*. Therefore,

FIGURE I
Three Stage Model of Choice
(after Roberts 1989)

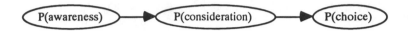

FIGURE II
Conceptual Model
Individual Choice with Visual Search

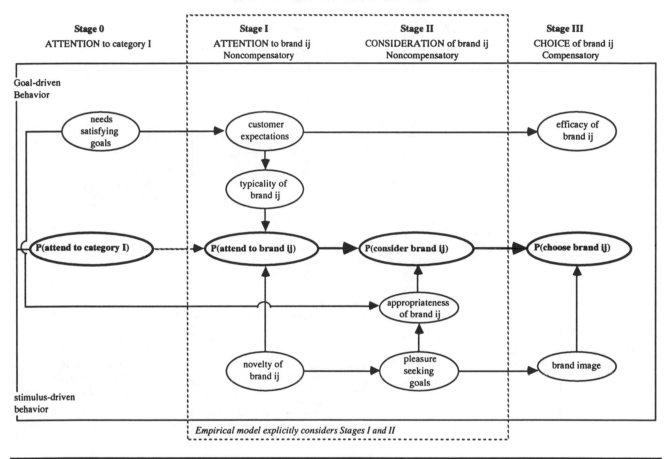

the effect of brands as visual stimuli is relative to a background comprised of competitor brands, all of whom are "shouting" for the shoppers's attention.

Visual Typicality and Novelty as Visual Attributes. Acknowledging the relative nature of visual stimuli in a competitive environment, the distinctiveness of stimuli must be defined and measured according to some notion of what is visually typical, or prototypical for a category. In this paper, it is argued that there are two possible visual strategies whose objective is to increase likelihood of inclusion in the consumer's attention set. The first strategy is to appear sufficiently visually typical for the category. The second strategy is the opposite of the first, or to appear sufficiently visually atypical, or novel. These ideas are represented graphically in Figure IV, where brands in a category are represented as points in a visual attribute space.

Each brand is defined relative to a category prototype. Perceived similarity or dissimilarity in a brand's appearance, relative to the category prototype, is represented on the map by its proximity or distance from a central point representing the point of visual prototypicality. For example, if a given brand falls relatively close to the prototype on all visual dimensions, then it is deemed relatively visually typical for the category. If a given brand falls relatively far from the category prototype on any visual dimension, it is deemed visually novel for the category. These notions are operationalized by conceiving of discrete zones fanning out concentrically from the position of the category prototype. Any brand that falls in the visually typical zone, depicted as the inner circle falling closely around the point of visual prototypicality, is declared visually typical for the category, as perceived by the consumer. Brand #1 is therefore declared typical. In contrast, any brand falling

FIGURE III
The Three-Stage Choice Process
with Visual Search at the Point of Purchase

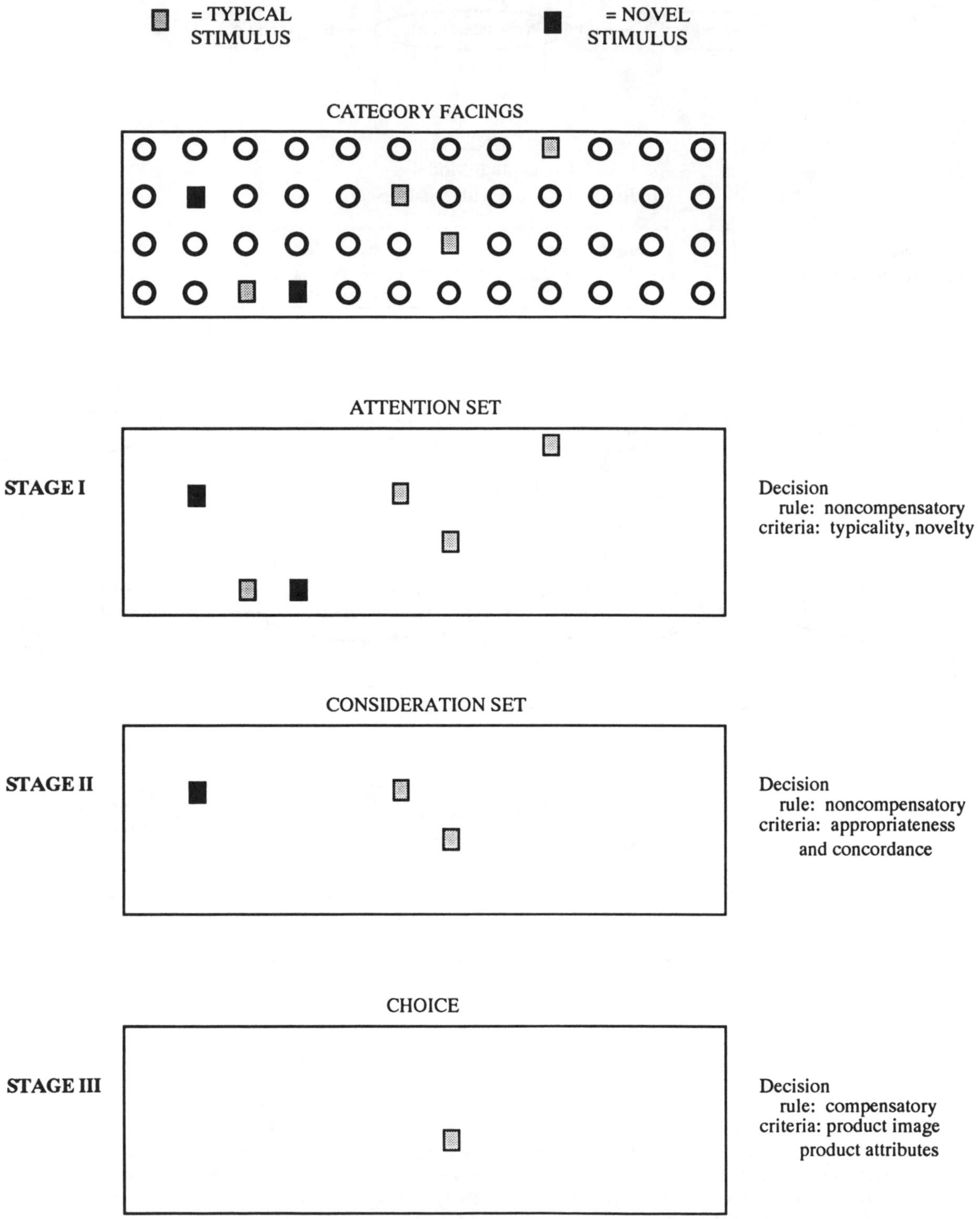

□ = TYPICAL STIMULUS   ■ = NOVEL STIMULUS

CATEGORY FACINGS

ATTENTION SET

STAGE I

Decision
 rule: noncompensatory
criteria: typicality, novelty

CONSIDERATION SET

STAGE II

Decision
 rule: noncompensatory
criteria: appropriateness
     and concordance

CHOICE

STAGE III

Decision
 rule: compensatory
criteria: product image
     product attributes

in the outermost zone is declared visually novel. Brands #3 and #4 are therefore declared novel. Any Brand falling into the doughnut-shaped zone between these two is declared neither visually typical nor novel. Brand #2 is therefore declared neither typical nor novel. In this way, all brands may be categorized according to where they fall relative to their distance from the point of visually prototypicality,

Visual typicality is defined as the look or appearance that most consumers would associate with a product category, and by which they identify brands that belong to the category. Examples would include the white bags associated with flour, as shown in *Figure V*, or the long, narrow boxes with a cellophane window associated with spaghetti. This definition is not to be confused with the more

FIGURE IV
Appearance Versus Probability of Attention or Consideration
The Graphical Representation of Package Appearance in Visual Attribute Space

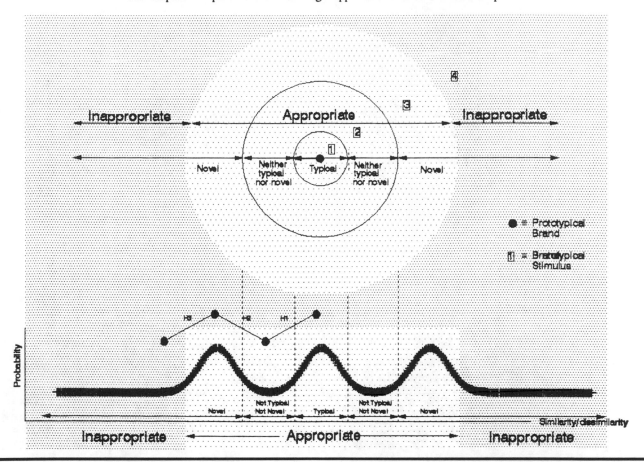

conventional notion of visual typicality found in the marketing literature, defined in terms of a sharing or commonality of performance attributes (Loken and Ward 1990). For our purposes, one may define visual typicality as a commonality or sharing of visual attributes. A visual strategy that employs a relatively visually typical package appearance may be thought of as a visual me-too strategy, one that emphasizes the brand's membership in the category. A visual strategy that employs a relatively novel package appearance may be thought of as a product differentiation strategy, one that emphasizes differences rather than similarities.

Attention to a visually typical brand is purposeful, the product of visual search and identification. By contrast, attention to a visually novel brand is involuntary: the eye cannot help but register the sensation of a vivid and unexpected visual element that enters its field of vision, such as a bizarre color or shape (Kahneman 1973).

The graph at the bottom of Figure IV relates perception of similarity to likelihood of attention or consideration. Put another way, a brand's position in visual attribute space, and relative to the category prototype and the zones of visual typicality and novelty that surround it, indicates the relative likelihood of attention and consideration on the part of a given consumer, according to the function that is specified. Specifically, those brands that fall within the zone of visual typicality are relatively likely to be attended to and considered. Those brands that fall within the zone of visual novelty are also relatively likely to be attended to. But those brands that fall between these zones, indicating that the brands that occupy this space are insufficiently visually typical or novel to be noticed, are therefore less likely to be attended to and considered.

Regardless of the differences by which visually typical versus novel brand stimuli have their effect, the strategic importance of the effect on likelihood of attention or consideration in both cases is as distractors to target brands at the point of purchase. Both kinds of brand stimuli may serve to distract the consumer away from some target brand, and may in turn cause him or her to add the distractor brand to their attention set. Accordingly, I propose the following hypotheses.

H_1: Brand packages which are sufficiently visually typical are more likely to enter the consumer's attention set, than are brand packages which are insufficiently visually typical and not novel.

H_2: Brand packages which are sufficiently novel are more likely to enter the consumer's attention set, than are brand packages which are insufficiently novel and not visually typical.

Hypothesis #3: Formation of the Consideration Set

Visual Novelty and Appropriateness. Appropriateness refers to the performance attributes or needs benefits that the consumer may infer about a product from its package. Having entered the attention set by dint of its appearance, it is argued that the brand may subsequently pass into the consideration set only if the brand is also deemed to perform sufficiently well.

All visually typical brands are by definition appropriate. Therefore, it is only with visually novel brands that appropriateness

FIGURE V
The Flour Category Display

FIGURE VI

as a screening device for consideration is relevant. Having attended to a visually novel brand precisely because it is novel, because of that very novelty its efficacy as a provider of needs benefits is called into question. Therefore, visually novel brands in the attention set must pass an appropriateness screen to gain entrance to the consideration set. Accordingly, I propose the following hypothesis.

H3   Novel packages which are appropriate to the category are more likely to pass from the attention set into the consideration set, than are novel brand packages which are inappropriate to the category.

The empirical results that these hypotheses indicate are represented graphically on Figure IV. The greater likelihood of a visually typical stimulus being attended to, relative to a stimulus that is not visually typical and not novel, is indicated by the positive slope of the line labeled "H1", on the graph showing the relationship between probability of attention or consideration, and package type. The greater likelihood of a visually novel stimulus being attended to, as opposed to a stimulus that is neither visually typical nor novel, is indicated by the negative slope of the line marked "H2". The greater likelihood of an appropriate visually novel stimulus being considered, as opposed to a novel stimulus that is not appropriate, is indicated by the positive slope of the line marked "H3".

EMPIRICAL METHOD

The empirical test of this model incorporates experiments in which subjects undertake a series of six computer-simulated shopping trips across four supermarket categories: flour, raisins, spaghetti and dry cereal. The parts of the theoretical framework to be tested are the elimination screens relating to Stages I and II of Figure II, the subject of the above three hypotheses.

The computer simulation to be employed has been developed and validated by Professor Raymond Burke of Harvard University (Burke, Harlam, Kahn and Lodish 1992). *Figure VI* shows a still photograph of the computer display. By this simulation, the subject is able to browse a set of supermarket facings, pull brands of interest from the shelf, turn and read the package, and select it for purchase. The computer accurately times and records all relevant behaviors.

To test the above hypotheses, I intend to manipulate the levels of visual typicality, novelty and appropriateness to measure their effect on attention and consideration. These manipulations will be introduced by systematically altering the packages of existing brands. These alterations are to be calibrated through pretesting to assure that they correctly represent the levels of visual typicality, novelty or appropriateness that are to be specified.

Stage O, selection of the product category, is not treated because it is assumed that the category is already selected, and the other stages are predicated on that. Stage III is also not treated, for three reasons. First, this step is seen as akin to a one-stage compensatory choice model, which has received ample treatment in the literature. Secondly, the effects of package appearance are hypothesized to effect choice only indirectly, through its effects on consideration set formation. And third, the current test is unlikely to have sufficient power to reliably detect the effects of these manipulations on choice.

The Calibration of Changed Packages by Pretesting

The stimuli in this experiment are existing brand packages that have all been changed in various ways, cleaned or altered, in order to be sure of the presence of certain visual attributes at certain levels, or to be sure of their absence. Pretesting is performed to calibrate the

packages according to these qualities, and otherwise to assure that the changed packages correctly represent the qualities that are intended of them, and do not introduce extraneous factors.

The Experimental Design

I am proposing a 4X4 latin square design as shown in the following table. 160 subjects — recruited by newspaper from the town of Cambridge, Ma., and paid an incentive fee of $20 — are assigned at random to one of four groups of forty. There are three factors: a product category factor (flour, spaghetti, raisins, dry cereal), a package alterations factor (visually typical, novel-appropriate, novel-inappropriate, and neither visually typical nor novel), and a group factor.

CONCLUSION

The subject of this research is how consideration sets are formed, and how visual perception plays a role in its formation at the point of purchase. The domain of the proposed model is the competitive purchase display, where all category brands are seen together, and competitor brands thus form the visual context for each other. It is suggested that the model of consideration set formation with visual search is general in nature, given the primacy of the visual sense and the constant use of visual search at the point of purchase.

The empirical model proposes a test of the elimination criteria of Stages I and II of the model: that a sufficiency of the visual attributes typicality and novelty will indicate a greater likelihood of attention, and that the appropriateness of a visually novel brand will indicate a greater likelihood of consideration. The theoretical model is itself more broad based, and if correct suggests a research stream. Topics for follow-up research may include: the effect of individual and cultural differences; how niche brands may exploit visual opportunities; and how the pioneer package may set the visual precedent for the category.

REFERENCES

Bettman, James R. (1979), *An Information Processing Theory of Consumer Choice*, Chicago: Addison-Wesley.

Nedungadi, Prakash, (1990), "Recall and Consumer Consideration Sets: Influencing Choice Without Altering Brand Evaluations," *Journal of Consumer Research*, 17 (December), 263-276.

Burke, Raymond R., Bari A. Harlam, Barbara E. Kahn and Leonard Lodish (1992), "Comparing Dynamic Consumer Choice in Real and Computer-Simulated Environments," *Journal of Consumer Research*, 19 (June), 71-82.

Kahneman, Daniel (1973), *Attention and Effort*, Englewood, N.J: Prentice- Hall.

Loken, Barbara and James Ward (1990), "Alternative Approaches to Understanding the Determinants of Typicality," *Journal of Consumer Research*, 17 (September), 111-126.

Roberts, John H. (1989), "A Grounded Model of Consideration Set Size and Composition," *Advances in Consumer Research*, 16, 749-57.

_____, and James M. Lattin (1991), "Development and Testing of a Model of Consideration Set Composition," *Journal of Marketing Research*, XXVIII (November), 429-40.

Shocker, Allan D., Moshe Ben-Akiva, Bruno Boccara, and Prakash Nedungadi (1991), "Consideration Set Influences on Consumer Choice: Issues, Models and Suggestions," *Marketing Letters* 1:3, 181- 197.

Toward the Development of Relationship Theory at the Level of the Product and Brand

Susan Fournier, Harvard Business School

Background on the Session

The "relationship" idea is not a new one to the marketing discipline. The relationship perspective has been accepted and encouraged in marketing theory (c.f., Groonroos 1991; Sheth 1994) and has become the norm for studying salesperson interactions in industrial marketing, services, and channel domains (c.f., Berry 1983; Dwyer et al 1987). Relationship thinking is also highly applicable to current marketing practices. Relationship-relevant marketing ideas such as addressable marketing (Blattberg and Deighton 1991) and the management of relationship life cycles (McCormack 1992) have taken hold in a business climate acutely attuned to the value of retaining versus attracting customers (Reichheld and Sasser 1990).

Despite increased acceptance in marketing theory and practice, the relationship perspective has not yet been maximized in the academic literature. No one has insightfully mined the interpersonal relationships literature for the conceptual contributions it has to offer. In particular, relationship theory at the level of the product and brand has been virtually ignored (for exception, see Ahuvia 1993 and Shimp and Madden 1988, in which isolated constructs from the relationship literature have been applied to products and brands). It is argued that such an exercise can greatly enhance our understanding of the interactions between consumers and their products or brands, illuminating existing theoretical conceptions in ways that are both relevant and meaningful to the study of consumer behavior.

The session takes a first step in this direction. The brand/product and the consumer are treated as "partners" in a dyadic relationship that is assumed to be conceptually similar to the relationships established between two people. Frameworks and theories from research on interpersonal relationships are then used to explore the enactment of person-brand/product relationships over time. Collectively, the papers address important issues of relationship formation, maintenance, and deterioration or breakdown. The session is intended to give the audience an organized and provocative glimpse into the issues involved in the conduct of consumer-product (brand) relationships; its overall goal is to stimulate research that can inform the development of relationship theory at the level of the product and brand.

Overview of Contributions

Aaron Ahuvia from the University of Michigan grounded the session with his paper, "Quasi-Social Relationships: The Love of Things." The paper investigates the question of what it means to have a relationship with a non-person: specifically, with an object, activity, or idea. Using a combination of 29 short and 10 depth interviews on emotionally-intense relationships, Aaron identified four themes that illustrate the meaning of person-object (activity or idea) relationships. These include: (1) responsiveness, the idea that relational members have a causal, reciprocal impact upon each other; (2) partnership; (3) personification, the attribution of life and energy to the object/activity/idea; and (4) exchanging love, especially in the form of comfort, warmth, and solace. In discussing the themes, Aaron drew comparisons with person-person relationships, highlighting where and how the relationship metaphor breaks down when it is applied in non-person situations. Aaron also discussed the personal significance of having a relationship with objects/activities/ideas, indicating how and why levels of importance differed across people.

The relationship maintenance stage was addressed in Fournier's paper, "Brand Relationship Quality: The Glue that Keeps the Relationship Together." The brand relationship quality (BRQ) notion was developed through qualitative life history interviews to explain the mechanisms through which brand-person relationships are maintained over time and at high levels of intensity (Fournier 1994). Seven facets of BRQ are identified: nostalgic attachment, self-concept connection, intimacy, personal commitment, interdependency, love/passion, brand-partner quality. Fournier shared the results of a survey in which a 37-item battery to measure BRQ was developed, and the hierarchical structure of the construct validated. Evidence of maintenance-enhancing outcomes encouraged by high levels of BRQ (e.g., repeat purchase intentions, resistance to competitive threats, enactment of supportive customer responses such as positive word-of-mouth and trial of brand extensions, tolerance of brand transgressions) was also provided. In closing, superiority of BRQ over traditional measures of brand association (e.g., brand attitude and satisfaction) was also established to provide insight into discriminant validity issues.

Mary Fajer and John Schouten from the University of Portland considered the relationship dissolution phase (see "Breakdown and Dissolution of Person-Brand Relationships," this volume). The authors drew upon a range of depth interviews in which informants shared stories of their brand relationship breakdown experiences. A typology of person-brand relationships was offered as a point of departure for discussing dissolution and break down issues. Stress factors precipitating breakdown, patterns of break-up, processes of dissolution, and consumer responses to dissolution were considered, especially as they varied by relationship intensity level. The authors examined several models of breakdown in the interpersonal relationship setting for their relevance in the marketing domain, providing conceptual starting points for the articulation of brand relationship deterioration models.

Gerald Zaltman from the Harvard Business School acted as session discussant. Gerry used a visualization task with session participants to provide fodder for discussion of the papers. As the session opened, Gerry encouraged participants to let images form and flow in response to the presentations, and to record these images for latter discussion. The images were revealed, captured on an overhead, and interpreted at the close of the session. They included, for example, a lump of clay, an unopened packet of sugar, a detached bystander—visuals reflecting an element of potential not yet realized. The intent of the exercise was to generate awareness of the powers and potential risks of metaphoric thinking, captured in Gerry's concluding caution that "metaphors may distort and hide as much as they reveal."

REFERENCES

Ahuvia, Aaron (1993), "Love as a General Construct: Understanding People's Love of Products," PhD dissertation, Kellogg Graduate School of Management, Northwestern University.

Berry, Leonard L. (1983), "Relationship Marketing," in *Emerging Perspectives in Relationship Marketing*, eds. Leonard L. Berry, G. Lynn Shostack, and Gregory Upah, Chicago, IL: American Marketing Association, 25-34.

Blattberg, Robert C. and John Deighton (1991), "Interactive Marketing: Exploiting the Age of Addressability," *Sloan Management Review*, Fall, 5-14.

Dwyer, F. Robert, Paul H. Schurr, and Sejo Oh (1987), "Developing Buyer-Seller Relationships," *Journal of Marketing*, 51 (April), 11-27.

Fournier, Susan (1994), "A Person-Brand Relationship Framework for Strategic Brand Management," PhD dissertation, University of Florida.

Groonroos, Christian (1991), "The Marketing Strategy Continuum: Toward a Marketing Concept for the 1990s," *Management Decision*, 29(1), 7-13.

McCormack, Kevin (1992), "American Express: Beyond Cars to Icons," *Adweek Eastern Edition*, June 1, 33(22), p. 9.

Reichheld, Frederick and W. Earl Sasser, Jr. (1990), "Zero Defections: Quality Comes to Services," *Harvard Business Review*, September-October, 105-111.

Sheth, Jagdish (1994), "Relational Marketing," talk given at the 1994 Winter Educator's Conference, St. Petersburg, FL, February.

Shimp, Terrence and Thomas Madden (1988), "Consumer-Object Relations: A Conceptual Framework Based Analogously on Sternberg's Triangular Theory of Love," in *Advances in Consumer Research*, Volume 15, ed. Michael Houston, Provo, UT: Association for Consumer Research, 163-168.

Breakdown and Dissolution of Person-Brand Relationships

Mary T. Fajer, University of Portland
John W. Schouten, University of Portland[1]

ABSTRACT

This theoretical paper examines several models of the dissolution of interpersonal relationships and explores their relevance to the context of person-brand relationships. From a grounding in interpersonal relationship theory we propose several integrative models to guide discussion and research in the area of person-brand break-ups. Topics addressed include types of person-brand relationships, latent causes and patterns of person-brand break-ups, processes of relationship dissolution, and affective and behavioral consumer responses throughout.

INTRODUCTION

Relationships between people and brands in some cases bear notable resemblances to interpersonal relationships (Fournier 1994). Feelings that are important in the development and maintenance of interpersonal relationships, such as attraction, intimate understanding, sensual enjoyment, and feelings of attachment, security, comfort, stability, and self-worth (Drigotas and Rusbult 1992), may also manifest as important characteristics of peoples' relationships with brands. Furthermore, the elements of interpersonal relationships that tend to give them longevity, such as investment, commitment, dependence, and integration in social networks (Lund 1985), may also constitute exit barriers to person-brand relationships.

The focus of this conceptual exercise is the dissolution of person-brand relationships. Understanding the breakdown and dissolution of person-brand relationships has practical relevance to marketers interested in issues of customer retention. Customer retention has a significant impact on a company's profitability. It is estimated that a 5% reduction in consumer defection can improve a business' long-term profits by 25-80% (Reichheld and Sasser 1990). The clear implication is that not only must we understand how relationships are formed between people and brands, we must also be aware of the factors that drive them (or allow them to drift) apart.

Our purpose here is to lay a foundation for understanding break-ups between people and brands using frameworks of interpersonal break-ups as a theoretical starting point. We examine several models of interpersonal break-ups and assess their potential relevance to the person-brand domain. We propose a model of person-brand break-ups that accounts for different types of relationships, different underlying causes, patterns, and processes of dissolution, and different consumer behaviors in the course of disengagement with a brand.

PERSON-BRAND RELATIONSHIPS

A meaningful discussion of relationship dissolution requires as a starting point an understanding of what kinds of relationships are dissolving. Fournier (1994) defines a person-brand relationship in terms of three key dimensions: 1) interdependence or reciprocation of action and benefit, 2) real or anticipated interaction over time, and 3) a bond that may be instrumental, affective, or both.

As with people, not all brands matter equally in psychological or social ways to consumers. Rodin (1978) suggests that, although we like all of our friends, we do not value them equally. There is

an ordering process which depends on 1) the importance of the liking criteria satisfied, 2) the substitutability of the friend, and 3) the pleasure/cost ratio of the friendship. We propose that people value brands for similar reasons, i.e., based on the satisfaction of certain liking criteria, perceived substitutability, and general assessments of costs versus benefits.

Although attraction brings people (and people and brands) together initially, the ability of a relationship to endure owes much to exit barriers. Observing that "empty shell marriages" often survive without affection, Lund (1985) proposes a barriers model of relationship longevity. Barriers to the dissolution of interpersonal relationships are, beyond and separate from love or attraction, a function of *investment* and *commitment* (Lund 1985). These barriers are comprised of such elements as effort, expenditure of resources, sacrifice of other interests, private pledges, and public announcements (Kanter 1972). In the person-brand domain investment and commitment are at least partially related to product categories. Consumables and packaged goods require little investment in money and time per purchase. Durables, on the other hand, are relatively expensive and may financially commit the consumer to years of ownership. Services occupy a special class of brands due to interpersonal dimensions and the possibility of truly dyadic communication between the consumer and the brand. Less tangible than time and money, yet also important as barriers to dissolution, are psychic investments such as the incorporation of the brand into one's personal or group identity.

Many kinds of interpersonal relationships merit scrutiny for their relevance to the person-brand context. Rose and Serafica (1986) identify various types of friendships such as "casual friends," "close friends," and "best friends" which vary in their levels of attraction, commitment, and exclusivity. Drawing upon models of attraction and commitment in interpersonal relationships we offer the following typology (Figure 1) of person-brand relationships as the focus of our discussion.

Higher-order relationships differ from lower-order relationships by consumer loyalty to the brand, a function of exit barriers of commitment and investment. The model presents a loyalty-ordered set of purchase behaviors and their interpersonal analogs.

Brand trying is the initial purchase of a brand. Like an experiment with a potential friendship, brand trying may lead to brand liking and, eventually, to a higher-order relationship. Lower levels of satisfaction may lead the consumer to regard the brand as an acquaintance (neither liked nor disliked) or to reject the brand altogether as a possible friend.

Brand liking occurs when a brand has been tried and has met a consumer's liking criteria. Like casual friends, brands at this stage have not yet formed the barriers of investment and commitment necessary to establish the person-brand dyad as a relationship.

Multi-brand resurgent loyalty (Sherry 1989) refers here to a person-brand relationship which has been tried, has met the consumer's liking criteria, and has progressed into an ongoing, loyal, but non-exclusive relationship of some duration. Analogous to close friends, such brands can be called upon and trusted but are not given exclusive best-friend status. Variety is sought, but the same brands are filtered in and out over time (Fournier 1994).

Brand loyalty refers to a "best-friend" relationship wherein the brand has been tried, has met the consumer's liking criteria, and has progressed into an ongoing, exclusive (from the consumer's point

[1]Acknowledgment: Special thanks to Susan Fournier for encouragement and guidance on this project.

FIGURE 1
Typology of Loyalty-Ordered Person-Brand Relationships

Lower-Order Relationships		Higher-Order (Loyal) Relationships		
Potential Friends	Casual Friends	Close Friends	Best Friends	Crucial Friends
Brand Trying	Brand Liking	Multi-Brand Resurgent Loyalty	Brand Loyalty	Brand Addiction

of view) relationship of some duration. An important factor in the stability of interpersonal relationships is the perceived quality or attractiveness of one's best alternative partner (Simpson 1987); in the case of brand loyalty no alternative is perceived as sufficiently attractive to override the barriers of investment and commitment to the brand.

Brand addiction defines an intensely brand-loyal relationship with the distinguishing component of psychological and/or physiological dependency (Solomon 1992). Brand-addicted relationships are characterized by a consumer's extreme reliance on the brand because of a perception of non-substitutability. The brand is like a crucial friend upon which the person relies for well being.

Summary

We have proposed a conceptual model of person-brand relationships as a point of departure for discussing the dissolution of such relationships. The model builds upon the metaphor of friendships for person-brand dyads of varying levels of loyalty. We propose that a higher-order person-brand relationship develops much like a friendship, beginning with a certain level of attraction and progressing to some degree of loyalty through increasing investment in and commitment to the relationship.

TERMINATING PERSON-BRAND RELATIONSHIPS

Interpersonal relationships may attenuate and dissolve for many reasons and through many different patterns and processes. We next examine several models of relationship dissolution for their potential relevance to the context of person-brand break-ups.

Interpersonal break-ups may be triggered by attitudes and actions of either or both partners. Duck (1982) identifies four latent causes of relationship dissolution which are potentially instructive in the person-brand context. 1) *Pre-existing Doom*: Certain inherent features enhance the chances of a satisfactory relationship and, conversely, relationships lacking these inherent features, or that fail to demonstrate them, will be likely to dissolve. Inherent incompatibilities between a person and a brand would fall into this category. 2) *Mechanical Failure*: Poor conduct within the relationship is the ultimate cause of dissolution. In the person-brand context this would include any loss of customer satisfaction due to poor brand performance. 3) *Process Loss*: A relationship fails to develop to its theoretical optimum. Brand management strategies that fail to reinforce or cultivate consumer commitment, or that do not keep pace with changing consumer needs, may leave consumers open to attractive alternatives. 4) *Sudden Death*: New, surprising, and negative information about a partner can hasten relationship dissolution. In the marketplace such information might include, for example, exposure of corporate malfeasance or product tampering.

Latent flaws in person-brand relationships may lead to several general patterns of break-up. The following examples are suggested by patterns of friendship termination identified by Rose (1984). 1) *Friends become physically separated*: The brand becomes unavailable to the consumer through some action of the marketer or because the consumer relocates to a region where the brand is not offered. 2) *New friends replace old*: A new brand replaces a former brand because it better meets a consumer's needs or liking criteria. 3) *One friend reveals or does something to alienate the other*: Some critical and disruptive aspect of brand performance leads to consumer dissatisfaction.

With some understanding of the latent causes and patterns of interpersonal break-ups, and reflecting on our loyalty-ordered model of person-brand relationships, we now advance a more integrative framework of person-brand break-ups. Depending on the nature of the relationship and the latent causes of dissolution we expect that break-ups will occur according to certain patterns and that customers will experience a variety of affective consequences.

The termination of a person-brand relationship may be initiated either by the consumer or by the brand. We assume that *brand-initiated break-up* follows one of two patterns: 1) the product is no longer manufactured or is no longer distributed to the consumer's region (process loss), or 2) service is revoked or a product is repossessed because the consumer fails to comply with the brand's requirements for use (consumer-side mechanical failure). Brand-initiated break-ups may occur at any level of the hierarchy of relationships described above; however, affective responses of the consumer will differ greatly according to the levels of liking, investment, and commitment associated with the brand. The differences conceivably range from the inconvenience of denied access to a potential friend to the grief associated with the sudden loss of a cherished, intimate relationship.

Consumer-initiated break-ups are more varied and probably much more common that those initiated by the brand. We use the term *brand switching* to designate a consumer-initiated, perhaps temporary deviation from the regular purchase of a brand. Brand switching may be facilitated by process loss on the brand side leading to mild consumer dissatisfaction. It may also reflect consumer boredom or variety seeking.

Brand spurning refers to a permanent, consumer-initiated dissolution of the relationship with no intent to repurchase the brand. The probable causes of brand spurning in lower-order relationships (i.e., "potential" or "casual" friendships) are pre-existing doom or mechanical failure. In the higher-order "best friend" and "crucial friend" categories exit barriers such as monetary investment, personal identification, integration into social networks, or even physiological or psychological dependencies, act as ballast that stabilize the relationship through times of consumer stress or poor brand performance. In these higher-order relationships brand-spurning behavior probably results only from compound mechanical failures or major changes in consumers' roles and/or liking criteria. In the case of serious or compound mechanical failures the break-up may be characterized by strongly negative consumer affect including anger, bitter disappointment, and/or vengefulness. Such feelings may culminate in complete brand alienation. We define *brand alienation* as a state of extreme, generalized dissatisfaction that goes beyond the spurning of a single product to encompass family brands and product line extensions.

Summary

We have conceptualized patterns of person-brand break-up taking our lead from observed patterns of friendship dissolution and accounting for prior levels of loyalty to the brand and different latent causes of break-up. In general we propose that at greater levels of loyalty the patterns of break-up become more complex and more disruptive or disturbing to the consumer. In order to deal with the complexity of such break-ups we next turn our attention to processes of relationship dissolution.

PROCESSES OF DISSOLUTION

"The most important observation for research is that we must avoid the risk of seeing relationship dissolution as an event...it is a process, and an extended one with many facets: affective behavioral, cognitive, intra-individual, dyadic and social." (Duck 1982)

The breakdown and dissolution of interpersonal relationships has a dynamic all its own that is not a mere linear reversal of the process of relationship formation (Duck and Lea 1983). Duck (1982) describes four separate but related processes inherent to interpersonal break-ups. We present them and recast them into the context of person-brand relationships. The process appears to occur more or less sequentially according to the following model:

Break-Down » Decline » Disengagement » Dissolution

Break-down refers to the attenuation of a relationship resulting from intentional or unintentional disruption in its conduct; breakdown may be temporary and may or may not lead to dissolution of the relationship. In the person-brand context break-down may result from unmet expectations for brand performance, changing consumer needs or liking criteria, or the appearance of potentially superior alternatives to the brand.

Decline is the next stage in the deterioration of an interpersonal relationship and refers to a diminishing of intimacy or liking for a partner or for the nature or form of the relationship. In the person-brand context we interpret decline as an affective reduction of liking or of loyalty which may involve a re-classification of the relationship to a lower level in our typology of person-brand relationships.

Disengagement refers to the interpersonal processes of communication and behavior that lead toward withdrawal from the relationship. Aspects of a consumer's disengagement from a brand-loyal relationship would include such behaviors as communication with other consumers (e.g., maligning the brand), and the active exploration and/or establishment of alternative brand relationships.

Dissolution refers to the termination or permanent dismemberment of the relationship, either through negotiation or unilateral withdrawal. In the terminology we have chosen for patterns of person-brand break-ups, dissolution can occur as brand-initiated separation, brand-switching, or brand-spurning behavior.

Loyalty effects on the dissolution process

In conceptualizing the process of person-brand break-ups it becomes evident that certain stages vary in importance and intensity depending in part on the antecedent level of loyalty to the brand. For example, break-down is probably less dangerous to a loyal than to a non-loyal relationship. Exit barriers of investment and commitment should provide consumers with some incentive to endure fluctuations in brand performance and, perhaps, to rationalize them away. In cases of the eventual dissolution of brand-loyal or brand-addicted relationships break-down may be a cyclic and/or prolonged process pushed along only by multiple failures in the conduct of the relationship.

Decline is an intra-psychic process of affect reduction. If we view decline as the erosion of exit barriers it stands to reason that the process should be more complex and involved where strong or multiple barriers exist. In cases where commitment to the brand is cemented in social relationships (e.g., in brand-dedicated clubs or users' groups), decline may require rituals of social withdrawal associated with disengagement.

Of all the stages in the dissolution process disengagement is perhaps the most ritualized and potentially damaging to the brand. It is in disengagement that consumers voice (and socially reinforce) their dissatisfaction with a brand and create social and/or psychological forces to counter the exit barriers that constitute brand loyalty. The more consumers invest in the brand, the more complex their disengagement activities must be. Disengagement from a higher-order relationship may therefore be characterized by a long period of rather subtle activities and affective changes, or alternatively by a short, intense conflagration of consumer response and emotion.

Dissolution or termination of a deteriorated person-brand relationship might seem straightforward: a simple, unilateral determination not to purchase the brand any more. For all the apparent simplicity of such a decision there may still be affective differences related to prior loyalty and resultant intensity and complexity of decline and disengagement. We would expect a low-investment relationship to dissolve with a whimper; the break-up of a high-investment relationship should be quite noisy by comparison.

Summary

We have advanced a model of the dissolution process as it may relate to person-brand relationships. We have elaborated the model somewhat with probable loyalty-related differences in consumer affect throughout the process. In order to further clarify some of the intricacies of the break-up process we next introduce a model of consumer responses to dissatisfaction in person-brand relationships.

CONSUMER RESPONSES TO DISSATISFACTION IN PERSON-BRAND RELATIONSHIPS

Dissatisfaction in a relationship appears to involve a fairly predictable set of behavioral responses, whether the relationship exists between a person and a social organization (Hirschman 1970), a person and a romantic partner (Rusbult, Zembrodt, and Gunn 1982), or a person and a brand (as we now propose). According to the model forwarded by Rusbult, et al (1982), dissatisfaction in a relationship elicits one or more of four responses: exit, voice, loyalty, and/or neglect.

Exit refers to the permanent termination of the (person-brand) relationship and corresponds to the dissolution stage in the process model suggested above. *Voice* refers to active communication of dissatisfaction to the partner (brand representative) with the intent

FIGURE 2

Break-Down	»	Decline	»	Disengagement	»	Dissolution

Loyalty	Voice (+)	Neglect	Voice (-)
Voice (+)	Neglect	Voice (-)	Exit

of improving the situation. We define such communication as *positive voice* and suggest that it would occur during breakdown or decline of the person-brand relationship. Conversely, we define *negative voice* as consumers' vocalizations of dissatisfaction to third parties during or after the process of disengagement. *Loyalty* manifests as continuing in the (person-brand) relationship while hoping that the situation will improve. Given that loyalty wanes during the decline process we expect it to function most strongly during break-down; however, loyalty may still operate during the decline stage until the consumer begins active disengagement. *Neglect* is a failure to care for or cultivate the relationship. In the person-brand context neglect would include reduced use of the brand and experimentation with alternatives.

Consumer response through the dissolution process

Understanding the nature and timing of consumer responses to dissatisfaction in person-brand relationships may be especially instructive for the purpose of identifying opportunities for brand-side intervention in the dissolution process. In Figure 2 we suggest the probable timing of responses with respect to the stages of the dissolution process.

In the perhaps inevitable periods of relationship break-down loyalty may carry consumers safely through lapses of brand performance (or through vacillations in consumer likes and dislikes) with no serious long-term damage to the relationship. Some consumers may be sufficiently motivated to voice their concerns about the brand or the relationship at this stage, but that seems unlikely *unless the relationship is truly dyadic*, i.e., unless it has an interpersonal component that facilitates two-way communication with a brand representative. Such an interpersonal component may be a firm's best first defense against customer defection.

Once the relationship is in decline loyalty is eroding by definition and will not compensate indefinitely for consumer dissatisfaction. The trajectory of the person-brand relationship is toward dissolution, and the brand side of the relationship may well be oblivious to the danger. The possibility exists that consumers will open channels of communication, voice their concerns to some brand representative, and thereby create the opportunity for brand-side remediation of the relationship. That possibility is lessened, however, if consumers have never received communication from the brand side indicating responsiveness to their concerns. Lacking confidence in brand-side responsiveness, or lacking the motivation to voice their concerns, consumers may instead neglect the relationship and begin experimentation with alternative brands, thus beginning the process of disengagement.

During disengagement consumers may already recognize or even desire the coming dissolution of the relationship. If they enter this stage in an attitude of neglect, then neglect is probably the attitude they will maintain through final dissolution. If consumers have been voicing grievances with expectations of remediation, and those expectations are unmet, then the voice may turn stridently negative. Complaining behavior will become directed to third parties with a vengeance, and negative word-of-mouth may proliferate. At this point of crisis some consumers may allow the brand side "one last chance" to address grievances and control damages,

but to expect anything less than a groveling CEO to assuage their feelings may be optimistic.

We expect that once dissolution is final and the consumer has exited the relationship, the exit door remains closed unless extraordinary circumstances reopen it. Ending a once loyal relationship is a high-involvement process in its own right and, therefore, should be subject to the same forces of attribution and dissonance reduction as any other high-involvement consumption decision.

Summary

We have adapted an exit-voice-loyalty-neglect model to the domain of person-brand relationships. We have then integrated it with a model of the dissolution process yielding potentially valuable insights for brand-side intervention. Close examination of our model argues for the value of developing, from the brand side, true dyadic (i.e., interpersonal) communication with a loyal customer base.

CONCLUSION

Interpersonal relationship theory offers many elegant and intriguing models with which to approach the topic of terminating person-brand relationships. We have advanced a comprehensive theoretical framework which may be valuable for heuristic purposes. The models should not be regarded as valid without empirical testing. We currently are in the process of exloring person-brand break-ups through depth interviews with adults who recently have terminated long-term usage of a wide variety of brands. Future research should also include stochastic testing.

The dissolution of an interpersonal relationship is not a perfect metaphor for brand-use termination. From a one-sided or monadic point of view the dynamics of an interpersonal break-up appear analogous in many ways to those of a person-brand break-up; yet an interpersonal relationship is dyadic in a way that person-brand relationships cannot be without the addition of a strong service component. We have attempted to acknowledge such differences in drawing our conclusions.

REFERENCES

Drigotas, Steven M. and Caryl E. Rusbult (1992), "Should I Stay or Should I Go? A Dependence Model of Breakups," *Journal of Personality and Social Psychology*, (62), 62-87.

Duck, Steve (1982), "A Topography of Relationship Disengagement and Dissolution," in *Personal Relationships 4: Dissolving Personal Relationships*, ed. S. Duck, London: Academic Press.

Duck, Steve and Martin Lea (1983), "Breakdown of Personal Relationships and the Threat to Personal Identity," in *Threatened Identities*, ed. G. Breakwell, John Wiley & Sons Ltd., 53-73.

Fournier, Susan (1994), "A Consumer-Brand Relationship Framework for Strategic Brand Management," Ph.D. Dissertation, University of Florida.

Hirschman, Albert O. (1970), *Exit, Voice and Loyalty: Responses to Decline in Firms, Organizations and States*, Cambridge, MA: Harvard University Press.

Kanter, R.M. (1972) *Commitment and Community*, Cambridge, MA: Harvard University Press.

Lund, Mary (1985), "The Development of Investment and Commitment Scales for Predicting Continuity of Personal Relationships," *Journal of Social and Personal Relationships*, (2), 3-23.

Reichheld, Frederick and W. Earl Sasser, Jr. (1990), "Zero Defections: Quality Comes to Services," *Harvard Business Review*, (Sep-Oct), 105-111.

Rodin, Miriam J. (1978), "Liking and Disliking: Sketch of an Alternate View," *Journal of Personality and Social Psychology*, (4), 473-478.

Rose, Suzanna M. (1984), "How Friendships End: Patterns Among Young Adults," *Journal of Social and Personal Relationships*, (1), 267-277.

Rose, Suzanna M. and Felicisima C. Serafica (1986), "Keeping and Ending Close and Best Friendships," *Journal of Social and Personal Relationships*, (3), 275-288.

Rusbult, Caryl E., Isabella M. Zembrodt, and Lawanna K. Gunn (1982), "Exit, Voice, Loyalty, and Neglect: Responses to Dissatisfaction in Romantic Involvements," *Journal of Personality and Social Psychology*, (43), 1230-1242.

Sherry, John F., Jr. (1989), "Cereal Monogamy: Brand Loyalty as Secular Ritual in Consumer Culture," paper presented at Annual Conference of the Association for Consumer Research, Boston.

Simpson, Jeffrey A. (1987), "The Dissolution of Romantic Relationships: Factors Involved in Relationship Stability and Emotional Distress," *Journal of Personality and Social Psychology*, (53), 683-692.

Solomon, Michael R. (1992), *Consumer Behavior*, Allyn and Bacon.

A Closer Look at the Influence of Age on Consumer Ethics

Barry J. Babin, University of Southern Mississippi
Mitch Griffin, Bradley University

ABSTRACT

Shoplifting is among the most serious and common aberrant consumer behaviors (ACB), yet has been largely ignored in the consumer behavior literature. This study empirically examines this topic, treating shoplifting as a behavior with ethical consequences, thus bringing together research on ACB with emerging research on ethical decision making. This research makes two important contributions to the current literature: (1) multiple age groups are considered to identify the differences between adolescents, young adults, and fully mature adults, and (2) individual difference characteristics are tested as mediators of the age—shoplifting relationship. The results support the position that adolescents are most prone to shoplifting behavior, but illustrate that this relationship is mediated by other factors.

INTRODUCTION

Shoplifting is among the most serious and common aberrant consumer behaviors (ACB) (Fullerton and Punj 1993). Statistics reflecting the magnitude of shoplifting are staggering (see Solomon 1994 for a detailed review). Most prominent among these statistics are figures representing shoplifting's pervasive impact on industry and society. For example, the total dollar value of goods shoplifted every year exceeds $30 billion (Fullerton and Punj 1993), over half of all U.S. consumers have shoplifted at some time (Klemke 1982), and shoplifting is a significant factor in many retail failures (Cole 1989). Considering these figures, shoplifting would classify as one of the developed world's leading industries.

Despite the pervasiveness of shoplifting as a consumer behavior and its profound impact on our society, consumer researchers have given very little attention to shoplifting behavior or, more broadly, ethical decision making among consumers (Tsalikis and Fritzsche 1989). An exception to this apparent oversight is recent research illustrating the prevalence of shoplifting among adolescent consumers and pointing out some potential contributory factors (Cox, Cox, and Moschis 1990). Specifically, this study reports that the percentage of the population who report shoplifting peaks during high school (see Cox et al. 1990, Figure 1).

Since shoplifting is purported to be most prevalent among adolescents, it could be argued that developing consumers become socialized over time and actually "learn" that this behavior is unacceptable. However, researchers have not generally examined multiple age groups or considered individual difference traits and their potential effects on shoplifting (Cox, Cox, Anderson, and Moschis 1993). Thus, it is difficult to determine the extent to which age actually *causes* shoplifting to be considered acceptable behavior.

The broad purposes of this paper are two-fold. First, the study treats shoplifting as a behavior with ethical consequences and thus ties in research on ACB with emerging research on ethical decision making. Second, the relationship between age (consumers varying in consumer socialization) and shoplifting is examined more closely. As Fullerton and Punj (1993, p. 570) point out, "The challenge for researchers is to identify those factors or interactions of factors which are likely to lead some consumers to misbehave some of the time." In the present study, we simultaneously consider several relevant personal traits of individuals. Thus, we examine the relationship between age and shoplifting compared to other traits that consumers develop over time.

CONCEPTUAL DEVELOPMENT AND RESEARCH HYPOTHESES

Shoplifting as an Ethical Decision

Ethical decision making usually involves consideration of potential personal, cultural, and/or legal sanctions that may be transgressed as a result of the decision (Robin and Reidenbach 1987). Ethical judgments can be explained along three dimensions rooted in moral philosophy (Reidenbach, Robin, and Dawson 1991): (1) *moral equity* captures an individual's perceptions of an act's "justness" or "fairness;" (2) *contractualism* represents perceptions of implied or explicit contracts that would be violated by performing a questionable act; and (3) *relativism* represents how culturally acceptable an act is or has become. Thus, these three dimensions are thought to underlie decisions and judgments involving moral or ethical dilemmas.

We believe shoplifting fits the requirements of an ethical judgment. There are multiple barriers-personal, cultural, and legal-that must be overcome before a shoplifting act can be performed. Further, recent research indicates that the three dimensions described above (i.e., moral equity, contractualism, and relativism) may underlie consumers' shoplifting judgments. More specifically, survey results suggest that consumers' ethical judgments are related to both attitudes toward shoplifting and intentions to shoplift positively, and that highly ethical judgments of shoplifting may represent consumers' attempts to rationalize the behavior (Babin, Robin, and Pike 1994). As consumers judge a shoplifting act as more ethical (on each dimension), he/she is predisposed more favorably toward it and becomes a more likely participant in that behavior. These findings are consistent with other research addressing ethical questions in nonconsumer contexts (Reidenbach et al. 1991).

Age and Shoplifting Judgements

Substantial evidence suggests that age is related to ethical judgments of shoplifting. For example, thirty-seven percent of high school students studied reported that they had shoplifted in the previous year (Cox et al. 1990), while nearly forty percent of shoplifters apprehended are adolescents (Baumer and Rosenbaum 1984). In speculating on potential reasons for this phenomenon, Cox et al. (1990) suggest that adolescents may lack the moral development necessary to deter stealing from retailers. As consumers become socialized, they gain the development necessary to judge such acts differently. Thus, the following basic relationship is suggested:

H1: Age is related negatively to moral equity, contractualism, and relativism ethical judgments of shoplifting.

Individual Difference Traits and Shoplifting Judgements

A growing body of evidence suggests that most ACB results from a combination of situational and individual variables (Fullerton and Punj 1993). When investigating shoplifting behavior, previous empirical research has focused primarily on situational factors such as a product's economic value, the type of product being considered, the number of people present, and the chance of being apprehended (Babin et al. 1994; Cole 1989; Cox et al. 1990).

Apart from age, individual difference traits have received little attention in comparison.

Although establishing a relationship between age and ethical judgments of shoplifting (H1) is useful descriptively, it fails to identify specific reasons for shoplifting. Interestingly, many individual traits that could be related to shoplifting attitudes and behavior tend to covary with age. Thus, the present study examines the partial contribution of age in predicting ethical judgments of shoplifting in light of these additional individual difference characteristics. The result is a test of mediation of the age-shoplifting judgment perceptions relationship by the individual difference characteristics considered. While space precludes a detailed analysis of each variable considered here, a brief discussion of each with respect to its potential mediating role follows.

Risk Aversion. Given the inherent risk associated with stealing, high levels of risk aversion may discourage someone from shoplifting. As analogous empirical evidence, Cox et al. (1990) found that shoplifting adolescents scored higher in measures of "rule breaking" than nonshoplifting adolescents. Although varying across all age groups, adolescents tend to be particularly low in risk aversion (Moschis 1987). Thus, there is the potential that part of the effect of age on shoplifting is due to risk aversion. Consequently, risk aversion should relate to ethical perceptions of shoplifting while controlling for the effect of age.

Self-Esteem. Shoplifters' self-esteem also may play a role in shoplifting decisions. Adolescents may view shoplifting as a way of fitting in or gaining acceptance among desired referents, a characteristic that may indicate low self-esteem (Brown and Lohr 1987). Self-esteem may also be a factor in adult shoplifting. Both adolescent and adult shoplifters tend to steal luxury items capable of enhancing self-esteem as opposed to necessity items whose need is more easily rationalized (Cameron 1964). This effect transcends social classes as well as age groups (Cox et al. 1990). Thus, self-esteem may be negatively related to shoplifting judgments. That is, consumers with low self-esteem will judge shoplifting acts to be relatively more ethical.

Susceptibility to Interpersonal Influence. Individual differences in susceptibility to peer influence can be captured along two dimensions (Bearden, Netemeyer, and Teel 1989). *Normative influence* refers to compliance with peers' expectations to help gain rewards or avoid punishment (e.g., buying the brand my friends approve of). Peer influence is also exerted through *informational influence*, where peer behavior is observed for information that is potentially useful in decision making (e.g., buying a brand because its what others are using).

Peer pressure has been hypothesized as a major influence on adolescent shoplifting (Klemke 1982). Adolescents with relatively high numbers of friends that shoplift report fewer moral objections to shoplifting and more frequent shoplifting behavior (Cox et al. 1993). One explanation for this observation is that adolescents are susceptible to interpersonal influence concerning shoplifting because it provides information allowing them to rationalize the behavior (i.e., "my friends are doing it, so it must be o.k. for me to do it too"). One might also argue that shoplifting is a way of gaining acceptance among peers. The former reason suggests a relationship between informational influence and shoplifting judgments, while the latter suggests a relationship between normative influence and shoplifting judgments. Based on the preceding discussion, we offer our second research hypothesis:

H2: Risk aversion, self-esteem, and susceptibility to interpersonal influence relate negatively to moral equity, contractualism, and relativism ethical judgments of shoplifting.

Individual Difference Traits as Mediators

We believe that an investigation of the personality variables presented above will extend our present knowledge of shoplifting. Furthermore, since these traits tend to covary with age, analyzing them simultaneously with age will provide a better understanding of the interrelationships among all variables. Specifically, we propose that these personality traits mediate the relationship between age and shoplifting judgements:

H3: The relationships between age and ethical judgments of shoplifting is attenuated when controlling for risk aversion, self-esteem, and susceptibility to interpersonal influence.

Summary

This study investigates three related hypotheses to test for mediation of the age—shoplifting relationship. In this case, three requirements must be met to establish mediation: (1) a direct relationship between age and ethical judgements of shoplifting (H1) must be shown, (2) a direct relationship between risk aversion, self-esteem, and susceptibility to interpersonal influence and shoplifting judgements (H2) must exist when controlling for age, and (3) the magnitude of the relationship between age and ethical judgments of shoplifting must be reduced by controlling for the individual difference traits (H3) considered here. The following section describes a study examining these hypotheses.

RESEARCH METHODS

Sample

A total of 168 respondents from the university community participated in the study in return for a small incentive. Variation in respondent age is required to test the hypotheses stated above. Thus, the study included three distinct age groups. Adolescent respondents were included as shoplifting has been considered particularly common among this age group. In the present study, local high school sophomores and juniors were interviewed at their school. Young adult respondents were students of junior and senior standing at the local university. This age group was selected to examine how rapidly consumers become socialized. Finally, a group of mature consumers was obtained from employers at a local manufacturing company. These respondents represented a wide range of demographic variables and included both blue and white collar workers. Forty-nine respondents were high school students (μ_{age}=16.0), 65 were college students (μ_{age}=21.7), and 54 were adult consumers (μ_{age}=40.1). The demographics of the sample were representative of the community with respect to family income levels and ethnic background.

Surveys were administered in group settings (15-25 respondents) within a single week. Given the potential sensitive nature of the questionnaire, several precautions were taken to help ensure respondent anonymity and confidentiality. Data collection closely followed the procedure described by Cox et al. (1990).

Data Collection and Measures

Respondents were handed a questionnaire booklet containing a brief shoplifting scenario and relevant measures. In the scenario, an ambiguously described consumer (Pat) is examining merchandise at a retail store in the local mall. When the clerk is distracted, the consumer shoplifts a small item worth about $25. Respondents then turned the page and were asked not to turn back to this page to respond to the items that followed.

Survey items that followed were assessed using a six point Likert format. Respondent perceptions of the ethicality of the

TABLE 1
Mean Scores By Age Group

Group	Variables [1]						
	Traits:				Ethicality:		
	Risk Aversion	Self-Esteem	Informational Influence	Normative Influence	Moral Equity	Contractualism	Relativism
Adults	17.2[a]	29.8[a]	15.3[a]	19.1	6.5[a]	7.5[a]	4.1[a]
College Students	15.0	29.7[b]	13.9	18.1	6.8[b]	7.7[b]	3.8[b]
Adolescents	14.0[a]	26.7[ab]	13.4[a]	18.2	10.8[ab]	9.1[ab]	5.3[ab]

[1]Means with matching superscripts are significantly different as indicated by Tukey's Studentized Range Test ($\alpha = .05$).

shoplifting situation were collected using an ethical judgment scale validated in numerous marketing and consumer contexts (e.g., Babin et al. 1994; Bearden, Netemeyer, and Mobley 1993; Reidenbach et al. 1991). Five items assessed moral equity, three items contractualism, and two items assessed relativism.

Following these judgments and some filler items, several individual difference characteristics were assessed. Six items assessed respondent risk aversion and were patterned after items found in Zuckerman (1979) that reflected tolerance of risk (e.g., "I consider myself a risk-taker"). Respondent self-esteem was assessed using six items taken from Heatherton and Polivy (1991; Bagozzi and Heatherton 1994). Finally, susceptibility to interpersonal influence was assessed along two dimensions (informational and normative) using twelve items developed and tested previously in a consumer context (Bearden et al. 1989).

The Appendix briefly describes each scale and gives the measurement results. Coefficient α ranged from .65 (relativism) to .92 (normative influence) and averaged .78. Thus, individual scale items were summed forming measures used in further analyses. The three ethical judgment scales were coded so that respondents with higher scores perceived the shoplifting act as more ethical. The four individual difference traits were scored positively so that higher scores represented higher levels of the construct.

The correlations between summated constructs were assessed to examine the extent of colinearity. The correlations were modest with relativism and moral equity being the most highly correlated scales (r=.49). Informational and normative susceptibility to interpersonal influence were the most highly correlated predictor variables used in the study (r=.39) with only two other significant correlations. Thus, the colinearity among predictors does not appear high enough to hamper interpretation of effects.

RESULTS

A series of ANOVA and ANCOVA models were used to test the research hypotheses. Age was treated as a three level predictor variable based upon group (adolescents, college students, and adults). Table 1 shows the mean scores on each interval level variable included in the study by age group. Although not directly pertinent to the hypotheses, age predicted risk aversion, self-esteem, and informational influence significantly (p<.05). Normative influence was not affected by age.

Hypothesis 1

Given the potential intercorrelation among ethical judgment dimensions (Reidenbach et al. 1991), a multivariate analysis of

variance was computed prior to analyzing individual effects. The results indicate that age affects ethical judgments significantly ($\Lambda = .72$; $F_{6,304} = 8.90$; p<.0001); thus, further analysis of each dependent variable is warranted.

Table 2 displays individual ANOVA results for each ethical judgment dimension. Moral equity (p<.001), contractualism (p<.05), and relativism (p<.001) all varied significantly with age. By comparing effect sizes, we can see that age has the strongest impact on perceived ethicality ($\omega^2 = .25$). Further, the means by age group suggest the relationship is in the hypothesized direction (see Table 1). In other words, high school respondents perceived the shoplifting act as significantly more ethical on each dimension than did either college students or adult respondents, providing support for H1. Interestingly, scores among college students and older adults did not differ significantly.

Hypothesis 2

Hypothesis Two examines the effect of several individual difference characteristics on respondents ethical judgments of the shoplifting episode. Table 3 shows the results of ANCOVA models testing each trait's effect while controlling for age. Individual parameter estimates are shown in Table 4.

The results show that self-esteem relates to perceived moral equity negatively ($b=-.17$; $F=8.50$; p<.01) while controlling for age. Contractualism is affected significantly by respondent risk aversion (p<.05) and susceptibility to interpersonal informational influence (p<.05). Increased risk aversion ($b=-.11$) and informational influence ($b=-.14$) decrease contractualism judgments. Finally, in addition to the effect of age, both risk aversion (p<.05) and self-esteem (p<.01) affect relativism significantly. Specifically, increased risk aversion ($b=-.10$) and high self-esteem ($b=-.13$) lower the perception that shoplifting behavior is culturally and/or traditionally acceptable. Thus, although not every potential relationship is significant, these five relationships are consistent with H2.

Hypothesis 3

Hypothesis Three requires a comparison of the strength of the relationship between age and ethical judgments of the shoplifting act before and after consideration of mediators (covariates). Effect sizes (ω^2) corresponding to these relationships are shown in Tables 2 and 4.

In all three cases, the effect size representing the direct relationship between age and perceived ethicality drops when the individual difference traits are added to the model. Specifically, the age—moral equity effect size drops from .25 to .15, the age—

TABLE 2
ANOVA Results Using Age As A Predictor

Dependent Variable	Model F	Variance Explained	ω^2	p value
Moral Equity	28.4	.26	.25	.0001
Contractualism	3.7	.05	.03	.03
Relativism	8.1	.09	.08	.0004

TABLE 3
Full Model (ANCOVA) Results Including Potential Mediators

Dependent Variable	Model F	R^2	Age	Independent Variable F's: Risk Aversion	Mediating Variables: Self-Esteem	Inf. Influence	Norm. Influence
Moral Equity	11.8 [a]	.32	18.28 [a]	1.10	8.50 [a]	1.30	0.02
Contractualism	3.4 [a]	.12	3.12 [b]	5.70 [b]	1.09	4.65 [b]	0.39
Relativism	5.8 [a]	.18	4.30 [b]	3.68 [b]	9.68 [a]	0.19	0.03

[a] $p < .01$
[b] $p < .05$

TABLE 4
Effect Size Estimates For Full Model

Dependent Variable	ω^2 Age	b Risk Aversion	Self-Esteem	Inf. Influence	Norm. Influence
Moral Equity	.15	-.04	-.17	-.07	.01
Contractualism	.02	-.11	.06	-.14	.03
Relativism	.03	-.10	-.13	.02	-.00

contractualism effect size drops from .05 to .02, and the age—relativism effect size drops from .08 to .03. The F-values representing the corresponding relationships indicate similar results. Likewise, the multivariate F drops to 4.82 (df$_{14,288}$) when the four individual difference traits are entered into the model.

Summary

The data reveal that five of twelve potential relationships between individual difference traits and perceived ethical judgments of the shoplifting act are significant. None of the relationships representing normative influence are significant. Thus, risk aversion, self-esteem, and susceptibility to informational interpersonal influence all play a role in predicting ethical perceptions of shoplifting.

Results also address the extent to which these individual difference traits mediate the relationship between age and perceived ethicality. Full mediation would require that age's direct effect become nonsignificant when the mediators are entered into the model. In the current case, since the levels of significance and effect sizes are only reduced, evidence of partial mediation is presented (Baron and Kenny 1986).

DISCUSSION

The study presented here extends earlier research on shoplifting by examining multiple age groups. Our findings are consistent with previous research suggesting adolescents are more prone to shoplift than older consumers. A series of ANOVA models indicates that adolescents view shoplifting as significantly more ethical than do either college students or older adults. However, no significant differences were found between college students (μ_{age}=21.7) and older adults (μ_{age}=40.1). This is consistent with Cox et al. (1990) who report that the percentage of students shoplifting peaks in tenth grade, then drops off rapidly. They did not, however, extend their study beyond high school aged consumers.

Why do perceptions of shoplifting change substantially between the ages of 16 and 21, but remain relatively constant thereafter? It may be that consumers rapidly become socialized during this period, experience moral development, and/or change their value structure. Each of these suggests that we become more "ethical" as we move from adolescence into adulthood. Alternatively, it is possible that our basic ethical makeup remains constant, but ACB is shifted from shoplifting to other arenas. For example, shoplifting and vandalism are largely the domain of adolescents, while insurance and credit card fraud is dominated by adults (Hirschi and Gottfredson 1983). Future research examining both multiple age groups and forms of ACB simultaneously may provide answers to this question.

While establishing a relationship between age and perceptions of shoplifting, our results also suggest that age may not be as strong a causal factor as the percentages may imply. Rather, there are numerous individual difference characteristics-also influenced by age-that are responsible for consumers' ethical perceptions of shoplifting. Risk aversion, self-esteem, and susceptibility to interpersonal influence were all shown to influence perceived ethicality to varying degrees. Analyzing these effects more specifically, by dependent variable, reveals some interesting results that relate closely to earlier research.

Our data suggests that both respondent self-esteem and age relate negatively to perceived moral equity. Thus, consumers with lower self-esteem see shoplifting as a more "just" or "fair" behavior than do those with higher self-esteem. One reason that adolescents are more prone to shoplifting may be the lower self-esteem that often accompanies this time in one's life (see Table 1). Across all age groups though, stealing luxury items may be a way of temporarily enhancing self-esteem. However, this may set up a vicious circle-much by like that associated with compulsive consumption-where the behavior leading to short-term improvements fails to improve self-esteem in the long term (O'Guinn and Faber 1989).

Both risk aversion and susceptibility to informational interpersonal influence also affect consumer perceptions of shoplifting. As consumers became more risk averse, they rated the shoplifting scenario lower on contractualism, implying increased perceptions of a violation of an implied or explicit rule or contract. As with self-esteem, adolescents exhibited less risk aversion than did college students or adults. Therefore, some of the effect formally attributed to age may more precisely be due to variance in consumer risk aversion.

The negative effect of informational influence is also interesting. It suggests that the more consumers rely on others' behavior for information, the less ethically they perceive shoplifting. The fact that informational, rather than normative, influence relates to contractualism suggests that Cox et al.'s (1993) speculation about the mechanism with which peer influence operates may be correct. They hypothesized that people consider other's shoplifting behavior as information in making judgements about the appropriateness

of the behavior, rather than shoplifting in an effort to win approval. Conversely, if shoplifting was done to gain approval, a positive relationship might be expected between these constructs. Under these conditions, the more you intended to seek approval through mimicking others' behavior, the more likely you would be to shoplift. These relationships, however, are dependent on the accepted behaviors of ones peer group.

Relativism, how culturally or traditionally acceptable a behavior is perceived, is affected by both risk aversion and self-esteem significantly. The negative relationship between risk aversion and relativism indicates that as a consumer becomes more risk averse, he/she is more likely to perceive shoplifting as an unacceptable behavior. In contrast, risk takers perceive it as a socially or traditionally acceptable act. The negative self-esteem—relativism relationship indicates that consumers reporting low self-esteem tend to view shoplifting as socially and/or culturally acceptable.

CONCLUSION

This study investigated an area of aberrant consumer behavior that has been largely ignored in the consumer research literature. By examining multiple age groups, we have additional evidence that adolescents perceive shoplifting differently than more mature consumers and are more likely to engage in this behavior. However, we also have evidence that the direct affect of age on shoplifting is mediated by individual difference variables. Thus, the factors influencing shoplifting are much more complicated than we sometimes recognize. Certainly we are only building the foundation of knowledge in regard our understanding of shoplifting. As consumer researchers, we must continue to investigate the aberrant as well as the typical elements of consumption behavior.

REFERENCES

Babin, Barry J., Donald P. Robin, and Kristi Pike (1994), "To Steal, or not to Steal? Consumer Ethics and Shoplifting," in *Marketing Theory and Application*, Vol. 5, eds. C. W. Park and D. C. Smith, American Marketing Association: Chicago, IL, 200-205.

Bagozzi, Richard P. and Todd F. Heatherton (1994), "A General Approach to Representing Multifaceted Personality Constructs: Application to State Self-Esteem," *Structural Equations Modeling*, 1 (1), 35-67.

Baron, Reuben M. and David A. Kenny (1986), "The Moderator-Mediator Variable Distinction in Social Psychological Research: Conceptual, Strategic, and Statistical Considerations," *Journal of Personality and Social Psychology*, 51 (June), 1173-1182.

Baumer, Terry and Dennis Rosenbaum (1984), *Combatting Retail Theft: Programs and Strategies*, Stoneham, MA: Butterworth.

Bearden, William O., Richard G. Netemeyer, and Mary F. Mobley (1993), *Handbook of Marketing Scales: Multi-Item Measures for Marketing and Consumer Behavior Research*, Newbury Park, CA: SAGE Publications.

Bearden, William O., Richard G. Netemeyer, and Jesse E. Teel (1989), "Measurement of Consumer Susceptibility to Interpersonal Influence," *Journal of Consumer Research*, 473-481.

Brown, B. Bradford and Mary Jane Lohr (1987), "Peer-Group Affiliation and Adolescent Self-Esteem: An Integration of Ego-Identity and Symbolic-Interaction Theories," *Journal of Personality and Social Psychology*, 52 (January), 47-55.

Cameron, M. O. (1964), *The Booster and the Snitch: Department Store Shoplifting*, New York: Free Press.

APPENDIX
Scale Descriptions

Scale	Sample Item	# of Items	α
Risk Aversion	Jumping out of an airplane sounds like fun. [1]	6	.72
Self-Esteem	I feel good about myself.	6	.85
Informational Influence	I often consult other people to help choose the best alternative available from a product class.	4	.79
Normative Influence	It is important that others like the products and brands I buy.	8	.92
Moral Equity	Pat's [the shoplifter described] behavior is just.	5	.85
Contractualism	Pat's behavior violates an unspoken promise. [1]	3	.70
Relativism	Considering the way things are, Pat's actions are culturally acceptable.	2	.65

[1]Reverse scored.

Cole, Catherine A. (1989), "Research Note: Deterrence and Consumer Fraud," *Journal of Retailing*, 65 (Spring), 107-120.

Cox, Dena, Anthony D. Cox, and George P. Moschis (1990), "When Consumer Behavior Goes Bad: An Investigation of Adolescent Shoplifting," *Journal of Consumer Research*, 17 (September), 149-159.

Cox, Anthony D., Dena Cox, Ronald D. Anderson, and George P. Moschis (1993), "Social Influences on Adolescent Shoplifting—Theory, Evidence, and Implications for the Retail Industry," *Journal of Retailing*, 69 (Summer), 234-246.

Fullerton, Ronald A. and Girish Punj (1993), "Choosing to Misbehave: A Structural Model of Aberrant Consumer Behavior," in *Advances in Consumer Research*, Leigh McAlister and Michael L. Rothschild, eds., Vol 20, Provo, UT: Association for Consumer Research, 570-574.

Heatherton, Todd F. and Janet Polivy (1991), "Development and Validation of a Scale for Measuring State Self-Esteem," *Journal of Personality and Social Psychology*, 60 (June), 895-910.

Hirschi, Travis and Michael Gottfredson (1983), "Age and the Explanation of Crime," *American Journal of Sociology*, 89 No. 3, 552-584.

Klemke, Lloyd W. (1982), "Exploring Adolescent Shoplifting," *Sociology and Social Research*, 67 (1), 59-75.

Moschis, George P. (1987), *Consumer Socialization: A Life Cycle Perspective*, Lexington, MA: Lexington.

O'Guinn, Thomas C. and Ronald J. Faber (1989), "Compulsive Buying: A Phenomenological Approach," *Journal of Consumer Research*, 16 (September), 147-157.

Reidenbach, R. Eric, Donald P. Robin, and Lyndon Dawson (1991), "An Application and Extension of a Multidimensional Ethics Scale to Selected Marketing Practices," *Journal of the Academy of Marketing Science*, 19 (Spring), 83-92.

Robin, Donald P. and R. Eric Reidenbach (1987), "Some Initial Steps Toward Improving the Measurement of Ethical Evaluations of Marketing Activities," *Journal of Marketing*, 51 (Winter), 44-58.

Solomon, Michael R. (1994), *Consumer Behavior*, Allyn and Bacon: Needham Heights, MA.

Tsalikis, John and David J. Fritzsche (1989), "Business Ethics: A Literature Review with a Focus on Marketing Ethics," *Journal of Business Ethics*, 8 (September), 695-743.

Zuckerman, Marvin (1979), *Sensation Seeking: Beyond the Optimum Stimulation Level of Arousal*, Hillsdale, NJ: Lawrence Erlbaum.

Older Consumers' Vulnerability to Bait-and-Switch

Anil Mathur, Hofstra University
George P. Moschis, Georgia State University[1]

ABSTRACT

The traditional view among researchers and public policy makers has been that the elderly are the most disadvantaged and most frequently victimized by consumer fraud. Contrary to this view some studies have found that the incidence of crime against the elderly is actually less than that against younger people. Based on a national telephone survey, this study found that age-related differences in experience of a common consumer fraud (bait-and-switch) could be explained by one's shopping behavior and knowledge of such practices rather than age per se.

INTRODUCTION

With the increase in the number of older population, public policy makers, marketers, consumer researchers, and social scientists have started paying attention to the needs of this segment. While marketers have seen this trend as an increasing opportunity to market products and services to meet the needs of the elderly, consumer researchers have attempted to understand the consumption patterns of the elderly that make them different from other segments of the population. Social scientists and public policy makers have focused their attention on the specific needs of the elderly, particularly on needs due to declining health and ability to care for themselves. Some unscrupulous operators might have also seen this demographic trend as an opportunity to profit.

It is widely believed that the elderly are the most disadvantaged group. It is also believed that they are the most victimized group (Butler 1975; McGhee 1983; Moschis 1992). Officers responsible for law enforcement have often reported that the elderly are frequent victims of consumer fraud (e.g., Friedman 1992). However, hard reliable data on the types of consumer fraud and the incidence of elderly victimization is scarce. Most of the information in this area is based on anecdotal evidence or surveys (Moschis 1992). The areas where the elderly are most susceptible to being victimized include housing, healthcare, insurance, automotive, appliance repair, general merchandise, utilities, and marketing methods (McGhee 1983; Alston 1986). Although previous research has contributed to our understanding of the situations experienced by the elderly in the marketplace, it has not focused on explanations of various types of crime and consumer fraud.

The purpose of this research is to examine the vulnerability of the elderly to one of the most common form of consumer fraud: bait-and-switch. Based on a field survey, reasons are sought to explain age-related differences in elderlys' experience of bait-and-switch.

BACKGROUND

Alston (1986) defines marketplace crime as "a broad category of crime which occurs in the context of buying and selling of goods and services." (p. 48). Marketplace crime may take several forms and may be directed toward businesses, government, or individuals. All marketplace crime adversely affects consumers. Consumer fraud is specifically directed toward consumers and affects them directly. It covers "a wide variety of behaviors, tactics, and practices detrimental to consumers" (Edelhertz et al. 1977). From a legal perspective such a fraud involves: knowingly making a false statement, assertion, or suggestion; deliberately suppressing facts to mislead; or making a promise with no intention of performing it (Newman, Jester, and Articolo 1978).

"Bait-and-switch" is a very commonly used form of consumer fraud (e.g., Zaltman, Srivastava, and Deshpande 1978). For example, in a study of the mail-order video camcorder market, Easley et al. (1992) found that 71.1% of the dealers misrepresented themselves as authorized dealers of a particular brand. Also, among unauthorized dealers who carried other brands, 25% attempted to use bait-and-switch on the prospective customer. Bait-and-switch involves advertising an item at a very low price, but when the potential customer arrives or calls to purchase that item, the salesperson may say a number of things disparaging the advertised item in an attempt to persuade the customer to purchase a more expensive substitute. Despite the advertisement and the offer of sale, in these cases the seller does not intend to sell the low-priced item. It is very easy for a marketer to engage in bait-and-switch, while it may be very difficult to catch and prosecute such unscrupulous marketers. However, when caught, companies engaging in this form of fraud have been subjected to legal action (e.g., Meeks 1990; Minkin 1990). In comparison to other types of crime, cases of consumer fraud are almost always nonviolent, yet they are viewed as very serious by the victims because they could involve large sums of money and may have serious consequences on the victims (Glick and Newsom 1974; Midwest Research Institute 1977).

Several studies have reported that the elderly are especially vulnerable to fraud and crime (e.g., Kosberg 1985). Also, both researchers and practitioners have reported that elderly are often victimized by businesses (Friedman 1992; Goldsmith and Goldsmith 1975; Hahn 1976). For example, several individuals representing victims, law enforcement authorities, and public policy makers recently testified in front of the Senate Committee on Aging that older Americans are seen as easy prey by unscrupulous marketers (U.S. Senate 1992). Moreover, it has been suggested that of all the crimes committed against the elderly, consumer fraud is the most frequent type. Consumer fraud against the elderly also ranks at the top in terms of the cost to the elderly (Hahn 1976).

While social service agencies have highlighted the plight of the elderly and have focused on the crime and fraud against them, some other empirical research has shown that the rate of victimization due to crime is actually less for the elderly than for the younger age groups (Hofrichter 1982; Lindquist and Duke 1982; Mawby 1982; Midwest Research Institute 1977). Some other studies have found that the rate of victimization of the elderly is not necessarily greater than those for the younger age groups (McGuire and Edelhertz 1980). Is this because elderly experience crime less than younger people, or is it because the crime against the elderly is not reported by them as often to the authorities? Could this reflect the older persons' inability to recognize crime?

According to Friedman (1992) there are four main reasons for elderly being victimized by consumer fraud in general: a) accessibility—elderly are easily found at home and in shopping malls; b) social isolation—i.e., a majority live alone and, therefore, may be eager to socialize with salespeople and strangers; c) declining physical and mental abilities—i.e., reducing the elderly's ability to identify the fraudulent situation and to protect himself or herself

[1]The authors wish to express their gratitude to the American Association for Retired Persons (AARP) for making the data for this study available to the Center for Mature Consumer Studies.

from such a fraud; and d) favorable financial circumstances contributing to targeting by unscrupulous businesses or organizations. For example, if a person experiences bait-and-switch and the victim does not know that such an action is illegal, chances are that this incidence will go unrecorded. Poor health and lack of consumer knowledge may make an elderly victim unaware of such a fraud. While accessibility of the potential victims is accounted by the frequency of store visits and major purchases, social isolation may not have any direct relationship to this particular type of consumer fraud. Biophysical declines associated with aging might reduce one's ability to comprehend complex information, thereby making elderly more vulnerable to consumer fraud. The problem is more complicated because in many cases victims might not realize that they have been targets of such a fraud if they do not understand the complexity of price-product feature relationships. Moreover, if the victims do not know that practices like bait-and-switch are illegal they may not complain. While potential swindlers may not know in advance who is knowledgeable, it is expected that those who know that bait-and-switch is illegal will mentally make a note of such experience and complain when opportunities arise.

METHODOLOGY

Data collection

The study consisted of 1,305 telephone interviews conducted by Market Facts' National Telephone Center in Evanston Illinois in December 1990 for AARP, which, in-turn, made the data available to the authors. Trained and experienced interviewers were briefed and monitored throughout the course of interviewing. The sample for the survey was selected from Market Facts' weekly omnibus telephone survey, TeleNation. This TeleNation survey is conducted on non-holiday weekends using random digit dialing to obtain a national sample of 1,000 households. The data from each week, including telephone numbers and demographic information for each respondent, are entered into a cumulative data base. The existing TeleNation data base allows interviewing of specific demographic groups without the need for expensive screening. For the present study, a disproportionately large number of interviews were conducted with older respondents. Using the TeleNation data base, which contains respondents' birthdays, Market Facts was able to identify respondents meeting the desired age characteristics.

To facilitate comparison across age groups quotas were set for five age groups; 25-49 (300), 50-64 (302), 65-74 (301), 75-84 (202), and 85+ (200). Within each age group, interviews were conducted for males and females proportionate to their distribution in the population. Although initial sample contained younger respondents too, those under 55 years of age were dropped from the analysis since the focus of this study was on older consumers. Thus, the analysis was carried out on the remaining 917 respondents. Demographic profile of the sample is given in Table 1.

Questionnaire development included pretesting and minor modifications due to pretest results. To measure the knowledge about bait-and-switch and to see if the respondents had experienced this form of consumer fraud they were read the following scenario:

"You read an ad in the paper for a television set on sale for $300. When you arrive at the store, the salesperson tells you that the advertised set is not a very good one. He advises you to buy a $500 set instead. What is your opinion of this selling technique?"

The above scenario explicitly included salesperson's action in disparaging the advertised item, a key component of bait-and-switch. Although intention not to sell the advertised item is another key aspect of bait and switch, the word "intention" was specifically not included in the scenario because most often persuasive communication from the salesperson sounds as if it is in the best interest of the potential customer. Therefore, the question of intention does not arise. Moreover, even if intention were specifically included, the respondents would have given their perception of salesperson's intention. The present scenario relied more on objective and observable aspects of the bait-and-switch tactic.

After the description they were asked: "Do you think it is a fair business practice?" and "Do you think it is legal?" with three response categories "yes," "no," and "don't know." They were also asked: "Has anything like this ever happened to you where you wanted to buy a less expensive product and were advised to buy the more expensive one?" Two response categories were given: "yes" or "no."

In order to measure *frequency of in-store purchasing*, respondents were asked: "On an average, how many times a week do you go to a store to purchase products or services other than food or drug items?" Response categories were: never go to the store, less than once a week, 1-2, 3-4, 5 or more times a week (responses were read, if necessary). Food and drug items were specifically excluded for several reasons: first food and drug purchase are essential purchases and do not reflect discretionary purchases; and second, a large proportion of cases of bait-and-switch involve major purchases other than food and drug items.

In order to measure the *number of major purchases* made, respondents were asked: "How many major purchases costing over $300 did you make in the past six months? Please include products as well as services such as repairs to your car, home, etc." Finally, to measure the number of prescription drug purchased, the respondents were asked: "How many purchases of prescription drugs did you make in the past six months? This would be the actual number of prescriptions filled."

ANALYSIS AND RESULTS

The first stage of the analysis was carried out to examine age-related differences in experience of bait-and-switch as well as certain shopping-related behaviors (Table 2). Cross tabulation and χ^2 test were used to test for the relationship between age and shopping-related variables, as well as between age and bait-and-switch experience. Age-related declines in general purchases are evident in the data. For example, there is a decline in the number of major purchases and frequency of in-store purchases with age. While 48.6 percent respondents in the 55-64 age group reported making at least one major purchase in the past six months, only 31.0 percent of the 75+ respondents made such a major purchase (χ^2=24.56, p<.001). Also, while 55.9 percent respondents in the 55-64 age group report making in-store purchases once a week or more often, only 30.7 percent of the 75+ respondents made in-store purchases once a week or more often (χ^2=53.33, p<.001). However, there is an age-related increase in the purchase of prescription drugs, suggesting that the health condition declines with age. For example, while 71.7 percent of the 55-64 age group reported making one or more prescription drug purchases in the past six months, more than four-fifth (82.8%) of the 75+ respondents made one or more prescription drug purchases in the past six months (χ^2=15.89, p<.001).

Almost 94 percent of people in 55-64 age group report that bait-and-switch is an unfair business practice, while only 85.6 percent of those in 75+ age group feel it is unfair (χ^2=10.85, p<.01). Almost 47 percent of the respondents in the 55-64 age group believe that bait-and switch is legal, however, there were no age-related

TABLE 1
Demographic Profile of the Sample

	Percentage (N=917)
Age	
55-64	23.2
65-74	32.7
75+	44.1
Sex	
Male	40.9
Female	59.1
Marital status	
Married	52.3
Widowed/divorced/separated	43.4
Single/never married	4.3
Living status	
Living alone	34.5
Employment status	
Employed (part time or full time)	18.3
Education	
Some high school or less	30.3
High school graduate	33.1
Some college or more	36.6
Income	
Less than $12,000	30.3
$12,000 - $19,999	29.8
$20,000 - $29,999	19.1
$30,000 - $39,999	10.5
$40,000 - $49,999	4.4
$50,000 or more	5.8
Experienced bait-and switch	32.1
Major purchases in the past 6 months (at least one)	40.0
In-store purchases (once a week or more)	44.2
Prescription drugs purchases in the past 6 months (at least one)	81.0

Note: Percentages may not add up to hundred percent due to rounding off

difference (χ^2=1.36,p=.506). The experience of bait-and-switch declines with age. While 53.1 percent of those in the 55-64 age group report having experienced bait-and-switch, only 20.3 percent of those in the 75+ age group report a similar experience (χ^2=68.55, p<.001).

Reported experience of bait-and-switch is also related to some other shopping behaviors. Table-3 shows the relationship between experiencing bait-and-switch and shopping-related variables. Experiencing bait-and-switch is related to the extent of shopping one engages in. For example, among those who had experienced bait-and-switch, 50.9 percent had made a major purchase in the past six months, compared with only 34.9 percent of those who had not

experienced such a practice had made a major purchase (χ^2=20.99, p<.001). Similarly, 53.4 percent of those with such an experience go to stores to purchase something at least once a week, compared with 39.9 percent of those who had not experienced bait-and-switch (χ^2=14.82, p<.001). There was no relationship between the health status of the respondents (as reflected in the purchase of prescription drugs) and experiencing bait-and-switch (χ^2=.72, p=.398). The question still remains to be answered: Is it that the elderly are victimized less or there is some other explanation?

To find answer to the above question, age-related differences in the reported experience of bait-and-switch was examined for those who had made at least one major purchase in the past six

TABLE 2

Relationships Between Age and Selected Variables Relating to Bait-and-Switch Experience

	55-64 % (N=213)	65-74 % (N=300)	75+ % (N=404)	Prob.
Major purchases in the past 6 months (% saying 1 or more)	48.6 [a]	46.0	31.0	.000
In-store purchases (% saying once a week or more frequent)	55.9	54.0	30.7	.000
Number of Prescription drugs purchased (% one or more in the past 6 months)	71.7	85.0	82.8	.000
Is bait and switch unfair business practice (% saying 'yes')	93.9	90.7	85.6	.004
Is bait and switch legal (% saying 'yes')	46.9	47.3	43.3	.506
Have you experienced bait and switch? (% saying 'yes')	53.1	33.0	20.3	.000
Have you experienced bait and switch? (% saying 'yes' among those who have made major purchases) (N=366)	61.2 [b]	38.4	26.4	.000
Experience: same as above but those who go to store once a week or more (N=196)	65.7	42.7	34.1	.000
Experience same as above but those who know that it is illegal practice (N=92)	50.0	47.5	50.0	.972

Note:

[a] read: among those who are in the 55-64 age group, 48.6 percent made at least one major purchase in the past six months.

[b] read: among those who made at least one major purchase in the past six months, and who are in the 55-64 age group, 61.2 percent reported experiencing bait-and switch.

months. The lower portion of Table-2 shows the results of this analysis. When controlled for major purchases, the proportion of the 75+ age group reporting bait-and-switch increased, however, it remains significantly below that of younger people reporting such an experience (χ^2=28.76, p<.001). When in-store purchases and the knowledge were also controlled for, age-related differences in reported experience of bait-and-switch disappear (χ^2=.06, p=.972).

Finally, multivatriate analysis was carried out to assess the relative importance of knowledge about bait-and-switch, shopping-related variables, and age in predicting bait-and-switch experience. Two multiple regression models were built and tested for the same. In the first model, all the variables were entered at the same time. In the second model, the interaction of age and shopping related behaviors were also included in addition to the variables included earlier. The results of these regression analysis are shown in Table 4. As shown in the table, both the regression models were significant (R^2=.09, F=15.08, p<.01 and R^2=.10, F=9.11, p<.01 respectively). When only shopping related variables, and knowl-

edge variables were entered in the equation, age was found to be the most important predictor (β=-.24, t-value=-7.15, p<.01). Major purchases was the next important predictor (β=.11, t-value=3.37, p<.01), and in-store purchase was marginally significant (β=.06, t-value=1.94, p<.10).

When additional terms representing interaction with age were entered in the equation, age continued to be the most important predictor (β=-.33, t-value=-2.62, p<.01). However, the interaction of age and the knowledge it is legal or not turned out to be the next important predictor (β=.12, t-value=2.78, p<.01). Major purchases continued to be another significant predictor (β=.10, t-value=3.21, p<.01). These findings confirm earlier results that experiencing bait-and-switch is a function of shopping related behavior rather than age per se. However, significant interaction term suggests that when older people lack specific knowledge about the legality of such practices they become more vulnerable to fraud than relatively younger people or those who are more knowledgeable.

TABLE 3
Relationships Between Selected Variables and Experience of Bait-and-Switch

	Experienced %	Not-experienced %	Prob.
Major purchases in the past 6 months (% saying 1 or more)	50.9 [a]	34.9	.000
In-store purchases (% saying once a week or more frequent)	53.4	39.9	.000
Number of prescription drugs purchased in the past 6 months (% saying 1 or more)	79.5	81.8	.398
Base	(N=294)	(N=622)	

Note: [a] read: among those who had experienced bait-and-switch, 50.9 percent made at least one major purchase in the past six months.

TABLE 4
Results of Multiple regression analysis

	Beta	t-value	Beta	t-value
Prescription drugs purchased	-.02	-.48	-.01	-.43
In-store purchases	.06	1.94 [b]	.06	1.83 [b]
Major purchases	.11	3.37 [a]	.10	3.21 [a]
Knowledge: is it legal	-.04	-1.21	-.04	-1.13
Knowledge: is it unfair	.01	.36	.01	.26
Age	-.24	-7.15 [a]	-.33	-2.62 [a]
Interaction terms				
Age * Prescription drugs			.05	.73
Age * In-store purchases			-.02	-.47
Age * Major purchases			-.03	-.76
Age * Knowledge: is it legal			.12	2.78 [a]
Age * Knowledge: is it unfair			.00	.01
R^2	.09		.10	
F	15.08 [a]		9.11 [a]	

Note:
[a] $p < .01$
[b] $p < .10$

SUMMARY AND IMPLICATIONS

One of the main findings of this research is that experiencing consumer fraud like bait-and-switch is related to shopping behavior rather than age per se. Although figures of reported cases indicate that among elderly, 'old-old' individuals are victimized less, it may be because they do not shop as often as their relatively younger counterparts, or they do not make major purchases as often. If such reasons are factored in, the older elderly's risk of being victimized by consumer fraud is the same as that for the relatively younger elderly person. Another factor that emerges from these findings is that when old age is associated with lack of consumer information (for example, regarding legality of practices like bait-and-switch) older-old adults become increasingly vulnerable to such consumer fraud. Also, the impact of such victimization on the elderly may be different from that on the younger people. Because of special economic circumstances (fixed income, impact of lower interest rates and inflation), social conditions (limited interaction, even isolation to some degree), and declining psychological well-being (negative self-concept) experienced by the elderly, the impact of such a victimization may be greater on older than on younger victims.

However, some other special circumstances may prevail in the case of the elderly that should be considered. Of great concern to public policy makers and consumer educators is the possibility that many elderly victims may not know that they have been victimized. This finding has important implications for public policy makers and consumer educators. Since there is a strong possibility that elderly may not know specific frauds or their legal rights, government agencies should focus on consumer education. Wider publicity and exposure of the businesses engaging in such practices could also increase awareness. Public policy makers should also consider stricter laws and their enforcement.

REFERENCES

Alston, Letitia A. (1986), *Crime and Older Americans*, Springfield, IL: Charles C. Thomas.

Butler, R. N. (1975), *Why Survive? Being Old in America*, New York: Harper and Row.

Easley, Richard W., James A. Roberts, Mark G. Dunn, and Charles S. Madden (1992), "Diagnosing Consumer Information Problems: An Investigation of Deception in the Mail-Order Video Camcorder Market," *Journal of Public Policy and Marketing*, 11(Fall), 37-44.

Edelhertz, H., M. Walsh, D. Berger, and M. Brintnall (1977), *Consumer Fraud and Abuse: Problems of the Elderly in the Marketplace: A Glossary of Terms and Bibliography*, Seattle, Washington: Batelle Law and Justice Study Center.

Friedman, Monroe (1992), "Confidence Swindles of Older Consumers," *The Journal of Consumer Affairs*, 26(1): 20-46.

Glick, Rush G. and Robert W. Newsom (1974), *Fraud Investigation*, Springfield IL: Charles C. Thomas.

Goldsmith, Jack and Sharon S. Goldsmith eds. (1975), *Crime and the Elderly: Challenge and Response*, National Conference on Crime Against the Elderly, Washington, DC: Lexington MA: Lexington Books.

Hahn, Paul H. (1976), *Crimes Against the Elderly: A Study in Victimology*, Santa Curz: C. A. Davis.

Hofrichter, R. (1982), "Impact of Crime Much Heavier on the Elderly," *Crime Control Digest*, 16, 6-7.

Kosberg, J. I. (1985), "Victimization of the Elderly: Causation and Prevention," *Victimology*, 10(1), 376-396.

Lindquist, John H. and Janice M. Duke (1982), "The Elderly Victim at Risk: Explaining the Fear-Victimization Paradox," *Criminology An Interdisciplinary Journal*, 20(1), May: 115-126.

Mawby, Rob I. (1982), "Crime and the Elderly: A Review of British and American Research," *Current Psychological Reviews*, 2(3) Sept-Dec: 301-310.

McGhee, Jerrie (1983), "The Vulnerability of Elderly Consumers," *International Journal of Aging and Human Development*, 17(3), 223-246.

McGuire, M. V. and H. Edelhertz (1980), "Consumer Abuse of Older Americans: Victimization and Remedial Action in two Metropolitan Areas," in G. Geis and E. Stotland eds. *White Collar Crime: Theory and Research*, Beverly Hills, CA: Sage Publications.

Meeks, Fleming (1990), "Upselling", *Forbes*, 145(1), Jan 8, 70-72.

Midwest Research Institute (1977), *Crimes Against the Aging: Patterns and Prevention*, (Grant number 93-p-75190/7-03 for the Department of Health, Education and Welfare, Office of Human Development), Kansas City Missouri, 1977.

Minkin, Gary (1990), "The Bait and Switch Pyramid," *Insurance Sales*, 133 (Feb), 14-19.

Moschis, George P. (1992), *Marketing to Older Consumers*, Westport CT: Quorum Books.

Newman, Graeme R., Jean C. Jester, Donald J. Articolo (1978), "A Structural Analysis of Fraud," in Edith Flynn and John P. Conrad eds. *The New and the Old Criminology*, New York: Praeger Publishers.

U.S. Senate (1992), *Consumer Fraud and the Elderly: Easy Prey? Hearing Before the Special Committee on Aging United States Senate*, 102 Congress, 2nd Session (S.HERG 102-987).

Zaltman, Gerald, Rajendra Srivastava, and Rohit Deshpande (1978), "Perception of Unfair Marketing Practices: Consumerism Implications," in K. Hunt et al eds. *Advances in Consumer Research*, Volume 5, Provo, UT: Association for Consumer Research, 247-253.

Tracking the Age Wave: Parsimonious Estimation in Cohort Analysis

Roland T. Rust, Vanderbilt University
Kary Wan-Yu Yeung, Vanderbilt University

ABSTRACT

The American population is experiencing major changes in its age distribution, and the burgeoning elderly market is capturing the attention of consumer researchers. The needs and wants of this segment change when different cohorts (generations) fill it at different time periods, and thus a knowledge of the impact of cohort membership, age, and period-specific factors on consumption behavior can help to identify potential marketing opportunities. Cohort analysis refers to research methodologies designed to estimate these effects. A new approach to cohort analysis, parsimonious cohort estimation (PACE), is proposed in this paper. Unlike the predominant existing approach, constrained multiple regression (CMR), PACE is based on a single, well-defined, theoretical criterion, and thus does not require ad hoc constraints. Instead of relying upon ad hoc constraints, PACE finds its solution based on a well accepted theoretical principle, the principle of parsimony, or Occam's razor. Besides its apparent theoretical advantage, PACE also performs better empirically, based on a simulation.

INTRODUCTION

The American population is undergoing widespread demographic changes as we approach the 21st century. Business strategies designed to achieve long run viability should take these projected demographic shifts in the market into consideration. Demographic shifts affect the definition, size, and characteristics of existing market segments. The changes occurring in its existing and potential target markets affect a firm's marketing strategies and profitability. One of the most important current demographic developments is the changing age distribution. Due to the graying of the baby boom generation, the declining fertility rate, and the rising life expectancy, the median age of the population in the year 2040 will be ten years older than the median age today (Leventhal 1990). The size of the 45-54 age group is projected to have an increase of 46% during the last decade of the 20th century (MRI 1990).

Not only is the relative size of the older population changing, but the characteristics of the members of this segment are also changing. The baby boomers, those born from about 1946 through 1964, will comprise the majority of the older population in the following decades. On average, members of the baby boom generation are better educated and more affluent than their parents. Hence their consumption behavior and response to marketing variables are very different from those of their parents, who typically experienced both the Great Depression and the Second World War. Therefore companies which are targeting the older population may find that they need to reevaluate their existing strategies. A study of soft drink consumption (Rentz, Reynolds and Stout 1983) showed that the soft drink industry was unlikely to suffer from the changing age distribution even though most of the consumers were younger people. The authors found that the consumption of soft drinks remained fairly stable over a person's life-course. Hence, the total amount of soft drink consumption should increase as the present older population is replaced by the baby boom cohort. The predictions of those researchers have so far been borne out. According to Beverage Industry Annual Manual (Edgell 1991), soft drink consumption has gone up 4% since 1983.

Since the wants and needs of the members of an age group may change as different cohorts fill it, a firm that is targeting an age group is at the same time also targeting a specific cohort. Therefore, to profit from the expanding elderly market, it is important for manufacturers and marketers of products and services to have a good knowledge of the changing needs and consumption behavior of this segment due to the cohort effect (factors that are peculiar to a particular cohort). Besides cohort- and age-based factors, a person's consumption pattern at a specific point in time is also influenced by the events happening during that time period. Hence time-specific factors should also be taken into consideration in formulating marketing strategy.

Estimating the age, cohort and period effects is problematic because the effects cannot be unambiguously determined. For instance, the change in the behavior of the baby boomers from their teenage stage to their mature stage is a function of both the age effect and the period effect. Only the combined effects of the two factors can be estimated unambiguously. In other words, there is no unique solution for each individual effect. Research methodology that formulates criteria for choosing the solution of the effect estimates is called cohort analysis. Cohort analysis has been applied in the areas of sociology, medical research, demographic and marketing research (Adams et al. 1990; Akers 1965; Clogg 1982; Frost 1939; Rentz et al. 1983; Rentz and Reynolds 1991; Sacher 1987; Sasaki and Susuki 1987). This paper proposes to use the principle of parsimony or Occam's razor (Cohen and Nagel 1934; Hempel 1966), a criterion which is widely applied in science, for choosing the solution of the cohort, period, and age effects. According to this principle, the simplest explanation among all competing explanations to the phenomenon of interest is preferred. The parsimonious solution is preferred because it is more readily falsified and therefore better testable.

Section 2 describes the essence of cohort analysis and Section 3 presents the parsimonious cohort estimation (PACE), its formulation and estimation procedure. In Section 4, the performance of PACE is compared to the performance of the predominant existing approach. Conclusions are given in Section 5.

COHORT ANALYSIS

The Conceptual Basis of Cohort Analysis

A cohort is an aggregation of people who enter a social system within the same time period. An alternative and more commonly used definition of cohort is a group of people who share an experience within the same time period (Glenn 1977). The experience used to delineate the population varies across studies. It can be marriage, education status, geographical location, or birth. Since the focus of this study is on birth cohorts, the term "cohort" will be used hereafter to mean "birth cohort". The boundary of the time period categorizing each cohort is arbitrary, with the interval length usually ranging from one to ten years. Homogeneity is not assumed within each cohort, but members of each cohort share the same macro-political, -cultural, -socio, -economic environment. Due to the differences in historical experience and peer group socializing process, each cohort has its unique characteristics. As a result, members of one cohort exhibit distinct behavioral patterns from members of other cohorts. The study of the differences in a phenomenon due to cohort effects (effects which are associated with cohort membership) is the domain of cohort analysis. Specifically, cohort analysis is a group of research techniques which

Advances in Consumer Research
Volume 22, © 1995

examine and estimate the relationships between cohort identification and the phenomenon of interest.

Demographic researchers have long been studying the extent to which cohort membership affects the fertility rate and mortality rate of certain age categories (Mason and Fienberg 1985). Medical researchers have found that the changes in the rate of tuberculosis mortality rate are cohort-based (Frost 1939; Mason and Fienberg 1985). In social science, there are studies of the impact of cohort membership on the changes in political sentiment (Adams et al. 1990; Hout and Knoke 1975; Mason and Fienberg 1985). In marketing, Rentz, Reynolds and Stout (1983) and Rentz and Reynolds (1991) have studied the impact of cohort membership on soft drink consumption.

Cross-sectional comparison of cohorts, without taking the age factor into consideration can be misleading. For instance, the difference in fertility rate between women in their 20's and women in their 40's is mainly age-related. Due to the differences in physiological condition caused by aging, younger women have a higher fertility rate than older women. The fact that the younger cohort is more educated, more mobile, more career oriented, and has access to advanced birth control devices contributes less to the difference in fertility rate. In general, an older person differs from a younger person in several dimensions, such as physical condition and the extent of exposure to social influence. Therefore, when two cohorts are compared at one point of time, their age difference has to be accounted for. Without including age effects (factors associated with aging), spurious findings may be obtained.

Investigating the aging effect is important not only for a better understanding of the cohort effect; it itself is the motivation of many cohort studies. The effects of aging are examined in many attitudinal and behavioral studies such as party identification, voter turnout, ideological conformity, church attendance, and alcoholic beverages consumption (Adams et al. 1990; Hout and Knoke 1974; Knoke and Hout 1975; Mason and Fienberg 1985). In these studies, the cohort effect is a nuisance variable that masks the aging effect.

In most cohort analyses, intra-cohort comparison is also used to measure the period effect. Period effect is the impact of factors that are associated with the time period under survey. The factors are events which have significant influence on individuals during that particular period. Period effect influences all cohorts at the same point in time and therefore at different lifestages of each cohort. Researchers measure characteristics of two or more cohorts at two or more points in time to examine the impact of the period-specific stimuli such as economic recession and political instability. In this paper, we are looking at both inter- and intra-cohort comparison.

The Cohort Analysis Model

Cohort analysis, due to its cross-sectional as well as longitudinal nature, is applied mostly to data in the form of age by period. A typical cohort data structure may be illustrated by a table in which age groups are rows and time periods are columns (see Table 1).

Each entry in the table is the measurement of a response variable of interest(Y) such as mortality rate, fertility rate, consumption rate. The ij entry is the measurement of Y of the sample segment that belongs to age category i at time j. The columns are equally spaced time periods. The rows are age categories with the same spacing as the time periods. Each of the I+J-1 diagonals corresponds to one cohort. The I by J cohort table contains information for both the inter- and intra-cohort comparisons. Information on inter- and intra-cohort comparisons can be traced by reading down the columns and the diagonals respectively. Time trends at each age level can be traced by reading across the corresponding row.

The cohort model assumes that the response variable Y is a linear function of the age effects, the cohort effects and the period effects. The basic model is formulated as:

$$(1) \qquad Y_{ijk} = \mu + A_i + P_j + C_k + e_{ijk}$$

$$with: \sum_{i=1}^{I} A_i = 0, \sum_{j=1}^{J} P_j = 0, \sum_{k=1}^{K} C_k = 0, \sum_{ij=1}^{IJ} e_{iik} = 0,$$
$$K = I + J - 1$$

where μ is the overall mean, A_i's are the age effects, P_j's are the period effects, C_k's are the cohort effects, and e_{ijk} is the random error which is assumed to be normally distributed with mean 0 and variance σ_e^2. The expected value of Y_{ijk} is:

$$(2) \qquad E(Y_{ijk}) = \mu + A_i + P_j + C_k$$

A_i, C_k and P_j are the deviations from the average due to aging, cohort membership, and effects of events happened at specific time periods respectively. They are the parameters to be estimated. The predominant method of estimating a cohort model is constrained multiple regression (CMR) (Mason et al. 1973).

There are a number of applications of CMR in cohort studies (e.g., Hout and Knoke 1974; Knoke and Hout 1975; Rentz et al. 1983; Rentz and Reynolds 1991). Rentz, Reynolds, and Stout (1983) and Rentz and Reynolds (1991) applied this method in their study of soft drink consumption in the United States. In the first paper, the variables which were of the least interest were chosen for the equality constraints. In the period models, the effects of two ages and the effects of two cohorts were set to be equal. The effects of two periods and the effects of two cohorts were set to be equal in the age models and the effects of two ages and the effects of two periods were set to be equal in the cohort models. The cohort models had the best fit. In the second paper, the use of prior knowledge and all available side information was emphasized. Specifically, the period effect of 1950 and 1960 were set to equal because there was substantial decline in coffee consumption due to concern about caffeine in the 1960's and 1970's. Since there was no specific prior knowledge about the age effects and cohort effects, minimum inter-class difference within each category was used as the criterion for choosing the equality constraints.

A NEW APPROACH TO COHORT ANALYSIS

Parsimonious Cohort Estimation (PACE)

The principle of parsimony (simplicity or Occam's razor) is one of the criteria used by scientists to determine the acceptability of a hypothesis or a theory, compared with that of alternative theories which would account for the same phenomenon. It is often illustrated by reference to the Copernican heliocentric theory which was considerably simpler than Ptolemy's geocentric theory (Cohen and Nagle 1934; Hempel 1966). Both theories can explain the apparent motions of the sun, moon, and planets, and in the sixteenth century, both produced the same predictions (except for the phases of Venus). The heliocentric theory was found to be simpler by Copernicus and his contemporaries and therefore was preferred.

A parsimonious theory does not have to be a familiar one. If familiarity is used as a criterion of parsimony, no new theory would be accepted and the choice would vary from person to person. Though the concept of parsimony is not well-defined, two criteria are suggested as indicators of complexity (Cohen and Nagle 1934; Hempel 1966): the number of independent concepts used and the number of assumptions used.

TABLE 1
Hypothetical Set of Data for a Cohort Analysis

	Time of measurement		
Age class	1970	1980	1990
40-49	20(c3)	25(c4)	30(c5)
50-59	30(c2)	35(c3)	35(c4)
60-69	35(c1)	35(c2)	40(c3)

c1 Cohort born 1901-1910.
c2 Cohort born 1911-1920.
c3 Cohort born 1921-1930.
c4 Cohort born 1931-1940.
c5 Cohort born 1941-1950.

For two competing theories, the one that uses fewer number of concepts or variables is simpler and therefore is preferred.

A theory is also simpler if it requires fewer assumptions. Heliocentric theory is simpler because it can account for astronomical phenomena in terms of its fundamental ideas without introducing assumptions ad hoc. Special assumptions have to be made, ad hoc, if the geocentric theory is used for explaining the same phenomena (Cohen and Nagel 1934).

There are several justifications for the preference given to simpler theories. Here the view advanced by Popper (Popper 1959) is presented. Popper argues that simpler theory is more readily falsified, if indeed it should be false, and therefore it is better testable. For instance, suppose that the following two functions are proposed to account for the variation in U:

U=2X + W
U=2X

If W is the true factor affecting U, but not X, the second function is more readily falsified by empirical evidence. In some cases, the simpler theory is stronger because it logically implies the more complex one. For example, suppose that a variable X is hypothesized as a linear function of another variable Y and two functions are proposed to account for the relationship:

X=aY + b
X=c(aY + b)

The first function is simpler and logically implies the second function. If the first one is falsified, the second function is automatically falsified.

The following section will present the technique used to achieve the parsimonious solution to the cohort problem according to the criteria mentioned above.

Cohort Analysis as a Nonlinear Programming Problem

The age-period-cohort problem is formulated in such a way that the solution obtained is maximally parsimonious. For a solution to be parsimonious, it has to have:

(a) the fewest number of variables, and/or
(b) the fewest number of assumptions.

In order to achieve the first criterion, a three-step approach is proposed:

1. Minimize the error sum of squares.
2. Require the fewest number of the independent variables to explain the dependent variable.
3. Have the smallest absolute values of the estimates.

To facilitate the understanding of the rationale behind the approach, the cohort model presented in Section 2 is reproduced:

$$(3) \qquad Y_{ijk} = \mu + A_i + P_j + C_k + e_{ijk}$$

$$with: \quad \sum_{i=1}^{I} A_i = 0, \ \sum_{j=1}^{J} P_j = 0, \ \sum_{k=1}^{K} C_k = 0, \ \sum_{ij=1}^{IJ} e_{iik} = 0,$$

$$K = I + J - 1$$

Minimizing the sum of squares error is an attempt to eliminate e_{ijk} from the equation. It is given the highest priority, not only because it directly corresponds to goodness of fit, but also because there is a unique error term associated with every response value Y_{ijk}. By eliminating e_{ijk}, we reduce the number of explanatory variables for the variation in Y by I*J. Step two attempts to further reduce the number of variables required for explaining the variation in Y. The fewer the number of effects are included in the equation, the more parsimonious the explanation is. For two competing models with the same number of explanatory variables, the one that has the smallest absolute value of the effect estimates is preferred according to step three. Finally, since having effect estimates equal to zero is maximally parsimonious (meeting the conditions of step two), we seek to make the model as parsimonious as possible by making the effect estimates as close to zero as possible in step three.

This three-step approach is lexicographic in nature. The three properties correspond to three ranked minimization objectives. To facilitate estimation, a compensatory model is specified to approximate the lexicographic minimum. The objectives are combined as if they are commensurable and weights are assigned to them so that they are expressed in a single performance measure. The weights are assigned in such a way that the preemptive priority structure is preserved. Accordingly, the following nonlinear programming problem is formulated to obtain the parsimonious solution which will have the three minimization objectives.

$$(4)\ Minimize\ h\ = M1[\sum_{i=1}^{I} A_i^2 + \sum_{j=1}^{J} P_j^2 + \sum_{k=1}^{K} C_k^2] +$$

$$+ M2[(\sum_{i=1}^{I} A_i^2) + (\sum_{j=1}^{J} P_j^2) + (\sum_{k=1}^{K} C_k^2) + (\sum_{j=1}^{J} P_j^2)(\sum_{k=1}^{K} C_k^2)] +$$

$$+ M3[(\sum_{i=1}^{I} A_i^2) + (\sum_{j=1}^{J} P_j^2) + (\sum_{k=1}^{K} C_k^2)] +$$

$$+ M4[\sum_{s=1}^{IJ} e_s^2]$$

$$with\ \sum_{i=1}^{I} A_i = \sum_{j=1}^{J} P_j = \sum_{k=1}^{K} C_k = \sum_{s=1}^{IJ} e_s^2 = 0$$

M1, M2, M3, and M4 are weights, with $0 << M1 << M2 << M3 << M4$ (<< symbolizes "much less than"). The e's are residuals. The function h is minimized with respect to the A_i's, P_j's, C_k's, and the e's. Step 1 is satisfied if (IV) is minimized. Step 2 is satisfied if (II) and (III) are minimized. (III) is minimized if all the effect parameters of one of the three variables (age effect, period effect, and cohort effect) are equal to zero. (II) is minimized if the effect parameters of two of the variables are equal to zero. Hence by minimizing line two and three, we are minimizing the number of variables required to explain the dependent variable (step 2). Step 3 is satisfied if (I) is minimized. The weights are assigned in such a way that the difference between two successive weights, for instance M3 and M4, is big enough to guarantee that (IV) is minimized first, followed by (III), (II) and (I) successively. Hence, the priority specified in the three-step process is achieved.
To achieve the second criterion of parsimony, no assumption external to the basic structure of the cohort model would be imposed in the estimation process.

Model Estimation

The nonlinear function h is solved using the subroutine NCONG, a Fortran code developed by Schittkowski(1986). It uses a successive quadratic programming method to solve the nonlinear function. No constraints are imposed other than that the estimates have to satisfy the conditions in (3). No information external to the data is used in the estimation of the effect parameters. To operationalize (4), we use 0.001, 2.5. 99, and 99999 to be the value of M1, M2, M3, M4, respectively. We have found these values to work well on trial data.
Starting values for the effect parameters and the error terms are required for searching the optimal solution. Since only local optima are found by NCONG, different sets of starting values should be used to generate solutions. There are many ways in which the starting values might be selected. For our analysis we choose starting values in such a way that each one of them is a desirable potential solution to the minimization problem. For example, one set of starting values would have only cohort effects and another set would have only time effects.

COMPARATIVE PERFORMANCE TESTING

The relative ability of PACE and CMR to represent the true process that generates the data is studied in this section. The testing consists of a simulation which compares the abilities of the two methods to recover true model parameters.

A Simulation of the Comparative Performance of PACE and CMR

A simulation is performed to compare the estimation accuracy of PACE and CMR. The design and results are described next.
Design. 240 random data sets are generated, reflecting 10 replications each for all combinations of three error variances (0, 10, 20) and eight true models. Thus we have 10 replications in a 3x8 full factorial design. The eight true models are:

(1) $Y = \mu + A + \varepsilon$
(2) $Y = \mu + P + \varepsilon$
(3) $Y = \mu + C + \varepsilon$
(4) $Y = \mu + A + P + \varepsilon$
(5) $Y = \mu + A + C + \varepsilon$
(6) $Y = \mu + P + C + \varepsilon$
(7) $Y = \mu + A + P + C + \varepsilon$
(8) $Y = \mu + \varepsilon$

All effect parameters are assumed to be normally distributed with mean 0 and variance 10. Thus we first sample the effect parameters, which we then assume to be constant across replications. We then sample an error term for each replication. For simple interpretation of results, we set $\mu = 0$. (This has no effect on the results.) Every data set is in the form of a cohort table with four age groups, four time periods, and seven cohort groups. In total 3840 data points are employed in the simulation.
To operationalize PACE, eight different starting points are constructed for each data set. We choose as our solution the one that generates the minimum value of h specified in Equation (10). As for CMR, equality constraints have to be set up for each data set. According to Rentz and Reynolds (1991), prior knowledge and all available side information should be used to determine the constraints. Since there is no prior knowledge, we assign a constraint in the commonly accepted manner: the two effect levels with the most similar means are set to be equal.
Results. The mean square errors of the effect estimates (calculated as deviations from the true parameter values) are used to compare the estimation accuracy of PACE and CMR. The degrees of freedom used for calculating the mean square error of an effect are:

(number of categories of the effect - 1) x 240

Therefore, the degrees of freedom for both the time and age effects are (4-1) x 240, and the degrees of freedom for the cohort effects are (7-1) x 240. The results are summarized in Table 2. In all three cases, PACE greatly outperforms CMR. The results should not be surprising. CMR imposes arbitrary assumptions on the data; therefore it does not perform well. In consumer research, researchers and practitioners mostly deal with data which do not have known and well-established prior knowledge. Using CMR for cohort analysis may result in erroneous findings.

CONCLUSIONS

The ability of a company to make accurate business forecasts is essential for the long term viability of the company. Knowledge of the changes taking place in the micro- and macro-environment is an important input in forecasting. One of the most important current shifts in the macro-environment is the changing age distribution. The American population is aging. The 45-54 bracket is expected to grow 46% by the year 2000. By contrast, the 25-34 bracket is expected to have a 15.4% decline (MRI 1990). Product

TABLE 2
MSE of Effect Estimates Obtained From Pace and CMR

Effect category	PACE	CMR	PACE/CMR
Age effect	3.38	73.3	0.046
Period effect	2.97	122.9	0.024
Cohort effect	3.00	511.8	0.006

categories targeting older audience will benefit as their universe of customers expands. However, the correlation between age and consumer behavior is complicated by the cohort phenomenon. The baby boomers, who will comprise the majority of the older population in the following decades, will carry some of their consumption patterns with them as they age. This is good news for marketers who have been targeting age groups that are shrinking. As for marketers who have been targeting the older audience, their traditional strategies may not be effective because the consumption behavior and response to marketing variables of the baby boom generation are very different from those of their parents. To identify opportunities in the growing elderly market, a knowledge of the cohort, age, and period effects on consumer behavior is crucial.

Estimating the effects is problematic because the effects cannot be unambiguously determined. There exists no unique solution for each individual effect. Cohort analysis is a group of methods designed to separate cohort, age, and period effects. This paper proposes a new approach, parsimonious cohort estimation (PACE), to the cohort estimation problem. A non-linear programming problem is formulated to operationalize the model. A simulation was performed to test the performance of PACE in comparison to the performance of CMR, the predominant existing approach in cohort analysis. The results suggest that PACE performs much better. Since PACE is an objective procedure (unlike CMR), has a clear theoretical basis (unlike CMR), and performed much better in a simulation test, we recommend the adoption of PACE (over CMR) as the standard method of conducting cohort analysis.

In conclusion, a new approach to cohort analysis is proposed in this paper. PACE has a theoretical advantage over the predominant existing approach and is demonstrated to be better empirically. The solutions obtained from PACE should aid researchers in understanding the cohort, age, and period effects on consumer behavior, and in formulating effective life-stage marketing oriented strategies.

REFERENCES

Adams, Wendy L., Philip J. Garry, Robert Rhyne, and James S. Goodwin (1990), "Alcohol Intake in the Healthy Elderly: Changes with Age in a Cross-Sectional and Longitudinal Study," *Journal of the American Geriatrics Society*, 38 (March), 211-216.

Akers, D.S. (1965), "Cohort Fertility Versus Parity Progression as Method of Projecting Births," *Demography*, 2 (1965), 414-428.

Clogg, Clifford C. (1982), "Cohort Analysis of Recent Trends in Labor Force Participation," *Demography*, 19 (November), 459-479.

Cohen, Morris R. and Ernest Nagel (1934), *An Introduction to Logic and Scientific Method*, New York, NY: Harcourt, Brace and Company.

Edgell Communications, Inc. (1991), *Beverage Industry Annual Manual*, Cleveland, OH: Magazines for Industry.

Frost, W.H. (1939), "The Age Selection of Mortality from Tuberculosis in Successive Decades," *American Journal of Hygiene*, 30 (1939), 91-96.

Glenn, Norval D. (1977), *Cohort Analysis*, Beverly Hills, CA: Sage.

Hempel, Carl Gustav (1966), *Philosophy of Natural Science*, Englewood Cliffs, NJ: Prentice-Hall.

Hout, Michael and David Knoke (1974), "Social and Demographic Factors in American Political Party Affiliations, 1952-1972," *American Sociological Review*, 39 (1975), 700-713.

_____ , _____ (1975), "Changes in Voting Turnout, 1952-1972," *Public Opinion Quarterly*, 39 (1975), 52-68.

Leventhal, Richard C. (1990), "The Aging Consumer: What's All the Fuss About Anyway?" *Journal of Services Marketing*, 4 (Summer), 39-44.

Mason, Karen Oppenheim, H.H. Winsborough, William M. Mason, and W. Kenneth Poole (1973), "Some Methodological Issues in Cohort Analysis of Archival Data," *American Sociological* Review, 38 (April), 242-258.

Mason, William and Stephen E. Fienberg (1985), *Cohort Analysis in Social Research*, New York, NY: Springer-Verlag New York Inc.

Mediamark Research Inc. (1990), *Targeting Consumers at the Crossroads of Their Lives*, New York, NY: Mediamark Research Inc.

Popper, Karl Raimund (1959), *The Logic of Scientific Discovery*, New York, NY: Basic Books.

Rentz, Joseph D., Fred D. Reynolds, and Roy G. Stout (1983), "Analyzing Changing Consumption Patterns with Cohort Analysis," *Journal of Marketing Research*, 20 (February), 12-20.

_____ , and _____ (1991), "Forecasting the Effects of an Aging Population on Product Consumption: An Age-Period-Cohort Framework," *Journal of Marketing Research*, 28 (August), 355-360.

Sacher, G.A. (1977), "Life Table Modification and Life Prolongation," in *Handbook of the Biology of Aging*, eds. C.E. Finch and L. Hayflick, New York, NY: Van Nostrand Rinehold, 582-683.

Sasaki, Masamichi and Tatsuzo Suzuki (1987), "Changes in Religious Commitment in the United States, Holland, and Japan," *American Journal of Sociology*, 92 (March), 1055-1076.

Schittkowski, K. (1986), "NLPQL: A FORTRAN Subroutine Solving Constrained Nonlinear Programming Problems," (edited by Clyde L. Monma), *Annals of Operations Research*, 5, 485-500.

The Institutionalized Consumer

T. Bettina Cornwell, University of Memphis
Terrance G. Gabel, University of Memphis

ABSTRACT

Despite rapid growth and increased levels of consumer choice within the institutionalized population in the United States, the consumer behavior of these 3.33 million individuals has been largely ignored. Through both analysis of pertinent literature, as well as the presentation of findings from multiple field studies, this paper provides a preliminary examination of the consumer behavior of institutionalized persons. Specifically, in light of constraints inherent in diverse institutionalized environments, the effects of institutionalization on both the current and future consumption behaviors of institutionalized individuals, their friends, and family members as well are discussed in regard to surrogate consumer usage and gift-giving behaviors.

"It has gotten to the point where jail is almost becoming an acceptable life style." - *New York Times*, July 24, 1992.

According to 1990 Census data, there are more than 6.6 million Americans living in non-household settings or "group-quarters" (U.S. Bureau of the Census 1990). Of these individuals, nearly half are classified as "institutionalized persons." In fact, in 1990, 1.34 percent of the total American population—over one out of every 100 persons—was institutionalized in some form or another.

Despite the large and growing number of institutionalized persons in the U.S., the consumer behavior of these individuals has been largely ignored by marketing and consumer behavior researchers. This is perhaps because much of the purchasing for persons confined to institutions, for whatever reason, has historically taken place at the institutional level, where little individual end-consumer choice was involved. While this may have been the case in the past, there is now evidence that consumer choice alternatives for the institutionalized are expanding, and will continue to do so to an even greater extent, in coming years. As a result, there will be an even greater need to understand the consumer behavior of institutionalized individuals.

The purpose of this paper is to provide a preliminary examination of the consumer behavior of institutionalized persons. Through both analysis of pertinent literature, as well as the presentation of findings from multiple field studies, we examine the pervasive effects of institutionalization on both the current and future consumption behaviors of institutionalized individuals, their friends, and family members. Specific consumer research issues discussed include both surrogate consumer usage, which is likely to be prevalent among the institutionalized due to the fact that direct purchase and consumption is restricted, and gift-giving behaviors, where surrogate usage may manifest itself. In this regard, a series of propositions is developed to both stimulate and guide future research efforts. Also, suggestions are offered concerning how marketers and public policy makers might best use this information to most effectively and responsibly meet the needs of the growing institutionalized consumer population.

INSTITUTIONALIZED CONSUMERS IN THE UNITED STATES

Examination of census information reveals that the number of institutionalized Americans has been growing for at least the last 20 years, increasing from a total of 2.13 million in 1970 (U.S. Bureau of the Census 1970) to 2.51 million in 1980 (U.S. Bureau of the Census 1980), then rising sharply to the current total of 3.33 million (U.S. Bureau of the Census 1990). Table 1 also illustrates other interesting trends with respect to the institutionalized population. Most notably, in 1970, census information included only three categories of institutionalized persons, with a staggering 36.4 percent of these individuals classified as "other inmates."[1] This possibly reflects a trend in recent years to better understand the heterogeneous nature of the institutionalized population. Also, the increasing number of nursing home patients over the last two decades is evident, due largely to the continuing aging of the American population. Moreover, note in Table 1 that both the absolute number and overall proportion of mental patients has dropped dramatically over the last twenty years, possibly indicative of public policy of the 1980s reflecting perceptions of mental problems not as organic illnesses, but rather as controllable, "deviant aspects" of the sufferer.

With both the increased focus of the Clinton Presidential Administration on social welfare reform programs (Andreasen 1993), as well as the aging of the American population, the size of the institutionalized population is likely to continue to escalate in coming years. Specifically, while the number of persons confined to correctional facilities is difficult to forecast due to ongoing ethical and economic debates regarding how to best deal with the problems of rampant crime and prison overcrowding, the number of individuals living in many other types of institutions, such as drug and alcohol rehabilitation centers and mental hospitals, is likely to increase dramatically.

In addition to the documented growth of the institutionalized population in recent years, also noteworthy is the fact that figures such as those reported in Table 1 tell but part of the story regarding the magnitude of institutionalization in the United States. In that persons often move in and out of institutions over the course of their lives, the reported numbers of persons living in institutions at any one time greatly understates the number of individuals that experience institutionalized living at some point in their lives. For example, although the percentage of the elderly in nursing homes is relatively small at any given time, nearly half of those people turning 65 in 1990 are likely to reside in a nursing home at some time in the future (Crispell and Frey 1993).

While the institutionalized population continues to grow, there is also strong evidence suggesting that consumer choice alternatives for many of these individuals are expanding. For example, increased personal freedoms among prison inmates such as cable and satellite television, more diverse meal choices, free phone calls and newspaper delivery, as well as the choice of wearing comfortable non-prison-issue clothing, have been well documented in recent years (see Helliker 1992; Henslik, et al. 1992; New York Times 1992). In light of these amenities, prison has been discussed as a viable life-style choice (New York Times 1992). As

---

[1] Given the title "other *inmate*" and the corresponding percentage of 1990 correctional institution inhabitants, it can be assumed that many of the 775,114 "other inmates" in 1970 were in fact incarcerated in jails and prisons of one form or another.

TABLE 1
Number of Institutionalized Individuals by Type of Institution (1990 and 1970)

TYPE OF INSTITUTION	1990 POPULATION	1990 PERCENT	1970 POPULATION	1970 PERCENT
NURSING HOMES	1,772,032	53.15	927,514	43.6
CORRECTIONAL INSTITUTIONS	1,115,111	33.45	NA	NA
MENTAL (PSYCHIATRIC) HOSPITALS	128,530	3.86	424,091	19.9
JUVENILE INSTITUTIONS	104,200	3.13	NA	NA
SCHOOLS, HOSPITALS, OR WARDS FOR THE MENTALLY RETARDED	103,713	3.11	NA	NA
HOSPITALS OR WARDS FOR THE CHRONICALLY ILL	40,980	1.23	NA	NA
WARDS IN GENERAL AND MILITARY HOSPITALS WITH PATIENTS WHO HAVE NO USUAL HOME ELSEWHERE	28,669	.86	NA	NA
SCHOOLS, HOSPITALS, OR WARDS FOR THE PHYSICALLY HANDICAPPED	20,654	.62	NA	NA
HOSPITALS OR WARDS FOR DRUG/ALCOHOL ABUSE	20,129	.60	NA	NA
OTHER INMATE	NA	NA	775,114	36.4
TOTAL	3,334,018	100.01	2,126,719	99.9

(Sources: U.S. Bureau of the Census (1990), *Census of Population: General Population Characteristics*. Washington, D.C.: U.S. Government Printing Office, p. 48; U.S. Bureau of the Census (1970), *Census of Population: Detailed Characteristics*. Washington, D.C.: U.S. Government Printing Office, p. 1-656.)

such, contrary to traditional perceptions of these individuals as non-consumers, totally isolated from society, institutionalized persons now represent an emerging consumer segment worthy of both consumer researcher and marketer attention.

Reported numbers of the institutionalized also fail to adequately address the impact of such living arrangements on millions of friends and family members. Moreover, as evidenced in numerous studies of the institutionalized elderly (see Baltes and Wahl 1992; High 1990; Novak and Guest 1992), the consumption behaviors of all affected individuals may be significantly influenced long after the period(s) of institutionalization. Following a brief discussion of the research methodology employed in this study, implications for both the current and future consumption behavior of institutionalized individuals are examined below.

RESEARCH METHODOLOGY
Several exploratory field studies eliciting testimony from either family-member informants or actual institutionalized persons, representing the four largest segments of the institutionalized population, were conducted in order to uncover distinct consumer behavior patterns. This highly humanistic research varied in specific methodology employed, ranging from totally emergent to semi-directed in nature. With emergent methods, the primary purpose was to find emergent patterns of behavior (i.e., phenomenological constructs) to serve as the basis for further investigation and analysis. The goal of the semi-directed interviews was to both ascertain the worth of several a priori assumptions, as well as to gain more in-depth knowledge of specific forms of institutionalized

consumer behavior. What follows is a brief discussion of the individual studies conducted.

Group Discussion with Juvenile Wards of the State
A series of discussions was held with a group of fifteen teens, ages 11 through 17. These individuals were temporary wards of the state and were participating in an educational program provided in conjunction with their living accommodation. Three of the fifteen—two female and one male—were parents themselves, with children living apart from them outside of the institutionalized environment. The researcher was allowed to talk with the children in a group setting while an assistant took notes. Tape recording of the discussions was not deemed appropriate by the institution.

Stressing contextualistic emergence in the existential-phenomenology tradition (Thompson, Locander, and Pollio 1989), the teens were asked general, open-ended questions regarding how they "earn" money, the products they buy, and the places they shop. They were allowed to talk freely about these matters with little further direction, other than to use some of their statements as the subject matter of subsequent, more specific, questions. General behavioral patterns were thus allowed to emerge as the discussions transpired.

In-depth Interviews with Family Members of Institutionalized Consumers
Individual in-depth interviews were conducted with three family members of both former and current institutionalized persons, including:

- the 65-year-old mother of a former drug and alcohol rehabilitation patient—a 40-year-old male—who spent a total of approximately three years in several different institutions
- the 62-year-old son of a woman who spent the last five to six years of her life in a number of nursing-home settings, and
- the sister-in-law of a current prison inmate—a 38-year-old male—convicted of larceny, who has been in and out of correctional facilities since the age of 14.

The interviews were structured around both the asking of several general open-ended questions, as well as more specific response-generated and a priori researcher inquiries. The interviews were tape-recorded and then analyzed in detail to both detect and examine emergent behavioral themes, as well as to assess the value of a priori researcher assumptions.

Interview with a Representative of a Community-Service Organization

A telephone interview was conducted with a representative of a community-service organization catering to both the spiritual and material needs of local prison inmates. This interview, prompted by researcher viewing of local television news coverage pertaining to the organization's activities, was conducted to clarify details of the service programs therein discussed, as well as to gain insight into additional services performed by the organization. As such, researcher questions included general inquiries about the organization's operations, as well as ones aimed specifically towards clarification of issues raised by television news reports. The interview was documented through the taking of notes by the researcher.

INSTITUTIONALIZED CONSUMER BEHAVIOR

Several existent areas of consumer behavior theory and research are applicable to the study of the consumption behavior of institutionalized individuals. While what might be called "normal" consumption behavior is irrefutably disrupted by institutionalization, "direct" purchase, consumption, and disposal of goods and services still occur in institutionalized environments. For example, the mother of the drug and alcohol rehabilitation patient we spoke to stated that she frequently gave her son "spending money" with which he was able to purchase goods (cigarettes) or services (haircuts) several hours each week, outside of institutional grounds, and with little or no supervision. Likewise, the teenage wards of the state interviewed were given several hundred dollars upon entering the institution with which to purchase clothing and other personal items. These individuals—both the teenagers and the rehabilitation patient—were also able to earn money through working at the institution, which could then be spent on goods and services.

In addition to "direct" consumption activity, other relevant consumer behavior issues among the institutionalized include the usage of surrogate consumers and the gift-giving behaviors of these individuals.

Surrogate Consumer Usage

With but few exceptions, surrogate consumer research has focused on those individuals most willing and able to formally employ the services of third-party "expert" agents to perform various consumption activities on their behalf. Researchers (e.g. Forsythe, Butler, and Schaefer 1990; Fuller and Blackwell 1992; Hollander 1971; Solomon 1986), have consistently found that consumers characterized by high levels of income and "upper"

social class affiliation are most likely to employ surrogates. As a result, what has emerged from this research is but a partial picture of surrogate consumer usage.

Because of their varying levels of inability to consummate consumption activities, 3.33 million institutionalized Americans must rely on some form of surrogate intervention. Our research suggests that friends and family members of the institutionalized individual are most likely to serve in this capacity. For example, the mother of the alcohol and drug rehabilitation patient we interviewed stated that she frequently—once a week—purchased for and delivered to her son toiletry products, items of clothing, and cigarettes. The son of the woman confined to a number of different nursing homes for the last several years of her life likewise told us that he and his six brothers often bought their mother food and clothing items, as well as selected over-the-counter medications. In a more restricted institutional setting, the sister-in-law of the prison inmate reported that she too—although less frequently so—acted as a surrogate consumer, purchasing and delivering "factory sealed" food products, toiletries, and items of clothing such as "tennis shoes" to wear in place of the ones provided by the institution. Interestingly, in regard to the food items—predominantly candy—requested by and purchased for the prisoner, our informant stated that she frequently had not heard of the products. She further stated that she assumed that her brother-in-law received his "cutting-edge" new product information as a result of frequent television viewing.

Virtually all institutionalized consumers are likely to rely on surrogates to some degree, with the identity and nature of the surrogate varying by type of institutional setting. While the above discussion has focused on the provision of surrogate services by family members, in the case of many institutionalized individuals, society itself, or charitable organizations may serve as the surrogate consumer. For example, as the sister-in-law of the prison inmate told us, if it were not for her and her husband's buying requested food and clothing items for the prisoner, he would have to make do with prison-provided goods. In the case of the latter, the institutionalized consumer must depend—by default—upon the surrogate services provided by society at large in order to meet basic consumption needs. Furthermore, it is not only those in the most restricted of institutionalized settings that depend on societally based surrogates. As the mother of the drug and alcohol rehabilitation patient we spoke to told us, her son and his fellow patients were allowed to go to local Salvation Army facilities once a month to "shop" for free donated goods. Also, these same individuals were often the recipients of food items such as cookies and donuts donated by charitable organizations.

Gift-Giving Behavior

Gift-giving behavior may manifest itself in either interpersonal or intrapersonal form (see Mick and DeMoss 1992), each of which are discussed separately below.

Interpersonal Gift Giving. Gift giving, as a form of reciprocity or exchange, is one of the processes that integrates a society (Sherry 1983). As such, it is often assumed that institutionalized individuals, given their supposed separation and isolation from society, engage in little or no gift-giving behavior. However, findings of our studies appear to refute this assumption. For example, two of the teenage wards of the state that are parents themselves told us that they buy their children gifts when they are financially able. One teen/parent described an instance in which she spent what she felt was far too much on her baby daughter, purchasing for her a $60 outfit and a $21 pair of "Barney" shoes. Another teenager in the group likewise stated that he had bought gifts for his mother.

Intrapersonal (Self) Gift Giving. Although there may be a general tendency towards decreased self-gift-giving among the institutionalized due to either inability to purchase such gifts because of confinement, or a relative lack of motivation due to low levels of control over their lives, there is evidence that self-gifting behavior nevertheless manifests itself in institutionalized environments. For example, among the teenage wards of the state we interviewed, many told us that they often buy themselves gifts such as "sweet" food items, clothes, cologne, and jewelry with the money that they earn by performing "chores" in and around their institutional facility. Also, it appears that the level of dependence encountered in the institutional setting may affect gift-giving behavior. The sister-in-law of the prison inmate we interviewed stated that he expected those people with money—i.e., her and her husband—to support him by giving him items that he requested as gifts. Here, the act of self-gifting is performed through a surrogate; even though the surrogate must pay for the gift, the act of gift giving was initiated by the prisoner himself. The inmate felt that he was deserving of these items, in part, because of the adverse circumstances with which he had had to deal with throughout his life. He felt, we were told, that he was not to blame for his "failure" in life, and that individuals "luckier" than himself should provide for his well-being. Interestingly, this individual was more concerned—almost solely so—with what his surrogate consumers would get him for Christmas, rather than with what his two teenage children would receive from him.

Given the above discussion, institutionalization may in many cases be perceived as a failure in its own right. Accordingly, taking the causal attribution perspective of intrapersonal gift-giving suggested by Faure and Mick (1993), one would expect attribution to external, uncontrollable causes to lead to relatively high levels of self-gift-giving, or at least to a desire to engage in such activity. While the "extreme-dependence" example of a prison inmate is given here, the likening of institutionalization to failed achievement outcome situations is similarly warranted in the case of drug and alcohol rehabilitation patients due to the social stigma commonly placed upon substance abuse.

Surrogate Gift-Giving. In addition to the surrogate-based self gift-giving behavior exhibited by the prison inmate in our field study, other examples serving to simultaneously illustrate both the surrogate consumer phenomenon and gift-giving behavior among the institutionalized emerge. For example, programs sponsored by church or community-service organizations exist which serve to facilitate the exchange of Christmas gifts between prison inmates and their children. According to the representative of the organization responsible for coordinating such projects that we spoke to, this is accomplished through the collection of the childrens' "wish lists," which is followed by consultation with the the inmate/parent, and then the delivery of the requested gifts to the children in a holiday atmosphere. Gift exchanges take place either at community centers, churches, or, in a limited number of cases, on prison grounds. Some gifts are also delivered directly to the homes of the children. Regardless of method of exchange, such programs function in surrogate fashion in order to facilitate the giving of gifts between institutionalized individuals and their loved ones. Likewise, the son of the woman confined to nursing homes told us that his mother "bought" her seven sons gifts by having them "surrogate shop" for each other on her behalf.

POST-INSTITUTIONALIZED CONSUMER BEHAVIOR AND RESEARCH PROPOSITIONS

The consumption behavior of institutionalized consumers is of interest not only while these individuals are actually confined in institutional settings but also behavior after leaving these restrictive environments is also of concern due to the likelihood that post-institutionalized consumption behavior may be affected by the period of limited consumer choice and dependence on others. While such behavioral effects may be expected to vary according to, among other things, the type of incapacitation and the length of stay, the possibility that the lingering effects of institutionalization might impact the behavior of millions of Americans is indeed worthy of consumer researcher consideration.

Researchers of institutionalized environments have consistently found that behavioral patterns developed and perpetuated in such settings may lead to the continuation of certain learned behaviors once the consumer is released into society. For example, in a study of the institutionalized elderly, Baltes and Wahl (1992) discuss what they term "the dependency-support script." Specifically, the authors maintain that institutionalized individuals learn to be dependent based upon the provision of positive reinforcement for dependent behavior, while independent behavior is ignored—and thus discouraged. Rationale cited for this scenario includes: persistent negative stereotypes of the elderly as incompetent, the caregiver ideal of helping, and social policy philosophies which dictate that independent behaviors be fostered in in-home, rather than in institutionalized, settings. The authors also contend that dependency is further reinforced by institutionalization, when in fact the stated purpose of such confinement is often to help these individuals become more self-dependent.

Just as they do during actual institutionalization, dependencies are likely to impact post-institutionalized consumer behavior in regard to both surrogate consumer usage and distinct gift-giving behaviors. These issues, and resultant research propositions, are discussed below.

Surrogate Consumer Usage

The continued usage of surrogates to perform a variety of consumption activities may occur in either direct or indirect fashion. Directly, the post-institutionalized consumer may stay in close contact with those who served as surrogates while confined in order to facilitate their being able to utilize the services of these individuals in a similar capacity after institutionalization. Indirectly, individuals may either resist direct personal dependencies, or more or less "give up" on making it on their own, becoming dependent instead on the larger society as their surrogate, through welfare or other social programs. Adopting Bagozzi and Warshaw's (1990) "theory of trying" framework, one might conclude, in this latter case, that the post-institutionalized consumer apathetically "quits trying to consume" in response to past failed attempts at independent consumption activity.

The findings of our exploratory research appear to both support and clarify the notion of continued high levels of surrogate usage. For example, the mother of the drug and alcohol rehabilitation patient we interviewed told us that her son both maintained close contact with her, as well as continued to rely on her for the consummation of certain acts of consumption, such as food purchase and preparation, immediately after actual institutionalization. However, several months after his release, and shortly after finding what was possibly a steady job, her son all but dropped out of sight. It seems that the period of post-institutionalized dependence lasted until her son was himself able to satisfy his consumption needs, at which time he became extremely independent, perhaps rebelling against his recently concluded institutionalized dependence.

The woman we interviewed who had acted as a surrogate consumer for her imprisoned brother-in-law shed additional light on the issue of post-institutionalized surrogate usage. Specifically, she told us that her brother-in-law was likely to cease contact for up to six months immediately after his release from prison. She explained that while he appeared to expect to be taken care of by surrogate consumers when in prison, he was highly independent when released, due at least in part to his being "fed up" with being dependent upon or controlled by other individuals. In fact, she stated that he invariably finds steady employment as a housepainter shortly after release, thus facilitating independent activity much in the same manner as the post-institutionalized drug and alcohol patient whose mother we interviewed. However, based on our research findings, it appears that the higher level of institutionalized dependence experienced by the prison inmate may have led to a more abrupt "rebellion" against his previous state of dependency.

This possible inverse relationship between the level of dependence while institutionalized and the level of post-institutionalized dependence should be tempered, however, with the understanding that some individuals leaving institutions are still not able to act on their own. Nursing home patients who return to the home of adult children, for example, are likely in many cases to continue to be highly dependent on the services of others. It may be then, that the inverse relationship between post-institutionalized surrogate usage and institutionalized dependence exists only for those consumers physically (or mentally) able to personally carry out consumption activities.

The above discussion suggests the possibility of the existence of two distinct forms of institutionalized dependency: *physical* dependency, as exemplified in the previous discussion of the nursing home patient being physically unable to perform consumption activities, and *societal* dependency, such as that seen in the case of the prison inmate whose sister-in-law we interviewed. This discussion suggests the following research propositions:

P$_1$: High levels of societal dependency while institutionalized are inversely related to post-institutionalized surrogate consumer usage.

P$_2$: High levels of physical dependency while institutionalized are positively related to post-institutionalized surrogate consumer usage.

Gift-Giving Behavior

As during actual periods of institutionalization, gift-giving behavior may manifest itself in either interpersonal or intrapersonal fashion in post-institutionalized consumer behavior. Our research findings offer little in this regard due to the fact that: (1) both the mother of the drug and alcohol rehabilitation patient and the sister-in-law of the prison inmate were unaware of gift-giving behavior of the post-institutionalized individual due to a lack of contact, and (2) there was no period of post-institutionalization with either the teenage wards of the state or the woman whose son we interviewed, who spent the last several years of her life in nursing homes. However, based on our findings applicable to actual institutionalized gift giving, the discussion of post-institutionalized gift-giving behaviors is nonetheless warranted.

Interpersonal Gift Giving. Given that gift giving appears to often persist throughout periods of institutionalization, it can be assumed that such behavior is likely to increase in post-institutionalized, as opposed to institutionalized, consumers. Not only are the physical constraints of the institutionalized environment lifted, but as in the case of both the prison inmate and drug and alcohol rehabilitation discussed in our field studies who found employment shortly after their respective releases, the possibility of having discretionary income is also a plausible antecedent of increased interpersonal gift-giving behavior. Stated more succinctly:

P$_3$: The incidence of interpersonal gift-giving is higher among post-institutionalized versus institutionalized individuals as a result of diminished physical and financial constraints.

Intrapersonal (Self) Gift Giving. Adopting the attributional perspective proposed by Faure and Mick, we contend that post-institutionalized self-gifting is likely to increase under situations where the released individual considers his or her release a success for which they themselves are responsible. More specifically, in accordance with Faure and Mick, the "achievement outcome" must be attributed by the post-institutionalized individual to internal, controllable, and unstable—"not likely to happen again soon"—causes. For example, the mother of the drug and alcohol rehabilitation patient we spoke to informed us that patients were not "released" from the last of the several institutions in which her son had lived, but that they rather "graduated," giving the post-institutionalized individual a sense of achievement. In such situations, increased self-gifting is likely to occur. In addition, this tendency towards higher levels of self-gifting is likely to be increased in situations where the post-institutionalized individual makes such internal attributions upon release from settings such as prisons and drug and alcohol rehabilitation hospitals that are characterized by high levels of societal dependence. This discussion suggests the following:

P$_4$: The incidence of intrapersonal or self gift giving is higher among post-institutionalized versus institutionalized individuals.

P$_5$: The probability of the incidence of intrapersonal or self gift giving being higher among post-institutionalized versus institutionalized individuals is increased under circumstances of societal—as opposed to physical—dependence during institutionalization.

DISCUSSION

Many of the 3.33 million Americans currently institutionalized increasingly have the ability to both make consumer decisions, as well as to engage in a variety of consumption activities. In fact, these individuals may have as many, if not more, consumption alternatives at a macro level (c.f. Firat 1987) than many non-institutionalized individuals, particularly the inner-city poor, who themselves have been characterized as no less than prisoners of their own surroundings (Alexis, et al. 1972). Unfortunately, the consumer behavior of institutionalized individuals is not well documented. Likewise, the ramifications of the rapid changes currently taking place within institutionalized environments are not fully understood. Clearly, however, there are substantial unmet consumer needs among the institutionalized which should be addressed only after first gaining a more thorough understanding of the complex relationships among social, financial, psychological, and physical dependence.

Not only does the current institutionalized population warrant consideration as a viable consumer segment, but with this population increasing in size while at the same time having higher levels of consumption choice, its recognition as such in the future appears all the more appropriate. This assertion, supported by our exploratory research findings, has direct and significant implications for both marketing practitioners and consumer researchers alike. For the practitioner, there is the opportunity to develop product and service offerings specifically for this growing segment of the American population. More importantly, however, is the fact that the vulnerability of institutionalized and post-institutionalized consumers necessitates that both marketers, as well as consumer researchers, pay greater attention to the social responsibility of these offerings and their promotion. Specifically, in regard to consumer researchers, the study of institutionalized consumers represents an opportunity to apply the principles of "critical theory," as suggested by Murray and Ozanne (1991), in an attempt to assist disadvantaged societal members in breaking free of potentially harmful societal constraints.

Future research into the consumer behavior of current and former institutionalized persons should strive to further clarify the findings of our research efforts. For example, research should explore the differences in consumer behavior between different segments of the institutionalized population, especially in consideration of varying levels of social, financial, psychological, and physical dependence. Areas of consumer research theory which hold specific promise in this regard are the continued usage of surrogate consumers and the nature of gift-giving behaviors among post-institutionalized individuals. To accomplish this, studies more longitudinal in nature than the ones conducted here are needed. As a result, the institutionalized population may be better understood to the benefit of all of American society.

REFERENCES

Alexis, Marcus, George Haines, Jr., and Leonard Simon (1972), "Consumption Behavior of Prisoners: The Case of the Inner City Shopper," in *Improving Inner-City Marketing*, Alan R. Andreasen (ed.), Chicago: American Marketing Association, 25-59.

Andreasen, Alan R. (1993), Revisiting the Disadvantaged: Old Lessons and New Problems," *Journal of Public Policy and Marketing*, 12 (Fall), 270-275.

Bagozzi, Richard P. and Paul R. Warshaw (1990), "Trying to Consume," *Journal of Consumer Research*, 17 (September), 127-140.

Baltes, Margaret M. and Hans-Werner Wahl (1992), "The Dependency-Support Script in Institutions: Generalization to Community Settings," *Psychology and Aging*, 7 (3), 409-418.

Crispell, Diane and William H. Frey (1993), "American Maturity," *American Demographics*, 15 (March), 31-42.

Faure, Corrine and David Glen Mick (1993), "Self-Gifts Through the Lens of Attribution Theory," in *Advances in Consumer Research*, Vol. 20, Leigh McAlister and Michael L. Rothschild (eds.), Provo, UT: Association for Consumer Research, 553-556.

Firat, A. Fuat (1987), "The Social Construction of Consumption Patterns: Understanding Macro Consumption Patterns," in *Philosophical and Radical Thought in Marketing*, A. Fuat Firat, Nikhilesh Dholakia, and Richard Bagozzi, Lexington, MA: D.C. Heath Company, 251-267.

Forsythe, Sandra, Sara Butler, and Robert Schaefer (1990), "Surrogate Usage in the Acquisition of Women's Business Apparel," *Journal of Retailing*, 66 (4), 446-469.

Fuller, Barbara K. and Suzannah C. Blackwell (1992), "Wardrobe Consultant Clientele: Identifying and Describing Three Market Segments," *Clothing and Textiles Research Journal*, 10 (Winter), 11-17.

Helliker, Kevin (1992), "On TV Today: Tips From Our Warden And the Lunch Menu," *The Wall Street Journal*, July 9, A1.

Henslik, Joseph, John Shinners and John Molenda (1992), "An Insider's Guide to America's Top Ten Jails," *Playboy*, 39 (July), 16.

High, Dallas (1990), "Old and Alone: Surrogate Health Care Decision-Making for the Elderly Without Families," *Journal of Aging Studies*, 4 (3), 277-288.

Hollander, Stanley C. (1971), "She 'Shops for You or With You': Notes on the Theory of the Consumer Purchasing Surrogate," in *New Essays in Marketing Theory*, George Fisk (ed.), Boston, MA: Allyn and Bacon, 218-240.

Mick, David Glen and Michelle DeMoss (1992), "Further Findings on Self-Gifts: Products, Qualities, and Socioeconomic Correlates," in *Advances in Consumer Research*, Vol. 19, eds. John F. Sherry and Brian Sternthal, Provo, UT: Association for Consumer Research, 140-146.

Murray, Jeff B. and Julie Ozanne (1991), "The Critical Imagination: Emancipatory Interests in Consumer Research," *Journal of Consumer Research*, 18 (September), 129-144.

New York Times (1992), "Secure Rooms, Imaginative Food And Lots of Bars," July 24, B1.

Novak, Mark and Carol Guest (1992), "A Comparison of the Impact of Institutionalization on Spouse and Nonspouse Caregivers," *Journal of Applied Gerontology*, 11 (December), 379-394.

Sherry, John F., Jr. (1983), "Gift Giving in Anthropological Perspective," *Journal of Consumer Research*, 10 (September), 157-168.

Solomon, Michael R. (1986), "The Missing Link: Surrogate Consumers in the Marketing Chain," *Journal of Marketing*, 50 (October), 208-218.

Thompson, Craig J., William B. Locander, and Howard R. Pollio (1989), "Putting Consumer Experience Back into Consumer Research: The Philosophy and Method of Existential-Phenomenology," *Journal of Consumer Research*, 16 (September), 133-146.

U.S. Bureau of the Census (1990), *Census of Population: General Population Characteristics*, Washington D.C.: U.S. Government Printing Office.

_____ (1980), *Census of Population: General Population Characteristics*, Washington D.C.: U.S. Government Printing Office.

_____ (1970), *Census of Population: Detailed Characteristics*, Washington D.C.: U.S. Government Printing Office.

Sad, Glad, and Mad: The Revealing Role of Emotions in Consumer Rituals

Julie A. Ruth, University of Washington

People regularly participate in ritualized activities (e.g., grooming) and ritual events (e.g., rites of passage such as weddings and funerals) that mark important and meaningful life experiences. While recent research has begun to investigate these activities and events, the experience of emotions concurrent with participation in rituals has received relatively little research attention. Because many rituals tend to accompany significant events in one's life (e.g., weddings, funerals, religious holidays), the concurrent emotional experiences also tend to be dramatic, intense, and likely to play fundamental roles in the ritual experience. The purpose of this session, then, was to bring together research focused on emotions as experienced, described, and displayed or managed in ritual events.

As part of the session, the three papers explored emotions in conjunction with three ritual contexts: planning and participating in weddings, funerals, and receiving a gift. The first paper, by Tina M. Lowrey (Rider University) and Cele Otnes (University of Illinois), focused on the "mixed emotions" or *ambivalence* experienced by brides as they plan and participate in weddings. The authors describe three types of ambivalence that emerged in their interviews with brides: psychological, sociological, and cultural ambivalence. These forms of ambivalence emerged as brides selected and shaped artifacts, performance roles, scripts, and audience to be included in their weddings. Psychological ambivalence typically involves inner tension resulting from contradictory and vacillating feelings about a person or object. Sociological ambivalence is characterized, not by internal conflict within an individual, but by the conflicting norms and expectations associated with different social roles including bride-to-be, daughter, and future daughter-in-law. Finally, cultural ambivalence stems from the existence of cultural or subcultural values that are incongruent. As brides proceeded through the complex assortment of tasks required to create their weddings, they experienced all three types of ambivalence.

The second paper, by Larry Compeau (Clarkson University) and Carolyn Nicholson (Clarkson University), addressed the experience of emotions in relation to the experience of death and the funeral ritual. Based on in-depth, long interviews, an existential-phenomenological approach was used to focus on the emotions experienced before, during, and after the funeral ritual. Detailed analysis of the transcripts of these interviews revealed several general themes about the "lived experience" of funerals: (1) detrimentality; (2) ritual as loss of agency; and (3) a distinct social/public funeral experience. The experiences associated with funerals are punishing—physically, emotionally, and mentally. Furthermore, attendance at funerals is deemed an obligation. Not only one's attendance but one's behavior is prescribed and compulsory. The ritual seems to engender a feeling of hopelessness and of being out of control. The funeral-goer is *forced* to attend and to *go through the motions*, which are unpleasant. The social/public aspects of the funeral were considered important by participants: funerals provide an opportunity to give comfort, to visit family and friends, and to reaffirm relationships—both with the deceased and the immediate family.

However, contrary to the "Received View" of funerals as useful mechanisms for expression of grief and commemoration of the life of the deceased person, it was observed that the essential nature of funerals varies depending on the funeral-goer's relationship with the deceased. For close loved ones, funeral-goers tend to be stoic and/or numb during the ritual itself, with periods of active and, importantly, private grief either preceding or following the funeral. In contrast, for those not close to the deceased, the funeral rite served a different role, one where the primary grief was experienced during the funeral itself and was oriented toward the family. Further, the acts and symbols of the ritual are signals for emotion or what is termed *ritualized emotions*. These *ritualized emotions*, prescribed as part of the script and performances associated with participation in the funeral experience, are used as communication tools to express feelings for the family left behind.

The third paper, by Julie Ruth (University of Washington), Cele Otnes (University of Illinois), and Frederic Brunel (University of Washington), probed deeply into the negative emotions which may be experienced by gift receivers. The research was based on critical incident reports regarding experiences where a gift was received and, at some point in the process, negative emotions were experienced. An interpretation of the data shows that components of the gift-exchange ritual itself characterize informants' interpretation of the "causes" of negative emotions. Negative emotions were oriented toward violations of expectations and norms associated with: (1) the nature of the gift artifact itself, particularly vis à vis the relationship of the giver and receiver, and (2) other elements of the ritual including presence of audience, anxiety associated with performance roles, and the ritual script. The authors interpreted the themes according to a Gestalt perspective, where the relationship between the gift, giver, and recipient were of foreground importance, and the other elements associated with the ritual provided an important background context to the emotional experience. Further, a theme that emerged with respect to performance roles was the recipients' ability to control their display of emotions. Respondents clearly recognized the importance of emotions as a form of communication with the giver and a critically important component of their performance as "gift recipient."

The session discussant, T. J. Olney (Western Washington University), highlighted the commonalities in the three papers and provided insightful comments with respect to each paper. Questions from the audience addressed the extent to which negative emotions, as a message from giver to recipient, were observed. Audience comments also addressed emotions and participation in funerals, both for close loved ones and those more distant to the deceased. Finally, the discussion acknowledged areas of opportunity for business in reducing or minimizing the ambivalence experienced by brides and others associated with the wedding planning process.

Illegal Adoption of a New Product: A Model of Software Piracy Behavior

Madhavan Parthasarathy, University of Nebraska
Robert A. Mittelstaedt, University of Nebraska

ABSTRACT

This paper is concerned with the decision process of computer software adopters, especially pirates. Based on past research, a model is proposed that contains two general normative constructs that influence the general attitude toward piracy. Other specific variables, e.g., perceived utility of the software, the tendency to rely on complementary products and on others (in order to reduce learning costs) are also included and the impact of all these variables on an individual's propensity to pirate a software program is investigated. Finally, implications, particularly managerial, of this analysis are presented.

INTRODUCTION

Modern communication and copying technologies have greatly enhanced the potential for the theft of intellectual property. Swinyard, Rinned and Keng Kau (1990) estimate that it now accounts for an annual loss to the American economy of over $40 billion. One form of this activity in which most average consumers can participate is the pirating of software. In spite of the impact of piracy has on computer software adoption, little attention has been given to this form of consumer behavior or to the consequences which follow from it.

The purpose of this paper is to investigate the variables which affect an individual's propensity to pirate. A model is proposed that contains general attitudinal and normative constructs regarding piracy; other constructs are suggested by Conner and Rumelt (1991) and Parthasarathy and Hampton (1993). These authors suggest that non-monetary costs associated with piracy (e.g., the time spent learning a specific software package and the efforts expended to acquire it illegally) could often overwhelm the monetray costs associated with the software. One of the objectives of this paper is, therefore, to ascertain if such non-monetary costs are systematically evaluated by individuals when they make a decision whether or not to pirate a particular software package. Thus, the proposed model contains general constructs regarding normative and attitudinal factors, and specific factors regarding the particular software being considered that, together, are expected to influence an individual's propensity to pirate a particular software package. The model is then tested using structural equation modelling with LISREL-7. Finally, the implications of the model are discussed.

THE NATURE OF PIRACY BEHAVIOR

For the purpose of this study, software piracy is defined as the act of making a nonlegal copy of a copyrighted or patented software for one's own use. Thus, it is a form of adoption behavior whose alternative is purchase. On the face of it, piracy carries a zero (or nearly zero) direct price to the pirate. However, there are other nonmonetary costs involved in adopting a software; to receive the benefit of the product one must invest time and effort in acquiring the copy and, more importantly, learning how to use it.

Parthasarathy and Hampton (1993) divided nonmonetary costs into those related to acquiring the software and the those related to learning the software. The cost of acquiring the software may be significant. The would-be pirate must locate a copy of the software and, possibly, some further software which makes it capable of being copied in a usable fashion. Since the person from whom one copies the program may have purchased it, and since pirating is both

illegal and unethical, there may be some embarassment or other negative feeling associated with the behavior. Note that these costs are born only by the pirate, not by a purchaser. These costs would be lower if a person knew others from whom he/she could copy the software. Thus, interpersonal influence and support among the adopters should be an important factor in deciding whether one pirates or purchases.

In a similar vein, learning a new software may involve significant nonmonetary costs. Manuals, tutorials, and on-line help services help to reduce these costs to the purchaser; generally, the cost of providing this form of help is part of the price of the software and, thus, is monetized to the purchaser. For the would-pirate, the market often provides tools such as independently produced manuals that make learning the pirate software easier (called complementary products). Friends who are well versed with the working of the program may also help reduce nonmonetary costs. However, the nonmonetary costs will be greater for the pirate and, for a relatively new and complex program, are likely to be very much higher.

In addition to the nonmonetary costs, piracy is a behavior which is both illegal and unethical, and the decision to pirate would be expected to be influenced by a person's subjective norms about the behavior. In sum, piracy is a conscious adoption decision in which the benefit of owning the software is influenced by the nonmonetary costs of using the product and the subjective norms about the nature of the behavior itself.

THE PROPOSED MODEL

General variables: The model on which this research is based contains elements corresponding to: the behavioral intention, the propensity to pirate (PP); the attitude toward piracy (APIRACY); and two subjective norms (NORMS1) and (NORMS2). NORMS1 involves the perception of the ethical nature of piracy itself. NORMS2 recognizes the possibility of "situational ethics" being involved in the decision. Preliminary research suggested that some people believe that the pricing policies of software developers are, themselves, unethical. NORMS2 captures these beliefs, which a person might use to justify piracy to him/herself.

This part of the model has some similarities to the theory of reasoned action (Ajzen and Fishbein 1980; Fishbein and Ajzen 1975) in that it contains a behavioral intention construct as well as attitudinal and normative constructs. However, in contrast to the original theory of reasoned action, the model proposed in this paper presumes that attitudes are largely a function of the normative factors. Indeed, research supports the contention that the theory of reasoned action is inadequate when applied to moral behavior and other behaviors (e.g., contraceptive use) that are largely private and concerned with non-visible consumption (e.g., Doll and Orth 1993; Vallerand et. al. 1992). These authors argue that in such a situation the normative factor would causally relate to the attitudinal factor since attitudes are largely a function of the norm. In addition, the normative variables used in this research are concerned with ethical beliefs and are therefore qualitatively different from those prescribed by the theory of reasoned action. Further, the attitudinal component is a general component (not specific to the particular software as would be indicated by the reasoned action model). Since the normative factors used in the model are general and will

FIGURE 1
Proposed Model

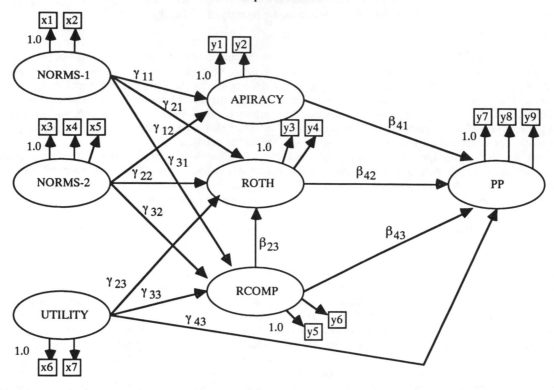

not vary between software packages, the attitudinal construct (which is a function of these normative beliefs) will have more meaning if meaured generally rather than specifically. However, the authors realize that specific factors associated with the particular software being tested could have strong influence on an individual's propensity to pirate that software package. Therefore, the model proposed also incorporates several specific factors, as discussed below.

Specific Factors: In addition to the general variables mentioned above, the proposed model includes two variables representing the nonmonetary costs of piracy. The perceived availability and usefulness of complementary products (as defined above) is incorporated into the variable "reliance on complementary products" (RCOMP.) The availability of informed other persons, and one's willingness to ask them for help, is incorporated into the variable "reliance on others" (ROTH.) A final variable (UTILITY) captures the perceived usefulness of the particular software under consideration.

Thus, the proposed model contains three general decision elements, the desirability of the particular software, the magnitude of nonmonetary costs of acquiring and learning how to use it, and the attitude toward piracy, with its normative components. Figure 1 shows the proposed model and the direction of the hypothesized relationships among the several constructs. The relationships among these variables are discussed, taking the three general decision elements in order.

Nature of the product: The greater the perceived desirability of the software, the more a consumer would wish to adopt it for use, thus enhancing the utility of both piracy and purchase. However, it is likely that, as a particular program is seen as being more desirable, its value to the purchaser is enhanced more than its value to the pirate. The key to this prediction lies in the nature of nonmonetary costs.

To the extent that programs which are more useful are also more powerful, the nonmonetary costs of adopting them are also rather high. Just as so-called "shareware" programs are relatively low-powered and generally very easy to use, powerful word processors or spreadsheet programs come with, and require, a sizeable package of support services. Thus, for highly desirable software packages, the nonmonetary costs are likely to be very high for the would-be pirate. Further, what often enhances the perceived utility of the program is the presence of the factors which are available to the purchaser as part of the program's price. Given this, greater desirability is likely to increase the *value* (i.e., the ratio of program benefit to the total of monetary and nonmonetary costs) for the purchaser more than for the potential pirate. Therefore, it would be expected that perceived utility of the particular program (UTILITY) would be inversely related to the propensity to pirate (PP).

Conversely, the greater the perceived usefulness of the software, the greater will a person be inclined to use tutorials to learn the software and ask others for help about it. Therefore, UTILITY should be expected to be positively related to both the reliance on others (ROTH) and the reliance on complementary products (RCOMP).

Attitudes toward Piracy: In keeping with the theory of reasoned action, the subjective norms about piracy (NORMS1 and NORMS2) combine with the generalized attitude toward piracy to affect the propensity to pirate in a straightforward way. Further, because the presence of knowledgable others and/or complementary products are almost necessary for one to make use of pirated software, the willingness to use these sources of help become the "situational" attributes which make "situational ethics" possible. Therefore, the subjective norms about piracy might be expected to be related to both the reliance on others and the reliance on complementary products.

TABLE 1
Questionnaire Items

NORMS-1
1. I do not think piracy is any more unethical than the exorbitant prices that software companies charge
2. I do not think that piracy is the same as stealing because the owner is not deprived when computer software is copied.

NORMS-2
1. I think that computer software packages are overpriced.
2. I think the cost of developing a good an average software package is no more than the cost of developing a good textbook.
3. I think that computer software manufacturers have much greater profit margins than textbook publishers.

UTILITY
1. I feel that an integrated package like *Integra* would be very useful to me.
2. I feel that integra will save me considerable time in performing computer related tasks.

APIRACY
1. I am against piracy.
2. I would never use a pirated copy of any computer software.

ROTH
1. If some of my friends know how to use the software, I would obtain the software and learn how to use it from them.
2. I would copy the software if I knew I could rely on my friends / classmates for help.

RCOMP
1. If I get a free copy, I would be willing to buy my own tutorials and / or manuals that make it easier to learn the software.
2. I would buy the software only if I knew that the manuals / tutorials were not easily available.

PP
1. I would purchase the software even if I could get a free copy easily.
2. I would be willing to ask my friends / classmates for a copy.
3. If the original was not in stock, I would wait till it is available rather than ask someone for a copy.

Reliance on Others and Complementary Products: Both the availability of complementary products and the presence of knowledgable others enhance the ability of the pirate to successfully use the product. Both would be expected to exert a positive influence on the propensity to pirate. However, the presence of others may substitute for complementary products, and vice versa; in this sense these two factors may be substitutes for each other and the relationship between the two could be inverse. As noted before, these variables would be affected by the perceived usefulness of the software and the subjective norms about pirating.

TESTING THE MODEL: METHOD

Data were supplied by a sample of 205 undergraduate students at a large Midwestern university. Sixty four respondents failed to answer the questionnaire completely (i.e., they skipped at least one question) and were excluded from the sample in order to keep the analysis unbiased. LISREL is especially sensitive to this issue and, since the sample size after excluding the incomplete questionnaires was still reasonably high (141), this approach was judged by the authors to be the most unbiased. The questionnaire presented the respondents with a hypothetical scenario involving a software package titled *Integra* that combined word processing, spreadsheet, and database applications in a single integrative package. Since most of the respondents were senior level students, they could identify with the usefulness of the package. It was mentioned that the university was trying to obtain student discounts that would make the package available to the students at $100. Also, it was mentioned that the package was not copy protected, that it was relatively easy to copy, and that the risk of being apprehended in the act of piracy was nil. The aim was to create a hypothetical scenario that reflected, as best as possible, a typical real-world situation. Following the introductory scenario, the the questionnaire requested the respondents to complete Likert type questions for each of the constructs used in the model. There were 26 items on the questionnaire corresponding to the constructs of interest. However, after an initial factor analysis (some items loaded strongly on more than one construct) and reliability tests (items with less than 0.7 coefficient alpha were dropped), sixteen items were used to measure the seven constructs, with each construct being assigned at least two items. As table-2 suggests, the chosen items loaded very strongly with their assigned constructs. The constructs and their respective items are contained in Table 1.

The Figure depicts the constructs and their relationships in graphical form. This model was tested using LISREL-7.

RESULTS

The results from the LISREL analysis are presented in Tables 2 and 3. Table 2 is concerned with the relationship of the constructs to their respective items (i.e., Lambda X and Lambda Y matrices and their significance levels, based on t-values). As an indication of construct validity, all the items are significant and of the expected sign.

Table 3 presents the overall fit of the model as well as the path coefficients and their respective significance levels. Of specific concern are the model chi-square, the goodness-of-fit index (GFI), the adjusted-goodness-of-fit-index (AGFI), and the root mean squared residual (RMR).

TABLE 2
Item-Construct Relationship

CONSTRUCT	ITEM	STANDARD VALUE	SIGNIFICANCE LEVEL
NORMS 1	LX 1 1	1.00	——
	LX 2 1	0.908	.01
NORMS 2	LX 3 2	1.00	——
	LX 4 2	0.478	.05
	LX 5 2	0.497	.05
UTILITY	LX 6 3	1.00	——
	LX 7 3	0.946	.01
APIRACY	LY 1 1	1.00	——
	LY 2 1	1.083	.01
ROTH	LY 3 2	1.00	——
	LY 4 2	1.124	.01
RCOMP	LY 5 3	1.00	——
	LY 6 3	0.804	.01
PP	LY 7 3	1.00	——
	LY 8 4	0.856	.01
	LY 9 4	1.101	.01

The chi-square value, though not of great concern in LISREL analyses, is (112.94 / df=88), thus indicating a reasonable fit of the model to the data. Traditionally, the GFI and RMR have been used as indicators of a model's fit (Tanaka, 1993). Bagozzi and Yi (1988) suggest that the GFI should be above 0.9 and the RMR below 0.05. Both these requirements are satisfied in this model, adding substance to the notion that the model is indeed a good fit.

The paths emanating from UTILITY were all in the correct direction, and those terminating at ROTH and RCOMP respectively were also highly significant. The negative relationship between UTILITY and PP was forecasted, although its strength was weaker than predicted.

A strong path from NORMS-1 to APIRACY was expected and confirmed. It suggests that attitude toward piracy is a function of existing long-term normative perceptions of the ethical nature of piracy (which are likely to vary between societies).

The paths emanating from NORMS-2 were all insignificant although in the direction forecasted. This strongly suggests that "situational ethics" are overshadowed by long-term perception of the nature of piracy itself. Put differently, the perception that computer software packages are overpriced and that software manufacturers make outrageously high profit margins does not seem to significantly enhance (or detract from) an individual's attitude toward piracy, or his/her reliance on either complementary products or on others.

The strong negative path between NORMS-1 and RCOMP was, however, surprising and not forecasted. While pirates have greater nonmonetary costs of adoption and therefore should be positively inclined toward the use of complimentary products, the results suggest that those who normatively support piracy are less likely to rely on complementary products. Perhaps their inclination to save money (by not purchasing complementary products) over-shadows their desire to reduce the nonmonetary costs of learning. It must also be remembered that the subjects were students who can easily find help with the operation of the software product, including that from friends. Additionally, most universities have help desks and lab assistants who can help. Therefore it seems reasonable to expect that in spite of a positive inclination to pirate, some of these individuals may favor reliance on others over reliance on complimentary products, especially since the former is free. The fact that most students are extremely price sensitive may add fuel to this contention. The notion that such individuals are likely to seek help from others is supported by the positive path between NORMS-1 and ROTH.

The path from APIRACY to PP, and from ROTH to PP were both positive and significant as predicted, suggesting that positive attitudes toward piracy as well as the degree of reliance on others is directly, and strongly, associated with a person's propensity to pirate. However, the path from RCOMP to PP, though positive as predicted, is insignificant, indicating that the use of complementary products does not necessarily result in enhanced piracy. There could be two reasons for this phenomenon: (1) the pirate's desire to save money (by not purchasing the complementary products) overrides his/her desire to ease the time and cost of learning (nonmonetary costs), and (2) those individuals who have a low propensity to pirate (likely purchasers) also purchase complementary products. Although nonmonetary costs are likely to be higher for the pirate than for the purchaser, they may be quite high for both of them (especially for a relatively complex package like Integra) and therefore the purchaser may also benefit strongly from the use of complementary products.

Finally the strong and negative path from RCOMP to ROTH confirms the prediction that individuals who rely more on complementary products rely less on others. To a large extent, these

TABLE 3
Results of the Path Model

PATH	ESTIMATED VALUE (Maximum Likelihood)	SIGNIFICANCE LEVEL
NORMS-1 TO APIRACY	0.585	0.01
NORMS-1 TO ROTH	0.125	Not Significant
NORMS-1 TO RCOMP	-0.388	0.01
NORMS-2 TO APIRACY	0.024	Not Significant
NORMS-2 TO ROTH	0.298	Not Significant
NORMS-2 TO RCOMP	0.150	Not Significant
UTILITY TO RCOMP	0.528	0.01
UTILITY TO ROTH	0.896	0.01
UTILITY TO PP	-0.664	Not Significant
APIRACY TO PP	0.635	0.01
ROTH TO PP	0.692	0.05
RCOMP TO ROTH	-1.529	0.01
RCOMP TO PP	1.067	Not Significant

Chi Square (with 88 degrees of freedom) = 112.94 (P= 0.038)
Goodness of Fit Index (GFI) = 0.913
Adjusted Goodness of Fit Index (AGFI) = 0.865
Root Mean Square Residual = 0.039

sources of reducing the nonmonetary costs of adoption are substitutable for each other; an individual who uses complementary products to learn the package may not have the need to seek help from others.

Although the model described above was satisfactory from a goodness-of-fit perspective, several theoretically meaningful paths were insignificant. While these may have enhanced understanding of the pirate adoption process, the quest for an even more parsimonious solution led to a partial trimming of the model through the removal of the NORMS-2 construct and the three nonsignificant paths that emanated from it. The results were more or less the same as that for the a priori model in that the significant paths in the previous model continued to remain significant (at the same levels) in the trimmed model and the insignificant paths (e.g., from UTILITY to PP and RCOMP to PP) were still insignificant. However, the chi square value dropped to 80.60 (p=0.014), the GFI went up to 0.921, the AGFI to 0.870, and the RMR to 0.041. This suggests that the trimmed model was a slightly better fit than the original one, although it changed none of the relationships.

DISCUSSION AND CONCLUSIONS

The general outline of the proposed model was confirmed. The propensity to pirate is influenced by the potential pirate's attitudes toward piracy, subjective norms about the act of piracy, the perceived utility of the software package, and the willingness to seek help from others or complementary products to reduce the nonmonetary costs.

Of course, the generalizability of the results is limited by the nature of the sample. While students are software users, their demographic and cultural homogeneity is likely to restrict the range of observed attitudes and, especially, subjective norms about piracy. Indeed, about three fourths of the respondents were willing to pirate the software in question and about two thirds saw no ethical problems with piracy. However, the strong effects of the desirability of the product itself and the role of the means for reducing nonmonetary costs suggest that there is little reason to believe that the nature of the relationships among the constructs would change much in a different sample.

To the extent the general nature of the model holds, the implications for software producers are not encouraging. First, the belief that software prices are unjustified did not appear to affect attitudes toward piracy nor encourage the propensity to pirate. Promotional efforts to justify prices would appear to be a relatively ineffective strategy to reduce piracy. Second, the a-priori model hypothesized that the relationship between perceived product utility and piracy would be negative, suggesting that enhancing product utility would be a piracy reducing strategy. However, the relationship, although in the right direction, was not significant. Rather, it seemed to affect the propensity to pirate only by acting through the constructs which reflect the ability to reduce the nonmonetary costs of pirating.

This brings us to the final issue; the roles of complementary products and knowledgable others appear to have a strong influence on piracy. Obviously, as a software product gains in popularity, the availability of complementary products and the likelihood of finding someone who can be of help in learning how to use the product increase. Further, one of the strongest paths in the tested model found that these two are seen as substitutable means for reducing nonmonetary costs. While a software manufacturer might take some means to limit the availability of complementary products, there is no way to limit access to helpful other persons. This may be another example of the winner's curse; one of the penalties of success in the software industry appears to be the increased likelihood of piracy.

REFERENCES

Ajzen, Icek and Martin Fishbein (1980), *Understanding Attitudes and Predicting Social Behavior*, Englewood Cliffs, NJ: Prentice Hall.

Bagozzi, Richard P. and Youjae Yi (1988), "On the Evaluation of Structural Models," *Journal of the Academy of Marketing Science*, 16 (Spring), 74-94.

Conner, Kathleen Reavis and Richard P. Rumelt (1991), "Software Piracy: An Analysis of Protection Strategies," *Management Science*, 37 (February), 125-39.

Fishbein, Martin and Ichek Ajzen (1975), *Belief, Attitude, Intention,Behavior: An Introduction to Theory and Research*, Ma: Addison-Wesley.

Parthasarathy, Madhavan and Ronald Hampton (1993), "The Role of Piracy in the Diffusion of a Software Product: A Propositional Framework", paper presented at the *Winters Educators Conference* of the American Marketing Association, Chicago: IL.

Sheppard, Blair H., Jon Hartwick, and Paul R. Warshaw (1988), "The Theory of Reasoned Action: A Meta-Analysis of Past Research with Recommendations for Modifications and Future Research", *Journal of Consumer Research*, 15 (December), 325- 343.

Swinyard, William R., Heikke Rinne and Ah Keng Kau (1990), "The Morality of Software Piracy: A Cross Cultural Analysis," *Journal of Business Ethics*, 9 (August), 655-64.

Tanaka, Jeff S. (1993), "Multifaceted Conceptions of Fit in Structural Equation Models," in *Testing Structural Equation Models*, Sage Publications, Bollen and Long (eds), 11-39.

A Consumer-Behavior Approach to Handgun Legislation and Regulation

Ronald Paul Hill, Villanova University
Debra Lynn Stephens, Villanova University

ABSTRACT

This paper examines gun-control from a consumer-behavior perspective. To this end, the history of gun control legislation in the United States is provided with a focus on handguns. The contribution of handguns to crime versus their deterrent effects are then discussed. Next is an exploration of the close ties between guns and America as a nation. The paper closes with public policy recommendations that are explicitly consumer-based and attempt to balance the needs of gun owners with the interests of society.

INTRODUCTION

In a city that sometimes seems hostile and threatening, many Philadelphians find comfort in having a gun. And they're buying them by the thousands.

Hollman and McCoy, *The Philadelphia Inquirer*, 1992

Firearms are one of America's leading consumer products (Ecenbarger 1993). More than 200 million, including rifles, shotguns, and handguns, are currently circulating, representing approximately four guns for every five consumers (Hollman and McCoy 1992). Four to five million new weapons are added to this arsenal annually, split evenly between long guns, such as rifles and shotguns which are used primarily for hunting, and handguns, the firearm of choice for citizens seeking self-protection as well as for drug dealers and other criminals.

In the 1980s amid declining sales for most types of guns, manufacturers responded to a shift in consumer preference due, in part, to media attention in programs such as *Miami Vice* that may have inadvertently increased the level of national violence, especially in urban areas (see Alexander and Stewart 1989). This shift was in the handgun of choice, from revolvers to semiautomatic pistols. Compared to standard revolvers that hold six rounds in a revolving cylinder, bullets in semiautomatic pistols are spring-loaded into the firing chamber with each shot for quick firing. Further, the magazines of such weapons often hold more rounds, and reloading can be done easily.

At the low end of this market are cheaply made low-caliber pistols that are semiautomatic versions of the "Saturday night special." Produced primarily by three California companies, these weapons accounted for 22 percent of all handgun sales in 1990 and 27 percent of all murders and other firearm-related crimes since 1986 (Freedman 1992). At the high end of the market are sophisticated and expensive assault-style semiautomatic pistols such as the Tec-9 that ordinarily come equipped with a magazine that holds 30 rounds (Rohter 1992). These weapons also are confiscated in violent crimes at rates disproportionate to their number in circulation.

These handguns may be purchased from any of the 270,000 dealers with a federal firearms license (Terry 1992). This easy-to-obtain license is good for three years, and allows the licensee to buy and sell guns across state lines. While such transactions are subject to local, state, and federal laws, violations are widespread as enforcement is difficult. For example, gun shop owners and other individuals with licenses will rent booths for $20 at gun shows across the nation to buy and sell weapons. Signs are posted at the shows warning that all laws must be obeyed; however, sales are poorly supervised and compliance is suspect. Also, federal laws traditionally have been weak due to the activities of the pro-gun lobby, and many states, including Arizona, Kentucky, and South Carolina, have few restrictions, leading to gunrunners selling weapons from lenient states in others with greater restrictions (see Mueller and Campbell 1993; Treaster 1992).

One result of easy access may be an increase in deaths by firearms. In 1991, there were 270,012 firearm-related robberies, 259,800 firearm-related assaults, and 12,408 handgun-related homicides (Bureau of Justice Statistics 1992). Nationally, if current trends continue unabated, guns will overtake automobiles as the leading cause of deaths by injury (Otto 1994). Nonetheless, the national debate over gun control remains one of the most contentious in our society. Kilborn (1992, p. A1) aptly summarizes the positions of the two primary adversaries (gun-control versus pro-gun groups) as follows: "...a gun, depending on one's view, is either an agent of evil that ought to be banned or restricted, or a constitutionally enshrined defense against evil."

The purpose of this paper is to examine this public policy issue from a consumer-behavior perspective (see Hill 1994 for an additional look at consumer matters). In order to accomplish this task, the history of gun control legislation in the United States is provided with a focus on handguns. Then, the origins and nature of America's attachment to guns are explored. The paper closes with public policy and marketer recommendations that are explicitly consumer-based.

HISTORY OF GUN CONTROL LEGISLATION

The Second Amendment to the U.S. Constitution, adopted in 1791 as part of the Bill of Rights, states that: "A well regulated Militia, being necessary to the security of a free State, the right of the people to keep and bear arms, shall not be infringed." Since that time, however, this country has experienced tremendous change. For instance, the founding of the first police department in the city of Boston in 1838 caused other major metropolitan areas to follow suit, offering protection to most citizens (Hart 1988). Further, movement from a rural agrarian to an urban industrial society reduced the need to use firearms for hunting purposes for survival.

These as well as other changes over the last 200 years have caused some observers to suggest that the ability to bear arms should be reinterpreted as a privilege rather than a right that is conferred upon a regular militia such as the National Guard (see Hart 1988; Joiner 1988). Known as the "collective" or "state's right" view, proponents interpret the amendment as responding to article I, section 8, clauses 15 and 16 of the original Constitution which gives Congress the power to organize, arm, and discipline a militia (Kates 1983). However, others, including former Attorney General Edwin Meese (1988, p. 10), disagree and invoke the words of the framers of the Constitution such as Patrick Henry who argued that "the great objective is that every man be armed...everyone who is able may have a gun." Thus, advocates of the "individual" right position interpret the amendment in the same fashion as the identically phrased first and fourth amendments, as a right that individuals (rather than the state) can assert (Lund 1987).

Nonetheless, beginning with the *United States v. Miller*, 307 U.S. 174 (1939), the Supreme Court has ruled that the Second Amendment does not prohibit gun control laws (Hardy 1986). The earliest firearm law with a national scope is the National Firearms Act (NFA) of 1934 (see Table 1 for a complete evolution of Federal legislation). This Act was passed to discourage the use of machine

TABLE 1
Evolution of Federal Firearm Laws

1934	The National Firearms Act was passed to discourage the use of machine guns and sawed off shotguns and rifles through registration and taxes. Handguns were exempt from the Act. Purpose: Banning high-risk firearms.
1938	Under the Federal Firearms Act, felons, persons under indictment, and persons who failed to have or meet local licensing requirements were prohibited from purchasing firearms. Purpose: Denying high-risk users access to firearms.
1954	The Mutual Security Act empowered the President to control the flow of firearms and ammunition. Purpose: Banning high-risk firearms, prohibiting high-risk uses of firearms, and denying high-risk users access to firearms.
1958	The Federal Aviation Act prohibited the carrying of any firearm, concealed or otherwise, on or about any person in a passenger aircraft. Purpose: Prohibiting high-risk uses of firearms.
1968	The Omnibus Crime Control and Safe Streets Act increased the list of persons prohibited from firearm purchase or possession to include veterans other than honorably discharged, mental incompetents, illegal aliens, and persons who have renounced their U.S. citizenship. Purpose: Denying high-risk users access to firearms.
1968	The Gun Control Act limited those who may engage in the firearms business by raising the standards for obtaining a license, regulating the interstate transportation of firearms between non-licensees, and increasing the minimum age to purchase firearms. Purpose: Denying high-risk users access to firearms.
1972	The Alcohol, Tobacco, and Firearms Division of the Treasury Department was separated from the Internal Revenue Service and elevated to Bureau status with the mission to curb the illegal use and trafficking of firearms, especially among repeat offenders and drug dealers. Purpose: Denying high-risk users access to firearms.
1984	The Armed Career Criminal Act required mandatory imprisonment of not less than 15 years with no parole for anyone possessing a firearm who had three previous convictions for a violent felony. This Act also required mandatory sentencing of 5 to 10 years for anyone who used or carried a firearm in the commission of a federal crime. Purpose: Prohibiting high-risk uses of firearms.
1986	The McClure-Volkmer Amendments to the Gun Control Act made interstate transactions easier, and defined requirements for becoming a dealer, manufacturer, or importer. Purpose: Denying high-risk users access to firearms.
1986	The Law Enforcement Officers' Protection Act banned the further manufacture or import of certain varieties of armor-piercing ammunition. Purpose: Banning high-risk firearms.
1988	The Terrorist Firearms Detection Act was signed into law, banning the import, manufacture, sale, or possession of firearms not meeting certain standards of detectability by security devices. Purpose: Banning high-risk firearms.
1988	The Anti-Drug Abuse Act required the Attorney General to develop a system accessible to gun dealers that would facilitate the identification of felons who attempt to purchase firearms. Purpose: Denying high-risk users access to firearms.

Source: *Congressional Digest*, June/July, 1991

guns and sawed off shotguns in the commission of crimes by requiring registration and levying taxes. As a concession to the parties that bitterly opposed this infringement on State's rights, handguns were removed from the Act.

Since that time, gun control legislation has been based on one of three strategies: banning high-risk firearms, prohibiting high-risk uses of firearms, or denying high-risk users access to firearms (Zimring 1991). The NFA of 1938 is an example of legislation designed to reduce the number of high-risk firearms in society, as are recent attempts to ban assault pistols. Regulations that prohibit high-risk uses of firearms include "place and manner" prohibitions and extra penalties for unlawful use. For instance, these laws often

TABLE 2
Highlights of the Brady Bill

Requires a five-business-day waiting period before an individual can buy a handgun. This waiting period ends after five years.

Requires local law enforcement agents to check whether the potential buyer is eligible to purchase a handgun. Those ineligible include minors, felons, fugitives, drug and alcohol addicts, and illegal immigrants.

Authorizes spending $200 million per year to help states update or improve criminal records for use in a national background check system.

Requires the local law enforcement agency to provide the reason for rejection of a buyer's bid to purchase a handgun within 20 days.

Requires notification of state and local police of multiple handgun sales.

Prohibits labeling packages in interstate commerce that show they contain firearms in order to deter thefts.

Makes it a federal crime to steal firearms from licensed gun dealers, punishable by a fine of $10,000 and 10 years in prison.

Increases fees for federal firearms licenses to $200 for the first three years and $90 for renewal.

Source: Associated Press, November 25, 1993.

forbid such high-risk uses as carrying firearms in a motor vehicle, discharging a firearm in populated areas, or concealing weapons on one's person (see the Federal Aviation Act of 1958 in Table 1 for an example). Also, the Comprehensive Crime Control Act of 1984 provides for mandatory imprisonment of not less than five years for anyone who uses or carries a firearm during the commission of a federal crime.

The third gun control strategy seeks to deny high-risk users access to firearms. The Omnibus Crime Control and Safe Streets Act of 1968, born of the riots of the sixties and assassinations of political figures such as Martin Luther King, Jr. and Robert F. Kennedy, prohibited felons, veterans other than honorably discharged, mental "incompetents," illegal aliens, and former citizens who have renounced their citizenship from purchasing or possessing firearms. However, the operational tactics used to implement this legislation rendered the bill ineffective (Hollman and McCoy 1992). To meet this federal law, gun dealers required buyers only to sign a pledge stating that they did not fall into one of these categories. This information was not checked before the sale was made. In fact, Congress expressly forbade the ATF from centralizing dealer records due to the activities of the pro-gun lobby (see Davidson [1992] for more on such activities).

Legislation placed before the 100th Congress by Senator Howard Metzenbaum attempted to correct this deficiency. This Bill, titled the Handgun Prevention Act of 1987, provided for a waiting period for the purchase of all handguns so that local law enforcement officials would have the time necessary to conduct background checks on potential buyers. Renamed the Brady Handgun Violence Prevention Act after Ronald Reagan's Press Secretary James Brady who was shot in 1981, it languished in the 100th, 101st, and 102nd Congresses. A modified version recently was passed in the House by a vote of 238-189, requiring a wait of five business days before a handgun buyer can receive a weapon. However, this requirement will be lifted whenever a national "instant check" database of criminal records is assembled or after five years. Following similar debate in the Senate the bill was passed, but the time period for the development of the instant check

system was reduced to four years. The complete bill, which emerged from a conference of House and Senate negotiators and signed into law by President Clinton on November 30, 1993, is contained in Table 2.

Proponents of the Bill often cite the experiences of high gun-control nations as indications of the effectiveness of the regulation of handguns. For example, 194 Canadians versus 13,035 U.S. citizens were slain with handguns in 1990 (Hollman and McCoy 1992). Given Canada has approximately one-tenth the population of the United States, this country experiences a murder rate from firearms that is higher by a factor of seven. The pro-gun lobby rejects such statistics and insists that waiting periods have never been a useful tool against crimes.

HANDGUNS AS A DETERRENT TO CRIME

Underlying defensive handgun ownership is the belief that the presence of guns is an effective deterrent to crime (Bankston and Thompson 1989). According to Kleck (1988), private gun use against violent criminals and burglars is about as frequent as legal actions such as arrests, and is a more prompt and severe form of social control. For instance, in 1980 guns used defensively by potential victims resulted in the deaths of approximately 2,800 felons and the injury of 16,000 others.

While these data suggest the *potential* for a deterrent effect, by themselves, they are insufficient for three reasons (McDowall, Lizotte, and Wiersema 1991, p. 543):

First, it is uncertain whether civilian gun ownership *deters* crime or *displaces* it from one victim to another. If an offender believes a potential victim is armed, he or she may simply find a substitute who is perceived to be less likely to possess a firearm.

Second, armed victim resistance is possible in relatively few criminal incidents. Most burglaries occur in unoccupied homes, and violent offenses, such as robberies, commonly involve an element of surprise.

Third, criminals have very limited information about whether a potential victim is armed.

Furthermore, Kleck and McElrath (1991) found that while the use of firearms during an attack reduces the probability of injury to victims as well as assailants, once injury occurs, their use increases the probability of death. Thus, the net effect of the use of handguns by victims on the overall probability of their injury or deaths may be very close to zero.

Any crime-reducing effects, however, must be balanced with other negative factors associated with handgun ownership (Green 1987). The increase in household ownership of handguns over the last 25 years has been linked with higher firearm suicide and homicide rates in this country (Boyd and Moscicki 1986; Lester 1989; Lester and Clarke 1991; Price, Desmond, and Smith 1991). Investigators in a case-controlled study of suicides in the Memphis and Seattle areas found that the risk of suicide in a home with a loaded gun was nine times greater than in a comparable home without guns (Herman 1992). Brent et al. (1991) found that this increased risk was constant across methods of firearm storage within the home, particularly for adolescents. Further, the majority of firearm homicides in this country involve family members or friends rather than criminals. In a six-year study of shootings in the home, Kellerman and Reay (1986) found that for every self-defense shooting in reaction to the perpetration of a crime, 43 family members were killed by guns. Such statistics suggest that domestic arguments that might otherwise have ended in a fist fight may lead instead to a gun fatality when such weapons are available (Alexander et al. 1985).

Increasingly the victims of gun fatalities are children. Vobejda (1994) states that between 1979 and 1991, almost 50,000 children were killed by guns, a figure roughly equivalent to the number of Americans killed in the Vietnam War. Furthermore, she notes, an American child is fifteen times as likely to be killed by gunfire as a child in Northern Ireland.

Non-fatal gunshot injuries have, until very recently, received little attention. It is estimated that for every fatality, there are five non-fatal wounds, or more than 150,000 injuries annually (American Academy of Pediatrics, cited in Larson 1994). A study of child gunshot victims by a group of medical researchers in Los Angeles details the non-fatal injuries of 34 children from one to nine years of age who were admitted to King/Drew Medical Center between 1980 and 1987 (Ordog et al. 1988). The children were shot in the head, neck, chest, leg, and rectum. A three year-old who was shot in the rectum underwent a colostomy. Other losses included hands, fingers, eyes, and brain tissue. The children were shot by family members, friends, robbers, snipers, and gang members.

In summary, it appears that any crime-reducing effects guns may have is more than offset by the deaths and injuries they cause. The question we must ask ourselves before we can effect a long-term solution to firearm-related violence is, why are Americans so quick to use guns to resolve conflict?

GUNS AND THE AMERICAN PSYCHE

Few consumer goods are tied so closely to the origin of this nation as firearms. Guns play a central role in stories of the Old West—stories that romanticize outlaws and lawmen alike. And these stories were born as the West was being "won." Even as outlaws went about robbing and killing, newspapermen and dime store novelists back East were recasting them as glamorous, heroic figures (Larson 1994). For example, Myra Belle Shirley, a woman outlaw better known as "the Bandit Queen," was portrayed as a beautiful heroine in the 1941 movie *Belle Starr*. In truth, Belle was a horse thief and stagecoach robber, and had an ongoing incestuous

relationship with her son, who eventually shot her to death (Lyon 1969). Billy the Kid, who was romanticized as a James-Dean like rebel, was once described by the *Silver City New Southwest and Grant Herald* as "a low-down vulgar cutthroat, with probably not one redeeming quality (Hollom 1974)." And the lawmen bore little resemblance to the television series *Gunsmoke's* brave and virtuous Matt Dillon. Lawman Wyatt Earp, a case in point, was a con man and gambler; he and his friend Bat Masterson were known around Dodge as "the Fighting Pimps" (Lyon 1969).

According to historian Richard Slotkin (1992), "Buffalo Bill's Wild West," a traveling show created in 1882 by William Frederick Cody, was the single most powerful commercial vehicle for the creation and diffusion of the Myth of the Frontier. Cody (Buffalo Bill) was a frontier scout who became a master at self-promotion; his show reached audiences throughout the U.S. and Europe. Not only did the gun play a starring role in the show, but Cody's showbill included the following discussion, entitled "The Rifle as an Aid to Civilization":

The bullet is the pioneer of civilization, for it has gone hand in hand with the axe that cleared the forest, and with the family Bible and school book. Deadly as has been its mission in one sense, it has been merciful in another; for without the rifle ball we in America would not be to-day in the possession of a free and united country, and mighty is our strength (quoted in Slotkin 1992, p. 77).

Hollywood and, later, television fueled the myth of the gun as tamer of the frontier. In the ensuing decades, the outlaws and sheriffs of the Old West were gradually supplanted on TV and in movies by equally glamorous urban criminals and their law-enforcer pursuers. The protagonists are still using bullets to resolve their differences. Indeed, it is often difficult to distinguish the "good" guys from the "bad"; bad has, in a sense, become good. And violence has become trivial, as reflected in the title song of the nightly TV show *Cops*. The song has an upbeat, reggae-like rhythm: "Bad boy, bad boy, whatcha gonna do, whatcha gonna do when they come for you?" It is as if what is at stake is nothing more than who will be "It" in a game of tag.

Marketers of firearms contribute to the gun's mystique, feeding into the American fascination with violence. An ad for Davis Industries firearms in *Hand Gunning* magazine (July/August 1994, p. 16) includes a quote by James Madison about citizens having the right to use arms in "private self-defense," along with the warning "Don't Tread On Us"; the tagline reads "The American Way." In the same issue (p. 87) is another Davis ad, this one quoting George Washington: "When firearms go, all goes. We need them every hour."

In *Modern Gun* magazine (August 1994, p. 3) is a four-color full-page ad for North American Arms, Inc., juxtaposing three shiny handguns with a poker hand and a pile of large coins that look old and valuable—shades of the Old West, and of the gun as the ultimate argument-winner. In the same issue (p. 13) is an ad for books from Paladine Press, featuring "training manuals" such as *The Ultimate Sniper: An Advanced Training Manual for Military and Police Snipers*. Minors can easily get on their mailing list—just as easily as they can buy any gun magazine. An ad for *Modern Gun* (p. 61) states that the magazine "is written for old hands at firearms and newcomers to the exciting world of shooting, whether men, women or supervised young people." Since anyone may send in the attached order form, it seems doubtful that the publisher has a way of determining whether the "young people" are in fact "supervised."

The following example shows the darkest and ugliest aspect of the American obsession with guns and violence:

> In July, 1989, [*Shotgun News*] carried an advertisement promoting the "Whitman Arsenal," consisting of the seven weapons and accessories that Charles Whitman brought with him on August 1, 1966, when he climbed the twenty-seven-story clock tower at the University of Texas and spent the next ninety minutes firing away at anyone who happened to fall within his sights. He killed sixteen people... [and] wounded another thirty-one...the *Life* magazine edition that covered the shooting called the incident "the most savage one-man rampage in the history of American crime." (quoted in Larson 1994, 182)

Given America's fascination with guns, it is not surprising that the domestic gun industry is among the least regulated of all consumer-products industries (Larson 1994). While products ranging from food processors to vitamins have been "childproofed," gun manufacturers have yet to design a childproof gun. And dealers are routinely party (knowingly or not) to straw-man purchases for juveniles and/or gun traffickers. Erik Larson, an investigative journalist, had this to say after extensive interviewing of dealers:

> One must be a cool customer to stay in business knowing that the products one sells are likely to be used to kill adults and children, or to serve as a terrorist tool in countless other robberies, rapes, and violent assaults. Yet gun dealers sell guns in America the way Rite Aid sells toothpaste, denying at every step of the way the true nature of the products they sell and absolving themselves of any and all responsibility for their role in the resulting mayhem (Larson 1994, p. 87).

The next section includes a discussion of firearms marketers' ethical obligations to American consumers.

PUBLIC POLICY RECOMMENDATIONS

Guns are potentially lethal weapons that empower individuals whether they are crime victims or criminals. These weapons are a source of both social order and disorder, depending on who uses them. Further, while all guns are deadly, some firearms are more harmful because they are more likely to be used in violent crimes. In the U.S., handguns fit this description since they are employed in more than 75 percent of firearm-related homicides and robberies, and a majority of the suicides where guns are the method of choice (Zimring 1991).

The findings of Tyler and Lavrakas (1983) suggest that the primary motivation for supporting or opposing gun control is the belief that such legislation would lessen or expand the crime rate. A 1992 *New York Times*/CBS News poll found that gun consumers as well as the general public support limited controls because they believe such laws deter criminals (Lewis 1992). For example, 82 percent of gun owners and 86 percent of the general population favor a national law that would require a seven-day waiting period between the time a person applies for a handgun and the time it is sold to allow for a background check. Further, 76 percent of gun owners and 79 percent of the general population agree with a complete ban on military-style assault weapons. Nonetheless, while the public is concerned about the misuses of firearms, there also is widespread support for uses such as hunting (Mauser 1990). Even with regard to handguns, a majority of the population (54 percent) is against a ban on their possession except by police or other authorized persons (Gallup 1993).

The pro-gun lobby in this country, which is led by the NRA, believes that any gun law is a foot in the door that eventually will lead to the wholesale confiscation of private firearms (Davidson 1992). One gun-control group has stated that this argument is "analogous to suggesting that the issuance of a driver's license and mandatory vehicle registration is the first step toward confiscating cars" (Executive Director's Report 1988, p. 8). In reality, legislation should be designed to meet the desires of the majority of the American public and gun consumers who favor limited controls, while simultaneously safeguarding the rights of lawful gun users.

To this end, groups such as the International Association of Chiefs of Police (1988) have recommended that the following features be included in a national screening program for handgun purchasers:

1. Positive verification of the identity of a prospective purchaser or permit applicant.
2. A waiting period to allow for a background check by local police agencies that also would provide a "cooling off" period for individuals pursuing crimes of passion.
3. The total costs related to this system would be supported by an appropriate fee charged to each applicant.

The records of states that have instituted similar programs argue for such a national policy. For example, in the 19 years that New Jersey has required a background check for handgun purchases, 10,000 convicted felons have been caught trying to purchase handguns. In California, the state's 15-day waiting period caused 1,200 prohibited gun buyers to be apprehended in one year alone. Further, this law does not include prohibitions on long guns such as shotguns and rifles used primarily for hunting and sport shooting. Thus, it maintains access to firearms by consumers for legitimate purposes while restricting access to guns that have a higher probability of being used for illicit aims.

Additionally, federal firearms licenses are far too easy to obtain. Applicants should undergo screening that could detect any psychopathological tendencies. Those who are not screened out should be given mandatory education on the uses and misuses of firearms. They also should be trained to spot suspicious customer behavior and buying patterns. And dealers who do not adhere closely to all regulations should have their licenses revoked.

As for firearms marketers, it is critical that any and all guns sold to civilians be childproofed. Whatever the cost of designing new models, it will be far outweighed by the lives saved and injuries prevented. Furthermore, marketers need to develop an ethical code that applies specifically to the advertising of dangerous products. Firearms advertising, for example, should not include attempts to associate guns with the "American Way," much less with criminals like Charles Whitman.

In the long run, it is essential that children be taught, from a young age, how to resolve conflicts peaceably. The Center to Prevent Handgun Violence, an education, research, and legal action organization (Brady 1992), is currently implementing a program to reduce the number of injuries and deaths that result from guns carried to schools each year by over 400,000 students. Their approach teaches children how to stay safe when encountering guns, how to distinguish between real-life and TV violence, and how to resolve conflict without hostility.

REFERENCES

Alexander, Andrew and Jim Stewart (1989), "'Miami Vice' the Trendsetter in Assault Weapons," *Atlanta Journal Constitution*, September 17, A13.

Alexander, Greg R., Ronnie M. Massey, Tyson Gibbs, and Joan M. Altekruse (1985), "Firearm-Related Fatalities: An Epidemiologic Assessment of Violent Death," *American Journal of Public Health*, 75 (2), 165-168.

American Academy of Pediatrics, Policy Statement, 20.

Bankston, William B. and Carol Y. Thompson (1989), "Carrying Firearms for Protection: A Causal Model," *Sociological Inquiry*, 59 (February), 75-87.

Boyd, Jeffery H. and Eve K. Moscicki (1986), "Firearms and Youth Suicide," *American Journal of Public Health*, 76 (10), 1240-1242.

Brady, James (1992), "Straight Talk About Children and Guns," *The New York Times*, March 30, A17.

Brent, David A., Joshua A. Perper, Christopher J. Allman, Grace M. Moritz, Mary E. Wartella, and Janice P. Zelenak (1991), "The Presence and Accessibility of Firearms in the Homes of Adolescent Suicides," *Journal of the American Medical Association*, 266 (21), 2989-2995.

Bureau of Justice Statistics (1992), *Sourcebook of Criminal Justice Statistics—1992*, Washington, DC: U.S. Government Printing Office.

Davidson, Osha Gray (1992), *Under Fire: The NRA and the Battle for Gun Control*, New York: Henry Holt.

Executive Director's Report (1988), "Special Issue: Guns and Violence—A National Tragedy," *The Police Chief*, March, 8.

Freedman, Alix M. 1992), "Fire Power: Behind the Cheap Guns Flooding the Cities Is a California Family," *The Wall Street Journal*, February 28, A1, A6-A7.

Gallup, George (1993), *The Gallup Poll Monthly*, 330 (March), Princeton.

Green, Gary S. (1987), "Citizen Gun Ownership and Criminal Deterrence: Theory, Research, and Policy," *Criminology*, 25 (1), 63-81.

Hand Gunning magazine (July/August 1994), 16, 87.

Hardy, David T. (1986), "Armed Citizens, Citizen Armies: Toward a Jurisprudence of the Second Amendment," *Harvard Journal of Law and Public Policy*, 9 (Summer), 559-638.

Hart, William L. (1988), "The Right to Bear Arms," *The Police Chief*, March, 32.

Herman, Robin (1992), "Suicide Risk Greater with Gun in the Home," *Washington Post Health*, August 18, 5.

Hill, Ronald Paul (1994), "A Consumer Perspective of Handgun Control in the U.S.," *Advancing the Consumer Interest*, 6 (1), 10-14.

Hollman, Laurie and Craig R. McCoy (1992), "The Growing Urban Arsenal," *The Philadelphia Inquirer*, August 2, E1, E4.

International Association of Chiefs of Police (1988), "Effective Firearm Management," *The Police Chief*, March, 21-24.

Hollom, W. Eugene (1974), *Frontier Violence: Another Look*, New York: Oxford University Press.

Joiner, Larry L. (1988), "Breaking the Cycle of Violence," *The Police Chief*, March, 34-35.

Kates, Don B. (1983), "Handgun Prohibition and the Original Meaning of the Second Amendment," *Michigan Law Review*, 82 (November), 204-273.

Kellerman, Arthur L. and Donald T. Reay (1986), "Protection or Peril? An Analysis of Firearm-Related Deaths in the Home," *New England Journal of Medicine*, 314 (24), 1557-1560.

Kilborn, Peter T. (1992), "The Gun Culture: Fun as Well as Life and Death," *The New York Times*, March 9, A1, A10.

Kleck, Gary (1988), "Crime Control Through the Private Use of Armed Force," *Social Problems*, 35 (February), 1-20.

Kleck, Gary and Karen McElrath (1991), "The Effects of Weaponry on Human Violence," *Social Forces*, 69 (March), 669-692.

Larson, Erik (1994), *Lethal Passage: How the Travels of a Single Handgun Expose the Roots of America's Gun Crisis*, New York: Crown Publishers, Inc.

Lester, David (1989), "Gun Ownership and Suicide in the United States," *Psychological Medicine*, 19, 519-521.

Lester, David and Ronald V. Clarke (1991), "Note on 'Suicide and Increased Availability of Handguns in the United States': The Influence of Firearm Ownership on Accidental Deaths," *Social Science Medicine*, 32 (11), 1311-1313.

Lewis, Neal A. (1992), "N.R.A. Meets Call for Gun Control With a Muzzle," *The New York Times*, March 12, D21.

Lund, Nelson (1987), "The Second Amendment, Political Liberty, and the Right to Self-Preservation," *Alabama Law Review*, 39 (Fall), 103-130.

Lyon, Peter (1969), *The Wild, Wild West*, New York: Funk and Wagnells.

Mauser, Gary A. (1990), "A Comparison of Canadian and American Attitudes Towards Firearms," *Canadian Journal of Criminology*, October, 573-589.

McDowall, David, Alan J. Lizotte, Brian Wiersema (1991), "General Deterrence Through Civilian Gun Ownership: An Evaluation of Quasi-Experimental Evidence," *Criminology*, 29 (4), 541-559.

Meese, Edwin (1988), "Attorney General's Forum: Safeguarding Both the Second Amendment and Public Safety," *The Police Chief*, March, 10.

Modern Gun magazine (August 1994), 3, 13, 61.

Mueller, Lee and Robert H. Campbell (1993), "Where Even the Flea Markets Crawl with Gun Dealers," *The Philadelphia Inquirer*, December 5, E2.

Ordog, Gary J. et al. (1988), "Gunshot Wounds in Children Under 10 Years of Age," *American Journal of Diseases of Children*, 142 (June), 618-622.

Otto, Mary (1994), "Survey: Guns May Outpace Cars as Killers," *Salt Lake Tribune*, January 28.

Price, James H., Sharon M. Desmond, Daisy Smith (1991), "A Preliminary Investigation of Inner City Adolescents' Perceptions of Guns," *Journal of School Health*, 61 (6), 255-259.

Rohter, Larry (1992), "Pistol Packs Glamour, Power and Reputation as a Menace," *The New York Times*, March 10, A1, A18.

Shotgun News (July 1989), cited in Larson (1994).

Slotkin, Richard (1992), *Gunfighter Nation*, New York: Atheneum.

Terry, Don (1992), "How Criminals Get Guns: In Short, All to Easily," *The New York Times*, March 11, A1, A20.

Treaster, Joseph B. (1992), "Teenage Murderers: Plentiful Guns, Easy Power," *The New York Times*, May 24, A1, A42.

Tyler, Tom R. and Paul J. Lavrakas (1983), "Support for Gun Control: The Influence of Personal, Sociotropic, and Ideological Concerns," *Journal of Applied Social Psychology*, 13 (5), 392-405.

Vobejda, Barbara (1994), "Advocacy Group Warns of Firearms Violence Against Youth," *The Philadelphia Inquirer*, June 21, A11.

Zimring, Franklin E. (1991), "Firearms, Violence, and Public Policy," *Scientific America*, November, 48-54.

The Impact of Framing, Anchorpoints, and Frames of Reference on Direct Mail Charitable Contributions

Gerald E. Smith, Boston College
Paul D. Berger, Boston University

ABSTRACT

Direct mail has long been an important tool to solicit charitable contributions. While consumers have become more comfortable using direct mail, they are deluged with ever more frequent direct mail solicitations. Direct marketers also have become increasingly sophisticated, which makes it difficult for traditional charitable direct mail appeals to cut through the clutter. The purpose of this paper is to examine three framing-related creative strategies in a charitable solicitation direct mail context: framing valence, suggested anchorpoints, and suggested frames of reference. It discusses the importance of considering these several framing heuristics *simultaneously* within the same research, and offers insights on how to test these effects using experimental design concepts.

Potential contributors to charitable organizations have become increasingly sophisticated and discerning in their giving. American companies have restructured, downsized, and emphasized efficient allocation of expenditures. Corporate contributors focus contributions strategically on fewer causes that relate more narrowly to the company's operations or marketing (O'Hare 1991). A recent study of the 100 largest corporate donation programs in the U.S. found that more than half have developed strategic plans for charitable giving (Therrien 1992; Zetlin 1990). Slower economic growth has had a similar effect on contributions by individuals. In the U.K., for instance, the British Charities Aid Foundation reported that individual contributions in 1991 were down significantly, almost 75% from 1989 contribution levels (Hamilton 1991).

Direct mail has long been an important tool to solicit charitable contributions. It also has become an increasingly prominent direct marketing channel for products and services. In 1990, direct mail dollar sales volume exceeded $23 billion, representing 18% of advertising expenditures (Kobs 1992). This has important implications for the direct mail efforts of charitable organizations. While consumers are more comfortable using direct mail, they are deluged with ever more frequent direct mail solicitations. Kobs (1992) reports that 53 percent of all mail a consumer receives is now advertising mail, versus only 27 percent eleven years ago (page 133).

Moreover, direct marketers have become increasingly sophisticated, through industry consultants, college and university direct marketing programs, and hundreds of books on the topic. Their use of advanced creative strategies to influence buyers makes it difficult for traditional charitable direct mail appeals to cut through the clutter.

A number of creative message strategies have been studied, tested, and applied in the consumer research literature, including framing strategies. In direct marketing, however, the literature on these strategies is less well developed. It is usually normative and offers practitioner guidelines. With respect to framing, for instance, one industry leader (Stone 1992) proposes that direct marketing appeals may be oriented toward one's desire to gain: to make money, to save time, to avoid effort, to achieve comfort, to have health, to enjoy pleasure, to be clean, to be praised, to be popular. Or, they may be oriented toward one's desire to avoid loss: to avoid criticism, to keep possessions, to avoid physical pain, to avoid loss of reputation, to avoid loss of money, or to avoid trouble.

The purpose of this paper is to examine three framing-related creative strategies in a charitable solicitation direct mail context: framing valence, suggested anchorpoints, and suggested frames of reference. The paper discusses the theory behind these framing-related concepts, their application to direct marketing, and their hypothesized effects.

The paper makes several important contributions to the direct marketing and consumer research literatures. It discusses how framing-related heuristics may be applied and tested in direct marketing. It also hypothesizes how these heuristics may influence behaviors in the field of charitable contributions, a topic that has been unexplored to date. It hypothesizes how framing influences actual donor behavior, i.e., likelihood of giving and average gift, rather than attitudinal measures, such as beliefs, affect, or intent to purchase. It discusses the importance of considering these several framing heuristics *simultaneously* within the same research, rather than independently, and offers insights on how to test these effects using experimental design concepts.

FRAMING, ANCHORPOINTS, AND FRAMES OF REFERENCE

We distinguish among three related effects on consumer decision making with respect to charitable direct mail appeals: framing, anchorpoints, and suggested frames of reference (see Smith and Wortzel 1993). All three flow from prospect theory (Kahneman and Tversky 1979; Tversky and Kahneman 1992), or from Tversky and Kahneman's (1974) anchor and adjustment effect.

Prospect theory proposes that under uncertainty decision makers employ heuristic processing. Decision outcomes are coded categorically as gains or losses relative to a neutral reference point. Decision makers are more responsive to losses than to gains, i.e., losses loom larger than gains. Certainty is overweighted, and uncertainty is underweighted. People are risk averse with respect to gains and risk seeking with respect to losses; that is, they prefer a small certain gain to a large uncertain gain, and they prefer a large uncertain loss to a small certain loss.

Applying Kahneman and Tversky's logic to the domain of charitable contributions suggests that there are three ways to influence a decision maker's frame of reference: (1) by influencing reference point formation; (2) by describing the valence of alternatives relative to the reference point, i.e., in positive or negative terms; and (3) by changing buyers' perceptions of decision certainty. In this research we focus on the first two effects.

We refer to *framing* as framing valence; that is, describing product performance information or decision outcomes in either positive or negative terms (Levin and Gaeth 1988; Meyerowitz and Chaiken 1987; Maheswaran and Meyers-Levy 1990). *Suggested anchorpoints* refer to the presentation of a specific starting value to make decision judgments, e.g., a suggested retail price or donation level (Tversky and Kahneman 1974). *Suggested frames of reference* evoke comparisons of more encompassing decision frames. In this research we test two types. Experiential frames of reference are consumer focused, and compare a consumer's predecision need status to a positive or negative post-decision outcome; the consequent outcome is contingent on the decision. Product frames of reference are product focused, and compare the product performance of one product to that of another, or compare product performance to some external performance standard.

The consumer research literatures for each of these effects offer important insights that help explain and predict how framing-related effects may influence consumer behavior towards charitable contributions. We next discuss each in turn.

HYPOTHESIZED EFFECTS ON CHARITABLE DIRECT MAIL APPEALS

The Effect of Framing

Empirical framing research gives evidence that buyers are motivated by the prospect of loss aversion. Meyerowitz and Chaiken (1987) framed the positive (negative) consequences of (not) performing monthly breast self-examinations (BSE) for cancer. Stressing BSE's negative consequences was more persuasive than emphasizing its positive consequences. Maheswaran and Meyers-Levy (1990) framed message content regarding cholesterol testing in terms of "you stand to gain (lose) important health benefits if you take (fail to take) the initiative to learn what your current cholesterol count is." Negatively framed messages were more persuasive with subjects who were more involved in health and cholesterol-related issues. Positively framed messages were more persuasive with less involved subjects.

Puto's work in industrial procurement (Puto 1987; Qualls and Puto 1989; Puto, Patton, and King 1985; see also Rowe and Puto 1987) found that framing influenced reference point formation, and hence buyers' perceptions of gains and losses. Consistent with prospect theory, positively framed sales messages led to risk averse buyer behavior; negatively framed messages led to risk seeking behavior. Levin and Gaeth (1988) found that labeling a product attribute in negative terms (25% fat) led to less favorable consumer evaluations than labeling in positive terms (75% lean); the framing effect was reduced after product trial.

These findings suggest that negatively framed direct mail appeals for charitable contributions will be more persuasive than positively framed appeals. Yet, direct mail appeals for charitable contributions differ from other product or service purchase decisions studied in previous framing research. With direct mail charitable appeals actual decision behavior is observed, whereas with most other framing studies attitudinal measures have been observed. Two behavioral measures are relevant to the success of charitable direct mail appeals: the likelihood of making a donation, and the magnitude of the gift.

In most previous framing studies the decision maker benefited directly from the decision: personal health benefits (Meyerowitz and Chaiken 1987; Maheswaran and Meyers-Levy 1990; Levin and Gaeth 1988); job performance as an industrial purchase agent (Puto 1987; Qualls and Puto 1989; Puto, Patton, and King 1985). Charitable contributions result in indirect benefits to the donor. Charitable organizations reinforce these benefits by prominently publicizing the donor's gift-giving status, by offering special organizational benefits, etc.

The framing literature also frequently addresses risky purchase contexts. Charitable contributions, by contrast, involve little or no risk, unless one is motivated by possible perceptions of social risk, i.e., the risk of being viewed unfavorably by one's peers. On the other hand, many charitable appeals attempt to make the donor feel like a member of the organization such that risk and loss to the organization affects all members of the organization. Hence, donors are motivated on behalf of the organization to take action to avoid organizational risk and loss.

The shared risk that donor-members of the organization perceive is likely to be felt most acutely by those who care most about and are most involved in the organization. These donors perhaps have been associated with the organization longer, or engage in lifestyles and activities that are consistent with the organization's mission, i.e., a form of enduring involvement (Bloch and Richins 1983; Houston and Rothschild 1978). Maheswaran and Meyers-Levy (1990) give evidence that involvement moderates response to framing. Thus, the greater the perception of potential organizational risk or loss the more likely these high involvement donors will increase the magnitude of their contribution. Nonetheless, this may have little effect on the number of donors responding to a direct mail appeal, particularly if donors on the margin are less involved, or only peripherally interested in the charity's mission.

Hence, we propose that

P$_{1a}$: Negatively framed direct mail appeals for charitable contributions will yield greater average donations than positively framed appeals.

P$_{1b}$: Negatively framed direct mail appeals for charitable contributions will not yield greater likelihood of response relative to positively framed appeals.

The Effect of Suggested Anchorpoints

Tversky and Kahneman (1974) gave early evidence of the effect of anchorpoints. They noted that people make heuristic judgments relative to specific anchorpoints to reduce decision processing and mental effort. Typically, subjects bias perceptual judgments in the direction of the anchorpoint. For example, when asked to estimate the percentage of African countries in the United Nations, subjects who were given higher starting values evoked higher estimates, and subjects given lower starting values evoked lower estimates.

A number of empirical papers in marketing have demonstrated anchor and adjustment in decision making. For example, Fraser, Hite and Sauer (1988), found that the presence of a $20 "suggested contribution level" on a donation request resulted in average gifts nearly three times the average gift of a control group that received no suggested anchorpoint appeal. Brockner et. al. (1984) found that when a specific dollar amount was mentioned in telephone and face-to-face fundraising, subjects were more likely to comply and make a pledge than when no amount was mentioned. Subjects also pledged greater amounts when exposed to higher suggested anchorpoint treatments. Reingen (1982) found that exposing potential donors to a list of other compliers significantly increased the number of donors, but not the average gift. In a related experiment, the size of compliers' donations was varied, which led to changes in the magnitude of donations.

In the pricing literature, Urbany, Bearden, and Weilbaker (1988) tested different levels of "advertised reference prices." They found that even though subjects attitudinally rejected exaggerated reference prices (150 percent greater than the actual sale price), these prices still positively influenced perceptions of value and estimates of market price. Berkowitz and Walton (1980) found that deeper price discounts relative to a comparison "regular price" evoked greater perceptions of value in three separate product categories. Della Bitta, Monroe, and McGinnis (1981) found that larger differences between sale price and regular price (differences ranging from 10 percent to 50 percent) led to greater perceived savings and perceived value for money. Mobley, Bearden, and Teel (1988) also found greater perceptions of value for larger "advertised price reductions."

The Fraser, Hite, and Sauer (1988), Brockner et. al. (1984), and Reingen (1982) studies give evidence that suggested anchors influence the magnitude of gifts in the direction of the anchor. This is consistent with the pricing literature where suggested reference prices influenced buyers perceptions of attitudinal measures such as perceived value and savings. Fraser, Hite, and Sauer (1988) tested the *presence or absence* of a suggested anchor. Brockner et. al. (1984) tested different *levels*, as well as presence or absence of a suggested anchor.

The Brockner et. al. (1984) study also gives evidence that providing subjects with a concrete suggested anchor influenced the magnitude of a pledge. This is consistent with the conceptualization of suggested anchors as a decision heuristic that allows donors to quickly infer approximately what would be a reasonable gift. Their results were inconclusive, however, about whether the size of the suggested anchor influences likelihood of making a pledge. If donations were seen as a form of price given in exchange for benefits derived from a charitable organization, it seems reasonable to suggest that smaller suggested anchorpoints would yield larger levels of compliance.

Hence we propose that the magnitude of the suggested anchor will have the following effects:

P2a: Greater suggested anchorpoints will yield greater average gifts.

P2b: Smaller suggested anchorpoints will yield greater likelihood of response.

The Effect of Suggested Frames of Reference

Direct marketing practitioners suggest several rules of thumb that relate to suggested frames of reference: (1) Specific episode narratives outpull statistics; (2) Examples are more credible than exhortation; (3) Coupling examples with exhortation geometrically expands the emotional impact of a message (Lewis 1992).

One type of suggested frame of reference involves episodic or narrative forms of information. It provides respondents with frames of reference that are holistic, experiential, or image oriented. We call these *experiential frames of reference.* They involve explicit comparisons of a personal need state (before) and a consequent outcome (after), which may be framed in positive or negative terms. The outcome is contingent on the decision. In advertising, for example, many weight loss advertisements provide vivid, and frequently visual, frames of reference to potential buyers. Other outcome frames of reference in advertising present explicit points of reference relating to personal emergencies (need state before), such as a fire, hurricane, flood, accident, theft, or illness. The consequent outcome (after), according to these advertisements, depends on the consumer's decision with respect to insurance, security systems, or safety equipment. See Wiener, Gentry and Miller (1986) and Gentry, Wiener and Burnett (1987) for examples in the literature.

The following excerpt from a Chrysler advertisement illustrates:

HEADLINE: "An open letter to Lee Iacocca."
COPY: "Dear Mr. Iacocca: I sat in an ambulance today looking at my 20 year old daughter Kelly's beautiful face. She still has her beautiful face and her life because of you... Today a truck hit her at about 60 mph. It took them 1/2 an hour to get her out of what was left of her new car. The police said she would surely be dead if not for her airbag... I thanked God for you and your deep appreciation and dedication to automobile safety.... [signed]"

Fortunately, relative to the need state (an automobile accident), for these buyers the outcome was positive because they had made the decision to buy a Chrysler car with an airbag.

Another type of suggested frame of reference focuses on product image and product performance. It provides respondents with comparative frames of reference that are concrete, factual, and product oriented, often along specific product attributes. We call these *product frames of reference.* Such frames often compare one product to another, or compare a product's performance to that of an established frame of reference in the industry. The decision is framed in terms of superior performance (e.g., our brand) relative to a known frame of reference (e.g., a leading brand). Comparative advertising of a challenger brand to a leader brand illustrates a commonly used product frame of reference.

Recent empirical research by Smith and Wortzel (1993) and Smith (1992) gives evidence that the presence of suggested frames of reference in advertising favorably influences intent to purchase consumer durables (video cameras). With respect to charitable direct mail appeals, however, the only trace of evidence we have that suggested frames of reference may be effective in such appeals is embodied in the rules of thumb highlighted at the beginning of this section. While not reported in the literature but most likely studied in unreported direct marketing tests, these rules imply that narrative episodic information, similar to our experiential frames of reference, appear to have been effective in influencing donor response to charitable direct mail appeals, although it is difficult to infer the extent to which compliance, average gift, or both were affected.

We propose that experiential frames of reference will be more effective at influencing compliance than product frames of reference. The reason for this is that donors with low involvement in the organization are more likely to attend to narrative, story-oriented copy than to statistical or exhortation copy. These low involvement donors are likely to be infrequent contributors. We expect that product frames will be effective in raising the average gift, particularly for donors who are more involved in the organization and its mission, and hence already relatively frequent contributors. These donors should relate more to statistical information about the institution and its performance and status relative to other institutions.

Hence, we propose that

P3a: The presence of an experiential frame of reference will yield greater compliance (i.e., higher response rate) than the presence of a product frame; this effect will be even greater for those who contributed less frequently in the past.

P3b: The presence of a product frame will yield a greater average gift than the presence of an experiential frame; this effect will be even greater for those who contributed more frequently in the past.

METHODOLOGICAL ISSUES

A number of methodological issues are particularly relevant to the study of these framing-related heuristics because of the possibility of potential interaction effects. Direct mail appeals, for instance, often employ not just one framing-related heuristic, but several simultaneously. For example, a charitable organization may frame an appeal in negative terms, as a potential loss to the organization if the respondent does not comply, while also suggesting either a low or high monetary amount as an anchorpoint. Consequently it is important to study not only the individual effects of these decision heuristics, but their interaction effects as well.

This has implications for the design of the experiment, as well as related issues such as experimental context and operationalization.

Selection of Experimental Context (Charitable Cause)

We refer to experimental context as the charitable cause in which to test framing-related heuristic effects. Two considerations are important. First, the researchers must be able to manipulate either positive or negative framing executions in the experimental context in such a way that these executions are viewed by respondents as credible and reasonably natural. Second, the experimental context must allow for simultaneous testing of both product frames of reference and experiential frames of reference.

From a framing valence perspective, charitable or non-profit organizations can be divided into satisfying two types of needs: those that enhance utility, and those that preserve utility (see Kahn and Meyer 1991 for a similar distinction of utility enhancing and utility preserving attributes; and Rossiter and Percy 1985, 1987 for a related discussion of transformational and informational communications).

Utility enhancing charities focus on positively valenced needs and motivations. They transform the recipient of the charity's services through sensory gratification, intellectual stimulation, or social or societal recognition or approval. Utility enhancing charities include, for example, the arts, literature, and many areas of scientific research such as space exploration or materials technologies. In such contexts positively framed appeals stress opportunities to gain; negatively framed appeals stress foregoing the opportunity to gain.

For example, college education may be framed as improving the quality of one's life by helping one fulfill a more satisfying lifestyle embodying career opportunity, income, and status. This emphasizes positive, gain-oriented, aspects of college education. College education also may be framed in terms of negative, loss-oriented dimensions. For example, a student's inability to complete a college education because of insufficient financial support may place him/her at a disadvantage relative to his/her peers. Consequently, the student struggles to get along on less income, with more career obstacles, and with fewer and less attractive opportunities.

Utility preserving charitable causes focus on negatively valenced needs and motivations. They preserve, protect, or remedy problems that affect recipients of the charity's services. These charities include, for example, research for serious diseases, such as cancer, heart, muscular dystrophy, or AIDS. They also address personal or societal needs such as hunger relief, disaster relief, environmental pollution, or resource depletion. In these contexts positively framed appeals stress the likelihood of avoiding a loss; negatively framed appeals stress the likelihood of incurring a loss.

Second, the choice of experimental context must also consider how to operationalize experiential and product frames of reference. College education, for example, offers opportunities to credibly operationalize experiential frames of reference using student experiences, e.g., a student with an acute financial need whose personal outcome is influenced by a donor's decision. The intercompetitive climate of university education also provides opportunities to operationalize product frames of reference, e.g., "our university's spending on educational programs versus other universities' spending".

Operationalizing Anchorpoints, Frames of Reference, and Framing

Operationalizing framing-related treatment manipulations involves several important considerations. These are particularly applicable in situations where the charity mails a solicitation appeal to a large number of previous donors, with a wide range of previous donations. For example, what level of donation should the charity suggest to the potential donor? For target respondents who *have never previously given* to the charity, a direct mail appeal may suggest a uniform suggested donation level, e.g., $100, or may suggest a range of anchorpoints in the same appeal, e.g., $25, $50, $75, $100, $_____.

For target respondents who *have previously given* to the charity the operationalization of the suggested anchor is more complex, and more important. To suggest an anchorpoint in the current appeal that is lower than last year's donation may be misinterpreted by respondents, e.g., the organization doesn't need more money, is poorly managed, didn't appreciate my previous gift. Direct mail appeals to previous donors virtually require a *customized* suggested donation that is consistent with the donor's previous giving history.

Fortunately, data processing technology allows the charity manager to easily customize suggested donation appeals. However, care must be taken to ensure that this is handled appropriately. For instance, for a person who gave $210 last year, a simple linear algorithm might suggest a 15% increase this year to $241.50. While customized, to the donor such computer automated appeals are not only transparent, but seem excessively precise, artificial, and, in the end, impersonal. A more natural appeal, of course, would be to round up to a suggested donation of $250.

The issue of rounding is more complex, since rounding levels may need to differ for different levels of suggested donation. For example, for a person who gave $60 last year, a suggested 15% increase this year to $69, rounded up to the nearest $10 increment, i.e., to $70, might be reasonable. However, to a donor who gave $2,500 last year, rounding up in similar $10 increments might seem trivially precise. Here, a calculated 15% increase to $2,875 would be rounded to $2,880. It might be more reasonable to round to a suggested anchorpoint of $3,000.

A number of operational rules are possible to address rounding. We propose one that may be useful for practical implementation, and for empirically testing different anchorpoint levels in an experimental context. To illustrate, assume that a charity solicits donations from previous individual donors. Previous donations may be categorized into groups, ranging from smaller gifts (under $50) to larger gifts (over $2,500). The calculated amount for the suggested anchor then may be rounded up by an appropriate category rounding level. Table 1 shows a summary of possible donation categories and their respective rounding levels. The rounding levels were determined by the following rule: Round to a multiple of 10% of the highest donation for the category. Thus, for a donor who gave $600 last year, a *calculated* 15% increase this year to $690 would be rounded to a suggested anchor of $700.

Table 2 shows examples of suggested anchorpoint calculations for two potential respondents, one exposed to a suggested anchor treatment 10% higher than the last donation, the other to a treatment 50% higher than the last donation. The range of suggested anchor amounts shown in the table (i.e., +10 percent to +50 percent) is consistent with previous price anchorpoint research. For example, Della Bitta, Monroe, and McGinnis (1981) tested price discounts ranging from 10 to 50 percent. Keiser and Krum (1976) tested discounts of 50 percent. At the extreme, Urbany, Bearden, and Weilbaker (1988) tested exaggerated reference prices of 150 percent greater than the sale price.

The operationalization of frames of reference is dependent on the context of the direct mail appeal. Experiential frames of reference involve explicit comparisons of a personal need state (before) and a consequent outcome (after); the outcome is contin-

TABLE 1
Suggested Anchorpoint Donor Categories and Rounding Levels

Donor Category	Anchor Rounded Up To Nearest
≤$50	$5
$51-$100	$10
$101-$250	$25
$251-$500	$50
$501-$1,000	$100
$1,001-$2,500	$250
$2,501+	$500

TABLE 2
Example of Suggested Anchorpoint Calculation for Two Potential Respondents

Previous Donation	Anchor Treatment	Calculated Anchorpoint	Rounded Up To Nearest	Suggested Anchorpoint
$260	+10%	$286	$50	$300
$70	+50%	$105	$10	$110

TABLE 3
Operationalizations of Experiential and Product Frames of Reference, With Framing Valence

	Experiential Frame of Reference	Product Frame of Reference
Positive	Imagine the following scenario. A dedicated student had a wonderful first year in college. She was on the Dean's List, having achieved high grades. But then something happened. She lost some federal financial assistance. *Without this aid it would be impossible to continue her education.* Fortunately, she was attending [University Name]. When members of the Office of Financial Assistance learned of her plight, they immediately contacted her at home and found additional financial aid. *Within days, she was back in class and engrossed in her studies.*	A hallmark of a great university is its spending on educational programs for students. *With the support of concerned alumni like you, our spending on educational programs can continue to increase and surpass other universities'.* A recent survey showed that [University name] spent *$15,997* per student on educational programs in 1992. By contrast, other, comparable national universities spent an average of *$13,796* during the same period.
Negative	Imagine the following scenario. A dedicated student had a wonderful first year in college. She was on the Dean's List, having achieved high grades. But then something happened. She lost some federal financial assistance. *Without this aid it would be impossible to continue her education.* Unfortunately, she attended a university where financial aid was in short supply. Instead of going back to school immediately, *she had to defer her education while earning additional money for the shortfall in tuition and expenses.*	A hallmark of a great university is its spending on educational programs for students. *Without the support of concerned alumni like you, our spending on educational programs may fall behind other universities'.* A recent survey showed that [University Name] spent *$15,997* per student on educational programs in 1992. By contrast, other, comparable national universities spent an average of *$13,796* during the same period.

gent on the decision. Table 3 illustrates the operationalization of an experiential frame of reference, for both positively and negatively framed conditions, for a potential educational institution's fundraising direct mail appeal. Here, potential donors are presented with an episodic narrative (in this case based on a true incident) that presents a sudden need state (before) of a student losing financial assistance, forcing her to discontinue her education. In the positively framed appeal the consequent outcome (after) is positive, i.e., she is quickly reinstated in school because the university has additional financial aid available to provide emergency assistance.

In the negatively framed appeal the consequent outcome is negative, i.e., she must defer her education, because financial aid was in short supply.

Product frames of reference compare one product to another, or compare a product's performance to that of an established frame of reference. The decision is framed in terms of superior performance (e.g., our brand) relative to the frame of reference. The other half of table 3 illustrates the operationalization of a product frame of reference, for both positively and negatively framed conditions, for an educational institution. The dimension used for performance comparison is money spent per student on educational programs for students. Respondents are presented with the university's per student spending ($15,997) versus the spending of "comparable national universities." Positively framed appeals emphasize that financial support will enable the university to "continue to increase and surpass other universities." Negatively framed appeals warn that failure to support may cause the university to "fall behind other universities."

Experimental Design Issues

As noted earlier, it is important to study the interaction effects as well as the individual effects of framing valence, frames of reference, and suggested anchorpoints. One way to achieve this is to design a simple 2x2x2 design with framing valence at two levels (positive, negative), suggested anchorpoint at two levels (high, low), and frame of reference at two levels (product frame, experiential frame). In addition to simplicity, this 8 cell design offers the ability to test all main effects, all 2-way interactions, and the 3-way interaction among the three major framing-related heuristics.

However, this design precludes the possibility of testing the potential interaction effect between presence/absence of product frame of reference and presence/absence of experiential frame of reference, or of testing the interaction effect of, say, presence/absence of experiential frame and level of framing valence, or presence/absence of product frame and level of framing valence. Moreover, charities employing direct mail may want to employ both product frame of reference and experiential frame of reference in the same appeal.

This requires experimentally treating presence/absence of product frame of reference as one factor and presence/absence of experiential frame of reference as another factor. In this case a two-way interaction between factors "Product Frame" and "Framing Valence" can be described by saying that "the impact of the presence of a product frame differs depending on the level of framing valence," or "the impact of framing valence differs depending on the presence/absence of a Product Frame." Both descriptions are numerically equivalent; one may be more contextually useful.

Treating product frame and experiential frame as two separate factors, each with two levels (present, absent), yields a four-factor *full factorial* design as follows:

Factor	Factor Definition	Levels
A	Suggested Anchorpoint	Low / High
B	Product Frame of Reference	Not Present / Present
C	Experiential Frame of Reference	Not Present / Present
D	Framing Valence	Negative / Positive

This design allows testing the interaction of product frame of reference and experiential frame of reference, BC. It also allows testing the remaining five 2-way interactions among the other factors, i.e., AB, AC, AD, BD, and CD, as well as the four 3-way interactions, i.e., ABC, ABD, BCD, ACD, and the 4-way interaction, ABCD.

A potential disadvantage of this design to charities using direct mail is the number of treatment cells required for implementation, 16. This may be unwieldy and costly. The experimental design literature offers several possible solutions. One is to utilize a *fractional factorial* design, rather than a full factorial design. For example, a 2^{4-1} fractional factorial design with defining relation/contrast I=ABCD results in each of the 4 main effects being aliased with a 3-factor interaction, and each of the 6 two factor interactions being aliased with another two factor interaction, as follows:

I =	ABCD
A	BCD
B	ACD
C	ABD
D	ABC
AB	CD
AC	BD
AD	BC

See Table 4 for detailed specification of cells and treatment levels for this design. For details of alias patterns in fractional factorial designs, see for example Davies (1984). Given the typical assumption that all 3-way and higher order interactions are zero (or negligible), the main effects thus may be cleanly (and orthogonally) estimated. The 2-way interactions, however, are aliased in pairs, which means that it is necessary to provide independent evidence, from other studies, or separate tests, that some of the two way interactions are in fact zero.

Previous framing research in an advertising context (Smith and Berger 1994) gives evidence of significant two-way interaction effects between product frames of reference and framing valence (BD), and between experiential frames of reference and framing valence (CD), but of *non-significant* two-way interaction effects between suggested anchorpoint and product frame of reference (AB), between suggested anchorpoint and experiential frame of reference (AC), and between product frame of reference and experiential frame of reference (BC). If it were reasonable to assume that these patterns held across experimental context, then the AB, AC, and BC 2-factor interaction effects could be assumed to be zero (or negligible). This would allow clean and orthogonal estimation of the remaining 2-factor interactions: AD, BD, and CD.

CONCLUSION

Direct mail has long been a staple fundraising technique for charitable organizations. In recent years, however, buyers have become more deluged with mail advertising appeals, while direct mail marketers have become increasingly sophisticated. This paper conceptualizes, hypothesizes, and describes how to test the effect of three creative strategies that should be useful to charities' direct mail efforts. The paper is part of a larger project designed to empirically test these effects.

Based on the consumer behavior literature we distinguished between framing, describing product performance or decision outcomes in positive or negative terms; suggested anchorpoints, the presentation of a specific starting value to make decision judg-

TABLE 4
Experimental Design

1	ab	ac	ad
Low Anchor PF Not Present EF Not Present Neg Framing	High Anchor PF Present EF Not Present Neg Framing	High Anchor PF Not Present EF Present Neg Framing	High Anchor PF Not Present EF Not Present Pos Framing
bc	**bd**	**cd**	**abcd**
Low Anchor PF Present EF Present Neg Framing	Low Anchor PF Present EF Not Present Pos Framing	Low Anchor PF Not Present EF Present Pos Framing	High Anchor PF Present EF Present Pos Framing

PF=Product Frame
EF=Experiential Frame

ments; and suggested frames of reference, the comparison of post-decision outcomes with a pre-decision need state for experiential frames, and the presentation of our product's performance versus other performance frames of reference for product frames.

This work complements related efforts in advertising and marketing communications, and hopefully will help stimulate further research in the fields of direct marketing and framing in general.

REFERENCES

Berkowitz, Eric N. and John R. Walton (1980), "Contextual Influences on Consumer Price Responses: An Experimental Analysis," Journal of Marketing Research, Vol 17 (August), 349-358.

Bloch, Peter H. and Marsha L. Richins (1983), "A Theoretical Model for the Study of Product Importance Perceptions," *Journal of Marketing* 47 (Summer), 69-81.

Brockner, Joel et. al. (1984), "Organizational Fundraising: Further Evidence on the Effect of Legitimizing Small Donations," *Journal of Consumer Research* 11 (June), 611-614.

Davies, O. L. (1984). *The Design and Analysis of Industrial Experiments.* New York: Hafner, Third Edition.

Della Bitta, Albert J., Kent B. Monroe, and John M. McGinnis (1981), "Consumer Perceptions of Comparative Price Advertisements," *Journal of Marketing Research,* Vol. 18 (November), 416-427.

Fraser, Cynthia, Robert E. Hite and Paul L. Sauer (1988), "Increasing Contributions in Solicitation Campaigns: The Use of Large and Small Anchorpoints," *Journal of Consumer Research,* 15 (September), 284-287.

Gentry, James W., Joshua L. Wiener, and Melissa Burnett (1987), "The Story, the Frame, and the Choice," in Melanie Wallendorf and Paul Anderson, eds., *Advances in Consumer Research,* Vol. 14. Provo, UT: Association for Consumer Research, 198-202.

Hamilton, Sally (1991), "Cashing In on Good Works," *Business-London* (July), 99-101.

Houston, Michael J. and Michael L. Rothschild (1978), "Conceptual and Methodological Perspectives in Involvement," in *Research Frontiers in Marketing: Dialogues and Directions,* S. Jain, ed. Chicago: American Marketing Association, 184-7.

Kahn, Barbara E., and Robert J. Meyer (1991), "Consumer Multiattribute Judgments under Attribute-Weight Uncertainty," *Journal of Consumer Research,* 17 (March), 508-522.

Kahn, Barbara E., and Robert J. Meyer (1991), "Consumer Multiattribute Judgments under Attribute-Weight Uncertainty," *Journal of Consumer Research,* 17 (March), 508-522.

Kahneman, Daniel and Amos Tversky (1979), "Prospect Theory: An Analysis of Decision Under Risk," *Econometrica,* 47 (March), 263-291.

Keiser, Stephen K. and James R. Krum (1976), "Consumer Perceptions of Retail Advertising With Overstated Price Savings," *Journal of Retailing,* Vol. 52 (Fall), 27-36.

Kobs, Jim (1992). *Profitable Direct Marketing, second edition.* Lincolnwood, IL: NTC Books.

Levin, Irwin and Gary J. Gaeth (1988), "How Consumers Are Affected by the Framing of Attribute Information Before and After Consuming the Product," *Journal of Consumer Research,* 15 (December), 374-378.

Lewis, Herschell Gordon (1992), "Fifty of the Easiest Ways to Begin An Effective Sales Letter," *Direct Marketing* (October), 16-19.

Maheswaran, Durairaj and Joan Meyers-Levy (1990), "The Influence of Message Framing and Issue Involvement," *Journal of Marketing Research,* 27 (August), 361-367.

Meyerowitz, Beth E. and Shelly Chaiken (1987), "The Effect of Message Framing on Breast Self-Examination Attitudes, Intentions, and Behavior," *Journal of Personality and Social Psychology,* Vol. 52, No. 3, 500-510.

Mobley, Mary F., William O. Bearden, and Jesse E. Teel (1988), "An Investigation of Individual Responses to Tensile Price Claims," *Journal of Consumer Research,* 15 (September), 273-279.

O' Hare, Barbara Clark (1991), "Good Deeds Are Good Business," *American Demographics* 13 (September), 38-42.

Puto, Christopher P. (1987), "The Framing of Buying Decisions," *Journal of Consumer Research,* Vol. 14 (December), 301-315.

Puto, Christopher P., Wesley E. Patton III, and Ronald H. King (1985), "Risk Handling Strategies in Industrial Vendor Selection Decisions," *Journal of Marketing 49,* 89-98.

Qualls, William J. and Christopher P. Puto (1989), "Organizational Climate and Decision Framing: An Integrated Approach to Analyzing Industrial Buying Decisions," *Journal of Marketing Research,* Vol. 26 (May), 179-192.

Reingen, Peter H. (1982), "Test of a List Procedure for Inducing Compliance with a Request to Donate Money," *Journal of Applied Psychology* 67 (February), 110-118.

Rowe, Debra and Christopher P. Puto (1987), "Do Consumers' Reference Points Affect Their Buying Decisions?" in Melanie Wallendorf and Paul Anderson, eds., *Advances in Consumer Research,* Vol. 14. Provo, UT: Association for Consumer Research.

Smith, Gerald E. (1992), "Prior Knowledge and the Effectiveness of Message Frames in Advertising," Unpublished dissertation, Boston University.

Smith, Gerald E. and Paul D. Berger (1994), "The Impact of Anchor Framing and Prior Knowledge on Advertising Effectiveness," Working Paper, Boston College.

Smith, Gerald E., and Lawrence H. Wortzel (1993). *Prior Knowledge and the Effect of Message Frames in Advertising.* Cambridge, MA: Marketing Science Institute.

Stone, Bob (1992). *Successful Direct Marketing Methods, Fourth Edition.* Lincolnwood, IL: NTC Business Books.

Therrien, Lois (1991), "Corporate Generosity is Greatly Depreciated," *Business Week* (November 2), 118-120.

Tversky, Amos and Daniel Kahneman (1974), "Judgment Under Uncertainty: Heuristics and Biases," *Science* 185, 1124-31.

Tversky, Amos and Daniel Kahneman (1992), "Advances in Prospect Theory: Cumulative Representation of Uncertainty," *Journal of Risk and Uncertainty.*

Urbany, Joel E., William O. Bearden, and Dan C. Weilbaker (1988), "The Effect of Plausible and Exaggerated Reference Prices on Consumer Perceptions and Price Search," *Journal of Consumer Research,* Vol. 15 (June), 95-110.

Wiener, Joshua L., James W. Gentry, and Ronald K. Miller (1986), "The Framing of the Insurance Purchase Decision," in Richard J. Lutz, ed., *Advances in Consumer Research,* Vol. 13. Provo, UT: Association for Consumer Research.

Zetlin, Minda (1990), "Companies Find Profit in Corporate Giving," *Management Review* 79 (December), 10-15.

Issues in Identifying Performance Measures for Social Marketing Programs

Teresa M. Pavia, University of Utah

Kotler (1987) suggests the following four step control process will maximize the probability that a social marketing organization will achieve its objectives: goal setting, performance measurement, performance diagnosis and corrective actions. The focus of this paper is to explore in depth the issues concerned with the second of these steps, performance measurement. Existing literature emphasizes methods for performing measurement rather than the problems with identifying the correct items to measure. This paper focuses on performance indicator selection as it applies to social marketing. An example of the complexity of this process, drawn from an existing advocacy group, is given.

Social marketing programs attempt to influence ideas, attitudes and/or behaviors in various arenas. Examples include non-smoking campaigns, organ donor programs, increasing environmental responsibility, advocacy for children, and safe sex campaigns. Sometimes organizations concerned with such causes have a specific goal that could, at least in theory, be measured, e.g., an increased awareness of condom benefits or condom usage. At other times the agency's stated goal is more difficult to quantify, such as improving child and maternal health or increasing someone's readiness for the job market. Whether the agency's goals appear straightforward or not, there are significant hurdles that must be overcome before an agency can successfully monitor the effect of its attempts at social marketing. This has lead some to suggest that "scarce resources are better invested in careful planning and meticulous execution than in evaluative research" (Fine 1990, pg. 299). Such problems notwithstanding, the need and the urge to monitor the effects of attempts at social marketing suggests establishing performance indicators for measuring the success or failure of these programs. The goal of this paper is to explore some of the critical decisions that must be made by an organization as it selects the indicators it will use to monitor its performance.

GOAL SETTING

Kotler (1987) suggests that a four step control process will maximize the probability that an organization will achieve its objectives. The steps are: goal setting (what are we trying to do), performance measurement (what is actually occurring), performance diagnosis (why are we seeing these results) and corrective actions (what should we do about it). Following this schema, it is premature to explore the issues surrounding performance measures before discussing the complexity of goal setting in social marketing. It is useful to think of goal setting at several levels. There is broad scale, macro level, *visionary* goal setting which generally corresponds to the overall mission. An example of a visionary goal could be to "Encourage self-sufficiency while helping those with special needs to lead productive, fulfilling lives" (Utah Tomorrow 1992). Visions like these are achieved when various *objectives* or *action level goals* are met such as "Provide needed mental health services for mentally ill adults and children" (Utah Tomorrow 1992). Objectives or action level goals can then be monitored by using *performance measures* or *benchmarks* to indicate movement towards or away from the goal. Continuing with the example provided above, a benchmark for mental health could be the "Number of seriously mentally ill adults and youth on waiting lists for services" (Utah Tomorrow 1992).

One step in establishing goals is developing a clear picture of what the organization considers success. The next decision is

whether success is measured by the absence of negative features or the presence of positive features. For example, if an agency has a vision of "promoting the well-being of children," it must have a clear picture of what a child with high well-being looks like. If one focuses on the absence of negative features one might suggest that action goals for this vision include reducing poverty rates and homelessness since a poverty stricken homeless child is probably not a child with high well-being. However, is a child with a home and with an income above the poverty level necessarily a child that rates high on "well-being"? That is, is it sufficient to measure risks that may impede the macro level goals and assume that anyone not in the risk group has met the goal? Instead of focusing on negative features, one could set goals of increasing positive features such as per capita household income 50% above the poverty level. Consequently, the first question raised in goal setting is: Given a particular vision, does one set an action goal of eliminating negative features or a goal of promoting positive features?

A second question that one may ask about goals is: To whom does the goal apply? Asking about the well-being of children is different from asking about the well-being of children at risk. The target of the social marketing campaign must be clearly identified before setting benchmarks or performance measures as it defines the sample frame to be assessed.

A third question to consider as goals are set are the values the agency brings to the social marketing program. The perception of a successful resolution of some problem may vary between social groups, and more importantly may vary between the agency and the audience targeted for social change. As Weilenmann (1980) describes in his discussion of social marketing programs in developing nations, "It should be clear that criteria for the assessment of what is happening with and to a society are closely related to the values that are held in the society ... [and] there are probably a large number of possible sources of values and corresponding goal images" (page 55). A clear example of a value clash may be seen in current efforts to curb world population growth. Actions to achieve this goal are heavily value laden. A performance measure such as "Number of women receiving subsidized contraception" may not be seen as a measure of success by all parties.

A fourth concern relative to the agency's goals is the extent to which the goals are action oriented. As Kotler and Roberto (1989) describe "many social change campaigns describe their objectives in qualitative terms, failing to operationalize such effects so they are measurable and researchable" (pg. 343-344). For example, a goal such as improving the well being of children provides very little direction for the actions that should follow.

A final comment on goal setting is to recognize the interplay between goals and performance indicators. While indicators are used to evaluate the success or failure of a social marketing program (e.g., the number of teens using condoms), they may also suggest new goals. This suggests that the indicator set may be dynamic, growing to reflect new programs that are instituted in response to the results of the initial set of indicators.

PERFORMANCE MEASURES

Ideally one seeks performance measures or indicators which are valid, reliable, and capable of measuring the effectiveness of programs instituted to meet the organization's goals. At the same time the indicators should be fairly easy to collect, timely, succinct, and comparable. Adding to this wish list, one may ask that the

Advances in Consumer Research
Volume 22, © 1995

indicators be contained in an accessible database. Not surprisingly, few sets of performance measures meet these criteria. Techniques for identifying good performance measures are still a subject for active research in areas as diverse as education (Henry and Dickey 1993), natural resources (Hayden 1991) and health status; and the broader area of program evaluation is very active in the social sciences (Chambers 1992, Mohr 1992).

The following discussion will focus on the types of strategic issues one must address before asking how the data can be generated or gathered. While some indicators may be derived from secondary sources such as the 10 year U.S. Census, other indicators may require primary data collection. The methodological details of data collection are beyond the scope of this paper, although some superficial discussion of aspects of data gathering are presented. The bulk of the following discussion will explore the issues that arise in the *selection*, rather than in the *gathering*, of a "good" set of performance measures. That is, this discussion will focus on asking the right questions, rather than getting the right answers, since "asking the right questions is an issue whose importance is widely recognized but whose accomplishment tends to be neglected in the methodology of evaluation" (Mohr 1992, pg 10).

How Many Indicators?: Although more data are often better than less, cost considerations, ensuring quality data, and the ability of the target audience to absorb the "message in the data," suggest that a small, select set of indicators is preferable. "The [performance monitoring system] must be geared to the selective acquisition of 'good' data with maximum potential for meaningful utilization (Poister 1983)." A small set of meaningful indicators will also reduce the likelihood of data "fishing expeditions" which may result in spurious findings. Further, a well defined set of indicators may help unite and focus the social marketing effort.

What, or Who, Is The Reference Group?: Raw numbers gain meaning relative to other numbers. Is five percent of a population recycling good or bad? If it was only three percent last year, perhaps it's good. If the adjoining community has a rate of fifteen percent, perhaps it's bad. Consequently, as indicators are selected, one must also select the reference group(s) that will be used for evaluation, and collect indicators based on the same methodology used for the reference group.

The audience for the data may also affect the reference group. For example, state legislators may find information on citizen health more compelling when comparisons are made to contiguous states than comparisons between their state and the national average (or vice versa).

What Is The Right Indicator To Use?: This is probably the most difficult question to resolve and will receive greater discussion than other performance measure issues. If an organization is attempting to improve the health status of citizens (a visionary goal), and has an action goal of decreasing heart disease among males over 45, how should progress towards this goal be measured? Is the incidence of heart disease appropriate? Or, perhaps, the mortality from heart disease? Maybe the number of people reporting changes in health habits conducive to healthy hearts? Five questions are provided below that may help in the selection of indicators.

1) The question of surrogates: The candidates for an indicator are only surrogates for whatever it is that really needs to be measured. A good surrogate is one that is closely related to the underlying dimension; this relationship implies a model, either explicit or implicit, supporting the correlation between the two measurements. For example, the number of adult smokers may be used as a surrogate for the number of adults at risk for heart disease because numerous studies have substantiated the link between smoking and heart disease. On the other hand, suppose the focus is on children at risk with the action goal of improving daycare for preschoolers. If one counts i) the number of preschoolers in families in which all the adults work outside the home, and ii) the number of preschoolers in licensed daycare programs, inferences will be difficult. The implicit model suggests that children not in appropriate daycare are at risk. But the measures suggested here *do not* track inappropriate daycare since parents with sequential work hours, grandparents watching children, in home babysitters, etc. are overlooked. Hence, these two measures are not good surrogates for this action goal, although the implicit model of "Children in licenced daycare receive appropriate daycare" may seem reasonable on the surface.

2) The question of availability: Given the limited resources of most social marketing agencies, the cost of generating primary data is prohibitive. Secondary data has great appeal, but comes with significant limitations. In secondary data the surrogates are selected by someone else, often to measure a slightly different underlying goal. Some organizations have successfully lobbied for minor changes in existing instruments to acquire indicators more closely matched to their needs.

3) The question of data quality: Often social marketing is aimed towards improving the situation of marginalized groups. The furious discussion surrounding counts of the homeless in the 1990 Census highlight some of the problems with generating or finding good secondary data on certain sample frames. Compounding the problem of access is the question of the validity of responses on emotionally charge issues such as domestic violence, incest, etc.

4) The question of context: Even if the indicator is a high quality measure, it may not be meaningful until it is placed in a particular context. The meaning of a birth to a teenager varies as the cultural and social network surrounding her changes. Should one measure all teen births, births to unwed teens, births to teens with no family support, etc.? The temptation is to say that all of these measures play a role and give critical information. But recall that the first issue raised above was the number of indicators and that, for a variety of reasons, the number of indicators should be constrained. Then, how should one choose? The following question provides some guidance.

5) The question of action: Generally, the purpose of indicators is performance diagnostics: Are our current programs working, Where are problem areas, and What changes should we make in current programs? Indicators should be evaluated from the perspective of whether they offer guidance for action. For example, if the goal is to decrease infant mortality, an action oriented indicator might be the number of women with access to prenatal care in the first trimester, as opposed to an outcome oriented indicators such as the number of low birth weight babies. Outcome indicators are valuable pictures of where "we are," but they provide only hints of "how to get where we want to be" or "are current interventions working?".

Mohr (1992) suggests forming a chain of related activities and outcomes (see also Kotler and Roberto 1989, Chapter 19 and Chambers et. al. 1992, Chapter 5). On the far left of the chain one places the basic action in which personnel engage (e.g., conducting a prenatal visit); at the far right one places the high level outcome (e.g., healthy, happy mother-baby pairs). Forming a chain between these are suboutcomes or subobjectives (e.g., the mother receives competent care, the mother returns for follow-up visits, the mother carries the baby to term, the delivery is low-risk, the baby is healthy, etc.). Mohr (1992) then suggests following the chain back from the highest level objective to the earliest precursor that is *in itself* inherently valued. In this example, the competency of care defined, perhaps, by the fit between the mother's needs/sophistication and the caregiver may be a better performance measure than simply counting the number of prenatal visits.

Having suggested that action oriented measures are best suited for the performance of social marketing programs, it is important to acknowledge that many organizations elect to gather outcome oriented measures. Outcome indicators are generally considered useful since they are considered to be correlated with an underlying need in the population (e.g., a high number of low birth weight babies is assumed to be correlated with the need for prenatal programs). However, from a social marketing viewpoint, if the number of low birth weight babies declines, it is a substantial leap to say that opening up a prenatal clinic for low income women (a "personnel action" in Mohr's model) caused a decline in low birth weight babies (a high level outcome) if measures were not taken on intervening subindicators. Something has caused a shift in the outcome indicator, but specific activities cannot be evaluated or redirected based on outcome indicators alone.

At What Level Should The Indicator Be Developed?: In an ideal setting should the indicators be developed at the individual level or an aggregate level? If aggregate, what are the appropriate groupings? Should data be sliced on a geographic basis (i.e., the percentage of poor by city or state), on a demographic basis (i.e., by ethnic group), by social unit (i.e., how many families are poor), etc.? The level of the indicator is also tied to the relationships between the indicators. If any comparative measures are available at only the aggregate level, the best comparisons between indicators will have to be done at an aggregate level. Consequently, if actions taken to solve the problem are taken at an individual level one might wish for very detailed level indicators; if action is taken at a broad program level, perhaps aggregate indicators are sufficient. In either case, exploring relationships between the indicators will be difficult if the indicators are gathered on different levels.

How Timely Are The Indicators?: If a social marketing program is only in place for a limited period of time, before and after measurements may be sufficient. However, most complex programs, such as the current AIDS awareness campaigns, are ongoing. Measurements of program performance must correspond in some way to the marketing program under evaluation.

How Related Are the Indicators?: If the number of indicators is limited each indicator must have a unique contribution to the profile of "success" defined by the agency. Suppose we consider a database supporting an agency concerned with the environment. The agency may have goals of improving environmental awareness, increasing recycling rates, supporting grass roots action for environmentally friendly legislation, etc. A database of performance indicators for this agency could include the number of homes actively recycling, the number of school programs given on recycling, the volume of material recycled in the area, the cost of recycling, etc. However, we may ask if these items provide a complete profile of successful social marketing, an incomplete profile, or overly complete profile (are the indicators so correlated that they are redundant in the information that can be used for meaningful actions). If the items are highly correlated, a composite measure (e.g., factor analysis) or a representative measure may free up space for other indicators that will round out holes in the existing profile.

How Do These Indicators Related To Indicators Used By Competing Causes?: Generally, an agency engaged in social marketing has a variety of competitors. Among these are causes vying for financial, emotional or some other support. Although all causes may be worthy, limited resources often mean that the cause with the best "position" will gain the greatest support. Consequently, agencies must be prepared to compare indicators with competing agencies. For example, if agencies dedicated to increasing support for cancer use statistics on the number of cancer deaths relative to HIV/AIDS deaths, then agencies dedicated to HIV/AIDS must be prepared to publicize their relevant indicators in some sort of comparison to cancer issues (e.g., yes there are more cancer deaths, but HIV is increasing at a faster rate than cancer).

Will The Indicators Measure Unintended Consequences?: Programs may achieve something other than their intended ends: involvement in Teacher Corps led to disillusionment and lower commitment by teachers (Kotler and Roberto 1992), smoking cessation may lead to weight gain, awareness of contact tracing for HIV infection may lead to people being less likely to be tested, etc. In addition to developing measures of progress towards the agency's goals, potential side effects should be actively sought and added, retrospectively, to the indicator set.

What Is The Best Format For Indicator Presentation And Access?: The indicators must be presented in some sort of format to the user. For example, the data may be available as summary statistics (i.e., the number of presentations given to local high schools), as raw data (i.e., annual activities for each volunteer), as reports (i.e., an executive overview of volunteer activities), or some other format entirely. Adding to this, the access to the indicators can range from an interactive format, wherein the user can crunch the raw numbers him/herself, to modem access to summary statistics and reports, to bound paper documents containing the relevant data. The presentation and access question should reflect anticipated users, their sophistication and their time constraints.

AN EXAMPLE

As an example of the complexity of the problems surrounding indicator selection, consider the development of performance measures by an organization dedicated to child advocacy. The following example is drawn from a real advocacy group and will be abbreviated due to space constraints.

Advocacy involves speaking for those with no political voice: children, political prisoners, ancient forests, wolves, etc. Advocacy theory suggest one way that an advocate may be successful is by bringing *attention* to given issues; in this case "sexy" or high shock-value media releases may be called for and measures of media coverage may be good performance measures. As an alternative advocacy strategy, advocates may instead emphasize *accountability* of governing/government bodies; in this case the indicators that form a report card on social services or legislative efforts may also be performance measures for the advocacy effort. That is, a trend towards better treatment of children's issues on the report card may indicate successful advocacy. Finally advocates may attempt to provide *tools* for change (e.g., providing networks of resources, grant writing support, lobbying efforts, etc.). In this case performance indicators are valuable if they measure movement towards a specific end such as passing favorable legislation.

Goals and High Level Issues: At the outset the advocates must evaluate their goals and articulate them in actionable terms. Are the advocates concerned with all children in the state or a subset of children? For example, are they trying to improve the status of all children but still leave a gap between the best and the worst off, or is it trying to decrease the size of the gap potentially at the expense of the welfare of the best off? Who is the reference group that these children should be compared to? They then must select the methods they will use to meet the goals (i.e., publicizing the situation, legislative activism, etc.). Finally, the agency should have a frank discussion about the implicit values they bring to their work (e.g., are out of wedlock pregnancies inherently "bad"?). Are these values shared by all citizens?

Target Audience: Who is the audience for the advocacy program? If the group does lobbying perhaps it is legislators or voters; if it does community action perhaps it is social service agencies or volunteer groups; if it does direct promotional campaigns perhaps it is parents and guardians; if it does grass roots activism perhaps it is local political figures and politically active voters. To what does this audience respond? What does successful advocacy look like when applied to this target?

What Are We Trying to Measure and Why?: The agency must decide what it would like to know and then decide what surrogates may be acceptable substitutes for this item. Recall that the selection of interest items should be driven by actions the agency can reasonably hope to take. For example, suppose the advocacy group has targeted domestic violence as an issue for legislation, community action, etc. A measure of the number of children witnessing domestic violence might be of interest, but what will the advocacy agency do with this? Does this measure evaluate the efficacy of programs for high risk families (i.e., is it an accountability measure)? Is it hoped that this measure is a surrogate for domestic violence in the community and that tracking this measure provides a sense of the advocate's impact? If the advocates implement specific strategies to curb domestic violence (e.g., lobbying for women and children's shelters) should a broad measure such as this be augmented by a measure of specific programs?

What Indicators Are Available: As this agency has limited funds, all the broad social indicators it gathers will be secondary (items such as the number of meetings with legislators can be generated within). Long term, the agency may be able to exert influence to prompt gathering of new, more topical indicators, but for the meantime they are limited to existing data. Data within the state is collected at a variety of levels (e.g., statewide, county, municipality,etc.) and by a variety of organizations (e.g., Vital Statistics, the Census, the Quality of Life Survey, the Bureau of Economic Research, etc.), most with slightly varying methodologies. Further, the different sources are all updated on different schedules (e.g., the Census will not be updated until the year 2000). As a first step, the agency should establish an inventory of potential performance measures relevant to their goals at state and private agencies with information on: the frequency of data updates, geographic breakdown, sample frame (e.g., children 3-18), quality of the data, relationship to other indicators, and contact person with a phone number.

DISCUSSION

As the above example begins to show, the issues involved with selecting indicators for a database for social marketing are complex and interrelated. Social marketing can learn some things about database construction from other field such as program evaluation and public policy. Innes (1990) suggests the movement in the 1970 to use social indicators to drive public policy failed, in part, because "the indicators were not selected explicitly to address defined policy objectives, nor were they linked to policy proposals in areas where there was public commitment to action" (pg 7). Social marketers may be able to avoid some of these pitfalls by carefully selecting indicators that are clearly associated with intended actions before forming the database.

This paper has drawn from a variety of literatures to attempt to spark a discussion of these issues. Increasingly, as social marketers measure the effect of their work, or attempt to do market research in advance of their work, questions such as the ones raised here must be addressed.

REFERENCES

Chambers, Donald E., Kenneth R. Wedel, et al. (1992), *Evaluating Social Programs*, Boston: Allyn and Bacon.

Fine, Seymore H. (1990), *Social Marketing: Promoting the Causes of Public and NonProfit Agencies*, Boston: Allyn and Bacon.

Hayden, F. Gregory (1991), "Instrumental Valuation Indicators for Natural Resources and Ecosystems" *Journal of Economic Issues* XXV (4), 917-935.

Henry, Gary T. and Kent C. Dickey (1993), "Implementing Performance Monitoring: A Research and Development Approach" *Public Administration Review* 53 (3), 203-212.

Innes, Judith Eleanor (1990), *Knowledge and Public Policy*, New Brunswick: Transaction Publishers.

Kotler, Philip and Alan R. Andreasen (1987), *Strategic Marketing for Nonprofit Organizations*, Englewood Cliffs, N.J.: Prentice-Hall, Inc.

Kotler, Philip and Eduardo Roberto (1989), *Social Marketing: Strategies for Changing Public Behavior*, New York: The Free Press.

Mohr, Lawrence (1992), *Impact Analysis for Program Evaluation*, Newbury Park, CA: Sage Publications.

The Utah Tomorrow Strategic Planning Committee (1992), Utah Tomorrow: 1992 Annual Report, Utah Office of Legislative Research and General Counsel.

Weilenmann, Alexander (1980), *Evaluation Research and Social Change*, Ghent, Belgium: Unesco.

Determinants of Marital Power in Decision Making

Cynthia Webster, Ph.D., Mississippi State University

ABSTRACT

Background, personality, and couple-related variables as possible explanations for marital roles in purchase decision making are explored for both wives and husbands. Marital roles in decisions reflecting various levels of purchasing involvement were related to component-score variables through discriminant function analysis. The most important factor for wives in determining the role structure for high-involvement purchases is modernity in sex-role orientation, whereas for husbands, the most powerful determinant is confidence in spouse. For both wives and husbands, the confidence in spouse factor is most important in determining relative influence for low-involvement purchases.

Although the importance of husband-wife decision making is well acknowledged in the psychological, sociological, and marketing literatures (e.g., Davis and Rigaux 1974; Corfman 1991), there have been few attempts to uncover explanations for marital power. In the main, three major theoretical tenets purporting to explain relative influence in decision making have been developed: resource theory, ideology theory, and involvement. Resource theory asserts that "the balance of power will be on the side of that partner who contributes the greatest resources to the marriage" (Blood and Wolfe 1960). Generally, husbands have had more power than wives because they have possessed more resources in the marriage (i.e., education, monetary contribution, occupational prestige, etc.). This theory has been supported in studies that found a significant relationship between marital power and education (Hempel 1975; Munsinger, Weber, and Hansen 1975; Rosen and Granbois 1983; Woodside 1975), job status (Hempel 1975; Rosen and Granbois 1983; Wolgast 1958; Woodside 1975), wife's reason for working (Rosen and Granbois 1983), whether or not the wife has her own bank account, social class (Rigaux-Briemont 1978), and income (Davis 1976; Green and Cunningham 1975; Huszagh and Murphy 1982; Munsinger et al. 1975; Sharp and Mott 1956; Wolgast 1958).

Rodman (1972) however, interpreted seemingly conflicting findings from different cultures regarding the relationship between the husband's resources and his power. His study suggested that not only do normative definitions about who *should have* power probably influence who actually *does have* power, but they also operate as a "contingent variable" influencing the effect that resources have on power. Rodman's synthesis (1967, 1972) referred to as a "theory of resources in cultural context" posits that in less developed societies, resource variables, like education, income, and occupational status, "are not merely resource variables in a power struggle, but are also positional variables in the social structure" (Rodman 1972).

The second theoretical paradigm, sex role orientation, posits that sex role preferences are indicative of culturally determined attitudes (traditionalism/modernity) toward the role of wife/husband in the household (Qualls 1987). Where the sex roles of Anglo-Americans have moved toward either autonomic or eqalitarian roles (Woodside and Motes 1979), the sex roles of U.S. Latin-Europeans are still primarily husband dominant (Canabal 1990). Several studies have found a significant relationship between sex-role orientation and relative influence in decision making (e.g., Green and Cunningham 1975; Rosen and Granbois 1983; Qualls 1987).

Finally, the concept of involvement postulates that the relative influence in a purchase decision is higher for a spouse who is highly involved in the purchase and desires that it reflect his or her individual interests and preferences (Corfman and Lehmann 1987; Qualls 1987). Thus, husbands have traditionally dominated in purchase decisions for such product categories as insurance (Bonfield 1978; Davis and Rigaux 1974; Green et al. 1983), automobiles (Burns and Granbois 1977; Green et al. 1983; Sharp and Mott 1956; Wolgast 1958), and televisions (Woodside and Motes 1979). On the other hand, wives have dominated in purchase decisions for products associated with the homemaker role, such as appliances (Green et al. 1983; Wolgast 1958), groceries (Bonfield 1978; Davis and Rigaux 1974: Green et al. 1983; Sharp and Mott 1956), and washers (Woodside and Motes 1979).

Although these theories have been supported and will not be ignored in the current study, the sociological and psychological literatures hints of other explanations of relative influence in husband/wife decision making such as personality (Sprecher 1986) and factors stemming from one's childhood (Acock and Yang 1986). Furthermore, an ethnographic study conducted by Webster (1992) supported the existing theories (resources and sex-role orientation) and also revealed ten additional explanations of marital power: years spent alone before marriage, childhood spoilness, aggressiveness, willingness to please, self-esteem, locus of control orientation, need for approval, confidence in spouse, decision-making power at work, and importance of marriage. The purpose of the current research is to determine which of these factors are most important in determining relative infuence in decision making for both husbands and wives.

METHOD

The sample consisted of married individuals from a major southern meteropolitan area. Due to the sensitive nature of the questionnaire items, privately questionning respondents was deemed necessary to facilitate frankness. Therefore, the respondents were contacted in their place of employment. To aid in having a representative group of respondents, a sample of firms from a wide range of business types (i.e., restaurants, product repair and maintenance shops, retail stores, manufacturing plants, financial and educational institutions, travel agents, etc.) was first randomly selected. Employees from various levels (from operational to top management) were randomly selected and contacted by telephone for an appointment. If contact with the selected individual could not be made after two attempts, another person was selected. No more than five individuals were selected from any one firm. The sampling process was completed in five weeks.

The interviewers were instructed to approach respondents until contact was made with 175 wives and 175 husbands who met the screening requirements (couples, per se, were not interviewed). The screening requirements were as follows: (1) the spouse had to be married for at least two years; (2) the respondent had to be both willing and confident of their ability to assess his or her own and the spouse's characteristics; (3) the respondent had to complete the questionnaire alone; and (4) with the exception of automobile and housing decisions, the consumer buying decisions had to have been made during the previous three years. From the 350 individuals with whom contact was made, 160 wives and 151 husbands agreed to participate in the study, which yielded 91.4% and 86.2% response rates for wives and husbands, respectively. During questionaire completion, 7 wives and 5 husbands terminated the survey because of either inability or unwillingness to continue. The final sample is comprised of 153 wives and 146 husbands.

The questionnaire was designed to measure marital roles in 25 durable goods/services purchase decisions, the extent to which the married respondent possessed each characteristic *relative to his or her spouse*, and purchasing involvement for each product. A summary description of each scale is provided in Table 1; references in the Table direct the reader to more detail (and evaluation of measurement issues) for those scales which have been developed and used in previous studies.

Respondents were asked to indicate whether each decision was handled by the wife mostly, husband mostly, or truly equally. To measure the independent variables, individuals were asked about the extent to which they possessed each characteristic *relative to their spouse*; thus, items were phrased accordingly (e.g., "Relative to your spouse, what is your level of willingness to please others?"). It should be noted that the extent to which a particular spouse possesses a characteristic is not of interest in this study. The objective here was to discover the extent to which one possesses a characteristic more or less than his or her spouse. These items were measured on a five-point scale, where 1="Much less," 2="Less," 3="Same," 4="More," and 5="Much more." Since these five categories refer only to the traits of husband and wife, the response to any given item represents a respondent's perception of the relative characteristic.

Since past research has shown that marital role patterns partially stem from the importance of the product category in question (Davis and Riguax 1974; Ferber 1973; Rosen and Granbois 1983), a method was used to determine whether involvement subgroupings existed within the product decisions. Product purchasing involvement data for all respondents were combined into one pool and factor analyzed. The analysis produced four factors with the eigenvalue greater than 1.0, explaining 76% of the total variance. However, an examination of the varimax rotated factor loadings matrix showed four items with poor (lower than .35) or ambiguous loading values on more than one factor. The subsequent factor analysis excluding these four items produced three distinguishable factors (with eigenvalues greater than 1.0) accounting for 73% of the total variance. The three groups of product categories were labeled as high-, medium-, and low-involvement decisions. The results from this three-factor solution are presented in Table 2.

The subscales of all the independent variables were submitted to a principal components analysis with varimax rotation to produce a set of uncorrelated variates. Twelve components were found with loadings higher than .49.

The analysis was intended to identify spousal characteristics that are important in determining marital roles for low-, medium- and high-involvement product decisions. A three-category coding system designated each product purchasing decision as predominately husband, wife dominant, or equal. A step-wise discriminant function analysis was then performed separately on the data for each of the six types of purchase decisions (from Table 2) to determine which of the independent variables were significant in determining husband or wife dominance in purchase decision making.

RESULTS AND DISCUSSION

Results of the discriminant function analysis were interpreted using a method (Klecka 1980; Rosen and Granbois 1983) to find those variables that were most important in determining marital roles for each of the three decision types. Table 3 shows results for these variables, including the contribution of each to the discriminant function (standarized coefficient), its correlation with the discriminant function (structure coefficient), and the statistical significance of the discriminant function with the listed variables

entered (Wilks lambda). The percentage classification accuracy of the discriminant functions ranged from 68 to 89 percent.

An examination of Table 3 shows that most of the independent variables discriminate among the marital role patterns in decision making for the different decision types. The only case where less than half of the components significantly discriminate among marital role patterns is the the effect of the husbands' relative on marital roles for low-involvement purchases. The last column of Table 3 also shows that the independent variables are significant in discriminating among the marital role patterns for each of the three decision situations for both wives and husbands. These findings indicate that there are many other important explanations for marital power in decision making other than the existing theoretical orientations of resource theory, sex-role orientation, and purchasing involvement.

There are some slight similarities in the wives' and husbands' data with respect to the power of the discriminating variables. For example, more factors are significant for discrimating among marital roles for medium-involvement products. Additionally, the factors which are particularly important for both wives and husbands in their discriminating power are relative modernity in SRO, resources, aggressiveness, confidence in spouse, decision-making power at work, and locus of control orientation.

On the other hand, there is a clear distinction between wives and husbands in marital roles among the decision types. First, the relative willingness to please and self-esteem components are particularly strong for wives in discriminating among the marital role groups. Furthermore, relative modernity in SRO has opposite effects for wives and husbands. For wives, it leads to an increase in relative influence. For husbands, however, an increase in SRO modernity leads to a decrease in relative influence. Obviously, as he becomes less traditional in SRO relative to his wife, he becomes less dominant. These findings support those of other studies that found a significant relationship between SRO and relative influence in decision making (Green and Cunningham 1975; Lee 1989; Qualls 1987).

There are both differences and similarities between wives and husbands with respect to the discriminating power of the factors on marital roles for the decision types. For the high-involvement purchase decisions, the wives' relative modernity in SRO, years alone before marriage, self-esteem, decision-making power at work, resources, and aggressiveness leads to joint decision making. And, finally, her relative confidence in spouse, willingness to please, and need for approval leads to husband dominance. Thus, none of these characteristics lead to her dominance for the relatively important product decisions. However, an increase in the husbands' relative traits (i.e., resources) is associated with husband dominance. Joint decision making exists for high-involvement products only when he has a relatively high level of modernity in SRO, need for approval, and places considerable importance on the marriage.

The marital role patterns change for the medium-involvement products. As the traits increase for wives relative to their husbands, wife dominance become the primary marital role pattern, followed by joint decision making. As the traits increase for husbands, wife dominance remains the most prominent pattern (for such traits as willingness to please), followed by joint decision making (e.g., relative childhood spoilness), and then husband dominance (e.g., resources).

For the low-involvement purchase decisions, the wives' increase in most of the traits leads to their dominance in decision making. The syncratic marital role pattern is next in importance. On the other hand, as the husbands' traits increase with respect to

TABLE 1
Summary Information Concerning Measures* Used and Relevant Source References

Construct Name (and reliability)	Description of Measure (and reference for additional details)
Decision making (alpha = .93)	Five-item scale measuring the more important aspects of the decision process, i.e., initiator of the decision process, alternative evaluation, and making the decision on which product to buy, how much to spend, and where to buy (Blood and Wolfe 1960; Hempel 1974). (Eigen = 3.21; 52.4% variance explained). An exception was made for two categories. First, relative influence for savings decisions was assessed with a three-item scale measuring marital roles in determining the amount to be contributed to savings, the types of savings plan, and what to do with leftover money (Eigen = 4.20; 60.1% variance explained). Second, relative influence in financial task implementation was measured with a three-item scale assessing marital roles for maintaining the checkbook, paying bills, reconciling the bank statements, and reconciling the checkbook (Eigen = 3.00; 62.0% variance explained). (Lee 1989)
Marital roles	One-item nominal scale to measure overall relative influence where 1 = Mostly wife, 2 = Mostly husband, 3 = Equal
Purchasing involvement (n = .96)	A composite measure of the purchase involvement associated with a particular product category. (Zaichkowsky 1985)
Sex-role orientation	A composite measure of a spouse's overall sex-role orientation measured as the average (alpha=.91) score of 23 items measuring attitudes toward men's and women's roles in the household, work situations, personality traits, and lifestyles (Osmond and Martin 1975). (Eigen = 2.77; 55.9% variance explained)
Time spent alone	One item measuring the length of time spouse spent alone before marriage.
Childhood spoilness (alpha = .84)	Five-item scale measuring the extent to which spouse got his/her way in childhood conflict situations, with siblings, parents, older relatives, and extent to which his or her life was attempted by others to be problem-free. (Eigen = 2.44; 48.7% variance explained)
Aggressiveness (alpha = .89)	Thirty eight-item scale measuring Type A/B behavioral tendencies such as ambitiousness, competitiveness, time urgency, impatience, hostility (Jenkins, Zyzanski, and Rosenman 1971). (Eigen = 2.54; 62.3% variance explained)
Willingness to please (alpha = .79)	Five-item scale measuring the desire to please others, the time devoted to doing things for others, the extent one goes out of one's way to please/help others, and the importance of the spouse's happiness. (Eigen = 2.38; 65.1% variance explained)
Self-esteem (alpha = .83)	Five-item scale measuring the degree, severity, or magnitude of a problem the spouse has with self-esteem or -confidence (Hudson 1982). (Eigen = 2.45; 48.8% variance explained)
Locus of control (alpha = .88)	Twenty-item scale measuring the extent to which a spouse makes attributions that the key events in their lives are the result of chance or factors beyond their control (Rotter 1966). (Eigen = 2.23; 47.9% variance explained)
Need for approval (alpha = .73)	Fourteen-item scale measuring the importance of social acceptance and approval in all environments (i.e., work and family), adapted and expanded from Crowne and Marlowe (1960). (Eigen = 2.39; 50.1% variance explained)
Confidence in spouse (alpha = .86)	Five-item scale measuring the degree of confidence one has in his/her spouse with respect to general competence, purchasing decisions, financial management. (Eigen = 2.09; 50.2% variance explained)
Decision-making power at work (alpha = .71)	Four-item scale measuring the extent of management and control of others at the workplace, independence at work, and the degree of control in decision making. (Eigen = 3.01; 62.0% variance explained)
Importance of the marital relationship (alpha = .75)	Four-item scale measuring the importance of harmony in the marriage, keeping the marriage intact, and of the spouse. (Eigen = 3.73; 59.8% variance explained)
Resources (alpha = .85)	Three-item scale measuring the level of education, occupational status, and financial resources. (Eigen = 2.32; 74.1% variance explained)

*All measures were measured on a relative-to-spouse basis.

TABLE 2
Component Loadings for Decision Cross-Product Matrix Following Varimax Rotation*

Decisions	Component 1 (Group 1)	Component 2 (Group 2)	Component 3 (Group 3)
Housing	.91		
Financial decisions	.88		
Automobiles	.85		
Children's school/study program	.73		
Family vacation	.68		
TV/stereo			
Wife's clothes		.86	
Housing upkeep		.85	
Living room furniture		.81	
Other insurance		.77	
Other furniture		.72	
Entertainment activities		.71	
Household appliances		.70	
Husband's clothes		.68	
Life insurance		.66	
Cosmetics/toiletries		.64	
Groceries		.63	
		.59	
Children's clothing			
Financial implementation			.93
Kitchenware			.87
Nonprescription drugs			.85
Children's toys			.80
Garden tools			.74
Alcoholic beverages			.69
Cleaning products			.63
			.60

*To facilitate interpretation, only loadings greater than 0.45 are shown.

low-involvement products, his dominance does not surface. Either the decisions are syncratic (as is the case for his external locus of control) or wife dominant (associated with his confidence in the wife and his relative resources).

Though the findings of this study provide insight into the nature of marital roles in decision making, there are related areas that could benefit from research attention. Future research might focus on determining if there are interaction effects of the factors on relative influence in decision making. Further, other analytical methods might be used—such a forward and backward stepwise regression—to determine if there are significant relationships between marital roles in purchase decision making and the various background, personality, and couple-related factors.

REFERENCES

Acock, Alan C. and Wen Shan Yang (1986), "Parental Power and Adolescents' Parental Identification," Journal of Marriage and the Family, 46 (May), 487-495.

Blood, Robert O. and Donald M. Wolfe (1960), *Husbands and Wives: The Dynamics of Married Living*, Glencoe, IL: The Free Press.

Bonfield, Edward H. (1978), "Perception of Marital Roles in Decision Processes: Replication and Extension," in *Advances in Consumer Research*, Vol. 5, ed. H. Keith Hunt, Chicago: Association for Consumer Research, 51-62.

Burns, Alvin C. and Donald H. Granbois (1977), "Factors Moderating and Resolution of Preference Conflict in Family Automobile Purchasing," *Journal of Marketing Research*, 14 (February), 77-86.

Canabal, Maria E. (1990), "An Economic Approach to Marital Dissolution in Puerto Rico," *Journal of Marriage and the Family*, 52 (May), 515-530.

Corfman, Kim P. (1991), "Perceptions of Relative Influence: Formation and Measurement," *Journal of Marketing Research*, 28 (May), 125-136.

_____ and Donald R. Lehmann (1987), "Models of Cooperative Group Decision-Making and Relative Influence: An Experimental Investigation of Family Purchase Decisions," *Journal of Consumer Research*, 14 (June), 1-13.

Crowne, Douglas P. and David Marlowe (1960), "A New Scale of Social Desirability Independent of Psychopathology," *Journal of Counseling Psychology*, 24 (4), 349-354.

Davis, Harry L. (1970), "Dimensions of Marital Roles in Consumer Decision-Making," *Journal of Marketing Research*, 7 (May), 168-177.

_____ (1976), "Decision-Making Within the Household," *Journal of Consumer Research*, 2 (March), 241-260.

_____ and Benny P. Rigaux (1974), "Perception of Marital Roles in Decision Processes," *Journal of Consumer Research*, 1 (June), 51-62.

Ferber, Robert (1973), "Family Decision Making and Economic Behavior: A Review," in *Family Economic Behavior: Problems and Prospects*, ed. Eleanor B. Sheldon, Philadelphia, PA: J.B. Lippincott, 29-61.

Green, Robert T. and Isabella C.M. Cunningham (1975), "Feminine Role Perception and Family Purchasing Decisions," *Journal of Marketing Research*, 12 (August), 325-332.

TABLE 3
Step-Wise Discriminant Analysis for Product Decision Making[a]

Type of Decision
I. WIVES

	Discriminating Variables	Standardized Coefficients [b]	Structure Coefficients [b]	Wilks Lambda
	Relative			
High involvement	Modernity in sex-role orientation	.88	.85	
	Resources	.67	.64	
	Years alone before marriage	.64	.60	
	Aggressiveness	.62	.58	
	Confidence in spouse	.60	.57	
	Self esteem	.59	.56	
	Decision-making power at work	.58	.55	
	Willingness to please	.58	.53	
	Need for approval	.57	.50	.781 [b]
Medium involvement	Modernity in sex-role orientation	.90	.87	
	Need for approval	.89	.86	
	Aggressiveness	.84	.80	
	Resources	.83	.79	
	Self esteem	.77	.74	
	Confidence in spouse	.75	.70	
	Childhood spoilness	.72	.68	
	Decision-making power at work	.68	.65	
	External locus of control	.64	.60	
	Importance of marriage	.61	.57	
	Willingness to please	.60	.56	
	Years spent alone before marriage	.56	.52	.632 [b]
	Confidence in spouse	.79	.77	
Low involvement	Need for approval	.77	.73	
	Decision-making power at work	.69	.65	
	Modernity in sex-role orientation	.67	.62	
	External locus of control	.64	.61	
	Self esteem	.62	.58	
	Aggressiveness	.61	.56	
	Willingness to please	.58	.55	
	Childhood spoilness	.55	.53	.744 [b]

II. HUSBANDS

	Discriminating Variables	Standardized Coefficients [b]	Structure Coefficients [b]	Wilks Lambda
	Relative			
High involvement	Resources	.67	.65	
	Decision-making power at work	.64	.60	
	Importance of marriage	.63	.59	
	Aggressiveness	.57	.54	
	Modernity in sex-role orientation	.56	.53	
	Need for approval	.56	.53	
	External locus of control	.55	.52	.852 [c]
Medium involvement	Self esteem	.88	.86	
	Childhood spoilness	.79	.77	
	Resources	.69	.65	
	Decision-making power at work	.66	.63	
	External locus of control	.66	.62	
	Aggressiveness	.65	.62	
	Willingness to please	.64	.61	
	Years alone before marriage	.64	.61	
	Need for approval	.63	.60	
	Confidence in spouse	.63	.59	
	Importance of marriage	.62	.58	
Low involvement	Modernity in sex-role orientation	.60	.56	.689 [b]
	Confidence in spouse	.86	.83	
	Resources	.78	.75	
	External locus of control	.62	.60	
	Childhood spoilness	.58	.55	.830 [c]
	Aggressiveness	.56	.53	

[a]Households with missing data on one or more discriminant variables were eliminated from the analysis. Degrees of freedom omitted to conserve space. [b]$p \leq .01$ [c]$p \leq .05$
[b]Signs have been omitted; the focus is on the weight of each variable.

_____, Jean-Paul Leonardi, Jean-Louis Chandon, Isabella C.M. Cunningham, Bronis Verhage, and Alan Strazzieri (1983), "Societal Development and Family Purchasing Roles: A Cross-National Study," *Journal of Consumer Research*, 9 (March), 436-442.

Hempel, Donald J. (1974), "Family Buying Decisions: A Cross Cultural Perspective," *Journal of Marketing Research*, 11 (August), 295-302.

Hudson, W. W. (1982), *The Clinical Measurement Package: A Field Manual*, Chicago, IL: Dorsey.

Huszagh, Sandra M. and Arthur D. Murphy (1982), "Patterns of Influence in the Purchase of Consumer Durables by Mexican Households," in *Educators' Conference Proceedings*, Vol. 48, eds., B.J. Walker et al., Chicago: American Marketing Association, 1-6.

Jenkins, C.D., S.J. Zyzanski, and R.H. Rosenman (1971), "Progress Toward Validation of a Computer Scored Test for the Type A Coronary Prone Behavior Pattern," *Psychosomatic Medicine*, 33, 193-202.

Klecka, William R. (1980), *Discriminant Analysis*, Beverly Hills, CA: Sage.

Lee, Wei-Na (1989), "The Mass-Mediated Consumption Realities of Three Cultural Groups," in *Advances in Consumer Research*, Vol. 16, ed. Thomas K. Srull, Honolulu, HI: Association for Consumer Research, 771-777.

Munsinger, Gary M., Jean E. Weber, and Richard W. Hansen (1975), "Joint Home Purchasing Decisions by Husbands and Wives," *Journal of Consumer Research*, 1 (March), 60-66.

Osmond, Marie W. and Patricia Y. Martin (1975), "Sex and Sexism: A Comparison of Male and Female Sex-Role Attitudes," *Journal of Marriage and the Family*, 37 (November), 744-758.

Qualls, William J. (1987), "Household Decision Behavior: The Impact of Husbands' and Wives' Sex Role Orientation," *Journal of Consumer Research*, 14 (September), 264-279.

Rigaux-Briemont, B. (1978), "Exploring Marital Influences in the Family Economic Decision Making," in *Research Frontiers in Marketing: Dialogue and Directions*, ed. S.C. Jain, Chicago, IL: American Marketing Association, 126-129.

Rodman, Hyman (1967), "Marital Power in France, Greece, Yugoslavia, and the United States: A Cross National Discussion," *Journal of Marriage and the Family*, 29 (May), 320-324.

_____ (1972), "Marital Power and the Theory of Resources in Cultural Context," *Journal of Comparative Family Studies*, 3 (Spring), 3-78.

Rotter, Julian B. (1966), "Generalized Expectancies for Internal Versus External Control of Reinforcement," *Psychological Monographs*, 80 (1), Whole No. 609.

Rosen, Dennis L. and Donald H. Granbois (1983), "Determinants of Role Structure in Family Financial Management," *Journal of Consumer Research*, 10 (September), 253-258.

Sharp, Harry and Paul Mott (1956), "Consumer Decisions in the Metropolitan Family," *Journal of Marketing*, 21 (October), 149-156.

Sprecher, Susan (1986), "The Relation Between Inequity and Emotions in Close Relationships," *Social Psychology Quarterly*, 49, 309-321.

Webster, Cynthia (1992), "Towards Furthering the Theoretical Orientation of Husband/Wife Decision Making: A Qualitative Approach," *Academy of Marketing Science Conference Proceedings*, (April),

Wolgast, Elizabeth H. (1958), "Do Husbands or Wives Make the Purchasing Decisions?," *Journal of Marketing*, (October), 151-158.

Woodside, Arch G. (1975), "Effects of Prior Decision-Making, Demographics, and Psychographics on Marital Roles for Purchasing Durables," in *Advances in Consumer Behavior Research*, 2, ed. M. Schlinger, Chicago, IL: Association for Consumer Research, 81-91.

_____ and William H. Motes (1979), "Perceptions of Marital Roles in Consumer Decision Processes for Six Products," in *American Marketing Association Proceedings*, eds. Neil Beckwith et al., Chicago, IL: American Marketing Association, 214-219.

Zaichkowsky, Judith L. (1985), "Measuring the Involvement Construct," *Journal of Consumer Research*, 13 (December), 341-352.

An Emotion-Based Perspective of Family Purchase Decisions

Jonghee Park, Dong-guk University, South Korea
Patriya Tansuhaj, Washington State University
Eric R. Spangenberg, Washington State University
Jim McCullough, Washington State University

ABSTRACT

Consumer behavior literature has largely ignored the role of emotion in family decision making in favor of more rational, economic based models of this process. This paper proposes and describes the components of a model incorporating emotion into the family decision making process. The model is based on the overarching proposition that emotion influences decisions by changing the relative influence of marital partners at various stages in the decision process.

"The more experience I have had, the more I am convinced that far more of life is governed by automatic emotional forces than man is willing to acknowledge (Bowen 1976, p. 60)."

This statement exemplifies the thoughts of many regarding the importance of emotion in human lives. Recent consumer behavior research has begun to examine feelings and emotions as elements influencing all aspects of human behavior (e.g., Allen, Machleit and Kleine 1992; Gardner 1985; Hirschman and Holbrook 1982; Holbrook, Chestnut, Oliva and Greenleaf 1984; Westbrook and Oliver 1991). The role of emotion in family purchase decisions has, however, been explored only minimally. Most studies of family decision making assume decisions are made in a rational manner by choosing among alternative courses of action with little regard for emotional factors. Park, Tansuhaj and Kolbe (1991, p. 651) offered a richer description of human interactions in a family setting:

"The relationships between family members which create notions of hearth and home are centered on the deep-seated affection members have for one another. The implications of such interpersonal affection pervades all family decisions."

Although often neglected by consumer behavior researchers, emotion-related constructs (such as love, affection, sympathy, anger and guilt) have taken a prominent place in the study of marriage and family relationships in other disciplines (e.g., Gottman and Levenson 1986; Sprecher 1986; Kerr and Bowen 1988).

This study suggests how the family purchase decision-making process and its outcomes are influenced by emotions. Specifically, we review the literature relevant to emotion and family decisions from various disciplines and propose relationships between emotion and the family purchase decision process in order to guide future research.

In this study, we refer to the family unit as consisting of the husband and wife. Future studies should extend this emphasis on emotion to include children who also play an important role in decision processes. Here, the decision process is seen as varying by product, depending upon the importance of, or preference for, a particular product to each spouse, (cf., Corfman and Lehmann 1987; Ekstrom et al. 1987; Gupta, et al. 1983).

EMOTION IN FAMILY DECISION RESEARCH

Previous Lack of Emotional Emphasis

Past family decision research has focused on issues such as: Who influences the decision (e.g., Cosenza and Davis 1981; Davis 1970; Ekstrom, Tansuhaj and Foxman 1989; Kelly and Egan 1969; O'Conner, Sullivan and Pogorzelsk 1985; Qualls 1982, 1984; Woodside 1975), or who makes the decision (e.g., Brinberg and Schwenk 1985; Davis 1971; Green and Cunningham 1975; Imperia, O'Guinn and MacAdams 1985; Munsinger, Weber and Hansen 1975; Sharp and Mott 1956; Walgast 1958; Wilkes 1975). Although a few studies have attempted to explain the entire decision making process such as Qualls' (1984) sex-role oriented model, Corfman and Lehmann's (1987) power-based group decision-making models, and Sheth's (1974) family decision model, research has not emphasized the role of emotion in joint family decisions. Emotional relationships between husbands and wives, parents and children, or among family members have been disregarded in decision process modeling.

Previous studies of group decision processes are influenced primarily by theories from sociology and economics (e.g., exchange theory, game theory, resource theory, and power theory), and focused more on non-family settings such as business and government. It is assumed the decision maker in these cases is rational, acting without emotion, and focused on efficiency or maximization of personal utility. These assumptions may hold for corporate entities making relatively impersonal decisions. Among families, however, familial goals, values and emotional needs certainly influence decisions. Park, Tansuhaj and Kolbe (1991) strongly suggested this in discussion of the care taking, nurturing and socialization roles of the family. Relative importance is viewed herein as the level of motivation to acquire a product or service derived from the product or service's ability to satisfy individual wants (Seymour and Lessne 1984). Each individual, husband and wife, is likely to hold different perceptions of importance for products because of different beliefs, values, and traits that individuals bring to a decision situation. Thus, emotion will likely be a factor in familial decision processes moderated by relative importance of the decision.

Although underresearched, there has been increasing attention toward emotion in marketing focusing on responses to products, advertisements, or emotion as an individual experience (e.g., Allen et al. 1992; Hirschman and Holbrook 1982; Westbrook and Oliver 1991). More closely related to the familial decision process are a few studies that explore components such as interpersonal needs (Seymour and Lessne 1984), empathy (Burns 1977; Burns and Granbois 1976), and support relationships (Corfman and Lehman 1987). Emotional need as a construct, however, has not been fully conceptualized and/or operationalized. For example, Burns (1977) conceptualized empathy as the ability to accurately recognize other's thoughts, feelings, and actions, and operationalized the construct as cognitive ability, rather than as an emotional response. One of the primary assumptions in previous studies of the family decision-making process was that each family member employs an economic model of rational or cognitive decision making, not taking into consideration how they are affected by personal feelings. That assumption, however, fails to incorporate the basic idea that humans are not wholly rational decision makers, but operate through emotion with its different rules and processes (Gelles and Straus 1979).

Similarly, little attention has been given to the family setting of these interactions. Family members, with intimate contact over extended periods of time, form strong emotional bonds (positive or negative). The emotional bond developed in a family relationship will undoubtedly influence the decision process and its outcomes. Emotional constructs (such as love, affection, sympathy, anger and guilt) may be associated with several stages of the family purchase decision making process.

CHARACTERISTICS OF EMOTION

Several terms are used to describe the effects of emotion on consumers. Among others, research on emotion has addressed the issues of how emotions change as physiological or bodily sensations change (Izard 1977; Tomkins 1982); how emotions have evolved (Hamburg 1963; Scott 1980); and emotions as psychological phenomena (Arieti 1970; Brenner 1980). This paper views emotion as an inclusive label viewing feelings, sentiments, and moods as states of emotional experience.

Several studies have attempted to clarify emotions at the individual level (Fehr and Russell 1984; Shaver and Schwartz 1984). An important issue in this area is whether or not some emotions are primary, or more fundamental (innate of biological nature) than others, or whether all emotions may be socially constructed as pride and shame are (Kemper 1987). Primary emotions proposed by many researchers include fear, anger, sadness, loneliness, joy, love, anxiety, satisfaction, and disgust (Epstein 1984, Fehr and Russel 1984, Plutchink 1980, and Scott 1980). Kemper (1987) proposed guilt, shame and pride as socially constructed emotions. The constructs of love, guilt, and shame are normally posited as emotional states. No less impactful, however, are emotional *traits* — personality characteristics that can vary across individuals in relationships. Empathy is one such trait that is of particular interest to researchers in the area of family decision processes. Because they occur more intensely in family settings than in other relationships or settings, this paper focuses on the emotional constructs of love, guilt and shame, and on the emotional trait of empathy. Conceptual definitions of the above emotions and explanations for how they may influence family decision making will be provided.

Positive and Negative Emotions

A recent study divided emotions broadly into two dominant, and relatively independent groups: 1) positive, and 2) negative (Watson, Clark and Tellegen 1988, p. 1063). They described positive emotion as "an energized and alert state of mind" and negative emotion as a state of "distress or aversive moods".

Previous studies have found that negative emotions are related to high stress and poor coping (Watson and Clark 1988; Schafer and Lazarus 1981), health complaints (Beiser 1974), frequency of unpleasant events (Stone 1981), and the use of coercion or withdrawal during interpersonal conflict (Downey and Coyne 1990). Attribution researchers have found that couples who experience more negative experiences are more likely to make casual attributions that undermine or neutralize positive spousal behavior and accentuate the impact of negative behaviors (e.g., Zelen 1987).

Averill (1982) reported that most people experience anger from several times a day to several times a week. In a later study, Averill (1983) showed that the target for one's anger was usually either a loved one or a friend. He suggested that people are more likely to become angry at friends and loved ones than at strangers, and disliked others because of more frequent contacts and a strong tendency to respond to the loved one's anger. This behavioral target and frequency suggests ample evidence that the state of negative

emotions can influence an individual's attitude and behavior, or influence the decision process and respective outcomes in a family setting.

Positive emotions are related to social activity and satisfaction (Watson 1988). Isen and Means (1982) found that subjects holding positive affect tend to use less information in decision making and are more likely to ignore information considered unimportant. They also found that subjects experiencing positive-affect are likely to use the strategy of "elimination by aspects" (eliminating from further consideration alternatives that did not meet a criterion on a single selected important dimension). Thus, although limited, existing evidence and logic suggest that positive emotions may also influence the process of decision making in a family environment since families are groups of individuals.

An important positive emotion influencing familial decisions is that of love. Diverse, and often conflicting, views exist concerning love. Freud (1955) viewed love as one's sexuality and sexual desires which have been converted by social and cultural norms from a primitive state to an acceptable state. Thus, he suggested that the emotion of love be viewed as an instinctive sexual desire. Fromm (1956), on the other hand, saw love as a need for overcoming separateness from others which is a source of guilt, shame, and anxiety. Because of these uneasy feelings, it was suggested that people try to maintain a close love relationship. A view developed later by Rubin (1973) conceptualized love more broadly as consisting of affiliative and dependent need, a predisposition to help, and exclusiveness and absorption; this conceptualization was adopted for our paper. Characteristics of love identified in previous studies imply that it is a critical variable in family decision making. For example, when a couple disagrees, the spouse more in love is likely to avoid engaging in conflict to maintain family solidarity. Therefore, it is reasonable to expect that the greater the feeling of love, the greater level of the consensus and joint decision making between husband and wife, because one spouse may be oriented toward subordinating his or her (decision) interests, and this orientation creates the environment of the joint decision making.

The negative emotions of guilt and shame occur during negative self-evaluation when an individual realizes his/her behavior does not conform to a given moral value (Ausubel 1955). Fromm (1956) suggested guilt and shame as a state of tension or anxiety caused by a loss of self-love or self-respect. Homans (1974) and Walster, et al. (1978) argued that guilt and shame are experienced by the family member who over-benefits in a relationship. The person who experiences guilt and shame tends to be depressed, and shows low self-esteem (Hoblitzelle 1987). According to attribution theory, it is suggested that the painful feeling and low self-esteem resulting from guilt or shame may be attributed to the partner (e.g., "how could you make me feel that way"), which, in turn, leads one to reject or disagree with their spouse's suggestions. Feelings of shame and guilt may lead one to withdraw from joint decision making.

Empathy

Shott (1984) described empathy as the ability to assume another's mental position and feeling; the ability to cognitively predict the thoughts, feelings and situations of another individual. Mehrabian and Epstein (1972) perceived empathy as emotional involvement in others' feelings. Several studies have demonstrated that empathy is a significant motivator of altruistic behavior (e.g., Aronfreed 1968; Krebs 1975). This construct could explain why Rodman's (1972) resource theory does not explain family decision making processes adequately. According to this theory, individuals with more resources have more decision making power. For

FIGURE 1
Proposed Relationships Within the Family Decision-Making Process

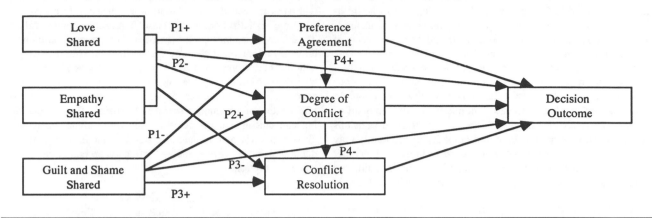

example, if one spouse has more education than the other, the more educated spouse should have more decision power. Yet, empathy from the more educated spouse could alter the manifestation of this power balance. That is, the potential for use of power may exist, yet not be exercised.

RELATIONSHIPS BETWEEN FAMILY DECISION MAKING STAGES AND EMOTION

It is apparent that the inclusion of the construct of emotion would further explain family decision making beyond existing research assumes rationality. Stages in the family decision model are adapted from Qualls' (1987) model, with the addition of the degree of conflict. Possible relationships between emotion and components or stages of the family decision process are discussed in this section. Elements include: Relative Importance, Preference Agreement, Conflict, Conflict Resolution, and Decision Outcome. Figure 1 shows posited relationships of these constructs within the family decision-making process. The arrows in the Figure show hypothesized relationships between emotion and relevant constructs discussed below. A plus sign indicates a direct relationship and a negative sign indicates an indirect relationship. In the interest of clarity, interactions between emotions and traits are not included.

Preference Agreement

Corfman and Lehmann (1987) found that individual preference is the most important variable in predicting who makes decisions. It can reasonably be assumed that each spouse's attitudes and values are developed and formed in different family backgrounds. These discrepancies can be sources of preference discord between spouses. When there is an incongruity of preference, a spouse can try to influence or control to get his or her way, or follow his or her partner's way. Thus, the difference existing between spouses' individual preferences will influence the degree of conflict and decision outcome. It is suggested that the level of preference agreement is affected by a spouse's emotions. Thus, two propositions are:

P1.1: The level of preference agreement is positively influenced by love and empathy.
P1.2: The level of preference agreement is negatively related to guilt and shame.

Conflict

Two persons living together are likely to face disagreement and conflict. When each spouse influences or exercises power to achieve their respective preferences, conflicts arise. Here, degree of conflict is conceptualized as the level of disagreement resulting from different philosophies and values, and the initiation of a joint purchase decision. Degree of conflict is related to the direction and intensity of emotions experienced. Frequent past disagreements may influence the marital relationship negatively, which in turn, will create more negative emotions. The experience of these negative emotions reinforces a spouse to maintain their preference and, as a result, enter into more disagreement or conflict. Related propositions are thus:

P2.1: Degree of conflict is negatively related to love, and empathy.
P2.2: Degree of conflict is positively related to guilt and shame.

Conflict Resolution

When a couple encounters disagreements or conflict of any sort, they will desire resolution before a decision can be reached. Conflict resolution refers to methods used by spouses in resolving a joint purchase conflict. It is expected that the mode of conflict resolution is influenced by the emotions experienced. It is reasonable to expect that with greater positive emotion and love experienced, less threatening conflict resolution will be implemented in the decision process. Coercion (punishments, threats, and authority) will occur when negative emotions are present as principal emotions and will not be found when love, and empathy dominate. Similarly, avoidance (withdrawal and egocentrism) should not accompany positive emotions, love, and empathy, but would be more common with negative emotion, guilt, and shame. Three propositions are then stated according to Nelson's (1988) conflict resolution type:

P3.1: The use of coercion (punishments, threats, and authority) is negatively related to love, and empathy.
P3.2: The use of coercion is positively related to guilt, and shame.
P3.3: The use of avoidance (withdrawal and egocentrism) is negatively related to love, and empathy.

Decision Outcome

Decision outcome has been conceptualized in previous studies as relative influence on the purchase within the family (cf., Burns and Granbois 1977; Qualls 1987). Information as to who influences, and who makes decisions, regarding purchases within families is very important to market researchers and the development of marketing strategies. Family decision process researchers have attempted to measure similar concepts as dependent variables although different terminology has been used. Relative influence between spouses is likely to relate to the intensity of emotion. In households where both spouses experience positive emotion or romantic love, couples are more likely to make final decisions jointly. Positive emotion, love and empathy in the family may result in more joint decisions, as opposed to individual member decision-making dominance, while negative emotion, guilt, and shame in the family may result in fewer joint decisions. Thus,

P4.1: Greater love and empathy in the family will result in more joint decisions, as opposed to individual dominated decision-making.

P4.2: More guilt, and shame in the family will result in fewer joint decisions and more individual dominated decision-making.

CONTRIBUTION OF EMOTION-BASED FAMILY DECISION STUDIES

Theoretical Contribution

Adding emotional constructs to the existing family decision making paradigm will provide further explanation for the complex set of phenomena in family settings. The introduction of emotions will help researchers look at different perspectives of the family, not only the rational aspects of a family. A family decision-making model describing decision processes and outcomes is proposed and propositions intended to measure how emotions influence decision processes and outcomes are suggested. An associated theoretical contribution would be new research directions such as the influence of parental emotions on children's purchase behavior and the influence of family socialization on children's emotional responses to products.

Practical Contribution

Sheth (1974) suggested that knowledge about family decision-making processes would be beneficial for marketers in persuading the appropriate decision-maker(s) or obtaining valid data about family preferences, intentions, or behaviors. Understanding the roles of emotion in family decision making might be helpful for marketers trying to predict attitudes and behavioral orientations of family members. This information would also help marketers select more effective marketing strategies (e.g., appeals of emotion rather than those emphasizing tangible attributes). For example, if negative emotions significantly affect processing information about tangible attributes of products, one could develop strategies to induce positive emotions within relationships. Similarly, if emotions are important factors in family purchase decision making, consumer contact people (e.g., retail salespersons, psychiatrists, and social workers) should recognize families' emotional levels, and attempt to produce and maintain positive emotional states in families by developing emotion-management skills for successful interpersonal interaction.

CONCLUSION

This paper offers thoughts on issues which are under-researched in the marketing discipline; we have discussed the importance of emotion in influencing family decision making processes. Researchers are urged to examine this topic further for empirical support of the propositions in our paper. Further conceptual work is needed to link emotion to other constructs (such as consumer socialization, sex roles, and family consumption values). These constructs incorporate the role of emotion of children and how they interact with those of the parents. Cross-cultural examinations of the aforementioned topics should also be given research attention. Additionally, the type of emotion displayed by each spouse and how it changes throughout the decision process will effect extent of information search, advertising effectiveness, timing and outcome of the decision, and post-purchase behaviors. Thus, marketing practitioners also stand to benefit from a more in-depth understanding of emotional influence on family purchasing and consumption.

REFERENCES

Allen, Chris T., Karen A. Machleit and Susan Schultz Kleine (1992), "A Comparison of Attitudes and Emotions as Predictors of Behavior at Diverse Levels of Behavioral Experience," *Journal of Consumer Research*, 18 (March), 493-504.

Arieti, Silvano (1970), "Cognition and Feeling," in *Feelings and Emotions: The Loyal Symposium on Feelings and Emotions* Magda B. Arnold. ed. New York: Academic.

Aronfreed, Justin (1968), *Conduct & Conscience*, New York: Academic Press.

Averill, James R. (1982), *Anger and Aggression: An Essay on Emotion.* New York: Springer-Veerlag.

_____ (1983), "Studies on Anger and Aggression," *American Psychologist*, (November), 1145-1160.

Beiser, Morton (1974), "Components and Correlates of Mental Well-Being," *Journal of Health and Social Behavior*, 15, 320-327.

Bowen, Murray (1976), "Theory in the Practice of Psychiatry," in *Family Therapy*, New York: Gardner.

Brenner, Charles (1980), "A Psychoanalytical Theory of Affects," in *Emotion: Theory, Research, and Experience*, Vol. I, Robert Plutchik and Kellerman eds. New York: Academic.

Brinberg, David and Nancy Schwenk (1985) "Husband-Wife Decision Making: An Exploratory Study of the Interaction Process," in E.C. Hirschman and M.B. Holbrook (eds.). *Advances in Consumer Research*, Vol. 12, Provo, UT: Association for Consumer Research, 487-491.

Burns, Alvin C. (1976), "Factors Moderating the Resolution of Preference Conflict in Family Automobile Purchasing," *Journal of Marketing Research*, 14 (February), 77-86.

_____ and Donald H. Granbois (1976), "Spousal Involvement and Empathy in Jointly Resolved and Authoritatively Resolved Purchase Subdivisions," in *Advances in Consumer Research*, Vol. 3, Beverlee B. Anderson, ed., Ann Arbor, MI: Association for Consumer Research, 199-220.

Corfman, Kim P. and Donald R. Lehmann (1987), "Models of Cooperative Group Decision-Making and Relative Influence: An Experimental Investigation of Family Purchase Decisions", *Journal of Consumer Research*, 14 (June), 1-14.

Cosenza, Robert M. and Duane L. Davis (1981), "Family Vacation Decision Making Over the Family Life Cycle", *Journal of Travel Research*, (Fall), 17-23.

Davis, Harry L. (1970), "Dimensions of Marital Roles in Consumer Decision Making", *Journal of Marketing Research*, 7 (May), 168-177.

_____ (1971), "Measurement of Husband-Wife Influence in Consumer Purchase Decisions", *Journal of Marketing Research*, 8 (August), 305-312.

Epstein, Seymour (1984), "Controversial Issues in Emotion Theory," in *Review of Personality and Social Psychology*, Vol. 5, Phillip Shaver, Beverly Hills eds., CA: Sage, 64-88.

Ekstrom, Karin M., Patriya S. Tansuhaj and Ellen J. Foxman (1987), "Children's Influence in Family Decision and Consumer Socialization: A Reciprocal View," in Wallendorf, M. and Anderson, P. (eds). *Advances in Consumer Research*, 14, Provo, UT: Association for Consumer Research, 283-287.

Fehr, Beverly and James A. Russell (1984), "Concept of Emotion Viewed from a Prototype Perspective," *Journal of Experimental Psychology: General*, (13), 464-468.

Freud, Sigmund (1955), "Group Psychology and the Analysis of the Ego," in *The Standard Edition of the Complete Psychological Works of Sigmund Freud*, J. Strachey ed., London: Hogarth, 18, 67-143.

Fromm, Erich (1956), *The Art of Loving*. New York: Harper.

Gardner, Meryl Paula (1985), "Mood States and Consumer Behavior: A Critical Review," *Journal of Consumer Research*, 12 (December), 281-300.

Gottman, John M. and Robert W. Levenson (1986), "Assessing the Role of Emotion in Marriage," *Behavioral Assessment*, 8, 31-48.

Green, Robert T. and Isabella C.M. Cunningham (1975), "Feminine Role Perception and Family Purchasing Decisions", *Journal of Marketing Research*, 12 (August), 325-332.

Gupta, Sunil, Michael R. Hagerty and John G. Meyers (1983), "New Directions in Family Decision Making Research," in R.P. Bagozzi, and A.M. Tybout, (eds). *Advances in Consumer Research*, vol. 10, Ann Arbor, MI: Association for Consumer Research, 445-450.

Hamburg, David (1963), "Emotions in the Perspective of Human Evolution," in *Expressions of Emotions in Man*, Peter H. Knapp (ed.), New York: International Universities, 300-317.

Hirschman, Elizabeth C. and Morris B. Holbrook (1982), "Hedonic Consumption: Emerging Concepts, Methods and Propositions," *Journal of Marketing*, 46 (Summer), 92-101.

Hoblitzelle, W. (1987), "Attempts to Measure and Differentiate Shame and Guilt," in H.B. Lewis (ed.), *The Role of Shame in Symptom Formation*, Hillsdale, NJ: Erlbaum, 29-50.

Holbrook, Morris B., Robert W. Chestnut, Terence A. Oliva, and Eric A. Greenleaf (1984), "Play as a Consumption Experience: The Roles of Emotion, Performance, and Personality in the Enjoyment of Games," *Journal of Consumer Research*, 11 (September), 728-739.

Homans, George C. (1974), *Social Behavior: Its Elementary Forms*. New York: Harcourt, Brace, Javonovich.

Imperia, Giovanna, Thomas C. O'Guinn and Elizabeth A. MacAdams (1985), "Family Decision Making Role Perceptions Among Mexican-American and Anglo Wives: A Cross-Cultural Comparison", in E.C. Hirschamn, and M.B. Holbrook, (eds). *Advances in Consumer Research*, vol. 12, Provo, UT: Association for Consumer Research, 71-74.

Isen, Alice M. and Barbara Means (1982), "The Influence of Positive Affect on Decision-making Strategy, *Social Cognition*, 2, 1, 18-31.

Izard, Carroll E. (1977), *Human Emotions*. New York: Plenum.

Kelly, Robert F. and Michael B. Egan (1969), "Husband and Wife Interaction in a Consumer Decision Process", in *Marketing Involvement in Society and the Economy*, AMA Proceedings, Chicago, (Fall), 250-258.

Kemper, Theodore D. (1987), "How Many Emotions Are There? Wedding the Social and the Automatic Components," *American Journal of Sociology*, 93, (September), 263-289.

Kerr, Michael E. and Murray Bowen (1988), *Family Evaluation: An Approach Based on Bowen Theory*, Michael E. Kerr and Murray Bowen, (eds.), New York.

Mehrabian, Albert and Norman Epstein (1972), "A Measure of Emotional Empathy," *Journal of Personality*, 40, 535-543.

Munsinger, Gary M., Jean E. Weber and Richard Hansen, (1975), "Joint Home Purchasing Decisions Between Husbands and Wives", *Journal of Consumer Research*, 1 (March), 60-66.

O'Conner, P.J., Gary L. Sullivan, and Dana A. Pogorzelski (1985),"Cross-Cultural Family Purchasing Decisions: A Literature Review," Elizabeth C. Hirschman and Morris B. Holbrook, (eds.), in *Advances in Consumer Research*, Vol 12, Provo, UT: Association for Consumer Research, 59-64.

Park, Jonghee, Patriya Tansuhaj and Rick Kolbe (1991), "The Role of Love, Affection and Intimacy in Family Decision Research," R.H. Holman and M.R. Solomon, (eds.), in *Advances in Consumer Research*, vol. 18, Provo, UT: Association for Consumer Research, 651-656.

Qualls, William J. (1982), "Changing Sex Roles: The Impact Upon Family Decision Making," in E.C. Hirschman, and M.B. Holbrook, (eds). *Advances in Consumer Research*, vol. 9. Provo, UT: Association for Consumer Research, 267-270.

_____ (1984), "Sex Roles, Husband-Wife Influence, and Family Decision Behavior," in T.C. Kinnear, (ed). *Advances in Consumer Research*, vol. 11. Provo, UT: Association for Consumer Research, 270-275.

_____ (1987), "Household Decision Behavior: The Impact of Family Decision Behavior," in *Journal of Consumer Research*, 14 (September), 264-279.

Rubin, Zick (1973), *Liking and Loving: An Invitation to Social Psychology*. New York: Holt, Rinehart and Winston.

Seymour, Daniel and Greg Lessne (1984), "Spousal Conflict Arousal: Scale of Development," in T.C. Kinnear, (ed). *Advances in Consumer Research*, vol. 11. Provo, UT: Association for Consumer Research, 810-821.

Sharp, Harry and Paul Mott, (1956), "Consumer Decisions in the Metropolitan Family", *Journal of Marketing*, 21, (October), 149-156.

Shaver, Phillip and Judith C. Schwartz (1984), "Prototypes and Examples of Fear, Sadness, Anger, Happiness, and Love," Paper presented at Society of Experimental Social Psychology Meetings, Snowbird, Utah.

Sheth, Jagdish N. (1974), "A Theory of Family Buying Decisions," in *Models of Buyer Behavior: Conceptual, Quantitative and Empirical*, J.N. Sheth, (ed.) New York: Harper and Row, 17-33.

Shott, Susan (1984), "Emotion and Social Life: A Symbolic Interactionist Analysis," *American Journal of Sociology*, 84, 6, 1317-1334.

Sprecher, Susan (1986), "The Relation Between Inequity and Emotions in Close Relationships," *Social Psychology Quarterly*, (49)4, 309-321.

Stone, Arthur A. (1981), "The Association Between Perceptions of Daily Experiences and Self-Rated Mood," *Journal of Research in Personality*, 15, 510-522.

Tomkins, Sylvan (1982), "Affect Theory," in *Emotion in the Human Face*, 2nd ed., Paul Ekman, (ed.) Cambridge University Press, 353-395.

Walgast, Elizabeth H. (1958), "Do Husbands of Wives Make the Purchasing Decisions?," *Journal of Marketing*, 23 (October), 151-158.

Walster, Elaine, G.W. Walster and Jane Traupmann (1978), "Equity and Premarital Sex," *Journal of Personality and Social Psychology*, 37, 82-92.

Watson, David (1988), "Intraindividual and Interindividual Analyses of Positive and Negative Affect: Their Relation to Health Complaints, Perceived Stress, and Daily Activities, *Journal of Personality and Social Psychology*, 54, 1020-1030.

_____and Lee Anna Clark (1988), "Positive and Negative Affectivity and Their Relation to Anxiety and Depressive Disorders," *Journal of Abnormal Psychology*, 97 (3), 346-353.

Watson, David, Lee Anna Clark, and Auke Tellegan (1988), "Development and Validation of Brief Measures of Positive and Negative Affect: The PANAS Scales," *Journal of Personality and Social Psychology*, 54 (6), 1063-1070.

Westbrook, Robert A. and Richard L. Oliver (1991), "The Dimensionality of Consumption Emotion Patterns and Consumer Satisfaction," *Journal of Consumer Research*, 18 (June), 84-91.

Wilkes, Robert E., (1975), "Husband-Wife Influence in Purchase Decisions: A Confirmation and Extension", *Journal of Marketing Research*, 12 (May), 224-227.

Woodside, Arch G., (1975), "Effects of Prior Decision-Making, Demographics and Psychographics in Marital Roles for Purchasing Durables," in *Advances in Consumer Research*, 2, 81-91.

Zelen, Seymour L. (1987), "Balance and Reversal of Actor-Observer Perspectives: An Attributional Model of Pathology," *Journal of Social and Clinical Psychology*, 5 (4), 435-451.

Coping With Household Stress in the 1990s: Who Uses "Convenience Foods" and Do They Help?

Judith J. Madill-Marshall, Carleton University
Louise Heslop, Carleton University
Linda Duxbury, Carleton University

Given the time pressures and stresses experienced by many women and men in coping with the pressures associated with work and family, and the importance of up-to-date knowledge of food consumption patterns, the purpose of this paper is to examine the use of convenience foods by women in families in the 1990s. Results show that women tend to be either fairly heavy users or non-users of the 6 types of convenience foods studied. A number of variables related to both the woman's work and family situation were found to be related to extent of use of these foods.

Much research attention has been paid to the changing roles of women over the past 20 years. In particular, researchers have examined the impact of women's employment outside the home on the lives of women who face the challenges of managing both work and family roles. Much of this research has reported high stress levels among working women largely attributable to the difficulties of coping with multiple roles in day to day life (Gupta and Jenkins 1985; Lewis and Cooper 1988). A mounting body of research is documenting the existence of a "second shift" for employed women who devote significantly more hours per day to unpaid household work than do employed men. For example, employed women with a partner and children under age 5 spend 4.9 hours per day doing unpaid household chores compared with 2.4 hour per day spent by their male counterparts (Barr, 1993). A major part of the unpaid work performed in virtually all households is the purchase and preparation of food (Marshall et. al., 1994).

Recognizing that women have traditionally been responsible for food shopping and preparation in the household, consumer researchers have demonstrated an interest in the effect of wives' employment on the purchase of food products with a focus on convenience food items (Bellante and Foster 1984; Bryant 1989; Douglas 1976; Jackson et al. 1985; Nickols and Fox 1983; Reilly 1982; Schaninger and Allen 1981; Roberts and Wortzel 1979; 1984; Strober and Weinberg 1980; Venkatesh 1980; Weinberg and Winer 1983).

The underlying philosophy behind this research has been that women who work outside the home experience greater time pressures than women who do not and therefore will consume in ways to alleviate this time pressure i.e. buy time (Jackson et al. 1985; Strober and Weinberg 1980; Reilly 1982). However, a quick glance at this research shows that much of it is very dated. Most of this research was conducted at a time when traditional family forms were still the norm. Strober and Weinberg (1980) and Weinberg and Winer (1983) based their findings on 1977 survey data. Bryant (1989) used data gathered in 1978-79, and Bellante and Foster (1984) used 1972-73 Consumer Expenditure data. The Roberts and Wortzel (1979) ground breaking work was also done in the 1970's. Social-cultural expectations have changed in the past 2 decades as the dual-earner family became the norm. It is probable, therefore, that working women in the 1990's will have different experiences, attitudes and responses to work and family roles and employ different consumption strategies than did women in the 1970's.

Given the need for food industry marketing practitioners to target "convenience" type foods to the most likely users and reach these consumers with communications based on a realistic under-standing of *current* consumer behaviour, the purpose of this paper is to examine the following questions:

(1) What types of "convenience" foods are consumed in the household of the 1990's to cope with food shopping and food preparation roles? Who are the heavy users of such foods?

(2) How much total meal preparation has been relegated outside the household? Who are the heavy buyers of meals prepared outside the household?

(3) Is the purchase of meals and the use of convenience foods related to work demands and time pressures and to stress and life satisfaction?

(4) Do those who enjoy the food-related tasks cope differently than those who do not?

BACKGROUND

Consumer Research and Food Consumption in Families

A review of the marketing and consumer behaviour literature shows that consumer researchers have been interested in the effect of wives' employment on three main areas of food consumption: (1) ownership of durables (Strober and Weinberg 1980; Weinberg and Winer 1983; Nickols and Fox 1983; Reilly 1982; Bryant 1989), (2) food expenditure patterns, with a focus on convenience food items (Douglas 1976; Jackson et al. 1985; Nickols and Fox 1983; Reilly 1982; Schaninger and Allen 1981; Strober and Weinberg 1980; Venkatesh 1980), and (3) purchase of services (Bellante and Foster 1984; Joag, Gentry and Hopper 1985; Nickols and Fox 1983). Previous research reveals a very complex picture, but, three key observations emerge from this literature.

First, as noted above, it is apparent that most of the consumer research on food shopping and preparation is very dated. This lack of recent research represents a glaring gap in consumer behaviour knowledge about current consumption practices and patterns in a very important consumer market - the food market. Evidence shows that food expenditures accounted for 16% of total household expenditures after personal taxes. Food consumption therefore represents the second largest category of expenses for Canadian families after shelter, for which Canadian families spend an average of 22% of their incomes after taxes (Statistics Canada, November 15, 1993). Further, the average total household food expenditure rose 22% between 1986 and 1992, resulting in an average household expenditure of $110 per week (Statistics Canada, December 2, 1993).

Secondly, it must be noted that food products have changed enormously over the past 20 years. Much of today's supermarket shelves are occupied by "convenience" type products that did not exist or existed in only very basic forms 20 years ago. For example, the number of prepared dinners and prepared meats (i.e. frozen Lasagna, frozen chicken Kiev or cabbage rolls) has increased dramatically, while the development of prepared sauces and mixes such as "Memories of Hong Kong", "Chicken Tonight" represent the development of a sophisticated category of products that one adds to basic ingredients to create exotic meals very quickly.

Convenience foods in the 1990's appear to strike a new balance between decreasing time and effort required and increasing the quality of the final food product. Given the time pressures of today's consumers, it is necessary to examine the use of these "convenience" type of products in North American households in the 1990's.

Third, many studies have compared working women to non-working women – a division found to be too simplistic in both the consumer behaviour and in the work-family literature (Bartos 1978; Reilly 1982; Schaninger and Allen 1981; Venkatesh 1980; Yogev and Brett 1985). As Schaninger and Allen (1981) found, work status or work involvement may be a key factor related to consumption strategies. Venkatesh (1980) reported significant differences on various demographic, life-style, and magazine readership characteristics among women identified as traditionalists, moderates and feminists.

The objectives of this paper are to examine the relationships between use of convenience foods and the purchase of meals prepared outside the household with (a) a number of predictor variables including (i) work status, (ii) role overload, (iii) role orientations, (iv) work involvement and hours in work, (v) education level, (vi) respondent and household incomes, (vii) stage of the family life cycle, as well as (b) two outcome variables - (i) stress and (ii) life satisfaction. A brief justification for including each of these variables is given below.

Work Status. The literature suggests that stress is experienced differently by families depending on the type of employment they are engaged in (Portner 1983). Schaninger and Allen (1981) found significant differences in food consumption across wives' occupation-status groups. They found that lower status families consumed convenience foods more frequently than other families, while higher status families tended to avoid instant convenience foods but put a greater emphasis on the evening meal as a stress-relieving pseudo-leisure activity. While Bartos (1978) and Douglas (1976) suggested that working wives will shop at fewer grocery stores and more convenience stores than non-working wives, Schaninger and Allen (1981) did not find support for this. In this study, the type of work performed by women was broadly classified into two categories - the professional/managerial career category, and the technical, clerical, semi-skilled earner category. Previous research has shown that each of these categories exhibits different psychological involvement and time spent on the work role (Yogev and Brett, 1985).

Role Overload. Since role overload can result in increased stress and decreased life satisfaction (Gupta and Jenkins 1985; Repetti, Matthews and Waldron 1989), it is expected that women will try to minimize these effects by utilizing more convenience foods. Reilly (1982) found moderate support for his model showing role overload as a result of wives' work involvement leading to purchase of more convenience foods and to ownership of time-saving durables. In this study, role overload was measured using Reilly's (1982) role overload scale.

Task Enjoyment. In households where the respondent does not enjoy food preparation, this task may be delegated to the market more often, whereas in households where the respondent enjoys the activity, she may employ it as a stress reducing activity (Hendrix and Qualls 1984; Roberts and Wortzel 1979). Enjoyment of the food preparation role was measured by a summed scale of six Likert scale items, and enjoyment of food shopping was measured by a summed scale of five Likert scale items.

Work Involvement and Hours in Work. Work involvement, defined as the extent to which a person identifies psychologically with work roles and the importance of work to an individual's self concept (Yogev and Brett 1985; Lodahl and Kehner 1965), has

received much research attention in the dual-earner family literature and some attention in the consumer behaviour literature (Joag, Gentry and Hopper 1985). Schaninger and Allen (1981) found that work involvement may be a key factor explaining variation in consumption patterns. Earlier consumer research that focused on the differences in consumption between women employed outside the home and those who were not, can be seen as laying the foundation for our understanding of the effects of hours of work and work involvement on food consumption patterns.

This research suggested that working and nonworking wives differ significantly in their perception of time pressures (Strober and Weinberg 1980), baking practices and price checking on grocery purchases (Strober and Weinberg (1980), and meals away from home (Nichols and Fox 1983). Douglas (1976) found that working wives tended to shop less frequently than non-working wives and made greater use of husbands in shopping activities. Jackson *et.al.*, (1985) reported that working wives tended to have a greater dislike for food shopping and cooking that seemed to stem primarily from time considerations. Nickols and Fox (1983) reported that employed women used more time buying strategies including purchased child care and meals away from home. Bellante and Foster (1984) reported that the number of hours a wife worked was positively associated with expenditure on food away from home, child care, and total services purchased.

It is expected that the higher the involvement with work and the longer hours one spends in employment, the more likely one will use convenience food products and consume meals purchased outside the home. Work involvement was measured using the Lodahl and Kehner (1965) scale. Hours in work was measured by asking for reports on hours spent in paid employment per week.

Education, Incomes and Stage of the Family Lifecycle. The literature indicates that two-earner parents experience more stress than nonparents and that the pressures are especially salient for parents of preschool children (Lewis and Cooper 1988; Googins and Burden 1987). Previous research in the consumer behaviour field has shown the importance of controlling for education, income, and stage of the family life cycle when attempting to examine how consumption patterns are related to work status (Strober and Weinberg 1980; Rubin, Riney and Molina 1990; Weinberg and Winer 1983). Measures of these variables were constructed from standard demographic questions.

Life Satisfaction and Perceived Stress. Previous consumer research has not examined the link between using convenience foods and life satisfaction and stress. This research examines how the level of usage of various types of convenience foods is associated with stress and life satisfaction levels. Perceived stress was measured via the 14-item Cohen, Kamarck, Miermelstekim (1982) scale. Life satisfaction was measured using the 5-item Diener et.al. (1985) measure.

Convenience Foods Purchased. On the basis of the qualitative phase of this research, a 6-item typology of convenience foods was used in this research. Respondents were asked how often they use: (1) prepared dinners that require only cooking, (2) purchased prepared meat (entrees that require only cooking), (3) prepared or frozen vegetables, (4) prepared or frozen baked goods, (5) mixes (cakes, biscuits, muffins etc.), (6) prepared items to be used in recipes (purchased sauces, hamburger helper type mixes). They were also asked how many dinners were purchased outside the home.

METHODOLOGY

Data were part of a recently completed study on the consumption strategies women use to help manage the pressures they experience in work and family and the outcomes associated with

TABLE 1
Frequency Of Use Of Convenience Foods

	Proportion(%) of Households Who Use		
	Weekly or More	Less Than Once/Week	Never
Prepared Dinners (i.e. pizza dinners requiring only cooking)	39.5	22.7	37.8
Prepared Meat (i.e. entrees that require only cooking, burger patties, frozen fish)	31.3	24.5	44.2
Prepared of Frozen Vegetables	52.5	25	22.5
Frozen or Prepared or Baked Goods	31.4	22.3	46.3
Mixes (i.e.cakes,muffins,biscuits)	17.9	35.5	46.6
Prepared Items Added to Food (i.e. purchased sauces, seasoning mixes)	39.1	25.3	35.5

each of these strategies. In the first phase of this research, twenty semi-structured depth interviews were conducted with women in their own homes. The second phase of the study gathered quantitative data on the food shopping and preparation practices and strategies used in Canadian families. During this phase a sample of women in five government departments were asked to complete a seventeen page self-administered questionnaire and return it using a postage paid self addressed return envelope. Eight hundred ninety-three responses were obtained for a response rate of 57%.

FINDINGS

Sample Description

To minimize the influence of non-measured confounds, and to make the population as homogenous as possible, the sample for the current study was limited to include only women who were engaged in full-time paid employment, were married or living with a significant other and who had children who were 18 years of age or less living at home at least 50% of the time. A total of 365 women met these sampling criteria.

Forty percent of these women were employed in managerial or professional careers (coded as careers for analysis below). Sixty percent were employed in technical, administrative, sales, skilled, semi-skilled and unskilled labour occupations (coded as earners for analysis below). The average age of the sample was 36 years, with 27% having high school or less, 23% community college and 50% with some university or higher qualification as their education. Approximately 28% of the women had one child, 49% had two, and 23% had three or more. Twenty-five percent of the respondents earned less than $30,000, 65% earned between $30,000 to 59,999, while only 10% earned $60,000 or more. Household incomes varied with five percent earning less than $30,000, 31% earning between $30,000 to 59,999, 36% earning between $60,000 to 89,999, and 28% earning $ 90,000 and more.
Comparing these demographic characteristics to the Statistics Canada 1991 census reports for Ottawa show that this sample was demographically very similar to the population of working women with

two exceptions: the women in the sample earned higher incomes and were more highly educated than average working women.

Use of Convenience Foods

Respondents were asked to indicate how often six types of "convenience" foods were used in their households. Table 1, which presents a summary of this information, indicates that there is considerable use of most categories of convenience type foods as between 30-40% of households use every category of products weekly or more (except frozen vegetables and mixes). Prepared or frozen vegetables appear to be used most frequently, (52.5% use weekly or more), while mixes are used the least (17.9% use weekly or more). Almost half of the study respondents reported that they never or almost never used frozen or prepared baked goods (46.3%) or mixes (46.6%) or prepared meats (44.2%). About 1/3 never use prepared dinners (37.8%), or prepared items added to foods (35.5%).

Respondents were also asked to report the number of times in the week prior to the study, that each family member consumed a meal that was purchased from a restaurant or deli. To account for differences in household size, mean numbers of purchased meals per person in the household was calculated. The median number of purchased meals consumed per week per household member was 2.2.

Convenience Foods and Purchased Meals: Predictors and Outcomes

Relationships between variables noted in the objectives of the research and use of six types of convenience foods are reported below and summarized in Table 2.

Work Status. Analysis of variance showed that career women use significantly more frozen or prepared baked goods than do earner women (t=2.08, p=.04); but they use significantly fewer mixes (t=-2.47, p=.01). There is no significant difference between the two groups in the use of any of the other types of convenience foods or in the number of purchased meals consumed. So, there is little support in this study for the earlier findings of Schaninger and

TABLE 2
Significant Correlates of Convenience Food Use

Types of Convenience Foods Used							
	Prepared Dinner	Prepared Meals/ Entrees	Prepared Vegetables	Baked Goods	Mixes	Prepared Items Used in Cooking	Purchased Dinners
Work Related Predictors :							
Work status (Earner vs. Career)				+	-		
Role Overload	+					+	
Work Involvement	-				-		+
Hours in Work	+						+
Role Orientation :							
Enjoy Food Preparation	-	-	-	-		-	
Enjoy Food Shopping	+	-	-	-		-	
Demographic :							
FLC -							
Young Children (<12)	+						+
Older Children (≥12)	-						-
Education		+			-		+
Income				+	-		+
Outcome Variables:							
Stress	+			-		+	
Life Satisfaction	-	-				-	+

Allen (1981) that work status was related to major differences in the use of convenience foods.

Role Overload. Role overload is positively correlated with use of prepared dinners (r=.10, p=.04) and use of prepared items in foods prepared at home(r=.11, p=.02).

Enjoyment of Food Preparation and Grocery Shopping. Enjoyment of food preparation is negatively related to usage of five of the six types of convenience foods, including use of prepared dinners (r=-.22, p=.00), prepared meats (r=-.16, p=.00), prepared vegetables (r=-.12, p=.01), prepared baked goods (r=-.14, p=.00), and prepared items added to food (r=-.10, p=.03). Similarly, enjoyment of grocery shopping is related to five of the types of convenience foods, including prepared dinners (r=-.12, p=.00), prepared meats (r=-.08, p=.02), prepared vegetables (r=-.09, p=.01), mixes (r=-.08, p=.04), and prepared items added to food (r=-.10, p=.01). These findings support the results of Hendrix and Quall (1984) concerning the importance of role orientation and enjoyment in affecting shopping behavior.

Work Involvement and Hours Spent in Paid Work. Work involvement is negatively correlated with use of prepared dinners (r=-.08, p=.02), and with use of mixes (r=-.13, p=.01) but positively with the number of purchased meals consumed (r=.09, p=.06). On the other hand, the more hours women spend in paid employment, the more prepared dinners they buy (r=.11, p=.02) and the more meals are purchased outside the home (r=.14, p=.00). These findings agree with earlier research on the significance of these two variables in explaining at least some types of convenience food consumption.

Education, Incomes, and Stage of the Family Life Cycle. Education is positively correlated with consumption of purchased meals (r=.16, p=.00), use of prepared meats (r=.10, p=.03), prepared baked goods (r=.10, p=.03) and negatively with use of mixes (r=-.10, p=.03). Both respondent and family incomes are positively correlated with consumption of purchased meals (r=.24, p=.00; r=.18, p=.00), use of prepared baked goods (r=.15, p =.00; r=.14, p=.00), but household income is negatively related with use of mixes (r=-.11, p=.02). Analysis of variance showed that stage of the family life cycle is related to use of prepared dinners. The highest usage is found in families with children aged 6-12, and under 6 years of age; lowest usage is found in families with children between 12 and 18 years of age. Consumption of purchased meals is also related to the stage of the family life cycle. Highest consumption is reported in households with children under age 6 (4.0), then in families with children 6-12 (2.6), and lowest in families with children aged 12-18 (2.0). Again, these results are in agreement with earlier research which has found that the presence and ages of children is highly predictive of convenience food use, and that income and education levels must be taken into account in analyzing consumption patterns.

Stress and Life Satisfaction. Perceived stress is positively related to use of prepared dinners (r=.10, p=.04), prepared items in food (r=.100, p=.03), but negatively with use of prepared baked goods (r=.08, p=.07). Life satisfaction is negatively related to use of many types of convenience foods including prepared dinners (r=-.21, p=.00), prepared vegetables (r=-.12, p=.03), and prepared items added to food (r=-.08, p=.06) but positively related to consumption of purchased dinners (r=.08, p=.02).

CONCLUSIONS

This research shows that working women in the 1990s tend to either not use each type of convenience food at all, or to use it quite frequently (weekly or more). The results show clearly that there are relatively high proportions of working women who are high users of each type of convenience food except mixes. However, there are also very high proportions who never or almost never use each type of convenience food (except for frozen vegetables). While there are some women who use each category about monthly, this proportion hovers around 1/4 or less for each category.

Several major patterns can be seen in the overall results. Firstly, it is apparent that all the variables in the study have important links to convenience food usage, suggesting that decisions about the use of these products is intricately linked to the entire life (work and family) circumstances of the woman. It is not just whether she works or not or enjoys cooking or not, but both of these and also how demanding her work is, how fulfilling, how stressful it and family life is, how many children and their ages, how much income there is, etc. However, the most useful predictor is orientation to food-related tasks. If these tasks are seen as pleasurable, even stress-relieving, they are much less likely to be delegated to the marketplace. Rather more cooking and shopping tasks will be done by the woman and convenience food usage of virtually all types, including eating meals prepared outside the home, will be lower.

In terms of the usefulness of convenience foods in overall stress reduction and life satisfaction, there does not seem to be a major impact. Generally, high stress is associated with delegating the whole task to the marketplace, and life satisfaction is negatively related to convenience food use, but, of course, the direction (or even the existence) of causal links can not be addressed in this type of study.

The results also reveal some very interesting *patterns of correlates* of use of types of convenience foods. Those who are high users of prepared dinners that are just heated in the home before use are earners, rather than career women, with high role overload, high number of hours of work, young children in the home, high stress levels and low life satisfaction, and they do not enjoy food tasks. They appear to be in a very difficult situation, with pressures on both the work and the family sides, and find little pleasure in meal preparation. Their decision appears to be to opt out of meal preparation all together by using "heat and serve" alternatives.

A different alternative is chosen by those women who also have long working hours and small children, but who are career workers with high incomes and education levels. These women are more likely to purchase meals outside the home. They have the resources to do so. This alternative is not associated with dislike of food preparation and food shopping tasks, but is associated with higher life satisfaction.

A similar difference in the choice with regards to baked goods can be seen. In this case, high users of both mixes and prepared baked goods do not enjoy food tasks. So how do they address the problem. Those who are career workers and with higher incomes buy fully prepared or frozen baked goods, whereas earners with more limited incomes and education use mixes instead.

Those who are heavy users of prepared meat entrees dislike food tasks and have higher education levels. Many of these types of food products are relatively new on the market and may appeal to the younger, more upscale "wannabe". "Prepared items used in cooking" follows a similar pattern in correlates to prepared dinners and may be seen as a close substitute.

Finally, prepared/frozen vegetables had the fewest correlates. It is likely that these products are no longer seen as convenience products, but are widely used by all consumers to reduce meal preparation tasks.

Notwithstanding the need for further analyses of the patterns of consumption observed in this research, the authors note several implications for marketing managers that emerge from this study. First, the study supports the need for the food industry to continue development of innovative "convenience" food products which can reduce time spent on food preparation tasks. A very high proportion of working women will continue to seek such products in trying to reduce role overload and stress by decreasing time spent on meal preparation and grocery shopping. Second, the marketing of such products is *extremely* complicated in the 1990's. Overall, messages targeted to women who do not see food preparation tasks as pleasurable, regardless of their work status, income, age, education and so on, are likely to be most successful. But, as noted in the discussion above, different types of convenience foods are attractive to women in different work/family life situations. Third, it is critical that advertisers recognize the high stress faced by women in the 1990's household and offer solutions aimed at alleviating this stress in effective advertising messages.

Additional research is needed to either support the use of the typology of convenience foods in this study or to develop other ones. This research supported the use of a typology that was built upon the idea that many different food products are currently available that can be labelled as 'convenience' foods for very different reasons. For example, some foods come fully prepared, one simply buys, then consumes them. Others come fully prepared but need to be heated. Others represent only portions of a meal that come prepared and require work at combining them with other foods for a meal. Others come with all the ingredients measured and in one box but require assembling and perhaps cooking in the home. Lastly, others are prepared items to be added to foods being prepared in the home.

Very little previous research has focused on categorizing convenience foods - yet this is an important first step in really understanding food consumption in North America in the 1990's. The authors are continuing the preliminary work reported in this paper by working on developing a theoretical model which will attempt to explain household food consumption strategies used to cope with the myriad of work and family demands facing families in the 1990's.

BIBLIOGRAPHY

Statistics Canada, *The Daily*, November 15, 1993.

Statistics Canada, *The Daily*, December 2, 1993.

Barr, Lynn (1993) *Basic Fact on Families in Canada, Past and Present*, Statistics Canada, Housing, Family and Social Statistic Division.

Bartos, T. (1978) "What Every Marketer Should Know About Women", *Harvard Business Review*, 56, 73-85.

Bellante, D. and Foster, A.C. (1984) "Working Wives and Expenditure on Services", *Journal of Consumer Research*, 11(2), 700-707.

Bryant, W.K. (1989) "Durables and Wives' Employment Yet Again", *Journal of Consumer Research*, 15(June), 37-47.

Cohen, S., Kamarck, T., and Mermelstein, R. (1983) "A Global Measure of Perceived Stress", *Journal of Health and Social Behavior*, Vol. 24, 385-396.

Diener, E., Emmons, R., Larsen, R. and S. Griffin (1985) "The Satisfaction with Life Scale", *Journal of Personality Assessment*, Vol. 49, 71-75.

Douglas, S.P. (1976) "Cross-National Comparisons and Consumer Stereotypes: A Case Study of Working and Non-Working Wives in the U.S. and France", *Journal of Consumer Research*, 3(1), 12-20.

Googins, B., and D. Burden (1987) "Vulnerability of Working Parents: Balancing Work and Home Roles", *Social Work*, 32, 295-300.

Gupta, N. and D. Jenkins (1985) "Stress, Stressors, Strains, and Strategies", in T. A. Beehr and R.S. Bhagat (Eds.), *Human Stress and Cognition in Organizations*, John Wiley, New York, 141-176.

Hendrix, P.E. and W.J. Qualls (1984) "Operationalizing Family Level Constructs: Problems and Prospects", in *Marketing to the Changing Household*, Roberts, M.L. and L.H. Wortzel (Eds.), Ballinger: Cambridge, Mass.

Jackson, R.W., McDaniel, S.W. and C.P. Rao (1985) "Food Shopping and Preparation: Psychographic Differences of Working Wives and Housewives", *Journal of Consumer Research*, 12(1), 110-113.

Joag, S.G., Gentry, J.W., and J. Hopper (1985) "Explaining Differences in Consumption By Working and Non-Working Wives", in *Advances in Consumer Research*, Vol. 12, 582-585.

Lewis,D. and C. Cooper (1988) "Stress in Dual-Earner Families', in B. Gutek, A. Stromber, and L. Larwood (Eds.) *Women and Work*, Volume 3, Sage Publications, New York, New York, 139-169.

Lodahl, T.M. and N. Kehner (1965) "The Definition and Measurement of Job Involvement", *Journal of Applied Psychology*, 49, 24-33.

Marshall, Judith J., Duxbury, L. and L.A. Heslop (1994) "Grocery Shopping and Food Preparation in Dual-Income Families: Implications for Marketing", Working Paper, School of Business, Carleton University, Ottawa, Canada.

Nickols, S.Y. and K.D. Fox (1983) "Buying Time and Saving Time: Strategies for Managing Household Production", *Journal of Consumer Research*, 10(2), 197-208.

Portner, J. (1983) "Work and Family, Achieving a Balance", in H. McCubbin and C. Figley (Eds.), *Stress and the Family Volume 1: Coping with Normative Transactions*, Brunner/Mazel, New York, 163-177.

Reilly, M.D. (1982) "Working Wives and Convenience Consumption", *Journal of Consumer Research*, 8(4), 407-418.

Repetti, R., Matthews, K., and I. Waldron (1989) "Employment and Women's Health: Effects of Paid Employment on Women's Mental and Physical Health", *American Psychologist*, 44, 1394-1401.

Roberts, M.L. and L.H. Wortzel (1979) "New Life-Style Determinants of Women's Food Shopping Behavior", *Journal of Marketing*, 43(3), 28-39.

Roberts, M.L. and L.H. Wortzel (1984) "A Dynamic Model of Role Allocation in the Household: Marketing Management and Research Implications", in M.L. Roberts and L.H. Wortzel (Eds.), *Marketing to the Changing Household*, Ballinger: Cambridge, Mass.

Rubin,R.M., Riney, B.J., and D.J. Molina (1990) "Expenditure Pattern Differentials Between One-Earner and Dual-Earner Households:1972-1978 and 1984", *Journal of Consumer Research*, Vol. 17(June), 43-52.

Schaninger, C.M. and C.T. Allen (1981) "Wife's Occupational Status as a Consumer Behavior Construct", *Journal of Consumer Research*, 8(2), 189-196.

Strober, M.A. and C.B. Weinberg (1980) "Strategies Used By Working and Nonworking Wives to Reduce Time Pressures", *Journal of Consumer Research*, 6(4), 338-348.

A. Venkatesh (1980) "Changing Roles of Women - A Life-Style Analysis", *Journal of Consumer Research*, 7(Sept), 189-197.

Weinberg, C.B. and R.S. Winer (1983) "Working Wives and Major Family Expenditures: Replication and Extension", *Journal of Consumer Research*, 10(2), 259-263.

Yogev, S. and J. Brett (1985) "Patterns of Work and Family Involvement Among Single and Dual Earner Couples", *Journal of Applied Psychology*, 70, 754-786.

Understanding Responses to Sex Appeals in Advertising: An Individual Difference Approach

Stephen M. Smith, North Georgia College
Curtis P. Haugtvedt, Ohio State University
John M. Jadrich, University of Georgia
and Mark R. Anton, University of Georgia

ABSTRACT

Although the use of partially nude models in advertising has increased in recent years (Soley and Reid 1988), how such ads influence consumer judgments and reactions is unclear. A review of existing research suggests complex relationships between the use of nudity in an advertisement and several measures of advertising effectiveness. In order to begin to better understand conditions under which the persuasive effects of nudity might be enhanced or diminished, we examined the moderating role of an individual difference factor expected to predict reactions to advertising containing partially nude models—sex guilt.

Consistent with earlier predictions by Kerin, Lundstrom and Sciglimpaglia (1979), recent evidence suggests that the use of nudity in advertising is more common than ever (Soley and Reid 1988). This is despite the fact that empirical work has produced inconsistent and sometimes negative results regarding the overall effectiveness of sexual stimuli in advertising.

For example, a number of studies have varied the sexual content of advertisements and examined brand recall effects. The most common finding in such studies is that nudity or sexual content actually reduces a consumer's probability of remembering the brand (e.g., Alexander and Judd 1979; Chestnut, LaChance and Lubitz 1977; Richmond and Hartman 1982; Steadman 1969). One explanation for such findings is that sexual stimuli draw attention away from brand information, and this is supported by findings that sexual content actually increases processing of ad execution factors, while undermining processing of brand information (Reid and Soley 1981; Severn, Belch and Belch 1990).

When measures other than brand recall are used to evaluate the effectiveness of sexual stimuli in advertising, a different picture has emerged. For example, nudity or sexual content in an ad increases consumer arousal (Belch, Holgerson, Belch and Koppman 1982; LaTour 1990). Increased arousal may be partially responsible for consumers' increased recognition of ads containing sexual content, when Starch scores are examined (Reid and Soley 1981). Of course, arousal per se is not necessarily a positive outcome, and could undermine ad and brand judgments if the arousal is negatively valenced or too extreme. Recent work by LaTour and his colleagues (LaTour 1990; LaTour, Pitts and Snook-Luther 1990) indicates that ad-based arousal is multidimensional, with some dimensions affecting ad evaluations in a positive manner, and some having a negative effect. In addition, arousal research indicates that extremely high levels of arousal undermine persuasion relative to lower levels (Sanbonmatsu and Kardes 1988). Since the arousal elicited by sexual content can apparently be a two-edged sword, it is important for advertisers to recognize when "good" or "bad" arousal is most likely.

Some important moderators of the valence of consumer reactions to sexual content have already been identified. Bello, Pitts and Etzel (1983) found that ads containing sexual suggestiveness were evaluated more favorably in the context of congruent programming (i.e., a program involving sexual content) than when viewed in the context of an incongruent, contrasting (i.e., nonsexual) program. In addition, several investigators have found that consumer gender is an important moderator of responses to ad nudity (e.g., Belch et al. 1982; Bello et al. 1983; LaTour 1990; LaTour and Henthorne 1993; Sciglimpaglia, Belch and Cain 1979). Specifically, it has been found that males respond more positively than do females to female nudity, and female subjects are more favorable toward male nudity than are male subjects. It seems reasonable to conclude that whatever arousal is elicited by viewing ads containing same-sex nudity will be more likely to be negative arousal than the arousal elicited by opposite-sex nudity (assuming, perhaps, a predominantly heterosexual sample). Finally, research suggests that product type is also a significant moderator of responses to nudity. A number of investigators have concluded that nudity works better for some products, such as alcoholic beverages or fragrances, than for others, such as a construction company (e.g., Peterson and Kerin 1977; Richmond and Hartman 1982; Steadman 1969), perhaps because sex is a relevant dimension of appeal for some products, but not others.

Responses to Ad Nudity: An Individual Difference Perspective

In recent years, consumer and social psychologists have begun to utilize specific individual difference variables to examine theoretical processes. For example, work by Snyder and his colleagues (e.g., Snyder and DeBono 1985) has employed the individual difference variable of self-monitoring to better understand attitude functions (e.g., Katz 1960; Shavitt, Lowrey and Han 1992). Likewise, work by Haugtvedt and his colleagues has employed the individual difference variable of need for cognition in order to gain insight into processes underlying the formation of strong attitudes (e.g., Haugtvedt and Petty 1992). In the case of both self-monitoring and need for cognition, the individual difference variables serve to operationalize a construct in a broader theoretical framework. In a recent ACR address, Bagozzi (1993) called for more research employing individual difference variables, citing specifically their power as moderator variables.

Given the hypothesized importance of the role of arousal in the effectiveness of ads containing nudity, the research presented in this paper represents our initial attempt to use a personality variable that may provide some insight into the effects of different kinds of arousal. The only previous study attempting to use an individual difference approach to understanding reactions to nudity in advertising is that by Sciglimpaglia, Belch and Cain (1979). In their work, Sciglimpaglia et al. compared respondents' scores on a social values scale to their evaluations of sexual and nonsexual ads. Sciglimpaglia et al. found that more conservative social values were moderately associated with less favorable responses to ads containing nudity, but only among male participants. The values of female subjects bore little relation to their evaluations of sexy advertisements.

Although personal social values should certainly be relevant to many consumers' responses to sexual advertising, such values are perhaps too broad to afford much predictive power for specific criteria such as responses to individual ads. One individual difference that would appear to be more directly relevant than overall social values is an individual's level of sexual guilt. As defined and measured by Mosher (1966), sex guilt is an individual difference in the extent to which people are comfortable with sexual matters, and more specifically, with sexual arousal. People who are high in sex guilt (SG) will tend to feel negatively about being sexually aroused, whereas people low in sex guilt feel positively about such arousal. Research has confirmed that differences in sex guilt are significantly related to the positivity of subjects' reactions to sexual stimuli, with high sex guilt associated with less favorable reactions (Kelley 1985). Thus consumers' level of sex guilt might serve to capture the likelihood of negative arousal.

In the present research, we examined the effects of subject gender and subject sex guilt on responses to ads containing one of three forms of nudity. Some participants viewed ads containing male nudity, some saw ads containing female nudity, and others saw ads containing both male and female nudity.

METHOD

Subjects and Design.

A total of 101 undergraduate psychology students (29 male) participated in exchange for extra credit in an introductory psychology course. They were randomly assigned to conditions on the manipulated variable of ad nudity. Subjects saw a target ad that contained either female nudity, male nudity, or both male and female nudity. About three weeks prior to participating, subjects completed the sex guilt (SG) items from the Mosher Guilt Inventory (MGI; Mosher 1966) along with several unrelated measures. Sample items from the MGI are, "Masturbation is wrong and a sin," and "When I have sexual dreams, I attempt to repress them." Respondents are asked to indicate their agreement with each of 48 statements on a scale ranging from 0 (*not at all true for me*) to 6 (*extremely true for me*). A median split on SG scores ($\alpha=.83$) created our low and high SG groups.

Procedure.

Subjects arrived at the experiment site in groups of two to six. They were informed that the experiment was about the use of emotional appeals in advertising. They were informed that their task was to look at some print ads and "let us know how they make you feel, and whether or not you think the ads are any good." They were further informed that some of the ads were designed to elicit emotional responses and some were not.

Each subject then received a bound folder containing four print ads, and a separate booklet containing four rating sheets. They were instructed to view and rate each of the ads in order. Ratings included the following information. First, subjects indicated their affective reactions to the ad on several 9-point scales, anchored by the following endpoints: *happy—sad*; *relaxed—aroused*; *threatened—safe*; *calm—excited*; *warm—cold*; *positive—negative*; *disgusted—contented*; and *not tired—tired*.

The next section of the ad response sheet asked subjects to list "whatever thoughts you had while looking at the advertisement, including favorable and unfavorable thoughts about either the ad or the brand itself." This was intended to provide an assessment of the valence or polarity of subjects' cognitive responses.

Following completion of the thought-listing measure, subjects were asked to indicate their attitudes toward the ad on five 9-point scales, anchored by the following endpoints: *effective—ineffective*; *good—bad*; *relevant—irrelevant*; *interesting—uninteresting*; and *uplifting—depressing*. Finally, subjects indicated their brand attitudes on three 9-point scales, anchored by: *good—bad*; *desirable—undesirable*; and *useful—useless*.

Subjects completed the same ratings for each of four, full-color print advertisements. Ads appeared in the same sequence in all conditions. The first was an ad for a liqueur, and the target ad

appeared second. Rather than attempt to create three parallel versions of the same ad to manipulate nudity type, we selected three existing ads that met the condition of being for the same type of product (a fragrance) and containing either female, male, or male and female nudity. Actual ads were used to increase the realism of the study. The three versions of the target ad were thus for three different brands of fragrance. The third and fourth ads were filler ads for an athletic shoe and a toothpaste, respectively.

Since our sample was fairly small, and included mostly females, some analyses were not likely to be reliable. Specifically, three-way interaction terms would be based on some extremely small cell sizes among male participants (ranging from a high of 9 to a low of 2). As a consequence, only two-way analyses involving gender are reported. The primary focus of the present paper is on examining the influence of sex guilt as a moderator of responses to nudity in ads. Thus we will limit our discussion of gender effects to a brief summary of these results.

RESULTS

Affective Reactions

Subjects' responses to the eight affect scales were submitted to a principle components factor analysis with varimax rotation. This analysis indicated a two-factor solution, with five of the measures loading primarily on the first factor, and the other three measures loading strongly on the second factor (see Table 1 below). The items loading on the first factor (which accounted for 43% of total variance) all appear to be related to the valence of responses, and the items on the second factor (accounting for about 29% of total variance) are arousal intensity items. Separate factor scores were thus created for Arousal Positivity and Arousal Intensity.

Arousal Positivity. First, a 3 (Ad Nudity: Male vs. Female vs. Both) X 2 (Subject Gender: Male vs. Female) ANOVA was performed on the factor scores for the positivity dimension. Results indicated significant main effects of both Nudity and Gender, as well as a significant interaction between these factors. The Nudity main effect, $F (2, 94)=11.29$, $p<.001$, reflected the fact that affective responses were more positive in response to the ad containing both male and female nudity ($M=0.76$) than in response to the other two ads (Ms=0.05, -0.19 for the male and female nudity versions, respectively). The main effect of Gender, $F (1, 94)=12.81$, $p<.01$, indicated that males had more favorable reactions overall ($M=0.48$) than did females ($M=-0.10$). These effects were qualified by a Nudity X Gender interaction, $F (2, 94)=34.90$, $p<.001$. The patterning of means suggested that females responded more favorably ($M=0.60$) to the ad containing male nudity than did males ($M=-0.59$), but males were more positive towards the ads depicting either female nudity ($M=0.62$) or both male and female nudity ($M=1.41$) than were female subjects (Ms=-1.00, 0.11, respectively, for female and male/female nudity ads).

The same pattern emerged on virtually all of our dependent measures. Specifically, male participants had more favorable thoughts and evaluations in response to the ads than did females when the ads contained either female nudity or both male and female nudity. When the ads contained male nudity, female subjects had more favorable thoughts and evaluations than did male subjects. These findings are consistent with a number of past investigations of nudity effects in advertising (e.g., Bello et al. 1983; LaTour 1990; LaTour and Henthorne 1993). Since complete elaboration of these data would occupy a great deal of space, and as they do not reflect the primary focus of the research, we do not discuss them further.[1]

---

[1] These data are available upon request from the first author.

TABLE 1

Item	Factor 1 Loading	Factor 2 Loading
Happy--Sad	-0.536	0.638
Relaxed--Aroused	0.210	-0.813
Threatened--Safe	0.743	0.075
Calm--Excited	0.333	-0.784
Warm--Cold	-0.734	0.321
Positive--Negative	-0.818	0.237
Disgusted--Contented	0.879	-0.156
Not Tired--Tired	0.365	0.629
Factor Eigenvalue	*3.109*	*2.268*
Variance Explained	*42.6%*	*28.9%*

Next we performed a 3 (Nudity) X 2 (Sex Guilt: High vs. Low) ANOVA on the arousal positivity scores. The same main effect of nudity emerged and needs no further discussion. A marginal Sex Guilt main effect, F (1, 94)=2.86, $p<.10$, reflects the fact that low sex guilt (SG) participants had somewhat more favorable affective reactions to the ads ($M=0.17$) than did high SG participants ($M=-0.14$). This was qualified by a Nudity X Sex Guilt interaction, F (2, 94)=2.89, $p<.04$. As can be seen in Table 2, this interaction is driven by responses to the ad containing female nudity. High SG subjects had highly unfavorable reactions to this ad, relative to the low SG participants, $F=7.92$, $p<.01$. High SG and low SG participants' reactions to the remaining versions of the ad did not differ significantly ($Fs<1$).[2]

Arousal Intensity. A 3 X 2 ANOVA of the intensity dimension of subjects' arousal responses yielded indicated no significant effects. This suggests that both low and high SG participants experienced the same degree of overall activation in response to the ads. It is worth noting here that subjects' arousal ratings were higher in response to the target ad than in response the nonsexual filler ads. For example, the mean rating on the *relaxed—aroused* item was 5.61 for the target ad, as opposed to 4.25 across the three filler ads.

Cognitive Responses

Subjects' responses on the thought-listing task were coded as either ad-related or brand-related and either positive (pro-ad or pro-brand) or negative (anti-ad or anti-brand). An index of subjects' net ad-related elaborations was constructed by subtracting the total number of negative ad elaborations from the total number of positive ad elaborations. A parallel index was also created for subjects' brand elaborations.

Ad Elaborations. A 3 X 2 ANOVA on the net polarity of subjects' ad elaborations yielded a main effect of Nudity, F (1, 96)=6.40, $p<.01$, as ad-related thoughts were more negative ($M=-0.79$) in response to the female nudity ad than in response to the male nudity ($M=0.02$) or male/female nudity version ($M=0.15$). This effect was qualified by a significant Nudity X Sex Guilt interaction, F (2, 96)=7.86, $p<.01$ (see Table 2 for means). This interaction was attributable the fact that low SG and high SG responses differed significantly only in the female nudity condition.

As expected the high SG respondents generated more unfavorable ad elaborations than the low SG participants in this condition, $F=11.25$, $p<.01$.

Brand Elaborations. An ANOVA performed on the net polarity of brand-related thoughts yielded no significant effects. As evidenced in the cell means (see Table 2), there were very few elaborations that referred specifically to the product.

Ad Attitudes

Responses to the five ad attitude measures were highly inter-related ($\alpha=.90$) and hence were averaged to form a single index. A 3 X 2 ANOVA on subjects' scores on the ad attitude index revealed several significant effects. First, a main effect of Nudity, F (2, 95)=11.24, $p<.001$, reflects the lower rating of the female nudity ad ($M=4.13$) than the male nudity ($M=5.72$) or male/female nudity ad ($M=5.90$). Second, a Sex Guilt main effect, F (1, 95)=8.27, $p<.01$, indicated that high SG participants rated the ads less favorably ($M=4.76$) than did high SG participants ($M=5.73$).

These effects were qualified by a significant Nudity X Sex Guilt interaction, F (2, 95)=6.00, $p<.01$, which was again due primarily to responses to the female nudity ad. Low SG and high SG participants gave approximately equal ad evaluations when the ad contained either male or male/female nudity ($Fs<1.50$, $ps>.20$), but high SG participants again were highly unfavorable towards the female-nudity version, relative to the low SG subjects, $F=23.85$, $p<.001$.

Brand Attitudes

Responses to the three brand attitude items were also highly interrelated ($\alpha=.85$) and averaged to form a single index. A 3 X 2 ANOVA on this index revealed no significant effects, although a marginal Sex Guilt effect did emerge, F (1, 96)=2.93, $p<.10$. High SG participants had slightly more negative attitudes toward the brand ($M=5.70$) than did low SG participants ($M=6.29$).

DISCUSSION

The present results are consistent with the suggestion that individual differences are important moderators of nudity effects in advertising. First, the present data add support to the notion that gender is an important moderator of responses to ad nudity. Consistent with numerous previous investigators (e.g., Belch et al. 1982; Bello et al. 1983; LaTour 1990; LaTour and Henthorne 1993; Sciglimpaglia, Belch and Cain 1979), we found that males were more receptive than females to ads containing female nudity, but females were more favorable than were males toward an ad containing a nude male.

The present data are limited, however, by weaknesses in the experimental design. Specifically, although the use of actual

---

[2]Although not central to the present study, we also analyzed subjects' responses to the nonsexual filler ads. High and low SG participants' responses to these ads did not differ significantly on any of our dependent measures, indicating that any differences between these subjects was limited to the ads containing nudity.

TABLE 2
Summary of Ad-Based Responses of Low and High Sex Guilt Subjects
(Means in Bold, Standard Deviations in Parentheses)

	Male Nudity Ad		Female Nudity Ad		Male & Female Nudity Ad	
	Sex Guilt		Sex Guilt		Sex Guilt	
	Low (N = 17)	High (N =18)	Low (N = 18)	High (N = 17)	Low (N = 14)	High (N = 17)
Arousal Positivity	**0.13** (0.71)	**0.23** (1.00)	**-0.02** (1.07)	**-0.99** (0.96)	**0.39** (0.89)	**0.34** (0.73)
Arousal Intensity*	**0.09** (0.70)	**-0.09** (0.84)	**-0.26** (1.19)	**-0.44** (0.91)	**-0.21** (1.07)	**0.01** (1.18)
Net Ad Elaborations	**-0.29** (0.85)	**0.33** (1.37)	**-0.16** (1.30)	**-1.41** (0.87)	**0.36** (1.34)	**-0.06** (1.20)
Net Brand Elaborations	**0.00** (0.35)	**0.00** (0.00)	**0.21** (0.42)	**0.00** (0.00)	**0.00** (0.56)	**-0.06** (0.24)
Ad Attitudes	**5.57** (1.53)	**5.87** (2.13)	**5.37** (1.77)	**2.88** (1.16)	**6.27** (1.78)	**5.53** (1.65)
Brand Attitudes	**6.08** (1.48)	**5.94** (2.09)	**6.68** (1.59)	**5.55** (2.16)	**6.12** (1.36)	**5.61** (1.54)

*Note: For Arousal Intensity, lower scores indicate higher levels of arousal.

advertisements added to the experimental realism in the present study, it also added potential confounds. The variations of nudity were confounded with brands (and as a consequence, with brand awareness, familiarity, etc.). Other characteristics of the ads which were not held constant (e.g., sexual suggestiveness of poses) could also be responsible for our results. However, it should also be noted that none of our participants spontaneously made a connection between the experimental session and the pretesting session in which they completed the sex guilt inventory.

Theoretical Implications

A more important contribution of the present research regards the use of the individual difference measure of sex guilt. Past research has identified important moderating variables that assist in understanding when nudity will be effective and when it will be ineffective in advertising. In particular, it appears that nudity should be avoided in situations where it is likely to elicit negative arousal (e.g., LaTour 1990), such as when it is used for an inappropriate product (e.g., Richmond and Hartman 1982). Whereas past research has utilized situational variables to study nudity effects, the present investigation identified an individual difference moderator of nudity effects. Specifically, participants with relatively high levels on an individual difference measure of sex guilt appeared to respond quite negatively to ads containing nudity, compared to individuals with lower levels of sexual guilt. This was especially true when the ads contained female nudity.

Both situational and individual difference factors can be used to test theory and better predict behavior (cf. Haugtvedt, Petty and Cacioppo 1992). Demonstrating parallel findings with both situational and individual difference variables increases our confidence in theoretical propositions regarding the influence of nudity in advertising. The present data shed additional light on the underlying processes leading to both positive and negative reactions to nudity in advertising.

Moreover, our data do seem to make clear that the intensity of the arousal elicited by an ad does not necessarily explain differences in the responses of different individuals (e.g., those high and low in sex guilt). Rather, it appears to be the manner in which that arousal

is interpreted. Past research suggests that high sex guilt individuals will experience relatively negatively valenced arousal when exposed to sexual stimuli, relative to low sex guilt individuals (e.g., Kelley 1985; Smith and Martin 1989), and our results appear to be consistent with such findings.

Practical Implications

On a global scale, the use of nudity in advertising has potentially harmful social consequences, characterizing people (especially women) as sexual objects. But even at a micro level, our data imply that marketers should beware of using nudity in advertising with the wrong people. The high sex guilt participants in our study were especially negative in their reactions to female nudity, which is becoming more and more frequently used in ads (see Soley and Reid 1988). Whatever positive effects such advertising may have on the thoughts and attitudes of low sex guilt consumers, they may be counteracted or even outweighed by the negative impact these ads have on high sex guilt consumers. It is therefore important to try to identify and avoid such consumers when using ads containing nudity.

Although perhaps all consumers will be aroused by ads containing sexual stimuli, it is important to recognize that not all arousal is beneficial to the advertiser. The present study seems to reinforce the notion that some arousal is good and some is bad, from a marketing perspective (see also LaTour 1990). However, no direct links were established between arousal and actual consumer behavior in this study, and it is conceivable that the negative reactions some consumers have to nudity in ads will not translate into changes in their consumption patterns. Future research might identify some of the characteristics that distinguish the consumers whose negative responses to an ad are relatively inconsequential, from those who will perhaps make a point of avoiding the advertised brand if and when it elicits negative affective reactions.

REFERENCES

Alexander, M. Wayne and Ben Judd (1978), "Do Nudes in Ads Enhance Brand Recall?" *Journal of Advertising Research*, *18*, 47-51.

Bagozzi, Richard P. (1993), "ACR Fellow Speech," *Advances in Consumer Research*, *21*, 8-11.

Belch, Michael A., Barbra E. Holgerson, George E. Belch and Jerry Koppman (1982), "Psychophysiological and Cognitive Responses to Sex in Advertising," *Advances in Consumer Research*, *9*, 424-427.

Bello, Daniel C., Robert E. Pitts and Michael J. Etzel (1983), "The Communications Effects of Controversial Sexual Content in Television Programs and Commercials," *Journal of Advertising*, *12*, 32-42.

Chestnut, Robert W., Charles C. LaChance and Amy Lubitz (1977), "The 'Decorative' Female Model: Sexual Stimuli and the Recognition of Advertisements, *Journal of Advertising*, *6*, 11-14.

Haugtvedt, Curtis P. and Richard E. Petty (1992), "Personality and Persuasion: Need for Cognition Moderates the Persistence and Resistance of Attitude Change," *Journal of Personality and Social Psychology*, *63*, 308-319.

_____, _____, and John T. Cacioppo (1992), "Need for Cognition and Advertising: Understanding the Role of Personality Variables in Consumer Behavior," *Journal of Consumer Psychology*, *1*, 239-260.

Katz, Daniel (1960), "The Functional Approach to the Study of Attitudes," *Public Opinion Quarterly*, *24*, 163-204.

Kelley, Kathryn (1985), "Sex, Sex Guilt, and Authoritarianism: Differences in Responses to Explicit Heterosexual and Masturbatory Slides," *The Journal of Sex Research*, *21*, 68-85.

Kerin, Roger A., William J. Lundstrom and Donald Sciglimpaglia (1979), "Women in Advertising: Retrospect and Prospect," *Journal of Advertising*, *8*, 37-42.

LaTour, Michael S. (1990), "Female Nudity in Print Advertising: An Analysis of Gender Differences in Ad Arousal and Response," *Psychology and Marketing*, *7*, 65-81.

_____and Tony L. Henthorne (1993), " Female Nudity: Attitudes Toward the Ad and the Brand, and Implications for Advertising Strategy," *Journal of Consumer Marketing*, *10*, 25-32.

_____, Robert E. Pitts and David C. Snook-Luther (1990), "Female Nudity, Arousal, and Ad Response: An Experimental Investigation," *Journal of Advertising*, *19*, 51-62.

Mosher, Donald L. (1966), "Development and Multitrait-multimethodMatrix Analysis of Three Measures of Guilt," *Journal of Consulting Psychology*, *30*, 25-29.

Peterson, Robert A. and Roger A. Kerin (1977), "The Female Role in Advertisements: Some Experimental Evidence," *Journal of Marketing*, *41*, 59-63.

Reid, Leonard N. and Lawrence C. Soley (1981), "Another Look at the 'Decorative' Female Model" The Recognition of Visual and Verbal Ad Components," *Current Issues and Research in Advertising*, 122-133.

Richmond, David and Timothy P. Hartman (1982), "Sex Appeals in Advertising," *Journal of Advertising Research*, *22*, 53-61.

Sanbonmatsu, David M. and Frank R. Kardes (1988), "The Effects of Physiological Arousal on Information Processing and Persuasion," *Journal of Consumer Research*, 15, 379-385.

Sciglimpaglia, Donald, Michael A. Belch and Richard F. Cain (1979), "Demographic and Cognitive Factors Influencing Viewers Evaluations of "Sexy" Advertisements, *Advances in Consumer Research*, *6*, 62-65.

Severn, Jessica, George E. Belch and Michael A. Belch (1990), "The Effects of Sexual and Non-sexual Advertising Appeals and Information Level on Cognitive Processing and Communication Effectiveness," *Journal of Advertising*, *19*, 14-22.

Shavitt, Sharon, Tina M. Lowrey and Sang-Pil Han (1992), "Attitude Functions in Advertising: The Interactive Role of Products and Self-Monitoring," *Journal of Consumer Psychology*, *1*, 337-364.

Smith, Stephen M. and Leonard L. Martin (1989), "The Effects of Erotica on Aggression in High Versus Low Sex Guilt Males," paper presented at the 1st Annual Meeting of the American Psychological Society, Alexandria, VA, June, 1989.

Snyder, Mark P. and Kenneth G. DeBono (1985), " Appeals to Image and Claims about Quality: Understanding the Psychology of Advertising," *Journal of Personality and Social Psychology*, *49*, 586-597.

Soley, Lawrence C. and Leonard N. Reid (1988), "Taking it Off: Are Models in Magazine Ads Wearing Less?," *Journalism Quarterly*, *65*, 960-966.

Steadman, Major (1969), "How Sexy Illustrations Affect Brand Recall," *Journal of Advertising Research*, *9*, 15-19.

Practicing Existential Consumption: The Lived Meaning of Sexuality in Advertising

Richard Elliott, Lancaster University UK
Mark Ritson, Lancaster University UK

ABSTRACT

The extent to which mundane consumption choices can be viewed as the exercising of existential freedom is explored through phenomenological interviews with one member of a small social group of young women. The portrayal of overt sexuality in an advertising campaign was adapted into the social practices of the group. This is discussed in relation to consumption-related symbolic creativity operating through the concept of "grounded aesthetics" being used in the creation and maintenance of social identity. Representations of sexuality in advertising may allow women to speak more easily of their desires through the consumption of advertising meaning and its use as a cultural commodity.

INTRODUCTION

More than a decade ago, Lannon & Cooper (1983) proposed a humanistic approach to advertising that instead of asking what advertising does to people, turns the question on its head and asks "what do people do with advertising?" More recently this perspective has been developed into a meaning-based model of advertising that focuses on the subjective lived experience of advertising (Mick & Buhl, 1992). This model is based on an existential-phenomenological interpretation of meaning as actualized through life themes and life projects (Thompson, Locander & Pollio, 1989). A key element in existential thought is a focus on freedom and choice, as it is only through the exercise of freedom and decision that we become truly human (Sartre, 1956). Even the mundane consumer choices made in the course of everyday life can shape how consumers understand themselves and the lives they lead (Thompson, Locander & Pollio, 1990).

The ability of consumers to resist the influence of advertising and thereby exercise freedom has been minimized by the Marxist analysis of its central role in the maintenance of capitalism which operates through the creation of "ideological hegemony" (Goldman, 1992). Marxists have also portrayed advertising as a "magic system" (Williams, 1962) of magical inducements and satisfactions which validates consumption, if only in fantasy, by association with social and personal meanings and thus transforms goods which had rational use-value into irrational symbols. This focus on the power of the symbolic is further developed by Williamson (1978) who argues that advertisements function at an unconscious level at which the consumer is unable to resist latent meaning transfer. More recent post-Marxist analyses have weakened their deterministic stance and recognised that "the meanings and uses of products cannot be entirely controlled" (Williamson, 1986). However, hegemony still exists, but now depends on affective gratifications provided by mass-mediated popular culture where "everyday life in amusement society proceeds within a dialectic of enfeeblement and empowerment" (Langman, 1992).

From a post-structuralist perspective limited freedom is allowed to the individual through consumption choices "for most members of contemporary society individual freedom, if available at all, comes in the form of consumer freedom" through which the individual must take responsibility to invent and consciously create a self-identity (Bauman, 1988). Through the "new existentialism" (Laermans, 1993) consumers can exercise the freedom to create new meanings for goods through their own idiosyncratic performance of everyday life (de Certeau, 1988). This freedom can be used for collective and individual resistance against the imposed meanings of the dominant cultural categories, particularly through the choice of style and the use of "bricolage" tactics (Hebdige, 1979; Fiske, 1989). A sustained argument for the active exercise of freedom through consumption is developed by Willis (1990) who characterizes the consumption choices of the young as the behaviour of "practical existentialists". The young are seen as exercising choice through consumption-related symbolic creativity which operates via the concept of "grounded aesthetics", a process which builds higher-level symbolic meaning structures from the mundane concrete experiences of everyday life. This allows the young a small creative space for making the received social world, to some extent, controllable by them. This process is very similar to the marginal "tactics" (de Certeau, 1984) by which the powerless make sense of consumption, and in relation to advertising would allow some control over the meaning of a text, but not control over the agenda within which the text is constructed (Morley and Silverstone, 1990). This is a limited freedom where we "make our own spaces within the place of the other" (Fiske, 1990) but yet it is potentially liberating in that to escape from dominant meanings is to construct our own subjectivity (Condit, 1989). Advertisements can be seen as cultural products in their own right, and young people consume them independently of the products and have a creative symbolic relationship with them. Although Willis (1990) sees advertising as manipulative to some extent, he emphasises the scope for individual choice and creativity in meaning and identity construction, as individuals use advertising images as personal and social resources. These are invested with specific meanings anchored in everyday life, via the process of grounded aesthetics, which are then used to construct or maintain personal and social identities.

The construction of social identity through "styles of consumption" is referred to in terms of lifestyle membership of "neo-tribes" by Bauman (1990), where one may join the tribe by buying and displaying tribe-specific paraphernalia. The neo-tribe is informal, without authority and only requires acceptance of the obligation to take on the identity-symbols of the tribe. The consumer may thus exercise the freedom to choose social groupings through existential consumption. The exercise of choice through consumption now flows across national boundaries in a global cultural economy through the operation of advertising "mediascapes" which are image-centred strips of reality which offer the consumer a series of elements "out of which scripts can be formed of imagined lives, their own as well as those of others living in other places" (Appadurai, 1990).

If aspects of advertising imagery can be appropriated at will by "practical existentialists" then they may, as Baudrillard (1983) suggested, "live everywhere already in an 'aesthetic' hallucination of reality," in which the real and the simulated are indistinguishable. However, the extent to which in a "mediacratic" age, advertising reflects reality or actually creates it is problematic. Are the "practical existentialists" using advertising or is it really using them? Schudson (1984) suggests that advertising is "capitalist realist art" and that although it does not have a monopoly of the symbolic marketplace, different social groups are differentially vulnerable especially during transitional states of their lives. This form of art idealizes the consumer and portrays as normative, special moments of satisfaction. It "reminds us of beautiful moments in our own lives or it pictures magical moments we would like to experience" (Schudson, 1984). This suggests that young people in particular, who are at a transitional state in their lives, may be subject to excessive influence by "buying-in" to advertising's depiction of a false reality. In contrast, young people may be exercising (limited) freedom in their use of advertising as a cultural commodity for "even as the market makes its profits, it supplies some of the materials for alternative or oppositional symbolic work" (Willis, 1990). This dichotomy between creativity and constraint (Moores, 1993) is, of course, an aspect of the structure/ agency debate in social theory which in the media context is represented by the problematic of hegemony, which sets parameters on the freedom to construct meaning (Ang, 1990). Hegemony does not dominate from outside but is a "thick texture" which interlaces resistance and submission, opposition and complicity (Martin-Barbero, 1988) and which therefore poses difficult problems for ethnographic analysis to unpick. Structuration theory (Giddens, 1984) offers a solution to the dualism of structure versus agency, by positing that the "structural properties of social systems are both medium and outcome of the practices they recursively organize". Thus the consumption of advertising can be both an active and creative practice yet is carried out within constraints imposed by material situation and ideological hegemony.

THE STARTING POINT FOR THIS STUDY

During the fieldwork for a study of consumer responses to advertisements using images of overt sexuality, (Elliott et al., forthcoming) one of the respondents mentioned that she knew of a group of young women who seemed to have incorporated into their lives some of the aspects of the advertising for Haagen-Dazs ice-cream (see Exhibit). This advertising features images of couples apparently using the product as an artifact during sexual activity. This overt use of sexuality in advertising has been termed commercial pornography (Stern, 1991), and been widely condemned in the British journalistic press. This serendipitous opportunity to explore the extent to which a small group of young people had exercised the freedom to create new meanings through their own idiosyncratic uses of consumer goods and to 'live-out' imagery from advertising prompted this research.

METHODOLOGY

The contact with the group was subsequently followed up, one of the group - Jessica - was identified and with great difficulty persuaded to agree to be interviewed. A group of five women university students, aged between 19 and 22 years, had formed a close friendship and shared accommodation in two rented houses in the city over a two-year period. But now the other four were currently in various European countries pursuing language studies and unavailable for interview. Therefore this study uses one respondent as both the subject of phenomenological interviews, and as a "key informant" (Phillips, 1981) on the behaviour of a social group. Although a single respondent study takes the call for increased use of personal interviews in advertising research (e.g. Mick & Buhl, 1992) to the extreme, single informants have proved useful in providing insight into unusual aspects of consumer behaviour (e.g. Pollay, 1987). Three depth interviews were carried out over a period of 4 weeks, following the guide-lines for phenomenological interviewing given by Thompson, Locander & Pollio (1989), where the focus was on obtaining subjective descriptions of lived experience. The interviews were audio-taped, transcribed, and analysed through the interpretive group method (Thompson et al., 1989). Excerpts from the interviews are reported at some length in order to best capture the subjective descriptions of experience.

PHENOMENOLOGICAL DESCRIPTION

Jessica described a typical day involving Haagen-Dazs ice-cream which developed into a "package" which was grounded in their quotidian behaviour involving music and conversations about sex:

Well, you normally arranged it the night before when we were going out drinking, and we'd say, come back, get up about 1 or 2 [pm], go straight round to their house, go into town, go to our favourite cafe, sit down put some music on, get some Haagen-Dazs and basically the whole conversation would be around Haagen-Dazs ice-cream, how much we enjoyed it, how much we liked the ice-cream and the ideas around the ice-cream and we'd talk about things other than the ice-cream but we associated it with the ice-cream like sex, and we'd talk about sex and how the music was associated with Haagen-Dazs and it would make a little package that we don't usually talk about.

Initially, all the women were not equally involved in the behaviour but it soon became a shared social practice which enabled them to define themselves as a group by adopting identity-symbols:

Some were more open than others. Some were very uhmmm... just went along and agreed and others initiated it a lot more. They were like the leaders of the Haagen-Dazs kind of thing. Like they'd collect all their pots [ice-cream containers] and they'd expose us to the advertising because they'd find the adverts then they would show us, and it became sort of a trendy thing to be, to have a pot in your room, an empty pot or something which said Haagen-Dazs on it perhaps, and when we found little spoons with Haagen-Dazs on we'd collect them as well.

Individuals differed in the extent to which they were prepared to practice actual sexual activities with the ice-cream and some exercised their freedom to ground the aesthetic of the brand in thinking about sex rather than doing it:

Somebody always initiated it, there was always one person who said "lets go and do it" [consume ice-cream] because she was the one who was really into her Haagen-Dazs and we just sort of went along with it, but got involved and then it became equal again. At the end of all this we were all equal. We were initiated and we said "lets go and out and do this...wouldn't it be nice if we could get some now" and others like... I think we were all on the same level really. 'Cos we were all really good friends and we had things in common we could speak openly anyway with each other so we all decided that this is what Haagen-Dazs is and this is what it means. We're all agreed on this. There's some more prepared to use it than others...with the sexual act than others. Others are more prepared to just think about it than do it.

Jessica described the "package" and its sexual meanings and function in allowing them to talk more easily about sex:

Basically its just the whole sexiness of the whole package. We talk about things that we'd like to do, yes? And how the ice-cream and the music and the talking would make us feel. We'd talk about that. I think on the whole, say, we spent about an hour and a half in there, we wouldn't talk about anything else

EXHIBIT

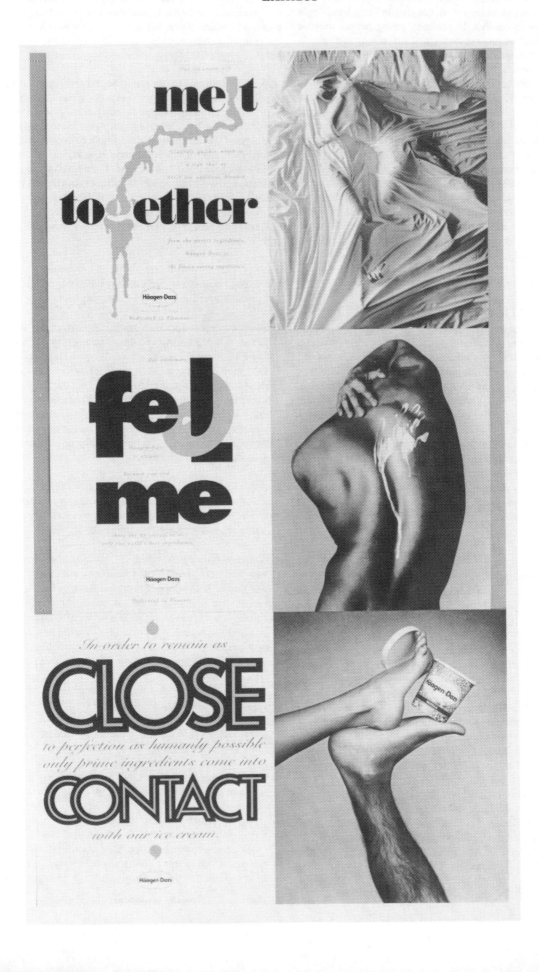

but the ice-cream, the music and the sex and men, you know and just all...dominated by, and it was the Haagen-Dazs that triggered it off because otherwise we wouldn't do that and if we did talk about sex we'd always say "Oh wouldn't it be good if we had some Haagen-Dazs and got the music and make a little kind of package together again", which made it an event. It allowed us to talk about it [sex]. It triggered it off. It sort of gave us an excuse to talk about it.

Jessica described the development of an association between sex and Haagen-Dazs through advertising, which suggests that there was both a conscious acceptance of the sexual meanings and an exercise of symbolic creativity which developed the product into a sign which was grounded in the concrete social life of the group. This allowed them to share knowledge of sexual activity whilst denying that knowledge to outsiders:

I think it must have been...it was very nice ice-cream, we really enjoyed the ice-cream and the advertising had a lot of sexual connotations in it and I think we basically liked the connotations of the ads and we liked the idea of that and we believed the idea that Haagen-Dazs was sexy because the ads told us it was sexy, so when we had the ice-cream in front of us we felt that the pot was very sexy, a sexy pot.

Basically, sometimes it was because we were bored and we wanted something to do...or if we'd been talking about sex and we'd go down and to just top it off we'd go down and get some Haagen-Dazs, sit in a cafe and continue the conversation, just things like that really. If a girl brought a boy back they would always go out and get some Haagen-Dazs and that would indicate what was going on. We'd all smile as she went into her room. It was like a secret thing. We knew but we didn't want other people to know. If we saw one of our friends going out getting a pot of Haagen-Dazs and bringing a boy back we knew exactly what was going to happen next, we had an idea what was going on but other people didn't. They just thought we were going to get some ice-cream.

The magazine advertising was eagerly consumed as a cultural product, but the group felt that they were in control of the meanings which they viewed as reflecting their lived experience not controlling it. They were in control because the aesthetics derived from the advertising were grounded firmly in their own social world:

Well, someone would come and say "Look what I've got" and then they'd just open up a magazine or they'd rip it out of a magazine and they'd pass it round and go "that's really nice." They'd discuss the ad and what it means and what they're trying to show in the ad and then we would stick it up on the wall along with the pots.

It didn't,... it wasn't separate from my ideas about, it was within our ideas of what we thought of Haagen-Dazs. It was just right to have that type of advertising. We would have said "Yes we want those kind of adverts" if we had to do it so that was our idea of how they should have...the whole thing about Haagen-Dazs, that's how it should have been portrayed and they did it correctly, we were quite pleased with their advertising, so it sort of like switched round. We felt we were the experts not them.

The group reflected a little on their behaviour but seemed unable to separate the influence of the consumption imagery on their representations of men as sex objects:

I think what we did was, we analyzed what we were doing, we never questioned, we never said "this is wrong, or why is this right?" We just thought it was right at the time,... but we analyzed it like. We took things apart. You know we associated certain things with things. The connection between Haagen-Dazs and sex...well it would be a part of sex, be used with sex. It would be added. It would be something, an added extra to sex.

I think we used to see men very much in sexual terms anyway and so it just increased our outlook, you know the way we used to see men. It just made it...cruder perhaps because we did see them as sexual objects a lot of the time and I think this was just a way of...this just came along with it, you know. We didn't think twice about what we were doing, making men into sexual objects. I mean we did stop and think "Oh my God this is really horrible," but we'd just laugh it off.

Jessica reflected on her own involvement in the group behaviour and seems to acknowledge the influence of the advertising, however she maintains that she adopted the meanings consciously and deliberately rather than unconsciously:

Sometimes I thought "what's the big deal about Haagen-Dazs?" and then I thought, well that was too serious for me to think "what am I doing?" Just go along with it. I just thought you know just...not go along with it for the sake of it but go along with it because I was enjoying eating my ice-cream anyway. It wasn't as if I was doing something I was forced to do...but I could stop and think sometimes, how can you know...what's this big thing about Haagen-Dazs....because sometimes it would annoy me when they'd go on and on about it.

Although the group is now dispersed in different countries, the meaning still persists for Jessica who defended her use of the advertising as a conscious and willing exercise of choice which she will continue to practice:

I still have the same beliefs but I just don't practice them as much as I did when they were around.. you know. So that's the only way... its changed in a way because now that I've analysed it, it sounds a bit silly but it only sounds silly because I have got to tell people but inside I still believe the same things and I know its just like consumerism and...their advertising's worked on me and everything but if I enjoy the product I'd still let the advertising work on me.

DISCUSSION

The young women certainly seem to have been "doing things with advertising" in that they had built on the ambiguous sexual meanings suggested in the advertising and incorporated them into the social practices and sexual activities of their small group. The "magic system" seems to have succeeded in "bringing the good things to life" (Williams, 1980), but not as the unconscious process suggested by Williamson (1978). This is a conscious exercise of freedom by a deliberate choice to accept and adapt the meanings of advertising through practical existentialism and symbolic creativity. They "ransack immediate experience for grounded aesthetics"

(Willis, 1990) which use the advertisements and the product as resources with which to construct and maintain their group identity. In doing this they use and display the neo-tribe-specific paraphernalia, and construct social reality from the scripts derived from the "mediascape".

But to what extent is this the conscious exercise of freedom as idealized by existentialism? Certainly there are limits to the freedom contained in consumption choices due to individuals having unequal access to the necessary resources. However, the lived experience described by Jessica conveys a strong sense of Sartre's "engagement" even if not at the level of decisional seriousness discussed by Kierkegaard (Macquarrie, 1972). Marxists may dismiss Jessica's claim to be making conscious choices about consumption as "false consciousness" but this is to deny the meaningfulness of everyday consumer experiences (Thompson, Locander and Pollio, 1990). The freedom of practical existentialism is real, even if it is constrained by inequalities in the economic system and by ideological hegemony. However, the fact that the group used only the advertised brand of ice-cream and did not exercise the freedom to transfer sexual meanings onto ice-cream per se suggests that the influence of ideological hegemony is difficult to escape. Sartre was able to reconcile existential freedom with the determinism of Marxist historical materialism through the recursivity of the progressive-regressive method (Poster, 1979) which allows some freedom to the individual through creativity. The creativity exercised by these young women is not the "semiotic democracy" celebrated by Fiske (1987) in which people freely construct their own meanings from texts, but is constrained to the tactical "poaching" of meaning described by de Certeau (1984). There are limits to the freedom of choice, and indeed it is only these limits which make freedom valuable. But each small act of existential choice, even if practiced through mundane consumption, can help us to play a part in constructing both our subjectivity and our social worlds.

CONCLUSION

The public language of advertising may be giving meaning to sexuality in a way that may act against the possibility that women "almost never speak of their sexual needs and desires as women" (Irigary, 1991). By articulating representations of sexuality in the mass media these manifestations of consumer culture may be allowing women to speak more easily of their desires through consumption choices. This may not be the "remodelling of existing language so as to give rise to a sexuate culture" that Irigary (1991) calls for, but advertising may be assisting women to achieve an "independence not just *of* sex, but *with* sex" (Davidson, 1992). However, the resulting discourse may be distorted with consumerist imagery and may thus impede consideration of the deeper nature of sexuality. Existential consumption provides an opportunity for the exercise of freedom through the consumption of advertising meaning and its use as a cultural commodity, but it may not necessarily lead to desirable social change.

REFERENCES

Ang, Ien (1990), "Culture and Communication: Toward an Ethnographic Critique of Media Consumption in the Transnational Media System," *European Journal of Communication*, 5, 239-260.

Appadurai, Arjun (1990), "Disjuncture and Difference in the Global Cultural Economy," *Public Culture* 2, 2, 1-24.

Baudrillard, Jean (1983), *Simulations*, New York: Semiotext(e).

Bauman, Zygmunt (1988), *Freedom*, Milton Keynes: Open University Press.

_____(1990), *Thinking Sociologically*, Oxford: Blackwell.

Condit, Celeste (1989), "The Rhetorical Limits of Polysemy," *Critical Studies in Mass Communication*, 6, 103-122.

Davidson, Martin (1992), *The Consumerist Manifesto: Advertising in Postmodern Times*. London: Routledge.

de Certeau, Michel (1988), *The Practice of Everyday Life*, Berkeley: University of California Press.

Elliott, Richard, Abbey Jones, Andrew Benfield and Matt Barlow (forthcoming), "Overt Sexuality in Advertising: A Discourse Analysis of Gender Responses," *Journal of Consumer Policy*, in press.

Fiske, John (1987), *Television Culture*. London: Routledge.

_____(1989), *Reading the Popular*, London: Routledge.

_____(1990), "Ethnosemiotics: Some Personal and Theoretical Reflections," *Cultural Studies*, 4, 1, 85-99.

Giddens, Anthony (1984), *The Constitution of Society: Outline of the Theory of Structuration*. Cambridge: Polity Press.

Goldman, Robert (1992), *Reading Ads Socially*, London: Routledge.

Hebdige, Dick (1979), *Subculture: The Meaning of Style*. London: Methuen.

Irigary, Luce (1991), "The Three Genres," in M. Whitford (ed.), *The Irigary Reader*. Oxford: Blackwell.

Laermans, Rudi (1993), "Bringing the Consumer Back In," *Theory, Culture & Society*, 10, 153-161.

Langman, Lauren (1992), "Neon Cages: Shopping for Subjectivity," in Rob Shields (ed.), *Lifestyle Shopping: The Subject of Consumption*, London: Routledge.

Lannon, Judy and Peter Cooper (1983), "Humanistic Advertising," *International Journal of Advertising*, 2, 195-213.

Macquarrie, John (1972), *Existentialism*. Harmondsworth: Pelican Books.

Martin-Barbero, Jesus (1988), "Communication from Culture: The Crisis of the National and the Emergence of the Popular," *Media, Culture, & Society*, 10 (4), 447-465.

Mick, David Glen and Claus Buhl (1992), "A Meaning-based Model of Advertising," *Journal of Consumer Research*, 19, 317-338.

Morley, David and Roger Silverstone (1990), "Domestic Communications: Technologies and Meanings," *Media, Culture, & Society*, 12 (1), 31-35.

Moores, Sean (1993), *Interpreting Audiences: The Ethnography of Media Consumption*. London: Sage Publications.

Phillips, Lynn(1981), "Assessing Measurement Error in Key Informant Reports: A Methodological Note on Organizational Analysis in Marketing," *Journal of Marketing Research*, 18, 395-415.

Pollay, Richard (1987), "It's the Thought That Counts: A Case Study in Xmas Excess," *Advances in Consumer Research*, 14, 140-143.

Poster, Mark (1979), *Sartre's Marxism*. London: Pluto Press.

Sartre, Jean-Paul (1956), *Being and Nothingness*, New York: Washington Square.

Schudson, Michael (1984), *Advertising, The Uneasy Persuasion: Its Dubious Impact on American Society*. London: Routledge.

Stern, Barbara (1991), "Two Pornographies: A Feminist View of Sex in Advertising," *Advances in Consumer Research*, 18, 384-391.

Thompson, Craig, William Locander and Howard Pollio (1989), "Putting Consumer Experience Back into Consumer Research: The Philosophy and Method of Existential-Phenomenology," *Journal of Consumer Research*, 16, 133-146.

_____(1990), "The Lived Meaning of Free Choice: An Existential-Phenomenological Description of Everyday Consumer Experiences of Contemporary Married Women, *Journal of Consumer Research*, 17, 346-361.

Williams, Raymond (1980), *Problems in Materialism and Culture*. London: Verso.

Williamson, Judith (1978), *Decoding Advertisements: Ideology and Meaning in Advertising*. London: Marion Boyars.

_____(1986), *Consuming Passions: The Dynamics of Popular Culture*. London: Marion Boyars.

Willis, Paul (1990), *Common Culture: Symbolic Work at Play in the Everyday Cultures of the Young*. Milton Keynes, UK: Open University Press.

Body and Soul: Beyond Physical Attractiveness—Implications for Consumer Behavior

Lynn Langmeyer, Northern Kentucky University
Matthew D. Shank, Northern Kentucky University

This study uses a qualitative research method (depth interviews) to examine the multidimensionality of beauty and ugliness and then uses a quantitative research technique (factor analysis) to propose a scale to measure beauty. Based on the results from these procedures, the authors conclude that beauty is certainly more than skin deep and ugliness, also, has more to do with non-physical than physical characteristics. Physical attractiveness may be the initial criterion on which people evaluate beauty (or ugliness) however, "someone could have tremendous physical attractiveness and I could say, 'Too bad he's a chump' " (CK). The evidence indicates that values, habits, personality, and behavior are the "soul" of beauty — essential ingredients in the creation of a truly beautiful person — and the "heart" of ugliness. The inside, in both cases, is truly much more important than the outside.

INTRODUCTION

Considerable evidence has accumulated that, regardless of cultural changes in its meaning, beauty is an effective sell. Beautiful people like Christie Brinkley, Cindy Crawford, and Cheryl Tiegs, are famous cover girls on whose looks ride "millions of dollars of advertising and marketing expenditures from companies for clothes and cosmetics" (Foltz 1992, p. 4F). Advertisers reportedly pay between $1 and $2 million dollars a year to have their products promoted by popular and glamorous women; their beauty is believed to add dazzle to the products.

Being physically attractive, however, doesn't seem to be enough — it seems to be a necessary yet not sufficient condition. For instance, Pepsi had to scrap its ultra-expensive endorsement deal with Madonna after she came out with a controversial video that didn't go over too well with the Catholic Church and a lot of other viewers (Miller 1991, p.2). It was not her attractiveness that was an issue. Then there was that "little faux pas of Cybill Shepherd, who announced that she didn't eat meat, yet she was a pitchwoman for the beef industry" (Miller 1991, p.2). Again, attractiveness was not the issue. Both blunders suggest that there is more to "beauty" than a simple "good/bad judgment of attractiveness" (Solomon, Ashmore, and Longo 1992, p.23) — "beauty" would seem to be more than skin deep.

It is remarkable therefore, that, despite the recognition that "being beautiful isn't enough" and that "stars have to have something special and almost indefinable" (Foltz 1992, p. 4F), attractiveness has been most frequently defined as, and/or assumed to be, *physical* attractiveness. Attractiveness studies concentrate on "physical attractiveness" (e.g., a small sample includes Baker and Churchill 1977; Belch, Belch and Villareal 1987; Bloch and Richins 1982; Caballero and Pride 1984; Dion, Berscheid and Walster 1972; Kahle and Homer 1985; Kamins 1990; Ohanian 1990; Patzer 1985; Solomon, Ashmore and Longo 1992). Even when multiple items are used to measure perceived attractiveness, (e.g., as in Ohanian's (1990) scale of source credibility), the items tend to be physically-based adjectives such as attractive, classy, beautiful, elegant, sexy, etc.

Furthermore, Ohanian's (1990) subscale is unusual because it does use multiple items. "Beauty" has been more typically defined as "attractiveness" in advertising literature and research, and has been measured, almost invariably, on a single "attractive/unattractive" dimension. For example, Kamins (1990) identified unattractive and attractive celebrity spokespeople (Telly Savalas and Tom Selleck) by asking respondents to evaluate twenty male celebrities on "a 7-point scale ranging from 'extremely physically attractive' to 'extremely physically unattractive' " (p.7).

Recently, Solomon et al. (1992) have argued that "beauty is a psychological multiplicity...replete with nuance" (p. 24). Using multidimensional scaling to analyze sorting data, their study revealed "six distinct types of good looks" (i.e., six categories of physical attractiveness). The study most assuredly pushes attractiveness research in the direction of recognizing that beauty is not a uni-dimensional construct. It does not, however, push it far enough because it investigates *multiple types of physical beauty* (e.g., cute, trendy, sex kitten, etc.), rather than investigating *multiple types of unbounded beauty* (e.g., physical, spiritual, etc.). This is analogous to investigating the multiple colors in which an automobile is produced (e.g., green, blue, black or red) — the interest being solely in the range of colors, contrasted to investigating the multiple attributes from which an automobile's features are selected and the available choices within each attribute. For example: is the automobile air-conditioned or un-air-conditioned; five-door, four-door, three-door, or two-door; automatic or manual shift; under $18,000 dollars or over $18,000 dollars (the interest being in the range of options as well as the differences within the options themselves). If we are to move beyond a simple notion of attractiveness as exclusively physical, then we must consider and explore all possible dimensions of beauty. This is particularly necessary when we are using beauty to assess the goodness of a match-up between an endorser and a product. We must go beyond *types* of physical beauty and explore the *whole range* of characteristics that encompass the concept of beauty. In addition, to balance the scales, so to speak, it seems appropriate (although certainly much less pleasant) to spend some time exploring the notion of ugliness. Is one necessarily the opposite of the other and if not, how are they alike?

The meager qualitative research that is available and the philosophical musings on beauty with which we are familiar, appear to be somewhat superficial; neither examine the multiple dimensions of unbounded beauty which appear to play an important role in the acceptance or rejection of endorsers as appropriate spokespeople. Therefore, this study was designed to probe beneath the surface of our conceptions of beauty, to explore the dimensionality of beauty, and to assess the possible implications for advertising and advertisers. Because much of the work on physical attractiveness has focused on the relationship between credibility and attractiveness for celebrity endorsers, it was determined to identify that context as the one in which the dimensionality of beauty would be examined.

METHOD AND RESULTS

Qualitative Research

This phase of the study was taken to identify and analyze emergent themes and thereby primarily expand our understanding of beauty and its importance and role in marketing. Definitions of beauty are highly complex, dependent on social and situational influences, and vary from highly abstract philosophical definitions (e.g., that which delights the senses or exalts the mind) to highly concrete applied definitions (e.g., a particularly good example of a thing). Therefore, the research required a method that would enhance and heighten our understanding of the phenomenon. Semi-structured depth interviews were designated as the appropriate technique and expert informants were identified and queried.

Informants

Ten key expert informants were ultimately selected because, given who they were and what they did, each one could provide a unique and singular perspective on "what beauty truly means" and "what ugly truly means." Each expert's occupation/ interests/ lifestyle was directly or indirectly linked with the study of beauty or an aspect of beauty. It is important to remember that we are proposing dimensions of beauty that go far beyond the physical attractiveness phenomena, particularly when thinking about the beauty of things. Therefore, we included a musician and a mathematician among our "experts" and ordinarily, we suspect, they would not be considered.

The ten individuals were recruited using a snowball sampling technique, starting with colleagues, friends, and relatives. Although the number of key informants may seem insufficient, previous researchers have endorsed using samples of ten or fewer, (assuming the research methodology is appropriate), to identify emergent themes (Fetterman 1989; Geertz 1973). The ten experts included: an athlete, a cosmetics consultant, a graphics artist, an interior designer, a landscape architect, a musician, a philosopher, a photographer, a studio artist, and a theoretical mathematician. Six of the ten informants were female, their ages ranged from 22 to 50, and one was African-American, the others white.

Interview Procedure

Each interview began with a relatively informal and non-technical discussion of the general purpose of the research and the types of questions that would be asked. Demographic data were also collected.

Human beauty: In the first section of the interview, respondents were asked to consider the meaning of *human beauty*. Specifically, they were asked, "When you describe a person as 'beautiful,' what dimensions of that person have you evaluated?" This question was used to probe the facets that people are thinking about when they label someone "beautiful." Respondents were then asked to furnish at least three words that "best describe a 'beautiful' person?" The words generated from this section of the interview were the foundation for the quantitative segment of the research which will be discussed in the next section. Finally, informants were asked to "provide some examples of people whom you consider 'beautiful' and then explain why you chose these people?" Respondents were asked the same questions regarding their perceptions of an "ugly person." This method has been used to study the sacred/profane consumption dichotomy and it was believed that a deeper understanding of beauty would result from a concurrent understanding of ugly (Belk et al. 1989 questioned nuns about profane consumption to obtain a richer meaning of sacred consumption).

Product beauty: The second part of the interview focused on *product beauty* rather than human beauty. Respondents were asked "Do you think products can be beautiful? Please explain," and "What are the characteristics of a 'beautiful' product?" The interview concluded with the question, "Can you provide some examples of products you consider 'beautiful'? Why did you choose these?"

Analysis of Depth Interviews

Interviews were audio taped when possible and then transcribed. Notes were also taken during all the interviews. Following the procedures recommended by Fetterman (1989), Hirschman (1986), McCracken (1989), and Wallendorf and Belk (1989), (amongst many others), key ideas and words were coded and then each interview was analyzed to identify emergent themes. The coded data were also compared and contrasted with respect to beauty versus ugly and human beauty versus product beauty. The analyses, comparisons, and contrasts ultimately produced two broad categories or dimensions of beauty.

Emergent Themes

The themes which emerge from the depth interviews do not support the age-old adage, "Beauty is only skin deep." Beauty, based on our interviews and experts, is more than skin deep — it is physical *and* non-physical; outward and visible *and* inward and non-visible, non-choice in certain aspects *and* high-choice others.

Physical Beauty: The meanings of physical beauty are dominated by what can be seen externally; this includes visible features such as face, body proportions, and body shape and visible traits such as poise, grace, and presence. As would be expected, BH, a female cosmetics consultant, started with the physical dimension (face and hair) to describe beauty. Make-up, body shape, clothing, jewelry, and polish followed — "before they even open their mouth...so there is no inner beauty involved in that even though I know it is important." For BH, Raquel Welch personifies physical beauty because she is "beautiful in her face." Physical attraction was the only dimension TS, a male graphics artist, talked about when he described a beautiful person until he got to the very end of his list. "Height has to be in proportion to weight; I am extremely offended by fat people."

LL, a male musician, focused on the external and internal features of a person when describing his pespective of beauty. However, the attributes he immediately contributed were abstract, "For a person to be beautiful, I usually know the person, they have a great outlook on life, are together, and warm, and share my values." Then he went on to say that clothes, body shape, style of dress, hairstyle, make-up (or lack thereof), and shoes were also important indicators of beauty.

KV, a female interior designer, started her description of beauty at facial features. Facial expression ("smiling, sparkling eyes") and appropriately proportioned facial features ("not too skinny or too fat") were the first dimensions and she admitted that "these lie at the most shallow level of beauty." DW, a male photographer, also notices facial features before anything else. "I look at the bone structure of the face — the eyes, nose, mouth, and the relationship amongst those features." Body proportions were next. If the proportions "fit my sense of beauty," then I think that person is beautiful." Beautiful people are physically attractive, poised, and well-proportioned. Examples of physically beautiful people for DW included: Lola Falana, his wife, and the older daughter of one of the co-authors. Why are these women beautiful to DW? They are "nicely proportioned pieces of sculpture."

BM, a female landscape architect, began her discussion of beauty by stating that beauty is based primarily on physical attractiveness and she pointed out, as did CK, a female studio artist, that "there is no one standard of beauty." Dimensions of beauty that were important to BM included an overall healthy appearance and intelligence. "Beauty is not being stupid rather than being smart."

Speech, posture, and deportment were important dimensions of beauty to BH and TS. Grooming habits, particularly those that are subject to smell, touch, and sight, are the important "choice" characteristics that help to determine beauty. Cleanliness may or may not be next to godliness; it is very close to beauty in our study —being clean is essential, as is being neat, not obese, finished, combed, well-shod, polished.

RG, a male philosopher, remarked that beauty and attractiveness are not the same thing — beauty is a much "deeper" construct than attractiveness and for him, attractiveness was the physical descriptor. However, he did go on to add, that if a person "achieved the unexpected or overcame a tremendous obstacle, then he/she could be beautiful." External physical dimensions, those aspects that one confronts directly and visually, are typically evaluated first. We have concluded, however, that after that first scan and determining "how well put together a person is," there has to be something else, something that transcends outward appearances and what we have chosen to call the non-physical or internal dimension.

Non-Physical Beauty: Non-physical dimensions of beauty are chosen and embrace the way one acts and the way one sees the world. Our experts delineated "spirituality" and "soul" as distinct and apparent characteristics without which a physically attractive person cannot be "beautiful." GE, a male athlete, had trouble articulating what beauty is and how to describe it without resorting to words such as "spiritual," "soul," "personality," and "intelligence," and TS added "a classy personality" and "an intriguing intellect." Similarly, NL, a theoretical mathematician, looks first at "the depth of character," then "at liveliness," and then "exoticness" before pronouncing a person "beautiful." Physical appearance is considered later and "unattractive people can be attractive because of their personality." Beautiful people, for NL, are "strong," "multifaceted," and "connected to me." She considers two of her friends "beautiful" because of who they are and not how they look; she also considers Katherine Hepburn beautiful for the same reason.

For BH, beautiful people are polished on the outside and loving on the inside and it is summed up in CK's statement, "Somebody could have tremendous physical attractiveness and I could say, 'Too bad he's a chump.' " That person could not be beautiful! Olivia Newton John is an example of a non-physically beautiful person for BH —"what makes her beautiful is the way she is with people...the person she is inside." RG went so far as to start his interview by saying, "I don't really think of people as being beautiful, I think of things like sunsets, art, sculptures as being truly beautiful. He thought about it for a moment and then said that a person's beauty stems from his/her character (internal and external features). He used words such as purity, unblemished, untarnished, and innocent to describe the inner and outer aspects of people. RG indicated that a person could have a beautiful face or body, and be an extremely ugly person. He had a more difficult time describing facets of an ugly prson than he had had describing a beautiful one.

KV described deep beauty as a beautiful personality: grace, charm, tolerance, wholesomeness, and other-centeredness." For her, the final and deepest dimension is "spiritual beauty" which transcends and exceeds attractiveness and personality and only after knowing someone can this be determined. Beautiful people, therefore, are beautiful on the inside as well as on the outside — their souls and their bodies are beautiful.

Ugliness: Our experts also agreed that people who are selfish, greedy, ignorant, uncultured, crass, unrefined, obnoxious, loud, nasty, hurtful, angry, vengeful, destructive, and self-centered cannot be beautiful. "Ugly people," according to KV, "are self-centered and have the power to inflict pain and do so. They are abusive, loud, and violent." For KV ugly does not have a physical dimension — "products can be physically ugly, people cannot!" NL agrees. "A person being ugly is not related to appearance. Ugly people are superficial, sneering, and hurtful." LL believes that a beautiful person "is not stressful to be around and can be identified by his/her "attitude." Therefore, he also believes that people who have "negative attitudes" are ugly. "All they care about is themselves and trying to impress other people. They have a lack of self-respect and usually a lack of respect for others. Ugliness is bitter and shallow people."

BM would not want to be around those types of people; she did not want to be around ugliness and it is largely because of personality that a person is ugly to her. However, she did indicate that an ugly person is also someone who is unkempt — the suggestion that there is, for her, a physical dimension to ugly in addition to a personal dimension. DW agrees. For him, an ugly person is disproportional, unpoised, and "lacks presence."

The examples of ugly people our informants gave us included: The Hunchback of Notre Dame, Adolph Hitler, Anthony Hopkins (in *Silence of the Lambs*), Jimmy Durante ("because of that big old red nose with all the bumps on it"), Charles Manson, Jesse Helms, Jerry Falwell, and Phyllis Schlafly, and The Creature from the Black Lagoon.

Beautiful Products: It was almost unanimous that products can be and are beautiful. RG responded, at once, that beautiful products are characterized "by the way they work." "My belt sander is beautiful because of the way it works...it is balanced just right...it is practical...it is functional...it has a certain unity about it." LL mentioned that a beautiful product is functional, well designed, high quality, and high tech, and that products have their own personalities. Each person, according to LL, has his or her own beliefs about which products are, in fact, beautiful. He suggested that the choice of a beautiful product is a function of the individual's level of involvement with it: the more involved a person is with a product, the more beautiful that product will be perceived by that person. Examples of beautiful products for him included a guitar with the shape, finish, and design that will permit the guitarist to easily reach high notes and a bike with a shiny, high-tech, customized frame and design. BH added lingerie, lace, eyeglasses, candles, vegetables, woods and cosmetics because they create beauty, are packaged beautifully, and smell good. For the majority of our experts, coffee makers and chairs are beautiful; perfume bottles and soaps are beautiful. Design, proportion, and shape are essential ingredients in a product's beauty.

GE, however, doesn't see products as beautiful because they have no "souls." His feelings about products are summarized in his comment: "products have no inner being therefore they cannot be beautiful." NL also initially indicated that products could not be beautiful because beauty is related to character, personality, and connectedness. "There are no emotional ties to a product therefore it cannot be beautiful although it can be attractive or appealing." Then she decided that "a beautiful product is one that is aesthetically pleasing and fulfills a function — objects that make me feel good when I look at them." Beautiful products, for her, are Tiffany lamps, fine china, fine crystal, and certain pieces of art.

Analogous to a person having to be "beautiful on the inside" in order to be considered "beautiful," a product, to be considered beautiful, must also promote a good purpose and function. Form is a necessary yet insufficient condition for a beautiful product; the product must also serve. "Form must follow function" according to TS. He likes modern and high tech things that are designed to be useful and elegant. Examples he gave of products he considered beautiful included a high-tech streamlined telephone, Ban deodorant's new package design, and a Honda CRX-XI. KV agreed. A product for her can be and is beautiful when it serves a good purpose and is physically elegant. It should be functionally useful also. If it is harmful to society or is environmentally unsafe, then it cannot be beautiful. Examples she gave of beautiful products are toys that serve a learning function and medical products that are not useless!

BM considers all products that are "properly designed" and "have the right shape" have an inherent beauty. On occasions when she has had a choice between two products that perform the same function, she always has always chosen the one that is physically more attractive. Products she considers beautiful include soap and one of her own bottle openers. "I could spend hours in the soap section looking at all the different colors and smelling the various soap scents." DW, adding the perspective of a photographer, expects beautiful products to be well-proportioned, well-textured, and well-designed. Products that are beautiful to him are: "architectural structures, like the Guggenheim Museum in New York, coffee makers, like the Braun, and anything that has been influenced by the De Still School (a Scandinavian avant-garde movement that has influenced things such as furniture, appliances, etc.)." Wood surfaces and wood grains can also be beautiful, "especially teaks and other hardwoods."

Packaging versus the product is an unresolved issue for some because a beautiful package can contain an environmentally harmful product. Some experts separated the packaging from the product in their evaluation, others did not; and some experts considered the visual aspects to be primary, for others it was touch and RG perhaps summed up the dilemma in saying "the packaging is often more beautiful than the product it contains."

The Interview That Taught Us The Most: CK, Studio Artist, Female 40: We have included a detailed description of our interview with CK because it is apparent that CK has done considerable thinking about beauty, it truly is an integral aspect of her life, and we learned the most from what she had to say to us.

"As a visual artist, naturally my first reaction is to evaluate the visual aspects of the person first — the physical notion first and then the 'inner beauty' of the person after the preliminary evaluation of physical beauty." Physical proportion was a key word. "The primary consideration is the face which is a fairly traditional response. Then the overall proportions of the person, and how they conform to different canons of beauty." CK also noted that physical beauty is culturally determined ("I always have this rather marvelous 'aha' about how the beauty of a particular culture, as seen in its sculptures and paintings, conforms to the actual physical types within that race and ethnic origin.") and it is a factor over which people have no control. After that, "the things a person makes some choices about."

A "beautiful person" for CK is graceful, spiritually balanced, well proportioned (which "doesn't have to be normal looking, it can be an exotic set of proportions"), and animated. Examples of "beautiful people": Elizabeth Taylor (who was also cited by NL), Dorothea Tanning ("a brilliant painter who was married to Max Ernst"), and Louise Nevelson, an artist, who was "exquisitely eccentric in what she wore including incredibly big false eyelashes which she wore in her 60's, 70's, and 80's."

"Ugly" uses the same set of criteria: proportions of the figure and face. CK adds other elements after those such as cleanliness and behavior. "It takes quite a bit of really bad behavior for me to see somebody as ugly on the inside. It's not something that I come to naturally. A person would have to work real hard for me to perceive him or her as ugly." An ugly person, therefore, is misproportioned, graceless, unkempt, and bad.

Well designed products are beautiful. "Well designed" is described as "coming back to proportion and that applies to very beautiful laws of nature...or science...or mathematics." Beautiful products are Braun coffee makers, the Barcelona Chair by Mies Van der Mier in the Museum of Modern Art, and Salvadore Dali's perfume bottle "Lips."

Evaluation of Qualitative Research Results

Our understanding of the meaning of "beauty" was significantly expanded and deepened by the results of the depth interviews with our "beauty" experts and, as their responses indicate, we were also expertly educated on the relationship between "beauty" and product marketing.

The second phase of the study was to turn our qualitative understanding into quantitative outcomes.

QUANTITATIVE RESEARCH

Scale Development

The qualitative research discussed in the preceding section served as the conceptual foundation for the development of the BEAUTY scale. In the initial phase of scale development, a list of adjectives describing beauty were compiled from the depth interviews and existing research. In addition, fifty undergraduate students were asked to respond to an open-ended question asking about their beliefs regarding beauty in general. Students were also asked to describe human and product beauty.

The findings resulted in 144 adjectives representing various facets of beauty. An instrument consisting of a ten-point, Stapel Scale ranging from -5 to +5 was then administered to 25 undergraduate students. Respondents were instructed to rate how accurately each of the adjectives described beauty by circling a plus number for words that describe beauty accurately and circling a minus number for those adjectives not describing beauty.

Scale Purification

The scale, designed to measure beauty, was purified in several stages. Initially, as suggested by Churchill (1979), the reliability of the instrument was assessed using coefficient alpha (Cronbach 1951). Adjectives having an item-to-total correlation of below .50 were deleted from the instrument. Based on this preliminary analysis, 81 items were deleted. Next, exploratory factor analysis was conducted to determine the dimensionality of the remaining 63 items. Based on the qualitative findings two factors were expected to emerge. However, the initial principle-component factor analysis resulted in over ten dimensions that were not easily interpreted.

To address the large number of dimensions and further purify the instrument, a second factor analysis using oblique rotation was performed on the 63 adjective pool. After several more iterations, a final set of 40 items loading on two factors emerged (see Table 1 for factor loadings and coefficient alpha on the final set of items). These two factors clearly represent the beauty construct definition as they included both the internal and the external aspects of beauty. As such, the dimensions subsequently named the Physical (Body) and the Non-Physical (Soul) dimensions of beauty.

DISCUSSION

Body and Soul

If any one cliché were to be chosen as the explanation for advertisers' selections of celebrity endorsers, then it would have to be "What is beautiful is good" (Dion, Berscheid and Walster 1972). Advertisers assume, (at least according to advertising researchers), that they can, at least, double their effects by combining celebrity status and physical attractiveness (Friedman and Friedman 1979; Kamins 1990; Singer 1983). Their assumption is not without strong support. As indicated in our Introduction, considerable evidence has accumulated, in the social sciences and in marketing, that beauty sells and that beauty changes attitudes towards products, people, and places (e.g., Belch, Belch and Villareal 1987;

TABLE 1
Exploratory Factor Analysis of Beauty Items

Item	Factor 1	2
Non-Physical:		
lively	.79	
poised	.49	
polished	.70	
sensitive	.85	
sensuous	.63	
sparkling	.63	
vivacious	.52	
warm	.66	
wholesome	.69	
appealing	.51	
charming	.69	
classic	.47	
confident	.66	
cultivated	.68	
decent	.60	
eloquent	.66	
energetic	.79	
engaging	.76	
enthusiastic	.73	
fascinating	.75	
friendly	.84	
funny	.74	
graceful	.57	
gracious	.68	
healthy	.59	
Physical:		
pretty		.71
proportionate		.88
smooth		.82
soft		.56
sultry		.54
attractive		.61
classy		.56
cute		.66
dainty		.85
delicate		.85
exhilarating		.71
glowing		.71
good-looking		.65
gorgeous		.90
handsome		.79
Reliability	**.95**	**.94**

Block and Richins 1992; Caballero and Pride 1984; Chaiken 1979; Kahle and Homer 1985; Kamins 1990; Ohanian 1990). However, that's not the whole story, it doesn't always work that way, and on occasion, advertisers have learned the hard way. The body beautiful may be necessary, it is not sufficient.

Our study revealed that, although the initial evaluation of an unknown quantity (i.e., person) appears to be based on physical appearance and attractiveness, real beauty goes beyond that part of the person that is physical. Values, habits, personality, and behavior are the "soul" of beauty. After all, our bodies are only a part of who we are and with judicious investments of time and money, they can be changed. We can change our hair color and hair style, lose weight or gain weight, surgically remove or add or alter features, and we will still be the same people. BH described it as "the inner person, the soul inside, what is offered to another person." CK described it as "inner spiritual balance that creates a kind of pulsation toward me." NL described it as "depth of character, strength, and kindness." And GE talked about "soul," "spiritual," "personality," and "what's inside." The qualitative evidence left little doubt that a truly beautiful person must be beautiful to the core.

The quantitative evidence of the factor analysis, the first step in the creation of what we have chosen to call the BEAUTY scale, contributes additional support to our contention that beauty consists of physical and non-physical dimensions — what we have chosen to call BODY and SOUL.

Endorser and Product "Soul" Compatibility

Products can be and have been examined based on their "body" attributes such as packaging, color, and size. Their "souls," however, have been ignored. Unquestionably, some products have personalities or "souls" that are as strong, if not stronger, than their endorser counterparts. For example, *Oil of Olay's* personality has been described as ..... "a secretary on the Riviera, by the swimming pool, in a silk bathing suit, reading Vogue, with her mink coat on the adjacent chair" (Plummer 1984/1985. p. 29). Moreover, understanding the personality of an individual product/service becomes particularly critical if "the person on the street" or a relatively unknown celebrity is used as the advertising endorser. For these matches, the "soul" of the established product/service may transcend the unfamiliar or unrecognized personality of the endorser. Given the potential implications of possible mismatches, researchers and practitioners may be obliged to acquire an understanding of the "soul" of the product.

That the match between endorser and product/service will have an effect, (positive or negative), on the celebrity and the product/service he or she endorses is, by now, an accepted truism. Bo Jackson's intensity and courage inspires us to *Just Do It* (with *Nike*), Cher's brazen and independent personality motivates us to get fit at *Bally's*, and Bill Cosby's bouncy and cheeful humor invites us to have fun eating *Jello*. Nevertheless, although researchers have labored to understand the effects of the endorser's "body" (i.e., attractiveness) and to some extent the endorser's "soul" (i.e., credibility) on the match, not much attention has been given to the effects of the product/service on the match — an intriguing and, as yet, unresearched question. Can the "soul" and/or "body" of a pure and unsullied product, for example, *Ivory Soap*, influence the image of an unchaste and sensual endorser, for example, *Madonna*?

Multi-Method Research

Most of us have followed the recent debates on quantitative versus qualitative research, positivistic versus post-modernistic research, and empirical versus interpretive research; some of us with considerable dismay about feeling forced to select one side and then, of course, vilify the other. For this study, multi-method research proved to be (in our opinion) far superior to an either/or strategy. The depth interviews, an accepted traditional qualitative research method, gave us a wide range of nuances of meanings and understandings of what people mean when they use the descriptors "beauty" and "beautiful." Without the interviews, we would have missed CK's discussion of the racial and ethnic determinants of beauty, DW's discussion of the role of proportion in beauty, KV's discussion of the spiritual beauty which transcends attractiveness, and LL's discussion of the beautiful person as one who is not stressful to be around. The multi-dimensionality of beauty would have been significantly understated without this aspect of the study. (For a full discussion of the interdependency of goals, assumptions, theories, and methodologies in positivism and interpretivism, please see Hudson and Ozanne 1988 and Ozanne and Hudson 1989.)

The quantitative component of the study confirmed and supported our notion of the "body and soul theory" of beauty. One can almost guess with 100 percent accuracy into which factor a particular adjective will fall and it is pleasing to be able to report the "hard numbers" we generated. For our results to be practical, in terms of assisting and benefiting advertisers, scale development is an appropriate endeavor. The quantitative results from this research will form the basis for further scale development and validation.

FUTURE DIRECTIONS

The present study is a preliminary (although indispensable) effort to understand the multi-dimensional nature of beauty. Improvements and extensions are planned for future research.

First: we developed the BEAUTY scale using a somewhat small and extremely convenient sample of marketing students. This sample contained a relatively narrow range of ages and, because it was all students, a relatively narrow range of incomes, occupations, and educational levels. There is, therefore, the potential for an age response bias and a "lifestyle" (for want of a more descriptive word) response bias. It is reasonable to assume that peoples' concepts of beauty are transformed as they age and their life circumstances change; a restricted sample on either and/or both these dimensions necessarily constrains the results. A larger, more diverse sample of respondents would improve the generalizability of the results and, perhaps of even more consequence, would expand the breadth and the enrich the depth of the results.

Second: we consider the scale developed in this study to be far from the final version of the BEAUTY scale. We see the present scale as a first step in a long march toward measuring "true beauty." The psychometric properties of the instrument (i.e., scale reliability and scale validity) require further examination and additional refinement. In addition, the scale needs to be tested by asking respondents to appraise the beauty of a specific person. Future studies should use an improved and refined version of the current BEAUTY scale to evaluate the "beauty" of Madonna, Tom Selleck, Bill Cosby, etc. The appropriateness, applicability, and "goodness" of the scale cannot be assessed without tests of this nature.

Third: we want this study to ignite interest in additional empirical "beauty" research. Beauty is a ubiquitous notion — it is constantly with us and around us in marketing and in everyday life. However, not much is known (empirically based, that is) about its impact. Future research should investigate positive and negative sides of beauty; economic, social, and psychological consequences of beauty; and male and female perspectives of beauty — all are extraordinary and fascinating subject matter for prospective studies.

Finally, and perhaps more relevant and pertinent to advertising/marketing researchers, we suspect that dimensions of beauty and standard variables such as salesperson effectiveness, ad effectiveness, and product involvement are related. We hope this study will inspire other studies which, along with our own, will support our contention.

REFERENCES

Baker, Michael J. and Gilbert A. Churchill, Jr. (1977), "The Impact of Physically Attractive Models on Advertising Evaluation," *Journal of Marketing Research*, 14 (November), 538-555.

Belch, George E. , Michael A. Belch, and Angelina Villareal (1987), "Effects of Advertising Communications: Review of Research," in *Research in Marketing*, Vol. 9, Jagdish Sheth, ed., Greenwich, CT: JAI Press, Inc.

Belk, Russell, Melanie Wallendorf, and John Sherry (1989), "The Sacred and Profane in Consumer Behavior: Theodicy on the Odyssey," *Journal of Consumer Research*, 16 (June), 1-38.

Bloch, Peter H. and Marsha L. Richins (1992), "You Look 'Mahvelous': The Pursuit of Beauty and the Marketing Concept," *Psychology & Marketing*, 9 (January), 3-15.

Caballero, Marjorie J. and William M. Pride (1984), "Selected Effects of Salesperson Sex and Attractiveness in Direct Mail Advertisements," *Journal of Marketing*, 48 (January), 94-100.

Chaiken, Shelly (1979), "Communicator Physical Attractiveness and Persuasion," *Journal of Personality and Social Psychology*, 37 (August), 1387-1397.

Churchill, Gilbert A., Jr. (1979), "A Paradigm for Developing Better Measures of Marketing Constructs," *Journal of Marketing Research*, 16 (February), 64-73.

Cronbach, Lee J. (1951), "Coefficient Alpha and the Internal Structure of Tests," *Psychometrika*, 16 (September), 297-334.

Dion, Karen K., Ellen Berscheid, and Elaine Walster (1972), "What is Beautiful is Good," *Journal of Personality and Social Psychology*, 24 (December), 285-290.

Fetterman, David M. (1980), *Ethnography: Step by Step*, Applied Social Research Methods Series, Newbury Park, CA: Sage Publications, Inc.

Foltz, Kim (1992), "Cover Girls: The Look That Sells is Both Girl-Next-Door and Celebrity," *The New York Times*, Sunday, May 24, 1992, 4F.

Friedman, Hershey H. and Linda Friedman (1979), "Endorser Effectiveness by Product Type," *Journal of Advertising Research*, 19 (October), 63-71.

Geertz, Clifford (1973), "Thick Description," in *The Interpretation of Cultures*, New York: Basic Books, 3-30.

Hirschman, Elizabeth (1986), "Humanistic Inquiry in Marketing Research: Philosophy, Method and Criteria," *Journal of Marketing Research*, 23 (August), 237-249

Hudson, Laurel Anderson and Julie L. Ozanne (1988), "Alternative Ways of Seeking Knowledge in Consumer Research," *Journal of Consumer Research*, 14 (March), 508-521.

Kahle, Lynn R. and Pamela M. Homer (1985), "Physical Attractiveness and the Celebrity Endorser: A Social Adaptation Perspective," *Journal of Consumer Research*, 11 (March), 954 961.

Kamins, Michael A. (1990), "An Investigation of the 'Match-Up' Hypothesis in Celebrity Advertising: When Beauty May be Only Skin Deep," *Journal of Advertising*, 19 (1), 4-13.

McCracken, Grant (1989), "'Homeyness': A Cultural Account of One Constellation of Consumer Goods and Meanings," in *Interpretive Consumer Research*, Elizabeth C. Hirschman, ed., Provo, UT: Association for Consumer Research, 168-183.

Miller, Cyndee (1991), "Even without HIV issue, using celebs can be risky," *Marketing News*, December 9, p. 2.

Nunally, Jum C. (1978), *Psychometric Theory*, New York: McGraw-Hill Book Company.

Ohanian, Roobina (1990), "Construction and Validation of a Scale to Measure Celebrity Endorsers' Perceived Expertise, Trustworthiness, and Attractiveness," *Journal of Advertising*, 19 (Number 3), 39-52.

Ozanne, Julie L. and Laurel Anderson Hudson (1989), "Exploring Diversity in Consumer Research," in *Interpretive Consumer Research*, Elizabeth C. Hirschman, ed., Provo, UT: Association for Consumer Research, 1-9.

Patzer, Gordon L. (1985), *The Physical Attractiveness Phenomena*, New York: Plenum.

Plummer, Joesph T. (1984/19485), "How Personality Can Make a Difference," *Journal of Advertising Research*, 24 (Number 6), 27-31.

Singer, Benjamin D. (1983), "The Case for Using 'Real People' in Advertising," *Business Quarterly*, 48 (Winter), 32-37.

Solomon, Michael R., Richard D. Ashmore and Laura C. Longo (1992), "The Beauty Match-Up Hypothesis: Congruence Between Types of Beauty and Product Images in Advertising," *Journal of Advertising*, 21 (December), 23-34.

Wallendorf, Melanie and Russell W. Belk (1989), "Assessing Trustworthiness in Naturalistic Consumer Research," in *Interpretive Consumer Research*, Elizabeth C. Hirschman, ed., Provo, Utah: Association for Consumer Research, 69-84.

Female Role Portrayals in Print Advertising: Talking with Women About Their Perceptions and Their Preferences

Patti Williams, University of California at Los Angeles

ABSTRACT

In-depth interviews using print advertisements as stimulus materials were conducted with women to assess perceptions of female role portrayals in advertising. This research highlighted three interpretive themes. Courtship images evoke strong reactions and projection on the part of informants. Perceptions of and "reading" of role portrayals are related to informants' gender and feminist self-schema and the centrality of those schema to their overall self-concept. The perceived appropriateness between product and female role portrayals is also linked with informants' self schema. Findings will be used in future experimental work to distinguish among clusters of women with similar self-schema, resulting in similar views toward stereotypical female role portrayals in advertising.

INTRODUCTION

Feminist critics have long been concerned that the portrayals of women in advertising will have negative impact upon the way adults and children view the role of women in society. Advertising portrayals are criticized for depicting women in a narrow range of primarily traditional roles, encouraging the view of women as sexual or decorative objects, and creating unrealistic and undesirable ideals for women to uphold.

The series of interviews presented in this paper is the first step in a project concerned with assessing whether women consumers are aware of the offensive portrayals cited by these critics. These interviews focus on the following questions: Do women recognize stereotypical role portrayals in advertising? Do different women notice them differently or "read" the same ads and portrayals differently, and if so, what accounts for those differences? And, how do women feel about these role portrayals? The answers to these questions presented in the remainder of this paper represent the initial exploratory work in this area. The findings from this exploration will be used to shape future empirical research to identify clusters of women who share similarities which lead to shared interpretations of the stereotypical role portrayals presented in advertisements and other media.

LITERATURE REVIEW

Beginning in the early 1970s with the high awareness of the women's movement, researchers began to empirically examine female role portrayals in advertising. The first phase of this research concentrated on content analysis, demonstrating the limited number of roles that female models in print advertising were likely to portray (Courtney and Lockeretz, 1971; Belkaoui and Belkaoui; 1976 among others). Later work focused on factors (such as education, age, and agreement with the tenets of the women's movement) that were believed to influence and explain individual differences in perceptions, and resulting preferences, for the female roles most often seen in advertising (such as Lundstrom and Sciglimpaglia, 1977; Cull, Marx and Hanson, 1977).

Analyses of the Roles Portrayed by Women in Print Advertising

Courtney and Lockeretz (1971) published the first major study in the marketing literature on female role portrayals in advertising. This content analysis demonstrated that women were generally portrayed in print ads in accordance with four primary stereotypes.

Women were depicted primarily as sexual objects, belonging in the home, and dependent on men. In addition, they were seldom shown making important decisions or doing important things.

At a time when this research was very popular in the field, other researchers corroborated their findings. Belkaoui and Belkaoui (1976) concluded that stereotypes from the pre-women's movement era had remained common in print advertisements in 1970 and 1972, and that advertising was not adequately portraying the diversity of women's real life roles. Venkatesan and Losco (1975) reported that while there had been an overall decline in the female images most offensive to women's groups during the period 1959-1971, advertisers remained insensitive to the reality of contemporary women. They found that the depiction of "Woman as a sexual object" declined after 1961, but nonetheless appeared more frequently than any other category in both men's and general interest magazines. This is followed closely by "Woman as dependent on man", which was found in nearly one out of every four magazine advertisements containing at least one woman.

Goffman (1979), in viewing advertisements as displays or pictures which demonstrate the structure of social reality, found similar results. In the ads he reviewed, the functional status of women was often portrayed as subordinate to men, with men and boys often serving the role of instructor to women and girls. The posture of women in advertisements was often seen as submissive and accepting of subordination, or childlike, unserious or even clownlike, while the same was not the case for men pictured in similar ads.

Perceptions of Female Role Portrayals in Print Advertisements

After the initial work demonstrating the narrow portrayals of women in print advertisements, researchers began to ask whether these portrayals were apparent to consumers, and if so, what factors could be used to predict awareness and resulting attitudes toward the ads and products within them.

Lundstrom and Sciglimpaglia (1977) reported that women generally have more critical attitudes toward role portrayals than do men. In their study, the women with the most critical attitudes were articulate, influential, younger, better educated, upper status women who had rejected the values and stereotypes of the traditional roles for women in society. Cull, Hanson and Marx (1977) provided evidence that recognition of sex stereotypes was correlated with reported agreement with the ideals of the women's movement.

Other researchers, however, were unable to predict role preferences or purchase behavior based upon feminist attitudes. Wortzel and Frisbie (1974) hypothesized that presenting products in conjunction with a woman in a career or neutral role would make the product appear more desirable to women than if the woman in the ad were depicted in a sex-object, family or fashion-object role. They believed this was likely to be especially true for women who strongly agreed with the tenets of the women's movement. In fact, however, the authors found that the role preference pattern for women with positive attitudes toward the women's movement were remarkably similar to the pattern for those with negative attitudes. They concluded that women react primarily to the product-use situation with which they are confronted and tend to "select role preferences on the basis of function rather than on the basis of ideology." These results were supported in a later study by Duker and Tucker (1977). Mazis and Beuttenmuller (1973) also found

Advances in Consumer Research
Volume 22, © 1995

only a weak relationship between women's liberation attitudes and perceptions of advertisements.

Authors have also attempted to correlate various demographic variables such as age and education, as well as geographic variables with preferences for role portrayals in advertising. However, of the many variables which have been studied with respect to their relationship to recognition of and preference for role portrayals in advertising, only gender of the respondent has consistently produced significant differences (Courtney and Whipple, 1983). This paper suggests that previous work has focused too much on prediction based on "external" variables rather than upon variables more "internal" and reflective of self, to the women viewing the ads.

Wilson and Moore (1979) previously suggested that in the context of sexually-oriented advertising, elements of self-concept are likely to influence perceptions. They posited that the stimulus presented in ads should be congruent with either actual or ideal self images of the consumer in order to serve as a link between the viewer and the product. They continued, "This theory may also explain the negative reaction of feminists to sex in ads. These critics are not likely to project themselves into the ad since their values are diametrically opposed to those embodied in the female model."

It is from the prior work in this area that research presented in this paper begins. Content analysis has demonstrated that role portrayals of women in advertising are limited and often stereotypical. It is certainly important, then, to ask whether consumers are as aware of these portrayals as are feminist groups. It is also important to understand whether this awareness translates into affect for the advertisements, the products they feature and perhaps even toward advertising in general. Further, it is important to consider whether or not, as suggested by feminist groups, these portrayals have an impact upon the self-images and self-esteem of individuals.

METHODOLOGY

The research reported in this paper was gathered via in-depth interviews with three female subjects. The depth interview was chosen as a method because of its unique ability to provide a large quantity of information that can be particularly useful when beginning the exploration of a new topic. While the number of informants in this project is small, their experiences and perceptions, as well as the reseacher's introspection regarding role portrayals in advertising, provide a remarkably rich understanding which was adequate to alter the researcher's thinking significantly enough to suggest new directions for future research into this area.

Because previous research on this topic (Lundstrom and Sciglimpaglia, 1977) indicates that those women with more education, higher social status and leadership positions are most likely to be critical of female role portrayals in advertising, this study focused exclusively on women who did not fit that description. It was the researcher's a priori belief that recognition, perception of and criticism for stereotypical portrayals is not exclusively the domain of upper class females, so a conscious decision was made to limit the sample of informants in this way.

Each of the three informants in this study is a white female between the ages of 33 and 45, living in a major metropolitan area in Southern California. Two were known to the author as neighborhood acquaintances, while the third was referred to the author by a friend. Two of the women do not have college degrees. Each informant is employed in a support-staff type role (accounts receivable supervisor, researcher, and program coordinator), and coincidentally, all work in similar industries. Two of the informants work for competing recruitment/employment advertising firms, while the third works for a cable television network.

Each interview lasted approximately one hour and was driven by the use of stimulus materials. These stimulus materials consisted of a set of 17 full-page, four-color print advertisements collected from various nationally published magazines. Initially, 44 advertisements were collected. This large set was then reduced to 17 in order to minimize fatigue of informants.

These 17 advertisements were selected to provide a cross-section of the roles most often identified in content analysis studies of female role portrayals, as well as to provide a spectrum of the roles of women and their relationships with men. As a result, the sample included women depicted as sexual objects, housewives and career women, as well as men and women depicted together in romantic relationships, working relationships, and familial relationships. It also included several depictions only of men which could be contrasted with similar depictions of women, such as professional role and parental role.

Before talking with the informants in this study, the researcher also engaged in introspection (Wallendorf and Brucks, 1993) for each of the advertisements chosen for the study. The researcher recorded her own impressions regarding the gender portrayals in each advertisement. As a feminist with a critical attitude toward female role portrayals in advertising, the researcher's opinions may be seen as representative of a certain interpretive community of critical feminism. Initially this introspection was meant to serve as an preliminary exploration of this topic and as an opportunity to further inform the researcher's work. As the interviews commenced, however, the author was often surprised to find how different her impressions were from those of her informants. Her introspection often provided a counterpoint to the words of the informants and led to a desire to understand the differences in reading these ads found in this small group of women. This desire has shaped the results reported in this work and where appropriate throughout the paper, the researcher's opinions will be compared to the reactions of the informants.

The development of the interview format was an iterative process, with adjustments made sequentially to enhance the informants' opportunities to view and discuss the advertisements. In order to facilitate the natural elicitation of gender-relevant information, informants were asked first to share their impressions of the people portrayed in the advertisements. If the ensuing discussion did not include gender-relevant perceptions, the interviewer more directly questioned the informants about this issue.

For the first interview, the advertisements were initially presented as a holistic set to encourage comparisons among the ads, and then each ad was discussed individually. As this process was rather cumbersome and resulted in tremendous repetition, for the second interview each ad was discussed only individually. Often, however, this individual presentation did not directly encourage informants to comment on gender in the ads. In the final interview, the researcher clustered the ads into groups of twos or threes that facilitated direct comparisons of the gender role portrayals in the ads in each cluster. While this comparison process seemed to be more effective than either of the previous methods, it was difficult to be certain as the final informant was also simply more aware of gender portrayals in advertising and required less prompting to approach this subject than did the first two.

In addition, for two of the interviews, a feminist deconstructionist methodology was employed to pursue the underlying gender conceptions of each informant. Informants were asked whether they could imagine the women in the ads as men, or vice versa, in order "to uncover traits and values so habitually defined as masculine or feminine that they are unimaginable in the other sex." (Stern, 1993)

Each interview was then transcribed and richly coded for meaning or ideas via a method of constant comparison (Glaser and Anselm, 1967). This encoding allowed for comparisons between interviews and the researcher's introspection, and for the development of larger interpretive themes linking the experiences, perceptions and ideas of the three informants.

INTERPRETIVE THEMES

Three major interpretive themes emerged from the words of these informants and will be outlined in this paper. The first theme, "The Power of Courtship", refers to the deep pleasure and intensity of self-projection which all three informants revealed in response to advertisements that contained images of romance and love.

The second theme points to the importance of internal self-structures in perceiving role portrayals in advertising. In particular, the centrality of gender self-schema to an individual's overall self-concept, as well as the inclusion in that self-schema of feminist values is important. Social psychologists have argued that an individual's self-schema impacts the perception of others. The responses of informants in this study indicate that elements of the self-schema, or valued self-traits, can have a substantial impact upon the way "others" presented in advertising are perceived. Informants also indicated, consistent with previous studies, that the appropriateness of role portrayals in ads often hinges upon the product being used. This "Match Between Product and Role" is the third theme, and is also impacted by self-schematic issues.

The Power of Courtship

In her 1991 paper, Stern characterized the romance genre as a form of soft-core pornography that women find arousing, socially acceptable and non-threatening. This feminine pornography is contrasted with traditional, "male" pornography that concentrates on sexual images and sexual gratification. Romances, Stern said, are the literature of courtship rather than of consummation. "Romances stop after foreplay because they have but one major theme"—courtship. They end with marriage and the image of living happily ever after.

Several advertisements in the set of stimuli for these interviews inspired reactions which resonate with this courtship theme. All three informants became emotionally involved in these ads, able to self-project to a tremendous degree and to create imaginative stories about the people portrayed in the ads. Also importantly, the role portrayals of women in these ads were never seen by any of the informants as sexist or inappropriate, contrary to the researcher's own introspection.

In response to a DeBeers Diamond advertisement which reads, "The first time I gave her a diamond ring her hug took my breath away", Janet (wf, single, 33) said:

"My absolute favorite ad of all times. I love this ad. It's so sexy because it doesn't show anything but these shadows and this glorious ring. Ohhh, I want to be the woman in this ad....It's just so, ohhh, it's sexy. I have a real emotional response to this. It makes me sort of step out of myself. I could be the person who has a guy like this. And he's lucky to have a gal like this. Oh, God, they're just so, I don't know. They're sexy. And they're in love...This is love, this has taken off. This is something new. I like that. 'Took my breath away.' Yeah, I want someone to feel like that when they look in my eyes and put a ring on my finger. That I took their breath away. That's why I'd like to be her. I'd like to experience that. This couple, I like them. I want to be them. They're young, healthy, and not only do they backpack, they have these exquisite evenings at home or at a restaurant. They look into each other's eyes a lot. And they like being together. And it runs the gamut the things they do together. They strike me as a couple that does everything. Everything."

She clearly has a very strong reaction to the image of love presented in this ad. She sees it as a powerful depiction of the kind of relationship she herself would like to have, and she is able to project her own ideal images for a relationship on to the two silhouettes presented in the ad.

Similarly, Riley, (wf, single, 45) contrasts an advertisement for Bic Twin Select disposable razors with one for Courvoisier, clearly illustrating the qualitative difference between a pornography of courtship with one of consummation. While one ad is seen to be about sex, the other is about love.

Riley: It (Bic Twin Select ad) doesn't have a risqué quality. It looks wholesome, it looks like they're married. So even though her legs are totally exposed, I didn't see it as sexy as this one (Courvoisier ad).
Interviewer: That one doesn't look like they're married?
Riley: No. (laughter)...it looks like a little holiday cheer could be involved there. The dark stockings, the glass of booze in the hand. This just makes me think of office couplings and things. And you can't really see their expression. These (Bic ad) look like they're smiling, and this (Courvoisier) just looks like they're into it. And it's sexier. The fact that she's facing him and he has his hand on her. They (Bic ad) could be relaxing and could fall asleep that way maybe. And the look on their faces renders it wholesome."

Whereas the courtship-oriented Bic ad is seen as "wholesome" and respectable because it implies commitment with romance, the Courvoisier ad is dirty. The dark stockings, the alcohol, the erotic orientation of the lovers pictured, all bring forth images of one night stands and sex for the sake of sex.

All three informants recalled the DeBeers ads from television and spoke of them as among their favorite commercials of all time. Similarly, each informant spontaneously mentioned the current Taster's Choice campaign featuring the ongoing relationship development between two neighbors through their shared enjoyment of the instant coffee. These ads successfully focus on romance and courtship leading to long-term, emotionally fulfilling commitment, and resonate with the deeply held desires of the women interviewed in this study.

Gender Self-Schema and the Perception of Role Portrayals

Previous research on female role portrayals in advertising attempted to correlate women's liberation attitudes with perceptions of the portrayals, but were unable to achieve statistical significance. As suggested by Wilson and Moore (1979), self-concept theory, and particularly, self-schema theory, may provide an explanation for these results. While previous researchers asked about agreement with feminist tenets, they did not attempt to estimate the degree to which those tenets were incorporated into their subjects' view of themselves. Agreement with feminist tenets may not be the same thing as incorporation into the self-concept in a way that will lead to behavioral consistency. Furthermore, while several individuals may all be schematic on "feminism", this self-schema will not be equally central (important) as a defining self characteristic to all of them. Differences in centrality lead to strong differences in the degree to which the schema is used to process incoming information.

The self-schema revealed by the informants in this study help us understand their perceptions of female role portrayals in the stimulus advertisements. In particular, these women's gender self-schema, and whether or not their schema includes a central feminist component, relates to their perceptions of and preferences for the advertisements presented in this study.

The excerpts presented from these interviews indicate that the informants "read" ads differently. Though there are some similarities in perceptions, there are also many differences which stem from their differences in self-concept. These differences illustrate that the meaning of ads, even the "gender meaning" presented in the ads' role portrayals, is not inherent (Stern, 1989, 1994; Scott, 1994). Meaning is created by readers and different readers may obtain different meanings from the same text.

Social psychologists have argued that schema, networks of memory-based associations that organize and guide an individual's perceptions, are the central cognitive units in the human information-processing system (Markus and Sentis, 1982). Individuals who are schematic in a particular domain should be able to encode schema-consistent information quickly, and organize incoming information in schema-relevant categories (Bem, 1981). Markus (1977) has argued that attempts to organize, summarize or explain one's own behavior in a particular domain will result in the formation of similar such cognitive structures about the self: self-schema. These schema represent the way the self has been differentiated and articulated in memory in particular domains (Markus, 1977).

Individuals vary enormously in the content and organization of their self-schema, developing them on dimensions which are important to them and which they thus choose to attend to, and not developing them on others. For instance, Markus (1982) states that though virtually all individuals develop some basic appreciation and understanding of their biological sex, only some people seem to construct an elaborate self-schema about their gender. She further asserts that behavioral consistency with self-description is most likely to occur for those individuals who base their self-descriptions upon a self-schema in the relevant domain. In contrast, those individuals who have no such clear schema about themselves are unlikely to exhibit such consistency in behavior.

The union of an individual's many domain-specific schemas make up the self-concept which can be seen as a system of substructures or a hierarchy of knowledge structures about the self (Markus and Sentis, 1982). Some self-conceptions receive repeated activation because of their importance in identifying or defining the self, and are likely to be strong, well-articulated and chronically accessible for the processing of incoming information. These views can be considered as the core self. Other, less central self-schema, will vary in their accessibility, and thus their influence on processing, depending on the individual's affective or motivational state, or on prevailing social conditions (Markus, 1986).

Markus and Smith (1981) have also argued that this self-schema based processing occurs not only for self-relevant information but for social cognition in general. Once established, schema function as selective mechanisms which determine whether information is attended to, how it is structured and what is done to it subsequently (Markus, 1977). As individuals accrue knowledge about themselves and generate self-schema in various behavioral domains, they become "experts" in that domain, particularly so in the case of highly central self-schema. The expertise that accumulates affects the processing of information relevant to that domain (Markus and Sentis, 1982). Markus (1985) argues that for schematics, the ability to use the information contained in the most central elements of their self-schema should allow them when perceiving others to do many of the things that experts can do: recognize when input is relevant to their domain; integrate this information with previously acquired information; and, make use of contextual cues to fill in incomplete or missing information in schema-consistent ways. When an individual has considerable expertise in a particular domain and obtains relatively low levels of knowledge about other

people being perceived, the self-concept is believed to provide a powerful frame of reference for social perception.

Based on Markus' conceptualization of self-schema and their varying centrality for individuals, a woman with a strong feminist self-schema should act as an "expert" when interpreting others in this domain. The research described in this study provided an opportunity to discover whether the informants interviewed did indeed possess that self-schematic expertise in the domains of gender and feminism. In the ads, only minimal information is imparted to the consumer about the individuals pictured. A woman with central feminist self-schema then, should be more likely than a woman without such a self-schema or with a less central such self-schema, to notice, react to and discuss stereotypical role portrayals in advertisements.

The following section of this paper will present a brief overview of the self-schema revealed by informants during the course of their interviews and demonstrate how those schema relate to their impressions of the stimulus advertisements.

Janet: Family, Friends, Love and then Feminism

Janet provided the most complete presentation of self-concept in the study. It is clear from her words that family and friends, which represent to her an extended family, are very important to her sense of self. She places a high value on them and responds quickly, both positively and negatively, to advertising images which feature these kinds of relationships.

"I'm a very family oriented individual and that's always appealed to me. Mom, dad and kids. I love that, I really do love that...And I love getting together with friends. It's one of my favorite things. Right behind being with family is being with friends, in a big way."

While focusing on depictions of these relationships, she often overlooks what other readers might see as sexist or stereotypical portrayals of women. In response to an ad for a recipe contest sponsored by Pillsbury and Green Giant featuring a family gathered around a pot of food, Janet says:

"I am moved by this family. Them all gathered around the meal makes me feel like they all participated in it. You know that it wasn't just mom in the kitchen doing stuff. It's a family in the kitchen making their dinner...Maybe it's the idea of food, that you have sustenance in order to live, but family is the sustenance you need for emotional things throughout life...And see, they weren't just in the kitchen cooking up dinner, they're cooking up a way to get $50,000."

This construal of what looked to the researcher as a stereotypical portrayal of a housewife presenting the evening meal to her family, is natural to Janet because of her value for family and the genuine family feeling she perceives in the ad.

Similarly, Janet has a strong desire to have a meaningful romantic relationship with a man that would lead to marriage and children. As a result, she had a strong reaction to these courtship advertisements, and did not focus on what might be construed as stereotypical portrayals.

"I want this (the DeBeers Diamond ad) to be the beginning of a relationship and this (Pillsbury/Green Giant family) to be the culmination, the family."

Further, Janet's yearning to achieve certain possible selves relates to the way she views women portrayed in advertising. In response to an ad for Hanes stockings, Janet says,

"And this ad, I would buy their stockings. Because this is so great...She's very classy. You only see three quarters of her, but you can tell. You can tell she is a very classy woman. She sits like I wish I could sit. Sometimes I think I'm very manly the way I sit. And she looks completely feminine and she's sophisticated...I suppose women who were more self-confident than I might not feel that way, but I do have some real work to do as far as self-confidence and I would easily switch places with her. Could I please switch places with her? She's so together. That whole look is completely together. She's classy and sophisticated...I want the legs too, the stockings and the legs...She reminds me that I'm not self-confident but it's not her fault. And there is a real feeling that this is what I could be if I could learn to sit like a lady. But not in a way that's demeaning. She's not doing it. Anything that's talking now is my lack of self-confidence. Not what she's doing to me."

While she indicates that she is aware of the feminist criticism for ads which make women feel physically inadequate, she rejects it here and takes complete responsibility for the feelings it produces in her. She seems to feel a sense of kindredness with the woman in this ad whom she wants to be able to emulate. She does not extrapolate from this ad to advertising or society as a whole perpetuating images that remind women of their "inadequacies." In contrast, the researcher saw this ad as presenting the headless, faceless body of a woman sitting alluringly with her legs prominently displayed. She is primarily a physical object, not much different from a sculpture of ideal femininity or beauty, with no sense of life, individuality or personality about her.

Yet Janet also considers herself to be a feminist and when the subject of women in advertising is directly mentioned she has a great deal to say.

Janet: I think there are too many ads that show women in bathing suits and that bugs me. And women in bathing suits selling cars and beer. I don't get it. If you drink a lot of beer, you don't have a shape like that.
Interviewer: Tell me about which ads cross the line. What sort of ads are offensive to you?
Janet: Almost all beer commercials. Oh and feminine protection ads infuriate me.
Interviewer: What about them makes you angry?
Janet: You know, it seems to me that woman's secretions are allowed to be a million dollar business, and that you can't...condom ads are controversial? Wait a minute. You can advertise for the early pregnancy test, 'Your doctor and the cure, she recommends Mycelex 7'. Fuck you, I won't even buy that stuff because they advertise it. How dare they. How dare women not be as sacred as men appear to be.

So while Janet does have a strong feminist view point, it is clear from the interview in its entirety, that her self-schema in this domain is less central to her self-concept than are her values for family, friends, love and yearning to achieve what she sees as a more desirable self. As a result, these other self-schema often supersede her feminist perspective in processing and evaluating female role portrayals in advertising.

Julie: Androgyny and the Interchangeability of Gender Roles

Julie's (wf, married, 35) sense of self is quite different from Janet's. Unlike Janet, who is very conscious of her "female-ness", Julie has an androgynous gender self-schema in that she has not sharply differentiated herself on the basis of gender, and has incorporated both masculine and feminine elements into her self-concept (Markus, 1982).

Julie: My husband and I kind of trade-off. In fact, he does a lot more cooking than I do. We're not the typical husband and wife type. And since he's out of work, he does all the housework and I do all the working. Sort of a role reversal there. We don't have male/female stigmas that, you know, 'You take out the garbage, I cook the food', thing. I think my children are similar. My son likes to cook, my daughter takes karate.
Interviewer: That seems to be an important value for you.
Julie: Yeah, I think so. My parents were that way too. A little more stereotypical than us, but not too much.

She believes that there are not many differences between the social roles that men and women can occupy, and that men and women are essentially "interchangeable". However, when asked to engage in feminist deconstructionist role reversal for an ad for Smirnoff Vodka featuring two men standing together, she is not always able to do so easily and she is bothered by this.

Interviewer: What if you saw two women standing holding lobsters in this same place at this time. Would that feel right to you?
Julie: You know what, probably no. I don't think it would and I hate to say that, because it should. You know, I mean, it should. But no I don't think so. Maybe it's the setting. I guess I still have a little bit of that stereotypical, you know, the men down at the docks.
Interviewer: You wouldn't see women standing on those docks holding lobsters saying they just met their dates for dinner?
Julie: No. If they were, they'd probably be looking at the lobsters in a tank, pointing. As opposed to touching them. I'm surprised I think that way.
Interviewer: Do you feel like you should always be able to see them as interchangeable?
Julie: Yes.

Despite her value for non-traditional sex roles, however, Julie does not have a feminist perspective, and feminist issues were not a concern with her when looking at the stimulus ads. Her responses to two advertisements are presented below. The first, for Learning International, shows an older man sitting at a conference table, clearly distressed over the state of his business. In the background are two other men. The second ad, for Hawaiian Tropic tanning lotion, features three women in bikinis.

Julie: Do I notice anything about women? I don't see any women in this ad (Learning International).
Interviewer: Does that matter to you?
Julie: No. It doesn't bother me. Sometimes you have women there, sometimes you don't. I don't think it's an intentional thing. It's just the way it is.
Interviewer: What if you saw these women (Hawaiian Tropic) in a different ad for a different product? Would you have a different feeling about it?

Julie: You mean like if these women were sitting in their bathing suits on top of a car? Okay. It's unnecessary, I think, because you're trying to sell a car. But that's a been there, done that kind of thing. There's always a woman on a car. It's typical. It doesn't bother me. I don't know why it doesn't bother me, but it doesn't. Obviously the girl knew what she was doing when she got up on the car. So, she made a conscious choice to do it. It's not like someone was standing there with a gun saying get up on the car.

While Julie has rejected stereotypical gender roles for herself and her family, she is not bothered by their continued propagation in advertising and as a result, does not react to the stereotypical portrayals of women as many feminists would. The absence of women in an ad about executives making important business decisions is not seen as part of a larger pattern of women missing from such environments. She also believes that absent physical coercion, sexual images are not forced upon women but are a matter of individual choice. She ignores or is unaware of the subtle influence of societal norms in perpetuating these images of women.

Julie clearly has a schema for gender for both herself and her family. Yet this does not insure perception of stereotypical role portrayals in advertising. And while she is aware of the feminist discourse on portrayals of women in advertising, this discourse is not a part of Julie's perceptions because these values are not a part of her self.

Riley: A Central Feminist Self-Schema

Unlike both Janet and Julie, feminist thought is very central to Riley's self concept. She has devoted a great deal of thought to the roles that women are assigned in society and the role of the hegemonic process. She says:

"Sometimes I think money is the bottom line and other times I think it isn't really. I think it's about maintaining that balance of power. Even though I know money is big, I think power is as big an issue as money. Those are the two biggies. Like Meryl Streep said recently that if there were an audience of people dying to see films about 50-year old women, we'd see them. I don't think we'd see them. Because it's about more than just making money. I think there probably is a whole audience out there, especially as my generation gets older. They could make a lot of money, but they won't. Because men produce and direct and cast. You know the thing about when a male actor is 20 he has a 20-year old as his leading lady. When he's 30 he has a 30-year old, but when he's 40 he has a 20-year old again. I think it's more about maintaining the status quo."

As a result of the importance of this issue to her sense of self, she is self-directed to notice gender-relevant information in her environment and is quick to pick it out in the stimulus materials. Often her first impressions are of the use of gender in an ad. This is her first response to an ad for Waterman pens featuring a family of siblings with one sister and four brothers:

"If I didn't know they were a family, I would think, 'Typical, four men and one woman.' There are always more men in ads and on TV shows and in movies and everything, except in real life in which there are more women than men. So I remember first seeing that and thinking uh-oh. You know my danger signals went off, and then I saw it was a family and I said what can you do."

The importance of gender to Riley's self-concept leads her to process information in this domain with the characteristics of expertise described by Markus (1985). She spontaneously goes to the domain of gender first when interpreting the stimulus ads, immediately recognizing the portrayals as domain relevant and using the contextual cues present in the ad to fill in incomplete information in a way that is consistent with her strong gender self-schema. It is clear that gender and feminism are chronically accessible, highly central, self-schema for Riley, used for interpreting much of the social world she sees around her.

The recognition and perception of stereotypical depictions of women in these ads is a function of the informants' internal self-structures. In the past, researchers have focused on measuring external variables such as demographics or agreement with feminist statements to predict perceptions of role portrayals. While these external factors may be related to the internal structures, they may not be the key variables needed for understanding this phenomenon. Focusing on the role that the self plays, and perhaps the relationships of potentially predictive external variables to that self, can provide a richer understanding. Future research will attempt to build upon this to distinguish among clusters of women with similar gender self-schema and importance to their overall self-concepts, which lead to similar views and reactions toward stereotypical role portrayals in advertising and other media.

The Match Between Product and Role

Wortzel and Frisbie (1974) concluded that women react to female role portrayals in advertising primarily with respect to product use situations rather than with respect to attitudes toward women's liberation. Similarly, Johnson and Satow (1978), found that the women they interviewed found the use of sex in ads acceptable in certain cases. The informants in this study also had rules about when using sexual images was appropriate to the product and when it was not. These rules, however, are related to the informant's gender self-schema and resulting views regarding depictions of women in advertising. In response to a Hawaiian Tropic ad featuring three young women in bikinis, Julie (wf, married, 35) commented:

"They are young and attractive, but for what it's for, this is probably the appropriate type of advertising"

In contrast, Riley (wf, single, 45) found this ad to be quite offensive.

Riley: Oh, boy. For this one I would just say, same old shit. Three girls in a bikini with long hair and smiling and not looking too bright.
Interviewer: Does it matter that it's an ad for suntan lotion?
Riley: No. Absolutely no. Same old shit. I can see them thinking, 'Oh we're justified in doing this because it's suntan lotion.' But to me it looks like you could put them anywhere. You know those ads where you think, why are there three half naked women here? They're selling spatulas. This looks like just that kind of ad. It doesn't make a bit of difference what it's for. I hate it. They look dumb and stupid and exploited. I hate the whole thing.

Yet Riley did not find the headless, leggy image in the Hanes stockings ads inappropriate at all. She said,

"They're selling hosiery so that's a very feminine image. I'm not offended by it. I think that's one mood of a woman."

While women are likely to evaluate the appropriateness of the product with the role of the female model being used to sell it before dismissing the role portrayal, not all women are likely to measure that appropriateness in the same way. This is again a call for researchers to more clearly understand the internal dimensions of self that lead to these impressions.

DISCUSSION

Though this research was conducted with a small number of informants, the richness of their comments revealed several important themes regarding women's perceptions of role portrayals in advertising. Awareness of stereotypical role portrayals and perceptions of them varies by individual, depending upon internal structures of self that reflect important values with respect to gender and feminism. Self-concept theory has much to add to our understanding of how women view the women they see in ads and how they measure the appropriateness of the portrayed roles with the products being promoted.

Each of the women interviewed for this paper had a different self-orientation regarding issues of gender and feminism. Julie, while rejecting traditional sex roles for herself and her family, has no feminist self-schema. As a result, she does not interpret role portrayals of women in the stimulus advertisements presented as critically as do the other two informants. While Janet clearly has a feminist self-schema, it is much less central to her overall self-concept than are family, friends and love. As a result, her feminist perspective was not the first view imposed on the incoming stimulus advertisements. Riley, in contrast, is not only schematic on feminism, but has placed such importance on that domain that feminism is very central to her self-concept as a whole. Her feminist self-schema works as an anticipatory structure, "providing a readiness for her to search for and to assimilate incoming information in schema-relevant terms" (Bem, 1981).

An understanding of the importance of self-schematicity in certain domains and the influence of centrality on schematicity, can provide a better understanding of the differences in perceiving and reacting to stereotypical portrayals of women in advertising. The application of self-concept theory may allow researchers to obtain more significant, stable results regarding which women are aware of such portrayals and which are not. While many of the variables measured in the past in attempts to understand this phenomena may be linked to differences in self-schema in relevant domains, they did not directly measure internal self structures.

The results of the research presented in this study will be used to fashion future empirical work to test the correlation between schematicity for gender and feminism and the centrality of those self-schema to the overall self-concept with recognition of and reactions toward stereotypical female role portrayals in advertising. As the findings in these interviews suggest, it is hypothesized that those women with central self-schema on gender and feminism will be more aware and critical of such portrayals.

This research, however, does leave some questions unanswered. With only three interviews, focusing on a particular subset of the population of women in America, this paper does not address the wider gender influences which advertisements and other media images can have upon men and women alike. Clearly such influences are likely to exist and are worthwhile subjects for future research.

In addition, some important questions remain unanswered with respect to the findings from the three women who were interviewed for this paper. The informants in this study revealed a number of inconsistencies in their feminist self-schema. It is not clear how Julie can so soundly reject traditional sex roles and at the same time not seem to object to the propagation of them in society at large through advertising. Similarly, Janet clearly felt a lack of confidence when confronted with "perfect" legs presented in the Hanes advertisement, but stated very emphatically that such a reaction was her own fault rather than the fault of the model featured in the ad. Finally, neither Janet nor Riley, who have feminist self-schema, found any of the courtship advertisements' portrayals of women to be offensive, in contrast to the introspection of the researcher. It is clear that not only are women holding or not holding feminist self-schema, but that they select some elements of feminist thought and reject others when fashioning their schema. Why this is done and how they discriminate among these elements is not clear, yet may have profound impact upon the viewing of stereotypical role portrayals. Understanding this phenomena is an important area of future research not only for fully comprehending the perceptions of female role portrayals in advertising, but also for gaining perspective on the spectrum of feminist thought among women.

REFERENCES

Alreck, Settle and Belch (1992), "Who Responds to Gendered Ads—And How? Masculine Brands v. Feminine Brands," Journal of Advertising Research, Vol. 22, No. 2, April/May

Barry, Gilly and Doran (1985), "Advertising to Women with Different Career Orientations," Journal of Advertising Research, Vol. 25, No. 3, April/May

Bem, Sandra Lipsitz (1981), "Gender Schema Theory: A Cognitive Account of Sex Typing," Psychological Review, Vol. 88, No. 4, pp. 354-364

Courtney, Alice E. and Sarah W. Lockeretz (1971), "Woman's Place: An Analysis of the Roles Portrayed by Women in Magazine Advertisements," Journal of Marketing Research, February, pp. 92-95

Courtney, Alice E. and Thomas W. Whipple (1983), *Sex Stereotyping in Advertising*, D.C. Heath & Company, New York

DeYoung, Susan and F. G. Crane (1992) "Females' Attitudes Toward the Portrayal of Women in Advertising: A Canadian Study," *International Journal of Advertising*, 11, pp. 249-255

Duker, Jacob M. and Lewis R. Tucker, Jr. (1977), "'Women's Lib-ers' Versus Independent Women: A Study of Preferences for Women's Roles in Advertising," *Journal of Marketing Research*, November, pp. 469-475

Fiske, Susan T. and Shelley E. Taylor (1991), *Social Cognition*, McGraw Hill

Glaser, Barney and Anselm L. Strauss (1967), "The Constant Comparative Method," *The Discovery of Grounded Theory: Strategies for Qualitative Research*, New York: Aldine De Bruyter, Chapter 5, 101-115

Goffman, Erving (1979), *Gender Advertisements*, Harvard University Press

Heisley, Deborah D. and Sidney J. Levy (1991), "Autodriving: A Photoelicitation Technique," *Journal of Consumer Research*, 18, December, pp. 257-272

Johnson, Deborah K. and Kay Satow (1978) "Consumers' Reactions to Sex in TV Commercials," *Advances in Consumer Research*, pp. 411-414

Leigh, T. W., A. J. Rethans, T. R. Whitney (1987), "Portrayals of Women in Advertising: Cognitive Responses and Advertising Effectiveness," *Journal of Advertising Research*, October/November, pp. 54-63

Markus, Hazel (1977), "Self-Schemata and Processing Information About the Self," *Journal of Personality and Social Psychology*, Vol. 35, No. 2, February, 63-78

Markus, Hazel and Keith Sentis, "The Self in Social Information Processing," *Psychological Perspectives on the Self*, J. Suls, Ed., 1982, pp. 41-70

Markus, Hazel and Paula Nurius (1986), "Possible Selves," *American Psychologist*, Vol. 41, No. 9, September, pp. 954-969

Markus, Hazel, Marie Crane, Stan Bernstein and Michael Siladi (1982), "Self-Schemas and Gender," *Journal of Personality and Social Psychology*, Vol. 42, No. 1, pp. 38-50

Markus, Hazel, Richard L. Moreland, Jeanne Smith (1985), "Role of the Self-Concept in the Perception of Others," *Journal of Personality and Social Psychology*, Vol. 49, No. 6, pp. 1494-1512

Mazis, Michael B. and Marilyn Beuttenmuller (1973), "Attitudes Toward Women's Liberation and Perception of Advertisements," *Advances in Consumer Research*, pp. 428-434

McCracken, Grant (1988) *The Long Interview*, Qualitative Research Methods, Volume 13, Sage Publications

Prakash, Ved (1992) "Sex Roles and Advertising Preferences," *Journal of Advertising Research*, May/June

Scott, Linda M. (1993), "Fresh Lipstick: A New Look at Images of Women in Advertising," *Media Studies Journal*

Scott, Linda M. (1994), "The Bridge from Text to Mind: Adapting Reader-Response Theory to Consumer Research," *Journal of Consumer Research*, 21, December (forthcoming)

Sharits, Dean and H. Bruce Lammers (1983), "Perceived Attributes of Models in Prime-Time and Daytime Television Commercials: A Person Perception Approach," *Journal of Marketing Research*, February, pp. 64-73

Stern, Barbara (1991), "Two Pornographies: A Feminist View of Sex in Advertising," *Advances in Consumer Research*, Vol. 18, pp. 384-391

Stern, Barbara (1993), "Feminist Literary Criticism and the Deconstruction of Advertisements: A Postmodern View of Advertising and Consumer Responses," *Journal of Consumer Research*, March, pp. 556-566

Venkatesan, M. and Jean Losco (1975), "Women in Magazine Advertisements: 1959-1971," *Journal of Advertising Research*, Vol. 15, No. 5, October, pp. 49-54

Wallendorf, Melanie and Merrie Brucks (1993), "Introspection in Consumer Research: Implementation and Implications," *Journal of Consumer Research*, Vol. 20, No. 3, pp. 339-359

Whipple and Courtney (1985), "Female Role Portrayals in Advertising and Communication Effectiveness: A Review," *Journal of Advertising Research*, Vol. 14, No. 3

Wilson, R. Dale and Noreen K. Moore (1979), "The Role of Sexually-Oriented Stimuli in Advertising: Theory and Literature Review," *Advances in Consumer Research*, pp. 55-61

Wortzel, Lawrence H. and John M. Frisbie (1974), "Women's Role Portrayal Preferences in Advertising: An Empirical Study," *Journal of Marketing*, October, pp. 41-4

Ethical Issues In Consumer Research: Consumer and Researcher Perspectives

Jill G. Klein, Northwestern University
N. Craig Smith, Georgetown University

Consumer research is an essential marketing tool that allows marketing decision-makers to identify opportunities, respond to consumer desires and needs, and to forecast sales success. It provides a vital communication link between the consumer and the marketing manager. Yet this link is open to abuse involving a variety of questionable practices (such as deception, breaches of privacy, and coercion) that ethical researchers would wish to avoid. Some practices also may bias research findings; for example, respondents providing short and incomplete answers to an overlong interview. Moreover, consumer goodwill is critical for most marketing research and unethical practices lessen the likelihood of consumer cooperation in an activity that rarely yields any direct benefit to the individual respondent. Increasing public distrust in market research practices is evidenced in reports in the business press of consumer reluctance to participate in market research (e.g., Honomichl 1991, Schlossberg 1989). Studies of the marketing research industry by Walker Research consistently report high levels of agreement with statements associating the industry with questionable practices, such as the use of overly-personal questions (47% agreement in 1990) and nondisclosure of the survey purpose (68% in 1986) (Laczniak and Murphy 1993: 58).

Despite the development of some reasonably comprehensive codes of conduct (reviewed in Smith and Quelch 1993: 145-88), ethical issues involving consumer respondents have received insufficient attention and are inadequately understood. There are noteworthy exceptions, such as the seminal paper by Tybout and Zaltman (1974), that identified consumer rights in research and how violations of these rights might be avoided. While recent contributions have raised the issue of ethical research practices from a conceptual viewpoint (Holbrook, 1994; Jacoby 1994; Sojka and Spangenberg 1994; Toy, Olson and Wright 1993), only a few studies of researcher perceptions of ethically questionable marketing research practices (e.g., Akaah and Riordan 1989; Hunt, Chonko and Wilcox 1984) and only one study of consumer perceptions of these practices (Schneider 1977) can be found in the literature. The purpose of the session, therefore, was to bring together empirical papers that examined ethical issues pertaining to the treatment of consumer respondents from the perspective of the respondents themselves and from the perspective of the practitioner.

Smith and Klein presented an overview of the ethical issues pertinent to marketing research based on a reveiw of codes of research ethics and the consumer behavior and psychology literature. This overview was followed by a discussion of an investigation of consumers' reactions to ethically questionable practices. The purpose of this study was to identify those practices that consumers find most bothersome, and to explore the effectiveness of attempts to avoid these practices or to minimize their negative impact if unavoidable. In a mall-intercept study, 352 adult consumers were asked to imagine that they were a participant in a given marketing research scenario and to indicate their response to the described event. The 35 scenarios (each respondent rated three unrelated scenarios) examined 7 major ethical issues involving consumer respondents: deception (study purpose and study sponsor), confidentiality (disclosure of respondent identity and data within the research organization and externally), privacy (research data merged with other data, covert observation, intrusive interviewer calling at dinner time and pushy interviewer), inconvenience/hindrance (over-long interview and follow-up interview), embarrassment (asking personal questions), coercion (monetary incentives), sugging (selling under the guise of research) and frugging (fundraising under the guise of research).

Results of the study indicated that the practices of most concern were: deception concerning the study sponsor, breach of confidentiality, frugging, videotaping without consent, and the concealment of a follow-up interview. Efforts to lessen the unfavorable impact of the practices examined were sometimes effective. For example, warning people of a follow-up interview led to positive ratings. Future investigations will examine more closely the efficacy of efforts to avoid or minimize the negative effects of research practices.

Zinkhan and Milberg examine managerial perceptions of deceptive survey research practices in three different countries: Spain, Switzerland, and the United States. These countries differ systematically on "uncertainty avoidance"—the extent to which individuals within the society feel threatened by uncertain and ambiguous situations. Based on Hofstede's (1980) theory of cultural values, the authors predicted that cultures high in uncertainty avoidance should place a high value on the findings of marketing research and may be tempted to engage in unethical practices to gain necessary information. MBA students in the three countries rated their approval of the ethically questionable actions taken by managers, including those taken by marketing research directors. Findings provide some support for the hypotheses as reported in more detail in the following paper.

Concluding comments and discussion focused on the importance of considering the perspective of both sides of the researcher - respondent relationship. The speakers argued for the integration of the empirical findings presented in the session into the discourse on how to address the serious ethical dilemmas of consumer research.

REFERENCES

Akaah, Ishmael P. and Edward A. Riordan (1989), "Judgments of Marketing Professionals About Ethical Issues in Marketing Research: A Replication and Extension," *Journal of Marketing Research*, Vol. 26, pp. 112-120.

Hofstede, Geert H. (1980), *Culture's Consequences: International Differences in Work-Related Values*. Beverly Hills: Sage Publications.

Holbrook, Morris B. (1994), "Ethics in Consumer Research: An Overview and Perspectus," In Chris T. Allen and Deborah Roedder John (Eds.) *Advances in Consumer Research*, Vol 21, Provo UT: Association for Consumer Research, pp. 566-571.

Honomichl, Jack (1991), "Legislation Threatens Research by Phone," *Marketing News*, (June), p. 24.

Hunt, Shelby D., Lawrence B. Chonko and James B. Wilcox (1984), "Ethical Problems of Marketing Researchers," *Journal of Marketing Research*, Vol XXI (August), pp. 309-24.

Jacoby, Jacob (1994), "Ethical Issues in Consumer Research," In Chris T. Allen and Deborah Roedder John (Eds.) *Advances in Consumer Research*, Vol 21, Provo UT: Association for Consumer Research, p. 565.

Laczniak, Gene R. and Patrick E. Murphy (1993), *Ethical Marketing Decisions: The Higher Road*, Boston: Allyn and Bacon.

Schlossberg, Howard (1989), "Right to Privacy Issue Pits Consumers Against Marketers, Researchers," *Marketing News*, (October), p. 23.

Schneider, Kenneth C. (1977), "Subject and Respondent Abuse in Marketing Research," *MSU Business Topics*, (Spring), pp. 13-19.

Smith, N. Craig and John A. Quelch (1993), *Ethics in Marketing*, Homewood, IL: Richard D. Irwin.

Sojka, Jane and Spangenberg, Eric (1993), "Ethical Concerns in Marketing Research," "Ethical Issues in Consumer Research," In Chris T. Allen and Deborah Roedder John (Eds.) *Advances in Consumer Research,* Vol 21, Provo UT: Association for Consumer Research, pp. 392-396.

Toy, Daniel R., Jerry C. Olson, and Lauren K. Wright (1993), "The Role of Deception and Debriefing in Consumer Research," Paper presented at the Association for Consumer Research Conference, Nashville, TN.

Tybout, Alice M. and Gerald Zaltman (1974), "Ethics in Marketing Research: Their Practical Relevance," *Journal of Marketing Research*, Vol. 12, pp. 234-37.

Deception in Survey Research: A Cross-Cultural, Managerial Perspective

George M. Zinkhan, University of Georgia
Sandra J. Milberg, Georgetown University

ABSTRACT

We surveyed 279 students in three countries to explore cross-cultural differences in ethical judgments. Overall, the pattern of results provides support for Hofstede's theory of cultural values. Five broad moral principles (beneficence, justice, nonmaleficence, nondeception, and nondiscrimination) are introduced to help survey researchers think about the ethical dilemmas which they face.

INTRODUCTION

Consumer researchers rely upon public opinion surveys to gain knowledge about a wide variety of behaviors and attitudes. In order to achieve success, such surveys depend upon a high level of consumer confidence. Consumer confidence (in the importance, seriousness, and validity of surveys) can be influenced by a number of factors, including: confidence in the marketing research industry; the introduction and phrasing of questions; the sponsor of the survey; and the (perceived) ethical practices of the researcher (e.g., is there full disclosure of a survey's sponsor?). The focus of this paper is on the last issue: the ethical practices and perceptions of research managers.

The purpose of this paper is to study perceptions of managerial practices, with respect to survey practices. This is an important topic, since unethical practices could lead to a decline of confidence in consumer surveys and such a decline could seriously threaten the validity of the forthcoming results.

Survey research, of course, consists of a broad set of conventions and techniques; and survey research is applied in a variety of disciplines, including: psychology, sociology, economics, marketing, consumer research and so on. One could argue, almost without limit, as to where the boundaries of these fields actually lie (Zinkhan, Roth, and Saxton 1992). Here, the terms, "consumer research," "marketing research," and "survey research" are used almost as synonyms. The authors are well aware that there are important differences between these approaches (e.g., differences between consumer research and marketing research); but the emphasis here is on describing ethical dilemmas which arise as marketing researchers apply survey methods to the problem of understanding consumer behavior.

There is a special problem in "ethics research" because there may be important cross-cultural differences about what is "right" and what is "wrong." We address this issue here by studying managerial perceptions about survey research in three cultures: Spain, Switzerland, and the U.S. These nations are chosen so as to differ systematically along Hofstede's (1980) "uncertainty avoidance" dimension. In general, Hofstede's theory of cultural values serves as the conceptual framework for this investigation. In addition, five broad moral principles are discussed, and the application of these principles to business problems are highlighted.

RESEARCH ON BUSINESS ETHICS BY ACADEMICS

Just as society's concerns about ethics in commerce have increased, academic research on business ethics has proliferated. For example, the *Journal of Business Ethics* was founded in 1982; and scholars use a wide variety of methods (including survey research) to contribute to knowledge in that publication. During its first twenty years of publication, the *Journal of Advertising* (JA) published at least 159 articles which were related to the specialized area of advertising ethics (including articles on tobacco advertising, advertising to children, and deceptive advertising). These 159 articles on ethics represent more than one third of all the articles published during the first twenty years of JA's history (Zinkhan 1994b). Thus, we have some evidence that ethics is not a neglected topic in marketing and advertising research. However, there has not been so much work done in the area defined by the intersection of ethics and survey research; and most of the academic studies which have been completed are primarily descriptive in nature.

COMMERCE AND ETHICS

Ethical issues arise in every area of human activity. The areas of commerce and industry are no exception. In the late 20th century, it is very difficult to separate a nation's culture from its business environment (Zinkhan 1994a). At the same time, ethical judgments are the product of a culture; and the subject-matter of ethics is "inherently shifting and unstable because of the phenomenon of social and historical change" (Warnock 1971, p. 2). That is, people's notions about what is right and what is wrong differ widely from one culture to another. These differences arise partly because of beliefs about the natural consequences of actions and perhaps because of beliefs about the supernatural consequences of actions.

Also, the nature of human conduct and character which is required for success in one society at one time period may be quite different from the conduct and character which promote success (or even survival) in another culture. For example, a prosperous commercial society experiencing a long period of peace may not value the same traits as societies of horse breeding nomads or rainforest dwellers (Warnock 1971). In fact, the ethical issues discussed here (i.e., marketing research practices) have meaning only within the context of twentieth century commerce.

A variety of philosophers (cf. Frankena 1973; Warnock 1971) argue persuasively that this diversity of cultural beliefs about ethics is amenable to explanation. That is, there may indeed be a set of "principles" which can guide decision makers who try to solve ethical dilemmas. It is quite important for researchers in consumer behavior to be aware of such principles, especially because of the cultural context of ethical decisions. Even if we observe cross-cultural differences in managerial attitudes toward practices in survey research, there may be a set of principles that can help managers to make difficult ethical decisions across a variety of settings and cultures.

Five broad principles are discussed here: beneficence, justice, nonmaleficence, nondeception, and nondiscrimination. Links are made between these principles and specific ethical problems which marketing research managers face (see Table 1). Specifically, Table 1 shows six ethical dilemmas which marketing researchers may face. After discussing the relationship of the five ethical principles to the moral dilemmas shown in the table, we proceed with an empirical examination of cross-cultural differences in ethical perceptions.

TOWARD A DEFINITION OF ETHICS

What is ethics? Some argue (or seem to argue by lack of explicit definition) that ethics is the same as morality. However, this approach raises the problem of tautology. What is morality? Can morality be distinguished from ethics? One approach is to define morality as moral principles which are directed at enhancing

Advances in Consumer Research
Volume 22, © 1995

TABLE 1
Six Survey Research Scenarios

Use of ultraviolet ink
1. A project director went to the Marketing Research Director's office and requested permission to use an ultraviolet ink to precode a questionnaire for a mail survey. The project director pointed out that although the cover letter promised confidentiality, respondent identification was needed to permit adequate cross tabulations of the data. The Marketing Research Director gave approval.

Hidden tape recorders
2. In a study intended to probe deeply into the buying motives of a group of wholesale customers, the Marketing Research Director authorized the use of the department's special attache cases equipped with hidden tape recorders to record the interviews.

One-way mirrors
3. One of the products of X Company is brassieres. Recently, the company has been having difficulty making decisions on a new product line. Information was critically needed regarding how women put on their brassieres. The Marketing Research Director therefore designed a study in which two local stores agreed to put one-way mirrors in the foundations of their dressing rooms. Observers behind these mirrors successfully gathered the necessary information.

Fake Research Firm
4. A Marketing Research Director wanted to interview a sample of customers about their reactions to a competitive product. He decided to invent an innocuous name (i.e., "The Marketing Research Institute") to interview people. This name change effectively camouflaged the identity of the sponsor of the study.

Sugging
5. A new Sales Manager was appointed for an encyclopedia company. She observed that a common way for encyclopedia representatives to get into homes was to pretend they were taking a survey. After finishing the survey, they switched to their sales pitch. This technique seemed to be very effective and was used by most competitors. The new Sales Manager decided to adopt this survey/sales-pitch tactic for her sales force.

Social Issues
6. The marketing research department of X Company frequently makes extensive studies of their retail customers. A federally supported minority group working to get a shopping center in their residential area wanted to know if they could have access to this trade information. Since the Marketing Research Director has always refused to share this information with trade organizations, the request was declined.

---

societal well-being. Following this reasoning, Frankena (1973) develops two moral principles: beneficence (doing good) and justice (being fair). Both of these principles have implications for survey researchers in consumer behavior, and both are discussed in the following two sections.

BENEFICENCE AND MARKETING RESEARCH

One may well ask, "Does marketing research do good?" One could, of course, adopt a macromarketing approach for answering such a question. By putting into practice the "marketing concept," marketing research provides a way for product planners to create services and features which customers want. Thus, a bountiful flow of new and improved products is the benefit ("the good") which the marketing research industry as a whole provides to society.

To adopt an alternative perspective, it could be argued that some societies (e.g., the former Soviet Union) provide sufficient goods and services without investing in a highly sophisticated (and expensive) marketing research system. It is true that the Soviet economic system no longer exists. But, at the same time, few would seriously argue that it was a lack of a fully developed system of consumer research which doomed the U.S.S.R to failure. And, similar systems (of state-determined production) may once more rise and flourish, again without the supposed benefits of consumer research.

At the micro level, individual consumer researchers could be concerned with the broad moral principle of "doing good." However, it is fortunate that the "marketing concept" (by specifying that

firms should achieve organizational goals by satisfying customers) provides a philosophical underpinning to justify much of what is done in survey research.

The institution and ideals of democracy also provide justification for the existence of the marketing research industry. Consumer surveys offer citizens a chance to make their preferences known, and marketing managers are urged to "hear the voice of the market" (Barabba and Zaltman 1992). Consumers "vote" with their cash and their credit cards as they purchase merchandise; but they also vote in consumer surveys, as they indicate product and attribute preferences. In fact, in print periodicals, United States residents are more frequently referred to as "consumers" than they are referred to as "citizens" (Zinkhan 1994a). Thus, consumer research promotes the ideals of egalitarianism and democracy and provides (economic) ways for citizens to vote.

Nonetheless, there is a potential problem raised by cultural differences. For example, in many Asian societies it is viewed as inappropriate to voice opinions publicly and answer surveys. It is seen as more appropriate to keep private personal opinions and beliefs. Thus, with this cultural milieu as background, it could be argued that marketing research does not work towards achieving the principle of beneficence.

JUSTICE AND MARKETING RESEARCH

As conceived by Frankena, justice is equivalent to fairness. The notion of fairness applies very well to a wide variety of ethical problems in marketing. For example, in the U.S., we believe that prices should be "fair." We believe that competition should be "fair." Thus, the Federal Trade Commission has a broad mandate to ensure that firms do not engage in unfair competitive practices.

Frankena's principle of justice has the potential to provide guidance for solving many day-to-day problems which are faced by consumer behavior researchers. This is important, because common approaches which have been proposed for solving ethical problems in marketing often do not apply directly to marketing research situations. For example, marketing operates as a boundary function; and marketing personnel often deal with parties who are outside of their organization (e.g., customers). Many ethical problems involve conflicts between two or more individuals. Potential conflicts may have more serious consequences (and may be relatively difficult to resolve) if the parties involved do not belong to the same organization (e.g., work for the same company).

Ethical problems which arise in marketing research may not be particularly amenable to easy solutions. For example, Nash (1989) has proposed "12 Questions for Examining the Ethics of a Business Decision." One of these questions is: "Can you discuss the problem with the affected parties before you make your decision?" Such discussion would typically not be possible in a survey research setting. In most cases, survey researchers make their first contact with respondents at the time of the actual survey. Excessive, prior contact would, most likely, bias survey results.

Negotiation

The principle of justice becomes even more useful to decision makers when it is combined with the technique of negotiation (French and Granrose 1995). Specifically, two parties with a potential ethical conflict could be encouraged to negotiate with the ultimate goal of creating a solution which is "fair." Through this negotiation approach, it is possible to move beyond principles and achieve new solutions to difficult problems. The five moral principles discussed here are especially useful to negotiating parties because they provide a framework and provide a goal to work toward. Nonetheless, such negotiation may not always be possible in survey research, since the parties in potential conflict (e.g., survey researcher and respondent) often do not meet face-to-face.

Justice Applied to the Ethical Scenarios: An Example

Frankena's principle of justice has important implications for the scenarios shown in Table 1. For instance, the sixth scenario describes a situation where a research firm is encouraged to share the results of a consumer survey with a federally-supported minority group hoping to establish a business in the local area (when such information typically isn't shared with trade organizations). The notion of fairness indicates that such information should not be shared, as such sharing wouldn't be "fair" to other trade organizations.

A counter argument would be that it is fair to compensate certain groups for past injustices, so that such sharing is fair. Thus, moral principles are useful; but it isn't always clear how these principles should be applied. Again, this is where the technique of negotiation could prove to be extremely valuable. In this particular situation, three parties may wish to participate in the negotiation process: the Research Director, representatives from the minority group, and representatives from other trade associations. In brief, negotiation provides the energy and focus to breathe life into moral principles.

NONMALEFICENCE AND MARKETING RESEARCH

The contemporary philosopher, Geoffry Warnock (1971) accepts the importance of Frankena's principle of beneficence; but he

argues that three others should be added to it: nonmaleficence (don't harm); nondeception; and nondiscrimination. These three all have implications for consumer research (and its cousin, marketing research).

Again from a macromarketing perspective, it could be argued that the survey research industry, as a whole, does harm. This harm could come from wasting (societal) resources. Douglas Adams, in his *The Restaurant at the End the Universe*, makes this point satirically. A group of (unwilling and unwitting) space travellers arrive on an uninhabited planet and are forced to re-invent civilization from scratch. One woman (who used to be a marketing expert on her home planet) is placed on a committee to invent fire. Before the invention process can proceed, she insists that the committee must conduct a series of focus group interviews with consumers: "When you've been in marketing as long as I have you'll know that before any new product can be developed it has to be properly researched. We've got to find out what people want from fire, how they relate to it, what sort of image it has for them." Just as marketing practice may unwittingly contribute to product proliferation and obsolescence, so too may the consumer research profession play a role in wasting society's resources (a maleficent activity).

As discussed above, the principles of beneficence and nonmaleficence are especially relevant for thinking about macro issues in consumer behavior research. However, the day-to-day problems of survey researchers do not so frequently involve decisions about life and death, decisions about good and evil. Rather, ethical dilemmas which arise in marketing research more often result from "lack of thought," from "misunderstanding" or from "compromise" (Smith 1989, p. 7). That is, survey researchers are not asked to handle "pure evil." They are not asked to make decisions such that they risk losing their souls as a consequence. Nonetheless, survey researchers do face moral dilemmas (in their day-to-day activities), and they need a framework for solving these kinds of problems.

NONDECEPTION AND MARKETING RESEARCH

Warnock's third moral principle (nondeception) is particularly relevant for guiding micro decision making in survey research. A number of scholars have attempted to generate a list or description of the ethical problems which marketing managers typically encounter. For example, Chonko and Hunt (1985) empirically identify 10 major ethical issues in marketing management, with "honesty" appearing as third most important (as rated by a sample of managers). Honesty includes misrepresenting services and lying to customers to obtain orders. Both of these "unethical" practices have counterparts in survey research. For example, researchers may misrepresent the purpose of customer contact (i.e., "sugging:" selling under the guise of research). Likewise, researchers may deceive a respondent about the true sponsor of a survey (so as to increase response rates). As Smith (1989) argues, trust, fairness, and honesty are key values both in business and in society. Warnock's principle of nondeception provides clear guidance as to how these research dilemma's (e.g., sugging) should be resolved. As such, these principles have the potential to be quite useful for developing solutions to day-to-day problems encountered by survey researchers.

NONDISCRIMINATION AND SURVEY RESEARCH

Warnock's fourth principle (nondiscrimination) also has practical implications for micro decisions made by marketing practitioners. For example, all hiring decisions should be made with the principle of nondiscrimination in mind. Akaah and Riordan (1989) create 11 "ethical scenarios" and ask marketing researchers and executives to indicate whether the behavior illustrated in the scenarios is ethical or not. One of their scenarios is shown as item number 6 in Table 1 and involves the sharing of research with a minority group (as discussed in the "fairness" section above). Again, Warnock's principle of nondiscrimination is relevant for dealing with this sort of micro issue. In 1989, only 13% of marketing researchers and only 10% of marketing managers felt that the survey research *should* be provided to the federally funded minority group.

CULTURE AND ETHICS

As discussed briefly above, culture can play an important role in determining ethical perceptions. Hofstede (1983) studied cultural values in the work place by surveying 116,000 respondents from 50 different countries. The employees studied were from their countries' middle class rather than from their lower or upper classes. Hofstede identified four major dimensions which accounted for country differences in his responses. These dimensions include: power distance, individuality, masculinity, and uncertainty avoidance. Only the last-mentioned dimension (uncertainty avoidance) is investigated here. Hofstede also developed and published index scores for the 50 countries which he studied. These index scores (related to uncertainty avoidance) are used here to make predictions about the ethical decisions that marketing researchers will make.

Hofstede's cultural dimensions have been found to be predictive of consumer behavior in other contexts. For example, Lynn, Zinkhan, and Harris (1993) found that uncertainty avoidance explained cultural differences in tipping behavior. Specifically, tipping was more prevalent in countries that were less tolerant of uncertainty. Zinkhan and Prenshaw (1994) applied Hofstede's theory to the prevalence of brand name associations in three cultures and found limited support for the notion that uncertainty avoidance explains the importance and prominence that brand names will have within a culture.

UNCERTAINTY AVOIDANCE

Uncertainty avoidance measures the extent to which a society feels threatened by uncertain and ambiguous situations and tries to avoid these situations (Hofstede 1980). Uncertainty avoidance describes how individuals deal with uncertainty and risk (Zinkhan and Prenshaw 1994). A culture's score on this dimension reflects individuals' need for security and their willingness to accept change and take risks. Uncertainty avoidance provides guidance in dealing with anxiety about the future and reflects the desire to find protection.

The three countries studied here rank as follows with respect to uncertainty avoidance: U.S. (lowest), Switzerland (middle), and Spain (highest). In other words, U.S. culture is the most risk taking; and Spanish culture is the most risk averse. These rankings lead to the following predictions about marketing research practices:

H1a: The percentage of respondents disapproving of "unethical" practices will be the highest in the U.S. (which has the lowest scores on Hofstede's dimension of uncertainty avoidance).

H1b: The percentage of respondents disapproving of "unethical" practices will be the lowest in Spain (which has the highest scores on Hofstede's dimension of uncertainty avoidance).

The rationale for these hypotheses is as follows.

A main purpose for gathering marketing research information is to reduce uncertainty. Thus, risk takers will not derive as much value from research information as will risk avoiders, who will value marketing research highly. Following this logic, risk avoiders will be willing "to bend the rules a little" in order to gain valued information. Risk takers will not care to bend the rules, because the information they are getting in return is not worth so much (to them).

An opposite argument would be possible. Specifically, one could argue that risk avoiders will not want to take the risk of "doing something wrong" (violating a religious law, for example). However, as discussed above, ethical dilemmas in marketing research do not typically involve profound questions of good vs. evil (as would be addressed by religious laws). Rather such dilemmas (as shown in Table 1) frequently involve the temptation to "bend the rules a little." Thus, the explanation offered in the preceding paragraph is the most plausible; and the hypotheses derived from this explanation are put forward in H1a and H1b.

METHOD

279 students were surveyed in three countries: Spain, the U.S., and Switzerland. The respondents from first two countries were graduate students, while the 53 respondents from Switzerland were equivalent to undergraduates. There were a total of 109 students in the U.S. and 117 from Spain.

Among other questions, the subjects responded to the first 5 scenarios shown in Table 1. The sixth scenario (from Table 1) was not used because it would not have direct meaning to European respondents. The first three scenarios in the table are derived from Akaah and Riordan (1989), while the last two are derived from Zinkhan, Bisesi, and Saxton (1989).

Following a procedure outlined by Akaah and Riordan (1989), respondents were asked to indicate their approval/disapproval of the action(s) of either the marketing research director or the sales manager in each scenario. A 5-point scale with descriptive anchors ranging from "disapprove," "disapprove somewhat," "neither approve nor disapprove," "approve somewhat," to "approve" was used for the evaluations. Respondents also wrote short essays to describe their reasoning in each scenario. Details concerning these open-ended responses are not reported here.

RESULTS

Results are shown in Table 2. To simplify the table, only disapproval rates (i.e., "disapprove somewhat" or "disapprove") are reported. In general, the results support both hypotheses. For all 5 scenarios, a greater percent of U.S. respondents disapprove of the "unethical" activities than their counterparts in other countries (thus supporting H1a). Similarly, the Spanish respondents were least likely to disapprove of unethical activities (as specified by H1b). Using chi square tests, both of these differences are significant ($p<.05$) for all 5 scenarios. In brief, support is found for the cultural predictions forthcoming from Hofstede's theory.

DISCUSSION

Despite the fact that business ethics has been studied in a variety of disciplines for the past 20 years, we still have much to learn. Here, Hofstede's theory of cultural values is used to understand differences between ethical decisions made in three countries. Hofstede's theory has value, since it provides a way to make predictions about human behavior in many countries (at least 50). This is important, because the vast number of cross-cultural studies in consumer behavior involve comparisons between only two cultures (Zinkhan 1994b). Following this pair-wise approach, it wold take researchers many years to recognize a pattern or construct

TABLE 2

Disapproval Ratings for the Five Scenarios[a]

		U.S. (n=109)	Switzerland (n=53)	Spain (n=117)
1.	Ultra Violet Ink	63.3	58.5	23.1
2.	Hidden Tape Recorder	78.9	69.8	38.5
3.	One-way Mirrors	94.5	71.7	53.0
4.	Fake Research Firm	41.3	34.0	12.0
5.	Sugging	30.3	28.3	9.4

[a]Cell entries indicate the percent who disapproved of a particular activity.

a theory about cross-cultural differences. Hofstede's theory applies particularly to values in the work place, so it is especially useful for thinking about the kinds of managerial issues highlighted here (e.g., in Table 1).

Given that there are important differences between cultures about accepted ethical practices in marketing research, the application of general moral principles is quite important. The five moral principles described here may be useful for guiding the resolution of ethical conflicts in marketing research. In addition, these five principles have the potential to aid decision makers whenever there is an ethical conflict, not just in marketing research situations.

There are a variety of weaknesses associated with the present study. The use of students subjects to simulate managerial judgments is a problem; but we are in the process of collecting data from managers to resolve this issue. Student subjects were selected using a convenience sample, and there were relatively few respondents from Switzerland. Decision-makers' intentions were measured, rather than actual behavior. A complete test of Hofstede's theory would involve recruiting (literally) thousands of respondents in many countries.

It may well be that attitudes toward business ethics are changing over time (Zinkhan, Bisesi, and Saxton 1989). A cross-sectional approach (as employed here) offers us little insight about such changes; and, as discussed above, the diversity of beliefs about ethics makes this a particularly tricky area for academic investigation.

In summary, we still have a lot to learn about business ethics. Three broad approaches are introduced here, including: Hofstede's theory of cultural values, the application of moral principles (e.g., justice), and the use of negotiation to resolve differences. A systematic application of these three approaches has the potential to change the way we think about ethics and human behavior.

REFERENCES

Akaah, Ishmael P. and Edward A. Riordan (1989), "Judgments of Marketing Professionals about Ethical Issues in Marketing: A Replication and Extension," *Journal of Marketing Research*, 26 (February), 112-21.

Barabba, Vincent P. and Gerald Zaltman (1992), *Hearing The Voice of the Market*, Boston: Harvard Business School Press.

Chonko, Lawrence B. and Shelby D. Hunt (1985), "Ethics and Marketing Management: An Empirical Examination," *Journal of Business Research*, 13, 339-59.

Frankena, William K. (1973), *Ethics*, New Jersey: Prentice-Hall, Publishers.

French, Warren and John Granrose (1995), *Practical Business Ethics*. New York: Prentice Hall.

Hofstede, Geert (1980), *Culture's Consequences: International Differences in Work-related Values*, Beverly Hills, CA: Sage.

Hofstede, Geert (1983), "National Cultures in Four Dimensions: A Research-based Theory of Cultural Differences among Nations," *International Studies of Management and Organization*, 8, (Spring/Summer), 46-47.

Lynn, Mike, George M. Zinkhan, and Judy Harris (1993), "Consumer Tipping: A Cross-Country Study," *Journal of Consumer Research*, 19 (December), 478-488.

Smith, N. Craig (1989), "Ethics and the Marketing Manager," *Ethics in Marketing*, Richard D. Irwin, Inc., 3-33.

Warnock, Geoffrey J., (1971), *The Object of Morality*, USA: Barnes & Noble.

Zinkhan, George M. (1994), "International Advertising: A Research Agenda," *Journal of Advertising*, 1 (March), 1-5.

Zinkhan, George M. (1994), "Advertising Ethics: Emerging Methods and Trends," *Journal of Advertising*, 3 (September), 2-6.

Zinkhan, George M., Martin Roth, and Mary Jane Saxton (1992), "Knowledge Development and Scientific Status in Consumer Behavior Research: A Social Exchange Perspective," *Journal of Consumer Research*, 18 (September), 282-291.

Zinkhan, George M., Mike Bisesi, and Mary Jane Saxton (1989), "MBAs' Changing Attitudes Toward Marketing Dilemmas: 1981-1987," *Journal of Business Ethics*, 8, 963-974.

AUTHOR INDEX